Newspaper Reports on

Big League Baseball in the Big Apple

The New York Yankees

from the beginning in 1901 to 1962

Thomas J. Antonucci and Eric Caren

From Ruth and Gehrig . . . to Joe DiMaggio . . . to Mantle and Maris, the New York Yankees were beyond doubt the best of the best, the creme de la Creme. While many teams had their glory years or their winning streaks the Yankees just seem to come up with best team(s) year in, year out and decade after decade. Yankee fans have traditionally been overwhelming in numbers and the most widespread. The Yanks had fans from Maine to Mexico, in North Dakota and South Carolina from sea to shining sea and from Tennessee to Toronto.

As you look through the historical and very entertaining newspaper pages in this book you can recall, (if you're old enough) the great glory years and the stories of the players who made them so glorious. If you're not old enough to recall, you will get the sense of what made the Yanks so great as you thumb through these pages.

Newspaper Reports on

Big League Baseball
in the Big Apple
The New York Yankees

Developed under agreement with **Historical Briefs, Inc.**, Box 629, Sixth Street & Madalyn Ave., Verplanck, NY 10596.

Orders by Visa or Master-1-800-732-4746

Holscher, at 25 to 1, Wins Brighton Cup.

The Sporting World

Baseball Season Ends in the East.

SHIELDS' HOLSCHER WINS CLASSIC BRIGHTON CUP

Beats Flip Flap in Drive and Distances Proper and the Clown.

OUTSIDER IN RING AT 25 TO 1.

Jimmie Lane Easy Victor Over Caller in Chantilly Steeplechase—Rain Mars Brighton's Getaway.

The Winners.

Tileing (Koerner), 12 to 1.
Jimmie Lane (Owens), even.
Belmere (Hennessy), 8 to 5.
Holscher (Noone), 25 to 1.
Arimo (Martin), 4 to 1.
Nannie Hodge (Miller), 9 to 5.

Holscher, son of Lamplighter—Princess Lorraine, until last Monday a despised maiden, a cast-off from the string of "Dimaond Jim" Brady, ridden by Harry Noone, still an apprentice jockey, won the Brighton Cup at the beach track yesterday in one of the best distance races seen in a decade. At his throatlatch, fighting gamely every step of the last half mile, was Flip Flap, winner of this year's Advance stakes, and accounted the crack 3-year-old filly of the year, while almost a sixteenth of a mile back staggered Proper, hero of many a handicap, and considered the "cinch of the

The Brighton Cup.

day" out to the last ounce. Far up the stretch came Miller on The Clown, raced off his feet by the superior class of the three other contenders.

Though few of the 10,000 or more spectators had bets on the winner which was at the wonderful price of 25 to 1 at post time, they cheered his game struggle. Noone received an ovation when he came back to the scales. His victory over Shaw on Flip Flap, the equally experienced Williams on Proper, and the crack of the year, Miller, who rode The Clown, particularly delighted the younger element about the jockey house.

It was a truly run race in spite of the apparent form upset indicated by the betting. Proper was at 3 to 5 all the time, and was taken for thousands by the plungers. Flip Flap, at 8 to 5, received the general public play, while the pikers and a few stable followers played Holscher from 30 to 1 to 25 to 1, and The Clown from 40 to 30.

The break was an even one. Miller, in his characteristic headlong fashion, took The Clown out in front, setting a hot pace, considering the mud. Before a mile had been run, The Clown was done, as Williams let Proper, which was fighting for his head, race up to him.

The slow beginning Flip Flap was a good third, three lengths back, at the mile, while Holscher, after being raced into two or three pockets, was two lengths behind her. Proper kept the field going full speed the second time around, and passing the stand, it looked as if the Jennings horse would surely crack. Flip Flap then looked the winner.

"The Favorite Beaten."

In the backstretch Flip Flap raced up to Proper and the usual cry, "The favorite is beaten," was heard on all sides. Noone again tried to bring Holscher up, but was cut off for the fifth time by Proper dropping back. Going to the outside, the son of Lamplighter raced up to Flip Flap and for the last half mile fought it out with her. His half length advantage turning into the stretch was held to the end, superior condition telling in the crucial stages of the final drive.

It was a fine performance for the winner and an excellent one for the second horse. The disappointing showing of Proper cannot be explained, while The Clown hardly was considered seriously. Holscher was bought by Will Shields from "Diamond Jim" Brady for $1,000. The latter was disgusted with the colt because he failed to run to his work. It was only on Monday last that Holscher succeeded in leaving the maiden ranks, after making so many fruitless efforts that his backers were wellnigh bankrupt. His showing of stake form to-day, therefore, surprised the talent greatly.

The Cup race marked the end of the six-day meet at the beach. The day was by no means a good one for racing, threatening rain all the afternoon, with some slight showers actually falling. The track was slow from the rain of yesterday and the fields that ran were of only fair size. Three favorites won, and the books lost handsomely on the day, though the defeat of Proper at odds-on and Belle of Iroquois in the first, also odds-on, helped them a lot.

Fully 10,000 were present at the getaway. The beach track, where every move in every race may be seen, always is popular, and the week's attendance has been most gratifying to the management. More than $60,000 was distributed among the horse owners during the week's session, James R. Keene, J. Curtis Van Ness and William Shields being the three largest winners (each upward of $11,000) by the victories of Court Dress, Electioneer and Holscher, respectively.

Only Three in the 'Chase.

The rain ruined the secondary feature, the Chantilly steeplechase, as four of the seven potential starters were scratched. Jimmie Lane was a poor favorite, receding from 3 to 5 to even money, but won handily from Caller, 7 to 2. Oro, which bid fair to be a contender until the second time around, refused the backstretch Liverpool. Ray forced him over and finished, thus securing the $150 third money.

Favorite players and Millerites began the day badly by installing Belle of Iroquois a 3 to 5 favorite. She romped to the front as usual, but Koerner, on Tileing, 12 to 1, caught her tiring in the stretch and won going away. Russell T., racing well up and at one time the pacemaker, was a good third. Allowmaise and Lady Vincent each was played by the wise few, but neither justified its backing.

Luck and superior class, many pounds of it, won for the O'Neil-Burlew combination in the third race, a mile and one-sixteenth, selling affair. Their Belmere was the medium of a tremendous plunge which forced the price from 2 to 1 and 6 to 5. But Hennessy, who had the leg up, almost tossed the race away. He ran Belmere into three pockets before the backstretch was reached and when he got clear raced into a three length lead. Then he took up and it looked as if he would surely lose.

Anneta Lady ran around her field and closed so strongly that she almost nipped the Buffalo Derby winner, but could not quite get up. Mandarin, which improved greatly as several expected, beat Deutschland, and the 13 to 5 second choice, for third place. It was a close squeak for the winner and the ring was hard hit by his victory.

Arimo, with Jack Martin up, won the fifth race, a six furlong dash for 2-year-olds, by himself. He took command before a quarter had been run and never was headed. Baringo, played from 10 to 1 to 5 to 1, was second, and Fish Hawk, the 3 to 1 favorite, was a head behind. James Crawford, plunged on by W. W. Darden and his following failed to get into the money.

The Darden crowd, however, landed Nannie Hodge in the last race of the day and meet, thanks to Miller's clever work in saving ground on both turns. Halifax looked all over the winner at the head of the stretch, but stopped so badly that he finished eighth. Gambrinus, well up all the way, was a good second and Robin Hood, running well with blinkers, hung on long enough to be third. Jack McGinnis tried to put over a killing with Aviston, played from 60 to 1 to 30 to 1, but the start settled his chances. Water Tank, Suffice, Monet and Dishabille also were backed.

Summaries.

FIRST RACE.

Selling, for 2-year-olds; $900 added. Five and a half furlongs.

Horse.	Wt.	Jockey.	Betting.		Fin.
Tileing	102	Koerner	12-1	5-1	1
Belle of Iroquois	101	Miller	3-5	1-4	2
Russell T.	102	Dillon	10-1	4-1	3
Ace High	104	Garner	15-1	5-1	4
Clements	102	Brussel	20-1	6-1	5
Our Own	94	Ross	100-1	40-1	6
Pungent	100	Harris	20-1	6-1	7
Joe Fallert	102	L. Smith	40-1	15-1	8
Allowmaise	112	Sewell	10-1	4-1	9
Donna Elvira	99	Horner	15-1	5-1	10
Daraban	102	Cochr'n	100-1	30-1	11
Lady Vincent	98	Hagan	10-1	4-1	12

Start fair; won easily. Time, 1:08 3-5. Winner, b. c., by Hastings—Futile. Owner, Palestine Stable; trainer, W. O. Scully.

SECOND RACE.

Chantilly Steeplechase; for 4-year-olds and upward; $1,500 added. Short course, about two miles.

Horse and age.	Wt.	Jockey.	Betting.		Fin.
Jimmie Lane, 6	156	Owens	1-1	out	1
Caller, a	145	Donohue	7-2	out	2
Oro, 4	140	Ray	3-1	out	3

Start good; won easily. Time, 4:20. Winner, ch. g., by His Grace—Anna Page. Owner, Mr. Cotton; trainer, M. Smart.

THIRD RACE.

For 3-year olds and upward; selling; $1,000 added. Mile and one-sixteenth.

Horse, age.	Wht.	Jockey.	Betting.		Fin.
Belmere, 3	95	Hennessy	8-5	3-5	1
Anneta Lady, 3	100	Koerner	5-2	4-5	2
Mandarin, 3	98	L. Smith	20-1	6-1	3
Deutschland, 6	108	Miller	13-5	9-10	4
Palm Tree, 4	106	Knapp	50-1	15-1	5
John F. Ahearn, 5	103	Harris	300-1	60-1	6
Cannon Ball, 6	107	Dickson	100-1	30-1	7
Ivanhoe, 4	103	Garner	40-1	10-1	8
Soufrere, 5	105	C. Miller	12-1	4-1	9

Start fair; won easily. Time, 1:48 1-5. Winner, b. g., Ogden—Nahma. Owner and trainer, F. Burlew.

FOURTH RACE.

Brighton Cup, for 3-year olds and upward; $10,000 and $1,000 gold cup added. Two miles and a quarter.

Horse, age.	Wht.	Jockey.	Betting.		Fin.
Hulscher, 3	111	Moore	25-1	3-1	1
Flip Flap, 3	109	Shaw	8-5	1-4	2
Proper, 6	124	Williams	3-5	out	3
The Clown, 3	111	Miller	30-1	4-1	4

Start good; won driving. Time, 3:59 1-5. Winner, br. c., Lamplighter—Princess Lorraine. Owner and trainer, W. Shields.

FIFTH RACE.

For 2-year-olds; $1,000 added; six furlongs.

Horse.	Wht.	Jockey.	Odds.		Fin.
Arimo	111	Martin	4-1	8-5	1
Baringo	105	Knapp	5-1	2-2	2
Fish Hawk	105	Miller	3-1	6-5	3
Victoria B.	105	Garner	10-1	4-1	4
Jas. Crawford	108	Radtke	7-2	7-5	5
Gen. Sherman	102	Brussel	100-1	40-1	6
Gild	105	Hennessy	5-1	2-1	7
Geo. S. Davis	114	Sewell	6-1	2-1	8
Pr. Nipissing	104	Pinn	100-1	40-1	9
Harry Gardner	99	L. Smith	100-1	40-1	10

Start good; won easily. Time, 1:15. Winner, ch. c., Solitaire II—Magdalenas. Owner, J. J. Walsh; trainer, J. R. Walker.

SIXTH RACE.

Handicap for all ages; $1,000 added; six furlongs.

Horse and age.	Wht.	Jockey.	Odds.		Fin.
Nannie Hodge, 5	123	Miller	9-5	7-10	1
Gambrinus, 4	108	Harris	7-1	5-2	2
Robin Hood, 5	106	Koerner	12-1	4-1	3
Deshabille, 4	126	Williams	7-1	5-2	4
Suffice, 4	99	Dillon	60-1	20-1	5
Water Tank, 3	90	Garner	20-1	8-1	6
Sir Caruthers, 3	97	Ross	60-1	20-1	7
Halifax, 3	127	Dugan	4-1	8-5	8
Listless, 3	89	P. Burns	60-1	20-1	9
Aviston, 3	92	Nother	30-1	10-1	10
Monet, 5	106	Hagan	12-1	4-1	11
T. Lex. Leader, 4	92	Mahon	200-1	80-1	12

Start good; won driving. Time, 1:14 4-5. Winner, ch. m., Rossington — Mrs. Lane. Owner and trainer, W. W. Darden. Weather showery; track slow.

BELMONT PARK ENTRIES.

Race Track, Belmont Park, October 6—The entries for the races here on Monday are as follows:

First race—For 3-year olds and up; selling; $1,000 added. One mile.

Name.	Wht.	Name.	Wht.
Hogan	98	Aucassin	101
Mandarin	108	Adbell	106
Lawsonian	98	Macy, jr.	93
Baron Esher	100	Mary Antoinette	90
Lady Ellison	98	Orly II	102
California King	95	Ladsarian	98
Runnels	106	Ivanhoe	103
Ebony	106	Consideration	103
Palm Tree	106	Givona Bolerio	93
Head Dance	101	Wizard	103
Belmere	105	Donna	105
Silver Wedding	95	Panique	103
Belle of Portland	98	Gypsy King	95
Merlingo	104		

Second race—The Eighth Matron; for colts and geldings; $5,000 added. Six furlongs.

Name.	Wht.	Name.	Wht.
McCarter	116	Hardshot	112
Flint Hill	109	Yankee Gun	116
Ballot	122	Don Enrique	117
Okenite	116	Rosemount	117

Third race—The Eighth Matron; for fillies; $5,000 added. Six furlongs.

Name.	Wht.	Name.	Wht.
Adoration	116	Fantastic	111
Yankee Girl	106	Common Sue	111
Glamor	114	Pope Joan	111

Fourth race—The Jerome Handicap; for 3-year-olds; $2,000 added. One and five-sixteenths miles.

Name.	Wht.	Name.	Wht.
Nealon	123	Ironsides	107
Running Water	122	Minnie Adams	113
Good Luck	114	Nifo	108

Fifth race—For 2-year-olds; $900 added. Six and a half furlongs.

Name.	Wht.	Name.	Wht.
Merrill	107	Baringo	107
Altuda	112	Arimo	110
Main Chance	110	Philander	104
Beaufort	107	Nancy	112
Oraculum	110	Stray	115

Sixth race—For 3-year-olds and upward; $1,000 added. One and five-eighth miles:

Name.	Wht.	Name.	Wht.
Martin Doyle	111	Cederstrome	98
Penrhyn	95	Jungle Imp	101
Cal'ia King	95	Bad News	116

ENGLISH RIFLEMEN CALL ON PRESIDENT.

Washington, October 6 — President Roosevelt to-day received the members of the rifle team and a regimental delegation of the Queen's Westminster Volunteers, headed by Sir Howard Vincent, aide-de-camp to King Edward, who are on a visit to the United States.

After being introduced to the President, Sir Howard presented to him in behalf of the executive committee of the Interparliamentary Conference, a magnificent silver medal bearing a likeness of King Edward and inscribed with the words "King Edward, the peacemaker."

NO PLAYERS TO BE SOLD—PRESIDENT EBBETS.

THE season of 1906 has been the most prosperous in both major and minor leagues during my twenty-five years experience. The Brooklyn Club is particularly grateful for the support accorded by the Brooklyn public. Starting off an apparent hopeless tail-ender, the players, by steady, persistent work, finally landed in the coveted position at the top of the second division.

We promise the Brooklyn public to keep our team intact. No player will be sold for a cash consideration; it will be our aim to strengthen the team, not to weaken it. We know the Brooklyn public appreciates good ball, and this we will use our best endeavors to give them in 1907.

CHARLES H. EBBETS.

YANKEES VICTORS IN THE FINAL GAME

Wind Up the Season by Defeating Bostons After a Hot Finish.

WHITE SOX LOSE AT LAST.

Beaten by the Clevelands, at Chicago. Browns Take Two From Detroit.

The Record.

Club.	W.	L.	PC.	Club.	W.	L.	PC.
Chicago	92	57	.619	St. Louis	76	72	.513
New York	89	61	.593	Detroit	70	78	.473
Cleveland	88	63	.582	Washington	55	95	.367
Phil'delphia	78	67	.538	Boston	49	104	.320

Results Yesterday.

New York, 5; Boston, 4.
St. Louis, 7; Detroit, 3.
St. Louis, 4; Detroit, 2.
Cleveland, 5; Chicago, 3.
Philadelphia vs. Washington—Rain.

Boston, October 6—New York closed the American League season here this afternoon by defeating Boston 5 to 4 in a rather poor game. Long hitting by both sides was the feature. Score:

New York.	r.	h.	po.	a.	e.	Boston.	r.	h.	po.	a.	e.
McGuire,1b	1	2	8	0	1	Hoey,lf	0	1	1	0	1
Conroy,3b	1	0	0	0	0	C'db'rne,ss	1	0	3	6	1
Yeager,ss	2	2	3	4	1	Stahl,cf	1	2	3	0	0
Chase,2b	1	2	3	3	0	Grimshaw1b	0	0	10	1	1
Laporte,lf	0	0	6	0	0	Wagner,2b	0	0	2	4	1
Hoffman,cf	0	2	0	0	0	Morgan,3b	0	0	1	3	1
Orth,rf	0	2	2	0	0	Freeman,rf	1	1	1	1	0
Thomas,c	0	0	5	1	0	Peterson,c	1	2	6	2	0
Hughes,p	0	1	0	0	0	Swormst'd,p	0	0	0	2	0
Totals	5	11	27	8	2	Totals	4	6	27	19	5

Score by Innings.

	1	2	3	4	5	6	7	8	9	
New York	1	0	4	0	0	0	0	0	0	—5
Boston	0	1	0	0	1	0	0	2	0	—4

Two base hits, McGuire, Yeager. Three base hits, Yeager and Hughes. Home runs, Stahl and Peterson. Stolen bases, Stahl, Freeman. First base on balls: off Hughes, 1. Struck out: by Hughes, 5; by Swormstead, 4. Double play, Wagner, Chadbourne and Grimshaw. Hit by pitched ball, Yeager. Time, 1:11. Umpire, Connolly.

CLEVELAND, 5; CHICAGO, 3.

Chicago, October 6—Cleveland bade farewell to Chicago to-day, defeating the new champions 5 to 3. Heavy hitting and sensational fielding were the features. Score:

Chicago. Name.	r.	1b.	p.o.	a.	e.	Cleveland. Name.	r.	1b.	p.o.	a.	e.
Hahn, r.f.	2	1	0	0	0	Caffyn, l.f.	2	0	1	0	0
O'Neil, c.f.	0	0	4	0	1	Stovall, 3b.	0	3	0	1	0
Rohe, 3b.	0	1	3	3	0	Turner, ss.	1	2	3	2	0
Don'hue,1b	0	3	9	0	0	Hess, c.f.	1	3	2	0	0
Do'erty,l.f.	0	2	1	0	0	Con'ton,r.f.	1	2	4	0	0
Towne, c.	0	0	2	0	0	Flick, 2b.	0	0	5	2	0
Roth, c.	0	3	2	1	0	Rossman,1b	0	1	8	0	0
Dundon,2b.	1	2	3	3	2	Clark, c.	0	0	1	1	0
Quillin, ss	0	0	3	3	2	Bemis, c.	0	1	3	0	1
Owen, p.	0	0	0	6	0	Rhoades,p.	0	0	0	3	0
Altrock, p	0	1	0	1	0	Total	5	12	27	9	1
Total	3	13	27	17	5						

Score by Innings.

	1	2	3	4	5	6	7	8	9	
Chicago	1	0	0	1	0	0	1	0	0	—3
Cleveland	3	0	0	1	1	0	0	0	0	—5

Two base hits—Stovall, Hess, 2; Donahue. Sacrifice hits—Owen, Rhoades. Stolen bases—Congalton, Caffyn, Altrock, Quillin. Struck out—By Owen, 1; by Rhoades, 2; by Altrock, 1. Bases on balls—Off Rhoades, 6. Double play—Owen, Rohe and Donohue. Hits—Off Owen, 8 in five innings; off Altrock, 4 in four innings. Left on bases—Chicago, 16; Cleveland, 10. Passed ball—Bemis. Time of game—1 hour and 35 minutes. Umpire—O'Loughlin.

BROWNS TWICE WINNERS.

St. Louis, Mo., October 6—St. Louis won both games from Detroit to-day. Jacobsen pitched excellent ball in the last game and held the visitors to four hits. Scores:

FIRST GAME.

St. Louis. Name.	r.	1b.	p.o.	a.	e.	Detroit. Name.	r.	1b.	p.o.	a.	e.
Niles, rf	0	2	1	1	0	McIntyre, lf	0	0	2	0	0
Jones, 1b.	1	1	7	1	0	Lindsay, 1b	1	2	12	0	0
Stone, lf.	1	1	5	0	0	Crawf'd, rf	1	0	1	0	0
H'phill, cf	0	0	3	0	0	Cobb, cf	0	1	1	0	2
Wallace,ss	1	2	3	1	1	Schaefer, 2b	0	0	3	5	1
O'Brien, 3b	1	0	2	0	0	O'Leary, ss.	0	1	3	4	0
R'k'nfi'd,2b	1	1	2	2	0	Schmidt, c	0	2	1	3	0
O'Conn'r, c	1	1	4	3	0	Keitling, 3b	0	1	1	2	0
Powell, p	1	2	0	3	1	Siever, p.	1	3	0	1	0
Total	7	10	27	11	2	Total	3	10	24	15	3

Score by innings:

	1	2	3	4	5	6	7	8	9	
St. Louis	0	0	1	4	0	0	2	0	..	—7
Detroit	0	0	0	0	0	0	0	0	3	—3

Two base hits—Wallace, 2; Lindsay. Three base hits—Powell, Schmidt. Home run—Stone. Sacrifice hit—O'Brien. Double play—O'Leary, Schaefer and Lindsay. Hit by pitched ball—By Siever, 1. Bases on balls—Off Powell, 1; off Siever, 1. Struck out—By Powell, 2; by Siever, 1. Left on bases—St. Louis, 4; Detroit, 7. Time of game—1 hour and 23 minutes. Umpire—Evans.

SECOND GAME.

St. Louis. Name.	r.	1b.	p.o.	a.	e.	Detroit. Name.	r.	1b.	p.o.	a.	e.
Niles, rf.	1	1	6	0	0	McIntyre,lf	0	0	1	1	0
Jones, 1b.	1	0	8	1	1	Lindsay, 1b	0	0	5	1	1
Stone, lf.	0	2	1	1	0	Crawf'd,rf.	0	2	0	0	0
Hemp'll,cf.	0	1	0	0	0	Cobb, cf	1	0	1	0	0
Wallace,ss	1	0	5	4	2	Schaefer,2b	1	1	2	1	0
O'Brien,3b.	1	1	1	3	0	O'Leary,ss.	0	0	1	1	0
Roc'n,ld,2b	0	2	1	4	1	Payne, c	0	1	12	3	1
Spencer, c.	0	1	5	3	0	Hoitling, 3b	0	0	2	0	0
Jacob'n,p	0	0	0	2	0	Willotts,p	0	0	0	3	0
Total	4	8	27	18	4	Total	2	4	24	10	

Score by Innings.

	1	2	3	4	5	6	7	8	
St. Louis	1	0	0	1	0	0	1	1	—4
Detroit	0	2	0	0	0	0	0	0	—2

Two base hit—Stone. Sacrifice hits—Jones, Stone, Rockenfield, 2; Lindsay, Schaefer. Passed ball—Payne. Stolen bases—O'Brien, Hemphill. Wild pitch—Willets. Bases on balls—Off Jacobsen, 2; off Willets, 4. Struck out—By Jacobsen, 3; by Willetts, 7. Left on bases—St. Louis, 9; Detroit, 3. Umpire—Evans. Time of game—1 hour and 45 minutes.

RAIN AT PHILADELPHIA.

Philadelphia, October 6—The two games between the Philadelphia and Washington American League teams which were to have been played here to-day were declared off on account of rain. As to-day closes the season in the East the games cannot be played off.

WOMEN GOLFERS OF EAST BEAT SISTERS OF WEST

Score 13 to 3 on Braeburn Links at West Newton, Mass.

TWO VERY EXCITING MATCHES

Miss Warren, of Chicago, Triumphs Over Mrs. Barlow After Playing Twenty-one Holes.

(Special to the Eagle.)

West Newton, Mass., October 6—The Woman's Eastern Golfing Association team this afternoon beat the Western Association team by 13 to 3 over the Brae Burn links. There were two exceptionally exciting matches. Mrs. R. H. Barlow, the Philadelphia crack, was defeated after a 21-hole struggle by Miss Marion Warren, of Chicago, while Mrs. S. F. Lefferts, of New York, was beaten on the nineteenth hole by Mrs. A. T. H. Brower, of Chicago, president of the Western Women's Association. Mrs. Lefferts laid he ropponent no less than three stymies.

One of the funniest things on record happened when Miss Frances Griscom, of Philadelphia, after finishing as she supposed, found she had one more hole to play and had to go back, find her opponent in the gathering darkness and supply the deficiency. The best medal scores reported were those of Miss Georgianna Bishop, ex-national champion, and Miss Fanny Osgood, Eastern Association champion, both 91.

It was something of a sop to the Westerners that they won both of the close matches, Mrs. Barlow was finally beaten by getting into deep woods from which, in extricating herself, she plunged into a bunker. Miss Warren got into a bunker on the same hole on her tee shot, but was well out and made the cup in 5 to her partner's 7.

Gallery Ignored Rain.

It rained smartly at intervals most of the afternoon, but that did not prevent a gallery of about 300 persons from following most of the play. Miss Bishop's card, which was two strokes over the women's local record, was:

Out	6	6	5	5	4	5	4	5	6	46	
In	7	6	4	5	4	5	5	4	5	45	91

Generally speaking, there was little choice between the two teams on the long game, but the Easterners were better around the cups. Miss Pauline Mackay, presen champion, had a medal card of 93, as did Mrs. G. Roope, of Chicago. About all the Westerners hail from Chicago, although some of them are also identified with St. Louis, Denver and Wisconsin clubs. The Eastern players were from New York, Philadelphia and Boston.

The Score.

Western Team. Name.	Points	Eastern Team. Name.	Points
Mrs. C. L. Dering	0	Miss Pauline Mackay	1
Miss Frances Everett	0	Miss Fanny Osgood	1
Miss Marion Warren	1	Mrs. R. H. Barloe	0
Miss Myra Helmer	0	Miss G. Bishop	1
Mrs. Franc Anderson	0	Miss Mary Adams	1
Mrs. G. Roope	1	Mrs. Caleb Fox	0
Miss Grace Semple	0	Miss Harriet Curtis	1
Mrs. E. Whitcomb	0	Miss Frances Griscom	1
Miss Isabelle Smith	0	Miss Louisa Wells	1
Mrs. A. T. H. Brower	1	Mrs. S. F. Lefferts	0
Mrs. H. A. Beidler	0	Mrs. M. D. Patterson	1
Mrs. E. C. Berriman	0	Miss M. Phelps	1
Miss Whitney	0	Mrs. E. F. Sanford	1
Miss Ruth Steele	0	Miss Julia Mix	1
Miss J. Sherman	0	Miss Eliza. Hurry	1
Mrs. Best	0	Miss E. Lockwood	1
Total	3	Total	13

The match play results were:

Mack, 3 up and 2 to go; Osgood, 2 up and 1 to go; Bishop, 5 up and 4 to go; Adams, 4 up and 3 to go; Rope, 5 up and 4 to go; Curtis, 6 up and 4 to go; Griscom, 4 up and 2 to go; Wells, 2 up and 1 to go; Warren, 1 up and 21 holes; Brower, 1 up and 19 holes; Patterson, 6 up and 5 to go; Margery Phelps, 8 up and 7 to go; Sanford, 2 up and 1 to go; Mix, 8 up and 6 to go; Hurry, 4 up and 3 to go; Lockwood, 5 up and 3 to go. The scoring system was simply a point for each winner.

LOUISVILLE RESULTS.

Louisville, Ky., October 6—Dolindo defeated a good field in the Louisville handicap to-day, Alma Dufour being only a nose back. Charlie Eastman and Creolin were winning favorites. Track fast; weather cool. Summaries:

First race—Selling, six furlongs. Potter, 109 (Gannon), 15 to 1, won; Orderly, 102 (J. Lee), 4 to 1, second; Matador, 115 (Nicol), 3 to 1, third. Time, 1:15. Petit Duc, Ara, Sorrel Top, Revolt, Miss Anxious, French Nun and Mayor Johnson ran.

Second race—Five and a half furlongs. Charlie Eastman, 108 (Mountain), 1 to 3, won; Invincible, 106 (Boland), 30 to 1, second; Marvel P., 98 (Swain), 4 to 1, third. Time, 1:07 3-5. Federal, Suzanne Rocamera, St. Tammany, S. A. B. and Great ran.

Third race—Steeplechase, short course. Creolin, 138 (Archibald), 5 to 2, won; Dr. Keith, 125 (Yourrell), 20 to 1, second; Madoc, 130 (Pierce), 12 to 1, third. Time, 3:01 2-5. Battle Creek ran. Ben Shaw, Weberfields, Gus Lanka, H. M. P., New Amsterdam, Evander ran out, Maverick fell.

Fourth race—Louisville handicap, mile and a sixteenth. Dolinda, 97 (J. Hunter), 15 to 1, won; Alma Dufeur, 116 (Nicol), 3 to 2, second, Charlatan, 108 (Moreland), 4 to 1, third. Time, 1:47 2-5. Miss Doyle and El Otres ran.

Fifth race—Five and a half furlongs. Western, 105 (Mountain), 4 to 1, won; Miss Officious, 97 (Keyes), 6 to 1, second; Timothy Wen, 108 (Dealy), 10 to 1, third. Time, 1:07 3-5. Le Veita, Elsie Janie, Charlie Mitchell, Cackler, Sister Huffman, Lens, Sam Cook and Montalban ran.

Sixth race—Selling; mile. Highbear, 104 (Mountain), 7 to 1, won; Colonel Bartlett, 94 (Sheridan), 11 to 5, second; Bitter Hand, 98 (Perkins), 6 to 1, third. Time, 1:41 3-5. Topsy Robinson, Chanida, Rubaiyat, Postman, Ingolthrift, Daring and Lazell ran.

LOUSIVILLE ENTRIES.

Louisville, Ky., October 6—Entries for Monday:

First Race—Five and a half furlongs, selling. Isabel Aimree, 97; Quarto, 100; Wee Kitty, Earl of Leicester, Nedra, Tybarnia, 102; Merry Patriot, 105; Two Bells, Lady Vimoni, Laura E., La Thorpe, 107; Von Vivant, Quagga, 110; Tanager, My Bessie, 112; San Ardo, 115.

Second Race—One mile, selling. Inflammable, Pacifico, Fleetwood, Gitfain, Joe Lesser, Falkiand, Sand Bath, Alcor, Helgerson, Auditor, Fotrero Grande, 103; Kleinwood, Whippoorwill, Prince Magnet, Elliott, St. George, jr., 112.

Third Race—Seven furlongs. Rolla, Azora, Marvel P., Oberon, Usury, 94; Telegrapher, 97; Alsono, 99; Rector, 104; Princess Orna, 105; Goldmate, 107; Pretension, Miss Dovie, 109.

Fourth Race—Short course, steeplechase. Battlecreek, Raveno, 125; Wilkey, 128; Gus Lanka, Weberfields, Ben Shaw, 132; St. Volma, 134; Pontotoc, 135; Lady Jocelyn, 136; John Dillon, Creolin, 138; Subador, 152.

Fifth Race—Six furlongs, selling. Temple, Moccasin Maid, Bitter Brown, 98; Sonny, 102; Airship, Sheen, The Pet, Frank Bill, 103; Gauze, 104; Ruby Right, Capitano, Florentine, Locket, 106; Miss Leeds, Exalted, 107; Orderly, 108.

Sixth Race—Mile and a sixteenth, selling. Larone, Dudley, 95; Eular, 96; Mae Lynch, Noel, 97; Speedmaker, 98; Belden, Daring, 102; Juba, Inspector Girl, 104; Missouri Lad, 105; Athena, 111; Chamblee, 112; Barkelmore, 112; Uncle Henry, 115.

FIRST DIVISION IN 1907—MANAGER DONOVAN.

IT HAS been the pleasantest and best season that I ever spent in baseball. From the very beginning until the end we have all worked together harmoniously, magnates and players alike, and the outcome has been extremely gratifying. It took time to get the team going. Every new machine has to get a trial of a month or so before it works easily, and the parts in unison. So it was with the Superbas. We started off altogether new. The players were not accustomed to one another. The machinery had to be well oiled. All was harmony, however, and when everything was running right, we showed the other fellows something. This was especially true of the last month or so, when we played as good ball as anybody else.

I feel highly confident regarding next season. We will come back ready to jump in and make a pace that while it may not land Brooklyn the pennant, will at least place us in the first division, barring accidents, of course. The outlook appears very bright to me.

P. J. DONOVAN

BASEBALL SEASON ENDS WITH REAL LOVE FEAST

President Ebbets Holds Impromptu Reception for Superba Players.

SIGNS MANY FOR NEXT YEAR.

Grand Stand Finish Gratified All Hands—Game With Phillies Off.

The Record.

Club.	W.	L.	PC.	Club.	W.	L.	PC.
Chicago	116	36	.763	Brooklyn	66	86	.434
New York	96	55	.636	Cincinnati	64	86	.427
Pittsburg	92	60	.605	St. Louis	52	98	.347
Phil'delphia	71	82	.485	Boston	48	102	.320

Results Yesterday.

At all cities, rain.

The lid was put on the local baseball season yesterday under very adverse conditions. It was a gloomy wind-up so far as the weather was concerned, but the spirits of the players were high and the attitude of the officials conspicuous for its cordiality. Instead of disappearing one by one as was the case last year, when the Superbas finished last, there was a jolly gathering in the office of President Ebbets, in which the head of the club, Treasurer Medicus, Manager Donovan, Secretary Watson, the players and reporters took part. It was a saengerfest in which all vied with one another in singing the praises of the Superbas and the partings were as cordial as one would expect at the breaking up of a family re-union. And such, according to all hands, had been the attitude of managers and players alike throughout the season.

For had not the team finished fifth in the race when at the beginning of the season a big majority of the baseball experts had picked them to repeat their performance of last year? Nosing out the Cincinnati Reds at the wire, so to speak, was the biggest feather in the cap of the locals, and they made much of the success of Patsy Donovan in taking up Ned Hanlon's burden and carrying it to a triumphant finish at the top of the first division. Patsy was congratulated on all sides and the wish was generally expressed that he experience even greater success next season.

Final Game Declared Off.

As soon as the final game of the season was declared off on account of rain the players gathered in the office and had a farewell fanning fest. All were there except Casey, Lumley and Maloney, who had departed for home the night before. President Ebbets took advantage of the unexpected invasion by signing those who were willing. To all appearances not one demurred. As a consequence the team will start off next spring apparently intact and in excellent spirits.

As each player departed to catch a train for home there was a cordial handshake all around and sincere expressions of hope for a winter's good luck. Several of the men remain here until next Sunday in order to play exhibition games with the Brightons and Visitations. They play the Brightons to-day at Brighton Oval, the team being made up of Eason, Scanlon, Jordan, Batch, Reardon, O'Neil, Jacklitsch and two others.

In the meantime an interesting event occurred in the secretary's office, where the ticket sellers and gatemen gathered around George Watson and presented him with a box of cigars as an evidence of the cordial feeling that had existed throughout the season among the lesser lights of the baseball campaign. Nothing like it has occurred in years.

Eason on the Stage.

Mal Eason will leave shortly to join the "Political Boss" company, a theatrical show in which he expects to secure an interest. Hummel, Ritter, Pastorius and Alperman took the same train for the West, the catcher going to Lancaster, Pa., and the others to Pittsburg. McCarthy left for Chicago, where he will attend the world's championship series.

Treasurer Medicus and Manager Donovan also will go to the Windy City for the series. Medicus picks the Cubs to win in five games, while Donovan thinks the series will go the limit of seven games. President Ebbets will remain in town cutting coupons.

The closing game at the Polo Grounds between the New Yorks and Bostons was also postponed. In fact, no games at all were played on the National League circuit, the Pittsburg-Chicago game being prevented by rain, while the Cincinnatis and St. Louis Cardinals were not scheduled.

HOPPE'S BRILLIANT PLAY.

Young Billiard Champion Averages 42 6-7 in Winning Game From Professor McLaughlin.

That Willie Hoppe is getting in splendid condition for his match with Jacob Schaefer in the Madison Square Garden Concert Hall, on October 17, was demonstrated last night in a match with Professor Edward McLaughlin at the Knickerbocker Billiard Academy.

Hoppe, playing at the 18-inch balk line style, one shot in balk, ran the necessary 300 points in seven innings, with an average of 42 6-7. His performance completely outclassed the veteran McLaughlin, who averaged 9 5-6 for six innings at the 18-inch balkline style, two shots in balk.

The young champion clicked off 35 points at the start, following it with 3, which was the poorest inning of the evening. Settling down to his real form, he displayed his remarkable skill by running off 121, 105 and 19, closing the match with 19. McLaughlin was unable to keep pace with his opponent, making 2 in each of his first two innings. After runs of 5 and 1, he gathered 42, his high run, and wound up with 7. The scores:

McLaughlin: 2, 2, 5, 1, 42, 7. Total, 59. Average, 9 5-6.

Hoppe: 35, 3, 121, 105, 17, 19. Total, 300. Average, 42 6-7.

NEW BOSTON TERRIER CLUB.

Thirty-nine Hub breeders recently met to form a new Boston terrier club, there being more or less opposition to the old organization.

SIGNING PLAYERS FOR NEXT SEASON—TREAS. MEDICUS.

We have experienced a very successful season, financially and otherwise. As far as the pennant race is concerned, I picked Chicago as a big factor at the beginning of the season. With the new material on the Brooklyn team, and the fact that most of the men had never played together before, I did not figure the Superbas to finish fifth. Consequently, the result has been very gratifying.

This is the best year the Brooklyn Club has experienced in several seasons, a fact that is made all the more evident when it is known that we have signed most of our players already, instead of waiting until next March. We consider it better to sign players personally than to do so by mail, which always causes delay. It is a new departure, which we have never attempted before.

I figure that we will be in the fighting class next season with the team we have and the new material we are developing. The team, as a whole, looks good. Everything has been harmonious between the management and the players, and there is no reason why it should not continue so. HENRY MEDICUS.

MORDECAI BROWN.

(Courtesy of the St. Louis Sporting News.)

IN all around playing ability, the Chicago Clubs, winners of the National League pennant, appear to outclass the Chicago White Sox, American League champions, for the world's championship series which begins next Tuesday, at the Windy City. In every department the National Leaguers seem to show up stronger, a fact that was exemplified last fall, when the Cubs easily won the post season series for the championship of Chicago. The Cubs are 40 per cent. stronger now than they were then, while the White Sox have not gained in proportion, despite the fact that they won the pennant this year and finished second last season.

The White Sox bank a great deal on their pitchers; but, man for man, the Cub twirling staff seems to be far away the superior. There is no pitcher in the White Sox array that stands out so prominently this season as Mordecai Brown, who won twenty-six out of thirty-two games, an average of .813. And this despite the fact that three of the fingers on his pitching hand are maimed.

Brown was born at Nyesville, Ind., 26 years ago. While a child, he playfully put his hand in a hay-cutter, and when he withdrew it the index finger was amputated below the second joint, the second finger was broken and the thumb and small finger frightfully crushed. In fielding, he grips the ball with his one good finger (third) his maimed thumb and shattered middle finger. Notwithstanding this handicap, he excelled his playmates at baseball, and in 1901 pitched for the Terre Haute team, of the I.-I.-I. League. He was with Omaha in 1902, and became a St. Louis Cardinal in 1903, being traded at the close of that season with Catcher Jack O'Neill, for Pitcher Jack Taylor. His team mates have always considered him a high class pitcher, but he never obtained pre-eminence until this year. He responds to the nickname "Miner," and is known in baseball as "Three-finger Brown." Like Mathewson, of the New Yorks, last fall, Manager Chance banks a great deal on Brown in the coming series.

HOWARD GEE WON CUP.

Defeated H. C. Richard for First 16 Trophy at Richmond County Country Club.

(Special to the Eagle.)

New Dorp, S. I., October 6—Two Princeton men, Harold C. Richard and Howard J. Gee, fought it out in the finals for the cup for the first sixteen at the Richmond County Country Club to-day. The golfers had to contend with a strong wind and frequent showers in the morning round. Richard was 1 up at the tenth hole, but losing six and halving two in the last eight holes, finished 5 down. In the afternoon Richard so far recovered as to be 1 up at the ninth, but took six for the "double ditches," making the score all even. Gee won the next hole and subsequently the cup by 1 up.

Richard won the medal for best gross scores with 87—84—171, and A. C. Paterson won the handicap with a card of 91—31—172, 18—154. Summaries:

First set, H. J. Gee beat H. C. Richard, 1 up.

Second set, P. W. Kendall beat N. S. Walker, 7 and 6.

Third set, R. Agar beat W. I. Seaman, 5 and 4.

Cup for beaten 8s: First set, L. H. Thomas beat B. T. Allen, 5 and 4; second set, B. F. Welton beat S. S. Smith, 12 and 11; third set, C. D. Simons, jr., beat H. D. Tucker.

Club handicap scores follow:

	Gross.	Hdp.	Net.
C. A. Blyth	89	7	82
C. W. Pierson	93	8	85
S. L. Davis	91	5	86
J. E. Faber	93	7	86
H. L. Williams	87	0	87
B. F. Welton	94	7	87
L. H. Thomas	89	1	88
H. Imbrie	93	5	88
A. Paterson	91	3	88
C. D. Simons, jr	99	10	89

BOUGHT RIPPLE HECTOR.

Fancier Weir, of Manhattan, has recently bought in England the bloodhound Ripple Hector. The dog has been highly successful on the English bench, adding many laurels to the collection of his late owner, Handley Spicer.

SOCKER AT BAY RIDGE.

Crescents Start Well at Association Football and Tie Freebooters.

Moved to initiate themselves into the mysteries of the association style of football, otherwise known as socker, a few brave spirits belonging to the Crescent Athletic Club, headed by L. J. Doyle, manager of the lacrosse team, and W. D. Andrews, the socker captain, indulged in an exhibition game with the Freebooters, of Bay Side, at the Crescent grounds yesterday afternoon. Owing to the disagreeable weather, there was a comparatively small gallery on hand, but, although few understood the finer points of the game, such was the open nature of the play that the onlookers voted it good outdoor sport.

Most of the players being practically strangers to this sort of football, it was not surprising that there were some bad breaks that caused much merriment. On the other hand, they exercised wonderful self-control in mastering the well nigh overpowering temptation to handle the ball. The fouls claimed for this infraction of the rules were for the most part conspicuous by their absence.

Awkwardness in controling the ball for dribbling purposes was due to inexperience, but this will soon wear off. The Crescents had good ideas of team work, and passing, which will greatly improve with steady practice. The Freebooters were composed largely of men hitherto accustomed to English Rugby, and they had but slight advantage in this respect over their opponents. As a matter of fact, honors in scoring were exactly even, each side tallying one goal.

During the first half the Freebooters did most of the pressing, but occasionally the Crescents got away from them. The latter, in fact, were the first to beat the opposing goalkeeper through a sharp shot from a scrimmage by Captain Andrews. Near the close of the first half Catty, captain of the Freebooters, squared the account.

There was no scoring in the second half on either side. Offside play deprived both teams of extra goals, and this, indeed, was the most glaring fault of which the players were guilty.

Andrews and Burney were conspicuous for their consistently good work on behalf of the Crescents. Ross and Cook, the halfbacks, excelled for the Freebooters.

Next Saturday the Crescents will play the Boys Club, of Manhattan, at Bay Ridge, and the week following they will entertain the crack eleven of the Belmont Cricket Club, of Philadelphia. Yesterday's lineup:

Crescent A. C. (1).	Position.	Freebooters (1).
Doyle	Goal	Taylor
Johnston	Right back	——
Bass	Left back	Heyman
Bonnar	Right halfback	Ross
Andrews	Left halfback	Cook
McIntyre	Outside right	Littlejohn
D. Kennedy	Inside right	Mutter
——	Center forward	Catty
Salter	Inside left	——
Burney	Outside left	Power

Goals—Andrews, Crescent; Catty, Freebooters. Time—Halves of 35 minutes.

PROFESSIONAL AND AMATEUR

THE EAGLE'S SPORTING SECTION

OTHER SPORTS ON NEXT PAGE

★★ NEW YORK CITY, MONDAY, OCTOBER 16, 1911.

DROP WORLD'S SERIES TO SAVE THE NATIONAL GAME?

LITTLE DANGER OF NEW YORK BEING LOST TO BASEBALL

More Likely That World's Series Will Be Abandoned as a Result of Ticket Scandal.

BY THOMAS S. RICE.

PRESIDENT Ban B. Johnson of the American League is quoted as saying that if collusion between the officials of the New York Baseball Club and the speculators who got hold of so many tickets for the world's series game between New York and the Philadelphia Athletics last Saturday can be proved, he would favor the expulsion of the New York Club from organized ball.

This sounds well, but, as a matter of fact, Mr. Johnson knows he is not going to oust the New York club. He was a member of the National Commission when that body agreed to a set of rules this year by which the officials of the two clubs, instead of representatives of the commission, were given charge of the sale of seats. To date we have not noted in the public press any violent protest from Mr. Johnson about his having been overruled when that change was made. He must have acquiesced, and must have had his reason for so doing.

So Much Smoke, Some Fire.

The general belief, and it is mighty general, and is not going to be dispelled, is that the ticket speculators of New York did get hold of seats in advance. Too many stories are told of people who saw world's series pasteboards in the hands of outsiders on Monday and Tuesday, when none were supposed to be delivered before Thursday. One man who knows the ways that are dark and tricks that are vain asserts that a certain party in New York had eight hundreds seats of consecutive numbers, or, in the altogether, as it were. It would have been an impossibility for a solitary soul to have acquired so many in a bunch if he had gotten them by the mail applications or by having men posted in line. Indeed, he is said to have had them before the sale opened. Another story is that twenty tickets were boastfully displayed by an employee of a sporting goods house last Monday, which would indicate that the lad had a large pull.

Where Politics Comes In.

Where politics comes in on a baseball deal is easily explained. Suppose you have such a large plant as the Polo Grounds and need hundreds of extra policemen off and on in the baseball season. Suppose there is a commission which has in hand the matter of opening streets. Suppose your plant cuts off the extension of one or more streets, as most baseball parks do. Having supposed that much, suppose that you were informed by politicians higher up that if you did not furnish tickets to be sold by speculators your million-dollar plant would be ruined by having a street cut through it, or, if that were too obviously absurd, that you would have police protection in its true sense withdrawn, and the crooks would be given the tip to go as far as they liked in the matter of robbing your patrons. The place would soon either be ruined by the street or the patronage killed off by the crooks. Is it not so? Aye, verily!

How It Is Worked.

When the American League first attempted to break into New York the threat was openly made that any man who dared to start an opposition to the New York National League Club would find a street being cut through his grounds before he could get started. That threat was based upon the influence of the owners of the National League club with Tammany Hall. It so happened that Frank Farrell became a baseball crank in a large degree, all of a sudden, and offered to back the efforts of the new organization to obtain a footing in Gotham. He had a pull that offset the one of his National League rivals, and no street has been run through the ballyard on the hilltop.

Another Holdup.

Followers of baseball will remember that a year or so ago a very prominent owner of a very powerful major league club was shaken down for so many tickets for politicians and their friends that he became aweary and finally refused to go further. The result was an ordinance introduced by one of the "city fathers" to charge him a license fee of $250 for every game played on his grounds. Can you conceive of any more typical holdup than that? We do not think you can. This particular magnate beat the grafters in some manner, but the case just goes to prove the effect that local politics can have on baseball.

Will Series Be Abolished?

The National Commission is threatening to investigate the ticket troubles in New York, and, in the same breath, declaring that there is no scandal. If the commission does find the publicly printed charges against New York Club have been proved it will do nothing except blow hot air, for the club is essential to the National League. But there will be another recourse. It will be perfectly possible to have the whole thing settled by calling off the series next year. This may seem a radical move, but the great American game for the whole United States should not be imperiled because of scandals arising from a particular series. Sensible ball players, who know that the existence of the sport depends upon its reputation for honesty, will agree with this view after second thought. It is better to be cut out of the profits of a series than to kill the profession to which you have devoted the best years of your life. At least, that is the way it appears to ordinary observers. Professional groaners will despair of the republic because of the slavery in baseball, but actual human beings will see the force of the argument.

Athletics Not All In Yet.

It is well to bear in mind that because the Athletics were beaten on Saturday, or may be beaten again today, they are not, therefore, necessarily and inevitably doomed to defeat in the series. It takes four out of seven to win the world's pennant. Neither team did anything on Saturday that was out of the ordinary. The Athletics failed to show much brilliancy or fancy teamwork, because the plays offered were so simple that any good ball club could have done the same. That statement applies to the Giants. It was a peculiar contest for such an important occasion. Collins made a rank error, but it is well known that unexpected heroes are developed in these big games, while the stars seldom deliver the goods of which they have shown themselves capable by their work in a long season. Ball players upon the field are prone to err, and likewise to errors. The miscue of Collins on Saturday in first booting a ball and then throwing badly to the plate, thereby allowing New York to score the first run of the two it made, does not imply that Collins is not a big leaguer. We have seen our little brother do the same when he was substitute on the freshman team at the agricultural college. He would have been allowed to play almost a whole game one day, too—that little brother—if the captain had not been jealous of his superior prowess in dancing.

PLAYERS WHO SHOULD STAR IN SECOND WORLD'S SERIES CLASH

Thomas. Merkle. Marquard. Coombs. Fletcher.

Collins. Meyers. Oldring. Doyle. Barry.

PUTTS AND DRIVES

Glen Cove, L. I., October 16—A field of seventeen golfers started in the Saturday event today at the Nassau Country Club, an eighteen hole medal play, handicap, in the Doubleday trophy point competition. Five cards were returned, the lowest being those of C. D. Smithers and Andrew Fletcher, who tied with net 73. The scores were:

	Gr.	H'p.	Net
C. D. Smithers	96	23	73
A. Fletcher	96	23	73
H. F. Whitney	78	3	75
W. L. Hicks	77	2	75
W. F. Richards	93	11	82

The first round of match play in the golf championship has been completed, as well as part of the second round. In the matches of the first round T. D. Hooper defeated A. W. Rossiter, 2 up and 1 to play; W. A. Engeman beat B. N. Busch, 4 up and 3 to go; F. C. Jennings defeated H. K. Hudson, 5 and 4; H. F. Whitney defeated Howard Maxwell, jr., 2 up; Guy Robinson beat A. E. Jones, 5 and 3; C. A. Dunning won from Herbert L. Pratt, 2 up and 1 to go; W. L. Hicks won from B. H. Tobey by default, and F. N. Doubleday beat W. F. Richards, 3 up and 2 to play. In the second round Hooper beat Engeman, 2 up and 1 to play; Whitney defeated Jennings, 4 and 3, and Hicks won from Doubleday, 5 and 4. There is still one match to be played in the second round—that between Guy Robinson and C. A. Dunning, the latter of whom returned the lowest score, that of gross 74, in the championship qualifying rounds.

Season Nearly Over.

The golf season of 1911 has drawn pretty much to a close, and although there are still two invitation tournaments in the metropolitan district, one might almost say that the season was finished. The Atlantic City Country Club and the Lakewood Club have arranged for competitions, and these will be the last. In the meantime most of the golfers have given up strenuous practice, and are contenting themselves with an occasional round of the links.

Was Twice Disappointed.

Miss Lillian Hyde was disappointed twice during the national women's tourney at Baltusrol last week. In the first place the defeat of Miss Dorothy Campbell by Miss Margaret Curtis prevented a match between the brilliant young Brooklyn player and the international champion, and Miss Curtis further added to the sorrow of the occasion, as far as local sympathizers are concerned, at least, by beating Miss Hyde rather decisively in the final match.

Carnegie Sends Clubs to Taft.

It is reported that Andrew Carnegie has sent from Skibo Castle a bag of golf clubs to President Taft, accompanied by the usual letter and the usual spelling, to the effect that "the Laird" hopes that plenty of golf will keep Mr. Taft in good condition to continue his work toward the furtherance of universal peace. Speaking of universal peace and golf, it has probably not been Mr. Carnegie's luck to see a match between two players who are quite convinced that each knows nothing about golf but is a "fool for luck."

A New Resolution.

At the conference of London captains, it was announced that the following resolution had been adopted at Sunbridge Park: "Golf balls found on any part of the club grounds are the property of the club, and the balls are to be marked with the initials of the player and a distinctive mark of the club." Nearly all golfers nowadays stamp their initials on their golf balls. They find that distinctive marks of the club are too readily imprinted on the balls in the course of play.

Many Golfers at Forest Park.

Autumn weather has brought quite a rush of golfers to the public course at Forest Park, and the greens are in decidedly better condition than at the early part of the season. There are many newcomers to the links taking advantage of the cooler weather, and the authorities are of the opinion that the locker space, already large, will have to have an addition before next spring.

Preserving the "Open Spaces."

A writer in Fry's Magazine directs attention to one of the many and far-reaching benefits of golf which are apt to be overlooked. "It is not more than a few years ago, in fact, that the game of golf in the South was the object of suspicion and agitation. The cry was that the golfer was appropriating the commons and open spaces to the exclusion of the multitude. Today the boot is on the other leg, for it is precisely the golfer who is preserving for the public, at all events the health value, of any number of open spaces."

Many Acres of New Lungs.

The writer reckons that golf courses have given to London new lungs extending over about 7,000 acres within the fifteen-mile radius. This area represents more than three new Richmond Parks or seventy new St. James Parks. He concludes that so far from encroaching on the freedom of the general public the golfer's sport is providing for the whole community incalculable benefits in the preservation of many large areas as permanent open spaces.

Invitation Event at Atlantic City.

The fall event at the Atlantic City Country Club will be an invitation tournament open to U. S. G. A. members, instead of an open affair. The playing dates are November 2, 3 and 4.

MOTOR RACES POSTPONED.

The motorcycle race meet that was scheduled to be held at the Guttenberg Motor Racing Association, was postponed until next Sunday at 2 p.m., because of the threatening weather. More than three thousand motorcycle enthusiasts were present when the postponement was announced, but to relieve their disappointment, no admission fee was charged, and they were entertained by exhibitions by Ralph De Palma in a Mercer car, and by J. U. Constant, the 10-mile amateur champion, and J. J. Cox, on their motorcycles.

PENN STATE WIN ENDED CORNELL'S AMBITIOUS PLAN

Ithaca Students Cannot Leave Premier Athletic Institution of the Country—Few Surprises in Saturday's Games.

There was little or no surprise at the result of the football games on Saturday. Even the defeat of Cornell was expected, as it was well known that several of the Ithaca players were on the sick list and that Pennsylvania State had an excellent team. However, the defeat is a bitter pill for the Ithaca students to swallow, particularly this year, as the upstaters had hoped for a world-beating eleven. Cornell practically has swept the intercollegiate world in every other sport this year, and with a championship football team the Ithaca institution could have claimed to be the premier athletic institution of the country.

Although included in what formerly was known as the "big five," Cornell never has had a really great football eleven. There have been years when the New York State boys have had teams that have been past the average, but it is hard to remember when the Ithaca college rightly ranked with Yale, Harvard or even Princeton or Pennsylvania. What is the matter with football at Cornell is a question. It generally is intimated that there is too much faculty interference. In fact, one head coach at Ithaca resigned on account of the opposition that he encountered from certain members of the faculty.

Princeton sprung the only real surprise by rolling up a 3—0 score on Colgate. Naturally the Tigers were expected to win, but after the game that Colgate played against Cornell and the exhibition that Princeton made against Lehigh, no one expected such a one-sided game. The result of the match has boomed the stock of the Tigers, which had taken a decided slump after the Lehigh game. However, the coaches in Jungletown know that the Tigers are far from being a first class team.

Yale Now Can Get Down to Work for West Point.

Yale's score of 33—0, against Virginia Poly means absolutely nothing as the Southern aggregation is a rank outsider in the football world and one that cannot be used in comparing Yale with any other team. The eleven from the South proved to be a very easy proposition and one that did little or no damage to the Eli players. As a result, the entire squad can get down to hard work for the game against West Point next Saturday, the first important contest of the year.

The score of 22—0 was just about the figure expected in the Pennsylvania-Villanova battle. There have been years when the latter aggregation have put up a snappy football game on Franklin Field, but throughout the present season, the "main liners" have not been playing classy football. Dartmouth's 6—0 score against Holy Cross left the impression that the Hanover lads have got to do some mighty fast stepping to be in a position to defeat Harvard this year.

Conference Colleges Passed Out of Preliminary Football Stages.

In the West, the "big eight" conference football passed out of the preliminary period and left the stage set for contests of championship importance for the remainder of the season. Chicago's 11 to 3 victory over Purdue and Illinois' 9 to 0 score against St. Louis University closed the early period in both camps, and put the next important conference question up to next Saturday's Chicago-Illinois contest in Chicago, when one of the 1911 contenders must drop out of the race.

All gridiron signs point to a fast game between Chicago and Illinois. The fact that Illinois defeated Chicago last year and has the shade in veteran material and individual stars gives encouragement to the state university team, but Chicago's fast games against Indiana and Purdue assured the Urbana eleven of worthy opposition. That this week's practice will tell the tale is the word from the two camps.

YOUNG MEN'S C. C. ARE EASY WINNERS.

At Hawthorn's Oval yesterday the Young Men's Catholic Club, champions of Greater New York, easily defeated the Acorn A. A. by the score of 17 to 0. Acorns were powerless before the great backfield of the Catholic boys, while the heavy purple and white's attack ripped the Acorn line to pieces. Next Sunday, Warlow A. C. of Whitestone plays the Y. M. C. C. Score:

Y. M. C. C. (17).	Position.	Acorn A. A. (0).
Corcoran	Left end	Locke
Hall	Left tackle	Syler
White	Left guard	Miller
Hettrick	Center	W. Nelson
O'Connor	Right guard	Gillen
Stergerwald	Right tackle	Ballaw
Ruckert	Right end	Weismiller
Burchill	Quarterback	McNally
Bisson	Left halfback	Nelson
Stallings (capt.)	Right halfback	Tamm
Coffey	Fullback	Spoerle (capt.)

Substitutes—Walsh for Corcoran, Planding for White, Goldfarb for Locke, Carlen for Ballaw. Touchdowns—Bisson, Stallings, Ruckert. Goals from touchdown—Bisson, 2. Referee—Mr. Halstead, Boys High. Umpire—Ed. Goate. Time of halves—15 and 10 minutes.

ROCHESTERS BEATEN.

The New Lots A. C. defeated the Rochesters yesterday by a score of 12 to 4.

DOC SCANLON LOST.

Doc Scanlon pitched for the Long Island Athletics against the Louisvilles yesterday and lost out in the ninth by 3 to 1.

CHAMPION JERSEYITES DOWN BROOKLYN AT SOCKER

Encountering the strong Jersey A. C., champions of the National League, the Brooklyn Football Club went down to defeat yesterday by the close score of 2 goals to 1. The game was played at Marquette Oval. Although the Brooklyns lost they made a splendid showing. Milnes was easily the star of the game, while he was helped greatly by Gillette and Williams. Smith and Stuart worked hard for the winners. The lineup:

Brooklyn.	Position.	Jersey A. C.
Halliwell	Goal	Leibert
Milne	Right back	Bosner
Williams	Left back	Rosenbauer
Gillette	Right half	Smith
Watts	Center half	Stuart
Matthews	Left half	E. Zehnbauer
Van der Weghe	Outside right	Best
McConville	Inside right	Waldron
Adamson	Center	A. Zehnbauer
McNeil	Inside left	Kettles
McKenzie	Outside left	Barber

At Blatt's Oval the Clan McDonalds disposed of the Yonkers F. C. by the score of 3 goals to 1. Two minutes after play started Porter tallied for the Yonkers eleven, but before the half ended Bell evened up matters.

The second half was decidedly in favor of the McDonalds. Peters received the ball on a pass from Thompson, thereby putting the McDonalds in the lead. Working the ball through from a scrimmage, Thompson was credited with the final goal of the day.

The Critchleys, champions of the New York State League, received an unexpected setback at the hands of the Camerons, at Van Cortlandt Park, by the score of 3 goals to 2. The first half, however, was the Critchleys, as they scored the only count in this period. L. Agar caught the Cameron goalkeeper out of his territory and easily tallied a goal.

Soon after the second half opened Welsh scored the tying goal for the Camerons. Through an infraction of the rules, in which a Critchley player fouled C. Pickford in the penalty area, the Camerons were granted a free kick. Welsh took it and converted it into a score. Seven minutes before the call of time E. Pickford added another point.

In a first section league game the McKenzies scored a victory over the Clan McDuff by the score of 2 goals to 1, at Harlem Oval, yesterday afternoon. A. B. Dunn scored two goals for the winners, while D. Ross was credited with the single point made by the losers. All the scoring was done in the first half.

OARSMEN READY TO QUIT; HOUSES ARE BEING CLOSED

What little rowing there might have been yesterday was put out by the weather, and the rain of the afternoon proved disappointing to several of the scullers who went to the boathouses prepared to pull a bit before the houses are closed. In several of the clubs there was quite a crowd to be in at the "death," but in only one or two was there even a shell pulled from the float.

At the Sheepshead Bay Boat Club, one of the Rogan boys was out for a short time and so was a double shell, but those were the only two craft immersed at all. At the Varuna Boat Club there was quite a crowd of members, but none of them cared to go out. It is likely that the house will be closed this week as far as rowing is concerned. The Nautilus Boat Club was quite active, with several gigs and doubles in impromptu races. The club will close this week.

Things were quiet at Flushing Bay. There were several members on hand at all of the houses excepting the Flushing Boat Club, which has been officially closed for the winter. The members congregated early in some of the clubrooms, hoping to pull an oar for the last time, but the rain put a damper on the enthusiasm, and except in one house there was no move made to row. Even then it was a case of canoeing rather than sculling.

At the Seawanhaka Boat Club it was decided to have a big beefsteak dinner to close the season and the date was set for November 4. It is expected that the affair will prove one of the most successful in the history of the club.

There will not be a single open house along Gravesend Bay after this week, although several of the clubs will keep their doors unlocked to allow for social gatherings. The floats will all be missing after this week and the boats housed permanently for the winter.

All of the members are interested in bowling, and theater parties are to occupy the time of several clubs.

At the Flushing Boat Club it was decided to go into active racing again next year, and Captain George Kelly announced that his men would be heard from with a vengeance, as the Seawanhakas and Wahnetahs have made the same announcements this fall, the rowing season in that section appears to be in for a big boom.

Fourteen clubs are ready to start the bowling tourney of the Long Island Navy tomorrow night, and several of them, prepared to drop out this year, have decided to again roll because the Brooklyn Eagle has put up a handsome trophy. The tourney will start at the Universal alleys tomorrow night, and all of the clubs will be strongly represented.

The Clifton Boat Club sent over a centipede yesterday to the Brooklyn Rowing Club for a call, and found that the float, which had loosened during a recent storm, had been already towed to Coney Island. The Cliftons will close house this week.

EXPERT RAISES OBJECTION IN BIG GOLF CONTROVERSY

Garden Smith Wants Royal and Ancient Club to Explain Statement Made to Silas Strawn of the U. S. G. A.

Since the visit to England of Silas H. Strawn, president of the United States Golf Association, and his memorable interview with the Royal and Ancient Club lawmakers at St. Andrews, there has been considerable agitation in the old country as a result. Garden G. Smith, the editor of a British golfing magazine, expresses "surprise" at the negotiations, which, it will be remembered, concluded by a promise that the R. and A. would send all new rules to the U. S. G. A., but only after Captain Burn had stated definitely that the Royal and Ancient Club legislated for itself alone.

In the interests of the uniformity of golf, Mr. Smith thinks that the Royal and Ancient Club should at once explain its attitude. He states that the St. Andrews body is and always has been the governing body for the rules of golf, and desires to know when the club began to limit itself to its own territory alone.

It is an interesting article, and should bring forth a reply from Captain Burn. This is what Mr. Smith had to say, in part:

A Remarkable Report.

"Circumstances have intervened to prevent us from commenting earlier on the report made to his Executive by S. H. Strawn, president of the United States Golf Association, on his recent interview with Captain Burn, chairman of the Rules of Golf Committee. But that report is so remarkable in itself and appears to have attracted so little attention that we may be excused, even at this late date, for referring to it. It is to be presumed that the object Mr. Strawn had in view was to prevent any recurrence of the unfortunate incidents which followed the St. Andrews prohibition of the Schenectady putter, when, it will be remembered, the United States Golf Association for the first time refused to accept the ruling of St. Andrews. We understand from those who had the pleasure of meeting him, that Mr. Strawn, by his attractive personality and evident desire to maintain a uniformity of rule and practice between American and British golf, created a most favorable impression, but we have regretfully to confess that a careful persual of his report does not afford any indication that the situation has been materially improved by his visit.

"In the first place it is a little difficult to understand what Mr. Strawn hoped to achieve, for, according to his report, he began by saying to Captain Burn that "we"—i.e., the Executive of the U. S. G. A.—"assumed that in the future as in the past the Royal and Ancient Club would not attempt to dictate or promulgate rules effective anywhere except at St. Andrew's.

"What Right Has the U. S. G. A. to Interfere?" He Asks.

"Having first stated his association's belief that the rules of golf as published by the Royal and Ancient Golf Club are only effective, and are only intended to be effective, at St. Andrews, Mr. Strawn then proceeded to ask that these same laws, framed for playing golf only at St. Andrews, should be submitted to the U. S. G. A. for their suggestion and opinions before they became law! The question that suggests itself is, what are the qualifications of the U. S. G. A. for teaching the people of St. Andrews how to play golf on St. Andrews links?

"We have no fault to find with the first part of Captain Burn's statement. It is courteous, dignified and non-committal. But when the chairman of the rules committee concludes by saying that 'the R. and A. expected in the future, as in the past, to enact rules and make interpretations applicable to the playing of golf only at St. Andrews,' we can only say that he completely misstates obvious and well-known facts, and insults the universal loyalty paid to the rule of the Royal and Ancient Club.

"It is true that for many years clubs made shifts with the rules of golf as played at St. Andrews, with such local modifications and additions as were necessary. But about 1890, when the game being to spread all over the world, an agitation began amongst other influential clubs to have the St. Andrews code revised in accordance with more modern ideas and rendered more applicable to courses where the conditions differed in many respects from those at St. Andrews. As the result of this agitation the Royal and Ancient Club formed the rules of golf committee, whose special function was to deal with proposals relating to, or questions of interpretation arising on, the rules and customs of golf. If it be said that the rules of golf committee was appointed to make rules and give interpretations for the Royal and Ancient Club alone, and not for the purpose of meeting the demand for a code of more universal application, it is only necessary to point out that in its first revision of the rules the committee removed all the local St. Andrews rules from the code where they had always stood; and if it be said that by appointing the rules committee the Royal and Ancient Club did not accept the position of ruling authority, it may be asked why the rules of golf committee was constituted the final authority on all questions of interpretation of the rules, and why, if the desire of the Royal and Ancient Club was not to secure the uniformity of golfing practice by the world-wide application and acceptance of its rules, has the rules of golf committee in successive revisions, invited and utilized outside opinion on alterations and additions to the code?

Desires Repudiation of Statement.

"If the view that the primary duty of the rules committee was to revise and frame rules applicable in the first instance, and more particularly, to St Andrews links, was regarded by the chairman and other members of the rule committee in 1900 to be 'altogether too parochial,' how comes it that in 1911 we find the new chairman of the committee, speaking, we presume, with the sanction of the other members, making the much stronger statement that the Royal and Ancient Club 'enact rules and make interpretations applicable to the playing of the game only at St. Andrews.' It would be interesting to know at what date and by whose authority the functions of the rules of golf committee and the scope of its rules were limited? We respectfully submit that this is a matter demanding the immediate attention of the Royal and Ancient Club. It is only by the prompt repudiation of the statement that the Royal and Ancient Club legislates for itself alone that the uniformity of golfing law, the continuity of golf tradition and the club's authority can be maintained. There can be no loyalty to a ruling body which neither desires nor exercises authority."

Cubs Give Giants a Final Kick, 4 to 0—Yankees Hand Sox a Surprise

RICHIE FLOPS LEADERS; CUBS LAND ON TESREAU

"Lurid Lew" Blanks McGraw's Men in Great Battle Before 25,000 at West Side.

ONE ROUND SETTLES GAME

Chance's Men Bunch Wallops in Sixth—Win Narrows Advantage of New Yorkers.

BY IRVING VAUGHAN.

"Lurid Lew" Richie continues as one of McGraw's undesirables. Chance's famed specialty man humbled, crumbled and otherwise humiliated the giants again yesterday at the West Side arena, the cubs copping the play-off of a postponed engagement by 4 to 0 and sending the leaders on their way to pirate town with a gloomy outlook and only four and one-half games between pursuer and pursued.

The battle that meant so much to the pennant chances of either team was practically settled in a single inning, but the exciting situations were so well scattered through the nine rounds that there was never a slack moment for the 25,000 spectators who crowded the stands and slopped over onto the confines of the playing field. The round that spelled defeat for the giants was the sixth, when four drives bunched on "Big Jeff" Tesreau, the king pin "spitter" from the Ozarks, sent three cub runs over the pan.

TESREAU STRONG AT START.

Tesreau was picked by McGraw as the logical man to trim the rising young West Siders. He took place over such a battle-scarred veteran as the peerless Christy Mathewson, but while he couldn't hold down the enemy it is even doubtful if "Big Six" himself could have accomplished more. Tesreau made the mistake of pitching himself out in the early rounds, working for as many strike-outs as there were to be had, and after the fourth round he showed symptoms of weakening.

In the early innings it looked as though McGraw had played the hunch right when he nominated this young twirler. In four sessions he was a bit wild, dishing up three passes, but always avoiding any treacherous spots. The cubs didn't get a hit off him until the start of the third, and he immediately disposed of the next three batters on strike-outs. The first man up in the fourth went the same way, then a pass and a single hinted at possible trouble, another two-bagger in the fifth pried him still further away from his effectiveness, and finally the lid blew open with a bound in the sixth. Then it was all over.

HEALTHY CLOUTS WIN.

There was nothing fluky about this stand, in which three men scampered across the plate with more than enough to win. It was the direct result of some healthy clouting, in which Tom Leach drove in two men after a single and double by Tinker and Zimmerman respectively. These two runs disconcerted the giant defense and some loose play gave the cubs further chances to score, but Tesreau tightened and only for his cutting loose with a wild pitch the third runner would never have crossed the pan.

After this there was no doubt as to the eventual outcome. Richie was mowing down the giant sluggers with monotonous regularity and McGraw soon concluded that there was no sign of a let-up. In the eighth he worked the old hunch that a pinch-hitter might possibly start something. He didn't reckon with the fact that Tesreau in two trips to the pan had driven out two singles. McCormick was sent forth to do the honors, but it did no good, so with Tesreau departed "Old Doc" Crandall was shoved into the limelight. He handled the cubs in the eighth and on Doyle's error and Archer's wallop the fourth run of the day was registered.

SCATTERED HITS OFF RICHIE.

Richie from the very start was so content with his job that he never faltered. He issued only one free ticket, this to the first man up, and was hit for seven safeties, two less than the cubs were able to bounce from the delivery of the giant twirlers. In only one inning did the visiting leaders get more than one wallop in a row, this being the fifth, when some great fielding held the giants away from the plate. Up to this inning there were runners on the bags in each the first, second and third, but nary a one of the lucky gents could find going beyond the first station.

The turn of affairs in the fifth gave the crowd a chill, as up to then Tesreau was pitching at his best and had been nicked only twice. Zimmerman was the particular stumbling block for the giants in this stand, and only his able assistance prevented Richie from undergoing some rough handling. For one thing he made a great play far behind third and retired Meyers at first for the second out. Then the hits followed, Fletcher and "Big Jeff" doing the unloading act.

What Zim pulled off with these two individuals racing the bags will long be remembered in the minds of McGraw and some of his athletes. Snodgrass poled a terrific drive directly at Zim, the ball sailing on a dead line about two feet above the third sacker's bean. Zim was wide awake for this occasion however, and with a daring leap into the air speared the flying pill with his gloved hand. It was a great play with an element of luck attached, but it cut off a run and possibly more, so the crowd cheered and whistled accordingly in honor of the Bronx Dutchman.

CUBS' SUPPORT IS STRONG.

Zimmerman was not alone in the limelight although it was his fielding and hitting that did as much as anything in the cub victory. Evers and Tinker put up their usually consistent game around the keystone sack, and among other things they divided between them the disposal of the only two giant base runners who dared to tempt the bullet-wing of Jim Archer.

While the above gents stood out in the defense because of some usually spectacular work, it was the cubs' machine as a whole that proved such a stumbler to the giants. Richie of course had the fellows from the big town guessing at every turn. When they did land against one it meant nothing, for Lew would tighten and it seemed impossible for the giants to get the ball beyond the infield unless it went via the aerial route to some keen-eyed outer-gardener.

The giants didn't work with the ease of the cub machine. They were plainly nervous over the thought that a pennant is slipping from them. It was especially noticeable in the sixth. Two of the three hits that counted runs might possibly have been knocked down had they not been uncorked at just such a critical spot. They were hard wallops nevertheless.

HERZOG BECOMES RATTLED.

After the runs scored the defense was worse than before, Herzog being especially bad in not knowing what to do with two successive bunts that came in his direction. One went for a hit, while the other failed to force a man at second when there was a world of time for the trick. The fact that Snodgrass was sent to first in place of the injured Merkle was of no help to the cubs.

After the cubs jumped to the lead the giants suddenly lost their fighting spirit, the same as happened in the games last week, when Richie beat them twice in three days. Even their offense weakened under the handicap, and with a big margin to nurse Richie just plowed through to the end, finishing without a single hostile getting beyond second base. Only two even got that far—Fletcher, who singled in the fifth, and Becker, who doubled in the sixth only to succumb to a double play in which Zim gave the crowd another thrill by tagging the runner as he raced up the line.

GAMES IN WESTERN LEAGUE

Healy Holds Des Moines to Four Hits, Denver Winning, 4 to 1.

DES MOINES, Aug. 21.—Healy held Des Moines to four scattered hits, while Denver bunched hits off Rogge in the eighth and won. Score:

										R.	H.	E.
Des Moines	0	0	0	0	0	0	0	1	0	1	4	1
Denver	0	0	0	0	0	0	0	3	1	4	12	0

Batteries—Rogge and McGraw, Healy and Block.

TOPEKA, Kan., Aug. 21.—St. Joseph hit Brandom hard in the sixth, scored four runs and defeated Topeka. Score:

										R.	H.	E.
Topeka	1	0	0	0	0	0	0	2	0	3	10	4
St. Joseph	0	0	0	0	0	4	0	0	0	4	7	0

Batteries—Brandom, Cochrehem and Smith; Crutcher and Gossett.

LINCOLN, Neb., Aug. 21.—Wolverton held Sioux City to four hits and Lincoln shut out the visitors. Score:

										R.	H.	E.
Lincoln	0	0	1	1	3	0	0	0	*	5	9	1
Sioux City	0	0	0	0	0	0	0	0	0	0	4	4

Batteries—Wolverton and Stratton, McAdams and Chapman.

OMAHA, Aug. 21.—Omaha had little difficulty shutting out Wichita, Robinson holding the visitors to five hits. Score:

										R.	H.	E.
Omaha	3	0	0	1	1	0	1	0	*	6	12	0
Wichita	0	0	0	0	0	0	0	0	0	0	5	1

Batteries—Robinson and Johnson, Scott and Clemons.

WHAT A DIFFERENCE A FEW YEARS MAKE

Copyright, 1912, by Henry Barrett Chamberlin.

Speeding the Slipping Giants Along

First Inning.

NEW YORK—Snodgrass walked and was caught stealing, Archer to Tinker. Doyle popped to Saier. Becker slammed a single to center. Leach camped under Murray's tall fly. NO RUNS, ONE HIT, NO ERRORS.

CHICAGO—Sheckard was out on a bounder to Snodgrass. Schulte fanned. Devore went to the edge of the crowd for Tinker's fly in far left. NO RUNS, NO HITS, NO ERRORS.

Second Inning.

NEW YORK—Devore was safe at first on Zimmerman's wide throw. Herzog flew to Leach. Zimmerman retired Meyers. Schulte raced in and grabbed Tesreau's low liner. NO RUNS, NO HITS, ONE ERROR.

CHICAGO—Zimmerman lifted an easy pop to Doyle. Leach walked and was out stealing, Meyers to Fletcher. Saier also drew a pass. Evers hit a long fly to Murray. NO RUNS, NO HITS, NO ERRORS.

Third Inning.

NEW YORK—Tesreau singled over short. Snodgrass popped to Leach. Doyle forced Tesreau, Evers to Tinker. Doyle died stealing, Archer to Evers. NO RUNS, ONE HIT, NO ERRORS.

CHICAGO—Archer lined a single to center. Richie struck out trying to bunt. Sheckard was called out on strikes. Schulte missed three swings. NO RUNS, ONE HIT, NO ERRORS.

Fourth Inning.

NEW YORK—Leach took Becker's fly. Richie nailed Murray's drive and threw him out at first. Devore bounded to Evers and was out at first. NO RUNS, NO HITS, NO ERRORS.

CHICAGO—Tinker struck out. Zimmerman walked. Leach dropped a single over first, Zim halting at second. Becker raced to the crowd in right center for Saier's long fly and Zimmerman made third after the catch. Herzog grabbed Evers' roller and retired him at first. NO RUNS, ONE HIT, NO ERRORS.

Fifth Inning.

NEW YORK—Herzog lifted to Evers. Zimmerman went back on the grass for Meyers' smash and threw him out at first by a brilliant peg. Fletcher singled between Zimmerman and Tinker. Tesreau pushed a hit into right. Snodgrass lined toward third and Zimmerman speared the ball with one hand. NO RUNS, TWO HITS, NO ERRORS.

CHICAGO—Archer was thrown out by Doyle. Doyle pulled a circus play by going back on the grass behind second and throwing Richie out at first. Sheckard doubled into the crowd in right. Schulte lofted to Murray. NO RUNS, ONE HIT, NO ERRORS.

Sixth Inning.

NEW YORK—Evers fumbled Doyle's grounder, but recovered in time to catch his man at first. Becker slammed a double into the right field crowd. Murray rammed a terrific bounder at Zimmerman, who swung at Becker as he ran out of the line, and then threw to Saier in time to double Murray at first. NO RUNS, ONE HIT, NO ERRORS.

CHICAGO—Tinker drove a liner over second for one bag. Zimmerman doubled through Herzog, Tinker going to third. Leach pushed a single past Tesreau, Tinker and Zimmerman scoring. Saier bunted, but Leach was safe at second on Herzog's late throw. Evers bunted toward third and beat the throw to first, filling the corners. Archer fouled to Herzog. Richie fouled to Meyers back of the plate. Tesreau's wild pitch got through Meyers and Leach slid home head first. Sheckard was out on a bounder to Snodgrass. THREE RUNS, FOUR HITS, NO ERRORS.

Seventh Inning.

NEW YORK—Tinker raced over into short left for Devore's fly. Herzog singled to left. Schulte rushed in to get Meyers' short fly. Fletcher forced Herzog, Evers to Tinker. NO RUNS, ONE HIT, NO ERRORS.

CHICAGO—Schulte doubled down the first base line. Tinker tried to sacrifice and bunted on the fly into Tesreau's hands. Zimmerman struck out. Leach flew to center. NO RUNS, ONE HIT, NO ERRORS.

Eighth Inning.

NEW YORK—McCormick batted for Tesreau and flew to Sheckard. Tinker went back into Sheckard's territory for Snodgrass' fly. Doyle singled past Evers. Becker forced Doyle, Evers to Tinker. NO RUNS, ONE HIT, NO ERRORS.

CHICAGO—Crandall pitching for New York. Saier was safe at first when Doyle let a ground ball get through him. Evers went out, Crandall to Snodgrass, Saier taking second. Archer singled to short, the ball bounding over Fletcher's head and Saier scoring. Richie popped to Doyle. Sheckard was thrown out by Herzog. ONE RUN, ONE HIT, ONE ERROR.

Ninth Inning.

NEW YORK—Murray flew to Leach. Devore hit to Tinker and was safe at first when Saier dropped the throw. Herzog hit to Tinker, whose heave to Evers forced Devore at second and Herzog was doubled at first, Evers to Saier. NO RUNS, NO HITS, ONE ERROR.

Figures on Cubs-Giants Clash

CHICAGO.

	ab.	r.	h.	tb.	bb.	sh.	sb.	po.	a.	e.
Schulte, lf	4	0	1	2	0	0	0	2	0	0
Sheckard, rf	5	0	1	2	0	0	0	1	0	0
Tinker, ss	4	1	1	1	0	0	0	6	1	0
Zimmerman, 3b	3	1	1	2	1	0	0	2	3	1
Leach, cf	3	1	2	2	1	0	0	5	0	0
Saier, 1b	3	1	0	0	1	0	0	8	0	1
Evers, 2b	4	0	1	1	0	0	0	3	6	0
Archer, c	4	0	2	2	0	0	0	0	2	0
Richie, p	4	0	0	0	0	0	0	0	1	0
Total	34	4	9	12	3	0	0	27	13	2

NEW YORK.

	ab.	r.	h.	tb.	bb.	sh.	sb.	po.	a.	e.
Snodgrass, 1b	3	0	0	0	1	0	0	7	0	0
Doyle, 2b	4	0	1	1	0	0	0	2	2	1
Becker, cf	4	0	2	3	0	0	0	2	0	0
Murray, rf	4	0	0	0	0	0	0	2	0	0
Devore, lf	4	0	0	0	0	0	0	1	0	0
Herzog, 3b	4	0	1	1	0	0	0	1	2	0
Meyers, c	3	0	0	0	0	0	0	7	1	0
Fletcher, ss	3	0	1	1	0	0	0	1	0	0
Tesreau, p	2	0	2	2	0	0	0	1	0	0
Crandall, p	0	0	0	0	0	0	0	0	1	0
*McCormick	1	0	0	0	0	0	0	0	0	0
Total	32	0	7	8	1	0	0	24	6	1

*Batted for Tesreau in eighth.

Chicago ....0[0] 0[0] 0[1] 0[1] 0[1] 3[4] 0[1] 1[1] * —4[9]
New York...0[1] 0[0] 0[1] 0[0] 0[2] 0[1] 0[1] 0[1] 0[0]—0[7]

Two-base hits—Sheckard, Becker, Zimmerman, Schulte. Struck out—By Tesreau, 7 (Schulte, 2; Richie, Sheckard, Tinker, Zimmerman). Bases on balls—Off Tesreau, 3. Double plays—Zimmerman to Saier, Tinker to Evers to Saier. Hits—Off Tesreau, 8 in seven innings. Wild pitch—Tesreau. Left on bases—Chicago, 9; New York, 6. Time—1:50. Umpires—Klem and Orth.

Notes of Cubs-Giants Game

Boston here this afternoon. Big scores will probably be the order for the next three days.

The giants have their hands full for the next three days. They have five games to settle with the pirates and if the latter are able to take three of the set, where will be the cubs' stand? Depend on Clark's men to put up a fight.

Sheckard was robbed of a homer in the fifth. He slammed the ball into the bleacher under the right field sign but the umps allowed him only two bases. It was plain to see that the ball went over the fence, as some of the fans stood up and reached for it. The cubs claimed the homer but there was nothing doing, and then to show that the umpires were wrong a "cop" recovered the ball and threw it out onto the field.

Tinker tried to sacrifice in the seventh and popped into Tesreau's mitt. Snodgrass wanted to make the catch also and crashed into the pitcher just as his fingers closed on the ball. Both fell to the ground with the force of the collision but were not injured.

Richie beat the giants in three full games in exactly a week. In after years this record will stand out among other "freaks" of the pastime.

With Herzog on first in the seventh Meyers lifted a short fly to Schulte. Herzog took a long lead off the bag and Schulte had a dandy chance for a double, but he preferred to hang on to the ball after a hard run to make the catch.

SWEENEY'S BATTING BEATS REDS

Boston Slugger Puts Braves in Lead and Cincinnati Drops Series.

CINCINNATI, Aug. 21.—Boston won the final game of the series here today, 7 to 4, making it three out of four from Cincinnati. Hard and timely hitting by Sweeney won the game for Boston. His double in the third inning with the bases full put the visitors in the lead and caused the retirement of Pitcher Frill. Humphries pitched good ball until the ninth, when four singles netted three runs. In the seventh Cincinnati tied the score when with two out Kirke threw wild to first, three runs scoring before Houser could return the ball. Score:

Boston.	R.	H.	P.	A.	E.	Cincin.	R.	H.	P.	A.	E.
Campb'll, cf	1	1	2	0	0	Bescher, lf	1	1	2	0	0
Kirke, 3b	1	1	1	4	1	Marsans, cf	0	0	0	1	0
Sweeney, 2b	1	2	1	3	0	H'litz'l, 1b	0	0	11	1	1
Jackson, lf	0	1	5	1	0	Mitchell, rf	0	1	1	0	0
Titus, rf	0	0	1	0	0	Phelan, 3b	0	1	2	2	1
Houser, 1b	1	1	5	0	0	Grant, ss	0	0	3	3	0
Bridwell, ss	1	0	2	0	2	Egan, 2b	1	2	2	5	0
Kling, c	2	3	10	2	1	McLean, c	1	1	5	2	1
Perdue, p	0	0	0	2	1	Frill, p	0	0	0	2	0
						Hump'es, p	1	1	1	1	1
Total	7	9	27	12	5	Total	4	7	27	17	4

Boston ....0 0 4 0 0 0 0 3—7
Cincinnati ....0 0 1 0 0 0 3 0 0—4

Two-base hits—Phelan, Sweeney, McLean. Hits—Off Frill, 4 in three innings; off Humphries, 5 in six innings. Sacrifice hits—Titus, Perdue, Marsans. Sacrifice fly—Jackson. Stolen bases—Mitchell, Sweeney, Egan (2). Double plays—Jackson to Kling; Grant to Egan to Hoblitzell. First base on balls—Off Perdue, 1; off Humphries, 2. Hit by pitched ball—By Frill (Campbell, Kirke). Struck out—By Perdue, 5; by Humphries, 4. Wild pitch—Humphries. Time—2:00. Umpire—Eason.

PIRATES ARE BLANKED

Rucker Holds Pittsburgh to Four Hits and Dodgers Take 1-to-0 Victory.

ONE MAN REACHES THIRD

PITTSBURGH, Aug. 21.—Wagner, who knocked a three-bagger in the ninth inning, was the only Pittsburgh player today to reach third base. Brooklyn won, 1 to 0. Rucker allowed the home team only four hits. Score:

Pittsb'gh.	R.	H.	P.	A.	E.	Brooklyn.	R.	H.	P.	A.	E.
Mensor, cf	0	0	6	0	0	Moran, cf	0	0	1	0	0
Carey, lf	0	2	1	1	0	Northen, rf	0	1	2	0	0
Byrne, 3b	0	0	1	0	0	Smith, 3b	0	0	0	2	0
Wagner, ss	0	1	3	0	0	Daubert, 1b	0	0	14	1	0
Miller, 1b	0	0	10	0	0	Wheat, lf	0	1	1	0	0
Wilson, rf	0	0	1	0	0	Cutshaw, 2b	0	1	4	6	0
Butler, 2b	0	1	1	5	0	Fisher, ss	1	2	1	5	0
Gibson, c	0	0	4	3	0	Erwin, c	0	1	4	0	0
Adams, p	0	0	0	2	0	Rucker, p	0	2	0	4	0
Warner, p	0	0	0	2	1						
Total	0	4	27	13	1	Total	1	8	27	18	0

Pittsburgh ....0 0 0 0 0 0 0 0 0—0
Brooklyn ....0 0 1 0 0 0 0 0 0—1

Two-base hit—Northen. Three-base hit—Wagner. Sacrifice hit—Rucker. Sacrifice fly—Moran. Double play—Smith to Cutshaw to Daubert. Bases on balls—Off Adams, 1; off Warner, 1; off Rucker, 3. Struck out—By Adams, 1; by Rucker, 4. Hits—Off Adams, 8 in eight innings; off Warner, none in one inning. Time—1:20. Umpires—Johnstone and Emslie.

GAMES IN "THREE I" LEAGUE

Bloomington and Davenport Break Even in a Bargain Attraction.

BLOOMINGTON, Ill., Aug. 21.—Bloomington dropped the first due to ragged support of Syfert. Nelson was hit hard in the second and Bloomington won easily. Bluejacket, late of Pekin, pitched effectively and, with proper support, would have registered a shutout. Score of first game:

Bloom'n.	R.	H.	P.	A.	E.	Dav'port.	R.	H.	P.	A.	E.
Bay, lf	0	0	1	0	0	Ohland, rf	1	0	0	0	0
Kohl, 2b	0	1	2	4	1	Godwin, lf	0	1	2	0	0
Hartford, ss	0	0	2	1	1	Koepping, 2b	1	1	4	4	0
Cuthbert, rf	1	0	1	0	0	Bromwich, 3b	0	1	2	0	0
Vinson, 1b	1	1	11	0	0	Clemens, cf	1	0	4	0	0
Riley, cf	1	2	5	0	0	Wilson, 1b	2	2	9	0	0
Erloff, c	0	2	3	1	1	Wilkes, ss	1	1	2	3	0
Burgwald, 3b	0	0	0	2	0	Coleman, c	0	1	4	0	0
Syfert, p	0	1	2	3	0	Hendrix, p	0	0	0	3	0
Total	8	7	27	11	3	Total	6	7	27	10	0

Bloomington ....0 0 0 0 0 0 2 0 1—3
Davenport ....0 0 0 6 0 0 4 0 2—6

Two-base hits—Kohl, Koepping, Wilson, Godwin. Struck out—By Syfert, 2; by Hendrix, 3. Bases on balls—Off Syfert, 2; off Hendrix, 3. Double play—Wilkes (unassisted). Stolen base—Clemens. Time—1:35. Umpire—Eddinger.

Second game:

										R.	H.	E.
Bloomington	1	0	3	0	0	0	1	2	*	7	14	1
Davenport	0	0	0	0	0	0	3	0	0	3	6	2

Batteries—Bluejacket and Erloff; Nelson and Coleman.

QUINCY, Ill., Aug. 21.—Elzi, a recruit, was wild and all of Springfield's hits counted. Schroeder was effective with men on bases after the first inning. Score:

Quincy.	R.	H.	P.	A.	E.	Spring'd.	R.	H.	P.	A.	E.
Kerwin, lf	2	3	1	1	0	Lofton, cf	1	1	3	0	0
Hill, ss	1	2	3	4	0	Vogel, 2b	2	2	3	1	0
Kahl, 3b	1	1	2	3	0	Kommers, rf	1	1	0	1	0
Mertens, rf	0	1	0	0	0	Smith, 1b	1	4	10	1	0
Rock'f'd, 2b	0	1	4	1	0	Collins, lf	1	1	1	0	0
Myers, 1b	0	1	10	0	0	Jacobs, c	0	0	7	0	0
Donahue, cf	0	0	2	0	1	Price, ss	0	0	1	2	0
Gard, c	0	0	4	3	1	Baird, 3b	1	1	1	3	0
Elzi, p	0	0	1	2	0	Schroeder, p	2	2	1	3	1
Total	4	9	27	14	2	Total	9	12	27	11	1

Springfield ....1 0 1 2 0 1 1 0 3—9
Quincy ....3 0 0 0 0 0 0 0 1—4

Stolen bases—Lofton, Kerwin. Sacrifice hits—Rockenfield (2), Baird, Kommers (2), Jacobs. Two-base hits—Rockenfield, Vogel, Collins. Three-base hit—Kommers. Bases on balls—Off Elzi, 5; off Schroeder, 4. Struck out—By Elzi, 3; by Schroeder, 7. Wild pitch—Elzi. Hit by pitcher—By Elzi, 2. Time—2:00. Umpires—Bannon and Cusack.

DANVILLE, Ill., Aug. 21.—Danville divided honors with Dubuque today, losing the first game, 4 to 2, and winning the second, 3 to 0. Score of first game:

										R.	H.	E.
Dubuque	0	3	0	0	0	0	0	1	0	4	6	3
Danville	0	0	0	1	0	0	0	0	1	2	5	0

Batteries—Webster and Boucher, Reynolds and Hildebrand.

SECOND GAME.

Dubuque.	R.	H.	P.	A.	E.	Danville.	R.	H.	P.	A.	E.
Swanson, cf	0	2	3	0	0	Kaylor, rf	0	0	1	0	0
Berraus, lf	0	1	2	0	0	Massing, c	0	1	2	0	0
R. Da'ger, ss	0	1	3	3	0	Sellers, cf	2	1	3	0	0
H. Da'ger, rf	0	0	1	0	0	Graham, lf	0	1	2	1	0
Beatty, 1b	0	0	3	1	0	Staley, 1b	1	0	7	1	0
Boucher, c	0	2	0	2	0	Blassuer, 3b	0	2	2	3	0
Frlewine, 2b	0	0	4	1	0	Falk, ss	0	1	3	3	0
Isaacs, 3b	0	2	1	1	0	Siner, 2b	0	0	0	1	0
Webster, p	0	0	0	0	0	Walsh, p	0	0	1	1	0
Total	0	8	*17	8	0	Total	3	6	21	10	0

*Blausser out for running out of line.

Dubuque ....0 0 0 0 0 0 0—0
Danville ....1 0 0 0 0 2 *—3

OVERCROWDING AT CUB PARK

Murphy Defendant in Two Suits for Alleged Violation of Fire Code.

Charles W. Murphy, president of the cubs, has been made defendant in a suit brought against him for alleged overcrowding of the stands at the West Side ball park during recent games. Two separate suits have been filed by the new bureau of fire prevention, which is operating under direction of Chief J. C. McDonnell.

The charge is overcrowding and blocking of aisles and exits, one suit resulting from an alleged violation Saturday, when the giants were here, and the other on Sunday, when the Philadelphia club played a double-header.

Murphy was notified by McDonnell, but claimed he was powerless to prevent the overcrowding. Notice was then served on the cub boss that the attendance will be limited to the seating capacity and no persons will be allowed to stand with the exception of employes and policemen. These are the first suits brought by the new bureau, and the fine for each offense is from $25 to $200.

HOSE SUFFER SETBACK BATTLING LOWLY YANKS

Wolverton Presents New Line-Up, Which Proves Effective Against Sox, Who Lose.

BENZ FAILS TO STAND PACE

Caldwell Uses Old-Time Jinx in Tumbling Invaders With Men on Bases.

BY HAROLD D. JOHNSON.

NEW YORK, Aug. 21.—Bunched swats and errors, coupled with the hurling effectiveness of "Big Ray" Caldwell, who at sundry times in his honorable career has jinxed the South Siders, beat the hose today. This lank hoodoo, though hammered no harder than was Joe Benz, our meatball manipulator, was air-tight in the pinches, holding the blasters of pennant ambitions in a one-sided victory, 6 to 1.

Some species of hard luck has pursued Benz in each of his recent slab starts, and "Cal," hoping against the worst, resolved to give the Batesville cadet another chance to shake off this nemesis. For three innings the sorrel-topped spitballer more than held his own, personally chucking out five of the first nine kilties to dally with his offerings. Then Childe Hal Chase set the trouble pot a-boiling with a single which, linked with two more wallops and Weaver's bungle, netted two markers.

This pair would have sufficed, but the made-over hill men swelled the count by scoring again in the fifth and mixing one hit with a pass and two fielding skips in the making of three more in the seventh. This last cluster was registered while Rescuer Oscar Casper Peters was floundering about in a near imitation of a major league twirler.

YANKS' LINE-UP SHIFTED.

Having broken even with the fast-going senators and with sweet recollections of three straight from the Athletics, a stupendous achievement and one that knocked the Mackmen out of the pennant shuffle, the Callahan clan anticipated another chain of successes in these four combats up the river. But Skipper Wolverton of the yankee camp was primed for a stern engagement and sent a strange-looking fighting front to grapple with the hose.

Tommy McMillan, one-time dodger, later with the reds and more recently with Rochester, went to shortstop, Ray Hartzell moved to right field, Bert Daniels nudged across to left and Sterrett sat in as center fielder. With Caldwell on the mound this combination looked fit and able to break our winning streak, but for costly bobbles by Weaver, Zeider and Peters the sox might have won, for they were giving Caldwell some anxious moments in the closing rounds.

CHASE SPOILS RALLY.

Prospects for early scoremaking flitted before the sox in their opener, when Rath beat out a dinky bunt to Caldwell and progressed to third on successive sacrifices by Mattick and Lord. Here the remarkable fielding of Chase smashed the opportunity, Hal rushing half way to second, knocking down Collins' liner, turning with a speedy throw in time to toss out Shano, who reached the bag a second behind Caldwell.

The yankees were on their good behavior in the first and second, and Caldwell, displaying marked improvement, found the hose easy victims in the third, fourth and fifth. After the strike-out of Sterrett in New York's third Ed Sweeney looped a single through Weaver's territory and stepped to second on Caldwell's infield out, but Benz steamed up and McMillan succumbed, lofting to Mattick. The fourth was a period of dire disaster and glooms for Benz. Chase welcomed him right off the reel with a shot to center and Daniels sacrificed, Paddock driving him home with a wallop over second.

Weaver, who had displayed a tendency to fight every ball poled his way, booted a grounder from Simmons, and Hartzell grassed out, Benz to Collins. Sterrett thereupon lent a hand with one of his most approved Princeton clouts to Weaver in deep short, Paddock scoring and Simmons falling at the plate when Buck made a lightning heave to Schalk.

CALDWELL WALLOPS TRIPLE.

With one down in the fifth Caldwell caught hold of a spit-ball and dropped it gently against the right field fence for three bases. He made the insane attempt to try for home, however, when McMillan slashed to Zeider, and Rollie's fast throw to Schalk nipped the rangy Yankee. Tommy immediately stole, and whizzed home on Chase's two-bagger to left. A brilliant diving play by Zeider disposed of Daniels at first.

The South Siders started something in the sixth session, bent on staging one of those old-fashioned rallies after Caldwell had eased away Benz and Rath, both on called strikes. Mattick rammed a single off Chase's shins, and raced to third on Lord's Texas League biff back of second. McMillan juggled Collins' liner, and Mattick registered, but Callahan, over-anxious to connect, missed the third strike, making three whiffers for Caldwell in this session.

Benz caught his second wind in the home sixth and fanned Paddock and Simmons, while Weaver nipped Hartzell at first. What smacked of another glorious opening went galley-west in our seventh after Zeider had nobly set the pace with a smash to left. Weaver missed fire, punting weakly to Caldwell, and the latter's heave forced Rollie, while McMillan and Chase coupled up Buck in the only double killing of the afternoon. Schalk got a freak single when Daniels and McMillan, doing the "After you, My Dear" act in short left, permitted the ball to drop safely between them. Easterly batted for Benz and was safe on McMillan's error.

SQUEEZE PLAY FAILS.

With runners on first and third Rath tried a squeeze play and his well-intended bunt went to Caldwell, who nailed Morris at first, snuffing out the opening. The Yankee half brought Peters to the hill, and the lanky fellow got away bad by passing Sterrett. Sweeney's out, Rath to Collins, put the former Princeton star on second, and he reached third safely when Zeider muffed Weaver's toss for a force-out after grabbing Caldwell's roller. The latter stole and scored with Sterrett on McMillan's drive to left, when Peters, taking the throw-in, loosed a crazy chuck past Schalk.

The Rube's error let McMillan reach third, and he easily tallied on Chase's sacrifice fly to Lord in deep center. Callahan and Zeider bunched singles with none dead in our ninth. Weaver lofted to Daniels and Pinch Hitters McIntyre and Bodie, swatting respectively for Schalk and Peters, failed to connect. The score:

Chicago.	AB.	R.	H.	TB.	BB.	SH.	SB.	PO.	A.	E.
Rath, 2b	4	0	1	1	0	0	0	0	1	0
Mattick, cf, rf	3	1	1	1	0	1	0	1	0	0
Lord, rf, cf	3	0	1	1	0	1	0	2	0	0
Collins, 1b	4	0	0	0	0	0	0	11	2	0
Callahan, lf	4	0	1	1	0	0	0	1	0	0
Zeider, 3b	4	0	2	2	0	0	0	0	3	1
Weaver, ss	4	0	1	2	0	0	0	1	3	1
Schalk, c	3	0	1	1	0	0	0	7	1	0
*McIntyre	1	0	0	0	0	0	0	0	0	0
Benz, p	2	0	0	0	0	0	0	0	7	0
†Easterly	1	0	0	0	0	0	0	0	0	0
Peters, p	0	0	0	0	0	0	0	1	0	1
‡Bodie	1	0	0	0	0	0	0	0	0	0
Total	34	1	8	9	0	2	0	24	17	3

*Batted for Schalk in the ninth. †Batted for Benz in the seventh. ‡Batted for Peters in the ninth.

New York.	AB.	R.	H.	TB.	BB.	SH.	SB.	PO.	A.	E.
McMillan, ss	4	2	1	1	0	0	1	1	2	2
Chase, 1b	3	1	2	3	0	1	0	14	1	0
Daniels, lf	3	0	1	1	0	1	0	2	0	0
Paddock, 3b	4	1	1	1	0	0	0	0	1	0
Simmons, 2b	4	0	0	0	0	0	0	0	3	0
Hartzell, rf	4	0	0	0	0	0	0	0	0	0
Sterrett, cf	2	1	1	1	1	0	0	2	0	0
Sweeney, c	3	0	1	1	0	0	0	7	1	0
Caldwell, p	3	1	1	3	0	0	1	1	4	0
Total	30	6	8	11	1	2	2	27	12	2

Chicago ......0[1] 0[1] 0[0] 0[0] 0[0] 1[2] 0[2] 0[0] 0[2]—1[8]
New York....0[1] 0[0] 0[1] 2[3] 1[2] 0[0] 3[1] 0[0] * —6[8]

Two-base hits—Weaver, Chase. Three-base hit—Caldwell. Struck out—By Caldwell, 4 (Benz 2, Rath, Callahan); by Benz, 3 (Sterrett, Paddock, Simmons); by Peters, 1 (Paddock). Base on balls—Off Peters, 1; off Benz, 0. Double plays—Caldwell to McMillan to Chase—Hits—Off Benz, 7 in six innings; off Peters, 1 in two innings. Left on bases—Chicago, 8; New York, 3. Time—1:43. Umpires—Dineen and O'Brien.

UMPIRES ARE RESTING EASY

Brennan and Owens Not Injured as Badly as First Reported.

PITTSBURGH, Aug. 21.—Umpires William Brennan and Clarence Owen, injured in the first Pittsburgh-Brooklyn game yesterday, are resting easy in the hospital, not as badly injured as was at first believed. An X-ray picture of Brennan's injury showed that a number of ligaments of the leg were torn. He will probably be able to leave the hospital tomorrow. Owen is more seriously hurt, but no bones are broken.

SOUTHERN ASSOCIATION.

New Orleans, 2; Nashville, 0.
Birmingham, 3; Atlanta, 4.
Montgomery, 0; Chattanooga, 6.

Baseball Standings and Results

GAMES FOR TODAY.

NATIONAL LEAGUE.

Boston at Chicago.
New York at Pittsburgh.
Philadelphia at Cincinnati.
Brooklyn at St. Louis.

AMERICAN LEAGUE.

Chicago at New York.
St. Louis at Philadelphia.
Detroit at Washington.
Cleveland at Boston.

NATIONAL LEAGUE.	W.	L.	Pct.	AMERICAN LEAGUE.	W.	L.	Pct.
New York	77	32	.706	Boston	79	36	.687
Chicago	**74**	**38**	**.661**	Washington	72	44	.621
Pittsburgh	66	44	.600	Philadelphia	67	46	.593
Philadelphia	53	57	.482	**Chicago**	**57**	**57**	**.500**
Cincinnati	53	61	.465	Detroit	55	63	.466
St. Louis	50	63	.442	Cleveland	52	63	.452
Brooklyn	41	72	.363	New York	40	73	.354
Boston	32	79	.288	St. Louis	37	77	.325

AMERICAN ASSN.	W.	L.	Pct.	WESTERN LEAGUE.	W.	L.	Pct.
Minneapolis	85	47	.644	Denver	72	51	.585
Columbus	84	48	.636	St. Joseph	66	53	.555
Toledo	77	53	.592	Omaha	68	55	.553
Milwaukee	63	66	.488	Des Moines	61	59	.508
Kansas City	63	67	.485	Sioux City	60	61	.495
St. Paul	60	74	.452	Lincoln	59	62	.488
Louisville	48	84	.364	Wichita	57	66	.463
Indianapolis	46	87	.346	Topeka	41	79	.342

"THREE I" LEAGUE.	W.	L.	Pct.	WIS.-ILL. LEAGUE.	W.	L.	Pct.
Springfield	72	32	.692	Racine	63	40	.612
Davenport	63	46	.578	Oshkosh	65	42	.607
Quincy	55	54	.505	Appleton	61	42	.592
Danville	52	54	.491	Wausau	54	55	.495
Decatur	53	61	.465	Green Bay	50	56	.472
Dubuque	49	62	.441	Rockford	49	56	.467
Bloomington	45	64	.413	Aurora	42	64	.396
Peoria	45	64	.413	Madison	40	69	.367

ILL.-MO. LEAGUE.	W.	L.	Pct.	SO. MICH. LEAGUE.	W.	L.	Pct.
Lincoln	66	39	.629	Battle Creek	65	40	.619
Pekin	54	47	.535	Adrian	59	44	.573
Canton	52	48	.520	Jackson	58	48	.547
Kankakee	48	56	.462	Flint	56	51	.523
Streator	46	60	.434	Lansing	53	49	.520
Champaign	44	60	.423	Kalamazoo	47	55	.461

CENTRAL LEAGUE.

	W.	L.	Pct.		W.	L.	Pct.
Fort Wayne	71	46	.607	Canton	59	60	.496
Springfield	64	44	.593	Grand Rap.	52	59	.468
Erie	69	48	.590	Akron	54	62	.466
Youngst'n	67	49	.578	Terre Haute	54	64	.458
Dayton	64	53	.547	Zanesville	47	72	.395
Wheeling	58	55	.513	South Bend	39	77	.336

RESULTS YESTERDAY.

NATIONAL LEAGUE.

Chicago, 4; New York, 0.
Pittsburgh, 0; Brooklyn, 1.
Cincinnati, 4; Boston, 7.

AMERICAN LEAGUE.

New York, 6; Chicago, 1.
Washington, 3; Detroit, 1.
Boston, 4; Cleveland, 9.
Philadelphia-St. Louis, rain.

AMERICAN ASSOCIATION.

Minneapolis, 6—9; Toledo, 0—1.
Milwaukee, 4; Louisville, 1.
St. Paul, 3; Columbus, 15.
Kansas City, 2—7; Indianapolis, 8—5.

CENTRAL LEAGUE.

Canton, 3; South Bend, 1.
Akron, 6; Dayton, 1.
Youngstown-Fort Wayne, rain.
Zanesville, 3; Springfield, 2.
Erie, 6; Terre Haute, 1.
Grand Rapids, 7; Wheeling, 5.

MICHIGAN STATE LEAGUE.

Boyne City, 7; Muskegon, 0.
Traverse City, 10; Ludington, 2.
Manistee, 3; Cadillac, 7.

ILLINOIS-MISSOURI LEAGUE.

Streator, 4; Lincoln, 1.
Champaign, 3; Kankakee, 2.
Canton, 12; Pekin, 6.

SOUTHERN MICHIGAN LEAGUE.

Adrian, 3; Flint, 4.
Lansing, 0; Battle Creek, 5.
Jackson, 6; Kalamazoo, 0.

"THREE I" LEAGUE.

Quincy, 4; Springfield, 9.
Peoria, 8; Decatur, 1.
Bloomington, 3—7; Davenport, 6—2.
Danville, 2—3; Dubuque, 4—0.

WISCONSIN-ILLINOIS LEAGUE.

Wausau, 6; Racine, 4.
Appleton, 8; Madison, 3.
Oshkosh, 4; Rockford, 6.
Green Bay, 0—6; Aurora, 1—3.

INTERNATIONAL LEAGUE.

Toronto, 5; Jersey City, 4.
Montreal, 2; Providence, 1.
Other games, rain.

WESTERN LEAGUE.

Omaha, 6; Wichita, 0.
Lincoln, 5; Sioux City, 0.
Topeka, 8; St. Joseph, 4.
Des Moines, 1; Denver, 4.

NAPS HALT RED SOX

Poor Pitching by O'Brien and Hall, Coupled With Errors, Defeat Leaders.

JACKSON STARS WITH BAT

BOSTON, Aug. 21.—Cleveland batted out an easy victory over the league leaders today, 9 to 1. Neither O'Brien nor Hall, who succeeded him, was effective. Boston's errors helped to make several Cleveland runs. Cleveland scored three runs off O'Brien in the first on a pass, doubles by Lajoie and Olson, Johnson's single and Carrigan's error. In the second, with Hall pitching, Peckinpaugh singled, Ryan was hit and three men scored when Hooper let Jackson's hit go through his legs. Jackson got four hits and four runs in four times at bat. Score:

Boston.	R.	H.	P.	A.	E.	Clevel'd.	R.	H.	P.	A.	E.
Hooper, rf	1	0	1	0	1	Ryan, lf	2	1	2	0	0
Ball, 2b	1	1	1	1	1	Birm'ham, cf	0	1	2	0	0
Speaker, cf	1	2	3	0	1	Jackson, rf	4	4	4	0	0
Lewis, lf	0	0	4	0	0	Lajoie, 2b	1	2	4	4	0
Gardner, 3b	1	2	2	1	0	Johnson, 1b	1	3	11	1	0
Engle, 1b	0	1	9	0	0	Olson, 3b	0	2	0	4	0
Wagner, ss	0	1	1	5	0	O'Neil, c	0	1	3	1	0
Carrigan, c	0	1	6	2	1	Peck'p'gh, ss	1	1	1	5	0
Nun'maker, c	0	0	0	0	0	Blanding, p	0	0	0	3	0
O'Brien, p	0	0	0	0	0						
Hall, p	0	0	0	1	0						
Total	4	8	27	10	5	Total	9	15	27	18	0

Boston ....2 0 0 1 1 0 0 0 0—4
Cleveland ....3 3 0 0 1 1 0 0 1—9

Two-base hits—Lajoie, Olson, Gardner, Ryan. Three-base hit—Carrigan. Hits—Off O'Brien, 3 in one inning; off Hall, 12 in eight innings. Sacrifice hits—Blanding, Olson, Lewis. Double play—Olson to Lajoie to Johnson. Stolen base—Speaker. Bases on balls—Off O'Brien, 1; off Blanding, 3. Hit by pitcher—By Hall, Ryan. Struck out—By Hall, 4; by Blanding, 3. Time—2:03. Umpire—O'Loughlin.

OPENING TILT TO NATIONALS

Groom Outpitches Lake and Tigers Lose by 3 to 1 Count.

WASHINGTON, Aug. 21.—Groom outpitched Lake today and Washington beat Detroit, 3 to 1. The batting of Gandil and base running of Moeller were features. Score:

Detroit.	R.	H.	P.	A.	E.	Wash'n.	R.	H.	P.	A.	E.
Jones, lf	0	0	5	0	0	Millan, cf	0	0	5	1	0
Bush, ss	1	1	4	0	0	Foster, 3b	0	1	0	2	0
Cobb, cf	0	2	3	0	0	Moeller, rf	1	2	2	0	0
Crawford, rf	0	0	0	0	0	Gandil, 1b	2	2	9	0	0
Vitt, 2b	0	0	0	3	0	Morgan, 2b	0	0	3	2	0
Onslow, 1b	0	0	7	0	0	Shanks, lf	0	0	2	0	0
Deal, 3b	0	2	2	3	0	McBride, ss	0	1	1	5	0
Kocher, c	0	2	3	1	2	Henry, c	0	2	4	1	0
Lake, p	0	0	0	3	0	Groom, p	0	0	1	3	0
Works, p	0	0	0	0	0						
Total	1	7	24	10	2	Total	3	8	27	14	0

*Batted for Lake in eighth.

Detroit ....0 0 0 1 0 0 0 0 0—1
Washington ....0 1 0 2 0 0 0 0 *—3

Two-base hit—Gandil. Three-base hit—Cobb. Hits—Off Lake, 7 in 7 innings; off Works, 1 in 1 inning. Sacrifice hit—Groom. Stolen bases—Moeller (3). Double play—Morgan to Henry. Sacrifice flies—Crawford, Shanks. First base on balls—Off Lake, 1. Struck out—By Lake, 3; by Groom, 3. Time—1:50. Umpires—Egan and Evans.

Notes of White Sox Game

NEW YORK, Aug. 21.—Fisher will probably oppose the sox tomorrow with Walsh the likely flinger for the sox. Cal does not want to work "Big Ed" too hard on the eve of the three-game series with the red sox, but the South Side leader is having success with only the spit-ball king and his recent acquisition, Cicotte.

Lord and Mattick switched outfield positions in the seventh when the sox captain complained that the sun hurt his eyes. Harry is fast picking up the fine points of fly chasing in the outer district.

Kid Gleason was injured five seconds after the contest started. Rath, swinging at the first ball, drove it foul and against the Buffer's right temple, all but knocking the kid cold. He was assisted to the sox habitat and later took treatment from old Doc Buckner.

Rain was falling downtown during the last three innings of play and in our half of the ninth black and threatening clouds settled over the highlanders' grounds, but the game was finished before rain descended.

Schalk handled Benz and Peters in steady fashion and is fast acquiring the tricks of a big league maskman. He has a habit of being on his toes at all times, and Managers Mack, Griffith and Wolverton say "Cal" has picked up a real comer.

"Cal" was disappointed with the showing of his lads in the battle today. In the three games at Philadelphia the hose gave a rattling exhibition of hitting and fielding, but the fighting pep was missing today.

COLONELS GET TWO HITS OFF MILWAUKEE HURLER

Nicholson Keeps Louisville in Line With a Pair of Scratch Bingles, Winning, 4-1.

COLUMBUS ROUTS ST. PAUL

Senators Hammer Two Slabmen at Will—Millers Win Over Hens in Double Bill.

MILWAUKEE, Aug. 21.—Nicholson held Louisville to two scratch hits today and the Milwaukee team won with ease, 4 to 1. Clemmons was touched up for twelve hits, but most of them were scattered. The score:

Louisville.	R.	H.	P.	A.	E.	Milw'kee.	R.	H.	P.	A.	E.
Burch, cf	0	1	0	0	0	Liebold, cf	0	1	2	0	0
Nelson, rf	0	0	1	0	0	Charles, 2b	1	1	2	9	0
Stansb'y, lf	0	0	0	1	1	Randall, rf	1	2	0	0	0
Hulswitt, 2b	0	0	6	1	0	Chap'lle, lf	0	2	1	0	0
Burke, 3b	1	0	0	2	0	Jones, 1b	1	2	19	0	0
Beum'r, ss	0	0	4	7	0	Clark, 3b	1	1	0	4	0
Fisher, 1b	0	0	10	2	0	Lewis, ss	0	1	1	3	0
Ludwig, c	0	0	3	0	0	Block, c	0	1	2	1	0
Clemmons, p	0	1	0	1	0	Nichol'n, p	0	1	0	2	1
Total	1	2	24	14	1	Total	4	12	27	19	1

Louisville ....0 0 0 0 0 0 1 0 0—1
Milwaukee ....0 2 0 0 1 0 1 0 *—4

Sacrifice hits—Lewis, Nicholson, Fisher. Stolen bases—Charles, Randall (2), Burch. Double plays—Charles to Jones, Clark to Charles to Jones, Fisher to Beumiller to Hulswitt. First on balls—Off Nicholson, 4; off Clemmons, 3. Hit by pitcher—Block. Struck out—By Nicholson, 3; by Clemmons, 1. Time—1:30. Umpires—Spade and Connolly.

KAWS AND HOOSIERS IN DRAW.

KANSAS CITY, Aug. 21.—Kansas City and Indianapolis divided a double-header, the visitors taking the first through hard hitting on their part and listless playing by the locals. The second game was won by Kansas City by bunching hits off Merz. Score of second game:

Indianap.	R.	H.	P.	A.	E.	Kan.City.	R.	H.	P.	A.	E.
E. Willi's, lf	1	1	2	0	0	Downey, cf	1	1	2	0	0
Wentz, ss	1	0	0	3	1	Coulson, lf	1	2	4	0	0
McCarty, cf	1	1	3	0	0	Barbeau, 3b	2	1	0	2	0
Veach, rf	0	1	0	1	0	Carr, 1b	1	1	14	0	1
Ingerton, 3b	1	1	1	0	0	Tannehill, ss	0	1	0	3	0
Keene, 1b	0	[illegible]	7	2	0	James, c	1	2	5	2	0
O. Willi's, 2b	0	0	3	2	0	Lennox, 2b	1	1	2	2	1
McKee, c	1	1	7	2	0	Fiene, rf	0	1	0	0	0
Merz, p	0	0	1	3	0	Schlitzer, p	0	[illegible]	[illegible]	5	0
Taylor, p	0	0	0	0	0						
Total	5	6	24	13	1	Total	7	11	27	14	2

Indianapolis ....0 0 0 0 4 1 0 0 0—5
Kansas City ....0 0 1 1 3 2 0 0 *—7

Stolen base—Coulson. Sacrifice hits—Wentz, Tannehill, O. Williams. Sacrifice fly—Downey. Two-base hit—E. Williams, McKee, Downey, Carr. Home runs—McCarty, James. Double plays—Merz to McKee to Keene, Wentz to O. Williams to Keene. Hits—Off Merz, 9 in 5 1-3 innings; off Taylor, 2 in 2 2-3 innings. Struck out—By Schlitzer, 3; by Merz, 2; by Taylor, 2. Bases on balls—Off Merz, 5; off Schlitzer, 1. Hit by pitched ball—Barbeau (by Taylor). Umpires—Ferguson and Handiboe. Time—2:00.

First game:

										R.	H.	E.
Indianapolis	0	0	0	0	0	0	0	6	2	8	9	2
Kansas City	0	0	1	0	0	0	1	0	0	2	11	6

Batteries—Link and McKee, Rhoades and O'Connor.

SENATORS TAKE BATFEST.

ST. PAUL, Aug. 21.—The senators pounded the ball hard and Columbus defeated St. Paul in the third game of the series here today. Score:

St. Paul.	R.	H.	P.	A.	E.	Columbus.	R.	H.	P.	A.	E.
McKechnie, ss	1	0	1	4	0	O'Rourke, 2b	2	1	5	2	1
H. H'hman, 2b	0	3	2	4	0	W. H'hman, lf	1	3	2	0	0
Flynn, rf	0	1	2	0	1	Johns, rf	1	1	1	0	0
Capron, lf	0	1	1	0	0	Perring, 3b	1	2	1	3	0
Autrey, 1b	0	1	12	0	0	Miller, 1b	3	0	5	0	1
Ralston, cf	1	0	5	0	1	Shelton, cf	3	1	4	0	0
Rehg, 3b	1	0	1	2	1	Gerber, ss	0	0	0	2	2
Marshall, c	0	2	3	0	0	Smith, c	2	2	7	1	0
LaRoy, p	0	0	0	2	0	Murphy, c	0	0	2	0	0
Fucik, p	0	0	0	2	0	Packard, p	2	3	0	1	0
						Bruck, p	0	1	0	0	0
Total	3	8	27	14	3	Total	15	14	27	9	4

St. Paul ....0 0 0 0 0 0 1 2— 3
Columbus ....1 0 1 5 6 2 0 0 0—15

Two-base hit—Packard, Flynn. Three-base hit—Perring. Home runs—Johns, W. Hinchman, Shelton. Stolen base—Miller. Bases on balls—Off LaRoy, 2; off Fucik, 3; off Burck, 2. Struck out—By LaRoy, 2; by Fucik, 1; by Packard, 6; by Bruck, 2. Passed ball—Murphy. Wild pitch—Fucik. Sacrifice hits—O'Rourke, Gerber. Sacrifice flies—Gerber, Flynn. Hits—Off LaRoy, 7 in four innings; off Fucik, 7 in five innings; off Packard, 4 in seven innings; off Bruck, 4 in two innings. Umpires—Hayes and Anderson. Time—2:05.

DOUBLE BILL TO MILLERS.

MINNEAPOLIS, Aug. 21.—Minneapolis took both ends of a double-header from Toledo today by scores of 6 to 0 and 9 to 1. Patterson and Liebhardt for Minneapolis pitched almost perfect ball, while Bill James, the righthander in the first, and Lefty James in the second, were easy for local hitters. Score of first game:

										R.	H.	E.
Minneapolis	1	2	0	2	0	1	0	0	*	6	14	1
Toledo	0	0	0	0	0	0	0	0	0	0	4	2

Batteries—Patterson and Owens; W. James and Land.

SECOND GAME.

Mpls.	R.	H.	P.	A.	E.	Toledo.	R.	H.	P.	A.	E.
Clymer, cf	2	1	1	0	0	Niles, lf	0	0	2	0	0
Altizer, ss	1	2	1	2	0	Congalton, rf	1	2	2	0	0
Williams, 2b	1	1	3	4	0	Burns, cf	0	1	1	0	0
J. Delahanty	1	1	0	0	0	Chapman, ss	0	0	4	3	1
Rossman, rf	0	2	1	0	0	Bronkie, 3b	0	0	3	3	1
Killifer, 3b	1	2	0	2	0	Derrick, 1b	0	0	7	0	0
Gill, 1b	1	0	12	2	0	Gardner, 2b	0	2	3	1	0
Owens, c	1	2	7	1	0	Land, c	0	0	2	2	1
Liebhardt, p	1	1	2	3	0	Walsh, c	0	0	0	0	0
						L. James, p	0	0	0	3	0
Total	9	12	27	13	0	Total	1	5	24	12	3

Minneapolis ....2 0 0 1 1 4 0 1 *—9
Toledo ....0 0 0 0 0 1 0 0 0—1

Home run—Congalton. Two-base hits—Congalton. Bases on balls—Off James, 4; off Liebhardt, 2. Struck out—By Liebhardt, 7; by James, 2. Hit by pitched ball—By James, 3. Wild pitch—James. Sacrifice hits—Gill, 2. Stolen bases—Gill, Owens, Williams. Double plays—James to Chapman to Derrick. Gardner to Derrick. Time—1:45. Umpires—Chill and Irwin.

M'INTOSH TO POST COIN HERE

Australian Promoter Willing to Put Up Forfeit for Johnson Bouts.

MILWAUKEE, Wis., Aug. 21.—"The statement by Jack Johnson in Chicago that Hugh McIntosh has not offered him (Johnson) $50,000 for his meetings with Langford and McVey in Australia is not correct," said T. S. Andrews, representative for Mr. McIntosh here today.

"The fact is," continued Andrews, "Johnson signed a contract to meet these two men for $45,000 and $5,000 expenses, also three tickets, which is the same as $50,000 for the two bouts. Mr. McIntosh wanted to deposit the $10,000 forfeit in a Chicago bank, but Johnson objected, insisting that Alderman Al Tearney be made stakeholder, and also insisting that $5,000 expenses be put up at once.

"Finally Mr. McIntosh agreed to post the money with Mr. Tearney, and all Jack has to do is to say the word and the money will be turned over to Mr. Tearney. All Mr. McIntosh asks is a guarantee that Johnson will go to Australia and carry out his part of the agreement."

ONE CENT EXTRA

LOS ANGELES EVENING HERALD

AN INDEPENDENT NEWSPAPER

LAST EDITION

VOL. XXXIX. WEATHER—FAIR TUESDAY, OCTOBER 15, 1912. WEATHER—FAIR NO. 12.

ROOSEVELT'S WOUND IS SERIOUS

NEW YORK AND SOX TIED; GIANTS WIN TODAY

PATIENT IN PAIN; ABSOLUTE QUIETUDE ESSENTIAL TO HIS RECOVERY, SAY PHYSICIANS

CHICAGO, Oct. 15.—The following official bulletin on the condition of Theodore Roosevelt on the second day was issued at Mercy hospital at 2:20 o'clock this afternoon:

"The examination at 1 o'clock shows his temperature is 98.8 and pulse 92, respiration normal. It pains him to some extent to breathe. He must have absolute quietude and cease from talking or seeing anyone until we give permission, as this is not a mere flesh wound, but a serious wound in the chest. Quietude is absolutely essential." (Signed) Drs. Murphy, Bevan, Terrell.

Daughters Hurry to the Side of Father

MILWAUKEE, Oct. 15.—Dr. Jancs, the X-ray expert who took the pictures of Roosevelt's wound here, has been called hastily to Chicago. This fact gave rise to the belief here that the colonel's condition might be more serious than was at first supposed.

CHICAGO, Oct. 15.—According to his own statement, made just after he left the operating table at Mercy hospital this morning, Colonel Roosevelt "feels bully."

The wound he received at Milwaukee last night from the bullet of a would-be assassin is of a superficial nature and Mr. Roosevelt ate a hearty breakfast and shows no indication of weakness.

Although Mrs. Roosevelt will not come to meet him here it is announced that the ex-president will return to his home in Oyster Bay and will abandon his speaking tour until such time as his physicians feel that all danger of complications has passed.

When he was first informed that it would be best to cancel his speaking dates Mr. Roosevelt demurred and it looked as though he would refuse, but he finally consented, adding that he would do as the doctors ordered, though he did not feel the necessity.

Hundreds of telegrams of sorrow have been received by him this morning and a great bundle of them was on hand at the station when his private car rolled into the station from Milwaukee this morning.

GOES UNDER X RAY

Colonel Roosevelt, who had insisted upon carrying through his speech at the Milwaukee auditorium after John Schrank, a political maniac, had shot him yesterday evening, was taken in an ambulance from his private car to Mercy hospital at 6:15 this morning.

Everything was in readiness and attending physicians at once began an X-ray examination to locate the bullet, which entered the left breast and lodged in the flesh.

Dr. Geo. Hochsin was in charge of the examination, Dr. W. B. McCaulkley, Dr. Philip Krausicher and Dr. John F. Golden assisting.

At the conclusion of the examination Dr. Scurry Terrill, the physician accompanying Roosevelt on his trip, issued a statement declaring the patient's condition to be "very good."

He stated that Roosevelt was weak after the strain of last night's meeting, but that the outlook was favorable unless complications ensued.

Nurses who were in the room when the examination was made said the bullet was located in the fleshy part of the chest and was not in the inner wall of the chest. The bullet is on the right side an inch and a half below the right nipple. It was decided to remove the bullet.

"Respiratory movement good, pulse normal; bullet in a safe place. Expectorate no blood."

This message was sent to Mrs. Roose-

(CONTINUED ON PAGE TWO)

Assailant in Court Pleads Guilty to Shooting

MILWAUKEE, Oct. 15.—Schrank today pleaded guilty to a charge of assault with intent to kill. He probably will be lodged in the state's prison before night.

MILWAUKEE, Oct. 15. — John Schrank, who attempted to assassinate Colonel Roosevelt, today made a new confession to the police and declared it had been his intention to keep shooting at Roosevelt until he was absolutely certain he was dead, but the crowd frustrated him.

The police are convinced Schrank is a maniac.

He is short in stature and shabbily dressed. The most remarkable features about him are his eyes. They are red-rimmed, blue and watery. At times they have a wild and incoherent look. He said he fired the shot because he was convinced Roosevelt was trying to be the first American king. He said the trouble in this country was too few people are on the square.

"There are probably a hundred thousand people who know it is their duty to keep this blatherskite from becoming king. All good Americans know we must have no kings.

"I wish I had been successful. If given another chance this afternoon I would take better aim and kill this man. He is the most dangerous man in the world today." Schrank said he felt no regret.

He was asked if he had a personal grudge against Roosevelt.

"Not what you would call a personal grudge," he said. "Of course, I remember how he enforced the closing ordinances in New York, when he was police commissioner. That put about a thousand places out of business and caused a heavy money loss to about 8000 saloon men. That was just another evidence of the tyrannical nature of the man. He is the greatest American political boss. He waves his hat and he sways thousands.

"Did you see him here? Did you see the people in the street? Did you watch them cheer when he waved his hat? I hate him, when he waves that hat of his. When the people shout he shows his teeth. They are like the teeth of an animal. He is trying to fasten them in the vitals of Americanism. He is hungry for power."

Schrank said that he felt when Roosevelt was police commissioner and he was a saloon keeper in New York that the colonel was a man of unusual power who could develop the same sort of power that Napoleon had held. Schrank said that he had money of his own that an uncle in New York had left him.

Twenty-five thousand of that was the money that was used in trailing the colonel from place to place in an effort to assassinate him.

"I am not irresponsible or a lunatic as people seem to think," said Schrank. "I know what I am doing and have been acting systematically. I expect I shall get fifteen years or so, maybe more. I fully anticipated a life sentence or hanging, and I would gladly have paid either penalty for a greater measure of success."

Schrank said he was not a drinking man and that he never used liquor even when he was a saloon keeper.

(CONTINUED ON PAGE TWO)

ELECTIONEERING LIVENS EASTERN STAR SESSION

Prominent members of the Eastern Star in session here. Standing from left to right they are: John E. Hartell, Pas[illegible] Patron of Pacific Chapter; B. A. Fassett, Post Patron Rosina Chapter and Candidate for Associate Grand Patron. Woman seated on left is Mrs. Emma C. Martin, Candidate for Grand Treasurer, and Past Matron of [illegible] Chapter of San Francisco. On Right Mrs. Miriam G. Davis, Past Matron of Santa Paula Chapter, and Candidate for Grand Matron for Southern California.

Seven Hundred Delegates Open Annual State Meeting in Shrine Auditorium

The fortieth annual session of the California grand chapter of the order of Eastern Star began with a rush this morning at 9 o'clock when more than 700 delegates appeared in the registration headquarters in the Hotel Alexandria to secure their official badges and programs. Five registration clerks were kept busy taking names and dealing out badges and at noon the registration had not been completed.

The majority of the delegates have arrived and the remainder from nearby chapters will have registered before 6 o'clock this evening, it is stated.

At 10 o'clock this moning the present officers gathered in the Shrine auditorium and went through the first of the preliminary initiatory drills which will be given frequently during the coming sessions, using dummy candidates to show the incoming officers how an initiation ceremony should be conducted.

WORK OF THE SESSION

According to officers this session will be confined chiefly to hearings of reports of lodge chapter work and work of the order in general.

Two plans, however, to be introduced before the delegates have been announced by prominent men and women in the order. The first is a move to have the Australian system of balloting introduced into the California chapter for future elections, and it is stated that the system will come up for approval at tomorrow's session, and if adopted will be put in use in the election of officers which takes place tomorrow morning. Only voting delegates will be admitted to the electoral session.

It is rumored that the plan of the Eastern Star lodge to acquire the present Masonic orphans home at San Gabriel and to make it essentially an Eastern Star home for orphans will also come up in one of the later business sessions. This plan is bitterly opposed by half of the delegates who

(CONTINUED ON PAGE NINE)

MRS. PHELPS' MOTHER ON STAND DEFENDS HER DAUGHTER'S CHARACTER

Careworn and suffering from the fatigue of the long journey, Mrs. Etta Feak, mother of Mrs. Alice Phelps, the principal witness against Guy Eddie, stepped to the witness stand in the court room today in the Eddie hearing to testify to the date of Mrs. Phelps' birth and to defend her character.

Mrs. Feak is 44 years old and of small stature. As she sat in the witness chair her feet hardly touched the floor. Quietly and showing no emotion except by a tenseness of the muscles of her face she recited the fact that Mrs. Alice Phelps was born in Lena, Wis., October 23, 1891.

"My daughter has never given me a care," she said simply. "If the assertions are true that detectives in the east have learned much about her, the facts they say they have learned are not known to me. I am 44 years old and the mother of 11 children. My husband was for many years a section foreman on a railroad in Wisconsin. We have by careful management saved from his wages enough to rear the children and purchase 160 acres of land. I have been in constant touch with my children from their infancy and never before this time have I ever heard a word against any of them."

TESTIMCNY NOT ATTACKED

Mrs. Feak's eyes moistened and her lips parted as if she were about to say more. She apparently changed her mind, however, and remained silent. Lewis R. Works in his cross-examination made no effort to impeach her testimony.

Mrs. Feak's trip to Los Angeles was due to a desire on her part to vindicate her daughter and a desire on the part of the prosecution to have her corroborate the daughter's statement of her age.

Officer Lloyd is on the witness stand this afternoon. The cross-examination of Lloyd will be conducted by Lewis R. Works. Earl Rogers, the chief counsel for the defense, will not be connected with the present proceedings. Rogers suffered a nervous breakdown while at his home in East Hollywood last night and was taken to the Good Samaritan hospital. Today he was removed to a sanitarium and will remain there, it is stated at his home, for fully a month.

EDDIE GREATLY DISAPPOINTED

Guy Eddie was greatly surprised and disappointed when he was told by an Evening Herald reported that Rogers was ill.

"That is indeed most unfortunate," he said. "Mr. Rogers has gained such a complete grasp of the situation that it is a big loss to me to have him stricken."

It was later stated that the rest of Eddie's attorneys asked for a continuance, but that Judge Wilbur denied it on the grounds that the prosecutor has sufficient other counsel to protect his rights.

Officer Lloyd is this afternoon relating his account of Eddie's arrest. He asserted that the hallway leading to Eddie's private office was vacant, with the exception of three Greeks who sat near the door of one of the police court rooms, and entirely away from all points from which a view of the interior of the office could have been obtained when the door was broken in.

His story corroborates that of other witnesses as to the alleged position of the defendant and his accuser.

IRON RAILING PERMITTED

The City Council today adopted the ordinance permitting contractors to use iron railing on the street sides of class A buildings instead of the fire wall now made compulsory.

WOOD DRIVEN FROM BOX IN FIRST; HALL HIT HARD; TESREAU HOLDS SOX SAFE

Facts About Game

WORLD'S SERIES STANDINGS

	Games	Won	Lost	Pct.
Red Sox	7	3	3	.500
Giants	7	3	3	.500

One tie game—does not figure in standings.

PLACE—Boston.

TIME—2 o'clock p. m.; 11 a. m. Los Angeles time.

TEAMS—Boston Americans and New York Nationals.

BATTERIES—For Boston: Wood, Hall, Cady; for New York, Tesreau, Meyers and Wilson.

UMPIRES—Klem, Evans, O'Loughlin, Rigler.

GATE RECEIPTS — Yesterday's game, $66,654.

PLAYERS' SHARES—First four games $147,571.10. If Boston wins, each man will receive $4000.

ATTENDANCE—First six games, 240,309.

BOSTON	NEW YORK
Hooper, rf.	Devore, lf.
Yerkes, 2b.	Doyle, 2b.
Speaker, cf.	Snodgrass, cf.
Lewis, lf.	Murray, rf.
Gardner, 3b.	Merkle, 1b
Stahl, 1b.	Herzog, 3b.
Wagner, ss.	Meyers, c.
Cady, c.	Fletcher, ss.
Wood, p.	Tesreau, p.
Hall, p	Wilson, c

SCORE BY INNINGS

GIANTS	6	1	0	0	0	2	1	0	[illegible]—11
Hits	6	1	2	0	1	1	2	1	1—15
RED SOX	0	1	0	0	0	0	2	1	0—4
Hits	0	1	1	2	1	1	2	1	0—9

BY SAM CRANE

(Every play in game dictated to operator at his side by Mr. Crane, greatest baseball expert in the world.)

BOSTON, Oct. 15.—The New York Giants today stopped the fast-going Boston Red Sox in the seventh game for the world's baseball championship and put themselves on even terms in the fight for the 1912 title. The score was 11 to 4.

The New Yorkers chose round one for the massacre of Joe Wood and before the inning closed they had knocked out six hits and scored as many runs. The entire team batted around.

A double steal and Wagner's fumble of a grounder helped to unnerve the lad who has twice defeated the Giants since the series began. After the first man singled it was evident that the "boy with the braided biceps" was not in his true form. The strain under which he has been laboring showed in his pitching for the first time.

Hall did little better than "Little Joe" and in the eight innings he was on the mound the Gothamites got nine hits and drove in five runs. He passed five men.

Tesreau was good in the pinches, with few exceptions, and allowed only nine safe swats. He struck out five Red Sox and walked three.

Not a Red Stocking stole a base, while three were pilfered by Giants. Devore got two of these.

Two home runs, one by Gardner and the other by Doyle, were the feature of the game. These were the first of the series.

That the New Yorkers have better than an even chance of winning the series is shown by their second "come back" in two successive days. They had been counted out of the race and their victory in Gotham on Monday only brought forth the statements that Marquard got away with a fluke victory. The defeat of Boston was attributed to Stahl for sending "Buck" O'Brien to the slab against the $11,000 lemon." This may be true in a degree, but the Giants showed that they had regained their batting eyes and the victory did a lot toward winning today's contest.

TAKE ON NEW LEASE OF LIFE

Now with two straight victories to their credit, McGraw's men have taken on a new lease of life and the encouragement they have had heaped on them has made them determined not to let the gonfalon get away from them after such a plucky fight from behind.

As the standings now read, New York and Boston have each won and lost three games. The eighth and deciding game will be played tomorrow.

A crowd like that which crowded Fenway park today has never been seen at a baseball game in Boston. Every available spot in the stands and on the grounds was occupied. The total attendance, as officially announced, exceeded 38,000.

A strong wind was blowing when the game started, but subsided before four innings had been played. Heavy black clouds hung over the field, but if old Jup. Pluvius had any intention of opening his water tanks he spared the feelings of several thousand baseball mad fans by delaying his action.

The Giants went after Joe Wood with a vengeance and before the third man went down in the first six Giants had cantered across the home plate. Devore, first man to face the Boston star, got to first on Wagner's fumble of his grounder. Doyle singled through second. While Snodgrass coaxed Wood to put one "down the groove" Devore stole third and Doyle second.

"Snoddy" then smashed out a double, sending Devore and Doyle home with the first runs of the game. Murray sacrificed to Stahl. Merkle slammed a double to center and the Giant center fielder counted. Herzog hit to Wood and the latter threw to Gardner, catching Merkle on the line. "Big Chief" Meyers sent a hot single to left and Herzog came home. Artie Fletcher picked out one of Wood's slow ones and turned it into a single, Meyers taking third. Tesreau scored Meyers with a neat single to right. Fletcher tallied as Stahl and Yerkes were throwing Tesreau out on the line between first and second.

TESREAU WALKS YERKES

Boston did not even get a hit in its half of the opener. Tesreau walked Yerkes, but fanned Hooper, and Speaker and Lewis were easy.

McGraw's men added another to their total in the second. Hall replaced Wood. Devore was walked and immediately pilfered second. Doyle, who followed him, also went to first when Hall failed to put the ball over. After Devore was caught asleep off second, Snodgrass singled, putting Doyle on second. Hall in trying to catch Doyle threw wild, the ball going to center field, and the New Yorker scored. Murray and Merkle went out and ended the inning.

Larry Gardner started off the second for the Red Sox by smashing the ball over the fence for the first home run of the series. It was a mighty drive, one of the longest ever made on the local grounds. His teammates could do nothing, and Stahl, Wagner and Cady went out in order.

HERZOG AND MEYERS SINGLE

Herzog and Meyers singled in order to open the third, but Fletcher, "Big Jeff" and Devore failed to advance them, being easy outs.

Hall got to second on Herzog's wild throw to first after getting his grounder. Hooper singled, sending Hall to third. Yerkes fanned and Speaker flied out, Devore doubling Hall at the plate.

Doyle, Snodgrass and Murray were easy victims for the Sox in the fourth,

(CONTINUED ON PAGE NINE)

Yankees Take Opener from Browns—Dodgers Lose—Giants Idle

Mrs. Hitchins In Final Round Of Tennis Tilt

Mexican Champion Faces Miss Gilleaudeau To-day at Staten Island

By FRED HAWTHORNE

Mrs. Charles Vernon Hitchins, champion of Mexico, who won the Middle States tournament at Staten Island last week, and Miss Helen Gilleaudeau, who was runner-up on that occasion, will renew their struggle this afternoon on the turf courts of the Crescent Athletic Club, at Bay Ridge, in the final round of the club's invitation lawn tennis tourney.

Mrs. Hitchins gained her final bracket by defeating Miss Edith Roberts in straight sets at 6—0, 6—2, and Miss Gilleaudeau vanquished Mrs. Robert Le Roy by a score of 6—2, 6—1.

Paired with her sister, Miss Grace, Miss Helen Gilleaudeau won a stirring match from Miss Ethel Tyndale and Miss Gladys Dowling in the semi-final round, scoring at 6—1, 10—8. In the other semi-final bracket Miss Marie Wagner and Miss Elisabeth H. Moore defeated Mrs. Hitchins and Mrs. Le Roy at 6—4, 6—2.

Collection for Red Cross

Mrs. Hitchins and Miss Gilleaudeau will face each other in the final round of the singles at 2 o'clock, and the final doubles match will be started immediately after the finish of the singles, before, during and after which a collection will be taken up for the Red Cross fund.

Before Miss Gilleaudeau and Mrs. Le Roy took the court yesterday it was believed that the latter would give the Barnard girl a hard fight for the honors. Mrs. Le Roy had been showing unusual strength in her deep driving game on the preceding days of the tournament and also cleverness in volleying from midcourt.

But Miss Gilleaudeau is gaining in courtcraft with every match she plays, and yesterday she tricked her opponent out of position with surprising ease. A session of hard driving from the back of the court would generally end with Miss Gilleaudeau winning the point by a quick change of pace, by means of which she would drop her return just over the net, while Mrs. Le Roy was hopelessly out of position at her base line.

Again, the Barnard champion would wait until her opponent started for the net position and then send up a soft, low lob to deep court. The slow playing surface proved more of a handicap to Mrs. Le Roy than to Miss Gilleaudeau under the circumstances, and the result of the match was never in doubt after the first couple of games.

Chop Strokes Effective

Mrs. Hitchins had an even easier task against Miss Roberts, her chop strokes working havoc with the latter's game. Try as she would, Miss Roberts could not get a game in the first set, but in the second she managed to win two, after deuce had been called several times. Mrs. Hitchins was placing her returns beautifully yesterday, picking her openings quickly and showing great cleverness in anticipating Miss Roberts's shots.

The Gilleaudeau sisters scored a triumph for the back court game as against the net attack, as exemplified by Miss Tyndale and Miss Dowling. The latter combination worked up their game considerably in the second set, flashing brilliantly at the net, Miss Dowling volleying sharply for the corners and Miss Tyndale smashing short lobs with spectacular force. But in the end the steadiness of the sisters told; they withstood the bombardment and kept hammering away with deep drives and lobs so successfully that Miss Tyndale and her partner finally broke under the strain and lost out on errors.

Voshell Too Much For Thockmorton On Flatbush Court

S. Howard Voshell, national indoor champion, worked his way into the final round of the Brooklyn patriotic singles lawn tennis tournament on the clay courts of the Terrace Club, of Flatbush, yesterday, defeating young George Throckmorton in the semi-final round by a score of 6—2, 6—1.

The champion's terrific smashing and his lightning volleying at the net were entirely too great an obstacle for the schoolboy to compete against.

Throckmorton, paired with Harold Taylor, the Brooklyn schoolboy, went into the final round of the doubles by defeating E. Cameron and E. A. Davis at 6—0, 6—4. Charles Chambers and Taylor will meet to-day in the semi-final round of the singles to determine who shall face Voshell in the final.

The final doubles match will be played this afternoon and the final singles to-morrow afternoon.

The summaries follow:

Singles (third round)—William Jennings defeated Dr. Morganthaler, 6—4, 6—2.

Fourth round—S. Howard Voshell defeated Count Otto Salm, 6—2, 6—4; Charles Chambers defeated Jennings, 6—3, 6—2; Harold Taylor defeated Edward Cameron, 6—4, 6—3.

Semi-final round — Voshell defeated George Throckmorton, 6—2, 6—1.

Doubles (third round)—Count Salm and Ingo Hartmann defeated Cecil Donaldson and Frank Anderson, 7—5, 6—2.

Semi-final round—George Throckmorton and Harold Taylor defeated E. Cameron and E. A. Davis, 6—0, 6—4.

Seaver Victor in Tennis Match Over Wheelwright

Boston, June 15.—A match between R. C. Seaver, several times champion of Massachusetts, and Josiah Wheelwright, New Hampshire title holder, was the feature of the play in the state lawn tennis singles championship tournament, which was advanced to the semi-final round to-day. Seaver won, 6—3, 6—8, 6—2.

Nathaniel Niles had a struggle in the second set in winning from A. G. Butler, 6—1, 10—8; Harold Bretsz defeated Horace Taylor, 8—6, 6—3, and S. L. Beals won from E. V. Page, 10—8, 6—0.

Spencer the Favorite

Arthur Spencer, the Toronto cyclist who has won the quarter and one-third mile national championships, is the favorite for the half-mile which will be decided at the Velodrome, in Newark, to-morrow afternoon.

Boxing Bill Defeated

Springfield, Ill., June 15.—A bill to legalize ten-round boxing exhibitions in Illinois failed to pass the state Senate to-day.

American Association

Milwaukee, 11; Minneapolis, 4.
Kansas City, 10; St. Paul, 7.
Indianapolis, 4; Toledo, 1.
Louisville at Columbus (cold).

Feature Facts For the Fans

The Phillies are again on even terms with the Giants.

Wally Pipp's home run won for the Yankees.

Al Walters made two hits in two times at bat.

The White Sox bunted Shore out of the box in the fifth.

Carlisle Smith made three hits in four times up, one a double.

Fred Merkle had a perfect day at bat. He made a single and two doubles.

Claude Williams shut out the Red Sox. He didn't allow a hit in seven innings.

Milan, of the Senators, made a single and a triple in two trips.

Walter Johnson struck out ten batsmen. He also gave eight bases on balls.

Ty Cobb got two hits in two times up, and also scored two runs.

Siebold gave only five hits. He made a single and a double in three times up, stole a base and scored a run.

Whitted made a triple and three singles in four times at bat.

Phillies Victors Over the Reds In Slug Fest

Cincinnati, June 15.—Philadelphia and Cincinnati indulged in an oldtime batting bee here to-day, the visitors finishing as winners, 12 to 8.

Lavender was effective until the ninth, when Cincinnati piled up six hits, and these, coupled with an error and a base on balls, netted the Reds six runs.

Previous to this, however, Knetzer had been hit hard and timely, while Eller, who preceded Knetzer, also proved ineffective, although errors behind him allowed three of the visitors' four runs to score while he was on the mound.

Whitted and Groh profited most at the bat, the former getting four hits out of four times at bat, while Groh obtained four hits out of five times up.

The score:

PHILADELPHIA (N. L.)	ab	r	h	po	a	e
Paskert, cf	5	1	3	3	0	0
McGaf'n, ss	4	1	1	2	4	0
Stock, 3b	2	3	1	0	1	0
Cravath, rf	5	3	2	1	0	0
Wh'ted, lf	4	2	4	1	1	1
Lud's, 1b	4	1	1	8	0	0
Niehoff, 2b	4	0	1	6	3	1
Killifer, c	4	0	0	6	0	0
Burns, c	0	0	0	0	0	0
Lav'der, p	3	1	1	0	1	0
*Dugey	1	0	0	0	0	0
Totals	36	12	14	27	10	2

CINCINNATI (N. L.)	ab	r	h	po	a	e
Groh, 3b	5	2	4	0	2	0
Kopf, ss	5	0	1	2	4	1
Roush, cf	3	1	0	7	0	1
Chase, 1b	5	1	2	11	1	1
Wi'go, c	5	0	1	1	1	1
Thorpe, rf	5	2	1	1	0	0
Neale, lf	4	0	2	1	0	1
Shean, 2b	5	1	2	2	2	0
Eller, p	0	0	0	0	1	0
Knetzer, p	1	0	0	0	2	1
†Griffith	1	0	1	0	0	0
‡Clarke	1	1	1	0	0	0
Totals	41	8	15	27	13	6

*Batted for Killifer in the ninth inning.
†Batted for Eller in the fourth inning.
‡Batted for Knetzer in the ninth inning.

Philadelphia	2	0	0	2	1	0	3	1	3	—12
Cincinnati	1	0	0	0	0	1	0	0	6	—8

Two-base hit—Thorpe. Three-base hits—Whitted, Cravath, Paskert, Clarke. Stolen bases—Neale, Shean, Chase, Groh (2), Roush. Sacrifice hits—Lavender, Stock, McGaffingan. Sacrifice flies—Whitted, Luderus, Niehoff. Double plays—Niehoff (unassisted); Kopf, Shea nto Chase. Left on bases—Philadelphia, 5; Cincinnati, 9. First base on errors—Philadelphia, 2. Bases on balls—Off Lavender, 3; off Eller, 1; off Knetzer, 1. Hits and earned runs—Off Lavender, 15 hits 5 runs in 9 innings; off Eller 6 hits 1 runs in 4 innings; off Knetzer, 8 hits 5 runs in 5 innings. Struck out—By Lavender, 4; by Knetzer, 1. Umpires—Harrison and O'Day. Time—2:02.

Siebold Wins Game For Connie's Men

Philadelphia, June 15.—Seibold's pitching and hitting played a big part in the game which Philadelphia won from Cleveland to-day, 3 to 2.

Seibold held his opponents to five hits. He scored a run after making a single and stealing second base, while he also drove in a run with a two-bagger.

The score:

CLEVELAND (A. L.)	ab	r	h	po	a	e
Graney, lf	3	0	0	1	0	0
Chapman, ss	4	1	1	1	3	1
Speaker, cf	4	1	1	0	0	1
Roth, rf	3	0	1	3	0	0
Wambs's, 2b	3	0	0	4	2	1
Harris, 1b	3	0	2	9	0	0
Turner, 3b	2	0	0	2	4	1
O'Neill, c	2	0	0	2	0	1
Billings, c	2	0	0	2	0	0
Coveleskie, p	3	0	0	0	2	0
*Evans	0	0	0	0	0	0
†Smith	1	0	0	0	0	0
Totals	30	2	5	24	11	5

PHILADELPHIA (A. L.)	ab	r	h	po	a	e
Witt, ss	4	0	0	1	4	0
Strunk, cf	4	1	0	2	0	1
Bodie, lf	4	0	1	4	0	0
Bates, 3b	4	0	2	2	2	0
McInnis, 1b	4	0	1	11	0	0
Schang, c	3	1	1	3	0	1
Johnson, rf	3	0	0	3	0	0
Lawry, 2b	3	0	0	1	1	0
Seibold, p	3	1	2	0	4	0
Totals	32	3	7	27	11	2

*Ran for Harris in the ninth inning.
†Batted for Coveleskie in the ninth inning.

Cleveland	1	0	0	0	0	0	0	1	0	—2
Philadelphia	0	0	0	0	0	2	1	0	x	—3

Two-base hits—Roth, Seibold. Stolen bases—Chapman, Seibold, Schang. Sacrifice hit—Turner. Double play—Wambsganss (unassisted). Left on bases—Cleveland, 7; Philadelphia, 5. First base on errors—Philadelphia, 3. Bases on balls—Off Seibold, 5. Earned runs—Off Coveleskie, 2; off Seibold, 1. Struck out—By Coveleskie, 3; by Seibold, 3. Wild pitch—Coveleskie. Passed balls—O'Neill, Billings, Schang. Umpires—Moriarty and Evans. Time—1:50.

Peace Minutes Cause Feds to Drop Big Suit

Baltimore Club Withdraws Its $900,000 Damage Action Against Organized Baseball

Philadelphia, June 15.—The Baltimore club of the defunct Federal League to-day withdrew its $900,000 anti-trust damage suit against organized baseball. This is the second time within two years that a legal action, brought in a United States court, involving the question of whether organized baseball, as operated under the national agreement, is a trust, has been withdrawn before a decision had been given.

The first suit was brought in the Federal Court in Chicago in January, 1915, and was withdrawn when the American and National leagues signed a peace agreement with representatives of the Federal League in December of the same year. The action of the Baltimore club in dropping the suit to-day was taken, counsel said, because it was convinced that the "representatives of organized baseball" had not entered into a conspiracy to destroy the business of the Baltimore club. Nothing was said in announcing the withdrawal regarding the question of whether organized baseball was being operated in violation of the anti-trust laws.

The members of the National Baseball Commission and attorneys for the defendants said they were not surprised at the action of the Baltimore club. The court was informed there had been no settlement out of court or suggestion of one. It was said by prominent members of organized baseball that the Baltimore club decided to withdraw the suit after its counsel had read the stenographic minutes of the peace meeting, held in New York in December, 1915. These minutes, called for and placed in the record by the plaintiff, showed that the Federal League representatives at the meeting had stated that they officially represented the league and had authority to act.

International League

GAMES TO-DAY

Toronto at Newark.
Buffalo at Baltimore (two).
Montreal at Providence.
Rochester at Richmond (two).

YESTERDAY'S RESULTS

Newark, 4; Toronto, 3.
Rochester, 4; Richmond, 1.
Montreal, 10; Providence, 9.
Buffalo at Baltimore (rain).

STANDING OF TEAMS

	W.	L.	Pct.		W.	L.	Pct.
Ne'ark	28	17	.622	Tor'nto	26	21	.553
Provid	29	19	.604	Buffalo	19	30	.388
Roch'r	28	20	.583	Montr'l	17	28	.378
Baltim	27	20	.574	Rich'nd	15	34	.306

Egan's Timely Blow Wins Close Game For Newark Bears

Ben Egan's hard smash to centre in the ninth inning, scoring "Brick" Eldred, enabled Newark to beat the Toronto Maple Leafs yesterday afternoon. The score was 4 to 3.

Jack Warhop weakened in the ninth, when, with the score tied, Eldred drove the ball to left for two bases, Gus Getz got an infield safety and Eldred reached third, to tally on Egan's timely clout.

Walter Smallwood started in the box for Newark, but was removed in the second frame in favor of Roy Wilkinson. Wilkinson allowed three runs in the second, but after this he settled down and held Toronto safe during the remainder of the game.

The score:

TORONTO (I. L.)	ab	r	h	po	a	e
Altenb'g, rf	3	0	0	1	0	0
Jacobson, cf	4	0	1	2	0	0
Whiteman, lf	4	0	1	7	2	0
Lajoie, 2b	4	0	0	1	2	0
Graham, 1b	4	0	0	9	0	0
Blackb'rne, 3b	3	1	2	1	1	0
Smith, ss	2	1	0	0	2	1
Kelly, c	4	1	1	3	1	0
Warhop, p	4	0	1	0	1	1
Totals	32	3	6	*24	9	2

NEWARK (I. L.)	ab	r	h	po	a	e
Fuller, 2b	3	1	0	0	3	0
Mowe, ss	3	1	1	3	3	1
Haas, lf	3	0	0	2	0	0
Callahan, cf	3	1	3	4	0	1
Russell, 1b	3	0	1	11	0	0
Eldred, rf	4	1	1	4	0	0
Getz, 3b	4	0	1	0	3	0
Egan, c	4	0	2	3	0	0
Smallwood, p	0	0	0	0	0	0
Wilkinson, p	3	0	0	0	2	0
Totals	30	4	9	27	11	2

*None out when winning run was scored.

Newark	2	0	1	0	0	0	0	0	1	—4
Toronto	0	3	0	0	0	0	0	0	0	—3

Two-base hits—Callahan, Eldred. Stolen base—Smith. Sacrifice hits—Haas, Russell, Lajoie. Sacrifice flies—Altenberg, Callahan. Double play—Whiteman and Kelly. Left on bases—Newark, 6; Toronto, 6. First base on errors—Newark, 1. Base on balls—Off Smallwood, 1; off Wilkinson, 2; off Warhop, 2. Hits and earned runs—Off Smallwood, 2 hits 1 run in 1 inning; off Wilkinson, 4 hits no runs in 8 innings; off Warhop, 9 hits 3 runs in 9 innings. Struck out—By Wilkinson, 2; by Warhop, 2. Umpires—Blackburne and Carpenter. Time—1:42.

"He Deserves All He Got," Says Tener of J. McGraw

National League Magnates to Meet Here Monday to Take Up Case

Philadelphia, June 15.—President John K. Tener of the National League to-day issued a call for a special meeting the board of directors of the parent major league to be held in New York next Monday. At this star chamber session the case of John J. McGraw, suspended manager of the Giants, will be reviewed.

From the talk of Mr. Tener and other National League magnates who were here to-day in the interests of organized baseball's suppressed litigation with the stockholders of the defunct Federal League club of Baltimore, it is probable that McGraw will be called on the carpet to explain certain interviews attributed to him in which he severely criticised the executive for discipline handed out in connection with McGraw's altercation with Umpire Byron. McGraw, who struck Byron in the dressing room just after the close of New York's last game in Cincinnati, was fined $500 and suspended for sixteen days by President Tener. The New York club, through President Harry N. Hempstead, has filed a protest against Tener's ruling, alleging that the discipline was too severe and that Umpire Byron was equally at fault in the rumpus.

The meeting of the National League board of directors is synonymous with a special meeting of the parent organization because all eight clug presidents are represented. Tener intimated that he was prepared to push the case against McGraw. The executive deeply resents McGraw's alleged insinuations that the National League is being run along Philadelphia sentiments. Tener, it is said, feels the slap from McGraw the more keenly because he shielded the Giant manager last winter when certain rival club presidents were bent upon investigating the near scandal of the last Brooklyn-New York series at Ebbets Field last October.

"I am willing to let my record stand beside that of McGraw," said Tener to-day. "He accuses me, I understand, of spoiling the Giants' chances for the pennant by suspending him. That is not my concern in the matter. I only desire to suppress rowdyism. McGraw deserved all he got. I am sure the National League will back my stand in the matter."

N. Y. A. C. Games To-day

The first series of eleven athletic competitions which have been arranged by the New York Athletic Club will be held at its Travers Island grounds this afternoon. The programme comprises a 100-yard run, 880-yard run, 120-yard high hurdles and javelin throw, and among the contestants will be George Bronder, Fred. Murray, William Gordon, Bernie Wefers, jr., and C. R. Erdman.

THIS is Walter Pipp, first baseman of the New York Yankees and champion clean-up batter of the American League. Pipp distinguished himself in yesterday's victory over the Browns with his first home run of the season at the Polo Grounds. With Hendryx and Maisel on the bases in the first inning Wally connected with one of Earl Hamilton's curves and raised a tall fly that dropped into the right field stand. Pipp's lusty clout really decided the game.

THE SPORT-LIGHT by Grantland Rice

"Conscientious Objectors"

1. Any ball player on any umpire's decision against him.
2. The enraged citizen who takes three putts.
3. The Hard Boiled Egg who is slipped the check.
4. Any pitcher when Cobb or Speaker comes to bat.

Beyond 40

"How many men," asks F. T. R., "have been stars in sport after passing forty? I mean by "stars" able to compete with the best in the game on fairly even terms."

We have no "Who's Who in Sport Beyond Forty" at our side. But in baseball Anson, Young, Wagner, Lajoie and Plank were, or still are, stars beyond the legal sportive limit.

In golf there are, or there were, Vardon, Braid, Taylor, Johnny Ball, Walter Travis and numberless others at their best above this age. Brookes and Larned were both stars around this age, or just short of the mark, in tennis.

Fitzsimmons at forty was still able to fire a salvo of wallops, but very few fighters have been any good beyond thirty-five.

For the Whites of Their Eyes

"The annual National Rifle Match has been cancelled." At first thought this seems a queer sport to cancel now.

But on second thought few American rifles can carry 3,000 miles, and the only interesting rifle targets for American guns are now fully that far away.

The Advance Guard

For those Americans who first left for the French front a year or more ago these lines, author unknown, are applicable—

"Jolly good fellows who die for the death of it;
Fight for the fun of it—live for the breath of it;
Catch at the instant and drink of the minute,
Thinking not, caring not what may be in it.

"All the good fellows who think not of wages;
Foreign, in part, to the thing that our age is;
Giving no heed to the weight of the coffer,
Taking what Fate and not men have to offer.

"They and the like of them, here's a health to them!
Taints of our lower aims never undo them;
They will survive us all, passed through the portal;
Life often jests at what death makes immortal!"

The Long Climb

Joe Jackson has never known what it was to bat below .300 for a year. But the Greenville Grenade is now well back of the mark, over 50 points back, and June is skidding rapidly toward July. He needs an early spurt to pass the old landmark, but the chances are that he will. For the .300 eye is hard to suppress, once it develops the habit.

Jackson was a .280 batsman down in the minors and he broke into the Main Show with .387 for a starter. Year before last he came near slipping below the mark for the first time, but finally wiggled a few points over the line in a driving finish.

With a full term average above .350 he must be classed among the great hitters of baseball, for only a few have ever known a five-year span above this mark.

Jackson has the eye, the punch and the speed, a combination productive of high class batting. Once he starts his rise will likely be rapid, for a few hits will bring back confidence, and confidence is about 24 per cent of any basehit output.

"Golf is five hundred years old." Which means that at least five hundred years have passed since any golfer was ever on his game.

Col. Miller—Many thanks for kindness in forwarding same along. The appreciation is 102 per cent.

Playing It Safe

Col. Charles Hanson Towne was inspecting a ball game recently. It was his first offence for a year. During the course of the game he leaped to his feet and began clamoring, "O you Mac"——

One of his friends was greatly surprised. "I didn't know," he said, "that you knew any of the players' names."

"I don't," remarked Col. Towne, "but I know enough about baseball to know there is always some Mac on a team, so there's no chance to go wrong."

"Umpire Byron Is Unpopular."—Exchange. Just how many popular umpires do you happen to know? How many umpires do you know who may be soaked upon the kneecap with a foul without inspiring the populace to rousing cheers?

Gonzales Beats Brooklyn Team By Fluke Bunt

Weird Hit in Twelfth Inning Snatches Game from Flatbush Dodgers

St. Louis, June 15.—Brooklyn was beaten by the Cardinals to-day in the twelfth inning by a score of 3 to 2. A fluke bunt hit by Gonzales, the Cuban, beat Leon Cadore out of a well pitched game.

With one out in the twelfth Baird tripled to deep left field. Leon Ames, who earlier had replaced Lee Meadows when the bespectacled pitcher suddenly lost control, was taken out to allow Bobby Bescher to bat. Bescher worked Cadore for a base on balls. This brought up Jack Smith, the cleanup hitter of the Cardinals. Robinson instructed Cadore to pass this dangerous hitter, filling the bases.

The Brooklyn manager had his infield play deep for a possible double play. Gonzales, next up, decided to "squeeze" home the winning run. Jack Daubert quickly realized the strategy and raced in at top speed with the pitch. But Gonzales met the ball harder than Jake figured he would and sent a twisting popup just a few inches higher than Jake could reach. This fluke hit ended the game.

The Dodgers played fine ball behind Cadore's clever pitching. Lee Meadows started the game against Cadore, but was taken out in the eighth inning. Leon Ames went in with the score tied and gets credit for the victory. Two were out in the eighth when passes to Stengel and Cutshaw, sandwiched round Wheat's single, filled the bases.

Meadows pitched two balls to Smyth, who was sent in to hit for Mike Mowrey. Ames completed the job of walking Smyth, which forced Stengel home with a run. Ames immediately settled and blanked the Dodgers the rest of the way.

The Dodgers got a run in the first inning rather cheaply. Ivy Olson doubled to left and got an extra base when Hornsby muffed Cruise's throw-in. Daubert singled to centre for the run. The next three Brooklyn batters were easy outs. Hornsby's bobble spoiled an otherwise wonderful afternoon.

The Dodgers could not hit Meadows in the pinches, and until Lee lost control in the eighth inning there didn't seem to be a chance for any further scoring by the visitors.

At the end of the fifth inning it looked as if the one cheap run might land the Dodgers in front. St. Louis tied the score in the sixth. Livingston led off with a single. He was forced by Meadows, after Fred Smith fouled to Mowrey. Jack Smith, however, doubled to centre, scoring the pitcher.

St. Louis took the lead by scoring again in the seventh, but Brooklyn evened the count with a second run in the eighth. From here to the twelfth the game proved a spirited pitching duel.

The failure to work a hit-and-run play cost Brooklyn heavily in the seventh. Chief Meyers singled, with one out, but was caught stealing when Cadore missed his swing. Cadore doubled off the next ball pitched.

BROOKLYN (N. L.)	ab	r	h	o	a	e
Olson, ss	5	1	2	2	6	0
Daubert, 1b	5	0	3	12	1	0
Hickman, cf	6	0	0	3	1	0
Stengel, rf	5	1	1	2	1	0
Wheat, lf	5	0	2	1	0	0
Cutshaw, 2b	3	0	2	6	6	0
Mowrey, 3b	3	0	0	2	1	0
Smyth, 3b	0	0	0	0	0	0
Meyers, c	3	0	1	2	0	0
*Johnston	1	0	0	0	0	0
O. Miller, c	0	0	0	3	0	0
Cadore, p	5	0	1	1	5	0
Totals	41	2	11	†34	21	0

ST. LOUIS (N. L.)	ab	r	h	o	a	e
J. Smith, cf	4	0	2	3	0	0
Gonzales, 1b	6	0	2	17	0	0
J. Miller, 2b	4	0	1	2	4	0
‡Betzel, 2b	1	0	0	0	0	0
Hornsby, ss	3	1	0	3	7	1
Cruise, lf	4	0	1	4	0	0
Long, rf	5	0	2	1	0	0
Livingston, c	2	0	1	2	1	0
Snyder, c	3	0	0	3	1	0
F. Smith, 3b	3	0	1	1	0	0
§Baird, 3b	2	1	1	0	1	0
Meadows, p	2	1	0	0	1	0
Ames, p	2	0	1	0	2	0
¶Bescher	0	0	0	0	0	0
Totals	41	3	12	36	17	1

*One out when winning run scored.
†Batted for Meyers in eighth inning.
‡Ran for J. Miller in ninth inning.
§Ran for F. Smith in eighth inning.
¶Batted for Ames in twelfth inning.

Brooklyn	1	0	0	0	0	0	0	1	0	0	0	0	—2
St. Louis	0	0	0	0	0	1	1	0	0	0	0	1	—3

Two-base hits—Cadore, J. Smith, Olson. Three-base hits—Long, Baird. Stolen base—Cutshaw. Sacrifice hits—J. Smith, J. D. Smyth, O. Miller, Daubert. Double plays—Hornsby to Miller; Olson, Cutshaw and Daubert (2). Left on bases—Brooklyn, 11; St. Louis, 10. Bases on balls—Off Cadore, 5; off Meadows, 5. Hits and earned runs—Off Cadore, 12 hits 3 runs in 11 1-3 innings; off Meadows, 9 hits 1 run in 7 2-3 innings; off Ames, 2 hits no runs in 4 1-3 innings. Struck out—By Cadore, 2; by Meadows, 2; by Ames, 2. Umpires—Klem and Bransfield. Time—2:21.

Braves Win Second In Row from Cubs

Chicago, June 15.—Boston won from Chicago to-day by bunching hits off Prendergast. The score was 6 to 3.

Prendergast started for the Cubs, but had three bad innings, and gave way to Reuther. Rudolph pitched his best ball in the pinches and received fine support.

BOSTON (N. L.)	ab	r	h	o	a	e
Bailey, cf	3	1	1	1	0	0
Fitpat'k, cf	1	0	1	0	0	0
Evers, 2b	5	0	1	1	5	0
Wilhoit, rf	3	1	1	0	0	0
Magee, lf	5	1	1	1	0	0
Konetc'y, 1b	3	0	0	14	0	0
Smith, 3b	4	2	3	2	1	0
Gowdy, c	3	0	2	3	3	0
M'nville, ss	3	1	1	5	1	0
Rudolph, p	3	0	1	0	5	0
Totals	33	6	12	27	15	0

CHICAGO (N. L.)	ab	r	h	o	a	e
Zeider, ss	3	2	1	2	3	0
Wolter, rf	5	0	0	1	1	0
Doyle, 2b	3	0	0	1	3	0
Merkle, 1b	3	1	3	11	0	1
Williams, cf	4	0	2	2	1	0
Mann, lf	4	0	1	4	0	0
Wilson, c	4	0	0	5	2	0
Deal, 3b	4	0	2	1	4	0
Prend'rast, p	2	0	1	0	4	0
Reuther, p	2	0	0	0	1	0
Totals	34	3	10	27	19	1

Boston	1	1	0	0	0	0	2	2	0	—6
Chicago	1	0	0	0	0	0	1	1	0	—3

Two-base hits—Merkle (2), Gowdy, Maranville, Magee, Smith. Sacrifice hits—Wilhoit, Gowdy, Zeider. Sacrifice flies—Wilhoit, Rudolph, Fitzpatrick. Double plays—Zeider to Doyle to Merkle; Williams to Prendergast to Zeider to Deal; Evers to Konetchy; Deal to Wilson to Merkle. Left on bases—Chicago, 7; Boston, 1. First base on errors—Boston, 1. Bases on balls—Off Rudolph, 2; off Prendergast, 1; off Reuther, 1. Hits and earned runs—Off Prendergast, 8 hits 4 runs in 6 1-3 innings; off Reuther, 4 hits 2 runs in 2 2-3 innings; off Rudolph, 10 hits 3 runs in 9 innings. Struck out—By Prendergast, 2; by Rudolph, 3; by Reuther, 1. Wild pitch—Rudolph. Passed ball—Wilson. Umpires—Byron and Quigley. Time—2:03.

New York State League

Elmira, 5; Reading, 3.
Binghamton, 2; Harrisburg, 1 (first).
Binghamton vs. Harrisburg (second, rain).
Wilkes-Barre, 9; Utica, 1.
Wilkes-Barre, 7; Utica, 2.
Scranton at Syracuse (wet gr'ds).

Southern Association

Atlanta, 6; Chattanooga, 0.
Little Rock, 6; Mobile, 0.
Memphis, 4; New Orleans, 2.
Birmingham, 7; Nashville, 0.

Yankees Off to Good Start with Browns

Walter Pipp's Home Run Drive Into Stand Takes All the Fight Out of Fielder Jones's Men —Score 5 to 1

By W. O. M'GEEHAN

The embattled Yanks kicked the remnants of the St. Louis Browns all over the lot at the Polo Grounds yesterday, as the score of 5 to 1 might indicate.

The hero of the brutal and sànguinary contest was Walter Pipp, one of the most earnest swatters in current baseball. Pipp located the right field stand at the Polo Grounds for the first time this season and dropped a homer among the spectators, scoring three runs in the first inning.

It was not a particularly impressive home run, however. It was one of those high flies that just volplaned into the stands. Pipp has soaked the ball much harder in that direction and got only a single for himself. But, whether the homer was deserved or not, it took all the fight out of the Browns. The other two runs come under the head of unnecessary slaughter.

The victory following two over the haughty White Sox seems to have put new life into the Yankees. Wild William Donovan, their stalwart leader, had been so depressed up to a few days ago that he had taken to literature in despair. He contracted the habit of reading all of the sporting pages, and it was beginning to tell upon him, souring his naturally sunny disposition.

When the swipe by Pipp descended gently on to the right-field stands Donovan decided that he would no longer be a bookworm. He threw his cheaters or glasses over the fence and began to take a new interest in the pennant race.

Wild Bill Optimistic

Although the field was still cluttered up with umpires, three of them—count 'em, three—still disfiguring Henry Fabian's lawn, Donovan took a bigger and a more cheerful view of life. A couple of decisions that made the stands give an imitation of a Roman mob did not even get a rumble out of William. He was so far ahead and so optimistic as to the chances for the Yankees yesterday that he would not deign to even address one of the trio.

The three runs which accrued to the Yankees in the first inning were gathered with ease and alacrity. Hendryx got a base on balls and went to second on Magee's sacrifice. Fritz Maisel placed a nice bunt along the third base line, sending Hendryx to third.

It was then that Walter Pipp recalled that he had not yet dumped the ball into the right field stands this season. In fact, Baker had been holding the Yankee home run record for the Polo Grounds this season. Pipp adjusted his sights and shot for the stands. The ball dropped in among the spectators, and the lean first sacker trotted around the route, bringing Hendryx and Maisel home ahead of him.

The Yankees got another run in their half of the second inning because of an error by Sisler, the perfect ball player who once had more teams claiming him than Homer had cities claiming him. This utterly superfluous tally came without the formality of a single hit.

Peckinpaugh got a base on balls and Walters sent him to second with a sacrifice. Robert Shawkey, the best golf player on the Yankee team, drove one at Sisler, who went after the ball with one mitt, but it got through him. Peckinpaugh came in from second before it could be retrieved.

Walters Beats Bunt

The Yankees got one more in the seventh. The consensus of opinion is that they should have had but two, but as Umpire Nallin decreed otherwise, it was an active and somewhat heated session. Walters laid down a nice bunt to Pratt and beat it to the bag. After Shawkey had popped out, Hendryx connected for a nifty swipe to left.

Leopold Hoernschmeyer, who has been fattening a once lean batting average of late, drove a pretty two-bagger to left, scoring Walters and sending Hendryx to third. Fritz Maisel grounded to Pratt, who threw to Severeid. It looked as though Hendryx had slid under the outstretched arm of Severeid. But Nallin called Hendryx out. That practically ended a drive that threatened to roll Fielder Jones's cripples into pancakes.

The Browns got their solitary run in the fourth inning. Severeid clouted a double to left. He scored on a neat single by Marsans, the corpulent Cuban insurrecto. Marsans was caught a second later while he was dozing peacefully a few yards off first base.

The Browns started in the sixth, but they got nowhere in particular because of a weird exhibition of base-running, combined with some commendable vigilance on the part of the Yanks.

Jacobson got on by forcing Sisler. Severeid was given a passport to the bag. Marsans singled to right, and Jacobson was rounding third when Fielder Jones gave him the office to halt. Marsans continued on his way, and Jacobson then started for home. Pipp, who was pursuing the insurrecto, threw to Walters, heading off Jacobson.

Walters started Jacobson back to third and tossed the ball to Baker, who nailed Jacobson right under the anguished eyes of Fielder Jones. That depressing occurrence took the last feeble kick out of the Browns. They were not in evidence to any extent after that.

Sisler, the perfect, showed some of his worth on the defensive yesterday. Magee, who had beaten a bunt, was holding a lead off first. Pipp drove a high and hard liner at Sisler, who speared the ball with one hand. Then Sisler tagged the bag, cutting off Magee from the return and achieving a very pretty double play unassisted.

Still Climbing!

ST. LOUIS (A. L.)	ab	r	h	o	a	e
W. Miller, lf	4	0	0	0	0	0
Austin, 3b	4	0	1	0	2	0
Sisler, 1b	4	0	2	8	1	0
Jacobson, rf	3	0	0	3	1	0
Sloan, rf	1	0	0	1	0	0
Severeid	3	1	2	2	2	0
Marsans, cf	4	0	2	1	0	0
Pratt, 2b	4	0	0	5	6	0
Johnson, ss	2	0	0	4	2	0
Hamilton, p	3	0	2	0	1	0
*Rumler	1	0	0	0	0	0
Totals	33	1	9	24	15	0

NEW YORK (A. L.)	ab	r	h	o	a	e
Hendryx, rf	2	1	1	0	1	0
Magee, cf	3	0	2	0	0	0
Maisel, 2b	4	1	2	1	7	0
Pipp, 1b	4	1	1	15	1	0
E. Miller, lf	3	0	1	2	0	0
Baker, 3b	3	0	0	3	3	0
Peck'ugh, ss	3	1	0	2	3	0
Walters, c	2	1	2	4	2	0
Shawkey, p	3	0	1	0	5	0
Totals	27	5	10	27	22	0

*Batted for Johnson in ninth inning.

St. Louis	0	0	0	1	0	0	0	0	0	—1
New York	3	1	0	0	0	0	1	0	x	—5

Two-base hits—Severeid, Magee. Home run—Pipp. Stolen base—Maisel. Sacrifice hits—Magee, Walters. Double plays—Johnson, Pratt and Sisler; Sisler (unassisted); Jacobson, Severeid and Johnson; Austin, Pratt and Sisler. Left on bases—New York, 5; St. Louis, 7. Bases on balls—Off Shawkey, 2; off Hamilton, 5. Earned runs—Off Shawkey, 1; off Hamilton, 5. Struck out—By Shawkey, 3; by Hamilton, 1. Wild pitch—Shawkey. Umpires—Nallin, O'Loughlin and Hildebrand. Time—1:50.

White Sox Add To Their Lead, Beating Boston

Boston, June 15.—Chicago increased its margin of leadership in the American League race by shutting out Boston, 8 to 0, to-day.

Claude Williams, the Chicago southpaw, pitched a well controlled game, allowing no hits until the eighth inning. Three of Boston's four hits were made in the ninth without score.

Chicago bunted Shore out of the box in the fifth inning, and immediately fell upon Pennock, who relieved him, a double by Weaver, with the bases filled, followed by a sacrifice fly and a single, accounting for four runs.

The score:

CHICAGO (A. L.)	ab	r	h	o	a	e
Leibold, rf	2	0	0	1	0	0
J. Collins, rf	3	3	1	1	0	0
Weaver, 3b	5	1	2	3	2	0
E. Col'ns, 2b	4	1	1	1	0	0
Jackson, lf	4	1	2	3	0	0
Felsch, cf	3	0	0	4	0	0
Gandil, 1b	4	0	0	6	0	0
Rissberg, ss	4	0	2	0	1	0
Schalk, c	4	1	1	7	0	0
Williams, p	2	1	0	1	0	0
Totals	38	8	9	27	3	0

BOSTON (A. L.)	ab	r	h	o	a	e
Hooper, rf	4	0	0	2	0	0
Barry, 2b	4	0	0	3	6	0
Gainer, 1b	3	0	1	10	1	0
Lewis, lf	3	0	1	2	0	0
Walker, cf	4	0	0	3	1	0
Gardner, 3b	4	0	0	2	2	0
Scott, ss	4	0	1	2	5	2
Agnew, c	3	0	1	3	0	1
Shore, p	1	0	0	0	0	0
Pennock, p	0	0	0	0	2	0
Bader, p	0	0	0	0	0	0
*Janvrin	1	0	0	0	0	0
Totals	31	0	4	27	17	3

*Batted for Pennock in the eighth inning.

Chicago	0	0	0	2	4	0	1	0	1	—8
Boston	0	0	0	0	0	0	0	0	0	—0

Two-base hits—Weaver, Agnew. Three-base hit—Jackson. Stolen bases—J. Collins, Weaver. Sacrifice hit—Williams. Sacrifice fly—E. Collins. Double play—Barry to Gainer. Left on bases—Boston, 8; Chicago, 4. First base on errors—Chicago, 2. Bases on balls—Off Shore, 1; off Williams, 4; off Bader, 1. Hits and earned runs—Off Shore, 4 hits 2 runs in 4 innings (none out in 5th); off Pennock, 5 hits 4 runs in 4 innings; off Bader, no hits, no runs in 1 inning. Struck out—By Shore, 1; by Williams, 6; by Pennock, 1. Wild pitch—Shore. Umpires—Connolly and McCormick. Time—2:05.

Tigers Take First Game from Senators

Washington, June 15.—Detroit took the first game of the series from Washington to-day, 4 to 3.

All the visitors' runs were directly traceable to the almost unprecedented wildness of Walter Johnson, who gave eight bases on balls, hit Veach twice, and made a wild pitch.

The score:

DETROIT (A. L.)	ab	r	h	o	a	e
Bush, ss	1	1	0	2	2	0
Young, 2b	2	1	0	6	3	0
Cobb, cf	2	2	2	5	0	0
Veach, lf	2	0	0	1	0	0
Hellman, rf	2	0	0	0	0	0
Crawford, rf	2	0	1	1	0	0
Burns, 1b	5	0	0	4	0	0
Vitt, 3b	4	0	1	3	0	1
Stanage, c	4	0	1	5	3	0
James, p	3	0	0	0	1	1
Boland, p	1	0	0	0	0	0
Totals	28	4	5	27	9	2

WASHINGTON (A. L.)	ab	r	h	o	a	e
Judge, 1b	4	1	1	8	0	0
Foster, 2b	5	1	1	1	1	0
Milan, cf	2	1	2	2	0	0
Rice, rf	4	0	3	2	0	0
Shanks, lf	4	0	0	2	1	0
Leonard, 3b	3	0	0	0	3	1
Ainsmith, c	3	0	0	11	1	0
Crane, ss	2	0	0	0	1	1
*Gharrity	1	0	0	0	0	0
McBride, ss	1	0	0	1	1	0
Johnson, p	2	0	0	0	0	0
†Menosky	1	0	0	0	0	0
Totals	32	3	7	27	8	2

*Batted for Crane in sixth inning.
†Batted for Johnson in ninth inning.

Detroit	0	0	1	0	2	0	1	0	0	—4
Washington	1	0	1	0	0	0	1	0	0	—3

Two-base hit—Stanage. Three-base hit—Milan. Stolen bases—Rice, Cobb. Sacrifice hits—Young, Cobb. Sacrifice flies—Veach, Crawford. Left on bases—Detroit, 11; Washington, 8. First base on errors—Washington, 1; Detroit, 2. Bases on balls—Off Johnson, 8; off James, 5; off Boland, 1. Hits and earned runs—Off James, 5 hits 2 runs in 6 innings (none out, one on base, in 7th); off Boland, 2 hits 1 run in 3 innings; off Johnson, 5 hits 3 runs in 9 innings. Hit by pitcher—By Johnson (Veach, 2). Struck out—By Johnson, 10; by James, 2; by Boland, 2. Wild pitch—Johnson (2). Umpires—Dineen and Owens. Time—2:16.

Engineers to Benefit By Big Baseball Game

Arrangements have been completed for the big patriotic demonstration and baseball game for the benefit of the 1st Reserve Engineer Regiment of New York at the Polo Grounds Sunday. There will be a drill by the engineer regiment, a band concert and a regular league baseball game between the Yankees and the St. Louis Browns.

The complete proceeds will be devoted to the mess fund of the New York engineers. As the idea was that of Captain T. L. Huston, who is now with the 6th Reserve Engineers at Detroit, it might seem a gracious thing on the part of the New York engineers to divide the fund with the Western unit which will leave for France at the same time.

Levinsky Defeats Madden

Battling Levinsky, the blond Hebrew light heavyweight, gave Bartley Madden a sound beating last night in the main bout at Bill Brown's Athletic Club, at Far Rockaway Beach. Madden was still on his feet at the end of the tenth session, but he was a badly mussed up young man when it was all over.

International League

At Richmond—

										R.	H.	E.
Rochester	0	1	0	2	0	0	0	0	1	—4	6	1
Richmond	0	0	0	0	0	0	1	0	0	—1	6	3

Batteries—Lohman and Wendell; Carmichael and Reynolds.

At Providence—

										R.	H.	E.
Montreal	0	0	1	9	0	0	0	0	0	—10	14	1
Providence	0	6	0	1	0	0	1	0	1	—9	12	1

Batteries—Lyons, Hersche and Madden; Schellenbach, Schultz and Allen.

At Baltimore—Buffalo vs. Baltimore (rain).

Eastern League

Lawrence, 2; New London, 1.
Portland, 2; Hartford, 1.
Springfield, 6; Bridgeport, 1.
Worcester, 6; New Haven, 3.

Standing of Major League Clubs

NATIONAL LEAGUE

GAMES TO-DAY

New York at Pittsburgh.
Brooklyn at St. Louis.
Philadelphia at Cincinnati.
Boston at Chicago.

YESTERDAY'S RESULTS

New York at Pittsburgh (wet gr'ds.).
Philadelphia, 12; Cincinnati, 8.
Boston, 6; Chicago, 3.
St. Louis, 3; Brooklyn, 2 (12 in.).

STANDING OF TEAMS

	W.	L.	Pct.		W.	L.	Pct.
N. York	29	16	.644	Cincin'ti	24	31	.436
Phila	29	16	.644	Boston	17	24	.415
Chicago	30	23	.566	B'klyn	17	25	.405
St. Louis	27	22	.551	Pittsb'h	16	32	.333

AMERICAN LEAGUE

GAMES TO-DAY

St. Louis at New York
Chicago at Boston
Cleveland at Philadelphia
Detroit at Washington

YESTERDAY'S RESULTS

New York, 5; St. Louis, 1.
Detroit, 4; Washington, 3.
Chicago, 8; Boston, 0.
Philadelphia, 3; Cleveland, 2.

STANDING OF TEAMS

	W.	L.	Pct.		W.	L.	Pct.
Chicago	34	17	.667	Detroit	22	25	.468
Boston	30	18	.625	St. Louis	20	29	.408
N. York	27	20	.574	Phila	17	28	.378
Clevel'd	26	27	.491	Wash'n	18	30	.375

Wild Bill's Men Win Two Games—Red Sox Lead Leagu

Yankees Come to Life Before Record Crowd

Twenty-eight Thousand Cleveland Fans Watch Fisher and Caldwell Baffle Indians—Home Run Baker Has Big Day with Stick

Cleveland, July 15.—In the presence of the greatest crowd that ever attended a major league baseball game in Cleveland Bill Donovan's fast sliding Yankees came to life here this afternoon and registered a double victory at the expense of Lee Fohl's Indians.

To-night the Donovan boys are within flirting distance of third place again, just at a time when it seemed that the Indians were about to distance them for good. The scores hung up by the invaders were 4 to 0 in the opener and 8 to 2 in the closing engagement.

According to the officials of the home club 26,431 paid to see the double bill this afternoon. Upwards of 1,500 more were within the gates, making a total attendance of about 28,000.

This is 10,000 above the seating capacity of the grandstand and bleachers, and an overflow gathering of many thousands encircled the playing field. All hits into the crowd were good for two bases.

The Indians did not hit one into the human fringe against Ray Fisher in the opener, and got only two such blows in the second game. The Yanks got four in the first game and one in the second. Two pitchers who make it a custom to beat Donovan's team had their opportunities to repeat this afternoon, and neither was able to tame the boys from Manhattan. In fact, neither remained to the finish.

A Heavy Bombardment

Stan Coveleskie was heavily bombarded in the opener, and finally gave way to a pinch hitter before the battle ended, Gould finishing the game. Otis Lambeth was driven off the hill in the second contest, and again Gould came on with the damage done. This time the Yanks continued the slaughter at the expense of the chubby boxman.

Ray Fisher held the home team helpless in the first game. He issued only one pass, and allowed four hits—two of them scratches which rolled only a few feet in front of the plate. His mates backed him up in faultless style, and not one of the Indians was able to get past second base. Tris Speaker, kingpin of the Cleveland attack, did not get on the bases in four trips to the plate against the big Vermonter.

The two teams went through six innings of scoreless baseball in the first game, and then Frank Baker opened things up with a double over the heads of the crowd in right field. A minute later Elmer Miller bounded one off the chalk line in right field, and the ball rolled into the crowd for another double, scoring Baker.

In the eighth the Yanks landed on Coveleskie hard. With one down, Peck hit to deep centre for two bases, and went to third on Baumann's one-base blow to centre, Paddy going to second on the throw-in. Pipp smashed a single into centre, scoring Peck and Baumann, and when Speaker threw to the plate Pipp raced to second. Baker followed with another double against the right-field fence, and Pipp counted with the last run of the game.

Yanks Keep at It

In the second game the Yankees were even stronger with the stick. Caldwell was by no means as effective in keeping the Indians tame as Fisher had been in the opener, but the slim telegrapher had the habit of tightening up after the home team got runners on the paths. The Indians nicked him for a total of nine hits, but the blows never arrived with runners on the paths.

It required a steal of the plate to score one Cleveland run and Elmer Miller's heave into the crowd behind third base to get the other. Cleveland scored in the first inning on Wamby's single, Chapman's sacrifice, an out and Wamby's steal home.

In the third Hendryx reached second on a fielder's choice and an error, and counted on Peck's single. Singles by Magee and Caldwell, a fielder's choice and Hendryx's sacrifice fly gave the Yanks two runs in the fifth. Maisel's single, a pass to Pipp and Baker's single added a run in the sixth and chased Lambeth out.

In the eighth Chapman's fumble on Maisel, singles by Pipp and Baker and Miller's double sent in three runs. Another arrived in the ninth on Hendryx's single and steal and a hit by Maisel. Graney's double and Miller's throw past Baker in the seventh gave the Indians their second run.

Well! Well!! Well!!!

FIRST GAME

NEW YORK (A. L.)	ab	r	h	po	a	e	CLEVELAND (A. L.)	ab	r	h	po	a	e
Hendryx, cf.	5	0	0	2	0	0	Wambs'ss, 2b	4	0	0	2	4	0
Peck'paugh, ss	4	1	3	4	3	0	Chapman, ss	4	0	1	0	3	0
Baumann, 2b	4	1	1	1	1	0	Speaker, cf..	4	0	0	1	0	0
Pipp, 1b....	4	1	2	10	1	0	Roth, rf....	4	0	2	2	0	0
Baker, 3b...	4	1	2	1	0	0	Guisto, 1b...	3	0	0	10	0	0
Miller, rf...	4	0	1	4	0	0	Graney, lf...	2	0	0	2	0	0
Magee, lf....	3	0	0	0	0	0	Evans, 3b...	3	0	1	2	4	0
Nunamaker, c	4	0	1	5	0	0	O'Neill, c...	1	0	0	5	0	0
Fisher, p....	4	0	0	0	3	0	Billings, c...	0	0	0	3	0	0
							Coveleskie, p	2	0	0	0	1	0
							Gould, p....	0	0	0	0	0	0
							*Smith......	1	0	0	0	0	0
							†Harris.....	1	0	0	0	0	0
Totals.....	36	4	9	27	8	0	Totals.....	29	0	4	27	12	0

*Batted for O'Neill in the eighth inning.
†Batted for Coveleskie in the eighth inning.

New York...........	0	0	0	0	0	0	1	3	0	—4
Cleveland	0	0	0	0	0	0	0	0	0	—0

Two-base hits—Baker (2), Miller, Peckinpaugh, Chapman, Roth. Sacrifice hits—Guisto, O'Neill. Left on bases—New York, 6; Cleveland, 5. Bases on balls—Off Fisher, 1; off Coveleskie, 1. Hits and earned runs—Off Fisher, 6 hits in nine innings; off Coveleskie, 9 hits and 4 runs in eight innings; off Gould, no hits and no runs in one inning. Struck out—By Fisher, 5; by Coveleskie, 4; by Gould, 2. Umpires—Dineen and O'Loughlin. Time—1:40.

SECOND GAME

NEW YORK (A. L.)	ab	r	h	po	a	e	CLEVELAND (A. L.)	ab	r	h	po	a	e
Hendryx, cf	4	2	1	0	0	0	Wambs'ss, 2b	4	1	2	0	3	1
Peck,ugh,ss	5	0	1	2	4	0	Chapman, ss	3	0	1	3	5	1
Baum'nn,2b	2	0	1	1	1	0	Speaker, cf..	4	0	1	2	0	0
Maisel, 2b.	3	2	2	3	1	0	Roth, rf.....	4	0	2	0	0	0
Pipp, 1b..	3	1	1	7	1	0	Guisto, 1b...	3	0	0	17	2	0
Baker, 3b.	4	1	3	2	3	1	Graney, lf...	4	1	1	1	0	0
Miller, rf.	4	0	1	3	0	1	Evans, 3b...	3	0	1	2	4	1
Magee, lf..	3	0	1	0	0	0	O'Neill, c...	3	0	1	1	2	1
Walters, c.	4	1	0	9	3	0	Lambeth, p..	2	0	0	0	1	1
Caldwell, p	4	1	1	0	2	0	Gould, p....	1	0	0	1	5	0
							*Smith......	1	0	0	0	0	0
Totals...	36	8	12	27	15	2	Totals.....	32	2	9	27	23	5

*Batted for Evans in the ninth inning.

New York...........	0	0	1	0	2	1	0	3	1	—8
Cleveland	1	0	0	0	0	0	1	0	0	—2

Two-base hits—Miller, Speaker, Graney. Stolen bases—Maisel (2), Hendryx, Wambsganss. Sacrifice hits—Magee, Chapman. Sacrifice fly—Hendryx. Double plays—Evans and Guisto; Wambsganss; Guito, Chapman and O'Neill; Baker, Maisel and Pipp. Left on bases—New York, 5; Cleveland, 5. Bases on errors—New York, 2. Bases on balls—Off Caldwell, 1; off Lambeth, 1; off Gould, 1. Hits and earned runs—Off Caldwell, 9 hits in nine innings; off Lambeth, 7 hits and 1 run in five innings, none out in sixth, pitched to three batters; off Gould, 5 hits and 1 run in four innings. Struck out—By Caldwell, 6. Umpires—O'Loughlin and Dineen. Time—2:05.

RAYS BRING RAYS OF HOPE TO OUR YANKEES

Rain Prevents Game For 69th Regiment

The baseball game between the Giants and Chicago Cubs, scheduled at the Polo Grounds yesterday for the benefit of the 69th Regiment, was cancelled because of the heavy downpour of the morning, which left the field in too soggy a condition for a contest.

It is expected that another attempt will be made by the management of the New York club to arrange for a concert and Sunday ball game, the proceeds to go to the same military organization.

Lee Magee Goes To Browns for Armando Marsans

Cleveland, July 15.—President Ban Johnson of the American League tonight notified Colonel Jacob Ruppert, president of the Yankees, that the St. Louis club owners had agreed to all the terms in the transfer of Lee Magee, outfielder, to the Browns in exchange for Armando Marsans, also an outfielder.

The deal goes into effect at once, and both players have been ordered to join their new clubs. To put the deal through the owners of the Yankees had to agree to pay the difference in money between the contracts of the two players. Magee is serving the last year under a contract calling for $8,333, which he signed for the Wards, of the Brooklyn Federal League Club. This contract the Yankees assumed when they purchased Magee through Harry F. Sinclair.

The price paid for Magee by Messrs. Ruppert and Huston was $22,500, and his work with the Yankees both last season and this has been a big disappointment.

Marsans is expected to report here to-morrow, and he will be assigned to a regular place in the New York outfield for the present, at least.

When High and Gilhooley are ready to play Marsans's standing as a regular or as a substitute will be determined by his stick work. Marsans has not batted well this season, but Donovan believes that a change of scene may help him. He still ranks with the best outfielders of the game in fielding.

American Association

Louisville, 5; St. Paul, 0.
Louisville, 11; St. Paul, 3.
Kansas City, 10; Toledo, 9.
Toledo, 4; Kansas City, 2.
Columbus, 8; Milwaukee, 2.
Columbus, 5; Milwaukee, 0.
Minneapolis, 2; Indianapolis, 1.
Indianapolis, 4; Minneapolis, 3.

Bush Pounds Ball As the Tigers Win

troit, July 15.—The defence of the delphia Athletics went to pieces eighth inning, and Detroit, scorur runs, won to-day's game, 7

and Myers were hit hard, but ger twirler was more effective en on bases. Bush was the batar.

score:

DELPHIA (A. L.)	ab	r	h	po	a	e	DETROIT (A. L.)	ab	r	h	po	a	e
an, rf	5	0	2	1	0	0	Bush, ss....	4	1	3	4	1	1
, cf.	3	1	1	0	0	0	Vitt, 3b....	4	1	2	3	4	0
, lf.	4	0	1	2	1	0	Cobb, cf....	4	1	2	1	0	0
s, 3b..	4	1	1	0	0	1	Veach, lf...	4	1	1	3	0	0
nnis, 1b	4	0	0	11	1	0	Heilman, 1b	3	0	0	8	1	0
nang, c.	4	0	2	3	2	1	Harper, rf..	3	2	1	0	0	0
gan, ss.	4	0	2	4	4	1	Young, 2b..	4	0	0	2	3	0
rover, 2b.	3	0	0	2	4	0	Stanage, c..	4	0	2	6	1	0
yers, p..	3	0	1	2	1	0	Dauss, p...	4	1	1	0	3	1
W.Johnson	1	0	0	0	0	0							
Totals...	35	2	10	24	13	3	Totals....	34	7	12	27	13	2

*Batted for Myers in the ninth inning.

Philadelphia	0	0	0	1	1	0	0	0	0	—2
Detroit	0	0	2	1	0	0	0	4	x	—7

Two-base hits—Harper, Cobb, Stanage. Three-base hits—Bodie, Vitt. Stolen bases—Strunk, Cobb, Veach, Harper, W. Johnson (2). Sacrifice hit—Strunk. Double plays—Bodie and McInnis; Bush, Young and Heilman; Dugan and McInnis. Left on bases—Philadelphia, 8; Detroit, 5. Bases on balls—Off Dauss, 1; off Myers, 1. Hits and earned runs—Off Myers, 3 runs and 12 hits; off Dauss, 1 run and 10 hits. Hit by pitcher—By Myers (Harper). Struck out—By Dauss, 8; by Myers, 2. Umpires—Nallin, Owens and McCormick. Time—1:49.

Weymouth Wins Golf Prize at Flushing

A. Weymouth won the 18-hole handicap tournament for the benefit of the Flushing Day Nursery on the links of the Flushing Country Club yesterday. The tournament was begun Saturday and over fifty members competed. By winning, Weymouth becomes possessor of a trophy presented by R. M. Littlejohn. The victorious card was 86—11—75. H. L. Bennett was second with 96—20—76, while W. A. Mantle and C. H. Stevick tied for third with 86—9—77, and 91—14—77.

R. H. Boyd beat F. B. Porter in a semi-final round for the Governors' Cup. After playing the first 18 holes they were all square, and in the extra round of 18 holes Boyd won by 2 and 1 to play. C. F. Watt beat A. S. Chatfield 3 and 2 and will meet Boyd in the final next week.

Southern Association

lanta, 5; Chattanooga, 3.
Atlanta, 4; Chattanooga, 2.
Memphis, 6; New Orleans, 3.
Birmingham vs. Nashville (wet gr'ds).

Red Sox Capture A Double Header From the Browns

St. Louis, July 15.—The Boston Red Sox twice defeated the St. Louis Browns to-day, the scores being 4 to 2 and 6 to 3. The double victory gave the visitors first place in the league race.

Boston won the first game with a batting rally in the tenth inning, after an error by Hoblitzell had enabled St. Louis to tie the score in the seventh. Hoblitzell and Gardner singled, and Lewis, who replaced Shorten in the seventh, tripled, scoring two runs.

Rogers's wildness lost the second game for the home team.

The scores:

FIRST GAME

BOSTON (A. L.)	ab	r	h	po	a	e	ST. LOUIS (A. L.)	ab	r	h	po	a	e
Hooper, rf.	5	0	2	0	0	0	Miller, lf...	3	0	0	0	0	0
Barry, 2b.	5	0	0	1	6	0	*Hartley.....	1	0	0	0	0	0
Hob'zell,1b	5	1	1	10	0	1	Johnson, ss.	1	0	0	1	1	0
Gardner, 3b	5	1	1	2	1	0	Austin, 3b..	3	0	0	0	0	0
Shorten, lf	3	0	1	2	0	0	Sloan, rf....	5	0	1	5	1	0
Lewis, lf..	2	0	1	0	0	0	Sisler, 1b...	4	0	2	13	2	0
Walker, cf.	4	0	0	5	0	0	Pratt, 2b...	3	1	0	2	8	0
Scott, ss..	5	0	1	4	6	0	Jacobson, cf.	4	1	1	1	0	0
Thomas, c.	3	2	1	6	0	0	Severeid, c..	4	0	1	6	0	0
Ruth, p...	4	0	3	0	2	0	Lavan, ss....	2	0	0	1	4	1
							†Rumler....	1	0	0	0	0	0
							‡Shotton....	1	0	0	0	0	0
							Sothoron, p.	4	0	0	1	0	0
Totals...	41	4	11	30	15	1	Totals.....	36	2	5	30	16	1

*Batted for Miller in the seventh inning.
†Batted for Lavan in the seventh inning.
‡Ran for Rumler in the seventh inning.

Boston	0	0	1	0	0	0	1	0	0	2	—4
St. Louis.........	0	0	0	0	0	0	2	0	0	0	—2

Two-base hits—Ruth, Sisler, Scott. Three-base hit—Lewis. Double plays—Sloan to Sisler to Severeid; Lavan to Sisler. Left on bases—Boston, 9; St. Louis, 7. Bases on balls—Off Ruth, 2; off Sothoron, 2. First base on errors—Boston, 1. Hits and earned runs—Off Ruth, 5 hits and 1 run in ten innings; off Sothoron, 11 hits and 3 runs in ten innings. Hit by pitcher—By Ruth (Austin). Struck out—By Ruth, 5; by Sothoron, 5. Passed ball—Severeid. Umpires—Evans and Hildebrand. Time—2:08.

SECOND GAME

BOSTON (A. L.)	ab	r	h	po	a	e	ST. LOUIS (A. L.)	ab	r	h	po	a	e
Hooper, rf..	3	1	1	1	0	1	Miller, lf....	3	1	1	1	1	0
Barry, 2b...	4	1	1	4	1	1	Austin, 3b..	4	1	2	1	6	0
Hoblitzell,1b	4	2	0	7	0	1	Sloan, rf....	4	1	2	1	0	0
Gardner, 3b.	4	0	3	0	1	0	Sisler, 1b...	4	0	2	17	1	1
Shorten, lf.	3	0	0	1	0	0	Pratt, 2b....	4	0	0	0	4	0
Lewis, lf...	1	0	0	0	0	0	Jacobson, cf.	4	0	0	2	0	0
Walker, cf.	4	1	2	4	0	0	Hale, c.....	3	0	0	2	0	0
Scott, ss....	4	0	0	4	5	0	Lavan, ss....	4	0	1	3	3	0
Agnew, c...	3	1	2	6	1	0	Rogers, p...	1	0	0	0	3	1
Shore, p....	1	0	0	0	2	0	*Shotton....	1	0	0	0	0	0
Pennock, p.	2	0	0	0	2	0	Koob, p.....	0	0	0	0	0	0
							†Rumler.....	1	0	0	0	0	0
							Molyneaux, p	0	0	0	0	0	0
							Martin, p...	0	0	0	0	1	0
							‡Severeid....	1	0	0	0	0	0
Totals....	33	6	9	27	12	3	Totals.....	34	3	8	27	18	2

*Batted for Rogers in the fifth inning.
†Batted for Koob in the seventh inning.
‡Batted for Martin in the ninth inning.

Boston	1	0	0	1	4	0	0	0	0	—6
St. Louis............	0	0	3	0	0	0	0	0	0	—3

Three-base hit—Gardner. Home run—Walker. Stolen base—Miller. Double plays—Sisler to Lavan; Lavan to Sisler; Miller to Sisler; Austin to Sisler. Left on bases—Boston, 6; St. Louis, 6. First base on errors—Boston, 1; St. Louis, 1. Bases on balls—Off Shore, 1; off Pennock, 1; off Rogers, 2; off Koob, 1; off Molyneaux, 2. Hits and earned runs—Off Shore, 5 hits and 2 runs in three innings; off Pennock, 3 hits in six innings; off Rogers, 7 hits and 4 runs in five innings; off Koob, 1 hit in two innings; off Molyneaux, 1 hit in one inning, none out in ninth; off Martin, no hits in 1 inning. Hit by pitcher—By Koob (Agnew). Struck out—By Shore, 1; by Pennock, 2; by Rogers, 1; by Koob, 1. Wild pitch—Martin. Umpires—Hildebrand and Evans. Time—2:12.

Standing of Major League Clubs

NATIONAL LEAGUE

GAMES TO-DAY

Chicago at New York
St. Louis at Brooklyn
Cincinnati at Philadelphia
Pittsburgh at Boston

YESTERDAY'S RESULTS

Chicago at New York (wet grounds)

STANDING OF TEAMS

	W.	L.	P.c.		W.	L.	P.c.
New York.	47	26	.644	Chicago	43	40	.518
Phila.....	39	32	.549	Br'klyn.	36	38	.486
St. Louis..	43	37	.538	Boston..	30	43	.411
Cincin'ti..	46	41	.529	Pittsb'h	24	51	.320

AMERICAN LEAGUE

GAMES TO-DAY

New York at Cleveland
Boston at St. Louis
Philadelphia at Detroit
Washington at Chicago

YESTERDAY'S RESULTS

New York, 4; Cleveland, 0
New York, 8; Cleveland, 2
Washington, 6; Chicago, 5
Detroit, 7; Philadelphia, 2
Boston, 4; St. Louis, 2 (10 innings)
Boston, 6; St. Louis, 3

STANDING OF TEAMS

	W.	L.	P.c.		W.	L.	P.c.
Boston...	50	30	.625	Detroit.	41	39	.512
Chicago...	51	31	.622	Wash'n.	33	45	.423
Cleveland.	45	40	.529	Phila...	29	47	.382
New York.	41	37	.526	St. L'uis	31	52	.373

Many Upsets in Games Of the Harlem League

Stars Fail to Overcome Handicaps—Glencoe A. C. Wins

By A. C. CAVAGNARO

Upsets came thick and fast in the annual outdoor handicap games of the Harlem Athletic League, held in the City College Stadium yesterday. The recognized champions of the association found it beyond human endurance to overcome the handicaps allotted, and the procession across the finish line was made up of competitors enjoying the limit allowances. Only one scratch contestant succeeded in winning a first place.

Victor Voteretsas, the big Greek of the Morningside Athletic Club, was one of those who went down with the landslide of stars. However, he went down with flying colors, as he made a gallant finish in the two-mile race, passing seven men on the final lap, to be beaten by ten yards. The victor was William Stokeley, the rangy St. Christopher Athletic Club runner, who had the big start of 125 yards.

The clubs of the league showed that they were developing much promising material, many novice runners scoring victories. As their capabilities in open competition were unknown, they were allowed liberal handicaps. The outstanding feats among these new athletic aspirants were furnished by Edward Maccanon, of the St. Christopher Club, and Edward Hunter, a Salem-Crescent runner. The latter won the 100-yard dash from 10 yards, in 0:09 4-5, while Maccanon defeated Hunter by one yard in the 300-yard event.

Whitehouse Big Aid

The team point trophy, donated by Congressman Murray Hulbert, went to the Glencoe Athletic Club principally through the great help afforded by Max Whitehouse, a new recruit. Whitehouse is a student at the High School of Commerce, and is the present broad jump champion among the high school boys.

Besides winning his specialty Whitehouse also captured the running hop, step and jump. The ten points he earned were responsible for his club pulling out a close victory, with 22 points. The St. Christopher Club followed with 19 points, while the Salem-Crescent Athletic Club had 17 and the Morningside Athletic Club 15.

Dave Rosenberg, winner of the shot-put event in the recent junior patriotic meet, was the only scratch winner, tossing the 12-pound missile 55 feet 7 inches. In capturing the 100-yard race for girls Miss Mae Kahl broke the league record by two seconds. Her time was 0:13 2-5.

How They Finished

880-yard run (handicap)—Won by S. Jackson, St. Christopher A. C. (20 yards); A. Meyerheim, Glencoe A. C. (35 yards), second; M. Cummings, Alpha P. C. C. (45 yards), third. Time, 2:02.

Putting 12-pound shot (handicap)—Won by D. Rosenberg, Glencoe A. C. (scratch), with 55 feet 7 inches; A. Kurzman, Morningside A. C. (1 foot), with 52 feet 4½ inches, second; J. Heim, Morningside A. C. (4 feet), with 49 feet 10 inches, third.

100-yard dash (handicap)—Won by E. Hunter, Salem-Crescent A. C. (10 yards); J. Anderson, St. Christopher Club (10 yards), second; C. Rosenberg, Morningside A. C. (10 yards), third. Time, 0:09 4-5.

Two-mile run (handicap)—Won by W. Stokeley, St. Christopher Club (125 yards); V. Voteretsas, Morningside A. C. (scratch), second; S. Jackson, St. Christopher Club (50 yards), third. Time, 9:52.

300-yard run (handicap)—Won by E. Maccanon, St. Christopher Club (20 yards); E. Hunter, Salem-Crescent A. C. (20 yards), second; R. Haden, Alpha P. C C. (14 yards), third. Time, 0:31 2-5.

100-yard run (special)—Won by Miss Mae Kahl; Miss Helen Benke, second; Mrs. Anna Paton, third. Time, 0:13 2-5.

Running broad jump (handicap)—Won by M. Whitehouse, Glencoe A. C. (3 feet), with actual jump of 20 feet 1 inch; A. Flourney, St. Christopher A. C. (3 feet), with 19 feet 2 inches, second; B. Louder, Salem-Crescent A. C. (1 foot 6 inches), with actual jump of 19 feet 10 inches, third.

Running, hop, step and jump (handicap)—Won by M. Whitehouse, Glencoe A. C. (4 feet), with actual jump of 40 feet 1¼ inches; D. Rosenberg, Glencoe A. C. (5 feet), with actual jump of 38 feet 9½ inches, second; F. Belsky, Morningside A. C. (3 feet), with actual jump of 39 feet 5 inches, third.

Medley relay race (handicap)—Won by St. Christopher Club (52 yards), with Jackson, Flourney, Levy and Maccanon; Salem-Crescent A. C. first team (30 yards), with White, Verwayen, Brown and Creed, second; Salem-Crescent A. C. second team (40 yards), with Mock, La Beet, Isaacs and Brunson, third. Time, 3:48.

Point score—Glencoe A. C., 22; St. Christopher Club, 19; Salem-Crescent A. C., 17; Morningside A. C., 15; Alpha P. C. C., 4.

Rose Marie Leads Yachts Over Line

Although the inclement weather of yesterday morning prevented many yachtsmen from bringing their craft to the Jamaica Bay Yacht Club, there was a satisfactory war-time entry of power boats for the annual open race of the organization.

Using as a basis the times made a week ago in the race of the Belle Harbor Yacht Club, the fleet was divided into two divisions. Both went over the same course that took them from the starting line off the Jamaica Bay Yacht Club, to a buoy off Rockaway Inlet, thence to Buoy No. 2, Grassy Point Buoy, and home. On both actual and corrected times the winner in Class A was the Rose Marie, the property of C. Scheiz.

Although Smarty II was the first home among the small power boats, on corrected time, the prize was annexed by the Mary Jones, owned by William Jones. Five sailboats started, but owing to light airs not a single one had finished one half hour after sundown.

Bugle Will Announce Starts of Trot Races

Cleveland, July 15.—The blast of a bugle, a new system of announcing that a race is on, will sound the call for the 2:10 trot on North Randall racetrack tomorrow, the opening event of the Grand Circuit season of 1917.

Harness horse experts say the fastest trotters and pacers in the world are now quartered at North Randall, and predict the greatest opening meeting in the history of the Grand Circuit. The races continue through to Friday, unless rain causes a postponement.

McVey Knocks Out Clarke

Panama, July 15.— Sam McVey, the American negro heavyweight pugilist, to-day knocked out Jeff Clarke, of Philadelphia, in the fifteenth round of a twenty-round match.

International League

GAMES TO-DAY

Newark at Rochester.
Richmond at Buffalo.
Baltimore at Montreal.
Providence at Toronto

YESTERDAY'S RESULTS

Providence, 6; Montreal, 2.
Providence, 3; Montreal, 2.

STANDING OF TEAMS

	W.	L.	P.c.		W.	L.	P.c.
Newark.	48	29	.623	Roch'ter	40	41	.494
Toronto.	47	33	.588	Buffalo..	33	49	.402
Provid...	47	33	.588	Richm'd.	31	47	.397
Baltim'e	45	34	.570	M'ntreal	26	51	.338

Triple by Foster In Ninth Inning Wins for Senators

Chicago, July 15.—Eddie Foster's triple in the ninth inning, when Washington had started a rally, drove in two runs and gave the visitors the first game of the series here to-day, 6 to 5.

Erratic playing by the visitors, coupled with opportune hitting, gave the White Sox their early runs, and they threatened to tie or win the game in the ninth when G. Harrity's error paved the way for a run.

Johnson's good judgment in passing Eddie Collins with the tieing run on third and the winning run on second probably saved the game for Washington.

The score:

WASHINGTON (A. L.)	ab	r	h	po	a	e	CHICAGO (A. L.)	ab	r	h	po	a	e
Judge, 1b..	4	0	0	5	0	0	Leibold, rf..	4	1	2	0	0	0
Gharrity, 1b	1	1	1	1	0	1	Weaver, 3b..	3	0	3	1	1	0
Shanks, ss..	5	1	2	3	1	0	E. Collins, 2b	4	1	0	2	3	0
C. Milan, cf	4	1	2	2	0	0	Felsch, cf...	5	0	0	2	0	0
Rice, rf....	4	0	1	0	0	0	Jackson, lf..	5	1	2	6	0	0
Foster, 2b..	4	1	1	5	4	1	Gandil, 1b..	4	0	2	7	1	0
Menosky, lf.	2	1	1	4	0	1	Risberg, ss..	4	1	1	2	1	0
*Morgan....	1	0	0	0	0	0	Schalk, c...	3	1	0	7	0	0
H. Milan, lf	1	0	0	0	0	0	Williams, p.	3	0	1	0	0	0
Leonard, 3b	0	0	0	0	0	0	Danforth, p.	0	0	0	0	0	0
McBride, 3b	3	0	0	1	3	0	†Murphy....	1	0	0	0	0	0
Ainsmith, c.	3	1	1	6	1	0							
Shaw, p....	2	0	0	0	2	0							
Johnson, p..	1	0	0	0	1	0							
Totals....	35	6	9	27	12	3	Totals.....	36	5	11	27	6	0

*Batted for Menosky in the eighth inning.
†Batted for Danforth in the ninth inning.

Washington	0	2	0	0	0	0	0	0	4	—6
Chicago	0	0	0	2	2	0	0	0	1	—5

Two-base hits—Jackson, Weaver (2). Three-base hits—Menosky, Foster. Stolen bases—E. Collins, Leibold, Rice, Schalk. Sacrifice hits—Weaver, C. Milan, Schalk. Double play—Ainsmith to Foster. Left on bases—Chicago, 9; Washington, 9. First base on errors—Chicago, 1. Bases on balls—Off Shaw, 2; off Williams, 5; off Johnson, 1. Hits and earned runs—Off Shaw, 9 hits and 1 run in eight innings; off Johnson, 2 hits and no runs in one inning; off Williams, 7 hits and 5 runs in eight and one-third innings; off Danforth, 2 hits and 1 run in two-third inning. Hit by pitcher—By Williams (McBride). Struck out—By Williams, 6; by Shaw, 4; by Johnson, 1. Umpires—Connolly and Moriarity. Time—2:20.

Joe Welling and Dundee To Battle Again Friday

By FRED HAWTHORNE

That bewhiskered old problem that we used to stump our teacher of physics with: "What would happen if an irresistible force should come into contact with an immovable body?" will be definitely decided on Friday night at the St. Nicholas Rink, when the "wonderfully willing" Joe Welling meets Johnny Dundee, the "wickedly walloping Wop," in a ten-round bout.

Jimjoy Johnston, the Bumptious Boy Bandit, who does the matchmaking for the Sixty-sixth Street icehouse, put these two slambang lightweights on at this club several weeks ago, and the result was one of the greatest battles seen since the Kaiser was forced to invade Belgium, 'way back in 1914.

The "willing" one was going along like a race horse in the first half of that bout, whipping over a beautiful right hand crusher to the Wop-Scot's jaw in a manner than threatened drastic action of some kind. Dundee's teeth rattled like castanets every time one of these punches landed on the button, and Scotty Monteith, his manager, was gulping feverishly as he mopped the beads from his clammy brow.

But a sudden change came over Welling along about the seventh stanza, and his right hand seemed to have lost its cunning and its charge of lyddite at the same time. Dundee kept piling in like the irresistible force that graces the first paragraph in our little story, and he piled in so hard and persistently that the honors of the bout were clearly his.

Bandit Johnston explained after the fight that Welling had injured his deadly right in the seventh round, else he would surely have flattened Dundee that balmy evening. We smeared a mustard plaster over Jimmie's heaving chest yesterday, and finally managed to draw out the following classic bit of English:

"One Joe Welling, formerly a cartoonist, will meet one Johnny Dundee, erstwhile farmer and fish pedler, known as Joseph Carora, in a ten-round duplicate battle of Vimy Ridge on Friday night at the St. Nicholas Rink.

"That deadly Welling right hand is in shape again, and I predict that it will land, very hard and rough, on Mister Dundee's chin before the tenth round ends. Spend your next day off by taking a trip to the top of the Woolworth Building, first filling a hod with Irish confetti, and then select some husky guy on the sidewalk below and sprinkle a few bricks on his head. If he stands up under the punishment, then Dundee will stay on his feet after taking one of Welling's rights to the jaw. You know about what a chance the gink on the sidewalk has. Dundee's will be just as sweet."

The Bandit had a few words to say about weights. Dundee and Welling will weigh in at 135 pounds, ringside, on Friday night. "And there won't be any trick scales, either. Anybody who wants to see the boys climb aboard the Fairbanks can walk right downstairs below the arena and watch them, and little James will be off by himself in a corner, with nothing up his sleeve.

"After the 'wonderfully willing' one puts the crusher on Dundee he will haunt that 142-pound lightweight champion of the world. I'm not mentioning any names, but you haven't noticed Benny Leonard weighing in at 133 pounds in public, have you?"

Giants Slump Badly But Cling to the To

McGraw Men Lose Three Out of Six Games Played Dur Last Week—Bitter Struggle On in American League

New York maintained its lead in the National League unimpai although winning only three out of six games the last week. Cincin and Brooklyn set the pace in the older organization by winning five ou seven games.

In the American Chicago forged to the front again, and on Satur was in first place, although winning only four out of seven. Boston sho little improvement, the world's champions being able to win only two of six games with Cleveland and Detroit. Yesterday, however, Boston two games from St. Louis while Chicago was losing to Washington, again took the lead.

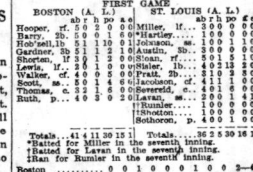

Record of Week In Big Leagues

The week's record in each league of games played, won and lost, with runs, hits, errors, men left on bases and runs scored by opponents, including the games of Saturday, July 14, is as follows:

NATIONAL LEAGUE

Clubs.	P.	W.	L.	R.	H.	E.	L.B.	O.R.
New York......	6	3	3	21	54	5	38	19
*Philadelphia ..	4	1	2	12	31	8	19	7
St. Louis.......	6	3	3	26	60	12	17	23
Cincinnati	7	5	2	31	69	6	32	23
*Chicago	6	3	2	9	43	6	42	16
Brooklyn	7	5	2	17	48	9	39	8
Boston	7	2	5	25	72	7	53	38
Pittsburgh	5	1	4	6	30	7	33	13

AMERICAN LEAGUE

Clubs.	P.	W.	L.	R.	H.	E.	L.B.	O.R.
Chicago	7	4	3	29	55	15	42	27
Boston	6	2	4	8	33	5	40	12
Cleveland	6	5	1	22	43	8	29	11
New York......	7	3	4	22	59	17	53	30
Detroit	8	4	4	28	59	14	42	29
Washington	8	3	5	32	73	6	65	38
Philadelphia ...	6	4	2	35	62	14	44	22
St. Louis.......	6	2	4	23	55	7	40	30

*Tie game, Saturday, July 14.

Rainy weather caused many dou headers late in the week in the tional. On Wednesday all the ga were postponed because of rain, Philadelphia did not take part in a test until Friday.

New York ended the series with Louis Monday by winning for fourth time in succession. The Gi were idle then until Thursday, Cincinnati took both ends of a dou header from the league leaders. Giants won Friday, but on Satu were only able to break even in games. Sallee, who beat St. Louis day and Cincinnati on Saturday, two out of the three victories cred to the Giants.

Reds Climb Ladder

Cincinnati started the week by ta two games from Boston, and in series with New York captured t out of five, advancing during the from fifth to fourth place. St. L broke even in six games and gaine Philadelphia, which is still in a sl Brooklyn had a good week, taking out of two from Chicago and four of five from Pittsburgh.

The week in the American bega Chicago regaining the lead, Boston ing to second place and Cleveland ing New York and taking third tion. The Chicago White Sox fini the series with Philadelphia, which team they gained only one tory out of four contests. Wedne the White Sox went back to se place, Boston taking the lead.

Thursday New York dropped tw Chicago, which again traded p with Boston. Chicago took three of four from New York, the only feat being an eleven-inning game day.

Senators Stop Indians

After the disastrous series Cleveland, in which it did not w game, Boston met Detroit, and wo Wednesday and Saturday. Thre Boston's defeats were shut-outs. C land continued its good work and its string of straight victories to s before it met defeat at the hand Washington Saturday.

Philadelphia did as well agains Louis as it did against Chicago went into seventh place ahead of Browns. Two of New York's three tories were in extra inning games, Yankees beating St. Louis 7 to seventeen innings Thursday and cago 6 to 5 in eleven innings Frid

Yesterday the Yankees took games from Cleveland and are within a half game of third again.

New Stymie Rule Is Found Wanting

Chicago, July 15.—The new rule of the Western Golf Association abolishing stymies was tried and found wanting at the Western amateur championship at Midlothian, and the rule was changed by the board of directors before the final rounds, in which Francis Ouimet yesterday won the title from Kenneth P. Edwards, of Chicago.

The rule had required that the nearer ball be played first when both balls were on the green, thus avoiding stymies. The plan worked well in medal play, as there was no lifting of the nearer ball, and an average of fifteen minutes time was taken off an eighteen-hole round without detriment to the players, as they were contesting the field instead of one man.

When the match play started, however, the contestants were loud in their clamor for a change in the rule, and President Charles F. Thompson, agreeing with the players, had a new one drafted.

The new one still abolishes stymies, whether due to the faulty play of the owner of the stymied ball or to the accidental position of his opponent's ball, but requires the ball further from the hole to be played first unless a stymie exists. In that case the nearer ball is to be played first or lifted, at the option of its owner.

Rain Stops Cycle Races

The programme of bicycle racing at the Newark Velodrome yesterday was postponed until next Wednesday evening on account of a wet track.

Fight Log

TO-NIGHT

Military A. C.—Battling Levinsky and Al Benedict.

TUESDAY

Pioneer S. C.—Georgie Maas and Danny Pavese.

Harlem S. C. (Hammel)—Frankie Burns and Young Marino.

THURSDAY

Clermont Rink—Leo Johnson and Billy Defoe.

FRIDAY

St. Nicholas Rink—Joe Welling and Johnny Dundee.

Brown's A. A. (Far Rockaway).—Albert Badoud and Marty Cross.

SATURDAY

Broadway S. C.—Dave Astey and Joe Tiplitz.

International League

At Montreal—First game:

										R.
Providence ..	0	0	1	1	0	3	1	0	0	—6
Montreal ...	0	0	1	0	1	0	0	0	0	—2

Batteries—Peters and Allen; Hersche and H

Second game:

										R.
Providence ..	0	0	0	0	0	0	0	1	2	—3
Montreal ...	0	0	0	0	0	0	1	1	0	—2

Batteries—McTigue and Allen; Gerner and ley.

Eastern League

Worcester, 3; Bridgeport, 1.

Empire City Entries

First race (two-year-olds; fillies; five and furlongs)—Arrowwood, 107; Empress, 111; Bonero, 111; Star Class, 111; Brocatelle, 107; sora, 111; Wawbeek, 111.

Second race (three-year-olds and upward; selling; one mile)—Favour, 114; *Lady Roths Margaret L., 93; *Dorcas, 109; Gingersnap II

Third race (three-year-olds and upward; iamsbridge Handicap; about six furlongs)—Ke 116; St. Isidore, 122; Thornhill, 113; Ed hee, 118; Kildee, 109; Milkman, 112; Bally Tom McTaggart, 114; Pan Zareta, 135.

Fourth race (three-year-olds; Tarrytown Stakes; one mile)—*Ed Roche, 106; *Kildee Straightforward, 111; *Brooklyn, 101; King got, 106; *Hanobala, 101; Ballad, 111; *Mac ray, 104.

Fifth race (three-year-olds and upward; cla one mile and seventy yards)—Intone, 122; 105; *Cliff Haven, 113; *Princess Janice, 108; dito, 110; Charmeuse, 108; *Spectre, 98; master, 110; Manganese, 118; *Muckross, 103; tery, 98; *Right, 98; *Spring Song, 90; Sosius Star Gaze, 118; Carlton G., 110; Armament,

Sixth race (two-year-olds; maidens; colts geldings; five furlongs)—Dr. Johnson, 114; craft, 114; Currency, 114; Cavan Boy, 114; A 114; Nepperham, 114; Caddy, 114.

*Apprentice allowance claimed.

Yankees Beat Senators in Twelfth Inning---Giants Win

Barnes' Debut as Giant Is Whitewash for Dodgers

itcher Faces the Celebrated Jack Coombs in Sharp Artillery Battle on Coogan's Bluff—Breaks Go Against the Flatbush Bunch

By W. J. Macbeth

Beating the 1918 Dodgers may be no man's sized job for a real cham- on baseball club, but it must take some ingenuity to vary the process in manner to hold the attention of the patrons till the last inning. Such genuity the Giants displayed yesterday afternoon at the Polo Grounds, hen they whitewashed the Flatbush team by a score of 2 to 0.

The fans would have had little op- ortunity to tire, even if this contest d not been one of the most interest- g and exciting that Coogan's Bluff ay expect to see 'fore dog days. It as reeled off in an hour and twenty- e minutes, which is going some for y major contest in these days of rategical deliberations. No daylight ving champion could establish a case ainst the noble athletes on yester- y's form.

Jess Barnes, the good right-hander ho so narrowly escaped exile to Bos- n on the eve of the championship ening, made a most successful début th the Giants. Mr. Barnes evidently appreciative of his transfer from hopeless trailer to the city of gay ghts and hope of a melon cutting some ne about the ides of October. If Mr. arnes's commendable behavior of yes- rday gave a true line on his conduct, en New York may forget Charles ncoln Herzog instanter.

The affable Mr. Doyle will be able take care of the pivot position of e infield, never fear. And a right- nded pitcher who is up to fifty-one arts in a season will lose mightly w of them at the hand of a clubbing ew such as the Giants, provided he erages anywhere close to the form of e Jess of yesterday.

Barnes Victor

BROOKLYN

	ab	r	h	o	a	e
Olson, ss	4	0	2	0	3	0
O'Mara, 3b	4	0	1	1	1	1
Daubert, 1b	4	0	0	15	0	0
Myers, cf	4	0	2	1	1	0
Johnston, lf	3	0	1	2	0	0
Hickman, rf	2	0	0	3	1	0
Schmandt, 2b	3	0	0	0	6	0
Miller, c	3	0	1	2	0	0
Coombs, p	3	0	0	0	4	0
Totals	30	0	7	24	16	1

NEW YORK

	ab	r	h	o	a	e
Young, rf	3	1	0	1	0	0
Kauff, cf	3	1	1	2	0	0
Burns, lf	3	0	1	1	2	0
Zimmerman, 3b	3	0	1	2	1	0
Doyle, 2b	3	0	0	3	4	0
Fletcher, ss	3	0	0	1	7	0
Holke, 1b	3	0	1	14	0	0
Rariden, c	3	0	1	3	0	0
Barnes, p	3	0	0	0	5	0
Totals	27	2	5	27	19	0

Brooklyn	0	0	0	0	0	0	0	0	0	—0
New York	0	0	0	2	0	0	0	0	x	—2

Two-base hits—Rariden, Olson, Burns, Myers. Stolen base—Myers. Double plays Fletcher, Doyle and Holke (2). Left on bases—New York, 2; Brooklyn, 4. Bases on balls—Off Barnes, 1; off Coombs, 1. Struck out—By Barnes, 3. Passed ball—Rariden. Umpires—Moran and Rigler. Time—1:24.

Barnes Faces Giant Killer

Nobody picked any soft assignment r the said Mr. Barnes. He was asked go in against no less a renowned ant killer than the sedate and ven- able Jack Coombs. Mr. Coombs, as hletic and Giant, won something like even dozen victories over the New rk Nationals before they finally agged him to defeat last year. New rk did manage to win two from ombs last season. But the score ood so far on the side of old "iron- les" there wasn't much crowing on is end of the bridge. In fact, Mr. ombs, even after yesterday's upset, likely to carry the due respect of e Giants next time he starts against em.

Probably if Coombs had traded uni- rms with Barnes before yesterday's me his name would be bracketed this orning. His work suffers nothing in mparison to that of his victorious al. The breaks went against the nnebunk veteran. True, the Giants ade the breaks for themselves, as nners invariably are in the habit of ing. Brooklyn wasted opportunities. Judged strictly by pure mathematics ombs had a shade the better of the ching duel. He held the slugging ants to five widely scattered hits. ooklyn clipped Barnes safely seven nes. Yet Coombs gummed the works letting escape his only pass of the me at a time when it could do the ximum of damage.

Ross Young, by the way, was largely strumental in keeping the Giants' 18 slate clean. This youngster, who n a home in the hearts of some rty-odd thousand rooters Tuesday, nply stole a run off Coombs in the urth inning and as it developed one n was all that Barnes needed.

Gives Fatal Pass to Young

t was to Young that Coombs issued fatal pass in question. Unfor- ately for Colby Jack this slight slip the new speed marvel of the Giants first with none out in the fourth. nny Kauff hopped a curve for a tty line single into right. It was a an, sharp blow directly at Hickman. t Young was off at the swing of the and sprinted around to third yards ead of Hickman's quick throw. Mara hurried his play for Kauff second. His throw was low and le. On the error Young scored while uff advanced to third. Benny scored second and last run of the game on rns' infield tap to Schmandt.

That lucky inning details fairly well w York's offensive punch of the af- noon. At only one other time did Giants threaten seriously. Walter lke hit safely to left with one out the fifth. Bill Rariden followed with double that glanced off Myers' glove Hickman. It looked another tally, e, but Hickman cut loose a wonder- throw from deep field as Holke nded first. Coombs intercepted this ow midway between the box and the te, as it was carrying a trifle wide, d by a lightning chuck to Miller gged Holke by a whisker at the plate. Fast fielding on the part of Jimmy nston held Burns' long drive to a ible in the sixth. Two were out at time. Heinie Zim fouled to Dau- t. Zim, by the way, hit safely to rt the second round. But he was ned back and run down on an at- npted steal for the third out after yle had popped to O'Mara and Hick- n had robbed Larry Doyle of an ra base hit by an unexpected, one- ided, blind stab after slightly mis- ging a wicked line drive.

Brooklyn Gets Regrets

The Brooklyn side of the picture is of regret over lost opportunities. less than six times the Dodgers e within striking distance of the te. That no score resulted testifies further to the excellence of nes, of course. Yet, if one were ashamed to claim allegiance to tbush, he might charge the over- nt to the breaks of the game rather n to superiority of New York's de- ce. Twice, in the ticklish moments, reliable captain, Artie Fletcher, othered wicked thrusts and started cious double plays.

till, it is possible to impugn Brook- 's base running judgment on sev- l occasions. The Flatbush lads med to press their luck just a bit far against the remarkable cun- g of the good right arm of Georgie ns. This king of the sun-field, who s snatching them out of the air, far near, with all the grace of a Speak- displayed also Tris's infield pro- ities in the pasture. He cut down Mara with a fine throw to Doyle in very first inning, when Ollie tried stretch a hit into a double. This med one bad time to gamble, as the e was so young. O'Mara was the ond battery, with the heavy artil- coming up.

Myers opened the seventh with a ble over Burns's head. But he was ght trying for third. This seemed lhardy base running, as Hi had the y in front of him, and Burns tched the ball on the first bound. course, it took perfect relaying on part of Georgie and Fletcher to d the runner, but it must be re- nbered that Myers was the first ter of the inning. As invariably pens, Jimmy Johnston followed with lean hit to centre. He was doubled h Hickman when the latter rapped Fletcher.

A wonderful one-handed catch by Kauff while on the dead run saved Barnes a whole lot of worry in the sixth. The clutch in deep centre ruined a triple for Coombs, the first batter. Olson a moment later dropped a fluke Texas League double in right among Holke, Young and Doyle. O'Mara hit wickedly to the box, but Barnes gamely threw himself onto the ball and nipped Olson on the lines.

Barnes showed his mettle as early as the second inning. Myers led off with a single to left and advanced on Johnston's out. Then he stole third, aided by a short passed ball. With what might have been the winning run on third (the Giants had not yet scored) Barnes fanned Hickman and held Schmandt to a puny tap toward the box.

Gossip of Giants

Jess Barnes showed his gameness on several occasions, notably when he took chances with smashed digits in going after two wicked clips from the bat of Jake Daubert.

Ross Young failed to get himself a safe blow, but he had about as much to do with the Giant victory as any man. His sprint from first to third on Kauff's single was the stuff of which Cobbs are made.

The fifth developed a rather unusual play. Hickman was on first, with one out, when Schmandt grounded to Doyle. Larry, in trying to run Hickman down for the first end of a double play, held the ball so long that when he finally threw for Schmandt the runner beat the play. Hickman had fallen down meanwhile, and Holke raced over to tag him for a force-out.

Miller's single in the eighth inning was rather fluky. Heinie Zimmerman made a wonderful pick-up of a slow roller and would have nailed the runner by yards had he not stumbled just as he came up with the ball.

Coombs is one of the most dangerous hitters among the major league boxmen, but Barnes had the good fortune to get away with him each time. Kauff's great catch of Coombs's wicked line drive in the sixth not only robbed Jack of a sure enough triple, but blocked Brooklyn's most spirited bid for the decision. Later Coombs had the additional mortification of hitting into a double play.

Larry Doyle's arm appears much stronger than when he was a member of the Cubs a year ago. His underpinning, too, has improved greatly. Larry was called upon to make two fast relays for double plays where the least handicap of props or wing would have spoiled the chances.

If Ross Young does not prove a flash in the pan Davey Robertson is likely to be forgotten by the Fourth of July. Young is quite as speedy as the departed Davis, is possessor of as accurate an arm and has a wonderful pair of hands. He knows how best to utilize his speed on the paths.

Rube Marquard is smarting under the unkind reception tendered him by the Giants' opening day and has asked Wilbert Robinson for a chance to avenge his honor. Richard is likely to be called upon this afternoon. Slim Sallee is due for the Giants.

Larry Doyle was the victim of poor fortune in his hitting. Johnston raced away back for a beautiful catch that ruined a triple in the fourth inning. Larry almost upset Jake Daubert with a wicked liner in the seventh, but the first sacker clung to the ball. Two feet either side and Laughing Larry would have had at least one extra base knock.

Both President Tener of the National League and President Hempstead of the Giants are lending every encouragement and help possible in the Liberty Loan campaign in progress at the Polo Grounds. The sales yesterday proved a decided improvement over those of the opening day despite the fact that the attendance was not half so large.

Killifer Denies He Plans To Enlist in Navy at Once

ST. LOUIS, April 17.—Reports that William Killifer intended to follow the lead of his battery mate, Alexander, and seek permission to join the navy were denied by the Chicago Nationals' catcher here to-day.

He stated he had received information that he had been placed in Class 1A in the army draft, but that he intended to wait for the call and would make no effort to get into any special branch of service.

Navy, 6; Maryland, 5

ANNAPOLIS, Md., April 17.—The Navy baseball team won a close game from Maryland State here to-day by a score of 6 to 5. Both teams fielded cleanly and scored the majority of their runs by bunching hits.

JESS BARNES made his debut as a Giant at the Polo Grounds and shut out the Robins. Barnes is a right-hander and came to McGraw with Larry Doyle in trade for Herzog. Jess allowed the visitors seven hits yesterday, but was given errorless support.

Over the Sport Trail

By Louis Lee Arms

The New Press Box

FOR the present the Polo Grounds press box is located atop the second tier, but how long it will stay there is a matter of debate; spirited, acrimonious debate, as it were.

Undoubtedly the removal to this eerie eminence has cut deeply into the social life of the writer. He has arisen on his hind legs and beefed about it. There are those who claim that a writer should go to a ground school first before being admitted to the present dizzying heights of the press box. There are others who refuse to sit in the extant quarters at all. These flit about the lower tier chasing the ghosts of yesterday, and kicking.

For one thing, the present press box isn't actor-proof. While it is true none but plutocrats ascend the second tier, there are times when an actor has money. There are other times when other people have, too. Thus the present press box gains in no measure over the old one, save that an outsider has to climb to get to it, whereas he could fall into it before, and did.

Personally, barring aerial raids, we prefer the new press box. It affords a better view of the field and every play is clean cut to the eye. Yet we are fair enough to admit that a man reared in a cellar would greatly prefer the old press box. It also gave a man many of the thrills of trench life.

The main trouble with the old press box is that it is impossible to see all plays clearly from it. This is a minor objection and would be raised only by those of us who persist in taking our baseball seriously.

Some Inside Baseball

ON THOSE days when little Benjamin Kauff failed to hit in the South—and there are times when he hooverizes in hits—some of the wise cracking birds said he was worrying over the draft, as it affected him. Far be it from such. Benny never worried over going to war. His direst fear was that the United States wanted him to PLAY BASEBALL.

"At $30 a month," murmured Benny. "Never . . . . Never!"

Now that it is officially announced that the quota in Kauff's district has been filled and there is no chance of his being called before the playing season is done, we violate no confidence in saying it is doubtful if Kauff will be called then.

Strange paradox. Here is a tremendously powerful youngster, much faster on his feet than the average, with arm muscles so well developed he could swing his way into the batting leadership of a baseball league. What an enraged Benjamin with a bayonet might do only can be imagined.

Yet the Marlin physician who examined Benny shook his head doubtfully at the conclusion of the physical appraisement. Benny's right arm is two inches shorter than his left, he has one weak knee and two feet that aren't according to Hoyle. The medic was sorry, but he feared Benny never would be accepted. He said as much.

Since Benny was there when he said it we doubt if the young coal miner's inability to hit ever could be attributed to the personal imminence of the draft.

One observer says Uncle Wilbert Robinson picked the wrong pitcher for his opening game. Yes, and he picked the wrong team, too.

Ty Cobb is away to an early start. He is now leading the American league in grip.

Not a Minute Under Fifty!

OLD as the Ancient Mariner,
Scarred as the aged tombs;
But in there yet with the hooks and smoke,
Will you ever quit, Jack Coombs?

As some of our athletes have found, the draft has a hop on its fast one.

Strangler Lewis says he will use his headlock against Joe Stecher. He could use a gun against him without arousing any of Lewis's followers.

In Dusty Texas

ALDRICH BLAKE, former Michigan athlete, who went to the Southwest, tells the following story of an Oklahoma "hill-billy" who was drafted.

"He had never been out of the hills," says Blake, "and he complained bitterly at the discipline of the training camp in Oklahoma. At length his regiment was sent to Camp Bowie, Texas, and after they were settled there the drafted man renewed his complaints.

"'This is nothing,' said a top sergeant. 'Wait until you get to France.'

"'My God,' answered the hill-billy, 'ain't this France?'"

Herzog Helps Braves Bury Phillies Alive

PHILADELPHIA, April 17.—Boston was so superior to Philadelphia in all departments to-day that the local team never had a chance, the score being 14 to 2. Both Philadelphia pitchers were hit hard and their support was poor.

Herzog played his first game for Boston and prevented two runs by a spectacular catch of a fly in short centrefield.

The score:

BOSTON (N. L.)

	ab	r	h	po	a	e
Massey, lf	6	2	5	2	0	0
Herzog, ss	5	1	1	6	2	0
Powell, cf	4	1	0	3	0	0
Konetchy, 1b	5	2	1	7	0	0
Smith, 3b	6	3	4	1	1	0
Wickland, rf	6	0	3	6	0	0
Conway, 2b	5	1	2	1	2	2
Henry, c	5	1	0	1	0	0
Nehf, p	3	3	1	0	5	0
Totals	45	14	17	27	10	2

PHILADELPHIA (N. L.)

	ab	r	h	po	a	e
Bancroft, ss	4	1	2	2	1	0
McCaffigan, 2b	4	0	[illegible]	2	4	1
Stock, 3b	4	0	2	2	1	1
Cravath, rf	4	0	0	3	0	1
Luderus, 1b	4	0	1	6	1	0
Whitted, lf	4	0	1	3	0	0
Meusel, cf	4	0	0	0	0	0
Burns, c	1	0	0	3	0	0
Dilhoefer, c	2	0	0	5	1	0
Tincup, p	1	0	0	1	1	1
*Pearce	1	0	0	0	0	0
Woodward, p	2	1	1	0	0	0
Totals	35	2	7	27	9	4

*Batted for Tincup in fifth inning.

Boston	4	5	0	0	1	4	0	0	0	—14
Philadelphia	0	0	0	0	0	0	0	2	0	—2

Two-base hits—Massey, Wickland, Nehf, Konetchy, Bancroft. Stolen bases—Massey, Dilhoefer. Sacrifice hit—Nehf. Left on bases—Boston, 10; Philadelphia, 7. First base on errors—Boston, 4; Philadelphia, 1. Bases on balls—Off Nehf, 1; off Tincup, 1; off Woodward, 4. Hits—Off Tincup, 11 in 5 innings; off Woodward, 6 in 4 innings. Struck out—By Nehf, 1; by Tincup, 3; by Woodward, 4. Wild pitch—Tincup. Losing pitcher—Tincup.

Pirates Beat the Reds With 7 Runs in Fourth

CINCINNATI, April 17. — Pittsburgh bunched hits off Regan in the fourth inning to-day and when the side was retired seven runners had crossed the plate, the visitors eventually winning, 8 to 1. Hamilton was also hit hard, but managed to keep the safeties well scattered.

Lee Magee carried off the premier hitting honors by gathering in two d[illegible]s and three singles out of five ti[illegible]p. Reuther strained his back in the first inning and was forced to retire.

The score:

PITTSBURGH (N. L.)

	ab	r	h	po	a	e
Caton, ss	4	0	1	4	1	0
Mollwitz, 1b	5	1	2	6	1	0
Carey, cf	4	1	1	3	0	0
Stengel, rf	4	1	2	1	0	0
Cutshaw, 2b	5	1	1	3	3	1
King, lf	4	1	1	2	0	0
M'Kechnie, 3b	3	1	0	1	4	0
Schmidt, c	4	1	1	7	2	0
Hamilton, p	4	1	2	0	1	1
Totals	37	8	11	27	12	2

CINCINNATI (N. L.)

	ab	r	h	po	a	e
Groh, 3b	4	0	1	3	3	0
L. Magee, 2b	5	1	5	3	5	0
Roush, cf	3	0	0	0	0	0
Chase, 1b	4	0	1	10	0	0
Griffith, rf	4	0	1	2	0	0
S. Magee, lf	3	0	0	3	0	0
Blackburne, ss	4	0	3	3	2	0
Allen, c	4	0	1	3	1	1
Reuther, p	0	0	0	0	0	0
Regan, p	1	0	0	0	0	0
Eller, p	2	0	0	0	1	0
*Smith	0	0	0	0	0	0
Totals	34	1	12	27	12	1

*Batted for Eller in ninth inning.

Pittsburgh	0	0	0	7	0	0	0	0	1	—8
Cincinnati	1	0	0	0	0	0	0	0	0	—1

Two-base hits—L. Magee (2), Cutshaw, Mollwitz. Stolen bases—Carey (2), Stengel, Groh. Sacrifice hits—Roush (2). Double play—Schmidt (unassisted). Left on bases—Pittsburgh, 7; Cincinnati, 11. First base on error—Cincinnati. Bases on balls—Off Hamilton, 3; off Reuther, 1; off Regan, 2; off Eller, 2. Hits—Off Reuther, none in 1 inning; off Regan, 5 in 2 1-3 innings; off Eller, 6 in 5 2-3 innings. Struck out—By Hamilton, 4; by Reuther, 1; by Eller, 1. Winning pitcher—Hamilton. Losing pitcher—Regan.

Nicholls and Barnes Win Exhibition Golf Match

LOUISVILLE, Ky., April 17.—In an exhibition golf match at the Audubon Country Club here to-day for the benefit of the Red Cross, Gil Nicholls, of New York, former amateur metropolitan champion, and James Barnes, of the Broadmoor Club, Colorado Springs, Western open champion, won in 3 up from Robert Craig, Audubon Country Club professional, and Harry Duff, Louisville Country Club professional.

At the close of the match the four balls used by the players were auctioned off, one bringing $200, one $150 and two $125 each. The play was followed by a large gallery.

Alexander May Be Called To-day to Camp Funston

LINCOLN, Neb., April 17.—Official notification summoning Grover Cleveland Alexander, pitcher for the Chicago National League club, to go to Camp Funston in the April draft contingent, probably will be mailed to Alexander to-morrow, according to a statement made to-day by K. D. Bahensky, member of the Draft Board of Howard County, the pitcher's home.

Bahensky also stated that a reply declining Alexander's request to be permitted to join the navy had been sent to navy officials in Chicago.

Havre de Grace Results

First race (two-year-olds; selling; four furlongs)—Agnes Cook, 108 (Mergler), $4.20, $3.30, $2.70, won; Cain Spring, 106 (J. McTaggart), $6.70, $4.10, second; Manœuvre, 110 (Rice), $6.90, third; Time, 0:49. John Powers, Green Mint, St. Quentin, Weston, Old Bill Bender, May Rustic, Vecneman and Sharp Practice also ran.

Second race (four-year-olds; steeplechase; selling; about two miles)—Fair Mac, 140 (Bryant), $9.10, $4.70, $3.60, won; Rhomb, 140 (O'Neil), $3.50, $3, second; High Flyer, 145 (Wilson), $3.80, third. Time, 4:26 2-5. Sea Coast II, Bob Redfield, Frijolee, Gloucester, Racebrook and Garter also ran. Sea Coast II, Bob Redfield and Gloucester fell.

Third race (three-year-old maidens and winners of one race only; claiming; five furlongs)—Our Nephew, 104 (Ericson), $12.70, $5.50, $3.70, won; Brocatelle, 99 (Bullman), $17.20, $8.90, second; Assign, 109 (McGraw), $3.20, third. Time, 1:01. Boy Blue, Blazonry, Pollyanna, Minto II, Marblehead, Brig o' Dee and Sir Oracle also ran.

Fourth race (three-year-olds and up; maidens and winners of one race only; claiming; five furlongs)—Coral, 110 (Mergler), $24.80, $11.40, $8.20, won; Pepper, 109 (Dominick), $13.90, $9.60, second; Grey Eagle, 109 (Kummer), $9.10, third. Time, 1:02 1-5. Generous, Priam, Royal Writ, P. G. King, Tolerance, Daybreak and Millrace also ran.

Fifth race (three-year-olds; selling; five and a half furlongs)—Jule, 106 (Ericson), $7.50, $5, $3, won; Harry Burgoyne, 115 (Obert), $14.90, $4.50, second; Onico, 101 (Rodriguez), $2.60, third. Time, 1:08 1-5. Bughouse, Fort Bliss, Royal Arch, Ideal and C. A. Comiskey also ran.

Sixth race (three-year-olds and up; six furlongs)—Dr. Campbell, 115 (Ericson), $10.20, $4.80, $2.90, won; Lazy Lou, 108 (Stalker), $6.10, $3.20, second; Preston Lynn, 115 (Rodriguez), $3.10, third. Time, 1:14. General, Curlicue, Stalwart Helen, George Roesch, Caro Nome and Hwfa also ran.

Seventh race (four-year-olds and up; claiming; one mile and seventy yards)—Highland Lassie, 101 (Humphrey), $39.90, $13.50, $10.90, won; Stir Up, 103 (Mergler), $17.10, $11.30, second; Ben Hampson, 98 (Enzor), $6.70, third. Time, 1:47 2-5. Jimmy Burns, Flare, Beautiful Morn, Monocacy, Lukemac, Great Dolly, Brando, Hickory Nut, Impression, Frim Harry and Darkey also ran.

Columbia Loses To Swarthmore In the Eleventh

Southpaw Koenig Goes Long Trail, but Weakens at Ffinish

After fighting for ten innings with the score tied Swarthmore finally took her game from Columbia yesterday afternoon by a hard-earned run in the eleventh. The final score was 3 to 2. Swathmore, after a fifteen-inning contest lost to Pennsylvania last week, seemed hardened to long-drawn out games and showed greater endurance than the Blue and White. However, it was only when Dutch Koenig, the Columbia southpaw, weakened in the eleventh session that Cornog was able to score, Houlihan missing a difficult fly from Carter.

Ogden, who twirled for Swartmore throughout, had control and speed enough to last eleven innings and struck out two of Columbia's heaviest hitters in the final inning. He allowed seven hits, but retired ten in the long game and gave only one base on balls.

Koenig, the Columbia twirler, was kept in the game for the entire eleven innings by Coach Coakley and showed no sign of slowing up until the very end of the game. His good infield support kept a second run from being scored in the last inning. He allowed one more hit than his rival twirler, but struck out only three men. Ogden excelled him in nothing except greater staying power.

Swarthmore started off the first inning by scoring two runs, but the local team tightened up in the next and held her scoreless for nine innings. Columbia evened the score with a run in the second and another in the sixth. Goodman and Lester made the Columbia runs.

The box score follows:

SWARTHMORE

	ab	r	h	po	a	e
Ewell, ss	5	0	1	1	1	0
White, 3b	5	1	1	1	1	0
Curnog, 2b	4	1	2	5	7	0
Carris, c	5	1	1	10	4	0
Carter, cf	5	0	0	0	0	0
H'lbarth, rf	2	0	0	1	0	2
Howell, rf	2	0	0	0	0	0
Webb, 1b	4	0	2	14	1	0
Larsin, lf	4	0	0	0	0	0
Ogden, p	3	0	0	1	3	0
Totals	39	3	7	33	17	2

COLUMBIA

	ab	r	h	po	a	e
Frisch, 3b	4	0	0	1	4	0
Lester, cf	5	1	1	5	2	0
Houlihan, lf	5	0	1	3	0	1
Ackerman, c	5	0	1	4	0	0
Buonaguro, ss	5	0	1	3	1	0
Houck, 2b	3	0	1	2	5	0
Goodman, 1b	4	1	1	13	0	0
Uris, rf	1	0	1	0	0	0
Weinstein, rf	3	0	0	2	0	0
Koenig, p	3	0	1	0	1	0
Totals	38	2	8	33	13	1

Swarthmore	2	0	0	0	0	0	0	0	0	0	1	—3
Columbia	0	1	0	0	0	1	0	0	0	0	0	—2

Two-base hits—Goodman, Houck. Stolen bases—Ewell, White. Sacrifice hit—Frisch. Double play—Webb and Curnog. Bases on balls—Off Ogden, 1; off Koenig, 2. Struck out—By Ogden, 10; by Koenig, 3. Hit batsman—By Ogden (Koenig). Umpire—O'Bryan. Time of game—2:20.

Red Sox Make Third Straight Over Athletics

BOSTON, April 17.—Schang's single to right in the ninth, with the bases full, scored two runs and gave Boston its third straight victory over Philadelphia here to-day, this time by a score of 5 to 4. It was Schang's first appearance in a Boston uniform.

Philadelphia twice held the lead. In seven innings Leonard was nearly invincible. He struck out nine men and allowed only four hits in that time, but weakened in the eighth and ninth.

The score:

PHILADELPHIA (A. L.)

	ab	r	h	po	a	e
Kopf, lf	5	1	0	4	0	0
Jamieson, rf	4	1	2	3	1	0
Gardner, 3b	4	1	1	2	2	1
Burns, 1b	5	1	2	9	0	1
Walker, cf	4	0	2	2	0	1
Shannon, 2b	2	0	1	2	1	1
Dugan, ss	3	0	0	1	0	0
McAvoy, c	3	0	1	1	2	0
Adams, p	4	0	0	0	2	0
Perry, p	0	0	0	0	0	0
Totals	34	4	9	*24	8	4

BOSTON (A. L.)

	ab	r	h	po	a	e
Hooper, rf	3	1	1	2	0	0
Shean, 2b	3	0	1	3	2	0
Strunk, cf	4	0	2	2	0	0
Hoblitzell, 1b	4	0	0	8	0	0
McInnis, 3b	4	2	2	1	1	0
Whiteman, lf	3	1	1	2	0	1
Scott, ss	3	1	0	0	3	0
Agnew, c	3	0	0	9	2	0
Leonard, p	3	0	0	0	2	1
†Ruth	0	0	0	0	0	0
‡Schang	1	0	1	0	0	0
Totals	31	5	8	27	10	2

*None out when winning run was scored.
†Batted for Agnew in ninth inning.
‡Batted for Leonard in ninth inning.

Philadelphia	0	0	0	0	0	0	0	2	2	—4
Boston	0	1	0	0	0	0	0	1	3	—5

Two-base hits—Jamieson, Burns, Strunk. Three-base hit—Hooper. Stolen base—Whiteman. Sacrifice hits—Gardner, Shannon, Dugan, Shean, Scott. Double play—Jamieson to Dugan. Left on bases—Philadelphia, 10; Boston, 7. First base on errors—Philadelphia, 2; Boston, 3. Bases on balls—Off Adams, 3; off Leonard, 4. Hits—Off Adams, 7 in 8 innings (none out in ninth); off Perry, 1 in no inning. Struck out—By Leonard, 9. Wild pitch—Leonard. Winning pitcher—Leonard. Losing pitcher—Adams.

Cochran Beats Schaefer Badly; Yamada Wins

Welker Cochran scored a decisive victory over Jake Schaefer by a score of 300 to 33 in the evening match of the special 18.2 balkline billiard tourney, which was continued at Daly's Academy yesterday. Schaefer was in woefully poor form, failing on several occasions to drive the balls out of balk. Cochran began poorly, but ended matters with two final efforts of 137 and 87 caroms. The match ended after eight innings.

However, Cochran suffered an afternoon defeat at the hands of Koji Yamada, the Japanese expert, who incidentally registered his first victory. The score was 30 to 88. Yamada's playing was steady throughout, while his final cluster of 205 (unfinished) contained a brilliant exhibition of close nursing and several 'round the table shots.

The scores follow:

AFTERNOON GAME

Koji Yamada—0, 7, 15, 0, 15, 60, 205. Total, 300. Average, 47 5-7. High run, 205.

Welker Cochran—2, 14, 41, 0, 5, 0, 26. Total, 88. Average, 12 4-7. High run, 41.

NIGHT GAME

Welker Cochran—10, 1, 10, 31, 15, 9, 137, 87. Total, 300. Average, 37 4-8. High run, 137.

Jake Schaefer—1, 1, 5, 3, 2, 12, 4, 5. Total, 33. Average, 6. High run, 12.

Standing of Major League Clubs

NATIONAL LEAGUE

GAMES TO-DAY

Brooklyn at New York.
Boston at Philadelphia.
Pittsburgh at Cincinnati.
Chicago at St. Louis.

YESTERDAY'S RESULTS

New York, 2; Brooklyn, 0.
Boston, 12; Philadelphia, 2.
Pittsburgh, 8; Cincinnati, 1.
Chicago at St. Louis (rain).

STANDING OF TEAMS

	W.	L.	P.C.		W.	L.	P.C.
N. York.	2	0	1.000	Boston ..	1	1	.500
St. Lo'is	1	0	1.000	Pittsb'h..	1	1	.500
Cin'nati.	1	1	.500	Chicago..	0	1	.000
Philad...	1	1	.500	B'klyn....	0	2	.000

AMERICAN LEAGUE

GAMES TO-DAY

New York at Washington.
Philadelphia at Boston.
St. Louis at Chicago.
Detroit at Cleveland.

YESTERDAY'S RESULTS

New York, 8; Washington, 7 (12 in.).
Boston, 5; Philadelphia, 4.
Detroit at Cleveland (rain).
St. Louis at Chicago (rain).

STANDING OF TEAMS

	W.	L.	P.C.		W.	L.	P.C.
Boston .	3	0	1.000	Detroit .	0	0	.000
St. Lo'is	1	0	1.000	Clevel'd.	0	0	.000
N. York.	2	1	.667	Chicago..	0	1	.000
Wash'n..	1	2	.333	Philad....	0	3	.000

Johnson, Called to Save Game, Loses to Yankees

New Yorkers Get Second Victory Over Senators After Twelve Innings of Assorted Baseball—Several Players Make Their Debut

By Charles A. Taylor

WASHINGTON, April 17.—The Yankees made it two games out of three here to-day with the Senators, but only after a struggle that went twelve innings. There is one satisfaction aside from the victory for the Huggins men—Walter Johnson will in all probability not face them to-morrow. Walter was called in to save the contest to-day, but instead of saving it he was charged with the loss of the game. This means that the Yanks have humbled the great Walter twice in three days, a fair enough percentage, to say the least.

It was not a good ball game so far as the playing was concerned, but it was brim full of lots of things to retain the interest of the fans. Before play was called Nick Altrock kept the crowd amused, but after the game started Nick was not needed. The players satisfied all demands. And what a bunch of players swarmed into the box score before hostilities were ended.

There are only two men in the New York lineup who have not been called upon so far in the series. They are Ed Monroe and Bob McGraw, the cub pitchers. As for Washington, the only player who failed to show himself is a fellow named Walbauer. It is safe to say that these three will appear to-morrow at some stage or other and then the fans here will have been properly intoduced to all the boys Miller Huggins and Clark Griffith have on their payrolls. It is nice to get acquainted with everybody so early in the season.

Thormahlen Bows

Herb Thormahlen was the first stranger to be introduced to-day. He was sent to the box by Huggins after a careful scrutiny of his demoralized pitching staff. In these times Miller has to pick at least two pitchers, one to start the game and the other to finish it. Sometimes it takes three to do the two jobs.

Well, Hig picked Herb to start and Griff, who is confronted with the same difficulties, picked a Mr. Shaw. Herb lasted long enough to give three bases on balls and hit a batsman, and Shaw lasted long enough to give three hits, including a triple by Pratt, walk one man and make a wild pitch.

The rest of the pitching array will be mentioned at the proper place in the exact order of their appearances on the stage, fitting reference also being made to the time and manner of their exit through the wings.

The Yankees, as hinted, fell upon the offerings of Mr. Shaw in the first inning. Gilhooley singled to centre, Miller sacrificed Pitcher to first, and Del Pratt drove out a triple to left field, tallying Gil with run No. 1. Pipp drew a base on balls. Baker hit to Lavan, who fumbled, and Pratt scored run No. 2. Ping Bodie singled to centre, tallying Pipp with run No. 3. Baker counted run No. 4 on Peck's out, Morgan to Judge. Ruel fouled out to Foster.

With these four runs back of him Herb Thormahlen entered the box for the Yankees. Shotton and Foster walked. Milan forced Foster and Shanks walked, filling the bases. Judge was hit and Shotton came home. Herb was gently removed from the mound by Hugg and Slim Love took up the duties there. Morgan sent a fly to Miller, on which Judge scored. Lavan went out, Pratt to Pipp. The Yanks' four-run lead had been cut in half in a jiffy.

Senators Get Another

The New Yorkers did nothing with Earl Yingling, the successor of Mr. Shaw, in the second inning, but it should be mentioned, perhaps, that Slim Love, first man up, got a single. This odd happening may have unnerved Slim a bit, for in the Senators' half he allowed one run by reason of a single by Ainsmith, the hitting of Yingling, a sacrifice hit and a single by Milan. This left the Yanks only one run to the good.

In the third New York picked up another run on a base on balls to Pipp, another single by Bodie and Peck's sacrifice fly to Milan. The Senators rested in their half, but in the fourth they climbed up a bit on the Yanks by adding another run. This came as a result of three hits, including a double by Milan. The Yanks got busy again in the fifth, when they scored two runs and apparently took a safe lead. A triple by Pipp aided greatly in this happy outcome.

In the sixth inning the Senators came within one run of tieing the score, and in the eighth spurted again and accomplishing the task. In the sixth, after Shotton had gone out, pitcher to first, Eddie Foster made his first hit of the series, a single to centre, and went to third when Milan hit to Pratt, who, with an easy double play in sight, let the ball go through his legs to right field. Milan, of course, dashed to second. Howard Shanks promptly doubled to left field, scoring the two base runners.

Slim Also Walks

In the eighth the tieing tally came. Slim Love walked Shoton, the first man up, and Hug thereupon told Slim to do some walking himself while Mogridge assumed the box burden. Foster hit to Peck, who, with another of those easy double plays in his grasp, fumbled and then threw wildly to first, Shotton landing on third and Foster on second.

Shotton might have scored, as the plate was left unguarded, but Altrock, who was coaching at third, was doing some tightrope walking. Nick was "called" good and proper by the gray-haired Griffith. Milan hit to Mogridge, who caught Shotton at the plate. Shanks drove a savage grounder at Mogridge, who deflected to Pratt for an out at first, but Foster sped over the plate with the run.

Now, with the opening of the ninth the great Walter Johnson went to the box amid the cheers of the hungry populace. (It was 7 o'clock.) Walter did nicely in the ninth, allowing only one hit, a fluke by Miller, and in the tenth he retired the Yanks in order. The Senators in the meantime had been just as easy for Mogridge. In the eleventh, however, the New Yorkers began to worry Walter.

The Yankees won the game in the twelfth. Pratt led off with a double to left field. Pipp attempted to sacrifice, but Johnson threw the ball to third to head off Pratt. Foster dropped the toss, and all hands were safe. Baker then came through with a fly to centre, which tallied Pratt. It seemed as though Johnson was attempting to pass Baker purposely, but Frank reached out and hit a wide one. Bodie went out, Lavan to Judge, and Peck lined out to Foster.

Won in Twelfth

NEW YORK

	ab	r	h	o	a	e
Gilhooley, rf	5	1	2	5	0	0
Miller, cf	5	0	1	4	0	0
Pratt, 2b	5	3	2	3	4	1
Pipp, 1b	4	3	1	17	0	0
Baker, 3b	5	1	1	0	6	0
Bodie, lf	6	0	2	1	0	0
Peckinpaugh, ss	4	0	0	2	2	1
Ruel, c	4	0	4	3	1	0
Thormahlen, p	0	0	0	0	0	0
Love, p	3	0	1	0	3	0
Mogridge, p	2	0	0	1	3	0
Totals	43	8	11	36	19	2

WASHINGTON

	ab	r	h	o	a	e
Shotton, rf	3	1	1	3	0	0
Foster, 3b	5	2	1	2	3	2
Milan, cf	6	2	2	3	1	0
Shanks, lf	5	0	2	4	0	0
Judge, 1b	4	0	0	15	1	0
Morgan, 2b	5	0	0	2	7	0
Lavan, ss	6	0	2	1	4	1
Ainsmith, c	5	1	1	4	2	0
Shaw, p	0	0	0	0	1	0
Yingling, p	3	1	1	1	3	0
Johnson, p	2	0	2	1	0	0
Totals	44	7	12	36	22	3

New York	4	0	1	0	2	0	0	0	0	0	0	1	—8
Washington	2	1	0	1	0	2	0	1	0	0	0	0	—7

Two-base hits—Milan, Shanks (2), Pratt. Three-base hit—Pratt. Stolen base—Milan. Sacrifice hits—Miller, Shotten (2), Judge. Sacrifice flies—Morgan, Peckinpaugh, Baker. Double play—Yingling to Morgan to Judge. Left on bases—New York, 7; Washington, 12. First base on errors—New York, 1; Washington, 2. Base on balls—Off Shaw, 1; off Thormahlen, 3; off Yingling, 3; off Love, 2; off Johnson, 1. Hits—Off Thormahlen, 0 in 1-3 inning, 3 men on base; off Love, 9 in 6 2-3 innings, one on base in 8th; off Mogridge, 3 in 5 innings; off Shaw, 3 in 1 inning; off Yingling, 5 in 7 innings; off Johnson, 3 in 4 innings. Hit by pitcher—By Thormahlen (Judge); by Love (Yingling). Struck out—By Love, 1; by Yingling, 4; by Johnson, 1. Wild pitches—Shaw, Yingling, Johnson (2). Winning pitcher—Mogridge. Losing pitcher—Johnson.

Marquard's Claim To Draft Exemption Is Denied by Board

THE district draft board in the Federal Building yesterday afternoon denied the claim to exemption from the draft of Riichard Marquard, known as "Rube" Marquard, one of the star pitchers of the Brooklyn National League club, and also his application for a change of his classification under the draft from 2A to 4A.

Marquard had registered at Local Board No. 146, at Broadway and 145th Street. After he had filed his questionnaire Marquard was placed in Class 2A. In his questionnaire he had stated that he had a wife, "Blossom Seeley," and a child. He said his wife had earned $1,200 in 1916, and that she had been out of work for a short period.

Heathcote to Go to Minors

ST. LOUIS, April 17.—Clifton Heathcote, an outfielder obtained by the St. Louis Nationals last year from Pennsylvania State College, is to be released to the minors for further training, according to announcement to-day.

Havre de Grace Entries

First race (two-year-old maidens; fillies; four furlongs)—Cresson, 112; Lindonia, 112; Marmon, 112; Mrs. Kate Leydecker, 112; Superba, 112; Ormonda, 112; Madam Byng, 112; Miss Inver, 112; *Alapa, 112. Superba and Ormonda, S. Ross entry.

Second race (four-year-olds and upward; steeplechase; selling; about two miles)—Kilwinning, 139; First Out, 137; Pandean, 139; Porin, 137; March Court, 149.

Third race (three-year-olds and upward; claiming; five and a half furlongs)—Tit for Tat, 99; Annie Edgar, 106; Jake Argent, 106; *Mae Murray, 108; Viley, 114; Paganini, 104; Encore, 119; *Green Tree, 103.

Fourth race (three-year-olds and upward; selling; handicap; six furlongs)—Pullux, 118; Berlin, 115; Gamecock, 111; Kohinoor, 117; George Starr, 120.

Fifth race (three-year-olds; The Wilmington Stakes; five and a half furlongs)—Compadre, 11; Sweep Up II, 114; Charlie Leydecker, 123; Jack Hare, jr., 123; High Cost, 120; Ballast, 114; Foreground), 114; Atthea, 99; Dr. Johnson, 111; Red Sox, 114. Foreground and Atthea, Ross entry. Dr. Johnson and Red Sox, Jeffords entry.

Sixth race (three-year-olds and upward; claiming; five and a half furlongs)—Veldt, 101; True as Steel, 109; *Mohioan, 94; General, 119; Dominion Park, 108; Peep Again, 103; *Fathom, 109; *Carbide, 109.

Seventh race (four-year-olds and upward; claiming; one mile and a sixteenth)—Arbitrator, 112; *Hesse, 99; Dundreary, 106; *Miss Fannie, 101; Tootsie, 101; *Say, 106; Waterproof, 114; *Senator James, 109; G. M. Miller, 117; *Charles Cannell, 99.

*Apprentice allowance claimed.

Cards Sign Two

ST. LOUIS, April 17.—Pitcher Vincent Molyneaux, released by the St. Louis Americans, and "Lefty" Grimm, first baseman, have been signed by the St. Louis Nationals.

Yankees Come Home To-day to Open Big Polo Grounds Season

Here are the Yanks as they look now. In the left-hand corner of the lay-out is Miller Huggins, the new manager, who has instilled a lot of "pep" in the team. The players in the three groups are: Slim Love, Ed Monroe, Bob McGraw, George Mogridge, Ray Caldwell, Walter Pipp and Harry Hannah. Second group: Herbert Thormahlen, Frank Baker, Elmer Miller, Allen Russell, D el Pratt, Aaron Ward and Roger Peckinpaugh. In the third group: Sam Vick, Zinn Beck, Pat O'Connor, Harold Ruel, Ping Bodie, Hugh High and Frank Gilhooley.

Royal Welcome Awaits Huggins in Debut As New Manager of the Yankee Team

THE YANKS ARE COMING! In fact, they are here.

They came from Boston early this morning, somewhat travel stained and worn, but ready to strike a real blow for democracy at the Polo Grounds this afternoon in the opening of the local American League season.

Miller Huggins, already firmly established in the hearts of local fandom because of his triumphs with the St. Louis Cardinals, makes his metropolitan debut as a power to be reckoned with in American League politics. Already in his short régime he has by judicious trading surrounded himself with a heavy hitting club and a great run getting club—something novel to American League rooters here.

But for the fact that his pitching has been away below the standard, which he had reason to expect, with a little affable weather Huggins's men would now be breezing away out in front, or mighty close to it, for no team of its company has shown a greater driving power. That the pitchers are beginning to respond to the edifying influences of their company there is good reason to believe. Herb Thormahlen's game against the Red Sox yesterday in Boston was the best omen of the season.

For to-day's official opening, in which Clark Griffith and his Washington team will take part, an elaborate programme, with a keen military flavor, has been arranged. Brigadier General William A. Mann will be present with his staff and will throw out the first ball.

A full company of soldiers from the general's command at Governor's Island, together with 250 Naval Militia from Pelham Bay Naval Training Station, will assist the players of the rival clubs in hoisting both the Stars and Stripes and club's service flag at 3 o'clock.

To stimulate the Liberty Loan drive, Colonel Ruppert, president of the club, will subscribe $50,000 to war bonds, in addition to the half million dollars' worth he has already purchased. The Liberty Loan campaign will be assisted by a number of Canadian troopers just returned from the front. Al Jolson, Jimmy Powers, Will Rogers and the Misses Rita Stanwood, Ina Claire, Pearl White, Edna Wallace Hopper, Sibyl Carmen and others.

Weather permitting, the big naval dirigible which recently flew over Manhattan will encircle the grounds, scattering Liberty campaign literature.

The gates will be opened at 1 o'clock and the game will be called at 3:30. Frank's band of sixty pieces will render a patriotic concert, beginning at 1:45.

Bunched Hits Help Indians Beat St. Louis

CLEVELAND, April 23.—The Indians bunched their hits off Gallia to-day and defeated St. Louis, 8 to 2. The locals made their long hits count for runs, most of them coming with men on the bases.

Coumbe, pitching his first game of the season, was scored upon in but one inning, the fourth, when Sisler walked and scored ahead of Gedeon when the latter hit for a home run to left. The hit would have been good for only two bases, but Left Fielder Graney made no effort to field it, believing it a foul ball.

The score:

ST. LOUIS (A. L.)	ab	r	h	po	a	e
Tobin, cf	4	0	0	3	0	0
Austin, 3b	3	0	2	1	0	0
Sisler, 1b	3	1	0	6	1	0
Smith, lf	3	0	0	1	1	0
Gedeon, 2b	4	1	3	4	2	0
Hendryx, rf	2	0	0	2	0	0
Nunamaker, c	4	0	1	7	0	0
Gerber, ss	4	0	1	0	3	0
Gallia, p	3	0	0	0	2	0
Totals	30	2	7	24	9	0

CLEVELAND (A. L.)	ab	r	h	po	a	e
Graney, lf	5	2	2	5	0	0
Chapman, ss	4	0	0	3	4	0
Speaker, cf	3	1	2	2	0	0
Roth, rf	4	1	1	2	0	0
Kavanagh, 1b	5	0	2	7	0	0
Turner, 2b	2	0	1	2	1	0
Getz, 3b	4	0	0	3	2	0
O'Neill, c	2	3	2	2	2	0
Coumbe, p	4	1	1	1	4	0
Totals	33	8	11	27	13	0

St. Louis	0	0	0	2	0	0	0	0	0	—2
Cleveland	0	0	0	0	2	0	4	2	x	—8

Two-base hits—Nunamaker, Graney, Kavanagh. Three-base hits—Speaker, Turner, O'Neill. Home run—Gedeon. Sacrifice hits—Smith, Turner. Double play—Smith, Sisler and Nunamaker. Left on bases—St. Louis, 6; Cleveland, 9. Bases on balls—Off Gallia, 6; off Coumbe, 4. Hit by pitcher—By Gallia (Chapman). Struck out—By Gallia, 2; by Coumbe, 2.

Hogg Pitches Phillies to Big Victory

PHILADELPHIA, April 23.—Bradley Hogg, recruit from Los Angeles, pitched Philadelphia to victory in his first game of the season to-day, 7 to 2. Brooklyn scored first, but the locals hammered Mamaux from the box soon afterward.

Captain Luderus's drive into the bleachers off Marquard was his second homer of the season. He also hit the right field wall twice, for a double and a single.

The score:

BROOKLYN (N. L.)	ab	r	h	po	a	e
Olson, ss	4	0	1	5	4	0
Daubert, 1b	4	0	1	9	1	0
Myers, cf	4	1	1	0	0	0
Mitchell, rf	4	0	1	0	0	0
Johnston, lf	3	0	0	1	0	0
O'Mara, 3b	4	0	0	2	2	0
Schmandt, 2b	4	1	1	2	4	0
Miller, c	2	0	2	5	0	0
Mamaux, p	1	0	0	0	3	0
*Hickman	1	0	0	0	0	0
Cheney, p	0	0	0	0	0	0
†Krueger	1	0	0	0	0	0
Marquard, p	0	0	0	0	0	0
Totals	32	2	7	24	14	0

PHILADELPHIA (N. L.)	ab	r	h	po	a	e
Bancroft, ss	5	1	3	3	3	2
M'Gaffig'n, 2b	3	1	1	1	5	0
Stock, 3b	3	2	3	1	3	0
Cravath, rf	4	0	0	1	0	0
Luderus, 1b	4	3	3	13	1	0
Whitted, lf	4	0	1	2	0	0
Meusel, cf	4	0	2	4	0	0
Burns, c	3	0	1	2	0	0
Hogg, p	4	0	1	0	3	0
Totals	34	7	15	27	15	2

*Batted for Mamaux in fifth inning.
†Batted for Cheney in seventh inning.

*Batted for Canavan in ninth inning.
†Burns out; hit by batted ball.

Brooklyn	0	1	0	0	0	1	0	0	0	—2
Philadelphia	0	1	3	0	0	0	3	0	x	—7

Two-base hits—Schmandt, Stock (2), Luderus, Meusel. Home run—Luderus. Sacrifice hit—McGaffigan. Sacrifice fly—Johnston. Double plays—Olson and Daubert; O'Mara and Daubert; Olson, Schmandt and Daubert; Luderus and Bancroft; Bancroft, McGaffigan and Luderus; Hogg, Bancroft and Luderus. Left on bases—Brooklyn, 5; Philadelphia, 6. First base on errors—Brooklyn, 2. Base on balls—Off Mamaux, 1. Hits—Off Mamaux, 9 in 4 innings; off Cheney, 1 in 2 innings; off Marquard, 5 in 2 innings. Hit by pitcher—Cheney (Burns); by Hogg (Miller). Struck out—By Mamaux, 2; by Cheney, 2; by Marquard, 1; by Hogg, 2. Losing pitcher—Mamaux.

Southern Association

Atlanta, 1; New Orleans, 1.
Birmingham, 3; Mobile, 5.
Little Rock, 3; Nashville, 1.
Memphis, 4; Chattanooga, 3.

"Lefty" Thormahlen Near No-hit Hall of Ball Fan[e]

Huggins Recruit From Baltimore Holds Red Sox Hi[tless] for Eight Innings and Loses Contest by 1 to 0 Score

By Charles A. Taylor.

BOSTON, April 23.—If ye Yankee fans have tears to shed, pre[pare] to shed them now, for Herbert Thormahlen. When the Bostonese [saw] Herb walk into the box to-day they were prepared to bury him, b[ut] inning after inning went by with this same Herb turning back the [Red] Sox sluggers without a hit they decided it was not a funeral they [were] attending. They had come to bury Herb, but they were forced to p[raise] him.

Thanking Shakespeare's Mark Antony for this introduction to a story of a baseball game, it should be said right now that this southpaw flinger Herb Thormahlen almost achieved one of those niches in baseball's hall of fame that are so coveted by big league twirlers.

And Herb is only a youngster. He pitched against the White Sox last year, when the season was ebbing to its close, and lost his game. He started one of the games against the Senators last week, and was so wild and unruly that he had to be removed before the first inning was ended. That was the major league experience of Herb until he faced the Red Sox to-day and held them hitless for eight innings. It would indeed seem that Herb is on his way to the heights.

Herb and his vain effort to reach the topmost rung constitute the whole tale of how the Red Sox beat the Yankees by a ninth-inning outburst to the tune of 1 to 0. And this doubly crucial ninth began in such fine fashio[n for] Herb it was a shame.

Still Fighting!

NEW YORK (A. L.)	ab	r	h	po	a	e
Gilhooley, rf	2	0	0	2	0	0
Peckin'gh, ss	4	0	0	2	5	1
Baker, 3b	4	0	0	1	4	0
Pratt, 2b	4	0	1	0	2	0
Pipp, 1b	1	0	0	14	0	0
Bodie, lf	3	0	2	0	0	1
Miller, cf	3	0	0	4	0	0
Hannah, c	2	0	0	2	0	0
Thor'len, p	3	0	0	0	4	0
Totals	26	0	3	*25	15	2

BOSTON (A. L.)	ab	r
Hooper, rf	3	0
Shean, 2b	2	0
Strunk, cf	4	1
Hoblitzell, 1b	3	0
McInnis, 3b	3	0
Whiteman, lf	3	0
Scott, ss	3	0
Agnew, c	2	0
Bush, p	3	0
†Ruth	1	0
Totals	27	1

*One out when winning run was scored.
†Batted for Hoblitzell in ninth inning.

New York	0	0	0	0	0	0	0	0
Boston	0	0	0	0	0	0	0	0

Two-base hit—Bodie. Stolen base—Strun[k]. [Sac]rifice hits—Pipp, Shean. Sacrifice fly—Wh[iteman]. Double plays—Bush to Scott to Hoblitzell; Hoblitzell to McInnis to Agnew. Left on [bases]—New York, 4; Boston, 7. First base on [errors]—Boston 2. Bases on balls—Off Thormah[len], off Bush, 4. Struck out—By Thormahlen, [...] Bush, 1.

Amos Singles to Left

Dave Shean politely flied out t[o ...]ler. Amos Strunk was the next [on the] list of those Thormahlen had t[o dis]pose of, and he of the Biblical [name] spoiled everything by smashing a [clean] cut single to left field. The [Boston] fans apparently were just as so[rry for] Herbert when this death-dealing [blow] came. Herb had won them by his [nerve] and gameness. They were all wi[th him].

Manager Ed Barrows seized th[is well] known and often-mentioned psyc[holog]ical moment to insert Babe Rut[h in] the batting order in place of Hob[litzell,] who had failed to make a hit in [twen]ty-one times at the plate, or [there]abouts. The Babe showed he [appre]ciated the compliment by bangi[ng the] first ball pitched to centre field [for] safety, on which the terrible [Amos] Strunk dashed to third. Her[b was] worried now over the outcome [of the] game, having tossed his no-hit [aspira]tions into the discard. He [walked] Stuffy McInnis purposely, and th[e situ]ation was—the bags full and on[e] man out.

George Whiteman appeared [on the] scene with his club and his whole [heart] set on driving out a sacrifice [at] least. Technically he achieved h[is am]bition, for he lifted the ball to [Bodie] in short left, and the merits of [Ping's] arm could not be tested, for the ["na]tive son," in his anxiety to ma[ke the] catch and whip the ball to the p[late to] shut off Strunk, made one of [the] most inglorious muffs.

Amos had hesitated long at th[e third] fore making his dash. He knew [Bodie's] ability in this line. But when [he saw] the ball rolling out of Bodie's [hands] he acted quickly and won the o[ld] game.

Herb Thormahlen does not [get] all the sobs we started this tale with. Tears, too, should be sh[ed for] Ping Bodie. Not alone because [of his] costly misplay in the ninth, bu[t] because of the strenuous attem[pts he] made in the earlier innings [to help] Thormahlen in his no-hit endeav[or and] at the same time win the strug[gle for] the Yanks. Ping is a ball pla[yer in] every sense of the word, and the fans at the Polo Grounds to-[day] will make no mistake if they gi[ve him] a royal welcome to his new e[nviron]ment.

Bush Worthy Opponent

The woes of Herb have now be[en de]scribed, save that no mention ha[s been] made of the fact that Joe Bu[sh was] doing the hurling for the Red S[ox. He] was certainly a fitting oppone[nt for] Thormahlen, for the statistics [show] that the New Yorkers gathere[d but] three hits from his slants. An[d that] leads us back to the tears that [should] be shed for Ping Bodie.

Ping took it upon himself to [make] two of these three safe wallops, [one of] them being a double, which he [deliv]ered with one man out and P[ipp on] first. Wally might have scored [on the] smash that shot past Hooper i[n right] field, but he failed to touch sec[ond as] he rounded the bag and was fo[rced to] go back, with the result that h[e only] reached third eventually. At th[is criti]cal period Miller was called [out on] strikes. Truck Hannah was pu[rposely] passed, filling the bases. Ping ch[ose this] occasion to take a nap somewh[ere be]tween second and third, and was [caught] through a quick throw by B[ush to] Scott. In the seventh Bodie, w[ith two] out, singled to centre, but w[as] stranded when Miller lined to [...] who made a shoestring catch.

Having mingled the tears fo[r Herb] and Ping, let us cover them all [for a] large period.

Standing of Major League Clubs

NATIONAL LEAGUE

GAMES TO-DAY

New York at Brooklyn.
St. Louis at Chicago.
Philadelphia at Boston.

YESTERDAY'S RESULTS

New York, 9; Boston, 2.
Philadelphia, 7; Brooklyn, 2.
Cincinnati, 3; Chicago, 2.
St. Louis, 6; Pittsburgh, 5.

STANDING OF TEAMS

	W.	L.	Pct.		W.	L.	Pct.
N. York	6	0	1.000	Chicago	2	3	.400
Phila.	5	1	.833	Pittsb'rgh	2	3	.400
Cin'nati	4	2	.667	Boston	1	5	.167
St. Louis	2	2	.500	Brooklyn	0	6	.000

AMERICAN LEAGUE

GAMES TO-DAY

Washington at New York.
Chicago at St. Louis.
Cleveland at Detroit.
Boston at Philadelphia.

YESTERDAY'S RESULTS

Boston, 1; New York, 0.
Philadelphia, 5; Washington, 0.
Cleveland, 8; St. Louis, 2.
Detroit at Chicago (rain).

STANDING OF TEAMS

	W.	L.	Pct.		W.	L.	Pct.
Boston	7	1	.875	Chicago	1	2	.333
Clevel'nd	4	1	.800	Wash'ton	2	4	.333
Detroit	1	1	.500	St. Louis	2	4	.333
N. York	3	5	.375	Phila	2	4	.333

Over the Sport Trail

By Louis Lee Arms

Look Who's Here!

YOU'VE heard that the Yankees are coming,
They have been for, lo! many years;
But though they have strived they've never arrived
Any place in this vale of tears.
There always is something or other
That keeps them from winning the flag—
It may be string beans or Hun submarines
But, anyhow, they always lag.

IN consequence, dear Yankee brethren,
We have an exception to-day;
Just glance at the schedule and when you have read you'll
Agree with the sense of my lay;
The Yankees are not only coming,
The sons-of-a-gun are in town,
Directed by Huggins, they've quit playing muggins,
They're out for a major league crown.

On Water Bucket Pitching

THE current production, labelled the New York Yankees, is strongly reminiscent of one club that once won American League pennants by the sheer power of a tremendous offensive, when it lacked finesse and fitness defensively. That club, of course, was the Detroit Tigers, which accomplished the miracle of winning ball games and pennants with subnormal pitching.

The late Addie Joss and other critics as well—among them, by the way, Miller Huggins—have said that pitching is from 60 to 80 per cent of winning baseball. A weak hitting club with a regular major league pitcher working always has a chance—remember Fielder Jones's Hitless Wonders in Chicago—but there never is any telling when a few tons of dynamite will be exploded under the team that is trying to get by with tank-town pitchers, whatever its offensive strength may be.

The Yankees have been averaging more than ten hits to the game and yet, after yesterday's game, they were on the shady side of the .500 average mark. This means only that their pitching has been blown full of holes while their fielding game is below normal.

Such a condition must worry Manager Huggins considerably. He is preëminently a pitching manager, one who, like Fielder Jones, tries to make one run go a long way. With pitching the Yankees have it in them to go far this season, but with the water bucket style of tossing Huggins has gotten so far we may look for a third or fourth place team at best and games that will be strung out as long as a bass solo. A bass solo is usually beginning when you think it's about over.

Under Orders

PRIVATE ARTHUR ROBINSON, former sports writer on "The New York American," attended the Officers' Training School at Spartanburg, S. C., and will soon be a commissioned officer in the United States Army. Robinson is now visiting in New York on a furlough.

"I am reminded of the private who was constantly petitioning for a furlough to visit his home," says Robinson. "One day he entered his captain's tent and renewed his request for a vacation.

"'About face! Forward, march!' bellowed the enraged captain.

"Two days later the captain received a telegram from his incorrigible private. It read:

"'Have just passed Albany. When shall I halt?'"

Captain Artie Fletcher scored from first on a single. That's shooting a shoe string into a saddle factory.

It begins to look as though the Dodgers didn't know the National League season was loaded.

Southern Memories

The panegyrics they write Burns must make Georgie blush;
My praise is for the way that sucker plays a four-card flush!

There'll be no Alaskan dog race this season. But they'll start at Jamaica in a few weeks.

Collins's Admirable Record

BY playing 473 consecutive games, Eddie Collins has excelled by one the record previously established by Wahoo Sam Crawford, of Detroit, and the White Sox Keystone King adds a new laurel to an already pretentious collection. Collins has not been out of a game since 1914, when he was with the Philadelphia Athletics.

One might say such a record could not be attributed largely to luck in escaping accident. The best of basemen are occasionally spiked and the great and sudden strains to which baseball muscles and joints are subjected often result in minor injuries that necessitate lay-offs.

But a record such as the one Collins has made, particularly on the part of an infielder, means more than mere luck in escaping accident. It bespeaks uncanny ability in muscular control and reflexes. It is the same quality that is found in the circus acrobat. It furthermore shows Collins, while he touches a runner deftly, does not try to "hog the baselines." Such infielders sooner or later come to spiking grief.

Zim's Triple Cleans Giant Bases Against Braves

McGraw's Men Make Sweep of Series With Hub Team and Are Still Undefeated—George Burns Also Star of Contest at Polo Grounds

By W. J. Macbeth

To about ten thousand onlookers, twenty-two players, Bill Klem and Bob Emslie yesterday's game at the Polo Grounds was just an idle afternoon. To Heini Zimmerman it was an event. To Heini, in helping to subjugate the Braves to the third application of a bitter pill, reached the heights of the players' heaven—a clean-up soak with the bases crowded. The score was 9 to 2.

Heine, like the rest of the Giants, began well and finished better. He was not quite so active as little Georgie Burns, it is true, for Georgie had a field day that would have gladdened the heart of any athlete. Still, field days are just common occurrences in the life of the sun god, while pinch triples with three on are occasions of rare delight even for sluggers of the well known proclivities of The Bronx's most famous native son. In passing, it may be said, Burns had a perfect batting day. Two passes were sprinkled in among his three safe swipes. He scored three runs and he stole third without assistance clean as a whistle. But this story is dedicated to Heine Zimmerman.

Heine's one smash in question netted as many bases as Burns's three totalled, and proved deucedly more provoking. It clinched the argument beyond recall at a time when the Braves were showing the slightest suspicions of resentment against the southpaw slants of Sheriff Slim Sallee. The champions had a commanding lead, but were not safely out of the woods when the mighty Zim broke into streamer type.

All in a Row!

BOSTON (N. L.)	ab	r	h	po	a	e
Massey, lf	5	0	1	0	0	0
Herzog, ss	2	0	0	3	2	1
Kelly, cf	4	0	1	1	0	0
Konetchy, 1b	4	0	0	10	1	0
Smith, 3b	4	1	2	3	2	0
Rehg, rf	4	0	1	2	0	0
Rawlings, 2b	4	1	1	1	3	0
Wilson, c	4	0	1	3	3	0
Crum, p	1	0	0	0	2	0
Canavan, p	2	0	0	0	5	0
*Tragesser	1	0	0	0	0	0
Totals	35	2	7	†23	18	1

NEW YORK (N. L.)	ab	r	h	po	a	e
Young, rf	3	2	1	1	0	0
Kauff, cf	4	2	2	4	0	1
Wilhoit, cf	1	0	0	2	0	0
Burns, lf	2	3	2	1	0	0
McCarty, c	1	0	1	0	0	0
Zim'man, 3b	4	0	2	1	1	0
Doyle, 2b	4	1	3	0	3	1
Fletcher, ss	2	0	0	2	4	1
Holke, 1b	3	0	1	7	3	0
Rodriguez, 1b	1	0	0	2	0	0
Rariden, c	2	0	1	2	0	0
Thorpe, lf	1	0	0	2	0	0
Sallee, p	4	1	0	3	4	0
Totals	32	9	13	27	15	3

Boston	0	0	0	0	0	2	0	0	0	—2
New York	0	1	3	0	1	3	0	1	x	—9

Two-base hits—Doyle, Kauff, Wilson. Three-base hit—Zimmerman. Stolen bases—Burns, Fletcher, Young. Sacrifice hits—Fletcher, Young. Double play—Fletcher and Holke. Left on bases—New York, 6; Boston, 8. First base on errors—Boston, 2. Bases on balls—Off Sallee, 2; off Crum, 3; off Canavan, 1. Hits—Off Crum, 6 in 2 1-3 innings; off Canavan, 7 in 5 2-3 innings. Hit by pitcher—By Crum (Fletcher). Struck out—By Sallee, 1; by Canavan, 3. Losing pitcher—Crum.

Stallings Very Nervous

We'll leave Heine in his glory for a minute and lamp the horrible carnage from a safe distance. Stallings, who wears out a set of trousers sliding up and down the bench in demonstrative prayer each afternoon, elected a young gentleman by the name of Crum to oppose the fire of the celebrated sheriff. We know little of Crum save that he looked the part of his monicker. He lasted less than three innings, and might not have gone half that far if there had been anything better among Stallings's débris to send to the rescue.

Succeeded Mr. Canavan, a port-sider of questionable size and jerky motion, who seemed now and then at his wit's end to propel the pellet as far as his catcher. Canavan, who finished like the tail end of a caravan, is the bird that set the sage for Heine Zim's knockout.

Old Heine made a bid to crumb Crum's game in the first inning, but his wicked smash on a hit-and-run play struck Burns, who had walked, with two out, before Georgie had a chance to duck. The technical hit retired the side, of course.

Doyle doubled to deep centre in the second and Fletcher sacrificed. Holke crashed a single through Red Smith, scoring Larry. Rariden drew his base. Sallee flied deep to centre, and on the out Holke sprinted to third. But he was nipped off that bag when he tried to protect Rariden in a delayed steal.

Ross Young, first up in the third, worked Crum for a pass. Kauff doubled to deep left centre, scoring him. Burns singled to left. Red Smith held the runners while he retired Zimmerman, after a pretty stop, but Larry Doyle lined a long single to right that counted both Kauff and Burns. When Crum hit Fletcher he was shown the gate. Canavan gathered Holke's weak splash and threw to Smith, forcing out Laughing Larry. Herzog then sprinted back for Rariden's twisting skyscraper.

Canavan, the colt southpaw, squeezed safely through the fourth, Kauff, who singled with two down, being pinched on an attempted pilfer. In the fifth the champs began to get this portsider's range. George Burns led off with a single. Zim's out sent him up, and he stole third, sliding around Smith nicely. Doyle's single, his third straight safety, got Georgie the rest of the way. Fletcher forced Doyle at second, then stole the midway, where he was left when Holke fanned.

Rariden Singles in Sixth

Wal Bill Rariden greeted Canavan with a clean single in the sixth. Sallee bunted, but Smith, who fielded the ball, threw wide to Herzog for a force play on the lumbering catcher, and all hands were safe. Thorpe ran for Rariden. Ross Young sacrificed. Kauff hit sharply to the box, and Rariden was pinched off third and run down. Stallings already had had enough of Burns and his trusty mace, so Canavan was told to feed the sun-god nothing to his fancy. The result was a base on balls that stifled the pillows.

It was the anti-climax of the game. Heine Zimmerman furnished the climax. He caught one on the end of his hefty bludgeon and slammed it far over toward the right field exit. For Young it would have been a homer easy enough, but Heine was laughing so hard that his limbs could not do justice to his courage. These three resulting runs proved the death blow to Boston's hopes. Heine was left on third when Doyle spoiled a perfect day with a hot shot to Herzog.

McGraw threw in his army of manœuvre in generous numbers for the purposes of exercise only after that. Thorpe, McCarty, Wilhoit and Rodriguez defended various sections of the pasture through the last three rounds, McCarty, in the ninth inning, distinguished himself with a sort of scratch Texas Leaguer to left that tallied Young with the final Giant run. Little Ross scratched a hit to Canavan with one out in this inning and stole second base. From that vantage point he watched Wilhoit whiff before McCarty extended a helping hand. McCarty allowed himself promptly to be caught off first in the interests of daylight saving.

Very fortunately for our friend, Sheriff Slim Sallee, the story on Boston's part, was just one sad chapter of misguided effort after another. The Braves spilled opportunity as lavishly as Squire Ebbets spills mixed metaphors at a baseball banquet. Stallings's tribe should have scored a-plenty; yet they were lucky to score at all.

Two Runs in Sixth

They got their two runs in the sixth simply because George Burns misjudged a line drive from Olaf Wilson's bat, handing his old pal a double on what should have been the third out. The two-sacker tallied Smith and Rawlings, who had singled earlier.

The first and fourth innings were particularly provoking to the Big Chief. With Massey and Herzog on and none out in the first, Kelly took his swing instead of laying down a bunt. Massey was forced at third as a result. Koney then wafted a gentle fly to Kauff, while Holke, after a wonderful stop on J. Carlisle Smith, retired him and the side with the assistance of Sallee.

Kelly opened the fourth with a clean single. Koney forced him. Doyle's error on Smith and Rehg's safety off Zim's glove filled the bases with only one gone. Rawlings splashed weakly in front of the plate, forcing out Konetchy at the home station. Wilson hit directly to Sallee.

The rest of the way—the sixth inning excepted—the gallant sheriff had the poor Braves up a tree.

Giants Pry Off Ball Lid To-day in Flatbush

Ceremonies Will Attend Opening of Season at Ebbets Field

Flatbush fans are assured of many exceptional attractions for the opening of the National League championship in that borough this afternoon. First of all, the champion Giants will furnish the Dodgers a target at which to shoot for a belated start in the flag race. Despite the many tough luck reverses of Wilbert Robinson's aggregation so far, his team is always able to make matters most interesting for New York, no matter how far the team standings may separate the old time rivals.

Charles H. Ebbets has arranged a most complete patriotic display on the side. As a first aid to the Liberty Loan boom all the employes of the park have been made agents of thrift stamp sales. Fronts of the boxes, ticket windows and entrances have been placarded with Liberty literature and the patrons will be asked to take their change in thrift stamps.

One thousand enlisted men from the navy yard, headed by their fife and drum corps, will give a drill at 2:15. Later six hundred drafted men from Fort Hamilton will also drill. Admirals Usher and McDonnell, with their staffs, will occupy boxes on the first base side of the field.

Mrs. Agnes Wheeler and Mrs. John A. Turner will have charge of about seventy-five women, who will solicit Liberty bond sales on behalf of the Flatbush branch of the Liberty Loan Committee. Lieutenant Marty McHale will assist the women.

Senator Robert R. Lawson, sponsor of the neglected Sunday baseball bill, will throw out the first ball for play at 3:30 o'clock. The gates will be opened at noon. Shannon's band will render an elaborate programme of patriotic music.

Olympic Field Games

On Sunday next at Olympic Field the well known Highbridge team, champions of The Bronx, will make their first appearance this season in the feature game of a double-header with the Lincoln Giants. The crack southpaw, Werneke, who has always been a puzzle to the colored players, will be in the box for the representatives of The Bronx.

Reds Wins Series From Chicago On Home Field

CINCINNATI, April 23.—By annexing to-day's game, 3 to 2, Cincinnati succeeded in winning the series from the Chicago team. To-day's contest was a pitcher's battle. Bressler was returned the winner through his ability to keep the hits made off him scattered combined with poor fielding by the Chicago team.

Chicago took a two-run lead in the third on passes to Barber and Paskert and singles by Mann and Kilduff. Cincinnati scored their first run on singles by Allen and Groh and Elliott's wild throw. The home team tied it up in the sixth on Hollocher's fumble, L. Magee's sacrifice, a pass to S. Magee and an error by Merkle, after S. Magee had been caught off first.

The Reds won the game in the seventh on a double by Blackburne and a single by Allen.

The score:

CHICAGO (N. L.)	ab	r	h	po	a	e
Hollocher, ss	5	0	3	0	6	1
Barber, rf	2	1	0	0	0	0
Mann, lf	3	1	2	3	0	0
Paskert, cf	2	0	0	1	0	0
Merkle, 1b	4	0	0	11	0	1
Kilduff, 2b	4	0	1	4	4	0
Deal, 3b	3	0	2	0	2	0
Elliott, c	4	0	0	3	0	1
Tyler, p	3	0	1	2	2	0
*Zeider	1	0	0	0	0	0
†Lear	1	0	0	0	0	0
‡McCabe	0	0	0	0	0	0
Totals	32	2	9	24	14	3

CINCINNATI (N. L.)	ab	r	h	po	a	e
Groh, 3b	4	1	1	1	1	0
L. Magee, 2b	3	0	0	3	3	0
Roush, cf	4	0	0	2	1	0
S. Magee, 1b	3	0	0	6	0	0
Griffith, rf	3	0	1	1	1	0
Neale, lf	3	0	0	3	0	0
Blackburne, ss	3	1	1	3	2	1
Allen, c	2	0	2	8	2	0
Bressler, p	3	1	0	0	2	0
Totals	28	3	5	27	12	1

*Batted for Tyler in ninth inning.
†Batted for Barber in ninth inning.
‡Ran for Lear in ninth inning.

Chicago	0	0	2	0	0	0	0	0	0	—2
Cincinnati	0	0	1	0	0	1	1	0	x	—3

Two-base hits—Mann, Blackburne. Sacrifice hits—Paskert, L. Magee. Double plays—L. Magee to S. Magee; Blackburne, L. Magee to S. Magee. Left on bases—Chicago, 10; Cincinnati, 4. First base on errors—Chicago, 1; Cincinnati, 1. Bases on balls—Off Tyler, 2; off Bressler, 5. Hit by pitcher—By Bressler (Barber). Struck out—By Tyler, 2; by Bressler, 5.

Schmidt's Error Gives St. Louis Close Vi[ctory]

ST. LOUIS, April 23.—A tri[ple by] Baird, followed by Schmidt's e[rror in] the seventh inning of to-day's [game] enabled St. Louis to defeat Pitts[burgh] 6 to 5. Pittsburgh got off to [a ...] run lead in the second, but St [Louis] tied the score in the third, when [...] was driven from the mound.

May replaced Doak for St. L[ouis in] the third and held his oppone[nts to] two hits, as did Sanders, who r[elieved] Steele.

PITTSBURGH (N. L.)	ab	r	h	po	a	e
Caton, ss	3	0	1	2	5	1
Mollwitz, 1b	5	1	2	11	1	0
Carey, cf	2	2	1	1	0	0
Stengel, rf	2	1	0	2	0	0
Hinchman, rf	1	0	0	0	0	0
Cutshaw, 2b	4	0	1	2	1	1
King, lf	3	0	1	2	0	0
M'K'hnie, 3b	4	0	0	1	2	0
Schmidt, c	4	0	0	2	0	1
Steele, p	0	1	0	0	1	0
Sanders, p	2	0	0	0	3	0
Totals	30	5	6	*23	13	3

ST. LOUIS (N. L.)	ab
Betzel, rf	4
Smith, cf	3
Baird, 3b	4
Hornsby, ss	4
Cruise, lf	3
Paulette, 1b	3
Niehoff, 2b	4
Gonzales, c	4
Doak, p	0
†Snyder	1
‡Menze	0
May, p	2
Totals	32

*Betzel out; hit by Smith's batted ball.
†Batted for Doak in second inning.
‡Ran for Snyder in second inning.

Pittsburgh	2	3	0	0	0	0	[...]
St. Louis	0	2	3	0	0	0	1 [...]

Two-base hit—Paulette. Three-base h[it ...]. Stolen bases—Carey, Stengel, King, Bair[d]. Sacrifice hits—Paulette, Caton. Doub[le plays ...] Hornsby and Paulette. Left on bases—P[ittsburgh,] 6; St. Louis, 7. First base on errors—[...] 3. Bases on balls—Off Steele, 3; off Sa[nders ...] off Doak, 3; off May, 4. Hits—Off Ste[ele ... in] 2 1-3 innings; off May, 2 in 7 innings; [off San]ders, 2 in 5 2-3 innings; off Doak, 4 in [...] Balk—Doak. Struck out—By Sanders, 2; [...] 2; by May, 3. Wild pitches—Doak, Sande[rs. Win]ning pitcher—May. Losing pitcher—San[ders].

Yankees Make It Three Straight Over Athletics—Giants Victors Against Quakers

Baker Offsets Error With Home-Run Clout

dwell Lucky to Best Gregg—Gardner and Peckinpaugh Offer Some Brilliant Fielding—Team Leaves for Chicago

By C. A. Lovett

Effecting a compromise with the dictator of precipitation, the kees contrived to put through one of the contemplated brace of games C. McGillicuddy's assiduous Athletics at the Polo Grounds yesterday. just to cap their profitable home stay, thus terminated, they made it e in succession over the Philadelphians, winning by 2 runs to 1, and ing half a game on the Red Sox, who were dividing honors with hington.

y B. Caldwell pitched his best of the season, but the Codydon rapher had less to show in the than the veteran Vean Gregg, who sed him. Both kept the hitting distributed and each had his spell wildness, but Gregg's support fal- frequently, and Jimmy Dugan ly kicked the game into the Yan- won column in the eighth, after of J. F. Baker's celebrated home had made restitution for an ex- ble error by the big third baseman he fourth that paved the way to Mackmen's marker.

here was a deal of sharp and long ng, but much of this was straight nanners of the inner defences or ered in by the outer fielding ps. Gardner, Peckinpaugh and er contributed fielding plays that ld have thrilled, had not the loyal 00 assembled been too benumbed to much of anything besides the p cold.

ack turned the hulking George ns into left field, where another athlete with the same names and iddle initial is accustomed to face lowering sun. The former Detroit sacker is destined to don khaki tly, and the boss of the A's started pon the operation of breaking in nch, a rangy youth from Atlanta, was a hold-out this spring, at the station.

uench singled to left, after Jamie- had rolled out in the first inning, was doubled up with Walker when er gathered in a stiff rap and put motion the two-ply elimination. nnon and Dugan walked when two out in the second, but Bodie came nd got McAvoy's low fly.

Baker Fumbles Bounder

lly Walker sent a high bounder rd Baker to start the fourth, and rapping the ball Frank fumbled. ker then stole second. Burns went swinging and saying things under breath. Gardner beat out a roller Peckinpaugh, Walker advancing to d. Murray Shannon flied fairly to Miller, whose throw to the e, but for a high bound, would have down Walker.

eanwhile Huggins's men had been ng Gregg little concern, although throwing by his battery mate, Mc- y, had him twice in trouble. Gil- ey was easy in New York's first. strolled. Baker chased Jamieson he remote end of the pavilion abut- t for a grab on which Peck might advanced had he expected the h. The Yankee captain negotiated layed steal after the first pitch to t, and continued to third when her Dugan nor Shannon covered for voy's low throw. Pratt went out ging, leaving Peck stranded.

urns made a neat catch off the sign ting the virtues of a new com- deered tobacco after Pipp struck in the second. The drive was e's and carried portentously high. er bunted in front of the heptagon, when McAvoy's throw glanced off shoulder he paddled to second, but non and Muench took care of Al ters.

ratt drew a pass in the fourth after er had gone, and beat Gregg's w to second for a force on Pipp's Bodie, however, elevated to Shan- and Miller fouled to McAvoy.

he Yanks failed to hit safely for and one-third innings. Then dwell turned a double into left near foul-line and reached third when sans, swinging for Gilhooley, went Gardner to Muench, Peck's effort a loft to Walker on one of the slow balls that Gregg was able to near the plate.

hree of Baker's trips to the plate rewarded with prodigious wallops. followed up his exceedingly long n the first with a line foul into the ng right-field stand at the outset he sixth. On the second subse- nt offering Baker drove just over barrier in right, a fan attempting tch and deflecting the ball back o the field. Pratt followed with a single to left, but Pipp forced him Bodie slashed into a double killing. he Athletics were pounding the ball he game's middle stages. In the Baker made a startling spearing slam by McAvoy and got his man irst, and Gilhooley ran over and ed for Jamieson's liner.

fter Muench fanned in the sixth ker justified his name. Burns d to Marsans before Gardner sin- into the same garden and went econd on the Cuban's vain throw Walker at third. Shannon tapped ow roller at Baker, whose inrush- pick-up and peg were perfection, ing the runner by the narrowest gin.

oth Jamieson and Muench lined into the rightfield stand near tape of demarcation before going Walker singled to centre and stealing.

Baker Sprawls on Turf

eckinpaugh fanned to get the New eighth under way. Baker oled down the right foul line. Pratt nded to Gregg, and Baker was ht in a run-up near the shortfield. home-run king finally got in the of a toss by Dugan, the ball roll- beyond third and near the field s. Baker rounded the third cor- and Truck Hannah, coaching there, him plateward. After going a few s Baker saw Gregg recover the ball, nged his mind, and in turning to rn to third sprawled on the soft In the ensuing run-up Gardner ed Baker out, but not before Pratt into third, whence he scored a mo- t later when Pipp rolled toward nd, and Dugan, with the easiest ginable play in sight, kneeled and the ball bound off his ankle.

fter Burns and Gardner had struck in the ninth Shannon doubled to fence in left, the Yankees vainly esting that the ball landed foul. idson, pinch-swinging for Dugan, ed punily to Walters and the day done.

he victory gave the Yanks a count en wins and six defeats in the stay the home field, not taking into ac- nt last Sunday's triumph over eland in the Forest City. Last t the Yanks entrained for Chicago, re they will open to-morrow their Western foray, involving sixteen es.

nsden Wins Trophy in Hackensack Golf Tourney

bout sixty members of the Hack- ck Golf Club competed in a thir- ix hole medal play handicap yes- lay for the vice-president's trophy. winner was W. M. Bansden, with a l of 200—52—148.

Climbing Again!

PHILADELPHIA

	ab	r	h	o	a	e
Jamieson, r. f.	4	0	0	1	0	0
Muench, 1b.	4	0	1	7	0	0
Walker, c. f.	3	1	2	1	0	0
Burns, l. f.	4	0	0	2	0	0
Gardner, 3b.	4	0	1	1	5	0
Shannon, s. s.	2	0	1	3	2	1
Dugan, 2b.	2	0	0	4	3	1
McAvoy, c.	3	0	0	5	1	2
Gregg, p	3	0	0	0	2	0
*Davidson	1	0	0	0	0	0
Totals	30	1	5	24	13	4

NEW YORK (A. L.)

	ab	r	h	o	a	e
Gilhooley, r. f.	2	0	0	1	0	0
Marsans, r. f.	2	0	0	1	1	0
Peckinpaugh, s. s.	3	0	0	1	5	1
Baker, 3b.	4	1	2	1	3	0
Pratt, 2b.	3	1	1	2	2	0
Pipp, 1b.	3	0	0	10	1	0
Bodie, l. f.	3	0	0	1	0	0
Miller, c. f.	3	0	1	2	0	0
Walters, c.	3	0	0	7	1	0
Caldwell, p	3	0	2	1	1	0
Totals	29	2	6	27	13	1

*Batted for Dugan in ninth inning.

Philadelphia	0	0	0	1	0	0	0	0	0	0—1
New York	0	0	0	0	0	0	1	0	1	x—2

Two-base hits—Caldwell, Baker, Shannon. Home runs—Baker. Stolen bases—Peckinpaugh, Walker. Sacrifice hit—Pipp. Sacrifice fly—Shannon. Double plays—Baker, Pratt, Pitt; Shannon, Dugan and Muench. Left on bases—New York, 6; Philadelphia, 6. First base on errors—New York, 1; Philadelphia, 1. Base on balls—Off Caldwell, 3; off Gregg, 2. Struck out—By Caldwell, 6; by Gregg, 4.

Red Sox Divide With Griffmen; Ayers in Form

BOSTON, May 30.—Boston to-day took the morning game, 9 to 1, and Washington the afternoon game, 4 to 0. Boston made five runs in the third inning of the morning game on three hits off Shaw and three errors behind him. Scott doubled three times and knocked over five runs.

The scores:

FIRST GAME

WASHINGTON (A. L.)

	ab	r	h	o	a	e
Shotton, rf.	0	0	1	3	0	0
Judge, 1b.	5	0	0	9	2	1
Foster, 3b	3	0	2	2	1	0
Milan, cf.	3	1	1	3	0	0
Shanks, lf.	2	0	1	1	0	0
Morgan, 2b.	4	0	2	2	2	0
Lavan, ss.	4	0	0	0	1	0
Ainsmith, c	3	0	1	3	1	1
Shaw, p.	2	0	1	1	2	2
Hanson, p.	0	0	0	0	3	0
*McBride	1	0	0	0	0	0
†Rice	1	0	0	0	0	0
Totals	33	1	9	24	12	4

BOSTON (A. L.)

	ab	r	h	o	a	e
Hooper, rf.	5	0	0	1	0	0
Shean, 2b.	4	1	1	1	3	0
Strunk, cf.	5	1	1	4	0	0
Whiteman, lf	5	0	1	2	0	0
McInnis, 1b.	2	3	2	8	0	0
Thomas, 3b.	2	3	2	1	1	0
Scott, ss	4	1	3	4	1	0
Schang, c.	2	0	2	6	2	0
Leonard, p.	4	0	0	0	2	0
Totals	33	9	12	27	9	0

*Batted for Shaw in sixth inning.
†Batted for Hanson in ninth inning.

Boston	0	1	5	0	2	0	1	0	x	—9
Washington	0	1	0	0	0	0	0	0	0	0—1

Two-base hits—Morgan, Scott (3), Schang (1). Stolen bases—Shean, Strunk, Thomas. Sacrifice hits—Shanks, 1; Shean, 1. Left on bases—Washington, 10; Boston, 7. First base on errors—Boston, 2. Bases on balls—Off Shaw, 3; off Hanson, 1; off Leonard, 4. Hits—Off Shaw, 9 in 5 innings; off Hanson, 3 in 3 innings. Sruck out—By Shaw, 2; by Hanson, 1; by Leonard, 4. Losing pitcher—Shaw.

SECOND GAME

WASHINGTON (A. L.)

	ab	r	h	o	a	e
Shotton, rf	5	0	1	0	0	0
Judge, 1b	4	0	0	12	2	0
Foster, 3b	3	0	1	2	2	0
Milan, cf	4	1	2	3	0	0
Schulte, lf	4	1	1	0	0	0
Morgan, 2b	3	1	2	1	7	0
Lavan, ss	4	1	2	5	4	1
Picinioh, c	4	0	2	4	0	0
Ayers, p.	3	0	0	0	1	0
Totals	34	4	11	27	16	1

BOSTON (A. L.)

	ab	r	h	o	a	e
Hooper, rf	4	0	0	2	0	0
Shean, 2b	4	0	2	4	1	0
Strunk, cf	4	0	1	2	0	0
Whiteman, lf	3	0	0	1	0	0
McInnis, 1b	3	0	1	10	4	0
Thomas, 3b.	3	0	0	1	0	1
Scott, ss	3	0	0	2	3	0
Agnew, c	2	0	1	4	1	1
Molyneaux, p	0	0	0	0	0	0
McCabe, p	2	0	0	1	3	0
Schang, c	1	0	0	0	0	0
*Ruth	1	0	0	0	0	0
Totals	30	0	6	27	12	2

*Batted for Agnew in eighth inning.

Washington	0	1	1	0	0	2	0	0	0	0—4
Boston	0	0	0	0	0	0	0	0	0	0—0

Two-base hit—Lavan. Stolen bases—Milan, Hooper. Sacrifice hit—Ayers. Double plays—Judge to Lavan to Judge (2); McInnis (unassisted); Scott to Shean to McInnis. Left on bases—Washington, 6; Boston, 3. First base on errors—Washington, 1; Boston, 1. Bases on balls—Off McCabe, 2. Hits—Off McCabe, 11 in 8 innings. Struck out—By Ayers, 3; by McCabe, 3. Losing pitcher—McCabe.

THIS is the famous "Murderers' Row" of the Yankees, so named because of its vicious attacks on the opposing pitchers. They are Wally Pipp, Frank Baker, Del Pratt and Ping Bodie (from left to right), and by their great stick work have helped to put the Huggins team safely in second position in the league race. In yesterday's game at the Polo Grounds Baker lived up to his reputation as the "Home Run King" by making a circuit hit in the sixth inning. His double in the eighth was the lead-off blow which preceded the counting of the winning tally, which was made by Pratt on Dugan's fumble of Pipp's grounder.

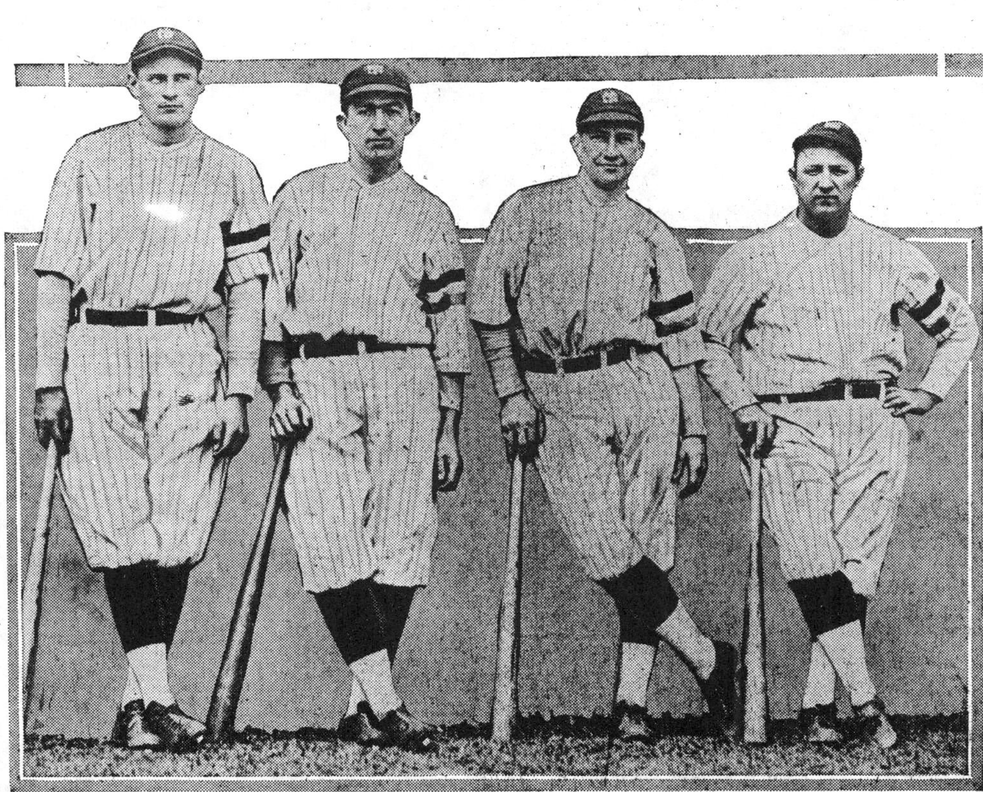

Walker's Single In Eighth Inning Beats Browns

DETROIT, May 30.—Walker's single in the eighth inning, with Veach on third base, gave Detroit a 2 to 1 victory over St. Louis this afternoon. Veach had reached third on his single, Heilmann's sacrifice and Dressen's out. The visitor's run resulted from Gallia's single and Tobin's two-base hit. Wet grounds caused the postponement of the game scheduled for this forenoon.

ST. LOUIS (A. L.)

	ab	r	h	o	a	e
Tobin, cf	4	0	1	3	0	0
Austin, 3b.	4	0	1	3	2	0
Sisler, 1b	4	0	1	12	3	0
Demmitt, rf.	3	0	1	0	1	0
Smith,	3	0	0	0	0	0
Gedeon, 2b.	3	0	0	2	5	0
N'nam'k'r, c	3	0	0	2	1	0
Gerber, ss.	3	0	0	2	4	0
Gallia, p	2	1	2	0	2	0
*Johns	1	0	0	0	0	0
†Maisel	0	0	0	0	0	0
Totals	30	1	6	24	18	0

DETROIT (A. L.)

	ab	r	h	o	a	e
Bush, ss	4	0	1	0	4	0
Young, 2b	4	0	2	4	3	0
Veach, lf	4	1	1	2	1	0
H'lm'nn, rf	2	0	1	3	0	0
Dressen, 1b.	3	0	1	12	0	0
Walker, cf.	4	0	2	3	0	0
Vitt, 3b	4	0	0	1	2	0
Yelle, c	3	1	2	2	3	0
Dauss, p	3	0	1	0	2	0
Totals	31	2	11	27	15	0

*Batted for Gallia in ninth innnig.
†Ran for Austin in ninth inning.

St. Louis	0	0	0	0	0	1	0	0	0	0—1
Detroit	0	1	0	0	0	0	0	0	1	x—2

Two-base hits—Tobin, Young. Stolen base—Young. Sacrifice hit—Heilmann. Left on bases—Detroit, 8; St. Louis, 2. Bases on balls—Off Gallia, 2. Struck out—By Gallia, 1; by Dauss, 1.

Bouts in Jersey Monday Night

The next show at the Armory A. A. of Jersey City will be held in the club's handsome stadium, on Hoboken, Oakland and Central avenues, next Monday night, with Soldier Bartfield, the slashing Brooklyn fighter, and Johnny Howard, of Bayonne, as the main eventers. On account of a local boy being one of the principals it is expected that this show will draw a big crowd.

Mrs. Edward W. Raymond Wins Semi-Final in Tennis

By Fred Hawthorne

Every contestant put in a full day's work yesterday on the clay courts of the Pelham Country Club, at Pelham Manor, where the women's annual invitation lawn tennis tournament is in progress. One match was played in the singles, Mrs. Edward W. Raymond defeating Mrs. Rawson L. Wood in the semi-final round by a score of 6—3, 6—3.

All the rest of the play was confined to the mixed doubles, with twenty-five strong pairs competing. Urged on by Mrs Benjamin F. Briggs's "will to play," the contestants went ahead at such a lively rate that only six teams were left in the competition at sundown.

This afternoon at 2 o'clock Miss Molla Bjurstedt, national champion, will meet Miss Marie Wagner, New York State champion, in the upper semi-final bracket, and at 3 o'clock the semi-finals in the women's doubles will be played, with Miss Caroma Winn and Miss Margaret Grove facing Miss Wagner and Mrs. Homer Stuart Green in one match and Miss Bjurstedt and Mrs. Johan Rogge opposing Mrs. George L. Chapman and her daughter, Miss Marian Chapman, in the other.

At 4 o'clock there will be a special men's doubles exhibition match, Frederick B. Alexander and Raymond D. Little meeting Beals C. Wright and William T. Tilden, jr., in what should prove one of the best matches of the season. Alexander and Little, the famour old Princeton pair, have both won countless national and international honors on the courts. Beals Wright, besides having held the national singles title, held the doubles crown for three years with Holcombe Ward, and defeated Norman Brookes in an international match. Tilden is to-day one of the most spectacular players in this country.

Mrs. Raymond's defeat of Mrs. Wood was not a surprise to those who have followed the progress of this tournament. The former metropolitan champion has been playing sound, consistent tennis, mixing up a strong back court driving game with a net attack sufficiently powerful to place her opponents on the defensive.

Mrs. Wood was not able to meet these tactics with much success, because her own drives from deep court were not going any too well, and when she attempted to go in to the net for the volleys it was generally to toss the points away on errors. After leading at 3—2 on games in the first set, she became erratic, and Mrs. Raymond, playing with splendid direction and "pace" in her strokes, won four out of the last five games, giving her the set at 6—3.

Again in the second set the former Florida champion was leading at 3—2, only to see Mrs. Raymond raise the power of her game and take the last four games in a row for the set at 6—3 and the match. The winner is certain to give her opponent, be it Miss Bjurstedt or Miss Wagner, a worthy battle for the honors in the final round at 2 o'clock to-morrow afternoon.

Pelham Country Club's Women's Invitation Singles (semi-final round)—Mrs. Edward W. Raymond defeated Mrs. Rawson L. Wood, 6—3, 6—3.

Mixed Doubles (first round)—Miss Marion Chapman and J. B. Hughes defeated Miss Clare Cassel and Jacques Thibaud, 6—1, 6—1; Mrs. Homer Stuart Green and J. S. O'Boyle defeated Mrs. W. H. Pritchard and H. A. Wyckoff, 6—0, 6—2; Miss Florence Ballin and W. T. Tilden, jr., defeated Mrs. S. F. Weaver, and W. A. Campbell, 6—3, 6—2; Miss Helene Pollak and Dr. William Rosenbaum won from Miss Bessie Holden and E. A. Walsh by default; Mr. and Mrs. E. W. Raymond defeated Mr. and Mrs. Ingo Hartmann, 9—7, 3—6, 6—4; Miss Elizabeth H. Moore and H. D. O'Boyle defeated Miss Molla Bjurstedt and J. S. Myrick, 7—5, 4—6, 6—4; Mrs R. S. Leachman and Elliott H. Binzen defeated Mrs. Albert Humphries and Embree Henderson, 6—4, 6—4; Mr. and Mrs. Thurber won from Miss Grace Gilleaudeau and partner by default; Miss Marie Wagner and Herbert W. Forster defeated Miss Margaret Grove and J. H. Steinkampf, 8—6, 7—9, 6—3.

Second Round—Mrs. E. W. Lynch and W. J. Toussaint defeated Miss Caroma Winn and Alexander Iler, 6—3, 6—4; Miss Chapman and Mr. Hughes won from Mrs. Marshall McLean and partner by default; Miss Ballin and Mr. Tilden defeated Mrs. Green and Mr. O'Boyle, 6—4, 6—3; Miss Pollak and Dr. Rosenbaum defeated Mrs. and Mr. Raymond, 6—3, 4—6, 6—4; Mrs. Leachman and Mrs. Einzen defeated Miss Moore and J. S. O'Boyle, 6—4, 7—5; Miss Wagner and Mr. Forster defeated Mrs. and Mr. Thurber, 6—2, 6—2; Mrs. and Mr. B. F. Briggs defeated Miss Edith Handy and Norman Johnson, 8—6, 6—3; Mrs. George L. Chapman and R. Clifford Black defeated Mrs. and Mr. L. G. Morris, 6—2, 5—7, 6—1.

Third Round—Miss Chapman and Mr. Hughes defeated Mrs. Lynch and Mr. Toussaint, 6—4, 7—5; Mrs. Chapman and Mr. Black defeated Mrs. and Mr. Briggs, 1—6, 6—3, 6—3.

Standing of Major League Clubs

NATIONAL LEAGUE

GAMES TO-DAY
New York at Philadelphia
Boston at Brooklyn
St. Louis at Pittsburgh

YESTERDAY'S RESULTS
New York vs. Phila. (1st, wet gds.)
New York 6, Philadelphia 3 (2d)
Boston 2, Brooklyn 1 (1st)
Boston 4, Brooklyn 3 (2d)
Pittsburgh 8, St. Louis 0 (1st)
St. Louis 4, Pittsburgh 0 (2d)
Cincinnati 9, Chicago 6 (1st)
Chicago 2, Cincinnati 1 (2d)

STANDING OF TEAMS

	W.	L.	P.c.		W.	L.	P.c.
N. York	24	11	.686	Boston	18	20	.474
Chicago	23	12	.657	Phila	15	19	.441
Cin'nati	21	18	.538	St. Louis	13	22	.371
Pittsbgh.	16	17	.485	Brklyn.	13	24	.351

AMERICAN LEAGUE

GAMES TO-DAY
St. Louis at Detroit
Washington at Boston
Chicago at Cleveland

YESTERDAY'S RESULTS
New York vs. Phila. (1st, wet gds.)
New York 2, Philadelphia 1 (2d)
Boston 9, Washington 1 (1st)
Washington 4, Boston 0 (2d)
Chicago 4, Cleveland 3 (11 in., 1st)
Cleveland 3, Chicago 2 (2d)
Detroit vs. St. L. (1st, wet gds)
Detroit 2, St. Louis 1 (2d)

STANDING OF TEAMS

	W.	L.	P.c.		W.	L.	P.c.
Boston	25	14	.641	Chicago	16	16	.500
N. York	22	15	.595	Wash'n.	16	23	.410
Clevel'd.	21	18	.538	Phila	14	21	.400
St. Louis	17	16	.515	Detroit.	11	19	.367

Dodgers Drop 2 to Braves After Hot Pitchers' Battle

G. Tweety Stallings, boss of the Boston Braves, chuckled with glee yesterday for a threefold reason. His team, nondescript and of minor league style on its last appearance here, yesterday looked like champions when they won two hard fought games from the lowly Dodgers, the first 2 to 1 and the second 4 to 3, which, incidentally, send the Hubbites into fifth place.

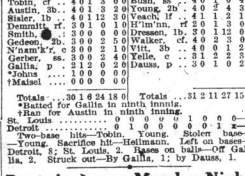

Reason three was that Memorial Day was featured by the return of the prodigal Bronxite—Dick Rudolph—to the Boston team. Believing the Braves have a chance for the pennant, Dick's terms, it is said, were met and he was out in uniform yesterday. He'll be ready to help the onrushing Braves by next week, he said yesterday.

Horseshoes surrounded both victories, for the Dodgers, staging a ninth inning rally in each game, were foiled just when it looked as if they were to emerge victorious. It was a sad day for Squire Ebbets and 8,000 of the faithful, who braved the drizzle and sat through two fast games.

Both Games Pitching Duels

Both games were pitchers' battles, the first between Art Nehf and Burleigh Grimes. Al Wickland, the Braves right fielder, was Burleigh's nemesis, for he drove in two of the runs for the visitors in the first game.

Bunn Hearn and Dan Griner hooked up in the twilight contest and Bunn emerged victor because all the luck was his. Rube Marquard twirled the ninth inning in both games after the Dodger pitchers had been replaced by pinch hitters.

The Braves were the first to score. With two out in the first, Powell singled and scored on Wickland's double to centre. The Robins tied up the score in the third when Miller flied to centre. Olson hit to the same spot and, when the ball went through Powell, the runners advanced a base. Hickman was purposely passed. Nehf then uncorked a wild pitch, scoring Miller.

The Braves stowed the game away in the eighth when Herzog was safe on Johnston's fumble. He started for second, but Miller's throw to Olson, It seemed, beat him to the bag. Quigley, however, called him safe. The decision was costly, for Wickland, with two down, tripled to the right field wall, scoring the Canteloupe King.

In the ninth Dodgers filled the bases only to be left stranded. Hickman skied to Wickland, but Wheat singled to centre. Myers doubled to centre, Buck negotiating the third sack. Jimmy Johnston was purposely pased, filling the sacks. Mique Doolan drove sharply to Smith, and the "Red 'Un," by a clever stop and throw, got Buck Wheat at the plate. It was up to Otto Miller to deliver the goods, but his best was a puny fly to Wickland.

Ollie O'Mara started to put the skids under Dan Griner in the second game when he foozled Henry's grounder. After Hearn and Rawlings had been retired Herzog was safe on Oliver's low throw to Johnston of Charley's grounder. Powell was equal to the emergency, for he singled to centre, scoring Amherst John.

It wasn't until the seventh that the Braves again found their way to the scoring pan. After Red Smith had fanned Koncy singled to left. Rehg and Henry singled in succession to right field, Koney scoring. On Henry's drive to right Hickman hurled in the direction of third base. The ball eluded O'Mara, and no one backing him up, Rehg, too, scored.

The Dodgers came back in their half with a run. O'Mara was safe on Herzog's error. Hickman sent him to second with a single to left. Jimmy was forced by Wheat, Ollie going to third and scoring on Johnston's drive to right.

One more tally was notched by the Braves in the eighth. Powell was passed and went to second on Krueger's sacrifice. Smith crossed the Dodgers' infield with a safe bunt, but was forced when O'Mara tossed Koney's grounder to Doolan, Powell scoring.

Again in the ninth the Dodgers staged a dying rally, and again they fell short. Hickman singled to center and Wheat doubled to right, Jimmy going to third. Johnston was there in the pinch with a single that scored Hickman and put a man on third for the tieing run. Mack Wheat batted for Doolan and did his best to break up the game, but his terrific drive was grabbed by Rawlings, who doubled Johnston off first. Krueger was at the bat, with two strikes and no balls when Myers tried to steal home. He was nicked just as he slid into the plate. That ended the inning, the game and the Dodgers' hopes.

E. Luther McGrath, the venerable Boston statistician, announced in the press box that most of the Boston navy yard team of former big league players are on active duty. One is in Tokio, another in Alaska and several are on the high seas. Rabbit Maranville is on a battleship.

The scores:

FIRST GAME

BOSTON (N. L.)

	ab	r	h	o	a	e
Rawlings, ss	4	0	0	1	4	0
Herzog, 2b.	3	1	0	3	3	0
Powell, cf.	4	1	3	2	0	1
Wickland, rf	4	0	2	5	0	0
Smith, 3b.	4	0	0	1	3	0
K'netchy, 1b	4	0	0	11	0	0
Rehg, lf	4	0	1	1	0	0
Henry, c	3	0	0	2	0	0
Nehf, p	3	0	0	1	1	0
Totals	33	2	6	27	11	1

BROOKLYN (N. L.)

	ab	r	h	o	a	e
Olson, ss.	4	0	1	0	5	0
O'Mara, 3b.	4	0	0	1	3	0
Hickman, rf.	3	0	1	0	0	0
Wheat, lf	4	0	1	2	0	0
Myers, cf	4	0	1	5	0	0
Johnston, 1b	3	0	1	14	0	1
Doolan, 2b.	4	0	1	3	0	0
Miller, c	4	1	1	2	0	0
Grimes, p	2	0	0	0	3	0
Marquard, p.	0	0	0	0	0	0
*Krueger	1	0	0	0	0	0
Totals	33	1	7	27	12	1

*Batted for Grimes in eighth inning.

Boston	1	0	0	0	0	0	0	1	0	—2
Brooklyn	0	0	1	0	0	0	0	0	0	0—1

Two-base hits—Wickland and Myers. Three-base hit—Wickland. Stolen base—Herzog. Double plays—Smith to Herzog to Konetchy; Doolan to Johnston. Left on bases—Boston, 6; Brooklyn, 7. First base on errors—Boston, 1. Bases on balls—Off Grimes, 2; off Nehf, 2. Hits—Off Grimes, 6 in 8 innings. Struck out—By Grimes, 1; by Nehf, 1. Wild pitch Nehf. Winning pitcher—Nehf. Losing pitcher—Grimes.

SECOND GAME

BOSTON (N. L.)

	ab	r	h	o	a	e
Rawlings, ss	5	0	1	2	5	0
Herzog, 2b	4	0	0	1	3	1
Powell, cf	3	1	1	2	0	0
Wickl'd, rf.	3	0	1	2	0	0
Smith, 3b	3	0	1	2	0	0
K'netchy, 1b	4	1	1	11	0	0
Rehg, lf	4	1	1	3	0	0
Henry, c	4	1	1	4	1	0
Hearne, p	3	0	0	0	1	0
Totals	33	4	7	27	11	1

BROOKLYN (N. L.)

	ab	r	h	o	a	e
Olson, ss.	4	0	1	1	3	0
O'Mara, 3b.	4	1	0	1	4	2
Hickman, rf	4	1	2	1	0	1
Z. Wheat, lf	4	1	1	3	0	0
Myers, cf	3	0	0	2	1	0
Johnston, 1b	4	0	3	11	0	0
Doolan, 2b.	3	0	0	4	2	1
Krueger, c.	3	0	1	4	3	0
Griner, p.	2	0	0	0	3	0
Marquard, p	0	0	0	0	0	0
*Miller	1	0	0	0	0	0
†M. Wheat	1	0	0	0	0	0
Totals	33	3	8	27	16	4

*Batted for Griner in eighth inning.
†Batted for Doolon in ninth inning.

Boston	0	0	1	0	0	0	2	1	0	—4
Brooklyn	0	0	0	0	0	0	1	0	2	—3

Two-base hits—Z. Wheat and Krueger. Stolen bases—Powell, Olson and Johnston. Sacrifice hits—Wickland, Smith and Hearne. Double plays—Rawlings and Konetchy; Myers, Olson and Doolan. Left on bases—Boston, 6; Brooklyn, 4. First base on errors—Boston, 3; Brooklyn, 1. Bases on balls—Off Hearne, 1; off Griner, 1. Hits—Off Griner, 8 in 8 innings. Struck out—By Hearne, 3; Griner, 5. Passed ball—Henry, 1 Losing pitcher—Griner.

Pirates Share Shutouts With St. Louis Cards

PITTSBURGH, May 30.—St. Louis and Pittsburgh split a double-header here to-day, the home team winning the morning game, 8 to 0, and the visitors taking the afternoon game, 4 to 0. Effective pitching by Doak brought victory to St. Louis in the latter game. Harmon was hit hard in the first inning when three singles and a wild throw gave the visitors three runs.

FIRST GAME

ST. LOUIS (N. L.)

	ab	r	h	o	a	e
Smythe, 2b.	3	0	0	2	1	1
Smith, cf	4	0	1	4	1	0
Baird, 3b	3	0	0	0	5	0
Hornsby, ss.	3	0	1	2	0	0
Cruise, lf	4	0	0	1	0	0
Paulette, 1b	3	0	1	11	1	0
Snyder, 1b.	0	0	0	1	0	0
Kavan'gh, rf	3	0	0	1	0	0
Gonzales, c.	3	0	1	1	4	0
Packard, p.	1	0	0	0	3	0
Tuero, p.	1	0	0	1	1	0
Totals	28	0	4	24	16	1

PITTSBURGH (N. L.)

	ab	r	h	o	a	e
Bigbee, lf.	5	1	1	2	0	0
Mollwitz, 1b	4	1	1	8	0	0
Carey, cf	2	3	2	1	0	0
Stengel, rf	3	1	1	4	0	0
Cutshaw, 2b	4	1	3	3	4	0
Caton, ss	3	0	0	1	5	0
McK'h'e, 3b	2	0	0	2	0	0
Schmidt, c.	4	1	1	6	2	0
Miller, p.	3	0	1	0	1	0
Totals	30	8	10	27	12	0

St. Louis	0	0	0	0	0	0	0	0	0	0—0
Pittsburgh	0	0	1	0	5	0	1	1	x	—8

Two-base hits—Mollwitz, Cutshaw. Three-base hit—Carey. Stolen bases—Paulette, Bigbee, Carey (2), Cutshaw, Schmidt. Sacrifice hits—Packard, Miller. Sacrifice fly—McKechnie. Double plays—Smith and Smythe; Cutshaw and Mollwitz. Left on bases—St. Louis, 5; Pittsburgh, 6. First base on balls—Off Packard, 3; off Tuero, 1; off Miller, 3. Hits—Off Packard, 6 in 4 1-3 innings; off Tuero, 4 in 3 2-3; off Miller, 4 in 9. Hit by pitcher—By Packard (McKechnie); by Tuero (Carey). Struck out—By Miller, 5. Winning pitcher—Miller. Losing pitcher—Packard.

SECOND GAME

ST. LOUIS (N. L.)

	ab	r	h	o	a	e
Smyth, 2b	4	1	1	3	1	0
Smith, cf	4	1	1	1	0	0
Baird, 3b.	4	1	1	1	4	0
Hornsby, ss.	4	1	1	1	6	0
Cruise, lf	4	0	1	2	0	0
Paulette, 1b	4	0	0	15	1	0
Kavanagh, rf	4	0	0	0	0	0
Gonzales, c.	3	0	1	4	1	0
Doak, p	3	0	1	0	6	0
Totals	34	4	7	27	19	0

PITTSBURGH (N. L.)

	ab	r	h	o	a	e
Bigbee, lf	4	0	1	3	0	0
Mollwitz, 1b	4	0	1	15	0	0
Carey, cf.	3	0	0	0	1	0
Stengel, rf	4	0	0	1	1	0
Cutshaw, 2b.	3	0	2	1	7	1
Caton, ss	3	0	0	4	4	0
McK'hnie, 3b	3	0	1	1	3	0
Blackwell, c	3	0	1	2	0	2
Harmon, p.	3	0	0	0	3	0
Totals	30	0	6	2	19	3

St. Louis	3	0	0	0	0	1	0	0	0	0—4
Pittsburgh	0	0	0	0	0	0	0	0	0	0—0

Two-base hit—Cruise. Three-base hits—Gonzales, Doak. Stolen bases—Carey, McKechnie. Left on bases—St Louis, 3; Pittsburgh, 4. First base on balls—Off Doak, 1. Struck out—By Doak, 4; by Harmon, 2. Winning pitcher—Doak.

Aviators' Field Meet At Mineola Postponed

A rain-soaked field forced a postponement of the scheduled triangular track and field meet between the members of the aviation service of Fields Nos. 1 and 2 and Camp Mills which was planned by the New York Athletic Club to be staged on the track at Field No. 2, at Mineola, yesterday. The games will be held to-morrow afternoon at 2 o'clock.

A number of the athletes entered were on hand for the fray, but after an investigation of the grounds by a committee from headquarters and the Winged Foot officials it was suggested that they be deferred until to-morrow. The members of the three camps will be granted a half haliday in order that they may compete.

Southern Association

New Orleans, 2; Chattanooga, 1.
New Orleans, 10; Chattanooga, 0.
Atlanta, 5; Little Rock, 4.
Nashville, 4; Mobile, 3.
Memphis, 5; Birmingham, 3.

Two Big Innings Give McGrawites 6-3 Win

Demaree, With Mother Looking On, Checks Club's Fall—McGraw's Men Bang Ball For Ten Safeties and Get Through Without An Error

By Charles A. Taylor

PHILADELPHIA, May 30.—The Giants took a decided brace to-day and defeated the Phillies by a score of 6 to 3. Not an error was made by the McGraw men and they banged the ball for ten safeties, one of them a triple by Walter Holke. Albertus Perfecto Demaree, who has flitted hither and yon about the National League circuit for several ages, did the pitching for the Giants, and in comparison with the recent efforts of the other McGraw slabmen Al Perfectus turned in a good game.

Al was found for nine hits, but in only one frame, the sixth, were they bunched to any damaging extent. Mrs. James Demaree sat right back of the Giant bench, and naturally Al just had to be on his best behavior.

Pat Moran nominated Joe Oeschger to do the box work for the Phillies, and the Giants appeared to be much pleased with Pat's selection. Joe stayed on the hill for one inning and two-thirds of another, or just long enough for the New Yorkers to gather five hits and all their six runs. The first two innings have been profitable for the Giants in practically every game played in the last three weeks, but the trouble has been that the runs usually accumulated then were insufficient in number to offset the tallies made by the opposition later on. To-day the McGrawites saw to it that Oeschger gave them a good enough start to carry them through.

Mule Watson was Moran's choice as relief twirler, and Mule got along nicely until the Phillie manager removed him in favor of Ben Tincup, who batted for Watson in the fifth and then took up Mule's job in the box. Tincup and his battery mate, Dilhoefer, who also got into the game in the sixth, join Uncle Sam's league to-morrow, so this was their final bow to the Quakertown fans. Tincup had the satisfaction of holding the Giants scoreless, but, as remarked before, the New York aggregation almost invariably closes its tally ledger after the second inning. Tincup, of course, did not know this and pitched his best, allowing three hits in the four stanzas he worked.

The Giants collected their runs in two bunches of three each. In the first inning Young was safe when Luderus dropped Stock's rather wide throw of the Giant outfielder's grounder. Benny Kauff singled to right field and Young raced to third, from which station he counted on a puny sacrifice fly to McGaffigan in short right. If Cravath had taken the ball, which really belonged to him, Young would have been snuffed out easily at the plate, but McGaffigan, with his back to the infield, was in no position to make the throw. Heinie Zimmerman expired, Stock to Luderus. Fletcher walked and Walter Holke came up with two on and two out. Holke smashed the ball far over Williams's head in left centre, scoring Kauff and Burns and pulling up at third. McCarthy lined to Meusel for the third out.

The Phillies picked up a run in their half of the first after two men had been retired. Stock singled and stole second and tallied on a double to right field by Luderus. Cravath took a mighty sweep at the ball, but Benny Kauff was under it when it descended.

In the second inning the Giants scored the runs that won the game. Niehoff singled to left and was safe at second when Oeschger threw Demaree's bunt too late for a force-out. Young hit to Bancroft, who stepped on second, forcing Demaree. Kauff made his second single in succession to right field and Niehoff scored. Burns banged the ball at Stock, who made a clever stop and got his man at first but was unable to prevent Young from crossing the rubber. Heinie Zimmerman hit safely to centre, bringing Kauff home.

The Phillies attacked stubbornly in the sixth, and for a time it looked as though Demaree would be driven from the mound. Al tightened just when "Red" Cecil Causey, who had been working vigorously in the warm-up pen, was awaiting the call to duty. Two men were out when Demaree suddenly lost all his "stuff." Luderus singled to the right field fence. Cactus Cravath aimed a terrific drive at the left field bleachers, which Burns managed to knock down as it was about to sail into the seats. Luderus scored on the mighty blow, and Cactus took up his perch on second. Meusel scored Cravath with a single to left field. Dilhoefer ended Demaree's worry by flying to Burns.

About Time!

NEW YORK

	ab	r	h	o	a	e
Young, r. f.	5	2	0	5	0	0
Kauff, c. f.	5	2	3	3	0	0
G Burns, l. f.	3	0	0	4	0	0
Zimmerman, 3b.	4	0	1	1	0	0
Fletcher, s. s.	3	1	1	1	1	0
Holke, 1b.	4	0	1	5	0	0
McCarty, c.	4	0	1	7	0	0
Niehoff, 2b.	4	1	2	1	2	0
Demaree, p.	3	0	1	0	2	0
Totals	35	6	10	27	5	0

PHILADELPHIA

	ab	r	h	o	a	e
Bancroft, s. s.	4	0	0	5	3	1
Williams, c. f.	4	0	0	1	0	0
Stock, 3b.	4	1	1	0	4	0
Luderus, 1b.	4	1	3	14	0	1
Cravath, r. f.	4	1	2	1	0	0
Meusel, l. f.	4	0	1	3	0	0
McGaffigan, 2b.	4	0	1	1	1	0
Adams, c.	1	0	0	1	1	0
*Fitzgerald	1	0	1	0	0	0
Dilhoefer, c.	2	0	0	1	1	0
Oeschger, p.	0	0	0	0	0	0
Watson, p.	1	0	0	0	3	0
Tincup, p.	2	0	0	0	3	0
Totals	35	3	9	27	16	2

*Batted for Adams in fifth inning.

New York	3	3	0	0	0	0	0	0	0	0—6
Philadelphia	1	0	0	0	0	2	0	0	0	0—3

Two-base hits—Luderus, Cravath. Three-base hits—Holke. Stolen bases—Kauff, Stock. Sacrifice hit—Demaree. Sacrifice fly—G. Burns. Left on bases—New York, 5; Philadelphia, 5. First base on errors—New York, 1 Base on balls—Off Oeschger, 1. Hits—Off Oeschger, 5 in 1 2-3 innings; off Watson, 2 in 3 1-3 innings; off Tincup, 3 in 4 innings. Struck out—By Demaree, 3; by Tincup, 1. Losing pitcher—Oeschger.

Reds and Cubs In Even Break; Players Fight

CHICAGO, May 30.—Chicago, by defeating Cincinnati, 2 to 1, in the afternoon game, broke even on the holiday bill to-day, the visitors having won the morning contest, 9 to 6.

The work of Jim Vaughn was the deciding factor in the afternoon game. He struck out twelve of the visitors and allowed only six hits. His three-base hit, which preceded a triple by Flack, scored the winning run.

The game was marked by an assault on Catcher Killifer by Outfielder Earl Neale. Bressler, in the seventh, hit a little pop-up in front of the plate. Killifer tried for the ball, but missed it and it went foul. Neale, who was coming up to bat, claimed it a fair ball and said that Killifer touched it before it went foul. Words were exchanged between the players, and while Killifer held his mask in one hand and his glove in the other Neale attacked the catcher, threw him to the ground and hit him in the face several times. Killifer had to leave the game. Neale was led off the field by Umpire Rigler.

The scores:

FIRST GAME

CINCINNATI (N. L.)

	ab	r	h	o	a	e
Groh, 3b.	3	2	1	0	2	0
L. Magee, 2b	5	2	2	1	4	0
Roush, cf.	4	0	2	5	0	0
S. Magee, 1b	4	1	1	11	0	0
Bressler, rf.	4	3	3	3	0	0
Neale, lf.	4	1	2	4	0	0
Blackb'e, ss	3	0	2	1	2	1
Wingo, c.	4	0	1	2	0	0
Toney, p.	4	0	1	0	2	0
Totals	35	9	15	27	10	1

CHICAGO (N. L.)

	ab	r	h	o	a	e
Flack, rf.	3	1	0	2	0	0
Hollocher, ss	5	1	3	3	3	0
Mann, lf.	5	0	0	1	0	0
Merkle, 1b.	5	2	2	13	1	0
Paskert, cf.	4	2	2	0	0	0
Deal, 3b.	3	0	1	1	5	0
Zeider, 2b.	4	0	2	4	4	0
Kilduff, 2b.	0	0	0	0	1	0
Killifer, c.	4	0	0	3	2	0
Tyler, p.	2	0	0	0	3	0
Weaver, p.	0	0	0	0	2	0
*Barber	1	0	0	0	0	0
Carter, p.	1	0	0	0	1	0
Totals	37	6	10	27	22	0

*Batted for Weaver in seventh inning.

Cincinnati	4	0	0	0	2	2	0	1	0	—9
Chicago	0	0	4	0	0	0	0	2	0	—6

Two-base hits—Bresler, Groh, Paskert. Three-base hits—Roush, Neale. Stolen bases—Deal (2). Paskert. Sacrifice hits—Roush, Neale. Sacrifice fly—Deal. Double plays—Tyler to Hollocher to Merkle; Deal to Zeider to Merkle. Left on bases—Cincinnati, 6; Chicago, 7. Base on error—Chicago, 1. Bases on balls—Off Tyler, 1; off Toney, 2; off Weaver, 1; off Carter, 3. Hits—Off Tyler, 9 in 4 2-3 innings; off Weaver, 4 in 2 1-3 innings; off Carter, 2 in 2 innings; off Toney, 10 in 9 innings. Struck out—By Tyler, 2; by Toney, 2. Passed ball—Wingo. Winning pitcher—Toney. Losing pitcher—Tyler.

SECOND GAME

CINCINNATI (N. L.)

	ab	r	h	o	a	e
Groh, 3b	4	0	2	1	5	0
L. Magee, 2b	4	1	1	1	3	0
Roush, cf	3	0	1	3	0	0
S. Magee, 1b	4	0	1	11	1	0
Bressler, rf	3	0	0	0	0	0
Neale, lf	2	0	1	2	0	0
Chase, rf	1	0	0	1	0	0
Bl'kb'rne, ss	3	0	0	3	5	0
Smith, c	3	0	0	2	0	0
Schn'der, p.	2	0	0	0	0	0
Eller, p	1	0	0	0	2	0
Totals	30	1	6	24	17	0

CHICAGO (N. L.)

	ab	r	h	o	a	e
Flauck, rf.	4	0	2	2	0	0
Holl'ch'r, ss.	3	0	0	2	1	0
Mann, lf	4	0	2	0	0	0
Merkle, 1b	3	0	2	5	0	0
Paskert, cf	3	0	0	1	0	0
Deal, 3b	3	1	1	3	0	0
Zeider, 2b	3	0	1	1	3	0
Killifer, c.	1	0	0	1	3	0
O'Farrell, c.	1	0	0	3	1	0
Vaughn, p	3	1	1	0	2	0
Totals	28	2	9	27	9	1

Chicago	0	0	0	1	0	0	0	1	0	x—2
Cincinnati	1	0	0	0	0	0	0	0	0	0—1

Two-base hits—S. Magee, Mann. Three-base hits—L. Magee, Vaughn, Flack. Stolen bases—Mann, L. Magee. Sacrifice hit—Paskert. Sacrifice fly—Killifer. Double plays—Killifer and Zeider; Blackburne and S. Magee; L. Magee, Blackburne and S. Magee; Schneider to Groh to Blackburne to L. Magee to Chase. Bases on balls—Off Schneider, 2; off Vaughn, 1. Hits—Off Schneider, 8 in 6 1-3 innings; off Eller, 1 in 1 2-3; off Vaughn, 5 in 9. Hit by pitcher—By Schneider, 1; by Deal, 1. Struck out—By Vaughn, 12; by Schneider, 1. Losing pitcher—Schneider.

American Association

Louisville, 1; Indianapolis, 0.
Louisville, 5; Indianapolis, 1.
Milwaukee, 2; Kansas City, 1.
Milwaukee, 8; Kansas City, 6.
Columbus, 1; Toledo, 0.
Columbus, 5; Toledo, 4 (10 in.).
Minneapolis, 2; St. Paul, 2.
Minneapolis, 8; St. Paul, 3.

White Sox Get First; Indians Take Second

CLEVELAND, May 30. — Cleveland and Chicago broke even to-day, the White Sox taking the morning game at 4 to 3 and the locals the afternoon contest, 3 to 2, winning in the last half of the ninth on Williams's double, O'Neill's sacrifice and Graney's sacrifice fly.

The score:

FIRST GAME

CHICAGO (N. L.)

	ab	r	h	o	a	e
Liebold, lf.	6	1	1	5	0	0
Murphy, rf	6	0	3	3	0	0
Collins, 2b	6	1	3	5	3	0
Felsch, cf.	5	1	3	4	0	0
Weaver, ss	3	0	1	1	5	0
Gandil, 1b	5	0	2	10	0	0
M'Mull, 3b	3	0	1	1	4	1
Schalk, c.	5	1	1	4	0	0
C. Wms, p.	1	0	0	0	0	0
Sh'll'b'k, p	3	0	0	0	2	0
Totals	43	4	15	33	14	1

CLEVELAND (A. L.)

	ab	r	h	o	a	e
Evans, 3b	5	1	1	2	3	1
Chapman, ss	5	1	1	2	4	0
Speaker, cf	6	0	1	5	0	0
Roth, rf	5	0	1	0	0	1
W'bsg'ns, 2b	5	0	2	2	4	0
Wood, lf	5	0	0	3	1	0
A. Wms, 1b	5	1	1	15	1	0
O'Neill, c	3	0	0	5	5	0
Enzmann, p	5	0	4	1	2	0
Totals	44	3	11	33	20	2

Chicago	2	0	0	0	0	0	1	0	0	0	1	—4
Cleveland	2	1	0	0	0	0	0	0	0	0	0	0—3

Two-base hits—Wambsganns, Roth. Three-base hit—Felsch. Stolen bases—Gandil, A. Williams. Sacrifice hits—Weaver, Shellenback. Double plays—E. Collins, Weaver and Gandil. Left on bases—Chicago, 11; Cleveland, 14. First base on errors—Chicago, 1; Cleveland, 1. Bases on balls—Off Shellenback, 4; off Enzmann, 2. Hits—Off C. Williams, 4 in 1 inning (none out in second inning); off Shellenback, 7 in 10. Hit by pitcher—By Williams, 2 (Chapman, O'Neill); by Enzmann, 1 (Weaver). Struck out—By Shellenback, 3; by Enzmann, 2. Wild pitches—Enzmann, 1. Winning pitcher—Shellenback. Losing pitcher—Enzmann

SECOND GAME

CHICAGO (A. L.)

	ab	r	h	o	a	e
Liebold, lf.	5	0	1	2	0	0
Murphy, rf.	3	0	2	1	1	0
E. Collins, 2b	2	0	0	4	2	0
Felsch, cf.	4	0	1	4	0	0
Weaver, ss.	4	0	0	2	4	0
Gandil, 1b.	4	0	1	8	1	0
McM'llin, 3b	0	0	0	0	0	0
Risberg, 3b.	4	1	0	1	0	0
Schalk, c.	3	1	2	3	1	0
Faber, p.	2	0	0	0	4	0
Benz, p.	0	0	0	0	0	0
Danforth, p.	0	0	0	0	0	0
Cicotte, p.	0	0	2	0	0	0
†J. Collins	1	0	0	0	0	0
‡Russell	1	0	0	0	0	0
Totals	33	2	9	*25	13	0

CLEVELAND (A. L.)

	ab	r	h	o	a	e
Evans, 3b.	4	0	2	0	1	0
Chapman, ss.	3	0	1	2	4	1
Speaker, cf.	2	0	0	2	0	0
Roth, rf.	3	1	0	2	1	0
Wam'nss, 2b.	3	1	1	5	4	0
Wood lf.	3	0	2	3	0	0
Williams, 1b	3	0	2	7	1	0
O'Neill, c.	3	0	1	5	2	0
Coveleskie, p	3	0	0	1	0	1
§Miller	0	1	0	0	0	0
¶Graney	0	0	0	0	0	0
Totals	27	3	9	27	13	2

*One out when winning run was scored.
†Batted for Faber in ninth inning.
‡Batted for Benz in ninth inning.
§Ran for Williams in ninth inning.
¶Batted for Coveleskie in ninth inning

Chicago	0	0	0	0	0	0	0	0	2	—2
Cleveland	0	1	0	1	0	0	0	0	0	1—3

Two-base hits—Murphy, Williams. Stolen bases—Chapman, 3. Sacrifice hits—O'Neill, Wood, Wambsganns, Williams. Sacrifice fly—Graney. Double plays—Weaver, E. Collins and Gandil; Wambsganns and Williams. Left on bases—Chicago, 8; Cleveland, 8. First base on errors—Chicago, 2. Bases on balls—Off Faber, 4; off Coveleskie, 4. Hits—Off Faber, 8 in 7 innings; off Danforth, 1 in 0. Struck out—By Faber, 1; by Benz, 1; by Coveleskie, 4. Losing pitcher—Danforth.

College Athletes Fight For Titles in Meet To-day

PHILADELPHIA, May 30.—College athletes from near and afar have already arrived here for the forty-second annual outdoor track and field championships of the Intercollegiate Associatoin of Amateur Atheletes of America, which will take place here to-morrow and Saturday. Franklin Field, where the games will be held, has been put in splendid shape and it is very likely that new standards will be set.

Although a number of the institutions terminated their studies several weeks ago, reports reaching here are that the track teams have been kept intact for the title meet. The entry for the games is especially gratifying in view of the drain on the athletic squads by the call to colors. Total nominations for the meet exceed 800, while the individual entry is well past the 350 mark. Of the twenty-eight colleges holding membership in the association only seven have failed to enter representatives.

The programme for to-morrow calls for the elimination of the athletes through a series of respective qualifying marks that will earn them the right to compete in the finals on Saturday. All the trials in the various events, with the exception of the one and two-mile runs and relay races, will be held on the opening day.

While the strength of the Cornell team is virtually an unknown quantity, the Ithacan athletes are looked upon to repeat their many victories in these important games. Coach Jack Moakley has high confidence in half a dozen of his charges capturing first places. He also looks to many of his other athletes to capture second, third and fourth places, which will compile an aggregate of points that should prove to be the highest of the contesting colleges.

Yankees Take Easy Game From Senators—Giants Beaten by Dodgers, 2 to 1

Tom McTaggart Wins Jamaica Feature Race

Captures Garden City Selling Stakes—Form Players Have Good Day

By W. J. Macbeth

Form players went home jubilant from the Jamaica racetrack yesterday, as four of the favorites in the card of six races showed their opponents the way home. The sport brought about a succession of close finishes, and only in the last race of the day was the winner a comfortable margin in the lead.

Tom McTaggart, the big Chuctanunda-Toplass colt, won his second race in succession for George W. McNamee, his new owner, in taking the Garden City Selling Stakes, the fourth race, at one mile and a sixteenth, from a field of fast opponents. The bay colt forced the issue the gerater part of the way, and, standing a hard drive gamely, led home by a length the fast coming Obolus, which failed to get away to a good start. Wise Man, the W. J. Starr horse, evidently set for a killing, weakened in the stretch run, but pulled down third honors.

The fanciers of the public choices began the day well when Pigeon beat home the two-year-olds in the opening event over the five-furlong route. However, it was not until the field was near the wire that Pigeon managed to answer Jockey McTaggart's urging with a rush to flash past Nan Knoehr and win going away.

Another victory would have been credited to those players of consistent winning horses had Kingfisher been able to enjoy fair luck in the second race. The favorite was forced to go around his field to obtain clear sailing, thereby losing much ground. With no rival to block his path, Kingfisher rushed to the front like a meteor, and just failed by a head to catch Starlike, the winner, at the finish.

Favorite Gets a Jolt

There was a sad blow for the backers of public favorites in the third event when Kirstie's Cub proved a good Santa Claus to the few that backed his chances. The Kriss Kringle colt swept past the judges' stand after a brilliant rush down the stretch to win by half a length for his admirers. Those few who wagered their American dollar on Kirstie's Cub are already in a position to purchase Christmas presents at such an early date, as he was quoted at 25 to 1.

As the field swung into the stretch Jockey Mergler, astride Kirstie's Cub, and who, incidentally, scored his second victory of the day, slipped his charge through an opening to gain the rail position. He went to the front quickly and won going away.

The field numbered fifteen starters, and the narrow track caused quite a jam at the start. In the mad rush to secure an advantageous position Star Spangled and Sweep Up II, the favorite, suffered the most interference. Jockey Ambrose, on Star Spangled, soon succeeded in getting his charge into a contending position, but Sweep Up II, cut off sharply, never had a chance. With more favorable racing luck, Star Spangled undoubtedly would have taken the measure of the unruly field, as he was by far the best. He managed gradually to increase his position to finish second to Kirstie's Cub.

Form Followers Win Again

However, the form followers again hit into a happy vein with the close victory of Sunflash II in the fifth race at one mile and a sixteenth. Sunflash II literally touched the sides of both rails of the track on his wide detour to victory. Jockey McTaggart had considerable difficulty in keeping the Sundridge-Naphthalia gelding on a straight line around the track, as he went wide on all the turns, but had enough left to get up and pass Dorcas in the last few strides.

A perfect day it was when Jusqu'au Bout, from the stable of J. E. Widener, captured the closing race at one mile and seventy yards. Those who had tried their luck on picking a long shot and failed in a majority of cases were again doomed to disappointment, as the horse of the French name was held at the prohibitive price of 2 to 5. The handicapping proved just, as Jusqu' au Bout merely enoyed a practice run. He was off quickly and always held command to win pulled up at the finish. First Troop showed a smart race by finishing second, after following the pace of Jusqu' au Bout from the barrier.

Jamaica Entries

FIRST RACE—Two-year-old maiden fillies; five furlongs.

22 Dahinda	112	151 *Doveridge	107
155 Queen of Spa	112	129 Milda	112
102 Polygon	112	161² Flyaway	112
169² *Danc. Carnival	107	— Milky Way II	112
129 Dixie Bird	112	169 Sweeplet	112

SECOND RACE—Three-year-old fillies; six furlongs.

127 Mary Maud	111	139² Helen Atkin	104
— Dawn Star	107	— Clarisse	101
— Parable	101	127 Jyntee	114
148³ Kate Bright	111	112 Enfilade	117
— Star Class	107	(99) Lady Gertrude	114
20³ Wheat Cakes	111		

THIRD RACE—Three-year-olds and upward; claiming; one mile and a sixteenth.

— *Coral	100	170 *Preston Lynn	106
174³ Little Cottage	107	— *Dundreary	106
149² Home S. Home	114	170³ Golding	96
65 Orderly	113	164 Sky Pilot	113
149 Daybreak	102	138 Napoleon	109
(131) Starry Banner	107	163 Poacher	101
170 Hesse	102	163 Babette	99
164³ *Say	111	171 Blazonry	108

FOURTH RACE—The Youthful; two-year-olds; five and a half furlongs.

114 War Mask	101	75³ Routledge	101
75 Lord Brighton	105	168² Grimalkin	101
(142) Hannibal	120	162³ Yurucari	101

FIFTH RACE—Three-year-olds; one mile and seventy yards.

148³ Kate Bright	115	116² Nutcracker	112
166 Trophy	112	135³ Tom Bolo	115
— Elmendorf	106	(156) Princeps	117
163² Magnetite	106	135 Orestes	120

SIXTH RACE—Claiming; four-year-olds and upward; one mile and seventy yards.

124 G. M. Miller	115	125 Captain Ray	105
64 *Nebraska	100	(174) Harwood II	115
164 *Burlingame	110	109 *Langden	105
149² Home S. Home	110	174³ Bill Simmons	105
164 Dervish	110	164 Sky Pilot	105

*Apprentice allowance claimed.

Latonia Entries

First race (two-year-olds; maidens, colts and geldings; claiming; purse, $700; five furlongs)—*George Meuhlenbach, 104; *Larry B., 104; Archie Alexander, 109; Buncrana, 109; Silent Bid, 109; Unomeal, 109; Buster Clark, 112; Linden, 112; Sun Myth, 112; Byrne, 112; Sir Beau, 112; Caballo, 112. Also eligible, Vivir, 112; Perigord, 112; Charley Rector, 112.

Second race (three-year-olds; claiming; purse $700; six furlongs)—*Stormbound, 97; *Vanessa Welles, 97; *Crystal Day, 97; *Capers, 97; *Dahadiah, II., 97; *Miss Wright, 102; Melilotus, 102; Koran, 102; Nib, 104; Gus Scheer, 104; Tom Goose, 104; *Clairvoyant, 99. Also eligible, Bandymo, 102; Nepe, 111; Brig o' War, 106; Azalea, 112; Peerless One, 113; Aztec, 114.

Third race (four-year-olds and upward; fillies and mares; claiming; purse, $800; mile and a sixteenth)—*Sophia Gatewood, 102; *Serenata, 105; Czar's Daughter, 107; Queen Apple, 107; Debra, 107; Guide Post, 107; Brown Velvet, 107; Nezib, 107; Tse Lai, 107; Fairy Legend, 110; Alda, 112.

Fourth race (four-year-olds and upward; fillies and mares; claiming, purse, $800; mile and a sixteenth)—*Eulogy, 105; *Jessie Louise, 105; *Baby Lynch, 107; *Madame Herrmann, 107; *Cora Lane, 107; Ardent, 107; Day Dream, 107; *Mary H., 107; Leonarra, 110; Black Front, 110.

Fifth race (three-year-olds and upward; purse $1,000; six furlongs)—Serenest, 100; Basil, 110; J. J. Murdock, 111; Prince of Como, 117.

Sixth race (handicap; for three-year-olds and upward; claiming, $800; mile and a sixteenth)—...n Heffering, 93; Dorothy Dean, 105; Regal Lodge (imp.), 107; Captain Rees, 112; Sansyming (imp.), ...; Dick Williams, 118; Faux Col (imp.), 118.

Seventh race (three-year-olds and upward; claiming; purse, $800; mile and a sixteenth)—*J. Walker, ...; Marauder, 95; Benefactor, 101; *Jack Lucas, ...; Fencer, 108; *David Craig, 109; Thorn Bloom, 111; Sun God, 114.

Murderers' Row Start Runs in First Inning

Fine Fielding Enables Allen Russel to Shut Out Visitors

By Charles A. Taylor

The Yankees celebrated their return to the Polo Grounds yesterday afternoon by defeating the Washington Senators with the utmost ease. The score was 9 to 0. The Griffith men, despite their appellation of Senators, failed to live up to the name. It was agreed in the Senate only a few days since that all Senators should argue and debate as long as they felt in the mood. Griffith's Senators yesterday stopped all argument and debate in the very first inning after the Yanks had tallied four runs.

Clark Griffith has ever been a welcome visitor to New York fandom, whether he brings his gang or comes alone. For it is well remembered by the local rooters, especially those who boast as many gray hairs as Griff, that he almost led the then Hilltop Yankees to a pennant in the days gone by.

The magnificent work of Griff in founding, sustaining and sweating for the bat and ball fund, the shekels from from which have brought loads of joy to the soldiers and sailors of the U. S. A., has added mightily to the popularity and prestige of the Washington manager. Not among the least of Griff's contributions to the national pastime has been his adoption of Nick Altrock at a time when Nick was a real baseball orphan with no place to go.

The sunny side of Nick appealed to Griff, who aims to scatter sunshine all along the way. And what a hit the antics of Nick on the coaching lines have made with the fans. Many a dull, monotonous game such as that of yesterday has been transformed by the comedian into a thing of delight.

Nick Altrock Busy

Griff brought his gang, including Nick, to the Polo Grounds yesterday and handed Huggins's men a game with they sorely needed in their desire to creep closer to the Red Sox. Griff seemingly had done just about all that a baseball manager could do to make the home town fans happy. But Griff is original. He is never satisfied. Nick Altrock got busy as per instructions immediately after the Yanks assumed a commanding lead. And Nick was going fine until Griff suddenly decided that the fans were going to sleep on the comedy king of baseball and that something further must be done.

The Washington manager thereupon waved Jim Shaw to the club house spray and summoned one Garland Buckeye, a big southpaw, to finish what was left of the game and send the fans home thoroughly awake and cheerful. Buckeye was there as a fun maker, but there were few garlands woven about his pitching.

Buckeye had no luck at all in mowing down the Yanks. He was new and polite, in fact so polite that he insisted on six Huggins men accepting free tickets to first in the two innings he occupied the centre of the diamond and the centre of the fans' attention.

It was learned that Buckeye came to the big show from Gary, Indiana. It is more than possible that he will soon be back in Gary unless Uncle Sam reaches out and grabs him. For Buckeye has the build of a mountaineer and although his pitching yesterday was poor he could undoubtedly lick a few Germans.

Yankees Start Early

The first inning was the big one, Murderers' Row swinging into action with a vim after their holiday. Little Gilhooley opened with a single to left field and raced to second when Shotton fumbled the drive. Peckinpaugh bunted to Pitcher Shaw and Gilhooley was caught between second and third. Gil finally dashed back to second, only to find Peck on the bag, and the latter was called out.

Home Run Baker walked and Del Pratt singled to right, scoring Gilhooley. Pipp hit safely to centre, tallying both Baker and Pratt. Bodie singled to right, sending Pipp to third. Marsans was safe on Rice's muff of the former's fly, but Bodie was forced at second as Pipp registered.

The Yankees made another run in the third as a result of Baker's single and Pipp's double, and then took full advantage of the advent of Garland Buckeye in the seventh when they put over three more runs. Gilhooley singled, Baker strolled, Pratt singled and both Bodie and Marsans drew passes from Buckeye, the ultimate damage being three tallies. In the eighth the unruly Buckeye gave two more passes and Baker put a run over by a single to right.

Russell Finds Holes

Allen Russell, pitching for the Yanks, was in difficulty on several occasions, but clever fielding on the part of his mates averted danger. Two double plays aided materially in enabling Allen to score a shut-out.

It was a grand day for Home Run Baker. He walked twice and hit three singles in his five appearances at the plate. It was not a grand day for Buckeye, but he made everybody happy.

NINE RUNS—COUNT 'EM

WASHINGTON (A. L.)	ab	r	h	o	a	e	NEW YORK (A. L.)	ab	r	h	o	a	e
Shotton, lf	4	0	1	3	0	1	Gilhooley, rf	4	3	2	1	0	0
Foster, 3b	4	0	1	1	3	0	Peck'augh, ss	4	0	0	2	3	0
Judge, 1b	4	0	1	4	0	0	Baker, 3b	3	3	3	2	4	0
Milan, cf	3	0	2	4	0	0	Pratt, 2b	4	1	2	6	2	0
Rice, rf	4	0	0	2	1	0	Ward, 2b	1	0	0	1	1	0
Morgan, 2b	3	0	2	1	0	0	Pipp, 1b	4	1	2	5	1	0
McBride, ss	4	0	0	3	3	0	Beck, 1b	1	0	0	2	0	0
Ainsmith, c	2	0	1	4	1	0	Bodie, lf	3	0	1	2	0	0
Shaw, p	2	0	0	1	2	0	Marsans, cf	2	0	1	1	0	0
*Shanks	1	0	0	0	0	0	Hannah, c	4	0	0	5	0	0
Buckeye, p	0	0	0	1	1	0	Russell, p	3	1	1	0	1	0
†Johnson	1	0	0	0	0	0							
Totals	32	0	8	24	11	1	Totals	33	9	12	27	12	0

*Batted for Shaw in the seventh inning.
†Batted for Buckeye in the ninth inning.

Washington	0	0	0	0	0	0	0	0	0	—0
New York	4	0	1	0	0	0	3	1	x	—9

Two-base hits—Morgan, Pipp. Stolen bases—Marsans, Baker and Morgan. Sacrifice fly—Marsans. Double plays—Peckinpaugh, Pratt and Pipp; Peck, Pratt and Pipp; Baker, Ward and Beck. Left on bases—New York, 8; Washington, 9. Struck out—By Russell, 5; by Shaw, 2; by Buckeye, 1. Bases on balls—Off Russell, 13; off Shaw, 1; off Buckeye, 6. Hits—Off Shaw, 9 in 6 innings; off Buckeye, 3 in 2. Hit by pitcher—By Russell (Milan). Losing pitcher—Shaw.

ALLEN RUSSELL, the Yankees' reliable southpaw, who pulled Miller Huggins's team nearer the league leading Red Sox by defeating the Washington Senators yesterday in the first game of the series. Russell was touched for eight safeties, but he was an enigma in the pinches.

Athletics Shut Out Red Sox in First of Series

BOSTON, June 19.—The Athletics won its first game of the season in this city from Boston to-day, 5 to 0. Geary held the home team to seven hits, while Bush was hit hard. Three hits, two passes and two errors gave Philadelphia four runs in the sixth. Only one Bostonian reached third base. Clever fielding by Walker and Gardner featured. Two games will be played to-morrow.

The score:

PHILADELPHIA (A. L.)	ab	r	h	o	a	e	BOSTON (A. L.)	ab	r	h	o	a	e
Shannon, ss	5	0	1	2	2	0	Hooper, rf	3	0	0	0	1	0
Oldring, lf	5	0	2	0	0	0	Truesdale, 2b	4	0	1	0	2	1
Walker, cf	5	0	1	3	1	0	Strunk, cf	3	0	1	5	0	1
Burns, 1b	5	2	3	8	1	0	Ruth, lf	3	0	0	1	0	0
Gardner, 3b	2	1	0	4	1	0	McInnis, 1b	4	0	0	14	1	0
McAvoy, c	4	0	2	6	1	0	Thomas, 3b	4	0	2	1	4	0
Davidson, rf	3	0	1	0	0	0	Scott, ss	3	0	1	1	5	0
Dugan, 2b	3	1	0	4	4	0	Agnew, c	3	0	1	4	0	1
Geary, p	3	1	0	0	1	0	Bush, p	3	0	1	1	3	0
Totals	35	5	10	27	11	0	Totals	29	0	7	27	16	3

Philadelphia	0	0	0	1	0	4	0	0	0	—5
Boston	0	0	0	0	0	0	0	0	0	—0

Sacrifice hits—Gardner (2), Davidson, Scott. Double plays—Burns to Shannon to Burns; Shannon to Dugan to Burns. Left on bases—Boston, 7; Philadelphia, 9. First base on errors—Philadelphia, 2. Bases on balls—Off Bush, 3; off Geary, 4. Struck out—By Bush, 3; by Geary, 3. Wild pitch—Geary.

Southern Association

Little Rock, 5; Atlanta, 4.
Atlanta, 7; Little Rock, 4.
Nashville, 7; Mobile, 4.
Memphis, 11; Birmingham, 3.
New Orleans, 1; Chattanooga, 0.
Chattanooga, 8; New Orleans, 2.

Racing Summaries

Jamaica, Twelfth Day, June 19

WEATHER CLEAR; TRACK FAST

175 FIRST RACE.—Selling; for two-year-olds; $761 added. Five furlongs. At post seven minutes; off at 2:38. Start poor. Won driving; place same. Time, 1:00 3-5. Winner, b. g., by Whiskbroom II—Tree Dove. Owner, Mrs. M. E. Williams. Trainer, J. Johnson.

Index.	Starter.	Wt.	Post Pos.	St.	⅛	¼	⅛	Fin.	Jockey.	Open.	High.	Close.	Place.	Sh.
(147)	Pigeon	111	2	2	4^n	4^h	2^1	$1^{1½}$	McTaggart	2	5-2	11-5	4-5	1-3
147	Nan Knoehr	108	3	1	1^1	1^n	1^1	2^1	Byrne	3	5	4	8-5	7-10
142	Zuleika	119	6	4	2^h	2^1	$3^{1½}$	3^1	Troxler	7	8	9-2	8-5	4-5
—	St. Quentin	109	4	6	6^2	6^2	4^4	4^4	Lyke	12	15	15	6	5-2
43	Dottie Vandiver	104½	7	8	6	7^1	5^1	5½	Ensor	8-5	5-2	5-2	1	2-5
82	Harry M. Stevens	110	8	7	8	8	8	6^5	Rowan	20	25	20	8	4
82	Jack Healey	105	1	3	$5^{1½}$	5^h	7^1	7^2	Ambrose	20	30	30	10	5
—	Jill	102	5	5	3^3	3^3	6^1	8	Callahan	20	30	30	10	5

Pigeon moved up fast coming around the home turn, caught Nan Knoehr at the eighth pole and won going away under a drive. The latter, off running, had a world of speed, but had nothing left when challenged. Zuleika had no excuse. Dottie Vandiver had no chance from where she got off.

176 SECOND RACE.—Selling; for four-year-olds and upward; $761 added. One mile and a sixteenth. At post one minute; off at 3:01. Start good. Won driving; place same. Time, 1:49. Winner, ch. c., by Star Shoot—Blakeslee. Owner, W. H. Travers. Trainer, R. A. Smith.

Index.	Starter.	Wt.	Post Pos.	St.	¼	½	1	Fin.	Jockey.	Open.	High.	Close.	Place.	Sh.
149	Starlike	99	4	3	2^h	2^1	1^1	1^h	Mergler	8	8	8	3	6-5
(138)	Kingfisher	114	3	1	6	6	$5^{1½}$	2½	Callahan	7-5	12-5	12-5	4-5	1-3
—	Paddy Dear	111	5	6	5^4	5^n	4^h	$3^{1½}$	Burger	3	3	11-5	4-5	1-3
14	Arbitrator	108	1	5	4^3	4^2	2^h	4^3	Jackson	12	15	15	5	5-2
95	Amalgamator	101	6	4	3^1	3¾	6	5^4	Stalker	3	4	4	7-5	2-5
164	Hondo	106	2	2	1^1	1^h	$3^{1½}$	6	Troise	6	8	8	3	6-5

Starlike saved a lot of ground at the head of the stretch and opened up a gap, but tired in the last sixteenth and just lasted. Kingfisher was best—had to run around the field at the head of the stretch, closed with a great burst of speed and would have won in another stride. Paddy Dear was poorly handled.

177 THIRD RACE.—Selling; for three-year-olds; $761 added; value to winners, $686, $100, $50. Six furlongs. At post two minutes; off at 3:32. Start good. Won driving; place easily. Time, 0:23 2-5, 0:47 4-5, 1:13 2-5. Winner, b. c., by Bearcatcher—Kirstie. Owner and trainer, William Martin.

Index.	Starter.	Wt.	Post Pos.	St.	¼	½	Str.	Fin.	Jockey.	Open.	High.	Close.	Place.	Sh.
157	Kirstie's Cub	108	4	1	3½	3^2	3^1	1½	Callahan	20	20	20	8	4
167	Star Spangled	108	1	2	$4^{1½}$	$2^{1½}$	2½	2^5	Ambrose	5	5	16-5	6-5	7-10
(37)	Nelsweep	116	2	5	2^2	1½	1^h	3^2	McTaggart	8	12	10	4	2
131	Common Law	108	11	13	10^2	7^1	4½	$4^{1½}$	Byrne	10	12	10	4	2
41³	Ideal	105	6	8	7½	5^1	5^1	5^1	Mergler	12	15	15	6	3
—	African Arrow	109	8	14	8^1	6½	6½	6½	Bell	10	15	10	4	2
—	Amackassin	111	5	10	11^1	10^1	9^1	7½	Rowan	10	15	12	5	5-2
37	Speedster	101	9	7	9^1	8½	8½	8^3	Willie	20	30	30	10	5
(157)	Sweep Up II	116	13	12	13	11^2	10½	9^1	Lkye	8-5	11-5	2	9-10	2-5
107	Grayson	106	3	11	12^1	9^1	11^1	10½	Ensor	20	30	30	10	5
—	Miss Sterling	101	15	6	6^1	4½	7^1	$11^{1½}$	Troise	30	40	40	15	6
20³	Thistle	107	7	3	1^h	13	12^2	12^2	Kelsay	4	6	5	2	1
121	Fidelis	107	14	9	5^h	12	13½	13^1	Schuttinger	30	40	30	10	5
—	Alf Vezina	109	12	4	14	14	14	14^2	Mara	50	60	60	20	10
156	Dublin Mary	113	10	15	15	15	15	15	Knapp	50	60	50	20	8

Winner entered for $600; bought in for $1,005.
Kirstie's Cub saved ground at the stretch turn. Star Spangled, off well, went wide at stretch turn and hung at the end. Sweep Up II, in close quarters, had no chance.
Overweight—Common Law, 1. Scratched—Golding, 101.

178 FOURTH RACE.—GARDEN CITY SELLING; for three-year-olds and upward; $2,000 guaranteed; value to winners, $1,575, $300, $200. One mile and a sixteenth. At post two minutes; off at 4:02. Start good. Won handily; place easily. Time, 0:24 4-5, 0:48 4-5, 1:14, 1:40, 1:47. Winner, b. c., 4, by Chuctanunda—Toplash. Owner, G. W. McNamee. Trainer, A. R. Bresler.

Index.	Starter.	Wt.	Post Pos.	St.	¼	½	¾	Str.	Fin.	Jockey.	Open.	High.	Close.	Place.	Sh.
145	Tom McTaggart	111	8	5	3^1	$2^{1½}$	$2^{1½}$	$1^{1½}$	1^1	Mergler	2	3	11-5	9-10	1-2
113²	Obolus	105	1	8	8	8	8	$3^{1½}$	2^2	Bell	8	12	12	5	5-2
34	Wise Man	113	6	4	2½	1½	1½	2^2	3^3	Knapp	12	15	15	6	3
70²	Whimsy	117	5	3	1½	3^h	3^1	4½	4½	Byrne	6	8	7	5-2	6-5
130	Flittergold	118	2	1	7^2	7^2	5^2	6^2	5^8	Schuttinger	5-2	3	13-5	1	1-2
(88)	Monomoy	109	4	6	5½	6½	7^2	7^{15}	6^2	Lyke	12	15	15	6	3
153	Air Man	108	3	2	4½	4^2	4½	5½	7^{15}	Ensor	7	9	8	3	6-5
(163)	Sands fo Pl'sure	108	7	7	6^2	5½	6½	8	8	A. Collins	5	7	6	2	1

Winner entered for $2,000; bought in for $2,705.
Tom McTaggart raced his field into submission and won easily. Obolus closed with a rush from far back. Flittergold ran a dull race.
Overweight—Monomoy, 2. Scratched—Ed Roche, 108; Barry Shannon, 106; Bar of Phœnix, 106; Royce Rolls, 99; Magnetite, 98; Prunes, 99; Ed Cudihee, 108; Menokin, 108.

179 FIFTH RACE.—MONTAGUE HANDICAP; for three-year-olds and upward; $961 added; value to winners, $851, $125, $75. One mile and a sixteenth. At post one minute; off at 4:32. Start good. Won driving; place easily. Time, 0:24 2-5, 0:48 3-5, 1:13 2-5, 1:39 4-5, 1:45 4-5. Winner, b. c., 4, by Sundridge—Napthalia. Owner and trainer, D. J. Leary.

Index.	Starter.	Wt.	Post Pos.	St.	¼	½	¾	Str.	Fin.	Jockey.	Open.	High.	Close.	Place.	Sh.
152²	Sunflash II	123	7	5	$1^{1½}$	1^1	2^4	2^4	1^h	McTaggart	6-5	7-5	13-10	2-5	—
(148)	Dorcas	108	5	4	$2^{1½}$	2½	$1^{1½}$	1^2	2^8	Byrne	9-5	2	9-5	1-2	—
130	Damrosch	115	6	6	$4^{1½}$	4^1	3^n	3^3	3^8	Lyke	6	8	8	5-2	1
89	Fizer	98	4	7	7	5^h	5½	$5^{1½}$	4^{10}	Rodriguez	15	15	15	5	5-2
81	Iron Cross II	97	2	2	5^1	6^2	6^8	4^h	5^8	Callahan	20	20	30	8	4
116	Decisive	97	1	1	3½	3½	4^2	6^4	6^{10}	Walls	20	20	20	6	5-2
141²	Red Sox	99	3	3	6^4	7	7	7	7	Ambrose	8	8	7	2	1

Sunflash II closed with a rush in the stretch and outgamed Dorcas. Byrne, on the latter, hurried his mount around the turns and she hung at the end. Damrosch outran the others.
Overweights—Dorcas, 1; Decisive, 2; Iron Cross II, 4. Scratched—Gex, 114; Sharpshooter, 104.

180 SIXTH RACE.—For maiden two-year-olds; $761 added; value to winners, $635, $100, $50. One mile and seventy yards. Off first break, at 4:58. Start good. Won eased up; place easily. Time, 0:24 3-5, 0:49, 1:15, 1:41 3-5, 1:46 1-5. Winner, b. c., by Ajax—Roquette. Owner, J. E. Widener. Trainer, T. Welsh.

Index.	Starter.	Wt.	Post Pos.	St.	¼	½	¾	Str.	Fin.	Jockey.	Open.	High.	Close.	Place.	Sh.
156²	Jusqu' au Bout	115	4	1	1^3	1^5	1^8	1^5	1^8	Knapp	3-10	2-5	7-20	—	—
109	First Troop	115	3	3	2^2	$2^{1½}$	2^2	2^4	2^5	Heupel	30	50	30	6	6-5
131	Sungold	115	2	4	4	4	3	3^{20}	3^{20}	Schuttinger	4	9-2	3	2-5	—
—	Impartiality	115	1	2	4	4	4	4	4	Lyke	10	15	12	5-2	—

Jusqu' au Bout just galloped in front. Sungold went wide at the turns and then tired.
Scratched—Elmendorf, 115; Man o' th' Hour, 115.

Yankees Buy "Ham" Hyatt

LITTLE ROCK, Ark., June 19.—"Ham" Hyatt, for several years with the Pittsburgh Nationals, has been sold by the Little Rock club of the Southern Association to the New York Americans, it was announced to-day. Hyatt leads the Southern Association in home run hitting, having made five this season.

American Association

Milwaukee, 7; Indianapolis, 4.
Indianapolis, 9; Milwaukee, 0 (forfeited).
Milwaukee, 9; Indianapolis, 2.
Toledo, 5; St. Paul, 3.
Kansas City, 7; Louisville, 5.

Eastern League

Bridgeport, 1; Waterbury, 0.
New London, 11; Hartford, 1.

Penn State's Coach Goes To Long Island Camps

STATE COLLEGE, Penn., June 18.—Bill Martin, Penn State's track coach and freshman football mentor, has been appointed district athletic director for the Long Island military camps. He took the position this week, with headquarters at the Mineola Y. M. C. A.

Martin's appointment, the first of the kind in this country, was made by the Fosdick Commission on Army Training Camp Activities. He will supervise the work of the Y. M. C. A. athletic directors throughout the Long Island district.

International League

At Baltimore—											R.	H.	E.
Rochester	0	3	0	1	0	0	0	0	0	—4	7	1
Baltimore	0	0	0	0	0	0	0	0	0	—0	4	0

Batteries—Hagen and Smith; Parnham and Egan.

Newark Treats Bisons "Rough" In New Series

International League

GAMES TO-DAY.
Toronto at Jersey City.
Buffalo at Newark.
Rochester at Baltimore.
Syracuse at Binghamton.

YESTERDAY'S RESULTS.
Newark, 7; Buffalo, 1.
Toronto, 9; Jersey City, 2.
Rochester, 4; Baltimore, 0.

STANDING OF THE TEAMS.

	W.	L.	Pct.		W.	L.	Pct.
Bing't'n	29	9	.763	Newark	20	19	.487
Roch't'r	25	15	.625	Buffalo	10	21	.323
B't'm're	22	20	.524	Syracuse	12	26	.316
Toronto	21	20	.488	Jer. City	9	25	.265

The Buffalo team met with a rough reception in the first game of the series with Newark at Wiedenmayer's Park, Newark, yesterday afternoon. The final score was 7 to 1.

Chief Meyers was in harness behind the plate and drove in the visitors' only run. Shay got around for Newark in the first inning on the first of his three singles, Jacobs's sacrifice and Cather's clean single.

The game was a draw until Newark broke loose in the fifth. Jenson singled. Shay, trying to sacrifice, forced him, but Jacobs hit to left for two bags, scoring Shay. Cather hit a triple to left, tallying Jacobs. Cather scored on Zinn's infield out.

There was another jambouree in the seventh, when Shay, Jacobs and Cather concocted singles, and then Zinn cleared the decks with a withering wallop to right.

NEWARK (I. L.)	ab	r	h	o	a	e	BUFFALO (I. L.)	ab	r	h	o	a	e
Shay, 2b	5	3	3	0	3	0	Don'dson, lf	4	0	1	1	0	1
Jacobs, ss	3	2	2	0	4	0	Harris, 2b	1	0	0	2	5	1
Cather, lf	4	2	3	3	0	0	McCabe, rf	4	0	0	1	0	0
Zinn, cf	4	0	1	2	0	0	Murphy, 2b	4	1	1	1	4	1
Schaefer, 1b	4	0	1	8	0	0	Meyers, c	4	0	2	4	1	0
Downey, 3b	4	0	0	0	1	0	Wiltse, 1b	4	0	1	10	0	0
Seymour, rf	4	0	1	3	0	0	Armstrong, ss	3	0	0	1	1	0
Madden, c	4	0	1	8	0	0	Schutz, cf	4	0	2	4	0	1
Jensen, p	3	0	1	0	3	1	Rose, p	3	0	0	0	2	0
							*Devinney	1	0	0	0	0	0
Totals	35	7	13	27	8	1	Totals	32	1	6	24	13	4

*Batted for Rose in ninth inning.

Buffalo	0	1	0	0	0	0	0	0	0	—1
Newark	1	0	0	0	3	0	3	0	x	—7

Two-base hits—Zinn, Murphy. Three-base hit—Cather. Sacrifice hits—Jacobs (2), Harris, Armstrong. Double plays—Murphy, Harris and Wiltse. Left on bases—Newark, 7; Buffalo, 8. First base on error—Buffalo, 1. Bases on balls—Off Jensen, 1; off Rose, 1. Hit by pitcher—By Jensen (Harris). Struck out—By Jensen, 4; by Rose, 4.

Toronto Swats Skeeters In First Round of Game

Erratic pitching by Jerry Mande, for Jersey City, in the opening inning of yesterday's game with Toronto, at West Side Park, gave the Maple Leafs a lead of four runs from as many bases on balls and a base hit.

With this advantage Howley's boys could not be headed. The added five more tallies in the remaining chapters.

The score:

TORONTO (I. L.)	ab	r	h	o	a	e	JERSEY CITY (I. L.)	ab	r	h	o	a	e
Reilly, lf	4	1	2	3	0	0	Brock, rf	4	0	1	4	0	0
Wagner, ss	4	2	1	1	4	0	Butler, ss	4	0	2	5	3	0
W'tehead, cf	3	3	1	4	0	0	McCarron, 3b	3	0	0	1	1	0
Lear, 2b	4	2	2	3	2	0	Bowman, 1b	4	0	1	6	1	1
Purtell, 3b	4	0	2	2	5	1	Felz, cf	4	0	1	1	1	0
Onslow, 1b	4	0	1	12	0	0	Menzel, lf	4	0	0	2	0	0
Thrasher, rf	2	0	1	0	0	0	Kromhaus, 2b	4	0	0	4	6	0
Howley, c	4	0	0	2	0	0	Carroll, c	3	2	1	4	1	0
Petersen, p	2	1	1	0	2	0	Maude, p	2	0	1	0	1	0
							Their, p	0	0	0	0	0	0
							LaBate, p	1	0	1	0	1	0
							*Edwards	1	0	0	0	0	0
Totals	31	9	11	27	13	1	Totals	34	2	8	27	15	1

*Batted for Maude in the seventh inning.

Toronto	4	0	1	0	1	0	0	3	0	—9
Jersey City	0	0	1	0	0	0	0	0	1	—2

Two-base hit—Carroll. Stolen bases—Lear, Purtell, Onslow, Carroll (2). Sacrifice hit—Petersen. Sacrifice flies—Thrasher. Double play—Kromhaus, Butler and Bowman. Left on bases—Jersey City, 8; Toronto, 5. First base on errors—Jersey City, 1; Toronto, 1. Bases on balls—Off Maude, 5; off Their, 2; off LaBate, 1; off Petersen, 2. Hits—Off Maude, 6 in 7 innings; off Their, 1 in 1-3 inning; off LaBate, 4 in 1 2-3 innings. Hit by pitcher—By Petersen (McCarron). Struck out—By Maude, 1; by Petersen, 3. Winning pitcher—Petersen. Losing pitcher—Maude.

Phillies and Pirates Swap Right-Handed Pitchers

PHILADELPHIA, June 19.—The Philadelphia National League baseball club announced to-night that it had traded Pitcher Erskine Mayer to Pittsburgh in exchange for Pitcher Elmer Jacobs, who made his entrance into the major league some years ago with the Philadelphia Club.

Both are righthanders. No cash or other players are included, the announcement said.

Scores Double Victory

The Murray Hill Vocational School was a double winner over the Brooklyn Vocational School in their annual track and field meet and baseball game at the Brooklyn Athletic Field yesterday afternoon. The score of the baseball game was 3 to 2. The fatal run was netted in the final inning on a double, single and an error.

Baseball Today, 3:30 P. M. N. Y. Yankees vs. Washington. Polo Grounds. Adm. 50c.

Young's Error In 13th Gives Dodgers Game

Giant Outfielder Muffs Daubert's Drive, Letting in Winning Run

Fortune frowned on Ross Young, the Giants' brilliant outfielder, as it was his dropping of Jake Daubert's long fly that sent McGraw's minions to defeat before the Dodgers in a thirteen-inning game at Ebbets Field yesterday.

The final score was 2 to 1. Young's error was an unfortunate climax to a game that was enriched by many sensational plays and with the pendulum of victory swinging frequently from side to side.

McGraw used all of his strategic powers and the Giants threatened on many occasions in the later innings. However, the airtight support given the Dodger twirlers checked the champions.

The fatal thirteenth saw Miller retired easily, but Steamer Al Demaree paved the way for his own defeat by passing Larry Cheney. Johnston then bounced a single off Zimmerman's shins. Olson popped to Zimmerman. Daubert smashed a hard drive to right centre. Young rushed after the ball when it appeared to be in Benny Kauff's territory. It was a long run, but Young managed to get his two hands to the pill. The Giant fans yelled in chagrin when the ball bounced out of Young's hands. Young showed his anger by throwing the ball over the fence.

Grimes Opens for Dodgers

Don Grimes opened on the mound for the Dodgers. The Giants had found him for five hits in the first three innings, but thereafter they were hitless until the ninth, when Grimes gave way to Cheney. Demaree was in hot water often and only the superfine Giant defence saved him on many occasions. Three singles gave the Giants their first run in the third. The Dodgers evened matters in the eighth on Miller's infield hit and Olson's double.

The score:

NEW YORK (N. L.)	ab	r	h	o	a	e	BROOKLYN (N. L.)	ab	r	h	o	a	e
Burns, lf	6	0	1	3	0	0	Johnston, rf	6	0	3	2	0	0
Young, rf	5	0	1	6	1	1	Olson, ss	6	0	1	2	5	0
Fletcher, ss	6	0	1	3	4	0	Daubert, 1b	6	0	0	16	0	0
Kauff, cf	4	0	1	1	0	0	Z. Wheat, lf	5	0	1	7	0	0
Zim'man, 3b	5	0	0	7	0	1	Myers, cf	5	0	2	4	1	0
Holke, 1b	5	0	1	9	1	0	O'Mara, 3b	5	0	1	0	4	1
McCarty, c	4	0	1	0	0	1	Doolan, 2b	5	0	1	3	5	0
Rariden, c	1	0	0	3	0	0	Miller, c	4	1	0	4	3	0
Rodriguez, 2b	2	0	0	5	2	0	Grimes, p	2	0	1	1	1	0
Sicking, 2b	1	0	0	1	1	0	Cheney, p	1	1	0	0	2	0
Demaree, p	5	1	2	0	5	0	§Hickman	1	0	0	0	0	0
*Thorpe	0	0	0	0	0	0							
†Wilhoit	1	0	0	0	0	0							
Totals	45	1	8	‡38	14	3	Totals	46	2	10	39	21	1

*Ran for McCarty in tenth inning.
†Batted for Rodriguez in tenth inning.
‡Two out when winning run was scored.
§Batted for Grimes in eighth inning.

New York	0	0	1	0	0	0	0	0	0	0	0	0	0	—1
Brooklyn	0	0	0	0	0	0	0	1	0	0	0	0	1	—2

Two-base hits—McCarty, Olson. Stolen base—Burns. Sacrifice hit—Miller. Double play—Fletcher and Holke. Left on bases—New York, 10; Brooklyn, 8. First base on errors—New York, 1; Brooklyn, 3. Bases on balls—Off Grimes, 2; off Cheney, 3; off Demaree, 1. Hits—Off Grimes, 5 in 8 innings; off Cheney, 3 in 5. Struck out—By Grimes, 2; by Cheney, 2; by Demaree, 2. Winning pitcher—Cheney.

Cubs Shut Out Pirates in Hot Pitchers' Duel

PITTSBURGH, June 19.—A hot pitchers' duel between Douglass and Harmon here to-day resulted in a Chicago victory over the Pirates, 1 to 0. The visitors scored the only run of the game in the opening inning on hits by Flack and Hollocher and Merkle's life, Harmon's throw to the plate being too late to get Flack.

The score:

CHICAGO (A. L.)	ab	r	h	o	a	e	PITTSBURGH (N. L.)	ab	r	h	o	a	e
Flack, rf	4	1	1	1	0	0	Caton, ss	4	0	0	5	8	1
Holloc'r, ss	4	0	2	0	4	0	Bigbee, lf	4	0	1	2	0	0
Mann, lf	3	0	1	2	0	0	Carey, cf	4	0	1	0	0	0
Merkle, 1b	3	0	0	17	0	0	Cutshaw, 2b	3	0	0	1	2	1
Paskert, cf	4	0	0	1	0	0	Mollwitz, 1b	3	0	0	16	2	0
Deal, 3b	4	0	1	1	3	0	King, rf	3	0	0	0	0	0
Zeider, 2b	3	0	1	1	3	0	McK'nie, 3b	3	0	1	3	2	0
Killifer, c	3	0	0	4	0	0	Schmidt, c	3	0	0	3	0	0
Douglass, p	3	0	1	0	4	0	Harmon, p	3	0	0	0	3	0
Totals	31	1	7	27	14	0	Totals	30	0	3	27	20	2

Chicago	1	0	0	0	0	0	0	0	0	—1
Pittsburgh	0	0	0	0	0	0	0	0	0	—0

Stolen bases—Hollocher, Bigbee, Carey. Sacrifice hits—Mann, Merkle. Double plays—Cutshaw, Caton and Mollwitz; McKechnie, Mollwitz and McKechnie. Left on bases—Chicago, 6; Pittsburgh, 4. First base on errors—Chicago, 2. First base on balls—Off Douglass, 1. Struck out—By Douglass, 4. Winning pitcher—Douglass. Losing pitcher—Harmon.

Pass by Oeschger Forces Winning Run for Phillies

PHILADELPHIA, June 19.—Oescher's base on balls to Wickland, after Boston had filled the bases on a single and two fumbles by McGaffigan, sent over the winning run in the opening game of the series here to-day. Score, 3 to 2. In each of seven of the nine innings only three men faced Rudolph and in each of six innings only three faced Oeschger. Double plays helped the visiting pitcher win his third straight game.

Score:

BOSTON (N. L.)	ab	r	h	o	a	e	PHILADELPHIA (N. L.)	ab	r	h	o	a	e
Rawlings, ss	5	1	1	2	4	0	Bancroft, ss	4	1	0	3	4	0
Herzog, 2b	4	0	0	3	2	1	Williams, cf	3	1	2	2	0	0
Powell, cf	3	1	0	2	1	0	Stock, 3b	4	0	1	0	2	0
Wickland, rf	3	0	1	2	0	0	Luderus, 1b	4	0	1	8	0	0
J.G.Smith, 3b	3	0	0	1	2	0	Cravath, rf	3	0	1	2	0	0
Konetchy, 1b	3	0	1	10	0	1	Meusel, lf	2	0	0	5	0	0
Rehg, lf	4	0	0	2	0	0	M'Gaf'n, 2b	3	0	0	2	0	2
Wilson, c	3	0	1	4	2	0	Adams, c	2	0	0	5	1	0
Rudolph, p	3	1	0	1	4	0	*Fitzgerald	1	0	0	0	0	0
							Burns, c	0	0	0	0	0	0
							Oeschger, p	2	0	0	0	2	0
							†Hogg	1	0	0	0	0	0
							Davis, p	0	0	0	0	0	0
Totals	31	3	4	27	15	2	Totals	29	2	5	27	9	2

*Batted for Adams in eighth inning.
†Batted for Oeschger in eighth inning.

Boston	0	0	0	2	1	0	0	0	0	—3
Philadelphia	2	0	0	0	0	0	0	0	0	—2

Two-base hits—Rawlings, Cravath. Home run—Williams. Stolen bases—Konetchy. Sacrifice hit—Rudolph. Sacrifice fly—Konetchy. Double plays—Rawlings and Konetchy; Herzog and Konetchy; Rudolph and Konetchy. Left on bases—Boston, 7; Philadelphia, 2. First base on errors—Boston, 2; Philadelphia, 2. Bases on balls—Off Rudolph, 2; off Oeschger, 4. Hits—Off Oeschger, 4 in 8 innings. Wild pitcher—Oeschger. Losing pitcher—Oeschger.

Miss Sears Wins By Brilliant Tennis

Defeats Miss Zinderstein After Losing First Set of Sensational Match in Women's National Title Tourney at Philadelphia Cricket Club

By Fred Hawthorne

ST. MARTIN'S, Penn., June 19.—Miss Eleanora Sears, of Boston won one of the most sensational matches ever contested in the women's national lawn tennis championhip singles tournament this morning when she defeated Miss Marion Zinderstein, also from the Hub, by a score of 6—8, 6—2, 6—4, in the third round of the great tuorney on the turf courts of the Philadelphia Cricket Club.

Playing really brilliant tennis from start to finish, Miss Zinderstein literally threw victory aside by serving the greatest number of double-faults ever made in a title match. Nineteen times did the young girl from Boston lose valuable points in this way, and the wonder was that she was able to make the match so close under the circumstances.

On placement aces she far outstripped her more experienced opponent, the tally standing of 30 to 11 in her favor, but Miss Sears, playing the game of her career to date, made no double faults and her service was always a mighty weapon of offence. The match was desperately played all the way and while Miss Zinderstein flashed with the greater brilliance and roused the big gallery to the topmost heights of enthusiasm, the cool, crafty playing of Miss Sears and her almost uncanny anticipation of shots made her triumph an earned one.

To-morrow morning at 10:30 o'clock Miss Sears will clash with Miss Clare Cassel, of New York, for a place in the semi-final bracket in the upper half. She is now regarded as the certain finalist in this section of the draw with Miss Eleanor Goss, the logical choice, in the other final bracket. As they played to-day Miss Sears should triumph over Miss Goss and earn the right to meet Miss Molla Bjurstedt, the great champion, in the challenge round.

Miss Pollak Defeats Girl

Three other players gained their semi-final brackets to-day, Miss Helene Pollak, of New York, defeating little Miss Dorothy Walker, the Philadelphia schoolgirl, at 6—1, 6—0; Miss Helen Le Doux, of Swarthmore, vanquishing Miss Barbara Hooker, of New York, at 6—4, 6—1, and Miss Goss taking the measure of Mrs. Spencer Fullerton Weaver by a score of 6—2, 6—4.

The girls' national singles reached the final round, with Miss Dorothy Walker, of the local club, defeating Miss Mary Heaton at 6—1, 6—0 in one semi-final match and Miss Katherine Porter eliminating Miss Louise Dixon at 6—2, 6—4 in the other. Miss Porter also plays under the Philadelphia Cricket Club standard.

Eight pairs are left in the women's doubles, with the favorites running true to form in every case. Mrs. George W. Wightman and Miss Sears crushed Miss Margaretta Dixon and Mrs. C. R. Wainwright at 6—1, 6—0 to gain their bracket in the round before the semi-final, while Miss Zinderstein and Miss Goss vanquished Miss Mildred Willard and Miss Deborah Seal, a local pair, by a score of 6—4, 6—0 in the same round. These matches were in the lower half of the draw.

In the upper section Mrs. Spencer Fullerton Weaver and Mrs. Rawson L. Wood, of New York, one of the most noted doubles combinations in the metropolitan district, defeated Mrs. J. B. Payne and Mrs. W. S. Calcott at 6—1, 6—2, while Miss Bjurstedt and Mrs. Johan Rogge, of Norway, eliminated the Misses Barbara and Helen Hooker at 6—4, 6—2. Mrs. Weaver and Mrs. Wood look like the eventual finalists against Mrs. Wightman and Miss Sears.

When Miss Sears and Miss Zinderstein began their match this morning on the clubhouse court they started where they left off yesterday, with the games at 5—4 in Miss Sears's favor and the points at 30—15, Miss Zinderstein serving. George Warder, the Eddie Conlin of referees in Philadelphia graced the official chair.

Miss Zinderstein started with a rush driving with great "pace" off her forehand and following up her forcing shots by swift dashes for the net, from where she volleyed with severity and success. She brought the games even at 5—all, and then made it 6—5, in spite of three glaring double faults that she committed in the eleventh game. Three wonderful placement aces, with the ball driven at sharp angles across forecourt, made amends for the errors.

Experts Admire Play

Miss Sears took the next game at love, owing to errors by her young opponent, but then Miss Zinderstein with a rare bit of sharp volleying and sizzling drives took the next two games and the set at 8—6. Irving Wright and George Wightman, who were among the spectators, both expressed admiration at the girl's dazzling display in that first set.

Miss Zinderstein looked more like a winner than ever when she swept through the first two games of the second set. Again she scored on beautiful placement aces, backhand shots played shoulder high, sending the ball slashing through Miss Sears's forecourt. The latter was putting up a courageous fight, making remarkable "gets" all over the court and showing wonderful anticipation as to the next point of attack.

FIRST SET

															Pts.
Miss Sears	1	4	3	6	2	5	1	4	2	4	5	0	4	7	—48
Miss Zinderst'n	4	2	5	4	4	3	4	0	4	1	3	4	2	5	—45

SECOND SET

Miss Sears	1	1	4	6	7	4	4	5	—32
Miss Zinderstein	4	4	0	4	5	1	2	3	—23

THIRD SET

Miss Sears	3	1	4	4	2	3	4	7	7	4	—39
Miss Zinderstein	5	4	1	0	4	5	2	5	5	2	—33

TOTALS

	Sets.	Games.	Points
Miss Sears	2	18	11[illegible]
Miss Zinderstein	1	14	10[illegible]

The summaries follow:

Women's national championship singles (third round)—Miss Eleanora Sears defeated Miss Marion Zinderstein, 6—8, 6—2, 6—4; Mrs. Spencer Fullerton Weaver defeated Mrs. R. B. Payne, 4—6, 11—9, 6—2.

Fourth round—Miss Helene Pollak defeated Miss Dorothy Walker, 6—1, 6—0; Miss Helen Le Doux defeated Miss Barbara Hooker, 6—4, 6—1; Miss Eleanor Goss defeated Mrs. S. F. Weaver, 6—2, 6—4.

Women's national championship doubles (second round)—Mrs. S. F. Weaver and Mrs. Rawson L. Wood defeated Mrs. R. B. Payne and Mrs. W. S. Calcott, 6—1, 6—2; Miss Molla Bjurstedt and Mrs. Johan Rogge defeated the Misses Barbara and Helene Hooker, 6—4, 6—2; Miss Marion Zinderstein and Miss Eleanor Goss defeated Miss Mildred Willard and Miss Deborah Seal, 6—4, 6—0; Mrs. George W. Wightman and Miss Eleanora Sears defeated Mrs. C. R. Wainwright and Miss Margaretta Dixon, 6—1, 6—0; Mrs. Robert Herold and Mrs. H. F. Kerbaugh defeated Miss Anne Townsend and Miss Rebecca Thompson, 5—7, 6—4, 7—5; Mrs. De oFrest Candee and Miss Florence Ballin defeated Miss Elizabeth Strubing and Miss Margaret Sharpless, 6—2, 6—3; Miss Dorothy Walker and Miss Louise Dixon defeated Mrs. J. F. Betz, 3d, and Mrs. John E. Bailey, 8—6, 6—2.

Girls' national championship singles (semi-final round)—Miss Dorothy Walker defeated Miss Mary Heaton, 6—1, 6—0; Miss Katherine Porter defeated Miss Louise Dixon, 6—2, 6—4.

National championship mixed doubles (first round)—Mrs. S. F. Weaver and Ensign Whelan defeated Mrs. H. F. Kerbaugh and A. J. Batz, 6—1, 6—...; Mrs. G. W. Wightman and Irving Wright defeated Miss Ansie Naylor and H. B. Endicott, 6—0, 6—...; Miss Helen Hooker and A. E. Van Pelt defeated Miss Deborah Seal and A. P. Holmes, 3—6, 6—2; Miss Mollie Bjurstedt and Frederick B. ...ander defeated Miss Eleanora Sears and ... Osborne, 6—1, 6—1; Miss Marion Zinderstein and W. H. Abbott defeated Mrs. J. O. Brown and D. Pratt, 6—0, 6—1.

Jeff Tesreau Deserts Giants For "Steel League"

BIG JEFF TESREAU is no more as a Giant pitcher according to the word flashed to the world of sport last night. Jeff deserted the McGraw forces last Saturday with the intention of going to work in the plant of the Bethlehem Steel Company and incidentally joining the regiment of former baseball stars who are now members of the "Steel League."

Big Jeff will be missed. He began this season in better trim than in many years past and although he was a bit disappointing in his last few starts all Jeff seemed to need was a goodly supply of hot weather to regain his skill and stamina. McGraw was counting heavily on the big fellow when the pennant race waxed more strenuous.

The baseball magnates and managers fully agree with the classic on war delivered by one Sherman some fifty years ago.

White Sox Waste Chances To Down Indian Sluggers

CHICAGO, June 19.—Cleveland's batting rally in the ninth inning enabled them to defeat Chicago, 6 to 5, to-day. The locals had several chances, but threw them away on the base lines. Erratic fielding behind Shellenbach aid the visitors in their scoring.

The score:

CLEVELAND (A. L.)	ab	r	h	o	a	e	CHICAGO (A. L.)	ab	r	h	o	a	e
Johnston, 1b	5	0	0	8	1	1	Murphy, rf	4	1	1	1	0	0
Chapman, ss	5	0	1	3	6	0	Liebold, lf	5	1	2	1	0	0
Speaker, cf	4	0	0	1	0	0	E. Collins, 2b	4	1	1	2	1	1
Roth, rf	2	1	1	2	0	0	Felsch, cf	4	0	1	5	0	0
Wam'nss, 2b	4	0	1	5	1	1	Gandil, 1b	5	0	1	10	0	0
Wood, lf	3	2	1	3	0	0	Weaver, ss	4	0	2	3	5	1
Evans, 3b	4	2	3	1	2	1	Risberg, 3b	4	1	1	1	3	0
Thomas, c	2	0	0	4	1	0	Jacobs, c	4	0	1	4	3	1
*Graney	0	0	0	0	0	0	Shel'bach, p	2	1	0	0	2	0
O'Neill, c	0	0	0	0	0	0	†Jourdan	1	0	0	0	0	0
Bagby, p	4	1	2	0	1	0							
Totals	33	6	9	27	12	3	Totals	37	5	10	27	14	3

*Batted for Thomas in ninth inning.
†Batted for Shellenbach in ninth inning.

Cleveland	0	3	0	0	0	0	0	0	3	—6
Chicago	1	1	0	0	0	0	1	0	2	—5

Two-base hits—Jacobs, Wood, Liebold. Three-base hit—E. Collins. Stolen base—Roth. Sacrifice hit—Thomas. Double play—Risberg, Jacobs and Gandil. Left on bases—Cleveland, 6; Chicago, 9. First base on errors—Chicago, 2; Cleveland, 1. Bases on balls—Off Shellenbach, 4; off Bagby, 4. Hits—Off Shellenbach, 9 in 9 innings; off Bagby, 10 in 9. Hit by pitcher—By Shellenbach (Roth). Struck out—By Shellenbach, 1; by Bagby, 3.

Tigers Make Clean Sweep Of Series With Browns

ST. LOUIS, June 19.—Detroit was more successful than St. Louis with its extra base hits and won to-day's game, 7 to 5, making a clean sweep of the three-game series. A home run by Veach with Bush on base in the fifth inning clinched the game for the visitors. Rogers's hitting was accountable for four of the local's five runs.

The score:

DETROIT (A. L.)	ab	r	h	o	a	e	ST. LOUIS (A. L.)	ab	r	h	o	a	e
Bush, ss	4	2	2	3	0	0	Tobin, cf	2	2	1	1	0	0
Vitt, 3b	4	1	1	0	3	0	Maisel, 3b	3	0	2	6	2	0
Cobb, cf	4	0	1	4	0	0	Sisler, 1b	5	0	0	12	2	0
Veach, lf	2	3	1	2	0	0	Demmitt, rf	4	0	1	0	0	0
Heilman, 1b	3	0	2	11	0	0	Smith, c	3	0	0	0	1	1
Cun'ham, rf	3	0	0	2	0	0	Gedeon, 2b	4	0	0	2	3	0
Young, 2b	3	0	0	3	6	1	Gerber, ss	2	0	1	1	1	0
Yelle, c	4	0	1	1	1	0	Johnson, ss	2	0	0	0	2	0
Kallio, p	3	1	0	1	1	0	Nuna'aker, c	4	0	0	3	0	0
Erickson, p	1	0	0	0	2	1	Rogers, p	3	3	3	1	4	0
							*Austin	0	0	0	0	0	0
Totals	31	7	8	27	13	2	Totals	32	5	7	27	15	1

*Batted for Rogers in ninth inning.

Detroit	0	0	4	0	2	0	0	1	0	—7
St. Louis	0	0	2	0	2	0	1	0	0	—5

Two-base hits—Rogers (2). Three-base hits—Heilman, Tobin. Home run—Veach. Stolen base—Heilman. Sacrifice hits—Tobin, Cunningham, Maisel. Sacrifice flies—Cobb, Maisel, Young. Left on bases—Detroit, 5; St. Louis, 8. First base on errors—St. Louis, 2. Bases on balls—Off Kallio, 3; off Erickson, 2; off Rogers, 5. Hits—Off Kallio, 5 in 5 innings; off Erickson, 2 in 4. Struck out—By Erickson, 1; by Rogers, 3. Winning pitcher—Kallio. Passed ball—Nunamaker.

Special 600-Yard Run Features Brooklyn Meet

Seven fast middle distance runners of the local district will vie for honors in the special 600-yard invitation race that will feature the members' games of the Brooklyn Athletic Association at the Brooklyn Athletic Field next Saturday afternoon. Among the starters are Jack Sellers, James O'Brien and Walter Powe, three speedy athletes.

Eight events have been set aside for the boys enrolled in the B. A. A. ranks. The club's sprinters, Sal Sanacore, Si Schuval and Joe Rubenstein, will back the low marks in the sprint races, while Eddie Mayo, Louis Kaufman and Andy Craw will start in the wake of big fields in the distance races.

Skeeters Buy Wyckoff

President Driscoll of the Jersey City New International League Club announced yesterday that he had bought Pitcher J. W. Wyckoff from the Boston Americans.

Standing of Major League Clubs

NATIONAL LEAGUE

GAMES TO-DAY
New York at Brooklyn.
Boston at Philadelphia.
Chicago at Pittsburgh.
Cincinnati at St. Louis.

YESTERDAY'S RESULTS
Brooklyn, 2; New York, 1 (13 in.)
Boston, 3; Philadelphia, 2.
Chicago, 1; Pittsburgh, 0.

STANDING OF TEAMS

	W.	L.	Pct		W.	L.	Pct
Chicago	35	15	.700	Cin'nati	23	28	.451
N. York	34	17	.667	B'klyn	21	29	.420
Boston	27	26	.509	Pitts'gh	20	30	.400
Phila	22	27	.449	St. Louis	19	29	.396

AMERICAN LEAGUE

GAMES TO-DAY
Washington at New York.
Cleveland at Chicago.
Philadelphia at Boston.

YESTERDAY'S RESULTS
New York, 9; Washington, 0.
Philadelphia, 5; Boston, 0.
Cleveland, 6; Chicago, 5.
Detroit, 7; St. Louis, 5.

STANDING OF TEAMS

	W.	L.	Pct		W.	L.	Pct
Boston	34	23	.596	Wash't'n	28	30	.483
N. York	31	22	.585	St. Louis	25	29	.463
Clevel'd	32	26	.552	Detroit	20	30	.400
Chicago	26	24	.520	Phila	20	32	.385

SMOKING-HOT RED SOX RAP YANKS, 6-3 — BRAVES BOW, 4-3

TWO-RUN HOMERS BY TED WILLIAMS, TEBBETTS BIG AID

Kinder Chalks Up 13th Victory and Third Straight; 35,691 Turn Out

By F. C. MATZEK

Boston, Aug. 9.—The old Providence College Friar, George "Birdie" Tebbetts, and the Bosockers' Mr. Slug, Ted Williams, provided motive power for the Red Sox victory chariot with a two-run homer apiece here at Fenway Park tonight and the rollicking Sockers beat the New York Yankees, 6 to 3, before 35,691 in the opener of a three-game Hub visit by the league leaders.

The Socker triumph, only the fourth in 12 tests against the Yanks this year, pared a full game from the Stengel crew's league lead which, however, still is a comfortable five and a half games over the third-place Sox and a somewhat less comfortable four and a half games over the second-place Cleveland Indians who shared in the paring by cuffing the hapless St. Louis Browns.

Tebbetts and Williams were the power performers but there were honors left over for Ellis "Old Grandad" Kinder, the Bosockers' leading right hander who notched his third triumph in a row and his 13th of the season.

Better Than Raschi

Old Grandad's 10-hitter wasn't brilliant but it was definitely better than the 10-hit stint turned in by Vic Raschi, Yankee ace right hander who went the full route, too, and for the fourth straight time missed racking up his 16th pitching victory of the campaign. Rather than that elusive No. 16 the husky Gothamite collected a seventh setback.

Tebbetts and Williams provided Kinder with his balance of power. Their homers, No. 4 of the year for Birdie the Friar in the second inning and No. 28 and the league lead for Williams in the third, were productive of two important markers each.

The Yanks got two circuit smashes, too, both by Hank Bauer for his sixth and seventh of the season but they came with no mates aboard in the sixth and eighth. Despite their towering proportions which at least matched the blows by Birdie and the Splinter they actually were too little and too late. Old Grandad and mates had the verdict in hand at the end of three frames.

It took some sharp chucking by the Socker moundsman to hold his early advantage but he had it when the blue chips were on the table and Raschi simply wasn't as efficient.

Dom's Streak Halted

The Yank righthander had one big stopper, however. He injected the one sad note of an otherwise happy evening for the Joe McCarthymen when he snapped Dom DiMaggio's long consecutive-game hitting string at 34 games. Tonight the Little Professor had five chances to continue his brilliant streak but it just wasn't in the cards for him to share in the abnormally large hit collection against Raschi. He grounded out a couple of times, flied out to big brother Joe twice and fanned once.

Oddly enough it was against the Yanks here on June 29 that he started his hitting skein. Over the span of that prolonged spree he went to bat 143 times, collected 51 hits including three homers, two triples and 10 doubles and spun along merrily at a .357 batting average. Those figures, of course, don't include tonight's goose-egging job by Raschi.

The Sox, as noted, grabed an early lead and clung doggedly to it. Junior Stephens, who shared only indirectly in the Boston triumph, paced a three run opening burst by the Sox in the Second inning. He led off that frame with one of three free tickets dealt by Raschi.

Only Error of Game

Bobby Doerr followed with a long fly to right and Billy Goodman all but killed the rally with a hopper to Jerry Coleman at second. Coleman's toss to Phil Rizzuto erased Stevie but Billy romped to the keystone sack as Rizzuto chipped in the only error of the game, a high throw past first and into the Boston dugout.

Al Zarilla promptly took advantage of the Yankee defensive lapse with a double into the left center which scored Goodman. Then Birdie unloaded his circuit jolt, a line-shot into the screen atop the left-field wall.

Johnny Pesky's blooper-double into left field which Johnny Lindell barely reached and couldn't hold and then Williams' long smash into the Boston pullpen in right center field boosted the Socker advantage to 5-0 in the third.

The Yanks then went to work and added suspense to the evening's entertainment. They started paring the Hub advantage in the fifth. Lindell was the pace guy with a single but he was forced at second by Coleman who then scored all the way from first on Raschi's two-bagger to center.

Bauer led off the sixth with his first homer, a high and long hoist into the left-field screen. And he led off the eighth with his second circuit wallop, a tremendous wallop which cleared the screen out beyond the left-field scoreboard. But that was all the productive power the Yanks could muster. The Sox had enough even at that point but they came up with one more tally in their half of the eighth.

Like the second-inning rally, that sortie started after two were out when Goodman strolled. Zarilla came up with his second double and his third hit of the game which pushed Goodman to third. Tebbetts drew an intentional walk, loading the cushions. Then Kinder aided his own cause with a smash back to the mound which bounced off Raschi's shin for a scratch single which scored Goodman.

That punch also brought Dom Di Maggio up for the fifth time in the game with a final opportunity to extend his batting string. But the Little Professor didn't save it. He flied out to broth Joe, who did little else to distinguish himself in this particular engagement.

STUFF AND STUFF—Tonight's triumph was Kinder's second against the Yanks while Raschi's loss was his first after three straight victories over the Sox. . . . Kinder's mound mark now is 13-5. . . . Bauer's two homers were Nos. 18 and 19 off Old Grandad . . . Williams' homer not only gave him the league lead in circuit hitting but it was his 250th homer under the Big Top. . . . His runs-batted-in total bounced to 111 and he is now one back of Stephens in that department. . . . Mr. Slug was that in name only in the fifth when he got his second hit of the evening—a bunt down the third-base line against the Yankee shift to the right.

The Yanks played tonight's game with two of their lustiest hitters, Tommy Henrich and Yogi Berra, sidelined by injuries. . . . Henrich has a lame elbow, result of being hit by a pitched ball, but it's likely he'll be ready to play tomorrow afternoon as the Yanks and Sox resume their crucial series here. . . . Joe Dobson and Ed Lopat are mound selectees. . . . Tonight's victory was the 12th for the Sox in 15 games during this current home stay.

The box score:

RED SOX	ab	r	h	po	a	YANKEES	ab	r	h	po	a
D.D'M'o cf	5	0	0	2	0	Rizzuto s	5	0	2	2	3
Pesky 3	4	1	2	1	2	Brown 3	5	0	1	1	2
Williams l	4	1	2	4	0	Bauer r	4	2	3	2	0
Stephens s	3	0	0	0	4	J.D'M'o cf	4	0	1	3	0
Doerr 2	4	0	1	5	1	Johnson 1b	4	0	0	8	0
G'dman 1b	3	2	0	8	0	Lindell l	4	0	1	1	0
Zarilla r	4	1	3	3	0	Coleman 2	3	1	1	0	2
Tebbetts c	3	1	1	4	0	Silvera c	3	0	0	7	0
Kinder p	4	0	1	0	1	aKeller	1	0	0	0	0
						Raschi p	2	0	1	0	1
						bWoodling	1	0	0	0	0
Totals	34	6	10	27	8	Totals	36	3	10	24	8

aFor Silvera in 9th, flied out.
bFor Raschi in 9th, fanned.

Red Sox	032	000	01x	—6
Yankees	000	011	010	—3

E—Rizzuto. RBI—Bauer 2, Raschi, Tebbetts 2, Williams 2, Zarilla, Kinder. 2BH—Raschi, Zarilla 2, Pesky, Doerr. HR—Bauer 2, Tebbetts, Williams. LOB—Yankees 8, Red Sox 7. BOB—Raschi 3, Kinder 2. SO—Raschi 6, Kinder 3. W—Kinder (13-5). L—Raschi (15-7). U—Boyer, Passarella, Stevens. T—2:24. A—35,691.

Doerr Doubles: Bobby Doerr, Red Sox second baseman, slides safely into second base in the third inning of last night's Fenway Park game with the Yankees. Doerr's drive off the left field wall was retrieved by Johnny Lindell, but the latter's throw to Jerry Coleman was not in time. Art Passarella calls the play. —Associated Press Wirephoto

Cardinals Bump Reds, 4-1

Brecheen Hurls 7-Hitter as St. Louis Keeps Pace With Brooks

St. Louis, Aug. 9.—(AP)—The St. Louis Cardinals kept pace with the Brooklyn Dodgers in the tight National League race by downing the Cincinnati Reds, 4 to 1, tonight. Harry Brecheen allowed seven hits and no walks for his ninth victory of the year.

The Dodgers scored an 8-to-1 triumph over the Phillies at Philadelphia.

Johnny Vander Meer was the victim, allowing seven of the 10 hits the Red Birds made. Previously Vander Meer had two shutout games against the Cardinals this season for two of his three victories. He was charged with his seventh loss tonight.

Successive doubles in the third inning by Nippy Jones and Enos Slaughter gave St. Louis its first run. The Cards added another in the fourth when Brecheen slammed out a triple and scored on Chuck Diering's single.

The Reds' lone run came in the sixth when Vander Meer opened with a single. With two out Jones fumbled Grady Hatton's grounder, Vander Meer going to third. Walker Cooper tingled the Reds' pitcher home.

The Cards gave the 13,759 fans two extra runs in the seventh.

The box score:

CARDINALS	ab	r	h	po	a	REDS	ab	r	h	po	a
Diering cf	5	0	3	2	0	Walker cfr	4	0	0	3	0
Sch'd'st 2	4	1	1	7	6	Lowrey l	4	0	0	2	0
Musial r	4	1	0	2	0	Hatton 3	4	0	1	1	1
Jones 1b	3	1	1	8	0	Cooper c	4	0	2	3	2
Nelson 1b	0	0	0	2	0	Stallcup s	4	0	0	3	2
Slaug'r l	2	0	2	1	0	Litwh'er l	3	0	1	1	0
Marion s	3	0	1	1	4	Wyrostek cf	1	0	0	0	0
D.Rice c	3	0	0	2	0	Klusz'ki 1b	4	0	1	8	0
Glaviano 3	3	0	0	0	2	Adams 2	2	0	0	3	4
Brecheen p	4	1	2	2	2	Vand'M'r p	2	1	1	0	1
						aBl'dw'th	1	0	1	0	0
						bFox	0	0	0	0	0
						Erautt p	0	0	0	0	0
Totals	31	4	10	27	14	Totals	33	1	7	24	10

aFor Vander Meer in 7th, singled.
bRan for Bloodworth in 7th.

Cardinals	001	100	20x	—4
Reds	000	001	000	—1

E—Jones. RBI—Slaughter, Diering, Cooper, Marion 2. 2B—Jones, Slaughter. 3B—Brecheen. S—Adams, Jones. DP—Adams, Stallcup and Kluszewski; Schoendienst and Jones. LOB—Reds 6, Cards 11. BOB—Vander Meer 4, Erautt 3. SO—Vander Meer 3, Brecheen 1. HO—Vander Meer 7 in 6; Erautt 3 in 2. W—Brecheen (9-8). L—Vander Meer (3-7). U—Barr, Ballanfant and Barlick. T—2:06. A—13,759 (paid).

EASTERN LEAGUE

Williamsport 18, Utica 8.

AMERICAN ASSOCIATION

Milwaukee 7, Columbus 5.
Indianapolis 4, Minneapolis 3.
St. Paul 8, Toledo 6.
Louisville 6, Kansas City 2.

Harry Brecheen

15 Walks Propel A's to Victory Over Senators

Washington, Aug. 9.—(AP)—Aided by 15 bases on balls, the Philadelphia Athletics defeated Washington, 8-3, tonight. Carl Scheib won his seventh game. He had a shutout until the ninth inning, when the Senators scored all their runs on four of their nine hits.

The Athletics, who won their fourth straight game, clipped Dick Weik for seven runs before he was shelled from the mound in the fifth inning. Weik yielded 10 walks and six of Philadelphia's eight hits.

Weik walked three A's in a scoreless first inning, but forced across two runs with five walks in the second inning. Three singles and an outfield fly fetched Philadelphia two runs in the third and Pete Suder doubled across two more in the fourth.

The box score:

ATHLETICS	ab	r	h	po	a	SENATORS	ab	r	h	po	a
Joost s	3	1	2	2	2	Coan cf	5	0	2	9	0
Moses r	4	0	0	1	0	Rob'tson 2	5	0	0	1	2
Valo l	3	0	0	4	0	Stewart l	4	0	0	2	0
Fain 1b	2	1	1	3	2	Lewis r	4	0	0	1	0
aBia'tti 1b	0	1	0	0	0	Rob'son 1b	4	0	3	6	0
Chap'an cf	5	1	2	8	0	Yost 3	3	0	0	2	0
Suder 3	5	0	1	4	1	Dente s	3	1	2	0	2
Fox 2	3	2	1	2	1	Early c	3	1	1	5	0
Guerra c	4	1	1	2	0	Weik p	2	0	0	0	1
Scheib p	4	1	0	1	2	Gonzales p	0	0	0	1	0
						bSimmons	1	0	0	0	0
						Welteroth p	0	0	0	0	0
						cVollmer	1	1	1	0	0
Totals	33	8	8	27	8	Totals	35	3	9	27	5

aRan for Fain in 8th.
bFor Gonzales in 7th, popped up.
cFor Welteroth in 9th, doubled.

Athletics	022	210	010	—8
Senators	000	000	003	—3

E—None. RBI—Valo, Fain, Scheib, Joost, Suder 2, Moses, Guerra, Vollmer, Coan 2. 2BH—Suder, Robinson, Vollmer, Coan. 3BH—Joost. S—Dente. DP—Dente, Robertson and Robinson. LOB—Athletics 14, Senators 10. BOB—Weik 10, Scheib 4, Gonzales 2, Welteroth 3. SO—Weik 3, Scheib 2, Welteroth 1. HO—Weik 6 in 4 (none out in 5th), Gonzales 0 in 3, Welteroth 2 in 2. HBP—Welteroth (Fox). WP—Welteroth. W—Scheib (7-8). L—Weik (1-5). U—McGowan, Hurley, Jones and McKinley. A—8946. T—2:24.

INDIANS WIN, 9-2, WITH BOB FELLER

Victory Over Browns 4th Straight for Cleveland Righthander

Cleveland, Aug. 9.—(AP)—Bob Feller pitched the Cleveland Indians to a 9-2 victory over the St. Louis Browns tonight for his fourth straight victory and 10th of the season against eight defeats.

Feller also paced the Indians' attack with a bases-loaded single in a five-run rally in the fourth, and a double in the eighth.

The victory gained the Tribe a full game on the league-leading New York Yankees, who lost to Boston tonight, 6-3, and now hold a 4½-game edge.

Each team made nine hits, but Cleveland bunched six blows in the fourth and fifth frames for eight runs. Catcher Johnny Moss got three of the Browns' hits, one a fifth-inning home run over the left field fence.

INDIANS	ab	r	h	po	a	BROWNS	ab	r	h	po	a
Mitchell l	5	0	1	3	0	Sullivan 3	4	1	1	2	0
Doby cf-r	5	0	1	4	0	Kokos r	4	0	1	1	0
Vernon 1b	5	1	1	7	1	Priddy 2	4	0	1	3	2
Boudreau s	2	2	0	3	4	Graham 1b	4	0	1	9	0
Keltner 3	2	2	0	0	1	Sievers cf	3	0	0	2	0
B'r'rdino 2	3	2	1	0	2	Platt l	4	0	1	2	1
R.K'n'dy r	2	0	2	3	0	Moss c	4	1	3	3	0
Tucker cf	1	0	0	2	0	cEmbree	0	0	0	0	0
Hegan c	3	1	1	3	0	Pellagrini s	3	0	1	2	5
Tresh c	1	0	0	1	0	bLehner	1	0	0	0	0
Feller p	3	1	2	1	1	Garver p	1	0	0	0	1
						W.K'n'dy p	0	0	0	0	0
						aElder	1	0	0	0	0
						Starr p	0	0	0	0	1
Totals	32	9	9	27	9	Totals	33	2	9	24	10

aFor W. Kennedy in 8th, struck out.
bRan for Moss in 9th.
cFor Pellagrini in 9th, hit into double play.

Indians	000	530	01x	—9
Browns	000	010	010	—2

E—Pellagrini. RBI—R. Kennedy 2, Hegan, Mitchell, Moss, Berardino, Feller 2, Graham, Doby. 2B—Moss, Berardino, Feller. HR—Moss. S—Keltner, Feller, W. Kennedy. DP—Berardino, Boudreau and Vernon; Boudreau and Vernon. LOB—Browns 6, Indians 6. BOB—Garver 2, W. Kennedy 3, Feller. SO—Garver, W. Kennedy 2, Feller 4. HO—Garver 5 in 3⅔, W. Kennedy 2 in 3⅓, Starr 2 in 1. W—Feller (10-8). L—Garver (7-13). U—Hubbard, Berry and Paparella. T—2:20. A—31,219.

Braves to Play Slaters In McCoy Stadium Tilt

The Boston Braves, including Manager Billy Southworth and his first-string lineup, will meet the Pawtucket Slaters, pacing the New England League, in an exhibition game Monday night at McCoy Stadium, according to an announcement yesterday by Bill Cousins, business manager of the Slaters.

The Braves may use their rookie 19-year-old battery of Johnny Antonelli and Del Crandall against the Slaters. The Boston club comes here on the tail end of their present road trip, playing in Brooklyn on the day before they meet Pawtucket.

Journal Nine at Quincy

Grennon and Dorgan May Be Starting Battery Tonight in Exhibition Game

Still seeking its initial triumph in the New England newspaper baseball program, the Providence Journal team will make its first out-of-state appearance when it meets the Quincy Patriot-Ledger nine at the Quincy Athletic Field today in an exhibition twilight game. The contest will start at 5:30.

Seeking additional batting strength to go along with what shapes up as a fairly strong defensive outfit, Coach Dona Maynard is expected to make several changes in the Journal's starting lineup. He shook up the bating order in the team's 5-2 loss to Quincy here Sunday but failed to obtain the hoped-for results.

Gene Dorgan, chunky Georgiaville catcher, may be the starting receiver. He's done well in several limited appearances and has shown signs of developing into a timely batter. Art Grennon, a promising hurler from Woonsocket, shapes up as Maynard's pitching choice.

The remainder of the opening lineup is expected to have Jim Shepherd, Frank Neri and Don Zanfagna in the outfield and Joe Carello, Coz Rampone, Frank McKitchen and Joe Corneau in the infield. Rampone and Neri are the leading stickers on the club but they'll need help from some of the other boys on the squad if the team is to snap its losing streak.

Quincy will have Ed Healy, Dick Welch, Barry Storrs and Howie Gaskill ready for pitching duty. The latter turned back the Journal at McCoy Stadium, Sunday and may get the call today.

Zack Taylor Says Rainy Sunday Caused Drews to Hit 3 Yankees

Cleveland, Aug. 9.—(UP)—Zack Taylor, manager of the St. Louis Browns today blamed a Sunday afternoon shower for the wildness which caused pitcher Karl Drews to bean three New York batters.

Yogi Berra, Yankee catcher suffered a broken thumb which will keep him out of the lineup for at least three weeks and first baseman Tommy Henrich was bruised on the right elbow.

"When Karl was out there pitching at Yankee Stadium there was a little shower and the ball was wet," Taylor said. "He had a hard time controlling it. Why, Bob Porterfield of the Yankees was having trouble, too. He threw two balls back to the screen."

Taylor said that pitcher Dick Starr, who hit Berra, starting a series of beanings in which four Yankees were hit, was merely rusty.

"Starr was wild because he had just come back into action from an injury," Taylor said.

"If there is any complaining to be done I've got a right to yelp, too. In the second game Porterfield hit Bob Dillinger, our third baseman and the second heaviest hitter in the league. He suffered a bruised arm and it won't help his hitting any."

DODGERS SUBDUE PHILLIES NINE, 8-1, BY 15-HIT ATTACK

Erskine Flings 3-Hit Game; Cox, Campanella, Robinson Lead at Plate

Philadelphia, Aug. 9.—(AP)—Carl Erskine hurled three-hit ball as Billy Cox, Roy Campanella and Jackie Robinson led a 15-hit attack which gave the Brooklyn Dodgers an 8-1 triumph over the Philadelphia Phillies tonight.

Campanella connected with two doubles, a single and drove in four runs. Cox also got three hits, including a triple. Robinson came through with a three-bagger and a single before injuring his left foot stealing home in the fifth. It was the fourth time this season Robinson stole home.

Erskine missed a shutout when Bill Nicholson tripled in the ninth and scored on an infield out.

The Dodgers got to Robin Roberts for a run in each of the first and second frames and drove him from the mound in the fourth with a three-run uprising with one of Campanella's doubles the big show.

Burt Shotton's men continued their attack at the expense of Ken Trinkle in the fifth, sending three more runs across on Robinson's three-ply blow, a pass, double steal and hit by Gil Hodges, Cox and Campanella.

Andy Seminick, Phils' catcher, was knocked out in a collision with Pee Wee Reese at the plate in the first inning. He was revived and walked to the bench but was replaced by Stan Lopata.

The box score:

DODGERS	ab	r	h	po	a	PHILLIES	ab	r	h	po	a
Reese s	4	1	1	1	3	Ashbu'n cf	4	0	1	2	1
Rackley l	5	0	1	4	0	Hamner s	4	0	0	2	4
Snider cf	5	0	1	2	1	Nichol'n r	2	1	1	2	0
Robin'n 2	4	1	2	2	1	Ennis l	4	0	1	3	0
Miksis 2	0	0	0	0	0	Jones 3	4	0	0	1	3
Herma'i r	3	2	1	3	0	Goliat 1b	3	0	0	11	1
Hodges 1b	4	2	2	4	0	Semin'k c	0	0	0	1	0
Cox 3	4	2	3	1	1	Lopata c	3	0	0	2	4
Campa'a c	4	0	3	9	0	Miller 2	1	0	0	3	1
Erskine p	4	0	1	1	0	aHollmig	1	0	0	0	0
						Blattner 2	0	0	0	0	0
						Roberts p	0	0	0	0	0
						Trinkle p	0	0	0	0	0
						Rowe p	1	0	0	0	0
						bSisler	1	0	0	0	0
						Meyer p	0	0	0	0	0
Totals	37	8	15	27	6	Totals	28	1	3	27	14

aFor Miller in 8th, flied out.
bFor Rowe in 8th, fouled out.

Dodgers	110	330	000	—8
Phillies	000	000	001	—1

E—Ashburn. RBI—Robinson, Campanella 4, Cox 2, Ennis. 2BH—Campanella 2. 3BH—Cox, Robinson, Nicholson. SB—Robinson, Hermanski. DP—Goliat, Hamner and Goliat; Robinson and Hodges. LOB—Dodgers 4, Phillies 4. BOB—Roberts 1, Erskine 4, Trinkle 1. SO—Roberts 1, Erskine 6, Rowe 3. HO—Roberts 9 in 3, Trinkle 4 in 1⅔, Rowe 1 in 3⅓, Meyer 1 in 1. WP—Roberts. W—Erskine (2-1). L—Roberts (10-11). U—Warneke, Stewart and Conlan. T—2:29. A—21,463.

SOUTHERN ASSOCIATION

Chattanooga 10-9, Little Rock 6-6.
Birmingham 3, Mobile 0.
New Orleans 4, Atlanta 0.
Memphis 8, Nashville 7.

TEXAS LEAGUE

Forth Worth 4, Beaumont 1.

Slaters Tally Twice In 12th, Down Springfield Cubs, 8-7

Walk, Fletcher's Triple and Heavern's Single Do It; Norwood Winner

By JOE McHENRY

Fireman Bill Norwood won his second game in two nights as the Pawtucket Slaters came from behind in the last of the 12th and scored an 8-to-7 victory over the Springfield Cubs last night at McCoy Stadium, sweeping the four-game series.

George Crowe, who reached five times on four hits and a walk, opened the 12th by drawing a base on balls off Wes Carr, who had pitched 5⅔ innings of shutout relief ball. Carr had two strikes on Ray Fletcher when Fletcher tagged one which hit the left field fence on the fly and bounded back towards the infield. Crowe scored from first and Fletcher ended up with a triple.

Bobby Heavern, a good clutch player in the field, was the next batter and with two strikes, he hit an outside ball into right field, just out of reach of Dwight Maxheimer, and Fletcher came in with the winning run.

The Cubs piled up a 3-0 lead on Johnny Fetzer, but Pawtucket went ahead with four runs in the fifth. Steve Kuczek, star on the Colgate baseball team this spring, tripled home three runs and later scored on Dick Keohane's fly. The Slaters picked up two more tallies in the sixth with Kuczek again coming through with the bases loaded. This time Kuczek doubled home two tallies, giving the Slaters a 6-to-3 lead.

Fetzer walked two men in the seventh and Dusty Rhodes walloped a homer over the right-field fence, tying the score at six-all. Norwood finally put out the fire in that inning, but ran into trouble in the top of the 12th. Maxheimer got his fourth hit and went to third on Hank Nasternack's blooper single. Here Norwood tried to pick Maxheimer off third and threw into foul territory, Maxheimer scoring.

Cliff Collins turned in some outstanding fielding in center for the Slaters, and Crowe hit safely in his 13th straight game. Manager Bob Peterson of the Cubs prevented a jam between umpire Jim Donahue and catcher Joe Sullivan in the eighth after Sullivan used some rugged language in addressing the umpire.

PAWTUCKET	ab	r	h	po	a	SPRINGFIELD	ab	r	h	po	a
Barbeau l	6	0	1	3	1	Klaus 3	6	1	2	2	1
Keohane 3	3	0	0	0	1	Mac'notis 2	4	2	0	2	3
aDavis 3	1	0	0	0	0	Rhodes cf	4	1	1	2	0
Montag r	6	0	3	4	0	Pugatch lf	6	1	1	3	0
Collins cf	5	0	0	7	0	M'heimer r	6	1	4	0	1
Crowe, 1b	5	3	4	10	0	Forbes 1b	5	0	0	14	0
Fletcher c	6	3	3	7	0	N'ternack s	5	1	3	5	4
Heavern 2	5	1	2	3	5	Wilkins c	5	0	0	4	2
Kuczek s	5	1	2	2	4	Kuncl p	2	0	1	1	3
Fetzer p	2	0	0	0	1	Giddens p	2	0	0	0	2
Wright p	0	0	0	0	0	Carr p	2	0	0	0	0
Norwood p	2	0	1	0	0						
Totals	46	8	16	36	12	Totals	47	7	12	33x	16

aFor Keohane in 9th, walked.
xNo outs when winning run scored.

Pawtucket	000	042	000	002	—8
Springfield	111	000	300	001	—7

E—Macrinotis, Giddens, Carr, Norwood. RBI—Maxheimer, Klaus, Nasternack, Kuczek 5, Keohane, Rhodes 3, Fletcher, Heavern. HO—Kuncl 9 in 5⅓, Fetzer 8 in 6⅔, Giddens 4 in 3⅓, Wright 0 in 0 (faced 2 batters), Norwood 4 in 5⅓, Carr 3 in 2⅓. 2BH—Kuncl, Crane, Pugatch, Maxheimer. 3BH—Kuczek, Crane, Fletcher. HR—Rhodes. DP—Kuncl to Forbes, Nasternack to Macrinotis to Forbes. SO—Fetzer 1, Kuncl 1, Giddens 2, Norwood 5, Carr 1. BOB—Fetzer 5, Kuncl 2, Giddens 2, Wright 2, Norwood 1, Carr 1. HBP—Giddens (Collins). W—Norwood. L—Carr. T—3:15. U—Donahue and Bolla. A—449.

He's Out at Home: Pittsburgh's Pete Castiglione, despite a smile on his face which would indicate he has safely crossed the plate, has just been tagged out by catcher Mickey Owen of the Cubs in the ninth inning of yesterday's game at Chicago. Castiglione tried to score on Dino Restelli's double to right fielder Hank Edwards, whose throw was relayed to the plate by first baseman Herman Reich. —Associated Press Wirephoto

MAJOR LEAGUE BASEBALL

AMERICAN LEAGUE

RESULTS LAST NIGHT

Boston 6, New York 3.
Cleveland 9, St. Louis 2.
Philadelphia 8, Washington 3.
Detroit 11, Chicago 5.

STANDING OF THE TEAMS

	Won	Lost	P.C.	G.B.
New York	65	38	.631	—
Cleveland	61	43	.587	4½
Boston	60	44	.577	5½
Philadelphia	59	47	.557	7½
Detroit	58	49	.542	9
Chicago	44	61	.419	22
Washington	37	65	.363	27½
St. Louis	34	71	.324	32

NATIONAL LEAGUE

RESULTS YESTERDAY

New York 4, Boston 3.
Brooklyn 8, Philadelphia 1.
Pittsburgh 8, Chicago 3.
St. Louis 4, Cincinnati 1.

STANDING OF THE TEAMS

	Won	Lost	P.C.	G.B.
St. Louis	65	39	.625	—
Brooklyn	65	39	.625	—
New York	54	50	.519	11
Boston	53	53	.500	13
Philadelphia	53	53	.500	13
Pittsburgh	47	56	.456	17½
Cincinnati	43	63	.406	23
Chicago	40	67	.374	26½

GAMES TODAY AND PROBABLE PITCHERS

New York at Boston—Lopat (10-5) vs. Dobson (9-8).
St. Louis at Cleveland (Night)—Fannin (4-8) vs. Lemon (13-7).
Philadelphia at Washington (Night)—Kellner (14-7) vs. Calvert (6-12) or Scarborough (8-8).
Chicago at Detroit—Haefner (6-6) vs. Newhouser (11-7).

Boston at New York—Spahn (13-9) vs. Jones (9-7).
Brooklyn at Philadelphia (night)—Branca (12-4) or Roe (9-3) vs. Simmons (3-10).
Pittsburgh at Chicago—Walsh (0-0) vs. Leonard (4-14) or Lade (1-2).
Cincinnati at St. Louis (night)—Raffensberger (11-12) vs. Brazle (12-5).

LEADING HITTERS

	G.	A.B.	R.	H.	P.C.
Williams, Red Sox	106	387	105	134	.346
Dillinger, Browns	94	371	51	128	.345
Kell, Tigers	96	384	70	131	.341
Robinson, Dodgers	106	414	87	151	.365
Slaughter, Cardinals	100	365	62	122	.334
Marshall, Giants	93	320	61	102	.319

HOME RUNS

Williams, Red Sox, 28; Stephens, Red Sox, 27; Joost, Athletics, 21.

Kiner, Pirates, 29; Sauer, Cubs, and Gordon, Giants, 24 each.

RUNS BATTED IN

Stephens, Red Sox, 112; Williams, Red Sox, 111; Wertz, Tigers, 92.

Robinson, Dodgers, 90; Hodges, Dodgers, 84; Gordon, Giants, 76.

RUNS FOR THE WEEK

	S	M	T	W	T	F	S	Tl
Boston	4	*	6					10
Chicago	4	*	5					9
Cleveland	6	*	9					15
Detroit	6	*	11					17
New York	22	*	3					25
Philadelphia	9	*	8					17
St. Louis	4	*	2					6
Washington	2	*	3					5

	S	M	T	W	T	F	S	Tl
Boston	14	*	3					17
Brooklyn	9	2	8					19
Chicago	4	*	3					7
Cincinnati	1	3	1					5
New York	2	1	4					7
Philadelphia	12	*	1					13
Pittsburgh	7	*	8					15
St. Louis	9	9	4					22

*-No Game.

MARCACCIO IN FIRST IN CEDAR Y.C. RACE

Ed Marcaccio sailed his Jet to a victory in the evening boat race held by the Cedar Tree Point Yacht Club last night. Ted Kroliki, in Sea Shell, was second. Nine boats started.

The summary:

1, Jet, Ed Marcaccio; 2, Sea Shell, Ted Korliki; 3, Merry-Bill, Dick Quinn; 4, Nausauket, Buddy Rogers; 5, Hi Ho, Ann Clarke; 6, Quinkid, Jack Quinn; 7, Dash, Don Hesketh; 8, Three B's, Frank Bain. Did not finish—Fibber, Phil McGee.

INTERNATIONAL LEAGUE

Syracuse 5-10, Rochester 4-3.
Jersey City 9-6, Toronto 6-3.
Buffalo 4-4, Baltimore 3-1.

7TH-INNING PUNCH BY GIANT HITTERS FLATTENS TRIBE

Braves' Rally in Seventh Ties Score, 3-3; Each Team Collects 2 Homers

New York, Aug. 9.—(AP) — Home runs by Bobby Thomson and Bill Rigney helped Larry Jansen and the New York Giants defeat Johnny Sain and the Boston Braves tonight, 4-3. It was Jansen's 12th victory and Sain's 12th defeat.

Thomson homered in the first with one on and Rigney in the second with the bases empty, giving the Giants a 3-0 lead but the Braves pecked away and tied the score in the seventh.

Successive singles by Willard Marshall, Rigney and Ray Mueller in the last of the seventh snapped the tie.

Jansen yielded 11 hits, including home runs by Jeff Heath and Bill Salkeld. Jansen was yanked in the ninth in favor of Al Zabala with two on and two out. The lefty fanned pinch hitter Ed Sauer and ended the game.

Bob Elliott, Boston third sacker, left seven mates stranded. He marooned three in the first, two in the fifth and two in the seventh.

GIANTS	ab	r	h	po	a	BRAVES	ab	r	h	po	a
Tho'pson 2	3	1	0	4	3	Stanky 2	5	0	1	2	3
Lockman l	4	0	0	4	0	Fletcher 1b	5	0	3	9	
Th'mson cf	4	1	2	1	0	dRyan	0	0	0	0	
Mize 1b	3	0	0	5	1	Reiser cf	3	0	2	4	0
Lafata 1b	1	0	1	2	0	cSauer	1	0	0	0	0
Marshall r	3	1	1	2	0	R.Elliott 3	4	0	0	1	0
Gordon 3	3	0	0	0	1	Heath r	4	1	1	1	0
Rigney s	3	1	2	2	1	Rickert l	4	0	0	3	0
R.Mu'ler c	3	0	1	7	1	Dark s	4	0	1	2	4
Jansen p	3	0	0	0	1	Salkeld c	4	1	1	2	1
Zabala p	0	0	0	0	0	Sain p	3	1	1	0	1
						aHolmes	1	0	1	0	0
						bSisti	0	0	0	0	0
Totals	30	4	7	27	8	Totals	38	3	11	24	9

aFor Sain in 9th, singled.
bRan for Holmes in 9th.
cFor Reiser in 9th, fanned.
dRan for Fletcher in 9th.

Giants	210	000	10x	—4
Braves	000	110	100	—3

E—Rigney. RBI—Thomson 2, Rigney, Heath, Salkeld, Reiser, R. Mueller. 2BH—Dark. HR—Thomson, Rigney, Heath, Salkeld. DP—Gordon, R. Mueller and Mize. LOB—Braves 9, Giants 3. BOB—Jansen 1, Sain 1. SO—Sain 1, Jansen 5, Zabala 1. HO—Jansen 11 in 8⅔; Zabala 0 in ⅓. W—Jansen (12-11). L—Sain (8-12). U—Pinelli, Gore, Robb and Ascoli. T—1:58. A—24,335.

JIM FUCHS COVERS 339 FEET IN 6 PUTTS

Stockholm, Aug. 9.—(AP)—James Fuchs of Yale University, holder of the world shot put record, covered a total distance of 339 feet, 7½ inches tonight with six mighty heaves in the international track and field meet at Malemoe.

He had throws of 56 feet, one inch; 55:09½; 57; 56:06; 57:08 and 56:07 in the series.

His world record, set in Oslo in July, is 58 feet, 4 27-64 inches. He also won the discus throw with a toss of 169 feet, 9 inches.

Now Everybody Can Make a Home Run as Babe Shows How to Do It

FOLLOWING BIG BABE RUTH, THE HOME RUN KING, THROUGH, ON ONE OF HIS LONG DRIVES, BY THE AID OF THE CAMERA

Here is the way Babe Ruth, the king of home run getters, swings at a ball when he knocks out one of his famous long drives that has made him the slugging wonder of baseball. Starting from right to left the pictures show just how he does it from the time he starts to meet the ball with his bat, until he completes the action and has sent the ball to the far corner of the ball park or over the fence. Babe posed himself for these photographs, which were taken by George Murray of the Boston Post staff. George tried to tell Babe how he wanted to catch him in action to show how he does the trick, but Babe wouldn't stand for it. "Your game is taking pictures, mine is poling home runs," says Babe. "I'll take the different poses myself as if it was for a movie. Then they'll be right. All you have got to do is shoot the camera." And George did.

Busting Babe and His Diadem

Clouting Hercules Is One of Celebrities of Country

By NEAL R. O'HARA

Boston's pretty proud of your 26th, Babe. As proud as it was of its own 26th last spring, when it came back from war. Honestly, we don't know but that our 26th Y. D. and your 26th H. R. are on the same level.

The way you've been whaling the ball all season has given you title to the Prince of Whales. But today you're the Home Run King. That ball you crowned yesterday certainly gives you the rank and throne.

HERE'S HOPING BABE DOES IT AGAIN.

Buck Freeman held the home run record long enough. And, believe us, we're all glad to see you passing the Buck. Not that Freeman wasn't a sweet hitter—they don't pack bonbons sweeter than that boy. But you've been clubbing the ball so hard this season you couldn't be denied. And we expect you to be the H. R. king for a long, long time—till next year, at least, when you'll probably make a whole lot more.

You are the mastodon of hitters, Babe—the dinosaur of slam artists. If you lived in the Stone Age, you'd doubtless be swinging an elm tree at every boulder they pitched to you.

But this is another age. Today you swing a mean club and get the same results. If the club that's surrounding you were only as good as the one you swing, they'd have a silk pennant for the Red Sox, instead of the lisle trophy, or whatever they give a second-division outfit.

However, we can't have everything. And although they may say we are sucking sour grapes, we don't know but that we'd rather have the world's champion slugger in Boston than the world's champion ball team.

We've got so used to winning pennants, it's a relief to have some other club win. Anyway, it's only fair to let the West have the best ball team once in a while. Besides, a world's champion ball club is made each season, but they don't produce champion sluggers that often.

IT WAS HARDER ON THE PITCHERS, WE'LL SAY.

You've had a hard and a soft time this season, Babe. Hard, because all the pitchers were working against you, and working hard. And soft, because you didn't do much running.

As we look back on the season, you haven't done much else than walk. For, as we recall it, you always got either a home run or a base on balls. If you got four balls, you walked to first; and, if you slammed the ball over the fence, you walked all the way around to home. Bryan has done more running than you.

You are the only 20th Century Express in Baseball, Babe. You never make local stops at second or third. The only place you stop for water is the dugout, after you've gone all the way around. You either make the whole trip on a single ticket, or else you go to first on the ticket some pitcher gives you.

Yea, bo—and you've put the ball over the top more times than any general. Many a day, when the Sox were having a zero at the bat, you stepped to the plate and put it over the top for at least one tally.

You've covered more ground going home than Ludendorff ever covered. You've given the ball more rides in the air than Eddie Rickenbacker ever took. And you've done more for the league than Henry Cabot Lodge—a lot more!

Hence, Babe, we take off our fall fedora to you. We'd have a medal struck out for you, but we know you wouldn't care for anything that's been struck out. We'd give you the freedom of the city, only there's been more bevo than freedom in Boston since last July. But, kid, we'll give you anything you ask for—anything at all. And all we ask in return is that you try for that 27th today:

Sure you've got the makings of another home run.

Mightiest hitter in baseball's history, more powerful than any of the great sluggers of the past, the undisputed home run king of all time, Big Babe Ruth, Boston battering ram, stands supreme among the big batters of the day.

HONORS ALL HIS OWN

No longer does he share honors with Buck Freeman, the home run champion of another generation. Today all baseballdom bows to Babe, with his world's record mark of 26 home runs.

Realizing his dream of years, eclipsing the mark at which he had aimed ever since Joe Lannin, the former Red Sox magnate, brought him to Boston from Baltimore, Big Babe Ruth yesterday shattered the record which has stood for two long decades when he caught hold of one of Thormahlen's fast ones and drove it into the right field pavilion at the Polo Grounds for his 26th home run of the year.

This terrific wallop, made in the eighth inning, when Boston led by the meagre margin of one run, settled the fate of battle apparently, just as most of his long distance drives this year have determined the result in the Red Sox' favor.

Surprised All Critics

In creating a new home run record and collecting most of his circuit drives on foreign fields, Ruth has accomplished the apparently impossible and excelled a mark which the wisest critics of the game firmly believed would stand for all time. And small wonder that the big crowd that packed the Polo Grounds yesterday in the hope that Ruth might realize his ambition went fairly frantic as the sphere disappeared from view and the mark that had stood unassailed for 20 long years was erased from world's record chronicles.

And long before Big Babe had finished shaking hands with his mates, even while the police were driving back from the Boston dugout the hundreds of fans who swarmed around in the hope of shaking the hand of Boston's burly Batterer, the fans began to appreciate the tremendous achievement that Babe had accomplished.

For, in wiping the mark of Buck Freeman from the official slate it must be understood that Ruth had to overcome the disadvantage of far larger parks, even more effective pitchers and pitching policies than ever existed in the days when Buck Freeman startled the baseball world by clouting out his 25 circuit wallops.

Harder to Make 'Em Now

In almost every instance the big league parks of today are nearly twice as large as those of 20 years ago. Were the same small parks that saw Freeman make his record standing today Ruth, without a doubt, would have eclipsed the official figures long since. Then, too, Ruth has been batting against some of the greatest twirlers that ever stood upon the rubber and in addition to this in nearly every game opposing pitchers have figured discretion as the better part of valor and walked him intentionally in the pinch.

Although Big Babe has been after the home-run record for many a long day no player in the American league, no well versed fan even, had the slightest idea that he had a chance of reaching the title of home run king until that memorable day in Chicago last month when he drove the ball into the right field bleachers at Comiskey Park—scored his 17th homer and wiped out Seybold's American League record of 16 home runs.

This was at that time supposed to be glory enough, but Babe didn't stop there. He kept right on hammering out the deadly four-baggers, bunched the circuit clouts at St. Louis and Detroit and with 23 to his credit came back to Fenway Park, two weeks ago, ready to wipe Freeman's figures off the slate.

Great Week's Work

On Labor Day afternoon, in the presence of nearly 30,000 people, he drove the ball far into the right field bleachers for his 24th. Last Friday afternoon, before an admiring crowd at Philadelphia, he evened the mark set 20 years ago. Yesterday's great achievement was the consummation of an entire season's battering.

And in no case was any home run that Ruth knocked out a gift. The greatest twirlers in the American league had to stand and watch the sphere driven by Babe's bat sink out of sight, Covaleskie, Ehmke, Dauss, Davenport, Shocker, Morton, Leonard, Shawkey, Johnson, Harper, Shaw, Thormahlen and Mogridge, right handers and southpaws, impartially, have been compelled to see their choicest offerings sent flying beyond the pale.

And in eclipsing the mark yesterday afternoon at the Polo Grounds Babe was compelled to face Thormahlen, one of the greatest southpaws in the business.

Today, against the St. Louis Browns on Fenway Park, Babe will make an effort to shatter his own record. It is nearly as good as an even bet that he will score 30 home runs before the season is brought to an end.

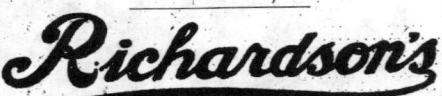

DAVE SHEAN IS COACHING TEAM

The Arlington Council, Knights of Columbus, baseball club, is to practice every evening this week to get in trim for the second of the series of games with the Winchester town team for the championship of the Mystic Valley. The contest is to be staged next Saturday afternoon on the Spy Pond Athletic Field, Arlington. Dave Shean, the former Red Sox second baseman, will coach the boys again this week. The Arlington outfit won the first game of the series, 2 to 0, in 11 innings at Winchester last Saturday, and another Arlington victory will give the series to the Spy Pond nine.

Meusel Brothers | stars of Yanks and Giants, contenders in world series, | To Write for | entertainment of vast army of readers who depend on | Evening Heral

U. S. Makes Clean Sweep in Sport Event

L. A. FANS ARE DIVIDED ON BIG GAMES

World Series Is Talk of Broadway; Many Ex-Coasters on Rival Championship Clubs

Will the Yankee sluggers hammer out enough runs to win?

Or will the pitching staff of the Giants carry the club through the series?

Up and down Broadway and Spring street the argument has started the hottest line of world's series talks in years.

Many of the fans are picking the Giants to win the world's series because of the strong manner the team finished the National league pennant race. The pitching staff is strong.

"BABE" AND PITCHERS

On the other hand, Yankee followers say that a two-man pitching staff 's enough to win a world's series.

They also say there is no such thing as a good pitching staff when "Babe" Ruth opposes it. Frank Chance, former Cub leader who went through four world's series, offers good advice.

"Pass Ruth whenever you have the opportunity," says Chance.

"I know that 35,000 fans would yell when you order your pitcher to pass the slugger. But that never bothered me. Perhaps my bum ear aided me in not paying any attention to the yells from the fans when I thought I was doing the right thing.

"If McGraw passes Ruth every chance he gets he will cut down the Yankee strength."

MANY PICK GIANTS

A surprisingly large number of ball players pick the Giants to win the world's series.

That is due to their belief that John J. McGraw, pilot of the Giants, is one of the real baseball leaders of the country. On the other hand, Miller Huggins, boss of the Yankees, has been "panned" by New York and other scribes for using poor baseball judgment.

No matter which way the series goes, 12 former Coast leaguers and another Native Son will come in for full shares of the money that is to be divided.

Phil Douglas, Dave Bancroft, Johnny Rawlings, "Irish" Meusel and Bill Cunningham helped make baseball history in the Pacific Coast league.

George Kelly, the first baseman, is a native of San Francisco. He is also a nephew of Bill Lange, one of the great stars of years ago. "Irish" Meusel, the outfielder, is hitting .334 for the Giants, according to late records, and is only two points behind Frank Frisch, the Fordham flash, who is leading the Giant batters.

MEUSEL BROTHERS

Opposed to "Irish" will be Brother Bobby Meusel, who has been clicking the baseball for a .328 average and who is leading the American league in home runs—outside of "Babe" Ruth.

Johnny Mitchell, Bill Piercy, Jack Quinn and Al DeVormer are all former Vernon players and many of the fans will be pulling for them to win.

Nelson Hawkes, formerly was with Oakland, while Roger Peckinpaugh played for Portland years ago.

SETS NEW RECORD FOR YEAR'S BATTING

LOUISVILLE, Ky., Oct. 3.—A new world's record for hits in a single season, was established here yesterday by Jay Kirke, first baseman of the Louisville team when he slammed out two bingles and brought his total for the year to 282.

The former record of 280 for a season was held by "Hack" Miller of the Oakland Coast league club.

CLIFF HERD WINS IN CHICAGO TENNIS

CHICAGO, Oct. 3.—Cliff Herd, former freshman coach at the University of Southern California, is the tennis champion of Chicago.

He won the title in the finals of the annual championship tournament staged here yesterday when he defeated Jerry Weber by a count of 6-1, 7-5, 6-3.

Club Standings

PACIFIC COAST LEAGUE

	W.	L.	Pct.		W.	L.	Pct.
Los Angeles	108	80	.574	Oakland	101	85	.542
Sacramento	105	80	.567	Vernon	96	90	.516
San Fran.	106	82	.564	Salt Lake	73	109	.400
Seattle	103	82	.556	Portland	51	134	.274

NATIONAL LEAGUE

	W.	L.	Pct.		W.	L.	Pct.
New York	94	59	.614	Brooklyn	77	75	.513
Pittsburg	90	63	.588	Cincinnati	70	83	.458
St. Louis	87	66	.569	Chicago	64	89	.418
Boston	79	71	.516	Philadelphia	51	103	.331

AMERICAN LEAGUE

	W.	L.	Pct.		W.	L.	Pct.
New York	98	55	.641	Boston	75	79	.487
Cleveland	94	60	.610	Detroit	71	82	.464
St. Louis	81	73	.526	Chicago	62	92	.403
Washington	80	73	.523	Philadelphia	51	104	.320

AMERICAN ASSOCIATION

	W.	L.	Pct.		W.	L.	Pct.
Louisville	98	69	.587	Milwaukee	81	86	.485
Minneapolis	92	72	.561	St. Paul	82	87	.485
Kan City	83	79	.512	Toledo	78	89	.467
Indianapolis	82	85	.491	Columbus	68	95	.417

TWO STARS OF YANKS, GIANTS

Mays Is Regarded as Best Pitcher of Year in American League. His Victory Saturday Clinched the Flag for Yankees

Two Stars Who Are Expected to Shine in Coming World Series Contests, Frank Snyder, on Left, Back-Stop of Giants, and Carl Mays, Ace of Yankee Twirlers

Baseball Results

At Los Angeles—

Sacs 10-1, Tigers 0-4

FIRST GAME

SACRAMENTO	AB	R	H	O	A	VERNON	AB	R	H	O	A
M'G'an,2b	5	1	1	2	1	Smith,3b	4	0	0	2	0
Kopp,lf	4	3	1	3	0	C'ourne,cf	4	0	1	2	0
M'lwitz,1b	4	2	8	10	1	Ed'gton,lf	4	0	2	5	0
Pick,3b	4	2	1	0	2	Hyatt,1b	4	0	0	8	1
Ryan,rf	3	1	2	4	0	S'neider,rf	3	0	1	0	0
Compton,cf	5	1	1	3	0	Murphy,c	2	0	0	5	1
Orr,ss	5	0	2	3	3	French,ss	3	0	0	2	1
Cook,c	4	0	0	1	0	Zeider,2b	3	0	0	3	1
Fittery,p	4	0	1	1	4	Faeth,p	0	0	0	0	0
						McGraw,p	2	0	0	0	3
Totals	38	10	12	27	11	Totals	29	0	4	27	7

SCORE BY INNINGS

Sacramento .....2 0 3 0 1 0 4 0 0—10
Vernon ....0 0 0 0 0 0 0 0 0— 0

SUMMARY

Errors—Edington, Murphy, French, Zeider. Two-base hits—McGaffigan, Kopp, Ryan. Stolen bases—Kopp, Mollwitz. Sacrifice hits—Mollwitz, Ryan. Struck out—By Faeth, 2; by McGraw, 2; by Fittery, 1.

SECOND GAME

SACRAMENTO	AB	R	H	O	A	VERNON	AB	R	H	O	A
M'G'an2b	4	0	0	2	3	Smith,3b	4	2	3	0	2
Kopp,lf	2	0	0	4	0	C'ourne,cf	2	0	0	4	0
M'lwitz,1b	4	0	1	12	0	Ed'gton,lf	3	0	1	4	0
Pick,3b	3	0	0	3	4	Hyatt,1b	3	0	2	8	0
Ryan,rf	3	0	1	2	0	S'neider,rf	3	0	0	1	0
Compton,cf	3	0	0	1	0	Hannah,c	3	1	2	4	0
Orr,ss	3	0	0	2	2	French,ss	3	0	0	3	3
Cook,c	2	0	0	1	0	Sawyer,2b	3	1	1	2	3
Kunz,p	0	0	0	0	0	Dell,p	3	0	0	1	2
Penner,p	1	0	0	0	0						
Schang,c	1	0	1	0	0						
Sheehan,x	1	1	0	0	0						
Prough,p	1	0	0	0	3						
Niehaus,p	0	0	0	0	0						
Totals	28	1	3	27	12	Totals	27	4	9	27	10

xBatted for Prough in eighth.

SCORE BY INNINGS

Sacramento .....0 0 0 0 0 0 0 1 0— 1
Vernon ....1 2 0 0 0 1 0 0 x— 4

SUMMARY

Error—Hannah. Two-base hit—Hannah. Stolen base—Kopp. Sacrifice hits—Schneider, Edington, Compton, French, Sawyer.

At Portland—

Angels 12-4, Beavers 3-5

First game:

LOS ANGELES	AB	R	R	O	A	PORTLAND	AB	R	R	O	A
Statz,cf	5	1	2	4	0	Genin,rf	4	0	0	3	0
McAuley,ss	3	4	3	2	8	Krug,2b	4	0	1	2	6
Carroll,lf	3	1	2	1	0	Hale, 3b	4	1	1	1	1
Griggs,1b	5	1	1	10	0	Poole,1b	4	0	0	10	0
Crwfrd,rf	5	1	2	2	0	Gnglrdi,cf	4	1	1	3	1
Niehoff,3b	4	1	1	2	2	Wolfer,lf	4	0	1	3	1
McCabe,2b	3	1	0	2	2	Grnthm,ss	4	1	1	0	0
Stanage,c	4	1	2	4	0	Fisher,c	3	0	0	4	0
Aldridge,p	5	1	1	0	0	Ellison,p	2	0	1	0	2
						Ross,p	2	0	0	1	1
Totals	37	12	14	27	12	Totals	35	3	6	27	12

SCORE BY INNINGS

Los Angeles .....0 0 2 0 1 5 0 4 0—12
Portland ....0 0 0 0 1 2 0 0 0— 3

SUMMARY

Errors—McCabe, 2; Hale, Poole, Ginglardi. Innings pitched—By Ellison, 6. Stolen bases—Carroll, Hale, 2. Home runs—Ginglardi, Niehoff. Two-base hits—Griggs, Crawford.

Second game:

LOS ANGELES	AB	R	R	O	A	PORTLAND	AB	R	R	O	A
Statz,cf	4	1	1	1	0	Genin,rf	5	0	2	0	0
McAuley,ss	5	1	1	3	5	Krug,2b	5	2	2	1	6
Carroll,lf	5	0	2	3	0	Hale,3b	4	1	1	0	2
Griggs,1b	5	0	1	8	2	Poole,1b	5	1	2	14	0
Crwfrd,rf	5	0	0	2	1	Gnglrdi,cf	4	0	0	4	0
Niehoff,3b	5	2	3	0	0	Wolfer,lf	5	0	3	1	0
McCabe,2b	2	0	0	3	0	Grnthm,ss	5	0	2	6	6
Stanage,c	5	0	2	7	3	Baker,c	4	0	2	7	0
Soria,p	4	0	0	0	1	Coleman,p	2	0	0	0	0
Lndmore,2b	2	0	1	3	1	Engle,x	1	0	0	0	0
						Johnson,p	2	1	2	0	0
Totals	42	4	11	31	13	Totals	42	5	16	33	14

One out when winning run scored.
x—Batted for Coleman in sixth.

SCORE BY INNINGS

Los Angeles.0 1 2 0 0 1 0 0 0 0 0—4
Portland ..2 0 0 0 2 0 0 0 0 0 1—5

SUMMARY

Errors—Griggs, Soria, Hale. Innings pitched—By Coleman, 6. Stolen bases—Wolfer, Poole, 2; Statz. Two-base hits—Niehoff, 2. Sacrifice hits—Genin, Krug.

AMERICAN LEAGUE

At Chicago— R. H. E.
Cleveland ....0 3 0 0 0 1 0 0 0—4 6 1
Chicago ....0 5 0 1 0 0 0 1 x—7 8 1
Batteries—Mails, Henderson and Sewell; Wilkinson and Yarvan.

At New York— R. H. E.
Boston ....0 0 0 2 3 0 0 1 0—6 9 0
New York ....0 2 3 0 0 0 0 0 2—7 10 3
Batteries—Fullerton and Chaplin; Piercy, W. Collins, Shawkey and De Vormer.

At Detroit— R. H. E.
St. Louis ....2 0 0 2 1 2 2 1 2—12 15 0
Detroit ....0 0 0 2 0 0 1 0 0— 3 11 2
Batteries—Davis and Severeid; Cole and Woodall.

At Washington— R. H. E.
Philadelphia ....0 0 0 0 0 1 3 2 0— 6 9 3
Washington .....3 0 3 0 0 3 2 0 0—11 8 2
Batteries—Keefe, Moore and Walker; W. Johnson and Picinich.

KOST IS WINNER OF SHOOT AT VERNON

C. L. Kost carried off the honors in the shoot staged over the traps of the Vernon Gun club yesterday when he broke 100 targets out of a possible 100.

At San Francisco—

Bees 8-0, Oaks 3-6

FIRST GAME

SALT LAKE	AB	R	H	O	A	OAKLAND	AB	R	H	O	A
Siglin,2b	5	0	1	2	0	Pinelli,3b	6	1	4	2	6
Lewis,lf	5	0	1	1	0	Willie,rf	5	0	1	0	0
Brown,3b	5	1	2	0	3	Cooper,cf	5	0	1	2	0
Sand,ss	4	0	0	4	4	Miller,lf	5	0	1	2	0
Strand,cf	5	0	0	4	1	Ruegg,2b	6	0	0	2	5
Mooney,rf	4	1	3	5	0	Guisto,1b	4	1	0	15	2
Reiger,1b	3	0	1	13	1	B'baker,ss	4	1	1	3	5
Lynn,c	5	0	0	3	1	Koehler,c	4	0	1	5	0
Kallio,p	3	1	1	1	4	Alten,p	4	0	2	1	3
						White,x	0	0	0	0	0
						Read,c	0	0	0	1	1
Totals	39	3	9	33	14	Totals	43	3	11	33	22

xRan for Koehler in ninth.

SCORE BY INNINGS

Salt Lake ....0 0 0 0 0 1 1 0 0 0 1—3
Oakland ....0 0 0 2 0 0 0 0 0 0 1—3

SUMMARY

Errors—Sand, Reiger, Ruegg. Two-base hits—Wilie, Kallio, Mooney 2, Pinelli, Cooper. Sacrifice hits; Wilie, Sand. Bases on balls—Off Kallio, 5; off Alten, 3. Stolen bases—Reiger, Pinelli, Cooper, Miller.

SECOND GAME

SALT LAKE	AB	R	H	O	A	OAKLAND	AB	R	H	O	A
Siglin,2b	4	0	1	1	4	Pinelli,3b	4	1	2	0	2
Lewis,lf	3	0	2	0	0	Willie,rf	3	0	0	1	0
Brown,3b	4	0	1	1	2	Cooper,cf	3	0	1	4	0
Sand,ss	2	0	0	2	3	Miller,lf	4	1	1	3	0
Strand,cf	4	0	2	4	0	Ruegg,2b	4	1	1	6	0
Mooney,rf	3	0	0	2	0	Cather,1b	4	1	0	8	1
Reiger,1b	2	0	0	11	0	B'baker,ss	3	0	0	0	5
Edwards,c	4	0	0	3	0	Read,c	4	1	1	5	2
Gould,p	3	0	0	0	5	Keiser,p	4	1	2	0	2
Jenkins,x	1	0	0	0	0						
Totals	30	0	6	24	14	Totals	33	6	8	27	12

xBatted for Reiger in ninth.

SCORE BY INNINGS

Salt Lake ....0 0 0 0 0 0 0 0 0—0
Oakland ....0 0 0 0 0 1 2 3 x—6

SUMMARY

Errors—Sand 3, Reiger 2, Gould. Stolen bases—Cooper 2, Strand, Pinelli, Keiser. Home run—Miller. Two-base hits—Keiser, Lewis, Strand. Sacrifice hits—Mooney, Wilie, Brubaker.

At Seattle—

Seals 9-5, Purps 1-6

FIRST GAME

SAN FRANCISCO	AB	R	H	O	A	SEATTLE	AB	R	H	O	A
Schick,lf	5	2	3	3	0	Middletn,lf	4	1	2	1	0
Kamm,3b	3	2	1	1	2	Peterson,3b	4	0	1	0	0
Caveney,ss	4	1	2	3	4	Murphy,1b	4	0	1	11	1
Ellison,1b	5	2	3	9	0	Eldred,cf	4	0	1	2	1
Kelly,cf	4	0	0	3	0	Knwthy,2b	2	0	0	4	6
Fitzgrld,rf	4	1	3	3	0	Lafay'te,rf	4	0	0	3	0
Walsh,2b	3	1	2	3	4	Stumpf,ss	3	0	0	2	2
Yelle,c	4	0	1	2	0	Adams,c	4	0	0	4	2
Scott,p	5	0	0	0	2	Jacobs,p	2	0	0	0	2
						Brenton,p	0	0	0	0	0
						Schorr,x	1	0	1	0	0
						Dailey,p	0	0	0	0	1
						Spencer,xx	1	0	0	0	0
Totals	37	9	15	27	12	Totals	33	1	6	27	15

x—Batted for Brenton in seventh.
xx—Batted for Dailey in ninth.

SCORE BY INNINGS

San Francisco ....1 0 0 1 4 0 1 2 0—9
Seattle ....0 0 1 0 0 0 0 0 0—1

SUMMARY

Errors—Peterson, Eldred, Adams 2. Innings pitched—By Jacobs 5, by Brenton 2. Stolen bases—Walsh, Schick. Home run—Fitzgerald. Three-base hit—Walsh. Two-base hits—Ellison, Walsh, Schick.

SECOND GAME

SAN FRANCISCO	AB	R	H	O	A	SEATTLE	AB	R	H	O	A
Schick,lf	4	0	1	2	0	Lane,lf	4	0	0	2	0
Kamm,3b	5	0	1	1	4	Pattrsn,3b	5	0	2	4	0
Caveney,ss	4	0	1	1	2	Eldred,cf	4	1	1	2	0
Ellison,1b	3	3	2	10	0	Knwthy,2b	4	1	3	3	4
Kelly,cf	4	1	2	1	0	Stumpf,ss	5	0	1	4	3
Fitzgrld,rf	4	0	1	1	0	Nixon,rf	3	1	2	0	0
Walsh,2b	3	0	1	5	4	Tobin,c	4	0	0	2	3
Yelle,c	4	1	2	5	0	Francis,p	4	0	2	0	4
O'Doul,p	2	0	0	0	2	Demaree,p	0	0	0	0	1
G'water,p	0	0	0	0	0						
Rath,xx	1	0	0	0	0						
Crumpler,p	0	0	0	0	0						
Totals	34	5	11	26	12	Totals	38	6	14	27	15

Two out when winning run scored.
xx—Batted for Gillenwater in ninth.

SCORE BY INNINGS

San Francisco ....0 1 0 1 1 2 0 0 0—5
Seattle ....1 0 0 0 0 0 0 4 1—6

SUMMARY

Errors—Caveney, Yelle, Nixon. Innings pitched—By O'Doul 7 1-3, by Francis 8 1-3, by Gillenwater 2-3. Stolen bases—Eldred, Bates. Home run—Kelly. Three-base hit—Nixon. Two-base hits—Kelly, Ellison, Fitzgerald, Kamm, Kenworthy 2, Caveney, Yelle.

NATIONAL LEAGUE

At Cincinnati (first game)— R. H. E.
Chicago ....0 0 0 3 0 0 1 1 0 0 0 2—7 14 2
Cincinnati ..0 0 0 1 1 0 2 1 0 0 0 0—5 11 1
Batteries—Jones, Freeman and O'Farrell; Markle, Rixey and Hargrave.

At Cincinnati (second game)— R. H. E.
Chicago ....0 0 7 0 0 0—7 7 0
Cincinnati ....0 0 0 0 0 0—0 4 2
Batteries—York, Cheves and O'Farrel; Clark and Douglas.

At St. Louis— R. H. E.
Pittsburg ....2 0 0 0 0 0 0 2 0—4 10 1
St. Louis ....0 0 0 0 2 0 1 0 0—3 11 0
Batteries—Cooper and Schmidt; North, Bailey, Pertica and Clemons.

At Brooklyn— R. H. E.
New York ....1 0 0 0 3 0 0 0 0—4 13 3
Brooklyn ....0 4 0 0 1 2 0 0 x—7 8 3

AMERICAN ASSOCIATION

Toledo, 5-3; Minneapolis, 11-8.
Louisville, 5-3; Milwaukee, 2-9.
Indianapolis, 9-5; Kansas City, 3-2.
Columbus, 9-0; St. Paul, 1-8.

WORLD TITLES CAPTURED BY YANKEES

Opposing Nations Shoved Into Discard by Americans; Rickard Pulls One on Middleweight Go

By ROBERT EDGREN

If you want to glance at the names of a few champions just turn the pages of the 1921 record book over in the direction of Uncle Sam.

Never in the history of sport events has one country swept opposing nations aside as has the United States during the past year. Practically every championship has been taken by the Yankees.

GRABS 'EM ALL

So far this year Uncle Sam has only won the international speed boat race, retained the heavyweight boxing championship, won back the American golf trophy, won the world's championships at rifle and trap shooting, lifted the polo cup in England, cleaned up visiting English athletic team, won the English tennis championship, won all five matches for the Davis cup in tennis, won the world's clay court championship in France, retained tennis and golf championships, won the British open golf championship, won the motoring Grand Prix in France, and completely busted up a varied lot of world's records in sprinting, distance running, broad jumping, auto horse racing, throwing a baseball, swimming, and so on.

And Babe Ruth has cracked his home run record again. He makes it tougher for himself year after year. Look at the job he has for next season.

MAKES ONE MISTAKE

Aside from that it has been a dull session.

Tex Rickard's one big mistake was the matching of Wilson and Downey. It only goes to show that sometimes the public is a better guesser than the best of promoters. Tex thought the Downey-Wilson go would be a good fight and draw a big house. The public guessed differently. So Tex lost about $50,000.

So far as I know, the only other sporting event Tex ever failed to cash on was the Dempsey-Brennan fight, and that was purely because he was too generous. Incidentally, Tex expected to see a good fight, and he outguessed the public, which didn't think Brennan would make much of a showing.

On an average, however, Rickard is a fairly successful promoter. If he didn't lose now and then his income tax would be a fright.

LOUISVILLE TO ENTER SERIES

CHICAGO, Oct. 3.—Louisville will represent the American association in the minor league championship series against the International league winners, President T. J. Hickey announced today.

The American association season closed yesterday. Louisville cinched the pennant in that circuit last week and wound up the season yesterday by taking the final game.

BASEBALL TEAMS TO PLAY FOR TITLE

The Haas-Cox nine and the A. Diamond squad will clash in a game Sunday for the Summer league championship. The two teams met yesterday and the contest resulted in a 6-to-1 victory for the Diamond nine.

C. W. TABLER WINS LOCAL CLUB SHOOT

Breaking 48 targets out of a possible 50, C. W. Tabler carried off the top honors in the shoot staged over the traps of the Los Angeles Gun club yesterday afternoon.

Martin Reese took second place honors by breaking 47x50, while Mrs. Greenfield and G. B. Warman tied for third with 45x50 each.

FIGHTING WORDS

BY Fane Norton.

The fans are taking kindly to the Jimmy Dundee-Bobby Ertle match at the Vernon arena tomorrow night, judging by advance reservations. It is doubtful if any boxer has appeared in more main events at Vernon than Dundee, and he has always proved to be a good drawing card. And Ertle himself is no weak box office attraction. The fans like a fellow who will get in and give his best, and that is what Ertle has always done at Vernon.

Dundee is favored to beat the youngster, but not without a mighty tough scrap. Dundee's habit of stepping just as fast as is necessary assures a good bout with a boy of the Ertle type, for Bobby will make him show his best every round to win.

One thing about Ertle that appeals to the fans is the fact that he can seemingly fight himself out, but still have a kick left for the finish. In previous matches Dundee, Coffey and other high class boys have found him a dangerous kid to take chances with.

Boxing semi-windups do not appeal to Young George. The local favorite was on top of the heap for so long that he got the habit and now he is out to stop Ray Neal and get back into the windup class. George promises to start his right hand working early and insists that he will keep it busy until Neal is knocked for a goal. All George needs to win back all his old following is to slam some tough gent for the count of 10, and he thinks he will turn the trick tomorrow night.

Chet Neff and Roy Sutherland are working easily for their main event bout at Hollywood Friday night. Both boys were ready to go last Friday, but the postponing of the show for a week necessitated their keeping on edge for an extra week. The entire Hollywood card has been held over and unless some boxer drops out will be staged just as originally planned.

COLLEGE GRID SQUADS AWAIT TOUGH GAMES AS REAL-SEASON OPEN

By RAY J. SMITH

With early practice games now a matter of history school and college football teams throughout the country tled down to hard work today in preparation for their struggles, which are on the schedule for Saturday afternoo

In most cases the college aggregations are ready for real tough battles, but on the other hand it is evident from recent showings that several squads will need a couple of more weeks' hard work before they reach perfection.

While it is a little early to secure a line on the true ability of the respective elevens it has been noticeable again this season that there undoubtdly will be few upsets. Teams which were figured as championship contenders two weeks are showing plenty of class, while some of the smaller schools, handicapped because of lack of material, are practically out of the running at the present time.

Teams in the Southern California conference will start on their 1921 schedule next Saturday. Two games are billed, Occidental meeting Whittier on the Quaker gridiron, and Redlands university, which defeated the Santa Fe shop team in their initial contest, 39-6, will stack up against the Southern Branch aggregation on the latter's field.

Coach Harry Trotter of the branch squad feels certain that he will have a winner this year. He has a dandy team and is pinning his main hopes on Rossell, a half. It will be remembered that Rossell threw quite a scare into the Redlands outfit a year ago, securing three touchdowns in the last 10 minutes of play.

"Gloomy Gus," Henderson's U. S. C. eleven, rated as the most powerful squad in the South, meets Cal. Tech. Saturday. The Trojans look like the goods again this year. They ran from the sailors at Bovard field urday, beating the U. S. S. Ar in the first struggle, 62 to 0, and ming the U. S. S. New York i other affair, 35 to 0.

The showing of the Universi California eleven against the Oly club Saturday was the talk of southern football world today. Bears scored but two touchd aganist the clubmen, winning b small score of 14 to 0.

Stanford, on the other hand away great, beating the Mare I Marines, 41-0.

Following are the score of so the important opening gridiron tests: U. of Washington 24, Army team 7; Oregon 7, Willia 3; Fleet 14, Nevada 13; Yale 14, mont 0; Harvard 3, Holy Cro Army 28, Springfield 0; New H shire State 10, Army 7, second Princeton 21, Swarthmore 7; cuse 38, Ohio University 0; State 24, Gettysburg 0; Lafaye Pittsburg 0; Dartmouth 26, Mi bury 0; Wisconsin 28, Lawren Michigan 44, Mt Union 0; Ohio 28, Ohio Wesleyan 0; Iowa 52, 14; Chicago 41, Northwestern 0; bash 9, Purdue 0; Notre Dam DePauw 10; Centre College 14, son 0; Cornell 41, St. Bonaventu Fordham 101, Washington 0; In 29, Kalamazoo 0; Minnesota North Dakota 0; Amherst 9, Co bia 7; Navy 13, North Carolina Bucknell 0.

Yankees Get Extension of Lease on Polo Grounds—Giants and Dodgers Win in West

Ban Johnson Comes to Aid Of Two 'Orphan Colonels'

Exact Terms Owners of Giants May Propose Not Known Yet, but They Are Expected To Be Reasonable; Ruth Will Be in Uniform To-day

By W. O. McGeehan

The Yankees will not be evicted from the Polo Grounds at the end of the year, as their crool landlords, Messrs. Stoneham, McGraw and McQuade at first threatened. Ban Johnson, president of the American League, came to the rescue of the two orphans, Colonels Ruppert and Huston, just as the landlords were bouncing them off the front porch and preparing to heave their trunks down on top of them.

While the two orphans were wondering who would cover them up with leaves yesterday a messenger dashed into the offices of the Yanks. "It is all off," sobbed Colonel Ruppert. "They are sending a truck to move Babe Ruth." With trembling fingers the colonel tore open the envelope and this is what he read:

"In conference with Mr. Stoneham yesterday and he agrees to let you stay at the Polo Grounds. He will arrive in New York next week to arrange final terms."

Last Gun of Strife

The message was signed Byron Bancroft Johnson. "We are saved," the two colonels shouted as they staggered down the stairs. And there you are. It looks as though the last gun had been fired in the internal strife in organized baseball and that the doves might as well start in nesting in the affidavit cannons.

Just what terms Charles A. Stoneham may propose the colonels cannot guess, but they are pretty confident that they will be reasonable enough. Ban Johnson came to the rescue of the Yankees as they were going down for the third time in the evictment seas, and he threw them a life preserver instead of an anchor.

It seems that among other things the late lamented Mays case started a lot of loose conversation. During the chatter there were a few threats about an abrogation of the national agreement and some wars that would cause organized baseball to do a more nervous shimmy than it did during the Federal League unpleasantness.

About that time the edict came from the Giant office that as soon as the Yanks worked out their current lease they would be thrown right out into the snow and that their household goods would be spilled right out on top of them. In keeping with this announcement the crool landlords of Coogan's Bluff came out recently with the ultimatum that after this season the Yanks would not be permitted to cavort over the nicely manicured lawns at the Polo Grounds.

Colonel Grabs Shovel

Whereupon Colonel Tillinghast L'Hommedieu Huston, vice-president of the Yanks and an engineer at heart, took off his coat and grasped his trusty shovel. The lust for building gleamed in his eyes and he called for bricks and mortar and cement and other toys that delight the soul of an engineer. But suddenly it seemed that the places for engineers to build in were scarce on the Island of Manhattan. The colonel had his shovel, but no room to work in.

In the meantime the Macedonian cry came up from the Yankee fans, "Who will save our orphans?"

"I will," Ban Johnson shouted. "I will save the two orphans from their crool landlords. They shall not be thrown into the raspberry bushes. I will save them." And he did.

The Yankee corps of physicians and surgeons visited convalescent row yesterday and brought back some more or less cheerful reports concerning the Yankee invalids.

Ruth, according to a consensus diagnosis, has recovered completely from the attack of housemaid's knee which first laid him low. But later he picked up a slight attack of croup from which he is still suffering. It seems that the slugger grew so rapidly that he never had time to accumulate the usual infantile diseases and they are all coming upon him now in a bunch.

Babe Smokes a Cigar

If this theory is correct Ruth will have to pass through measles, mumps, whooping cough, chicken pox and cholera infantum. When visited yesterday by Truck Hannah, the pale and interesting invalid was sitting up in bed and taking light nourishment from a cigar of his own manufacture. Despite the ravages which housemaid's knee have wrought upon his once massive form, the Babe asserts that he will be in uniform to-day and that on Sunday afternoon he will be poling them out of the lot. The news that Hap Felsch is within one of his home run record for the coming year is dragging the Babe out from his cot of pain.

Chick Fewster, another Yankee invalid, was setting on the front porch of the Yankee hospital eating tobacco and breathing defiance. Fewster announces that he will be out for practice on the first and that along about the fifteenth of June he will be actively engaged in assisting the Yanks toward the pennant.

There was no game at the Polo Grounds yesterday. Wind and weather permitting, there wil lbe a duel between Urban Shocker and Carl Mays this afternoon.

Moran Stops Another English Heavyweight

LONDON, May 21.—Frank Moran, of Pittsburgh, to-night knocked out Frank Goddard, the English heavyweight, in the second round of what was to have been a twenty-round bout. The fight took place in the Holborn Stadium.

The bout started with both men going at a fast pace. In the second round Goddard was floored twice for counts respectively of nine and eight, and then Moran landed a terrific right on the Englishman's jaw and he was counted out.

Kingsley Wins Track Meet

Kingsley School easily defeated the West Orange High School in a dual track and field meet on the former's New Jersey field yesterday by a score of 57 to 39.

Syracuse Wins at Lacrosse

SYRACUSE, May 21.—Syracuse defeated Cornell at lacrosse, 5 to 3, in an extra period game here to-day.

Colonel Huston Gets Citation From Pershing For Services Abroad

COLONEL Tillinghast L'Hommedieu Huston, part owner of the New York Yankees, yesterday received a citation from General J. J. Pershing, commander of the American Expeditionary Forces, for "exceptional and meritorious services" in the world war. The citation was dated March 15, 1920.

Colonel Huston was the first man in professional baseball to join the colors when the United States entered the war. He had seen previous service as a captain of engineers during the war with Spain. This time he entered the service with his old rank of captain, and was honorably discharged as a lieutenant colonel after serving eighteen months and in many major engagements overseas.

Four More Homers As Athletics Lose To Indians, 9 to 4

PHILADELPHIA, May 21.—Four home runs during to-day's 9 to 4 victory of Cleveland over Philadelphia ran the week's total of four base hits in the local park to thirteen, a record here for five playing days. Walker, who registered the first of the local team's two circuit drives to-day, has made three of the thirteen.

The Athletics bunched hits off Caldwell and took the lead in the first inning, but Smith's home run in the second tied the score and Manager Speaker's home run drive in the third scored two runners ahead of him and decided the game.

CLEVELAND (A. L.)	ab	r	h	po	a	e
Graney, lf	5	1	2	2	0	0
Chapman, ss	3	1	0	4	2	1
Speaker, cf	5	1	2	0	1	0
Smith, rf	5	1	1	2	0	0
Gardner, 3b	5	1	1	2	5	0
Wamsg's, 2b	4	0	1	4	1	0
Johnson, 1b	4	1	3	8	0	0
O'Neill, c	3	1	1	5	0	0
Caldwell, p	2	2	0	0	0	0
Totals	36	9	11	27	9	1

PHILADELPHIA (A. L.)	ab	r	h	po	a	e
Dykes, 2b	5	2	2	0	5	0
Thomas, 3b	5	0	3	1	5	0
Walker, lf	5	1	2	1	0	0
Witt, rf	3	0	1	3	0	0
Dugan, ss	4	0	0	2	1	0
Welch, cf	4	1	0	0	0	0
Perkins, c	3	0	1	2	1	0
Styles, c	1	0	0	0	0	0
Griffin, 1b	3	0	2	15	2	0
Bigbee, p	2	0	1	1	2	0
Hasty, p	1	0	0	1	1	0
*Burrus	1	0	0	0	0	0
Totals	37	4	12	27	17	0

*Batted for Hasty in ninth inning.

Cleveland	0	1	3	0	1	3	1	0	0	—9
Philadelphia	1	0	0	1	1	0	0	0	1	—4

Two-base hits—Johnston, Speaker, Gardner, Dykes, Witt, Bigbee. Home runs—Smith, Speaker, Walker, Dykes. Stolen base—Thomas. Sacrifices—Chapman, Witt. Double play—Gardner and Johnston. Left on bases—Cleveland, 5; Philadelphia, 8. Bases on balls—Off Caldwell, 1; off Bigbee, 3; off Hasty, 1. Hits—Off Bigbee, 9 in 5 1-3 innings; off Hasty, 2 in 3 2-3. Struck out—By Caldwell, 4; by Bigbee, 2. Wild pitches—Bigbee, Hasty. Losing pitcher—Bigbee. Umpires—Hildebrand and Evans. Time—1:52.

Brown Qualifies 15 and Tech 12 In College Meet

CAMBRIDGE, Mass., May 21.—A lively scramble for points which will decide the championship of the New England Intercollegiate Association to-morrow was indicated by the preliminary events of the annual title meet, which were held on Tech Field to-day.

Brown qualified fifteen men for the finals; Technology, 12; Boston College, Bowdoin, Williams and Wesleyan, 7 each; Amherst, 6; New Hampshire, 5; Holy Cross, 4; Tufts, 3; Vermont, Trinity and Massachusetts Agricultural College, 2 each; Bates, Middlebury and Maine, 1 each.

In the quarter-mile J. W. Driscoll, of Boston College, the champion, bettered his last year's time, winning in 51 seconds. Thomas King, of Holy Cross, in winning his heat in the half-mile, improved by a full second the winning performance of last year. King's time was 1 minute 58 3-5 seconds.

U. S. Amateur Golfers And Rules Body to Sail

The executive committee of the United States Golf Association, consisting of G. H. Walker, F. S. Wheeler and H. F. Whitney, who are going abroad for the rules conference with the committee of the Royal and Ancient Club of England, together with the contingent that will compete in the British amateur meet and against the Oxford and Cambridge Society, will sail to-day on the Coronia. The other members of the party are Robert A. Gardner, who is also on the rules committee; J. F. Byers, Nelson Whitney, Sam Graham, F. C. Newton, F. S. Douglas, Howard Maxwell and Stewart Stickney.

The Americans will be met at Plymouth by Mansfield and A. C. Croome, of the Royal and Ancient Club, and will proceed to London, where they are to be entertained by a committee of which Lord Riddell is chairman. The sub-committee of the Royal and Ancient Club on golf ball standardization is John L. Low, chairman; A. C. Croome, Stewart Paton, Angus Hambro and Cecil Hutchinson.

Record of Major League Clubs

NATIONAL LEAGUE

GAMES TO-DAY

New York at St. Louis.
Brooklyn at Pittsburgh.
Philadelphia at Chicago.
Boston at Cincinnati.

YESTERDAY'S RESULTS

New York, 2; Chicago, 1.
Brooklyn, 3; Cincinnati, 0.
Pittsburgh, 9; Boston, 0.
St. Louis, 3; Philadelphia, 1.

STANDING OF TEAMS

	W.	L.	Pct.		W.	L.	Pct.
Cin'nati	17	11	.607	Boston	11	12	.478
Pitt'gh	15	11	.577	St. Louis	12	15	.444
Brooklyn	13	10	.565	N. York	11	14	.440
Chicago	15	15	.500	Phila	11	17	.393

AMERICAN LEAGUE

GAMES TO-DAY

St. Louis at New York.
Detroit at Boston.
Cleveland at Philadelphia.
Chicago at Washington.

YESTERDAY'S RESULTS

Chicago, 11; Washington, 9 (10 ins.)
Boston, 8; Detroit, 3.
Cleveland, 9; Philadelphia, 4.
N. York-St. Louis (wet grounds).

STANDING OF TEAMS

	W.	L.	Pct.		W.	L.	Pct.
Cleve'd	20	8	.714	Wash'ton	13	15	.464
Boston	18	9	.667	St. Louis	12	14	.462
Chicago	15	11	.577	Phila	9	17	.346
N. York	14	13	.519	Detroit	7	21	.250

Ain't It a Grand and Glorious Feelin'? . . . By BRIGGS

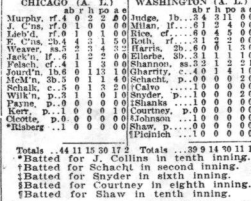

-AFTER YOU'VE SHOT THE PILL INTO EVERY TRAP AND BUNKER ON THE COURSE
- AND YOU'VE MISSED A LOT OF SHORT AND EASY PUTTS
- AND YOU'VE LOST A LOT OF BRAND NEW BALLS IN THE ROUGH
-AND ON THE 11TH YOU PUT ONE IN THE BROOK
PLUNK
- AND AS YOU WEARILY CLIMB THE STEEP HILL ON THE 18TH DECIDING TO GIVE UP THE GAME FOREVER -
- YOU MARCH RIGHT INTO THE LOCKER HOUSE AND GET UNDER THE SHOWER AND SOME-ONE HOLLERS THERE'S SOME-THING WAITING FOR YOU
OH-H-H- BOY!! - AIN'T IT A GR-R-R-RAND AND GLOR-R-R-RIOUS FEELIN'?
TA TATA TYA
Copyright N. Y. Tribune Inc.
BRIGGS

White Sox Again Take Extra-Inning Tilt From Senators

WASHINGTON, May 21.—The Chicago White Sox began hitting the ball in the first inning, kept it up through the tenth and won from Washington to-day, 11 to 9. Each team used four pitchers. A pass to Liebold, Eddie Collins's single and doubles by Weaver and Jackson gave the visitors their winning margin in the tenth.

The score:

CHICAGO (A. L.)	ab	r	h	po	a	e
Murphy, rf	4	0	2	2	0	0
J. C'ns, rf	0	1	0	0	0	0
Lieb'd, rf	0	1	0	1	0	0
E. C'ns, 2b	4	4	3	1	5	0
Weaver, ss	5	2	3	4	3	2
Jack'n, lf	6	1	2	2	0	0
Felsch, cf	4	1	1	3	0	0
Jourd'n, 1b	6	0	1	13	1	0
McM'n, 3b	5	0	1	1	4	0
Schalk, c	5	0	1	3	2	0
Wilk'n, p	3	1	1	0	1	0
Payne, p	0	0	0	0	0	0
Kerr, p	1	0	0	0	1	0
Cicotte, p	0	0	0	0	0	0
*Risberg	1	0	0	0	0	0
Totals	44	11	15	30	17	2

WASHINGTON (A. L.)	ab	r	h	po	a	e
Judge, 1b	3	4	3	11	0	0
Milan, lf	6	1	2	4	0	0
Rice, cf	6	0	4	5	0	0
Roth, rf	3	1	2	2	0	0
Harris, 2b	6	0	0	1	3	0
Ellerbe, 3b	3	1	1	1	1	0
Shannon, ss	3	2	1	2	2	1
Gharrity, c	4	0	1	4	1	0
Schacht, p	0	0	0	0	2	0
†Calvo	1	0	0	0	0	0
Snyder, p	1	0	0	0	2	0
‡Shanks	1	0	0	0	0	0
Courtney, p	0	0	0	0	0	0
§Johnson	1	0	0	0	0	0
Shaw, p	0	0	0	0	0	0
¶Picinich	1	0	0	0	0	0
Totals	39	9	14	30	11	1

*Batted for J. Collins in tenth inning.
†Batted for Schacht in second inning.
‡Batted for Snyder in sixth inning.
§Batted for Courtney in eighth inning.
¶Batted for Shaw in tenth inning.

Chicago	3	1	1	1	0	0	0	2	0	3	—11
Washington	1	0	0	2	0	3	0	2	0	1	— 9

Two-base hits—Judge, Weaver (2), Gharrity, Rice, E. Collins (2), Jackson. Three-base hits—Wilkinson, Felsch. Stolen bases—Rice (2), Felsch. Sacrifices—E. Collins, Gharrity. Double plays—Schacht, Gharrity and Judge; Weaver, E. Collins and Jourdan; E. Collins, Weaver and Jourdan. Left on bases—Chicago, 11; Washington, 11. Bases on balls—Off Schacht, 2; off Wilkinson, 6; off Snyder, 2; off Payne, 1; off Courtney, 1; off Kerr, 3; off Shaw, 1. Hits—Off Schacht, 5 in 2 innings; off Shaw, 3 in 2; off Snyder, 3 in 4; off Courtney, 4 in 2; off Wilkinson, 5 in 5 (none out, 2 on bases in sixth); off Payne, 3 in 1; off Kerr, 6 in 3 2-3; off Cicotte, none in 1-3. Struck out—By Snyder, 1; by Wilkinson, 1; by Payne, 1; by Courtney, 2; by Kerr, 1. Hit by pitcher—By Snyder (Felsch). Wild pitch—pitcher—Shaw. Umpires—Moriarity and Connolly. Time—2:38.

Red Sox Pound Pitchers Again and Defeat Tigers

BOSTON, May 21.—The Red Sox continued their heavy hitting to-day, pounding Dauss and Ayers and defeating Detroit, 8 to 3. Owens put eight of the visiting players off the bench for boisterous talk.

The score:

DETROIT (A. L.)	ab	r	h	po	a	e
Young, 2b	4	0	1	1	2	0
Ainsmith, c	5	0	2	5	3	0
Cobb, cf	5	0	0	1	0	0
Veach, lf	5	1	1	3	0	0
Heilman, 1b	4	0	2	11	0	0
Shorten, rf	2	0	0	0	0	0
Bush, ss	2	1	0	0	1	0
Jones, 3b	4	0	1	3	1	0
Dauss, p	2	0	0	0	3	0
Ayers, p	0	0	0	0	1	0
*Hale	1	0	0	0	0	0
†Flagstead	1	1	1	0	0	0
Totals	35	3	8	24	11	0

BOSTON (A. L.)	ab	r	h	po	a	e
Hooper, rf	4	2	2	1	0	0
McNally, 2b	4	1	3	1	1	2
Menosky, lf	4	1	2	3	0	0
Hendryx, cf	3	0	0	0	0	0
Hunter, cf	1	0	0	0	0	0
McInnis, 1b	4	1	3	9	0	0
Foster, 3b	4	1	3	4	1	0
Scott, ss	4	1	0	2	3	0
Walters, c	2	1	0	6	1	0
Russell, p	4	0	0	1	2	0
Totals	34	8	13	27	8	2

*Batted for Dauss in sixth inning.
†Batted for Ayers in ninth inning.

Detroit	0	0	0	0	0	1	0	1	1	—3
Boston	0	0	4	0	1	0	0	3	x	—8

Two-base hits—Jones, Flagstead, McNally, McInnis. Three-base hits—Hooper, Foster. Stolen bases—Veach. Sacrifice hits—Shorten, Walters, McNally. Double play—Walters and Foster. Left on bases—Detroit, 10; Boston, 6. Bases on balls—Off Dauss, 1; off Ayers, 1; off Russell, 4. Hits—Off Dauss, 7 in 5 innings; off Ayers, 6 in 3. Struck out—By Dauss, 3; by Ayers, 3; by Russell, 4. Wild pitch—Russell. Losing pitcher—Dauss. Umpires—Owens and Chill. Time of game—2:08.

Captain of Shamrock IV Arrives Here on Adriatic

Captain William P. Burton, who will be in command of Sir Thomas Lipton's Shamrock IV in the coming international yacht race, arrived here yesterday on board the steamship Adriatic. He was accompanied by his wife Emily, whom Captain Burton termed the best yachtswoman abroad, and Claude A. Hickman, who will also be aboard the Shamrock. It is Captain Burton's first trip to this country since 1894.

Robert McLean, the American professional champion ice skater, was also an arrival along with D. R. Scanlon, his manager. McLean did not offer any alibi for the loss of his world title to Oscar Mathiesen, of Norway, which competition, along with the other exhibitions in which he took part, netted McLean the sum of $51,000.

Johnston Headed East

SAN FRANCISCO, May 21.—William Johnston, tennis singles champion of the United States, left here yesterday for New York to join the American team that will compete for the Davis cup. The team will sail May 29.

American Association

St. Paul, 5; Louisville, 3.
Minneapolis, 9; Indianapolis, 1.
Milwaukee, 10; Toledo, 9.
Columbus, 6; Kansas City, 0.

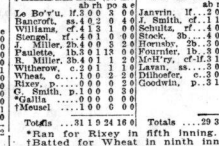

The SPORTLIGHT by Grantland Rice

(Copyright, 1920, New York Tribune Inc.)

Leading to a New One

Come, gather round me, little ones,
And give heed to my song;
I may detain you quite a while,
Or maybe not so long;
I have no idea just now
What I intend to say,
And yet I feel the time is ripe
To kick in with this lay.

There's nothing new on Speaker now,
Moran or John McGraw;
The Johnson boost is overplayed
And should be stopped by law;
The Babe Ruth punch is ancient stuff,
Like jeering at the Reds,
And panning magnates long ago
Was good for big type heads.

So, little ones, you may disperse;
I've had my little say;
There may be something new to shoot,
But not by me to-day;
To-morrow? Well, perhaps by then
We'll have a new, fresh crack—
Some sprightly dope in which we'll moan
For "Ty Cobb going back."

Proving What You Will

At the exact middle of May the Cleveland and St. Louis clubs of the American League were batting .290, with Cincinnati and St. Louis of the National League at .284.

This being above the average, it is evident that ballplayers hit harder in the spring than later on, when pitchers unfurl their kinks.

But on that same date the hard hitting Detroit club was registered at .213, with the supposedly hard hitting Giants and Pirates at .235.

Proving, in the main, that spring dope is full of knots, and that May is a long, long way from October.

Carpentier's Case

"Why should boxing fans have hissed Carpentier's name in a moving picture announcement?" questions a reader.

After Jess Willard won the championship from Jack Johnson he boxed but ten rounds between the spring of 1915 and July, 1919.

He spent most of his time in a circus, and from a chance for great popularity he fell to extreme unpopularity.

Jack Dempsey was never very popular with 4,000,000 members of the A. E. F. and the American Legion, and a good many others.

He lost additional friends when he left the boxing game after his Willard conquest to clean up in the movies.

Carpentier says that he came over to fight Dempsey and fulfill a motion picture and vaudeville contract.

The situation that he faced was a rasping one. Dempsey was held in check by his own government, and it was difficult to expect Carpentier to meet a second choice, where he had little to gain and everything to lose.

On the other wing, fight fans, recalling the careers of Willard and Dempsey, look for something different from the eminent Frenchman.

The multitude at large had grown weary of seeing champions desert their profession to mop up on the side.

Probably most of the complaining multitude would have done the same. But this doesn't alter the status of the squawk.

When they found there was little chance for Carpentier to fight over here a large peevishness immediately developed.

"Same old story" was the general comment.

It wasn't quite the same old story, with Dempsey, his main opponent, barred.

A Complicated Affair

It is a complicated affair all along.

The only victory that can add to Carpentier's credit is a victory over Dempsey.

The next best in sight looks to be Fred Fulton.

But Dempsey trimmed Fulton in less than 20 seconds. If Carpentier beat Fulton just how much added glory would he gain?

And yet there are large flocks of the populace who are not inclined to cheer the idea of any visitor coming over here to clean up a fortune without striking a blow.

One good battle over here would revive all his early popularity. But with him it is still a question as to whether this popularity is worth the chance of being beaten by a second choice—by some one who isn't champion.

"Have you made your reservations for the next world series?" writes an Ohio fan. "It will be very simple this fall, as the trip between Cleveland and Cincinnati is a simple one, requiring only a short ride." We'll bear the suggestion in mind and get busy accordingly.

Cadore Shuts Out Champions; Eller Batted From Box

CINCINNATI, May 21.—Buoyed by the reassurance of early help on the part of Outfielder Tommy Griffith, the Dodgers tore into the world's champion Reds here this afternoon and handed them a coat of kalsomine, 3 to 0. Lieutenant Leon Cadore, who figured all the way in the celebrated 26-inning tie at Boston a couple of weeks ago, pitched his first full game since that effort and proved conclusively that his good right wing was not damaged.

Cadore found no soft spot, for he had the tough assignment of taking on "Hod" Eller, one of the heroes of the last world's series. For Cadore it was simply a case of his side getting a run. Leon was never better, and he has often been great. He was invincible in the pinches, and there were plenty of pinches in the early innings. Cincinnati got five of the half dozen hits from Cadore in the first four innings.

The Dodgers won the game in the fifth by making five hits in a row for three runs. This feat knocked Eller right out of the pastime. Koney led off with a triple and tallied on Kilduff's single. Krueger singled to right. Then Cadore himself weighed in with a single that counted Kilduff. Krueger scratched a single through the box and Krueger scored. Ward hit into a double play; then Johnston skied to Neale.

The score:

BROOKLYN (N. L.)	ab	r	h	po	a	e
Olson, 2b	4	0	2	5	6	0
Ward, ss	4	0	1	2	4	0
Johnston, rf	4	0	0	3	0	0
Wheat, lf	2	0	0	0	0	1
Myers, cf	3	0	0	4	0	0
Konetchy, 1b	4	1	2	10	0	0
Kilduff, 3b	3	1	1	0	2	1
Kreuger, c	3	1	1	3	3	0
Cadore, p	4	0	1	0	4	0
Totals	31	3	8	27	19	2

CINCINNATI (N. L.)	ab	r	h	po	a	e
Rath, 2b	4	0	2	4	1	0
Daubert, 1b	4	0	1	11	0	0
Groh, 3b	3	0	0	2	4	0
Roush, cf	3	0	0	4	0	0
Duncan, lf	2	0	1	0	1	1
Kopf, ss	3	0	1	0	4	0
Neale, rf	3	0	0	2	0	0
Wingo, c	3	0	1	3	2	0
Eller, p	1	0	0	0	1	0
Luque, p	1	0	0	1	3	1
*Ruether	1	0	0	0	0	0
Totals	28	0	6	27	16	2

*—Batted for Luque in ninth inning.

Brooklyn	0	0	0	0	3	0	0	0	0	—3
Cincinnati	0	0	0	0	0	0	0	0	0	—0

Two-base hit—Ward. Three-base hit—Konetchy. Sacrifice—Myers. Double plays—Eller, Groh and Rath; Kilduff, Olson and Konetchy (2), Cadore, Ward and Kontechy. Left on bases—Brooklyn, 6; Cincinnati, 2. Bases on balls—Off Eller, 2; off Luque, 1; off Cadore, 1. Hits—Off Eller, 7 in 5 innings; off Luque, 1 in 4. Hit by pitcher—By Eller, 1. Struck out—By Eller, 2; by Luque, 1; by Cadore, 2. Losing pitcher—Eller. Umpires—O'Day and Quigley. Time—1:23.

Pirates Clout Eayrs And Win by 9 to 0

PITTSBURGH, May 21.—Eayrs was hit hard to-day by the Pirates, who defeated the Boston Braves by a score of 9 to 0.

After being touched up for fifteen hits and nine runs in five innings, Eayrs was relieved by Watson, a recruit pitcher, who held Pittsburgh hitless for the last three innings.

Carlson was effective at all times and received sensational support in the field.

The score:

BOSTON (N. L.)	ab	r	h	po	a	e
Powell, cf	4	0	0	2	0	0
Pick, 2b	3	0	1	1	2	0
Mann, lf	4	0	2	3	0	0
Cruise, rf	4	0	2	0	0	0
Holke, 1b	4	0	0	8	0	0
Boeckel, 3b	4	0	0	3	2	0
Maranv'e, ss	4	0	0	2	2	1
Gowdy, c	2	0	0	5	4	0
Eayrs, p	2	0	1	0	2	0
Watson, p	1	0	0	0	1	0
Totals	32	0	6	24	13	1

PITTSBURGH (N. L.)	ab	r	h	po	a	e
Bigbee, lf	3	1	2	2	0	0
Nicholson, lf	1	0	0	1	0	0
Carey, cf	5	0	1	3	0	0
Southw'h, rf	4	1	2	4	0	0
Whitted, 3b	4	2	1	0	1	0
Cutshaw, 2b	3	2	2	4	5	0
Caton, ss	4	0	1	1	8	0
Grimm, 1b	4	1	3	12	1	0
Schmidt, c	3	1	1	0	0	0
Lee, c	1	0	0	0	0	0
Carlson, p	4	1	2	0	1	0
Totals	36	9	15	27	16	0

Boston	0	0	0	0	0	0	0	0	0	—0
Pittsburgh	4	0	1	0	4	0	0	0	x	—9

Two-base hits—Carey, Cutshaw, Carlson. Three-base hits—Bigbee, Whitted. Double plays—Eayrs, Gowdy and Holke; Caton, Cutshaw and Grimm. Left on bases—Boston, 7; Pittburgh, 5. Bases on balls—Off Eayrs, 2; off Carlson, 2. Hits—Off Eayrs, 15 in 5 innings; off Watson, none in 3; off Carlson, 6 in 9. Struck out—By Eayrs, 1; by Watson, 1. Winning pitcher—Carlson. Losing pitcher—Eayrs. Umpires—Klem and Emslie. Time—1:30.

Jeff Tesreau to Pitch

Jeff Tesreau, former pitcher of the New York Giants, will appear on the mound in the opening game of a double-header at Dyckman Oval to-morrow afternoon, when Jeff's Bears will meet the Bacharach Giants. Tesreau's opponent in the box will be "Cannonball" Dick Redding.

Lowdermilk Released

CHICAGO, May 21.—Grover Lowermilk, pitcher of the Chicago White Sox, to-day was released to the Minneapolis Club of the American Association.

Gerner Quits Champions

CINCINNATI, May 21.—Pitcher Edward Gerner, a left-hander, jumped the champion Reds to-day to join the outlaw club at Franklin, Pa.

Toney Pitches McGraw Men To 2-1 Victory

Lefty Tyler Also Makes Good Showing on Mound; Robertson's Error Is Costly

Special Dispatch to The Tribune

CHICAGO, May 21.—Manager McGraw and his New York Giants wound up their four-game series with the Chicago Cubs here to-day with a close victory at 2 to 1. The game brought out a pitchers' battle between Fred Toney, of the invaders, and Lefty Tyler, with the Giant representative giving the more impressive performance. Although defeated, Tyler showed Manager Mitchell of the Cubs that he was rapidly rounding to form. It was Tyler's first appearance in the box since the middle of April.

The Giants scored their winning run in the ninth inning after Tyler had tied matters in the eighth with a triple. Killefer's poor throw to catch Young napping at second in the opening inning gave the Giants their first run. Although the Giant batsmen nicked the local twirler for a total of ten hits it was not until the final frame that they could bunch their hits to record the winning tally.

Two triples were among the seven hits gathered from the offerings of Toney, one of which was accounted for by Robertson, the former Giant outfielder. Toney was invincible in the pinches. But it was an error by Robertson in the ninth that aided King Lear to reach home with the winning tally.

The Giants' run in the first was started on its way when Young singled. Killifer threw high to catch Young attempting to steal second and the runner reached third. Fletcher then doubled to right, scoring Young, but when Artie attempted to stretch the hit into a triple he was out, Paskert to Terry to Deal.

The Cubs gathered three hits in the second but nary a run was the fruit therefrom, as Toney caught a runner off first. Barber singled and Robertson flied to Young. A snap throw from Toney caught Barber napping and he was run down. Deal and Terry singled in succession but Toney forced Killefer to fly out to Burns.

From here on Tyler and Toney settled down to a pitching duel. Toney held the local batters in check until the eighth, when Tyler drove a three bagger to center field and had barely caught his wind when Flack chased him home with a single to left.

The series proved a profitable one for the Giants, for they captured three of the four, losing only to Alexander, who, incidentally, thereby recorded his eighth straight victory. Immediately after the game the Giants left for St. Louis to play their last series of the Western trip before returning home.

The score:

NEW YORK (N. L.)	ab	r	h	po	a	e
Burns, lf	4	0	1	5	0	0
Young, rf	3	1	1	2	0	0
Fletcher, ss	4	0	1	4	3	0
Doyle, 2b	4	0	2	1	1	0
Kauff, cf	2	0	0	1	0	0
Lear, 3b	4	1	1	0	2	0
Kelly, 1b	3	0	2	7	1	0
Snyder, c	2	0	1	7	2	0
Toney, p	3	0	1	0	2	0
Totals	29	2	10	27	11	0

CHICAGO (N. L.)	ab	r	h	po	a	e
Flack, rf	4	0	1	2	1	0
Hollocher, ss	2	0	0	4	4	0
Paskert, cf	4	0	0	2	0	0
Barber, 1b	4	0	2	9	0	0
Robertson, lf	3	0	1	0	0	1
Deal, 3b	4	0	1	2	6	0
Terry, 2b	4	0	1	3	4	0
Killefer, c	3	0	0	5	4	1
Tyler, p	3	1	1	0	4	0
Totals	31	1	7	27	23	2

New York	1	0	0	0	0	0	0	0	1	—2
Chicago	0	0	0	0	0	0	0	1	0	—1

Two-base hit—Fletcher. Three-base hits—Robertson, Tyler. Stolen base—Young. Sacrifices—Kauff, 2; Flack. Double plays—Deal to Terry to Barber; Deal to Hollocher to Barber. Left on bases—Chicago, 6; New York, 6. Base on balls—Off Tyler, 4; off Toney, 2. Struck out—By Tyler, 2; by Toney, 4. Umpires—Moran and Rigler. Time—1:42.

Umpire Banishes Rixey And Cards Beat Phillies

ST. LOUIS, May 21.—St. Louis took three out of four from Philadelphia by winning to-day's game, 3 to 1, bunching three hits with two passes of Smith in the sixth for two runs. Umpire Hart ordered Rixey out of the game in the fifth, when the latter, after being hit by a pitched ball, hurled his bat on top of the visitors' dugout, whence it bounded into the grandstand.

The score:

PHILADELPHIA (N. L.)	ab	r	h	po	a	e
Le Bo'v'u, lf	3	0	0	3	0	0
Bancroft, ss	4	0	2	0	4	0
Williams, cf	4	1	3	1	0	0
Stengel, rf	4	0	1	0	0	0
J. Miller, 2b	4	0	0	3	2	0
Paulette, 1b	3	0	1	13	0	0
R. Miller, 3b	4	0	1	1	2	0
Witherow, c	2	0	1	1	1	0
Wheat, c	1	0	0	2	2	0
Rixey, p	0	0	0	0	2	0
G. Smith, p	1	0	0	0	3	0
*Gallia	0	0	0	0	0	0
†Meusel	1	0	0	0	0	0
Totals	31	1	9	24	16	0

ST. LOUIS (N. L.)	ab	r	h	po	a	e
Janvrin, lf	2	0	0	2	0	0
J. Smith, cf	1	1	0	2	0	0
Schultz, rf	4	0	0	0	0	0
Stock, 3b	4	0	1	1	2	0
Hornsby, 2b	3	0	2	2	5	0
Fournier, 1b	3	0	2	9	0	1
McH'ry, cf-lf	3	1	0	5	1	0
Lavan, ss	3	0	2	4	0	0
Dilhoefer, c	3	0	0	2	2	0
Goodwin, p	3	1	1	0	4	0
Totals	29	3	8	27	14	1

*Ran for Rixey in fifth inning.
†Batted for Wheat in ninth inning.

Philadelphia	0	0	0	1	0	0	0	0	0	—1
St. Louis	0	1	0	0	0	2	0	0	x	—3

Two-base hit—Lavan. Three-base hit—Williams. Stolen base—Dilhoefer. Sacrifices—Le Bourveau, Rixey. Double plays—G. Smith, Wheat and Paulette; Hornsby and Fournier. Left on bases—Philadelphia, 7; St. Louis, 4. Bases on balls—Off G. Smith, 2; off Goodwin, 1. Hits—Off Rixey, 4 in 4 innings; off G. Smith, 4 in 4. Hit by pitcher—By Goodwin (Rixey). Struck out—By Rixey, 1; by G. Smith, 1; by Goodwin, 1. Losing pitcher—G. Smith. Umpires—Hart and McCormick. Time—1:55.

May Be No Observation Train for Big Regatta

POUGHKEEPSIE, N. Y., May 21.—Because of the car shortage and unless the West Shore Railroad reconsiders its decision there will be no observation train for the intercollegiate regatta here on July 1, for the first time in the history of the local races.

The railroad officials say they cannot tie up the main line of the road for eight or ten hours, in addition to taking so many cars away from business which the observation train uses. Efforts are now being made to induce the officials to reconsider this decision.

Word has been received here that the Wisconsin University crews will not be represented in the regatta this year.

Eastern League

All ames postponed; rain.

Five Leading Batters In Two Big Leagues

NATIONAL LEAGUE

Player, Club.	G.	AB.	R.	H.	PC.
Hornsby, St. L.	27	107	19	44	.411
Groh, Cinn.	27	108	24	41	.380
Daubert, Cinn.	26	101	17	36	.356
Le Baurveau, Phil.	20	67	7	22	.328
Myers, Bklyn.	24	93	12	30	.323

AMERICAN LEAGUE

Player, Club.	G.	AB.	R.	H.	PC.
Johnson, Cleve.	26	92	8	39	.424
Jackson, Chic.	26	105	12	40	.381
Jacobson, St. L.	26	93	14	34	.366
Weaver, Chic.	26	112	23	40	.357
Gerber, St. L.	26	84	8	30	.357

Willard in Town Seeking Another Dempsey Match

Jess Willard arrived yesterday to attend a banquet to former champions given by the International Sporting Club, also to tell the world that he wants a return match with Jack Dempsey. What he will do with it when he gets its remains to be seen. Those who saw the Willard-Dempsey bout at Toledo do not think that he will do much with it.

Always secretive, Willard refuses to admit that the return match is what he is after, but he has been in conference with Tex Rickard for some time. Jess announces that he weighs 270 pounds and that he is in the best of condition. He admits that he has been hankering for another chance when he says, "My farming and roughing it in the oil wells has kept me in fine shape so that I can regain the necessary ring condition should I decide to resume boxing at some later date."

There is no doubt that an effort will be made to bring Dempsey and Willard together again in New York when the new boxing bill becomes a law. The proposal of a Dempsey-Carpentier bout does not seem to be creating the interest it did at first.

Willard declared some time ago that he wanted the return match with Dempsey, but then he dropped back to his farm at Lawrence, Kansas. Now he is loose again and there is more than a likelihood that, Rickard will book the two actors of Toledo, provided, of course, Dempsey comes clean on the draft evasion charges.

Southern Association

Little Rock, 13; Mobile, 5.
Birmingham, 2; Chattanooga, 1.
Memphis, 5; New Orleans, 10.
Nashville, 2; Atlanta, 6.

Yankees Win Twice; Ruth Adds Another Homer—Giants Lose Holiday Games to Dodgers

Eight in Row for Hugmen; Rallies Defeat Senators

Babe Gets Twelfth Circuit Clout Off Walter Johnson in Second Game; Lewis, Hannah and Picinich Also Make Homers; Scores Are 7—6 and 10—7

By W. O. McGeehan

The Yankees came from behind twice yesterday and pounded the entire pitching staff of Clark Griffith's Senators into a state of insensibility, winning both games at the Polo Grounds. At the afternoon performance there were 38,688 customers—cash and otherwise—which makes a new record for attendance in the field below Coogan's Bluff. The stuffed stands and bleachers caused young Rip Collins, who saved the second game for the Yanks, to remark: "Gosh, what a lot of folks!"

Yesterday's performance made it eight straight for the Yankees and put them just a small fraction of a game behind the Boston Red Sox. It begins to look as though George M. Cohan, the sweet singer of Forty-second Street and Broadway, had chirped a mouthful when he warbled "The Yanks are coming." The scores were 7 to 6 and 10 to 7, respectively.

To make it a perfect day with the pièce de resistance, the happy ending and all that sort of thing, Babe Ruth got his twelfth home run of the season in the eighth inning of the second game. He plastered the ball against the frieze over the upper right field stands, scoring a couple of superfluous runs after Peckinpaugh and Meusel had won the game by hitting Walter Johnson for a couple of triples. This makes seventeen homers to go to the last year's record, and the season is still a mere infant.

"Speed King" Is Victim

The demonstration that followed will make anything that the most powerful lungs of the nation may do at the Chicago convention sound like a husky whisper. The wallop came just as the pessimists were beginning to remark, "Ruth ain't had a home run all day." As a matter of fact he hadn't and he was getting peevish about it until he finally landed it against Walter Johnson, who did not allow one homer last year.

The games were both a trifle loose, but filled with melodrama. The fact that the Yanks won both after they looked fairly well mussed up and much depressed figures well for the future of the team. They just naturally rubbed their way out.

Nearly everything that could happen in a couple of ball games happened out at the Polo Grounds yesterday. The Yanks once had to use a couple of singles and a double to move the ponderous Truck Hannah all the way around for a run. It the first game Babe Ruth did some right fielding that was more spectacular than any homer when he ran for the right center field gate and stopped a triple by Judge, catching the ball over his shoulder. Ping Bodie shocked the stands into a state of insensibility by bunting and beating the bunt.

But the sensation of the afternoon was Rip Collins, former inmate of Texas and late captain in the United States Army. Oldest inhabitants say that he is another Amos Rusie, and this time the oldest inhabitants may not be lying. He came in with the game lost for the Yanks, with Thormahlen and Shore beaten to a frazzle, and he stopped the Senators abruptly. He was so calm and matter-of-fact about it all that he seemed to put nerve into the whole Yankee team just when they appeared to have shuddered themselves right out of the ball game.

Three Homers in Morning

In the morning there were three home runs, and Ruth was not among the participants in the pasting. Lewis and Hannah got a couple for the Yanks, starting a little rally that just naturally tired Pitcher Shaw of the entire proceedings and caused him to retire to the showers in an effort to make the fit of ennui. Picinich got one in a ninth inning onslaught by the Senators that almost cost George Mogridge the victory. But the consistent pasters of the day were Peckinpaugh and Meusel. In the afternoon Peckinpaugh got a single, two doubles and a triple, which is considered a fair afternoon's work anywhere.

There were thousands turned away in the afternoon, but the crowd was handled in an admirable fashion by Inspector Cornelius Cahalane, of the Harlem district. There was not the slightest confusion and every ticket holder got into the grounds comfortably and got to his seat. When you consider the fact that over 60,000 were trying to reach the entrances, it was some feat.

In the morning game George Mogridge kicked his jinx in the slats again, though one careless inning nearly cost him the game and caused considerable anxiety to the early risers at Coogan's Bluff. There were about 15,000 of these, which comes fairly close to being a record for a morning Polo Grounds crowd for a ball game.

Peckinpaugh and Meusel started their breaking into the extensive rash of base hits in the first inning of the matutinal game. Peckinpaugh shot a double to left field and scored on Meusel's single to the same territory.

Pratt's Errors Costly

In the sixth the visiting Solons started to come across. Shaw was beaned by a fast one and got his base. Judge got a single and Milan shot one down to Pratt, who made a bad throw to Peckinpaugh. The runner was safe. Shaw scored and Judge went to third. A long fly by Rice scored Judge. Roth lifted a double to left and scored Milan.

The Yanks clubbed their way out of the hole in their half of the same inning and they clubbed with such vehemence that Shaw probably never will look the same. The inning started very inauspiciously, for Ruth struck out, but up came the reserves.

Bodie forced Pratt, who singled, and made it two out as the carnage started. Duffy Lewis drove a homer into the left field stands. It was so close to the foul line that the Senators came in to debate the issue, but the hit was a homer and all protests were vetoed. Immediately afterward Truck Hannah lashed a homer into the same stands and there was no argument about this one.

George Mogridge wanted to make it certain and slammed a triple against the right field wall. Peckinpaugh pushed a hit past third, scoring Mogridge. Peck stole second. Meusel lifted a triple to left center, scoring Peckinpaugh and sending Shaw right away from vicinity of Coogan's Bluff.

Tie It Up in Ninth

It looked like a cinch for the Yanks after that until the ninth, when the Senators came from under the pile and tied it up in a melodramatic fashion. Ellerbe got a base on balls and "River" Shannon just made one flow into right for a single. Picinich then dug his toes into the grit and swung. The ball went into the left field bleachers and the score was tied.

But the Yanks came bobbing up again in their half of the ninth. Meusel did it once more. He got a single to right. Then Pipp laid down a neat bunt and beat it to first. Ellerbe, making a desperate effort to cut him off, made a wild throw and Meusel continued to trip around the bases until he crossed the plate with the winning run.

The afternoon game was another thriller. The Yanks looked so badly beaten at one point that the big crowd started to jeer and the two doughty colonels, Ruppert and Huston, were looking for the nearest exit. In the eighth inning their equanimity was entirely restored and the multitude was busily engaged in repairing the cracked pedestal of the Yanks. That is the way of the game. The bum of the first inning may be the idol of the ninth, and vice versa.

Thormahlen looked soft for the Senators as early as the second inning, when Ellerbe, Shannon and Gharrity had pasted him for a hit for one run. But the Yankees came right back in their half with three runs. Pratt got a base on balls and Ping Bodie sent him to third with a double. Pratt might have come home on the blow, but Ellerbe tricked him into pulling up by making motions as though he were about to receive the throw. Duffy Lewis came through with a double to left and Pratt and Bodie scored.

Peckinpaugh put his first double of the second game into the dial of the Ingersoll clock and Lewis scored. This caused Clarke Griffith to remove Courtney from the box with some abruptness.

In the third inning the Senators retaliated by giving young Herbert Thormahlen the beating of his career. Milan beat a hit to the box. With Rice out, Roth singled to right, sending Milan to third. Then George Duffy Lewis encountered a calamity that seemed to stun him. Harris singled to right and Duffy let the ball go through him. It went so rapidly that Duffy stood there paralyzed, while the entire trio of Senators romped across the plate as Ping Bodie pursued the elusive pellet through the tall green grass. Thormahlen knocked off for the afternoon and Long Ernie Shore took up the load of misfortune that he flung behind him.

Wake Up in Fourth

More terrible things happened in the fourth. Judge got a hit to left, and got to third on a couple of outs. Roth scored him with a hit to center. Roth proceeded to steal second and third from directly under the two noses of the Yankee battery. Harris got a base on balls. Then Roth and Harris tried the double steal. Shore stood and held the ball as though the play were something new to him, and he was still holding it in amazement as Roth crossed the plate. Ellerbe cracked a double to left and scored Harris.

The Yanks quickly disposed of Snyder in their half of the fourth. Lewis hit to left, Hannah walked and Collins advanced with a sacrifice. Peckinpaugh was passed and Meusel scored two runs with a hit to left. The Washington battery was switched to Johnson and Picinich.

In the sixth the Yanks tied it up and accomplished the difficult feat of driving Truck Hannah all the way around with hits. Truck started with a single. Peckinpaugh tried to ram him along to third, but Truck made second. Meusel propelled Hannah all the way to third with another mighty blow. Pipp drove him home with Peckinpaugh right behind, tieing it up with a hit to left.

The last onslaught on the overworked Walter Johnson came in the eighth, when Peckinpaugh and Meusel tripled in turn and Ruth made it official with the daily home run.

The Scores

MORNING GAME

WASHINGTON (A. L.)

	ab	r	h	po	a	e
Judge, 1b	5	1	2	6	1	0
Milan, lf	4	1	0	3	0	0
Rice, cf	3	0	1	4	0	0
Roth, lf	4	0	1	2	0	0
Harris, 2b	4	0	0	1	1	0
Ellerbe, 3b	3	1	0	3	3	1
Shannon, ss	4	1	1	0	3	0
Picinich, c	4	1	1	4	0	0
*Carlson	2	0	1	0	0	0
Shaw, p	1	1	0	1	1	0
†Shanks	0	0	0	0	0	0
‡Schacht	0	0	0	0	0	0
Totals	34	6	7	§24	9	1

NEW YORK (A. L.)

	ab	r	h	po	a	e
Peck'gh, ss	5	2	2	2	2	0
Meusel, 3b	5	1	3	1	2	0
Pipp, 1b	5	0	2	12	0	0
Ruth, rf	3	0	0	3	0	0
Pratt, 2b	4	1	1	2	4	2
Bodie, cf	4	0	2	2	0	0
Lewis, lf	4	1	1	2	0	0
Hannah, c	4	1	2	3	0	0
Mogridge, p	4	1	1	0	2	0
Totals	38	7	14	27	10	2

*Relieved Shaw in sixth inning (2 out).
†Ran for Carlson in ninth inning.
‡Relieved Carlson in ninth inning.
§None out when winning run was scored.

Washington.. 0 0 0 0 0 3 0 0 3—6
New York... 0 0 1 0 0 5 0 0 1—7

Two-base hits—Rice, Peckinpaugh, Roth. Three-base hits—Hannah, Meusel, Mogridge. Home runs—Lewis, Hannah, Picinich. Stolen base—Peckinpaugh. Sacrifice—Rice. Left on bases—New York, 8; Washington, 4. Bases on balls—Off Shaw, 1; off Mogridge, 1. Hits—Off Shaw, 11 in 5 2-3 innings; off Carlson, 1 in 2 1-3; off Schacht, none in 1. Hit by pitcher—By Mogridge (Shaw). Struck out—By Mogridge, 2; by Shaw, 3; by Carlson, 1. Winning pitcher—Mogridge. Losing pitcher—Schacht. Umpires—Chill and Owens. Time of game—2 hours.

AFTERNOON GAME

WASHINGTON (A. L.)

	ab	r	h	po	a	e
Judge, 1b	5	1	1	11	1	0
Milan, lf	5	1	1	1	0	0
Rice, cf	3	0	0	3	0	0
Roth, rf	5	2	3	2	0	0
Harris, 2b	4	2	1	1	2	0
Ellerbe, 3b	4	1	2	1	1	0
Shannon, ss	4	0	2	0	3	0
Gharrity, c	2	0	1	2	1	0
Courtney, p	1	0	0	0	1	0
Snyder, p	1	0	0	0	1	0
Johnson, p	1	0	0	0	1	0
Picinich, c	2	0	1	3	0	0
Totals	37	7	12	24	11	0

NEW YORK (A. L.)

	ab	r	h	po	a	e
Peck'p'h, ss	4	2	4	2	4	0
Meusel, 3b	5	1	3	1	2	1
Pipp, 1b	5	0	2	14	2	0
Ruth, rf	5	1	1	1	0	0
Pratt, 2b	4	1	1	0	5	0
Bodie, cf	4	1	1	0	0	1
Lewis, lf	4	2	2	4	0	1
Hannah, c	3	2	1	3	0	0
Thorm'n, p	1	0	0	1	0	0
Shore, p	0	0	0	0	2	0
Collins, p	2	0	0	1	3	0
Totals	37	10	15	27	18	3

Washington. 0 1 3 3 0 0 0 0 0—7
New York.. 0 3 0 2 0 2 0 3 x—10

Two-base hits—Peckinpaugh (2), Bodie, Lewis, Ellerbe, Picinich. Three-base hits—Peckinpaugh, Meusel. Home run—Ruth. Stolen bases—Rice, Roth (4), Harris. Sacrifice—Collins. Double play—Collins and Pipp. Left on bases—Washington, 7; New York, 7. Bases on balls—Off Shore, 2; off Courtney, 1; off Snyder, 2; off Collins, 1. Hits—Off Courtney, 5 in 1 2-3 innings; off Thormahlen, 6 in 2 1-3; off Snyder, 3 in 1 2-3; off Shore, 3 in 1 1-3; off Johnson, 7 in 4 2-3; off Collins, 3 in 5 1-3. Hit by pitcher—By Thormahlen (Rice). Struck out—By Thormahlen, 1; by Courtney, 1; by Johnson, 1; by Collins, 2. Wild pitch—Courtney. Winning pitcher—Collins. Losing pitcher—Johnson. Umpires—Owens and Chill. Time of game—2:20.

St. John's Nine Wins

St. John's College defeated Brooklyn Polytechnic Institute at baseball yesterday on St. John's Field by a score of 12 to 2.

Five Leading Batters In Two Big Leagues

AMERICAN LEAGUE

Player, Club.	G.	AB.	R.	H.	PC.
Speaker, Cleve....	37	136	39	53	.390
Jackson, Chicago.	32	129	16	48	.372
Johnston, Cleve....	35	128	12	47	.367
Judge, Wash'ton...	37	158	31	56	.354
Hendryx, Boston..	37	141	24	50	.353

NATIONAL LEAGUE

Player, Club.	G.	AB.	R.	H.	PC.
Hornsby, St. Louis.	39	155	31	62	.400
Groh, Cincinnati..	38	149	30	54	.362
Robertson, Chicago	34	125	17	45	.360
Daubert, Cin'nati.	37	142	26	48	.338
Williams, Phila...	38	154	26	51	.331

Yankee Home Run Hitters of Yesterday

Leading Indians Outscore Tigers In Both Contests

CLEVELAND, May 31.—The Indians made it two straight from the Detroit Tigers to-day, winning the morning game 9 to 5 and the afternoon contest 7 to 3.

In the morning game the Indians came up from behind and won by terrific hitting. Speaker and Gardner excelled at the bat, the former making a double and three singles in four times up, while Gardner made two doubles and a home run, driving in five runs. Detroit knocked Myers out of the box but as stopped by Niehaus.

The scores:

MORNING GAME

DETROIT (A. L.)

	ab	r	h	po	a	e
Young, 2b	5	1	1	1	6	0
Jones, 3b	2	1	0	0	5	0
Cobb, cf	3	2	2	2	0	0
Veach, lf	2	0	1	2	0	0
Heilman, 1b	4	0	1	11	0	0
Flagstead, rf	3	0	0	1	0	0
Bush, ss	3	1	1	[illegible]	4	0
Stanage, c	2	0	0	5	2	0
Dauss, p	3	0	2	0	2	0
*Ellison	1	0	0	0	0	0
†Pinelli	1	0	0	0	0	0
Totals	29	5	8	24	19	0

CLEVELAND (A. L.)

	ab	r	h	po	a	e
Jamieson, lf	5	1	1	4	0	0
Chapman, ss	5	1	3	2	4	0
Speaker, cf	4	2	4	3	0	1
Smith, rf	5	1	1	2	0	0
Gardner, 3b	4	2	3	1	3	0
Wambs's, 2b	3	0	0	3	2	0
Johnston, 1b	4	1	1	11	0	0
O'Neill, c	4	1	2	1	0	0
Myers, p	0	0	0	0	3	0
Niehaus, p	3	0	2	0	0	0
Totals	37	9	17	27	12	1

*Batted for Dauss in ninth inning.
†Batted for Jones in ninth inning.

Detroit...... 2 1 0 0 2 0 0 0 0—5
Cleveland... 2 0 0 0 1 2 2 2 x—9

Two-base hits—Young, Speaker, Gardner (2), Jamieson. Three-base hit—O'Neill. Home run—Gardner. Stolen base—Veach. Sacrifices—Young, Stanage (2), Veach, Wambsganss, Speaker. Double plays—Chapman (unassisted); Chapman, Wambsganss and Johnston (2); Young, Bush and Heilman. Left on bases—Detroit, 6; Cleveland, 9. Bases on balls—Off Dauss, 3; off Niehaus, 5. Hits—Off Myers, 5 in 1 1-3 innings; off Niehaus, 3 in 7 2-3. Struck out—By Dauss, 4; by Niehaus, 1. Wild pitch—Myers. Winning pitcher—Niehaus. Umpires—Nallin and Dinneen. Time of game—2:05.

AFTERNOON GAME

DETROIT (A. L.)

	ab	r	h	po	a	e
Young, 2b	3	0	1	2	0	0
Jones, 3b	5	1	0	3	1	0
Cobb, cf	5	1	3	2	0	0
Veach, lf	4	0	0	2	0	0
Heilman, 1b	4	1	3	8	0	0
Shorten, rf	3	0	3	3	1	0
Bush, ss	4	0	1	1	4	1
Ainsmith, c	2	0	0	2	0	0
Stanage, c	1	0	0	0	0	1
Ayers, p	2	0	1	0	1	0
Alten, p	0	0	0	0	0	0
Glaizier, p	0	0	0	1	0	0
*Flagstead	1	0	0	0	0	0
†Ellison	1	0	1	0	0	0
‡Pinelli	1	0	0	0	0	0
Totals	37	3	13	24	7	2

CLEVELAND (A. L.)

	ab	r	h	po	a	e
Jamieson, lf	4	0	1	2	0	0
Chapman, ss	3	1	0	4	2	0
Speaker, cf	4	2	2	7	0	0
Smith, rf	3	1	1	1	0	0
Wood, rf	0	0	0	1	0	0
Gardner, 2b	2	0	1	0	2	0
Wam'nss, 2b	2	1	1	1	4	0
Johnston, 1b	4	0	1	9	0	0
O'Neill, c	3	0	0	2	0	0
Bagby, p	3	1	1	0	1	0
§Burns	1	1	0	0	0	0
Totals	29	7	8	27	9	0

*Batted for Ainsmith in sixth inning.
†Batted for Ayers in seventh inning.
‡Batted for Alten in eighth inning.
§Batted for Smith in seventh inning.

Detroit...... 0 0 0 0 0 0 0 1 2—3
Cleveland... 0 0 0 2 2 1 2 0 x—7

Two-base hits—Cobb, Ellison, Shorten, Heilman. Home run—Speaker. Stolen bases—Chapman, Burns, Gardner. Sacrifices—Shorten, Bush, Young, Gardner, Jamieson. Double plays—Bush and Heilman; Shorten, Bush and Heilman. Left on bases—Detroit, 13; Cleveland, 6. Bases on balls—Off Ayers, 3; off Alten, 2; off Bagby, 3. Hits—Off Ayers, 7 in 6 innings; off Alten, 1 in 1; off Glaizier, none in 1. Hit by pitcher—By Ayers (Wambsganss). Struck out—By Ayers, 2; by Bagby, 2. Passed ball—Stanage. Losing pitcher—Ayers. Umpires—Dinneen and Nallin. Time of game—1:50.

Britton Beats Griffiths

AKRON, Ohio, May 31.—Jack Britton, champion welterweight, won the newspaper decision over Johnny Griffiths in a fifteen-round open air boxing contest here this afternoon.

American Association

Milwaukee, 10; Kansas City, 1 (a. m.)
Milwaukee, 4; Kansas City, 3 (p. m.)
Indianapolis, 2; Louisville, 1 (a. m.)
Indianapolis, 2; Louisville, 1 (p. m.) (16 innings).
Minneapolis, 12; St. Paul, 3 (a. m.)
Minneapolis, 4; St. Paul, 3 (p. m.)
Columbus, 3; Toledo, 2 (a. m.)
Toledo, 10; Columbus, 7 (p. m.)

Eastern League

Springfield, 2; Worcester, 1 (a. m.)
Springfield, 8; Worcester, 1 (p. m.)
Hartford, 5; Waterbury, 4 (a. m.)
Waterbury, 2; Hartford, 1 (p. m.)
New Haven, 6; Bridgeport, 2 (a. m.)
Bridgeport, 6; New Haven, 4 (p. m.)
Pittsfield, 5; Albany, 1 (a. m.)
Pittsfield, 8; Albany, 7 (p. m.)

Southern Association

New Orleans, 11; Nashville, 5 (1st).
Nashville, 2; New Orleans, 0 (2d).
Mobile, 6; Chattanooga, 3 (1st).
Chattanooga, 3; Mobile, 2 (2d).
Little Rock, 3; Birmingham, 2 (1st).
Little Rock, 1; Birmingham, 0 (2d).
Memphis, 0; Atlanta, 0 (6in., rain).

Pirates Triumph After Dropping First to Cards

PITTSBURGH, May 31.—The St. Louis Cardinals and Pirates divided honors to-day, the visitors winning the morning game by a score of 5 to 4 and losing the afternoon contest, 7 to 4. The scores:

MORNING GAME

ST. LOUIS (N. L.)

	ab	r	h	po	a	e
Shotten, lf	5	0	1	1	0	0
*Janvrin	1	0	0	0	0	0
McHenry, lf	1	0	0	2	0	0
Smith, cf	4	1	1	2	0	0
Heathc'e, cf	0	0	0	0	0	0
Stock, 3b	4	0	1	0	1	0
Hornsby, 2b	4	0	0	1	6	0
Fourn'r, 1b	4	0	2	12	1	0
Schult, rf	4	1	1	5	0	0
Lavan, ss	3	0	1	2	3	0
Clemons, c	4	1	4	1	1	0
Sherdel, p	3	0	0	1	2	0
Jacobs, p	0	0	0	0	1	0
Totals	36	5	11	27	15	0

PITTSBURGH (N. L.)

	ab	r	h	po	a	e
Southw'h, rf	4	0	1	0	0	0
Carey, cf	3	1	1	5	0	0
Cutshaw, 2b	3	0	0	2	3	0
Whitted, 3b	4	1	1	1	5	0
Nicholson, lf	4	1	2	1	0	0
Caton, ss	3	0	1	1	3	0
Grimm, 1b	4	1	1	12	1	0
Schmidt, c	4	0	2	4	1	0
Ponder, p	1	0	0	0	0	0
†Lee	1	0	0	0	0	0
Meador, p	0	0	0	1	1	0
‡Hinchman	1	0	1	0	0	0
§Bigbee	0	0	0	0	0	0
Watson, p	0	0	0	0	0	0
Cooper, p	1	0	0	0	0	0
Totals	33	4	10	27	14	0

*Batted for Shotton in ninth inning.
†Batted for Ponder in fifth inning.
‡Batted for Meador in seventh inning.
§Ran for Hinchman in seventh inning.

St. Louis.... 0 2 0 1 1 0 0 1 0—5
Pittsburgh... 0 0 0 0 0 0 1 3 0—4

Two-base hits—Shotton, Fournier, Carey, Clemons (2). Three-base hits—Smith, Nicholson. Stolen base—Southworth. Sacrifices—Cutshaw, Caton, Jacobs. Double play—Lavan, Hornsby and Fournier. Left on bases—St. Louis, 6; Pittsburgh, 7. Bases on balls—Off Sherdel, 2; off Jacobs, 1; off Watson, 1. Hits—Off Sherdel, 10 in 7 1-3 innings; off Jacobs, none in 1 2-3; off Ponder, 7 in 5; off Meador, 1 in 2; off Watson, 3 in 1 1-3; off Cooper, none in 2-3. Struck out—By Sherdel, 1; by Ponder, 2; by Cooper, 1. Wild pitch—Ponder. Winning pitcher—Sherdel. Losing pitcher—Ponder. Umpires—Hart and McCormick. Time of game—2:01.

AFTERNOON GAME

ST. LOUIS (N. L.)

	ab	r	h	po	a	e
Janvrin, lf	4	1	0	1	0	0
*Smith	1	0	0	0	0	0
Schultz, rf	5	1	1	1	0	0
Stock, 3b	2	0	0	1	2	0
Hornsby, 2b	5	1	3	2	6	0
Fournier, 1b	3	1	1	15	1	0
McHenry, cf	4	0	2	2	0	0
Lavan, ss	2	0	0	2	5	0
Clemons, c	2	0	0	0	3	0
Doak, p	4	0	1	0	1	0
Totals	32	4	8	24	17	0

PITTSBURGH (N. L.)

	ab	r	h	po	a	e
Southw'h, rf	4	2	1	1	0	0
Carey, cf	3	2	1	5	0	0
Cutshaw, 2b	2	1	1	4	2	0
Whitted, 3b	4	0	1	3	3	0
Nicholson, lf	4	1	3	0	0	0
Caton, ss	4	0	2	2	2	2
Grimm, 1b	4	0	0	6	1	0
Schmidt, c	3	1	1	6	4	2
Hamilton, p	0	0	0	0	0	0
†Hood	1	0	0	0	0	0
Cooper, p	1	0	0	0	1	0
‡Hinchman	0	0	0	0	0	0
§Bigbee	0	0	0	0	0	0
Carlson, p	0	0	0	0	0	0
Totals	30	7	10	27	13	4

*Batted for Janvrin in ninth inning.
†Batted for Hamilton in third inning.
‡Batted for Cooper in eighth inning.
§Ran for Hinchman in eighth inning.

St. Louis.... 0 1 2 0 0 1 0 0 0—4
Pittsburgh— 1 0 2 0 0 0 0 4 x—7

Two-base hit—Caton. Three-base hits—Hornsby, McHenry, Schmidt. Home run—Southworth. Stolen bases—Fournier, Carey (2), Cutshaw, McHenry, Lavan. Sacrifices—Stock, Clemons, Cutshaw. Double plays—Whitted (unassisted); Hornsby and Fournier. Left on bases—St. Louis, 9; Pittsburgh, 3. Bases on balls—Off Doak, 2; off Hamilton, 2; off Cooper, 3; off Carlson, 1. Hits—Off Hamilton, 4 in 3 innings; off Carlson, none in 1; off Cooper, 4 in 5. Hit by pitcher—By Doak (Hinchman). Struck out—By Hamilton, 2; by Cooper, 1. Winning pitcher—Cooper. Umpires—McCormick and Hart. Time of game—2:07.

Yale Beats Harvard at Golf

PROVIDENCE, May 31.—The Yale golf team defeated Harvard on the Rhode Island Country Club links here this afternoon, 6 matches to 3. Yale got all three points in the foursomes matches and three of the six in the individual play. The Yale freshman team beat the Harvard freshmen 11 to 7.

Home Run by Alex Extends His String To Eleven Straight

CHICAGO, May 31.—The Cubs and the Cincinnati Reds broke even today in the holiday double-header, the locals winning the morning game 3 to 2 in ten innings and the visitors taking the afternoon contest, 4 to 2.

Alexander's home run with two out in the last half of the tenth won in the morning. It also gave Alexander his eleventh straight victory and made it nine straight for the Cubs. Deal made a home run in the seventh which put Chicago in the lead temporarily, but the Reds tied the score in the eighth, when Alexander lost control for a few minutes.

Jim Vaughn, who started the afternoon game, was forced to quit because of a sore shoulder. Rallies in the seventh and eighth innings, when Cincinnati bunched hits, won for them.

The scores:

MORNING GAME

CINCINNATI (N. L.)

	ab	r	h	po	a	e
Rath, 2b	5	0	1	4	5	0
Daub't, 1b	4	0	2	13	0	0
Groh, 3b	5	1	1	0	6	0
Roush, cf	3	0	0	3	0	0
Duncan, lf	4	1	2	1	0	0
Kopf, ss	4	0	1	6	5	1
Neale, rf	4	0	2	0	0	0
Wingo, c	3	0	1	0	1	0
Fisher, p	4	0	0	0	3	0
Totals	36	2	10	*29	20	1

CHICAGO (N. L.)

	ab	r	h	po	a	e
Flack, rf	3	0	0	0	0	0
Twombly, rf	1	0	0	1	0	0
Hollocher, ss	4	0	0	7	6	0
Paskert, cf	3	0	1	1	0	0
Barber, lf	4	0	1	1	0	0
Merkle, 1b	3	0	0	15	1	1
Deal, 3b	4	1	1	2	1	0
Terry, 2b	4	1	1	2	7	0
Killefer, c	4	0	0	1	3	0
Alexander, p	4	1	2	0	4	0
Totals	33	3	6	30	22	1

*Two out when winning run was scored.

Cincinnati........ 0 1 0 0 0 0 0 1 0 0—2
Chicago........... 0 0 1 0 0 0 1 0 0 1—3

Two-base hits—Duncan, Daubert (2). Home runs—Deal, Alexander. Stolen bases—Duncan, Neale. Sacrifice—Killefer. Double plays—Kopf and Daubert (2). Left on bases—Chicago, 4; Cincinnati, 8. Bases on balls—Off Alexander, 4; off Fisher, 2. Struck out—By Alexander, 1. Umpires—Quigley and O'Day. Time of game—2:00.

AFTERNOON GAME

CHICAGO (N. L.)

	ab	r	h	po	a	e
Twombly, rf	3	0	0	1	0	0
*Flack	1	0	0	0	0	0
Friborg, rf	0	0	0	0	0	0
Hollocher, ss	3	1	0	2	4	0
Paskert, cf	3	0	1	0	0	0
Barber, lf	3	0	0	2	0	0
Merkle, 1b	2	1	1	15	1	0
Deal, 3b	4	0	1	1	4	0
Terry, 2b	4	0	3	1	7	0
Killefer, c	4	0	0	4	1	0
Vaughn, p	0	0	0	0	1	0
Martin, p	3	0	0	1	0	0
*O'Farrell	1	0	0	0	0	0
Totals	31	2	6	27	18	0

CINCINNATI (N. L.)

	ab	r	h	po	a	e
Rath, 2b	4	0	2	1	3	0
Daubert, 1b	5	0	0	12	1	0
Groh, 3b	5	0	1	1	2	0
Roush, cf	4	2	1	4	0	0
Duncan, lf	4	1	1	1	0	0
Kopf, ss	3	1	2	1	5	1
Neale, rf	3	0	1	3	0	0
Rariden, c	1	0	0	1	0	0
Wingo, c	3	0	1	3	1	1
Ring, p	4	0	1	0	2	0
Totals	35	4	10	27	14	2

*Batted for Twombly in eighth inning.
†Batted for Martin in ninth inning.

Cincinnati... 0 1 0 0 0 0 1 2 0—4
Chicago...... 0 0 0 0 0 1 0 0 1—2

Two-base hits—Paskert, Kopf (2), Merkle. Stolen base—Hollocher. Sacrifices—Barber, Merkle, Neale. Left on bases—Chicago, 7; Cincinnati, 8. Bases on balls—Off Ring, 3; off Martin, 3. Hits—Off Vaughn, 3 in 2 1-3 innings; off Martin, 7 in 6 2-3. Struck out—By Martin, 3; by Ring, 3. Losing pitcher—Vaughn. Umpires—O'Day and Quigley. Time of game—1:52.

Bears Split Double Bill

Jeff Tesreau's Bears broke even with the Paterson Silk Sox in a double header at Dyckman Oval yesterday afternoon.

The scores by innings:

		R.	H.	E.
Paterson Silk Sox.	0 0 0 1 2 0 0 1 3	7	9	2
Tesreau's Bears...	0 0 0 0 0 0 2 0 0	2	5	3

Batteries—Gaston and Wiley; Hanstein and Smith. Umpires—Tone and Adler.

		R.	H.	E.
Paterson Silk Sox.	0 1 0 0 0 0 0 1 0	2	8	2
Tesreau's Bears...	0 0 1 0 0 0 2 0 x	3	6	1

Batteries—Raymond and Pickering; Fullerton and Hebblewaite. Umpires—Tone and Adler.

Ledoux Knock Out Briton

LONDON, May 31.—Charles Ledoux, of France, to-night knocked out Jim Higgins, of England, in the eleventh round of a twenty-round bout. The bout was for the bantamweight championship of Europe, which is held by Ledoux.

Burns an Easy Victor

Frankie Burns, the Jersey bantamweight, easily defeated Freddie Jacks, of England, in the feature twelve-round bout at the Armory A. A., Jersey City, last night. In the semi-final Johnny Buff knocked out Willie Burns in the sixth round.

Record of Major League Clubs

NATIONAL LEAGUE

GAMES TO-DAY

New York at Brooklyn.
Boston at Philadelphia.
Cincinnati at Chicago.
St. Louis at Pittsburgh.

YESTERDAY'S RESULTS

Brooklyn, 5; New York, 2 (a. m.)
Brooklyn, 5; New York, 1 (p. m.)
Boston, 4; Philadelphia, 1 (a. m.)
Philadelphia, 3; Boston, 2 (p. m.)
Chicago, 3; Cincinnati, 2 (10 ins.) (a. m.)
Cincinnati, 4; Chicago, 2 (p. m.)
St. Louis, 5; Pittsburgh, 4 (a. m.)
Pittsburgh, 7; St. Louis, 4 (p. m.)

STANDING OF TEAMS

	W.	L.	Pc.		W.	L.	Pc.
Bklyn...	21	14	.600	Boston..	16	19	.457
Chicago.	24	16	.600	St. Louis.	17	22	.436
Cin'nati.	23	16	.590	N. York..	15	21	.417
Pittsb'g.	19	17	.528	Phila....	14	24	.368

AMERICAN LEAGUE

GAMES TO-DAY

Washington at New York.
Philadelphia at Boston (two).
Detroit at Cleveland.
Chicago at St. Louis.

YESTERDAY'S RESULTS

New York, 7; Washington, 6 (a. m.)
New York, 10; Washington, 7 (p. m.)
Boston, 3; Philadelphia, 1 (1st).
Philadelphia, 9; Boston, 4 (2d)
Cleveland, 9; Detroit, 5 (a. m.)
Cleveland, 7; Detroit, 3 (p. m.)
St. Louis, 2; Chicago, 0 (1st)
Chicago, 5; St. Louis, 3 (10 ins., 2d)

STANDING OF TEAMS

	W.	L.	Pc.		W.	L.	Pc.
Cleve...	26	11	.703	Wash....	19	18	.514
Boston..	22	14	.611	St. Louis.	14	22	.389
N. York..	23	15	.605	Phila....	13	25	.342
Chicago.	20	18	.526	Detroit..	11	25	.306

Douglas and Barnes Fail; Brooklyn in Tie for Lead

New York Pitchers Driven From Box in Both Games; Errors by Doyle and Fletcher Help Grimes and Mamaux Win by 5–1 and 5–2

By R. J. Kelly

Wilbert Robinson's Dodgers maltreated John McGraw's Giants at Ebbets Field yesterday by taking both ends of the holiday bill from the Manhattanites. The score of the morning game was 5 to 2, and that of the afternoon 5 to 1. The two-ply triumph made it five straight for the Flatbush aggregation and put them in a tie for first place with the Chicago Cubs. The Giants dropped back to seventh position.

The Giants were guilty of many errors of omission as well as commission and their poor playing was largely responsible for their double setback. The veterans, Doyle and Fletcher, were the chief offenders.

About 7,000 fans turned out to witness the morning tilt and 23,000 more were on hand for the matinee. The home rooters had many opportunities to exercise their lung power, as their favorites outclassed the visitors in all departments of the game.

The Dodgers drove Shufflin' Phil Douglas from the box under a fusilade of hits in the second inning of the mornig contest and shoved three runs across the plate. They nicked Jess Winters for two more in the fourth and had little difficulty in retaining their early lead.

Grimes Also Hits

Burleigh Grimes occupied the mound for the Brooklyns and, although he was found for eleven safeties, he was very effective in the pinches, and fanned seven. He also wielded his bat with a vengeance and got three hits in as many trips to the plate.

The Dodgers had no trouble in solving the curves of Jesse Barnes in the afternoon game, and they fell on him for nine hits during his seven-inning stay in the box. Three of these were bunched in the seventh, when the home players registered three runs. Douglas succeeded him in the eighth and prevented further scoring.

Al Mamaux was well nigh invincible in the afternoon engagement. He had the Giants completely at his mercy and allowed them only five hits. The former Pirate deserved a shut out, but two hits, coupled with a wild pitch, gave McGraw's men their run in the fifth inning.

The Brooklyn players ran wild on the bases as the New Yorkers threw the ball around with reckless abandon. Fletcher and Doyle failed to cover second base on several occasions when Smith threw to the bag to check an advancing runners. Three lightning a double steal Neis scored and Wheat critical stages.

Dodgers Start Well

The Dodgers got off to a good start in the second game and tallied in the first inning. After Olson had flied out to Burns, Neis singled to center. Johnston followed with a hit to right and Neis pulled up at second. Wheat then forced Johnston at second, Doyle to Fletcher, and Neis took third. On a doupble steal Neis scored and Wheat went to second as Smith made a poor throw to Fletcher.

Two successive fumbles by Doyle and a wild throw by Smith in attempting to catch Myers napping off second, gave the Flatbush clan another run in the sixth.

The Dodgers added three more runs in the seventh. Mamaux led off with a single over second base and scored a moment later on Olson's triple to deep center field. Neis drew a base on balls. Johnston flied out to Kauff and Olson scored after the catch. Wheat sent Neis to third with a scorching single to right center. Myers then grounded to Fletcher. The latter hit Neis on the head in attempting to throw him out at the plate, and the youngster was safe.

Giants Threaten in Ninth

The Giants threatened to stage a rally in the ninth, but a double play nipped it in the bud. Young, the first batter, singled over second. He was doubled off first a moment later when Fletcher hoisted a fly to Neis in right field. Doyle singled to center but Kauff ended the game by hitting a long fly to Myers.

The dodgers lost no time in getting under way in the morning game and they had chalked up four runs in the second inning. Wheat started the bombardment of Douglas with a single to right field. Myers sacrificed him to second. Mitchell smashed a triple to center, scoring Wheat. Kilduff's single sent Mitchell home. After Miller reached first on Fletcher's fumble, Grimes hit to right field, scoring Kilduff.

Shufflin' Phil was sent to the showers and Winters undertook to hold the Brooklyn sluggers in check. He fared little better and the Flatbush clan bumped him for two runs in the fourth. Hubbell relieved him in the seventh inning.

The Brooklyn aggregation suffered two near-casualties. Otto Miller was hit on the back of the head in the fourth inning of the morning contest and Zack Wheat twisted his ankle at second base in the second game. Both continued to play, however.

The Brooklyn club started a drive against ticket speculators and three were arrested by members of the detective bureau.

The Scores

MORNING GAME

NEW YORK (N. L.)

	ab	r	h	po	a	e
Burns, lf	5	1	2	4	0	0
Young, rf	4	0	2	2	0	0
Fletcher, ss	4	0	0	3	5	2
Doyle, 2b	4	0	1	0	3	0
Kauff, cf	4	0	1	0	1	0
Sicking, 3b	4	0	2	1	0	0
Kelly, 1b	4	1	1	10	0	0
Snyder, c	4	0	1	4	1	0
Douglas, p	0	0	0	0	1	0
Winters, p	2	0	0	0	1	0
Hubbell, p	0	0	0	0	0	0
*McCarty	1	0	1	0	0	0
†E. Smith	1	0	0	0	0	0
Totals	37	2	11	24	12	2

BROOKLYN (N. L.)

	ab	r	h	po	a	e
Olson, ss	4	0	0	4	3	0
Neis, rf	4	0	1	3	0	0
Johnst'n, 3b	4	0	2	1	2	0
Wheat, lf	4	1	1	0	0	0
Myers, cf	3	0	0	4	0	1
Mitchell, 1b	4	1	1	9	1	0
Kilduff, 2b	3	2	2	0	4	0
Miller, c	3	1	0	6	1	0
Grimes, p	3	0	3	0	3	0
Totals	32	5	10	27	14	1

*Batted for Winters in seventh inning.
†Batted for Hubbell in ninth inning.

New York... 0 0 1 0 0 0 0 0 1—2
Brooklyn.... 0 3 0 2 0 0 0 0 x—5

Two-base hits—Johnston, Burns. Three-base hits—Mitchell, Kilduff. Sacrifice—Myers. Double plays—Fletcher and Kelly; Miller and Johnston. Left on bases—New York, 8; Brooklyn, 6. First base on errors—Brooklyn, 2. Base on balls—Off Winters, 1. Hits and earned runs—Off Douglas, 4 hits, 3 runs in 1 2-3 innings; off Winters, 5 hits, 2 runs in 4 1-3; off Hubbell, 1 hit, no runs in 2. Hit by pitcher—By Winters (Miller). Struck out—By Grimes, 7. Umpires—Klem and Emslie. Time of game—1:35.

AFTERNOON GAME

NEW YORK (N. L.)

	ab	r	h	po	a	e
Burns, lf	4	0	0	4	0	0
Young, rf	3	0	1	0	0	0
Fletcher, ss	4	0	1	0	3	0
Doyle, 2b	4	0	1	4	1	2
Kauff, cf	3	1	1	1	0	0
Sicking, 3b	3	0	0	2	4	1
Kelly, 1b	2	0	1	7	1	0
Smith, c	3	0	0	6	1	1
Barnes, p	2	0	0	0	2	1
Douglas, p	0	0	0	0	0	0
*McCarty	1	0	0	0	0	0
Totals	29	1	5	24	12	5

BROOKLYN (N. L.)

	ab	r	h	po	a	e
Olson, ss	5	1	1	3	2	0
Neis, rf	3	2	1	2	2	0
Johnston, 3b	3	0	1	1	1	0
Wheat, lf	4	0	2	5	0	0
Myers, cf	4	1	0	6	0	0
Mitchell, 1b	4	0	2	5	0	0
Kilduff, 2b	3	0	0	3	1	1
Miller, c	3	0	0	2	1	0
Mamaux, p	4	1	2	0	0	0
Totals	33	5	9	27	7	1

*Batted for Barnes in eighth inning.

New York... 0 0 0 0 1 0 0 0 0—1
Brooklyn.... 1 0 0 0 0 1 3 0 x—5

Three-base hit—Olson. Stolen bases—Neis, Wheat, Myers, Mitchell. Sacrifices—Johnston, Kilduff, Miller. Double plays—Fletcher, Doyle and Kelly; Johnston and Mitchell; Miller and Olson; Neis and Mitchell. Left on bases—New York, 4; Brooklyn, 8. Bases on balls—Off Barnes, 1; off Mamaux, 3. Hits—Off Barnes, 9 in 7 innings; off Douglas, none in 1. Struck out—By Barnes, 4; by Douglas, 1; by Mamaux, 2. Wild pitch—Mamaux. Losing pitcher—Barnes. Umpires—Klem and Emslie. Time of game—1:43.

Braves and Phillies Get an Even Break

MORNING GAME

BOSTON (N. L.)

	ab	r	h	po	a	e
Powell, cf	3	0	0	2	0	0
Pick, 2b	4	1	2	4	6	0
Eayres, lf	3	1	3	0	0	0
Cruise, rf	2	0	1	1	0	0
Sullivan, rf	0	0	0	0	0	0
Holke, 1b	4	1	1	9	0	0
Boeckel, 3b	4	0	0	1	0	0
Maran'le, ss	4	1	1	5	4	1
Gowdy, c	4	0	1	5	2	0
Oeschger, p	4	0	0	0	2	0
Totals	32	4	9	27	14	1

PHILA. (N. L.)

	ab	r	h	po	a	e
Bancroft, ss	4	0	2	6	2	1
Williams, cf	4	1	2	4	0	0
Stengel, rf	4	0	2	4	1	1
Meusel, lf	4	0	1	0	1	0
J. Miller, 2b	2	0	0	2	6	2
Paulette, 1b	4	0	0	6	2	1
R. Miller, 3b	3	0	0	1	1	0
Witherow, c	3	0	1	4	3	0
Smith, p	2	0	0	0	1	0
*L'Bour'au	1	0	0	0	0	0
Weinert, p	0	0	0	0	1	0
Totals	31	1	8	27	18	5

*Batted for Smith in eighth inning.

Boston...... 1 0 1 0 0 0 0 0 2—4
Philadelphia. 0 0 0 0 0 0 0 1 0—1

Two-base hit—Cruise. Three-base hit—Eayrs. Home run—Williams. Sacrifices—Eayrs, J. Miller. Double plays—Maranville, Pick and Holke; Stengel, Witherow, J. Miller, Paulette, Witherow, R. Miller and Bancroft; Bancroft, J. Miller and Paulette. Left on bases—Boston, 5; Philadelphia, 5. Bases on balls—Off Oeschger, 1; off Smith, 2; off Weinert, 1. Hits—Off Smith, 7 in 8 innings; off Weinert, 2 in 1. Struck out—By Oeschger, 4; by Smith, 2. Losing pitcher—Smith. Umpires—Rigler and Moran. Time of game—1:43.

AFTERNOON GAME

BOSTON (N. L.)

	ab	r	h	po	a	e
Powell, cf	3	0	0	3	0	0
Pick, 2b	4	0	1	2	1	0
Mann, lf	4	0	1	1	0	0
Cruise, rf	4	0	2	3	1	0
Holke, 1b	4	1	1	6	0	0
Boeckel, 3b	4	0	1	2	1	1
Maranv'le, ss	4	0	1	3	6	1
O'Neill, c	1	0	0	0	0	0
*Christ'b'y	1	0	0	0	0	0
Gowdy, c	0	0	0	1	0	0
Eayrs, p	3	1	1	0	3	0
Hearne, p	0	0	0	0	1	0
Totals	33	2	9	24	14	3

PHILADELPHIA (N. L.)

	ab	r	h	po	a	e
Bancroft, ss	4	0	2	2	5	0
Williams, cf	4	1	1	0	1	0
Stengel, rf	3	0	1	1	0	0
Meusel, lf	4	1	1	4	0	0
J. Miller, 2b	2	1	1	2	3	0
Paulette, 1b	4	0	0	7	2	0
R. Miller, 3b	4	0	2	2	1	0
Tragresser, c	4	0	0	7	1	1
Meadows, p	3	0	0	2	2	0
Totals	32	3	8	27	15	1

*Batted for O'Neill in eighth inning.

Boston...... 0 0 0 1 0 0 0 1 0—2
Philadelphia. 0 0 3 0 0 0 0 0 x—3

Two-base hits—R. Miller, J. Miller, Holke, Maranville. Home run—Williams. Sacrifice—J. Miller. Left on bases—Boston, 5; Philadelphia, 8. Bases on balls—Off Eayrs, 1; off Meadows, 1. Hits—Off Eayrs, 8 in 7 innings; off Hearne, none in 1. Hit by pitcher—By Eayrs (Stengel). Struck out—By Eayrs, 4; by Meadows, 4. Losing pitcher—Eayrs. Umpires—Moran and Rigler. Time of game—1:57.

Red Sox-Athletics Divide the Honors In Double Header

BOSTON, May 31.—The Red Sox and Philadelphia Athletics divided honors in their double-header this afternoon. Pennock's superior pitching and his own single, which drove over two runs, accounted for Boston winning the first game 3 to 1. The visitors won the second game, 9 to 4.

The scores:

AFTERNOON GAMES

PHILA. (A. L.)

	ab	r	h	po	a	e
Dykes, 2b	4	1	1	3	2	1
Thomas, 3b	4	0	1	0	1	0
Walker, lf	4	0	0	3	0	0
Welsh, cf	3	0	0	0	0	0
Dugan, ss	3	0	2	4	4	0
Witt, rf	3	0	0	1	0	0
Griffin, 1b	3	0	0	7	0	0
Perkins, c	2	0	1	6	3	0
Naylor, p	3	0	0	0	1	0
*Styles	1	0	0	0	0	0
†Galloway	1	0	0	0	0	0
Totals	31	1	5	24	11	1

BOSTON (A. L.)

	ab	r	h	po	a	e
Hooper, rf	3	0	0	2	0	0
McNally, 2b	3	1	1	2	2	0
Menosky, lf	3	0	1	1	0	0
Hendryx, cf	2	0	1	1	0	0
McInnis, 1b	3	0	0	10	0	0
Foster, 3b	3	0	0	2	3	0
Scott, ss	3	1	1	2	3	0
Walters, c	3	1	1	7	0	0
Pennock, p	3	0	1	0	3	0
Totals	26	3	6	27	11	0

*Batted for Welsh in ninth inning.
†Batted for Witt in ninth inning.

Philadelphia. 0 0 0 0 0 1 0 0 0—1
Boston...... 0 0 0 1 2 0 0 0 x—3

Two-base hits—Dugan, Perkins. Three-base hit—McNally. Stolen base—Dugan. Double play—Dykes, Dugan and Griffin. Left on bases—Philadelphia, 4; Boston, 1. Bases on balls—Off Naylor, 2; off Pennock, 1. Struck out—By Naylor, 4; by Pennock, 7. Umpires—Hildebrand and Evans. Time of game—1:40.

PHILADELPHIA (A. L.)

	ab	r	h	po	a	e
Dykes, 2b	4	3	3	5	2	0
Thomas, 3b	4	1	1	2	0	0
Walker, lf	4	2	2	2	0	0
Welsh, cf	5	0	1	0	0	0
Dugan, ss	4	1	0	3	3	2
Witt, rf	5	1	3	3	0	0
Burrus, 1b	4	0	1	8	1	1
Perkins, c	5	1	1	3	2	0
Perry, p	4	0	1	1	1	0
Totals	39	9	13	27	9	3

BOSTON (A. L.)

	ab	r	h	po	a	e
Hooper, rf	5	0	0	1	0	0
McNally, 2b	5	0	0	3	3	1
Menosky, lf	5	0	1	0	0	0
Hendryx, cf	5	1	0	3	1	1
McInnis, 1b	4	0	3	10	0	0
Foster, 3b	3	0	3	1	3	0
Scott, ss	4	0	0	4	3	1
Schang, c	4	2	2	5	1	0
Harper, p	0	0	0	0	1	1
Karr, p	4	1	2	0	0	0
Totals	39	4	11	27	12	4

Philadelphia. 1 0 3 0 0 2 0 0 3—9
Boston...... 0 0 0 0 0 1 1 0 2—4

Two-base hits—Dykes (2), Walker, Welsh, Foster, McInnis. Three-base hit—Schang. Home run—Schang. Stolen bases—Dykes, Perkins. Sacrifice—Walker. Double plays—McNally and Schang; Hendryx and McInnis. Left on bases—Philadelphia, 8; Boston, 9. Bases on balls—Off Perry, 1; off Harper, 2; off Karr, 1. Hits—Off Harper, 3 in 3 innings; off Karr, 10 in 6. Hit by pitcher—By Karr (Burrus). Struck out—By Perry, 2; by Harper, 1; by Karr, 2. Wild pitch—Harper. Losing pitcher—Harper. Umpires—Evans and Hildebrand. Time of game—1:58.

White Sox Lose and Win

FIRST GAME

CHICAGO (A. L.)

	ab	r	h	po	a	e
Leibold, rf	4	0	1	3	0	0
E. Collins, 2b	4	0	1	2	3	0
Weaver, 3b	4	0	1	1	3	0
Jackson, lf	3	0	0	0	0	0
Felsch, cf	3	0	0	4	0	0
Jourdan, 1b	2	0	0	9	2	0
Risberg, ss	4	0	1	0	1	0
Schalk, c	4	0	1	3	1	0
Faber, p	3	0	0	2	1	0
*Murphy	1	0	1	0	0	0
†J. Collins	1	0	0	0	0	0
Totals	33	0	6	24	11	0

ST. LOUIS (A. L.)

	ab	r	h	po	a	e
Tobin, rf	4	0	0	2	0	0
Gedeon, 2b	4	0	2	1	3	0
Sisler, 1b	4	0	1	12	2	0
Jacob'n, cf	3	0	1	2	0	0
Williams, lf	3	2	1	2	0	0
Austin, 3b	3	0	0	0	2	0
Gerber, ss	3	0	1	3	5	1
Severeid, c	3	0	1	3	1	0
Shocker, p	3	0	0	2	2	0
Totals	30	2	7	27	15	1

*Batted for Jourdan in ninth inning.
†Batted for Faber in ninth inning.

Chicago..... 0 0 0 0 0 0 0 0 0—0
St. Louis.... 0 1 0 0 0 0 0 1 x—2

Three-base hit—E. Collins. Home run—Williams. Left on bases—Chicago, 9; St. Louis, 4. Bases on balls—Off Shocker, 3. Struck out—By Faber, 1; by Shocker, 1. Umpires—Connolly and Moriarty. Time of game—1:40.

SECOND GAME

CHICAGO (A. L.)

	ab	r	h	po	a	e
Leibold, rf	5	2	3	3	0	0
E. Col'ns, 2b	5	2	2	6	4	0
Weaver, 3b	5	0	2	4	1	0
Jackson, lf	6	0	1	3	1	0
Felsch, cf	6	0	3	1	0	0
Jourdan, 1b	4	0	0	6	0	0
Risberg, ss	3	1	1	4	4	0
Lynn, c	4	0	0	2	0	0
C. Wil'ms, p	3	0	0	1	4	0
Totals	41	5	12	30	14	0

ST. LOUIS (A. L.)

	ab	r	h	po	a	e
Tobin, rf	4	1	0	2	0	0
Gedeon, 2b	5	2	3	2	5	0
Sisler, 1b	5	0	4	12	1	0
Jacob'n, cf	5	0	1	6	0	0
K. Wil'ms, lf	3	0	0	2	0	0
Austin, 3b	4	0	2	1	2	0
Gerber, ss	5	0	1	1	3	1
Billings, c	5	0	4	3	1	0
V. Gilder, p	1	0	1	0	0	0
Davis, p	1	0	0	1	0	0
Burwell, p	0	0	0	0	1	0
Sanders, p	0	0	0	0	0	0
*Severeid	1	0	0	0	0	0
†Collins	1	0	0	0	0	0
Totals	40	3	16	30	13	1

*Batted for Davis in sixth inning.
†Batted for Burwell in eighth inning.

Chicago.. 0 0 2 1 0 0 0 0 0 2—5
St. Louis. 1 0 0 0 0 0 0 0 2 0—3

Two-base hits—Felsch, Gedeon, Sisler. Stolen base—Felsch. Sacrifices—Lynn, C. Williams, K. Williams. Double plays—E. Collins, Risberg and Jourdan; Williams, E. Collins and Jourdan; Williams and Jourdan. Left on bases—Chicago, 15; St. Louis, 11. Bases on balls—Off Williams, 3; off Van Gilder, 1; off Davis, 3; off Burwell, 1; off Sanders, 2. Hits—Off Van Gilder, 4 in 2 1-3 innings (one out in third); off Davis, 3 in 3 2-3; off Burwell, 2 in 2; off Sanders, 3 in 2. Struck out—By Williams, 1; by Burwell, 1; by Sanders, 1. Losing pitcher—Sanders. Umpires—Moriarty and Connolly. Time of game—2:15.

RECORD CROWD SEE YANKEES SHUT OUT RED SOX BY 14 TO 0 SCOR

RIP COLLINS HOLDS FOE TO ONE HIT

Young Texan Gives Brilliant Exhibition of Pitching at Polo Grounds—Police Close Gates

By Arthur Robinson.

ASSASSINS' ALLEY held a red carnival at the Polo Grounds yesterday, and up and down the full length of Dynamite Walk a fury of base hits raged. Rip Collins, picturesque Texas League, ex-army captain and Southwestern football star, pitched for the Yanks, and held the Red Sox to one hit. And the Yankees won by the score of 14 to 0.

There were no home runs, and save for the blast of Yankee bats against the ball a singular calm descended upon the crowd after a succession of scoring outbreaks.

Almost forty thousand spectators saw the game and thousands were turned away.

Bullet Joe Bush was driven to cover in the Yankee assault and was replaced by Karr, a youngster, who failed to quell the carnage.

ONE HIT FOR RED SOX.

The only hit which Collins allowed came in the second inning. It was made by Foster, when Ping Bodie, running toward second, in a desperate effort to make a shoestring catch, failed to snatch the ball. The hit went for a double.

Throughout the game Collins, making his third big league start, went about his work with the calm deliberation of a veteran. In the presence of the biggest crowd which he ever saw this young giant of the Texas plains appeared as cool as ice.

Occasionally his face broke out into a smile, when at the end of an inning he came to the bench and was greeted with a salvo of applause, but when he emerged from the dugout his face took on the expression of a stoical Indian, and he resumed the business of mowing down the Red Sox one after the other.

GATES ARE CLOSED.

A current of world's series enthusiasm ran through the crowd as it watched the game, and an atmosphere peculiar to a conflict between the two league champions hung vibrant over the field. Thousands came as early as 1 o'clock, and shortly after a police force of 150, under Inspector Cahalane, arrived to take charge of the crowd.

Ropes were strung along Eighth avenue and the Speedway and spectators passed through the aisles of uniformed men on the way to the entrances for which their tickets called. At game time the gates were closed, and only ticket holders were allowed to enter.

The curtains over the center field fence were rolled up and the crowd in the right field bleachers surged to the seats. There is a frenzied desire to get away from the spot where Ruth hit the first of his home runs the day before.

"Assassins Alley" warmed up to their murderous ways in the first inning scored two runs and gave indications of the outbreak which was to come later.

Peck, the first man up walked. Vitt fumbled Ward's grounder and after Pipp and Ruth had been retired Meusel was hit by a pitched ball filling the bases. Bodie then singled to center scoring Peck and Ward.

The Yanks got two more runs in the second on Hannah's single, Collins' sacrifice, Peck's single and Ward's hit to left and in the fifth they got four more.

Ruth missed a terrific swipe at the ball, he spun around twice from the force of the swing, a moment later drove a liner to right. By good base running stretched it into a double. Meusel was again hit by a pitched ball and Bodie bunted along the third base line. Walter's throw to third failed to get Ruth and the bases were filled. Pratt then singled to center scoring Futh and Meusel and Hannah followed with a double driving in Bodie and Pratt.

In the sixth the Yanks made two triples, two doubles and two singles, and the outbreak resolved in a total of five runs. Bush was driven from the box in the course of the assault and was replaced by Karr.

PIPP STARTS THE TROUBLE.

Pipp precipitated the onslaught with a triple to right centre. He scored on Ruth's infield out and Meusel singled. Bodie tripled scoring Meusel, and Pratt singled driving Bodie in. Bush was taken out of the box at this point and Collins greeted Karr with a double, scoring Pratt.

And still the offensive raged. For Peck doubled bringing Collins in, and Ward, the ninth man up in the inning was called out on strikes, ending the slaughter.

The Yankees fourteenth run came in the seventh on Ruth single and Meusel's triple. The blow carried on a line to the fence in right centre but Meusel was out at the plate trying to make it a home dun.

The score:

BOSTON.	ab	r	h	o	a	e	NEW YORK.	ab	r	h	o	a	e
Hooper,rf	3	0	0	2	1	1	Peck,ss	4	2	3	3	2	0
Vitt,2b	4	0	0	2	8	1	Ward,3b	5	1	2	2	8	0
M'nosky,lf	4	0	0	2	1	0	Pipp,1b	5	1	1	12	1	0
Schang,cf	2	0	0	1	0	1	Ruth,lf	4	2	2	1	0	0
M'I'nis,1b	2	0	0	9	1	0	Meusel,rf	3	2	2	4	0	0
Foster,3b	3	0	1	0	3	0	Bodie,cf	5	2	3	2	0	0
Scott,ss	3	0	0	0	2	0	Gleich,cf	0	0	0	0	0	0
Hiller,ss	0	0	0	1	1	0	Pratt,2b	5	2	2	0	3	0
Walters,c	3	0	0	6	0	0	Hannah,c	4	1	2	3	0	0
Bush,p	1	0	0	0	2	0	Collins,p	4	1	1	0	1	0
Karr,p	1	0	0	1	0	0							
Totals	26	0	1	24	14	3	Totals	39	14	18	27	10	0

Boston	0	0	0	0	0	0	0	0	0	—0
New York	2	2	0	0	4	5	1	0	x	—14

Two-base hits—Foster, Ruth, Hannah, Peck, Collins. Three-base hits—Pipp, Bodie, Meusel. Sacrifice hits—Collins. Stolen bases—Ward, Ruth. Double plays—Peck (unassisted), Pipp to Peck; Foster to Veit to McInnis. Left on bases—Boston, 3; New York, 7. Bases on balls—Off Bush, 3; off Collins, 4. Struck out—By Bush, 2; by Collins, 4. Hit by pitched balls—By Bush, 2; by Karr, 1. Time of game—Two hours. Umpires—Chill and Moriarity. Attendance—35,000.

WILSON HERE TO-MORROW

Johnny Wilson, recently crowned world's middleweight champion, will arrive here to-morrow to finish training for his twelve-round match with Soldier Bartfield at the Newark Sportsmen's Club next Thursday night. The champion will work out at Marshall Stillman's gymnasium in Harlem. He is bringing with him a staff of sparring partners. He planned to round out his training at Grupp's gymnasium, but as Bartfield had pre-empted those quarters he was obliged to establish his camp elsewhere.

REDDY AWAITS LEDOUX

Battling Reddy, the sensational Harlem featherweight, is anxiously waiting to hear from Charlie Dedoux, claimant of the French featherweight championship, whom he challenged immediately after Ledoux's bout with Joe Burman in Philadelphia recently.

ROWING coaches agree that Cornell's sturdy freshman eight would make a worthy representative for Uncle Sam in the Olympic contests. At the intercollegiate regatta, held recently on Lake Cayuga, the Ithaca youngsters won an easy victory. Their time ove rthe course was seconds faster than that made by the Syracuse crew in winning the varsity race; to be exact 10:45 2-5, as compared with 11:02 3-5.

Such expert judges as Coach Rice, of Columbia, and Coach Wright, of Pennsylvania, are of the opinion that the Cornell freshman crew form a combination that can defeat almost any other eight in the country, and say that the Ithacans would do well to enter the Olympic tryouts, in which they would probably meet the strong oarsmen from Annapolis.

BASEBALL SUMMARY

AMERICAN LEAGUE.

YESTERDAY'S RESULTS.

New York, 14; Boston, 0.
Chicago, 12; Cleveland, 7.
Washington, 4; Philadelphia, 3.
Detroit, 5; St. Louis, 2.

STANDING OF THE CLUBS.

	W.	L.	P.C.		W.	L.	P.C.
Cleveland	39	21	.650	Boston	29	28	.509
New York	40	23	.635	St. Louis	29	31	.483
Chicago	35	25	.583	Detroit	21	39	.350
Wash'ton	30	26	.536	Philadel'a	16	45	.262

GAMES TO-DAY.

Boston at New York.
Philadelphia at Washington.
Detroit at St. Louis.
Cleveland at Chicago.

NATIONAL LEAGUE.

YESTERDAY'S RESULTS.

New York, 9; Philadelphia, 6 (11 innings, first game).
Philadelphia, 8; New York, 1 (second game).
Boston, 1; Brooklyn, 0 (first game).
Boston, 7; Brooklyn, 2 (second game).
Pittsburgh, 9; Chicago, 4.
St. Louis, 5; Cincinnati, 0 (first game).
St. Louis, 4; Cincinnati, 3 (second game).

STANDING OF THE CLUBS.

	W.	L.	P.C.		W.	L.	P.C.
Cincin'ati	32	25	.561	Chicago	30	29	.508
St. Louis	33	28	.541	Boston	26	28	.481
Brooklyn	31	27	.534	New York	27	33	.450
Pittsb'gh	27	26	.509	Philadel'a	25	35	.417

GAMES TO-DAY.

New York at Brooklyn.
St. Louis at Cincinnati.
Pittsburgh at Chicago.
No other games scheduled.

INTERNATIONAL LEAGUE.

YESTERDAY'S RESULTS.

Akron, 7; Jersey City, 4.
Buffalo, 4; Syracuse, 1 (first game).
Buffalo, 5; Syracuse, 3 (second game).
Baltimore, 8, Rochester, 2 (first game).
Toronto, 11; Reading, 6.

STANDING OF THE CLUBS.

	W.	L.	P.C.		W.	L.	P.C.
Balt.	40	22	.645	Reading	31	32	.492
Buffalo	40	22	.645	Jersey C.	25	38	.397
Toronto	41	24	.631	Rochester	23	41	.359
Akron	36	25	.590	Syracuse	15	47	.242

GAMES TO-DAY.

Akron at Jersey City (two games).
Rochester at Baltimore.
Buffalo at Syracuse.
Toronto at Reading

Pirates Defeat Cubs by Rally in Eighth

PITTSBURGH, June 26.—Pittsburgh won from Chicago here to-day, 9 to 4, in a game featured by heavy hitting.

The visitors scored one run off Hamilton in the first inning and three in the second. Meador and Ponder held Chicago scoreless for seven innings. In the eighth Pittsburgh came from behind, scoring six on six hits and two walks.

The score:

CHICAGO.	ab	r	h	o	a	e	PITTSBURGH.	ab	r	h	o	a	e
Flack,rf	4	1	1	1	1	1	Bigbee,lf	5	1	1	2	0	0
Hol'her,ss	4	0	1	3	1	0	Carey,cf	5	1	1	3	0	0
Terry,2b	4	0	0	0	2	1	S'worth,rf	5	2	5	2	0	0
Merkle,1b	5	0	2	6	0	0	Whitted,3b	4	1	1	0	0	1
Barber,lf	4	0	0	2	0	0	C'shaw,2b	0	0	0	0	1	0
O'F'rell,c	3	1	2	6	1	0	Meador,p	2	0	0	0	1	0
Herzog,3b	3	1	0	3	3	0	Grimm,1b	5	0	1	13	0	0
Paskert,cf	4	1	3	3	1	0	Caton,ss	3	2	1	1	6	0
Vaughn,p	4	0	1	0	1	0	Schmidt,c	2	0	1	1	0	0
							Lee,c	1	1	1	1	0	0
							Hamilton,p	0	0	0	0	5	0
							Barbare,2b	4	1	4	3	3	0
							aNicholson	1	0	0	0	0	0
							Ponder,p	1	0	1	1	0	0
							bMcKech'e	1	0	0	0	0	0
							Hoeffner,c	0	0	0	0	0	0
Totals	35	4	10	24	10	2	Totals	39	9	17	27	14	1

a Batted for Meador in seventh inning.
b Batted for Lee in eighth inning.

Chicago	1	3	0	0	0	0	0	0	0	—4
Pittsburgh	0	0	1	0	0	2	0	6	x	—9

Two-base hits—Lee, Merkle. Three-base hits—O'Farrell, Paskert, Southworth. Stolen bases—Bigbee, O'Farrell, Southworth, Hollocher. Sacrifices—Flack, Hollocher. Double plays—Caton, Barbare and Grimm; Herzog and Merkle. Left on bases—Chicago, 9; Pittsburge, 10. Bases on balls—Off Vaughn, 4; off Hamilton, 1; off Ponder, 2. Hits—Off Vaughn, 17 in 8 innings; off Hamilton, 2 in 2 innings; off Ponder, 8 in 2 innings; off Meador, 4 in 5 innings. Struck out—By Vaughn, 4; by Ponder, 1. Wild pitch—Ponder. Winning pitcher—Ponder. Losing pitcher—Vaughn. Umpires—Rigler and Moran. Time of game—Two hours and seven minutes.

Wildness of Davis Causes Browns' Downfall, 5-2

ST. LOUIS, June 26.—Timely hitting, Davis's wildness and an error by Billings resulted in Detroit defeating St. Louis, 5 to 2, to-day.

The score:

DETROIT.	ab	r	h	o	a	e	ST. LOUIS.	ab	r	h	o	a	e
Young,2b	5	0	1	2	4	0	Tobin,rf	4	0	0	2	0	0
Bush,ss	5	1	1	2	7	0	Gedeon,2b	2	0	0	1	3	0
Shorten,cf	4	0	0	2	0	0	Sisler,1b	3	1	2	8	0	0
Veach,lf	3	1	1	2	1	0	Jacobson,cf	2	0	0	5	1	0
H'lman,rf	4	1	2	2	0	0	Williams,lf	4	0	0	5	1	0
Ellison,1b	3	1	1	13	0	0	Austin,3b	4	0	0	2	1	0
Pinelli,3b	3	1	0	2	2	0	Gerber,ss	4	0	0	2	5	0
A'smith,c	2	0	0	2	1	0	Billings,c	3	1	2	2	1	1
Dauss,p	2	0	0	0	0	0	Davis,p	3	0	2	0	1	0
							xSmith	1	0	0	0	0	0
Totals	31	5	6	27	15	0	Totals	30	2	6	27	13	1

xBatted for Davis in ninth inning.

Detroit	2	2	0	0	0	0	0	1	0	—5
St. Louis	0	0	0	0	0	0	1	1	0	—2

Two-base hits—Heilman, Sisler, Davis. Three-base hits—Billings, Sisler. Home run—Heilman. Stolen bases—Bush and Jacobson. Sacrifices—Pinelli, Ainsmith, Jacobson. Double plays—Young, Bush and Ellison; Jacobson and Gerber. Left on bases—Detroit, 6; St. Louis, 7. Bases on balls—Off Dauss, 4; off Davis, 5. Hit by pitcher—By Dauss (Billings). Struck out—By Dauss, 2; by Davis, 1. Umpires—Connolly and Nallin. Time of game—One hour and twenty-five minutes.

WILSON TAKES HONORS

R. C. Wilson yesterday won two-thirds of the ball sweepstakes at the Baltusrol Club, with the score of 89—14—75, and Dr. Granoury the remaining third.

HARVARD DOWNS YALE, 6 TO 3, IN DECIDING GAME OF SERIES

BOSTON, June 26.—Emulating the example of the Crimson varsity crew the Harvard nine crashed through Yale's baseball defense this afternoon at Fenway Park, winning a 6 to 3 game, which gave them the series, and brought about a deadlock in the triangular championship, as Yale recently defeated Princeton two out of three and the Tigers beat Harvard two straight.

Lefty Coxe looked like a winner for five rounds, with his team mates working Felton for two runs, aided by ragged fielding. The Crimson batters broke through in their half of the sixth and put the game on ice. Conlon walked and took second on Perkins' single to right. Captain Emmons sacrificed and Jeff Jones' single to left registered Conlon. Perkins and Jones scored when Fritz Janin doubled to left. Lincoln pushed Janin home on a long single, after Hallock had flied to Parsons, and Lincoln took second after the catch, coming home himself on Blair's drive off Coxe's shins. Felton ended the inning by striking out.

Yale scored one in the first, one in the second and another in the eighth inning. A pass to Murphy, an error by Jones, with Blair's passed ball, produced the first run. An error by Lincoln, a hit by Peters and Blair's error at the plate on an attempted double steal accounted for the second. A pass to Murphy, Sawyer's single and two outs registered the former for the final Yale tally.

Felton, who was beaten two straight by the Blue last year, got sweet revenge, winning last Wednesday at Yale by the count of 4 to 1 and again to-day.

The score:

YALE.	ab	r	h	o	a	e	HARVARD.	ab	r	h	o	a	e
Murphy,rf	2	2	0	1	0	0	Conlon,ss	2	2	1	3	3	0
Sawyer,2b	4	0	2	2	2	0	Perkins,rf	3	1	1	0	1	0
Aldrich,ss	4	0	0	1	4	0	H'lowell,rf	0	0	0	0	0	0
Faherty,cf	4	0	1	0	0	0	Emons,2b	2	0	0	1	1	0
Helmes,3b	4	0	0	2	3	0	Jones,1b	4	1	2	3	1	2
D'mond,1b	4	0	0	8	1	1	Janin,lf	4	1	1	1	0	0
Parsons,lf	4	1	1	2	0	0	Hallock,cf	4	0	2	4	0	0
Peters,c	3	0	1	8	1	0	Lincoln,3b	4	1	1	2	1	1
Coxe,p	2	0	0	0	2	0	Blair,c	4	0	1	9	1	1
Selleck,p	1	0	0	0	0	0	Ga'mack,c	0	0	0	1	0	0
xFred'cks	1	0	0	0	0	0	Felton,p	3	0	0	3	1	0
Totals	33	3	5	24	13	1	Totals	30	6	9	27	9	4

x Batted for Coxe in seventh inning.

The score:

Yale	1	1	0	0	0	0	0	1	0	—3
Harvard	0	0	0	0	0	5	1	0	x	—6

Two-base hits—Parsons, Sawyer, Janin. Stolen bases—Aldrich, Murphy, Peters. Sacrifice hits—Emons. Base on balls—Off Coxe, 1; off Felton, 3; off Selleck, 2. Struck out—By Coxe, 5; by Felton, 8; by Selleck, 1. Double plays—Peters to Aldrich. Hits—Off Coxe, 8 in six innings; off Selleck, 1 in two innings. Passed ball—Blair. Wild pitches—Felton. Hit by pitched ball—Emons. Umpires—McBride and McCormick. Attendance, 17,000.

White Sox Wallop Four Indian Hurlers; Win, 12-7

CHICAGO, June 26.—Chicago hit four Cleveland pitchers hard to-day and won 12 to 7. Cleveland made a belated rally in the ninth when Gardner tripled with the bases full, but it availed them nothing. Weaver and Gardner both hit well. Faber was effective except in the final inning when he apparently eased up, having a nine run lead at that time.

The score:

CLEVELAND.	ab	r	h	o	a	e	CHICAGO.	ab	r	h	o	a	e
Evans,lf	5	0	0	3	0	0	Leibold,rf	5	2	1	4	0	0
C'pman,ss	3	2	2	1	2	0	E.C'llns,2b	4	2	2	2	3	0
Speaker,cf	5	1	3	1	0	1	Weaver,3b	4	2	3	1	2	1
Smith,rf	3	1	1	2	0	0	Jackson,lf	4	1	2	1	0	0
G'dner,3b	4	1	3	0	1	0	Felsch,cf	5	1	2	5	0	0
W'anss,2b	5	0	2	1	4	0	J.C'lins,1b	3	1	0	9	1	0
J'nston,1b	4	0	0	10	2	0	Risberg,ss	4	1	1	2	4	1
O'Neill,c	4	0	1	5	0	1	Schalk,c	4	1	2	8	2	0
C'dwell,p	1	1	1	0	0	0	Faber,p	3	1	1	0	0	0
Faeth,p	0	0	0	0	0	0							
Myers,p	1	0	0	0	0	0							
Niehaus,p	1	0	1	0	0	0							
aBurrus	1	0	0	0	0	0							
bWood	0	1	0	0	0	0							
Totals	37	7	14	24	9	2	Totals	36	12	14	27	12	2

a Batted for Niehaus in ninth inning.
b Ran for O'Neill in ninth inning.

Cleveland	0	0	1	1	0	0	0	1	4	—7
Chicago	0	0	0	7	0	4	0	1	x	—12

Two-base hits—Risberg, Speaker. Three-base hits—Wambsganss, Chapman, Jackson, Gardner (2). Stolen base—E. Collins. Sacrifice—Faber, U. Collins, Smith, Weaver, Jackson. Double plays—E. Collins to Risberg to U. Collins to E. Collins; Schalk to Risberg. Left on bases—Cleveland, 8; Chicago, 5. Bases on balls—Off Faeth, 1; off Faber, 4. Hits—Off Caldwell, 6 in 3 innings (none out in fourth); off Faeth, 3 in 2-3 innings; off Myers, 3 in 1 1-3 innings (none out in sixth); off Niehaus, 2 in 3 innings. Struck out—By Caldwell, 2; by Myers, 1; by Faber, 1. Losing pitcher—Caldwell. Umpires—Hildebrand and Evans. Time of game—Two hours thirteen minutes.

Berrien and Sanderson to Meet in Final Round

Stephen Berrien and R. Sanderson came through to the final round of the club championship on the links of the Upper Montclair Country Club yesterday. In the semi-final round Berrien eliminated A. E. Betteridge by the meagre margin of one up, while Sanderson won from S. M. Harding by two up and one to play.

In the weekly sweepstakes event C. T. Taylor, with an allowance of sixteen strokes, turned in the low net score of 68. C. T. Woodward was second, one stroke behind, with 94-25-69. R. R. Lauckler was third, with 85-12-73.

EASTERN LEAGUE.

Springfield, 8; New Haven, 7.
Albany, 3; Hartford, 1.
Pittsfield, 7; Bridgeport, 1 (first game). Pittsfield, 14; Bridgeport, 7 (second game).
Waterbury, 3; Worcester, 1.

AMERICAN ASSOCIATION.

Louisville, 6; Toledo, 4 (first game).
Indianapolis, 5; Columbus, 3.
Minneapolis, 17; Kansas City, 5.
St. Paul, 7; Milwaukee, 6.

Luque Attacks Klem During Ball Game

CINCINNATI, June 26.—St. Louis went to second place in the National League race to-day by winning both games of a double-header from the champions, 5 to 10 and 4 to 3. Both teams played perfect ball in the field, but the hitting of the visitors was much more effective than the Reds. Ruether was pounded hard in the first game, while Haines pitched perfectly, allowing only three hits. In the second game long drives by the Cardinals gave them the victory.

In the eighth inning of the second game Pitcher Luque, of the Reds, attacked Umpire Klem and dealt him several hard blows about the head. The assault took place while Luque was in the box with no one on base, and the pitcher claims that it was due to vicious language used by the official. Luque and Catcher Allen, of the Reds, both made affidavit that Klem had used such language.

If the claims are proved the club will bring charges against Klem. Luque was put out of the game and Eller finished it. Previous to this incident a shower of pop bottles fell around Klem when he called Fournier safe at the plate in the sixth inning. Wingo was put out of the game this time for abusive language.

The score:

First Game.

ST. LOUIS.	ab	r	h	o	a	e	CINCINNATI.	ab	r	h	o	a	e
Janvrin,lf	4	1	1	4	0	0	Rath,2b	4	0	0	2	2	0
Schultz,rf	4	0	1	3	0	0	Groh,3b	4	0	1	2	2	0
Stock,3b	5	2	3	0	1	0	Roush,1b	3	0	0	11	1	0
H'nsby,2b	4	0	0	1	3	0	Duncan,lf	3	0	0	1	0	0
F'rnier,1b	4	1	2	10	1	0	Kopf,ss	3	0	1	1	2	0
M'H'ry,cf	4	1	1	2	0	0	Neale,rf	3	0	0	3	0	0
Lavan,ss	3	0	1	3	6	0	See,cf	2	0	0	5	0	0
Dilh'fer,c	4	0	2	4	1	0	Wingo,c	3	0	0	2	2	0
Haines,p	3	0	0	0	3	0	Ruether,p	3	0	1	0	1	0
Totals	35	5	11	27	15	0	Totals	28	0	3	27	10	0

St. Louis	2	0	0	0	0	0	0	3	0	—5
Cincinnati	0	0	0	0	0	0	0	0	0	—0

Two-base hits—Kopf, Janvrin, Stock, McHenry. Three-base hits—Fournier, Dilhoefer. Sacrifices—Schultz, Haines. Left on bases—St. Louis, 7; Cincinnati, 3. Base on balls—Off Reuther, 2; off Haines, 1. Hit by pitcher—By Haines, 1. Struck out—By Reuther, 1; by Haines, 1. Umpires—Klem and Emslie.

Second Game.

ST. LOUIS.	ab	r	h	o	a	e	CINCINNATI.	ab	r	h	o	a	e
Shotten,lf	3	1	0	2	0	0	Rath,2b	3	0	1	1	4	0
H'hcote,cf	3	0	1	0	0	0	Groh,3b	1	1	0	0	2	0
Stock,3b	4	0	2	0	1	0	Roush,1b	3	0	0	13	1	0
H'nsby,2b	4	0	1	4	4	0	Duncan,lf	4	0	2	0	0	0
F'rnier,1b	4	1	1	13	0	0	Kopf,ss	4	1	1	3	4	0
Schultz,rf	3	1	1	3	0	0	Neale,rf	4	0	1	0	0	0
Lavan,ss	4	0	1	2	7	0	See,cf	3	0	1	1	0	0
Clemons,c	4	1	1	3	2	0	xCrane	1	0	0	0	0	0
Doak,p	3	0	1	0	2	0	Wingo,c	2	0	0	4	1	0
Sherdel,p	1	0	0	0	2	0	Allen,c	1	1	0	3	0	0
							Luque,p	2	0	0	2	3	0
							Eller,p	1	0	0	0	1	0
Totals	33	4	9	27	18	0	Totals	29	3	6	27	19	0

xBatted for See in ninth inning.

St. Louis	1	0	0	2	0	1	0	0	0	—4
Cincinnati	0	0	0	2	0	0	1	0	0	—3

Two-base hit—Lavan. Three-base hits—Heathcote, Fournier, Clemons. Stolen bases—Heathcote, Schultz. Sacrifices—Rath, Groh. Double plays—Stock to Hornsby to Fournier. Left on bases—St. Louis, 5; Cincinnati, 6. Bases on balls—Off Luque, 3; off Doak, 5. Hits—Off Luque, 8 in 7 2-3 innings; off Eller, 1 in 1 1-3 innings; off Doak, 6 in 6 innings; off Sherdel, 0 in 3 innings. Struck out—By Luque, 3; by Eller, 2; by Doak, 2. Wild pitch—Luque. Winning pitcher—Doak. Losing pitcher—Luque. Umpires—Klem and Emslie. Time of game—Two hours ten minutes.

FRUSH TO MEET O'LEARY

A pair of top-notch featherweights, each considered in boxing circles as a very probable successor to Johnny Kilbane's eagerly sought title, will furnish the stellar attraction at the Bayonne A. A., Fiftieth street on the Hudson boulevard, next Friday night. The two ring gladiators signed are Danny Frush, England's classy featherweight, and Artie O'Leary, the aggressive Metropolitan entry, and a whirlwind battle seems certain to be the outcome, with possibly a knockout ending it.

HOWARD HIGH GUNNER

J. A. Howard was the high scratch gunner in the weekly shoot of the Bergen Beach Gun Club yesterday. He took the event with a card of 96 out of a possible 100 targets. He also was tied for the high handicap trophy along with E. B. Magnus and I. J. Kauder. The trio all had 100 targets. As Howard was not eligible for both cups, the other two only shot off for the handicap trophy. It was won by Magnus, Kauder taking third prize.

ARCHERS HOLD TOURNEY

The fortieth annual tournament of the National Archery Association of the United States will be held on the athletic field of St. Luke's School at Wayne, Pa., (14 miles from Broad street station, Philadelphia, on the main line of the Pennsylvania Railroad) on Tuesday, Wednesday, Thursday and Friday, August 24th to 27th, inclusive. Events for both men and women are scheduled.

COLLEGE BASEBALL.

Boston College, 10; University of Vermont, 3.

Runs for the Week

NATIONAL LEAGUE.

Club	S	M	T	W	T	F	S	Tls.
New York	8	*	4	2	3	9	10	36
Brooklyn	2	*	7	5	6	7	2	29
Pittsburgh	0	*	9	2	2	6	9	28
Philadelphia	*	5	1	3	3	1	14	27
Boston	*	*	3	6	4	5	8	26
Chicago	4	*	10	1	1	3	4	23
St. Louis	*	*	2	2	7	*	9	20
Cincinnati	*	1	3	0	5	*	3	12

AMERICAN LEAGUE.

Club	S	M	T	W	T	F	S	Tls.
Cleveland	9	3	13	7	*	3	7	42
Chicago	7	*	2	7	*	6	12	34
New York	4	*	3	6	*	3	14	30
Boston	10	2	5	6	*	6	0	29
Washington	9	*	6	5	*	4	4	28
St. Louis	3	*	9	3	0	10	2	27
Detroit	4	*	1	2	5	6	5	23
Philadelphia	5	*	1	6	*	2	3	11

INTERNATIONAL LEAGUE.

Club	S	M	T	W	T	F	S	Tls.
Akron	29	3	5	11	5	15	7	75
Reading	15	*	20	4	4	15	6	64
Jersey City	11	*	0	18	2	11	4	46
Baltimore	2	5	6	11	4	7	8	43
Toronto	3	*	4	6	6	13	11	43
Rochester	9	*	3	7	1	2	10	32
Buffalo	6	*	11	1	2	2	9	31
Syracuse	13	*	3	6	1	1	4	28

Geo. Sisler Boosts Batting Average

"Babe" Ruth, the New York slugger, has eighty-seven games in which to wallop out eight home runs to shatter the record of twenty-nine, established by himself last season, when a member of the Boston Americans.

In his remarkable drive toward a new world's record, Ruth crashed out his twenty-second homer Friday in the game with Boston, giving him a total of twenty-two. He is sixth in batting, with an average of .355, according to averages, including games of Wednesday.

George Sisler, the St. Louis star, who is leading the American League, boosted his average to .416—eight points within a week. Tris Speaker, of Cleveland, managed to cling to second place with .384. Speaker tops the league in scoring, having counted 57 runs in 58 games. Ruth has crossed the plate 55 times in 54 games.

Rice, of Washington, is running away with honors in base stealing. He has stolen twenty-five, while Bobby Roth, his team-mate, is next in line with nineteen. Sisler is third with fifteen.

Other leading batters are: Johnson, Cleveland, .362; Milan, Washington, .359; Weaver, Chicago, .352; Felsch, Chicago, .343; Jacobson, St. Louis, .341; Judge, Washington, .339; Rice, Washington, .338; Hendrix, Boston, .330.

St. Louis, which has been clamoring for baseball distinction for years, is finding solace in the batting performances of Sisler and Roger Hornsby. The latter is in no immediate danger of being ousted from the batting leadership of the National League, the averages, including Wednesday's games, giving him .391. Nicholson of Pittsburgh is trailing him in second place with .350. Roush of Cincinnati is third with .337.

Hornsby and Robertson, of Chicago, are giving Cy Williams, of Philadelphia, a close rub for home run honors. Williams has belted out seven, while the St. Louis star and Robertson have made six each.

Max Carey, of Pittsburgh, in setting the pace for the base stealers, has a total of nineteen. Roush, of Cincinnati, and Hollocher, of Chicago, are next up, with fourteen each.

Other leading batters: Robertson, Chicago, .335; Daubert, Cincinnati, .333; Smith, New York, .333; Flack, Chicago, .325; Duncan, Cincinnati, .323; Kelly, New York, .317; Myers, Brooklyn, .317; Young, New York, .316; Groh, Cincinnati, .311.

Senators Trounce Macks in Pitching Duel, 4 to 3

WASHINGTON, June 26.—Washington defeated Philadelphia here today in the ninth inning by 4 to 3, in a pitcher's battle between Zachary and Perry.

The score:

PHILADELPHIA.	ab	r	h	o	a	e	WASHINGTON.	ab	r	h	o	a	e
Th'mas,3b	5	1	2	4	1	0	Judge,1b	4	1	2	13	0	0
Griffin,1b	4	0	0	6	1	0	Milan,lf	4	0	2	1	0	0
Walker,lf	3	0	1	3	0	1	Rice,cf	4	0	1	1	0	0
Dugan,ss	4	1	2	0	1	2	Roth,rf	4	1	1	0	0	0
Strunk,cf	4	0	0	4	0	0	Shanks,3b	3	1	1	3	2	0
P'k's,c.2b	3	1	0	3	1	0	Shannon,2b	4	0	2	0	5	0
Welch,rf	4	0	2	3	0	0	O'Neill,ss	4	0	0	3	4	1
G'oway,2b	1	0	0	1	2	0	Gharrity,c	4	1	1	6	1	0
Myatt,c	2	0	1	2	1	0	Zachary,p	4	0	0	0	4	0
Perry,p	4	0	2	0	1	0							
Totals	34	3	10x26		8	3	Totals	35	4	10	27	16	1

xTwo out when winning run was scored.

Philadelphia	1	0	0	2	0	0	0	0	0	—3
Washington	0	1	1	1	0	0	0	0	1	—4

Two-base hits—Judge, Dugan, Milan (2). Stolen bases—Gharrity (2), Rice, Walker, Judge. Sacrifices—Griffen, Shanks, Milan, Myatt, Walker. Left on bases—Philadelphia, 10; Washington, 8. Base on balls—Off Zachary, 2; off Perry, 1. Hit by pitcher—By Zachary (Perkins). Struck out—By Zachary, 4; by Perry, 1. Umpires—Friel and Dineen. Time of game—One hour and fifty minutes.

MATHEY ANNEXES TITLE

WILMINGTON, Del., June 26.—Dean Mathey, West Side Tennis Club, Long Island, and New York State tennis champion, sprang a surprise to-day when he won the singles championship of Delaware by defeating Wallace Johnson, Philadelphia, the Pennsylvania State title holder, 6—4, 6—4, 1—6, 6—4.

SMITH SOUTHERN VICTOR

NEW ORLEANS, June 26.—Carlton Smith, of Atlanta, defeated Frank T. Payne, New Orleans, for the men's singles tennis championship of the South here to-day. Scores, 6—3, 6—2, 3—6, 6—4.

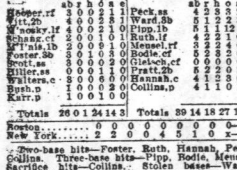

DODGERS LOSE TWO TO BRAVES

Oeschger Holds Brooklyn to Three Hits and Wins, 1 to 0. Boston Annexes Second by 7-2

BOSTON, Mass., June 26.—Brooklyn lost the first game of the double-header to-day to the Braves by 1 to 0 and the second by 7 to 2. Oeschger held the Dodgers to three hits in the opener, and they never had a chance.

Smith was reached for nine hits in the first seven innings and was the loser. Oeschger singled in the third inning and was forced by Powell. The bases were filled by Pick's single and McCabe's fumble of Sullivan's grounder. Cruise's short single over second scored Powell.

In the second game Burleigh Grimes gave the six thousand fans an exhibition of temper when three runs were made off him in the fifth inning after the Braves had batted home three in the third with the aid of loose fielding.

Eayres opened the fifth round of the second game with a single off Grimes and Cruise walked. Holke drove to Grimes who made a bad throw to McCabe at second to start a double play. Grimes's throw was wild and pulled McCabe off the bag, leaving all three runners safe, but the pitcher put all the blame on the shortstop.

He threw his hat and glove on the ground and bawled out McCabe, while other Dodgers tried to pacify him. Boeckel's force of Holke scored Eayres, Maranville's hit through McCabe scored Cruise and O'Neil's single to left scored Boeckel.

Grimes was still kicking against his support when he went to the bench, and Uncle Robbie took him out of the game, or Grimes took himself out, with eight hits and six runs off him in five innings.

John Miljus lasted three innings and Maranville's infield single, with Johnston's two-base wild throw and O'Neil's single, counted a run off Miljus.

Brooklyn's runs in the second game were lucky, as Fillinim held the Dodgers to six hits. Wheat went all the way to third on Fillingim's wild throw in the third inning and scored on Myers's hit. Myers doubled in the ninth and scored on Konettchy's hit.

The scores:

First Game.

BROOKLYN.	ab	r	h	o	a	e	BOSTON.	ab	r	h	o	a	e
Kilduff,2b	4	0	0	3	0	0	Powell,cf	4	1	1	2	0	0
J'nston,3b	4	0	1	1	3	0	Pick,2b	3	0	1	1	7	0
Griffith,rf	4	0	1	1	0	0	aMann	1	0	0	0	0	0
Wheat,lf	2	0	0	2	0	0	Ford,2b	0	0	0	0	0	0
Myers,cf	2	0	0	0	0	0	Sullivan,lf	4	0	2	3	0	0
Koney,1b	3	0	0	14	0	0	Cruise,rf	3	0	1	0	0	0
M'Cabe,ss	3	0	0	1	6	1	Holke,1b	3	0	1	10	1	0
Krueger,c	3	0	1	2	0	0	Boeckel,3b	3	0	0	0	3	0
Smith,p	2	0	0	0	7	0	M'nville,ss	4	0	0	8	1	0
bMitchell	1	0	0	0	0	0	Gowdy,c	3	0	1	2	2	0
Miljus,p	0	0	0	0	0	0	Oeschger,p	3	0	3	1	0	0
Totals	28	0	3	24	16	1	Totals	30	1	10	27	14	0

aMann batted for Pick in the seventh inning.
bMitchell batted for Smith in the eighth inning.

Brooklyn	0	0	0	0	0	0	0	0	0	—0
Boston	0	0	1	0	0	0	0	0	x	—1

Sacrifice hits—Cruise. Left on bases—Brooklyn, 2; Boston, 6. Bases on balls—Off Smith, 1; off Meyus, 1; of Oeschger, 2. Time—1:40. Umpires—Quigley and O'Day.

Second Game.

BROOKLYN.	ab	r	h	o	a	e	BOSTON.	ab	r	h	o	a	e
Kilduff,2b	4	0	0	3	3	2	Powell,cf	4	1	0	3	0	0
J'nston,3b	4	0	1	1	1	1	Pick,2b	5	1	1	2	3	0
Griffith,rf	3	0	0	1	0	0	Eayrs,lf	5	2	3	0	0	0
Wheat,lf	2	1	0	3	0	0	Cruise,rf	4	1	1	0	0	0
Neis,lf	1	0	0	1	0	0	Holke,1b	4	0	0	10	2	0
Myers,cf	4	1	2	2	0	0	Boeckel,3b	3	1	1	1	3	1
K'tchy,1b	4	0	1	5	1	0	M'nville,ss	4	1	2	4	4	0
McCabe,ss	4	0	0	2	4	0	O'Neill,c	4	0	2	6	1	0
Miller,c	3	0	1	4	0	0	Fillingim,p	4	0	2	1	1	1
Elliott,c	1	0	0	1	0	0							
Grimes,p	1	0	0	1	1	1							
Miljus,p	1	0	1	0	0	0							
Boston	32	2	6	24	10	4	Totals	37	7	12	27	14	2

Brooklyn	0	0	1	0	0	0	0	0	1	—2
Boston	0	0	3	0	3	0	1	0	x	—7

Two-base hits—Cruise, Eayres, Myers. Three-base hit—Miljus. Sacrifice hits—Powell, Holke. Stolen bases—Wheat, Boeckel. Left on bases—Brooklyn, 6; Boston, 9. Bases on balls—Off Grimes, 2; off Fillingim, 3. Struck out—By Grimes, 2; by Fillingim, 4. Umpires—O'Day and Quigley. Attendance—6,000.

Many Feature Races on Tap for Aqueduct This Week

The Queens County Jockey Club, whose meeting began so auspiciously last Thursday with the running of the Brooklyn Handicap, will continue until Tuesday, July 18, when a transfer will be fade to the Empire City course at Yonkers. Much of the spirit which prevailed in the management of the Brooklyn Jockey Club, which made the Gravesend course a success under the leadership of Phil J. Dwyer, is found in the Queens County directorate.

The features for the coming week include the Rockaway Selling Stakes, for three-year-olds and upward, at six furlongs, which will be run to-morrow; the Canarsie Selling, for two-year-olds, at five furlongs, which will be decided on Tuesday; the Gazelle Handicap, at one and one-sixteenth miles, for mares three years old and upward, on Wednesday; and the Union Selling Stakes, for three-year-olds, at seven furlongs, on Thursday.

Saturday's programme is an exceptionally rich one, as on that day the crack two-year-olds will meet in the Great American, a $6,000 race at five furlongs, while the best of the handicap division will be seen in the historic Brookdale Handicap, $2,500 added, at one mile and a furlong.

LOSS OF WACHTER FELT

WILLIAMSTOWN, June 26.—Williams College is bemoaning the loss of Ed Wachter, of Troy, as basketball coach for next year. He will not return to take charge of the quintet as he has been engaged to coach at Harvard. Wachter was well on the road to restore basketball to the same high place it enjoyed at Williams a decade ago when his services were snatched away by the Cambridge university.

GOLFERS PLAY TO TIE

The Moraff prizes were in competition yesterday at the Fox Hills Golf Club. In Class A there was a tie at 73 net between E. T. Villareal and E. Heikel, who must play off in consequence. In Class B, A. M. Kerr won at 68 net.

INGHRAM LOW ON LINKS

Two Saturday golf handicaps at 18-holes were held yesterday at the Gedney Farms Country Club. In the morning James Ingham, Jr., won with 87—15—72, and in the afternoon A. L. Trunk with 95—20—75.

JAMES AND TAYLOR LOSE

TORONTO, June 26.—R. L. James and Harold Taylor, of New York, were defeated to-day in the final for the Eastern Canadian doubles tennis championship by R. A. Burns and A. Ross, of Toronto, 9—7.

Giants Divide with Phill Win First in Eleven Inning

Barnes and Nehf Pitch Opener—Benton W loped Hard in 2d Game—Umpire Mobbed.

PHILADELPHIA, June 26.—The Giants and Phillies split up a do header to-day, the Giants winning the first game, 9 to 6, in el innings, and losing the second, 8 to 1. In the first game Um Harrison was showered with pop bottles by irate fans in the grandst Jess Barnes and Art Nehf hurled this game for the Giants.

Harrison put Lee Meadows, who started the game for the Phillies, off the field in the third inning. Meadows was succeeded by Bert Gallia, Eppa Rixey and George Smith.

In the second game, Rube Benton was hit hard all the way, while Cecil Causey turned the Giants away with three hits.

The Phillies were the first to score in the opening game, grabbing off a run in the second inning. Meusel walked, moved upon Fletcher's sacrifice and scored on a single by Paulette. In the second inning Tragesser led off with a double, took third on Gallia's sacrifice and scored on a one-base blow by Williams.

The Giants broke through in the fifth inning. Kelly walked and stole second as Kauff fanned, and continued on to third on Tragesser's wild peg past the middle bag. After Sicking had fanned Smith singled to left and Kelly scored.

Kelly opened the seventh with a double to left. Kauff's sacrifice put him on third. Here Doyle was injected as a pinch hitter for Sicking and doubled to right, scoring Kelly. Smith singled to left and Doyle scored.

GIANTS TIE SCORE.

In the eighth Burns singled, and on a hit-and-run play Bancroft singled to right, putting Burns on third. Burns scored on Young's sacrifice fly to Williams. This run apparently clinched the game for the Giants, but in their half of the inning the Phillies hung up three runs on a pass to Gallia, a single by Rawlings and an error by Young, and doubles by Williams and Stengel.

The Giants tied the score in the ninth. Doyle singled to centre and Smith singled to deep short. Gallia gave way to Rixey, and Snyder, batting for Barnes, moved the runners along with a sacrifice. Burns was called out on strikes, but Rixey let go a wild pitch with Bancroft at the bat and Doyle scored. Fletcher then threw out Bancroft.

The Giants got a run in the tenth on a single and a stolen base by Frisch and a single by King, who batted for Kauff. The Phillies again tied the score in their half of the inning on doubles by Williams and Cravath, who batted for Stengel.

The game was broken up in the eleventh with George Smith pitching for the Phillies. The Giants counted three times on a single by Earl Smith, a pass to Nehf, a sacrifice by Burns, singles by Bancroft and Young and a sacrifice fly by Frisch.

YOUNG STARTS TROUBLE.

An error by Ross Young paved the way for the hanging up of a lead by the Phillies in the second inning of the second game. Young muffed a fly from Paulette's bat, Paulete reaching second, and scoring on a double by Wheat. The Phillies increased their lead in the fourth, when, with two out, R. Miller doubled to centre and scored on a single by Wheat.

A pass to Rawlings and a triple by Williams, singles by Stengel and Meusel, a sacrifice by Fletcher and a double steal netted the Phillies three runs in the fifth. Doubles by Stengel and Meusel, a wild pitch, a triple by Fletcher and a single by Paulette were woven into three runs by the Phillies in the seventh. The Giants got their lone run in the ninth on a single by Bancroft, a pass to Young and a single by Kauff.

The scores:

First Game.

NEW YORK.	ab	r	h	o	a	e	PHILADELPHIA.	ab	r	h	o	a	e
G.Burns,lf	4	1	2	3	1	0	Rawl'gs,2b	5	1	1	4	6	0
B'ncroft,ss	6	1	2	2	2	0	Williams,cf	5	2	4	4	0	0
Young,rf	5	0	1	3	0	1	Stengel,rf	4	0	2	2	0	0
Frisch,3b	6	1	2	0	2	0	Cravath	1	0	1	0	0	0
Kelly,1b	4	2	2	13	1	0	Leb'rveau	0	0	0	0	0	0
Kauff,cf	4	0	0	4	0	1	Meusel,lf	4	1	1	1	0	0
King,cf	1	0	1	1	0	0	Fletcher,ss	4	0	0	5	2	0
Sicking,2b	3	0	1	2	8	0	P'lette,1b	5	0	1	9	2	0
Doyle,2b	3	2	2	0	3	0	R.M'ler,3b	5	0	0	1	2	0
E.Smith,c	6	1	5	4	0	0	Tragesser,c	4	1	1	7	0	1
Barnes,p	4	0	1	0	4	0	Meadows,p	0	0	0	0	0	0
Snyder	0	0	0	0	0	0	Gallia,p	1	1	0	0	1	0
Nehf,p	0	1	0	0	0	0	Rixey,p	1	0	0	0	0	0
							R.M'ler,3b	4	1	1	1	5	0
							G.Smith,p	0	0	0	0	2	0
Totals	46	9	19x32		16	2	Totals	39	6	11	33	15	1

New York	0	0	0	0	1	0	2	1	1	1	3	—9
Phila	0	1	1	0	0	0	0	3	0	1	0	—6

Smith out, hit by batter once.
Snyder batted for Barnes in ninth inning.
J. Miller batted for Rixey in tenth inning.
Cravath batted for Stengel in tenth inning.
Lebourveau ran for Crasath in tenth inning.

Two-base hits—Stengel (2), Kelly, Doyle, Williams (2), Cravath. Sacrifice hits—Fletcher, Gallia, Kauff, Snyder. Sacrifice fly—Young. Stolen bases—Kelly, Frisch. Double plays—Sicking to Kelly; Sicking to Bancroft to Kelly; Rawlings to Fletcher. Left on bases—New York, 14; Philadelphia, 2. Bases on balls—Off Barnes, 2; off Meadows, 5; off Gallia, 3. Struck out—By Barnes, 8; by Gallia, 4; by Rixey, 2. Wild pitch—By Rixey, 1. Time of game—Two hours and ten minutes. Umpires—Hart and Harrison. Attendance—12,000.

Second Game.

NEW YORK.	ab	r	h	o	a	e	PHILADELPHIA.	ab	r	h	o	a	e
Burns,lf	4	0	0	0	0	0	Rawl'gs,2b	4	1	2	2	2	0
B'ncroft,ss	3	1	1	1	5	1	Williams,cf	5	1	3	4	0	0
Young,rf	3	0	1	3	0	1	Stengel,rf	5	1	2	2	0	0
Frisch,3b	3	0	0	0	2	0	Meusel,lf	4	2	2	2	0	0
Kelly,1b	4	0	0	12	2	0	Fletcher,ss	3	1	1	1	2	1
Kauff,cf	3	0	1	2	0	0	Paulette,1b	4	1	1	8	0	0
Sicking,2b	3	0	0	0	4	0	B.M'ler,3b	4	1	1	1	5	0
Snyder,c	3	0	0	5	0	0	Wheat,c	4	0	2	7	0	0
Benton,p	3	0	0	1	2	0	Causey,p	4	0	0	0	0	0
xDoyle	1	0	0	0	0	0							
Totals	30	1	3	24	15	2	Totals	37	8	14	27	9	1

*Batted for Sicking in ninth inning.

New York	0	0	0	0	0	0	0	0	1	—1
Philadelphia	0	1	0	1	3	0	3	0	x	—8

Two-base hits—Wheat, Miller, Stengel, Meusel. Three-base hits—Williams, Fletcher. Sacrifice hits—Stengel, Fletcher. Stolen bases—Meusel, Paulette. Left on Bases—New York, 4; Philadelphia, 3. Bases on balls—Off Benton, 1; off Causey, 2. Struck out—By Benton, 1; by Causey, 6. Hit by pitched ball—Kauff. Wild pitches—Causey, 1; Benton, 1. Umpires—Hart and Harrison. Attendance—21,000.

INTERNATIONAL LEAGUE.

AT JERSEY CITY—

Akron	0	0	1	0	2	0	0	4	0—7	14	2
Jersey City	0	0	0	0	0	2	0	0	2—4	11	2

Flaherty, Walker and Smith; Wilhelm, Biemiller and Freitag.
Umpires—Carpenter and Derr.

AT BALTIMORE—

FIRST GAME.

Rochester	0	0	0	1	0	0	0	0	1—2	7	1
Baltimore	0	1	0	3	1	0	0	3	x—8	16	5

Sherman and Manning; Kneisch and Egan.
Umpires—Corcoran and Stockdale.

AT SYRACUSE—

FIRST GAME.

Buffalo	2	0	1	0	0	0	1	0	0—4	6	1
Syracuse	0	1	0	0	0	0	0	0	0—1	6	3

Martin and Bengough; Perryman and Niebergall. Umpires—Moran and McGowan.

SECOND GAME.

Buffalo	2	0	0	1	0	0	1	1	0—5	6	0
Syracuse	1	0	2	0	0	0	0	0	0—3	4	4

Cardonier, Carruthers and Bruggy; Tipple and Niebergall.
Umpires—McGowan and Moran.

AT READING—

Toronto	1	1	0	3	1	0	2	1	2—11	19	2
Reading	0	0	0	2	1	2	0	0	1—6	10	2

Quinn, Ryan and Sandberg; Barnhardt, Karpp and Konnick. Umpires—O'Brien and Warner.

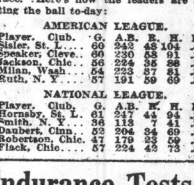

Five Leading Batters in Major Leagu

BY making five hits in five times at bat Earl Smith, the Giant catch is now in second place in the batt race. Here's how the leaders are ting the ball to-day:

AMERICAN LEAGUE.

Player.	Club.	G.	A.B.	R.	H.
Sisler,	St. L.	60	242	48	104
Speaker,	Cleve.	60	230	58	91
Jackson,	Chic.	56	224	35	86
Milan,	Wash.	54	223	37	81
Ruth,	N. Y.	57	191	59	69

NATIONAL LEAGUE.

Player.	Club.	G.	A.B.	R.	H.
Hornsby,	St. L.	61	247	44	94
Smith,	N. Y.	36	113	7	41
Daubert,	Cinn.	52	204	34	69
Robertson,	Chic.	47	179	23	59
Flack,	Chic.	57	224	42	73

Endurance Tests at N. Y. Velodro

Endurance tests, in which al tions will be represented, will b of the features to be inaugurat the $250,000 cycle racing stdiu the New York Velodrome Compa Two Hundred and Twenty-fifth and Broadway. There will be usual short distance sprint races for the first time in recent ye great deal of attention will be to outdoor tests of enduranc brance of racing that is so popu foreign countries.

Some of the best riders now peting in this country were deve in Australia. These riders g their experience and built up a fect physique by competition o greater distance than one mile o miles. France, Italy, Belgium Switzerland have sent over cycle racing stars, and all wer veloped in long distance classic

More attention will be direct the amateurs at the New York drome than was ever accorded at any other track in the cou It is from the unknown am that our future champions and this latent talent c be developed unless racing grammes are arranged so as to the embryo a chance to displa racing qualities. The New Yor lodrome plans to develop all-a cycle racers. Aspirants for c pionship honors will have the a tage of working out with such rienced riders as Spencer, Goullet and a flock of other sta

Eight Fistic Champs i A. A. U. Boxing Tryo

With three National title ho three Metropolitan and two New State champions entered, the York, New Jersey and Conne Olympic boxing tryouts, which be conducted by the Metropolita sociation of the Amateur At Union in the Twenty-third Reg Armory, on Tuesday and Thu evenings, June 29 and July 1, p ises to be the best held in thi trict in many months. The bout being held to select the compe to represent this association in the Olympic tryouts to be held on 12 and 13.

Sol Seeman, 125 pound Na and Metropolitan Champion, w the favorite in the featherw class. A bout that will be while seeing will be in the weight 135 pound class betwee champions, Frank Cassidy, Oz Association, and Sam Mosberg, M politan welterweight champion, will make the lightweight limi this tournament. The other com tors in the lightweight class a Ponteau, St. Christopher Club, Crozier, Bronxdale A. C.; J. H Paulist A. C.; J. Florio, Paulist and H. Addonizio, Stamford, William Spengler, New York Club, Metropolitan heavyw champion, will be pitted against don Munce, of Bayonne, N. J.

Mrs. Barlow Nabs Gol Title for Seventh T

Shawnee-on-the-Delaware, Pa., 26.—Mrs. Ronald H. Barlow, Phi phia, woman's Eastern golf cham to-day for the seventh time wo annual tournament of the local try Club when she defeated Charles Knight, of Garden City former English star, in the match, 7 up and 6 to play.

Their cards:

Mrs. Barlow—
Out 4 4 5 4 5 5 4 8
In 6 6 3 4 5 5 8 9
Mrs. Knight—
Out 5 5 6 7 5 5 5 4 5
In 8 7 4 4 5 4 4 6 3

Ole Anderson Stopped by Brennan in Eig

CLEVELAND, O., June 26.—Ba Levinsky, of Philadelphia, w newspaper decision over Sergean Smith, of New York, in a ten- bout here this afternoon, the f event of a boxing show for the land Olympic games fund. The are light-heavyweights.

Bill Brennan, of Chicago, kn out Olie Anderson of New Yo the eighth round of a schedule round contest. The men are h weights.

HOVEY WINS TITLE G

BRIDGEPORT, Conn., June Roger H. Hovey, of Shuttle Me won the Connecticut golf cham ship for the third time this afte when he defeated Reginald Lew Greenwich, 5 up and 4 to play. was never hard pressed, finishin morning play, 5 up.

ARDSLEY CLUB BEA

The Gedney Farms Country yesterday defeated Ardsley Club ers in a team match on the named course by 7 points to 2 the system of scoring each counted a point.

240 VETERANS ENTE

There are 240 entries, for th nual father and son golf ha contest, to-morrow, at the Hollow Country Club.

SOUTHERN ASSOCIATION

Birmingham, 9; Memphis, 8.
Nashville, 8; Mobile, 2.
Chattanooga, 5; New Orleans, 3.
Atlanta, 5; Little Rock, 1.

ABE RUTH'S 27TH HOME RUN AIDS YANKS IN TROUNCING TIGERS

,000 ENJOY EAVY HITS BY MEUSEL

ornian Thrills Big Crowd n His Timely, Hard Swats. ays Tightens in the Pinches

By Arthur Robinson.

'HE Yankees beat the Tigers at the Polo Grounds yesterday by the score of 6 to 5, and outstanding features of the were as follows:

Babe Ruth was deliberately d three times, and on his other at bat drove the ball into the r tier of the right field grand- for his twenty-seventh home of the season;

Bob Meusel, following Ruth in atting order, made two doubles, in three runs, scored one him- and was deprived of a third le as the result of a spectacular ing catch by Ty Cobb after walked for the third time;

Howard Ehmke, who pitched for Tigers, was continually hooted hissed by the crowd because of imidity;

Ping Bodie stole two bases, and pinch-hitting for Pinnelli in ninth, hit the ball into the left bleachers for a home run. Cobb got a homer; and—

Carl Mays, pitching for the s, was hit freely, and save in ixth, when the Tigers made five and scored three runs, was ive in the pinches and preserved ead which the Yankees gave him e early innings.

WATCH STRUGGLE.

crowd of 35,000 saw the game. y seat in the grandstand and s was sold a half-hour before started, and several thousand n the stone steps on the sides of aisles. Others stood three deep d the last row of seats and d over the shoulders of those ed on the iron railings high in stand.

ny turned away from the park r than sit in the bleachers. As s, there were only a few small es of unoccupied seats out there the true democrats of the game in the sun day after day, and reds of women and their escorts hed the game with them rather forego the pleasure of watching and Cobb in action at the same

e hundred and fifty policemen lled the outside of the park a squad of mounted bluecoats led the pedestrian and automo- traffic. Early arrivals were en- ined by the antics of Ruth, who a turn at second, short and after going through the regu- period of fielding and batting ise with the Yanks.

e Tigers scored a run in the first g, and Hughey Jennings blew elf to a tuft of choice grass. He red acute indigestion in the sec- half of the first, however, when Yanks scored two runs, went into ead and retained it until the end.

TO RUTH JEERED.

e Tigers' first run was the result ngles by Jones and Cobb and an d out. In the Yanks' portion of same inning Vick walked and to third on Pipp's double. Ruth purposely passed for the first filling the bases, and the crowd red Ehmke a large and ripe berry in the form of sustained g, hissing and whistles.

Meusel, he of the celebrated Twins, responded to the on accorded him, drove a double ft, scoring Vick and Pipp.

the third Ruth got his homer, Colonel T. L. Huston, vice-presi- of the Yanks, uttered a dirthy- ic groan and fell back limp into eat.

, my gosh!" he cried. "My athlete is going back. He only the ball into the lower tier of stand, and that's the first time done that this season. Oh, my He's always hit the ball into bleachers, into the upper tier or the roof. Oh, my gosh!"

Colonel, however, recovered composure at length, and felt what relieved when Ruth walked e fifth and was again brought by a double by Meusel. The t Terrible committed some ex- nt base running on that hit, and he and Meusel, the other Bust Twin, were cheered to the echo e great crowd. Ping Bodie, the ely and Magnificent Pizzola, then through with a modest single to and Meusel scored.

WALLOPS A HOMER.

at made the score 5 to 1, but in ixth the Tigers got to Mays for its and three runs, and the crowd e a bit uneasy. Bush precipi- the annoyance with a single scored on Cobb's homer into the r tier of the right field grand- . Veach and Shorten singled and nced a base on Ellison's out, and inelli's infield out Veach scored. the eighth Cobb walked and ad- ed a base on an infield out, but the tying run on second Ellison hed the ball at Mays, who defied by catching it. He was spun letely around by the force of blow and quickly got rid of the ing ball. He threw to Ward, doubled Cobb off second and ltaneously prevented a tie.

e Yankees got their last run in ighth. Veach lost Pratt's drive e left field fence in the sun, and it went for a double. He went to on Mays' long fly to Cobb, and d on Cobb's poor throw to the d.

the ninth Hale, batting for elli, hit a homer and again cut the Yanks' lead to a run. Flag- , batting for Ehmke, doubled to , but with the tying run again econd Bush flied to Vick for the out.

e score:

DETROIT.	ab	r	h	o	a	e	NEW YORK.	ab	r	h	o	a	e
ss	5	1	1	0	2	0	Ward,ss	5	0	0	3	5	0
,2b	4	1	1	2	0	1	Vick,rf	3	1	0	2	0	0
cf	3	1	2	0	0	0	Pipp,1b	4	1	1	13	0	0
,lf	4	1	2	2	0	0	Ruth,lf	1	2	1	1	0	0
en,rf	4	0	1	2	0	0	Meusel,3b	4	1	2	0	2	0
n,1b	4	0	0	5	3	0	Bodie,cf	3	0	1	0	0	0
ll,3b	3	0	1	0	0	0	Pratt,2b	4	1	1	5	6	1
ith,c	4	0	1	6	2	0	Ruel,c	3	0	1	2	2	0
ke,p	3	0	0	2	1	0	Mays,p	3	0	0	1	3	0
e	1	1	1	0	0	0							
tead	1	0	1	0	0	0							
als	36	5	11	24	8	1	Totals	30	6	7	27	18	1

atted for Pinelli in ninth inning.
atted for Ehmke in ninth inning.

it	1	0	0	0	0	3	0	0	1	—5
York	2	0	1	0	2	0	0	1	x	—6

o-base hits—Meusel (2), Pipp, Pratt, tead. Home runs—Ruth, Cobb, Hale. n bases—Bodie (2), Ruth. Sacrifice— Double plays—Pratt to Ward to Pipp; to Ward. Left on bases—Detroit, 5; York, 7. Bases on balls—Off Mays, 1; hmke, 6. Struck out—By Mays, 1; by ke, 4. Umpires—Evans and Hildebrand. of game—One hour and fifty minutes.

PO KNOCKS OUT JIRSA

UENOS AIRES, July 10.—Luis An- Firpo, heavyweight boxing cham- of South America, knocked out nio Jirsa in the first half of the round of a scheduled ten-round at the University Club here ight. The winner has challenged South American fighter to meet

BRINGING UP FATHER By George McManus

KRAZY KAT By Herriman

GIANTS COME FROM BEHIND TO NOSE OUT CUBS BY 3-2 SCORE

CHICAGO, July 11.—The Giants got an even break in their series with the Cubs by winning to-day's game, 3 to 2, Rube Benton earning a decision over Jim Vaughn in a splendid pitching duel. A crowd of 20,000, part of which found accommodation on the field, saw the game, making ground rules necessary.

Both pitchers started strong, and for two and a half innings the batters didn't have much of a chance to make much headway, but in the Cubs' half of the third Benton suddenly weakened and yielded a brace of runs. After Killifer had been disposed of, Vaughn shot a single through the box and Twombly poked a one-base blow to left. Hollocher was retired on a hopper to Doyle, but Benton couldn't keep the ball over the plate for Terry, who walked, and the bases were filled.

MERKLE SWATS DOUBLE.

This brought up Merkle, who always is a dangerous hitter against left-handed pitchers. Fred laced a double into the crowd in right field, and Vaughn and Twombly scored, Terry stopping at third. Robertson ended the inning by grounding to Kelly.

In the fourth inning Larry Doyle incurred the wrath of Umpire Bill Klem and in consequence got an early start to the shower. Larry kicked on a third strike and Bill waved him out of the pastime. He was replaced by Al Lefevre.

The Giants made a bid for a run in the sixth, when Young, first man up, drew a pass and Frisch rapped a single past Terry. Kelly, however, flied to Paskert and King hit into a rapidly consummated double play.

TIE GAME IN SEVENTH.

In the seventh the Giants stepped out in earnest and tied the score. Herzog made a fine play on Lefevre's grounder and threw him out, but Snyder beat out a bunt down the third-base line. Herzog booted Benton's grounder into the crowd back of third base, Snyder going to third and Benton to second, Burns scoring both men with a double into the crowd in right field. He was left stranded at the middle bag when Bancroft popped to Hollocher and Young struck out.

The tie was broken in the eighth. Frisch led off with a drive into the crowd along the fence in right centre for two bases. Kelly moved him along to third with a sacrifice, and King sent a sacrifice liner to Paskert on which Frisch scored.

The score:

NEW YORK.	ab	r	h	o	a	e	CHICAGO.	ab	r	h	o	a	e
Burns,lf	5	0	2	1	0	0	Twombly,rf	4	1	2	2	0	1
Banc'ft,ss	4	0	0	3	3	1	Hol'cher,ss	4	0	1	2	3	0
Young,rf	3	0	1	2	0	0	Terry,2b	3	0	1	2	2	0
Frisch,3b	4	1	2	1	4	0	Merkle,1b	4	0	1	9	0	0
Kelly,1b	3	0	1	15	0	0	Rob'tson,lf	4	0	2	0	0	0
King,cf	3	0	0	0	0	1	Paskert,cf	4	0	0	3	0	0
Doyle,2b	2	0	1	1	1	0	Herzog,3b	4	0	0	1	4	0
Lefevre,2b	2	0	0	2	6	0	Killifer,c	4	0	0	8	1	0
Snyder,c	4	1	1	2	2	0	Vaughn,p	3	1	1	0	0	0
Benton,p	4	1	0	0	3	0							
Totals	34	3	8	27	22	2	Totals	34	2	8	27	?	2

New York	0	0	0	0	0	0	2	1	0	—3
Chicago	0	0	2	0	0	0	0	0	0	—2

Two-base hits—Young, Merkle, Burns (2), Hollocher, Frisch. Sacrifices—Kelly, King. Double plays—Herzog to Merkle; Lefevre to Bancroft to Kelly. Left on bases—New York, 7; Chicago, 6. Bases on balls—Off Benton, 1; off Vaughn, 1. Struck out—By Benton, 1; by Vaughn, 8. Wild pitch—Benton. Umpires—Klem and Emslie. Time of game—One hour and fifty minutes.

Star Ball Players on "House of David" Team

When the "House of David" baseball team starts its series with the Bronx Giants this Saturday the fans will witness one of the greatest clubs that ever came out of the West. Baseball to this sect is more than a fancy; it is almost part of their religion. Whenever the opportunity presents itself the team is out on the diamond perfecting in the national pastime.

That the major league owners consider the "House of David" players far above the ordinary can be judged by the enticing proffers made to obtain the services of some of the players that will be seen in action Saturday. Mooney, who will twirl, has been sought repeatedly by the Chicago Cubs, and has an offer of $25,000 waiting for him if he cares to consider it.

When the team was in this city last Winter entertaining in vaudeville with its famous band, the members created quite a furore when it was seen that each one wore a full beard. That is one of the tenets of their faith, and it is an odd sight to watch them when in play on the diamond. Each man on the team is a wizard in his position and there isn't the least doubt that the "House of David" team would give most of the major league clubs a stiff battle.

EASTERN LEAGUE.

Albany, 7; Pittsfield, 3.
Worcester, 3; Bridgeport, 2.
Springfield, 10; Waterbury, 2 (first game).
Springfield, 11; Waterbury, 7 (second game).
Hartford, 8; New Haven, 6.

BASEBALL SUMMARY

AMERICAN LEAGUE.

YESTERDAY'S RESULTS.

New York, 6; Detroit, 5.
Cleveland, 4; Washington, 0.
No other games scheduled.

STANDING OF THE CLUBS.

	W.	L.	P.C.		W.	L.	P.C.
Cleveland	51	26	.662	Boston	35	37	.486
New York	52	27	.658	St. Louis	36	39	.480
Chicago	46	29	.613	Detroit	23	50	.315
Wash'ton	37	35	.514	Philadel'a	21	58	.266

GAMES TO-DAY.

Chicago at Philadelphia.
St. Louis at Boston.
No other games scheduled.

NATIONAL LEAGUE.

YESTERDAY'S RESULTS.

New York, 3; Chicago, 2.
Brooklyn, 2; St. Louis, 1.
Cincinnati, 6; Boston, 3.
No other game scheduled.

STANDING OF THE CLUBS.

	W.	L.	P.C.		W.	L.	P.C.
Brooklyn	44	32	.579	Pittsburgh	35	36	.493
Cincin'ati	41	31	.569	Boston	31	35	.470
Chicago	39	38	.506	New York	35	40	.467
St. Louis	39	39	.500	Philadel'a	30	43	.411

GAMES TO-DAY.

New York at St. Louis.
Brooklyn at Chicago.
Philadelphia at Cincinnati.
Boston at Pittsburgh.

INTERNATIONAL LEAGUE.

YESTERDAY'S RESULTS.

Akron, 4; Jersey City, 1.
Buffalo, 7; Baltimore, 5.
Rochester, 5; Syracuse, 3.
No other game scheduled.

STANDING OF THE CLUBS.

	W.	L.	P.C.		W.	L.	P.C.
Baltimore	51	24	.680	Reading	38	40	.487
Buffalo	51	27	.654	J'sey City	30	48	.385
Toronto	52	28	.650	Rochester	24	53	.312
Akron	47	30	.610	Syracuse	17	60	.221

GAMES TO-DAY.

Jersey City at Akron.
Baltimore at Buffalo.
Syracuse at Rochester.
Reading at Toronto (2 games).

Many Enter Singles Event in Greenwich Net Play

The entries for invitation tennis tournament at the Greenwich Field Club on July 15, 16 and 17 closed yesterday at Greenwich, Conn. The drawings for the doubles will be announced as soon as the committee is advised as to the make-up of the teams.

These entries have been received thus far:

Women's Singles—Miss Edith Sigourneym, Miss Eleanor Goss, Mrs. Lewis G. Morris, Mrs. De Forest Cande, Mrs. Rawson Wood, Miss Edith B. Handy, Mrs. H. Pritchard, Miss Katherine Lauder, Miss Mary Heaton, Miss Florence Ballin, Mrs. Robert Leroy, Miss Carona Winn, Mrs. S. H. Waring, Miss Bessie Holden, Miss Katherine Force, Mrs. David C. Mills, Mrs. Dorothy Tenant, Mrs. Clara Cassel, Mrs. Welth, Mrs. Thomas Bundy and Miss Helen Baker.

Men's singles—Harold A. Throckmorton, Theodore R. Pell, Lyle Mahan, Walter H. Hall, Aldrich H. Mahan, Jr., H. S. Parker, Dun Mathey, Cedric A. Major, Robert Leroy, Francis Hunter, Dwight P. Robinson, Allen J. Lowrey, Willard J. Botsford, William Rosenbaum, S. H. Boshell, Watson M. Washburn, Wallace Rovol, William Rand, Jr., Robert C. Rand and Leonard Beckman.

Hall and Voshell Win Doubles in Net Tourney

Walter Merrill Hall and S. Howard Voshell, runner-up for the Metropolitan title, proved a very good combination on the courts of the Atlantic Yacht Club, at Sea Gate, yesterday, and romped off with the invitation tennis doubles tournament. In the final round they defeated the team of Frank T. Anderson, the Brooklyn champion, who won the singles event on Saturday, and Willard Bottsford in three out of four sets after having dropped the opener, a deuce set, 5—7, 6—4, 6—0, 6—0.

In the semi-final round Anderson and Bottsford gained their way to the final by triumphing over Frederick C. Anderson and Ben Letson, the New Jersey State doubles champions, in two out of three sets, 6—2, 8—10, 6—4. The surprise registered in this match was in the fact that the winners are a new combination while the New Jersey champions have been playing together for quite some time.

TOOTS AND CASPER By J. E. Murphy

Daubert's Circuit Drive in Ninth Crushes Braves

CINCINNATI, Ohio, July 11.—Daubert's home run in the ninth inning to-day broke a tie score and gave Cincinnati an even break in the series with Boston. The drive sent in two runners ahead of Daubert, and all three tallies counted under the new rules. Sallee and Rudolph were both hit freely.

The score:

BOSTON.	ab	r	h	o	a	e	CINCINNATI.	ab	r	h	o	a	e
Powell,lf	5	0	0	3	0	0	Rath,2b	5	2	1	1	4	0
Pick,2b	4	0	1	2	4	0	Daubert,1b	4	1	1	8	0	0
Mann,lf	3	1	0	4	0	0	Groh,3b	4	1	3	3	2	0
Sullivan,rf	2	0	1	1	0	0	Roush,cf	4	0	2	6	0	0
Cruise,rf	1	0	0	0	0	0	Duncan,lf	3	0	0	1	1	0
Holke,1b	3	0	1	9	3	1	Neal,rf	4	0	1	5	1	0
Boechel,3b	4	1	1	2	0	1	Sicking,ss	4	0	1	2	4	1
Mrnvile,ss	3	1	2	3	2	0	Wingo,c	4	1	3	1	0	1
Gowdy,c	3	0	1	1	2	0	cCrane	0	0	0	0	0	0
Rudolph,p	3	0	1	0	4	0	Sallee,p	2	0	0	0	1	0
aEayrs	1	0	1	0	0	0	dSee	1	0	1	0	0	0
M'Quilln,p	0	0	0	0	0	1	Eller,p	1	1	0	0	1	0
Totals	32	3	9	b25	15	3	Totals	36	6	13	27	14	2

a Batted for Rudolph in ninth inning.
b One out when winning run was scored.
c Ran for Wingo in ninth inning.
d Batted for Sallee in seventh inning.

Boston	0	0	0	0	1	1	1	0	0	—3
Cincinnati	1	0	0	0	0	1	1	0	3	—6

Two-base hits—Wingo, See, Sullivan, Boeckel, Maranville (2). Three-base hit—Roush. Home run—Daubert. Sacrifices—Daubert, Holke, Maranville. Double plays—Rath to Sicking to Daubert (2); Groh to Roth to Daubert; Neale to Daubert; Maranville to Holke; Pick to Holke to Maranville. Left on bases—Boston, 7; Cincinnati, 7. Bases on balls—Off Sallee, 2; off Eller, 1; off Rudolph, 1. Hits—Off Sallee, 7 in 7 innings; off Eller, 2 in 2 innings; off 1-3 inning. Struck out—By Eller, 1; by Rudolph 1 inning. Struck out—By Eller, 1; by Rudolph, 1. Winning pitcher—Eller. Losing pitcher—McQuillen. Umpires—Rigler and Moran. Time of game—One hour and forty-five minutes.

PHILLIES TRIUMPH, 3-2

TOLEDO, Ohio, July 11.—The Philadelphia Nationals bunched hits off Ralph Comstock, former Detroit and Louisville pitcher, and won from the Rail-Lights, an independent outfit by a score of 3 to 2 here to-day. Manager Cravath injected himself into the game as a pinch hitter and hit a foul.

Phila. Nationals	0	0	0	1	0	0	0	2	0	—3	9	4
Rail-Lights	0	0	0	2	0	0	0	0	0	—2	7	2

Batteries—Gallia and Withrow; Comstock and Brennegan.

Runs for the Week.

NATIONAL LEAGUE.

Club	S	M	T	W	T	F	S	Tls.
Cincinnati	6							6
New York	3							3
Boston	3							3
Brooklyn	2							2
Chicago	2							2
St. Louis	1							1
Philadelphia	*							*
Pittsburgh	*							*

AMERICAN LEAGUE.

Club	S	M	T	W	T	F	S	Tls.
New York	6							6
Detroit	5							5
Cleveland	4							4
Washington	0							0
Boston	*							*
Philadelphia	*							*
Chicago	*							*
St. Louis	*							*

INTERNATIONAL LEAGUE.

Club	S	M	T	W	T	F	S	Tls.
Buffalo	7							7
Rochester	5							5
Baltimore	5							5
Akron	4							4
Syracuse	3							3
Jersey City	1							1
Reading	0							0
Toronto	0							0

*No game played.

Eddie Summers Joins Burke's Training Camp

Eddie Summers, New York featherweight, will become a stablemate of Marty Burke's upon the "Stringbean's" arrival in Gotham.

Burke has a lot of respect for Gene Tunney, the Greenwich Village star, whom he opposes at John Jenning's Armory Club on the night of July 19.

To the end of making the Tunney battle a decisive victory, Burke is working hard for his engagement with Gene. Summers will be the only New York boy who will work with Burke. Eddie has signed a contract with John Cox, Marty's Eastern representative. Summers will go South with Burke and Cox after the Tunney party.

Summers will box some good featherweight on the Tunney-Burke card.

Larkin's Home Run Trips St. Aloysius Nine, 8-6

Washington Heights Catholic League Club scored its fifth straight victory by defeating the St. Aloysius nine yesterday afternoon at Van Cortland Park, by a score of 8 to 6.

With two runs behind as they entered the ninth, Larkin, of the Washington club, knocked a homer, with the bases full, and chalked up three markers for his team, thereby downing the St. Aloysius squad.

The score:

Washington	8	11	0
St. Aloysius	6	9	1

Noonan and Coughlin; Dunn and Walker.

AMERICAN ASSOCIATION.

Louisville, 3; Kansas City, 2.
Toledo, 4; Minneapolis, 2.
St. Paul, 10; Columbus, 4.
Milwaukee, 9; Indianapolis, 3 (first game).

Five Leading Batters in the Major Leagues

BABE RUTH has averaged more than one run per game as a member of "murderers' row." In the 73 games "Bustin' Babe" has crossed the pan 78 times, seven more than that of Tris Speaker, his nearest run-scoring rival. Babe collected his 76th homer in the American League to-day, making his lifetime average over 12 four-sackers a year.

AMERICAN LEAGUE.

Player	Club	G.	A.B.	R.	H.	P.C.
Sisler,	St. L.	75	302	59	127	.421
Speaker,	Cleve.	77	298	71	121	.406
Jackson,	Chic.	71	284	47	113	.398
Ruth,	N. Y.	73	247	78	95	.385
Weaver,	Chic.	75	318	60	115	.362
Player	Club	G.	A.B.	R.	H.	P.C.
Hornsby,	St. L.	78	309	60	114	.369
E. Smith,	N. Y.	44	137	10	47	.343
Roush,	Cinn.	69	255	34	84	.329
Konetchy,	Bkn	63	243	27	79	.325
J. Smith,	St. L.	50	153	31	49	.320

Indians Daub Whitewash on Senators; Score, 4-0

WASHINGTON, July 11.—Cleveland made it 5 out of 6 from Washington by winning to-day, 4 to 0, Morton scoring his second victory of the series. It was the second shutout of the season for the locals.

The score:

CLEVELAND.	ab	r	h	o	a	e	WASHINGTON.	ab	r	h	o	a	e
Jam'son,lf	5	1	3	2	0	0	Judge,1b	4	0	0	13	0	0
C'pman,ss	5	1	2	1	4	0	Milan,lf	4	0	0	3	0	0
Speaker,cf	4	1	1	2	0	0	Rice,cf	3	0	1	2	0	0
Smith,rf	5	0	2	5	0	0	Roth,rf	4	0	1	0	0	0
G'dner,3b	5	0	1	0	1	0	Harris,2b	4	0	0	2	4	0
Wambs,2b	4	0	0	1	4	0	Shanks,3b	3	0	2	1	6	0
J'nston,1b	4	0	0	14	0	0	Ellerbe,ss	4	0	2	1	2	1
O'Neill,c	4	0	1	2	1	0	Picinich,c	1	0	0	3	1	0
Morgan,p	4	1	1	0	1	0	xGh'rrity,c	3	0	0	2	0	1
							Johnson,p	3	0	1	0	2	0
							Erickson,p	0	0	0	0	1	0
Totals	40	4	11	27	11	0	Totals	33	0	7	27	16	2

xBatted for Picinich in fifth inning.

Cleveland	1	1	0	0	0	0	2	0	0	—4
Washington	0	0	0	0	0	0	0	0	0	—0

Two-base hits—Shanks, Jamieson. Three-base hits—Chapman, Speaker. Left on bases—Cleveland, 11; Washington, 8. Bases on balls—Off Johnson, 2; off Morton, 2. Hits—Off Johnson, 10 in 7 innings; off Erickson, 1 in 2 innings. Struck out—By Johnson, 3. Losing pitcher—Johnson. Umpires—Moriarity and Chill. Time of game—One hour and fifty-six minutes.

HAWK IS CLOSE WINNER

A feature of the races among Arrow class yachts over the Indian Harbor Yacht Club, shorter course, at Greenwich, Conn., yesterday was the close finish time between the four yachts entered. Ralph E. Slaven's Hawk crossed the line just two seconds ahead of the Snapper, owned by Frank H Page. In the Indian Harbor one design class, N. H. Whittelsey's Saleny won by a good margin over the June Bug, belonging to J. H. Martin. There was a moderate wind blowing from the northeast when the yachts started over the course and in each class the yachts made fast time.

MARQUARD'S SLANTS STOP CARDS, 2 TO 1

Dodgers Win Four Out of Five Games in St. Louis—Elliott's Hit Scores the Winning Run

ST. LOUIS, July 11.—Brooklyn made it four out of five from the Cardinals on their second visit here by winning to-day's game, 2 to 1, before 10,000 fans.

Rube Marquard was in top form and held the Cardinals to six hits. He made a long hit over first base in the ninth inning that would have been a double, but Rube did not like the idea of running with only one inning to go. He had to run when Schultz kicked the ball around and he reached second, but allowed himself to be tagged out at third when Olsen drove to Lavan.

ELEVEN HITS OFF DOAK.

Doak allowed the Dodgers eleven hits, but fast fielding made most of them worthless. The winning run was started by one base on balls and pushed along by another. Lavan's clever work at short robbed the Dodgers of two runs and Milton Stock's fielding at third stopped another one.

The Cardinals put over their one run in the first inning when Janvrin tripled to left centre and scored on Schultz's fly. Myers singled for Brooklyn in the fourth inning and scored on Konetchy's double to left. Kilduff sacrificed, but Elliott was thrown out by Doak to Hornsby on a beautiful play, and Marquard grounded out to Fournier.

Wheat walked in the sixth inning. Myers bunted toward first and was out for interfering with his own hit. Konetchy walked. Kilduff flied to Schultz in short right. Elliott's single to left scored Wheat with the winning run.

A NARROW ESCAPE.

The Dodgers pulled out of a bad hole in the fourth. Stock singled with one out. Hornsby drove to Olson and both runners were safe when Kilduff muffed the throw for a force. Fournier beat out a bunt filling the bases. McHenry drove to short and a double play of Olson to Kilduff to Konetchy retired the side.

The Dodgers left to-night for Chicago where they play double headers on Monday and Wednesday and single games on Tuesday and Thursday.

The score:

ST. LOUIS.	ab	r	h	o	a	e	BROOKLYN.	ab	r	h	o	a	e
Janvrin,lf	4	1	2	2	0	1	Olson,ss	5	0	1	2	6	[illegible]
Schultz,rf	3	0	1	1	0	1	J'nston,3b	4	0	2	0	1	[illegible]
Stock,3b	4	0	1	1	2	0	Griffith,rf	5	0	1	1	0	[illegible]
H'nsby,2b	4	0	0	4	4	0	Wheat,lf	3	1	0	4	0	[illegible]
F'rnier,1b	4	0	1	8	0	0	Myers,cf	4	1	2	2	0	[illegible]
McH'ry,lf	4	0	0	5	0	0	Koney,1b	3	0	1	8	1	[illegible]
Lavan,ss	3	0	0	2	4	0	Kilduff,2b	3	0	2	4	5	1
lemons,c	3	0	1	2	0	0	Elliott,c	4	0	1	4	1	[illegible]
Doak,p	2	0	0	0	2	0	M'rquard,p	4	0	1	2	0	[illegible]
Dilh'fer,c	0	0	0	1	0	0							
aSmith	0	0	0	0	0	0							
Totals	31	1	6	b26	12	2	Totals	35	2	11	27	14	1

aRan for lemons in eighth inning.
bMyers called out for interference.

Brooklyn	0	0	0	1	0	1	0	0	0	—2
St. Louis	1	0	0	0	0	0	0	0	0	—1

Two-base hit—Koney. Three-base hit—Janvrin. Sacrifice hits—Schultz, Kilduff, Johnston. Caught stealing—Janvrin. Double plays—Lavan to Fournier; Olson to Kilduff to Koney. Bases on balls—Off Doak, 2; off Marquard, 1. Struck out—By Doak, 3; by Marquard, 3. Left on bases—St. Louis, 5; Brooklyn, 9. Umpires—McCormick and Harrison.

Freeman Leads Cyclists in Final Olympic Tryouts

J. D. Freeman, of St. Louis, Mo., captured the final Olympic bicycle race tryout at Floral Park yesterday. Leading home a field of thirty-five starters, he covered the 108.74 miles in 5 hours 24 minutes 50 seconds, hanging up a new record for the course. The former mark of 5:24:46 was set up by A. Nieminsky, of the Acme Wheelmen, at the Eastern tryouts over the same course on June 27.

A. Nogara, of Washington, D. C., was second, being timed in 5:27:51, with J. Otto, of Newark, third, in the time of 5:28:30. The start was made at 6 o'clock in the morning, and it was close to 1 in the afternoon when the first starter came in.

E. Kockler, of Chicago, Ill., was the first rider to come through, but the time elapsed between his start and finish was greater than that of the first three men and he was placed fourth. R. Grasing, of New York, finished fth, but his status is being invesigated, and in the event of disqualification Nieminsky, who finished seventh, will make up the sixth man to go over. C. Stockholm, of Chicago, was sixth.

WELSH TRAINS WITH BEAR

Freddie Welsh, ex-champion lightweight of the world, has injected a decided novelty into his training methods. He has secured a big black bear weighing two hundred and fifty pounds and daily he wrestles with the animal for fifteen or twenty minutes. According to Freddie, it's got medicine ball stuff and weight-pulling "beaten to a frazzle."

THE WEATHER.
Western Pennsylvania, Ohio and West Virginia—PROBABLY SHOWERS Thursday. Sun rises, 5:55; sets, 6:43.

The Pittsburgh Post

GOOD MORNING!
Possum' Whitted likes Bambino,
Ruth, the greatest slugger of 'em all.
That explains why our third baseman
Let the 'Demon's' foul fly fall.

78TH YEAR—NO. 365. THURSDAY MORNING, SEPTEMBER 9, 1920. *** TWO CENTS A COPY.

G. O. P. FUND PROBE WITNESSES ADMIT COX'S "QUOTA" CHARGES TRUE

'BABE' RUTH HITS OVER WALL
26,000 FANS SEE HOME-RUN KING SHINE

CLEVELAND "DRIVE" FOR BIG SUM TO AID HARDING DESCRIBED

Workers Rapidly Building Up Fund With $400,000 as Goal, as Charged by Cox, Probers Are Told by Blossom.

SCRAMBLE TO BOOST GEORGIA TOTAL AIRED

CHICAGO, Sept. 8.—Governor Cox's "quota" figures on the amount the Republicans sought to raise in Cleveland were substantiated and an admission made that the Nationa committee had sought to raise more than Georgia's $25,000 quota when the Senate committee investigating campaign expenditures resumed its hearing today.

Dudley S. Blossom, one of the leaders in the Cleveland fund raising drive, testified the Cuyahoga county quota was fixed at $400,000, although the testimony of Fred W. Upham, Republican National treasurer, fixed the goal for the entire state of Ohio at $400,000 for the National committee and $250,000 for state purposes.

O. W. McClure of Atlanta, Ga., said Upham sent C. F. Taylor, a paid field worker, to him last month with a letter stating that Taylor was delegated to raise more money in that state. McClure quoted Dr. J. C. Stockbridge of Atlanta, who assisted him, as saying Taylor had told Dr. Stockbridge that he wanted to raise $25,000 in Atlanta alone.

Blossom said they actually raised $74,000 in Cuyahoga county and McClure said his committee obtained pledges of about $11,000 in the state of Georgia, on which $6.015.75 had been paid.

Failing to get any other Ohio witnesses, Senator Kenyon called C. W. McClure of Atlanta, Ga., who was chairman of the state ways and means committee.

McClure testified Georgia's quota was $25,000, of which $11,000 was subscribed and about $6,000 collected. An attempt was made, however, by the Republican National treasurer, he said, to get more money out of Georgia, and for this purpose C. F. Taylor, a paid field worker, was sent to Atlanta with a letter from Treasurer Upham to McClure explaining the purpose.

HAD LONG LIST.

Taylor was given a list of 20 prospects but after visiting four gave up in disgust and left the state, the witness said. McClure quoted his chief assistant, Dr. J. C. Stockbridge, as saying that Taylor had told him he wanted to get $25,000 in the city of Atlanta alone.

McClure's testimony brought up the vagaries of Republican politics in the South, a question that was gone into some time ago when the committee heard Henry Lincoln Johnson, Negro Republican National committeeman from Georgia, who received $9,000 from the pre-convention campaign chest of Governor Lowden.

Dr. Stockbridge, it was brought out, was a Democrat up until last year and his son is now directing the campaign of Governor Dorsey, Democrat, for senator. Senator Kenyon attempted to bring out that records and information from McClure's office had found their

(Continued on Page Two, Col. Two.)

Wounded Woman Identifies Negro

Fugitive Caught in Glassmere by Detectives.

Lying in her bed in the Citizens' Hospital, New Kensington, where she is believed to be recovering from gunshot wounds in the head, inflicted by a Negro whom she had discovered rifling the cash register in her husband's restaurant last Saturday, and which it was thought would prove fatal, Mrs. Rose Lolusa yesterday morning positively identified as her assailant Tuesday Dixon, a Negro arrested at Glassmere by county detectives.

Dixon was taken to the New Kensington police station, where he was recognized as a Negro who had escaped from the New Kensington police after having been arrested on a minor charge.

Thearrest was made by County Detectives Harry Barker and T. A. Sidenstricker, who were assigned to the case when Westmoreland county authorities requested the Allegheny county detective bureau for assistance in running down the culprit.

Sleeping Sickness Cause Found

Filterable Virus Origin, SaysColumbia Medical Man.

SARATOGA SPRINGS, N. Y., Sept. 8.—Discovery of the cause of "sleeping sickness" was reported today by Dr. I. S. Wechler, of Columbia University to the state conference of health officers and public health nurses, in session here. The origin, he said, was found to be a filterable virus, which, in experiments, has transmitted the disease from man to monkeys.

Horsemen on Strike

Owners Refuse to File Entries; Till Purse Is Increased.

MONTREAL, Sept. 8.—The latest thing in strikes occurred here today, when owners of horses on the program to complete in the fall meeting of the Montreal Jockey Club tomorrow, refused to file their entries unless the size of purses were increased.

Colonel Roosevelt Has Two Narrow Escapes From Death

First Comes When Plane to Carry Him From Joplin to Vinita, Mo., Runs Away, Second When Another Machine, on Arrival, Hits Fence.

OKLAHOMA CONGRESSIONAL CANDIDATE SHAKEN UP

VINITA, Okla., Sept. 8.—Lieutenant Colonel Theodore Roosevelt escaped injury in an airplane accident a second time today, when the airplane carrying him from Joplin, Mo., to Vinita to fill a speaking date, crashed into a fence and a tree at the fair grounds here. None of the four passengers in the plane was hurt.

"Accidents will happen," Roosevelt said, as he left the scene of the second smashup and jumped into another plane to continue his trip to Okmulgee.

JOPLIN, Mo., Sept. 8.—Lieutenant Colonel Theodore Roosevelt had a narrow escape from death here today while preparing for an airplane flight to Vinita Okla., to fill speaking dates. The plane ran away with Colonel Roosevelt before the pilot had boarded it. Colonel Roosevelt managed to jump from the fusilage and land free of the rudders.

Colonel Roosevelt was entering the front seat of the plane in which Bert Chandler, candidate for Congress from in First Oklahoma district, was sitting, while Paul Meng, the pilot, gave the propeller blade a twist. The throttle was too high and the big machine tore wildly down the field.

The machine struck a high place on the ground and was wrecked. Chandler was badly shaken up.

MODIFICATION OF TELEPHONE RATES AGREED TO BY USERS AND COMPANY

Means $500,000 Reduction in Firm's Revenue, Estimate.

ACCEPTED BY COMMISSION

HARRISBURG, Sept. 8.—Modification of charges put into effect by the Bell Telephone Company in Pennsylvania last spring, an estimated reduction of $500,000 in receipts of the company, were agreed to by counsel for the corporation and more than 100 municipalities, chambers of commerce, commercial organizations, business firms and individuals and submitted to public service commissioners today as a basis for settling complaints. The commission accepted the proposals for consideration with the understanding that no rights of any complainant would be prejudiced or the "door be closed on complaints." Testimony was then ordered taken in complaints which attorneys claimed were not covered by the tentative agreement.

ACCEPTED BY COMPANY.

This was the result of a series of meetings held today by counsel for the numerous complainants and the telephone company. The proposition was submitted by Charles K. Robinson of Pittsburgh, chief of counsel for complainants, and accepted by the counsel for the company.

The proposed settlement includes:

New classifications outside of Philadelph'a and Pittsburgh and to include among others Reading, Lancaster, New Castle, McKeesport, Jeannette, Rochester, Duquesne and some smaller places with modification of business and residential rates.

Modification of the exchange areas of 243 exchanges and a reclassification which restores about 50 per cent of the former free area with

(Continued on Page Two, Col. Four.

Lenroot Leading Rival in Wisconsin

Oddie Wins in Nevada; Arizona Race Tight.

MILWAUKEE, Wis., Sept. 8.—Additional returns in the Republican senatorial contest from yesterday's state wide primary, today increased the lead of Senator Irvine L. Lenroot, over James Thompson, of La Crosse.

Complete unofficial returns from the First congressional district show Representative Randall defeated by former Representative Henry Allen Cooper.

RENO, Nev., Sept. 8.—Brewster Adams, nearest competitor to Tasker L. Oddie, one of the five Republican candidates for United States senator from Nevada, late today conceded Oddie's nomination in yesterday's primaries.

PHOENIX, Ariz., Sept. 8.—With less than one-third of the 450 precincts in the state heard from in yesterday's primaries, races still undecided include that between Senator Marcus A. Smith and R. C. Stanford for Democratic nomination for senator.

Simms had an apparent majority of 1,900 for the Democratic nomination for governor.

Masonic Emblem Lost Nine Years Is Recovered From Ohio River Catfish

HUNTINGTON, W. Va., Sept. 8.—A Masonic emblem worn as a watch charm, lost here by Herbert C. Reed of Milford, O., nine years ago, has been returned to him by a Cannelton, Ind., fisherman, who claims to have found the pin in a three-pound catfish he took from the Ohio river. Reed, who was leaning over the side of the steamer Greenland at the local wharf when the charm dropped into the water, is the auditor of Clermont county, Ohio.

WINE AND BEER ACT WOULD KILL DRY LAW, SAYS M'ADOO

NEW YORK, Sept. 8.—(By Universal Service.)—In a statement issued today, William Gibbs McAdoo made a sweeping attack upon any leniency in the prohibition amendment. He declared that the amendment will become dead letter once a beer and light wine law is passed, and called upon every man and woman voter "who puts welfare of children and humanity above mere gratification of harmful appetites" to see that Congress does not restore breweries and wineries to "political power" and re-establish "debasing and immoral liquor traffic."

In his declaration the ex-secretary of the treasury said:

"I know from my experience as secretary of the treasury that no law which provides for a drink containing a certain percentage of alcohol can be successfully enforced. If the law should permit thousands of breweries and wineries to be re-opened throughout the land and to manufacture beverages with specified alcoholic content, it would be impossible to prevent the manufacture of those beverages with a larger percentage of alcohol than prescribed, or to prevent adulteration after manufacture, and the effect would be to nullify the prohibition amendment.

"Even if the saloon were not reopened, light wines and beer would be sold at every soda fountain, at every lunch counter and in every restaurant and every hotel. It is a notorious fact that drunkards begin by drinking light wines and beer when young, and as the appetite grows the desire for stronger drink is developed. If we turn loose upon the country light wines and beer we will have destroyed the prohibition amendment and brought back upon humanity a curse greater than war itself. The greatest victory ever achieved for helpless women and children would be thrown to the winds.

"It required a two-thirds vote of the Congress to submit the prohibition amendment to the states; it then required three-fourths of the states to put the amendment in the constitution. Forty-five states have ratified the amendment.

"If Congress can, by mere majority vote, with the approval of a favoring President to license beer and light wine, then prohibition, which required a two-thirds vote and a presidential approval, plus the consent of three-fourths of the states, can be nullified by a majority of the Congress with the approval of the President and the breweries and wineries know this fact."

"CARRY YOUR LUNCH" PLAN INDORSED BY CONGRESS OF WOMEN'S CLUBS

Campaign to Reduce Restaurant Prices Approved.

CLUBS TO TAKE UP MOVEMENT

The "Carry Your Lunch" plan and the campaign of the fair price committee against profiteering restaurant men of Pittsburgh were indorsed yesterday afternoon by the executive board of the Congress of Women's Clubs.

The meeting, which was held in the Hotel Chatham, was attended by Mrs. C. E. Cosolowsky, Mrs. John S. Sloan, president of the Women's Club; Mrs. W. L. Ferson, secretary of the congress; Mrs. Davis Scott of the Bellevue Women's Club, Mrs. R. W. Johnston of the Tourists' Club, Miss Mathilda Orr Hays of the Pittsburgh Forum, Mrs. I. L. Gillespie of the Travelers' Club, and Dr. Laura Shorm of the Women's Medical Society. Miss Helen Grimes, president of the congress, presided

The vote to indorse the movement to reduce the high cost of restaurant food came after an hour's discussion during which the great majority of the women declared themselves not only in favor of the "Carry Your Lunch" idea, but as also willing to do all in their power to make it successful.

HUSBANDS APPROVE.

Many of the women stated that the matter had long been under consideration in their homes and that their husbands and sons heartily approved of it.

Discussion of the methods of putting the plan into general operation will be taken up at regular meetings of the various clubs. The Housekeepers' Club of Pittsburgh will make the matter the chief business of its meeting this afternoon in the home of Mrs. Joseph C. Heckman, 327 Home street. It is hoped that by the time the first general meeting of the congress is held, October 1, plans will have reached the final stage of formulation.

WOMEN IN EARNEST.

The various advantages and disadvantages of carrying lunches were taken into consideration at the meeting yesterday. One of the women brought up the matter of the difficulty in supplying and need of having hot drinks with the mid-day meal. Other members told of experiments with the vacuum bottles which, it was declared, would clear up that stumbling block.

All of the women were thoroughly in earnest regarding the fight against the gouging restaurant-keepers, many of them citing examples that had come to their attention of outrageous profiteering.

PIRATES LOSE 7-3 IN FEATURE CLASH

WHAT "BABE" DID

First time up—Got base on balls.
Second time up—Flied to Bigbee.
Third time up—Singled to center.
Fourth time up—Struck out.
Fifth time up—Hit homer over right field wall.

Here's the Mighty "Babe" Ready to "Lose" the Ball

—By Walter Thiesen, Post Staff Photographer.

Whitted Intentionally Misses Babe's High Foul in Ninth, Making Spectacular Smash Over Right Field Bleachers Possible and Bringing Chorus of Cheers.

BODIE'S ANKLE DISLOCATED; HAROLD CARLSON IS BEANED

By EDWARD F. BALINGER.

Babe Ruth bundled his mighty war-club into Forbes Field yesterday, and after several attempts, finally succeeded in the ninth inning in doing exactly what 26,000 fans were howling for, when he soaked the sphere completely out of the lot. Incidently, the New York Americans defeated the Pirates 7-3, in an exhibition game.

George Whitted divided honors with Ruth for the role of hero. George had a splendid chance to prevent the home-run king from performing his famous specialty. Babe sent up a foul which went so high the spectators began to think it never would return to earth. Whitted stepped to the edge of the overflow crowd and set himself to make the catch.

"Let it drop!" and "don't catch that ball!" were the principal words that poured into the third baseman's ears as he stood there ready to retire the swatting celebrity of the baseball world. The Pirates were behind, with little hope of overcoming their lost lead. It was nothing but an exhibition game anyway, and the multitude had paid good money to see Ruth smite that apple. All these thoughts flashed through the quick-thinking Whitted and as the ball descended, he suddenly decided to let it fall.

The foul smacked against the sod at George's feet and Umpire Klem called it strike two. The fans gave vent to a rousing cheer. Whitted had made a perfect hit with them. Ruth caught the next offering and sent it high and far. At first it looked as if it might drop in right field, but it didn't. As it started its downward course, it threatened to alight inside the bleacher, but it did no such thing. That ball fell from the sky and plunked against the hill, perhaps 15 feet on the outside of the fence. Chick Fewster scored ahead of the Babe.

Big Demonstration.

Ruth's homer was followed by a wave of cheering that was deafening. Straw hats were shied upon the playing field and the crowd fairly went wild with delight. The applause did not subside for fully five minutes. Prior to yesterday, the only batter to knock a fly over the right field wall was Ham Hyatt. He made the smash on the afternoon of May 29, 1913, when one was on, and this drive tied up the score and enabled the Pirates to win out in the ninth. The Cubs were the visitors and Humphries was in the box for them. Hyatt's memorable thump was a liner which sailed far back in the direction of the hollow.

In addition to the thrill produced by Babe's bat, yesterday's game had a serious feature. Ping Bodie, the great center fielder of the Yankees, met with an accident that will keep him off the field during the rest of the season. The mishap is most unfortunate, for the reason that Manager Miller Huggins has his Yanks fighting for the lead in

(Continued on Page Eight, Col. Seven.)

PIRATE BOX SCORE

NEW YORK.	AB.	R.	B.	P.	A.	E.
Fewster, ss	5	1	1	0	3	0
Pipp, 1b	4	1	0	14	1	0
Ruth, rf	4	1	2	5	1	0
Pratt, 2b	5	1	1	1	8	1
Meusel, lf	4	1	1	0	0	0
Vick, lf	1	0	1	0	0	0
Bodie, mf	1	1	1	1	0	0
Lewis, mf	2	1	1	3	0	0
Gleich, mf	0	0	0	0	0	0
Ward, 3b	4	0	0	0	1	0
Hofmann, c	2	0	1	3	1	0
Ferguson, p	4	0	1	0	0	0
Totals	36	7	10	27	15	1

PITTSBURGH.	AB.	R.	B.	P.	A.	E.
Bigbee, lf	4	0	1	2	0	0
Carey, mf	2	0	0	1	0	0
Lee, rf	1	0	0	0	0	0
Cutshaw, 2b	3	1	0	3	3	0
Nicholson, rf-mf	4	1	1	1	0	0
Whitted, 3b	3	0	0	1	1	1
Grimm, 1b	3	0	1	10	1	0
McKechnie, ss	4	1	0	2	4	0
Haeffner, c	2	0	0	7	2	0
Zinn, p	3	0	0	0	1	0
Totals	29	3	3	27	12	1

New York	010	004	002	—7
Pittsburgh	001	200	000	—3

Earned runs—New York 5, Pittsburgh 2.
Two-base hit—Bigbee.
Three-base hits—Bodie, Lewis.
Home run—Ruth.
Stolen bases—Pratt, Bigbee.
Double play—Ruth to Hofmann.
First base on balls—Off Ferguson 2 (Haeffner, Cutshaw); off Zinn 5 (Ruth, Pipp, Hofmann 2, Lewis).
Wild pitches—Zinn, Ferguson.
Passed ball—Hofmann.
Hit with pitched ball—By Ferguson 1 (Carey).
First base on errors—New York 1, Pittsburgh 1.
Sacrifice bunt—Whitted.
Sacrifice fly—Grimm.
Left on bases—New York 7, Pittsburgh 4
Struck out—By Ferguson 2 (Nicholson, Zinn); off Zinn 6 (Fewster, Lewis, Ward, Ruth, Ferguson, Pipp).
Time of game—1:46.
Umpires—Klem and Emslie.

Italian Earthquake Death Toll Grows

FLORENCE, Italy, Sept. 8.—Graver news from the area affected by Tuesday's earthquake was received today, the number of victims being put at several hundred dead and injured. The quake caused great damage in the provinces of Florence, Lisa, Leghorn, Lucca, Massa Carrara, Reggio d'Emilia, Modena and Piacenza. The shock was felt in the surrounding provinces as far as Milan, but there was no injury to life or property.

Fivizzano, where the damage to buildings was especially heavy, was a flourishing little town perched on the slopes of the Apennies. It possessed an old town hall and also the ruins of a castle. The whole scene is one of ruin, with hundreds of the inhabitants buried under the debris. Groans and cries were heard on all sides as rescuers worked feverishly.

LONDON, Sept. 8.—The "Epocha" of Rome estimates 300 people were killed in Tuesday's earthquake, says a Stefian news agency dispatch this evening.

Trans-Continental Mail Planes Reach Cleveland En Route To San Francisco

CLEVELAND, Sept. 8.—The airplane piloted by R. G. Page arrived here at 12:45 p. m., completing the first leg of the Inaugural Transcontinental Air Mail Service between New York and San Francisco.

William Hopson's machine arrived at 1:17 p. m.

After taking a supply of gasoline, Page continued his journey to Chicago at 1:17 p. m., saying he hoped to reach Iowa City before night. He reported slow progress between Mineola and Cleveland because of a heavy head wind, his actual flying time being five hours and 59 minutes.

Hapson brought the regular mail, 16,000 letters, from New York, according to air service officials here. These included letters from Senator Warren G. Harding, G. O. P. nominee, to friends in San Francisco. Others were from Postmaster General Burleson and Assistant Postmaster General Praeger to San Francisco newspapers.

The Aerial League of America announced it had sent letters to Senator Harding and Governor Cox. Each presidential candidate was asked if he would favor extension of aerial mail service if elected.

One stop was made en route to Cleveland, at Bellefonte, Pa., where both machines took on gasoline.

The machine piloted by Page arrived at Bellefonte at 8:59, and left for Cleveland at 10:05 a. m., and Hopson's machine arrived at Bellefonte at 9:47, and left at 1:34.

Page carried letters to the mayors of six cities along the route.

The trip is expected to be completed in three days, arriving at San Francisco 42 hours ahead of the time regularly required for mail trains.

The flight mapped out is 2,651 miles in length. The establishment of the service places at the disposal of the United States military forces what is probably the greatest system of regularly maintained landing fields and facilities in the world, according to the postoffice department.

In addition to Cleveland, stops en route to the coast were scheduled for Chicago Omaha, Cheyenne, Salt Lake City and Reno, the latter being the lst before San Francisco.

RING, TRACK, FIELD AND GAMES

Evening Herald to Have Best Service on World Series

BOBBY, IRISH MEUSEL AND OTHER STARS TO WRITE OF BIG GAMES

With the close of the Pacific Coast league season tomorrow ttention of local baseball fans will be turned to the world's eries games between the Yankees of the American league and ie Giants, National league, both clubs representing New York.

The big league pennant winners ill stage their first game at the Polo rounds Wednesday afternoon and e series will continue until one of e clubs has taken five games.

Realizing that the world's series is e all-important event in the sport orld, The Evening Herald has arnged to handle the big games in a g way.

Opposing each other on the two ubs are two Los Angeles boys, Bobe and "Irish" Meusel, the former ing with the Yankees and the later with the Gians. Bobbie was gradted to the major leagues from the ernon club and his brother went to e big show from the Los Angeles am. Each is recognized as one of e stars of his club.

DAILY STORIES

Because the sympathies of the local ns will be divided between the two rmer local stars, The Evening Herd has arranged to publish daily ories by the two players. Bobbie d "Irish" will write of the big mes just as diligently as they play the ball field.

Then, too, as for the past several ars, Frank Chance will analyze ch game for The Evening Herald. iance, who managed the famous d Chicago Cubs when they won ree National league pennants and o world's series, will tell just how ch game was won and lost. Chance considered one of the world's great baseball authorities. The former ib manager was the one fellow in seball who could beat John Mcaw, the man who will pilot the ants in the coming series. Chance ows the McGraw system and his mment on the performances of the ational leaguers will be interesting.

OTHER STAR WRITERS

Another big star who will write for ie Evening Herald is Sid Mercer, e of the best known baseball exrts in the game today and a brilnt writer. Tad, the best "kidder" iong all writers, will also have a ily column of clever paragraphs. Jack Veiock, Henry L. Farrell and ier baseball writers of big league liber will be on hand at every game d will look after the details of the ries.

Not only will The Evening Herald ve a great corps of writers, but it s arranged to give the fans every tail of the series the instant the me is over each day. In order to ure speed in transmission of news o leased wires will be used, each nning from the Polo grounds dit to the office of this paper.

The moment the last man is out in ch game The Evening Herald's failities for handling big news with e utmost dispatch will make posle special editions that will give e fans the last word in up-to-thenute baseball service.

TWO SCOREBOARDS

But the fans will not be compelled wait for extras telling the news. e Evening Herald will operate two scoreboards showing every play moment it is completed. One oreboard will be in front of The ening Herald, between First and cond streets, on Broadway, and the ier will be at the Tufts-Lyon Arms at Sixth and Olive. Both scoreard exhibitions will be free to the blic and every baseball fan is ined to witness the big games as ests of The Evening Herald.

Remember—there will be two scoreards.

A staff of expert writers, special wire service, two scoreboards and arrangements for special editions giving all the details of play will make The Evening Herald's world series service supreme.

Depend upon your Evening Herald for it will be

FIRST WITH THE LATEST.

KEEPING FIT

By Al Treloar

Physical Director, L. A. Athletic Club

Some of the old timers may remember the vaudeville team of Barker and Levy, "Comedy Strong Men." Albert Geyer says that to him all strong men are comedy strong men. They all hand him a laugh. It has long been a moot question in the gymnasium which kind of work most quickly topples Reason from her throne, weight lifting, tumbling or swimming, so those interested must make the decision for themselves.

Barker and Levy did an act that was half serious and half alleged comedy. Barker was the unhurtable rubber man. As one of their funniest tricks, Barker lay on his back on the floor while Levy jumped from a chair on a table down onto Barker's face. Max Levy's old mother always objected to this trick, saying that she was sure sooner or later Maxie would sprain his ankle doing that!

ALL TO BARKER

Max Levy was very neat and precise in his work and left the clowning all to Barker. When the team was with the Fitzsimmons show Barker and Fitz put up a job on Levy. It was on the occasion of the show opening at the old Star theater in Brooklyn, Levy's home neighborhood. Levy would lift a large single-handed dumbbell in three different ways, lecturing and explaining the lifts to the audience as he did so. He had the bell loaded to about 135 pounds weight, light enough so he could lift it easily.

On this opening day Fitz and Barker sent out and bought a large quantity of lead shot. They then, unknown to Levy, loaded up his dumbbell till it weighed nearly 1000 pounds. Few men could lift it from the floor with both hands, to say nothing of bringing it to the shoulder, or putting it above the head.

At the night show many of Levy's relatives and friends were out in front, and he got a reception when he came on. Finally he came to his routine with the single dumb-bell, and Barker rolled the weight out into position in the middle of the stage as usual.

AH, SOFT MUSIC

Levy gave a longer lecture than usual on his three styles of lifting, explaining that accuracy of movement should count for as much as the amount of weight lifted. He then stated his own records for the "swing-lift," the "snatch-lift" and the "jerk." Having signaled the orchestra leader to play soft music he struck a pose, standing over the dumb-bell. Then he seized the dumb-bell and tugged. It never moved. Thinking, perhaps, that it was nailed to the floor, he rolled it a little, with difficulty, to the side. Then he strained at it again till the veins stood out on his forehead, but it never budged. And Levy was a real strong man, too.

It evidently dawned on him about that time that there was something wrong. He stood up and looked about him, and saw the crowd collected in the wings. Old Fitz was laughing so that he nearly strangled. Levy turned toward the weight again, but thought better of it and quietly walked off the stage.

QUESTIONS AND ANSWERS

Q.—Please tell me if sciatic rheumatism, as other kinds of rheumatism, is caused by focal infection? Had all my teeth out three years ago, but have been a martyr to what the doctors call sciatic rheumatism for several years. Would have tonsils removed if sure it would help. M. N. R.

A.—In all probability your trouble is caused by focal infection. You should have your tonsils examined, and if they are bad have them removed. If that fails you should have a good physician continue the search for any focus of pus infection which may exist anywhere in the body.

Q.—I have weak lungs and would like to know what particular exercise would help me regain my health the quickest, and if there is any to improve my appetite? E. F. F.

A.—If you have any fever, don't try to exercise at all. In fact, when you have any temperature the best thing is to lie down and be still. When you have no temperature, do a little easy walking. Your appetite will come back when your general condition improves.

Three Who Will Compete in Champ Series

Three stars of the Yankees and Giants who will play in the world series, which opens Wednesday afternoon in New York. On left is Fred Toney, one of the aces of the Giant pitching staff. Waite Hoyt, right, youthful pitching star of the Yankees, and below, Frank Frisch of the Giants, considered one of the best third-sackers in the National league.

Special Shoot Is Scheduled at Vernon Gun Club Tomorrow

Even if the rain continues until tomorrow, local and visiting trapshooting experts intend to get in on the big century shoot to be held at "Pop" A. W. Bruner's Vernon Gun club.

Bruner scheduled the shoot in order to give all shooters a last whack at practice before the registered tournament starts on Oct. 6 and continues for four days.

The event tomorrow will be at regulation 16-yard targets with four trophies up for the four high guns and a like number of awards up for the last four low guns. The shot is expected to attract over 50 gun pointers.

Colleges and High Schools

The San Pedro high football team looms up as a strong contender for the Bay league flag this season. Gene Mahoney, who watched the boys work out yesterday, declares that the eleven should stack up well against any in the beach circuit this season.

Coach Overin, who was connected with Venice high school during last season, has been assigned to Pomona college. He has been made line coach and assistant to Coach Eugene W. Nixon. Overin should be a big help to Nixon in setting the Sagehen eleven into championship shape.

The lightweight football league of the Los Angeles city schools should be a close race. Hollywood, Los Angeles, Lincoln, Pasadena, Manual and Jefferson will all have strong lightweight aggregations and some close contests should be brought out during the coming season.

Lieut. Williams of the U. S. S. Nevada is getting a football team into shape that should stack up with the best in Southern California this season. He is anxious to line up games with any high school or college squad, it is understood.

The light Jefferson football team will play its opening game against Hollywood on Oct. 7, meeting the Hilltoppers on their home grounds. Coach Tipton believes that his lads will give the Hollywood aggregation something of a surprise.

Poly will tackle Lincoln high in their opening game, while Pasadena and Manual Arts play on the Toilers' field. Los Angeles high drew a bye for the first round and will probably remain idle on that day. Glen Whittle, however, is arranging for several out-of-town practice contests.

LEWIS WINS MATCH

SAN JOSE, Oct. 1.—Ed "Strangler" Lewis threw Nick Daviscourt in 1 hour and 15 minutes at an American Legion benefit show last night.

TEAM GETS PLAYER

Manuel Leon has been signed by the Terminal team.

FOOTBALL TEAMS PLAY SECOND CONTESTS

94 Games Billed in U. S.; Trojans Meet Sailors in L. A.; Oxy Battles Manual Arts

By RAY J. SMITH

Old King Football, shoved into the discard for the past ten months, came back today.

College and high school teams throughout the country, having completed their tough training grinds, stepped out and entered the second week of the 1921 gridiron schedule this afternoon.

Something like 94 contests were on the schedule, 50 of them being between fairly big teams. The majority of games today were of the practice variety and figured merely to give football fans a line on the true ability of the respective aggregations.

FIELDS ARE WET

Old Jupe Pluvius took a hand in entertaining the fans in Southern California. Despite soggy fields, games to the number of six were billed for this section. The feature affair of the day around Los Angeles was slated for Bovard field, the husky U. S. C. eleven being scheduled to play a double-header against teams from the U. S. S. Arizona and the U. S. S. New York.

Joe Pipal's Occidental college machine, the "dark horse of the Southern California conference, was slated to go into action against Manual Arts high on the former's field. Other affairs listed this afternoon in this territory were Whittier college vs. Sherman Indians at Whittier; Fullerton high vs. Santa Monica at Fullerton, and San Bernardino high vs. Hollywood high at San Bernardino.

The remainder of the schools in the Southern California conference took things easy today, preparing for their opening contests on Oct. 8.

California, the wonder team of 1920, meets the strong Olympic club at Berkeley. The Bears, it was figured, were due to win easily.

BIG TEN STARTS

In the Middle West the Big Ten squads got down to work, Michigan meeting Mt. Union, Minnesota playing North Dakota, Iowa battling Knox, Ohio State tackling Ohio Wesleyan, Wisconsin meeting Lawrence, Purdue meeting Wabash, Indiana going against Kalamazoo, and Chicago swinging into action against Northwestern.

Other games of importance staged in the East follow: Colgate vs. Allegeny, Yale vs. Vermont, Brown vs. Colby, Amherst vs. Columbia, Princeton vs. Swarthmore, Cornell vs. St. Bonaventure, Dartmouth vs. Middlebury, Holy Cross vs. Harvard, Lafayette vs. Pittsburg, Notre Dame vs. DePauw, Navy vs. North Carolina, Pennsylvania vs. Franklin and Marshall, Gettysburg vs. Penn State, Syracuse vs. Ohio University, and the Army vs. New Hampshire.

NEW YORK GAME AIDS MATHEWSON FUND

NEW YORK, Oct. 1.—The testimonial fund being raised for Christy Mathewson was larger by several thousand dollars today as a result of the exhibition game staged here yesterday.

The Old Timers, composed of oldtime baseball players, defeated the New York Giants by a count of 2 to 0 in a five-inning game.

PLAY 1ST ROUND IN GOLF TOURNEY

MONTEREY, Oct. 1.—First round of matches in the annual championship golf tournament of the Olympic club were staged here today.

The qualifying round was played yesterday and resulted in a win for Eddie Twiggs. Close to 60 teed off yesterday.

DUNDEE PUTS OVER K. O. ON COAST BOY

CHICAGO, Oct. 1.—Frankie Tucker of San Francisco was knocked out in the first round of a 10-round bout here last night by Mike Dundee of Rock Island, Ill.

The bout was staged on the United States training ship Commodore a few miles out on Lake Michigan.

CALL OFF BALL GAME

The contest slated for tomorrow between the Standard Oil nine and the submarine base team was called off today.

I'LL SAY SO

BY REED HEUSTIS.

Turk, 146, named Zaro, gets his twenty-fifth wife, and you might say it's her "Zaro" hour.

* * *

Zaro hour for the dame and the Turk because she gets nothing, and so does he. Zero plus Zero means Zaro and Mrs. Zaro No. 25.

* * *

Lou Berrien, the golf pro, was speaking of a fellow's mid-iron shots. But he didn't mean it; he was talking as you might say, "mid-ironically."

* * *

Grand opera is sung over the wireless. Sailors at sea immediately reefed the sails.

* * *

"T. J. Dunnigan, the hotel man," says the newspaper, "battled a gigantic fish for three and a half hours." Leading one to believe the fish must have been behind in his room rent!!

* * *

Here's a guy films a play and the belief is he may have had an eye to the box office. MAY HAVE HAD, huh?

* * *

Have you seen Jack Warner play golf? If you have, there is no need to tell you about it. If you haven't, we couldn't.

* * *

Hank Ford is still trailing that guy Newberry. Never let Hank get after you or he'll run you ragged.

* * *

Two police judges pinched for L. A. traffic violations. They will sentence themselves to long, hard terms on the L. A. farm. Har! har!

* * *

WARNING

Tough life for someone. Cafeteria cashier shortly to wed. When this is accomplished she'll feed her lesser half his breakfast then dash to the door and collect the amount of the check before he hies himself to work.

* * *

If you must marry a cafeteria worker, get the dame who runs an eye over your tray and punches the ticket. Get a firm control of the punch and you can always eat, drink and be merry.

* * *

"Hickman," says the newspaper, "opened at the Ambassador." But what did he open?

* * *

Hutt Martin is back. Hutt is present holder of the Southern California open championship and national champion of the open vowels league.

* * *

This "Beans" Reardon boy is going great as a Coast league umpire. Today "Beans" has failed to spill 'em.

* * *

Jess Willard is still eager to meet Jack Dempsey over the box-office route.

FOOTBALL TEAMS IN PRACTICE CONTEST

REDLANDS, Oct. 1.—The Santa Fe Athletic club and the Redlands university eleven clashed in a practice game here this afternoon.

It was the first game of the season for the Bulldogs, who are expected to be strong contenders for the Southern California conference crown this season.

RAIN WELCOMES HUNTERS IN SO. CAL.

Showers Fail to Halt Sportsme as Duck Season Is Opened; Birds Are Plentiful

A drizzling rain, which at time promised to develop into a real st rn welcomed hundreds of Los Angele hunters early today when the seaso on ducks opened in California.

The rain, which started falling yesterday and continued throughout th night, failed to halt the usual larg turnout of hunters. All of the loc gun clubs, located around Anaheir Sunset Beach and Naples, wer crowded to capacity, while Big Bea lake and Baldwin lake took care numerous of the Southern Californ nimrods.

Buena Vista lake, near Taft, wher ducks are reported in large number attracted hundreds of hunters. Eliza beth lake also took care of many.

The rain, which, according to re ports, was rather heavy in Sa Joaquin valley, was expected to driv thousands of new birds into South ern California.

A number of limits were brough into town by noon and by night man of the hunters were expected to home with opening day bags.

GOLF FINALS TO BE STAGED TOMORROW

FAR ROCKAWAY, L. I., Oct. 1.—Walter Hagen will meet either Ji Barnes or Emmett French in th finals of the annual profession golfers' championship tournamen here tomorrow.

Hagen won his way into the fina yesterday by defeating Cyril Walke amid a pouring rain.

French and Barnes will finish their 36-hole match here this after noon.

SIGN JOE STECHER TO PLAY WITH BEES

SAN FRANCISCO, Oct. 1.—Jo Stecher, former heavyweight wrest ing champion, has been signed to fi ish the season with Salt Lake as th result of the showing he made in th game yesterday.

Stecher handled nine chances first base without an error. slammed out a single in the four inning that scored two runs.

PEN STADIUM DRIVE MONDAY

The state-wide campaign for the ction of California's mammoth morial stadium at Berkeley will en with a bang Monday.

The stadium, according to the hitect's plans, will be able to acmmodate 60,000 spectators when npleted, but, due to the enormous nand which is being expressed for kets from all parts of the state, it ll be necessary to apportion a limd number of unit subscriptions to ch county of the state.

Only 10,000 unit subscriptions, or 000 seats, will be allotted to the mni of the University of Califor and the general public of the te, the balance of the seats being d for California students and for dents and alumni of Stanford.

ANS IN ST. LOUIS HONOR HORNSBY

Roger Hornsby, who will manage Los Angeles club in the Winter gue, was presented with two diand rings, a diamond stickpin and 00 worth of Liberty bonds at St. uis yesterday.

One of the rings was presented by Masonic lodge, another from a fund tributed by fans and the diamond kpin was given him by the Chamof Commerce.

Hornsby hit a home run and two ibles. He will leave Monday for Angeles.

OOTBALL CIRCUIT OPENS OCTOBER 6

Opening football games in the Los geles City Lightweight league will played on October 6, it was annced today. The first contests re announced as follows: Lincoln Poly high, Manual Arts at Pasana, Hollywood at Jefferson, and A. high bye.

TEAMS WILL PLAY

A fast independent ball game is ked for tomorrow afternoon when ie Murphy's nine clashes with diaid performers from the New York re at Exposition park.

The Evening Herald Has the Largest Circulation of Any Daily Newspaper in the Entire West

SECTION 2
WANT ADS
Average Temperature in L. A. Yesterday Was 67 Degrees

LOS ANGELES
EVENING HERALD
AN INDEPENDENT NEWSPAPER
Reg. U. S. Pat. Off.
The Evening Herald Grows Just Like Los Angeles

THREE CTS.
CITY AND COUNTY
Average Temperature in L. A. Yesterday Was 67 Degrees

VOL. XLVI. "THE PAPER THAT GOES HOME" Weather—SHOWERS TUESDAY, OCTOBER 4, 1921 Weather—SHOWERS "THE PAPER THAT GOES HOME" NO. 289

HERALD TO DESCRIBE WORLD SERIES CONTESTS OVER TWO LEASED WIRES

These Men Will Be Closely Watched in Games Between Yankees and Giants

Babe Ruth, the Yankee's star batter.

George Kelly, the Giant's star first baseman.

"Erin" Ward, the Yankee's star second baseman.

Bobby Meusel, the Yankee's star outfielder.

Al DeVormer, the Yankee's star catcher.

Roger Peckinpaugh, the Yankee's star shortstop.

"Irish" Meusel, the Giant's star outfielder.

Here Are Some of Stars Who Will Play in Big Series

'DOOMED TO DIE' BY SPOOKS, MAN SURVIVES TO PAY ALIMONY

Charges Wife Told Him Spirits Had Sealed His Fate for Certain Day

OCCULT SENTENCE FOILED

Judge Grants His Spouse Allowance Pending Suit for Divorce Decree

Despite the alleged statement of his wife that the spiritualists told her he would die in May, 1921, Lewis T. Stowells, a fish merchant of Sawtelle, was very much alive today when he appeared before Judge McLucas in temporary alimony proceeding in connection with the suit for divorce he filed against Lilly Stowells.

Her purported statement relative to the insight into his future was set up in Stowells' complaint as one of the instances of alleged cruelty on the part of his wife.

"I do not care for my husband," he quoted her as saying to another woman. "The spiritualists told me he would die in May, 1921."

Mrs. Stowells had filed a cross-complaint, it developed, in which she denied her husband's charges that she caused him mental suffering by continually associating with Lawrence A. Fields. She accused her husband of striking her with his fists on several occasions and falsely accusing her.

GRANTED ALIMONY

Mrs. Stowells was represented in court by Attorney A. W. Sorensen, and after a spirited hearing, Judge McLucas ordered the husband to pay his wife $50 a month alimony, $25 costs and $250 as an attorney's fee.

The order was made after Stowells admitted under questioning by the court that he and his wife had entered into a property settlement by which he took about $4000 and his wife the furniture valued not to exceed $1000.

Stowells declared in his complaint that once in his absence she and Fields embraced and kissed each other. Once when he found them walking together, he and Fields engaged in an altercation, the complaint recited, whereupon the wife was declared to have said:

ATTORNEY OBJECTS

"There is no use scrapping over me. I don't care for you, Mr. Stowells, at all."

"Where is your wife living?" Stowells was asked on the witness stand.

"She is living with the man who broke up my home—" he began, but was interrupted by an objection from his wife's attorney, which shut off further testimony along this line.

An effort was made to show that the property settlement precluded the wife from seeking alimony, but after hearing the terms of the settlement, the court refused to recognize it and made an order without reference to the agreement.

Food Prices Drop in Ten Cities in Sept.

WASHINGTON, Oct. 4.—Food prices in 10 cities in the country showed a decrease for the month of September, according to a report made public here by the labor department. The decrease in the month ranged from 3 per cent in Chicago and Baltimore to one-half of 1 per cent in Washington and Peoria, Ill., the report stated.

FINANCIAL NEWS

All of the Financial News up to going to press will be found on pages 12 and 13 of this section. If you don't read The Evening Herald financial pages you don't get the financial news.

OFFICERS LEAVE FOR ROUND-UP OF INDIANS

One of the biggest roundups of Indians in Southern California since early bandit days in pueblo times, was on today when United States Deputies Dolph Bassett and Vincent Monteleone left Los Angeles for the several Indian reservations in the vicinity of Temecula, Pala, Warner Hot Springs, Santa Ysabel, Mesa Grande and Escondido.

The deputy marshals went armed with federal warrants and heavy revolvers, prepared to arrest 31 Mission Indians named in the indictment charging them and Jonathan Tibbets, Riverside realtor, with conspiracy to defraud the government and to antagonize the Indians against the government.

Last Friday the deputy marshals rounded up 15 Indians in the Riverside-Banning-San Jacinto country.

CHARGES WIFE CASHED $6000 IN SECURITIES

With each side promising to carry the case to the court of last resort, preliminary hearing of Mrs. W. T. Groff, formerly known as Mrs. H. A. Canfield, charged with the embezzlement of $6000 worth of bonds belonging to her husband, was to be held in justice court today.

If it is carried to the supreme court of the state, it will be the first time of record that such a case has been heard there. Thus the legal battle that was to begin today promised to be hotly contested.

According to the complaint filed against the wife on the charges made by her husband, Mrs. Groff is said to have forged her husband's name to securities valued at about $6000 and then to have sold them and appropriated the money to her own use.

Spain Claims Big Morrocan Victory

MADRID, Oct. 4.—A report from Gen. Berenguer, Spanish high commissioner in Morocco, tells of the capture of Sebt, which gives the Spanish troops command of the valley of Saganan, a tactical base for further operations.

Meusel Brothers and Chance Will Write Stories of Big Diamond Battle

The world series, crowning event of the baseball season, will open in New York tomorrow with the New York clubs of the American and National leagues competing.

While 40,000 or more fans will see each game played on the Polo grounds, millions of fans are intensely interested in the outcome of the games, and will have to depend on the newspapers and bulletin boards to furnish them with details of the contests.

That Los Angeles fans may not want for quick and accurate reports of the big games, The Evening

(CONTINUED ON PAGE FOUR)

Postmaster Speeds Up Window Service for Waiting Crowds

Postmaster P. P. O'Brien took quick action today when he espied crowds of patrons of the central postoffice standing in the corridors waiting to obtain service at the one open parcel post window, and other crowds waiting to pay their quarterly letter box rent.

"That custom and kind of slow service ends right here," said the postmaster, as he issued orders to open additional parcel post windows and box rent windows. "When I took charge of this office I promised the public it would have service."

A few minutes later additional parcel post windows were open and the waiting crowd vanished.

TO CONFER ON PEACE

WASHINGTON, Oct. 4.—Senator Hitchcock, ranking Democrat on the foreign relations committee, plans to confer with former President Wilson here within a few days regarding the German peace treaty.

MAN BRANDED AS 'ABYSMAL BRUTE' GETS TWO YEARS

'Three-Time Loser' in Police Court Will Go to San Quentin

FIRED AT ANOTHER, CLAIM

Is Convicted of Making Attack Following Heated Dispute

Arraigned by the prosecution as an "abysmal brute" and convicted of having made an attack with a deadly weapon on a man with whom he had an argument, Roy L. Jones, a "three-time loser" in police court, was sentenced to two years in San Quentin today by Judge Reeve.

Jones, according to the authorities, has a record of assaults on which he has been previously brought into police court on battery charges.

FIRED SHOTS, CHARGE

In the present case, however, he is said to have gone further than just a mere attack with his fists in that he fired two shots from a pistol at a man named Davita.

The shooting took place, it was brought out at his hearing, after he and Davita had been engaged in an heated argument.

It was charged by the prosecution that the argument began with a physical encounter and that Jones had Davita on the ground and was choking him into unconsciousness when Davita managed to draw a knife with which to defend himself.

RETURNS WITH GUN

Jones is then said to have gone to his home, obtained the revolver and then to have returned and fired two shots at the other man. A passerby interfered and took the weapon away from Jones.

According to the law under which Jones was sentenced, he must spend two years in San Quentin in place of the usual term of from one to five years.

Demand Extension of L. A. Breakwater

Admiral Eberle's demand for increased facilities for the Pacific fleet in Los Angeles harbor has reawakened the demand for an extension of the breakwater to the outlet of the Long Beach flood control channel.

A survey and estimate of cost for this extension was provided in the federal river and harbor bill more than a year ago, the amendment being offered by Congressman Charles H. Randall in the house of representatives. It is proposed now to demand action upon this provision of the law. Estimates of cost have been reduced from $20,000,000 to about $8,000,000, since the Randall amendment became a law.

70-Year-Old Pair Licensed to Wed

Giving their age as 70 years each, Dr. Lyman Gregory, 528 West Vernon avenue, this city, and Miss Waity E. Brayton, also of Los Angeles, obtained a license to marry from the county clerk in San Jose, according to advices received today from that city. Dr. Gregory is a retired physician and school teacher and reputed wealthy.

BOBBY MEUSEL SAYS HIS BROTHER'S TEAM TO LOSE

By BOBBY MEUSEL.

Former star of Vernon Coast league club, who will play for Yankees in world's series starting tomorrow.

NEW YORK, Oct. 4.—The big scrap starts tomorrow and there is only one fellow in the world facing the same situation I find myself in and that is my brother, known to the fans as "Irish."

I've got to play for the Yankees tomorrow against the Giants and my brother will be playing with the Giants against the Yankees.

DEFENSIVE CLUB

I believe the Yankees will win because they are a better ball club. Hitting counts in baseball and you know there is only one Babe Ruth. We have players who get on base pretty regularly. You have probably noticed that while Babe was piling up his home run record he was continually driving in runs and he made a lot of singles, doubles and triples that counted heavily but did not cause much comment.

When it comes to attack I am confident the Yankees have it on the Giants. Defensively we have just as good a ball club and when it comes to pitching we can hold our own with any of them. The Giants didn't have any easy time winning the pennant. We had tougher opposition than the National league could furnish them, hit better pitching than the Giants had to face and our pitchers stood up in great shape.

Don't worry about the Yankee pitchers when fellows like Mays, Quinn, Hoyt and Shawkey are ready to work.

EVENED UP

Individually there are spots where either club may have the edge. It has been said that Frisch is far better than McNally at third. I'm not admitting it, but just suppose it is true, it's but one position.

Then I'll claim for the sake of the argument that Peckinpaugh has it all over Bancroft at short. That makes the two clubs appear even again. It's the way a club averages up that counts and the way they fight that makes a winner.

I believe hitting will win the series and when it comes to hitting we won't take off our caps to any of them. A ball player has to be good to be in the major leagues so you can gamble there are no weak spots on either club. Two clubs may play game after game without a situation coming up that couldn't be handled by an ordinary minor league club, but it takes slugging to win ball games and it takes pitchers to check the sluggers.

NO FAMILY AFFAIR

Our pitchers will check the Giants and the Giants' pitchers aren't going to stop us from hitting. That's the way I dope it out.

I want to tell the world that the

(CONTINUED ON PAGE FOUR)

YANKS MAKE IT TWO STRAIGHT

THREE CENTS CITY AND COUNTY

LOS ANGELES EVENING HERALD
AN INDEPENDENT NEWSPAPER
Reg. U. S. Pat. Off.
The Evening Herald Grows Just Like Los Angeles

BOX SCORE EDITION

VOL. XLVI. THREE CENTS Hotels and Trains Five Cents THURSDAY, OCTOBER 6, 1921 THREE CENTS Hotels and Trains Five Cents NO. 291

FRISCH STARS IN FIELD

'Liquor Witness' Against Arbuckle Missing

RUTH GETS BASE ON BALLS BUT MEUSEL POPS OUT IN PINCH

POLO GROUNDS, NEW YORK, Oct. 6.—With sunny weather, the Polo grounds were jammed today, between 38,000 and 40,000 witnessing the second world series game between the Yankees and Giants.

The Yanks had won the opening contest 3 to 0 and the Giants were out today to even things up if they could.

Hoyt pitched for the Yankees and Nehf for the Giants. The catchers were Smith for McGraw's men and Schang for Miller Huggins.

The Yanks were the home team today.

Burns, the first Giant batter to face Hoyt, fanned out, swinging hard and grunting.

With one on Nehf walked Babe Ruth in the opener and the strategy proved good, for no Yank got near the plate. Kelly made a wonderful one-hand stop of Smith's wild throw and prevented an error. But Smith got an error anyway when he muffed Miller's foul.

Bob Meusel was the victim of a double play in the Yanks' half of the first. Frisch leaped high in the air to make the play.

Hoyt fanned "Slugger" Kelly in the second, while the Giants' home run king stood with the bat on his shoulder. The crowd cheered wildly.

Nehf, who was wild, walked Pipp in the second, but fast playing by Frisch held the Yankees scoreless. Frisch was easily the star for the Giants and was given a wild ovation as he left the field.

Rawlings got the first hit of the game in the third inning but could not score.

Nehf was nervous in the last of the third when with two on and two out Babe Ruth came to the bat. He had two strikes on Babe, but gave him an unintentional base on balls, filling the bags. There was a wild argument over the gairness of the decision on the "fourth ball." Bob Meusel popped out, ending the tension.

The Game Play by Play

FIRST INNING

GIANTS—Burns up. Ball one. Ball two. Strike one called. Foul strike two. Burns fanned. Bancroft up. Strike one, swung. Bancroft out, Hoyt to Pipp. Frisch up. Ball one. Strike one called. Foul strike two. Frisch out, Ward to Pipp. NO RUNS. NO HITS, NO ERRORS.

YANKEES—Miller up. Ball one. Foul strike one. Smith drew an error when he muffed Miller's high foul. Ball two. Ball three. Miller walked. Peck up. Ball one. Ball two. Strike one called. Strike two called. Smith tried to catch Miller off first base and Kelly saved him from a wild throw by a one-handed stab. Peck sacrificed, Nehf to Kelly. Ruth up. Ball one. Ball two. Ball three. Ruth walked. He took the base on four straight balls while the crowd booed Nehf. R. Meusel up. Strike one called. Ball one. R. Meusel lined into a double play, Frisch to Rawlings. NO RUNS, NO HITS, ONE ERROR.

SECOND INNING

GIANTS—Young up. Strike one called. Strike two called. Ball one. Pipp, unassisted. Kelly up. Ball one. Ball two. Ball three. Young out. Strike one called. Foul, strike two. Kelly fanned, standing with the bat on his shoulder when Hoyt grooved one. Meusel up. Strike one called. Ball one. Strike two called. Ball two. Foul. Ball three. E. Meusel out, Pipp, unassisted. NO RUNS, NO HITS, NO ERRORS.

YANKEES—Pipp up. Ball one. Ball two. Strike one called. Strike two swung. Ball three. Pipp walked. Ward up. Strike one called. Ball one. Ward out, Bancroft to Kelly. Pipp pulled up at second. McNally up. Foul strike one. Ball one. Ball two. Frisch took McNally's grounder and tagged Pipp out on the base line for a very smart play. Schang up. Ball one. McNally out stealing, Smith to Rawlings. NO RUNS. NO HITS. NO ERRORS.

THIRD INNING

GIANTS—Rawlings up. Rawlings singled to left. It was a measly little pop fly that neither Ruth nor Peck could get under. Smith up. Smith popped to Peck. Nehf up. Ball one. Strike one called. Strike two called. Nehf fanned, swinging, and Rawlings nearly nipped off first, but made the bag in a slide. Burns up. Ball one. Strike one, swung. Foul, strike two. Burns forced Rawlings, Peck unassisted. NO RUNS, ONE HIT, NO ERRORS.

YANKEES—Schang up. Strike one called. Ball one. Schang popped to Bancroft. Hoyt up. Ball one. Ball two. Strike one called. Strike two swung. Hoyt reached first on a single. It was a pop fly which Rawlings ran back to get and dropped after making the catch. Miller up. Foul strike one. Strike two swung. Ball one. Miller flied to Burns, Hoyt holding first. Peck up. Ball one. Ball two. Foul strike one. Foul strike two. Ball three. Foul. Foul. Foul. Peck walked. Ruth up. Ball one. Ball two. Ball three. Strike one called. Foul strike two. Ruth walked, filling the bases. R. Meusel up. R. Meusel popped to Bancroft. NO RUNS, NO HITS, NO ERRORS.

(Continued in Columns 7 and 8)

BOX SCORE of TODAY'S GAME

GIANTS—	AB	R	H	2b	3b	Hr	Sb	Sh	PO	A	E
Burns, cf	3	0	0	0	0	0	0	0	1	0	0
Bancroft, ss	4	0	0	0	0	0	0	0	3	3	0
Frisch, 3b	4	0	0	0	0	0	0	0	3	2	[illegible]
Young, rf	3	0	0	0	0	0	0	0	2	0	0
Kelly, 1b	3	0	0	0	0	0	0	0	12	2	0
E. Meusel, lf	2	0	0	0	0	0	0	0	0	0	0
Rawlings, 2b	3	0	1	0	0	0	0	0	2	1	0
Smith, c	3	0	0	0	0	0	0	0	1	1	1
Nehf, p	2	0	0	0	0	0	0	0	0	3	1
	0	0	0	0	0	0	0	0	0	0	0
	0	0	0	0	0	0	0	0	0	0	0
	0	0	0	0	0	0	0	0	0	0	0
	0	0	0	0	0	0	0	0	0	0	0
	0	0	0	0	0	0	0	0	0	0	0
Totals	27	0	1	0	0	0	0	0	24	12	1

YANKEES—	AB	R	H	2b	3b	Hr	Sb	Sh	PO	A	E
Miller, cf	3	0	0	0	0	0	0	0	1	0	0
Pec'paugh, ss	2	0	0	0	0	0	0	1	3	1	0
Ruth, lf	1	1	0	0	0	0	2	0	0	0	0
B. Meusel, rf	4	1	1	0	0	0	0	0	1	0	0
Pipp, 1b	3	0	0	0	0	0	0	0	16	0	0
Ward, 2b	3	1	1	0	0	0	0	0	2	5	0
McNally, 3b	3	0	0	0	0	0	0	0	0	2	0
Schang, c	2	0	0	0	0	0	0	0	4	2	0
Hoyt, p	3	0	1	0	0	0	0	0	0	2	0
	0	0	0	0	0	0	0	0	0	0	0
	0	0	0	0	0	0	0	0	0	0	0
	0	0	0	0	0	0	0	0	0	0	0
	0	0	0	0	0	0	0	0	0	0	0
	0	0	0	0	0	0	0	0	0	0	0
Totals	23	3	3	0	0	0	2	1	27	12	0

Giants	0 0 0	0 0 0	0 0 0	— 0
Yankees	0 0 0	1 0 0	0 2 X	— 3

WE'LL OUTSLUG 'EM, SAYS BOB MEUSEL

By BOBBY MEUSEL

Former Vernon star, now playing for New York Yankees

NEW YORK, Oct. 6.—Just before we left the hotel for the opening game "Irish" showed me a wire from the folks in Los Angeles that said "The best team will win." After the game I told "Irish" the telegram was right, score 3 to 0.

The Yankees got away to the kind

(CONTINUED ON PAGE FIFTEEN)

YANKS 10 TO 7 FAVORITES ON SERIES

POLO GROUNDS, NEW YORK, Oct. 6.—The Yankees were 10 to 7 favorites to win the series when today's game began, but the Giant rooters had rallied from their momentary panic of yesterday—when the McGrawites were beaten 3 to 0—and there were plenty of takers for what bets were offered.

The weather was clear and cool

(CONTINUED ON PAGE FIFTEEN)

KISS OF DEATH IS THEORY IN BLUEBEARD GIRL TRIAL

Defense Works Up to Contention Mrs. Southard Is Typhoid 'Germ Carrier'

TWIN FALLS, Idaho, Oct. 6.—The "kiss of death" became the dominant feature today of the trial of Mrs. Lyda Southard, alleged Bluebeardess, on trial for poisoning her fourth husband, Edward F. Meyer.

In the questioning of physician witnesses today it became apparent that Mrs. Southard's attorneys will base her defense on the contention that the woman's four husbands, including Meyer, did not die of poison administered to them but died as a result of her kisses.

Foundation was laid to show that Mrs. Southard was a "typhoid carrier" and that the germs of death lay in her kisses. The more she loved the greater the peril to the loved one. Already in cross-questioning the defense had elicited some testimony regarding the woman's alleged passionate love for Meyer, the man she is now alleged to have slain by poison.

DEFENSE TACTICS

Today the questioning of physicians who attended Meyer was directed by defense attorneys toward proving that Meyer actually came to his death through typhoid fever and that previous to his fatal sickness he had a case of "walking typhoid."

The prosecution had set up the claim that Mrs. Southard purchased poison flypaper, soaked it in water and brewed a potion which she gave him in a drink that caused his death.

The defense will attempt to show that Meyer, on the day that his wife arrived at the Blue Lakes ranch with the poison flypaper, ate some decomposed food, which illness so weakened his constitution that the typhoid germs, already sown in his body by the love of his "typhoid carrier" wife, got in their deadly work and caused his death through intestinal hemorrhage.

DOCTOR'S THEORY

Questioned by District Attorney Frank Stephan as to how he accounted for Meyer's great improvement on the morning before his death, Dr. J. F. Coughlin, who attended Meyer, replied:

"I believed that his body had rid itself of the offending matter which had originally poisoned him."

The defense then made strenuous efforts to show that typhoid fever was the direct cause of Meyer's death,

(CONTINUED ON PAGE ELEVEN)

MAN IN FILM STAR'S CASE LEAVES U.S. IS REPORT

Warrant Out for Jack Lawrence on Charge of Violating Dry Law

By United Press

SAN FRANCISCO, Oct. 6.—Jack Lawrence, star witness for the state in the investigation of the prohibition angles surrounding the Roscoe Arbuckle manslaughter case, was listed as missing today.

Rumore were circulated that he had left for Australia, whence he came last April.

A warrant for Lawrence, charging him with violation of the prohibition laws, was placed in the hands of the United States marshal today.

GAVE EVIDENCE

Lawrence was said to have given evidence to Special Assistant Attorney General Robert McCormick, in charge of the federal investigation of the Arbuckle case, showing where Arbuckle secured the liquor used at his Labor Day party, which preceded the death of Virginia Rappe.

Withdrawal of Frank Dominguez as counsel for Arbuckle on the eve of the film comedian's arraignment on a manslaughter charge caused a stir here.

WIDE DIVERGENCE

Dominguez said other business demanded his attention, but it was said differences over fees caused his withdrawal. It was said the attorney demanded $50,000, while Arbuckle thought $5000 more reasonable as a retainer.

Milton Cohen and Charles Brennan are now handling Arbuckle's case.

Arbuckle was expected here late today to plead personally to the manslaughter charge in connection with **the death of Virginia Rappe** during **a party** in Arbuckle's apartment. **Judge Louderbach** had refused to allow **Arbuckle** to plead through his **lawyers.**

ARBUCKLE PREPARES FOR APPEARANCE IN ARRAIGNMENT COURT

Roscoe "Fatty" **Arbuckle today** prepared to leave **his West Adams** street mansion to **appear for arraignment** in the **superior court in San** Francisco **tomorrow morning on the** charge of **manslaughter against him** in connection **with the death of Virginia Rappe.**

At the **Arbuckle home, it was stated, "Fatty" will leave for the North this evening. It was not stated whether Minta Durfee Arbuckle,** his

(CONTINUED ON PAGE ELEVEN)

LATEST NEWS

YANKEE-GIANT GAME—(Continued)

FOURTH—Giants—Bancroft struck out. Frisch out, Peck to Pipp. Young out, McNally to Pipp.—NO RUNS.

Yanks—Pipp flied to Young. Ward singled to right and reached second on Neff's wild throw. Schang walked, filling the bases. Hoyt out, Rawlings to Kelly, Ward scoring. McNally out trying to score.—ONE RUN.

FIFTH—Giants—Kelly out, Schang to Pipp. E. Meusel walkel. Rawlings flied to R. Meusel. Smith flied to Miller. NO RUNS.

Yanks—Miller out, Frisch to Kelly. Peck out, Bancroft to Kelly. Ruth walked and stole second and third. R. Meusel out, Bancroft to Kelly.—NO RUNS.

SIXTH—Giants—Nehf walked. Burns popped to Ward. Bancroft out, Hoyt to Pipp. Frisch out, Pipp unassisted.

Yanks—Pipp out, Nehf to Kelly. Ward out, Kelly, unassisted. McNally popped to Frisch.—NO RUNS.

SEVENTH—GiantsYoung walked. Kelly forced Young. McNally to Ward. E. Meusel forced Kelly, Ward to Peck. Rawlings out, Ward to Pipp—NO RUNS.

Yanks—Schang up. Ball one. Ball two. Strike one, called. Schang flied to Young, who made a nice catch in deep right. Hoyt up. He was given a big hand when he came to the plate. Ball one. Hoyt popped to Kely. Miller up. Strike one, called. Miller out, Nehf to Kelly.—NO RUNS.

EIGHTH—Giants—Smith up. Smith out, Ward to Pipp, on the first ball pitched. Nehf up. Strike one, swung. Strike two, called. Foul. Ball one. Nehf out, Ward to Pipp. Burns up. Ball one Ball two. Foul strike one Ball three Foul. Strike two Burns walked. Bancroft up. uBrns out, stealing, Schang to Peck.—NO RUNS.

Yanks—Peck up. Ball one. Strike one, called. Foul, strike two. Peck safe at first on Frisch's muff of an easy pop fly back of the box. Frisch was given an error. Ruth up. Ball one. Ruth forced Peck at second, Kelly to Bancroft. R. Meusel up. Ball one. R. Meusel singled to center, Ruth taking third and Meusel reaching second on the throw to catch Ruth Pipp up. Pipp out, Rawlings to Kelly, Ruth scoring and R. Meusel taking third. Ward up. R. Meusel stole home. Smith dropped Nehf's hurried throw. Ball one on Ward. Ward fouled to Kelly—TWO RUNS.

Giants—Bancroft out, Ward to Pipp Frisch singled. Young walked. Kelly hit into a double play.—NO RUNS.

NEW GUN FIGHTS BREAK IRISH ARMISTICE

DUBLIN, Oct. 6.—The armistice truce was broken today both in North and South Ireland.

From Belfast it was reported that there were half a dozen separate instances of disorder, when Orangemen and Catholics fought revolver duels.

A bomb hurled into one Catholic home failed to explode.

There was a more serious breach of the truce in Dunmanway in the western part of County Cork. There auxiliary police claimed they were fired upon and replied in kind, killing one person.

Later the auxiliary crown forces appeared in force and began firing wildly. They roughly treated known republicans and entered some Sinn Fein dwellings. Sinn Feiners charged that the auxiliary **forces were drunk.**

A strong **protest will be made by** Sinn Fein **military leaders to British** authorities **demanding punishment** of the **auxiliaries involved.**

PROBE FRENCH RAIL COLLISION FATAL TO 35

By United Press

PARIS, Oct. 6.—Official **investigation was begun today of the rear-end collision in the St. Lazare railroad station tunnel last night, in which 35 persons lost their lives and a considerable number were injured.**

Two suburban trains collided in the half-mile tunnel and flames, spread by a terrific gas reservoir explosion made the disaster one of the most horrible in French railway history.

Poisonous gases forming in the tunnel when the flames consumed the wooden railway coaches made rescue work by **firemen difficult and dangerous.**

SHACKLETON AT LISBON

LISBON, **Oct. 6.—Sir** Ernest Shackleton **and his party arrived here** aboard the **vessel Quest, which was** damaged **in a storm off the west coast** of **Portugal.**

BETTING ODDS ON YANKS DROP

THREE CENTS

Home Delivery and by mail, 65 cents a month. Published every day except Sunday in the Chamber of Commerce Building, Los Angeles, Cal., Guy B. Barham, President. Frank F. Barham, Publisher.

LOS ANGELES EVENING HERALD

AN INDEPENDENT NEWSPAPER

Reg. U. S. Pat. Off.

The Evening Herald Grows Just Like Los Angeles

EVENING NEWS EDITION

VOL. XLVI. Entered as second-class matter Nov. 2, 1911, at the post-office at Los Angeles, Cal., under act of March 3, 1879. SATURDAY, OCT. 8, 1921 THREE CENTS NO. 293

2 DYING IN AUTO CRASH

Father Jails L. A. Spender as Thief

BABE RUTH OUT OF GAME AS INJURED ARM GROWS WORSE

POLO GROUNDS, NEW YORK, Oct. 8.—In spite of threatening weather the crowds came out early and packed the Polo grounds for the fourth game of the 1921 world series today.

They came under promise of the management that the contest would be staged unless a drenching downpour halted the struggle.

And they came, enthusiastic over the rehabilitated Giants' chances of taking the series in spite of their two early defeats, both to the tune of 3 to 0—for yesterday's 13 to 5 victory had brought the McGrawites back almost to even money in the betting and had reinstated them first in the hearts of the rooters.

It was announced early that Babe Ruth was officially out of the game. His left elbow was so badly infected that the doctors would not permit him to play, though the big "Bambino" begged to be allowed to go in.

"Babe's illness will not greatly handicap us," said Manager Huggins before today's game. "We will win the series anyhow."

LINE-UP CHANGED

The absence of Ruth made necessary a sharp change in the line-up and batting order of the Yankees.

The day was another threatening one, but in spite of the mist and lowering clouds the fans came out in flocks and droves. With the series at a critical stage no mere freak of the weather could keep them away.

It was announced early that the game would be played unless rain fell in such quantities as to make the grounds unfit for use.

The Yanks sent Mays back to the hill today, and the Giants, as in the opening contest, pinned their faith to Douglas.

SLEEPLESS NIGHT

Mrs. Ruth spent a sleepless night caring for her husband, and Dr. Stewart, attending physician, said:

"From Mr. Ruth's condition last night I would advise against his playing today. His arm is badly infected and even in the event that he should play it would be very painful for him." It was stated, however, that he might be used as a pinch hitter in case of extreme emergency.

Ruth's left arm was injured in the final game of the Cleveland series two weeks ago. He slid into second and tore the flesh from his elbow. Little was thought of the injury until the arm began to swell yesterday. It became so painful that after Ruth walked in the eighth inning he was replaced by Fewster.

With hope born anew and determ-

(CONTINUED ON PAGE FIFTEEN)

PLAY BY PLAY AS 'MRS. BABE' SEES IT

By PAUL R. MALLON
Staff Correspondent United Press

BOX 138, POLO GROUNDS, NEW YORK, Oct. 8.—This is the play by play description of Mrs. Bambino Ruth, watching the third game of the world's series:

Mr. Babe Ruth comes walking across the field, doffing his cap to the cheering fans. Some batteries or other are announced.

FIRST INNING—Mr. Babe Ruth comes to bat with two men out and one on base. Mrs. Ruth—"I think my hubby is about due for a home run." Ball one. Mrs. Ruth—"I think somebody ought to pull Mr. Toney's hair if he don't pitch to Babe." Ball two. Mrs. Ruth—"Boo-o-o-o!" Strike one. The Babe took a hefty swing. Mrs. Ruth—"I dare Mr. Toney to put it there again." Strike two—a heftier swing. Silence. Another, heftier than the one before, and the Babe struck out. Mrs. Ruth—"Gee whiz!"

NOTHING TO DO

SECOND INNING — Mr. Ruth stands out in left field with nothing to do.

THIRD INNING—Mr. Ruth steps to the plate with the bases full and nobody out. Mrs. Ruth—"He'll smack it a mile!" Somebody put a sweater on Shawkey as he stood on third. Mrs. Ruth—"I think they ought to furnish sweaters for all the players." Ball one. "Oh, gee, they're going to walk him again." Foul. "They ought to give him a sweater. He'll catch more cold if they don't." Ball two. A peanut vendor steps in front of Mrs. Ruth. "Down in front." Ball three. "The suspense is terrible." Ruth singled to center, scoring Shawkey and Miller. "It's a good thing he did hit

(CONTINUED ON PAGE FIFTEEN)

Hitless Hero

"Home Run" Kelly, the only Giant "regular" who hasn't got a hit during present world series games.

GIANTS SURE BET, CLAIMS MEUSEL

By IRISH MEUSEL

Former Los Angeles High school boy who started the batting rally which won yesterday's game for the Giants.

NEW YORK, Oct. 8.—Yesterday Bob and I rode out to the Polo grounds with a fellow who also came here from Los Angeles. I won't mention his name but he and Bob were doing a little kidding about the hitless champions of the National league.

It's very peculiar how both Bob and this fellow were missing after the game, and I had to go back to the hotel alone.

Great ball club, these Yankees. They're out of the picture now and don't figure it any other way. We

(CONTINUED ON PAGE FIFTEEN)

MACHINE AND STREET CAR COLLIDE

Woman and Youth Are Seriously Hurt; Man Is Also Injured

Two persons were perhaps fatally injured and another was painfully hurt today at Twenty-first street and Vermont avenue when an automobile operated by Arthur L. Chandler, 47, of 1052 West Sixty-third street crashed into the front end of a street car.

Chandler's son, aged 24, suffered a fractured skull and was believed to be dying at the receiving hospital. Mrs. A. Blabon, 24, a neighbor of Chandler, suffered a fractured skull and other serious injuries and may die, according to Polise Surgeon Norman A. Dorn.

According to Arthur L. Chandler sr., he was driving north on Vermont avenue and a motor truck forced him to drive onto the tracks of the outbound street car.

SWERVES TO LEFT

In a desperate effort to prevent a collision, he told the police, he swerved the automobile to the left, but not quick enough to prevent a head-on collision with the street car.

The elder Chandler suffered severe scalp lacerations and other injuries.

The University police were summoned and Officers J. W. Church and W. P. Powers removed the two men and the woman to the receiving hospital.

According to Dr. Dorn, Mrs. Blabon suffered a severe scalp laceration and evidently received a depressed skull fracture. Chandler jr. and Mrs. Blaban were unconscieus when picked up by the University police officers, and police surgeons said their chances for recovery were unfavorable.

ACCEPTS INVITATION

According to the elder Chandler, Mrs. Blabon lives in a house adjoining his home and moved into the place a few days ago. When he and his son started for their places of business today Mrs. Blabon accepted their invitation to ride into the city in their automobile.

After the two men and the woman were treated at the receiving hospital they were removed to private institutions.

U. S. Competes in Egyptian Shipping

WASHINGTON, Oct. 8.—Forcing competition with the British shipping board through independent companies, the United States shipping board has brought about a shipping rate for Egyptian cotton to American ports, 10 shillings below the British rate.

CALLS POLICE WHEN SON RETURNS

Reveal How Pretty Bride of Robber Lived Luxurious Life Here

Revealing how he squandered $45,000 in Los Angeles, where he purchased diamonds, airplanes and racing cars and became a "stunt" aviator, Carl Steiler jr., one of four men who stole $234,000 from the Standard Oil Co. at Whiting, Ind., in September, 1919, was under arrest in Chicago today.

With Steiler when he was arrested was his youthful and pretty bride, Bessie Jasiak Steiler, who came to robbery and lived like a princess here while he threw his money away.

SPENDS LAVISHLY

In Los Angeles Steiler studied aviation at the Sydney Chaplin aviation school and became a "stunt" flyer. Later he organized the International Aircraft Corporation of California in this city and a few months later the concern went into bankruptcy.

While he was here Steiler spent money lavishly. He bought diamonds by the dozens, a new racing car every month and an airplane whenever one struck his fancy.

When he left Los Angeles Steiler and his bride went to Texas. Most of the $45,000 was gone, squandered, and Steiler earned a living as a "stunt" flyer. One day he smashed his airplane, however, and, without money to pay for repairs, he sold the wreck and went to Memphis.

JAILED BY FATHER

There, in Memphis, Steiler and his girl-wife were "flat broke." Mrs. Steiler even scrubbed floors to get money for food. Her costly garments, her furs, her rings, purchased for her by Steiler in Los Angeles, were all pawned many months before.

Penniless and with Mrs. Steiler an expectant mother, Steiler returned to Chicago and went to the home of his father. As soon as his son stepped into the house Steller sr. took down the telephone and called the police.

Steiler's three partners in the $234,000 theft, John Wedja and Leo and Walter Filpkowski, are in the penitentiary serving prison sentences. They were arrested shortly after the robbery. Steiler, however, managed to throw detectives off his trail by hurrying with the Jasiak girl to Los Angeles.

American to Wed Russian Princess

PARIS, Oct. 8.—When William J. Leeds jr., son of the late American "tin plate king," and Princess Xenia of Russia are married here tomorrow, a French civil ceremony, an American church ceremony and a Russian church ceremony will be performed.

Line-Up of Fourth Game of Big Series

GIANTS—	YANKEES—
Burns, cf.	Miller, cf.
Bancroft, ss.	Peck, ss.
Frisch, 3b.	Fewster, lf.
Young, rf.	B. Meusel, rf.
Kelly, 1b.	Pipp, 1b.
E. Meusel, lf.	Ward, 2b.
Rawlings, 2b.	McNally, 3b.
Snyder, c.	Schang, c.
Douglas, p.	Mays, p.

Angels and Tigers Tangle in Opening Of Winter Circuit

VERNON—	LOS ANGELES—
Smith, 3b.	Statz, cf.
Cooper, cf.	High, lf.
Knight, 2b.	Cox, rf.
Sisler, 1b.	Hornsby, 2b.
Schneider, rf.	Brown, 3b.
Hannah, c.	Brubaker, ss.
Wolfer, lf.	Anheir, 1b.
Kingdon, ss.	Baldwin, c
Hughes, p.	Reiger, p.

With Sisler's Tigers meeting Hornsby's Angels at Washington park this afternoon the first annual season of the California Winter league opened today.

Roger Hornsby, premier batter of the National league, and George Sisler, who hit .371 for the St. Louis Browns, managed the opposing clubs.

Elmer Reiger was the pitcher selected by Hornsby to work the opening game, while Sisler picked Tom Hughes for Vernon.

Dry Forces Start Liquor Cleanup of National Capital

By International News Service

WASHINGTON, Oct. 8.—Under the personal direction of prohibition Director Haines a large force of prohibition officers started a systematic series of raids here today. Officials refused to state the number of arrests, but it was said that 30 warrants had been issued and more than 20 places had been raided.

Prohibition officials stated the raid is aimed at a "rum ring" which has been running liquor by automobile from Pennsylvania and maintaining a regular rum route, serving customers in the national capital.

NEW U. S. RIFLE

ABERDEEN PROVING GROUNDS, Oct. 8.—Experiments conducted here before army experts with a 16-inch, 5-caliber rifle mounted on a "barbette" carriage showed that the new gun planted shells 20 miles away. The "barbette" carriage allows a maximum elevation of 65 degrees and will probably eliminate the disappearing gun carriage for coast defense rifles.

IRISH ENVOYS OFF TO PEACE PARLEY

By United Press

DUBLIN, Oct. 8.—Sinn Fein delegates, who will open the Irish peace conference with Premier Lloyd-George in London on Tuesday, left for that city today. They were given a great ovation as they boarded the steamer.

Michael Collins, commander-in-chief of the Irish republican army, was the only one of the delegates not included in the party. He will arrive in London on Monday.

PARENTS LOSE RACE TO HALT ELOPING COUPLE ON HONEYMOON IN S. F.

Mingled with reports of robberies and other crimes on the "blotter" at the sheriff's office was a report early today that placed one "Daniel Cupid" in the role of victor in a love plot.

The report stated that Lloyd Cogier of Glendale and his bride, formerly Gertrude M. Wyckoff, aged 17, were en route to San Francisco on their honeymoon.

At the same time it was revealed that Mr. and Mrs. W. C. Wyckoff of 600 South Adams street, Glendale, parents of the bride, had lost a race to the sheriff's office in an effort to halt the honeymoon trip.

When informed the authorities could do nothing to halt the couple Mrs. Wyckoff fainted and became so hysterical that Deputy Sheriff Hotz found it necessary to remove her to the receiving hospital for treatment.

According to the girl's father the elopers telephoned during the evening that they had been married and were on their way to San Francisco for a honeymoon trip of a few days.

The race of the bride's parents to the sheriff's office began a few minutes later, but Cupid was the winner.

Paris Says Stork Hovering Over Mary

PARIS, Oct. 8.—That the reported nervous breakdown of Mary Pickford Fairbanks which is keeping her from attending the many social functions here with her husband is a diplomatic illness, pending the imminent arrival of the stork, is the belief of intimate friends in Paris.

LATEST NEWS

RAIN THREATENS WORLD SERIES GAME

POLO GROUNDS, NEW YORK, Oct. 8.—At 12:30 o'clock a few drops of rain fell on the diamond, the sky was overcast and a rainstorm threatened. Preparations to play the game continued, however.

TWO KILLED IN OIL PLANT BLAST

BEAUMONT, Texas, Oct. 8.—Two men were killed and one man was seriously burned this morning following a flash explosion in a still at the Magnolia Oil Co.'s refinery here.

FEAR FOR VESSEL 24 DAYS OVERDUE

SAN FRANCISCO, Oct. 8.—Although greatest anxiety is felt for the safety of the Santa Clara, a windjammer, with 100 cannery workers and a crew of 22 on board, now 24 days overdue from Karluk, on Bristol Bay, Alaska, hope has not entirely been given up in marine circles. She left 34 days ago from San Francisco and under present conditions the voyage should have been made in 10 days.

$500,000 FIRE AT VERNON IS PROBED

With practically the entire plant of the H. F. Lewis Packing Co., at East Vernon avenue and the Salt Lake tracks, a mass of smouldering ruins today as the result of a fire that started in the smoke house and swept rapidly through the place during the night, a thorough investigation was in progress to determine the cause of the fire.

The loss was estimated at $200,000, and practically was covered by insurance, according to officials of the concern.

It was announced by representatives of the company that the work of rebuilding the plant would be started immediately and that there would be no halt in the conduct of business. Slaughtering was in progress at a neighboring plant and it was an-

(CONTINUED ON PAGE FIVE)

MANY ARE HELD IN HUGE MAIL TRUCK HOLDUP

By United Press

DETROIT, Mich., Oct. 8.—Seven suspects were held by police today in connection with the robbery here of a Canadian government truck of mail pouches. Authorities today checked up on the loot, which they believed would total close to $300,000. Three of the pouches contained registered mail matter.

One of the stolen pouches is believed to have contained the day's receipts of the Kenilworth race track in Windsor. Other pouches carried valuable securities consigned from Canadian banks to Detroit financial institutions.

Authorities are convinced the bandits had information from someone inside the mail service regarding the value of the mail sacks on the truck

RUTH ILL, UPSETS YANK PLANS

HREE CENTS

ne Delivery and by mail, 65 cents a month. ublished every day except Sunday in the mber of Commerce Building, Los Angeles, , Guy B. Barham, President, Frank F. ham, Publisher.

LOS ANGELES EVENING HERALD
AN INDEPENDENT NEWSPAPER

Reg. U. S. Pat. Off.

The Evening Herald Grows Just Like Los Angeles

EVENING NEWS EDITION

VOL. XLVI. Entered as second-class matter Nov. 2, 1911, at the post-office at Los Angeles, Cal., under act of March 3, 1879. TUESDAY, OCTOBER 11, 1921 THREE CENTS NO. 295

2 DEAD IN LOVE TRAGEDY

State Report Aids P. E. Rate Raise

IANTS ARE VEN BET TO WIN SERIES TITLE

Up of Huggins' Men for Remainder of Contest Is Changed

LO GROUNDS, NEW YORK, 11.—There was a shift in the p of the Yanks today, due to act that Babe Ruth has been dden by his physicians to play in the 1921 world series.

Yankees and their supporters in deep gloom as a result of nd because of the serious con- of their pitching staff.

weather was fine and the ls turned out early.

ler Huggins sent "Lefty" Harp- t to warm up, as soon as the rs took the field.

Graw selected Jess Barnes to lay's twirling.

was with fear and trembling Huggins made his choice, but could not be called on again with only a single day of rest, Shawkey's arm is in such con- that he cannot be expected a full game at any time.

IANTS "EVEN MONEY"

the other hand, McGraw had all warmed up and ready to if Barnes showed signs of fal- and with this pitching ad- ge to their credit, the Giants still even money for the series in spite of the fact that the s have won three games to their

umpires today were Moriarty e plate, Quigley at first base, at second and Rigler at third.

STRIKE STRIDE

swollen arm of big Babe Ruth so painful he today that he not get into the game. The rs forbade him playing yester- out he disregarded their orders, h he fainted twice during the st from the pain of his injury.

Giants seem to have struck batting stride, for they an- 10 hits off Hoyt yesterday and m hard, even though they did in the game.

ere was a big attendance, larger yesterday, for the weather was t and the sun gave promise of ing things up early and making oats an unnecessary evil.

Yankees and the crowds will Ruth sorely. He practically won fth game. It was not one of omerun acts—just a little bunt, e bowled the Giants over with d before they got to their feet ll game was gone.

Babe out of the game Fewster

NTINUED ON PAGE FIFTEEN)

GEORGE BURNS, STAR OF N. Y. GIANTS IN SERIES WITH YANKS

RUTH GAMEST PLAYER, SAYS MEUSEL

By BOBBY MEUSEL

Former Los Angeles High school boy, whose great playing yesterday enabled the Yankees to beat the Giants.

NEW YORK, Oct. 11.—This story is not about a ball game, but about the gamest and most unselfish fellow I have ever had the privilege of knowing.

For weeks Yankee fans as well as the boys on the club have looked forward to seeing the great big, good natured Babe Ruth in the world series.

With pain and injuries increasing every day he has dragged himself through five games and been a leading factor in our three victories. But now it looks as though he is through and all because of his anxiety to keep up the spirits of the club despite torn ligaments in his leg and poison in his arm and that has now gone from his elbow up under his arm pit.

The doctor had just left when I visited Babe's apartment and the

(CONTINUED ON PAGE FIFTEEN)

COMMISSION SAYS ROAD IS LOSING CASH

Blame Heavy Competition of Bus and Truck Lines in Hearing Statement

With the chambers crowded with officials and experts engaged by the railway and by the state, the state railroad commission today opened the hearing to determine the future fares and operation of the Pacific Electric railway system.

A detailed report of the commission's engineers, in which it was pointedly stated that the electric railway was facing financial ruin because of automobile bus competition, was presented as the "opening gun" of the important hearing.

At the same time it was disclosed that the Pacific Electric will ask an immediate increase both in city and suburban fares.

BIG FIGHT LOOMS

The contents of the report as bared today were recognized by all parties to the hearing as the most startling facts yet revealed in connection with the company's petition to increase its fares, and the document as a whole presages a coming death fight between the electric lines and the motor operated lines in Southern California.

In their report, engineers of the commission state that rates during the past four years have nicreased less than 3 8per cent, while operating expenses have increased over 100 per cent.

They estimate that the bus and truck competition has diverted over $1,000,000 revenue from the Pacific Electric annually in business which is tributary to the electric line.

PASSENGER INCREASE

Referring to the federal census of 1920, the engineers point out that while the population in the four counties served by the Pacific Electric increased 78 per cent over that of 1910, passenger travel only showed an increase of 16.5 per cent over the totals of 1914.

Chambers of commerce in cities located along the system, city officials and other organizations prepared to make a vigorous protest to the commission when the hearing opened today before Commissioner H. L. Brundige and Chester H. Rowell.

The proceedings were originally set to be heard before the commission sitting en banc, but owing to the illness of Commissioner H. D. Loveland, and also due to the fact that other members of the body were called out of the city by business duties, it was agreed to stage the hearing before the two mentioned members.

ZONING SYSTEM

The increase in the local fare schedule which it was expected Frank Karr, attorney for the railway would ask this morning, is in line with the company's suggestions relative to the Hollywood case, which

(CONTINUED ON PAGE TEN)

IRISH PEACE PARLEY IS OPENED

New Plan to Halt Strife in Erin Is Launched; Oppose Parliament Proposal

LONDON, Oct. 11.—The first session of the momentous Irish peace conference to settle the quarrel of seven centuries between Irlaend and England lasted barely two hours.

The Irish delegates and the British envoys left Premier Lloyd George's official residence at 10 Downing street just before 1 o'clock. They were smiling and apparently satisfied.

The police had trouble in clearing a way through the crowd of Sinn Feiners with motor cars. The Irish got a big reception.

The Sinn Fein delegates, who were hailed by cheering, flag-waving crowds, both when they arrived and departed from the conference chambers, were to return at 4 o'clock.

PROGRESS DIFFICULT

The Irish delegates, five in number, drove up to the prime minister's residence in the narrow little street of Whitehall and were received by Lloyd George.

The British delegates, a cabinet committee appointed by the prime minister while in Scotland, arrived shortly before the Sinn Fein plenipotentiaries. The latter came to Downing street in a luxurious limousine and made their way with difficulty through the crowd.

The conference, which today was most formal in nature, opened shortly before noon. Lloyd George introduced the Irish plenipotentiaries to his colleagues of the Briish cabinet.

CHAMBERLAIN ILL

Arthur Griffith, Sinn Fein foreign minister, spoke.

Austen Chamberlain, former chancellor of the exchequer, who was to have been one of the British delegates, was taken suddenly ill and was unable to attend today's conference.

Sir Gordon Bewart, attorney general, was present in his place.

The first real business of the conference was not expected today. This, it was indicated, would begin tomorrow.

The meeting got under way shortly after 11 o'clock with the full Sinn Fein delegation, headed by Arthur Griffith, present.

Premier Lloyd George altered his original decision to open the parley with a speech. Instead he put the convention on a "conversational basis" at once.

SHOW ARMY TRAINING

It was announced that no communique would be issued until night, and that it would be very brief.

A few minutes after 11 o'clock and just before Winston Churchill, secretary of state for the colonies, had appeared, four magnificent limousines drove up in front of No. 10 Downing street and two commandants of the

(CONTINUED ON PAGE SIX)

Line-Up of Sixth Game of Big Series

GIANTS—	YANKEES—
Burns, cf.	Miller, cf.
Bancroft, ss.	Peck, ss.
Frisch, 3b.	Schang, c.
Young, rf.	B. Meusel, rf.
Kelly, 1b.	Pipp, 1b.
E. Meusel, lf.	Ward, 2b.
Rawlings, 2b.	McNally, 3b.
Snyder, c.	Fewster, lf.
Barnes, p.	Harper, p.

Heinman's Missions Open Seven-Game Ball Series in L. A.

MISSIONS—	ANGELS—
Siglin, 2b.	Statz, cf.
Kamm, 3b.	High, lf.
Caveney, ss.	Cox, rf.
Heilman, 1b.	Hornsby, 2b.
Miller, lf.	Brown, 3b.
Compton, cf.	Anheir, 1b.
O'Doul, rf.	Brubaker, ss.
Agnew, c.	Baldwin, c.
Faeth, p.	Reiger, p.

Tony Faeth was the pitcher Harry Heilman, manager of the San Francisco Mission club, picked to oppose Rogers Hornsby's Angels at Washington park this afternoon in the opening game of the series of seven.

Hornsby ordered Elmer Reiger, Salt Lake spitball pitcher, to be ready to oppose Heilman and his crew.

Ted McGrew and Billy Phyle will umpire.

Sailor Is Held on Narcotics Charge

Recent activities of Eugene d'Artenay, quartermaster of the steamship Venezuela, under arrest at San Pedro on a charge of violating the Harrison drug act and smuggling, were investigated today by police. The man was arrested after officers said d'Artenay offered to sell them 112 bottles of morphine and cocaine for $1375. The Venezuela arrived in the local port yesterday from Baltimore.

Robbed of $90 by 'Infant Bandits'

Two young bandits early today held up Jue Hong, a Chinese, of 330 Marchassault street, at Eleventh street and Maple avenue, robbing him of $90. Hong was driving his vegetable wagon towards the market when the "baby" bandits stepped from the curb and with drawn revolvers, commanded him to halt.

Convicted Minister Leaves for Prison

LAKEPORT, Cal., Oct. 11.—With a deputy from the sheriff's office, the Rev. J. A. Spencer, retired minister convicted of murdering his wife, today left for San Quentin to serve a life sentence. He refused to make an appeal of the decision of Judge Sayre of the superior court here.

"DRY" CHIEF SATISFIED

WASHINGTON, Oct. 11.—Prohibition Commissioner Haynes today asserted that his office had the "wet spots" of the nation well in hand.

SPURNED MAN KILLS GIRL AND HIMSELF WHILE WIFE WAITS OUTSIDE IN AUTO

KANSAS CITY, Oct. 11.—"What was that noise? Did a tire blow out on my machine?"

That was the question asked a passing policeman by Mrs. H. H. Slick as she sat in her automobile in front of a beauty parlor here today.

The officer investigated and found that the explosions which had excited Mrs. Slick's curiosity were two revolver shots fired by her husband.

Leaving his wife in the auto at the curb, Slick had entered a manicure shop and shot beautiful Hazel Masten, aged 24, through the head, then turned the smoking weapon upon himself.

He fell dead instantly with a bullet through his brain.

Miss Masten cannot recover.

A probe instantly instituted by the police developed that there had been a love affair of long standing between Slick and the manicurist, which was on the verge of being broken off by the girl, who had transferred her affections to another man.

Slick had been threatened with divorce by his wife and had promised that he would "end the affair."

So while Mrs. Slick waited for him in the car today he shot the girl and took his own life.

LEAVES NOTE

He left a note, which was found after the tragedy, stating that it was "his only way out, because he loved the other woman so much."

"I did not even know that my husband had entered the building for the purpose of seeing the Masten girl," Mrs. Slick said after the killing. "I was waiting in the machine and when I heard the reports of the pistol, I thought a tire had exploded."

LATEST NEWS

URGES 100 TRAFFIC OFFICERS TO HUNT BANDITS

Advocating temporary disbandment of the police traffic division of 100 officers and other so-called 'second line" departments, Capt. R. Lee Heath, commander of Central precinct, caused a sensation in police and civic circles today by urging that all police officers be detailed in the roundup of burglars, bandits and thugs.

BRITAIN INVITES PERSHING FOR MEDAL CEREMONY

LONDON, Oct. 11.—The British government has decided to invite Gen. Pershing to come to London to lay the congressional medal of honor on the tomb of the unknown soldier in Westminster Abbey next Friday, the Evening Star said today.

KU KLUX IMPERIAL WIZARD FACES HOUSE QUIZ

WASHINGTON, Oct. 11.—Imperial Wizard William Joseph Simmons of the Ku Klux Klan appeared before the house rules committee today ready to defend his "invisible empire."

Suit Against Santa Monica to Stand

By a decision of Judge Burnell, entered today in the superior court records, a demurrer to the suit of John W. Mitchell and the Los Angeles Trust & Savings bank against the City of Santa Monica was sustained. The suit involved the title to the property known as the Palisades, and the question as to whether the deed to the city required the municipality to devote the property to park purposes was an issue.

Georgia Society to Meet Saturday

The Georgia society will hold its first fall meeting Saturday evening, Oct. 15, at Barton's hall, Sixteenth and Main streets. Special entertainment has been arranged. Plans for the winter meetings are to be formulated and an invitation is extended to all Alabamians and Floridians as well as Georgians to be present.

MORALS RAIDS ARE PLANNED BY POLICE

With two score men and women in custody as a result of a series of morals raids conducted during the night under direct supervision of Police Commissioner C. A. De Coo, Police Captain Lee Heath of central division today mapped out a number of new raids to be made by the vice squad, probably tonight.

Squads of police operated in the downtown district, in Chinatown and in many residence sections in the series of raids last night and early today.

AID POLICE

Special investigators employed by Commissioner De Coo and by the morals efficiency commission have been aiding the police in gathering evidence against gambling dens and other alleged resorts.

Some of these officers participated

(CONTINUED ON PAGE TEN)

MAN IN ATTACK CASE BURNED AT STAKE

LEESBURG, Tex., Oct. 11.—Wylie McNealy, a negro, was burned at the stake here last night by a mob estimated at 500 after he had been taken from the Mount Pleasant jail and brought here in an automobile.

McNealy had been indicted for an attempt to assault and an attempt to murder an 8-year-old white girl.

Firemen Near Death in $500,000 Blaze

By United Press

CHICAGO, Oct. 11.—Fifteen firemen were overcome here today in a fire at the hay warehouse of the Union Stockyards and Transit Co. The loss was estimated at $500,000. The fire will smoulder for at least two weeks, officials believed.

Baseball, Golf, Tennis, Turf, Track, Boxing, Wrestling—all expertly reported by expert re'porters, Best in the West.

SPORT NEWS

Los Angeles Examiner

TUESDAY, SEPTEMBER 19, 1922 SECTION I—PAGE

The Examiner carries the most complete Sporting Section of any newspaper West of Chicago.

YANKEES RALLY AND DEFEAT BROWNS, 3 TO 2

Vernon Expects to Lead as Seals Meet Angels

Tigers Open Against Oakland Here Today

Essick Hopes to See Los Angeles Down Seals; Killefer's Club Still in Race

BY MAXWELL STILES

DEAR WADE:

I take back all I ever said about you. Wade, you are a gentleman, after all. And so are your Angels, every one of them. I want you to know that the Vernon club is backing you to the limit against San Francisco. We hope that you win every game and let the Seals down a peg in the percentage column. Los Angeles forever!!

BILL ESSICK.

IF Bill Essick didn't send that note to Wade Killefer last night, be sure that he feels it in his heart today. Of course, Bill figures that his Vernon Tigers will lay the Oaks out for a stretch at Washington Park this week, and if the Angels succeed in stopping the Seals, then—

Vernon will jump ahead of San Francisco in the race for the pennant.

But it is quite likely that Wade Killefer does not wish Bill Essick so much luck as Bill Essick wishes Wade Killefer. The sorrel-topped manager of the Angels still believes that his club has a fighting chance for the pennant. Now, according to Wade's philosophy, if the Los Angeles club can take about six out of seven from San Francisco, with Oakland handing out the same kind of medicine to the Tigers, then—

ANGELS' CHANCE

Before the season ends the Angels will be in first place.

So there you are. Take your choice.

Vernon is just one full game behind the Seals. The Angels are ten games behind Vernon and eleven back of San Francisco. There are four weeks to go. Vernon has yet to meet Oakland twice and Seattle and Los Angeles once. San Francisco meets Los Angeles twice and Sacramento and Oakland once. Los Angeles is to clash with the Seals twice, Salt Lake once and wind up the season with Vernon at Washington Park.

The Tigers, apparently, have the easiest schedule. While the Angels are far behind, this is minimized by the fact that in three out of four weeks they meet their pennant rivals. Every game which they win—if, indeed, they do win—will bring their opponents down while they climb. It is, therefore, a three-cornered race, with the team getting the breaks having the best chance.

LOOK OUT FOR TIGERS

At the rate things are going now, the Tigers should be in first place before the end of the week. San Francisco showed signs of cracking when the club dropped four out of seven to Portland last week. The Angels took four out of seven from Seattle and seem primed to give the Seals a terrible battle, especially as their last pennant hopes hinge on their showing this week.

The Tigers took five out of seven from Sacramento, and the week before let Salt Lake down heavily. Salt Lake won six games from Oakland, which does show that the Tigers seem to be a much stronger ball club than the Oaks.

If the dope runs true to form Los Angeles will win four out of seven from the Seals and Vernon will take five games from Oakland. This will put Bill Essick's crew in first place.

Pacific Coast League

	W.	L.	Pct.	W.	L.
San Francisco	110	62	.640	.642	.636
VERNON	109	63	.634	.636	.630
LOS ANGELES	99	73	.576	.578	.572
Salt Lake	83	90	.480	.483	.477
Oakland	77	96	.445	.448	.443
Seattle	74	95	.438	.441	.435
Portland	67	103	.394	.398	.392
Sacramento	67	104	.392	.395	.390

TODAY'S GAMES

Oakland at VERNON.
LOS ANGELES at San Francisco.
Portland at Sacramento.
Seattle at Salt Lake.

ABOVE—Mollwitz, Sacramento first baseman, tried to steal third base, in the fourth inning of the second game at Washington Park Sunday and was out when May, Vernon pitcher, threw to Smith and the Strawberry blonde, of the Tigers, ran him down.

BELOW—Rod Murphy, Sacramento infielder, safe at first base when Zeider's throw to Locker was slow. Eighth inning of the first Vernon-Sacramento game, Sunday.

George Shade Gets Decision at Boston

BOSTON, Sept. 18.—George Shade of San Francisco won the judges' decision in a ten-round bout with Harry Silva of Boston here tonight. The men are middleweights.

Bradshaw and Steers to Play Here on Nov. 11

ARRANGEMENTS have been virtually completed for an Armistice Day football game between the Olympic Club of San Francisco and the Multnomah A. C. of Portland, to be played November 11 at Pasadena's new stadium, it was announced yesterday.

Among the stars who will play are "Rabbit" Bradshaw, famous Nevada quarterback, who will captain the Olympic Club; Bill Steers, former Oregon star, and Mike Moran, Washington State fullback, who will play for Multnomah.

Killefer Says Seals Have Cracked

PORTLAND, Ore., Sept. 18.—"Red" Killefer, manager of the Los Angeles baseball club, while in Portland today enroute to San Francisco where the Angels open a series against the Seals Wednesday, gave out a belligerent statement of his intentions.

"Red" Killefer

"Los Angeles can't win the pennant now," said Killefer. "We are ten games behind, which is too much, but what we can and will do is beat San Francisco out of the flag. Anything to beat the Seals is my motto and my players all feel the same way.

"To my notion the Seals have cracked. The tail-end Beavers started it last week by taking four out of seven and what they started we will finish in the two series we have against the Seals.

"I sent Pitchers Lyons and Hughes on ahead of us from Seattle to San Francisco so they will be in perfect condition, and Elmer Ponder will join us and pitch if he is able. If I can be the humble means of causing San Francisco to lose the pennant and thereby make the Seal owners squirm, I will be the happiest manager in the Coast League."

Anglo-American Polo Four Wins

PHILADELPHIA, Sept. 18.—Better team work, coupled with good stroking, gave Eastcott, the Anglo-American polo team, a fine victory over Averill Harriman's Orange county four at the Philadelphia Country Club today by the score of 12 goals to 11. The winning team had conceded Orange four goals by handicap.

The defeat of Orange eliminates that team from the present tournament and gives Eastcott the right to meet next Saturday, in the final, the winner of Wednesday's match between Argentine Federation and Devereaux Milburn's Meadow Brook team.

YOUNG BROWN A FAVORITE OVER GOOZEMAN TONIGHT

By SOL PLEX

WHAT figures to be one of the toughest four-round bouts staged in Southern California in several weeks will be held at the Vernon arena tonight when Ernie Goozeman, local 125-pounder, meets Young Brown in the main event of the weekly boxing show.

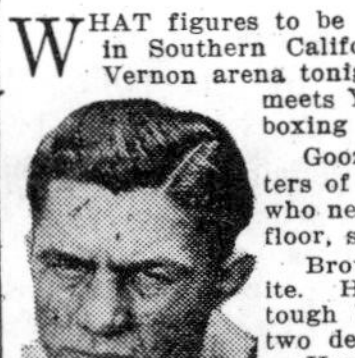

Ernie Goozeman

Goozeman is regarded as one of the hardest hitters of his weight on the Coast. Brown is a fighter who never stops until he's on the winning end or the floor, so it figures to be some scrap.

Brown will probably enter the ring a slight favorite. He defeated Southpaw Danny Kramer in a tough bout a short time ago, while Goozeman lost two decisions to the portsider.

However, Goozeman is more rugged than Kramer and there are a lot of fans who believe he will punch too hard for the Mexican.

Unless all signs fail, the semi-windup will crowd the main event when it comes to real action. Larry Murphy, the youngster who has made such an impressive showing at the old arena, will tackle George Sirey in this affair.

The bout is a rematch, but it looks to be one that won't miss fire. A week ago Sirey slipped over a finisher on the tough youngster, but before he landed his k. o. wallop Murphy had sent him to the canvas twice for fairly long counts.

If Murphy can get by in winning fashion tonight he is practically set for a main event in the very near future.

Johnny Tyman and Louie Garcia are down for the feature preliminary. They will step into the ring at 135 pounds. It will be Garcia's second bout in Southern California since he returned from a tour of Australia.

A couple of bantamweights are down for the fourth battle of the evening. They are Georgie Rivers and Frankie Novie.

Other bouts scheduled and the order in which they will be staged follow:

Lucky Lugo vs. Eddie Watson, 145 pounds.

Joe Mandot vs. Johnny LaRose, 118 pounds.

Ernest Owens vs. Jack Moore, 150 pounds.

George Blake will referee.

BASEBALL RESULTS STANDINGS SCHEDULES

National League

	W.	L.	Pct.		W.	L.	Pct.
New York	86	55	.610	Chicago	75	66	.532
Pittsburg	81	61	.570	Brooklyn	69	73	.486
St. Louis	78	63	.553	Philadel	50	88	.362
Cincinnati	77	66	.538	Boston	47	91	.341

YESTERDAYS RESULTS

St. Louis, 6; Boston, 4.
New York, 7; Cincinnati, 2.
Chicago 4; Brooklyn, 3.
Pittsburg, 11-2; Philadelphia, 3-5.

TODAY'S GAMES

St. Louis at Boston.
Pittsburg at Philadelphia.

Western League

	W.	L.	Pct.		W.	L.	Pct.
Tulsa	101	58	.635	Sioux Cty	80	77	.510
St. Joseph	92	67	.579	Okla Cty	77	87	.470
Wichita	87	71	.551	D Moines	61	97	.386
Omaha	85	74	.535	Denver	58	101	.365

YESTERDAY'S RESULTS

Sioux City, 9; Denver, 8.
Other games postponed, rain.

American Association

	W.	L.	Pct.		W.	L.	Pct.
St. Paul	97	55	.638	Milwake	79	77	.506
Minneapo	84	68	.553	Louisvill	74	82	.474
Kan Cty	82	72	.532	Toledo	60	94	.390
Indianapo	71	72	.529	Columbu	58	95	.379

YESTERDAY'S RESULTS

Milwaukee, 10; Louisville, 9.
Kansas City, 1; Indianapolis, 1 (called in fifth, rain).
Other games, postponed; rain.

International League

	W.	L.	Pct.		W.	L.	Pct.
Baltmre	114	50	.695	Toronto	75	84	.472
Rochstr	100	61	.621	Reading	70	90	.437
Buffalo	93	67	.581	Syracuse	60	100	.375
Jersy Cty	81	81	.500	Newark	51	110	.317

YESTERDAY'S RESULTS

Jersey City, 7; Newark, 6.
Reading, 3; Baltimore, 3 (10 innings, called, darkness).
Toronto, 2; Rochester, 1 (11 innings).
Only games played.

American League

	W.	L.	Pct.		W.	L.	Pct.
New York	88	56	.611	Clevelnd	71	73	.493
St. Louis	87	58	.600	Washgtn	63	78	.447
Detroit	77	69	.527	Philadel	59	83	.415
Chicago	73	72	.503	Boston	57	86	.399

YESTERDAY'S RESULTS

Chicago, 7; Boston, 0.
Philadelphia, 4; Cleveland, 3.
Detroit, 11; Washington, 5.
New York, 3; St. Louis, 2.

TODAY'S GAMES

Washington at St. Louis.
Philadelphia at Chicago.
New York at Detroit.
Boston at Cleveland.

Cobb Makes It 200 Hits for 8th Season

DETROIT, Sept. 18.—Ty Cobb made his 200th hit of the season in the fourth inning of today's game with Washington. It was a triple, with one man on. With that hit, the Detroit Manager completed eight seasons in which he has clouted 200 or more safeties.

Ty Cobb

His record equals that made years ago by "Wee Willie" Keeler. Keeler's record, however, was made in consecutive seasons.

With the close of this season the famous Georgian will have tied another old time record—that of Hans Wagner, who batted .300 or better for 17 years. Cobb's percentage now assures him of better than a .300 average.

Ty Cobb Congratulates Sisler on Hit Record

ST. LOUIS, Sept. 18.—(By the Associated Press.)—George Sisler, of the St. Louis Americans, who yesterday broke Ty Cobb's record of hitting in 40 consecutive games, today received the following telegram from Cobb:

"Congratulations upon your success. You have been a rare credit to the game of baseball and I am delighted to see you win your latest honors."

Sisler hit safely in his 41st consecutive game yesterday.

Fine Squad of Frosh Turns Out at U. S. C.

FRESHMEN of the University of Southern California turned out in a body to learn the fundamental principles of collegiate football yesterday. Coach Hess, formerly of the Sherman Indian Institute, is filling the shoes of Coach Ofstie, last year's frosh mentor.

Among the former prep stars who reported are: Loustalot and Green from Bakersfield, quarterback and half respectively; Scott of Manual Arts, fullback, and LeFebvure of Long Beach, halfback.

Bringing Body of Roscoe Sarles to L. A. for Burial

His Pals Will Present Excess Prize Money to Widow; Others Will Recover

ROSCOE SARLES, "one of the greatest" of race kings, will make his last homecoming Thursday afternoon. His body with be brought to Los Angeles by his parents and by Fred Oomer and Tommy Milton, his friends of the roaring road. Sarles' parents are expected to reach Kansas City this morning from LaFayette, Ind. He was burned to death there Sunday afternoon when his car overturned and caught fire during races dedicating the new Kansas City Speedway. Mrs. Sarles, his widow, mourns alone in a darkened room of her apartment at 312 South Hoover street. Hundreds of friends, calling yesterday, were met by Mrs. J. Wesley Jones, her mother, who told them the widow seemed unable to rally from the terrible shock.

KANSAS CITY, Mo., Sept. 15.—Excess prize money of $6000 may be presented to the widow of Roscoe Sarles, Los Angeles driver, killed in the 300-mile automobile race here yesterday, Tommy Milton, winner, announced. Milton and the other five who finished the race arranged a conference late today to consider disposition of prize money which was NOT claimed because cars dropped out of the contest.

Twelve prizes were offered, aggregating $30,000. The prizes were claimed by the six finishing the race:

Tommy Milton, $10,000; Frank Eliot, $3250; Ralph Mulford, $2750; Jerry Wonderlich, $2250; Bennett Hill, $1750.

Hospital physicians this afternoon reported the seven injured drivers and mechanicians improved with recovery certain.

Speedway officials estimate receipts from yesterday's race at $175,000.

Three Other Drivers Injured Will Recover

KANSAS CITY, Sept. 18.—Reports from hospitals today indicated that the three motor car drivers injured seriously yesterday in the dedication race of Kansas City's new half-million dollar speedway would recover.

Christopher V. Pickup, Los Angeles, mechanician for Sarles; Ed Hefferman, Chicago, mechanician for Eddie Hearne, and Harry Henning of Independence, Mo., mechanician of Pete de Paolo, suffered the most serious injuries. They sustained concussions of the brain besides cuts and bruises. They also may be injured internally, physicians said.

The less seriously injured include Hearne, De Paolo, Joe Thomas and Jimmy Murphy.

N.Y. ANNEXES GAME IN 9TH; COPS SERIES

Yankees Increase Lead Over St. Louis to Game and a Half, but Race Is Still Close

ST. LOUIS, Mo., Sept. 18.—After holding a lead on the New York Americans, the Browns permitted the visitors to come from behind in the last inning and take today's game, 3 to 2, thus increasing New York's lead to one and one-half games.

The Browns' four errors figured in the visitors' three runs.

Up to the last inning, the contest was a pitchers' battle, with Davis of the Browns getting the best of his battle with Bush. He weakened however, in the ninth and the visitors took advantage of two hits and an error, and scored the tying and winning runs.

The Browns scored the first run in the fifth inning on Jacobson's double, McManus' single, and Severeid's sacrifice fly, and added another in the seventh on Williams' double, Jacobson's sacrifice, and McManus' double.

The visitors made the first run in the eighth inning, when Dugan who had doubled raced home as McManus threw over Sisler's head on Pipp's infield single. The tying and winning tallies came in the last inning.

DOUBLE PLAY

Schang reached first base on an infield hit and went to second on a passed ball. Smith was sent in to bat for Ward, but was removed in favor of McNally, when Pruett relieved Davis. McNally, attempting to sacrifice went to first as Severeid threw low to catch Schang on third. Scott walked and Shocker relieved Pruett. Bush forced Schang at the plate. Witt's single brought in McNally and Scott. Dugan hit into a double play, ending the rally.

By taking today's game the visitors also took the series, having won the first game Saturday. The Browns' only victory of this crucial series was due to Pruett's great pitching in Sunday's game. Having lost today's game, the Browns are now conceded but little chance to win the pennant. Sports writers agreed that this series would decide the pennant winner of the American League.

SISLER FAILS TO HIT

Sisler, the Browns' first baseman, broke his string of hitting in consecutive games after getting at least one hit in forty-one successive contests thus establishing a new modern major league record.

The previous modern record was made by Cobb when he hit safely in forty consecutive games in 1911.

This series between the Yankees and Browns referred to as a "little world's series," drew a capacity crowd. At all three games the spectators were admitted to the playing field and ground rules were enforced. It has been estimated by the Browns' management that at least 85,000 attended the three games.

Although the Browns are scheduled to meet the weaker teams of the league while the leaders will play Detroit and Cleveland, it is believed unlikely by followers of the national pastime that the Yankees will lose their lead of one and one-half games. Score:

NEW YORK	AB	H	O	A	E	ST. LOUIS	AB	H	O	A	E
Witt,cf	4	3	0	0	0	Tobin,rf	4	1	2	0	0
Dugan,3b	5	1	2	0	0	Foster,3b.	4	0	1	3	0
Ruth,lf	4	0	4	1	0	Sisler,1b	4	0	10	1	1
Pipp,1b	4	1	13	0	0	Wiliams,lf	4	1	2	0	0
Meusel,rf.	4	0	0	0	0	Jacobsn,cf	2	1	3	0	0
Schang,c.	4	1	2	2	0	M'Mns,2b	3	2	2	5	1
Ward,2b	2	0	2	6	0	Severeid,c.	1	0	4	0	1
Smith	0	0	0	0	0	Gerber,ss.	3	0	3	2	0
M'Naly,2b	0	0	1	1	0	Davis,p	2	0	0	2	1
Scott,ss	2	0	2	4	0	Pruett,p.	0	0	0	0	0
Bush,p	4	0	1	3	0	Shocker,p.	0	0	0	0	0
Totals	33	6	27	17	0	Totals	27	5	27	13	4

Smith batted for Ward in ninth.
McNally batted for Smith in ninth.

New York	0	0	0	0	0	0	0	1	2—3
St. Louis	0	0	0	0	1	0	1	0	0—2

Two-base hits—Jacobson, Williams, Dugan, McManus. Sacrifice hits—Davis, Scott, Severeid, McNally, Jacobson. Double plays—Ruth to Schang to Ward to Pipp, Foster to McManus to Sisler. Base on balls—Off Bush, 1; off Davis, 2; off Pruett, 1. Struck out—By Bush, 2; by Davis, 3. Innings pitched—By Davis, 8; by Pruett, 0; by Shocker, 1. Hit by pitcher—By Bush (Jacobson). Passed ball—Severeid. Losing pitcher—Pruett.

Macks, 4; Indians, 3

CLEVELAND, O., Sept. 18.—Philadelphia made it two out of three from Cleveland today, winning 4 to 3. Score:

PHILADELPHIA	AB	H	O	A	E	CLEVELAND	AB	H	O	A	E
M'Gown,cf	4	0	4	0	0	Jamison,lf	4	1	4	1	0
Perkins,c.	3	0	2	2	0	Wamby,ss.	4	0	1	2	0
Walker,rf.	3	0	2	0	0	Summa,rf.	4	1	1	0	0
Hauser,1b	3	1	9	0	1	Gardnr,3b	3	0	1	0	0
Miller,rf.	4	3	2	0	0	J.Sewel,2b	4	1	2	1	0
Galoway,ss	3	1	3	3	0	McNuty,cf	4	2	2	0	0
Dykes,3b	2	0	1	0	1	McInis,1b	4	1	6	1	0
Scheer,2b.	4	0	4	4	0	L.Sewell,c	1	0	9	1	0
Rommel,p	3	0	0	3	0	O'Neill,c.	2	1	0	1	0
Heimach,p	0	0	0	0	0	Edwards,p	2	0	1	0	0
						Lindsey,p.	0	0	0	0	1
						Speaker	0	0	0	0	0
						Stephensn	1	1	0	0	0
						Wood	1	0	0	0	0
Totals	29	5	27	12	2	Totals	34	8	27	7	1

Speaker batted for Edwards in 8th.
Evans ran for Speaker in 8th.
Stephenson batted for Lindsey in 9th.
Sorrels ran for O'Neill in 9th.
Wood batted for Jamieson in 9th.

Philadelphia	0	1	0	0	0	0	2	0	1—4
Cleveland	0	0	0	0	0	0	0	1	2—3

Two base hits—Miller, J. Sewell, McInnis. Bases on balls—Off Rommell, 4; Edwards, 2; Lindsey, 1. Struck out—By Rommell, 2; Heimach, 1; Edwards, 7; Lindsey, 1.

What Say?

—By Ed Sullivan—

CHICAGO, Sept. 18.—For some reason, which the promoters and general muddlers of boxing don't seem to see the need of, there is a tendency in sport to give the spectator all the best of it. It is a very proper tendency.

Ed Sullivan

The most spectacular recent evidence of it is, of course, the lively ball, which needs but to be tickled to vanish from the ball parks. Babe Ruth took to clouting the old soulless hosshide a few seasons back and the national fan went cuckoo. He liked it, and straightway those clouters who lacked the back muscles of Babe Ruth were aided in their budding ambitions by a new and frisky pell . The fans like it and get apl .ty of it.

The most important change in the football rules for the season of 1922 has to do with the spectators' viewpoint. The open game, which succeeded the mass formation type of play, was a concession to sense and the spectator. Under the new rules, the kicking of goal after a touchdown becomes an event rather than a mere incident.

The team scoring is permitted to bring the ball out to any point not less than five yards from the goal line, and may attempt to score from a run forward pass place or drop kick.

It represents new action, and if there is anything a spectator at any sporting event desires it is just that. What say?

Two Eastern Teams May Meet Jan. 1

PASADENA, Sept. 18.—Pasadena is going to have a big football game this New Year which will attract as much attention as any ever played in Pasadena and which will completely fill the new stadium now building in the Arroyo Seco. This game in all probability will be another East-West contest—then, again, it may be an all-East game, for Pasadena is not without an ace in the hole.

This is the word which comes from Tournament of Roses officials in relation to alleged controversies with officials of the Pacific Collegiate Conference. Not that the officials of the tournament admit there is any controversy with the conference. They merely smile and say negotiations are proceeding satisfactorily. Nor will they allow their names to be quoted. But they have let it be known that the Pasadena football situation stands about so.

THE ALLOTMENTS

A New Year's game is to be played and it will be one that will fill the Stadium, which at the announced scale of prices will bring in $185,000. Of this $35,000 will be allowed to each of the competing colleges and they will pay their own expenses out of that. There will be an allowance of $5000 for incidental expenses of the tournament. The balance of the receipts will be applied toward paying for the new stadium.

"By allowing $50,000 to University of California last year we helped them finance their new stadium. It is only right the college help the Tournament, which started this New Year idea, finance the stadium," say the Pasadenans. They expect a Pacific Coast Conference team to play here on New Year's.

If another East-West game is also scheduled for the Stanford stadium, all well and good. There are two cities in California, each capable of furnishing a capacity New Year's football crowd, Pasadenans say.

PENN STATE IS SIGNED

The real joker in Pasadena's confidence is here: Penn State is already under contract to play here next New Year's, if desired. Likewise, the winner in a group of colleges, which includes Washington and Jefferson, the Eastern contender of last year, is also signed up, to whichever team it may be to play here if desired. If the Pacific Conference gets too "uppy" the Tournament of Roses has but to bring on two Eastern elevens.

Inasmuch as the actual floral festival of the Tournament of Roses brings approximately 250,000 people to Pasadena every New Year's, tournament officials do not feel much worry over whether or not 60,000 of these will stay over in the afternoon for any football game that is going to be a good one—East vs. West or just East vs. East.

GIANTS' AND YANKEES' PERSONNEL CHANGED SINCE LAST WORLD SERIES

National League Leaders Have Lost Burns, Toney and Douglas Since 1921

'ades, Sales and Expulsions Deprive McGrawmen of Services of Three Players Who Figured Largely in Result of Last Year's Fight With Rival New York Aggregation—Scott Has Four Series.

Of the Giants who took part in the world series with the Yankees last ·r three are gone. These are George Burns, who was traded to the Reds t winter; Fred Toney, who was released to the Braves in the McQuillan l last July, and Phil Douglas, who wrote himself out of the majors. In ce of Douglas and Toney on the pitching staff John McGraw has Mc-illan; Jack Scott, who was signed after he had been released by the Reds; ·men Hill, purchased from Indianapolis; Claude Jonnard, acquired from tle Rock, and Virgil Barnes, recalled from Milwaukee.

)f the Yankees who played last ·r against the National League ·mpions no fewer than eight have ·e from the club. They are Jack ·nn, Bill Piercy, Rip Collins, Elmer ler and Chick Fewster, who now with the Red Sox; Harry Harper, o was released unconditionally this son; Roger Peckinpaugh, who was ded to the Red Sox and thence to ·shington last winter, and Tom gers, the pitcher, who has been t back to the minors.

n place of the somewhat tatterde-lion bunch of flingers who have ·e Miller Huggins has two stars. Bush and Sam Jones were acquired m the Red Sox along with Everett ·tt, the shortstop. George Murray, ·t hander, was realled from Roch-er. Lefty O'Doul still is with the nkees, but he did not work last fall l it is not likely that he will be d this time, unless it be to finish

ries veteran of the field. The classic will be his fifth. He played in three with the Red Sox. Everett Scott was in three with the Red Sox, so this will be his fourth. His world series record in the field is phenomenal. Sam Jones was with the Red Sox in 1918.

For John McGraw the series which will open next Wednesday will be his seventh. He has won eight pennants with the Giants but in 1904 there was no series with the Red Sox, who won the American League pennant. In 1905, mainly through the remarkable pitching of Matty, the Giants won their first world series, beating the Athletics four games to one.

HOW PARTICIPANTS FARED IN WORLD SERIES SINCE 1884

Year.	Winners.	Games Won	Losers.	Games Won
1884	Providence, National League	3	Metropolitan, American Association	0
1885	Chicago, National League	3	St. Louis, American Association	2
1886	St. Louis, American Association	4	Chicago, National League	2
1887	Detroit, National League	10	St. Louis, American Association	4
1888	New York, National League	10	St. Louis, American Association	1
1889	New York, National League	6	Brooklyn, American Association	3
1890	Louisville, National League	3	Brooklyn, American Association	3
1892	Boston, National League	5	Cleveland, National League	0
1894	New York, National League	4	Baltimore, National League	0
1895	Cleveland, National League	4	Baltimore, National League	1
1896	Baltimore, National League	4	Cleveland, National League	0
1897	Baltimore, National League	4	Boston, National League	1
1903	Boston, American League	5	Pittsburgh, National League	0
1905	New York, National League	4	Philadelphia, American League	1
1906	Chicago, American League	4	Chicago, National League	2
1907	Chicago, National League	4	Detroit, American League	0
1908	Chicago, National League	4	Detroit, American League	1
1909	Pittsburgh, National League	4	Detroit, American League	3
1910	Philadelphia, American League	4	Chicago, National League	1
1911	Philadelphia, American League	4	New York, National League	2
1912	Boston, American League	4	New York, National League	3
1913	Philadelphia, American League	4	New York, National League	1
1914	Boston, National League	4	Philadelphia, American League	0
1915	Boston, American League	4	Philadelphia, National League	1
1916	Boston, American League	4	Brooklyn, National League	1
1917	Chicago, American League	4	New York, National League	2
1918	Boston, American League	4	Chicago, National League	2
1919	Cincinnati, National League	5	Chicago, American League	3
1920	Cleveland, American League	5	Brooklyn, National League	2
1921	New York, National League	5	New York, American League	4

No series was played in 1891, 1893, 1898 to 1902, and 1904. From 1884 to 1890 National League vs. American Association. 1894 to 1897 Temple cup series. 1903 to present time National League vs. American League.

released to Montgomery, April, 1912; recalled by Brooklyn, August, 1912; Brooklyn, 1913-14-15-16-17; traded to Pittsburgh, N. L., January, 1918; Pittsburgh, 1918-19; traded to Philadelphia, N. L., 1919; Philadelphia, 1919-20-21; traded to New York N. L., 1921; New York, N. L., 1922.

BASEBALL FANDOM AGAIN VISITS MECCA

Thousands Arrive This Week —Vanguard Already Worries Hotel Clerks.

New York again is the mecca of the baseball world this week. The well known countless thousands will be on hand and, as a matter of fact, they have already begun to add to the worries of bizarre hotel clerks, to say nothing of adding to the bankrolls of their employers.

Thousands will come to New York to attend the world series, and the Hagen-Sarazen golf match on the 7th will bring more sportsmen. The American Bankers' Association will hold its annual convention, which will bring at least 7,000 delegates to the big hotels of the city. On Monday, the 9th, representatives of 300,000 women will convene in what is expected to be the largest women's conference ever held in the State, when delegates from every part of New York will attend the convention of the New York State Federation of Women's Clubs.

The "furthest from home" fan to date is Eugene S. Cochran, who has come to the McAlpin from Hayti. He has never missed a world series, and he started several weeks ago in order to be here for the event. The Waldorf already has registered William N. Cubben and his son, Nace, from Cleveland.

Rooms Will Be at Premium.

It is safe to say that there will not be an available room in any of the largest hotels on Tuesday night, but it is equally certain that no baseball fan will be forced to sleep in the park because of lack of accommodations. At the time of the Dempsey-Carpentier fight it was predicted, by all sure signs, that there would be no available rooms. As a result thousands stayed away from New York. The hotel men are anxious to assure America's baseball public that their plans need not be given up, even if their favorite hotel has wired "sold out" to their plea for reservations.

The hotel men will cooperate with the fans and plan to direct them to one of the horde of smaller hotels in the city. These, they say, can take care of almost any number. The Pennsylvania had a small number of double rooms left yesterday, but was accepting no single reservations. The Astor, Commodore, Biltmore, Waldorf and McAlpin will have rooms only for those with early reservations. It should be remembered, however, that the hotel district has scores of small hotels, while there are hundreds elsewhere in the city.

The world series is of more interest in the hotel lobby to-day than the weightier bankers' convention, but no betting was reported and opinion as to the outcome is divided. A clerk at the McAlpin reported that several St. Louis men, who were in town on business, had declared their opinion of the result of the season in no uncertain tones. Nevertheless they planned to see the series.

Commodore Writers' Headquarters

The Commodore will be the headquarters of the two leagues, and also of the American Baseball Writers' Association, which comprises the leading baseball reporters of the country. The large writing room on the main floor will be turned into a great newspaper office, with typewriters, copypapers, pencils, telegraph facilities, and everything that goes with a big newspaper office. The Giants will hold forth at the Waldorf, while the Yankees are expected to make their headquarters at the Martinique with Col. Huston.

While the great majorty of the out-of-town fans will not arrive until Tuesday, Judge Landis and other notables are expected Monday to look over the ground. The advance guard, however, turned up yesterday.

Two Scranton men, who have never missed a series since they were old enough to attend, are Harry W. Clark and Stanley P. Callory of Scranton, who reached the Martinique at noon. They are strong Yankee fans. W. S. Bunting of Jacksonville, Fla., took no chances on railroad tieups, and likewise arrived early.

Kinsella Calls It a Season.

Dick Kinsella, chief scout of the Giants, has called it a season and has come from Springfield, Ill., to the Waldorf. With him was Roger Bresnahan, former Giant backstop in Matty's time, who is now manager of the Toledo American Association team.

The first fans at the McAlpin were M. J. Sawyer and W. A. Prescott of Boston, Allen D. Jones of Newport News, Va.; James U. Jackson, Augusta, Ga.; C. T. Symons, Saginaw, Mich., and A. J. Richardson, San Antonio.

At the Biltmore the first request for reservations was received from John P. Rice, Geneva, N. Y., and C. J. Maloy of Rochester. They are respectively president and secretary of the Ornamental Growers Association. Another room is ready for George Morris, a State Boxing Commissioner, who is coming from Amsterdam, N. Y.

A number of prominent cotton men, who have been in convention at Atlantic City, will come to New York for the big battle.

Rural Folk on Hand.

Hotel clerks point out that many men from the rural districts, who never come to New York except at the time of the series, are taking their annual holiday at this time.

To the Astor will come the following: Edwin G. Beal, Syracuse, Ohio; Sol Barnett, Boston; J. M. Beck, South Fallsburg, N. Y.; Leo J. Drum, Montgomery, Ala., S. H. Wood, Monroe, Mich.; Max Anderson, Providence; Dr. W. W. S. Butler, Jr., Roanoke, Va.; H. J. Bander, Philadelphia; Clark Howell, Atlanta; Mr. and Mrs. Edward Rohr, Norfolk, Va.; R. W. Sheegog, Dallas, Texas, and A. L. Shuman of the Fort Worth *Star-Telegram*, Fort Worth, Texas. A resident of Birdseye, Ind., also wired that he would be on hand.

The Pennsylvania has these reservations for the days of the series: Charles H. McGann, Electra, Texas; W. Eliot Dunwody, Jr., Macon, Ga.; James F. Sullivan and party, Seneca Falls, N. Y., and James O. Watson, Fairmont, W. Va.

American League Leads in World's Baseball Classic.

World's series play began thirty-eight years ago, when the Providence Grays, led by George Wright and with the famous Radborune as their leading pitcher, defeated the Metropolitans, champions of the American Association, three straight games in post season competition. There have been interruptions since then in the succession of annual series, so that the coming event between the Giants and the Yankees will be the thirty-first. Incidentally, it will be the nineteenth between the National and American leagues.

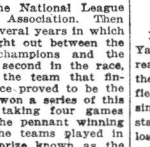

From 1884 to 1890 the rivals in the world's series were the respective pennant winners in the National League and the American Association. Then came a period of several years in which the series was fought out between the National League champions and the team that finished second in the race, and several times the team that finished in second place proved to be the winner. Cleveland won a series of this character in 1895, taking four games out of five from the pennant winning Baltimore club. The teams played in those days for a prize known as the Temple cup.

The year 1897 saw the end of the Temple cup series, and for five years following there were no post season games, baseball being disturbed by the war between the National and American leagues. In 1903 the American League had established itself unquestionably as a lasting organization, the hatchet was buried and the series betwen the two major leagues was begun. The Red Sox and the Pirates had the distinction of playing in the first of the latter series and the American League team gained all the honors, winning five games in a row.

There was no series in 1904, but the National Commission took charge of the event in 1905 and has controlled it ever since. To date the American League holds a big lead in the matter of world's series victories with eleven championships out of sixteen played for. The victory of the Giants a year ago was the first in five years for the National League and the second in ten years. The Red Sox have won five world's titles since 1903, the Athletics three, the White Sox two, the Cubs and Giants two, Pirates, Braves, Reds and Indians one each.

Since the modern series began between the two major leagues world's series titles, with few exceptions, have been won easily. In three of the sixteen cases the losers failed to win a game; in six cases the winners dropped only one game and in five other cases two games.

In only four instances did the title hinge on the last game of the series. The first of these was the Pirate-Tiger series in 1909, won by the former, and the second occasion was the famous 1912 series in which an equally famous error by Fred Snodgrasss in center field prevented the Giants from scoring a victory over the Red Sox.

HEINIE GROH, 3D BASE

IRISH MEUSEL, LEFT FIELDER

Some of the Reasons Why Betting Odds Are 7 to 5

Giants Must Inspire Pitchers With New Life.

Betting men offer 7 to 5 that the Yankees will conquer the Giants. The reasons? It is generally believed that the Giants have improved in batting, fielding, base running and steadiness since last year, but that their pitching staff has been greatly weakened by the loss of Douglas. The Yankees, on the other hand, have five high class pitchers instead of two, and have been remarkably strengthened by Witt, Dugan and Scott.

In the 1921 series the Yankees, weaker in fielding and pitching than now, prolonged the struggle with the Giants to eight games. Two of the five defeats sustained by the American League champions were attributed to unfortunate errors, McGraw's men winning as a result of those mistakes by scores of 2 to 1 and 1 to 0.

Although the Giants are noted for their bulldog courage, it would seem that they will have nothing on the Hugmen in this respect. During the recent Western trip the Yankees played with great pluck, particularly in St. Louis, where the baseball public treated them with outrageous unfairness.

To take the Yankees' measure, therefore, the Giants will have to inspire their pitchers with new life, for the Hugmen are preparing to go to the bat with neither fear nor lack of confidence.

Among the Giants, who now have time to think over what has happened, the impression prevails that they have overcome more strenuous opposition in the National League than the Yankees have encountered in the Johnson circuit. McGraw's men rate the Browns below the Pirates and consider the Cardinals and Reds more formidable than the Tigers, White Sox and Clevelands. They believe that the Cubs outclass the Washingtons and that the Brooklyns would finish higher than the Athletics. Of course, this is merely a matter of opinion, but few experts will deny that the National League teams, collectively, excel in pitching.

The Giants have beaten the competent boxmen of the Pirates, Cardinals, Reds, Cubs and Robins, which is worth recalling when the chances of Bush, Shawkey, Hoyt, Mays and Jones of the Yankees are figured in the coming interleague tussles.

'EXPECT TO GET PITCHING OF WINNING KIND'

By JOHN J. M'GRAW, Manager of the Giants.

I am absolutely certain that outside of the pitching staff the Giants are a far stronger aggregation than the Yankees in every way. As to the pitching I think that out of the squad of hurlers we have I will be able to get two or three to settle down and give us some real pitching. We hit harder, we field better, we run bases faster, and I do not see why we should not have as good a chance as the other fellows.

Of course, the breaks are the things. The team which gets the breaks and knows enough to make the most of them will win the series. Just now I have no idea who will do the pitching for the Giants, nor have I any idea in what order my men may work. I have not decided who will pitch the first game. Our pitchers have not been running to form of late and it is hard to pick out any one man and say with certainty that he will be the opening selection.

I am going to ponder quite a bit over that first nomination, for I believe that if we win the first game there will be no stopping the Giants. It's a great, courageous club we have.

JOHN McGRAW, MANAGER

FRANKIE FRISCH 2ND BASE

BILL RYAN, PITCHER

It was not until 1911 that McGraw got into another world series, and again the Athletics met the Giants. But this time Connie Mack's great machine won by 4 to 2. In 1912 the Red Sox beat the Giants, 4 to 1, with one tie. In 1913 the Athletics again beat the Giants, 4 to 1. In 1917 the Giants lost again, the White Sox winning by four games to two. Last year McGraw won over the Yankees, 5 to 4.

Huggins never was in a world series until last year, when he led the Yankees in their fight against the Giants. Hughey Jennings, as manager of the Detroits, was in three world series in a row—in 1907, 1908 and 1909. Hughey lost all three but broke into the winning class last fall with the Giants. In all three defeats for the Tigers Charley O'Leary, now assistant to Huggins, figured as a player.

Thumbnail biographies of the Giants follow:

CLAUDE JONNARD, PITCHER

FRANK SNYDER, CATCHER

CARMEN HILL, PITCHER

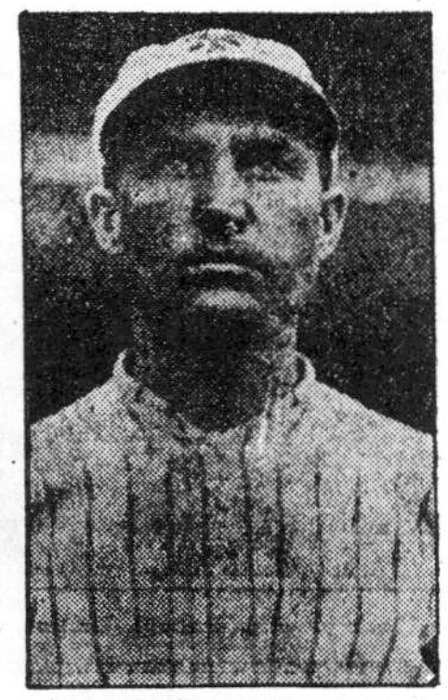

DAVE BANCROFT, SHORT STOP AND CAPTAIN

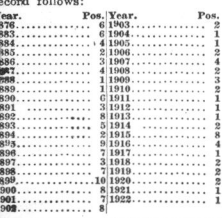

CASEY STENGEL, CENTER FIELDER

·opeless task if any such contingency ·uld arise.

None Remains From 1917.

·mong the Giants there is not a sin-player who took part in the world ·ies with the White Sox in 1917. ·rge Kelly and Ross Young were ·h the Giants then, but they were ·ngsters just recalled from the mi-·s and were not in that fight. Davy ·ncroft was in the world series of with the Phillies, who won only game from the Red Sox, so this l be his third appearance in the ·ssic.

·oe Bush faced the Giants—and beat ·m—in 1913 as a member of the Ath-·cs. He was with the Athletics in 1914 series with the Braves and ·h the Red Sox in 1918 against the ·bs. This will be his fourth world ·ies. Babe Ruth will be the world se-

What Giants Have Done In Forty-one Seasons

THE Giants finished first for the tenth time in the forty-one seasons that they have represented New York in the National League. Since 1903, when John J. McGraw took charge, they have finished in the second division only once, while on only three other occasions were they worst than second.

Since 1876 the Giants have finished first ten times; second, ten times; third, four times; fourth, four times; fifth, once; sixth, thrice; seventh, thrice; eighth, four times, and in ninth and tenth positions, when there were ten clubs in the league, each once. The Giants' record follows:

Year.	Pos.	Year.	Pos.
876	6	1903	2
883	6	1904	1
884	4	1905	1
885	2	1906	2
886	3	1907	4
887	4	1908	2
888	1	1909	3
889	1	1910	2
890	6	1911	1
891	3	1912	1
892	8	1913	1
893	5	1914	2
894	2	1915	8
895	9	1916	4
896	7	1917	1
897	3	1918	2
898	7	1919	2
899	10	1920	2
900	8	1921	1
901	7	1922	1
902	8		

LEE KING, OUTFIELDER

DAVIS ROBERTSON.

OUTFIELDER—Born at Norfolk, Va., June 10, 1889; bats and throws left handed; height, 6 feet; weight, 185 pounds; A. and M. College, 1911; Elizabeth City, 1911; New York, N. L., 1912-13; farmed out to Mobile, April, 1913, and recalled August, 1913; New York, 1914-15-16-17-19; traded to Chicago, N. L., July, 1919; Chicago, 1920-21; traded to Pittsburgh, N. L., July, 1921; sold to New York, N. L., 1922.

EARL N. SMITH.

CATCHER—Born at Hot Springs, Ark., February 14, 1897; bats left handed; throws right handed; height, 5 feet 10½ inches; weight, 170 pounds; Dallas, 1916; Tulsa-Ardmore, 1917; Rochester, 1918; traded to New York, N. L., September, 1918; New York, 1919-20-21-22.

FRANK SNYDER.

CATCHER—Born at San Antonio, Tex., May 27, 1893; bats and throws right handed; height, 6 feet 1 inch; weight, 192 pounds; Victoria, 1910; Floraville, 1911; San Antonio, 1911; Flint, 1912; sold to St. Louis, N. L., August, 1912; St. Louis, 1913; farmed out to Springfield, May, 1913, and recalled August; St. Louis, 1914-15-16-17-18-19; traded to New York, N. L., 1919; New York, 1920-21-22.

CHARLES A. STENGEL.

OUTFIELDER—Born at Kansas City, Mo., July 30, 1890; bats and throws left handed; height, 5 feet 8 inches; weight, 175 pounds; Kansas City, 1910; farmed out to Kankakee, April, 1910; transferred to Maysville, July, same year; recalled by Kansas City and farmed out to Aurora, 1911; drafted by Brooklyn, 1911, and released to Toronto, November, 1911;

ROSS YOUNG.

OUTFIELDER—Born at Shiner, Tex., April 10, 1897; bats left handed and throws right handed; height, 5 feet 8 inches; weight, 162 pounds; Austin, 1914; released to Lampasas, 1914; signed by Benham at close of 1914 season; Houston, 1915-16; released, March, 1916, to Sherman; sold to New York, N. L., August, 1916, and farmed out to Rochester, April, 1917; recalled by New York, October, 1917; New York, N. L., 1918-19-20-21-22.

JESSE L. BARNES.

PITCHER—Born at Guthrie, Okla., August 26, 1892; bats left handed and throws right handed; height, 6 feet; weight, 160 pounds; Keokuk, 1912; sold to Davenport, 1913; on trial with Chicago, N. L., 1914; returned to Davenport, May, 1914; Davenport, 1914-15; sold to Boston, N. L., July 1915; Boston, 1916-17; traded to New York, N. L., January, 1918; New York, 1918-19-20-21-22.

JOHN WILLIAM SCOTT.

PITCHER—Born at Ridgeway, N. J., April 18, 1894; bats left handed and throws right handed; height, 6 feet 2½ inches, weight, 200 pounds; Macon, 1916; sold to Pittsburgh on trial, August, 1916, and returned to Macon, September of same year; released to Columbia, 1917, and turned over to Nashville immediately after; sold to Boston, N. L., August, 1917; Boston, 1917-19-20-21; traded to Cincinnati, December, 1921; dropped by Cincinnati and signed by New York, July, 1922.

ROSS YOUNG, RIGHT FIELDER

HUGH A. M'QUILLAN.

PITCHER—Born at New York city, September 15, 1897; bats and throws right handed; height, 6 feet; weight, 170 pounds; began with Toronto, 1916; released to Bridgeport (afterward Worcester), May, 1916; Worcester, 1916-17-18; sold to Boston, N. L., July, 1918; Boston, 1918-19-20-21-22; traded to New York, N. L., July, 1922.

FRANK F. FRISCH.

THIRD BASEMAN—Born at Ozone Park, L. I., September 9, 1898; height, 5 feet 10 inches; weight, 165 pounds; Fordham College, 1918; New York, N. L., 1919-20-21-22.

ARTHUR N. NEHF.

PITCHER—Born at Terre Haute, Ind., July 31, 1892; bats and throws left handed; height, 5 feet 9 inches; weight, 170 pounds; began with Negawnee, 1912; Kansas City, 1913; released to Sioux City, August, 1913; released to Kansas City and sent to Terre Haute, July, 1914; sold to Boston, N. L., August, 1915; Boston, 1916-17-18-19; traded to New York, N. L., August, 1919; New York, 1920-21-22.

GEORGE LANGE KELLY.

FIRST BASEMAN—Born at San Francisco, Cal., September, 10, 1895; bats and throws right handed; height, 6 feet 3½ inches; weight, 198 pounds; California Polytechnic School; Spokane, February, 1914; released to Victoria, March, 1914; reserved for 1915; sold to New York, N. L., July, 1915; New York, 1916-17; released on waivers to Pittsburgh, August, 1917; returned to New York, N. L., and sent to Rochester, August, 1917; recalled by New York, N. L., September, 1917; released to Rochester, May, 1919; recalled by New York, August, 1919; New York, 1920-21-22; in United States army, 1918.

DAVID JAMES BANCROFT.

SHORTSTOP—Born at Sioux City, Iowa, April 20, 1892; bats right and left handed; throws right handed; height, 5 feet 8 inches; weight, 150 pounds; Duluth and Superior, 1909; Superior, 1910-11; Portland, P. C. L., 1912; Portland, N. W. L., by optional agreement, 1913; recalled by Portland, P. C. L., 1914; transferred to Philadelphia, N. L., under club agreements, 1915; Philadelphia, 1915-16-17-18-19-20; traded to New York, N. L., summer, 1920; New York, 1921-22.

HENRY KNIGHT GROH.

THIRD BASEMAN—Born at Rochester, N. Y., September 18, 1890; bats and throws right handed; height, 5 feet 7 inches; weight, 157 pounds; Oshkosh, 1908-09-10; drafted by Cleveland, 1910, and sold to Decatur, May 11, 1910; Decatur, 1911; sold to New York, N. L., July 20, 1911; farmed out to Buffalo, 1911; recalled by New York, 1912; New York, 1912; traded to Cincinnati, N. L., May, 1913; Cincinnati, 1914-15-16-17-18-19-20-21; traded to New York, N. L., December, 1921; New York, N. L., 1922.

JOHN WILLIAM RAWLINGS.

INFIELDER—Born at Bloomfield, Ill., August 17, 1892; bats and throws right handed; height, 5 feet 8 inches; weight, 158 pounds; Long Beach, 1910; Los Angeles, 1910; Boise, 1911; Victoria, 1912; sold to Cincinnati, February, 1913; released to Minneapolis, July, 1914; jumped to Kansas City, F. L., July, 1914; reserved for 1915; released to Toledo in peace agreement, January, 1916; drafted by Boston, N. L., September, 1916; Boston, 1917-18-19; sold to New York, N. L., June, 1920; traded to Philadelphia, N. L., June, 1920; traded to New York, N. L., July, 1921; New York, 1922.

BILL CUNNINGHAM, CENTER FIELDER

WILLIAM D. RYAN.

PITCHER—Born at Worcester, Mass., March 15, 1898; bats and throws right handed; height, 6 feet; weight, 185 pounds; Holy Cross College, 1918; New York, N. L., 1919; released to Buffalo, April, 1919; recalled by New York, August, 1919, released to Toronto, April, 1920; recalled by New York, September, 1920; reserved for 1921; New York, 1922.

EMIL FREDERIC MEUSEL.

OUTFIELDER—Born at Oakland, Cal., June 9, 1893; bats and throws right handed; height, 6 feet; weight, 180 pounds; Fresno, 1913; Los Angeles, 1913; drafted by Washington, A. L., 1913; Washington, 1914; farmed out to Elmira, April, 1914; sent to Minneapolis, January, 1915; transferred to Los Angeles and released to Elmira, May, 1915; drafted by Birmingham, 1916; drafted by Chicago, N. L., 1917; and released to Los Angeles, May, 1917; drafted by Philadelphia, N. L., 1918; Philadelphia, 1919-20-21; traded to New York, N. L., July, 1921; New York, 1922.

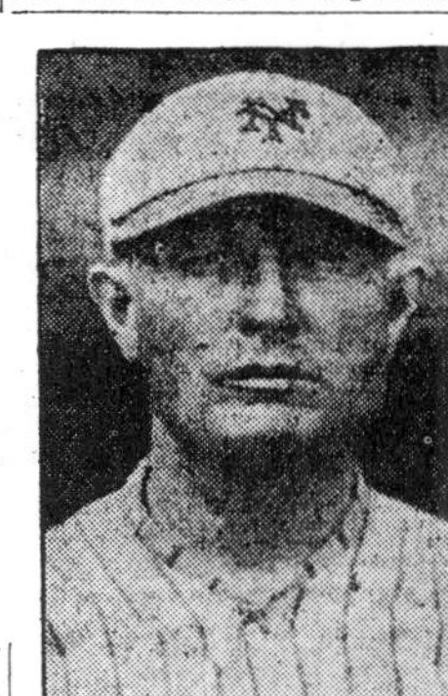

EARL SMITH CATCHER

JOHNNY RAWLINGS, IN FIELDER

ALECK GASTON, CATCHER

GEORGE KELLY 1ST BASE

GIANTS AND YANKEES TIE AT THREE ALL

$120,554 Gate Sets Record in Baseball

DRAW CONTEST IS THIRD HELD IN HISTORY OF SERIES

New York, Oct. 5.—(By the Associated Press.)—The Yankees and the Giants fought furiously but to no avail to-day in the second game of the World Series. They had the score tied at three runs each at the end of the 10th inning when the umpires, seeing the approach of twilight, called an armistice. When hostilities break out anew to-morrow the teams will be in the same position as before to-day's game, the Giants having one victory and the Yankees none.

Thousands of the 37,020 spectators who paid to see the thrilling encounter and others who rolled the attendance to approximately 40,000 were angered when the umpires ruled it was a no-decision bout. They had come to see a knockout, these fans had, and as they swamed over the field they screeched their disgust to the high heavens and to every person they encountered who was of any importance in baseball affairs.

Had they know of the baseball officials' contemplated gift of the entire gate receipts to the charities of New York city, announced a few hours later, they would have saved their imprecations, but as it was they told Manager McGraw of the Giants they wouldn't come back to his old Polo Grounds for anything in the world. They hurled mean words upon the umpires, saying that anybody with good eyes could see it was still light enough to keep on playing. Then they rushed to the box where Baseball Commissioner Landis sat with Mrs. Landis.

The leading actors in the crowd barked questions and comments at the Commissioner, and the chorus behind them booed with vigor. To hear them, it seemed they wanted to know what kind of an outrage the Commissioner thought the Giants and Yankee clubs could get away with.

Unmoved, Mr. Landis put his old black hat over his flowing white locks and started to walk across the field to return to his hotel. The crowd surrounded him, hurling taunts and insults. A dozen special policemen rushed in to clear the way for him, and the commissioner sought to wave them away, saying he could get through any New York crowd. Mrs. Landis, too, seemed unperturbed. The howling hundreds dogged their footsteps until Mr. and Mrs. Landis had reached the Polo Grounds office. Later, the commissioner walked unguarded to his automobile, refusing protection.

From the commissioner the mob turned its fountains of advice upon the writers working in the press box. They wanted the world informed what an awful thing it is to see a ball game that nobody wins.

The other thousands who went straight home seemed to feel they had seen one of the most remarkable battles in the history of the titular autumn baseball classic.

They had seen the Giants rush into the lead in the first inning when Irish Meusel belted the ball into the bleachers for a home run with two men on bases. They had witnessed the dogged, relentless uphill climb of the Yankees, first cutting down the Giant lead to two runs at the end of the first inning, then to one run in the fourth when Aaron Ward lashed a home run over the fence above the left field bleachers. And finally, with Bob Shawkey, getting better and better so that the Giants could not even threaten to score, they had seen the Yankees tie the game in the eighth inning on two base blows from bats of Babe Ruth and Bob Meusel, brother of the home run hero of the first inning.

Nor were the innings that brought scores the only ones of high endeavor. Several times the crowd had the fine thrill of watching an infielder hurl himself at a hard-hit ball, be knocked to the ground by the force of it, and then jump up and throw out the batsman at first base.

This experience came three times to Frankie Frisch, the fast second baseman for the Giants. Another time he went far back of second base and pulled down a drive from Everett Scott's bat with his bare hand. It bowled him over, but he came up with his grip still tight on the ball.

Once Heinie Groh, the Giants' third baseman, leaped after a ball and caught it while sliding in the dirt. It was in the first inning, from the bat of Whitey Witt. Groh hopped up from the dust and threw Witt out at first. This may have saved the Giants from defeat, for a moment later, through an error by Bancroft and a single off Pipp's bat, the Yankees scored a run.

Meusel Brothers, Sluggers Par Excellence

Emil Who Hit Homer in First Round

Bob Who Tied Score

The game was a pitchers' battle between Jess Barnes, the tall Giant righthander, who twice defeated the Yankees during the 1921 World Series, and Shawkey, one of the stellar Yankee veterans. Shawkey, after the second inning, improved steadily and the Giants made but three hits off his service in the last eight innings.

Barnes, spotted to a three-run lead before he even walked into the box, was often in trouble. But with perfect support at all times he would have won, as the Yanks earned but two of thir runs, while the Giants cleanly hammered all three of their counters across the plate. Both Groh and Frisch had got on bases with singles before Meusel's homer sent them across the plate.

It would have been a heart-breaking game for either Shawkey or Barnes to lose. Each was found for eight hits, although four off Barnes went for extra bases; each issued two passes and the detailed pitching analysis reveals that Shawkey pitched 146 balls while Barnes threw only one more to the plate.

But Shawkey, hit hard in the first inning, when the Giants scored all their runs on Meusel's homer, and wobbly for the next two frames, steadied and was practically invincible for the remaining seven innings. A double play, Scott to Ward, to Pipp, killed off a Giant rally in the second, after Stengel, who retired because of a charley horse, was left on third when Bancroft flied out.

Shawkey passed Groh and Young in the third, but whiffed Kelly for the final out. Thereafter, for seven innings, only four Giants reached first base, three on hits and but one of them got as far as third base. Frisch beat out a bunt in the fifth, stole second with the aid of a wild pitch and got to the far corner on another wild toss, but Scott grabbed Irish Meusel's

Champions Thrill Crowd of 40,000

BARNES AND SHAWKEY WAGE HOT DUEL WITH HONORS EVEN

smash and threw him out to end the inning.

Only three batters faced Shawkey in each of the last four innings and the Giants' last faint chance to win went glimmering in the 10th when Bancroft was thrown out at second trying to stretch his hit to centre.

Barnes, on the other hand, pulled himself out of several tight places by his skilful change of pace. Mixing his tantalizing slow ball with a curve that cut the corners sharply, he choked off several budding rallies, whiffing Ward in the sixth and Dugan in the ninth with a man on second each time.

Jess was hit harder than Shawkey toward the close of the game. But, except for the fourth, when Ward belted his homer, and a brace of doubles by Ruth and Bob Meusel in the eighth that tied the score, he held his rivals in check.

Barnes pulled himself together in the sixth after apparently losing control. He issued three straight balls to Pipp before forcing Wally to fly out, walked Meusel and fanned Ward on a called strike after the count had reached two and three.

The Yankees threatened in the ninth, but again Barnes rose to the emergency. Scott singled, after Ward fanned, but was forced by Shawkey. Witt then singled to left and Yankee hopes were high until Dugan fanned with the count two and two.

The Giants made a strong threat in the 10th, when Bancroft drove to centre field. Witt grabbed the ball on the first bounce and with a fine throw caught Bancroft as he tried to make two bases on the hit. Then the Yanks went out one, two, three, and the umpires called off the fight.

It was just the day for a pitchers' battle, hot and sultry as midsummer. Almost every rooter in the bleachers peeled off his coat, and so did the fans in the upper grandstand. But those in the more select seats down below kept their coats on.

The crowd was bigger than on any day during the 1921 series, and the money paid to sit in on to-day's session—$120,554—was the highest sum ever deposited into baseball's coffers for one game. It was the third crowd that has seen a tie World Series game. The first was in 190[illegible] when the Chicago Nationals and Detroit Americans quit fighting after 12 innings had produced a 3-3 deadlock in the first game of the series. In 1912 the Giants and the Boston Americans played their second clash to a 6-6 tie in 11 innings.

Both Shawkey and Barnes took their time this afternoon and the game dragged along for two hours and 41 minutes. Shawkey managed the ball with great care before every pitch and Barnes's lazy floater reminded one of the slow motion pictures. It was the best thing he had. Shawkey relied on a curve that broke beautifully after the third inning.

Barnes tried exceedingly hard to fool Babe Ruth with his slow ball. For a time he succeeded, but in the eighth inning, the Babe choked his bat and when Jess eased one of his slow ones toward the plate, the famous home run slugger hooked it to left field for two bases. Pipp's long fly to centre field permitted him to reach third, from where he scored when Bob Meusel slapped a two-bagger flying close to the turf, into centre field.

Ruth attempted to steal home, just before scoring on Meusel's hit in the eighth. He dashed in as Barnes started his windup and appeared to have succeded in his daring attempt until Meusel fouled the pitch against the right field stand.

Ruth and Frisch stood out among their teammates in all-round work. The Fordham flash was the only Giant to knock out two hits. On the defence he had another spectacular day, robbing Scott twice of hits, once in the second on a great diving stop of the shortstop's smash toward right field and again in the fourth when he nailed a fly in short centre after a hard run, rolling over after the catch.

Details of the pitching analysis show that Barnes pitched 57 balls and 3[illegible] strikes while Shawkey twirled 50 balls and shot over 32 strikes. Twenty-two foul strikes were knocked off Shawkey's delivery and 12 off the Giant moundsman.

The Yankee outfield gathered in seven flies to but three for the Giant defensive workers, while 17 infield outs were credited to the Yankees and 21 to the Giants.

BROWN COACHES EASE OFF ON HEAVY WORK

Sweet and Swaney Get Long Session Under Reggie Brown in Punting.—Ends Receive Special Attention from Robinson

The exceedingly hot weather forced Coach Ed Robinson to call off the scrimmage that he had scheduled for the Brown 'Varsity yesterday afternoon. With the sturdy Colby eleven coming to Andrews Field to-morrow afternoon the Brunonian mentor does not want to give his men too much work. Since the sorry showing against Rhode Island State the practice sessions have been filled with the hardest kind of drills.

Reggie Brown, backfield coach, spent much time with the kickers yesterday. He had Sweet and Swaney practicing spirals, and with Adams in his usual form the Bears should have the edge in the punting Saturday. Adams seems the "class" of the Hill punters, but if yesterday's practice can be taken as a reliable indication, both Sweet and Swaney are capable of taking their regular turn in the kicking department of the game.

The ends are still bothering the Bruin coaches. At present it seems that Jim Sheldon is headed on his way to a regular position on the left flank of the line. The position on the other end of the line is still uncertain, as Johnstone is bothered with a bad ankle that may cause him all kinds of trouble and so far this season he has not been in a position to even engage in scrimmage. Reynolds, Sayward, Monk and Spellman are men who can step into the game at any minute, but their work does not seem to satisfy the coaches.

Yesterday Coach Robinson had his line and ends running down the field under punts. It was surprising to see how Capt. Gulian, Eckstein, Spellman and H. Metzger, all big men, weighing in the neighborhood of 200 pounds, covered these kicks. Much of the attention of the coaches, however, was directed on the ends, who are expected to show a decided improvement against Colby.

A long signal drill also came in for part of the afternoon's programme, with Eisenberg, Myers and Higgins all taking a turn at calling the signals. The quarterback position is causing the Bruin mentor no trouble, as, in the Sophomores mentioned, he has three field generals who are perfectly capable of directing the attack of the Brown eleven against the best defence that any college team can offer.

Sweet, Paasche, Pohlman, Adams, Swaney and Foulkner all took their turns in the backfield. These men constitute a first-class cast and all have been under actual fire in the intercollegiate game for at least a season. From present indications it seems that Reggie Brown is grooming this material into two distinct sets of backs. Adams, Paasche and Faulkner have been working constantly together, as have Sweet, Swaney and Pohlman.

With Syracuse, Lehigh, Yale, Harvard and Dartmouth on the schedule, Brown will need all the backfield men that are listed on the 'Varsity squad. From the showing made the last week, it seems that for the first time in many years the Hilltoppers have two elevens that are nearly on a par, and this fact is causing the fans to claim a successful season for Capt. Gulian and his men.

CRIMSON LINEUP FOR HOLY CROSS CONTEST SHAKEN UP

Coach Fisher Makes Many Changes. Defence Work Features Practice.

Special to the Journal.

Cambridge, Oct. 5.—Following this afternoon's secret practice, Coach Fisher of the Harvard eleven announced a decided shakeup in the eleven for the game with Holy Cross on Saturday. Roscoe Fitts will play left end instead of halfback, Fisher deeming it necessary to play him in Jenkins's place, the latter being on the injured list. Hartley will be at right end in place of Gordon. Tunker has supplanted Theopold at left tackle. Eastman will be at right tackle, Hubbard and Grew at guards, and probably Kernan at centre, while Capt. Buell is down for quarter, with Owen, Gehrke and Coburn in the backfield, the last named getting into his first game. Pfaffman will be held in reserve to take Buell's place if necessary.

These radical changes show that Fisher does not intend to let Holy Cross get away with the game if he can muster an eleven strong enough to prevent it.

During the two hours practice this afternoon, the coaches laid great stress on defensive tactics. They realized that the Purple backs will bear the closest kind of watching and also realize that Harvard must show a decidedly better defensive game than it has yet displayed to hold the Worcester boys in check. There was also a long signal drill and a blackboard talk.

TIE GAME WILL COUNT AS COMPLETE ONE IN SERIES

Tickets for Third Battle Will Be Honored To-day.

New York, Oct. 5.—To-day's tie game between the New York Giants and the New York Yankees, the second of the World Series, counts as a complete contest and to-morrow the "third" game, with the National League club technically "at home," will be played, it was officially announced from the office of Commissioner Landis to-night.

This statement was made after a conference of the Commissioner with Secretaries Barrow and Tierney of the two clubs. The decision was designed to avoid confusion of the public, especially ticket holders. Only tickets marked "third" game will be accepted to-morrow.

Many fans purchased tickets intending to attend Saturday's and Sunday's games and should to-day's tie game be replayed to-morrow a bad ticket mix-up would result, it was pointed out.

Since the 10 innings of play count as a complete game, the players' share of the receipts will not be affected in any way by the fact that the result was a tie. To-day's contest counts as one of the four games from which their share is derived.

Every play made to-day counts in the records and averages of the series and the ultimate victor still must win four games—the Giants three more, since they won the first yesterday.

TWO DIAMONDS KEEP THIS WORCESTER MISS VERY BUSY

One Represents Engagement to Pitcher Ryan of Giants.

Worcester, Mass., Oct. 5.—Announcement was made to-day of the engagement of Miss Anna H. Reidy, daughter of Mr. and Mrs. Cornelius J. Reidy of this city, and Wilfred ("Rosy") Ryan, the Giant pitcher, who held the Yankees scoreless in the last two innings of the first game of the World Series.

Miss Reidy attended the first game, and was also present at the Polo Grounds to-day, but her attntion was divided between the diamond and a sparkling solitaire on the proper finger of the proper hand. With Miss Reidy was Ryan's sister, Mary, and his father, Patrick Ryan, all of Worcester.

The wedding is expected to take place in the fall of 1923. The young people met first when Ryan was attending Holy Cross College and was starring for the Purple baseball nine.

TIE GAME RECEIPTS GO TO CHARITIES

Commissioner Landis Announces New York Clubs Will Turn Over $120,554.

DISABLED "VETS" TO SHARE

Statement Issued to Newspaper Men Does Not Take Umpires to Task. Records Will Be Included in Series

New York, Oct. 5.—The entire receipts from to-day's World Series game between the New York Giants and the New York Yankees will be given to disabled soldiers and charities of New York city, Commissioner Landis announced to-night. The total receipts amounted to $120,554, a record for a World Series game.

In a statement issued to newspapermen, who had been called to his hotel room, Commissioner Landis gave no direct explanation for the decision. He referred, however, to the fact that "many spectators" were dissatisfied with the ending of the game. He made no reference to the mistreatment accorded him by a large number of fans when he was leaving the field.

His statement is as follows:

"Under baseball law the umpires are charged with the sole authority of calling a game on account of darkness. In exercise of this authority, to-day's game was called by them at the end of the 10th inning. Many spectators were of the opinion that the game might have continued.

"Of course, the umpires on the field are in much better position to judge conditions that affect play. But, regardless of any question whether this decision was erroneous, the two New York clubs, acting for themselves and their teams, have decided, with the approval of the Commissioner, that the entire receipts of to-day's game shall be turned over to funds for the benefit of the disabled soldiers and to the charities of New York city."

This will give the players, the clubs and the baseball commission a share in the next three games. The records made in to-day's game, however, will be included in the records of the series.

Official Box Score of Second World Series Game

GIANTS

	ab	r	bh	po	a	e
Bancroft, s	5	0	1	1	0	1
Groh, 3b	4	1	1	1	3	0
Frisch, 2b	4	1	2	1	4	0
E. Meusel, l	4	1	1	0	0	0
Young, r	3	0	1	1	0	0
Kelly, 1b	4	0	0	15	0	0
Stengel, m	1	0	1	0	0	0
*Cunningh'm, m	2	0	0	2	0	0
King, m	0	0	0	0	0	0
Snyder, c	4	0	1	9	1	0
J. Barnes, p	4	0	0	0	4	0
**Earl Smith	1	0	0	0	0	0
Totals	36	3	8	30	12	1

YANKEES

	ab	r	bh	po	a	e
Witt, m	5	0	1	1	1	0
Dugan, 3b	5	1	2	3	0	0
Ruth, r	4	1	1	5	0	0
Pipp, 1b	5	0	1	11	0	0
R. Meusel, l	4	0	1	1	0	0
Schang, c	4	0	0	5	0	0
Ward, 2b	4	1	1	4	5	0
Scott, s	4	0	1	0	3	0
Shawkey, p	4	0	0	0	2	0
Totals	39	3	8	30	11	0

Innings	1	2	3	4	5	6	7	8	9	10	
Giants	3	0	0	0	0	0	0	0	0	0	—3
Yankees	1	0	0	1	0	0	0	1	0	0	—3

(Called at end of 10th inning, darkness.)

Runs—Groh, Frisch, E. Meusel—3; Dugan, Ruth, Ward—3.

Two-base hits—Dugan, Ruth, R. Meusel. Home runs—E. Meusel, Ward. Stolen base—Frisch. Double play—Scott, Ward and Pipp. Left on bases—Yankees 8, Giants 5. First base on balls—Off Shawkey 2 (Groh, Young); off Barnes 2 (Ruth, R. Meusel). Struck out—By Shawkey 4 (Kelly, Cunningham, J. Barnes, Smith); by Barnes 6 (Schang, Ward 2, Shawkey, Witt, Dugan). Wild pitch—Shawkey 2. Umpires—Hildebrand (A), umpire in chief, at plate; McCormick (N), first base; Owens (A), second base; Klem (N), third base. Time of game—2:41.

*Ran for Stengel in second.

**Batted for Cunningham in ninth.

ANNUAL ARMY-NAVY FOOTBALL GAME IN BALTIMORE DEC. 2

Contest Will Open Venable Stadium. Capacity 40,000 Persons.

Baltimore, Oct. 4.—The annual Army-Navy football game will be played here on Dec. 2. At the same time a reunion of the men of the four World War divisions from the territory comprised in the Third Corps area—the Twenty-eighth, Twenty-ninth, Seventy-eighth and Seventy-ninth Divisions—will be held in Baltimore.

The football game will open Venable Stadium, now under construction, with a seating capacity of 40,000 persons.

To-day's Jamaica Entries.

First race, selling, for 2-year-olds, maidens, 5½ furlongs—Brother Pat 107, xSir Sidney 100, Keenan 115, Homestretch 107, Ruddy 109, Leloba 104, Satellite 108, xChief Flynn 100.

Second race, 3-year-olds and upward, claiming, 1 1-16 miles—xCarmencita 104, xService Star 107, xThistle Bloom 98, Witchwork 105, Horeb 112, xLiberty Girl 112, Scottish Chief 112, Wylie 106, Lord Herbert 112, Orderly 112, xSearchlight 3rd 106, Consort 110.

Third race, 2-year-olds, selling, 5½ furlongs—Rock Salt 112, xPeter Brown 97, Cape Clear 114, Roseate 2nd 104, Prince of Umbria 108, Lady Inez 108, Sequel 99, Prima Donna 104, Rigel 108.

Fourth race, 3-year-olds and upward, the Brunswick Selling Handicap, 1 mile and 70 yards—Wild Heather 110, Tufter 114, Georgie 120, Broomflax 106, Wynnewood 108.

Fifth race, 3-year-olds and upward, claiming, 1 mile and 70 yards—Wild Heather 116, xCanyon 106, xThistle Bloom 95, Scotland Yet 106, Bridesman 116, King Albert 122, xVendor 108, Dunce Cap 102.

Sixth race, the Cherry Valley, 3-year-olds, maidens, six furlongs—Supercargo 115, Belski 112, Poe 115, The Hottentot 115, Good Time 115, Anna M. 112, Miss Finn 112, Occidenta 115, Lucky Antoine 115, Fitzgibbon 115.

Weather clear; track fast.

xApprentice allowance claimed.

TRANSYLVANIA GOES TO PETER THE BREWER

Son of Peter the Great Equals Record of 2:02½ for the Event, Set by Peter Manning in 1920. E. Colorado is Second

Lexington, Ky., Oct. 5.—The 34th renewal of the Transylvania was won to-day by Peter the Brewer. The big son of Peter the Great in winning the event equalled the record of 2:02½ for the stake set by Peter Manning in 1920. He was clearly the best and responded readily to the call of his driver, Nat Ray, when he was asked for the supreme effort in the stretch.

The consistent cripple, E. Colorado, secured second money, trotting a good race, while Bill Sharon, the Canadian-bred trotter from the Murphy barn, was third.

Great Britton was a top-heavy favorite in the betting, but the brown stallion was not in form and finished last in the summary. He got the worst of the start in the first heat and in the second heat made two breaks.

The day was full of surprises. Dottie Day was expected to win the 2:09 trot, but the New York trotter, Pluto Watts, landed the event in straight heats, with second money going to Dottie Day and third to Amarilla McKinney.

Lon McDonald won his first race of the meeting with Wilaska, the daughter of The Northern Man narrowly missing the 2:05 list in the first heat. Finvarra, that won on the opening day, furnished most of the competition.

The 2:17 pace went to Peter Cleo, driven by Pallin.

First race, 2:09 trot, 2 in 3, purse $1000:

Pluto Watts, b. h., by General Watts, Rose Bengen (W. Dickerson) 1 1
Dottie Day, br. m. (McDonald) 3 2
Amarilla McKinney, b. g. (Erskine) 2 6
Eunice Bell, b. f. (Macey) 11 3
Tolus Boy, blk. h. (Brietenneeld) 4 4

Prodigal Watts, Don De Lopez, Tallahatchie, Mary D., Noble Argot, Fay Mathews, Franc Sterling also started.

Time—2:06½, 2:07¼.

Second race, The Transylvania, 2:05 trot, 2 in 3, purse $5000:

Peter the Brewer, b. c., by Peter the Great-Zombrewer (Ray) 1 1
E. Colorado, b. h. (Cox) 3 2
Bill Sharon, ch. g. (Murphy) 2 4
Escotillo, br. g. (H. Fleming) 10 3
Kilo Watts, b. m. (M. Childs) 4 6

The Great Rose, Peter Coley, The Consequence, Favonian, Prince Loree, Great Britton also started.

Time—2:02½, 2:03¼.

Third event, 2:13 trot, 2 in 3, purse $1000: (First Division.)

Wilaska, blk. h., by The Northern Man (McDonald) 1 1
Finvarra, br. h. (H. Fleming) 3 2
Major Riser, blk. g. (Hinds) 2 3
Peter Alation, ch. g. (Loomis) 4 4
Alta Evans, ro. m. (Whitehead) 5 5

Alice G., also started.

Time—2:05¼, 2:06.

Fourth race, 2:17 pace, 2 in 3, purse $1000:

Peter Cleo, b. g., by Peter McKlyo (Palin) 1 1
Walter M., b. g. (Leith) 2 3
Northern Earl, br. g. (Lewis) 4 2
Russell Ongale, br. g. (Valentine) 3 5
Princess Marion, blk. m. (Edman) 5 4

Lambetto also started.

Time—2:06¾, 2:05½.

The following new marks were made to-day:

To beat 2:12½ trotting: All Worthy, b. c. (3) by Lee Axworthy (McDonald), 2:09½.

To beat 2:30¼ trotting: Anna Branford's Girl, b. f. (2) by The Northern Man (White, 2:08¾.

To beat 2:06¾ trotting: Guaveta, b. f. (4 by Etawah (Rodney), 2:04¾.

To beat 2:07¼ trotting: Zombro Dillon b. g., by Dillon Axworthy (Serrill), 2:04¾.

To beat 2:08¾ trotting: Lee Wynolot, b. (3) by Lee Axworthy (H. Fleming), 2:05½.

To beat 2:08 trotting: Philura, b. m., by Si Harvester (S. Caton,) 2:07¼.

To beat 2:10 trotting: Geers, b. g. (4), b Etawah (S. Caton), 2:07½.

Jamaica Results

First race, all ages, maidens, non-winners this year, other than selling race, purse $1000, 5½ furlongs — Dolores, 12[illegible] (Sande), 3 to 1, even, 1 to 2, first; Mawrcoron, 125 (Robinson), 2 to 1, even, second; Humboldt, 105 (Parke), even, third. Time 1:06. Spread Eagle, Blue Teal, Passamaria, Mary Patricia, Deep Sinker, Flamion, also ran.

Second race, 3-year-olds and upward, claiming, purse $1000, $1\frac{1}{16}$ miles—Huonec 108 (Miller), 4 to 1, 7 to 5, 1 to 2, first; Lackawanna, 105 (Fator), 1 to 4, even, second; Horeb, 121 (Jelly), even, third. Time 1:47. Maize, Witchwork, Pansy also ran.

Third race, 3-year-olds and upward, selling, purse $1000, six furlongs—The Peruvian, 115 (McCoy), 7 to 1, 5 to 2, [illegible] to 5, first; Nightboat, 111 (Hammond), 5 to 1, 5 to 2, second; Evil, 113 (Sande), 4 to 5, third. Time 1:12 4-5. Pastora, Shaffer, Sling, Swift Grass, Eager Eyes, Blazed Trail, Jug, Pierre Rhue also ran.

Fourth race, 2-year-olds, The Oceanus handicap, $2500 added, six furlongs—Cyclops, 117 (McAtee), 3 to 1, even, 1 to [illegible] first; Tall Timber, 117 (Butwell), 6 t[illegible] 5, 1 to 2, second; Cherry Pie, 118 (Lyke), even, third. Time 1:11 1-5. Heremon, Osprey, Dreammaker, Bud Lerner, Bayonet also ran.

Fifth race, 2-year-olds, maidens, claiming, purse $1000, 5 furlongs—Chile, 11[illegible] (Sande), 5 to 2, 6 to 5, 3 to 5, first; Faithful Girl, 109 (Miller), 2 to 1, even, second; Winnipeg, 112 (Fairbrother), even, third. Time 1:01. Temptress, Gandida, Runmath, Patsy B., Sophia, Goldman, Ella C., Bargain, Dream Day, Margaret Loretta, Wigee, Lucidus, Conundrum, Soviet also ran.

Sixth race, 3-year-olds and upward, handicap, purse $1200, 1 mile and 70 yards—Tangerine, 103 (Bell), 5 to 1, 8 to 5, 1 to 2, first; Pilgrim, 110 (Parke), 2 to 5, 1 to 5, second; Story Teller, 103 (Thomas), even, third. Time 1:43. June Grass, John Paul Jones also ran.

Ohio State Player Ineligible.

Columbus, O., Oct. 5.—Noel Workman, who probably would have held down the quarterback job on this year's Ohio State University football team, has been declared ineligible.

It was found that Workman has lost a season of conference competition by playing as a Freshman at Bethany College, W. Va., in 1917. As he has played two years at Ohio State, he is technically ineligible for future participation.

Jack Scott's Airtight Pitching Gives National League Champions a Two-Game Advantage

Victory of Big Right-Hander Puts New Aspect on Series

Giants Now Hold Safe Lead Over Their American League Rivals, Who Face Difficult Task; Cast-Off Twirler Allows Only Four Hits and No Runs

By John Kieran

From a fixed point south-southeast of the diamond, it looked as if he Yankees were a lot of tall young fellows headed toward the short end of the purse as they stood in a row and were neatly whitewashed by John Scott in the third game of the world's series. As a nine-cylinder baseball nachine they are flivering fatally. As shock absorbers they are magnificent. Their only consolation is that the experts who figured the series n advance are taking a worse beating than the Yanks themselves.

If that's any consolation, they are naking the most of it. With coal high and a hard winter coming on, the oser's end of the purse has no attractions for the armed forces of the paying Colonels, but it seems that John McGraw is going to be paymaster unless the Hugmen hit their batting stride n three shakes of a lamkin's tail. The helpless Huggins' outfit has used ıp its three leading hurlers and has yet to win a game. The outlook is not propitious from an American League point of view.

On the other hand, from the roosting place of John Joseph McGraw, never was there such a pleasing expanse of autumn scenery. From his bay window in the Giant dugout he can plainly see his third world's series pennant floating proudly over the domains of Stoneham. The early frosts are ready to turn the forest leaves to a golden hue, indicative of the current coin of the realm that the winners of the big series will have forced upon them by a kindly fate. Running happily in the foreground are several rosyheek-cy pitchers who were nursed along on the Stoneham homstead under the watchful eye of John J. himself. They had been given up by the best doctors in baseball as hopeless paralytics and congenital cripples. But see them now!

Wonderful Change in Scott

The Little Napoleon effected a wonderful cure with John Scott of Ridgeway, North Carolina. John was overhauled by an ivory expert early this season. He had been traded from Boston to Cincinnati in the deal that sent Larry Kopf to Hubtown. After his arrival in Porkopolis, he pitched two innings and the game was halted to enable the authorities to discover where that terrible creaking noise was coming from. A diligent investigation showed that it was the oscillation of Jack Scott's pitching arm that was causing all the confusion. It grated, squeaked, creaked and groaned as he threw up an assortment of basehits to the enemy batters.

"Call the doctor" shrieked Garry Herrmann, "Someding is los mid him." Placed under an anaesthetic, Scott was subjected to a scientific examination and the following results were tabulated: His arm was unhinged in at least three vital places, he had the mental developments of a twenty-eight-year old child, his curve ball had been lost in transit, some previous operation had removed the hop from his fast one, in fact, he was a total wreck. Herrmann broke down and wept, he felt so sorry for himself. He opened the door of the Cincinnati clubhouse and gently tossed the prostrate form out into the gutter.

The John McGraw Bowery Mission for Homeless Hurlers happened to be passing at that moment, and John Scott took his place among the rescued. He was able to beat a drum and shake a tambourine in a short while after eating at the McGraw table d'hote. Yesterday he reached the point in his come-back career where he led the whole band in a grand concert by the Mission troupe. Thirty-nine thousand persons voted it a howling success.

Scotty Strong in Pinch

That's baseball to the ueen's taste, if any reigning regal female has a taste for our national pastime. Kicked out of the league as a hopeless cripple, Jack Scott returns to hold the American League champions to four hits in a world's series contest. The Hugmen never had a chance against the clever twirling of the rejuvenated hurler except for a fleeting moment in the seventh when a Yankee hit would have tied the score. Then Scott showed at his best. He fanned Elmer Smith, who was striking out for Aaron Ward, and he retired Deacon Scott on a harmless grounder.

While the Giant flinger was fast-balling the Yanks up into a series of double-bow knots, young Master Waite Hoyt was being knocked about the campus in disconcerting style. It is true that his support wavered, and that two of the three runs chalked against his record were unearned, but even with the most defiant defense, he would have been beaten by the score of 1 to 0. The National League tally in the eighth inning could be laid right on the doorstep of the Flatbush flinger, from which point of vantage it could call him "Papa, papa!" with every chance of proving its parentage.

The first break in the Yankee defense system came in the third inning of yesterday's game. After Jack Scott had opened for the Giants with a single to center, Bancroft scaled a skipping grounder in the second base area. Aaron Ward tried to catch it with his shinbone, which is a difficult feat under the most favorable circumstances. The ball bounded into left field, Scott going to third and Bancroft being safe on first. The "Man from Arkansas" was debited with an error, though it was a difficult chance.

Frisch Sends in First Run

Heinie Groh hit straight to Hoyt, and the Giant hurler was an easy victim on the third base line, but Frank Frisch was waiting at the plate to deliver a sacrifice fly to send Bancroft home with the first run of the game. With the Fordham Flash a sacrifice fly is just a matter of form. He always has them in stock ready for instant delivery. He left this one at the residence of Whitey Witt, and Bancroft just ambled over the plate.

The second run of the inning came over as the result of further operations by the devastating Irish of the Meusel Brigade. This desperate and brutal character has been viciously assaulting the upright young men of Colonels Ruppert and Huston for the last three days in an evident effort to knock them into a horizontal position. He landed only one clean blow yesterday, btu it came in this third inning and enabled Heine der Groh to scramble over the scorig dish with the second Giat run. It would seem that the Irish of the species is more deadly than the Bob. If this thing goes much further, Miller Huggins may put in a claim that the boys were switched on him at an early age.

The Giants had been firing at Hoyt since the start of the game with fair success. They wounded him at the rate of twice an inning for the first four stanzas, but only in the fatal third did the hits bring in their harvest of runs and then only because of the gap in the defense. The only soul-stirring moment in the long afternoon for the Yankee rooters came in the seventh. Bob Meusel beat out a puny hit to Bancroft and Wally Schang smote the first ball pitched to him against the right field wall for a pair of bases, Meusel stopping at third. A hit would tie the score at 2 all. Aaron Ward started for the plate, but was waved back by the lightweight manager. One man was out. Colonel Tillinghast L'Hommedieu Huston, seated in the front row of the press box, encouraged his formerly merry men with a sonorous "Hurroar!" Huggins picked Elmer Smith, left-handed slugger, to bat against Jack Scott, a right-handed twirler. This is according to Hoyle's Helpful Hints to Melancholy Managers, but the guide book has been all torn apart by this series to date. Another chapter was declared null and void yesterday as a result of the debacle that overwhelmed Hoyt while Scott rode on prosperously to victory.

Last Hope of Yankees Fades

Elmer Smith was as willin' as Barkis, but Jack Scott was as deceitful as sin. Elmer's act was short and tragic. It was one strike, two strikes, three strikes and fare thee well! Deacon Scott then grounded to Bancroft, and the threatened Yankee rally was as extinct as the dodo. For all practical purposes the game ended right there and then. A walk to Bancroft and successive singles by Groh and Frisch scored the final run for the Giants in the seventh, but it was for ornamental purposes only.

After the game Miller Huggins repulsed a suggestion from the populace that he rename his Murderers' Row and call it Dream Street. He admitted that his hired men looked more like peramulating somnambulists than cheery champions, but he hoped for a change for the better, beginning to-day at 2 p. m. If the Giants dash off with the world's series bunting while the Yankees are in their present condition the Hugmen can set up a claim that they were robbed while they slept.

The Yankee board of strategy was in session long into the night devising ways and means for the improvement of the scoring methods used in the bitter battles of this hectic struggle. Huggins himself seemed to think that better days were at hand. "We can still win," said the Dusty Miller. "It'll be more interesting to win the last four games than the first four."

It will be, indeed. The only impediment to this ambitious program is the corpulent figure of John Joseph McGraw. The way the helpless Yankees run up against this Nemesis every which way they turn recalls the ancient tale of the inebriated gentleman who tried three times to reach his own front door and each time ended up with his arms around the lone little maple tree in his dooryard plot, whereupon he wailed: "Losht! Losht, by God, in misht of impen'trable foresh!" It doesn't even seem to profit the Yankees to know that the moss grows on the north side of all Giant pitchers. In fact, they now suspect this information was issued with intent to deceive. They are out for r-r-revenge!

Frank Baker was hauled out of a back seat on the Yankee bench to bat for Hoyt in the eighth, but the veteran Trappe mauler died peacefully on a roller to Kelly.

Ross Young welcomed "Squire" Jones to the mound in the eighth with a snappy single to center. It was the third hit of the day for the little right fielder.

Casey Stengel is so badly affected with an attack of "charley horse" that he may not play again in the series. The ancient mariner is limping sadly about the field these soulful days.

Standing of Clubs In World's Series

THE Giants now hold a decided advantage over the Yankees as a result of their second victory of the series, with one game ending in a tie. The standing to date is as follows:

	Won	Lost	Tied	Pct.
Giants	2	0	1	1,000
Yankees	0	2	1	.000

The total in runs, hits and errors for the three games is as follows:

FIRST GAME

	R.	H.	E.
Yankees	2	7	0
Giants	3	11	3

Bush, Hoyt and Schang; Nehf, Ryan and Snyder.

SECOND GAME

	R.	H.	E.
Giants	3	8	1
Yankees	3	8	0

J. Barnes and Snyder; Shawkey and Schang.

THIRD GAME

	R.	H.	E.
Yankees	0	4	1
Giants	3	12	1

Hoyt, Jones and Schang; J. Scott and E. Smith.

FACTS ON TO-DAY'S GAME.

Game starts at 2 p. m.

Probable pitchers—Nehf or McQuillan for Giants; Bush for Yankees.

Umpires — Owens, American League, behind plate; Klem, National League, first base; Hildebrand, American League, second base; McMormick, National League, third base.

The Yankees will be the "home" team to-day, wearing white uniforms, using the home team's dugout and batting last. The Giants will wear gray uniforms, occupy the visitors' dugout and bat first.

This will be the second home game for the Yankees and tickets marked No. 4 will be honored.

The 22,000 unreserved seats in bleachers and upper tier of the grand stand will be on sale at 10 a. m. as usual.

Play-by-Play Account of The Giants' Second Victory

By Joseph Val

Manager McGraw, of the Giants, had the big crowd guessing as to his probable pitching selection up until ten minutes before game time. Shortly after 1:40 p. m. Hughie McQuillan and Jack Scott were testing their arms and it was broadly hinted that McQuillan would be selected. Hughie's leg proved stiff, however, from the injury he received in the last practice session Tuesday and Scott finally went to the trial pitching slab at 1:50.

Scott was ready and willing. He had had practically a whole afternoon of practice in the bull pen during the tie game of Thursday. Scott had a world of stuff in his preliminary work yesterday.

No one was surprised when Huggins selected young Waite Hoyt. There was an outside chance that Sam Jones might be chosen, but Hoyt got the call because of his impressive work as relief pitcher in the opening game.

FIRST INNING

YANKEES—Scott started well, retiring the side in order. Witt, the first Yankee to face the big right hander, dropped a bunt along the first base line. Scott pounced on it and his throw to Kelly retired the runner. Dugan's fly was easy for Young and Ruth went out on a weak tap to Frisch. No runs, no hits.

GIANTS—Hoyt was lucky to get by this inning, a double play saving him with two runners on the bases. Bancroft grounded to Pipp, but Groh singled to right, his fifth hit of the series. Frisch singled over second, Groh stopping at the midway. Irish Meusel was then in just such a position as on Thursday when he hit his home run. Yesterday, however, he lined to Ward and Frisch was doubled up. No runs, two hits.

SECOND INNING

YANKEES—Pipp got the first hit off Scott, a clean single to right. Meusel sent an easy pop fly to Kelly and Schang's fly fell right into Cunningham's hands. With Ward at bat Pipp stole second, being aided by Earl Smith's low throw. Ward's best was a grounder to Bancroft on which he was tossed out. No runs, one hit.

GIANTS—The McGrawmen got two more hits off Hoyt, but no scoring resulted. Young singled to left field and was out at second trying to stretch it. Meusel's throw to Ward was perfect and the play was not very close. Kelly was easy for Scott and Pipp. Cunningham singled to right for the second hit of the inning, but was forced by Smith, Ward and Scott handling the ball.

THIRD INNING

YANKEES—Jack Scott was still going strong, facing only three men here. Everett Scott flied to Young. Fritsch threw out Hoyt. Witt drew a pass, but spoiled his opportunity for further travel by taking a nap off first base. Smith to Kelly was the order of Whitey's finish. No runs, no hits.

GIANTS—Two more hits for the National Leaguers and two runs, which practically decided the ball game. Scott opened with a bounder over second. Ward booted Bancroft's grounder across the diamond and Scott reached third, while Bancroft roosted on first. Scott was caught off third on Groh's tap to the box. Hoyt and Dugan ran down the pitcher, but so slowly Bancroft went to third and Groh to second on the play. Frisch lifted a long sacrifice fly to Witt, scoring Bancroft and putting Groh on third. Meusel's line hit to right scored Groh. Young forced Meusel, Ward to Scott. Two runs, two hits.

FOURTH INNING

YANKEES—Dugan was thrown out by Groh. After taking one ball Ruth was hit on the ankle and ambled to first. Pipp could do nothing, striking out on a ball which cut the heart of the plate. Meusel drove a grounder toward second, which Frisch fumbled. Ruth tried to make third on the misplay, but was out on Frisch's toss to Groh. The Babe crashed into Groh head-on, knocking Heinie and the little fellow's headgear into the dust. This collision precipitated a strong argument, and the players almost came to blows. Umpire Hildebrand intervened and Ruth went to his post amid a chorus of intermingled cheers and boos. No runs, no hits.

GIANTS—Two more hits were wasted by the Giants. After singling to center Kelly was out stealing, Schang to Scott. Cunningham grounded out to Dugan. Earl Smith raised a hit into short field for his first hit of the series. Jack Scott struck out. No runs, two hits.

FIFTH INNING.

YANKEES—The side was retired in order. Kelly and Scott disposed of Schang. Ward flied to Cunningham and Scott fouled to Groh, the latter taking the ball near the visiting players' dugout. No runs, no hits.

GIANTS—An easy inning for Hoyt. He fanned Bancroft and Groh was tossed out by Dugan. Frisch was out stealing after drawing a pass. Schang's toss was handled by Scott. No runs, no hits.

SIXTH INNING.

YANKEES—Hoyt delivered the second Yankee hit of the game when he lined one to center. Witt forced Hoyt, Scott to Ward. Witt was left as Dugan flied to Meusel and Ruth grounded to Kelly. No runs, one hit.

GIANTS—Irish Meusel raised an easy fly to brother Bob. Young hit to left for his second single of the day. He was left stranded, however, as Kelly fouled to Pipp and Cunningham was tossed out by Ward.

SEVENTH INNING.

YANKEES—The Hugmen had their best chance to score here when they had runners on second and third with only one out. Pipp was the first out, dying on a grounder to Frisch. Meusel's slow roller past the box was too slow for Bancroft to handle and it went as a hit. Schang got the biggest hit of the day, driving to the right field wall for a double, which put Meusel on third. Elmer Smith, a left handed batter, got a chance to bat for Ward. He failed to do anything, striking out ingloriously. Yankee hopes faded when the next batsman, Scott grounded to Bancroft. No runs, two hits.

GIANTS—Hoyt yielded the last run of the game after two were out. Waite retired Earl Smith and Dugan threw out Scott. Bancroft then walked, went to third on Groh's single to right and scored when Frisch pushed a one-bagger to the same territory. McNally, who had taken Ward's place, threw out Meusel.

EIGHTH INNING

YANKEES—Scott was invincible. Home-run Baker, batting for Hoyt, was expunged on a grounder to Groh; Witt flied to Cunningham and Dugan was retired by Groh. No runs, no hits.

GIANTS—Sam Jones went in to pitch for the Yankees. Young opened with a single to center and advanced when Kelly sacrificed, Jones to Pipp. Cunningham walked, but Smith and Scott popped out, the catcher flying to McNally and Scott skying to Dugan. No runs, one hit.

NINTH INNING

YANKEES—The last stand of the Hugmen was a weak one. None of the three Yankee batsmen could put the ball out of the infield. Ruth's puny tap was converted into an out by Frisch and Kelly. Bancroft tossed out both Pipp and Meusel. No runs, no hits.

New World's Series Hero

Jack Scott, who shut out Yankees

Bleachers' Four Million Confer Rawsberry on Witt and Ruth

Nearly all the social leaders listed in "Regular Guys"—the Blue Book of New York's four million—visited the bleachery at the Brush Stadium yesterday to attend the debut of Mr. Jack Scott's debutante daughter Miss Fame. Any one who has not attended a bleacher reception at a world's series debutante party knows little or nothing about real baseball society. In the bleacher social world introductions are ignored. The pet formal expressions are "Oooooo—" and "Atta Boy!" Disagreement with a mere statement calls—not for silence—but a barrage of newspapers.

In the bleachers if some one stands up and you think that person is between you and the object of your eye you yell: "Sit down!" If that does not bring the some one to his seat you holler: "Sit down, you big bum!" If that doesn't work you repeat the latter remark until your companions have heard you once or twice, and then they will assist you in drawing attention of the stander by hitting him on the head with some of those mysterious objects which loom up from everywhere in bleacher sections.

By 12:30 o'clock yesterday there wasn't a vacant seat in the bleachers. Harry Stevens's waiters, dressed in their white yachting suits, were serving luncheon in a la Ritz style. The conversation centered around Judge Landis. Evidently those who had attended Thursday's game did not announce the fact, because it was openly announced in the bleachers that only "hoodlums" could jeer an old man who was trying to do all he could for baseball. Articles by favorite sporting writers were quoted to prove that it was probably best that Thursday's game had been called at the end of the tenth inning. When Judge Landis arrived just before the game four million of the bleachers gave him a rousing cheer.

Jimmy Collins, Nyack's postman and weather prophet, was about the last of the 4,000,000 to be let in the gate. Jimmy explained that he had flivvered from Nyack and had carburetor trouble or something and was delayed. He also said Nyack would get its mail O. K. tomorrow morning and nobody would holler, because he would tell 'em all about the game when he brought the mail.

Joseph E. K. Timmins, of St. Paul, sat in the center field stand and announced the Yankees would win. Jeb Calkins, who hails from Coxsackie, N. Y., and who sat in the left field bleachers, told Joe whenever he could be heard that only a guy from St. Paul would be fool enough to think the Yanks would win.

The order of the Rawsberry—a sacred degree in the bleacher world—was first conferred upon Whitey Witt when he was caught flat-footed off first in the third. When Witt came out into the gardens to chase the Giants' hits the 4,000,000 told him a few things about Smith's arm, which would have been god advice if given before the game. But Whitey was ignored after Babe hit Heine Groh for a bumpety bump in the fourth. Babe was then installed into the 32d chapter of the Royal Order the Rawsberries. The installation ceremonies continued each inning as Babe took to fly chasing.

The main difference between the 4,000,000 of the bleechers and the 400 of the reserved section is $4.40 and also a natural vividness of speech that would delight a Kipling. In the left field section a fan announced about the eighth inning that he had bet on the Yanks. This called for a newspaper barrage. When the last man was out all available ammunition was brought into use and the final shelling sent hats flying and hastened the steps of the slow-moving fans up front.

Jay Kirke Is Traded To Indianapolis Club

LOUISVILLE, Ky., Oct. 6.—Jayson Kirke, first baseman of the Louisville Colonels, who last year set a world's record for hits made during a regulation season, has been traded to the Indianapolis club of the American Association, it was announced to-day. The Colonels will receive Tex Covington, first baseman of the Indianapolis team, in exchange.

Kirke never has batted under .300 since coming here seven years ago. Last year he led the league with a mark of .386, while in the past season he batted .355.

Curtin Defeats London

FALL RIVER, Mass., Oct. 6.—Irish Johnny Curtin, of Jersey City, was awarded the decision over Harry London at the Casino A. C. here to-night when the latter boxer fouled Curtin in the second round of a scheduled twelve-round bout. Curtin had all the beter of the fight in the first round.

Yankees Shut Out by Scott; Giants Win, 3-0

Game Heart and Good Arm of "Come-Back" Pitcher Put McGrawmen 2 Games to Good in World's Series

(Continued from page one)

By Grantland Rice

that drove Meusel to third as Wally slid in safely to second base.

The slaughter was about to take place after all. The crowd scented the first whiff of blood, and after the manner of all crowds upon such an occasion one of those wild, ripstering roars beat back and forth across the field. Scott had made a brave start, but he was now standing on the rim of doom. Yankee bats were back again and the tide was running their way.

In a flash Huggins lifted Aaron Ward, who hadn't been hitting a lick to make way for Elmer Smith, the left-handed hitter with the eagle's eye. Since Scott was breaking up, one more heavy shot would tie the count and drive John William from the reservation, to seek solace under the cooling shower and think how closely he had come to beating his way back to the fashionable marts of his trade.

But as we suggested just above there was nothing the matter with John Scott's heart. Facing Elmer Smith he looked as cool as a thin slice of cucumber on ice. He must have known that the long slog back would be about ended by another blow, and Hugh McQuillan was warming up in center field.

Crowd Roars Tribute

The second largest crowd that ever saw a world's series game in the Polo Grounds sat in breathless interest as Smith took his place at bat, while Scott, taking his time, looked the batter over before bending over the first strike. Three balls followed, and then Scott turned on two perfect strikes, and Smith stalked back to the bench as 38,000 voices paid their tribute to a good arm and a game heart.

But Scott had another Scott to handle, and the Yankee deacon is no piker in a pinch. This time he, too, was helpless, as Bancroft threw him out and the Yankee rally went to seed.

This was the only time throughout the battle where the Yankees ever threatened to spoil the story of a derelict turned into a man o' war. They never had a chance against the combination of Giant pitching and Giant infield play, where Groh, Bancroft and Frisch continued to back up their pitching mate with an impregnable defense. Four hits, only two of which were bunched, tell the story of Scott's greatness and the second Yankee defeat. For they were beaten in that third inning, where none other than our hero, viz., John William Scott, led off with a single to Hoyt's astonished disgust. Ward booted Bancroft's hard, low grounder into left and Scott, by unexpected speed, raced on to third. Groh grounded to Hoyt and Scott was run down, but Bancroft and Groh kept on running until they reached third and second, waiting for a hit. Frisch scored Bancroft with a long sacrifice fly and Irish Meusel's busy bat scored Groh with all the runs Scott needed to complete his day of triumph.

Giants Add One in Seventh

Hoyt yielded another tally in the seventh before Sam Jones replaced him in the eighth, but the battle was already over. It was over when Bancroft scored the first run, although no one except the Giant pitcher seemed to know it then. The beauty of his pitching was the perfect ease and lack of effort which stayed with him all the afternoon. He knew that nine-tenths of those present expected his complete demolition at almost any moment. He knew that the message had gone forth that after Nehf and Barnes the Giants had no one left to stop the Yankee attack, which was now about due to resume its chorus from the Opera of Swat. But knowing all this, the lanky one from the Carolina pines proved that the broken blossom was blooming again in the garden of the game's acclaim.

Scott had not only stopped the Yankees, but there came another dent for the soft and yielding dope in the Giants' heavy assault upon Waite Hoyt, who only a year ago had stopped them effectively at almost every turn. They socked Hoyt with carefree abandon, bunching their blows in two innings, which is usually quite enough. It is always enough when the other pitcher is turning in a shutout. Save in a few spicy instances the crowd was strangely quiet. It must have been remembering that uncalled for outbreak against Judge Landis the day before when a headless mob proved how headless, unfair and cowardly a mob can be when it starts to work.

Yankees Not Yet Crushed

Those in the big demonstration must have known the judge had no part in the umpire's lack of judgment, but few mobs ever go far enough to call upon any function of the brain.

As a result of two defeats Yankee hopes are dimmed, but they are not yet entirely crushed to earth. For the Yankees today are just where the Giants were a year ago after Carl Mays and Waite Hoyt had wrenched away the first two games.

After these two defeats the Giants then rallied and fought their way safely through, winning five of the last six games through superior strength in the box. The Yankees still look to have their share of pitching supremacy left if Bullet Joe Bush can only stand the strain upon his wounded heel, thereby proving himself to be a better man than Achilles from another day.

But so far it must be admitted that the supposed Yankee margin in the box has failed to show up. Bob Shawkey has turned in the best stuff so far from the American League camp and the best he could get was a ten inning draw. Both Bush and Hoyt were outpitched, proving again that the dope can break in more directions than a piece of shrapnel. Anyway, with the shorter series, this next game is a vital affair and Carl Mays must drag his ball club back into the jubilee unless it is to be demolished in four out of five games.

Looks Like Mays.

Huggins is almost certain to rush Mays to the pit, while McGraw figures on McQuillan, Ryan or Nehf. It may be that McGraw's pitching staff is weak. It may be that he has no one around who can hold a hard hitting club at bay. But you can no longer prove this by three world's series crowds who have seen Nehf, Barnes and Scott under fire. And no one can make the Yanks believe it. They have been hammering away for three days nof without getting anywhere and the moment has about arrived when they either start or else stand out as one of the greatest upsets that ever overturned the dope, as big an upset if they are beaten quickly as the Braves-Athletic series developed just eight years ago.

Babe Ruth Roundly Hissed for Purposely Bumping Into Groh

Famous Slugger Charges Into Midget Third Baseman With Such Force as to Send Him Crashing to Ground; Thousands Turned Away at the Gates

By W. J. Macbeth

The third game of the current series between the Giants and Yankees for the championship of the world furnished a number of striking sidelights on mob psychology. The rabid masses which congregated before the box of Commissioner Kenesaw Mountain Landis the previous afternoon and hissed him soundly for what was interpreted as bland and blatant commercialism were all on hand again, but in a more pleasant frame of mind. Baseball as the national institution which it is had been forgiven. But the multitude just naturally had to have its "goat" and instead of the Commissioner singled out "Babe" Ruth against whom to vent its spleen.

A fine object lesson was furnished Mr. Ruth, if he has the sense to appreciate the change of heart which seems to have affected the fan. He was roundly hissed for having selected little Heinie Groh as the object of a display of unnecessary roughness. In the fourth inning Ruth was on first with two out. Frisch fumbled a hard drive from the bat of Bob Meusel. The Babe kept on for third base in spite of the fact that the Fordham Flash made a rather quick recovery on the bobble. Ruth had no possible change to beat the play, and Frisch's throw had the ball in Groh's hands before Ruth got within fifteen or twenty feet of the midget third sacker.

It is true that Ruth, as base runner, had the right to the lines. But it is equally true that Ruth deliberately bumped Groh with such force as to flatten him. Ruth's "charge" seemed deliberate unsportsmanship. There was no possibility for him to benefit.

Babe Is Soundly "Razzed"

As a result, Babe Ruth was submitted to the humiliation of a general "razzing" the rest of the afternoon. Each time as he strutted out to his position or pedalled the reverse way toward the bench he was hissed and booed pretty freely. It is true that some of the partisans handed him a handicap, but the good-will generally was drowned by the voice and invective of general disapproval. And on the two occasions when he came to bat afterward—particularly as he did nothing to vindicate his reputation—he was soundly "razzed."

All of which should make Mr. Ruth realize the fickleness of so-called public esteem and popularity. A year ago the then king of home-run hitters was lionized at every appearance while he continued in the series, for it was known he was struggling under the great handicap of a badly infected arm. Yesterday the thumbs were turned down in a manner to show what is in store for the battering Bambino once he starts on the down grade after having passed the crest.

In passing, however, it may be mentioned that Ruth evidently considered he had provocation for bumping off a midget rival. At the time of the bumping Groh and Ruth made hostile demonstrations, but were split by the third base umpire. In the next inning Ruth, as he passed Groh on the way to the bench renewed the argument and did an impromptu fancy high kick as if to illustrate a point he was evidently making as to the fact that Heine in the first game had intentionally "ridden high" into Aaron Ward when he attempted to steal second.

There probably never was a greater number of disappointed baseball fans than attempted to storm . Brush Stadium in the shadows of Coogan's Bluff yesterday afternoon. It goes without saying, of course, that the crowd was up to capacity or so much of it as the police and fire departments would admit. An hour before the time of play the police cordons had cut off from all entrance below 155th Street everyone but the holders of box or reserved seat tickets. At that time the upper grand stand and bleacher spaces were entirely filled with many standees in the back reaches and no few of the favored in the aisles.

A Fitting Testimonial.

No more fitting testimonial to the popularity of the sport could be imagined, and this despite the fact that the crowd on quitting the field the day previously had gone away in bad temper vowing it was through with this form of professional sport forever. Undoubtedly the wise counsel of Commissioner Landis and the owners of the Giants and Yankees in giving the receipts of the tie game of Thursday to charity saved the face of a sport which might have been injured unwittingly.

In the cool reason of the day after few could be found who would not admit that there was every justification for the calling of the game Thursday afternoon at the end of the tenth inning. Dusk was falling. It might have been possible to play a couple more innings provided the contest moved with the speed that had been shown up to that time. But a long half inning for the Giants, and especially one in which they would have scored, would have brought the Yankees to bat in practical darkness; certainly there was every reason to fear discrimination against the American Leaguers had the contest been prolonged.

However that may be, the fact that the club owners and the commissioner so promptly and plainly brought forth the point that organized baseball did not intend to profit by a chance of error of judgment on the part of an umpire satisfied every spectator of the innate honesty of the promoters. The result was such an assault against the baseball field as had never before been witnessed. It is safe to say that half as many as watched the battle were turned back from the approaches.

Even the most ardent admirers of the American League admitted with little reluctance after yesterday's game that the cause of the junior major to win the premier honors of baseball was little but a sad-eyed hope at best.

Usually the team that wins the first game annexes the blue ribbon classic. There have been only two exceptions since 1903, when the Red Sox had to come from behind with three straight victories to snatch the laurels from the Pirates, and last year, when McGraw's men finally beat out the Yankees after dropping the first two to the Hugmen.

The Yankees to-day stand just where the Giants stood after the first two games of the 1921 classic, for, of course, there was no tie game last year. The American League supporters are hoping that history may repeat itself and that, after all, supposedly superior pitching must triumph for the Ruppert-Huston forces. They figure the Yankees have been in a slump—a bad hitting slump—ever since they returned out of the West, and that the team must eventually come back to something like its normal hitting form.

Colonel Bill Fleischman, the rabid Yankee rooter, wandered around the field after the game moaning "Oh, Death, where is thy sting?"

Hawaiians Face Extinction

Native Hawaiians are said to be facing extinction, and if the present ratio of births and deaths is maintained the remaining life of the race will be only about seventy-five years.

Picked Up at Polo Grounds

By John Kieran

In spite of Thursday's near-tragedy, the fans again filled the stands at an early hour. In honor of the auspicious revival the band struck up "Hail, Hail, the Gang's All Here"

Nick Altrock and Al Schacht were reinforced yesterday with a performing monkey. They staged a new act with their acquisition entitled "The Three of Us."

John Harrison Dempsey the Manassa Mauler, blocked traffic around the field just before hostilities began when he posed with Cosy Dolan in front of the Giant dugout. About two hundred photographers took eight pictures apiece.

The portly person of Cap. Huston was seen moving majestically through the aisles, giving utterance to his battle cry at stated intervals "Every cent for the disabled soldiers! Every cent! Are you with me, or against me?"

Garry Herrmann got his first close-up of Matty at the ball game yesterday. "I've been looking for you for three days," said Garry. "You've grown so fat I wouldn't know you without a guide. Here's to your very good health!"

Both pitchers started work by slipping a strike across the plate. Hoyt went even further. He retired the first Giant batter unassisted when he took Bancroft's bunt and beat the runner to the bag.

The Yankee hurlers are becoming afflicted with Groh-ing pains. The frequency with which Heinie pours hits out of his bottle bat is getting to be a heavy strain on their constitutions.

Bob Meusel struck a lady in the eye. It was not exactly a case of intentional assault and batery. Bob fouled a ball into the upper stand in batting practise and all the gentlemanly fans stood aside to let the lady make the catch. The human eye is not adapted to this operation as the fair fan discovered. Luckily the injury was not serious and the lady remained to witness the fary.

The Yanks got a break in the first inning when Irish Meusel lined to Ward and Frisch was doubled off first. Irish meant that to be a base hit and made no secret of it.

With two down in the Yanks' third Whitey Witt drew a pass, strolled to first and fell into a profound slumber about six feet off the bag. He was rudely awakened when Earl Smith snapped the ball to Kelly and Long George plastered Whitey with the pellet between two snores.

Aaron Ward made the first Yankee error of the series, when he booted Bancroft's hot grounder in the third. It was a costly kick he gave the ball. Two Giant runs were rushed over the plate as the attack continued.

In the first three innings the Giants got six hits and the Yanks got one. The pre-series dope on the respective pitching staffs is working at full speed in a reverse direction. Figures are lying fluently this season.

Babe Ruth tore into third base in the fourth and knocked Heinie Groh for a circular row of revolving butter-tubs. It reminded the aged spectators of their school days and the merry game of "Johnnie dump the apple cart."

The chunky third sacker wanted to chaw the Bambino up on the spot, hide, hair and all. Umpire Hildebrand suggested that this project be postponed to a later day, when a separate admission might be charged.

Looked as though Frank Frisch had stolen second in the fifth inning, but Bill Klem said "No," and after a brief debate the Fordham Flash accepted the verdict with the best grace he could muster. Klem calls them against friend and foe alike.

The first real "Meusel to Meusel" play of the series came in the sixth inning yesterday, when Irish, of the Giants, sailed a soft fly to Yankee Bob. The lanky lad had to wag his No. 10 shoes at a rapid pace to make the catch.

Claude Jonnard kept right on warming up, even though the total Yankee damage to Jack Scott was two hits in six innings. John McGraw was not caught napping by the Yankee attack in the seventh.

As it turned out, Jack Scott rescued himself by fanning Elmer Smith, who batted for Ward, with runners on second and third. Deacon Scott grounded to short, and the dangerous inning was over.

The box score might be labelled "Initials Only." There was R. Meusel and E. Meusel, J. Scott and E. Scott, Earl Smith and Elmer Smith, just to make the scoring difficult.

The Giants put on a perfect hit-and-run play in the seventh when Groh placed a clean single in right as Bancroft dashed for second. Bancroft tallied on another hit by Frisch. All this trouble descended on Hoyt after two men were out. A walk to Bancroft did the trick.

The last turn at bat for S. Herman Ruth was the signal for three rousing jeers from the Giant rooters. The fans were "riding" him all afternoon after he tumbled Groh in the dust.

"Self-reverence, self-knowledge, self-control,—
These three alone lead life to sovereign power."

The Boston Post

EIGHTEEN PAGES—TWO CENTS | *Established 1831* | SA U ' 7 1922 ** | *Copyright, 1922, by Post Publishing Co.* | EIGHTEEN PAGES—TWO CENTS

THE NEW WEDDING BELLS

HERE COMES THE BRIDE
SCORE CARD
SCORE CARD
EXTRAS
PA
MA
CADDIE ATTENDANTS
THE RECENT "KNICKERBOCKER" WEDDING SUGGESTS THAT SOON WE MAY HAVE THE GOLF BUGS WEDDING—ALL RIGGED FOR THE LINKS
JUSTICE OF THE PEACE
FEE
MARRIAGE CERTIFICATE
RICE
CON-FETTI
BEST MAN
BRIDES MAID
NO DOUBT THE TENNIS NUPTIALS, APPROPRIATELY COSTUMED WILL BE THE NEXT IN LINE
NORMAN
DO YOU TAKE THIS MAN FOR YOUR HUSBAND?
AND THE BASKETBALL ROMANCERS MAY HELP THE INNOVATION ALONG

SCOTT THE DISCARD SHUTS OUT YANKEES

Pitcher Traded by Braves And Turned Loose by Cincinnati Twirls Magnificent Game, Holding American League Champions to Four Scattered Hits —Hoyt Hit Hard by Giants Who Score Three Runs For Victory

Giants Play Brilliant Ball Whil Yankees Seem To Be In Pronounced Slump

Ruth Bowls Over Heinie Gro And Is Booed By Throng Of Former Admirers

Dempsey to Announce for Post

Jack Dempsey, heavyweight champion of the world, boxes at Mechanics Building tonight under the auspices Faneuil A. C., will be the official announcer at the Post board this afternoon. Jack will megaphone the play in th game of the series to the big crowd that will pack Ne Row. And maybe there will not be a jam. The Post has se Dempsey as announcer through the courtesy of the champ himself, Manager Kearns, and John F. Mahony of the Fan Club.

BY PAUL H. SHANNON

POLO GROUNDS, Oct. 6.—Baseball's hall of fame—the goal of all world's series entrants, threw wide its portals to a newly crowned hero this afternoon, and as the slipping, shattered idols of the New York Yankee crew fell from grace again, the pitching derelict of a few weeks back won his golden spurs by a 3 to 0 victory over the American league champions.

Continued on Page 14—First Col.

BABE RUTH OUT ON THIRD AFTER COLLIDING WITH GROH
The photo shows the Babe "dying" on third base in the fourth inning, having capsized Heinie Groh of the Giants in the third game of the world series in New York.

NO LIQUOR ON ANY STEAMER

Daugherty Rules Foreign Shipping Must Come in Dry---Barred on All American Craft

WASHINGTON, Oct. 6 (by the Associated Press).—All vessels, American and foreign owned, are prohibited from having liquor on board in American territorial waters under an interpretation of the prohibition amendment and the enforcement handed down today by the Department of Justice.

Moreover, the transportation or sale of intoxicants on American craft, wherever operated, was held to be forbidden.

TERRITORIES INCLUDED

American territorial waters were construed to include those not only within

Continued on Page 8—First Col.

PRISON MADE TOO INVITING

Blames Bail Bond Evil for Crime Wave

NEW YORK, Oct. 6.—That "too much tennis, football and baseball" at Sing Sing makes "crime too inviting" was the belief expressed by Dr. Perry Lichtenstein, chief physician of the Tombs prison in a speech at the Elks' Club in Freeport.

"The so-called crime wave in New York," declared Dr. Lichtenstein, "is not due to any inefficiency on the part of the police. The bail bond evil is to blame and the attractiveness of Sing Sing. I have seen cases in which a man sentenced to the Elmira reformatory preferred to go to Sing Sing and lose his citizenship because of the good times he knew awaited him there."

SEEK SIGNERS IN CAMBRIDGE

Must File Petition for Charter Change Today

Only a Harvard-Yale game or a vacant flat with a low rental could create as much excitement and interest in Cambridge as the race against time that the "petitioners" are making to have the charter of the city changed at the next election.

Before 4 o'clock this afternoon petitions bearing the names of about 3500 voters must be filed with City Clerk Frederick H. Burke, or the question of changing the charter from plan "B" to "C" will not be placed on the ballot. Not a name had been filed when the city clerk's office closed at 4 o'clock yesterday afternoon.

The entire voting population of Cambridge, to say nothing of two dozen office-holders, are watching the race from the sidelines.

According to the statute covering the procedure, the filing must take place one month before the November election. The proposed change of charter would mean a commissioner form of government with five commissioners, one of whom would be Mayor. The five commissioners would constitute the City Council. Under its present charter the city has a Mayor and 15 councillors, 11 representing wards and the others elected at large.

The Cutest Animal Pictures Yet

In the next Boston Sunday Post Magazine will appear a 16-page booklet of "Animal Cuties," one of the cutest collections of animal pictures ever published.

TURKISH SITUATION CRITICAL

Turks Insist on Immediate Occupation of Thrace

LONDON, Oct. 6 (by the Associated Press).—Despatches received here tonight give even a graver aspect to the Near Eastern situation than that of earlier in the day.

The Kemalists are insisting on the right to the immediate occupation of eastern Thrace and have given the allies a time limit, expiring this evening, for a reply on this question.

TURKS INSIST ON DEMAND

The Turks have refused to accept the proposal for allied occupation of Thrace or any allied control, and apparently they are supported in this stand by the French and Italian governments.

Everything seems now to depend on the British cabinet reply to the report of Brigadier General Harington, which

Continued on Page 8—Second Col.

WOMAN OF 75 STRUCK BY CAR

Rib Broken While Crossing Street

Mrs. Margaret Dugan, 75, of 357 Columbia road, Dorchester, was struck by a street car late yesterday afternoon while crossing the street in front of her home. She sustained a fractured rib on the right side and contusions to her back and was taken to her home.

According to Motorman Thomas Splain and Conductor G. D. Byrne, in charge of the car, Mrs. Dugan, crossing the street after alighting from an outbound car, stepped directly in the path of the inbound car and was thrown to the ground.

BLUENOSE FAVORITE FOR RACES

First of Elimination Contests Starts Today

SECOND TRIAL TO BE HELD MONDAY

The Mahaska's Crew Confident She Will Win

BY HERBERT L. BALDWIN

HALIFAX, N. S., Oct. 6.—Four Nova Scotia fishing schooners, cream of Canada's fleet, were ready tonight for the first of the Nova Scotia fishing vessel championship races which commence at 10 o'clock tomorrow morning for the double purpose of naming the queen of the dominion's fleet and choosing the boat that will go to

Continued on Page 8—Fourth Col.

BOY KILLED BY TROLLEY CAR

Carried Under Fender and Skull Broken

Robert Seeley, 6 years old, of 1 Lexington place, East Boston, was fatally injured last night when he fell beneath the forward end of a Lexington street tunnel elevated car, opposite 38 Lexington street, East Boston.

The boy, in running across the busy street, stepped from behind one car into the other. Before Motorman John Collins, 31, of 91 White street, East Boston, could stop his car, the boy was carried under the fender close to the wheels. Spectators and a wrecking crew worked feverishly to raise the heavy vehicle from the tracks, and when it was finally jacked up, the boy was rushed in a waiting ambulance to the East Boston Relief Station.

At the hospital, he was pronounced dead by Dr. George E. Allen. Death was due to a fracture of the skull. Collins was arrested by the East Boston police and charged with manslaughter.

MONOPLANE IN AIR 35 HOURS

Army Fliers Break All Known Records

SAN DIEGO, Calif., Oct. 6.—Lieutenants John A. MacReady and Oakley Kelly who had been flying over San Diego since 5:56 a. m. yesterday in the great monoplane T-2, landed at Rockwell Field 5:11:30 p. m. today, having broken all known records for sustained flight in the heavier than air flying machine. They were in the air 35 hours 18 minutes 30 seconds.

LAWSON LEASES FLAT IN FENWAY

Secures 8-Room Suite at No. 90 Formerly Occupied by Gov. Cox at $275 Per Month

From $2,500,000 Dreamwold which, in its prime, cost nearly $200,000 a year to maintain to an eight-room and two baths apartment in the Fenway for which he pays $275 per month is the extent of the financial drop in the living conditions of Thomas W. Lawson, erstwhile copper "king," sportsman and author.

AT 90 FENWAY

It was learned yesterday that Lawson, who has offered his palatial estate

Continued on Page 9—Fifth Col.

THIEVES ROB SCOTLAND YARD

Take Store of Overcoats From Property Room

LONDON, Oct. 6.—Provident thieves, mindful of the long, rainy autumn just ahead, robbed Scotland Yard, the most famous police headquarters in the world, of a big store of overcoats and umbrellas early today. The police are investigating. There are said to have been no arrests.

The robbers broke into the lost property office, which is detached from the main building, but close enough to make the exploit daring.

'WALLINGFORD' IS IN AGAIN

Proprietors of Boston Hostelry His "Hosts"

NEW HAVEN, Oct. 6.—Dillon C. Willoughby, who on account of his many illegal plans for gaining riches and because of imaginative talk representing himself to be of the British nobility, has been arrested dozens of times in Boston, Brookline, New York and other places, was turned over to local authorities today by Massachusetts officials. He was recently released from the Psychopathic Hospital, Boston.

"Get Rich Quick Wallingford" is the monniker generally applied to him by police officials. His latest trouble is the result of an attempt to defraud the proprietors of the Garde Hotel here. He will be arraigned tomorrow.

First Mail Aeroplane Lands at Hartford, Conn.

HARTFORD, Conn., Oct. 6.—United States mail aeroplane number 213 arrived at Brainard Field here today in the first aerial mail trip from New York to this city. The plane came from Hazlehurst, Long Island, in one hour and 32 minutes.

Yale Graduate Refused Citizenship Papers

NEW HAVEN, Conn., Oct. 6.—Citizenship papers were refused by Judge E. S. Thomas in the United States district court today to Morris N. Bailey of New Britain, a graduate of the Sheffield Scientific School at Yale, class of 1915, because he had never seen a copy of the United States constitution and knew nothing about it. The court told Bailey to take time and study the document.

HIGH TIDE TODAY

A. M. | P. M. 12:03

SUN Rises 5:47 Sets 5:17 **MOON** Rises at 6:18 p. m.

Light all vehicles tonight at 5:47.

TODAY'S ANNIVERSARIES, ETC.

James Whitcomb Riley born, 1853.
Austro-German invasion of Serbia begins, 1915.
Uruguay breaks with Germany, 1917.
German war submarine U-53 entered Newport harbor, 1916.
French take Barry-au-Bac, 1918.
One year ago today—British court of inquiry found collapse of R-38 balloon due to structural weakness.—New U. A. army 16-inch, 50-calibre gun threw shell 20 miles at Aberdeen, Md.

UNSETTLED

Forecast for Boston and vicinity—Unsettled Saturday and Sunday; probably showers; moderate easterly winds.

WASHINGTON, Oct. 6.—Forecast for northern New England: Unsettled, probably showers Saturday and Sunday; cooler in Vermont Saturday.

Southern New England: Unsettled Saturday and Sunday; probably showers; cooler in Connecticut and Western Massachusetts Saturday.

Winds: North of Sandy Hook—Moderate to fresh easterly and weather overcast, probably showers Saturday.

Sandy Hook to Hatteras—Moderate winds mostly southerly and weather overcast, possibly showers Saturday.

The Old Farmer's Prediction

It looks to me as if today's weather will be overcast and unsettled and continue rather cool.

CHILDREN VICTIMS OF POISONIN

Near Death—Moth in Psychopathic Hospital

Two children of Mr. and M Walter Stafford of 1273 Massa setts avenue, Roxbury, hover tween life and death at the Hospital, victims of poisoning, w their mother, her mind weakened an all winter illness which minated in influenza, is a patien the Psychopathic Hospital.

STILL UNCONSCIOUS

Louise, aged four, and Eleanor, five, were unconscious at the City pital last evening, 24 hours after b admitted to the institution, suffe from the toxic effects of a slow wor poison.

The illness of three members of a few short weeks ago was one of happiest of happy families, constit one of the most pathetic of life's t edies which hospital authorities come into contact with for m months.

How the children secured the p —believed to have been medicinal prescribed for Mrs. Stafford's use— mystery which baffles the bereaved band and father. He is torn by d as to whether they, accomplishin seemingly impossible task, secured pills themselves or whether Mrs. S ford, still in a weakened mental dition, gave the pills to the childre the belief that the medicine would in curing the babies' colds even helped her.

The mother was taken to the Psy pathic Hospital at the end of a siege of illness. On Monday last woman expressed a desire to go h hospital authorities considered her dition satisfactory, and the hus took his wife home.

The Cutest Animal Pictures Ye

In the next Boston Sunday Magazine will appear a 16-p booklet of "Animal Cuties," one the cutest collections of animal tures ever published.

Baseball, Golf, Tennis, Turf, Track, Boxing, Wrestling—all expertly reported by expert reporters, Best in the West.

SPORT NEWS

Los Angeles Examiner

MONDAY, OCTOBER 9, 1922 SECTION I—PAGE 11

The Examiner carries the most complete Sporting Section of any newspaper West of Chicago.

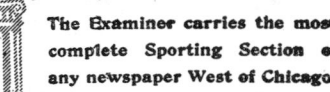

YANKS TOSS AWAY WORLD SERIES

Seals Drive Spike in Pennant Flagpole

SPLIT EVEN BUT TIGERS DROP A PAIR

S. F. Loses Series to Seraphs, but Gain One Game in Race for Flag; Enter Final Week

By Mark Kelly

THIS here now old pennant ought to flap from the breeze at Recreation Park, San Francisco, next year. Yesterday's doings would indicate as much. Not positivile, y'understand, but probabible, very probabible.

"Lindy" Lindimore

Yesterday's red letter day for baseball did a lot of things that a man could rave over, cheer over or get a laugh out of. For instance:

San Francisco split even with Los Angeles in two games at Washington Park. Seals took first one 3 to 0, and dropped second 2 to 1.

Up Oakland way Vernon dropped two more games to the Oaks.

Vernon trails San Francisco two full games, with but seven to go.

Attendance at Washington Park established the year's record to date, 15,028 cash customers decorating the exchequers. Mr. Gawge Alfie Putnam took a lot of jack out of this man's town with him last night, and the athletes will eat regularly for another month.

The day's amusement was furnished by Yellowtail and Tuna, two cops of the Keystone aroma. The two had a great day snagging balls that went into the crowds that overflowed the stands and decorated the baselines.

THRONG FLOODS GROUNDS

Tuna was outdone by Yellowtail. Tuna lost three decisions and won two to the crowd, while Yellowtail batted .500. Yellowtain relieved Tuna once, dived into the crowd and produced the errant pill that Tuna had been arguing over for ten minutes. Shoulders back, head erect and his classic map radiating supreme satisfaction with itself, Yellowtail deliberated, walked to the center of the diamond and threw the ball to the umps. He got a hand. He should have gotten a foot. This must have peeved Tuna all up, for his work improved thereafter. While Tuna and Yellowtail were battling their way to unpopularity by their picayunish parsimony with baseballs, two ginks were held up a block away. Great is the law—of averages.

But getting back to the athletes.

The opening game got under way five minutes late while the frantic ushers tried to squeeze two bodies in space allotments that were intended for but one. It proved unsuccessful and finally the fish broke over the barriers and into the field. It made ground rules necessary.

Lefty Thomas, our jinxed southpaw, was opposed to Bob Geary. Lefty got his usual quota of breaks against him—and dropped the verdict on one three-run rally. The Angels could do nothing with Geary. The pudgy Seal flinger tossed avoirdupois, but he whizzed the pellet smack past the batters with annoying regularity. He was touched for four hits. Babe Twombly got three of them and Deal the other, so you know just how much the Angels had in the line of punch.

McAULEY BOOTS APLENTY

Geary outpitched Thomas, all right, but of the Seals' eleven hits five were the kind that beat Carl Mays and started that civil war in the Yankee bailiwick, according to the prints. On top of that the three runs weren't earned, but came on two slipups of Jim McAuley's.

The Seals ought to have won that game on several opportunities. The Angels never had but one look-in and failed to do anything about it.

The second game was the better of the two. Nick Dumovich turned in his second win of the week over the Seals and cinched the series by outpitching Oliver Mitchell, the Northerner's ace. If O. Twist had that Angel outfit to hurl against very much he would be one of the league's leading twirlers—reading from south to north.

Mitchell lost his own game on a balk, technically speaking. The teams were tied at one all when the Angels came up for their ninth. Deal spanked a double into the crowd. After much fumdoodelums and many whisperings between the Seals' infield, it was decided to put

(Continued on Page 12, Column 2)

Huston and Ruppert Yank Battery Today

So Says

Ring W. Lardner

Special to the Los Angeles Examiner

NEW YORW, Oct. 8.—WELL, boys, it looks like it was all over and the only complaint I have got to make is that the traffic regulations was not handled right.

Ring W. Lardner

The next time the Yankees take part in a world serious they should ought to have a traffic policeman stationed between 1st and 2d bases and another traffic policeman stationed between home and 1st.

The former should tell the boys when it is O. K. to run to 2d. And the latter must inform them that when a ground ball is hit to the infield in a world serious the general theory which has never been disproved is to run on high speed to 1st base which is the base towards right field from the home plate.

The lack of adequate stop and go system is what lost this serious on the part of the Yanks. The final game of the serious was marked by the only incedence of brains exhibited by the Yanks during the whole serious.

In the second inning with two boys on the bases and one out, Joe Bush passed Arthur Nehf to 1st btse so as to get the head of the batting order up and not confuse the official scorers. This bit of thinking probably was responsible for nothing.

Those Boys From Detroit Must Have Their Sights

(Will not any dilate on the rest of the serious only to say that Charles A. Hughes and Eddie Batchelor of Detroit spent this a. m. at the Bronx zoo to try and see more animals. It is hard to satisfy the boys from Detroit.)

All as I know what to write about on a occasion like this kind is little incedence that come off. The 1st incedence that calls to mine is in regards to Tommy Rice of the Brooklyn eagle. Tommy wrote 7000 words in regards to the 1st game of the serious and page by page it blew out of the window in the costly apartment building in which Brooklyn experts lives. There is no telling what the loss to the world is on account of not being able to read Tommy's story to say nothing about the readers of the eagle.

Now, boys, I suppose they is a few interested in whether the little woman is going to get a costly fur coat. The only day I wrote a story to the general effects that we was going to kill our cats and use their fur to make the costly garment. This story was not appreciated in the heavily mortgaged home. After a long argument the master of the house compromised and decided to not to doom the little members of the finny tribe to death.

Instead of that we are going to use a idear furnished by the same Eddie Batchelor of Detroit mentioned a few thousands words ago. Eddie's idears is to start a chain letter to all our friends and readers asking them to look around the old homestead and find their family albumens and take the plush off of the covers and send it to the undersigned and make a plush coat which everybody tells me is the most fashionable fur on the green foot stool.

Harry Frazee's Life Story Nothing Much After All

The little woman can wear plush and a specially the red pigment but black and tan plush covers will be welcome and this man tells me they's nothing more attractive than a black and red and tan blocked coat made out of plush albumens.

I was going to say further in regards to the plush albumens, but Harry Frazee has just butted in with the story of his life. It seems like when Harry was a young man in Peoria his father said to him, if you don't be wild and go into the theatrical business and stay around Peoria you will be as big a man as your uncle. So Harry looked at his uncle, who was getting $125 per month staring at books.

"Well," says Harry. "I can get more than that catching runaway horses." So he is now catching runaway horses and selling them to the New York baseball club.

As I now sit here and write I am surrounded by a corpse of experts just as ignorant as me and they don't seem to be none of them able to tell who is going to pitch tomorrow. Personally, I think it will be Col. Ruppert and Huston.

HOYT AGAIN HAS A SLAP AT HUGGINS

His Desire to Pitch to Young Against Orders

BY WAITE HOYT

Hero of the 1921 World Series
Special Correspondent Universal Service
(Copyright, 1922, by Universal Service)

NEW YORK, Oct. 8.—The nightmare is over. The Giants are a better team than the Yankees—that's why we didn't win one game of the series. It's a bitter pill to swallow—it's brutal.

Joe Bush

I don't even want to talk about, but I want to review today's game briefly, especially that eighth inning.

Joe Bush was certainly in a hole when Young came to bat. Joe told me after the game that he was confident he could have disposed of Ross, but orders are orders in baseball or any other kind of business and when Huggins said pass him, there was nothing else for "Bullet" to do.

I know just how Joe felt, for I have been in that position many times. I think he lost confidence when Kelly faced him, so when Long George cracked out a single which brought in two runs I wasn't surprised.

WHO IS MASTER?

I am not criticizing Huggins. His judgment was probably right—but I want to tell you it's disheartening when you want to do one thing and have to do the other.

Throughout the series we have had good pitching. As a matter of fact the game I twirled in an ordinary series would have been a victory. The same goes for Mays and Bush. It was simply a case of "too much Giants." Little more can be said.

It cannot be denied that Babe Ruth was the series' biggest disappointment from our and the spectators' point of view. It was a case of the big Bam trying too hard, I think, and no one can deny that he tries hard every minute he is on the field. Ruth probably feels his slump during the series more than any one else.

DID NOT PLAY BEST GAME

As I said in my previous articles, we did not play the kind of ball during the series that we did when we won the pennant. I certainly thought that we would come out of our slump today, but we didn't, getting only five hits.

If we could play the series over again—but I guess we'll have to wait until next year for that. It's tough to have so much depending on such a short series.

Pipp's work during the series certainly stands out in bold relief. He hit often and timely and his fielding was faultless.

Ward's two homers furnished the biggest thrills. Aaron has played great ball all year and I look for him to be the sensation of the league next year.

Scott was not quite up to par, but he played a great game nevertheless. Dugan was all over the infield with his flashy fielding and he also hit well. Witt, Bob Meusel

(Continued on Page 12, Column 8)

Bush, Peeved, Lobbed Ball Kelly Hit

Yanks Deserved to Lose Series; Badly in Need of Firm Hand at Wheel

By Ed Sullivan

(Special Examiner Correspondent)

POLO GROUNDS, NEW YORK, Oct. 8.—A combination of beautiful left-handed pitching by Artie Nehf and ugly left-handed baseball by Miller Huggins' helpless Yankee champions aided and abetted by some horny-handed hitting by John McGraw's game Giants gave the National League champions a World Championship today in four straight wins.

Among the outstanding features of the Yankee playing was the usual world-beating stupidity on the bases, a difficulty in hitting during the pinches or otherwise and a fine sample of insubordination by Joe Bush. Bush may be the most successful pitcher in either league, but today he was no pitcher at all and his conduct on the field was all that it should not be, although the Yankees all energetically did what they could on occasion to kick victory in the chin.

Bush may be said to be the principal offender. On the extreme other net the Giants played up and up ball behind Nehf all the way and he turned in a sweet exhibition of pitching. He allowed but five hits, fanned two and passed three, while Bush permitted ten whistling hits, passed four and fanned three.

BOOT VICTORY

At no time during the innings which followed a grand Yankee opening was there great likelihood of the Giants winning and anything like championship plays would have kept the Yankees in the party, but, as it is their regular custom, they booted it away almost deliberately.

The Giants on the other hand went along in a smooth fashion, which has characterized their play from start to finish of this series. They were unperturbed by an early Yankee lead and did not lose confidence when that lead was re-established as late as the seventh inning, which is pretty late in any World Series contest. They proved themselves just what they have been in this series and throughout the tough finish of the National League scrap, a club with gameness as its principal asset.

The Yankees outgamed, outsmarted, out hit and outpitched, made a sorry showing as the final incident in a series of sorry showings. They had no right to this ball game; they had no right to this series. If ever a ball club showed the need of management, the Yanks did and nothing could more clearly demonstrate it than the antics of Bush in the Giants' big eighth inning. With Frisch and Meusel on third and second, Huggins signalled for him to walk

(Continued on Page 12, Column 6)

Who? What?

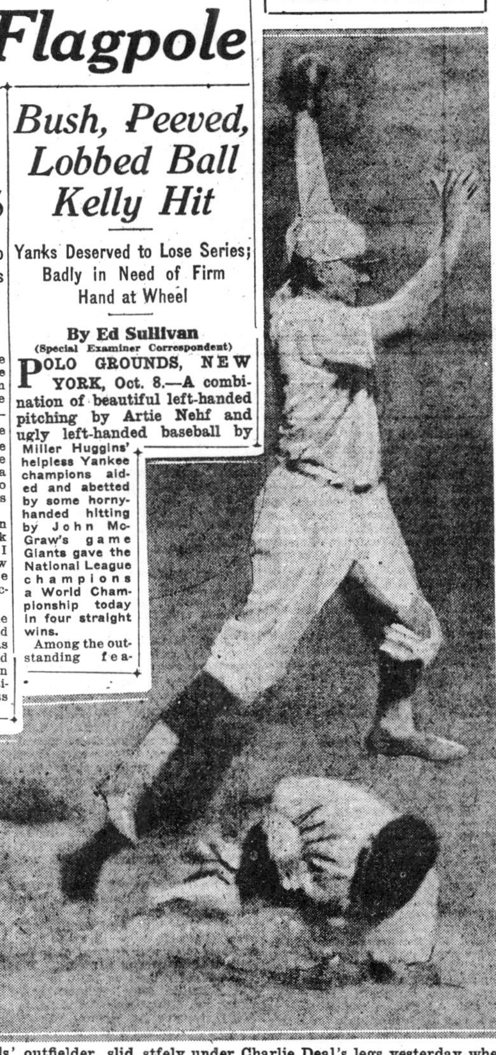

Joe "Chin-Chin" Kelly, Seals' outfielder, slid stfely under Charlie Deal's legs yesterday when McCabe threw high to nail him going from first to third on Kamm's single.—Examiner Photo.

New Record for Receipts Set by 1922 World's Series

Each Giant Receives $4451.57, While Every Yank Must Be Satisfied With $2967.71

NEW YORK, Oct. 8.—The fifth and last game of the World's Series today saw 38,551 fans paying their way in to see the Giants clinch the world's championship over the Yankees, and a new record for the classic in receipts. A total of $125,147 was taken in today.

This amount for paid attendance broke the record-making figures in the third game, Friday, when a total of $122,354 was taken in.

The advisory board received $18,772.05 of today's receipts. Each club received $21,274.99, and the players' share was $63,824.

As the receipts of the second game, which resulted in a ten-inning tie, were turned over to charities—a total of $120,544—the total players' share is for the first, third, fourth and fifth games.

This amount, $247,309.81, is divided as follows:

The Giants and Yankees receive 75 per cent of the players' share, which is divided 60 per cent to the winners, or $111,289.42, to the Giants, and 40 per cent to the losers, or $74,202.94, to the Yankees.

Figuring on 25 full shares for each club, each Giant will thus receive $4,451,57, while each Yankee on the basis of 25 full shares, will receive $2,967.71.

As the regular players vote as to the amounts allowed coaches, substitutes and players joining the team after the season opened, these divisions will come in for a change, but a general idea is provided as the amount to be given.

The Cincinnati Reds and St. Louis Browns, second teams in each league, will divide 15 per cent of the players' share, amounting to $37,096.47, and 10 per cent among the third teams, $24,730.98, to be divided between the Pirates and Cardinals, who tied in the National League, and the Detroit Tigers in the American League.

The total paid attendance was 185,651, and total receipts $605,471, exclusive of the tie game on the second day.

Torrance Ties Legion No. 8

ONE of the feature games in yesterday's schedule of the Southern California Managers' Association was played at Torrance when the American Legion Post 8, and the Torrance nine hooged up in a 12-inning battle. Bill Shackleton's legionaires took the fracas 2 to 1. Both Barnett and Bell went the full distance. The latter allowed but seven hits. Second Baseman McClain came through with three hits for the winners.

A few weeks ago these clubs played a seventeen inning tie game at Torrance.

POST 8, AMER. LEG.	AB	H	O	A	E	TORRANCE	AB	H	O	A	E
Bartlet,rf	5	1	1	0	0	Thmpsn,cf	5	1	2	0	0
Forbes,3b	5	2	2	3	0	B.McCn,2b	5	3	4	4	0
DiPorto,ss	5	0	1	1	1	Deal,1b..	5	1	14	1	0
Colter,c..	5	1	8	0	0	R.McLn,c.	5	1	9	2	1
Vogue,1b.	4	0	13	0	0	Bell,p....	4	0	0	2	1
Cully,lf...	5	0	4	0	0	Leonrd,ss	5	1	0	1	0
Sturm,2b	5	2	2	2	0	Loge,3b..	5	1	2	3	0
Walters,cf	5	1	5	4	0	Grant,lf..	4	1	3	0	0
Barnett,p	4	0	0	2	0	Hatzer,rf	5	1	2	0	0
Totals.	43	7	36	12	1	Totals.	43	10	36	13	2

Post 8, Amer. Leg. 0 0 0 1 0 0 0 0 0 0 0 1—2
Torrance .... 0 0 0 0 1 0 0 0 0 0 0 0—1

Firpo Kayoes Tracey in 4th

By Associated Press

BUENOS AIRES, Oct. 8.

LUIS ANGELO FIRPO, champion heavyweight of South America, this afternoon knocked out Jim Tracey, the Australian fighter, in the fourth round.

Shift Vernon Main Event

BY SOL PLEX

JIMMY CALLAHAN and Young Farrell have been matched for the main event at the Vernon arena tomorrow night to replace the Danny Kramer-Solly Seaman bout. Kramer has contracted a heavy cold and found it impossible to get in good shape for Tuesday.

Young Farrell

Callahan has had great success in the north and is expected to prove a sensation against any of the local four rounders. Jimmy has beaten Eddie Macy and Joe Lynch and boxed a draw with Tod Morgan in the last three weeks and declares he is now ready to clean up the best in the south.

* * *

BOBBY ALLEN and Jimmy Marcus, 145 pounders are slated for the semi-windup. Marcus can be depended on to do the heavy slugging, while Allen resorts to clever boxing at all times.

* * *

LOUIE STEGMEYER and Eddie Roberts are matched for the feature preliminary. Roberts has won his last three starts and is improving rapidly. Stegmeyer trounced Ernest Owens in a toe to toe battle last Tuesday.

Long George Kelly Last Game's Hero

His Single in Eighth Hands Giants 5 Victory; Four in a Row

By Damon Runyon

Special to The Los Angeles Examiner
Copyright, 1922, by Universal Service

POLO GROUNDS, New York, Oct. 8.—"Hello, Frisco, h... Put old Bill Lange, who was baseball's "Little Ev... auld lang syne, on the wire.

He will be pleased to hear these tid...

George Kelly

The world's series of 1922 is over. New York Giants are still champions of baseball world and old Bill's favorite nep... Long George Kelly, is the lad who finish... it up.

Long George "leaned" on one of "Bull... Joe" Bush's high-power shoots in the eig... inning of the last game today, much as "Litt... Eva" used to "lean" on the pitching of ... long ago.

Long George produced a single that drove in the tying and the winning runs, and blew up a billow of hats and torn paper all over the Polo Grounds as most of 38,000 persons expressed their emotions.

The final score of the game was 5 to 3, Giants getting another run on top of those made by Long George's hit. They won four out of the five games played, one being the famous tie, caused by an umpirical error.

There was a lot of fussing in the Yankee clubhouse after the game over that hit of Kelly's. Eavesdroppers heard angry voices seeping out of the chinks and one voice they claimed to identify as the voice of "Bullet Joe" Bush.

One could imagine small Miller Huggins, manager of the American Leaguers standing in the center of his players in the big room that always reeks with the odor of liniment and steaming human bodies, and defending his judgment in that eventful eighth.

Huggins on the Pan

Huggins ordered "Bullet Joe" Bush to pass Ross Young, the slugging Texan, with two men on second and third, with two out. Huggins thought long George Kelly would be easier game than Young, an opinion that in seven instances out of ten would probably be correct.

The crowd began filtering out of the yard when a young chap of mild demeanor came to the press stand unnoticed. Few recognized him.

"Gimme a match," he requested mildly. It was Johnny Rawlings, hero of the World's Series of 1921, who never got a chance to play in the World's Series of 1922, which made heroes of John Scott, the third, of the bottle legged Heinie Groh, of long George Kelley, and many others.

Not even old "Eppy," of the Harry Stevens forces, gathering up the empty bottles in the big stand and silently gloating, seemed to remember Johnny. Such is World Series fame.

What the Giants did to the Yanks is approximately what the Boston Braves did to the Philadelphia Athletics in 1914, when George Stallings and his supposedly rag-tag outfit swept through Connie Mack's mighty machine for four straight games.

The Yankees were the hot favorites in the betting when this series started, the odds being based on their pitching staff. In pitching and in everything else, however, the Giants had it on the American Leaguers. "Bullet" Joe Bush, a memory of the series of 1913, when he was with the Athletics and beat McGraw's Giants, pitched fairly well in spots today, but the Giants hit for ten safe blows. Meantime Arthur Nehf, the only left hander in the series, was holding the sluggers of the Yankees to five hits. Last year, in three games, Nehf was the hard luck pitcher of the series.

Babe Ruth, the highest priced baseball man, fell down in the series. The Giant pitchers pitched to him without fear and the big fellow could do no hitting. Outside of one base running lapse, Bob Meusel was the star of the Yankees, while Ward, who was not expected to do much hitting, made two home runs. Walter Pipp also played good ball for the American Leaguers.

"Bullet Joe" had pitched one ball at Young when he got his orders and he acted mightily displeased. He yelled something in to the bench. Orders are orders, however, and it is not a ball player's place to reason why.

So "Bullet Joe" tossed four balls at Young in such manner that there was no chance for Young to hit at them and this filled the bases with Giant runners. In the world's series last year, "Long" George struck out ten times. He almost busted his galluses swinging at the ball. He had fanned three times in the series this year and perhaps it was the memory of the air that misled Miller Huggins.

Bush pitched one ball to Long George, as the runners jockeyed along the base lines and the crowd bubbled and roared. On the next pitch Kelly smashed a single to center, and to all intents and purposes the game, and the world series was over.

The crowd boiled out into the damp field as Ross Young took the last ball of the series out of the air as it left Ward's bat and threw it into the stand.

The ball players ran off the scene rapidly and the excited fans could not catch up with them, but McGraw, now the holder of his third world's championship with a string of eight National League pennants fluttering behind him, walked leisurely out from the bench into the crowd.

Cheers for McGraw

He was in street dress, but the portly, gray-haired man who but a few years ago was a wispy looking, fiery tempered fellow, stormy petrel of baseball, was quickly recognized and surrounded. The crowd cheered him time and again, and it was some minutes before McGraw could get to the clubhouse.

Over at the third base, Henry Fabian, the old ground keeper of the Giants, proud as Punch, held forth to a big gathering of pop eyed fans after running up the tiny blue streamer on the center field pole that always means the Giants have won.

Under the grandstand, Colonel Tillinghast l'Hommedieu Huston vice president of the Yankees, held forth with sympathizing friends, the last survivor of the day of the American League contingent.

Some good guessers thought McGraw might send "Rosie" Ryan or Jonnard after this game in view of the fact that he held a three-game jump on the Yanks, but Mac led with his left-handed ace, showing that he wanted to get it over.

A stout little shower was falling as Whitey Witt faced Nehf. The

(Continued on Page 12, Column 3)

Giants 5, Yanks 3

FIFTH GAME

YANKEES.	AB	R	H	O	A	E
Witt, cf.	2	0	0	0	0	0
McMillan, cf.	2	0	0	1	0	0
Dugan, 3b.	3	1	1	0	1	0
Ruth, rf.	3	0	0	2	0	0
Pipp, 1b.	4	0	1	8	0	0
R. Meusel, lf.	4	1	1	0	0	0
Schang, c.	3	0	0	4	0	0
Ward, 2b.	2	1	0	3	1	0
Scott, ss.	2	0	1	5	5	0
Bush, p.	3	0	1	1	3	0
Totals	28	3	5	24	10	0
GIANTS.	**AB**	**R**	**H**	**O**	**A**	**E**
Bancroft, ss.	4	0	0	2	5	0
Groh, 3b.	4	0	2	1	3	0
Frisch, 2b.	4	1	2	2	4	0
E. Meusel, lf.	4	2	1	1	0	0
Young, rf.	2	2	0	2	1	0
Kelly, 1b.	3	0	2	14	0	0
Cunningham, cf.	2	0	1	2	0	0
King, c.	1	0	1	0	0	0
Snyder, c.	4	0	1	3	3	0
Nehf, p.	1	0	0	0	2	0
Earl Smith	1	0	0	0	0	0
Totals	30	5	10	27	18	0

McMillan batted for Witt in fifth.
Earl Smith batted for Cunningham in seventh.

By Innings:

Yankees .... 1 0 0 0 1 0 1 0 0—3
Giants ...... 0 2 0 0 0 0 0 3 x—5

Two-base hit: Frisch. Sacrifice hits: Ruth, Scott, Kelley, Schang. Double plays: Bush to Scott to Pipp (2); Ward to Scott to Pipp. Base on balls: Of Bush, 4 (Young 2, Nehf 2); off Nehf, 2 (Ward 2). Struck out: By Bush, 3 (Groh, Earl Smith, Snyder); by Nehf, 3 (Ruth, R. Meusel and Schang). Wild pitch: Nehf, 1. Hit by pitched ball: By Nehf, 1 (Dugan). Left on bases: Yankees, 4; Giants, 6. Umpires: Klem (National umpire-in-chief), at plate; Hildebrand (American), at first base; McCormick (National), at second base; Owens (American), at third base. Time—2:01.

Baseball, Golf, Tennis, Turf, Track, Boxing, Wrestling—all expertly reported by expert reporters, Best in the West.

CHARACTER · QUALITY · AMERICA FIRST · ACCURACY · ENTERPRISE

Los Angeles Examiner Sports

AN AMERICAN PAPER FOR THE AMERICAN PEOPLE · THE GREAT NEWSPAPER OF THE GREAT SOUTHWEST

The Examiner carries the most complete Sporting Section of any newspaper West of Chicago.

THURSDAY, APRIL 19, 1923 · SECTION III—PAGE 1

74,200 SEE RUTH SMASH FIRST HOMER

Yanks Beat Red Sox; Dodgers Cop in Ninth

Greatest Ball Crowd in History Sees Chance Lose, 4-1

By Thomas L. Cummiskey
Universal Service Sports Editor

NEW YORK, April 18.—Seventy-four thousand, two hundred persons saw Babe Ruth hit a home run that won the opening game for the Yankees from the Boston Red Sox today at the dedication of the gigantic new Yankee Stadium.

The score was 4 to 1. Babe's homer came with two on base in the fourth inning, and went like a shot from a rifle into the right field bleachers.

The sensation of that hit, working on the emotions of far and away the biggest crowd baseball has ever known, was something well nigh indescribable. The game's greatest figure came into his own at the psychological moment. A genius in drama could not have thought of anything more thrilling. It was stupendous, tremendous, moved past compare, that homer, and the spectacle it cast into being.

A fat book of colorful adjectives, used with little or no discretion, could be rapped out on typewriters and still fail to portray in any omprehensive degree the wonder f it all. Baseball reached its zenith thrills when the Babe got that llop. In unison the 74,000 arose heer, to shout, to give a demonation hysterical in its aspects.

RAMATIC DEDICATION

Truly, the Yankee Stadium, $3,000,000 edifice in baseball in the greatest city in the world, was dedicated in a manner beyond the fondest dreams of Colonels Ruppert and Huston, the owners, the "gambling colonels." Some sages have said: "Baseball is in its infancy," but today they must have been wrong. Today baseball came into a glorious manhood.

The fourth inning:

Aaron Ward, first up, got the Yankees' first hit in the Stadium, and Everett Scott sacrificed him to second. Bob Shawkey, honored in pitching the opening game, hit to Pitcher Ehmke of the Sox, and Ward was trapped between second and third, but delayed his demise long enough for Shawkey to reach second.

"Whitey" Witt got a pass. Joe Dugan dropped a short fly safe in center and Shawkey scored, while Witt scurried to third. Then, up came Babe Ruth, the Sultan of Swat, the Bambino, the Monarch of Maul.

LIKE RIFLE BULLET

It was his second appearance at the plate. The first time, in the opening inning, he had flied to right, with no one on. Now was his chance, the crowd told him, long and loud, as if the Babe didn't know it. He fouled one. He fouled another, strike two. Two balls came over, the Babe looking them over. Then he socked it, viciously, vengefully, with a herculean follow-through swing. On the line the pellet shot, not more than thirty feet from the ground, into the right field bleachers.

Witt, Dugan and the Babe paraded the bases, while the crowd was lost to sanity in its enthusiasm. Babe jogged around, his homely face in smiles, until he reached the plate. There he took off his cap, uplifted his face to the towering stands and bowed. He lifted his cap, he smiled from ear to ear.

TICKLED TO DEATH

The Babe had made his homer, the earliest he has ever made in a big league season, and there was none more thrilled, more joyoue than he. As he tarried briefly at the plate, he was the greatest hero baseball has known, with the most tremendous adultation a player has known. It was a demonstration deserved, and whole-heartedly given.

Except for this inning, the game was rather listless. That fourth inning was largely to blame. Nothing thereafter could have at all approached it. The poor Red Sox, fighting valiently under a fighting leader, Frank Chance, got a run in the seventh. It came on a pass to Harris and a triple by McMillan, ex-Yankee. Otherwise, he had the Sox at his mercy, got brilliant fielding and Ehmke performed strongly for the visitors.

CROWD BREAKS RECORDS

The biggest crowd before today was in Boston, in 1917, in a world's series game between the great Red Sox of that day.

Sox of that day. It was approximately 42,000.

The 90,000 that saw Jack Dempsey knock out Georges Carpentier and the 77,000 that attended a Yale-Harvard football game are the only sport crowds that have surpassed today's vast throng in this country.

Today's crowds in colorful aspects and demonstration can only be likened to the throngs we read about in ancient history—the throngs of the Coliseum of Rome. They say it was of 350,000 capacity. They must have made some noise. Yet it is hard to think they rivaled the 75,000 of today.

Judge Landis, Gov. Smith, Col.

(Continued on Page 3, Column 3)

Williams and Heilman Also Get 1st Homers

ST. LOUIS, April 18.

KEN WILLIAMS of the Browns hit a circuit drive in the seventh inning of today's opening game with Detroit. Francis was pitching for the Tigers. No one was on base. Williams lead the American League in homers last year.

Ken Williams

ST. LOUIS, April 18.—Rightfielder Heilman of Detroit knocked a homer in the sixth inning of today's game with the Browns, driving in Cobb ahead of him. Danforth was pitching for the locals.

Wilshire Golf Team Humbles Los Angeles, 3-2

CAPT. GEORGE CLINE of the Wilshire Country Club golf team yesterday led his followers out to the Los Angeles Country Club and defeated Major Karnes and the Los Angeles golfers, 3 to 2, in one of the best contested interclub matches of the season. This was the first match of the year in which Cline played and he celebrated his return to tournament ranks by shooting the last nine of the North Course in 34. He and Frank Deleot defeated Harley Moore and E. K. Brown, 3 and 1.

The feature match of the day at Los Angeles was that in which Norman Macbeth and Elmer Ralphs defeated A. D. S. Johnston and Everett Seaver, 2 and 1. In accomplishing this Macbeth turned in a card of 69 for the eighteen holes.

Annandale defeated Midwick, 3 to 2, at Midwick in an interclub match that was replete with thrills. Scotty Armstrong and Les Gordon of Midwick won a marathon match from Dr. Paul Hunter and H. B. Ingalls of Annandale, defeating that distinguished duo 1 up on the twentieth hole.

Annandale, 3; Midwick, 2.
E. S. Armstrong and L. S. Gordon (M.) defeated Dr. Paul Hunter and H. B. Ingalls, 1 up, 20 holes.
W. P. Herbert and J. L. Mothershead (M.) defeated C. M. Ransome and C. P. Erdman, 4 and 3.
Nate Mears and Frank Chaffee (A.) defeated W. B. Tait and C. G. Lathrop (M.), 6 and 5.
Bob Finkbine and W. J. Bowman (A.) defeated S. C. Fertig and A. F. Halstead (M.), 4 and 3.
R. M. Modisette and L. Barnes (A.) defeated J. S. Cravens and H. Coppell (M.), 3 and 2.
Wilshire, 3; Los Angeles, 2.
Norman Macbeth and E. Ralphs (W.) defeated A. D. S. Johnston and E. H. Seaver (L. A.), 2 and 1.
W. D. Whelan and M. E. McLoughlin (W.), defeated C. H. Palmer and Frank Tatum (L. A.), 2 up.
George Thomas and H. T. Major (L. A.) defeated Pat Higgins and Dr. H. C. Humes (W.), 2 and 1.
J. T. Gilmer and W. H. Spinks (L. A.) defeated W. G. Nevin and J. C. Hodge (W.), 6 and 5.
George Cline and Frank Deleot (W.) defeated E. K. Brown and H. A. Moore (L. A.), 3 and 1.

Gastine Draws With Don Davis

SAN DIEGO, April 18.—Henry Gastine of Los Angeles and Don Davis of San Diego drew in the main event at Dreamland tonight after four hard-fought rounds.

Frisco Lewis knocked out Joe Chaney of Los Angeles in the third.

Al Shapiro won from Kid Sweeney.

Sammy Sandos, Navy, drew with Packy McMullin of Los Angeles.

Billy Wilson, Navy, knocked out Charley Gall of San Diego in the third round.

Murphy, 2-Miler, Lost to Cards in Bears' Meet

STANFORD UNIVERSITY, Cal., April 18.

PAUL MURPHY, Stanford's crack two-miler, was ruled ineligible here today to participate in next Saturday's track and field meet with the University of California.

The decision, under the conference rules, is based on the fact that Murphy has not put in a sufficient number of hours in study according to the announcement of the scholarship committee.

Murphy has covered the eight laps in 10:7, but it was figured that he would come close to Hayes' time of 9:53. in competition next Saturday.

Stanford had figured on him for sure place points.

Cubs Even Series With Pirates; Score, 7 to 2

BROOKLYN, April 18.—The Brooklyn Dodgers staged a riotous ninth inning today to beat out the Phillies, 6 to 5. The visitors apparently had sewed up the game in the ninth when Sand boosted a homer over the wall, driving in Walker to make the score 5 to 1. Wheat greeted Ralph Head, who had held the Dodgers to three hits in eight innings, with a circuit swat over the right field wall. Schleibner singled and Barber walked. Hubbell relieved Head and after passing Reuther and allowing DeBerry a hit, was sent to the showers. Meadows then passed Grimes and Olson's single won the game without a Dodger being retired in the inning.

Giants Win Again

BOSTON, April 18.—Long hits off Watson and Oeschger enabled the world champion Giants to beat Boston, 7 to 4, today. Scott was given brilliant support and his home run to right center in the fourth also scored Snyder. When Scott walked Gowdy in the last of the ninth, Barnes relieved him. Bagwell hit the left field wall on the fly, getting only a double for this unprecedented feat.

Cubs Square Series

CHICAGO, April 18.—Boehler weakened in the eighth inning and Chicago pounded out six hits, including two doubles and a triple, broke a tie score and defeated Pittsburg 7 to 2 in the second game of the series. Johnny Kelleher of Chicago knocked the ball into the newly erected left bleachers for a home run, the first in the new park. Grimm of Pittsburg duplicated the feat a little later. Alexander pitched in fine form.

Toney Beats Reds

CINCINNATI, O., April 18.—Fred Toney outpitched Rixey in the second game of the season here today and St. Louis evened up the series by beating Cincinnati, 4 to 2.

Rixey was wild and was hit safely in every inning, but one. Mann made the first home run of the local season on a long drive to right center inside the grounds in the third inning. Score:

Buick Sets Up 108-Mile Record

OVER the bed of Roger's dry lake, a remarkable natural race course in the Mojave desert, one mile from Murock, Joe Nikrent, veteran race driver on Tuesday made a straightaway record of better than 108 miles an hour with a Buick Special Six from the Howard Automobile Company, over a measured mile.

The speed test was made under the sanction of the A. A. A. and was supervised by officials of that body. Fred J. Wagner handled the flags and Val Haresnape and Hal Weller did the timing with the official electric timing device.

Three trials were made to a flying start. The first resulted in a score of 33.49 seconds, an average of 107.48 miles per hour. The second dash with the motor well warmed up was done in 33.26 seconds making the remarkable record for a car said to be 90 per cent stock of 108.24 miles per hour. The [illegible]st trial developed a speed of 33.3[illegible] r the mile, an average of 108 per [illegible]our.

Plan Veteran Golfers Union

CHICAGO, April 18.—(By The Associated Press.)—Tentative plans were made today for the formation of a National golf association of players more than fifty years old, and recommendations were made for a meeting, to be held in Chicago within a couple weeks, to formulate plans for the organization.

It was suggested that the body be known as Seniors' Golf Association and that State bodies be created, so that there eventually would be forty-eight regional associations, which would hold annual tournaments. The champions of these State organizations would then meet in a National championship for men past the half century milestone.

It was recommended that the senior golfers be divided by periods of five years in age, so that all those between 50 and 55 years old would constitute one class and the succeeding classes would range in age from 55 to 60 and so on to the Octogenarians.

Veteran New York Fight Manager Reported Dying

CHICAGO, April 18.—Charley Harvey of New York, pioneer manager of boxers, was reported to be dying in a hospital here tonight as the result of an automobile accident today in which three others were injured. He suffered a triangular fracture of the skull over the left eye and has not gained consciousness.

Babe's No.1

Babe Ruth

BASEBALL RESULTS STANDINGS SCHEDULES

Coast League Standing

	W.	L.	Pct.	If Win	If Lose
San Francisco..	9	5	.643	.667	.600
Sacramento	8	5	.615	.643	.578
VERNON	7	5	.583	.615	.538
Salt Lake City	7	5	.583	.615	.538
Portland	6	8	.429	.467	.400
LOS ANGELES.	5	7	.417	.462	.385
Seattle	5	7	.417	.462	.385
Oakland	4	9	.308	.357	.286

YESTERDAY'S RESULTS

Sacramento, 6; Oakland 4.
San Francisco, 4; Portland 1.
Seattle, 1; LOS ANGELES, 0.
VERNON and Salt Lake, rain.

GAMES TODAY

Salt Lake at VERNON.
Sacramento at Oakland.
LOS ANGELES at Seattle.
San Francisco at Portland.

American Legaue

	W.	L.	Pct.		W.	L.	Pct.
New York	1	0	1.000	Boston..	0	1	.000
Philadl..	1	0	1.000	Wash'ngtn	0	1	.000
Clv'land.	1	0	1.000	Chicago..	0	1	.000
Detroit..	1	0	1.000	St. Louis	0	1	.000

YESTERDAY'S RESULTS

New York, 4; Boston, 1.
Philadelphia, 3; Washington, 1.
Cleveland, 6; Chicago, 5.
Detroit, 9; St. Louis, 6.

TODAY'S GAMES

Chicago at Cleveland.
Detroit at St. Louis.
Washington at Philadelphia.
Boston at New York.

National League

	W	L	Pct.		W	L	Pct.
New York	2	0	1.000	St. Louis	1	1	.500
Brooklyn.	1	0	1.000	Chicago..	1	1	.500
Cincinnati	1	1	.500	Philadel..	0	1	.000
Pittsburg.	1	1	.500	Boston...	0	2	.000

YESTERDAY'S RESULTS

Brooklyn, 6; Philadelphia, 5.
New York, 7; Boston, 4.
Chicago, 7; Pittsburg, 2.
St. Louis, 4; Cincinnati, 2.

TODAY'S GAMES

New York at Boston (2 games).
Philadelphia at Broklyn.
Pittsburg at Chicago.

Western League

	W.	L.	Pct.		W.	L.	Pct.
Wichita..	6	0	1.000	Sioux City	2	4	.333
Okl. City.	5	1	.833	Omaha...	2	5	.286
Tulsa.....	5	2	.714	D. Moines	1	5	.167
St. Joe..	4	2	.667	Denver...	0	6	.000

YESTERDAY'S RESULTS

Wichita, 9; Omaha, 3.
Sioux City, 8; Oklahoma City, 5.
St. Joseph, 11; Denver, 2.
Tulsa, 17; Des Moines, 7.

Minnesota House Kills Small Town Boxing Bill

ST. PAUL, April 18.—The Minnesota House tonight killed the Senate bill which would have permitted boxing in cities of the second, third and fourth class when ten members objected to its consideration. Boxing is permitted in Minneapolis, St. Paul and Duluth.

American Ass'n Opens Up Today

By Associated Press
CHICAGO, April 18.

FACING the brightest prospects in its twenty-one years of unbroken campaigning, the American Association will open its season tomorrow with Columbus playing at Toledo, Louisville at Indianapolis, Minneapolis at Milwaukee and St. Paul at Kansas City.

Southern Golfers Win; Angels Shut Out, 1-0

Miss Cameron and Miss Kavanagh Take Matches

SAN FRANCISCO, April 18.—The women golfers claim to have fixed the "weather man" and Old Sol was on the job, smiling his brightest. So that's that.

Mrs. Brent Potter shocked the "talent" by defeating Mrs. Robert A. Roos in the second round of the State championship on the Ingleside links by a margin of two and one.

Despite her impressive victory over Mrs. Albert B. Swinerton on Tuesday, the San Jose and Lincoln Park player was conceded little chance to defeat the Beresford golfer, who has always made such a good showing in representative events. But a golfer who can win a match on the long eighteenth with a five as Mrs. Potter did against Mrs. Swinerton must not be overlooked.

It was a thrilling match from the start and there was never more than two holes margin separating the two players. Both of them played daring and sporty golf, taking chances when necessary despite the high wind that prevailed. And Mrs. Roos is no "wind player" as has been demonstrated on several occasions.

WEARIES OPPONENT

They were all square at the turn, but the local player gradually wore down her opponent to the dormy stage and all Mrs. Roos could do on the seventeenth was to earn a half. The approaches to the sixteenth green would have done justice to any man golfer.

Miss Doreen Kavanagh, title holder, and Miss Margaret Cameron, challenger, the representatives from Southern California, emerged successfully in the semi-final round, but the State champion looked to have quite a battle on her hands in the early stages of the match.

As a matter of fact, Mrs. Charles F. Ford of Claremont held her to an even basis to the turn and a crowd gather to witness a close finish. But the end was surprisingly near, as Miss Doreen commenced one of her streaks of putting and took the next five holes in succession. The twelfth was surely stolen by the Los Angeles player after it looked as though Mrs. Ford had the edge.

MISS HANCHETT LOSES

Mrs. W. C. Van Antwerp had a walkover from Miss Alice Hanchett, who was expected to give her a much closer argument. But there was no denyin the Burlingame player today, and six and five just about represents the difference between the two golfers on the day's play.

Mrs. Van Antwerp was sinking her putts persistently. She averaged two less than par on the greens played.

Miss Margaret Cameron was not caught napping by Mrs. H. A. Prole today and was in excellent form, winning in easy fashion.

Miss Mildred Landreth defeated Mrs. Herbert Schmidt in the second flight.

CHAMPIONSHIP FLIGHT

Miss Doreen Kavanagh defeated Mrs. C. Ford, 5 and 4.
Mrs. W. C. Van Antwerp defeated Miss Alice Hanchett, 6 and 5.
Mrs. Brent Potter defeated Mrs. Robert A. Roos, 2 and 1.
Miss Margaret Caremon defeated Mrs. H. A. Prole, 7 and 6.

English Fight Title to Yank

LONDON, April 18.—(By the Associated Press.)—Edward P. Eagan, the American student at Oxford, who holds the Olympic light heavyweight boxing championship, tonight defeated F. J. Hulks of St. Pancras, in the third round at Alexander Palace, thus winning the boxing association heavyweight championship.

Eagan trained for the bout in Dublin, acting as sparring partner for Mike McTigue. Tonight was the thirty-ninth time the championship had been contested and Eagan is the first American to win it.

Eagan competed also in the light heavyweight class, but was beaten on points in this event by H. J. Mitchell, holder of the title.

Man Falls, Badly Hurt, at Seals-Beavers Game

PORTLAND, Ore., April 18.—Falling in some unexplained manner from the grandstand of Recreation Park, where a game was in progress this afternoon between the Portland and San Francisco clubs of the Pacific Coast Baseball League, Louis E. Geer, a Portland postal clerk, struck upon his head on a cement approach outside the gate and suffered injuries which a doctor summoned from the crowd feared might prove fatal.

Geer was hastened to a hospital. The game was not interrupted.

ASTORIA REGATTA AGAIN

ASTORIA, Ore., April 18.—The rejuvenation of the old Astoria regatta, which for many years was among the leading water carnivals on the Pacific Coast, is being planned and committees have been named to arrange for the feature next August.

Chance Gets Excited When Season Opens

NEW YORK, April 18.

FRANK CHANCE, once peerless leader of the old Chicago Cubs, sat among his Red Sox in the visitors' dugout at the Yankee stadium today trembling like an oak leaf in the late fall.

Frank Chance

"What's the matter, boss, cold?" asked "Chick" Fewster, the Red Sox shortstop.

"Cold, nothing," smiled Chance. "Excited, like a fish that's been hauled out on a river bank, then thrown back into the stream."

Tennessee Nine Nosed Out by New Mexico, 4-3

THE U. S. S. NEW MEXICO ball team downed the Tennessee nine, 4 to 3, in the feature attraction of Pacific Fleet baseball yesterday afternoon at San Pedro. The hitting of Peckerick for the winners and the hurling of Jacoby for the Rebel Ship featured the day.

In the second game of the afternoon the U. S. S. California nosed out the U. S. S. Idaho, 4 to 2. Sailor Arrow Smith, the Prune Barge's new backstop, showed up in great style, both behind the plate and at bat. The fielding of Pat Phelan of the winners also featured.

The Pennsylvania walloped the U. S. S. Arizona, 13 to 6, in the third game at the Athletic Field. The contest was slowed up by poor fielding on the part of the losers.

The Lone Star State ship, Texas, defeated the Oklahoma, 6 to 1. Hinson pitched excellent ball for the losers, striking our 14 opposing batsmen, but was given poor support by his teammates.

The scores:

New Mexico	4	9	2
Tennessee	3	7	1

Langley and Davis; Jacoby and Morganroth.

California	4	5	2
Idaho	2	6	3

Hanlon and Arrowsmith; Smith and Correlia.

Pennsylvania	13	7	1
Arizona	6	6	2

Colburn and Kingsley; Fletcher and Lewis.

Texas	6	10	2
Oklahoma	1	5	6

Miller and Kelly; Hinson and Suflick.

Ad Wolgast, or Double, Is Dead

PEORIA, Ill., April 18.—While Ad Wolgast is claimed to be alive in Los Angeles, death last night of "Ed" Wolgast at the State Insane Asylum brings to light one of the greatest cases of similarity on record.

Frances Wolgast, a sister of Ad, telephoned from Cadillac, Mich., tonight inquiring about the dead man and furnished a complete description of her brother. This had a broken nose, a scar on one of his legs, and had a broken arm. So had this man. Ad had a scar from an operation for appendicitis and so had this man. Both are the same age, same weight and same height. Ad never had "cauliflower ears" neither has this man. The dead man was taken into the asylum about three months ago. Little is known of him. He has the appearance of having been a prize fighter. The body is being held.

Anzacs Out of Davis Cup Play; Net Minus 2 Stars

By Associated Press
MELBOURNE, Australia, April 18.

AUSTRALIA will not participate in the Davis cup lawn tennis competition ths year, it has been decided, owing to the inability of Gerald L. Patterson and Pat O'Hara Wood, members of last year's team, to go to Honolulu for the initial test with Hawaii.

HONOLULU, April 18.—(By Associated Press.)—A. L. Castle, president of the Hawaii Tennis Association, today said that in the event Australia defaults with Hawaii in the Davis cup match play, the Hawaiian team would go to the mainland to play the winner of the Canada-Japan match.

Yaryan Smashes Out Home Run for Victory

By Mark Kelly

SEATTLE, April 18.—Smack! It sounded like that, did Yama Yaryan's home run into the water-soaked bleachers. It came about in the ninth inning of an air-tight game of ball, and it brought to a spectacular close the interesting opener between Seattle and Los Angeles. It gave a rosy finish to what started out as a duel, drab afternoon, and it gave Seattle victory in the first opening day engagement that this city has won since it advent into the Coast League.

It wasn't much of an opening, if you consider the crowd and the weather. The crowd was about seven thousand—about half of the throng that would have checked through the turnstiles had it been fair. And the weather was awful. But the ball game was the neatest opening day contest the Queen City has ever ben privileged to game upon. And the swet part of it is, the tribe won.

Today when Harry Gardner and Tom Hughes, the rival slabsters squared away for their duel it was raining hard. For three and one half scoreless innings the clubs played. Umpire Jimmy Toman finally called a halt to wipe the rain drops from his red neck and change his dripping socks. After a fifteen minute wait, Old Sol, just three hours late, came out in all his glory and the clubs knuckled down to an exhibition of very fancy baseball.

As has ben stated, Yam Yaryan won it; won it in such a sudden and unexpected manner that it was a full five seconds before the fans realized the meaning of Yam's wallop. The score was nothing-all, as the broad shouldered catcher ankled to the plate in the ninth.

A young right hander named Hanna and Harry Gardner were treating the crowd to a neat exhibition of pitching. Well nigh perfect defense work by the opposing forces had blocked what few chances there were for scores. That's how things stood when Yaryan cleaned the mud from his cleaks, pounded his bat on the log and faced the pitcher.

Smack! The first ball pitched was met squarely by Yam's club and it whistled straight and fair halfway up in the left fiend bleachers. It was a real home run. It broke up the party right there and it sen tthe customers home to their cold suppers quite contented and satisfied with their ball club.

Two bits of fielding by Red Baldwin, Wolverton's sensational young third sacker, and by Golvin, the Los Angeles first baseman, ranked as exceptional plays. Both were turned into double plays and Golvin's in particular was as pretty a bit of fielding as one would see in a long spell. The Angel infielder dashed headlong, scooping Billy Orr's bunt as it was about to settle onto the grass and doubled Eldred at first. A truly great play it was.

GARDNER WEAKENS

Gardner had easy sailing until the sixth, when he began to weaken a trifle. McAuley and Daly both singled in the seventh, after two were down and Harry threw one wild to Hanna, McAuley and Daly advancing. But the crafty Gardner struck out the pitcher and saved himself much trouble.

The Tribe was in position to score in the same inning. Gardner walked. Lane hit the first ball. Johnson drove a single past third base. Rohwer waited until there was three and two on him, and then lifted one to center.

More trouble for Harry in the eighth, some poor base running on the part of Twombly robbing the Angels of a golden opportunity.

The eighth inning saw Golvin's great play. Eldred, first up, had singled and Orr's sacrifice attempt looked like a success until Golvin pulled a "Houdini" and converted it into a double play. Janvrin beat out a scratchy hit in the same inning, but Baldwin's hard bounder was flagged by Charley Deal at third, who forced the runner at second.

And the next incident worth mentioning was Mr. Yaryan.

LOS ANGELES	AB	H	O	A	E	SEATTLE	AB	H	O	A	E
Twmby,rf	4	2	0	0	0	Lane,lf..	3	0	1	0	1
McCabe,lf	3	1	4	0	0	Jhnton,1b	4	2	13	0	0
Deal,3b..	4	1	1	1	0	Rohwer,rf	4	1	0	0	0
Griggs,1b	1	0	2	0	0	Eldred,cf	4	2	2	0	0
Hood,cf..	4	0	2	0	0	Orr,ss...	4	0	1	6	0
Krug,2b.	3	0	3	1	0	Jnvrin,2b.	4	1	4	6	0
McAly,ss.	3	1	1	1	0	Bldwin,3b	4	1	2	8	0
Daly,c...	4	2	8	1	0	Yaryan,c.	4	2	3	1	0
Hughes,p	1	0	0	0	0	Gardner,p	2	1	1	1	0
Hanna,p..	3	0	0	1	0						
Golvin,1b	2	0	3	1	0						
Totals	32	7	*24	6	0	Totals	33	11	27	17	1

*None out when winning run scored.

Los Angeles ...	0	0	0	0	0	0	0	0	0	—0
Hits	0	0	0	0	0	1	2	3	1	—7
Seattle	0	0	0	0	0	0	0	0	1	—1
Hits	2	3	0	0	2	0	1	2	1	—11

Innings pitched—By Hughes, 2. Home run—Yaryan. Bases on balls—Off Hughes, 1; Hanna, 1; Gardner, 4. Struck out—By Hughes, 3; Hanna, 4; Gardner, 4. Double plays—Baldwin to Johnston; Golvin to Krug. Runs responsible for—Hanna, 1. Charge defeat to Hanna. Wild pitches—Gardner, Hanna. Time—2:05. Umpires—Toman and Becker.

INDOOR BALL GAMES START

REDLANDS, April 18.—Teams representing Notchers' clubs of the Methodist, Baptist, Christian, Presbyterian and Yucaipa churches will compete in an indoor baseball league, games starting this week and continuing to May 24. The games will be at the Y. M. C. A. gymnasium.

Willie Kamm

This Coast League youngster, for whom the Chicago White Sox paid $100,000, made his major league debut yesterday fielding, cleaning two balls for assists and smashing out a two-base hit. Below we have an International Newsreel actiongraph of this stellar third-sacker.

Sudden Returns to Card Track

STANFORD UNIVERSITY, Cal., April 18.—Eddie Sudden, star track man and winner for Stanford of the 100 and 220-yard dashes in the California Stanford University track meet last year, registered at the University today. His registration fee has not yet been paid, but it is anticipated the fee will be paid tomorrow.

ankees Lose Series to the Red Sox, Going Down to Defeat in Final Game at Boston, 5 to 3

rray Outpitches Joe Bush, Holding Hugmen to Five Hits

ner Yankee Hurler Is Invincible After Opening Inning; Reichle Comes Through With Timely Hit That Drives in Two Tallies in the Fifth

By John Kieran

OSTON, April 28.—Under threatening skies and before a holiday of only seven thousand more or less hardy citizens wrapped in , the Red Sox defeated the Yankees at Fenway Park here to-day score of 5 to 3. "Smiler" Murray, the Southern collegian, who was om the varsity to the scrubs during a winter trade for Pennock, fair and square decision over none other than "Bullet Joe" Bush. ox thereby took the honors in the short series, two games to one.

e start it seemed that Murray omed to suffer defeat through dness. The Hugmen scored a tallies in the first inning when threw the ball everywhere but e plate, and Nemo Leibold con- d a two-base error in the out- After that the "Smiler" was in- . He permitted only five hits , and the final Yankee tally in hth. was allowed to drift over te, while the Bostonians cut off of further damage.

ing a two-run lead to Joe Bush rly considered as equivalent to g up one complete game for the clan. It was not so to-day, and hangs a sad tale. Bullet Joe no less than eight of the enemy d them to the same number of it for once the Hubtown team d the hits when they could do t damage. Up until to-day they own more ability in bringing rrors at such times. Two bad , the fifth and seventh, brought d tribulation on the head of Sir The Sox gathered all their these stanzas. However, there ankee alibi for the game, Mur- played the New York fast ball nd earned the decision.

Yanks Off to Lead

Hugmen popped away to a two- d in the opening stanza, through 's wildness and a devastating y Nemo Leibold in center field. Witt had grounded out Dugan walk and Ruth persuaded Brick that Murray had grazed his arm lose ball. Wally Pipp lined a to center which Leibold allowed through him to the fence while nd Dugan tallied. The Red Sox ontent to take the goose eggs out by Joe Bush until the fifth, hey pounded the Bullet person errily and took the lead at 3 to k Fewster started the attack on mer playmate with a double to icinich walked and Murray sac- the runners up a peg. Leibold noved to permit Dick Reichle to it for him. The rookie pinched style. His double sent two runs e pan and he scored the third hen Harris smote the ball safely t.

Fenway Fusileers added two n the seventh. Shano Collins d one off the left center wall air of bases and Joe Bush mas- Harris on the top of the head pitched ball. A double steal y a short passed ball, put the s where they could score when l Shanks singled sharply to

inal tally for the Hugmen came eighth on singles by Pipp and and Schang's infield out on Pipp was allowed to saunter the pan. Elmer Smith and Har- endrick were inserted as pinch for Scott and Bush in the ninth, rray found them apple pie for He got three men out on four balls.

Briefs

Bambino drove a soaring ball e right field bleachers in prac- nd sent Fewster and Picinich reboard. The crowd of two men boy applauded vigorously.

track was so heavy from the g rain that the ball took on the ance and resiliency of a soggy after minutes of skidding over ss and mud.

k Fewster has been playing a ful game afield for the Red Sox y young season. Even Miller s, who traded him, has com- on it. "That boy may fool ody yet," said Hug, "And I hope ."

e first inning Ruth put in a hat "Smiler" Murray had nicked th a ball inside. He got away , too, and Brick Owens permit- n to trot down to first as the ave him the raspberry chorus.

Yanks filled the bases with no- ut in the third, but Murray set own without a run. He fanned eusel and made Schang tap into double play.

k Chance turned up an ace he sent Reichle in to bat for Leibold in the fifth. The rookie ler doubled down the first base nd sent Fewster and Picnich o tie the score.

y Frazee was disconsolate over ather that spoiled the expected crowd. "Tell me not the ul numbers," he murmured to Graver as the Beau Brummel of ries came in with the turnstile

score:

ON (A.L.)	ab	r	h	po	a	e	NEW YORK (A.L.)	ab	r	h	po	a	e
cf..	2	0	0	0	0	1	Witt, cf.....	4	0	0	0	0	0
cf..	2	1	1	1	0	0	Dugan, 3b...	3	1	1	0	1	0
rf..	3	1	1	2	0	0	Ruth, lf.....	2	1	0	2	0	0
f...	3	1	1	0	0	0	Pipp, 1b.....	3	1	2	7	0	0
....	3	0	1	9	2	0	Meusel, rf....	3	0	1	1	0	0
3b.	4	0	1	5	1	0	Schang, c....	3	0	0	8	1	0
2b..	4	0	1	1	4	0	Ward, 2b....	3	0	0	4	4	0
ss..	3	1	1	3	1	1	Scott, ss.....	3	0	1	2	3	0
c...	2	1	0	5	2	0	Bush, p.....	3	0	0	0	1	0
p...	3	0	1	1	4	0	*Smith	1	0	0	0	0	0
							†Hendrick ..	1	0	0	0	0	0
...29		5	8	27	14	2	Totals ...29		3	5	24	10	0

ed for Scott in ninth inning.
ed for Bush in ninth inning.

....	000	030	20x	—5
rk.............	200	000	010	—3

ase hits—Dugan, Burns, Fewster, Collins. Stolen bases—Fewster, Harris. Sacrifices—Pipp, Murray, Double plays—Scott, Ward and Murray, Picinich and Burns. Left s—New York, 7; Boston, 7. Bases s—Off Bush, 5; off Murray, 4. Hit her—By Murray, 2 (Ruth, Ward); h (Harris). Struck out—By Bush, Murray, 4. Wild pitch—Bush. ball—Schang. Umpires—Owens and Time—1:42.

Title Soccer Games On Schedule To-day

championship games in the of the American Soccer League wn for decision this afternoon, ork being pitted against Harri- New York Oval, and the Brook- anderers against Philadelphia at orne Field.

apic Field, at Clifton, N. J., will n attraction in the A. F. A. semi- etween Paterson, national cham- and the Fleischer Yarn soccer of Philadelphia. The Tyrconnell and Overseas Wanderers will in the third round of the Na- Amateur Cup competition at orne Field at 4:30 o'clock.

Williams Stars As Phils Beat Robins, 3-2

Cy Drives Out Homer in Fourth Inning and Plays Brilliantly in Outfield

PHILADELPHIA, April 28.—Dazzy Vance was a victim to-day of Cy Williams and of his own error that let in a run in the fourth inning that was responsible for the Phillies winning the last game of the three-game series by 3 to 2. Vance allowed six hits and three runs in the six innings he pitched before Neis batted for him in the seventh, and Arthur Decatur finished the game.

It was a dark and stormy day, and rain fell for the last three innings, but 8,000 fans were there to encourage the Phillies, who had lost the first two games of the series to the Robins. They saw Williams make four catches that were as good as ever seen here and also saw him hoist a home run over the right field fence in the fatal fourth inning. Curtis Walker abetted Williams by making a one-handed catch off High in the eighth inning that robbed High of a triple and Brooklyn of two runs. Wheat was on third and Barber on second, with two out when Walker did his bit.

Turner Barber in the seventh made a jumping one-hand catch off Williams, after Holke had doubled with one out, and it led to the doubling of Holke off second. That catch cost the Phillies a run. Williams's catches of Schliebner and Deberry in the Brooklyn fourth, at the edge of the center field bleachers cost those batters and their team two home runs.

Jimmy Ring, who pitched so successfully for the Phillies to-day, was bombarded off the mound by the Robins in three innings on Thursday, and in the first inning to-day he seemed to be due for another hasty exit. Olson opened the first inning with a double to center. Johnston flied out, but Tom Griffith singled to center, scoring Olson.

Zack Wheat had hit safely in all of Brooklyn's ten National League games up to this point and he singled in the first inning to-day, but Barber hit into a double play. Wheat singled again in the third inning and was the one visitor to get more than two hits off Ring. He has made twenty-two hits in eleven games and most of them have been timely.

Dazzy Vance held the Phillies to one hit for the first three innings, but his finish began when Williams opened the fourth with a homer over the right field fence. Walker followed with a pass and Lee fouled to Schliebner. Heinie Sand, who had a great day in the field, doubled to right, sending Walker to third. Wrightstone grounded to Vance, who had a simple throw to the plate, but the throw was so wide it eluded De Berry nd Walker scored with a costly run.

Lee opened the sixth with a single to center off Vance and scored the winning run on Sand's sacrifice and Wrightstone's single.

Brooklyn looked like a possibe winner in the eighth until Curtis Walker's catch put the Robins out of the running. Johnston opened the eighth with a single to center. Wheat walked. Barber singled to left, scoring Johnston and putting Wheat on second. Williams robbed Schliebner of a hit by his running catch, but the out advanced Wheat and Barber. Walker made his one-hand grab of High's fly along the left foul line and the Robins were through.

The score:

PHILA. (N.L.)	ab	r	h	po	a	e	BROOKLYN (N.L.)	ab	r	h	po	a	e
Rapp, 3b...	4	0	1	2	2	0	Olsen, 2b...	5	1	1	4	3	0
Holke, 1b...	4	0	1	8	1	0	Johnst'n, ss.	4	1	1	1	4	0
Williams, cf.	4	1	2	7	0	0	Griffith, rf...	4	0	1	1	1	1
Walker, lf..	3	1	1	3	0	0	Wheat, lf...	3	0	2	1	0	0
Lee, rf	4	1	2	0	0	0	Barber, cf...	4	0	1	2	1	0
Sand, ss....	3	0	1	3	5	0	Schl'bner, 1b	4	0	1	12	0	1
Wr'gtson, 2b.	3	0	1	4	4	0	High, 3b....	4	0	0	1	1	0
Henline, c..	0	0	0	0	0	0	De Berry, c.	3	0	0	2	2	0
Ring, p.....	4	0	0	0	1	0	Vance, p....	1	0	1	0	2	1
							*Neis	1	0	0	0	0	0
							Decatur, p..	0	0	0	0	1	0
							†Bailey	0	0	0	0	0	0
Totals ...29		3	9	27	13	0	Totals ...33		2	8	24	15	3

*Batted for Vance in seventh inning.
†Batted for Decatur in ninth inning.

Philadelphia.........	000	201	00x	—3
Brooklyn..............	100	000	010	—2

Two-base hits—Olson, Schliebner, Sand, Holke. Home run—Williams. Stolen base—Sand. Sacrifices—Sand, Henline. Double plays—Johnston, Olson and Schliebner; Vance, De Berry and Schliebner; Barber, Olson and Johnston; Sand, Wrightstone and Holke; Sand and Holke. Left on bases—Brooklyn, 8; Philadelphia, 9. Bases on balls—Off Vance, 2; off Decatur, 2; off Ring, 4. Struck out—By Vance, 1. Hits—Off Vance, 6 in 6 innings; off Decatur, 3 in 2. Hit by pitcher—By Vance (Henline). Losing pitcher—Vance. Umpires—Klem and Derr. Time—1:37.

Harlem Tennis Tourney Will Begin on May 12

The singles open tournament of the Harlem Tennis Club, at 136th Street and Eighth Avenue, will begin on Saturday, May 12, and continue on Sunday and the remainder of the following week. Play will start at 1:30 o'clock on the opening day. Entries close on Thursday, May 10, at 5 p. m., with Louis Bry, 242 Fourth Avenue, and must be in writing.

The Harlem challenge cup will be in competition and standard gold and silver medals will be awarded to the winner and runner-up. The following compose the tournament committee: Louis Bry, chairman; Paul Goold, H. H. Galbraith, Edwin Bry, C. H. Nannes, Colgate Baker, Ben Landau, R. J. Sommer and J. Minster. Goold will act as referee.

Evans Visits Reese

MORGANTOWN, W. Va., April 28.—"Dick" Evans, one of the most dependable hurlers on the West Virginia University squad, was sent to see "Bonesetter" Roose, the famous Youngstown, Ohio, specialist, to-day. Evans has been suffering with a bad arm all season, and it is hoped the "Bonesetter" can put him in shape to join the mountaineer squad on its Eastern trip at Washington Monday.

Southern Association

Mobile, 5; Atlanta, 2.
Birmingham, 8; New Orleans, 1.
Nashville, 10; Little Rock, 4.
Memphis-Chattanooga (wet grounds).

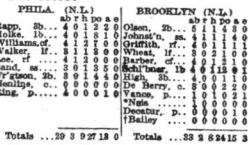

Everett Scott, Who Is Nearing His 1,000th Consecutive Game

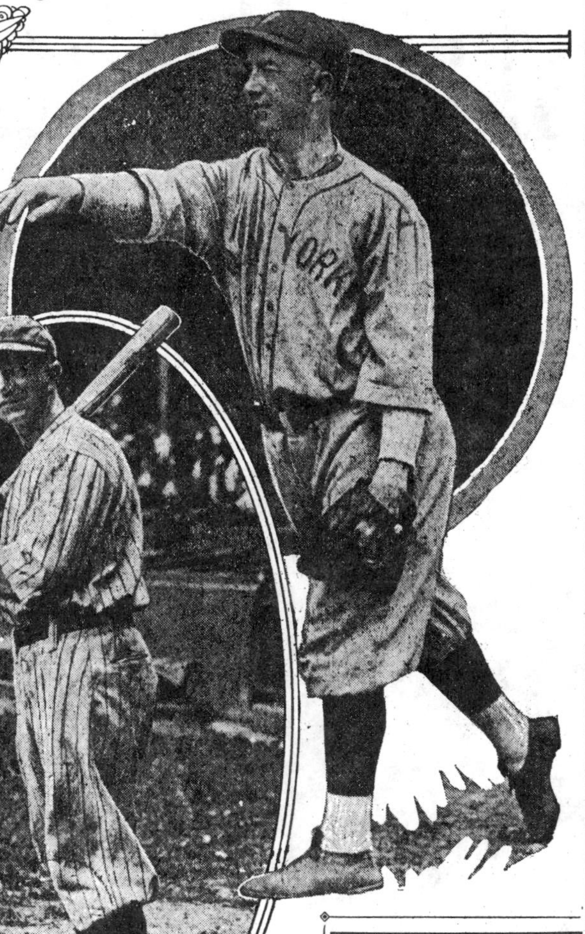

P. & A. Photo

Five Leading Batsmen In Each Major League

NATIONAL LEAGUE

Player and Club.	G.	AB.	R.	H.	Pct.
Wheat, Brooklyn...	11	45	7	22	.489
Traynor, Pittsburgh	11	40	10	19	.475
Grimm, Pittsburgh.	11	36	9	16	.444
Hartnett, Chicago..	7	21	6	9	.429
Hargrave, Cincinnati	7	24	1	10	.417

AMERICAN LEAGUE

Player and Club.	G.	AB.	R.	H.	Pct.
Heilmann, Detroit..	11	44	11	24	.545
Devormer, Boston..	6	22	3	10	.455
Williams, St. Louis.	10	41	7	17	.415
Burns, Boston......	10	39	5	16	.410
Collins, Chicago....	10	37	4	15	.405

Tigers Beat Browns Behind Pillette's Good Hurling, 4–1

DETROIT, April 28.—Herman Pillette beat the St. Louis Browns for the first time in his major league career today, Detroit winning, 4 to 1. Elam Van Gilder was hit freely when hits meant runs, allowing, besides Veach's home run, doubles by Cobb, Haney, Heilmann and Woodall. It was the eleventh consecutive game in which Heilmann has hit safely.

Pillette wobbled only in the seventh, when singles by McManus and Severeid and a double by Gerber resulted in one run. A fast double play, Rigney to Pratt to Blue, broke up the threatened St. Louis rally.

(DETROIT (A. L.)	ab	r	h	po	a	e	ST. LOUIS (A. L.)	ab	r	h	po	a	e
Blue, 1b....	3	0	0	12	1	0	Rob'tson, 3b.	4	0	0	0	1	0
Haney, 3b...	4	0	2	1	5	1	Foster, 2b...	4	0	0	2	3	0
Cobb, cf....	3	0	2	1	0	0	Tobin, rf...	4	0	1	2	0	0
Veach, lf....	4	1	2	3	0	0	Williams, lf..	3	0	1	3	1	1
Heilmann, rf	3	1	2	4	0	0	M'Manus, 1b	4	1	1	12	0	0
Pratt, 2b....	1	0	1	2	4	0	Severeid, c..	4	0	1	1	1	1
Rigney, ss..	4	0	0	1	2	0	Jacobson, cf..	3	0	0	1	0	0
Woodall, c..	3	1	1	2	0	0	Gerber, ss...	4	0	3	3	4	0
Pillette, p...	3	1	1	1	2	0	Van Gilder, p	3	0	0	0	2	0
							*Collins....	1	0	0	0	0	0
Totals ..28		4	11	27	14	1	Totals ..34		1	7	24	12	2

*Batted for Van Gilder in ninth inning.

Detroit.............	002	002	00x	—4
St. Louis...........	000	000	100	—1

Two-base hits—Gerber, Haney, Cobb, Heilmann (2), Woodall. Home run—Veach. Sacrifices—Blue, Cobb, Pratt (3). Double plays—Van Gilder, Foster and McManus; Rigney, Pratt and Blue. Left on bases—St. Louis, 8; Detroit, 7. Bases on balls—Off Van Gilder, 2; off Pillette, 2. Struck out—By Pillette, 2. Umpires—Hildebrand, Ormsby and Dinneen. Time—1:44.

White Sox Hit Hard And Beat Indians, 6–3

CHICAGO, April 28.—The Chicago White Sox won their second game of the season to-day when they defeated Cleveland 6 to 3. The locals hit Boone hard, and this, combined with erratic support, made it easy or Charlie Robertson to pitch his mates to victory.

Robertson pitched in fine form until the eighth, when he weakened and walked three men. F... fielding by Collins and McClellan, who replaced Johnson at short, however, checked the rally.

The score:

CHICAGO (A. L.)	ab	r	h	po	a	e	CLEVELAND (A. L.)	ab	r	h	po	a	e
Elsh, lf.....	3	0	1	4	0	0	Jamieson, lf..	5	0	2	3	0	0
Kamm, 3b...	3	2	0	1	1	0	Wamby, 2b..	5	1	1	10	0	0
Collins, 2b...	3	2	1	3	5	0	Speaker, cf..	5	0	1	3	0	1
Hooper, rf...	1	1	1	4	0	0	Guisto, 1b...	3	1	1	5	1	0
Sheely, 1b...	3	1	1	7	0	0	Summa, rf...	4	1	1	0	0	0
Mostil, cf....	4	0	1	3	0	0	J. Sewell, ss..	2	0	1	0	5	0
M'Clellan, ss	4	0	1	2	2	0	Lutzke, 3b...	2	0	0	1	1	1
Schalk, c....	4	0	0	3	1	0	Gardner, 3b..	2	0	2	1	0	0
Robertson, p.	3	0	1	0	0	0	*Hogan.....	0	0	0	0	0	0
							Morton, p....	0	0	0	0	1	0
							Myatt, c.....	3	0	1	0	1	1
							Boone, p....	1	0	0	0	1	0
							Edwards, p..	1	0	0	1	1	0
							†Brower.....	1	0	0	0	0	0
							Winn, p.....	0	0	0	0	0	0
							Step'h'son, 3b	1	0	0	0	0	0
Totals ...28		6	7	27	9	0	Totals ..35		3	10	24	11	3

*Batted for Edwards in seventh inning.
†Ran for Gardner in eighth inning.

Chicago.............	103	020	00x	—6
Cleveland...........	010	000	020	—3

Two-base hit—Summa. Three-base hit—Hooper. Stolen bases—Kamm, Elsh. Sacrifice hits—Hooper, Sheely, Roberftson. Double plays—Wamby (unassisted); Collins and Sheely. Left on bases—Cleveland, 9; Chicago, 6. Bases on balls—Off Boone, 2; off Robertson, 4; off Edwards, 2; off Winn, 1. Struck out—By Robertson, 2. Hits—Off Boone, 5 in 2 1-3 innings; off Edwards, 2 in 3 2-3; off Winn, 0 in 1; off Morton, 0 in 1. Losing pitcher—Boone. Umpires—Rowland and Moriarty. Time—2:00.

Hutchison's Coldstream Engagement Confirmed

CHICAGO, April 28.—Reports that Jock Hutchison, professional at the Glenview Country Club, and former American open and British open champion, would go to the Coldstream Club at New York next year, were confirmed to-day by E. A. Engler, president of the former club. Hutchison came to Glenview a half dozen years ago from the Alleghanie Country Club at Pittsburgh.

Hutchison did not ask for his release from the contract with the Glenview club, which was not to expire until until the end of 1924, but showed the Coldstream offer to President Engler. In order not to stand in his way, Mr. Engler said the club decided to release him at the close of this season.

Deacon Scott Needs Three More Games to Reach Thousand Mark

By Joseph Val

Unless the gods of fate unite to perform one grand miracle within the next few days, Everett W. ("Deacon") Scott, Yankee shortstop, will be the proud possessor of a record which probably never will be equaled. For during the coming week this steady, hard-warking infifielder will have played his one-thousandth consecutive big league ball game.

Scott's record even now stands unparalleled in the annals of baseball. When the 1922 season closed Deacon had played his seventh consecutive season without a day off—a total of 986 games. Including the game played by the Yankees yesterday Scott has now appeared in 997 consecutive games. Barring postponements Scottie's goal of 1,000 will be reached when the Yankees play the Senators in Washington Thursday.

Little short of death itself can stop Scottie. One might think in virtue of his great record, that he has been lucky enough to escape the numerous injuries sustained by ball players in the pursuance of their duty. Nothing of the kind. Fate has dealt with Deacon even more harshly than with the average ball player. He has suffered injuries and illness, but an indomitable will has overcome all difficulties.

Close Shave This Season

For a time it looked as if Scott's great record was about to be shattered this season, when he suffered an injury in a pre-season exhibition game. It was so serious in fact that he was carried off the field. Scottie spent several days in bed, but when the Stadium was opened he was on hand, playing at short for the American League champions as if nothing had happened.

This is but one of a dozen instances where Scott's record seemed on the verge of being shattered. Only last season during the Yankees' last Western trip, Scott spent $40 in order to reach Chicago in time to participate in a game there after his train had been wrecked. He spent seven hours' journey in taxicabs and trolleys, but finally arrived to play in the closing innings.

"I guess I must be lucky," he said in discussing the incident. "That was another time I almost made a miss of it. The first time was back in 1918, after I had played about 550 consecutive games with the Boston Red Sox. I was going pretty good at the time and hadn't been hurt or anything, but one morning I bobbed up with a boil over my right eye, which was not only extremely painful, but practically closed my eye.

Rain Saves the Day

"I doubt if I could have played if I had wanted to, but Manager Ed. Barrow gave me no choice in the matter. He told me to stay away from the ball park and I did. Just as luck would have it, however, it rained like all possessed that afternoon, the game was postponed and by the following day I was ready to resume my accustomed duties.

"Another time we were playing in Philadelphia, and Wykoff was pitching to us in batting practice. He threw me a couple of wild ones which almost knocked me down, and as I started back to the bench I turned my head to tell him he ought to practice pitching through a barrel. While my head was turned I walked between Waite Hoyt and the catcher with whom he was warming up and a fast one hit me back of the ear. I was 'out' for twenty minutes, but recovered in time to play the entire game.

"Then when I was train-wrecked and had to spend about seven hours and $40 on interurban trolleys and taxicabs to keep my record intact."

Deacon Scott's Great Eight-Year Record

Year.	Club.	Games.
1916	—Red Sox	103
1917	—Red Sox	157
1918	—Red Sox	126
1919	—Red Sox	138
1920	—Red Sox	154
1921	—Red Sox	154
1922	—Yankees	154
1923	—Yankees	11
Total		997

Ward, of Syracuse, Blanks Skeeters

Bill Ward, the Syracuse young port sider, held the Jersey City Skeeters to two hits on the latter's home field yesterday, shutting them out, while the "stars" batted Deam Barnhardt, the Jersey City veteran, for a collection of twelve hits and a victory, 8 to 0.

The score:

SYRACUSE (I. L.)	ab	r	h	po	a	e	JERSEY CITY (I. L.)	ab	r	h	po	a	e
Keatin, 2b...	5	1	1	3	4	0	Donelson, rf.	4	0	0	4	0	0
Taggert, cf..	5	3	2	2	0	0	Wolf, ss.....	4	0	0	4	2	1
Holm, ss....	5	2	2	1	2	0	Jacobs, lf....	3	0	1	5	0	0
M'Carty, rf..	4	1	3	2	0	0	Holt, 1b.....	2	0	0	6	0	1
Denoville, 1b	5	1	1	13	0	0	Cobb, cf.....	3	0	0	3	0	1
Makin, 3b...	5	0	0	0	6	0	Wagner, 3b..	3	0	0	1	1	0
Mason, lf....	3	0	1	1	0	0	Freitag, c....	1	0	0	0	0	0
Nieb'r'g'l, c.	4	0	2	5	0	0	M'Crea, c...	2	0	0	1	1	0
Ward, p.. ..	4	0	0	0	1	0	Ray, 2b.....	3	0	0	3	4	0
							Barnhardt, p	3	0	1	0	3	0
Totals ..40		8	12	27	13	0	Totals ..28		0	2	27	11	3

Syracuse............	410	000	102	—8
Jersey City.........	000	000	000	—0

Two-base hits—Keating, Denoville, Niebergall, Taggert, Jacobs. Stolen base—Holm. Double play—Makin, Keating and Denoville. Left on bases—Jersey City, 2; Syracuse, 7. Bases on balls—Off Barnhardt, 2; off Ward, 1. Struck out—By Ward, 4. Umpires—McBride and Phyle. Time—1:25.

Graham Is Coaching Williams Freshman Nine

WILLIAMSTOWN, April 28.—Charlec L. Graham is coachig the Williams freshman baseball nine this spring. He has a large list of candidates who are working out daily in preparation for the hard schedule of games which has been arranged.

Mr. Graham is assistant athletic director at Williams. He coached the freshman football team last fall and the varsity swimming team last winter. In both cases he met with good success. He is a former Springfield College athlete.

Penn State Lacrosse Team Beats Bklyn Poly

STATE COLLEGE, Pa., April 28.—Penn State was much too strong for Brooklyn Poly Tech in lacross this afternoon, the Nittany Lions scoring a lopsided victory, 19 to 0. Rain fell steadily during the contest and the wet sticks made shooting uncertain and prevented an even greater score.

Standing of Clubs in International League

YESTERDAY'S RESULTS

Syracuse, 8; Jersey City, 0.
Buffalo, 6; Newark, 5.
Rochester, 12; Reading, 6.
Baltimore, 6; Toronto, 2.

STANDING OF THE CLUBS

	W.	L.	Pct		W.	L.	Pct
Roch'ter..	10	1	.909	Buffalo....	5	6	.455
Bal'more...	8	3	.727	Newark....	4	7	.364
Jer. City....	5	6	.455	Reading.	4	7	.364
Toronto....	5	6	.455	Syracuse.	3	8	.273

GAMES TO-DAY

Buffalo at Jersey City (2).
Syracuse at Newark (2).
Toronto at Reading (2)
Rochester at Baltimore (2).

Wladek Zbyszko Is Ready to Take On Plestina to Finish

Wladek Zbyszko has signed a contract with Matty Zimmerman, the wrestling promoter, agreeing to tackle any grappler in the world, barring no one. Zbyszko now has the sum of $2,500 filed with his challenge to "Strangler" Ed Lewis in the hands of the State Athletic Commission. The recent winner of the Graeco-Roman title is ready to turn over the money now held by the commission to Lewis the moment he signs a contract, and further Zbyszko stands ready to turn over his end of the purse to charity.

As a further evidence of the fact that he fears no man Zbyszko is even ready to take on Marin Plestina, who has been ducked by all the stars of the wrestling trust. Plestina was given only one chance here, when he met Pezek, and the latter was permitted to gough and use such tactics that he was barred for life in this state by William Muldoon. Colonel Zimmerman, as an evidence that he has no respect for the wrestling trust powers, is ready to give Plestina an opportunity to prove to the world just how good he really is.

"If Plestina signs up to meet Zbyszko," says Zimmerman, "it must be under conditions that insure a decision if such a thing is possible. For one thing, the match would have to start at 9 o'clock, which would give the men two and one-half hours to fight it out. In addition I would seek special permission from the Boxing Commission to prolong the bout, if necessary, so that it would be to a finish. There is always the suggestion of a hippodrome where no decision is reached. Wladek Zbyszko is willing to take on Plestina to a finish. Plestina has been claiming for years that the wrestling stars fear him; if he is the terror he is touted he will not be afraid to go to a decision."

Hurley-Duane Bout Is Feature at Fairmount

Five six-round events and the usual four-round curtain raiser are carded for to-morrow night at the Harlem Fairmount Club.

In the main bout of the evening Lew Hurley will try conclusions with Carl Duane, of the Bronx. Sammy Vogel, former A. A. U. champion, is paired with Joe Saviola in another event. Sid Terris tackles Louis Gugimaine. Jack Snyder faces Lou Sigli and Joe Ryder will meet August Pisano.

Goebel Traded to Tigers

BOSTON, April 28.—Manager Frank Chance, of the Boston Red Sox, tonight announced the trade of Outfielder Goebel to Detroit for Utility Man Flagstead. Pitcher Fowlkes to-day was sent back to the Memphis club by Manager Chance.

Schapiro Meets 22 Chessmen

In his first exhibition of simultaneous play at the Manhattan Chess Club, Morris A. Schapiro, club champion, was opposed by twenty-two players and made a score of 15 wins, 3 draws and 4 losses. S. Ginsburger, Caleb Levy, P. Wolfson and Dr. F. C. St. John were the winners. The drawn games were scored by Dr. A. A. Bryant, N. Lederer and S. Sladkus.

Lacrosse at Hoboken

Johns Hopkins defeated Stevens at lacrosse yesterday at Hoboken, 14 to 1.

Home Run Hitters In Games Yesterday

		Season's Total.
Williams, Phillies.......	1	3
Blades, Cardinals.......	1	3
Frisch, Giants..........	1	1
Bagwell, Braves........	1	1
McInnis, Braves........	1	1
Veach, Tigers..........	1	1

THE LEADERS

Williams, Browns	4
Hartnett, Cubs	4
Blades, Cardinals	3
Kelleher, Cubs	3
Williams, Phillies	3
Grimm, Pirates	3
Ruth, Yankees	2
Dykes, Athletics	2
Miller, Cubs	2
Friberg, Cubs	2

LEAGUE TOTALS TO DATE

National League

Chicago	14
Pittsburgh	7
St. Louis	6
New York	5
Philadelphia	5
Brooklyn	3
Boston	3
Cincinnati	1
Total	44

American League

St. Louis	6
New York	4
Philadelphia	4
Washington	3
Detroit	3
Boston	2
Cleveland	—
Chicago	—
Total	22

TOTALS THIS DATE LAST YEAR

National League	38
American League	35

HOME RUNS LAST YEAR

National League	530
American League	524
Total	1,054

Toney Holds Reds To Four Hits and Cards Win, 4 to 3

ST. LOUIS, Mo., April 28.—Toney allowed the Cincinnati Reds but four hits, and St. Louis took the odd game of the series to-day. The score was 4 to 3.

Blades hit over the left field fence in the third inning for his third homer of the season. The four-bagger came off Luque with the bags empty. Jake Daubert, who suffered an attack of pneumonia early this year, was back on first base for the Reds.

The score:

ST. LOUIS (N.L.)	ab	r	h	po	a	e	CINCINNATI (N.L.)	ab	r	h	po	a	e
Blades, lf...	3	1	1	1	0	0	Burns, rf....	3	0	0	1	0	0
Flack, rf....	4	1	1	3	0	0	Daubert, 1b..	3	0	1	9	0	0
Hornsby, 2b.	3	2	2	1	1	0	Duncan, lf...	4	1	0	1	0	0
Bottomley, 1b	3	0	2	9	1	0	Roush, cf...	3	1	0	3	0	0
Stock, 3b...	3	0	1	2	2	0	Bohne, 2b..	4	1	1	4	5	0
Myers, cf...	4	0	1	4	0	0	Pinelli, 3b...	2	0	0	0	3	0
Freigau, ss...	3	0	1	3	3	0	Caveney, ss..	4	0	2	4	4	1
Clemons, c..	3	0	0	4	0	0	Wingo, c...	3	0	0	1	4	0
Toney, p....	3	0	0	0	2	0	Luque, p....	1	0	0	0	0	0
							Keck, p....	2	0	0	1	2	0
Totals ...29		4	9	27	9	0	Totals ...29		3	4	24	18	1

St. Louis.............	102	000	01x	—4
Cincinnati............	000	300	000	—3

Two-base hits—Hornsby, Stock, Caveney (2), Daubert. Home run—Blades. Stolen base—Bottomley. Sacrifices—Pinelli, Bottomley. Double play—Caveney and Daubert. Left on bases—Cincinnati, 4; St. Louis, 5. Bases on balls—Off Toney, 4; off Luque, 1; off Keck, 1. Struck out—By Toney, 4; by Luque, 1. Hits—Off Luque, 7 in 2 1-3 innings; off Keck, 2 in 5 2-3. Hit by pitcher—By Luque (Blades). Losing pitcher—Keck. Umpires—Moran and Finneran. Time—1:29.

American Association

Toledo, 5; Indianapolis, 1.
Kansas City, 7; St. Paul, 5.
Milwaukee, 6; Minneapolis, 5.
Louisville-Columbus (rain).

Eastern League

All games postponed, rain.

Newark Fans Punch Dye, of Buffalo Club

Bison Player Throws Ba at See and Is Roughl Handled by the Crow

Buffalo came back in the thi game of their series at Newark yeste day and won out, 6 to 5, in a te inning game. A mix-up occurred the last frame, in which Dye, Buff left fielder, received a few blows fro spectators.

The rumpus came about when Ch See, of Newark, was trapped betw first and second in the tenth with two out and Newark one hind. He held the Bisons at a long time and nearly the e was strung along the base at first got the ball and but See couldn't stop him and gave Dye a bump.

The collison knocked S Dye remained on his fee angered at what he consi tempt to knock him over, I ball at See while he was ground and hit him in t crumpled up and lay th fans and players swarme Dye's face was bloody w corted by a bodyguard bench.

In the tenth Buffalo s on singles by Webb an an error by Miller. N to pinch hitters in its got two on bases. Alter down between third and tired. A batter groundeo was caught off first. W being retired Honig scored

The score:

BUFFALO (I. L.)	ab	r	h	po	a	e
Dye, lf......	5	0	3	3	1	0
Burns, cf....	5	0	1	2	0	0
Webb, 3b....	5	1	1	2	5	0
Butler, 2b....	5	1	0	0	5	0
Kane, rf.....	4	1	1	6	0	0
Kelly, 1b....	4	2	3	13	2	0
Sheehan, ss..	4	0	0	2	6	0
Stearns, c....	2	0	0	1	0	0
Akins, c.....	1	0	0	1	0	0
Weineke, p...	1	1	1	0	1	0
Heitmann, p..	1	0	1	0	0	0
Reddy, p.....	0	0	0	0	0	0
*Spencer.....	1	0	0	0	0	0
Totals ..38		6	11	30	20	0

NEWA[RK] (I. L.)	
Zitman, lf....	[illegible]
See, rf.......	[illegible]
Brainerd, cf..	[illegible]
Anderson, 3b	[illegible]
Miller, 1b....	[illegible]
Devine, c.....	[illegible]
Sheridan, ss.	[illegible]
Benes, 2b....	[illegible]
Ellis, p......	[illegible]
Kneisch, p...	[illegible]
Woodhead, p	[illegible]
†Altenburg..	[illegible]
‡Honig......	[illegible]

*Batted for Stearns in seven
†Batted for Benes in tenth i
‡Batted for Woodhead in ter

Buffalo............ 001 01...
Newark............ 013 00...

Two-base hits—Brainerd, K Three-base hits—Dye, Kelly. —Dye, Miller, Brainerd. Sacr See, Kane. Double plays— and Webb; Anderson and on bases—Buffalo, 9; Newark, 7 balls—Off Weineke, 6; off Kne Heitman, 2; off Reddy, 1; off Struck out—By Heitman, 1; b by Kneisch, 1. Hits—Off Wei 2 1-3 innings; off Ellis, 9 in Kneisch, 2 in 1 1-3; off Woodhead off Heitman, 1 in 5 2-3; off Reddy Hit by pitcher—By Kneisch (Akin pitch—Weineke. Winning pitcher— Losing pitcher—Woodhead. Umpir penter, Hett and Magerkurch. Time

Other I. L. Games

AT BALTIMORE

Baltimore...... 200 101 20x—...
Toronto......... 010 100 ...

Batteries—Ogden and McAvoy; Tay and Vincent.
Second game—Rain.

AT READING

Rochester...... 040 610 10...
Reading........ 010 100 11...

Batteries—Milous and Lake; Hus and Clarke.
Second game—Rain.

Cornell Wins at Lacrosse

NEW HAVEN, Conn., April 28.—Cornell defeated Yale at lacrosse he to-day, 2 to 1. The game was play on a muddy field.

United States Now an Active Member of Tennis Federation

By Fred Hawthorne

After more than ten years of dickering, the United States Lawn Tennis Association has become an active member of the International Lawn Tennis Federation, thus bringing the game under the world-wide domination of a central controlling body, with uniform rules, standard and weighted balls, and a general welding together of associations, clubs and players in all countries where lawn tennis is played.

The action of our national body in allying itself with the international association was practically consummated a month ago, when formal application to the international federation was made by the U. S. L. T. A., but no announcement was made until yesterday, when official acknowledgment of the application and the favorable action taken thereon, was received by the secretary of the national body, in a letter from M. Henry Wallet, president of the international federation.

M. Wallet, in his letter to President Dwight F. Davis, said the U. S. L. T. A. had been elected to membership on March 16, and added: "In conferring, by way of exception, such a power on the Consulting Commission, the General Assembly evidenced the great importance attached to the U. S. L. T. A. becoming a member of the international federation.

"The pleasure of greeting you in the name of all my colleagues is the greater for me, Mr. President, as I am thoroughly convinced that the adhesion of your powerful association will considerably increase the authority that the International Federation exercises over the whole world."

The International Federation was organized on March 1, 1913, with the following nations as members: Great Britain, France, Italy, Spain, Belgium, Australia, South Africa, Holland, Hungary, Sweden, Switzerland, Denmark, Russia and Germany. The United States was asked to join at that time, but, because of the fact that the federation had awarded the world's turf court championship tournaments to the Wimbledon Club of England, and the hard court championships to France, both in perpetuity, our national association refused to become a member of the federation while such a condition existed, feeling these awards were against the best interests of the game.

Then began a correspondence between our national body and the international federation which lasted for years. Watson M. Washburn, R. Norris Williams 2d and Henry W. Slocum at various times acted as intermediaries in the negotiations between this country and the federation. Some months ago the English and French associations succeeded in having the world's championship awards revoked, to take effect after January 1, 1924. This left the door open for the entry of the United States into the international body, and the game should be the gainer thereby.

Probably the largest gallery that ever witnessed a tennis match will on hand next Wednesday afternoon the courts in Central Park, oppos Ninety-third Street and the W Drive, when Tilden, Johnston and Richards, the three leading players of world, appear in a round-robin ser of exhibition one-set singles match

The schedule calls for Tilden to f Johnston in the opening match, to followed by Johnston and Richards posing each other, and Tilden meeti Richards in the last event. Play scheduled to start promptly at o'clock, daylight saving time, and tickets or cards of any kind will required. Dwight F. Davis, preside of the U. S. L. T. A.; George W. Wig man, vice-president, and many oth officials and famous players will present, as well as Mayor Hylan, Co missioner Hulbert and other city ficials.

Bunce Is High Gun

F. Bunce was both the high scra and the high handicap gunner in monthly shoot of the Northport G Club. He finished with a card of straight targets. As he could not ta both prizes, the handicap cup went H. L. Brush, who only won after shoot-off against six other gunners

JAIL MAN AS CRASH KILLS GIRL

THREE CENTS CITY AND COUNTY

LOS ANGELES EVENING HERALD — AN INDEPENDENT NEWSPAPER

EVENING NEWS EDITION

Reg. U. S. Patent Office. Copyright, 1923, by Evening Herald Publishing Company

The Evening Herald Grows Just Like Los Angeles

VOL. XLVIII THREE CENTS Hotels and Trains, Five Cents WEDNESDAY, OCTOBER 10, 1923 THREE CENTS Hotels and Trains, Five Cents NO. 294

WORLD SERIES OPENED IN N. Y.

Nab 'Badge' Bandit Suspect

Babe Ruth, Home Run Slugger, and One of New York Yankees' Mainstays in Today's Game with Giants Opened World Series

The Bambino, Batting Hero, in His Characteristic Pose. The Yanks Pin a Great Amount of Their Confidence on Ruth's Ability to Slam the Pill for Circuit Runs.

70,000 PACK STADIUM TO WATCH FIRST CLASH OF YANKS AND GIANTS

YANKEE STADIUM, NEW YORK, Oct. 10.—A crowd estimated at 70,000 packed the stadium today when the Giants, representing the National league, and the Yankees, flag winners in the American league, trotted on the field for the first game of the world's series. It was the third successive time the series has been entirely a New York affair.

More than 36,000 fans filed through the general admission gates which were thrown open at 10 o'clock. Many of the fans had waited in line throughout the night in order to be among the first to enter the unreserved sections. The reserved spaces filled more slowly, but there was scarcely a vacant seat an hour before game time.

Both teams received an ovation when they came onto the field. The Yankees, being the home club, were last to go through their preliminary workout.

PIPP AT FIRST

Babe Ruth, the greatest slugger of them all, was in his accustomed place in right field and Bobby Meusel, his slugging teammate, was in center. Walter Pipp, limping slightly because of a weak ankle, was at first base, but handled himself in a way that assured the fans he is in shape to go through the series in good form.

Although the Yankees entered the game slight favorites, the Giants got the biggest reception when they took the field. Ross Young, who has been on the hospital list, showed a lot of speed in right field and Cunningham, former Coast league star, worked out in center.

PITCHERS WORK OUT

The pitchers for both clubs worked out easily. Pennock and Hoyt started tossing the ball over to warm up for the Yanks and Ryan and Nehf warmed up for McGraw. Snyder and Gowdy handled the offerings of the Giants' pitchers, while Schang and Hoffman were the receiving stars in the Yankee bull pen.

Babe Ruth, voted by a committee of baseball critics the most valuable player to his club in the American league, was the center of all eyes when the clubs took the field.

After the greatest year of his

(CONTINUED ON PAGE THIRTEEN)

Nehf and Hoyt to Pitch Opener

NEW YORK, Oct. 10.—Arthur Nehf, Giants' star southpaw, and Waite Hoyt, youthful righthander of the Yankees, were tentatively picked today to start the world's series. The probable batting order of the team follows:

GIANTS—Bancroft, ss.; Groh, 3b.; Frisch, 2b.; Young, rf.; Meusel, lf.; Cunningham, cf.; Kelly, 1b.; Snyder, c.; Nehf, p.

YANKEES—Witt, cf.; Dugan, 3b.; Ruth, lf.; Pipp, 1b.; Meusel, rf.; Ward, 2b.; Schang, c.; Scott, ss.; Hoyt, p.

N. Y. Showgirl in Court on Charge Of Stabbing Man

NEW YORK, Oct. 10.—Pretty Moravia Balfour, showgirl who is alleged to have stabbed Andre Sherri, producer, in the arm in front of the Victoria theater, was to appear in the Washington Heights police court today on a charge of assault with a deadly weapon.

Miss Balfour said Sherri threatened to kill her when she demanded two months' pay she declared is due her; that he struck her with a cane and that she defended herself with a nail file. Sherri alleges she stabbed him with a pair of scissors. Miss Balfour further alleges that Sherri is "Tony" Macalus, notorious underworld character, who was involved in the Carl Fischer Hanson extortion and bribery case of 15 years ago.

Hold L. A. Youth in Street Fight Death

Charged with manslaughter for the death of Roy W. Root, age 27 years, who died of injuries received in a street fight, R. W. Rousey, age 19 years, 217 East Forty-second street, was held by the police today. Rousey is said to have attempted to become peacemaker in the fight and was struck by Root. He retaliated, knocking Root down and inflicting fatal injuries.

WARM IN THE YUKON

DAWSON, Yukon Territory, Oct. 10. — The oldest settlers here cannot remember another year when the city was not icebound in October. The last steamer of the summer sailed for the south today and no trace of the freeze has yet appeared.

JAIL MAN AS GIRL KILLED IN CRASH

Tragedy today brought an abrupt close to what the police describe as a thrilling early morning joyride by two young Los Angeles couples in an automobile when the heavy car, careening down a narrow, little-used road in Beverly glen, near Sawtelle, skidded and turned over, the accident resulting in the death of pretty Miss Florence Duncan, 24, of the Hoffman apartments, 1241 Ingraham street, Los Angeles.

The three other persons, George Robinson of 719 Whittier boulevard, Lillie Viral of 840 South Flower Xstreet and Louis J. Vaughn of 2222 West Eighth street, were slightly injured when the car hurtled from the road and pinned Miss Duncan beneath it.

MAN ARRESTED

The victim of the accident died without regaining consciousness and before an ambulance could reach the scene from Sawtelle.

Robinson, companion of Miss Duncan, was alleged to have been driving the automobile when he lost control of it. He was arrested by Police Officers A. L. Peterson and R. C. Rasmusses of Sawtelle and placed in the city jail on a charge of suspicion of manslaughter.

According to the arresting officers, Robinson apparently had been drinking before the accident occurred. They said they were greeted with a scene of desolation when they reached the place where the accident occurred.

The body of the dead woman was pinned beneath the heavy au-

(CONTINUED ON PAGE TWELVE)

Tigers, Angels Open Last Series of Year

Frank Shellenback and Jakie May, two of the pitchers left at home by the Tigers, were told to warm up for the opening game of the series against the Angels at Washington park today.

Marty Krug ordered Ote Crandall and Roy Hannah to warm up for his squad.

Today's game marked the opening of the final series of the season. The line-up:

TIGERS—	ANGELS—
H. High, lf	McCabe, lf
Schneider, rf	Jacobs, ss
Gillespie, cf	Twombly, rf
Burke, 1b	Hood, cf
Zanic, c	Smith, 3b
Rader, 2b	Golvin, 1b
Warner, 3b	Lindimore, 2b
Slade, ss	Rego, c
May, p	Crandall, p

$77,000 Shortage Found in Bank; Doors Are Closed

ERIE, Pa., Oct. 10.—The Citizens Bank of Alban, Erie county, was closed today by state bank examiners. A shortage of $77,000 has been found.

Ralph J. Griswold, cashier, has been taken into custody on complaint of State Bank Examiner Beckman, charged with being responsible for the shortage.

Woman Slayer of Boy, 13, Hanged

By International News Service

GLASGOW, Oct. 10.—Mrs. John Newell, convicted of the murder of 13-year-old John Johnstone, was hanged here today.

PRISONER CONFESSES HIGHWAY HOLDUP

Check Story in Attempt to Solve Forty Other Robberies

The notorious "badge bandit," who has operated in Los Angeles county for months with more than two score of holdups, and 12 attacks on women at the point of a pistol, is believed by the police to have been captured.

His description said to conform closely to that of the "badge bandit," a man giving the name of C. S. Hammock, was taken into custody at dawn today near Redondo Beach, following the wrecking of an automobile he is alleged to have used in the holdup and robbery of the Burton oil station, Market street and Redondo boulevard.

SIGNS CONFESSION

Boastful of his career of crime, and proud that he "always works alone," the suspected "badge bandit" made a signed and written confession of his night of banditry to Chief of Police Henry of Redondo Beach, the chief reported. In an effort to verify his suspicion that Hammock is the "badge bandit," Chief Henry planned to bring him to the sheriff's office for a close examination.

Hammock was captured when a Redondo Beach motorcycle officer and the constable of Gardena hurried to Riverside and Western avenue where an automobile was reported to have been wrecked against a telegraph pole. Hammock and a man giving the name of Shirley Shephard were taken into custody.

BREAKS UNDER GRILLING

For more than an hour Hammock refused to talk to Redondo Beach police, Chief Henry said. Attracted by the close resemblance of his pris-

(CONTINUED ON PAGE TWELVE)

FRENCH REJECT BERLIN RUHR PARLEY PLAN

By International News Service

PARIS, Oct. 10.—Premier Poincare today flatly rejected the German proposal for a French, Belgian and German commission to settle the Ruhr problem through direct negotiations. It had previously been rejected by Belgium.

By International News Service

BERLIN, Oct. 10.—Communist charges of disloyalty against Hugo Stinnes, Germany's foremost industrial magnate, were exploded today by Stinnes' official explanation of his visit to Dusseldorf to confer on Ruhr affairs with General deGoutee, commander of the French army in the Ruhr. It was stated that the Stresemann cabinet did not object to Stinners' visit.

Stinnes did not see Chancellor Stresemann before his departure, but he has an alibi. He tried to see the chancellor, but the latter was too busy with the ministerial crisis to grant an audience.

Stinnes knew that no Socialist minister could accede to his demands, but he evidently hoped to create dissention in the cabinet.

The industrial magnate had been

(CONTINUED ON PAGE TWELVE)

SEVERE EARTH TREMORS IN MALAY ARE RECORDED

SYDNEY Australia, Oct. 10.—An earthquake disturbance, believed to center in the north Malay archipelago, was recorded by the observatory seismograph today.

LONDON, Oct. 10.—Earth tremors were recorded by the West Bromwich observatory seismograph this morning.

DUBLIN, Oct. 10.—The seismograph at Rathfarnham Castle observatory registered severe earthquake shocks this morning. The

(CONTINUED ON PAGE TWELVE)

WORLD SERIES EXTRA

SPORTS 32 PAGES

Los Angeles Evening Express — Associated Press Service

VOL. LIII, NO. 171 | FIFTY-THIRD YEAR | THURSDAY, OCTOBER 11, 1923

Entered as second-class matter March 4, 1918, at the postoffice at Los Angeles, Calif., under act of congress of March 8, 1879. Published daily except Sunday

YANKEES WINNERS

BIG CROWD AGAIN TURNS OUT TO SEE WORLD SERIES TILT

POLO GROUNDS, NEW YORK, Oct. 11.—The Yankees, American League pennant winners, tied up world series contests today when they defeated Giants, National League. The Giants won the game yesterday.

POLO GROUNDS, NEW YORK, Oct. 11.—Grim determination was apparent in every move of Yanks today as they warmed up for the second game of Gotham's third annual baseball classic.

Facing defeat for the third straight year, Miller

Huggins' American loop champions swatted the ball savagely in batting practice and displayed snap and ginger as they tossed the ball around the bags for infield practice.

The batteries were announced as follows:

Giants—McQuillan and Snyder.

Yanks—Pennock and Schang.

There was just a ripple of applause when the Giants and the Yankees came on the field almost simultaneously at 12:30.

The Giants were trim and neat in freshly laundered white and black striped uniforms that they have worn all season at home. The Yankees were attired in their blue-gray road outfits.

The crowd, slowly filling the stands because of the threatening weather this morning, watched Babe Ruth knock long flies to the far wall in practice.

HOPE TO BREAK JINX

"We'll break that jinx today," said Ruth, between swings. "We have a better team than the Giants and luck can't always go their way."

The Giants felt sure of reaching the half-way mark today. They were sure they have it on the Yanks. They were confidence personified as they unlimbered. Playing on their own field and with Art Nehf, southpaw ace, and Jack Scott warming up they looked for nothing but victory.

Miller Huggins, mite manager of the Americans, had Herb Pennock, veteran left-hander, and Sam Jones, the no-hit hero, remove their

(CONTINUED ON PAGE SIX)

EMIL MEUSEL, L. A. BOY, HITS HOME RUN

Game by Innings

By Associated Press

FIRST INNING

YANKEES—Witt up. There was a delay until the photographers could be cleared from the field. McQuillan tossed out Witt. Dugan walked on four straight balls. Ruth walked and the crowd howled. Meusel hit into a double play, Bancroft to Frisch to Kelly. NO RUNS, NO HITS, NO ERRORS.

GIANTS—Scott threw out Bancroft. Pennock took Groh's grounder and threw him out. Ward robbed Frisch of a hit with a one-hand stop and a quick throw to first. NO RUNS, NO HITS, NO ERRORS.

SECOND INNING

YANKEES—Groh threw out Pipp, making a nice play of Pipp's hot grounder. Ward hit a home run into the upper left field stand. Schang lofted out to Snyder. Scott flied out to Meusel. ONE RUN, ONE HIT, NO ERRORS.

GIANTS—Young popped to Dugan. Emil Meusel hit a home run into left field, tying the score. Cunningham flied out to Ruth. Kelly singled into right. Snyder sent up a high fly to Ward. ONE RUN, TWO HITS, NO ERRORS.

THIRD INNING

YANKEES—Frisch tossed out Pennock. Frisch also got Witt at first. Dugan flied out to Meusel. NO RUNS, NO HITS, NO ERRORS.

GIANTS—Dugan made a wonderful play on McQuillan's roller and threw him out. Bancroft flied to Meusel. Groh got a base on balls. Frisch singled into centerfield, Groh holding second. Young lined out to Ruth. NO RUNS, ONE HIT, NO ERRORS.

FOURTH INNING

YANKEES—Ruth up. Ball one. Strike one. Ball two. Ruth got a homerun over the right field stand. Meusel fanned. Pipp singled into right. Ward popped to Kelly. Schang shot a hot single into right field, Pipp going to third. Young jugled the ball and got an eror on the play. Pipp scored on Scott's single to center Schang going to second. McQuillan was knocked out of the box at this stage and Bentley went in. Pennock was hit by a pitched ball. He fell to the ground, his face was contorted with pain, and the players of both clubs gathered around him. The crowd cheered when he rose to his feet and limped to first base. The bases were filled. Witt flied out to Cunningham. TWO RUNS, FOUR HITS, ONE ERROR.

GIANTS—Ward threw out Meusel at first. Cunningham flied out to Ruth. Kelly fanned. NO RUNS, NO HITS, NO ERRORS.

(CONTINUED IN COLUMNUS 7 AND 8)

IMPEACHMENT LEGISLATURE IN OKLA. MEETS

Anti-Klan Message Is Presented

ASKS TEETH IN LAW

By Associated Press

OKLAHOMA CITY, Oct. 11.—The Oklahoma legislature, called into extraordinary session by Gov. J. C. Walton, convened today. The house was called to order at 9:11 a. m. by D. A. Stovall, representative from Choctaw county, who was chosen majority floor leader at a caucus last night. The session was called to consider impeachment charges against the governor.

The senate convened and both branches then recessed for a joint session and to receive the message of the governor.

A committee of the joint session informed Governor Walton that the legislature was ready to hear him. The governor did not appear personally, however, and Aldrich Blake, executive counselor, brought the message to the joint assembly and delivered it to the clerk of the senate with the brief statement:

PRESENTS MESSAGE

"Gentlemen, herewith is presented the governor's message to the legislature."

The clerk then began reading the message.

Governor Walton called upon the Oklahoma legislature today to enact an anti-Ku Kluk Klan law to save the state from the disaster he says it faces through existence of the secret organization.

In his address, opening an extraordinary session of the assembly, the executive charged the klan with responsibility for hundreds of outrages. "This all-powerful and most demoralizing 'super-government' is undermining the very cornerstone and foundation of our government and sapping life blood of our citizenship," Governor Walton declared.

FEARS ANARCHY

"It must be either killed or the government itself must finally give way to anarchy and revolution. There is no alternative or middle ground.

"The conflict between the visible and invisible government must be brought to a close with a complete victory for the visible government or Oklahoma will face indefinite turmoil and strife, the results of which are bound to be disastrous," he said.

"This invisible, insidious and terrorizing empire represents in an ex-

(CONTINUED ON PAGE SIX)

PUPILS HURLED TO DEATH BY FAST TRAIN

Bodies Thrown in Every Direction

BOUND FOR SCHOOL

By United Press

ATWATER, O., Oct. 11.—Eight children were killed, three injured severely and several others hurt today when a bus crowded with school children was demolished by "the Clevelander," the fastest train on the Pennsylvania railroad between New York and Cleveland.

The accident occurred at Lamberts Crossing, a short distance from here.

Calls were sent for doctors and nurses for miles around.

SAW BUS TOO LATE

The engineer of the train saw the vehicle too late to jam on the brakes. A second later there was a terrific crash.

The children, some instantly killed, some dying and others badly injured, were hurled in all directions.

The locomotive plowed through the wreckage, scattering it along the right of way for several hundred feet.

As soon as the train came to a stop members of the train crew and passengers began picking up the victims.

While a score of passengers picked up the little victims, laying their maimed and battered bodies at the trackside, others rushed to the nearest farm house to send in telephone calls for help.

RUSHED TO RAVENNA

The bus was used by the county to convey children to and from schools.

A few minutes after the crash the dead, dying and injured were placed on the train and rushed into Ravenna, where doctors and nurses were waiting at the station.

The children who survived the accident were so dazed that their stories were incoherent.

The different versions of the crash revealed a second of terror, a second when the front wheels of the bus were on the rails and the children heard the roar of the oncoming train.

Through the windows they saw the great bulk of the locomotive

(CONTINUED ON PAGE SIX)

SCORE-BY-INNINGS

YANKS—

1	2	3	4	5	6	7	8	9	10	11	12	13	14
0	1	0	2	1	0	0	0	0					

GIANTS—

1	2	3	4	5	6	7	8	9	10	11	12	13	14
0	1	0	0	0	1	0	0						

Corrected up to and including the eighth inning.

YANKS—	AB	R	H	PO	A	E
Witt........cf	4	0	0	1	0	0
Dugan.......3b	3	0	0	2	2	0
Ruth........rf	2	2	2	3	0	0
R. Meusel.... lf	4	0	1	3	0	0
Pipp........1b	3	1	1	11	0	0
Ward........2b	4	1	2	3	4	0
Schang.......c	4	0	1	1	0	0
E. Scott.....ss	4	0	2	0	5	0
Pennock.....p	2	0	0	0	1	0
	0	0	0	0	0	0
	0	0	0	0	0	0
	0	0	0	0	0	0
	0	0	0	0	0	0
	0	0	0	0	0	0
Totals	30	4	9	24	12	0

	1	2	3	4	5	6	7	8	Total
Runs	0	1	0	2	1	0	0	0	4
Hits	0	1	0	4	2	1	0	1	9

GIANTS—	AB	R	H	PO	A	E
Bancroft.....ss	4	0	0	0	5	0
Groh........3b	3	1	1	0	1	0
Frisch.......2b	4	0	2	2	4	0
Young......rf	4	0	2	0	0	2
E. Meusel....lf	4	1	2	3	0	0
Cunningham .cf	3	0	0	1	0	0
Kelly.......1b	3	0	1	14	0	0
Snyder.......c	3	0	0	4	1	0
McQuillan....p	1	0	0	0	1	0
Bentley......p	2	0	1	0	2	0
Gowdy.........	1	0	0	0	0	0
	0	0	0	0	0	0
	0	0	0	0	0	0
	0	0	0	0	0	0
Totals	32	2	9	24	14	2

	1	2	3	4	5	6	7	8	Total
Runs	0	1	0	0	0	1	0	0	2
Hits	0	2	1	0	0	3	1	2	9

Babe Ruth Knocks 2 Home Runs

SECOND GAME GIANTS AND YANKEES—(Continued)

FIFTH INNING—Yankees: Bancroft threw out Dugan at first. Ruth hit his second home run to left field stand. Bob Meusel singled to right, and continued to second when Young fumbled the ball. Pipp grounded out to Kelly, Meusel going to third. Ward fouled out to Kelly. One run, two hits, one error.

Giants: Snyder flied out to Meusel. Ward threw out Bentley at first. Scott threw out Bancroft at first. No runs, no hits, no errors.

SIXTH INNING—Yankees: Bancroft threw out Schang at first. Scott singled past Bancroft. Pennock hit into a double play, Bancroft to Frisch to Kelly. No runs, one hit, no errors.

Giants: Groh singled over second. Frisch singled to left, Groh going to third. Young singled to left, Groh scoring. Meusel forced Young at second, Scott to Ward, Frisch going to third. Cunningham hit into a double play, Scott to Ward to Pipp. One run, three hits, no errors.

SEVENTH INNING—Yankees: Bentley threw out Witt at first. Bentley threw out Dugan. Ruth walked. Ruth was caught off first, Snyder to Kelly to Bancroft to Kelly. No runs, no hits, no errors.

Giants: Kelly fouled out to Pipp. Snyder sent high fly to Meusel. Bentley doubled to left. Bancroft fouled out to Dugan. No runs, one hit, no errors.

EIGHTH INNING—Yankees: Meusel fouled out to Snyder. Pipp walked on four straight balls. Ward singled to center. Schang flied out. Scott fanned. No runs, one hit, no errors.

Giants: Dugan threw out Groh at first. Scott threw out Frisch at first. Young singled to center. Meusel singled to left. Gowdy, batting for Cunningham, out. No runs, two hits, one error.

HAWKERS REAP PROFIT FROM MARKS

NEW YORK, Oct. 11.—Peddlers on lower Broadway are doing a big business and making a handsome profit selling German paper marks at 10 cents for 100,000 and throwing in a "made in Germany" tin whistle. Marks were quoted at 5,000,000,000 for $1 today.

MAY CLOSE INTERNATIONAL BRIDGE AT EL PASO

WASHINGTON, Oct. 11.—Advisability of closing at night the international bridge at El Paso, Texas, is being considered by treasury officials, as a result of requests from El Paso citizens that this be done in an effort to curb smuggling.

First Legal Bout Victory for Wife

Involved in two legal bouts, Mrs. W. Dingeldein today won a preliminary skirmish.

Seeking support from her husband, Charles C., pending her divorce action, Mrs. Dingeldein was awarded $15 temporary alimony by Judge Clock.

After buying all the provisions for the household and doing his own cooking, Dingeldein lost his wife's affections, he asserted in a $...00 heart balm suit which he recently filed against his wife's employer, W. N. Katz.

Crew Quits Sinking Ship for Life Boats

By Associated Press

KEY WEST, Fla., Oct. 11.—The crew of the tank steamer City of Everett, reported sinking west of Tortugas, has taken to lifeboats, according to wireless messages received here. The steamer Comal, en route to Galveston, reports she is nearing the sinking vessel. The coast guard cutter Saukee has left Key West to aid the ship.

The City of Everett sailed from New Orleans September 24.

MAID TESTIFIES IN STOKES TRIAL

Gives Testimony in Plaintiff's Favor

By Associated Press

NEW YORK, Oct. 11.—Mrs. Lillian Payne, Negress maid in the East Thirty-first street apartment of Edgar T. Wallace from July to December, 1917, and a visitor there on errands for six months previous, today testified at the retrial of W. E. D. Stokes' divorce action against Mrs. Helen Elwood Stokes, that she had seen Mrs. Stokes in the apartment in company with Wallace, who is named co-respondent.

Mrs. Stokes, she said, came in with Wallace through a kitchenette entrance and accidentally came face to face with her.

Adjournment of yesterday's dramatic hearing, which was enlivened by sensational insinuations subsequently retracted by Elmer

(CONTINUED ON PAGE SIX)

POLICE PROBE IS THREATENED

Grand Jury May Act in Long Beach Case

Action that may result in grand jury investigation involving officials of the Long Beach police department was the plan announced by District Attorney Asa Keyes today concerning a clash between the district attorney's office and Long Beach police officials over the proposed extradition of H. B. Freidman, wanted in Long Beach on a charge of passing a bogus check on a beach bank.

ACTION OF CAPTAIN

Today's announcement followed the asserted action of Captain of Detectives J. B. Worley of Long Beach, who is said to have telegraphed New York authorities to release Freidman to Virginia au-

(CONTINUED ON PAGE SEVEN)

Express Scores Big 'Beat' on Series

The spirit of speed and efficiency which has always characterized the Evening Express was again demonstrated yesterday during the first game of the world series. Not only did thousands gather in Broadway to listen to the Evening Express megaphone man announce the plays FIRST, but the printed result of the game was on the street 10 minutes ahead of the extras of the nearest competitor.

Watch the Evening Express maintain its batting average each day of the series.

Crandall and Alten Picked to Toss in Angel-Tiger Clash

HOW THEY LINE UP

ANGELS—	TIGERS—
McCabe lf.	High lf.
Beck ss.	Chad'rne cf.
Twomhly rf.	Gillespie rf.
Hood cf.	Murphy 1b.
Smith 3b.	Whitney c.
Griggs 1b.	Gorman 2b.
Lindimore 2b.	Warner 3b.
Rego c.	Slade ss.
Crandall p.	Alten p.

Los Angeles and Vernon staged the second game of the final Coast League series at Washington Park this afternoon. Otis Crandall wsa selected to work for the Angels and Ernie Alten for the Tigers.

Finney and Reardon umpired.

Baseball, Football, Golf, Tennis, Track, Boxing, Turf and Amateur Sports expertly reported by the best sporting writers in the West

CHARACTER · QUALITY · AMERICA FIRST · ENTERPRISE · ACCURACY

Los Angeles Examiner Sports

AN AMERICAN PAPER FOR THE AMERICAN PEOPLE · THE GREAT NEWSPAPER OF THE GREAT SOUTHWEST

The Examiner carries the most complete Daily Sports Section of any newspaper west of New York

FRIDAY, OCTOBER 12, 1923 — SECTION III—PAGE 1

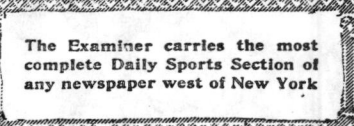

Ruth Hits Twin Homers to Win

"BUGS" BAER SAYS

NEW YORK, Oct. 11.—Yanks nominated Even Stephen on their ticket today. Stephen was elected.

SERIES is now balanced like a cat on a back fence.

McGRAW'S justly established strategy failed to stratt.

HUGHEY JENNINGS was back on his diet of home grass. While Hughey was grazing at third base, he saw those Yanks turn Giants' base lines into parade grounds.

FOUR spectators got assists on home runs.

IT was Yanks' first win in ten series games. Ruth helped with two lobbs over the net.

WARD knocked another excursion into the stands. So did Meusel for the Giants.

THERE were so many home runs wasted that the base umpires look like quarter mile posts.

PENNOCK started for the Yanks and finished for the Yanks. McQuillan started for the Giants and finished for the Yanks, too.

AFTER three home runs had been caromed off McQuillan's bowling McGraw looked at McQuillan like he was a mouse in a sugar bowl.

M'QUILLAN got out.

THEN Jack Bentley took his place in the throwing depot and sniped Pennock with a wild pitch in the back. Bentley's wind up is all arms and legs. He looks like an Egyptian dancer in the wiggle season.

CASEY STENGEL kept his running feet on the bench. Casey is nursing a bonus bruise on his heel. Casey is always reserved for trouble. He didn't get into the game until the ninth, although the police whistle was blowing all afternoon.

WHEN McQuillan started passing out the old-fashioned home runs in the second inning, all the Yanks held out their dishes for more.

THEY certainly loved his cooking.

STENGEL spoiled a home run for Ruth when he chased Babe's slap across the prairies. Casey runs like a piano trying to escape from Paderewski. But he gets there.

YOUNG and Ward boxed a preliminary on Young's force at second. Ward claimed Ross interfered with his throw on Meusel. Ross got a red nose in the mix-up.

THE crowd booed Ross, but it isn't Young's fault if his nose bleeds too easily.

JUDGE LANDIS went through all of today's motions for the photographers. If he's got to make any more balk motions with that baseball he ought to put on a uniform.

IN nine straight world's series games, all the Yanks got out of the turkey was wishbone. Today's win was the first since October, 1921.

BENTLEY, RYAN AND JONNARD were warming up all afternoon. After McQuillan got busier than a Chinaman with a hot iron, Bentley was called upon to throw the meat to the lions.

YANKS refused to stumble over McGraw's master mind. They said it with flowers. Four bases to a bouquet.

PENNOCK got into a bunker in the sixth. Three on and nobody dead. Nobody even sick. A double play pulled him out of the panic while the Yankee rooters brushed down the fur on their bankrolls.

THE game proves that the Yanks are through opening oysters for the Giants.

THOSE two games made the rooters get rid of their chewing tobacco to make room for their hearts.

THE umpires examined every baseball pitched. They seemed to think the Yankees were putting something on the ball.

THEY were putting something on the ball. Plenty of wood.

Orioles Even Junior Series

KANSAS CITY, Mo., Oct. 11.—(By International News Service.)—The Baltimore Orioles this afternoon evened up the count in the "little world series" by taking the second game from Kansas City, 3 to 1. Each team has now won a game.

Willie O'Brien Draws With Joe Layman

Joe Layman and Willie O'Brien fought a draw in the Pasadena armory last night. Four knockouts featured the program.

Other results follow: Tuffy Jinks beat Young Goodwin. Kid Carr knocked out Young Sales. Benny Klagge knocked out Kid Alvarez. Ernie Hood knocked out S. Kaya. Pete Dickson knocked out Young Kullus.

Yankees Finally Win; Landis Doubts Legality

By Ring W. Lardner

POLO GROUNDS, New York, Oct. 11.—This article may sound kind of embarrassed, as I am writing it in the press box and they's a large crowd of beauty lovers standing in front of the screen, giving we newspaper boys a long and admiring look, and this in spite of the fact that a little ways off is seated two other movie queens, George Ade and Thomas Meighan. But will try and forget myself long enough to tell the fans that the score is said to of been 4 to 2 in favor of the Yankees, though it seems so improbable that Judge L——s has called a meeting of the umpires and official scorers to go over the game inning by inning and see if it was legal.

They's a man in our crowd of admirers that says this is not the first time the Yankees ever win from the Giants but he has got a long gray beard and may be all through from a mental standpoint.

The thing that probably beat the Giants today, if the report is true that they were beaten, was the terror struck in their hearts by this man Pennock. Before the World Champions bat against a pitcher who they have never faced, Mr. McGraw makes them go to the library and look up all the books that bear on the subject. Well, they learned that Pennock is a man who has a country estate in Kenneth Square, Pennsylvania, and when he ain't pitching he rides to hounds.

"What does it mean," asked Casey Stengel, "when it says a man rides to hounds?"

"All it means," replied Cozy Dolan, "is that you ain't going to hit against him."

A great many of the Giants, after witnessing Pennock's exhibition has made up their mind to spend the winter riding to hounds no matter what it is.

Will say in this connection that Great Neck is a great place for riding to hounds and practically every time I go out in my costly motor I run over a couple of them.

Last year I predicted that Babe Ruth was going to be the hero of the World Serious, and a good many people thought I meant the World Serious which I was then writing about. They must of been crazy.

Arthur Robinson says that the Babe is now two up on Cy Williams and Cy ain't got no chance to catch up this season unlest he can get some Shelby, Mont., banker to arrange a City Serious in Philadelphia.

Well, when Mr. Pennock took his turn in the Yankee batting practice indicating that he was going to pitch, Casey Stengel's dogs was heard to give a loud bark of relief, knowing they would not be sent on another long trip as long as a left-hander was working. The dogs was probably pulling for Pennock to last through the game, but Casey was not. The official announcement that Herb was going to start caused quite a discussion on the Giant bench. Some of the boys wanted to go up to bat without their bats, as the only Yankee left-hander they had ever faced before was Harry Harper.

The experts who had picked Arthur Nehf to work was greatly surprised when the well-known organist never even warmed up. Bentley and McQuillan worked out and in McQuillan's first inning it looked like the Yankees was the ones that might as well of left their bats on the bench, but after Hugh had throwed eight of the wildest balls ever seen to Dugan and Ruth somebody pointed out the plate to him and he made Meusel hit into a double play. By the time the next inning started the Giant hurler's control was so good that he hit Ward's bat right in the middle. He done the same thing to the Babe's big bludgeon in the fourth. If anybody had been riding on the ball Babe hit they could of got right on the elevated without climbing the stairs. Before this round was over word was sent to McQuillan from the clubhouse saying that his tub was ready. The Yankees was leading by three runs at the end of the fifth and the game began to look like an even bet with the Giants a slight favorite.

Along about this time it was announced that Mrs. Caroline Dorsey, the Traverse City, Mich., fan, was still in her seat at the Yankeee stadium, thinking the game was being played there. It is thought that standing in lnie so long has infected the lady's mind, which wasn't so good to start with. It was even whispered that her ambition is to become a pinch base runner for the Yankees.

The monotony of the general situation was relieved somewhat in the Giant half of the sixth by the interspersal of a bit of football. With Young on first base, Emil Meusel tried to hit into a double play. Scott tossed the ball to Ward and forced Young, but Ward couldn't throw to first as Young was setting on him. The Yanks claimed interference, but the umpires refused to allow same, and for a time the fans thought he was the same party that refereed the Dempsey-Firpo fight.

Mr. Stengel's dogs begin to whine in the eighth, when Manager McGraw sent Gowdy to bat for Cunningham, and they knew that Casey would have to work at least one inning. They were obliged to carry the old boy on two defensive trips, the second of which landed him under Ruth's long fly which would of been the Babe's third homer if he had aimed it pretty near any other direction.

After the game the writer visited the rival clubhouses to interview the rival managers.

"Mr. Huggins," I said, "have you anything to say about the game?"

But it seems that Mr. Huggins had left the clubhouse. So had Mr. McGraw.

FRED BARBER LEADS FIELD AT WILSHIRE

Former Inglewood High Boy Carries Own Clubs and Beats Stars by Six Strokes

By Darsie L. Darsie

FREDDY BARBER, a simon-pure Los Angeles product, knocked the folks cold at Wilshire yesterday when he nonchalantly turned in a card of 71 in the qualifying round of the annual Wilshire tournament. Far behind Freddy, six and seven strokes to be exact, came such renowned players as Willie Hunter, former British champion, Scotty Armstrong, former Southern California title holder, and Harlow Hurley, now of Annandale and once Kansas champion.

But Barber's faultless play is but half the story of this great qualifying round. The other half is of the throngs that crowded the Wilshire course from daylight till an hour after dark—a crowd so great that close to 100 golfers were unable to finish the round and will be permitted to wind up their eighteen holes early this morning.

TO QUALIFY TODAY

Never before has such a huge field attempted to qualify in one day on a single course. A total of 298 teed off and when the players were halted about 6:30 last night something like eighty had from two to ten holes to play. These belated ones will be at the course promptly at 7 a. m. this morning and will start where they finished last night. The pairings will then be made up and match play will start with the seventh flight at 9:30 a. m.

The Wilshire course was in admirable shape for the tournament yesterday, although the closely cropped, keen greens caused many of the boys to take three and four putts. True to advance dope, the great barranca that runs through the course, making a natural hazard for almost every hole, took its full toll of strokes. Even Willie Hunter was not immune. He was out in 36 and was progressing nicely until he hit the long sixteenth hole. His third shot was in the depths and twice he did his best to play out. Then he saw the error of his way and lifted back, taking a nine on the hole.

WRIGHT HAS CHANCE

Freddy Wright still has a good chance to get down with Barber. He reached the seventh hole just

(Continued on Page 3, Column 2)

Ruth Makes Good

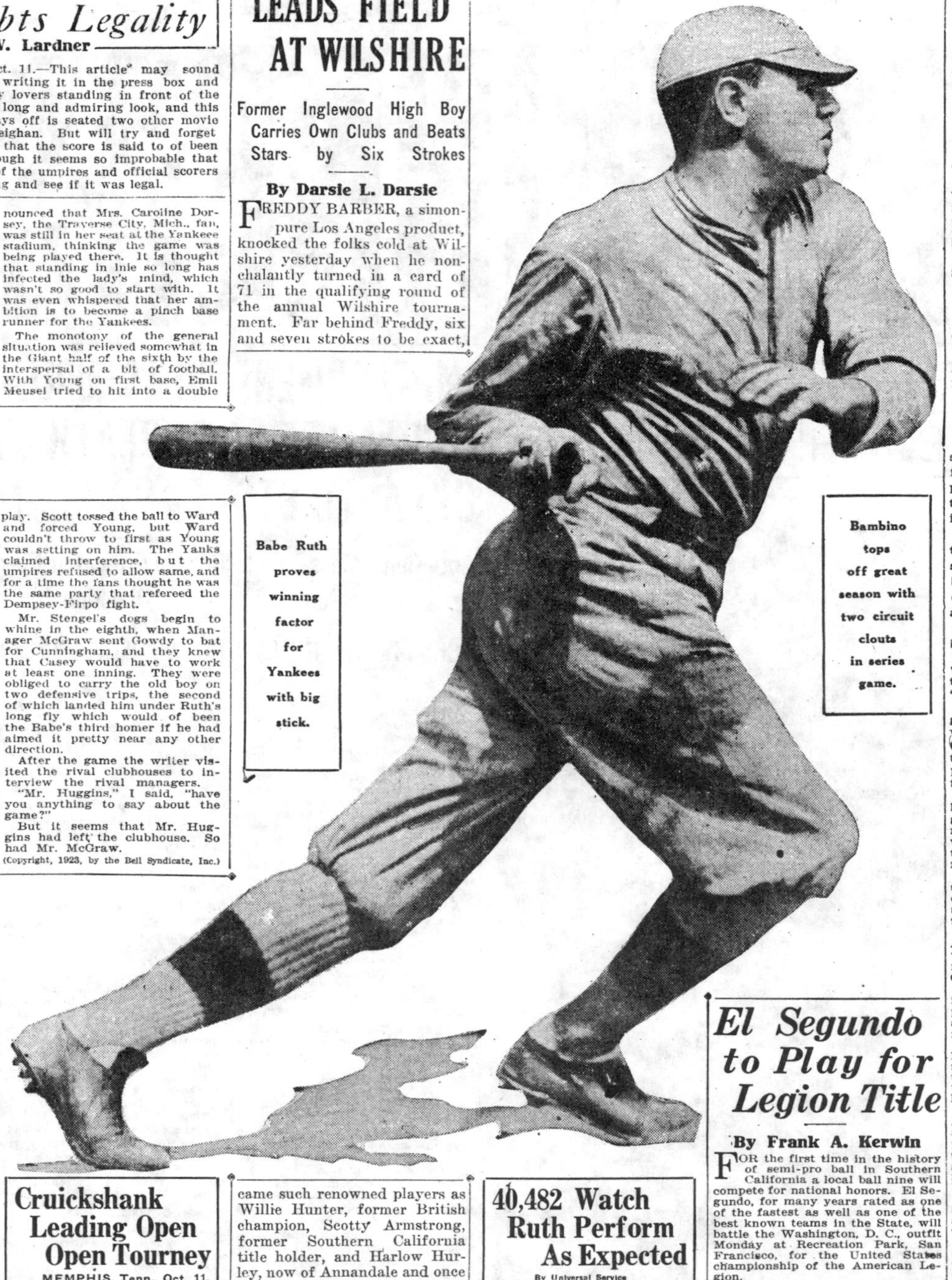

Babe Ruth proves winning factor for Yankees with big stick.

Bambino tops off great season with two circuit clouts in series game.

Brute Force Better Than 'Master Mind'

Bambino Outslugs Crafty McGraw To Give Yanks Even Break On Series

By Damon Runyon

Staff Correspondent Universal Service
(Copyright, 1923, by Universal Service)

POLO GROUNDS, N. Y., Oct. 11.—It has been written that the World's Series of 1923 is a struggle between brute force and a master mind, the first represented by Babe Ruth, huge, ponderous, formidable, the second by John J. McGraw, pudgy, gray and crafty.

That being true, it must be set down that the score of the second game at the Polo Grounds this afternoon was:

Brute force 4.

Master Mind 2.

Socrates, Aristole, and all the heavy thinkers of the ages couldn't have stopped Ruth today.

The mighty hitter of the New York Yankees slugged the American Leaguers to victory over the Giants with two home runs, those runs proving the margin of the Yankee triumph.

Poor McGraw

McGraw, sitting back in the shadow of the Giants' bench, thinking, thinking, thinking, could not produce a single thought to offset the fierce lunges of the big fellow in the fourth and fifth innings.

Once Ruth smashed the ball into the upper tier of the right field stand. Again he drove it into the lower tier. Twice he got his base on balls, and in his fifth and final appearance at bat he brought a roar from the 45,000 people packed in the green stands by hitting a ball so hard and so high that it was almost lost in the mist above the field before it settled in "Casey" Stengel's glove.

Brute force was loose in that game. Nothing could hold it. Ruth was Ruth, mammoth, majestic. The thinker on the Giant bench seemed to dwindle into nothing more important, nothing more impressive than a short, fat old gentleman.

It was the first game the Yanks have won from the Giants in nine games played since they began meeting in the world series, which was in 1921. It was their first victory after eight consecutive defeats, with a tie game among them.

It was the first time in this long stretch that brute force really became unfettered, which is surely not an impressive record for brute force.

It was a game of home runs. Aaron Ward, the Arkansas man who plays second for the Yanks, made one. "Irish" Meusel of the Giants made another.

These home runs were both hit into the left field stand. They were perhaps as important in their way as Ruth's home runs but they did not evoke the same cheering.

That is the curious thing about Ruth's home run hitting—his home runs always seem more terrific than any other home runs, though they may be hit no farther, or harder.

It would be just as easy to pick Aaron Ward's home run as the run that won the game for the Yanks, perhaps, counting Ruth's two home runs as merely part of the Yankee general score, but Ruth's two home runs will be remembered long after Ward's one has been forgotten.

That is another curious thing about Ruth's home runs—they are always the ones that seem to count the most.

A spidery young man named Herbert Pennock, a young man with thin arms and thin legs, and not much body, who pitched with his left hand, held the Giants in check after Ruth and Ward had made their home runs.

Pennock came to the Yankees from Boston Red Sox, whence so many other Yanks have come, in a trade last winter. He was once with the Philadelphia Athletics. In the winter he is said to be a gentleman farmer residing at a place called Kenneth Square, not far from Philadelphia, where he rides to the hounds and does other things gentlemen farmers are supposed to do.

Fragile Young Man

Herbert Pennock has the distinction of having pitched before the King of England, of having shook the kingly hand. That was during the war, when he pitched for a team of American sailors against a team of American soldiers in London, holding the soldiers to one hit and winning the game.

Pennock is a fragile young man. He needs four or five days' rest between ball games. Then he can generally pitch as he pitched today, with intelligence and effectiveness. His thin left arm tossed a slow ball at the Giants that seemed to quite befuddle them. Occasionally he varied this with a whizzing pitch that caught McGraw's sluggers quite unprepared.

The Yankees soon drove Hugh McQuillan, a Giant righthander, from the box, then big Jack Bentley, said to have cost McGraw $65,000, came in.

Had Bentley started the game for the Giants and pitched as effectively as he pitched after relieving McQuillan, "brute force" might have had a hard time. He held the Yankees to five scattered hits.

The game lacked the high spots of the opening game. At times it was draggy and slow, but the Yanks played with more confidence than at any time since 1921.

"As Ruth goes, so the Yankees go," says Miller Huggins.

Perhaps their new spirit today was due to the fact that Ruth found himself, that Ruth was Ruth.

A heavy handicap was placed on the big hitter when it was said before the series started that it was "all up to Ruth."

He met his handicap today and overcame it grandly, majestically, in a manner befitting Ruth.

It was a murky day, the sky gray and watery looking. There was little breeze, the forty-eight flags on the roof of the grandstand clinging limply to their staffs.

The crowd came late. The centerfield bleachers which look rather skimpy filled soon after the gates

(Continued on Page 2, Column 1)

Official Score

THE official box score tells how the world's series was evened by the American Leaguers by a score of 4 to 2.

YANKEES

	AB	R	H	O	A	E
Witt,cf	5	0	0	1	0	0
Dugan,3b	4	0	1	2	3	0
Ruth,lf	[illegible]	2	2	3	0	0
R. Meusel,lf	4	0	1	4	0	0
Pipp,1b	3	1	1	13	0	0
Ward,2b	4	1	2	3	4	0
Schang,c	4	0	1	1	0	0
Scott,ss	4	0	2	0	6	0
Pennock,p	3	0	0	0	1	0
Totals	34	4	10	27	14	0

GIANTS

	AB	R	H	O	A	E
Bancroft,ss	4	0	0	0	6	0
Groh,3b	3	1	1	0	1	0
Frisch,2b	4	0	2	2	6	0
Young,rf	4	0	2	0	0	2
E. Meusel,lf	4	1	2	4	0	0
Cunningham,cf	3	0	0	1	0	0
Kelly,1b	4	0	1	16	1	0
Snyder,c	4	0	0	3	1	0
McQuillan,p	1	0	0	0	0	0
Bentley,p	2	0	1	0	2	0
Gowdy	1	0	0	0	0	0
Stengel,cf	0	0	0	1	0	0
Jackson	1	0	0	0	0	0
Totals	35	2	9	27	17	2

Gowdy batted for Cunningham in 8th.
Jackson batted for Bentley in 9th.

Yankees	0	1	0	2	1	0	0	0	0	—4
Giants	0	1	0	0	0	1	0	0	0	—2

Two-base hits—Bentley, Dugan. Home runs—Ward, E. Meusel, Ruth, 2. Double plays—Bancroft to Frisch to Kelly, 2; Scott to Ward to Pipp. Left on bases—Yankees, 8; Giants, 8. Bases on balls—Off McQuillan, 2; Pennock, 1; Bentley, 2. Struck out—By McQuillan, 1 (R. Meusel); Pennock, 1 (Kelly). Hits—Off McQuillan, 5 in 3 2-3 innings; Bentley, 5 in 5 1-3 innings; Pennock, 9 in 9 innings. Hit by pitcher—By Bentley (Pennocw). Winning pitcher—Pennock. Losing pitcher—McQuillan. Umpires—O'Day at plate, Nallin at first, Hart at second, Evans at third. Time, 2:07.

Hose Falter and Cubs Win Second Game

CHICAGO, Oct. 11.—The National Leaguers made it two straight over the Americans in the Chicago city series today when the Cubs won the second game of the set from the Sox, 4 to 3.

Vic Aldridge pitched tight ball and was afforded brilliant support for seven innings, but after yielding two runs in the eighth and passing Mostil, first up in the ninth, he was removed in favor of Fussel, Hollis Thurston toiled the route for the Sox and was hit hard in spots.

Catcher Ray Schalk of the Americans was chased from the game in the second inning for throwing a handful of dust at Umpire Ormsby in protesting a close decision in which Schalk was called out at second. Score:

CUBS	AB	H	O	A	E	WHITE SOX	AB	H	O	A	E
Statz,cf.	5	2	1	0	0	Strunk,cf.	4	0	1	0	0
Adams,ss.	4	0	0	1	1	Hooper,rf	4	1	2	0	0
Gnthm,2b	5	2	4	2	0	Colins,2b	4	1	4	0	1
Grimes,1b	4	1	8	1	0	Sheely,1b.	4	0	10	0	0
Fribrg,3b	3	1	5	2	0	Falk,lf...	2	0	3	0	0
Miller,lf.	4	0	1	0	0	Barrett,lf	2	1	1	0	0
Heathe,rf	4	1	4	0	0	Kamm,3b	4	2	1	7	0
Hartnet,c	4	1	4	1	0	M'Clan,ss	4	1	2	5	1
Aldridg,p	4	2	0	2	0	Schalk,c.	1	1	1	0	0
Fussell,p.	0	0	0	1	0	Crouse,c.	3	2	2	2	0
						Thurstn,p	3	1	0	3	0
						Mostil...	0	0	0	0	0
						Elsh....	0	0	0	0	0
Totals	37	10	27	10	1	Totals	35	10	27	17	2

Mostil batted for Thurston in ninth.
Elsh batted for Strunk in ninth.

Cubs	1	0	0	2	0	1	0	0	0	—4
White Sox	0	0	0	0	0	0	1	2	0	—3

Two base hits—Grantham, Statz, Grimes, McClellan, Kam. Three base hits—Hooper, Barrett. Stolen bases—Hooper, Heathcote, Grantham. Sacrifice hits—Adams, Friberg, Elsh. Double plays—Friberg to Grimes. Bases on balls—Off Aldridge, 3. Struck out—By Thurston, 2; Aldridge, 2. Innings pitched—By Aldridge, 8; Fussel, 1. Winning pitcher—Aldridge. Umpires—Holmes at plate, Quigley at first base, Ormsby at second, Klem at third. Time 2 hours.

Pink Mitchell Wins Verdict

MILWAUKEE, Oct. 11.—Pinkey Mitchell of Milwaukee outpointed Joe Simonich, Butte, in a ten-round no-decision bout here tonight, in the opinion of newspaper men at the ringside. Mitchell led by a wide margin during the early rounds, when Simonich absorbed heavy punishment and landed some hard blows, which did not overcome Mitchell's lead.

Simonich was substituted for Sailor Friedman of Chicago, who was to have boxed Mitchell, but was confined to a hospital recovering from the effects of a beating he received here last night at the hands of three men, none of whom have been located by the police. Friedman's condition was reported much improved tonight.

Dempsey Challenger Knocks Out Smith

NEW YORK, Oct. 11.—Harry Wills, negro, challenger of Jack Dempsey, knocked out Homer Smith, Michigan heavyweight, in the second round of their bout at the Queensboro Stadium tonight. The end came after two minutes and six seconds of the round had elapsed. Smith was on the floor most of the time.

Cruickshank Leading Open Open Tourney

MEMPHIS, Tenn., Oct. 11.

"WEE BOBBY" CRUIKSHANK of Westfield, N. J., small of statue, but mighty of wrist, literally ironed his way to premier qualifying honors today in the Western Open Golf Tournament with a score of 140 for the two days of qualifying play, topping a field of 110 entrants in the battle for the Western classic.

"Jock" Hutchison equalled the course record of 67, four under par, in today's eighteen holes, and tied with Wilbur Oakes, Chattanooga, Wilfred Reid, Detroit, and Walter Hagen, New York, as runner-up to Cruikshank for low qualifying score.

Zev Struts His Stuff on Track for Railbirds

NEW YORK, Oct. 11.—Papyrus, English derby winner which is to run against Zev in the $100,000 international race at Belmont Park, October 20, had a good workout at Belmont today.

Although never forced to extend himself he easily out-distanced Bar Gold, who had a handicap of one-sixteenth of a mile and proved himself a real runner.

The English horse covered the mile and an eighth in 1:54 4-5 after being eased up at the mile.

Zev covered the distance in 1:52 3-5.

40,482 Watch Ruth Perform As Expected

By Universal Service

NEW YORK, Oct. 11.

FANS, 40,482 strong, paid $158,498 to see the second game of the world's series:

Today's figures:
Paid attendance, 40,482.
Receipts, $158,498.00.
Advisory Board, $23,774.70.
Each club's share, $26,944.66.
Players' share, $80,833.98.
Total two games:
Paid attendance, 95,789.
Receipts, $340,410.00.
Advisory Board, $51,661.50.
Each club's share, $26,944.66.
Players' share, $173,609.10.

Lieb Again Will Head Association of B. B. Writers

NEW YORK, Oct. 11.—Friedrich G. Lieb of New York today was re-elected president of the Baseball Writers' Association of America. Directors elected included H. P. Edwards, Cleveland. Edwards succeeds Oscar C. Reichow of Chicago, now business manager of the Los Angeles Baseball Club, who was given an honorary membership in the association.

ST. L. BROWNS' PITCHER HERE

Herb Pruitt, star St. Louis Browns hurler, has arrived in the city and expects to spend the winter here. Pruitt may take part in several exhibition games this winter. Frank Isbell, owner of the Wichita club of the Western League, is also in town.

El Segundo to Play for Legion Title

By Frank A. Kerwin

FOR the first time in the history of semi-pro ball in Southern California a local ball nine will compete for national honors. El Segundo, for many years rated as one of the fastest as well as one of the best known teams in the State, will battle the Washington, D. C., outfit Monday at Recreation Park, San Francisco, for the United States championship of the American Legion.

With the national convention in session and no opposition from a Coast League game Monday's fracas will no doubt attract enough interest to fill the home of the San Francisco Seals to capacity. According to statements of local American Legion officers the crew that hails from the Nation's capital is an aggregation of ball gamers capable of holding its own with the best semi-pro clubs in the State.

Even though the ability of the Easterners is not exaggerated they will find that in bumping up against the El Segundo nine they are meeting a foe that knows what it's all about. The crowd from the oil refining town proved its baseball strength last month when it came within an ace of trimming the big time Richmond team in a series for the State oil title.

Keltas, a young right hander, who had turned in splendid results for George Duncan's club, will be given the hurling assignment, with Lefty Bell to fall back on in case the former falters. Duncan will don the mask and pad for the Southerners. Smith, Daniels, Rodax and Brown will cover the infield, with Cramer, Thomson and Bell taking care of the outer garden. Bo Barkley, commander of El Segundo Post, and Billy Wilson, secretary of the club, will make the trip North.

Should the El Segundo legionaires cop the big title they will undoubtedly exploit their laurels to the extent of pastiming in one of the Managers' Association's winter leagues.

A special meeting for the purpose of reorganizing the double A division of the winter will be held tonight at the B. H. Dyas Log Cabin, Seventh and Olive streets. Managers of the Pasadena Merchants, Arcadia Merchants, Colton, San Bernardion, Palms and A. B. Ellis clubs will be present

FOREST FIRE DEATHS GROW

3 CENTS
OLDEST LOS ANGELES DAILY :: :: FOUNDED 1871 :: ::

Los Angeles Evening Express
ASSOCIATED PRESS SERVICE

SIX P·M· CLOSING FINANCIAL

VOL. LIII, NO. 174 | FIFTY-THIRD YEAR | MONDAY, OCTOBER 15, 1923 | Weather: Fair

Entered as second-class matter March 4, 1918, at the postoffice at Los Angeles Calif., under act of congress of March 8, 1879. Published daily except Sunday

YANKS WIN 1923 PENNANT

German Food Rioters Killed in Police Clash

THREE MORE ARE VICTIMS OF BIG BLAZE

Search of Hills Is Given Impetus

LOSS IS $1,000,000

The bodies of three more men, urned and charred by the intense eat, found shortly before noon to- ay near Montrose, have raised the nown death list to five persons the great fire than injured 50 nd did large property damage. The odies have not been identified.

According to a telephone mes- age from Forest Ranger Flintham om the scene of the fire this fternoon a search is still being ade over all the scorched and harred area for further victims. The finding of the five bodies the forest fire ruins brought the oll of death to six in fires that ave swept the outskirts of Los ngeles and a portion of the in- ustrial section near Vernon.

In the last named district a man as seen to enter the office of a urning structure. He never re- urned, and firemen today were earching the ruins for his body. he total loss by fire in this vicin- y in the past 48 hours is about ,000,000.

The fire in the neighborhood of lendale and Eagle Rock City was eported practically extinguised, ough the lines are being patrolled insure against another outbreak. erdugo canyon was not burned, but choll and Sycamore canyons were id waste.

NDER CONTROL

In Los Flores canyon the fire, hich is reported to have destroyed everal homes yesterday, today is nder control.

It was reported today that the res in the vicinity of Glendale did ss than $500,000 damage and about e same loss was suffered in the re that threatened Vernon last ight.

Trapped by the brush fire in Ver- ugo canyon, which more than 2000 en battled for hours when it reatened Montrose, Eagle Rock nd Glendale, Joseph McGahan and larence Edwards were burned to eath while trying to fight through e wall of flame.

WO BODIES RECOVERED

Dashing into the flaming office of e Wohlman Manufacturing Com- any at Alameda and Twenty-sixth reets last night, an unidentified an became separated from his ompanions when the fire threat- ned to cut off their retreat and it believed that he stumbled blind- to his death.

The bodies of Joseph McGahan, plumber living in Sycamore rove, and Clarence Edwards, ged 34, a plumbing inspector of 59 West California street, were ecovered yesterday, and the search or the other three bodies was arted this morning.

Last night's fires, which de- troyed the Ganahl Lumber Com- any and the Wohlman Manufac- uring Company plant at Alameda nd Twenty-sixth street; the Pa- fic Coast Glass Company build- g at Twenty-fifth and Santa Fe reets; the Calori Brothers Plan-

(CONTINUED ON PAGE FIVE)

BORAH SCORES LAW DEFIANCE ON WETS' PART

Says Wealth, Society Block Dry Law

POLITICS IS BLAMED

By Associated Press

WASHINGTON, Oct. 15.—The framing of recommendations as to the most effective means of arousing public opinion for a more rigid enforcement of the Volstead act constituted the most important work today before the citizenship conference at the closing sessions.

Wealthy Americans who violate the eighteenth amendment and "reds" who denounce constitutional provisions designed to protect property, Senator Borah of Idaho declared in an address here today, "are both traveling the road to lawlessness, sowing the seeds of destruction and undermining the whole fabric of law and order." The senator spoke before the citi-

(CONTINUED ON PAGE FOUR)

MEUSEL'S HIT SENDS IN RUN THAT WON

LOS ANGELES BOY GAINS NEW HONOR IN 1923 CONTESTS

YANKEE STAR LEFT FIELDER PLAYS BIG PART IN GIVING NEW YORK AMERICANS FIRST WORLD'S CHAMPIONSHIP.

BOB MEUSEL, YANKEE

ALL READY FOR IMPEACHMENT

By Associated Press

OKLAHOMA CITY, Oct. 14.—At least a full week of intensive investigation with possibly every member assigned to some committee faces the lower house of the Oklahoma legislature. Preliminary details virtually complete, the house is ready to begin the real work of its impeachment program looking to the trial before the senate of all elective state officials who may be found delinquent.

Heads of every bank in the city have been before this committee.

SHIP HITS BANK

SAN FRANCISCO, Oct. 15.—The steamer Bidwell, San Pedro for New York, is being towed to Colon leaking badly after having struck one of the banks of the Panama canal, according to a message received here today by the marine department of the Chamber of Commerce.

LEGIONNAIRES GIVE OVATION TO COMMANDER

Alvin Owsley Is Honored At S. F. Convention

KLAN QUESTION UP

By Associated Press

SAN FRANCISCO, Oct. 15.—Borne through the Civic Auditorium by the red-shirted delegates from Texas, Alvin Owsley, national commander of the American Legion, was given an enthusiastic ovation by the thousands who gathered here from every state in the Union and many foreign lands to attend the opening session of the fifth annual legion convention.

Secretary of Labor James J. Davis, representing President Coolidge; Admiral R. E. Coontz, commander in chief of the United States fleet, and Gen. Josef Haller, commander of the army of the republic of Poland, were scheduled to address the convention today.

AMERICA FIRST, SAYS DAVIS

A purely American immigration bill administered solely by Americans is needed in the United States today, Secretary of Labor Davis told the delegates. The United States can have no divided allegiance, no double loyalty and America must be for America against the world, he said.

The secretary of labor said in part:

"I recently told the chairman of the congressional immigration committee that if he had courage to put through a bill restricting immigration that we have a President with the courage to sign such a bill. If treaties have to be drawn up with other nations it will be time enough to do that when all aliens are barred from the United States.

IMMIGRATION POLICY NEEDED

"We are faced in America with the necessity of determining upon an immigration policy. At present our immigration from all coun-

(CONTINUED ON PAGE FOUR)

Lila Lee's Father Under Indictment

By United Press

CHICAGO, Oct. 15.—The [illegible] grand jury today [illegible] an indictment charging [illegible] Appel, father of Lila Lee, [illegible] with larceny.

The charge was [illegible] E. M. George, an investme[illegible] connection with a de[illegible]

Judge Caverty of [illegible] court fixed Appel's bo[illegible]

Appel is now in Los [illegible]

UNEMPLOYED FORCE STORE DOOR CLOSING

Berlin Merchants Try to Save Stocks

GUARD IS REINFORCED

By CARL D. GROAT
United Press Staff Correspondent

BERLIN, Oct. 15.—Unemployed stormed the public markets of Leipsig this morning and marched in great crowds throughout the city, breaking into stores wherever they could get past the cordons of poilce.

Many stores have bolted and barred their doors in an attempt to protect their dwindling supplies from the plunderers.

All available police have been called out to disperse the crowds by splitting them up into small groups so they can be more easily handled and prevented from engaging in fatal clashes.

TWO CIVILIANS KILLED IN CLASH AT MEININGEN

By Associated Press

BERLIN, Oct. 15.—Two civilians are reported killed and several others injured at Meiningen Saturday night, when the reichswher was called upon to help the police clear the streets of rioters. Three persons were injured in a food riot at Frankfort-on-Main on Saturday.

Involve 4 Officers In Cases of Girls

Criminal complaints against four Long Beach police officers were issued today by Judge Edwin F. Hahn charging the officers with contributing to the delinquency of Zelma Chambers, aged 14, and Clara Skipp, 17, both of Long Beach. The complaints were requested by Deputy District Attorney Joos, after an investigation by the district attorney's office and by Judge Hahn. The four officers involved in the charges are George M. Sheffield, Frank G. Henderson, Charles E. Guthrow and Otto Faulkner.

White Sox Win; Series Now 3-2 Their Favor

CHICAGO, Oct. 15.—The White Sox took today's game from the Cubs in the City series by the score of 7 to 4, giving them the edge now, three games to two for the Cubs.

Score:

	R.	H.	E.
White Sox	7	7	1
Cubs	4	5	0

Diplomats Attend Tsao-Kun Reception

By Associated Press

PEKIN, Oct. 15.—The entire diplomatic body attended the reception this morning to Marshal Tsao-Kun, the new president of China.

SMASHING RALLY IN 8TH MAKES HUGGINS MEN WORLD CHAMPS

By Associated Press

POLO GROUNDS, New York, Oct. 15.—The New York Yankees are the kings of the baseball universe for 1923. Coming from behind in the eighth inning when the score was 4 to 1 the American League champions crushed McGraw's last pitching ace, Artie Nehf, and scored five runs. The final score was 6 to 4.

SOUTHPAWS BATTLE

Southpaws—Herb Pennock for the New York Americans and Arthur Nehf for the New York Nationals opposed each other at the start.

In the three previous games the Yankees had won, brute force was the deciding factor, but today Manager Miller Huggins, emulating Manager John McGraw of the Giants, mixed in some strategy and so bewildered Arthur Nehf that the Giants' southpaw went completely to pieces and the game was lost.

FIVE RUNS IN EIGHTH

Huggins threw in two pinch hitters and two extra runners in the decisive eighth inning and the Yankees scored five runs on two hits, three bases on balls and a third hit, helped along by the error of Cunningham, Giant centerfielder who overthrew the ball in trying to get a runner.

Nehf had pitched wonderful baseball, allowing only two hits and striking out two men. He was given the most brilliant support by the Giant infield, particularly by Frank Frisch, "the Fordham flash," who made three brilliant features of fielding. Frisch also distinguished himself at bat, making three consecutive hits and scoring two runs.

BAT ALL AROUND

The Giants went to the field in the eighth inning with the game on ice. They had rolled up a lead of three runs, one of them a homer by Frank Snyder in the fifth inning that matched the circuit clout that Babe Ruth made in the first inning. But in the eighth the Yanks batted all around, the second time in the series that "murderers' row" has accomplished this feat.

The official figures of attendance and receipts for the sixth and last game of the series today are:

Attendance, 34,172.
Receipts, $139,252.
Advisory council share, $20,887.80
Each club share, $59,182.10.

It was the first time that a New York American League team had won a world's series.

GIANTS GET LEAD

Opportune hitting by Giant batsmen and after the first inning, airtight pitching by Arthur Nehf coupled with brilliant support by the Giant infield, gave the Giants a three-run lead at the end of the sixth inning. The score then was 4 to 1.

Frankie Frisch, the Fordham flash, was one of the stars of the contest, getting three hits, his first three times up, one instrumental in scoring another runner, another single on which Cunningham scored him and the third a triple on which

(CONTINUED ON FIRST SPORT PAGE)

BOX SCORE

YANKS—	AB	R	BH	PO	A	E
Witt, cf	3	0	0	3	1	0
Dugan, 3b	3	1	0	2	1	0
Ruth, rf	3	1	1	1	0	0
R. Meusel, lf	4	0	1	1	0	0
Pipp, 1b	4	0	0	12	0	0
Ward	4	0	1	0	7	0
Schang, c	4	1	1	7	0	0
E. Scott, ss	4	1	1	1	2	0
Pennock, p	2	0	0	0	1	0
Hofmann	0	0	0	0	0	0
Haines, cf	0	1	0	0	0	0
Bush	0	0	0	0	0	0
Johnson	0	1	0	0	0	0
Jones, p	0	0	0	0	1	0
Totals	31	6	5	27	13	0

Hofmann batted for Pennock in eighth.
Haines ran for Hofmann in eighth.
Bush batted for Witt in eighth.
Johnson ran for Bush in eighth.

GIANTS—	AB	R	BH	PO	A	E
Bancroft, ss	4	0	0	1	7	0
Groh, 3b	4	1	1	1	2	0
Frisch, 2b	4	2	3	1	5	0
Young, rf	4	0	2	0	0	0
E. Meusel, lf	4	0	1	1	0	0
Cun'gham, cf	3	0	1	0	0	1
Kelly, 1b	4	0	0	19	0	0
Snyder, c	4	1	2	4	0	0
Nehf, p	3	0	0	0	5	0
Ryan, p	0	0	0	0	0	0
Stengel, cf	1	0	0	0	0	0
Bentley	1	0	0	0	0	0
Totals	38	4	10	27	19	1

Stengel batted for Cunningham in eighth.
Bentley batted for Ryan in ninth.

Yankees	100 000 050—6
Giants	100 111 000—4

Three-base hit—Frisch. Home runs—Ruth, Snyder. Double plays—Nehf, Bancroft to Kelly. Left on bases—Yankees, 2; Giants, 5 Bases on balls—Nehf, 3; Ryan, 1. Struck out—Nehf, 3 (R. Meusel, Pennock, Ruth); by Pennock, 6 (E. Meusel, Snyder, Nehf 3, Kelly); by Ryan, 1 (Ruth). Hits—Off Nehf, 4 in 7 1-3; Ryan, 1 in 1 2-3; Pennock, 9 in 7; Jones, 1 in 2. Winning pitcher—Pennock. Losing pitcher—Nehf. Umpires—O'Day at plate, Nallin at first, Hart at second, Evans at third. Time—2:07.

YANKEES WON BY GAMENESS

By HENRY L. FARRELL
United Press Staff Correspondent

POLO GROUNDS, NEW YORK, Oct. 15.—Game and as stout hearted as any team that ever walked, the surprising New York Yankees

(CONTINUED ON FIRST SPORT PAGE)

YANKS WIN WORLD SERIES

3 CENTS in San Francisco and Oakland ELSEWHERE 5¢

THE SAN FRANCISCO CALL AND POST — AN INDEPENDENT NEWSPAPER

FINAL HOME EDITION

CALL AND POST, VOL. 114, NO. 86
SAN FRANCISCO CALL, VOL. 134, NO. 86

TWENTY-FOUR PAGES—SAN FRANCISCO, MONDAY, OCTOBER 15, 1923

PRICE ON TRAINS AND HOTEL NEWSSTANDS 5¢ | DELIVERED BY CARRIER 75c a Month

LEGION CONVENTION OPENS HERE

$5000 JEWEL LOOT IN THIRD ST. HOLDUP

THUG PAIR HOLD UP ATTELL'S STORE

Held up at the point of a revolver while hundreds of pedestrians passed by and a policeman stood on the opposite corner, Caesar Attell, owner of the Atlas Jewelry Company, 101½ Third street, was robbed of $5000 in jewelry and cash early today by two desperadoes who escaped. A large sum of money in a cash drawer was overlooked by the robbers.

Whipping out a pistol as he stepped in the store, one of the robbers leveled the weapon at Attell and ordered him to scoop gold watches, diamond stickpins and other jewelry into a bag.

"Work fast and gimme your watch and stickpin," commanded the robber, who then grabbed a $125 diamond ring from Attell's finger.

The bandit then emptied the cash till of $90 and ordered Attell into a rear room.

"I'm going to clean you out now," the thug growled, "and if you make one peep I'll drill you."

Attell remained in the rear room until Harry Schwartz, foreman of the store, entered five minutes later.

Attell describes the robber as being about 26 years old and the lookout as about 40. The "inside man" wore a light gray suit and a cap, while his companion wore a dark suit.

This is the second time Attell, who is a brother of Abe and Monte Attell, prizefighters, has been victimized.

Four months ago Attell was robbed of $3800 in cash and a $500 ring by two men who had offered to sell him a grip full of platinum, which turned out to be copper wire.

Baltimore-K. C. Game Off; Rain

By Associated Press.

KANSAS CITY, Oct. 15.—Today's game between Baltimore and Kansas City, the fourth of the junior world series, was postponed on account of rain. It will be played tomorrow, weather permitting.

Legion Head = = By Argens

Alvin Owsley, National Legion Commander

CONVICT FELLS JUTE MILL GUARD

Special Dispatch to The Call.

SAN QUENTIN, Oct. 15.—Arthur Fyfe, guard at San Quentin, was struck over the head with an iron bar by Roberto Diez, a convict, in the ujte mill today, sustaining probably a fractured skull. Diaz, a burglar from Imperial County, was locked in solitary confinement pending investigation. Fyfe was instructing a new prisoner in the use of a loom when struck from behind.

Citizens and Reichswehr in Battle; 3 Die

BERLIN, Oct. 15 (By the Associated Press).—Three persons are dead and many wounded at Meiningen, in the duchy of Saxe-Meiningen, following a violent battle between citizens and reichswehr, said a dispatch from that place this afternoon.

Disorders continue at Erfurt, in Prussian Saxony.

CUBS' STADIUM BLAST

CHICAGO, Oct. 15.—Damages in excess of $6000 was caused by the explosion of a dynamite time bomb at the entrance of the Cubs' baseball stadium here yesterday.

OWSLEY OUSTS LEGION OFFICIAL

Joseph Sparks, chairman of the national rehabilitation committee of the American Legion, has been summarily removed by Alvin Owsley, national legion commander, it became known from an authoritative source today.

The dismissal, it was said, came swiftly yesterday on the eve of the opening of the national legion convention in San Francisco.

"Conduct unbecoming a legionnaire" was given as the reason.

YANK CREW COMES FROM BEHIND IN EIGHTH INNING, DEFEATING GIANTS 6 TO 4

POLO GROUNDS, NEW YORK, Oct. 15 (By the Associated Press).—Coming from behind with a great batting attack that drove Arthur Nehf from the mound the New York Americans scored five runs in the eighth inning of today's world series game at the Polo Grounds and led the New York Nationals at the end of the eighth inning . Nehf had allowed only two hits up until the eighth, and then went to pieces. With Ward down, Schan and Scott singled, Hoffman, batting for Pennock, was walked, filling the bases, and Nehf passed Bush, batting for Witt, forcing in a run. Nehf was yanked and "Rosey" Bill Ryan, who went in to relieve him, walked Dugan, forcing in another run.

RUTH FANS

With the bases full, Babe Ruth fanned on four pitched balls(but Bob Meusel sent a long double to center, scoring Hoffman and Bush. Dugan was stopping at third, but Cunningham, Giant center field, threw the ball to the grand stand and "Jumping Joe" came in. Pipp made the last out.

The Giants had a chance in their half of the eighth. After Frisch went out, Young singled, but Emil Meusel forced him at second and Casey Stengel, who went in in place of Cunningham, fouled out to Dugan, who ran dowon to the plate to get the ball.

The score today was 6 to 4.

The official figures of attendance and receipts for the game today are: Attendance, 34,172; receipts, $139,252; advisory council's share, $20,887.80; each club's share, $59,182.10.

HUGGINS STRATEGY

In the three previous games the Yankees had won, brute force was the deciding factor; but today Manager Miller Huggins, emulating Manager John McGraw of the Giants, mixed in some strategy and so bewildered Arthur Nehf that the Giant southpaw went completely to pieces and the game was lost.

Huggins threw in two pinch hitters and two extra runners in the decisive eighth inning and the Yankees scored five runs on three hits, three bases on balls, helped along by the error Cunningham, Giant centerfielder, who overthrew the ball in trying to get a runner.

Nehf had pitched wonderful baseball, allowing only two hits and striking out two men. He was given the most brilliant support by the Giant infield, particularly by Frank Frisch, "the Fordham flash," who made three brilliant features of fielding. Frisch also distinguished himself at bat, making three consecutive hits and scoring two runs.

RUTH HITS HOMER

he Giants went to the field in the eighth inning with the game on ice. They had rolled up a lead of three runs, one of them a homer by Frank Snyder in the fifth inning that matched the circuit clout that Babe Ruth made in the first inning. But in the eighth the Yanks batted all

Continued on Next Page, Col. Four

LEGIONERS OPEN FIFTH CONVENTION

Color—a riot of it! Music—a dozen bands blaring forth the tunes of the trenches, the trenches of 1917. Legionnaires standing on chairs and cheering, singing, thumping each other on the back. Youth—exuberant, a hundred friendships renewed in a polite civilization which seemed 5000 years away from the primitive struggle of Flanders field. A band! A hip-hip-hooray! And "the old gray mare, she ain't what she used to be, she ain't what she used to be—"

That is the way the fifth annual convention opened today in the Exposition Auditorium.

It was forty minutes before order could be restored. Alvin Owsley of Texas, national commander, rapped for order at 10:10 a. m., and finally brought the conclave to order.

CHEER ROLPH, JOHNSON

There were cheers for Mayor James Rolph Jr. and for Senator Hiram W. Johnson—ovations which lasted for several minutes.

The Texas delegation whooped it up in true wild West style.

Clad in their colorful red shirts with the green trimming, they paraded the auditorium bearing Alvin Owsley of their state, national commander of the legion, on their shoulders.

Owsley was greeted with a tremendous barrage of cheers and applause.

SEA OF FLAGS

Arizona came in with its bronze-helmeted delegates. Color everywhere. A dozen bands playing at once.

The huge auditorium was a sea of flags of all nations, and on the stage were photographs of the late Warren G. Harding and Frederick W. Galbraith Jr., late national commander of the legion.

A sea of faces greeted National Commander Owsley.

The color guard presented the col-

Continued on Page Three, Col. One

BOX SCORE

YANKEES

Player, Position—	AB.	R.	BH.	PO.	A.	E.
Witt, center field	3	0	0	3	1	0
Dugan, third base	3	1	0	2	1	0
Ruth, right field	3	1	1	1	0	0
R. Meusel, left field	4	0	1	1	0	0
Pipp, first base	4	0	0	12	0	0
Ward, second base	4	0	1	0	6	0
Schang, catcher	4	1	1	7	0	0
Scott, shortstop	4	1	1	1	2	0
Pennock, pitcher	2	0	0	0	1	0
Hoffman	0	0	0	0	0	0
Haines, center feild	0	1	0	0	0	0
Bush	0	0	0	0	0	0
Johnson	0	1	0	0	0	0
Jones	0	0	0	0	0	0
Totals	31	6	5	27	11	0

GIANTS

Player, Position—	AB.	R.	BH.	PO.	A.	E.
Bancroft, shortstop	4	0	0	1	7	0
Groh, third base	4	1	1	1	2	0
Frisch, second base	4	2	3	1	5	0
Young, right field	4	0	2	0	0	0
E. Meusel, left field	4	0	1	1	0	0
Cunningham, center field	3	0	1	0	0	1
Kelly, first base	4	0	0	19	0	0
Snyder, catcher	4	1	2	4	0	0
Nehf, pitcher	3	0	0	0	5	0
Stengel, center field	1	0	0	0	0	0
Ryan, pitcher	0	0	0	0	0	0
Bentley	1	0	0	0	0	0
Total	36	4	10	27	19	1

RUNS AND HITS BY INNINGS

Yankees	1	0	0	0	0	0	0	5	0—6
Hits	1	1	0	0	0	0	0	3	0—5
Giants	1	0	0	1	1	1	0	0	0—4
Hits	3	0	0	2	1	2	1	1	0—10

SUMMARY

Home runs—Ruth, Snyder. Three-base hit—Frisch. Double plays—Nehf, Bancroft, Kelly. Left on bases—Yanks 1, Giants 4. Struck out—By Nehf 3, Ryan 1, Pennock 4. Bases on balls—Off Nehf 2, Ryan 1. Credit victory to Pennock. Charge defeat to Nehf. 25 at bat, 3 runs, 4 hits off Nehf in 7 2-3 innings.

BATTING AVERAGES FOR SERIES

YANKEES

Player, Position—	G.	AB.	R.	BH.	2B.	3B.	HR.	SH.	SB.	Pct.
Ward, second base	6	24	4	10	0	0	1	0	1	167
Bush, pitcher	4	7	2	3	1	0	0	0	0	428
Ruth, right field	6	19	8	7	1	1	3	0	0	368
Schang, catcher	6	22	3	7	0	0	0	2	0	318
E. Scott, shortstop	6	22	2	7	0	0	0	0	0	318
Shawkey, pitcher	1	3	0	1	0	0	0	0	0	333
Dugan, third base	6	25	5	7	2	1	1	0	0	280
Pipp, first base	6	20	2	5	0	0	0	1	0	250
Witt, center field	6	25	1	6	2	0	0	1	0	240
R. Meusel, left field	6	26	1	7	1	2	0	0	0	269
Pennock, pitcher	3	6	0	0	0	0	0	0	0	000
Jones, pitcher	2	2	0	0	0	0	0	0	0	000
Hoyt, pitcher	1	1	0	0	0	0	0	0	0	000
Haines	2	1	1	0	0	0	0	0	0	000
Hendricks	1	1	0	0	0	0	0	0	0	000
Hoffman	2	1	0	0	0	0	0	0	0	000
Johnson	2	0	1	0	0	0	0	0	0	000

GIANTS

Player, Position—	G.	AB.	R.	BH.	2B.	3B.	HR.	SH.	SB.	Pct.
Bentley, pitcher	5	5	0	3	1	0	0	0	0	600
Stengel, center field	6	12	3	5	0	0	2	0	0	416
Frisch, second base	6	25	2	10	0	1	0	0	0	400
Nehf, pitcher	2	3	0	1	0	0	0	0	0	333
Young, right field	6	23	2	8	0	0	1	0	0	347
E. Meusel, left field	6	25	3	7	1	1	1	0	0	280
Kelly, first base	6	22	1	4	0	0	0	0	0	125
Groh, third base	6	22	3	4	0	1	0	0	0	125
Bancroft, shortstop	6	24	1	2	0	0	0	0	1	083
Snyder, catcher	5	17	1	2	0	0	1	0	0	117
Cunningham, center field	3	7	0	1	0	0	0	0	0	142
Gowdy, catcher	3	4	0	0	0	0	0	0	0	000
McQuillan, pitcher	2	3	0	0	0	0	0	0	0	000
Ryan, pitcher	3	2	0	0	0	0	0	0	0	000
O'Connell	2	1	0	0	0	0	0	0	0	000
J. Scott, pitcher	2	1	0	0	0	0	0	0	0	000
Jonnard, pitcher	2	1	0	0	0	0	0	0	0	000
Barnes, pitcher	2	1	0	0	0	0	0	0	0	000
Jackson	1	1	0	0	0	0	0	0	0	000
Maguire	2	0	0	0	0	0	0	0	0	000

GAME IN DETAIL BY INNINGS

By Associated Press.

FIRST INNING

YANKEES—Witt up. Strike 1. Ball 1. Ball 2. Foul, strike 2. Witt sent up a high fly to Groh. Dugan up. Strike 1. Ball 1. Ball 2. Foul, strike 2. Foul. Frisch tossed out Dugan. Ruth up. Strike 1. Ball 1. Ball 2. Foul, strike 2. Ball 3. Ruth scored on a home run into the upper right field stand. Meusel up. Ball 1. Strike 1. Ball 2. Foul, strike 2. Foul. Ball 3. Meusel fanned. **One run, one hit, no errors.**

GIANTS—Bancroft up. Strike 1. Strike 2. Ball 1. Foul. Bancroft flied out to Witt. Groh up. Ball 1. Ball 2. Ball 3. Strike 1. Strike 2. Groh singled into left. Frisch up. Foul, strike 1. Frisch got a single off Pennock's leg, Groh going to second. Young up. Strike 1. Ball 1. Ball 2. Ball 3. Strike 2. Foul. Groh scored on Young's single to center and Frisch was thrown out at third, Witt to Dugan. Meusel up. Strike 1. Ball 1. Foul, strike 2. Ball 2. Meusel struck out. **One run, three hits, no errors.**

SECOND INNING

YANKEES—Pipp up. Strike 1. Strike 2. Ball 1. Nehf threw out Pipp. Ward up. Foul, strike 1. Ball 1. Ball 2. Ward crashed a single into left. Schang up. Foul, strike 1. Ball 1. Ball 2. Strike 2. Schang hit into a double play, Nehf to Bancroft to Kelly. **No runs, one hit, no errors.**

GIANTS—Cunningham up. Ball 1. Strike 1. Cunningham flied out to Witt. Kelly up. Kelly fouled out to Schang. Snyder up. Foul, strike 1. Strike 2. Snyder whiffed. **No runs, no hits, no errors.**

THIRD INNING

YANKEES—Scott up. Nehf threw out Scott. Pennock up. Strike 1. Strike 2. Ball 1. Ball 2. Nehf also threw out Pennock. Witt up. Strike 1. Foul, strike 2. Witt flied out to Meusel. **No runs, no hits, no errors.**

GIANTS—Nehf up. Foul, strike 1. Ball 1. Ball 2. Strike 2. Nehf struck out. Bancroft up. Ball 1. Ball 2. Ball 3. Strike 1. Strike 2. Dugan threw out Bancroft.

Continued on Next Page, Col. Three

NEWS DOWN TO THE LAST MINUTE

TWO KILLED IN CAR CRASH

By Associated Press

DENISON, Neb., Oct. 15.—August Hansen and Henry Grawman, farmhands, were caught at a crossing one mile east of here last night by a Chicago Northwestern fast mail while riding in an auto and both were killed instantly.

5:30 P. M.

SPORTING EXTRA
The Evening Bulletin.

5:30 P. M.

VOLUME LXI. NO. 242. TUESDAY: Fair. PROVIDENCE, MONDAY, OCTOBER 15, 1923 32 PAGES TWO CENTS 14 Cents Per Week Delivered by Carrier.

YANKS WIN WORLD'S BASEBALL CHAMPIONSHIP

"BOB" MEUSEL

Yankee Outfielder Who Won World Series for His Team To-day When He Drove Tieing and Winning Runs Across in the Eighth

COMPLETE BOX SCORE OF SIXTH WORLD SERIES GAME

YANKEES

	AB	R	H	PO	A	E
Witt, m......	3	0	0	3	1	0
Haines, m.....	0	1	0	0	0	0
Dugan, 3......	3	1	0	2	1	0
Ruth, r.......	3	1	1	1	0	0
R. Meusel, l...	4	0	1	1	0	0
Pipp, 1b......	4	0	0	12	0	0
Ward, 2.......	4	0	1	0	7	0
Schang, c	4	1	1	7	0	0
Scott, s......	4	1	1	1	2	0
Pennock, p ...	2	0	0	0	1	0
*Hofman, ...	0	0	0	0	0	0
‡Bush, ...	0	0	0	0	0	0
xJohnson, ...	0	1	0	0	0	0
Jones, p......	0	0	0	0	1	0
Totals.....	31	6	5	27	13	0

GIANTS

	AB	R	H	PO	A	E
Bancroft, s ...	4	0	0	1	7	0
Groh, 3	4	1	1	1	2	0
Frisch, 2......	4	2	3	0	6	0
Young, r......	4	0	2	0	0	0
E. Meusel, l...	4	0	1	1	0	0
Cun'gham, m ...	3	0	1	0	0	1
Stengel, m....	1	0	0	0	0	0
Kelly, 1b.....	4	0	0	20	0	0
Snyder, c.....	4	1	2	4	0	0
Nehf, p	3	0	0	0	5	0
Ryan, p	0	0	0	0	0	0
†Bentley ...	1	0	0	0	0	0
Totals.....	36	4	10	27	29	1

INNINGS	1	2	3	4	5	6	7	8	9	R	H	E
YANKEES	1	0	0	0	0	0	0	5	0	6	5	0
GIANTS	1	0	0	1	1	0	1	0	0	4	10	1

Hits—Off Nehf 4 in 7 1-3 innings; off Pennock 9 in 7 innings.
Three base hit—Frisch.
Home runs—Ruth, Snyder.
Double plays—Nehf to Bancroft to Kelly.
Struck Out—By Nehf 3, by Pennock 5, by Ryan 1.
Bases on Balls—Off Nehf 3, off Ryan 1.
Left on bases—Yankees 2, Giants 4.
Time of game—2h. 8m.
Umpires — Evans, Nallin, Hart, O'Day.

*Hofmann batted for Pennock in seventh.
†Bentley batted for Ryan in ninth.
‡Bush batted for Witt in seventh.
xJohnson ran for Bush in seventh.

GEORGE "BABE" RUTH

The Mighty Bambino, Who Created New World Series Record To-day When He Got a Home Run in the First Inning, Making Three Circuit Clouts for the Series.

TWELVE INDICTED HERE ON GAMBLING CHARGES

Nearly Score of Secret Bills Are Also Returned as Grand Jury Reports in Superior Court

The crusade against gamblers which has been conducted in different sections of the State hit Providence County to-day when the September grand jury, which has been in session the past few weeks in the Superior Court building, returned indictments against the following:

George B. Briggs of Warwick, charged with being a common gambler in Cranston and Pawtuxet Valley.

Joseph Payan, alleged manager of the Pilgrim Club in Cranston, charged with being a common gambler and with maintaining a nuisance.

John F. Hennessey of East Providence, charged with being a common gambler and with maintaining a nuisance.

James Cianci, alleged proprietor of the Silver Lake Hotel in Cranston, which recently burned, charged with being a common gambler and with maintaining a nuisance.

William Riley of North Providence, charged with being a common gambler.

Joseph Lizard of North Providence, alleged to be in the employ of William Riley, charged with being a common gambler.

Bessie Cook, alias Ramsey, alleged proprietor of the Admiral Inn, Cumberland, which was raided Friday night by Sheriff Jonathan Andrews and Deputy Thomas, charged with being a common gambler and with maintaining a nuisance.

Briggs, Riley and Lizard are alleged to be the owners or operators of slot machines.

Bertha Koch of Foster, two indictments, alleging maintaining gambling nuisances.

Jacob Kulze, alleged proprietor of the Sunnyside Hotel, Johnston, maintaining common gambling nuisance.

James P. Cahill, Foster, alleged proprietor of the Hartford Pike House, two indictments, alleging common gambler and maintaining gambling unisance.

Joseph George, alias Blind Joe, Woonsocket, maintaining common nuisance.

Cornelius Keating, alleged proprietor of the St. Cloud Hotel, Johnston, maintaining nuisance.

Nineteen secret indictments were also returned, a large number of which were said to be the result of the crusade of the Attorney General's office against gambling.

The report of the grand jury shows that thus far 26 gambling indictments have been filed against 12 different persons, in addition to the secret indictments.

No indictments were found against the following: James E. Spelman, charged

Continued on Page 2, Col. 5.

SIX, TRAPPED IN ATTIC, BURN TO DEATH IN BROOKLYN

Firemen Find Charred Bodies in Ruins Two Hours After Blaze is Discovered.—Investigation of Cause Ordered.

[*By the Associated Press*]

New York, Oct. 15.—Six persons were trapped in an attic and burned to death, and a seventh, a woman, suffered grave injuries in leaping from the flames in a fire which early to-day destroyed a frame three-story dwelling in the Bensonhurst section of Brooklyn.

The dead are:

Mrs. Lillian Andrews, her nephew, Charles, and niece, Margaret.
Geo Kyne, playwright.
Fr .s Poncho Fowler.
M Roberta Wigert.
M Anna Andrews, who was trapped wit the others in the attic of the building, leaped through a window, sustaining internal injuries which may prove fatal.

Neighbors, seeing smoke rolling from the basement of the dwelling house, rushed to the spot just in time to see Mrs. Anna Andrews leap from a window of the attic apartment. Two hours later firemen found the charred bodies of the six victims. They apparently had been overcome after escape had been cut off by the flames.

The body of Charles Andrews, 19-year-old athlete and student at Polytechnic Institute, Brooklyn, lay just inside of a rear window. Near him lay his aunt, Mrs. Lillian Andrews. The body of 12-year-old Margaret was found clasped in the arms of Miss Wigert, a maid, in an adjoining room.

The ruins of a third bedroom disclosed the body of Fowler. Kyne had been trapped in the bathroom in an attempt to reach a window. They were roomers in the Andrews home.

A dozen occupants of the first and second floor apartments of the burned building were awakened and led through the flames to safety by Dr. Thomas McNickle, a dentist, and his brother, whose four nieces were among the rescued.

Heads of the fire department have ordered an investigation to determine the origin of the fire.

TWO CIVILIANS KILLED IN MEININGEN, GERMANY

Troops Aid Police in Clearing Streets of Rioters.

[*By the Associated Press*]

Berlin, Oct. 15.—Two civilians are reported to have been killed and several others injured at Meiningen Saturday night when the Reichswehr was called upon to help the police clear the streets of rioters.

Three persons were injured in a food riot at Frankfort-on-Main on Saturday.

NO IDLENESS IN FRANCE, LABOR STATISTICS SHOW

Only 66 in All Paris Out of Work; 1275 in Whole Country.

[*By the Associated Press*]

Paris, Oct. 15.—The French Government has no unemployment problem on its hands. Statistics compiled by the Ministry of Labor show that only 1275 persons are out of work in all France, of whom 66 are in Paris, whereas in March, 1921, the number of unemployed was 91,225. Of this number 45,100 were in Paris.

Series Results

FIRST GAME
GIANTS 5—YANKEES 4

SECOND GAME
YANKEES 4—GIANTS 2

THIRD GAME
GIANTS 1—YANKEES 0

FOURTH GAME
YANKEES 8—GIANTS 4

FIFTH GAME
YANKEES 8—GIANTS 1

SIXTH GAME
YANKEES 6—GIANTS 4

4 MEN SEIZED WITH LIQUOR-LADEN CARS FAIL TO RAISE BAIL

Quartet Apprehended Early Yesterday Morning in East Providence is Jailed.—464 Bottles of Whiskey Found in Two Machines Are Valued at $5000.

Four alleged rum runners, piloting two liquor-laden touring cars, fell victims to the vigilance of Patrolmen Frederick Hancock and John Estes of the East Providence police after an exciting chase at 3 o'clock yesterday morning. The haul aggregated 464 bottles of Scotch whiskey, valued at $5000, and the prisoners, W. B. Bradley and Bertram M. Armstrong of Albany, King Johnson of Riverside and Alex Carron, formerly of East Providence, arraigned before Judge Malcolm D. Champlin in the Seventh District Court, East Providence, yesterday forenoon, were jailed in default of bail. Trial was set for next Saturday.

All entered not guilty pleas. Bradley was charged with carrying a concealed weapon and transporting liquor. Bail was set at $500 on the first charge and $1000 on the second.

Armstrong's case was similarly disposed of. Johnson and Carron were charged with transporting liquor only. Their bail was $1000 each.

Signal Unheeded

Hancock, on duty in Riverside, signalled a touring car to stop when he saw it speeding into Turner avenue. The big automobile hurtled on, unheeding, how-

Continued on Page 3, Col. 4.

NEW PRESIDENT OF CHINA IS TENDERED RECEPTION

Pekin, Oct. 15.—(By the Associated Press.))—The entire diplomatic body attended the reception this morning to Marshal Tsao Kun, the new President of China.

BABE RUTH GETS THIRD HOME RUN, NEW RECORD

Mighty Swatsmith Sets Mark That May Stand for All Time

Special to the Evening Bulletin.

Polo Grounds, New York, Oct. 15.—All hail the Yankees, new baseball champions of the world. After two years of dismal failure the American League crew under Miller Huggins came into its own to-day. The result of to-day's final set-to of the 1923 struggle was:

Yankees 6, Giants 4

Starters in the blue ribbon classic of baseball the past three years, each year against "Jawn" McGraw and his Giants, the Yankees landed the bacon this year for the first time. Two years ago the Yankees obtained an early lead and it looked as though there was nothing to it but the American Leaguers. Then, in one of the most sensational rallies ever witnessed in the fall classic, the Giants took three straight and the series, making monkeys out of Babe Ruth and the other big sticks of the Yankee crew.

Last year the Yanks made their punkiest showing, falling down miserably in five games, the best they could do being to tie the Giants in one of the games and losing the other four. But this year it was a different story. Losing the first game, the Yankees came back in the second and evened the series. Casey Stengel gave the Giants a 2 to 1 lead in the third game when his home run was the only run scored in the set-to.

But in the fourth battle the Yankees unlimbered their heavy artillery and when the smoke of battle had cleared away they were out on the long end of an 8 to 4 score, the clan of Huggins having crushed to a pulp the Giant firing squad. Hit after hit of every description rolled off the bats of the American Leaguers. Yesterday it was almost a repetition of the day before, Babe Ruth et al., taking kindly to everything

CHARACTER QUALITY AMERICA FIRST ENTERPRISE ACCURACY

Los Angeles Examiner Sports

AN AMERICAN PAPER FOR THE AMERICAN PEOPLE — THE GREAT NEWSPAPER OF THE GREAT SOUTHWEST

N. Y. YANKEES 1923 WORLD CHAMPIONS

TOD SLOAN PICKS PAPYRUS OVER ZEV

Coast League Season Financial Bust for Five of Eight Clubs

War on Draft Gave Inferior Class to Game

By Mark Kelly

THE Coast League's 1923 season goes into the little red book as a triple bust—a flivver in class, financial gain and warfare on the majors. The defeat is admitted on all sides and the magnates' moans are not hushed.

W. H. McCarthy

Three of the eight clubs in the league made a little money—San Francisco, Sacramento and Portland. None of them got rich. The pennant winning Seals made profit because they led the league for 23 of the 28 weeks in the season. Sacramento made a little money because they get a better "cut" on the road than other clubs and also because they managed to finish second. Portland made a slight profit because their club finished third and for a time threatened to give the Seals a battle. After those three clubs—period.

The season just ended has been disastrous from many angles and for many causes. The fans tired of baseball that was below mediocrity. The class of baseball was fully 35 per cent beneath that of previous seasons and as there was no remedy to be had, weak teams went through the season without succor from their major league brethren. Strong teams—and there were but two—waxed fat.

POLITICS ENTER

Petty political bickering opened the season. Personal acrimony closed it. The filling for the sandwich was public apathy. Perhaps the moguls will profit from the lesson; perhaps harmony and better baseball will be the sunrise of 1924's baseball; perhaps hatchets will be buried elsewhere than in the scalps of the rival factions, but in any event unless 1924 produces better baseball than 1923 did the Coast League is due for a flop.

The Coast League in annual meeting last January voted to refuse to accept the major leagues' draft clauses. The draft is one of the workings of baseball whereby young ball players get a chance for major league careers by being "drafted" at the end of the playing season from minor league clubs. The majors agreed to give the Coast League clubs $7500 for each player so commandeered. No more than one player was to be taken from a Coast League club in one year.

This, the minority of the Coast League voted down. Because several phenoms had been turned up by San Francisco—O'Connell and Kamm and Caveney—this outfit wanted no draft but fat purchase prices. They succeeded—with the aid of a friendly league president—in forcing the issue in their favor. When this was done the Seals already had lined up the most powerful club in the circuit and had plenty of reserve strength to carry them through to a pennant.

SEATTLE ROW

Then came the Seattle row. James Boldt sold the Indians' franchise to Wade Killefer, James J. Sullivan and Charles Lockhard. Killefer and Lockhard had been Wrigley employees and connected with the Los Angeles club, so the cry was raised of syndicate baseball. President McCarthy ordered a probe to determine whether Wrigley money had purchased the club. He refused to recognize either Lockhard or Killefer and refused to grant Seattle a vote in the directorate, further gumming up the cards.

This controversy had a bad effect on the game's popularity. Yet in the heat of argument the moguls played politics and forgot baseball. Vernon went to pieces and dropped to eighth place where they finished. Los Angeles, a high-priced organization, did another flop and finished sixth. Oakland, a cheap outfit, finished seventh. Salt Lake finished fifth. Portland and Seattle finished in the first division. The failure of the Angels to make a better showing may be attributed to the failure of its pitching staff to come up to advance notices. Or it may be attributed to the internal strife. We are inclined to the former theory while we admit that there will have to be at least seven changes on the club next year if Krug, the manager, is to have a harmonious ball club.

The program ahead looks doubtful. If McCarthy, the San Francisco, Vernon and Sacramento owners hang together again and refuse to allow Seattle a vote there is no relief in sight—merely a continuation of the class of baseball that made the game odious this year. If Los Angeles, Salt Lake, Portland and Oakland can force the recognition of Seattle the "Big Five" becomes a fact; McCarthy is out as president; the draft is restored; the relationships with the major leagues is resumed and all will be "jake" for 1924.

The annual meeting is in November at Catalina. On the outcome of that session depends baseball's future on the Pacific Coast. Continuation of a fat-headed policy will wreck the structure. A sane, sensible effort to get together and quit petty wrangling in the interests of baseball and the chap whose six bits a day makes it possible will be appreciated.

But 1923 goes into the books as a "bust." Can't get away from it.

Positions Occupied by Coast Clubs Week by Week for Season of 1923

	1	2	3	4	5	6	7	8	9	10	11	12	13	14	15	16	17	18	19	20	21	22	23	24	25	26	27	28
San Francisco	6	3	5	4	3	1	1	1	1	1	1	1	1	1	1	1	1	1	1	1	1	1	1	1	1	1	1	1
Sacramento	2	2	1	6	5	5	2	3	2	2	2	2	2	2	2	2	2	2	2	2	2	2	2	2	2	2	2	2
Portland	7	5	6	3	1	3	5	2	4	6	5	3	3	3	4	3	3	3	3	3	3	3	3	3	3	3	3	3
Seattle	8	7	4	5	6	7	8	8	7	7	7	7	7	5	3	5	7	7	4	5	5	5	4	4	4	4	4	4
Salt Lake	1	4	2	2	4	2	3	5	6	5	4	5	5	6	6	7	5	4	5	4	4	4	6	7	6	5	5	5
Los Angeles	4	6	8	8	8	6	6	6	5	4	6	6	4	4	5	4	4	5	7	6	6	6	5	5	5	6	6	6
Oakland	5	8	7	7	7	8	7	7	8	8	8	8	8	8	8	8	8	8	8	8	8	7	7	6	7	7	7	7
Vernon	3	1	3	1	2	4	4	4	3	3	3	4	6	7	7	6	6	6	6	7	7	8	8	8	8	8	8	8

(Compiled by Leo Moriarty.)

Pale Hose In Another Win Over Bruins

CUBS PARK, CHICAGO, Oct. 15. (By Associated Press.) — A five-run attack in the fourth inning put the White Sox out in front today with a lead that never was threatened and the Americans won the fifth game of the Chicago city series from the National Leaguers, 7 to 4.

Home runs featured the contest, Willie Kamm, $100,000 beauty purchased by the Sox last spring from San Francisco, leading with two four-baggers, while Ed Collins hit one. Friberg and Vogel hit for circuit drives for the Cubs.

Charley Robertson pitched the route for the Sox and always had a good lead. Four pitchers, Aldridge, Fussell, Osborne and Dumovich, toiled for the National League nine.

WHITE SOX	AB	H	O	A	E	CUBS	AB	H	O	A	E
Brtt,cf-lf	4	0	3	0	0	Statz,cf	3	0	1	0	0
Hooper,rf	3	2	4	0	0	Osborne,p	0	0	0	1	0
Collins,2b	3	1	2	2	0	Heathcote	1	0	0	0	0
Sheely,1b	4	0	10	0	1	Dmovch,p	0	0	0	1	0
Falk,lf	2	1	0	0	0	Adams,ss	4	1	5	5	0
Mostil,cf	2	1	3	0	0	Gnthm,2b	4	0	0	4	0
Kamm,3b	4	2	1	2	0	Grimes,1b	4	0	15	1	0
McClln,ss	3	0	1	5	0	Fribrg,3b	3	2	0	0	0
Crouse,c	2	0	3	0	0	Miller,lf	3	0	2	0	0
Rbertsn,p	3	0	0	0	0	Grigsby,rf	4	0	1	0	0
						O'Farrll,c	3	2	2	0	0
						Aldrdge,p	1	0	0	1	0
						Fussell,p	0	0	0	0	0
						Vogel,cf	2	1	1	0	0
Totals	30	7	27	9	1	Totals	32	6	27	13	0

Heathcote batted for Osborne in eighth.

White Sox	0	0	0	5	0	2	0	0	0	—7
Cubs	0	1	0	0	0	0	1	2	0	—4

Two-base hit—O'Farrell. Home runs—Friberg, Collins, Kamm (2), Vogel. Sacrifice hits—Collins, Friberg. Double plays—Grantham to Adams to Grimes; Grimes to Adams to Grimes; Grimes (unassisted). Bases on balls—Off Aldridge, 3; Fussell, 2; Osborne, 4; Robertson, 1. Struck out—By Aldridge, 1; Robertson, 3; Osborne, 1. Innings pitched—By Aldridge, 3 1-3; Fussell, 2 2-3; Osborne, 2; Dumovich, 1. Losing pitcher—Aldridge. Umpires—Klem, Holmes, Quigley and Ormsby. Time—1:57.

Pilots Sing Swan Songs for Season

By Miller Huggins

Manager World's Champions New York Yankees

Statement Given to Universal Service

NEW YORK, Oct. 15.—The Giants had some tough breaks in the eighth inning I know, but in the pinch my boys came through wonderfully, just as I expected them to do. Wally Schang and Everett Scott started it, and Bob Meusel finished it.

The Giants are still one up on us though and I hope we even it up next year. It was a great series. I think the greatest that ever was played. I knew my team would come through. I'm proud of them all.

By John McGraw

Manager of the New York Giants, World's Champions in 1905, 1921 and 1922

Statement Given to Universal Service

NEW YORK, Oct. 15.—I have no alibis. We beat them twice, in 1921 and 1922. Maybe they were entitled to win. I congratulate them and I hope we will meet again next year. It will be a different story if we do.

I want to say one thing to clear up something—Babe Ruth walked eight times during the series, more than any other man, it is true, but not once did I order any pitcher of mine to pass him. But he's a dangerous hitter. There's no getting away from that.

Donoghue to See English Horse Today

NEW YORK, Oct. 15.—Zev and Papyrus, who will have their day next Saturday, cantered out of the sports limelight today so that it might shine with full candlepower on the world's series.

Both the star of the Rancocas stables and the English Derby winner, who are to race at Belmont Park, for a $100,000 purse, exercised lightly, but no real time tests were attempted.

Tomorrow Papyrus will get under saddle in earnest with a stiff workout scheduled for him by his trainer, Basil Jarvis. The American colt tonight wandered around his commodious stall, not knowing what tomorrow night might bring forth, for Sam Hildreth had not whispered his training plans in his ear.

JOCKEY HERE TODAY

The English thoroughbred tomorrow will be reintroduced to his jockey, Steve Donoghue, champion of the British turf, who will arrive on the Olympic to ride the Derby winner in the international classic.

The little English rider thinks highly of his mount as he made plain when he sailed with the statement that "Papyrus is a generous, game horse."

Zev, already is well acquainted with his rider, Earl Sande, recognized as the premier jockey on American tracks. Sande has been in the saddle since Zev has been working out at Belmont Park, although exercise boys have been put up when the colt has not been sent romping his fastest.

Although both Donoghue and Sande have the same faultless hands and an almost hypnotic power over their horses, they got their starts in very different fashion.

TRAINING VARIES

The American was born in Groton, S. D., and he had for his first mounts the stocky little cow ponies of the Western ranges. Sande, who now is 25, raced at first at local fairs. It was not until 1917 that he got his chance to become a real jockey. The Britisher, on the other hand, first began earning his daily bread in an English wire works, devoting his spare time to the study of horses. He now is 39, and during his career in the track he has piloted five Derby winners to victory and been congratulated by the King.

Sande took his post-graduate course in riding under the tutelage of Sam Hildreth, Sinclair's trainer.

Donoghue, the idol of England, got his first chance at 13, when he ran away from home and won a mount from John Porter, the famous Chester trainer. He lost his first race by a neck, but won his second. Donoghue has ridden for years in England and France. His Derby winners were Pommern, Gay Crusader, Humorist, Captain Cuttle and Papyrus.

A $50,000 rain insurance policy has been taken out by the Westchester Racing Association for October 20, the day of the Zev-Papyrus race.

Under the terms of the contract the association will receive $50,000 if the rainfall between 9 a. m. and 1 p. m. exceeds one tenth of an inch.

Tacoma Tennis Star Wins Way to Final Play

BERKELEY, Oct. 15.—Wallace Scott, of Tacoma, Pacific Northwest champion, and Manuel Alonso, champion of Spain, were the only seeded players to appear on the Berkeley club's courts in the California State championship tennis tournament today and they advanced, Scott into the fourth round and Alonso into the round of eight. They are in opposite halves.

Alonso was opposite W. O. Jens, a San Francisco player, who was nervous, apparently not playing his usual game because of his ranking opposition. The score was 6-0, 6-1 and the Spanish champion was not forced to cover the court for which he is known.

THORP RATES ROCKNE DEAN OF FOOTBALL

Famous Eastern Official Says Notre Dame's Mentor Stands Forth as Greatest of Coaches

By Tom Thorp

(Former All-American Tackel and Leading Eastern Football Official and Authority)

NEW YORK, N. Y., Oct. 15.—Knute Rockne stands today at the head of the football coaching world.

Knute Rockne —Keystone Photo.

The sensational win that his Notre Dame pupils put across on the husky Army outfit at Ebbets Field on Saturday was enough to give the South Bend mentor the upper hand on his various rivals. Any individual that can reach the grade of gridiron sport that Rockne's charges put up in the sixty minutes of playing last Saturday is worthy to take his place at the head of his profession.

Many coaches have made football history in the past. Warner, Haughton, Jones, Bezdek, Sutherland, Neale, Dobie, Daly and such experts have been singled out at various times as the best we have in the gridiron sport. The achievements of their pupils have kept the sport world buzzing for months. Quite a few have gone so far as to predict that the heights that their teams reached would never be attained by any rivals.

GREATEST EXHIBITION

To all of this we make answer that the quality of game that Notre Dame put up at Ebbets Field on

(Continued on Page 3, Column 2)

CLASS COUNTS, JOCKEY'S TIP FOR BIG RACES

Dirt Track No Handicap and Running to Left Is Nothing New to Great British Colt

By Sam Hall

(Copyright, 1923, by Los Angeles Examiner)

TOD SLOAN, the master mind of his day in a saddle, thinks Papyrus, the English horse, will beat Zev, the American entry, in the $100,000 match race for three-year-olds at Belmont Park next Saturday. Tod does not consider it a cinch by any means, but believes that a great English colt is better than a great American colt and that the conditions are not so much against the English Derby winner as most folks imagine.

Tod Sloan

Sloan knows horses like Dempsey knows boxing gloves. He was the Earl Sande of his time and few old-timers around race tracks today will concede that Sande knows how to judge pace and boot bad horses home in front the way Sloan did.

Tod's judgment on English horses is worth pondering over because Sloan is the American jockey who taught the English boys how to ride. He rode four straight years on the best English tracks and also much in France.

FRENCH HORSES BEST

Here is one statement we got from Tod today:

"A great English horse will beat a great American horse most any time and a great French horse will beat either one of them. The European horses are bigger and stronger and faster than ours and

(Continued on Page 3, Column 4)

Composite Box Score

YANKEES' BATTING

Player—	AB	R	H	2B	3B	HR	TB	BB	SH	SO	SB	RBI	Pct.
Witt, c	25	1	6	2	0	0	8	1	1	1	0	4	.240
Dugan, 3b	25	5	7	2	1	1	14	3	0	0	0	4	.280
Ruth, rf and 1b	10	8	7	1	1	3	19	8	0	6	0	3	.368
R. Meusel, lf	26	1	7	1	2	0	12	1	0	3	0	8	.269
Pipp, 1b	20	2	5	0	0	0	5	3	1	1	0	1	.250
Ward, 2b	24	4	10	0	0	1	13	1	0	3	1	2	.417
Schang, c	22	3	7	1	0	0	8	1	2	2	0	0	.318
E. Scott, ss	22	2	7	0	0	0	7	0	1	1	0	3	.318
Hoyt, p	1	0	0	0	0	0	0	0	0	1	0	0	.000
Bush, p and x	7	2	3	1	0	0	4	1	0	1	0	0	.429
Pennock, p	6	0	0	0	0	0	0	0	0	2	0	0	.000
Jones, p	2	0	0	0	0	0	0	0	0	1	0	0	.000
Shawkey, p	3	0	1	0	0	0	1	0	1	0	0	1	.333
Johnson, ss and xx	0	1	0	0	0	0	0	0	0	0	0	0	.000
Haines, rf and xxx	1	1	0	0	0	0	0	0	0	0	0	0	.000
Hendrick xxx	1	0	0	0	0	0	0	0	0	0	0	0	.000
Hofman, xxxxx	1	0	0	0	0	0	0	1	0	0	0	0	.000
Totals	205	30	60	8	4	5	91	20	6	22	1	26	.293

xBatted for Witt in 6th game.
xxRan for Bush in sixth game.
xxxRan for Hofmann in sixth game.
xxxxBatted for Scott in first game.
xxxxxBatted for Jones in third game, and for Pennock in sixth game.

GIANTS' BATTING

Player—	AB	R	H	2B	3B	HR	TB	BB	SH	SO	SB	RBI	Pct.
Bancroft, ss	24	1	2	0	0	0	2	1	0	2	1	0	.182
Groh, 3b	22	3	4	0	1	0	6	3	0	1	0	2	.123
Frisch, 2b	25	2	10	0	1	0	12	0	0	0	0	1	.400
Young, rf	23	2	8	0	0	1	11	2	0	0	0	3	.391
E. Meusel, lf	25	3	7	1	1	1	13	0	0	2	0	2	.290
Stengel, cf	12	3	5	0	0	2	11	4	0	0	0	3	.417
Cunningham, cf	7	0	1	0	0	0	1	0	0	1	0	1	.143
Kelly, 1b	22	1	4	0	0	0	4	1	0	2	0	0	.136
Snyder, c	17	1	2	0	0	1	5	1	0	2	0	1	.118
Gowdy	4	0	0	0	0	0	0	0	0	0	0	0	.000
Watson, p	0	0	0	0	0	0	0	0	0	0	0	0	.000
Ryan, p	2	0	0	0	0	0	0	0	0	1	0	0	.000
McQuillan, p	3	0	0	0	0	0	0	0	0	1	0	0	.000
Bentley, p	5	0	3	1	0	0	4	0	0	0	0	1	.600
Nehf, p	6	0	1	0	0	0	1	0	0	4	0	0	.167
Scott, p	1	0	0	0	0	0	0	0	0	0	0	0	.000
Jonnard, p	1	0	0	1	0	0	0	0	0	0	0	0	.000
Barnes, p	1	0	0	0	0	0	0	0	0	1	0	0	.000
Maguire	0	1	0	0	0	0	0	0	0	0	0	0	.000
Jackson	1	0	0	0	0	0	0	0	0	0	0	0	.000
Gearin	0	0	0	0	0	0	0	0	0	0	0	0	.000
O'Connell	1	0	0	0	0	0	0	0	0	1	0	0	.000
Totals	202	17	47	2	3	5	70	12	0	18	1	14	.233

Stengel batted for Cunningham in sixth. Cunningham batted for Stengel in fourth game. Gowdy batted for Cunningham in escond game. Bentley batted for Watson in first game, McQuillan in fourth and Ryan in sixth game. Maguire ran Gowdy in first game and Bentley in fourth game. Jackson batted for Bentley in second game. Gearin ran for Bentley in first game. O'Connell batted for Jonnard in fourth game and Barnes infifthgame.

COMPOSITE SCORE BY INNINGS

Innings	1	2	3	4	5	6	7	8	9	
YANKEES	5	13	1	4	1	0	1	5	0	—30
GIANTS	1	2	4	1	1	2	1	3	2	—17

SUMMARY

Double plays—Yankees: Scott, Ward, Pipp 3; Jones, Scott, Pipp, 1; Shawkey, Dugan, Pipp, 1; Dugan, Pipp, 1.

Giants: Bancroft, Frisch, Kelly, 2; Ryan, Groh, Frisch, 1; Frisch, Snyder, 1; Frisch, Bancroft, Kelly, 1; Bancroft, Frisch, 1; Nehf, Bancroft, Kelly, 1.

Left on bases—Yankees, 42; Giants, 35.

Bases on balls—Off Hoyt, 1; of Bush, 4; off Pennock, 1; off Jones, 2; off Shawkey, 4; off Watson, 1; off Ryan, 4; off McQuillan, 4; off Bentley, 4; off Nehf, 6; off Jonnard, 1; off J. Scott, 1.

Struck out—By Bush, 5 (Ryan, Snyder, Barnes, O'Connell and Bancroft); by Pennock 8 (Nehf, 3 ;Kelly, 2; E. Meusel, Snyder and Cunningham); by Jones, 3 (Nehf, Bancroft and Groh); by Shawkey, 2 (E. Meusel and McQuillan), by Watson, 1 (Hoyt); by Ryan, 3 (Ward, E. Scot and Ruth); by McQuillan, 3 (R. Meusel, 2, and Ruth); by Nehf, 7 (Ruth, 2; Jones, Witt, R. Meusel, Pennock and Ward); by J. Scott, 2 (Ruth and Bush); by Barnes, 4 (Schang, Pennock, Ward and Ruth); by Bentley, 1 (Schang); by Jonnard, 1 (Pipp).

Hits and runs—Off Hoyt, 4 and 4 in 2 1-3 innings; off Bush, 7 and 2 in 16 2-3; off Pennock, 19 and 4 in 17 1-3; off Jones, 5 and 1 in 10; off Shawkey, 12 and 3 in 1 2-3; off Watson, 4 and 3 in 2; off Ryan, 11 and 6 in 9 1-3; off McQuillan, 11 and 5 in 9; off Bentley, 10 and 7 in 7 2-3; off Nehf, 13 and 4 in 16 1-3; off J. Scott, 9 and 4 in 3; off Jonnard, 1 and 0 in 2; off Barnes, 4 and 0 in 4 2-3.

Wild pitch—Ryan, 1.

Hit by pitched ball—By Bentley (Pennock); by Shawkey (O'Connell).

Winning pitchers—Ryan, first game; Pennock, second game; Nehf, third game; Shawkey, fourth game; Bush, fifth game; Pennock, sixth game.

Losing pitchers—Bush, first game; McQuillan, second game; Jones, third game; J. Scott, fourth game; Bentley, fifth game, and Nehf, sixth game.

Come From Behind to Win After Trailing Giants for Six Innings

Nehf Falters, Walks 3 Men, Yanks Cop 6-4

By Damon Runyon

Staff Correspondent Universal Service (Copyright, 1923, by Universal Service)

POLO GROUNDS, NEW YORK, Oct. 15.—"Long Bob" Meusel knocked the championship of the baseball world from Harlem over into The Bronx this afternoon.

The big pennant that has fluttered so proudly for two years on the tall staff at the foot of Coogans Bluffs will next year kiss the breezes over the gray and green walls of the Yankee Stadium just across the river.

The World's series of 1923 is all over, the Yankees, of the American League, taking the sixth game by a score of 6 to 4 at the Polo Grounds, home of their National League rivals.

It is the first time since the American League came to New York twenty years ago that its club has won the big tilt, and the proudest man leaving the field this afternoon, with an eager crowd swirling about him, was Colonel Jacob Ruppert, owner of the Yankees.

PROUD OF HUGGINS

He was proud of himself, he was proud of his manager, the diminutive Miller Huggins, who had long since sneaked from the scene by way of the tunnel from the players' bench under the stand. He was proud of his ball players.

He was most especially proud of "Long Bob" Meusel, who knocked the championship across the river.

Colonel Jacob Ruppert considers that a much more important feat than George Washington's throwing of a silver dollar across the Delaware, even though the Delaware is wider than the Harlem.

"Long Bob" Meusel is the taller of the California Meusels, the sleepier looking one—the one with the great arm.

"Long Bob" can throw a baseball almost as far as he knocked the championship today, certainly much farther than he hit the ball in lifting the title from the island of Manhattan to the Bronx.

JUST A SINGLE

The hit was a simple little drive over second base, a single—no more.

But it produced both the tying and the winning runs for the Yankees. It gave each American League player something like $2000 more out of the first million dollar baseball pot than they might have received had the Giants won the game and the series gone over until tomorrow.

The hit came in the eighth inning, after the mighty Ruth had fanned with furious sweeps for the second out with the bases full, and the Yankees a run behind.

The Giants went into the inning three runs ahead, and with Arthur Nehf, the great left hander of the McGraw forces, pitching remarkable ball. The Yankees had but two hits off Nehf as the eighth opened, then Nehf suddenly lost control—"blew up" completely.

Tall Wilfrid Ryan, the Holy Cross collegian, came in and struck out Ruth, while the smallest crowd of the series seemed to be making the most noise. Ruth seemed to be too anxious. He swung wildly at the final pitch, which was wide of the plate.

While Ruth was at bat, McGraw seemed to have resumed his master minding on the bench. Lank Hank Gowdy rushed out to Ryan with some order, and it was Ryan's next pitch after that order on which Ruth fanned. McGraw didn't have time to do any master thinking on "Long Bob" Meusel, however.

Bob hit too quickly. A bad throw from the outfield by Cunningham permitted an extra run to score on Meusel's hit and advanced "Long Bob" to third, but the Yankees didn't need the run. The championship was on its way to The Bronx with Meusel's punch.

NERVELESS BOB

"Long Bob" Meusel is a nerveless young man, so nerveless that he seems indolent. He has about him a calm of manner that is somewhat exasperating to Yankee fans at times. Your baseball fan loves the nervous, peppery type of ball player. "Long Bob" never seems excited, never hurries unduly.

Perhaps his disposition runs in the Meusel family. Bob's brother, Emil, who plays left field for the Giants, is the unhurried type.

"Long Bob" seemed most phlegmatic as he stood at the plate in the eighth inning today waiting for Ryan to pitch. He seemed no part of the wild excitement that raged about him.

He did not lash his bat at the ball with any semblance of fury, as Ruth had lashed just before him.

He merely met it with his bat, giving it a good solid crack, without that violent unleashing of all his muscles that characterizes Ruth.

When he saw Cunningham's throw going wild, Meusel ran to third with a stately stride, then stood on the bag and watched his teammates over in front of the Yankee bench jumping up and down, and shrilling their joy, as if

(Continued on Page 2, Column 1)

Who Said Master Mind?

The score of games now standing: Ash and Willow, Deep Thought, 2. Miller Huggins is looking for more cogitato[rs] to conquer. His Yankees yesterday won the world baseba[ll] championship from the Giants.

Gate Totals Million for Big Series

NEW YORK, Oct. 15—(By International News Service.)—The "million-dollar" world's series became a reality today when, with the paid receipts of this afternoon's game between the Yankees and Giants at the Polo Grounds, the total receipts at all six games played reached $1,063,815.

This is the greatest sum ever taken in at any world's series in the history of the game. The official figures for this afternoon's game were announced as follows:

Attendance, 34,172.
Receipts, $139,252.
Commission's share, $20,887.80.
Club owners' share, $118,364.20.

The figures for the entire series are as follows:

Attendance, 301,430.
Receipts, $1,063,815.
Players' share, $362,783.04.
Commission's share, $160,170.25.
Club owners' share, $535,459.70.

Angelenos Wins $50,000 on Yanks

"NICK THE GREEK" is reported to have established a new record for rewards in sporting events, taking the title from Jack Dempsey, who received about $125,000 a minute for his recent fight wtih L. Angel Firpo.

"Nick" is said to have obtained $8,333.33 1-3 a thought during the World Series which closed yesterday. This is how—

"Nick" thought the Yankees would win. He thought so before each of the six games and backed his thoughts with coin. He bet $10,000 on each of the first three games, winning once and losing twice. Then he thought harder and bet $20,000 on each of the last three contests. As the Yanks copped the second game and the fourth, fifth and sixth, "Nick's" thoughts netted him $50,000.

At any rate that was the report yesterday from wagering folk who said they knew how "Nick," one of "our best known gamblers," followed the series.

Supplant Bush as Senators' Mgr.

WASHINGTON, Oct. 15.—Donie Bush will be supplanted as manager of the Washington American League baseball team next season, it was announced today by President Griffith. No successor has been chosen, and no reason was given for the change.

Yankees Cop

YANKEES	AB	R	H	PO	A	E
Witt,cf	3	0	0	3	1	0
Dugan,3b	3	1	0	2	1	0
Ruth,rf	3	1	1	1	0	0
R. Meusel,rf	4	0	1	1	0	0
Pipp,1b	4	0	0	12	0	0
Ward,2b	4	0	1	0	7	0
Schang,c	4	1	1	7	0	0
Scott,ss	4	1	1	1	2	0
Pennock,p	2	0	0	0	1	0
Hoffman	0	0	0	0	0	0
Bush	0	0	0	0	0	0
Haines,cf	0	1	0	0	0	0
Johnson	0	1	0	0	0	0
Jones,p	0	0	0	0	1	0
Totals	31	6	5	27	13	0

Hoffman batted for Pennock in 8th.
Bush batted for Witt in 8th.
Johnson ran for Bush in 8th.

GIANTS	AB	R	H	PO	A	E
Bancroft,ss	4	0	0	1	7	[illegible]
Groh,3b	4	1	1	1	2	[illegible]
Frisch,2b	4	2	3	1	5	[illegible]
Young,rf	4	0	2	0	0	[illegible]
Meusel,lf	4	0	1	1	0	[illegible]
Cunningham,cf	3	0	1	0	0	1
Stengel,c	1	0	0	0	0	[illegible]
Kelly,1b	4	0	0	19	0	[illegible]
Snyder,c	4	1	2	4	0	[illegible]
Nehf,p	3	0	0	0	5	[illegible]
Ryan,p	0	0	0	0	0	[illegible]
Bentley	1	0	0	0	0	[illegible]
Totals	36	4	10	27	19	[illegible]

Stengel batted for Cunningham in 8th.
Bentley batted for Ryan in 9th.

BY INNINGS

Yankees.. 1 0 0 0 0 0 0 5 0—6
Giants.... 1 0 0 1 1 1 0 0 0—4

SUMMARY

Three-base hit—Frisch. Home runs—Ruth, Snyder. Double play—Nehf to Bancroft to Kelly. Left on bases—Yanks, 2; Giants, 5. Bases on balls—Off Jones, 0; Nehf, 3; Ryan, 1. Struck out—By Pennock, 6; Jones, 0; Nehf, 3; Ryan, 1. Hits—Off Pennock, 9 in 7 innings; off Jones, 1 in 2 innings; off Nehf, 4 in 3 innings; off Ryan, 1 in 2 2-3 innings.

Redlands Golf Prodigy Hon[ored]

REDLANDS, Oct. 14.—Phil Finlay, 15-year-old son of Mr. and Mrs. J. R. Finlay, has returned to the home of the family on Redlands Heights with an assortment of trophies that make the youth appear almost a prodigy. He won most of his medals and cups on Long Island courses, though his showcase was taken in the Redlands Invitation Tournament for the low gross score. In twelve rounds of eight courses that were new to Finlay he averaged 82½. He made 'scores of 76 on the Engineers and Garden City courses. His worst score was a 95 on the Shinnecock course, made in a heavy wind storm.

Bob Meusel's Single in Pinch Gives Yankees 6-4 Victory and 1923 World Series Crown

Art Nehf Fails in Eighth; Yankees Win

Continued from Page One

That was a wonderful inning, taht eighth. It was like an earthquake. Then it was like a bull fight with the matador flunking at his big moment, after the bull had been baited and weakened and made ready for the masterful death thrust.

Meusel Came Through

The Yanks provided the earthquake. Babe Ruth himself, not a movie hero, played the part of the bungling matador, and a tall, sullen, right-handed hitter from the Pacific Coast, name of Robert Meusel, took up the matador's sword and slew the bull with little uppercut through the tonsils, instead of the classic overhand blow Babe Ruth by all tradition should have administered.

Here's the scenario:

For seven innings today, Arthur Nehf, who white-washed the mighty Yanks last Friday, cowed them completely, and for seven innings the Giants kept pecking at Herb Pennock, their conqueror of last Thursday.

A battle of southpaws, this, by the way, first time two left-handers hove c shed on World Series battlefields since 1920 when Buster Mails, of Cleveland, won that 1-0 battle from Sherrod Smith, of Brooklyn.

But today, neither southpaw saw the ninth inning. Pennock was not the Pennock of last Friday. The Giants pecked and punched and their nine hits in even innings netted them four runs. Pennock was a defeated pitcher, 4 to 1, when a pinch hitter went to bat for him in the eighth. The fox-hunter of Kennett Square had ridden to hounds too soon after his last kill.

Pennock Was Beaten

He was beaten, 4 to 1, and when Aaron Ward, first Yank to bat in the eighth, popped a high fly to Kelly back of first base they were checking off the putouts between that moment and a Giant victory. Five of them, five little putouts. It seemed as simple as rolling down hill off the proverbial log.

Ward popped weakly to Kelly. There was no chance. Two hits the Yanks had made against Nehf in seven and one-third innings, a home run by Ruth in the first, a single by Ward in the second, and after that single only once did a Yank hit the ball out of the infield between second inning and eighth. And that once was an easy fly to left field.

The multitude, many thousands less than the week-end gatherings, was almost silent. The Giant fans had watched with outspoken joy the steady increase, one by one, of the National League tally sheet. The Yanks' fans were ready to wait until the morrow.

Then the whole situation changed. Wallie Schang, hitting right-handed, reached above his head and hammered a single to right. Everett Scott lashed out at the first ball pitched and drove a single to the same place. Schang dashed aroun dto third. Hofmann, a right-handed hitter, went to bat in place of Pennock. The stands were in an uproar; a rally, but nobody dreamed how that rally would spin itself out.

Art Nehf Falters

Hofmann is no mighty hitter, but Nehf, for all his trying, was unable to pitch. Four in a row missed home plate and Hofmann galloped to first, here to be supplanted by a pinch runner, Hinkey Haines, Penn State football hero of other years.

In a thrice, it seemed, the bases had sprouted with Yankee baserunners. The score was still 4 to 1, but what a difference. Nehf, the only varsity pitcher who had subdued the Yanks at any time since the classic rung up its curtain, was fidgety and furtive as he stood on the pitching eminence. Captain Bancroft, Groh, Frisch, communed with him and slapped him on the back; he was their only hope, their forlorn hope.

He tried to pull himself together. They pointed out that it was Whitie Witt's turn to hit, and Whitie is no strong force against left-handed pitching.

The Big Collapse

But when Nehf turned toward the plate he confronted a right-handed hitter, "Bullet" Joe Bush, pinch-hitting for Witt. "Bullet" Joe was Sunday's winning pitcher. And has been a pretty good hitter in the series.

He didn't hit in this clinch. He didn't have to. Nehf pitched three swift balls and it seemed that he aimed them all at Bush's knees. Three balls, the fourth was wide of the plate, very wide.

A base on balls with the bases filled, a run scored by a gift. The Giants faced the facts. The pitcher was shot to pieces. He had pitched his heart out those five inning when the Yanks could not hit the ball out of the infield.

Exit Nehf, a sad farewell for last Friday's hero. Enter Wilfred "Rosy" Ryan, who was the heroic rescuer in the very first game of the series, the man who agged the Yankee flails when Watson went the voyage.

Here was a real man's job of rescuing. Wilfred "Rosy" Ryan was in a position to be the toast of New York town. He faced Joe Dugan, and if he made Joe Dugan pop up, Wilfred "Rosy" Ryan would face Ruth with two out. If Joe Dugan rolled a grounder anywhere around the Giant infield chances were 10 to 1 that a double play would wipe the bases clear and save the whole situation with the loss of only one run.

The Bambino Fails

So close were the Giants to escaping but Ryan was not the man to save the day. The master mind was betrayed. Joe Dugan did not pop up. He did not hit into a double play. He held his bat on his shoulder and, although one strike hooked over the plate, Joe Dugan had self-possession enough to receive the third straight base on balls.

Everett Scott ambled across the plate. Score 4 to 3. Only one run was needed to tie now. Pinch runner Hinkey Haines proceeded to third. Ernie Johnson, sub infielder running for Bush, went to second. Joe Dugan danced on first. Thus was assembled the matador scene, for the next batter was Babe Ruth.

Of all the siege guns in baseball, who better to strike the deciding death-stroke of the season than the Bambino?

So sensed the mighty multitude, and pandemonium reigned as Babe Ruth faced Wilfred "Rosy" Ryan. It was a bull fight. The bull, tortured and taunted to the limit of endurance, was ready for the matchless matador to run home his shining steel.

The death-stroke, with the populace aroar, the matador balancing his weapon in the white light of the world's watching. The stage was never more elaborately arranged for the denouncement.

Wilfred "Rosy" Ryan is the losing pitcher. That is the Ryan family's business. But Wilfred "Rosy" Ryan had his moment, and when memory has mellowed the loss of the world's championship Wilfred "Rosy" Ryan and family can say, "We struck out Babe Ruth in the biggest pinch of the World Series."

For a fact the Bambino expected to be passed gratuitously; you could see that when Ryan's curve hooked the plate for a strike bellowed by ancient Hank O'Day. The second pitch was low and inside, a curve, which Ruth nicked for a foul along the ground past the first base coacher's box.

Two strikes and nothing. The mighty Bambino wouldn't let that ball go by again. The next pitch was another curve, inside, and the Babe leti t pass. Two strikes and one ball.

From the iFeld Marshal

The lank Hank Gowdy, World's Series star since his National League inception, loped across the lawn from the Giants' cave to the pitcher's box. A courier, Hank, with sealed orders from the master mind. Snyder, the catcher, gathered round and Gowdy transmitted his message to Wilfred "Rosey" Ryan.

That was a gret pitch, the next one. Low it was, fast as a bullet, and over the outside corner of the plate. The great Bambino had it figured for a curve. You could see that, because he swung mightily at it, and because it wasn't a curve he missed it by a good twelve-inch foot. Three strikes and out.

The world expected a home run, such as Babe had smitten in the first inning, and such as he had won the second game with. Babe Ruth struck out, and you would have said, right there is the World Series.

Up Lame Meusel

But, unfortunately for the National League, Ruth's strike out was only the second out. Up Came Bob Meusel, the anticlimax of the drama. Ruth, the matador, had missed fire. What chance was there for Meusel? Bring him up, anyhow. And the fans, taking a long breath after Ruth's third strike, were framing encomiums for Wilfred "Rosy" Ryan, when, suddenty, the bat of Robert Meusel spoke its piece.

No triple or double. Just an ordinary one-base hit, a low thing which raked the pitcher's box and kept on rolling and rambling till it passed second and penetrated center field. Pandemonium.

The fateful ball sizzled through the outfield grass. Pinch runner Hinkey Haines crossed home plate and the score was tied. Pinch runner Ernie Johnson turned third and crossed the plate with the run that made it 5 to 4. Jumping Joe Dugan galloped around second and on toward third. Bill Cunningham, a great center fielder, eclipsed because he hits right-handed and most National League pitchers are right-handed, scooped up the fli ting pill and threw to third in a frantic attempt to nail Jumping Joe.

Frantic and also wild. Heinie Groh, great third-sacker, dove for that throw and missed it. The ball rolled to the concrete grandstand wall. Dugan scored the sixth run. Robert Meusel, running out his single, rounded second and tore to third.

And there it was. The ball was retrieved from the waste spaces, but what did it matter Ernie Johnson had scored the winning run and Dugan had crossed the plate and had danced with wide-spread jaws toward the Yankee bench. The World Series of 1923 was over.

It was over, though the next batter, Wally Pipp, rolled an easy grounder to second base. It was over, though Ryan cowed three Yanks in a row in the ninth inning. It was over, because in the ninth inning, Giants, Sad Sam Jones kept Stengel, Snyder and Pinch-hitter Jack Bentley from knocking the ball out of the infield.

All that went before that eighth inning was of no importance. Kelly made a World Series record by accepting nineteen chances at first base, but the Giants lost.

Statistics of the Series Attendance and Receipts

First Game

Attendance, 55,307.
Receipts, $181,912.
Players' share, $92,775.10.
Each club's share, $30,925.05.
Commission's share, $27,286.80.

Second Game

Attendance, 40,402.
Receipts, $158,498.
Players' share, $74,835.98.
Each club's share, $29,944.66.
Commission's share, $23,774.70.

Third Game

Attendance, 62,430.
Receipts, $201,072.
Players' share, $102,546.72.
Each club's share, $34,182.24.
Commission's share, $30,160.80.

Fourth Game

Attendance, 46,302.
Receipts, $181,622.
Players' share, $92,627.22.
Each club's share, $30,875.74.
Commission's share, $27,243.30.

Fifth Game

Attendance, 62,817.
Receipts, $201,459.
Each club's share, $85,620.07.
Commission's share, $30,218.85.

Sixth Game

Attendance, 34,172.
Receipts, $139,252.
Each club's share, $59,182.10.
Commission's share, $20,887.80.

Total

Attendance, 301,430.
Receipts, $1,063,815.
Each club's share, $267,729.86.
Commission's share, $165,572.25.
x Players' share, $362,873.04.
x Share only in first four games.

It's All Over, Boys!

YANKEES

	AB.	R.	H.	TB.	O.	A.	E.
Witt, cf.	3	0	0	0	3	1	0
Dugan, 3b	3	1	0	0	2	1	0
Ruth, rf.	3	1	1	4	1	0	0
R. Meusel, lf.	4	0	1	1	1	0	0
Pipp, 1b.	4	0	0	0	12	0	0
Ward, 2b.	4	1	1	1	0	7	0
Schang, c.	4	1	1	1	7	0	0
E. Scott, ss.	4	1	1	1	1	2	0
Pennock, p.	2	0	0	0	0	1	0
*Hofmann	0	0	0	0	0	0	0
Haines, cf.	0	1	0	0	0	0	0
‡Bush	0	0	0	0	0	0	0
†Johnson	0	1	0	0	0	0	0
Jones, p.	0	0	0	0	0	1	0
Totals	31	6	5	8	27	13	0

*Batted for Pennock in eighth.
†Ran for Hofmann in eighth.
‡Ran for Bush in eighth.

GIANTS

	AB.	R.	H.	TB.	O.	A.	E.
Bancroft, ss.	4	0	0	0	1	7	0
Groh, 3b.	4	1	1	1	1	2	0
Frisch, 2b.	4	2	3	5	1	5	0
Young, rf.	4	0	2	2	0	0	0
E. Meusel, lf.	4	0	1	1	1	0	0
Cunningham, cf.	3	0	1	1	0	0	1
Kelly, 1b.	4	0	0	0	19	0	0
Snyder, c.	4	1	2	5	4	0	0
Nehf, p.	3	0	0	0	0	5	0
Ryan, p.	0	0	0	0	0	0	0
§Stengel	1	0	0	0	0	0	0
‖Bentley	1	0	0	0	0	0	0
Totals	36	4	10	15	27	19	1

§Batted for Cunningham in eighth.
‖Batted for Ryan in ninth.

Yankees	1	0	0	0	0	0	0	5	0	—6
Giants	1	0	0	1	1	1	0	0	0	—4

Three-base hit—Frisch. Home runs—Ruth, Snyder. Double play—Nehf, Bancroft and Kelly. Left on bases—Yankees 2; Giants, 5. Bases on balls—Off Nehf, 3; off Ryan, 1. Struck out—By Nehf, 3 (R. Meusel, Pennock, Ruth); by Pennock, 6 (E. Meusel, Snyder, Nehf, 3; Kelly); by Ryan, 1 (Ruth). Hits—Off Nehf, 4 in 7 1-3 innings; off Ryan, 1 in 1 2-3 innings; off Pennock, 9 in 7 innings; off Jones, 1 in 2 innings. Winning pitcher—Pennock. Losing pitcher—Nehf. Umpires—O'Day at plate, Nallin at first, Hart at second, Evans at third. Time of game—2:07.

EACH YANKEE WILL GET $6530 SHARE

Giants Will Receive $4363 Per Player—Receipts and Attendance Records Are Broken

New York, Oct. 15.—Three hundred and one thousand, four hundred and thirty persons paid $1,063,815 to see the World Series of 1923, ended with the sixth game today. These figures shatter all previous records, the old record having been established in 1921, when the Giants and Yankees, in an eight-game series attracted 269,977 persons with receipts of $900,233.

Today's figures:
Attendance, 34,172.
Receipts, $139,252.
Advisory Council's share, $20,887.80.
Each club's share, $59,182.10.
Figures for six games:
Attendance, 301,430.
Receipts, $1,063,815.
Advisory Counncil's share, $165,-.572.25.
Each club's share, $267,729.86.

The players' pool this year, $362,-873.04, was more than $100,000 larger than ever before. Seventy-five per cent of this amount is to be divided among the Yankees and Giants. The Yankees, for their victory, will receive 60 per cent, and the Giants 40 per cent. Figured on a basis of twenty-five eligible players, each Yankee will receive about $6530, and each Giant about $4,363.

Each second-place club will receive about $27,208, and each third-place club about $18,139.

LOW MARK REACHED IN PITCHED BALLS IN FINAL SERIES' GAME

New York, Oct. 15.—The low mark in pitched balls for the 1923 World Series was recorded in the sixth and last game today, when but 232 deliveries were made by the opposing pitchers. Of that number eighty-one were called balls; sixty called strikes; twenty-eighth foul strikes; six fouls; thirty-six resulted in infield outs; six in outfield outs and fifteen were hit safely.

As in all other games of the series, Giant pitchers registered a higher total than the Yankee boxmen, 117 pitched balls being the combined total of Nehf and Ryan, and 115 for Pennock and Jones.

The individual records of the four pitchers who worked in today's game follow:

Art Nehf, of the Giants, in seven and one-third innings, threw ninety-four balls; thirty-seven were called balls, twenty-two called strikes, eleven foul strikes, two fouls, seventeen infield outs, one outfield out, four safe hits.

Bill Ryan, of the Giants, ine one and two-thirds innings, tossed twenty-three pitched balls; nine were called balls, seven called strikes, two foul strikes, four infield outs and one safe hit.

Herb Pennock, of the Yankees, in seven innings, hurled ninety-seven pitched balls; twenty-nine were called balls, twenty-eight called strikes, fourteen foul strikes, three fouls, nine infieul outs, five outfield outs and nine safe hits.

Sam Jones, of the Yankees, in two innings, delivered eighteen pitched balls; six were called balls, three called strikes, one foul strike, one foul, six infield outs and one hit.

Scenes From the Final Act

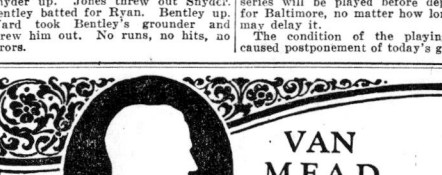

BOB MEUSEL (in Circle) Photo © P.E.A. THE DOUBLE KILLING

MILLER HUGGINS

It was a single by Bob Meusel yesterday that gave the 1923 World Series crown to the Yankees, led by Miller Huggins. In the second inning the Giants nipped a Yank threat by a double play. After Ward singled, Schang hit to Nehf, who threw to Banc:oft for a force-out of Ward. Banny's toss to Kelly doubled up Schang at first

WALKER MAKES APPEAL

Welterweight Champion Asks Revocation of Year's Suspension in New Jersey

Trenton, N. J., Oct. 15.—Mickey Walker, welterweight champion, today made a personal appeal to State Comptroller Newton A. K. Bugbee, in charge of boxing in New Jersey, for revocation of the year's suspension invcked against him for alleged "talling" in his bout with Jimmie Jones, of Youngstown, O., in Newark a week ago.

Mr. Bugbee said he would consider the testimony offered at today's hearing in the State House and render a decision Wednesday.

Walker's story, told in a straightforward manner, was commended by Commissioner Bugbee. His manager, Jack Gugler, came in for some criticism from the Commissioner for what was characterized as an attitude "a little too eager for money."

Evidence was produced to indicate that Walker's hands were crippled as a result of a previous bout and an X-ray photograph was shown indicating that bones in one of his hands had been fractured and on the night of the fight caused him considerable pain each time he punched. It was also brought out that because of the condition of Walker's hands the bout had been postponed for one week, from October 10.

The champion contended that he never put on a show that wasn't on the level and always tried his best to please the fans.

Composite Box Score of Six World Series Game

YANKEES

Player	G.	AB.	R.	H.	2B.	3B.	HR	TB.	SH.	SB.	Bat. Avg.	PO.	A.	E.	Fld. Avg.
Witt, rf.	6	25	1	6	2	0	0	8	1	0	.240	18	1	0	1.000
Dugan, 3b.	6	25	5	7	2	1	1	14	0	0	.280	7	13	0	1.000
Ruth, rf, 1b.	6	19	8	7	1	1	3	19	0	0	.370	17	0	1	.944
R. Meusel, lf.	6	26	1	7	1	2	0	12	0	0	.270	14	0	0	1.000
Pipp, 1b.	6	20	2	5	0	0	0	5	1	0	.250	63	3	0	1.000
Ward, 2b.	6	24	4	10	0	0	1	13	0	1	.417	11	27	0	1.000
Schang, c.	6	22	3	7	1	0	0	8	2	0	.318	21	2	1	.960
E. Scott, ss.	6	22	2	7	0	0	0	7	1	0	.318	8	20	1	.965
Hoyt, p.	1	1	0	0	0	0	0	0	0	0	.000	0	0	0	.000
Bush, p.	4	7	2	3	1	0	0	4	0	0	.429	2	3	0	1.000
Pennock, p.	3	6	0	0	0	0	0	0	0	0	.000	0	2	0	1.000
Jones, p.	2	2	0	0	0	0	0	0	0	0	.000	0	3	0	1.000
Shawkey, p.	1	3	0	1	0	0	0	1	1	0	.333	1	2	0	1.000
Johnson	2	0	1	0	0	0	0	0	0	0	.000	0	1	0	1.000
Haines, rf, cf.	2	1	1	0	0	0	0	0	0	0	.000	0	0	0	.000
(a)Hendrick	1	1	0	0	0	0	0	0	0	0	.000	0	0	0	.000
(b)Hoffmann	2	1	0	0	0	0	0	0	0	0	.000	0	0	0	.000
Totals	6	205	30	60	8	4	5	91	6	1	.288	162	77	3	.987

GIANTS

Player	G.	AB.	R.	H.	2B.	3B.	HR	TB.	SH.	SB.	Bat. Avg.	PO.	A.	E.	Fld. Avg.
Bancroft, ss.	6	24	1	2	0	0	0	2	0	1	.083	10	24	0	1.000
Groh, 3b.	6	22	3	4	0	1	0	6	0	0	.182	4	17	0	1.000
Frisch, 2b.	6	25	2	10	0	1	0	12	0	0	.400	18	18	1	.973
Young, rf.	6	23	2	8	0	0	1	11	0	0	.347	6	1	2	.778
E. Meusel, lf.	6	25	3	7	1	1	1	13	0	0	.280	13	0	0	1.000
Cunningham, cf.	4	7	0	1	0	0	0	1	0	0	.143	2	0	1	.667
Stengel, cf.	6	12	3	5	0	0	2	11	0	0	.417	10	0	0	1.000
Kelly, 1b.	6	22	1	4	0	0	0	4	0	0	.182	63	4	1	.985
Snyder, c.	5	17	1	2	0	0	1	5	0	0	.117	24	3	0	1.000
Gowdy, c.	2	4	0	0	0	0	0	0	0	0	.000	7	0	0	1.000
Watson, p.	1	0	0	0	0	0	0	0	0	0	.000	0	1	0	1.000
Ryan, p.	3	2	0	0	0	0	0	0	6	0	.000	1	2	0	1.000
McQuillan, p.	2	3	0	0	0	0	0	0	0	0	.000	0	1	0	1.000
Bentley, p.	5	5	0	3	1	0	0	4	0	0	.600	0	2	0	1.000
Nehf, p.	2	6	0	1	0	0	0	1	0	0	.167	0	6	0	1.000
J. Scott, p.	2	1	0	0	0	0	0	0	0	0	.000	0	0	1	.000
Jonnard, p.	2	0	0	0	0	0	0	0	0	0	.000	0	1	0	1.000
Barnes, p.	2	1	0	0	0	0	0	0	0	0	.000	1	2	0	1.000
(c)Maguire	2	0	1	0	0	0	0	0	0	0	.000	0	0	0	.000
(d)Jackson	1	1	0	0	0	0	0	0	0	0	.000	0	0	0	.000
(e)Gearin	1	0	0	0	0	0	0	0	0	0	.000	0	0	0	.000
(f)O'Connell	2	1	0	0	0	0	0	0	0	0	.000	0	0	0	.000
Totals	6	201	17	47	2	3	5	70	0	1	.234	159	79	6	.975

(a), (b), (c), (d), (e), (f): Pinch hitter and pinch runner.

Score by Innings

YANKEES	5	13	1	4	1	0	1	5	0	—30
GIANTS	1	2	4	1	1	2	1	3	2	—17

Summaries:

Double plays—(Giants) Nehf to Bancroft to Kelly; Bancroft to Frisch to Kelly, 2; Ryan to Groh to Frisch; Frisch to Bancroft to Kelly; Bancroft to Frisch. (Yankees) Scott to Ward to Pipp, 3; Jones to Scott to Pipp; Shawkey to Dugan to Pipp; Dugan to Pipp. Left on bases—Yankees, 42; Giants, 35.

Base on balls—Off Hoyt, 1; off Bush, 4; off Pennock, 1; off Jones, 2; off Shawkey, 4; off Watson, 1; off Ryan, 4; off McQuillan, 4; off Bentley, 4; off Nehf, 6; off Jonnard, 1; off J. Scott, 1.

Struck out—By Bush, 5 (Ryan, Snyder, Barnes, O'Connell and Bancroft); by Pennock, 8 (Kelly, 2; Cunningham, E. Meusel, Snyder, Nehf, 3; by Jones, 3 (Nehf, Bancroft and Groh); by Shawkey, 2 (E. Meusel and McQuillan; by Watson, 1 (Hoyt); by Ryan, 3 (Ward, Scott and Ruth); by McQuillan, 3 (R. Meusel, 2, and Ruth); by Nehf, 7 (Jones, Witt, Ruth, 2; Ward, Pennock, 2); by J. Scott, 2 (Ruth and Bush); by Barnes, 4 (Schang, Pennock, Ward and Ruth); by Bentley, 1 (Schang); by Jonnard, 1 (Pipp).

Hits—Off Hoyt, 4 in 2 1-3 innings; off Bush, 7 in 16 2-3 innings; off Pennock, 19 in 17 1-3 innings; off Jones, 5 in 10 innings; off Shawkey, 12 in 7 2-3 innings; off Watson, 4 in 2 innings; off Ryan, 11 in 9 innings; off McQuillan, 11 in 9 innings; off Bentley, 10 in 7 2-3 innings; off Nehf, 13 in 16 1-3 innings; off J. Scott, 9 in 3 innings; off Jonnard, 1 in 2 innings; off Barnes, 4 in 4 2-3 innings. Wild pitch—Ryan. Hit by pitched ball—By Bentley, Pennock; by Shawkey, O'Connell.

Winning pitchers—First game, Ryan; second game, Pennock; third game, Nehf; fourth game, Shawkey; fifth game, Bush; sixth game, Pennock. Losing pitchers—First game, Bush; second game, McQuillan; third game, Jones; fourth game, J. Scott; fifth game, Bentley; sixth game, Nehf.

HOME RUNS GIVE SOX THIRD VICTORY

Kamm Hits Pair and Collins One in City Series Triumph

Chicago, Oct. 15.—A five-run attack in the fourth inning put the White Sox out in front with a lead that never was threatened and the Americans won the fifth game of the Chicago city series from the National Leaguers, 7 to 4. The series now stands: Cubs, 2; Sox, 3.

Home runs were the feature of the contest. Willie Kamm, $100,000 third baseman purchased by the Sox from San Francisco last spring, hit two four-baggers, while Ed Collins hit one. Friberg and Vogel hit circuit drives for the Cubs.

Charley Robertson pitched for the Sox and always had a good lead. Four pitchers toiled for the National Leaguers. Aldridge, Fussell, Osborne and Dumovich pitched in order.

Total paid attendance, 16,562. Receipts, $16,061.92. Commission's share, $2409.29. Each club's share, $6826.31.

The box score:

WHITE SOX

	ab	r	h	o	a
B'rett,cf,lf	4	0	0	3	0
Hooper,rf.	3	1	2	4	0
Collins,2b.	3	1	1	2	2
Sheely,1b.	4	1	0	10	0
Falk,lf.	2	1	1	0	0
Mostil,cf.	2	1	1	3	0
Kamm,3b.	4	2	2	1	2
McCy'n,ss.	3	0	0	1	5
Crouse,c.	2	0	0	3	0
Rob'tson,p	3	0	0	0	0
Totals	37	7	7	27	9

CUBS

	ab	r	h	o	a
Statz,cf.	3	0	0	1	0
Osborne,p.	0	0	0	0	1
*Heathcote	1	0	0	0	0
Du'ovich,p	0	0	0	0	1
Adams,ss.	4	1	1	5	5
Gran'm,2b	4	0	0	0	4
Grimes,1b	4	0	0	15	1
Friberg,3b	3	1	2	0	0
Miller,lf	3	0	0	2	0
Grigsby,rf.	4	0	0	1	0
O'Farrell,c	3	1	2	2	0
Aldridge,p	1	0	0	0	1
Fussell,p.	0	0	0	0	0
Vogel,cf.	2	1	1	1	0
Totals	32	4	6	27	13

*Batted for Osborne in eighth.

White Sox	0	0	0	5	0	2	0	0	0	—7
Cubs	0	1	0	0	0	0	1	2	0	—4

Error—Sheely. Two-base hits—O'Farrell. Home runs—Friberg, Collins, Kamm 2; Vogel. Sacrifices—Collins, Friberg. Double plays—Grantham, Adams and Grimes; Grimes, Adams and Grimes; Grimes, unassisted. Left on bases—White Sox 7; Cubs, 3. Base on balls—Off Aldridge, 3; Fussell, 2; Osborne, 4; Robertson, 1. Struck out—By Aldridge, 1; Robertson, 3; Osborne, 1. Hits—Off Aldridge, 4 in 3 1-3 innings; Fussell, 3 in 2 2-3; Osborne, none in 2; Dumovich, none in 1. Hit by pitcher—By Osborne, Hooper. Wild pitch—Robertson. Losing pitcher—Aldridge. Umpires—Klem, Holmes, Quigley and Ormsby. Time—1:57.

HARD WORK AT STATE

Bezdek Puts Squad Through Stiff Drill

State College, Pa., Oct. 15.—Instead of the customary light workout this afternoon, Penn State grid boys were treated to a stiff dose of scrimmage by Coach Hugo Bezdek. The Nittany mentor made no effort to conceal his disappointment with the work of the Gettysburg game on Saturday, and he told the players in no uncertain tones just what was in store for them when they meet the Navy on Saturday unless there is a sudden turn for the better this week.

Several of the Blue and White linemen failed to show the form that was expected of them against Gettysburg, an dthey must show to better advantage in the next few days or else lose their varsity berths. The game with the Middies this week is expected to be one of the hardest of the season and Penn State must display top-notch football to even hold Folwell's eleven on even terms.

Details of Sixth Game, Ball by Ball

FIRST (YANKEES)—Witt up. Strike one. Ball one. Ball two. Foul, strike two. Witt sent up a high fly to Groh. Dugan up. Strike one. Ball one. Ball two. Foul, strike two. Foul. Frisch tossed out Dugan. Ruth up. Strike one. Ball one. Ball two. Foul, strike two. Ball three. Ruth scored on a home run into the upper right field stand. Meusel up. Ball one. Strike one. Ball two. Foul, strike two. Foul. Ball three. Meusel struck out. One run, one hit, no errors.

GIANTS—Bancroft up. Strike one. Strike two. Ball one. Foul. Bancroft flied out to Witt. Groh up. Ball one. Ball two. Ball three. Strike one. Strike two. Groh singled into left. Frisch up. Foul, strike one. Frisch got a single off Pennock's leg, Groh going to second. Young up. Strike one. Ball one. Ball two. Ball three. Strike two. Foul. Groh scored on Young's single to center and Frisch was thrown out at third, Witt to Dugan. Meusel up. Strike one. Ball one. Foul, strike two. Ball two. Meusel fanned. One run, three hits, no errors.

SECOND (YANKEES)—Pipp up. Strike one. Strike two. Ball one. Nehf threw out Pipp. Ward up. Foul, strike one. Ball one. Ball two. Ward crashed a single into left. Schang up. Foul, strike one. Ball one. Ball two. Strike two. Schang hit into a double play, Nehf to Bancroft to Kelly. No runs, one hit, no errors.

GIANTS—Cunningham up. Ball one. Strike one. Cunningham flied out to Witt. Kelly up. Kelly fouled out to Schang, who ran to the Giants' bench to make the catch. Snyder up. Foul, strike one. Strike two. Snyder whiffed. No runs, no hits, no errors.

THIRD (YANKEES)—Scott up. Nehf threw out Scott. Pennock up. Strike one. Strike two. Ball one. Ball two. Nehf also threw out Pennock. Witt up. Strike one. Foul, strike two. Witt flied out to Meusel. No runs, no hits, no errors.

GIANTS—Nehf up. Foul, strike one. Ball one. Ball two. Foul, strike two. Nehf struck out. Bancroft up, Ball one. Ball two. Ball three. Strike one. Strike two. Dugan threw out Bancroft. Groh up. Strike one. Strike two. Groh sent a long liner to Meusel. No runs, no hits, no errors.

FOURTH (YANKEES)—Dugan up. Frisch robbed Dugan of a hit by a remarkable running catch. Ruth up. Ball one. Strike one. Ball two. Foul, strike two. Ball three. Ruth got a base on bals. Meusel up. The Giants protested. Ball one. Foul, strike one. Ball two. Bancroft threw out Meusel at first, Ruth going to second. Pipp up. Bancroft threw out Pipp at first. No runs, no hits, no errors.

GIANTS—Frisch up. The crowd cheered Frisch. Frisch beat out a bunt. Young up. Ball one. Strike one. Ward threw out Young, Frisch sliding safely into second. Meusel up. Meusel flied out to Witt. Cunningham up. Frisch scored on Cunningham's single to right. Kelly up. Foul, strike one. Strike two. Ball one. Ward threw out Kelly. One run, two hits, no errors.

FIFTH (YANKEES)—Ward up. Ball one. Ball two. Strike one. Ward went out, Bancroft to Kelly. Schang up. Frisch threw out Schang, robbing him of a hit. Scott up. Strike one. Ball one. Foul, strike two. Frisch tossed out Scott. No runs, no hits, no errors.

GIANTS—Snyder up. Snyder got a home run into left-field stands. It was his first hit of the series. Nehf up. Foul, strike one. Ball one. Foul, strike two.

Nehf was a strike-out victim. Bancroft up. Ball one. Foul, strike one. Ball two. Scott got Bancroft at first.

Groh up. Foul, strike one. Ball one. Groh sent a fly out to Ruth. One run, one hit, no errors.

SIXTH (YANKEES)—Pennock up. Strike one. Ball one. Strike two. Pennock struck out. Witt up. Ball one. Nehf took Witt's hopper and got him at first. Dugan up. Strike one. Dugan was thrown out at first, Groh to Kelly. No runs, no hits, no errors.

GIANTS—Frisch up. Foul, strike one. Ball one. Foul, strike two. Frisch got a long hit into left field for three bases. Young up. Ward threw out Young at first, Frisch holding third. Meusel up. Ball one. Frisch scored on Meusel's single past Ward. Cunningham up. Ball one. Strike one. Cunningham went out to Pipp, unassisted, Meusel going to second. Kelly up. Strike one. Strike two. Ball one. Kelly struck out. One run, two hits, no errors.

SEVENTH (YANKEES)—Ruth up. Strike one. Foul, strike two. Ball one. Ball two. Ruth struck out. Meusel up. Groh took Meusel's grounder and got him at first. Pipp up. Strike one. Strike two. Bancroft tossed out Pipp at first. No runs, no hits, no errors.

Nehf was pitching a superb game, his curves were breaking sharply, and a bewildering change of pace.

GIANTS—Snyder up. Strike one. Snyder sent a liner into left field for a single. Nehf up. Foul, strike one. Foul, strike two. Ball one. Ball two. Nehf struck out. Bancroft up. Ball one. Strike one. Bancroft was thrown out on a grounder that bounced from Pennock's gloved hand to Ward, who made a quick throw to first. Snyder went to second. Groh up. Ball one. Foul, strike one. Strike two. Groh went out, Scott to Pipp. No runs, one hit, no errors.

EIGHTH (YANKEES)—Ward up. Ward's fly fell into Kelly's mitt. Schang up. Schang pushed a hit into left for a single. Scott up. Scott hit into right field for a single, Schang going to third. Hoffmann batted for Pennock. Hoffmann up. Ball one. Ball two. Ball three. Hoffmann walked and the bases were filed. Haines ran for Hoffmann. Bush batted for Witt. Bush up. Bal one. Ball wo. Ball three. Bush walked and Schang scored. Nehf was taken from the box. Johnson ran for Bush. Ryan went into the box for the Giants. Dugan up. Ball one. Ball two. Ball three. Dugan walked and Scott scored. Ruth up. The stands were in a turmoil. Strike one. Foul, strike two. Ball one. Ruth struck out. Meusel up. Strike one. Haines and Johnson scored on Meusel's single to center, and Dugan scored when Cunningham threw wildly to the grandstand, Meusel going to third. Pipp up. Strike one. Ball one. Frisch threw out Pipp. Five runs, three hits, one error.

GIANTS—Frisch up. Haines went into center field for the Yankees and Jones went into the box. Ball one. Ball two. Strike one. Foul, strike two. Foul. Ward took Frisch's hot smash and threw him out. Young up. Ball one. Ball two. Strike one. Young singled through the box. Meusel up. Strike one. Meusel forced Young, Ward to Scott. Stengel batted for Cunningham. Stengel up. Ball one. Stengel sent a high fly to Dugan. No runs, one hit, no errors.

NINTH (YANKEES)—Stengel went into centerfield for the Giants. Ward up. Ball one. Ball two. Ball three. Strike one. Strike two. Bancroft threw out Ward. Schang up. The game was delayed by a conference at the home plate to determine the correct Yankee batting order. Strike one. Frisch tossed out Schang. Scott up. Foul, strike one. Bancroft robbed Scott of a hit and threw him out. No runs, no hits, no errors.

NINTH (GIANTS)—Kelly up. Ball one. Kelly sent up a high fly to Pipp. Snyder up. Jones threw out Snyder. Bentley batted for Ryan. Bentley up. Ward took Bentley's grounder and threw him out. No runs, no hits, no errors.

The Standings

World Series

	Won	Lost	Pct.
Yankees	4	2	.667
Giants	2	4	.333

Junior Series

	Won	Lost	Pct.
Kansas City	2	1	.667
Baltimore	1	2	.333

Chicago Series

	Won	Lost	Pct.
Sox	3	2	.600
Cubs	2	3	.400

PRINCETON SQUAD IN SPLENDID SHAPE

Roper Omits Scrimmage—Plan Strong Defense Against Notre Dame Attack

Princeton, N. J., Oct. 15.—Trainer Keene Fitzpatrick reported the Princeton varsity football squad in excellent condition after the Georgetown encounter, and the Tigers started a week of grueling training this afternoon in preparation for the Notre Dame game in Palmer Stadium next Saturday. Except for Charlie Caldwell, first-string center, who may not be able to play Saturday, Fitzpatrick said that his charges are in better shape than at this time any previous season.

Bill Roper omitted scrimmage this afternoon, but, starting tomorrow, three hard scrimmages lay ahead of the Orange and Black warriors. As the varsity was being drilled in fundamentals and signals today Net Poe was teaching his Omelettes the Notre Dame aerial and ground attack, which they will use in scrimmage against the regulars. The coaches realize that the Knute Rockne system is different than anything they have met before, the South Benders depending upon precision and speed of execution rather than any surprise and strategy, and on this account they plan a strong defense, based on their knowledge of the Westerners' game gained from the contest with Army Saturday.

Signal drill, kicking, forward passing and blocking intereference was on the program for the varsity today. Maury Ledgendre, Powell Vangerbig and Gibson spent fifteen minutes punting under the watchful eye of Trainer Fitzpatrick, but none did as well as Ledgendre in the Georgetown encounter. Don Lourie, All-American quarterback of the 1921 eleven and a member of the Graduate Football Advisory Committee, was on hand today for the first time this year in order to help shape up the backfield for Notre Dame. Another newcomer in the ranks of Bill Roper's assistants was Jim McCormick, of the class of 1907, former freshman coach.

The varsity eleven lined up as follows: Ends, Drews and Stout; tackles, Hills and Rutan; guards, Bedell and Howard; center, Bergen; quarter, Dinsmore; halfbacks, Snively and Ledgendre; fullback, Crum.

JUNIOR SERIES CHECKED

Rain Forecast for Today—Fourth Game at Kansas City

Kansas City, Oct. 15.—With rain forecast for tomorrow, it seemed unlikely tonight hat the fourth game of the junior World Series, between the Kansas City Club, of the American Association, and Baltimore, of the International League, would be played before Wednesday.

It was announced that the concluding game of the Kansas City section of the series will be played before departure for Baltimore, no matter how long rain may delay it.

The condition of the playing field caused postponement of today's game.

Double Defeat Drops Pirates From Lead; 40,000 See Athletics Beaten in the 15th

PIRATES LOSE TWO; TOPPLED BY PHILS

Meet Defeat in Opener, 3-2, and Final, 4-2, Dropping Both Games in Eighth.

HENLINE'S HOMER WINS 1ST

Carey's Error in Second Game Costs Two Runs — Friberg's Four-Bagger Helps Victors.

PITTSBURGH, Aug. 1 (AP).—The Pirates lost two games to the Phils today, 3 to 2 and 4 to 2. The eighth inning of each game spelleddef eat for Pittsburgh.

Henline's home run decided the first game. In the eighth inning of the second Carey muffed Ring's long fly and Wilson and Friberg romped home. Friberg hit a home run in the closing contest.

The double defeat cost the proud Pirates first place in the torrid National League race and they now trail the Giants by two points.

The score:

FIRST GAME.

PHILADELPHIA (N)	Ab	R	H	Po	A	PITTSBURGH (N.)	Ab	R	H	Po	A
Sands,ss	5	0	3	4	2	Carey,cf	4	0	1	3	1
Leach,cf	5	0	1	8	0	Moore,2b	4	0	1	4	1
W'gt'stne,lf	1	1	0	0	0	Cuyler,rf	4	0	0	4	0
Mokan,lf	2	0	0	3	0	Barnhart,lf	4	0	0	2	0
Harper,rf	4	0	1	2	0	Traynor,3b	4	0	0	0	3
Henline,c	3	1	1	1	0	Wright,ss	4	1	2	1	5
Fonseca,1b	4	1	1	7	0	McInnis,1b	4	1	2	9	1
Huber,3b	3	0	2	0	1	Gooch,c	4	0	3	4	0
Friberg,2b	4	0	2	2	4	Kremer,p	1	0	0	0	0
Decatur,p	4	0	1	0	0	Morrison,p	2	0	0	0	0
						aSmith	1	0	0	0	0
Total..35	3	12	27	7		Totals..36	2	9	27	11	

Errors—Philadelphia 2 (Leach, Henline), Pittsburgh 0.

a Batted for Morrison in ninth.

Philadelphia ....1 0 0 1 0 0 0 1 0—3
Pittsburgh ....0 2 0 0 0 0 0 0 0—2

Two-base hits—Wright, Gooch, Moore, Sands. Three-base hits—Harper, McInnis, Fonseca. Home run—Henline. Sacrifice—Huber. Double plays—McInnis, Wright and McInnis; Traynor, Moore and McInnis. Left on bases—Philadelphia 8, Pittsburgh 8. Bases on balls—Off Kremer 1, Decatur 1. Struck out—By Morrison 3, Decatur 1. Hits—Off Kremer 8 in 3 2-3 innings, Morrison 4 in 5 1-3. Hit by pitcher—By Kremer (Henline). Losing pitcher—Morrison. Umpires—McCormick and Rigler. Time of game—1:31.

SECOND GAME.

PHILADELPHIA (N.)	Ab	R	H	Po	A	PITTSBURGH (N.)	Ab	R	H	Po	A
Sand,ss	5	0	0	3	2	Carey,cf	3	0	1	3	1
Leach,cf	5	1	3	3	0	Bigbee,lf	4	1	0	1	0
Mokan,lf	4	0	1	2	0	Moore,2b	2	0	2	5	5
Harper,rf	4	0	1	1	0	Cuyler,rf	3	0	0	1	0
Wilson,c	3	1	0	1	2	Traynor,3b	4	1	1	2	3
Fonseca,1b	4	0	0	14	2	Wright,ss	4	0	1	0	0
Huber,3b	4	1	1	2	2	McInnis,1b	2	0	0	9	0
Friberg,2b	3	1	1	1	3	Smith,c	2	0	0	5	0
Ring,p	4	0	0	0	5	Meadows,p	2	0	0	1	1
Total....36	4	7	27	16		Total....27	2	5	27	10	

Errors—Philadelphia 1 (Fonseca); Pittsburgh 4 (Carey, Moore, Wright, Smith.

Philadelphia ....0 1 0 0 1 0 0 2 0—4
Pittsburgh ....0 1 1 0 0 0 0 0 0—2

Two-base hits—Leach (2), Carey, Mokan. Home run—Friberg. Sacrifices—Cuyler, Smith. Double plays—Sand, Friberg and Fonseca; Wilson and Fonseca. Lef on bases Philadelphia 8, Pittsburgh 5. Bases on balls—Off Meadows 2, Ring 5. Struck out—By Meadows 4. Hit by pitcher—By Meadows (Mokan). Umpires—Rigley and McCormick. Time of game—1:34.

ROBINS GET 17 HITS OFF CUB SOUTHPAW

Continued from Page 1, This Section.

the frame ended when Freigau was thrown out at the plate. Adams led off with a single and died trying to steal his way to second. Maranville was tossed out by Grimes and Freigau singled. Griffith followed with a double to right and Freigau tried to score from first. Cox relayed the ball to Grimes, who threw to Taylor in time to nail Fregau as he slid into the plate.

Cubs Escape a Shutout.

After that the Cubs did not have a chance to score until the last inning, when they escaped being shut out. Freigau led off with a single and was allowed to walk to second. He took third on Griffith's infield out and carried the lone Cub tally over the plate after Cox caught Grigsby's fly against the right field screen.

Rabbit Maranville is finding it difficult to make base hits since he was made a manager. The Rabbit went hitless this afternoon, and has only four safeties in his last thirty-seven times at bat.

The fans gave the Rabbit the razz after he batted in the eighth inning.

Tom Griffith was the only Cub who made any headway against Grimes's slants. The former Robin made a double and two singles.

Wheat may allow his rookie southpaw, Arthur Brown, to start his first game when the series is resumed tomorrow. Wilbur Cooper is slated to pitch for the Cubs.

The Robins hope to take two of the three games that remain to be played here. Wheat said today that he may not use Dazzy Vance in this series. The speed ball king will pitch the first game in Pittsburgh, the next stop on the Western trip.

The score of today's game:

BROOKLYN (N.)	Ab	R	H	Po	A	CHICAGO (N.)	Ab	R	H	Po	A
Mitchell,ss	6	1	3	4	5	Adams,2b	4	0	1	0	2
Stock,2b	5	1	2	1	5	M'r'nville,ss	4	0	0	2	3
Wheat,lf	5	2	5	0	0	Freigau,3b	4	1	2	0	2
Fournier,1b	3	0	0	5	0	Griffith,rf	4	0	3	2	0
Tierney,3b	2	0	0	0	0	Grigsby,lf	3	0	0	2	0
Cox,rf	4	2	2	3	1	Brooks,cf	3	0	0	2	0
E.Brown,cf	5	1	3	3	0	Grimm,1b	4	0	1	10	0
J'nson,3b-1b	4	0	1	7	2	Hartnett,c	1	0	0	9	0
Taylor,c	5	0	1	3	1	Jones,p	2	0	0	0	1
Grimes,p	5	0	1	1	3	aWeis	1	0	0	0	0
						Brett,p	0	0	0	0	0
Totals.44	7	17	27	17		Total...30	1	7	27	8	

Errors—Brooklyn 0; Chicago 1 (Brooks).

a Batted for Jones in eighth.

Brooklyn ....0 0 2 0 0 0 0 5 0—7
Chicago ....0 0 0 0 0 0 0 0 1—1

Two-base hits — Griffith, Wheat (2), Grimm, E. Brown. Home runs—Cox, E. Brown. Sacrifice—Grigsby. Double play—Mitcell and Fournier. Left on bases—Brooklyn 12, Chicago 6. Bases on balls—Off Jones 2, Grimes 2. Struck out—By Jones 6, Grimes 2, Brett 1. Hits—Off Jones 17 in 8 innings, Brett 0 in 1 inning. Hit by pitcher—By Grimes (Hartnett). Losing pitcher—Jones. Umpires—Wilson and Klem. Times of game—1:55.

ROBINSON WINS GOLF TITLE.

Beats Brearley in Yorkshire Amateur Final by 5 and 3.

J. Robinson of Halifax recently won the amateur golf championship of Yorkshire by defeating T. Brearley of Yorkshire in the 36-hole final at Ganton, England, 5 and 3. It was quite a good set-to in the morning and when the players stopped for lunch they were all square. Robinson was the steadier, though his golf was never particularly brilliant. On the other hand, Brearley showed remarkable power of recovery, but was too often erratic and in trouble.

In the second round Robinson started with a bang, winning three of the first four holes and halving the other. His opponent improved afterward for a time, but he could never wipe off arrears.

BASEBALL

YESTERDAY'S RESULTS.

AMERICAN LEAGUE.

New York 8, Cleveland 3.
Chicago 5, Philadelphia 3.
(Fifteen innings.)
Washington 9, Detroit 5.
St. Louis 5, Boston 2.

NATIOAL LEAGUE.

New York 5, St. Louis 1.
Brooklyn 7, Chicago 1.
Philadelphia 3, Pittsburgh 2.
(First game.)
Philadelphia 4, Pittsburgh 2.
(Second game.)
Cincinnati 6, Boston 5.
(Thirteen innings).

STANDING OF THE CLUBS.

AMERICAN LEAGUE.

	Won.	Lost.	P.C.
Philadelphia	62	33	.653
Washington	61	35	.635
Chicago	55	46	.545
Detroit	49	50	.495
St. Louis	49	50	.495
Cleveland	46	54	.460
New York	42	55	.433
Boston	29	70	.293

NATIONAL LEAGUE.

	Won.	Lost.	P.C.
New York	58	39	.598
Pittsburgh	56	38	.596
Cincinnati	52	44	.542
Brooklyn	47	45	.511
Philadelphia	44	48	.478
St. Louis	45	53	.459
Chicago	41	55	.427
Boston	39	60	.394

WHERE THEY PLAY TODAY.

AMERICAN LEAGUE.

Cleveland at New York.
(Game starts at 3 P. M.)
Detroit at Washington.
Other clubs not scheduled.

NATIONAL LEAGUE.

New York at St. Louis.
Brooklyn at Chicago.
Boston at Cincinnati.
Other clubs not schedueld.

YANKEES DEFEAT INDIANS, 8 TO 3

Continued from Page 1, This Section.

first when Ruth stung a single to centre while the Injun outfield was hanging on the back fences for his rockets. Bob Meusel tilted a high fly into the left field sun veranda for a homer, Ruth jogging home in front.

The Redskins got one in the third. After Smith fanned and Jamieson rolled to Gehrig Lee got an infield hit, beating Shanks's toss to first. Speaker's single to left sent Lee to second. Joe Sewell belted a single in short right, Lee scoring. Speaker also tried to cross the dish, but was nipped at the plate. Tris probably can't gallop as he did half a dozen years ago.

Engrave three more for the Ruppert boys in the third. Pennock singled to centre and Combs hopped a single off Lutzke's tender shins, Pennock going to third and Combs to second when the play at third failed to cut down the Yank pitcher. Ward's slap to right sent Pennock and Combs to the home station.

Queer noises of disappointment rumbled through the stands when Ruth fanned. Meusel displayed a feeling of violent hate toward the ball and soaked a single to centre which scored Wardie.

Pennock was seized with a philanthropic impulse in the fourth and showed alarming indications of giving the game away. With one out, Fewster got an infield hit and Lutzke walked. Luke Sewell singled to centre, scoring Fewster. Smith rolled one to Pennock who tossed to Bengough, and Lutzke was out at the plate on an extremely close decision. Jamieson walked and filled the bases. Pennock was overgenerous, passed Lee and forced Luke Sewell home. He repented for that and pitched so well to Speaker that Tris merely lofted to Ward.

Two hands had been exterminated in the fifth when Lou Gehrig catapulted a home run into the left field bleachers. Shanks followed with a double to right which came close to sinking into the bleachers. Bengough singled to right, tallying Shanks, but Benny died trying to act like rubber and stretch his way to second.

Ward skipped to single off Joe Sewell's glove in the seventh and went to third on Ruth's two-bagger to right. Speaker tried to get his clutches on it and ran almost to the wire screen but missed the ball. Meusel's sacrifice fly to Speaker scored Ward with the final run of the game.

The score of yesterday's game:

CLEVELAND (A.)	Ab	R	H	Po	A	NEW YORW (A.)	Ab	R	H	Po	A
Jamieson,lf	4	0	1	2	0	Combs,cf	4	1	1	4	0
Lee,rf	4	1	2	2	1	Ward,2b	4	2	2	1	2
Speaker,cf	4	0	2	2	0	Ruth,rf	4	1	2	2	1
J.Sewell,ss	4	0	1	2	3	Meusel,lf	3	1	2	2	0
Burns,1b	4	0	0	9	1	Gehrig,1b	4	1	1	12	0
Fewster,2b	4	1	1	3	1	Shanks,3b	4	1	1	1	1
Lutzke,3b	3	0	1	0	2	Bengough,c	3	0	1	4	0
L.Sewell,c	4	1	1	4	0	W'ninger,ss	4	0	0	1	2
Smith,p	4	0	0	0	4	Pennock,p	4	1	2	0	4
Total..35	3	9	24	12		Total..34	8	12	27	10	

Errors—New York 0, Cleveland 1 (Lee).

New York ....2 0 3 0 2 0 1 0 ..—8
Cleveland ....0 0 1 2 0 0 0 0 0—3

Two-base hits—Shanks, Ruth. Home runs—Meusel, Gehrig. Sacrifice—Meusel. Left on bases—New York 4, Cleveland 9. Bases on balls—Off Pennock 4, Smith 1. Struck out—By Pennock 1; Smtih 3. Umpires—Rowland, Evans and Dinneen. Time of game—1:52.

CUTHBERT BATTERS CURLEY

Sheffield Boxer in London Bout Repeats Surprising Victory.

When Johnny Cuthbert of Sheffield obtained the decision over Johnny Curley of Lambeth, the featherweight champion of England, in a fifteen-round bout the surprise was great among boxing experts across the water. But the pair met again recently at Premierland, London, over the same distance, and again Cuthbert won on points. The stipulated weight was 128 pounds, and as both were announced to have scaled inside that poundage it was assumed that Curley was fit.

Cuthbert was a dominant figure throughout most rounds, and only in the seventh and eighth did he have slightly the worst of the argument. At all other points he outboxed the Londoner, who at times appeared to be on the verge of collapsing. Occasionally Curley tried to make a toe-to-toe fight of it, but on every occasion he was forced to retreat before the onslaughts of Cuthbert, who would then go after his man in a most businesslike manner until Curley clinched, for which he was frequently admonished by the referee.

Rain Halts Trotting Derby.

AURORA, Ill., Aug. 1 (AP).—Because of a sloppy track yesterday, the $25,000 American Trotting Derby, feature of the Grand Circuit meeting here, has been postponed to next Thursday. The race, run under the three-heat plan, will carry an entry list of a dozen of the fastest trotters on American tracks.

PENNOCK SAFE AT THIRD IN GAME AT YANKEE STADIUM YESTERDAY.

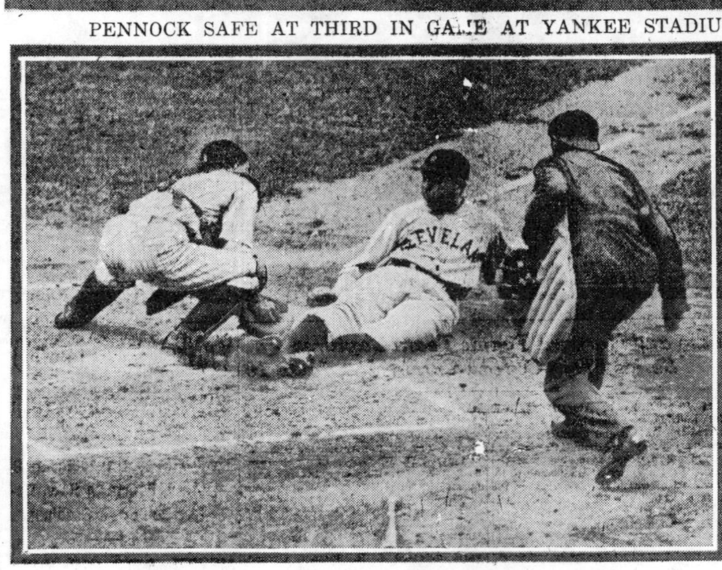

SPEAKER OUT AT THE PLATE IN THIRD INNING.

Wide World Photos.

FEWSTER REACHING FIRST SAFELY IN THE FOURTH.

Pickups and Putouts.

No, the Yanks cannot get into the world's series, but they may be able to make life miserable for some of their baseball enemies.

A new pitcher reported to the club yesterday. His name is Marquis and he hails from St. Joseph of the Western League. What's he Marquis of?

The Yankess have also bought the king pin shortstop of the minors, Tony Pasqual, Lazerre of Salt Lake City. As three or four other major league clubs were bidding for him, it is believed that he cost enough money to fill a bushel basket. He won't report till Spring.

More news: The Yanks have bought Catcher Jack Smith from Scottdale of the Middle Atlantic League and Pitcher Joe Bloomer of the Salina, Kan., club.

Just as though the housing situation in New York wasn't acute enough without the Yanks shipping ball players here by the carload.

Wallie Pipp is out practicing every day and is in shape to get into the game any time. The worst of it is Gehrig, who is understudying Wallie, knocks out too many home runs.

In the sixth inning Gehrig got busy and retired the side without a bit of help from anybody.

The Indians are here again today and many of the home folks will be out to see if what they are saying about the Yankees these days is true.

REDS AGAIN WIN; TRIUMPH IN 13TH

Take Eighth Straight Game When Holke Singles and Bohne Crashes Out Triple.

CINCINNATI, Aug. 1 (AP).—The Reds ran their winning streak up to eight straight games when they triumphed over the Boston Braves here this afternoon in the thirteenth inning of a torrid and hard-fought battle, 6-5. The teams went into the ninth tied at 2-2 but in the tenth the Braves suddenly ran wild and snared three tallies and apparently had the game sewed up.

However, the fighting Reds came back in their half of the session and matched the Braves' three with three of their own. In the Reds' half of the thirteenth Holke singled and Bohne drove him in with a smashing triple to right after Critz had fouled out.

STENROOS IS BEATEN BY HENNIGAN IN RUN

Dorchester A. C. Athlete Leads Finn and De Mar in 15-Mile Marathon in 1:25:54¼.

BOSTON, Aug. 1 (AP).—Jimmy Hennigan of the Dorchester A. C. won in 1 hour 25 minutes 54 1-5 seconds, the fifteen-mile marathon run today under the auspices of the seventy-second annual Scotch picnic at Caledonian Grove. He led Albin Stenroos, Finn distance star, by half a lap, and Clarence De Mar of Melcose by three laps.

The race was run on a track with eight laps to the mile.

ACHILLES CLUB IS VICTOR.

Repeats Its Triumph of Last Year in British Relay Meet.

Seven clubs took part in the annual interclub contest for the 500 Guineas Challenge Cup, in aid of the Woolwich War Memorial Hospital, held recently in the Army Stadium in England. There were twelve events on relay and team lines, and the Achilles Club, winner last year by a large margin, again was successful, but only after a great struggle with the Polytechnic Harriers, who were beaten by only eight points. The Herne Harriers were third, the Blackheath Harriers fourth and the Woolwich Garrison A. C. fifth.

The Achilles Club won seven events and was placed in four others, while the Polytechnic Harriers won three and placed in seven. Herne Hill, which took the trophy for the best local club, was strong in distance runners, winning the four-mile relay in 18:46 3-5, and the three-mile team race by capturing the first three places. In the team race Herne Hill was unlucky in that E. A. Montague, the old Oxford Blue, miscalculated the laps and started to sprint

WOMEN NET STARS AT RYE TOMORROW

All of Leading Players to Compete for State Title—Draw Is Announced.

The women tennis stars who have been at Seabright during the past week will be seen tomorrow at the Westchester Biltmore Country Club when the women's New York State tennis championship begins. The title is now held by Miss Helen Wills, national and Olympic champion, and Miss Elizabeth Ryan, who defeated her at Seabright yesterday, is also entered. Miss Mary K. Browne, second ranking player in the country; Mrs. Molla Bjurstedt Mallory, seven times national champion; Miss Eleanor Goss, Mrs. Marion Zinderstein Jessup, Mrs. May Sutton Bundy, Helen Jacobs, junior champion, and Charlotte Hosmer, who was the finalist against Miss Wills in the Pacific Coast championship, are others who will appear.

While they are not entered in the tournament, the English women's tennis team, which will oppose the American women at Forest Hills later this month, will probably be seen in exhibitions. Several of them will be at the club during the week. Should Miss McKane and her team mates play at Rye it will be their first appearance in this district.

Miss Wills, Miss Ryan, Miss Browne, Miss Goss, Mrs. Mallory and Mrs. Jessup all will play tomorrow. Miss Ryan and Miss Goss will appear in the morning and the others in the afternoon. At 10:30 A. M. Miss Goss will play Florence Sheldon and an hour later Miss Ryan will oppose Mrs. W. H. Pritchard.

Beatrice Kuokol will be Helen Wills's opponent at 4 P. M. and Miss Browne will play Elizabeth Irving at 3 P. M. Mrs. Mallory will meet Gertrude Dwyer at 4 P. M. and Mrs. Jessup will play Mrs. George B. Stanwix at 3 P. M.

The draw:

Miss Helen Wills vs. Miss Beatrice Koukol, Miss Alice Francis vs. Miss Janet Campbell, Miss Penelope Anderson vs. Miss Peggy Loughman, Miss Hermine Kuhn vs. Miss Margaret Dwyer, Miss Mary K. Browne vs. Miss Elizabeth Irving, Miss Charlotte Hosmer vs. Miss Helen McKenzie, Miss Elizabeth Labartat vs. Mrs. Theodore Cassebeer, Mrs. Warren Lewis vs. Miss Carona Winn, Miss Eleanor Goss vs. Miss Florence Sheldon, Miss Dorothy Brand vs. Mrs. John E. Bailey, Miss Marion Williams vs. Miss Marion Van Colt, Miss Elizabeth Ryan vs. Mrs. W. H. Pritchard, Mrs. Richard Ewers vs. Miss Louise Wilson, Miss Isabelle Mumford vs. Miss Edith O'Brien, Miss Edith Guiler vs. Mrs. Arthur M. Duncan, Mrs. May Sutton Bundy vs. Miss Martha Ewers, Miss Helen Hooker vs. Miss Helen Johnson, Mrs. Molla Bjurstedt Mallory vs. Miss Gertrude Dwyer, Miss Helen Kolman vs. Miss Marguerite Landini, Mrs. Marion Zinderstein Jessup vs. Mrs. George B. Stanwix, Mrs. George Chapman vs. Miss **Helen Jacobs.**

Major League Schedule.

AMERICAN LEAGUE.

Aug. 3, 4—Cleveland at New York, Detroit at Washington, St. Louis at Boston.

Aug. 5, 6, 7, 8—Detroit at New York, Cleveland at Philadelphia, St. Louis at Washington, Chicago at Boston.

Aug. 9—Chicago at New York, Cleveland at Washington.

NATIONAL LEAGUE.

Aug. 3—New York at St. Louis, Brooklyn at Chicago, Philadelphia at Pittsburgh, Boston at Cincinnati.

Aug. 4—New York at St. Louis, Brooklyn at Chicago, Philadelphia at Pittsburgh.

Aug. 5, 6—New York at Cincinnati, Brooklyn at Pittsburgh, Boston at St. Louis, Philadelphia at Chicago.

Aug. 7—Brooklyn at Pittsburgh, Philadelphia at Chicago, Boston at St. Louis.

Aug. 8—New York at Cincinnati, Brooklyn at Pittsburgh, Boston at St. Louis, Philadelphia at Chicago.

Aug. 9—New York at Cincinnati, Boston at Chicago, Philadelphia at St. Louis.

Indians Buy Canadian Catcher.

CLEVELAND, Aug. 1 (AP).—The Cleveland Indians have purchased Catcher McCrea of the Hamilton (Ontario) Michigan-Ontario League team. McCrea will join the Indians late next Summer.

Five Leading Batsmen In Each Major League

AMERICAN LEAGUE.

Player and Club.	G.	A.B.	R.	H.	P.C.
Hornsby, St. Louis	90	328	83	129	.393
Stock, Brooklyn	85	350	61	134	.383
Wilson, Philadelphia	63	198	29	75	.379
Bottomley, St. Louis	98	401	57	150	.374
Fournier, Brooklyn	89	333	66	123	.369

Figures include yesterday's game.

NATIONAL LEAGUE.

Player and Club.	G.	A.B.	R.	H.	P.C.
Speaker, Cleveland	93	368	71	148	.402
Rice, St. Louis	70	220	59	89	.389
Heilmann, Detroi	94	350	55	136	.386
Cobb, Detroit	83	319	60	123	.386
Sisler, St. Louis	97	428	77	158	.369

BUSH HELPS MATES BEAT RED SOX. 5-2

Holds Boston Batsmen to Eight Hits, Aids in Making Four Runs for Browns.

BOSTON, Aug. 1 (AP).—Bush's hitting was as big a factor as his pitching in the first game of the Browns-Red Sox series today. The visitors won, 5 to 2. He held the Sox to eight hits and had a part in themakingof four runs for his team when he singled twice and doubled.

The score:

ST. LOUIS (A.)	Ab	R	H	Po	A	BOSTON (A.)	Ab	R	H	Po	A
Bennett,lf	5	0	1	2	2	Flagst'd,cf	3	1	0	6	0
Lamotte,ss	5	0	0	3	3	Ezzell,3b	3	0	1	3	1
Tobin,rf	5	0	3	0	0	Boone,rf	3	0	1	1	0
Rice,1b	5	0	2	8	0	Carylye,lf	4	0	1	3	0
M'Manus,2b	4	1	1	3	3	Wambs'a,1b	4	0	1	6	1
Jacobson,cf	4	1	2	0	0	Prothro,ss	3	0	1	0	3
Rob'son,3b	4	0	0	4	2	Rogell,2b	4	0	1	1	2
Dixon,c	4	2	2	7	3	Picinich,c	3	1	1	6	0
Bush,p	4	1	3	0	[illegible]	Ruffing,p	2	0	0	0	0
						aVache	1	0	1	0	0
						Fuhr,p	0	0	0	1	0
						bWilliams	1	0	0	0	0
Total...40	5	14	27	13		Total....31	2	8	27	7	

Errors—None.

a Batted for Ruffing in seventh.

b Batted for Fuhr in ninth.

St. Louis ....0 0 1 1 0 2 1 0 0—5
Boston ....0 0 2 0 0 0 0 0 0—2

Two-base hits—McManus, Dixon, Bush, Ezzell, Carlyle. Stolen bases—Rice, Bush, Flagstead, Picinich. Double plays—Prothro, Rogell and Wambsganss. Left on bases—St. Louis 8, Boston 7. Bases on balls—Off Bush 5. Struck out—By Bush 2, Ruffing 2. Hits—Off Ruffing 14 in 7 innings, Fuhr 0 in 2. Passed ball—Picinich. Losing pitcher—Ruffing. Umpires—Owens and McGowan. Time of game—1:32.

SENATORS ADVANCE ON 9 TO 5 VICTORY

Gain Full Game on Athletics by Beating Tigers With Four-Run Rally.

WASHINGTON, Aug. 1 (AP).—The Senators gained a full game on Philadelphia by defeating the Detroit Tigers, 9 to 5, while the Athletics were losing an extra-inning contest to Chicago. The game was a free-hitting affair enlivened by spectacular catches by Rice. A four-run rally in the fourth clinched the game for Washington.

The score:

DETROIT (A.)	Ab	R	H	Po	A	WASHINGTON (A.)	Ab	R	H	Po	A
Rigney,ss	4	0	2	3	2	McNeely,cf	1	2	1	4	0
O'Ro'rke,2b	4	0	0	6	3	S.Harris,2b	4	2	2	5	3
F'th'rg'il,lf	5	1	1	2	0	Rice,rf	4	2	1	3	0
Cobb,cf	4	1	2	3	1	Goslin,lf	4	1	3	3	0
H'lmann,rf	4	1	2	1	0	Judge,1b	4	0	0	7	0
Blue,1b	3	1	1	8	1	Bluege,3b	3	0	1	0	2
Jones,3b	4	1	1	0	3	P'paugh,ss	4	0	0	0	2
Woodall,c	2	0	0	1	0	Ruel,c	4	0	0	5	1
Stoner,p	2	0	0	0	3	Reuther,p	4	2	3	0	1
Doyle,p	0	0	0	0	1						
aHaney	1	0	0	0	0						
bNeun	1	0	1	0	0						
Total	34	5	10	24	14	Total	32	9	11	27	[illegible]

Errors—Washington 2; Detroit 0.

a Batted for Stoner in sixth.

b Batted for Doyle in ninth.

Washington ....3 0 0 4 0 0 0 2 ..—9
Detroit ....0 3 1 0 1 0 0 0 0—5

Two-base hits—Fothergill, Goslin. Stolen bases—Rice, Bluege, S. Harris. Sacrifices—Blue, McNeely. Double play—Ruether, S. Harris and Judge; Bluege, S. Harris and Judge. Left on bases—Detroit 7, Washington 8. Bases on balls—Off Stoner 5, Ruether 4. Struck out—By Ruether 3. Hits—Off Stoner 7 in 5 innings, Doyle 4 in 3. Hit by pitcher—By Stoner 3 (Rice, Bluege, McNeely). Losing pitcher—Stoner. Umpires—Geisel, Moriarty and Hildebrand. Time of game—2 hours.

RIFLEMEN WILL BE BUSY.

N. Y. U. May Schedule Matches With 100 Teams Next Season.

The program for New York University's rifle team for the coming season will be an ambitious one, according to a memorandum addressed to the members of the team by Captain Wallace E. Hackett, coach. Teams from colleges and universities throughout the East, South and Middle West have been challenged, and while it is not expected that more than one hundred of the challenges will be accepted, this number will probably give the Violet marksmen complete schedule in the country.

In addition the method of scheduling matches has been changed. Instead of shooting against single teams each week, New York University will now have weekly matches with about seven teams entered in each match. In order to add to the interest the schedule is arranged to include teams from all over the United States.

Furthermore, from time to time, matches will be undertaken under the auspices of the National Rifle Association, in which individual members of the university team may compete for trophies. The season will begin on Nov. 2 and close on April 10.

ATHLETICS BEATEN IN 15-INNING GAME

40,000 See White Sox, With Lyons on Mound, Oerthrow the League Leaders, 5-3.

PASS STARTS FINAL RALLY

Scalk's Double, Single by Lyons and Sacrifice Bring About Walberg's Downfall.

PHILADELPHIA, Aug. 1 (AP).—The pace-making Athletics went down to defeat at the hands of the Chicago White Sox today after a stirring battle of fifteen innings. The score was 5 to 3.

Ted Lyons, youthful Chicago twirler from Baylor University, Texas, outpitched both the veteran Quinn, who was taken out in the seventh inning for a pinch hitter, and Walberg, the lefthander Lyons started to weaken in the fifteenth with men on bases and was relieved by Connally.

The fifteenth inning was a hummer with nearly 40,000 persons wildly shouting for victory. Kamm opened it for Chicago by walking and came home with the winning run on Schalk's double. Lyons singled and Schalk scored on Davis's sacrifice fly.

The league leaders in their half made a desperate effort to win. Lamar singled and after Welch flew out, Simmons singled. Here Chicago switched pitchers and the inning ended quickly, for Hale struck out and Lamar was caught trying to steal third.

The Mackmen tied Chicago's two-run lead in the sixth inning, but the White Sox forged ahead again in the seventh when Sheely singled and scored on Falk's double. Welch of the Athletics sewed up the game again in the eighth when he hit a home run into the left field seats.

This was the second time this season the White Sox had beaten the Athletics in an extra-inning game. On the first Western trip, the Mackmen, after winning nine, lost to Chicago in sixteen innings.

The score:

CHICAGO (A.)	Ab	R	H	Po	A	PHILADELPHIA (A)	Ab	R	H	Po	A
Mostil,cf	7	1	1	7	0	Bishop,2b	5	1	0	2	6
Davis,ss	1	0	1	1	4	Lamar,lf	7	1	3	8	0
Collins,2b	7	0	1	2	6	Miller,rf	2	0	0	1	0
Sheely,1b	6	1	4	18	0	aBagwell	1	0	0	0	0
Falk,lf	6	0	1	7	0	Welch,rf	4	1	1	2	0
Barrett,lf	1	0	0	0	0	Simmons,cf	6	0	3	6	0
Hooper,rf	6	1	2	4	0	Hale,3b	7	0	2	0	1
Kamm,3b	5	1	4	2	2	Poole,1b	6	0	1	15	2
Schalk,c	6	1	3	4	1	Galloway,ss	6	0	0	5	3
Lyons,p	7	0	1	0	5	Perkins,c	6	0	2	8	2
Connally,p	0	0	0	0	0	bHeimach	0	0	0	0	0
						Cochrane,c	0	0	0	1	0
						Quinn,p	2	0	0	2	2
						cFrench	1	0	0	0	0
						Walberg,p	2	0	1	0	4
Total..58	5	18	45	18		Total..56	3	13	45	20	

Errors—Chicago 0; Philadelphia 2 (Hale, Perkins).

a Batted for Miller in sixth.

c Batted for Perkins in fourth.

c Batted for Quinn in seventh.

Chicago ....1 0 0 1 0 0 1 0 0 0 3 H. . R 1
Chicago ....1 0 0 cvmfwyp a oemfwyp aopp
Chicago ....1 0 0 1 0 0 1 0 0 0 0 0 0 0 2—5
Philadelphia ....0 0 0 0 0 2 0 1 0 0 0 0 0 0 0—2

Two-base hits—Kamm (2), Lamar, Falk, Hooper, Poole, Schalk. Home run—Welch. Sacrifices—Collins, Davis. Double plays—Poole and Perkins; Kamm, Collins and Sheely; Schalk and Kamm. Left on bases—Chicago 16, Philadelphia 11. Bases on balls—Off Lyons 6, Quinn 1, Walberg 4. Struck out—By Lyons 2, Quinn 1, Walberg 4. Connally 1. Hits—Off Lyons 13 in 14 1-3 innings, Connally 0 in 2-3. Quinn 11 in 7. Walberg 7 in 8. Hit by pitcher—By Quinn (Schalk). Winning pitcher—Lyons. Losing pitcher—Walberg. Umpires—Nallin, Ormsby and Connolly. Time of game—3:04.

MACKMEN BUY TWO MAYS.

Kit and Orie, Blue Ridge League Brothers, Obtained for $2,500.

MARTINSBURG, W. Va., Aug. 1 (AP).—Kit and Orie May, brothers, of Staunton, Va., both pitchers for Martinsburg in the Blue Ridge League, have been sold to the Philadelphia Athletics. Martinsburg club officials, announcing the deal today, said the brothers would report to Philadelphia at the end of the present Blue Ridge season. The consideration, they said, was $2,500.

MARTIN SETS FOUR MARKS.

Fleet Swiss Runner Stars in Five Meets in France.

Paul Martin, the fleet Swiss runner, who is expected to come to the United States either this Fall or next Spring at the invitation of Paddock and Murchison, has been creating quite a sensation on the tracks of France. In Paris he ran two races in one afternoon, the first at 800 meters and the second at 400. In both of these he lowered the national French records.

Later he went to other French cities and in five meets he set two more new records. It seemed that whenever he found a track that was in good condition he broke a record. Since his trip through France he has returned home, and while he has issued no statements it is generally understood that he is very anxious to race in the United States. Friends of his have said that all that is holding him back is receipt of an official invitation from an athletic organization in the United States which would have power to ask him to compete here.

It is understood that he plans to practice high jumping again, the specialty at which he first attracted major attention. When in school he was performing well in the jumps and began to win titles. Then it was discovered that he could run and since that time he has been devoting his time to racing, but it is said that he likes jumping better and intends to see if there is not a chance that he may become a Harold Osborn.

LATEST RESULTS AT ALL RACE TRACKS

SPORTING FINAL
(Racing—All Sports)
★ ★ ★ ★ ★ ★ ★

Calendar, Tides and Steamships Scheduled on Page 11.

The New York Telegram

SPORTING FINAL
(Racing—All Sports)
★ ★ ★ ★ ★ ★ ★

LOCAL FORECAST:—Fair and warmer tonight; probably thunderstorms tomorrow.

NO. 29,966.—DAILY. NEW YORK, FRIDAY, AUGUST 7, 1925. Entered as second class matter, Post Office, New York, N. Y. PRICE THREE CENTS.

		R.
GIANTS	. . 000 010 000 —	1
REDS	. . . 000 002 00X —	2

		R.
TIGERS	. . 200 001 000 —	3
YANKEES	. . 000 010 000 —	1

GEORGE DAUSS BEATS YANKEES; GIANTS AGAIN BEATEN BY REDS

Baseball, Racing Results

DODGERS LOSE

Brooklyn	0	0	0	5	0	0	2	2	0	— 9
Pittsburg	1	0	0	1	1	1	3	0	3	—10

BATTERIES—GRIMES AND TAYLOR; MEADOWS AND GOOCH.

AMERICAN LEAGUE

Cleveland (1st)	0	4	0	1	1	0	1	3	0	—10
Philadelphia	2	0	0	1	0	0	0	0	1	— 4

BATTERIES—BUCKEYE AND MYATT; QUINN AND COCHRANE.

Cleveland (2d)	0	0	0	0	0	0	0	0	0	— 0
Philadelphia	0	0	0	0	0	0	2	0	x	— 2

BATTERIES—UHLE AND MYATT; ROMMEL AND COCHRANE.

Chicago	0	0	0	0	0	1	1	0	0	— 2
Boston	0	0	0	0	0	0	0	0	0	— 0

BATTERIES—LYONS AND SCHALK; RUFFING AND PICINICH.

St. Louis	0	0	1	0	2	0
Washington	0	0	0	0	0	0

BATTERIES—GIARD AND HARGRAVE; COVELESKIE AND RUEL.

NATIONAL LEAGUE

Philadelphia	0	0	0	1	0	0	0	0	0	— 1
Chicago	1	0	0	0	0	1	0	3	x	— 5

BATTERIES—CARLSON AND HENLINE; BLAKE AND HARTNETT.

Boston at St. Louis—Postponed on account of rain.

INTERNATIONAL LEAGUE

Jersey City	0	0	0	0	3	0	0	2	3	— 8
Rochester	0	6	3	3	1	2	0	4	0	—19

BATTERIES—HORNE AND LAKE; KEIFER AND FREITAG.

Syracuse (1st)	0	0	0	0	0	0	2	0	0	— 2
Providence	0	0	0	0	0	0	0	0	0	— 0

BATTERIES—MILLER AND NEIBERGALL; SWANEY AND LYNN.

Syracuse (2d)	1	0	0	1	0	0	2	— 4
Providence	0	0	0	0	0	2	0	— ?

BATTERIES—GRABOWSKI AND KOPSHAW; MATTESON AND LYNN.

Toronto	0	1	0	0	0	0
Reading	1	0	0	0	0	0

BATTERIES—STEWART AND MANION; MANGUM AND O'NEILL.

SEVENTH RACE AT CONEY ISLAND.

SIXTH (A.P.)—BONA VERA, $12.30, $4.80, $2.90, first; BUTTIN' IN, $3.90, $3.10, second; VALLEY LIGHT, $4.80, third. Time, 1:44 1-5. No scratches.

SEVENTH (A.P.)—MIDNIGHT ROSE, first; KIT, 2d; COL. WAGNER, 3d. Scratched—Payman, Spellbinder, Poor Sport, Lierre, My Colleen.

SIXTH RACE AT HAWTHORNE.

SIXTH RACE (A. P.)—MARY ELLEN O., 8-1, 3-1, 8-5, first; ORPHEUS, 9-5, 3-5, 1-5, second; BLACK BART, 7-1, 5-2, 1-1, third. Time, 1:46. Scr.—Elizabeth K., Jubal Early, Arabian, Alex. Moore, King's Ransom.

LATEST RACELAND RACING RESULTS.

HAWTHORNE RESULTS.

FIRST RACE (A. P.).—Claiming; purse $1,000; two-year-olds; five and a half furlongs.
Greenwoods, 112 (L. Schaefer), 6-5, 2-5, 1-5.
Josephine Weidel II., 109 (R. Yelton), 20-1, 8-1, 4-1.
Sannatuga, 110 (Petzold), 20-1, 8-1; 4-1.
Time, 1:08.
Also ran:—Turner, Frazer, Runerva, Outlawed, Viking, Nona Marie, Private Seth, Cas Welch.

SECOND RACE—Purse $1,000; claiming; three-year-olds and upward; six furlongs.
Fausto, 113 (D. Froggatte), 3-1, 1-1, 1-2.
June Day, 93 (J. Jones), 20-1, 8-1, 4-1.
Irish Lace, 96 (A. Mortensen), 5-1, 2-1, 9-10.
Time, 1:13. Also ran—Whirlwind, Boys Believe Me, Dorothy Pop, Full of Pep, and Battleshot.

THIRD RACE—Purse $1,000; three-earolds and upward; six furlongs.
Conway, 104 (N. Burger), 12-1, 5-1, 5-2.
Put and Take, 105 (J. Smith), 5-1, 2-1, 1-1.
Jim Daisy, 101 (R. Creese), 12-1, 5-1, 5-2.
Time 1:13. Also ran—Lew Pope, Royal Dick, Plenty Coos, aJck Trout, Wawona, Elusive, Gold Grafton, and Voogaria.

FOURTH RACE—Purse $1,000; claiming; three-year-olds and upward; six furlongs.
Gold Mount, 107 (A. Mortensen), 4-1, 8-5, 4-5.
Meddling Mattie, 105 (D. Froggatte), 6-1, 2-1, 1-1.
Lorena Marcella, 103 (L. Schaefer), 6-5, 2-5, 1-4.
Time, 1:02 3-5.
Also ran—Keegan, Venus, San Isabel Little Smoke, Modna.

FIFTH RACE—Purse $1,500; the East End purse; three-year-olds and up; one mile and seventy yards.
Flagstaff, 108 (L. Schaefer), 1-2, out, out.
Max Brick, 108 (A. Mortensen), 6-1, 6-5, out.
Rival, 108 (K. Hoagland), 4-1, 4-5, out.
Time, 1:42 2-5. Also ran—King's Ransom.

Falls Four Stories to Death.

Hyman Bredamknapp, of 97 Hart street, Brooklyn, fell to his death today while repairing the roof atop the building at No. 603 Bedford avenue, Brooklyn. Bredamknapp leaned too far out over the gable, lost his balance and plunged headforemost to the areaway, four stories below.

CONEY ISLAND RESULTS.

FIRST RACE (A. P.).—Purse, $1,300; for maiden two-year-old fillies; five and a half furlongs.
Symphony, 112 (L. Canfield), $3.60, $2.70, $2.30.
Susan Rebecca, 112 (D. Connelly), $14.20, $6.90.
Blue Sprite, 112 (H. Taylor), $5.20.
Time, 1:07 3-5. Also ran—Little Trump, Impact, Twinola, Traplin, Specialist, Farceuse, Susanne B.

SECOND RACE—Purse $1,400; for two-year-olds; five furlongs.
Gentry, 109 (H. Burke), $41.80, $14.50, $9.60.
Caroline, 109 (J. McCoy), $7.20, $5.60.
Longport 112 (K. Noe), $7.60.
Time, 1:00 3-5. Also ran—Brown Leaf, Moon Dove, Oak, Smoot Bar, Herbert, Bonny Castle, and Queen Anna Marie.

THIRD RACE—Purse $1,400; for three-year-olds; six furlongs.
Cup Bearer, 108 (G. Noel), $6.80, 4.10, $2.80.
Clonaslee, 98 (A. Lacoste), $6.10, $3.80.
Alice Lang, 101 (K. Hoffman), $4.80.
Time, 1:12. Also ran—Foyle, Lady Glassen, Quick Lunch, Million, Mad Boy, Betty Star and Beverely.

FOURTH RACE—Purse $1,400; for two-year-olds; five furlongs.
Margaret Gaut, 106 (H. Meyer), $80.50, $23.20, $8.60.
Flicker, 109 (E. Scobie), $8.40, $3.70.
Jet, 104 (L. Geving), $4.20.
Time, 1:00 4-5. Also ran—Golden Mary, Anquince, Gunny Sack, Selective, High Joy, The Missus.

FIFTH RACE — The Montgomery; purse $1,600; three-year-olds and up; one mile.
Sanutar, 104 (D. Connelly), $3.50, $2.20, $2.20.
Foreign Relations, 103 (C. Hooper), $2.30, $2.20.
Bob Cahill, 110 (H. Meyer), $2.90.
Time, 1:37. Also ran—Setting Sun and Gloria Quayl.

RACELAND RESULTS.

FIRST RACE—Purse $800; three-year-olds and upward; claiming; five and a half furlongs. Ege, $3.50, $2.80, first; Rambler, $5.80, second; Black Mask, $6.70, third. Time, 1:07 4-5. No scratches.

SECOND RACE—Purse $800; three-year-olds and upward; claiming; five and a half furlongs. Wee Dear, $5.10, $3.20, first; Belle Woods, $7.60, second; Pearl Boots, $2.40, third. Time, 1:08. No scratches.

THIRD RACE—Purse $800; three-year-olds and upward; claiming; six furlongs. Maude Harvey, $8.40, $4.00, first; Green Spring, $4.10, second; New Moon, $2.90, third. Time, 1:13 1-5. No scratches.

Telegram Daily Charts.

(COMPILED BY THE ASSOCIATED PRESS.)

AT SARATOGA.

SARATOGA SPRINGS, N. Y., Friday, August 7, 1925.—Seventh day of the twenty-six day summer meeting of the Saratoga Association for Improvement of the Breed of Horses.

1,047.—FIRST RACE—Two-year-olds; claiming; five and a half furlongs; purse $1,000. Time 1:08. At post 3:04; off 3:05. Start good, won ridden out; place driving. Winner, b. f., 2, by Trompe la Mort—Inver Belle. Trainer, E. Fred.

Index.	Starters.	Wt.	P.	St.	¼	⅜	½	Fin.	Jockeys.	Open.	High.	Close.	Place.	Sh.
1030²	Sweet Inver	109	4	3	1¹	1⁸	1¹½	1¹	Thompson	8	8	6	5-2	6-5
—	Nettie Sweep	114	10	10	9⁸	5¹	5⁴	2½	Thomas	15	15	8	3	8-5
1003²	Tea Ball	112	5	6	7ʰ	6¹½	3¹	3ʰ	Stevens	3	6	6	5-2	6-5
1027	Frances Rock	109	1	1	4	4	2	4	Hudgins	15	15	15	6	3
1035	Fascjste	112	9	7	2	2	4	5	Carter	10	12	12	5	5-2
1030⁶	Green Blazes	114	8	9	8	7	7	6	McAuliffe	10	12	12	5	5-2
968	Cherub	117	3	2	5	9	8	7	Robbins	15	20	20	8	4
—	Golden Glen	112	6	8	10	10	9	8	Barnes	30	30	30	12	6
979	The Seer	114	7	5	6	8	6	9	Sande	3	4	3	6-5	3-5
883⁴	Prodigal	107	2	4	3	3	fell		Pierce	8-5	9-5	8-5	3-5	1-8

Track fast.
Scratched—Anchester, Marie Baker, Tempest.
Owners—1, A. Locacono; 2, T. J. Pendergast; 3, B. G. Lewis; 4, J. E. Madden; 5, J. L. Holland; 6, Brookmeade Stable; 7, T. O. Webber; 8, Chula Vista Stable; 9, The Village Stable; 10, Ebenbury Stable.
Sweet Inver held her opposition safe for speed, lost ground by coming wide entering the stretch, but maintained her position under pressure. Nettie Sweep, off slowly, closed a big gap. Tea Ball raced evenly.

1,048. SECOND RACE—Spring Steeplechase, four-year-olds and upward; about two miles; purse $1,000. Time, 4:21 2-5. At post, 3:31; off, 3:32. Start good; won easily; place driving. Winner, b. g., 4, by Sunnyland—Naisha. Trainer, A. Escott.

Index.	Starters.	Wt.	P.	St.	½	M.	1½	Fin.	Jockeys.	Open.	High.	Close.	Place.	Sh.
—	His Lordship	130	3	4	5¹½	2½	1⁴	1⁶	Escott	5-2	5-2	2	7-10	1-3
—	Away II.	139	1	1	6	5¹	3⁵	2½	McNair	6	7	6	2	1
1018	Moseley	142	4	3	3¹	4²	2¹	3¹²	C. Smoot	6	7	7	2	1
1018	Fredden Rock	144	2	2	1	1	4	4	Kennedy	6	7	7	2	1
689²	Barleycorn	134	5	5	4	3	5	5	Byers	7-5	2	7-5	7-10	1-3
—	Helsdelite	137	6	6	2	6	lost rider		Veitch	20	30	30	8	4

Track fast.
Scratched—Grenadier II., Rip, Silver Threads, Boatman.
Owners—1, W. A. Read; 2, T. H. McCreery; 3, W. A. Read; 4, Brookmeade Stable; 5, J. E. Widener; 6, A. Case.
HisLordship assumed an easy lead after going on the first turn of the field, winning as his rider pleased. Away II. finished gamely and outlasted Moseley. Byers rode Barleycorn very weakly and permitted him to drop out of contention after taking twelfth jump.

1,049.—THIRD RACE—Three-year-olds and up; claiming; seven furlongs; purse $1,000; Time, 1:26 1-5. At post 4:05; off 4:07. Start good; won easily; place ridden out. Winner, ch. f., 4, by Pennant—Whisk By. Trainer, W. M. Wallace.

Index.	Starters.	Wt.	P.	St.	¼	½	¾	Fin.	Jockeys.	Open.	High.	Close.	Place.	Sh.
731	Fly By	108	10	1	6	1	1	1	Malben	[illegible]	[illegible]	[illegible]	[illegible]	[illegible]
502	Roman B'helor	114	11	6	5ʰ	6½	5⁴	2³	Ponce	8	15	12	3	5-2
918⁵	Sarsaparilla	123	4	5	4¹	4¹½	4½	3½	Johnson	8	10	7	5-2	6-5
951²	Emissary	102	3	4	1	2	2	4	Richards	8-5	8-5	3-2	7-10	1-3
1017²	Dream Maker	118	1	7	2	5	3	5	Catrone	8	8	6	5-2	6-5
1023	Wild Bill	119	6	10	9	9	6	6	L. Fator	30	30	30	12	6
951	Who Knows Me	112	9	2	7	8	7	7	Mathews	30	40	40	15	8
1029	Wild Lane	112	8	8	6	7	8	8	Turner	15	20	20	8	4
(803)	Comic Artist	118	2	9	10	10	10	9	Tammaro	20	20	20	8	4
1014	Delmor	113	5	3	3	3	9	10	F'rbrother	8	8	6	2	1
—	Omar T'tmaker	109	7	11	11	11	11	11	Robbins	30	40	40	15	8

Track fast.
Scratched—Batter Up, Banner Bearer, Revoke, Johnny Campbell, Jibe.
Owners—1, Log Cabin Stud; 2, F. A. Clark; 3, E. J. Strasner; 4, R. L. Gerry; 5, A. C. Bostwick; 6, Shoshone Stable; 7, Everglade Stable; 8, G. A. Marshall; 9, A. Mounce; 10, C. H. Thieriot; 11, T. Jones.
Fly By, off forwardly, bolted toward the outer rail and Maiben was unable to straighten her out for an eighth of a mile. She gained rapidly when fully in stride, opened up a long lead and won in hand. Roman Bachelor was well up all the way and closed stoutly under punishment. Sarsaparilla outclassed Emissary.

1,050.—FOURTH RACE—Expectation Handicap; maiden three-year-olds; one mile; purse $3,000. Time, 1:40. At post, 4:34; off, 4:37. Start good; won ridden out; place driving. Winner, ch. g., 3, by Omar Khayyam—Deliverance. Trainer, J. Fitzsimmons.

Index.	Starters.	Wt.	P.	St.	¼	½	¾	Fin.	Jockeys.	Open.	High.	Close.	Place.	Sh.
1020³	Marconi	120	2	2	2½	1¹½	1²	1¹	Stevens	2-5	1-2	2-5	—	—
880²	*Zeebrugge	111	3	3	4	4	2⁵	2¹²	Barnes	4	7	5	1	—
645	Forward Pass	115	4	4	3⁵	3⁸	3⁴	3⁸	Sande	6	10	8	2	—
1001	Jibe	114	1	1	1	2	4	4	Maiben	10	10	8	8-5	—

*Added starter.
Track fast.
Scratched—Bruns.
Owners:—1, Belair Stud; 2, W. L. Hernstadt; 3, L. Rosenberg; 4, J. Butler.
Marconi took command at his leisure, but was under mild pressure to withstand Zeebrugge's challenge. The latter outpaced the early running and closed with a rush in the stretch. Forward Pass tired and was pulled up.

1,051.—FIFTH RACE—Three-year-olds and upward; one mile; purse $1,500. Time, 1:39 2-5. At post, 5:04; off, 5:05. Start good; won easily; place driving. Winner, b. g., 5, by Sun Briar—Contessina. Trainer, F. M. Bray.

Index.	Starters.	Wt.	P.	St.	¼	½	¾	Fin.	Jockeys.	Open.	High.	Close.	Place.	Sh.
(1026)	Sunsini	108	1	4	4²	4²	1³	1⁴	Barnes	6-5	8-5	8-5	1-3	—
1026²	Reparation	109	5	3	2ʰ	2¹½	2¹	2²	Maiben	4-5	11-10	4-5	1-4	—
985²	Sun Tess	94	4	5	5	5	4¹	3²	Thomps'n	6-5	8-5	8-5	1-3	—
964²	Washington	100	3	1	1	1	3	4	Harvey	6	8	8	8-5	2-5
(964)	McAuliffe	101	2	2	3	3	5	5	Callahan	6	12	12	3	1

Track fast.
Scratched:—Fraternity II. and Flames.
Owners:—1, Liliane Stable; 2, J. E. Davis; 3, W. S. Kilmer; 4, M. L. Davis; 5, J. Livingston.
Sunsini saved ground entering the stretch and easily disposed of his opposition. Reparation was used up racing Washington into defeat. Sun Tess closed going gamely.

1,052.—SIXTH RACE—Two-year-olds; allowances; five and a half furlongs; purse, $1,000. Time, 1:06 4-5. At post 5:34; off 5:36. Statr good; won easily; place ridden out. Winner, ch. c., 2, by North Star III.—Beaming Beauty. Trainer, H. J. Thompson.

Index.	Starters.	Wt.	P.	St.	¼	⅜	½	Fin.	Jockeys.	Open.	High.	Close.	Place.	Sh.
—	Bubbling Over	119	4	1	2½	2³	1³	1⁴	Johnson	7-5	7-5	4-5	2-5	1-5
(706)	Federal	113	6	4	3¹½	3³	2ʰ	2⁸	Sande	4	5	5	2	4-5
961	Rock Slide	110	10	7	5¹½	4½	4¹	3¹	Legere	20	30	30	10	5
—	Rhinock	110	5	6	7	7	6	4	Coltiletti	15	15	12	5	5-2
764	Crossfire	107	7	8	9	9	9	5	Maiben	8	10	7	2	1
—	Token	107	8	10	8	5	5	6	McAtee	8	15	15	6	3
998	Sandy Man	114	1	3	6	8	7	7	Schuttinger	4	6	6	2	1
1016	Jeff	107	11	9	10	10	10	8	Callahan	30	30	30	12	6
998²	Tiff	110	9	11	11	11	8	9	Pierce	20	30	30	12	6
644²	Lachen	110	2	2	1	1	3	10	M. Fator	8	12	12	5	5-2
759	Irresistible	110	3	5	4	6	11	11	Harvey	20	20	20	8	4

Track fast.
Scratched:—Cinema, Marche Militaire.
Owners:—1, Idle Hour Stock Farm; 2, J. E. Widener; 3, J. E. Madden; 4, Parkview Stable; 5, Log Cabin Stud; 6, H. P. Whitney; 7, La Brea Stable; 8, A. Barklie; 9, H. W. Sage; 10, Rancocas Stable; 11, Greentree Stable.
Bubbling Over followed the pace closely under restraint until straightened out in the stretch, where he assumed an easy lead and won in hand. Federal, hard urged, finished well. Rock Slide saved ground all the way.

SONS OF ITALY SECEDE

New York Lodge Rejects Fascism and Bolts Organization.

The New York State Lodge of the Free Sons of Italy, by a vote of 249 to 1, has rejected Fascism in their organization and, in protest against the policies of the national body of the organization, has seceded, acording to an announcement made today at the general convention, being held in the Star Casino, 107th street and Park avenue.

Coast Guard Seaman Killed by Staten Island Train

N. S. Goland, boatman's mate on the United States Coast Guard cutter No. 204, was killed by an electric train of the Staten Island Rapid Transit Railway at the Norwood avenue, Clifton, today.

The Norwood avenue crossing is a private one, used by employes of an electric plant and sometimes as a short cut by the crews of the Coast Guard boats when they are tied up at Pier No. 17, Clifton. Goland's view was obstructed by a brick building.

TEST VOTING MACHINE

Two Different Devices Set Up at Albany for Tryout.

Special Dispatch to The New York Telegram.
The New York Telegram Bureau, Albany, Friday.

Machines representing two different methods of automatically tabulating votes, one of which may be used in New York city this autumn, have been set up in the Capitol and were examined today by Mrs. Florence E. S. Knapp, Secretary of State, who is charged with the duty of installing voting machines in the metropolis.

The types are the Cummings voting machine, manufactured in Knox, Ind., and the automatic registry machine made in Jamestown, N. Y.

It is understood that before any choice of a voting machine is made by Mrs. Knapp other machines will be tested, including the American, manufactured in Massachusetts, and the Shoupe, manufactured at Hoboken.

India Liberal Leader Dead.

CALCUTTA, India, Friday (A. P.).—Sir Surendranath Banerjea, leader of the Indian Liberal party in Bengal, popularly regarded as the "Father of Indian Nationalism," died her yesterday.

GRIMES, CAREY PUT OFF FIELD FOR FIST FIGHT

DODGERS.

	A.B.	R.	H.	O.	A.	E.
Mitchell, ss	4	1	1	3	2	0
Stock, 2b	5	1	2	2	2	0
Loftus, lf	5	1	1	2	0	0
Fournier, 1b	4	0	3	5	0	0
Cox, rf	5	1	2	0	1	0
E. Brown, cf	5	2	1	4	0	0
Johnston, 3b	3	2	1	2	1	0
Taylor, c	4	1	1	0	1	0
Grimes, p	3	0	1	0	1	0
Oeschger, p	0	0	0	0	0	0
Wheat	1	0	0	0	0	0
Ehrhardt, p	0	0	0	0	1	0
Hubbell, p	0	0	0	0	0	0
Totals	39	9	13	*25	13	1

*One out when winning run was scored.

PITTSBURG.

	A.B.	R.	H.	O.	A.	E.
Carey, c.f	3	2	2	2	0	0
Grantham, 1b	4	0	1	7	0	0
Cuyler, r.f	3	2	2	4	0	0
Barnhart, l.f	5	2	1	1	0	0
Traynor, 3b	4	2	3	1	5	0
Wright, s.s	3	0	1	2	0	0
Moore, 2b	3	0	0	3	3	1
Gooch, c	3	0	1	6	0	0
Meadows, p	3	0	0	0	1	0
Adams, p	0	0	0	0	0	0
Bigbee, c.f	1	0	0	1	0	1
McInnis	1	0	0	0	0	0
Smith, c	1	0	1	0	0	0
Yde	0	0	0	0	0	0
Morrison, p	0	0	0	0	0	0
Spencer, c	1	0	1	0	0	0
Totals	39	10	18	27	9	2

SCORE BY INNINGS

Dodgers	0	0	0	5	0	0	2	2	0	— 9
Pittsburg	1	0	0	1	1	1	3	0	3	—10

Two base hits—Cox, Taylor, Cuyler, Traynor. Three base hits—Grimes, Stock, Fournier. Sacrifice hit—Traynor. Stolen bases—Carey, Grantham. Left on bases—Brooklyn, 4; Pittsburg, 7. Double plays—Traynor to Moore to Grantham (2); Stock to Fournier. Struck out—By Meadows, 4; by Adams, 1. Bases on balls—By Meadows, 2; by Grimes, 1; by Morrison, 1.
Umpires—Pfirman, McLaughlin and Hart. Attendance—6,000.

PITTSBURG, Friday.—Grimes. Dodger pitcher, and Carey, Pirate outfielder, were banished from the game in the seventh inning today when they staged a fist fight. They exchanged punches until other players pulled them apart. Carey had collided with Grimes on the base line. The Pirates then went on to win a free-hitting game.

The Game in Detail.

FIRST INNING—Mitchell flied to Cuyler. So did Stock. Loftus singled to left. Fournier popped to Wright. NO RUNS, ONE HIT.

Carey singled to right. Carey stole second. Grantham singled to centre, scoring Carey. Grantham stole second. Cuyler hit to Mitchell and Grantham was out at third, Mitchell to Johnston. Barnhart hit in front of the plate and was thrown out by Taylor. Traynor flied to Brown. ONE RUN, TWO HITS.

SECOND INNING—Cox singled to left. Brown flied to Carey. Johnston hit into a double play, Traynor to Moore to Grantham. NO RUNS, ONE HIT.

Wright flied to Loftus. Moore popped to Mitchell. Gooch did likewise. NO RUNS, NO HITS.

THIRD INNING—Taylor struck out. Grimes struck out. Mitchel grounded to Grantham. NO RUNS, NO HITS.

Johnston threw out Meadows. Carey flied to Brown. Grimes tossed out Grantham. NO RUNS, NO HITS.

FOURTH INNING — Traynor threw

Continued on Page Twelve.

EDWARD QUINN GETS POLICE CAPTAINCY

Enright Gives Appointment to Hylan's Bodyguard.

Edward J. Quinn, personal bodyguard to Mayor Hylan and since 1920 in charge of the City Hall police detail, was appointed a captain this afternoon by Police Commissioner Enright. For some time he has held the rank of Acting Captain.

Quinn was apppinted to the police force on May 4, 1902. He became a sergeant in 1909 and a lieutenant in 1914. Since October 4, 1920, he has been the Mayor's personal bodyguard and has charge of the police detail in City Hall. He succeeded Lieutenant William Kennel as the Mayor's bodyguard.

Quinn was born in 1878 in Greenwich Village. He was educated in Public School No. 3, at Grove and Hudson streets. When he applied for membership in the police force he was a clerk for Austin, Nichols & Co., wholesale provision merchants.

The new captain lives at No. 362 Eighty-fourth street, Brooklyn.

Insane Patient Escapes.

Brooklyn police broadcast an alarm for Waino Wasarenen, twenty-five, a patient at the Brooklyn State Hospital for the Insane, who slipped away from a guard while walking about the hospital grounds on Clarkson avenue. He was described as harmless.

Two Errors by Johnson Give Tigers Edge on Pennock

Tough Battle for Herb to Lose, but It Would Have Been Worse For Rival.

YANKEE STADIUM, Friday.—The Yankees were beaten by the Tigers today, George Dauss outpitching Herb Pennock in a great exhibition.

Two errors by Ernie Johnson were responsible for two Tigers' runs. Without these errors the game might still be going on.

The Game in Detail.

FIRST INNING—Haney rolled to Johnson. O'Rourke flied to Meusel. Fothergill doubled down the third base line and scored when Johnson booted Manush's grounder. Heilmann tripled to deep centre, scoring Manush. Blue popped to Shanks. TWO RUNS, TWO HITS.

Combs bounded to Haney. Johnson popped to Tavener. Ruth walked. Meusel rolled to Blue. NO RUNS, NO HITS.

SECOND INNING—Tavener flied to Ruth. Bassler popped to Shanks. Dauss walked. Haney singled to centre. Shanks grabbed O'Rourke's grounder and tagged Dauss as he was running to third. NO RUNS, ONE HIT.

Gehrig grounded to Tavener. Shanks grounded to O'Rourke. Schang lifted to Fothergill. NO RUNS, NO HITS.

THIRD INNING—Fothergill flied to Meusel. Manush lifted to Ruth. Heilmann bounded to Johnson. NO RUNS, NO HITS.

Wanninger flied to Fothergill. Pennock lifted to Heilmann. Fothergill backed up for Combs' fly. NO RUNS, NO HITS.

FOURTH INNING—Shanks and Gehrig disposed of Blue. Tavener dropped a short single in right. Ruth ran over near the foul line to grab Bassler's hoist. Dauss struck out. NO RUNS, ONE HIT.

Blue took Johnson's bounder and beat him to first. Ruth rolled to O'Rourke. Meusel flied to Manush. NO RUNS, NO HITS.

FIFTH INNING—Haney struck out. Combs came in for O'Rourke's fly. Fothergill singled to left. Fothergill died stealing, Schang to Wanninger. NO RUNS, ONE HIT.

Gehrig fouled to Haney. Shanks singled to centre. Schang forced Shanks, O'Rourke to Tavener. Wanninger got a lucky triple when his fly in deep right near the foul line fell safely in front of Heilmann, scoring Schang. Pennock popped to Blue. ONE RUN, TWO HITS.

SIXTH INNING—Manush doubled to right. Wanninger threw out Heilmann, Manush going to third. Johnson fumbled Blue's grounder, Manush scoring. Tavener was disposed of by Johnson and Gehrig. Bassler fanned. ONE RUN, ONE HIT.

Combs rolled to Blue. Johnson flied to Fothergill. Ruth lined to Heilmann. NO RUNS, NO HITS.

SEVENTH INNING—Dauss tapped in front of the plate and was thrown out by Schang. Johnson threw out Haney. O'Rourke grounded to Wanninger. NO RUNS, NO HITS.

Tavener threw out Meusel. Gehrig beat out a hit to O'Rourke. Shanks singled past third. Schang fouled to Bassler. Wanninger grounded weakly to Blue. NO RUNS, TWO HITS.

EIGHTH INNING—Wanninger took Fothergill's fly. Johnson made a diving attempt for Manush's drive, but it went for a single. Heilmann hit into a double play, Wanninger to Johnson to Gehrig. NO RUNS, ONE HIT.

Veach batted for Pennock and grounded to Dauss. Combs singled to left. Johnson struck out. Ruth grounded to O'Rourke. NO RUNS, ONE HIT.

NINTH INNING—Shocker went to the mound. Ruth made a great shoestring catch with his gloved hand at the expense of Blue. Tavener popped to Wanninger. Bassler walked. Wanninger threw out Dauss. NO RUNS, NO HITS.

Meusel flied to Manush. Gehrig walked. Shanks walked. Shang lined to Fothergill. Pipp batted for Wanninger. It was his first appearance since he was beaned in practice on July 2. Pipp forced Shanks, Tavener to O'Rourke. NO RUNS, NO HITS.

QUAKE AT MEXICO CITY

Two Shocks Felt, but Damage Is Confined to Cracking Walls.

MEXICO CITY, Friday (U. P.).—Two distinct earth shocks were felt here early today, but no damage was reported beyond he cracking of a few walls.

FAENZA, Italy, Friday (U. P.).—A terrific earthquake 1,500 kilometers distant was registered today on the seismographs of Raffaele Bendandi, earthquake prophet.

Bendandi predicts more shocks on the tenth and twelfth.

CHICAGO, Friday (A. P.).—A rather severe earthquake of an indicated distance of 1,840 miles in a southerly direction from Chicago was recorded at six minutes to two A. M. on the United States Weather Bureau seismograph at the University of Chicago.

Yankee Box Score

YANKEES.

	A.B.	R.	H.	O.	A.	E.
Combs, cf	4	0	1	1	0	0
E. Johnson, 2b	4	0	0	1	5	2
Ruth, rf	3	0	0	4	0	0
Meusel lf	4	0	0	2	0	0
Gehrig, 1b	3	0	1	11	0	0
Shanks, 3b	3	0	2	3	1	0
Schang, c	4	1	0	3	2	0
Wanninger, ss	3	0	1	2	5	0
Pennock, p	2	0	0	0	0	0
Veach	1	0	0	0	0	0
Shocker, p	0	0	0	0	0	0
Pipp	1	0	0	0	0	0
Totals	32	1	5	27	13	2

DETROIT.

	A.B.	R.	H.	O.	A.	E.
Haney, 3b	4	0	1	1	1	0
O'Rourke, 2b	4	0	0	1	3	0
Fothergill, l.f	4	1	2	5	0	0
Manush, c.f	4	2	2	2	0	0
Heilmann, r.f	4	0	1	2	0	0
Blue, 1b	4	0	0	12	0	0
Tavener, s.s	4	0	1	2	3	0
Bassler, c	3	0	0	2	0	0
Dauss, p	3	0	0	0	1	0
Totals	34	3	7	27	8	0

SCORE BY INNINGS.

Detroit	2	0	0	0	0	1	0	0	0	— 3
Yankees	0	0	0	0	1	0	0	0	0	— 1

Two-base hits—Fothergill, Manush. Three-base hits—Heilmann, Wanninger. Left on bases—Yankees, 7; Detroit, 6. Double plays—Wanninger to Johnson to Gehrig. Struck out—By Dauss, 1; by Pennock, 3. Bases on balls—By Dauss, 3; by Pennock, 1; by Shocker, 1.
Umpires—Ormsby, Nallin and Moriarty. Attendance 6,000.

11 INDICTED IN PLOT TO SELL FAKE STOCK

Charged with False Representations to Induce Purchases.

The Federal Grand Jury today handed down to Judge Bundy an indictment hcarging the use of the mails to bring about fraudulently the sale of stock against Louis C. Van Riper, Charles E. Van Riper, William C. Ish, William W. Sweet, Harry Hedrick, Henry D. Brown, alias "Henry G. Smyth"; Roy Hatch, alias "J. A. Thompson"; Fred A. Maloney, Thomas J. McCluskey, Alexander Ackerson, alias "Martin Sands," and Abraham Rabinowitz, alias "Edwin Lenrock."

The indictment charges that the accused men conspired to make false representations and promises for the purpose of inducing various persons to buy securities of the Ertel Oil Company and the Parco Oil Company; that their acts were committed on and about May 15, 1925; that they engaged offices at No. 15 Moore street and elsewhere; and that they sent out a publication called the "Financial Analyst," of which Hedrick was the editor, to S. J. Racquet, of Clarence Center, N. Y.

MOB LYNCHES NEGRO

Assaulter of Missouri Girl Is Dragged from Prison to Street.

EXCELSIOR SPRINGS, Mo., Friday.—A mob of 700 persons dragged Miller Mitchell, negro assaulter of Miss Maude Holt, eighteen years old, from the county jail here this afternoon and lynched him.

The mob entered the jail shortly before three o'clock and brought the negro into the street, where he was hanged.

Mitchell was identified by Miss Holt as the man who kept her escort, Leonard Utt, at bay with a revolver while he dragged her from an automobile on a road near here early today and attacked her.

A crowd milled around the jail all morning and reinforcements were rushed here from hurrounding towns in an endeavor to hold the mob at bay. An earlier attempt to storm the jail was frustrated by police.

Boy, 18, Found Guilty in Taxi Driver Hold-Up

Albert James, eighteen years old, was today found guilty of second degree assault by a jury before County Judge McLaughlin in Brooklyn, and will be sentenced on August 17. He was charged with robbery, assault and grand larceny in connection with the hold-up by four young men, on June 11 last, of William Ballentyne, a taxi driver, at Tenth avenue and Twentieth street, Brooklyn, at which time one of the young men drew a gun, while another robbed the chauffeur of $6.

Joseph Byrne, another youth held in Raymond Street Jail in connection with the hold-up, is now awaiting trial.

PETE DONOHUE TRIMS BARNES IN MOUND DUEL

GIANTS.

	A.B.	R.	H.	O.	A.	E.
Southworth, cf	4	1	2	1	0	0
Frisch, ss	4	0	1	4	5	1
Young, rf	4	0	1	3	0	0
Meusel, lf	3	0	0	1	0	0
Terry, 1b	4	0	1	9	0	0
Kelly, 2b	4	0	1	2	3	0
Lindstrom, 3b	2	0	0	0	2	0
Gowdy, c	3	0	0	4	2	0
V. Barnes, p	3	0	1	0	1	0
Bentley	1	0	0	0	0	0
Totals	32	1	7	24	13	1

CINCINNATI.

	A.B.	R.	H.	O.	A.	E.
Zitzmann, lf	4	0	1	2	0	0
Pinelli 3b	4	0	1	0	2	0
Roush, c. f	3	1	2	7	0	0
Walker, rf	4	1	2	6	0	0
Holke, 1b	3	0	1	7	0	0
Critz, 2b	3	0	1	2	3	0
Caveney, s. s	3	0	0	1	1	0
Hargrave, c	3	0	1	2	1	0
Donohue, p	3	0	1	0	0	0
Totals	30	2	10	27	7	0

SCORE BY INNINGS.

Giants	0	0	0	0	1	0	0	0	0	— 1
Cincinnati	0	0	0	0	0	2	0	0	x	— 2

Two-base hits—Terry, Kelly, Young. Three-base hit—Walker. Stolen base—Roush. Left on bases—Giants, 7; Cincinnati, 5. Double plays—Frisch to Kelly to Terry. Struck out—By Donohue, 2; by Barnes, 3. Bases on balls—By Donohue, 2; by Barnes, 1. Passed ball—Hargrave.
Umpire—Rigler, Wilson and Klem. Attendance 7,500.

CINCINNATI, Friday.—The Reds cut down the Giants' lead by another full game today. Pete Donohue kept the Giants' hits well scattered. Barnes was effective except in the sixth, when the Reds bunched two hits for a pair of runs.

The Game in Detail.

FIRST INNING—Critz threw out Southworth. Frisch singled to left. Young flied to Roush. Roush made a fine catch of Meusel's short fly. NO RUNS, ONE HIT.

Zitzmann singled to centre. Pinelli hit into a double play, Frisch to Kelly to Terry. Roush beat out a hit to Frisch. Walker forced Roush, Frisch unassisted. NO RUNS, TWO HITS.

SECOND INNING—Terry doubled to centre. Kelly popped to Critz. Lindstrom flied to Zitzmann. Gowdy was passed. Barnes fanned. NO RUNS, ONE HIT.

Barnes tossed out Holke. Critz beat out a high bounder in front of the plate. Critz was out stealing, Gowdy to Frisch. Caveney fanned. NO RUNS, ONE HIT.

THIRD INNING—Southworth singled to left. Frisch sent a long fly to Walker and Southworth took second after the catch. Young flied to Roush. A passed ball put Southworth on third. Pinelli threw out Meusel. NO RUNS, ONE HIT.

Hargrave singled to deep short and reached second when Frisch threw the ball over Terry's head. Donohue raised a short fly to Young. Zitzmann flied to Southworth. Kelly threw out Pinelli. NO RUNS, ONE HIT.

FOURTH INNING—Terry struck out. Kelly doubled to centre. Lindstrom grounded to Holke. Gowdy flied to Walker. NO RUNS, ONE HIT.

Roush struck out. Walker singled to right. Holke singled to left. Critz flied to Meusel. Caveney flied to Young. NO RUNS, TWO HITS.

FIFTH INNING—Barnes flied to Roush. Southworth singled to centre. Frisch sent a long fly to Roush, Southworth taking second after the catch. Young double to right, scoring Southworth. Critz threw out Meusel. ONE RUN, TWO HITS.

Frisch threw out Hargrave. Donohue singled to centre. Zitzmann forced Donohue Lindstrom to Kelly. Zitzmann was out stealing, Gowdy to Frisch. NO RUNS, ONE HIT.

SIXTH INNING—Critz threw out Terry. Kelly flied to Roush. Lindstrom walked. Lindstrom out stealing, Hargrave to Caveney. NO RUNS, NO HITS.

Frisch threw out Pinelli. Roush shot a hit through the box. Roush stole second. Walker tripled over Southworth's head, scoring Roush. Kelly threw out Holke, Walker scoring. Frisch threw out Critz. TWO RUNS, TWO HITS.

SEVENTH INNING—Gowdy flied to Walker. Barnes singled to left. Southworth flied to Walker. Frisch forced Barnes, Critz unassisted. NO RUNS, ONE HIT.

Frisch threw out Caveney. Hargrave fanned. Frisch got Donohue's high fly. NO RUNS, NO HITS.

EIGHTH INNING—Young flied to Roush. Meusel flied to Roush. Terry flied to Walker. NO RUNS, NO HITS.

Lindstrom threw out Zitzmann. Pinelli singled to left. Roush walked. Walker sent a long fly to Young. Roush dashed for second base, and as Gowdy pulled back for a throw Holke stepped in front of him and was promptly called out for interference. NO RUNS, ONE HIT.

NINTH INNING—Pinelli threw out Kelly. Bentley batted for Lindstrom and flied to Walker. Caveney threw out Gowdy. NO RUNS, NO HITS.

For Today's Radio Program See Page 5.

Babe's 25th Helps Yanks Win; Reds Massacre Pirates

BEES OFF TO MACON TO CUT DOWN PEACHES' LEAD

LEFTY WILSON ON MOUND IN FIRST CLASH

Undisputed captain of fourth place as a result of a pleasing record during the past week, the Hornets, steamed up with new life, are once again off for other fields of battle.

The Bees attained first division last week by playing that sort of baseball. Before good crowds of Wearn field customers they stuck their fingers three times in a row in to Bill Purtell's Columbia Comers and administered the same medicine three times out of four attempts to the merry Kels from Spartanburg.

CLUB IN GOOD TRIM.

Winning six out of seven on their home stay, and with the club in excellent shape to further carry the progress, hopes for the 1926 Hornets, which were going stale hereabouts, have revived in no mean fashion.

The fans are whooping it up, and the Insects promise to make their whoops stand for something besides so much empty ballyhoo.

To Macon trek the Hornets the first three days of this week to tackle the Macon Peaches, one of the brightest clubs in the loop which may yet make it exceedingly warm for the flag contenders.

The Peaches at present are perched one step ahead of the fast stepping Hornets, and the series will give the Bees an opportunity to cut down the lead the Peaches now hold.

After a three day engagement with the Burke brigade, the Kennedymen mix it up with Gabby Street's Tygers who recently paraded their wares in Charlotte.

WILSON ON PEAK.

Lefty Wilson is slated to pitch against the Burkemen today. He has ths far hurled two games for the Hornets and won them both. It is considered extremely likely that he will be rtained as a regular although as yet the moguls have not done the necessary cutting down to point to what pitchers will go through the long summer grind.

Jack Leroy has been pitching find of the season. After scouring the woods for more talent to supplement the tottering Insect hurlers who were finding it extremely difficult to get opposing batsmen out, Ray Kennedy took a look at his own club and decided, as last resort, to give Jack a turn or too on the mound. The Irishman has pitched four games and has a 1.000 percentage.

Two minor casualties on the Hornet club were reported as being considerably improved for the road trip.

WHITE SOX BEAT BROWNS.

CHICAGO, June 27.—(AP)—Chicago bunched hits off C. Falk and Vangilder and defeated St. Louis 6 to 3 today.

St. Louis.	AB	R	H	O	A	Chicago.	AB	R	H	O	A
Durst,cf	5	0	1	5	0	Mostil,cf	3	1	1	4	0
Melillo,2b	3	1	0	3	7	H'field,ss	4	1	1	2	4
xxxE.R's'n	1	0	0	0	0	Collins,2b	2	1	1	3	5
Sisler,1b	5	1	2	10	0	Sheely,1b	4	0	2	9	0
M'Man's,3b	4	0	1	0	3	B.Falk,lf	4	0	0	1	0
Miller,lf	4	1	1	1	1	Barrett,rf	3	1	1	3	0
Rice,rf	4	0	0	2	0	Kamm,3b	4	0	2	2	2
H'grave,c	3	0	2	2	2	Schalk,c	4	1	2	3	1
Gerber,ss	4	0	3	1	2	Bl'ship,p	2	1	1	0	2
C.Falk,p	2	0	0	0	0						
xWilliams	1	0	0	0	0						
Vangild'r,p	0	0	0	0	0						
xxBennett	1	0	1	0	0						
Totals	37	3	11	24	15	Totals	30	6	11	27	14

xBatted for C. Falk in 6th.
xxBatted for Vangilder in 9th.
xxxBatted for Melillo in 9th.

St. Louis	000 102 000—3
Chicago	003 011 10x—6

Errors, none. Two-base hits, Hunnefield, Sheely 2, McManus, Durst, Collins, Sisler. Stolen base, Hunnefield. Double plays, Melillo to Gerber to Sisler; McManus to Melillo to Sisler. Base on balls off C. Falk 1; Blankenship 2; Vangilder 1. Struck out by Blankenship 3. Hits off C. Falk 7 in 5; Vangilder 4 in 3. Losing pitcher, C. Falk. Umpires, Ormsby, Owens and McGowan.

BAM! THERE GOES 25

BABE RUTH, sultan of swat, poled his 25th homer of the season against the Red Sox yesterday. He is now three drives behind his 1925 record.

Titles Of Three Ring Champions At Stake

NEW YORK, June 27.—(AP)—Three pugilistic diadems, the featherweight, lightweight and welterweight crowns, will be dangled before the eyes of challengers this week.

Louis (Kid) Kaplan, of Meriden, Conn., featherweight pride of the nutmeg state, will defend his 126-pound title against Bobby Garcia, United States army champion, at Hartford, tomorrow night in a 15-round match, referee's decision.

LATZO VS. HARMON.

Pete Latzo, newly-crowned king of the welters, will step into the ring at Dreamland Park, Newark, N. J., Tuesday night, against Willie Harmon, of New York, in a 12-round, no-decision contest, which twice has been postponed by rain.

Chicago will inaugurate boxing under its new control Saturday night with a lightweight championship contest between Rocky Kansas, of Buffalo, N. Y., and Sammy Mandell, of Rock Island, Ill.

M'TIGUE BACK AGAIN.

The headliner at New York will be fought Thursday night when Mike McTigue, former world's light-heavyweight champion, will meet Johnny Risko, rugged Cleveland heavyweight, in a 10-rounder at Madison Square Garden.

As a counter attraction to the Latzo-Harmon fight, promoters of the Queensboro A. C., have announced a return match between Dave Shade and Maxie Rosenbloom for their Long Island City staudium, Tuesday night.

Burns First To Get 100 Hits This Year

CLEVELAND, June 27.—(AP)—George Burns, of the Indians, is the first major league player to make 100 hits this season. He made his 100th blow, a single, in the second game at Detroit today.

In 68 games Burns has been at bat 273 times and scored 43 runs and 100 hits for an average of .366.

THREE STRAIGHT FOR NEW YORK OVER BOSTON

NEW YORK, June 27.—(AP)—The New York Americans made it three straight over the Red Sox today by wining 7 to 1, Babe Ruth lifting his 25th home run of the season into the left field bleachers in the seventh inning. None was on base.

Ruth now is three games behind his 1921 record.

Tony Lazzeri hits his 11th homer with Paschal aboard in the eighth. Score:

Boston.	AB	R	H	O	A	New York.	AB	R	H	O	A
Fl'stead,cf	3	0	0	4	0	Combs,cf	3	0	2	2	0
Herrera,3b	3	0	0	1	4	Koenig,ss	4	0	1	1	1
Todt,1b	4	0	0	8	2	Gehrig,1b	4	0	1	9	1
J'bson,cf	4	0	1	1	0	Ruth,lf	3	1	2	1	0
Regan,2b	4	0	0	4	0	Paschal,rf	4	2	1	1	0
F'gerald,lf	3	1	1	0	0	Lazzeri,2b	3	2	2	2	2
Rigney,ss	3	0	1	2	4	Gazella,3b	3	1	0	0	2
Stokes,c	4	0	1	2	0	B'gough,c	4	1	0	11	1
Heimach,p	3	0	1	2	4	Beall,p	3	0	0	0	1
Totals	31	1	5	24	14	Totals	31	7	9	27	8

Boston	000 000 001—1
New York	000 000 52x—7

Errors, Todt, Heimach, Gazella. Two-base hit, Combs. Three-base hits, Stokes, Koenig. Home runs, Ruth, Lazzeri. Stolen base, Paschal. Sacrifices, Gazella, Combs. Double play, Heimach, Rigney and Todt. Base on balls off Beall 4; off Heimach 2. Struck out by Beall 9; by Heimach 2. Umpires, Evans, Connolly and Rowland.

TIGERS RALLY TO WIN.

DETROIT, June 27.—(AP)—Scoring three runs in the eighth after trailing since the third inning, Detroit defeated Cleveland, 5 to 4 today to register its seventh consecutive victory.

Cleveland.	AB	R	H	O	A	Detroit.	AB	R	H	O	A
Eichrodt,lf	2	0	0	0	0	Blue,1b	3	2	2	10	0
Jam'son,lf	2	0	1	1	0	O'R'ke,2b	4	1	3	3	3
Spurg'n,2b	4	2	3	2	3	Manush,cf	4	1	1	3	0
Speaker,cf	3	0	2	3	1	Cobb,lf	4	0	1	0	0
Burns,1b	4	1	[illegible]	11	0	F'gill,rf	3	0	1	2	0
Sewell,ss	4	0	2	8	5	Warner,3b	4	0	2	2	2
Summa,rf	4	0	0	[illegible]	0	Tavener,ss	4	0	1	1	4
Lee,c	3	0	0	1	0	Woodall,c	3	0	0	6	1
Myatt,c	0	0	0	0	0	W'hill,p	0	0	0	0	2
Lutzke,3b	3	0	1	1	2	Dauss,p	1	0	0	0	2
Smith,p	3	1	1	0	3	Hol'way,p	0	0	0	0	0
zMcNulty	1	0	0	0	0	xH'worth	1	0	0	0	0
zzKnode	1	0	0	0	0	xxNeun	1	1	1	0	0
Totals	34	4	10	24	14	Totals	32	5	12	27	14

zBatted for Lutzke in 9th.
zzBatted for Smith in 9th.
xBatted for Whitehill in 3rd.
xxBatted for Dauss in 8th.

Cleveland	003 010 000—4
Detroit	100 001 03x—5

Two-base hits, Spurgeon, Blue. Three-base hit, Sewell. Stolen base, Sewell. Double plays, Sewell to Burns; Smith to Spurgeon to Burns; Sewell to Spurgeon to Burns; Tavener to O'Rourke to Blue. Base on balls off Whitehill 1; Dauss 1; Smith 2. Struck out, by Dauss 5; Holloway 1. Hits off Whitehill 5 in 3; Dauss 4 in 5; Holloway 1 in 1. Winning pitcher, Dauss. Umpires, Dineen and Nallin.

BUNCHED HITS WIN.

WASHINGTON, June 27.—(AP)—Washington bunched hits off Ehmke to take the fourth straight game from Philadelphia here today, 6 to 2.

Philadelphia.	AB	R	H	O	A	Washington.	AB	R	H	O	A
Bishop,2b	5	0	1	2	2	Rice,cf-rf	2	1	1	0	0
French,rf	4	1	2	2	0	S.Harris,2b	3	0	1	4	2
Sim'ns,cf	4	0	2	2	0	Goslin,lf	3	1	0	3	0
Lamar,lf	4	1	0	4	0	J.Harris,rf	4	1	2	1	0
Dykes,3b	3	0	2	2	1	M'Neely,cf	0	0	0	2	0
Pool,1b	4	0	2	5	1	Judge,1b	4	1	2	8	1
Perkins,c	4	0	1	6	0	Bluege,3b	4	0	0	0	1
Cochrane,c	0	0	0	0	0	P'paugh,ss	3	1	0	3	3
Gay'way,ss	3	0	0	1	2	Ruel,c	3	1	1	6	1
Ehmke,p	2	0	0	0	0	Ruether,p	4	0	1	0	1
Rommell,p	0	0	0	0	0						
xHale	1	0	0	0	0						
xxWelch	1	0	1	0	0						
Totals	35	2	11	24	6	Totals	31	6	8	27	9

xBatted for Ehmke in 6th.
xxBatted for Rommell in 9th.

Philadelphia	000 101 000—2
Washington	000 500 10x—6

Two-base hits, Ruel, Rice, Welch. Double plays, S. Harris to Judge; Ruel to S. Harris; Bluege to S. Harris to Judge. Base on balls off Ehmke 3; Ruether 2. Struck out by Ehmke 5; Ruether 5. Hits off Ehmke 5 in 5; off Rommell 3 in 3. Losing pitcher, Ehmke. Umpires, Moriarity, Geisel and Hildebrand.

CINCINNATI WOMEN WIN NET TOURNEY

INDIANAPOLIS, June 27.—(AP)—Clara Zinke and Mrs. Olga Weil, both of Cincinnati defeated Helen Canfield and Marion Pearson, both of Detroit, in the women's doubles final of the western clay court tennit tournament. The score was 7-5, 6-3.

BASEBALL SUMMARY

SALLY LEAGUE

GAMES MONDAY.
Charlotte at Macon.
Greenville at Augusta.
Asheville at Spartanburg.
Knoxville at Columbia.

CLUB STANDINGS.

Team	W	L	Pct
Greenville	40	24	.625
Asheville	40	25	.615
Macon	35	29	.547
HORNETS	35	32	.522
Augusta	31	30	.508
Spartans	32	35	.478
Knoxville	29	35	.453
Comers	16	48	.250

American League.

GAMES TODAY.
Athletics at Washington.
Boston at New York.
St. Louis at Chicago

CLUB STANDINGS.

Team	W	L	Pct	Team	W	L	Pct
N. York	47	20	.701	Wash'ton	33	32	.508
Chicago	39	31	.557	Cleveland	35	34	.507
Detroit	36	32	.529	St. Louis	27	42	.397
Athletics	35	33	.515	Boston	18	47	.277

RESULTS YESTERDAY.
New York 7; Boston 7.
Chicago 6; St. Louis 3.
Washington 6; Athletics [illegible].
Detroit 5; Cleveland 4.

National League.

GAMES TODAY.
Chicago at St. Louis.
Pittsburgh at Cincinnati.
Phillies at Brooklyn.
Boston at New York.

Team	W	L	Pct	Team	W	L	Pct
Cincin'ati	40	26	.606	Chicago	32	33	.492
St. Louis	33	29	.557	N York	32	33	.492
Pitts'urgh	34	27	.557	Phillies	25	39	.391
Brooklyn	33	30	.524	Boston	23	40	.365

RESULTS YESTERDAY.
Cincinnati 16; Pittsburgh 0.
Phillies 2; Brooklyn 1.
St. Louis 3-0; Chicago 2-5.
Only three scheduled.

Southern Association.

GAMES TODAY.
Atlanta at Birmingham.
Chattanooga at Little Rock.
Nashville at Memphis.
Mobile at New Orleans.

CLUB STANDINGS.

Team	W	L	Pct	Team	W	L	Pct
N Orleans	52	22	.703	Atlanta	35	35	.500
Bir'ing'm	42	28	.600	Mobile	31	41	.431
Memphis	43	31	.581	Chattan.	24	46	.343
Nashville	40	35	.533	L. Rock	21	50	.296

RESULTS YESTERDAY.
Atlanta 13; Chattanooga 0
New Orleans 5; Mobile 2.
Nashville 4; Memphis 2.
Only three scheduled.

INTERSTATE LEAGUE.
Scores Saturday.

	R	H	E
Marlboro	7	7	5
Entwhistle	5	7	6

Autry and Hamer; Vaughn and Kirby.

	R	H	E
Cheraw	0	6	2
Laurinburg	7	8	1

Benfield and West; Norton and Benton.

CLUB STANDINGS.

Team	W	L	Pct	Team	W	L	Pct
Laur'nb'rg	2	0	1,000	Marlboro	1	1	.500
Entw'istle	1	1	.500	Cheraw	0	2	.000

PIEDMONT LEAGUE

GAMES MONDAY.
Raleigh at Winston.
Durham at Greensboro.
High Point at Salisbury.

CLUB STANDINGS.

Team	W	L	Pct	Team	W	L	Pct
Greensbo	44	24	.647	Raleigh	28	38	.424
H. Point	42	26	.618	Winston	28	39	.418
Salisbury	35	33	.515	Durham	25	42	.373

WESTERN CAROLINA LEAGUE.

Team	W	L	Pct
Newton	8	2	.800
Hickory	7	2	.778
Valdese	6	3	.667
Morganton	4	5	.444
Lenoir	3	6	.333
Toylorsville	0	9	.000

COLUMBIA ASKS WAIVER ON FOUR

Special to The Observer.

COLUMBIA, June 27.—Columbia has waivers on four players including Arnett, Voyles and Steggerd. Knoxville has secured a new short fielder Don Rutherford from Louisville of the American association. Skippers Moffitt and Gabby Street of Augusta are dickering with a view of sending George Rhinehart, Smokey rightfielder to the Tigers. Moffitt announced that unless this trade is consummated waivers will be asked on Rhinehardt, who has been a great disappointment here.

Reas Still Show Other Clubs Their Heels

NEW YORK, June 27.—(AP)—Consistent hitting behind steady pitching, which has marked Cincinnati's advance as pacemaker in the National League pennant scramble, carried the Reds through severe tests with front rank contenders, figures for the past week show.

Jack Kendrick's club amassed the greatest number of hits for both big league circuits—37—in winning five of seven contests.

Cincinnati was also at the top in both batting and fielding for the season. According to the latest team records, the Reds had a batting percentage of .288 and a fielding mark of .792.

PIRATE THREAT FADES.

The close of the week folnd the Pittsburgh threat to the peak position temporarily sidetracked as the Corsairs were compelled to yield the runner up place to the Cardinals.

Cincinnati took toll of Lee Meadow' untarnished pitching slate for the year by landing on the Buccaneer twirler for a 9 to 1 triumph. Meadows had won eight games.

Brooklyn became intrenched in the first division by tying the Reds in games won and lost while the Cubs were sharing the fifth rung with the Giants.

A new acquisition to the Robins lineup was infielder Sammy Bohne of Redland. Bohne's real name is Cohen.

BRAVES MAN HANDLED.

Boston's Braves were tossed about unceremoniously with seven reserves in eight starts and were obliged to retreat into the cellar while the Phillies emerged from the pit into seventh place.

Detroit turned in the best performance for the week in the American with five victories and no setbacks, thereby rising from the second division to tie the Athletics for third place. Tris Speaker's Indians continued their eratic course climbing into second place early in the week but dropping back to fifth in the standing at the conclusion.

The Yankees and Browns gained an even break by winning three out of six games apiece.

However, the New Yorkers suffered a hard blow in the injury to Bob Muesel who broke a small bone in his left ankle in an attempted steal in a game with the Red Sox. He probably will be lost to the Yankees for at least a month.

George Sisler furnished one of the brilliant plays of the season by stealing home from third in the ninth to win a game for the Browns from the White Sox.

The Hugmen headed the Cubs in the majors for high runs with 47. The Phillies had first honors in the home run column with six. There were were 486 hits in the National against 467 in the American. Off 33 circuit drives 18 were made in the National circuit.

Last Week's Record

The week's major league record of games won and lost, runs, hits, errors, opponents' runs and home runs, including games of Saturday, follow:

NATIONAL LEAGUE.

	W.	L.	R.	H.	E.	HR.
Cincinnati	5	2	38	87	9	0
Brooklyn	5	2	33	77	14	0
Philadelphia	4	3	38	79	12	6
St. Louis	3	3	38	61	3	3
Pittsburgh	3	3	38	68	12	3
New York	3	3	35	68	9	4
Chicago	2	4	24	62	4	1
Boston	1	7	35	84	11	1

AMERICAN LEAGUE.

	W.	L.	R.	H.	E.	HR.
Detroit	5	0	34	49	7	1
Washington	4	2	27	50	6	2
Chicago	5	3	38	84	9	2
New York	3	3	47	66	9	1
St. Louis	3	3	32	57	5	3
Cleveland	2	5	20	68	5	0
Philadelphia	1	4	19	40	7	1
Boston	1	4	18	58	7	2

Ruth And Bottomley Lead Major Home Run Races

CHICAGO, June 27.—(AP)—A home run by Babe Ruth today gave the Babe his 25th homer of the season, and brought him to within three games of his 1921 schedule.

Ruth and his team mate, Anthony Lazzeri, were the only notables in the American competition to make base circuits in one blow last week, but helped the average by scoring three each. Lazzeri's three home runs brought his total of 11 to rank second only to Ruth for the major honors.

Rogers Hornsby of the Cardinals and Glenn Wright of the Pirates delivered two home runs each to join the ranks of the choice while all others were idle.

Leading home-run hitters:

American league—Ruth, New York 25; Lazzeri, New York 11; Simmons, Philadelphia, 10; Meusel, New York, 9; Williams, St. Louis, 8; P. Collins, New York, 7; Hauser, Philadelphia, 7; Cochrane, Philadelphia, 7.

National league—Bottomley, St. Louis, 10; Wilson, Chicago, and Kelly, New York, 7; Hornsby, St. Louis, 7; Bell, St. Louis, 7; Wright, Pittsburgh, 7.

Texas League.

Dallas 4; Houston 6.
Fort Worth 2; Waco 6.
Shreveport 1; Beaumont 4.
Wichita Falls-San Antonio, rain.

37,000 Fans See Chicago And St. Louis Divide

ST. LOUIS, June 27.—(AP)—Chicago and St. Louis split a double bill here today, the Cardinals winning the first, 3 to 2, and the Cubs the second, 5 to 0.

Grover Cleveland Alexander, recently released by the Cubs held his former team-mates to four hits in the opener. The locals were helpless before the pitching of Blake in the second, getting but one hit.

A record crowd of 37,000 persons attended the games.

FIRST GAME.

Chicago.	AB	R	H	O	A	St. Louis.	AB	R	H	O	A
Adams,2b	4	0	1	0	3	Blades,lf	4	0	1	2	0
H'cote,rf	3	0	0	1	0	Douthit,cf	4	0	0	0	0
Freigau,3b	4	0	0	1	0	Hornsby,2b	3	0	1	3	7
Wilson,cf	4	0	0	1	0	Bot'ley,1b	5	0	2	18	0
Ste'son,lf	4	1	1	2	0	S'worth,rf	3	2	1	1	0
Grimm,1b	4	1	2	10	2	L.Bell,3b	4	1	2	1	2
Cooney,ss	4	0	0	4	4	O'Farrell,c	3	0	0	5	0
H'tnett,c	4	0	0	7	3	Th'now,ss	4	0	2	0	5
Osborne,p	3	0	0	1	3	Alex'der,p	4	0	0	0	1
Totals	34	2	4	x29	15	Totals	34	3	9	30	15

xTwo out when winning run scored.

Chicago	000 000 200 0—2
St. Louis	000 010 100 1—3

Error, Freigau. Two-base hit, Thevenow. Home runs, Southworth, Grimm. Double play, Osborne, Cooney and Grimm. Base on balls off Osborne 10; Alexander 1. Struck out by Osborne 6; Alexander 5. Umpires, Quigley, Moran and Reardon.

SECOND GAME.

Chicago.	AB	R	H	O	A	St. Louis.	AB	R	H	O	A
Adams,2b	4	0	0	2	3	Blades,lf	3	0	0	0	0
H'cote,rf	4	1	1	1	0	Douthit,cf	3	0	0	4	0
Freigau,3b	3	0	0	0	1	Hornsby,2b	4	0	0	1	5
Wilson,cf	4	0	0	3	0	Bot'ley,1b	2	0	0	13	0
Ste'son,lf	4	1	1	2	0	S'worth,rf	4	0	1	2	0
Grimm,1b	4	2	1	7	0	L.Bell,3b	3	0	0	1	3
Cooney,ss	4	1	3	1	2	Warwick,c	3	0	0	5	2
Gonzales,c	4	0	1	10	1	Th'now,ss	3	0	0	1	3
Blake,p	3	0	0	0	1	H.Bell,p	1	0	0	0	1
						Reinhart,p	1	0	0	0	0
						Johnson,p	0	0	0	0	0
						xT'porcer	1	0	0	0	0
Totals	34	5	7	27	8	Totals	28	0	1	27	14

xBatted for Reinhart in 8th.

Chicago	000 212 000—5
St. Louis	000 000 000—0

Errors, Adams, Cooney, Douthit, Hornsby 3, H. Bell. Two-base hits, Grimm, Cooney. Stolen bases, Heathcote, Freigau. Double plays, Gonzales and Adams, Cooney, Adams and Grimm. Base on balls off Blake 4; off H. Bell 1. Struck out by Blake 10; Bell 3; Reinhart 1; Johnson 1. Hits off H. Bell 7 in 6; Reinhart none in 2; Johnson none in 1. Losing pitcher, H. Bell. Umpires, Moran, Reardon and Quigley.

AMERICAN BOAT THIRD.

LONDON, June 27.—(AP)—British motorboats won first and second in the first of a series of international races on the Thams for the Dupke of York's Trophy. The United States came in third.

FOUR PITCHERS HAMMERED IN 16-0 ROUT

CINCINNATI, June 27.—(AP)—Four Pittsburgh pitchers were hammered for 18 hits today and Cincinnati won from the champions 16 to 0.

Pittsburgh.	AB	R	H	O	A	Cincinnati.	AB	R	H	O	A
Moore,3b	4	0	0	1	2	Dressen,3b	5	3	2	3	1
Carey,cf	1	0	0	1	0	Walker,rf	4	2	2	5	0
B'hart,lf	2	0	1	0	1	Roush,cf	5	1	3	1	0
Waner,rf	4	0	0	3	0	C'st'sen,cf	1	0	0	2	0
C'yler,lf-cf	3	0	0	1	0	Bressler,1b	3	2	2	5	0
Bigbee,cf	1	0	0	0	0	Pipp,1b	5	2	3	5	1
Traynor,ss	4	0	3	4	6	Allen,lf	0	0	0	0	0
Gr'tham,1b	2	0	2	10	0	Critz,2b	5	2	2	1	4
Rhyne,2b	1	0	0	1	1	Picinich,c	3	1	0	0	0
R'lings,2b	1	0	0	1	1	Emmer,ss	4	2	3	5	3
Gooch,c	3	0	0	1	1	Donohue,p	4	1	1	0	1
Songer,p	0	0	0	0	1						
Yde,p	1	0	0	1	0						
Morrison,p	0	0	0	0	0						
Adams,p	2	0	0	0	2						
Totals	29	0	6	24	15	Totals	39	16	18	27	10

Pittsburgh	000 000 000—0
Cincinnati	405 043 00x—16

Errors, Traynor, Rhyne. Two-base hits, Roush, Emmer, Bressler, Walker, Traynor. Three-base hits, Pipp, Bressler, Emmer, Donohue, Walker. Home run, Critz. Double play, Donohue, Emmer to Pipp. Triple play, Emer, Dressen to Bressler. Bases on balls off Songer 2; Yde 1; Morrison 1; Adas 1; Donohue 2. Struck out by Yde 1. Hits off Songer 3 in 1-3; Yde 5 in 2 1-3; Adams 10 in 5; Morrison 0 in 1-3. Losing pitcher, Songer. Umpires, McCormick, Hart and Rigler.

PHILLIES STOP DODGERS.

BROOKLYN, N. Y., June 27.—(AP)—Philadelphia stopped Brooklyn's five game winning streak today by coming out on the long end of a 2 to 1 score, Wayland Dean holding the Robins to five hits.

Philadelphia.	AB	R	H	O	A	Brooklyn.	AB	R	H	O	A
Sand,ss	4	0	2	2	5	Stand't,2b	4	0	2	2	[illegible]
Leach,cf	4	0	0	1	0	Witt,cf	3	0	0	5	0
Mokan,rf	4	0	0	[illegible]	0	Herman,1b	4	0	0	6	0
Nixon,cf	1	1	0	2	0	Wheat,lf	4	0	0	8	0
Grimes,1b	3	1	2	12	1	Cox,rf	3	0	1	1	0
Henline,c	4	0	1	6	0	O'Neil,c	2	0	0	2	1
Huber,3b	4	0	1	0	1	zJ'bson	0	1	0	0	0
Friberg,2b	4	0	1	3	3	H'gr'ves,c	1	0	0	3	0
Dean,p	3	0	0	0	0	Mar'tt,3b	4	0	1	1	1
						Butler,ss	2	0	1	4	5
						zzFournier	0	0	0	0	0
						[illegible],ss	0	0	0	0	0
						Petty,p	2	0	0	0	0
						[illegible]x	1	0	0	0	0
						Ehrh'dt,p	0	0	0	0	0
Totals	34	2	7	27	10	Totals	30	1	5	27	9

zBatted for O'Neil in 7th.
zzBatted for Butler in 7th.
zzzBatted for Petty in 7th.

Philadelphia	000 000 200—2
Brooklyn	000 000 100—1

Errors, Wheat, Maranville, Petty. Two-base hit, Cox. Three-base hit, Butler. Double plays, Butler, Standaert and Herman; Butler (unassisted); Standaert, Butler and Herman; Grimes, Sand and Grimes. Base on balls off Petty 1; Dean 3. Struck out by Petty 3; Dean 3; Ehrhardt 2. Hits off Petty 6 in 7; off Ehrhardt 1 in 2. Losing pitcher, Petty. Umpires, Pfirman, O'Day and Sweeney.

EVENING HERALD SPORTS

HUGGINS' TEAM 5 TO 4 FAVORITE IN BIG SERIES

WELTERS CLASH TONIGHT AT WINSOR'S ARENA

Morrie Lux and Joe Conway in Feature Bout at Reopening of Club

Morrie Lux, Portland welterweight, who has met many of the topnotchers in the country, and Joe Conway, who hails from Buffalo, N. Y., will meet tonight in the main event to be staged at Fred Winsor's Madison Square Garden arena.

It will be the first show to be put on by Winsor at the Madison Square Garden arena in several weeks and will mark the beginning of Monday night boxing in Los Angeles. Hereafter the shows will be held on Monday evenings instead of Wednesday.

Tommy Carter, a lightweight with a wallop, who boxed some good bouts at Vernon two years ago, will trade punches with Baby Gans in the semiwindup. Battling O'Dell and Young Sam Langford are billed for the feature spot. Both are 130-pound sluggers and the fans are expected to see some action when they mix.

Other bouts are: Ted Frenchie, colored, vs. Barney Tooley, 150 pounds; Terry Brown vs. Battling Vega, 158 pounds; Boy Wonder vs. Frank O'Connell, 125 pounds, and Jeffries vs. Billy Plimmer, featherweights.

LOCAL LEAGUE WILL HOLD MEET TONIGHT

The regular weekly meeting of the Greater Southern California baseball association will be held tonight at the organization's headquarters at 435 South Spring street. President Weinreich requests that all managers be present as several winter leagues are to be formed.

Random Shots by Bill Smith

"K. O." BOBBY DYSON is one eastern boxer who has lived up to the advance notices. Dyson came here heralded as a bantam of class who had mingled with the best boys of his weight in the east, and he displayed the goods when he beat Dick Griffin at Hollywood Friday night.

After watching such former good ones as Ritchie Mitchell, Jack Sharkey, Midget Smith and even Bobby Ward try to get over here as four-rounders, it was something of a relief to see Dyson. He is the first boy with an eastern reputation to show the Los Angeles fans that the highly touted lads from the Atlantic coast ase not all false alarms.

HERE'S some inside information about Dyson which was slipped to us by Fred Winsor, who is managing the boy. Dyson wouldn't have been Dyson at all if it were not for the knockout kick he carries in his left mitt.

He started out in life at Adams, Mass., 23 years ago under the euphonious name of Anthony Chicoine. At New Bedford liver a boxer who called himself Bobby Dyson and who was doing so well that his manager dug up a match for him in Boston with a lad named Young Benny.

TWO days before the match Dyson became ill, and his manager, who never liked to break a date when there was any coin in sight, enlisted Anthony Chicoine to play the role of Bobby Dyson and meet the Boston boy.

The pseudo Bobby Dyson did his part. He slammed Young Benny on the chin in the first round and for about 15 minutes thereafter the birds were chirping for the Boston slugger.

ON his return to New Bedford, Chicoine met the original Bobby Dyson, who was slightly peeved at having had his name swiped. But he was game enough to risk his moniker if Chicoine would fight him for it.

So the boys battled.

Chicoine knocked him out in the second round, gained undisputed title to the name, and then to avoid any future mixups inserted "K. O." in front of it.

DYSON is aiming for a match with Joe Lynch, world's bantamweight champion, and according to Winsor, is so eager for a crack at the title that he will give his services for nothing if he is not returned the winner.

That's some offer in these days when even ordinary boxers are getting all kinds of fancy medals. Furthermore Winsor intimates that Joe Burman and Carl Tremaine want none of Dyson's game.

FORM LEAGUES AT MEETING TONIGHT

The last chance for clubs to enter the Triple A league of the Southern California Managers' association will be at tonight's meeting at the B. H. Dyas Log Cabin, announced Les Taylor today.

Managers wishing to enter their clubs in the circuit can do so by handing their application in to Frank Kerwin, accompanied by $100 forfeit money. Several other leagues are to be formed at tonight's confab and all managers are requested to be present.

CHICAGO BOXER TO UNDERGO OPERATION

Eddie Brown, Chicago boxer, is in Los Angeles today following an invasion of San Diego, where he knocked out Joe Larson in the third round of a four-round bout. Brown will undergo a minor operation here, after which he will seek matches with the welterweights who are doing business in the four-round game.

L. A. Fans Split on Chances of Giants and Yanks

OPINIONS ARE 50-50 ON BIG BALL GAMES

"Always String With Champions," Is Expert Advice of Dempsey

Los Angeles baseball fans are about fifty-fifty in their opinons on the outcome of the New York Giants-New York Yanks world's championship series which is scheduled to open Wednesday afternoon.

Many of the followers of the diamond sport here in Los Angeles are confident that John McGraw will lead his band of baseball athletes to another world's series title, while just as many believe that Miller Huggins will step out and carry off the honors.

Here is the way a few of the Angeleno fans and visiting guessers expressed themselves when asked who they figured as the next world's baseball champions:

OSCAR VITT'S OPINION

Oscar Vitt, third baseman of the Salt Lake club—Although I am an American league man I believe McGraw's strategy will win the series. McGraw is one of the greatest leaders of all times. He directs the entire play of the club and his little moves here and there will win for him.

Harry Trotter, coach at the University of California, southern Branch—The law of averages says the Yankees should win.

JACK DEMPSEY'S TIP

Jack Dempsey, world's heavyweight champ—Always string with the champions. You can only lose once.

Billy Ferrier—I figure the pitchers will win the series for the Yankees.

Billy Oates—I've won every bet with the Giants, so why stop now.

John Dugan—It looks like the Yanks this time.

WHAT GOLFERS SAY

"Pat" Patterson, Griffith Park golf professional—Watch the Giants. They look good to me.

Mel Smith, Pasadena professional golfer—The Giants won't be the world's champions after this series.

Lou Berrien, Wilshire professional—I think the Giants will turn the trick without any trouble.

Pat Higgins—It will be as easy for the Giants as the Australian crawl stroke for an expert swimmer.

MIKE DONLIN LOYAL

Mike Donlin, ex-Giant star—McGraw will kid the Yanks out of it for the third time.

Jesse Smith, Glendale golfer—I string with my friend, Mike Donlin.

E. A. O'Donnell, L. A. A. C.—The Yanks in a walk. Watch their smoke.

Rex Anglin—Think the Giants will win again.

Elmer Henderson—The Yanks should have a fair chance.

Charlie Keppen—Haven't gone wrong in 10 years on the series, so to keep up the record I'll pick the Yankees.

J. Cameron Smith—New York will win.

Harry Brand—These ball games ruin me. I won't pick one. If I hit it right they'll say I had the inside dope and if I miss it I still will be a sap.

Jack Scanlon—I never have missed one yet, so put me down for the Seals.

Charlie Dillard—The Yankees.

Jack Doyle—Guess I'll string with the Giants.

Tom Kennedy—I like the Yankees this time.

George Stanley—It's a tossup, but I like the Giants.

Tom Andrews—The Yankees look stronger, but McGraw figures to outguess them.

Fred Winsor—I'll take the Giants.

HOPE, ADAMS WILL TANGLE AT VENICE

Boxing fans of the bay district will witness another card full of action at the Venice Athletic club, according to Matchmaker "Pop" Nealis.

For the main event Willie Hope, the Denver flash, is to meet Johnny Adams, the San Bernardino bear cat.

The semi-windup has Marty Burman, who knocked out Stanley Frye last week, hooked up with "Red" Burke of San Francisco. The rest of the card is as follows: Jack Spencer vs. Jerry Clark, Gilbert Gallant vs. Johnny McGraw, Billy Kelly vs. "Sailor" Ashford, Ivan Unger vs. "Young" Siki.

FIRST LINE OF DEFENSE

Yankees' infield, from left to right—Everett Scott, shortstop; Mike McNully, utility; Wallie Pipp, first base; Aaron Ward, second base and Joe Dugan, third base.

Ruth to Cover Big Series for Evening Herald

Do you want to know why John McGraw will use certain pitchers against the Yankees in the great world's series games?

Or do you want the inside information as to the system of play of the YankeesZ

If you do, let Babe Ruth, baseball's most famous star, tell it to you through The Evening Herald.

Dave Bancroft, captain of the New York Giants, will tell it to you from the National league viewpoint, and Shortstop Everett of the Yankees will write a daily story from the American league angle.

Frank Chance, who managed the Boston Red Sox during the past season, will analyze the games for The Herald readers.

Three big news agencies, the International, the Cosmopolitan and the United Press will carry special features and the play by play description of every game.

For authentic news of the world's series games read The Evening Herald. FIRST WITH THE LATEST.

JORDAN TO BOX BROWN

Johnny Jordan and Young Brown, lightweights, will meet in the main event of the weekly boxing show at the Hollywood American Legion stadium Friday night, it was announced by Matchmaker Tom Kennedy today.

Jimmy Hackley and Frankie Dean, 130 pounders, are billed for the semi-windup while Bert Meyers and Tom Kelley, middeweights, will swap punches in the feature bout.

Other bouts follow: Freddie Ellis vs. Johnny Reno, 135 pounds; Jack Spencer vs. Young Leddy, 128 pounds; Johnny Doyle vs. Tobey Montoya, 121 pounds.

NEW WESTERN BALL LEAGUE IS FORMED

KANSAS CITY, Oct. 8.—A new western association baseball league was formed here, it was announced today. Towns in the new league were selected from those comprising this year's Southwestern league and Western Association.

BEES CINCH TO FINISH 5TH THIS YEAR

By MATT GALLAGHER

Duffy Lewis and his hard hitting Salt Lake club arrived in Sacramento today with five victories out of the seven games played against the Los Angeles club.

That practically assured the Bees of fifth place in the Coast circuit and also the Angels sixth.

After winning the first two contests the Los Angeles club was unable to hold Salt Lake. Paul Strand came back yesterday after a two days' rest and drove in five runs in the first game. He hit his forty-third home run of the season.

FINAL SERIES

The final series of the year starts Wednesday when the Vernon squad tangles with the Angels.

Bill Essick's squad is on its way home after a dizzy road trip. The youngsters lost everything but their uniforms.

Portland's victories over Vernon put that club within striking distance of Sacramento for second place. The Seals showed that they can beat Sacramento any time they want to start. Bert Ellison has his club 12 games in front of Sacramento and there is no chance for his squad to lose.

BEHIND BEAVERS

The rivalry between the Seattle and Portland fans is almost as keen as that between the Tiger and Angel rooters. Seattle finishes behind the Beavers this year.

Bert Neihoff, manager of the Mobile club in the Southern association, has arrived here to pass the winter. Neihoff won the Southern league pennant last season and had his club fighting for first place this year. He says that Bill James, former Vernon pitcher whom he bought the latter part of the season, had a hard time getting started in his league. Neihoff has been mentioned for other managerial berths.

Bill Lane, owner of the Salt Lake club, will return to Los Angeles early next month to prepare plans for the annual Coast league meeting. Lane claims William H. McCarthy will not contest the election and that a local man will be named head of the circuit.

HARRY GREB MEETS LOUGHREN THURSDAY

BOSTON, Oct. 8.—Harry Greb of Pittsburg, middleweight champion of the world, will clash with Tommy Loughren of Philadelphia in a 10-round decision bout here Thursday night, it became known today.

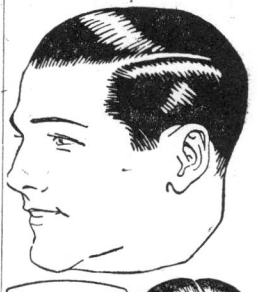

Club Standings

COAST LEAGUE STANDING

	W.	L.	Pct.	If Win	If Lose
San Francisco	121	73	.624	.626	.621
Sacramento	108	84	.563	.55	6.506
Portland	104	86	.547	.550	.545
Seattle	96	94	.505	.508	.503
Salt Lake	91	101	.474	.477	.472
Los Angeles	88	107	.451	.454	.448
Oakland	87	108	.446	.449	.444
Vernon	75	117	.391	.394	.389

AMERICAN LEAGUE

	W.	L.	Pct.		W.	L.	Pct.
New York	98	54	645	Washington	74	78	487
Cleveland	82	70	.539	Philadelphia	69	83	.454
Detroit	83	71	.539	Chicago	68	85	.444
St. Louis	74	78	.487	Boston	61	90	.404

NATIONAL LEAGUE

	W.	L.	Pct.		W.	L.	Pct.
New York	95	58	.621	St. Louis	79	74	.516
Cincinnati	92	63	.594	Brooklyn	76	78	.494
Pittsburg	87	68	.561	Boston	54	100	.351
Chicago	83	71	.539	Philadelphia	50	1$4	.325

AMERICAN ASSOCIATION

	W.	L.	Pct.		W.	L.	Pct.
Kansas City	112	54	.675	Milwaukee	75	91	.452
St. Paul	111	57	.661	Minneapolis	74	92	446
Louisville	91	77	.542	Indianapolis	72	94	.434
Columbus	79	89	.470	Toledo	54	114	.321

Final Averages of Leading Players in Two Major Leagues

Copyright, 1923, by Cosmopolitan News Service

LEADING SLUGGERS

Player	Club	G	AB	R	H	Pct.
Heilmann,	Tigers	144	525	120	211	.402
Ruth,	Yankees	152	520	151	205	.394
Hornsby,	Cardinals	107	424	89	163	.385
Speaker,	Indians	150	573	132	218	.380
Wheat,	Dodgers	98	349	63	131	.375

LEADING HOME RUN HITTERS

Ruth, Yankees	41
Williams, Phillies	41
Williams, Browns	29
Fournier, Dodgers	22
Miller, Cubs	20

LEADING RUN MAKERS

Ruth, Yankees	151
Speaker, Indians	132
Jamieson, Indians	130
Young, Giants	121
Carey, Pirates	120

LEADING PITCHERS

	W.	L.	Pct.
Luque, Reds	27	8	.771
Ryan, Giants	16	9	.762
Pennock, Yankees	19	6	.760
Jones, Yankees	21	8	.724
Cole, Tigers	13	5	.722

Baseball Scores

At Los Angeles—

Bees 13, Angels 4

First game:

SALT LAKE	AB	R	H	O	A	LOS ANGELES	AB	R	H	O	A
Wilhoit,rf	4	3	3	2	0	W.M'c,lf	4	1	2	2	0
Vitt,3b	5	2	3	0	1	Jacobs,ss	4	0	0	2	8
Lewis,lf	4	1	1	0	0	Tw'bly,rf	2	0	0	4	0
Strand,cf	4	2	2	5	0	Hood,cf	4	0	1	1	0
Leslie,1b	3	1	1	6	0	Smith,3b	3	0	0	3	3
S'ehan,2b	5	0	2	3	3	Griggs,1b	4	2	1	8	1
Lazzeri,ss	4	2	2	2	0	L'more,2b	4	0	0	3	2
R.M'h,p	5	0	0	1	1	Baldwin,c	4	0	1	3	0
Coumbe,1b	2	0	0	1	0	Jones,p	2	0	0	1	2
Fred'ks,lf	2	1	1	1	0	Hughes,p	0	0	0	0	0
						xCarroll	1	0	1	0	0
						Rob'son,p	0	0	0	0	0
						xxGolvin	1	1	1	0	0
Totals	43	13	16	27	6	Totals	33	4	7	27	16

x Carroll batted for Hughes in seventh.
xx Golvin batted for Robertson in ninth.

SCORE BY INNINGS

Salt Lake ....3 0 0 0 0 5 2 0 3—13
Los Angeles ...1 0 0 0 0 0 1 0 2— 4

At Los Angeles—

Bees 7, Angels 4

Second game:

SALT LAKE	AB	R	H	O	A	LOS ANGELES	AB	R	H	O	A
Fred'ks,lf	3	2	2	2	0	Carroll,lf	4	2	2	2	0
Lazzeri,ss	4	0	0	2	2	Jacobs,ss	4	1	3	1	3
Wilhoit,rf	4	1	2	2	0	Twmbly,rf	4	0	1	2	0
Vitt,3b	3	1	1	0	5	Hood,cf	4	0	1	2	0
Coumbe,1b	4	1	2	12	0	Smith,3b	3	0	0	1	2
Sheeh'n,2b	4	0	0	2	1	Golvin,1b	3	0	1	5	0
Strand,cf	4	1	1	1	0	Lin'me,2b	3	0	1	0	1
Peters,c	3	1	1	2	0	Regan,c	3	0	0	2	2
Myers,p	2	0	1	0	1	Lyons,p	1	0	0	0	1
						Douglas,p	2	1	1	0	3
Totals	31	7	10	21	9	Totals	31	4	10	21	12

Game called end of seventh account of darkness.

SCORE BY INNINGS

Salt Lake ....4 1 1 1 0 0 0—7
Los Angeles ....2 0 0 0 0 0 2—4

At Seattle—

Seattle, 7; Oakland, 2

First game:

OAKLAND	AB	R	H	O	A	SEATTLE	AB	R	H	O	A
Massey,2b	3	0	0	3	5	Lane,cf	5	0	1	4	0
Cooper,cf	4	0	0	5	0	Merkle,2b	3	0	0	4	2
Cather,3b	4	0	2	1	3	Johnstn,1b	4	0	0	8	1
Arlett,rf	4	0	1	0	0	Eldred,rf	3	0	0	0	0
Laf'yte,lf	4	1	2	10	1	Rohwer,lf	4	3	3	3	0
Read,c	3	1	1	0	0	Crane,ss	3	3	2	2	7
Lepsiich,lf	3	0	1	1	0	Bldwin,3b	3	1	2	1	0
[illegible]						[illegible]					

Oaks 10, Seattle 4

[illegible]

At San Francisco:

Senators, 12; Seals, 6.

[illegible]

Leading Facts Regarding 1923 World Series

Here are the leading facts regarding the world series:

Principals—New York Giants and New York Yankees.

Number of Games—Four out of seven.

Series Begins—Wednesday, Oct. 10.

Games Start—2 p. m. (New York time) 11 a. m. (Los Angeles time).

First Game — Yankee stadium.

Manager of Giants—John McGraw.

Manager of Yankees—Miller Huggins.

Probable Batteries—For the Giants, Nehf and Snyder; Yankees, Hoyt and Schang.

Umpires — National league, "Hank" O'Day and Bob Hart; American league, Billy Evans and Dick Nallin.

Capacity Polo grounds, 56,000; Yankee stadium, 70,000.

At Portland—
First game:

Portland 10, Tigers 5

VERNON	AB	R	H	O	A	PORTLAND	AB	R	H	O	A
H.High,lf	5	1	3	1	0	King,lf	4	2	3	0	0
Schn'd'r,rf	4	1	3	1	0	Stumpf,2b	5	1	0	2	3
Gil'spie,1b	5	1	1	13	1	C.High,rf	4	1	1	1	1
Ch'd'ne,cf	4	1	1	2	0	Poole,1b	4	2	4	11	2
Whitney,c	4	0	1	4	2	Cox,cf	5	2	2	2	0
Rader,2b	2	1	0	2	5	Brazill,3b	5	1	3	2	1
Warner,3b	4	0	2	0	0	Jones,ss	5	0	2	2	4
Slade,ss	4	1	0	1	0	Onslow,c	2	0	0	2	0
[illegible]						[illegible]					
Totals	35	6	11	24	17	Totals	38	10	15	27	13

x—Ran for Onslow in sixth.

SCORE BY INNINGS

Vernon [illegible]—6
Portland [illegible] x—10

Second game:

Portland 7, Tigers 4

VERNON	AB	R	H	O	A	PORTLAND	AB	R	H	O	A
H.High,lf	[illegible]					Wolfer,lf	[illegible]				
Sch'd'r,rf	4	2	2	0	0	Stumpf,2b	5	1	1	2	3
Gil'spie,1b	5	0	1	14	2	C. High,rf	5	1	2	0	0
Ch'db'e,cf	5	0	3	1	0	Poole,1b	4	1	1	10	0
Zanic,c	3	0	0	1	0	Cox,cf	3	2	2	5	0
Rader,2b	4	1	1	3	4	Brazill,3b	4	1	3	1	4
Warner,3b	3	0	1	2	2	Jones,ss	4	0	1	2	2
Slade,ss	4	0	1	1	7	Daly,c	4	0	1	6	0
Tiner,p	2	0	0	0	1	Leverenz,p	4	0	2	0	1
Gilder,p	2	0	0	0	1						
Totals	37	4	11	24	17	Totals	33	7	17	27	10

SCORE BY INNINGS

Vernon .... 0 0 2 0 0 1 1 0 0—4
Portland ...... 0 0 1 2 4 0 0 0 x—7

AMERICAN LEAGUE

At New York—		R.	H.	E.
Philadelphia	0 0 0 1 3 1 0 0 4	9	12	2
New York	2 0 0 0 5 0 0 0 0	7	10	1

Batteries—Harris, Rommel, Meeker and Perkins; Hoyt, Pipgras, and Schang, Hoffman.

At Cleveland—		R.	H.	E.
Chicago	1 0 2 0 0 0 0 1 2	6	11	2
Cleveland	2 0 1 2 0 2 1 1 x	9	13	2

Batteries—T. Blankenship, Thurston and Graham; Shaute and N'Neill.

At Detroit—		R.	H.	E.
St. Louis	1 1 0 3 0 1 0 0 0	6	12	1
Detroit	0 0 4 0 0 1 1 0 1	7	10	2

Batteries—Kolp and Collins; Whitehill, Dauss, Cole and Bassler.

At Washington—		R.	H.	E.
Boston	0 0 1 0 0 1 0 0 0	2	7	2
Washington	0 1 0 0 0 3 1 0 x	5	U	2

Batteries—Fullerton, Howe and Walters; Mogridge and Ruel.

NATIONAL LEAGUE

At St. Louis—
First game:

		R.	H.	E.
Chicago	3 0 1 0 0 2 3 0 1	10	16	1
St. Louis	1 1 0 0 0 0 0 0 1	3	12	1

Batteries—Collins, Fussell and Hartnett; Haines, Stone and Beibergal.

Second game:

		R.	H.	E.
Chicago	1 0 0 0 0 2 0 0 0	3	6	1
St. Louis	0 0 0 2 4 0 0 0 x	6	12	4

Batteries—Osborne, Dumovich and Wirth; Stuart and McCurdy.

At Cincinnati—		R.	H.	E.
Pittsburg	0 0 2 0 5 0 0 0 0	7	12	1
Cincinnati	0 0 1 0 0 0 2 2 0	5	11	3

Batteries—Morrison and Gooch; Donohue, Harris, Keck and Sandberg

At Brooklyn—		R.	H	E.
New York	0 0 0 0 0 0 0 0 1	1	9	2
Brooklyn	0 0 0 2 4 0 0 0 x	6	11	1

Batteries—Watson, Hunsinger and Gaston; Henry and Hargraves.

FERRIS TO CONFER ON RACING PLANS

Dick Ferris, general manager of the Culver City race track, will leave this week for San Francisco to confer with the officials of the Tanforan track.

Ferris is anxious to work in harmony with that organization.

Horses that will race at Tanforan can come south for the Culver City meet which will start about Christmas day.

Want Ads are the people's advertising. Put them in The Evening Herald, which is the people's preference.

BASEBALL 'DOPE' AGAIN FAVORS 'RUTH AND COMPANY'

For Third Time American League Champions Are Figured 'Sure Things'

(CONTINUED FROM PAGE ONE)

edly crushed last year by practically all of the accidental breaks going against them.

They should find Babe Ruth a big asset this year. Ruth was a positive handicap in the world's championship games of 1921 and 1922.

Yanks Made 5-4 Favorites in L. A.

Although the New York Giants easily defeated the Yankees during the past two world's series, local men who back their opinions with money have made the American league pennant winners a 5 to 4 favorite over the world's champions.

One man has posted $400 to bet on the Giants. He wanted to place it against $500 of the Yankee money. The man who put up the $400 lost several thousand dollars betting on the field against the Giants in the pennant race.

Hundreds of smaller wagers have been reported. Most of them were between friends and were made at even money.

WEBER, HUNEFELD TO CLASH AT LYCEUM

Dick Donald will have to conjure up a whirlwind card this week to better that classy bill at the Lyceum club Saturday night, but he has already made a start by naming Willie Hunefeld and Johnny Weber for next Saturday's main event.

Benny Diaz received his first setback in months in the main event Saturday night. Pico Ramies, a clever little southpaw, had the hard-hitting Diaz puzzled throughout the fight and gave him a four-round trimming.

Sailor Buel hurt his right wrist in the semi-windup and he forfeited to Joe Pimenthal at the end of the third round.

Other results follow: Young Bruno lost to Young Moran, 125 pounds; Larry Murray defeated Kid Morey, 138 pounds; Pete Wagner whipped Kid Payo in the best slugging match of the evening, and Peanut Jensen drew with Kid Howard, 105 pounds.

PARKER BEATS GRIFFIN

SAN JOSE, Oct. 8.—C. J. "Peck" Griffin was defeated by William Parker of San Francisco in the all-comers tennis tournament being held by the San Jose Tennis club.

Grover Alexander Outguesses Rival Batters and Yankees Let Numerous Good Balls Go By

Control and Quick Curve Prove Main Assets of Cardinal Hurler

One-Sidedness of Game Entirely Due to Alec's Superiority to Shawkey and Shocker; Fielding by Both Teams Fast and Gritty in Face of Hot Fire

By W. B. Hanna

The Cardinals had al lthe better of it at the Yankee Stadium yesterday in the sixth game of the world series and carried off the day's laurels from the Yankees by the gaping score of 10 to 2. This, like the 10 to 5 victory of the Yankees in St. Louis, was one of the decisively won games, in which the loser was a lcser indeed and the winner a world beater. 'Twas ever thus; nothing succeeds like success.

The series now has become practically a one-game series. Everything depends on to-day. Each side has won three games, and except for the gate receipts and the statistical fodder the other games might as well not have been played. To day it will be Hoyt vs. Haines pitching, and with the out look even. Hoyt is as good as Haines, Haines is as good as Hoyt. Alexander is out of the way, and a pitching edge is non-existent. One man is as good as the other.

It was a question of pitching yesterday, and Grover Alexander, in winning his second game of the week-long ruction, so far excelled either Bob Shawkey or Urban Shocker as to be the main influence in the one-sidedness of the game. Alexander's pitching was met more squarely and hit more freely than last Sunday, but inasmuch as he could bear down whenever it was urgent to do so, and had sprightly suport when needed, he was always the master of the Yankee batters.

Alec Outguesses Yankees

The man whom Joe McCarthy, Cub manager, didn't want on his ball club, preferring discipline to the presence of a star, outguessed the batters largely, for one thing. They let numerous good ones go by. His control any and all the time was of priceless value to the Missouri melange, and his quick though narrow curve was all the more valuable for that reason.

His screw ball took the desired skid as it faded in and low across the plate. His fast one, not so wonderful, was rammed with some viciousness, but his repertoire and his savvy were easily adequate for the undoing of any opponent he could have met.

Ruth, who is hitting in streaks in this red-letter clash, could not get hold of the Alexandrian service except to pour hot shot at Bottomley, and that rakish gentleman took care of it niftily. The Cardinals rapped Shawkey for three runs in the first inning, and then Bob, keeping his fast ball high, straightened himself out and pitched tellingly until the seventh inning. His support sagged a bit in the seventh, and then he was taken out after two hits had been made off of him, one of these, a two-bagger by Southworth, being a hit solely because it traversed the slanting sun's rays to left and was lost by Bob Meusel when he tried to outstare Old Sol.

The other miscue behind Shawkey in the seventh, in which run-flecked inning the Cardinals tallied five times and salted the game away indubitably, was a dropped assist at first base by Tony Lazzeri. Yet nobody will socld Tony. He has played splendid baseball in this series, showing heart and stomach for controversy, and it may be mentioned just here that though the fielding was slightly ragged pro and con yesterday by our boys and by the strangers within the Gotham gates, it was tidy, fast and gritty most of the time and nervy in the face of some lively peppering. All of which applies to both teams.

Shocker Ineffective

Shocker, who relieved Shawkey in the seventh, was less effective than Bob an dlasted no further than the end of the inning. He was cudgelled for a single by Hornsby, a home run into the left-field seats by Lester Bell and a two-bagger by Hafey. Myles Thomas pitched pretty nice ball in his two innings of work in a cause already batted into the limbo of the lost by the rapacity of the Cardinals' clubs. Eleven hits were made off Shawkey and Shocker and of there three were bunched in the first inning and five in the seventh.

In the first inning Umpire Hank O'Day, National Leaguer, saw Shawkey wetting his finers, and he wanted to know. He called Umpire Bill Dinneen and Dinneen told him that in the American League, where no rosin ball is used, they permitted what few pitchers that wanted to to wet their fingers provided they then dried them on their shirts so they wouldn't be pitching a spitball. Shawkey and Slim Harriss, of the Red Sox, are the only pitchers who do this. They do it to get a purchase.

The first inning went to a tedious length, but was spiced by the hitting of the Cardinals. Shawkey took his time—and some of the spectators'. Holm opened with a hit to right and Southworth forced him. Hornsby waited it out and Jeems Bottomley, who is putting no end of spirit into his play in this series, whacked a long double to left which scored Holm and sent the Cardinals away with heels flying. Lester Bell, who has quite redeemed himself for his previous weak hitting, did what Bottomley did, he banged a liner past Dugan.

Bell Scores Two

The Bell hit sent in two more runs, and on the first of these liners past Dugan the latter was none too agile. Three years ago he would have at least knocked down a whizzer of that sort between himself and the cushion. Shawkey pluckily stoked up and stopped stopped the foray by striking out Hafey and O'Farrell. The New York pitchers had O'Farrell's number. He went hitless.

Combs gave the ball a nasty prod the first time up, but Alexander checked it and allowed Thevenow to make a good play on it. Alexander struck out Koenig with a curve, and Ruth trundled to Bottomley after a bad strike had been called on him.

The Cardinals didn't make a hit in the second, third or fourth. In this barren interval was a clinking catch by Combs of a liner from Southworth. Earle came in on it, juggled it, then grabbed it again. Bell enjoyed a walk in the fourth and Severeid, whose throwing to bases was capital and who has handled the backstopping like a little man, threw him out stealing third.

Meusel Doubles and is Left

Alexander's ability to bear down, to put on the screws, was seen in the second and in the third. Meusel hit a high double into left in the third. This, presumably, was a "break" against the Cardinals, since so much they don't get is a "break." When the Yankees do things of that kind it is it appears, bad ball. Gehrig nor Lazzeri nor Dugan could bring Meusel in All died on infield grassers.

In the third inning the opportunity was there for business, and fairly big business. Huggins, had he elected, could have gone after one or two runs and have made at least one. Severeid began with a hit. It was a case of step up and slam, to rush Alexander before he could get set. Shawkey hit out at once and Trevenow bungled his grounder. Two on and none out.

Huggins went for a batch of runs. He could have had Combs sacrifice and gone for two runs, or even one, and as there were still six innings to come he wouldn't have been so badly off. A score of 3 to 2 at this stage wouldn't have been the worst that could have happened. However, that wasn't the Lilliput leader's idea, and he had to do the ordering. He resorted to the more vigorous though not necessarily the more sagacious course. Combs swung and hit to Alexander, who threw out Honest Hank Severeid.

Gehrig Drives in Meusel

The rest of the attack folded up in a fly from Koenig to Southworth and a clinging clip from Ruth to Bottomley. The Yankees made their first run in the fourth on a triple by Meusel down the left foul line and Gehrig's grounder to Hornsby.

The Cardinals made two hits off Shawkey in the fifth. Thevenow singled to left. Alexander bunted to Gehrig, who touched him on the line. Holm singled to center and scored Thevenow. Dugan came in and handled Southworth's grounder nicely. Lazzeri made a fine play over toward first on Hornsby's grounder. Bottomley began the sixth with a two-bagger and was held at second by Shawkey's rally. Robert the Gobbert struck out Bell and Hafey, and O'Farrell high fouled to Dugan.

The New York sixth started with Alexander passing Ruth. Previously there had been some senseless booing of Alexander by unknown intellects who thought he wasn't pitching to the Babe. Ruth's appearance on base this time was merely indulgence, for Meusel flied high to Holm on lunging at a sinker, Gehrig fanned after letting a good one go and Lazzeri flied high to Holm.

Alec's Quick Return

Alexander made one of those quick return pitches to Gehrig in the sixth, which is or is not ethical, according to how you look at it. The writer never had any overpowering admiration for this procedure. It wasn't quite in keeping with the admirable spirit which has prevailed in this series.

The cruel seventh began with Thevenow's second liner to left. Alexander dropped a sacrifice in front of the plate, and Severeid had it quickly. He glanced toward second, decided it was too late for a play there and threw to first. Lazzeri covered, and on the throw, not the straightest in the world, Tony made his first error of the series. He dropped the ball. Severeid picked up Holm's bunt and used it to force Thevenow at third.

Whereat the hits began to pop. Southworth lined crisply toward Meusel, and that tall subaltern found himself looking into the sun. When he saw the ball it was passing him. Which was quite too late to hop aboard. Alexander scored on the hit, Holm reached third. Southworth reached second. Shawkey dropped out, giving the Cardinals a chance to see what subsitence there was in Shocker's wet ball work.

Bell Clouts Distant Homer

Koenig came up with Bottomley's grounder and forced Hornsby, who had singled past Lazzeri and batted in Holm and Southworth. Bell hit far and fatally. He followed Bottomley with a homer and a good one. It fell in the left field extension of the grand stand and herded home the fifth run of the most injurious inning. Hafey's clean double to left created a little additional pain but nothing serious, for O'Farrell struck out and the worst was over.

Dugan's single in the seventh opened the way for a run. Severeid smashed violently to Bell, who found the ball too hot to handle. Then he overthrew first, letting Dugan take third. In the writer's opinion, Bell should have been charged with an error for letting Dugan reach third, which he was, and Severeid should have been credited with a hit, which he was not.

Southworth's triple in the ninth, followed by a wicked lick by Hornsby, on which Dugan made a difficult play, concocted a run.

Summary of Contests In Big Series to Date

THE St. Louis Card'nals drew up on even terms in the world series with the New York Yankees yesterday at the Yankee Stadium, winning by 10 to 2 and tying the series at 3 all. The seventh and deciding game will be played at the Yankee Stadium to-day. The summary of the six games to date, with runs, hits, errors and batteries, follows:

FIRST GAME

	R.	H.	E.
New York (A. L.)	2	6	0
St. Louis (N. L.)	1	3	1

Batteries—Pennock and Severeid; Sherdel, Haines and O'Farrell.

SECOND GAME

	R.	H.	E.
St. Louis (N. L.)	6	12	1
New York (A. L.)	2	4	0

Batteries—Alexander and O'Farrell; Shocker, Shawkey, Jones and Severeid, Collins.

THIRD GAME

	R.	H.	E.
St. Louis (N. L.)	4	8	0
New York (A. L.)	0	5	1

Batteries—Haines and O'Farrell; Ruether, Shawkey, Thomas and Severeid.

FOURTH GAME

	R.	H.	E.
New York (A. L.)	10	14	1
St. Louis (N. L.)	5	14	0

Batteries—Hoyt and Severeid; Rhem, Reinhart, H. Bell, Hallahan, Keen and O'Farrell.

FIFTH GAME

	R.	H.	E.
New York (A. L.)	3	9	1
St. Louis (N. L.)	2	7	1

(Ten innings.)

Batteries—Pennock and Severeid; Sherdel and O'Farrell.

SIXTH GAME

	R.	H.	E.
St. Louis (N. L.)	10	13	2
New York (A. L.)	2	8	1

Batteries—Shawkey, Shocker, Thomas and Severeid, Collins; Alexander and O'Farrell.

Hago and Santasiere Tie

Martin D. Hago and A. Edward Santasiere divided the first and second prizes in the weekly rapid transit tournament at the Marshall Chess Club. There were nine competitors and each of the leaders made scores of 7—1. The third prize was divided between C. S. Howell and H. Helms, who scored 5—3 each.

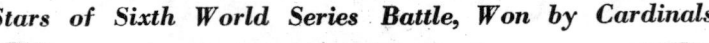

Stars of Sixth World Series Battle, Won by Cardinals

Lester Bell, who delivered yesterday's big blow, a homer in the seventh inning

Grover Cleveland Alexander, who scored his second vitory of the series

Billy Southworth, who played a spectacular game in the field

Decisive Series Test Expected to Draw Record Attendance

Despite the general opinion among baseball devotees that the weather man had hardly given them a fair break some 50,000 fans poured into the Yankee Stadium yesterday to see the home team walloped by the Cardinals in their second invasion of enemy territory. Disregarding the co'd, a goodly number displayed the faithfulness and fortitude which has made New York grandstand patrons famous, and stood nearly all night shivering or dozing against the chilly walls of the stadium untli the gates opened yesterday morning at 9 o'clock.

Cheered by forecasts of higher temperatures and southerly winds to-day, a little band of the faithful had already begun to make preparations for another all-night vigil beside the walls at 7 o'clock last night. Some retired to closed cars beside the gates, and others, wrapped in blankets and overcoats, settled themselves on wooden boxes they had purchased from youthful captains of trade.

The more prosperous followers of the game, hoping to secure reservations, were disappointed when it was announced that all seats would go on sale at the same time to-day.

At the end of the game those experienced handlers of crowds, the taxi drivers, estimated that if weather conditions become better as promised by the Whitehall Building authorities, to-day's crowd would break the record for attendance at any world series game.

"Nothin' will keep 'em away, with the series tied," explained one, between bites of a well known hot delicacy furnished by nearby concessionaires. "Boys, I'm sure gonna make arrangem'nts to be here to-morrow."

There was general rejoicing among all of those who make money out of the crowd which comes up to the stadium for purposes of observation. At one stand, when the news came that St. Louis was leading the Yankees by a scor of 10 to 2a heavy-handed lady, who had been variously called "You" and "Hey, you," throughout the afternoon by prospective customers, made a great gesture of generosity in honor of the occasion.

"Everybody at the counter gits a free cuppa cawfee," she answered, whereupon there was a general scramble to get near the counter.

The stadium management is also expecting a record crowd. The gates to the grandstand and bleachers will be opened at 8 o'clock this morning.

Haines and Hoyt Will Pitch in Crucial Battle

(Continued from page three)

gave him a slow one inside which forced the Babe to rap it to Bottomley.

Babe Anxious to Hit

"I kept feeding him slow ones outside," said Alex, "because I know he was anxious to hit, and I thought I could get him to swing at the bad ones. It's pretty hard to keep the Babe from hitting into right field, no matter what you do, but I managed, by keeping the ball close to him, to make him hit them on the ground where somebody could get them. I walked him once, but I'd rather walk him than give him a good ball and a chance to drive it a couple of miles."

Alex said that Meusel got his two hits by accident.

"The balls he hit," he said, "were low and inside, but they were not far enough inside. It was my mistake. I intended them to be closer to him, but they got away from me and he smacked them into left field. One of them should have been caught." (The first one which Thevenow went after. Hafey should have had it.)

Alexander said he had difficulty keeping his arm warm during the longer innings.

"It was chilly on the bench," he said, "and I'd go out there cold. But after the seventh inning it did no make much difference. I eased up and I think they got four hits in the las' three innings."

Hornsby was happy. He agreed that Alex had pitched a great game, but he was quick to say:

"Don't forget to mention that Thevenow played a beautiful ball game A couple of those balls he came up with were hit, and don't let any one tell you they weren't."

About Southworth's spectacular catch of Dugan's liner in the eighth, with which he doubled Meusel off second Hornsby said what a lot of the old Giant rooters probably thought.

"He could have caught that ball standing up," he said. "It was all right, but—no, I don't know what Meusel was thinking of letting himself get caught like that."

Lester Bell, the third baseman who hit the home run, was satisfied. And Jess Haines was kidding him because after he hit his home run in the third game, Bell had joshed him. Now, paraphrasing Bell, Haines was saying:

"Gee, it must be great to be able to hit home runs."

So what with one thing and another much of the grimness about the Cardinal team was relieved by a sense of security. They are sure they can go out there to-day and take this final game.

Down the hall in the Yankees' club house, Huggins sat on a stool with his heels drawn up under him and his head sunk on his chest, looking for all the world like a little medicine man brooding over certain forms of deadly magic.

"There's nothing to say," he muttered without raising his head. "They were getting their base hits and we weren't. The pitching was all right, but they just happened to be hitting. It's up to us now Hoyt, to-morrow."

On the way out, Hornsby paused in sight of the close pressed throng waiting on the street to glimpse the ball players and said:

"You may not see me to-morrow."

Immediately one suspected he was not going to play, and voiced the question.

"Oh, yes," he said; "but I'm going away right after the game. You'll have to hurry if you want to see me. I've got to bury my mother."

Composite Score of First Six Games

NEW YORK YANKEES

	G.	AB.	R.	H.	2B.	3B.	HR.	SH.	SB.	BB.	SO.	Bat's Ave.	PO.	A.	E.	Field Ave.
Combs, cf	6	23	3	8	2	0	0	0	0	5	2	.348	15	0	0	1.000
Koenig, ss	6	28	2	4	1	0	0	0	0	0	0	.143	10	20	3	.909
Ruth, rf, lf	6	19	5	5	0	0	3	0	1	7	2	.263	6	2	0	1.000
Meusel, lf, rf	6	17	3	4	1	1	0	3	0	6	1	.235	10	0	0	1.000
Gehrig, 1b	6	21	1	8	[illegible]	[illegible]	[illegible]	1	0	3	4	.381	67	1	0	1.000
Lazzeri, 2b	6	22	2	5	1	[illegible]	0	2	0	1	3	.227	12	18	1	.968
Dugan, 3b	6	20	1	6	[illegible]	0	0	0	0	1	1	.300	6	11	0	1.000
Gazella, 3b	1	0	0	0	0	0	0	0	0	0	0	——	1	2	0	1.000
Severeid, c	6	13	1	4	0	0	0	1	0	1	2	.211	34	6	0	1.000
Collins, c	2	1	0	0	0	0	0	0	0	0	1	.000	1	0	0	1.000
Pennock, p	2	6	1	1	1	0	0	1	0	0	0	.167	0	5	0	1.000
Shocker, p	2	2	0	0	0	0	0	0	0	0	2	.000	0	2	0	1.000
Shawkey, p	3	2	0	0	0	0	0	0	0	0	1	.000	0	1	0	1.000
Jones, p	1	0	0	0	0	0	0	0	0	0	0	——	0	0	0	——
Ruether, p	3	4	0	0	0	0	0	0	0	0	0	.000	0	2	0	1.000
Thomas, p	2	0	0	0	0	0	0	0	0	0	0	——	0	2	0	1.000
Hoyt, p	1	4	0	0	0	0	0	1	0	0	1	.000	0	0	0	——
*Paschal	4	3	0	1	0	0	0	0	0	1	2	.333	0	0	0	——
†Adams	1	0	0	0	0	0	0	0	0	0	0	——	0	0	0	——
Totals	—	191	19	46	9	1	3	9	1	25	28	.241	162	72	4	.983

ST. LOUIS CARDINALS

	G.	AB.	R.	H.	2B	3B	HR.	SH.	SB.	BB.	SO.	Bat's Ave.	PO.	A.	E.	Field Ave.
Douthit, cf	4	15	3	4	2	0	0	0	0	3	2	.267	4	2	0	1.000
Southworth, rf	6	25	6	10	1	1	1	2	1	0	0	.400	8	3	0	1.000
Holm, rf, cf	4	11	1	2	0	0	0	0	0	1	2	.182	5	0	0	1.000
Hornsby, 2b	6	24	2	5	1	0	0	1	1	2	2	.208	11	21	0	1.000
Bottomley, 1b	6	26	3	9	3	0	0	0	0	1	2	.346	65	1	0	1.000
L. Bell, 3b	6	23	3	7	1	0	1	1	0	2	5	.304	7	13	2	.909
Hafey, lf	6	23	1	3	2	0	0	2	0	0	6	.130	18	1	0	1.000
O'Farrell, c	6	20	2	7	1	0	0	0	0	2	2	.350	32	6	0	1.000
Thevenow, ss	6	20	5	8	1	0	1	1	0	0	1	.400	9	23	2	.941
Sherdel, p	2	5	0	0	0	0	0	0	0	0	2	.000	2	5	0	1.000
Haines, p	2	3	1	2	0	0	1	0	0	0	0	.667	0	2	0	1.000
Alexander, p	2	6	1	0	0	0	0	2	0	0	2	.000	0	6	1	.857
Rhem, p	1	1	0	0	0	0	0	0	0	0	1	.000	0	1	0	1.000
Reinhart, p	1	0	0	0	0	0	0	0	0	0	0	——	0	0	0	——
H. Bell, p	1	0	0	0	0	0	0	0	0	0	0	——	0	0	0	——
Hallahan, p	1	0	0	0	0	0	0	0	0	0	0	——	1	0	0	1.000
Keen, p	1	0	0	0	0	0	0	0	0	0	0	——	0	1	0	1.000
*Flowers	3	3	0	0	0	0	0	0	0	0	1	.000	0	0	0	——
*Toporcer	1	0	0	0	0	0	0	1	0	0	0	——	0	0	0	——
Total	—	205	28	57	12	1	4	10	2	11	28	.278	162	85	5	.980

*Pinch hitter. †Pinch runner.

Runs batted in—L. Bell (6), Bottomley (5), Ruth (4), Southworth (4), Hornsby (4), Gehrig (3), Thevenow (3), Lazzeri (3), Combs (2), Dugan (2), Koenig (2), Haines (2), Paschal (1), Toporcer (1), Douthit (1), O'Farrell (1), Holm (1).

Double plays—Thevenow, Hornsby and Bottomley; Alexander, Thevenow and Bottomley; Koenig, Lazzeri and Gehrig; Hornsby, Thevenow and Bottomley (2); Hornsby and Bottomley; Lazzeri, Koenig and Gehrig; Gehrig and Koenig; Southworth and Thevenow.

Left on bases—St. Louis, 36; New York, 45.

PITCHING RECORDS

	G.	Ins.	Hits off.	Runs off.	B.B.	S.O.	W.P.	H.B.	W.	L.
Pennock	2	19	10	3	4	8	0	0	2	0
Sherdel	2	17	15	5	8	3	1	1	0	2
Alexander	2	18	12	4	3	16	0	0	2	0
Haines	2	10	5	0	4	3	0	0	1	0
Hoyt	1	9	14	5	1	8	0	0	1	0
Shocker	2	10⅔	13	7	0	3	0	0	0	1
Shawkey	3	10	13	7	2	7	0	0	0	1
Ruether	1	4⅓	7	4	2	1	0	0	0	[illegible]
Jones	1	1	2	1	2	1	0	0	0	[illegible]
Thomas	2	3	3	1	0	0	0	1	0	0
Rhem	1	4	7	3	2	4	0	0	0	0
Reinhart	1	2	1	4	4	0	0	0	0	1
H. Bell	1	2	4	2	1	1	0	0	0	0
Hallahan	1	2	2	1	3	1	0	0	0	0
Keen	1	1	0	0	0	0	0	0	0	0

Balk—H. Bell.

Umpires—O'Day and Klem (National League); Dinneen and Hildebrand (American League).

Time of games—1:48 (first game); 1:57 (second game); 1:41 (third game); 2:39 (fourth game); 2:28 (fifth game); 2:05 (sixth game).

Random Briefs Picked Up at World Series

By J. P. Abramson

The one brightt spot, or spots, in the vast top-coated assemblage were the red-garbed ushers. Many a coat collar was turned up in the chilly confines and inner recesses of the second tier.

What a day for football! The coolish atmosphere deterred any extraordinary rush for unreserved tickets to see the American Leaguers atttempt to clinch the honors. A half hour before game there were still thousands of vacant seats in the bleachers and upper tier. They remained vacant for the most part.

A banner entitled "Everybody sing 'Along Came Ruth'" was unfurled to the autumn breezes and a chorus of ten male song pluggers showed 'em how, to the accompaniment of the brass band. This was one of the songs born of the world series strife.

Gene Tunney viewed his first world series game from the box of Mr. and Mrs. Bernard F. Gimbel on the Cardinal side of the field. Dudley Field Malone, his legal adviser, also was a guest of the Gimbels.

Jack Dempsey was there, viewing the proceedings from a front row box close to the St. Louis dugout.

The ex-champion, smoking a cigar, was the cynosure of many eyes, while the king heavy himself passed to his seat hardly noticed. Not until the eighth inning did a cameraman spot the champion. Recognition by many fans followed.

Southworth did a beautiful tumbling act in snaring Dugan's liner at his shoetops. He rolled over and over and came up to double Meusel at second.

When the Babe trotted to his position for fie ding practice the bleacherites in right recalled those three homers of Wednesday. They cheered. How they cheered!

The sketpical shook their heads sadly when Shawkey appeared on the hill for his pre-game workout. He was purely a hot-weather pitcher, said they, and the Cardinals would murder him.

Shawkey's red flannels were more than ornaments yesterday.

Judge Landis uncovered his head for a few minutes at 1:28 and the eagle eyed newsreel cameramen were there on the spot to put the glistening white mop on a roll of film. The Commissioner had a front seat in a box hard by the Cardinals' dugout.

The national anthem at 1:30 suspended a l activities but the ceaseless clicking of the telegraphers, who told their story by dots and dashes standing up.

Bob the Gob worked hard on Sherlock Holm, first batter up, but Holm, after dilly-dallying for a spell, smote a clean single to Ruth's sector.

From the cheers that greeted Bottomley's double and Southworth's run in the first one would have thought St. Louis had taken possession of the Stadium for the sixth game. But the noise increased five-fold when L. Bell walloped his hit and drove in two.

Koenig evidently wanted to assure himself of the strikeout record (inversely) for the series. His sixth such in the opening inning was accomplished in the twinkling of an eye.

Thevenow sprinted a mile for Meusel's mile-high fly in the second, then ran around in circles and the ball dropped between Thevenow and Hafey for a two-bagger.

Thevenow more than made up for that by robbing Lazzeri on a scorcher back of second a moment later.

Then Thevenow mussed up Shawkey's grounder in the third when he had a double play in front of him. Tommy certainly scaled the heights and plumbed the depths in his fielding.

The Cardinal rooters in the working men's row were torn between their faith in the National Leaguers and their desire to have the thing done, what with a Sunday in the offing.

The distance champions of the series were Mr. and Mrs. W. B. Glenn, who came on from Sacramento, Calif., for yesterday's game.

Nick Altrock and Al Schacht, baseball comics, were submerged in the masses yesterday afternoon. They were merely spectators. They were "working" on the series. Last night, however, they appeared at the Garden with a new and old line of fun for the tennis fans.

Collins, batting for the first time in his first series, struck out, and walked back to the bench as dejected as could be.

Five runs in one inning constituted a record fo ra world series.

Play-by-Play Description of Sixth World Series Game

By Rud Rennie

Hornsby sent Grover Alexander in to pitch the sixth game of the world series for the Cardinals and Huggins used Bob Shawkey. The weather was sunny and brisk.

The play by play account of the game follows:

FIRST INNING

CARDINALS—Holm led off with a single into right field. Southworth forced Holm at second, Koenig to Lazzeri. Hornsby walked. Bottomley hit along the third base line for two bases, scoring Southworth and putting Hornsby on third. Bell drove a single into left field, scoring Hornsby and Bottomley. Hafey struck out. O'Farrell also struck out. Three runs, three hits, no errors.

YANKEES—Thevenow threw out Combs. Koenig struck out. Bottomley handled Ruth's grounder unassisted. No runs, no hits, no errors.

SECOND INNING

CARDINALS—Thevenow flied out to Combs. Alexander flied out to Meusel. Holm lifted a foul to Severeid. No runs, no hits, no errors.

YANKEES—Meusel lifted a fly back of third base which went for two bases. Thevenow threw out Gehrig, holding Meusel on second. Thevenow went over to his left and made a beautiful stop of Lazzeri's grounder to catch him at first, Meusel taking third on the play. Bell threw out Dugan. No runs, one hit, no errors.

THIRD INNING

CARDINALS—Southworth drove a liner at Combs, who caught it twice, the ball jumping out of his hands the first time. Koenig threw out Hornsby. Bottomley flied to Gehrig. No runs, no hits, no errors.

YANKEES—Severeid singled cleanly to center. With a double play in front of him, Thevenow let Shawkey's grounder go through his legs, leaving men on first and second. Combs drove a grounder at Alexander, who used it to force Severid at third. Koenig flied to Southworth, the runners holding their bases. Ruth drove a grounder at Bottomley, who ended the inning by putting him out unassisted. No runs, one hit, one error.

FOURTH INNING

CARDINALS—Bell walked. Hafey sacrificed, Bell stopping at second. Bell was caught trying to steal third, Severeid to Dugan. O'Farrell flied to Meusel. No runs, no hits, no errors.

YANKEES—Meusel again started off, driving the ball along the left foul line for three bases. Hornsby threw out Gehrig, Meusel scoring on the play. Thevenow threw out Lazzeri. Dugan shot a single past Thevenow. Severeid struck out. One run, two hits, no errors.

FIFTH INNING

CARLINALS—Thevenow singled to left. Alexander sacrificed Thevenow to second, Gehrig making the put-out unassisted. Holm singled to center, scoring Thevenow. Dugan made a fast play on Southworth's slow grounder, catching him at first. Holm meanwhile alvanced to second. Lazzeri went over to his left and came up with Hornsby's hard hit grounder just in time to throw him out. One run, two hits, no errors.

YANKEES—Shawkey struck out. Combs flied out to Hafey, Koenig lifted a fly to Holm. No runs, no hits, no errors.

SIXTH INNING

CARDINALS—Bottomley drove a long fly over Ruth's head against the right field stands for a two-bagger. Bell struck out. Hafey also struck out and O'Farrell, with two and three against him, lifted a foul to Dugan. No runs, one hit, no errors.

YAUKEES—Ruth walked. It was Alexander's first base on balls. Meusel sent a high fly to Holm. Ruth remaining on first. As Gehrig struck out, Ruth stole second. Lazzeri flied to Holm. No runs, no hits, no errors.

SEVENTH INNING

CARDINALS—Thevenow led off and again singled to left. Again Alexander bunted, but this time Lazzeri, who came over to cover first, dropped Severeid's throw and all hands were safe. Holm then tried to sacrifice, but succeeded only in forcing Thevenow at third, Severeid to Dugan. Meusel lost Southworth's fly in the sun and it went for two bases, scoring Alexander and putting Holm on third. Shawkey was taken out and Urban Shocker was summoned to take his place. With the infield in, Hornsby singled between Lazzeri and the ba, scoring Holm and Southworth. Bottomley hit a grounder to Koenig, forcing Hornsby at second. Bell drove a home run into the center of the left field stands, scoring Bottomley. Hafey hit into left field for two bases, coming into second sliding. O'Farrell struck out. Five runs, five hits, one error.

YANKEES—Dugan drove a grounder at Bell which was too hot for him to hold and which was credited as a single. Severeid also shot a hot one at Bell, who fumbled it and then made a wild throw past Bottomley, allowing Dugan to go third. Adams ran for Severeid and Paschal batted for Shocker. Alexander struck out Paschal. Combs drove a single past Thevenow, scoring Dugan and putting Adams on second. Bottomley put out Koenig unassisted while Adams went to third and Combs went to second. Thevenow, playing near second for Ruth, had no trouble handling the grunder which the Babe hit over the bag. One run, two hits, one error.

EIGHTH INNING

CARDINALS—The new battery for New York was Myles Thomas pitching and Pat Collins catching. Thomas hit Thevenow on the back, putting him on first. Alexander forced Thevenow at second, Thomas to Koenig. Holm hit a grounder to Gehrig, who touched first and then doubled Alexander at second, Alec making no effort to run. No runs, no hits, no errors.

YANKEES—Meusel walked. Hornsby made a beautiful stop of Gehrig's hit near first base, but he was unable to catch him at first. Meusel stopped at second on the play. Lazzeri flied to Holm, the runners holding their bases Southworth came in for Dugan's low liner and made a great diving catch turning completely over and doubling Meusel off second, Thevenow taking the throw. No runs, one hit, no errors.

NINTH INNING

CARDINALS—Southworth drove a hard single into center field, where it took a bad bounce over Combs's head permitting him to get three bases Hornsby drove a grounder straight at Thomas. The ball bounced out of his glove toward Dugan, who made a fast play to get his man at first. Meantime, Southworth had scored. Gehrig put out Bottomley unassisted. Bell drove a single into right center, but was out trying to stretch it into a double. Ruth to Koenig. One run, two hits, no errors.

YANKEES—Collins struck out. Ruether batted for Thomas and Hornsby threw him out. Combs hit into right field for two bases. Koenig hit a long fly to Holm. No runs, one hit, no errors.

Cards Pound Two Yank Hurlers For 10-2 Victory, Tying Series

By W. O. McGeehan

(Continued from page three)

Francisco, is very sure-fingered. He never has yet let a string of spaghetti escape his unerring fork, but his fingers slipped and the ball went through and Alexander was safe. Holm forced Thevenow.

William Southworth, discarded by John Joseph McGraw as shopworn ivory early this season, lifted a high one to left. Mr. Lank Robert Meusel gauged its descent somewhat inaccurately and it rolled along for a two-base hit, scoring Mr. Alexander.

Shocker Steps Into Trouble

At this point Mr. Urban Shocker, who had been making motions with a baseball in the bull pen, came in to take his punishment, and not too enthusiastically, while Mr. Robert Shawkey retired to the clubhouse to hang up his red flannel undershirt for the winter.

Mr. Shawkey is contradictory that way. He dons the red flannels in the summer and doffs them in the winter. You may now take it that this is the time to lay in the winter coal, for the last red flannel shirt of the baseball is now carefully packed in camphor balls.

Mr. Shocker, who wears a more conservative flannel shirt, stepped right into trouble. Mr. Hornsby drove one of his infrequent world series hits through second, scoring Holm and Southworth. Bottomley forced Hornsby.

It was at this point that Mr. Tinker Bell (no relation of the pitcher, Jingle Bell) lifted a homer into the customers in the left field bleachers which scored Bottomley in front of him. This hit did not seem to register at the Yankee Stadium. To get the proper effect of it one would have to be somewhere in St. Louis—say, in the vicinity of the Hotel Jefferson. The sock was heard with considerable more distinctness there than it was at hte Yankee Stadium.

At this point several of the customers yawned and remarking, "Well, the Yanks seem to have blown another ball game," moved languidly toward the exits.

Combs Drives Dugan Home

The second run of the Yankees was escorted across the plate by Mr. Jumping Joseph Dugan, the alert Westchester realtor. Mr. Dugan hit past Mr. Tinker Bell, got to third when Mr. Bell made a bad forward pass to Bottomley on Severeid's grounder and came home on a single by Mr. Combs, the tall Kentuckian.

The tenth run for the Cardinals was piloted by Will'am Southworth, the useful castoff. He got a three-bagger past Colonel Combs and arrived on Hornsby's out. By this time it did not seem to matter whether Mr. Alexander's dogs held out or not. It was certain that the series would have the record gate receipts, but it was not at all certain as to how they would be cut.

You can not manufacture any melodrama out of a ball game like that. If the relic of the Cleveland administration, Mr. Alexander had been forced to work his soupbone to any extent it might have made a nine-reel thriller, "The Last Stand of Alexander." But it was about the least strenuous afternoon that Grover Cleveland Alexander has passed since the Chicago Cubs decided that all he was all through.

It was just one of those baseball games that crop up during the course of the regular season when the boys are not going anywhere in particular. Of course, in St. Louis, is was a glorious victory, for when the St. Lousians expect a rout of the enemy they want them routed right, as the Yankees were yesterday.

There was considerable uneasiness among the Yankees last night. If they lose again to-morrow it will mean a deficit of $2,000 for each Yankee and that is a considerable deficit, especially after the athlete has already counted it.

One might say that the Cardinals will have a moral advantage, or something of the sort to-day, especially as they seem to have the stronger supply of reserve soupbones. This will hold unless Mr. George Herman Ruth should start hitting, in which case no advantage, moral or immoral, amounts to much.

Only the weather can prevent a decision in the Battle of the Harlem and the ississippi this afternoon, the longest series in the matter of mileage and probably in the matter of gate receipts.

Important Facts About To-day's Series Game

THERE has been no advance sale on tickets for to-day's deciding game. The 60,000-odd reserved and unreserved tickets available will be placed on sale at the Yankee Stadium starting at 8 o'clock this morning. The game will start at 2 o'clock

Only WJZ will broadcast to-day's game. The station will go on the air with the series starting at 1:45 p. m.

The Stadium can be reached by way of the Jerome Avenue line on the East Side subway, by the Bronx line, changing at 149th Street and Mott Avenue, on the West Side subway, by Sixth Avenue elevated and by 163d Street cross-town trolley.

Prices for to-day's game remain the same—$6.60 for box seats, $5.50 for reserved seats, $3.30 for unreserved seats in the grandstands, $1.10 for bleachers.

White, 21, Youngest Manager in Baseball

By The Associated Press

Iowa this year provided the youngest team manager in professional baseball.

George (Dutch) White, an infielder and .300 hitter, took over the management of the Cedar Rap'ds Club in the Mississippi Valley League for the last two months of the season after two previous leaders had failed to bring the club out of a slump. He was just twenty-one when he took the team in hand. He was sold at the close of the season to the Danville Club of the Three I League.

Section II SPORTS NEW YORK Herald Tribune SPORTS Section II

TWELVE PAGES SUNDAY, OCTOBER 10, 1926 TWELVE PAGES

Cardinals Defeat Yankees, 10 to 2 and Tie the Series; Princeton Held to 7 to 7 Tie by Washington and Lee; Holy Cross Downs Harvard, 19 to 14, in Final Minute

Stories on Page 3

The Sixth Game of the World Series between the New York Yankees and the St. Louis Cardinals is shown in this general view of the first inning, in which Lester Bell, of the Cardinals, is pectured running to first on his single, which scored Hornsby (about to cross the plate) and Bottomley (leaving third base for home). *Herald Tribune Photos—Acme*

Bell Crossing the Plate in the Seventh Inning in the only home run of the game, which scored Bottomley. With two strikes on him Bell hit the ball into the left field stands. The Cardinals scored five runs in this inning. *Herald Tribune Photo—Steffen*

Holm, of the Cardinals, Forced Out at second on Koenig's throw to Lazzeri in the first inning of Southworth's grounder. Holm, the first man up, drove a single into right field when Shawkey tried t osneak over a third strike. *Herald Tribune Photo—Steffen*

Meusel Scoring the First Yankee Run in the fourth inning on Gehrig's sacrifice after hitting the first triple of the series into left field. *Herald Tribune Photo—Steffen*

The Last Cardinal Out in the ninth inning was Lester Bell, shown being tagged at second base by Lazzeri after he had tried to beat Babe Ruth's return of his single. *Herald Tribune Photo—Freudy*

Keen Judgment of Yankees' Manager Nets Pennant

TRADES MADE BY HUG HELP RUPPERT MEN

Despite Much Criticism, Miller Puts Club at Top of Heap; His Decisions Stand Test

By Bill Slocum

NEW YORK, Sept. 24.—When one stops to consider how many mistakes a baseball manager can make over a stretch of ten years in sizing up talent as it comes to him—very frequently in the rough, there is only one way to figure Miller Huggins, the pint-sized boss of the most spectacular ball club of recent years.

Miller Huggins

Huggins has IT.

The IT in this case is the ability to judge keenly, save what may be most valuable and let the remainder move along. For baseball law limits club managers to specified numbers, and the big trick comes in picking the proper players—the ones who will be best in building up a winner.

Huggins is spending these September afternoons looking at his ball club step along to new records, with the 1927 pennant already won. At the same time he is closing his tenth year as boss of the Yankees. Ten years ago this month, he was leading the St. Louis Cardinals to third place in the National League race, a point reached by only one other St. Louis entry over a stretch of twenty-six successive years. The 1914 Cardinals, also bossed by Mr. Huggins, had finished third.

FORTUNATE FOR BOTH

Considerable has happened in the American League since Huggins came in. And his keen judgment was responsible for a lot of prosperity in the junior circuit. This is not meant to imply that the league would have foundered if Ban Johnson had not taken a fancy to the Cardinals' leader along in 1916 and 1917, this fancy leading Ban to look und for a place in his league for such a capable leader. He found an opening in New York, and the Yankees were, and are, as much to be congratulated over the connection as Huggins ever was.

It seems the easiest thing in the world to manage a ball club which carries the strength of the present-day Yankees. There surely are plenty of jobs in baseball that are more difficult. But assembling such a club is not always a success. Moves must be made which, at times, could make or break the best conducted campaign of building up a winner. There have been some decisions by Huggins which earned him criticism at times, but he was willing to trust his own judgment, and time has vindicated him.

Perhaps 300 player have been passed along by Huggins in his ten years with the Yankees. Besides those who have come under his control and who were let out, he has had to pass on various trading propositions that have been offered to him. He couldn't go wrong on many of them and build up the club which he has today.

There was much criticism that Aaron Ward was shunted off second base when he seemed to be so good a defensive player. Lazzeri was an unknown quantity then, but Huggins had faith in him. So, too, he stuck to Mark Koenig after the disastrous season of 1926, when the critics decided unanimously that Mark owuld never do as a shortstop.

STUCK BY GEHRIG

He took Wally Pipp off first base and installed Gehrig there, when he was very green as a fielder and very much a stranger to major league pitching. He refused to consider taking either Ty Cobb or Tris Speaker, last winter, because that would mean the benching of Earle Combs.

These re but a few instances in which Huggin's judgment was questioned. His decisions have stood the test.

Whether a manager is popular is very often unimportant. Whether his judgment commands respect is very important. It can be said for Huggins that he is well liked by his men, though he is not a kidder or a back-slapper. But most of all, every last one of them respects his judgment above any personal idea.

The Yankee leader has had some squabbles, including some very celebrated ones with Babe Ruth. But in a quiet and effective way, he proved himself boss without humiliating anybody, and today Babe is among Hug's strongest boosters.

Huggins is seldom on view when the Yanks are playing. It takes only a small portion of the bench corner to hide him, and he usually remains hidden. He went out on the coaching lines once this year—because he did not believe his players were showing fight enough.

He knew them well enough to believe there would be the desired reaction. And there was.

He is no driver while a game is in progress, nor does he ride players when their work disappoints. There is no hip-hip hooray as games are won, no abusing if things do not please. He is as keen a student of player-disposition as he is of baseball strategy, because he regards it as important enough to make or break a player. He takes his baseball seriously and expects his players to do the same. Those who don't take it seriously don't stay. When his team slumps, and there have been such things under Huggin's leadership, he can usually tell you why. He has stuck to players through their poorest playing when he believed in them, and generally they proved that his confidence was justified. When teams are winning, he can see glaring weaknesses, and does not hesitate to trade, as he has done after each championship season.

There have been years, since Huggins reached New York, when he was criticised to a turn. He took it all gamely, with no grouching, no sulking, no disposition to abuse his critics. He believed in his own judgment, and now he is sitting on the top of the world without a harsh feeling for those who were certain that he was all wrong.

When the going was bad, he had no alibis, nor was he ever inclined to pass the buck.

Some argue that the Ruppert bankroll is a big factor. That bankroll, helped, yes, but it would not have been worth a dime in baseball returns if there wasn't sound judgment by the man who had to decide who would stay and who would go. Other millionaires in baseball also have the rubber off, but they have not been up on top five times in seven years as the Yankees have been since 1920. Huggins has been as keen in his choice of scouts as of players.

Quite a big man in the world of baseball is this little Mr. Huggins of the Yankees.

What Any Pitcher Wants----

Lou Gehrig Tony Lazzeri Mark Koenig Joe Dugan

HERE'S THE YANKEE INFIELD that has turned back many an opponent's rally during the American League season. First on the left is the young gentleman who has won lots of publicity this season—Gehrig, first sacker. Lazzeri, former Pacific Coast Leaguer, plays second with Koenig at short and Dugan at third.

BUILD ROMAN TEAM AROUND VETERAN TRIO

Levy, Quaglino, Bowles Return; Line Untried; Meet Lincoln in First City League Game

THREE letter men form the nucleus around which Coaches Ed Rich and Herb White will build the 1927 Los Angeles High football machine. Art Levy, end; Joe Quaglino and Clark Bowles, halfbacks, are the returning regulars. Quaglino and Bowles are to have a hard time holding their positions, as there is a good turnout of backfield material. The Romans play at Lincoln October 14 in their first City League game.

Three red-haired lads are out this season seeking backfield positions. They are Jimmie Owens, Frank Houck and Bob Beaver. The three possess plenty of speed, having been members of last year's relay squad.

At quarterback Phil Wilson is the leading candidate. Dick McKey and Aubrey Grossman are seeking the fullback berth and a hard battle is being waged between them. Both have the beef, the line-plunging ability and are good kickers.

The line is an unknown quantity. Art Levy is almost a cinch to land one wing berth. Kearns Hampton may garner the other. At tackle Coaches Rich and White have Ritchie Chapman and Stan Lloyd. Bud Pozzo, Del McKee and Dick Leslie are fighting for the guard posts. At center Ackley Quirck appears as the likely candidate.

Rutgers Drills in Use of Lateral Pass

NEW BRUNSWICK, N. J., Sept. 24.—That Rutgers University is going to make liberal use of the lateral pass in its 1927 football campaign is evident from the amount of time which Lionel Conacher, famous Canadian athlete and rugby player, is spending with the Scarlet gridiron backfield.

The Canadian star showed up for duty recently and was immediately put in charge of the backfield men. The speedy backs gave a splendid exhibition in tossing and handling the ball.

These Men Supporting Him

Earl Combs Babe Ruth Bob Meusel

OPPOSING HURLERS FIND TROUBLE in quelling the members of this outfield at the plate and in the field they cover a lot of ground. Of course, the great Ruth, home run maker supreme, tops the trio as an attraction, but Combs, Yank leadoff man and center fielder, and Meusel, left gardener, are skilled workmen.

McGraw Pins Hopes on National League Boxmen

Hurlers in Older Circuit Rated Better Than American Moundsmen

By John J. McGraw
Manager, New York Giants

PITTSBURGH, Sept. 24.—Whether the Pirates, Cards or Giants play in the world's series against the Yankees, in my opinion, Huggins' club will have a tough job on their hands winning the big championship. I hear that the American League team is to be a strong favorite on account of their easy time in the pennant race, their naturally hard punch and the presence of Ruth and Gehrig, the home run hitters. This thing of making this or that club favorite doesn't mean a thing. The so-called favorites, selected in advance, have lost just as often in the past as the others.

John McGraw

Against any of the strong National League teams the recognized punch of the Yankees will not be as threatening as against the other American League clubs in a pennant race.

PITCHING DIFFERS

In the first place the National League pitching is different—quite different—and in the second place the concentration of pitching in a seven-game series is always a different matter from the steady run of battery defense during a long season. That, of course, works both ways. The Yanks, you know, are also equipped with a strong staff of pitchers, including Hoyt, Pennock, Shocker and this new man, Wilcey Moore.

The marked difference in pitching styles when pitted against each other in a limited number of games, generally tends to check the normal hitting strength of both clubs. In other words, the odd situation is somewhat new to both teams. Usually it cuts down the long hitting considerably. Nearly all batters are more or less tense and tightened up in such important games. That is one reason why it is so difficult to figure on what may happen.

I think most baseball people agree that the National League pitching has been better this season than the American. Many prominent American League players have remarked on this. Now when it comes down to a fine point that is bound to tell in the result.

YANKS HAVE POWER

Anybody would be foolish to discount the batting of the American League champions. The Yankees have one of the most powerful line-ups of hitters ever put together. It has been powerful enough as a scoring machine to win even when the defense went bad. Despite this, I have held all along during the amusing summer controversy that the present day Yanks would not have beaten the old Orioles in a pennant race, because the Baltimore club was what we call a snappier and smarter ball club. Neither is there a club in the National League as smart and hustling as the old Orioles. But we can play that mythical series on paper only. This one must be played on the diamond with a lot at stake for each player.

Pitching usuallly decides these seven-game series for the championship. The slightest wobbling may mean a game. That is why I expect to see a very close fight and can see no reason for making either club a big favorite. Naturally the question will arise as to whether the pitchers should pitch to Ruth and Gehrig. As a matter of fact, there is little alternative. I have never believed in letting reputation guide the pitching. I believe in pitching to any batter as the situation arises, whether he be Ruth, Gehrig, Hornsby or anybody else. There are times, of course, when it is advisable to pass any batter.

My one prediction at this early stage is that the Yanks won't find the pitching as easy as they have all this pennant season.

Pat Collins Benny Bengough John Grabowski

GOOD CATCHERS ARE AS IMPORTANT as good pitchers, for a poor maskman can spoil the effectiveness of any moundsman. That's why this trio are so prominent in the Yanks' scheme of things.—International Newsreel Photos.

YANKEE SERIES PLAYERS NAMED

NEW YORK, Sept. 24.—Now that the Yankees are certain of a place in the World's Series, it is only a matter of time before the list of eligible players will be announced officially.

There will be no surprises in the official list as only one player now with the club was not with the Hugmen when the season opened. The exception is Pitcher Don Miller, who came to the Yankees from the University of Michigan at the close of the college season. The official list will include the following:

Pitchers—Hoyt, Pennock, Shocker, Ruether, Moore, Shawkey, Pipgras, Thomas, Giard, Miller.

Catchers—Bengough, Collins, Grabowski.

Infielders—Gehrig, Lazzeri, Koenig, Dugan, Gazella, Morehart, Wera.

Outfielders—Ruth, Meusel, Combs, Paschal, Durst.

The above list includes twenty-five players. Manager Huggins and Coaches O'Leary and Fletcher will be listed as eligibles for coaching duties.

Lake Forest College Signs Up MacIntosh

CHICAGO, Sept. 24.—Ira D. MacIntosh, graduate of Rhode Island State College and former halfback of the Providence Steam Rollers of the National Professional Football League, has been appointed backfield coach at Lake Forest College to fill the vacancy left by the resignation of Elmer Kershaw. He will take up his duties at once.

Semi-Pro Schedule

ELKS LEAGUE

Pasadena Elks vs. Long Beach Elks, at Signal Hill.

Glendale Elks vs. Los Angeles Elks, at White Sox Park.

INDEPENDENT GAMES

Murphy's Comedians vs. Chanslod-Canfield Midway Oil, at C. C. M. O. Park, Torrance.

Pacific Electric vs. Pasadena Eagles, at Tournament Park, Pasadena.

Prep Stars. vs .Temple Merchants, at Temple.

L. A. Nippons vs. West Coast Theater, at San Bernardino, 1:30 p. m.

Torrance Merchants vs. West Coast

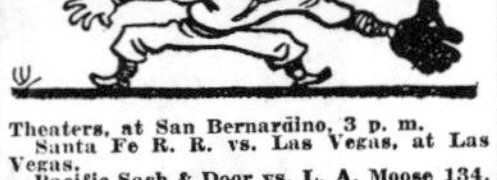

Theaters, at San Bernardino, 3 p. m.

Santa Fe R. R. vs. Las Vegas, at Las Vegas.

Pacific Sash & Door vs. L. A. Moose 134, at Glimore Park, Third and Fairfax.

North Hollywood Cubs vs. Crown City, at Brookside Park, Pasadena.

Universal City vs. First National Studio, at North Hollywood (Lankershim).

Eastern Outfitting Co. vs. Palms Merchants, at Palms.

Balmorals vs. Pomona Blue Birds, at Pomona.

Decimo Club vs. Lawndale A. C., at Lawndale.

Santa Paula vs. San Fernando Fire Department, at San Fernando.

Radiant Comedy vs. Pacific Steamship Co., at Pacific avenue and Harbor boulevard, San Pedro.

Cleanwell Dye Works vs. Monterey Park Chamber of Commerce, at Monterey Park.

Standard Oil of Torrance vs. Standard Oil of Taft, at Taft.

United Cleaners vs. Manchester Heights Knights of Columbus, at Eighty-first and Vermont.

L. C. M. Tigers vs. Santa Monica Postoffice, at Twentieth and Colorado, Santa Monica.

Beverly Hills Merchants vs. Newhall Saugus, at Saugus.

Mack Trucks vs. Glendale Merchants, at Glendale.

Grand Central Market vs. Graham Merchants, at Graham.

Palos Verdes vs. William Lane Cubs, at Manchester Playground.

Alhambra All Stars vs. Highland Park Merchants, at Arroyo Seco Playground.

El Paso White Sox vs. Echo Park at Echo Park.

L. A. Firemen vs. Ventura Shell Oil at Ventura.

South Gate vs. Norwalk at Norwalk.

Mission Bell Soaps vs. Soldiers' Home at Sawtelle.

Yellow Cabs vs. L. A. White Sox at White Sox Park (two games).

Santa Rita vs. Monolith Cement Co. at Monolith.

Pasadena All-Stars vs. Valley Lumber Co. at San Gabriel.

Ortiz Fords vs. Home Gardens at Home Gardens.

Belvedere Athletics vs. Reseda at Reseda.

Buick Autos vs. Artesia at Artesia.

New York Hats vs. North Long Beach Merchants at Virginia City.

El Patio Auto Laundry vs. Maywood Merchants at Bell.

Sarnis Cubs vs. Union Rock at Duarte.

Carpenteria vs. El Paso Shoes at San Gabriel.

White Mysteries vs. Centrals at San Bernardino.

Alhambra Merchants vs. Olinda at Olinda.

Maravilla Park vs. Anaheim Tigers at Anaheim.

Ocean Park vs. Belvedere Gardens at Belvedere, 1 o'clock.

Harold Lloyd's Romans vs. Belvedere Gardens at Belevedere, 3 o'clock.

Felix Chevrolets vs. Hynes at Hynes.

Calif. Laundry vs. Modern Woodmen of America at Hazard.

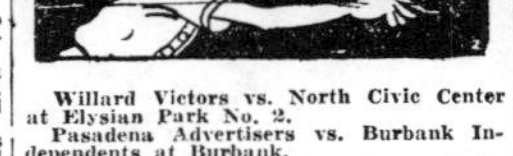

Willard Victors vs. North Civic Center at Elysian Park No. 2.

Pasadena Advertisers vs. Burbank Independents at Burbank.

Cahuenga Athletic Club vs. Preps at Alhambra.

Larry's Cubs vs. El Monte at El Monte.

Lieut. Walsh Will Coach Navy Crews

ANNAPOLIS, Md., Sept. 24.—It was announced at the Naval Academy that Lieut. Charles Walsh of the 1922 and 1925 academy crews had been appointed assistant rowing coach there and would resign from the Navy for his new duties.

Firemen to Oppose Heavy Navy Team at San Diego

Casey Shifted From Lie to Backfield by Blewett, Smoke-Eanters' Coach

EXPECTING their hardest game of the season, members of the Los Angeles Fire Department football team are at San Diego where this afternoon they meet the heavy United States Naval Training Station eleven.

Coach Bill Blewett announced a last-minute shift in his lineup when he left with the team yesterday, deciding to use Lawrence Casey, regular lineman, at fullback.

Blewett gave Casey a try at the line-smashing berth in scrimmage the past week, and the former Lincoln star came through in great style. Casey started the season at center, but was later moved to tackle because of his ability to fathom plays. At fullback, Blewett declares, he is the real find of the season.

The starting lineup will see Herb Wheeler and Weise at ends; Zumwalt and Ewers, tackles; Hardy and Hauseneur, guards; Morris, center; Capt. George Dyer, quarterback; McCarter and Danks, halfbacks,

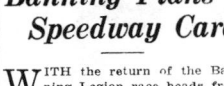

and Casey, fullback. Royce Wheeler, 195-pound end; Jim Dyer and Eddie Tyler, halfbacks, will be on the side lines because of injuries.

The firemen, with four triple-threat men in the backfield, plan to open up early with passes, believing it well nigh impossible to make yardage through the heavy San Diego line.

Banning Plans Speedway Card

WITH the return of the Banning Legion race heads from a hunting trip, arrangements are being completed for a series of

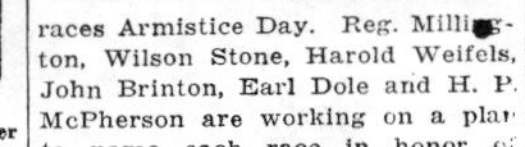

races Armistice Day. Reg. Millington, Wilson Stone, Harold Weifels, John Brinton, Earl Dole and H. P. McPherson are working on a plan to name each race in honor of some Southern California post and have the adjutant or the commander wave the red flag to start the pilots.

ELK TEAM NAMED

DEL MONTE, Sept. 24.—Oroville Lodge 1484, B. P. O. E., has entered the following team for the Elks' state convention tournament here, October 6-8: S. R. Baker, V. M. Damon, R. M. Nurse and R. H. Butler.

Japanese Five May Play Bear Squad on Trips

BERKELEY, Sept. 24.—The first Japanese basketball team ever to visit the United States will arrive in San Francisco about December 15 for a barnstorming tour which will probably include a series of games with the University of California. William W. Monahan, graduate manager of California, was notified of the projected trip by F. H. Brown, coach of the Waseda team, which is considered the best in Japan.

In requesting a place on the California schedule, the Waseda coach said, "As you no doubt know, Waseda is Japan's ranking team. But our idea in coming to America is not to teach, but to be taught, and therefore to improve the standard of the game in the East."

Brown said that his team will stay in the United States until February 15, playing as many games as possible on the Pacific Coast.

Waseda and Keio, its sister university, are the Yale and Harvard of Japan. Both schools have been represented in this country by baseball teams upon several occasions, and the University of California had games with both during the Bears' tour of the Orient this summer.

Basketball, while not a new sport in the Orient, has been superseded

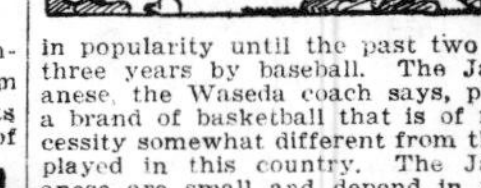

in popularity until the past two or three years by baseball. The Japanese, the Waseda coach says, play a brand of basketball that is of necessity somewhat different from that played in this country. The Japanese are small and depend in the main upon their cat-like swiftness. A Japanese, when dribbling, is but three or four feet from the floor.

It will be a strange sight to see a Waseda center jumping against Vern Corbin, California's varsity center, who is an even six feet high and weighs in the neighborhood of 180 pounds.

"HALL OF FAME"

DEL MONTE, Sept. 24.—The Hotel Del Monte sports room has become a "Hall of Fame." Photographs of many of the former state golf champions and those of famous golfers and polo stars have been given places of honor in this room. The latest addition to the Del Monte "Hall of Fame" is the picture of John J. McHugh of San Francisco winner of the recent California Amateur golf championship

CHARACTER QUALITY AMERICA FIRST ENTERPRISE ACCURACY

Los Angeles Examiner Sports

AN AMERICAN PAPER FOR THE AMERICAN PEOPLE — THE GREAT NEWSPAPER OF THE GREAT SOUTHWEST

RUTH EQUALS RECORD

Wham! Wham! The Bam's a Wow

TWO LUSCIOUS HOME RUNS and his record of 1921 was tied by that great swat Sultan Babe Ruth yesterday when he pickled the pill for his fifty-eighth and fifty-ninth homers of the season. He still has two days to get another and break the mark.—International Newsreel photo.

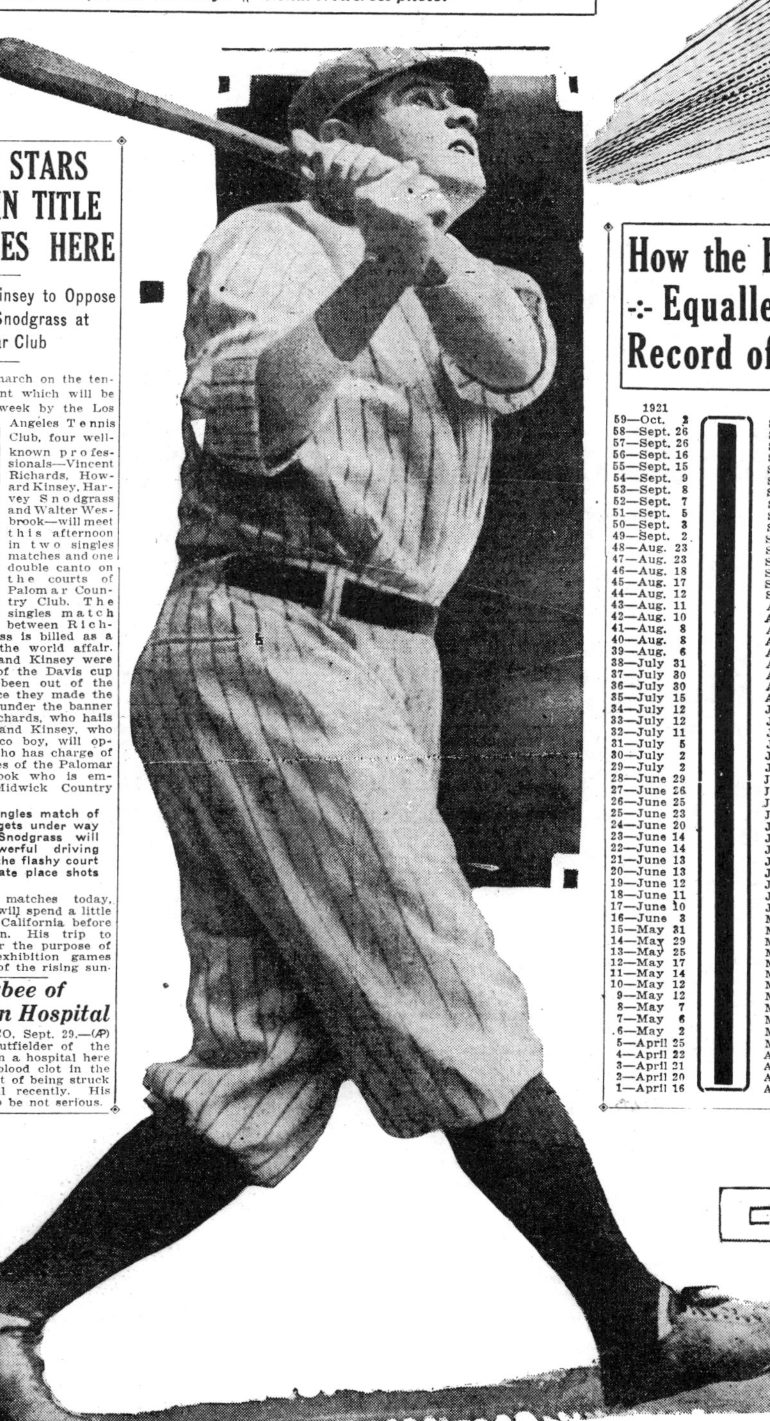

WHAT NOTS

by Mark Kelly

REMEMBER Johnny Mack Brown, that good-looking halfback of Alabama's Crimson Tide who two years ago against Washington ran the Huskies' ends bow-legged and played a big part in Washington's downfall?

The boy had the speed of an antelope and the fight of a tiger. He took more rough handling than a house-mover can give a baby grand and kept bouncing back for more. Once, I recall, George Wilson stood Mr. Brown on his head near the side-lines, twisted his leg and gave him quite tackle. Two plays later Mr.

Johnny Mack Brown Back in Limelight

George Wilson was present but not voting.

Johnny Mack Brown made the All-Southern twice and that he failed of All-American rating is due to the fact that the boys selecting that mythical organization know little of their geography and believe that the South is just a place to sing mammy songs about.

* * *

When he finished his collegiate term Johnny Mack Brown was taken in hand by Champ Pickens, the granddaddy of Dixie football.

"With that classic pan of yours, my boy, we'll go to Hollywood and bust into those pictures. I'm your manager," says Mr. Champ Pickens, who forthwith made the grade.

Metro-Goldwyn-Mayer accepted Johnny Mack Brown at one-fifth of Champ Pickens' rating, and even that percentage was unusually high.

* * *

JOHNNY MACK BROWN made good.

As a cinema player he bids fair to equal his football brilliance. It is rarely that a "green pea" ascends with the speed that Johnny Mack Brown has generated. He was cast in the leading male role opposite Miss Marion Davies in her starring picture, "The Fair Co-ed," a college picture which is said to be one of Miss Davies' very best cinema attainments. The picture is on exhibition next week at the Metropolitan.

And Johnny Made Good in Pictures

Of a modest, likeable demeanor Johnny Mack Brown was given every opportunity to "make" himself.

* * *

Recently Al Green was casting for a new picture and somebody told him that Johnny Mack Brown would make a good leading man for the cast.

Mr. Green yowled, "No experience," but reluctantly

consented to look at some of Mr. Brown's work in rushes of "The Fair Co-ed."

"Quit cranking," he yelled when they were halfway through. "I've seen enough—get me that baby at any cost."

And when the Fox folks tried to borrow Johnny Mack Brown from Metro-Goldwyn-Mayer they were politely given the bird. Mr. Brown's services were not for hire.

* * *

I BELIEVE that it was "The Fair Co-ed" which gave several other football players a lot of summer work and winter spending money. I know that Capt. Morley Drury of U. S. C. was given a minor role at fat pay and Jess Hibbs and other U. S. C. stars are in the cast. If you want to get a closeup of your favorite football player such as you cannot get on the football field where the boys wear gas masks, get a load of that picture next week. They say it really has college atmosphere and is faithful to detail in every regard. Most of the campus scenes were taken at Pomona College in Claremont.

Other Stars Appear in 'Fair Co-ed'

* * *

But to get back to Mr. Champ Pickens and Dixie football.

Mr. Pickens has a new idea which constant polishing has made fairly brilliant. It is Mr. Pickens' idea that an all-southern eleven, picked from the entire Southland and

(Continued on Page 17)

PRO NET STARS CLASH IN TITLE MATCHES HERE

Richards and Kinsey to Oppose Wesbrook, Snodgrass at Palomar Club

STEALING a march on the tennis tournament which will be staged next week by the Los Angeles Tennis Club, four well-known professionals—Vincent Richards, Howard Kinsey, Harvey Snodgrass and Walter Wesbrook—will meet this afternoon in two singles matches and one double canto on the courts of Palomar Country Club. The singles match between Richards and Snodgrass is billed as a championship of the world affair.

Vincent Richards

Both Richards and Kinsey were former members of the Davis cup teams, but have been out of the amateur class since they made the world tennis tour under the banner of C. C. Pyle. Richards, who hails from New York, and Kinsey, who is a San Francisco boy, will oppose Snodgrass, who has charge of the tennis activities of the Palomar Club, and Wesbrook who is employed at the Midwick Country Club.

In the first singles match of the day, which gets under way at 1 o'clock, Snodgrass will match his powerful driving strokes against the flashy court work and accurate place shots of Richards.

Following the matches today, Vincent Richards will spend a little time in Southern California before leaving for Japan. His trip to Japan is taken for the purpose of playing several exhibition games while in the land of the rising sun.

Carson Bigbee of Ducks in Hospital

SAN FRANCISCO, Sept. 29.—(AP) Carson Bigbee, outfielder of the Portland club, is in a hospital here suffering from a blood clot in the right leg, the result of being struck by a pitched ball recently. His condition is said to be not serious.

How the Babe -:- Equalled -:- Record of 59

1921	1927
59—Oct. 2	Sept. 29—59
58—Sept. 26	Sept. 29—58
57—Sept. 26	Sept. 27—57
56—Sept. 16	Sept. 22—56
55—Sept. 15	Sept. 21—55
54—Sept. 9	Sept. 18—54
53—Sept. 8	Sept. 16—53
52—Sept. 7	Sept. 13—52
51—Sept. 5	Sept. 13—51
50—Sept. 3	Sept. 11—50
49—Sept. 2	Sept. 7—49
48—Aug. 23	Sept. 7—48
47—Aug. 23	Sept. 6—47
46—Aug. 18	Sept. 6—46
45—Aug. 17	Sept. 6—45
44—Aug. 12	Sept. 2—44
43—Aug. 11	Aug. 31—43
42—Aug. 10	Aug. 28—42
41—Aug. 8	Aug. 27—41
40—Aug. 8	Aug. 22—40
39—Aug. 6	Aug. 20—39
38—July 31	Aug. 17—38
37—July 30	Aug. 16—37
36—July 30	Aug. 10—36
35—July 15	Aug. 5—35
34—July 12	July 28—34
33—July 12	July 26—33
32—July 11	July 26—32
31—July 5	July 18—31
30—July 2	July 12—30
29—July 2	July 9—29
28—June 29	July 9—28
27—June 26	July 8—27
26—June 25	July 3—26
25—June 23	June 30—25
24—June 20	June 22—24
23—June 14	June 22—23
22—June 14	June 16—22
21—June 13	June 12—21
20—June 13	June 11—20
19—June 12	June 11—19
18—June 11	June 7—18
17—June 10	June 5—17
16—June 3	May 31—16
15—May 31	May 31—15
14—May 29	May 30—14
13—May 25	May 29—13
12—May 17	May 28—12
11—May 14	May 23—11
10—May 12	May 22—10
9—May 12	May 17—9
8—May 7	May 11—8
7—May 6	May 10—7
6—May 2	May 1—6
5—April 25	May 1—5
4—April 22	April 29—4
3—April 21	April 25—3
2—April 20	April 23—2
1—April 16	April 15—1

HIBBS PUTS 'BIG KICK' IN U. S. C. DRILL

Jesse Shows Skill in Punting and Mentors Are Astounded; Broncos Reach City Today

By Martin Burke

A REAL kick was added to the Southern California football team yesterday. It was a 100 per cent kick to pep up a squad that has been floundering along on less than the legal one-half of 1 per cent.

Jesse Hibbs

Jesse Hibbs furnished the kick. Handsome Hibbs they call him at U. S. C. because he is good-looking enough to grab off junior leads in some of our very best Hollywood pictures.

Kicking in the face of a charging line, Hibbs got off some of the finest punts ever delivered at Bovard Field. Long, wriggling spirals with a skid at the finish that handcuffed the waiting safety man. Forty, fifty, fifty-five, sixty yards and better that ball traveled.

Coach Howard Jones has been moaning the absence of a real kicker to put the kick in his team. He found one yesterday in his versatile, vigorous tackle—Jesse Hibbs.

MENTORS ASTOUNDED

When Hibbs got off his first long drive after Drury, Elliott and Williams had taken their turn, the Trojan mentors were a bit astounded. Cliff Herd, who attends to the booting department and who has been bringing Hibbs along, told him to try again.

Zowie! And off there floated a sky-scraper, high enough for any end to cover and long enough to keep the best team in its own territory. Another was tried. The tackles slipped through in a concentrated effort to block the drive. Right off their outstretched hands it shot and well-placed in the corner of the field.

Still another and another until the truth finally dawned on every one. U. S. C. had finally found a punter after years without one.

Hibbs is not a fast kicker. But with practice he's getting quicker and is bound to improve. He is as steady as a rock and has the leg drive and strength that is essential to a first-class punt producer.

DRURY SHIFTS

When Hibbs dropped back to the rear position Captain Drury shifted to tackle to plug the gap. Having once played in the line, Drury can take care of the job in fancy style.

The varsity worked on defense against Notre Dame plays for an hour and then polished up on the booting and covering of kicks. To offset the uncovering of Hibbs was an unfortunate and possibly serious injury to Johnny Fox, the leading light in the race for the center position.

In blocking a line charge Fox rapped his right arm on Ward's head with such telling effect that he couldn't use his arm afterwards. An X-ray will be taken today to determine whether or not any bones have been broken. Ward reported no damage to his head, which is something of a pointer on how hard his head really is. All kidding aside, Ward is coming as fast as any of the green men on the squad and may win himself a steady berth at center or tackle.

Santa Clara arrives here today and will work out this afternoon at the Coliseum in preparation for the contest Saturday.

National League -:- Standings -:-

Pittsburgh	93	58	.616
St. Louis	91	61	.599
New York	90	61	.596
Chicago	85	67	.559
Cincinnati	73	77	.487
Brooklyn	63	87	.420
Boston	57	93	.380
Philadelphia	51	99	.340

YESTERDAY'S RESULTS

Cincinnati, 3; St. Louis, 2.
Philadelphia, 7; Boston, 1.
Only games scheduled.

GAMES TODAY

Philadelphia at Boston.
Pittsburgh at Cincinnati.
Only games scheduled.

CARDS' PENNANT HOPES BLASTED

Lose to Reds, 3-2, and Fall 2 1-2 Games Behind League Leading Pirates

CINCINNATI, Sept. 29.—(AP)—The Cincinnati Reds dealt the Cardinals a crushing blow in their pennant pursuit today by hanging up a 3 to 2 victory in the final of a three-game series. As the Pirates were not scheduled, the St. Louis club fell back to 2½ games behind Pittsburgh.

As the Cardinals now have only two games left to play, the best they can do is to force the Corsairs to a tie, granting they win both contests while Pittsburgh drops three. St. Louis held on to second place by a half game over the idle Giants.

But a scant crowd of 340 witnessed the contest on a soggy field drenched by two days of rain.

Frankhouse, Card hurler, had one bad inning, the fourth, when he contributed a wild throw which, with three hits and a sacrifice, brought in three runs.

Jakie May came through as the winning pitcher, allowing eight hits, one of which was a homer by Frisch. The Reds made only five safeties.

St. Louis	AB	H	O	A	Cincinnati	AB	H	O	A
Douthit,cf.	4	1	6	0	Dressen,3b.	4	0	1	1
Frisch,2b.	4	2	3	2	Walker,rf.	4	0	0	0
Hafey,rf.	4	1	1	0	Pipp,1b.	3	1	10	0
Botomley,1b	3	0	8	0	Bressler,lf.	2	0	2	0
Blades,lf.	2	1	2	0	Allen,cf.	4	2	5	0
Holm,2b.	3	0	1	1	Ford,ss.	4	1	3	5
Snyder,c.	4	1	2	0	Critz,2b.	2	0	3	4
Maranvil,ss	3	1	1	4	Picinich,c.	3	1	3	2
L.Bell	1	0	0	0	May,p.	3	0	0	1
Frankhse,p.	3	1	0	1					
Totals	31	8	24	8	Totals	29	5	27	13

L. Bell batted for Maranville in ninth.

St. Louis.... 0 0 0 0 1 1 0 0 0—2
Cincinnati... 0 0 0 3 0 0 0 0 x—3

Errors—Maranville, Frankhouse.

Two-base hits—Douthit, Pipp, Picinich, Allen. Home run—Frisch. Sacrifices—Bressler, Critz, Holm. Double plays—Critz to Ford to Pipp (2); Picinich to Ford. Left on bases—St. Louis, 6; Cincinnati, 6. Bases on balls—Off Frankhouse, 2; off May, 2. Struck out—By Frankhouse, 2; by May, 4. Hit by pitcher—Bottomley by May. Umpires—McCormick, O'Day and Reardon. Time—1:27.

Major League -:- Leaders -:-

(By Associated Press)
(Including Games of September 28)

NATIONAL LEAGUE

Batting—P. Waner, Pirates .382
Runs—Hornsby, Giants, 132; L. Waner, Pirates 132
Hits—P. Waner, Pirates 234
Doubles—Stephenson, Cubs 47
Triples—P. Waner, Pirates 18
Homers—Williams, Phillies 30
Stolen Bases—Frisch, Cardinals 49
Pitching—Kremer, Pirates, won 19, lost 8

AMERICAN LEAGUE

Batting—Simmons, Athletics .389
Runs—Ruth, Yankees 228
Doubles—Gehrig, Yankees 53
Triples—Combs, Yankees 23
Homers—Ruth, Yankees, 57; Gehrig, Yankees 46
Stolen Bases—Sisler, Browns 28
Pitching—Pipgras, Yankees, won 10, Lost 3; Rommsell, Athletics, won 10, lost 3.

BABE SPANKS TWO TO KNOT MARK OF 59

2 Washington Pitchers Victims of Bambino's Outburst; One in Advance of Big Output

NEW YORK, Sept. 29.—(AP)—Carrying on in a furious September finish, Babe Ruth today knocked out two mammoth home runs to tie his great record of 59, accomplished in 1921. The mighty slugger of the New York Yankees stands on the brink of establishing a new mark, since he has two more days left in the campaign.

Miller Huggins

The king of the swat is one home run in advance of his output in 1921, for at that time No. 59 fell during the Yanks' 153d game, while today was New York's 152d.

Horace Lisenbee of the Senators was the victim of Babe's first rap today. It came in the first inning with the sacks empty. In the fifth, Paul Hopkins, a young pitcher, who just joined the Washington Club, received a baptism of fire when Ruth drove out No. 59, with the bases full. That gave Ruth three homers in the last two games, two of which dropped with the sacks loaded.

GETS RECEPTION

Some 5000 fans rejoiced with Ruth and gave him a great ovation when he equalled his former standard. Lou Gehrig, his teammate and rival for home run honors, this season, was the first to congratulate Ruth with a handshake at the plate. At the Yanks' dugout a warm reception awaited him from his co-players and Manager Miller Huggins.

This has been the greatest month in Ruth's home run career. With fifteen thus far, his best previous maonthly assortment was thirteen in June, 1921.

Ruth started the month still battling with Lou Gehrig and well behind the 1921 record. Gehrig had led him during the greater part of the season and the speculation was about even that the young Columbia product would beat Ruth out.

LOU FALLS BACK

The first three months of the current season found Ruth and Gehrig deadlocked, with twenty-five apiece. Early in the present month, they were running neck and neck again, when Gehrig clipped a homer in Boston. That was on Labor Day, and tied the sluggers at 45. Then Ruth started stepping out and Ruth has hit 14 while Gehrig made but one. The Yanks won today's game by a score of 15 to 4.

Washington	AB	H	O	A	New York	AB	H	O	A
Rice,rf.	3	0	0	0	Combs,cf.	5	1	4	0
Hopkins,p.	1	0	0	2	Koenig,ss.	5	3	0	2
Harris,2b.	4	2	1	3	Ruth,rf.	5	3	3	0
Stewart,2b.	1	0	0	1	Paschal,rf.	0	0	1	0
Ganzel,cf.	4	2	3	0	Gehrig,1b.	3	1	9	0
Goslin,lf.	5	1	3	2	Durst,1b.	0	0	0	1
Judge,1b.	4	2	7	1	Meusel,lf.	5	3	3	0
Speaker,1b.	0	0	2	0	Lazzeri,2b.	1	1	0	0
Tate,c.	4	2	5	0	Dugan,3b.	3	1	1	3
Bluege,3b.	4	0	0	0	Gazella,3b.	2	0	0	1
Reeves,ss.	4	1	2	4	Collins,c.	2	2	5	0
Lisenbee,p.	1	0	0	0	Shocker,p.	1	0	0	0
Marberry,p.	0	0	0	0	Ruether,p.	2	1	0	0
Barnes,rf.	3	0	2	1	Shawkey,p.	1	0	1	0
Totals	38	10	24	14	Totals	38	19	27	8

Washington ... 0 2 0 0 2 0 0 0 0—4
New York ..... 1 7 0 3 4 0 0 0 *—15

Errors—Koenig, Reeves, Stewart.

Home runs—Ruth, 2; Reeves, Ganzel. Three-base hits—Ruth, Meusel. Two-base hits—Collins, Meusel, 2. Stolen bases—Lazzeri. Double plays—Judge to Harris; Reeves to Judge; Barnes to Judge. Bases on balls—Off Lisenbee, 3; Marberry, 1; Hopkins, 1; Shocker, 1; Ruether, 1. Struck out—By Lisenbee, 1; Marberry, 1; Hopkins, 1; Ruether, 1; Shawkey, 3. Wild pitch—Lisenbee. Winning pitcher—Shocker. Losing pitcher—Lisenbee. Umpires—Dineen, Connolly and Owens.

French Tourney Won by Duncan

PARIS, Sept. 29.—(AP)—George Duncan of Great Britain won the French open golf championship today with a score of 299 for the seventy-two holes. Aubrey Boomer of France was second with 301. Archie Compston, Great Britain, third, 304; Arthur Havers, Great Britain, fourth, 306, and Arnaud Massey, France, fifth, 307.

AUTO RACER INJURED

FRESNO, Sept. 29.—(AP)—In the first few minutes of automobile racing car tryouts on the half-mile dirt track at the Fresno district fair, Bill Paige of Reno was seriously injured this afternoon when his car crashed through the fence on the south turn of the dirt track. A large sliver of wood was driven into Paige's leg and his pelvis and several ribs were broken.

Terris Handed Pummeling by Spanish Star

NEW YORK, Sept. 29.—(AP)—Hilario Martinez, hard-punching Spanish lightweight, scored a sensational ten-round victory over Sid Terris, crack New York title contender, in the feature match at the Queensboro Stadium tonight. Terris was knocked down for three counts of nine in the second round and barely kept his feet under Martinez' merciless attack in several others.

Davy Arad, Panama bantamweight, lost to Milton Cohen of New York on a foul in the first round of a ten-round semi-final.

HACKLEY SCORES K. O.

DAYTON, Ky., Sept. 29.—(AP)—Jimmy Hackley, Los Angeles junior lightweight, knocked out Carl Schmadel, Indianapolis, in the first round of a scheduled ten-round bout here tonight.

Capacity Attendances Forecast for Net Meet

CAPACITY attendance every day of the big tournament to be held next week at the Los Angeles Tennis Club under the auspices of the Tennis Patrons' Association of Southern California was forecast yesterday by officials of the latter organization as a result of the first four days' sale of season tickets.

Arrival here this week of Big Bill Tilden, famous American net star; Miss Kea Bouman, champion of Holland, and plans to greet Molla Mallory, Francis T. Hunter, Jean Washer, champion of Belgium; Alonso, Spanish champion, and others tomorrow and Sunday has greatly stimulated interest in the matches, which will begin at 2 o'clock Monday afternoon.

Plans have been completed for the dinner-dance to be given Saturday night at the Tennis Club in honor of the visiting and local players to participate in the tourney, according to Harold H. Braley, president of the patrons' organization; Clif Herd, president of the L. A. Tennis Club, and E. Avery McCarthy, chairman of the entertainment committee.

Society women of the city are arranging a series of dinners and other receptions for the noted players for the next week. Patronesses of the tourney include some of the most socially prominent women of Southern California. Radio talks will be made from 9 to 10 o'clock Monday night by Tilden and other stars of the courts.

Pittsburgh Can Cinch Rag With Victory Today

NEW YORK, Sept. 29.—(AP)—The Pirates were shoved virtually into the National League championship today without a struggle, as the Cardinals were cut down by the Reds to diminish the St. Louis' flag possibility to the event of a tie. The Corsairs stand a chance of definitely capturing the bunting tomorrow by a victory over the Reds. All Pittsburgh needs to take the banner is one triumph in three remaining starts. However, if the Buccaneers drop the three games and the Cards and Giants sweep all their encounters, the clubs will be tangled in a triple tie with the standing as follows:

	W.	L.	Ave.
Pittsburgh	93	61	.604
St. Louis	03	61	.604
New York	93	61	.604

Reach Semi-Finals in Squash Event

Semi-finals of the A. A. U. doubles championship, in a tournament which is being played at the Pasadena Athletic Club, will be held this afternoon at 5 o'clock, with the finals following at eight.

The L. A. A. C. team of Butler and Schaumer is favored to win, although Redwine and Dan Jones threaten. They defeated Cooper and Klawiter, 21-16, 19-21 and 21-17 last night.

In the semi-finals tonight Kline and Keller meet Butler and Schaumer, while Redwine and Da nJones face A. Jones and W. O'Brien.

1926 Officials Handle Stanford, U. S. C. Game

THE same quartet of officials that functioned in last year's Trojan-Stanford game will again handle the contest, it was officially announced yesterday at the University of Southern California offices. The officials are:

Evans, former Stanford coach, referee.
Ralph McCord, Illinois, umpire.
Badenoch, Chicago, head lineman.
Dud Clark, Oregon, field judge.

The list of officials for the U. S. C.-California game … played in the Los Angeles Coliseum on October 29 is as follo…

George Varnell, Chicago, referee.
McCord, umpire.
Fitzpatrick, head lineman.
Badenoch, field judge.

Babe Ruth Hits Sixtieth Homer, Breaking 1921 Record, as Yankees Down Senators, 4 to 2

Record-Breaking Home Run Off Zachary Is Fair by Six Inches

Pitcher's Attempt to Outwit Slugger With Screw Ball Fails When Babe Drives Ball Into Bleachers; Pipgras and Pennock Effective for Hugmen

By W. B. Hanna

The home-run record for the season and for major leagues, went into the discard yesterday when Babe Ruth lined the ball, sprouting wings as it does when he hits it, into the right field bleachers of the Yankee Stadium. Then and there another record was created. The Babe coined his sixtieth in the eighth inning of the tilt with the Senators and won the game with it, 4 to 2.

His record homer eclipsed his own performance of fifty-nine, made in 1921 and tied day before yesterday. It was made off Tom Zachary, with Mark Koenig on third and one out, and broke a tie score. Zachary had been pitching well and was keeping a tight rein on our boys, but he hadn't been holding Ruth much, for two singles and a base on balls was the Babe's grist up to that time.

In the eighth Zachary sought to outwit Ruth with a screw ball, "a slow screw ball," as Ruth described it. The ball broke in to Ruth as a left-hander's screw ball would to a left-handed batter. The screw ball once upon a time was known as a fadeaway. A right-hander breaks it in to a right-handed batter and a southpaw breaks it in to left-handed hitter. The idea was to break it in and down past the Babe.

Homer Fair by Six Inches

This one broke over the plate and was a screw ball until it met the Babe's unruly bat. After that it was a minie ball. It didn't go high, and it did go on a line. Bill Dinneen, the umpire, crouched on the foul line and peered carefully into the distance to see whether it was fair or foul. It buried itself in the bleachers fifteen rows from the top and was fair by not more than six inches. Still, it was fair, and the record was broken. Count 'em—sixty!

Nobody ever got a livelier reception per capita than Ruth did as he paced around. Fletcher's cap went up in the air first, then O'Leary's—and O'Leary hates to expose his bald head—and the other players rushed to congratulate the Babe. All of the fans, grandstand, bleachers and boxes, stood and cheered and waved their handkerchiefs. The crowd was small, the ovation deafening.

When the Babe crossed the plate he lifted his cap high and with the other hand waved a salute. He held his hand there in midair: "Well, folks, here we are. How about it, folks?"

The bleachers gave him an ovation all their own when he went out there after the inning, and he gave them a salute and a bow no less genuine and punctilious.

The Yankee infielding was somewhat ragged, with a muffed throw by Koenig and bad throws by Gehrig and Lazzeri, but also was done with a good deal of style and lots of ground covered. The outfield play was fast and far flung. Pipgras and Pennock both did their work effectively, though Pipgras's control was wayward now and then.

Zachary Pitches Cleverly

The only alien hitting of any consequence was in the fourth inning, in which Goslin, Ruel and Bluege bunched hits for two runs. The Yankees didn't pulverize Zachary by a good deal. In fact they had no slight amount of trouble with his clever pitching, but they hit him timely.

Ruth and Gehrig singled in the fourth. The Babe took third on Lou's single to right center, and Henry Lou took second on the throw to third. Said sprightly base running earned a run for the Yankees, for Ruth tallied on Meusel's fly to Goslin. Ruth, Gehrig and Meusel singled in the sixth, and Ruth tallied.

Koenig hit Zachary for a triple to left in the eighth. Next came Ruth's sixtieth to write its challenge across the baseball skies.

Briefs

The first ball hit gave our young-old third baseman a chance to show his peerless skill at coming in on a ball. He threw out Sam Rice by a whisker, and thus does the trial of Joey Dugan proceed satisfactorily.

Emerson Douglas—In the world series last year is the only time Ruth has made three homers in one game.

Koenig had an easy chance to retire Bluege on Bengough's perfect throw, but muffed it for a plain, unadorned error. It was no fault of Pipgras's that the runner was safe, but the next time it was, for he gave the runner a big start.

Moore and Hoyt will pitch for the Yankees in to-day's finale, and the chances are one of them will open the world series.

The score:

WASHINGTON (A. L.)	ab	r	h	po	a	e	NEW YORK (A. L.)	ab	r	h	po	a	e
Rice, rf	3	0	1	2	0	0	Combs, cf	4	0	0	3	0	0
Harris, 2b	3	0	0	3	4	0	Koenig, ss	4	1	1	3	5	0
Ganzel, cf	4	0	1	1	0	0	Ruth, rf	3	3	3	4	0	0
Goslin, lf	4	1	1	5	0	0	Gehrig, 1b	4	0	2	10	0	1
Judge, 1b	4	0	0	8	0	0	Meusel, lf	3	0	1	3	0	0
Ruel, c	2	1	1	2	0	0	Lazzeri, 2b	3	0	0	2	2	0
Bluege, 3b	3	0	1	1	4	0	Dugan, 3b	3	0	1	1	1	0
Gillis, ss	4	0	0	2	1	0	Bengough, c	3	0	1	1	2	0
Zachary, p	2	0	0	0	1	0	Pipgras, p	2	0	0	0	2	0
*Johnson	1	0	0	0	0	0	Pennock, p	1	0	0	0	1	0
Totals	30	2	5	24	10	0	Totals	30	4	9	27	13	1

*Batted for Zachary in ninth inning.

Washington .... 000 200 000—2
New York .... 000 101 02x—4

Two-base hit—Rice. Three-base hit—Koenig. Home run—Ruth. Stolen bases—Ruel, Bluege, Rice. Sacrifice—Meusel. Double play—Harris and Bluege; Gillis, Harris and Judge. Left on bases—New York, 4; Washington, 7. Bases on balls—Off Pipgras, 4; off Pennock, 1; off Zachary, 1. Struck out—By Zachary, 1. Hits—Off Pipgras, 4 in 6 innings; off Pennock, 1 in 3. Hit by pitcher—By Pipgras (Rice). Winning pitcher—Pennock. Umpires—Dinneen, Connolly and Owens. Time—1:38.

U. S. L. T. A. Honors Lacoste at Luncheon

On the eve of his departure for France, Jean Rene Lacoste, ace of the recent Davis Cup challenge round matches and winner for the second time of the national singles title, was tendered a farewell luncheon yesterday afternoon by the U. S. L. T. A., at the Bankers' Club. Lacoste sailed on the French liner Ile de France shortly after midnight this morning.

Locoste was seated in the position of honor at the luncheon table, between Julian S. Myrick, chairman of the Davis Cup Committee of the U. S. L. T. A., and Jones W. Mersereau, president of the association. Myrick presided as toastmaster. Among others seated at the table were former Davis Cup and national champions and officers of the association, including George T. Adee, Malcolm D. Whitman, Charles S. Garland, Bernon S. Prentice, Albert J. Gibney, Harold H. Hackett, Franklin I. Mallory, Beals Coleman Wright, Edward B. Moss, Louis B. Dailey, Henry W. Slocum, J. S. Cushman, Benjamin H Dwight and Harold H. Hackett.

The hope was expressed by many of the speakers that Lacoste would return to the United States next year to compete in the national singles tourney, and the little champion said he hoped to defend his championship.

Fellowship Is Jones's Definition for Golf

ATLANTA, Ga., Sept. 30 (AP).—Having exhausted their vocabulary in praise of his golfing record, admirers of Bobby Jones called upon the American amateur and British open titleholder to tell himself what the game has meant to him at the "annual dinner" in his honor here last night.

Without mentioning any of the seven titles he has acquired since 1923, the champion told the gathering consisting of the elite of Atlanta sportdom and society what the game had meant to him.

"Golf means fellowship," he declared. "It bridges the gap of generations. It is the only game I know where a father and his son may meet on exactly an equal basis; where the good player and the duffer may compete on the keenest terms. Golf to me has meant and always will mean a list of real friendships."

Falk's Hitting Helps White Sox to Win Two From Tigers

CHICAGO, Sept. 30 (AP).—Chicago took both games of a double-header from Detroit here to-day, by scores of 5 to 4, and 4 to 1, respectively. Bib Falk's batting was the winning factor for the White Sox. He broke up the first game with a single in the thirteenth inning, which enabled Tommy Thomas to register his eighteenth victory of the season.

Falk's single in the third inning of the second game drove in two runs, putting the locals in front. The game was called in the sixth because of darkness.

Heilmann's batting featured for the visitors.

The scores:

FIRST GAME

DETROIT (A. L.)	ab	r	h	po	a	e	CHICAGO (A. L.)	ab	r	h	po	a	e
Blue, 1b	5	1	2	17	0	0	Hunnefi'ld, ss	6	1	2	5	0	0
Gehringer, 2b	6	1	1	3	6	1	Kamm, 3b	4	1	2	2	4	0
Manush, cf	5	1	0	6	0	0	Barrett, rf	5	0	1	1	0	0
Heilman, rf	5	0	3	4	0	0	Falk, lf	6	0	2	4	0	0
Ruble, lf	2	0	0	2	0	0	Neis, cf	5	0	0	6	1	0
*Neun	1	0	0	0	0	0	Clancy, 1b	5	1	1	11	1	0
Fothergill, lf	1	0	0	1	0	0	Ward, 2b	4	1	0	2	4	0
McManus, 3b	5	1	3	0	0	0	McCurdy, c	5	1	1	7	2	0
Tavener, ss	4	0	0	0	4	1	Thomas, p	5	0	0	1	2	0
Bassler, c	5	0	0	5	2	0							
Gibson, p	5	0	0	0	6	0							
Totals	44	4	9	†38	18	2	Totals	45	5	9	39	14	0

*Batted for Ruble in eighth inning.
†Two out when winning run was scored.

Detroit ..... 000 012 010 000 0—4
Chicago ..... 000 031 000 000 1—5

Two-base hits—Heilmann (2), Blue, McManus. Three-base hits—Hunnefield, Clancy. Home run—McManus. Stolen base—Gehringer. Sacrifices—Kamm, Ruble, Tavener, Barrett. Double play—Neis, McCurdy, Kamm and McCurdy. Left on bases—Detroit, 5; Chicago, 6. Bases on balls—Off Thomas, 2; off Gibson, 2. Struck out—By Thomas, 3; by Gibson, 4. Umpires—McGowan, Evans and Hildebrand. Time—2:14.

SECOND GAME

DETROIT (A. L.)	ab	r	h	po	a	e	CHICAGO (A. L.)	ab	r	h	po	a	e
Blue, 1b	3	0	1	7	0	0	Hunnefi'd, ss	3	0	1	0	2	0
Gehringer, 2b	3	0	0	1	3	0	Kamm, 3b	1	2	1	4	1	0
Manush, cf	3	1	2	2	0	0	Barrett, rf	2	1	0	1	0	0
Heilmann, rf	2	0	1	1	0	0	Falk, lf	3	0	1	0	0	0
Ruble, lf	2	0	0	1	0	0	Neis, cf	3	0	0	1	0	0
McManus, 3b	2	0	0	0	0	0	Clancy, 1b	2	0	0	4	1	0
Tavener, ss	2	0	1	3	1	0	Ward, 2b	2	0	2	1	0	0
Woodall, c	2	0	1	0	1	0	Crouse, c	2	0	0	6	2	0
Stoner, p	2	0	0	0	2	0	Faber, p	1	1	1	1	3	0
Totals	21	1	6	15	7	0	Totals	19	4	6	18	9	0

Detroit .... 000 100—1
Chicago .... 003 01x—4

Sacrifices—Kamm, Ruble, Faber. Double play—Gehringer, Tavener and Blue. Left on bases—Detroit, 5; Chicago, 5. Bases on balls—Off Faber, 2; off Stoner, 3. Struck out—By Faber, 4. Wild pitch—Stoner. Umpires—Hildebrand, Evans and McGowan. Time—1:03.

Only 2 Home Games for Providence College Five

PROVIDENCE, R. I., Sept. 30 (AP).—A sixteen-game basketball list which includes but two home games, one being with Brown University, has been announced by graduate manager John E. Farrell for the Providence College quintet.

Ten new-comers are slated to oppose the Dominicans in their second season in the court game.

The complete schedule is as follows:

Dec. 7, Clark University at Worcester, Mass.; 10, Dartmouth College at Hanover, N. H.; 16, Upsala College at East Orange, N. J.; 17, Seton Hall College at South Orange, N. J.; 19, Columbia College of Pharmacy at New York City; 20, St. John's College at Brooklyn.

Jan. 7, Trinity College at Hartford, Conn.; 13, Springfield College at Providence; 21, Connecticut State College at Storrs, Conn.

Feb. 4, U. S. Coast Guard Academy at New London, Conn.; 7, University of New Hampshire at Durham, N. H.; 10, Boston University at Boston, Mass.; 18, Massachusetts Institute of Technology at Cambridge, Mass.; 24, New York State Collefe at Albany, N. Y.; 25, Union College at Schenectady, N. Y.

March 3, Brown at Providence, R. I.

Movie of a Raffle : : : : : : : : : By BRIGGS

Indians Win First From Browns, 5–4, Lose Second, 9–4

ST. LOUIS, Sept. 30 (AP).—St. Louis and Cleveland divided a double-header here to-day, the Indians winning the first, 5 to 4, and the Browns taking the second, 9 to 4. The games were played before only 200 persons, largely as a result of the inclement weather and yesterday's disaster.

J. Sewell's homer in the sixth with two on was the feature of the first game. In the second game Wright held the visitors to five hits, while his teammates were garnering thirteen.

The scores:

FIRST GAME

CLEVELAND (A. L.)	ab	r	h	po	a	e	ST. LOUIS (A. L.)	ab	r	h	po	a	e
Gill, lf	5	0	1	0	0	0	Adams, 3b	4	1	1	1	0	0
Orsatti, 3b	3	0	0	0	2	0	Rice, rf	4	2	2	4	0	0
Summa, rf	4	1	1	2	0	0	Sturdy, 1b	4	0	3	9	1	0
Hodapp, 1b	4	1	2	12	0	1	Williams, lf	4	0	1	0	1	0
J. Sewell, ss	4	1	1	5	2	0	E. Miller, cf	4	0	1	3	0	0
L. Sewell, c	4	0	1	6	1	0	Schang, c	4	0	0	3	1	0
Langford, cf	3	2	2	1	0	0	Melillo, 2b	3	0	0	4	3	0
Lind, 2b	1	0	0	1	3	0	Kress, ss	4	1	1	2	4	0
Hudlin, p	3	0	0	0	4	0	Blaeholder, p	3	0	1	1	3	0
							*Bennett	1	0	0	0	0	0
Totals	31	5	8	27	12	1	Totals	35	4	10	27	13	1

*Batted for Blaeholder in ninth inning.

Cleveland .... 000 003 101—5
St. Louis .... 100 100 200—4

Two-base hits—E. Miller, Kress, Langford (2), Blaeholder. Home run—J. Sewell. Sacrifices—Hudlin, Melillo. Stolen base—Sturdy. Double plays—Schang, Kress and Sturdy; Melillo and Sturdy. Passed ball—Schang. Hit by pitcher—By Blaeholder (Lind). Bases on balls—Off Hudlin, 2; off Blaeholder, 4. Struck out—By Hudlin, 3; by Blaeholder, 2. Left on bases—St. Louis, 7; Cleveland, 5. Umpires—Rowland and Geisel. Time—1:24.

SECOND GAME

CLEVELAND (A. L.)	ab	r	h	po	a	e	ST. LOUIS (A. L.)	ab	r	h	po	a	e
Gill, lf	3	1	0	2	0	0	Allen, 2b	3	3	1	3	2	1
Ussatti, 3b	4	1	1	1	1	0	Rice, 3b	4	2	2	0	1	0
Summa, rf	3	1	0	0	0	0	Sturdy, 1b	5	2	3	8	1	1
Hodapp, 1b	3	0	1	9	0	1	Williams, lf	4	1	2	5	0	0
J. Sewell, ss	4	1	1	1	1	1	E. Miller, cf	3	0	1	1	0	0
Myatt, c	4	0	1	7	0	0	Bennett, rf	4	0	2	4	0	0
Langford, cf	4	0	0	2	1	0	Kress, ss	5	0	2	2	6	0
Lind, 2b	4	0	1	2	6	0	Dixon, c	3	0	0	3	0	0
Underhill, p	1	0	0	0	0	0	Wright, p	3	1	0	1	0	0
McKain, p	2	0	0	0	3	0							
*Burnett	1	0	0	0	0	0							
Totals	33	4	5	24	12	2	Totals	34	9	13	27	10	2

*Batted for Underhill in fifth inning.

Cleveland .... 400 000 000—4
St. Louis .... 220 400 10x—9

Two-base hits—J. Sewell, Myatt, Allen, Kress, Rice. Sacrifices—E. Miller, Bennett. Double plays—Ussatti, Lind and Hodapp. Left on bases—St. Louis, 10; Cleveland, 5. Bases on balls—Off Wright, 3; off Underhill, 6; off McKain, 1. Struck out—By Wright, 3; by McKain, 3; by Underhill, 2. Hits—Off Underhill, 8 in 4 innings; off McKain, 5 in 4. Wild pitch—McKain. Losing pitcher—Underhill. Umpires—Geisel and Rowland. Time—1:27.

Tiger Flowers Wins Over Pete Latzo in 10 Rounds

WILKESBARRE, Pa., Sept. 30 (AP).—Tiger Flowers, former middle champion to-night battled his way to a ten-round judges' decision over Pete Latzo, of Scranton, former welterweight titleholder. Latzo made his middleweight debut after surrendering his welterweight crown to Joe Dundee, of Baltimore, a few months ago.

Newspapermen at the ringside gave Latzo an even break in two rounds, the second and the fifth, but aside from that the fight was all Flowers. Short choppy blows by the Georgian puzzled Latzo throughout the contest.

Flowers weighed 168 pounds and Latzo 164.

Ruiz Retains European Title

MADRID, Sept. 30 (AP).—Anoulio Ruiz, featherweight champion of Europe, successfully defended his title by outpointing Barbens, the challenger, in a ten-round bout to-night.

Standings in Major Leagues

SATURDAY, OCTOBER 1, 1927

American League

YESTERDAY'S RESULTS

New York, 4; Washington, 2.
Chicago, 5; Detroit, 4 (1st, 13 ins.).
Chicago, 4; Detroit, 1 (2d).
Cleveland, 5; St. Louis, 4 (1st).
St. Louis, 9; Cleveland, 4 (2d).
Other game postponed.

STANDING OF THE CLUBS

	New York	Phila'phia	Washington	Detroit	Chicago	Cleveland	St. Louis	Boston	Won	Lost	Percentage
New York	—	14	13	14	17	12	21	18	109	44	.712
Phila'phia	8	—	12	13	14	12	16	14	89	62	.589
Wash'ton	8	9	—	11	12	14	12	18	84	68	.553
Detroit	8	9	11	—	8	13	14	17	80	71	.530
Chicago	5	8	10	13	—	8	13	11	68	82	.453
Cleveland	10	10	8	7	14	—	10	7	66	85	.437
St. Louis	1	6	10	8	6	11	—	16	58	92	.387
Boston	4	6	4	5	11	15	6	—	51	101	.336
Gms. lost	44	62	68	71	82	85	92	101	—	—	

GAMES TO-DAY

Washington at New York (3 p. m.).
Boston at Philadelphia (2).
Cleveland at Detroit.
St. Louis at Chicago.

National League

YESTERDAY'S RESULTS

Brooklyn, 10; New York, 5.
Cincinnati, 2; Pittsburgh, 1.
Boston, 12; Philadelphia, 2.
Other clubs not scheduled.

STANDING OF THE CLUBS

	Pittsburgh	St. Louis	New York	Chicago	Cincinnati	Brooklyn	Boston	Phila'phia	Won	Lost	Percentage
Pittsburgh	—	14	11	13	13	14	13	15	93	59	.612
St. Louis	8	—	10	11	14	14	15	19	91	61	.599
New York	11	12	—	12	15	11	15	14	90	62	.592
Chicago	9	9	10	—	14	15	15	13	85	67	.559
Cincinnati	7	8	7	8	—	10	18	16	74	77	.490
Brooklyn	8	8	10	7	11	—	9	11	64	87	.424
Boston	9	7	7	7	4	12	—	12	58	93	.384
Phila'phia	7	3	7	9	6	11	8	—	51	100	.338
Games lost	59	61	62	67	77	87	93	100	—	—	

GAMES TO-DAY

New York at Brooklyn (3 p. m.).
Pittsburgh at Cincinnati.
Chicago at St. Louis.
Philadelphia at Boston.

Giants' Chances for Flag End as Robins Pound Out 10-5 Victory

By Rud Rennie

Before the Giants went to Brooklyn yesterday to play off last Sunday's tie game, there was a mathematical possibility of their finishing the season in a tie with Pittsburgh. After playing the Robins, there wasn't any possibility, mathematical or otherwise, of the Giants finishing any better than second, if at all.

The Robins went on a wild batting spree in two innings, making four runs in the fifth, and batting all the way around in the seventh to score six more and break up a tie score. Dazzy Vance, who was pitching, looked at his teammates in amazement and wondered why under the sun they had not thought of doing something like that earlier in the season.

So what with all this unusual stick work and Vance's pitching, the Robins beat the Giants by a score of 10 to 5 and pushed them a little deeper into third place.

Defeat Ends Suspense

If the Giants had won the suspense would only have been prolonged, because the Pirates lost and the Cardinals were not playing. As things turned out, however, the Cards gained half a game on the Pirates and are now only two games out of first place and one game ahead of the Giants. And there are only two more games to play.

The Robins were up to all their old tricks yesterday. They made five errors and some of them were ridiculous. But their new trick of hitting all at once offset all their bad playing. They made nine hits, four of them were in the fifth and four more came in the seventh.

Dutch Henry started for the Giants. It was he who worked so well against the R obins in the tie game last Sunday. He would have been all right yesterday if it had been a four-inning game, because Flowers was the only Robin to hit him in the first four frames and the R obins had thrown away three runs.

Giants Get Gift of Two Runs

Vance chucked two runs at the Giants in the first inning. He hit Mueller with the first ball he pitched and then hurled Reese's little hit so far into right fiel dthat Mueller scored and Reese moved along to second. Roush's single brought Reese in a moment later.

A lot of Robins collaborated in giving the Giants their third run in the second inning. It started when Statz took Harper's single and returned it to the infield. Nobody bothered to pick up the ball. It rolled past Flowers, Vance and De Berry, while Harper pounded around the bags and came to rest on third. Cummings's sacrifice brought him in.

After this deplorable beginning it didn't seem that the Robins would ever make up that three-run deficit. To all intents and purposes the Giants would win the game. But the Robins got wise to whatever Henry was tossing at them in the fifth. Flowers and Butler hit and De Berry walked. So the bases were filled when Vance sent a sacrifice fly to Mueller and the Robins said their first run with Flowers. Then Statz lofted a double into left field, bringing in two more runs, and Carey drove in Statz with another double.

Another Run on Error

With Harper on second and Mann on first, in the seventh, Flowers took a ground ball and hit Harper with it as he was going to third. The ball rolled to the edge of the Giants' dug-out and Harper kept going until he was home. That tied the score at 4 to 4 and the Giants still had two men on bases.

At this time Vance showed the world what kind of pitcher he is. You could see him bearing down. First he fanned Mueller. Then he fanned Reese. And Roush was an easy infield out. It was great pitching, to have two men on bases and none out and to get out of it without any more runs being scored.

Virgil Barnes took Henry's place in the Robins's part of that inning and did nothing but fill the bases. He walked two men and Reese bobbled a grounder. That was the end of Barnes. Fred Fitzsimmons was called upon to try to stop any of those three men from scoring. All the luck he had wouldn't get you safely across a deserted street at midnight.

Statz hit him for a single and brought in Butler. Then Carey doubled into left field and cleared the bases of everyone but himself. Herman doubled and brought him in. Partridge singled and sent Herman around. Then Fitzsimmons hit Butler when he came up for the second time and there were two men on bases when De Berry ended the inning with a fly to Mueller.

After that, there was nothing to Harper scored in the ninth, hamm[ering] a triple over Statz's head and c[ame] home when Butler reached in the wrong place for the throw-in. But that was all. Isn't it enough?

Robins' Score

NEW YORK (N. L.)	ab	r	h	po	a	e	BROOKLYN (N. L.)	ab	r	h	po	a	e
Mueller, lf	4	1	0	2	0	0	Statz, cf	4	2	2	3	0	1
Reese, 3b	3	1	1	1	1	1	Carey, rf	5	1	2	1	0	0
Roush, cf	4	0	1	2	0	0	Felix, lf	3	0	0	3	0	0
Hornsby, 2b	2	0	0	1	2	0	Herman, 1b	3	1	1	10	0	0
Terry, 1b	4	0	1	9	1	0	Flowers, ss	4	1	2	0	2	1
Jackson, ss	4	0	0	2	3	0	Partridge, 2b	4	0	1	5	2	1
Harper, rf	2	3	2	3	0	0	Butler, 3b	2	2	1	1	2	1
Cummings, c	3	0	1	2	0	0	DeBerry, c	2	2	0	4	1	0
*Mann	0	0	0	0	0	0	Vance, p	2	1	0	0	1	1
Taylor, c	1	0	0	2	0	0							
Henry, p	2	0	0	0	0	0							
†Ott	1	0	0	0	0	0							
Barnes, p	0	0	0	0	0	0							
Fitzsim'ns, p	0	0	0	0	1	0							
‡Devormer	1	0	0	0	0	0							
Totals	31	5	6	24	8	1	Totals	29	10	9	27	8	5

*Ran for Cummings in seventh inning.
†Batted for Henry in seventh inning.
‡Batted for Fitzsimmons in ninth inning.

New York .... 210 000 101— 5
Brooklyn .... 000 040 60x—10

Two-base hits—Statz, Carey (2), Herman. Three-base hit—Harper. Sacrifices—Hornsby, Cummings, Vance, Felix, Deberry. Double plays—Terry, Jackson and Terry; Hornsby and Terry; Flowers, Partridge and Herman. Left on bases—New York, 5; Brooklyn, 4. Bases on balls—Off Vance, 3; off Henry, 3; off Barnes, 2. Struck out—By Vance, 4; by Henry, 1; by Fitzsimmons, 2. Hit by pitcher—By Vance (Mueller); by Fitzsimmons Butler). Hits—Off Henry, 5 in 6 innings; off Barnes, 0 in 0 (none out in seventh); off Fitzsimmons, 4 in 2. Losing pitcher—Barnes. Umpires—Moran, Rigler and Wilson. Time—1:45.

Briefs

The Robins are now only sixteen games out of first place. It's too bad the season ends to-morrow.

Three of the Robins's five errors were made on Harper. He scored three of the Giants's five runs. We should have more Harpers Or more errors.

The new Roosevelt Hotel in Pittsburgh will probably hang crepe upon its front if the Pirates don't win to-day or to-morrow.

There is a large excavation adjacent to Forbes Field in Pittsburgh which will accommodate a losing Pirate team quite comfortably.

In place of bats, Mueller and Reese should have had a piece of paper and a pencil when they went to bat in the seventh. They needed something besides bats to figure out what the Dazzler was throwing.

If the Robins beat the Giants again to-day, they will get an even break on the season—eleven games each.

Statz evidently never heard of Lot's wife. If he had he wouldn't have turned around in the first inning while on his way from first to second. By this turn of the head the Jigger got himself caught in a snappy double play begun and ended by Bill Terry.

Penn Meets Swarthmore To-day With New Line-Up

Special to the Herald Tribune

PHILADELPHIA, Sept. 30.—With four changes in the line-up since the opening game last week, Pennsylvania will meet Swarthmore on Franklin Field to-morrow.

Gene Kuen, a sophomore, has taken the place of John Smith at right tackle, the latter having a head injury. Joe Lenzner will be at right end in place of Ralph Monk, who has been shifted to utility guard. Johnny Shober will start his first game at quarterback, and Paul Murphy, regular signal caller, has been moved to halfback in Carroll's place. Penn worked out to-day under a hot sun.

The probable line-up:

Pos.	Penn	Swarthmore
L. E.	F. Scull	Haviland
L. T.	Hake	Hallowell
L. G.	Utz	E. McFeely
C.	Olexy	W. McFeely
R. G.	McGinnis	Dellmuth
R. T.	Kuen	Wiegand
R. E.	Lenzner	Petriken
Q. B.	Shober	McGuire
L. H. B.	P. Scull	Maxwell
R. H. B.	Murphy	Wilding
F. B.	Wascolonis	Castle

Referee—Chas. G. Eckles, W. & J. Umpire—E. E. Miller, Penn State. Field judge—[?]. Sangree, Haverford. Linesman—G. [?]kard, Dartmouth.

Mud Hens Defeat Bisons in 1st Junior Series Battle, 5 to 2

TOLEDO, Sept. 30 (AP).—The Toledo Mud Hens, champions of the American Association, upholding the honor of their circuit in the junior world series for the first time in twenty-six years, defeated the Buffalo Bisons, of the International League, 5 to 2 to-day in the twice-postponed inaugural of the series.

It was almost a personal victory for Bobby Veach, who drove in three Toledo runs with a fence-clearing homer, and Jess Barnes, the Toledo twirler, who held the Bisons to five scattered hits. Veach opened the attack with Toledo's first hit, a long triple in the second inning; and the two following singles gave the Mud Hens a two-run lead. Lebourveau led off Toledo's third inning with a single; Marriott was safe on an error, and Veach, a former veteran of the Detroit Tigers, picked out a good one and drove it over the left field wall.

That settled the ball game, the way Barnes was turning back the Bisons, but the International League titleholders managed to squeeze across several runs. In the fourth inning Fisher and Bissonette opened with singles, and Fisher dashed home when Maguire threw wild to first on Andy Cohen's grounder. In the eighth Devine began the inning with a single; Chester Falk, pinch hitting for Stryker, was walked, and Devine came home on Tyson's scorching grounder over second. Maguire dived to catch the ball and tossed it to Cote for a force play at second, but both Toledo players were flat on the ground and there was no chance to head off the Bisons' second and last run.

The official attendance was 9,890. At midnight to-night the two teams and about 500 Toledo rooters left on special trains for Saturday and Sunday games at Buffalo. They will return here Tuesday to resume the series, until one team has won five games.

The score:

BUFFALO (I. L.)	ab	r	h	po	a	e	TOLEDO (A. A.)	ab	r	h	po	a	e
Tyson, cf	4	0	2	1	0	0	Lebourv'u, rf	3	1	1	1	0	0
Carter, lf	3	0	0	0	0	1	Maguire, 2b	3	0	0	3	4	1
Fisher, rf	4	1	1	1	0	0	Marriott, 3b	4	1	0	0	4	0
Bissonett, 1b	4	0	1	11	1	0	Veach, lf	4	2	3	1	0	0
Cohen, ss	4	0	0	1	4	1	Grimes, 1b	3	1	0	12	2	0
Huber, 3b	4	0	0	2	4	0	Koenier, cf	3	0	1	4	0	0
Malone, 2b	3	0	0	5	4	1	O'Neil, c	3	0	0	3	0	0
Devine, c	3	1	1	3	1	0	Cote, ss	3	0	2	2	7	0
Mangum, p	1	0	0	0	0	0	Barnes, p	3	0	0	1	1	0
Stryker, p	1	0	0	0	2	0							
*Falk	0	0	0	0	0	0							
Leverenz, p	0	0	0	0	0	0							
Totals	31	2	5	24	16	3	Totals	29	5	7	27	18	1

*Batted for Stryker in eighth inning.

Buffalo .... 000 100 010—2
Toledo .... 023 000 00x—5

Three-base hit—Veach. Home run—Veach. Left on bases—Toledo, 2; Buffalo, 4. Sacrifice hits—Carter, Maguire. Double plays—Huber, Malone and Bissonette. Struck out—By Barnes, 2; by Mangum, 1; by Stryker, 1. Hits—Off Mangum, 5 in 1 1-3 innings; off Stryker, 1 in 5 2-3; off Leverenz, 1 in 1. Bases on balls—Off Barnes, 1; off Leverenz, 1. Umpires—Guthrie and Finneran. Time—1:36.

Braves Collect 18 Hits And Drub Phillies, 12–2

BOSTON, Sept. 30 (AP).—Boston fell upon the offerings of Tabor and Scott for eighteen hits to-day, and the Braves took the second game of the series from Philadelphia, 12 to 2. Brown's three doubles featured the Boston attack Neither team made an error.

The score:

PHILADELPHIA (N. L.)	ab	r	h	po	a	e	BOSTON (N. L.)	ab	r	h	po	a	e
Sand, 3b	3	1	0	1	3	0	Richbourg, rf	4	2	2	1	0	0
Thompson, 2b	4	0	2	4	4	0	Gautreau, 2b	3	3	1	1	5	0
Williams, rf	4	0	2	1	0	0	J. Smith, cf	4	2	3	3	0	0
W'htstone, 1b	3	0	0	8	0	0	Brown, lf	4	2	3	2	0	0
Leach, cf	4	0	0	5	0	0	Fournier, 1b	2	0	1	13	1	0
Mokan, lf	1	0	0	1	0	0	Farrell, ss	4	1	2	3	2	0
Holman, lf	2	0	1	0	0	0	[illegible], 3b	5	1	2	0	3	0
Jonnard, c	2	0	0	0	1	0	Hogan, c	5	1	3	3	0	0
O'Donnell, c	2	0	0	2	0	0	Genewich, p	4	0	1	1	2	0
Cooney, ss	2	1	1	0	2	0							
Dietrich, ss	1	0	0	0	1	0							
Tabor, p	1	0	0	1	1	0							
Scott, p	2	0	0	1	0	0							
Totals	31	2	6	24	12	0	Totals	35	12	18	27	13	0

Philadelphia .... 100 010 000— 2
Boston .... 340 103 10x—12

Two-base hits—Cooney, Brown (3), J. Smith, Hogan, Genewich. Stolen bases—J. Smith, Brown, Fournier. Sacrifices—Wrightstone, J. Smith, Brown, Farrell, Genewich. Double plays—Thompson and Wrightstone; Dietrich, Thompson and Wrightstone; Genewich, Farrell and Fournier. Left on bases—Philadelphia, 5; Boston, 9. Bases on balls—Off Tabor, 2; off Scott, 3; off Genewich, 2. Struck out—By Scott, 2; by Genewich, 3. Hits—Off Tabor, 6 in 1 1-3 innings; off Scott, 12 in 6 2-3. Hit by pitcher—By Tabor (Fournier). Umpires—Pfirman and McLaughlin. Losing pitcher—Tabor. Time—1:40.

Football Results

Furman, 20; North Carolina State, 0.
Still College, 7; Midland, 0.
Buena Vista, 7; Doane College, 0.
Alabama, 31; Southwestern, Memphis, 0.
North Plainfield H. S., 25; Union, 0.
Central Normal, 66; Vincennes U., 0.
St. Olaf, 14; Augsburg, 7.
St. Cloud Teachers, 7; Moorehead Teachers, 0.
West Orange H. S., 12; Roselle High, 6.
Chattanooga, 44; Western Ky. Teachers, 6.
Hendrix, 27; Little Rock, 10.

Reds Prolong Pennant Fight By Defeating Pirates, 2 to 1

Lucas Holds Leaders to Six Hits Aided by Critz's Sparkling Fielding; Dressen Scores Winning Run on Double Off Aldridge and Two Sacrifices

By The Associated Press

CINCINNATI, Sept. 30.—Checked in all but one inning by the brilliant twirling of Red Lucas and the sensational defensive work of Hughie Critz around second base, the league leading Pittsburgh Pirates lost to Cincinnati 2 to 1, to-day, thereby prolonging the settlement of the superheated National League pennant race, with only two days to go.

Lucas held the Buccaneers to six hits, two of which were bunched in an eighth-inning rally that fell one run short of knotting the score after the Cincinnati clan had fallen on Vic Aldridge in the sixth and sevent frames for the tallies that turned out to be the deciding margin.

The set-back left the Pirates "Dormie two," to borrow a golfing phrase, on the St. Louis Cardinals. Pittsburgh holds a two-game lead and each club has two more to play. One victory for the Pirates will clinch the pennant to-morrow or Sunday in the closing games with the Reds here, while a defeat for St. Louis in either remaining game with the Cubs would put the Cards out of the battle.

While the pitching slants of Lucas were poison for the usually heavy-hitting Pirates to-day, Critz was also constantly annoying to the league leaders. The crack little second sacker was all over his side of the field, dazzling particularly with running stops that choked off Grantham in the fourth and Aldridge in the fifth innings. Hughy also shone at bat, getting a pop-fly double in short right center in the sixth inning that brought Allen over with the first Red run, after Allen and Ford had singled in succession. Although Picinich walked, filling the bases, the scoring ended there as Aldridge fanned his pitching rival, Lucas.

Aldridge yielded the second run in the seventh inning on Dressen's double and successive sacrifice flies by Walker and Pipp. He was replaced by a pinch hitter in the eighth and Miljus twirled against the Reds in their final turn at bat.

The only successful Pirate sortie, in the eighth, was started with a walk to Joe Harris. Brickell, batting for Gooch, forced him, but Earl Smith, batting for Aldridge, singled to center. Brickell was called safe at third after nearly being caught on a snap throw by Pininich, who let out so vigorous a protest that he was ejected from the game. When the storm subsided and Hargrave had gone behind the plate, Brickell scored on L. Waner's force-out of Comorosky, who was running for Smith. Barnhardt revived Pirate hopes with another hit, but Paul Waner, the League's leading batter, failed in the pinch, tapping to Ford and forcing Barnhardt.

The Pirates got one hit in each of the first four innings, but their only scoring chance, coming in the third when Lloyd Waner tripled with two out, went glimmering as Barnhardt skied to Walker.

The score:

PITTSBURGH (N. L.)	ab	r	h	po	a	e	CINCINNATI (N. L.)	ab	r	h	po	a	e
L. Waner, cf	4	0	1	2	0	0	Dressen, 3b	3	1	2	1	1	0
Barnhart, lf	4	0	2	2	0	0	Walker, rf	3	0	0	2	0	0
P. Waner, rf	4	0	0	5	0	0	Pipp, 1b	3	0	0	11	2	0
Wright, ss	4	0	0	1	3	0	Bressler, lf	4	0	0	3	0	0
Traynor, 3b	4	0	2	1	2	0	Allen, cf	4	1	1	4	0	0
Grantham, 2b	4	0	0	0	2	0	Ford, ss	4	0	2	2	6	1
Harris, 1b	2	0	0	10	0	0	Critz, 2b	4	0	3	3	5	0
Gooch, c	2	0	0	2	0	0	Picinich, c	1	0	0	0	0	0
*Brickell	1	1	0	0	0	0	Hargrave, c	0	0	0	0	0	0
Spencer, c	0	0	0	1	0	0	Lucas, p	3	0	0	1	3	0
Aldridge, p	2	0	0	0	2	0							
†E. Smith	1	0	1	0	0	0							
‡Comorsky	0	0	0	0	0	0							
Miljus, p	0	0	0	0	0	0							
Totals	32	1	6	24	9	0	Totals	29	2	8	27	17	0

*Batted for Gooch in eighth inning.
†Batted for Aldridge in eighth inning.
‡Ran for E. Smith in eighth inning.

Pittsburgh .... 000 000 010—1
Cincinnati .... 000 001 10x—2

Two-base hits—Critz, Dressen. Three-base hit—L. Waner. Sacrifices—Picinich, Walker, Pipp. Double play—Ford, Critz and Pipp. Left on bases—Pittsburgh, 5; Cincinnati, 8. Bases on balls—Off Aldridge, 1; off Lucas, 1. Struck out—By Aldridge, 1; by Miljus, 1. Hits—Off Aldridge, 8 in 7 innings; off Miljus, 0 in 1. Hit by pitcher—By Aldridge (Dressen). Umpires—Reardon, McCormick and Quigley. Losing pitcher—Aldridge. Time—1:36.

Leading Five Batsmen In Each Major League

AMERICAN LEAGUE

Player and club.	G.	AB.	R.	H.	Pct.
Heilmann, Detroit	139	493	104	192	.389
Simmons, Phila.	103	394	82	152	.386
Gehrig, N. Y.	154	581	148	218	.375
Fothergill, Detroit	140	519	91	187	.360
Ruth, N. Y.	150	537	157	192	.358

Leader a year ago to-day—Manush, Detroit, .378.

NATIONAL LEAGUE

Player and club.	G.	AB.	R.	H.	Pct.
P. Waner, Pitts.	154	617	113	234	.379
Hornsby, N. Y.	153	562	132	202	.359
L. Waner, Pitts.	148	619	132	217	.350
Stephenson, Chi.	151	576	99	197	.342
Traynor, Pitts.	148	568	92	193	.340

Leader a year ago to-day—Hargrave, Cincinnati, .354.

Johnson Berates Landis, White Sox For Opposition

CHICAGO, Sept. 30 (AP).—Ban Johnson, president of the American League trained his guns on the Chicago White Sox and Commissioner Landis to-day, berating them for lack of co-operation and accusing them of deliberately attempting to embarrass the league.

The former "czar of baseball," who refused to say when his resignation as head of the league would become effective, praised the seven other members of the American League for "their common sense and business judgment in maintaining their ordinary relations with their presidential office.

"The only club which has given evidence of deliberate intent to embarrass the league, as conducted from headquarters has been the Chicago organization, which might have been expected to grasp at such an opportunoty, since it has been almost continuously out of step with the majority of the league for a period of years," the statement declared.

"The childish spite and rebellion on the part of the Chicago club has been matched, even outdone, by petty action of the office of the commissioner of baseball."

"Nothing to say, nothing at all," said Landis. "I have a copy of his statement."

The American League head's complaint of lack of co-operation was for the period since he offered his resignation as president last July. He said he would not quit the office until he had the business of the league in good shape.

Charles A. Comiskey, president of the White Sox, said he was amused with Johnson's statement and issued the following reply:

"The outburst of Johnson to-day is amusing. In view of his usual procedure, he probably will do the verbal somersault and deny to-morrow what he said to-day."

Hagenlacher Wins Second Block in 18.2 Match With Cochran

CHICAGO, Sept. 30 (AP).—Eric Hagenlacher, of Germany, to-night strengthened his grip on Welker Cochrane's world 18.2 blakline billiard crown, by winning the second block of their titular 1,500-point match to gain a lead of 1,000 to 708. Hagenlacher won the second 500-point block, 500 to 370. He also won the first, played last night, 500 to 332.

Starting from his unfinished run of last night, Hagenlacher scored only four before he missed an easy left-handed draw shot; thus at the end of the seventeen innings, the total score was: Hagenlacher, 504; Cochran, 332.

Mingling an assortment of pretty bank, time and masse shots, Cochran clicked off 54 points for a grand match total of 386 in the eighteenth inning, or the first of to-night's block. Hagenlacher ran three in that inning for a grand total of 507, bobbling on a kiss shot.

Gathering the ivories by a remarkable three-cushion shot in the nineteenth inning, Hagenlacher scored a run of 135 for a match total of 642. Time and again the challenger nursed the balls, and when apparently befuddled, he used masse and bank shots to group them. He missed his 136th try with a two-cushioned draw.

Cochran was in poor form, and in the nineteenth and twentieth innings scored but ten points for a total match score of 396. Hagenlacher bagged only ten in the twentieth inning for a total of 652.

Cochrane failed to tally in the twenty-first inning, but gathered 45 points in the next four, to total 441. He averaged only 21 4-5 points an inning to-night, as compared with Hagenlacher's average of 46 4-5. Hagenlacher scored 84 in the twenty-first and 2 in the twenty-second, for a grand total of 738. A long two-cushion draw shot along the length of the table by Cochran in the twenty-second drew the loudest applause of both nights.

The grand total score at the end of the twenty-fifth inning was: Cochrane, 527; Hagenlacher, 907. The champion scored 22 in the twenty-third; 22 in the twenty-fourth, and 38 in the next, while Hagenlacher picked up 113, 17 and 39 in the same innings.

The champion's stroke improved in the next two frames and he scored his two best runs of the match, 85 and 94, bringing his total to 706. Hagenlacher missed two easy shots after running 20 in the twenty-sixth inning and 11 in the twenty-seventh.

After sparring for an opening, Hagenlachere won the second block with a run of 59 in the thirtieth inning.

Ferguson Knocks Out Pultz

PITTSFIELD, Mass., Sept. 30 (AP).—Tracy Ferguson, of Northford, Conn., knocked out Oscar Pultz, of Philmont, N. Y., in the fifth round of a scheduled ten-round bout here to-night. Pultz was knocked down six times in the three rounds before the knockout.

PACIFIC COAST LEAGUE

Hollywood, 8; Seattle, 7.
Oakland, 11; San Francisco, 2.
Sacramento, 10; Los Angeles, 4.
Portland, 8; Missions, 1.

STANDING OF THE CLUBS

	W.	L.	Pct.		W.	L.	Pct.
Oakland	118	74	.615	Portland	93	94	.497
San Fran.	105	88	.544	Hollyw'd	90	103	.466
Seattle	97	90	.519	Missions	85	108	.440
Sac'mento	98	94	.510	L. Angeles	79	114	.409

Voigt Keeps D. C. Golf Title

WASHINGTON, Sept. 30 (AP).—George J. Voigt, of Washington, whose amateur golf standing was contested this summer unsuccessfully by the District of Columbia links authorities, captured the District's amateur championship yesterday for the third consecutive time.

YANKS RULE 6 TO 5 FAVORITES ON EVE OF SERIES

HOYT P. • MOORE P. • LAZZERI INF. • RUTH OF. • HUGGINS MGR. • GEHRIG INF. • PENNOCK P. • MEUSEL OF. • REUTHER P.

YANKS

EVENING HERALD SPORTS

AN INDEPENDENT NEWSPAPER

VOL. LII 3 CTS. TUESDAY, OCTOBER 4, 1927 Hotels and Trains Five Cents NO. 289

SHOCKER P. • GRABOWSKI C. • PASCHAL OF. • COMBS OF. • SHAWKEY P. • KOENING INF. • DUGAN INF. • BENGOUGH C. • THOMAS P. • COLLINS C. • PIPGRAS P.

Saints' Defeat of Cards Arouses Trojan Spirit

RIVAL SQUADS ON EDGE FOR OPENER TOMORROW

By JAMES L. KILGALLEN

International News Service Staff Correspondent

PITTSBURG, Pa., Oct. 4.—With Babe Ruth and his slugging ball club in town, swinging bats in menacing fashion in practice at Forbes field, hotels crowding up with visitors from nearby cities and ticket speculators operating on all sides, the bustling city of Pittsburg was as excited today over the impending world series, which opens tomorrow, as Chicago was on the eve of the Tunney-Dempsey fight.

"Pittsburg will take those Yanks," was the confident prediction of the home town rooters.

YANKEES FAVORITES

New York was a 6 to 5 favorite to win the series in the odds quoted by the gambling element this morning, and unless the National league partisans come to the scratch with heavier financial support in the next 24 hours the Yankees will rule even stronger favorites when they take the field tomorrow.

Every train into Pittsburg today brought more visitors eager to see the annual baseball classic. Judge Kenesaw M. Landis, the silver-haired commissioner of baseball, is here; so are scores of big league players, an army of sports writers and the usual run of sports luminaries.

Hotel rooms are unavailable, even at $15 a day. Guests are glad to sleep in hallways of the hotels, and most rooms quarter from two to six persons.

Manager Miller Huggins of the New York club and Donie Bush, the Pirates' leader, both expressed themselves as confident of victory. Huggins indicated he would use Waite Hoyt as his pitcher in the opening game and Bush said he would start either Ray Kremer, his great right hander, or Vic Aldridge.

Bush gave the impression that he would send out on to the field tomorrow the same lineup that won the pennant. This would mean that Kiki Cuyler, his great outfielder and a star of the 1925 world series, will sit on the bench and that Clyde Barnhart will hold down the left field position.

THE CUYLER CASE

There is considerable feeling in Pittsburg over the Cuyler matter. Many Pittsburg fans think Bush should play Cuyler. But Bush seems to be adamant. He has been "off" this sensational performer since he was forced to fine him $50 for failing to slide to second in a game nearly two months ago.

The fans, however, are looking to the spectacular Waner brothers, Paul and Lloyd, to more than hold up the outfield strength of the Pirates. They think, in fact, that the Waners will hit as hard in this series as will Ruth and the other New York home run hitter, Lou Gehrig.

HEAVY HITTING

No series in baseball history has brought into the limelight heavier hitting clubs than the Pirates and the Yanks and great will be the disappointment if the fences of Forbes field and the Yankee stadium are

(CONTINUED ON NEXT PAGE)

Fans Line Up to Purchase Bleacher Tickets for Game

PITTSBURG, Oct. 4.—While the statisticians and dopesters busied themselves with forecasts as to the likely winner of the world series, the average fan ranked this as secondary. His main and only concern at present was getting hold of one of the 40,000 pastboards.

At an early hour this morning dozens of youths formed outside Forbes field to be first in line when the 4000 bleacher tickets go on sale at $1.10. Few of them expected to see the games, but Pittsburg is a city of business and its youth have an eye for business. They will sell their places later at a premium.

U. S. Golf Stars Lead in Canadian Women's Tourney

TORONTO, Oct. 4.—Glenna Collett if Providence, R. I., had a 77 yesterday to lead the field in the qualifying round of the Canadian women's open golf championship.

Two other players from the United States, Helen Payson of Portland, Me., and Virginia Van Wie of Chicago, were second and third with rounds of 80 and 83 respectively. Mrs. Harry Pressler of Los Angeles qualified with an 88.

DRAKE ELEVEN IN FINAL PRACTICE

By International News Service

DES MOINES, Oct. 4.—The Drake university Bulldogs were to take their final workout on the home field this afternoon, after which they will entrain for the east for their meeting Saturday with the navy at Annapolis. The Bulldogs will stop over at Harper's Ferry, Va., for practice Thursday, according to plans.

5 ST. MARY'S STARS ON HOSPITAL LIST

By Pacific Coast News Service

OAKLAND, Cal., Oct. 4.—Five members of the St. Mary's football team which defeated Stanford Saturday by a score of 16 to 0, were on the hospital list today.

Fair and Cool Prospect for Opening Game

By International News Service

PITTSBURG, Oct. 4.—"Fair and moderately cool" weather was forecast today for the opening game of the world series here tomorrow. Ideal weather will continue through Thursday, the local weather bureau predicted.

Crisp air and clear skies greeted the Pirates and Yankees today as they prepared for their practice workouts, curtailed by rain yesterday.

Willie Hunter Is Winner in Tourney at Fox Hills Club

Willie Hunter, Brentwood professional, who recently won the Southern California open championship continues to play spectacular golf. In the pro sweepstakes staged yesterday at the Fox Hills Country club Hunter shot an even 70 to finish first and win most of the $100 in cash offered by officials of the Fox Hills club.

Second honors went to Ed Dudley who had 74, while Tom Stevens, Dick Linares and Ted Lampton tied for third with 75 each.

The pros all agreed that Fox Hills was a very delightful test of golf.

LLOYD WANER SETS TWO NEW RECORDS

PITTSBURG, Oct. 4.—Lloyd Waner, sensational young Pittsburg outfielder, broke two major league records and almost equaled another his first year as a member of the Pittsburg Pirates. The Oklahoma phenom was the first player in the history of the major leagues to get 200 hits his first season. He broke Johnny Tobin's record for singles by getting 198. The old mark was 179.

S. F. RING STAR PASSES BAR TEST

SAN FRANCISCO, Oct. 4.—Armand Emanuel, local light heavyweight, who made quite a hit with eastern fight fans when he fought the anti-climax bout at the Tunney-Dempsey show, was today informed that he had passed the California state examinations for admission to the bar.

RYAN DEFEATED BY CANZONERI IN BOUT

NEW YORK, Oct. 4.—Tony Canzoneri of Brooklyn handed Tommy Ryan of Buffalo a one-sided defeat here last night in a 10-round bout. Canzoneri had an edge in every round of the match.

EXPECT 75,000 AT CAL., ST. MARY'S GAME

By Pacific Coast News Service

BERKELEY, Oct. 4.—The California-St. Mary's football game here next Saturday is expected to draw a crowd of 75,000 spectators.

S. C. WILL FACE TOUGH FIGHT WITH STANFORD

By HARRY CULVER

THEY'VE clamped the lid down on football at University of Southern California. Almost bowled over by St. Mary's defeat of Stanford but realizing on second thought that their job in the Cardinal game at Palo Alto Oct. 15 has been made harder by the upset of Stanford's highly touted steam roller, the Trojan gridiron master minds have closed like clams and issued orders for strictly secret drill against a squad using Stanford plays for the next two weeks at Bovard field.

Howard Jones, the big boss of the outfit, isn't overlooking the opening conference game with the Oregon Aggies Saturday at the Coliseum, but he doesn't fear the Farmers. The O. A. C. squad uses Notre Dame plays and the Trojans ruined that system in the Santa Clara game. So most of the time in the three-hour drills at the Trojan stamping ground are being spent priming for the Cardinal steamroller.

TOUGHER SITUATION

"St. Mary's victory only makes it tougher for us," is the cry you hear all around the Southern California campus. And Jones echoes the tune to the close harmony of Cliff Herd, Leo Calland and Bill Hunter, his assistants in coaching the Trojan hopefuls.

Cliff Herd, Jones' righthand man, who has largely made the Trojan backs what they have appeared to be in the two Coliseum games, and one of the keenest students of the game, went north to scout the Cardinals in their game with St. Mary's, which turned out disastrously for "Pop" Warner's favored athletes.

And here is what Cliff Herd had to say before the lid went down in yesterday's practice:

"Stanford still has the greatest team on the coast, in my estimation!"

Don't think that Herd is just trying to cover up a bad situation and convince the Trojan following that the St. Mary's victory was nothing at all, spreading around a lot of propaganda to make the Trojans short-enders. Read on:

'LICK ANY TEAM'

"St. Mary's could have licked any team on the coast last Saturday. They were 'right.' But I maintain that Stanford could come back and bury them next Saturday.

"The Cardinals under-rated St. Mary's. They really didn't think the Saints had much. But St. Mary's went in there fighting from the opening whistle. Stanford didn't have her dauber up. And that 16 to 0 upset was the result.

"St. Mary's was what we call 'hot.' They put on the best exhibition of ball hawking I ever saw. You know, on Warner's reverse plays, several backs handle the ball. Well, St. Mary's players would come through fighting and tackle the Cards so hard they would drop that ball. Thirteen fumbles in all were made that way, and they weren't ordinary fumbles. St. Mary's hit their man before he could get the ball, and the pigskin just popped up in the air. Every time it fell, there was a black sweater on top of it.

"St. Mary's never let down. They were fighting for that first victory over Stanford, and they got it. There was one turning point of the game. After the Saints had a 13 to 0 lead, Wilton returned the kickoff 75 yards up the field, but a Saint grabbed him before he got across the goal line.

"Then the Saint line rose up and held like a stone wall. Stanford worked the ball to the one-foot line and then gave it to Hoffman. 'Biff' failed to make an inch, and right there Stanford's back was broken. They could not match St. Mary's great spirit.

"But get this. 'Pop' Warner and Stanford are fightin mad right now. They are laying for us a week from next Saturday, and our chances were hurt 50 per cent by St. Mary's victory and our lopsided win over Santa Clara. The Broncos had a lot of fight taken out of them in that stiff California game of theirs last week, and that's why they didn't give us the competition.

"We really didn't want a score like that. I guess Howard made a lot of substitutions, putting in second, third and fourth stringers to keep the score down, but the Broncos were all tired out.

WILL COME BACK

"Stanford will come back a million in the next two weeks and Warner will have the best team he has ever had at Palo Alto ready to trot out against us Oct. 15.

"Don't let anybody kid you that we can beat Stanford. They have the edge on us mentally now, for while our boys think they're pretty good after that Santa Clara showing, Stanford's boys are out to beat us if it is the last thing they ever do.

"Our only chance is to fight Stanford like St. Mary's did. If the boys show the spirit and will to win that the Saints did, we stand a chance."

Howard Jones echoed Herd's thought.

"It only makes it tougher for us," said the Trojan boss. "I wouldn't detract from St. Mary's victory, but I will say that I consider Stanford just as tough, no, even tougher, than I ever did, and all summer I've been thinking about how good they were going to be.

HAVE TO FIGHT

"The boys will have to fight with everything they've got to beat Stanford, because Warner will have a changed squad up there in two weeks.

"And don't for a minute think he won't. Warner is pointing for us now."

Just then, Herd came over to see if Jones wanted the varsity squad to run against the "Oregon Aggie Juniors," a goof squad using Aggie plays as brought back by Scout Jeff Cravath.

"No sirree, run 'em against Stanford plays. You might just warm them up a bit against Aggie plays, but when they get going, use the Stanford stuff," hollered Jones.

And that's just an indication of

(CONTINUED ON NEXT PAGE)

Grid Star, Boxer Become Bar Members

SAN FRANCISCO, Oct. 4.—Two famous athletes will be admitted to the California bar Friday, it was learned today. They are Armand Emmanuel, heavyweight boxer who fought in one of the preliminaries to the Tunney-Dempsey fight at Chicago, and Don Nichols, who was captain of the University of California football team in 1923.

HUNTER BEATS POOLEY AT L. A. NETS

(CONTINUED FROM PAGE ONE)

an easy opponent in Lee Yates, Manual Arts high school boy.

Miss Kea Bouman, women's champion of Holland and one of Europe's leading tennis players, defeated Mary Taylor of Pasadena, 6-0, 6-1, putting her in the third round of the woman's singles.

Ed Berry of U. S. C. beat Hardy, 3-6, 6-4, 6-2 in another man's single match.

Marion Williams, Southern California champion and lone local hope against the two invading stars, drew a bye today after showing remarkable form in defeating Miss Ruth McCabe, 6-0, 6-3, yesterday. Mrs. May Sutton Bundy, veteran of the courts, and women's national champion of years ago, was also slated to rest after eliminating Mrs. Neville, a non-ranking player, 6-0, 6-1.

BRILLIANT TENNIS

Brilliant tennis marked the opening of the greatest tennis tournament ever staged on the coast yesterday at the local club.

Both Alonso and Hunter cut loose on their opponents and showed no mercy in mowing them down. Alonso especially played as though he were in a championship match instead of the first round, and seemed to take delight in showing up Vic DeLory of Palomar Tennis club his opponent, by 6-1, 6-0 scores. DeLory tried hard and engaged the Spaniard in some brilliant rallies, but was no match for the hard-playing invader.

Hunter got away to an easy start over Rivierre in his opening match, but became nettled over Rivierre's easy serve, which barely cut over the net with a peculiar slice, in the second set, and dropped three games to the local player. Hunter displayed a wonderful forehand drive that supplied a thrill for the gallery during the match.

Molla Mallory, seven times women's national champion, cut down diminutive Dorothy Robinson of Pasadena, 6-0, 6-1, running her opponent ragged with well-placed shots to the base line. The Pasadena girl gave Mrs. Mallory an excellent rally on each point, but the veteran always won out in the end.

WORLD'S SERIES FANS IN L. A. ARE DIVIDED

As the time approaches for the start of the world's series Los Angeles fans are very evenly divided as to the outsome of the battle between the Pittsburg Pirates and New York Yankees.

Those favoring the Yankees are depending upon the slugging of Combs, Ruth, Gehrig and Lazzeri to make their predictions stand up, while the followers of the Pirates place their faith in the greater speed of the Pittsburg club, splendid pitching and the belief that Paul and Lloyd Waner, former coast league players, will be the outstanding stars of the series.

Following are the expressions of a number of local fans concerning the outcome of the series:

CHARLES A. WEBER, secretary Los Angeles baseball club—I have a lot of respect for the Pirates, but the Yanks have too much power for them. Any club with Ruth, Gehrig, Meusel, Lazzeri and Combs must be given an edge over any opponent. I am backing the Yanks for the cakes and coffee at odds of 7 to 5.

OSCAR P. REICHOW, business manager Los Angeles baseball club—In a short series give me the club that is at fighting pitch. The Pirates have had to battle every step of the way and their momentum will carry them into the series at top speed. They have an edge on pitching, I believe, and that is a big factor. I like Pittsburg.

MARTY KRUG, manager Los Angeles baseball club—It should be a hard fought series with both sides a bit rough on the pitchers. The Yanks have a little more punch and their pitching and fielding is on a par with the Pirates, so I think it is logical to make them favorites. They figure to win.

CHARLES A. BAUM, secretary Hollywood baseball club—The Yanks have the wallop and in modern baseball it's the wallop that counts. Barring Ray Kremer, I don't give any of the Pirate pitchers a chance to check them. Ray might win one game. Otherwise I wouldn't be surprised to see it over in four contests.

LES HENRY, well known local A. A. U. official—I'll take Pittsburg. They look like a good bet to me.

GEORGE BLAKE, Los Angeles boxing authority—It should be a great series with Pittsburg on top.

FRED OLNEY, Los Angeles A. C. athlete—Ruth and Gehrig are sure to bring victory to the Yanks. Don't believe the Pirate pitchers can stop them.

MICKEY REID, well known local sportsman—Give me the Yanks.

CHARLEY KEPPEN, athletic director, L. A. A. C.—With the short series Pittsburg should win. Donie Bush has a mighty smart ball club.

GEORGE KLAWITER, handball star—Miller Huggins should have no trouble in bringing home the bacon. I think the Yanks are entirely too strong for Bush's boys.

CHARLEY PADDOCK, famous sprinter—Pittsburg for mine.. Waner's speed should offset the hitting of Ruth and Gehrig.

DEAN SNYDER, Olympic Boxing association—I'll take the Yanks.

EDDIE O'CONNELL, Thatcher school athletic instructor—Pittsburg has an edge in the pitching department. This should offset the hitting power of the Yanks. I like the Pirates.

HARRY SHINN, well known local sportsman—New York for mine.

ZACK FARMER, general manager Los Angeles Coliseum—Why bring that up? U. S. C. looks good to me.

ERNIE CLARK, well known boxing referee—Yanks. Watch 'em wade through. I don't think the Pirates will have a look-in. New York, with its tremendous hitting power, is too strong for the Pirates.

GUY GIFFIN, Los Angeles sportsman—I like the Yanks.

HARRISON HANSHUE, Western Air Mail official—Give me the punch in the Yankees.

BILL RANFT, L. A. A. C. handball star—Huggins has too much experience in world's series. He'll skipped the Yanks to another victory.

DR. WALLACE DODGE, well known sportsman—Pittsburg. I like those short-end bets.

HAL ROACH, motion picture producer—New York.

GEORGE CULVER, L. A. A. C. member—Donie Bush should put up a good fight. He has a smart ball club and a fast one. They should outmaneuver the Yanks.

NYE WILLIAMS, well known sportsman—I'll take the Pirates.

Bar Minor League Stars From Playing Winter Baseball

OAKLAND, Oct. 4.—All minor league ball players are prohibited from playing winter ball under penalty of expulsion from organized baseball, the Oakland management was advised today by Commissioner K. M. Landis. The commissioner's ruling came in answer to a query from the Oakland owners relative to certain youngsters owned by the clubs who desired to play winter ball with their home-town clubs during the off season.

HOTEL GOLFERS IN DEL MONTE EVENT

DEL MONTE, Oct. 4.—The annual California Hotel Men's golf tournament will feature the convention of the California State Hotel association at Hotel Del Monte, Oct. 13-14.

Del Monte links will be the scene of action Oct. 13 and the divot digging will be transferred to Pebble Beach on the following day.

JOHNNY M'CORY TO FACE PABLO DANO

By Pacific Coast News Service

SAN FRANCISCO, Oct. 4.—Johnny McCory, San Antonio flyweight, will clash with Pablo Dano, Filipino boxer, in a scheduled 10-round bout here tomorrow night.

RAIN GIVES YANKS ADDED EDGE IN SERIES

All Set for Your Games Returns

New York, American League champions, open at Pittsburgh, National League champions, in the first game of the 1927 world series tomorrow. The game will start at 10:30 a. m. Pacific coast time and the Evening Express has arranged to lead the entire Western field in covering the event for its subscribers and local sport fans. Two score boards equipped with "megaphones" will be in operation. The usual free Express board will be on Broadway, between Second and Third, in the window of Scott's Department Store. The other will be a pay affair run in conjunction with the Philharmonic Auditorium on a Play-O-Graff board. Then there will be the Express extras. Always First—All Ways.

Los Angeles Evening Express
SPORTS SECTION
LOS ANGELES, CAL., TUESDAY, OCTOBER 4, 1927

Yanks Enter 5th World Series

When Miller Huggins leads his band of New York Yankee fence busters into the world series, starting tomorrow, it will be his fifth classic in seven years. The Yankees have been victorious only once in their four previous attempts at lifting the big prize. That was in 1923 when Babe Ruth got the range with his big bat, and "brute" force won over the master mind of John McGraw. The Yanks hope to revive the prestige of the American circuit by breaking the two-time hold of the National Leaguers. Pittsburgh won in 1925 and St. Louis won last year. It has taken seven games to decide the championship in the last three series.

MEUSEL

SHOCKER

KOENIG

GEHRIG

RUTH

PENNOCK

PASHAL

BENGOUGH

HOYT

SHAWKEY

LAZZERI

COLLINS

COMBS

DUGAN

PIPGRAS

HUGGINS

The INSIDE TRACK With Sid Ziff

REMEMBER "Uncle" Charley Moran? Coached the "Praying Colonels" of Centre College some years back. Just a dinky, little place buried somewhere in Kentucky. Couldn't ever find it on the map without help. Comes a game one season with lordly old Harvard, full of tradition and all that sort of thing. What happens? Centre wins. And how they did make over "Uncle" Charley. Papers all over the country carried reams about him.

'POP' WARNER

Across the bay from San Francisco there is a diminutive seat of learning called St. Mary's College. Endowed by Irish Catholics. Turn back to 1920. A bashful institution, taking what it could get athletically. A baseball player coached the football team. A handful of candidates.

There was a game that year with the University of California. It was just one of those things. Score, 127 to 0. St. Mary's blushed in humiliation. Where was that Irish dander? About this time a young man named "Slip" Madigan was looking around for more worlds to conquer. He had graduated from Notre Dame, an all-American center who only weighed 145 pounds. Went on to Columbia High School in Portland and was splashing modestly in his little puddle.

"Slip" Madigan discovered St. Mary's and St. Mary's discovered "Slip" Madigan about one and the same time. They decided to cast lots together for better or for worse. Not much salary. Not much glory. Just expectation. For "Slip" Madigan and St. Mary's College.

That year California again defeated St. Mary's. The score was 46 to 0. Not so terrible. The following year it was 27 to 0, then 17 to 7, then 6 to 0, and last year the worm turned completely. It was 26 to 6 in St. Mary's favor. "Slip" had come steadily forward. His teams were better and better. By 1926 the "Little Brother" had trounced the "Big Brother."

All the while Madigan was making his bid into bigger things. He kept tab upon the opposition that was supposed to be St. Mary's size. He made beating Santa Clara an annual affair. He won six times out of seven.

"Slip" Madigan was accomplishing things. He managed to work his way into the Stanford schedule. Got licked 9 to 0. Close score. Took three place kicks to beat him. U. S. C. lost a game with Stanford. It was the year of the big athletic break. Ever on the alert, Madigan begged for the emergency date. "We'll play you," he implored.

U. S. C. was primed for its biggest year. St. Mary's flogged Troy. The score was 14 to 10. Here was Madigan, a man steadily doing things. Still his row was no easier to hoe than ever. True, several Eastern colleges began to hear of him and made him flattering offers. But no universal appeal.

Last Saturday St. Mary's defeated Stanford. The score was 16 to 0. Think of it. Terribly decisive. But is much credit coming Madigan's way? Is he being acknowledged as was "Uncle" Charley Moran? Not so as you could notice. The man is being positively ignored. Nine people out of 10 do not know who he is. Madigan is the most versatile coach on the coast. Given California, Stanford and Southern California material he would be a wizard.

Why, he goes out for football practice and discovers a score or so candidates. California, Stanford and U. S. C. have armies. He dresses up students in the uniforms of substitutes so as to "have a moral effect." He has no substitutes. He defeated Stanford with only two changes in his entire lineup. They were halfbacks.

"Slip" could go elsewhere and get more money, more fame.

(CONT. ON THIRD PAGE, SPORTS SEC.)

Big Ticket Scandal Hits World Series

BASEBALL FANS RAVE, SCALPERS GRAB 'DUCATS'

By LEMUEL F. PARTON

Special Correspondent of the Los Angeles Evening Express. (Copyright, 1927)
By Consolidated Press Association

PITTSBURGH, Oct. 4.—Baseball writers assembled here in legion for the world series of 1927 were guileless enough yesterday to write optimistically about the ticket situation and the weather.

Ti[illegible]ll bets were "coppered" when a rearing big ticket row and a rainstorm came over the horizon together.

MILLER HUGGINS

The rain seems to be just about as wet as that which made the series here a swimming tournament two years ago. The big fuss over the tickets appears to be something more than the annual squawk emanating from the world series. Ticket speculators have blossomed suddenly everywhere, with advertisements in the papers, and apparently with a fat share of choice tickets on hand.

But the rain and the ticket row have not in the least dampened Pittsburgh's enthusiasm for its winning ball team or its conviction that it will be astride the world after it meets the Yankees.

Owen J. (Donie) Bush, manager of the Pirates, can lay claim to anything laying around loose in Pittsburgh. This earnest, energetic and sagacious little man has climbed clear to the top in his year

(CONTINUED ON NEXT PAGE)

Want a Laugh? Read Lardner in Express

Ring Lardner, the greatest basegall humorist in the country, will cover the funny side of the 1927 world series for the Evening Express readers.

The first article will appear in the sport section of the Evening Express tomorrow.

Lardner knows baseball as well as any writer in the game today. He possesses that heaven gift faculty of being able to pick the humor out of pathos; to see the comical angle in a serious play and to make you laugh even if your favorite team lost.

In addition Lardner is an author of note—not bank notes, as that would be counterfeiting.

The addition of Ring Lardner to the great list of writing stars will give the Evening Express the champion and allow it to retain its title of

Always First—All Ways.

Odds Going Down On Yanks to Win

PITTSBURGH, Oct. 4.—The Yankees are the favorites in the betting here, with the odds at 8 to 10 that the Huggins crew will win the world series, starting tomorrow. A week ago it was thought that the odds would be about 10 to 7. Since Saturday the home guard has been getting steamed up and Pirate money is less gun shy. It is thought plenty of even-money bets will be placed by tomorrow. The hide-busting Waner brothers have been picked by the Pittsburgh fans to offset the heavy clouting of Babe Ruth and Lou Gehrig. These lads from Oklahoma, in their first season with the Pirates, have attained popularity with the fans comparable to that of Hans Wagner in his best days.

Paul Waner, with a batting average of .379, leads the National League. Lloyd Waner, batting .355, was the surprise of the season. Slight of stature, a self-effacing lad with no spectacular appeal, he was lost in the shuffle at the start. His brilliant fielding and hitting brought him rapidly to the front.

WOMEN BATTLE IN TORONTO GOLF

By Associated Press

TORONTO, Oct. 4.—The possibility of another meeting between Miss Glenna Collett of Providence, R. I., and Mrs. Alexa Stirling Fraser, now of Ottawa, Ontario, stood out today in the pairings for first-round matches in the Canadian women's golf championship being played over the Lambdon Country Club. Miss Ada McKenzie of Toronto is the defending champion.

The two former American champions are in the upper half of the draw, and if they are successful in their first two matches will come together in one of the semi-final attractions.

Injuries Hit Bears Before Saint Game

By Associated Press

BERKELEY, Oct. 4.—The injury hoodoo that has been following the University of California football team around all season, made itself felt again last night when Don Koch, guard, and Ned Green, tackle, **were added to the hospital list.**

Koch, who played a great game in the Nevada contest last Saturday, received a broken jaw and probably will be out for several weeks, while Green, who was injured in the third play of the contest with the wolfpack, is laid up with a bruised side. Koch's place has been taken by **Louis Pitto, who has recovered** from early season hurts, while Green's shoes at tackle have been filled by Elmer Gerken of Modesto.

Indications are that there will be an attendance of 75,000, a complete sell-out for Saturday's game with St. Mary's, the Saints' great game against Stanford, and the improved **play of the Bears against Nevada.**

SOGGY FIELD EXPECTED TO SLOW UP BUCS

Kremer for Pirates and Hoyt For New York Favored as Opening Pitchers

PENNOCK IS READY

By JOHN B. FOSTER

Special Leased Wire to Evening Express (Copyright, 1927)

PITTSBURGH, Oct. 4.—All the experts were out with their magnifying glasses today at the Pirates baseball park for careful inspection to determine whether the diamond will be soggy or dry by the time the first world series game is played on Wednesday.

Rain and the world series are coincident in Pittsburgh. That means something more than rain in some cities. The Pittsburgh baseball ground absorbs moisture and holds it tight. The composition of the earth is pasty — black paste that is slewy and slippery.

JOE HARRIS

The playing field of the diamond can bake hard in summer when there is no rain, but even then cuts up badly. Unfortunately it has rained hard at the start of the week. There should be two days of good sun to make the field snappy again. If there are not two good drying days the field will be slow, and if it is slow it will help the fielders.

PLAY SYSTEM DIFFERS

The condition of the field may be a small thing, but it is not. The styles of the Yankees and Pirates as batters are contingent somewhat upon the surface of the ground. The Pirates bat a great many ground hits and they beat some of them out, because of their speed as runners. If the field is sluggish the fielders will be able to handle the ball well and the runners have less edge to do their sprinting.

Babe Ruth wishes to observe that he is all fed up on this psychology stuff, to which so much attention is paid by his fellow literary artists.

"I've batted against all these guys," he announced to the writer. "If they don't pitch 'em inside and around the knee I can hit 'em. Besides that. I never heard of any Cy Young on this Pittsburgh team. I've

(CONTINUED ON NEXT PAGE)

Ruth Shines in Series' Records

Babe Ruth's home-run hitting has made him an outstanding star of two world's series, 1923 and 1926, but the Bambino shows the rather slim batting average of .252 for his seven appearances in the annual fall baseball classic.

Nevertheless the Yankee slugger's terrific clouting, even if spasmodic, has helped him establish or share in eleven world's series batting records. He has collected the most extra bases on long hits, and has also been passed more times than any other batsman. The brightest spot in his record is the mark of three home runs in a single game, made in the fourth game of the 1926 series.

Here is Ruth's world's series record in detail:

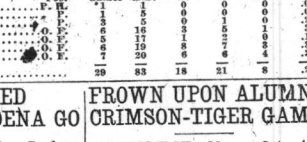

	Pos.	Games	A.B.	R.	H.	H.R.	Avg.
1915—Boston	P. H.	1	1	0	0	0	.000
1916—Boston	P.	1	5	0	0	0	.000
1918—Boston	P.	3	5	0	1	0	.200
1921—New York	O. F.	6	16	3	5	1	313
1922—New York	O. F.	5	17	1	2	0	.118
1923—New York	O. F.	6	19	8	7	3	.368
1926—New York	O. F.	7	20	6	6	4	.300
Totals		29	83	18	21	8	.253

CARDOZA SIGNED FOR PASADENA GO

Ham Jenkins and Joe Cardoza, middleweights, are billed in the 10-round main event at Pasadena Thursday night.

The six-round semi-final promises a lot of punching between Marcelino Lomeli and Tony Escalente. Four-rounders on the card will be: Dud Eales vs. Joe Parras; Big Boy Samson vs. Billy Boaz and Jack Stephens vs. Johnny Riley, 120 pounds.

FROWN UPON ALUMNI CRIMSON-TIGER GAME

CAMBRIDGE, Mass., Oct. 4.—Announcement of plans for a football game in New York City between alumni of Harvard and Princeton, whose traditional undergraduate athletic relationships were severed last year, evoked little enthusiasm here today.

With the exception of Al Miller, speedy halfback for the last three Harvard teams, prominent former players saw little to be gained

-5 CHOICE OVER PIRATES

THE CALL SPORTS

SAN FRANCISCO, TUESDAY, OCTOBER 4, 1927

NINE COAST STARS' NAMES WRITTEN ON PITTSBURGH'S ROLL

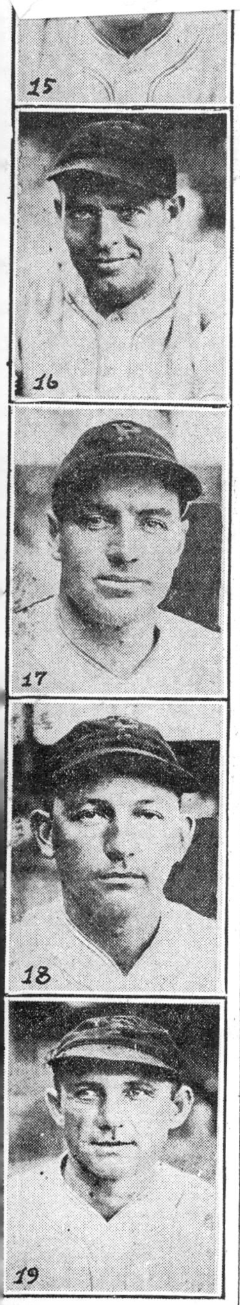

...n the ...er at ...f lo-..., for ...uers, ...rsair ...men ...her; ... but who is one of the greatest outfielders in the game; 16, Glenn Wright, shortstop; 17, Pie Traynor, third baseman; 18, Clyde Barnhart, outfielder, and, 19, Heinie Groh, utility infielder and coach.

Including Aldridge and Groh, the players in the center constitute the reason why local fans will root for the Pirates. They are, 4, John Miljus, Seattle; pitcher; 5, Wiz Kremer, Oakland, pitcher; 6, Paul Waner, Seals, outfielder; 7, Hal Rhyne, Seals, shortstop; 8, Donie Bush, manager; 9, Lloyd Waner, Seals, 10, George Grantham; 11, Joe Cronin, Sacred Heart High, and second baseman. Others are, 12, Yde; 13, Cvengros; 14, Meadows; 20, Harris; 21, Smith; 22, Spencer; 23, Gooch; 24, Bucrell. Many are series veterans.

KREMER OR ALDRIDGE TO START FOR BUCS; HOYT YANKEE CHOICE

By JAMES L. KILGALLEN
Staff Correspondent International News Service

PITTSBURGH, Pa., Oct. 4—With Babe Ruth and his slugging ball club in town, swinging bats in menacing fashion in practice at Forbes Field, hotels crowding up with visitors from nearby cities and ticket speculators operating on all sides, the bustling city of Pittsburgh was as excited today over the impending world series, which opens tomorrow, as Chicago was on the eve of the Tunney-Dempsey fight.

New York was a 6 to 5 favorite to win the series in the odds quoted by the gambling element this morning, and unless the National League partisans come to the scratch with heavier financial support in the next twenty-four hours, the Yankees will rule even stronger favorites when they take the field tomorrow.

Landis Arrives

Every train into Pittsburgh today brought more visitors eager to see the annual baseball classic. Judge Kenesaw M. Landis, the silver-haired commissioner of baseball, is here; so are scores of big league players, an army of sports writers and the usual run of sports luminaries.

Hotel rooms are unavailable, even at $15 a day. Guests are glad to sleep in hallways of the hotels, and most rooms quarter from two to six persons.

Manager Miller Huggins of the New York club and Donie Bush, the Pirates' leader, both expressed themselves as confident of victory. Huggins indicated he would use Waite Hoyt as his pitcher in the opening game and Bush said he would start either Ray Kremer, his great right-hander, or Vic Aldridge.

Bush gave the impression that he would send out on to the field tomorrow the same lineup that won the pennant. This would mean that Kiki Cuyler, his great outfielder and a star of the 1925 world series, will sit on the bench and that Clyde Barnhart will hold down the left field position.

The fans, however, are looking to the spectacular Waner brothers, Paul and Lloyd, to more than hold up the outfield strength of the Pirates. They think, in fact, that the Waners will hit as hard in this series as will Ruth and the other New York home run hitter, Lou Gehrig.

Record Crowd Expected

No series in baseball history has brought into the limelight heavier hitting clubs than the Pirates and the Yanks and great will be the disappointment if the fences of Forbes Field and the Yankee Stadium are not wrecked by heavy cannonading. It is a striking commentary on the equality of the two clubs hitting that the records show that the

Cont'd on Next Page, Column Four

BUC PITCHERS GIVEN EDGE ON YANKS

PITTSBURGH, Oct. 4 (AP).—Pitching is usually an uncertain, although decisive, factor in world's series' competition.

Victory, on the average, has gone to the club with one or two twirling aces. The records are full of the triumphs that come in baseball's classic through the feats of Mathewson, Coombs, Adams, Coveleskie and Alexander.

If pitching is to be the turning influence in this week's battle the Pirates seem to have a better chance of victory than the Yankees. Ruth, Gehrig and their mates may mow down the Corsair curvers, but on form, both for the season as well as during the past month, the Pirate pitchers appear a better equipped lot than the Yankee staff.

The average of earned runs off the Pirate hurlers for the last month has been only 2.46 a game, off the Yankees, 3.34.

Kremer Finished Strong

It will be chiefly a battle of right handers, at any rate. Dutch Ruether isn't likely to try his southpaw slants at all against the Bucs and Herb Pennock, although he never has been beaten in a world's series, has not measured to the usual form. The Pirate southpaws, Yde and Cvengros, are both reservists.

Two right handers, Ray Kremer for the Pirates and Waite Hoyt for the Yankees, are expected to start and the second game probably will witness another starboard exhibition, between Wilcy Moore and Vic Aldridge.

Kremer, with seven victories in a row in September, has the best record of any of the contending pitchers in the last month. Strong and with lot of stuff, the Californian is the main Buccaneer bet.

Miljus in Great Form

Aldridge, the Hoosier schoolmaster, and John Miljus, late season acquisition from Seattle, ranked next to Kremer in recent form.

Both may get preference over Lee Meadows, veteran moundsman, and Carmen Hill, bespectacled star, in Manager Bush's selections.

Against these five aces the Yankees will toss Hoyt, Moore, Urban Shocker, Pennock and probably George Pipgras, who has shown as brilliant form as any of his older and more experienced mates in the last month. Moore, one of the 1927 sensations, is a veteran even though in his first year as a major leaguer.

Pirates-Yanks To Clash Early Sunday

NEW YORK, Oct. 4 (AP).—When ...e Pirates and Yankees clash in ...e stadium on Sunday, the game ...ll start at one minute past 2 o'clock because of the state law of ...me years' standing which provides ...at no baseball game can be started on the Sabbath before 2 o'clock. ...he statute, making Sunday ball playing in this city legal; was sponsored by Mayor James J. Walker when he was a member of the state senate and had the approval of Governor Smith.

Fair, Cool Weather For Series

PITTSBURGH, Oct. 4 (INS). "Fair and moderately cool" weather was forecast today for the opening game of the world series here tomorrow. Ideal weather will continue through Thursday, the local weather bureau predicted.

Crisp air and clear skies greeted the Pirates and Yankees today as they prepared for their practice workouts, curtailed by rain yesterday.

Warner Vs. West Aided Grid Here

This is a third of a series on Coast football, written by Edward P. ("Slip") Madigan, coach of the St. Mary's College football squad, rated as one of the West's best by its victory over Stanford.

By EDWARD ("SLIP") MADIGAN

IN THE Spring fo 1921 we came to Saint Mary's, fresh from instruction at Notre Dame by Jesse Harper and Knute Rockne, and ready to teach to others what we had learned from these two originators of the Notre Dame system. We were rather young in those days, a fledgling coach. We were sensitive, too, and criticism, that would not bother us now, hurt and rankled in those days. We didn't feel of course that we were above criticism, but we knew that the system that we were instilling had been a success in the East and the Middle West against some of the greatest teams in the country and we found it rather hard to take without a murmur the adverse stand that many took towards our style.

Since then we have grown older, less impetuous. We have come to realize that perhaps Harper and Rockne were simply ahead of their day and that they and their followers, like all innovators, had to stand the laughs and the destructive criticism that comes to any who dare to differ with the reactionaries.

Yet in the East at the very time was another great football mentor, one who had coached for many years, yet one who was not too old in football ways to try anythnig new. We refer, of course, to Glenn S. Warner, who has been to progressive football what Teddy Roosevelt was to politics. Warner's coming to the coast made a tremendous change in the attitude of coaches in these parts towards departure from cut and dried styles, towards time worn and ancient plays.

"Pop" has recently stated that football in the West has been more progressive than football in the East. Since he has coached in both localities, the veteran of Carlisle, Cornell and Stanford assuredly knows what he is talking about. It is true, no doubt, that such is the case today, but it was not so in 1921.

Then, as we have stated in a previous story, Andy Smith alone had originality; Andy alone, with his flair for the dramatic, had the courage to try the new, to do the unexpected. Yet even Andy, with all his departures from football rule and custom, was an extreme conservative when compared to Warner.

Certain it is that football in these parts is more progressive than it has been; certain it is that today there are more opportunities for open play, for thrills, than formerly. And for all this, we exponents of the same idea and you lovers of the great old game can thank the Old Fox of the Gridiron, Glenn Scobey Warner.

STANDING ROOM FOR CALIFORNIA, SAINTS CONTEST

"STANDING room only" will greet the late comers at the California Memorial Stadium Saturday when the Golden Bears meet St. Mary's, according to Jack McKenzie, stadium manager at Berkeley.

Advance sale of seats for the contest has already broken all records, according to McKenzie, and it has been almost impossible for the athletic officials at Berkeley to keep the San Francisco and Oakland sporting goods houses supplied with pasteboards.

About 65,000 persons will be seated in the big bowl for the game, McKenzie believes, and he today began making plans to take care of a large overflow crowd.

Last year about **60,000** persons stood in the rain for the contest and **interest is far greater today.**

FRIDAY'S FIGHT CARD CANCELED, VARGAS SICK

The entire card of the Observatory Club's Friday night fight show at Golden Gate ball room was called off today by Promoter Frank Schuler when it was learned that Joe Vargas was stricken with tonsilitis and would be unable to meet Bill Adams in the ten round main event.

Vargas is purportedly in a hospital and sufficiently ill to make the bout an impossibility, although his condition is not serious. Efforts to match someone else were unsuccessful.

Efforts were made to get Joey Silver reinstated to meet Adams, but the boxing commission refused the pleas.

KASPEROWICZ, O'GORMAN OUT OF ST. MARY'S, BEAR GAME SATURDAY

By PAT FRAYNE

THE possibility of an entire new array of Galloping Gaels in the backfield as the result of injuries to the first string ball carriers, and the likelihood of the loss of two stars of the Seven Stubborn Stalwarts of the famous front line of the 1927 St. Mary's varsity today heightened the hopes of the University of California securing a victory over St. Mary's in the coming Saturday grid classic.

Kasperowicz, fullback, and O'Gorman, halfback, are definitely out of the game.

Simas, quarterback, Merrick, halfback, Bettencourt, center and captain, and Illia, tackle, are on the doubtful list of injured.

Had Rough Time

Kasperowicz is suffering from a broken clavicle (shoulder bone) from an injury sustained in the Stanford game last Saturday.

O'Gorman is suffering from a hemorrhage of the eyeball and is unable to see out of one of his eyes.

If Simas and Merrick are out of the California game, Madigan will have to start with an entirely new set of backs, although it is certain now that he will have to start with two new ball carriers.

Driscoll will probably replace Simas, Joe Rooney also being placed in the backfield to do the punting. Bogan will replace O'Gorman with Pitchford starting in Kasperowicz' place.

The change of the line-up of the forward wall if Bettencourt and Illia are lost to Madigan is serious to the hopes of St. Mary's. It is believed certain that hould either of the pair be started substitutions will be made before the game is over. Against Stanfo d the seven linemen played the entire game.

Madigan's injury list has cast a cloud of gloom over the Galloping Gaels' campus. If the team had come through unscathed it was felt certain that it would be the winner over California. Now there is some doubt.

John Scarlett and Malcolm Frankain, right and left ends respectively, have recovered from the Stanford onslaught and will be important factors again in the defense of the Gael goal. Their playing against Stanford, particularly that of Frankain, lists them as the best pair of ends on the Pacific coast.

Changes Odds

While California is now on the short end of the two-to-one betting the odds are expected to take radical changes before game time if Madigan's front line is broken.

Madigan will determine just what his chances are tonight after his practice is through and a medical report made on the condition of the doubtful list of injured.

Joe Rooney, who played against the Army team for the Gaels, has been punting well of late and Madigan believes that Rooney will be called upon to do the kicking for his team next Saturday.

Dick Scarlett, Bogan, McIntyre and Rooney are Madigan's substitute halfbacks.

Pitchford, Porrella and Greerherty are his fullback substitutes, while Driscoll, Haley and Johnson are his second string signal callers.

Harding Women In Golf Tourney

First round matches in the Harding Park Golf Club women's championship are being contested today. Mrs. A. H. Campion won low net with 95-12—83.

LOM, RIEGELS, PHILLIPS READY

By ROY CUMMINGS

FOUR powerful searchlights illuminated the California Memorial Stadium last night and for an hour after darkness had fallen two white ghost balls came spiralling back from perspiring centers to fast moving backfields as Coach "Nibs" Price started the Golden Bear varsity on its final five day drive for the St. Mary's College game.

Things good and bad for California shone through the brilliant light.

One could see in the incandescent glow the slippery form of Benny Lom, working with the first eleven for the first time since his injury in the Santa Clara game. And Irvine Phillips at end, completely recovered from his attack of the "flu." Joe Pitt was back at guard and there was Roy Riegels completely well and ready to take his place at center today.

On the second team Lee Eisan snapped out the signals, still favoring his weak ankles, but appearing able to take his place at the quarterback position with the varsity Saturday.

All of this brought smiles to Coach Price.

Koch Injured

But there also was Don Koch, California's latest serious injury. Koch, his jaw covered with bandages, will be out of the game three weeks from a broken jaw which he received in the Nevada game. And Ned Green, limping badly from a bone bruise in his side. Dr. Donald, without much enthusiasm, reported that Green probably would play Saturday, but the big tackle looked to be in a bad way.

However, with the new injuries, California is stronger today than it has been any time this season. If Ned Green is ready the Golden Bears will be able to present their strong-

Continued on Next Page, Col. Three

California Bar Wins 2 Famed Sports Figures

Two famous athletes were admitted to the California bar Friday, it was learned today. Trey are Armand Emmanuel, heavyweight boxer, who fought in one of the preliminaries to the Tunney-Dempsey fight at Chicago, and Don Nichols, who was captain of the University of California football team in 1923.

Tiger, Crimson Alumni Game Causes Trouble

CAMBRIDGE, Mass., Oct. 4 (AP). Announcement of plans for a football game in New York city between alumni of Harvard and Princeton, whose traditional undergraduate athletic relationships were severed last year, evoked little enthusiasm here today.

With the exception of Al Miller, speedy halfback for the last three Harvard teams, prominent former players saw little to be gained by the projected game.

The Only Evening Newspaper in St. Louis With the Associated Press News Service

PAGES 19—24 | ST. LOUIS, THURSDAY EVENING, OCTOBER 6, 1927. | PRICE 2 CENTS

YANKS WIN SECOND IN ROW FROM PIRATES, 6-2

Aldridge Blows Up, Wild Pitch Letting In Run

American Leaguers Bunch Four Safeties In the Third Inning

Ruth and Paul Waner, Batting Heroes, of First Day, Both Strike Out in Opening Frame — Brother Lloyd Triples First Time Up.

By the Associated Press.

PITTSBURG, Oct. 6.—The New York Yanks made it two straight over the Pittsburg Pirates by winning the second world series game here this afternoon, 6 to 2.

The Yankees were pitched to victory by George Pipgras, a newcomer to the classic, who held the Pirates to seven hits and was not in danger after his mates gave him three runs in the third inning. They added three more in the eighth for good measure.

Vic Aldridge, Pittsburg's starting pitcher, blew up and was removed from the mound in the eighth.

The game:

FIRST INNING.

YANKEES—Coombs flied to Barnhart near the scoreboard. Koenig singled to center. Ruth struck out. Gehrig walked on four pitched balls. Aldridge tossed out Meusel. NO RUNS. ONE HIT. NO ERRORS.

PITTSBURG—L. Waner tripled to left. **L. Waner scored on Barnhart's sacrifice to Ruth.** P. Waner was called out on strikes. Wright flied to Ruth. ONE RUN. ONE HIT. NO ERRORS.

SECOND INNING.

YANKEES—Lazzeri bounced a single off Aldridge's glove. Dugan fouled to Gooch. Bengough also fouled to Gooch. Pipgras lined to Grantham. NO RUNS. ONE HIT. NO ERRORS.

PIRATES—Pipgras tossed out Traynor. Grantham singled to center. Harris grounded out to Gehrig. Gooch fouled to Bengough near the Yankees' bench. NO RUNS. ONE HIT. NO ERRORS.

THIRD INNING.

YANKEES—Combs singled to right. **Koenig singled to center, and when the ball got past Lloyd Waner, Combs scored and Koenig went to third. Koenig scored on Ruth's sacrifice fly to L. Waner.** Gehrig doubled to right. Meusel beat out a grounder to Wright, Gehrig going to third. **Gehrig scored on Lazzeri's sacrifice fly to P. Waner,** Meusel going to second on the throw in. Dugan flied to P. Waner. THREE RUNS. FOUR HITS. ONE ERROR

PIRATES—Aldridge lined to Lazzeri. Gehrig tossed out L. Waner. Barnhart singled to center. P. Waner flied to Meusel. NO RUNS. ONE HIT. NO ERRORS.

FOURTH INNING.

YANKEES—Bengough lined to L. Waner. Pipgras struck out. Combs also struck out. NO RUNS. NO HITS. NO ERRORS.

PIRATES—Wright flied to Combs. Traynor doubled to left center, Dugan leaned over into the temporary boxes and caught Grantham's foul with one hand. Harris flied to Ruth. NO RUNS. ONE HIT. NO ERRORS.

FIFTH INNING.

YANKEES—Koenig flied to Paul Waner. Ruth walked on four pitched balls. Gehrig sent a sacrifice fly to L. Waner. Meusel struck out. NO RUNS. NO HITS. NO ERRORS.

PIRATES—Pipgras threw out Gooch. Aldridge fouled to Bengough. L. Waner flied to Combs. NO RUNS. NO HITS. NO ERRORS.

SIXTH INNING.

YANKEES—Lazzeri lined deep to P Waner. Dugan singled to left. Bengough flied to L. Waner. Pipsingled to right, Dugan stopping at second. L. Waner robbed Combs of an extra-base hit by going to the flag pole in deep center for his long fly. NO RUNS. TWO HITS. NO ERRORS.

PIRATES—Barnhart flied to Combs. P. Waner singled past Dugan. Wright flied to Combs. Traynor forced P. Waner, Koenig unassisted. NO RUNS. ONE HIT. NO ERRORS

SEVENTH INNING.

YANKEES—Koenig flied to P. Waner. Ruth grounded to Harris. Aldridge tossed out Gehrig. NO RUNS. NO HITS. NO ERRORS.

PIRATES—Grantham doubled against the right-field fence. Koenig threw out Harris. Gooch lined to Lazzeri and Grantham was doubled off second, Lazzeri to Koenig. NO RUNS. ONE HIT. NO ERRORS.

EIGHTH INNING.

YANKEES—Meusel singled to center. On the hit-and-run Lazzeri singled to right, Meusel going to third. **Meusel scored on a wild pitch,** Lazzeri going to second. Dugan bunted and Lazzeri was out at third, Gooch to Traynor. Bengough walked. Pipgras also drew a pass, filling the bases. Cvengros replaced Aldridge. **Combs was hit by a pitched ball, forcing Dugan across the plate. Bengough scored when Koenig singled to right. Ruth hit a grounder to Grantham and Pipgras was forced at the plate, Grantham to Gooch.** Gehrig forced Koenig at third, Traynor unassisted. THREE RUNS. THREE HITS. NO ERRORS.

PIRATES—Smith batted for Cvengros and grounded to Gehrig. L. Waner walked. Barnhart singled to center, L. Waner going to third. **L. Waner scored on P. Waner's sacrifice fly to Meusel.** Wright forced Barnhart, Koenig unassisted. ONE RUN. ONE HIT. NO ERRORS.

NINTH INNING.

YANKEES—Dawson went to the box for Pittsburg Meusel got to first on Wright's fumble. Lazzeri flied to L. Waner. Dugan went out the same way. Meusel stole second, but was out trying for third when the ball got away from Wright, Grantham to Traynor. NO RUNS. NO HITS. ONE ERROR.

PIRATES—Traynor flied to Combs. Grantham struck out. Pipgras took Harris' grounder and ran over and touched first. NO RUNS. NO HITS. NO ERRORS.

Runs Batted In

Gehrig, 2.
Lazzeri, 2.
P. Waner, 2.
Barnhart, 2.
Wright, 1.
Harris, 1.
Ruth, 1.
Koenig, 1.

TWO TICKET SCALPERS ARRESTED BY AGENTS FOR BOOSTING PRICES

By the Associated Press.

NEW YORK, Oct. 6.—Operators of two Broadway theater ticket agencies were arrested by Federal agents today on charges of boosting to $15 and $18 the prices of $5.50 tickets to the fourth world series game scheduled for Saturday at the Yankee stadium.

Agents for the Internal Revenue Department said one scalper had sold them four tickets at $15 each and the other had taken $18 each for two tickets. The maximum penalty which may be imposed is $100 fine for each ticket sold.

MIKE McTIGUE MEETS LOUGHRAN TOMORROW

Special to the Post-Dispatch.

NEW YORK, Oct. 6.—A $100,000 gate is expected at Madison Square Garden tomorrow night when Mike McTigue meets Tommy Loughran. Tex Rickard is holding the bout.

TOLEDO WINS LITTLE WORLD SERIES, 5 TO 1

Defeat of Buffalo by a Score of 4 to 0 in Sixth Game Clinches Title for Mud-Hens.

By the Associated Press.

TOLEDO, O., Oct. 6. — Toledo won the minor league championship of the baseball world here today when it defeated Buffalo, of the International League, 4 to 0.

Toledo, American Association champions, won five out of the six games in the series and completely outclassed Buffalo. Palmero won his second game of the series today.

BUFFALO (INTE).)

	AB.	R.	H.	O.	A.	E.
Tyson cf.	4	0	2	0	0	0
Fisher rf.	4	0	1	2	0	0
Brainard lf-2b.	3	0	2	1	0	0
Bissonette 1b.	4	0	0	12	0	0
Cohen ss.	4	0	2	3	6	0
Malone 2b.	1	0	0	2	5	1
Anderson 3b.	2	0	1	0	0	0
Taylor 3b.	2	0	0	0	1	0
Carter lf.	2	0	0	0	0	1
Pond c.	2	0	0	4	1	0
Proffitt p.	2	0	1	0	3	0
*Ogden	1	0	0	0	0	0
Hollingsworth, p.	0	0	0	0	0	0
Leverenz p.	0	0	0	0	0	0
Totals	31	0	9	24	16	2

TOLEDO (A. A.)

	AB.	R.	H.	O.	A.	E.
Leberveaux rf.	4	1	3	1	0	0
Maguire 2b.	3	0	0	6	8	1
Marriott 3b.	4	0	1	0	1	0
Veach lf.	4	0	1	0	0	0
Grimes 1b.	4	0	0	6	1	0
Kochler cf.	4	1	3	1	0	0
O'Neil c.	3	1	1	6	0	0
Cote ss.	3	0	0	7	3	0
Palmero p.	3	1	1	0	2	0
Totals	32	4	10	27	15	1

*Batted for Proffitt in the seventh.

Innings—	1	2	3	4	5	6	7	8	9	
Buffalo	0	0	0	0	0	0	0	0	0	— 0
Toledo	0	2	0	0	0	0	2	0	x	— 4

Stolen bases—Marriott, Lebourveau. Sacrifice hits—Malone, Maguire, O'Neill. Double plays—Maguire to Cote to Grimes (2); Malone to Cohen to Bissonette. Struck out—By Palmero, 4; by Proffitt, 1. Hits—Off Proffitt, 7 in 6 innings; off Hollingsworth, 2 in 1-3 inning; off Leveernz, 1 in 1 2-3 innings. Bases on balls—Off Proffitt, 1; off Palmero, 1; off Hollingsworth, 1. Wild pitch—Proffitt. Left on bases—Buffalo, 8; Toledo, 8. Losing pitcher—Proffitt. Umpires—Finneran and Guthrie. Time of game, 1h. 56m.

World Series Sidelights

By the Associated Press.

Ruth Strikes Out.

Babe Ruth's first strikeout of the series, in the opening inning of the second game, was done with the usual Ruthian eclat. Aldridge's sharp-breaking curves had the Babe guessing. He let one slip by, fouled off another and missed a third, while the crowd cheered wildly.

Tony Lazzeri, Yankee second-sacker, played the game with a bandaged left wrist, which he sprained in a mix-up with George Grantham in the opening game. There was doubt whether Tony would start the game, but once in it, his play did not seem affected by the injury.

Lloyd Waner, in manhandling Koenig's single in the third inning, displayed the same nervousness afield that brother Paul had in the first game, in spite of being taken to task overnight on this score by "Dad" Waner. The father of the two boys, after watching the Yankee sluggers, gave some advice on how to play them. Lloyd atoned for his early mistake by grabbing Combs' long fly on the run in the sixth, with two on base.

Aldridge Fans Pipgras and Combs.

After being laced for four hits, resulting in three Yankee runs in the third inning, Aldridge came back to whiff Pipgras and Combs in succession in the fourth. Combs swung at and missed the last three balls. Vic also fanned Bob Meusel for the third out in the fifth, with Ruth on second.

HOYT AND JOE DUGAN ROBBED OF $400

By the Associated Press.

PITTSBURG, Oct. 6.—Waite Hoyt and Joe Dugan of the New York Yankees had their satisfaction at winning the first game of the world series dimmed last night when robbers entered their room and took away $400 of their money.

PITCHED YANKS TO VICTORY

GEORGE PIPGRAS.

The Yanks twirler surprised fans by holding the Pirates to 7 hits in the second game of the series. Pipgras' record for the regular season was 10 victories and 3 defeats.

RACE RESULTS

At Creve Coeur.

Weather cloudy, track fast.

FIRST RACE—Five furlongs:
Out of Sight (C. Eames) 7.20 3.60 4.20
Fallen Leaf (L. Aron) 5.60 4.60
Carriebelle (McCabe) 4.20
Time—:58. Nowata, Double Rainbow, Calzon, Cluricaune also ran.

SECOND RACE—Six furlongs:
Illinois King (P.McCabe) 15.20 6.60 3.00
Manipulator (E. Rea) 9.00 3.40
Viking (C. Eames) 2.40
Time, 1:17. Macedonian, True Worth, Cuban Flag also ran.

THIRD RACE—Six and one-half furlongs:
Request (Holecko) ...16.60 4.40 2.60
Rotarian (Eams) 2.80 2.40
Gus R. (McCabe) 2.20
Time—1:26 1-5. Spats, Argento and Mary Ruth also ran.

Ring On, Irish Lord, Goulash, Warrior Bold, Super Star also ran.

SECOND RACE—Mile and a sixteenth:
Overlook (Ambrose) ..4.80 3.20 2.80
Parchesie (Josiah).... .... 5.60 4.50
Highland Daisy (Bulcroft)........... .... 5.08
Time 1:48 3-5. Hobson, Zeod, Fire Boy, Selfish and White Marsh also ran.

THIRD RACE—Six furlongs:
Femight (Bullman) ...8.30 4.50 3.80
Blaze (Peternell)...... .... 10.00 7.00
*Courser (Smith).... .... 5.30
Time, 1:13. Harry Heilman, Ortlieb, Leatherwood, *Venus, Missionary, *Miss Sand, Alex Woodlitie, Word of Honor, Subtle also ran. *Field.

FOURTH RACE—Six furlongs:
Honker (Josiah) 14.20 6.90 4.50
Polish (Hull)....... .... 5.00 3.50
Inquisitor (Harvey).. .... 3.70
Time, 1:12 1-5. Fairy Girl, Bridegroom, Wellet Timekeeper, Black Beetle and Congress also ran.

FIFTH RACE—One mile:
Fair Star (Callahan).. 6.90 2.90 2.40
Edith Cavell (Ambrose) 2.60 2.30
Glister (Richards) 4.00
Time—1:37 4-5. Krick, F. Bette, Be Fair also ran.

SIXTH RACE—One mile and 70 yards:
Purple Pirate (Richards) 19.40 7.80 3.80
Signola (Harvey) 5.90 3.30
Alifey (Barnes) 2.40
Time—1:44 1-5. Golden Powder, Brown Study and Candy Fox also ran.

SEVENTH RACE—One mile and one-eighth:
Tazewell (D. Mergler).12.30 6.60 3.90
Speedy Prince (Emery) 9.00 4.20
Eric (Ellis) 2.70
Time—1:54. Mayne, Fire Rock, Sun Rajah and Frewell also ran.

CREVE COEUR SCRATCHES.

1—Monsoon, Spartan Boy, Richard Andrews. 3—Pet Cat. 6—War Boy.

At Jamaica.

Weather clear, track fast.

By the Associated Press.

FIRST RACE—Six furlongs:
Forget Me Not (Allen) 5-1 2-1 even
Reprisal (Walls)........ ... even 1-2
Cyclamen (Stevens)........ ... 6-1
Time, 1:14. Wild Aster, Knight of Merci II, Miss Crump, Joan Grier, Gumdrop, Foxy Peter, Pichonne, John S. Mosby, Big Heart, Gorget, Red Curl and Clodomir II also ran.

SECOND RACE—Six furlongs:
bCharm (Watters) 10-1 4-1 2-1
Okay (Gotterup)....... ... 4-1 2-1
Inca (Walls) 8-5
Time, 1:14 1-5. bRhyme and Reason, Omrah, Paige, Star Rocket, Golden Gloss, Broom Whisk, Campo Bello, Miss Boyd, Matchmaker II, Last Spot, Philip's First, Golden Slumber and Royal Lot also ran. bArlington entry.

THIRD RACE—Mile and a sixteenth:
Florian (Catrone) ....9-20 out out
Maelstrom (M. Garner)....... 2-1 out
Ceylon Prince (Kelsay)........ ... out
Time, 1:45 2-5. Only three starters.

FOURTH RACE—Mile and one-sixteenth:
Kentucky II (Fator)..... 9-10 2-5 1-5
Cherry Pie (Burke)........ ... 4-1 2-1
Light Carbine (Garner).. 1-2
Time—1:45. Cloudland, High Star, Premier and Black Panther also ran.

FIFTH RACE—Five furlongs:
Lace (Garner) 7-2 7-10 1-4
Valkyr (Kelsay) .... 1-4 out
Ratification (Weiner).. 7-5
Time, 1:00. Belmona, Heloise, Sailor Maid, Play Well, Jacque Minot also ran.

SIXTH RACE—One mile and seventy yards:
Priceman (Barceno) ..6-1 2-1 even
McAuliffe (Hicks)...... ... 1-2 1-5
King Jimmy (McGovern) 1-2
Time, 1:44 3-5. Fire Opal, Resourceful, Prattle, Captain Martin also ran.

At Laurel.

Weather clear, track fast.

By the Associated Press.

FIRST RACE—Six furlongs:
Sun Kin (Warner) ...18.40 6.70 5.20
Royal Cause (Barnes) 4.00 2.60
Alma (Williams)...... .... 5.70
Time, 1:13 4-5. Dear Lady, Steroptican,

At Hawthorne.

Weather cloudy, track fast.

By the Associated Press.

FIRST RACE—Six furlongs:
Dr. Maxon (R. Jones).5.60 4.12 3.60
Common Denominator (Philpot) 15.94 11.88
*Kendall (Luther).. .... 24.26
Time. 1:16 2-5. Billy Beer, *Richeleu, Bad Luck Aileen P., Neat Girl, Note O' Love and The Poet also ran. *Field

SECOND RACE—Six furlongs:
Best Friend (Philpot). 7.98 4.10 3.28
Laska (Hebert) 4.18 3.48
Monday Morning (Burke) 3.70
Time—1:17 4-5. Bonny Castle, Edith D. and Jeannette S. also ran.

THIRD RACE—Six furlongs:
Voshell (Pendergrass)..54.00 12.32 4.94
Estin (Bowden) 4.20 3.00
Gotham (Hebert) 3.50
Time—1:16 3-5. Papa Blinks, Medley, Post Mistress, George Groom and Great Sport also ran.

FOURTH RACE—Five and one-half furlongs:
William P. (Hebert)... 9.50 6.02 4.38
Peggy Taylor (Francis) 4.56 3.34
Shasta Sand (Philpot).. .... 3.16
Time—1:10 4-5. Kischief Macher, Quicken, Go Away, Glint o' Gold, Al Garnet, Woollatt, Princely and Halside Guy also ran.

FIFTH RACE—One mile and one-eighth:
Hopeless (Philpot) ... 6.84 4.10 3.65
Up and Down (Francis) 4.90 2.98
Heed (Allen) 5.32
Time—1:57 4-5. Jack Horgan, Pathan, Samaron, Cartoon and Fire Under also ran.

PIPGRAS BAFFLES BUSH'S MEN AND MATES BAT OUT VICTORY

The Box Score

NEW YORK.

	AB.	R.	H.	O.	A.	E.
Combs cf	4	1	1	5	0	0
Koenig ss	5	1	3	3	1	0
Ruth rf	3	0	0	3	0	0
Gehrig 1b	3	1	1	6	0	0
Meusel lf	5	1	2	2	0	0
Lazzeri 2b	4	0	2	2	2	0
Dugan 3b	5	1	1	1	0	0
Bengough c	3	1	0	4	0	0
PIPGRAS P	3	0	1	1	2	0
Total	35	6	11	27	5	0

PITTSBURG.

	AB.	R.	H.	O.	A.	E.
L. Waner cf	3	2	1	7	0	1
Barnhart lf	3	0	2	1	0	0
P. Waner rf	3	0	1	5	0	0
Wright ss	4	0	0	0	0	1
Traynor 3b	4	0	1	3	0	0
Grantham 2b	4	0	2	1	2	0
Harris 1b	4	0	0	3	0	0
Gooch c	3	0	0	7	1	0
ALDRIDGE P.	2	0	0	0	2	0
CVENGROS P.	0	0	0	0	0	0
DAWSON P.	0	0	0	0	0	0
Smith	1	0	0	0	0	0
Total	31	2	7	27	5	2

Smith batted for Cvengros in the eighth.

	1	2	3	4	5	6	7	8	9	T
NEW YORK.	0	0	3	0	0	0	0	3	0	6
PITTSBURG.	1	0	0	0	0	0	0	1	0	2

Two-base hits—Gehrig, Traylor, Grantham. Three-base hit—L. Waner. Stolen base—Meusel. Sacrifices—Barnhart, Ruth, Lazzeri, Gehrig, P. Waner. Double play—Lazzeri to Koenig. Left on bases—New York, 10; Pittsburg, 5. Bases on balls—Off Aldridge, 4 (Gehrig, Ruth, Bengough, Pipgras); off Pipgras, 1 (L. Waner). Struck out—By Aldridge, 4 (Ruth, Pipgras, Combs, Meusel); by Pipgras, 2 (F. Waner, Grantham). Hits—Off Aldridge, 10 in 7 1-3 innings; off Cvengros, 1 in 2-3 inning; off Dawson, none in 1 inning. Runs scored—Off Aldridge, 5. Hit by pitcher—By Cvengros (Meusel). Wild pitch Aldridge. Losing pitcher—Aldridge. Umpires—Nallin (American) at plate; Quigley (National), third; Ormsby (American), second base; Moran (National), first base. Time of game—2h 20m.

MISS MACKENZIE ELIMINATED FROM CANADIAN GOLF

Defending Champion Loses to Mrs. W. S. Frazer, 5 and 4, in Third Round of Women's Tourney.

By the Associated Press.

TORONTO, Ontario, Oct. 6.—Mrs. W. G. Fraser of Ottawa, the former Alexa Stirling of Atlanta, Ga., today defeated the defending champion, Miss Ada Mackenzie of Toronto, 5 and 4, in the third round of the Canadian women's open golf championship tournament.

Miss Fritzi Stifel of Wheeling, W. Va., entered the semifinal bracket with Mrs. Fraser by defeating Miss Helen Paget, Ottawa, by a 1-up margin. It was Miss Paget who yesterday scored a sensational upset by eliminating Miss Glenna Collett, a leading United States contender.

Granite City Prospects Good

Early indications are that Granite City High School w... strong football team present campaign. In tests so far the team Greenville High School and the Alton High, 13

Youngster Pitches Steadily, Holding Opponents to Seven Safeties—Lloyd Waner Makes Brilliant Catch of Long Drive by Gehrig.

By J. Roy Stockton.
Of the Post-Dispatch Sport Staff.

PITTSBURG, Oct. 6.—The baseball world thought that Miller Huggins, manager of the Yankees, was joking when he announced that George Pipgras would pitch for the American League champions in the second game of the world series. But this evening the critics of the morning are patting the mite manager on the back with columns of praise.

Pipgras, a righthanded son of Minnesota, held year after year despite his failure to arrive as a regular starting pitcher, finally "get there" in his sixth season as a Yankee. He held the slugging Pittsburg Pirates to seven hits, doled out not more than one to an inning, and hurled the Yankees into commanding lead in the struggle for the world championship by beating the National League flag winners 6 to 2.

Yankees Show Real Attack.

Pipgras' brilliant pitching and a concentration of the Yankee attack in two big innings gave the men of Huggins their victory. The Pirate defense cracked again, but even had their fielding been perfect, it would have made no difference. The American League machine made enough solid hits to win the ball game, with Pipgras breezing along so steadily.

The Pirates scored first, pushing over a run in the opening inning on Lloyd Waner's triple to left and a sacrifice fly by Barnhart, but in the third inning the Yankees scored enough runs to win.

Earl Combs, the Yankee leadoff man, singled to left for his first hit of the series to start the frame and he scored when Lloyd Waner missed Koenig's bounding single to center. Koenig continued to third on the error and scored when Ruth flied deep to Lloyd Waner. Gehrig crashed a double against the right field wall, moved to third on Meusel's single to deep short and scored the third New York run on Lazzerie's sacrifice fly to Paul Waner.

Three More in Eighth.

Before the Pirates could score their second run, the Yankee doubled their total by driving in three more in the eighth.

Victor Aldridge, Indiana school master and hero of the Pirates' 1925 world series victory, was knocked out of the box in this inning and Mike Cvengros, a little lefthander, also was treated roughly.

Bob Meusel started the eighth inning rally, punching a single over second that Grantham reached, but could not stop. Meusel went to third on Lazzeri's single to right and then Aldridge made a wild pitch. Gooch half stopped the ball, but Meusel has a reputation for laziness and the Pirate catcher did not expect the big Yankee to exert himself to the extent of trying to score. But the Yankees are hustling in this series. They have been in five title struggles and they have won only one and they want the long end of the swag.

Meusel raced for the plate and before Gooch could get the ball Bob slid safely home.

Aldridge Blows Up.

Lazzeri took second on the pitch, but overslid third on Dugan's intended sacrifice bunt. Aldridge, however, was up in the air now. He walked Bengough and when he also passed Pipgras—an unpardonable crime to walk a pitcher—he was waved from the slab and Cvengros went to the rescue with the bases loaded. Cvengros nicked Combs in the ribs with a pitched ball, forcing Dugan home with a run and on Koenig's single to left, Bengough scored.

The stands roared their appreciation of the dramatic situation as Ruth strode to the plate with the bases loaded. The game appeared to be hopelessly lost now and the fans wanted to se the big fellow hit one of his home run. But Babe

the stands were emptying now and those who stayed yelled for Kiki Cuyler, boohed Manager Donnie Bush and jeered Earl Smith when he batted for Cvengros and grounded to Gehrig. A pass to Lloyd Waner, Barnhart's single to center and Paul Waner's sacrifice fly, a line drive straight to Bob Meusel, produced the run.

The Yankees needed only two more victories now to win the series.

Third Game in New York.

The scene of battle will shift for tomorrow's game, the teams moving to New York tonight to play tomorrow, Saturday and Sunday, if necessary, at the Yankee Stadium.

Manager Huggins has announced that either Herb Pennock or Wilcy Moore will pitch for the American Leaguers, while Donie Bush has named Meadows as his probable hurler.

If the Yankees win tomorrow and Saturday, the series will end. If a fifth game is played at New York and the series is still undecided, the teams will return to Pittsburg to play the sixth and seventh contests.

The attendance at the second game exceeded that of the first contest by nearly 200, the total paid having been announced as 41,634 and the receipts as $182,978.

Series Facts

STANDING.

Club.	W.	L.	Pct.
New York	2	0	1.000
Pittsburg	0	2	.000

RESULTS.

First game—New York, 5-6-1; Pittsburg 4-9-2. Batteries—New York—Hoyt, Moore and Collins; Pittsburg — Kremer, Miljus and Smith.

Second Game—New York, 6-11-0; Pittsburg, 2-7-2. Batteries: New York—Pipgrass and Bengough; Pittsburg—Aldridge, Cvengros, Dawson and Gooch.

TOMORROW'S GAME.

Pittsburg at New York, 1:30 p. m. Eastern Standard Time. (12:30 p. m. St. Louis Time.)

Probable batteries—New York Shocker or Pennock and Collins; Pittsburg Hill and Gooch.

ATTENDANCE AND FINANCES.

SECOND GAME.

Attendance, 41,634.
Receipts, $182,978.
Players' Pool, $93,318.78.
Advisory Council, $27,446.70.
Each Club, $15,553.13.
Each league, $15,553.13.

Players' pool divided as follows: $65,323.15 to contending teams, $13,997.83 to second-place teams, $9,331.87 to third-place clubs, $4,665.93 to fourth-place clubs.

TOTAL FOR SERIES.

Attendance, 83,101.
Receipts, $365,455.
Players' pool, $186,382.05.
Advisory Council, $54,818.25.
Each club, $31,063.67.
Each league, $31,063.67.

Players' pool divided as follows: $130,466.44 to contending teams, $27,957.82 to second-place teams, $18,638.53 to third and $9,319.26 to fourth.

RUTH AND P. WANER BOTH STRIKE OUT FIRST TIME AT BAT

Aldridge walked a man and was touched for a single in the first inning but he was master of the ... game as he ... fly to left ... ed a single

20, Col. 2.

YANKEES AGAIN BEAT PIRATES; SCORE IS 6 TO 2

PIPGRAS IS WINNER FOR NEW YORK IN 2ND

Aldridge Fails to Get Away With Win; Is Driven From Mound

(CONTINUED FROM PAGE ONE)

second by grounding to Pipgras on the first ball and the Yank hurler tossed him out at first. The National league champions were cutting at the first pitch whenever it was over the plate.

George Grantham clicked his first hit of the series, a single to short cent r, which Combs played safe. Harris hit a hot bouncer to Gehrig, who beat him to the bag with the ball, Grantham taking second. Gooch could not fathom Pipgras when a hit meant a run and his foul to Bengough retired the side.

YANKS REPEAT

The Yanks had their second big third inning in as many days and looked fairly secure when it was over with a 3 to 1 lead. Earl Combs came to life long enough to slam out his first hit of the series, a single to right.

Koenig singled through the middle of the diamond and Combs scored when Lloyd Waner let the ball get through him, the batter going all the way to third. It was scored as a single and an error for Lloyd Waner. The ball rolled to the fence, Paul Waner recovering in time to hold Koenig at third.

Ruth hoisted a fly to Lloyd Waner and Koenig scored after the catch, Ruth receiving credit for a sacrifice. Lou Gehrig slashed a hard drive to right center for two bases. It was a sizzling liner Meusel hit a hot one to Wright which the Pirate shortstop could not handle and it went for an infield single, Gehrig taking third.

LOOSE FIELDING

Lazzeri lifted a sacrifice fly to Paul Waner, who made a great throw to the plate which Gehrig barely beat by a hook slide. Joe Dugan ended the agony for the Pirate adherents when he flied to Paul Waner. Loose fielding contributed to Aldridge's downfall just as it had in the same inning the preceding day with Kremer on the mound.

Aldridge was the first Pirate out in the third on a line drive to Lazzeri. Lloyd Waner received a big hand from the crowd as he came to bat. Lazzeri took his roller and threw him out at first.

Clyde Barnhart hit a sharp single over second, the ball clinging closely to the ground. Paul Waner failed to produce once more, going out on a long fly to Meusel.

Manager Bush conferred with Aldridge before the latter resumed his duties on the mound in the fourth No one knows what Bush said to his pitcher, but it apparently had a stimulating effect for he retired the Yanks in order, two of them fanning.

ALDRIDGE TIGHTENS UP

Bengough looked at one wide pitch and then busted a liner to center which Lloyd Waner took care of. Pipgras worked the count to three and two and then went out swinging at the third strike. After throwing one ball high and wide to Combs, Aldridge cut loose with three strikes, all of which Combs swung at and missed. Aldridge's fast ball was cutting the plate in fine style.

A double by Capt. "Pie" Traynor gave Yankee followers a few anxious moments in the Pirates' half of the fourth but Pipgras managed to emerge unscathed from this round.

Wright lifted a towering fly to Combs for the first out. The count was 3 and 2 on Traynor when "Pie" caught one squarely on the nose and sent it to left-center on a line. He hustled for second and beat Combs' throw to that bag by a beautiful slide.

RALLY NIPPED

Grantham fouled to Dugan, who reached into the crowd back of third and made the catch with his gloved hand. Harris flied to Ruth, who caught the ball near the right field boxes. It was still 3 and 1 with the Yanks on the long end.

Ruth drew his first pass of the series in the fifth but it was not altogether intentional apparently.

The count was 1 and 1 on Koenig when he sent a fly to Paul Waner for the first out of the inning. Aldridge threw four straight balls to Ruth The first was wide, the second inside, the third and fourth wide. Aldridge was not anxious to give Ruth a good ball and "Babe" declined to swing at anything he saw.

MEUSEL SWINGS

Gehrig hit a long fly to Lloyd Waner in deep center and received credit for a sacrifice when Ruth

(CONTINUED ON THIRD SPORT PAGE)

Second Game

By International News Service

FORBES FIELD, PITTSBURG, Pa., Oct. 6.—Official figures for the second game of the world series were:

Total attendance, 41,634.

Total receipts, $182,978.

Commissioner's share, $27,446.70.

Club owners' share, $62,212.52.

Players' share, $93,318.78.

BASEBALL FANS ✠ SEE WORLD SERIES ✠ AS HERALD GUESTS

Photograph showing part of the huge crowd that saw the opening game of the world's series at The Evening Herald's scoreboard at 128 South Broadway. Similar boards are being operated by The Evening Herald at 746 South Hill street and at the Tufts-Lyon Arms Co., Sixth and Olive streets. The boards will be operated every day except Sunday.

THRONGS SEE GAMES ON HERALD BOARDS

Thousands Entertained as Pirate-Yankee Battles Are Played for Fans

A BANKER came out of his mahogany furnished office and sat down on the curb in Hill street beside a freckle faced messenger boy, whose bicycle sprawled forgotten in the sun.

A negro elevator operator won a 50-cent bet from a taxi driver when Babe Ruth and Lou Gehrig both failed to knock home runs.

Street car motormen tolled their bells dismally, hoping that traffic cops would drive back enough men off the tracks for them to pass without an accident.

Twenty-five hundred or so men and a few women clapped or shouted or groaned or sighed or said "I told you so" as each inning, each play, was megaphoned to them from the scoreboard of the world series game, operated in the Lincoln building, between Seventh and Eighth streets, in Hill street, by The Evening Herald, keeping up its reputation of being in this, as in all other instances—

FIRST WITH THE LATEST!

HUGE CROWDS

And anybody who was foolish enough to doubt the fact that baseball is still the most popular of all American national games should have stopped before this scoreboard, or at one of the other two operated by The Evening Herald at 128 South Broadway, or at Sixth and Olive streets, to have had his misapprehensions removed.

The men were there in numbers—thousands of them gathering before the first ball was pitched, staying, most of them, until the last Yankee or Pirate in the ninth inning had been called out by the

(CONTINUED ON THIRD SPORT PAGE)

EVENING HERALD SPORTS
AN INDEPENDENT NEWSPAPER

VOL. LII | Hotels and Trains Five Cents | 3 CTS. | THURSDAY, OCTOBER 6, 1927 | 3 CTS. | Hotels and Trains Five Cents | NO. 291

The Figures

PITTSBURG, Oct. 6.—Official figures for the first world series game:

Paid attendance, 41,467.
Total receipts, $182,477.
Players' pool, $93,063.27.
Advisory council, $27,371.55.
Each club, $15,510.54.
Each league, $15,510.54.

RUTH PRAISES PIRATES

Box Score of First Game

NEW YORK (AMERICAN)

	AB.	R.	H.	PO.	A.	E.
Combs, cf	4	0	0	4	0	0
Koenig, ss	4	2	1	2	2	0
Ruth, rf	4	2	3	5	0	0
Gehrig, 1b	2	1	1	9	0	0
Meusel, lf	3	0	0	2	0	1
Lazzeri, 2b	4	0	1	2	5	0
Dugan, 3b	3	0	0	0	0	0
Collins, c	2	0	0	3	0	0
Hoyt, p	3	0	0	0	0	0
Moore, p	1	0	0	0	2	0
Totals	30	5	6	27	9	1

PITTSBURG (NATIONAL)

	AB.	R.	H.	PO.	A.	E.
L. Waner, cf	4	2	1	1	0	0
Barnhart, lf	5	0	1	3	0	0
P. Waner, rf	4	0	3	3	0	0
Wright, ss	2	1	1	1	5	0
Traynor, 3b	4	0	1	1	2	0
Grantham, 2b	3	0	0	5	3	1
Harris, 1b	4	0	1	8	2	0
Smith, c	4	0	0	4	1	1
Kremer, p	2	1	1	0	0	0
Miljus, p	1	0	0	1	2	0
Brickell	1	0	0	0	0	0
Totals	34	4	9	27	15	2

Brickell batted for Miljus in the ninth.

SCORE BY INNINGS

New York	1	0	3	0	1	0	0	0	0	—5
Pittsburg	1	0	1	0	1	0	0	1	0	—4

SUMMARY

Two-base hits—P. Waner, Kremer, Koenig, L. Waner, Lazzeri Three-base hit—Gehrig.. Sacrifice hits—Wright 2, Gehrig, Dugan. Double plays—Lazzeri to Gehrig; Wright to Grantham to Harris. Left on bases—New York, 4; Pittsburg, 7. Bases on balls—Off Hoyt, 1 (Grantham); off Kremer, 3 (Collins, Gehrig, Meusel); off Miljus, 1 (Collins). Struck out—By Hoyt, 2 (Kremer, Miljus); by Kremer, 1 (Koenig); by Miljus, 3 (Combs, Meusel, Moore). Hits—Off Hoyt, 8 in 7 1-3 innings; off Moore, 1 in 1 2-3 innings; off Kremer, 5 in 5 innings (none out in sixth); off Miljus, 1 in 4 innings. Hit by pitched ball—By Hoyt (L. Waner). Winning pitcher—Hoyt. Losing pitcher—Kremer Umpires—Quigley and Moran (National), Ormsby and Nallin (American). Time of game—2:04.

16,000 EXPECTED FOR EUGENE GAME

By Pacific Coast News Service

EUGENE, Ore., Oct. 6.—More than 16,000 football fans were expected here for the Oregon-Idaho clash Saturday. In the 18 games already played between the two teams, Idaho has won but two, three having been tied and the Webfooters have been victorious in the rest.

SCHIKAT, VASSEL IN MAT BOUT TONIGHT

By Pacific Coast News Service

SAN FRANCISCO, Oct. 6.—Richard Schikat, German grappler, and George Vassel will meet here in a wrestling match tonight. Renato Gardini, Italian wrestler, will try conclusions with Higami, a jui jitsu champion.

41,000 SEE 2ND GAME IN SERIES

FORBES FIELD, PITTSBURG, Oct. 6.—A capacity crowd of more than 41,000 enthusiasts watched the New York Yanks and the Pittsburg Pirates battle through the second game of the world series here today.

No whit less enthusiastic than the mob of 41,461 ball fans who witnessed the opener yesterday, today's crowd wore a decidedly more business-like aspect than was manifest in the holiday spirit of yesterday's throngs.

They cheered their favorites with grim determination, forming a mighty echo to the determination of the teams playing on the field below.

HOWL ENCOURAGEMENT

The crowds, sensing the fact that the Yanks went into this game grimly resolved to sweep on to victory in one-two-three order, while Pittsburg as eagerly sought revenge for the 5-to-4 broadside hurled into the bow of the Pirate craft yesterday, howled encouragement in the same spirit.

The weather was ideal for the second world series game. It was like a mid-summer day, the sun shining brightly into the towering steel stands and upon the carefully manicured diamond. The atmosphere was balmy and the breeze across the ball park was so faint it barely ruffled the American flag atop the pole in center field. The mercury hovered around 70 degrees.

FRENZY LACKING

The lack of frenzy which motivated yesterday's patrons was evident long before the game started In fact, there had been no all night vigil of fans at the gates, and the mad stampede toward the windows when they closed yesterday was also lacking today.

But by 12:45 the bleachers were entirely filled, and the grandstands and boxes were also registering capacity when batteries were announced and the game on.

Betting at game time today had switched to 10 to 7 in favor of the Yanks, with even money on the day's contest. The odds were not because New York was deemed a better team, a survey of opinion showed, but because they had the edge of one game safely tucked

(CONTINUED ON NEXT PAGE)

BILL TILDEN BEATS BEN GORCHAKOFF IN HOT TENNIS BATTLE

(CONTINUED FROM PAGE ONE)

dropped the final after coming from behind to even the game count.

Manuel Alonso of Spain had little trouble in trimming Leonard Dworkin, local junior player, 6-0, 6-0.

A sensational upset was recorded in women's ranks when Marion Williams, Southern California champion, lost out to Midge Gladman, 16-year-old Santa Monica girl, holder of the national girls' title, 2-6, 6-4, 6-2. Miss Gladman played far above her usual good game to take Miss Williams into camp.

Kea Bouman, women's champion of Holland, registered an easy 6-0, 6-1 victory over Louise McFarland of Pasadena, former girls' national champion.

Francis T. Hunter of New York faced another hot battle at the hands of Phil Neer. Hunter wiped out a couple of college stars yesterday, trimming Lionel Ogden of Stanford 6-4, 6-3, and Bob Laird of U. C. L. A., 6-1, 6-2.

Another interesting women's match was on tap when Mrs. Mallory faced the winner of the Jessie Grieve-Louise Hoyt match. Marion Williams, Southern California champion, was pitted against Midge Gladman, the Santa Monica juvenile who won the national girls' championship this year. Miss Williams defeated Miss Gladman for the Southland title earlier this year.

Gerald Stratford, the Berkeley meteor who turned in two victories yesterday, looms as opposition for the invading stars. Stratford, who holds the Southern California championship, faced Hinckley today after defeating Ralph Sindorf and Merle Manning yesterday. Ray Casey, the slugging southpaw from San Francisco, was also slated to see action, meeting Gail Warrick.

It was announced that two night matches would be played on the lighted exhibition court at the club tonight. Tilden and Hunter will play Ogden and Green, while Stratford and Davies will meet Warren and Sindorf in two doubles matches.

A group of navy officers from the fleet with their ladies were guests of the club in boxes this afternoon.

Baseball Stars to Play Benefit Game At Wrigley Sunday

Two of the greatest line-ups of young ball players that was ever gathered together for a ball game in Southern California will clash in the benefit game next Sunday at Wrigley field for the sick fund of the Professional Ball Players association.

These young players all learned their baseball on the sand lots of Los Angeles and vicinity. After a successful season on eastern fields they are home for the mid-winter season and will come out for the benefit game Sunday. The official line-ups will be announced tomorrow.

BRETONNEL, ROMERIO IN 10-ROUND DRAW

PARIS, Oct. 6.—Fred Bretonnel and Emil Romerio, leading French welterweights, boxed a 10-round draw here last night. Bretonnel, former European lightweight champion, can no longer make the weight limit for that class.

Terris Takes on McGraw in Bout at Ebbets Field

By International News Service

NEW YORK, Oct. 6.—The long-standing fistic debate between Sid Terris, east side lightweight, and Phil McGraw of Detroit, on the question of who is better suited to meet Sammy Mandell for the lightweight championship, is expected to be decided at Ebbets field tonight.

The fight is a critical one for both battlers. Terris hopes to wipe out the defeat administered him recently by Hilarie Martinez, and McGraw is equally anxious to square up for Terris' close victory over him on Aug. 24.

TENDLER TO INVADE COAST; SEEKS BOUTS

PHILADELPHIA, Oct. 6.—Lew Tendler is planning another boxing invasion of the Pacific coast. He expects to leave soon for Los Angeles.

BUCS PROVE HARD CLUB TO BEAT

By BABE RUTH
Baseball's Greatest Batter

PITTSBURG, Oct. 6.—Well, the first one is in. It was not easy to get. The Pirates put up a gerat game and they were fighting just as hard at the finish as they were at the start. But we won and the edge is ours.

Personally, I never enjoyed a game more. I'll hand it to the Pirate pitchers. They didn't seem to fear our heavy guns and they pitched to every man on the club. Honestly, the way those balls were sailing up there I thought sure I'd soak three of them into the stands.

The thing that pleased me most in the whole game was the fact that Lou Gehrig drove in two runs. Lou is our big siege gun when it comes to driving runners over the plate, and when he smacked those two runners home it proved to me that he is himself again after that long slump he had.

BOTH CAREFUL

So far as fine points of baseball are concerned, the first game didn't have any. Both clubs played careful old-fashioned baseball, and I think each club went home feeling a lot of added respect for each other.

The pitching was not exactly what either side expected. Waite Hoyt was not himself. He's a lot better than he showed out there and the next time he starts I've got a hunch that he'll show the Pirates something. I suppose the same thing is true of Kremer. But just the same, I doubt if Remy does much in this series. He's not the sort of stuff the Yankees like.

MILJUS GREAT

But this fellow Miljus showed us plenty. His relief pitching was corking and so was Cy Moore's. When you come to think of it, there is quite a stunt—two first-year men going into their first world series and pitching ball like that against hitters who are supposed to be poison.

And believe me, the Pirates have a couple of real ball players in those Waner boys. Those two kids are great. Believe me, they're tough eggs up there at the plate, and I'll have to join right in with the chorus

(CONTINUED ON NEXT PAGE)

DE LA HUERTA BROTHER SLAIN IN MEX.

Col. Drake Hurt in Crash

THREE CENTS

LOS ANGELES EVENING HERALD
AN INDEPENDENT NEWSPAPER

The Evening Herald Grows Just Like Los Angeles

'OL. LII THREE CENTS H 'els and Trains e Cents FRIDAY, OCTOBER 7, 1927 Hotels and Trains Five Cents THREE CENTS NO. 292

SPORTS AND RACES

LOUISVILLE RESULTS

First race, 3-year-olds and upward, claiming, $1200, seven furlongs—Gale (Root), won; Dark Angel (Guerra), second; Jolly Boy (Boganowski), third. Time, 1:30 3-5. Princess Darrell, Sincerely, Resolute, Watchful, Stinson and Realtor also ran.

Second race, 2-year-old maiden fillies, $1200, six furlongs—Concession (D. Smith), won; Coloratura (Pichon), second; Virginia Beauty (Crump), third. Time, 1:17. Goldiva, Spot Light, Echolight, Runaway, Princess, Perle D'Or and Fana Omarack also ran.

Third race, 3-year-olds and upward, claiming, $1200, seven furlongs—Abstract (G. Johnson), won; San San (Roberts), second; Shasta Love (McClair), third. Time, 1:30. Prospect, The Rove, Berry Picker, Black Cyclone, Queen of Sheba and Bob Johnston also ran.

Fourth race, 3-year-olds and upward, claiming, $1200, one and one-sixteenth miles—

(CONTINUED ON THIRD SPORT PAGE)

NIGHT EDITION

YANKS BEAT PIRATES, 8-1, WIN THIRD SERIES GAME

R̶BEL GENERAL'S BODY ʟACED IN PLAZA AT NOGALES AS WARNING

By International News Service

NOGALES, Ariz., Oct. 7.—Gen. Manuel Aguirre, whose tros killed Alfonso de la Huerta and his aide, Gen. Barron Mena, in a surprise attack 70 miles below the border, was toc pursuing a band of 40 Yaqui Indians in the vicinity where the rebel leaders were slain. A battle was imminent.

NOGALES, Ariz., Oct. 7.—The bullet-riddled body of Alfonso de la Huerta, brother of the former provisional president of Mexico, was brought to Nogales, Sonora, opposite here, today, and propped up against an umbrella tree in the public plaza with a placard on the breast reading, "A rebel general," while near him was placed the equally lead-torn body of Pedro Medina, a Yaqui general and ally.

The two men were killed in battle at sundown yesterday, according to federal officers who accompanied the bodies, when government troops discovered them apparently en route to enlist Yaqui Indian tribes to the Mexican revolution.

CROWDS VIEW BODY

However, reports, wholly unconfirmed, gained circulation to the effect that De la Huerta was not killed in battle but was arrested and executed. The rumors stated that he had been hanged and his body then mutilated to create the impression that he had been slain in fighting. Many who viewed the body were of the opinion that it gave evidence of having been hanged.

Still other rumors declared De la Huerta had been spirited across the border from the United States some time ago and that both he and Medina have been held in jail until now, when their death was decreed as an object lesson to revolutionists.

The bodies were brought here early this morning from Ojo de Agua, Sonora, 30 miles southeast of here, where the battle was reported to have taken place.

PLACED IN PLAZA

Just as the sun started to light up the skies they were removed from a military escort car attached to the northbound passenger train. A guard of four soldiers took the bodies from the coach, depositing

(CONTINUED ON PAGE TWENTY)

TLDEN AND HUNTER WIN ʟT NETS

B Tilden, six times holder of the natial tennis championship, and Frais Hunter, Davis cup player of NewYork, won their way into the fina of the Pacific southwestern chamionship tennis tournament today n the courts of the Los Angele Tennis club and will meet Sum in the final and deciding mat of the tournament.

Bi were in top form and displa much spectacular tennis.

Then defeated Gerald Stratford of Bekely, holder of the Southern Califrnia tennis title, 6-2, 6-3, 6-2, whi Hunter won over Manuel Alono, the Spanish "ace," 6-2, 6-2, -1.

Mge Gladman, 16-year-old Santa Mora tennis star, was defeated by KeaBouman, leading player of Hollandin a semi-finals match of the wom's division

Tl set scores were 6-4, 6-8, 6-4 MisGladman carried the Europeanstar o 4-2 games score in the first set, ut was unable to maintain her gan under the hot pace set by her oppent. She went out in front in

(COMINUED ON FIRST SPORT PAGE)

Herald First and Best Again Today

Once again today, The Evening Herald's would-be competitors were left far behind.

FIRST WITH THE LATEST, this newspaper presented the final result, complete detail of play and box score of the world series game before any other Los Angeles newspaper could reach the street.

Mystifying and confusing their readers, other newspapers issued incomplete extras, sacrificing accuracy and comprehensive description in an ineffectual attempt to beat The Evening Herald.

This newspaper not only was first, but its extra was complete and fully comprehensible.

The public is invited to see the world series games free of cost at The Evening Herald scoreboards, 128 South Broadway, 746 South Spring and at the Tufts Lyon store, at Sixth and Olive. These scoreboards will be operated every day except Sunday and are connected with the Evening Herald's double leased wire service, which spans the continent, direct from the baseball grounds where the series is being played. These games begin at 10:30 o'clock, Los Angeles time.

Babe Ruth, the world's greatest hard-hitting baseball player, writes exclusively for The Evening Herald.

FIRST WITH THE LATEST. AND THE BEST.

Hindu Is Found Guilty as Slayer Of 2 Countrymen

Mohammed Jack, Hindu, today was convicted of the first degree murder of Mohammed Box and Mohammed Gulam, Hindus, by a jury in Judge Charles W. Fricke's court after a deliberation of 1 hour and 10 minutes.

The jury recommended leniency to the extent of life inprisonment. Sentence is to be passed Tuesday.

Jack was alleged to have murdered the two men during an argument over a fertilizer contract, on a ranch one mile east of Glendora.

Lord Iveagh, 2nd Wealthiest Man In England, Dies

LONDON, Oct. 7.—Lord Iveagh (Edward Cecil Guinness), reputed to be the second ri-st man in England, died today. Lord Iveagh, who came of a famous family of brewers, was 80 years old.

RICH BEACH HOTEL MAN INJURED

Col. Charles Rivers Drake, 84, president of the corporation which owns the fashoinable Virginia hotel in Long Beach and a large part of the amusement concessions on the Long Beach "pike," and rated as one of the wealthiest men in the beach city, was seriously injured today in an automobile accident in Los Angeles.

Colonel Drake was rushed to the Georgia street receiving hospital after the accident, which took place in front of 1642 West Adams street when an automobile in which he was riding collided head-on with a car driven by Tom Asadumon, 5626 Gerr street, Beverly Hills.

SERIOUSLY HURT

At the Receiving hospital it was stated the wealthy man had little chance for recovery because of his serious injuries and his age, which had lowered his vitality.

Police Surgeon Jack Renfrew said Colonel Drake had suffered a possible fracture of the cervical spine, two long, deep lacerations of the head, severe abrasions and contusions and a sprained ankle.

Following first aid treatment at the Receiving hospital he was removed to the California Lutheran hospital for an X-ray examination of his injuries and further treatment.

CIVIC WORKER

Relatives were notified immediately of the accident.

Colonel Drake is widely known throughout California. He is chairman of the Long Beach park commission and has been an active civic worker from the time of his arrival in 1901, when Long Beach had a population of only 2200 persons, to the present time.

Colonel Drake was riding in an automobile driven by C. E. Meyers of the Hotel Virginia, Long Beach, when the accident occurred this afternoon.

According to reports of witnesses to the police, Asadymon's car accidentally swerved toward the center of the street as he was going east on Adams street and Meyers was driving west.

THROWN FROM CAR

The automobiles collided and were wrecked. Asadymon was not injured, but Meyers was thrown from the car and fell on his face in the street 10 feet away, being injured and narrowly escaping death.

(CONTINUED ON PAGE TWENTY-TWO)

World Box Score

PITTSBURG	AB	R	H	O	A	E
L. Waner, cf	4	0	1	1	1	0
Rhyne, 2b	4	0	0	0	6	0
P. Waner, rf	4	0	0	0	0	0
Wright, ss	3	0	0	3	2	0
Traynor, 3b	3	1	1	0	3	1
Barnhart, lf	3	0	1	0	0	0
Harris, 1b	3	0	0	11	0	0
Gooch, c	2	0	0	9	0	0
Meadows, p	2	0	0	0	1	0
Cvengros, p	0	0	0	0	0	0
Spencer, c	1	0	0	0	0	0
Groh	1	0	0	0	0	0
Totals	30	1	3	24	13	1

Groh batted for Cvengros 9th.

NEW YORK	AB	R	H	O	A	E
Combs, cf	4	2	2	5	0	0
Koenig, ss	4	2	2	1	2	0
Ruth, rf	4	1	1	1	0	0
Gehrig, 1b	3	0	2	12	0	0
Meusel, lf	4	0	0	2	0	0
Lazzeri, 2b	4	1	1	1	7	0
Dugan, 3b	4	1	1	1	2	0
Grabowski, c	2	0	0	3	0	0
Pennock, p	4	1	0	1	1	0
Durst	1	0	0	0	0	0
Bengough, c	1	0	0	0	0	0
Totals	35	8	9	27	12	0

Durst batted for Grabowski 7th.

SCORE BY INNINGS

										R.	H.	E.
Pittsburg	0	0	0	0	0	0	0	1	0	1	3	1
New York	2	0	0	0	0	0	6	0	x	8	9	0

SUMMARY

Runs batted in—By Ruth 3, Gehrig 2, Pennock 1, Combs 1, Koenig 1. Two-base hits—Koenig, Barnhart. Three-base hit—Gehrig. Home run—Ruth. Sacrifice—Dugan. First base on errors—New York 1. Left on base—Pittsburg 2, New York 4. Base on balls—off Meadows 1. Struck out—by Meadows 5, Pennock 1, Cvengros 2. Hits—Off Meadows 7 in 6 1-3 innings, off Cvengros 2 in 1 2-3 innings. Losing pitcher—Meadows. Time—2:04. Umpires—Moran at plate, Ormsby at first, Quigley at second and Nallin at third.

Play by Play

FIRST INNING

PIRATES—L. Waner out, Koenig to Gehrig. Rhyne flied to Meusel. P. Waner flied to Meusel on the first ball. NO RUNS, NO HITS, NO ERRORS.

YANKEES—Combs sent a single through the box. Koenig was safe at first and Combs took second on an infield hit. Rhyne fumbled the ball but it was scored as a hit for Koenig. Ruth flied to Wright. Gehrig tripled, scoring Combs and Koenig, but was caught at the plate, L. Waner to Wright to Gooch. Meusel fanned, swinging. TWO RUNS, THREE HITS, NO ERRORS.

SECOND INNING

PIRATES—Wright flied to Combs. Traynor out, Lazzeri to Gehrig. Barnhart out, Lazzeri to Gehrig. NO RUNS, NO HITS, NO ERRORS.

YANKEES—Lazzeri was out on strikes, the third being called. Dugan was out, Wright to Harris, who had to dig it out of the dirt. Grabowski out, Traynor to Harris. NO RUNS, NO HITS, NO ERRORS.

THIRD INNING

PIRATES—Harris flied to Combs Gooch was out on strikes, the third being called. Meadows out, Lazzeri to Gehrig. NO RUNS, NO HITS, NO ERRORS.

YANKEES—Pennock out, Rhyne to Harris. Combs flied to L. Waner. Wright made a beautiful running catch in left center of Koenig's fly NO RUNS, NO HITS, NO ERRORS.

FOURTH INNING

PIRATES—L. Waner out, Lazzer to Gehrig. Rhyne flied to Koenig P. Waner flied to Dugan. NO RUNS NO HITS, NO ERRORS.

YANKEES—Ruth fanned, swinging. Gehrig walked. Meusel hit to Traynor, who threw over Harris head into the stands, Gehrig going to third and Meusel to second on the error. With two and three on Lazzeri he fanned, swinging. Dugan out, Traynor to Harris. NO RUNS, NO HITS, ONE ERROR.

FIFTH INNING

PIRATES—Wright popped to Grabowski. Traynor fouled to Grabowski. Barnhart flied to Combs. NO RUNS, NO HITS, NO ERRORS.

YANKEES—Grabowski popped to Wright. Pennock was called out on strikes. Combs out, Meadows to Harris, on a bunt. NO RUNS, NO HITS, NO ERRORS.

SIXTH INNING

PIRATES—Harris out, Pennock to Gehrig. Gooch flied to Ruth. Meadows flied to Combs. NO RUNS NO HITS, NO ERRORS.

YANKEES—Koenig out, Rhyne to Harris. Ruth out, Rhyne to Harris. Gehrig doubled to right center, making the bag by a nice headlong dive. Meusel fanned, swinging. NO RUNS ONE HIT, NO ERRORS.

SEVENTH INNING

PIRATES—L. Waner out, Lazzeri to Gehrig. Rhyne out, Dugan to Gehrig. P. Waner out, Lazzeri to Gehrig. NO RUNS, NO HITS, NO ERRORS.

YANKEES—Lazzeri singled to center. Dugan bunted and was safe at first when Meadows threw too late to second to catch Lazzeri. Durst batting for Grabowski. Durst out, lined to Harris. Pennock hit to Rhyne, scoring Lazzeri, Dugan going to third. Pennock reached first on a fielder's choice when the

(CONTINUED ON SECOND SPORT PAGE)

PENNOCK BAFFLES BUC HITTERS; RUTH SLAMS FIRST HOMER

YANKEE STADIUM, NEW YORK, Oct. 7.—The New York Yankees made it three straight over the Pittsburg Pirates today when Herb Pennock, star southpaw, held the National leaguers to three hits, and Babe Ruth pounded out a long homer with two on base to provide the finishing touches to a crushing 8 to 1 defeat.

Such masterly pitching as Pennock delivered for seven innings today never has been bettered in a championship series since the first ball was tied up from horsehide.

For seven innings not a single Pirate reached first base and it seemed as though Herbie was about to join those immortals who have delivered a no-run, no-hit, no-man-reach-first-base ball game.

Pennock, who was injured in the leg before the series opened in Pittsburg, tired in the eighth and the Pirates got to him for two hits and a run.

They added another hit in the ninth which did no damage.

The American league champions hammered Lee Meadows from the mound in the seventh inning and Mike Cvengros, who relieved him, came to the box with two men on and Babe Ruth at bat.

The big punch of the current series followed when the Babe wound up and smashed one into the right field stands.

More than 60,000 cheering fans went wild when the Babe's bat sounded the old familiar home run tune.

Cvengros finished out the game and the Yanks made no more runs.

GEHRIG GETS TRIPLE

Lou Gehrig was the secondary batting star with a triple that scored two New York runs in the first inning. He also hit a double in the Sixth.

A fielding feature of the game was Dugan's one-hand pick and rifle throw to first on Rhyne's perfect bunt in the seventh inning, when Pennock was still pitching hitless ball.

Gehrig missed a homer by an eyelash in the first. He tried to stretch a triple into a homer but

(CONTINUED ON FIRST SPORT PAGE)

TOPLITZKY IS CLEARED IN 'PETE' CASE

Six indictments against person charged with conspiracy to commi usury in connection with Julian Petroleum pools were dismissed today by Superior Judge Charles W. Frick on motion of Harold L. Davis, chie deputy district attorney, who stated the defendants had established complete innocence of criminal intent in the transactions.

The persons thus exonerated were Joe Toplitzky, real estate broker Albert Lane, head of the Lane Mortgage Co; Abe Prell, broker; E Bastheim, wholesale jeweler; L Horowitz, broker, and S. F. Pruett merchant.

MADE RESTITUTION

Each of the six defendants, Mr Davis said, went into pools believing it was a legitimate move to refinance the Julian corporation and that he would receive valid stock for his investment. Those who made profits in the transaction made full restitution when they learned the true nature of the deal, the chief deputy declared.

Mr. Toplitzky, it was stated, went into a pool on the advice of his banker and went to New York immediately thereafter, so he had no knowledge of subsequent operations. He made no profit, all he

(CONTINUED ON PAGE TWENTY-TWO

AGGIES, S. C. BOTH SCORE

NIGHT EDITION

LOS ANGELES EVENING HERALD
AN INDEPENDENT NEWSPAPER
Reg. U. S. Patent Office. Copyright, 1927, by Evening Herald Publishing Company
The Evening Herald Grows Just Like Los Angeles

VOL. LII THREE CENTS Hotels and Trains Five Cents SATURDAY, OCTOBER 8, 1927 Hotels and Trains Five Cents THREE CENTS NO. 293

LATEST NEWS

S. C. OPENS UP IN THIRD PERIOD

The Trojans snapped out of it in the third period and made four first downs to O. A. C.'s none. Morley Drury tore loose for several long gains featured by a 27-yard runback of a punt. This put the ball in mid-field, but penalties interrupted the Trojans march here. Logan intercepted a forward pass from Drury and raced to the Trojan's 42-yard line before they downed him.

U. C. L. A. DEFEATS WHITTIER, 24 TO 6

Final—U. C. L. A. 24, Whittier 6.

CANYON FIRE NEAR BEVERLY HILLS

A brush fire, which broke out in Stone canyon between Beverly Hills and the ocean, was spreading rapidly toward nearby property late today with 50 firemen attempting to control the flames. The blaze was reported to be a short distance off Beverly boulevard.

U. of C. Scores Against St. Mary's

N. Y. WINS WORLD SERIES BY BEATING PIRATES, 4-3

5,000 SEE TROJANS IN TILT WITH BEAVERS

lastered hither, thither and yon r the landscape by a fast charg- Aggie line, Southern California's jans barely managed to eke out to 6 lead over the fighting Ore- Aggie grid squad this afternoon the end of the first half of their ning coast conference game at Coliseum.

oth teams were fighting des- ately during the half and the touchdowns came as the result reaks. Thirty-five thousand rav- football fans witnessed the hot tle.

oth teams got away to a slow rt in the first quarter, failing to much on the offensive and ding but small yardage on the ensive.

AGGIES WARM UP

he Aggies trotted out on the d first, attired in white jerseys. ey spent 15 minutes kicking, sing and warming up in all de- tments.

oward Maple, star Aggie quar- back, was busy attempting field ls from the 15-yard line.

he Trojans took the field next. ey were given a rousing hand by colorful assemblage. In the pre- inary game the Trojan Spartans eated the U. S. C. freshmen, 15 6.

FIRST PERIOD

oreley Drury of the Trojans the tossup and chose to kick the Aggies defending the east l. Elliott then started in place Drury.

lliott kicked off to Maple, who urned the ball to the 27-yard , a return of 15 yards. Maple de two yards over left guard. It s a spin play.

lliott made another over the e spot.

hitlock kicked off at the 22- d line to Saunders, who caught ball on the 34-yard line and s downed in his tracks by Luce. loyd Palmer made 13 yards und left end.

. S. C. was penalized 5 yards the 30 second stop rule. First n and 15 to go. Elliott made 8

NTINUED ON FIRST SPORT PAGE)

Again Today Herald First on World Series

The Evening Herald was first again this afternoon with the result, box score and details of the world series game.

Frantically but fruitlessly attempting to beat The Evening Herald, another Los Angeles newspaper published an incomplete box score, only a partial account of the game and enigmatical figures on the result, which left its readers floundering for the facts.

The Evening Herald extra was complete in all details and gave a full and comprehensive story of the game, with all plays and box score.

The Evening Herald score boards also were first with the news.

Babe Ruth is writing exclusively for this newspaper, giving the inside facts and gossip of the world series games.

THE EVENING HERALD FIRST WITH THE LATEST AND BEST

CRISIS NEAR IN MEX., BATTLE LOOMS

Adolfo de la Huerta, former provisional president of Mexico, today announced from his home in Hollywood that he had concluded a formal alliance with Gen. Arnulfo Gomez, southern revolutionary leader, whose troops were reported today near battle with large Calles forces.

MEXICO CITY, Oct. 8.—Federal forces were expected to establish contact with the principal rebel band commanded by General Arnulfo Gomez and Hector Almada today, and, according to government sources here, the coming 12 hours may tell the story of whether the revolution started last Sunday will be snuffed out within the week or whether it will drag along indefinitely.

A bulletin issued from presidential headquarters in Chapultepec castle last night predicted a decisive battle between federals and the rebel forces probably will get under way some time today near Perote, Vera Cruz state. Approxi-

(CONTINUED ON PAGE FOUR)

BEARS GET JUMP ON SAINTS

MEMORIAL STADIUM, BERKELEY, Oct. 8.—The Golden Bear had the advantage of a 13-point lead today at the end of the first half of play against the St. Mar's Gaels, conquerors of Stanford last Saturday.

After both teams had tried ineffective attacks during the first seven minutes of play, California pierced its way into St. Mary's territory after a punting duel. Lom of the Bear backfield then threw a forward pass to Jimmy Dougery that was good for a 33-yard gain and placed the ball on the galloping Gaels' 11-yard mark.

Lom followed up the attack with a wide sweep around right end that was good for 10 yards. With the Gaels fighting gamely to stave off a touchdown, Ralph Dougery pierced the line for the necessary yard gain. Evans failed to convert.

Football Results

Third period—Pomona 13, Cal. Tech 6.
First half—San Diego 6, Redlands 0.
First half—Stanford 14, Nevada 0.
Third period—Loyola 12, Arizona State 0
First half—California 13, St. Mary's 0.
First Half—Oregon 0, Idaho 0.
Pasadena Jr. College 18, Occidental Frosh 12.
First Hal—Occidental 28, Santa Barbara Teachers 0.
Colgate 0, Virginia Polytechnic Institute 6.
Holycross 18, Dayton 0.
Notre Dame 20, Detroit 0.
St. Johns 0, St. Marys 6.
Northwestern 13, Utah 6.
New York University 65, Alfred 0.
Purdue 19, Harvard 0.
Middlebury 12, Mass. Agri. 0.
Amhurst 14, Haverford 0.
Dartmouth 38, Allegheny 7.
Penn 14, Brown 6.
St. Francis 3, Westminster 0.
Thiel 0, Waynesburg 0.
R. I. State 26, Lowell Textile 0.
Providence 7, Norwich 7.
Georgia 14, Yale 10.
Washington and Jefferson 31, Bethany 0.
U. C. L. A. Frosh 27, Fullerton Junior College 0.
Cornell 53, Richmond 0.
Michigan 21, Michigan State 0.
Minnesota 40, Oklahoma Aggies 0.
Franklin-Marshall 13, Dickinson 8.
Temple 58, Juanita 0.
Williams 12, Vermont 0.
Lafayette 58, Rutgers 0.
Villanova 32, Lebanon Valley 7.
Syracuse 21, Johns Hopkins 6.
Wisconsin 26, Kansas 6.
Ohio State 13, Iowa 6.
Springfield 7, Union 7.
Navy 35, Drake 6.
Connecticut Aggies 13, Maine 14.
Clarkson 7, R. P. I. 0.
Indiana 0, Chicago 13.
Wabash 12, Milliken 7.
Penn State 7, Bucknell 13.
Denison 19, Case 0.
Colorado Aggies 6, Brigham U. 0.
Denver U. 7, Wyoming U. 12.
Army 21, Marquette 12.
John Carroll 7, Grove City 0.
Michigan 21, Michigan State 0.
California Freshmen 14, St. Mary's Freshmen 7.
Illinois 58, Butler 0.

FIRE RAZES $250,000 L. A. PLANT

Fire starting shortly before noon today completely destroyed the plant of the Miller Box and Lumber Co., 107 North Avenue 18 doing $250,000 damage there and partially burning eight neighboring dwellings.

The blaze started when an electrical shaving machine operated by E. Telles short circuited, throwing a spark into a pile of dry sawdust, it was stated by Detective Lieutenant George Price. The sawdust burst into flame like an explosion, it was stated.

Eight houses adjacent to the factory were partially burned and 12 more were threatened. The plant is located at the intersection of Avenue 18 with the Union Pacific tracks, near the Broadway bridge.

Three alarms turned in brought nine fire companies to the scene. Dry lumber in the plant burned like tinder and the firemen were unable to do anything but try to protect surrounding property.

The plant was almost surrounded by dwellings, the occupants of which dragged out furniture as sparks sprayed about their roofs.

The plant of the Graves Sash and Door Co., opposite the box factory on Avenue 18, was also in danger and the firemen deluged it in their endeavor to keep the flames from spreading.

Milton Metzler, manager, and L. H. Sweet, superintendent of the Miller plant, said about 90 per cent of the loss was covered by insurance.

Purdue Defeats Harvard, 19 to 0; New Back Stars

CAMBRIDGE, Mass., Oct. 8.—Playing his first college game of football before 30,000 spectators here this afternoon, W. R. Welch, a new Purdue left halfback, ran the ball and tossed it around Harvard for a 19-to-0 victory for the Lafayette, Ind., Boilermakers.

Welch scored two touchdowns and hurled a 50-yard forward pass to Hutton for another.

World Box Score

PITTSBURG	AB	R	H	O	A	E
L. Waner, cf	4	1	3	0	0	1
Barnhart, lf	5	0	1	2	0	0
P. Waner, rf	4	0	1	0	0	0
Wright, ss	4	0	1	1	6	0
Traynor, 3b	4	0	0	1	3	0
Grantham, 2b	4	0	2	0	2	0
Harris, 1b	4	0	2	13	0	0
Smith, c	3	0	0	6	0	0
xYde	0	1	0	0	0	0
Gooch, c	0	0	0	3	0	0
Hill, p	1	0	0	0	0	0
xxBrickell	1	1	0	0	0	0
Miljus, p	1	0	0	0	0	0
Totals	35	3	10	z26	11	1

zTwo out when winning run was scored.

NEW YORK	AB	R	H	O	A	E
Combs, cf	4	3	2	2	0	0
Koenig, ss	5	0	3	0	3	0
Ruth, rf	4	1	2	1	0	0
Gehrig, 1b	4	0	0	15	1	0
Meusel, lf	5	0	0	2	0	0
Lazzeri, 2b	3	0	0	4	5	1
Dugan, 3b	4	0	1	1	4	0
Collins, c	3	0	3	2	1	0
Moore, p	4	0	1	0	3	1
Totals	36	4	12	27	17	2

Yde ran for Smith in 7th.
Brickell batted for Hill in 7th.

SCORE BY INNINGS

										R	H	E
Pittsburg	1	0	0	0	0	0	2	0	0	3	10	1
New York	1	0	0	0	2	0	0	0	1	4	12	2

SUMMARY

Runs batted in— By Ruth 3, Wright 1, Barnhart 1, P. Waner 1. Two-base hit—Collins. Home run—Ruth. Sacrifice—L. Waner, P. Waner. Stolen base—Ruth. First base on errors—Pittsburg 2. Double plays—Lazzeri to Gehrig, Dugan to Lazzeri to Gehrig, Traynor to Wright to Harris. Left on base—Pittsburg 8, New York 11. Base on balls—Off Hill 1, off Miljus 3, off Moore 2. Struck out—By Hill 6, by Miljus 3, by Moore 2. Hits—Off Hill 9 in six innings, off Miljus 3 in two and two-thirds innings. Wild pitch—Miljus 2. Losing pitcher—Miljus. Time—2:15. Umpires—Ormsby at plate, Quigley at first, Nallin at second and Moran at third.

STANFORD 14, NEVADA 0, IN 1ST HALF

PALO ALTO, Oct. 8.—Stanford was leading Nevada 14 to 0 at the end of the first half of their football game here today.

PALO ALTO, Cal., Oct. 8.—Stanford was unable to score on Nevada during the first quarter of the game at Stanford stadium today. Coach Pop Warner started his second team with a surprise backfield consisting of Hoffman as quarterback, Frentrup and Padgett, halves, and Fleischacker at fullback. Although Stanford was unable to score, the play was all in Nevada territory.

Notre Dame Eleven Beat Detroit, 20-0

DETROIT, Oct. 8.—Notre Dame's football team today triumphed over the University of Detroit by a 20 to 0 score. The charging Notre Dame backfield time and again tore through Detroit's line for substantial gains.

YALE DEFEATED BY GEORGIA, 14 TO 10

By International News Service

YALE BOWL, NEW HAVEN, Conn., Oct. 8.—The University of Georgia with a gritty, fighting eleven defeated Yale by a score of 14 to 10, here today in game that was crowded with thrilling plays and equally dumb football. Georgia crossed Yale's coal line twice and kicked the goals from touchdown each time, while the Blue scored one touchdown, a goal from touchdown and three points on a drop-kick.

In the last two minutes of play Yale had the ball on Georgia's five-yard line and apparently had victory in its grasp as Loud hurled a forward pass to Scott over the goal line but Scott was beyond the end zone and outside the field of play so that the touchdown was denied the Blue.

CARDINAL SERIOIUSLY ILL

BELFAST, Ireland, Oct. 8.—Cardinal O'Donnell, head of the Catholic church in Ireland, was seriously ill today at Carlingford, suffering from an attack of pleurisy.

WILD PITCH IN 9TH INNING GIVES YANKS 4TH STRAIGHT GAME

YANKEE STADIUM, NEW YORK, Oct. 8.—The New York Yankees won the championship of the baseball world today. They won by defeating the Pittsburg Pirates for the fourth consecutive time, winning out, 4 to 3, in a dramatic ninth-inning rally.

A wild pitch by John Miljus, Pittsburg relief hurler, with the bases filled and two out, let Earl Combs dash home with the winning tally.

The Yankees made a clean sweep of four straight games, the first time this feat has been accomplished since the Boston Braves won four in a row from the Philadelphia Athletics in 1914.

The Pirates fought harder today than ever before in the series but that final destructive wild fling cost them all chance of gaining as much as a single victory.

RUTH HITS HOMER

Early in the game Babe Ruth put a tremendous homer into the distant right center stands, scoring Combs ahead of him. This came in the fifth inning and seemed to put the game on ice.

Wilcy Moore was working well for the Yanks but the Yank defense cracked twice in the seventh and the Pirates tied the score.

Carmen Hill, who started for Pittsburg, was not much better than any of the other pitchers Donie Bush has tried during the series.

Hill gave way to a pinch hitter in the seventh when the Pirates scored two runs.

Moore kept the Pira' hits well scattered but was touched safely 10 times while the Yanks made 12 hits off Hill and Miljus.

RUTH PASSED

The last half of the ninth inning provided drama seldom seen in even the most exciting of world series games. Earl Combs had walked and Mark Koenig reached first on an infield hit.

With two on and none out, Babe Ruth was purposely passed, filling the bases and none out. Then and

(CONTINUED ON FIRST SPORT PAGE)

Fourth Game Play by Play

FIRST INNING

PIRATES—L. Waner beat out an infield hit to Koenig. He hit the first ball pitched and made the bag by his wonderful fleetness of foot. Barnhart was thrown out by Koenig, L. Waner taking second. P. Waner out, Dugan to Gehrig, L. Waner holding second. Wright singled to right, scoring L. Waner, and took second on the throw to the plate. Traynor hit to Dugan, who tagged Wright on the base line. ONE RUN, TWO HITS, NO ERRORS.

YANKEES—Combs hit past Grantham into right field for a single. Koenig singled to right, Combs stopping at second. Ruth singled to right, scoring Combs and sending Koenig to third. Gehrig fanned, swinging at the last one. Rain began falling. Ruth stole second. Meusel was called out on strikes. Lazzeri fanned. ONE RUN, THREE HITS, NO ERRCRS.

SECOND INNING

PIRATES—Grantham out, Dugan to Gehrig, on an attempted bunt. Harris singled past Koenig, who just managed to stop the ball but could not get it away. Smith filed to Ruth. Hill walked. L. Waner beat out a hit to Moore, filling the bases. Barnhart hit to Lazzeri, forcing L. Waner at second. NO RUNS, TWO HITS, NO ERRORS.

YANKEES—Dugan out, Wright to Harris. Collins hit into left field for

(CONTINUED ON SECOND SPORT PAGE)

Gehrig Slams Homer as Yankees Defeat Red Sox, 7-2

FIVE-RUN RALLY IN 3RD INNING STOPS BOSTON

Pipgras Holds Bean-Eaters While Mates Freeze Out Victory in Chilly Game

By Bill Slocum.

BOSTON, April 16.—Yankees and Red Sox played baseball here today in weather that would drive a fan to drink, and many of them did. The champions emerged on top, as was to be expected, the chilling blasts having no apparent effect on the Titanic thumping which has been in evidence in their limited opportunities since the season opened. The score was 7 to 2.

SOME SOLID THUMPING.

One solid session of socking against Danny MacFayden was all the Hugmen needed, but they broke out in two other innings for a run each time. They picked off ten hits against a trio of Boston moundsmen, and half of the hits were for extra bases.

With George Pipgras holding the under control, there wasn't a thing to worry about after the five-run rash in the third inning.

Lou Gehrig moved a bit farther ahead of his home-runless rival, the Bambino. Gehrig hit high and far

WHAT RUTH DID.

FIRST INNING—Popped to Todt near first base.
THIRD INNING—Walked, after count of three and two, filling the bases.
FIFTH INNING—Grounded out. Regan to Todt.
SEVENTH INNING — Grounded out, Rothrock to Todt.
NINTH INNING—Doubled to centre.

WHAT GEHRIG DID.

SECOND INNING—Hit over fence in left centre for home run.
THIRD INNING—Called out on strikes after count of two and two.
FIFTH INNING—Grounded out. Regan to Todt.
SEVENTH INNING—Out at first base on slow roller to Settlemire.
NINTH INNING—Hit sacrifice fly to Taitt, Ruth going to third.

away in the second inning, the ball passing from view behind the left field barrier, far out toward centre field. It was the sort of hit that could be appreciated properly only on a field where the outfields are outfields, and fences are unknown.

Ruth hit only one ball beyond the infield today. In the ninth inning he sizzled one down the right field line and pulled up at second base. Meusel and Pipgras also connected for doubles and Grabowski for a triple. One never knew where the hitting rash would break out when the batterymen were going to such lengths to get on the bases.

Pipgras had to do some efficient pitching in the pinches to keep the Sox down to a pair of runs.

LOU SOCKS ONE.

Gehrig got the only hit off MacFayden in the first two innings but what a sock it was. A high fence perches atop a bank in left centre and the ball cleared it while still humming away from there.

MacFayden got a lot of experience and the Yanks a flock of runs in the third. Grabowski opened with a single to centre and got the decision over MacFayden's throw to second when Pipgras bunted. Combs popped out and both Koenig and Ruth drew passes, forcing Grabowski home. After Gehrig had been called out in strikes, Meusel slapped a single to centre, scoring Pipgras and Koenig. Dugan and Durocher came through with two more singles, each good for a run.

That made it six for the Yankees and a day's work for MacFayden. His successor brought in the name of Merle Settlemire and a pretty fair southpaw delivery which put an efficient check on the Yankee sluggings. The left-hander worked four innings and the only run scored against him was the result of two resounding smacks—Grabowski's triple and Pipgras's double to centrefield in the sixth.

SOX ESCAPE SHELLACKING.

This same inning saw the Sox escape the threatened kalsomine bath. Ken Williams smacked to centre for a base; Buddy Myer was safe when Koenig tried to throw a ball before he fielded it, and Bill Regan delivered Boston's soundest sock of the day, a triple to deep centre.

NEW YORK.	ab	r	h	o	a	BOSTON.	ab	r	h	o	a
Combs.cf	5	0	0	2	0	R'rock.ss	5	0	0	1	3
Koenig.ss	4	1	0	2	3	Todt.1b	4	0	0	13	0
Ruth.lf	4	1	1	1	0	F'stead.cf	4	0	0	0	0
Gehrig.1b	4	1	1	11	0	K.W'ms.lf	3	1	1	3	0
Meusel.rf	4	1	2	1	0	Myer.3b	2	1	1	1	1
Dugan.3b	4	0	1	3	4	Regan.2b	4	0	1	1	4
D'cher.2b	4	0	2	1	3	Taitt.rf	4	0	2	2	1
G'owski.c	4	2	2	6	1	Hoffm'n.c	3	0	0	5	0
Pipgras.p	3	1	1	0	1	Heving.c	0	0	0	1	0
						M'F'den.p	0	0	0	0	0
						S'ttlem'e.p	1	0	0	0	3
						G'rrison.p	0	0	0	0	1
						aD.W'ams	1	0	0	0	0
						bRollings	1	0	0	0	0
						cRogell	1	0	0	0	0
						dBerry	1	0	0	0	0
Totals	36	7	10	27	12	Totals	34	2	5	27	13

a Batted for McFayden in fourth inning.
b Batted for Settlemire in seventh inning.
c Batted for Hoffman in eighth inning.
d Batted for Garrison in ninth inning.

Yankees	0	1	5	0	0	1	0	0	0	—7
Boston	0	0	0	0	0	2	0	0	0	—2

Errors—Combs, Koenig, Rothrock. Two-base hits—Taitt, Pipgras, Meusel, Ruth. Three-base hits—Grabowski, Regan. Home run—Gehrig. Stolen base—Myer. Left on bases—Yankees, 4; Red Sox, 9. Bases on balls—Off Pipgras, 4; off McFayden, 2. Struck out—By Pipgras, 6; by McFayden, 1; by Settlemire, 3. Sacrifice hits—Pipgras (2), Gehrig. Wild pitch—Pipgras. Umpires—Geisel, Campbell, Owens. Time of game—Two hours and two minutes. Attendance—5,000.

Gehrig Scoring Second Home Run

This picture, telephotoed to The American from Boston yesterday, shows First Baseman Lou Gehrig, of the Yankees, scoring his second home run of the season. He banged it off Pitcher McFadden in the second inning. Gehrig is two homers ahead of his 1927 record. He did not score his first homer last year until after the fourth game.

A. T. & T., International Newsreel.

Senators Hand Athletics Third Defeat in Row, 5-4

PHILADELPHIA, April 16 (AP).—The Washington Senators defeated the Philadelphia Athletics in the first of a three-game series today 5 to 4. It was the third straight defeat for the Mackmen.

Buckey Harris.

Singles by "Goose" Goslin and Ossie Bluege that drove three runs over the plate in the eighth inning broke a 2 to 2 tie and gave the Senators the victory. In the fourth inning Goslin lifted the ball over the right field wall for a home run.

Two errors by Bobby Reeves, who is filling in for Manager Harris, helped the Athletics to two of their runs.

Score:

WASHINGTON.	ab	r	h	o	a	PHILADELPHIA.	ab	r	h	o	a
Sisler.lf	5	0	0	1	0	Bishop.2b	4	0	1	3	6
West.cf	0	0	0	0	0	Cobb.rf	4	1	1	3	0
Gillis.ss	4	2	2	1	2	Speaker.cf	5	0	0	3	0
Judge.1b	4	1	2	13	0	Miller.lf	4	1	2	2	0
Goslin.l-rf	4	2	2	2	0	Hauser.1b	4	1	0	9	0
G'zel.r-cf	3	0	1	4	0	Cochr'ne.c	4	0	1	6	0
Bluege.3b	3	0	1	3	4	Hale.3b	3	0	2	0	1
Ruel.c	4	0	0	1	1	Boley.ss	3	0	0	1	1
Reeves.2b	4	0	1	2	5	Dykes.ss	0	0	0	0	0
Lis'nbee.p	3	0	1	0	4	Walberg.p	4	1	1	0	4
						aCollins	1	0	0	0	0
Totals	34	5	10	27	16	Totals	36	4	8	27	12

a-Collins batted for Boley in eighth.

Washington	1	0	0	1	0	0	0	3	0	—5
Philadelphia	0	0	0	0	2	0	0	2	0	—4

Errors—Reeves (2), Lisenbee, Boley, Speaker. Two-base hits—Gillis, Miller, Bishop, Ganzzel, Judge, Hale 2). Home run—Goslin. Stolen base—Cochrane. Sacrifices—Lisenbee, Ganzel. Double play—Hale to Bishop to Hauser. Left on bases—Washington, 5; Philadelphia, 9. Bases on balls—Off Lisenbee, 3; off Walberg, 10. Hits—Off Lisenbee in 9 innings, 8; of Walberg in 9 innings, 10. Hit by pitcher—By Lisenbee (Hale). Struck out—By Walberg 3. Winning pitcher—Lisenbee. Losing pitcher—Walberg.

Uhle Hurls Indians to Victory Over Tigers, 5-4

DETROIT, April 16.—The Indians evened matters with the Tigers here today, 5 to 4.

Uhle, pitching the full game for the tribe, allowed ten hits. Whitehill stuck it out for Detroit until the ninth, when Smith went in for him. Together, they also gave ten.

The score:

DETROIT.	ab	r	h	o	a	CLEVELAND.	ab	r	h	o	a
Neun.1b	4	1	1	5	0	Ja'ieson.lf	5	1	3	2	0
G'nger.2b	4	2	2	5	1	Lind.2b	5	1	1	1	9
Rice.cf	3	1	1	5	1	Gerken.cf	5	1	2	4	0
H'ilm'n.rf	4	0	1	3	0	J.S'well.ss	4	0	1	3	1
M'M'us.3b	4	0	1	3	3	Burns.1b	4	0	0	11	1
F'ergill.lf	3	0	1	1	0	Summa.rf	4	0	0	0	0
T'vener.ss	4	0	2	0	0	Hod'pp.3b	4	0	2	1	4
Woodall.c	2	0	0	4	0	L.Sewell.c	3	1	1	4	1
aH'gr've.c	3	0	0	1	0	Uhle.p	3	1	0	1	0
W'tehill.p	2	0	0	0	2						
Smith.p	0	0	0	0	0						
bEasterl'g	1	0	1	6	0						
cSweeney	1	0	0	0	0						
Totals	34	4	10	27	7	Totals	37	5	10	27	16

a Batted for Woodall in seventh.
b Batted for Whitehill in eighth.
c Batted for Smith in ninth.

Cleveland	0	0	1	0	4	0	0	0	0	—5
Detroit	0	0	0	1	0	0	0	3	0	—4

Errors—Gehringer, McManus (2). Two-base hits—Gehringer, Jamieson, Gerken, Hodapp, Rice, McManus. Three-base hits—Gerken, Heilmann, L. Sewell. Sacrifice hit—Rice. Double play—Hodapp to Lind to Burns. Left on bases—Detroit, 5; Cleveland, 7. Bases on balls—Off Whitehill, 1; off Uhle, 1. Struck out—By Whitehill, 3; by Smith, 1; by Uhle, 2. Losing pitcher—Whitehill. Umpires—Guthrie, Hildebrand and Ormsby. Time of game—One hour and fifty-eight minutes.

Cards Bow to Cubs Again, 6-3

ST. LOUIS, April 16.—Timely wallops behind Guy Bush's high-powered pitching gave the Cubs, a 6-to-3 win over the Cardinals here this afternoon. The game put McCarthy's contingent two up in the local series.

Bush held the slugging Cardinals to seven wallops and fanned seven men. The Bruins drove Jess Haines from the slab in five innings, countin five times in the fourth on three hits, two passes and an error. Little John and Tony Kaufman later took their turns in the box.

Webb sent the apple over the right field pavilion for a homer in the fifth.

The score:

CHICAGO.	ab	r	h	o	a	ST. LOUIS.	ab	r	h	o	a
English.ss	5	1	1	1	3	Douthit.cf	3	1	0	2	0
McG'e.2b	5	0	2	1	4	Holm.3b	4	0	1	1	1
Cuyler.cf	4	0	2	1	0	Frisch.2b	3	0	0	2	5
Webb.rf	5	1	2	0	0	Bot'ley.1b	4	1	2	16	0
Steph'n.lf	4	1	2	1	1	Hafey.rf	4	0	0	2	0
Kelly.1b	3	1	0	12	0	Roett'r.cf	3	0	1	1	0
Hartnett.c	3	1	1	7	0	Thev'w.ss	3	0	0	1	7
Butler.3b	2	1	0	3	4	O'Farrell.c	3	1	1	2	1
Bush.p	4	0	0	1	2	Haines.p	1	0	0	0	1
						Littlej'n.p	0	0	0	0	1
						Kaufm'n.p	0	0	0	0	1
						High.3b	2	0	1	0	1
						bMartin	1	0	[illegible]	0	0
Totals	35	6	10	27	14	Totals	31	3	7	27	18

aBatted for Haines in fifth inning.
bBatted for Littlejohn in seventh inning.

Cubs	0	0	0	5	1	0	0	0	0	—6
Cardinals	1	0	0	1	0	0	1	0	0	—3

Errors—English, Holm (2) Two-base hits—Stephenson, Bottomley. Three-base hits—Hartnett, Bottomley. Home Run—Webb. Sacrifice hits—Frisch, Thevenow, Roettger, Kelly. Stolen bases—Maguire, O'Farrell, High. Bases on balls—Off Bush, 2; off Haines, 2. Struck out—By Bush, 7; by Kaufman, 1. Hit by pitcher—By Kaufman (Butler). Passed ball—Hartnett. Umpires—Stark, Quigley and Pfirman. Time, 1 hour and 51 minutes.

Pirates Win Second Straight from Reds, 8-1

CINCINNATI, April 16. — The Pirates made it two in a row from the Reds here today. The score was 8 to 1.

Grimes gave the Hendricks crew but six hits. In the fifth Cincinnati changed both pitcher and catcher, Edwards going on the mound for Rixey and Sukeforth going behind the bat for Hargraves.

CINCINNATI.	ab	r	h	o	a	PITTSBURGH.	ab	r	h	o	a
D'ssen.3b	4	0	0	1	3	L.W'ner.cf	5	2	1	2	0
C'ghan.cf	3	0	0	4	0	Adams.2b	5	1	3	1	2
Purdy.lf	4	0	1	5	0	P.W'ner.rf	5	0	1	3	0
Kelly.1b	4	0	0	8	1	Wright.ss	5	1	1	3	6
Walker.rf	3	0	1	3	0	T'ynor.3b	5	1	1	1	1
Critz.2b	4	0	1	0	2	G'tham.1b	4	1	2	11	0
Ford.ss	4	1	1	1	2	B'nhart.lf	3	0	0	5	0
H'grave.c	1	0	0	1	0	Gooch.c	4	1	1	1	1
Suke'th.c	3	0	0	2	0	Grimes.p	4	1	1	0	5
Rixey.p	1	0	0	1	1						
Edw'rds.p	3	0	2	1	0						
Totals	34	1	6	27	9	Totals	40	8	11	27	15

Pittsburgh	3	0	0	3	1	1	0	0	0	—8
Cincinnati	0	0	0	0	1	0	0	0	0	—1

Errors—Dressen, Walker, Ford, Wright, Grantham. Two-base hits—P. Waner, Traynor, Barnhart. Double play—Grimes to Wright to Grantham. Struck out—By Grimes, 2; Rixey 1; Edwards, 2. Bases on balls—Off Grimes 2; Edwards, 1. Losing pitcher—Rixey. Left on bases—Pittsburgh, 6; Cincinnati, 8. Umpires—McCormick, Magee and Klein. Time, 1:55.

The Play That Won The Game

By Lou Gehrig

(Yankee First Baseman).

BOSTON, April 16.—A throw by Danny MacFayden in the third inning when George Pipgras laid down a bunt in front of the plate was the turning point in today's game between the Yankees and the Red Sox.

It was a difficult play to make, and I understand it was not scored as an error, but if the throw had been just a little lower, there would not have been any five run rally in that inning.

Those five runs were the difference between the Yankees and the Sox, so it can be seen how important an effect that throw had on the game.

Grabowski had opened the inning with a single and Pipgras bunted, to put Grabowski on second and give Combs a chance to chase him in. The throw was a bit high, pulling the receiver from the bag, and Grabowski was safe instead of being the first out.

Combs popped out to Myer, but MacFayden still had two on bases to think about, and only one out, when Koenig came up. Mark finally worked him for a pass and then Ruth, coming up with three on, was enough to rattle any pitcher. Babe's walk forced in the first run of the inning, and when I went out on strikes, which should have retired the side, it didn't do any such thing. Meusel, Dugan and Durocher followed with singles, and four more runs were in.

After that we couldn't do much in the way of hitting, but with Pipgras going as he was, there wasn't much needed. Both Settlemire and Garrison, who were strangers to us, did not suffer any from the fact that we also were strangers to them. Only once after the third inning could we get two hits in the same session. That was in the sixth, when our last run grew from Grabowski's triple and a double by Pipgras.

Runs for the Week.

NATIONAL LEAGUE.

Teams.	M	T	W	Th	F	S	Su	Tl.
Pittsburgh	8							8
Chicago	7							7
Philadelphia	7							7
New York	5							5
Boston	3							3
Brooklyn	2							2
Cincinnati	1							1
St. Louis	0							0

AMERICAN LEAGUE.

Teams.	M	T	W	Th	F	S	Su	Tl.
New York	7							7
Chicago	6							6
Washington	5							5
Cleveland	5							5
Philadelphia	4							4
Detroit	4							4
St. Louis	3							3
Boston	2							2

SAMMY BAKER DEFEATS ALGER IN TEN ROUNDS

Welters in Lively Scrap at St. Nicholas Athletic Club; Nickfer and Kelly in Draw

Sammy Baker won the decision over Billy Alger in a lively ten-round bout last night at the St. Nicholas A. C.

A small-sized Phil Scott, Bert Stanley, also an Englishman, couldn't take 'em on the jaw and was put to sleep by Bobby Brady, of Jersey City, lightweight, in the 2:40 of the fifth round. Stanley was clearly superior at long range, but wasn't quite as good when they got close.

DELAY IN COUNT.

Rushing in with a volley of blows to the jaw, Brady stumbled over Stanley when the knockdown occurred. Referee Donovan disentangled the pair and wasn't able to pick up the timekeeper's count until eight.

Considerable commotion resulted among the customers, as Stanley indicated his dissatisfaction, but it was a clean knockout. He couldn't have reached his feet. Brady weighed 132¾, Stanley 128¾.

Jimmy Kelly, New York State National Guard champion, fought a draw with Georgie Nickfor, Sheepshead Bay featherweight, in the six-round semi-final. Nickfor went down for an eight count in the fifth round, but had the better of the early sessions. He weighed 126 pounds to Kelly's 129½.

McNAMARA WINS.

Jimmy McNaJmara added to the prestige of Greenwich Village as an art centre by artistically outboxing Jimmy Becker, of Bayonne, in the first six-rounder. It was close, but McNamara was just a trifle too fast. Both weighed 132½ pounds.

Tony Liguroi, a stiff puncher from Iowa, registered a technical knockout over Frank Zavoella, of Brooklyn, in the third round. The bell saved Zavoella at the count of six i nthe second round, and after 20 seconds of fighting in the third session Referee Arthur Donovan decided the punishment was already enough. This was scheduled for four rounds. Liguroi scaled 136½ pounds, Zavoella 139¾.

The four-rounder that opened the bill saw Sam Fillipo, 141¾ pounds, and Sid Goldie, 146½, both Brooklynites, battle to a fast, perfect draw.

It's a Gentle Sport Of a Playful Sort

By George E. Phair

THE hockey star comes limping home,
And he is bruised and lame,
With bandages around his dome
And splints about his frame.

Those divots blasted from his hatch,
Those fractures in his neck,
Remind us that a hockey match
Is like a railroad wreck.

* * *

Our Rangers won the Stanley Cup in Montreal, where there are plenty of ingredients to fill said cup. There was method in their madness.

* * *

It may be okay with the hockey fans, but can you imagine the Yanks playing a world's series away from home? Neither can we.

* * *

Reports from the wide open spaces of Cleveland indicate that the Indians are on the warpath. Baseball fans in Detroit will tell you that the only good Indian is a dead Indian.

* * *

If the aforementioned Indians keep up their warlike habits they will be a great help to the American League exchequer. Competition is the life of baseball, and the Yanks won't get much of it from the Athletics or the Senators.

* * *

Mr. Pyle announces that his Bunion Derby is half finished, but the last thousand miles are the hardest.

* * *

Over the hills and far away
They hike on weary feet,
And oftentimes I fear that they
Are crazy with the heat.

* * *

Twenty thousand Spaniards turned out to cheer Paulino Uzcudum when he returned after discovering the American dollar. And they threw Columbus into jail.

* * *

"Watch the Browns," advises President Barnard, and he might have added: "Do it now." You won't be able to see them in July.

* * *

There ain't many thrills
In the spiritless Phils
Whose playing is full of paralysis,
To win from the same
Seems a sin and a shame
But it counts in the final analysis.

P. S. A. L. Gunners Will Hold Shoot Saturday

Due to a renovated schedule, the Winchester P. S. A. L. rifle shoot will take place this Saturday at the Wingate Athletic Field, formerly known as the Brooklyn Athletic Field, and the New York State shoot will follow a week later, Rowland A. Patterson, of the P. S. A. L. announced yesterday. According to the original plans the Winchester shoot was scheduled for March 31 and the New York State meeting for this Saturday.

Owing to the death of General George W. Wingate, first and only president of the Public Schools Athletic League, one of the shoots was postponed a week prior to the Easter holidaps, causing a change in programme to be made by the high school games committee.

I THINK SO

By Damon Runyon

Continued from Page ..

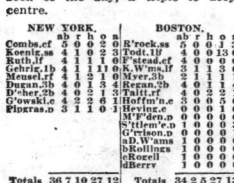

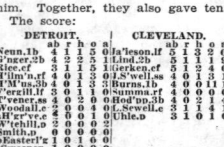

takes to follow the Stribling trail on pugilistic purpose bent is in tough luck.

In Florida, Georgia, Alabama, Tennessee and the Carolinas, the wayfarer encounters only devastation, so far as gate receipts are concerned, for the Striblings live off the country as they march, like General Sherman's boys on his well-known amble to the sea.

And as there are plenty of Striblings who feel that they must live, the ruin in their wake is complete, so Mr. Cox says. There is not only Young Stribling himself, and Mr. "Pa" Stribling, but all the other Striblings, including Little Bill Stribling, the Third.

Plenty of Them in This Family

Little Bill is no bigger than a pint of peanuts, but Mr. "Paw" Stribling has already made him a consumer of gate receipts. It takes a mighty prosperous pugilistic community to support all the Striblings in the affluence to which they are accustomed.

"You can give the cash clients free ringside tickets to see a show following one of Stribling's exhibitions," reports Mr. Cox, sadly. "He comes in and grabs a third of the house. Fights some cracker peach grower, or farm hand, and makes home-loving folks out of the clients."

I FORGOT to mention that Mr. Cox's welterweight, Farmer Joe Cooper, of Terra Haute, Ind., was with Mr. Cox in the cypress swamp.

I presume Mr. Cox was trying to find useful employment for Farmer Joe in the wake of the Stribling caravan, but it was like trailing Big Hearted Charley Murray, the Buffalo promoter, with the idea of picking up any spare change that Mr. Murray might shed.

Looking Over the Heavies in South

Meantime, Mr. Cox viewed the heavyweight crop of the Southland, inspecting sprouts here and there, and making chemical tests whenever possible, and he tells me that the outlook is very glum. He says the best looking heavyweight he saw in the South is a fellow named Tunney.

The prospects of the region below the Mason and Dixon line include Addison (Knock Out) Warren, of the university of North Carolina; Big Sid Terris, of Chapel Hill, N. C., whose right name is Sid McIver; Big Bill Middlekaupf, of Tampa, Fla., and Big Ben Pound, of Rollins College, in Florida. They all seem to come big down hat way.

The most promising, in Mr. Cox's opinion, is Addison (Knock Out) Warren. It is said that Jimmy Bronson, the man with the soft voice, has a contract on Addison (Knock Out).

BIG SID TERRIS, or McIvor, was once flattened by Big Ben Pound, but came back and won a decision over Benjamin. Recently Big Sid went out to Wichita, Kans., and was stretched by one Babe Hunt.

This Hunt, by the way, is the most promising heavy out that way just now. He comes from Ponca City, Okla., and is a huge young man. Angus Snyder, a Canadian, who is making his home at Dodge City, Kans., is another up and coming youth.

Some Likely Looking Boxers

Despite the fact that he was stopped by Hunt, Terris may yet be heard from, so Mr. Cox thinks. He lives near Allison (Knockout) Warren at Chapel Hill, in North Carolina, which also contributed to this union that well-known side-winder of the old Giants, Bunny Hearn.

Big Ben Pound and Big Ben Middelkaupf are stablemates, both managed by Jim Downing, the Tampa boxing promoter. Middelkaupf and Pound are being schooled for Downing by Dan O'Dowd, the Boston heavyweight, who fought 'em all in his day—not always successfully, perhaps, but earnestly.

Pound must be a dead game fellow. He broke his hand in the third round of his fight with Big Sid at Jacksonville, but kept right on plugging to the finish. Middelkaupf is a former football star at the University of Florida, and Mr. Cox reports that he, too, seems to have plenty of "moxie," as we say at the club, meaning courage.

And that seems to be about all from Mr. Cox for the time being.

Heeney Says He Has 50-50 Chance To Defeat Tunney

LONDON, April 16 (AP).—Tom Heeney, the New Zealand challenger picked to fight Gene Tunney for the heavyweight championship in July, thinks he has at least an even chance of winning the title.

"It's a fifty-fifty break on my chances," he said today. "I gave Tunney full credit for not picking a lemon when given the choice of three opponents."

Heeney said he had done no serious training since leaving the United States for a short vacation here, but will sail for America in about ten days to set up training quarters either at Atlantic City or some other seaside resort.

COMPSTON IS CONFIDENT OF BEATING HAGEN

They Are to Meet in a Seventy-two-Hole Match for "Big Money" in London

BELFAST, Northern Ireland, April 16 (AP).—Archie Compston, long-hitting British golfer, who meets Walter Hagen in London in a 72-hole match for "big money" April 27-28, is looking forward with confidence to the test.

The British star expects to have his hands full in disposing of the

American professional champion, but he is on his game and believes he will win.

"NEVER PLAYED BETTER."

"I never played finer golf than in private matches I have played recently," said Compston today, in discussing his chances with the hard fighting Hagen.

"I am particularly pleased with the accuracy of m yiron play.

"Hagen is among the coolest and bravest of match fighters. In a match for a big stake there is something more required than ability to play the game. Hagen's personality has won him many money matches, and personality plays a big part in golf."

Granham and Meusel Lead in Batting Race

NATIONAL LEAGUE.

Player and Club.	G.	AB.	R.	H.	P.C.
Grantham, Pitts.	5	19	2	11	.579
Cohen, New York	4	15	4	8	.533
Frisch, St. Louis	5	17	7	9	.525
Hendrick, Brklyn	3	8	3	4	.500
Brown, Boston	4	13	1	6	.462

AMERICAN LEAGUE.

Player and Club.	G.	AB.	R.	H.	P.C.
Meusel, New York	3	12	5	7	.583
Reynolds, Chicago	3	8	1	4	.500
J. Sewell, Cleveland	6	22	2	10	.455
K. Williams, Boston	6	20	4	9	.450
Rice, Washington	5	16	3	7	.438

The Angler & Hunter

High Water Chart for Local Anglers

	Sandy Hook A.M.	Sandy Hook P.M.	Governors Island A.M.	Governors Island P.M.	Willets Point A.M.	Willets Point P.M.	Jamaica Bay (Canarsie) A.M.	Jamaica Bay (Canarsie) P.M.	Great South Bay (Babylon) A.M.	Great South Bay (Babylon) P.M.
April 17	5:04	5:38	5:33	6:08	8:28	8:56	5:49	6:23	7:19	7:53
April 18	5:57	6:27	6:23	6:54	9:22	9:46	6:42	7:12	8:12	8:42
April 19	6:47	7:15	7:12	7:40	10:13	10:33	7:32	8:00	9:02	9:30
April 20	7:36	8:03	8:00	8:25	11:02	11:20	8:21	8:48	9:51	10:18
April 21	8:26	8:52	8:49	9:12	11:51	—	9:11	9:37	10:41	11:07

BEAM TRAWLERS HAVOC.

The early flounder fishing off the Rockaways and the inshore grounds has already started the depredation done by the beam trawler. Last week one of the Sheepshead Bay skippers watched through the glasses at an arrival which tied up to the Manhattan Beach Bulkhead after having completed a day's dragging of the bottom.

It was clearly seen the depredation done by one, not alone a dozen or so such craft, as green crab, wreck and most every form of crustacea were treated as refuse and thrown over the side on ground that was not fertile, polluted with debris of other sorts. It seemingly is of no concern to the trawl fishermen as to how they deprive the denizens of their feed, driving fish elsewhere and killing the sporting chances of anglers from getting a day's fishing.

The commercial fishermen along the coast are beginning to realize their little end of the programme in showing more co-operation with the conservation commissions, as the depletion of various marketable species is causing alarm. Their methods of netting have been preached against for many years, but, like the "Doubting Thomas," they could not see where any redemption could come about with the methods that were asked of them.

Jersey has been most active in this respect and is getting better co-operation from the commercial fishermen. Something must be done to amend the present laws that give the beam trawlers and illegal netters the scope of inshore ground.

CHIPPERS SOUND FLOUNDERS

It was a tough break for the Long Island Sound anglers on Sunday, not that they did not get their share of flounder fishing, but that the blow was on, which made the boats take to more sheltered quarters.

The Clason Point contingent of the Long Island Sound Boatmens' Association carried capacity crowds, who on making their landings, to be greeted by other anglers who were on the dock to inquire into conditions, seemed from their chilled appearance to be singing in unheard unision that old-time Scotch ballad "Oh wer't thou in the cauld blast!" Nevertheless, the cold elements did not chill the spirits of the anglers, who were prepared for anything that might come.

Captain Bill Byers, of the Chipper, carried a jubilant lot, probably on account of having their supply of flounders, especially Isadore Miller, who collected a ten dollar note for the taking of a flounder which tipped the balance scale resembling 2½ pounds.

Joseph Siniscalchi ran Mr. Miller a close second with a fair sized fish, but the scale naturally favored the larger flounder.

The cold blow that has extended through last week has deterred many from making the trip up the Sound waters, but with havens like Lloyds Harbor, Huntington Harbor, Hempstead Harbor and other coves which afford shelter, some splendid catches are being registered.

Yankees Pound Out 7-2 Victory Over Tigers by Bunching Hits in First and Eighth Innings

Pennock Pitches Smooth Game As Teammates Make 15 Hits

Four Runs in First and Three in Eighth Spoil Day for Gibson; Koenig and Ruth Are Batting Stars; Fothergill Has Very Busy Time in Left Field

By W. B. Hanna

Always an artist to his finger tips, Herbert Pennock never was more so yesterday, disposing of a team which in the past has made more trouble for him than enough. He held the Tigers, who can claw roughly on occasion, to seven hits while the Yankees were winning, 7 to 2.

The Yankee output of hits was fifteen and Pennock pitched one of those ...e, superior games of his, never in trouble, or working out of it before it went far. It was his sixth victory. The Yankees applied their hitting to good bunched purposes in the first and eighth times up, and what ...uning of profit they did with the ...and supple Gibson was in those ...ds.

Gibson, in between, pitched good ball with men on bases and worked hard and faithfully to hold the Yankees so his mates could always have a chance to catch up. He succeeded up to the eighth inning, when the Yanks ...ned the game. Four adverse runs were bad enough, but seven were insurmountable with the skilled server, Pennock, beguiling the Detroiters with his wiles. His control, his hook which shaded the corners, his deceptive ... made them pliable as clay.

Yankees Excel in Field

...had in a fielding way the busy afternoon in left field of Bob Fothergill, ...got as even as he could for inability to hit by smothering all the balls he could get his hands on. He ... off a good deal of weight, but ... slowed up as a rover.

Gehrig's deft work at first base also ...ed. The Yankees were far cleverer in the field, and the Tigers had an ...ss way of throwing the ball ...d which was a good deal more ...eurish than Tigerish. Koenig and ... had an assiduous afternoon hitting the ball.

The Yankees strung up four hits in the first inning, and with the Tigers ...ng the ball here and there and ...where, as if engaged in a new sort of game, the Yankees converted the ... hits into as many runs. Koenig, ... Gehrig and Robertson did the ...g, and each was a belt on the hose ...t Gehrig's fly. Rice was playing so ...t for Gehrig that he was hoist by ...wn and Lou's petard. He couldn't ...n to it.

...vener tripled in the second, with ...out, and ran in on a slow grasser ...ea, which Robertson didn't scoop. Yankees went along hitting steadily but without scoring, as Gibson did work in pinches and showed himself not one to be fussed up easily.

Meusel Hits Foul Into Stands

...Meusel slugged a foul home run ... the left-field seats in the fifth, ... was foul by the span of your ... and the next minute he blistered ... fingers on Warner's hand with a ... down the base line. A lot of New ...s long hitting was deep into left, where Fothergill could get it, and caught such a one off Lazzeri be... Meusel's single. Robertson hit ... the same maw. Warner gathered ... one from Collins, so that this ...g really saw four viciously hit ...ut any reward.

...e in the sixth broke up a monot... of zero innings by lining a home ...nto the right-field seats. Ruth ... move for it. No use. Besides, ... wasn't room for him in that ...

The homer set something go... which soon grew forbidding. Heil... singled and Pennock, working ...dges on Gehringer, wound up by ...ng that efficient Tiger.

...re was one out, and the fat and ...ing Fothergill was up next. He ...it them a mile, but sometimes ...hem less than that. This was one ...ose times. He merely ticked the ...nd was doubled, Pennock to Rob... to Gehrig.

...ergill Catches Three in Seventh

...hergill caught all hands out in the ...d half of the seventh—Pennock, ...s and Koenig. His catch off ...s was a classic and made with ...and, but the one off Koenig was ...stand, pure and simple. He ...ed in the air for it when there ...o need whatsoever of any appeal ...e calcium. However, said theatri... went over big. The crowd gave the ...y little man a hand, and his ...d catch was entitled to that dis...on.

...h struck out in the seventh. ... missed the strike, but threw the ... out in a headlong attempt to go ...cond on the misplay. Therefore a ...agger by Gehrig through Rice ...wasted. Our boys were wasting ...lmost profligately.

...e Yankees did their scoring first ...ast; in other words, they played ... ends against the middle. Four ...n their first inning, three in their ... The three eighth inning runs ... from a single by Robertson, ...e by Collins, triple by Koenig and ...e—to left—by Ruth.

Leading Five Batsmen In Each Major League

NATIONAL LEAGUE

Player	Club	G.	A.B.	R.	H.	Pct.
Grantham,	Pittsburgh	25	88	19	38	.432
P. Waner,	Pittsburgh	25	104	23	41	.394
Roettger,	St. Louis	23	87	7	32	.368
Bottomley,	St. Louis	27	107	24	39	.364
High,	St. Louis	21	83	14	30	.361

Leader year ago to-day, High, Boston, .390.

AMERICAN LEAGUE

Player	Club	G.	A.B.	R.	H.	Pct.
Kress,	St. Louis	24	85	19	35	.412
Rice,	Washington	23	98	18	37	.378
Hale,	Philadelphia	20	72	14	27	.375
Miller,	Philadelphia	19	70	10	26	.371
Meusel,	New York	24	97	14	36	.371

Leader year ago to-day, Fothergill, Detroit, .424.

Reds Lead League After 11-4 Victory Over Philadelphia

CINCINNATI, May 13 (AP).—Cincinnati went into first place in the league race to-day by defeating Philadelphia 11 to 4 while New York lost to Chicago.

The game was a hitting bee, the visitors greeting Carl Mays with a single and two triples which with an error gave them three runs in the first inning. The Reds scored six runs after two were out in the same inning.

Mays settled down after the initial round and permitted only one other run, in the eighth inning.

Donald Hurst, a recruit, joined the Phillies to-day and did well, both at bat and in the field.

The score:

PHILADELPHIA (N. L.)	ab	r	h	po	a	e	CINCINNATI (N. L.)	ab	r	h	po	a	e
Southern, cf	5	0	3	4	0	0	Critz, 2b	4	1	1	3	4	0
Thompson, 2b	5	1	1	2	3	0	Callaghan, lf	4	0	4	1	0	0
Leach, lf	4	1	3	2	0	0	Pipp, 1b	4	1	0	9	1	0
Whitney, 3b	5	1	0	0	2	0	Walker, rf	3	2	2	1	0	0
Hurst, 1b	2	1	2	6	1	0	Allen, cf	4	2	2	4	0	0
Nixon, rf	3	0	0	4	0	0	Dressen, 3b	3	1	1	1	1	1
Sand, ss	4	0	1	3	2	0	Hargrave, c	4	2	2	2	0	0
Schulte, c	4	0	0	3	1	0	Ford, ss	5	2	3	6	6	0
Walsh, p	0	0	0	0	0	0	Mays, p	4	0	2	0	3	0
McGraw, p	2	0	0	0	2	0							
Mitchell, p	2	0	1	0	2	0							
Totals	36	4	12	24	13	0	Totals	35	11	17	27	15	1

Philadelphia .... 300 000 010—4
Cincinnati .... 600 121 01x—11

Runs batted in—Leach, Hurst, Schulte, Hargrave (3), Ford (2), Mays (2), Callaghan, Dressen. Three-base hits—Leach, Hurst, Ford. Stolen bases—Southern, Thompson, Critz (3), Hargrave, Callaghan. Sacrifices—Pipp, Walker, Dressen, Allen. Double plays—Ford, Critz and Pipp; Pipp, Ford and Pipp; Ford and Pipp. Left on bases—Philadelphia, 9; Cincinnati, 9. Bases on balls—Off Walsh, 1; off McGraw, 4; off Mays, 4. Struck out—By McGraw, 1; by Mays, 2. Hits—Off Walsh, 5 in 2-3 innings; off McGraw, 5 in 5; off Mitchell, 7 in 2 1-3. Wild pitch—Mitchell. Losing pitcher—Walsh. Umpires—McCormick, Magee and Klem. Time—2:02.

Di Angelis Pitches Erasmus to Top in P. S. A. L. Baseball

Up to date the outstanding figure in the Public Schools Athletic League chase for the Herald Tribune baseball trophy is Vinny DiAngelis, star Erasmus Hall pitcher, who has pitched his team to five successive league victories and has yet to drop a game to a Brooklyn division nine. DiAngelis's sensational twirling has kept the team on top, ahead of New Utrecht and James Madison, the city champion. Whatever doubt remained as to the right of the Buff and Blue to lead the division was dispelled when DiAngelis added New Utrecht and Madison to his string during the week.

Evander Childs is the only other undefeated team and needs but one more victory to win its way into the playoffs. Its victory over George Washington Saturday was its fourth straight in league competition. James Monroe, last year a finalist, is second in the Bronx division, with four victories and one defeat.

Jamaica and Curtis are now favored to win in the Queens and Manhattan-Richmond divisions, respectively, having gained substantial leads during the week. Richmond Hill, which won in the Queens section last year, is in second place this season and still has a chance of successfully defending its title.

The standing of the schools:

Brooklyn

Erasmus	5	0	1.000	Boys'	2	3	.400
N. Utrecht	4	1	.800	Hamilton	2	3	.400
Madison	3	2	.600	Bkln. Tech.	2	4	.250
Manual	3	2	.600	Lane	1	4	.200
Bushwick	3	3	.500	Jefferson	0	3	.000

Manhattan

Curtis	3	0	1.000	Seward	1	2	.333
Stuyvesant	1	0	1.000	Commerce	0	2	.000
Clinton	2	1	.667	Haaren	0	3	.000
Textile	2	1	.667				

Bronx

Evander	4	0	1.000	Washington	1	2	.333
Monroe	3	1	.750	Harris	0	2	.000
Morris	2	1	.667	Roosevelt	0	4	.000

Queens

Jamaica	4	1	1.000	Bryant	2	3	.400
Richmond	2	1	.667	Flushing	1	3	.250
Newtown	2	3	.400				

TEXAS LEAGUE

Houston, 6; Shreveport, 1.
Waco, 7; Fort Worth, 6 (10 innings).
Dallas, 4; Beaumont, 3.
San Antonio, 3; Wichita Falls, 2.

Briefs

...Dugan was absent again. The ... which Carroll winged for him ...day was not fit for contest.

...my Connolly, the dean, was pre... at first base yesterday. Tommy's ...ing can't be too close to you to ...good. At umpiring he is not only ...n but a virtuoso.

...ce Gehrig raised deep flies with ...on bases and two out. There ...n't have been but one out the ...d time if Combs hadn't tried to ...—Earle had singled and Koenig followed with a two-bagger.

...a absolved himself of a passed ...when Ruth's third strike got away ... him, but as the Babe got to first ...on the misplay, Shea had to ac... an error instead. He also got an ... by throwing the Babe out at ...d. In other words, a strike out, ... and assist all on one pitched ...

...pped third strikes, which let bat... get to first base used to be scored ...ssed balls. Now they are scored ...rors. It would be neither equi... nor sanctioned by rule to score ... as both.

The score:

DETROIT (A. L.)	ab	r	h	po	a	e	NEW YORK (A. L.)	ab	r	h	po	a	e
...ib.	4	0	1	8	0	0	Combs, cf	5	0	1	4	0	0
..., 3b.	3	0	0	2	2	0	Koenig, ss	5	2	4	3	5	0
...ill	1	0	0	0	0	0	Ruth, rf	4	1	3	0	0	0
...ay, 3b	0	0	0	0	0	0	Gehrig, 1b	4	1	2	15	0	1
...f	3	1	1	3	0	0	Meusel, lf	3	1	1	0	0	0
...an, rf	3	0	1	0	0	0	Lazzeri, 2b	4	0	1	3	5	0
...ger, 2b	3	0	0	0	3	0	Robertson, 3b	4	1	2	2	1	0
...ill, lf	4	0	0	7	0	0	Collins, c	4	1	1	0	0	0
...r, ss.	4	1	2	2	0	0	Pennock, p	3	0	0	0	4	0
...	4	0	1	2	2	1							
...p.	3	0	1	0	2	0							
Totals	32	2	7	24	9	1	Totals	36	7	15	27	15	1

...tted for Warner in eighth inning.

Detroit .... 010 001 000—2
New York .... 400 000 03x—7

Runs batted in—Gehrig, Lazzeri, Shea, Robertson (2), Pennock, Koenig, Ruth. Two-base hits—Koenig, Gehrig, Collins, ... Three-base hits—Tavener, Koenig. Home run—Rice. Sacrifices—Lazzeri, Pennock. Double plays—Pennock, Robertson and Gehrig; Koenig, Lazzeri and Gehrig. Left on bases—New York, 11; Detroit, 6. Bases on balls—Off Gibson, 4; off Pennock, ... Struck out—By Gibson, 2. Umpires—...van, Connally and Van Graflan. Time ...

BASEBALL, Today, Yankee Stadium. Yankees vs. Detroit. Game starts 3 P. M.—Advt.

The Days of Real Sport : : : : : : By BRIGGS

Richbourg Is Star At Bat as Braves Beat Cards, 6 to 5

ST. LOUIS, May 13 (AP).—Lance Richbourg, Braves' rightfielder, crashed out a homer and a double to score four of the runs which defeated the St. Louis Cardinals, 6 to 5, here to-day. Hornsby's nine in so doing halted the six-game winning streak of the Cardinals.

Hornsby and Bell, former Card performers, assisted in the defeat, the onetime St. Louis pilot connecting with a pair of singles and a double, while the Boston third baseman collected two singles.

Genewich, except for a bad fifth inning, held the Cardinals at his mercy.

The score:

BOSTON (N. L.)	ab	r	h	po	a	e	ST. LOUIS (N. L.)	ab	r	h	po	a	e
Richbourg, rf	4	1	2	1	0	0	Douthit, cf	4	1	2	1	0	0
J. Smith, rf	0	0	0	2	0	0	High, 3b	5	0	0	0	0	0
Moore, lf	5	1	1	3	0	0	Frisch, 2b	4	1	1	5	5	0
Hornsby, 2b	4	1	3	0	2	0	Bottomley, 1b	4	1	1	9	0	0
Brown, cf	5	0	1	3	0	0	Hafey, lf	4	0	0	4	0	0
Bell, 3b	4	0	2	2	0	0	Harper, rf	4	0	1	3	0	0
Farrell, ss	3	0	0	3	4	2	Wilson, c	3	0	0	4	2	0
Burrus, 1b	3	1	2	10	0	0	Thevenow, ss	3	1	1	1	4	0
Taylor, c	3	2	2	3	0	1	Frankhouse, p	1	0	0	0	0	0
Genewich, p	2	0	0	0	4	0	Johnson, p	2	1	1	0	1	0
*Urban	1	0	0	0	0	0	Sherdel, p	0	0	0	0	0	0
							†Blades	1	0	0	0	0	0
							‡Roettger	1	0	0	0	0	0
Totals	34	6	13	27	10	3	Totals	36	5	7	27	12	0

*Batted for Richbourg in eighth inning.
†Batted for Thevenow in ninth inning.
‡Batted for Sherdel in ninth inning.

Boston .... 003 021 000—6
St. Louis .... 000 050 000—5

Runs batted in—Richbourg (4), Hornsby, Bell, Johnson, Douhit, Frisch, Bottomley (2). Two-base hits—Moore, Hornsby, Richbourg. Three-base hit—Thevenow. Home runs—Richbourg, Bottomley. Stolen base—Harper. Sacrifices—Genewich (2). Double plays—Frisch, Thevenow and Bottomley; Frisch and Bottomley; Thevenow, Frisch and Bottomley. Left on bases—Boston, 7; St. Louis, 6. Bases on balls—Off Genewich, 1; off Johnson, 1. Struck out—By Genewich, 2; by Frankhouse, 3; by Johnson, 1. Hits—Off Frankhouse, 8 in 4 1-3 innings; off Johnson, 5 in 3 1-3; off Sherdel, 0 in 1 1-3. Hit by pitcher—By Frankhouse (Taylor, Burrus); by Sherdel (Hornsby); by Genewich (Douthit). Wild pitches—Johnson, Genewich. Losing pitcher—Johnson. Umpires—Hart, Jorda and Rigler. Time—1:59.

Double-Headers for American League Clubs

By The Associated Press

May 21—At Philadelphia (Washington).
May 21—At New York (Boston).
May 24—At Philadelphia (New York).
May 25—At Philadelphia (New York).
May 26—At Boston (Washington).
May 28—At Boston (Washington).
May 29—At New York (Washington).
June 19—At Cleveland (Chicago).
June 19—At Cleveland (Chicago).
June 19—At Washington (Boston).
June 19—At New York (Philadelphia).
June 23—At Washington (Philadelphia).
June 23—At New York (Boston).
June 25—At Washington (Philadelphia).
June 30—At Boston (New York).
July 2—At Chicago (St. Louis).
July 2—At Philadelphia (Boston).
July 14—At New York (Cleveland).
July 19—At Washington (Detroit).
July 19—At Philadelphia (St. Louis).
Sept. 6—At Boston (Philadelphia).

Uhle Shuts Out A's With One Hit as Indians Triumph, 2 to 0

By The Associated Press

CLEVELAND, May 13.—George Uhle held Philadelphia to one hit and the Cleveland Indians won their second straight game from the Athletics here to-day, 2 to 0.

It was Uhle's sixth victory of the season and he fanned six of the visitors. Mickey Cochrane, Philadelphia catcher, garnered that team's only hit, a double to right in the second inning. Thereafter only one other visitor saw first and he was passed.

Eddie Rommel held Cleveland to five hits, three of which were made by Fonseca, but he contributed a wild pitch which helped the locals get their first run.

The game was played before a crowd of 26,000 fans, the largest to witness a contest here this season.

The score:

PHILADELPHIA (A. L.)	ab	r	h	po	a	e	CLEVELAND (A. L.)	ab	r	h	po	a	e
Bishop, 2b	4	0	0	3	1	0	Jamieson, lf	3	0	0	4	0	0
Cobb, rf	3	0	0	0	0	0	Lind, 2b	3	0	0	0	2	0
Speaker, cf	3	0	0	3	0	0	Langford, cf	3	0	0	4	0	0
Hauser, 1b	3	0	0	8	0	0	J. Sewell, ss	3	1	1	1	4	0
Cochrane, c	3	0	1	2	0	0	Fonseca, 1b	3	0	3	7	1	0
Miller, lf	2	0	0	7	0	0	Summa, rf	3	0	0	2	0	0
Hale, 3b	3	0	0	0	1	0	Hodapp, 3b	2	0	0	2	1	0
Boley, ss	1	0	0	1	2	0	L. Sewell, c	3	1	1	6	0	0
Rommel, p	2	0	0	0	5	0	Uhle, p	2	0	0	1	1	0
*Foxx	1	0	0	0	0	0							
†Haas	1	0	0	0	0	0							
Totals	26	0	1	24	9	0	Totals	25	2	3	27	9	0

*Batted for Boley in ninth inning.
†Batted for Rommel in ninth inning.

Philadelphia .... 000 000 000—0
Cleveland .... 000 001 10x—2

Two-base hits—Cochrane, Fonseca. Sacrifices—Miller, Uhle, Lind, Hodapp. Double plays—Bishop and Hauser; Uhle, J. Sewell and Fonseca. Left on bases—Philadelphia, 1; Cleveland, 3. Bases on balls—Off Uhle, 1; off Rommel, 1. Struck out—By Uhle, 6; by Rommel, 2. Wild pitch—Rommel. Umpires—Nallin, Barry and Dinneen. Time—1:13.

Senators Batter Three Pitchers to Win, 10-3

WASHINGTON, May 13 (AP).—The Washington Senators sallied into three Chicago White Sox pitchers for sixteen hits to-day and took the second game of the series, 10 to 3. Kayes led the batsmen with three hits, including a three bagger.

The score:

CHICAGO (A. L.)	ab	r	h	po	a	e	WASHINGTON (A. L.)	ab	r	h	po	a	e
Mostil, cf	5	1	1	2	1	1	West, lf	4	1	1	3	0	0
Cissell, ss	4	0	1	1	3	1	Rice, rf	5	2	2	2	0	0
Hun'field 2b	3	0	0	2	2	1	Judge, 1b	3	1	2	10	0	0
Barrett, rf	4	0	1	1	0	0	Barnes, cf	3	0	2	3	0	0
Falk, lf	4	1	1	3	0	0	Gillis, 3b	4	0	2	0	2	0
Kamm, 3b	3	0	1	1	2	0	Tate, c	5	1	0	4	0	0
Clancy, 1b	3	0	0	11	1	0	Harris, 2b	5	1	2	2	6	0
Crouse, c	3	1	2	3	1	0	Hayes, ss	4	2	3	2	2	1
Barnabe, p	0	0	0	0	1	0	Hadley, p	3	2	2	1	4	0
Cox, p	2	0	0	0	4	0							
Connally, p	0	0	0	0	0	0							
*Moore	1	0	0	0	0	0							
†McCurdy	1	0	0	0	0	0							
Totals	33	3	7	24	15	3	Totals	36	10	16	27	14	1

*Batted for Fox in seventh inning.
†Batted for Connally in ninth inning.

Chicago .... 002 100 000—3
Washington .... 140 004 01x—10

Runs batted in—Gillis, Hayes, Hadley, West, Judge, Barnes (2), Mostil, Cissell, Rice (2), Gillis. Two-base hits—Mostil, Hadley, Judge. Three-base hit—Hayes. Stolen bases—Cissell, Rice. Sacrifices—Barnes, Crouse, Gillis, Judge. Double plays—Hadley, Hayes and Judge; Cissell, Hunnefield and Clancy. Left on bases—Chicago, 7; Washington, 9. Bases on balls—Off Cox, 3; off Hadley, 2. Struck out—By Connally, 1; by Hadley, 3. Hits—Off Barnabee—6 in 1 inning (none out in second); off Cox, 7 in 5; off Connally, 3 in 2. Hit by pitcher—By Barnabee (Barnes); by Hadley (Clancy). Winning pitcher—Hadley. Losing pitcher—Barnabee. Umpires—Guthrie, Hildebrand and Ormsby. Time—1:45.

Latzo Meets Conley at St. Nicholas Rink To-night

Pete Latzo, former world's welterweight champion, but now in the ranks of the light heavyweights, will oppose Bill Conley at the St. Nicholas Arena to-night in the last bout before he tackles Tommy Loughran on Memorial Day. Conley, who comes from Lewiston, Me., has not been seen here since he dropped a decision to Paul Berlenbach a year ago.

Georgie Nickfor and Al Singer, bantamweights, will meet in the six-round semi-final. Four other bouts are on the card.

Standings in Major Leagues

MONDAY, MAY 14, 1928

American League

YESTERDAY'S RESULTS

New York, 7; Detroit, 2.
Cleveland, 2; Philadelphia, 0.
Washington, 10; Chicago, 3.
Other clubs not scheduled.

STANDING OF THE CLUBS

	New York	Phila'phia	Cleveland	St. Louis	Washington	Detroit	Boston	Chicago	Won	Lost	Percentage
New York	—	2	2	—	5	2	4	4	19	5	.792
Phila'phia	2	—	0	3	1	3	4	—	13	7	.650
Cleveland	1	2	—	3	—	6	2	4	18	10	.643
St. Louis	—	0	4	—	2	4	0	4	14	15	.483
Washington	1	2	—	2	—	1	3	1	10	14	.417
Detroit	0	0	2	3	2	—	1	4	12	19	.387
Boston	1	1	1	1	3	0	—	2	9	15	.375
Chicago	0	—	1	3	1	3	1	—	9	19	.321
Games lost	5	7	10	15	14	19	15	19	—	—	

GAMES TO-DAY

Detroit at New York (3:00).
Cleveland at Philadelphia.
Chicago at Washington.
St. Louis at Boston.

National League

YESTERDAY'S RESULTS

Chicago, 6; New York, 5.
Brooklyn, 8; Pittsburgh, 5.
Cincinnati, 11; Philadelphia, 4.
Boston, 6; St. Louis, 5.

STANDING OF THE CLUBS

	Cincinnati	New York	Chicago	St. Louis	Pittsburgh	Brooklyn	Boston	Phila'phia	Won	Lost	Percentage
Cincinnati	—	2	4	5	2	—	3	2	18	11	.621
New York	2	—	0	—	2	3	4	2	13	9	.591
Chicago	3	2	—	4	2	3	—	3	17	12	.586
St. Louis	2	—	3	—	4	2	1	4	16	12	.571
Pittsburgh	3	1	5	0	—	1	3	—	13	12	.520
Brooklyn	—	0	0	2	1	—	3	6	12	13	.480
Boston	1	2	—	1	1	2	—	2	9	15	.375
Phila'phia	0	2	0	0	—	2	1	—	5	19	.208
Games lost	11	9	12	12	12	13	15	19	—	—	

GAMES TO-DAY

New York at Chicago.
Brooklyn at Pittsburgh.
Philadelphia at Cincinnati.
Boston at St. Louis.

Minor League Baseball

INTERNATIONAL LEAGUE

YESTERDAY'S RESULTS

Jersey City, 7; Toronto, 3 (1st).
Jersey City, 6; Toronto, 4 (2d).
Newark, 5; Montreal, 1 (1st).
Newark, 8; Montreal, 1 (2d).
Reading, 8; Buffalo, 1.
Rochester, 12; Baltimore, 5.

STANDING OF THE CLUBS

	W.	L.	Pct.		W.	L.	Pct.
Toronto	15	9	.625	Jersey City	11	12	.478
Rochester	12	8	.600	Buffalo	9	12	.429
Montreal	11	9	.550	Reading	7	10	.412
Newark	11	11	.500	Baltimore	9	14	.391

GAMES TO-DAY

Jersey City at Buffalo.
Newark at Rochester.
Reading at Toronto.
Other clubs not scheduled.

EASTERN LEAGUE

At Bridgeport— R. H. E.
Waterbury 5 4 6
Bridgeport 19 22 2
Batteries—Sedgewick, Walsh and McCrae; Vincent, Pollinger, Boswell and McCarthy.

At Hartford— R. H. E.
Hartford 4 13 4
Springfield 0 5 1
Batteries—Levy and Eisemann; Bloomer and Niebergall.

At Albany— R. H. E.
Pittsfield 3 8 2
Albany 4 6 1
Batteries—Metevier, Enzmann and Wilder; Marty, Johnson and Akins.

New Haven, 13; Providence, 8.

At New Haven— R. H. E.
Providence 8 20 2
New Haven 13 15 0
Batteries—Morrison, Spear, Jones and Cronin; Loftus, North, Hyman, Kemner and Smith.

STANDING OF THE CLUBS

	W.	L.	Pct.		W.	L.	Pct.
N. Haven	14	6	.700	Springfield	9	11	.450
Hartford	12	7	.632	Pittsfield	9	13	.409
Bridgeport	11	7	.611	Waterbury	8	13	.381
Providence	11	9	.550	Albany	5	13	.278

AMERICAN ASSOCIATION

At Toledo— R. H. E.
Columbus ....000 000 020—2 10 3
Toledo ......010 200 30x—6 8 0
Batteries—Meyers and Vickes, Bird; Scott and O'Neill.

At Minneapolis— R. H. E.
St. Paul.......000 002 002—4 8 4
Minneapolis ....102 210 20x—8 13 2
Batteries—McQuaid, Hopkins and Gaston; Liska and Kenna.

At Milwaukee— R. H. E.
Kansas City....000 000 000—0 5 1
Milwaukee .....003 025 02x—12 15 0
Batteries—Morrison, Sheehan, Davis and Peters; Eddleman and McMenemy.

At Louisville (first game)— R. H. E.
Indianapolis ....000 000 000—0 7 1
Louisville ......002 000 00x—2 4 1
Batteries—Burwell and Spencer; Deberry and Shinault.

Second game— R. H. E.
Ind'pls ...000 000 100 001—2 12 1
L'sville ..000 010 000 000—1 9 1
Batteries—Yde and Spencer; Moss, Tincup and Shinault.

STANDING OF THE CLUBS

	W.	L.	Pct.		W.	L.	Pct.
St. Paul	19	11	.633	Ind'polis	14	14	.500
Kan. City	18	11	.621	Toledo	12	17	.414
Minn'pls	17	12	.586	Louisville	12	18	.400
Mil'wkee	17	12	.586	Columbus	8	22	.267

NEW YORK-PA. LEAGUE

At York— R. H. E.
Williamsport 6 9 0
York 0 3 1
Batteries—Farquhar and Wilson; George and O'Brien.

At Binghamton— R. H. E.
Wilkes-Barre 2 12 5
Binghamton 3 5 2
Batteries—Dixon and Thompson; Auer, Oliver and Trout.

At Elmira (ten innings)— R. H. E.
Scranton 7 13 1
Elmira 6 10 5
Batteries—Kelly, Samuels, Stiley and Hartline; Pritchard and Ennis.

At Syracuse— R. H. E.
Harrisburg 12 14 1
Syracuse 0 4 2
Batteries—Brown and Johnson; Blake, Milligan and Artus.

STANDING OF THE CLUBS

	W.	L.	Pct.		W.	L.	Pct.
Harrisburg	8	4	.667	Bing'ton	6	7	.462
Wil'sport	8	4	.667	Syracuse	5	8	.385
Scranton	8	5	.615	York	5	8	.385
W.-Barre	7	6	.538	Elmira	4	9	.308

PACIFIC COAST LEAGUE

Oakland, 4; San Francisco, 3 (1st).
Oakland, 11; San Francisco, 8 (2d).
Los Angeles, 3; Sacramento, 1 (1st).
Sacramento, 7; Los Angeles, 5 (2d).
Portland, 3; Missions, 2 (1st).
Missions, 3; Portland, 1 (2d).
Hollywood, 7; Seattle, 0 (1st).
Hollywood, 5; Seattle, 4 (2d).

STANDING OF THE CLUBS

	W.	L.	Pct.		W.	L.	Pct.
Hollywood	28	14	.667	Missions	18	22	.450
Sacramento	26	16	.619	Portland	18	23	.439
San Fr'isco	24	18	.571	Oakland	17	25	.405
Los Angeles	22	20	.524	Seattle	13	28	.317

WESTERN LEAGUE

Omaha, 8; Wichita, 6.
Oklahoma City, 6; Denver, 4.
Tulsa, 10; Pueblo, 8.
Des Moines—Amarillo, rain.

STANDING OF THE CLUBS

	W.	L.	Pct.		W.	L.	Pct.
Oklah. City	17	10	.630	Des Moines	12	12	.500
Pueblo	15	12	.556	Wichita	13	15	.464
Amarillo	12	10	.545	Omaha	11	16	.407
Denver	14	13	.519	Tulsa	10	16	.384

SOUTHERN ASSOCIATION

At Nashville— R. H. E.
Burmingham 8 13 2
Nashville 9 10 3
Batteries—Roy, Judd and Yaryan; Fuhr, Alten and Mackey, Knox.

At Chattanooga— R. H. E.
Atlanta 6 7 0
Chattanooga 7 10 3
Batteries—Pence, Rogers and Brock; Pyle, Horan and Minetree.

At Mobile— R. H. E.
Memphis 7 11 4
Mobile 4 12 2
Batteries—Caldwell, Sheppard and Barrett; Friday, Pierce and Coubineau.

At New Orleans— R. H. E.
Little Rock 4 9 1
New Orleans 3 10 1
Batteries—Robinson, Woolfolk, Turpin and Grace; Underhill, Danforth and Stahlman.

STANDING OF THE CLUBS

	W.	L.	Pct.		W.	L.	Pct.
Birming'm.	23	9	.719	Nashville	14	17	.452
Memphis	21	11	.656	Little Rock	13	18	.419
Mobile	17	14	.548	Chat'nooga	11	20	.355
N. Orleans	16	15	.516	Atlanta	10	21	.323

Bears Win, 5-1, Lose, 8-2, in Twin Bill With Royals

MONTREAL, May 13 (AP).—Newark closed its first visit to Montreal by splitting a double bill with the Royals this afternoon. The Bears won the first game, 5 to 1, and lost the second, 8 to 2. The division gave Newark the series, three games to two.

Bentley was wild in the first game, but the Royals could not cash in on his generosity in giving passes, failing badly in the pinches when hits meant runs. Bentley was going strong at the end.

Excellent hurling by Bill Bailey gave the Royals a victory in the second. Bailey held the slugging Bears to two hits, while the Royals c[illegible]ted five off Russell and Fischer, four of them for extra bases. Fowler, with a homer and a triple, batted in six of the Montreal runs.

The scores:

FIRST GAME

NEWARK (I. L.)	ab	r	h	po	a	e	MONTREAL (I. L.)	ab	r	h	po	a	e
Conlan, cf	5	1	2	0	0	0	Haines, lf	2	0	0	0	0	0
Kingdon, ss	4	0	1	2	6	0	Fewster, 2b	4	1	0	2	4	0
Lamar, lf	5	0	1	0	0	0	Gaudette, cf	3	0	0	3	0	0
Fournier, 1b	4	1	2	12	0	0	Holt, 1b	4	0	1	11	2	0
Lee, rf	3	0	1	2	0	0	Shannon, rf	4	0	0	0	0	0
Lutzke, 3b	4	1	0	2	3	1	Fowler, 3b	3	0	0	1	0	0
Mackin, 2b	3	1	2	4	2	0	Fabre, ss	3	0	1	4	5	0
Jenkins, c	2	0	0	5	0	0	Daly, c	4	0	0	4	0	0
Bentley, p	4	1	1	0	4	0	R. Smith, p	2	0	0	2	7	0
							*F. Smith	1	0	0	0	0	0
Totals	34	5	10	27	15	1	Totals	30	1	2	27	18	0

*Batted for R. Smith in the ninth inning.

Newark .... 000 200 003—5
Montreal .... 100 000 000—1

Runs batted in—Holt, Mackin (2), Bentley, Fournier (2). Three-base hit—Mackin. Stolen base—Fewster. Sacrifice—Lee. Double plays—Fewster, Fabre and Holt (2). Left on bases—Newark, 9; Montreal, 10. Bases on balls—Off R. Smith, 5; off Bentley, 8. Struck out—By R. Smith, 4; by Bentley 3. Hit by pitcher—By R. Smith (Kingdon). Umpires—Gaston and Clark. Time—2:10.

SECOND GAME

NEWARK (I. L.)	ab	r	h	po	a	e	MONTREAL (I. L.)	ab	r	h	po	a	e
Conlan, cf	4	1	1	0	0	1	Whitman, lf	2	0	0	0	0	0
Kingdon, ss	4	0	0	0	1	1	Haines, lf	1	0	0	0	0	0
Lamar, lf	3	0	1	2	0	0	Fewster, 2b	2	1	0	3	4	0
Fournier, 1b	3	0	1	8	0	0	Gaudette, cf	3	2	2	3	1	1
Lee, rf	3	0	0	2	0	0	Holt, 1b	2	0	0	6	0	1
Lutzke, 3b	3	1	1	0	3	1	Gulley, rf	1	1	0	2	0	1
Mackin, 2b	2	0	0	0	1	0	Shannon, rf	1	1	0	1	0	0
Jenkins, c	3	0	1	6	0	0	Fowler, 3b	3	2	2	0	4	0
*Uzmann	0	0	0	0	0	0	Fabre, ss	3	0	0	3	1	0
Russell, p	1	0	0	0	1	0	F. Smith, c	2	1	0	2	0	0
†Carlyle	1	0	0	0	0	0	Bailey, p	2	0	1	1	0	0
Fischer, p	0	0	0	0	1	0							
‡Fitzgerald	1	0	0	0	0	0							
Totals	28	2	5	18	7	3	Totals	22	8	5	21	10	3

*Ran for Jenkins in the seventh inning.
†Batted for Russell in the fourth inning.
‡Batted for Fischer in the seventh inning.

Newark .... 001 100 0—2
Montreal .... 400 130 x—8

Runs batted in—Fowler (6), Lamar, Jenkins, Holt, Haines. Two-base hits—Conlan, Haines. Three-base hits—Fowler, Lutzke, Gaudette. Home run—Fowler. Sacrifice—Holt. Left on bases—Newark, 6; Montreal, 3. Bases on balls—Off Bailey, 1; off Russell, 3; off Fischer 3. Struck out—By Bailey, 1; by Russell, 2; by Fischer, 4. Hits—Off Russell, 2 in 3 innings; off Fischer, 3 in 3. Wild pitch—Bailey. Losing pitcher—Russell. Umpires—Clark and Gaston. Time—1:40.

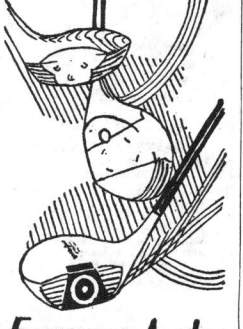

Miss Wills Returns to Paris After 2 Victories

The Hague, May 13 (AP).—Victorious in the first matches of her European tour, Miss Helen Wills, American women's tennis champion, left here for Paris at 12:20 this afternoon. Richard M. Tobin, American Minister to The Netherlands, who was host to Miss Wills and her mother during their stay in The Hague, was present to say farewell.

Miss Wills was successful in two of the three matches she played in Holland, defeating Miss Rollin Couquerque, the Dutch woman champion, in the first singles match, and overwhelming Miss Kea Bouman in the second.

In the doubles Miss Wills, with Miss Penelope Anderson as her partner, lost to Miss Bouman and Miss Couquerque. Miss Anderson had less success in her singles match, losing to both of the Dutch girls.

Children Present 2,000 Pennies to Olympic Fund

Two thousand children of the Holy Innocents Lyceum have contributed 2,000 pennies to the American Olympic Fund. The donation has just been received by the Metropolitan Association of the A. A. U. from the Rev. Joseph G. Murray, director of the Lyceum. Father Murray declared the 2,000 children who contributed a penny each all use the facilities afforded by the Lyceum. This is the first donation of its kind to the Olympic fund.

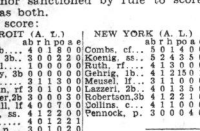

Other Olympic contributions just received include $250 from the Westchester Biltmore Country Club of Rye, $200 from the Staten Island Elks, $210 profits from the benefit swimming meet conducted recently at the Park Central Hotel, and $548 profits of a boxing tournament in an Orange armory. With these additions the Metropolitan Association has obtained $44,000 of its quota of $50,000. It expects to hit the top before June 1.

Pirates Contribute 7 Errors to Help Robins End Losing Streak

Grimes Blasted for Eleven Hits, Which, With Enemy Misplays, Gain 8-5 Victory; Elliott Blows Up in Seventh and Clark Finishes; 15 Passes Issued

By Murray Tynan

In a comedy of seven errors that had the added flavor of fifteen bases on balls to make it even more foolish, the Robins finally managed to win a ball game yesterday and brought their losing streak of five straight to an end. They outfought the Pirates and beat them, 8 to 5, to the immense satisfaction of 20,000 howling fans who turned out to see a ball game at Ebbets Field and wound up by looking at a circus.

Oddly enough, it was the Pirates who made the seven errors while the Robins were playing championship baseball in every section except the pitching box. Their reputation suffered badly there when Big Jim Elliott went from the sublime to the ridiculous in the seventh inning and started to give away the profits the Robins had accumulated through the Pittsburgh errors.

Elliott had handed out free passage to first twice each in the second and fourth, but Charley Hargreaves had pulled him out of one of those tight places when the Pirates set out to test the Brooklyn catcher's arm. Charley tossed out two larcenous Pirates in the fourth, and Jim squeezed out of the spot in the second himself. But there was no getting out of the trouble in the seventh.

Elliott Runs Into Trouble

The Robins had piled up a three-run lead off Burleigh Grimes when the Pirates came up to hit in the seventh, and Elliott was feeling at peace with the world. He had reason to feel that way about it, for it isn't often the Robins are so kind to their pitchers. But prosperity went to James's head, and that expansive smile was soon wiped off his face.

Elliot walked Scott, the first man up, and Mulligan, batting for Gooch, singled to left. There was a deal of talking and fussing on the Pittsburgh bench at this happening, and after a long conference they decided to let Grimes bat for himself. Burleigh also walked and the wave of excitement swept over the Brooklyn dug-out. It reached its crest when Elliott also walked Lloyd Waner, forcing in Scott, and in the backwash Big Jim was swept from the mound.

William Watson Clark, who pitched so well against the Pirates for three innings on Saturday, was sent in to test his southpaw curve against the Pirates and started in just where Elliott left off. Clark walked Adams, forcing in Mulligan. Then Paul Waner looped a single over second that brought in Grimes and brother Lloyd. The Pirates were one run ahead and the hopes of the Robins took on a deep blue hue.

Robins Get Lead Back

Things seemed a little better in the home half of the seventh when Herman led off with a single. When Bressler followed with another single the fans took to yelling again. Bissonette attempted to sacrifice and placed his bunt so well that Grimes couldn't field it in time to make the out. The turnings were filled with none out.

Riconda popped up and Grimes walked Bancroft, forcing in Herman with the tying run. The fate of the Robins was in the hands of Hargreaves and he rose to the occasion with a sizzling smash past Traynor that scored Bressler and Bissonette. The Pirates threw Charley out at second when he attempted to stretch his good fortune, but noboby minded that. The Robins were ahead once more and Clark was pitching as though he intended to keep them there.

All told, Grimes was struck for eleven hits, but with better fielding he probably would have won. Wright and Gooch each made two errors and Grantham and Hemsley made one apiece. Grimes also booted one. With that kind of fielding it was inevitable that the Robins would score, and they did.

Four Unearned Runs

Singles by Bissonette and Riconda and a wild throw made a run in the fourth, and a hit by Statz, Wright's fumble on Partridge, a walk to Herman and Bresslers single made two more in the fifth. All these tallies were unearned.

Grantham muffed Riconda's foul in the sixth and Harry promptly tripled. He scored on Grimes's own error. A fourth unearned run.

Elliott had perfect fielding to help him out in the early innings and had no trouble holding the Pirates to one hit in the first five innings. He started to slide, though, in the sixth, when Lloyd Waner maced him for a triple and Adams and Paul Waner singled. There was a suspicion in this inning that Jim was due for the skids, which was verified by the business in the seventh.

old days that they still cheer for him. Here and there you could hear a "Come on Burleigh!" There was also a chorus of boos.

Not a bad catch by Partridge in the second. Jay pranced over to the foul line and snatched Traynor's fly with his back to the stands.

"The Babe's only two ahead of you" yelled the fans at Bisonette. Whereupon Del bounced one to Grimes.

There were odd doings in the fourth. Paul Waner walked and died stealing. Wright also strolled and went out the same way. Then Elliott regained his control and fanned Traynor.

Grimes has been called a fifth infielder, and he looked like one in the fifth when he pounced on Elliott's bunt for a double play. Burleigh, however, was not so elegant on Elliott's tap in the sixth. The ball rolled between Grimes's legs and a run scored.

The Robins skipped back to Pittsburgh last night to complete their Western trip. They play three more with the Pirates, three with the Reds, and return to Ebbett's Field next Sunday.

The score:

PITTSBURGH (N. L.)	ab	r	h	po	a	e	BROOKLYN (N. L.)	ab	r	h	po	a	e
L. Waner, cf	4	2	1	1	0	0	Statz, cf	3	1	1	2	0	0
Adams, 2b	4	0	1	5	4	0	Partridge, 2b	5	1	0	5	2	0
P. Waner, rf	4	0	3	1	0	0	Herman, rf	3	1	1	1	0	0
Wright, ss	3	0	0	2	2	2	Carey, rf	0	1	0	1	0	0
Traynor, 3b	3	0	0	0	2	0	Bressler, lf	5	1	2	0	0	0
Grantham, 1b	3	0	0	12	0	1	Bissonette, 1b	5	2	3	8	2	0
Scott, lf	2	1	0	0	1	0	Riconda, 3b	5	1	2	0	6	0
Gooch, c	2	0	1	2	1	2	Bancroft, ss	3	0	0	2	2	0
*Mulligan	1	1	1	0	0	0	Hargraves, c	2	0	2	8	2	0
Hemsley, c	1	0	0	0	0	1	Elliott, p	3	0	0	0	0	0
Grimes, p	3	1	0	1	6	1	Clark, p	1	0	0	0	0	0
Totals	30	5	7	24	16	7	Totals	35	8	11	27	14	0

*Batted for Gooch in seventh inning.

Pittsburgh .... 000 001 400—5
Brooklyn .... 000 121 31x—8

Runs batted in—Bressler (2), Bancroft, Hargreaves (2), Bissonette, Adams (2), P. Waner (2), L. Waner. Three-base hit—L. Waner, Riconda. Stolen bases—Grantham, Riconda, Partridge, Carey. Sacrifices—Traynor, Wright. Double plays—Grimes, Wright and Grantham. Left on bases—Pittsburgh, 9; Brooklyn, 10. Bases on balls—Off Grimes, 6; off Elliott, 7; off Clark, 2. Struck out—By Grimes, 2; by Elliott, 4; by Clark, 2. Hits—Off Elliott, 5 in 6 innings (none out in seventh); off Clark, 2 in 3. Hit by pitcher—By Grimes (Statz). Balk—Grimes. Winning pitcher—Clark. Umpires—Wilson, Reardon and Moran. Time—2:18.

Amateurs to Box To-night

The Unison Club will conduct the New York County boxing championships to-night at the Manhattan Casino, 155th Street and Eighth Avenue. Full teams have been entered by the Newsboys' Club, Seward Gymnasium, Clark House A. A., Ascension Parish House and the Holy Name Club. Eight classes will be contested.

Briefs

Harvey Hendrick hasn't been hitting so well. A day or two off may bring him around.

Some of the Flatbush fellows became so used to rooting for Grimes in the

Ruth Hits 45th as Yanks Lose to White Sox; Giants Halted

YANKS BEATEN, 8-4, AS RUTH HITS 45TH

White Sox Pound Pipgras, Johnson and Moore, While Faber Halts Hugmen.

LOSERS' LEAD UNAFFECTED

Chicago Scores 4 Runs in 3d, While Crouse's Homer in 4th Counts 2 More—Victors Star Afield.

By JAMES R. HARRISON.

Thanks to the Detroit Tigers, who again knocked the Athletics into a very horizontal position, the Yankees managed to maintain their lead of four and a half games over the merry Mackmen yesterday. This, however, was no fault of the Yankees, who again lost to the White Sox, this time by 8 to 4.

The Sox did everything to our boys except to tweak their noses. Outside of pitching, batting, fielding and base running, the Yanks were clearly the superior of the White Sox.

Old Red Faber, who was pitching baseballs when some of the Yanks were rolling hoops, held the champions to eight hits, while George Pipgrass, Hank Johnson and Wilcy Moore, handicapped by wretched fielding, were taking everything that the Chicago bats had to offer and were coming back for more.

Ruth and Dugan Hit Homers.

Two of the Yankee runs took the form of homers by the estimable Mr. Ruth and the no less eminent Mr. Dugan. The Babe's forty-fifth slap, in the fourth inning, was one of the longest he has ever hit into the right-field stand. The ball landed only a few rows from the rear of the stand, and the clients applauded furiously thereat.

Dr. Dugan's blow was a synthetic concoction. Johnny Mostil lost a line drive in the sun and the ball rolled to the fence while Mr. Dugan jogged homeward.

These, however, were only minor joys in a day of major griefs. Take a look at the third inning. Pipgras walked Cissell and then Crouse hit to Dugan and a double play was in sight. But Josephus threw miserably to Lazzeri, who was back in the game after several weeks' absence, and both hands were safe.

Faber singled to left and scored Cissell. Crouse should have been out at third, but Pipgras, backing up, threw the pill into the dirt. It was terrible, mates. Mostil tripled to centre, Swanson singled, Metzler was hit by a pitched ball, Pipgras went out and the Sox had four runs.

Crouse's Homer Counts Two.

They made a couple more in the fourth on Cissell's single and a homer into the right field seats by Crouse. In the sixth the venerable Mr. Faber crashed one off the fence, and the rest was just aimless Yankee sniping.

Professor Huggins had his regular nine on the field, with Lazzeri at second and Dugan at third, but they didn't look so good as the junior varsity.

Bill Dickey, the catcher from Little Rock, had something to write home about last night. The tall lad made his début as a Yankee, pinch hitting for Bengough in the seventh and then going in to catch.

Dickey won't get much work this season, but don't be a bit surprised if he is in there regularly with the mask and wind pad next year.

Metzler Causes Commotion.

Metzler's bat slipped from his hands and sailed into the Chicago dugout, grazing the ear of a bench-warmer and causing the boys to scatter nimbly.

Every time the Yanks threatened to start something, a Windy City fellow would make a startling one-hand catch. Cissell did it on Dugan and Mostil went back to the running track for a magnificent catch of Coombs's drive. It was all very discouraging.

The box score:

CHICAGO (A.)	ab.	r.	h.	po.	a.	e.
Mostil, cf	4	2	2	4	1	0
Swanson, 2b	4	0	1	3	3	0
Metzler, rf	4	0	0	1	0	0
Falk, lf	5	0	1	1	0	0
Kamm, 3b	5	0	1	5	0	0
Clancy, 1b	3	0	0	7	2	0
Cissell, ss	3	2	1	4	3	1
Crouse, c	4	2	1	2	0	0
Faber, p	4	2	2	0	1	0
Total	36	8	9	27	10	2

NEW YORK (A.)	ab.	r.	h.	po.	a.	e.
Combs, cf	2	0	1	4	0	0
Koenig, ss	4	0	1	3	4	0
Ruth, lf	3	1	1	3	0	0
Gehrig, 1b	3	0	2	11	1	0
Meusel, lf	4	0	0	1	0	0
Lazzeri, 2b	4	0	0	0	4	0
Dugan, 3b	3	2	2	0	1	1
Bengough, c	2	0	0	3	0	0
Dickey, c	2	0	0	0	0	0
Pipgras, p	0	0	0	0	0	1
Johnson, p	2	1	1	1	0	0
aHeimach	1	0	0	0	0	0
Moore, p	0	0	0	1	1	0
bRob'tson	1	0	0	0	0	0
Total	31	4	8	27	11	2

aBatted for Johnson in seventh.
bBatted for Moore in ninth.

Chicago ....0 0 4 2 0 1 0 0 1—8
New York ....0 0 0 1 0 1 1 0 1—4

Runs batted in—Mostil 2, Faber 2, Swanson 2, Crouse 2, Ruth 1, Combs 1, Gehrig 1, Falk 1, Dugan 1.
Three-base hits—Mostil, Kamm. Home runs—Crouse, Ruth, Faber, Dugan. Stolen base—Falk. Sacrifices—Combs, Swanson. Double plays—Swanson and Clancy; Cissell, Swanson and Clancy; Clancy (unassisted). Left on bases—New York 5, Chicago 6. Bases on balls—Off Pipgras 1, Johnson 1, Moore 1, Faber 4. Struck out—By Pipgras 1, Faber 1. Hits—Off Pipgras 3 in 2 innings (none out in third), Johnson 5 in 5, Moore 1 in 2. Hit by pitcher—By Pipgras (Metzler). Losing pitcher—Pipgras. Umpires—Owens, Geisel and McGowan. Time of game—2:05.

INTERNATIONA LLEAGUE.

Jersey City 3, Montreal 2 (1st game).
Jersey City 4, Montreal 3 (2d).
Rochester 10, Newark 7.

AT READING.
First Game.

		R.	H.	E.
Toronto	3 1 0 0 0 1 1 0 1—7		14	1
Reading	0 0 0 4 1 2 0 1 ..—8		10	2

Batteries—Prudhomme and Styles; Welch, Harrison and Legett.

Second Game.

Toronto	0 0 0 1 0 0 1—2	7	1
Reading	0 2 2 0 0 0 ..—4	9	0

(7 Innings).

Batteries—Collins and Phillips; Hubbell and Lake.

AT BALTIMORE.
(First Game).

Buffalo	0 1 1 2 0 1 0 2 0—7	13	0
Baltimore	3 0 0 0 0 0 0 0 0—3	8	1

Batteries—Williams and Barnes; Johnson, Allen and Dixon.

(Second Game).

Buffalo	2 0 1 0 0 3 3—9	13	0
Baltimore	3 0 1 0 0 0 2—6	11	4

(7 Innings).

Batteries—Ogden, Proffitt, Signor and Barnes; Chambers, Allen and Devine.

STANDING OF THE CLUBS.

	Won	Lost	P. C.
Toronto	68	55	.553
Reading	63	56	.529
Baltimore	62	58	.517
Montreal	63	59	.516
Rochester	59	57	.509
Newark	60	61	.496
Buffalo	61	63	.492
Jersey City	49	76	.392

WHERE THEY PLAY TODAY.
Montreal at Jersey City.
Rochester at Newark.
Buffalo at Baltimore.
Toronto at Reading.

Five Leading Batsmen Of Each Major League

AMERICAN LEAGUE.

	G.	AB.	R.	H.	P.C.
Goslin, Wash	96	303	52	116	.383
Simmons, Phila	80	304	51	114	.375
Gehrig, New York	114	418	102	153	.366
Manush, St. Louis	116	477	73	172	.361
Lazzeri, New York	88	316	52	112	.354

Leader year ago—Simmons, Philadelphia, .393.

NATIONAL LEAGUE.

	G.	AB.	R.	H.	P.C.
Hornsby, Boston	94	332	66	126	.380
P. Waner, Pitts	108	435	96	157	.361
Lindstrom, N. Y.	104	438	67	156	.356
Sisler, Boston	65	282	46	99	.351
Grantham, Pitts	90	316	68	110	.348

Leader year ago—P. Waner, Pittsburgh, .383.

ATHLETICS JOLTED BY DETROIT AGAIN

Tigers Prevent the Mackmen From Gaining in Race, Pounding Out 6-3 Victory.

Special to The New York Times.

PHILADELPHIA, Aug. 15.—By hammering the veteran Jack Quinn in the last two innings, Detroit not only beat the Athletics again today, winning 6-3, but again prevented the Mackmen from gaining on the Yanks. The Tigers brought the Athletics' winning streak to a stop yesterday.

With Mayor Harry A. Mackey and members of his Cabinet looking on, the Athletics held a 1-0 lead going into the eighth, only to have the Tigers score six runs in the next two innings on six hits and errors by Ossie Orwoll and Bing Miller.

For seven innings Quinn, who was seeking his seventeenth victory of the season, engaged in a keen duel with Sam Gibson. Quinn yielded but three hits in the seven rounds while Gibson held the A's hitless until the sixth.

The Mackmen finally scored in the seventh on Jimmy Foxx's single, a force-out by Miller and Orwoll's two-bagger.

While the crowd was watching the scoreboard and saw the Yanks were losing to Chicago again, Quinn wabbled in the eighth and singles by Hargrave, McManus and Gehringer, coupled with Orwoll's error and a wild throw by Miller, gave the Tigers four runs and the game.

In the ninth Detroit increased its total to six, scoring two runs on singles by Rice and Wingo and Fothergill's two-bagger.

Consecutive singles by Foxx, Miller and Orwoll raised the fans' hopes in the ninth, but Gehringer and Tavener came through with flashy stops and the rally was stopped with two runs.

Harry Heilmann, Tiger right-fielder, was banished from the game by Umpire Ormsby in the second inning for protesting a decision at first base.

The box score:

DETROIT (A.)	ab.	r.	h.	po.	a.	e.
Sweeney, 1b	4	0	2	9	0	0
McManus, 3b	4	1	1	0	1	0
Gehr'ger, 2b	4	0	2	2	7	0
Rice, cf	4	1	1	5	1	0
Heilmann, rf	1	0	0	0	0	0
Fothergill, lf	3	1	1	2	0	0
Hargrave, c	3	0	1	2	1	0
aWarner	0	1	0	0	0	0
Smith, p	1	0	0	0	0	0
Wingo, lf-rf	3	0	1	1	0	0
Tavener, ss	4	1	0	5	2	0
Gibson, p	2	0	0	0	0	0
Shea, c	2	1	0	1	0	0
Total	35	6	8	27	12	0

PHILADELPHIA (A.)	ab.	r.	h.	po.	a.	e.
Bishop, 2b	5	0	0	2	1	0
Haas, cf	4	0	2	2	0	0
Cochrane, c	3	0	0	4	2	0
Simmons, lf	4	0	0	1	0	0
Foxx, 3b	3	1	2	0	1	0
Miller, rf	4	2	1	2	0	1
Orwoll, 1b	4	0	2	13	0	1
Boley, ss	1	0	0	2	3	0
bCollins	1	0	0	0	0	0
Quinn, p	3	0	0	1	8	0
cFrench	1	0	0	0	0	0
Total	33	3	7	27	18	2

a Ran for Hargrave in eighth.
b Batted for Boley in ninth.
c Batted for Quinn in ninth.

Detroit ....0 0 0 0 0 0 0 4 2—6
Philadelphia ....0 0 0 0 0 0 1 0 2—3

Runs batted in—Shea 1, McManus 1, Gehringer 1, Wingo 2, Orwoll 1, Collins 1, French 1.
Two-base hits—Sweeney, Orwoll, Fothergill. Three-base hit—Gehringer. Stolen base—Cochrane. Sacrifice—Wingo. Left on bases—Detroit 3, Philadelphia 6. Bases on balls—Off Gibson 3. Struck out—By Gibson 1, Smith 1, Quinn 2. Hits—Off Gibson 3 in 7 innings, Smith 4 in 2. Winning pitcher—Gibson. Umpires—Guthrie, Ormsby and Hildebrand. Time of game—1:58.

SENATORS TOP BROWNS, 4-3.

Rally in Fifth Enables Washington to Take Second of Series.

WASHINGTON, Aug. 15 (AP)—A rally in the fifth inning, which netted two runs, enabled Washington to take the second game of the series today from St. Louis, 4 to 3. Braxton for the Senators and Gray for the Browns were hit freely, but they tightened with men on bases.

The box score:

ST. LOUIS (A.)	ab.	r.	h.	po.	a.	e.
Blue, 1b	5	0	1	9	0	0
O'Rourke, 3b	5	0	0	1	2	0
Manush, lf	3	1	1	0	0	0
Schulte, cf	4	1	4	3	0	0
Kress, ss	3	1	1	1	5	0
McNeely, rf	4	0	2	1	0	0
Mellilo, 2b	3	0	2	4	2	0
Brannon, 2b	0	0	0	0	0	0
Schang, c	3	0	0	4	0	0
Gray, p	2	0	0	1	1	0
aManion	1	0	0	0	0	0
bBet'court	1	0	0	0	0	0
Total	35	3	11	24	11	0

WASHINGTON (A.)	ab.	r.	h.	po.	a.	e.
West, cf	4	1	1	4	0	0
Rice, rf	4	1	2	4	0	0
Goslin, lf	3	1	2	1	0	0
Judge, 1b	3	0	1	9	0	0
Reeves, 3b	4	0	1	1	1	1
Cronin, ss	3	1	2	0	1	0
Harris, 2b	4	0	0	2	2	0
Ruel, c	4	0	1	6	1	0
Braxton, p	3	0	0	0	2	0
Total	32	4	10	27	8	1

aBatted for Mellilo in eighth.
bBatted for Gray in ninth.

St. Louis ....0 2 1 0 0 0 0 0 0—3
Washington ....1 0 0 1 2 0 0 0 ..—4

Runs batted in—Goslin 1, Mellilo 1, Schang 1, Schulte 1, Ruel 1, Judge 1, Reeves 1.
Two-base hits—Goslin 2, Schulte 2, Ruel, McNeely. Stolen base—Cronin. Sacrifices—Schang, Kress. Double plays—Kress, Mellilo and Blue; Kress and Mellilo. Left on bases—St. Louis 8, Washington 8. Bases on balls—Off Gray 4, Braxton 1. Struck out—By Gray 2, Braxton 3. Umpires—Van Graflan, Connolly and Campbell. Time of game—1:44.

EASTERN LEAGUE.

AT NEW HAVEN.
First Game.

		R.	H.	E.
Waterbury	0 1 0 0 0 0 0 0 0—1		9	1
New Haven	2 0 0 0 0 0 3 0 ..—5		11	0

Batteries—Bailey and O'Connell; Zubris and Danning.

Second Game.

Waterbury	0 0 1 1 1 0 0 0 0—3	12	1
New Haven	0 0 2 1 4 0 0 0 ..—7	11	0

Batteries—Head and Moller; Richardson and Danning.

AT BRIDGEPORT.
First Game.

Springfield	2 3 0 3 0 1 0 0 0—9	12	0
Bridgeport	1 0 1 0 1 2 0 1 0—6	13	1

Batteries—Page and Niebergall; Hyman, Auer, Lynch and Rangnow, Jacobs.

Second Game.

Springfield	4 0 0 0 0 0 0 0 0—4	9	0
Bridgeport	0 3 0 3 0 0 0 0 ..—6	15	0

Batteries—Fortune, Moriarty and Niebergall; O'Neal and Rangnow.

AT ALBANY.

Providence	0 0 0 0 0 0 0 0 0— 0	3	1
Albany	2 0 1 3 1 0 10 2 ..—19	23	0

Batteries—Morrison, Wiltsie, Bader and Pond; Styborski and Munn.

AT PITTSFIELD.

Hartford	2 0 0 0 0 3 0 0 0—5	11	0
Pittsfield	0 0 2 0 0 0 0 0 0—2	10	1

Batteries—Cannon, Smith and Redman; Cascarella and Wilder.

STANDING OF THE CLUBS.

	W.	L.	PC.		W.	L.	PC.
N. Haven	76	43	.639	Albany	61	57	.517
Pittsfield	61	51	.545	Bridgeport	59	59	.500
Provid'nce	60	55	.522	Springf'ld	56	57	.496
Hartford	61	57	.517	Waterbury	29	84	.257

CUBS' RALLY IN 9TH CHECKS GIANTS, 6-5

After McGrawmen Make 2 Runs in Last Frame to Take 5-3 Lead Victors Score Thrice.

GENEWICH ROUTED IN NINTH

Gives Way to Faulkner, Who Yields Deciding Run—Giants Now Trail Cards by 3½ Games.

By RICHARDS VIDMER.

Special to The New York Times.

CHICAGO, Aug. 15.—In 1871 Chicago was swept by fire and putting it out was quite a feat. About nine years ago a cyclone blew through the Windy City and there was joy and relief when it subsided. But it is doubtful if the City of Chicago felt as much satisfaction or as great relief on either occasion as when the Cubs stopped the Giants this afternoon as the Cards won, the Giants lost a full game in the race and are now three and a half games behind.

The Nomadic New Yorkers had won five games in a row and sixteen out of their last twenty when they faced the Cubs today. They were moving so fast that they were expecting a warrant any minute for exceeding the speed limit. They even had this contest won three times, and then in the last of the ninth the Cubs came from behind like a thief in the night and the triumph turned into tragedy.

When that final inning started the score was tied, 3-3. When the first half of it was over the Giants were leading by two runs, but when the last half was completed the Cubs were out in front for the first but most important time and the concluding figures were 6 to 5.

Melvin Ott did all he could to make it six straight for the Giants. He drove in a couple of runs with a single in the first inning and, after the Cubs had tied the count, put the New Yorks ahead again with a home run in the fifth.

McMillan Matches Ott.

But every step Ottie took was matched by Norman McMillan, a former Yankee, substituting at third for the Cubs. After Ott's homer, Norman hit one in the seventh and that tied the score for the second time. In the ninth he singled with men on second and third, knotting the count once more. Freddy Maguire did the rest.

When the Giants took their final turn at bat Guy Bush was pitching in a most pleasant manner, if viewed from the Chicago angle. He struck out the first man who faced him, but Welsh and O'Doul singled and Percy Lee Jones was injected to face Ott.

But Ott had done his work for the day and Les Mann stepped up instead. Mann was just as good, though. He singled to centre and drove Welsh home, whereupon Sheriff Blake appeared in the box. Lindstrom singled to left and sent O'Doul home, giving the Giants a two-run lead, 5-3, which at the time seemed one more than necessary. It wasn't even enough.

Genewich Weakens in Ninth.

Two runs behind, the Cubs came up for their final fling against Joe Genewich, who had allowed only six hits up to that point. Stephenson immediately made it seven with a single and Grimm made it exciting by walking. Hartnett sacrificed both runners a base and then McMillan drove them home.

That merely tied the score, though, and still undismayed, McGraw ordered Faulkner to keep it that way. He couldn't do it. Blake hit safely, sending McMillan to second, and a bad throw by Jackson put him on third. On Beck's grounder, McMillan was retired at the plate for the second out, and there was still hope, but Maguire singled to right and Blake scored from second with the winning run.

Artie Nehf received a live rattlesnake from friends in the Southwest this morning. It was accompanied by the suggestion that Artie turn it loose on the Cubs' bench and put some life in the team.

Ray Schalk, former manager of the White Sox, was at large in the park. Ray is running a bowling alley and says he doesn't expect to form any new baseball connections until next Spring. It wouldn't be surprising to see him in a Giant uniform.

The box score:

NEW YORK (N.)	ab.	r.	h.	po.	a.	e.
Welsh, cf	4	2	2	0	0	0
O'Doul, lf	5	2	3	1	0	0
Ott, rf	3	1	2	1	0	0
Mann, lf	1	0	1	0	0	0
Lindstr'm, 3b	5	0	3	0	3	0
Terry, 1b	5	0	1	13	1	0
Jackson, ss	4	0	0	1	7	2
Cohen, 2b	3	0	0	4	2	0
Hogan, c	4	0	0	5	0	0
Genewich, p	4	0	1	1	2	0
Faulkner, p	0	0	0	0	0	0
Total	38	5	13	*26	15	2

CHICAGO (N.)	ab.	r.	h.	po.	a.	e.
Beck, ss	5	0	0	4	4	0
Maguire, 2b	5	0	1	3	2	0
Cuyler, rf	4	1	1	3	0	0
Wilson, cf	4	1	2	2	0	0
Steph'son, lf	4	1	1	3	1	0
Grimm, 1b	3	1	1	8	1	0
Hartnett, c	3	0	0	3	0	0
McMillan, 3b	4	1	3	0	1	0
Bush, p	3	0	0	1	0	0
Jones, p	0	0	0	0	0	0
Blake, p	1	1	0	0	0	0
Total	36	6	10	27	9	0

*Two out when winning run was scored.

New York ....2 0 0 0 1 0 0 0 2—5
Chicago ....1 0 0 1 0 0 1 0 3—6

Runs batted in—Wilson 1, Hartnett 1, McMillan 3, Maguire 1, Terry 2, Ott 1, Mann 1, Lindstrom 1.
Three-base hits—Cuyler, Wilson. Home runs—McMillan, Ott. Sacrifice—Hartnett. Double play—Maguire, Beck and Grimm. Left on bases—Chicago 6, New York 9. Bases on balls—Off Bush 3, Genewich 1. Struck out—By Bush 2, Genewich 3. Hits—Off Bush 10 in 8 1-3 innings, Blake 2 in 2-3, Genewich 8 in 8 1-3, Jones 1 in 0 (pitched to one batter in ninth), Faulkner 2 in 1-3. Winning pitcher—Blake. Losing pitcher—Genewich. Umpires—Rigler, Hart and Jorda. Time of game—2:00.

AMERICAN ASSOCIATION.

AT MILWAUKEE.

		R.	H.	E.
Columbus	1 0 3 0 3 0 0 0 0— 7		14	4
Milwaukee	3 0 5 2 0 1 3 0 ..—14		18	1

Batteries—Winters, Harris and Ferrell; Gearin, Fons and McMenemy.

AT KANSAS CITY.

Toledo	1 0 0 0 0 1 0 1 1—4	7	1
Kansas City	3 0 0 0 0 2 3 1 ..—9	14	1

Batteries—Huntzinger, McNamara and O'Neil, Hamby; Murray, Morrison and Peters.

AT ST. PAUL.

Indianapolis	1 0 1 3 0 0 0 0 1—6	14	2
St. Paul	0 2 0 2 0 0 0 1 0—5	14	1

Batteries—Yde and Spencer; Betts, Kirsch, Hopkins, Shealey and Gaston.

First Game.
AT MINNEAPOLIS.

Louisville	0 0 1 0 2 0 0 0 0—3	7	1
Minneapolis	0 2 0 0 0 0 0 0 0—2	11	1

Batteries—Cullop and Thompson, Bird; Benton, Van Alstyne and Mancuso, McMullen.

Second Game.

Louisville	0 0 0 0 0 0 2 1 0—3	7	3
Minneapolis	0 0 3 0 0 2 1 0 ..—6	13	3

Batteries—Moss, Creson and Bird; Lisenbee and McMullen.

STANDING OF THE CLUBS.

	W.	L.	PC.		W.	L.	PC.
Indianapolis	73	52	.584	St. Paul	64	63	.504
Minneapolis	71	57	.555	Toledo	61	66	.480
Milwaukee	69	57	.548	Louisville	51	73	.411
Kans. City	65	61	.516	Columbus	50	75	.400

MAJOR LEAGUE BASEBALL

AMERICAN LEAGUE.

YESTERDAY'S RESULTS.
Chicago 8, New York 4.
Detroit 6, Philadelphia 3.
Cleveland 7, Boston 0.
Washington 4, St. Louis 3.

STANDING OF THE CLUBS.

	Won.	Lost.	P.C.
New York	77	37	.675
Philadelphia	72	41	.637
St. Louis	59	57	.509
Chicago	53	61	.465
Cleveland	53	62	.461
Detroit	50	62	.446
Washington	51	64	.443
Boston	41	72	.363

WHERE THEY PLAY TODAY.
Chicago at New York (3:20 P. M.).
Detroit at Philadelphia.
Cleveland at Boston.
St. Louis at Washington.

NATIONAL LEAGUE.

YESTERDAY'S RESULTS.
Chicago 6, New York 5.
Brooklyn 6, Pittsburgh 5.
Cincinnati 11, Philadelphia 4.
St. Louis 7, Boston 3.

STANDING OF THE CLUBS.

	Won.	Lost.	P.C.
St. Louis	70	42	.625
New York	63	42	.600
Chicago	64	50	.561
Cincinnati	62	49	.559
Pittsburgh	58	50	.537
Brooklyn	55	57	.491
Boston	32	69	.317
Philadelphia	29	74	.282

WHERE THEY PLAY TODAY.
New York at Chicago.
Brooklyn at Pittsburgh.
Philadelphia at Cincinnati.
Boston at St. Louis.

CARDS BEAT BRAVES AND INCREASE LEAD

Win, 7-3, as Sherdel Allows 7 Hits and Swell Margin Over Giants to 3½ Games.

ST. LOUIS, Aug. 15 (AP).—Sherdel held the Braves to seven hits in the second game of the series here today and, as the Giants lost, the St. Louis Cardinals increased their National League leadership to three and a half games with a 7-3 victory.

Three Boston hurlers were found for a dozen hits, including a home run by Bottomley with two on base. This advanced his total to twenty-six, which is within one of Hack Wilson's aggregate number.

The box score:

BOSTON (N.)	ab.	r.	h.	po.	a.	e.
Richbourg, rf	4	0	2	4	0	1
Brown, lf	4	0	1	2	0	1
Sisler, 1b	4	2	1	10	2	0
Hornsby, 2b	1	1	0	2	2	0
Clark, cf	4	0	1	2	0	0
Bell, 3b	4	0	1	1	3	0
Farrell, ss	4	0	1	2	5	0
Spohrer, c	3	0	0	2	2	0
R. Smith, p	2	0	0	1	1	0
Barnes, p	0	0	0	0	0	0
Edwards, p	0	0	0	0	0	0
aFreigau	1	0	0	0	0	0
Total	31	3	7	24	15	2

ST. LOUIS (N.)	ab.	r.	h.	po.	a.	e.
Douthit, cf	5	1	2	4	0	0
High, 3b	4	1	1	1	2	0
Frisch, 2b	3	2	1	1	3	0
Bot'mley, 1b	4	2	3	10	2	0
Hafey, lf	3	0	1	1	0	0
Harper, rf	3	0	0	1	1	0
E. Smith, c	4	1	2	2	0	0
Thevenow, ss	4	0	1	7	5	0
Sherdel, p	3	0	1	0	0	0
Total	33	7	12	27	13	0

aBatted for Barnes in eighth.

Boston ....0 0 0 1 0 0 0 0 2—3
St. Louis ....2 0 0 2 3 0 0 0 ..—7

Runs batted in—Frisch 1, Hornsby 1, E. Smith 1, Sherdel 1, Bottomley 3, Bell 2.
Two-base hit—Bell. Three-base hit—Sisler. Home run—Bottomley. Stolen base—Douthit. Sacrifices—Hornsby, Hafey. Double plays—Bottomley, Thevenow and Bottomley; High, Frisch and Bottomley; Sisler, Farrell and Sisler. Left on bases—St. Louis 6, Boston 4. Bases on balls—Off R. Smith 2, Sherdel 3, Barnes 1. Struck out—By Sherdel 1. Hits—Off R. Smith 9 in 4 innings (none out in fifth), Barnes 3 in 3, Edwards none in 1. Losing pitcher—R. Smith. Umpires—Pfirman, Quigley and Stark. Time of game—1:49.

SHAUTE BLANKS RED SOX.

Keeps 8 Hits Well Scattered and Indians Win by 7 to 0.

BOSTON, Aug. 15 (AP).—Joe Shaute, Cleveland southpaw, kept Boston's eight hits well scattered today and had an easy time winning from the Red Sox, 7 to 0. Johnny Hodapp knocked in three of the Indians' runs. Griffin was forced to give way in the box in the fourth inning.

The fielding play was Summa's catch of Taitt's long drive into the right field corner, in which he crashed against the fence, suffering injuries which led to his retirement later.

The box score:

CLEVELAND (A.)	ab.	r.	h.	po.	a.	e.
Langford, lf	5	1	1	2	0	0
Lind, 2b	4	3	3	3	5	0
J.Sewell, ss	4	1	0	2	2	0
Hodapp, 3b	5	0	3	1	3	0
Summa, rf	3	1	1	1	0	0
Caldwell, rf	1	0	1	0	0	0
Morgan, 1b	4	0	2	10	2	0
Harvel, cf	5	0	0	2	0	0
L.Sewell, c	5	1	0	6	0	0
Shaute, p	4	0	0	0	2	0
Total	37	7	11	27	14	0

BOSTON (A.)	ab.	r.	h.	po.	a.	e.
Rothrock, 3b	5	0	3	1	3	0
Rogell, ss	4	0	1	3	3	4
Flagstead, cf	3	0	0	5	0	0
K.Wil'ms, lf	4	0	0	2	0	0
Regan, 2b	4	0	2	3	1	1
Taitt, rf	3	0	0	1	0	0
Todt, 1b	3	0	1	8	0	0
Berry, c	2	0	0	4	2	2
aSumner	0	0	0	0	0	0
Griffin, p	1	0	0	0	1	0
Harriss, p	2	0	0	0	1	0
bHeving	1	0	1	0	0	0
Total	32	0	8	27	11	3

a Ran for Berry in ninth.
b Batted for Harriss in ninth.

Cleveland ....0 1 2 2 0 2 0 0 0—7
Boston ....0 0 0 0 0 0 0 0 0—0

Runs batted in—Hodapp 3, Morgan 2, Lind 1, Summa 1.
Two-base hits—Lind, Regan, Todt. Three-base hit—Summa. Stolen base—Lind. Sacrifices—Lind, J. Sewell, Shaute, Rogell. Double plays—Hodapp, Lind and Morgan 2. Left on bases—Cleveland 11, Boston 11. Bases on balls—Off Shaute 4, Griffin 3, Harriss 1. Struck out—By Shaute 3, Griffin 1, Harriss 1. Hits—Off Griffin 6 in 3 2-3 innings, Harriss 5 in 5 1-3. Hit by pitcher—By Shaute (Todt), Harriss (Summa). Losing pitcher—Griffin. Umpires—Dinneen and Nallin. Time of game—1:44.

REDS' 7-RUN RALLY WINS.

Attack in Eighth Inning Routs the Phillies, 11 to 4.

CINCINNATI, Aug. 15 (AP).—Cincinnati scored seven runs in the eighth inning here today and defeated the Phillies, 11 to 4. The victory gave the Reds the edge on the series, two to one.

The box score:

CINCINNATI (N.)	ab.	r.	h.	po.	a.	e.
Critz, 2b	5	1	2	2	3	0
Zitzmann, lf	4	1	2	2	0	0
Walker, rf	4	1	2	2	0	0
Kelly, 1b	3	1	1	9	1	0
Stripp, 3b	3	0	0	1	1	0
Pit'ger, 3b	0	0	0	1	0	0
Allen, cf	4	2	2	3	1	0
Picinich, c	5	2	2	3	1	0
Ford, ss	3	2	3	3	3	0
Kolp, p	2	0	0	1	1	0
bZipp	0	0	0	0	0	0
Rixey, p	1	1	0	0	1	0
Total	34	11	14	27	11	0

PHILADELPHIA (N.)	ab.	r.	h.	po.	a.	e.
Sothern, cf	4	0	0	4	0	0
Th'pson, 2b	4	0	0	1	4	3
Hurst, 1b	4	1	1	11	2	0
Klein, rf	4	1	2	1	0	0
Leach, lf	4	2	2	0	0	0
Whitney, 3b	4	0	3	0	0	1
Sand, ss	4	0	0	2	1	0
Davis, c	4	0	0	4	2	0
Ring, p	2	0	0	1	2	0
Ferguson, p	0	0	0	0	1	0
aDeitrick	1	0	1	0	0	0
McGraw, p	0	0	0	0	2	0
Total	35	4	9	24	14	4

a Batted for Ferguson in eighth.
b Batted for Kolp in seventh.

Philadelphia ....0 0 0 0 0 0 2 0 2— 4
Cincinnati ....0 1 0 0 0 0 3 7 ..—11

Runs batted in—Picinich 1, Pipp 1, Walker 1, Allen 1, Ford 1, Zitzmann 1, Walker 1, Kelly 1, Leach 2, Whitney 2.
Two-base hits — Klein, Whitney, Allen. Stolen bases—Critz, Walker, Kelly, Pittenger. Sacrifices — Zitzmann, Ford, Pipp, Stripp. Double plays—Sand, Thompson and Hurst. Left on bases—Philadelphia 4, Cincinnati 8. Bases on balls—Off Ring 2, McGraw 2. Struck out—By Ring 3, Kolp 3. Hits—Off Ring 9 in 6 2-3 innings, Ferguson 0 in 1-3, McGraw 5 in 1, Kolp 4 in 7, Rixey 5 in 2. Hit by pitcher—By McGraw (Stripp). Winning pitcher—Kolp. Losing pitcher—Ring. Umpires—Reardon, Moore and Magee. Time of game—1:45.

Matsuyama Wins Two.

Kinrey Matsuyama defeated two opponents in exhibition three-cushion matches at the Hoppe Billiard Academy yesterday. In the afternoon he beat H. Bradbury, 30 to 16, in 32 innings, making a high run of 5 to one of 3 for Bradbury. At night Matsuyama vanquished R. Randall, 30 to 8 in 27 innings. The high runs were 5 for the winner and 3 for the loser.

ROCHESTER AGAIN CONQUERS NEWARK

Batters Four Hurlers to Defeat Walter Johnson's Team by 10 to 7 Count.

Walter Johnson's Newark Bears lost their second game in as many days when they fell before the Rochester Red Wings yesterday at the stadium in Newark by a score of 10 to 7. It was a free-hitting contest, with the Bruins garnering eleven hits and the Red Wings fourteen.

In the eighth inning Newark made four of its seven runs. Lutzke hit for a home run with Jacobson and Fournier on bases.

Newark used four hurlers—Harold Goldsmith, who started; Doc Sheridan, Jim Bagby and Harvey Reese.

The box score:

ROCHESTER (I.)	ab.	r.	h.	po.	a.	e.
Brown, 3b	5	1	2	1	0	0
Urban, 2b	4	1	2	1	3	0
Gelbert, ss	5	1	2	3	2	1
Duncan, lf	4	1	0	3	0	0
Felix, cf	4	3	2	7	1	0
I.Smith, rf	5	2	2	1	0	1
Monahan, 1b	5	1	3	7	0	0
Morrow, c	3	0	1	4	2	0
Keen, p	4	0	0	0	1	0
H.Smith, p	0	0	0	0	0	0
Total	39	10	14	27	9	2

NEWARK (I.)	ab.	r.	h.	po.	a.	e.
Conlan, cf	4	0	0	2	0	1
Kingdon, ss	5	1	1	2	5	1
Jacobson, rf	4	1	1	1	1	1
Fournier, 1b	4	1	2	11	0	0
Lutzke, 3b	4	2	3	2	3	0
Lamar, lf	3	0	0	1	0	0
Mackin, 2b	3	0	1	4	4	0
Malone, 2b	0	1	0	1	0	0
Jenkins, c	3	1	1	3	0	0
Goldsmith, p	1	0	0	0	3	0
Sheridan, p	0	0	0	0	0	0
Bagby, p	0	0	0	0	0	0
Reese, p	0	0	0	0	0	0
aBentley	1	0	1	0	0	0
bCarroll	1	0	0	0	0	0
cFleming	1	0	1	0	0	0
Total	34	7	11	27	16	3

a Batted for Goldsmith in fifth.
b Batted for Sheridan in seventh.
c Batted for Bagby in eighth.

Rochester ....0 0 1 2 3 1 3 0 0—10
Newark ....0 1 0 0 1 1 0 4 0— 7

Runs batted in—Lamar 1, Urban 1, Monahan 4, Gelbert 1, Bentley 1, I. Smith 3, Morrow 1, Lutzke 3, Fleming 1.
Two-base hits—Urban, Fournier, Jenkins, Brown, I. Smith. Three-base hits—Lutzke, Gelbert. Home runs—Monahan, Lutzke. Stolen base — Brown. Sacrifices — Lamar, Fournier, Morrow, Urban. Double play—Morrow and Brown. Left on bases—Newark 6, Rochester 6. Bases on balls—Off Goldsmith 2, Keen 4. Struck out—By Keen 3, Sheridan 1. Hits—Off Goldsmith 6 in 5 innings, Sheridan 6 in 2, Bagley 1 in 1, Keen 10 in 7 1-3, Reese 1 in 1, H. Smith 1 in 1 2-3. Winning pitcher—Keen. Losing pitcher—Goldsmith. Umpires—Fyfe, Gaston and Clark. Time of game—2:00.

JERSEY CITY TAKES TWO FROM MONTREAL

Victor, 3 to 2 and 4 to 3, Shoffner Allowing Only Three Hits in Opening Game.

Jersey City defeated Montreal in both ends of a doubleheader in Jersey City yesterday, 3 to 2 and 4 to 3, and scored their fourth and fifth consecutive victories. Lefty Shoffner and Bill Henderson pitched fine ball for the victors, Shoffner holding the Royals to three hits in the opener. Head's hit in the fifth counted two Jersey City players and decided the issue.

The second contest, scheduled for seven innings, was tied at 2—2 in that frame. Each club counted once in the eighth, and then Jersey City tallied again with one out in the ninth to make it a clean sweep for the day.

The box scores:

FIRST GAME.

MONTREAL (I.)	ab.	r.	h.	po.	a.	e.
Stapleton, 1b	4	1	1	14	0	0
Urbanski, 2b	4	1	2	1	4	1
Haines, cf	2	0	0	2	0	0
Shannon, lf	4	0	0	1	1	0
Daly, c	4	0	0	4	0	0
Gaudette, cf	2	0	0	0	0	0
Helgeth, 3b	2	0	0	1	3	0
Schreiber, ss	2	0	0	1	3	1
Thorm'len, p	2	0	0	0	3	0
Buckalew, p	1	0	0	0	0	0
aD.Smith	1	0	0	0	0	0
Total	28	2	3	24	14	2

JERSEY CITY (I.)	ab.	r.	h.	po.	a.	e.
Gilhooley, cf	4	1	1	4	0	0
Kunesch, rf	3	0	1	1	0	1
Manger, 2b	3	2	2	3	3	0
Walsh, lf	2	0	0	0	0	0
Head, c	4	0	2	2	2	0
J.Smith, 1b	4	0	0	14	0	0
Martin, ss	4	0	1	1	3	0
Calleran, 3b	3	0	0	2	3	0
Shoffner, p	3	0	0	0	2	0
Total	30	3	7	27	13	1

a Batted for Thormahlen in eighth.

Montreal ....0 0 0 0 0 2 0 0 0—2
Jersey City ....1 0 0 0 2 0 0 0 ..—3

Runs batted in—Head 2, Urbanski 1, Haines 1.
Three-base hit—Urbanski. Sacrifices—Kunesch, Walsh, Haines. Left on bases—Montreal 3, Jersey City 8. Bases on balls—Off Shoffner 4, Thormahlen 2. Struck out—By Shoffner 1, Thormahlen 3. Hits—Off Thormahlen 7 in 7, Buckalew 1 in 1. Losing pitcher—Thormahlen. Umpires—Solodar and Myers. Time of game—2:00.

SECOND GAME.

MONTREAL (I.)	ab.	r.	h.	po.	a.	e.
Stapleton, 1b	5	0	0	9	0	0
Urbanski, 3b	4	1	2	3	6	0
Haines, cf	2	1	1	1	0	0
Murphy, rf	2	1	1	0	1	0
Gulley, rf,lf	4	0	3	0	0	0
D. Smith, c	4	0	1	7	1	0
G'dette, lf,cf	4	0	1	4	0	0
Helgeth, 3b	3	0	0	1	2	0
Schreiber, ss	3	0	0	0	5	0
Miller, p	3	0	2	0	2	0
Total	34	3	11	*25	17	0

JERSEY CITY (I.)	ab.	r.	h.	po.	a.	e.
Gilhooley, cf	4	0	0	3	0	0
Kunesch, rf	4	1	1	4	0	0
Manger, 2b	[illegible]	2	2	3	5	0
Walsh, lf	3	0	2	4	0	0
Head, c	4	0	0	1	2	0
J. Smith, 1b	4	1	2	9	1	0
Martin, ss	3	0	1	3	1	0
Calleran, 3b	4	0	2	0	0	0
Henderson, p	3	0	0	0	2	0
Total	31	4	10	27	11	0

*One out when winning run was scored.

Montreal ....2 0 0 0 0 0 0 1 0—3
Jersey City ....1 0 1 0 0 0 0 1 1—4

Runs batted in—Calleran 2, Head 2, Haines 1, Gulley 1, D. Smith 1.
Two-base hits—Urbanski, Gulley 2, Calleran. Three-base hits—Walsh (2). Stolen bases—Urbanski, Manger. Sacrifices—Walsh, Martin, Schreiber. Double plays—D. Smith, Urbanski and Stapleton. Left on bases—Montreal 6, Jersey City 6. Bases on balls—Off Henderson 1, Miller 2. Struck out—By Miller 1. Passed ball—Head. Umpires—Myers and Solodar. Time of game—2:00.

WESTERN LEAGUE.

Omaha 3, Amarillo 2.
Des Moines 14, Wichita 0.
Oklahoma City 2, Pueblo 0.
Denver 4, Tulsa 0.

STANDING OF THE CLUBS.

	W.	L.	P.C.		W.	L.	P.C.
Okla. City	26	17	.605	Denver	23	20	.535
Tulsa	26	18	.591	Omaha	19	24	.442
Pueblo	25	20	.555	Des Moines	16	27	.372
Wichita	25	20	.555	Amarillo	14	28	.333

NEW YORK-PENN. LEAGUE.

Harrisburg 4, Syracuse 0 (1st game).
Syracuse 5, Harrisburg 3 (2d, 7 innings).
York 7, Binghamton 5 (1st).
Binghamton 4, York 1 (2d, 7 innings).
Scranton 8, Elmira 5.
Williamsport 7, Wilkes-Barre 2.

ROBINS WIN BY 6-5 FROM THE PIRATES

Vance, Although Rescued by Petty in Eighth, Captures His Sixth in Row.

DAZZY STARS ON ATTACK

Robbie Changes His Line-Up and Harris Rsponds With Homer and Brilliant Fielding.

By JOHN DREBINGER.

Special to The New York Times.

PITTSBURG, Aug. 15.—Deeply incensed over something or other, the Robins gave the Pirates a terrific battle here this afternoon, and on the strength of a number of early knockdowns managed to stagger through to the final bell with enough points in hand to win the decision.

The score was 6 to 5, and left all Pittsburgh speechless, including Manager Donie Bush, who was silenced in the eighth round by Umpire McCormack and run out of the game for making so much noise the good umpire could not hear himself think.

This was slam bang battle from gong to gong, with the Robins running up a lead of 6 to 2 inside of five innings and knocking the left-handed Fred Fussell out of the box in the fifth, only to see their own peerless flinger, Dazzy Vance, overcome with shortness of breath in the closing rounds and go down in a heap in the eighth when it became necessary for Jess Petty to come to his rescue.

Vance Stars With Bat.

However, the collapse of the dazzler was excusable as in the early frames he had performed heroic deeds not so much with his famed right arm but with his bat. Determined to win this game at any cost, Vance had blazed away with a single and two doubles on his first three times up and had helped materially in piling up the early Robin lead.

But though his dignity was ruffled somewhat by the fact that he had to be removed in the middle of an inning, Vance nevertheless had the satisfaction of seeing his co-star Petty preserve a one-run margin to the end. Vance was thus enabled to record his sixth successive triumph and his tenth victory in his last eleven starts.

There were other contributing factors to this Dodger success, not the least being an elaborate shake-up which Uncle Robbie gave the team before the game and which resulted in Joe Harris performing in right field. Old Joe saved the game twice, once in the eighth with a spectacular throw to the plate which cut down what would have been the tying run and again in the ninth when he hauled down a mighty wallop by Traynor in right centre for the final put out. Also old Joe hit a homer.

A double by De Berry and a single by Vance gave the Robins their first run in the second, which the Pirates matched immediately on hits by Brickell and Hargreaves. Bressler's single, a pass to Harris and a single by Riconda gave the Flock another in the third and they added still another in the fourth on the double by Vance, an out and a sacrifice fly by Flowers.

Hillis Hits Homer.

By this time the Pirates were plainly worried, though in the lower half of the fourth young Hillis helped to put them a run closer to the Robins by bouncing a homer between Statz and Bressler.

However, in the fifth the Robins gave Fussell a fearful hiding. Harris hit the ball a tremendous blow over the high scoreboard in right field. Bissonette doubled, took third on a misplay by Paul Waner, and Fussell took the air. Joe Dawson came on and was greeted by a pair of doubles by Bancroft and Vance and the Robins had three for the inning.

Here the Dodgers stood pat, figuring doubtless that Vance easily would hold that four-run advantage. But the dazzler soon encountered stormy going. In the sixth two passes and a single by Traynor gave the Pirates a run. They got another in the seventh on hits by Dawson and Adams, and in the eighth they brought the dazzler down and almost tied the score.

Traynor singled and Brickell walked. Hillis sacrificed, and then Hargreaves took a mean poke at his old pals by lining a single to right. It scored Traynor, but Harris's fine throw nailed Brickell on a close decision which so enraged Donie Bush that McCormack fired him out too.

This finished Vance, and Petty came in. He stopped the Pirates dead.

The box score:

BROOKLYN (N.)	ab.	r.	h.	po.	a.	e.
Statz, cf	4	0	0	3	0	0
Flowers, 2b	4	0	1	4	5	0
Bressler, lf	5	1	1	0	0	0
Harris, rf	3	1	1	3	1	1
Bis'nette, 1b	4	1	2	6	2	0
Riconda, 3b	4	1	1	1	2	0
Bancroft, ss	3	1	1	5	2	0
DeBerry, c	4	1	1	5	1	0
Gooch, c	0	0	0	0	0	0
Vance, p	4	1	3	0	0	0
Petty, p	0	0	0	0	0	0
Total	35	6	11	27	13	1

PITTSBURGH (N.)	ab.	r.	h.	po.	a.	e.
Adams, ss	5	0	1	2	7	0
L.Waner, cf	5	0	1	2	0	0
P.Waner, rf	4	1	2	2	0	1
Granth'm, 1b	3	0	0	13	0	1
aBarnhart	1	0	0	0	0	0
Traynor, 3b	5	1	2	3	1	0
Brickell, lf	3	1	1	2	1	0
Hillis, 2b	3	1	1	3	5	0
Hargreaves, c	4	0	2	2	2	0
bMulligan	0	0	0	0	0	0
Hemsley, c	0	0	0	0	0	0
Fussell, p	1	0	0	0	0	0
Dawson, p	2	1	1	0	0	0
Total	35	5	12	27	16	2

a Batted for Grantham in ninth.
b Ran for Hargreaves in eighth.

Brooklyn ....0 1 1 1 3 0 0 0 0—6
Pittsburgh ....0 1 0 1 0 1 1 1 0—5

Runs batted in—Vance 2, Riconda 1, Hargreaves 2, Flowers 1, Harris 1, Hillis 1, Bancroft 1, L. Waner 1.
Two-base hits—DeBerry, Vance 2, Bissonette, Bancroft. Home runs—Hillis, Harris. Stolen bases—Flowers, Brickell, Hargreaves. Sacrifices—Grantham, Flowers, Hillis. Double play—Hargreaves and Adams. Left on bases—Brooklyn 7, Pittsburgh 9. Bases on balls—Off Fussell 4, Vance 4. Struck out—By Fussell 1, Vance 3. Hits—Off Fussell 8 in 4 innings (none out in fifth), Dawson 3 in 5, Vance 11 in 7 2-3, Petty 1 in 1 1-3. Winning pitcher—Vance. Losing pitcher—Fussell. Umpires—McCormick and Klem. Time of game—2:13.

SOUTHERN ASSOCIATION.

AT NASHVILLE.

		R.	H.	E.
Atlanta	0 1 0 0 1 0 0 1 0—3		10	3
Nashville	0 0 0 1 0 0 0 0 0—1		6	2

Batteries—Oldham and Brock; Alten and Bool.

AT LITTLE ROCK.

Mobile	0 0 0 0 0 0 0 0 0—0	1	1
Little Rock	0 0 0 0 1 0 1 0 ..—2	6	2

Batteries—Welzer, Morton and W. Moore; Turpin and Grace.

AT MEMPHIS.
First Game.

New Orleans	0 0 0 0 0 0 0 1 0—1	6	0
Memphis	3 0 0 0 0 0 0 1 0—4	7	2

Batteries—Collins and Stahlman; Griffin and Berger.

Second Game.

New Orleans	0 3 0 1 0 0 0—4	9	0
Memphis	0 0 0 0 0 0 0—0	3	0

Batteries—Karr and Anderson; Griffin, Shepherd and Berger.

STANDING OF THE CLUBS.

	W.	L.	PC.		W.	L.	PC.
Birm'ham	28	17	.622	Memphis	24	26	.480
Atlanta	31	19	.620	Mobile	21	25	.457
Little Rock	27	23	.540	Chatt'n'ga	20	27	.416
N. Orleans	23	23	.500	Nashville	15	32	.360

Telephoto Reel -:- Bottomley Hits Triple -:- Gehrig Goes Him One Better

These pictures, transmitted to the International Newsreel, show actual play in the third World Series game in St. Louis yesterday, in which the Yanks won by 7 to 3. At the right is a general view of the park and crowd when Bottomley tripled in the first inning. High and Frisch scored on this long wallop of Jim's.

Babe Ruth is seen crossing the plate ahead of Lou Gehrig on the latter's second homer of the game in the fourth inning. This, incidentally, was Columbia Lou's third four-base smack of the series.

St. Louis Gets Look At Baseball 'Clinic'

By Arthur "Bugs" Baer

ST. LOUIS, Mo., Oct. 7.—The old Mississippi looks like Cripple Creek tonight .

* * * *

The limping Yanks limped wider and longer when they crawled over the Cards for the third time.

* * * *

This series has been a very successful clinic.

* * * *

St. Louis should have had an infield of doctors and an outfield of surgeons.

* * * *

Lou Gehrig was swinging his crutch nicely. He connected with a couple of hot water bags and dropped them for homers.

* * * *

AFTER seeing Babe Ruth run the bases like a coward in a war, the St. Louis fans could hardly realize that the Babe is being kept alive by artificial respiration.

* * * *

Nothing but gloom was reported from the Yanks' headquarters tonight. Huggins said: "My team is very sick. I hope they don't recover."

* * * *

But Huggins became happy when Hoyt reported that his arm is so sore he will have to carry it in a sling. Huggins gave Hoyt ten dollars and told him to buy two slings.

* * * *

Gehrig sprained his back smacking that second homer. The trouble with the Cards is that they are too healthy.

* * * *

It doesn't pay to be in the pink of condition these days. Even Strangler Lewis will tell you that a slight dash of halitosis has won many a close wrestling match.

* * * *

ALL the Yanks have to do now is to get into a train wreck to make it four straight.

* * * *

After suffering for nine terrible innings, the Yanks drove away from the park in their four-passenger ambulances.

* * * *

The Missouri Board of Health warned Huggins not to put those patients on the field today. It is open gossip that the Yanks are in the last stages of world seritis.

* * * *

One more sustained slump and the series is over.

* * * *

Durocher and Durst did very well when you consider that neither man is badly hurt.

CARDS LOST OWN GAME, SAYS LOU

Huggins Told Players Before Contest That Red Birds Would 'Collapse.'

Continued from Page 7.

team in the world has ever won a World Series in straight games twice in succession—but believe me the Yankees are apt to do it tomorrow.

Hug probably will send Waite Hoyt in there for that fourth game and I know and the Yankees know and the Cardinals know, too, that if Hoyt is right it's all over but the shouting. Waite is unbeatable when he's right—and in that fourth game he'll go in with everything to gain and nothing to lose.

I suppose the Cards will start Sherdel. He's about all they have. And it will be no easy spot for Willie or any one else. Believe me, any pitcher who goes out there to the mound tomorrow with the knowledge that he's leading a forlorn hope will be in a tough spot.

It takes nerve to pitch in that sort of place. Sherdel has it, I know, and he'll be a tough nut to crack.

But we've already beaten him—and it's history with the Yankees that no pitcher ever goes as well in his second start against us as he does in the first.

COMPOSITE BOX SCORE

NEW YORK (A. L.).

	G.	AB.	R.	H.	2B.	3B.	HR.	TB.	SH.	SB.	SO.	BB.	BA.	O.	A.	E.	F.A.
Durst, cf......	3	7	2	2	0	0	0	2	0	0	1	0	.286	8	0	0	1.000
Paschal, cf...	2	6	0	1	0	0	0	1	0	0	0	1	.167	0	0	0	1.000
Koenig, ss....	3	14	2	2	0	0	0	2	0	0	1	0	.143	4	9	1	.929
Ruth, rf., lf...	3	11	5	7	3	0	0	10	0	0	2	1	.636	6	1	0	1.000
Gehrig, 1b....	3	9	4	5	1	0	3	15	0	0	0	3	.556	26	0	0	1.000
Meusel, lf., rf.	3	10	4	2	1	0	1	6	0	2	3	2	.200	5	0	0	1.000
Lazerri, 2b...	3	8	1	0	0	0	0	0	1	1	0	1	.000	1	5	2	.750
Durocher, 2b..	3	1	0	0	0	0	0	0	0	0	1	0	.000	1	1	0	1.000
Dugan, 3b....	2	3	0	0	0	0	0	0	1	0	0	0	.000	3	0	0	1.000
Robertson, 3b.	2	6	1	1	0	0	0	1	0	0	0	1	.167	2	1	1	.750
Bengough, c...	3	10	1	2	0	0	0	2	0	0	1	1	.200	25	1	0	1.000
Hoyt, p.......	1	3	0	0	0	0	0	0	0	0	0	0	.000	0	1	0	1.000
Pipgras, p....	1	2	0	0	0	0	0	0	1	0	0	0	.000	0	1	0	1.000
Zachary, p....	1	4	0	0	0	0	0	0	0	0	1	0	.000	0	1	0	1.000
Totals		94	20	22	5	0	4	39	3	3	10	10	.234	81	21	4	.962

ST. LOUIS (N. L.).

	G.	AB.	R.	H.	2B.	3B.	HR.	TB.	SH.	SB.	SO.	BB.	BA.	O.	A.	E.	F.A.
Douthit, cf....	3	11	1	1	0	0	0	1	0	0	2	1	.091	6	1	0	1.000
High, 3b......	3	12	1	2	1	0	0	3	0	0	2	1	.167	2	4	0	1.000
Frisch, 2b....	3	9	1	3	0	0	0	3	1	1	1	2	.333	5	12	0	1.000
Bottomley, 1b.	3	11	1	3	0	1	1	8	0	0	4	1	.273	25	1	0	1.000
Hafey, lf......	3	12	0	2	0	0	0	2	0	0	3	0	.167	7	0	1	.875
Harper, rf....	2	6	1	1	0	0	0	1	0	0	1	1	.167	3	0	0	1.000
*Holm, rf.....	2	5	0	1	0	0	0	1	0	0	2	0	.200	4	0	0	1.000
Wilson, c.....	3	11	1	1	1	0	0	2	0	0	2	0	.091	14	2	2	.889
Maranville, ss.	3	9	1	2	0	0	0	2	0	0	1	1	.222	8	2	1	.909
Thevenow, ss..	1	0	0	0	0	0	0	0	0	0	0	0	—	1	0	0	1.000
Sherdel, p....	1	2	0	0	0	0	0	0	0	0	1	0	.000	0	3	0	1.000
Alexander, p..	1	1	0	0	0	0	0	0	0	0	0	1	.000	0	1	0	1.000
Johnson, p....	2	0	0	0	0	0	0	0	0	0	0	0	—	0	0	0	—
Mitchell, p....	1	2	0	0	0	0	0	0	0	0	0	0	.000	0	1	1	1.000
Haines, p.....	1	2	0	0	0	0	0	0	0	0	0	0	.000	0	1	0	1.000
Rhem, p.......	1	0	0	0	0	0	0	0	0	0	0	0	—	0	0	0	—
*Orsatti	3	2	0	0	0	0	0	0	0	0	0	1	.000	0	0	0	—
*Blades	1	1	0	0	0	0	0	0	0	0	0	0	.000	0	0	0	—
Totals		96	7	16	2	1	1	23	1	1	19	8	.168	75	47	5	.961

*Pinch hitters and runners.

SCORE BY INNINGS.

NEW YORK...........	4	2	4	4	0	3	2	1	0—20
ST. LOUIS...........	2	3	0	0	1	0	1	0	0— 7

Runs batted in—By Gehrig, 8; by Meusel, 3; by Durst, 1; by Bengough, 1; by Paschal, 1; by Pipgras, 1; by Dugan, 1; by Robertson, 1; by Ruth, 1; by Bottomley, 3; by Wilson, 1; by Alexander, 1; by Douthit, 1; by High, 1.

Double plays—Koenig, Lazzeri to Gehrig; Koenig, Durocher to Gehrig; Frisch, Maranville to Bottomley; High, Frisch to Bottomley.

Hit by pitcher—By Mitchell (Pipgras); by Zachary (Douthit).

Left on bases—New York, 13; St. Louis, 18.

PITCHERS' RECORDS.

	G	INS	AB	R	H	SO	BB	HB	WP	BK	W	L	PC
Hoyt	1	9	29	1	3	6	3	0	0	0	1	1	1.000
Pipgras	1	9	32	3	4	8	4	0	0	0	1	0	1.000
Zachary	1	9	35	3	9	7	1	1	0	0	1	0	1.000
Sherdel	1	7	26	3	4	2	0	0	0	0	0	1	.000
Alexander	1	2⅓	12	8	6	1	4	0	0	0	0	1	.000
Haines	1	6	23	6	11	3	3	0	0	0	0	1	.000
Mitchell	1	5⅔	16	1	2	2	2	1	0	0	—	—	—
Johnson	2	2	11	1	4	1	1	0	0	0	—	—	—
Rhem	1	2	6	0	0	1	0	0	0	0	—	—	—

Umpires—Rigler and Pfirman (N. L.); McGowan and Owens (A. L.).

Time of games—First game, 1:49; second game, 2:04; third game, 2:09.

FORDHAM NEXT ON N. Y. U. LIST

Coach Meehan of Violet Grid Forces Plans Busy Week for His Charges.

HAVING turned back a stubborn West Virginia Wesleyan eleven, the New York University varsity football squad will launch a trying week of practise on Ohio Field this afternoon in preparation for the annual game with Fordham at the Polo Grounds next Saturday.

Fortunately for Meehan, there were no injuries in Saturday's fracas,

outside of a minor bump here and there. Today's drill will be devoted to a correction of whatever faults were evident in the West Virginia Wesleyan game, while the initial scrimmage will be held tomorrow afternoon.

The Fordham game will be the ninth meeting of the two institutions. The Maroon eleven leads with five victories to their credit.

Purchase of Zachary Proves 'Not So Bad'

By BILL SLOCUM.

Continued from Page 7.

the second of the three games which Huggins dreamed about in August. Then he went to Cleveland, shut out the Indians in the final game of the set, and sent the Yanks into Detroit for the final series of the year with a good lead. And two days later the pennant was in.

"I'm not sure that Huggins wants me to pitch in the series," remarked Zachary while en route from New York to St. Louis on the Yankee special Friday morning. "If he does I will be ready and I hope I can win for him and the other Yanks. You know those boys were awful nice to me for the little work that I did for them. They voted me a full share just the same as if I had been with the club all season."

SHOWS APPRECIATION.

Then he turned again to gaze out the window at the fleeting picture of dryed and faded cornstalks, miles and miles of them, in the ride through Indian October. It was a long speech for Zachary, who is anything but loquatious. As he saw it his part in the pennant fight had been a minor one, but Huggins and the players and the newspaper men, who had seen that ball club stagger through July and August, knew better. Zachary was too modest in rating those performances when every slip meant so much.

Today Tom got his chance to show those Yankee players how he ap-

preciated that consideration shown him when the shares were being voted.

He was not a stranger to world series competition when he stepped out today, as he had been in the scuffle with the Giants in 1924 and with the Pirates in 1925 while wearing a Washington uniform. Today he eased his way to a victory over the Cardinals that should have been much simpler than it was. Only one run should have been scored by the Red Birds. And that could be measured with a micrometer.

KOENIG FUMBLES.

A pitched ball flicked Douthit's shirt in the fifth and High bounced a hit along the right field foul line. It hit the chalk and rolled into the corner for a double on which the speedy Douthit registered. An inch or two, and it would have been foul.

The two runs in the first inning were due to a fumble by Koenig which escaped the records when High's grounder was ruled a hit. Even Andy must have snickered to hear about the veridct. If Koenig grabbed that one and Durst had taken Bottomley's fly, which he misjudged, there would have been no scoring.

But the misplays didn't ruffle Zach in the slightest. He hitched his belt, straightened his cap and kept Bottomley on third while getting the next two men. He allowed nine hits, but only that foul-line double by High could be charged against him. Old Tom was still pitching when High flied to Ruth in the ninth. In the pitching scale Zachary had not been rated as high as Jess Haines, the big right-hander, with the speed and the knuckle ball who started for the Cards. But Tom

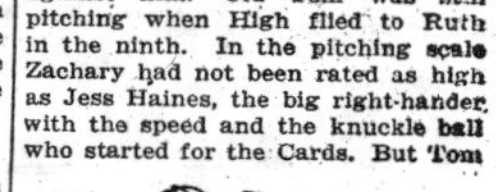

was there at the finish and three pitchers appeared for the home team.

And when Huggins moved to the clubhouse, after shaking Zach's hand, he probably recalled that sultry afternoon in August when the only thing certain about his Yanks was that they still were in the American League.

Chicago Cardinals Win in Pro Grid Game

CHICAGO, Oct. 7 (AP).—The Chicago Cardinals defeated the Dayton Triangles, 7 to 0, in a National Professional Football League game today.

Erickson, Cardinal halfback, intercepted a Dayton pass at the start of the third period, and ran forty yards for the only touchdown of the game. Grant, Cardinal quarterback, kicked for the extra point.

PRO-FOOTBALL RESULTS.

Pottsville, 9; New York Yankees, 7.
New York Giants, 6; Green Bay, 0.
Chicago Cards, 7; Dayton Triangles, 0.
Columbus, 13; Cleveland, 6.
Chicago Bears, 12; Minneapolis Marines, 6.

Lavender Junior Varsity Called

The first of a series of long practice sessions for the City College junior varsity football team in preparation for the game with the Columbia University freshmen at South Field a week from tomorrow starts this afternoon, when Coach Ally Dreiband takes his jayvees in hand and drills them in their new plays for the Lion cubs. The season of the juniors opened on Saturday in the game with Stuyvesant, and there will be no more contests until that with the Columbians.

This is the first time in the history of the college that a Lavender eleven of any kind has met Columbia University, and Coach Dreiband is therefore doubly anxious to score a victory over the Lions. C. C. N. Y. does not meet Columbia in any sport excepting swimming, and the under graduates are therefore attaching more importance to the jayvees' game than they would ordinarily attach to a junior contest. Practice every day right up to the game is the C. C. N. Y. schedule.

Laurries Next Lavender Foe

THE opening game a matter of history now, City College will bend its eforts during the next five days toward preparing for the game with St. Lawrence University, which is scheduled to be played at the Lewisohn Stadium next Saturday.

Coach Parker does not intend to give his men any rest tomorrow after their exertions yesterday against Lebanon Valley College and will drive them hard for the contests with the up-Staters.

St. Lawrence held City College to a 14—14 tie last Fall, and was only deprived of a victory over the Lavender by a sensational run in the last few minutes of the game by Lester Barckman, City College's star halfback.

The Lauries, who have never won from the Lavender in New York, are coming down here Saturday determined to break up their Lewisohn Stadium "jinx" and will be "loaded for bear" when they take the field against the Lavender.

Port Chester Marathon Attracting Many Stars

Requests for entries are coming in from every part of the United States, and from Canada as well, for the Fourth Annual Port Chester national marathon, being conducted under the auspices of the Port Chester Chamber of Commerce.

The course will cover the full 26 miles from Columbus Circle, New York City to Summerfield Park at Port Chester, N. Y. on Columbus Day, Friday, October 12. The race starts at 12 o'clock noon.

Entry blanks can be had from Louis McEvoy, Chamber of Commerce, Port Chester, N. Y.

Warehouseman Is Best Choice At Ravenna

FIRST RACE — Foundation, One Gold Buck, Rose Stark.

SECOND RACE — Warehouseman, Enjoyment, Kings Court.

THIRD RACE—Young April, My Ally, Needy.

FOURTH RACE—Steinway, Blue Caddy, Realtor.

FIFTH RACE—Post Mistress, Stuart's Draft, Go Through.

SIXTH RACE—King's Row, Happy Hobo, Escort.

SEVENTH RACE—The Tailor, Miss Lou, Foolscap.

Roller Skating Marathon In Brooklyn Oct. 12

Competition for the County Clerk William E. Kelly trophy, the chief prize for the modified roller skating marathon to be staged in Brooklyn, Columbus Day, Oct. 12, promises to develop into a thrilling three cornered fight.

The entries include Charley Gregory of the Brooklyn Roller Skating Rink; Murray Gorman, newly crowned one mile champion of Eastern United States, and Eddie Jervis, of Newark, N. J.

Star French Amateur Runners Disqualified

PARIS, Oct. 7—(A.P.)—Seraphim Martin and Jules La Doumegue French middle distance running stars, have been disqualified from all amateur events for three months and barred from representing France in foreign competition for one year.

This ruling was handed down after the two stars had refused to accompany a French team to Japan.

Joie Ray Here to Talk With A. A. U. and Tex

Joie Ray, America's premier long distance runner, arrived from his home in Gary, Ind., this morning for a conference with the A. A. U. authorities and Tex Rickard, scheduled for tomorrow morning regarding his competing in the promoter's international indoor marathon programme at the Garden.

BOYS' BASEBALL PILOTS TO MEET

The managers of the following teams are invited to meet the boys' baseball chairman, in Room 275 at No. 1834 Broadway, Thursday afternoon at 4 p. m. Only one representative from a team will be permitted at this important meeting and managers must bring their identification cards.

In case the team manager cannot come he should give his identification card to the team captain or representative.

It is important to attend this meeting, but only one member from the teams listed below should report:

Yankee Granges, Chelseas, Eddie All-Stars, York Avenue Boys, El Reys, Emeralds Junior, Prospects B. C., New York Maroons, Lances White Eagles, St. Athanasius, Diamonds A. C., Laramie Cubs, Foster A. C., Eurekas, Rosebank Yankees, Paterson Emblems, Remsens Columbians, Ossining Juniors, Bell Harbor Midgets Coney Island All-Stars, Marnes A. C. Dalton Club Gleason A. C., Arrow B. C., Condors, Combines, Royal Aces, Alwyns Jefferson Juniors Silver Foxes, Cubs of the Catholic Boys' Clubs, Veronas Crotona All-Stars, Webster A. C. Bell A. C., Meteors Keltons, Christie All-Stars, Majestics, Common wealths, Braves Junior, Forest Cubs Raiders Kingsway Midgets.

Managers who have not mailed in the names of their two most valuable players should do so at once. Address to The Boys' Baseball Chairman, care The New York American 1834 Broadway, New York City.

HOOVER LEADS IN KENTUCKY STRAW VOTE

For Details of National Vote, See Page 6.

REGISTER THIS WEEK

CHARACTER · QUALITY · AMERICA FIRST! · ENTERPRISE · ACCURACY

New York American

AN AMERICAN PAPER FOR THE AMERICAN PEOPLE

FINAL

IN TWO SECTIONS—SECTION ONE.

No. 16,518.—DAILY. Copyright, 1928, by New York American, Inc. Registered in U. S. Patent Office. EDITORIAL PHONE, DRY Dock 8000 MONDAY, OCTOBER 8, 1928—26 PAGES BUSINESS PHONE, COLumbus 7000. Entered as second class matter, Post Office, New York, N. Y. ★★★ THREE CENTS Within 200 Mile Radius | Elsewhere Four Cents

YANKS WIN, 7-3; GEHRIG HITS 2 HOMERS

ZEPPELIN IN LAST TEST FOR U. S. HOP

Today

Thanks, Mr. Wilbur.
The South Sees Hoover.
Cheerful Mr. Simpson.
Old Hearts Need Care.

—By Arthur Brisbane—

CONGRATULATIONS to Secretary Wilbur, who has ordered for our navy two dirigibles that will be the biggest in the world.

They will be three times as big as the Los Angeles, one third bigger than the German giant Count Zeppelin and each will carry, under the great gas bag, five airplanes for scouting.

The Goodyear Zeppelin Corporation will build them and friendly nations abroad are informed that we do not intend to be taken by surprise.

A fleet of such dirigibles, each carrying fifty tons of explosives and modern war gas, able to unleash one hundred fast destructive planes, could leave with Uncle Sam's compliments a visiting card in Europe or Asia that would not soon be forgotten.

We make war on no nation, but we should be ready and able to fill with subsequent regret any one attacking us.

Mr. Hoover was warmly received in Tennessee and elsewhere in the South. His declarations in favor of a protective tariff and protective immigration laws were heavily applauded.

The South becomes more and more an industrial region, with immense natural wealth in coal, iron, water power and climate. It has long been said that many Southerners vote the Democratic ticket and pray for the Republican ticket.

This year many will vote as they pray.

Anything approaching a free-trade Democratic policy would crack the Solid South, with no other complication.

This year, however, as Mr. Raskob says, the Democratic party advocates high tariff and high wages.

James Simpson, head and owner of Marshall Field & Co. in Chicago, starting for Europe, says he is for Hoover and, "The purchasing power of the country is increasingly great. Our sales are bigger this year than for any like period in the history of our firm."

Mr. Simpson can judge conditions. His retail and wholesale departments each do the biggest business of any individual concern in this country. His wholesale department puts him in touch with business conditions everywhere in the United States.

Mr. Simpson also says: "I do not think the election of Governor Smith would injure the business of the United States. He is a very fine man and very human in his conduct toward his fellow men."

Governor Smith is the first Democratic candidate in many years not feared by big business interests.

William W. Breck, retired business man, fell dead while playing golf last Saturday. He was sixty-four years old.

At sixty-four, make no violent effort, unless a good doctor has pronounced your heart "fool proof."

Golf is good for old men that play, as they should, talking, laughing, walking slowly. It's dangerous for those that strain and strive to better their game.

Remember, old gentlemen, that whether you go around in 130 or 103, the cosmos will roll on, just the same. Treat an old heart as you would a delicate vase, not as you would treat an old rubber boot.

A dirigible, the "Puritan," made by Goodyear, landed gently yesterday on a roof in Washington, remained five minutes, flew away.

That will interest Postmaster New and President Coolidge, who have made the postoffice efficient in aviation development.

They will want postoffices in big cities with air mail landings on the roofs. That should begin with gigantic postoffices in New York and Chicago.

SOME of the mail now goes by airplane. ALL first class mail will go by airplane soon.

Also passengers will travel more and more by air. Colonel Lindbergh announces that the cross country trip by Pullman car and airplane will hereafter include "Pullman sleeping planes." Pullman cars will take passengers to Columbus, Ohio, via the Pennsylvania Railroad, thence will fly to the coast, sleeping in the plane at night, making the trip from ocean to ocean in forty-eight hours. That is flying progress.

Big New York, with about seven million population, and on its way to twenty millions, has about 125,000 new babies born each year, including 1,052 sets of twins on the average, and only nine sets of triplets.

The population problem would be complicated, but for nature's wisdom that holds down increase, in the higher ranks of animal life. A mouse has 100 children in a year, an elephant lives 100 years and has only one or two children.

HUGMEN MAKE IT 3 STRAIGHT OVER ST. LOUIS

Zachary, Left-Hander, Twirls Invincible Game; Bad Plays on Field Prevent Shutout

By DAMON RUNYON.

SPORTSMAN PARK, St. Louis, Oct. 7.—It wouldn't be inappropriate, though it might not be in good taste, for the congregation to rise at this moment and join in the famous civic lullaby of St. Louis:

"Got the Blues—
Got the Blues—
Got the St. Louis Blues."

Memory halts us there. Possibly the reader will recall the words of the Grand Old Moan in toto. In the interests of variety and detail, ye scribe dispatched Mr. Al Schacht, the well-known harlequin of baseball, among the dour-looking natives to gather all the lyric this afternoon, but as the New York Yankees had just finished lambasting the St. Louis Cardinals by a score of 7 to 3—the Yanks' third consecutive victory in the world's series of 1928—all Mr. Schacht met with was rebuff.

"NOBODY KNOWS."

He reported:

"They seem to want to keep them words a secret. I asked nine gentlemen and eight ladies, and six of the nine gentlemen wished to put the slug on me, while four of the ladies said, 'Mind your own business.' One line goes something like this."

Here Mr. Schacht leaned over and crooned softly in ye scribe's ear:

"St. Louis won with a diamond ring-lah-de-dah-lah-de-dah."

"That's enough," ye scribe protested, turning to the tally sheets to scan more closely the record of Jonathan Thompson Zachary, the vintage left-hander of the Yanks, who was largely responsible for the big towners's triumph today—or at least as much responsible as any one else. But Mr. Schacht persisted:

"St. Louis woman
"Made a wreck outa me—
"Lah-de-dah-lah-de-dah."

Thus he continued moaning gutturally, until a kindly copper came and led him away, leaving ye scribe to a peaceful contemplation of the Zacharian exploit.

A YOUNGISH HERO.

The Yanks got Jonathan Thompson out of a claiming race, so to speak. A tall, angular, slab-sided son of North Carolina, Jonathan

Continued on Page 8, Column 5.

13,000 BRITONS VIE TO HEAR AIMEE TALK

LONDON, Oct. 7.—Only 10,000 of 13,000 well dressed Londoners who struggled and almost fought, succeeded in gaining admittance to Mrs. Aimee McPherson's first London meeting tonight in the vast Albert Hall. The great hall proved entirely too small to hold the crowds who wanted to hear the evangelist.

The revivalist, who entered the hall on the arm of her sixteen-year-old son, Rolf, was greeted with cries of "Hallelujah," "Praise the Lord," and other expressions of fervor. Aimee wore a white silk gown and stockings partly concealed by a black cloak.

Potenziani Pinks Prince In Long Duel

Lancelotti Thrice Wounded by Rome Governor's Sword.

By PRINCE PIGNATELLI,
Universal Service Staff Correspondent.

ROME, Oct. 7.—A duel of thirty-one rounds was fought just before noon today by Prince Potenziani, former Governor of Rome, and Prince Lancellotti, victor of yesterday's contest with Count Di Sambuy. Efforts of the police to prevent the encounter failed, as the principals and their seconds did not spend the night at their homes and traveled separately to the scene, meeting at Villa St. Ame at 11:30.

PRINCE POTENZIANI
Thrice Wounds His Foe in Long Duel

Prince Potenziani spent the night at the cavalry school. Tor di Quinto, after an evening at the theatre.

WOUNDS FOE THRICE.

The fight began at 11:30 exactly and lasted for thirty-one rounds of two minutes each. In the third round Prince Lancellotti was wounded slightly in the wrist. In the fifteenth round he received a more serious wound in the elbow, but after it was bandaged he was allowed to continue. In the twenty-first round he received a thrust in the shoulder, Prince Potenziani's sword penetrating an inch and a half.

The doctors declared then that the wounded man was unable to continue. Both duelists refused to shake hands. Prince Potenziani led the fight all the way. The encounter did not end until 3:45.

MUST FACE COURT.

It is understood that the participants in both yesterday's and today's duels have been summoned to appear before a court of honor presided over by Senator Colonna, also a former Governor of Rome, and will be questioned about their respective parts in the duels.

It was reported tonight that Cardinal Gasparri, Papal Secretary of State, has offered to Prince Potenziani and Count Di Sambuy to perform the blessing function which would save them from excommunication of the Church. Such action would amount to a decision in their favor in the dispute between them and Prince Lancellotti, who made the original charges against Prince Potenziani leading to the duels.

'FULL OF PEP,' ROOSEVELT HOME AGAIN

Fellow-Townsmen Greet Nominee with Cheers on His Arrival to Begin Campaign

Campaign Highlights

By WILLIAM E. LAWBY,
Staff Correspondent New York American.

HYDE PARK, Oct. 7.—Franklin D. Roosevelt came to Crum Elbow, his ancestral home and estate near here, this afternoon to be welcomed and cheered by several hundreds of his friends and neighbors.

Leaning on a post on the spacious veranda of the old stone mansion, the Democratic gubernatorial candidate told those friends and neighbors gathered in the driveway and lawns:

"I come home full of pep and vigor, to go through the next four weeks."

HOLDS RECEPTION.

Following that he held an impromptu reception and then, with political advisers and intimate friends of his family, the candidate presided over a luncheon party, with his wife, Mrs. Eleanor Roosevelt, sitting at his left, and his mother, Mrs. James Roosevelt, at his right.

The reception given him was a complete surprise, as his time of arrival from Cleveland, where he spoke last night, was not definitely known until a few hours before his train made a special stop at Hyde Park to permit him to alight.

At the station rousing cheers greeted him, led by Dr. Alban Richey, Jr., rector of St. James Episcopal Church. Then, with a motor escort of twenty cars, piloted by a squad of State police, he was driven to Crum Elbow.

HIS DUTY TO ACCEPT.

To the assemblage at the home Roosevelt said that two days will always stand out in his memory—one eight years ago, when he returned after being nominated for the Vice-Presidency by his party's convention at San Francisco, and the day when his party again chose him, this time as the standard bearer in the State. He said:

"To come back home and to be so handsomely greeted by the friends and neighbors who have known this boy from his youth, is worth more to me than the nomination itself. If elected Governor I promise you now that I shall be a non-partisan Governor, a Governor of all the people—not only of one political party.

"As you know, I had made up

Continued on Page 6, Column 5.

Grand Opera Lil

OH, IMMIGRATION, OH, MR. VOLSTEAD, IF WE COULD LOWER THE TARIFF,
OH EQUALIZATION, OH FARM RELIEF!
RASKOB
DUPONT
WOODIN
HARK-
WALL ST. SUGAR DADDIES
WHAT DO YOU THINK?
A LOTTA SOUR NOTES!
THINKER
P.

PULLING a Ganna Walska, Diamond Lil, Queen of the Democracy, empress of Wall Street, beloved of the "Brown Derby Boys," Raskob, du Pont, Woodin and Harkness, has taken to grand opera.

Two things in grand opera you must have, a voice and a combination of melody and soul.

Diamond Lil has the VOICE.

Her four diamond-studded financial caddies, otherwise known as the "Wall Street Sugar Daddies," can see nothing wrong about her. In [illegible] Patti, Jenny Lind, Calve, Schalchi, and Lillian Russell all boiled down into one couldn't sing as well as their beloved Diamond Lil.

Others think differently.

The average opinion will be recorded in November.

U. S. NAVY SOON BRITISH EQUAL, COOLIDGE TOLD

By WILLIAM P. FLYTHE,
Universal Service Staff Correspondent.

WASHINGTON, Oct. 7.—The incoming session of Congress will authorize enough construction and appropriate sufficient funds to give the United States a well-rounded-out fleet, the equal of the British, it was learned in a high official quarter today.

President Coolidge was assured of this in conference with Senator Hale, Maine, Chairman of the Senate Military Affairs Committee, and Representative Fred Britten, Illinois, Chairman of the House Committee dealing with the Navy, it was learned. Britten is just back from Europe.

Due to the expose by the Hearst papers of the secret alliance or understanding between the French and the British, it was stated this action is essential.

PLAN 23 CRUISERS.

Both Senator Hale and Representative Britten declare funds will be set aside for immediate completion of

Continued on Page 4, Column 4.

1,200 HELP BISHOP STAGE CHURCH RIOT

LOWELL, Mass., Oct. 7 (Special).—Battling with pieces of lead pipe and paving stone, 1,200 men and women rioted inside and out of Holy Trinity Greek Church here today

More than fifteen persons were felled by clubs in the wild battle with police, and eight arrests were made.

The riot began when Bishop Vailios Kimvopoulis and the Rev. Consodine Harmantis, deposed pastor, strove to enter the church, which was guarded by a policeman.

Treasury Must Pay 4¾ Per Cent On New U.S. Loan

By M. L. RAMSAY,
Universal Service Staff Correspondent.

WASHINGTON, Oct. 7.—High interest rates today forced Secretary Mellon to offer 4¾ per cent for a loan for the Government with the soundest credit on earth.

This rate will be paid on $300,000,000 of United States Treasury certificates to be issued October 15, Mellon announced. It is the highest rate paid on a like issue since September, 1921, and on any issue since 1923. Billions were borrowed by the Government to finance the World War at 4¼ per cent.

SHORT TERM LOAN.

The new loan will be for only eleven months, being repaid next September 15.

Proceeds will be used to pay off $150,000,000 of third Liberty loan bonds still outstanding and to meet $150,000,000 of interest payments on the public debt falling due on October 15.

With this operation Mellon will carry out his programme for the paying off and refunding of the $4,175,000,000 of third Liberty loan bonds originally issued. The bonds paid 4¼ per cent. Last month's issue of certificates, partly in exchange for the Liberties, paid 4½.

SAVINGS COVER LOSS.

Although the last two stages of the programme thus show at least a temporary loss, the great bulk of the bonds were either paid off or refunded earlier at lower rates, with a huge saving in interest charges.

The third Liberties matured, ceasing to bear interest, on September 15. Just before that date $955,000,000 were outstanding.

Knowing that many holders would be slow in surrendering them, Mellon limited his borrowing to actual needs.

With the new loan the Treasury will be prepared to pay off the remaining bonds, some immediately and others as they dribble in.

KILLS 10 HERE; POISON LIQUOR 49 IN HOSPITAL

Ten persons died and forty-nine others were admitted to Bellevue Hospital yesterday as a result of another stream of poison liquor in Manhattan.

All the deaths occurred between midnight and noon within a radius of a few blocks on the lower East Side. Police are investigating the source of the liquor. Chief Medical Examiner Norris expressed the suspicion wood alcohol had found its way back into the city's cheap bootleg supply. City chemists will make examinations today.

The forty-nine cases of acute alcoholism admitted to Bellevue yesterday brought the week's total to 208 patients. Other hospitals were called on to help handle alcoholic cases in the emergency.

THE VICTIMS.

Altogether, ten men died, four of them unidentified. The death list of the identified follows:

FLORENCE KELLY, thirty-seven, of No. 334 Pearl street.

MICHAEL SHANKEY, twenty-nine, of No. 181 Third street, found at No. 285 Water street, suffering from delirium tremens; rushed to Bellevue, where he died.

JOHN KESSLER, sixty-five, of No. 6 Chatham Square.

FREDERICK STROM, forty-five, and EINAR SWAMBER, forty-seven, both seamen, of No. 24 Peck Slip. Swamberg died en route to Bellevue; Strom, an hour after admission to the hospital.

PETER VOLKA, fifty, of No. 94 Division street; taken to Bellevue Hospital, where he died from alcoholic poisoning.

FOUR UNIDENTIFIED.

Of the four unidentified men, one about fifty-five, was found at No. 109 Madison street; another, about forty-five, in front of No. 13 Allen street; the third, about sixty-five at No. 285 Water street, and the fourth at No. 44 Pike street.

Autopsies will be performed today

Continued on Page 6, Column 7.

WE'LL BE OFF TO LAKEHURST BY TOMORROW, SAYS ECKENER

Big Ship's Crew Busy Taking on Large Supply of Fuel, Enough to Make Round Trip

Officers' Wives Honor Guests on Final Trial Flight Today, to Pacify Women's Protest

When the super-dirigible Graf Zeppelin starts on its epochal flight from Friedrichshafen to New York the representatives of only one newspaper and picture service will be allowed aboard—the Hearst Publications representatives.

And to get the real inside story of the history-making flight—from the moment the huge ship [illegible] from its hangar in Germany to the landing at Lakehurst, N. J.—you will have to read the New York American.

The American will print daily the EXCLUSIVE story of the Zeppelin's flight as it is radioed from the control cabin of the huge ship while the flight is in progress.

By KARL H. VON WIEGAND.

FRIEDRICHSHAFEN, Oct. 7.—"The Graf Zeppelin will be clear for Lakehurst Tuesday afternoon. Tomorrow noon we expect to go out for several hours in a final tune-up and to satisfy a few more of those who have deluged us with requests for a ride. Our guests tomorrow will be taken from among those to whom we are somewhat indebted, and that includes the wives of our officers."

This statement was made to me this afternoon by Dr. Eckener as he sat before a mountain of mail and telegrams when I came to his office to find him putting in a hard Sunday's work dictating. He said:

Sure of Success.

"At the present moment conditions look promising for getting away early Wednesday, but we will see what tricks the weather gods are playing on the Atlantic

The Weather

MONDAY, OCTOBER 8, 1928.

NEW YORK AND VICINITY—Fair today. Tomorrow increasing cloudiness and warmer; gentle, moderate east winds.

NEW JERSEY — Fair today, increasing cloudiness tomorrow, followed by showers.

NEW ENGLAND—Fair today, increasing cloudiness tomorrow, followed by showers.

COOLER · CLOUDY · WARMER · RAIN

TEMPERATURES IN NEW YORK.

3 A. M.	55	4 P. M.	68
6 A. M.	53	5 P. M.	66
8 A. M.	57	6 P. M.	64
9 A. M.	59	7 P. M.	61
10 A. M.	61	8 P. M.	59
11 A. M.	64	9 P. M.	57
12 Noon	67	10 P. M.	57
1 P. M.	68	11 P. M.	57
2 P. M.	68	12 Midnight	56
3 P. M.	68		

Average temperature, 61. Average same date last year, 70. Barometer, 8 a. m., 30.25; 1 p. m., 30.06; 8 p. m., 30.12. Wind, 8 a. m., N. W., 3; 1 p. m., N. W., 26; 8 p. m., N., 22.

For detailed weather report see page 11.

Ruth and Gehrig Hit Homers as Yankees Open Season Before 35,000 by Beating Red Sox, 7-3

Pipgras and Heimach Limit Boston Visitors to Three Hits

World's Championship Flag Unfurled, McKee, Aldermanic President, Throws Out First Ball, Landis Presents Watches to Champions; Crowd Shivers

By Rud Rennie

The grand opening finally took place yesterday and the New York Yankees started in right where they left off last fall. The Babe socked one; Gehrig socked one, and the Yankees defeated the latest edition of the Red Sox by a score of 7 to 3 in the presence of 35,000 highly frapped fans at the Stadium.

The start was two days late and Mayor Walker could not be there. No matter how late anything is, he can be later. So Joe McKee, president of the Board of Aldermen, threw out the first ball. The players, all out of step but Miller Huggins, followed Lieutenant Sutherland's 7th Regiment Band to the flag pole to listen to the "Star-Spangled Banner" and watch the national emblem and the world's championship flag unfurled to a cold breeze. Commissioner Landis, wearing a funny new hat which is absolutely no improvement on the old one, presented diamond-studded wrist watches to the members of last year's championship team. And the game began.

It was a good game and it was not a good day for a game. But the crowd did not shiver in vain. It had no sooner become reconciled to death by slow freezing than Ruth, the most important bridegroom of the day, neatly labeled with a large "3" on his broad back, took hold of a curve ball outside and whacked it into the lower part of the left field stands.

Babe's Homer Goes to Left

The crowd roared its astonishment and joy. It was a joy to see the Babe start off in such a noble manner, but it was astonishing to see him poling them into left field. The constant customers in the right field bleachers, who have been handling the Babe's homers for years, began to wonder if, at this late date, they would have to move to the other side of the park.

But the right field fans still have a friend in Gehrig. Five and a half innings elapsed before he hit one, but when he did, the ball sailed fair and square into the right field stands.

So the home run twins got away to an even start in their quest of home run honors. And the 35,000 fans got the thrill they had hoped for.

Such events as these would have been better if the sun had been warm and smiling. The bright flags festooning the boxes semed less bright under the cold, gray sky. The grounds looked cold, the players looked cold, even though there was something gay and colorful in the sight of them as they followed the keen blue capes of the band to the flag pole, the Red Sox in their red windbreakers and red and white stockings, and the Yankees in blue and white making up the rear.

Crowd Besieges Ruth

There was something, too, in the scene which followed the final put-out of the game, when men and boys poured out of the stands to swarm around the Babe long before he could run from his position in right field to the exit under the Yankee dugout. They had him stopped. There he was, the big man of baseball, helpless in the press of an admiring mob. His hat was gone. His big, brown face was red with exertion as he pushed and shoved, only to be carried, like a stick on a swirling river, this way and that, until he managed to escape.

By that time it seemed at least a week since they had raised the flags to the tune of "The Star-Spangled Banner." It was a slowly played game. George Pipgras started for the Yankees and Charlie Ruffing for the Red Sox. Both are right handers. Neither finished.

Pipgras looked great while pitching to the first two batters. He fanned the first one and the next was an easy infield out. Then he began a spell of wildness, which lasted until Huggins yanked him in the sixth.

Pipgras Walked Nine Batsmen

In that time the Red Sox made only three safe hits off Pipgras, and three were all they got in the entire game. But Pipgras walked nine men and was lucky not to be scored against more heavily than he was. His work was not nearly so good as that of his successor, Fred Heimach, who took the task after one-third of the sixth had been played and held the Red Sox hitless for three and two-thirds innings. Not a man reached first while he was pitching and he faced the minimum of batters—eleven.

Ruffing was another three-hit pitcher who had to be taken out. He was not so wild as Pipgras, but he was behind in runs, owing to some heavy and timely hitting, and left in favor of a pinch hitter in the sixth. Milton Gaston worked the last three innings and it was off him that Gehrig hit his homer and the Yankees made their last three runs to clinch their victory.

Pipgras walked three men in the first inning and had them all on bases when the inning fortunately ended.

There were two men away in the Yankees' part of the first and the count was two and two against the Babe when he reached for an outside curve and eased it into the stands.

Red Sox Go Into Lead

Both teams went out, one-two-three in the second, Pipgras fanning two of the hitters. But the third was bad for the Yankees. Rothrock, the first man up, slipped a single into right field and Pipgras walked the next two batters. With the bases full, Flagstead rapped a grounder at Koenig who let Rothrock ramble home while he whipped the ball to Lazzeri for a double play ending at first. Then Regan singled, making Pipgras duck from a line drive into center which sent Rhyne home with a second run. But for Gehrig's great catch of Koenig's high throw, the inning might have continued indefinitely.

Those two runs wiped out the early Yankee lead and left them one run behind. If Ruffing could have skipped the fourth, the game would have had a different ending. In that inning Ruffing began to act like Pipgras. He walked Ruth and Gehrig; then Meusel doubled to right. Ruth came home and Gehrig pulled up in a hurry at third.

In these circumstances Lazzeri fanned for his second time, and Durocher rapped a grounder at Reeves which resulted in Gehrig's being rushed back to third and Meusel's being tagged for creeping up and occupying the same bag. Grabowski's grounder to Reeves brought Gehrig home, because Todt failed to squeeze the well-known American League apple. It rolled past him and Grabowski was advised to continue toward second. He did, but got caught at it. Before they caught him, however, Durocher scored. So the Yankees made three more runs and had a two run lead.

Pipgras walked two more men in the fifth, but escaped. He walked two more in the sixth, but this time he escaped right out of the ball game.

He had one man away and the singling Todt on first when he walked Berry and Bigelow, who took Ruffing's place at bat when the latter had a strike and two balls called against him. Once Bigelow walked, Narlesky ran for him.

With the bases full, Pipgras was slowly but surely walking Rothrock when Huggins opened the door of the dugout and said "Scat!" Pipgras "scatted" and Heimach entered. He got Rothrock to hoist a fly to Meusel which went as a sacrifice for Todt to score. Then he closed the inning by getting rid of Rhyne.

From then on Heimach got rid of everyone. Nobody hit him. He was invincible and the boys stepped around and gave him sweet support, Durocher and Koenig especially.

Meantime, the Yankees took advantage of Gaston to enlarge their lead from one to four runs. Gehrig led off with his home run into the right-field bleachers. Lazzeri singled. Then Gaston walked two men and fanned Heimach. There were two out and the bases were full when Combs drove in two runners with his one and only hit of the day, a single to left field when went past Reeves like a rabbit.

The Yankees had another chance to score in the seventh when Gehrig and Muesel singled after Ruth had walked. But the coach held the Babe at third and let Gehrig go tearing past second to fall into an easy out. Then Lazzeri hit into a double play.

But by that time the Yankees had the game safe in their grasp. The season was open. And they were on their way, hopefully, toward their fourth consecutive pennant.

Yankees' Score

BOSTON (A. L.)	ab	r	h	po	a	e
Rothrock, cf	4	1	1	2	0	0
Rhyne, ss...	3	1	0	2	1	0
Scarritt, rf.	1	0	0	2	1	0
Flagstead, lf	1	0	0	1	0	0
K.Will'ms lf	2	0	0	0	0	0
Regan, 2b...	3	0	1	3	2	0
Reeves, 3b..	4	0	0	0	3	0
Todt, 1b....	3	1	1	3	2	1
Standaert 1b	1	0	0	0	0	0
Berry, c....	3	0	0	10	0	0
RUFFING,p.	2	0	0	0	1	0
*Bigelow ...	0	0	0	0	0	0
†Narlesky ..	0	0	0	0	0	0
M.GAST'N,p	0	0	0	1	0	0
‡Barrett ...	1	0	0	0	0	0
Totals....	28	3	3	24	10	1

NEW YORK (A. L.)	ab	r	h	po	a	e
Combs, cf..	4	0	1	4	0	0
Koenig, 3b..	4	0	0	1	5	0
Ruth, rf....	2	2	1	1	0	0
Gehrig, 1b..	3	2	2	12	1	0
Meusel, lf..	4	0	2	2	0	0
Lazzeri, 2b..	4	1	1	3	2	0
Durocher, ss	3	2	0	0	5	0
Gabros'ki, c	3	0	1	3	1	0
PIPGRAS, p	1	0	0	1	0	0
HEIMACH,p	2	0	0	0	0	0
Totals....	30	7	8	27	14	0

*Batted for Ruffing in sixth inning.
†Ran for Bigelow in sixth inning.
‡Batted for M. Gaston in ninth inning.

Boston	002	001	000—3
New York	100	303	00x—7

Runs batted in—Ruth, Meusel, Flagstead, Regan, Gehrig, Rothrock, Combs (2). Two-base hit—Meusel. Home runs—Ruth, Gehrig. Sacrifice—Rothrock. Double plays—Koenig, Lazzeri and Gehrig; Rhyne, Regan and Todt. Left on bases—New York, 5; Boston, 8. Bases on balls—Off Pipgras, 9; off Ruffing, 3; off Gaston, 3. Struck out—By Pipgras, 2; by Heimach, 1; by Ruffing, 5; by Gaston, 2. Hits—Off Pipgras, 3 in 5 1-3 innings; off Heimach, 0 in 3 2-3; off Ruffing, 3 in 5; off Gaston, 5 in 3. Winning pitcher—Pipgras. Losing pitcher—Ruffing. Umpires—McGowan, Van Graflan and Connolly. Time—2:25.

Briefs

The Yankees have won the American League pennant so often they did not even bother to hoist it.

Both teams looked very neat in their new uniforms, the Yankees, with large black numbers on their backs, resembling an unusually tidy football team.

The photographers had no difficulty keeping warm. They were running all over the park, taking pictures of the new Mrs. Ruth, Judge Landis, E. S. Barnard, president of the American League; Colonel Ruppert, Joe McKee, the two teams, the two managers, Gehrig, the Babe, the flagpole and the crowd.

Landis, Barnard and Ruppert ducked the parade to the flagpole by hiding under the left field bleachers and emerging just as it came to a halt.

Huggins finished a bad last in the parade. He lost ground at every step and was still marching after every one else had come to a halt. He likes to march to waltz music; it is more restful—hesitation waltz music.

The left field bleachers were empty.

Two cops escorted McKee to the flagpole. Once an alderman, always an alderman.

Mike Gazella, the wolf of Wall Street, came up to get his wrist watch. He insisted he will not play for the price the Newark club has offered him.

While Pipgras was pitching, Scarritt did nothing but walk. Pipgras should have led the parade. He made lots of people walk yesterday.

Meusel and Rothrock each made a spectacular catch in the outfield, Meusel going back after one and Rothrock taking a dive to come up with a short one.

Today, if the season continues, the Yankees will play their most serious rival—the A's.

Miss Ryan to Play With Miss Nuthall in Doubles

LONDON, April 18 (AP).—Miss Elizabeth Ryan, former California star much sought after as a partner for the coming women's doubles championships at Wimbledon, announced definitely today she would team with Miss Betty Nuthall, youthful British star.

Miss Ryan said she would refrain from competitive play until May 1.

Seen at Stadium as Yankees Opened Season With Victory

Herald Tribune photos—Acme

Above: Joseph V. McKee, Colonel Jacob Ruppert, Commissioner Kenesaw M. Landis and E. S. Barnard, president of the American League. Right: Babe Ruth (note No. 3 on Ruth's back, which will be his number throughout the season). Below, left: Strike one, as Ruth stepped to the plate in the first inning. At right he is shown receiving handshake from Lou Gehrig as he crossed the plate after his home run.

Herald Tribune photo—Steffen

Browns Capture 3d Straight Game From White Sox by 4 to 1

ST. LOUIS, April 18 (AP).—The St. Louis Browns bunched hits today and chalked up their third consecutive victory over the Chicago White Sox to make a clean sweep of the opening series of the season. The score was 4 to 1.

Ogden held the visitors to six hits, while Lyons limited the Browns to five. Blue kept up his sensational hitting, knocking a home run in the third inning and clipping in a double during a three-run rally in the fifth. A walk, an error and two singles also contributed to the three runs.

The score:

CHICAGA (A. L.)	ab	r	h	po	a	e
Metler, cf...	3	0	0	3	0	0
Kerr, 2b....	5	1	1	1	4	0
Clancy, 1b...	4	0	2	11	2	0
Reynolds, lf.	4	0	1	0	0	1
Kamm, 3b....	3	0	0	2	1	0
Watwood, rf	3	0	1	1	0	0
Cissell, ss....	4	0	0	1	4	0
Autry, c.....	4	0	0	3	0	0
LYONS, p..	3	0	1	2	4	0
*Hunnefield.	1	0	0	0	0	0
Totals....	34	1	6	24	15	1

ST. LOUIS (A. L.)	ab	r	h	po	a	e
Blue, 1b....	4	1	2	9	1	0
O'Rourke, 3b	3	0	0	3	2	0
Manush, lf..	3	0	0	3	0	0
Schulte, cf..	3	0	0	2	0	0
Kress, ss....	3	0	0	2	2	2
McGowan, rf	2	1	1	4	0	0
Melillo, 2b..	2	0	0	3	4	0
Schang, c....	3	1	1	1	0	0
OGDEN, p..	3	1	1	0	4	0
Totals....	26	4	5	27	13	2

*Batted for Lyons in ninth inning.

Chicago	001	000	000—1
St. Louis	001	030	00x—4

Runs batted in—Reynolds, Blue (2), Schang, Ogden. Two-base hits—Reynolds, Blue. Home run—Blue. Sacrifice—Melillo. Double plays—Kerr and Clancy; Kerr, Cissell and Clancy. Left on bases—Chicago, 10; St. Louis, 2. Struck out—By Lyons, 2; by Ogden, 4. Bases on balls—Off Lyons, 3; off Ogden, 4. Umpires—Campbell, Owens and Ormsby. Time—1:32.

A's Beat Senators With Six-Run Rally In Fifth Inning, 8-2

WASHINGTON, April 18 (AP).—A six-run rally in the fifth inning by the Philadelphia Athletics was the margin of their victory over the Washington Senators today as they took the second game of the opening series, 8 to 2.

Walberg toiled the entire nine innings for the Mackmen and gave up only seven hits. The score:

PHILADELPHIA (A. L.)	ab	r	h	po	a	e
Bishop, 2b..	2	1	1	1	2	0
Summa, rf...	4	0	1	2	0	0
Cochrane, c.	4	1	1	7	1	0
Haas, cf.....	4	0	0	3	0	0
Hale, 3b.....	5	1	2	4	2	0
Foxx, 1b....	3	1	0	8	0	0
Miller, lf....	5	1	3	1	0	0
Dykes, ss....	3	2	1	1	2	0
WALBERG,p	4	1	2	0	0	0
Totals.....	34	8	11	27	7	0

WASHINGTON (A. L.)	ab	r	h	po	a	e
West, cf.....	4	1	1	2	0	0
Myer, 3b....	4	0	1	3	3	0
Goslin, lf....	4	0	2	1	0	0
Barnes, rf....	4	0	0	0	0	0
Bluege, ss....	3	1	2	3	3	0
Judge, 1b....	3	0	0	11	0	0
Hayes, 2b....	4	0	1	1	4	0
Ruel, c......	2	0	0	5	2	0
Spencer, c...	1	0	0	1	0	0
HADLEY, p..	2	0	0	0	0	0
BROWN, p...	0	0	0	0	2	0
CAMPB'L, p.	0	0	0	0	0	0
BURKE, p...	0	0	0	0	0	0
*Gooch	1	0	0	0	0	0
Totals.....	32	2	7	27	14	0

*Batted for Brown in seventh inning.

Philadelphia	000	060	020—8
Washington	100	100	000—2

Runs batted in—Bluege, Ruel, Dykes, Summa (2), Cochrane (2), Hale, Miller, Bishop. Two-base hits—Miller (2), Hale (2), Bluege. Sacrifices—Ruel, Haas. Double play—Bluege and Hayes. Left on bases—Philadelphia, 8; Washington, 6. Struck out—By Walberg, 3; by Hadley, 3; by Burke, 1. Bases on balls—Off Walberg, 2; off Hadley, 4; off Brown, 2; off Campbell, 2. Hits—Off Hadley, 5 in 4 1-3 innings; off Brown, 2 in 2 2-3; off Campbell, 1 in 0; off Burke, 3 in 2. Passed ball—Spencer. Losing pitcher—Hadley. Umpires—Guthrie, Moriarity and Hildebrand. Time—2:00.

College Baseball

Columbia, 3; Seton Hall, 0.
Western Normal, 10; Chicago, 2.
Springfield, 14; Clark U., 5.
Kentucky, 5; Minnesota, 1.
Penn, 16; Swarthmore, 2.
C. C. N. Y., 5; Stevens, 4.
Catholic U., 4; Bucknell, 0.
B. C.-Vermont, wet grounds.

Standings in Major Leagues

FRIDAY, APRIL 19, 1929.

American League

YESTERDAY'S RESULTS

New York, 7; Boston, 3.
Philadelphia, 8; Washington, 2.
Cleveland, 8; Detroit, 4.
St. Louis, 4; Chicago, 1.

STANDING OF THE CLUBS

	W.	L.	Pct.		W.	L.	Pct.
St. Louis..	3	0	1.000	Detroit.	1	2	.333
Phila'phia	2	0	1.000	Boston...	0	1	.000
N. York...	1	0	1.000	Wash'n.	0	2	.000
Cleveland.	2	1	.666	Chicago.	0	3	.000

GAMES TODAY

Philadelphia at New York (3:15 p. m.).
Boston at Washington.
Chicago at St. Louis.
Detroit at Cleveland.

National League

YESTERDAY'S RESULTS

New York, 11; Philadelphia, 9.
Boston, 13; Brooklyn, 12.
St. Louis, 3; Cincinnati, 1.
Chicago, 11; Pittsburgh, 1.

STANDING OF THE CLUBS

	W.	L.	Pct.		W.	L.	Pct.
N. York...	1	0	1.000	Pittsb'h.	1	2	.333
Boston...	1	0	1.000	Cincin'ti	1	2	.333
St. Louis..	2	1	.666	B'klyn...	0	1	.000
Chicago..	2	1	.666	Phila...	0	1	.000

GAMES TODAY

New York at Philadelphia.
Brooklyn at Boston (2).
Pittsburgh at Chicago.
St. Louis at Cincinnati.

Haines Holds Reds In Check as Cards Bat Out 3-1 Victory

CINCINNATI, April 18 (AP).—Jess Haines's tight pitching baffled the Reds here today and the Cardinals won the odd game of the series, 3 to 1. Haines also drove in the first run of the game with a single in the second inning. Loose fielding behind Luque's rather erratic pitching saw the Cardinals sew up the contest in the first inning. Douthit, St. Louis center fielder, gathered in eight flies.

The score:

ST. LOUIS (N. L.)	ab	r	h	po	a	e
Douthit, cf..	5	0	1	8	0	0
Haney, 3b...	4	1	2	1	1	0
Frisch, 2b...	4	1	2	2	1	0
Bot'mly, 1b.	4	0	0	5	0	0
Hafey, lf....	4	1	1	2	0	0
Roettger, rf.	4	0	1	3	0	0
Gelbert, ss..	4	0	0	1	2	0
Smith, c....	4	0	1	5	0	0
HAINES, p..	3	0	1	0	2	0
Totals.....	36	3	9	27	6	0

CINCINNATI (N. L.)	ab	r	h	po	a	e
Crit, 2b.....	5	1	1	4	1	1
Purdy, lf....	4	0	2	5	0	0
Kelly, 1b....	3	0	1	8	0	0
Walker, rf...	4	0	0	0	0	0
Allen, cf....	4	0	0	1	0	0
Pittenger, 3b	4	0	2	1	2	1
Ford, ss.....	4	0	0	2	1	0
Dixon, c.....	2	0	1	5	2	0
*Crabtree ..	1	0	0	0	0	0
Sukeforth, c.	1	0	1	1	0	0
LUQUE, p...	2	0	0	0	2	0
†Lucas	1	0	0	0	0	0
ASH, p......	0	0	0	0	1	0
‡Swanson ..	1	0	1	0	0	0
Totals.....	36	1	9	27	9	2

*Batted for Dixon in seventh inning.
†Batted for Luque in seventh inning.
‡Batted for Ash in ninth inning.

St. Louis	012	000	000—3
Cincinnati	000	000	010—1

Runs batted in—Haines, Frisch, Hafey, Purdy. Two-base hits—Haney, Swanson. Three-base hits—Haney, Critz. Sacrifice—Haines. Left on bases—St. Louis, 7; Cincinnati, 9. Struck out—By Haines, 4; by Luque, 5; by Ash, 1. Base on balls—Off Haines, 1. Hits—Off Luque, 8 in 7 innings; off Ash, 1 in 2. Losing pitcher—Luque. Umpires—Quigley, Moran and McLaughlin. Time—1:54.

Indians Defeat Tigers, Miljus Winning, 8 to 4

CLEVELAND, April 18 (AP).—The Indians scored their second victory in three days by nicking Owen Carroll and Frank Barnes for fourteen hits in six innings for an 8 to 4 decision over Detroit.

John Miljus, former National Leaguer, went the route for Cleveland, and, although he was wild and issued eight passes, was able to stop the Detroiters whenever they threatened.

Fonseca, the Indians' first baseman, led the local attack with four singles. He also stole three bases.

The score:

DETROIT (A. L.)	ab	r	h	po	a	e
Rice, cf.....	2	1	0	1	0	0
Gehringer,2b	4	1	3	3	6	0
Heilmann, rf	4	0	0	1	1	0
Alexander,1b	2	0	1	11	0	0
Fothergill, lf	4	0	1	1	0	0
McManus, 3b	3	1	0	2	1	0
Rich'son, ss.	3	1	1	1	1	0
†Johnson ...	1	0	0	0	0	0
Schuble, ss..	0	0	0	0	1	0
‡Stone	1	0	0	0	0	0
Phillips, c...	4	0	3	4	0	0
CARROLL, p	1	0	1	0	0	0
*Hargrave...	1	0	0	0	0	0
BARNES, p..	1	0	0	0	1	0
YDE, p.....	1	0	0	0	0	0
Totals....	32	4	10	24	11	0

CLEVELAND (A. L.)	ab	r	h	po	a	e
Tavener, ss..	4	0	1	3	6	0
Lind, 2b.....	5	1	1	4	4	0
Averill, cf...	3	1	2	2	0	0
J. Sewell, 3b.	5	1	1	1	3	1
Porter, rf...	4	2	2	1	0	0
Fonseca, 1b.	5	1	4	14	0	0
Jamieson, lf.	2	1	1	1	0	0
L. Sewell, c..	4	0	1	1	0	0
MILJUS, p..	4	1	2	0	4	0
Totals....	36	8	14	27	17	1

*Batted for Carroll in fourth inning.
†Batted for Richardson in seventh inning.
‡Batted for Schuble in ninth inning.

Runs batted in—Fonseca (4), Lind, Jamieson, Miljus, Alexander (2), Phillips, Carroll. Two-base hits—Miljus (2), Gehringer (2), Porter. Stolen bases—Fonseca (3), Richardson, Porter. Sacrifices—Alexander (2), Fothergill. Double plays—Miljus, Lind and Fonseca; McManus, Gehringer and Alexander; Tavener, Lind and Fonseca; Richardson, Gehringer and Alexander; Tavener and Fonseca. Left on bases—Cleveland, 12; Detroit, 12. Bases on balls—Off Miljus, 8; off Carroll, 2; off Barnes, 2; off Yde, 2. Struck out—By Barnes, 2; by Yde, 2. Hits—Off Carroll, 9 in 3 innings; off Barnes, 5 in 3; off Yde, 1 in 2. Hit by pitcher—By Carroll (Tavener); by Barnes (Porter). Wild pitch—Yde. Balk—Barnes. Losing pitcher—Carroll. Umpires—Geisel, Dinneen and Nallin. Time—2:21.

Robins Trade Battery To Reds for Picinich

Special to the Herald Tribune

BOSTON, April 18.—The Robins announced tonight that they had traded pitcher Rube Ehrhardt and catcher Johnny Gooch to the Cincinnati Reds for Val Picinich, veteran backstop, who was unable to come to a salary agreement with the Cincinnati club this year. Ehrhardt and Gooch left tonight to join the Reds.

Picinich has been in the big leagues for a number of years. Last season he was used regularly for the first time and hit .302, a surprisingly good average for him. His heavy batting attracted the attention of Wilbert Robinson, who lost no time making a deal for the catcher when it became apparent that he would not sign with the Reds. Robinson said the Brooklyn club expected no trouble signing their new man.

Cubs Batter Pirates Again, 11-1, Blake Allowing Only Four Hits

By The Associated Press

CHICAGO, April 18.—Sheriff Blake oiled up his handcuffs, his vicious mates snapped them shut and the Chicago Cubs handed the Pittsburgh Pirates another unmerciful 11 to 1 beating today.

It was a repetition of yesterday's massacre, and the result gave McCarthy's heavy hitters a 2 to 1 edge over the Pirate brigade in their opening series.

Blake, ordinarily a slow starter, was invincible today. He allowed but four scattered singles, while his mates crashed out two home runs, three doubles and eight singles off the southpaw deliveries of Jess Petty and Larry French. One of these four-ply clouts was blasted by Charlie Grimm in the fourth inning with the bases jammed.

The Pirates got their only run in the first inning on a single by Lloyd Waner, an error by English, Cub shortstop, and two walks. The Cubs tied it up in their half on errors by Adams and Hemsley, a base on balls and a single by Cuyler.

The next inning was scoreless and then the fury of the Cub bats broke out. With two men on base and two out, Petty purposely passed Stephenson for Grimm. After taking a strike, Grimm hammered the ball into the right field bleachers, scoring Beck, Wilson and Stephenson and giving the Cubs a 5 to 1 advantage.

In the fifth inning, another bombardment shook the Pirate brigade to pieces. Hornsby drew his third consecutive base on balls and Wilson connected with his first home run of the season.

French stepped on the mound for Pittsburgh, but an error by himself and one by Adams filled the bases again and he forced in another by walking English.

"Murderers' Row" fired another salvo in the eighth, and it was good for three runs. Cuyler walked, Hornsby singled and Wilson scored them both with his two-bager. Stephenson doubled and Wilson trotted home with the final run.

Only 8,000 fans braved the frigid temperature to watch the game.

The score:

PITTSBURGH (N. L.)	ab	r	h	po	a	e
Adams, ss...	4	1	0	1	1	2
L. Waner, cf	4	0	2	3	0	0
P. Waner, rf	3	0	0	3	0	0
Traynor, 3b..	3	0	1	2	2	0
Gr'ntham, lf	2	0	0	0	0	0
Sheely, 1b...	4	0	0	6	0	0
Bartell, 2b...	4	0	0	3	2	0
Hemsley, c...	4	0	1	6	1	1
PETTY, p...	1	0	0	0	1	0
FRENCH, p.	1	0	0	0	1	1
*Brickell ...	1	0	0	0	0	0
Totals.....	31	1	4	24	8	4

CHICAGO (N. L.)	ab	r	h	po	a	e
English, ss..	4	1	2	2	4	1
Beck, 3b....	5	1	1	0	2	0
Cuyler, rf...	4	1	1	6	0	0
Hornsby, 2b.	2	2	1	2	4	0
Wilson, cf...	5	3	3	2	0	0
St'nson, lf..	4	2	2	1	0	0
Grimm, 1b..	5	1	1	13	0	0
Gonzales, c.	5	0	1	1	0	0
BLAKE, p..	5	0	1	0	4	0
Totals....	39	11	13	27	14	1

*Batted for French in ninth inning.

Pittsburgh	010	000	000— 1
Chicago	104	030	03x—11

Runs batted in—Grimm (4), Wilson (4), Cuyler, Stephenson. Two-base hits—English, Wilson, Stephenson. Home runs—Grimm, Wilson. Stolen bases—English, Beck, Wilson. Double play—English, Hornsby and Grimm. Left on bases—Chicago, 10; Pittsburgh, 8. Struck out—By Blake, 1; by Petty, 1; by French, 4. Bases on balls—Off Blake, 5; off Petty, 3; off French, 3. Hits—Off Petty, 9 in 4 innings (none out in 5th); off French, 4 in 4. Losing pitcher—Petty. Umpires—Klem, Jorda and Magerkurth. Time—1:45.

Princeton Elects Hockey And Swimming Captains

Special to the Herald Tribune

PRINCETON, N. J., April 18.—Princeton's hockey and swimming teams today elected their respective captains for next season.

Leading the Tiger sextet will be Warren S. Adams 2d, of Newton, Mass., who has played at right defense on the varsity for the last two seasons. This year he teamed up with Johnny Jones, an All-American selection, for left defense, to form one of the best combinations in the East.

John H. Brooks, also a junior, of Scranton, Pa., was named captain of the Princeton swimming team. During the last season he won the intercollegiate diving championship and two weeks later added to his laurels by taking fourth place in the national collegiate swimming championships at St. Louis. Brooks is the first diver selected to lead a Princeton swimming team in recent years. He is also manager of the 1929 football team.

Robins Make 19 Hits, but Drop Opening Game to Braves, 13-12

Pattison Only One of Four Brooklyn Hurlers to Make Good Showing; Hendrick, Herman and Bissonette Drive Out Homers; Clark, of Boston, Badly Hurt

By Murray Tynan

BOSTON, April 18.—In a competitive sense, the Boston Braves opened the baseball season today in a most successful manner. The Robins played their part nobly and though they made nineteen hits, three of them homers, they still managed to make the home side, richly attired in scarlet and yellow trappings, appear like a good team.

But, sad to relate, there were so few persons present to see the Braves scuttling the Brooklyn ship, the affair must be set down as a financial flop, or even calamity. The final score was 13 to 12.

Less than 4,000 people turned out to see the Braves, assisted by Governor Frank Allen and his military staff, open the season. The weather, however, undoubtedly was responsible for the slim attendance. It was cold, the sky was gray, and save for the fact that it wasn't raining, the weather was no improvement over the past two days. The sun came out for a few moments after the game started, but shortly afterwards the gray clouds closed in again and rain or snow seemed imminent.

The Governor led the march to the flagpole, helped raise the national colors, threw out the first ball, and did most everything save break into the game. It seemed a pity that the Robins didn't have an extra uniform with which to equip Governor Allen, for he certainly would have been an improvement on the pitchers they used. The throw he made to start the game was proof enough of that.

Governor Better Than Clark

The Governor's pitch had more on it than William Watson Clark, who started for the Robins, could get on the ball, and was far more accurate than any Clise Dudley made.

Clark was unable to throw anything but base hits, while Dudley had great difficulty locating the plate. To make the situation worse, Bancroft and Bissonette made wild throws that were costly, and Hendrick fumbled a grounder.

While the Bostonians drew many a "lucky break" during the course of the long afternoon, they also had one bad one. Earl Clark, their nimble-footed centerfielder, crashed into the metal fence while chasing a long drive from Nick Cullop's bat and was knocked unconscious. He was carried from the field and attended by Dr. Ferguson, of the Brooklyn club. A later examination showed that he had received a concussion of the brain and he probably would be out of the game for three weeks at least. Clark was confined to his room in the hotel rather than being sent to a hospital.

Bob Smith, who acted as master of ceremonies for the Braves, was hammered fairly hard by the Robins, but always had the presence of mind to be at his best in the pinches. He fanned Bressler and Wright, who were sent in to hit with men on the bases, and despite the constant pecking of the Robins, always was able to protect his lead.

Pattison Makes Debut

Young Jimmy Pattison, the fourth Brooklyn pitcher to get into the game, probably did the best job of the day. He retired the side in order in the sixth and seventh, which was a vast improvement. But by that time it was getting dark, which may have aided the youngster somewhat.

After Hendrick and Bissonette had made homers and Herman and Cullop had helped out with long wallops, Smith finally had to be taken out in the eighth. Cullop, first up, smashed a long two-bagger to the center field fence and Judge Fuchs decreed that his man had had sufficient. All told Smith was rapped for sixteen hits by the Robins, which was far more than the Braves made off the combination of Brooklyn pitchers.

By dint of a lot of hitting the Robins finally drew up to within one run of the Braves in the eighth inning, but even then their pitching fell down. Jim Elliott replaced Pattison, who stepped out for a pinch hitter and started off by walking Dugan. Meuller doubled, scoring Dugan and raced in himself when Maranville's roller went through Bancroft for an error.

The Robins made their final bid in the ninth when Frederick opened on Johnny Cooney with a two-bagger and Herman knocked a home run into the center field stands. But after Mueller had hauled in Bissonette's long fly to end the game they were still one run behind and had to go home content with the knowledge that if they had had any pitching worth the name they would have won easily.

Robins' Score

BROOKLYN (N. L.)	ab	r	h	po	a	e
Frederick,cf.	6	2	2	6	0	0
Hendrick,3b.	6	2	2	0	2	1
Herman, lf.	6	2	4	1	0	0
Cullop lf...	5	3	2	2	0	0
Bissonette,1b	6	1	1	7	0	1
Flowers, 2b.	2	2	1	2	2	0
Bancroft, ss	7	0	4	4	3	2
De Berry c.	4	0	3	2	0	0
W.CLARK,p	1	0	0	0	0	0
*Bressler ..	1	0	0	0	0	0
MOSS, p...	0	0	0	0	0	0
†Wright	1	0	0	0	0	0
DUDLEY, p.	0	0	0	0	1	0
‡Gooch	1	0	0	0	0	0
PATTIS'N,p.	0	0	0	0	0	0
§Carey	1	0	0	0	0	0
ELLIOTT,p.	0	0	0	0	0	0
Totals...	47	12	19	24	9	4

BOSTON (N. L.)	ab	r	h	po	a	e
Richbourg,rf	5	2	1	6	[illegible]	[illegible]
Maguire, 2b.	4	2	1	3	[illegible]	[illegible]
Sisler, 1b...	5	3	3	4	[illegible]	[illegible]
Harper, lf...	4	1	2	2	[illegible]	[illegible]
Dugan, 3b..	3	2	1	0	[illegible]	[illegible]
E. Clark, cf.	2	0	1	3	[illegible]	[illegible]
Mueller, cf..	2	1	1	4	[illegible]	[illegible]
Maranville,ss	5	1	2	2	[illegible]	[illegible]
Collins, c...	2	1	0	7	[illegible]	[illegible]
R.SMITH, p	3	0	0	0	[illegible]	[illegible]
COONEY, p.	1	0	0	0	[illegible]	[illegible]
Totals...	36	13	12	27	[illegible]	[illegible]

*Batted for W. Clark in fourth inning.
†Batted for Moss in fifth inning.
‡Batted for Dudley in sixth inning.
§Batted for Pattison in eighth inning.

Brooklyn	001	034	022—12
Boston	203	150	02x—13

Runs batted in—Bissonette (3), Deberry (2), Bancroft (2), Hendrick, Herman (2), Cullop, Sisler (2), Maguire, Harper, Dugan, Clark, Mueller, Maranville, Collins. Two-base hits—Frederick (2), Cullop, Deberry, Harper, Sisler, Maranville, Herman (2), Mueller. Three-base hits—Cullop, Richbourg, Maguire. Home runs—Bissonette, Hendrick, Herman. Sacrifices—Deberry, Collins (2), R. Smith. Left on bases—Brooklyn, 1[illegible]; Boston, 9. Bases on balls—Off W. Clark, [illegible] off Moss, 1; off Dudley, 3; off Elliott, 1; [illegible] R. Smith, 3; off Cooney, 1. Struck out—[illegible] W. Clark, 1; by Dudley, 1; by R. Smith, [illegible] by Cooney, 1. Hits—Off W. Clark, 7 in [illegible] innings; off Moss, 2 in 1; off Dudley, 2 in [illegible] off Pattison, 0 in 2; off Elliott, 1 in 1; [illegible] R. Smith, 16 in 7 (none out in 8th); [illegible] Cooney, 3 in 2. Wild pitches—W. Clark, Moss. Winning pitcher—R. Smith. Losing pitcher—W. Clark. Umpires—Rigler, Ha[illegible] and Stark. Time—2:42.

Briefs

Solomon in all his glory was never attired in such splendid raiment as the Braves. With their red and yellow stockings, caps the same and a brown and green Indian head on their backs the Braves are positively gaudy.

Maranville looks more like an old jockey with each passing year. Especially with that red cap perched on his head.

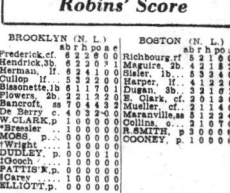

Robinson and Judge Fuchs added some distinction to the parade. They are the only president-managers known to man or science.

Governor Allen and Robbie did some light sparring before the march to the flagpole. They weren't really fighting, however. Just trying to keep warm.

It's too bad Methuselah was waived out of the league so long ago. With him at second, Maranville at short, Dugan at third and Sisler at first, the Boston infield could play in any museum.

Memories of 1914 and a great Boston team. Maranville, Hank Gowdy and Johnny Evers posed for the movies while the band played "Auld Lang Syne."

The Braves will celebrate Patriots' Day tomorrow by working morning and afternoon. McWeeney will pitch the morning game and Vance in the afternoon.

Section IV SPORTS NEW YORK Herald Tribune SPORTS Section IV

TEN PAGES SUNDAY, JUNE 23, 1929 TEN PAGES

Yanks Win Second, 4-3 in Fourteen Innings, After A's Score, 7-3; Columbia's 150-Lb. Crew Wins Marlow Eights by Brilliant Spurt

Lion Fifties Win 3 Races In England

Columbia Comes From Behind in Last 100 Yards to Defeat Twickenham by Length and a Quarter

Victors Clocked in 4:20 for 7/8 Mile

U. S. Crew Also Triumphs in Semi-Final and 1st Heat Races at Henley

By The Associated Press

MARLOW, England, June 22.—The crack 150-pound crew of Columbia University today won the Marlow Eights, defeating Twickenham by a length and a quarter in the final after winning two preliminary heats. The time for the seven-eighths of a mile was 4 minutes 20 seconds.

Columbia won only after staging a brilliant spurt to come from behind in the final hundred yards of a thrilling struggle.

Both crews shot off the mark at a high stroke with Twickenham a shade in front. Passing bisham Abbey, a quarter mile down the course, the British eight led by half a length and held this advantage at the halfway mark.

Along Stoney Weir, close to home, the Columbia Youngsters spurted and the crews waged a terrific fight amid great excitement. A scant hundred years from the finishing posts, Twickenham cracked under the pace and Columbia swept over the line victorious.

Lions Beat Kingston, Vesta.

In the semi-final, Columbia conquered the Kingston and Vesta eights by one and one-half lengths. Columbia's time for the seven-eights of a mile brush was 4 minutes 25 seconds, two seconds slower than the time for the first winning heat.

Columbia shot away from the mark at the start, pulling a high stroke that soon brought a clight lead over Kingston. Toward the finish of the dash, a much shorter race than the American crew is accustomed to rowing, the Kingston eight staged a terrific spurt, but failed to close the gap.

Drawing to the finish line, Columbia drew away again to win by open water. The Vesta crew was last, two lengths behind Kingston.

United States Crew Wins First Heat

In the first heat Columbia won by a length from the Lensdury eight and a crew from the Henley-on-Thames Rowing Club. The time for the seven-eighths of a mile was 4 minutes 23 seconds.

Starting out with a fast stroke, Columbia rowed smoothly all the way, taking the lead in the first few hundred feet and won without being extended. The Lensbury eight made a fine showing, but could do no better than come within a length of the flying Americans. The Henley eight was more than a length back of Lensbury.

J. E. Styles's Hyatter 2d Wins Race on Delaware

Owner Pilots Outboard Motor to Score in Two Heats

Special to the Herald Tribune

PHILADELPHIA, June 22.—Hyhatter II, piloted by John E. Styles, of the Delaware River Outboard Association, carried off the leading honors today at the Delaware River Yacht Club, in Torresdale.

Styles took the first and third heats and finished second in the other to win from a good field that included Duke's Folly, owned by Carl Vogt, of Ardmore; W. J. Hewitt's Bo Bo, of the Delaware River Yacht Club; Gulf Pride, owned and driven by David Entricken, of Hammondton, and Francis Bentz's Noname, from Trenton. The races were over a five-mile course, Styles's boat making the fastest time of 6 minutes 10 seconds.

Hyhatter also won both heats in the free-for-all class, with Gulf Pride second. Carl Vogt suffered slight cuts when his boat upset after the start of the second heat.

Miss Miller and Partner Win N. J. Doubles Title

Teams With Mrs. Letson to Score in Straight Sets

Special to the Herald Tribune

WESTFIELD, N. J., June 22. — Miss Charlotte Miller and her partner, Mrs. Frederick Letson, won the women's doubles championship of New Jersey this afternoon by defeating Mrs. Mary Keller and Miss Grace Surber in straight sets, 6—3, 6—2, at the Westfield Tennis Club.

Miss Miller's slashing drives and stops of high lobs at the net, and Mrs. Letson's fine back-court game were the outstanding features of the final match.

Tomorrow Miss Miller will meet Mrs. Mary Keller in the final round of the singles competition.

The latter advanced today as a result of a 6—1, 6—2 victory over Miss Martha Havemeyer in their belated semi-final contest.

Polo Match Postponed

On account of the death Friday of Colonel Perrin L. Smith, of Governors Island, the polo game scheduled for this afternoon on the island between the post team and the Saddle River team has been postponed, according to an announcement from the headquarters of the Second Corps area yesterday. The Governors Island Rover team will play as scheduled at Massapequa, L. I., against the Fort Point tomorrow afternoon.

Burke Takes N. Y. Open by Four Strokes

Retains Lead in Final 36 Holes to Finish With 73-74 for 287 Total; Christ Second Over Rye Links

Henry Ciuci Wins 3d Money With 294

Six Tie for Fourth at Westchester Biltmore; Macfarlane Climbs to 79

By Kerr N. Petrie

RYE, N. Y., June 22.—Playing seventy-two holes of the long West course at the Westchester Biltmore Country Club in one stroke under seven 4s, Willie Burke, of Westport, N. Y., scored a runaway victory today in the New York State open golf championship, winning with four strokes to spare with a score of 287.

Something of a sensation a season or two ago when he first broke loose in the South, Burke came back into the winning column with as brilliant a flourish as he has ever shown, evidently reinvigorated and rejuvenated by a few months spent on the shores of Lake Champlain. Leading the field by four strokes at the end of the first thirty-six holes with rounds of 72 and 68, Burke put on a 73 and then a 74. The 73 increased his lead to five estrokse at the end of the fifty-four holes, but George Christ, of Rochester, who finished in runner-up position, regained one of these with a 73 in the afternoon. Cooper, with a 75, scored 295, being tied for fourth place by five others—Mike Brady, of the Winged Foot; Macdonald Smith, of Lakeville; Tony Manero, unattached; Joe Turnesa, of Elmsford, and Herman Barron, of Tamarack. Before these and in third place was Henry Ciuci, of Mill River, Conn., who finished with a 72 for a total of 294.

Cooper Loses Second Place

The round-up for the third round found the tie for second place broken. Cooper and Christ had started the eighteen holes together at 144. Christ, who had done 74 and 70, broughti n another 74. Cooper had a 76 and was even out of third place, displaced by Massie B. Miller, of Norwich, Conn., until that moment practically unknown.

Miller is one of those midgets, built somewhat on the lines of Cyril Walker. Like the former national open champion he is also a mighty atom and one to remember when the guns begin to thunder along the front in the battle of the Winged Foot the latter part of this week. When Miller added his morning 72 to his 73 and 74 of the previous day he was one stroke in front of Cooper at 219 and one one behind Christ.

Gene Sarazen, who had overcome the handicap of a 7 at the third and a 6 at the fourth, was tied with Cooper at 220, having done a 73 despite his two bad holes. Joe Turnesa, with a 75, stood at 221, and Willie Klein, last year's champion, Henry Ciui, of Mill River, Conn.; Mike Brady, of the Winged Foot; Tony Manero and Macdonald Smith each had 222. George Voigt, ranking amateur of the metropolitan district, had 223, thereby ranking at that point with Roland Hancock, Mike Turnesa, Herman Barron and Whiffy Cox, of Dyker Beach.

Manero Wins Low-Round Prize

Tony Manero had the distinction of winning the prize for low round in the morning, scoring a 71, with a 36 out and 35 home. A number of those in the running soared badly, notably Willie Macfarlane, of Oak Ridge, who, after his brilliant 69 of the second round, climbed to a 79 and piled up an 8 at the ninth, where he was in more traps than he usually sees in the course of a round.

Voigt was another who lost something of his keen edge, taking 77 where he had been 74 and 72 on the opening day. However, in the afternoon the amateur was back in form, shooting up among the leaders with a 74, which gave him 297.

The garrey today had no difficulty keeping in touch with the leading players, inasmuch as Burke, Christ and Cooper were paired. In the afternoon, therefore, the tournament became a race between these three. At the first hole Christ surprised his companions by pushing his tee shot away off the line and then approaching up for the only birdie 3 of the trio. Burke recovered from a bunker, but took two putts, while Cooper, after driving the green indulged in three putts.

At the second hole Burke regained this stroke with a perfect 4. Christ was in the rought with his drive and over the green into a bunker with his second. A bunker also cost Cooper an extra stroke.

Burke Regains a 6

After finishing out on the third, Burke probably felt gratified that he had started with a lead of five strokes. He required three shots to get within ten feet of the pin and from that point three more to get down. As he started to putt, a group of onlookers appeared to unsettle him. He putted eighteen inches over the cup and missed coming back, taking six for the hole. Christ and Cooper each had a 5 here, Christ being short with his second and Cooper in the rough.

The trio played the next three holes in regulation figures. There were several features at the short seventh, however, where Christ and Burke had their par 3s and Cooper a 4.

Burke was the only one of the party on the green, but Christ recovered cleverly for a single putt after placing his tee shot to the right of the green. Bunkered with his tee short, Cooper had to pay the penalty.

The eighth saw Cooper drop another shot when his approach failed to hold the green. At the ninth he and Burke

(Continued on page four)

Grattan Winning the Great American Two-Year-Old Race at Aqueduct

Rancocas Stable two-year-old is shown leading H. P. Whitney's Prometheus, with Sarazen running third

Herald Tribune photo—Steffen

Grattan Scores In Last Stride At Aqueduct

Rancocas Colt, Topweight of Field, Leads Prometheus; Diavolo Wins Brookdale

By W. J. Macbeth

The Rancocas Stable's Grattan, by grace of a million-dollar ride on the part of apprentice jockey E. Steffen, who is now subbing for the suspended master of the craft, Laverne Fator, won the thirty-fourth running of the Great American, which figured as a twin feature to the Brookdale Handicap at Aqueduct yesterday afternoon. Grattan, a black son of Lucullite, which some years ago was one of the best sprinters hereabout, ran the five furlongs against a strong wind in the good time of one minute flat. He got up in the very last stride to beat Harry Payne Whitney's Prometheus by the proverbial nod.

Yesterday's Great American, which was worth $15,650 to the winner, attracted a field of eleven of the best two-year-olds in the East, barring only Harry Payne Whitney's Boojum, a suspected new Man o' War, which is being reserved for the richer stakes of Saratoga. The Whitney interests thought they had a formidable enough trick in Prometheus, which, indeed, might have won had Sonny Workman not taken just a little too much for granted after he had put away the early pacemaker, William Ziegler's Sumair.

Sumair Knocked Off Stride

It was a break in racing luck that cost this same Sumair at least a look-in for the main pot, for after breaking smartly from his rail position and cutting out all the early pace he seemed well within himself under Mack Garner, and a half length ahead of the driving Prometheus when, approaching the furlong pole, Workman cut the Broomstick colt sharply with the whip. Prometheus swerved sharply under the lash and hit Sumair so hard as almost to stave in his hindquarters. In one short instant from a possible winer Sumair became a million to one shot. He was knocked so completely off his stride that he never did recover and was running lopsidedly as he passed the judges in fifth place.

Evidently the officials looked upon the swerving of Prometheus as an accident, the bumping being between the two front ones, and Garner evidently took the same philosophical view, for he made no claim. A disqualification would not have put him in the money and Prometheus lost the decision in the long run. There was one jockey in the stand, but he was called up. This was Johnny McTaggart, who carried the banner all the way with Wrestler. The stewards wished an explanation of why he did not do better.

Gives Weight to All

Grattan, which previously had won the Hudson, and as a result of this double becomes one of the really pretentious juveniles of the season to date, closed out like a good, game colt under his impost of 125 pounds, giving ten pounds or more to everything opposed to him save Doc Cassidy's Crack Brigade and W. R. Coe's Black Majesty. Black Majesty was among the front runners as far as the elbow where he experienced some interference and quickly dropped out of it evidently disturbed by the weight.

Crack Brigade, which broke from second position, had plenty of excuse. He was sluggish and pinched off in the natural jam for position. Sarazen 2d, which finished third, was running strongly at the end. The Whitney entry of Prometheus and Frumper was the heavily played favorite of the field, with Sumair second choice at 7 to 2, and Crack Brigade third choice at 9 to 2. As a result of the play on the others, the price against Grattan receded to 7 to 1. The esteem in which Sam Hildreth held Grattan was expressed through the fact that he scratched Mokatam, winner of the Keene Memorial, to put it strictly up to the son of Lucullite. Each had been assigned top weight of 125 pounds.

The Wheatley Stable's Diavolo won the Brookdale Handicap of a mile and a furlong in smart fashion. Like a runaway steam engine he came through the stretch to pick up the pack one by one and draw off by a length from Light Carbine. Diavolo ran the mile and an eighth in the good time of 1:51 flat, under 120 pounds. His winning

(Continued on page six)

Myers Breaks Javelin Record As N. Y. A. C. Keeps Met. Title

New Yorkers Score 109 Pts; Swedish-American A. C. 2d; Newark A. C. 3d

By J. P. Abramson

NEWARK, N. J., June 22.—The New York Athletic Club easily defended its metropolitan senior A. A. U. track and field championship today, scoring 109 points in the annual meet at Weequahic Park. The Swedish-American A. C., of New York, was runner-up with 22 and Newark A. C. third with 18.

The only record-breaking performance of the day was turned in by Dave Myers, New York University all around athlete, who hurled the javelin 192 feet, 3¼ inches, shattering the metropolitan mark of 186 feet, 7 inches set by J. C. Lincoln jr. in 1917.

Moore Wins Senior Met. Mile

Gus Moore, the slim, smooth-striding Brooklyn Negro youth, scored his first major triumph at the mile when he won the senior metropolitan mile championship in 4:23 1-5, one of the fastest district title races since Abel Kiviat set his metropolitan record of 4:30 4-5 fifteen years ago and beat Loring McMillen, of the New York A. C., by thirty yards, with Joe Hickey, of N. Y. U., the intercollegiate champion, ten yards back in third place. In his only other start in these championships three years ago, just out of Boys' High School, Moore had run third, beaten by Johnny Theobald and Dick Halton.

Moore went out to run the same sort of sensational mile that he produced last Monday night at the Yankee Stadium. He slammed through the first quarter in 0:58 3-5, passed the half in 2:04 2-5, waving his skinny arms up and down (he said later they felt stiff), and went on through the three-quarters in 3:13. Pursued by Hickey most of the way, Moore had a 10-yard lead at 440, fifteen yards at 880 and forty yards at the three-quarters, and then madly coasted in thirty yards ahead as McMillen, the former Union College runner, sprinted around the last turn to catch and pass Hickey for second place.

Misses Chance for Record

For the first half of the mile Moore was five seconds faster than he was up at the Stadium. But he did not have Leo Lermond to drive him onward after the half, and quite naturally he loafed after picking up an unbeatable lead. And so hemissed a new district record where he had it easily in his grasp. He had stepped the mile at the Stdaium in 4:15 2-5, and had plenty left in winning by thirty yards. Wilbur C. Getz, of the Millrose A. A., the National Collegiate A. A. mile champion, did not start. An infected toe kept him out of the race.

Carl Ring, giant Harvard law student, carried the New York A. C. colors to the first record performance when he twice equaled the championship standard of 15 1-5 seconds in heat and final in the 120-yard high hurdles, going against slight breeze. Ring beat Bill Edwards, ex-Halstead, by a yard, with Earle McDonald, formerly of Holy Cross, third, and Eddie Knoblock, of Pitt, fourth. All four finalists wore the colors of the New York A. C.

Hurth Defaults Hurdles Title

Sol (Happy) Furth, versatile N. Y. U. star, competing for the Swedish-American A. C., was a sideline spectator as Ring succeeded him as hurdles champion and tied his record. The stocky Violet athlete, however, did not remain a specator long. Because of an injured knee he defaulted his hurdles crown. Concentrating in the jumps his performance was excellent, considering the bad knee for he cleared 23 feet 2 1-4 inches, the best jump of his life to win the long jump title.

Everett Utterback, of the University of Pittsburg, competing for the Brooklyn Harriers, was second at 23 feet, ⅛ inches and Stanley Potter, of the New York A. C., former champion, third at 22 feet, 11½ inches.

Furth came from behind in his fifth and last jumps to win, clearing 23 feet 6 inches, then 23 feet 8¼ inches. He was only 3¼ inches short of the district record that has stood for twenty-five years.

The 100-yard dash, run in one heat, went to arl Wildermuth, little Georgetown sprinter and intercollegiate champion, who beat Henry H. Cumming, of the University of Virginia and the Newark A. C., by a foot, Kenneth Wibecan of the Brooklyn Harriers, and Bobby Wiese, of the New York A. C., were third and fourth, with Jimmy Quinn, 1928 intercollegiate champion, unplaced. Because the sprint was run in one heat, giving the sprinters no opportunity for a tune-up, Wildermuth's time, 10 1-5 seconds, was comparatively slow for a field of this class.

Furth came back to score a double when he won the hop, step and jump, beating Utterback on an extra jump after both had tied at 45 feet, 4 inches. In the jump off Furth triple-jumped 46 feet, ½ inches.

Eddie Roll, of Colgate, competing unattached, lost his twice-won laureis in the 440 when Victor Bieslakiewicz, of the Millrose A. A., former Stuyvesant High School champion, came from behind in a bitter stretch duel to beat him by five feet in a fast fifty seconds that was only three-fifths of a second from Maxey Long's thirty-two-year-old record.

Two Run Even for First Fifty Yards

The two were neck and neck for nearly fifty yards after the bespectacled Beesey caught the 1927 and 1928 champion half way down the homestretch. His greater power earned him his winning margin in the last twenty yards. Oliver Proudlock, of the Newark A. C., and George Simons, of Fordham, and the New York A. C., were third and fourth.

Johnny Gibson, of Bloomfield Lyceum, came home a winner in the 440-yard hurdles for the fifth straight year, spread-eagling his field in 56 4-5 seconds—slow time for the man who holds the world's record of 52 3-5 seconds. Erick Kjellstrom, of Georgetown, winner at the Penn relays, was second, fifteen yards behind Gibson, and Charles Kelly, of the Newark A. C., the met junior champion, pulled down the bronze.

Hinkel Defends His Title

Another champion to defend his title successfully for the fourth straight year was Harry Hinkel, of the New York A. C., beating Mack Weiss, of the Newarks, in the three-mile walk by seventy-five yards in 22:53 4-5. The venerable Pat McDonald, the portly lieutenant of police, lost his shot put title, placing third behind Leo Sexton, of Georgetown, the winner, and Charley Smith, of N. Y. U., and Sylvan Scholpp, of the New York A. C., winner of the pole vault title six years in a row, bowed to William A. Cone, Yale junior. Cone cleared 12 feet 4½ inches, and Scholpp, old Yale star, was next at 12 feet.

One of the biggest upsets of the meet came in the defeat of Ben Hedges, of Princeton, intercollegiate champion, by the schoolboy sensation, George Spitz, of Flushing High School. Spitz, clearing 6 feet 2 inches in his third successive meet, was first, and Hedges, beaten for the first time this season, was second at 6 feet. Tom Halleran and Sexton tied for third at 5 feet 11 inches, and the former took the bronze medal on a jump-off.

This was Spitz's third triumph in eight days. He cleared 6 feet 2⅞ inches for a new record on the P. S. A. L. championships a week ago, then jumped 6 feet 2⅛ inches for a new mark (displacing Hedges as record holder) in the metropolitan junior championships last Sunday, and continued his brilliant performances to beat Hedges in person today.

The summaries:

100-yard dash—Won by Karl Wilderman, New York A. C.; Henry C. Cumming, Newark A. C., second; Kenneth Wibecan, Brooklyn Harriers A. A., third; Robert S. Wiese, New York A. C., fourth. Time, 0:10 1-5.

120-yard high hurdles—Won by Carl Ring, New York A. C.; William S. Edwards, New York A. C., second; Earl C. McDonald, New York A. C., third; Ed Knoblock, New York A. C., fourth. Time, 0:15 1-5 (equals meet

(Continued on page three)

Barry Sculls to Victory Over Relay Team of 3

LONDON, June 22 (Canadian Press [illegible]).—Bert Barry, world's professional sculling champion, achieved [illegible] triumph on the River [illegible] today by defeating three [illegible] course from Putney to Mortlake. His opponents were S. Perrin, Putney; R. Dowson, Barnes, and H. Walford, Kew. Barry won by a length in 24 minutes and 24 seconds.

The famous professional is now coaching Joe Wright jr., Toronto holder of the Diamond Sculls, who is defending his title at Henley next month.

Giants Defeat Phillies Twice For Six in Row

Ott Hits Three Homers in 12-6 and 12-5 Victories; Thevenow Rejoins Club

By W. B. Hanna

PHILADELPHIA, Pa., June 22.—The baseball extravaganza engaging the Giants and Phillies in a six-game turmoil of slugging and poor pitching, ended this evening, six games to none in favor of the Giants. They won the day's double-header, 12 to 6 for the first game and 12 to 5 for the second.

Dutch Henry served a right good game in the second, and though hit often, did well in keeping the hits scattered. Few of the pitchers in the series have been efficient, in that detail. After the game the fans waited around the telegraph instruments anxiously to get the result of the second game in New York.

In the series here the Giants made 65 runs and 84 hits. There were thirteen home runs, one three-bagger and seventeen two-baggers in their harvest. Home runs today were made by Ott, three; Leach, two; Lindstrom, Terry, Jackson, O'Doul, Thompson and Friberg.

Tommy Thevenow played for the first time since he was smashed up in Florida in the spring. He jumped in in the ninth inning o fthe first game and played all of the second. He made a single the first time at bat, and his fielding was clean, fast and the work of the artist.

Ott Is Strong at Bat

Melvin Extraordinary Ott began hitting home runs in the first inning of the first game and in the course of that plodding and plastering struggle, he made two home runs, one two-bagger, took a pitched ball on the arm and walked once. He batted in five runs and on the occasion when the pitched ball hit him, the Phillies kindly let Genewich run for him until he was taped up.

Both homers flitted over the right field fence full panoplied and winging. The second was his nineteenth and tied him with Lou Gehrig for the major league lead. The second rate Philly pitching and the correlative slugging of the Giants made them easy winners. They drove Lefty Sweetland from the redoubt.

O'Doul and Jackson also hit home runs, both off the starting pitcher. The Phillies flogged Mays from the box in the fifth in a sequence of slitting singles, but Mays thought he had Thompson struck out instead of passed, and held converse with the umpire on the subject as he left the game. The decision preceded two hits which lifted Carl and contributed no calm to his state of mind.

Captain Thompson, a philosophic lad on the whole, was ejected in the ninth inning by Pfirman for kicking, but he stayed out there. Pfirman walked over to McGraw and spoke to McGraw, and at the latter's request presumably, Thompson stayed. McGraw didn't want to be rude to a fellow ball man who had granted him a

(Continued on page three)

Moles Beats Yale With 5 Hits, 10 to 4

Princeton Takes Annual Series With Elis in Polo Grounds Games, Making 16 Hits Off 3 Pitchers

Tigers Score Four Runs in 1st and 4th

Sawyer, Loud and Thompson Are Hit Hard; Hoben Vincent, Wittmer Star

Ted Moles, Princeton pitcher, who yielded Yale three runs and a victory last Saturday in the second game of the annual series of the two colleges, came back to beat the Elis in the rubber game at the Polo Grounds yesterday, 10 to 4, holding the Blue batters to five hits.

While Moles was pitching a sturdy, courageous game and aiding his own cause with two smartly hit singles, Princeton was treating Sawyer, Loud and Thompson with impartial levity. Sawyer, who won one game from Harvard, worked three innings, and Loud, who won the other, lasted only one. So while the Big Three series is actually that nolonger, Princeton had the satisfaction of taking the series from the team that took two straight from Harvard and of battering the two pitchers who humbled the Crimson.

Sawyer Yields Four Runs

Sawyer and Loud each yielded four runs in an inning, Sawyer in the first and Loud in the fourth. Thompson, who finished the game, was fairly effective and his one bad inning, the seventh, gave the Orange and Black only two runs, which wound up the Princeton scoring.

Only a few scattered thousands saw the close of the series but gave fair imitations occasionally of the bellows that rolled over from the Yankee Stadium. Most of the crowd appeared Princeton rooters.

Moles's victory yesterday was only his second of the season, but he made it good. Vincent, Eli first baseman, found him none too mystifying, making a lusty triple and almost as tremendous a double, and Johnny Hoben hit a home run to deep left center in the second, but otherwise the Princeton hurler kept the Elis hitting straight grounders to the infielders or lofty, easy flies to the outfield.

Princeton gathered sixteen hits in all, Johnny Wittmer, with four singles, and Lebhar, with two singles and a double, leading an attack which saw every regular in the batting order with the exception of the keystone combination of Swift and O'Toole driving out at least one safety.

Errors in First Hurt Sawyer

Sawyer was badly treated in the first inning when four Princeton runs crossed the plate, but slipshod fielding helped to effect his ruin. After the first he held Princeton scoreless during the time he worked and the defeat might not have been so overwhelming had he been left on the mound. Smokey Joe Wood evidently figured on Loud pitching a similar three innings and Thompson finishing.

Strubing, Lebhar, Wittmer and Ebbets, the first four to face Sawyer, singled. Lebhar sent Strubing to third with his hit and then stole second, scoring behind Strubing on the first of Wittmer's four safeties. Bennett walked after Ebbets had singled, filling the bases. Swift flied out for the first out and Sawyer showed signs of settling down. O'Toole hit a slow roller to Vincent, who fumbled the ball and then fell, allowing Wittmer to cross the plate. Carter hit to Aldrich and Ebbets scored, aided by a throw that was none too good. Moles ended the misery by hitting into a double play, which went from Sawyer to Hoben, nipping Bennett at the plate, and then to Vincent to catch Moles at first.

Hoben Hits Homer in Second

Hoben's home run, a mighty crack to left center, came in the second inning and in the third Yale cut down farther on the Princeton lead when Grove, center fielder, singled, stole second and came all the way home when Carter threw into the outfield in a vain effort to catch him. While Yale was creeping closer in these innings, Sawyer was pitching a much better game and kept the Tigers away from the plate.

The scoring broke loose again in the fourth, but Yale had to be content with but one run to set against four for Princeton. Vincent drove a fast one from Moles far out to the right field bull pen and raced around to third while Princeton was executing a somewhat sluggish relay. Vincent was halted at third when O'Toole turned to

(Continued on page three)

Yankees Win Thriller for Even Break

Defeat Athletics in Fourteenth as Lazzeri's Hit Scores Combs; Walberg Turns Back New York

Pipgras Hurls Fine Game for Victory

Blank A's After First; Visitors Cut Down Late Rallies With Great Play

By Rud Rennie

If too much excitement is bad for a person, then the 67,000 who attended yesterday's double-header between the Yankees and the Athletics at the Stadium are undoubtedly in a bad way this morning.

There was nothing exciting in the first game, which the Yankees lost by the simple process of going without runs until the last inning, when they made three, which were not enough. The A's won this game with two timely home runs, a couple of doubles and an untimely Yankee error. The score was 7 to 3.

But the second game—people were hoarse from shouting and limp from having one thrill after another for fourteen consecutive innings. Six times in the closing innings the Yankees had the winning run on base. Twice in this frenzied period of play the A's stopped the winning run at the plate with spectacular plays. Once did the great Ruth and the powerful Lazzeri come to bat with the bases full and fail. Always were the Yankees ominous.

Lazzeri Breaks Up Game

But it was not until the fourteenth inning that they were able to bring home the winning run. Combs started it with a single. Gehrig and Ruth were walked. There were two out and Lazzeri, who had not made a hit all day, was the hitter. With the bases full and the frenzied shouts of the crowd roaring out of the stands turning dark in the twilight, Lazzeri singled to center and won the game for the Yankees by a score of 4 to 3.

This game was a master piece of pitching by the Yankees' tall right-hander, George Pipgras. Away back in the beginning of things, in the first inning, he had a few minutes' wildness. He walked Bishop and Cochrane and made a ball too good for Al. Simmons, who promptly slugged a home run into the right field bleachers to make three runs.

From then until the end of the game Pipgras was a master pitcher. For thirteen innings he held the leading club in the league scoreless and nearly hitless. Haas beat out a little bunt in the third, Fox singled in the seventh and Miller singled in the tenth. Pipgras issued one base on balls. Those three hitters and the lonely walker were the only men to reach first base. No one reached second, three of the men being caught in double plays and the other being picked off first base. He faced the minimum of three batters an inning for thirteen innings. And when he was through he had won a four-hit, fourteen-inning ball game.

Quinn Canny in Pinches

While he was pitching so perfectly and the boys were giving him beautiful support, all hands joined in the task of overcoming an early three-run lead. It was hard work, because old John Quinn, the Philadelphia pitcher, was canny in the pinches and was being supported beautifully.

It was Pipgras who came in with the first of the Yankee runs, forcing the singling Dickey in the third and moving around on hits by Combs and Lary.

(Continued on page three)

Yankees' Scores

FIRST GAME

PHILA. (A. L.)	ab	r	h	po	a	e
Bishop, 2b	4	0	0	2	4	0
Haas, cf	5	1	2	5	0	0
Cochrane, c	5	1	1	3	0	0
Simmons, lf	4	2	2	4	0	0
Foxx, 1b	2	2	1	10	0	0
Miller, rf	3	1	1	2	0	0
Dykes, 3b	4	0	1	1	3	1
Boley, ss	4	0	2	0	2	1
WAL'RG, p	4	0	0	0	2	0
Totals	35	7	10	27	11	2

NEW YORK (A. L.)	ab	r	h	po	a	e
Combs, cf	3	0	0	1	0	0
Byrd, cf	1	1	1	3	0	0
Robert'n, 3b	2	0	0	0	0	0
Lary, 3b	2	1	1	1	2	0
Gehrig, 1b	2	1	0	13	0	0
Ruth, rf	4	0	1	0	0	0
Lazzeri, 2b	5	0	0	3	5	0
Meusel, lf	5	0	1	1	0	0
Grabow'i, c	5	0	1	2	0	1
Durocher, ss	4	0	3	3	4	0
HEIM'CH, p	0	0	0	0	0	0
SHERID, p	3	0	0	0	1	0
Totals	36	3	8	27	12	1

Philadelphia .... 020 320 000—7
New York .... 000 000 003—3

Runs batted in—Foxx (2), Boley (2), Cochrane (2), Byrd, Lary, Meusel. Two-base hits—Ruth, Simmons, Boley. Home runs—Foxx, Cochrane, Byrd, Lary. Sacrifice—Miller. Double plays—Lazzeri, Durocher and Gehrig; Boley, Bishop and Foxx; Sherid, Lazzeri and Gehrig. Left on bases—New York, 13; Philadelphia, 5. Bases on balls—Off Heimach, 1; off Sherid, 2; off Walberg, 7. Struck out—By Sherid, 1; by Walberg, 2. Hits—Off Heimach, 8 in 4 innings (none out in fifth); off Sherid, 2 in 5. Losing pitcher—Heimach. Umpires—Moriarty, McGowan and Campbell. Time—2:10.

SECOND GAME

PHILA. (A. L.)	ab	r	h	po	a	e
Bishop, 2b	4	1	0	8	2	0
Haas, cf	5	0	1	6	1	0
Cochrane, c	4	1	0	4	0	0
Simmons, lf	5	1	1	4	0	0
Foxx, 1b	4	0	1	13	2	0
Miller, rf	5	0	1	3	1	0
Dykes, 3b	4	0	0	1	7	0
Boley, ss	5	0	0	1	5	0
QUINN, p	5	0	0	1	2	0
Totals	41	3	4	*41	20	0

NEW YORK (A. L.)	ab	r	h	po	a	e
Combs, cf	6	2	5	4	0	0
Lary, 3b	5	0	2	0	1	0
Gehrig, 1b	5	0	1	11	1	0
Ruth, rf	5	0	2	3	0	0
Lazzeri, 2b	7	0	1	6	3	0
Meusel, lf	6	0	0	5	0	0
Dickey, c	4	1	3	6	1	0
†Robertson	0	0	0	0	0	0
Koenig, ss	2	0	1	1	1	0
Durocher, ss	3	0	1	2	2	0
‡Durst	1	0	0	0	0	0
Grabow'i, c	2	0	1	3	0	0
PIPGRAS, p	5	1	1	1	2	0
Totals	51	4	18	42	11	0

*Two out when winning run was scored.
†Ran for Dickey in ninth inning.
‡Batted for Durocher in ninth inning.

Philad'phia. 300 000 000 000 00—3
New York.. 001 010 010 000 01—4

Runs batted in—Simmons (3), Lary, Combs, Ruth, Lazzeri. Two-base hits—Combs (2). Three-base hit—Dickey. Home run—Simmons. Stolen base—Combs. Sacrifices—Combs, Lary (2), Gehrig. Double plays—Dickey and Durocher; Boley, Dykes and Foxx; Durocher and Gehrig; Boley, Bishop and Foxx; Lazzeri and Gehrig; Pipgras and Gehrig; Haas and Cochrane; Miller and Foxx. Left on bases—New York, 14; Philadelphia, 0. Bases on balls—Off Pipgras, 4; off Quinn, 4. Struck out—By Pipgras, 6; by Quinn, 2. Passed ball—Cochrane. Umpires—McGowan, Campbell and Moriarty. Time—2:58.

Standings in Major Leagues

SUNDAY, JUNE 23, 1929

American League

YESTERDAY'S RESULTS

Philadelphia, 7; New York 3 (1st).
New York, 4; Philadelphia, 3 (14 ins, 2d).
Washington, 3; Boston, 2 (1st).
Washington, 5; Boston, 1 (2d).
Cleveland, 4; Detroit, 3.
St. Louis, 11; Chicago, 3.

STANDING OF THE CLUBS

	Phila'phia	New York	St. Louis	Detroit	Cleveland	Washington	Chicago	Boston	Won	Lost	Percentage
Phila'phia	—	5	3	4	4	13	5	8	42	15	.737
New York	4	—	6	4	1	3	7	10	35	23	.603
St. Louis	1	1	—	7	7	3	10	5	34	24	.586
Detroit	3	3	5	—	6	4	6	6	33	30	.524
Cleveland	2	4	3	6	—	4	4	4	27	29	.482
Washington	1	5	3	2	3	—	4	5	23	33	.411
Chicago	2	0	2	5	6	3	—	4	22	39	.361
Boston	2	5	2	2	2	3	3	—	19	42	.311
Games lost	15	23	24	30	29	33	39	42	—	—	

GAMES TODAY

Philadelphia at New York (3 p. m.).
Boston at Washington.
Detroit at Cleveland.
Chicago at St. Louis.

National League

YESTERDAY'S RESULTS

New York, 12; Philadelphia, 6 (1st).
New York, 12; Philadelphia, 5 (2d).
Brooklyn, 3; Boston, 0 (1st).
Boston, 5; Brooklyn, 0 (2d).
Pittsburgh, 7; Chicago, 4.
St. Louis, 11; Cincinnati 8.

STANDING OF THE CLUBS

	Pittsburgh	Chicago	St. Louis	New York	Brooklyn	Phila'phia	Boston	Cincinnati	Won	Lost	Percentage
Pittsburgh	—	7	7	4	4	3	4	7	36	21	.632
Chicago	7	—	7	2	6	4	4	4	34	22	.607
St. Louis	2	4	—	2	5	5	4	14	36	25	.590
New York	3	4	4	—	5	10	6	2	34	24	.586
Brooklyn	2	0	1	6	—	6	4	5	24	34	.414
Phila'phia	3	2	1	1	5	—	8	3	23	33	.411
Boston	1	2	3	5	8	2	—	2	23	34	.404
Cincinnati	3	3	2	4	1	3	4	—	20	37	.351
Games lost	21	22	25	24	34	38	34	37	—	—	

GAMES TODAY

New York at Brooklyn (3 p. m.).
Pittsburgh at Chicago.
St. Louis at Cincinnati.
Philadelphia at Boston (2).

Ruth Hits His 500th Major League Homer, but Yanks Lose; Giants and Robins Win

YANKS BEATEN, 6-5; RUTH HITS HIS 500TH

Babe's Smash Off Hudlin Is 30th of Season and Clears Cleveland's Rightfield Wall.

GETS POSSESSION OF BALL

Gives $20 and 2 Autographed Spheres to the Finder—Cy Williams Next With 237.

GEHRIG ALSO MAKES HOMER

Overflow Crowd of 25,000 Sees the Game, Decided by Indians' 2 Runs in the Sixth.

By WILLIAM E. BRANDT.

Special to The New York Times.

CLEVELAND, Aug. 11. — Babe Ruth's 500th major league home run and a subsequent four-bagger by Lou Gehrig represented about all the glory the Yanks gleaned against Cleveland today. Their own erors, some visible in the box score and others represented only in Cleveland's run column, helped the Indians to their 6—5 victory.

The fans overflowed from the stands to form a crescent across left field. The attendance numbered upward of 25,000, making a proper setting for Ruth's achievement of his most important homer numerically thus far this year. He made it on the first ball pitched by Willis Hudlin in the second inning, a high, fast ball, wihch left home plate much higher and ten times faster than it arrived. It cleared the right-field fence near the foul line, and was the first run of the afternoon.

Ruth Far Ahead of Rivals.

Ruth not only became the first player in history to hit 500 home runs, but he has raised his total to the point where it is more than double the aggregate number of circuit blows made by any other player. Cy Williams, veteran outfielder of the Phillies, is his nearest rival with 237. Williams had made 234 up to the start of the present season.

Ruth has served notice that he will put up a great fight before being deposed as home run monarch this season. In his last seven games the Babe has smashed six homers. His present total of thirty puts him on even terms with Hack Wilson of the Cubs. Only Chuck Klein of the Phillies now leads Ruth.

Babe dispatched a courier in quest of the priceless ball he knocked out of the park to place the major league all-time homer-hitting record at the half-thousand mark. Ten minutes later there reported at the Yankee bench Jake Geiser, aged 46, of New Philadelphia, Ohio. He was visiting relatives near the ball park, and at the moment Babe Ruth's 500th home run dipped over the fence he was on his way to catch a bus for New Philadelphia.

Ball Retriever in Spotlight.

He was just a passerby, but his capture of the baseball after it ricochetted off a Lexington Avenue doorstep put him in fame's spotlight for a moment. The Emperor of Swat shook hands with him in the Yankee dugout, traded him a pair of autographed baseballs in exchange for the historic sphere he fielded off the doorstep, then presented him with a $20-bill, unautographed.

Mr. Geiser decided to miss the New Philadelphia bus, but after watching Ruth miss the fence in three subsequent efforts, and ascertaining that Ruth's 600th homer is not likely to happen here this week, he left for his home tonight, richer by $20, to say nothing of the two baseballs.

Edwin Wells was today's severest sufferer. After Gehrig lofted his twenty-seventh homer of the season along the pathway taken by Ruth's thirtieth of the year, the Yanks enjoyed a 2—0 lead. It vanished in the fourth. After a couple of fluke singles and a sacrifice, Meusel allowed a fly to drop safe near his feet for a single, scoring two runs.

Indians Take Lead.

Two minutes later Luke Sewell's single put Cleveland ahead because Meusel threw wild to the plate to catch Hodapp scoring from second. The Yanks tied it on Gardner's wild throw in the fifth, but after two were out in Cleveland's half Koenig's muff turned a pop fly into a scratch single. Two real singles put the Tribe ahead again.

Meusel's double with the bases filled in the sixth put the Yanks in front, 5—4, then in Cleveland's half Lazzeri muffed a throw which should have retired the side runless. The Indians scored two runs and Wells retired to the seclusion of the showers.

The box score:

NEW YORK (A).	ab.	r.	h.	po.	a.	e.
Combs, cf.	4	0	0	3	1	0
Robert'n, 3b.	5	0	0	1	1	0
Gehrig, 1b.	3	2	1	9	0	1
Ruth, rf.	4	2	2	2	0	0
Lazzeri, 2b.	3	0	0	2	2	1
Meusel, lf.	4	0	1	3	0	1
Dickey, c.	3	0	2	2	1	0
aLary	0	0	0	0	0	0
Koenig, ss.	4	1	1	2	3	1
Wells, p.	3	0	1	0	1	0
Sherid, p.	0	0	0	0	0	0
bDurst	1	0	0	0	0	0
Total	34	5	8	24	9	4

CLEVELAND (A).	ab.	r.	h.	po.	a.	e.
Morgan, rf.	5	1	0	1	0	0
J.Sewell, 3b.	5	0	1	1	2	0
Averill, cf.	5	2	3	3	0	0
Fonseca, 1b.	4	1	2	14	4	0
Falk, lf.	2	0	1	1	1	0
Hodapp, 2b.	4	1	2	0	7	0
Gardner, ss.	4	0	1	1	3	1
L.Sewell, c.	4	1	2	3	0	0
Hudlin, p.	4	0	1	3	2	0
Total	37	6	13	27	19	1

aRan for Dickey in sixth.
bBatted for Sherid in ninth.

New York	0	1	0	1	1	2	0	0	0	—5
Cleveland	0	0	0	3	1	2	0	0	.	—6

Runs batted in—Hodapp 2, J. Sewell 1, Averill 1, Falk 1, L. Sewell 1, Meusel 2, Ruth 1, Gehrig 1.

Two-base hits—Meusel, Averill. Home runs—Ruth, Gehrig. Sacrifice—Falk. Double play—Combs and Gehrig. Left on bases—New York 6, Cleveland 9. Bases on balls—Off Hudlin 4, Wells 1. Struck out—By Hudlin 2, Wells 1. Hits—Off Wells 12 in 5 2-3 innings, Sherid 1 in 2 1-3. Losing pitcher—Wells. Umpires—Nallin, Dinneen and McGowan. Time of game—2 hours.

International League.

Jersey City 6, Toronto 4 (first).
Toronto 3, Jersey City 1 (second).
Newark 4, Rochester 3 (first, 12 innings).
Rochester 7, Newark 2 (second).
Baltimore 7, Buffalo 2 (first).
Buffalo 6, Baltimore 4 (second).
Reading 11, Montreal 4.

STANDING OF THE TEAMS.

	Won.	Lost.	P.C.
Rochester	73	47	.608
Toronto	69	55	.557
Baltimore	65	53	.551
Reading	62	55	.530
Buffalo	60	63	.4879
Montreal	59	62	.4876
Newark	55	64	.462
Jersey City	38	82	.317

WHERE THEY PLAY TODAY.
Rochester at Newark.
Toronto at Jersey City.
Buffalo at Baltimore.
Montreal at Reading.

Ruth's 500 Homers Recorded Over Period of Fifteen Years

In addition to the 500 home runs Ruth has recorded during his major league career with the Boston and New York clubs in American League regularly scheduled games, he has driven out thirteen four-baggers in world series engagements. Ruth's complete rome-run record covers fifteen seasons of play, he having made no homer in 1914, his first year in the majors. Ruth was purchased by the Yankees prior to the 1920 season.

His record follows:

1915	4	1923	41
1916	3	1924	46
1917	2	1925	25
1918	11	1926	47
1919	29	1927	60
1920	54	1928	54
1921	59	1929	30
1922	35		
Total			500

HUBBELL SUBDUES REDS WITH 5 HITS

Giants Hammer Luque for Four Runs in the 1st and Triumph Easily by 6 to 1.

JACKSON DRIVES HOME RUN

Circuit Wallop Accounts for Three Tallies—Cincinnati Escapes Shut-out in the Ninth Inning.

By JOHN DREBINGER.

Carl Hubbell, tall, lean and somber of appearance, stepped out on the mound at the Polo Grounds yesterday and confided to his Giant comrades that he did not think much of the Reds.

"As a matter of fact," remarked Carl, who usually is a conservative and extremely modest fellow, "I think I can beat these birds with my left hand."

Whereupon Carl proceeded to prove his point to the complete satisfaction of a gathering of 15,000 spectators, who saw Hubbell pitch a five-hit game while the Giants stalked off with an easy 6-to-1 victory over the Reds, who left the field doubtless wondering what would have happened to them had Hubbell pitched with his right hand.

The fact, of course, that Hubbell is normally left-handed is beside the point and merely heightened the joke he perpetrated on the unsuspecting Reds, who seemed not to know with which hand he was throwing or what he was throwing. Later they admitted frankly they seldom saw the ball.

Simplify Hubbell's Task.

By way of making the task as simple as possible for Hubbell, the Giants rushed off to a four-run lead in the opening round that at once put the Reds in a somnolent state from which they were unable to arouse themselves. Adolfo Luque was the victim of this swift attack that overwhelmed the distinguished Cuban before he even had a chance to adjust himself to the situation.

The good Señor, once upon a time one of the most feared foemen the Giants ever had to face, has not been so successful against the McGrawmen recently and yesterday he was less so than usual. He started by passing Fullis, and though he induced Leach to pop out, Doc Farrell lashed a double to left and Fullis scored.

Then Luque fanned Terry, but passed Ott, and immediately after this misfortune struck him all in a lump. Travis Jackson wafted a homer against the railing of the upper left field tier. That gave the Giants three in a bunch and four for the round.

Ehrhardt Is Effective.

The margin was ample, though the Giants prodded Luque for two more runs in the third and fourth before the good Señor decided to retire in favor of Rube Ehrhardt, who did an excellent though unprofitable piece of relief pitching the rest of the way.

Meanwhile, Hubbell, pitching continuously with his left hand despite the fact that Manager Jack Hendricks had carefully selected a 100 per cent right-handed batting order to oppose him, held the Reds spellbound. He allowed them only three hits in the first eight innings and not a Redleg reached third.

In the ninth Hubbell lost his shutout chiefly because Andy Cohen fumbled a grounder by Zitzmann. Two outs put Zitzmann on third and a single by Allen put him over the plate. The run seemed to put the Reds in better humor and they promised to be back again today.

The box score:

CINCINNATI (N).	ab.	r.	h.	po.	a.	e.
Swanson, lf.	3	0	0	2	0	0
Zitzmann, rf.	4	1	0	0	0	0
Stripp, 3b.	4	0	0	0	1	0
Kelly, 1b.	4	0	1	7	0	0
Allen, cf.	4	0	1	3	0	0
Pittenger, ss.	4	0	2	5	4	0
Ford, 2b.	4	0	0	4	4	0
Gooch, c.	3	0	1	2	4	0
Luque, p.	2	0	0	1	0	0
aDressen	1	0	0	0	0	0
Ehrhardt, p.	1	0	0	4	1	0
Total	34	1	5	24	14	0

NEW YORK (N).	ab.	r.	h.	po.	a.	e.
Fullis, cf.	3	1	1	2	0	0
Leach, lf.	4	0	0	3	0	0
Farrell, 3b.	3	2	1	0	3	0
Terry, 1b.	3	0	2	10	1	0
Ott, rf.	3	1	0	1	0	0
Jackson, ss.	4	1	4	1	6	0
O'Farrell, c.	4	0	1	6	0	0
Cohen, 2b.	3	1	1	3	1	1
Hubbell, p.	2	0	0	1	1	0
Total	29	6	10	27	12	1

aBatted for Luque in fifth.

Cincinnati	0	0	0	0	0	0	0	0	1	—1
New York	4	0	1	1	0	0	0	0	.	—6

Runs batted in—Farrell 1, Jackson 4, Fullis 1, Allen 1.

Two-base hits—Farrell, Pittenger, Gooch. Home run—Jackson. Stolen base—Ott. Sacrifice—Hubbell. Double play—Ford, Pittenger and Kelly. Left on bases—New York 4, Cincinnati 6. Bases on balls—Off Hubbell 1, Luque 4. Struck out—By Hubbell 6, Luque 1, Ehrhardt 1. Hits—Off Luque 6 in 4 innings, Ehrhardt 4 in 4. Losing pitcher—Luque. Umpires—McCormick and Pfirman. Time of game—1:35.

MAJOR LEAGUE RECORDS.

Show What Each Club Did During Week in Pennant Races.

Major league records for the past week including games won and lost, runs, hits, errors, opponents' runs and home runs, as compiled by the Associated Press, follow:

AMERICAN LEAGUE.

	W.	L.	R.	H.	E.	OR.	HR.
New York	5	3	60	83	8	38	10
Washington	5	3	61	94	10	51	4
Deroit	4	3	61	92	10	59	5
Philadelphia	4	4	41	77	9	50	8
Boston	2	2	22	40	8	14	2
Chicago	2	3	22	51	5	33	2
St. Louis	3	5	41	83	8	45	2
Cleveland	2	4	32	69	7	50	4

NATIONAL LEAGUE.

	W.	L.	R.	H.	E.	OR.	HR.
Chicago	4	1	35	56	7	24	4
New York	3	2	28	54	6	25	4
Pittsburg	4	3	38	80	5	36	2
Cincinnati	2	2	21	39	5	17	0
Brooklyn	2	3	27	57	3	28	1
Philadelphia	2	3	30	57	9	37	1
St. Louis	2	4	24	50	6	33	4
Boston	1	2	6	23	1	9	0

OTT OF THE GIANTS OUT AT PLATE ON ATTEMPTED DOUBLE STEAL IN THIRD INNING YESTERDAY.

Times Wide World Photo.

ATHLETICS BEATEN BY DETROIT IN 11TH

Johnson's Homer Tops Mackmen, 9-8, After Losers Take Five-Run Lead in First.

DETROIT, Aug. 11 (AP).—Detroit spotted the Athletics five runs in the first inning today and then with the aid of timely home runs by Red Hargrave and Roy Johnson, won by 9 to 8 in the eleventh. The Mackmen's pennant lead of eleven and a half games was not affected as the Yanks also lost.

Hargrave's homer came in the ninth with two on base when the Tigers were trailing by four runs. Quinn came to the aid of Earnshaw, but was unable to prevent the tying run, scored on Cronin's wild throw. He also was removed. Johnson's homer came in the eleventh with two out and won the game.

The box score:

PHILADELPHIA (A.).	ab.r.h.po.a.e.
Cronin, 3b.	6 0 1 1 5 1
Haas, cf.	4 0 0 3 0 0
Cochrane, c.	6 1 1 6 1 1
Simmons, lf.	[illegible]
Foxx, 1b.	[illegible]
Miller, rf.	[illegible]
Hale, 3b.	[illegible]
Boley, ss.	[illegible]
Earnshaw, p.	[illegible]
Quinn, p.	[illegible]
Orwell, p.	[illegible]
Total	44 8 13 *32 16 3

DETROIT (A.).	ab.r.h.po.a.e.
Johnson, lf-cf.	7 1 2 7 0 0
Harris, 3b.	4 1 1 1 4 1
Gehringer, 2b.	[illegible]
Rice, cf-3b.	[illegible]
Heilmann, rf.	[illegible]
Alexander, 1b.	[illegible]
M'M'us, 3b-ss.	[illegible]
Hargrave, c.	[illegible]
Schuble, ss.	[illegible]
Fothergill, lf.	[illegible]
Sorrell, p.	[illegible]
Carroll, p.	[illegible]
Whitehill, p.	[illegible]
aYde	1 0 1 0 0 0
Total	46 9 15 33 15 1

*Two out when winning run was scored.
aBatted for Carroll in ninth.

Philadelphia ....5 0 1 1 0 1 0 0 0 0 0—8
Detroit ....0 1 1 1 1 0 0 0 4 0 1—9

Runs batted in—Simons 1, Miller 2, Boley 3, Hargrave 4, Haas 1, Heilmann 2, Hale 1, Johnson 1.

Two-base hits—Cochrane, Simmons, Hargrave 2. Three-base hits—Boley, Rice. Home runs—Miller Hargrave, Johnson. Stolen base—Miller. Sacrifices—Haas, Hale. Double play—Hale, Cronin and Foxx. Left on bases—Philadelphia 11, Detroit 13. Bases on balls—Off Sorrell 3, Carroll 3, Earnshaw 8. Struck out—By Sorrell 11, Earnshaw 5, Whitehill 1, Orwell 1. Hits—Off Sorrell 5 in 1 2-3 innings, Carroll 6 in 7 1-3, Whitehill 1 in 2, Earnshaw 11 in 8 1-3, Quinn 3 in 0 (pitched to three batters in ninth), Orwell 1 in 2 1-3. Winning pitcher—Whitehill. Losing pitcher—Orwell. Umpires—Moriarty, Geisel and Van Graflan. Time of game—2:37.

PACIFIC COAST LEAGUE.

AT SAN FRANCISCO.

		R.	H.	E.
San Francisco	0 0 0 1 0 2 0 0 1	—4	8	0
Missions	0 0 3 1 2 0 1 0 .	—7	14	0

Batteries—Mails and Reed; Cole and Baldwin.

San Francisco	3 0 1 0 0 0 1 0 0	—5	8	0
Missions	0 0 0 2 4 5 0 0 .	—11	19	0

Batteries—Gomez and Reed; Ruether, Pillette and Hoffman.

AT OAKLAND.

Seattle	0 0 0 0 1 0 0 0 0	—1	5	0
Oakland	0 0 0 0 0 0 0 0 0	—0	4	1

Batteries—Pitgras and Borreani; Dumovich and Lombardi.

Seattle	0 1 0 0 0 2 1 1 0	—5	15	3
Oakland	1 4 0 3 6 0 0 1 .	—15	28	1

Batteries—Smith, Lamanski, Dahlberg, Fisch and Borreani; Edwards and Lombardi.

AT SACRAMENTO.

Portland	0 4 1 0 0 1 0 1	—7	9	1
Sacramento	0 0 2 2 0 0 0 0	—4	9	2

(Eight innings by agreement.)

Batteries—Ortman, Fullerton and Tomlin; Rachac, Gould and Harris.

Portland	0 0 0 1 1 1 0 0 0	—3	6	1
Sacramento	0 0 0 0 2 0 0 0 0	—2	12	0

Batteries—Fullerton, Chesterfield and Woodall; Keating, Cano and Koehler.

AT LOS ANGELES.

Hollywood	1 1 0 0 1 0 2 2 2	—7	13	1
Los Angeles	1 0 1 0 0 1 0 0 0	—3	4	0

Batteries—Peters, Baecht and Hannah, Sandberg; Shellenbach and Severeid.

Hollywood	2 0 0 0 0 0 0	—2	5	1
Los Angeles	0 0 0 1 0 0	—1	5	1

Batteries—Roberts and Sandberg; Johns and Bassler, Severeid.

STANDING OF THE LEAGUE.

	W.	L.	P.C.		W.	L.	P.C.
Missions	27	16	.628	Oakland	21	22	.488
S. Fr'ncisco	27	16	.628	Portland	20	22	.476
Hollywood	26	16	.619	Sacramento	15	26	.366
L. Angeles	25	18	.581	Seattle	9	34	.209

SOUTHERN ASSOCIATION.

AT CHATTANOOGA.

		R.	H.	E.
Atlanta	1 2 1 2 0 0 2 0 0	—8	9	1
Chattanooga	0 0 3 0 0 0 0 0 0	—3	9	4

Batteries—Kiefer and Yelle; Pyle, Settlemire and Brock.

AT MOBILE.

Memphis	1 1 0 0 0 0 0 0 0	—2	8	2
Mobile	0 2 0 0 0 1 0 0 .	—3	9	0

Batteries—Griffin and Berger; Maple and Mackey.

Memphis	0 1 0 1 3 0 0 0 0	—5	8	0
Mobile	0 0 0 0 0 0 1 0 0	—1	6	1

Batteries—Weinert and Palm; Harmon, Thomas and Moore.

AT NASHVILLE.

Birmingham	3 0 0 0 0 0 1 0 0	—4	9	2
Nashville	0 0 4 3 1 0 2 0 .	—10	13	1

Batteries—Van Alstyne, C. Moore, Hearn and Gibson; Sanders and Kreuger.

AT NEW ORLEANS.

Little Rock	0 0 0 2 0 0 0 1 1 0 0	—5	11	1
New Orleans	0 0 0 0 0 0 0 3 1 0 0	—4	14	3

Batteries—Moore, Woolfolk, Hughes, Moon and Whitney; Harder, Danforth and Brown.

STANDING OF THE CLUBS.

	W.	L.	PC.		W.	L.	PC.
Birmingham	69	47	.595	Atlanta	63	56	.529
Nashville	65	51	.560	Little Rock	50	67	.427
N. Orleans	63	50	.558	Mobile	47	66	.416
Memphis	62	54	.534	Chattanooga	43	71	.377

MAJOR LEAGUE BASEBALL

NATIONAL LEAGUE.

YESTERDAY'S RESULTS.
New York 6, Cincinnati 1.
Brooklyn 5, Pittsburgh 3.
Chicago 3, Boston 1.
Other clubs not scheduled.

STANDING OF THE CLUBS.

	Won.	Lost.	P.C.
Chicago	70	32	.686
Pittsburgh	63	41	.606
New York	60	48	.556
St. Louis	54	53	.505
Brooklyn	46	60	.434
Cincinnati	44	61	.419
Boston	43	63	.406
Philadelphia	41	63	.394

WHERE THEY PLAY TODAY.
Cincinnati at New York (3:15 P. M.).
Pittsburgh at Brooklyn (3:20 P.M.).
St. Louis at Philadelphia.
Chicago at Boston.

AMERICAN LEAGUE.

YESTERDAY'S RESULTS.
Cleveland 6, New York 5.
Detroit 9, Philadelphia 8.
(11 innings.)
Chicago 6, Boston 3.
Washington 7, St. Louis 5.

STANDING OF THE CLUBS.

	Won.	Lost.	P.C.
Philadelphia	78	31	.716
New York	65	39	.625
Cleveland	56	51	.523
St. Louis	56	52	.519
Detroit	52	55	.486
Washington	44	60	.423
Chicago	43	65	.398
Boston	32	73	.305

WHERE THEY PLAY TODAY.
New York at Cleveland.
Philadelphia at Detroit.
Washington at St. Louis.
Boston at Chicago.

THOMAS, WHITE SOX, BEATS BOSTON, 6-3

Yields Only Five Hits and Chicago Captures Second Game of the Series.

CHICAGO, Aug. 11 (AP).—Alphonse Thomas held the Red Sox to five hits today and the White Sox won the second game of the series. The score was 6 to 3. Charlie Ruffing was also an efficient workman, limiting the Chicago team to seven blows, but the White Sox bunched their hits in the fourth and seventh innings to win.

Triples by Shires and Reynolds and a double by Taitt were the blows that hurt Ruffing most. Thomas issued three passes, one of which resulted in a run. The Red Sox made two hits in the second chapter, but in no other inning did they count more than one hit.

The box score:

BOSTON (A).	ab.	r.	h.	po.	a.	e.
Reeves, 3b.	1	1	0	1	1	0
Scarritt, lf.	4	0	0	0	0	0
Rothrock, cf.	4	1	1	5	0	0
Barrett, rf.	4	0	1	3	0	0
Regan, 2b.	4	0	1	2	1	0
Todt, 1b.	3	1	1	6	0	0
Berry, c.	4	0	1	2	1	0
Rhyne, ss.	3	0	0	1	4	0
Ruffing, p.	3	0	0	0	1	0
aBigelow	1	0	0	0	0	0
Total	30	3	5	24	7	0

CHICAGO (A).	ab.	r.	h.	po.	a.	e.
Metzler, lf.	4	1	1	4	0	0
Cissell, ss.	4	0	1	0	3	0
Reynolds, cf.	3	1	1	3	0	0
Shires, 1b.	4	1	1	10	0	0
Kamm, 3b.	3	1	0	1	1	0
Taitt, rf.	4	0	1	1	0	0
Kerr, 2b.	4	1	1	4	2	0
Berg, c.	2	0	0	4	1	0
Thomas, p.	3	1	1	0	2	0
Total	31	6	7	27	9	0

aBatted for Berry in ninth.

Boston	0	1	0	0	0	2	0	0	0	—3
Chicago	0	0	0	3	0	0	3	0	.	—6

Runs batted in—Shires 1, Taitt 2, Berry 1, Rothrock 2, Thomas 1, Reynolds 2.

Home run—Rothrock. Three-base hits—Berry, Shires. Two-base hits—Taitt. Cissell, Reynolds. Sacrifices—Berg, Todt. Stolen base—Kamm. Struck out—By Thomas 5, Ruffing 4. Bases on balls—Off Ruffing 1, Thomas 3. Left on bases—Boston 4, Chicago 5. Umpires—Dineen, Hildebrand and Ormsby. Time of game—1:34.

BROWNS DROP TO 4TH PLACE

Descend From Third as Senators Win by Score of 7 to 5.

ST. LOUIS, Aug. 11 (AP).—The Browns lost to Washington, 7 to 5, today and dropped from third to fourth place as Cleveland beat the Yankees. Blaeholder yielded eleven hits, one a homer by Cronin, while the Browns hammered Burke for nine before he retired in the ninth.

The box score:

WASHINGTON (A).	ab.	r.	h.	po.	a.	e.
Judge, 1b.	3	1	0	6	0	0
Rice, rf.	4	2	2	2	0	0
Goslin, lf.	3	0	2	7	0	0
Myer, 2b.	4	1	2	2	1	0
West, cf.	4	0	0	4	0	0
Tate, c.	4	1	2	3	2	0
Cronin, ss.	2	1	2	2	2	0
Haines, 3b.	3	1	1	1	4	0
Burke, p.	2	0	0	0	0	0
Thomas, p.	0	0	0	0	0	0
Total	29	7	11	27	10	0

ST. LOUIS (A).	ab.	r.	h.	po.	a.	e.
O'Rourke, 3b.	4	0	1	0	0	0
McNeely, rf.	4	0	0	2	0	0
Manush, lf.	5	0	1	1	0	0
Kress, ss.	3	1	1	3	3	0
Schulte, cf.	3	1	2	5	1	0
Melillo, 2b.	3	1	1	2	4	3
Roetz, 1b.	3	1	1	9	2	0
Ferrell, c.	3	1	1	2	2	0
Blaeholder, p.	3	0	1	0	3	0
aDondero	1	0	0	0	0	0
bBadgro	1	0	0	0	0	0
Total	34	5	9	27	13	0

aBatted for Blaeholder in ninth.
bBatted for McNeely in ninth.

Washington	0	1	0	0	4	1	0	0	1	—7
St. Louis	0	1	0	1	0	0	0	0	3	—5

Runs batted in—Tate 1, Roetz 1, Melillo 1, Cronin 1, Goslin 3, Myer 1, Burke 1, Ferrell 2, O'Rourke 1.

Two-base hits—Myer, Kress, Schulte, Rice, Ferrell. Home run—Cronin. Sacrifices—West, Schulte, Melillo, Myer, Hayes, Burke 2. Double play—Roetz and Kress. Left on bases—Washington 6, St. Louis 8. Bases on balls—Off Burke 4, Blaeholder 6. Struck out—By Burke 2, Blaeholder 1. Hits—Off Burke 9 in 8 1-3 innings, Thomas 0 in 2-3. Winning pitcher—Burke. Umpires—Campbell and Owens. Time of game—1:55.

NEW ENGLAND LEAGUE.

Lynn 3, Lewiston 2.
Fitchburg 3, Portland 2.
Portland 3, Fitchburg 1.
Other games postponed, rain.

STANDING OF THE CLUBS.

	W.	L.	PC.		W.	L.	PC.
Manchester	25	11	.694	Fitchburg	16	20	.444
Lynn	24	12	.667	Nashua	15	21	.417
Lewiston	20	16	.556	Brockton	14	21	.400
N. Bedford	17	14	.548	Portland	12	28	.300

BEARS WIN IN 12TH, THEN LOSE, 7 TO 2

Defeat Rochester, 4 to 3, When Stevens Triples, Scoring Lutzke With the Deciding Run.

After winning a 4 to 3 twelve-inning game, the Bears dropped the second contest to Rochester at Newark yesterday afternoon, 7 to 2.

Bobby Stevens won the opening game by tripling off the right field bleacher fence to score Rube Lutzke, who had walked, with the winning run. It was the third time within a week that Stevens had decided a game with a safety.

Lefty Fischer and Tex Carleton had a pitching duel until the latter gave way to Lingrel in the eleventh. Fischer allowed seven hits and had ten strikeouts for a total of 128 for the season. Collins's homer was his thirty-first of the season.

In the second game Berly pitched great ball for Rochester, allowing only four hits.

The box scores:

FIRST GAME.

ROCHESTER (I).	ab.	r.	h.	po.	a.	e.
Brown, 3b.	4	1	0	2	4	0
Toporcer, 2b.	5	0	1	4	7	0
Felix, lf.	5	0	0	1	0	0
Watkins, cf.	5	0	1	5	0	0
W'hington, rf.	4	1	1	0	0	0
Collins, 1b.	3	1	2	16	1	0
Sand, ss.	3	0	0	2	5	1
Florence, c.	5	0	0	2	5	0
Carleton, p.	4	0	0	1	3	0
Lingrel, p.	0	0	0	0	0	0
aCunningham	1	0	1	0	0	0
Total	39	3	7	*35	20	1

NEWARK (I.).	ab.	r.	h.	po.	a.	e.
Conlan, lf.	4	1	0	0	0	0
W'stone, lf.	3	0	0	3	0	0
Speaker, rf.	4	1	2	3	0	0
Pipp, 1b.	4	1	1	9	2	0
West, cf.	6	1	2	2	0	0
Lutzke, 3b.	5	1	1	1	3	0
Kingdon, 2b.	6	0	2	6	0	0
Stevens, ss.	6	0	3	1	2	0
Hungling, c.	5	0	0	12	0	0
Fischer, p.	5	0	0	0	2	0
Total	45	4	12	36	9	0

aBatted for Carleton in eleventh.
*Two out when winning run was scored.

Rochester	0	1	0	1	1	0	0	0	0	0	0	0	—3
Newark	1	0	0	1	1	0	0	0	0	0	0	1	—4

Runs batted in—West 1, Collins 1, Florence 1, Stevens 2, Watkins 1, Lutzke 1.

Two-base hits—Pipp, Collins, Speaker 2, Three-base hit—Stevens. Home run—Collins. Sacrifices—Toporcer, Speaker, Collins. Double plays—Fischer, Stevens and Pipp; Collins and Toporcer. Left on bases—Newark 12, Rochester 8. Bases on balls—Off Fischer 7, Carleton 4, Lingrel 2. Hits—Off Carleton 10 in 10 innings, Lingrel 2 in 2. Struck out—By Fischer 10, Carleton 4. Wild pitch—Fischer. Winning pitcher—Fischer. Losing pitcher—Lingrel. Umpires—Holmes and Westervelt. Time of game—3 hours.

SECOND GAME.

ROCHESTER (I).	ab.	r.	h.	po.	a.	e.
Brown, 3b.	3	1	1	0	1	0
Toporcer, 2b.	2	1	0	3	4	0
S'thw'th, lf.	4	1	1	5	0	0
Watkins, cf.	4	1	1	2	0	0
W'thgton, rf.	3	1	1	0	0	0
Collins, 1b.	2	2	2	6	0	0
Sand, ss	2	0	0	1	1	0
Florence, c.	3	0	1	4	0	0
Berly, p.	3	0	0	0	1	0
Total	26	7	7	21	7	0

NEWARK (I.).	ab.	r.	h.	po.	a.	e.
W'thstone, lf.	3	0	1	1	0	0
Speaker, rf.	2	0	0	3	0	0
Pipp, 1b.	3	0	0	7	1	0
Jacobson, cf.	1	0	0	1	0	0
West, cf.	1	0	0	2	0	0
Lutzke, 3b.	3	0	1	0	1	0
Kingdon, 2b.	3	0	0	1	2	0
Stevens, ss.	3	0	0	2	0	0
Stahlman, c.	3	1	1	4	0	0
Bush, p.	0	0	0	0	0	0
Harvin, p.	1	0	0	0	4	0
Fallenstin, p.	0	0	0	0	0	0
aConlan	1	0	0	0	0	0
Total	23	2	4	21	8	0

aBatted for Harvin in sixth.

Rochester	4	0	0	1	2	0	0	—7
Newark	0	0	0	0	0	2	0	—2

(Seven innings by agreement.)

Two-base hit—Wrightstone. Three-base hit—Collins. Home runs—Southworth, Collins. Sacrifices—Sand, Worthington, Speaker. Double play—Brown, Toporcer and Collins. Left on bases—Newark 3, Rochester 4. Bases on balls—Off Bush 1, Harvin 2. Hits—Off Bush 1 in 3 innings, Harvin 5 in 4, Fallenstin 1 in 0. Hit by pitcher—By Berly (Conlan). Fallenstin (Toporcer). Struck out—By Harvin 3. Losing pitcher—Bush. Umpires—Westervelt and Holmes. Time of game—1:30.

TEXAS LEAGUE.

Wichita Falls 5, Fort Worth 2.
Beaumont 10, San Antonio 1 (1st).
Beaumont 5, San Antonio 1 (2d).
Waco 14, Houston 6 (1st).
Waco 4, Houston 2 (2d).
Dallas 6, Shreveport 4 (1st).
Dallas 4, Shreveport 0 (2d).

STANDING OF THE CLUBS.

	W.	L.	PC.		W.	L.	PC.
Wich. Falls	27	14	.659	Houston	21	21	.500
Fort Worth	25	19	.568	Beaumont	20	20	.500
Shreveport	22	19	.537	Dallas	21	23	.470
Waco	23	21	.523	San Antonio	11	33	.250

HORNSBY'S 3 HITS WIN FOR CUBS, 3-1

Homer and 2 Singles Account for All Chicago Tallies Against Braves.

BOSTON, Aug. 11 (AP).—Rogers Hornsby hit a home run, a single and a double today and they accounted for all the scoring the Chicago Cubs did to defeat the Boston Braves, 3 to 1.

Hornsby smashed the ball into the right field pavilion with two out and nobody on his first time up in the first inning. In the sixth, again with two out, he singled to right, scoring English from second with what proved to be the winning run. His double in the eighth sent Taylor home with another run for good measure.

The Braves reached Charley Root for eight safe blows, while the Cubs garnered only six off Bob Smith. McMillan was spiked by Lester Bell at third base in the second inning and will be out for several days.

The box score:

CHICAGO (N).	ab.	r.	h.	po.	a.	e.
English, ss.	4	1	0	6	4	1
Heathcote, rf.	3	0	1	0	0	0
Hornsby, 2b.	4	1	3	1	4	0
Wilson, cf.	4	0	0	4	0	0
Stephe'son, lf.	4	0	0	1	0	0
Grimm, 1b.	4	0	0	11	0	0
McMillan, 3b.	1	0	1	0	0	0
Blair, 3b.	2	0	0	0	2	0
Taylor, c.	3	1	2	3	2	0
Root, p.	3	0	0	0	3	0
Total	32	3	6	27	15	1

BOSTON (N).	ab.	r.	h.	po.	a.	e.
Richbourg, rf.	4	0	1	3	0	0
Mara'ville, ss.	4	0	1	4	5	0
Sisler, 1b.	4	0	0	8	2	0
Bell, 3b.	4	1	1	0	1	0
Harper, lf.	2	0	1	1	0	0
Welsh, cf.	4	0	3	6	1	0
Maguire, 2b.	3	0	1	3	2	0
Spohrer, c.	3	0	0	1	6	0
R.Smith, p.	3	0	0	1	5	1
Total	31	1	8	27	16	1

Chicago	1	0	0	0	0	1	0	1	0	—3
Boston	0	0	1	0	0	0	0	0	0	—1

Runs batted in—Hornsby 3, Welsh 1.

Two-base hits—Hornsby, Taylor, Maranville, Bell. Home run—Hornsby. Sacrifices—Harper, Maguire. Double play—Hornsby, English and Grimm. Left on bases—Chicago 3, Boston 6. Bases on balls—Off Root 1, R. Smith 1. Struck out—By Root 1. Umpires—Magerkurth, Rigler and Jordan. Time of game—1:35.

QUELLICH SETS MARK WITH 13 HITS IN ROW

Reading Outfielder Breaks Speaker's Record of 11 Straight—Keys Beat Montreal, 11-4.

READING, Pa., Aug. 11 (AP).—George Quellich, Reading outfielder, set a new record for most hits in succession when he ran his streak to thirteen in a row here today, when Reading beat Montreal, 11 to 4. The old record of eleven was held by Tris Speaker. Quellich, who started his streak Friday, hit four straight, two of which were home runs today. He hit three in a row Friday and six straight yesterday. Quellich has hit four home runs, a double and eight singles in his streak.

The Keys pounded Elon Hogsett, Indian pitcher, off the hill in the sixth to defeat the Royals, and continued their attack on Hartman. Stryker held the Royals to seven hits to win easily.

The box score:

MONTREAL (I.)	ab.	r.	h.	po.	a.	e.
Gaudette, lf.	4	1	1	3	0	0
Henry, 1b.	4	1	2	11	0	0
Haines, cf.	4	0	3	1	0	0
Gulley, rf.	3	0	0	0	0	0
Urbanski, ss.	4	0	1	0	2	4
Fowler, 3b.	4	0	0	2	0	1
Gautreau, 2b.	4	0	1	3	4	0
Nisbergall, c.	3	0	0	3	2	0
Hogsett, p.	2	0	0	0	0	0
Hartman, p.	1	0	0	0	1	0
aTice	1	0	0	0	0	0
Total	33	4	7	24	12	4

READING (I.)	ab.	r.	h.	po.	a.	e.
Walsh, 2b.	3	2	1	4	4	0
Hawks, 1b.	5	1	2	9	0	1
Whitman, rf.	5	1	4	3	0	0
Taylor, cf.	4	1	2	2	0	0
Quellich, lf.	4	3	4	2	0	0
Mullan, 3b.	5	0	0	2	1	0
Jurges, ss.	4	0	0	3	6	0
Smith, c.	3	2	1	2	2	0
Stryker, p.	4	1	2	4	2	0
Total	37	11	16	27	15	1

aBatted for Gautreau in ninth.

Montreal	3	0	1	0	0	0	0	0	0	—4
Reading	0	1	0	0	2	3	1	4	.	—11

Runs batted in—Walsh 3, Whitman 2, Taylor 2, Quellich 3, Hawks 1, Jurges 1, Fowler 2, Haines 1, Gulley 1.

Two-base hits—Hawks, Taylor, Stryker. Three-base hit—Whitman. Home runs—Quellich 2, Haines. Double plays—Urbanski, Gautreau and Henry; Gautreau and Henry (2); Jurges, Walsh and Hawks. Left on bases—Reading 7, Montreal 3. Bases on balls—Off Hogsett 3, Stryker 1, Hartman 1. Struck out—By Stryker 2, Hartman 1. Hits—Off Hogsett 14 in 5 1-3 innings, Hartman 4 in 2 2-3. Hit by pitcher—By Stryker (Gulley). Losing pitcher—Hogsett. Umpires—Clarke, Parker and Finneran. Time of game—1:55.

Home Run Hitters.

YESTERDAY'S HOMERS.

Ruth, New York Americans	1
Gehrig, New York Americans	1
Miller, Philadelphia Americans	1
Rothrock, Boston Americans	1
Johnson, Detroit	1
Hargrave, Detroit	1
Cronin, Washington	1
Jackson, New York Nationals	1
Frederick, Brooklyn	1
Hendrick, Brooklyn	1
Bissonette, Brooklyn	1
Hornsby, Chicago Nationals	1

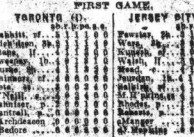

The Leaders.

AMERICAN LEAGUE.

Ruth, New York	30	Alexander, Detroit	19
Gehrig, New York	27	McManus, Detroit	14
Foxx, Phila.	26	Heilmann, Detroit	14
Simmons, Phila.	26	Haas, Phila.	14

NATIONAL LEAGUE.

Klein, Phila.	33	Hornsby, Chicago	25
Ott, New York	30	Hurst, Phila.	24
L. Wilson, Chicago	30	Hafey, St. Louis	23
Bottomley, St. L.	25	O'Doul, Phila.	20

League Totals.

National League	587
American League	449
Total	1,036

Five Leading Batsmen In Each Major League

NATIONAL LEAGUE.

	G.	AB.	R.	H.	Pct.
Herman, Brooklyn	102	401	80	165	.411
O'Doul, Phila	105	427	98	164	.384
Terry, New York	109	443	73	168	.379
Hendrick, Brooklyn	80	284	54	104	.366
Hornsby, Chicago	106	411	106	150	.365

Leader a year ago, Hornsby, Boston, .378.

AMERICAN LEAGUE.

	G.	AB.	R.	H.	Pct.
Foxx, Philadelphia	110	389	97	150	.386
Simmons, Phila	106	433	89	165	.381
Manush, St. Louis	108	450	72	166	.369
Fonseca, Cleveland	107	413	74	152	.368
Heilmann, Detroit	96	382	77	138	.361

Leader a year ago, Goslin, Washington, .384.

3 HOMERS IN EIGHTH WIN FOR ROBINS, 5-3

Frederick, Hendrick and Bissonette Connect and Herman Hits Double With Two Out.

KREMER VICTIM OF ATTACK

Pittsburgh Leads, 3-1, Before Onslaught—Moss Mound Star—Straw Hats Flood Field.

By ROSCOE McGOWEN.

Three Robin home runs in the eighth inning scattered straw hats and Pirate hopes all over Ebbets Field yesterday, brought the Robins from behind to win the third game of the series by the score of 5 to 3, gave Ray Moss his sixth victory of the season and added a sixth defeat to the impressive record of the astonished Remy Kremer.

Going into the eighth trailing, 3 to 1, the Flatbush cause looked hopeless after Rube Bressler, pinch-hitting for Moss, had grounded out and Wally Gilbert had been deprived of a hit by Lloyd Waner's shoestring catch of a line drive. But at this moment Johnny Frederick inserted his sixteenth home run of the season, a drive over the wall into Bedford Avenue, the Robins came back in the ball game and the straw hat barrage began.

Herman Hits Safely.

Amid the wild shouts and pleadings of the 12,000 fans Babe Herman came up and slashed the ball against the right-field wall for a double—a double that he just made by fast running and something of a lucky break.

Harvey Hendrick, who, with both Frederick and Herman, had been held hitless until this inning, then added to the excitement by dropping another home run just over the right-field wall to put the Robins one run in the lead.

This should have been enough, for it required several minutes to remove from the field the débris of straw hats that had descended in a veritable cloud from the stands, but Del Bissonette, the only one of the slugger aggregation who had made a hit off Kremer previously, hit the noblest homer of them all, the ball going on a line far over the right-field wall. Eddie Moore, who had two singles to his credit, ended the great rally with an infield pop fly to Pie Traynor.

Morrison Goes On Hill.

Johnny Morrison went to the mound to turn back the enemy in the final frame and did it, but not until the Pirates had threatened mightily. Both Paul Waner and Traynor slashed hot grounders at Gilbert and were retired only by two fine stops and throws by the Robin third-baseman. Comorosky dropped a double near the foul line in right field, but Billy Rhiel took a grounder from George Grantham, batting for Hemsley, and tossed him out easily to end the game.

Bartell was responsible for the first run of the game when he tripled to open the fourth and scored on the younger Waner's sacrifice fly to Herman. In the fifth the home boys tied it up on singles by Moore and DeBerry and an intervening out by Rhiel, but the Pirates went into a two-run lead in the seventh by the simple process of Lloyd Waner's single and theft of second, Traynor's triple and Comorosky's single.

The box score:

PITTSBURGH (N.)	ab.	r.	h.	po.	a.	e.
Bartell, 2b.	4	1	2	3	2	0
L.Waner, cf.	3	1	1	3	0	0
P.Waner, rf.	4	0	0	1	1	0
Traynor, 3b.	4	1	1	1	0	0
Com'sky, lf.	4	0	2	2	0	0
Hemsley, c.	3	0	0	4	0	0
aGrantham	1	0	0	0	0	0
Sheely, 1b.	2	0	0	8	0	0
Clarke, ss.	3	0	0	2	3	0
Kremer, p.	3	0	0	0	3	0
Total	31	3	6	24	9	0

BROOKLYN (N.)	ab.	r.	h.	po.	a.	e.
Gilbert, 3b.	4	0	0	0	4	0
Frederick, cf.	3	1	1	2	0	0
Herman, rf.	4	1	1	1	0	0
Hendrick, lf.	4	1	1	1	0	0
Bissonette, 1b.	4	1	2	13	0	0
E.Moore, ss.	4	1	2	2	3	0
Rhiel, 2b.	3	0	0	2	5	0
DeBerry, c.	3	0	2	7	0	0
Moss, p.	2	0	0	0	0	0
bBressler	1	0	0	0	0	0
Morrison, p.	0	0	0	0	0	0
Total	32	5	8	27	12	0

aBatted for Hemsley in ninth.
bBatted for Moss in eighth.

Pittsburgh	0	0	0	1	0	0	2	0	0	—3
Brooklyn	0	0	0	0	1	0	0	4	.	—5

Runs batted in—Hendrick 2, Frederick 1, Bissonette 1, DeBerry 1, L. Waner 1, Traynor 1, Comorosky 1.

Two-base hits—Herman, Comorosky. Three-base hits—Bartell, Traynor. Home runs—Frederick, Hendrick, Bissonette. Stolen base—L. Waner. Sacrifice—L. Waner. Double plays—E. Moore and Bissonette, P. Waner and Sheely. Left on bases—Pittsburgh 3, Brooklyn 5. Bases on balls—Off Kremer 2, Moss 1. Struck out—By Moss 7, Kremer 3. Hits—Off Moss 5 in 8 innings, Morrison 1 in 1. Winning pitcher—Moss. Wild pitch—Moss. Umpires—Stark, Hart and Klem. Time of game—1:35.

AMERICAN ASSOCIATION.

AT INDIANAPOLIS.

		R.	H.	E.
St. Paul	0 0 0 0 0 0 1 0 1	—2	8	1
Indianapolis	0 0 1 0 0 0 0 0 0	—1	9	1

Batteries—Polli and Fenner; Jonnard and Sprinz.

St. Paul	2 2 0 1 0 0	—5	6	4
Indianapolis	1 0 0 0 8 2	—11	8	4

(Called end sixth, rain).

Batteries—Harriss, Van Atta and Nargrave; Love, Speece and Riddle.

AT COLUMBUS.

Milwaukee	3 0 4 0 1 0 0 0 3	—11	13	1
Columbus	0 0 0 3 1 0 2 0 1	—9	9	2

Batteries—Ryan, Cobb and Young; Johnson, Winters and Devine.

Milwaukee	0 1 0 1 0 0 0 2 0	—4	9	2
Columbus	0 0 0 0 3 1 0 1 .	—5	9	1

Batteries—Robertson, Cobb and McMenemy; Miller, Wysong and Shinault.

AT LOUISVILLE.

Minneapolis	0 0 0 0 0 0 1 0 0	—1	9	1
Louisville	0 0 0 0 0 2 0 2 0	—4	8	2

Batteries—Benton and McMullen; DeBerry and Tesmer.

Minneapolis	0 0 0 0 0 0 0 0 0	—0	8	1
Louisville	0 0 0 1 1 1 1 2 .	—6	9	2

Batteries—Buckeye, Middleton and McMullen; Tincup and Thompson.

AT TOLEDO.

Kansas City	4 0 0 0 1 0 0 2 0	—8	11	2
Toledo	0 0 3 1 0 0 0 0 0	—4	10	2

Batteries—Thomas and Peters; Lucas, McQuillan and Heyworth.

Kansas City	0 2 4 1 0 5 1 1 1	—12	15	3
Toledo	3 0 1 0 1 3 2 0 0	—10	16	2

Batteries—Murray, Nelson, Davis and Angley; Pfeffer, Ferguson, McQuillan, Doyle and McCurdy.

STANDING OF THE CLUBS.

	W.	L.	P.C.		W.	L.	P.C.
Kan. City	77	37	.675	Louisville	52	62	.456
St. Paul	70	45	.609	Columbus	50	65	.435
Min'polis	65	48	.575	Milwaukee	46	68	.404
Ind'polis	54	61	.470	Toledo	41	69	.373

2-RUN RALLY IN 8TH WINS FOR N. Y. A. C.

Dongan Caseys Bow by 6 to 4 After Having Tied Score in the Eighth.

ALEXANDER LEADS ATTACK

Bats in Three Runs and Scores One for Victors—Quinn of Losers Gets Four Hits.

The New York Athletic Club baseball team scored two runs in the eighth inning to defeat the Dongan Caseys yesterday at Travers Island, 6—4. Bill Alexander, New York A. C. right fielder, led the attack, getting two singles and one double in three times at the bat, sending in three runs and scoring once himself. Quinn of the losers made four hits.

The Caseys were trailing until the eighth inning when they scored three runs to tie the score on two singles, a double and two passes.

The Winged Foot nine settled matters in their half. Howard Miller and Ryan opened the inning with singles and they were advanced by Dzigan's neat bunt. Miller scored on a sacrifice fly to centre field and Ryan was sent across on Cremmins's single to right field.

The box score:

DONGAN CASEYS.	ab.r.h.po.a.e.
Garvey, 3b.	5 0 0 0 0 1
Howard, 1b.	5 0 0 7 0 1
Schirling, ss.	4 1 2 2 1 0
J.Quinn, c.	4 1 4 1 1 0
Clough, lf.	3 1 0 1 0 0
Myers, cf.	4 0 0 0 0 0
McMahon, 2b.	3 1 1 3 2 0
Charles, rf.	4 0 0 2 0 1
N.Quinn, p.	4 0 2 3 5 0
Total	36 4 11 24 10 3

NEW YORK A. C.	ab.r.h.po.a.e.
Belchert, 3b.	[illegible]
Norton, lf.	[illegible]
Alexander, rf.	[illegible]
Graham, 1b.	[illegible]
Miller, cf.	[illegible]
Ryan, 2b.	[illegible]
Dzigan, ss.	[illegible]
Hector, c.	[illegible]
Rosner, p.	[illegible]
Cremmins, p.	[illegible]
Total	[illegible]

Dongan Caseys ....0 0 0 0 1 0 0 3 0—4
New York A. C. ....[illegible]—6

Two-base hits—J. Quinn 2, Schirling, Alexander. Three-base hits—Norton. Sacrifices—Dzigan 2, Hector. Stolen bases—Alexander 2, Norton, Dzigan, Garvey. Left on bases—New York A. C. 8, Dongans 6. Struck out—By Rosner 3, Cremmins 2, Quinn 1. Bases on balls—Off Rosner 1, Cremmins 1, Quinn 2. Passed ball—J. Quinn. Hits—Off Rosner 11 in 7 2-3 innings, Cremmins 0 in 1 1-3. Umpires—Murray and Fitzsimmons. Time of game—2:10.

JERSEY CITY SPLITS TWO WITH TORONTO

Captures Opening Contest, 6-4, but Loses the Second Game by 3 to 1.

Toronto divided a double-header with Jersey City at Jersey City yesterday, dropping the opening contest by a score of 6 to 4, but coming back in the nightcap to win, 3 to 1. The Leafs took the series by winning two out of three.

Paul Zahniser held Jersey City hitless for the first four frames of the first, and with the score in Toronto's favor, 4 to 0, in the fifth, Jersey City [illegible] to score three runs on singles by Head, Selkirk, Hopkins, Manger and Fewster. That started Jersey City on the way.

The box scores:

FIRST GAME.

TORONTO (I).	ab.r.h.po.a.e.
Rabbitt, rf.	[illegible]
Rich'dson, 2b.	[illegible]
Stone, lf.	[illegible]
Sweeney, 1b.	[illegible]
Burke, 3b.	[illegible]
Shinners, cf.	[illegible]
Cote, ss.	[illegible]
O'Neill, c.	[illegible]
Zahniser, p.	[illegible]
Cantrell, p.	[illegible]
aArchdeacon	[illegible]
bBedore	[illegible]
Total	32 4 7 *23 11 0

JERSEY CITY (I).	ab.r.h.po.a.e.
Fewster, 2b.	[illegible]
Wera, 3b.	[illegible]
Kunesh, cf.	[illegible]
Walsh, lf.	[illegible]
Head, c.	[illegible]
Jourdan, 1b.	[illegible]
Selkirk, rf.	[illegible]
M.H'pkins, ss.	[illegible]
Rhodes, p.	[illegible]
Roberts, p.	[illegible]
cManger	[illegible]
dV.Hopkins	[illegible]
Total	31 6 8 27 14 0

*Head out, hit by own batted ball.
aBatted for Cantrell in ninth.
bRan for O'Neill in ninth.
cBatted for Rhodes in fifth.
dRan for Manger in fifth.

Toronto ....2 0 0 1 1 0 0 0 0—4
Jersey City ....0 0 0 0 3 0 3 0 .—6

Runs batted in—Stone 2, O'Neill 1, Sweeney 1, H. Hopkins 1, Manger 2, Selkirk 1, Wera 1, Kunesh 1.

Three-base hits—Burke, Selkirk. Home run—Stone. Sacrifice—Richardson. Double plays—Hopkins, Fewster and Jourdan; Richardson and Burke; Cote and Burke. Left on bases—Toronto 6, Jersey City 5. Bases on balls—Off Rhodes 2, Zahniser 2, Cantrell 1, Roberts 2. Struck out—By Zahniser 1, Rhodes 2, Roberts 1, Cantrell 2. Hits—Off Rhodes 7 in 5 innings, Roberts 0 in 4, Zahniser 3 in 6 (none out in seventh), Cantrell 2 in 2. Winning pitcher—Roberts. Losing pitcher—Cantrell. Umpires—Derr, Michaels and Carroll. Time of game—1:50.

SECOND GAME.

TORONTO (I).	ab.r.h.po.a.e.
Rabbitt, rf.	3 0 0 2 0 0
Rich'dson, 2b.	3 1 2 1 1 0
Stone, lf.	3 1 1 1 0 0
Sweeney, 1b.	3 0 1 2 0 0
Burke, 3b.	[illegible]
Shinners, cf.	[illegible]
Cote, ss.	3 0 0 0 3 1
Rensac, c.	3 1 1 5 0 0
Page, p.	3 0 0 0 0 0
Total	26 3 5 21 4 2

JERSEY CITY (I).	ab.r.h.po.a.e.
Fewster, 2b.	[illegible]
Wera, 3b.	[illegible]
Kunesh, cf.	[illegible]
Walsh, lf.	[illegible]
Jorgens, c.	[illegible]
Jourdan, 1b.	[illegible]
Selkirk, rf.	[illegible]
Hopkins, ss.	3 1 0 2 4 0
Bream, p.	[illegible]
Rhodes, p.	[illegible]
aManger	[illegible]
bHead	1 0 1 0 0 0
Total	[illegible]

a Batted for Bream in fifth.
b Batted for Rhodes in seventh.

Toronto ....0 0 3 0 0 0 0—3
Jersey City ....0 0 0 0 1 0 0—1

Runs batted in—Wera 1, Sweeney 2, Richardson 1.

Two-base hits—Stone, Walsh, Selkirk. Sacrifice—Wera. Left on bases—Toronto 3, Jersey City 4. Bases on balls—Off Page 4, Rhodes 1. Struck out—By Page 4, Bream 1, Rhodes 3. Hits—Off Bream [illegible] in 6 innings. Losing pitcher—Bream. Umpires—Michaels, Carroll and Derr. Time of game—1:45.

NEW YORK-PENN. LEAGUE.

AT BINGHAMTON.

		R.	H.	E.
Williamsport	0 0 0 0 0 0 0 1 1	—2	[illegible]	[illegible]
Triple Cities	0 2 0 0 6 3 0 0 .	[illegible]	[illegible]	[illegible]

Batteries—Clagett and Trout; Miner and O'Brien.

AT HAZLETON.

Harrisburg	2 1 1 0 0 0 0 0 0	—4	6	3
Hazleton	0 0 0 1 0 2 2 0 .	—5	10	1

Batteries—Knetsch and McCarthy; Pempster and Glenn.

AT YORK.

Wilkes-Barre	0 3 0 1 0 0 0 0 0	—4	7	0
York	1 0 2 0 0 0 2 0 .	—5	10	1

Batteries—Tyson and Wilson; Tennant and Uzmann.

Wilkes-Barre	1 1 0 0 2 0 0	—4	5	3
York	0 3 2 0 0 0 .	—5	9	3

Batteries—Ross and Wheat; Vincent and Uzmann.

AT ELMIRA.

Scranton	0 0 0 0 7 0 2 0 0	—9	5	1
Elmira	1 0 0 0 0 0 0 0 0	—1	7	3

Batteries—Reitz and Rangnow; Foster and Jenkins.

STANDING OF THE CLUBS.

	W.	L.	PC.		W.	L.	PC.
Triple Cities	62	41	.602	Hazleton	53	57	.477
Williamsp't	65	44	.596	Elmira	45	60	.429
Harrisburg	58	46	.558	Scranton	44	58	.431
York	57	51	.528	W.-Barre	39	65	.375

EASTERN LEAGUE.

AT ALBANY.

		R.	H.	E.
Pittsfield	0 2 0 0 0 1 0 0 0	—3	[illegible]	2
Albany	0 0 0 0 0 0 2 0 .	—4	12	0

Batteries—Douglas and Connolly; Andrews and Munn.

Pittsfield	0 1 0 1 0 0 1 0 0	—3	13	1
Albany	0 0 0 0 1 1 0 0 0	—2	8	[illegible]

Batteries—Wilson and Ashy; Styborski and Eisemann.

AT ALLENTOWN.

Providence	3 0 0 0 0 0 0 2 0	—5	17	1
Allentown	0 2 2 0 0 0 0 0 0	—4	16	2

Batteries—Touchstone and Pond; Dunnegan and Evans.

Providence	0 1 0 0 0 0 0 3 0	—4	11	1
Allentown	0 0 0 0 1 0 0 1 3	—5	9	2

Batteries—Touchstone and Pond; Hyman and Kennick.

Bridgeport at New Haven, rain.
Hartford at Springfield, rain.

STANDING OF THE CLUBS.

	W.	L.	P.C.		W.	L.	P.C.
Bridgeport	74	42	.638	New Haven	50	61	.450
Albany	72	43	.626	Springfield	48	65	.425
Providence	66	49	.574	Hartford	47	67	.412
Pittsfield	56	57	.496	Allentown	42	71	.372

RUTH HITS NOS. 43, 44 AS YANKS-TIGERS SPLIT

CHARACTER · QUALITY · AMERICA FIRST · ACCURACY · ENTERPRISE
New York American Sports
AN AMERICAN PAPER FOR THE AMERICAN PEOPLE
WEDNESDAY, SEPTEMBER 11, 1929

Believe It Or Not!

—By Ripley—

On request, sent with stamped, addressed envelope, Mr. Ripley will furnish proof of anything depicted by him.

THE WATERMELON IS A BERRY!
FRED FITZSIMMONS (Giants) SHUT OUT CINCINNATI 4 TIMES IN SUCCESSION 1929
RALPH ANDERSON —of Milwaukee COULD WHISTLE LOUDLY AT THE AGE OF 11 MONTHS
IT RAINED SALT WATER Martha's Vineyard Is. Mass. Aug 19, 1896
PLACE A SQUARE PENCIL ON A ROUND ONE Point it to the right — PUSH IT AND IT WILL MOVE TOWARD THE LEFT INSTEAD OF THE DIRECTION POINTED.
RIP
9-11
© 1929, King Features Syndicate, Inc., Great Britain rights reserved.

TOMORROW—WHERE WHITE IS BROWN

ALLISON DOWNS LOTT; BIG BILL BEATS SHIELDS

Texan Humbles Davis Cup Player, 6-3, 6-3, 3-6, 3-6, 7-5; Tilden Wins by 2-6, 6-1, 14-12, 6-4.

By Paul Gardner.

THE trail that winds from Texas led Wilmer Allison to the conquest of George Lott, of Chicago, American Davis Cup hope, in the blazing accomplishment that marked the third round of the men's national singles tennis championships yesterday. The fleet Austin player overpowered the third ranking expert of the United States, 6-3, 6-3, 3-6, '-6, 7-5, as twilight hemmed in the West Side Club Stadium, Forest Hills, L. I.

This reversal, occasion by the Davis Cup doubles - master, dimmed, but did not subordinate, the victory of William T. Tilden, 2nd, over Franx X. Shields, 2—6, 6—1, 14—12, 6—4, earlier in the afternoon.

Allison, who, by some whimsical prank of the U. S. L. T. A. committee, went unseeded, although listed as No. 5, emerged from 3—5 in the final set to topple Lott from a tournament in which the latter, besides Tilden, stood as co-favorite.

OUTVOLLEYS LOTT.

Volleying like a robot trained to the purpose, Allison counteracted the effects of Lott's wonderful lobbing in their test. Unwilling to concede anything, straining for every point, tumbling on severla occasions over the slippery soil, Allison earned his win.

Along with Tilden the Philadelphian, H. W. "Bunny" Austin of England, Frank Hunter of New Rochelle, John H. Doeg, of Santa Monica, Cal., Julius Seligson of New York, R. Norris Williams, 2nd, of Philadelphia, John Van Ryn of Orange, N. J., and Wilbur F. "Junior" Coen of Kansas City, several highly considered contestants, progressed to the fourth-round bracket.

Shields won the first set against Tilden for two reasons —one the exceptional severity of the Roxbury school youngster's drives and, secondly, the indifference of the Philadelphian internationalist. Unable, or deeming it unstrategical to reveal his hand, overhitting, experimenting, studying, setting, and generally slumping, it was no wonder that Shields apportioned himself the introductory chapter despite Tilden's efforts.

TILDEN STILL CONFIDENT.

After 2-all, the New Yorker attained four consecutive games. Still Tilden did not seem worried Placid, confident, Tilden took his stand in the second set. He accounted for a game on service, solved Shields's leads, profited on his own in the third of cross-fire shots, and dropped the fourth game. Shields at this junction was the batter of 1928 who reached the semi-finals, the boy who overcame Jacques Brugnon. Tilden, however, lacked for nothing, and his superlative ability enabled him to attach the set, 6-1

What a third set. What action. Tilden, ahead at 3-1 and 5-3, wilted, and Shields deuced the chapter at 5-5. Shields forged in front, 6 to 5. Tilden retrieved the twelfth game. Shields acquired the thirteen on love. They were pro and con until the eleventh game. Shields was at set point, 10 to 9, 30-40. Tilden serving. The embattled youth whipped a forehand out by a foot which would have meant the set. Tilden reached set point in the twentieth game, but double faulted. Shields was the more fatigued of the two Tilden held advantage point twice in the twenty-third game. After an Alphonse and Gaston argument as to a double fault, Shields achieved the game. He had the vantage, 12 to 11.

Behind at 0 — 30, Tilden brought the twenty-fourth game out of the fire. He broke through Shield's service. in the twenty-fifth game after remonstrating because a ball boy disturbed him. The crowd was noticeably pro-Shields and plainly did not give Tilden credit for his splendid exhibition in the dramatic moments. A scathing placement in the right hand corner, followed by a screaming ace and the venerable warrior closed the third set 14 to 12. It was the longest chapter ever undergone by Tilden in an American title competition.

In the fourth set Shields slapped back Tilden's service tremendously in the sixth game to advance to a 4—2 standing in his

Continued on Page 11, Column 5.

THEME SONGS

Toddlin' Town
One Real Blues
In Memphis, Tenn.
Near Sleepy Valley

By Damon Runyon.

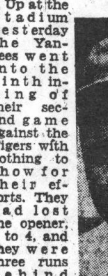

WHEN the newsreel turns on a Chicago view, what is almost invariably the incidental music, my little organ grinders? That is, what is the incidental music if the incidental musicians have an ear to the fitness of things?

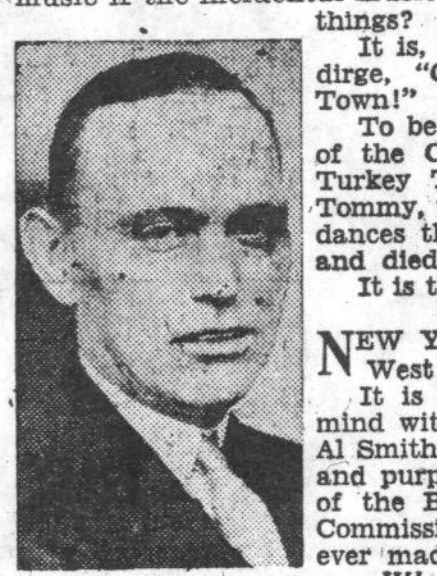

DAMON RUNYON.

It is, as you well know, that triumphant dirge, "Chicago! Chicago! That Toddlin' Town!"

To be sure, the Toddle has gone the way of the Charleston, the Black Bottom, the Turkey Trot, the Grizzly Bear, the Texas Tommy, the Pas-sa-ma-la, and all the other dances that bloomed briefly, then withered and died, but the music remains.

It is the theme song of the western town.

NEW YORK'S theme song is "East Side, West Side."

It is so closely identified in the public mind with the big city, especially since Mr. Al Smith's campaign, that it is to all intents and purposes the civic ditty, though no act of the Board of Aldermen, or the Boxing Commission, or Chief of Police Whalen has ever made it officially such.

When the first strains of the music incidental to the news reel reach your ear with "East Side, West Side," you know you're in New York. In the news reel, I mean. It is the song nearest and dearest the hearts of the older generation of New Yorkers, and was brought back to the younger folks by Mr. Smith.

GIVE MY REGARDS TO BROADWAY!

BUT there is another song second only to "East Side, West Side," as the theme song of New York, and I don't mean "Tammany." I mean, "Give My Regards to Broadway."

A thousand and one songs of Broadway have been written since George Cohan turned out his, but his alone endures. More than any other Broadway song ever written, it voices the yearning of the wanderer far from the big street, though its locale—Herald Square, and Forty-second street—doesn't mean much to the modern-day Broadway guy.

St. Louis probably doesn't feel greatly flattered by the fact that its accepted theme song is "The St. Louis Blues," but it is none the less a fact. And while thousands of different "blues" have been composed in the past few years, "The St. Louis Blues" remains the bluest blues of them all—Oh. man, how blue!

The incidental music for San Francisco is usually "My Chinatown," though this song probably had specific reference in the minds of its New York authors, Jean Schwartz and Bill Jerome, to New York's Chinatown, and anyway, San Francisco's real themie is an old one that runs: "When I First Met Kate by the Golden Gate, 'Way Out in San Francisco Bay." Maybe the incidental musicians overlook that one, because "Chinatown" is more familiar to the general public.

CALIFORNIA, HERE I COME!

FOR Los Angeles, though the song would appear to apply equally well to the entire State of California, you invariably get Buddy de Sylva's "California, Here I Come!"

During the boom in Florida, the song writers were turning out Florida melodies by the dozen, yet "Miami Shore," written long before the realtors took charge down yonder, lingers on as Miami's theme song, with the newer "Lovely Florida," assigned to Palm Beach.

For Mobile, Alabama, in particular, we have long had "Mobile Bay," and for Alabama in general a hundred ditties, none of which seems to have endured.

"The Memphis Blues" go with Memphis, Tenn., sometimes varied by "The Beale Street Blues," but a raft of Tennessee songs have been written, generally by young men who never were in

Continued on Page 14, Column 1.

GEHRIG SLAMS 31ST HOMER IN FINAL CONTEST

Hugmen Lose Opener, 8 to 4, but Win Nightcap in Ninth Inning by 10 to 9 Score

By Bill Slocum.

CHALK up another conquest and two more home runs for the battering Bambino.

Up at the Stadium yesterday the Yankees went into the ninth inning of their second game against the Tigers with nothing to show for their efforts. They had lost the opener, 8 to 4, and they were three runs behind after the Tigers finished swinging in their half of the ninth inning in the after piece. Then things happened fast.

BABE RUTH
Smacks Two Homers.

Combs drew a pass. Lary unleashed his fourth hit.

"Then up stepped our hero of ever so many battles, G. Herman Ruth. As soon as George had finished swinging everybody in that 20,000 crowd knew that another home run was on its way. It was No. 44 for George, who had parked No. 43 in the same right field bleachers during the first battle. Ruth followed Combs and Lary over the plate with the run that tied the score and then the Yanks went on to gather another run to win the ball game, 10 to 9.

THEN FOUR FULL PASSES.

A walk to Durst started the winning run. Then Lazzeri sacrificed and out went Carroll. Yde walked Gehrig, both advanced on Dickey's infield out and Koenig was purposely walked, filling the bases. Yde couldn't get the ball across for Meusel and Durst was forced home with the winning run.

The Yankees picked up an early six-run lead in this game, most of it being due to Gehrig's thirty-first home run with the bases filled in the first inning. But the Tigers kept clawing away and they finally overtook the passing champs in the eighth. They batted Pipgras and Zachary out in this advance and drove Heimach out in the ninth when two hits and a walk buit up what seemed to be a winning lead.

The Tigers got four homers during the afternoon. Gehringer and Whitehill delivered in the first game, and Alexander and Graham in the second.

YANKS SCORE FIVE.

Five Yankees had crossed the plate and only one had been retired when Page was taken out in the first inning. He pitched to only six batsmen. Combs singled, Lary doubled and Ruth was hit, filling the bases. Paschal scored Combs with a long fly to centre, Lazzari's walk filled the bases again and Gehrig hit into the bleachers for a homer which swept four runs across. Lary's single and a double by Ruth added a run in the second and made the score 6—0.

Two were out in the third when Graham got the first hit off Pipgras, a homer into the right field bleachers. Two were out in the fourth when Alexander walked, Rice doubled and McManus scored the pair with a single to centre. Gehringer shut off two Yankee runs in the fifth with a great stop off Koenig with two out and runners on second and third.

When Alexander opened the sixth with a homer into the right field seats Huggins called Pipgras in and sent Zachary to the pen. The next three Tigers went out in order . . .

Singles by Fothergill, Gehringer and Heilmann added another run in the seventh for the Tigers.

The Yanks finally were over

Continued on Page 14, Column

Cubs Granted First Game of World Series

Judge Landis Decides on Dates at Meeting with Officials of League Leaders.

CHICAGO, Sept. 10 (AP).—The first game of the world series will be played October 8 in the city winning the National League pennant, it was announced today at the office of Kenesaw Mountain Landis, commissioner.

The date for the baseball classic, prices of admission and other details were agreed on today at a meeting presided over by Mr. Landis.

Granting that the Cubs and Athletics are the pennant winners, the world's series schedule will read as follows:

October 8, at Chicago.
October 9, at Chicago.
October 10, traveling.
October 11, at Philadelphia.
October 12, at Phiadelphia.
October 13, open (Sunday).
October 14, at Philadelphia.
October 15, traveling.
October 16, at Chicago.
October 17, at Chicago.

Thomas Shibe, president of the Athletics, and Robert Shroeder, secretary, represented the Philadelphia club.

Fugazy Asserts Garden Tried to Buy Campolo

Promoter Charges Argentinian Was Offered $600,000 for Four Bouts.

By Ed Frayne.

INSISTENT reports that the Victorio Campolo-Phil Scott fight would never come off crystallized yesterday in a wild denunciation of Madison Square Garden and its officials by Promoter Humbert J. Fugazy.

HUMBERT FUGAZY
Turns Orator.

Talking before a roomful of perspiring interviewers, the little Brooklyn promoter declared he would ask the State Athletic Commission to examine the activities of Frank Bruen, vice-president of the Garden, and Tom McArdle, its macthmaker.

Bruen and McArdle called on Campolo within the last twenty-four hours and offered him $600,000 to sign with the Garden for a series of four matches, Fugazy charged. He placed on the witness stand Prometeo Mazzanti, interpreter and secretary for Campolo, who said he had been present at the conference, which he said was held at Campolo's apartment in New York on Monday afternoon. Mazzanti said Bruen and McArdle had offered Campolo the sum of $100,000 to sign the contract.

While both Mazzanti and Fugazy admitted that no direct effort had been made to have Campolo drop the Scott fight, both declared that Campolo had been

Continued on Page 13, Column 6.

U. S. Boats Star In Italy Races

VENICE, Italy, Sept. 10 (AP).—American-made boats made the biggest impression today in the opening of the international speedboat regaata here. Gar Wood, with his Miss America VII and Major Segrave's Miss England are to meet later in the week in the outstanding race of the regetta.

The German, Richard Busse, won the first heat for the Tatler Cup, with a Hacker Detroit cruiser. A Baby Gar turned out by Gar Wood and owned by Count Beistecuie of Spain won the first heat of the Lloyd Sabaudo Cup race.

ATTELL WINS BOUT IN JAMAICA COURT

"THAT is another fight that you have won," said Justice Healy in the Court of Special Sessions in Jamaica, to Abe Attell, former featherweight champion of the world, after he was acquitted of a charge of ticket speculating.

When the case came before Justices Healy, Caldwell and Solomon, it was alleged that in June Attell had attempted to sell two tickets outside the Queensboro sporting arena for two cents more, than they would cost at the box office. He was arrested by Detective George Rinchey of the Fifteenth Division.

Attell claimed that he had bought the tickets for two friends who had failed to put in an appearance. He had then attempted to sell the tickets. He was acquitted.

Macks Tighten A. L. Flag Lead; Pirates Advance

Standing of the Clubs.

AMERICAN LEAGUE.

1928	W.	L.	P.C.	G.B.
2 Philadelphia	92	42	.687	——
1 NEW YORK	77	56	.579	14½
7 Cleveland	70	61	.534	20½
3 St. Louis	69	64	.519	21½
6 Detroit	62	72	.463	30
5 Washington	60	72	.455	31
4 Chicago	53	78	.405	37½
8 Boston	49	87	.360	44

G. B.—Games behind leader.

NATIONAL LEAGUE.

1928	W.	L.	P.C.	G.B.
2 Chicago	90	43	.677	——
4 Pittsburgh	78	56	.582	12½
3 NEW YORK	70	61	.534	19
1 St. Louis	63	67	.485	25½
6 BROOKLYN	62	72	.463	28½
8 Philadelphia	60	73	.451	30
5 Cincinnati	55	77	.417	34½
7 Boston	51	80	.389	38

G. B.—Games behind leader.

Yesterday's Results.

AMERICAN LEAGUE.

Detroit ..... 8; NEW YORK . 4
NEW YORK 10; Detroit 9
Philadelphia . 6; Cleveland 5
St. Louis ... 6; Boston 1
St. Louis ... 1; Boston 0
Chicago at Washington, Rain.

NATIONAL LEAGUE.

Cincinnati .. 7; NEW YORK . 4
Pittsburgh . 7; BROOKLYN . 6
Only games scheduled.

Games Today.

AMERICAN LEAGUE.

St. Louis at NEW YORK
Chicago at Philadelphia
Cleveland at Washington
Detroit at Boston

NATIONAL LEAGUE.

NEW YORK at Pittsburgh (2)
BROOKLYN at Cincinnati
Boston at St. Louis
Philadelphia at Chicago

Black Skies Postpone Queensboro Fight Card

Threatening weather last night caused the postponement of the weekly boxing show at the Queensboro Stadium in which Pal Silvers and Tony Vaccarelli were to box inthe main event.

Kozak, Met. Champ, Fails In U. S. 'Pro' Tourney

Craigwood Leads Golf Qualifiers at Knollwood; Joe Turnesa Put Out.

By Lester Rice.

THAT annual pastime of showing a quart of something in a pint bottle, prescribed by the National Professional Golfers' Association as a bromide for squally nerves, was indulged in yesterday by a field of 84 Metropolitan Business Golfers, over the Knollwood Country Club links at White Plains.

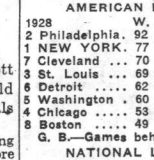

WALTER KOZAK
Fails to Qualify.

Inasmuch as there were so few as eleven places in the December championship at La Combra, Cal., allotted to the vast New York district, you are right in surmising that there were many casualties.

Most of the stars, troubled as they were with thoughts of possible failure, made the grade, but the number that didn't again proved that he Metropolitan quota is palpably inadequate.

Those that qualified for the Winter trip to the Pacific Coast were Craig Wood, of Forest Hill, who led the field with a rather fanciful double round of 145; Johnny Golden, his burly contemporary from North Jersey; the renowned Walter Hagen, the anxious Johnny Farrell, clustered at 146; the tempestuous "Wild Bill" Mehlhorn and the picturesque Wiffy Cox, of Dyker Meadows, at 149; Tom Kerrigan, of Simanoy; Herman Barron, of Tamarack; George McLean, of

Continued on Page 11, Column 6.

Young Ketchall Outpoints Polo

YOUNG KETCHALL, of Chester, Pa., battered Fredie Polo, of Bloomfield, N. J., to win a ten-round decision by a decisive margin at Newark Veledrome last night.

Ketchall staggered Polo in the second, third, eighth and tenth rounds. In the eighth he rocked Polo with a right to the chin and stuck over another right which cut Polo's left eye into a crimson blotch. It was the second fight between them. Ketchall knocked out Polo in Newark several weeks ago. About ten thousand saw the bout.

Bob Lavery, of Newark, drew with Mickey Bottone, of Nutley, in four rounds, whiel in the opener Johnnie Diaz, of Newark, outpointed Joe Levinson.

AWED SHARKEY HAILS ZAZZY AS SUCCESSOR

JACK SHARKEY, who ranks as a conversationalist with such immortals as "Windy" Winsor, "Wild Bill" Lyons and Bob Brill, has voluntarily relinquished his championship. He quit after trying to get a word in edgewise with Young Zazzarino, the Jersey lightweight.

"I hope I was never anything like that guy," was Sharkey's awed comment. "I used to think I could talk about myself pretty good, but I don't think I was ever anything like like him. I asked him how he thought he would do with Al Singer.

"'THINK!' he says scornfully. 'I don't think. I know. I'll knock that mug out in seven rounds, and if he gets fresh, I'll knock him out in three!'"

EXPRESS SPORTS

BEST SPORTS STAFF ON PACIFIC COAST

Start World Series in Home of Yankees

HERE is an airplane view of the Yankee stadium, where the world series gets under way tomorrow. Infielder Travis Jackson is shown on the lower left. He kept the Giants on top by playing shortstop and third base when Dave Bancroft and Heinie Groh were out. This Southern League product will get into the series if Bancroft, Groh or Frisch is injured. On the lower right is a closeup of Art Nehf, who will probably start the first game for John McGraw. Nehf finished the season in fine form and is the Giants' best bet.

Figures Reveal Real Strength Of Two Great New York Clubs

NEW YORK GIANTS

Player-Pos.	B.	G.	AB.	R.	H.	2B.	3B.	HR.	TB.	SB.	SH.	Pct.	PO.	A.	E.	Pct.
Bentley, p. ..	L	50	84	9	35	6	1	1	46	0	2	.417	5	37	1	.977
Frisch, 2b ...	B	136	571	105	198	27	9	11	276	23	12	.347	291	448	18	.976
Young, rf.....	L	136	537	114	183	31	12	3	247	14	11	.341	256	21	12	.958
Stengel, cf...	L	67	192	36	65	9	4	5	97	6	6	.338	99	3	2	.981
Scott, p.	L	38	75	11	24	4	0	1	31	1	2	.320	3	42	2	.957
Bancroft, ss..	R	91	370	70	115	25	3	1	149	7	5	.308	238	344	33	.946
Groh, 3b.....	R	109	408	81	122	19	5	4	163	2	10	.299	120	202	8	.976
Meusel, lf ...	R	130	534	89	157	22	10	16	247	6	9	.294	238	10	15	.943
Kelly, 1b ...	R	130	498	68	146	20	5	11	209	11	9	.293	1388	54	11	.992
Jackson, ut...	R	90	315	44	89	13	7	4	128	3	2	.282	96	238	20	.944
Cun'gham, cf.	R	64	162	16	43	5	0	4	60	3	4	.265	108	8	0	1000
Gowdy, c.....	R	67	149	17	39	3	4	1	53	3	8	.262	139	28	2	.988
O'Connell, ut.	L	84	248	40	64	11	2	6	97	7	2	.258	198	3	4	.980
Snyder, c....	R	111	381	35	98	11	6	5	136	6	6	.257	402	80	7	.986
Nehf, p	L	32	58	5	12	2	0	0	15	0	1	.207	14	46	1	.984
Maguire, ut..	R	38	29	11	6	1	0	0	1	1	2	.207	21	31	7	.881
Watson, p....	R	25	44	3	9	1	0	0	10	0	1	.205	5	24	1	.967
Ryan, p......	L	42	51	3	10	2	0	0	12	0	6	.196	9	30	1	.975
M'Quillan, p..	R	39	79	9	14	2	0	0	16	1	3	.177	7	46	2	.964
Shinners, ut..	R	33	13	6	2	1	0	0	3	0	0	.154	8	0	0	1000
Gaston, c.....	R	17	26	1	3	1	0	0	4	0	0	.115	24	9	0	1000
Jonnard, p...	R	44	26	1	1	0	0	0	1	0	0	.038	3	16	1	.950
Gearin, p.....	L	5	4	0	0	0	0	0	0	0	0	.000	0	4	1	4.800
Barnes, p....	L	20	11	0	0	0	0	0	0	0	0	.000	1	6	0	1000
Grand total.			4865	774	1435	216	68	73	2006	94	95	.295	3673	1730	149	.973

Passed balls—Snyder, 5; Gowdy, 1.

NEW YORK YANKEES

Player-Pos.	B.	G.	AB.	R.	H.	2B.	3B.	HR.	TB.	SB.	SH.	Pct.	PO.	A.	E.	Pct.
Ruth, rf.....	L	129	440	126	172	35	10	38	329	14	2	.391	321	15	8	.977
Witt, cf.....	L	123	500	94	159	16	10	6	213	2	16	.318	315	11	8	.976
Pipp, 1b.....	L	129	514	72	160	18	7	6	210	4	17	.311	1307	76	11	.992
Meusel, lf....	R	114	400	51	122	26	8	6	182	12	6	.305	182	16	10	.952
Smith, ut....	L	62	152	26	45	5	1	7	73	2	3	.296	75	6	7	.920
Hoffman, c...	R	65	220	22	65	9	4	3	91	2	2	.295	255	29	6	.970
Ward, 2b....	R	129	486	67	138	21	9	9	204	6	11	.284	329	384	13	.982
Johnson, ut..	B	24	68	6	19	3	0	0	19	0	4	.279	4	65	0	1000
Dugan, 3b...	R	127	562	96	154	2	1	1	26	2	0	.279	35	45	8	.909
Schang c....	R	67	217	29	9	27	7	5	210	4	12	.274	127	254	7	.982
Bush, p......	R	36	107	11	29	5	1	1	69	1	5	.272	226	47	7	.975
Scott, ss.....	R	129	461	42	118	15	1	5	150	1	16	.256	224	251	23	.962
McNally, ut..	R	23	24	3	6	5	3	2	46	0	0	.271	13	69	3	.965
Hendrick, ut.	L	29	44	5	10	6	0	0	6	1	2	.250	6	18	2	.923
Shawkey, p...	R	34	93	8	19	3	1	0	15	1	0	.227	6	1	0	1000
Pennock, p...	B	33	79	11	16	1	1	0	22	0	2	.204	8	58	1	.985
Jo[illegible] p.....	R	35	76	12	15	3	0	0	18	0	3	.197	4	61	1	.985
H[illegible] p......	R	33	75	6	14	0	1	0	16	0	4	.187	15	50	3	.956
Mays, p......	L	22	25	2	4	0	1	1	9	0	1	.169	7	31	1	.974
Haines, ut...	R	25	21	8	3	2	0	0	5	0	1	.143	12	1	0	1000
Bengough, c..	R	19	53	1	7	2	0	0	9	0	1	.132	55	13	2	.971
Roettger, p...	R	4	1	0	0	0	0	0	0	0	0	.000	3	3	0	1000
Pipgrass, p...	R	5	3	0	0	0	0	0	0	0	0	.000	0	5	0	1000
Gazella, ut...	R	5	4	1	0	0	0	0	0	0	0	.000	1	5	0	1000
Grand totals....			4625	699	1334	198	66	90	1922	52	108	.288	3530	1514	121	.977

Passed balls—Schang 8; Hoffman, 7; Bengough, 1.

WILLIAMS, BIG LINCOLN BACK, IS INJURED

FRIDAY'S PREP GAMES
Los Angeles at Franklin.
Jefferson at Lincoln.
Manual Arts, Hollywood.
Polytechnic, bye.

By TOM STIMSON

Hundreds of ardent followers of [...]y league prep football are im[pat]iently awaiting the two open[ing] games that will start off the [192]3 championship Friday. When [the] sun is beginning to set, they [alw]ays start the prep games when [the] crows turn in, Coach Costel[lo's] light Jefferson squad meets [Lin]coln at Lincoln, and Los An[gel]es plays at Franklin.

[C]oach George Costello, prepdom's "[Gl]oomy Gus," acknowledges his [ligh]test team in years and cau[tio]ns his supporters not to expect [mu]ch this Friday. By Costello's [me]asurement the Jefferson line [tip]s the beam around 135 pounds. [Hi]s ends, Greenfield and Leiter, [are] fast but as light as feathers.

[U]nfortunately Coach Frank "[Ra]bbit" Mallette, the former Uni[ver]sity of Southern California cap[tai]n, has several of his best Lin[col]n men on the side lines for [the] tussle. Clarence Williams, big [...]-pound fullback, has hurt his [sho]ulder and must decorate the [ben]ch for a couple of weeks.

[MA]LLETTE'S LINEUP

[M]allette intends to start Milt [...]an, Vern Hafenfeld and Hob [Gri]swold in the backfield. The [oth]er party is yet to be selected. [Thi]s trio will average 160 pounds. [Cap]tain Long and Russ Striff, the [yo]ungster, will play the ends. Jud[...] Cornwall and Vincent Arlosky [wil]l be stationed at tackle with [...]an Cromwell, jr., offspring of [U.] S. C.'s great dean the senior, [on] hand to fill in.

[L]os Angeles will likely base its [atta]ck on the forward pass against [the] crippled Franklin champions. [Coa]ch Herb White has had them [stu]dy the aerial method assiduous[ly] this fall. Janick is cinched to [star]t at quarter with Smith, Austin [and] Middleton as partners behind [the] line. Bruce Kirkpatrick, who [wor]ries about the forward wall, is [sati]sfied with Captain Bill Saun[der]s at tackle and Al Krause op[pos]ite him.

[F]ranklin is weak. That much is [tru]e. Sam Tenison's gang lost [thei]r first game in two years to [Gle]ndale last week.

[RH]INEHART AND JONES

[D]ick Rhinehart and Bob Jones, [bac]kfield men, are out with injuries [...]y, but will have to be back in [the] contest Friday if they are at [all] able to hobble about. Don Tay[lor,] captain and 175-pound end, and [Geo]rge Fusco, 160-pound end, are [the] nucleus of the outfit. If Frank[lin] does anything you can lay the [res]ponsibility to these two live [wir]es. "Lad" Stevens, 185-pound [gua]rd, will play at that position, [wit]h Gordon Newell at center.

[Fa]ir Weather for Series Predicted

[N]EW YORK, Oct. 9. — World [seri]es fandom is promised agree[abl]e weather conditions for the [firs]t two games of the Yankee-[Gia]nts series in a bulletin issued [by] the local weather bureau today. [The] bulletin follows:

"Fair today, Wednesday and [Thu]rsday; little change in temper[atu]re; gentle to moderate north [to] northeast winds."

REISELT VICTOR

[C]LEVELAND, Oct. 9.—Otto Rei[selt], Philadelphia, defeated Jess [...]an, Cleveland, in two national [cha]mpionship three-cushion billiard [gam]es here. The score in the aft[ern]oon game was 50 to 39 in 43 [inn]ings; the night result was 50 to [...] in 50 innings.

RICKARD SAYS 'BLACK PANTHER' EASY FOR FIRPO

NEW YORK, Oct. 9.—Tex Rickard thinks that Firpo, despite his defeat by Dempsey, can whip Harry Wills.

"Firpo is stronger than is Wills," stated Rickard, "and he can hit harder; he's younger and faster.

"Wills has a habit when he's fighting of holding an opponent. If he tried that with Firpo he'd be shaken off.

"I really think Firpo would whip Wills quicker than would Dempsey.

"I'm not saying this to help make a Wills-Firpo match. That match is already made so far as public interest is concerned.

"I'm saying what I actually think. Everybody can't whip Firpo as Dempsey did."

Angels Must Trim Vernon to Remain In Sixth Place

Only a few points ahead of the Oakland club, Marty Krug has ordered his Angels to bear down this week and defeat the Vernon Tigers. The two teams open a seven-game series tomorrow, closing the season Sunday.

Bill Essick of the Tigers would like to get Ernie Vache, the big Dallas outfielder, who winters here. Vache, whom Dallas obtained from the St. Louis Browns, had a big year in the Texas League. It is said that Essick offered Don Rader and Ping Bodie for Vache, also a couple of other players.

Oscar Reichow, business manager of the Angels, has recommended Joe Becker and Perle Casey, Coast League umpires, to Ban Johnson, president of the American League.

ALTROCK, SCHACHT ON JOB

NEW YORK, Oct. 9.—Nick Altrock and Al Schacht, baseball clowns, arrived in town today, and began rehearsals of some of the stunts they will do for world series crowds. Altrock said they had some dumb assistants, including the Washington goat.

Jersey Officials Suspend Walker For Poor Fight

TRENTON, N. Y., Oct. 9.—Mickey Walker, welterweight champion, and his manager, Jack Bulger, today were suspended for one year by the state boxing commissioner, as a result of the unsatisfactory fight in Newark last night, between Walker and Jimmy Jones of Youngstown, Ohio, the recognized titleholder in New York.

NEWARK, N. J., Oct. 9.—Elizabeth, N. J., will have a new home for crippled children because Jimmy Jones, welterweight champion of the world in the state of New York, and Mickey Walker, welterweight champion of the world outside of New York state, "did not try" in their bout last night. More than 22,000 fans were present, according to official figures, and $22,000 was taken in through advance sales alone.

Soon after the fight started the cry of "stalling" was taken up by the crowd, and in the ninth round Chief Boxing Commissioner Adams called a halt. No decision was given. The bout was scheduled for 12 rounds. The proceeds were ordered given to the Elizabeth home after the match had been declared "no contest."

The bout, originally scheduled for a week ago yesterday, was postponed because of an injury to one of Walker's hands. He stated that he had not sufficiently recovered and that every blow he struck hurt him more than it did Jones.

STRIBLING BOXES BURNS

MACON, Ga., Oct. 9.—"Pa" Stribling, father-manager of W. L. "Young" Stribling, announced that Young Stribling will fight Tommy Burns in Detroit, October 15, 12 rounds no-decision.

Lux Kayoes Conway in Two Rounds

Morrie Lux, former Kansas City welterweight championship contender, made an impressive comeback last night when he completely outclassed Joe Conway of Buffalo, stopping him in two rounds at Fred Winsor's Madison Square Garden arena.

Lux landed rights and lefts at will.

Baby Gans, colored lightweight, won from Jim Stanley in the semi-windup.

Other results:

Young Sam Langford defeated Battling O'Dell.
Ted Frenchie defeated Barney O'Toole.
Jimmy Brown won from Jim Smith.
Frankie O'Connell defeated Bobby Jones.
Jim Jefford won from Bill Plimmer.

Bucketshop Probe Brings Up Series Scandal Again

NEW YORK, Oct. 9.—The scandal in which the Chicago White Sox and the world championship series of 1919 was brought into the Fuller-Magee bucketshop investigation when Arnold Rothstein, who was prominently mentioned as a gambler at the time of the series, was a witness before Harold P. Coffin, referee in bankruptcy.

The scandal was mentioned almost as soon as Rothstein had taken his place on the witness stand. At the reference to it Rothstein became angry and several times joined in wordy tilts with William Chadbourne, the attorney representing the Fuller creditors, who was questioning him.

EUGENE CRIQUI FRACTURES HIS HAND IN BOUT

PARIS, Oct. 9.—Eugene Criqui fractured his left hand in winning a decision over Henri Hebrans, the Belgian, last Saturday, and will be unable to fight for months.

It is estimated that Criqui has foregone purses totaling close to 1,000,000 francs in order that he may keep his word to fight for charity. These bouts included three no-decision 8-round matches in the United States. His exhibition tours in October and November have been abandoned.

Benjamin Wants To Meet Leonard In Tijuana Ring

Joe Benjamin wants to meet Benny Leonard at Tijuana on December 24. He has asked his manager, Jack Kearns, to get him the match. Jim Coffroth, who has signed Leonard, has not named the champion's opponent as yet.

Joe is sure he has a chance with the champion, inasmuch as he thinks Benny has lost his former knockout punch.

Umpire Burnside Visits This City

Bill Burnside, veteran Western League umpire, arrived in Los Angeles today. Bill resides in Oakland but will spend several days in Southern California before returning home. Mrs. Burnside is with him.

COAST LEAGUE

	W.	L.	Pct.	If Win	If Lose
San Francisco	121	73	.624	.626	.621
Sacramento	108	84	.563	.565	.560
Portland	104	86	.547	.550	.545
Seattle	96	94	.505	.508	.503
Salt Lake	91	101	.474	.477	.472
LOS ANGELES ...	88	107	.451	.454	.448
Oakland	87	108	.446	.449	.444
VERNON	75	117	.391	.394	.389

TODAY'S GAMES

Vernon at Los Angeles postponed; team traveling.
Oakland at San Francisco.
Salt Lake at Sacramento.
Portland at Seattle.

Hendricks in Left Field if Ruth Plays First for Huggins' Outfit

NEVADA ARRIVES ON MORNING OF U.S.C. GAME

By SID ZIFF

Football, the kind of game where one team has to play the best that's in it for 60 full minutes, hits Los Angeles next Saturday afternoon.

On that day "Corky" Courtwright's great pack of Nevadans tangle with the University of Southern California varsity in their annual tussle. Remember last year when the squads battled desperately, neither giving ground until Chet Dolley went over for the only score of the game on a quarterback sneak.

CHET DOLLEY

Think about that and then make a hasty trip to the mammoth Los Angeles Coliseum at Exposition park. There are two reasons to get into your seats early. First, the freshman game has been moved up to 1 o'clock sharp. Coach Leo Calland's yearlings mangling with the Long Beach high team. This has been done so that the varsity game will start promptly at 3. Kickoff will be earlier if at all possible. Nevada arrives in Los Angeles early Saturday morning.

LEAVE AFTER GAME

University of Southern California has made arrangements to board train for Seattle, Wash., immediately after the Nevada conflict. The game will be over around 5 or 5:30. The boys will hop out of their moleskins into civics and board limited for the land of rain and mud about 6:30 or 7 o'clock.

This step has been taken so that the team will arrive in Seattle Tuesday morning. This will give them four days to get acquainted with the gridiron upon which they'll meet Enoch Bagshaw's powerful University of Washington team Saturday, October 20.

U. S. C. WON 6 TO 0

Saturday's game should be a genuine treat. That 6 to 0 score of last year will act as a mighty magnet to the throngs and the stadium's high water mark, set in its very first game of 15,000 should go by the boards.

The fans will undoubtedly see Coach Elmer C. Henderson's gang work everything in them except the secret plays laid aside for California, November 10. The varsity first string men will have plenty to do with the Nevadans.

Nevada is far stronger this season than last despite the fact that Stanford was able to defeat them, 20 to 0. The line and backfield work machine like and the whole business is "pointed for U. S. C." This game is the same with Nevada that the California classic is to the Trojan.

GUTTERIN AT QUARTER

Gutterin at quarter has made a hit with Nevada fans. They say he has everybody skinned but the one and only "Rabbit" Bradshaw. He's a wonderful tackler and a formidable offensive power.

Captain Scranton and Jones are halfbacks; Lowry, the man who played full against the Trojans last year, will again face Troy Saturday. Carlson, a huge 215-pound right tackle, is starring on the line.

Captain Dolley, Gordon Campbell, Johnny Riddle, "Indian" Newman, Otto Anderson and the sophs, LeFevbre and Adams, will have to do some tall playing back of the line to beat that bunch.

STARK AND DORSEY

What looks like a mighty fine battle for one of the end jobs has developed at U. S. C. Its Stark vs. Gene Dorsey at Bovard field now and the man who draws the assignment will have much to boast about. These two gridders are as good as they make them. Andy Smith would smile if either had reported to the Golden Bear this fall.

Burke Stops Martin In Seventh Round

NEW ORLEANS, Oct. 9. — The scheduled 15 rounds between Bob Martin of New York, heavyweight champion of the A. E. F., and Martin Burke of New Orleans was stopped in the seventh round here last night and Burke awarded the decision. The New York fighter apparently was unsteady on his legs in the seventh round and the referee stopped the bout. Martin weighed 200 pounds and Burke 176.

SPEARS ENRAGED AS TEAM BECOMES ALL PUFFED UP

NEW YORK, Oct. 9.—"Collective magalomania" is the way Bob Spears, the University of West Virginia's football coach, describes the mental attitude of most of the star veterans of the great 1922 eleven.

The know-it-all spirit has become so pronounced that Spears cannot tell his veterans anything.

So he is forming a new eleven which will leave most of the great ones upon the sidelines. Meditation throughout a period of enforced inactivity is expected to produce the desired results in bringing the chesty ones to even keel.

West Virginia played Gonzaga in San Diego last Christmas day.

PHIL SALVADORE MEETS HOPPE TONIGHT

TONIGHT'S CARD

Phil Salvadore vs. Dick Hoppe, 135 pounds.
Young Fisher vs. "Speedy" Sparks, 158 pounds.
Kid Moha vs. Larry Murphy, 130 pounds.
Fred Murphy vs. Billy Ketchell, 145 pounds.
Packy McMullin vs. Sammy Santos, 128 pounds.
Alfred Ellis vs. Harry Ritzer, 145 pounds.
"Mushy" Callahan vs. Sailor Buell, 125 pounds.

By STUB NELSON

Papa Petie Wadhams, a bit disappointed at the showing two foreign lightweights made against Phil Salvadore, has picked an opponent right out of our own back yard for tonight's main event at the Vernon Coliseum and he is confident that Phil will have a lot more trouble than he experienced in the Richie Mitchell and Bobby Ward arguments.

Dick Hoppe, the Glendale kid, is the man Wadhams is counting on to break up the smooth and serene waters that Salvadore is now enjoying.

HOPPE AGGRESSIVE

Hoppe is just the type to give the clever Phil, who is going at his fastest clip, trouble. Dick never quits trying and is always swinging. We doubt if Phil has the sock to stop his aggressiveness. Hoppe is a greatly improved boy and don't be surprised if he crowds Salvadore all the way. At least he has a better chance to do so than Phil's recent victims.

Young Fisher, the pudgy Syracuse, N. Y., middleweight, makes his bow against "Speedy" Sparks. Fisher will get a top shot if he goes over tonight. He has been boxing around Oakland, where he met with only fair success. Judging from the left hand Sparks displayed a couple of weeks back Fisher is liable to run second best.

MOHA AND MURPHY

Old rivals in the 130-pound class, Kid Moha and Larry Murphy should throw a lot of leather in the special spot. They have staged several good melees in the past.

Fred Murphy, former amateur welterweight champion from San Francisco, will show his wares against Billy Ketchell, the San Diego lad.

The first three prelims look good.

HOYT AND NEHF, PRIMED FOR OPENER

NEW YORK, Oct. 9.—Just where ardent supporters of the New York Yankees and John J. McGraw's world champion Giants stand in the coming world series may be determined at today's final practice sessions in the Yankee stadium and the Polo Grounds.

Both clubs are hoping that all of their men will be on hand and in shape for their third successive world series, but some qualms are felt about the reported injuries of several of Miller Huggins' most reliable stars.

Huggins will know his position today on Babe Ruth, Wally Pipp and Bob Meusel, all of whom have been ailing from more or less serious although temporary injuries. Pipp and Meusel both have injured ankles. If Wally is unable to break into the lineup, Babe will have to desert the gardens and romp around the initial sack.

SMITH IN SLUMP

Manager Huggins said today that Harvey Hendricks would draw the left field assignment over Elmer Smith. Hendricks has been hitting with considerable regularity of late, whereas Smith has been in a bad slump. If Meusel will have to sit on the bench it will come as a serious blow to the Yanks. The big Californian is one of Huggins' best offensive bets. Hinkey Haines, former Penn State football star, will swing the leg for Meusel in case Bob is out.

HOYT VS. NEHF

Predictions as to the rival pitchers for tomorrow's game generally name Waite Hoyt as the probable Yankee twirler and Art Nehf as the man who will oppose him, although several were of the opinion that Jack Scott, if he proves to have recovered from his cold, would be McGraw's selection.

White Sox and Cubs Open Chicago City Series Tomorrow

CHICAGO, Oct. 19.—Urban Faber and Ray Schalk, members of the Chicago American baseball team, who have been out of the game because of injuries, will probably appear in the lineup of the team in the city series with the Chicago Nationals beginning tomorrow.

EVENING HERALD SPORTS

YANKEES REAL BALL CLUB IS VERDICT OF FANDOM

HUGGINS' TEAM PROVES CLASS OVER GIANT COHORTS

McGraw's Men Outplayed in All Branches of Game, Fans of Gotham Admit

By HENRY L. FARRELL
United Press Staff Correspondent

NEW YORK, Oct. 16.—World's champions for the first time in history, the New York Yankees are now holding the throne occupied for two years by the proud Giants of John McGraw.

The Yankees are real champions by a hard earned, well deserved victory over the best team in the National league.

With a game heart that carried them through seven innings of the final contest when Art Nehf was making their big guns puff like pop guns, the Yankees crashed through in the eighth and won the deciding game, 6 to 4.

The motor which propelled the frail arm of Nehf started missing in the eighth, with one down and before McGraw could do anything to stop the rush, five runs were over the plate and the championship was gone.

PITCHING HANDICAP

Terrible pitching which caused the Giants to go down two games to four in the series that meant so much to them, was the handicap that they carried all through the series against one of the most savage hitting teams in baseball. Throughout the entire series the Giants battled hard and clean and played fine baseball, but they couldn't get the pitching. The Yanks had everything.

There are some who scoff at the thought of sentiment in professional baseball, where the purse is supposed to have as much appeal as it has among boxers.

SENTIMENT IN GAME

There is sentiment in baseball. No one could have doubted had he been able to see Art Nehf walk to the dugout with tears streaming down his cheeks, had they been able to look at him on the Giants' bench with his head in his hands and his frame shaken with sobs.

Sorrow over the loss of the money representing the difference between the winners' and losers' end of the series does not bring out emotions like that.

Sentiment, almost like college boy stuff, was pulled by the Yanks at the end of the game. They jumped about and acted like crazy kids.

CLUBHOUSE SCENE

The most touching scene was enacted in the Yankee clubhouse. It will be remembered that Miller Huggins once was the joke manager of the club who occupied the manager's office and nothing else.

When the Yanks were coming out of the showers, Babe Ruth jumped to the rubbing board and shouted for silence.

"Fellows," he said, "we've just won the world's championship and we owe everything to 'Hug' for pulling us through and sticking behind us in everything for years. He has done a fine thing this year and we all know it. Mr. Huggins, we want to present this to you as a little token of our respect and admiration."

He handed Huggins a beautiful diamond ring and the team gave three cheers for "Hug."

Box Score of Final Game

YANKEES

	AB	R	H	O	A	E
Witt, cf.	3	0	0	0	1	0
Dugan, 3b.	3	1	0	2	1	0
Ruth, rf.	3	1	1	1	0	0
R. Meusel, lf.	4	0	1	1	0	0
Pipp, 1b.	4	0	0	1	2	0
Ward, 2b	4	0	1	2	7	0
Schang, c.	4	1	1	7	0	0
E. Scott, ss.	4	1	1	1	2	0
Pennock, p.	2	0	0	1	0	0
xHoffman	0	0	0	0	0	0
xxHaines, cf.	0	1	0	0	0	0
xxxBush	0	0	0	0	0	0
xxxxJohnson	0	1	0	0	0	0
Jones, p.	0	0	0	0	1	0
Totals	31	6	5	27	13	0

GIANTS

	AB	R	H	O	A	E
Bancroft, ss.	4	0	0	1	7	0
Groh, 3b.	4	1	1	1	2	0
Frisch, 2b.	4	2	3	1	5	0
Young, rf.	4	0	2	0	0	0
Meusel, lf.	4	0	1	1	0	0
Cunningham, cf.	3	0	1	0	0	1
Kelly, 1b.	4	0	0	1	9	0
Snyder, c.	4	1	2	4	0	0
Nehf, p.	3	0	0	0	0	1
Ryan, p.	0	0	0	0	0	0
zStengel	1	0	0	0	0	0
zzBentley	1	0	0	0	0	0
Totals	36	4	10	27	19	1

xBatted for Pennock in eighth. xxRan for Hoffman in eighth. xxxBatted for Witt in eighth. xxxxRan for Bush in eighth. zBatted for Cunningham in eighth. zzBatted for Ryan in eighth.

SCORE BY INNINGS

	1	2	3	4	5	6	7	8	9	
Yankees	1	0	0	0	0	0	0	5	0	—6
Giants	1	0	0	1	1	1	0	0	0	—4

SUMMARY

Three-base hit—Frisch. Home runs—Ruth, Snyder. Double play—Nehf to Bancroft to Kelly. Left on bases—Yankees, 2; Giants, 5. Bases on balls—Off Nehf, 3; off Ryan, 1. Struck out—By Nehf, 3 (E. Meusel, Pennock, Ruth); by Pennock, 6 ("Irish" Meusel, Snyder, Nehf 3, Kelly); by Ryan, 1 (Ruth). Hits—Off Nehf, 4 in 7 innings; off Ryan, 1 in 2 innings; off Pennock, 9 in 7 innings; off Jones, 1 in 2 innings. Winning pitcher—Pennock. Losing pitcher—Nehf. Time—2 hours 7 minutes.

RAIN AGAIN HALTS LITTLE WORLD SERIES

By International News Service

KANSAS CITY, Mo., Oct. 16.—The fourth game of the Baltimore-Kansas City post-season series was again postponed today because of a muddy field.

What They Say on Last Tilt in Champ Series

MILLER HUGGINS
Manager of the Yankees.
Manager of the Yankees.

"We won because we had the better pitchers and hitters. But we had to beat a great club."

JOHN McGRAW
Manager of the Giants.
Manager of the Giants.

"I have no alibis. The better team won. All honor to it."

R. MEUSEL
Whose Hit Won the Game.
Whose Hit Won the Game.

"I got the thrill of my life when I saw the ball going into center field."

BABE RUTH
Who Fanned with the Bases Full.
Who fanned with the bases full.

"It was awful, that strikeout. I never felt worse about anything. However, I'm tickled to death that Bob Meusel got the honor of winning the series. He deserves it."

ART' NEHF
Giant Pitcher, Whose Collapse Cost the Giants the Game.
Giant pitcher, whose collapse cost the Giants the game.

"The arm went fine for seven innings. It couldn't go any further."

RUTH TELLS OF SPIRIT THAT WON TITLE

(CONTINUED FROM PAGE ONE)

by sheer nerve and grit pounded out a thrilling victory.

The world's championship belongs to everybody because no particular pitcher or batter did any more than his team mates. To John McGraw goes the credit of being as game a loser as he is a winner.

Fifteen minutes after Jack Bentley was tossed out in the ninth inning, John McGraw was shaking hands with Mill Huggins in the Yank dressing rooms. He met me first because I was nearest to the door. He joshed Joe Bush a little and then made his way to the man who had taken away his championship.

RIVALRY GONE

The rivalry of a terrific series had disappeared almost immediately and there stood baseball's two great managers shaking hands, smiling and exchanging good wishes. It was a lesson in character to every ball player in the room. As they parted someone yelled, "Three cheers for McGraw," and as Mac went through the door he left a lot of new friends behind him in the Yankee clubhouse.

Bob Meusel was the boy who slugged us to victory after I had tried and failed just before him. In fact, it seemed everybody figured in that eighth inning scoring deluge except the right-fielder of the Yankees. Heaven knows I never tried harder, swung harder or missed harder.

TELLS OF STRIKE OUT

In the first inning, with two strikes and three balls, Nehf, who always gives me trouble, put one close to my belt and an easy, well-timed swing drove the ball far into the bleachers. The facts are, I was in a hole and was only trying to meet the ball just enough for a safe swat. Then comes the eighth, with three on base, the stage all set for a killing, and I go up there and miss three beauties, but that's baseball for you!

My reward came later. The greatest pleasure of the entire series was not on the ball field, but in the Yankee clubhouse, where to me was given the privilege of presenting a token to Miller Huggins, as well loved today by each player on our club as any manager in the history of baseball.

A handsome diamond ring, representing every player who has labored these long, hard months and years with Hug, was our way of showing this wonderful little leader that to him, more than any member of the team, goes the glory of victory, just as he had to carry the worry and disappointment in the days of defeat.

SPIRIT OF CLUB

Early this season the baseball writers discovered a spirit on the Yankee ball club unlike anything in the past and equal to the spirit of any other ball club in days gone by.

That was the spirit that won the American league pennant and then carried us through to the championship of the world—even when we were running behind the Giants and according to many early experts, ready to repeat our performance of 1922. It was the spirit that prompted us to get that diamond ring for Miller Huggins even before we won the final game.

When I got through saying a few words, that didn't anywhere near tell Hug what the boys wanted me to say or what I was trying to say, he climbed on a chair and smiling as he accepted the gift, told us that the ring with all its beauty was only a small incident to the spirit of comradeship that it represented.

LASTING FRIENDSHIP

"It's mighty nice to win pennants," said Hug, "and the greatest think a ball club can accomplish is to win a world series, but I'd sooner win and maintain the friendship of you fine fellows than win a dozen pennants. That's what this token represents to me—that spirit of unselfishness, loyalty and team work that you have given since early spring. I shall always prize it for its beauty, but if it's beauty ever dims I will still treasure it as evidence of a lasting friendship."

Newly Crowned World Champs

Miller Huggins' team which gained baseball's highest honor by defeating the Giants four games to two. Top row, left to right, are Doc Woods, trainer; Haines, Smith, Pennock, Hoffman, Meusel, Ruth, Pipp, Dugan, Jones, Scott, Shields. Center row left to right, Bush, Shawkey, Witt, Coach O'Leary, Manager Miller Huggins, Schang, Mays, Ward, Roettger. Front row, Johnson, Bengough, Pipgras, Mascot Eddy Bennett, McNally, Gazella and Hendricks.—Internation 1 Newsreel photo.

PITCHING WON SERIES, SAYS BANCROFT

By DAVE BANCROFT
Captain of the New York Giants—Copyright, 1923, by Cosmopolitan News Service

NEW YORK, Oct. 16.—The Yankees whipped us fairly and squarely.

And we doff our caps to the new champions of the baseball world.

There is no excuse to offer beyond the fact that the Yankees showed pitching effectiveness beyond our own—and that is why we lost.

The final game of the series was a heart-breaking loss. For seven full innings Art Nehf pitched a most wonderful game. Only three balls were hit out of the infield in those innings, and Nehf, in addition to making the Yankee sluggers look like bush leaguers, fielded his position in superb style.

It seemed to us as the Yankees went to bat in the eighth that the game would be ours and that on Tuesday there would come for us the golden opportunity to win the seventh and the final game. And then things began to happen.

GROWS WILD

There is no explanation for Art's sudden collapse. He seemed to be going along just as well in the early part of the eighth as he was throughout the other seven innings. But after those two hits were made Art, one of the steadiest pitchers in baseball, found it difficult to locate the plate.

Everybody knows what happened then.

Nehf walked two men in a row and forced in a run. Then Ryan, who took his place, forced in another, making it 4 to 3, with the bases filled and Bob Meusel at bat.

Then came Meusel's hit which won a world's championship for the American league.

GOT BIG LEAD

We gave to Art Nehf everything we had. We punched out hits when hits meant runs and we gave him a three-run lead in the eighth inning. We fielded behind him to the limit of our endeavor and the finish of the game and the series came not because the Giant team cracked but because Art went to pieces for some inexplicable reason at the critical moment.

Any time our ball club is whipped fairly and squarely every Giant is willing to concede it. And today we gladly yield the laurels to our ancient enemies. If our pitching had been a bit better the series perhaps would have ended differently. But it was not better; the men who had to carry us through to the National league championship probably worked out their arms in that pennant struggle and came into the classic minus the something necessary to win ball games from the slugging Yankees.

TICKETS ON SALE

PASADENA, Oct. 16.—Membership tickets in the Tournament of Roses association, which entitles the holders to pasteboards for the annual New Year's day football game here, were placed on sale today.

Composite Score of Series

YANKEES' BATTING

Player—	AB	R	H	2B	3B	HR	TB	BB	SH	SO	SB	RBI	Pct.
Witt, c	25	1	6	2	0	0	8	1	1	1	0	4	.240
Dugan, 3b	25	5	7	2	1	1	14	3	0	0	0	4	.280
Ruth, rf and 1b	19	8	7	1	1	3	19	8	0	6	0	3	.368
R. Meusel, lf	26	1	7	1	2	0	12	1	0	3	0	8	.269
Pipp, 1b	20	2	5	0	0	0	5	3	1	1	0	1	.250
Ward, 2b	24	4	10	0	0	1	13	1	0	3	1	2	.417
Schang, c	22	3	7	1	0	0	8	1	2	2	0	0	.318
E. Scott, ss	22	2	7	0	0	0	7	0	1	1	0	3	.318
Hoyt, p	1	0	0	0	0	0	0	0	0	1	0	0	.000
Bush, p and x	7	2	3	1	0	0	4	1	0	1	0	0	.429
Pennock, p	6	0	0	0	0	0	0	0	0	2	0	0	.000
Jones, p	2	0	0	0	0	0	0	0	0	1	0	0	.000
Shawkey, p	3	0	1	0	0	0	1	0	1	0	0	1	.333
Johnson, ss and xx	0	1	0	0	0	0	0	0	0	0	0	0	.000
Haines, rf and xxx	1	1	0	0	0	0	0	0	0	0	0	0	.000
Hendrick, xxxx	1	0	0	0	0	0	0	0	0	0	0	0	.000
Hofman, xxxxx	1	0	0	0	0	0	0	1	0	0	0	0	.000
Totals	205	30	60	8	4	5	91	20	6	22	1	26	.293

Bush batted for Witt in sixth game. Johnson ran for Bush in sixth game. Haines ran for Hofmann in sixth game. Hendricks batted for Scott in first game. Hofmann batted for Jones in third game and for Pennock in sixth game.

GIANTS' BATTING

Player—	AB	R	H	2B	3B	HR	TB	BB	SH	SO	SB	RBI	Pct.
Bancroft, ss	24	1	2	0	0	0	2	1	0	2	1	0	.182
Groh, 3b	22	3	4	0	1	0	6	3	0	1	9	2	.123
Frisch, 2b	25	2	10	0	1	0	12	0	0	0	0	1	.400
Young, rf	23	2	8	0	0	1	11	2	0	0	0	3	.391
E. Meusel lf	25	3	7	1	1	1	13	0	0	2	0	2	.290
Stengel, cf	12	3	5	0	0	2	11	4	0	0	0	3	.417
Cunningham, cf	7	0	1	0	0	0	1	0	0	1	0	1	.143
Kelly, 1b	22	1	4	0	0	0	4	1	0	2	0	0	.136
Snyder, c	17	1	2	0	0	1	5	1	0	2	0	1	.113
Gowdy	4	0	0	0	0	0	0	0	0	0	0	0	.000
Watson, p	0	0	0	0	0	0	0	0	0	0	0	0	.000
Ryan, p	2	0	0	0	0	0	0	0	0	0	0	0	.000
McQuillan, p	3	0	0	0	0	0	0	0	0	1	0	0	.000
Bentley, p	5	0	3	1	0	0	4	0	0	0	0	1	.600
Nehf, p	6	0	1	0	0	0	1	0	0	0	0	1	.167
Scott, p	1	0	0	0	0	0	0	0	0	0	0	0	.000
Jonnard, p	1	0	0	1	0	0	0	0	0	0	0	0	.000
Barnes, p	1	0	0	0	0	0	0	0	0	1	0	0	.000
Maguire	0	1	0	0	0	0	0	0	0	0	0	0	.000
Jackson	1	0	0	0	0	0	0	0	0	0	0	0	.000
Gearin	0	0	0	0	0	0	0	0	0	0	0	0	.000
O'Connell	1	0	0	0	0	0	0	0	0	1	0	0	.000
Totals	202	17	47	2	3	5	70	12	0	18	1	14	.233

Stengel batted for Cunningham in sixth. Cunningham batted for Stengel in fourth game. Gowdy batted for Cunningham in second game. Bentley batted for Watsen in first game, McQuillan in fourth, and Ryan in sixth game. Maguire ran for Gowdy in first game and Bentley in fourth game. O'Connell batted for Jonnard in fourth game and Barnes in flith game.

COMPOSITE SCORE BY INNINGS

Innings	1	2	3	4	5	6	7	8	9	
YANKEES	5	13	1	4	1	0	1	5	0	—30
GIANTS	1	2	4	1	1	2	1	3	2	—17

SUMMARY

Double plays—Yankees: Scott, Ward, Pipp, 3; Jones, Scott, Pipp, 1; Shawkey, Dugan, Pipp, 1; Dugan, Pipp, 1.

Giants: Bancroft, Frisch, Kelly, 2; Ryan, Groh, Frisch, 1; Snyder, 1; Frisch, Bancroft, Kelly, 1; Bancroft, Frisch, 1; Nehf, Bancroft, Kelly, 1.

Left on bases—Yankees, 42; Giants, 35.

Bases on balls—Off Hoyt, 1; off Bush, 4; off Pennock, 1; off Jones, 2; off Shawkey, 4; off Watson, 1; off Ryan, 4; off McQuillan, 4; off Bentley, 4; off Nehf, 6; off Jonnard, 1; off J. Scott, 1.

Struck out—By Bush, 5 (Ryan, Snyder, Barnes, O'Connell and Bancroft); by Pennock, 8 (Nehf, 3; Kelly, 2; E. Meusel, Snyder and Cunningham); Jones, 3 (Nehf, Bancroft and Groh); by Shawkey, 2 (E. Meusel and McQuillan); by Watson, 1 (Hoyt); by Ryan, 3 (Ward, E. Scott and Ruth); by McQuillan, 3 (R. Meusel, 2, and Ruth); by Nehf, 7 (Ruth, 2; Jones, Witt, R. Meusel, Pennock and Ward); by J. Scott, 2 (Ruth and Bush); by Barnes, 4 (Schang, Pennock, Ward and Ruth); by Bentley, 1 (Schang); by Jonnard, 1 (Pipp).

Hits and runs—Off Hoyt, 4 and 4 in 2 1-3 innings; off Bush, 7 and 2 in 16 2-3; off Pennock, 19 and 4 in 17 1-3; off Jones, 5 and 1 in 10; off Shawkey, 12 and 2 in 7 2-3; off Watson, 4 and 3 in 2; off Ryan, 11 and 6 in 9 1-3; off McQuillan, 11 and 5 in 9; off Bentley, 10 and 7 in 7 2-3; off Nehf, 13 and 4 in 16 2-3; off J. Scott, 9 and 4 in 3; off Jonnard, 1 and 0 in 2; off Barnes, 4 and 0 in 4 2-3.

Wild pitch—Ryan, 1.

Hit by pitched ball—By Bentley (Pennock); by Shawkey (O'Connell).

Winning pitchers—Ryan, first game; Pennock, second game; Nehf, third game; Shawkey, fourth game; Bush, fifth game; Pennock, sixth game.

Losing pitchers—Bush, first game; McQuillan, second game; Jones, third game; J. Scott, fourth game; Bentley, fifth game, and Nehf, sixth game.

Jack Dempsey to Referee Bout for Delhi 4-Rounders

With Jack Dempsey scheduled to referee, Jack Thompson will tackle Sam Isman in the main event of the boxing show to be staged at Delhi, near Orange, Oct. 22, according to Tommy McFarland, former star lightweight, who is managing the club.

Terry Adams and Young Terry, a couple of 142-pounders, will meet in the semi-windup. Other bouts on the card follow:

Toby Montoya vs. Pete Golinda, Billy Craig vs. K. O. Montoya. Young Joe Rivers vs. Speed McFarland.

WILLIE KAMM HERO OF CHICAGO SERIES

By United Press

CHICAGO, Oct. 16.—The sixth game in the Chicago championship series was to be played today with the White Sox having a 3 to 2 edge over the Cubs as a result of yesterday's win.

Willie Kamm knocked in three deciding runs with two circuit clouts and the Sox won, 7 to 4. Friberg, Vogel and Collins also made four-base hits.

I'm to Blame, Says Nehf When Giants Lose Last Contest

By United Press

NEW YORK, Oct. 16.—Although urged by his teammates to forget it, Arthur Nehf, Giant southpaw, has assumed the full responsibility for the loss of the world's championship by the Giants.

"I can't explain it," Nehf said today. "My arm suddenly failed me when I was sure that I was perfectly sage. It wouldn't respond and I couldn't get a thing out of it."

Nehf was distressed beyond expression, although the Giant players hold him he was the hero for trying so hard to win. He was disappointed also, because in the stands were his father from Indiana, his wife and his two children.

TEN SCHOLARSHIPS TO INSURANCE COURSE GIVEN

NEW YORK, Oct. 16.—Ten annual scholarships of $100 each have been given New York university for young men and women students in the life insurance training course, by Joseph D. Bookstaver, general agent in New York for a well known company.

GAMES WON ON MERIT, SCOTT DECLARES

By EVERETT SCOTT
Captain of the New York Yankees—Copyright, 1923, by Cosmopolitan News Service

NEW YORK, Oct. 16.—The revenge we sought is ours today. The Yankees dominate the heights of the baseball world because they outplayed the enemy in every department of baseball in the 1923 world's series.

There was nothing flukish about our triumph; there is no possibility for any real alibi on the part of the beaten Giants. We outhit them, we outfielded them, we outslugged them and certainly our pitchers displayed infinitely more ability than did those from the National league.

The element of luck did not figure in any consequential way in this series. The battles were decided largely upon sheer merit. And because they were the Yankees proved to the baseball world that their team is infinitely superior to the opposition.

'MADE US STEP'

The Giants fought us as best they could—and they certainly made us step to win the final combat. But the Giants have no complaint to offer over anything that happened. They were beaten fairly and squarely and that the series went as far as six games was due only to the fact that Casey Stengel hit out two spectacular home runs at critical moments, something that Stengel probably could not duplicate in another 100 world's series games.

In triumph we are not forgetful of the feeling of sympathy for Art Nehf, the Giant southpaw. Art pitched one of the most beautiful games that we have ever looked at for seven innings. It seemed to the Giant admirers that we were doomed to defeat. But even the fact that the Giants had a three-run lead didn't discourage us for a single minute.

FELT CONFIDENT

We felt that sooner or later we would begin to smash Nehf's offerings through the wonderful Giant defense—and that's exactly what we did.

I have known many happy moments in my baseball career—and so have the other Yankees, but none of us has ever experienced quite such a delirious bit of joy as came to us when Bob Meusel punched out the hit in the eighth inning which cleared the bases, put us in the lead and won for us the sixth and final game in the world's championship of 1923.

Matlock to Box Rockson in Star Event at El Rio

Leo Matlock and Mickey Rockson, 160-pounders, will meet in the main event at El Rio Thursday night. The remainder of the card will be: Jack Martin vs. K. O. Kid Lewis; Harry Ritzer vs. Fred Murphy; Joe Garcia vs. Young Moha; Charley Dalton vs. Tony Marco; Cy Cooper vs. Arizona Kid; Paddy McKeen vs. Joe Silver.

Series Gate Receipts Reach Million Mark

NEW YORK, Oct. 16.—More than 301,430 baseball fans paid $1,063,915 to watch the six world's series games which came to an end yesterday with the Yanks winning, it was announced today by officials.

Of this amount the players get $362,783.04, the commission will get $160,170.25 and the club owners $535,459.70.

This is the first time in the history of world's series games that the gate for the series went over the million mark.

SPECIAL MATCH TO DECIDE GOLF TITLE

SAN DIEGO, Oct. 16.—Tied for first place in the annual San Diego championship golf tournament, A. E. Childs and Nelson Barker will meet here Sunday afternoon in a special playoff match for the title.

Barker and Childs ended the tourney with counts of 387. They played an extra 80 holes, but were still tied at the end of the round.

BEST CLUB WON CHAMP SERIES SAYS FRANK CHANCE

Huggins Must Be Given Credit as Smart Manager, Claims Peerless Leader

By FRANK L. CHANCE
Who Won Four National and Two World Championships.

NEW YORK, Oct. 16.—The best team won.

The Yankees showed they possessed the fighting heart by coming from behind in the final game of the series.

Critics who have been "panning" Miller Huggins now will have to proclaim him the leader of the world's champions.

I always have maintained that it is the ball club that makes the manager and not the manager the ball club.

But the manager has to make the right moves and that is where Huggins gets the credit.

ALL ON NEHF

The Giants staked all on Art Nehf. He went good for a time, but could not stand up under the strain. I have heard some fans trying to criticize McGraw for taking Nehf out in the eighth inning, but that is foolish. Here was a pitcher who had a three-run lead and then he fills the bases and even walks a man over the plate. If he was going to settle down he would have done it before walking in a marker. It was time to make the change.

Ruth's home run in the opening inning put his team out in front. The big fellow hit up to his standard during the present series. He struck out later with men on the bases, but he did his share toward making his club victorious.

Three singles scored a run off Pennock in the first, but Frisch was out trying to take third, and that helped the Yankees.

HAVE NICE LEAD

The Giants kept on adding a marker in the fourth, fifth and sixth innings. That put the club out in front with the score 4 to 1. It looked like an easy Giant victory.

Snyder's home run in the fifth was a hard blow, but Miller Huggins was waiting for the big inning.

It came in the eighth. Ward popped out to Kelly and then Schang singled. Scott followed with another hit. Hoffman was sent in to bat for Pennock and Nehf, who lost his control, walked him, filling the bases.

Bush, who has been hitting the ball hard, batted for Witt and he was walked and in came a run. Nehf was taken out and Ryan went to the mound.

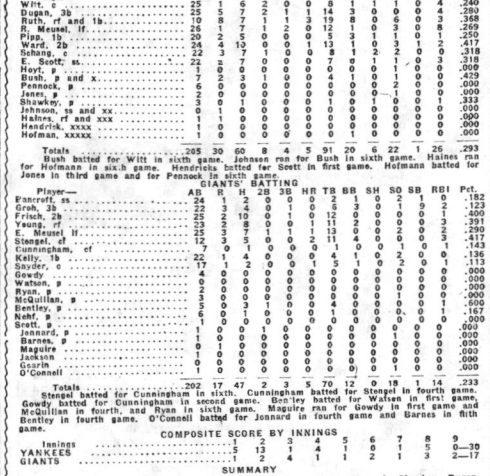

Ruth's Homer Enables American League to Down National, 4 to 2, in "Game of Century"

49,000 See Babe Score 2 With Drive Off Hallahan

Smash in 3d Inning Decides 1st Clash in History Between All-Stars of Rival Circuits; Frisch Hits 4-Base Blow; Gomez Knocks in Run

By Rud Rennie

CHICAGO, July 6.—When the "dream game" of countless fans came into being in Comiskey Park here this summery afternoon before a comfortably seated crowd of 49,000 persons, it was not long before all the assembled stars of both major baseball leagues were dimmed by the effulgent power of one planet.

There were cheers for Vernon Gomez, the Yankee pitcher, who started for the American League team. There was applause for Bill Terry, of the Giants, playing first base for the National League team. Al Simmons, the slugging White Sox outfielder, was noisily received. He was the most popular man in the balloting by which the teams were selected. But when the ball game was played, a bulky, pigeon-toed man in the plain white home uniform of the New York Yankees was the life of the party.

When it was all over there were no stars on this ball field, only Ruth, the old Bambino. Ruth, thirty-nine years old, playing his twentieth season of major league baseball, approaching the end of his long and spectacular career, stepped into the only game of its kind ever held, and ruled it with a regal swish of his mighty bat.

He Meets Everybody's Hopes

The American League team won the game by a score of 4 to 2. But in this convention of celebrated ballplayers, where personalities had an important effect upon the sentiments of the crowd, Ruth was the main show. He did what every one expected him to do. He hit a home run and virtually won the ball game.

Frank Frisch, of the St. Louis Cardinals, playing second base for the National League, also made a homer. But it was just a homer, whereas the Babe's hit was the fulfillment of a hope, a kingly gesture made by the king himself.

The Babe became headman of this galaxy of stars in the third inning. Bill Hallahan, the lefthander of the St. Louis Cardinals, had walked Charley Gehringer, of the Detroit Tigers. It was Hallahan's fourth base on balls. He was wild. He had pitched two balls and one strike to Ruth. The fourth was a cripple coming up and an American League rabbit going away. The Babe smacked it solidly on a line into the lower right-field stands. The crowd stood up and roared.

Gehringer and Ruth circled the bases. And the score was 3 to 0. That hit decided the game, because the National League made two runs in the sixth off Alvin Crowder, a right-hander representing the Washington Senators.

Gomez, .093 Hitter, Singles

Excepting Ruth's homer, a single he made in the fifth and a catch he made in the eighth, the most interesting thing about this game was the batting of two pitchers—Gomez and Lon Warneke, a righthander from the Cubs, who took Hallahan's place in the midst of the third inning.

The great Gomez, a .093 hitter, singled clean into center field on his only time at bat and drove in the American League's first run after Hallahan had walked two men in the second.

Warneke, coming to bat with one out in the National League's half of the sixth, dumped a triple alongside the right-field foul line and scored his side's first run. It was in this inning that Frisch hit his homer. All told, the National's made eight hits off Gomez, Crowder and Bob Grove, the star lefthander of the Philadelphia Athletics, but those two hits were all that counted in the scoring.

Hallahan Walks Five Men

The American League players started off in front, encouraged by Hallahan's wildness, and they remained there, warding off attacks in the sixth and seventh. No sooner had the National League scored in the sixth than the American League got back a run on hits by Joe Cronin, manager and shortstop of the Senators, and Earl Averill, of the Cleveland Indians, batting for Crowder.

The Americans made nine hits off Hallahan, Warneke and Carl Hubbell, the New York Giants' ace left-hander. But they profited by Hallahan's liberality. He walked five men. Two of his walkers scored. Then, of course, there was Ruth's homer.

There was not so much hitting in this game as one might expect from a gathering of so many powerful batsmen. If Hallahan had not been wild it would have been a different ball game.

No one knew until game-time who was going to pitch. The batting orders previously announced were made up by the votes of the fans and were not adhered to either by Connie Mack, the veteran manager of the Philadelphia Athletics, who guided the American League team, or by John McGraw, retired manager of the Giants, who directed the National League team.

All Big League Games Off

The American League stars appeared dressed in the uniforms of their respective teams. They were the home team. The National League men were dressed alike in gray uniforms, with blue caps and socks, all supplied for this occasion. And it was an occasion. All league games were called off today and some of yesterday's were postponed to give the players time to travel here and home again.

World Series regulations prevailed in the seating arrangements. No spectators were allowed on the field and no one stood in the back or sat in the aisles. There were four umpires, two from each league. The American League ball was used in the first four and a half innings and the National League ball in the last four innings. An American League umpire officiated behind the plate for the first half of the game and a National League umpire for the last half. The proceeds of the game will be turned over to the Association of Professional Baseball Players of America. The athletes received nothing except their expenses.

Looking back, it is regrettable from a National League standpoint that Hallahan started. He walked Gehringer in the first. He walked Dykes and Cronin in the second. Two men were out and it seemed reasonable to suppose that Gomez, who had made only

(Continued on page eighteen)

Game Nets $42,000 For Needy Players

CHICAGO, July 6 (AP).—Needy, retired baseball players were the real winners of today's all-star game between the National and American Leagues.

Gross receipts totaled $52,000, with net receipts estimated at approximately $42,000, which will go to the National Association of Professional Baseball Players, which was formed to help old players in want. The official attendance was 49,200.

Regular admission prices—55-cent bleachers, $1.10 grandstand tickets and $1.65 box seats—were charged, accounting for the low gross.

Score of All-Star 'Game of Century'

National League

	AB.	R.	H.	O.	A.	E.	HR.	3B.	2B.	BB.	SB.	SO.	Ave.
Martin, 3b., St. Louis	4	0	0	0	3	0	0	0	0	0	0	1	.000
Frisch, 2b., St. Louis	4	1	2	5	3	0	1	0	0	0	0	0	.500
Klein, rf., Philadelphia	4	0	1	3	0	0	0	0	0	0	0	0	.250
P. Waner, lf., Pittsburgh	0	0	0	0	0	0	0	0	0	0	0	0	.000
Hafey, lf., Cincinnati	4	0	1	0	0	0	0	0	0	0	0	0	.250
Terry, 1b., New York	4	0	2	7	2	0	0	0	0	0	0	0	.500
Berger, cf., Boston	4	0	0	4	0	0	0	0	0	0	0	0	.000
Bartell, ss., Philadelphia	2	0	0	0	3	0	0	0	0	0	0	1	.000
†Traynor, Pittsburgh	1	0	1	0	0	0	0	0	1	0	0	0	1.000
HUBBELL, p., New York	0	0	0	0	0	0	0	0	0	0	0	0	.000
‡Cuccinello, Brooklyn	1	0	0	0	0	0	0	0	0	0	0	1	.000
J. Wilson, c., St. Louis	1	0	0	2	0	0	0	0	0	0	0	0	.000
*O'Doul, New York	1	0	0	0	0	0	0	0	0	0	0	0	.000
Hartnett, c., Chicago	1	0	0	2	0	0	0	0	0	0	0	1	.000
HALLAHAN, p., St. Louis	1	0	0	1	0	0	0	0	0	0	0	0	.000
WARNEKE, p., Chicago	1	1	1	0	0	0	0	1	0	0	0	0	1.000
English, ss., Chicago	1	0	0	0	0	0	0	0	0	0	0	0	.000
Totals	34	2	8	24	11	0	1	1	1	0	0	4	.235

*O'Doul batted for Wilson in sixth inning.
†Traynor batted for Bartrell in seventh inning.
‡Cuccinello batted for Hubbell in ninth inning.

American League

	AB.	R.	H.	O.	A.	E.	HR.	3B.	2B.	BB.	SB.	SO.	Ave.
Chapman, lf., rf., New York	5	0	1	1	0	0	0	0	0	0	0	1	.200
Gehringer, 2b., Detroit	3	1	0	1	3	0	0	0	0	2	1	0	.000
Ruth, rf., New York	4	1	2	1	0	0	1	0	0	0	0	2	.500
West, cf., St. Louis	0	0	0	0	0	0	0	0	0	0	0	0	.000
Gehrig, 1b., New York	2	0	0	12	0	1	0	0	0	2	0	1	.000
Simmons, cf., lf., Chicago	4	0	1	4	0	0	0	0	0	0	0	0	.250
Dykes, 3b., Chicago	3	1	2	2	4	0	0	0	0	1	0	0	.667
Cronin, ss., Washington	3	1	1	2	4	0	0	0	0	1	0	0	.333
R. Ferrell, c., Boston	3	0	0	4	0	0	0	0	0	0	0	0	.000
GOMEZ, p., New York	1	0	1	0	0	0	0	0	0	0	0	0	1.000
CROWDER, p., Washington	1	0	0	0	0	0	0	0	0	0	0	0	.000
§Averill, Cleveland	1	0	1	0	0	0	0	0	0	0	0	0	1.000
GROVE, p., Philadelphia	1	0	0	0	0	0	0	0	0	0	0	0	.000
Totals	31	4	9	27	11	1	1	0	0	6	1	4	.290

§Averill batted for Crowder in sixth inning.

National League	0 0 0	0 0 2	0 0 0	—2
American League	0 1 2	0 0 1	0 0 x	—4

Runs batted in—Martin, Frisch, Ruth (2), Gomez, Averill. Sacrifice—R. Ferrell. Double plays—Bartell, Frisch and Terry; Dykes and Gehrig. Left on bases—National League, 5; American League, 10. Bases on balls—Off Hallahan, 5; off Hubbell, 1. Struck out—By Hallahan, 1; by Warneke, 2; by Hubbell, 1; by Gomez, 1; by Grove, 3. Hits—Off Hallahan, 2 in 2 (none out in third); off Warneke, 6 in 4; off Hubbell, 1 in 2; off Gomez, 2 in 3; off Crowder, 3 in 3; off Grove, 3 in 3. Winning pitcher—Gomez. Losing pitcher—Hallahan. Umpires—Dinneen (A. L.) at the plate, Klem (N. L.)

Stars of the All-Stars in Inter-League Baseball

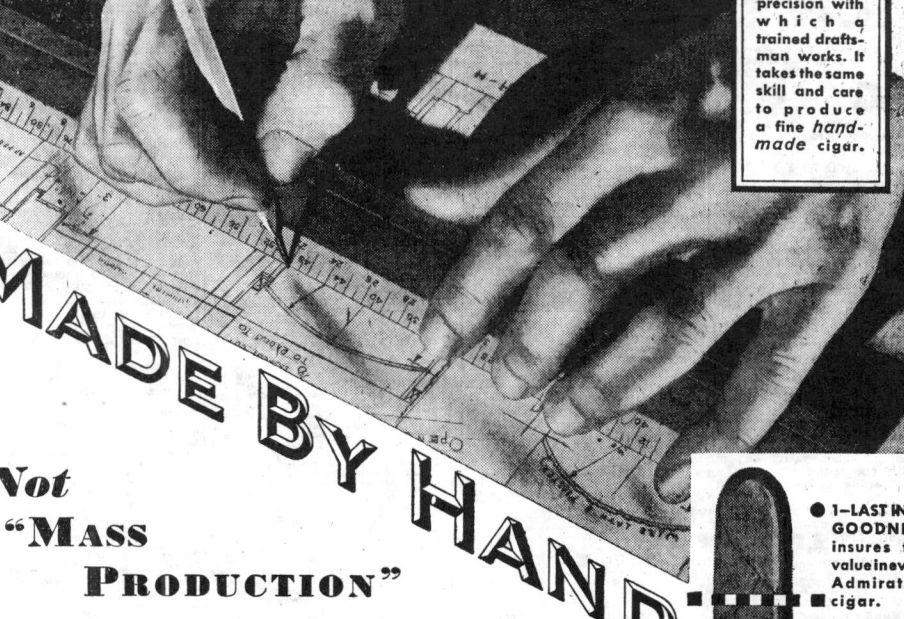

Babe Ruth, whose crashing home run clinched the game for the American League team, and, surrounding him in insets, Gomez (upper left), who pitched three innings for the American Leaguers and drove in one run; Terry (upper right), who made two hits in four times at bat for the National League team, and Frisch (lower right), who made a home run for the National Leaguers, but a home run which did not count as heavily as Ruth's

Play-by-Play Description Of Inter-League Struggle

* * *

CHICAGO, July 6 (AP).—The play-by-play detail of the game today between all-star teams of the American League and the National League, which was won by the American League, 4—2, follows:

First Inning

National League—Martin grounded out, Cronin to Gehrig. Frisch went out the same way. Cronin made a fine running, one-handed catch of Klein's short fly. No runs, no hits, no errors, none left.

American League—Chapman was thrown out by Martin. Gehringer was the first player to reach base, drawing a walk with a three and two count as Hallahan's slant zoomed in above his neck. The crowd roared as Ruth came to bat. After feeding Ruth three straight balls, Hallahan got him with three straight strikes, the last one called. On the last strike Gehringer stole second. Gehrig was out, Terry to Hallahan, who covered first. No runs, no hits, no errors, one left.

Second Inning

National League—Hafey's pop fly fell safe for a single back of second as Gehringer missed it after a hard run backward. Terry hit the first pitch for a single to left, Hafey stopping at second. Berger lined to Dykes, who threw to Gehrig to double Terry. Bartell struck out on three pitched balls, missing Gomez's curves by a wide margin. No runs, two hits, no errors, one left.

American League—Simmons flied high to Berger. Dykes walked. Cronin also walked on a count of 4 to 1. The National League infield gathered about Hallahan as McGraw waved two pitchers into action in the bullpen. Rick Ferrell flied to Klein and both runners stuck to their bases. Lefty Gomez drew first blood by slapping a hard single to short left center, scoring Dykes. Cronin stopped at second. Chapman forced Gomez, Bartell to Frisch. One run, one hit, no errors, two left.

Third Inning

National League—Dykes took J. Wilson's slow roller and threw him out. Hallahan got a big hand as he came to bat. Simmons made a fast dash to right center to get Bill's high one. Cronin went back on the grass to catch Martin's high pop fly. No runs, no hits, no errors, none left.

American League—Gehringer drew another walk with a 4—1 count. Ruth, with the count 2 and 1, hoisted one of Hallahan's slants into the lower right field grandstand seats for a home run, scoring Gehringer ahead of him. The crowd gave the Babe a tremendous ovation as he doffed his cap and cantered around the bases with a wide grin on his face. Eddie Collins, coach of the Americans, did an Indian dance as Ruth strutted his specialty. Gehrig drew still another walk and Hallahan went to the showers. Out of the bullpen strode Lonnie Warneke, pride of the Chicago Cubs pitching staff, to replace him. Simmons hit into a lightning double play, Bartell to Frisch to Terry. Dykes singled sharply past Martin. Cronin flied to Berger. Two runs, two hits, no errors, one left.

Fourth Inning

National League—Alvin Crowder, right-handed star of the Washington Senators, replaced Gomez on the mound for the American League. Simmons made a running catch in left center to haul down Frisch's long drive. Klein tapped along the first-base line and was out, Gehrig, unassisted. Hafey fouled out to Dykes. No runs, no hits, no errors, none left.

American League—Rick Ferrell flied to Klein in short right. Frisch tossed out Crowder. Martin threw out Chapman on a fast play. It was the first time the Americans had gone out in order. No runs, no hits, no errors, none left.

Fifth Inning

National League—Gehringer threw out Terry. Cronin stopped Berger's hard smash and tossed to Gehrig, who made a stretching one-hand catch for later and hung on to the ball. No run, no hits, one error, none left.

American League—The National League ball was now put into play and Bill Klem, dean of the National League umpires, went behind the plate. Gehringer flied deep to Berger. Babe Ruth got another big ovation and responded by dumping a short fly to center field for a single. Gehrig struck out, swinging from the heels at the last strike. Simmons sent Ruth to second with a sizzling single past Martin. Dykes forced Simmons, Bartell to Frisch. No runs, two hits, no errors, two left.

Sixth Inning

National League—Lefty O'Doul, of the New York Giants, 1932 National League batting champion, batted for Wilson and was an easy victim, rolling to Gehringer, who got him at first. Warneke dropped a high one to Ruth in short right and the Babe missed it after a mighty lunge. Seeing the break, Warneke dashed all the way to third for a triple, giving the National League fans their first real chance to cheer. Warneke scored as Dykes threw out Martin. Frisch hit a long home run over Ruth's head into the rightfield grandstand seats. Klein kept the rally alive with a whistling single to centerfield. Dykes threw out Hafey. Two runs, three hits, no errors, one left.

American League—Gabby Hartnett, Chicago Cubs' backstop, went in to catch for the Nationals. Cronin singled past second. Rick Ferrell sacrificed and was out, Terry to Frisch, who covered first. Earl Averill, of Cleveland, batted for Crowder. Averill singled through the box, scoring Cronin. Chapman caught the National infield asleep and laid down a perfect bunt along the third-base line, making first easily as Martin stumbled after fielding the ball. Averill stopped at second. Klein made a fine catch of a long foul by Gehringer, and Averill had lots of time to make third after the catch. Chapman stayed on first. Ruth struck out as the crowd howled. One run, three hits, no errors, two left.

Seventh Inning

National League—Lefty Grove, of the Athletics, took the mound for the Americans with his fire ball. Terry greeted him with a looping single to left center. Berger forced Terry, Cronin to Gehringer. Pie Traynor, of the Pirates batted for Bartell. Traynor hit a long double to center that Simmons lunged at and just missed. Berger stopped at third. Hartnett, a notorious victim of Grove's slants in the 1929 World Series, struck out. Woody English, Cub shortstop, batted for Warneke. English hit a high fly to Simmons. No runs, two hits, no errors, two left.

American League—Carl Hubbell, Giants' southpaw, took up the pitching for the Nationals; English replaced Bartell at short. Gehrig walked on four pitched balls. Simmons forced Gehrig, Martin to Frisch. Dykes singled past third, Simmons halting at second. Cronin fouled to Terry. Frisch threw out Rick Ferrell. No runs, one hit, no errors, two left.

Eighth Inning

National League—Martin was called out on strikes. Frisch, batting right-handed, sent a hot grounder toward Gehrig, but it bounded away from him with a freak hop for a single. Klein flied deep to Simmons. Ruth leaned back against the right-field wall to make a pretty catch of Hafey's long drive. No runs, one hit, no errors, one left.

American League—Paul Waner, of Pittsburgh, went to right field for the Nationals, replacing Klein. Grove was out, Terry unassisted. Chapman struck out. Hubbell was clipping the corners

Louis, went to center field, Chapman moved to right and Simmons to left for the Americans. Gehringer threw out Terry. Chapman came in fast with a nice run and speared Berger's low drive. Tony Cuccinello, of Brooklyn, batted for English. Cuccinello struck out. No runs, no hits, no errors, none left.

Weather and Setting Perfect For Baseball's Day of Days

* * *

CHICAGO, July 6.—Fortune smiled on baseball today. Perfect weather, a perfect setting and a perfect crowd all awaited the all-star teams of the American League and the National League, when they moved out on Comiskey Field for the "game of the century." There were 49,000 paid admissions—the capacity of the park. And it was a crowd that came from every corner of the land.

The National League players were dressed alike in specially made gray uniforms, with dark blue caps and blue sox. The American Leaguers wore the white uniforms of the teams to which they belong.

The uniform dress of the National League was swanky; but the individual costumes of the American Leaguers were more in keeping with the spirit of the game.

* * *

Neither John McGraw nor Connie Mack wore a uniform. McGraw was dressed in a brown sack suit, Mack in a dark suit with panama hat.

* * *

While the National Leaguers were posing for a group picture, Ben Chapman, of the Yankees, hit four consecutive balls into the left field stands and Jimmy Foxx, of the A's, hit one up against the front of the left field balcony. The massed photographers had trouble getting the Nationals to "look right here, please."

* * *

Ed Rommel, of the A's, pitched in batting practice for the American Leaguers. Bill Walker, of the Cardinals, pitched to the National Leaguers.

* * *

Arthur Fletcher, of the Yankees, and Eddie Collins, of the Red Sox, were Connie Mack's assistants. Collins, who is general manager of the Red Sox, wore a uniform for the first time since he left the A's.

* * *

McGraw's assistants were Bill McKechnie, manager of the Braves, and Max Carey, manager of the Dodgers. Andy Lotshaw, of the Cubs, acted as trainer for the National League team. Ed Schacht, of the White Sox, did the rubbing for the American League.

* * *

Bill Walker, the batting practice pitcher, was the only National Leaguer who was out of style. He wore his Cardinal uniform.

* * *

The Yankees had six men on the American League team. The pickers might as well have picked three more and let the Yankees play the National League.

* * *

Each team had a manager playing in the infield—Joe Cronin at shortstop for the Americans, manager of the Senators, and Bill Terry at first for the Nationals' manager of the Giants.

* * *

McGraw and Mack have matched wits three times in World Series. Connie won two of them.

* * *

Connie Mack did not enter his team's dressing room before the game. He never does, even at home in Philadelphia.

* * *

Other major league stars, not playing in this game, paid to see it.

* * *

Tickets were mailed to people in forty-six states and Canada.

* * *

The National Leaguers took fielding practice first. Both Traynor and Martin worked at third base. Max Carey wielded the bat.

* * *

Eddie Collins batted to the American League fielders.

* * *

Bill Terry acted as captain of the Nationals. Eddie Collins represented the Americans.

* * *

Joe Cronin handled the National Leaguers in the first inning. He threw out Martin and Frisch and went to left to catch Klein's liner in his gloved hand.

* * *

As was expected, both line-ups, as previously announced, were changed. Martin played third for the Nationals and led off. Ben Chapman led off for the Americans.

* * *

Gehringer was the first player to reach first. He walked in the first inning.

* * *

This was the first time Ruth played right field in this park. It also was the first time Chapman played in left field in this park.

* * *

It was perhaps fitting that the first home run in this "ball game of the century" should be made by the greatest home-run hitter of all time—Babe Ruth. He drove the ball on a line into the right field stands in the third inning.

* * *

After walking Gehringer, throwing a home-run ball to Ruth and walking Gehrig, Hallahan was taken out. Lon Warneke, of the Chicago Cubs, took his place on the mound.

* * *

Alvin Crowder, a right-hander of the Washington Senators, replaced Gomez in the fourth inning for no reason except to keep Vernon from doing too much work.

* * *

Frisch, batting left-handed, made Simmons hurry to catch his line drive in the fourth. Klein, a slugger, bunted and was tagged out by Gehrig.

* * *

Cronin bobbled Berger's grounder in the fifth, but Gehrig made a fine play, picking the throw out of the dirt for a put-out.

* * *

Five hits were made with the American League ball. The American Leaguers made three, including Ruth's home run. The National leaguers made two singles. With this ball Hallahan issued five bases on balls and Gomez and Crowder issued none.

* * *

Martin slipped and sat down with Chapman's bunt in the sixth. Even if he had not slipped, the speedy Chapman would have been safe.

* * *

Babe Ruth retired from the game in the ninth and the American League outfield shifted. Simmons went to left field, Chapman to right and Sam West of the Browns, came in and played center. As far as the National Leaguers were concerned, Ruth left the game seven innings too late.

RUD RENNIE.

Bisons Defeat Bears, 5 to 2, Square Series

Wilson Betters Weaver to Score His 7th Victory; Victors Steal Five Bases

By The Associated Press

BUFFALO, July 6.—Johnny Wilson bested Big Jim Weaver to score his seventh victory here this afternoon as the Buffalo Bisons squared their series with the league-leading Newark Bears through a 5-to-2 triumph. Timely hitting by Carnegie and Koenecke and some fast base running which saw the Bisons pilfer five bases, three of them by Koenecke, were outstanding.

The score:

NEWARK (I. L.)	ab	r	h	po	a	e
Neun, 1b.	4	0	0	7	0	0
Saltzgvr, 3b	5	0	3	2	0	0
Rolfe, ss.	4	1	1	1	2	1
Hoag, cf.	4	0	0	3	0	0
Selkirk, rf.	3	1	0	2	0	0
Watwood, lf.	4	0	2	1	1	0
Olsen, 2b.	4	0	1	1	1	0
Kies, c.	4	0	1	7	1	0
WEAVER, p	3	0	1	0	1	0
*Barton	1	0	0	0	0	0
Totals	36	2	9	24	6	1

BUFFALO (I. L.)	ab	r	h	po	a
Mulleavy, ss	4	2	2	1	1
Thompsn, 2b	4	0	1	2	0
Koenecke, cf	4	1	2	4	0
Tucker, rf.	3	1	0	3	0
Carnegie, lf	3	1	1	2	0
Crouse, c.	3	0	1	9	0
English, 3b.	3	0	0	1	1
Tarr, 1b.	3	0	0	4	1
WILSON, p	3	0	0	1	1
Totals	30	5	7	27	4

*Batted for Weaver in ninth inning.

Newark	011	000	000	—2
Buffalo	000	400	01x	—5

Runs batted in—Watwood, Koenecke (2), Carnegie (2), English, Weaver. Two-base hits—Saltzgaver, Weaver, Mulleavy. Stolen bases—Mulleavy, Koenecke (3), Tucker. Sacrifice—Hoag. Double plays—Watwood and Kies; Kies and Saltzgaver. Left on bases—Buffalo, 2; Newark, 11. Bases on balls—Off Wilson, 3; off Weaver, 1. Struck out—By Weaver, 5; by Wilson, 7. Umpires—Parkre and Powell. Time—2:03.

Skeeters Collect 14 Hits, Rout Montreal, 11 to 3

MONTREAL, July 6 (AP).—Jersey City evened its four-game series with the Montreal Royals today by humbling the Canadians 11 to 3.

The Skeeters pounded Warren Ogden and McKeithan for fourteen hits.

The score:

JERSEY CITY (I. L.)	ab	r	h	po	a	e
Baker, ss.	5	1	2	4	6	0
Walker, cf.	3	2	3	2	0	0
Clancy, 1b.	4	2	2	13	2	0
Rosenfi'd, lf.	5	1	2	0	0	0
Fitzger'd, rf.	4	1	2	2	0	0
Brown, 3b.	4	0	1	1	3	0
Rensa, c.	5	0	0	3	0	0
Calleran, 2b.	4	2	1	0	3	0
CASC'LA, p	5	2	1	2	1	0
Totals	30	11	14	27	15	0

MONTREAL (I. L.)	ab	r	h	po	a
Gautreau, 2b	5	0	1	1	6
Finney, 1.	3	0	0	2	1
Ripple, cf.	4	0	1	1	0
Roettger, 1b	4	2	3	12	1
Winsett, rf.	4	0	1	1	1
Tate, c.	4	1	2	3	1
Regan, 3b.	4	0	0	3	1
Goldman, ss.	3	0	2	3	2
OGDEN, p.	1	0	0	0	1
McKeith'n, p	1	0	0	1	2
*Shiver	1	0	0	0	0
Totals	34	3	10	27	17

*Batted for McKeithan in ninth inning.

Jersey City	003	006	020	—11
Montreal	010	001	001	—3

Runs batted in—Walker (2), Clancy (2), Rosenfeld (3), Fitzgerald (3), Tate, Winsett, Goldman. Two-base hits—Walker, Fitzgerald, Roettger (3), Winsett, Rosenfeld. Three-base hits — Baker, Tate. Stolen bases—Fitzgerald, Brown. Double plays—Baker and Clancy; Brown, Baker and Clancy; Calleran, Baker and Clancy. Left on bases—Jersey City, 7; Montreal, 7. Bases on balls—Off Ogden, 4; off McKeithan, 2; off Cascarella, 3. Struck out—By Ogden, 1; by Cascarella, 2; by McKeithan, 1. Hits—Off Ogden, 9 in 5 innings (none out in sixth); off McKeithan, 5 in 4. Passed ball—Rensa. Losing pitcher—Ogden. Umpires—Hubbard and Jorda. Time—2:01.

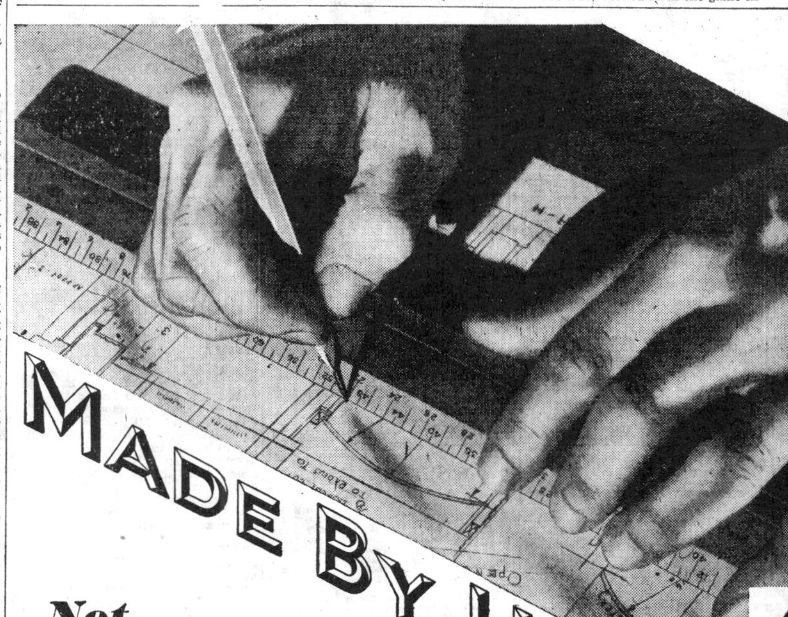

Leslie's 'Wicket Error' Ruins Beck and Dodgers Bow to Braves by 2 to 1

TRIPLE BY LEE BIG FACTOR IN BOSTON'S WIN

Rosy Ryan Used as Finishing Pitcher for 3d in Row; Hogan, Nicked on Wrist, Retires

By SID MERCER.
N. Y. American Staff Correspondent.

BOSTON, Mass., Aug. 5—Elmer The Great Beck, functioning in his finest form, staged a one-man insurrection against the Braves today but at the finished was propped up against the execution wall and slain by a poisoned bullet fired by one of his own men.

The Braves thus made it five out of six on the Flatbush diet by a count of 2 to 1? taking the last four scores almost as anaemic as today's figures. Like vultures they picked on Brooklyn bones and managed to glut themselves on starvation rations.

Tonight the Dodgers fled the city but they are not goin- anywhere except into more trouble for they encounter the Giants twice tomorrow at Ebbets Field.

Beck went the way of other Brooklyn pitchers after he had scored the run that would have earned him a shut-out with good support. Sambo Leslie was the scalawag who tripped Elmer up with a timely error which let in the second and winning Boston run in the sixth inning. Elmer must accept part of the blame himself for with two out and none of the Braves off the reservation he opened the stockade gate by walking Pinkey Whitney.

LEE DELIVERS TRIPLE.

Hal Lee followed with a drive to right field which caromed off the fence and shadow boxed with Joe Hutcheson until Whitney had delivered the tieing run and Lee was safe on third base. It was a legitimate triple and set the stage for Hargrave, the Boston catcher, who slapped a smart grounder toward first base. Leslie squatted but not far enough. His legs formed a wicket through which the ball bowled out to right field and Lee strolled in with the bad news.

Our brave boys contributed greatly to the glory of Boston pitchers in this series. In the last four games they collected just two runs. They had gone 32 consecutive innings with only one run when they scored in the sixth inning today. Their record in reverse is now 23 out of the last 30. They outhit the enemy, 10 to 6, today and still wound up behind the eight-ball.

Not only did Elmer pitch with great aplomb, but he seemed to be the only Dodger who could do any serious business with the ancient Huck Betts, who was flipping them for the other side. Elmer doubled in the third inning for Brooklyn's first hit, but was left on third base when Buzz Boyle grounded to Betts and Frederick flied to Moore.

Again in the sixth he led off with a base knock to left, moved up on a sacrifice and scored on a lusty double by Johnny Frederick. There was only one out and prospects were bright but Stripp grounded to Maranville and Old Hutch fouled to Hargrave. Hutch made two of Brooklyn's ten hits but they were wasted.

OUTEN SWINGS FOR BECK.

With a perfect hitting record Elmer was benched in the seventh with runners on first and second bases with two out. Chick Outen swung for him and poled a fly to Moore. That brought Rosy Ryan in as a finishing pitcher in his third consecutive game. Rosy did his part but the Dodgers could not quite reach far enough in the eighth and ninth.

With two gone in the eighth, Stripp and Hutcheson singled, but Leslie's effort was a fly to Berger.

One was out in the ninth when Hack Wilson delivered a single as a pinch hitter for Wright. It was Ladies' Day with an attendance of 7,000 and Hack is the ladies' favorite. Lopez followed with a single to left field and that was all, there wasn't any more. With the tieing run once more languishing on second base, Taylor, batting in Ryan's spot, reared a tall fly for Jordan and Boyle, after getting a 3 and 2 count, splashed weakly to Betts.

There was one Boston casualty. Shanty Hogan was nicked on the wrist in the fifth inning and forced to discontinue. His substitute, Hargrave, drove in the winning run.

Heigh, Ho. Alackaday. Things go along that way for the Dodgers and when they change they change for the worse.

Southern Association.

New Orleans	...0000100312	—7 13 1
Atlanta	4000100000	—5 10 0

Galehouse, Ferrin, Messenger and Autry; Holloway, Moore and Neisler.

Birmingham	000000003	—3 5 0
Knoxville	000200120	—5 7 0

Touchstone and Berres; Hulvey and Head.

Little Rock	102100012	—7 10 1
Chattanooga	000002021	—5 14 2

Willoughby, Sharpe, Nugent and Wise; Dudley, Barfoot, McColl and Maple.

Second game:

Little Rock	0000000	—0 4 3
Chattanooga	.........000007x	—7 9 1

Nugent and Goebel; Linke and Klumpp.

Memphis	000002111	—5 14 1
Nashville	......30203061x	—9 16 1

Griffin, Bean and Berger; Cuoto; Chaplin, Reid and Baker.

It's Our Mr. Babe Ruth, Stealing His Fourth Base of the Season

YANKEE STADIUM—The old master gave the Yankee fans a thrill as he completed this slide in the sixth inning of yesterday's game with the Athletics. He was safe. He rarely tries any antics on the bases these days, and this was only his fourth steal of the year. If he had only stolen "Lefty" Gomez instead of second base, it would have been much better, for "Lefty" blew up in the eighth inning and the A's won, 8 to 3.

N. Y. American Staff Photo.

Elmer Great, but—

BROOKLYN	ab	r	h	o	a
Boyle,lf	4	0	0	1	0
Fred'k,cf	4	0	1	6	0
Stripp,3b	4	0	1	3	0
Hutch'n,rf	4	0	2	2	0
Leslie,1b	4	0	1	5	0
Cuc'lo,2b	3	0	0	4	2
Wright,ss	3	0	1	1	1
b-Wilson	1	0	1	0	0
c-Flowers	0	0	0	0	0
Lopez,c	4	0	1	2	1
Beck,p	2	1	2	0	2
a-Outen	1	0	0	0	0
Ryan,p	0	0	0	0	1
d-Taylor	1	0	0	0	0
Totals	35	1	10	24	7

BOSTON	ab	r	h	o	a
Urb'ski,ss	4	0	0	1	1
Jordan,1b	4	0	1	9	0
Berger,cf	4	0	1	4	1
Moore,rf	4	0	1	4	0
Whitney,3b	3	1	1	1	2
Lee,lf	4	1	1	4	0
Hogan,c	1	0	0	1	0
e-Cantwell	0	0	0	0	0
Hargrave,c	2	0	0	1	0
Mar'lle,2b	2	0	0	2	2
Betts,p	2	0	1	0	3
Totals	30	2	6	27	9

a-Batted for Beck in 7th.
b-Batted for Wright in 9th.
c-Ran for Wilson in 9th.
d-Batted for Ryan in 9th.
e Ran for Hogan in fifth.

Brooklyn	0	0	0	0	0	1	0	0	0	—1
Boston..	0	0	0	0	0	2	0	0	x	—2

Errors—Leslie, Beck. Runs batted in—Frederick, Lee. Two-base hits—Beck, Frederick. Three-base hit—Lee. Sacrifices—Boyle, Maranville. Double play—Berger to Jordan. Left on bases—Brooklyn, 9; Boston, 8. Base on balls—Off Beck, 2; off Betts, 1. Struck out—By Ryan, 1; by Betts, 1. Hits—Off Beck, 4 in 6 innings; off Ryan, 2 in 2 innings. Hit by pitcher—By Beck (Hogan). Losing pitcher—Beck. Umpires—Moran, Reardon and Powell. Time—1:31.

Tigers Trim Indians, 7-1, After Losing by 15-6

DETROIT, Aug. 5 (AP).—Detroit won the secnod game of a twin bill with the Cleveland Indians here today, 7 to 1. Carl Fischer went all the way for the Tigers, allowing only six hits. Detroit knocked Hudlin out of the box as the sixth inning ended. Cleveland won the first game, 15 to 6.

FIRST GAME

CLEVELAND	ab	r	h	o	a
Porter,rf	7	2	1	1	0
Burnett,ss	7	2	2	2	5
Boss,1b	5	1	1	12	0
Averill,cf	6	4	3	8	1
Vosmik,lf	6	1	2	2	1
Hale,2b	5	2	3	8	9
Kamm,3b	6	1	1	1	4
Pytlak,c	6	1	2	5	1
Brown,p	2	0	0	0	2
Bean,p	3	1	2	0	0
a-Galatzer	1	0	1	0	0
Totals	54	15	18	39	23

DETROIT	ab	r	h	o	a
Rogell,ss	7	1	2	6	7
Owen,3b	5	0	0	0	3
Gr'n'g,1b	6	0	2	16	2
Stone,rf	6	1	1	1	0
Fox,cf	6	1	2	6	0
Doljack,lf	6	1	3	1	2
Green'g,1b	6	0	2	15	2
Hayw'h,c	6	1	5	7	0
Bridges,p	4	0	0	0	1
Hoggett,p	0	0	0	0	1
Herring,p	0	0	0	0	0
b-White	1	0	0	0	0
Totals	52	6	17	39	23

a-Batted for Brown in eighth.
b-Batted for Herring in thirteenth.

Cleveland	000	200	103	000	9	—15
Detroit	003	120	000	000	0	— 6

Errors—Burnett 2, Hale, Rogell, Gehringer. Runs batted in—Doljack 3; Hale 3; Porter 2; Pytlak 2; Kamm 2; Gehringer, Greenberg, Vosmik, Boss, Burnett, Averill. Two base hits—Hale 2; Averill 2; Rogell, Doljack, Porter. Three base hits—Doljack, Hayworth. Home run—Hale. Stolen bases—Gehringer, Kamm. Sacrifices—Owen, Bridges. Double plays—Doljack to Gehringer to Greenberg; Gehringer to Rogell to Greenberg; Bridges to Rogell to Greenberg; Rogell to Greenberg; Burnett to Hale to Boss. Left on bases—Cleveland 4; Detroit 11. Base on balls—off Bridges 2; Herring 2; Brown 1; Bean 1. Struck out—by Bridges 6; Bean 3; Brown 1. Hits—off Brown, 13 in 7 innings; Bean, 4 in 6 innings; Bridges, 10 in 10 innings, none out in eleventh; Hogsett, 3 in 2 1-3 innings; Herring, 5 in 2-3 inning. Winning pitcher—Bean. Losing pitcher—Hogsett. Umpires—Owens and Dinneen. Time—2:58.

SECOND GAME

CLEVELAND	ab	r	h	o	a
Porter,rf	4	0	1	2	0
Cissell,ss	5	0	2	2	5
Boss,1b	4	0	1	13	0
Averill,cf	4	0	0	0	0
Vosmik,lf	3	0	1	1	0
Hale,2b	4	0	0	4	4
Kamm,3b	2	0	0	0	2
Spencer,c	4	1	1	2	0
Hudlin,p	1	0	0	0	3
Connally,p	0	0	0	0	0
a-Oulliber	1	0	0	0	0
b-Ferrell	1	0	0	0	0
Totals	33	1	6	24	14

DETROIT	ab	r	h	o	a
Rogell,ss	4	1	2	1	3
Owen,3b	3	1	1	4	3
Geh'ger,2b	4	0	2	2	1
Stone,rf	5	0	1	3	0
Fox,cf	5	1	2	4	0
Doljack,lf	5	1	1	1	0
Green'g,1b	5	2	3	9	0
Pasek,c	5	1	2	3	0
Fischer,p	5	0	0	0	1
Totals	41	7	14	27	8

a Batted for Hudlin in seventh.
b Batted for Connally in ninth.

Cleveland	0	0	0	0	1	0	0	0	0	— 1
Detroit	0	2	0	0	0	2	2	1	x	— 7

Errors—Hale (3), Pasek. Runs batted in—Rogell (2), Gehringer, Stone, Doljack, Pasek, Boss. Two-base hits—Owen, Fox. Sacrifice—Porter. Left on bases—Detroit, 16; Cleveland, 10. Base on balls—Off Fischer, 4; Hudlin, 3; Connally, 3. Struck out—By Fischer, 2; Hudlin, 1. Hits—Off Hudlin, 8 in 6 innings; Connally, 6 in 2. Losing pitcher—Hudlin. Umpires—Dinneen and Owens. Time—2:11.

GIANTS AND PHILS SPLIT TWIN BILL

Continued from Page 17.

Bartell gave the Phils their last tally in the fourth, whereupon O'Doul nullified it with his first home run.

Liska was pitching in the eighth when our side made the game safe with a three-run attack. James opened with a two-bagger, Terry bunted safely and Liska made a wild heave, allowing James to cross the plate. Ott struck out on three slow balls but the same trick failed to work against O'Doul. Lefty picked out a slow one and whanged it over the fence.

Freddie Fitzsimmons did a good job of pitching in the second game and deserved a better fate. He allowed only one run, but two errors of his own making in the fatal eighth inning helped to bring about his downfall.

The Giants took an early lead of three runs when Vergez smacked his homer with two runners aboard in the fourth, but after that they were completely foiled by the southpaw pitching of Roy Hansen.

The Phils picked up an unearned tally in the fifth, largely the result of a misplay by Vergez. Chuck Klein added another to the Philadelphia string with a homer in the sixth—his nineteenth.

The eighth started with a pass to McLeod, who moved ahead on a sacrifice, and took third when Fitz made a wild heave to second. Another wild throw by Fitz put Fullis on base and Klein tied the score with an infield hit. James gummed up another play, filling the bases, and Schulmerich emptied them with a two-bagger to center. Davis drove in the final run with a single against the right wall.

O. K. Then K. O.!

NEW YORK	ab	r	h	o	a
J.Moore,lf	6	2	1	0	0
James,2b	6	2	2	3	8
Terry,1b	6	3	3	10	2
Ott,cf	5	1	2	1	0
O'Doul,rf	5	2	2	2	1
Vergez,3b	4	0	1	3	3
Manc'so,c	4	0	2	3	1
Ryan,ss	5	0	3	3	3
Schum'r,p	5	1	3	2	0
Totals	46	11	19	27	18

PHILADELPHIA	ab	r	h	o	a
McLeod,3b	3	0	1	0	0
b-McCurdy	1	0	0	0	0
Knothe,3b	1	0	0	0	0
Bartell,ss	5	1	2	3	2
Fullis,cf	4	1	2	3	0
Klein,rf	3	0	2	0	0
Schul'h,lf	4	0	1	0	0
Davis,c	4	0	0	10	0
Dugas,1b	4	0	0	9	3
Warner,2b	3	1	2	1	5
Collins,p	2	0	0	1	0
a-Hurst	1	0	1	0	0
Liska,p	1	0	0	0	0
Totals	36	3	11	27	10

a Batted for Collins in sixth.
b Batted for McLeod in sixth.

New York......	2	5	0	0	1	0	0	3	0	—11
Philadelphia....	2	0	0	1	0	0	0	0	0	— 3

Errors—Bartell, McLeod, Liska. Runs batted in—Terry 2, Ott 5, O'Doul 3, Klein, Schulmerich, Bartell. Two-base hits—Ott, Warner, James. Home runs—Ott, O'Doul 2. Double plays—Vergez, James to Terry; Dugas (unassisted). Left on bases—New York, 11; Philadelphia, 9. Base on balls—Off Schumacher, 3; Collins, 3. Struck out—By Schumacher, 3; Collins, 2; Liska, 3. Hits—Off Collins, 12 in 6 innings; Liska, 7 in 3. Passed ball—Davis. Losing pitcher—Collins.

SECOND GAME

NEW YORK.	ab	r	h	o	a
James,2b	3	0	0	3	5
Peel,lf	4	0	0	1	0
Terry,1b	4	1	2	10	1
Ott,cf	4	1	2	2	0
Vergez,3b	4	1	1	0	1
O'Doul,rf	4	0	1	4	0
Rich'rds,c	4	0	1	3	1
Ryan,ss	4	0	0	1	1
Fitz'ns,p	3	0	0	0	3
Bell,p	0	0	0	0	0
Totals	34	3	7	24	12

PHILADELPHIA	ab	r	h	o	a
McLeod,3b	3	1	1	0	3
Bartell,ss	3	0	1	1	3
Fullis,cf	4	1	0	4	0
Klein,rf	3	2	2	2	0
Hurst,1b	4	1	0	16	0
Schul'h,lf	4	2	2	0	0
Davis,c	4	0	1	4	0
Warner,2b	4	0	0	0	6
Hansen,p	3	0	0	0	3
Totals	32	7	7	27	15

New York	0	0	0	3	0	0	0	0	0	—3
Philadelphia	0	0	0	0	1	1	0	5	x	—7

Errors—James, Vergez, Fitzgibbons 2. Runs batted in—Vergez, 3; McLeod; Klein, 2; Schulmerich, 3; Davis. Two base hits—Richards, Schulmerich. Home runs—Vergez, Klein. Sacrifice—Bartell. Double play—Ryan, James to Terry. Left on bases—New York, 5; Philadelphia, 4. Base on balls—Off Hansen, 1; Fitzsimmons, 2. Struck out—By Hansen, 4; Fitzsimmons, 2. Hits—Off Fitzsimmons, 7 in 7 1-3 innings; Bell, 0 in 2-3. Losing pitcher—Fitzsimmons. Umpires—Rigler, Stark and Barr. Time—1:41.

Runs for the Week.

NATIONAL LEAGUE.

Team	S.	M.	T.	W.	T.	F.	S.	Tls.
NEW YORK....	3	x	1	24	x	18	14	60
Pittsburgh	13	x	9	3	1	5	6	37
St. Louis	14	x	3	4	4	4	5	34
Boston	5	x	3	9	3	7	3	30
Philadelphia	3	x	x	14	x	1	10	28
Cincinnati	10	x	1	6	1	x	7	25
Chicago	7	x	3	10	2	x	2	24
BROOKLYN	1	x	x	8	6	1	1	17
Daily totals ..	56	0	20	78	11	36	48	249

AMERICAN LEAGUE.

Team	S.	M.	T.	W.	T.	F.	S.	Tls.
Cleveland	1	8	2	16	7	x	16	50
St. Louis	9	12	5	8	3	x	[illegible]	[illegible]
Chicago	23	x	x	6	x	3	[illegible]	[illegible]
Philadelphia	8	x	x	16	7	x	6	[illegible]
NEW YORK ...	7	13	x	3	0	x	2	[illegible]
Detroit	6	x	x	4	x	9	13	[illegible]
Washington	2	9	x	2	8	x	[illegible]	[illegible]
Boston	6	x	x	1	4	x	2	[illegible]
Daily totals ..	59	42	7	56	28	5	64	261

INTERNATIONAL LEAGUE.

Team	S.	M.	T.	W.	T.	F.	S.	Tls.
NEWARK	14	0	5	9	13	11	15	67
Albany	11	8	1	9	x	16	19	64
Baltimore	21	2	18	5	x	10	4	60
Rochester	13	8	2	11	x	6	3	43
JRESEY CITY ..	10	2	1	13	x	10	5	41
Buffalo	4	7	4	6	x	10	10	41
Montreal	8	0	11	5	6	7	2	39
Toronto	5	4	10	4	x	6	6	35
Daily totals ..	86	31	52	62	19	76	69	395

x—No game.

BEARS TAKE TWO FROM TORONTOS

NEWARK, N. J., Aug. 5 (AP).—The Newark Bears sent their winning streak to eight in a row here today when they captured both ends of double-header from Toronto, 11-3 and 4-3.

The league leaders came from behind in each contest, raking Brame for eleven hits in the opener for five-run rallies in the fifth and eighth frames.

In the nightcap, the Bears tied the score with a three-run rally in the sixth and won out in the seventh when Saltzgaver hit a home run after two out. Neun and Hoag hit for the circuit in the first game.

FIRST GAME

TORONTO	ab	r	h	o	a
Blue,1b	4	0	0	5	1
Lawr'e,cf	4	1	1	1	0
Boone,rf	4	0	1	2	0
Howell,lf	4	1	1	4	0
Mallon,2b	3	1	1	4	5
Rich'on,ss	4	0	0	2	3
Sax,3b	3	0	1	3	1
Smith,c	4	0	2	2	2
Brame,p	3	0	0	1	3
a-Heving	1	0	0	0	0
Totals	34	3	7	24	15

NEWARK	ab	r	h	o	a
Neun,1b	5	2	3	7	0
Rolfe,ss	4	0	1	2	1
Hoag,cf	4	1	1	7	0
Saltzg'r,3b	4	0	1	0	1
Pucc'lli,lf	4	0	0	2	0
Barton,rf	3	2	0	2	0
Schalk,2b	3	2	2	2	2
Kies,c	4	2	2	5	1
Deshong,p	2	2	1	0	1
Totals	33	11	11	27	6

a—Batted for Sax in 9th.

Toronto........	2	0	0	1	0	0	0	0	0	—3
Newark.........	0	0	0	0	5	0	1	5	x	—11

Errors—Sax, Barton. Runs batted in—Howell, Mallon, Sax, Neun (6), Hoag (3), Kies. Two-base hits—Howell, Kies. Three-base hits—Lawrence, Neun. Home runs—Hoag, Neun. Sacrifices—Richardson, Deshong. Double play—Richardson, Mallon, Blue. Left on bases—Toronto, 6; Newark, 4. Base on balls—Off Deshong, 1; Brame, 5. Struck out—By Deshong, 4; Brame, 1. Umpires—Jorda and Nallin. Time—2:05.

SECOND GAME

TORONTO	ab	r	h	o	a
Blue,1b	3	0	1	10	0
Lawr'e,cf	3	0	0	3	0
Boone,rf	4	1	2	0	1
Howell,lf	4	1	0	0	0
Mallon,2b	3	1	1	1	6
Rich'n,ss	2	0	0	1	3
Sax,3b	3	0	0	1	1
Heving,c	2	0	1	4	0
Collier,p	3	0	0	0	1
Totals	27	3	5	x20	12

NEWARK	ab	r	h	o	a
Neun,1b	4	0	1	5	1
Rolfe,ss	3	0	0	2	1
Hoag,cf	4	0	1	5	0
Saltzg'r,3b	3	2	2	1	3
Pucc'lli,lf	3	0	0	0	0
Barton,rf	2	0	1	4	0
Schalk,2b	3	1	2	1	2
Stack,c	3	1	1	2	0
Jablon'ki,p	3	0	1	1	1
Totals	28	4	9	21	7

x—Two out when winning run scored.

Toronto	0	0	3	0	0	0	0	—3
Newark	0	0	0	0	0	3	1	—4

Errors—Puccinelli, Jablonowski. Runs batted in—Mallon 2, Stack 2, Jablonowski, Saltzgaver. Two base hits—Barton, Schalk, Jablonowski. Home runs—Mallon, Saltzgaver. Stolen base—Richardson. Sacrifice—Lawrence. Left on bases—Toronto 7, Newark 7. Base on balls—off Collier 3, Jablonowski 3. Struck out—by Collier 3, Jablonowski 2. Umpires—Nallin and Jorda. Time—1:53.

A'S 7 IN EIGHTH ROUT YANKEES, 8-3

Continued from Page 17.

and Lazerri had contributed another boot.

It was the third straight setback for the Yanks and they now have lost as many home games as they did all last season—fifteen. They are beginning to look even worse under pressure of a tight race than the Cubs looked in the big series last Fall. The last seven meetings with the A's have showed one New York victory, since which they have dropped five in a row to the Mackmen.

Gomez finally blew his own chance of winning by his wildness and the infield cracked with him. The A's needed only five hits to pile up an easy victory with the Yanks going so completely haywire in the clinches.

Mahaffey held the Yankees well in hand, no more than one hit in any inning, until the seventh, when they clustered three hits together for a pair of runs. Then the blow-up, during which Bing Miller swung for Mahaffey. Rube Walberg finished and the Yanks were just as easy for him.

YANKS TAKE LEAD.

Gomez got through the first two innings safely despite the fact that he walked two in each session. He buzzed through the third inning in snappy fashion and then the Yanks picked up a one-run lead in their half. A walk to Combs, Sewell's infield out and Ruth's double to right center were the ingredients.

Another walk by Gomez did no damage in the fourth but it was apparent that he couldn't go on forever and escape. A pass to Bishop in the fifth led up to the tying run. Cramer reached first while Bishop was being retired at second, raced to third on Cochrane's single—the first hit for the A's—and then a walk by Foxx filled the bases.

Gehrig fumbled Coleman's grounder, but could have got his man at first and ended the inning if Gomez had covered the bag. Lefty was dozing, so Coleman was safe and the tying run went over the plate.

The tie persisted until the seventh, when Dickey doubled to right, and scored on Crosetti's double to center. Gomez slapped another run in with a single past second.

GOMEZ EXPLODES.

The two-run lead took a fast fadeout. Gomez opened the door with walks to Johnson and Higgins after Coleman had started the eighth with a fly to Ruth. Williams scored Johnson and sent Higgins around to third with a single which flecked Crosetti's glove. Bing Miller, hitting for Mahaffey, brought Higgins across with a long fly to Combs. This tied the score at 3-3. Bishop's single to right sent Williams to third and Gomez over the hill to the clubhouse, Van Atta replacing him.

A fumble by Crosetti on Cramer's slow grounder kept the rally in motion as Williams streaked home. When Van Atta walked Cochrane, filling the bases, Moore was called in to pitch to Foxx, a right-hand hitter. Jimmy welcomed Cy with a triple to deep center, which swept three runs across, and Foxx followed with the seventh run of the inning when Lazzeri fumbled Coleman's grounder.

Errors Help Senators To Trip Red Sox, 3-2

WASHINGTON, Aug. 5 (AP).—With the aid of two Boston errors and some air-tight pitching in the pinches by Monte Weaver, the Washington Senators today set down the Red Sox for the third successive time, 3 to 2, and rose to the eminence of a four-game lead over the stumbling New York Yankees.

"Dusty" Rhodes, for Boston, allowed only eight hits to the nine given by Weaver, but his own wild throw and one by Hodapp in the third, coupled with singles by Weaver and Myer, contributed directly to the scoring of two Washington runs.

Joe Judge, playing his first full game in the Capital in a foreign uniform after gracing the first base station for the Senators for seventeen years, scored the first Sox run after singling in the first. He crossed the plate on Ferrell's single.

The Sox tied the score in the fourth on singles by Hodapp and Rhodes, but the Senators pushed over the deciding run in the next inning.

Myer, who captured batting honors with three singles for the day, pushed one safely to right. Manush's bunt bounced off Rhodes when he stumbled, sending Myer to third, from where he scored on Dave Harris' single.

BOSTON	ab	r	h	o	a
Werber,ss	4	0	1	2	2
Judge,1b	3	1	1	5	1
Cooke,cf	4	0	1	3	0
R.Joh'n,lf	3	0	1	2	0
Ferrell,c	4	0	2	6	0
Hod'p,2b	4	0	1	3	3
Jolley,rf	4	1	1	1	0
Walters,3b	3	0	0	2	1
Rhodes,p	3	0	1	0	2
a-Seeds	0	0	0	0	0
Totals	32	2	9	24	9

WASHINGTON	ab	r	h	o	a
Myer,2b	4	2	3	7	6
Manush,lf	3	0	2	1	1
Cronin,ss	3	0	0	2	4
Harris,rf	4	0	1	1	0
Schulte,cf	4	0	0	0	0
Kuhel,1b	3	0	1	10	1
Bluege,3b	3	0	0	2	3
Sewell,c	3	0	0	4	2
Weaver,p	3	1	1	0	1
Totals	30	3	8	27	18

a—Ran for Jolley in 9th inning.

Boston 1	0	0	1	0	0	0	0	0	—2	
Washington 0	0	2	0	1	0	0	0	x	—3	

Errors—Hodapp, Walters, Rhodes, Myer. Runs batted in—Ferrell, Cronin, Harris, Rhodes. Two base hit—Werber. Sacrifices—Judge, Manush. Double plays—Werber to Hodapp to Judge; Bluege to Myer to Kuhel; Rhodes to Hodapp to Judge; Bluege to Myer to Kuhel. Left on bases—Boston, 5; Washington, 7. Base on balls—Off Rhodes, 2: Struck out—By Rhodes, 4; Weaver, 4. Hit by pitcher—By Weaver (R. Johnson). Rhodes (Bluege). Passed ball—Ferrell. Umpires—Summers and McGowan. Time—1:48.

Wells' Double in 12th Wins for Browns, 10-9

ST. LOUIS, Aug 5 (AP)—Pitcher Ed Wells' double in the twelfth inning, scoring Jim Levey, who had singled, gave the St. Louis Browns a 10 to 9 victory over the Chicago White Sox in the series opener here today. The Browns scored two runs on three hits in the ninth to tie the count and to prolong the game.

CHICAGO	ab	r	h	o	a
Swa'on,rf	7	1	1	3	0
Haas,cf	5	2	2	5	0
Webb,1b	5	1	1	14	0
Sim'ns,lf	6	1	1	3	0
Ap'ing,ss	6	3	5	3	4
Dykes,3b	5	1	2	0	2
Hayes,2b	6	0	2	2	8
Berry,c	6	0	1	4	1
Durham,p	2	0	1	0	0
Heving,p	3	0	0	0	0
Faber,p	1	0	0	0	1
Totals	52	9	16	x34	16

ST. LOUIS	ab	r	h	o	a
Storti,3b	5	1	1	1	4
West,cf	5	3	4	4	0
Reyn'ds,lf	6	1	1	5	0
Campb'l,rf	5	0	1	5	0
Burns,1b	5	2	3	17	0
Melillo,2b	6	2	3	1	7
Shea,c	6	0	0	2	1
Levey,ss	6	1	1	1	2
Hadley,p	2	0	1	0	1
McDon'd,p	0	0	0	0	0
Stiles,p	0	0	0	0	0
Wells,p	2	0	1	0	0
a-Garms	1	0	0	0	0
b-Gullic	1	0	0	0	0
Totals	50	10	16	36	15

a-Batted for McDonald in 6th.
b-Batted for Stiles in 9th.
x-One out when winning run scored.

Chicago.	1	0	0	1	4	3	0	0	0	0	0	0	— 9
St. Louis	1	0	2	2	0	2	0	0	2	0	0	1	—10

Errors—Webb, Appling 2, Storti 2. Runs batted in—Appling 3, Reynolds, West 2, Hayes 2, Levey 2, Hadley, Dykes 2, Hadley, Dykes 2, Berry, Simmons, Burns, Shea, Wells. Two base hits—Appling 3, Reynolds, Hadley, Swanson, Simmons, West, Wells. Three base hits—West 2. Home run—West. Sacrifice—West. Double play—Dykes, Hayes and Webb. Left on bases—Chicago 10; St. Louis, 10. Base on balls—off Faber, 3; Hadley, 3. Struck out—by Heving, 4; Hadley, 1. Hits—off Durham 6 in 3; Heving 7 in 5 2-3; Faber 3 in 2 2-3; Hadley 13 in 5 2-3; McDonald 1 in 1-3; Stiles 2 in 3; Wells 0 in 3. Winning pitcher—Wells. Losing pitcher—Faber.

Skeeters Break Even With Rochester Wings

JERSEY CITY, N. J. Aug. 5 (AP)—Rochester and Jersey City divided a doubleheader here today, the Red Wings took the first game, 7 to 4, but the Skeets came back to cop the second, 3 to1.

Jim Lindsey forced in all three of Jersey Citys runs in the first inning of the scond game with three bases on balls and two hit batsmen.

Mize and Pepper hit home runs for the Wings in the first game.

FIRST GAME

ROCHESTER	ab	r	h	o	a
Carey,ss	4	0	0	2	4
Gilbert,3b	3	1	1	3	1
Selkirk,cf	5	1	2	2	0
Mize,1b	3	1	1	10	0
Pepper,lf	4	1	1	2	0
Good'n,rf	5	1	1	2	0
Wilson,2b	4	1	1	6	3
Hinkle,c	4	1	2	3	0
Henry,p	3	0	0	0	4
Totals	35	7	11	27	13

JERSEY CITY	ab	r	h	o	a
Walker,cf	5	0	1	3	0
Benes,ss	4	0	0	1	4
Clancy,1b	2	1	0	12	3
Ros'feld,lf	4	0	2	1	0
English,3b	4	0	1	0	1
Baker,2b	4	0	0	2	2
Gross'n,rf	4	0	0	2	0
Rensa,c	4	1	2	4	3
Bartulis,p	2	0	2	2	2
a-Emerson	1	0	1	0	0
Totals	34	2	9	27	15

aBatted far Bartulis in 9th.

ROCHESTER 0	0	0	3	2	1	0	1	0	—7	
JERSEY CITY ..0	0	0	1	0	0	1	0	0	—2	

Errors—Carey, Rosenfeld, Rensa, 3. Runs batted in—Mize, Pepper, Hinkle, Selkirk, Gilbert, English, Walker. Two-base hits—Goodman, Wilson. Three-base hit—Selkirk. Home runs—Mize, Pepper. Stolen base—Pepper. Sacrifices—Henry. Double plays—Carey, Wilson and Mize, 2. Left on bases—Rochester, 8; Jersey City, 8. Bases on balls—off Bartulis, 6; Henry, 3. Struck out—by Bartulis, 5; Henry, 3. Passed ball—Rensa. Umpires—Hoblitzell and Carroll. Time—2.02.

SECOND GAME

ROCHESTER	ab	r	h	o	a
Carey,ss	3	0	1	0	1
Gilbert,3b	3	1	1	3	1
Selkirk,cf	3	0	0	2	0
Mize,1b	3	0	0	5	1
Pepper,lf	3	0	1	1	0
Good'n,rf	2	0	0	1	0
a-Crabtree	0	0	0	0	0
Wilson,2b	3	0	1	1	1
Florence,c	2	0	0	4	1
Lindsey,p	2	0	0	1	2
Totals	24	1	4	18	7

JERSEY CITY	ab	r	h	o	a
Walker,cf	1	1	0	2	1
Benes,ss	3	0	1	0	4
Clancy,1b	2	1	1	11	0
Ros'feld,lf	1	1	0	0	0
English,3b	1	0	0	1	3
Baker,2b	2	0	0	0	5
Gross'n,rf	3	0	0	1	0
Emerson,c	2	0	1	5	1
Pipgras,p	3	0	0	1	1
Totals	18	3	3	21	15

a-Batted for Goodman in seventh.

Rochester 1	0	0	0	0	0	0	—1	
JERSEY CITY.......3	0	0	0	0	0	x	—3	

Errors—None. Runs batted in—Mize, English, Baker, Emerson. Two-base hit—Wilson. Sacrifice—English. Left on bases—Rochester. 3; Jersey City, 7. Bases on balls—Off Lindsey, 7; Pipgras, 1. Struck out—By Lindsey, 4; Pipgras, 5. Hit by pitcher—By Lindsey (Rosenfeld), (Emerson). Passed ball—Florence. Umpires—Hoblitzell and Carroll. Time—1:23.

International League.

STANDING OF THE CLUBS.

Team.	W.	L.	Pct.	Team.	W.	L.	Pct.
NEWARK	75	49	.605	Albany...	59	64	.480
Rochester.	67	57	.540	Buffalo...	58	66	.466
Baltimore.	67	59	.532	Monteral.	57	67	.460
Toronto..	62	61	.504	JER. CITY	49	71	.408

YESTERDAY'S RESULTS.

NEWARK .....11; Toronto........... 3
(First game.)
NEWARK.......4; Toronto........... 3
(Second game.)
Rochester.......7; JERSEY CITY.... 2
(First game.)
JERSEY CITY...3; Rochester......... 1
(Second game.)

Buffalo....	101101000	—4	10	1
Baltimore...	001001000	—2	7	2

Lucas and Legett; Melton, Day and Sprinz.

(Second game.)

Buffalo.........	4010100	—6	11	1
Baltimore.......	0020000	—2	5	1

Elliott and Crouse; Mattingly, Prudhomme and Linton.

Montreal....	000001000	—1	8	1
Albany......	00300101x	—5	8	0

Dietrich, Fisher, Grabowski and Tate; Filley and Padden.

(Second game.)

Montreal......	0001000	—1	4	5
Albany........	620240x	—14	14	0

R. Phelps, McKeithan, Roettger and Ttate; Miner and Padden.

GAMES TODAY
Rochester at JERSEY CITY.
Toronto at NEWARK.
Montreal at Albany.
Buffalo at Baltimore.
(2 games in each city).

PIRATES UPSET CUBS, 6-2, AND CLIMB 1-2 GAME

Smith Outpitches Warneke, Allowing Only 5 Safeties; Traynor Gets Three Singles

CHICAGO, Aug. 5 (AP).—Hal Smith, first year Pittsburgh righthander, held the Cubs to five hits today and the Pirates took the opening game of the series, 6 to 2. The victory enabled the second-place Bucs to climb a half game nearer the league leading Giants, whom they now trail by three games.

Lonnie Warneke, on the mound for the Cubs, made a third start in search of his season's 13th victory, but wound up with his eighth defeat, two more than he was charged with all last season. The Pirates found him for ten hits in eight innings and combined these with four cub errors for four of their runs. They scored their scored their other two tallies on a pair of hits off Lynn Nelson in the ninth.

Smith shut out the Chicagoans with three singles until the ninth, when Demaree's triple, preceded by a single by Babe Herman and followed by Hartnett's long fly, accounted for the Cubs' two tallies.

Pie Traynor led the Pittsburgh attack with three singles. He scored the first run in the second inning when Demaree let Suhr's single go through him and he advanced Vaughan, who had walked, from first to third in the fourth inning. Vaughan then scored on Suhr's second single. Singles by Smith and Comorosky, plus errors by Koehig and Billy Herman, gave the Bucs two more runs in the seventh.

PITTSBURGH	ab	r	h	o	a
L.W'r,cf-lf	5	1	1	4	0
P.Wa'r,rf	5	2	2	3	0
Com'sky,lf	4	0	1	1	0
Lind'm,cf	0	1	0	1	0
Vaug'n,ss	4	1	1	2	5
Tray'r,3b	5	1	3	0	2
Suhr,1b	5	0	2	10	2
Piet,2b	4	0	1	3	8
Finney,c	4	0	0	2	0
Smith,p	4	0	1	1	0
Totals	40	6	12	27	12

CHICAGO	ab	r	h	o	a
Koenig,3b	4	0	0	0	[illegible]
W.Her'n,2b	4	0	0	5	1
Cuyler,lf	4	0	0	2	0
F.Her'n,rf	3	1	1	1	0
Demaree,cf	4	1	1	[illegible]	[illegible]
Hartnett,c	4	0	2	[illegible]	[illegible]
Grimm,1b	4	0	0	[illegible]	[illegible]
Jurges,ss	3	0	1	[illegible]	[illegible]
Warneke,p	2	0	0	[illegible]	[illegible]
a-Moselt	1	0	0	[illegible]	[illegible]
Nelson,p	0	0	0	[illegible]	[illegible]
Totals	33	2	5	27	[illegible]

a—Batted for Warneke in 8th.

Pittsburgh	0	1	0	1	0	0	2	0	2	—6
Chicago	0	0	0	0	0	0	0	0	2	—2

Errors—Suhr, Smith, Koenig, W. Herman, Damaree, Jurges. Runs batted in—Vaughan, Traynor, Suhr, Demaree, Hartnett. Two-base hit—Piet. Three-base hit—Demaree. Stolen base—Cuyler. Double plays—Vaughan to Piet to Suhr; W. Herman to Jurges to Grimm. Left on bases—Pittsburgh, 9; Chicago, 6. Bases on balls—Off Smith, 1; Warneke, 1; Nelson, 1. Struck out—By Smith, 2; Warneke, 5. Hits—Off Warneke, 10 in 8 innings; Nelson, 2 in 1. Hit by pitcher—By Smith (Jurges). Losing pitcher — Warneke. Umpires—Magerkurth and McGrew. Time—1:57.

Reds Conquer Cards, 6-3, Then Meet Defeat, 2-1

CINCINNATI, Aug. 5 (AP).—Glorying in the basehits and bases on balls "Wild Bill" Hallahan yielded liberally, the Cincinnati Reds ended a ten-game losing streak today by defeating the Cardinals, 6 to 3, in the first game of a double header, and then got the worst of a pitching battle between Vance and Benton, losing the second, 2 to 1.

Vance held the Reds hitless in the second contest until the seventh when Bottomley scratched a fruitless single. He yielded his only run on a walk to Manion, an infield out, and Adams' single in the eighth.

The Cards, meanwhile, jammed over a tally in the fourth as Crawford doubled and Medwick singled, and another in the seventh, when they registered four hits, two of them doubles.

FIRST GAME

ST. LOUIS	ab	r	h	o	a
Martin,3b	5	0	1	0	2
Allen,rf	5	1	2	2	1
Collins,1b	4	0	1	8	0
Craw'd,2b	4	1	1	1	4
Medw'k,lf	4	0	2	6	0
Orsatti,cf	4	0	2	0	0
Wilson,c	4	1	2	3	0
Dur'her,ss	4	0	0	2	2
Hal'han,p	1	0	0	0	1
Johnson,p	1	0	0	0	0
a-Frisch	1	0	1	0	0
b-Lewis	0	0	0	0	0
Totals	37	3	10	24	10

CINCINNATI	ab	r	h	o	a
Adams,3b	4	1	2	0	3
Mor'sey,2b	5	2	3	1	2
Hafey,cf	5	2	2	7	0
Moore,lf	4	0	0	2	0
Bot'ley,1b	2	1	0	10	0
Roett'r,rf	3	0	1	3	0
Manion,c	3	0	1	2	0
Bluege,ss	4	0	1	2	3
Rixey,p	4	0	0	0	1
Totals	34	6	10	27	9

a-Btted for Johnson in 9th.
b-Ran for Frisch in 9th.

St. Louis	0	0	0	1	0	0	2	0	0	—3
Cincinnati	0	0	3	0	0	3	0	0	x	—6

Errors—Martin, Frederick. Runs batted in—Allen, Collins, Orsatti, Moore, Bottomley, Roettger, 2; Manion. Two-base hits—Medwick, 2. Stolen bases—Adams. Left on bases—St. Louis, 8; Cincinnati, 10. Base on balls—Off Hallahan, 5; Rixey, 1; Johnson, 1. Struck out—By Hallahan, 2; Rixey, 2; Johnson, 1. Hits—Off Hallahan, 7 in 5 innings; Johnson, 3 in 3 innings. Losing pitcher—Hallahan. Umpires—Pfirman, Quigley and Klem. Time—2:04.

SECOND GAME

ST. LOUIS	ab	r	h	o	a
Martin,3b	4	0	0	1	1
Watkins,rf	4	0	0	2	0
Collins,1b	4	0	0	7	0
Craw'd,2b	4	1	2	1	1
Medw'k,lf	4	1	2	5	0
Orsatti,cf	3	0	3	6	0
O'Farrell,c	3	0	0	1	1
Dur'her,ss	3	0	1	3	3
Vance,p	3	0	1	1	2
Totals	32	2	9	27	8

CINCINNATI	ab	r	h	o	a
Ada's,3b-ss	4	0	1	2	2
Mor'sey,2b	4	0	1	1	2
Hafey,cf	4	0	0	5	1
Moore,lf	4	0	0	3	0
Bot'ley,1b	4	0	2	11	0
Roett'er,rf	4	0	0	2	0
Manion,c	2	1	0	3	2
Bluege,ss	2	0	0	0	3
a-Lucas	1	0	0	0	0
Hunter,3b	0	0	0	0	0
Benton,p	2	0	0	0	2
Frey,p	1	0	0	0	0
Totals	32	1	4	27	13

a—Batted for Bluege in 9th.

St. Louis	0	0	0	1	0	0	1	0	0	—2
Cincinnati	0	0	0	0	0	0	0	1	0	—1

Errors—Martin, Bottomley. Runs batted in—Medwick, Orsatti, Adams. Two base hits—Crawford, Medwick, Vance. Stolen base—Morrissey. Sacrifices—Orsatti, O'Farrell. Left on bases—St. Louis 5, Cincinnati 5. Base on balls—off Vance 1. Struck out—by Vance 1, Benton 2. Hits—off Benton, 8 in 8 innings; Frey, 1 in 1. Losing pitcher—Benton. Umpires—Quigley, Klem, and Pfirman. Time—1:50.

45,000 See Yankees Beat Senators, 6-5, 5-4, Both in Ninth, and Climb to One Game From Lead

Winning Runs Driven in By Chapman and Sewell

Champions Come From Behind in Opener and Drive Out Crowder; Home Runs by Gehrig and Ruth Help New York to Victory in Second Game

By Richards Vidmer

The Yankees moved onward and upward so fast and so far yesterday that they almost penetrated the stratosphere.

By winning both games of a double-header before a week day crowd of 45,000 at the Stadium against the leading Senators, they moved right up to a spot where they are now right on the heels of the pace-setters, just one game behind, and the peak may be reached this afternoon.

They had a four-run deficit to overcome in the first game, but behind the pitching of Russell Van Atta they whittled it down to one tally and then came through in the ninth to win, 6 to 5, with Ben Chapman driving the ball between Joe Cronin's legs and the tying and winning runs over the plate.

Again in the second game they came through in the ninth, after the Senators had tied the count in the first half of that last inning. This time it was Joe Sewell who drove the winning run across the plate with a sharp single to right that gave the Yankees a 5—4 victory.

Relief Pitchers Triumph

Both triumphs were credited to relief pitchers, Cy Moore and Herb Pennock gaining the verdicts, although each pitched only to three batters. Moore turned back the Senators in order in the ninth inning of the first game after Van Atta had given way to a pinch hitter, and Pennock checked the Senators in the ninth inning of the second contest when Red Ruffing, who had allowed only seven hits, walked two pinch hitters.

Until that latter streak of wildness it looked as though the power supplied by the twin thrillers, Babe Ruth and Lou Gehrig, had done enough to assure the Yankees of success, for Gehrig had hit his twentieth homer of the season in the first inning, and Ruth had hit his twenty-sixth in the eighth, but those two walks in the ninth let the Senators tie the score, and it was Joe Sewell and his single instead of Babe Ruth and his homer that won the ball game.

The Yankees seemed lost when the Senators scored five runs in the second inning of the first game, but Van Atta saw that they scored no more; and while the Yankees were in the process of catching up they knocked Alvin Crowder out of the box. It was off Jack Russell that Chapman got the hit that gained a triumph that had the crowd chattering excitedly until the second game was well under way.

Four in Row for Yankees

The double victory gave the Yankees four in a row over Washington, two in the capital and two here. Apparently the old spell that the Senators held over McCarthy's men has been broken at last.

Cronin wasn't charged with a fielding error, but a managerial mistake when Chapman drove home the winning run in the first game. With Combs on third, Byrd on second and two out it looked as though the thing to do was walk Chapman, filling the bases, not so much because Lazzeri was less to be feared, but because it would give the Senators a chance to retire a man at any base.

Chapman slapped the ball on the ground between second and short, and Cronin went over and down for it. But he came up empty handed and the tying and winning runs scored. It was ruled a hit and not an error, because Chapman had more than an even chance of beating it out, even if Cronin had fielded the ball cleanly.

Had Chapman been purposely passed and Lazzeri had hit the same kind of ball, if Cronin had come up with it he would have had an easy force play at second base. If he had handled it the way he did, however, the tying and winning runs would have scored anyway, so it makes no difference in the final analysis.

Giants Take Notes

Apparently convinced that they will have to play one of the teams in the World Series, most of the Giants were scouting the Senators and Yankees from front row boxes. Bill Terry, Hal Schumacher, Blondy Ryan, Glenn Spencer and Paul Richards were taking notes.

Bill McKechnie and Judge Emil Fuchs, of the Braves, also were present, but not taking notes. They don't anticipate meeting any American League club this year.

Frank Dole, the dog expert, also was noticed among the spectators. He said he had heard the Yankees were "dogging it" and figured he might be able to find a remedy quicker than a mere baseball man.

Neither the Yankees nor Senators had the names of their clubs on their shirts and some one wanted to know if they had to win a pennant to get their letter.

The only echo from the battle of the Potomac was a tame scrimmage between Gehrig and Cronin in the first game. Gehrig slid into second base none too gently and Cronin was much perturbed because he could not complete a double play.

Gehrig at least should have won some sort of insignia by this time. He completed 1,300 consecutive games yesterday.

Kuhel tried to kick himself a hit in the first contest and almost got away with it, but Lazzeri called the umpire's attention to the fact that the ball had received more momentum from Kuhel's foot than his bat and the Senators' first baseman was automatically retired.

Ruth, the man who plays on a dime, covered right field adequately and no small part of center besides, showing once more that money is being inflated.

Yankees' Scores

FIRST GAME

WASHINGTON (A. L.)	ab	r	h	po	a	e	NEW YORK (A. L.)	ab	r	h	po	a	e
Myer, 2b	5	1	2	4	8	0	Combs, cf	5	2	3	3	0	0
Manush, lf	3	1	1	1	0	0	J.Sewell, 3b	4	0	2	1	5	0
Cronin, ss	5	0	1	3	3	0	Ruth, rf	2	0	0	3	0	0
Harris, rf	5	0	0	0	0	0	§Byrd	0	1	0	0	0	0
Rice, rf	0	0	0	0	0	0	Gehrig, 1b	5	0	1	10	0	0
Schulte, cf	3	1	0	3	0	0	Chapman, lf	5	0	2	2	0	0
Kuhel, 1b	3	1	1	11	0	1	Lazzeri, 2b	4	0	0	5	3	1
Bluege, 3b	4	1	2	0	1	0	Dickey, c	4	1	1	3	0	0
L.Sewell, c	3	0	0	4	0	0	Crosetti, ss	3	2	2	0	3	1
CROWD'R, p	2	0	0	0	1	0	†Ruffing	1	0	0	0	0	0
RUSS'L, p	2	0	1	0	2	0	Farrell, ss	0	0	0	0	0	0
							V. ATTA, p	2	0	1	0	3	0
							‡Walker	1	0	0	0	0	0
							MOORE, p	0	0	0	0	0	0
Totals	35	5	8	*26	15	1	Totals	36	6	12	27	14	2

*Two out when winning run was scored.
†Batted for Crosetti in eighth inning.
‡Batted for Van Atta in eighth inning.
§Ran for Ruth in ninth inning.

Washington	050	000	000	—5
New York	120	100	002	—6

Runs batted in—Gehrig, Bluege, J. Sewell, Cronin (2), Combs (2), L. Sewell, Chapman (2). Two-base hits—Bluege, Manush. Sacrifices—Van Atta, Manush, J. Sewell. Double plays—J. Sewell, Lazzeri and Gehrig; Myer, Cronin and Kuhel. Left on bases—New York, 9; Washington, 8. Bases on balls—Off Crowder, 1; off Van Atta, 4; off Russell, 2. Struck out—By Russell, 2; by Van Atta, 1; by Moore, 1. Hits—Off Crowder, 8 in 3 1-3 innings; off Russell, 4 in 5 1-3; off Van Atta, 8 in 8; off Moore, 0 in 1. Balk—Russell. Winning pitcher—Moore. Losing pitcher—Russell. Umpires—Ormsby, Summers and McGowan. Time—2:04.

SECOND GAME

WASHINGTON (A. L.)	ab	r	h	po	a	e	NEW YORK (A. L.)	ab	r	h	po	a	e
Myer, 2b	5	0	3	4	7	0	Combs, cf	5	0	2	1	0	0
Goslin, rf	5	1	1	2	0	1	J.Sewell, 3b	4	1	1	1	3	0
Berg, c	0	0	0	1	0	0	Ruth, rf	4	1	2	2	0	0
Manush, lf	5	0	1	1	0	0	Byrd, rf	0	0	0	0	0	0
Cronin, ss	4	1	1	4	1	0	Gehrig, 1b	3	1	2	15	0	0
Schulte, cf	4	0	1	3	0	0	Chapman, lf	4	0	0	1	0	1
Kuhel, 1b	4	0	1	9	3	0	Lazzeri, 2b	4	1	2	4	5	0
Bluege, 3b	2	0	0	1	0	0	Dickey, c	4	0	1	3	0	0
*Rice	1	0	0	0	0	0	Crosetti, ss	4	1	0	0	5	0
L.Sewell, c	3	0	0	1	0	0	RUFFING, p	3	0	2	0	4	0
Harris, rf	0	1	0	0	0	0	PENNO'K, p	0	0	0	0	0	0
CROW'ER, p	0	0	0	0	0	0	§Walker	1	0	0	0	0	0
STEW'RT, p	2	1	0	0	2	0							
†Bolton	0	0	0	0	0	0							
Boken, 3b	0	0	0	0	0	0							
Totals	35	4	8	*26	13	1	Totals	36	5	12	27	17	1

*Two out when winning run was scored.
†Batted for Bluege in ninth inning.
‡Batted for Stewart in ninth inning.
§Batted for Pennock in ninth inning.

Washington	101	001	001	—4
New York	210	000	011	—5

Runs batted in—Cronin, Gehrig (2), Ruffing, Manush, Bluege, Ruth, Myer, J. Sewell. Two-base hits—Goslin, Myer, Kuhel. Home runs—Gehrig, Ruth. Sacrifice—Bluege. Double plays—Cronin, Myer and Kuhel. Left on bases—New York, 7; Washington, 8. Bases on balls—Off Stewart, 2; off Ruffing, 3. Struck out—By Ruffing, 3; by Stewart, 1; by Pennock, 1; by Crowder, 1. Hits—Off Ruffing, 7 in 8 1-3 innings; off Pennock, 1 in 2-3; off Stewart, 9 in 8; off Crowder, 3 in 2-3. Winning pitcher—Pennock. Losing pitcher—Crowder. Umpires—Summers, McGowan and Ormsby. Time—2:14.

Orioles Beat Booth's Nine

NEW HAVEN, Conn., Aug. 7 (AP).—The Baltimore Orioles, of the International League, defeated the New Haven Chevies, led by Albie Booth, former Yale star, 10 to 2, today in a twilight exhibition game.

Buzz Artlett, an outfielder, pitched for the Orioles. Leo Stroner and Jules Solters, each knocked out a home run and a double. The score by innings:

					R.	H.	E.
Baltimore	013	011	040	—	10	14	2
New Haven	000	002	000	—	2	7	2

Batteries—Arlett and Linton; Klarman and Rueb.

Temple Signs Usilton Again

Jimmy Usilton, veteran basketball mentor at Temple University, has renewed his contract for next winter. Temple, a member of the intercollegiate basketball conference, which also includes Pittsburgh, Carnegie Tech, Georgetown, Bucknell and West Virginia, play a twenty-game schedule

Exciting Moments as Yankees Twice Defeated Senators

Byrd, running for Ruth, scoring winning run for Yankees in the ninth inning of the first game. Combs, who also scored, is seen holding hands up to keep Byrd from sliding, and Lazzeri, who was ready to bat, is walking back to the bench

Herald Tribune photos—Frank

Lou Gehrig congratulating Babe Ruth as he crosses the plate following his home run in the eighth inning of the second game

Skeeters Beat Leafs, 10-1, After Losing First, 2-1

TORONTO, Aug. 7 (CP).—Toronto broke even with Jersey City today in a civic holiday double-header. The Leafs captured the opener, 2 to 1, but were swamped under a 10-1 count in the abbreviated second game.

Ralph Birkhofer outpitched Roger Hanlon in the first game, the local southpaw holding the visitors to four hits and striking out seven batters. Hanlon yielded only six hits, but three of them were bunched in the first inning for Toronto's two runs.

Neither Keith Frazier nor Earl Cook could check the Skeeters in the nightcap. They pounded out sixteen hits, including a home run by Rosenfeld. Mike Meola held the Leafs to five hits.

The scores:

FIRST GAME

JERSEY CITY (I. L.)	ab	r	h	po	a	e	TORONTO (I. L.)	ab	r	h	po	a	e
Merville, rf	4	0	0	1	1	0	Blue, 1b	4	0	0	10	0	0
Benes, ss	4	0	0	1	5	0	Lawrence, cf	3	1	2	3	0	0
Clancy, 1b	4	0	0	12	0	0	Boone, rf	1	1	1	0	0	0
Rosenfeld, lf	4	0	1	2	0	0	Howell, lf	3	0	1	1	0	0
Fitz'rald, cf	4	1	2	1	0	0	Mallon, 2b	3	0	0	3	2	0
English, 3b	3	0	1	0	2	0	Rich'son, ss	3	0	0	3	6	0
Baker, 2b	2	0	0	4	4	0	Sax, 3b	2	0	0	0	1	1
Emerson, c	1	0	0	2	1	0	Heving, c	3	0	1	7	0	0
HANLON, p	3	0	0	0	1	0	BIRK'ER, p	2	0	1	0	1	0
Rensa, c	1	0	0	1	2	0							
Totals	30	1	4	24	16	0	Totals	24	2	6	27	10	1

Jersey City	000	010	000	—1
Toronto	200	000	00x	—2

Runs batted in—Boone, Howell, Rensa. Two-base hit—Lawrence. Three-base hit—Boone. Sacrifice—Birkofer. Double plays—English, Baker and Clancy; Merville and Emerson; Benes, Baker and Clancy; Mallon, Richardson and Blue (2). Left on bases—Jersey City, 4; Toronto, 3. Bases on balls—Off Hanlon, 4; off Birkofer, 2. Struck out—By Birkofer, 7. Umpires—Parker and Hubbard. Time—1:33.

SECOND GAME

JERSEY CITY (I. L.)	ab	r	h	po	a	e	TORONTO (I. L.)	ab	r	h	po	a	e
Walker, cf	4	0	1	1	0	1	Blue, 1b	4	0	0	9	0	0
Benes, ss	5	0	0	0	3	0	Lawrence, cf	2	0	2	1	0	0
Clancy, 1b	5	1	1	6	0	0	Boone, rf	3	0	0	0	0	0
Rosenfeld, lf	4	3	2	1	0	0	Howell, lf	2	0	1	1	0	0
Merville, rf	2	1	1	4	0	0	Mallon, 2b	3	0	0	4	6	0
English, 3b	3	3	2	0	2	0	Rich'son, ss	3	1	1	0	3	0
Baker, 2b	4	1	3	3	1	0	Sax, 3b	3	0	1	2	2	1
Rensa, c	3	1	3	6	0	0	R. Smith, c	3	0	0	4	2	0
MEOLO, p	4	0	3	0	0	0	FRAZIER, p	1	0	0	0	0	0
							COOK, p	1	0	0	0	0	0
							*M. Smith	1	0	0	0	0	0
Totals	34	10	16	21	7	1	Totals	26	1	5	21	13	1

*Batted for Cook in seventh inning.

Jersey City	023	011	3	—10
Toronto	010	000	0	— 1

Runs batted in—Walker, Rosenfeld, English, Baker (3), Rensa (2), Meola (2), R Smith. Two-base hits—Rensa (2), Richardson. Three-base hit—English. Home run—Rosenfeld. Sacrifice—English. Left on bases—Jersey City, 8; Toronto, 6. Bases on balls—Off Meola, 2; off Frazier, 2; off Cook, 1. Struck out—By Meola, 3; by Frazier, 1; by Cook, 2. Hits—Off Frazier, 4 in 2 1-3 innings; off Cook, 12 in 4 2-3. Losing pitcher—Frazier. Hit by pitcher—By Cook (Walker). Losing pitcher—Frazier. Umpires—Parker and Hubbard. Time—1:45.

Red Sox Beat Athletics, 8-5; Walters Stars

Philadelphia Boy Smashes Homer and Triple in Debut Before Home Folks

By The Associated Press

PHILADELPHIA, Aug. 7.—Bucky Walters, a Philadelphia boy with the Boston Red Sox, made his debut before his home folks today and led the Sox to an 8 to 5 victory over the Athletics

Presented with a chest of silver and a cup before the game, Walters hit a home run with one on base in the second inning and in the sixth broke up a 4 to 4 tie by tripling with the bases filled. The score:

BOSTON (A. L.)	ab	r	h	po	a	e	PHILADELPHIA (A. L.)	ab	r	h	po	a	e
Werber, ss	4	2	1	0	3	0	Bishop, 2b	3	0	2	1	4	0
Walters, 2b	4	2	2	5	3	0	Cramer, cf	4	0	2	2	0	0
Cooke, lf	5	0	3	5	0	0	Cochrane, c	4	0	0	7	1	0
R.John'n, rf	5	1	1	2	0	0	Foxx, 1b	4	0	0	11	0	0
Ferrell, c	5	0	2	5	0	0	Coleman, rf	5	0	1	1	0	0
Judge, 1b	3	0	2	5	1	0	B.John'n, lf	4	2	3	5	1	0
McManus, 3b	5	1	1	1	0	0	Higgins, 3b	5	1	2	0	3	0
Oliver, cf	3	1	0	3	0	0	Williams, ss	4	1	2	0	2	0
WEIL'D, p	1	1	1	0	0	0	EARN'W, p	1	0	0	0	0	0
ANDRE'S, p	3	0	0	1	0	0	COOMBS, p	1	1	0	0	1	0
							*Miller	1	0	0	0	0	0
							WALB'G, p	0	0	0	0	2	0
							†McNair	1	0	0	0	0	0
Totals	38	8	13	27	7	0	Totals	37	5	12	27	14	0

*Batted for Coombs in seventh inning.
†Batted for Walberg in ninth inning.

Boston	220	003	010	—8
Philadelphia	000	400	001	—5

Runs batted in—R. Johnson, Ferrell, Walters (5), Cooke, B. Johnson, Williams (2), Cramer, Higgins. Two-base hits—Cooke (2), Ferrell, McManus, Werber. Three-base hits—Walters, Cooke, Judge, B. Johnson. Home runs—Walters, B. Johnson, Williams. Stolen base—R. Johnson. Sacrifice—Cramer. Double play—Werber, Walters and Judge. Left on bases—Boston, 9; Philadelphia, 13. Bases on balls—Off Weiland, 4; off Andrews, 3; off Earnshaw, 1; off Coombs, 4. Struck out—By Weiland, 2; by Coombs, 3. Hits—Off Weiland, 5 in 3 1-3 innings; off Andrews, 7 in 5 2-3; off Earnshaw, 5 in 2; off Coombs, 5 in 5; off Walberg, 3 in 2. Hit by pitcher—By Earnshaw (Walters). Winning pitcher—Andrews. Losing pitcher—Coombs. Umpires—Moriarty and Geisel. Time—2:08.

Broaca Fans 10 as Bears Vanquish Red Wings, 4-0

ROCHESTER, N. Y., Aug. 7 (AP).—The Rochester Red Wings inaugurated night baseball here this evening by dropping a verdict to the Newark Bears before 15,000 fans. Johnny Broca, on the mound for Newark, was master of the situation, yielding only six scattered blows and striking out ten men. Sheriff Blake worked eight innings for Rochester and then gave way to McAfee. The score:

NEWARK (I. L.)	ab	r	h	po	a	e	ROCHESTER (I. L.)	ab	r	h	po	a	e
Neun, 1b	4	0	2	5	1	0	Carey, ss	4	0	1	1	3	1
Rolfe, ss	4	0	1	5	1	0	Crabtree, cf	4	0	3	4	0	0
Hoag, cf	5	0	0	1	0	0	Selkirk, rf	3	0	0	2	0	0
Saltz'ver, 3b	4	1	1	3	1	0	Mize, 1b	4	0	1	12	0	1
Puccin'li, lf	4	1	2	2	0	0	Pepper, lf	4	0	0	2	0	0
Barton, rf	4	0	0	1	0	0	Goodman, 3b	4	0	0	0	1	1
Schalk, 2b	4	1	0	0	3	0	Wilson, 2b	4	0	1	1	6	1
Kies, c	4	0	1	10	0	0	Hinkle, c	3	0	0	5	0	0
BROACA, p	2	1	0	0	0	0	BLAKE, p	3	0	0	0	2	0
							M'AFEE, p	0	0	0	0	0	0
							*Parham	0	0	0	0	0	0
Totals	35	4	7	27	6	0	Totals	33	0	6	27	12	4

*Batted for Blake in eighth inning.

Newark	002	000	020	—4
Rochester	000	000	000	—0

Runs batted in—Rolfe, Puccinelli, Kies. Two-base hits—Rolfe, Puccinelli. Three-base hit—Saltzgaver. Double play—Wilson and Mize. Left on bases—Newark, 8; Rochester, 7. Bases on balls—Off Blake, 4; off Broaca, 1. Struck out—By Broaca, 10; by Blake, 5. Hits—Off Blake, 7 in 8 innings; off McAfee, 0 in 1. Wild pitch—Blake. Losing pitcher—Blake. Umpires—Donnelly and Jorda. Time—2:00.

5 Double Plays by Browns Help Stiles Blank White Sox, 6 to 0

Third Victory in 4 Games Gives St. Louis First Series Under Hornsby

By The Associated Press

ST. LOUIS, Aug. 7.—Roland (Lena) Stiles, with the aid of five double plays by his companions, shut out the Chicago White Sox today, 6 to 0, and took the four-game series from the Sox, three games to one.

It was the first series victory by the Browns since Rogers Hornsby took over the managership.

Whitlow Wyatt who started for the White Sox, pitched sterling ball for three innings. In the fourth the Browns got five hits which were good for five runs. The score:

CHICAGO (A. L.)	ab	r	h	po	a	e	ST. LOUIS (A. L.)	ab	r	h	po	a	e
Swanson, rf	3	0	1	2	0	0	Storti, 3b	3	0	0	0	1	0
Haas, cf	3	0	1	1	0	0	West, cf	3	0	1	0	0	0
Kress, 1b	3	0	1	9	0	0	Garms, lf	3	1	1	5	0	0
Simmons, lf	4	0	1	2	0	0	Campbell, rf	3	1	0	0	0	0
Appling, ss	4	0	1	3	5	1	Burns, 1b	4	1	1	11	0	0
Dykes, 3b	4	0	1	0	0	0	Melillo, 2b	3	2	1	5	8	0
Hayes, 2b	2	0	1	3	4	0	Shea, c	3	1	2	4	1	0
Berry, c	3	0	0	3	1	0	Levey, ss	4	0	2	2	5	0
Sullivan, c	0	0	0	1	0	0	STILES, p	2	0	1	0	1	0
WYATT, p	1	0	0	0	0	0							
HEVING, p	1	0	0	0	3	0							
FABER, p	0	0	0	0	0	0							
*Lyons	1	0	0	0	0	0							
Totals	29	0	7	24	13	1	Totals	28	6	9	27	16	0

*Batted for Heving in eighth inning.

Chicago	000	000	000	—0
St. Louis	000	500	01x	—6

Runs batted in—Burns, Melillo, Shea (3), Levey. Two-base hits—Garms, Shea. Sacrifices—Stiles, Garms, Storti. Double plays—Levey, Melillo and Burns (3); Hayes, Appling and Kress; Levey and Melillo; Appling, Hayes and Kress; Storti, Melillo and Burns. Left on bases—Chicago, 6; St. Louis, 6. Bases on balls—Off Wyatt, 3; off Heving, 1; off Stiles, 4. Struck out—By Wyatt, 2; by Faber, 1; by Stiles, 3. Hits—Off Wyatt, 5 in 3 1-3 innings; off Heving, 2 in 3 2-3; off Faber, 2 in 1. Hit by pitcher—By Wyatt (Stiles). Losing pitcher—Wyatt. Umpires—Kolls, Hildebrand and Van Graflan. Time—1:47.

Tigers Commit 6 Errors, But Beat Indians, 6 to 3

By The Associated Press

DETROIT, Aug. 7.—Although the Tigers made six errors, four in one inning, they batted out a 6-3 victory over Cleveland today in the final of a series that went to Detroit, four games to one.

Vic Sorrell went the route for Detroit and was in trouble only in the eighth when Oulliber singled, Burnett was safe on Davis's error and Averill cracked out a home run, driving in all the Cleveland runs.

A five-run attack in the fourth gave the Tigers all the runs they needed. Detroit batted around in that frame, obtaining five hits and a walk. Mel Harder lasted out that assault, but gave way to a pinch batter in the fifth and Clint Brown finished.

The score:

CLEVELAND (A. L.)	ab	r	h	po	a	e	DETROIT (A. L.)	ab	r	h	po	a	e
Oulliber, rf	5	1	2	0	0	0	Rogell, ss	5	1	2	1	3	1
Burnett, ss	5	1	1	4	7	1	Owen, 3b	4	1	1	5	2	1
Boss, 1b	5	0	1	9	2	0	Gehr'ger, 2b	4	0	2	2	1	1
Averill, cf	4	1	2	2	0	0	Stone, rf	4	1	1	3	0	0
Vosmik, lf	4	0	0	0	0	0	Fox, cf	4	1	3	2	0	1
Hale, 2b	4	0	0	3	1	0	Doljack, lf	3	0	1	2	0	1
Kamm, 3b	4	0	2	1	0	0	Davis, 1b	3	1	0	10	1	1
Spencer, c	4	0	0	4	1	0	Hayworth, c	4	1	2	1	1	0
HARDER, p	1	0	0	1	2	0	SORRELL, p	4	0	1	1	2	0
BROWN, p	1	0	0	0	1	0							
*Galatzer	1	0	0	0	0	0							
†Porter	0	0	0	0	0	0							
Totals	38	3	8	24	14	1	Totals	35	6	13	27	10	6

*Batted for Harder in fifth inning.
†Batted for Brown in ninth inning.

Cleveland	000	000	030	—3
Detroit	000	500	10x	—6

Runs batted in—Averill (3), Gehringer (2), Fox, Hayworth, Rogell, Owen. Two-base hits—Gehringer, Stone. Home run—Averill. Stolen base—Fox. Sacrifice—Doljack. Double play—Boss and Burnett. Left on bases—Detroit, 8; Cleveland, 9. Bases on balls—Off Sorrell, 1; off Harder, 1. Struck out—By Harder, 1; by Brown, 2. Hits—Off Harder, 7 in 4 innings; off Brown, 6 in 4. Hit by pitcher—By Harder (Owen). Losing pitcher—Harder. Umpires—Owens and Dinneen. Time—2:12.

Miss Wall's 79 Wins Medal in Western Golf

31 Qualify in Field of 160 Over Oak Park's Course; Miss Van Wie Cards 83

By The Associated Press

CHICAGO, Aug. 7.—Over the tricky Oak Park Country Club course today, Miss Bernice Wall, of Oshkosh, Wis., led more than 160 feminine golfers in the qualifying round of the Women's Western Golf Association tournament today with a 79, one over par.

The Wisconsin girl who has yet to win a major golf title, played the first nine in 39 one under par, and finished her day on the course with 40, two over par.

Thirty-one of the leading women golfers in the Middle West qualified for the championship flight with scores ranging to 92. A playoff was necessary for the last place. The well-trapped course was held responsible for the higher average than usual among the qualifiers, but lower figures were expected tomorrow with the opening of match play.

Two strokes behind the medal winner was Miss Jean Armstrong, youthful Chicagoan, who carded 41—40—81.

The defending champion, Mrs. Opal S. Hill, of Kansas City, who played a courtesy round, scored an 82 as did Mrs. Leon Solomon, crack Memphis player; the Iowa champion, Lucille Robinson, of Des Moines, and Elizabeth Abbott, of Los Angeles. Mrs. Hill took a 43 on the outgoing nine, but recovered on the incoming trial to shoot a 39, one over par.

The national champion, Miss Virginia Van Wie of Chicago, qualified easily with 42—41—83.

The leading cards:

Miss Wall, out	5 3 5 5 5 3 4 5 4—39	
Miss Wall, in	4 4 5 2 5 6 6 3 5—40—79	
Miss Armstrong, out	4 2 5 5 5 3 5 5 5—41	
Miss Armstrong, in.	5 4 5 2 5 5 5 4 5—40—81	
Mrs. Hill, out	6 3 5 6 4 4 5 5 5—43	
Mrs. Hill in	3 4 4 4 4 5 6 4 5—39—82	

The scores:

Miss Bernice Wall, Oshkosh, Wis.	39—40— 79
Miss Jane Armstrong, Chicago	41—40— 81
Miss Elizabeth Abbott, Los Angeles	40—42— 82
Mrs. Leon Solomon, Memphis	41—41— 82
Mrs. O. S. Hill, Kansas City	43—39— 82
Miss Lucille Robinson, Des Moines	44—38— 82
Miss Virginia Van Wie, Chicago	42—41— 83
Miss Helen Lawson, Los Angeles	41—42— 83
Mrs. Gregory Lifur, Los Angeles	42—42— 84
Miss Mildred Green, Los Angeles	45—40— 85
Mrs. John. Arends, Detroit	41—44— 85
Mrs. S. L. Reinshardt, Chicago	46—39— 85
Miss I. J. Grabbe, Terre Haute, Ind.	44—42— 86
Miss Rena Nelson, Chicago	42—44— 86
Mrs. C. B. Harbaugh, Cleveland	43—43— 86
Miss Jane Weiler, Chicago	45—41— 86
Mrs. Austin Pardue, Chicago	46—41— 87
Mrs. Melvin Jones, Chicago	47—41— 88
Miss Helen MacMorran, Chicago	43—45— 88
Miss June Beebe, Chicago	46—43— 89
Mrs. Lee Mida, Chicago	43—46— 89
Mrs. John Wittig, Los Angeles	45—45— 90
Mrs. R. T. Kohn, St. Louis	47—44— 91
Mrs. Chas. Dennehy, Chicago	45—46— 91
Mrs. Robert I. Bullard, Springfield, Ill.	47—44— 91
Miss Mary Ford, Kansas City	45—47— 92
Miss Betty Lord, Peoria, Ill.	47—46— 93
Miss Mary K. Browne, Cleveland	47—46— 93
Miss Betty Botterill, Salt Lake	47—46— 93
Mrs. Lewis Kaye, Louisville	49—46— 95
Mrs. Joseph Palma, Hawaii	46—49— 95
Miss Merle Nickels, Madison	47—48— 95
Miss Marie Reimer, Milwaukee	44—52— 96
Mrs. A. W. Clapp, St. Paul	50—47— 97
Miss Rose Adley, Los Angeles	50—47— 97
Mrs. A. H. Means, Salt Lake City	50—47— 97
Mrs. Chas. McGrew, Louisville	52—49—101
Miss Kay Daugherty, Los Angeles	52—51—103
Mrs. Frank Briggs, Kansas City	55—50—105
Mrs. Robt. Greenlease, Kansas City	59—46—105
Mrs. F. A. Dowling Kansas City	60—51—111

Leading Five Batsmen In Each Major League

NATIONAL LEAGUE

Player and Club	G.	AB.	R.	H.	Pc.
Klein, Phila	102	408	68	156	.382
Terry, New York	76	292	46	104	.356
Davis, Philadelphia	96	345	34	121	.351
Schulmerich, Phila	76	274	41	92	.336
Fullis, Phila	101	442	68	148	.335

Leader a year ago today, Hurst, Philadelphia, .360.

AMERICAN LEAGUE

Player and Club	G.	AB.	R.	H.	Pc.
Simmons, Chicago	104	436	69	155	.356
Foxx, Phila	99	376	88	133	.354
Manush, Wash	103	446	79	151	.339
Cronin, Wash	102	409	66	138	.337
Hodapp, Boston	92	340	44	113	.332

Leader a year ago today, Foxx, Philadelphia .357.

Home Runs		Runs Batted In	
Foxx, Athletics	31	Foxx, Athletics	101
Ruth, Yankees	26	Simmons, W. Sox	97
Gehrig, Yankees	20	Klein, Phillies	95
Berger, Braves	20	Gehrig, Yankees	91
Klein, Phillies	19	Campbell, Br'ns	83

New York Printers Win Twice in Baseball Meet

DETROIT, Aug. 7 (AP).—With the field reduced by three eliminations, Washington, New York and Chicago were out in front tonight with two victories apiece in the Union Printers Baseball League tournament. Buffalo, Indianapolis and Baltimore were eliminated in their first and second round games.

Washington, defending champion, shut off a ninth-inning rally with two runs scored to defeat Cincinnati, 4 to 2, today. New York just nosed out Detroit, 7 to 6, and Chicago won a free-hitting game from Pittsburgh, 13 to 11.

Minneapolis-St. Paul eliminated Baltimore, 9 to 8; Cleveland ended Indianapolis's hopes, 10 to 5, and St. Louis overwhelmed Buffalo, 20 to 1, in a game that was called at the end of six innings.

Detroit, Cincinnati, Cleveland, St. Louis, Twin Cities and Pittsburgh have won one and lost one game.

Semi-finals will be played Thursday and the championship decided Friday, both at Navin Field, home of the Detroit Tigers.

Washington Club Again Wins National Canoe Title at Chicago

Paddlers From Capital Take Three Events, Boosting Regatta Total to 55 Pts.

CHICAGO, Aug. 7 (AP).—Scoring victories in three events today, the Washington Canoe Club retained the national championship of the American Canoe Association's annual regatta, with 55 points. The Breeds Club, of Roxbury, Mass., which led after the single-blade events yesterday, finished second, with 28 points.

The Washington club won the junior double blade single, H. Houghton outpaddling the field in the final, and Houghton, paired with Schultz, took the junior double-blade tandem. Knight and Rodman won the senior double-blade tandem.

The summaries:

All Double Blade Events

Junior single—Won by H. Houghton, Washington Canoe Club; second, Howard La Brant, Columbia Canoe Club, Chicago; third, J. Hassenfus, Breeds Canoe Club, Roxbury, Mass. Time, 4:07.

Intermediate single—Won by Ed Balko, Yonkers Canoe Club; second, M. Young, Washington Canoe Club; third, J. Zaboy, Samoset Canoe Club, Boston. Time, 4:02.4.

Senior Single—Won by G. Moser, Crescent Canoe Club, Waltham, Mass.; second, H. Bruns, Yonkers C. C.; third, C. Sawling, Knickerbocker Canoe Club, New York. Time 3:58.4.

Junior Tandem—Won by Washington C. C. (Houghton and Shults); second, Yonkers C. C. (Lysak and Krajeski); third, Philadelphia C. C. (Smith and Kreier). Time, 3:56.4.

Intermediate Tandem—Won by Cacawa C. C., Philadelphia (Cinicowski and Krick); second, Breeds C. C. (Volante and Blackman); third, Washington C. C. (Miller and Jones). Time, 3:58.6.

Senior tandem—Won by Washington C. C. (Knight adn Rodman); Second, Samoset C. C. (Zaboy and Zaboy); third, Cacawa C. C. (Holland and Haas). Time, 4:03.6.

Junior fours—Won by Yonkers C. C. (Balko, Sullivan, Lysak, Krajeski); second, Edison C. C., Schenectady, N. Y.; third, Lincoln Park Boat Club, Chicago. Time, 3:32.6.

Intermediate fours—Won by Wanda Canoe Club, Edgewater, N. J. (Ryan, Norman, Kennedy, Franz); second, Philadelphia Canoe Club; third, Lincoln Park Boat Club, Chicago. Time, 3:33.6.

Senior fours—Won by Cacawa C. C., Philadelphia (Cinicowski, Krick, Holland, Haas); second, Wanda C. C., Edgewater, N. J.; third, Potomac C. C., Washington. Time, 3:22.5.

Standings in Major Leagues

TUESDAY, AUGUST 8, 1933

American League

YESTERDAY'S RESULTS

New York, 6; Washington, 5 (1st)
New York, 5; Washington, 4 (2d)
Boston, 8; Philadelphia, 5
Detroit, 6; Cleveland, 3
St. Louis, 6; Chicago, 0

STANDING OF THE CLUBS

	Washington	New York	Phila'phia	Detroit	Cleveland	Chicago	Boston	St. Louis	Won	Lost	Percentage
Wash'gton	—	9	10	7	9	8	11	10	64	38	.628
New York	7	—	9	9	9	9	11	9	63	39	.618
Phila'phia	6	6	—	7	10	5	7	10	51	50	.505
Detroit	6	4	6	—	10	9	6	11	52	54	.491
Cleveland	4	5	4	10	—	9	10	10	52	57	.477
Chicago	6	5	8	7	7	—	2	13	48	56	.462
Boston	4	5	9	8	5	9	—	5	45	55	.450
St. Louis	5	5	4	6	7	7	8	—	42	68	.382
Gms. lost	38	39	50	54	57	56	55	68	—	—	

GAMES TODAY

Washington at New York, 3:15
Boston at Philadelphia
Chicago at St. Louis
Other clubs not scheduled

National League

YESTERDAY'S RESULTS

No games scheduled

STANDING OF THE CLUBS

	New York	Pittsburgh	Chicago	St. Louis	Boston	Phila'phia	Cincinnati	Brooklyn	Won	Lost	Percentage
New York	—	8	7	6	5	12	10	13	61	41	.598
Pittsburgh	5	—	8	10	7	8	12	9	59	46	.562
Chicago	7	10	—	5	11	8	8	8	57	47	.548
St. Louis	8	6	10	—	5	9	11	6	55	50	.524
Boston	9	7	5	10	—	7	8	9	55	51	.519
Phila'phia	4	5	4	5	9	—	10	7	44	58	.431
Cincinnati	4	6	9	7	6	4	—	8	44	63	.411
Brooklyn	4	4	4	7	8	10	4	—	41	60	.406
Gms. lost	41	46	47	50	51	58	63	60	—	—	

GAMES TODAY

New York at Brooklyn, 3:20
St. Louis at Chicago
Other clubs not scheduled

Olin Dutra Starts Title Defense Against 100 in P. G. A. Today

Hagen, Wood, Shute Out of Milwaukee Tourney; Joe Turnesa Cards a 67

By The Associated Press

MILWAUKEE, Aug. 7.—Rocked by a revolt that caused withdrawal of several Ryder Cup stars, the 1933 National Professional Golfers Association championship opens over the watersoaked Blue Mound Country Club course tomorrow with a field of 100 out to topple Olin Dutra off his throne.

Repercussions of the revolt were evident today as the professional marksmen from all sections of the nation finished drills amid rain and later under a hot sun. Three Ryder Cup players—Walter Hagen, Craig Wood and Denny Shute—were definitely out of the tournament. After it had been predicted that Gene Sarazen and Paul Runyan would pass up the event they showed up late in the day for practice rounds.

Exciting Golf Assured

Dutra, back on the game that enabled him to spreadeagle a greater starting field last year at St. Paul, and four other Ryder Cup players were ready for action, however, to insure a week of heavy, exciting golf. The other Ryder Cup players at peace with the P. G. A. are Billie Burke, Ed Dudley, Horton Smith, and Leo Diegel, two-time winner of the title.

There were other star members of the "old guards" and "freshmen," too, to give Dutra a rousing battle. Among the veterans are Bobby Cruickshank, Johnny Farrell, Willie Klein, John Golden, Harry Cooper and Abe Espinosa. While the "freshmen," packing a wallop in the pretournament picking, include Johnny Revolta, rising young star from Menominee, Mich.; Jimmy Foulis, of Chicago, winner of the recent St. Paul open, and Ralph Guldahl, of St. Louis, runner-up to Johnny Goodman in the national open at Glenview. The home town brigade boasted several threats, among them Francis Gallett, who promised to be a keen factor because of his game and his thorough knowledge of one of golf's trickiest courses.

Blue Mound Short Layout

As the field winds up practice today it was an almost unanimous opinion that Blue Mound—an expanse of 6,270 yards—would be "taken apart" by the par-shelling field tomorrow. Although the course is protected by tricky, rolling greens, it is one of the shortest championship layouts for the P. G. A. championship. Practice rounds, ranging from 68 and upwards, indicated low scoring. Par is 35—35—70 and the course record a 65, shot by Gallett. Clarence Hackney, of Atlantic City, toured the course in 34—35—69 today, while Revolta shot a 68 in practice yesterday. Golden and Burke turned in 71s despite a heavy downpour.

Joe Turnesa, of New York, came in later with the prize practice round—a 67. Joe took 36, one over par, on his outward trip, but shelled the course with a 31, four under perfect figures, coming back. On the back nine he had five birdies.

Other doubtful ones were Pat Circelli, New Rochelle, N. Y., and Tom Kerrigan, Mount Vernon, N. Y.

Tomorrow's qualifying round will be over thirty-six holes, after which the thirty-one low scorers and Dutra open fire for the title over the arduous match-play route of thirty-six holes a day through to the final Sunday.

Par and Yardage In P. G. A. Play

MILWAUKEE, Aug. 7 (AP).—Par and yardage of the Blue Mound Country Club, scene of the 1933 Professional Golf Association championship tomorrow:

Holes	Yds.	Par	Hole	Yds.	Par
1	440	4	10	400	4
2	325	4	11	410	4
3	440	4	12	220	3
4	190	3	13	370	4
5	365	4	14	470	5
6	390	4	15	320	4
7	325	4	16	130	3
8	165	3	17	400	4
9	560	5	18	350	4
			In	3,070	35
Out	3,200	35	Tot.	6,270	70

Red Star Triumphs Over Natty Bumpo In Upstate Regatta

Less Than a Minute Separates Sloops in Opening of Lake Yachting Season

Special to the Herald Tribune

FAIR HAVEN, N. Y., Aug. 7.—Red Star, international star class yacht skippered by Dr. J. Greenough, of Otsego Lake, Cooperstown, N. Y., was victor in the first day of the Lake Yacht Racing Association regatta here today. Red Star nosed out Natty Bumpo, skippered by Samson Smith of the same club. Natty Bumpo is last year's champion of the central New York star class fleet.

Less than a minute separated the two sloops at the finish of a nine-mile triangular course that provided plenty of weather work. There were no casualties among the stars, but one of the Class R sloops, Banshee, of Buffalo, was dismasted just before reaching the finish line. Shifty winds that turned squally provided rail-down conditions for the fleet of forty-three boats.

Winners in other classes included Conewago, eight-meter from the Rochester Yacht Club, defending her right to the George H. Gooderham Trophy, and Nirie, of the Buffalo Canoe Club, which stole the honors in Class R competing for the Sir Thomas Lipton Trophy. In this case, with eleven starters, Buffalo took the first three places. Kathea II, of Rochester, winner of the distance cruise from Coburg, was fourth, first Rochester boat home.

Patricia, Class P sloop from the Royal Canadian Yacht Club, defeated two sister ships, including the Cara Mi from Kingston, in class two.

579 Amateurs Tee Off In National Golf Today

A total of 579 amateur golfers, cream of the American crop, will tee off today on twenty-two courses from New York to Honolulu in battle for the 165 qualifying places for the national amateur championship at Cincinnati, September 11 to 16.

Only C. Ross (Sandy) Somerville, Canadian holder of the American title, is exempt from the sectional qualifying play, which is at thirty-six holes with qualifying places allotted districts on the basis of entries.

In the metropolitan district eighty-four will tee off at the Siwanoy Country Club, Mt. Vernon, in quest of the twenty-two qualifying places. Chicago, with seventy-four entries, has been allotted nineteen places.

Standing of Clubs In Minor Leagues

INTERNATIONAL LEAGUE

YESTERDAY'S RESULTS

Toronto, 2; Jersey City, 1 (1st)
Jersey City, 10; Toronto, 1 (2d)
Newark, 4; Rochester, 0 (night game).
Albany, 4; Buffalo, 0 (night game).
Other clubs not scheduled

STANDING OF THE CLUBS

	W.	L.	Pct.		W.	L.	Pct.
Newark	77	50	606	Albany	60	66	.476
Rochester	68	59	.535	Montreal	59	67	.468
Baltimore	68	60	.531	Buffalo	59	68	.465
Toronto	64	63	.504	Jersey City	51	73	.411

GAMES TODAY

Newark at Rochester
Jersey City at Toronto
Albany at Buffalo
Baltimore at Montreal

AMERICAN ASSOCIATION

At Toledo—

					R.	H.	E.
Milwaukee	000	000	301	—	4	10	1
Toledo	004	000	12x	—	7	12	1

Batteries—Hillin, Gregory and Young, Bengough; Winegarner and Healy.

At Columbus—

					R.	H.	E.
Kansas City	000	001	003	—	4	10	2
Columbus	011	000	102	—	5	10	2

Batteries—Mails and Brenzel, Gaston; Lee and Gonzales.

STANDING OF THE CLUBS

	W.	L.	Pct.		W.	L.	Pct.
Columbus	73	39	.652	Toledo	56	59	.487
*Minn'p'lis	63	53	.543	*Louisv	55	58	.487
*St. Paul	64	54	.542	Milw'kee	47	66	.416
*India'plis	55	55	.500	K. City	45	74	.378

* Night game.

SOUTHERN ASSOCIATION

At New Orleans—

					R.	H.	E.
Atlanta	000	000	012	—	3	10	4
New Orleans	200	000	11x	—	4	7	1

Batteries—Durham, C. Moore and Neisler; Galehouse and Autry.

At Knoxville—

					R.	H.	E.
Birmingham	000	000	000	—	0	5	1
Knoxville	000	023	20x	—	7	10	1

Batteries—Lisenbee, White and Berres; Rabb and Head.

Little Rock-Nashville, night game.
Other clubs not scheduled.

STANDING OF THE CLUBS

	W.	L.	Pct.		W.	L.	Pct.
Knoxville	26	15	.634	Chat'nooga	21	22	.488
N. Orleans	24	18	.571	Lit. Rock	19	23	.452
Nashville	19	18	.514	Birm'ham	17	21	.447
Memphis	20	20	.500	Atlanta	16	25	.390

NEW YORK-PA. LEAGUE

At Elmira—

					R.	H.	E.
Harrisburg	141	000	000	—	6	7	0
Elmira	000	010	002	—	3	8	2

Batteries—C. Eckert and Karlon; Lyons, A. Eckert and Chervinko.

York at Binghamton, night game.
Other clubs not scheduled.

STANDING OF THE CLUBS

	W.	L.	Pct.		W.	L.	Pct.
Bingha'ton	60	40	.600	Elmira	47	50	.485
Reading	53	45	.541	Harrisburg	49	55	.471
Wilkes-B.	53	51	.510	Williams't.	46	54	.460
Scranton	52	51	.505	York	42	56	.429

PACIFIC COAST LEAGUE

No games scheduled.

STANDING OF THE CLUBS

	W.	L.	Pct.		W.	L.	Pct.
Portland	75	51	.595	Oakland	56	70	.444
Hollywood	74	51	.592	San Fran.	52	75	.409
L. Angeles	75	52	.591	Missions	52	76	.406
Sac'mento	75	53	.586	Seattle	46	77	.374

Yankees Overpower Red Sox, 16-12, With 23 Hits, Gehrig and Ruth Collecting Home Runs

Pennock Wins At Boston, but Fails to Finish

New York Scores 6 Times in Third; Farrell Gets 3 Hits in First 4 Innings

Special to the Herald Tribune

BOSTON, Sept. 23.—The Yankees aren't going either up or down before the current baseball campaign comes to a close, but they still have plenty to play for. Perhaps the heavy hitting they turned loose against the Red Sox this afternoon served only to win a futile ball game, 16 to 12, on the surface, but their twenty-three hits also served as ammunition for winter arguments against salary cuts.

The Yankees may have finished their fighting for the dear old pennant, but they were in there today hammering away with a right good will for themselves, building up batting averages at the expense of the Red Sox pitching staff that they hope to use as an argument when the times comes to sign contracts for 1934.

Gehrig and Ruth Hit Homers

Like the Yankees, neither Babe Ruth nor Lou Gehrig is going any place in the home run derby, for Jimmy Foxx is as far out of reach as the Washington Senators. Still, there's something in finishing second, and both were after that for debating purposes, if nothing else. Gehrig hit his thirty-first of the season in the first inning and was runner-up momentarily, but Ruth hit his thirty-first in the fourth and they were tied again.

In between the Yankees put on a six-run storm that should have pulled them well out of danger from the Boston bats, but the Red Sox apparently had some ideas about the coming winter themselves, and hung on to the finish of a battle where a four-run lead was as fragile as a cellophane bathing suit.

Herb Pennock and Lloyd Brown, a couple of left-handers, were first to face the firing squads, but no respect was given the age of the former and no bows were made to the youth of the latter. Both were hit with abandon. Pennock was credited with the victory.

Three Hits for Farrell

The most important bid for consideration next year was made by Eddie Farrell, who singled three times in the first four innings. Chapman also boosted his average and Ruth got over the .300 mark.

Ben Chapman put on some speed and brought his base thefts to twenty-six for the year. It still is something short of Ben's record, which is 61, but good enough to lead the league.

Among one of the most unexpected bids for recognition next year is that of George Rensa, the Yankee catcher obtained merely as a substitute for Bill Dickey when Arndt Jorgens fell ill toward the end of August. No one took Rensa very seriously until he stepped in and started hitting. Nor has he slowed down his pace.

Tomorrow will be Charlie Devens's Day and the former Harvard pitcher and halfback will do the hurling for the Yankees. He had been looking forward to the occasion until he got a good view of the way the Red Sox were hitting today. Now he wonders if it wouldn't be better to postpone the celebration.

Boston gets a break in having the Yankees at Fenway Park over the week end, for that's the only time the customers get a chance to see Babe Ruth these days. The score:

NEW YORK (A. L.)	ab	r	h	po	a	e
Byrd, cf, rf	5	2	3	2	0	0
Farrell, 2b	5	3	3	5	2	0
Ruth, lf	5	2	2	0	0	0
Combs, lf, cf	1	0	1	2	0	0
Gehrig, 1b	5	4	4	8	0	0
Chapman, rf	5	2	3	4	0	0
Sewell, 3b	0	0	0	0	0	0
Lary, 3b, lf	3	1	1	0	4	1
Rensa, c	5	0	2	5	1	1
Crosetti, ss	5	2	3	1	3	3
PEN'OCK, p	3	0	0	0	2	0
MOORE, p	1	0	1	0	0	0
V. ATTA, p	0	0	0	0	0	0
Totals	43	16	23	27	12	5

BOSTON (A. L.)	ab	r	h	po	a	e
Werber, ss	5	2	1	3	7	0
Stumpf, cf	6	0	2	3	0	0
Cooke, rf	4	1	0	1	0	1
§Oliver	1	0	0	0	0	0
Jolley, lf	2	0	0	3	0	0
Almada, lf	2	3	2	0	0	0
¶McManus	1	0	0	0	0	0
Ferrell, c	6	0	3	5	5	2
Judge, 1b	2	2	1	4	0	0
Seeds, 1b	3	0	1	3	1	0
Walters, 3b	5	1	1	1	1	0
Muller, 2b	5	1	3	4	1	0
BROWN, p	0	0	0	0	0	0
WELCH, p	1	0	0	0	0	0
*Leggett	1	0	0	0	0	0
KLINE, p	0	0	0	0	1	0
†Alexander	1	1	1	0	0	0
FULL'ON, p	1	0	0	0	0	0
Hodapp	1	1	1	0	0	0
Totals	47	12	16	27	16	3

*Batted for Welch in fourth inning.
†Batted for Kline in sixth inning.
‡Batted for Fullerton in ninth inning.
§Batted for Cooke in ninth inning.
¶Batted for Almada in ninth inning.

New York .... 2 0 6 3 1 1 2 1 0—16
Boston .... 0 0 1 3 1 4 0 2 1—12

Runs batted in—Gehrig (3), Rensa (3), Farrell, Chapman (2), Ruth (3), Byrd, Crosetti, Moore, Muller, Almada, Werber, Ferrell (2), Seeds (2). Two-base hits—Rensa, Chapman, Byrd, Gehrig (2), Crosetti, Combs, Muller. Three-base hit—Byrd. Home runs—Gehrig, Ruth, Almada. Stolen bases—Chapman (2). Sacrifices—Pennock, Farrell. Double play—Kline, Werber and Seeds. Left on bases—New York, 7; Boston, 11. Bases on balls—Off Pennock, 1; off Moore, 2; off Brown, 1; off Welch, 1; off Fullerton, 2. Struck out—By Pennock, 3; by Van Atta, 1; by Brown, 2; by Kline, 1; by Fullerton, 1. Hits—Off Pennock, 12 in 5 2-3 innings; off Moore, 4 in 2 1-3; off Van Atta, 0 in 1; off Brown, 7 in 2 1-3; off Welch, 5 in 1 2-3; off Kline, 5 in 2; off Fullerton, 6 in 3. Hit by pitcher—By Kline (Chapman). Wild pitches—Pennock, Welch. Winning pitcher—Pennock. Losing pitcher—Brown. Umpires—Moriarty and Ormsby. Time—2:25.

West Chester Teachers Lose to Villanova, 45-0

VILLANOVA, Pa., Sept. 23 (AP).—Profiting by some of their opponents' mistakes, the Villanova College football team opened the season today with a 45 to 0 victory over West Chester Teachers' College.

The winners scored six touchdowns, four points after touchdowns, a safety and a field goal.

Captain Whitey Randour, Carroll Cook, Frank Wetzler, Joe Weisenbaugh, Ed Michaels and Johnny Higgins scored the touchdowns and Bill Cavanaugh drop kicked the field goal from the 22-yard line.

Vincent Renshaw, of the Teachers' team, suffered a leg injury and was taken to a hospital where an X-ray was taken to determine whether he received a fracture. He is a halfback and his home is in Wilkes-Barre, Pa.

Today's Sports

BASEBALL

New York Giants vs. Boston Braves, two games, National League games, at Polo Grounds, Eighth Avenue and 157th Street, 2 p. m.

Brooklyn Dodgers vs. Philadelphia, National League game, at Ebbets Field, Bedford Avenue and Sullivan Street, Brooklyn, 3 p. m.

POLO

Open championship game, Aurora vs. Hurricanes, at Meadow Brook Club, Westbury, L. I., 3:30 p. m.

Open championship game, Sands Point vs. Westbury, at Sands Point Club, Port Washington, L. I., 3:30 p. m.

Fort Hamilton vs. West Point, at Fort Hamilton, Fort Hamilton Parkway and 99th Street, Brooklyn, 3 p. m.

GOLF

Invitation tournaments at Nassau Country Club, Glen Cove, L. I., 9 a. m.

TENNIS

Invitation tournament, at Pelham (N. Y.) Country Club, 2 p. m.

SOCCER

Brooklyn vs. Hakoah Americans, at Starlight Park, East 177th Street, Bronx, 3 p. m.

TRACK

Round Tower A. C. games, at Brooklyn Sports Stadium, 2 p. m.

Late 1933 Model of Pennant-Winning Giants' Infield

Associated Press photo

Inner defense of the National League champions which is expected to start against the Senators in the World Series. Left to right: Travis Jackson, third base; Blondy Ryan, shortstop; Hughie Critz, second base, and Bill Terry, manager, first base. Jackson, a shortstop in normal times, is filling in at third for Johnny Verges, out of play as the result of an operation for appendicitis

Ghosts of Old Champion Giants Parade as Pennant Flies Again

By Richards Vidmer

THE Giants—champions of the National League!

Through the rich romance of the game, since baseball was organized into leagues and became the pastime of a nation, that phrase occurs and recurs, bringing back thrilling memories to those who are not so young as once they were.

The Giants—champions of the National League!

There have been intervals when other clubs came thundering to the fore to take their place at the peak when the pennants fly. There have been lan years at the Polo Grounds, but only once since they won their first championship just forty-five years ago, have nine years passed without the Giants being champions of the National League.

What dramatic pictures the names of Jim Mutrie, Tim Keefe, Mike Welch, Buck Ewing, Roger Connor and the dapper James Montgomery Ward must recall to those who were young in another century.

These were the men who first wrote that sentence across an early page in the game's history: The Giants—Champions of the National League. Twice they won the only big league pennant that flew in those days, in 1888 and 1889. The game still was young and victory wasn't of national importance, but it marked the beginning of New York's oft repeated rule.

Success Returns in 1904

The late eighties give way to the gay nineties and the century fades before another flag flies at the Giants' field. Then, with the arrival of the fiery little Napoleon, John McGraw, success returns in 1904 and 1905.

A fair-haired youngster named Mathewson, Joe McGinity, called the Iron Man; Roger Bresnahan, Mike Donlin, Billy Gilbert, Arthur Devlin—these write their names across a horizon as horse cars clatter and clang along Broadway, hand organs grind out giddy tunes at Forty-second Street. The Flatiron Building rises high above the skyline and men toil in the fields of the Bronx. Automobiles are "horseless buggies" and Teddy Roosevelt, the President, is a Giant fan.

New York is baseball conscious by now an dthis swaggering, fighting, two-fisted group of athletes that parades to the park in tallyhos each day is cheered along the way, the heroes of the city, the gods of the baseball world.

Half a dozen years pass. Then another crew slips before the spotlight to take its bow. Matty is in his prime, Donlin is slowing down, but Rube Marquard, "the $11,000 lemon," who turned out to be a peach; Chief Meyers, the big and bulky Indian; Fred Merkle, Larry Doyle, Red Murray, Jeff Tesreau and Tillie Shafer have come to take the places of the departed great.

Rule for Three Years

For three years they rule, 1911, 1912 and 1913. Jim Thorpe is the hero of the Olympic Games. The Castles are the dancing sensations of the city. Automobiles are accepted as common carriers and taxicabs clutter up Broadway. Hazel Dawn is the star of the stage, "Seven Keys to Baldpate" is a theatrical hit and a song-plugger bellows the "International Rag" through a megaphone at the World Series.

The Braves, the Phillies and the Dodgers each step in and win a pennant through the next three seasons, then once more it's the Giants—champions of the National League. Georgie Burns and Buck Herzog, Heinie Zimmerman and Arthur Fletcher, Benny Kauff and Dave Robertson drive in the runs behind the pitching of Ferdie Schupp, Slim Sallee and Rube Benton. But for the moment they are secondary heroes.

War drums are sounding in the distance and most of the spectators are men in uniform. Hank Gowdy and Eddie Grant have deserted their teams and enlisted. The Lusitania has gone down. Gynemer, the Frenchman, is the war's greatest air ace. A youngster from St. Paul's School has joined the Lafayette Escadrille, his name, Tommy Hitchcock. They are playing "Over There" in the streets and song hits from "Leave It to Jane" in the cabarets. Shanley's, Churchill's and the Ziegfeld Roof are packing in the crowds.

Four More Flags in Row

Five years later. The war is over. Prohibition has brought new words and new ways, but another great Giant crew is assembled with McGraw, now silvery haired, still at the head. He has won six pennants since taking hold way back there in 1904. Now he wins four more in a row.

Long George Kelley, Li'l Arthur Nehf, Beauty Bancroft, Shufflin' Phil Douglas, Frisch, the Fordham Flash; Heine Groh, with his bottle bat; Casey Stengel, the clown, and Pep Young pass in the parade of memory as those three World Series with the Yankees were played and one with the Washington Senators. Here were more names rich with romance to add to the collection who had helped, from time to time, to make them the Giants—champions of the National League.

And now the roll of honor will include Bill Terry, Carl Hubbell, Hal Schumacher, Mel Ott and Blondie Ryan, the raw rookie who typified the spirit of this year's Giants in a seven-word telegram which he sent as he hurried to join them in the midst of a losing streak:

"They cannot beat us enroute."

As it turned out, they couldn't.

Columbus Plays Bisons Today In Little World Series Opener

Red Birds, Winners of First Pennant in 26 Years, to Start With Lee in Box

By The Associated Press

COLUMBUS, Ohio, Sept. 23.—After twenty-six years of waiting and sixteen years of hoping, the Columbus Red Birds will meet the Buffalo Bisons in the first game of the 1933 Little World Series here tomorrow afternoon.

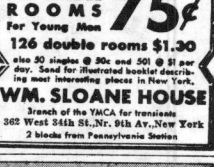

It has been twenty-six years since Columbus won a pennant in the American Association and the first time in the sixteen-year history of the series that the Ohio team has participated.

Four games will be played here—Sunday and Monday at 3 p. m. (E. S. T.) and Tuesday and Wednesday beneath the arc lights starting at 8 p. m. (E. S. T.)—before the clubs shuffle off to Buffalo to conclude the classic of the minor leagues.

Rivals Picked in Playoffs

Columbus won the right to play in the series by finishing far out in front at the end of the regular season and then went on to whip the Minneapolis club in a playoff.

Buffalo finished fourth at the end of the season, defeated Baltimore three straight games in the first playoff and last night won its third contest in five starts from the Rochester Red Wings. This was the first year the International League and American Association had used the playoff system to determine the champions.

The series will bring together two former major league players as managers of the teams. Ray Schalk, former catching star, will guide the Bisons, while Ray Blades will be at the helm of the Red Birds.

The Buffalo club arrived today, and plans for a workout in the Red Bird Stadium was abandoned as a result of rain. Columbus had its final workout last night in an exhibition game at Zanesville against the Mid-Atlantic League champions. Zanesville won, 8 to 6.

Lee to Pitch Opener

Blades has selected Bill Lee for his starting pitcher tomorrow. Lee, who has been sold to the Chicago Cubs for spring delivery, was one of the Birds' leading hurlers last summer and won the opening game in the play-off series with Minneapolis. Bill De Lancey will be behind the bat. The rest of the line-up will be the same as started the majority of regular games—Heath, Whitehead, Borgman and Riggs in the infield, and Cullop, Rothrock and Anderson in the outfield.

Schalk was non-commital on his starting pitcher and said he would make no announcement until he saw them work out tomorrow.

Red Bird officials announced that if favorable weather prevailed they expected a sellout for the four home games. The stadium will seat 20,000 persons.

Senators Shift Line-Up, Lose To Athletics, 3-1

Victors Bunch Four of Five Hits Off Monte Weaver in 6th and 7th Innings

By The Associated Press

WASHINGTON, Sept. 23.—The Senators, American League champions, took a 3-to-1 beating today from the Philadelphia Athletics.

Monte Weaver held the Athletics to five hits, but four of these came in the sixth and seventh to net enough tallies to win.

Joe Cronin, manager, began easing up on his Senators, who meet the New York Giants in the World Series. He shifted his line-up from time to time, Boken relieving Myer, Rice going in for Manush and Harris for Schulte.

The score:

PHILADELPHIA (A. L.)	ab	r	h	po	a	e
Bishop, 2b	4	1	1	0	5	0
Cramer, cf	4	0	0	1	0	0
Cochrane, c	3	0	1	4	0	0
Foxx, 1b	4	0	1	9	0	0
McNair, ss	4	0	0	4	2	1
Johnson, lf	3	1	0	8	0	0
Higgins, 3b	4	1	1	1	2	0
Finney, rf	3	0	1	0	0	0
CAIN, p	3	0	0	0	1	0
Totals	32	3	5	27	10	1

WASHINGTON (A. L.)	ab	r	h	po	a	e
Myer, 2b	3	1	1	2	1	0
Boken, 2b	2	0	0	0	2	0
Goslin, rf	4	0	0	0	0	0
Manush, lf	2	0	1	2	0	0
Rice, lf	2	0	1	2	0	0
Cronin, ss	4	0	0	1	6	0
Schulte, cf	2	0	0	2	0	0
Harris, cf	1	0	0	1	0	0
Kuhel, 1b	4	0	1	14	0	0
Bluege, 3b	4	0	2	0	2	0
Bolton, c	4	0	1	3	0	0
WEAVER, p	3	0	0	0	0	0
*Travis	1	0	0	0	0	0
Totals	36	1	7	27	11	0

*Batted for Weaver in ninth inning.

Philadelphia ..... 0 0 0 0 0 1 2 0 0—3
Washington ..... 0 0 0 0 1 0 0 0 0—1

Runs batted in—Goslin, Cochrane, Finney, Cain. Two-base hits—Manush, Bishop, Cochrane, Finney. Three-base hit—Myer. Left on bases—Philadelphia, 4; Washington, 9. Bases on balls—Off Cain, 1; off Weaver, 2. Struck out—By Cain, 2; by Weaver, 3. Umpires—Summers and McGowan. Time—1:35.

Chicago Beats Indians, 6 to 5, in 11th Inning

By The Associated Press

CLEVELAND, Sept. 23.—Clint Brown's pass of Al Simmons in the eleventh inning today enabled the Chicago White Sox to nose out the Cleveland Indians, 6 to 5, in a nip-and-tuck struggle.

Appling followed Simmons's walk with a single and Brown purposely passed Swanson, whereupon Berry sent a fly to the outfield to score Simmons.

Brown had relieved Mel Harder in the sixth inning when the Sox staged a three-run uprising, and had pitched effectively against Joe Heving, who had succeeded Leslie Tietje in the same inning.

The score:

CHICAGO (A. L.)	ab	r	h	po	a	e
Stone'm, rf	3	0	0	2	0	0
Hayes, 2b	1	0	0	0	4	0
Haas, cf	5	1	1	4	0	0
Dykes, 3b	4	1	0	1	2	1
Simmons, lf	5	2	2	4	0	0
Appling, ss	5	0	3	2	5	0
Kress, 1b	5	0	1	14	0	0
English, 2b	2	0	0	2	2	1
Swanson, rf	2	0	0	1	0	0
Berry, c	6	0	0	3	0	0
TIETJE, p	1	1	0	0	1	0
*Roeck	1	1	1	0	0	0
HEVING, p	3	0	1	0	1	0
Totals	43	6	9	33	15	2

CLEVELAND (A. L.)	ab	r	h	po	a	e
Porter, rf	4	0	0	4	0	0
Knickb'r, ss	4	0	0	2	1	0
Burnett, 2b	4	1	0	2	1	1
Averill, cf	4	1	1	8	0	0
Trosky, 1b	5	1	1	10	2	0
Hale, 3b	5	2	2	1	4	2
Ferrell, lf	4	0	[illegible]	1	0	0
Pytlak, c	5	0	1	5	0	0
HARDER, p	2	0	0	0	2	0
BROWN, p	2	0	0	0	2	0
Totals	39	5	6	33	12	3

*Batted for Tietje in sixth inning.

Chicago .... 0 0 1 0 1 3 0 0 0 0 1—6
Cleveland ...... 0 1 3 0 0 0 0 1 0 0 0—5

Runs batted in—Appling (3), Haas, Simmons, Berry, Trosky, Hale, Ferrell, Pytlak. Two-base hits—Hale, Kress, Haas. Three-base hit—Simmons. Stolen base—Swanson. Sacrifices—Haas, Hayes. Double play—English, Appling and Kress. Left on bases—Chicago, 15; Cleveland, 6. Bases on balls—Off Harder, 5; off Brown, 3; off Tietje, 5. Struck out—By Brown, 2; by Tietje, 2; by Heving, 1. Hits—Off Tietje, 4 in 5 innings; off Heving, 2 in 6; off Harder, 6 in 5 2-3; off Brown, 3 in 5 1-3. Hit by pitcher—By Harder (Dykes). Winning pitcher—Heving. Losing pitcher—Brown. Umpires—Owens and Geisel. Time—2:45.

ST. LOUIS (A. L.)	ab	r	h	po	a	e
Scharein, 3b	4	0	0	0	1	0
West, cf	4	1	2	2	0	0
Reynolds, lf	5	0	0	2	0	0
Campbell, rf	5	0	1	2	0	0
Melillo, 2b	4	1	0	2	5	0
Gullic, 1b	2	1	1	12	0	0
Helmsley, c	3	0	2	4	0	0
Levey, ss	3	0	1	0	4	0
BLA'DER, p	2	0	1	1	2	1
†Storti, 3b	1	0	0	0	0	0
BRAXT'N, p	0	0	0	0	0	0
*Hornsby	1	0	0	0	0	0
Totals	34	3	8	24	12	1

DETROIT (A. L.)	ab	r	h	po	a	e
Rogell, ss	3	2	2	2	2	0
Fox, cf	4	1	1	4	1	0
Gehr'ger, 2b	4	0	1	1	5	0
Stone, rf	4	1	1	1	0	0
Greenb'g, 1b	4	0	0	14	1	0
Walker, lf	4	0	1	1	0	0
Schuble, 3b	3	0	0	0	[illegible]	0
Hayworth, c	3	0	0	4	0	0
HAMLIN, p	3	1	1	0	0	2
MARB'Y, p	0	0	0	0	0	0
Totals	32	5	7	27	12	2

*Batted for Levey in eighth inning.
†Batted for Blaeholder in eighth inning.

St. Louis .... 0 1 1 1 0 0 0 0 0—3
Detroit .... 0 0 0 0 0 4 0 1 x—5

Runs batted in—Stone (2), Greenberg, Fox, Rogell, Blaeholder, West Levey. Two-base hits—Walker, Blaeholder, Hamlin. Three-base hits—Campbell, Rogell, Stone. Home run—West. Sacrifices—Hemsley, Blaeholder. Double play—Gehringer, Rogell and Greenberg. Left on bases—Detroit, 4; St. Louis, 10. Bases on balls—Off Hamlin, 4; off Braxton, 1. Struck out—By Hamlin, 3; by Marberry, 1; by Blaeholder, 3; by Braxton, 1. Hits—Off Hamlin, 7 in 7 1-3 innings; off Marberry, 1 in 1 2-3; off Blaeholder, 6 in 7; off Braxton, 1 in 1. Winning pitcher—Hamlin. Losing pitcher—Blaeholder. Umpires—Van Graflan, Hildebrand and Dinneen. Time—1:47.

Phillies Split With Braves By 5-4 Scores

Klein, Davis and Moore Hit Homers in First; Boston Rally in 8th Wins Second

By The Associated Press

PHILADELPHIA, Sept. 23.—The Phillies and Braves divided a double-header today, the locals winning the first game, 5 to , and the visitors taking the second, also by 5 to 4.

Both games were "see-saw" contests in which the lead changed several times. Chick Fullis provided the winning hit for the Phillies in the first game. eH singled to right field with a man on third base.

A two-run rally by the Braves in the eighth inning, with the score 4 to 3 in favor of the Phils, turned the tide in the nightcap.

Chuck Klein hit his twenty-eighth home run of the season in the opening encounter. Spud Davis and Randy Moore also hit for the circuit in the first game.

The scores:

FIRST GAME

BOSTON (N. L.)	ab	r	h	po	a	e
Thomp'n, cf	4	0	2	2	0	0
Lee, cf	1	0	0	0	0	0
Mowry, lf	5	0	0	0	0	0
Urbanski, ss	4	0	0	3	7	0
R. Moore, rf	4	1	1	0	0	0
Jordan, 1b	4	0	2	12	1	0
Whitney, 3b	4	2	3	0	1	0
Maran'le, 2b	3	0	0	3	3	0
Hoan, c	4	0	2	4	0	0
*Gyselman	0	0	0	0	0	0
SMITH, p	0	0	0	0	1	0
FRANK'E, p	3	1	2	0	5	0
†Harrave	0	0	0	0	0	0
Spohrer, c	1	0	0	0	0	0
Totals	37	4	12	24	18	0

PHILADELPHIA (N. L.)	ab	r	h	po	a	e
Fullis, cf	5	1	2	4	0	0
Bartell, ss	4	0	1	2	5	1
Klein, rf	3	1	3	1	0	0
Hurst, 1b	3	0	0	12	2	0
Davis, c	3	1	2	1	1	0
Schul'ch, lf	4	1	3	2	0	0
Haslin, 2b	1	1	0	3	2	0
McLeod, 3b	3	0	1	1	2	0
GRAB'KI, p	2	0	1	1	0	0
ELLIOTT, p	1	0	0	0	0	0
Totals	29	5	13	27	12	1

*Ran for Hogan in eighth inning.
†Batted for Frankhouse in eighth inning.

Boston .... 0 0 1 1 1 0 0 1 0—4
Philadelphia .... 0 0 0 2 0 0 2 1 x—5

Runs batted in—Mowry, Frankhouse, R. Moore, Hogan, Davis, McLeod, Klein (2), Fullis. Two-base hits—Jordan, Whitney, McLeod. Home runs—Davis, R. Moore, Klein. Sacrifices—Haslin (2), Bartell, Maranville, MvLeod. Double plays—Maranville, Urbanski and Jordan (2); Jordan, Urbanski and Jordan; Hurst and Haslin. Left on bases—Philadelphia, 9; Boston, 9. Bases on balls—Off Frankhouse, 4; off Smith, 1; off Grabowski, 1. Struck out—By Frankhouse, 3; by Elliot, 1. Hits—Off Frankhouse, 12 in 7 innings; off Smith, 1 in 1; off Grabowski, 12 in 7 1-3; off Elliott, 0 in 1 2-3. Hit by pitcher—By Grabowski (Urbanski). Passed balls—Davis. Winning pitcher—Smith. Umpires—Quigley and Stark. Time—1:40.

SECOND GAME

BOSTON (N. L.)	ab	r	h	po	a	e
Urbanski, ss	5	1	2	2	2	0
Thom'n, cf	4	1	2	1	0	0
Spohrer, c	0	0	0	0	0	0
Jordan, 1b	4	1	2	12	1	0
R. Moore, rf	5	0	1	0	0	0
Whitney, 3b	4	0	2	2	6	0
Mowry, lf	4	0	1	6	1	0
Hoan, c	3	0	1	1	1	0
*Gyselman	0	0	0	0	0	0
Maran'le, 2b	5	1	0	3	5	0
CANT'L, p	2	0	0	0	0	0
†Harrave	0	0	0	0	0	0
MANGUM, p	0	0	0	0	0	0
Lee, cf	0	1	0	0	0	0
ZACHARY, p	1	0	0	0	0	0
BETTS, p	0	0	0	0	0	0
Totals	37	5	11	27	16	0

PHILADELPHIA (N. L.)	ab	r	h	po	a	e
Fullis, cf	4	0	0	2	0	0
Bartell, ss	4	1	1	1	4	0
Klein, rf	4	1	3	5	0	0
Hurst, 1b	3	0	2	13	2	0
Davis, c	3	1	0	1	0	0
Schul'ch, lf	2	1	1	1	0	0
Haslin, 2b	4	0	1	2	4	0
McLeod, 3b	1	0	0	0	1	0
‡McCurdy	1	0	1	0	0	0
Warner, 3b	2	0	1	1	1	0
HOLLEY, p	3	0	0	0	2	0
ELLIOTT, p	0	0	0	1	0	0
§Todd	1	0	0	0	0	0
Totals	32	4	10	27	14	0

*Ran for Hogan in eighth inning.
†Batted for Cantwell in sixth inning.
‡Batted for McLeod in fourth inning.
§Batted for Elliott in ninth inning.

Boston .... 2 0 0 0 1 0 0 2 0—5
Philadelphia .... 0 0 0 3 1 0 0 0 0—4

Runs batted in—R. Moore, Whitney, Jordan (2), Urbanski, Haslin, McCurdy (2), Hurst. Sacrifices—Mowry, Hurst. Double plays—Whitney, Maranville and Jordan (2); Mowry and Jordan. Left on bases—Philadelphia, 6; Boston, 12. Bases on balls—Off Cantwell, 2; off Zachary, 1; off Holley, 3; off Elliott, 1. Struck out—By Mangum, 1; by Holley, 1. Hits—Off Holley, 10 in 7 1-3 innings; off Elliott, 1 in 1 2-3; off Cantwell, 8 in 5; off Mangum, 0 in 2; off Zachary, 2 in 1 (none out in ninth); off Betts, 1 in 1. Hit by pitcher—By Cantwell (Davis). Winning pitcher—Mangum. Losing pitcher—Holley. Umpires—Stark and Quigley. Time—2:00.

Pirates Beat Cards, 9-3; Second Game Called Off

ST. LOUIS, Sept. 23 (AP).—A steady attack gave the Pirates a 9-to-3 victory over the Cardinals here today in a game delayed two hours by rain. The second game of what was to have been a double-header could not be played because of darkness.

The score:

PITTSBURGH (N. L.)	ab	r	h	po	a	e
Jensen, lf	5	2	3	2	0	0
Linds'm, cf	5	1	2	2	0	0
P. Waner, rf	5	1	2	2	0	0
Traynor, 3b	4	1	1	0	0	0
Vaughan, ss	3	2	2	4	4	0
Suhr, 1b	4	0	0	7	1	0
Theve'w, 2b	5	1	3	3	3	0
Padden, c	4	1	1	7	1	0
BIRK'ER, p	5	0	1	0	2	0
Totals	40	9	15	27	11	0

ST. LOUIS (N. L.)	ab	r	h	po	a	e
Martin, 3b	4	0	1	1	1	3
Watkins, rf	2	1	1	3	0	0
Frisch, 2b	4	0	0	8	6	1
Medwick, lf	4	1	2	0	1	0
Collins, 1b	3	1	1	6	0	0
Moore, cf	4	0	2	2	0	0
Durocher, ss	3	0	0	2	5	0
Lewis, c	3	0	0	5	0	0
HALLA'N, p	3	0	1	0	3	0
*Allen	1	0	0	0	0	0
Totals	31	3	8	27	16	4

*Batted for Hallahan in ninth inning.

Pittsburgh .... 0 1 1 1 1 1 2 1 2—9
St. Louis .... 0 0 0 3 0 0 0 0 0—3

Runs batted in—Lndstrom (2), Thevenow (2), Traynor, Jensen, Suhr, Birkofer, Medwick, Collins, Moore. Two-base hits—Jensen, Traynor, Medwick. Three-base hit—Collins. Home run—Lindstrom. Sacrifices—Lewis, Padden, Traynor, Suhr. Double plays—Durocher, Frisch and Collins; Thevenow, Vaughan and Suhr; Martin, Frisch and Collins; Vaughan, Thevenow and Suhr. Left on bases—Pittsburgh, 10; St. Louis, 6. Bases on balls—Off Birkofer, 4; off Halahan, 3. Struck out—By Birkofer, 7; by Hallahan, 4. Wild pitch—Birkofer. Umpires—Klem, Pfirman and Barr. Time—2:10.

Cubs Shatter Derringer as Reds Lose, 7-1

Cincinnati Pitcher Suffers His 27th Setback of Season; Bush Wins 19th

CHICAGO, Sept. 23 (AP).—Paul Derringer, the majors' "losingest" pitcher, suffered his twenty-seventh defeat of the season today as the Chicago Cubs defeated the Cincinnati Reds, 7 to 1, in the opening game o ftheir series.

Guy Bush went the route for the Cubs for his nineteenth victory and was deprived of a shut out only by Jim Bottomley's home run with one out in the ninth.

After Derringer pitched perfect ball the first three innings, he was nicked for a run in the fourth on Mark Koenig's triple and a fly and then was chased in the sixth as successive singles by Koenig, W. Herman, Cuyler and F. Herman opened the inning by scoring two and leaving two men on.

After Demaree sacrificed and Grimm was purposely passed, filling the bases, Ray Kolp, Derringer's successor, was the victim of a home run by Gabby Hartnett. It was the sixteenth of the season for the big Cub catcher.

The score:

CINCINNATI (N. L.)	ab	r	h	po	a	e
Adams, 3b	4	0	1	0	2	0
Moore, lf	4	0	0	3	0	0
Hafey, cf	4	0	0	2	0	0
Bottom'y, 1b	4	1	2	11	0	0
Rice, rf	4	0	1	3	0	0
Lombardi, c	4	0	1	2	0	0
Morris'y, 2b	3	0	1	1	8	0
Bluege, ss	3	0	0	2	2	0
DER'GER, p	2	0	0	0	2	0
KOLP, p	0	0	0	0	1	0
*Roettger	1	0	1	0	0	0
STOUT, p	0	0	0	0	0	0
Totals	33	1	7	24	15	0

CHICAGO (N. L.)	ab	r	h	po	a	e
Koenig, 3b	4	2	2	0	1	0
W. Her'n, 2b	4	1	1	3	7	0
Cuyler, lf	3	1	1	2	0	0
F. Her'n, rf	4	1	2	2	0	0
Demaree, cf	3	0	0	1	0	0
Grimm 1b	3	1	0	14	1	0
Hartnett, c	3	1	1	1	0	0
Jurgess, ss	3	0	1	4	5	0
BUSH, p	3	0	0	0	2	0
Totals	30	7	8	27	16	0

*Batted for Kolp in eighth inning.

Cincinnati .... 0 0 0 0 0 0 0 0 1—1
Chicago .... 0 0 0 1 0 6 0 0 x—7

Runs batted in—Bottomley, W. Herman, F. Herman (2), Hartnett (4). Three-base hit—Koenig. Home runs—Hartnett, Bottomley. Stolen base—F. Herman. Sacrifice—Demaree. Double plays—Morrissey, Bluege and Bottomley; W. Herman, Jurges and Grimm. Left on bases—Cincinnati, 5; Chicago, 2. Base on balls—Off Kolp, 1. Struck out—By Derringer, 1; by Kolp, 1. Hits—Off Derringer, 6 in 5 innings (none out in sixth); off Kolp, 1 in 2; off Stout, 1 in 1. Hit by pitcher—By Derringer (Cuyler). Losing pitcher — Derringer. Umpires — Rigler, Magerkurth and McGrew. Time—1:19.

Harris Resigns As Manager of Detroit Tigers

BuckyTells NavinSomeOne ElseShouldHaveChance; Successor Not Yet Named

By The Associated Press

DETROIT, Sept. 23.—Explaining that he felt somebody else should have a chance to see what he could do with the Detroit Tigers, Stanley R. (Bucky) Harris today submitted his resignation to Frank J. Navin, the club's president.

Navin reluctantly announced his manager's resignation at the close of the game with the St. Louis Browns, adding that he had been unable to persuade Harris to change his mind.

Harris said he was resigning because he felt it only fair to Navin that he step aside and give someone else an opportunity to direct the team. "Perhaps he can do better," said Harris, referring to his successor, who, Navin said, he had not yet selected.

"I am not going to sit around and blame the breaks," Harris said. "I dislike to sever my connections with the Tigers, but under the circumstances feel that it is the only fair thing to do."

Harris said he had no plans for next season, but hoped to remain in the American League.

The Tiger's retiring manager came to Detroit in 1929, succeeding George Moriarty as the team's pilot. Although he won two American League championships and one World Series for the Washington Senators before coming to Detroit, Harris was unable to make any headway toward giving Detroit a winning team.

During the five seasons Harris has managed the Tigers he has virtually rebuilt the team. Despite his efforts fifth is the highest the Tigers have finished under him. That was in 1932.

Navin said Harris's resignation had come to him so suddenly that he had not had time to even consider candidates for the managership.

International League Records

CLUB BATTING

Club.	G.	AB.	R.	H.	RBI.	SB.	Pct.
Buffalo	173	5804	1004	1712	913	123	.295
Baltimore	169	5570	969	1597	902	103	.287
Rochester	171	5700	856	1624	779	118	.285
Newark	170	5573	830	1556	763	96	.279
Albany	166	5489	783	1532	703	103	.279
Montreal	165	5289	744	1453	671	68	.275
Toronto	169	5415	741	1474	674	47	.272
Jer. City	165	5350	654	1389	594	61	.258

CLUB FIELDING

Club.	G.	PO.	A.	E.	DP.	TP.	Pct.
Montreal	165	4229	2000	146	152	1	.977
Newark	170	4351	1714	163	105	0	.974
Toronto	169	4191	1740	160	125	0	.974
Albany	166	4179	1954	180	156	0	.971
Baltimore	169	4248	1966	200	144	1	.969
Buffalo	173	4381	2084	212	152	0	.968
Jer. City	165	4143	2093	204	137	0	.968
Rochester	171	4315	1870	203	168	0	.968

INDIVIDUAL BATTING

Player, club.	G.	AB.	R.	H.	RBI.	SB.	Pct.
Mamaux, Nwk.	18	11	1	5	1	0	.455
Dugas, Albany	37	129	24	50	21	3	.388
Boone, Tor.	157	556	99	199	104	1	.3579
Solters, Balt.	150	537	123	192	158	19	.3575
Mize, Roch.	44	164	27	57	28	2	.348
Mulleavy, Buf.	158	631	129	216	70	20	.342
Arlett, Balt.	162	542	135	183	150	20	.338
Koen'cke, Buf.	166	620	119	209	102	29	.337
Clabaugh, Bal.	128	375	83	126	78	14	.336
Tate, Mont.	118	348	31	117	46	2	.335
Rolfe, Nwk.	160	621	118	204	78	21	.329
Stack, Jer. C.-Nwk.-Mont.	53	150	14	49	21	1	.327
Gallivan, Buf.	59	104	21	34	18	0	.327
Prim, Albany	41	68	6	22	12	0	.324
Tucker, Buf.	157	539	106	174	119	9	.323
Hinkle, Roch.	104	301	46	96	39	0	.319
Taylor, Alb.	144	529	87	166	42	12	.314
Carnegie, Buf.	152	538	106	168	121	9	.312
Redfern, Balt.	90	336	45	104	50	7	.310
Selkirk, N.-R.	160	560	106	173	108	25	.309
Howell, Tor.	138	449	65	138	71	4	.307
Shiver, Mont.	146	449	70	138	83	3	.307
Roettger, Mnt.	165	657	90	201	113	6	.306
S'ltzgaver, Nk.	169	635	109	193	191	20	.304
Neun, Nwk.	161	618	101	188	69	14	.304
Mills, Roch.	106	414	65	126	67	15	.304
Ripple, Mont.	157	602	97	182	83	7	.302
Thompson, Jer. C.-Buf.	167	641	115	192	95	36	.300
Hoag, Nwk.	154	579	87	173	108	10	.299
Toporcer, Rch.	137	495	96	147	37	19	.297
Moore, Nk.-Al.	138	455	66	135	75	4	.297
Lawrence, Tor.	145	537	77	159	68	6	.296
Rosenfeld, J.C.	132	480	65	142	70	8	.296
Watwood, Nk.	113	379	53	112	35	3	.296
Pepper, Roch.	149	573	77	169	104	4	.295
Carey, Roch.	171	706	97	207	61	9	.293
Fitzgerald, J.C.	81	284	44	83	42	4	.293
Kreevich, Alb.	162	599	107	175	82	26	.292
Puccinelli, Roch.-Nwk.	144	524	78	153	92	8	.292
Stroner, Balt.	141	508	64	148	73	6	.291
King, Albany	138	457	66	133	75	3	.291
Sprinz, Balt.	78	258	25	75	34	3	.291
Heffner, Balt.	167	642	123	186	66	12	.290
Kies, Nwk.	96	279	38	81	30	0	.290
Clancy, Jer. C.	161	605	67	175	89	2	.289
Benes, Jer. C.	76	251	32	72	16	6	.287
Gilbert, Roch.	79	283	40	81	34	8	.286
Linton, Balt.	90	273	43	78	44	0	.286
Brewer, Buf.	33	35	4	10	3	0	.286
McGow'n, Bal.	131	444	91	126	70	8	.284
Winsett, Mont.	114	314	47	89	61	2	.283
Kaufm'n, Rch.	45	99	15	28	10	1	.283
Brown, Roch.-J. C.-Buf.	150	550	86	155	48	17	.282
Florence, Roch.	94	257	32	72	39	1	.280
English, Buf.	133	466	63	130	74	2	.279
Olsen, Nwk.	85	244	34	68	27	3	.279
Brame, Tor.	58	86	6	24	19	0	.279
Jabl'wski, Nk.	27	68	10	19	5	0	.279
Walker, JC-M.	141	454	98	126	49	18	.278
Porter, Alb.	59	72	15	20	11	1	.278
Mallon, Tor.	167	625	87	171	78	10	.274
Smith, Buf.	165	613	100	168	87	6	.274

PITCHING RECORDS

Pitcher, club.	G.	H.	BB.	SO.	W.	L.	Pct.
Wilson, Buf.	42	253	61	89	15	6	.714
Smythe, Balt.	56	242	63	98	21	9	.700
Broaca, Nwk.	11	71	35	67	7	3	.700
Osterm'ler, Rch.	27	186	86	94	16	7	.696
Weaver, Nwk.	42	245	99	183	25	11	.694
Henry, Roch.	16	104	44	33	9	4	.692
Pomorski, Mont.	38	236	71	48	14	7	.667
Fisher, Mont.	53	106	57	26	10	5	.667
Filley, Albany	16	89	37	25	7	4	.636
Murphy, Nwk.	42	97	53	54	10	6	.625
Jablon'ski, Nwk.	23	162	62	55	13	8	.619
Deshong, Nwk.	36	250	127	115	16	10	.615
Brennan, Nwk.	11	70	24	41	6	4	.600
Gallivan, Buf.	51	298	99	110	16	11	.593
Melton, Balt.	40	285	110	127	16	11	.593
Prim, Albany	37	197	66	68	14	10	.583
Gould, Buf.	41	227	53	53	14	10	.583
Ggden, Balt.	19	87	52	21	7	5	.583
Ogden, Mont.	25	144	48	30	8	6	.571
Michaels, Mont.	52	236	91	85	17	13	.567
Fussell, Buf.-Al.	24	122	42	41	9	7	.563
Brame, Tor.	31	179	38	29	9	7	.563
Lucas, Buf.	27	153	75	33	9	7	.563
Miner, Nwk.-Al.	33	129	45	52	10	8	.556
Elliott, Buf.	35	147	97	60	10	9	.526
Blake, Roch.	24	157	74	59	10	9	.526
Perkins, J.C.-Bf.	43	233	140	135	15	13	.519
Kaufmann, Rch.	35	243	82	69	15	15	.500
Smith, Roch.	35	209	52	54	11	11	.500
Duke, Alb.-Nwk.	32	119	60	58	6	6	.500
Pr'homme, Balt.	39	213	85	50	12	13	.480
Campbell, Alb.	35	194	81	75	9	10	.474
Phelps, JC-Mont	35	234	92	79	13	16	.448
Porter, Albany	31	149	39	31	4	5	.444
Dietrich, Mont.	30	157	104	70	11	14	.440
Shealy, Albany	32	208	56	83	11	14	.440
Marrow, Tor.	41	240	60	64	11	15	.423
Cascarella, J. C.	32	198	85	75	10	14	.417
Claset, Balt.	28	196	82	55	7	10	.412
Mattingly, Balt.	36	199	71	46	8	12	.400
Mooney, Roch.	8	47	34	7	2	3	.400
A. Smith, Tor.-Mont.	38	210	51	42	7	12	.368
Meola, Jer. C.	35	158	97	60	7	13	.350
Pipgras, Jer. C.	35	181	54	39	7	13	.350
Collier, Tor.	41	240	88	60	9	17	.346
Hanlon, Jer. C.	20	123	56	30	5	10	.333
McAfee, Roch.	18	80	33	11	2	4	.333
Frazier, Tor.	36	135	80	30	4	9	.308
Milstead, Al.-Bf.	41	224	61	67	5	14	.263
Bartulis, Buf-JC	48	197	76	47	4	12	.250
Lindsey, Roch.	24	111	63	40	3	9	.250
Brewer, Buf.	33	137	64	47	2	7	.222
Slaalien, Jer. C.	8	68	22	8	1	4	.200
Cantrelli, Tor.-Balt.	21	100	29	39	2	9	.182

Major League Averages

National League

CLUB BATTING

Club.	G.	AB.	R.	H.	RBI.	SB.	Pct.
Pittsburgh	147	5174	630	1470	583	33	.284
St. Louis	148	5179	666	1430	615	95	.276
Chicago	149	5082	613	1372	574	56	.270
Phila'phia	141	4903	574	1326	542	51	.270
New York	147	5150	612	1367	572	30	.265
Brooklyn	145	4960	567	1296	519	77	.261
Boston	145	4873	489	1219	470	21	.250
Cincinnati	148	4983	480	1225	443	27	.246

CLUB FIELDING

Club.	G.	PO.	A.	E.	DP.	Pct.
Boston	145	3867	1751	131	131	.977
St. Louis	148	4086	1589	151	111	.974
New York	147	3988	1979	166	146	.973
Pittsburgh	147	3929	1741	160	130	.973
Cincinnati	148	3918	1882	169	128	.972
Chicago	149	3958	1799	164	155	.972
Brooklyn	145	3807	1742	166	112	.971
Philadelphia	141	3734	1713	168	143	.970

INDIVIDUAL BATTING

Player, club.	G.	AB.	R.	H.	RBI.	SB.	Pct.
Klein, Phila	141	562	94	207	115	13	.368
Frey, Bklyn	25	96	94	207	10	4	.354
Hack, Chi.	20	66	6	21	2	4	.350
Davis, Phila	131	465	46	158	56	2	.240
Brandt, Bos.	42	89	8	29	5	0	.326
Terry, N. Y.	119	460	67	149	57	3	.324
Piet, Pitts.	107	362	45	117	42	12	.323
Stephenson, Chi.	95	337	41	109	48	5	.323
Cuyler, Chi.	65	240	35	77	34	5	.321
Martin, St. L.	139	575	119	184	57	25	.320
Schlumerich, Bos., Phila	115	149	59	134	68	1	.320
Thevenow, Pitts.	66	225	17	72	31	2	.320
Vaughan, Pitts.	144	548	80	173	94	3	.316
Berger, Bos.	136	526	83	164	100	1	.312
Hafey, Cinn.	139	546	77	169	61	3	.310
Lindstrom, Pitts.	132	522	65	160	53	1	.310
Fullis, Phila	140	604	87	186	44	17	.308
P. Waner, Pitts.	147	589	98	181	66	3	.307
Medwick, St. L.	142	570	85	174	95	5	.305
Frisch, St. L.	141	563	71	171	63	18	.304
Frederick, Bklyn.	139	529	60	161	63	7	.304
Warneke, Chi.	37	92	8	28	11	0	.304
Collins, St. L.	126	469	63	142	65	7	.303
Orsatti, St. L.	117	433	54	130	38	13	.300
Young, Pitts.	24	20	3	6	0	0	.300
Traynor, Pitts.	148	596	82	177	78	5	.297
Leslie, N. Y., Bln.	127	475	59	141	71	0	.297
Moore, N. Y.	126	497	56	147	40	4	.296
Boyle, Bklyn.	83	304	38	90	26	5	.296
Hendrick, Chi.	68	186	29	55	24	4	.296
Moore, Bos.	125	455	58	134	62	2	.295
Lopez, Bklyn.	119	354	35	104	37	11	.294
Grace, Pitts.	86	276	21	79	43	0	.286
Ott, N. Y.	146	447	99	158	101	1	.284
Campbell, Chi.	44	88	11	25	10	0	.284
Taylor, Bklyn.	98	339	69	96	36	11	.283
Jordan, Bos.	141	546	70	154	42	4	.282
F. Herman, Chi.	132	486	70	137	86	6	.282
Koenig, Chi.	77	206	30	58	24	7	.282
W. Herman, Chi.	148	589	78	168	43	6	.281
O'Doul, Bln., N.Y.	116	377	44	106	55	2	.281
Comorosky, Pitts.	59	161	18	45	16	2	.280
Lucas, Cinn.	72	118	14	33	14	0	.280
Watkins, St. L.	132	503	64	140	62	11	.278
Lombardi, Cinn.	103	335	28	93	45	2	.278
Jensen, Pitts.	63	162	21	45	8	1	.278
L. Waner, Pitts.	116	481	56	133	24	3	.277
Hartnett, Chi.	135	473	52	129	83	1	.275
Demaree, Chi.	131	507	67	139	51	5	.274
Bartell, Phila	141	544	74	148	37	6	.272
Suhr, Pitts.	147	541	67	147	70	1	.272
Mosolf, Chi.	31	81	13	22	8	0	.272
Stripp, Bklyn.	133	519	66	146	48	5	.270
Vergez, N. Y.	123	459	57	124	72	1	.270
Crawford, St. L.	90	223	24	60	21	1	.269
Jurges, Chi.	138	468	47	125	46	4	.267
Moore, Cinn.	131	495	59	133	43	4	.265
Hurst, Phila	136	510	54	134	72	3	.263
Rice, Cinn.	128	495	43	130	50	4	.263
Mancusco, N. Y.	140	468	38	123	54	0	.263
Luque, N. Y.	34	19	0	5	1	0	.263
Outen, Bklyn.	85	130	17	24	14	1	.262
Davis, N. Y.	120	414	57	108	34	10	.261
Spohrer, Bos.	60	186	11	46	12	3	.261
Jackson, N. Y.	50	115	11	30	11	1	.261
Adams, St.L., Cin.	140	546	60	142	23	3	.260
English, Chi.	103	389	51	101	37	5	.260
Wilson, Bklyn.	109	341	40	89	48	7	.258
Cuccinello, Bklyn.	126	456	54	117	61	4	.257
Rixey, Cinn.	15	35	2	9	6	0	.257
Wilson, St. L.	112	364	34	93	44	6	.256
McCurdy, Phila	67	47	9	12	9	0	.255
Durocher, Cinn., St. L.	133	421	50	107	41	2	.254
Grimm, Chi.	105	372	36	94	37	1	.253
Jordan, Bklyn.	64	194	15	49	15	3	.253
Swift, Pitts.	33	75	8	19	4	0	.253
Hogan, Bos.	87	299	14	75	26	0	.251
Urbanski, Bos.	133	520	60	130	33	3	.250
Frey, Cinn.	35	36	2	9	1	0	.250
Shaute, Bklyn.	39	34	3	6	0	0	.250
Nelson, Chi.	29	20	5	5	1	0	.250

PITCHING RECORDS

Pitcher, club.	G.	B.	BB.	SO.	W.	L.	Pct.
Luque, N. Y.	34	76	21	22	8	2	.800
Vance, St. L.	26	103	28	66	6	2	.750
Tinning, Chi.	32	170	60	58	13	6	.684
Cantwell, Bos.	37	216	47	51	19	9	.679
Rixey, Cinn.	16	118	12	9	6	3	.667
Meine, Pitts.	21	219	52	47	15	8	.652
Parmelee, N. Y.	31	185	75	124	13	7	.650
Hubbell, N. Y.	44	248	50	154	22	12	.647
Schumecher, N.Y.	34	188	77	90	19	11	.633
Carleton, St. L.	42	252	90	144	16	10	.615
French, Pitts.	44	269	54	83	18	12	.600
Bush, Chi.	39	244	68	81	18	12	.600
Haines, St. L.	31	112	35	37	9	6	.600
Birkofer, Pitts.	7	27	13	11	3	2	.600
Warneke, Chi.	34	248	69	126	17	12	.586
Root, Chi.	34	227	62	86	14	10	.583
Fitz'mons, N. Y.	35	233	72	60	15	11	.577
Hallahan, St. L.	34	222	97	87	16	12	.571
Smith, Pitts.	27	140	30	39	8	6	.571
Brandt, Bos.	38	224	69	94	17	13	.567
Dean, St. L.	46	257	72	189	20	16	.556
Chagnon, Pitts.	38	99	18	39	5	4	.556
Frey, Cinn.	35	133	20	11	5	4	.556
Swift, Pitts.	33	202	35	55	12	10	.545
Bell, N. Y.	38	93	19	21	6	5	.545
Mungo, Bklyn.	38	209	76	101	15	14	.517
Frankhouse, Bos.	39	231	73	73	15	15	.500
Moore, Phila	34	168	40	51	8	8	.500
Smith, Cinn., Bos.	26	129	16	30	6	6	.500
Nelson, Chi.	24	65	30	20	5	5	.500
Harris, Pitts.	30	68	14	19	4	4	.500
Pearce, Phila	18	69	27	14	4	4	.500
Mangum, Bos.	24	93	11	27	3	3	.500
Johnson, St. L.	35	90	16	28	3	3	.500
Shaute, Bklyn.	39	118	30	24	3	3	.500
Swetonic, Pitts.	29	162	60	35	11	12	.478
Benton, Cinn.	34	165	36	33	10	11	.476
Betts, Bos.	32	209	40	36	10	11	.476
Holley, Phila	28	200	55	55	12	14	.462
Carroll, Bklyn.	31	243	51	43	12	15	.444
Walker, St. L.	27	158	64	34	8	10	.444
Zachary, Bos.	24	128	33	22	7	9	.438
Kolp, Cinn.	28	165	22	26	6	8	.429
Lucas, Cinn.	27	229	18	36	10	14	.417
Malone, Chi.	31	186	59	71	10	14	.417
Thurston, Bklyn.	29	154	29	21	5	7	.417
Hoyt, Pitts.	35	119	19	44	5	7	.417
Berly, Phila	12	61	19	4	2	2	.400
Stout, St.L., Cinn.	23	85	26	29	2	3	.400
Clark, Blyn., N.Y.	26	115	17	24	5	8	.385
Collins, Phila	41	180	56	38	8	13	.381
Beck, Bklyn.	39	240	36	82	11	18	.379
Benge, Bklyn.	35	221	50	67	10	17	.370
Hansen, Phila	31	176	29	45	6	13	.316
Grimes, Chi., StL.	21	87	37	16	3	7	.300
Rhem, Phila	27	176	33	26	5	12	.294
Elliott, Phila	32	181	46	35	4	10	.286
Johnson, Cinn.	33	205	58	51	7	18	.280
Ber'ger, StL. Cin.	35	258	60	81	7	26	.212

American League

CLUB BATTING

Club.	G.	AB.	R.	H.	RBI.	SB.	Pct.
Washington	147	5296	819	1526	774	65	.289
Philadel	144	5060	833	1456	796	31	.288
New York	144	4998	871	1407	796	74	.281
Chicago	146	5139	654	1400	611	44	.273
Boston	143	4981	654	1342	598	46	.269
Detroit	150	5353	702	1434	646	73	.268
Cleveland	146	5060	628	1321	581	35	.261
St. Louis	148	5116	660	1314	602	69	.258

CLUB FIELDING

Club.	G.	PO.	A.	E.	DP.	Pct.
Washington	147	4006	1744	132	136	.977
St. Louis	148	3962	1795	145	162	.976
Cleveland	146	3913	1821	146	122	.975
New York	144	3857	1543	149	116	.973
Chicago	146	3977	1848	183	136	.970
Detroit	150	3957	1797	178	160	.970
Boston	143	3741	1791	193	126	.966
Philadelphia	144	3792	1644	195	118	.965

INDIVIDUAL BATTING

Player, Club.	G.	AB.	R.	H.	RBI.	SB.	Pct.
Bolton, Wash.	27	26	4	11	5	0	.423
Hebert, St. L.	33	22	3	8	3	0	.364
Foxx, Phil.	141	541	121	191	153	2	.353
Knott, St. L.	19	21	3	7	0	0	.333
Coombs, Phil.	21	6	1	2	3	0	.333
Manush, Wash.	147	639	112	212	88	6	.332
Simmons, Chi.	142	590	83	195	114	5	.331
Gehrig, N. Y.	144	566	130	185	130	9	.327
Gehringer, Det.	150	608	100	198	97	6	.326
Kuhel, Wash.	147	580	90	186	103	17	.321
Appling, Chi.	146	592	88	189	81	6	.319
Higgins, Phil.	144	540	83	172	99	2	.319
Dickey, N. Y.	129	476	58	152	99	4	.319
Cochrane, Phil.	126	416	98	132	54	7	.317
Garms, St. L.	78	189	35	60	24	3	.317
R. Johnson, B.	133	483	91	151	94	13	.313
Cronin, Wash.	146	581	87	181	112	5	.312
Hodapp, Bos.	114	412	53	128	52	1	.311
Pytlak, Cleve.	78	241	34	75	33	3	.311
Stumpf, Bos.	16	13	5	4	2	0	.308
Judge, Bos.	29	88	17	27	13	2	.307
Swanson, Chi.	140	531	98	162	63	18	.305
Chapman, N. Y.	139	541	105	164	90	24	.303
Williams, Phil.	110	390	52	110	72	1	.303
Myer, Wash.	127	511	89	154	53	6	.302
Cramer, Phil.	144	625	105	188	73	5	.301
Greenberg, Det.	114	438	58	132	82	5	.301
Boken, Wash.	50	123	19	37	26	0	.301
Averill, Cleve.	146	580	79	174	87	3	.300
West, St. L.	128	499	90	149	46	1?	.299
Melillo, St. L.	127	479	49	143	78	11	.299
Rogell, Det.	150	571	64	170	53	7	.298
Schulte, Wash.	138	530	96	158	87	9	.298
Goslin, Wash.	126	524	92	156	59	5	.298
Lazzeri, N. Y.	139	521	94	155	101	15	.298
Ruth, N. Y.	129	433	88	129	95	4	.298
Combs, N. Y.	115	407	84	121	60	6	.297
Johnson, Phil.	135	514	96	152	91	6	.296
Pennock, N. Y.	22	17	8	5	1	0	.296
Bishop, Phil.	113	380	76	112	40	1	.295
Farrell, N. Y.	35	61	9	18	4	0	.295
Reynolds, St. L.	130	459	80	135	70	4	.294
Ferrell, S. L., B.	134	467	51	137	68	4	.293
Lyons, Chi.	48	89	11	26	10	0	.292
Burns, St. L.	144	555	89	160	73	12	.289
Fox, Det.	121	508	76	147	50	11	.289
Cooke, Bos.	114	439	79	127	53	7	.289
Webb, D., Chi.	62	114	16	33	10	0	.289
Finney, Phil.	64	208	26	60	30	1	.288
Jolley, Bos.	115	404	47	116	64	1	.287
Doljack, Det.	42	147	18	42	22	2	.286
Miller, Phil.	62	112	22	32	18	4	.286
Rice, Wash.	66	77	18	22	12	0	.286
Burnett, Cleve.	78	239	37	68	28	3	.285
Haas, Chi.	142	571	93	162	52	0	.284
Campbell, St. L.	141	544	86	154	103	7	.283
Walker, Det.	120	457	65	129	63	25	.282
Kamm, Cleve.	133	447	59	126	47	6	.282
Madjeski, Phil.	47	131	16	37	15	0	.282
McManus, Bos.	104	363	51	102	35	2	.281
Stone, Det.	141	550	81	154	75	2	.280
Hale, Cleve.	93	330	46	92	60	1	.279
Alexander, Bos.	94	315	39	86	39	1	.279
Coleman, Phil.	100	385	49	107	66	0	.278
Brown, S. L., B.	39	65	5	18	11	0	.277
Walker, N. Y.	97	327	68	90	49	2	.275
Harris, Wash.	75	164	31	45	34	3	.274
Sewell, N. Y.	132	502	87	142	53	2	.273
Van Atta, N. Y.	24	59	7	16	4	0	.271
Boss, Cleve.	111	437	54	118	52	2	.270
McNair, Phil.	79	270	52	73	42	2	.270
Oulliber, Cleve.	21	74	9	20	2	0	.270
Rhyne, Chi.	37	78	8	21	9	1	.269
Porter, Cleve.	127	478	69	128	39	4	.268
Ferrell, Cleve.	56	120	24	32	24	0	.267
Rhodes, Bos.	35	86	9	23	16	1	.267
Berry, Chi.	80	250	24	66	28	0	.264
Dykes, Chi.	145	536	48	141	66	5	.263
Bluege, Wash.	134	486	61	128	68	6	.263
Werber, N.Y., B.	106	401	60	105	37	12	.262
Owen, Det.	137	548	79	143	63	2	.261
Vosmik, Cleve.	119	441	53	115	54	0	.261
Pearson, Cleve.	19	50	6	13	4	0	.260
Hemsley, St. L.	26	81	8	21	12	0	.259
Sewell, Wash.	136	457	58	118	58	8	.258
Oliver, Bos.	89	244	25	63	23	0	.258
Ruffing, N. Y.	53	110	9	28	14	0	.255
Byrd, N. Y.	77	68	19	17	7	0	.250

PITCHING RECORDS

Pitcher, Club.	G.	H.	BB.	SO.	W.	L.	Pct.
Uhle, Det., N. Y.	11	55	18	23	6	0	1.000
Kimsey, Chi.	28	123	36	19	4	1	.800
Grove, Phil.	43	262	77	107	23	7	.767
Van Atta, N. Y.	24	154	58	73	12	4	.750
Whitehill, W.	38	273	92	96	21	8	.724
Allen, N. Y.	24	167	83	117	15	6	.714
Stewart, Wash.	33	219	57	67	15	6	.714
Weaver, Wash.	21	130	45	52	9	4	.692
Russell, Wash.	49	119	31	28	12	6	.667
Pearson, Cleve.	19	111	54	49	10	5	.667
Burke, Wash.	25	64	31	27	4	2	.667
Crowder, Wash.	50	297	79	101	24	13	.649
Rowe, Det.	19	129	31	73	7	4	.636
Gray, St. L.	38	130	45	35	7	4	.636
Connally, Cleve.	39	110	48	29	5	3	.625
Hildebrand, Cl.	35	196	85	86	16	10	.615
Gomez, N. Y.	34	210	100	158	15	10	.600
Durham, Chi.	23	133	45	59	9	6	.600
Pennock, N. Y.	22	82	20	19	6	4	.600
MacFayden, N.Y.	23	116	35	27	3	2	.600
Devens, N. Y.	12	50	43	22	3	2	.600
Marberry, Det.	36	232	77	75	16	11	.593
Johnson, Bos.	25	156	73	64	8	6	.571
Mahaffey, Phil.	32	194	74	62	13	10	.565
Barrett, Phil.	14	74	49	26	4	3	.571
Bridges, Det.	32	190	101	110	14	11	.560
Heving, Chi.	39	112	26	46	6	5	.545
Pipgras, N.Y., B.	26	172	57	70	11	10	.524
Brown, Cleve.	31	190	30	44	11	10	.524
Cain, Phil.	37	234	135	38	12	12	.500
Frasier, Chi., D.	30	161	70	32	6	6	.500
Ferrell, Cleve.	28	223	70	40	14	12	.478
Harder, Cleve.	42	248	62	78	15	17	.469
Thomas, Wash.	34	145	42	32	7	8	.467
Kline, Bos.	44	116	65	14	6	7	.462
Jones, Chi.	26	179	65	59	10	12	.455
Hebert, St. L.	32	113	35	18	5	6	.455
Miller, Chi.	25	126	45	30	5	6	.455
Rhodes, Bos.	33	241	94	87	12	15	.444
Hadley, St. L.	44	305	140	140	15	19	.441
Blaeholder, S.L.	37	277	69	60	14	18	.438
Faber, Chi.	35	86	28	18	3	4	.429
Sorrell, Det.	36	233	77	75	11	15	.423
Ruffing, N. Y.	33	220	90	116	9	13	.409
Gaston, Chi.	30	177	60	40	8	12	.400
Earnshaw, Phil.	21	152	58	40	6	9	.400
Moore, N. Y.	33	78	18	17	4	6	.400
Walberg, Phil.	39	219	94	63	8	13	.381
Fischer, Det.	33	169	77	85	9	15	.375
Hogsett, Det.	45	136	55	37	6	10	.375
Wyatt, D., Chi.	34	104	52	38	3	5	.375
Brown, S. L., B.	39	220	78	40	9	16	.360
Weiland, Bos.	37	190	91	80	7	14	.333
Stiles, St. L.	30	143	45	27	3	6	.333
Welch, Bos.	45	134	64	63	4	9	.308
Lyons, Chi.	34	256	72	69	9	21	.300
Wells, St. L.	36	229	61	59	6	14	.300
Gregory, Chi.	22	118	47	17	4	10	.288
Peterson, Phil.	29	102	33	17	2	5	.286
Hudlin, Cleve.	33	159	61	47	5	13	.278
Andrews, Bos.	32	151	60	30	5	13	.278
McDon'd, P., S.L.	28	96	36	22	1	5	.167
Knott, St. L.	19	84	31	17	1	7	.125

3-Cushion Cue Carnival Arranged for Amateurs

Amateur three-cushion billard players of all classes will participate in a billiard carnival at Greenleafs Recreation, starting tomorrow, and continuing for the next two or three weeks. Tournaments have been formed for three grades of players ranked as A, B and C.

Three prizes will be given for first, second and third places in each class. The first and second players in class B also will automatically be graduated to Class A for further competition, and the same applies to first and second in Class C, who will graduate into Class B.

Three tables have been set aside for the competition and to increase the carnival spirit it will be required that three games, one in each class, be played simultaneously.

Stamford Public Links Play

Special to the Herald Tribune

STAMFORD, Conn., Sept. 23.—The Stamford public links golf championship will be held here next Sunday, October 1. The course selected is the Hubbard Heights Country Club.

St. Stanislaus Nine Wins Title

PITTSBURGH, Sept. 23 (AP).—The St. Stanislaus team of Youngstown, Ohio, won the national baseball Federation championship today by defeating Immaculate Heart of Herron Hill, Pa., 6 to 5, in the second of a series of three games. St. Stanislaus won the first game, 4 to 3, last night.

Yankees Defeat Browns, 6-2; Dodgers Drubbed by Pirates, 15-2; Giants Vanquish Reds, 6-4

Gehrig's 16th Helps Gomez Win His 10th

New York First Baseman Also Poles Triple and Single as Left-Hander Holds Rivals to Six Hits

By Murray Tynan

"What is holding back the Yankees?" Rogers Hornsby asked on his arrival here a couple of days ago, but the question is still unanswered. Nothing whatever was holding back the Yankees yesterday as they beat the Browns, 6 to 2, behind the stylish pitching of Vernon Gomez.

This was the tenth victory of the season for Senor Gomez against only one defeat, a point which may be almost as interesting as the game itself. It may be recalled that the lone defeat charged against the slender left-hander was the one-hit game Earl Whitehill pitched for the Senators and which the Yankees lost, 1 to 0. For the time being Gomez seems to be the closest thing to the unbeatable in baseball, and if he continues to pitch at his present gait he may win thirty or more games.

With any pitcher other than Gomez the Yankees yesterday might have trembled on occasions. He was in trouble twice, but pitching with grace and style and his head as well as his arms, he slipped past dangers that would have capsized most pitchers. He actually made it look easy.

Gehrig Hits No. 16

In the fourth, for example, after the Yankees had established a one-run lead in the first on a walk to Babe Ruth and Lou Gehrig's sixteenth homer, Gomez had men on first and second with none out. A sacrifice advanced each runner a base, but there they stayed. Gomez fanned Melillo, walked Hemsley and induced Bejma, the shortstop, to ground out.

It was almost the same way in the seventh, when Melillo reached first on Crosetti's fumble and took third on Bejma's double to the left-field corner. Hornsby batted for Bump Hadley, the pitcher, and walked. Three were on with none out, but only one runner scored. Clift, badly fooled, looked at three straight strikes; West hit into a force play, scoring Melillo, and Burns grounded out to Gehrig.

Gomez spread six hits over the nine innings, and he certainly spread them lightly. A single by Pepper and Melillo's double in the second provided the Browns with their first run, and only once after that were they able to make as many as two hits in an inning.

While the pitching of Gomez tended to overshadow other items, the Yankees had handsome help from Gehrig, who reaped a harvest of three hits, a homer, a triple and a single. During the first four innings the Yankees made only three hits off Hadley, and the big first basemen accounted for two of them as well as having a hand in all three runs they scored. His homer in the first also scored Ruth and his three-bagger in the fourth was converted into another tally when Chapman followed it with a single.

Gomez Drives in Run

Gomez batted in a run in the sixth with a single, and the Yankees picked up their last brace of runs in the seventh after Hadley had been replaced by McAfee.

The attendance of nearly 10,000 was surprisingly good for a week day. Navy men made up a large part of the crowd, and many of them seemed to be for the gallant Brownies. They gave Hornsby a generous hand when he came up to hit, and they razzed Gomez when he walked the Rajah.

Ruth hit in hard luck. His liner in the fourth went directly into the waiting hands of Burns at first base, and his drive into the stands in fifth drifted out over the foul line.

The Yankees discussed a trade with the Browns before the game, but nothing came of it. Joe McCarthy feels that he could use another pitcher, but who couldn't?

Gomez may have set a record for a fast strikeout when he disposed of Clift in the seventh. His first pitch was a fast ball, and Clift merely stared at it. The next one was a curve, and Clift also stood motionless. The third strike was a fast ball right down the middle, after which Clift departed for the bench, his bat still on his shoulder.

The score:

ST. LOUIS (A. L.)	ab	r	h	po	a	e	NEW YORK (A. L.)	ab	r	h	po	a	e
Clift, 3b	4	0	0	2	2	0	Cro'te, 3b	4	0	0	3	4	1
West, cf	4	0	1	4	2	1	Rolfe, ss	3	1	1	1	3	0
Burns, 1b	4	0	1	8	0	0	Ruth, rf	2	1	1	1	0	0
Pepper, lf	4	1	2	3	0	0	Byrd, rf	0	1	0	0	0	0
Garms, rf	3	0	0	1	0	0	Gehrig, 1b	4	2	3	9	0	0
Melillo, 2b	4	0	1	4	2	0	Chapman, lf	4	0	2	2	0	0
Hemsley, c	3	1	0	2	0	0	Dickey, c	4	0	0	7	0	0
Bejma, ss	4	0	1	0	1	0	Hoag, cf	4	1	1	3	0	0
HADLEY, p	2	0	0	0	3	0	Heffner, 2b	3	0	1	1	2	0
*Hornsby	0	0	0	0	0	0	GOMEZ, p	3	0	1	0	2	0
McAFEE, p	0	0	0	0	0	0							
†Grube	1	0	0	0	0	0							
Totals	33	2	6	24	10	1	Totals	31	6	10	27	11	1

*Batted for Hadley in seventh inning.
†Batted for McAfee in ninth inning.

St. Louis	010	000	100	—2
New York	200	101	20x	—6

Runs batted in—Gehrig (2), Melillo, Bejma, Chapman (2), Gomez, Ruth, West. Two-base hits—Melillo, Bejma, Ruth. Three-base hit—Gehrig. Home run—Gehrig. Stolen bases—Heffner, West. Sacrifices—Garms, Gomez. Left on bases—St. Louis, 7; New York, 6. Bases on balls—Off Hadley, 4; off Gomez, 2. Struck out—By Gomez, 6. Hits—Off Hadley, 6 in 6 innings; off McAfee, 4 in 2. Losing pitcher—Hadley. Umpires—Owens and McGowan. Time—1:55.

Athletics Collect 14 Hits, Routing Indians, 11 to 2

PHILADELPHIA, June 13 (AP).—Cracking out fourteen hits and clubbing Monte Pearson out of the box, the Athletics defeated the Cleveland Indians, 11 to 2, today.

The Athletics batted Pearson for eleven of their blows, scoring seven runs off him in the sixth inning.

Bob Johnson hit his fourteenth home run of the season with one on base in the big inning. Sugar Cain went the distance for the Athletics and held the Indians to five hits.

The score:

CLEVELAND (A. L.)	ab	r	h	po	a	e	PHILADELPHIA (N. L.)	ab	r	h	po	a	e
Rice, rf	3	0	0	2	0	0	Cramer, cf	4	2	2	0	0	0
Knick'er, ss	4	0	0	3	3	0	Warstler, 2b	4	1	1	1	3	0
Averill, cf	2	1	0	2	0	0	Johnson, lf	4	1	1	2	0	0
Hale, 2b	4	0	1	2	2	0	Foxx, 1b	4	1	3	15	2	0
Trosky, 1b	4	1	0	7	1	0	McNair, ss	5	1	1	2	4	0
Pytlak, c	3	0	2	4	0	0	Coleman, rf	5	3	2	1	0	0
WINEG'R, p	1	0	0	0	0	0	Higgins, 3b	4	1	3	1	5	0
Seeds, lf	4	0	0	0	0	0	Hayes, c	3	1	1	4	0	0
Kamm, 3b	3	0	1	1	4	1	CAIN, p	3	0	0	1	2	0
Burnett, 3b	0	0	0	1	0	0							
PEARS'N, p	2	0	0	0	1	0							
Myatt, c	1	0	1	2	0	0							
Totals	31	2	5	24	11	1	Totals	36	11	14	27	16	0

Cleveland	000	000	200	— 2
Philadelphia	021	007	10x	—11

Runs batted in—Pytlak, Seeds, Coleman, Higgins (3), Foxx, Warstler, Johnson (2), Cramer. Two-base hits—Pytlak (2), Coleman, Kamm, Hayes, Higgins. Home run—Johnson. Sacrifices—Warstler, Cain. Double play—Warstler, McNair and Foxx. Left on bases—Cleveland, 5; Philadelphia, 7. Bases on balls—Off Pearson, 3; off Winegarner, 1; off Cain, 3. Struck out—By Pearson, 4; by Winegarner, 1; by Cain, 3. Hits—Off Pearson, 11 in 6 innings; off Winegarner, 3 in 2. Losing pitcher—Pearson. Umpires—Dinneen, Hildebrand and Summers. Time—2:08.

Out at the Plate Trying to Score From First on a Single

Herald Tribune photo—Frank

Heffner caught sliding into home at the Stadium yesterday in the fifth inning of the game in which the Yankees defeated the Browns, 6 to 2. He tried to complete the circuit of the bases after Gomez singled. Hoag (No. 28) has just counted on the play, Hemsley has tagged the runner and Brick Owens, the umpire, is calling him out. Crosetti (No. 5) is coming up to bat, but the out was the third one

Red Sox Yield 22 Hits, Down Tigers, 15-13

Grove Is Hammered for 13; Boston Scores 8 in 2d in Beating League Leaders

By The Associated Press

BOSTON, June 13.—The Boston Red Sox bunched hits in three innings today and turned back the league-leading Detroit Tigers, 15 to 13, in a slugging match. The visitors belted three Boston pitchers for twenty-two hits, making thirteen off Bob (Lefty) Grove, who was credited with the victory despite the fact he worked only four and two-thirds innings.

The Sox sent twelve men to the plate in the second inning, when they scored eight runs on seven hits, including two doubles by Carl Reynolds, a triple by Roy Johnson and two-baggers by Bill Werber and Rick Ferrell.

They got two more tallies on three hits in the third inning and five in the eighth on three hits and Owens's wild throw on Reynolds's grounder. Two runners scored when the Tiger third-sacker threw into the Red Sox dugout.

The score:

DETROIT (A. L.)	ab	r	h	po	a	e	BOSTON (A. L.)	ab	r	h	po	a	e
Fox, rf	7	3	3	2	0	0	Cissell, 2b	4	2	1	0	2	0
C'rane, c	3	0	1	3	1	0	Werber, 3b	4	2	3	1	1	0
H'worth, c	3	1	1	2	1	0	Morgan, 1b	3	1	0	9	0	0
Goslin, lf	6	2	4	0	0	0	R. J'son, lf	5	2	3	4	0	0
G'ringer, 2b	4	3	3	2	1	0	Reyn's, cf	5	2	2	4	0	0
Rogell, ss	5	0	1	1	3	0	Porter, rf	4	1	2	2	0	0
G'berg, 1b	6	1	3	8	0	0	R. F'rell, c	5	1	1	5	1	0
Walker, cf	5	1	3	5	0	0	Lary, ss	3	3	1	2	1	0
Owen, 3b	4	0	1	1	1	1	WELCH, p	1	1	1	0	0	0
MARB'Y, p	0	0	0	0	1	0	GROVE, p	3	0	0	0	1	0
FRASIER, p	2	2	2	0	2	0	RHODES, p	0	0	0	0	0	0
*Doljack	1	0	0	0	0	0							
H'SETT, p	2	0	0	0	0	0							
†White	1	0	0	0	0	0							
Totals	49	13	22	24	10	1	Totals	37	15	14	27	6	0

*Batted for Frasier in fifth inning.
†Batted for Hogsett in ninth inning.

Detroit	003	200	026	—13
Boston	082	000	50x	—15

Runs batted in—Cochrane, Goslin (2), Gehringer, Rogell (4), Greenberg (2), Owens (2), White, Cissell, Werber (4), Morgan, R. Johnson, Reynolds, Porter, Ferrell, Welch. Two-base hits—Rogell, Werber, R. Johnson, Reynolds (2), Ferrell. Three-base hits—Cissell, R. Johnson. Stolen base—Werber. Sacrifices—Welch, Cissell. Left on bases—Detroit, 15; Boston, 7. Bases on balls—Off Marberry, 2; off Frasier, 3; off Welch, 3; off Grove, 3; off Hogsett, 2. Struck out—By Marberry, 1; by Frasier, 1; by Hogsett, 2; by Welch, 2; by Grove, 2; by Rhodes, 1. Hits—Off Marberry, 5 in 1 1-3 innings; off Frasier, 5 in 2 2-3; off Welch, 8 in 3 2-3; off Grove, 13 in 4 2-3; off Hogsett, 4 in 4; off Rhodes, 1 in 2-3. Wild pitch—Welch. Balk—Frasier. Winning pitcher—Grove. Losing pitcher—Marberry. Umpires—Geisel and Moriarty. Time—2:28.

St. Ann's Nine Defeats Mt. St. Michael's, 5 to 4

St. Ann's Academy defeated the Mount St. Michael's High School nine, 5 to 4, yesterday in a Manhattan division C. H. S. A. A. game at the Mount St. Michael's field. The winners scored all five runs in the fifth inning on a double by Joe Wallace and a home run by Bill Murray with two on.

The score by innings:

Mt. St. Michael's	100	020	1	—4
St. Ann's	000	050	x	—5

Batteries—Pagano, Ernano and Burke; Finnegan and McGee.

Lou Gehrig, who kept his place in the van of home-run hitters by poling his sixteenth yesterday

Brown Wins 8th As Buffalo Bows To Newark, 3-2

Kowalik's Wild Pitch in 8th Permits Barton to Tally Deciding Run for Bears

By The Associated Press

NEWARK, N. J., June 13.—Walter Brown bested Fabian Kowalik in a pitching duel today and the Newark Bears took the series opener from Buffalo, 3 to 2. It was Brown's eighth victory of the season.

Kowalik had the better of the argument for six innings, limiting the Newark club to one hit. Spencer's home run gave the Bisons a 1-0 margin in the seventh, but Kowalik was touched for five hits in the seventh and eighth. His wild pitch permitted Barton to score the winning run in the eighth after Barton's single scored Hill with the tying count.

The score:

BUFFALO (I. L.)	ab	r	h	po	a	e	NEWARK (I. L.)	ab	r	h	po	a	e
Mulleavy, ss	4	1	1	2	1	1	Farrell, 3b	3	0	0	1	1	0
Regan, 2b	4	0	1	1	5	0	Selkirk, lf	4	0	0	1	0	0
Plummer, cf	4	0	1	1	5	0	Hill, cf	4	1	1	1	0	0
Tucker, rf	4	0	2	2	0	0	Alex'der, 1b	4	0	0	9	0	0
Carnegie, lf	3	0	1	2	0	0	Barton, rf	4	1	2	1	0	0
Smith, 1b	3	0	0	9	1	0	Glenn, c	4	1	2	10	1	0
Spencer, c	3	1	1	7	0	0	Schalk, 2b	3	0	0	3	3	0
Myers, 3b	3	0	1	0	0	2	Gibson, ss	4	0	1	1	3	0
KOW'LIK, p	3	0	0	1	3	0	BROWN, p	2	0	0	0	4	0
*Outen	1	0	0	0	0	0							
Totals	32	2	8	24	10	3	Totals	32	3	6	27	12	0

*Batted for Kowalik in ninth inning.

Buffalo	000	000	110	—2
Newark	000	000	12x	—3

Runs batted in—Spencer, Gibson, Carnegie, Barton. Two-base hits—Barton, Carnegie. Home run—Spencer. Stolen base—Farrell. Double plays—Gibson, Schalk and Alexander; Schalk, Gibson and Alexander. Left on bases—Buffalo, 8; Newark, 8. Bases on balls—Off Brown, 5; off Kowalik, 2. Struck out—By Kowalik, 7; by Brown, 9. Hit by pitcher—By Kowalik (Farrell). Umpires—Jorda and Collins. Time—1:58.

Baseball Results in Minor Leagues

* * *

INTERNATIONAL LEAGUE

YESTERDAY'S RESULTS

Newark, 3; Buffalo, 2.
Montreal, 8; Baltimore, 7 (10 innings).
Syracuse, 7; Rochester, 4 (1st).
Syracuse, 3; Rochester, 2 (2d).
Toronto, 13; Albany, 11 (night game, 10 inns).

STANDING OF THE CLUBS

	W.	L.	Pct.		W.	L.	Pct.
Newark	39	19	.672	Syracuse	23	28	.451
Rochester	34	22	.607	Albany	22	28	.440
Toronto	33	23	.589	Buffalo	23	30	.434
Montreal	28	27	.509	Baltimore	13	28	.317

GAMES TODAY

Buffalo at Newark.
Toronto at Albany.
Rochester at Syracuse.
Montreal at Baltimore.

AMERICAN ASSOCIATION

At St. Paul—

					R.	H.	E.
Milwaukee	000	000	100	— 1		9	5
St. Paul	315	001	00x	—10		10	0

Batteries—Pressnell, Walkup and Young; Phelps, Walenowski and Guiliani.

At Minneapolis—

					R.	H.	E.
Kan. City	010	001	210	00—5		12	0
Minn'polis	311	000	000	01—6		12	1

Batteries—Carson and Orandall; Holsclaw, Ryan, Tauscher and Hargrave.

STANDING OF THE CLUBS

	W.	L.	Pct.		W.	L.	Pct.
Minn'polis	36	21	.632	St. Paul	27	27	.500
Mil'w'kee	30	26	.536	*Louisville	25	30	.455
*Ind'polis	27	24	.529	Kan. City	24	31	.436
*Col'mbus	27	27	.500	*Toledo	23	33	.411

*Night game.

SOUTHERN ASSOCIATION

At Nashville—

					R.	H.	E.
Chattanooga	100	100	400	— 6		9	0
Nashville	530	030	00x	—11		17	4

Batteries—Gould and Holbrook, Chandler; Gabler and Wise.

At Atlanta—

					R.	H.	E.
Knoxville	300	001	010	— 5		11	1
Atlanta	520	004	01x	—12		17	4

Batteries—Moon, Biethen and Head. West; Schmidt and Palmisano.

At Memphis—

					R.	H.	E.
New Orleans	001	100	000	— 2		7	5
Memphis	141	220	23x	—15		16	1

Batteries—Milnar, Ragland and Autry; Boward and Powell.

STANDING OF THE CLUBS

	W.	L.	Pct.		W.	L.	Pct.
Nashville	37	17	.685	Chat'nooga	25	29	.463
Atlanta	30	23	.566	Knoxville	25	29	.463
N. Orleans	31	24	.564	Birm'gham	25	32	.437
Memphis	25	28	.472	Little Rock	20	36	.354

NEW YORK-PA. LEAGUE

At Elmira—

					R.	H.	E.
Harrisburg	000	000	001	—1		7	2
Elmira	001	100	00x	—2		7	1

Batteries—Eckert and Maple; Lyons and P. Chervinko.

At Wilkes-Barre—

					R.	H.	E.
Scranton	160	002	000	—9		11	0
Wilkes-Barre	000	001	200	—3		9	1

Batteries—Shaute and Reilly; Reitz, Andrews, Keifer and Wasem.

At Binghamton (first game)—

					R.	H.	E.
Reading	000	000	000	—0		4	0
Binghamton	000	200	000	—2		3	2

Batteries—Browning and Moss; Wicker and Collins.

Second game—

					R.	H.	E.
Reading	021	000	04	—7		4	1
Binghamton	100	002	00	—3		4	1

Batteries—Niggeling and Moss; Tobin and Collins.

At Williamsport (first game)—

					R.	H.	E.
Hazleton	010	022	010	—6		9	0
Williamsport	000	012	010	—4		9	2

Batteries—Krider and Uzmann; Myllykangas and Baker.

Second game—

					R.	H.	E.
Hazleton	101	110	8	—12		15	2
Williamsport	310	000	0	— 4		7	0

Batteries—Parkes, Wydallis and Connell; McNamara, Thomas and Baker.

STANDING OF THE CLUBS

	W.	L.	Pct.		W.	L.	Pct.
Bing'mton	24	21	.533	Elmira	24	24	.500
Reading	24	22	.522	Scranton	23	23	.500
Hazleton	24	22	.522	Harrisburg	22	25	.468
Wil'msport	24	23	.511	Wilkes-B.	21	26	.447

PACIFIC COAST LEAGUE

At Los Angeles—

					R.	H.	E.
Portland	000	000	100	—1		6	0
Hollywood	001	000	001	—2		6	1

Batteries—Wilson and Doerr; Shechan and Bassler.

STANDING OF THE CLUBS

	W.	L.	Pct.		W.	L.	Pct.
*Los Ang.	57	15	.792	Hollywood	32	38	.457
*Missions	42	29	.592	*Oakland	31	41	.431
*Sac'mento	36	35	.507	*Seattle	27	42	.391
*San Fran	34	37	.479	Portland	23	45	.338

*Night game.

TEXAS LEAGUE

Tulsa, 4; Galveston, 3.

STANDING OF THE CLUBS

	W.	L.	Pct.		W.	L.	Pct.
*Dallas	34	24	.586	Galveston	29	30	.492
*S. Antonio	34	25	.576	*Ft. Worth	26	32	.448
Tulsa	30	26	.536	*Okla. City	25	32	.439
*Beaumont	30	29	.508	*Houston	24	34	.414

*Night game.

Frankhouse Blanks Cardinals As Braves Register 9-0 Victory

Leading Five Batsmen In Each Major League

AMERICAN LEAGUE

Player and club	G.	AB.	R.	H.	Pct.
Gehringer, Detroit	51	195	47	80	.410
Manush, Washington	51	214	42	85	.397
Vosmik, Cleveland	42	166	29	63	.379
Hemsley, St. Louis	[illegible]	[illegible]	[illegible]	[illegible]	.362
Knickerbocker, Cleve.	45	188	29	67	.356

Leader a year ago today—Simmons, Chicago .373.

NATIONAL LEAGUE

Player and club	G.	AB.	R.	H.	Pct.
Terry, New York	52	203	42	74	.365
Medwick, St. Louis	49	203	42	74	.365
Leslie, Brooklyn	52	199	27	72	.362
Vaughan, Pittsburgh	47	169	34	61	.361
Urbanski, Boston	49	213	42	76	.357

Leader a year ago today—Martin, St. Louis, .367.

Home Runs		Runs Batted In	
Bonura, Wh. Sox	16	Gehrig, Yankees	61
Gehrig, Yankees	16	Ott, Giants	54
Klein, Cubs	15	Cronin, Senators	51
Ott, Giants	15	Bonura, Wh. Sox	48
Foxx, Athletics	14	Suhr, Pirates	47
Collins, Cardinals	14		
Johnson, Athletics	14		

Boston's Triumph Increases Lead of the Giants Over St. Louis to 2½ Games

By The Associated Press

ST. LOUIS, June 13.—A pest to the Cardinals ever since they sent him away, Fred Frankhouse was even more bothersome than usual today as he pitched shutout ball, and the Boston Braves even dthe series with a 9 to 0 victory.

The Cardinals' defeat enabled the Giants, who defeated Cincinnati, to increase their lead to 2½ games, but the Cardinals remained in second place, ahead of the Cubs, who lost to Philadelphia.

Frankhouse allowed only six hits, all of them singles, while his teammates were collecting thirteen off Wild Bill Hallahan, Jesse Haines and Jim Winford.

It was Frankhouse's third victory of the season over the Cardinals. The Cardinals made five errors, four of them by Leo Durocher, the shortstop.

Hallahan, who started for the Cardinals, was in trouble from the start, although he managed to keep the Braves away from the plate until the third inning, when Boston scored three runs.

The score:

BOSTON (N. L.)	ab	r	h	po	a	e	ST. LOUIS (N. L.)	ab	r	h	po	a	e
Urbanski, ss	0	1	0	2	2	0	Martin, 3b	4	0	0	0	1	0
M'Manus, 3b	6	2	2	0	0	0	Rothrock, rf	4	0	1	0	0	0
Jordan, 1b	4	2	3	12	0	1	Frisch, 2b	3	0	0	5	3	1
Berger, cf	4	0	2	1	0	0	White'd, 2b	1	0	1	3	2	0
R. Moore, rf	5	0	0	3	0	0	Medwick, lf	4	0	2	2	0	0
Lee, rf	5	0	1	3	0	0	Collins, 1b	4	0	0	6	2	0
Whitney, 2b	4	2	1	3	3	0	Delancey, c	3	0	0	4	1	0
Hogan, c	5	0	2	3	0	0	Orsatti, cf	4	0	0	3	0	0
FRANK'E, p	4	2	2	0	5	0	Durocher, ss	4	0	1	4	4	4
							HALLA'N, p	0	0	0	0	0	0
							HAINES, p	1	0	1	0	1	0
							WINF'RD, p	0	0	0	0	2	0
							*V. Davis	0	0	0	0	0	0
							†Carleton	0	0	0	0	0	0
							‡Mills	1	0	0	0	0	0
							§Crawford	1	0	0	0	0	0
Totals	37	9	13	27	11	1	Totals	34	0	6	27	16	5

*Batted for Hallahan in third inning.
†Ran for V. Davis in third inning.
‡Batted for Haines in seventh inning.
§Batted for Winford in ninth inning.

Boston	003	103	101	—9
St. Louis	000	000	000	—0

Runs batted in—Jordan (2), Berger (2), Lee, McManus, Frankhouse (2). Two-base hits—Berger, Jordan, McManus. Sacrifices—Urbanski (2), Frankhouse. Double plays—Frisch, Durocher and Collins; Whitehead, Durocher and Collins; Winford, Whitehead and Collins. Left on bases—Boston, 11; St. Louis, 9. Bases on balls—Off Frankhouse, 2; off Hallahan, 3; off Haines, 2; off Winford, 1. Struck out—By Frankhouse, 3; by Hallahan, 3. Hits—Off Hallahan, 6 in 3 innings; off Haines, 6 in 4; off Winford, 1 in 2. Hit by pitcher—By Winford (Berger). Wild pitches—Frankhouse, Haines. Losing pitcher—Hallahan. Umpires—Quigley and Reardon. Time—2:17.

Senators Twice Vanquish White Sox, 11-3, 13-11

WASHINGTON, June 13 (AP).—The Senators slugged it out with the Chicago White Sox this afternoon and won both games of a double-header, 11 to 3 and 13 to 11.

Joe Cronin, Washington's manager, cracked out six hits in nine times at bat, including a timely home run in the second contest.

Bonura, Chicago's first baseman, and Simmons also hit homes. It was Bonura's sixteenth of the season.

Washington took an early lead in each game. In the opener Lyons was knocked out of the box in the first inning. Whitehill held the Sox to eight hits and struck out five.

The teams matched hits in the final, with Russell, McColl and Crowder well pounded by Chicago, and Gaston and Heving trying vainly to stem the rush of Washington blows.

The scores:

FIRST GAME

CHICAGO (A. L.)	ab	r	h	po	a	e	WASHINGTON (A. L.)	ab	r	h	po	a	e
Swanson, rf	5	0	2	2	0	1	Myer, 2b	2	3	1	3	1	0
Haas, cf	5	0	0	4	0	0	Stone, rf	3	2	1	5	0	0
Bonura, 1b	5	1	2	9	0	0	Manush, lf	4	3	3	3	0	0
Simmons, lf	4	1	2	3	0	0	Harris, lf	1	0	0	1	0	0
Boken, 2b	4	0	0	1	0	0	Cronin, ss	4	1	3	1	1	0
Dykes, 3b	1	1	0	0	0	0	Travis, 3b	4	1	1	0	1	0
Cham'lin, ss	3	0	1	2	5	0	Kuhel, 1b	4	0	1	6	0	0
Madjeski, c	4	0	1	3	1	0	Schulte, cf	3	0	0	2	0	0
LYONS, p	0	0	0	0	0	0	Sewell, c	4	0	0	5	0	0
TIETJE, p	3	0	0	0	3	0	WH'HILL, p	2	1	0	1	0	0
G'VAN, p	0	0	0	0	1	0							
*Shea	1	0	0	0	0	0							
Totals	35	3	8	24	10	1	Totals	31	11	10	27	3	0

*Batted for Tietje in eighth inning.

Chicago	000	100	020	— 3
Washington	530	001	02x	—11

Runs batted in—Manush (2), Kuhel (3), Cronin (5), Chamberlin, Simmons, Madjeski, Harris. Two-base hits—Stone, Kuhel, Cronin (2), Swanson, Chamberlin, Madjeski. Three-base hits—Simmons, Bonura. Sacrifices—Schulte, Travis. Left on bases—Chicago, 11; Washington, 6. Bases on balls—Off Lyons, 3; off Tietje, 3; off Gallivan, 2; off Whitehill, 6. Struck out—By Whitehill, 5. Hits—Off Lyons, 4 in 0 inning; off Tietje, 5 in 7; off Gallivan, 1 in 1. Wild pitch—Gallivan. Losing pitcher—Lyons. Umpires—Ormsby, Kolls and Donnelly. Time—2:00.

SECOND GAME

CHICAGO (A. L.)	ab	r	h	po	a	e	WASHINGTON (A. L.)	ab	r	h	po	a	e
Uhalt, rf	5	1	0	2	0	1	Myer, 2b	5	1	4	2	2	0
Haas, cf	6	2	3	3	1	0	Stone, rf	4	2	0	2	0	0
Bonura, 1b	4	3	3	8	1	1	Travis, 3b	3	2	1	2	4	0
Simmons, lf	5	3	3	1	0	0	Cronin, ss	5	3	3	1	3	0
Boken, 2b	5	1	2	3	4	2	Kuhel, 1b	4	2	3	8	1	0
Dykes, 3b	5	0	1	1	5	0	Harris, lf	4	2	2	5	0	0
Chamb'n, ss	4	0	1	1	3	1	Schulte, cf	5	1	1	1	0	0
Madjeski, c	5	0	1	3	3	0	Phillips, c	4	0	1	5	0	0
GASTON, p	3	1	1	2	0	1	RUSSELL, p	2	0	0	1	0	0
HEVING, p	3	1	1	2	0	1	McCOLL, p	2	0	0	0	0	0
*Lyons	1	0	0	0	0	0	CRO'DER, p	0	0	0	0	0	0
Totals	42	11	15	24	17	1	Totals	38	13	15	27	10	0

*Batted for Heving in ninth inning.

Chicago	004	001	033	—11
Washington	640	000	03x	—13

Runs batted in—Cronin (5), Schulte, Phillips (3), Simmons (4), Boken (2), Dykes, Madjeski, Bonura (2). Two-base hits—Kuhel, Haas, Simmons. Home runs—Simmons, Cronin, Bonura. Stolen base—Uhalt. Sacrifices—Travis (2). Double plays—Chamberlin, Boken and Bonura; Dykes, Madjeski and Boken. Left on bases—Chicago, 13; Washington, 6. Bases on balls—Off Gaston, 2; off Heving, 1; off Russell, 5; off McColl, 3; off Crowder, 1. Struck out—By Heving, 2; by McColl, 2; by Crowder, 1. Hits—Off Gaston, 7 in 1 innings (none out in second); off Russell, 6 in 3 1-3; off Heving, 8 in 7; off McColl, 6 in 3 2-3; off Crowder, 3 in 2. Wild pitches—Gaston, McColl. Passed ball—Madjeski. Winning pitcher—McColl. Losing pitcher—Gaston. Umpires—Kolls, Donnelly and Ormsby. Time—2:24.

Miss Pearson Is Beaten In Pennsylvania Tennis

PHILADELPHIA, June 13 (AP).—Miss Kathryn Pearson, of Houston, Texas, today became the victim of the first upset of the women's Pennsylvania and Eastern States tennis championships, losing to Miss Alison Harriman, of Philadelphia, 2—6, 6—3, 8—6.

The defending champion, Mrs. Marion Z. Jessup, of Wilmington, also reached the quarter-final bracket, eliminating Miss Marian Janney, of Merion, 6—1, 6—1.

Other third round victors included Mrs. De Lloyd Thompson, Washington, Pa., who defeated Miss Cecile Bowes, Cynwyd, 6—2, 6—2, and Mrs. John Van Ryn, Philadelphia, who eliminated Mrs. Alfred Hunter, Philadelphia, 6—2, 6—2.

Syracuse Twice Breaks Rochester Spell, 7-4, 3-2

SYRACUSE, N. Y., June 13 (AP).—The Chiefs today shattered the jinx which Rochester has held over them this season, taking both ends of a double-header, 7 to 4 and 3 to 2. Previously the Red Wings had won six in a row from Syracuse.

A four-run blast in the first inning of the opener set the Chiefs off to a lead which they never relinquished, and Estel Crabtree's homer in the sixth inning, his tenth of the season, marked the main threat of the Wings against Fred Fussell.

A single by Foots Blair with the bases loaded in the last of the sixth scored two runs and brought the Chiefs from behind to win the abbreviated second game.

The scores by innings:

First game—

					R.	H.	E.
Rochester	200	002	000	—4		8	0
Syracuse	410	200	00x	—7		9	0

Batteries—Harrell, Liska and Lewis; Fussell and Taylor.

Second game—

					R.	H.	E.
Rochester	000	101	0	—2		8	0
Syracuse	000	102	x	—3		7	0

Batteries—Potter and Florence; Merena and Taylor.

Standings in Major Leagues

THURSDAY, JUNE 14, 1934

American League

YESTERDAY'S RESULTS

New York, 6; St. Louis, 2.
Boston, 15; Detroit, 13.
Washington, 11; Chicago, 3 (1st).
Washington, 13; Chicago, 11 (2d).
Philadelphia, 11; Cleveland, 2.

STANDING OF THE CLUBS

	Detroit	New York	Cleveland	Washington	St. Louis	Boston	Phila'phia	Chicago	Won	Lost	Percentage
Detroit	—	2	5	2	3	6	3	9	30	21	.588
New York	3	—	1	3	6	3	8	4	28	20	.583
Cleveland	2	3	—	[illegible]	6	4	4	3	24	21	.533
Wash'ton	3	3	3	—	1	5	5	7	27	25	.519
St. Louis	1	2	4	5	—	2	2	5	24	23	.511
Boston	3	4	1	8	3	—	3	3	25	25	.500
Phila'phia	3	4	4	3	2	3	—	1	20	28	.417
Chicago	3	2	3	2	2	2	3	—	17	32	.347
Gms. lost	21	20	21	25	23	25	28	32	—	—	

GAMES TODAY

St. Louis at New York, 3:15.
Detroit at Boston.
Chicago at Washington.
Cleveland at Philadelphia.

National League

YESTERDAY'S RESULTS

New York, 6; Cincinnati, 4.
Pittsburgh, 15; Brooklyn, 2.
Boston, 9; St. Louis, 0.
Philadelphia, 2; Chicago, 1.

STANDING OF THE CLUBS

	New York	St. Louis	Chicago	Pittsburgh	Boston	Brooklyn	Phil'phia	Cincinnati	Won	Lost	Percentage
New York	—	2	3	3	6	6	8	6	34	18	.654
St. Louis	5	—	2	5	5	2	5	6	30	19	.612
Chicago	2	6	—	4	2	4	5	8	31	21	.596
Pit'sburgh	3	6	2	—	2	5	4	5	27	20	.574
Boston	2	3	4	1	—	8	3	4	25	23	.521
Brooklyn	1	2	3	3	4	—	5	3	21	30	.412
Phila'phia	3	0	3	2	2	4	—	3	17	30	.362
Cincinnati	2	0	4	2	2	1	0	—	11	35	.239
Gms. lost	18	19	21	20	23	30	30	35	—	—	

GAMES TODAY

New York at Cincinnati.
Brooklyn at Pittsburgh.
Boston at St. Louis.
Philadelphia at Chicago.

17-Hit Barrage By Pittsburgh Fells Brooklyn

Suhr Leads Attack on Herring, Munns, Beck With Double and 3 Singles

By Arthur E. Patterson

PITTSBURGH, June 13.—The Carnera-Baer fight has been the main subject of conversation wherever the Brooklyn Dodgers have gathered recently, and perhaps the fact that the bout is only a day off can be blamed for the groggy condition of the pitching staff here this afternoon. If there is as much heavy hitting at Madison Square Garden Bowl tomorrow night as there was today at Forbes Field, the big crowd will get a run for its money.

Sad to relate, most of the clouting was done by the opposition, so the Dodgers went down to defeat, 15 to 2, thereby ending a three-game losing streak for the Buccaneers and evening the current series here. When Brooklyn players arrived here they were regaled with tales of numerous batting slumps in the Pirate ranks, but they were not evident today, as the offerings of Art Herring, Les Munns and Walter Beck were combed for no less than seventeen safeties of various proportions. What with four bases on balls and two wild pitches tossed in for good measure, this represented the Dodger hurling at its lowest ebb.

Four Hits for Suhr

Gus Suhr was supposed to be the most afflicted batter in the Pirate line-up, but when Drs. Herring, Munns and Beck went to work on him he was miraculously cured, and he led the winning team's slugging with a double and three singles. Arky Vaughan was right behind with two triples and a double, and Paul Waner did not do so badly for his batting average, either, with a single, double and triple. All the starting Pittsburgh players made at least one hit, and Woody Jensen and Bill Swift, the pitcher, were the only runners who did not cross the plate.

Swift, incidentally, turned in a fine pitching performance, in which he was touched for three hits and two runs in the first inning, and then coasted in. Brooklyn was able to make only six hits after the opening frame, and Clyde Sukeforth, who doubled in the seventh, was the only Dodger to reach third. A long fly by Beck advanced him, but after Boyle walked the rally was halted by Suhr's unassisted double play on Jimmy Jordan's liner.

Successive singles by Taylor and Koenecke and Sambo Leslie's liner to the right center field fence for a triple gave Brooklyn a two-run lead in the first, but the Pirates evened the count on two walks and Suhr's double. Then they sent eleven men to the plate in the second for seven runs and the ball game. In this splurge were included a double by Padden, a single by Swift, a triple by P. Waner, a double by Traynor, a double by Vaughan and a single by Suhr off Herring, and a double by Lavagetto and a single by Jensen off Munns.

Munns Routed in Sixth

It did not matter much thereafter, but the Pirates were hit-hungry, so they picked up a run in the fourth, another in the fifth and then sent Munns to the showers amid a four-run surge in the sixth. Beck relieved Munns and one of his early acts was to put Lloyd Waner out of the game with a bruised shin, an accident which occurred with the bases loaded. Brother Paul's single scored two more runs, but Beck took Traynor's grounder for a double play to end the session and he was unmolested in the seventh and eighth.

With the game hopelessly lost, Stengel gave Taylor, Koenecke and Lopez a rest soon after the big rally.

A stolen base by Lavagetto was the first the Pirates have seized in twenty-two games.

Owen Carroll's finger injury, suffered in the last game at home, was diagnosed as a fracture today.

Wilson had an active afternoon in right field. He dived as gracefully as possible in two gallant but unsuccessful tries for low liners.

Van Lingle Mungo, ace of the staff, will hurl for Brooklyn tomorrow, and Tom Zachary probably will get the call the last day here.

The score:

BROOKLYN	ab	r	h	po	a	e	PITTSBURGH (N. L.)	ab	r	h	po	a	e
Boyle, rf, cf	3	0	0	0	0	0	L. Waner, cf	4	2	1	3	0	0
Jordan, ss	5	0	0	1	1	0	Roettger, lf	1	0	0	1	0	0
Taylor, lf	3	1	1	2	0	0	P. Waner, rf	5	2	3	4	0	0
Fred'ick, lf	2	0	0	1	0	0	Traynor, 3b	5	1	1	0	2	0
Koenecke, lf	2	1	1	0	0	0	Vaughan, ss	4	4	3	3	2	0
Wilson, rf	1	0	1	3	1	0	Suhr, 1b	5	2	4	7	0	0
Leslie, 1b	4	0	1	10	0	0	Lavag'to, 2b	5	2	1	5	1	0
Cucci'llo, 2b	4	0	1	1	4	1	Jensen, lf, cf	5	0	1	4	0	0
Stripp, 3b	4	0	1	1	0	2	Padden, c	3	2	2	0	0	0
Lopez, c	1	0	0	0	0	0	SWIFT, p	4	0	1	0	1	0
Sukeforth, c	2	0	1	2	1	0							
Berres, c	1	0	1	3	0	0							
HER'ING, p	0	0	0	0	3	0							
MUNNS, p	1	0	1	0	0	0							
BECK, p	1	0	0	0	0	0							
*Smythe	1	0	0	0	0	0							
Totals	35	2	9	24	10	3	Totals	41	15	17	27	6	0

*Batted for Beck in ninth inning.

Brooklyn	200	000	000	— 2
Pittsburgh	270	114	00x	—15

Runs batted in—Leslie (2), Suhr (4), Swift, P. Waner (3), Traynor, Vaughan, Lavagetto, Jensen (2), L. Waner. Two-base hits—Suhr, Padden, Traynor, Vaughan, P. Waner, Sukeforth, Lavagetto. Three-base hits—Leslie, P. Waner, Vaughan (2). Stolen base—Lavagetto. Double plays—Wilson and Leslie; Back, Sukeforth and Leslie; Suhr (unassisted). Left on bases—Brooklyn, 10; Pittsburgh, 8. Bases on balls—Off Herring, 2; off Swift, 4; off Munns, 2; off Beck, 1. Struck out—By Beck, 2; by Munns, 1. Hits—Off Herring, 7 in 1 2-3 innings; off Munns, 8 in 3 2-3; off Beck, 2 in 2 2-3. Hit by pitcher—By Beck (L. Waner). Wild pitches—Herring, Munns. Losing pitcher—Herring. Umpires—Stewart, Barr and Klem. Time—2:03.

Champions Take 4th Straight With Four-Run Assault in 7th

Castleman and Hubbell Foil Cincinnati After Bowman Is Driven Out of Box in 5th

By Rud Rennie

CINCINNATI, June 13.—Just when it seemed as if the Reds might be on the verge of winning a ball game the Giants beat them with a four-run rally in the seventh here this afternoon for a 6—4 victory. It was the Giants' fourth straight triumph.

Each team made thirteen hits and used three pitchers. The Giants gave the Reds a treat. They let them look at Carl Hubbell's bruised thumb for three innings. It apparently was pliant enough to control the Reds at the tag-end of the game.

Joe Bowman started for the Giants, and Bob O'Farrell, the Reds' manager, drove in a run with a double in the second inning. The Giants made two runs in the third after two men were out. Bowman started the scoring action by beating out a bunt. Moore, Critz and Terry followed with singles, completing the job.

Then the Reds tied it up. Adams doubled and scored on Koenig's single. Bottomley also doubled, but Koenig had been caught off first by a quick throw from Mancuso, and there was no more scoring until the fifth.

Bowman Routed in Fifth

In this inning Homer Peel let Adams's single pass him for three bases. Koenig drove Adams home with a single and at the same time drove Bowman out of the box. Clyde Castleman came in. With two out Pool singled, scoring Koenig. The small crowd perked up, thinking the Reds were about to win one for a change. It was a pretty thought while it lasted, but it did not last long.

The Giants belted Kleinhans and his successor, Ray Kolp, in the seventh, made four runs and put the Cincinnati citizenry back into a normal frame of mind.

Harry Danning, pinch hitting for Castleman in this inning, wielded a helping bat. With two men on bases, he doubled, scoring Ryan, and putting Schumacher, who was running for Mancuso, on third. Then Kleinhans made a wild pitch and Schumacher came home. When Joe Moore singled sending Danning across the platter, Kleinhans was relieved by Kolp. The latter got Critz to force Moore, and he induced Terry to fly out, but Ott whacked a double to center, scoring Critz.

To add to the Reds' discouragement, Terry called in Hubbell to pitch the last three innings. Carl hurt his left thumb in Philadelphia and was not supposed to work here. It would have been all right with the Reds if he hadn't. Hubbell shut out the Reds with three hits.

Castleman's First Victory

It was Castleman's first victory of the season. He has been in four games and has not yielded a run in the eight and two-thirds innings he has pitched.

Terry charged into the railing of the stands behind first base in pursuit of Comorosky's foul in the eighth and bruised his left thigh. The bruise was all he got. The ball escaped.

Slade handled his nine chances without an error.

There is a vast apathy toward the Reds. There were only about 1,000 persons out to see them today.

After driving in a run in the third Koenig was too impetuous. He started for second with the pitch and before he could get back to first Mancuso picked him off with a snap throw. As a result, the Reds got only one run out of two doubles and a single.

Bob O'Farrell was active catching fouls. He snared five. Chasing one behind first base with Bottomley's assurance that he had "a lot of room," O'Farrell was surprised to find himself bouncing off the railing of the stands after he caught the ball. He wasn't hurt.

Giants' Score

NEW YORK (N. L.)	ab	r	h	po	a	e	CINCINNATI (N. L.)	ab	r	h	po	a	e
Moore, lf	5	1	3	2	0	0	Adams, 3b	5	2	3	0	2	0
Critz, 2b	5	1	1	2	2	0	Koenig, ss	5	1	3	2	2	0
Terry, 1b	5	0	3	12	0	0	Hafey, cf	4	0	0	2	0	0
Ott, rf	5	0	1	2	0	0	Bott'm'y, 1b	5	0	1	14	1	0
Jackson, ss	4	0	1	2	3	0	Pool, lf	4	1	2	1	0	0
Peel, cf	3	0	0	4	0	1	Com'sky, rf	3	0	0	1	0	0
Watkins, cf	1	0	0	2	0	0	Slade, 2b	4	0	2	1	8	0
Ryan, 3b	4	1	1	1	3	0	O'Farrell, c	3	0	2	6	0	0
Manucso, c	2	0	1	0	3	0	KLEIN'S, p	2	0	0	0	3	0
*Schumac'r	0	1	0	0	0	0	KOLP, p	0	0	0	0	0	0
HUBBE'L, p	1	0	0	0	0	0	†Lombardi	1	0	0	0	0	0
BOWMAN, p	1	1	1	0	0	0	DER'GER, p	0	0	0	0	0	0
CASTL'N, p	0	0	0	0	2	0							
Danning, c	2	1	1	0	0	0							
Totals	38	6	13	27	13	1	Totals	36	4	13	27	16	0

*Ran for Mancuso in seventh inning.
†Batted for Kolp in eighth inning.

New York	002	000	400	—6
Cincinnati	011	020	000	—4

Runs batted in—Hoore, Critz, Terry, Ott, Danning, Koenig (2), Pool, O'Farrell. Two-base hits—Ott, Danning, Adams, Bottomley, Slade, O'Farrell. Sacrifices—Bowman, Hafey, Comorosky, Kleinhans. Double play—Bottomley, Koenig and Bottomley. Left on bases—New York, 7; Cincinnati, 9. Bases on balls—Off Castleman, 1; off Kleinhans, 1. Struck out—By Castleman, 1; by Kolp, 1. Hits—Off Bowman, 9 in 4 innings (none out in fifth); off Castleman, 1 in 2; off Hubbell, 3 in 3; off Kleinhans, 10 in 6 (none out in seventh); off Kolp, 1 in 2; off Derringer, 2 in 1. Wild pitches—Kleinhans (2). Passed ball—Mancuso. Winning pitcher—Castleman. Losing pitcher—Kleinhans. Umpires—Magerkurth and Rigler. Time—2:15.

Exeter Nine Elects Woodman

Special to the Herald Tribune

EXETER, N. H., June 13.—Everett M. Woodman, of Franklin, N. H., was elected captain of the 1935 Exeter baseball team at a meeting today. Woodman has been a regular third baseman for the last two years. William M. Canby, of Wilmington, Del., was awarded the managership.

Phils Subdue Cubs, 2-1, On Home Run by Allen

CHICAGO, June 13 (AP).—Ethan Allen's homer with Dick Bartell on base gave Philadelphia a 2 to 1 victory over the Cubs today that evened the series at one game each.

The same blow gave Curt Davis the decision over Charley Root in a pitchers' duel. Davis pitched five-hit ball until the ninth and then squelched a Chicago rally by setting down Billy Jurges on a tap in front of the plate after the Cubs had put men on third and on first on singles by Gabby Hartnett and Don Hurst.

Root, pitching his first complete game since April 21, allowed eight hits, but, given splendid infield assistance, was in trouble only twice.

The score:

PHILADELPHIA (N. L.)	ab	r	h	po	a	e	CHICAGO (N. L.)	ab	r	h	po	a	e
Fullis, lf	3	0	1	0	0	0	W. H'an, 2b	4	0	0	5	2	0
Bartell, ss	3	1	1	3	3	0	English, 3b	4	0	0	0	2	0
Allen, cf	4	1	2	3	0	0	Klein, lf	4	1	0	1	1	1
J. M're, rf	4	0	0	1	0	1	F. H'an, rf	4	0	1	2	0	0
Clancy, 1b	4	0	0	13	0	0	Cuyler, cf	3	0	1	2	0	0
Wilson, c	4	0	2	4	2	0	*Phelps	1	0	0	0	0	0
Haslin, 3b	3	0	1	1	2	0	H'nett, c	3	0	3	6	3	0
J'ries, 2b	4	0	1	2	4	0	†Galan	0	0	0	0	0	0
DAVIS, p	3	0	0	0	4	0	Hurst, 1b	4	0	1	8	1	0
							Jurges, ss	4	0	1	3	3	0
							ROOT, p	3	0	0	0	2	0
Totals	32	2	8	27	15	1	Totals	34	1	7	27	14	1

*Batted for Cuyler in ninth inning.
†Ran for Hartnett in ninth inning.

Philadelphia	000	000	020	—2
Chicago	000	100	000	—1

Runs batted in—Allen (2), Hartnett. Two-base hit—Haslin. Home run—Allen. Stolen base—Fullis. Double plays—English, Hartnett and Hurst; Klein and W. Herman. Left on bases—Philadelphia, 6; Chicago, 7. Bases on balls—Off Davis, 1; off Root, 2. Struck out—By Davis, 4; by Root, 4. Hit by pitcher—By Root (Fullis). Umpires—Pfirman and Moran. Time—1:43.

Montreal Nips Baltimore In 10th on Wild Pitch, 8-7

BALTIMORE, June 13 (AP).—A wild pitch by Cliff Melton, which enabled Ripple to score from second base with the winning run, gave Montreal an 8-7 victory over Baltimore in a ten-inning struggle today.

Baltimore enjoyed a 6-3 lead in the seventh, but Pete Appleton cracked and the Royals took a 7-6 lead in the eighth on five hits, two being homers by Thompson and Riel.

Puccinelli's fifth homer since he became an Oriole, delivered with two mates on bases, was the clout that gave the Birds their temporary lead. Olson hit the other Bird four-bagger.

The score by innings:

						R.	H.	E.
Montreal	300	000	040	1	—8		11	0
Baltimore	001	002	310	0	—7		12	0

Batteries—Fritz, Savleson and Reiber; Appleton, Grainger, Melton and Asby, Picinich.

Ruth Hits 699th Homer on 20th Big League Anniversary as Yanks Win, 6-3; Giants Victors

Babe Adds Lusty Double; Retires After Batting In 4

Feats Dim Two Circuit Clouts by Manush for Senators and Pitching of Deshong, Whose Second Victory in Three Starts Gives N. Y. Series

By Rud Rennie

It was the twentieth anniversary of the sale of Babe Ruth by the Baltimore Orioles to the Boston Red Sox. Ruth does not remember it clearly. He thinks he stepped off a train and pitched a game for the Sox. Anyway, he is a great hand at doing a little something of a spectacular nature on occasions like all-star games, world series, crucial games and anniversaries.

He hit a home run and a double and knocked in four runs in the Stadium yesterday afternoon. He had an idea something was expected of him. So he won the ball game before departing, as usual, in the seventh. The score was 6 to 3, and the Yankees won the series from the Washington Senators, three games to one. In the only other series between the teams in the Stadium this year the Senators won, two out of three.

It would have been a nice touch if the Babe had hit two homers. The one he hit was his thirteenth of the season and his 699th of his major-league career. On his twentieth anniversary the 700th homer would have been rather decorative.

Just Misses 700th

The Babe took a healthy swing at one in the seventh, aiming for the necessary homer, but he drove it straight into the vacant space in center field and got only two bases because of fast fielding by Manush. If he could have pulled it toward the stands he would have had his 700th.

As it was, Ruth on his anniversary dimmed the fine performance of young James Brooklyn Deshong, making his third start of the season and winning his second straight game. He also overshadowed the bat work of Heinie Manush, who hit two home runs into the right-field stands and was responsible for two of his team's three runs.

Manush hit his first one in the first inning with two out. This hit and a single by Travis in the second were all Deshong allowed until the seventh. Meanwhile Crosetti scored while Ruth was being caught in a double play along with Saltzgaver in the first inning.

The tie was broken in the third when the Yanks got one run out of a conglomeration of two hits, a sacrifice, two bases on balls and two wild pitches. Heffner started it with a hit, took second on a wild pitch, third on Deshong's sacrifice and came home on Saltzgaver's single.

Weaver Ended in Fifth

The Babe's homer happened in the fifth, with Saltzgaver on first. Monte Weaver was pitching for the Senators. It was his last inning. Al Thomas followed him, and Alex McColl followed Thomas.

The Senators' third hit of the game was Manush's second homer. He led off with it in the seventh. It just eased into the stands. Ruth climbed the screen in an attempt to reach it and hung, suspended like a monkey.

In the last part of the inning the Yanks made two more runs. Deshong started it with a hit. Crosetti sacrificed. Saltzgaver came through with his fourth straight single, scoring Deshong. Then the Babe belted his double into center field and called it a day. Byrd ran for him and played left field, Hoag moving to right. It was a good performance for a man who had been burning up the major leagues for twenty years and is supposed to be through.

Deshong got lots of help from Crosetti and Heffner, particularly the former, in the seventh and eighth. Heffner started a double play for him in the seventh, and Crosetti rambled back into center field and caught an awkward fly in the eighth, and then came up with a grounder which Stone had knocked whizzing off Deshong's glove for a glittering force play at second.

Ken Auer, former Fordham pitcher, has been signed by Binghamton, a Yankee farm.

Chapman had a busy day afield and hit .500, getting a single and two bases on balls out of four trips to the plate.

This is an open date in the schedules of both major leagues. It is opened to permit the players from out of town to come here for the All-Star game tomorrow. The writers will have their annual outing at Huntington today.

Yankees' Score

WASHINGTON (A. L.)	ab	r	h	po	a	e
Myer, 2b	4	0	1	2	5	0
Stone, cf	4	0	1	2	0	0
Manush, lf	4	2	2	0	0	0
Cronin, ss	4	0	0	2	6	0
Travis, 3b	4	0	2	1	0	0
Harris, rf	4	0	1	0	0	0
Kress, 1b	4	0	1	15	0	0
Sewell, c	4	0	0	2	0	0
WEAVER, p	1	0	0	0	1	0
*Bluege	1	0	0	0	0	0
THOMAS, p	0	0	0	0	3	0
†Schulte	1	1	1	0	0	0
M'COLL, p	0	0	0	0	1	0
Totals	35	3	9	24	16	0

NEW YORK (A. L.)	ab	r	h	po	a	e
Crosetti, ss	3	1	1	3	2	0
Saltz'ver, 3b	4	2	4	0	1	0
Ruth, rf	3	1	2	2	0	0
Byrd, lf	0	0	0	0	0	0
Gehrig, 1b	3	0	0	9	0	0
Chapman, cf	2	0	1	7	0	0
Dickey, c	4	0	0	2	0	0
Hoag, lf,rf	4	0	0	3	0	0
Heffner, 2b	4	1	1	1	3	0
DESH'G, p	3	1	1	0	4	0
Totals	30	6	10	27	10	0

*Batted for Weaver in sixth inning.
†Batted for Thomas in eighth inning.

Washington .... 1010 000 110—3
New York .... 101 020 20x—6

Runs batted in—Manush (2), Ruth (4), Saltzgaver (2), Stone. Two-base hit—Ruth. Home runs—Manush (2), Ruth. Sacrifices—Deshong, Crosetti. Double plays—Myer, Cronin and Kress (2); Heffner, Crossetti and Gehrig. Left on bases—New York, 6; Washington, 5. Bases on balls—Off Weaver, 2; off Thomas, 2. Struck out—By Deshong, 2; by Weaver, 1; by Thomas, 1. Hits—Off Weaver, 7 in 5 innings; off Thomas, 3 in 2; off McColl, 0 in 1. Wild pitches—Weaver (2). Losing pitcher—Weaver. Umpires—McGowan, Moriarty and Hildebrand. Time—1:48.

Ruth pitching for a school team in the days before he became famous as the game's outstanding player

Now and Then—20 Years in Baseball

Associated Press photos

Babe Ruth, the New York Yankees' home run hitter, who yesterday marked the twentieth anniversary of his advent into major leagues

Standings in Major Leagues

MONDAY, JULY 9, 1934

American League

YESTERDAY'S RESULTS

New York, 6; Washington, 3.
Boston, 7; Philadelphia, 4 (1st).
Boston, 7; Philadelphia, 2 (2d).
Detroit, 5; St. Louis, 4.
Cleveland, 5; Chicago, 1 (1st).
Cleveland, 10; Chicago, 5 (2d).

STANDING OF THE CLUBS

	New York	Detroit	Boston	Cleveland	Washington	St. Louis	Phila'phia	Chicago	Won	Lost	Percentage
New York	—	5	5	4	8	8	8	8	46	27	.630
Detroit	4	—	7	8	6	7	5	10	47	29	.618
Boston	6	3	—	3	8	7	8	7	42	35	.545
Cleveland	4	4	5	—	4	4	7	11	39	35	.527
Wash'ton	5	4	6	6	—	6	6	6	39	38	.506
St. Louis	2	6	3	4	5	—	5	6	31	39	.443
Phila'phia	4	4	6	4	5	4	—	3	30	45	.400
Chicago	2	3	3	6	2	3	6	—	25	51	.329
Gms. lost	27	29	35	35	38	39	45	51	—	—	

GAMES TODAY

No games scheduled.

National League

YESTERDAY'S RESULTS

New York, 2; Brooklyn, 0.
Philadelphia, 5; Boston, 3.
Pittsburgh, 11; Chicago, 4 (1st).
Chicago, 12; Pittsburgh, 3 (2d).
St. Louis, 6; Cincinnati, 1 (1st).
Cincinnati, 8; St. Louis, 7 (2d).

STANDING OF THE CLUBS

	New York	Chicago	St. Louis	Pittsburgh	Boston	Brooklyn	Phila'phia	Cincinnati	Won	Lost	Percentage
New York	—	4	4	6	9	10	8	7	48	28	.632
Chicago	5	—	8	8	3	8	6	8	46	30	.605
St. Louis	7	4	—	5	6	5	7	9	43	31	.581
Pit'sburgh	3	4	6	—	5	5	8	7	38	33	.535
Boston	3	7	4	3	—	8	7	7	39	37	.513
Brooklyn	4	3	3	5	4	—	7	5	31	45	.408
Phila'phia	3	4	2	3	7	6	—	5	30	47	.390
Cincinnati	3	4	4	3	3	3	4	—	24	48	.333
Gms. lost	28	30	31	33	37	45	47	48	—	—	

GAMES TODAY

No games scheduled.

Indians Hand White Sox Double Reverse, 5-1, 10-5

CLEVELAND, July 8 (AP).—The Indians won their first double-header of the year today, defeating the White Sox 5 to 1 in the opener and 10 to 5 in the second game.

Willis Hudlin won his eighth game in the early battle, outpitching sad Sam Jones and allowing the Sox only seven hits. Chicago scored in the first inning, but from then on not a runner reached third base. The Indians sewed up the game in the fourth inning by bunching four hits.

Unsteady in the early innings of the second game, Monte Pearson checked the Sox in the last five rounds and won his tenth victory. A four-run attack on Whitlow Wyatt gave the Indians their winning margin in the third inning.

The double victory put Cleveland back in the first division.

The scores:

FIRST GAME

CHICAGO (A. L.)	ab	r	h	po	a	e
Conlan, rf, cf	4	1	2	3	0	0
Haas, cf	1	0	0	0	0	0
Swanson, rf	2	0	0	0	0	0
Dykes, 2b	4	0	2	3	4	0
Bonura, 1b	4	0	2	12	0	0
Simmons, lf	3	0	0	2	0	0
Boken, ss	3	0	1	1	4	0
Chamb'n, 3b	3	0	0	0	0	2
Madjeski, c	3	0	0	3	1	0
JONES, p	3	0	0	0	1	0
Totals	30	1	7	24	10	2

CLEVELAND (A. L.)	ab	r	h	po	a	e
Rice, rf	4	0	4	1	0	0
Burnett, ss	3	0	1	3	3	0
Averill, cf	4	0	0	2	0	0
Vosmik, lf	4	0	0	0	0	0
Trosky, 1b	4	1	1	17	1	0
Hale, 2b	4	1	2	2	6	0
Kamm, 3b	3	1	1	0	6	1
Pytlak, c	3	2	0	2	0	0
HUDLIN, p	3	0	0	0	2	0
Totals	32	5	9	27	18	1

Chicago .... 100 000 000—1
Cleveland .... 001 040 00x—5

Runs batted in—Rice (2), Burnett (2), Pytlak, Dykes. Two-base hits—Conlan, Bonura. Sacrifices—Haas, Burnett. Double plays, Hale, Burnett and Trosky (2); Trosky and Burnett; Hudlin, Hale and Trosky; Bonura (unassisted). Left on bases—Chicago, 3; Cleveland, 5. Base on balls—Off Jones, 1. Struck out—By Jones, 2; by Hudlin, 1. Umpires—Kolls, Donnelly and Dinneen. Time—1:29.

SECOND GAME

CHICAGO (A. L.)	ab	r	h	po	a	e
Conlan, cf	4	2	2	3	0	0
Swanson, rf	3	0	1	2	0	0
Dykes, 2b	5	0	1	5	2	0
Bonura, 1b	4	0	0	7	2	0
Simmons, lf	5	2	3	1	0	0
Boken, ss	5	0	1	3	6	0
Chamb'n, 3b	4	0	0	1	0	1
Shea, c	3	0	1	2	1	0
WYATT, p	3	1	1	0	1	0
TIETJE, p	0	0	0	0	1	0
*Boken	1	0	0	0	0	0
GALLI'N, p	0	0	0	0	0	0
Totals	37	5	10	24	13	1

CLEVELAND (A. L.)	ab	r	h	po	a	e
Rice, rf	5	0	2	3	0	0
Burnett, ss	4	2	2	0	2	0
Averill, cf	1	2	0	4	0	0
Vosmik, lf	3	1	0	2	0	0
Seeds, lf	0	0	0	0	0	0
Trosky, 1b	4	2	2	8	0	0
Hale, 2b	3	1	1	2	1	0
Kamm, 3b	3	1	2	0	1	1
Wyatt, c	5	1	1	8	0	0
PEARSON, p	5	0	1	0	1	0
Totals	33	10	11	27	5	1

*Batted for Tietje in eighth inning.

Chicago .... 011 210 000—5
Cleveland .... 204 030 01x—10

Runs batted in—Hale (3), Trosky (2), Kamm (2), Wyatt (2), Pearson, Swanson (2), Dykes, Chamberlain, Shea. Two-base hits—Trosky, Shea, Conlan, Burnett, Swanson, Simmons. Three-base hit—Wyatt. Stolen base—Conlan. Sacrifice—Swanson. Double plays—Boken, Dykes and Bonura; Boken and Bonura. Left on bases—Chicago, 10; Cleveland, 11. Bases on balls—Off Wyatt, 6; off Tietje, 2; off Gallivan, 4; off Pearson, 4. Struck out—By Wyatt, 1; by Tietje, 1; by Pearson, 8. Hits—Off Wyatt, 8 in 1 2-3 innings; off Tietje, 2 in 2 1-3; off Gallivan, 0 in 1. Wild pitches—Pearson, Gallivan. Losing pitcher—Wyatt. Umpires—Donnelly, Dinneen and Kolls. Time—2:31.

Tigers Shade Browns, 5 to 4, On 2 Hits and 2 Errors in 9th

Melillo's Miscues and Pass to Cochrane Send Three Across in Series Final

By The Associated Press

DETROIT, July 8.—Two errors by Melillo and a pair of singles, all in the ninth inning, gave the Tigers a 5—4 victory over the St. Louis Browns in their series final here today.

Trailing, 4 to 2, as the final inning opened, the Tigers got to Blaeholder for two singles which sent that pitcher to the showers. The singles were hit by Owen and Rowe. Newsom supplanted Blaeholder and the first man to face him was Fox, who hit a grounder which Melillo booted, filling the bases. Cochrane walked, forcing Owen across the plate, and Wells went in for Newsom. At this juncture Goslin bounced to Melillo and the latter threw wildly to the plate trying to catch Rowe, but both Rowe and Fox scored.

The scores:

ST. LOUIS (A. L.)	ab	r	h	po	a	e
Clift, 3b	4	1	1	2	1	0
West, cf	3	1	1	2	0	0
Burns, 1b	4	0	1	7	1	0
Garms, lf	4	1	1	1	0	1
Campbell, rf	3	1	1	2	0	0
Melillo, 2b	4	0	0	2	5	2
Hemsley, c	3	0	0	3	2	0
Strange, ss	4	0	1	5	3	0
BLAE'ER, p	3	0	1	0	1	0
NEWSOM, p	0	0	0	0	0	0
WELLS, p	0	0	0	0	0	0
Totals	32	4	6	*25	12	3

DETROIT (A. L.)	ab	r	h	po	a	e
Fox, rf	5	1	0	3	0	0
Cochrane, c	2	1	1	7	0	0
Goslin, lf	5	0	0	1	0	0
Gehr'ger, 2b	3	0	0	1	3	0
Rogell, ss	4	0	3	2	3	0
Green'g, 1b	4	1	1	10	1	1
White, cf	4	0	0	2	0	0
Owen, 3b	4	1	2	0	2	0
MARB'Y, p	1	0	0	1	2	0
ROWE, p	2	1	2	0	0	0
†Doljack	1	0	1	0	0	0
Totals	35	5	10	27	11	1

*One out when winning run was scored.
†Batted for Marberry in sixth inning.

St. Louis .... 000 021 010—4
Detroit .... 000 000 113—5

Runs batted in—Strange (2), Garms, Burns, Rowe, Rogell. Two-base hits—Burns, Rogell. Three-base hit—West. Sacrifices—Blaeholder, West. Double plays—Melillo, Strange and Burns. Left on bases—Detroit, 9; St. Louis, 5. Bases on balls—Off Marberry, 1; off Rowe, 1; off Blaeholder, 3; off Newsom, 1. Struck out—By Marberry, 4; by Rowe, 1; by Blaeholder, 2. Hits—Off Marberry, 4 in 6 innings; off Rowe, 2 in 3; off Blaeholder, 10 in 8 1-3; off Newsom, 0 in 0; off Wells, 0 in 0. Winning pitcher—Rowe. Losing pitcher—Newsom. Umpires—Geisel and Ormsby. Time—2:20.

Syracuse Wins 1st, 5-4; Montreal Takes 2d, 3-2

MONTREAL, July 8 (AP).—The Montreal Royals and the Syracuse Chiefs split a double-header today, the Chiefs winning the thirteen-inning first game, 5 to 4, and the home forces taking the second, 3 to 2. Pomorski, who finished both games for Syracuse, was charged with the loss in the extra-inning contest, but got credit for the second game.

The scores by innings:

First game— R. H. E.
Syracuse ... 000 000 100 020 2—5 10 0
Montr'l ..... 000 001 000 020 1—4 12 1
Batteries—Pickrel, Coombs and Taylor; Smythe, Pomorski and Outen.

Second game— R. H. E.
Syracuse .... 000 200 00—2 9
Montreal .... 100 000 11—3
Batteries—Liska and Cronin; Myllykangas, Pomorski and Outen.

Dizzy Dean Gains Glory, Paul Woe as Cards Split

ST. LOUIS, July 8 (AP).—The Dean brothers act started brilliantly and ended dismally here today as the St. Louis Cardinals split a double-header with Cincinnati, winning the first game, 6 to 1, then dropping the nightcap, 8 to 4.

Dizzy Dean, the elder of the pitching duo, got his fourteenth victory of the season as he fanned ten Reds.

In the second game Paul Dean, the kid brother, started for the Cardinals, but after hurling six strikeouts in three innings, was met by a homer by Pool with the bases loaded. In the same inning Piet doubled to score two more runs. The scores:

FIRST GAME

CINCINNATI (N. L.)	ab	r	h	po	a	e
Piet, 3b	4	0	1	0	3	0
Slade, 2b	4	0	0	1	2	0
Koenig, ss	4	1	2	6	3	1
Hafey, cf	4	0	2	2	0	0
Bottom'y, 1b	4	0	2	6	0	1
Lombardi, c	4	0	0	6	2	0
Schul'ch, lf	3	0	0	1	0	0
Comor'ky, rf	3	0	0	2	0	0
DERRI'R, p	2	0	0	0	2	0
KLEINH'S, p	0	0	0	0	0	0
*Shevlin	1	0	0	0	0	0
Totals	33	1	7	24	12	2

ST. LOUIS (N. L.)	ab	r	h	po	a	e
Whiteh'd, 3b	4	2	2	0	4	0
Rothrock, rf	4	2	2	2	0	0
Frisch, 2b	4	0	3	1	2	0
Medwick, lf	4	0	1	0	0	0
Collins, 1b	3	1	1	8	0	0
Davis, c	4	0	1	11	1	0
Orsatti, cf	4	0	2	4	0	0
Durocher, ss	4	0	1	1	1	0
J. DEAN, p	4	1	0	0	0	0
Totals	35	6	13	27	8	0

*Batted for Derringer in eighth inning.

Cincinnati .... 100 000 000—1
St. Louis .... 001 030 11x—6

Runs batted in—Bottomley, Frisch (4), Medwick. Two-base hits—Bottomley, Frisch, Hafey. Stolen base—Orsatti. Double play—Slade, Koenig and Bottomley. Left on bases—Cincinnati, 6; St. Louis, 6. Bases on balls—Off Derringer, 1; off J. Dean, 1. Struck out—By Derringer, 6; by J. Dean, 10. Hits—Off Derringer, 11 in 7 innings; off Kleinhans, 2 in 1. Wild pitch—Kleinhans. Losing pitcher—Derringer. Umpires—Klem and Pfirman. Time—1:38.

SECOND GAME

ST. LOUIS (N. L.)	ab	r	h	po	a	e
Whit'd, 3b, ss	5	0	0	2	3	1
Rothrock, rf	5	0	1	0	0	0
Frisch, 2b	4	2	3	1	6	0
Medwick, lf	4	0	1	3	0	0
Collins, 1b	4	1	1	8	0	0
Davis, c	4	0	1	9	0	0
Orsatti, cf	3	1	1	2	0	0
Durocher, ss	1	0	0	1	0	0
Martin, 3b	3	0	1	1	0	0
P. DEAN, p	0	0	0	0	0	0
HAINES, p	0	0	0	0	0	0
VANCE, p	0	0	0	0	0	0
LINDSEY, p	0	0	0	0	0	0
*Fullis	1	0	1	0	0	0
†Delancey	1	0	0	0	0	0
‡Healey	1	0	0	0	0	0
§Crawford	1	0	0	0	0	0
Totals	37	4	10	27	9	1

CINCINNATI (N. L.)	ab	r	h	po	a	e
Piet, 3b	6	1	2	3	5	0
Slade, 2b	5	1	1	2	4	0
Koenig, ss	5	1	2	0	3	0
Hafey, cf	5	1	2	4	0	0
Bottom'y, 1b	4	1	2	12	0	0
Pool, lf	5	1	3	6	0	0
Lombardi, c	4	1	1	0	0	0
Schul'ich, rf	4	1	1	0	0	0
FREY, p	4	0	1	0	2	0
Totals	42	8	15	27	14	0

*Batted for P. Dean in third inning.
†Batted for Haines in fourth inning.
‡Batted for Vance in seventh inning.
§Batted for Lindsey in ninth inning.

Cincinnati .... 106 000 010—8
St. Louis .... 000 110 020—4

Runs batted in—Martin, Medwick, Collins (2), Koenig, Pool (5), Piet (2). Two-base hits—Koenig, Piet, Orsatti, Martin, Frisch (2), Medwick, Davis. Home runs—Pool, Collins. Left on bases—Cincinnati, 11; St. Louis, 7. Bases on balls—Off Frey, 1; off P. Dean, 3. Struck out—By P. Dean, 6; by Vance, 2; by Lindsey, 1. Hits—Off P. Dean, 7 in 3 innings; off Haines, 1 in 1; off Vance, 3; off Lindsey, 3 in 2. Hit by pitcher—(Frey). Losing pitcher—P. Dean. Pfirman and Klem. Time—2:05.

Red Sox Take Double-Header From Athletics, 7 to 4, 7 to 2

Foxx's 25th, 26th Homers and Bob Johnson's 25th Fail to Save First Game

By The Associated Press

BOSTON, July 8.—The Boston Red Sox today took both ends of a double-header from the Philadelphia Athletics before a crowd of 24,018, winning the first game 7 to 4, despite three Athletic home runs, and the second 7 to 2.

Henry Johnson pitched the opener for the Sox, striking out seven. The Athletics outhit the Red Sox, 12 to 7, but Dietrich's wildness cost him the game. He walked nine Boston batters and hit one.

Fred Ostermueller hurled effectively in the second game and was never in danger after the Sox gave him a four-run lead in the first inning.

Jimmie Foxx, Athletics' first baseman, hit his twenty-fifth home run of the season in the seventh inning and his twenty-sixth in the ninth inning of the first game. His teammate, Bob Johnson, smashed out his twenty-fifth in the final inning of the first game. All three came with the bases unoccupied.

Max Bishop, Sox second baseman, walked four times in each game. Roy Johnson drove in three runs in the first game and four in the second.

The scores:

FIRST GAME

PHILADELPHIA (A. L.)	ab	r	h	po	a	e
McNair, ss	5	0	1	2	3	1
Cramer, cf	5	0	2	2	0	0
R. Joh'n, lf	4	1	1	4	0	0
Foxx, 1b	4	2	3	7	1	0
Higgins, 3b	4	1	0	1	2	0
Miller, rf	4	1	1	2	0	0
Warstler, 2b	4	0	0	2	5	1
Berry, c	3	0	2	5	1	0
DIETR'H, p	4	0	1	0	1	0
Totals	36	4	12	24	13	2

BOSTON (A. L.)	ab	r	h	po	a	e
Bishop, 2b	1	1	0	2	1	0
Werber, 3b	4	1	1	1	1	1
Morgan, 1b	4	1	1	7	2	0
R. John'n, lf	5	0	1	3	0	0
Reynolds, cf	4	0	0	0	0	0
Porter, rf	4	0	1	0	0	0
R. Ferrell, c	2	2	1	7	2	0
Lary, ss	2	1	1	4	3	0
H. JOH'N, p	4	1	2	3	1	0
Totals	29	7	7	27	10	1

Philadelphia .... 000 001 102—4
Boston .... 010 011 04x—7

Runs batted in—Foxx (2), Rob Johnson, Warstler, Roy Johnson (3), Bishop, Werber, Morgan, H. Johnson. Two-base hits—Morgan, H. Johnson. Three-base hit—Miller. Home runs—Foxx (2), Rob Johnson. Stolen base—Warstler. Sacrifices—Miller, Werber, Lary. Double plays—McNair, Warstler and Foxx; H. Johnson and Morgan; Bishop, Lary and Morgan. Left on bases—Philadelphia, 11; Boston, 10. Bases on balls—Off Dietrich, 9; off H. Johnson, 5. Struck out—By Dietrich, 2; by H. Johnson, 7. Hit by pitcher—By Dietrich (Morgan). Umpires—Summers and Owens. Time—2:21.

SECOND GAME

PHILADELPHIA (A. L.)	ab	r	h	po	a	e
McNair, ss	4	0	0	0	2	0
Cramer, cf	4	0	1	1	0	0
B. John'n, lf	4	0	1	1	0	0
Foxx, 1b	4	0	2	8	1	1
Higgins, 3b	4	0	1	1	4	0
Miller, rf	4	1	1	0	0	0
Warstler, 2b	4	0	0	3	5	0
Berry, c	4	1	2	3	1	0
MARCUM, p	2	0	0	0	2	0
BENTON, p	0	0	0	0	1	0
*Moss	1	0	0	0	0	0
Totals	35	2	8	24	13	2

BOSTON (A. L.)	ab	r	h	po	a	e
Bishop, 2b	1	1	0	2	2	0
Werber, 3b	5	2	2	0	2	0
Morgan, 1b	5	3	3	10	0	0
R. John'n, lf	4	1	2	0	0	0
Reynolds, cf	4	0	0	6	0	0
Porter, rf	3	0	1	0	0	0
R. Ferrell, c	4	0	1	5	0	0
Lary, ss	3	0	1	2	5	0
OSTER'R, p	4	0	0	0	2	0
Totals	33	7	10	27	11	0

*Batted for Benton in ninth inning.

Philadelphia .... 000 110 000—2
Boston .... 401 000 20x—7

Runs batted in—Cramer, Foxx, Roy Johnson (4), Reynolds (2), Porter. Two-base hits Rob Johnson, Morgan (2), Roy Johnson, Porter. Stolen bases—Roy Johnson, Porter, Lary. Double plays—Higgins, Warstler and Foxx. Left on bases—Philadelhia, 7; Boston, 8. Bases on balls—Off Marcum, 4; off Benton, 2; off Ostermueller, 1. Struck out—By Marcum, 2; off Ostermueller, 1. Hits—Off Marcum, 9 in 6 innings (none out in 7th); off Benton, 1 in 2. Losing pitcher—Marcum. Umpires—Owens and Summers. Time—1:55.

Reading Buys George Ferrell

ASHEVILLE, N. C., July 8 (AP).—George Ferrell, leading Piedmont League slugger, was sold by Asheville today to Reading, of the New York-Pennsylvania Circuit. Ferrell, an outfielder, is a brother of Wesley and Rick Ferrell, of the Boston Red Sox. At the latest compilation of averages he was hitting .395.

NEW YORK-PA. LEAGUE

At Reading (first game)— R. H. E.
Hazleton ...... 103 020 010—7 7 0
Reading .... 000 012 030—6 8 3
Batteries—Parkes, Krider and Maynard; Niggeling, Turner, Simmons and Savino.

Second game— R. H. E.
Hazleton .... 000 412—7 10 1
Reading .... 006 002—8 9 2
Batteries—Harrison and Uzmann; Gilvary, Simmons, Niggeling and Moss.

At Wilkes-Barre (first game)— R. H. E.
Binghamton ...... 000 000 001—1 9 2
Wilkes-Barre ..... 001 140 40x—10 13 4
Batteries—Wicker, Laflamme and Straub; Willis and Stats.

Second game— R. H. E.
Binghamton ...... 010 100 0—2 10 2
Wilkes-Barre ..... 000 201 x—3 7 3
Batteries—Tobin and Collins; Reitz and Wasem.

At Scranton (first game)— R. H. E.
Elmira .... 000 000 010—1 4 1
Scranton .... 210 000 00x—3 8 1
Batteries—Brown and Chervinko; Shoffner and Steinecke.

Second game— R. H. E.
Elmira .... 010 000 000 0—1 8 1
Scranton .... 000 000 100 1—2 5 2
(Called in tenth inning; Sunday 6 o'clock law.)
Batteries—Lyons and Munson; Shaute and Reilly.

At Harrisburg (first game)— R. H. E.
W'ms'pt 001 100 240 000 11—10 23 0
Ha'burg 070 000 000 100 10—9 16 1
Batteries—McNamara, Mills, W. Thomas and Baker; Montague, Heffleringer, Lake, Cooney and Maple.
(Second game called in fourth inning; Sunday 6 o'clock law.)

STANDING OF THE CLUBS

	W.	L.	Pct.		W.	L.	Pct.
Willi'msport	3	1	.750	Wilkes-B'rre	2	4	.333
Reading	3	2	.600	Hazleton	2	4	.333
Scranton	3	2	.600	Harrisburg	2	4	.333
Bingh'mton	2	3	.400	Elmira	1	3	.250

Leading Five Batsmen In Each Major League

AMERICAN LEAGUE

Player and Club.	G.	AB.	R.	H.	PC.
Manush, Washington	75	320	63	129	.403
Gehringer, Detroit	76	294	74	112	.381
Gehrig, New York	73	286	67	105	.367
Travis, Washington	60	234	38	84	.359
Higgins, Philadelphia	76	278	46	99	.356

Leader a year ago, Simmons, Chicago, .373.

NATIONAL LEAGUE

Player and Club.	G.	AB.	R.	H.	PC.
Terry, New York	76	294	61	108	.367
P. Waner, Pittsburgh	70	290	56	102	.352
Cuyler, Chicago	68	267	45	94	.352
Leslie, Brooklyn	77	299	44	105	.351
Medwick, St. Louis	75	318	68	111	.349
Vaughan, Pittsburgh	72	258	69	90	.349
Traynor, Pittsburgh	55	209	34	73	.349

Leader a year ago, Klein, Philadelphia, .368.

Home Runs		Runs Batted In	
Foxx, Athletics	26	Gehrig, Yankees	92
Johnson, Athletics	25	Ott, Giants	84
Gehrig, Yankees	24	Cronin, Senators	73
Ott, Giants	21	Bonura, Wh. Sox	70
Klein, Cubs	19	Collins, Cards	67
		Berger, Braves	67

Bisons Pummel Bears For 14 Hits and Win, 11-5

BUFFALO, N. Y., July 8 (AP).—Rearing up to pound three Newark pitchers for fourteen hits that netted twenty-six bases, the Bisons crushed the Bears here this afternoon, 11 to 5.

The score:

NEWARK (I. L.)	ab	r	h	po	a	e
Neun, lf	4	0	1	1	0	0
Far'ell, 3b, ss	5	1	2	1	2	0
Hill, cf	5	0	0	2	0	0
Alex'der, 1b	4	1	1	7	0	0
Barton, rf	4	0	0	4	0	0
Kies, c	3	0	1	7	0	0
Schalk, 2b	4	1	3	2	2	1
Gibson, ss	3	1	1	0	2	1
MAK'SKY, p	1	0	0	0	1	0
LAROCCA, p	2	0	0	0	0	0
DUKE, p	0	0	0	0	0	0
Muller, 3b	2	1	1	0	0	0
Totals	37	5	10	24	7	2

BUFFALO (I. L.)	ab	r	h	po	a	e
Meyers, 3b	5	1	2	0	4	1
Mallon, 2b	5	1	3	4	3	0
McGowan, cf	5	3	3	1	0	0
Carnegie, lf	4	2	1	3	0	0
Clancy, 1b	5	0	1	8	0	0
Tucker, rf	4	2	1	2	0	0
Mulleavy, ss	4	2	3	1	3	0
Crouse, c	5	1	2	8	0	0
KOW'LIK, p	3	0	0	0	2	0
Totals	38	11	14	27	10	1

Newark .... 200 200 001—5
Buffalo .... 020 423 00x—11

Runs batted in—Kies (2), Tucker, Mulleavy (2), Gibson (2), Myers (2), Mallon (2), Crouse, Carnegie (2), Clancy, Farrell. Two-base hits—Kies, Mallon (3), Schalk, Clancy. Three-base hit—Carnegie. Home runs—Tucker, Mulleavy, Gibson. Stolen bases—Mallon, McGowan. Left on bases—Buffalo, 9; Newark, 9. Bases on balls—Off Kowalik, 4; off Larocca, 4; off Duke, 1; off Makosky, 1. Struck out—By Kowalik, 6; by Larocca, 3; by Duke, 2; by Makosky, 2. Hits—Off Larocca, 8 in 4 1-3 innings; off Duke, 5 in 1 2-3; off Makosky, 1 in 2. Umpires—Jorda and Carroll. Losing pitcher—Larocca. Time—1:46.

47,138 See Pirates, Cubs Split Twin Bill

Chicago Loses First, 11-4, Wins Second, 12-3; Billy Herman Extends Record

By The Associated Press

CHICAGO, July 8.—An overflow crowd of 47,138 saw the second-place Cubs divide a double-header with Pittsburgh today, winning the second game, 12 to 3, after losing the first, 11 to 4. They slipped another half game back of the Giants, whom they now trail by two games.

After the Pirates employed rough-house tactics in batting Bill Lee and Roy Joiner from the mound in the sixth inning of the first game, scoring six runs and wiping out a four-run disadvantage and then winning "going away" behind the fine relief pitching of Ralph Birkofer, the Cubs adopted similar mauling measures in the afterpiece.

Paul Waner led the Pirate offense in the opener with a home run, three singles and a walk. Gabby Hartnett hit a home run for the Cubs in the second game. Billy Herman, Cub second baseman, got a single in the opener and a pair of ground-rule doubles and a single in the second game, stretching his new hit streak to nineteen consecutive games.

The Cubs started the first game with a four-run lead by picking up single tallies off Larry French, but Lee, after pitching shut-out ball for five and two-thirds innings, weakened with two out in the sixth. Before Charley Root could stem the assault that drove Joiner, as well as Lee, from the mound, six runs had been recorded on eight hits, two of which Cuyler juggled for errors.

The Cubs wasted no time in making amends in the second game, driving Bill Swift from the mound with a four-run attack in the first inning that included Hartnett's homer with Cuyler on base, and then picked up four more in the second off French who tried an unsuccessful comeback.

It was Weaver's fifth straight triumph since joining the Cubs.

The scores:

FIRST GAME

PITTSBURGH (N. L.)	ab	r	h	po	a	e
L. Waner, cf	5	1	1	2	0	0
P. Waner, rf	5	2	4	2	0	0
Traynor, 3b	6	0	1	2	2	0
Vaughan, ss	6	2	2	3	2	0
Suhr, 1b	3	2	2	10	1	0
Theven w, 2b	4	1	1	1	5	0
Jensen, lf	5	1	2	1	0	0
Padden, c	4	1	1	6	0	1
FRENCH, p	2	0	0	0	1	0
*Lucas	1	1	1	0	0	0
BIRK'ER, p	2	0	1	0	2	0
Totals	43	11	16	27	13	1

CHICAGO (N. L.)	ab	r	h	po	a	e
W. Her'n, 2b	4	1	1	2	1	1
English, ss	5	1	1	5	3	0
Klein, lf	4	0	1	3	0	1
F. Her'n, rf	4	0	1	3	0	0
Cuyler, cf	4	1	2	0	0	1
Hartnett, c	4	1	2	4	0	0
Grimm, 1b	3	0	2	9	2	0
‡Warneke	0	0	0	0	0	0
Hack, 3b	3	0	0	0	1	0
§Galan	1	0	1	0	0	0
LEE, p	2	0	0	1	1	0
JOINER, p	0	0	0	0	0	0
ROOT, p	0	0	0	0	1	0
†Stainback	1	0	0	0	0	0
TINNING, p	0	0	0	0	0	0
¶Stephen'n	1	0	0	0	0	0
Totals	36	4	11	27	9	3

*Batted for French in sixth inning.
†Batted for Root in seventh inning.
‡Ran for Grimm in ninth inning.
§Batted for Hack in ninth inning.
¶Batted for Tinning in ninth inning.

Pittsburgh .... 000 006 032—11
Chicago .... 111 100 000—4

Runs batted in—L. Waner, P. Waner (3), Vaughan, Thevenow, Jensen (2), Lucas, Klein (2), Hartnett, Lee. Two-base hits—English, Klein, F. Herman, Cuyler. Home run—P. Waner. Stolen bases—P. Waner, Suhr, W. Herman. Double plays—Thevenow, Vaughan and Suhr (2); English and Grimm. Left on bases—Pittsburgh, 11; Chicago, 7. Bases on balls—Off Birkofer, 2; off Lee, 4; off Root, 1; off Tinning, 1. Struck out—By French, 4; by Lee, 2; by Root, 1; by Tinning, 1. Hits—Off French, 8 in 5 innings; off Birkofer, 3 in 4; off Lee, 7 in 5 2-3; off Joiner, 2 in 0 (pitched to two batters in sixth); off Root, 2 in 1 1-3; off Tinning, 5 in 2. Wild pitch—French. Winning pitcher—Birkofer. Losing pitcher—Lee. Umpires—Reardon, Magerkurth and Stewart. Time—2:11.

SECOND GAME

PITTSBURGH (N. L.)	ab	r	h	po	a	e
L. Waner, cf	1	0	0	0	0	0
Roettger, lf	4	1	2	3	0	0
P. Waner, rf	3	0	1	0	0	0
Traynor, 3b	2	0	1	0	0	0
Lavag'to, 2b	1	0	0	3	0	0
Vaughan, ss	3	0	0	4	1	1
Suhr, 1b	4	0	1	6	1	0
The'w, 2b, 3b	4	0	0	0	1	0
Jensen, lf, cf	4	1	2	1	0	0
Grace, c	3	0	0	6	0	0
Veltman, c	1	0	0	2	0	0
SWIFT, p	0	0	0	0	0	0
FRENCH, p	0	0	0	0	0	0
MEINE, p	1	0	0	1	1	0
CHAGN'N, p	1	0	0	0	0	0
*Lucas	1	0	0	0	0	0
HARRIS, p	0	0	0	0	1	0
†Padden	1	0	0	0	0	0
Totals	34	3	7	24	8	1

CHICAGO (N. L.)	ab	r	h	po	a	e
W. Her'n, 2b	5	3	3	2	4	0
English, ss	6	1	3	2	1	0
Klein, lf	5	1	2	2	0	0
F. Herm'n, rf	5	2	1	2	0	0
Cuyler, cf	4	2	3	2	0	0
Hartnett, c	3	1	1	3	0	0
Phelps, c	1	0	0	1	2	0
Grimm, 1b	5	1	3	12	1	0
Hack, 3b	2	1	0	0	2	0
WEAVER, p	5	0	0	1	2	0
Totals	41	12	16	27	12	0

*Batted for Chagnon in seventh innnig.
†Batted for Harris in ninth inning.

Pittsburgh .... 000 002 100—3
Chicago .... 440 112 00x—12

Runs batted in—Roettger, Suhr (2), W. Herman, English, Klein (2), Cuyler (3), Hartnett (2), Grimm (2). Two-base hits—Roettger, Suhr, Jensen, W. Herman (2), English, Klein (2), F. Herman, Cuyler. Home run—Hartnett. Stolen base—Hack. Left on bases—Pittsburgh, 7; Chicago, 13. Bases on balls—Off Swift, 1; off French, 2; off Meine, 2; off Chagnon, 1; off Harris, 2; off Weaver, 3. Struck out—By Swift, 1; by French, 2; by Meine, 2; by Chagnon, 1; by Harris, 2; by Weaver, 6. Hits—Off Swift, 3 in 2-3 inning; off French, 4 in 2-3; off Meine, 4 in 2 2-3; off Chagnon, 4 in 2; off Harris, 1 in 2. Wild pitches—Swift, Harris. Balk—Harris. Losing pitcher—Swift. Umpires—Magerkurth, Stewart and Reardon. Time—2:25.

Results in Minor Leagues

* * *

INTERNATIONAL LEAGUE

YESTERDAY'S RESULTS

Buffalo, 11; Newark 5.
Rochester, 5; Baltimore, 1 (1st).
Rochester, 4; Baltimore, 3 (2d).
Syracuse, 5; Montreal, 4 (1st).
Montreal, 3; Syracuse, 2 (2d).
Other clubs not scheduled.

STANDING OF THE CLUBS

	W.	L.	Pct.		W.	L.	Pct.
Newark	54	29	.651	Montreal	41	40	.506
Rochester	51	35	.593	Buffalo	35	46	.432
Toronto	47	33	.588	Syracuse	33	45	.423
Albany	41	38	.519	Baltimore	21	56	.273

GAMES TODAY

Albany at Montreal
Baltimore at Buffalo
Syracuse at Rochester
Other clubs not scheduled.

SOUTHERN ASSOCIATION

At Nashville (first game)— R. H. E.
New Orleans... 010 001 200—4 8 0
Nashville...... 000 000 000—0 7 3
Batteries—Milnar and George; Brillheart and McAdams.

Second game— R. H. E.
New Orleans...... 000 020 0—2 8 1
Nashville......... 010 300 x—4 7 0
Batteries—Bryant and Autry; Gabler and O'Malley.

At Birmingham (first game)— R. H. E.
Atlanta....... 000 100 000—1 4 2
Birmingham... 000 001 11x—3 5 0
Batteries—Schmidt and Palmisano; Scott and Neisler.

Second game— R. H. E.
Atlanta.......... 000 000 0—0 7 1
Birmingham....... 304 312 x—13 18 0
Batteries—Casey, Nelson and Vance; Griffin and Redmond.

At Chattanooga (first game— R. H. E.
Knoxville...... 000 000 000—0 10 0
Chattanooga... 000 010 00x—1 4 1
Batteries—Moon and Head; Linke and Holbrook.

Second game— R. H. E.
Knoxville......... 13 001 0—5 8 1
Chattanooga....... 003 002 1—6 8 3
Batteries—Wetherel and West; Thormahlen and Holbrook.

At Memphis (first game)— R. H. E.
Little Rock. 000 020 101 1—5 11 2
Memphis... 002 001 100 0—4 12 3
Batteries—Scheussler and Whitney, Rice; Kelley and Powell.

Second game— R. H. E.
Little Rock....... 000 200 0—2 10 3
Memphis.......... 001 011 x—3 7 1
Batteries—Sharpe and Rice; Bayne, Swayze and Cuoto.

STANDING OF THE CLUBS

	W.	L.	Pct.		W.	L.	Pct.
Memphis	6	2	.750	Atlanta	3	4	.429
Little Rock	5	2	.714	New Orleans	3	5	.375
Nashville	5	2	.714	Chattanooga	2	4	.333
Birmingham	3	3	.500	Knoxville	0	5	.000

TEXAS LEAGUE

Oklahoma City, 4; Dallas, 3.
Dallas, 8; Oklahoma City, 6.
Three night games.

STANDING OF THE CLUBS

	W.	L.	Pct.		W.	L.	Pct.
S. Antonio	50	36	.581	Dallas	42	45	.483
Tulsa	44	38	.537	Ft. Worth	40	43	.482
Galveston	45	39	.536	Houston	38	46	.452
Beaumont	45	40	.529	Okla. City	34	51	.400

AMERICAN ASSOCIATION

At St. Paul (first game)— R. H. E.
Toledo....... 200 003 001—6 13 1
St. Paul..... 600 000 11x—8 11 0
Batteries—Perrin Lawson, Sewell, Nekola and Garbark; Claset and Giuliani.

Second game— R. H. E.
Toledo....... 000 010 000—1 6 2
St. Paul..... 000 001 10x—2 8 0
Batteries—Uhle and O'Neil, Garbark; Phelps and Fenner, Giuliani.

At Minneapolis (first game)— R. H. E.
Columbus.... 004 100 011—7 14 2
Minneapolis. 000 880 02x—18 21 2
Batteries—Teachout, Spencer and Odea; Starr and Hargrave, Young.

Second game— R. H. E.
Columbus........ 000 110 0—2 7 0
Minneapolis..... 002 011 x—4 8 0
Game called end of seventh inning account of 6 o'clock law.
Batteries—Klinger and Angley; Starr and Hargrave.

At Kansas City (first game)— R. H. E.
Indianapolis.. 100 111 012—7 14 2
Kansas City.. 000 201 003—6 11 2
Batteries—Burwell, Butzberger, Chamberlain and Riddle; Carson, Shealey and Crandall.

Second game— R. H. E.
Indianapolis.. 021 000 100—4 7 0
Kansas City.. 000 100 000—1 9 2
Batteries—Page and Sprinz; Hockette and Brenzel.

At Milwaukee (first game)— R. H. E.
Louisville.... 000 000 003—3 10 0
Milwaukee... 106 011 02x—11 19 2
Batteries—Hatter, Penner and Thompson, Ringhofer; Braxton and Susce.

Second game— R. H. E.
Milwaukee.. 000 013 60x—10 15 1
Louisville.... 000 000 012—3 12 0
Batteries—Bass, McLean and Thompson; Stine and Rensa.

STANDING OF THE CLUBS

	W.	L.	Pct.		W.	L.	Pct.
Ind'polis	45	35	.563	Milwaukee	41	41	.500
Minn'polis	45	37	.549	St. Paul	39	39	.500
Columbus	42	38	.525	Kan. City	35	46	.432
Louisville	41	40	.506	Toledo	36	48	.429

Fitzsimmons Blanks Dodgers With 3 Safeties for 2-0 Triumph

Hurler Also Drives Triple and Scores; Turns Back Foe With 3 on in Fourth

By Richards Vidmer

They've been going around for a long time asking "Who killed Cock Robin?" and if the Dodgers hadn't changed their nickname a couple of years ago, Freddy Fitzsimmons might be the answer.

He beat them again at Ebbets Field yesterday, which makes his fourth victory this year over what were once known as the Robins. Of these four triumphs, though, yesterday's probably was the most convincing. He not only beat them, but he shut them out, 2 to 0, allowing only three hits, which is considerable pitching against anybody.

There were a couple of times when the Dodgers threatened to score, but on each occasion Fitz held them off from the plate, once ending their hopes with the bases filled and another time fanning Boyle and Wilson with a man on third.

As Tom Zachary was doing a rather neat job of pitching himself, holding the Giants to eight scattered hits, the crowd of 15,000 worked up considerable excitement when the Dodgers threatened to score. They cheered and howled encouragement as only a Brooklyn crowd can, but in the end they were forced to limit their noise to respectful applause for the Giant pitcher.

Terry Doubles and Scores

The visitors from across the bridge laid two of their hits off Zachary end to end in the first inning when Terry doubled with two out and Ott drove him home with a single. They put another run across the plate in the fifth when Fitzsimmons's drive got past Koenecke for a triple and Frey made a wild heave to first, allowing him to score. But otherwise Terry's team of destiny was almost as helpless as Brooklyn.

But Terry's team seldom wastes any runs. If two runs are enough to win, that's about what they get. And if it takes a dozen they're quite frequently capable of making that many too. They had to supply a stonewall defense in view of the fact that Zachary was curbing their bats, but they built up a defensive barrier that couldn't be broken down.

Critz made a couple of brilliant plays at second and Johnny Vergez came up with a bare hand clutch of a drive by Johnny Frederick that might have completely changed the result.

That was in the fourth, which Boyle opened with a single. Frey fanned, but then Frederick hit a ball that almost sizzled as it sped toward left field, just inside the third base line. It started off with all the sound of a double, at least, but Vergez dug his right hand into the dust and came up with the ball.

Three Dodgers Left

Vergez was too far out of position to throw to first and no one was covering second, but he shot the ball toward that bag anyway and Critz arrived just in time to force Boyle. As Koenicke followed with a single and Fitzsimmons followed with a wild pitch, it is easily imagined what the situation would have been at about this point had Frederick's drive escaped Vergez. As it was Leslie was purposely passed, filling the bases, Cuccinello flied to Ott for the third out, three men were left on the bags and no harm was done.

The only other gesture of a serious uprising by the Dodgers came in the eighth, when Ryan made a wild throw past Terry, and Jordan, the first man up in that inning, went all the way to second. However, Fitz retired the next three men and Jordan's final stop was third. Fitz covered first and took Terry's toss when Zachary grounded to the Skipper, and then he proceeded to fan Boyle and Wilson.

Some statistician figured it out that the Giants have won thirty-four of their forty-eight victories against the second division teams, but that's like the story of why the black horses eat more than the white horses. The Giants have played more games against the second division teams.

Hank Leiber played like a fish in the seventh. He spent the entire inning catching flies.

Lefty O'Doul, who started setting off explosions with his bat on the Fourth of July, finally ran out of fireworks yesterday. He had made a dozen hits in five straight games, but was blanked by Zachary.

Terry, Ott and Vergez divided six of the Giants eight hits among them, each getting two.

PACIFIC COAST LEAGUE

At Seattle (first game)— R. H. E.
Los Angeles... 002 000 002—4 7 0
Seattle ...... 000 000 002—2 9 2
Batteries—Kallio, Radonits and Bottarini; Meola and Hannah.

Second game (7 innings)— R. H. E.
Los Angeles..... 003 010 0—4 8 2
Seattle .... 311 007 x—12 12 2
Batteries—Ward, Henshaw, Nelson, Lightfoot and Hannah; Craghead, H. Pillette and Bradbury.

At Portland (first game)— R. H. E.
San Francisco. 000 300 000—3 5 0
Portland ..... 000 000 010—1 6 0
Batteries—Mails, Stutz and McMillen; Ulrich and Cox.

Second game— R. H. E.
San Fran.... 030 300 013—10 18 1
Portland .... 000 012 000—3 8 1
Batteries—Herrmann and Woodall; Turpin and Cox.

At San Francisco (first game)— R. H. E.
Oakland ..... 002 002 002—6 10 2
Missions ..... 010 000 300—4 11 0
Batteries—Udolph and Raimondi; Daglia and Fitzpatrick.

Second game (7 innings)— R. H. E.
Oakland .... 000 001 0—1 4 0
Missions .... 300 300 x—8 10 1
Batteries—Rego, Salinsen, Douglas and Pasek; Osborne and Duggan.

At Los Angeles (first game; 12 innings)— R. H. E.
Sac'to.. 000 100 101 000—3 9 5
Hol'w'd. 100 000 101 001—4 7 2
Batteries—Flynn, Gregory and Salkeld, Mayer; Campbell, Hebert and Hershberger.

Second game (6 innings)— R. H. E.
Sacramento .... 021 102—6 11 2
Hollywood .... 300 14x—8 8 1
Batteries—Vinci, Horne and Mayer; Densmore, Hebert and Bassler.

STANDING OF THE CLUBS

	W.	L.	Pct.		W.	L.	Pct.
H'wood	10	3	.769	Missions	8	7	.533
San Fran.	11	4	.733	Sac'to	6	9	.400
*Los Ang.	9	6	.600	Oakland	4	10	.286
*Seattle	8	7	.533	Portland	2	12	.143

Giant-Dodger Score

NEW YORK (N. L.)	ab	r	h	po	a	e
Critz, 3b	4	0	0	2	1	0
O'Doul, lf	4	0	0	3	0	0
Terry, 1b	4	1	2	7	1	0
Ott, rf	4	0	2	1	0	0
Leiber, cf	4	0	1	6	0	0
Vergez, 3b	4	0	2	2	4	0
Ryan, ss	3	0	0	0	1	1
Mancuso, c	4	0	0	5	0	0
FITZ'NS, p	3	1	1	1	1	0
Totals	34	2	8	27	8	1

BROOKLYN (N. L.)	ab	r	h	po	a	e
Boyle, lf	4	0	1	2	0	0
Frey, ss	3	0	0	1	4	1
*Wilson	1	0	0	0	0	0
Chapman, 2b	0	0	0	0	0	0
Frederick, rf	4	0	1	4	1	0
Koenecke, cf	4	0	1	3	0	0
Leslie, 1b	3	0	0	10	0	0
Cucc'n'lo, 3b	3	0	0	0	2	0
Lopez, c	3	0	0	5	0	0
Jord'n, 2b, ss	3	0	0	2	3	0
ZACHA'Y, p	3	0	0	0	4	0
Totals	31	0	3	27	14	1

*Batted for Frey in eighth inning.

New York .... 100 010 000—2
Brooklyn .... 000 000 000—0

Runs batted in—Ott. Two-base hit—Terry. Three-base hit—Fitzsimmons. Sacrifice—Ryan. Left on bases—New York, 6; Brooklyn, 5. Bases on balls—Off Fitzsimmons, 1. Struck out—By Zachary, 4; by Fitzsimmons, 5. Wild pitches—Fitzsimmons (2). Umpires—Barr, Moran and Rigler. Time—1:40.

Euel Moore Wins First Major Start for Phils, 5-3

PHILADELPHIA, July 8 (AP).—Euel Moore, Indian hurler recently obtained by the Phillies from Baltimore, won his opening major league start by defeating the Boston Braves, 5 to 3, today. Moore allowed ten hits, but was well supported by his mates. He did not issue a walk.

The Phillies made only seven hits off Barrett, but bunched them in the first and sixth innings.

The score:

BOSTON (N. L.)	ab	r	h	po	a	e
Urbanski, ss	4	1	1	6	3	0
M'Manus, 3b	4	1	2	2	3	1
Thomp'n, rf	4	0	2	1	0	0
Berger, cf	4	0	2	0	0	0
Lee, lf	4	0	0	0	0	0
Jordan, 1b	4	0	2	8	0	0
Whitney, 2b	4	0	0	1	2	0
Spohrer, c	2	0	0	4	1	0
*Worth'ton	1	0	0	0	0	0
Hogan, c	1	0	1	2	0	0
BARRE'T, p	2	0	0	0	2	0
†R. Moore	1	1	1	0	0	0
SMITH, p	1	0	0	0	0	0
Totals	36	3	10	24	11	1

PHILADELPHIA (N. L.)	ab	r	h	po	a	e
Bartell, ss	4	0	1	2	3	0
Chiozza, 2b	4	1	0	3	3	0
Allen, lf	4	2	2	1	0	0
J. Moore, rf	3	1	2	7	0	0
Camilli, 1b	3	1	1	11	0	0
G. Davis, cf	3	0	0	3	0	0
Walters, 3b	3	0	2	0	5	0
Wilson, c	3	0	0	1	0	0
E. MOORE, p	3	0	0	0	0	1
Totals	30	5	8	27	11	1

*Batted for Spohrer in eighth inning.
†Batted for Barrett in eighth inning.

Boston .... 000 000 030—3
Philadelphia .... 200 003 00x—5

Runs batted in—McManus, Thompson, Berger, J. Moore (3), Camilli (2). Two-base hits—McManus, Allen (2), Walters. Home run—Camilli. Double plays—Barrett, Urbanski and Jordan; Walters, Chiozza and Camilli (2). Left on bases—Boston, 6; Philadelphia, 2. Bases on balls—Off Barrett, 1. Struck out—By Barrett, 4; by Smith, 2; by E. Moore, 1. Hits—Off Barrett, 8 in 7 innings; off Smith, 0 in 1. Balk—Barrett. Losing pitcher—Barrett. Umpires—Stark and Quigley. Time—1:37.

Rochester Twice Beats Baltimore, 5-1 and 4-3

ROCHESTER, N. Y., July 8 (AP).—Rochester came out of its batting slump today and defeated Baltimore in both ends of a double-header, 5 to 1 and 4 to 3.

The Orioles put up a bitter fight in the second game, forcing the Wings to go an extra round to take the decision. The scores by innings:

First game— R. H. E.
Baltimore....... 000 001 000—1 4 0
Rochester....... 100 010 03*—5 7 2
Batteries—Mellon and Asby; Kleinke and Lewis.

Second game— R. H. E.
Baltimore....... 012 000 00—3 9 1
Rochester....... 002 010 01—4 5 1
Batteries—Bucher, Richmond, Granger and Atwood; Kaufmann, Winford and Florence, Lewis.

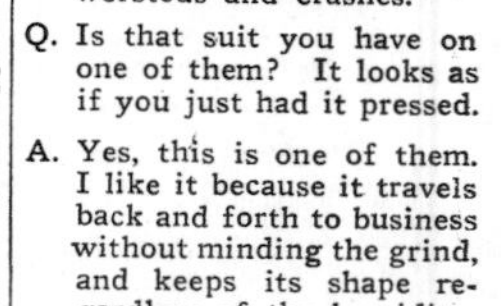

Gomez Wins 24th Game as Yankees Beat A's, 11-7, Then Drop Final, 10-3; Dodgers Lose 2

Southpaw Salvages 10th In Row After Shaky Start

Ruth Raps 21st Homer and Single, Scores 3 Runs in Rain Before 34,228; Foxx Hits 40th, While 3 N. Y. Hurlers Toil in Home Stay Wind-Up

By Rud Rennie

The Yankees home stand came to a gloomy end yesterday in a drizzle of rain and base hits. They split a double-header with the Philadelphia Athletics, dropping the second game 10 to 3 after winning the first, 11 to 7.

Once again the Yankees disappointed their supporters. The front-running Tigers were rained out. If the Yankees won both games, they would gain a full game and be only four and a half out of first place. Many of the 34,228 persons present were hoping the Yankees would take this forward step on the eve of their departure for Chicago and a final campaign in the West.

This hope was encouraged by the forceful manner in which the Yankees came from behind and won the first game despite some erratic pitching by the great Gomez. But hope turned to gloom as the A's battered Johnny Broaca and Charley Ruffing and pecked at Johnny Allen throughout nine damp innings of the second game.

Babe Ruth hit his twenty-first home run. Jimmy Foxx hit his fortieth. And Gomez won his twenty-fourth game of the season.

Tenth in Row for Gomez

Gomez lasted until the end even though he walked three men, forced in a run and let the A's score five in the second inning. It was his tenth in succession. He has lost only three. But he did not look impressive, even though he fanned nine men.

"I guess," he said after the game, "that was just about as bad a game as I've pitched all season."

He yielded eleven hits, but he really wasn't so bad after the second inning. That was a discouraging experience. It put the Yankees four runs behind.

Ruth, who was as frisky as a puppy, had supplied the Yankees with a run in the first inning, hoisting the ball into the right-field stands with two out. He walked twice thereafter and made a single. Every time up he got on base. He scored three runs and would have scored four if Hoag had not run for him in the eighth. He also moved around like a youngster in the outfield and caught one foul close to the stands. He was tired when he was through—tired but happy. His legs ached from activity and his ears tingled from applause.

Yankees Forge Ahead

The entire Yankee team seemed to partake of the Babe's enthusiasm in the first game. After Rabbit Warstler had hit a double with the bases filled, scoring three men in the A's big second inning, the Yankees proceeded to catch up as in the old days when they had a vast contempt for the A's. Jorgens tripled and scored, and Gehrig knocked in two runs with a double in the third.

The A's made another run in the first when Gomez threw Warstler's bunt into right field. But the Yankees came up and made three more runs in the sixth and took the lead, 7 to 6. The A's tied it up in the eighth with two hits and a long fly. That same inning, the Yankees got four runs, two scoring when Bill Dietrich, the Philadelphia pitcher, threw Chapman's bunt to first. It was the right play, but no one was covering the bag. It looked rather ridiculous. Chapman reached third and scored on Lazzeri's triple, which Miller played like a timid lady dipping herself in the ocean. Selkirk came through with a single, scoring Lazzeri, and completing a conquest which in the second inning, seemed highly unlikely.

Foxx's Homer Scores Three

Roger Cramer and Jimmy Foxx annoyed the Yankees considerably in the second game. The former made three hits, drove in four runs, got on base five times, and scored thrice. Foxx hit his fortieth home run with two men on bases in the third. The Yankees made three errors behind inferior pitching and were smothered under continued scoring.

The A's made one run in the first, three in the third and two in the fourth off Broaca; two in the sixth and two in the seventh off Ruffing, and none off Allen in the last two innings.

All the Yankees got off Merritt Cain was two in the third and one in the ninth.

So they ended three weeks at home with a record of fourteen victories and eleven defeats, five and a half games behind the Tigers. They go from here into the West and will not be back before the end of the month.

Allen looked good making his first appearance since August 14. He strained his arm striking out twelve A's August 3, and has not been much use since then.

Gehrig, the home run leader, with forty-two, put one into the right field stands in the first game, but it was foul. He then hit for two bases and was thrown out trying to make it three.

Johnny Broaca nearly got his second hit of the year in the second inning. He hit a line drive which would have been it, if Warstler had not been so agile and had not caught it.

George Selkirk caught the fancy of the fans in the fifth inning of the second game. He also caught a ball which Bob Johnson knocked into the left field stands. Selkirk was folded over the rail like an ailing voyager, with nothing visible but his legs when he caught the ball.

This has been a remarkable year for the Yankees in that they have not lost a Saturday, Sunday or holiday date at home. The same cannot be said for the games played.

Yankees' Scores

FIRST GAME

PHILADELPHIA (A. L.)	ab	r	h	po	a	e	NEW YORK (A. L.)	ab	r	h	po	a	e
Cramer, cf.	4	1	1	1	1	0	Crosetti, ss.	5	0	0	2	0	0
Warstler, 2b	5	2	2	3	3	0	Rolfe, 3b.	4	1	1	2	1	0
Johnson, lf	5	0	3	1	0	0	Ruth, rf.	2	3	2	3	0	0
Foxx, 3b.	4	0	0	4	0	0	Hoag, rf.	0	1	0	0	0	0
McNair, ss.	4	0	1	1	4	0	Gehrig, 1b.	3	2	2	7	0	1
Miller, rf.	4	1	2	3	0	0	Chapman, cf	3	2	3	1	0	1
Finney, 1b.	4	1	2	7	0	0	Lazzeri, 2b.	4	1	1	1	3	0
Berry, c.	3	1	0	4	0	0	Selkirk, lf.	4	0	2	2	0	0
DIET'ICH, p	3	1	0	0	1	1	Jorgens, c.	4	1	1	9	0	0
							GOMEZ, p	4	0	0	0	2	1
Totals	36	7	11	24	9	1	Totals	33	11	12	27	6	3

Philadelphia ...... 030 010 010—7
New York .... 103 003 04x—11

Runs batted in—Cramer, Warstler (3), Johnson, Ruth, Crosetti, Foxx, Gehrig (2), Chapman, Lazzeri (2), Selkirk (2), Berry. Two-base hits—Warstler, Gehrig. Three-base hits—Jorgens, Lazzeri. Home run—Ruth. Double plays—Warstler and Finney; Rolfe, Lazzeri and Gehrig. Left on bases—Philadelphia, 5; New York, 2. Bases on balls—Off Gomez, 3; off Dietrich, 4. Struck out—By Gomez, 8; by Dietrich, 4. Umpires—Summers and McGowan. Time—1:47.

SECOND GAME

PHILADELPHIA (A. L.)	ab	r	h	po	a	e	NEW YORK (A. L.)	ab	r	h	po	a	e
Cramer, cf.	5	3	3	2	0	0	Crosetti, ss.	5	2	2	4	2	1
Warstler, 2b	4	0	0	4	2	0	Rolfe, 3b.	5	0	2	0	1	1
Johnson, lf	4	1	3	2	0	0	Chapman, cf	5	1	1	2	1	0
Foxx, 3b.	5	1	2	0	2	0	Gehrig, 1b.	3	0	1	5	1	0
McNair, ss.	5	1	1	0	4	0	Selkirk, lf.	3	0	1	5	0	0
Miller, rf.	5	2	1	5	0	0	Lazzeri, 2b	3	0	1	3	1	0
Finney, 1b.	5	1	3	10	0	0	Hoag, rf.	4	0	2	0	0	0
Hayes, c.	4	1	1	4	0	0	Jorgens, c.	3	0	0	8	1	0
CAIN, p.	2	0	0	0	1	0	BROACA, p	1	0	0	0	2	0
							RUFFI'G, p	2	0	0	0	1	1
							ALLEN, p.	0	0	0	0	1	0
							*Ruth	1	0	0	0	0	0
Totals	39	10	14	27	9	0	Totals	35	3	10	27	11	3

*Batted for Allen in ninth inning.

Philadelphia ...... 103 202 200—10
New York .... 002 000 001—3

Runs batted in—Johnson (2), Foxx (3), Chapman (2), Lazzeri, Cramer (4). Two-base hits—Johnson, Rolfe, Crosetti (2). Home run—Foxx. Sacrifices—Wartler, Cain (2). Double plays—McNair, Warstler and Finney; Foxx, Warstler and Finney; Jorgens and Crosetti. Left on bases—New York, 10; Philadelphia, 9. Bases on balls—Off Cain, 5; off Broaca, 3; off Ruffing, 1. Struck out—By Broaca, 2; by Cain, 3; by Ruffing, 2; by Allen, 2. Hits—Off Broaca, 7 in 3 2-3 innings; off Ruffing, 5 in 3 1-3; off Allen, 2 in 2. Losing pitcher—Broaca. Umpires—McGowan and Summers. Time—1:58.

Gehrig Slides Home With a Run in Yankees' Big Inning

One of the runs which scored on Dietrich's wild throw into right field following Chapman's bunt. Ruth preceded Gehrig home on the play

Herald Tribune photos—Steffen

Indians Twice Topple Browns In Cold Rain

Cleveland Is Victor, 9-5, and 6-4; Hudlin Scatters Nine Hits in Nightcap

By The Associated Press

ST. LOUIS, Sept. 3.—The Cleveland Indians took both games of today's double-header with the Browns, sweeping the first, 9 to 5, when the St. Louis defense collapsed, and marking up the second, 6 to 4, behind Willis Hudlin's pitching.

About 2,000 fans shivered in the stands as the players labored in a cold drizzle on a muddy field. Hudlin allowed nine hits in the nightcap, but they were scattered well.

George Blaeholder failed to finish the first freak inning of the opening contest. With two men out, Cleveland scored seven runs, five of them directly attributed to three Brownie errors. The scores:

FIRST GAME

CLEVELAND (A. L.)	ab	r	h	po	a	e	ST. LOUIS (A. L.)	ab	r	h	po	a	e
Galatzer, rf	4	0	1	3	0	0	Clift, 3b.	4	0	0	0	3	1
Averill, cf.	5	1	1	4	0	0	Garms, lf.	4	0	1	1	0	0
Trosky, 1b.	4	2	3	5	0	0	Burns, 1b.	5	0	0	12	2	1
Vosmik, lf.	4	1	1	1	0	0	Pepper, cf.	5	1	1	0	0	0
Hale, 2b.	4	1	2	4	2	0	Campbell, rf	5	1	1	4	0	0
Burnett, 3b	4	1	0	1	0	0	Melillo, 2b.	2	3	1	6	7	0
Knick'er, ss	4	1	1	0	1	1	Hemsley, c.	2	0	0	2	1	1
Berg, c.	4	1	1	9	0	0	Strange, ss.	3	0	2	2	4	1
PEARS'N, p	4	1	1	0	2	0	BLAE'ER, p	0	0	0	1	0	0
							McAFEE, p	2	0	0	0	1	0
							ANDRE'S, p	0	0	0	0	0	0
							HADLEY, p	0	0	0	0	0	0
							*Bejma	1	0	0	0	0	0
							†Grube	1	0	0	0	0	0
Totals	37	9	11	27	5	1	Totals	34	5	6	27	18	4

*Batted for McAfee in seventh inning.
†Batted for Andrews in eighth inning.

Cleveland .... 700 000 200—9
St. Louis .... 020 000 120—5

Runs batted in—Hale (2), Pearson (2), Campbell, Strange (3), Averill, Trosky, Garms. Two-base hits—Hale, Melillo. Three-base hit—Hale. Home runs—Pearson, Campbell, Averill, Trosky. Double plays—Strange, Melillo and Burns (2); Melillo, Strange and Burns. Left on bases—Cleveland 3; St. Louis, 9. Bases on balls—Off Pearson, 7; off Blaeholder, 1; off McAfee, 1. Struck out—By Pearson, 7. Hits—Off Blaeholder, 4 in 2-3 innings; off McAfee, 6 in 6 1-3; off Andrews, 1 in 1; off Hadley, 0 in 1. Wild pitch—Pearson. Losing pitcher—Blaeholder. Umpires—Geisel and Owens. Time—1:40.

SECOND GAME

CLEVELAND (A. L.)	ab	r	h	po	a	e	ST. LOUIS (A. L.)	ab	r	h	po	a	e
Galatzer, rf.	4	1	0	1	0	0	Clift, 3b.	5	0	1	0	3	0
Averill, cf.	4	2	3	0	0	0	Garms, lf	3	1	1	2	0	0
Trosky, 1b.	4	1	0	7	2	0	Burns, 1b.	4	2	2	13	0	0
Vosmik, lf.	4	0	1	6	0	0	Pepper, cf.	4	0	0	3	0	0
Hale, 2b.	4	1	1	3	2	0	Campbell, rf	3	0	2	1	0	0
Kamm, 3b.	3	1	1	1	4	0	Melillo, 2b.	4	0	0	4	3	0
Knick'er, ss	4	0	3	1	2	0	Hemsley, c.	4	0	2	2	0	1
Garbark, c.	1	0	0	2	0	0	Strange, ss.	3	1	0	1	5	0
Berg, c.	2	0	0	5	0	0	WELLS, p.	2	0	0	1	4	0
HUDLIN, p	4	0	0	1	0	0	HADLEY, p	1	0	0	0	0	0
							*Bejma	1	0	1	0	0	0
Totals	34	6	9	27	10	0	Totals	34	4	9	27	15	1

Cleveland .... 000 104 100—6
St. Louis .... 000 110 020—4

Runs batted in—Trosky, Garms, Hale, Kamm (2), Knickerbocker, Vosmik, Campbell (2). Two-base hits—Hemsley, Averill, Burns, Hale. Three-base hits—Averill, Campbell. Stolen bases—Burns, Campbell. Sacrifices—Strange, Berg. Double plays—Strange, Melillo and Burns; Hale, Knickerbocker and Trosky. Left on bases—Cleveland, 6; St. Louis, 6. Bases on balls—Off Hudlin, 2; off Wells, 3; off Hadley, 1. Struck out—By Hudlin, 7; by Hadley, 2. Hits—Off Wells, 6 in 5 1-3 innings; off Hadley, 3 in 3 2-3. Losing pitcher—Wells. Umpires—Owens and Geisel. Time—2:03.

Cronin, Senators Pilot, Breaks Arm in Game Against Red Sox

Crashes With Wes Ferrell in Play at First; Out for Season; Nats Lose, Tie

By The Associated Press

WASHINGTON, Sept. 3.—The Washington Senators, one of the hard-luck teams of the current season, today dropped the first game of a double-header to Boston, 6 to 3, had the second game called with the score tied at 4—all on account of darkness, and lost the playing services of their manager for the rest of the season.

Joseph Cronin, Washington shortstop and pilot, fractured a bone in his right arm in the eighth inning of the first game. He was forced to turn over the management of the team to Al Shacht, third-base coach, and remained here with his arm in a cast when the team left tonight for St. Louis.

The manager, latest of a long list of injured that have caused the American League champions to fall far down in the second division, was running out an infield hit to Morgan, first baseman. Wesley Ferrell, Sox pitcher, ran over to cover first base and he and Cronin tangled. Cronin was thrown to the ground. He finished out the first game, but his arm caused him such pain that he was rushed to the hospital before the start of the second contest.

An X ray showed a fracture of the radius, larger of the two bones in the forearm, near where it is joined to the wrist.

Ferrell won his game handily, allowing the Senators only nine hits while his colleagues were belting Monte Weaver and Alec McColl.

Both games were played under cloudy and at times drizzling skies. The Sox had just reached Jack Russell for two runs and tied the score in the eighth inning of the second game, when it became so dark the play was halted. The scores:

Joe Cronin

FIRST GAME

BOSTON (A. L.)	ab	r	h	po	a	e	WASHINGTON (A. L.)	ab	r	h	po	a	e
Bishop, 2b.	4	2	3	3	5	0	Bluege, 3b.	4	1	0	0	3	0
Werber, 3b.	3	1	2	5	0	1	Stone, rf.	3	0	2	2	0	0
R. John'n, lf	5	0	1	1	0	0	Cronin, ss.	4	0	2	1	3	0
Porter, rf.	4	0	1	0	0	0	Manush, lf.	4	0	1	0	0	0
Solters, rf.	1	0	0	0	0	0	Bolton, c.	4	0	0	4	1	0
Cooke, cf.	3	1	1	2	0	0	Schulte, cf.	4	1	1	1	0	0
R. Ferrell, c	4	0	0	3	0	0	Susko, 1b.	3	0	1	14	3	1
Morgan, 1b	3	1	0	7	2	0	Kerr, 2b.	3	0	1	3	5	0
Lary, ss.	3	0	1	4	3	0	WEAVER, p	1	0	0	1	0	0
W. FER'L, p	4	1	1	2	0	0	McCOLL, p	1	1	1	1	2	0
							*Myer	1	0	0	0	0	0
							†Travis	1	0	0	0	0	0
							‡Sewell	1	0	0	0	0	0
Totals	34	6	10	27	10	1	Totals	34	3	9	27	17	2

*Batted for Weaver in sixth inning.
†Batted for Kerr in ninth inning.
‡Batted for McColl in ninth inning.

Boston .... 011 012 001—6
Washington .... 000 000 021—3

Runs batted in—Morgan, R. Johnson, Porter, W. Ferrell, Werber (2), Stone, Cronin, Susko. Three-base hits—Cooke, Schulte. Home run—Werber. Sacrifices—Werber, Lary. Double plays—Lary, Bishop and Morgan; Bishop and Morgan. Left on bases—Boston, 7; Washington, 6. Bases on balls—Off Weaver, 4; off W. Ferrell, 2. Struck out—By W. Ferrell, 3; by Weaver, 2; by McColl, 1. Hits—Off Weaver, 8 in 6 innings; off McColl, 2 in 3. Winning pitcher—W. Ferrell. Losing pitcher—Weaver. Umpires—Kolls and Dinneen. Time—2:00.

SECOND GAME

BOSTON (A. L.)	ab	r	h	po	a	e	WASHINGTON (A. L.)	ab	r	h	po	a	e
Bishop, 2b.	2	0	0	1	1	0	Bluege, ss.	4	1	1	1	4	0
Werber, 3b.	4	0	0	2	1	0	Stone, rf.	5	0	0	3	1	0
R. John'n, lf	4	2	3	3	0	0	Travis, 3b.	5	1	1	1	2	1
Porter, rf.	3	1	0	3	0	2	Harris, lf.	4	0	3	4	0	0
Cooke, cf.	3	1	2	1	0	0	Schulte, cf.	3	0	1	3	0	0
Loggett, c.	3	0	1	5	1	0	Susko, 1b.	3	2	1	6	0	0
R. Fer'ell, c	1	0	0	2	0	0	Sewell, c.	4	0	2	2	1	0
Morgan, 1b.	4	0	1	5	0	0	Kerr, 2b.	2	0	1	4	2	0
Lary, ss.	4	0	1	2	0	0	THOMAS, p	2	0	0	0	0	0
WALB'G, p	2	0	1	0	1	0	RUSSELL, p	0	0	0	0	0	0
H. JOH'N, p	0	0	0	0	0	0							
OSTER'R, p	0	0	0	0	0	0							
*Reynolds	1	0	0	0	0	0							
Totals	31	4	9	24	4	2	Totals	32	4	10	24	10	1

*Batted for Walberg in seventh inning.

Boston .... 010 001 02—4
Washington .... 200 001 10—4

Runs batted in—Harris, Susko, Sewell, Kerr, Cooke, Morgan. Stolen bases—Bishop, R. Johnson. Sacrifices—Thomas, Kerr. Double play—Travis and Susko. Left on bases—Boston, 7; Washington, 11. Bases on balls—Off Walberg, 4; off Thomas, 4. Struck out—By Walberg, 3; by Thomas, 1; by H. Johnson, 2; by Ostermueller, 2. Hits—Off Walberg, 8 in 6 innings; off H. Johnson, 2 in 1; off Ostermueller, 0 in 1; off Thomas, 9 in 7 2-3; off Russell, 0 in 1-3. Hit by pitcher—By H. Johnson (Susko). Umpires—Dinneen and Kolls. Time—1:55.

Newark Beats Syracuse, 2-0; Then Bows, 5-2

Brown Totals 28 Scoreless Innings in Row With 5-Hit Shutout in Opener

By The Associated Press

NEWARK, N. J., Sept. 3.—Newark divided a double-header with Syracuse here today, taking the opener, 2 to 0, behind Walter Brown's five-hit pitching and losing the seven-inning second game, 5 to 2.

Brown's victory was his nineteenth of the year and his third shut-out in a row, sending his scoreless inning record to twenty-eight consecutive frames. Vince Barton's thirty-second home run also came in the first game, providing the winning margin.

The Chiefs were more effective behind Fred Fussell in the second game and walloped Chandler for all their runs during the first five innings. The scores:

FIRST GAME

SYRACUSE (I. L.)	ab	r	h	po	a	e	NEWARK (I. L.)	ab	r	h	po	a	e
Maruska, lf	4	0	0	3	0	0	Gibson, ss.	3	1	0	5	1	0
Cihocki, ss.	3	0	1	0	3	0	Carlyle, cf.	4	0	1	2	0	0
Watwood, cf	4	0	0	4	0	0	Hill, lf.	4	0	1	4	0	0
Blair, 1b.	4	0	0	13	0	0	Alexand'r, 1b	3	0	1	8	1	0
Rosenfeld, rf	4	0	2	1	0	0	Muller, 3b.	3	0	0	2	0	0
Cronin, c.	3	0	0	3	0	0	Barton, rf.	3	1	1	2	0	0
Murphy, 3b	3	0	1	1	3	0	Glenn, c.	3	0	1	4	0	0
Taylor, 2b.	3	0	1	2	2	0	Schalk, 2b.	3	0	0	2	0	0
COOMBS, p	3	0	0	0	3	0	BROWN, p	3	0	0	0	1	0
Totals	31	0	5	24	11	0	Totals	29	2	5	27	5	0

Syracuse .... 000 000 000—0
Newark .... 100 010 00x—2

Runs batted in—Alexander, Barton. Two-base hits—Hill, Murphy. Home run—Barton. Left on bases—Syracuse, 2; Newark, 3. Bases on balls—Off Combs, 10; off Brown, 1. Struck out—By Brown, 3; by Combs, 3. Wild pitch—Brown. Umpires—Kearney and Parker. Time—1:18.

SECOND GAME

SYRACUSE (I. L.)	ab	r	h	po	a	e	NEWARK (I. L.)	ab	r	h	po	a	e
Maruska, lf	4	0	3	1	0	0	Gibson, ss.	3	0	1	0	3	0
Cihocki, ss.	4	1	1	0	1	0	Carlyle, cf.	3	1	1	2	0	0
Watwood, cf	3	1	1	4	0	0	Hill, lf.	4	0	0	2	0	0
Blair, 1b.	4	0	1	3	0	0	Alex'der, 1b	3	0	2	11	0	0
Rosenf'ld, rf	4	1	2	1	0	0	Muller, 3b.	3	1	1	0	2	0
Laviano, c.	2	1	0	6	0	0	Barton, rf.	3	0	0	0	0	0
Murphy, 3b	3	1	1	4	1	0	Kies, c.	2	0	0	1	0	0
Taylor, 2b.	3	0	1	2	0	0	Neun, 1b.	1	0	0	3	0	0
FUSSELL, p	3	0	0	0	0	0	Schalk, 2b.	3	0	2	2	4	0
							CHAND'R, p	1	0	0	0	2	0
							McDON'D, p	1	0	1	0	3	0
							Glenn, c.	0	0	0	0	0	0
							*Farrell	1	0	0	0	0	0
							†Tamulis	0	0	0	0	0	0
Totals	30	5	10	21	2	0	Totals	28	2	8	21	14	0

*Batted for Chandler in fifth inning.
†Ran for Alexander in sixth inning.

Syracuse .... 030 020 0—5
Newark .... 100 100 0—2

Runs batted in—Alexander, Fussell, Maruska, Muller, Blair, Rosenfeld. Two-base hits—Alexander (2), Maruska, Taylor. Home run—Muller. Sacrifices—Carlyle, Watwood. Left on bases—Syracuse, 6; Newark, 6. Base on balls—Off Fussell, 1. Struck out—By Fussell, 6. Hits—Off Chandler, 8 in 5 innings; off McDonald, 2 in 2. Hit by pitcher—By Chandler (Laviano). Winning pitcher—Fussell. Losing pitcher—Chandler. Umpires—Parker and Collins. Time—1:25.

Three Errors By McCarthy Assist Braves

Recruit's Misplays Aid in Defeat of Babich, 4-2, After Benge Bows, 1-0

By Arthur E. Patterson

BOSTON, Sept. 3.—Time was this season when the chief detriment to winning baseball with the Dodgers was their lack of high-class pitching. That was the only classy thing about them here today, however, as the Stengel forces bowed on both ends of a double-header with the Braves, 1 to 0 and 4 to 2.

In game No. 1 Ray Benge hurled his second four-hit game in a week, yet was no more successful than in his duel last Tuesday with Paul Dean at St. Louis. In the second game young Johnny Babich, the $37,500 recruit from the Missions, once again proved that luck was not one of the attributes he brought up with him from the minors when he did not allow a single earned run, but lost nevertheless.

Benge can blame only the lack of hitting by his mates. Babich's defeat, however, must be put to a severe case of the jitters, into which Johnny McCarthy, the newcomer from Dayton, ran at first base. Hailed as one of the classiest guardians of that bag by numerous experts, he committed three errors and was directly the cause of the first, third and fourth tribal tallies.

McCarthy Starts Error Streak

In the first inning McCarthy dropped Babich's throw of Moore's grounder, so Thompson, who had walked, scored on Hal Lee's single. In the second, McCarthy was mixed up in another misplay, but not charged with it. McManus's line drive bounced off the ex-Dayton Duck's glove toward Jimmy Bucher, stationed at second, and Bucher threw wild past Babich, who covered first. McManus went to third and scored on a squeeze bunt by Huck Betts, the second game's winning pitcher.

Babich kept the error-an-inning streak going in the third, but brilliant support saved him. In the fourth, however, the prize boner of the day was enacted again by the unfortunate McCarthy. He failed to hold Joe Stripp's throw of Pinkey Whitney's infield hit. Then when he retrieved the ball he tossed it, without permission from the umpire, toward the Braves' ball collector behind home plate. Whitney scampered around to third as Ray Berres chased the errant pellet, and Shanty Hogan's fly scored what proved to be the winning run.

Again in the sixth McCarthy was at fault. With Lee on first base as the result of a single, McManus sent a popper down toward first base. McCarthy had an easy double play in front of him, but in his anxiety to get the play started he made a bad throw, hitting Lee in the back as he ran toward second. Whitney's single added another run.

Hogan's Single Wins First

The Braves had the novel experience of scoring a run on two singles to win the first. Of course the second single, a fierce grounder over first, was by the ponderous Hogan, and his singles are doubles or triples for any one else. Whitney, who had preceded him with a single in the third, beat Boyle's throw to the plate, standing up. Benge then was touched for a pop fly double by Urbanski but hurled no-hit, no-run ball for the next four innings until he was taken out for a pinch hitter and replaced by the equally successful Les Munns.

Fred Frankhouse, although he allowed two more hits than Benge, scored his sixteenth victory.

Rabbit Maranville sat in a box during the game. He plans to watch his teammates as often as possible.

The scores:

FIRST GAME

BROOKLYN (N. L.)	ab	r	h	po	a	e	BOSTON (N. L.)	ab	r	h	po	a	e
Boyle, rf.	4	0	2	3	1	0	Urbanski, ss	4	0	1	2	3	0
Frey, ss.	4	0	1	1	2	0	Thomp'n, rf	3	0	1	1	0	0
Taylor, lf.	2	0	0	1	0	0	R. Moore, 1b	2	0	0	14	0	0
Fred'rick, lf	2	0	0	0	0	0	Berger, cf.	3	0	0	2	0	0
Cucci'llo, 2b	2	0	0	1	3	0	Lee, lf.	3	0	0	0	0	1
Bucher, 2b.	1	0	0	0	0	0	M'Manus, 2b	3	0	0	4	3	0
Koenecke, cf	3	0	1	4	0	0	Whitney, 3b	3	1	1	0	3	0
Stripp, 3b.	3	0	2	0	2	0	Hogan, c.	3	0	1	2	2	0
Lopez, c.	2	0	0	3	0	0	FRANK'E, p	2	0	0	2	3	0
BENGE, p.	2	0	0	0	3	0							
*Leslie	1	0	0	0	0	0							
MUNNS, p.	0	0	0	0	1	0							
Totals	29	0	6	24	12	0	Totals	26	1	4	27	14	1

*Batted for Benge in eighth inning.

Brooklyn .... 000 000 000—0
Boston .... 001 000 00x—1

Run batted in—Hogan. Two-base hits—Boyle, Urbanski. Sacrifice—Frankhouse. Double plays—McManus, Urbanski and Moore; Urbanski, McManus and Moore. Left on bases—Brooklyn, 3; Boston, 3. Bases on balls—Off Benge, 1; off Frankhouse, 1. Struck out—By Benge, 2; by Munns, 1; by Frankhouse, 2. Hits—Off Benge, 4 in 7 innings; off Munns, 0 in 1. Passed ball—Hogan. Losing pitcher—Benge. Umpires—Moran and Barr. Time—1:29.

SECOND GAME

BROOKLYN (N. L.)	ab	r	h	po	a	e	BOSTON (N. L.)	ab	r	h	po	a	e
Boyle, rf.	3	0	1	2	1	0	Urbanski, ss	4	0	0	3	4	0
†Leslie	1	0	1	0	0	0	Thomp'n, rf	3	1	1	3	0	0
‡Chapman	0	0	0	0	0	0	Moore, 1b.	4	0	0	9	1	0
Frey, ss	4	1	2	4	5	0	Berger, cf.	4	0	0	4	0	0
Frederick, lf	4	1	1	0	0	0	Lee, lf.	4	1	3	1	0	0
McCarthy, 1b	4	0	1	10	1	3	McManus, 2b	4	1	1	1	2	0
Bucher, 2b.	4	0	0	5	7	1	Whitney, 3b	3	1	2	1	0	0
Koenecke, cf	3	0	0	1	0	0	Hogan, c.	2	0	0	4	0	0
Stripp, 3b.	3	0	0	2	0	0	BETTS, p.	3	0	1	1	2	0
Berres, c.	2	0	0	0	0	0							
*Tremark	1	0	0	0	0	0							
Lopez, c.	0	0	0	0	1	0							
BABICH, p.	3	0	0	0	5	1							
Totals	32	2	6	24	20	5	Totals	31	4	8	27	10	0

*Batted for Berres in eighth inning.
†Batted for Boyle in ninth inning.
‡Ran for Leslie in ninth inning.

Brooklyn .... 000 200 000—2
Boston .... 110 101 00x—4

Runs batted in—Frederick, Bucher, Lee, Betts, Whitney, Hogan. Two-base hit—Frey. Three-base hit—Frederick. Double plays—Frey, Bucher and McCarthy (2); Betts, Urbanski and Moore. Left on bases—Brooklyn, 3; Boston, 5. Base on balls—Off Babich, 1. Struck out—By Betts, 4. Hit by pitcher—By Babick (Hogan). Umpires—Barr and Moran. Time—1:20.

Pirates Scuttle Dean Brothers, Beating Cards Twice, 12-2, 6-5

Paul Routed in 1st by 8 in 3d; Dizzy Fails as Relief in 2d; Giant Lead Grows

By The Associated Press

PITTSBURGH, Sept. 3.—Beating each of the Dean brothers in a Labor Day double-header, the Pittsburgh Pirates dealt two hard blows to the pennant aspirations of the St. Louis Cardinals today before 20,000 fans.

Paul Dean was chased in an eight-run, third-inning uprising of the first game, which Pittsburgh won, 12 to 2.

Brother Jerome was charged with the 6—5 defeat in the second, although he pitched to only four batters. Rushed into the game after the Redbirds had suddenly driven Waite Hoyt to cover with a three-run, ninth-inning rally that put them in the lead, 5 to 3, Dizzy retired the first batter.

Then Grace, pinch hitter, and Lloyd Waner singled and Freddie Lindstrom came through with his seventh safety of the afternoon, a double, that counted a run. Hallahan relieved Dean and Vaughan's long fly brought in the tying run. Traynor then singled to score Lindstrom with the winning tally.

The double defeat, while Chicago was splitting a double-header, put the Cardinals and Cubs in a tie for second place, six full games behind the giants.

The scores:

FIRST GAME

ST. LOUIS (N. L.)	ab	r	h	po	a	e	PITTSBURGH (N. L.)	ab	r	h	po	a	e
Martin, 3b.	4	1	2	1	1	0	L. Waner, cf	5	2	3	0	0	0
Rothrock, rf	4	0	0	3	0	0	Lindst'om, lf	5	2	4	3	0	0
Frisch, 2b.	3	0	0	2	2	0	P. Waner, rf	5	1	2	1	0	0
Crawford, 2b	0	0	0	0	2	0	Vaughan, ss	4	2	1	2	8	1
Medwick, lf.	3	0	0	0	0	0	Traynor, 3b	4	2	1	0	4	0
Collins, 1b.	4	0	1	7	1	1	Suhr, 1b.	5	1	2	12	1	0
V. Davis, c	4	0	1	2	0	0	Thev'ow, 2b	5	0	1	6	2	0
Fullis, cf.	4	0	2	5	0	1	Grace, c.	4	1	0	3	0	0
Whiteh'd, ss	3	1	0	4	2	1	FRENCH, p	3	1	0	0	1	0
P. DEAN, p	0	0	0	0	0	0							
VANCE, p.	1	0	0	0	0	0							
*Healy	1	0	0	0	0	0							
HAINES, p	0	0	0	0	0	0							
Totals	31	2	6	24	8	3	Totals	40	12	14	27	16	1

*Batted for Vance in eighth inning.

St. Louis .... 000 000 020—2
Pittsburgh .... 008 004 00x—12

Runs batted in—P. Waner, Vaughan, Traynor (3), Suhr (3), Thevenow (2), Martin, Rothrock. Two-base hits—L. Waner, Suhr, Davis, Fullis. Three-base hit—Martin. Sacrifice—P. Dean. Double plays—French, Vaughan and Suhr; Thevenow, Vaughan and Suhr. Left on bases—St. Louis, 6; Pittsburgh, 7. Bases on balls—Off P. Dean, 1; off Vance, 1; off French, 3. Struck out—By French, 3. Hits—Off Dean, 7 in 2 innings (none out in third); off Vance, 7 in 5; off Haines, 0 in 1. Hit by pitcher—By Dean (Traynor). Losing pitcher—P. Dean. Umpires—Stewart, Pfirman and Magerkurth. Time—1:36.

SECOND GAME

ST. LOUIS (N. L.)	ab	r	h	po	a	e	PITTSBURGH (N. L.)	ab	r	h	po	a	e
Martin, 3b.	5	1	2	0	5	0	L. Waner, cf	5	1	2	4	0	1
Rothrock, rf	3	0	1	2	0	1	Lindst'om, lf	5	2	3	4	0	0
Frisch, 2b.	5	0	2	0	7	0	P. Waner, rf	4	0	1	3	1	0
Medwick, lf	5	0	1	1	0	0	Vaughan, ss	3	1	0	3	2	0
Collins, 1b.	5	1	2	14	2	0	Traynor, 3b	4	0	1	0	3	0
Delancey, c	4	1	2	0	1	0	Suhr, 1b.	4	0	1	7	0	0
Orsatti, cf.	3	0	0	1	0	0	Theve'w, 2b	4	1	2	0	2	0
Whiteh'd, ss	4	1	1	7	3	0	Padden, c.	1	0	0	9	0	0
WALKER, p	3	0	0	1	1	0	HOYT, p.	3	0	0	0	0	0
*Crawford	1	0	1	0	0	0	MEINE, p.	0	0	0	0	0	0
†Fullis	0	1	0	0	0	0	¶Jensen	1	0	0	0	0	0
J. DEAN, p	0	0	0	0	0	0	§Grace	1	0	1	0	0	0
HALLA'N, p	0	0	0	0	0	0	‖Young	0	1	0	0	0	0
Totals	38	5	12	‡26	19	1	Totals	35	6	11	27	7	1

*Batted for Walker in ninth inning.
†Ran for Crawford in ninth inning.
‡Two out when winning run was scored.
¶Batted for Padden in ninth inning.
§Batted for Meine in ninth inning.
‖Ran for Grace in ninth inning.

St. Louis .... 000 002 003—5
Pittsburgh .... 100 100 103—6

Runs batted in—Vaughan (2), Thevenow, Whitehead, L. Waner, Martin (2), Medwick, Lindstrom, Traynor. Two-base hits—Delancey, Martin, Rothrock, Thevenow, Lindstrom. Three-base hit—Martin. Stolen bases—Frisch, Collins. Sacrifice—Padden. Double play—Frisch, Whitehead and Collins. Left on bases—St. Louis, 9; Pittsburgh, 9. Bases on balls—Off Hoyt, 2; off Walker, 4; off Meine, 1; off J. Dean, 1. Struck out—By Hoyt, 6. Hits—Off Hoyt, 12 in 8 innings (none out in ninth); off Walker, 7 in 8; off Meine, 0 in 1; off J. Dean, 3 in 1-3; off Hallahan, 1 in 1-3. Winning pitcher—Meine. Losing pitcher—J. Dean. Umpires—Pfirman, Magerkurth and Stewart. Time—2:42.

Cubs Beat Reds In 10th, 6 to 3; Then Lose, 6-4

Hartnett's Homer Ties Count in 9th of Opener; Triple by Koenig Scores 3 in 2d

By The Associated Press

CINCINNATI, Sept. 3.—Trailing by four runs and seemingly whipped, the Cincinnati Reds came back to take the second game of a double-header from the Chicago Cubs, 6 to 4, today after dropping the first game, 6 to 3, in ten innings.

Koenig's triple with the bases filled tied the score in the seventh inning of the second game and Bottomley's triple drove in Koenig to put the Reds ahead. Lombardi's homer in the eighth made the victory more secure.

The Reds were having the best of a pitching duel between Frey and Warneke in the first game until Gabby Hartnett tied the score at three-all with his homer in the ninth. The Cubs bunched three singles, a sacrifice and a hit batsman for three runs in the tenth. The scores:

FIRST GAME

CHICAGO (N. L.)	ab	r	h	po	a	e	CINCINNATI (N. L.)	ab	r	h	po	a	e
Hack, 3b.	4	1	1	2	2	0	Adams, 2b.	4	1	2	3	5	0
Galan, 2b.	5	1	2	1	5	0	Slade, ss.	5	0	1	6	1	0
Cuyler, cf.	4	1	1	1	0	0	Koenig, 3b.	5	0	2	1	1	1
F. Her'n, rf	4	0	0	3	1	0	Bottom'y, 1b	5	0	0	11	0	0
Stainb'k, rf.	1	0	1	0	0	0	Hafey, cf.	5	1	3	4	0	0
Klein, lf.	5	0	0	2	0	0	Pool, lf.	5	1	1	3	1	0
Hartnett, c.	5	1	2	7	0	0	Lombardi, c	4	0	1	3	0	0
Grimm, 1b.	4	0	1	12	0	0	Como'sky, rf	4	0	2	5	0	0
Jurges, ss.	4	1	1	1	4	0	FREY, p.	4	0	1	0	4	0
WARN'E, p.	4	1	2	1	3	0	FREITAS, p	0	0	0	0	0	0
Totals	40	6	11	30	15	0	Totals	41	3	13	30	12	1

Chicago .... 000 100 101 3—6
Cincinnati ...... 010 100 100 0—3

Runs batted in—Cuyler, Stainback (2), Klein, Hartnett, Warneke, Koenig, Comorosky (2). Two-base hits—Jurges, Warneke, Adams, Koenig, Hafey, Pool. Three-base hits—Hack, Grimm. Home run—Hartnett. Sacrifice—Hack. Left on bases—Chicago, 6; Cincinnati, 9. Base on balls—Off Warneke, 1. Struck out—By Warneke, 5; by Frey, 2. Hits—Off Frey 9 in 9 1-3 innings; off Freitas, 2 in 2-3. Hit by pitcher—By Frey (Cuyler). Losing pitcher—Frey. Umpires—Sears and Klem. Time—1:55.

SECOND GAME

CHICAGO (N. L.)	ab	r	h	po	a	e	CINCINNATI (N. L.)	ab	r	h	po	a	e
Hack, 3b.	4	0	1	2	3	0	Adams, 2b.	4	1	2	3	2	0
Galan, 2b.	5	1	1	1	1	0	Slade, ss.	3	1	1	1	1	1
Cuyler, cf.	4	0	3	2	0	0	Koenig, 3b.	4	1	1	0	4	0
F. Her'n, rf	5	0	2	1	0	0	Bottom'y, 1b	3	0	2	8	1	0
Klein, lf.	3	1	1	0	0	0	Hafey, cf.	4	0	1	2	0	0
Stainba'k, lf	1	1	0	1	0	0	Pool, lf.	4	0	1	2	0	1
O'Farrell, c	3	1	2	7	0	0	Com'sky, rf	4	1	0	3	0	0
*Lee	0	0	0	0	0	0	Manion, c.	2	0	1	5	1	0
Hartnett, c.	1	0	0	0	0	0	Lombardi, c	2	2	2	3	0	0
Grimm, 1b.	3	0	1	9	0	0	STOUT, p.	2	0	0	0	2	0
Jurges, ss.	3	0	0	1	5	0	†Marshall	1	0	0	0	0	0
WEAVER, p	3	0	0	0	0	0	DER'GER, p	1	0	0	0	0	0
MALONE, p	1	0	1	0	0	0							
Totals	38	4	12	24	9	0	Totals	34	6	11	27	11	2

*Ran for O'Farrell in eighth inning.
†Batted for Stout in seventh inning.

Chicago .... 021 001 000—4
Cincinnati .... 000 000 51x—6

Runs batted in—Hack, F. Herman, O'Farrell, Grimm, Adams, Koenig (3), Bottomley, Lombardi. Two-base hits—O'Farrell, F. Herman, Cuyler, Adams, Hafey. Home run—Lombardi. Sacrifices—Cuyler, Stainback. Double play—Jurges and Grimm. Left on bases—Chicago, 12; Cincinnati, 6. Bases on balls—Off Weaver, 1; off Stout, 2; off Derringer, 1. Struck out—By Weaver, 7; by Stout, 5; by Derringer, 3. Hits—Off Weaver, 9 in 6 2-3 innings; off Malone, 2 in 1 1-3; off Stout, 8 in 7; off Derringer, 4 in 2. Hit by pitcher—By Weaver (Slade). Winning pitcher—Stout. Losing pitcher—Weaver. Umpires—Klem and Sears. Time—2:0?.

Piet, Hurt in Collision, Lost to Reds for Season

CINCINNATI, Sept. 3 (AP).—Injured in colliding with a teammate several days ago, Tony Piet will be out of the game for the rest of the season, the Cincinnati Reds made known today.

Piet, at second base, crashed into Adam Comorosky, outfielder, in trying to field a hit by George Berger during the recent series with Boston here.

Standings in Major Leagues

TUESDAY, SEPTEMBER 4, 1934

American League

YESTERDAY'S RESULTS

New York, 11; Philadelphia, 7 (1st).
Philadelphia, 10; New York, 3 (2d).
Cleveland, 9; St. Louis, 5 (1st).
Cleveland, 6; St. Louis, 4 (2d).
Boston, 6; Washington, 3 (1st).
Boston, 4; Washington, 4 (8 ins., darkness, 2d).
Detroit-Chicago, postponed, rain.

STANDING OF THE CLUBS

	Detroit	New York	Cleveland	Boston	St. Louis	Washington	Phila'phia	Chicago	Won	Lost	Percentage
Detroit	—	10	16	12	10	11	10	15	84	44	.656
New York	8	—	9	10	14	11	13	15	80	51	.611
Cleveland	6	8	—	11	11	8	11	12	67	60	.528
Boston	6	9	6	—	12	12	11	11	67	63	.515
St. Louis	6	4	6	6	—	12	11	14	59	68	.465
Wash'gton	7	9	9	9	8	—	7	8	57	70	.449
Phila'phia	7	7	7	8	6	9	—	8	52	72	.419
Chicago	4	4	7	7	7	7	9	—	45	82	.352
Gms. lost	44	51	60	63	68	70	72	83	—	—	

GAMES TODAY

Detroit at Chicago (2).
Cleveland at St. Louis.
Other clubs not scheduled.

National League

YESTERDAY'S RESULTS

Boston, 1; Brooklyn, 0 (1st).
Boston, 4; Brooklyn, 2 (2d).
Pittsburgh, 12; St. Louis, 2 (1st).
Pittsburgh, 6; St. Louis, 5 (2d).
Chicago, 6; Cincinnati, 3 (10 ins., 1st).
Cincinnati, 6; Chicago, 4 (2d).
New York-Philadelphia, postponed, rain.

STANDING OF THE CLUBS

	New York	St. Louis	Chicago	Boston	Pittsburgh	Brooklyn	Phila'phia	Cincinnati	Won	Lost	Percentage
New York	—	8	8	13	12	14	18	13	81	47	.633
St. Louis	10	—	9	14	8	11	12	11	75	53	.586
Chicago	10	12	—	7	10	11	12	13	75	53	.586
Boston	5	5	11	—	9	14	10	13	67	61	.523
Pittsburgh	6	12	5	9	—	6	11	13	62	65	.488
Brooklyn	6	7	6	5	12	—	10	9	55	72	.433
Phila'phia	5	4	6	8	7	8	—	9	47	77	.379
Cincinnati	5	5	8	5	7	8	9	—	47	81	.367
Gms. lost	47	53	53	61	65	72	77	81	—	—	

GAMES TODAY

New York at Philadelphia (2).
Brooklyn at Boston.
Other clubs not scheduled.

Giants, Phillies to Play Postponed Games Today

Special to the Herald Tribune

PHILADELPHIA, Sept. 3.—The double-header scheduled for today between the New York Giants and Phillies was postponed until tomorrow because of rain. Both teams happen to have an open date. The Giants came to Philadelphia without so much as a tooth-brush in the party and went shopping in drugstores when it became necessary to stay overnight.

Jimmy Wilson, manager of the Phillies, said that he will use Curtis Davis and Euel Moore, his two best pitchers, in the double-header. Carl Hubbell and Fred Fitzsimmons are scheduled to pitch for the Giants.

TEXAS LEAGUE

Ft. Worth, 7; Oklahoma City, 6 (1st).
Oklahoma City, 3; Ft. Worth, 2 (2d).
Houston-Galveston, rain.

STANDING OF THE CLUBS

	W.	L.	Pct.		W.	L.	Pct.
*S. Antonio	86	60	.589	*Dallas	74	71	.510
Galveston	84	60	.583	Houston	72	74	.493
*Beaumont	76	66	.535	Ft. Worth	57	88	.393
*Tulsa	74	70	.514	Okla. City	56	90	.384

*Night game.

Leading Five Batsmen In Each Major League

AMERICAN LEAGUE

Player and Club.	G.	AB.	R.	H.	Pct.
Gehrig, N. Y.	129	506	111	183	.362
Gehringer, Det.	128	504	120	182	.361
Manush, Wash.	119	474	80	170	.360
Simmons, Chi.	115	469	82	164	.350
Foxx, Philadel.	125	453	105	156	.344

Leader a year ago today—Foxx, Philadelphia, .356.

NATIONAL LEAGUE

Player and Club.	G.	AB.	R.	H.	Pct.
P. Waner, Pitts.	125	520	104	191	.367
Terry, N. Y.	128	497	102	175	.352
Ott, New York	128	489	105	169	.346
Cuyler, Chi.	120	469	71	160	.341
Allen, Philadel.	124	510	81	173	.339

Leader a year ago today—Klein, Philadelphia, .380.

Home Runs		Runs Batted In	
Gehrig, Yankees	42	Gehrig, Yankees	157
Foxx, Athletics	40	Ott, Giants	131
Ott, Giants	32	R. Johns'n, R. Sox	117
Berger, Braves	31	Trosky, Indians	115
Collins, Cards	31	Greenb'g, Tigers	109

Results and Standings in Minor Leagues

INTERNATIONAL LEAGUE

YESTERDAY'S RESULTS

Newark, 2; Syracuse, 0 (1st).
Syracuse, 5; Newark, 2 (2d).
Montreal, 7; Rochester, 6 (1st).
Montreal, 10; Rochester, 9 (8 ins., 2d).
Buffalo, 1; Toronto, 0 (1st).
Toronto, 8; Buffalo, 7 (2d).
Albany, 14; Baltimore, 8 (1st).
Albany, 4; Baltimore, 2 (2d).

STANDING OF THE CLUBS

	W.	L.	Pct.		W.	L.	Pct.
Newark	90	58	.608	Buffalo	73	75	.493
Rochester	86	62	.581	Montreal	73	75	.493
Toronto	83	65	.561	Syracuse	59	89	.399
Albany	76	71	.517	Baltimore	51	96	.347

GAMES TODAY

Syracuse at Newark.
Rochester at Montreal.
Buffalo at Toronto.
Baltimore at Albany.

AMERICAN ASSOCIATION

At Toledo (first game)— R. H. E.
Columbus .... 010 002 020—5 7 1
Toledo .... 000 022 000—4 9 1

Batteries—Elliott, Klinger and Odea; Bowler and Oneill.

(second game)— R. H. E.
Columbus .. 400 010 002 1—8 15 2
Toledo .... 411 100 000 0—7 14 3

Batteries—Greer, Sims, Klinger and Odea; Nekola, Lawson, Perrin, Uhle and Desautels.

At Indianapolis (first game)— R. H. E.
Louisville .... 200 001 005—8 10 2
Indianapolis . 141 010 000—7 14 3

Batteries—McLean, Bass, Hatter and Thompson; Turner, Logan and Sprintz.

Second game postponed, rain.
St. Paul-Minneapolis, rain.
Milwaukee-Kansas City, rain.

STANDING OF THE CLUBS

	W.	L.	Pct.		W.	L.	Pct.
Minn'polis	79	57	.581	Louisville	71	68	.511
Columbus	75	64	.540	Toledo	64	76	.457
Milwaukee	73	64	.538	St. Paul	62	76	.449
Indian'olis	72	67	.518	Kan. City	57	81	.413

SOUTHERN ASSOCIATION

At Chattanooga (first game)— R. H. E.
Atlanta .... 000 000 010—1 7 0
Chattanooga .. 020 001 00x—3 9 5

Batteries—Kelly and Palmisano; Cohen and Holbrook.

Second game— R. H. E.
Atlanta .... 100 012 0—4 10 0
Chattanooga ..... 010 002 0—3 7 1

Batteries—Lindsey and Vance; Porter and Chandler.

At New Orleans (first game)— R. H. E.
Little Rock .... 100 300 000—4 13 3
New Orleans ... 000 010 013—5 9 0

Batteries—Sharpe and Van Grofski; Galehouse and George.

Second game— R. H. E.
Little Rock .... 000 022 0—4 9 2
New Orleans ...... 103 004 x—8 12 0

Batteries—Scheussler and O'Malley; Ragland, Bryant and George.

At Knoxville (first game)— R. H. E.
Nashville ..... 030 300 020—8 13 0
Knoxville ..... 010 101 200—5 13 2

Batteries—Stafford and Crouch; Blethen, Wetherell and West.

Second game— R. H. E.
Nashville .... 010 200 0—3 5 0
Knoxville .... 000 002 0—2 10 0

Batteries—Pessulo and O'Malley; Couzens, Moon and Head.

At Birmingham (first game)— R. H. E.
Memphis ..... 111 000 250—10 11 1
Birmingham .. 000 000 000—0 3 [illegible]

Batteries—Touchstone and Cuoto; Moore and Redmond.

Second game— R. H. E.
Memphis .... 000 000 2—2 4 1
Birmingham ...... 000 000 0—0 5 3

Batteries—Boward and Cuoto; Hughes and Parrish.

STANDING OF THE CLUBS

	W.	L.	Pct.		W.	L.	Pct.
N. Orleans	46	22	.676	Knoxville	30	34	.469
Chattan'ga	38	26	.594	Atlanta	31	37	.456
Nashville	36	33	.522	Little Rock	25	40	.385
Memphis	35	34	.507	Birmingh'm	24	39	.381

NEW YORK-PA. LEAGUE

At Elmira (first game)— R. H. E.
Binghamton .. 130 001 010—6 11 2
Elmira ...... 100 100 003—5 8 2

Batteries—Tobin and Straub; Ogrodowski, Vaicek and Chervinko.

At Reading (first game)— R. H. E.
Harrisburg .... 100 000 400—5 12 0
Reading .... 100 010 000—2 6 3

Batteries—Klarman and Maple, Mueller; Eckert, Gilvary and Moss, Savino.

Second game— R. H. E.
Harrisburg .... 030 00—3 5 1
Reading .... 430 00—7 10 0
(Called—rain.)

Batteries—Montague, Pipgras and Maple; Monroe and Savino.

At Hazleton (first game)— R. H. E.
Williamsport . 000 311 000—5 13 2
Hazleton ..... 300 000 003—6 13 1

Batteries—W. Thomas and Baker; Krider and Uzmann.

Second game— R. H. E.
Williamsport ..... 002 110 1—5 10 1
Hazleton .... 000 000 3—3 5 1

Batteries—Miner and Baker; Simmons and Maynard.

At Wilkes-Barre (first game)— R. H. E.
Scranton ..... 301 001 000—5 13 0
Wilkes-Barre .. 001 001 000—2 7 3

Batteries — Vandermeer, Ahearn and Stack; Willis and Stats.

Second game— R. H. E.
Wilkes-Barre .. 001 001 000—2 8 1
Scranton ...... 031 101 00x—6 12 0

Batteries—Reitz and Stats; Shaute and Kenny.

STANDING OF THE CLUBS

	W.	L.	Ptc.		W.	L.	Pct.
W'msport	37	27	.578	Wilkes-B're	29	31	.483
Scranton	37	27	.578	Hazleton	28	33	.459
Reading	34	31	.523	Harrisburg	27	34	.443
*B'hamton	31	32	.492	*Elmira	27	35	.435

*Night game.

PACIFIC COAST LEAGUE

At San Francisco (first game) R. H. E.
Hollywood ..... 000 000 000—0 7 0
San Francisco 010 000 03x—4 7 1

Batteries—Sullivan and Bassler; Stutz and Woodall.

Second game— R. H. E.
Hollywood .... 010 001 0—2 8 1
San Francisco ... 010 211 x—5 7 0

Batteries—Herrmann and Monzo; Densmore and Hershberger.

At Los Angeles (first game)— R. H. E.
Missions ..... 250 000 100—8 10 0
Los Angeles .. 100 000 020—3 8 4

Batteries — Lieber and Fitzpatrick; J. Campbell, Nelson, McDougal and G. Campbell, Goebel.

Second game— R. H. E.
Missions ..... 000 000 000—0 3 1
Los Angeles . 004 202 05x—13 15 0

Batteries—Osborne, Horne and Fitzpatrick; Ward, J. Campbell and G. Campbell.

At Sacramento (first game)— R. H. E.
Portland ..... 000 210 000—3 10 0
Sacramento .. 000 000 001—1 3 0

Batteries—Wilson and Cox; Salvo and Wirts.

Second game— R. H. E.
Portland .... 103 300 1—8 15 0
Sacramento ..... 000 000 2—2 6 2

Batteries—Caster and Doerr; Hartwig, Gabler and Skalkeld.

At Oakland (first game)— R. H. E.
Seattle ...... 010 014 001—7 19 0
Oakland ..... 000 110 000—2 10 1

Batteries—Piilette and Bottarini; Douglas, Haid and Sinabaldi.

Second game— R. H. E.
Seattle .... 000 110 0—2 6 0
Oakland .... 020 010 x—3 8 1

Batteries — Craghead, Vinci, Radonitz, Yerkes, Kallio and Bottarini; Rego and Raimondi.

STANDING OF THE CLUBS

	W.	L.	Pct.		W.	L.	Pct.
L. Angeles	47	26	.644	Missions	36	37	.493
Seattle	42	31	.575	Oakland	36	37	.493
Hollywood	39	34	.534	Portland	29	44	.397
San Fran.	39	34	.534	Sacramento	24	49	.329

Tigers Rout Browns Twice, 8-3, 15-1, Moving to Within 2 Games of American League Flag

Detroit Scores 11 Runs in 7th Of Final Game

Bridges Chalks Up 20th Victory in First Contest; Fischer Takes Second

By The Associated Press

ST. LOUIS, Sept. 22.—The Detroit Tigers thrashed the St. Louis Browns in both ends of a double-header today and moved still closer to the American League pennant, 8 to 3 and 15 to 1.

Mickey Cochrane's men now have a lead of six and one-half games over the New York Yankees and have only seven games to play. Even should the Yankees win all their remaining games, the Tigers need only two more victories to clinch the pennant.

The Tigers have another double bill with the browns tomorrow.

In the opener Tommy Bridges outpitched Hadley, Andrews and Walkup to record his twentieth victory. A home run by Jack Burns accounted for the Browns' three runs.

The Tigers went completely berserk in the seventh inning of the second game, scoring eleven runs. Darkness halted the slaughter after the seventh. Carl Fischer had the situation under control throughout.

The scores:

FIRST GAME

DETROIT (A. L.)	ab	r	h	po	a	e	ST. LOUIS (A. L.)	ab	r	h	po	a	e
White, cf.	5	2	1	2	0	0	Clift, 3b.	4	1	2	0	0	0
Cochrane, c	5	1	2	3	1	0	Garms, lf.	3	1	1	2	1	1
Gehr'ger, 2b	4	0	2	0	5	0	Burns, 1b.	4	1	2	8	0	0
Green'g, 1b	5	0	2	13	1	1	Pepper, cf.	4	0	0	5	0	0
Owen, 3b.	4	0	0	3	2	0	Campbel, rf	4	0	0	1	0	0
Goslin, lf.	4	1	2	3	0	0	Melillo, 2b.	4	0	2	2	7	1
Rogell, ss.	3	2	0	1	6	0	Hemsley, c.	4	0	0	5	1	0
Fox, rf.	2	1	0	0	0	0	Strange, ss.	4	0	0	4	2	0
BRIDGES, p	3	1	1	2	0	0	HADLEY, p	0	0	0	0	1	0
							ANDRE'S, p	2	0	0	0	0	0
							*Bejma	1	0	0	0	0	0
							WALKUP, p	0	0	0	0	0	0
Totals	35	8	10	27	15	1	Totals	34	3	7	27	12	2

*Batted for Andrews in seventh inning.

Detroit	150	000	020	—8
St. Louis	000	003	000	—3

Runs batted in—By Cochrane (2), Bridges (3), Greenberg (2), White, Burns (3). Two-base hits—Bridges, Goslin, Garms. Three-base hit—White, Clift. Home run—Burns. Stolen base—Rogell. Double plays—Strange, Melillo and Burns; Hemsley and Melillo; Gehringer, Rogell and Greenberg. Left on bases—St. Louis, 5; Detroit, 7. Bases on balls—Off Hadley, 3; off Bridges, 1; off Walkup, 4. Struck out—By Bridges, 3; by Andrews, 3; by Walkup, 2. Hits—Off Hadley, 4 in 1 2-3 innings; off Andrews, 5 in 5 1-3; off Walkup, 1 in 2. Wild pitch—Walkup. Losing pitcher—Hadley. Umpires—Ormsby and Kolls. Time—1:40.

SECOND GAME

DETROIT (A. L.)	ab	r	h	po	a	e	ST. LOUIS (A. L.)	ab	r	h	po	a	e
Fox, rf.	5	1	2	3	0	0	Clift, 3b.	4	0	0	0	1	0
White, cf.	3	3	2	3	0	0	Garms, lf.	3	0	0	1	0	0
Gehr'ger, 2b	5	2	3	3	2	0	Burns, 1b.	2	1	0	7	0	1
Green'g, 1b	4	1	2	5	0	0	Pepper, cf.	3	0	3	1	0	0
Owen, 3b.	5	1	1	1	1	0	Bejma, rf.	2	0	0	3	0	0
Goslin, lf.	5	3	5	3	0	0	Melillo, 2b.	3	0	1	5	4	0
Rogell, ss.	5	2	3	0	4	0	Hemsley, c.	3	0	0	1	2	1
Hayworth, c	3	1	0	3	0	0	Strange, ss.	3	0	0	3	1	1
FISCHER, p	3	1	0	0	0	0	COFFM'N, p	2	0	1	0	1	0
							McAFEE, p.	1	0	0	0	1	0
Totals	38	15	18	21	7	0	Totals	26	1	5	21	10	3

Detroit	100	102	11	—15
St. Louis	001	000	0	—1

Runs batted in—Gehringer (4), Melillo, Hayworth, Greenberg (2), Goslin, Fox, Owen, Fischer. Two-base hits—Greenberg (2), Coffman. Three-base hits—White, Gehringer, Owen. Sacrifices—White, Fischer. Double plays—Melillo and Strange; Strange, Melillo and Burns. Left on bases—Detroit, 9; St. Louis, 7. Bases on balls—Off Fischer, 3; off Coffman, 4; off McAfee, 1. Struck out—By Fischer, 1. Hits—Off Coffman, 15 in 6 1-3 innings; off McAfee, 3 in 2-3. Wild pitch—McAfee. Losing pitcher—Coffman. Umpires—Kolls and Ormsby. Time—1:37.

Cochrane Picks Rowe To Start World Series

ST. LOUIS, Sept. 22 (AP).—Figuring that his Detroit Tigers are "in" in the American League pennant race, Mickey Cochrane said definitely today he would start Lynwood (Schoolboy) Rowe in the first game of the World Series.

"That's easy—Rowe," Mickey said when asked as to his selection. "I don't care who the other manager picks. It may be bad bridge, but it's good baseball to lead your ace and that's what I'm going to do.

"If the Giants win, they'll use Hubbell, won't they? If the Cardinals should nose the Giants out, they'll use Dizzy Dean, won't they? That's sound judgment; so we'll use Rowe. Why, if we used any but our best against their best, we'd be in the position of conceding the game and the Tigers aren't conceding anybody anything."

Right now, Cochrane said, he figures Rowe, the veteran Alvin Crowder and Tommy Bridges will be his three starters in the series. Maybe, he said, Auker will start one. Marberry, Fischer, Hogsett, Sorrell and Hamlin will be ready for relief roles.

'I don't intend to start a left-hander against the Giants—if they win," he said.

Indians Forced to Rally To Best White Sox, 9-8

CHICAGO, Sept. 22 (AP).—Spotted five runs in the first two innings, three of them on Hal Trosky's thirty-fourth homer, the Cleveland Indians nevertheless were forced to put on a four-run eighth-inning rally today to turn back the White Sox, 9 to 8, in the first game of their series and hand the cellar Chicagoans their sixth straight defeat.

Aided by homers by Zeke Bonura and Marshall Mauldin, the former's twenty-seventh of the season, the Sox batted Oral Hildebrand out of the box and fought their way to a 7-to-5 lead in the seventh, only to have George Earnshaw fail in a relief role in the eighth, the Indians pounding him for five hits and four runs.

The score:

CLEVELAND (A. L.)	ab	r	h	po	a	e	CHICAGO (A. L.)	ab	r	h	po	a	e
Galatzer, rf	6	3	3	2	0	0	Conlan, cf.	5	0	1	7	0	0
Averill, cf.	3	3	1	4	0	0	Mauldin, 3b	5	3	3	1	1	1
Trosky, 1b.	4	2	2	11	2	0	Simmons, lf	4	1	2	3	0	0
Vosmik, lf.	5	0	3	1	0	0	Bonura, 1b.	3	1	3	7	0	0
Hale, 2b.	4	0	0	3	4	1	‖Hopkins	0	0	0	0	0	0
Kamm, 3b.	4	0	2	1	3	0	Appling, ss.	5	0	1	0	1	0
Knick'er, ss	4	0	0	2	3	0	Radcliff, rf.	4	0	0	5	0	0
Brenzel, c.	5	0	0	2	0	0	Hayes, 2b.	4	0	0	1	2	0
HILDE'D, p	3	0	0	1	1	0	Shea, c.	2	0	0	3	0	0
HUDLIN, p	0	0	0	0	1	0	†Haas	1	0	1	0	0	0
HUDLIN, p.	0	0	0	0	1	0	‡Uhlir	0	1	0	0	0	0
*Burnett	1	1	1	0	0	0	Madjeski, c.	1	1	1	0	0	0
C. BRO'N, p	1	0	0	0	0	0	KLAER'R, p	0	0	0	0	0	0
							GAL'AN, p.	2	0	0	0	1	0
							§Swanson	1	1	0	0	0	0
							EARN'W, p.	0	0	0	0	0	0
							¶Lyons	1	0	0	0	0	0
							HEVING, p.	0	0	0	0	0	0
Totals	40	9	12	27	14	1	Totals	28	3	12	27	5	1

*Batted for Hudlin in eighth inning.
†Batted for Shea in seventh innnig.
‡Ran for Haas in seventh innnig.
§Batted for Gallivan in seventh inning.
¶Batted for Earnshaw in eighth inning.
‖Ran for Bonura in ninth inning.

Cleveland	320	000	040	—9
Chicago	010	101	410	—8

Runs batted in—Averill, Trosky (4), Vosmik (3), Kamm, Conlan, Mauldin (2), Bonura (2), Appling (2), Radcliff. Two-base hits—Galatzer, Kamm, Mauldin, Simmons, Haas. Home runs—Trosky, Mauldin, Bonura. Double plays—Hudlin, Knickerbocker and Trosky; Trosky, Knickerbocker and Trosky. Left on bases—Cleveland, 11; Chicago, 6. Bases on balls—Off Hildebrand, 3; off Klaerner, 2; off Gallivan, 3; off Earnshaw, 2. Struck out—By Hildebrand, 2; by Gallivan, 1. Hits—Off Hildebrand, 8 in 6 1-3 innings; off Hudlin, 1 in 2-3; off C. Brown, 3 in 2; off Klaerner, 5 in 1 1-3; off Gallivan, 2 in 5 2-3; off Earnshaw, 5 in 1; off Heving, 0 in 1. Wild pitch—Gallivan. Winning pitcher—Hudlin. Losing pitcher—Earnshaw. Umpires—Donnelly, Summers and Hildebrand. Time—2:03.

Rain Halts Rochester-Toronto

ROCHESTER, Sept. 22 (UP).—The fourth game of the series between Rochester and Toronto to decide an International League representative against the American Association champions was postponed today by rain. Toronto needs one victory to clinch the series, having won the first three games.

Last Local Appearance and Those Who'll Miss Him Most

Above, the mighty swing of the one and only Babe Ruth; inset at left, back in 1923, the heyday of his career; lower inset, a close-up as he is today; below, surrounded by boys, of whom Ruth always has been sincerely fond and not merely for publicity purposes

Fordham Alumni to Pay Tribute To Murphy at Stadium Today

Pitcher, Star in His First Year, to Receive Present; Ruth Farewell Tomorrow

By Rud Rennie

Johnny Murphy will be picked out of the wavering Yankee ranks and honored today in the Stadium if it does not rain. Not so long ago he was a pitcher for Fordham University. The Fordham alumni have a present for him, in recognition of his achievements in this, his first full year of major league baseball.

Murphy deserves something more than empty words of praise. In a year in which some of the more experienced Yankee pitchers did not carry their share of the pitching burden, Murphy, Johnny Broaca, of Yale, and Jimmy Deshong—all young and right-handed, and freshmen in the post-graduate school of baseball—shouldered the load and kept the Yankees at the top of the league or close to it until August. Murphy has won fourteen ball games.

If these three first-year twirlers had not performed so well, the Yankees might not be ensconced in second place. It is no small accomplishment for any pitcher to be rated as a regular starting pitcher in his first season in the majors.

Due to the rain yesterday, Babe Ruth's farewell appearance here as an active player has been postponed to tomorrow. There will be two games in the Stadium today and the Yankees last home game of the season will be played tomorrow.

Meanwhile the Giants, leaders of the National League, come panting down the stretch, closely pursued by the sprinting Cardinals. That race is not yet over.

The Detroit Tigers, comfortably leading the American League by five and a half games, are rooting for the Giants.

"I hope nothing happens to keep the Giants from winning," said Mickey Cochrane, the Tiger-man, in the clubhouse in Detroit last Thursday. "I think we can beat the Giants. I'm not so sure about the Cards. They're tough—those Deans, Martin, Frisch, Medwick." He shuddered. "I'd rather play the Giants."

Which brings to mind something Bill Terry said one sunny forenoon on Flamingo Field, where the Giants trained last spring in Miami Beach.

"The Cardinals should beat us," he said, "but they won't."

"Why?" he was asked.

"There'll be dissension on that club," he answered.

And there was. The same men who have done most to bring the Cardinals along until they are almost on the Giant's heels, went on strike. The team had to do without their valuable services until they were pacified. The Deans—Jerome and Paul—while striking for more money may have gypped themselves and their companions out of the larger sum to be gained in a World Series. They are marvelous pitchers, but neither is very bright.

Leading Five Batsmen In Each Major League

NATIONAL LEAGUE

Player and Club	G.	AB.	R.	H.	Pct.
P. Waner, Pitts.	141	582	119	208	.357
Terry, New York	146	579	108	202	.349
Ott, New York	147	558	118	190	.341
J. Moore, Phila.	122	458	70	156	.341
Moore, New York	133	555	102	188	.339

Leader a year ago—Klein, Philadelphia, .366.

AMERICAN LEAGUE

Player and Club	G.	AB.	R.	H.	Pct.
Gehrig, New York	146	555	123	198	.357
Gehringer, Detroit	146	577	128	205	.355
Manush, Wash.	134	543	98	193	.355
Simmons, Chicago	131	530	97	182	.344
Foxx, Phila.	142	513	116	174	.339

Leader a year ago—Foxx, Philadelphia, .353.

Home Runs		Runs Batted In	
Gehrig, Yankees	46	Gehrig, Yankees	163
Foxx, Athletics	43	Trosky, Indians	138
Ott, Giants	35	Ott, Giants	136
Collins, Card.	34	Gr'nberg, Tigers	127
Trosky, Indians	34	Foxx, Athletics	122
		R. J'son, R. Sox	122

INTERNATIONAL LEAGUE PLAY-OFFS

Toronto-Rochester, rain.

STANDING OF THE CLUBS

	W.	L.	Pct.		W.	L.	Pct.
Toronto	3	0	1.000	Rochester	0	3	.000

AMERICAN ASS'N PLAY-OFFS

No game scheduled.

STANDING OF THE CLUBS

	W.	L.	Pct.		W.	L.	Pct.
Columbus	2	1	.667	Minneapolis	1	2	.333

SOUTHERN ASS'N PLAY-OFFS

No games scheduled.

STANDING OF THE CLUBS

	W.	L.	Pct.		W.	L.	Pct.
New O'leans	2	1	.667	Nashville	1	2	.333

Giants Lose, Lead Falling To 2½ Games

(Continued from page one)

Dodgers shifting games in order to play the Cards twice Friday. They think the White Sox shouldn't allow the use of the American League's Monday date for a play-off of the last Card-Cub game. They are talking of the Deans, Hallahan, Walker and Carlton. In short, they are fast losing confidence of their own ability, despite the fact that they've been leading since June 8.

The defeat today put the Giants just one game, 55 to 56, in front of St. Louis in the all-important "lost" column, and that is where the pennant fight may be decided. If, however, the Cards are unable to play all their games, the unusual situation of a championship club with more defeats than the runner-up is likely to be produced.

What a ball game was today's! The Giants peppered Rhem for eleven hits, while Schumacher allowed only nine. Still, it was the Braves, not the Giants, who were continually threatening to end the ball game. They had chances galore, but had to have the last run handed to them eventually.

Giants First to Score

The Giants scored first in the third. Johnny Vergez doubled and was sacrificed to third by Ryan. Schumacher then drove him home with a single to center. The Braves tied it up in the fourth on successive singles by Buck Jordan, Wally Berger and Randy Moore. Then in the seventh they went ahead on singles by Bill Urbanski and Pinky Whitney and Mallon's fly to Leiber. Just before he flied to drive in the run Mallon had sent a long foul to Joe Moore in left, but Moore allowed the ball to drop so as to keep alive the chance for a double play to end the inning. Urbanski would have scored then if Moore had caught it.

The Giants tore back into the game in the eighth when Moore singled on the first pitch and went to second on a sacrifice. This time Ott drove him in.

Schumacher worked himself out of a hole in the ninth when, after one out, Randy Moore bounced a single over his head on which Critz could make no play. Moore went to second on a wild pitch, so Whitney was walked intentionally. On that occasion Mallon also brought the count to three and two, but bounced out to Ryan, the latter making a low throw which Terry dug out of the dirt amid gasps from the Giants' bench and New York correspondents in the press box.

All the eleventh-inning trouble started after two out. R. Moore got his third hit, a single to right. Urbanski singled to left and Whitney topped a ball down the third-base line on which Schumacher did not even try to make a throw to first. Then came the game-losing walk to Mallon.

Braves Fight for Fourth

The Braves were fighting for fourth place. Before they took the field the scoreboard showed the Pirates had beaten the Cubs, 2 to 1, in the first game of a double-header.

Friends from Providence gave Bill McKechnie a shot gun and there was a suggestion that he use it on Pfirman and Stark when the umpires complained of the manner in which Rehm was stepping off the rubber in the fifth.

Pfirman threatened to clean the Braves's bench when they continued heckling him while Schumacher was pitching in the same session.

Adhering to an old custom, Terry refused an interview by a woman reporter in the coffee shoppe at the hotel this morning. The girl was rather peeved, but not half as much as was Terry when she and her photographer met him again in the lobby and the picture man snapped Terry as he waved her away.

The weather was dark and dank, indeed, and it was unnecessary for the train-yard engine to lay down a smoke screen across the diamond in the ninth. Through it, Mancuso shot a single to center, but was doubled on Vergez's grounder to short. Vergez missed two attempts to bunt.

Just to add luster to the extra innings Joe Moore, Ott and Whitney made greot stops of liners to rob Hogan, Thompson and Ryan.

The score:

NEW YORK (N. L.)	ab	r	h	po	a	e	BOSTON (N. L.)	ab	r	h	po	a	e
J. Mo're, lf, cf	5	1	3	1	0	0	Thomps'n, rf	5	0	0	2	0	0
Critz, 2b.	3	0	0	3	6	0	Jordan, 1b.	5	1	1	12	2	1
Terry, 1b.	4	0	1	15	3	0	Berger, cf.	5	0	1	5	0	0
Ott, rf.	4	0	2	1	0	0	R. Moore, lf	5	1	3	3	0	0
Leiber, cf.	4	0	0	4	0	0	Urbanski, ss	4	1	2	1	4	0
‡O'Doul	1	0	0	0	0	0	Whitney, 3b	4	0	2	2	3	0
Weintra'b, lf	0	0	0	0	0	0	Mallon, 2b.	4	0	0	5	6	0
Mancuso, c.	4	0	2	1	0	0	Hogan, c.	4	0	0	3	0	0
†Watkins	0	0	0	0	0	0	RHEM, p.	4	0	0	3	0	0
Danning, c	1	0	0	2	0	0							
Vergez, 3b.	4	1	1	1	3	0							
Ryan, ss.	4	0	1	1	4	0							
SCHU'ER, p	4	0	1	3	3	0							
Totals	38	2	11	*32	19	0	Totals	40	3	9	33	18	1

*Two when winning run was scored.
†Ran for Mancuso in ninth inning.
‡Batted for Leiber in tenth inning.

New York	001	000	010	00	—2
Boston	000	100	100	01	—3

Runs batted in—Schumacher, Ott, R. Moore, Mallon (2). Two-base hits—Vergez, Ott. Sacrifices—Ryan, Vergez, Critz (2). Double plays—Ryan, Critz and Terry; Rhem, Urbanski and Jordan; Urbanski, Mallon and Jordan (2). Left on bases—New York, 9; Boston, 8. Bases on balls—Off Schumacher, 3; off Rhem, 2. Struck out—By Schumacher, 3; by Rhem, 3. Wild pitch—Schumacher. Umpires—Pfirman, Stark and Magerkurth. Time—2:22.

World Series Jinx Stalks Vergez, Injured Jackson Slated for Third

Infielder, Benched by Illness in 1933, May Be Kept Out by Captain's 'Trick Knee'

BOSTON, Sept. 22.—It is almost worth your head to mention the World Series in the Copley Plaza, off-field camping grounds of the Giants, during the current series with the Braves. The boys are fumbling with lucky pieces. Bill Terry is wearing the same crazily colored tie put on last week and promises to wear it until the pennant is in, whether it matches his shirt or not. Just for luck the infield practice between innings is conducted with a red ball, which none but Carl Hubbell can touch off the field.

As the players go out on the diamond they keep an eye on the scoreboard in right field to see what the Cardinals are doing. Nevertheless, one must begin thinking of the World Series, anyway, and that brings up the subject of this story, one Johnny Vergez, a tough-luck guy if ever there was one in the major leagues.

Johnny isn't likely to be a starter against the Tigers on October 3. And this time it will be an injury to someone else which probably will keep him off third base. In the past it has been his own ills, or death or illness in his family which has forced Vergez out, about .107, and if it were not for fashion after the loss of a child. Another was born and died. Then his wife became very ill. Then, to cap it all, when the Giants were playing here last August, Johnny was stricken with appendicitis and had to be hurried to a hospital and out of the series.

Perhaps this string of misfortunes is responsible for Vergez's poor showing this season. He's hitting at or about .1[illegible] and, if it were not for Blondy Ryan's almost equal importence at bat Vergez wouldn't be playing third base even now. There is no secret that Vergez is spending his last season in a Giant uniform, but it is tragic that he will not end it in the big series.

Instead, the Giants will present that same infield which last year beat the Senators. Travis Jackson hurt his left knee last Sunday and isn't likely to return to the line-up until (and if) the Giants get into the series. Then, because he cannot patrol his usual ground at the shortfield, he will be shifted to third. Terry has intimated this move in casual conversation. He yields batting power in replacing Jackson at short with Ryan, but he adds offensive strength with Jackson at third instead of Vergez.

That's baseball. Still, its tough on Vergez. And, on the other hand, extremely lucky for John C. (Blondy) Ryan, apparently a child of fortune—all good.

ARTHUR E. PATTERSON.

Major League Averages

National League

CLUB BATTING

Club	G	AB	R	H	RBI	SB.	Pct
Pittsburgh	142	5064	700	1469	643	40	.290
St. Louis	145	5196	753	1495	703	66	.288
Philad'phia	139	4870	635	1373	601	53	.283
Chicago	143	4937	670	1410	635	54	.282
Brooklyn	145	5127	702	1437	656	52	.280
New York	146	5149	737	1424	687	20	.277
Boston	143	5050	663	1377	607	26	.273
Cincinnati	145	5120	573	1368	545	29	.268

CLUB FIELDING

Club	G	PO	A	E	DP	Pct.
Pittsburgh	142	3744	1500	138	116	.978
Chicago	143	3848	1675	131	116	.977
St. Louis	145	3917	1582	159	139	.972
New York	146	3915	1925	173	138	.971
Boston	143	3825	1682	160	109	.971
Brooklyn	145	3838	1745	170	130	.970
Cincinnati	145	3870	1735	173	127	.969
Philadelphia	139	3644	1582	183	140	.967

INDIVIDUAL BATTING

Player, club.	G.	AB.	R.	H.	RBI.	SB.	Pct.
P.Waner, Pitts.	139	575	116	207	85	7	.360
Danning, N. Y.	48	88	8	31	7	1	.352
Terry, N. Y.	145	575	108	201	79	0	.350
W'traub, N. Y.	27	72	13	25	15	0	.347
Padden, Pitts.	76	228	25	78	21	3	.342
J.Moore, C-Ph.	122	458	70	156	96	8	.341
Ott, N. Y.	146	554	118	188	135	1	.339
Moore, N. Y.	132	550	101	185	57	5	.336
Cuyler, Chi.	134	527	76	177	63	14	.336
Vaughan, Pit.	141	530	105	177	86	8	.334
Collins, St. L.	145	568	111	188	120	2	.331
Allen, Phil.	138	556	85	183	82	6	.329
Leslie, Bklyn.	140	520	69	169	93	6	.325
Todd, Phil.	84	278	33	90	39	3	.324
O'Doul, N. Y.	78	174	27	56	44	2	.322
Medwick, St.L.	140	584	100	186	97	3	.319
Stripp, Bklyn.	98	360	48	115	38	2	.319
Pool, Cin.	92	332	35	106	50	2	.319
Jordan, Bos.	116	456	66	145	53	3	.318
K'necke, Bklyn.	116	432	76	137	70	8	.317
Delancey, St.L.	85	224	37	71	33	1	.317
Traynor, Pit.	111	415	58	131	56	2	.316
[illegible]							

PITCHING RECORDS

Pitcher, club.	G.	H.	BB.	SO.	W.	L.	Pct.
[illegible]							

American League

CLUB BATTING

Club	G	AB	R	H	RBI	SB	Pct
Detroit	145	5144	892	1538	788	116	.299
Cleveland	146	5143	778	1473	732	52	.286
Phila'phia	145	5044	743	1424	679	55	.282
Wash.	146	5147	697	1437	637	43	.280
New York	146	5072	809	1416	752	67	.279
Boston	146	5120	794	1417	732	111	.278
St. Louis	146	5016	656	1348	608	43	.270
Chicago	144	4994	658	1303	616	32	.262

CLUB FIELDING

Club.	G	PO	A	E	DP	Pct.
Detroit	145	3892	1681	149	141	.974
New York	146	3923	1501	152	135	.973
Washington	146	3878	1786	152	152	.973
Cleveland	146	3677	1750	163	157	.971
St. Louis	146	3849	1665	173	151	.969
Chicago	144	3833	1703	188	127	.967
Philadelphia	145	3789	1716	184	161	.967
Boston	146	3791	1692	188	130	.967

Triple plays—Detroit, 2.

INDIVIDUAL BATTING

Player, club.	G.	AB.	R.	H.	RBI.	SB.	Pct.
Andrews, St. L.	32	38	5	14	8	0	.368
Legett, Boston	17	30	3	11	1	0	.367
Gehrig, N. Y.	146	555	123	198	163	9	.357
Manush, W'sh.	134	543	89	193	87	9	.355
Gehr'ger, Det.	144	568	126	200	114	11	.352
Simmons, Chi.	130	526	96	180	100	2	.342
Vosmik, Cleve.	96	372	68	127	69	1	.341
Foxx, Phila.	142	513	116	174	122	11	.339
Greenb'g, Det.	144	556	110	187	123	8	.336
Higgins, Phila.	136	511	86	170	84	7	.333
Trosky, Cleve.	146	593	113	195	134	2	.329
Cochrane, Det.	124	421	69	137	67	7	.325
West, St. L.	122	482	90	156	56	3	.324
R. J'nson, Bos.	140	566	85	183	122	13	.323
Werber, Bos.	145	597	125	192	63	38	.322
Dickey, N. Y.	104	395	56	127	69	0	.322
Knick'b'r, Cl.	138	562	79	180	64	5	.320
Owen, Det.	144	539	78	172	91	2	.319
Travis, Wash.	106	387	46	123	50	1	.318
Hornsby, St. L.	23	22	2	7	10	0	.318
[illegible]							

PITCHING RECORDS

Pitcher, club.	G.	H.	BB.	SO.	W.	L.	Pct.
[illegible]							

International League Averages

CLUB BATTING

Club.	G.	AB.	R.	H.	RBI.	SB.	Pct.
[illegible]							

CLUB FIELDING

Club.	G.	PO.	A.	E.	DP.	TP.	Pct.
[illegible]							

INDIVIDUAL BATTING

Player, club.	G.	AB.	R.	H.	RBI.	SB.	Pct.
[illegible]							

PITCHING RECORDS

(Five decisions or more)

Pitcher, club.	G.	H.	BB.	SO.	W.	L.	Pct.
[illegible]							

Pirates Defeat Cubs Twice to Tie for Fourth

Win Second Double-Header in Row by Attack in 6th of Nightcap, 2-1, 11-7

By The Associated Press

PITTSBURGH, Sept. 22.—The Pirates defeated the Cubs twice today, 2—1 and 11—7, for their fourth victory in two days.

As a result Pittsburgh moved into a tie with Boston for fourth place in the National League standings, the winner of which, the Buccaneers have figured, will distribute about $400 each to its players, out of the World Series pool.

Jensen's single, sending two mates home in the sixth frame of the first contest gave the verdict to Ralph Birkofer over Hal Lee.

Tinning and Bush were victims of another Pirate sixth-inning uprising that counted seven runs and clinched the second game. The Bucs close their home season tomorrow against Chicago.

The scores:

FIRST GAME

CHICAGO (N. L.)	ab	r	h	po	a	e	PITTSBURGH (N. L.)	ab	r	h	po	a	e
Hack, 3b.	4	0	1	0	0	0	Roettger, lf	3	0	1	2	0	0
W.Her'n, 2b	4	0	2	2	1	0	Jensen, cf.	3	0	1	2	0	0
Cuyler, cf.	3	0	0	1	0	0	P. Waner, rf	3	0	0	1	0	0
Stephen'n, lf	4	0	0	1	1	0	Vaughan, ss	3	0	0	1	4	0
F. Her'n, 1b	3	0	0	10	1	1	Traynor, 3b	3	0	0	0	3	0
Hartnett, c.	3	0	0	4	2	0	Suhr, 1b.	3	0	0	11	0	0
Stainba'k, rf	3	1	1	2	0	0	Thev'ow, 2b	3	1	1	4	5	0
Jurges, ss.	3	0	0	3	5	0	Padden, c.	3	1	2	6	1	0
LEE, p.	3	0	1	1	3	0	BIRK'ER, p	3	0	0	0	0	0
Totals	30	1	5	24	13	1	Totals	27	2	5	27	13	0

Chicago	000	001	000	—1
Pittsburgh	000	002	00x	—2

Runs batted in—Hack, Jensen (2). Two-base hit—Stainback. Stolen base—Hack. Double plays—Hartnett and Jurges; W. Herman, Jurges and F. Herman; Thevenow, Vaughan and Suhr. Left on bases—Chicago, 3; Pittsburgh, 1. Base on balls—Off Birkofer, 1. Struck out—By Birkofer, 4; by Lee, 3. Passed ball—Padden. Umpires—Rigler, Sears and Klem. Time—1:30.

SECOND GAME

CHICAGO (N. L.)	ab	r	h	po	a	e	PITTSBURGH (N. L.)	ab	r	h	po	a	e
Hack, 3b.	5	1	1	2	2	0	Roettger, lf	5	1	1	4	0	0
W.Her'n, 2b	4	2	3	2	2	0	Jensen, cf.	5	1	2	2	0	0
Cuyler, cf.	5	1	3	2	1	0	P.Waner, rf	4	2	2	1	0	0
Klein, rf.	5	1	2	2	0	1	Vaughan, ss	3	3	2	3	3	0
F. Her'n, 1b	4	2	0	9	1	0	Traynor, 3b	4	2	1	1	4	0
O'Farrell, c	4	0	1	3	1	0	Suhr, 1b.	2	2	0	5	0	0
*Phelps	1	0	1	0	0	0	Thev'ow, 2b	4	0	0	4	3	0
Steinback, lf	4	0	3	1	0	0	Grace, c.	3	1	2	7	1	0
Jurges, ss.	4	0	1	2	4	0	HARRIS, p.	1	0	1	0	0	0
TINNING, p	3	0	1	1	2	0	FRENCH, p	0	0	0	0	0	0
BUSH, p.	0	0	0	0	0	0	‡Lucas	1	0	0	0	0	0
WEIDE'R, p	0	0	0	0	0	0	SMITH, p.	1	0	0	0	1	0
ROOT, p.	0	0	0	0	0	0	§Padden	1	0	0	0	0	0
†Galan	1	0	0	0	0	0	HOYT, p.	1	0	0	0	1	0
JOINER, p.	0	0	0	0	0	0							
Totals	41	7	16	24	14	1	Totals	34	11	12	27	9	0

*Batted for O'Farrell in ninth inning.
†Batted for Root in eighth inning.
‡Batted for French in fifth inning.
§Batted for Smith in sixth inning.

Chicago	101	020	003	— 7
Pittsburgh	010	007	30x	—11

Runs batted in—Cuyler (2), Harris, O'Farrell, Steinback, P. Waner, Vaughan, Traynor, Thevenow (2), Grace (3), Klein (2), Phelps, Jensen (2). Two-base hits—W. Herman, P. Waner (2), Vaughan, Cuyler. Three-base hits—Cuyler, Traynor, Phelps. Stolen bases—P. Waner, Vaughan. Sacrifice—W. Herman. Double play—Jurges and F. Herman. Left on bases—Chicago, 9; Pittsburgh, 3. Bases on balls—Off Harris, 1; off Tinning, 1; off Bush, 1; off Weidemeyer, 2. Struck out—By Harris, 1; by French, 1; by Tinning, 2; by Smith, 1; by Hoyt, 2. Hits—Off Harris, 5 in 2 1-3 innings; off Smith, 0 in 1; off Bush, 3 in 1; off Weidemeyer, 0 in 1-3; off Joiner, 1 in 1; off French, 6 in 2 2-3; off Tinning, 7 in 5 (none out in sixth); off Hoyt, 5 in 3; off Root, 1 in 2-3. Winning pitcher—Smith. Losing pitcher—Tinning. Umpires—Sears, Klem and Rigler. Time—2:15.

Watts Wins Skeet Cup In Nassau Club Shoot

A rainstorm kept down the field at the Mineola traps of the Nassau Trapshooting Club yesterday. Twelve gunners competed in the skeet shoot, the best work being done by W. A. Ketcham, who broke 50 straight targets. However, he was shooting for targets only, so J. H. Carl and G. B. Watts shot off for the prize, as they tied with 49. On the first shoot-off they again tied with 23 targets each. Due to the heavy rain, they decided to toss for the cup, which was taken by Watts.

Six gunners tied for the high handicap cup, each with a full score of 50 targets. On the shoot-off A. S. Bayles broke 25 straight targets and took the trophy. In the regular shoot R. Marano broke 50 straight targets and took the high scratch cup. There was a tie for the high handicap cup between F. C. Chapman and T. Kilpatrick. Each had a full card of 50 targets. On a toss Kilpatrick won.

The scores:

Skeet Shoot—50 Targets

	Hit	H'cap	Total
W. A. Ketcham	50	0	50
G. B. Watts	49	4	50
J. H. Carl	49	3	50
A. S. Bayles	48	2	50
W. J. Bode	46	5	50
R. Marano	47	3	50
T. H. Lewis	42	12	50
H. A. Echenbach	48	3	50
F. Dickerson	47	2	49
P. G. Gossler jr.	45	4	49
I. Richards	47	1	48
W. Tyson	44	4	48

Regular Shoot—50 Targets

	Hit	H'cap	Total
R. Marano	50	1	50
T. Kilpatrick	37	13	50
F. C. Chapman	46	4	50
J. Pulido	33	15	48
F. Wise	43	5	48

YANKEES BEAT A'S, 8-5; PHILLIES LOSE

Moody, Jacobs Win in Wimbledon Tennis

Dooly:

Tips Off Big League Scouts to Pitcher Who Has Allowed One Run in 11 Games and Another Who Has Fanned 150 in 16.

STEPPING out today and turning the slide down the pillar to the trade. In other words, giving the readers a chance to talk to themselves. The first oration is by one "Germantown Charlie," who, we take it, hides his handle iest its revealing rock the universe.

A modest authority on schoolboy baseball, Germantown Charlie's contribution, with some few deletions of the parsley, runs: When it comes to baseball, the high schoolers are generally chumps, but in a number of cases this ranking is reversed.

Mentioning a few that I've seen play, and I'm willing to bet will make the major leagues within the next six or seven years, I'll take first Jack Benninghoff, the Doylestown High pitcher. I'll admit high schools don't boast of Jimmy Foxxes and Bob Johnsons, but anybody that allows only one run in 11 games is a good pitcher even if he's tossing them up for the 40-pound team at some kindergarten. His earned-run mark was .011 and he heaved something like nine or 10 shutouts. Two were no-hit games.

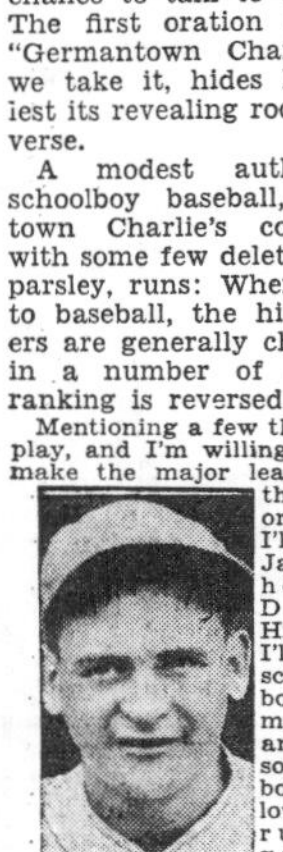

Bob Johnson

When it came to strikeouts, Jack knew what to do. He fanned them like the circus fat lady fans herself when the circus is playing an August engagement in St. Louis.

Next, we'll take that guy Carter, who heaved for Olney during the past two or three seasons. Pretty good, he won a heap of ball games by using not only his arm and head but by wielding a mighty willow. I don't know much about him except that he beat Tommy Watts, the Germantown High moundsman, who is next in my list of high schoolers who will get somewhere.

Watts is good. He doesn't think so, but everyone else does. He's worked out with both the Phillies and Boston Braves, and if he weren't so young and small he would have been signed. They told him to come back later, meaning when he's grown up.

Watts teamed up with Pete Stranges, rated as the best youngster behind the plate in the city. He struck out something like 150 opponents in 16 games in two years; won 16 and lost 5. No one knows how many other games he won on the sandlots.

Now we'll take another Germantown High player—Harry Piper, who covered third base last year and short this season. Now playing third for the Germantown Artisans, he socks the ball like Babe Ruth used to hit it.

Against Wissinoming, which is rated as one of the strongest semipro teams in the vicinity, he cracked the longest hit of the day and worked efficiently around third. The Artisans won, 4-3, and Piper's playing nipped a rally and clinched the victory.

* * *

(Editor's note — Thanks, Charley. And don't forget to write again and remind us—when the six or seven years are up.)

* * *

Basibola in Venezuela

The following is an excerpt from a letter originating in Maracaibo, Venezuela. Contributed by a go-between, whose identity we have awkwardly forgotten and who neglected to attach the name of the writer, it deals with the popularity of baseball among yon Latins:

The people here (in Maracaibo) are baseball crazy, going so far as to put their games on the air. I was listening in on one of the broadcasts recently. It was, naturally, made in Spanish.

They use most of the American baseball terms and it is amusing to hear them, in their excitement, yelling, "Un hit," or "Un basibolas," "Strike out, el peetcher," etc.

There are two announcers for the games. As soon as one finishes the description of a play the other chips in with some advertising propaganda, such as "flume Capitolio" (smoke Capitolio cigarettes), or "tome rom Ibarra" (drink rum Ibarra), etc. During the broadcast as many as 50 different articles are plugged.

The game I listened to ended with the mob wanting (showing the yearning must be universal) to lynch the umpire. The score was 9-7, but the side trailing had men on second and third with one out in the ninth.

The batter was thrown out at first and the runner on third was caught at home, according to the umpire. But the crowd didn't seem to agree with him.

Some of the players are imported from Puerto Rico, Cuba and Santo Domingo, but most of them are local talent, and they like the spectacular. The first baseman, for instance, likes to take the ball one-handed, so he will appear clever.

All the big-wigs of society turn out for the games, and there is always a band in attendance—which is more than you get at Shibe Park even in a World Series. Also, there is plenty of betting on all phases of the game.

* * *

Baseball has been played here for the past 10 years by men connected with the oil companies, the majority of whom are Texans, with Californians running a close second. Among them, it might be mentioned, are a few former minor leaguers.

ALLEN COMES THROUGH

Johnny Allen, one of the New York Yankees' four "dollar-a-year" men at the start of spring training, won six of his first eight pitching starts,

GEHRIG'S TENTH HOMER IN 8TH STARTS RALLY

New Yorkers Push Over 5 Runs in Last Two Innings.

2 LEADS WIPED OUT

Mack Pitchers Fail After Given Early Advantages.

No Pitching Again

NEW YORK.	ab	r	h	o	a	ATHLETICS.	ab	r	h	o	a
Combs, lf.	5	2	2	2	0	Moses, rf.	5	2	2	1	0
Rolfe, 3b.	3	1	0	1	5	Cramer, cf	3	0	0	3	0
C'pman, cf	5	0	1	1	0	Johnson, lf	3	0	2	1	0
Gehrig, 1b	4	2	2	14	0	Foxx, 1b..	4	0	0	14	1
Lazzeri, 2b	4	2	2	1	3	Higgins, 3b	4	0	0	0	2
Selkirk, rf	5	0	2	4	0	W'stler, 2b	4	1	3	2	6
Crosetti, ss	4	0	1	2	4	N'some, ss.	4	2	1	4	6
Jorgens, c	4	0	1	2	0	Richards, c	4	0	1	2	0
Broaca, p.	2	0	1	0	0	B'holder, p	2	0	0	0	3
*Hill	1	0	0	0	0	‡Marcum.	1	0	1	0	0
Murphy, p	1	1	1	0	1	Dietrich, p	0	0	0	0	0
						†Berry....	1	0	0	0	0
						Caster, p.	0	0	0	0	0
						Benton, p	0	0	0	0	1
Totals	38	8	13	27	13	Totals	35	5	10	27	18

* Batted for Broaca in seventh.
‡ Batted for Blaeholder in sixth.
† Batted for Dietrich in eighth.

New York ...	0	0	0	0	0	3	0	3	2	—8
Athletics	1	0	0	1	1	2	0	0	0	—5

Errors—Rolfe, Crosetti. Runs batted in—Lazzeri, 2; Selkirk, 2; Gehrig, 2; Combs, Chapman, Johnson, Richards, Marcum, 2. Two-base hits—Crosetti, Newsome, Richards, Warstler, Murphy. Three-base hits—Lazzeri, Marcum, Combs. Home run—Gehrig. Stolen base—Moses. Sacrifices—Cramer, 2. Double plays—Foxx to Newsome to Foxx; Blaeholder to Newsome to Foxx; Lazzeri to Crosetti to Gehrig. Left on bases—New York, 7; Athletics, 8. Base on balls—Off Broaca, 1; Murphy, 2; Blaeholder, 1; Dietrich, 2; Benton, 1. Struck out—By Broaca, 1; Murphy, 1; Dietrich, 1; Benton, 1. Hits—Off Broaca, 9 in 6 innings; Murphy, 1 in 3; Blaeholder, 8 in 6; Dietrich, 2 in 2; Caster, 2 in 0 (none out in 9th); Benton, 1 in 1. Wild pitch—Broaca. Winning pitcher—Murphy. Losing pitcher—Dietrich. Umpires—Dineen, Kolls and Donnelly. Time—2.15.

By BILL DOOLY

Resorting to their timeworn pitching trick of converting themselves into stooges for the Yankee slugging artists, the Athletics' curvers brought back misery en scenes of bygone days at Shibeshire yesterday afternoon, the while they permitted New York to beat them 8 runs to 5.

The Mack hitsmiths had no hand in the denouement. They twice fashioned leads for their so-called pitchers, piling up a handle of 3-0 in five innings and finding it lost in a 3-3 tie in the sixth, promptly building a fresh one of 5-3 in the closing half of the sixth.

Before going further it might be added that a three-bagger by Johnny Marcum, pinch-hitting in the grand manner, fashioned this second margin. But, heh, heh, it was no match for the A's chuckers, who countered with the kind of pitches the enemy loves to touch.

Dietrich Is Victim.

Bill Dietrich was in the box by this time, George Blaeholder having started and been lifted to make room for Footsy Marcum to enter his brogans in the batting box. Dietrich held the lead through the seventh and then came through.

Doing a Professor Picard, he led off the eighth by issuing a pass to Red Rolfe. Ben Chapman he disposed of and then seeing Lou Gehrig at the plate pitched himself into a three-and-two spot. You guessed it the first time, Montmorency!

He heaved the next one right down the middle and the guy they called Lou whaled it right on the old proboscis, slapping it with such vigor that the ball dropped on the rooftops across the way from rightfield, his tenth of the season.

Selkirk Scores Lazzeri.

That tied the score and Bill renewed his efforts by walking Signor Tony Lazzeri and tossing one George Selkirk couldn't resist. George banged it to the furthest corner of leftfield. Selkirk had to retrace his steps to tag first-base and was held to a single on the hit, but Lazzeri negotiated three bags to cross the plate.

This was enough, as events were to prove, to win the day for Marse Joe McCarthy's league leaders, but to add a bit of comfort to their margin they banged George Caster for a double and triple in the ninth and George's rescuer, Al Benton, for a single that netted two surplus tallies.

Meanwhile, the Mack apple knockers, who had made the afternoon miserable for Johnny Broaca,

Continued on Page 15, Column 6.

This Yank Foils A's ✶ Warstler Gets Double

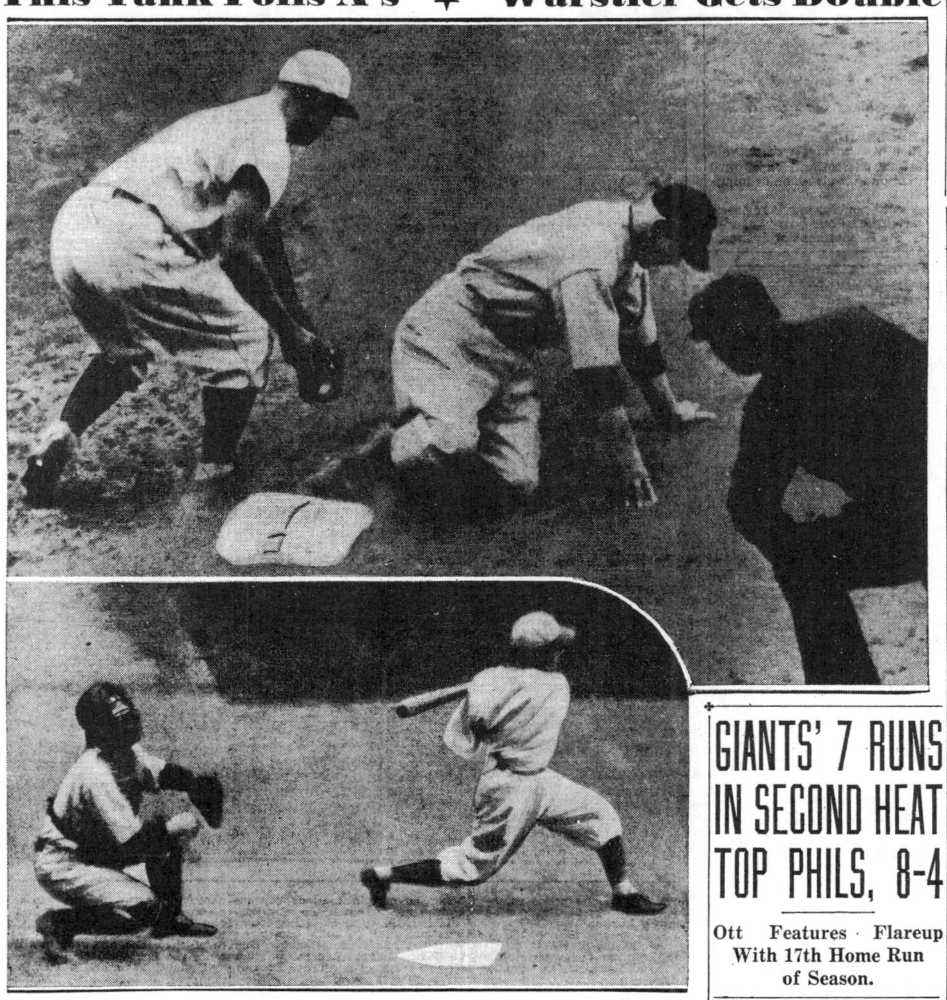

Even the Athletics, who are more or less noted for turning back a league leader when least expected, failed to check the drive of the pace-setting New York Yankees at Shibe Park yesterday. At top, Red Rolfe, who was wide awake when Pitcher Blaeholder tried to catch him napping at the first bag with a throw to Jimmy Foxx. Below, Hal Warstler hammering out a two-bagger in the eight inning. This was his third hit of the game.

Detroit Takes Second Place As Bridges Nips Indians, 8-3

Tigers Pass Cleveland to Trail Yankees by Three Games; Winners Pound Stewart and Winegarner for 12 Hits.

By Associated Press

DETROIT, July 2.—The Detroit Tigers climbed over Cleveland into second place in the American League pennant race today by shellacking the Tribe for the second time in as many day, 8-3.

The victory gave the Tigers an 11-point edge over Cleveland in the pursuit of the speeding Yanks who continued their winning ways by taking the Athletics into camp today. The Tigers trail the Yanks by three games.

Tommy Bridges hurled the distance for the winners and let the Tribe down with seven hits, two of them homers. Winegarner, who relieved Walter Stewart on the mound in the sixth, connected for a circuit clout in the seventh and Campbell clouted one over the fence in the eighth.

Fox Continues Streak.

Cleveland's other run came as a result of early wildness by Bridges. He walked the first two men to face him, Galatzer and Knickerbocker. Vosmik singled to fill the bases and Galatzer scored when Campbell forced Vosmik.

The Tigers evened things in the third, when Fox singled and came home on an infield out and a single. It was the 22d consecutive game in which Fox has hit safely.

They went on a hitting rampage in the fifth and before Stewart finally retired the 10th man to face him in the inning, the Detroiters had scored five runs.

Goslin Clears Sacks.

With one out, Fox singled. Cochrane flied out and Gehringer pushed Fox to third with a single. Stewart passed Greenberg to get at Goslin and the Goose responded with a double that cleared the bases.

Rogell walked and Walker singled to score Goslin, Rogell scoring on Owens' single.

Bridges lined to Vosmik to end the inning, but not before the injury-haunted Manager Walter Johnson saw Vosmik plow into the scoreboard after the drive. Vosmik was out for a few minutes, but resumed play.

Gehringer finished the Tiger scoring in the sixth when he homered with Cochrane ahead of him.

CLEVELAND.	ab	r	h	o	a	DETROIT.	ab	r	h	o	a
Galatzer, cf.	3	1	1	1	0	Fox, rf...	5	2	2	1	0
K'bocker, ss.	3	0	1	3	3	Cochrane, c	3	1	1	3	0
Vosmik, lf..	4	0	1	2	0	B'inger, 2b	5	2	4	4	3
Campbell, rf.	4	1	2	2	0	G'berg, 1b	4	1	0	11	1
Trosky, 1b...	3	0	0	10	1	Goslin, lf	4	1	1	2	0
Hale, 3b....	4	0	0	0	2	Rogell, ss.	3	1	1	1	6
Berger, 2b...	4	0	0	1	3	Walker, cf	4	0	1	3	0
Pytlak, c....	4	0	0	4	0	Owen, 3b.	4	0	2	1	1
Stewart, p...	2	0	1	1	1	Bridges, p	4	0	0	1	2
W'garner, p.	2	1	1	0	1						
Totals.	33	3	7	24	11	Totals	36	8	12	27	13

Cleveland ...	1	0	0	0	0	0	1	1	0	—3
Detroit	0	0	1	0	5	2	0	0	x	—8

Runs batted in—Gehringer, 3; Goslin, 3; Campbell, 2; Winegarner, Walker, Rogell. Two-base hit—Goslin. Home runs—Gehringer, Winegarner, Campbell. Double play—Bridges to Rogell to Greenberg. Left on bases—Cleveland, 6; Detroit, 8. Bases on balls—Off Bridges, 3; Stewart, 2; Winegarner, 2. Struck out—By Bridges, 2; Winegarner, 3. Hits—Off Stewart, 10 in 5 innings; Winegarner, 2 in 3 innings. Losing pitcher—Stewart. Umpires—Moriarty, Marberry and Owens. Time—1.46.

Minor Leagues

INTERNATIONAL LEAGUE

Yesterday's Results.

Montreal-Rochester, not scheduled.
Other games at night.

Standing of the Teams.

	W.	L.	P.C.		W.	L.	P.C.
Baltimore..	42	32	.568	Newark..	37	35	.514
Montreal...	41	33	.554	Syracuse	39	37	.513
Toronto....	41	33	.554	Rochester	30	44	.405
Buffalo.....	37	32	.536	Albany...	27	48	.360

NEW YORK-PENNA. LEAGUE

Yesterday's Results.

Elmira, 13; Scranton, 0.
Wilkes-Barre, 6; Binghamton, 4.
Reading, 2; Williamsport, 1.
Hazleton-Harrisburg, night game.

Second Half.
Standing of the Teams.

	W.	L.	P.C.		W.	L.	P.C.
Wilkes-B're.	1	0	1.000	Harrisb'g	0	0	.000
Elmira......	1	0	1.000	Reading.	1	0	1.000
Hazleton....	0	0	.000	Bingh'ton	0	1	.000
Wil'msport..	0	1	.000	Scranton	0	1	.000

AMERICAN ASSOCIATION

Milwaukee, 6; Louisville, 4.
Columbus, 8; Minneapolis, 5 (1st).
Minneapolis, 7; Columbus, 5 (2d).
Toledo, 10; St. Paul, 9.
Indianapolis-Kansas City, night game.

SOUTHERN ASSOCIATION

Knoxville, 4; Chattanooga, 3 (12 innings).
Memphis, 6; Little Rock, 4.
New Orleans, 8; Birmingham, 4.
Nashville at Atlanta, night game.

Big League Baseball Facts

AMERICAN LEAGUE

Yesterday's Results.

New York, 8; ATHLETICS, 5.
Boston, 6; Washington, 5.
Detroit, 8; Cleveland, 3.
St. Louis at Chicago, postponed, rain

Standing of the Teams.

	W.	L.	P.C.	*G.B.
New York	41	24	.631	——
Detroit	40	29	.580	3
Cleveland	37	28	.569	4
Chicago	33	28	.541	6
Boston	34	33	.507	8
Washington	29	37	.439	12½
ATHLETICS ...	26	36	.419	13½
St. Louis	19	44	.302	21

* Games behind.

Today's Schedule.

New York vs. ATHLETICS, at Shibe Park.
Washington at Boston.
St Louis at Chicago.
Cleveland at Detroit.

NATIONAL LEAGUE

Yesterday's Results.

New York, 8; PHILLIES, 4.
Brooklyn, 5; Boston, 0.
Chicago, 9; Cincinnati, 3.
St. Louis, 7; Pittsburgh, 0.

Standing of the Teams.

	W.	L.	P.C.	*G.B.
New York	45	18	.714	....
Chicago	38	28	.576	8½
St. Louis	37	29	.561	9½
Pittsburgh	39	31	.557	9½
Brooklyn	30	34	.469	15½
Cincinnati	29	38	.433	18
PHILLIES	26	39	.400	20
Boston	20	47	.299	27

* Games behind.

Today's Schedule.

PHILLIES at New York.
Pittsburgh at St. Louis.
Boston at Brooklyn.
Chicago at Cincinnati.

GIANTS' 7 RUNS IN SECOND HEAT TOP PHILS, 8-4

Ott Features Flareup With 17th Home Run of Season.

Knocked Out in 2d

PHILLIES.	ab	r	h	o	a	NEW YORK	ab	r	h	o	a
Allen, cf...	4	0	0	3	0	JoeM're, lf	4	2	1	0	0
Watkins, lf.	5	0	1	1	0	Bartell, ss.	3	1	1	4	3
J.M're, rf...	3	1	0	1	0	Terry, 1b..	5	1	3	12	0
Camilli, 1b.	4	1	2	6	0	Ott, rf.....	4	1	1	0	1
Vergez, 3b.	4	0	2	0	2	Leiber, cf..	5	1	2	4	0
Haslin, ss..	4	1	2	1	1	J'kson, 3b.	4	1	2	0	4
Chi'zza, 2b.	4	1	0	5	1	C'c'n'llo, 2b	2	0	0	2	2
Wilson, c..	4	0	1	6	0	Mancuso, c.	3	1	0	5	0
E.M're, p..	0	0	0	0	1	P'm'lee, p..	4	0	0	0	5
J'gens, p...	1	0	0	1	2						
*Boland...	1	0	0	0	0						
Pezzullo, p.	0	0	0	0	0						
†Todd.....	1	0	0	0	0						
Totals	35	4	8	24	7	Totals	34	8	10	27	15

*Batted for Jorgens in 7th.
†Batted for Pezzullo in 9th.

Phillies	0	0	0	0	0	2	0	0	2	—4
New York	0	7	0	0	0	0	0	1	x	—8

Errors—Vergez, Watkins, Parmelee, Bartell. Runs batted in—Joe Moore, 2; Terry, 2; Ott, 3; Camilli, Todd. Two-base hits—Camilli, Haslin. Home run—Ott. Stolen base—Bartell. Sacrifice—Cuccinello. Double play—Jackson, Cuccinello and Terry. Left on Bases—Phillies, 7; New York, 9. Bases on balls—E. Moore, 2; Parmelee, 3; Jergens, 3. Strikeouts—E. Moore, 2; Parmelee, 3; Pezzullo, 2. Hits—Off E. Moore, 5 in 1 2-3 innings; Jorgens, 4 in 4 1-3; Pezzullo, 1 in 2. Hit by pitcher—By Pezzullo (Joe Moore), by Jorgens (Cuccinello). Passed ball—Mancuso. Losing pitcher—E. Moore. Umpires—Stark, Rigler and Pinelli. Time—2.09.

NEW YORK, July 2.—The Giants bunched eight hits, including Mel Ott's 17th home run of the season and two singles each by Hank Leiber and Travis Jackson, in the second inning of today's game with the Phillies and coasted to an 8 to 4 victory before about 2000 fans.

Euel Moore, who started for the Quakers, was routed in the second-inning uprising when seven runs crossed the plate, and was replaced by Orville Jorgens, who twirled four scoreless innings until removed for a pinch-hitter in the seventh.

Pretzels Pezzullo then took the box and finished, allowing an unearned run in the eighth as Joe Moore was hit, Terry singled and Watkins fumbled.

Parmelee Notches 9th Victory.

Roy Parmelee, league-leading pitcher, went the route for the New Yorkers and was credited with his ninth victory against one defeat. After five scoreless innings he yielded a pair in the sixth as John Moore walked, Camilli doubled, Vergez singled and Haslin hit into a double play.

The Phils got their final two in the ninth. Haslin opened with a

Continued on Page 17, Column 8.

BENGE BLANKS BRAVES BY 5-0; ALLOWS 3 HITS

Dodger Hurler Walks Five; Brown Nicked for Eight Bingles.

By Associated Press

BROOKLYN, July 2. — Ray Benge, pitching a complete game for the first time since May 17, held the Boston Braves to three hits as the Brooklyn Dodgers won the first game of the series, 5 to 0, today.

The Braves, with Wally Berger getting the only extra-base hit, a double in the fourth, did not get a runner as far as third until the ninth, when Benge handed out two of his five walks.

Bob Brown was touched for eight blows, seven of which came in the first three innings when the Dodgers scored four of their runs.

BROOKLYN.	ab	r	h	o	a	BOSTON.	ab	r	h	o	a
Bord'ray, rf.	4	0	0	1	0	U'anski, ss.	3	0	0	1	2
Bucher, 3b..	4	2	2	3	2	Lee, lf.....	4	0	0	1	0
Frey, ss.....	4	1	1	2	7	Berger, cf..	3	0	1	8	0
Leslie, 1b...	4	1	2	12	0	Moore, rf..	2	0	0	3	1
Taylor, lf...	4	0	0	2	0	B.Jord'n, 1b	4	0	0	7	0
Koenecke, cf	3	1	2	1	0	Whitney, 3b	3	0	0	1	0
Phelps, c....	3	0	1	1	0	Mallon, 2b..	4	0	1	1	2
J.Jordan, 2b.	3	0	0	5	2	Spohrer, c..	3	0	1	2	0
Benge, p....	3	0	0	0	2	Brown, p..	3	0	0	0	1
Totals...	32	5	8	27	13	Totals....	29	0	3	24	6

Boston	0	0	0	0	0	0	0	0	0	—0
Brooklyn	1	1	2	0	1	0	0	0	x	—5

Error—Urbanski. Runs batted in—Leslie, 3; Koenecke, Phelps. Two-base hits—Berger, Bucher, Phelps, Leslie. Three-base hit—Frey. Double plays—Benge, Frey and Leslie; Moore and Spohrer. Left on bases—Boston, 7; Brooklyn, 5. Bases on balls—Benge, 5; Brown 2. Umpires—Reardon, Sears and Stewart.

LOU RECOVERS QUICKLY

In recovering from his baffling and persistent batting slump, Lou Gehrig, of the Yankees, gained 43 percentage points in the month of June to hop over the .300 mark.

America's Net Aces Advance With Straight-Set Victories; May Clash Again for Diadem

Mrs. Moody Given Fine Chance to Beat Joan Hartigan, but Helen Jacobs Meets Tourney's Steadiest Player in Mrs. Sperling, Denmark; Kay Stammers, Dorothy Round Bow in Upsets.

By JOHN R. TUNIS

Copyright, 1935, by Universal Service

WIMBLEDON, England, July 2.—Helen Wills Moody and Helen Hull Jacobs, America's hopes for the Wimbledon women's singles championship, blasted their way into the semifinal round with straight-set victories today to make the settling of their old feud a possibility.

Mrs. Moody crushed Mme. Rene Mathieu, ranking French star, 6-3, 6-0, in a battle of "errors," while Miss Jacobs chop-stroked to a 6-1, 9-7 triumph over Hedwig Jedrzejowska, of Poland.

Although the possibility of an all-American final is present, critics believe that either one or both of the Helens will fall in the semifinal round on Thursday.

Miss Jacobs May Lose.

Mrs. Moody, because of her greater experience, is given a fine chance of getting past Joan Hartigan, of Australia, but few look for Miss Jacobs to beat the brilliant Hilda Krahwinkel Sperling, of Denmark, who has been playing the steadiest tennis of any woman in the tournament.

Miss Hartigan accounted for the major upset of an unusually thrill-less day by eliminating Dorothy Round, England's defending champion, 6-4, 4-6, 6-3. The Australian's victory was well-deserved.

Her relentless and accurate forehand repeatedly left Miss Round standing helplessly as the ball swept by, and her resourceful fleet-footedness foiled Miss Round's attempt to expose her weak backhand.

Kay Stammers Bows.

Frau Sperling disposed of Katherine Stammers, England's third-ranking player, 7-5, 7-5, in the best match of the afternoon from every viewpoint. Both girls played a brilliant, resourceful game.

Miss Stammers' left-handed drives to the corners were countered by the Frau Sperling's persistent retrieving, each taking the net in turn and playing a fine all-court game.

Miss Stammers, after dropping the first, had a 5-2 lead in the second set, but faded under the persistent rain of her opponent's shots toward the end.

Mrs. Moody's driving today, the speediest she has shown yet in her comeback attempt, was the only bright spot of her game and should help her in her match with the 19-year-old Miss Hartigan. But it was the errors of her French opponent which enabled the Californian to come through as easily as she did.

Little Trouble for Mrs. Moody.

Mme. Mathieu attempted to swap drives from the baseline, resulting in endless rallies and usually finishing with nets or outs on one side or the other. At the finish of the set, Mrs. Moody made 28 errors to Mme. Mathieu's 35, in nine games, showing the poor quality of the play.

Mrs. Moody regained control in the second set, although she was not putting her first service over the net, and scored point after point with unassilable placements.

The French veteran tried heroically to slow up the game, lobbing over continuously, but to no avail.

Miss Jacobs had too much experience for her Polish opponent. Mlle. Jedrzejowska was nervous in the first set, misjudging the spin of the American's shots, but she recovered in the second, and scored frequently with her tremendous forehand drive.

Budge, Mako Advance.

Miss Jacobs, however, used her chop-shots with great effect, cross-volleyed beautifully and pulled up from 2-4 to 6-all and then set and match.

Red-haired Donald Budge and Gene Mako, America's Davis Cup "frehmen" advanced to the fourth round of the men's doubles with a victory over the English combination of I. J. Collins and Frank H. D. Wilde, 6-3, 6-2, 12-14, 6-4.

Mako was erratic in the first two sets, double-faulting frequently, but Budge's sterling play made up for his partner's occasional lapses.

McGrath, Turnbull Beaten.

There was a big surprise earlier in the day when the highly-rated Australian team of Vivian McGrath and Don Turnbull fell before Max Bertram and Walter Musgrove, a South African pair, 7-5, 2-6, 6-3, 2-6, 6-4, in a second round match.

Sidney B. Wood, Jr., of New York and the American Davis Cup team, and his Spanish partner, Enrique Maier, gained the third round, defeating Martin Legeay and J. Lesueur, of France, 2-6, 3-6, 6-4, 6-4, 6-2.

Umpire O'Day Called 'Out' by Great Arbiter

HANK O'DAY IN HEYDAY

Death Claims Man Who Gave Verdict on Merkle's 'Boner.'

CHICAGO, July 2 (AP).—The Great Arbiter called a great arbiter "out" today as Hank O'Day closed his eyes in death.

Loser in a courageous battle for life, a fight destined to be lost at the start of his illness months ago, O'Day, one of baseball's greatest umpires, died in the Presbyterian Hospital of cancer and bronchial pneumonia.

The man whose eyes saw 1,000,000 plays on the diamond in his 50 years' connection with the game, including the never-to-be-forgotten "bonehead" play of Fred Merkle, first baseman for the New York Giants, that cost the Giants the National League championship in 1908, passed on peacefully.

No one knew his exact age, but the best guess is that he was 74 years old. He was born in 1861, according to baseball record books, but he never would admit it. He lived in hotels most of his life and had no close relatives, so far as is known.

He Was "The Reverend."

The picturesque figure, with a somber face that caused him to be called "The Reverend" in baseball circles, O'Day was best known as an umpire in the National League, but he interrupted his career calling balls and strikes long enough to manage the Cincinnati Reds in 1912 and the Chicago Cubs in 1914.

He started his career as a pitcher and played with New York, Washington and Pittsburgh, besides minor league clubs, before joining the National League as an umpire in 1895. He served as umpire-in-chief until retired in 1927. He was on the payroll of the league at the time of his death.

Called "Bonehead" Play.

As long as baseball is played, perhaps long after the exploits of the game's greatest heroes have faded in memory, the famous "bonehead" play of Fred Merkle, first baseman of the New York Giants, will linger as the never to be forgotten legend of the diamond.

O'Day, a product of the old

Continued on Page 17, Column 4.

Breadon Sees Cardinals Winner in Stretch

* * *

Expects St. Louis Club to Repeat Its 'Punch' Finish of 1934

ST. LOUIS, July 2 (AP).

SAM BREADON, the Cardinals' No. 1 worrier, today still was confident his slipping world champions would launch one of their famous "home stretch" spurts and capture the 1935 National League pennant.

The volatile club president, undismayed by the Redbirds' disastrous road tour and their drop from second to fourth place rank, found his chief consolation in history—which he hopes will repeat itself.

"We've been farther behind than this in other years and won pennants," said Breadon, waxing statistical. "In 1930 we were 12 games behind in August and we went on to the championship and last season we were seven behind on Labor Day and still we won."

"But Sam, don't you think your pitching staff then was better than it is this season?"

The seer's "y-e-e-s" was a little reluctant.

"But we have more power this year," he countered. "We are making more runs than we ever made and the pitchers won't have to show any tremendous improvement to put us back in stride.

"If Paul Dean and Bill Walker were old men it would be different. You might conclude that they were washed up. But Paul's arm is as strong as ever and Walker is still a young pitcher."

With the season only at the halfway mark, Breadon thought the fanfare and catcalls about the Cardinals being on the downgrade somewhat premature. He looks for Manager Frankie Frisch and his temperamental followers to uncork a "punch" finish.

"Teams and pitchers have been in slumps before and it is still early," he said. "We have two long stands at home and I look for a winning streak that will put us back in the thick of competition."

Except for recalling Dick Ward from Rochester, Breadon said there was little likelihood of adding further to the Cardinal hurling strength this season. Ward joined the Red Birds yesterday,

Cubs Trounce Dodgers Again, 10-4, Behind Carleton, Scoring 6 Runs in 6th, Routing Clark

Brooklyn's Laxity Afield Speeds Chicago to Victory

Bordagaray, After Poling Homer in First, Helps Rivals to Score by Sitting Down in Vain Effort to Catch Fly; Frey Also Connects for Circuit

By Arthur E. Patterson

CHICAGO, June 6.—They laughed when Frenchy Bordagaray sat down to field a fly ball at Wrigley Field this afternoon. But, unlike the correspondence school piano player, the Dodger outfielder and his teammates had nothing to show the Cubs and some 7,000 fans to halt their merriment.

Instead they continued to amuse and eventually bowed gracefully—one of the few things they do gracefully—by a 10-to-4 score.

Perhaps it is silly to mix melodrama with such fun, but the fact remains that William Watson Clark, the sad-faced southpaw, was more morose than ever this evening and not without reason, for he had hurled in high-class fashion until the moment Bordagaray provided the Cubs with the break of the game. No defeat he has suffered or will suffer this season will be more difficult for him to forget.

Carleton Gains Control

As a matter of fact, Clark, a few minutes before, had smashed out a single and put the Dodgers in front, 3 to 2, when it began to look as though pitching, alone, would not do. The Dodgers had made three hits, including a home run, and had received a walk in the first inning for the minimum total of one run. They had scored another in the second, but once again left the bags fully inhabited. But after that Tex Carleton gained control of the situation and became embroiled in a mound duel with Clark.

In the fourth Clark allowed the second hit of the game, a single to center by Billy Herman. Tossing just the right ball to Augie Galan for a double-play roller to Ben Geraghty, Clark watched his shortstop lose the ball. Hartnett also rolled an easy grounder to Lonnie Frey and once more a double play seemed assured, but this time Geraghty didn't get over to cover second base so Frey and Clark had to be satisfied with a single out. Eventually a fly to left scored the inning's only run. Phil Cavarretta's home run out of the park tied the count, but Brooklyn went out in front again when Ray Berres doubled and Clark singled to right in the sixth.

After that the storm. Clark walked Hartnett after Galan had been tossed out by Frey. Demaree then lifted a towering fly to center field. Suddenly it was apparent that Bordagaray had misjudged the ball and as he put on the brakes he slid to a sitting position, the ball just missing his head and dropping for a single. Unnerved, Clark walked Ethan Allen and when Cavarretta doubled the bases were cleared and Clark walked dejectedly to the dugout.

Twelve Hits for Cubs

George Earnshaw, George Jeffcoat and Emil Leonard assisted the Cubs to their third successive day of double figures for hits, raising the total to an even dozen. Earnshaw was tagged for three runs before the sixth inning was over. Jeffcoat chipped in with a balk in a two-run seventh and Leonard squeezed through the eighth after yielding a single and a double. Little did it matter that Frey rammed his third home run of the season into the right-field bleachers in the eighth.

The Dodger first was, in itself, something of a madcap affair. Bordagaray started like a hero with a homer to right, his second of the season. When Watkins and Stripp singled Charlie Root and Roy Henshaw warmed up feverishly in the bull pen. Attempting a sacrifice bunt, Hassett hit into a force play at third, then Bucher forced Hassett. A base on balls to Frey filled the bags but Geraghty flied to left.

The punch was missing at the right moment in the second, too, when Gene Lillard muffed Berres's liner at third. Clark forced Berres but Bordagaray bunted safely and Watkins singled to right, crowding the corners. The Cubs missed a double play by inches on Stripp's grounder and a run came over. After Hassett walked Bucher was an easy out, Herman to Cavarretta.

Infielders Rob Each Other

Lillard and Stripp exchanged great catches in the fifth when the Cub third baseman robbed the Brooklyn guardian of that station of a sure two-bagger and vice versa.

The snappiest play of the game, however, was Herman's stop and throw on Bucher's slow grounder behind the box.

Stan Hack was out of the line-up and may be on the side lines for a few days. He took one of Red Corriden's infield-drill balls between the eyes just before the game and is sporting a pair of blacked orbs.

The Dodgers have lost Johnny Cooney for a few days. His heel is bruised.

Before the sixth-inning travesty Bordagaray was in line to be something of a star for the day. His two hits in the early frames put him at .300. He had batted .181 as late as May 26.

The score:

BROOKLYN (N. L.)	ab	r	h	po	a	e
Bordag'y, cf	5	1	2	1	0	0
Watkins, rf	5	0	2	3	0	0
Stripp, 3b	4	0	1	1	1	0
Hassett, 1b	3	0	1	8	0	0
Bucher, lf	4	0	0	3	0	0
Frey, 2b	3	1	1	3	4	0
Geraghty, ss	4	0	0	1	4	1
Berres, c	4	1	1	5	0	0
CLARK, p	3	1	1	0	0	0
EARNS'W, p	0	0	0	0	0	0
JEFFC'T, p	0	0	0	0	0	0
LEON'D, p	1	0	0	0	0	0
Totals	36	4	9	24	9	1

CHICAGO (N. L.)	ab	r	h	po	a	e
Lillard, 3b	5	1	1	2	2	1
Herman, 2b	4	1	1	3	6	0
Galan, cf	5	0	2	2	0	0
Hartnett, c	4	1	1	3	2	0
Demaree, rf	4	2	2	1	0	0
Allen, lf	3	2	1	3	0	0
Cavar'ta, 1b	3	2	2	11	0	0
English, ss	4	0	0	2	4	0
CARLE'N, p	4	1	2	0	0	0
Totals	36	10	12	27	14	1

Brooklyn .... 110 001 010—4
Chicago .... 000 116 20x—10

Runs batted in—Bordagaray, Stripp, Frey, Clark, Galan (2), Demaree, Cavarretta (4), English, Carleton. Two-base hits—Berres, Hartnett, Cavarretta. Home runs—Bordagaray, Cavarretta, Frey. Stolen base—Galan. Double play—Herman and Cavarretta. Left on bases—Brooklyn, 7; Chicago, 8. Bases on balls—Off Clark, 3; off Earnshaw, 1; off Jeffcoat, 2; off Carleton, 2. Struck out—By Clark, 2; by Jeffcoat, 1; by Leonard, 1; by Carleton, 3. Hits—Off Clark, 6 in 5 1-3 innings; off Earnshaw, 3 in 2-3; off Jeffcoat, 1 in 1; off Leonard, 2 in 1. Balk—Jeffcoat. Losing pitcher—Clark. Umpires—Klem, Sears and Ballanfant. Time—2:02.

Leading Five Batsmen In Each Major League

AMERICAN LEAGUE

Player and Club	G.	AB.	R.	H.	Pct.
Sullivan, Cleveland	30	100	15	42	.420
DiMaggio, New York	31	148	34	55	.372
Radcliff, Chicago	31	118	22	43	.365
Appling, Chicago	36	139	22	50	.360
Gehrig, New York	40	184	58	66	.359

NATIONAL LEAGUE

Player and Club	G.	AB.	R.	H.	Pct.
Terry, New York	28	75	16	30	.400
S. Martin, St. Louis	37	121	30	47	.388
Medwick, St. Louis	47	194	28	70	.361
J. Moore, Phila	43	172	38	62	.360
Jordan, Boston	51	208	34	74	.356

Tigers Defeat Senators, 10-4, Behind Rowe

Reiber, Catching for Ailing Cochrane, Leads 13-Hit Attack With 3 Singles

By The Associated Press

WASHINGTON, June 6.—Yielding only seven hits, Schoolboy Rowe held the Washington Senators in check today while his Detroit Tiger teammates clubbed out a 10-to-4 victory.

Three Washington pitchers tried unsuccessfully to tame the Tigers, who again were playing without their ailing manager, Mickey Cochrane. The visitors collected thirteen hits, three of which were singles by Reiber, catching in place of Cochrane, in four times up.

Rowe was making his first pitching start since May 30, when he was charged with his second straight loss and dropped out of the regular mound order because of a tooth ailment. Buddy Lewis's double was the only extra base hit he allowed today, while striking out two and allowing three bases on balls.

The score:

DETROIT (A. L.)	ab	r	h	po	a	e
Rogell, ss	4	1	2	2	5	0
Fox, rf	5	3	1	2	0	0
Gehri'r, 2b	4	0	2	6	4	0
Goslin, lf	4	0	1	1	0	0
Walker, cf	5	1	1	3	0	1
Burns, 1b	4	0	1	8	2	1
Owen, 3b	5	1	1	1	0	0
Reiber, c	4	3	3	2	0	0
ROWE, p	2	1	1	2	3	0
Totals	37	10	13	27	14	2

WASHINGTON (A. L.)	ab	r	h	po	a	e
Powell, cf	4	1	1	1	0	0
Lewis, 3b	5	1	2	0	2	1
Bluege, 2b	3	1	1	5	2	0
Stone, lf	3	0	1	7	0	1
Travis, rf	4	1	0	2	0	0
Kuhel, 1b	4	0	1	7	0	0
Kress, ss	4	0	0	2	4	0
Bolton, c	4	0	1	3	1	0
DE S'G, p	2	0	0	0	2	0
RUSS'LL, p	0	0	0	0	1	0
LINKE, p	0	0	0	0	1	0
*Reynolds	1	0	0	0	0	0
†Miles	1	0	0	0	0	0
Total	35	4	7	27	13	2

*Batted for De Shong in seventh inning.
†Batted for Russell in eighth inning.

Detroit .... 100 104 031—10
Washington .... 002 000 020—4

Runs batted in—Gehringer (3), Lewis, Rogell (2), Fox (3), Kuhel, Bolton, Owen. Two-base hits—Lewis, Gehringer, Fox, Walker. Three-base hit—Goslin. Stolen base—Powell. Sacrifices—Bluege, Rowe, Burns. Double play—Kress, Bluege and Kuhel. Left on bases—Detroit, 8; Washington, 8. Bases on balls—Off Rowe, 2; off De Shong, 6. Struck out—By Rowe, 2; by De Shong, 2. Hits—Off De Shong, 8 in 7 innings; off Russell, 3 in 1; off Linke, 2 in 1. Passed ball—Reiber. Winning pitcher—Rowe. Losing pitcher—De Shong. Umpires—Hubbard, Dinneen and Geisel. Time—2:35.

A's Rally, Win First, 6-5; Browns Take Second, 5-3

PHILADELPHIA, June 6 (AP).—The Athletics and the St. Louis Browns divided a double-header today, the Mackmen taking the first game, 6 to 5, and the Missourians the second, 5 to 3.

The Athletics scored their triumph with a six-run rally in the seventh inning. Dean, a pinch-hitting role, doubled three runners across the plate and Warstler came up later with two on and hit for the circuit, wiping out Al Thomas's 5-to-0 lead.

Earl Caldwell won his own game in the nightcap by hitting a ninth-inning home run after a double by Carey. Frankie Hayes had hit for the circuit in the previous inning, tying the score at 3 to 3.

The scores:

FIRST GAME

ST. LOUIS (A. L.)	ab	r	h	po	a	e
Lary, ss	5	0	1	0	4	0
Clift, 3b	4	0	1	0	1	0
Solters, lf	4	0	0	3	0	0
Bottom'y, 1b	4	1	2	8	0	0
Bell, rf	4	1	1	2	0	0
West, cf	5	1	2	2	0	0
Hemley, c	3	0	1	4	0	0
Carey, 2b	4	2	3	5	2	2
THOMAS, p	1	0	0	0	2	0
*Coleman	0	0	0	0	0	0
KNOTT, p	0	0	0	0	0	0
Totals	34	5	11	24	9	2

PHILADELPHIA (A.L.)	ab	r	h	po	a	e
Finney, f	3	1	1	11	1	0
Warstler, 2b	3	1	2	2	3	0
Moses, cf	4	0	0	1	0	0
Puc'nelli, rf	4	0	0	1	0	0
Higgins, 3b	4	1	2	1	0	0
Johnson, lf	4	0	1	1	0	0
Niemiec, ss	4	1	1	4	2	0
Hayes, c	3	1	0	6	0	1
FINK, p	1	0	0	0	0	0
†Dean	1	1	1	0	0	0
DIET'CH, p	0	0	0	0	1	0
Totals	31	6	8	27	7	1

*Batted for Thomas in eighth inning.
†Batted for Fink in seventh innnig.

St. Louis .... 011 300 000—5
Philadelphia .... 000 000 60x—6

Runs batted in—Clift, West, Carey, Lary, Dean (3), Warstler (3). Two-base hits—Bottomley, Carey, Clift, West, Warstler, Hemsley, Dean. Three-base hit—Johnson. Home run—Warstler. Stolen base—Lary. Sacrifices—Thomas (2), Warstler, Hemsley, Bottomley. Double plays—Lary, Carey and Bottomley (2); Warstler, Niemiec and Finney. Left on bases—St. Louis, 10; Philadelphia, 4. Bases on balls—Off Thomas, 1; off Fink, 2; off Dietrich, 2. Struck out—By Thomas, 1; by Fink, 4; by Dietrich, 2. Hits—Off Thomas, 7 in 7 innings; off Knott, 1 in 1; off Fink, 9 in 7; off Dietrich, 2 in 2. Hit by pitcher—By Thomas (Fink). Winning pitcher—Fink. Losing pitcher—Thomas. Umpires Moriarty, Basil and Kolls. Time—2:02.

SECOND GAME

ST. LOUIS (A. L.)	ab	r	h	po	a	e
Lary, ss	5	1	1	4	6	0
Clift, 3b	5	0	1	1	2	0
Solters, cf.lf	5	2	1	1	0	0
Bottom'y, 1b	4	0	1	13	0	0
Bell, lf.rf	4	0	2	1	0	0
Coleman, rf	4	0	1	1	0	0
West, cf	0	0	0	0	0	0
Hemsley, c	4	0	1	6	2	1
Carey, 2b	4	1	1	0	2	0
CALD'L, p	4	1	2	0	2	0
Totals	39	5	11	27	14	1

PHILADELPHIA (A. L.)	ab	r	h	po	a	e
Finney, 1b	4	0	0	15	0	0
Warstler, 2b	4	1	2	1	9	0
Moses, cf	2	1	0	1	0	0
Pucci'li, rf	4	0	0	2	0	0
Higgins, 3b	4	0	1	0	1	0
Johnson, lf	3	0	1	1	0	0
Niemiec, ss	4	0	0	4	6	0
Hayes, c	3	1	2	3	1	0
KELLEY, p	3	0	0	0	0	0
Totals	31	3	6	27	17	0

St. Louis .... 200 001 002—5
Philadelphia .... 100 100 100—3

Runs batted in—Solters, Bottomley, Bell, Caldwell (2), Moses, Higgins, Hayes. Two-base hits—Hemsley, Caldwell, Carey. Three-base hits—Solters, Warstler, Coleman. Home runs—Hayes, Caldwell. Double play—Carey, Lary and Bottomley. Left on bases—St. Louis, 8; Philadelphia, 4. Bases on balls—Off Caldwell, 3; off Kelley, 1. Struck out—By Caldwell, 4; by Kelley, 3. Umpires—Basil, Kolls and Moriarty. Time—1:45.

Seeds Paces Montreal As Baltimore Bows, 12-9

BALTIMORE, June 6 (AP).—Montreal closed its series today by winning from the Orioles, 12 to 9, for the only victory in the series.

The Royals, led by Bob Seeds, who hit a homer and three doubles, belted four Bird hurlers for fifteen hits, while the flock nailed three Royal heavers for an even dozen.

Bill Cissell paced the Oriole attack with a homer, double and three singles.

The score by innings:

				R.	H.	E.
Montreal	[illegible]	[illegible]	[illegible]	12	15	1
Baltimore	[illegible]	[illegible]	[illegible]	9	13	2

Batteries—Johnson, Wade, Smythe and Tate; Pearce, Lohrman, Bivin, Berly and Savino, Florence.

Los Angeles Gets Stephenson

CHICAGO, June 6 (AP).—In answer to manager Jack Lelivelt's personal visit the Chicago Cubs today turned over their third-string catcher, Walter Stephenson, to the Los Angeles club of the Pacific Coast League, a Cub farm. Stephenson, consigned on option, departed for the coast tonight.

Four Players Who Are Helping to Keep the Yankees in Lead

Herald Tribune photo—Acme

Left to right, Frank Crosetti, Lou Gehrig, Joe DiMaggio and Ben Chapman, whose batting has carried the team to many victories when the pitchers have failed. DiMaggio, the sensational coast recruit, is leading the team in hitting and on occasion has been leading the league

Harder Halts Yankees, 4-2, For Indians

(Continued from page one)

that the Yankee captain had an easy play at the plate.

A clean-cut Indian run came over in the sixth, when Earl Averill doubled and Sullivan, the league's leading hitter, scored him with his second of three hits. In the eighth Sullivan, Trosky and Vosmik singled successively with two out, and Sullivan scored.

Roy Johnson came within a few feet of putting the Yankees back in the running when he batted for Arndt Jorgens in the seventh with Selkirk on second. He hit a tremendous drive into the right-field bleachers just to the wrong side of the foul mark. Having done that, he popped out.

Steve O'Neill, the Indians' manager, made a radical shift in his batting order, moving Sullivan to the clean-up position. The latter hit the ball fiercely four times, but once Chapman came in fast enough and caught the ball at the level of his knees.

Selkirk missed a chance for a smart play in the ninth. With a man on first he came in and caught Harder's short fly. If he had dropped it he had an easy force play at second, and would have made the enemy pitcher run bases.

DiMaggio made up for his early faux pas with a great catch of Odell Hale's clout in the sixth, taking the ball over his shoulder on the running track.

Joe Gould, manager of Jimmy Braddock, the heavyweight champion, wired Jim Kahn, the official scorer, protesting that Chapman should have been given a hit on a double play ball which Hughes mangled Friday. Gould should stick to boxing.

Joe McCarthy is maneuvering so that he will have his three best pitchers, Gomez, Pearson and Ruffing, to throw at the Detroit Tigers when they come in Thursday. Ruffing will work today, probably against Johnny Allen.

DiMaggio will give the New York police ball team a lesson in batting before tomorrow's game. The minions of the law are getting ready for their annual game with the fireman in the Polo Grounds on June 13.

The score:

CLEVELAND (A. L.)	ab	r	h	po	a	e
Galatzer, rf	1	0	0	1	0	0
Hughes, 2b	5	0	0	2	3	0
Averill, cf	4	1	1	0	0	0
Sullivan, c	4	2	3	4	0	0
Trosky, 1b	4	1	2	11	1	0
Vosmik, lf	3	0	1	2	0	0
Hale, 3b	3	0	0	4	2	0
Knick'er, ss	4	0	1	2	5	0
HARDER, p	4	0	1	1	0	0
Totals	32	4	9	27	11	0

NEW YORK (A. L.)	ab	r	h	po	a	e
Crosetti, ss	4	0	1	2	2	0
Rolfe, 3b	4	0	1	2	3	0
DiMaggio, lf	4	0	0	2	0	0
Gehrig, 1b	4	1	1	8	1	0
Selkirk, rf	4	0	2	4	0	0
Chapman, cf	3	0	0	3	0	0
Lazzeri, 2b	3	1	1	2	3	0
Jorgens, c	2	0	0	3	1	0
*Johnson	1	0	0	0	0	0
Glenn, c	0	0	0	0	0	0
PEARS'N, p	2	0	0	1	1	0
†Ruffing	1	0	0	0	0	0
HADLEY, p	0	0	0	0	0	0
Totals	32	2	6	27	11	0

*Batted for Jorgens in seventh inning.
†Batted for Pearson in eighth inning.

Cleveland .... 010 101 010—4
New York .... 020 000 000—2

Runs batted in—Trosky, Gehrig, Lazzeri, Vosmik (2), Sullivan. Two-base hits—Rolfe, Averill. Three-base hits—Sullivan, Trosky. Home runs—Gehrig, Lazzeri. Stolen base—Galatzer. Sacrifices—Galatzer, Chapman. Double play—Lazzeri, Crosetti and Gehrig. Left on bases—New York, 4; Cleveland, 7. Bases on balls—Off Pearson, 3; off Hadley, 2. Struck out—By Pearson, 3; by Harder, 4. Hits—Off Pearson, 9 in 8 innings; off Hadley, 0 in 1. Losing pitcher—Pearson. Umpires—Summers, Owens and Johnston. Time—2:07.

Syracuse Gets 4 in 8th And Beats Toronto, 11-7

SYRACUSE, June 6 (AP).—The Chiefs spotted Toronto's Maple Leafs four runs in the second inning and one more in the third, came from behind twice to tie the score and then slugged their way to an 11 to 7 victory this afternoon, clinching the verdict with a four-run splurge in the eighth.

Babe Dahlgren collected a homer for the Chiefs, while Nick Dallessandro blasted out two doubles and a triple in four trips to the plate.

The score by innings:

				R.	H.	E.
Toronto	041	000	110	7	10	2
Syracuse	000	122	24x	11	12	3

Batteries—Hermann, Mooty, Lucas, Nekola, Cooke and Erickson; Starr, Fussell and Heving, Legett.

David Jones Wins Abroad

HARPENDEN England, June 6 (AP).—David N. Jones, former Columbia University tennis star, took the singles title in a local tennis tournament today. The American defeated the Chinese Davis Cup player, Gordon Lum, 6—1, 9—7, in the final. In the mixed doubles Jones and Mrs. W. J. Dyson defeated K. Chartikavant and Miss J. Saunders, 6—2, 6—1.

Giants Win 2 Games From Cards And Cut Their Lead to 2 Games

(Continued from page one)

off the center-field wall. Whitehead rapped a single off Durocher's glove, scoring Moore. Leslie walked. Then Ott hit his eleventh homer of the season and his fourth in three days onto the right-field roof.

Frisch threw out Leiber, but Mancuso doubled to left. When Parmelee walked Mayo he was through. Bill Cox, a right-hander acquired from Columbus at the time Munns was brought up from Rochester, emulated Munns by coming in and stopping a rally. But the Giants picked up four runs that inning to lead, 6 to 0.

Giants Score in Sixth

In the sixth the Giants scored again. Whitehead doubled to right and Leslie brought him in with a single. It began to rain.

Cox was removed for a pinch hitter and old Jess Haines faced the Giants in the seventh. They were leading, 7 to 0, and Smith had a one-hit game until Pepper Martin knocked a double off the right-field screen in the seventh. The rain was coming down hard by this time, in drops so large they looked like snow. After Medwick and Collins were retired ending the inning, time was called.

The wind rose. The rain turned to hail and sounded like pebbles on the roof. Thunder rumbled. As suddenly as it had gathered force, the storm subsided, leaving puddles on the infield. Ground keepers went to work with brooms, sweeping water and also obliterating the foul lines. Then they dumped buckets of molders' sand on the infield.

The Cardinals died hard. Seven runs behind and only two innings to go against a pitcher off whom they had made only two hits, the Gas House Gang did everything possible to keep the game going.

At the end of one hour and three minutes Ernie Quigley, the umpire, called the game off.

Hubbell Wins Opener

Hubbell was nicked for twelve hits while winning the opener.

It was a tie game until the seventh, when Durocher, the captain of the Gas House Gang, failed to stop Hank Leiber's hard grounder and let Whitehead come in with the winning run.

It wasn't Durocher's day. After letting in the winning run, he had a chance to tie the score in the Cards' seventh. He led off with a prodigious triple against the center-field wall. Frisch followed with one of those high-bounding grounders which cannot be hurried. Durocher could have scored easily, but Mike Gonzales, the coach, held him on third while Bartel was making a close play to get Frisch. Hubbell then fanned Leslie Munns, the pitcher, and got Terry Moore to pop to Bartel.

After that Hubbell was in no great danger. Pepper Martin made his fourth straight hit in the eighth, but he was caught a moment later in a double play, Whitehead neatly avoiding Martin's efforts to sweep him off his feet. Durocher got his third hit in the ninth, but there were two out and Frisch made it three, hoisting a fly to Joe Moore.

Except for the Giants' winning run in the seventh, all the scoring was done in the first three innings. The Giants made one in the first inning. So did the Cardinals. Ed Heusser was pitching then for the Cards.

Heusser Routed in Second

The Giants routed him with a two-run attack in the second. In this, Eddie Mayo hit his first major-league home run, a line drive into the right center-field pavilion. Bartell walked and was forced by Hubbell, who scored from first on Joe Moore's double. Moore made four hits in a row before the Cards got him out in the ninth.

Davis hit a double off the left-field wall, scoring Collins in the second, and Stu Martin banged a triple into left center field and scored on J. Martin's single in the third, tying it up.

Munns, a former Dodger recently acquired from Rochester, did a splendid job of relief pitching. He replaced Heusser with one out and a man on second in the second inning and stopped the Giant rally. Going on from there Munns yielded only two hits in the next seven innings. His most worrisome inning was the fourth, when he started the inning by walking Mayo and Bartell. But Munns escaped as Hubbell forced Mayo at third. Moore made an infield hit. But Whitehead forced Bartell at the plate and Terry forced Whitehead at second.

In the seventh Munns was betrayed by his captain. Joe Moore had opened the inning with his fourth hit only to be forced by Whitehead. Terry flied out. Then Whitehead made victory possible by stealing second. Ott walked. Then came Leiber's grounder and the error which cost the Cards the ball game.

It was Danning's first participation in a game since the knuckle of his right forefinger was fractured in Hubbell's seventeen-inning game here on April 29.

The Giants got nothing out of two singles and a double in the second inning of the second game. Leiber, who in this series has looked from time to time like a farmer on relief in center field, was on second base when Mayo hit a double off the right-field wall. Stu Martin got the ball on the rebound and threw Leiber out at the plate. Either Stu Martin is awfully good, or Leiber is awfully slow. There is not much argument about Martin's being good.

Giants' Scores

* * *

FIRST GAME

NEW YORK (N. L.)	ab	r	h	po	a	e
J. Moore, lf	5	1	4	3	0	0
Whiteh'd, 2b	5	1	1	4	4	0
Terry, 1b	5	0	0	8	1	0
Ott, rf	2	0	1	2	0	0
Leiber, cf	4	0	1	2	0	0
Danning, c	4	0	0	3	2	0
Mayo, 3b	3	1	1	4	2	0
Bartell, ss	2	0	0	1	2	0
HUBB'L, p	4	1	0	0	1	0
Totals	34	4	8	27	12	0

ST. LOUIS (N. L.)	ab	r	h	po	a	e
T. Moore, cf	4	1	1	1	0	0
S.Martin, 2b	3	1	1	1	11	0
J. Martin, rf	4	0	4	0	0	0
Medwick, lf	4	0	0	1	0	0
Collins, 1b	3	1	1	15	0	0
Davis, c	4	0	1	2	1	0
Durocher, ss	4	0	3	4	4	1
Frisch, 3b	4	0	1	3	0	0
HEUSSER, p	0	0	0	0	0	0
MUNNS, p	3	0	0	0	6	0
Totals	33	3	12	27	22	1

New York .... 120 000 100—4
St. Louis .... 111 000 000—3

Runs batted in—Ott, Mayo, J. Moore, J. Martin (2), Davis. Two-base hits—J. Moore, Davis. Three-base hits—S. Martin, Durocher. Home run—Mayo. Stolen base—Whitehead. Sacrifice—S. Martin. Double plays—S. Martin, Durocher and Collins; Bartell, Whitehead and Terry. Left on bases—St. Louis, 5; New York, 8. Bases on balls—Off Munns, 4. Struck out—By Hubbell, 2; by Munns, 1. Hits—Off Heusser, 6 in 1 1-3 innings; off Munns, 2 in 7 2-3. Hit by pitcher—By Heusser (Bartell); by Hubbell (Collins). Winning pitcher—Hubbell. Losing pitcher—Munns. Umpires—Magerkurth, Quigley and Moran. Time—2:07.

SECOND GAME

NEW YORK (N. L.)	ab	r	h	po	a	e
J. Moore, lf	4	2	2	1	0	0
Whiteh'd, 2b	5	2	3	0	2	0
Leslie, 1b	3	1	2	5	0	0
Ott, rf	4	1	1	3	0	0
Leiber, cf	4	0	1	4	0	0
Mancuso, c	4	0	3	8	0	0
Mayo, 3b	3	0	1	0	0	0
Bartell, ss	4	0	1	0	2	0
SMITH, p	2	1	0	0	1	0
Totals	33	7	14	21	5	0

ST. LOUIS (N. L.)	ab	r	h	po	a	e
T.Moore, cf	3	0	1	4	0	0
S.Martin, 2b	3	0	0	1	2	0
J.Martin, rf	3	0	1	2	0	0
Medwick, lf	3	0	0	4	0	0
Collins, 1b	3	0	0	6	0	0
Duro'r, ss	2	0	0	0	1	0
Frisch, 3b	2	0	0	1	2	0
Vergez, 3b	0	0	0	0	0	0
Ogrod'ski, c	2	0	0	3	0	0
PARM'E, p	1	0	0	0	0	0
COX, p	0	0	0	0	0	0
HAINES, p	0	0	0	0	2	0
†Gelbert	1	0	0	0	0	0
Totals	23	0	2	*21	7	0

*Game called at end of seventh inning.
†Batted for Cox in sixth inning.

New York .... 002 041 0—7
St. Louis .... 000 000 0—0

Runs batted in—Leslie (2), Ott (4), Whitehead. Two-base hits—Mayo, T. Moore, Mancuso, Whitehead, J. Martin. Three-base hit—J. Moore. Home run—Ott. Sacrifice—Smith. Left on bases—St. Louis, 2; New York, 10. Bases on balls—Off Parmelee, 2; off Haines, 1. Struck out—By Smith, 6; by Parmelee, 1; by Cox, 1. Hits—Off Parmelee, 10 in 4 1-3 innings; off Cox, 2 in 1 2-3; off Haines, 2 in 1. Hit by pitcher—By Parmelee (Smith). Wild pitch—Parmelee. Winning pitcher—Smith. Losing pitcher—Parmelee. Umpires—Quigley, Moran and Magerkurth. Time—1:42.

Rochester Beats Newark With 5 Runs in 4th, 8-3

NEWARK, N. J., June 6 (AP).—Rochester won the odd game of a three-game series with the Newark Bears today, 8 to 3. A five-run splurge in the fourth inning sewed up the decision for the Red Wings.

Spud Chandler started on the hill for Newark and was hit freely until he was replaced in the eighth by Al Piechota. Ray Harrell, who has yet to go the route for the Wings this season, was credited with his second victory.

The score:

ROCHESTER (I. L.)	ab	r	h	po	a	e
Brown, ss	5	1	2	2	2	0
Cuccin'lo, 2b	5	1	1	3	2	0
Rothrock, rf	5	0	2	2	0	0
Weintr'b, 1b	4	1	3	11	1	0
Mills, cf	2	1	0	4	0	0
Sturdy, 3b	4	2	2	3	4	0
Scoffic, lf	4	1	1	1	0	0
Poland, c	3	1	2	1	0	1
HARR'L, p	2	0	1	0	1	0
KLING'R, p	0	0	0	0	2	0
Totals	34	8	14	27	12	1

NEWARK (I. L.)	ab	r	h	po	a	e
May, 3b	4	0	3	1	1	0
Boyle, rf	4	1	2	0	0	1
Schalk, 2b	5	0	1	2	7	0
Koy, cf	4	0	1	1	0	0
McCar'y, 1b	4	1	2	17	1	0
Baker, c	3	1	2	3	1	0
Rosen'ld, lf	3	0	0	0	0	0
Rich'son, ss	5	0	0	3	3	0
CHAND'R, p	3	0	0	0	5	0
DUKE, p	0	0	0	0	1	0
*Piechota	1	0	0	0	0	0
Totals	35	3	11	27	19	1

*Batted for Chandler in eighth inning.

Rochester .... 100 500 011—8
Newark .... 000 002 100—3

Runs batted in—Weintraub, Scoffic (2), Poland (3), Brown, Baker (2), Boyle, Rothrock. Two-base hits—Cuccinello, Harrell. Home runs—Baker, Boyle. Stolen bases—Baker, Mills, Sturdy. Sacrifices—Harrell, Scoffic, Brown. Double plays—Schalk, Richardson and McCarthy; Sturdy and Weintraub; Cuccinello and Weintraub; Richardson, Schalk and McCarthy. Left on bases—Newark, 11; Rochester, 6. Bases on balls—Off Harrell, 5; off Chandler, 2; off Piechota, 1; off Klinger, 3. Struck out—By Chandler, 5. Hits—Off Harrell, 8 in 6 innings; off Klinger, 3 in 3; off Chandler, 13 in 8; off Piechota, 1 in 1. Winning pitcher—Harrell. Losing pitcher—Chandler. Umpires—Jorda, White and Tobin. Time—2:35.

Red Sox Down WhiteSox, 10-6, For 5 Straight

Victory Cuts New York Lead to 1½ Games; Bonura Hits 2 Homers, Piet One

By The Associated Press

BOSTON, June 6.—The home run slugging of Zeke Bonura and Tony Piet availed the Chicago White Sox but little today when they dropped their eighth straight game to the Boston Red Sox, 10 to 6, before a crowd of 16,000.

It was Boston's fifth victory in a row and it pulled them to within a game and a half of the league-leading Yankees, who were humbled by the Indians.

Bonura laced out his fifth and sixth homers of the season to account for four tallies. Piet brought in the other Chicago runs with his four-bag smash in the fifth inning. Bonura's first homer came with none on in the second, but Piet and Merritt (Sugar) Cain, who ran for Mule Haas after the right fielder singled and was banished for talking back to Bill McGowan, were on base when Bonura belted out his second.

The Red Sox got to Vernon Kennedy early. Dusty Cooke led off with a homer and Rog Cramer followed with a double. Heinie Manush scored him with a single. Kenendy lasted only two-thirds of the second frame, when the Red Sox blasted him for three more hits and two passes and pulled into a 6-1 lead.

The Boston sluggers, who piled up fourteen hits against three Chicago pitchers, also scored single runs in the fourth and sixth. They unleashed a two-run burst in the eighth, against Ray Phelps and Italo Chelini.

The score:

CHICAGO (A. L.)	ab	r	h	po	a	e
Radcliff, lf	3	0	0	1	0	0
Piet, 2b	3	2	2	0	5	1
Haas, rf	5	0	1	2	1	0
*Cain	0	1	0	0	0	0
Bonura, 1b	5	2	3	9	0	0
Kreevich, cf	4	0	0	0	0	0
Hayes, ss	5	0	1	5	5	0
Dykes, 3b	5	0	1	1	2	1
Sewell, c	1	1	0	6	1	0
KEN'EDY, p	0	0	0	0	0	0
PHELPS, p	3	0	0	0	2	0
†Wash'gton	1	0	0	0	0	0
CHELINI, p	0	0	0	0	1	0
Totals	35	6	8	24	17	2

BOSTON (A. L.)	ab	r	h	po	a	e
Cooke, rf	5	3	3	1	0	0
Cramer, cf	5	3	4	4	0	0
Manush, lf	4	2	1	2	0	0
Foxx, 1b	4	0	0	8	1	0
McNair, 2b	5	0	3	2	2	0
Cronin, ss	4	0	1	3	1	0
Werber, 3b	3	1	1	1	1	0
R. Ferrell, c	4	1	1	5	0	0
HENRY, p	4	0	0	1	2	0
MARC'M, p	0	0	0	0	1	0
Totals	38	10	14	27	8	0

*Ran for Haas in ninth inning.
†Batted for Phelps in eighth inning.

Chicago .... 010 020 003—6
Boston .... 240 101 02x—10

Runs batted in—Bonura (4), Piet (2), McNair (4), Manush (2), Cooke, Cramer, Foxx. Two-base hits—Cramer (2), McNair (2), Cooke (2), Cronin. Home runs—Bonura (2), Piet, Cooke. Left on bases—Chicago, 10; Boston, 8. Bases on balls—Off Kennedy, 2; off Phelps, 2; off Henry, 6; off Marcum, 1. Struck out—By Kennedy, 2; by Phelps, 3; by Henry, 4. Hits—Off Kenedy, 6 in 1 2-3 innings; off Phelps, 5 in 5 1-3; off Chelini, 3 in 1; off Henry, 8 in 8 1-3; off Marcum, 0 in 2-3. Hit by pitcher—By Henry (Piet). Wild pitch—Phelps. Winning pitcher—Henry. Losing pitcher—Kennedy. Umpires—McGowan, Quinn and Ormsby. Time—2:30.

Phils Down Pirates, 5-1, Routing Weaver in First

PITTSBURGH, June 6 (AP).—The Phillies drove Big Jim Weaver from the mound today with a four-run assault in the first inning, and scored a 5 to 1 victory over Pittsburgh behind Orville Jorgen's four-hit pitching.

Ralph Birkofer relieved Weaver in the first after the Phillies had touched him for four hits. Birkofer stopped the uprising, but was replaced by Guy Bush after Philadelphia had pushed another marker across in the third. Bush limited the Phillies to one hit in six innings. Cy Blanton hurled the ninth.

Arky Vaughan ran his hitting streak to eighteen consecutive games.

The score:

PHILADELPHIA (N.L.)	ab	r	h	po	a	e
Chiozza, cf	5	1	1	3	0	0
Sulik, lf	4	1	2	0	0	0
Klein, rf	5	1	1	2	0	0
Camilli, 1b	2	2	1	12	2	0
Whitn'y, 3b	4	0	1	0	0	0
Norris, ss	4	0	2	5	6	0
Grace, c	2	0	1	4	1	0
Gomez, 2b	4	0	0	1	4	1
JORG'S, p	4	0	0	0	0	0
Totals	34	5	9	27	13	1

PITTSBURGH (N. L.)	ab	r	h	po	a	e
Jensen, lf	4	0	2	2	0	0
L.W'n'r, cf	4	0	0	4	0	0
P.W'n'r, rf	4	1	0	1	0	0
Vaug'n, ss	4	0	1	3	4	0
Suhr, 1b	4	0	1	9	2	0
Brub'er, 3b	3	0	0	1	0	1
Lavag'o, 2b	3	0	0	3	4	0
Todd, c	3	0	0	3	4	0
W'AV'R, p	0	0	0	0	0	0
BIRK'R, p	1	0	0	0	0	0
BUSH, p	1	0	0	1	1	0
*Lucas	1	0	0	0	0	0
BLAN'N, p	0	0	0	0	0	0
Totals	32	1	4	27	15	1

*Batted for Bush in eighth inning.

Philadelphia .... 401 000 000—5
Pittsburgh .... 100 000 000—1

Runs batted in—Sulik, Klein, Norris (2), Suhr, Whitney. Three-base hits—Sulik, Camilli. Double play—Todd and Lavagetto. Left on bases—Philadelphia, 7; Pittsburgh, 4. Bases on balls—Off Weaver, 1; off Birkofer, 1; off Bush, 2; off Blanton, 1. Struck out—By Jorgens, 2; by Bush, 2. Hits—Off Weaver, 4 in 1-3 innings; off Birkofer, 4 in 1 2-3; off Bush, 1 in 6; off Blanton, 0 in 1. Losing pitcher—Weaver. Umpires—Barr, Goetz and Reardon. Time—1:47.

Major League Averages

* * *

American League

CLUB BATTING

Club.	G.	AB.	R.	H.	RBI	SB.	Pct.
New York	47	1690	336	517	313	23	.307
Chicago	44	1546	253	446	243	18	.288
Washington	48	1673	266	479	237	34	.286
Boston	48	1652	276	465	248	17	.281
Cleveland	45	1593	243	446	222	16	.280
St. Louis	45	1599	228	442	214	12	.276
Detroit	48	1690	268	463	244	18	.274
Philadelphia	43	1481	193	375	171	9	.253
Washington	41	1434	228	417	203	28	.291

CLUB FIELDING

Club.	G.	P.	A.	E.	DP.	Pct.
Detroit	48	1288	588	43	49	.977
Boston	48	1267	487	45	37	.974
New York	47	1257	501	54	38	.970
Washington	48	1252	574	61	53	.969
Cleveland	45	1213	539	57	50	.968
St. Louis	45	1182	555	56	47	.968
Chicago	44	1169	564	57	..	.967
Philadelphia	43	1145	523	67	46	.961

INDIVIDUAL BATTING

Player, club.	G.	AB.	R.	H.	RBI.	SB.	Pct.
Tietje, Chi.St.L.	11	1	3	1	1	0	1.000
Sullivan, Cleve.	28	96	13	39	16	1	.406
White, Det.	14	10	1	4	1	0	.400
DiMaggio, N.Y.	30	144	34	55	33	2	.382
Radcliff, Chi.	30	115	22	42	29	0	.374
Galatzer, Clev.	18	58	10	21	5	0	.362
Gehrig, N. Y.	47	100	57	65	34	1	.361
Appling, Chi.	36	139	22	50	31	1	.360
Kroner, Bos.	11	25	5	9	9	0	.360
Dickey, N. Y.	37	151	39	54	50	0	.358
Gehringer, Det.	48	203	46	71	31	1	.350
Dean Phila.	21	20	1	7	5	0	.350
Auker, Det.	10	20	1	7	6	0	.350
Greenberg, Det.	12	46	10	16	15	1	.348
Crosetti, N. Y.	47	188	41	64	30	7	.340
Campbell, Clev.	14	53	8	18	8	1	.340
Lewis, Wash.	43	189	28	63	18	1	.339
Puc'nelli, Phil.	43	161	28	54	35	0	.335
Bell, St. L.	45	177	24	59	31	0	.333
Averill, Cleve.	43	171	30	57	35	0	.333
R. Ferrell, Bos.	40	139	24	46	22	0	.331
Moses, Phila.	43	173	34	57	23	1	.330
Bonura, Chi.	39	155	25	51	34	1	.329
Cooke, Bos.	40	138	24	45	26	1	.326
Pepper, St. L.	26	37	3	12	6	0	.324
Berg, Bos.	11	34	4	11	7	0	.324
Goslin, Det.	48	194	44	62	46	0	.320
Clift, St. L.	44	181	40	57	20	3	.315
Werber, Bos.	47	170	33	53	26	9	.312
Trosky, Cleve.	45	181	36	56	45	2	.309
Coleman, St.L.	31	65	7	20	19	0	.308
Foxx, Bos.	48	171	38	52	46	4	.304
Dykes, Chi.	39	135	24	41	19	0	.304
Walker, Det.	33	115	21	35	17	1	.304
Hale, Cleve.	43	175	39	53	20	3	.303
Johnson, N. Y.	21	66	11	20	5	0	.303
Glenn, N. Y.	10	33	4	10	3	0	.303
Hoag, N. Y.	23	86	9	26	20	0	.302
Finney, Phila.	41	176	28	53	11	2	.301
Bejma, St. L.	13	10	2	3	0	0	.300
Kress, Wash.	28	97	15	29	13	2	.299
Stone, Wash.	32	104	23	31	24	1	.298
Selkirk, N. Y.	43	158	36	47	38	4	.297
Walker, NY, Chi.	22	81	14	24	17	2	.206
Owen, Det.	48	180	22	53	33	5	.294
Carey, St. L.	45	177	23	52	19	2	.294
Manush, Bos.	39	160	22	47	23	1	.294
McNair, Bos.	48	188	33	55	26	0	.293
Powell, Wash.	47	192	36	56	29	10	.292
Haas, Chi.	44	179	28	52	17	1	.291
Travis, Wash.	45	175	26	51	31	1	.291
Hemsley, St. L.	42	141	16	41	18	1	.291
Reynolds, Wsh.	32	117	11	34	17	3	.291
Hill, Wash.	31	110	19	32	13	5	.291
Kuhel, Wash.	48	173	28	50	40	2	.289
Lazzeri, N. Y.	47	166	28	48	40	4	.289
Chapman, N.Y.	30	112	17	32	18	1	.286
Higgins, Phila.	35	131	21	37	15	1	.282
Simmons, Det.	44	192	28	54	33	1	.281
Bott'ley, St. L.	44	167	26	47	27	0	.281
Rolfe, N. Y.	47	208	42	58	22	1	.279
Cochrane, Det.	39	120	24	33	16	1	.275
Bolton, Wash.	31	99	16	27	13	0	.273
Lary, St. L.	45	184	30	50	16	4	.272
Almada, Bos.	27	85	12	23	8	0	.271
Myer, Wash.	38	131	29	35	13	7	.267
Solters, St. L.	42	162	26	43	37	1	.265
K'bocker, Clev.	45	198	18	52	16	3	.263
Miles, Wash.	15	42	6	11	3	0	.262
Vosmik, Cleve.	43	157	29	41	28	1	.261
Burns, St.L.Det.	43	142	16	37	16	1	.261
Fox, Det.	30	104	24	27	7	1	.260
Pytlak, Cleve.	26	77	9	20	7	1	.260
Sewell, Chi.	42	147	22	35	24	2	.259
Piet, Chi.	44	159	33	41	26	9	.258
Ruffing, N. Y.	13	35	3	9	1	0	.257
Pearson, N. Y.	11	33	4	7	8	0	.212

PITCHING RECORDS

Pitcher, club.	G.	H.	BB.	SO.	W.	L.	Pct.
Broaca, N. Y.	11	76	17	29	3	0	1.000
Henry, Boston	8	19	9	8	3	0	1.000
Brown, Chicago	8	29	11	4	2	0	1.000
Grove, Boston	12	66	18	44	8	1	.889
Gomez, N. Y.	10	57	34	33	6	1	.857
Pearson, N. Y.	11	52	57	50	8	2	.800
Sorrell, Det.	10	61	26	21	4	1	.800
Deshong, Wash.	9	59	29	24	6	2	.750
Hadley, N. Y.	9	39	16	20	3	1	.750
Malone, N. Y.	10	53	16	29	3	1	.750
Whitehill, Wash.	6	52	11	9	4	2	.667
Blaeholder, Clev.	9	50	20	10	4	2	.667
Phillips, Det.	5	34	4	1	2	1	.667
Wilson, Bos.	12	42	24	20	2	1	.667
Crowder, Det.	5	41	12	7	2	1	.667
W. Ferrell, Bos.	14	107	41	29	7	4	.636
Harder, Cleve.	11	86	22	34	6	4	.600
Bridges, Det.	12	88	29	47	6	4	.600
Russell, Wash.	16	52	22	6	3	2	.600
Cain, St.L.-Chi.	10	72	23	16	4	3	.571
Appleton, Wash.	12	73	31	31	4	3	.571
Kennedy, Chi.	9	58	38	28	4	3	.571
Phelps, Chi.	10	63	36	12	4	3	.571
Hildebra'd, Clev.	10	65	34	23	5	4	.556
Newsom, Wash.	14	107	48	59	6	5	.545
Ruffing, N. Y.	10	67	24	29	5	5	.500
Oster'ler, Bos.	17	63	30	41	4	4	.500
L. Brown, Cleve.	11	61	23	17	4	4	.500
Rowe, Detroit.	11	58	15	30	4	4	.500
Marcum, Bos.	8	39	14	6	3	3	.500
Hogs't, L.-St.L.	13	77	27	9	3	3	.500
Dietrich, Phila.	13	65	28	26	3	3	.500
Murphy, N. Y.	7	20	15	12	2	2	.500
Thomas, St. L.	12	54	17	13	2	2	.500
Kimsey, Det.	11	18	13	8	2	2	.500
Fink, Phila.	5	26	4	5	1	1	.500
Weaver, Wash.	9	21	11	3	1	1	.500
Lee, Cleve.	12	40	16	13	1	1	.500
Kleinhans, N.Y.	7	11	8	4	1	1	.500
Auker, Det.	10	80	22	18	4	5	.444
Whitehead, Chi.	12	78	40	21	4	5	.444
Allen, Cleve.	10	75	24	42	4	5	.444
Kelley, Phila.	10	72	31	23	3	4	.429
Rhodes, Phila.	10	68	39	12	4	6	.400
Mahaffey, St. L.	12	46	24	8	2	3	.400
Lyons, Chi.	7	53	12	10	2	4	.333
Brown, N. Y.	6	37	12	7	1	2	.333
Tietje, Chi.-St.L.	10	28	23	6	1	2	.333
Walberg, Bos.	8	26	20	12	1	2	.333

National League

CLUB BATTING

Club.	G.	AB.	R.	H.	RBI.	SB.	Pct.
Chicago	43	1529	233	449	216	16	.294
Philadelphia	47	1695	252	487	239	16	.287
St. Louis	45	1601	252	459	233	23	.287
Pittsburgh	46	1671	264	478	237	9	.286
New York	45	1601	228	448	217	7	.280
Boston	49	1766	214	488	202	7	.276
Brooklyn	48	1687	192	448	170	13	.266
Cincinnati	45	1592	231	421	211	23	.264

CLUB FIELDING

Club.	G.	PO.	A.	E.	DP.	Pct.
New York	45	1225	632	56	43	.971
Pittsburgh	46	1232	489	55	30	.969
Boston	49	1330	633	63	51	.968
St. Louis	45	1222	471	56	47	.968
Chicago	43	1143	474	53	43	.968
Brooklyn	48	1295	539	71	39	.963
Cincinnati	45	1211	542	69	45	.962
Philadelphia	47	1246	558	82	44	.957

INDIVIDUAL BATTING

Player, club.	G.	AB.	R.	H.	RBI.	SB.	Pct.
Leonard, Bklyn.	13	4	1	2	0	0	.500
Terry, N. Y.	27	70	16	30	14	0	.429
S. Martin, St. L.	35	115	29	46	19	8	.400
Ripple, N. Y.	17	28	7	11	6	0	.393
O'Dea, Chi.	16	18	7	7	4	0	.389
Medwick, St. L.	45	187	28	70	49	1	.374
J. Moore, Phil.	43	172	38	62	31	1	.360
Jordan, Bos.	49	200	33	71	23	1	.355
Suhr, Pitts.	46	169	37	59	40	0	.349
Camilli, Phil.	47	173	36	60	36	3	.347
Demaree, Chi.	43	180	28	61	23	0	.339
Herman, Chi.	43	185	33	62	37	1	.335
King, St. L.	19	21	7	7	2	1	.333
Cuccinello, Bos.	46	172	25	57	28	0	.331
P. Waner, Pitts.	39	155	27	51	21	2	.329
Durocher, St. L.	40	146	17	48	17	1	.329
Schulte, Pitts.	19	64	8	21	7	0	.328
Leslie, N. Y.	35	129	25	42	20	0	.326
Klein, Chi.-Phil.	39	154	31	50	34	0	.325
Lombardi, Cin.	36	117	15	38	18	0	.325
Chapman, Cin.	32	80	15	26	8	3	.325
Moore, N. Y.	45	202	35	65	13	1	.322
Hassett, Bklyn.	48	188	23	60	27	0	.319
Allen, Phil.-Chi.	42	176	25	56	14	4	.318
Hartnett, Chi.	41	155	17	49	32	0	.316
Lavagetto, Pitts.	21	86	14	27	18	0	.314
English, Chi.	25	74	9	23	9	0	.311
Grimm, Chi.	17	61	10	19	9	0	.311
Haslin, Phil.-Bos.	25	84	10	26	10	0	.310
Taylor, Bklyn.	28	71	9	22	11	1	.310
Jurges, Chi.	20	58	16	18	6	1	.310
Mize, Chi.	35	117	21	36	29	0	.308
Collins, St. L.	23	72	12	22	12	0	.306
Ott, N. Y.	44	154	35	47	43	1	.305
Lucas, Pitts.	17	23	5	7	4	0	.304
Norris, Phil.	47	179	23	54	36	1	.302
Moore, N. Y.	49	213	34	64	25	2	.300
Brubaker, Pitts.	35	140	19	42	31	2	.300
Leiber, N. Y.	44	105	18	49	37	1	.297
Bordagaray, Bklyn.	34	95	17	28	4	1	.295
Todd, Pitts.	21	78	13	23	9	0	.295
Watkins, Phil.-Bk.	37	133	21	39	13	3	.293
L. Waner, Pitts.	24	82	14	24	3	0	.293
Vaughan, Pitts.	46	175	42	51	20	2	[illegible]
Ogrodowski, St. L.	27	62	12	18	8	0	[illegible]
Chiozza, Phil.	43	170	31	49	10	2	.288
Whitney, Bos.-Ph.	41	160	22	46	32	0	.288
Myers, Cin.	44	140	24	40	14	5	.286
Thompson, Bos.	28	63	9	18	8	1	.286
Sherrin, Phil.	19	35	3	10	5	0	.286
Warneke, Chi.	13	28	5	8	3	0	.286
Jensen, Pitts.	46	215	24	61	22	1	.284
J. Martin, St. L.	44	183	42	52	27	9	.284
Bucher, Bklyn.	45	166	24	47	16	3	.283
Lee, Bos.	45	170	16	48	24	3	.282
Phelps, Bklyn.	32	61	3	17	10	0	.279
Hack, Chi.	43	166	25	46	25	6	.277
Urbanski, Bos.	49	222	27	61	11	0	.275
Cuyler, Cin.	42	171	34	47	18	4	.275
Earnshaw, Bklyn.	12	22	3	6	2	0	.273
Galan, Chi.	43	150	30	49	22	6	.272
Mancuso, N. Y.	43	158	12	43	27	0	.272
Davis, St. L.	31	107	7	29	15	0	.271
Berres, Bklyn.	40	119	9	32	6	1	.269
Whitehead, N. Y.	45	183	33	49	11	3	.268
Riggs, Cin.	39	153	20	41	24	2	.268
Bartell, N. Y.	37	131	18	35	10	1	.267
Gautreaux, Bklyn.	17	15	1	4	4	0	.267
Stripp, Bklyn.	29	117	10	31	13	2	.265
Cooney, Bklyn.	39	146	20	38	14	0	.260
Geraghty, Bklyn.	32	85	9	22	7	2	.259
Schumacher, N.Y.	14	32	2	8	6	0	.250
Frey, Bklyn.	45	158	19	39	17	1	.247
Brandt, Bklyn.	12	25	2	6	1	0	.240
Gumbert, N. Y.	14	17	2	4	4	0	.235
Jordan, Bklyn.	29	84	3	18	9	0	.214
Koenig, N. Y.	12	24	3	5	4	0	.208
Jackson, N. Y.	41	149	12	30	13	0	.201

PITCHING RECORDS

Pitcher, club	G.	H.	BB.	SO.	W.	L.	Pct.
Winford, St. L.	9	21	14	21	2	0	1.000
J. Dean, St. L.	13	104	15	50	10	2	.833
Weaver, Pitts.	12	78	25	37	7	2	.778
Schumacher, N.Y.	12	89	26	27	6	2	.750
Hollingsworth, Cn.	11	77	25	28	6	2	.750
Cantwell, Bos.	14	38	17	12	3	1	.750
Gumbert, N. Y.	14	57	19	22	5	2	.714
Carleton, Chi.	10	45	19	20	5	2	.714
Smith, N. Y.	14	48	18	28	5	2	.714
Hubbell, N. Y.	14	83	19	36	6	3	.667
Johnson, Phil.	15	60	8	15	4	2	.667
Brown, Pitts.	15	35	13	12	2	1	.667
E. Moore, Phil.	11	42	6	11	2	1	.667
Brennan, Cin.	17	50	12	18	2	1	.667
Lucas, Pitts.	6	23	5	7	2	1	.667
French, Chi.	12	78	20	28	2	1	.667
Warneke, Chi.	13	86	28	33	5	3	.625
Benge, Bos.	13	94	25	24	5	3	.625
Birkofer, Pitts.	12	62	22	17	3	2	.600
Walker, St. L.	9	42	10	10	3	2	.600
MacFayden, Bos.	13	76	21	26	7	5	.583
Swift, Pitts.	13	74	21	23	4	3	.571
Lee, Chi.	12	61	36	27	4	3	.571
P. Dean, St. L.	12	85	13	22	5	4	.556
Parmelee, St. L.	10	80	37	36	5	4	.556
Derringer, Cin.	14	103	10	32	5	5	.500
Walter, Phil.	13	78	39	22	4	4	.500
Henshaw, Chi.	11	46	15	18	3	3	.500
Clark, Bklyn.	8	59	10	13	3	3	.500
Hoyt, Pitts.	8	23	6	11	2	2	.500
Hallahan, S.L.-Cn.	9	58	16	16	2	2	.500
Passeau, Phil.	13	38	3	20	1	1	.500
Grissom, Cin.	5	27	8	11	1	1	.500
Jeffcoat, Bklyn.	8	12	15	10	1	1	.500
Gabler, N. Y.	10	21	8	7	1	1	.500
Mungo, Bklyn.	15	94	41	64	6	7	.462
Brandt, Bklyn.	12	58	23	33	3	4	.429
Lanning, Bos.	8	43	17	10	2	3	.400
Reis, Bos.	9	65	25	11	2	3	.400
Coffman, N. Y.	12	47	9	14	2	3	.400
Schott, Cin.	11	62	31	17	3	5	.375
Davis, Phil.-Chi.	13	97	26	25	3	6	.333
Earnshaw, Bklyn.	12	74	20	27	3	6	.333
Chaplin, Bos.	11	84	14	31	2	6	.250
Frankhouse, Bk.	13	78	30	24	2	6	.250
Castleman, N. Y.	8	60	25	17	1	5	.167

International League Averages

* * *

CLUB BATTING

Club	G.	AB.	R.	H.	RBI.	SB.	Pct.
Rochester	40	1385	238	438	219	17	.316
Buffalo	46	1626	308	494	286	23	.304
Newark	40	1634	292	459	259	23	.278
Albany	47	1562	178	426	173	9	.273
Baltimore	48	1671	285	456	249	19	.272
Toronto	49	1625	191	437	166	12	.269
Montreal	46	1522	214	397	200	9	.261
Syracuse	40	1380	190	340	168	11	.246

CLUB FIELDING

Club	G.	PO.	A.	E.	DP.	Pct.
Montreal	46	1183	561	37	40	.980
Newark	49	1250	612	49	68	.976
Buffalo	45	1210	511	42	36	.976
Toronto	49	1238	558	53	52	.967
Syracuse	40	1043	434	52	27	.967
Baltimore	48	1263	566	71	26	.962
Rochester	40	1032	406	71	40	.952
Albany	47	1190	564	89	32	.951

Triple play—Newark.

INDIVIDUAL BATTING

Player and club	G.	AB.	R.	H.	RBI.	SB.	Pct.
Dickshot, Buf.	22	83	28	34	24	6	.410
McGowan, Buf.	42	166	38	67	44	0	.404
Weintraub, Rch.	23	76	24	30	19	0	.395
Vandenberg, Syr	11	19	0	7	2	0	.368
Olson, Buffalo	46	180	33	66	30	5	.367
Jolley, Albany	47	178	22	63	32	0	.354
Crabtree, Roch.	36	134	22	47	7	2	.351
Harris, Buffalo	13	37	6	13	10	0	.351
Pattison, Tor.	16	20	3	7	5	0	.350
Powers, Nk-Balt.	25	63	13	22	10	1	.349
Mills, Rochester	40	161	27	56	49	6	.348
Brown, Roch.	35	135	29	47	15	2	.348
Rothrock, Roch.	25	104	22	36	11	0	.346
Dahlgren, Syr.	40	160	32	55	48	1	.344
Wright, Balt.	32	135	20	46	30	0	.341
Sturdy, Roch.	40	152	24	51	29	1	.336
Boyle, Newark	39	156	35	52	23	1	.333
Myllykangas, Mt	11	21	4	7	4	0	.333
Smythe, Mont.	16	21	4	7	2	0	.333
Kaufman, Roch.	11	15	1	5	5	0	.333
Fletcher, Buffalo	46	170	33	56	29	2	.329
Heath, Toronto	31	92	11	30	11	0	.326
Crouse, Buffalo	26	92	18	30	20	1	.326
Schalk, Nwk.	47	166	37	54	39	2	.325
King, Montreal	42	126	23	41	22	0	.325
Abernathy, Balt.	44	154	30	49	31	2	.318
Phillips, Buffalo	28	88	11	28	14	0	.318
Cissell, Balt.	48	190	31	60	22	3	.316
Koy, Newark	47	185	43	58	50	6	.314
Funk, Toronto	22	80	9	25	12	0	.313
Thompson, Mont	46	186	25	58	29	0	.312
McCarthy, Nwk.	48	203	34	63	31	1	.310
Baker, Newark	36	117	11	36	18	2	.308
Heving, Syr.	22	62	4	19	5	1	.306
Rhiel, Montreal	25	49	5	15	8	0	.306
Boone, Toronto	31	69	9	21	6	0	.304
Boland, Alb-Buf.	42	129	23	39	28	0	.302
Loane, Albany	35	117	19	35	12	0	.299
Oliver, Toronto	48	182	28	54	18	3	.297
Blackerby, Alb.	35	111	15	33	13	1	.297
Mulleavy, Buf.	46	179	45	53	34	3	.296
Roettger, Balt.	40	152	22	45	17	0	.296
Pool, Toronto	49	185	24	54	24	2	.292
Cuccinello, Roch	23	96	16	28	15	4	.292
Tate, Montreal	26	55	7	16	4	0	.291
Seeds, Montreal	43	176	23	51	28	3	.290
Bell, Albany	40	124	16	36	10	2	.290
Porter, Newark	39	142	25	41	21	5	.289
De La Cruz, Alb.	19	14	2	4	0	0	.286
Barton, Syr.	19	67	11	19	8	0	.284
Martin, Balt.	22	82	21	23	12	0	.280
Wilson, Mont.	29	68	7	19	6	2	.279
Griffith, Syr.	11	36	8	10	3	0	.278
Burnett, Toronto	48	191	29	53	17	3	.277
Dallesandro, Syr	39	153	30	42	16	1	.275
Savino, Alb-Balt	38	125	15	34	16	0	.272
Scoffic, Roch.	18	59	8	16	5	1	.271
Cazen, Balt-Syr.	39	115	19	31	21	3	.270
Poland, Roch.	35	100	10	27	22	0	.270
Redmond, Alb.	12	37	4	10	11	0	.270
Rosenfeld, Nwk.	24	67	10	18	12	0	.269
Richardson, Nk.	48	195	40	52	8	2	.267
Bates, Montreal	43	169	36	45	23	3	.266
Davis, Albany	20	61	7	16	7	0	.262
O'Farrell, Roch.	19	46	9	12	7	0	.261
Williams, Syr.	40	150	24	30	21	2	.260
McFarl'd, Buf-Al	43	146	23	38	13	2	.260
Mowry, Buffalo	27	96	19	25	9	0	.260
Weiland, Roch.	15	13	1	8	2	0	.258
May, Newark	48	171	27	44	28	3	.257
Bissonette, Mont	46	172	25	44	21	1	.256
Carnegie, Buf.	20	55	6	14	10	0	.255
Dugas, Montreal	44	135	22	34	22	0	.252
Snyder, Albany	34	103	13	26	7	1	.252
Barton, Roch.	27	68	10	17	10	1	.250
Johnson, Mont.	12	24	3	6	1	0	.250
James, Syracuse	35	138	27	34	3	1	.246
Miller, Toronto	48	165	16	40	10	1	.242
Oana, Syr-Balt.	39	150	19	36	25	1	.240
Chapman, Balt.	45	153	21	36	31	5	.235
Blakely, Toronto	46	133	14	31	12	0	.233
Molesw'th, Blt-Sy	27	82	20	19	8	2	.232
Piechota, Nwk.	15	35	5	7	5	0	.200
Makosky, Nwk.	15	11	3	1	1	0	.091
Wicker, Newark	15	28	0	0	0	0	.000

PITCHING RECORDS

Pitcher and club.	G.	H.	BB.	SO.	W.	L.	Pct.
Spittler, Newark	6	24	7	4	2	0	1.000
Wilson, Buffalo	12	58	16	25	6	1	.857
Weiland, Roch.	15	73	26	43	8	2	.800
Michaels, Roch.	11	36	17	8	4	1	.800
Johnson, Mont.	6	43	17	22	4	1	.800
Jacobs, Buffalo	11	22	7	16	4	1	.800
Mooty, Toronto	9	39	14	14	4	1	.800
Murray, To-Rch.	12	38	15	6	3	1	.750
Makosky, Nwk.	15	29	18	24	5	2	.714
Piechota, Nwk.	16	74	38	[illegible]	7	3	.700
Melton, Balt.	15	74	23	35	7	3	.700
Harris, Buffalo	13	79	24	39	7	3	.700
Ash, Buffalo	14	88	25	25	6	3	.667
Poli, Montreal	11	53	13	20	6	3	.667
Wicker, Newark	15	63	20	34	6	3	.667
Blake, Balt.	10	99	26	57	6	3	.667
Kleinke, Roch.	14	79	25	15	4	2	.667
Bivin, Balt.	12	56	21	17	4	2	.667
Phebus, Albany	6	30	15	22	2	1	.667
Pearce, Balt.	17	81	26	27	5	3	.625
Chandler, Nwk.	[illegible]	81	25	21	5	3	.625
Smythe, Mont.	16	72	13	16	5	3	.625
Sewell, Buffalo	8	48	26	14	4	3	.571
Duke, Newark	12	82	20	14	4	3	.571
Chagnon, Mont.	10	75	24	18	4	4	.500
Pattison, Tor.	13	61	20	15	3	3	.500
Nekola, Toronto	11	52	19	23	3	3	.500
Kaufman, Roch.	11	47	20	13	3	3	.500
Matuzak, Albany	10	51	25	17	3	3	.500
Da La Cruz, Alb	19	51	12	19	2	2	.500
Bowers, Syr.	5	32	6	6	1	1	.500
Brown, Syr.	4	8	13	4	1	1	.500
Hensiek, Mont.	9	19	8	6	1	1	.500
Herrmann, Tor.	11	74	32	22	4	5	.444
Myllykangas, Mt	12	67	27	28	4	5	.444
Mangum, Syr.	10	51	13	13	2	3	.400
Kline, Buffalo	13	101	16	17	3	5	.375
Pettit, Albany	12	69	24	19	3	5	.375
Burke, Albany	11	76	19	18	3	5	.375
Starr, Syracuse	14	89	46	39	4	7	.364
Meola, Syracuse	6	37	9	11	1	2	.333

British Cricket Results

LONDON, June 6 (CP).—Closing scores in first-class cricket matches started today:

Middlesex, 192 (Robins, 77; Clark, seven wickets for 68 runs); Northampton, 55 for five wickets; at Lord's.

Essex, 171 (O'Connor, 55; Voce, five for 54; Larwood, four for 47); Nottinghamshire, 11 for one wicket; at Nottingham.

Leicestershire, 127 for nine wickets; vs. Sussex at Loughborough.

Kent, 165 (Wellard, seven for 61); Somerset, 81 for six wickets; at Frome.

Gloucestershire, 328 for seven wickets (Barnett, 132, Dacre, 64 not out); vs. Warwickshire at Bristol.

Surrey, 161 (Hopwood, seven for 53); Lancashire, 61 for one wicket; at Manchester.

Hampshire, 110 for four wickets; vs. Glamorgan at Swansea.

India, 86 (Smailes, four for 26); Yorkshire, 182 for seven wickets; at Bradford.

Terry Says World Series Will End Playing Days; Ruffing Wins 20th as Yanks Beat A's, 6-5

Won't Even Be Reserve, Giants' Manager Insists

1937 Plans Include Replacement of Jackson and Koenig, Acquisition of Pitcher and Catcher; McCarthy's Homer Wins Final Against Bees, 3-2

By Arthur E. Patterson

BOSTON, Sept. 25.—There had been a party—champagne and speeches by all the Giants—but in the small hours of this morning all was quiet and Bill Terry, the manager, sat sipping coffee and smoking a brown pipe. He was content with life. He had just won his second National League pennant and, within a few days, he can put his signatures to contracts which will mount well into the important five figures.

He wasn't keeping an athlete's hours because today's game with the Bees, which the Giants won, 3 to 2, didn't mean a thing to him. For the immediate future his only plans were to cure a head cold, rest his hobbled knees and ready himself for his last fling on the ball field in the World Series.

"I hope I go out on top," he mused, "because this is to be my last year as a player."

Now, correspondents had heard Terry announce his retirement before. As late as the third Western trip he told the press he didn't plan to finish the season. A hurried visit to his physician in Memphis, Dr. J. Spencer Speed, had been discouraging. Further action on the field, the doctor told him, would endanger his natural walking for life. Those knees might stiffen without warning. The stories were wired back to New York that Terry was through.

Plays Next Day

Yet, the very next day Terry saw a chance to win a ball game by substituting a runner for Sambo Leslie. Mark Koenig was kept on the bench for later use as a pinch-hitter and Terry, himself, stripping off a splint which guarded a broken finger and revolting against his doctor's orders went out and played. A few days later he began the Giants' surge July 15 by whaling a single, a double and triple at Pittsburgh. He has played dozens of games since.

Small wonder, then, that your correspondent, chatting with Terry this morning, offered to bet him a hat—the conventional wager in baseball—that he would be zipping around first base next April.

"Well, I'll tell you what I'll do," was the pilot's quick rejoinder. "I'll make that $500 to $100 that I won't even be on the reserve list in 1937."

It was a convincing statement.

Already Terry is making plans to stay on top next season. He says he wants a few younger, faster men. Such players as Travis Jackson and Mark Koenig know they are through, of course.

"Old Jax doesn't have to worry, though; he's set with us as long as he wants to work for the Giants."

This means either a minor league manager's job, coaching duties or, perhaps, utility infield for another season for the Giants' captain.

Not Scared by Yankees

"I'm [illegible]g to go along with this young McCarthy and Sam (Leslie) at first base next year and I'd like to pick me up a fast third baseman and another second-string catcher to help Gus (Mancuso) out. Then maybe a pitcher, and I'd be set."

The conversation shifted to the World Series and the Yankees.

"You can bet one thing," remarked Terry. "They haven't scared us. If every one wants to build up the myth that they're unbeatable that's just fine by me. My boys don't scare very easily. I never saw more spirit.

"They're just big kids. You know that Coffman couldn't wait to send a wire to Hornsby thanking him for kicking him into a World Series. And that Whitehead must have a million friends. He had to place orders for $2,100 worth of series tickets. He was running around like an accountant before we got it straightened out."

Terry revealed several interesting details. Did you know, for instance, that the National League scouts the American League each year before the World Series and brings information on play formation to the winning manager? He also said that the Giants are bringing their own scouts, Heinie Groh and Hank De Berry, as well as Frank Brazil, manager of their winning Greenwood, Miss., team in the Cotton States League, to the series as guests of Horace Stoneham for their fine work this season.

Hit .401 in 1930

If this is to be Terry's last World Series it means he will close his career with fourteen years in the majors, all spent in the uniform of the Giants. He started with Atlanta in 1914 and came from Toledo to New York late in 1923 in time to sit in on the last clash between the Yankees and the Giants. This will be his third active series and he carries a batting average of .333 for series play into action. When he started his 1936 campaign he had a major league life-time mark of .352, the peak of which was reached in 1930, when he cudgeled the ball at a .401 clip for John J. McGraw, his managerial predecessor.

Starting with his first full season as boss of the club, 1933, Terry has been the National League's most successful manager if success is measured by the number of days a season in first place. None can challenge his record in that respect and he hasn't done badly in the final standings, either—two championships, one second and one third in four full years after starting with a last-place ensemble.

Terry was more certain than ever tonight that he has his first baseman for 1937, for McCarthy took care of hitting Hank Gumbert into his eleventh triumph today. After seven innings of a 1-to-1 deadlock with Arthur Doll, a reformed catcher, Gumbert won on McCarthy's 350-foot homer into the right field pavilion. Mel Ott, who had doubled to the left-field line, scored ahead of him.

Before that homer McCarthy singled in the fourth, the ball hitting Joe Moore in the leg. It was no fluke hit, however, for it was far beyond the reach of both first and second basemen. The homer, before, was McCarthy's sixth hit in his first two games with the Giants. He went four for four yesterday.

Both teams scored in the first inning, the Giants on a single by Mayo, a double by Bartell and Ripple's fly to center, and the Bees on a single by Moore and a double by Cuccinello which Ripple allowed to get by in an attempt at a shoestring catch. Gumbert then proceeded to hurl two-hit ball until the ninth, when a single by Moore, two infield outs and Rupert Thompson's single tallied the second Hub run. It was Gumbert's first complete game since May 26.

The Giants will work out Monday at the Polo Grounds and Tuesday will exchange parks with the Yankees. Pitching plans for the next few days are uncertain, but Terry thinks he will start Hubbell Sunday and let him go as long as he wants up to four innings against Brooklyn. It is possible, then, that Hubbell will gain credit for his seventeenth successive triumph.

Giants' Score

* * *

NEW YORK (N. L.)	ab	r	h	po	a	e	BOSTON (N. L.)	ab	r	h	po	a	e
Mayo, 3b	5	1	2	0	3	0	Urb'ski, 3b	3	0	0	4	3	0
Bartell, ss	4	0	2	2	7	0	Jordan, 1b	4	0	0	8	0	0
Ripple, cf	5	0	1	2	0	0	E. M're, rf	4	2	2	0	0	0
J. M're, lf	1	0	1	0	0	0	Cuc'lo, 2b	4	0	1	4	3	0
Ott, rf	3	1	1	1	0	0	Lee, lf	4	0	1	2	0	0
McC'y, 1b	4	1	2	17	1	0	Th'son, cf	3	0	1	4	0	0
D's, rf, lf	4	0	1	0	0	0	W'stler, ss	4	0	0	3	6	0
W'head, 2b	3	0	1	3	6	1	Lewis, c	3	0	1	2	0	0
Danning, c	3	0	0	2	0	0	DOLL, p	2	0	0	0	1	0
G'BERT, p	4	0	2	0	4	0	*Haslin	1	0	0	0	0	0
							BUSH, p	0	0	0	0	0	0
Totals	36	3	13	27	21	1	Totals	32	2	6	27	13	0

*Batted for Doll in eighth inning.

New York.......... 100 000 020—3
Boston.............. 100 000 001—2

Runs batted in—Ripple, McCarthy (2), Cuccinello, Thompson. Two-base hits—Bartell, Mayo, Whitehead, Ott, Cuccinello, Gumbert. Home run—McCarthy. Sacrifice—Bartell. Double plays—McCarthy, Bartell and McCarthy; Mayo, Whitehead and McCarthy; Doll, Warstler and Jordan; Cuccinello, Warstler and orda. Left on bases—New York, 10; Boston, 5. Bases on balls—Off Gumbert, 2; off Doll, 2. Struck out—By Gumbert, 2; by Doll, 2. Hits—Off Doll, 11 in 8 innings; off Bush, 2 in 1. Hit by pitcher—By Doll (Danning). Losing pitcher — Doll. Umpires — Magerkurth, Parker and Klem. Time—1:42.

Davis, of Reds, Ends Rally of Cardinals, 3-2

Pitcher Stops Gas House Gang in Ninth; Medwick Hits His 64th Double

By The Associated Press

ST. LOUIS, Sept. 25.—The Cincinnati Reds—troublesome all season—kept the St. Louis Cardinals from assuring themselves second place in the National League today by winning their only victory of the present series, 3 to 2.

A three-run attack in the second brought the victory that seemed slipping in the ninth when a pinch hitter, Rip Collins, first up, doubled and a typical gas house rally seemed imminent. But Ray "Peaches" Davis bore down and snuffed out the next three batters on two infield blows and a foul fly.

In the second Scarsella led off with a single and went to second on an infield out. Riggs walked. Gilbert tossed out Thevenow, but Kampouris was passed purposely, loading the bases. Then Bill McGee, who had a good year with Columbus, of the American Association, before he returned to the Cardinal fold, uncorked a wild pitch which allowed Scarsella to score. Davis then surprised with a single to center, scoring Riggs and Kampouris. That was all, but it was enough.

Joe Medwick, of the Cards, who set a new National League record for doubles when he hit his sixty-third yesterday, added his sixty-fourth today in the third. But two already were out and John Mize, slugger, couldn't bring him home.

The score:

CINCINNATI (N. L.)	ab	r	h	po	a	e	ST. LOUIS (N. L.)	ab	r	h	po	a	e
Walker, cf	4	0	0	3	0	0	T. M'e, cf	4	0	1	0	1	0
G'men, rf	3	0	0	1	0	0	Gar'di, 2b	4	0	0	2	7	0
Cuyler, lf	3	0	2	2	0	0	J. M'n, rf	5	0	2	1	0	0
Scar'la, 1b	4	1	1	11	1	0	Medwick, lf	4	0	2	2	0	0
Campbell, c	2	0	0	2	0	0	Mize, 1b	4	0	1	11	0	0
Riggs, 3b	3	1	0	1	1	0	Gelbert, ss	4	0	0	4	3	0
Th'now, ss	4	0	2	1	7	0	G'ridge, 3b	4	2	2	2	1	0
Kam'ris, 2b	3	1	0	5	3	0	Ogro'ski, c	4	0	1	5	2	0
RAY D'S, p	4	0	2	1	1	0	M'GEE, p	0	0	0	0	0	0
							H'SER, p	0	0	0	0	0	0
							E'SHAW, p	0	0	0	0	0	0
							PAR'EE, p	0	0	0	0	0	0
							*King	0	0	0	0	0	0
							†Fullis	1	0	1	0	0	0
							‡V. Davis	1	0	0	0	0	0
							§Collins	1	0	1	0	0	0
							¶S. Martin	1	0	0	0	0	0
Totals	30	3	7	27	13	0	Totals	37	2	11	27	14	0

*Batted for McGee in second inning.
†Batted for Heusser in fourth inning.
‡Batted for Earnshaw in sixth inning.
§Batted for Parmelee in ninth inning.
¶Batted for Garibaldi in ninth inning.

Cincinnati.......... 030 000 000—3
St. Louis........... 000 101 000—2

Runs batted in — Ray, Davis (2), T. Moore, V. Davis. Two-base hits—Medwick, Collins, Gutteridge. Stolen base—Scarsella. Double plays—Thevenow, Kampouris and Scarsella; Gutteridge and Mize; Gelbert and Mize. Left on bases—Cincinnati, 6; St. Louis, 1. Bases on balls—Off Ray, 2; off McGee, 2; off Heusser, 2; off Parmelee, 2. Struck out—By Davis, 1; by McGee, 3; by Earnshaw, 1. Hits—Off McGee, 3 in 2 innings; off Heusser, 1 in 2; off Earnshaw, 2 in 2; off Parmelee, t1 in 3. Wild pitch — McGee. Losing pitcher — McGee. Umpires—Barr, Moran and Pinelli. Time—2:07.

Golfers to Tour Argentina

BUENOS AIRES, Sept. 25 (AP).—The Argentine Golf Association announced today that Johnny Revolta, of Chicago, and Tony Manero, of Greensboro, N. C., United States professional and open champion, respectively, will make a three-week tour of Argentina and other South American countries next month. They will leave Miami October 6.

Standings in Major Leagues

* * *

SATURDAY, SEPTEMBER 26, 1936

National League

YESTERDAY'S RESULTS

New York, 3; Boston, 2
Cincinnati, 3; St. Louis, 2
Other clubs not scheduled

STANDING OF THE CLUBS

	New York	St. Louis	Chicago	Pittsburgh	Cincinnati	Boston	Brooklyn	Phila'phia	Won	Lost	Percentage
New York	—	10	11	15	13	13	13	17	92	60	.605
St. Louis	12	—	13	13	12	9	13	15	87	65	.572
Chicago	11	7	—	10	10	16	15	16	85	67	.559
Pit'sburgh	7	9	12	—	11	14	13	15	81	68	.553
Cincinna'i	9	10	12	6	—	9	13	13	72	80	.474
Boston	9	13	6	8	13	—	10	11	70	82	.461
Brooklyn	7	9	7	9	9	12	—	12	65	87	.428
Phila'phia	5	7	6	7	9	9	10	—	53	99	.349
Gms. lost	60	65	67	68	80	82	87	99	—	—	

GAMES TODAY

Brooklyn at New York, 3:00
Chicago at St. Louis
Pittsburgh at Cincinnati
Boston at Philadelphia

American League

YESTERDAY'S RESULTS

New York, 6; Philadelphia, 5 (10 ins.)
Washington, 9; Boston, 3
St. Louis, 8; Cleveland, 2 (1st)
Cleveland, 7; St. Louis, 6 (2d)
Other clubs not scheduled

STANDING OF THE CLUBS

	New York	Detroit	Washington	Chicago	Cleveland	Boston	St. Louis	Phila'phia	Won	Lost	Percentage
New York	—	14	12	14	16	15	14	16	101	50	.669
Detroit	8	—	11	14	13	9	11	17	83	69	.546
Wash'gton	8	11	—	5	8	14	19	16	81	70	.536
Chicago	7	8	16	—	12	10	11	15	79	70	.530
Cleveland	6	7	14	10	—	13	15	13	78	74	.513
Boston	7	13	8	12	9	—	12	12	73	79	.480
St. Louis	8	11	3	8	7	10	—	10	57	93	.380
Phila'phia	6	5	6	7	9	8	11	—	52	99	.344
Gms. lost	50	69	70	70	74	79	93	99	—	—	

GAMES TODAY

New York at Washington
St. Louis at Chicago (2)
Detroit at Cleveland
Philadelphia at Boston

Pennant Smiles as Giants Quit Field After Victory

Associated Press photo

After retiring the last Boston batter in the ninth inning of Thursday's first game, Dick Bartell, left, Hal Schumacher, center, and Gus Mancuso, of the New York Giants, show exhilaration of having clinched the National League pennant as they leave the diamond

Rolfe's Homer in Tenth Defeats Edgar Smith, Sandlot Southpaw

Big Right-Hander Reaches Score of Triumphs After Eleven Years of Trying

By Rud Rennie

PHILADELPHIA, Sept. 25.—Charley Ruffing, the big, red-headed Yankee right-hander, achieved an ambition this chilly afternoon. He turned in his twentieth victory of the season, the only season in the twelve of his major league career that he has won twenty games.

It was Ruffing's last workout before he appears in the World Series. It was a long one. He had to go ten innings to beat the last-place Philadelphia Athletics, 6 to 5. Red Rolfe won the game with a home run in the tenth off Edgar Smith.

Smith, a young left-hander from the sandlots of New Jersey who has been gaining experience with Williamsport, gave the Yankees a battle. They hit him in every inning except the first, but they had trouble scoring. Three of their runs were unearned. Observers, looking at every left-handed pitcher with Carl Hubbell and Al Smith in mind, shook their heads. If a kid left-hander could hold the Yankees.

Crosetti Hits Hard

Anyway, they beat him. Crosetti hit a triple and a home run. DiMaggio went hitless. Gehrig got a single. Selkirk made two hits. And Ruffing weathered the storm and won. His teammates shook his hand and slapped him on the back as he walked off the field.

The Yankees now can boast one pitcher who has won twenty games. Ruffing is the first Yankee right-hander to turn the trick since Waite Hoyt in 1928. He had failed in his last two attempts. He has lost twelve.

Crosetti got Ruffing in trouble in the first inning by making two errors and letting the A's pick up an unearned run.

Puccinelli hit a home run to make one of the two scored off Ruffing in the second.

Bob Johnson, besides hitting a scoring triple in the third, made two singles and a home run, tying the score after the Yankees made two in the first half of the eighth to take a 5-to-4 lead.

Ruffing Misses Chance

Ruffing had a chance to win his own game in the ninth. He came up with the bases filled and two out, but forced Lazzeri at second.

Rolfe's homer was his tenth of the season and the team's 181st. Crosetti's was his fourteenth.

The A's made twelve hits off Ruffing.

This was the A's last home game of the season and their last with the Yankees. The New Yorkers have beaten them in sixteen of the twenty-two games.

Monte Pearson, the Yankee right-hander who was overcome in the midst of yesterday's ball game by a pain in his back, did not accompany the team. He is home, in care of a physician. McCarthy thinks he will be all right in time for the World Series. Pearson says he had the same thing happen to him in 1929 and he was in bed for seventeen days.

Bill Dickey started, but his hand bothered him, so he retired in the second inning and let Glenn do the catching.

Wins Twentieth Game

Charles (Red) Ruffing

Smith fanned DiMaggio for the third out in the first and Gehrig and Dickey, the first two men up in the second.

Gehrig singled and Glenn doubled in the fourth with none out, but Smith got Selkirk and Powell to hoist flies to the third baseman, and Puccinelli ran to the fence and caught Lazzeri's line drive, leaving two men on bases a long time.

Bob Johnson went to the end of the line and made a backhand catch of Powell's long foul in front of the bullpen to help keep the Yankees from scoring in the sixth.

The Yankees made three double plays.

The Yankees moved on to Washington tonight to finish their schedule in Washington with two games against the Senators. The score:

NEW YORK (A. L.)	ab	r	h	po	a	e	PHILADELPHIA (A.L.)	ab	r	h	po	a	e
Crosetti, ss	6	2	2	4	4	2	Finney, cf	5	0	1	5	0	0
Rolfe, 3b	6	1	3	4	3	0	Culler, 2b	5	1	1	2	1	2
DiMag'o, cf	6	0	0	1	0	0	Dean, 1b	5	1	2	5	1	0
Gehrig, 1b	5	0	1	8	2	0	John'n, lf	5	1	4	3	0	0
Dickey, c	1	0	0	0	0	0	Higgins, 3b	4	0	0	4	0	0
Glenn, c	3	0	1	5	1	0	Pucc'li, rf	3	1	1	4	0	0
Selkirk, rf	4	0	2	1	0	0	Peerson, ss	4	1	1	3	3	0
Powell, lf	5	1	2	2	0	0	Hayes, c	4	0	2	4	1	0
Lazzeri, 2b	4	1	2	5	2	0	SMITH, p	4	0	1	0	3	0
RUFF'G, p	4	1	0	0	1	0							
Totals	44	6	13	30	13	2	Totals	39	5	13	30	9	2

New York....... 001 010 120 1—6
Philadelphia...... 121 000 010 0—5

Runs batted in—Johnson (3), Puccinelli, Finney, DiMaggio, Crosetti, Ruffing, Rolfe (2). Two-base hit—Glenn. Three-base hits—Crosetti, Johnson. Home runs—Puccinelli, Crosetti, Johnson, Rolfe. Sacrifice—Puccinelli. Double plays—Rolfe, Lazzeri and Gehrig; Lazzeri, Crosetti and Gehrig; Ruffing, Crosetti and Gehrig. Left on bases—New York, 13; Philadelphia, 6. Bases on balls—Off Smith, 5; off Ruffing, 1. Struck out—By Smith, 4; by Ruffing, 2. Umpires—Johnston, McGowan and Dinneen. Time—2:11.

Senators Beat Red Sox Behind Deshong, 9 to 3

WASHINGTON, Sept. 25 (AP).—Aided by Jimmy Deshong's eight-hit pitching, plus nine walks and a balk by Boston pitchers, the Senators beat the Red Sox today, 9 to 3.

It was Deshong's eighteenth victory and gave the Senators a full game hold on third place and put them but a game and a half out of second.

The score:

BOSTON (A. L.)	ab	r	h	po	a	e	WASHINGTON (A. L.)	ab	r	h	po	a	e
Melillo, 2b	4	1	2	0	2	0	Chap'n, cf	3	2	1	0	0	0
Werber, 3b	4	1	1	4	1	0	Lewis, 3b	3	1	1	0	2	0
Cramer, cf	4	0	2	2	0	0	Kuhel, 1b	4	1	0	12	0	0
Foxx, rf	3	1	1	2	0	0	Stone, lf	4	1	2	3	0	0
Almada, rf	0	0	0	0	0	0	Travis, ss	5	0	0	2	7	0
Kroner, ss	1	0	0	1	0	0	Sington, rf	3	1	1	5	0	1
McNair, ss	3	0	0	2	3	0	Mihalic, 2b	2	0	0	3	3	0
Gaffke, lf	4	0	0	0	0	0	Hogan, c	4	1	2	2	0	0
Dahlg'n, 1b	4	0	2	8	1	0	D'HONG, p	3	2	2	0	0	0
Dickey, c	4	0	0	5	0	2							
HENRY, p	1	0	0	0	0	0							
WILSON, p	1	0	0	0	0	0							
BOW'RS, p	0	0	0	0	0	0							
*Marcum	1	0	0	0	0	0							
Totals	34	3	8	24	7	2	Totals	31	9	9	27	12	1

*Batted for Wilson in eighth inning.

Boston.............. 000 100 110—3
Washington......... 004 100 40x—9

Runs batted in—Stone (2), Sington, McNair, Dahlgren, Hogan, Chapman (2), Cramer. Two-base hits—Cramer, Chapman, Werber, Dahlgren. Three-base hit—Cramer. Stolen bases—Kuhel (2), Stone (2), Chapman. Sacrifice—Deshong. Double plays—Lewis, Mihalic and Kuhel; Mihalic, Travis and Kuhel; Werber (unassisted). Left on bases—Boston, 5; Washington, 9. Bases on balls—Off Henry, 5; off Deshong, 1; off Wilson, 4. Struck out—By Henry, 1; by Wilson, 3; by Deshong, 2. Hits—Off Henry, 1 in 2 innings (none out in third); off Wilson, 8 in 5; off Bowers, 0 in 1. Hit by pitcher—By Henry (Lewis). Wild pitch—Wilson. Balk—Wilson. Losing pitcher—Henry. Umpires—Quinn, Owens and Summers. Time—2:05.

Indians Lose Chance to End In 1st Division

Split With Browns Settles Cleveland in Lower Half; Averill Hits 28th Homer

By The Associated Press

CLEVELAND, Sept. 25.—The Cleveland Indians lost their last mathematical chance to finish in the American League's first division today when they divided a double-header with the St. Louis Browns.

The Tribe won the second game, 7 to 6, after the Browns took the opener, 8 to 2.

Roy Weatherly, Cleveland's hard-hitting recruit outfielder, collided with a right-field wall and was knocked unconscious in the fourth inning of the nightcap, but he caught Clift's foul and retired the St. Louis third baseman before he "passed out." He revived and walked unassisted from the field.

Earl Averill connected for his twenty-eighth homer of the season with two on base in the third inning of the second game.

The scores:

FIRST GAME

ST. LOUIS (A. L.)	ab	r	h	po	a	e	CLEVELAND (A. L.)	ab	r	h	po	a	e
Lary, ss	4	3	3	2	7	0	Hughes, 2b	4	0	1	3	6	0
Clift, 3b	3	2	2	0	2	1	Hale, 3b	4	1	2	1	2	2
Solters, lf	5	1	1	1	0	0	Averill, cf	3	1	2	3	0	0
Bell, rf	5	1	2	1	0	0	Trosky, 1b	3	0	1	12	0	0
Bot'ley, 1b	4	0	0	17	0	0	Vosmik, lf	4	0	0	0	0	1
West, cf	5	0	1	4	0	0	Weath'y, rf	3	0	0	2	0	0
Hemsley, c	5	0	2	2	0	0	Kn'ker, ss	4	0	0	3	4	1
Carey, 2b	4	0	1	0	7	0	George, c	4	0	0	3	0	0
H'SETT, p	3	1	0	0	1	0	ZUBER, p	3	0	0	0	1	0
							*Pytlak	1	0	0	0	0	0
Totals	38	8	12	27	17	1	Totals	33	2	6	27	13	4

*Batted for Zuber in ninth inning.

St. Louis............ 203 200 100—8
Cleveland........... 002 000 000—2

Runs batted in—Bell (2), Clift (2), Bottomley, Hemsley, Trosky. Two-base hits—Clift (2), Hale, Carey. Stolen bases—Lary (2). Double plays—Hughes and Trosky; Carey, Lary and Bottomley; Hale and Trosky. Left on bases—St. Louis, 8; Cleveland, 7. Bases on balls—Off Hogsett, 2; off uber, 5. Struck out—By Hogsett, 2; by Zuber, 3. Hit by pitcher—By Hogsett (Trosky). Umpires—Kolls, Hubbard and Ormsby. Time—1:35.

SECOND GAME

ST. LOUIS (A. L.)	ab	r	h	po	a	e	CLEVELAND (A. L.)	ab	r	h	po	a	e
Lary, ss	5	0	0	4	1	0	Hughes, 2b	4	1	1	1	2	0
Clift, 3b	3	2	1	1	1	1	Hale, 3b	3	2	3	3	0	1
Solters, lf	5	2	2	1	0	0	Averill, cf	4	1	2	3	0	0
Bell, rf	5	2	4	2	0	0	Trosky, 1b	3	0	0	9	0	0
Bot'ley, 1b	5	0	2	3	1	0	Weath'y, rf	1	0	0	2	0	0
Pepper, cf	5	0	1	3	0	0	Gal'zer, rf	3	0	0	2	0	1
Hemsley, c	5	0	2	7	1	0	Heath, lf	4	0	0	1	0	0
Carey, 2b	3	0	1	2	3	0	Kn'ker, ss	4	0	0	0	6	0
V. ATTA, p	2	0	0	1	0	0	Becker, c	2	2	0	6	0	0
*Bejma	0	0	0	0	0	0	MILNAR, p	4	1	3	0	1	0
JAK'KI, p	0	0	0	0	0	0							
†West	1	0	0	0	0	0							
C'WELL, p	0	0	0	0	0	0							
‡Coleman	1	0	0	0	0	0							
Totals	40	6	13	24	7	1	Totals	32	7	9	27	9	2

*Batted for Van Atta in fifth inning.
†Batted for Jakucki in eighth inning.
‡Batted for Caldwell in ninth inning.

St. Louis............. 201 010 020—6
Cleveland............ 003 010 30x—7

Runs batted in—Averill (4), Hale (2), Trosky, Bell (3), Solters, Bejma. Two-base hits—Solters, Hughes. Home run—Averill. Sacrifice—Hughes. Left on bases—St. Louis, 13; Cleveland, 6. Bases on balls—Off Van Atta, 1; off Jakucki, 2; off Milnar, 6. Struck out—By Van Atta, 6; by Caldwell, 1; by Milnar, 5. Hits—Off Van Atta, 3 in 4 innings; off Jakucki, 5 in 3; off Caldwell, 1 in 1. Hit by pitcher—By Jackucki (Trosky). Passed ball—Hemsley. Losing pitcher — Jakucki. Umpires — Hubbard, Ormsby and Kolls. Time—2:04.

Mrs. Patton's 91 Is Low Gross In Jersey Golf

Suburban Player Wins by 6 Strokes 1-Day Event at Upper Montclair Club

By Janet Owen

MONTCLAIR, N. J., Sept. 25.—Mrs. James Patton, Suburban Golf Club champion, carried off the low gross prize in the Women's New Jersey Golf Association one-day tournament at the Upper Montclair Country Club today by a margin of six strokes over her two nearest rivals, Mrs. Ralph Watson and Miss Josephine Merrill, both of Montclair.

Playing the south course going out and the east course coming in, the two longer stretches among the club's three nines, Mrs. Patton carded 46—45—91. Mrs. Watson and Miss Merrill went around in 97.

Mrs. Watson won the first low net prize, her handicap of 12 enabling her to make up all but one stroke on Mrs. Patton. When the club champion accepted the gross prize for her 91—7—84, Mrs. Watson was awarded the net prize with 97—12—85.

Four other net prizes were won, in order, by Mrs. Farleigh S. Dickinson, of Yountakah, who carded 100—14—86; Mrs. Joseph Coult, of Rockaway River, 100—14—86; Mrs. G. Lovel Parker, of Baltusrol, 98—12—86, and Mrs. Charles Horne, of Arcola, 106—19—87. Mrs. Horne won the fifth prize by matching cards with Miss Alice Gregg and Mrs. H. E. Smith, both of the home club, who also had 87s.

Sixty-one players teed off for the contest, a smaller number than usual in New Jersey one-day tournaments because many New Jersey golfers are concentrating on practice for next week's national championship at the Canoe Brook Country Club. Mrs. William Hockenjos jr., of Crestmont, New Jersey match and medal-play champion; Miss Charlotte Glutting, of Rock Spring, and Mrs. Maureen Orcutt Crews, of White Beeches, were among the large number threading their way through Canoe Brook's water-laced course today.

Slow fairways and fast greens at Upper Montclair, the result of recent heavy rains and today's sunny morning, which dried the short grass, gave the one-day tourney players a stiff challenge. Forty-seven of the original sixty-one found the need for switching from hard driving to cautious approaching and putting too much for them and did not turn in cards. Only fourteen were left in the running for prizes.

Mrs. Patton showed keen judgment and control in adjusting to the difficulty on the start of the outward nine and later on the last three holes of the east course. She had birdies on the 210-yard fourth and 410-yard eighteenth.

Her card:

Women's par, out. 5 5 4 4 5 4 5 3 4—39
Mrs. Patton, out.. 5 5 5 3 6 5 6 6 5—46
Women's par, in.. 5 5 4 3 5 4 5 3 5—39—78
Mrs. Patton, in... 7 6 5 4 6 5 5 3 4—45—91

The scores:

Mrs. James Patton, Suburban	91— 7—84
Mrs. R. M. Watson, Montclair	97—12—85
Mrs. Farleigh S. Dickinson, Yountakah	100—14—86
Mrs. Joseph Coult, Rockaway River	100—14—86
Mrs. G. Lovel Parker, Baltusrol	98—12—86
Mrs. Charles Horne, Arcola	106—19—87
Mrs. H. E. Smith, Upper Montclair	107—20—87
Miss Alice Gregg, Upper Montclair	111—24—87
Mrs. H. A. Trax, Upper Montclair	107—19—88
Mrs. A. G. Hupfel, Hackensack	98— 9—89
Mrs. J. H. A. Williams, Echo Lake	105—16—89
Mrs. George R. Griffith, Green Brook	104—14—90
Miss Josephine Merril, Montclair	97— 6—91
Mrs. W. W. Povey, Crestmont	99— 8—91

Eileen Whittingstall To Wed Horse Trainer

LONDON, Sept. 25 (AP).—Mrs. Edmund Owen Fearnley Whittingstall, formerly Eileen Bennett, the tennis player, today filed notice of her forthcoming marriage to Marcus Marsh, racehorse trainer.

Mr. and Mrs. Whittingstall were divorced last year in a suit in which Marsh was named as co-respondent. Marsh was the trainer of the horse Windsor Lad, winner of the Derby in 1934. The tennis player was formally presented at a royal court in Buckingham Palace in 1932 and the same year married Whittingstall, a portrait painter, in fashionable St. Margaret's, Westminster, London. In 1931 she lost to Mrs. Helen Wills Moody in the finals of the United States national championship at Forest Hills.

Lack of Funds Imperils Ross Fight in Australia

CHICAGO, Sept. 25 (AP).—The world's welterweight championship between Barney Ross, titleholder, and Jack Carroll, Australian challenger, scheduled for Sydney December 8, was on the verge of collapse today in consequence of Ross's failure to receive $7,000 in advance for expenses.

Sam Pian, co-manager of Ross, said he had received no word from Charles Lucas, Sydney promoter, after he had promised to cable the money two days ago. Ross, with his handlers, had planned to leave for Vancouver next Thursday, sailing on October 7.

Pian declared that unless he received the $7,000 by Monday he would call off the match and seek opponents in this country. Ross had been guaranteed $45,000 to defend his title in a fifteen-round bout, with $7,000 for expenses. The articles provided that the $45,000 be deposited in a Chicago bank September 1.

Evens and Creel Reach Final In National Left-Handed Golf

Former Upsets Antonio by 1 Up at St. Louis as Latter Crushes Alpert

By The Associated Press

ST. LOUIS, Sept. 25.—There will be no more battles in the national left-handers golf tournament between Alexander Antonio and his caddy. The colorful Antonio is out.

Antonio — Linden, N. J., Italian, whose caddy orders him around like a schoolmaster and resorts to force, if necessary, to calm the temperamental golfer who brought him to the tournament all the way from the East coast—lost to Fred Evens, St. Louis dark horse, by one hole in a thirty-six-hole semi-final struggle today.

And so tomorrow the imperturbable Evens will play the tournament medalist, steady Howard Creel, of Pueblo, Col., for the championship. Creel advanced with 9 and 8, over Samuel G. Alpert, of La Salle, Ill.

Evens came from behind in the morning eighteen to square the match on the fourteenth after being four down, but lost his putting touch directly after that and was two down at the halfway mark.

In the afternoon he started by losing the nineteenth, but won four of the next five holes from the faltering Easterner and went one up. After that it was a dog fight. They came to the thirty-sixth tee with Evens one up.

They were both to the right of the fairway off the tee and neither made a good second shot. Both rolled on to the green, Evens within fifteen feet and Antonio twelve feet away, with their thirds. They both took two putts to halve the hole and leave Evens with the margin he had held since the thirty-first.

Creel held an 8-up advantage at the end of eighteen and took it easy in the ten holes he had to play in the afternoon. His afternoon thirty-nine going out was his worst nine-hole round of the tournament, but Alpert didn't take advantage of his opponent's lapses.

Kinder and Whitehead Card 67 For Jersey Pro-Amateur Medal

Plainfield Team Is 5 Under Par; Simon Pure Takes 71, Low Score for Day

By Fred Hawthorne

PLAINFIELD, N. J., Sept. 25.—Two representatives of the home club, John Kinder, professional, and Charles Whitehead, amateur, came home with a record-breaking 33—34—67, this afternoon to lead a field of sixty players in the qualifying round of the first pro-amateur New Jersey State best-ball foursome championship tourney.

The achievement of the winners was hailed with enthusiasm by the entire membership of the Plainfield Country Club gathered around the scoreboard as the last pairs came straggling in this evening. The card returned by the home club pair was five under the 72-par figures for the 6,757-yard course.

In second place, with 34—36—70, were Victor Ghezzi, professional of the Deal Country Club, and Dr. Harold V. Garrity. Next in line were Bert McDougall, pro, and Dr. Stephen G. Lee, of Essex Fells, 33—38—71, and Johnny Farrell, former national open champion, and A. F. Kammer jr., of Baltusrol, were fourth with 35—37—72.

Qualifying Play-Off Necessary

So low was the scoring that three pairs were tied at 76 for last place in the qualifying field of sixteen teams and a play-off was necessary.

The program for tomorrow calls for the start of the first round of match play at eighteen holes, with the first pair teeing off at 9 a. m. The second round will start at 1:30 p. m. On Sunday the two eighteen-hole semi-final round matches will start at 9:30 a. m., and the final, also at eighteen holes, will begin at 2 o'clock.

The amateur, Whitehead, who has evidently been hiding his light under a bushel until today, was credited with the lowest individual score of the day, finishing one under par with a sparkling 71.

Whitehead and Kinder chalked up five birdies on their card, going under par on the third, fifth, seventh, eleventh and twelfth holes and scoring par figures on all the rest.

Winners Never Over Par

The medalists played their round with Victor Ghezzi and Dr. Garrity, and after the ninth hole carried the major portion of the gallery. Both Whitehead and Ghezzi were long on their tee shots, frequently getting over 250 yards straight down the fairway, and the amateur was a bit more than holding his own in this respect. It is obvious with such low scoring that few mistakes were being made by any one of the four, but Whitehead and Ghezzi had the edge on their partners. If Ghezzi made any mistakes, it was in his approaches and on the greens.

Bert McDougall and Dr. Stephen G. Lee, of Essex Fells, after reaching the turn in 33, and being even with par through the fifteenth hole coming in, faltered on the last three to finish with 5, 5, 5, and spoil their chances of finishing in second place with a 69.

Par and the winning card:

Par, out.......... 4 4 3 4 5 3 4 5 4—36
Par, in........... 4 3 5 4 3 4 5 4 4—36—72
Whitehead-Kinder, out........ 4 4 2 4 4 3 3 5 4—33
Whitehead-Kinder, in.......... 4 2 4 4 3 4 5 4 4—34—67

Qualifiers

John Kinder-Charles Whitehead, Plainfield	33—34—67
Victor Ghezzi-Dr. Harold V. Garrity, Deal	34—36—70
Bert McDougal-Dr. Stephen G. Lee jr., Essex Fells	33—38—71
John Farrell-A. Fred Krammer jr., Baltusrol	35—37—72
Maurice O'Connor-John Cunniff, Branch Brook	39—34—73
Harold Sanderson-Dr. R. P. Lauckner, Canoe Brook	37—36—73
Jack Forrester-Robt. H. Landsdell, Hackensack	35—39—74
William Malcolm-Paul De B. Scott, Essex County	37—37—74
Chet Irwin-Al Nichols, White Beeches	35—39—74
John Showler-Joseph Ghezzi, Swimming River	35—39—74
Al Nelson-Ray Peeney, Hopewell Valley	39—35—74
John Hoctor-Robert Wilkinson, Locust Grove	35—40—75
Thomas J. Harmon jr.-William Y. Dear jr., Montclair	36—39—75
Dan Williams-Gene Hampson, Shackamaxon	36—39—75
Byron Nelson-Ernest F. Thomas jr., Ridgewood	37—39—76
Martin Wallach-C. H. Hall jr., Twin Brooks	37—39—76

Non-qualifiers

*Bruce Heatley-Edward Down, Echo Lake	39—37—76
Alec Ternyer-Edward Buckley, Elmwood	38—39—77
Tom O'Connor - Phil Ohlson, Bloomfield	37—40—77
Harry Smith-Frank K. Montgomery jr., Green Brook	39—38—77
Rudy Sexton-Reginald Rollinson, Plainfield	42—36—78
Tony Farese-J. William Thomas, Penn Brook	39—39—78
Peter Kosky-Kenneth Walcott, Trenton	38—40—78
Dave O'Connell-Donald S. Case, Essex Fells	39—39—78
Frank Siciliano - Mike Elko, Sunny Field	40—39—79
Jim Dante - Clayton Farris, Braidburn	41—38—79
Ken Milne-Don Van Houten, Mount Tabor	37—42—79
Andrew Lapola-Oscar Straub, Florham Park	40—41—81
Herbert Gaskill-Harold James, Monmouth County	41—41—82

*Lost on play-off.

First-round pairings:

Upper bracket — John Kinder-Charley Whitehead vs. Al Nelson-Ray Peeney; Maurice O'Connor-John Cunniff vs. Tom Harmon-Billy Dear; Chet Irwin-Al Nichols vs. Jack Forrester-Bob Lansdell; Bert McDougall-Dr. S. G. Lee jr. vs. John Hoctor-Bobby Wilkinson.

Lower bracket—Johnny Farrell-Freddie Kammer vs. Bill Malcolm-Paul Scott; John Showler-Joe Ghezzi vs. Byron Nelson-Ernie Thomas; Harold Sanderson-Bob Lauckner vs. Danny Williams-Gene Hampson; Marty Wallach-C. H. Hall vs. Victor Ghezzi-Dr. H. V. Garrity.

Leading Five Batsmen In Each Major League

NATIONAL LEAGUE

Player	G.	AB.	R.	H.	PC.
P. Waner, Pitts.	146	577	106	215	.373
Phelps, Brooklyn	113	309	35	115	.372
Medwick, St. Louis	152	623	115	219	.352
Demaree, Chicago	152	598	90	207	.346
Herman, Chicago	151	625	100	210	.336

AMERICAN LEAGUE

Player	G.	AB.	R.	H.	PC.
Appling, Chicago	135	520	110	202	.388
Averill, Cleve.	148	599	131	225	.376
Dickey, New York	109	419	98	150	.358
Gehrig, New York	152	571	167	203	.356
Walker, Detroit	132	546	106	194	.355

Home Runs		Runs Batted In	
Gehrig, Yankees	49	Trosky, Indians	158
Trosky, Indians	42	Gehrig, Yankees	151
Foxx, Red Sox	39	Medwick, Card.s	139
Ott, Giants	33	Foxx, Red Sox	138
Averill, Indians	30	Ott, Giants	134

MacDonald Smith Sets Scoring Pace on Links

CHICAGO, Sept. 25 (AP).—Macdonald Smith, the veteran Glendale, Calif., stylist, is leading the country's professional golfers in the shooting for average low-scoring honors, with Harry Cooper, of Chicago, and Ralph Guldahl, of St. Louis, fractions of strokes behind. Smith, who has played more tournament golf than in many seasons, still has a lot of playing to do to qualify for the Harry E. Radix cup, the prize for low average scoring. He has averaged 71.12 strokes for thirty-three rounds. A minimum of forty rounds is required to qualify.

Cooper, runner-up to Tony Manero in the United States open championship last June, has shot seventy-two rounds at an average of 71.65. Neil Christian, of Yakima, Wash., ranks third with a 71.75 average, but has played only twelve rounds. Guldahl has an average of 71.78 strokes for fifty-seven rounds.

Other rankings:

	Rounds	Average
Henry Picard, Hershey, Pa.	50	72.14
Paul Runyan, White Plains, N. Y.	50	72.16
Tony Manero, Greensboro, N.C.	48	72.33
Byron Nelson, Ridgewood, N.J.	82	72.36
Ky Laffoon, Chicago	54	72.37
Jimmy Thomson, Shawnee on Delaware, Pa.	81	72.56
Horton Smith, Chicago	78	72.61
Victor Ghezzi, Rumford, N. J.	54	72.63
Johnny Revolta, Chicago	48	72.85
Harold McSpaden, Boston	38	72.92

Miss Marble Vanquishes Mrs. Van Ryn in Tennis

LOS ANGELES, Sept. 25 (AP).—Miss Alice Marble, national women's single champion, survived a three-set struggle with Mrs. Marjorie Van Ryn, of Orange, N. J., today and entered the women's singles final of the Pacific Southwest tennis tournament. The scores were 2—6, 6—3, 9—7.

Three times during the match the Eastern matron reached match point, but each time Miss Marble turned back the threat of the former Santa Monica girl. Miss Marble will face the winner of the match between Miss Carolin Babcock and Miss Gracyn Wheeler set for tomorrow.

Men's singles semi-finalists, Fred Perry and Francis X. Shields, and Donald Budge and Jack Tidball, will settle their respective issues tomorrow.

In the men's doubles, Budge and Gene Mako, California's young national doubles champions, defeated John Van Ryn and Henry Culley, of Santa Barbara, 3—6, 6—3, 6—4, 6—2, and gained the final round.

In women's doubles Miss Dorothy Bundy, of Santa Monica, and Miss Dorothy Workman, of Pasadena, defeated Dr. Esther Bartosh and Miss Josephine Cruickshank, of Los Angeles, 6—2, 6—3.

Ward Loses to Mitchell In Golf at Philadelphia

PHILADELPHIA, Sept. 25 (AP).—Bill Ward, of Syracuse, medalist and defending champion, was eliminated from the Spring Haven cup invitation golf tournament today by C. Bayard Mitchel, of Pine Valley, N. J., Country Club, 2 and 1.

Sam Wilcox and W. H. Morpeth jr., both of Wilmington, also dropped out of the running. Morpeth lost to Jack Buchanan, of Philadelphia, 3 and 1, as Wilcox fell before Jack Stein, of Philadelphia, 5 and 3.

Another Wilmington entry, George Hoopes, won his first match by defeating Bill Robinson, of Philadelphia, 1 up, on the nineteenth hole.

Governor Horner Attends Funeral of McFarland

JOLIET, Ill., Sept. 25 (AP).—Friends from the sports, business and professional worlds paid final tribute today to Patrick (Packey) McFarland, member of the Illinois Athletic Commission, who died Wednesday, after an illness of two months.

Funeral services for the one-time famous lightweight boxer were held at St. Raymond's Catholic Church. Among the hundreds who attended were Governor Henry Horner and Joseph Triner and George Getz, of the state athletic commission. McFarland, who was forty-eight, was named to the commission by Governor Horner in 1933.

Mrs. Mulqueen Wins in Golf

POINTE CLAIRE, Que., Sept. 24 (CP).—Mrs. F. J. Mulqueen, of Toronto, won the Canadian women's closed golf championship today by defeating Mrs. A. B. Darling, of Montreal, 3 and 2. Mrs. Darling won the Canadian open last week.

LAZZERI HOMERS WITH 3 ON

News Views

By CLEVELAND RODGERS

Al Smith and Party Loyalty—Roosevelt Not So Good—Baseball and Politics—Trolley Bells and Whistles—New York Realty Values

IN COMING out for Governor Landon, Alfred E. Smith is wholly consistent and within his rights as an American citizen who heartily disagrees with the New Deal. There is not much sense in opposing Roosevelt and not supporting Landon unless one happens to be a Communist.

But as a Democrat and former candidate of that party Mr. Smith's position is anomalous. Millions of Democrats voted for him in 1928 merely because he was the Democratic nominee. What will these Democrats think of his present attitude?

MR. SMITH paid a deserved tribute to Senator Glass last night. The Senator was only one of many Democrats who battled for Smith in sections where it took real courage to do so. It is true, as the former Governor said, that Senator Glass has been a severe critic of the New Deal, but he is supporting Roosevelt.

This is not a defense of blind party loyalty. Mr. Smith is showing characteristic courage. But when he bases his opposition to the New Deal on the ground that it is not Democratic and makes a speech for the Republican candidate his logic becomes mixed. He shouldn't be too hard on Roosevelt for accepting Progressive Republican support and putting some Progressives in office. Mr. Smith has sought and secured Republican support many times and has appointed many good Republicans to office.

PRESIDENT ROOSEVELT'S speech at Pittsburgh was not so effective as his Syracuse address. He was on the defensive and he was entirely too vague regarding the important issue of public spending. We may concede that the real deficit is not so large as it is represented to be and that the huge expenditures were necessary and have produced results, but what we want to know is where we go from here.

True, the President promised that we should have a balanced budget in a year or so, to be attained by revenue derived from increased national income, but there can be no justification for continuing waste and inefficiency, no matter how great the national income. He might have made out a better case if he had asked Governor Landon, point blank, how he proposed to economize.

WE HAVE never understood how public officials and candidates for office get so much time to attend baseball games. It takes us so long to read their speeches and in trying to keep track of what they are doing in the various branches of the government no time is left to get to the ball parks.

Not that we begrudge the President the pleasure of seeing a World Series game. He needs the diversion, and it must be a relief for him to sit in the grandstand and have the crowd ignore him while it watches the game.

IN SPITE of all the talk about violating the Constitution, the only forthright blow delivered against the Constitution in a long time was the action of the Chief of Police of Terre Haute, Ind., in arresting Earl Browder, the Communist candidate for President, to prevent him from speaking.

It simply doesn't make sense to legalize the Communist party and then to put its candidates in jail. Those who insist that no such freedom would be accorded an opponent of the Soviet system in Russia are quite right, but they miss the point. There is nothing to fear from Communism so long as the appeal of its supporters is made peaceably and force is not used to suppress their legal rights.

ONE of the best things about the new B. M. T. trolleys is that they are quiet. Half the clanging of street car bells is unnecessary. Having motormen use up their energy working the foot contraption that rings a bell, when everything else about the trolley is automatic, is a sheer waste.

In the Union station in Washington they have done away with the ringing of train bells and the blowing of shrill steam whistles. Instead, there is a purring whistle that is just as effective and it spares the nerves.

ACCORDING to the Department of Taxes and Assessments, the real estate of New York City is worth $47,000,000 more than it was last year, the total being $16,000,000,000. It is still over $4,000,000,000 less than it was at the peak a few years ago.

Why New York realty should be worth less today than it was in 1929 may be explained in many ways, but it is not a sound or a logical condition. Assessments were run up to the high peak in anticipation of the rise in values due to the new city subway. The money was [illegible] and spent before the subway was finished. [illegible] the transit system is now nearing [illegible]

[illegible]

THE WEATHER

By U. S. Weather Bureau

FAIR TONIGHT AND TOMORROW. NOT MUCH CHANGE IN TEMPERATURE. LIGHT LOCAL FROSTS IN NEARBY INTERIOR TONIGHT

Tempeature, noon —— 64
Year ago, clear —— 55
Mean average for the day —— 62

BROOKLYN DAILY EAGLE

95th YEAR—No. 274

Entered at the Brooklyn Postoffice as 2d Class Mail Matter—(Copyright 1936 The Brooklyn Daily Eagle)

NEW YORK CITY, FRIDAY, OCTOBER 2, 1936

34 PAGES

THREE CENTS

WALL STREET
Stocks and Curb Closing Prices
★ ★ ★ ★ ★

7,000,000 Put To Work, Says U. S. Chamber

Unemployment Total Greatly Exaggerated, Directors Are Told

Washington, Oct. 2 (AP)—Directors of the Chamber of Commerce of the United States were told today that private employment had increased steadily during the Summer and that at least 7,000,000 had been put back to work since the low point of the depression.

In a preliminary outline of its activities, John W. O'Leary, chairman of the chamber's committee on employment, said this estimate had been obtained from members in their own communities and fields of business.

"Using the material furnished from these reports and other data which upon analysis has been found to be dependable," O'Leary said, "it is clear that private employment has steadily increased during the Summer of 1936, and at mid-September there were in private employment in all of its forms at least 7,000,000 more wage and salary workers than when employment was lowest in the depression.

"It is clearly evident that estimates which have been made of unemployment have been greatly exaggerated; that estimates of unemployment on a national basis are necessarily inaccurate and useless for practical purposes."

U. S. Baseball Fan Number 1

Roosevelt Arriving in Town on Way to See Series Game

Eagle Staff Photo

Smiling President Roosevelt, at Pennsylvania Station, in rear of car which took him to Jersey City dedication ceremony.

Schumacher and Smith Routed; Yanks Score 7 Runs in 3d Inning

400,000 Throng Hails President In Jersey City

Queens Ready for Gala Welcome to Chief Executive After Ball Game

President Roosevelt came to town today to see a baseball game, dedicate a medical building in Jersey City and break ground for the $58,000,000 Queens-Midtown Tunnel in Long Island City.

Fresh from his fighting campaign speech in Pittsburgh last night, he smiled at a throng of cheering admirers in the Pennsylvania Station when his special train brought him there at 10 a.m. He was driven by way of the Holland Tunnel to Jersey City and found that Democratic city's streets packed with over 400,000 men, women and children to welcome him.

It took the Presidential party, preceded by a police escort, half an hour to make its way to the Jersey City Medical Center, where a new building was dedicated. Speaking to the assembled doctors and others there, the President gave his assurance that the hand of politics would never be laid on the medical profession by the Government in putting the social security program into effect.

"The overwhelming majority of the doctors of the nation want medicine kept out of politics. On occasions in the past attempts have been made to put medicine into politics. Such attempts have always failed and always will fail.

"Government, State and national, will call upon the doctors of the nation for their advice in the days to come."

Cites Support of Plan

"The American Medical Association, the American Public Health Association and the State and Territorial Health Officers Conference came out in full support of the public health provisions. The American Child Health Association and the Child Welfare League indorsed the maternal and child health provisions.

"This in itself assur[illegible] that the

Continued on Page 2

WORLD SERIES

											R.	H.	E.
Yanks	2	0	7	0	0					—			
Giants	0	1	0	3						—			

Batteries—Gomez and Dickey; Schumacher, Smith and Mancuso.

BOX SCORE

(Second Game)

YANKEES

3½ Inning Box Score

	AB.	R.	H.	O.	A.	E.
Crosetti, ss. .	3	2	2	0	0	0
Rolfe, 3b. . . .	1	2	0	2	0	0
DiMaggio, cf.	2	1	1	1	0	0
Gehrig, 1b. . .	3	1	2	0	0	0
Dickey, c. . . .	2	1	1	6	0	0
Selkirk, rf. . .	1	0	0	2	0	0
Powell, lf. . . .	1	1	0	0	0	0
Lazzeri, 2b. .	2	1	1	0	0	0
Gomez, p. . .	2	0	0	0	0	0
Totals	17	9	7	11	0	0

GIANTS

	AB.	R.	H.	O.	A.	E.
Moore, lf. . .	3	0	0	1	0	0
Bartell, ss. . .	1	0	0	2	1	0
Terry, 1b. . .	2	0	1	2	0	0
Leiber, cf. . .	1	0	0	2	1	0
Ott, rf.	2	0	0	2	0	0
Mancuso, c. .	0	1	0	2	2	0
Whiteh'd, 2b.	2	0	0	1	0	0
Jackson, 3b. .	2	0	1	0	1	1
Schumach'r, p	0	0	0	0	0	0
Smith, p.	0	0	0	0	0	0
Coffman, p. .	0	0	0	0	1	0
Davis	1	0	1	0	0	0
Totals	14	1	3	12	6	1

Bronx Bombers Put on a Big Assault Before President Roosevelt—Giants Tally on Wild Pitch by Lefty Gomez

Game in Detail

First Inning

YANKEES—Hal Schumacher and Lefty Gomez had nothing on President Roosevelt when it came to warming up. The National Executive practiced his pitches several times for the cameramen. The vast multitude stood up to the strain of the national anthem, the President did his stuff in hurling out the first ball, the Giants dashed out on the greensward and the game was on.

Schumacher's first pitch was for the purpose of giving the pellet to the President as a souvenir. Time was called when the umpires chased the photographers off the field.

Crosetti stepped to the plate, cut at the first ball and sent it screaming to center for a single. Rolfe took a ball that almost got away from Mancuso. A second ball was high and inside. Schumacher came in with a half speeder over the middle for a called strike. Ball three was low and Mancuso threw to first trying to pick Crosetti off the bag, but Frank scrambled back safely. Rolfe walked, the fourth pitch being low and inside.

DiMaggio swung from the heels and missed for a strike. In came ball one that was wide. DiMaggio bunted down the third-base line and beat it out, getting to first ahead of Jackson's throw. This filled the bags.

Gehrig hit the first pitch for a

Continued on Page 22

Last-Minute Game in Detail

FOURTH INNING

YANKEES—Rolfe tried to bunt the first pitch, but the ball caromed behind the plate for a foul and strike one. After taking a ball that was low, Red bunted between first and the box and was tossed out by Coffman on a pretty play. DiMaggio sent the first pitch on an arch to Moore, who gathered in the ball. Gehrig looked over a called strike, followed by three balls low and inside. He swung for a second strike and then singled past Terry.

Dickey ignored a wide ball and a second that was low and Gehrig was nipped attempting to steal, Mancuso to Bartell.

No runs, one hit, no errors, none left.

GIANTS—Mancuso walked on four straight balls, all wide of the target.

Whitehead took a called strike, fouled into the lower stands for a second, put another foul in the upper deck behind the Giant dugout. He then missed a curve ball that broke across the outside corner to sit down a strikeout victim.

Plaza Payment Begins Today

All Awards Ready by Oct. 15, Taylor Says —First 25 Disbursed

Controller Frank J. Taylor announced today as payment was begun on awards for property condemned by the city for the Brooklyn Bridge Plaza, that all the payments would be ready by Oct. 15.

A total of 160 awards, amounting to $3,586,847.60 have been granted for holdings on the Plaza, which extends from Fulton and Washington Sts. to the bridge entrance. Controller Taylor's plan to complete payments by Oct. 15 superseded a previous arrangement to make them at the rate of about 25 a week.

The first payment made today following an announcement that 25

Continued on Page 2

Fall Down Stairs Kills Queens Woman

Mrs. Carrie Mehling, 50, of 79-36 67th Road, Middle Village, Queens, was fatally injured today when she fell down a flight of stairs in her home. She slipped on the top step of the stairway leading from the first floor hallway to the cellar. Her groans brought her niece, Anna Mehling, who summoned an ambulance, but Mrs. Mehling was dead when the surgeon reached her.

Rockingham Park Results

FIRST RACE — Six furlongs, off 1:42. First, PLAYMORE, 114 (Porter), $33.70, $13.20, $7.20; second, QUEEN VIC, (Barba), $5.80, $4.00; third, SQUAWKER, 106 (Rosen), $4.20. Time, 1:16 3-5. Eddie Helck, Gold Clip, Memphis Lass, Radiator, Rolling Along, Zulu Lad, Mount Auburn, Starogan, Falermian also ran.

SECOND RACE—One mile; off 2:13. First, WELL DONE, 112 (Taylor), $48.30, $20, $13.30; second, REIGH TETRARCH, 111 (Stevenson), $4.90, $3.40; third, YANKEE PRINCE, 112 (Jackson), $3.50. Time, 1:45. Cutie Girl, Johns Son, Harry Bernard, Sweet Beauty, Black Selma, Hasty Hanna, Bay Streak, War Chase, Hold Out also ran.

Woodbine Park Results

FIRST RACE—Six furlongs. Off, 2:03½. First, BOSCOBEL, 110 (Remillard), $5.20, $3.60, $2.80; second, SUGAR JAR, 110 (Mann), $5.15, $3.90; third, HANNAH ANNE, 110 (Barnes), $36.20. Time, 1:13 2-5. aThe Miner, Safari, aThermal, Uvira, Solid, Ardawn, Nell Kuhlman, Governor Bill, Lorraine S. also ran. aN. Hlynsky and F. Hammer entry.

Lincoln Fields Results

FIRST RACE—Six furlongs. Off, 2:20. First, LE MISERABLE, 113 (Dickinson), $6.80, $4.40, $3.20; second, MISS FLICKER, 110 (McClellan), $41.60, $28.60; third, fKAPENA, 113 (Cowley), $8.00. Time, 1:15. Yes Polly, fKissie, Royal Bird, Shuffle Off, fRoundabout, Lo, Coffee Cup, Mighty Quick, Dance Princess also ran. fField.

1937 Tax Levy Budget $8,530,093 Over 1936

LaGuardia Gives Estimate Board Request for $554,071,935 After Pruning Figures for City Needs

A 1937 executive budget of $554,071,935 for tax levy appropriations, an amount greater by $8,530,093 than the 1936 budget for the same purposes, was submitted by Mayor LaGuardia today at a special meeting of the Board of Estimate and Apportionment. The 1936 budget for tax levy purposes was $545,541,842.

The budget submitted by the Mayor by no means indicates the total asked by the various departments of the city government to carry on their work next year. Using the pruning knife judiciously Mr. LaGuardia trimmed away $22,097,104 from the total before he took his request to the Board of Estimate.

In addition to the $554,071,935 for tax levy appropriations, the sum upon which will be based the taxpayers' burden for 1937, the Mayor also told the board that $82,259,082 will have to be raised by borrowing for capital outlay. The sum required for this purpose in 1936 was $67,827,564. Such moneys are used for bridge building and similar improvements.

Including this $82,259,082 the

Continued on Page 2

Board of Estimate O.K's Relief Fund

The Board of Estimate at a special meeting today approved an expenditure of $27,357,000 for the Emergency Relief Bureau during the months of October, November and December, of which $1[illegible],528,000 is being appropriated by the city, the balance coming from the State.

In requesting the appropriation, Mayor LaGuardia appealed to businessmen to co-operate with the city in eliminating chiselers from the home relief rolls. He expressed the fear that some employers were developing the technique of hiring home relief people on part time, thus in effect receiving a subsidy from the city.

"In a small city," said the Mayor, "these instances would soon be reported, but in a large city the cooperation of industry is required to reduce the relief rolls."

River Downs Results

FIRST RACE—Six furlongs; off 2:26½. First, MAIN MAN, 115 (Meloche), $3.60, $3.40, $2.60; second, aEYE JAY, 115 (Thornton), $8, $4.80; third, BOOKMARK, 115 (Cheatham), $2.80. Time, 1:13. Job Printer, Overplay, aEli W., Black Sergeant, fO'Bantam, Rhiniz, Oddesa Boy, fBold General also ran. fField. aI. J. Collins entry.

Franco Pledges Minimum Wage

Rebel Chieftain Also Promises Peasants Land in 'New Spain'

Lisbon, Oct. 2 (AP)—Reports from the Spanish insurgent strongholds of Valladolid today said several Spanish Cabinet Ministers had left Madrid, by way of Alicante, aboard the Argentine warship 25 De Mayo, en route to Marseille, France.

(Informed sources at Buenos Aires last week said the wife of President Manuel Azana of Spain and the wives and daughters of other Cabinet Ministers had been taken to Alicante under the protection of the Argentine Ambassador to be put aboard the Argentine cruiser. There also were reports in Buenos Aires that President Azana himself had asked asylum aboard the cruiser,

Continued of Page 15

War Hero Executed For Holdup Slaying

Florence, Ariz., Oct. 2 (AP)—Roland H. (Jerry) Cochrane, former U. S. Marine who served in the Nicaraguan rebellion, calmly went to his execution in the lethal gas chamber at the State Penitentiary at dawn here today in payment of a $2.40 holdup slaying.

Cochrane, decorated for war service by the Nicaraguan Government and by his own country, smiled once just before his body became rigid. Thelma Martin, his sweetheart, claimed the body.

Mother Would Take Killer's Place in Jail

Chicago, Oct. 2 (AP)—Pleading she was old and likely to die soon, a mother today asked to be placed in jail in place of her son, held on assault charges in the fatal shooting of his father.

Mrs. Bertha Roth, 50, said her son, Joseph, 27, "was merely protecting his family" when he shot his father after the elder Roth had thrown three bricks through the window of his home in a rage.

Mayor Is Defied On Snow Removal

In the face of a warning from Mayor LaGuardia that charges would be made that some Aldermen might be fixed if his request were denied, the Board of Aldermen late today refused to exempt from public letting, as requested by the Mayor, the purchase of $956,000 worth of snow removal equipment.

To make the exemption the city charter requires 49 of the 65 votes in the board. The exemption proposal received only 31 affirmative votes and 20 negative votes. The remaining members were either absent or not voting.

After the vote, several Aldermen said they would have voted in favor of the proposal if the Mayor had stayed away from the meeting. The Mayor's speech before the board today was denounced by several members as a tactless, careless tirade. The Mayor had reviewed the story of the arrest of two men charged with attempted extortion in connection with an attempt to shake down one of the contractors who was trying to sell snow removel equipment to the city. Then he said: "The honor of this board is at stake. These two were selling you."

Esquirol Is Promoted To 9th District Court

Chief Clerk Joseph H. Esquirol Sr., of the Coney Island Court, received word today from the office of Chief Magistrate Jacob Gould Schurman that, beginning Oct. 16, he is to be transferred to the Ninth District Magistrate's Court in Bay Ridge.

Esquirol has frequently been complimented by magistrates sitting in Coney Island Court for his efficiency in handling the large number of cases coming up there, including hundreds of daily complaints on vagrants and beach peddlers in the Summer months. His transfer to the Ninth District Court is regarded as a promotion.

Ruth Etting Walks Out of Donahue Cast

London, Oct. 2 (AP) — Ruth Etting quit the harassed cast of "International Rhythm" today to go home.

Felix Ferry, co-producer of the tempestuous musical with Jimmy Donahue, heir to the American five-and-ten-cent-store millions, announced, however, the show which opened last night would go on.

The excitement of yesterday, when some of the players threatened to bolt because of unpaid salaries while the first night curtain waited, had simmered down.

Relief Fraud Sends Man and Wife to Jail

Justices Perlman, Voorhees and Nolan in Brooklyn Special Sessions Court today convicted George Smith, 50, and his wife, Ethel, of taking $1,000 relief money over a period of two years when Mrs. Smith had $5,524.18 in the bank.

The Smiths live at 821 57th St. Sentenced to three months in the workhouse or to pay a fine of $500, they chose the prison term, saying they no longer had any money.

J. Stuart Blackton To Wed Again at 61

Hollywood, Oct. 2 (AP)—Thrice a widower, Commodore J. Stuart Blackton, formerly of Brooklyn, has filed notice of intention to wed Evangeline Russell, screen actress. Blackton, who helped Thomas Edison form Edison-Vitascope in 1896, is 61. His fiancee is 34.

48,000 Jam Polo Grounds

By TOMMY HOLMES

Staff Correspondent of The Eagle

Polo Grounds, Oct. 2—For the first time the sun shone on the 1936 World Series here

Continued on Page 22

N. J. Girl, 15, Is Shot; Companion, 17, Held

Dover, N. J., Oct. 2—Samuel Miller, 17, was held on open charges today following the shooting and wounding of Jean Nash, 15, a freshman in Dover High School. The girl is in Dover General Hospital suffering from a bullet would in the abdomen. Physicians said her condition was fair.

Police said Miller and Miss Nash visited the home of Miller's brother-in-law, James Ferrone The Ferrone family went to the theater, leaving the boy and girl in the house. Some time later, police said, the boy appeared on the street carrying the girl in his arms. He hailed a passing motorist who took the girl to the hospital with Miller accompanying her.

Hospital authorities informed them, police said, that on arriving at the hospital the girl threw her arms around Miller and said:

"I know you didn't mean to do it."

Official Count Gives Brunner 263,544

The Board of Elections made public today the official canvass of the Democratic primary votes for President of the Board of Aldermen, showing that William F. Brunner received 263,544 votes to 238,314 votes for Frank J. Prial. This gave a plurality of 25,230 votes for Brunner, as compared to an earlier estimated plurality of 24,714.

CHICAGO BASEBALL

Cubs 0 1
White Sox. . 3 . . 0

Batteries—Warneke and Hartnett; Stratton and Sewell.

In Today's Eagle

Belmont Park Results

FIRST RACE. Six furlongs. Off, 2:33½. Time, 1:13.

	Gold Cross	Snap Judgment	Cherry Chic
Prices	5 1 2 1 1-1	5-2 6-5	7-5

Scratched: Highmost.

TONY CALLS TURN ON DICKEY

Tony Lazzeri called the turn on Bill Dickey's home run in the ninth inning yesterday. Tony hit a fast ball for his homer, but Dickey pounded a slow curve into the stands. Harry Gumpert tried to fool him on a change of pace, but Bill saw it coming. "They were throwing me slow balls all afternoon," revealed Bill. "By the ninth inning I was getting so that I expected them."

DAILY EAGLE SPORTS

6 NEW YORK CITY, SATURDAY, OCTOBER 3, 1936 MI

ED. HUGHES' COLUMN

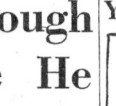

Lazzeri Comes Through In Crisis Where He Failed Ten Years Ago

By TOMMY HOLMES

Shadows ten years old hovered over the Polo Grounds yesterday as Tony Lazzeri came to the bat in the third inning. Old and very painful shadows they were for Tony. He sees again, in his mind's eye the menacing figure of Grover Cleveland Alexander looming up in the pitcher's box, and there is the weight of the burden of Atlas on his shoulders. It is the final game of the 1926 series and Tony comes up in a desperate, soul-searing situation. The bases are loaded with his own Yankee colleagues and it is up to him to write Yankee success or failure.

Fate is unkind to Lazzeri. It draws a wafery line between conquest and defeat, glory and humiliation. Tony raps the second ball pitched into the stands. A sure homer had it been fair, a world championship payoff clout. But the ball flew foul. The fortunate Alexander, shifting his quid of tobacco to the other cheek, again takes up the Cardinal gauge of battle against Tony. He fans out Tony with a curve, converting a near hero into the abject shape of a "goat." The game is over. The Cardinals have won the championship.

It took ten long years for Tony to catch up with his failure, but catch it he did yesterday. The third inning it is, and the bases are again loaded with Tony at bat. Coffman is in there this time, not Alexander, and the Giants are the anxious parties, not the Cardinals. Again he raps the second ball pitched and the sphere, this time, wings to the right field stands. It is a gloriously fair swat. Four runs amble across the plate. This feat has not been accomplished since the 1920 series, when Earl Smith delivered such a blow for the Cleveland Indians against our pennant-winning Dodgers. There is a great commotion about this, but before the saturnalia of swatting is ended the fans will have more to talk about. Lazzeri is credited with five runs batted in—a series record. Oddly enough, ere the hammering is done, Billy Dickey equals it. Both his homers and drive in five runs.

SHATTERING OF SIX OLD MARKS

In all six old marks are shattered and four others are tied. Frankie Crosetti equals the feat of Babe Ruth and Earl Combs by scoring four runs. In this amazing exhibition every Yankee gets at least one hit and scores one run.

Gomez, one of the world's worst hitters, had the distinction of batting in the 13th tally. This tied the previous record of runs scored in any one World Series game by a single club. A few seconds later he carried the run across the plate that established a new record for the Yankees in this matter. Another record we must not overlook. Yesterday's game was also the longest on record in a World Series, the boys consuming two hours and 49 minutes on the field.

The field' hero was undoubtedly Joe DiMaggio. He gave the Giant sluggers a collective headache with his graceful spearings of wallops. Joe snared them from almost every angle, grabbing them off his shoelaces as neatly as he took them over a shoulder on the run. In the Giants' last turn at bat it was DiMaggio who attended to all their threatening gestures. He accounted for all three putouts, and one of them was decidedly more than a gesture. This was the Herculean rap of burly Hank Leiber. It sailed 455 feet—the longest and most violently cuffed ball of the whole afternoon.

GOMEZ HURLED A SHODDY GAME

Lefty Gomez won his game all right, but he wasn't any dazzling hero at that. The fact of the matter is El Goofy pitched a shoddy game when you think of Carl Hubbell's magnificent flipping. He was in plenty of three-and-two hot water, and he was about as steady as an old woman crossing the street.

To point the obvious, when you lamp the box score, the big factor yesterday was not the heaving of El Goofy but the Herculean power in the Yankee bats. They entirely wrecked five Giant pitchers with a bombardment of 17 hits—count 'em—that piled up the grotesque and humiliating score of 18 to 4. All appearance of a ball game vanished into thin air after the third inning. In this explosive session the Yanks slugged seven runs across the plate.

The clients must have enjoyed it, for the roars sounded like the waters of Niagara. They forgot all about the loss of competition in the whirl of record-breakings and Jovian clouting.

It was a New Deal for the revengeful Yankees, still smarting from their previous day humiliation at the hands of the wizardous Carl Hubbell. They showed everybody they could take over the Giants—and how!

Speaking of the Yankees' New Deal reminds you of another New Dealer who sat in on the Giant rout—President Roosevelt. The President seemed to enjoy the Yankee interpretation of the New Deal. He remained to the very end of it.

Burman Proves No Match for Lewis

Chicago, Oct. 3 (AP)—Whatever hopes Clarence (Red) Burman held of climbing to the front rank as a heavyweight contender were badly dented today by the smashing fists of John Henry Lewis of the Phoenix, Ariz., Negro, world's light heavyweight boxing champion.

More than 11,000 spectators at the Stadium here last night saw Lewis drop the Baltimore, Md., red head three times in the first round and then stop him for a technical knockout in the second.

Bill Terry Calls DiMaggio Best Yankee Player

'He's Dynamite,' Avers Giants' Manager in Praise of Outfielder

By HAROLD PARROTT

Roosevelt was there, Al Smith, the Giants' pitcher, took a walk (after giving one too many) and George Magerkurth, the umpire at first base, is Herbert Hoover's double, facially. And, oh yes, those Giants played like a crew of WPA workers.

Politics was in the air, you see, at the Polo Grounds yesterday and perhaps Colonel Terry was just being diplomatic and politic when he said all those glowing things about the Yankees.

But say them he did, after the game. "That club, from top to bottom, has more power than any I've ever seen," said the Giant pilot. "It's fatal to let them get ahead of you."

How about Joe DiMaggio?

"A wow," said Terry, with enthusiasm very unlike his saturnine self. "I can see now why they say he 'made' their club. He never looks as if he's trying hard, but with that easy, loping stride he gets everything. He's a dandy young ball player, the best to come up in years, and as far as I can see he hits about everything. He's dynamite!"

"You can't pitch like that to a powerful club like the Yanks and get away with it," said Terry. "Our pitchers were all in the hole, and they had to come through with it after being behind the batters, they were murdered. But the Yanks CAN be pitched to, and when we pitch to 'em for nine innings, as we did Wednesday, we'll beat 'em."

Official Score of 2d World Series Game

YANKEES (A. L.)

	ab	r	h	po	a	e
Crosetti, ss...	5	4	3	0	1	0
Rolfe, 3b.....	4	3	2	2	0	0
DiMaggio, cf.	5	2	3	6	0	0
Gehrig, 1b...	5	1	2	6	0	0
Dickey, c.....	5	3	2	8	0	0
Selkirk, rf...	5	1	1	2	0	0
Powell, lf....	3	2	2	2	0	0
Lazzeri, 2b...	4	1	1	1	3	0
Gomez, p....	5	1	1	0	0	0
Totals.....	41	18	17	27	4	0

GIANTS (N. L.)

	ab	r	h	po	a	e
Moore, lf.....	5	0	0	2	0	0
Bartell, ss....	3	0	1	2	2	0
Terry, 1b.....	5	0	2	6	1	0
Leiber, cf....	4	0	0	7	1	0
Ott, rf.......	4	0	0	4	0	0
Mancuso, c...	2	2	1	3	2	0
Whiteh'd, 2b.	4	0	0	2	1	0
Jackson, 3b..	4	1	1	0	2	1
Sch'mach'r, p	0	0	0	0	0	0
Smith, p.....	0	0	0	0	0	0
Coffman, p..	0	0	0	0	1	0
aDavis	1	1	1	0	0	0
Gabler, p....	0	0	0	1	0	0
bDanning ...	1	0	0	0	0	0
Gumbert, p..	0	0	0	0	0	0
	33	4	6	27	10	1

aBatted for Coffman in fourth inning.

bBatted for Gabler in eighth inning.

Yankees	2 0 7 0 0 1 2 0 6—18
Giants	0 1 0 3 0 0 0 0 0— 4

Runs batted in—Gehrig (3), Dickey (5), Lazzeri (5), Bartell, Terry (2), DiMaggio (2), Gomez (2), Rolfe. Two-base hits—DiMaggio, Mancuso, Bartell. Home runs—Lazzeri, Dickey. Stolen base—Powell. Sacrifice—DiMaggio Double play—Leiber, Jackson and Bartell. Earned runs—Yankees, 17; Giants, 4. Left on bases—Yankees, 6; Giants, 9. Bases on balls—Off Schumacher, 4 (Rolfe, 2; Selkirk, Lazzeri); off Smith, 1 (Powell); off Gomez, 7 (Leiber, Mancuso, 2; Schumacher, Bartell, 2; Gabler); off Gabler, 3 (Crosetti, Dickey, Gehrig); off Gumbert, 1 (Powell). Struck out—By Gomez, 8 (Moore), 2; Bartell, Terry, Leiber, Whitehead, Mancuso, Danning); by Schumacher, 1 (Gomez); by Coffman, 1 (Gomez). Hits—Off Schumacher, 5 runs, 3 hits in 2 innings (none out in third); off Smith, 3 runs, 2 hits in 1-3 inning; off Coffman, 1 run, 2 hits in 1 2-3 innings; off Gabler, 3 runs, 5 hits in 4 innings; off Gumbert, 6 runs, 5 hits in 1 inning. Wild pitches—Schumacher, Gomez. Losing pitcher—Schumacher. Umpires—Geisel, Magerkurth, Summers and Pfirman. Time of game—2:49.

Yankee Stars Scatter Stars - - - - - - - - - By Ed Hughes

Niagara of Hits In Keeping With Season's Pace

Yankees' Barrage Is Answer to Giants' Sneer of Pitching in A. L.

By FRANK REIL

The display of power and fancy batting which awed and panicked the Giants yesterday was really nothing out of the ordinary—that is for the Yankees. All season they have been hitting at such a pace and yesterday's record-breaking Niagara of runs was merely in keeping with their usual form.

However, the big batting show was a direct answer to the sneers the Giants made at the remarkable achievements of their rivals before the Series started.

"Why, there's no pitching in that league," poo-pooed the Giants. "They'll see some real pitching in the Series."

So far the only one the Yankees have seen who resembles a pitcher is Carl Hubbell and the Yanks have sworn that the next time he starts, he'll look as woe-begone as the five fellows who pitched yesterday. Hubbell is due to pitch tomorrow and the Yanks say his "number is up."

Until further evidence is submitted the Giants will have to admit that the Yankees can really hit or else confess that their marvelous pitching staff which won the pennant for them is over-rated.

A Convincing Homer

This observer, who has seen the Yankees make as many as 25 runs in a single game, is inclined to believe that the Yankees can hit—and hit any kind of pitching when they are in the right mood. Not even a Hubbell would have stood them off yesterday once they got under way. Bill Terry must have sensed it after Tony Lazzeri had hit his best relief pitcher, Dick Coffman, for a home run with the bases filled. The base-clearing wallop was the finish of the game as far as Terry was concerned.

Not only was the hitting typical of the Yankees but also the pitching

Continued on Following Page

Results and Standing In the World Series

The standing, results and schedule of the World Series between the Yankees and the Giants follow:

Standing

	W.	L.	Pct.
New York Giants (N. L.).	1	1	.500
New York Yankees (A. L.).	1	1	.500

Results

At Polo Grounds (Sept. 30)—

		R.	H.	E.
Yankees ...	0 0 1 0 0 0 0 0 0	1	7	2
Giants	0 0 0 0 1 1 0 4 x	6	9	1

Batteries — Ruffing and Dickey; Hubbell and Mancuso.

At Polo GrGounds (Oct. 2)—

		R.	H.	E.
Yankees ...	2 0 7 0 0 1 2 6	18	17	0
Giants ..	0 1 0 3 0 0 0 0 0	4	6	1

Batteries — Gomez and Dickey; Schumacher, Smith, Coffman, Gabler, Gumbert and Mancuso.

Schedule

Third game today at Yankee Stadium, 1:30 p.m.

Fourth game tomorrow at Yankee Stadium, 2 p.m. and fifth game Monday at Yankee Stadium, 1:30 p.m.

Sixth and seventh games (if necessary), Tuesday and Wednesday, 1:30 p.m.

Composite Box Score of World Series

New York Yankees (A. L.)

	G	AB	R	H	2B	3B	HR	RBI	BB	SO	FAv	PO	A	E	FAv
Crosetti, ss	2	9	4	4	1	0	0	0	1	0	.444	1	4	1	.833
Rolfe, 3b	2	7	3	3	0	0	0	1	2	0	.429	4	1	0	1,000
DiMaggio, cf.	2	9	2	4	1	0	0	2	0	1	.444	9	0	0	1,000
Gehrig, 1b	2	8	1	2	0	0	0	3	1	1	.250	13	0	0	1,000
Dickey, c.	2	9	3	2	0	0	1	5	1	1	.222	16	0	1	.941
Selkirk, rf.	2	9	2	2	0	0	1	1	1	2	.222	2	0	0	1,000
Powell, lf.	2	7	2	5	1	0	0	0	2	0	.714	4	0	0	1,000
Lazzeri, 2b.	2	7	1	1	0	0	1	5	2	2	.143	2	5	0	1,000
Ruffing, p.	1	3	0	0	0	0	0	0	0	2	.000	0	1	0	1,000
Gomez, p.	1	5	1	1	0	0	0	2	0	2	.200	0	0	0	.000
Totals	2	73	19	24	3	0	3	19	10	11	.329	51	11	2	.969

New York Giants (N. L.)

	G	AB	R	H	2B	3B	HR	RBI	BB	SO	FAv	PO	A	E	FAv
Moore, lf.	2	10	0	0	0	0	0	0	0	3	.000	2	0	0	1,000
Bartell, ss.	2	7	1	3	1	0	1	2	2	1	.429	3	4	0	1,000
Terry, 1b.	2	9	1	4	0	0	0	2	0	1	.444	18		0	1,000
Ott, rf.	2	6	2	2	1	0	0	0	2	0	.333	4	0	0	1,000
Leiber, cf.	1	4	0	0	0	0	0	0	1	7	.000	7	1	0	1,000
Ripple, cf.	1	2	0	0	0	0	0	0	0	1	.000	0	0	0	.000
Mancuso, c.	2	5	3	2	1	0	0	1	3	2	.400	12	3	0	1,000
Whitehead, 2b.	2	7	1	0	0	0	0	1	1	2	.000	5	5	0	1,000
Jackson, 3b.	2	8	1	1	0	0	0	1	0	1	.125	1	3	1	.800
Hubbell, p.	1	4	0	2	0	0	0	1	0	0	.500	1	2	1	.750
Schumacher, p.	1	0	0	0	0	0	0	0	1	0	.000	0	0	0	.000
Smith, p.	1	0	0	0	0	0	0	0	0	0	.000	0	0	0	.000
Coffman, p.	1	0	0	0	0	0	0	0	0	0	.000	0	1	0	1,000
Gabler, p.	1	0	0	0	0	0	0	0	1	0	.000	1	0	0	1,000
Gumbert, p.	1	0	0	0	0	0	0	0	0	0	.000	0	0	0	.000
aDavis	1	1	1	1	0	0	0	0	0	0	1,000	0	0	0	.000
bDanning	1	1	0	0	0	0	0	0	0	1	.000	0	0	0	.000
Totals	2	64	10	15	3	0	1	8	11	13	.234	54	22	2	.974

aBatted for Coffman in the fourth inning, second game.

bBatted for Gabler in the eighth inning, second game.

Pitching Records

	G	CH	IP	H	R	ER	BB	SO	WP	HR	W	L	Pct.
Ruffing	1	1	9	9	6	5	4	5	0	0	0	1	.000
Gomez	1	1	9	6	4	4	7	8	1	0	1	0	1,000
Hubbell	1	1	9	7	1	1	1	8	0	1	1	0	1,000
Schumacher	1	0	2	3	5	4	4	1	1	0	0	1	.000
Smith	1	0	1-3	2	3	3	1	0	0	0	0	0	.000
Coffman	1	0	1 2-3	2	1	1	0	1	0	0	0	0	.000
Gable .r...........	1	0	4	5	6	6	1	1	0	0	0	0	.000
Gumbert	1	0	1	5	6	6	1	1	0	0	0	0	.000

SCORE BY INNINGS

New York (A. L.)	2	0	8	0	0	1	2	0	6—19
New York (N. L.)	0	1	0	3	1	1	0	4	0—10

Stolen base—Powell.

Sacrifices—Rolfe, DiMaggio, Ripple (2).

Double plays—Whitehead and Terry; Leiber, Jackson and Bartell.

Left on base—Yankees, 13; Giants, 16.

Umpires—Geisel and Summers, American League; Pfirman and Magerkurth, National League.

Sportpourri

The 'Nut' for Jasper-Holy Cross Grid Tilt Much Steeper Than St. John's

That tune they played thrice at the Polo Grounds yest'y, dubbed the "Franklin D. March," was written by Chas. Ryan, a Queens man...Manhattan College is running an excursion to Worcester, Mass., next week, so Jasper fans can follow their team...including a reserved seat at the game, the tab will be $8.50...We can remember when St. John's men by the hundreds made it on a dollar, a toothbrush and a three-cylinder Ford, to see their heroes play Holy Cross...Charley Dressen has grabbed Lonny Frey for the Reds (no foolin') because he used to play beside the youngster at Nashville in the Southern, and thinks he has the stuff...Lonny fielded just as jittery then, too, however...Another shift you can mark in the book right now is Riper Collins, who's around town putting the rap on the Cards and the way they're run...He'll bring plenty of gold on the market, which is another reason he can't stay with St. Loo...St. John's has re-hired that capable press-agent, for which bravo...Buck Freeman, whose Iona Prep gridders opened with a 39—0 win, starts next week to promote pro basketball in White Plains with Bill O'Brien, the pro tennis sachem...O'Brien has wrestling and boxing there, too, and owns Scranton and McKeesport in the minor leagues, if you please!...Top price since 1928 was paid for a polo pony at the East Williston (L. I.) sale yest'y, Jock Whitney laying out $14,500 for one nifty on four legs...What will that ciggie gal at the Garden City hotel do when Roberto Cavanagh of the Argentine polo outfit, sails back?...Walter Stewart is favored to win, hands up (to his mouth) in the newspapermen's eating contest at World Series baseball hdqtrs.

HAROLD PARROTT.

Batting Records Fall in Yankees Rout of Giants

Lazzeri and Gomez Add Their Names to World Series Hall of Fame

By GEORGE CURRIE

Records fell by the wayside . . . The Yankees had 17 hits for 18 runs . . . Thereby running every statistic that had been tucked away in the Judge Kenesaw Mountain Landis billfold . . . As our Tommy Holmes will tell you, Tony Lazzeri cleaned the bases in the third inning to hit a home run with the bases full for the first time since Elmer Smith did it away back in 1920 . . . The Giants used up all their quarterbacks, excepting Freddy Fitzsimmons . . . And they might as well have used him up, too, for all that their pitchers could hold those Yankee batters. They didn't seem to have a running guard . . . In fact, Mr. Casey Stengel told me a story that Ed Hughes, Tommy Holmes, Harold Parrott and Frank Reil had already told me about Cottreaux, who ate a dozen oysters, washed down with a pint of beer . . . And Mr. Casey Stengel told him that he could eat his oysters—but the hell with the beer!

Tony Lazzeri was the big hero of the game . . . But he had to share it with President Roosevelt, who received an organized ovation from the reserved seats . . . And a GREAT ovation from the bleachers—where the votes are.

Lefty Gomez went all through the motions of a great and bad ball game . . . He had his worst time in the fourth inning, when he probably pitched the worst ball that was ever served up in a World Series . . . In the ninth he had his inning, so to speak . . . He batted in a run and scored a run.

Lefty broke a series record when he batted in his run . . . Then he went on to break the record by scoring himself.

Lefty bows to his batters very politely . . . Apologizing for striking out eight of them.

Lazzeri, after getting a cheap home run in the right field stands, also hit probably the longest ball that was ever walloped in the Polo Grounds, only to have DiMaggio

Continued on Following Page

Official Series Figures For First Two Games

The official figures for the second game of the World Series and the totals for two games, as compared with the same figures last year, follow:

Second Game Totals

	1936	1935
Paid attendance...,	43.543	46.742
Receipts	$184,962.00	$144,725.00
Players' share	94,330.62	73,809.75
Commission's share.	27,744.30	21,706.75
Club's share	31,443.54	24,603.14
League's share.....	31,443.54	24,603.14

Totals for Two Games

	1936	1935
Paid attendance....	82.962	94.133
Receipts	$357,119.00	$290,157.00
Players' share	182.130.69	147.980.07
Commission's share.	53.567.85	43.521.55
Club's share	60,710.23	49,276.58
League's share.....	60,710.23	49,276.58

The Power of Suggestion

THE POWER of suggestion is a mighty potent business, sometimes as persuasive as were those Yankee bats yesterday. There was a deal of slugging power as well as dire suggestion ringing off Yankee maces while the hits fell like shrapnel around a bevy of misguided Giant pitchers. One could be pardoned for wondering just what emotions were passing through the gaunt frame of an idle Giant pitcher who will shortly have another experience with the deadly Yankee artillery. I mean Carl Hubbell, of course. Hubbell watched the unholy slaughter of his colleagues of the mound, saw the Yankee siege guns booming for the first time.

The Giant ace is a stolid, imperturbable fellow, but it would be interesting to know what was going on inside his skull during all this. It is a fair guess that he was musing: "Well, these fellows don't look a lot like the birds I tamed the other day!" And it is just possible that Carl doesn't feel quite so sure today as he did Wednesday night that he has the Yankees' number. The Yanks were dispensing quite a lot of discomforting suggestion at the Polo Grounds yesterday.

Remember Mr. Brickley?

SPEAKING of the power of suggestion, do you recall a little stratagem of Charlie Brickley some years back? I mean Brickley the great Harvard kicker, of course. Remember how the burly Brickley deliberately walked out in front of a Yale team and began practicing drops and placements, just to impress on them what he could do in that line? Brickley kicked some half doze ngoals in succession from various distances while the Elis looked on in pop-eyed wonderment.

I don't say this sly exhibition of skill and power licked Yale before the game started. But it is a fact that Brickley, in the game itself, did lick them single-handed, single-footed would be better. It looked like a combination of the power of suggestion and the nower in Brickley's right hoof.

Herr Schmeling's Conviction

SOMETIMES, though, the power of suggestion takes a happier turn for the onlooker. Hard by the ringside the night Joe Louis knocked tough Paulino addel-brained with one deadly, clean-driven punch, sat another fighter. Ringsiders felt sorry for him. In the then near future he was scheduled to face this same master-puncher, Louis. This interested onlooker was Max Schmeling.

He made a hasty getaway from the scene of Paulino's paingul collapse. A scribe near me predicted "Max is heading for Germany and I'll bet you anything you want that he'll never come back to fight Mr. Louis." If you didn't agree with him, you at least felt that Schmeling would be exercising the better part of wisdom if he didn't come back.

However, it is a matter of record that Schmeling did come back, and he brought with him a curious conviction. Did it worry him, that picture of the menacing young Negro cashiering the hitherto punch-proof Paulino? Not at all, it seems.

In fact Herr Schmeling explained that he had really profited a great deal by witnessing Louis in action that particular time. He had discovered, so he said, a flaw in the Louis fighting machinery. That is, he had figured out a way, on the spot, to beat Joe. No, he wasn't kidding; he really meant it. He thought it not extraordinary that Paulino had been knocked out, but he was really amazed that someone, ere that, hadn't whippd Joe Louis.

Suggestion in Reverse

IT IS a fact that few people took this tongue-wagging of Schmeling seriously. They asked him what it was that he saw that made him sure Louis wasn't a world-beater but rather a fighter who was begging to be whipped.

Schmeling wouldn't say anything about that—until after the fight. Then he explained, and it was all very simple. Louis was a "sucker" for a right hand punch to the chin. He held his left very low and was really slow in getting away from a quick right. At least Schmeling figured that he would be, and the interesting part of it is that Max proved that such was the case. He rattled whizzing righthanders off Joe's chin until the brown boy crumpled to the floor thoroughly beaten.

The power of suggestion worked in reverse the night Max Schmeling studied Louis from that ringside seat. Louis didn't suggest defeat and pugilistic ruin to Schmeling, no matter how fearful a fighting machine he looked to the paying customers. His style suggested a brilliant conquest for the observing Max, wherein he was the one man in all that gathering who received that particular suggestion.

Another Schmeling?

CARL HUBBELL has the encouraging knowledge that he can at least beat the Yankees on occasion, for he has already performed that feat. It is not improbable that, like Max Schmeling, he discovered further weaknesses in the Yanke eattack as he observed them in homicidal action against his team-mates yesterday.

But offhand, I'd say it's fortunate for Hubbell that he isn't of a fretful disposition, is not inclined to let his imagination have too much rein. Because there was a copious supply of uncomfortable suggestion being batted out by those Yanks—for anyone who was inclined to let his mind run to depressing thoughts.

How They Will Line Up for the Rich Futurity at Belmont

Belmont Park Race Track, N. Y., Oct. 3 (AP)—Following are the lineups for the $25,000 added six and a half furlong Futurity (estimated value $80,990) and the $5,000 added, two-mile Jockey Club Gold Cup (estimated value, $9,010), to be decided here today, with prospects for a fast track prevailing. Post positions for the futurity will be drawn 30 minutes before post time.

FUTURITY

Horse	Wt.	Jockeys	Owner	Prob. Odds
Pompoon	127	H. Richards	J. H. Louchheim....	3—2
Apogee	127	E. Steffen	H. P. Headley.....	30—1
Privileged	125	E. Arcaro	Calumet Farm......	7—1
aReaping Reward......	125	No boy	Milky Way Farm....	20—1
aDogaway	122	A. Robertson	Milky Way Farm....	20—1
Billionaire	122	D. Brammer	E. R. Bradley......	5—1
bCharing Cross	122	E. Yager	M. Field	10—1
bSir Damion	122	G. Seabo	M. Field	10—1
Flying Cross..........	122	R. Workman	C. V. Whitney.....	20—1
Flying Scot	122	J. Gilbert	J. H. Whitney.....	20—1
John P. War..........	122	E. Litz'ger	Mrs. W. H. Hurst..	15—1
Optic	122	W. D. Wright	J. E. Widener.....	4—1
cMelodist	122	No boy	Wheatley Stable....	30—1
cRiparian	122	J. Stout	Belair Stud	30—1
Sun Capture	122	C. Kurtsinger	W. S. Kilmer......	50—1
dEli Yale.............	122	No boy	Greentree Stable....	30—1
dTattered	117	No boy	Greentree Stable....	30—1
Dawn Play............	119	I. Hanford	King Ranch	20—1
Cosmic Ray...........	117	M. Corona	Brookmeade Stable..	100—1

aMilky Way Farm entry.
bMarshall Field entry.
cTrainer J. Fitzsimmons entry.
dGreentree Stable entry.

BOUTS LAST NIGHT

Chicago—John Henry Lewis, 178½, Phoenix, Ariz., stopped Clarence (Red) Burman, 176¼, Baltimore, Md. (2).

San Diego—Baby Jack Thomas, 141½, Houston, Texas, and Frenchy Proulx, 145, Chicago, drew (10).

Atlantic City—Johnny Hutchinson, 127, Philadelphia, won on technical knockout over Johnny De Foe, 128½, New York (3).

Philadelphia—Danny Hassett, 181½, outpointed Terry Mitchell, 187½, Brooklyn (10).

Providence, R. I.—Ralph Zennelli, 144, Providence, won on technical knockout over Eddie Holmes, 142¾, Providence (3).

Manual Socecrites Stop Tilden, 3 to 0

The Manual Soccer team started its P. S. A. L. season with a 3—0 victory over Tilden, at Manual's field yesterday. The spearhead of the Manual attack was little Milio Elustando who scored tw ogoals. Manual was kept from running wild by the numerous and brilliant saves of goalie Saul Markin of Tilden.

The lineup:

MANUAL (3)		TILDEN (0)
G.	Agoglia	Markin
R.F	Rappalie	Gansin
L.F	Bruce	Korba
R.H	Brybrough	Koslow
L.H	Naverson	Andrews
C.	Mulholland	Bernstein
R.O	Whalen	Getland
L.O	Elustando	Beaker
I.	Powell	Goldberg
C.F	Basso	Malick

Substitutes—Manual: Cutael, Fields, Lee, Boulas, Olhson: Tilden: Reichberg, Haas, Halpern. Scoring—Manual: Elusstando 2, Powell.

YANKEES BEAT GIANTS IN 3D GAME, 2-1

ANY ICE TODAY, TEAM?

The ice man is a very important person in Michigan State. He is an assistant student manager. It is his duty to rush out with cracked ice when Spartan warriors are hurt. The ice is always on hand. Coach Charley Bachman says prompt application of ice prevents long sojourns on the sidelines.

Sports BROOKLYN Financial
DAILY EAGLE

PERAMBULATING PLAINSMEN

Coach Jack Meagher's Alabama Poly gridders this season play just exactly one game on their home sod at Auburn. They do play two games at Montgomery, Ala., however. But they will travel 9,664 miles, including trips to Detroit to play Detroit University and to San Francisco to meet Santa Clara.

POMPOON TAKES RICH FUTURITY STAKES

N. Y. U. Crushed—Lovelock Loses—Barton Wins Golf

Jerome Louchheim Colt Sets Record, Winning $56,790

By W. C. VREELAND

With long, sweeping strides, which gained in speed and power as his swinging motion carried him down the Widener course, Pompon, giant two-year-old son of Pompey—Conagh, carried home the orange white sleeves, black cap colors of J. H. Louchheim four lengths to the good in the race for the 47th running of the Futurity at Belmont Park yesterday.

So fast did he travel the last 6½ furlongs of the straight away that he hung up a new track record of 1:16 2-5, beating the previous mark made by Balladier by a fifth of a second. And that flight of speed netted the big bay juvenile $56,790, the first portion of the rich prize which grossed $72,990.

Behind Pompoon, in a cluster, followed the Calumet Farm's Privileged, which beat C. V. Whitney's Flying Cross a neck for second money, $9,800. Flying Cross, by the margin of his head, earned third money, $5,400, from Marshall Field's Sir Damion, which saved his starting fee of $1,000.

—o—

NEVER UP IN FINAL QUARTER

It was not until the final quarter of a mile that Pompoon showed his superiority over the other colts. Up to that stage of the race he raced with the pack of five leaders—Charing Cross, Pompoon, Billionaire, John P. War, Sir Damion and Privileged. All were in a cluster, heads apart. Up to that time Harry Richards, his jockey, was holding him under stout restraint. Then Richards made one move—and the race was over, all but the gleeful shouting of 25,000 racegoers.

Among the crowd of delighted racing fans who bet on Pompoon, which was favorite at 8 to 5, were just two who had great fait in the colt's speed and stamina.

—o—

NEGRO ATTENDANT SWEEPSTAKES WINNER

One was Roger Johnson, the Negro attendant of the field glasses owned by club members. He had invested $2 in a sweepstakes and in the draw his ticket corresponded with the name of Pompoon.

The other interested onlooker was Herbert Bayard Swope, chairman of the State Racing Commission. Swope purchased a half interest in Johnson's sweep ticket, paying $3,000 for it. Its total value was $12,500. Swope last year had been equally fortunate in buying a prize. He paid $800 for a ticket held by John Sanford on Tintagel. And when Tintagel flashed home the winner of the Futurity in 1935 Swope cashed in $8,500.

Sixteen juvenile colts and one filly made up the field of starters for the bi gevent. It was an open betting race with Pompoon always an outstanding favorite. Billionaire was second choice at 5 to 1. Optic was next at 6 to 1. The Field pair at post time was backed from 15 to 1 to 8 to 1.

There was a short delay at the post due to John P. War's fractiousness. He was placed on the outside. Pompoon drew No. 11 position. Cassidy sent them away in a line. Billionaire was the first to show, followed closely by Pompoon, Charing Cross, John P. War and Sir Damion. Cosmic Ray was last with Privileged just in front of him.

Mrs. John D. Hertz's Count Arthur, winner of the Saratoga Cup in 1935, romped home the winner of The Jockey Club Gold Cup, $6,750 net, two miles, the longest race of the year by four lengths.

With Firethorn and Esposa scratched, Count Arthur opened even money favorite in the odds but at post time Memory Book replaced him, closing first choice at 13 to 10. Count Arthur receded to 8 to 5.

For a mile and a half Jean Bart showed the way on sufferance by open daylight. Count Arthur and Memory Book raced in company, a neck apart.

Giant Killer trailed six lengths in the rear. In the last half mile Count Arthur easily moved to the front and won under a pull by four lengths. Memory Book was second three lengths in front of Giant Killer. Jean Bart stopped badly in the last half mile.

Bushranger was crowned king of the inner field when he romped home the winner of the Grand National Steeplechase, three miles, value $5,750 net. Carrying 172 pounds, a weight never before on the back of a winner for this notable cross-country event [illegible]

Continued on Page 2

N.Y.U. Crushed By Ohio State Eleven, 60-0

Record 73,000 Crowd Sees Violets Suffer One of Worst Losses

Columbus, Oct. 3—Helpless in the face of a punishing Ohio State attack, the New York University football team fell easy prey to the Buckeyes, 60 to 0, here today. The home team Savaged every Violet combination relentlessly and allowed the losers little time to collect their own offense.

A crowd of 72,948, a new attendance record for an opening game, packed Ohio Stadium and saw Willitm (Tippy) Dye, dynamic little quarterback, run and pass his mates to a smashing victory.

State scored its first touchdown with the game barely 30 seconds old. After winning the toss, the Buckeyes elected to kick. Bill Booth's punt to Mike Stelmach on the Violet 7-yard line was returned to the 22-yard marker.

Stelmach, in an attempt to catch his opponents napping, faded back and threw a pass, which was intercepted by Jim McDonald. Not a hand was laid on McDonald as he sped 33 yards over the goal line.

The second Scarlet and Gray score came in the middle of the first period. An exchange of punts had brought the ball to N. Y. U.'s 23-yard stripe. Joe Williams, on a reverse around left end, carried it to the visitors' 4-yard line and plunged over two plays later to raise the count to 13 to 0.

Completely Outclassed

After that, Dyke took almost complete charge of the Buckeye offensive. Alternating long passes with short running gains, he was responsible for three of his team's scores.

Only once in th efirst half was the Violet in possession of the ball in State territory, and then but for one play. Mike Dabealo kicked to Bernie Bloom from his own 4-yard line to N. Y. U.'s 46.

After running the ball to State's 49, Bloom essayed a pass, which was intercepted by Merle Wendt, Buckeye captain, on his 47-yard stripe.

It wasn't until the last quarter that the Violets entered enemy territory again. Bloom threw a 33-yard pass to Howard Dunney, who took it on State's 20-yard line.

Dunney raced across the Buckeye goal line, but was called back because he had stepped out of bounds after receiving the pass. It was the nearest they came to scoring all day.

Continued on Page 2

This Dickey Was a Dead Bird

Bill Dickey, Yankee catcher, gunned down at second b ase in the first part of a double play into which Ja[illegible] hit in the second inning at Yankee Stadium yesterday.

Record Crowd Sees Crosetti's Hit Win Keen Mound Duel

Continued From Page 1, Main Section

up their first series victory. The 17 Yankee hits at the Polo Grounds, laid end to end, would reach from Borough Hall to Times Square.

Yesterday they were able to get only four hits and won with a single which dribbled no more than 10 feet past the pitcher's box.

Before 64,842 paying guests, the largest crowd ever to witness a World Series ball game, the two teams staged a terrifically tense struggle through seven and one-half innings of a perfect baseball day.

When the Yankees came to bat in the eighth inning the score was tied at 1 to 1. One of the two hits the American Leaguers had obtained off the whirling delivery of Fitzsimmons was a home run planted in the right field bleachers by Lou Gehrig, the burly Yankee first baseman, who probably is the most consistently dangerous hitter in baseball today. Gehrig came through with his blast in the second inning.

Jim Ripple, tawny-thatched center fielder of the Giants, hit another home run into that same sector in the fifth inning to tie the score. Before and after Ripple's poke the Giants pecked away consistently at Bump Hadley, the righthanded flinger, who trod the tee for the American Leaguers. The Giants seemed sure to score eventually. On the other hand, it seemed as though the Yankees might be forced to wait until next week for their next hit the way Fitzsimmons was whizzing the ball through the slot.

—o—

SELKIRK'S SINGLE IS PAY-OFF BALL

But George Selkirk changed all that with a single to right, and Jake Powell, the next Yankee batter, received the second and last base on balls issued by Fitz in the jolly ball game.

To the eye of this writer, peering from the cavernous depths of the mezzanine press box, the next play seemed the real break of the ball game rather than the things that happened later.

Poosh-'em-up Tony Lazzeri, stolid San Francisco Italian who has played second base for the Yankees for 11 seasons, stepped to the plate to drop down a sacrifice bunt and advanced both runners. Bunting against Fitzsimmons is an extremely risky proposition, for that barrell chested, hammered down citizen is perhaps the best fielding pitcher in baseball.

No one will know whether the success of the Lazzeri maneuver was accidental or not. Technically, the ball was hit too hard to be a perfect bunt in ordinary circumstances. But the bunt fitted this situation perfectly. Fitz couldn't get to it in time, Travis Jackson had to move off third base to field the ball and though Lazzeri was thrown out at first, Selkirk gambolled to third and Powell steamed to second

—o—

FITZ STARTS TO BEAR DOWN

Fitzsimmons was bearing down now and bearing down hard. Red Ruffing batted for Hadley and topped a ball back toward the box. As agile as a beagle, the sturdy Fitzsimmons fielded the ball and threw it to Gus Mancuso, who blocked Selkirk off the plate for the second out.

Powell reached third and Ruffing got to first on the play. The followers of the Giants relaxed. Two men were out and somehow Frankie Crosetti, the Yankee shortstop, up at the plate, didn't seem dangerous.

But, as Jimmy Durante would put it, Crosetti—another Italian from San Francisco—meant the gallows for the deserving Fitzsimmons. He hit one back a little to the left of the pitcher's box.

—o—

DESPERATE TRY IS IN VAIN

Instinctively Fitz lunged for the ball. It struck his glove, but broke through and rolled behind him. Burgess Whitehead, the second baseman of the Giants, raced in and desperately tried a bare hand stab of the ball and a throw to first with one motion. He missed his first attempt, then grabbed the ball and threw. But in that important split second Powell had charged across the plate with the run that proved the payoff, while the speedy Crosetti was sprinting over first.

That was the ball game, pure and simple. Red Rolfe, the next batter

Continued on Page 6

Pamela Barton Wins Women's U.S. Golf Crown

English Girl Defeats Mrs. Orcutt Crews in Final Round, 4 and 3

By RALPH TROST

Summit, N. J., Oct. 3—A woman succeeded where main failed when stout 19-year-old Pamela Barton, a young woman of many freckles and the glint of new copper in her hair, won the national woman's golf championship by defeating Mrs. Maureen Orcutt Crews, 4 and 3, in the 36-hole final.

The finishing touch was electric, Pam, whose putting from beyond 25 feet having been so uncertain, sinking a 30-footer for a 4.

In winning, Miss Barton becomes the first Britisher to capture the crown since Miss Gladyce Ravenscroft defeated Long Island's Miss Marion Hollins at Wilmington 23 years ago; the first Britisher since then to hold both British and American titles in the short span of a single year. The tall, thistle-adorned trophy Miss Barton takes back to London is a British-presented (the Indian givers) cup, donated by Robert Cox exactly 30 years ago and in competition for the first time at Morris County, just a few brassie shots away from this loggy course where Pam won it.

Maintained Pace

A Briton, with out national amateur crown within his grasp a fortnight ago at Garden City, kicked his chance away. No rabbit, the husky Pam had to go 17 holes this morning before getting a grip on it, but once her neatly manicured chubby hand grabbed hold it hung on, never permitting the taller, slimmer Maureen to wedge her away from it.

Miss Barton, a girl with a swing as hearty as the Ole Ale and Roast Beef of merrie England, won as a champion should. Starting at the 12th hole in the morning and carrying through clear to the very finish, the winner played golf far exceeding the anticipated attainments of a woman on so long and heavy course as this. Aided by a chip shot holed for a birdie on the 18th, Pam played the last 18 holes in three over even fours, five strokes better than the medal winners score on Monday.

For the first five holes the 157-pound champion was as wobbly as any invitation tournament finalist. From there on she was superb.

Mrs. Crews, five times a metropolitan title holder, who reached the final of this championship at Cherry Valley in 1927, the last time it was played in this section, had her opportunity at the start. Miss

Continued on Page 7

Princeton Mile To San Romani; Lovelock Is 2d

By ED HUGHES
(Staff Correspondent of The Eagle)

Palmer Stadium, Princeton, N. J., Oct 3—With a sustained finishing spurt that failed of its objective, Jack Lovelock, Olympic 1,500-meter hero, bowed in defeat here this afternoon as Archie San Romani resisted the New Zealander's desperate effort and led him across the tape by eight yards in the Princeton invitation mile. Glenn Cunningham,

Continued on Page 7

College Football Results

LOCAL

City College 6	Brooklyn 0
Fordham 66	F. and M. 7
Columbia 34	Maine 0
Jamaica 20	Brooklyn J.V. 0

EAST

Army 28	W. and L. 0
Navy 13	Davidson 6
Yale 23	Cornell 0
Princeton 27	Williams 7
Penn 35	Lafayette 0
Penn State 45	Muhlenberg 0
Dickinson 20	Lehigh 6
Boston College 26	Northeastern 6
Boston Univ. 40	Amer. Inter. 0
Brown 7	Rhode Island 6
Colgate 54	Ursinus 0

Continued on Page 5

Lions Defeat Maine on Grid By 34-0 Count

Lou Little's Co[illegible] football team, with Sid [illegible], former Erasmus Hall [illegible] the lead, had a successfu[illegible] yesterday by cavorting th[illegible] round and over the Univers[illegible] f Maine eleven to win, 34 to 0, before a crowd of 7,000 at Baker Field.

Columbia's first string tallied three times after sustained marches of 75, 80 and 57 yards, while the second team carried through to its lone score after covering 79 yards.

It remained for Jimmy Hudasky

Continued on Page 7

Yale Gridders Crush Cornell By 23-0 Score

By GEORGE CURRIE
Staff Correspondent of The Eagle

New Haven, Conn., Oct. 3—Yale took its 1936 edition of a football scoring machine out of the mothballs today for a good airing, chasing Cornell up and down the field to the tune of 23—0 and twice bringing to a halt detenmined Ithacan drives

Continued on Page 2

Gurske, Dulkie Lead Rams to Easy Win, 66-7

By JOSEPH J. GOREVIN

Fordham's fine football team made its initial appearance of the 1936 season at Randall's Island yesterday afternoon and certainly lived up to all the nice bits written about it during the past three weeks.

The big Ram simply gritted its teeth, dug its cleats and rolled over a greatly outclassed Franklin-Mar-

Continued on Page 7

Amherst Eleven Is Victim In Harvard Opener, 38-6

Cambridge, Mass., Oct. 3 (AP)—Harvard's well-drilled football team, miles ahead of the one that launched Dick Harlow's coaching career here last ye , opened its season with a 38-6 victory over the hard-fighting Lord Jeffs from Amherst today before a 15,000 crowd.

The Crimson, although unable to do much with the simple passing attack it attempted, cashed in six of the nine scoring chances that came its way while battling the sturdy (Little Three) collegians in intelligent fashion.

Full-Back Vernon Struck was the outstanding ground-gainer for Harvard. George Roberts plunged over for three of the six touchdowns.

Harvard scored but once in the opening period, added another in the second when Bobby Jones, its center blocked an Amherst punt that was recovered in the Lord Jeffs end zone, 20 yards back, by Left End Gib Winter, and twice in each of the last two quarters.

Early in the final session Harvard's second-string backs marched 53 yards before Bob Stuart drove over from the one-foot line on his second try from that distance. About midway in the period, Ken Booth, a tackle replacement, recovered an Amherst fumble on the latter's 40, and George Ford supplied most of the gains that enabled him to jaunt ten yards off his left tackle for Harvard's final touchdown.

SCORE BY PERIODS

Amherst	0	0	6	0	6
Harvard	7	6	12	13	38

Amherst scoring: Touchdown, Joys (sub for K. Pattengill).

Harvard scoring: Touchdowns, Roberts 3, Winter, Stuart (sub for Roberts), Ford (sub for McTernen); points after touchdown: Kavorkian (place kick), Boston (sub for Wilson) (place kick).

Officials: Referee, W. D. Maginnes Lehigh; umpire, J. E. Coogan, Annapolis; head linesman, J. N. Young, Adams; field judge, J. F. Farrell, Michigan.

Hobart Eleven Turns Back nion, 26-0

Geneva, N. Y., Oct. 3 (AP)—Before a homecoming day crowd, Hobart scored in every quarter but the second today to defeat Union 26 to 0.

Miller scored the first Hobart touchdown on an end run after King galloped 35 yards to the Union 45-yard line on the first series of Hobart plays. Union came back to penetrate to Hobart's 4-yard line on a series of short runs by Thomas and Brown only to lose out on its biggest scoring chance when the Genevans held.

Catholic U. Gridders Score 81-0 Victory

Washington, Oct. 3 (AP)—Catholic University's grid team galloped off with an 81 to 0 win over Shenandoah College today by running up the Cardinal's highest scoring in four seasons.

An even dozen touchdowns went into the score. Nine points went spinning over the cross bar after the touchdowns. Five scores were made by way of the air route from as far as midfield. Catholic University made 20 first downs to one for the Dayton, Va., college.

Met. Golf Assn. Combine Leads In Lesley Cup Links Tourney

Special to The Eagle

Cedarhurst, L. I., Oct. 3—The representatives of the Metropolitan Golf Association started off in excellent fashion at the Rockaway Hunting Club today in the 30th Lesley Cup competition. Rolling up a total of 38 points out of a possible 45, the local golfers had an overwhelming advantage over the three other teams in the event at the end of the two-day tournament.

The Massachusetts aggregation, winners of the event last year, are in second place tonight with 27½ points, while the Pennsylvania Golf Association follows with 22½ points. The Province of Quebec Association, the fourth team taking part, was far in the rear, with only 1½ markers.

This year's team to represent the M. G. A. was captained by T. (Tommy) Suffern Tailer Jr. of Piping Rock and Meadow Brook, former metropolitan titleholder, boasting a powerhouse lineup, which included former national titleholders and present and former New York State, metropolitan as well as district champions, they seemed assured of their 15th triumph since the play got under way back in 1905 at Garden City.

George Voigt, who reached the semi-final round in the National amateur at Garden City two weeks ago; Ray Billows, the cinderella kid, who won the State title last year; Edmund Driggs Jr., another former State titleholder; Charles Mayo Jr. of Lido, the Long Island champion, and Charles Whitehead of Westchester each registered three vfiictories for the M. G. A. in the afternoon singles play.

It All Happened as Yankees Captured World Series From Giants

On left—Umpire Harry Geisel calling Joe DiMaggio safe at plate in ninth inning of World Series finale as ball popped out of glove of Catcher Ike Danning of Giants. In center is celebration in Yankees' clubhouse after American Leaguers settled the question of baseball supremacy in the Fall Blue Ribbon Classic. The occasion is observed by Coach Arthur Fletcher, Manager Joe McCarthy Col. Jacob Ruppert, owner of winning club; Joe DiMaggio and Timothy O'Sullivan, bat boy. On the right is Red Rolfe of the Yankees sliding safely into third base in third inning on DiMaggio's single.

Granville Is Retired To Farm for Balance Of the Racing Season

By W. C. VREELAND

Back to the farm—Granville. The King of the Turf has run his last race—this season.

The son of Gallant Fox, which achieved fame and a goodly portion of fortune this year, has recovered from the "cuffing" of his ankle which prevented him from starting in The Jockey Club Gold Cup.

"Ganville is all right now," said Sunny Jim Fitzsimmons in reply to my query as to the physical condition of the $100,000 winner of the season. "If the Gold Cup were scheduled to be run off this Saturday he would have been ready to race.

—o—

ENGLISH TRAINER HIGH ON OMAHA

"I just didn't care to take a chance with Granville when he showed signs of soreness after his race in the Lawrence Realization Stakes. His ankles had always troubled him more or less, and I was afraid if I raced him in the Cup that he might rupture a tendon. Rather than take any chances Mr. Woodward and I decided to keep him out of the race."

And then the conversation veered around to Omaha. How was he? "Fine," said Fitz. "Mrs. George D. Widener, just returned from Europe, told me that while she was in England she saw Omaha and that he looked splendid—had improved very much in looks, having filled out considerably. I wouldn't be at all surprised if he started in a handicap pretty soon. Captain Boyd-Rochefort, who trains Omaha in England, told Jack Hare, who looks after the horses on the ocean liner which carries them to England, that Omaha is the best colt he has ever trained."

—o—

CAMBRIDGESHIRE HANDICAP

Fitz wasn't certain what race Omaha is eligible for. But putting two and two together—"in a handicap pretty soon"—and knowing that the Cambridgeshire Handicap will be run off at Newmarket on Oct. 28, it's possible that "the big express" will go to the post for that event.

The Cambridgeshire is one one of the most notable races in England. It had its inaugural in 1839, the same year as the Cesarewitch Stakes, which is also run off at Newmarket. The distance of the Cambridgeshire is one mile and a furlong; that of the Cesarewitch, two and a quarter miles.

There is no other course in the world quite like that at Newmarket. There are 29—count 'em, 29—different courses at Newmarket with four stands at which the horses finish. We who get the "Gumps" now and then about the straightaway of the Widener course, and grumble and growl over the fact that the finish is at a different point from that of the regular winning post, in front of the grandstand, should take a trip to Newmarket. There we would be on a hop, skip and a jump going to the different courses.

The Cambridgeshire is practically straightaway—all the way. Where the Cambridgeshire ends is the finishing post of just four courses—Cambridgeshire, Cesarewitch, Rowley Mile and Rous Mile. In the race for the Cesarewitch the start is at an angle with the main course—what we would call a chute, but it's a long one. And then after a dash of a mile and a furlong, the main track is reached for the other mile and a furlong, straightaway.

—o—

GRANVILLE HAS EARNED VACATION

Granville has well earned his rest. He began the season of 1936 practically unheralded and unsung—except by yours truly. He had won only one race, an overnight purse, as a juvenile. But he showed me in all of his races, particularly his last two, in whch he was beaten, that he was a colt which needed a route and that he would do better after he had fully developed. Then, too, knowing that Sunny Jim never hurries a backward colt, I wrote about Granville in the Winter as being as good a prospect as Brevity for the three-year-old events of '36.

And now Granville, after meeting with poor racing luck in his early start is—the King of the Turf.

ERIE FEEDS DETROIT SQUAD

Detroit (AP)—It's rather an unusual coincidence, but both the University of Detroit's regular tackles—Dave Crotty and Joe Cieslak—come from East High School of Erie, Pa. Still another Erie boy on the Titan team is John Krkoska, who alternates at left end with Roy Larson.

ED. HUGHES' COLUMN

Continued from Preceding Page

folks do really think it interesting—as well as significant. Would you believe it that these skeptics are saying that the Dodger bigwigs planned the bombshell for that particular moment? Why? Well, the figuring hath it that the Flatbush moguls thought the fanfare of the series would take some of the curse off the announcement. The idea being that the fans were so absorbed in the World Series that they wouldn't have time to realize what they had done to the popular Casey!

Can such things be? Hardly. It must be the ravings of the incurable, unreasoning skeptics. Such business is always an open book at Ebbets Field—just as was the Casey Stengel affair a week before the beheading. Nobody knew anything about it then—not even the people who should have known, so to speak. They made up their minds suddenly—right during the World Series.

In Ten Years

The books at Ebbets Field also show that many employes have passed there, one way or another, during the last ten years. Offhand here are a few entries and the manner in which they departed:

President Charles H. Ebbets, deceased; Vice President Ed J. McKeever, deceased; Secretary Charles H. Ebbets Jr., released; Director John H. Scholl, deceased; Director Walter (Dutch) Carter, released; Manager Wilbert Robinson, released; Scout Nap Rucker, released; Business Manager Dave Driscoll, released; Coach Ivy Olson, released.

President Frank B. York, released; manager ticket office, Mrs. A. R. Archer, released; assistant manager ticket office, Mrs. E. Myers, released; head of cleaners, Mrs. M. Walsh, released; Traveling Secretary Fred Hanlon, deceased; Chief Clerk William Byrne, released; Groundkeeper Lee Meyers, released; Groundkeeper Len Schwab, released; Manager Max Carey, released; Scout Larry Sutton, retired; Business Manager Bob Quinn, preparing to quit when he grabbed Boston job; superintendent of park help, Robert Blau, released.

Casey Stengel, released.

But the burning question with Dodger fans are still the same: When will the present Dodger club magnates be released?

When will a new, up-and-coming outfit get in there to give Flatbush fans a winner?

Owens, Olympic Ace, Turns Grid Scout

Columbus, Ohio (AP)—Jesse Owens, Olympic sprint and broad jump champion, has turned football scout for his alma mater—Ohio State. He saw Pittsburgh play West Virginia last week and yesterday told the Buckeyes what he learned of the Panthers, who travel to Columbus to meet Francis Schmidt's powerful outfit Saturday.

KILMERTO SELL BROODMARES

h W. S. Kilmer, Virginia and New York sportsman, will sell 24 of his royally-bred broodmares at auction at Lexington, N. Y., Oct. 19. The group includes several daughters of the famous miler Sun Briar and others by St. James, Ultimus, Sun Beau, Ben Brush, Celt and Gay Crusader.

Yankee Victory Fulfills Prediction

Continued from Preceding Page

had been bounced from the Polo Grounds across the river to the Bronx to the music of a 13—5 score.

It is particularly difficult to select an outstanding hero in this World Series.

—o—

TERRY AND BARTELL SHINE FOR GIANTS

For the Giants, there was Bill Terry, whose gameness in playing through the Series under the handicap of a badly damaged knee, must have been an inspiration to his outclassed team. Manager Bill also drove in the run that clinched Monday's game in the tenth inning and kept the Giants in the World Series business. But then Terry pulled an apparent piece of cock-eyed master-minding that was the turning point in yesterday's game.

It wasn't any of the Giants pitchers. Hubbell hurled beautifully to get the Giants off to a running start but was hammered hard as he tried to repeat. Schumacher pitched the most courageous game of the series on Monday but he was virtually slaughtered by the Yankees previously. Fitzsimmons was horribly unlucky to lose his first start, but had his ears pinned back quite properly yesterday.

The Giant who played the most consistently good ball throughout the series was Shortstop Dick Bartell. But after the first game, Bartell's hitting was not particularly conspicuous in the scoring rallies of the National Leaguers.

—o—

GEHRIG IN SPOTLIGHT FOR THE YANKEES

For the Yankees Lou Gehrig was the only player, other than George Selkirk, to pound out two home runs in the series. One of them helped win Saturday's 2 to 1 game, the other completed the ruin of Mr. Hubbell. But the series would have ended with the fifth game had not Gehrig pulled an uncertain and costly bit of poor baserunning that made the boys think of numerous and sundry Dodger basepath specialists of the past and present.

Al of the other Yankees contributed some fair country hitting but no one was a standout. Joe DiMaggio was more impressive to us National Leaguers who hadn't seen him more because of his style than because of his actual performance. I thought the veteran second baseman Tony Lazzeri did a grand job. He didn't drive in so many runs but he perhaps clicked in more important rallies than any other hitter in the series.

Monte Pearson turned in the best Yankee pitching performance, but Pearson appeared only in one game. Vernon Gomez alone won two games, but Gomez was taken out yesterday and he would have been taken out in his other start if the Yankees had not given him those 18 runs to play with.

Strategy had nothing much to do with this World Series. It was merely a question of how long the Giants could carry on. In view of later events the Yankees would probably have won anyhow, but the prize boner of master-minding in the series was undoubtedly pulled by Terry yesterday.

—o—

LEIBER'S BUNT A TERRY BONER

This isn't one of the wrong raps that unfriendly baseball writers love to hang on Terry. Actually, nobody could guess how on earth his mind was working when he ordered Hank Leiber to bunt in the seventh inning.

The Yankees led by 5 to 3 as the inning started. Bartell blasted a double down the left field foul line and Terry brought him in with a line single to center. DiMaggio fumbled the ball and Terry reached second with the tying run. If ever a pitcher seemed on the verge of shell-shock it was Gomez. Joe McCarthy, the Yankee boss, could not have been criticized if he had yanked the left-hander right there. Certainly another base hit would have driven him right across the lawn to the clubhouse.

But to the amazement of one and all, Terry had Leiber, his longest and strongest right-hand hitter, his fourth-place clean-up hitter against left-handed pitchers, sacrifice. Which Leiber did successfully. Terry was safe at third as Rolfe threw Leiber out.

I think the Yankees were more astonished than anybody else—and pleased, too. They immediately grasped the way out of the jam. Gomez walked Mel Ott purposely. Then Johnny Murphy, a right-hander, replaced Gomez.

Terry threw three left-handed pinch hitters in succession into the breech to redeem the situation, but the Yankees laughingly went to town. Sam Leslie, No. 1, popped out. Jim Ripple, No. 2, walked. Then Mark Koenig, No. 3, was called out on strikes.

There just didn't seem to be any sense to Terry's maneuver. Granting that Leiber had not hit one out of the infield against Gomez previously, why sacrifice a putout.

The Giant manager will be criticized for the play, but he can't call it second-guessing because astonishment was general as soon as what the Giants were trying to do became evident. The play hadn't even the virtue of being unexpected, because Leiber bunted foul before he dumped one in fair territory.

Composite Box Score of World Series

By the Associated Press

NEW YORK YANKEES (A. L.)

	G	AB	R	H	2B	3B	HR	RBI	BB	SO	Bat. Avg.	PO	A	E	Fldg. Avg.
Crosetti, ss	6	26	5	7	2	0	0	3	3	5	.269	11	14	2	.926
Rolfe, 3b	6	25	5	10	0	0	0	4	3	1	.400	14	7	1	.955
DiMaggio, cf	6	26	3	9	3	0	0	3	1	3	.346	18	0	1	.947
Gehrig, 1b	6	24	5	7	1	0	2	7	3	2	.292	45	2	0	1.000
Dickey, c	6	25	5	3	0	0	1	5	3	4	.230	38	4	1	.977
Selkirk, rf	6	24	6	8	0	1	2	3	4	4	.333	9	0	1	.900
Powell, lf	6	22	8	10	1	0	1	5	4	4	.455	12	0	0	1.000
Lazzeri, 2b	6	20	4	5	0	0	1	7	4	4	.250	13	17	0	1.000
*Ruffing, p	3	5	0	0	0	0	0	0	1	2	.000	1	3	0	1.000
Gomez, p	2	8	1	2	0	0	0	3	0	3	.250	0	3	0	1.000
Hadley, p	1	2	0	0	0	0	0	0	0	1	.000	0	3	0	1.000
Malone, p	2	1	0	1	0	0	0	0	0	0	1.000	0	2	0	1.000
Pearson, p	1	4	0	2	1	0	0	0	0	0	.500	1	2	0	1.000
Murphy, p	1	2	1	1	0	0	0	1	0	1	.500	0	0	0	.000
†Johnson	2	1	0	0	0	0	0	0	0	1	.000	0	0	0	.000
‡Seeds	1	0	0	0	0	0	0	0	0	0	.000	0	0	0	.000
Totals	6	215	43	65	8	1	7	41	26	35	.302	162	57	6	.973

*Batted for Hadley in eighth inning, third game.

†Ran for Ruffing in eighth inning, third game; batted for Ruffing in sixth inning, fifth game.

‡Ran for Dickey in ninth inning, fifth game.

NEW YORK GIANTS (N. L.)

	G	AB	R	H	2B	3B	HR	RBI	BB	SO	Bat. Avg.	PO	A	E	Fldg. Avg.
Moore, lf	6	28	4	6	2	0	1	1	1	4	.214	9	0	0	1.000
Bartell, ss	6	21	5	8	3	0	1	3	4	4	.381	8	13	1	.955
Terry, 1b	6	25	1	6	0	0	0	5	1	4	.240	45	8	0	1.000
Ott, rf	6	23	4	7	2	0	1	3	3	1	.304	12	0	1	.923
Leiber, cf	2	6	0	0	0	0	0	0	2	2	.000	13	1	0	1.000
Ripple, cf	5	12	2	4	0	0	1	3	3	3	.333	8	0	0	1.000
Mancuso, c	6	19	3	5	2	0	0	1	3	3	.263	40	5	0	1.000
§Danning c	2	2	0	0	0	0	0	0	0	1	.000	3	0	1	.750
Whitehead, 2b	6	21	1	1	0	0	0	2	1	3	.048	14	20	1	1.000
¶Koenig, 2b	3	3	0	1	0	0	0	0	0	1	.333	1	0	0	1.000
Jackson, 3b	6	21	1	4	0	0	0	1	1	3	.190	2	8	3	.769
Mayo, 3b	1	1	0	0	0	0	0	0	0	0	.000	0	0	0	.000
Hubbell, p	2	6	0	2	0	0	0	1	0	0	.333	2	2	1	.800
Schumacher, p	2	4	0	0	0	0	0	0	1	3	.000	0	2	0	1.000
Smith, p	1	0	0	0	0	0	0	0	0	0	.000	0	0	0	.000
Coffman, p	2	0	0	0	0	0	0	0	0	0	.000	0	1	0	1.000
Gabler, p	2	0	0	0	0	0	0	0	1	0	.000	1	0	0	1.000
Gumbert, p	2	0	0	0	0	0	0	0	0	0	.000	0	0	0	.000
Fitzsimmons, p	2	4	0	2	0	0	0	0	0	1	.500	1	2	0	1.000
Castleman, p	1	2	0	1	0	0	0	0	0	0	.500	0	0	0	.000
**Davis	4	2	2	1	0	0	0	0	0	0	.500	0	0	0	.000
***Leslie	3	3	0	2	0	0	0	0	0	0	.667	0	0	0	.000
Totals	6	203	23	50	9	0	4	20	21	33	.246	159	62	7	.969

§Batted for Gabler in eighth inning, second game.

¶Batted for Jackson in ninth inning, third game; batted for Whitehead in ninth inning, fifth game.

**Batted for Coffman in fourth inning, second game; ran for Leslie in ninth inning, third game; ran for Leslie in eighth inning, fourth game; batted for Castleman in eighth inning, sixth game.

***Batted for Fitzsimmons in ninth inning, third game; batted for Hubbell in eighth ipning, fourth game; batted for Mancuso in seventh inning, sixth game.

PITCHING RECORDS

	G	CG	IP	H	R	ER	BB	SO	WP	HB	W	L	Pct.
Gomez	2	1	15 1-3	14	8	8	11	9	1	0	2	0	1.000
Pearson	1	1	9	7	2	2	2	7	0	0	1	0	1.000
Hadley	1	0	8	10	1	1	1	2	0	0	1	0	1.000
Ruffing	2	1	14	16	10	8	5	12	0	0	0	1	.000
Malone	2	0	5	2	1	1	1	2	0	0	0	1	.000
Murphy	1	0	2 2-3	1	1	1	1	1	0	0	0	0	.000
Hubbell	2	1	16	15	5	4	2	10	1	1	1	1	.500
Schumacher	2	1	12	13	9	9	10	11	2	0	1	1	.500
Fitzsimmons	2	1	11 2-3	13	7	7	2	6	0	0	0	2	.000
Smith	1	0	1-3	2	3	2	1	0	0	0	0	0	.000
Coffman	2	0	1 2-3	5	4	5	1	1	0	0	0	0	.000
Gabler	2	0	5	7	4	4	4	0	0	0	0	0	.000
Gumbert	2	0	2	7	10	8	4	2	0	0	0	0	.000
Castleman	1	0	4 1-3	3	1	1	2	5	0	0	0	0	.000

COMPOSITE SCORE BY INNINGS

Yankees	2	5	13	2	0	3	2	3	13	0—43
Giants	5	1	0	4	3	2	1	6	0	1—23

Final game standing—New York (A.L.) 4, New York (N.L.) 2.

Stolen base—Powell.

Sacrifices—Ripple (2), Bartell (2), Mancuso, Terry, Leiber, Rolfe, DiMaggio, Lazzeri.

Double plays—Whitehead and Terry; Leiber, Jackson and Bartell; Mancuso and Whitehead; Bartell, Whitehead and Terry (3); Schumacher, Terry and Mancuso; Crosetti and Gehrig; Crosetti, Lazzeri and Gehrig.

Left on bases—Yankees 43, Giants 46.

Umpires—Geisel and Summers, American League; Pfirman and Magerkurth, National League.

Time of games—2:40, 2:49, 2:01, 2:12, 2:45, 2:50.

BASEBALL MEN GO HUNTING

Tom Yawkey and Eddie Collins left the Series flat to fly to Wyoming for a big game hunting expedition with Mickey Cochrane and Tris Speaker.

SHOT-PUTTERS ON GRID SQUAD

Baton Rouge (AP)—Three shot-putters, all of whom placed in the 1936 Southeastern Conference track and field meet, are on the Louisiana State football team. They are Bill Cross, 200-pound halfback; "Big Ben" Friend, 245-pound tackle, and Gordon (Lefty) Lester, 195-pound tackle.

Romatowski Scores Unpopular Victory

Vic Romatowski of the Roman Sports Club was awarded an unpopular decision over Frank Parker, unattached, in the final of the 130-pound class, at the amateur boxing show at the Jamaica Arena last night. The decision was booed.

In the semi-final of the four-man class Romatowski had defeated Pedro Guanill, unattached, while Parker had won the nod over Leroy Saunders, unattached.

Kelly Scores Technical K. O.

Veteran Amateur Boxer Halts Gene Dosai in Ridgewood Grove Ring

Being an amateur fighter for 12 years, Billy Kelly has seen some of the lads he met during that period turn professional with very few of them getting any place in this art. The fighters who failed to make the mark had no other alternative but to retire.

Billy believes he did the right thing by staying with the simonpires as he has won many prives and can still follow the fighting business which he loves. Kelly added another prize to his collection when he was awarded a technical knockout over Gene Dosai, representing the Lenox Hill A. A. in 1:38 of the fourth round in a special 147-pound event at the Ridgewood Grove, last night.

When he first started as a boxer, Kelly fought an exhibition bout with Tony Canzoneri, former lightweight champion of the world, when the latter held the Metropolitan bantamweight title. He also fought one of the cleverest colored welterweight fighters in fistiana, Canada Lee. Kelly fought Lee three times in the amateurs and gained one decision.

Kelly then signed up with the Coast Guards. He stayed in for two years and during that time captured the welterweight title of the service.

For a lad who has fought so long, Kelly is by no means a whirlwind of a fighter. He is still an amateur and boxes like one. Dosai didn't have a change as the Bushwick lad broke through his guard landing with hard right hand uppercuts. One of these blows sent the mouthpiece flying from Dosai's mouth. Kelly hooked two lefts to the mouth and cut it badly. The referee, Frank Morris, examined the cut which bled profusely and halted the bout.

Summaries:

115-pound semi-final—Chas. Scottrone, unattached, defeated Samuel Weinstein, unattached, three rounds. Wilfred Minnis, unattached, knocked out Max Krause, unattached, 2:06 first round. Final—Minnis defeated Scottrone, three rounds.

170-pound semi-final—Charles Jackson, Salem Crescent, knocked out William Addison, unattached, third round. Daniel Roberts, Salem Crescent, defeated Jack Erickson, First Avenue Boys Club, three rounds. Final—Jackson knocked out Roberts, 1:46 first round.

138-pound class—Ray Fudge, unattached, defeated Harry Cooper, Salem Crescent, three rounds. Thomas Padovane, unattached, defeated Harry Tramontone, unattached, three rounds. Final—Padovane won from Fudge by default.

147-pound special—Billy Kelly(unattached, knocked out Gene Dosai, Lenox Hill A. A., 138 fourth round.

Italian Speed Demon Holds Test

Continued from Preceding Page

during the race next Monday, and Lord Howe, England's most aristocratic knight of the roaring road.

Mayor Fiorello H. LaGuardia, has accepted an invitation to attend the Columbus Day spectacle, President George P. Marshall of the Raceway announced this morning. The brisk advance sale of tickets indicates a big crowd, but raceway officials stated today that an ample supply of tickets is still available in clubhouse, stands and stadium. Meanwhile, large crowds are watching each day's speed trials and qualification tests starting at 1 p.m.

WAGGONER PICKING UP FOALS

E. Paul Waggoner, who with his brother, Guy L. Waggoner, operates Arlington Downs, will leave next week for Kentucky, where he will pick up nine 1936 foals belonging to the brothers' Three D's Stock Farm. Three of the youngsters, says an Associated Press writer, are from three mares, while the other six were purchased this year. Included in the sextet are two by Ariel and four by Display.

West Point Team Seeks Its First Victory Over Columbia on Gridiron

By GEORGE CURRIE

Army's invasion of Yankee Stadium this coming Saturday to give battle to Columbia is the oldest major game on the city's weekend schedule, but there is the matter of Manhatan vs. North Carolina State Friday night at Ebbets Field, and Fordham vs. Southern Methodist at the Polo Grounds the following afternoon.

Those intent upon hitting the heavy traffic should be entertained by the Yale-Penn game in the New Haven Bowl and, of course, history fairly gets in one's hair in contemplation of the Princeton-Rutgers renewal in Palmer Stadium. They were the pair that started the excitements of Saturday's millions, away back in 1869, though in these latter years, the Outlanders, whose ivy has just begun to make a showing on their stadiums, have undertaken to finish the business. How well they are succeeding may be judged by Ohio's 60 points to N. Y. U.'s nothing; but that is a game we loyal New Yorkers do well to write off to profit and loss.

The unblushing Vialets, bloody but unbowed, debauch upon the turf of Ohio Field against Penn M. C., a tougher outfit than some of the experts are willing to concede. Should Mal Stevens' men catch the soldiery on a rebound, the result might well be terrific. On the other hand, if the military janissaries should hit N. Y. U. in the throes of a University Heights depression, alack and alas! The first 10 minutes of this game will be momentous to the local forces. N. Y. U.'s ability to bounce back from an awful pasting is the issue on the fire.

—o—

FULL CADET CORPS AT YANKEE STADIUM

Both C. C. N. Y. and Brooklyn College have decided that life is too tame in these parts. The Beavers plan to journey to Reading to encounter Albright; the Pearl Street Dodgers will be going to Troy, to meet up with Renssalaer Poly.

Southern Methodist comes to town with a record of much frightfulness behind it. It and Fordham accounted for 127 points all by themselves last Saturday, of which 66 were supplied by the Rams. They are a pair of atrocity-Committers and their meeting again illustrates the old saying that he who lives by the sword shall perish by it. The Mustangs, as usual, are air-conscious, but the locals from Rose Hill are all het up over the fact that their team seems to be score-conscious this year. You pay-off on what the scoreboard says, not on what the Monday quarterbacks second-guess.

But the two ivy-meetings of the Eatsern zone are Army-Columbia and Yale-Penn. So festooned with Hedera helix is the former, indeed, that the Cadet Corps will attend en masse, band and all.

—o—

ARMY HAS YET TO BEAT COLUMBIA

For some reason West Point has never been able to beat Columbia.

Their first meeting was in 1899, when the immortal Harold Weekes, Wild Bill Morley, Hoevnbrg, Slocovich, Smythe, Berrien et al were just getting their bearings before putting th fear of the Lion into the great powers of the gridiron. The score was 16—0.

After a lapse of 25 years, they got togethr again and played a tie, right after the death of Percy D. Haughton, the Morningside coach, in mid-season. The next year George Pease led the squad to a 21—7 triumph. The 1924 squad was led by Walter Koppisch, then captain for the third year in a row. The 1925 victory was the first major red-letter ecstacy after restoration of football at Morningside Heights in 1915. One of its glories was a 60-yard run for a touchdown by Ray Kirchmeyer.

—o—

CADETS FAVORED, BUT SO WAS STANFORD

To the paying guests, the battle of course, is Sid Luckman, the Columbia iron-man, vs. Monk Meyer 145-pound ball-carrying star of whom it has been said he could take the pigskin through a key-hole.

Crosetti Raps Two Homers, But Browns Stop Yanks, 7-6

VOSMIK'S HIT IN NINTH WINS FOR ST. LOUIS

By JAMES CANNON,
N. Y. American Staff Writer.

ST. LOUIS, Mo., June 12.—Frankie Crosetti took two Golden Gate swings at curve balls this sultry afternoon and almost knocked them home to San Francisco.

But Frankie's two home runs and another circuit wallop by Lou Gehrig were petty thrills as the Browns beat the Yankees, 7-6, in a ball game which was an intermission for a country fair.

The Yankees wabbled behind Lefty Gomez and a five-run lead and lost out in the ninth when tow-headed Joe Vosmik hit a two-run double off of Pat Malone after Crosetti's second homer of the afternoon and his fourth of the season had put the New Yorkers ahead going into the last reel.

TWELVE BROWN HITS.

We guess the Browns figured to win, because they maced Rodeo Slim Gomez and Malone for twelve hits while the Yankees were fiddling around with eight base knocks as Elon Hogsett was burning his lefty under-handed curve with a dogged skill.

As all this was coming off nine American Legion bands made their fifes whine and their drums roll thunderously in the stands after a two-hour jamboree of noisy strutting before and after the game.

After Gomez and Hogsett had pitched placidly scoreless ball for three innings, the Yanks smacked five runs into the scorboard in the fourth. Gehrig, the first man up in the big inning, clouted his tenth home run of the season into the right field pavilion shed.

Bill Dickey then doubled, Myril Hoag drooled a sacrificial bunt and Powell doubled. After Tony Lazzeri had walked and Gomez had gone out to the infield, Crosetti busted his first home run of the game, scoring Powell and Lazzeri ahead of him.

BROWNS TALLY.

The Browns chipped their first run off Rodeo Slim in the fourth. Singles by Sammy West, Beau Bell and Harlon Clift made the trouble.

They returned with sinister intent in the fifth to get three runs on Rollie Hemsley's double, Crosetti's error on Tommy Carey's infield roller, Harry Davis' single and West's fly to DiMaggio.

Another error figured in the Browns' tying run in the eighth because Jakey Powell fumbled Vosmik's single, Joe going to second and scoring on Clift's single as Gomez shambled out of the ball park to take his bath and Malone came in.

As a silence choked the wheedling fifes and the drums stopped their clatter, the San Francisco shortstop cracked his second home run into the center field bleachers, breaking the tie.

VOSMIK ON JOB.

But the Browns had a ninth-inning lick, too. Carey bulleted a single off Red Rolfe's chest and Ethan Allen, pinch-hitting for Hogsett, sacrificed him to second with a bunt that dribbled into Malone's glove. Pat lost his control and walked Davis, but West flied harmlessl y to Hoag. There were two out.

Up came Vosmik as the American Legion troubadours started for the gates. Pat let go. Vosmik banged it into center field, Carey and Davis running home with the tying and winning runs as Joe stopped at second.

NEW YORK	ab	r	h	o	a	ST. LOUIS	ab	r	h	o	a
Cros'tti,ss	4	2	2	1	2	Davis,1b	4	1	2	12	2
Rolfe,3b	5	0	0	1	3	West,cf	5	1	1	1	0
DiM'io,cf	4	0	1	4	0	Vosmik,lf	5	1	1	2	0
Gehrig,1b	3	1	1	10	0	Bell,rf	4	0	2	3	0
Dickey,c	4	1	2	4	1	Clift,3b	4	0	2	2	1
Hoag,rf	2	0	0	1	0	Knick'r,ss	4	0	0	0	2
Powell,lf	4	1	2	2	0	Hemsley,c	4	1	1	5	0
Lazz'i,2b	3	1	0	3	4	Carey,2b	4	2	1	1	5
Gomez,p	3	0	0	0	2	Hogsett,p	3	1	1	2	1
Malone,p	1	0	0	0	1	aAllen	0	0	0	0	0
T't'ls	33	6	8	x26	13	T't'ls	37	7	12	27	11

a-Batted for Hogsett in ninth.
x-Two out when winning run scored.

New York	0	0	0	5	0	0	0	0	1	—6
St. Louis	0	0	0	1	3	0	0	1	2	—7

Errors—Crosetti, Powell. Runs batted in—Powell, Crosetti (4), Clift, Hogsett (2), West, Bell, Vosmik (2), Gehrig. Two-base hits — Dickey, Powell, Hemsley, Hogsett, Vosmik. Home runs—Gehrig, Crosetti (2). Sacrifices—Hoag, Allen. Double play—Lazzeri to Crosetti to Gehrig. Left on bases—New York, 4; St. Louis, 6. Bases on balls—Hogsett, 3; Malone, 1. Strikeouts—Gomez, 4; Hogsett, 5. Hits—Off Gomez, 9 in 7 2-3 innings; Malone, 3 in 1 1-3. Winning pitcher—Hogsett. Losing pitcher—Malone. Umpires—Summers, Kolls and Basil. Time—1:51.

BLACK YANKS BOW

The Pittsburgh Crawfords stood off a four run rally in the ninth to defeat the Black Yankees, 11-8 in an Negro National League game at Recreation Park yesterday.

Crawfords	2	2	5	1	1	0	0	0	0	—11	—16	—2
B. Yankees	2	0	1	1	0	0	0	0	4	—8	—10	—3

Strong, Harvey, Morris and Ruffin; Stanley, Brown and Clark.

BRACK SAFE AT THIRD!

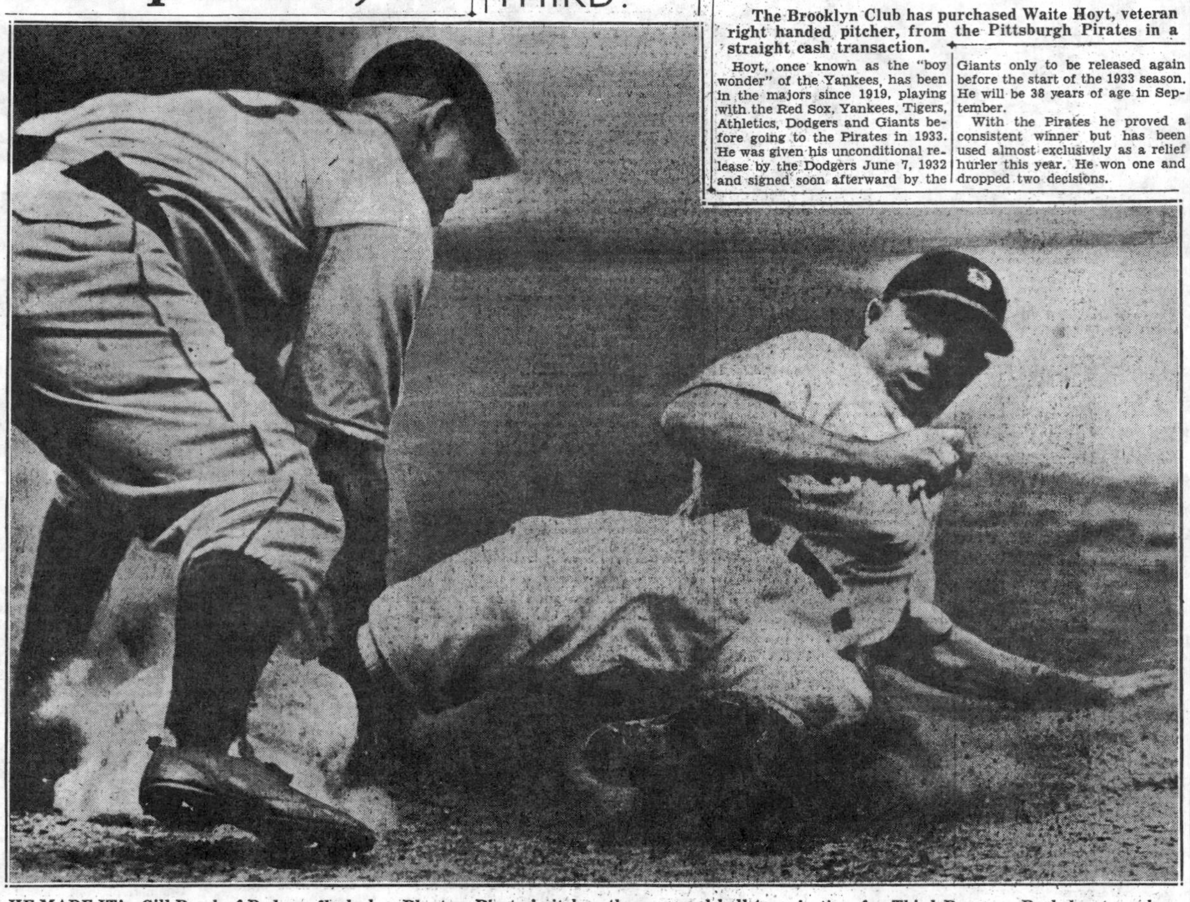

HE MADE IT!—Gill Brack of Dodgers flashed from second to third yesterday in nick of time. Blanton, Pirates' pitcher, threw passed ball to Catcher Todd, but Todd got ball to third almost in time for Third Baseman Brubaker to make putout. Pittsburgh beat the Dodgers, 8—3.
N. Y. American Staff Photo.

Dodgers Get Hoyt in Straight Cash Deal

The Brooklyn Club has purchased Waite Hoyt, veteran right handed pitcher, from the Pittsburgh Pirates in a straight cash transaction.

Hoyt, once known as the "boy wonder" of the Yankees, has been in the majors since 1919, playing with the Red Sox, Yankees, Tigers, Athletics, Dodgers and Giants before going to the Pirates in 1933. He was given his unconditional release by the Dodgers June 7, 1932 and signed soon afterward by the Giants only to be released again before the start of the 1933 season. He will be 38 years of age in September.

With the Pirates he proved a consistent winner but has been used almost exclusively as a relief hurler this year. He won one and dropped two decisions.

Hayworth Breaks Arm as Bad Luck Follows Tigers

DETROIT, June 12 (AP).—Ray Hayworth, catcher of the Detroit Tigers, suffered a broken arm in the second game against Boston today when hit by a ball pitched by Louis (Buck) Newsom.

Hayworth is the second Tiger catcher to be injured this season.

Manager Cochrane, hit on the head by a pitched ball May 26, is in Ford Hospital here with a triple skull fracture.

George (Birdie) Tebbetts, a rookie, the only available catcher on the Detroit roster, replaced Hayworth.

Marvin Owens, third baseman, suffered a fracture in his left hand several days ago.

CHICAGO DOWNS PHILLIES, 10 TO 5

PHILADELPHIA, June 12 (AP).—The Chicago Cubs pounded out a 10-to-5 victory over the Phillies today to remain half a game behind the league leading Giants.

The Cubs knocked Wayne La Master out of the box with a 7-hit attack in two innings and then went on to win easily behind Larry French's southpaw pitching. French yielded a run in the first on three successive singles and the remaining four Philly runs came on homers by Chuck Klein and Morrie Arnovich.

CHICAGO	ab	r	h	o	a	PHILADELPHIA	ab	r	h	o	a
Galan,lf	5	2	2	1	0	Norris,2b	4	0	0	2	6
Her'an,2b	5	0	1	4	2	Martin,cf	5	0	0	3	0
Collins,1b	5	2	4	7	1	Klein,rf	4	3	4	1	0
Dema'e,rf	5	1	2	1	0	Camilli,1b	4	0	1	14	0
Hack,3b	4	1	0	2	2	W'tney,3b	4	1	3	1	0
Bott'ini,c	4	1	0	5	1	Arnov'h,lf	4	1	1	1	0
Marty,cf	4	1	1	5	0	Grace,c	3	0	1	4	1
Jurges,ss	4	2	4	1	4	Schar'n,ss	4	0	0	1	3
French,p	4	0	1	1	0	Lam'ter,p	1	0	0	0	1
						Jorgens,p	1	0	0	0	1
						aAtwood	1	0	0	0	0
						Johnson,p	0	0	0	0	1
						bWilson	1	0	0	0	0
T'ls	40	10	15	27	10	T't'ls	36	5	10	27	13

a-Batted for Jorgens in seventh.
b-Batted for Johnson in ninth.

Chicago	1	3	2	1	0	1	1	1	0	—10
Philadelphia	1	0	0	0	1	0	0	3	0	— 5

Errors—Herman, Camilli. Runs batted in—Whitney 1, Arnovich 3, Klein 1, Collins 3, Marty 1, Galan 2, Jurges 2, Demaree 1. Two base hits—Galan, Demaree, Jurges, Collins, Klein. Home runs—Marty, Galan, Collins, Arnovich, Klein. Stolen base—Hack. Sacrifices—Hack, French. Double plays—Bottarini to Herman; Norris to Camilli; Hack to Herman to Collins. Left on base—Chicago 9, Philadelphia 6. Base on balls—Off French 2, Jorgens 3, Johnson 1. Hits—Off Lamaster 7 in 2 innings; Jorgens 5 in 5; Johnson 3 in 2. Losing pitcher—Lamaster. Umpires—Goetz, Reardon and Pinelli. Time—2.03.

BLANTON FANS 11 AS PIRATES TRIP DODGERS

Those happy days when all pint-sized Roy Henshaw had to do to defeat the Pittsburgh Pirates was arrive promptly at the park are gone. Roy, Burleigh Grimes and 8,137 denizens of Flatbush found that out at Ebbets Field yesterday much to the chagrin, disappointment and pain of all concerned.

For Roy, after being spotted a three-run lead in the first inning found he couldn't exert his old time superiority and by the time the last lingering wail of the populace had ceased to ring, the Pirates had notched an 8 to 3 decision over the Dodgers.

LEAD SHRINKS.

The three-run bulge started shrinking in the second inning to two, and by the end of the third had disappeared altogether.

Al Todd was the No. 1 menace, plastering three trouble and run-making singles before unloading a game-winning home run. After the eruption Luke Hamlin held the Buccos scoreless.

It didn't matter though, what the Pirates failed to do after that. Cy Blanton settled down after the first inning, allowing no runs and fanning eleven of the hapless home folks. He was touched for eleven hits, but outside of the over the fence blast by Heinie Manush, none meant anything.

Good old Heinie drew the approbation of the early arrivals with one of those rare events—a Dodger home run with men on the paths. Gibby Brack had greeted Blanton with a blistering double down the third base line.

Then, after Jimmy Bucher had vainly attempted to sacrifice and had succeeded in striking out, Joe Stripp drew a walk. Heinie then hit his homer.

The Pirates wasted no time in cutting into that three-run deficit. Arkie Vaughan planked a double off the right center cement to open the second. Gus Suhr's best was a towering foul to Spencer, but Al Todd poked a single into right that sent Arkie home.

BUCS TIE IT UP.

Returning to the task at hand, the Corsairs evened the balance in the third. Cookie Lavagatto aided his old mates not a little by booting Lloyd Waner's lead-off roller. Woody Jensen smacked back through the box. Waner going to third and Woody to second when Brack slipped in fielding the ball.

Paul Waner's single just out of Bucher's reach scored brother Lloyd and Jensen registered while English was tossing out Vaughan.

The deadlock came to its end in the seventh. Suhr lifted a fly to right, but Brack and Manush couldn't catch it. The result was a two-base hit and Todd then hit his home run.

That didn't end the fireworks. Lee Handley squeezed a single into right field and then Cookie Lavagetto committed a ghastly error on a certain double play, dropping Jimmy Bucher's perfect throw. Handley reached second and Brubaker first. Blanton fanned, but both runners were advanced on a wild pitch.

It seemed Henshaw might again escape without severe damage when Woody English copped Lloyd Waner's clipper, held the runners on the spot and tossed Little Poison out. But this was not to be. Jensen crashed a low drive to left center for a triple, scoring Handley and Brubaker, and when English dropped the relay out in short center, the Pirate left fielder also tallied.

PITTSBURGH	ab	r	h	o	a	BROOKLYN	ab	r	h	o	a
L.W'er,cf	5	1	0	0	0	Brack,cf	5	1	1	5	0
Jensen,lf	5	2	2	1	0	Bucher,3b	5	0	2	1	3
P.W'er,rf	5	0	1	0	0	Stripp,1b	3	1	1	6	0
V'ghan,ss	5	1	1	3	1	Manush,rf	4	1	2	3	0
Suhr,1b	4	1	1	7	1	Winsett,lf	4	0	0	3	0
Todd,c	5	1	4	11	2	Lava'o,2b	4	0	2	1	2
H'dley,2b	5	1	2	4	4	English,ss	4	0	1	2	2
Brub'r,3b	5	1	1	1	0	Spencer,c	4	0	2	6	0
Blanton,p	4	0	1	0	3	Hensh'w,p	2	0	0	0	0
						aMorgan	1	0	0	0	0
						Hamlin,p	0	0	0	0	0
						bMalino'y	1	0	0	0	0
T't'ls	43	8	13	27	11	Totals	37	3	11	27	7

a-Batted for Henshaw in 7th.
b-Batted for Hamlin in 9th.

Pittsburgh	0	1	2	0	0	0	5	0	0	—8
BROOKLYN	3	0	0	0	0	0	0	0	0	—3

Errors—Lavagetto 2, English. Runs batted in—Todd 3, P. Waner, Vaughan, Jensen 2, Manush 3. Two-base hits—Vaughan, Jensen, Brubaker, Suhr, Brack, English. Three-base hit—Jensen. Home runs—Todd, Manush Stolen base—Handley. Left on bases—Pittsburgh, 12; Brooklyn, 8. Bases on balls—Henshaw 3, Hamlin 1, Blanton 1. Strikeouts—Henshaw 3, Blanton 11. Hits off—Henshaw, 12 in 7 innings; Hamlin, 1 in 2. Wild pitches—Blanton, Hamlin. Losing pitcher—Henshaw. Umpires — Sears, Ballanfant and Klem. Time—2:20. Attendance—8,137.

TIGERS DIVIDE BEFORE 40,250

DETROIT, June 12 (AP).—The Boston Red Sox lost the first game of a doubleheader here today, 3 to 2, but overcame Detroit's four-run lead to win the 10-inning nightcap, before 40.250 fans.

The defeat stopped the Tigers' winning streak at six games.

Colonel Mills, who had walked, scored the winning run in the second game after a single by Eric McNair.

Roxie Lawson held Boston to four hits in the first game to win his ninth victory. Detroit got six hits in the second game off Newsom.

BOSTON	ab	r	h	o	a	DETROIT	ab	r	h	o	a
Mills,lf	3	0	0	2	0	Fox,cf	5	1	2	5	0
C'pm'n,cf	4	0	0	3	0	Rogell,ss	3	1	1	3	2
Cronin,ss	2	1	0	0	1	Gehri'r,2b	4	0	1	3	1
Foxx,1b	3	1	2	7	0	G'nb'g,1b	4	0	3	2	0
M'N'ir,2b	4	0	1	2	4	Walker,rf	3	0	1	5	0
Higg's,3b	4	0	0	0	0	Laabs,lf	3	0	0	4	0
Gaffke,rf	4	0	0	6	0	Tebbetts,c	4	0	0	4	1
Des'ltels,c	3	0	1	4	0	Clifton,3b	4	0	1	1	3
Walb'rg,p	0	0	0	0	0	Lawson,p	4	1	2	0	1
Oster'er,p	2	0	0	0	0						
aD'llesa'o	1	0	0	0	0						
Totals	30	2	4	24	5	Totals	34	3	11	27	8

a-Batted for Ostermueller in ninth.

Boston	0	0	0	2	0	0	0	0	0	—2
Detroit	1	2	0	0	0	0	0	0	x	—3

Errors—Rogell 2. Runs batted in—Gehringer 2, Foxx 2, Rogell. Two base hits—Greenberg 2, Foxx. Home runs—Rogell, Foxx. Stolen base—Foxx. Sacrifice—Ostermueller. Double plays—Gehringer, Rogell to Greenberg; McNair to Foxx. Left on base—Detroit 10, Boston 7. Bases on balls—Lawson 5, Walberg 1, Ostermueller 2. Strikeouts—Lawson 3, Ostermueller 3. Hits—Off Walberg 6 in one and two-thirds innings; Ostermueller 5 in six and one-third innings. Losing pitcher — Walberg. Umpires — Dinneen, Quinn and Hubbard. Time—2:05.

SECOND GAME

BOSTON	ab	r	h	o	a	DETROIT	ab	r	h	o	a
Mills,lf	2	2	0	2	0	Fox,cf	4	1	1	4	0
C'pm'n,cf	5	1	1	5	2	Rogell,ss	4	1	1	5	4
Cronin,ss	4	0	0	2	3	Geh'er,2b	3	0	1	1	5
Foxx,1b	4	1	1	7	1	G'nb'g,1b	5	0	0	8	0
M'N'ir,2b	5	0	1	3	1	Walker,rf	5	0	1	2	0
Higg's,3b	5	0	0	1	1	Laabs,lf	4	1	1	5	0
Gaffke,rf	4	0	0	0	0	Hayw'h,c	1	0	0	1	0
Des'ltels,c	4	0	1	10	0	Tebbetts,c	2	0	0	3	0
News'm,p	4	1	2	0	1	Clifton,3b	4	0	1	1	0
						Wade,p	2	1	0	0	1
						Russell,p	0	0	0	0	2
Totals	37	5	6	30	9	Totals	34	4	6	30	12

Boston	0	0	0	0	0	0	0	4	0	1	—5
Detroit	1	0	0	1	0	0	2	0	0	0	—4

Errors—Greenberg, Clifton, Fox, Rogell, Laabs. Runs batted in—Foxx, 2; McNair, Chapman, Gehringer Rogell, Walker, Cronin. Two-base hits—Newsom, Laabs. Home run—Foxx. Sacrifice—Russell. Left on bases—Detroit, 7; Boston, 7. Bases on balls—Wade, 2; Russell, 1; Newsom, 5. Strikeouts—By Wade, 2; by Russell, 1; by Newsom, 10. Hits—Off Wade, 5 in 7 1-3 innings; off Russell, 1 in 2 2-3 innings. Bit by pitcher—By wade (Mills); by Newsom (Hayworth); by Russell (Cronin). Balk—Newsom. Losing Pitcher—Russell. Umpires—Quinn, Hubbard and Dineen. Time—2:35. Attendance—40,250.

Rowe Ready for Easy Workouts

MIAMI, Fla., June 12 (AP).—Pitcher Lynwood (Schoolboy) Rowe of the Tigers planned to leave tonight for Detroit with a tentative "O. K." stamped on his ailing right arm.

Dr. Cecil B. Ferguson, who has been treating Rowe for a pulled tendon, said he advised the pitchworkouts for a few days before rejoining the team.

Wes Ferrell Wins, 6-2, In Washington Debut

CHICAGO, June 12 (AP).—Wes Ferrell, repeatedly rough-housed by the White Sox with Boston, made his debut in a Washington uniform here today and held the Chicagoans to four hits for a 6-2 victory.

A liner off Jonathan Stone's bat bounced past center Fielder Mike Kreevich for an inside-the-park homer with two on in the eighth to break a 2-2 tie and give Ferrell, who was traded to the Senators in a five-man deal Thursday, his fourth victory of the season.

His brother, Rick, also included in the deal, caught him. Wes Ferrell contributed a double and a single to the Senators' 14-hit attack, 13 of which came off Johnny Rigney, local freshman, who had been feted before the game by admirers and given, beside the usual traveling bag, a gold watch and flowers.

The Box Score

WASHINGTON	ab	r	h	o	a	CHICAGO	ab	r	h	o	a
Alm'da,cf	5	0	1	1	0	Radc'ff,lf	4	1	1	1	0
Lewis,3b	5	1	2	1	3	Kreev'h,cf	4	0	1	4	0
Kuhel,1b	5	1	1	9	1	Walker,rf	4	0	0	1	0
Stone,rf	4	2	2	7	0	Bon'ra,1b	3	0	0	12	2
Simm's,lf	4	1	1	3	0	Appling,ss	3	0	1	3	4
Travis,ss	4	1	2	2	1	Hayes,2b	4	0	0	2	5
Myer,2b	4	0	3	2	2	Piet,3b	3	0	1	0	1
R.Ferr'l,c	4	0	0	2	1	Sewell,c	2	1	0	3	0
W.F'rel,p	4	0	2	0	2	Rigney,p	1	0	0	1	0
						Brown,p	1	0	0	0	0
T't'ls	39	6	14	27	10	Tot'ls	29	2	4	27	12

Washington	0	0	0	2	0	0	0	4	0	—6
Chicago	0	0	2	0	0	0	0	0	0	—2

Errors—Radcliff 2. Runs batted in—Stone 3, Travis, Myer, W. Ferrell, Radcliff, Walker. Two-base hits—W. Ferrell, Kreevich. Home run—Stone. Stolen base—Almada. Sacrifice—Rigney. Double plays—Myer, Travis and Kuhel; Bonura and Appling; Appling, Hayes and Bonura. Left on base—Washington 7, Chicago 4. Base on balls—Off W. Ferrell 3, Rigney 1. Strikeouts—By W. Ferrell 2, Rigney 2. Hits—Off Rigney, 13 in 7 1-3 innings; Brown, 1 in 1 2-3. Losing pitcher—Rigney. Umpires—Owens and Ormsby. Time—1:56.

WARNEKE WINS FOR CARDS, 4-1

BOSTON, June 12 (AP).—Lon Warneke, the Cardinals' righthander, today held the Bostons to five hits as his mates pounded out a 4-1 victory.

The Cards, who found Danny MacFayden facing off against them at the start, clinched the game in the third frame by blasting the veteran for three runs.

ST. LOUIS	ab	r	h	o	a	BOSTON	ab	r	h	o	a
J.M'tin,cf	4	1	2	4	0	Garms,3b	4	0	1	1	4
Brown,2b	4	1	1	1	3	Wars'er,ss	3	0	0	1	2
Padg'tt,rf	4	0	1	0	0	aEnglish	1	0	1	0	0
Medw'k,lf	3	0	0	3	0	Thev'w,ss	0	0	0	0	1
Mize,1b	4	0	2	12	1	E.M'ore,rf	4	0	1	3	0
Bord'y,3b	4	0	2	0	3	Cucc'io,2b	4	0	1	3	4
Duroc'r,ss	4	0	0	1	3	Berger,lf	4	0	0	4	1
Ogrod'l,c	4	2	2	5	0	DiMa'c,cf	4	0	0	2	0
Warn'e,p	3	0	0	1	1	Fletc'r,1b	3	0	0	10	1
						Lopez,c	2	0	1	3	0
						M'F'den,p	2	0	0	0	2
						bJohnson	1	1	0	0	0
						Lanning,p	0	0	0	0	0
T't'ls	34	4	10	27	11	Totals	32	1	5	27	15

a-Batted for Wartsler in 8th.
b-Batted for Macfayden in 8th.

St. Louis	0	0	3	0	0	0	1	0	0	—4
Boston	0	0	0	0	0	0	0	1	0	—1

Errors—Warstler. Runs batted in—Brown (2), J. Martin, Padgett, English. Two base hits—J. Martin (2). Three base hits—Brown. Sacrifice—Warneke. Double plays—Warstler to Cuccinello to Fletcher. Left on bases—St. Louis, 5; Boston, 5. Bases on balls—Warneke, 1; Macfayden, 1. Strikeouts—Warneke, 5; Macfayden, 2.

Indians Rally in Ninth Falls Short, A's Triumph, 3 to 2

CLEVELAND, June 12 (AP).—A ninth inning rally, which filled the bases three times, produced only one run for the Cleveland Indians today as Philadelphia won, 3 to 2.

The rally was made up of three bases on balls, a hit, and an error.

Cleveland scored in the fourth on Solters' double and Hale's single. A double by Moses, who scored on Dean's single in the fifth, helped the Athletics tie the score.

Hale's bad throw helped the Athletics to a run in the sixth, and after Galehouse had been removed in the eighth, Philadelphia added the winning run off Mel Harder in the ninth.

PHILADELPHIA	ab	r	h	o	a	CLEVELAND	ab	r	h	o	a
R'tr'ck,cf	5	0	0	3	0	Lary,ss	4	0	0	5	4
Moses,rf	5	0	3	1	0	W'herly,rf	3	0	0	0	0
Werb'r,3b	5	0	0	2	3	Averill,cf	4	0	0	3	0
Johns'n,lf	4	0	3	2	0	Trosky,1b	3	0	0	5	0
Hayes,c	3	1	2	6	2	Solters,lf	4	1	2	1	1
Peters,2b	4	0	1	0	4	Hale,2b	3	0	2	4	2
Dean,1b	4	1	1	9	1	Pytlak,c	3	0	1	5	1
News'e,ss	4	0	2	3	1	Hugh's,3b	3	0	0	3	1
Kelley,p	4	1	1	1	1	Galeh'se,p	2	0	2	1	3
						Harder,p	0	0	0	0	0
						aCampbell	1	0	0	0	0
						bSullivan	0	1	0	0	0
						cKroner	0	0	0	0	0
T't'ls	38	3	13	27	12	Totals	30	2	7	27	12

a-Batted for Galehouse in 8th.
b-Ran for Trosky in 9th.
c-Batted for Harder in 9th.

Philadelphia	0	0	0	0	1	1	0	0	1	—3
Cleveland	0	0	0	1	0	0	0	0	1	—2

Errors—Dean, Newsome, Hale. Runs bated in—Moses, Werber, Hale, Pytlak. Two-base hits—Solters, Pytlak, Moses. Stolen base—Pytlak. Sacrifices—Weatherly, Pytlak. Double plays—Hayes to Werber; Newsome to Dean; Hale to Lary to Trosky. Left on bases—Philadelphia 9, Cleveland 8. Base on balls—Off Kelley 5, Galehouse 1. Strikeouts—By Kelley 4, Galehouse 3, Harder 1. Hits—Off. Galehouse, 11 in 8 innings; Harder, 2 in 1. Wild pitches—Galehouse. Losing pitcher — Galehouse. Umpires—McGowan and Moriarty. Time—2:20. Attendance—5,000.

SENATORS SIGN COLLEGE PITCHER

RICHMOND, Va., June 12 (AP).—Newton "Bucky" Jacobs, the slim pitching ace who hurled three no-hit no-run games for the University of Richmond this Spring, has signed a contract to join the Washington Senators this season.

Runs for the Week

NATIONAL LEAGUE.

Teams.	S	M	T	W	T	F	S	Tls.
Chicago	8	x	x	8	9	x	10	35
St. Louis	16	x	x	10	x	x	4	30
Cincinnati	9	4	4	2	6	x	3	28
Pittsburgh	5	2	8	1	4	x	8	28
Boston	9	x	0	10	5	x	1	25
NEW YORK	9	5	x	4	x	x	4	22
Philadelphia	2	x	1	8	5	x	5	21
BROOKLYN	2	5	x	4	3	x	3	17
Totals	60	16	13	47	32	x	38	206

AMERICAN LEAGUE.

Teams.	S	M	T	W	T	F	S	Tls.
Cleveland	7	17	8	12	x	3	2	49
Chicago	12	12	5	x	3	14	2	48
Boston	8	6	10	6	x	5	7	42
NEW YORK	4	3	4	x	10	10	6	37
Washington	8	5	x	x	3	8	6	30
Detroit	5	4	6	x	4	6	7	32
St. Louis	8	9	x	x	6	0	7	30
Philadelphia	6	6	0	x	3	11	3	29
Totals	58	62	33	18	29	57	40	297

INTERNATIONAL LEAGUE.

Teams.	S	M	T	W	T	F	S	Tls.
Jersey City	14	0	x	1	x	x	3	18
Montreal	4	9	3	x	x	4	12	32
Newark	4	8	6	10	x	11	10	40
Baltimore	8	6	0	5	x	5	9	33
Toronto	4	3	x	4	5	x	2	18
Rochester	10	6	2	x	2	5	12	37
Buffalo	5	6	x	1	7	3	5	27
Syracuse	3	2	x	5	7	4	18	39
Totals	52	40	11	26	21	32	71	253

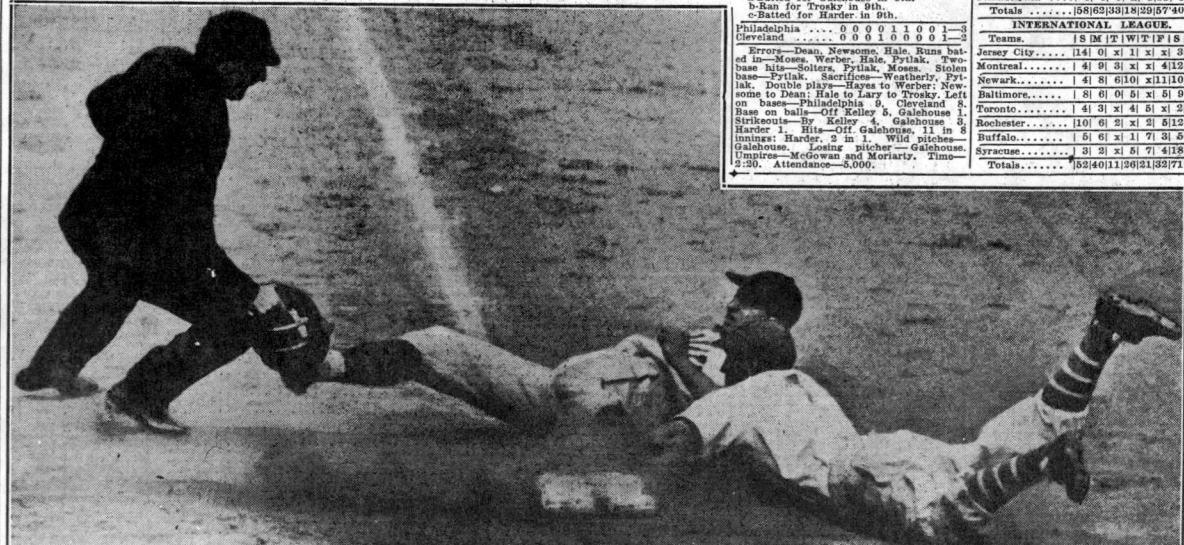

CLOSE DECISION AT THIRD BASE

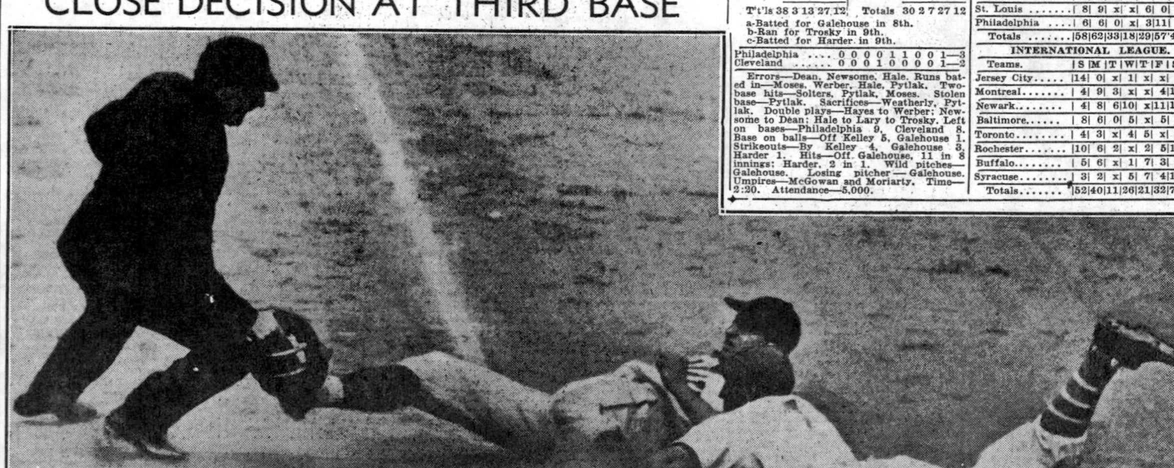

POLO GROUNDS—Weintraub, of the Reds, ran into trouble in the third inning of the game with the Giants yesterday. He drew a pass and then tried to reach third after Jordan shot a single to right. Ott made a quick recovery and whipped the ball to Chiozza. Both players made a slide for the bag and Chiozza won by an eyelash.
N. Y. American Staff Photos.

BRADDOCK WEIGHS 197; JOE LOUIS 197 1-4

SPORTING FINAL
★★★★★★
RACING CHARTS
Temperatures—Min., 61; Max., 75.
(Detailed weather report on page 22.)

The Sun

Copyright, 1937, by The Sun Printing and Publishing Association.

SPORTING FINAL
★★★★★★
7th RACE RESULT
United States Official Weather Forecast:
Partly cloudy tonight and tomorrow.

VOL. CIV—NO. 248—DAILY. NEW YORK, TUESDAY, JUNE 22, 1937. PRICE THREE CENTS.

YANKEES WHIP BROWNS, 8-5; LEE OF CUBS PUZZLES GIANTS; LUKE HAMLIN OPPOSES HAINES

YANKEES

ST. LOUIS.

	AB	R	H	PO	A	E
Davis, 1b	4	0	0	13	1	0
West, cf	3	2	2	0	0	0
Vosmik, lf	4	0	2	1	0	0
Bell, rf	4	0	0	1	0	1
Clift, 3b	3	0	0	2	4	0
Knickerbocker, ss	4	0	0	1	0	0
Hemsley, c	4	0	0	4	2	0
Carey, 2b	2	1	0	2	6	1
Knott, p	0	0	0	0	0	0
Walkup, p	2	1	0	0	0	0
Thomas, p	0	0	0	0	0	0
Allen	1	1	1	0	1	0
Huffman	1	0	0	0	0	0
Bottomley	1	0	0	0	0	0
Total	33	5	5	24	14	2

YANKEES.

	AB	R	H	PO	A	E
Crosetti, ss	4	1	0	1	2	1
Rolfe, 3b	5	2	2	0	3	0
DiMaggio, cf	4	0	1	2	0	1
Gehrig, 1b	3	2	0	9	0	0
Dickey, c	4	1	2	7	0	0
Selkirk, rf	3	1	2	3	0	0
Powell, lf	3	1	1	3	0	0
Heffner, 2b	4	0	2	2	2	0
Malone, p	4	0	0	0	0	0
Total	34	8	10	27	7	2

Allen batted for Walkup in 7th.
Bottomley batted for Thomas in 9th.
Huffman batted for Carey in 9th.

SUMMARY.

Home runs—Dickey, West.
Three-base hits—Vosmik, Rolfe.
Two-base hit—Selkirk.
Bases on balls—Off Knott 3, off Malone 4.
Struck out—By Knott 1, by Malone 7.
Runs batted in—Vosmik, Dickey (3), Powell (2), Rolfe, DiMaggio, West (3).
Hits—Off Knott 5 in 1 2-3, off Walkup 5 in 4 1-3, off Thomas 0 in 2.
Hit by pitched ball—Crosetti (Knott).
Left on bases—Browns 5, Yankees 6.
Umpires—Moriarty, Johnson and McGowan.
Attendance—6,000.

By EDWARD T. MURPHY.

YANKEE STADIUM, June 22.—Pat Malone, in his first starting assignment of the season, held the Browns in check here today and the Yankees won the first of a three-game series, 8 to 5.

As a result of the victory the Yankees increased their lead over

Continued on Page 29.

BASEBALL

AT YANKEE STADIUM.

											R.	H.	E.
ST. LOUIS	1	0	0	0	2	0	2	0	0	—	5	5	2
YANKEES	2	4	0	0	2	0	0	0	x	—	8	10	2

Knott, Walkup (2), Thomas (7) and Hemsley; Malone and Dickey.

AT CHICAGO.

											R.	H.	E.
GIANTS	0	0	0	0	0	0	0	0	0	—	0	7	1
CHICAGO	2	1	1	1	0	0	0	0	X	—	5	9	0

Gumbert, Baker (4) and Mancuso; Lee and Hartnett.

AT ST. LOUIS.

		R.	H.	E.
BROOKLYN	—			
ST. LOUIS	—			

Brooklyn-St. Louis game starts at 5 P. M., New York daylight time.

AMERICAN LEAGUE

AT PHILADELPHIA.

											R.	H.	E.
CHICAGO	0	0	0	1	0	1	0	0	0	—	2	6	1
ATHLETICS	0	0	0	0	0	0	0	0	0	—	0	3	1

Stratton and Shea; Ross, Smith (7) and Conroy.

AT WASHINGTON.

					R.	H.	E.
CLEVELAND	0	0	0	—			
WASHINGTON	3	0	0	—			

Whitehill and Pytlak; Fischer and R. Ferrell.

Detroit-Boston game postponed; rain.

NATIONAL LEAGUE

AT PITTSBURGH.

											R.	H.	E.
BOSTON	0	0	0	0	1	0	0	0	0	—	1	4	1
PITTSBURGH	0	0	0	0	2	1	1	0	x	—	4	17	0

Turner and Lopez; Blanton and Todd.

AT CINCINNATI.

								R.	H.	E.
PHILADELPHIA	0	0	0	0	0	0	—			
CINCINNATI	0	0	5	1	0	0	—			

Passeau and Atwood; Grissom and V. Davis.

INTERNATIONAL LEAGUE

AT JERSEY CITY. FIRST GAME.

												R.	H.	E.
ROCHESTER	0	0	0	0	0	0	0 2	1	1	—	4	12	1
JERSEY CITY	0	1	0	1	1	0	0 0	0	0	—	3	10	0

Walker, Doyle (8) and Poland, O'Farrell (9); Stiles, Cantwell (9) and Klumpp.

AT JERSEY CITY. SECOND GAME.

									R.	H.	E.
ROCHESTER	0	1	0	0	0	0	0	—	1	4	1
JERSEY CITY	0	3	0	1	0	0	x	—	4	5	1

Doyle, Smith (5) and O'Farrell, Poland (5); Gabler and Redmond.

AT BALTIMORE. FIRST GAME.

											R.	H.	E.
BUFFALO	0	1	0	2	0	0	1	0	0	—	4	6	3
BALTIMORE	1	0	0	4	2	2	0	1	x	—	10	12	4

Ash and Grube; Lohrman, Hibbs (6) and Crouse, Phillips (6).

AT BALTIMORE. SECOND GAME.

						R.	H.	E.
BUFFALO	0	0	0	2	—			
BALTIMORE	0	3	0	8	—			

Kline, Jacobs (2), Kowalik (4) and Grube; Vandenberg and Crouse.

Other teams play night games.

College Baseball Scores will be found on Page 29.

GIANTS

By WILL WEDGE.

WRIGLEY FIELD, Chicago, June 22.—Twenty thousand fans assembled for the opener of a three-game series between the Cubs and Giants here today. Harry Gumbert was picked for mound duty, Manager Bill Terry having come to the conclusion that Carl Hubbell needed a little more rest, before trying to break his three-weeks' slump, which had cost the New York ace four straight defeats. Bill Lee hurled for Chicago.

Gumbert was making his thirteenth appearance of the season, but he had only two complete jobs to his credit. His record was two won and three lost. Lee went to work with a mark of six won and five lost.

The batting order:

Giants.	Cubs.
Bartell, ss.	Galan, lf.
Chiozza, 3b.	Herman, 2b.
Moore, lf.	Collins, 1b.
Ripple, cf.	Demaree, rf.
Ott, rf.	Hack, 3b.
Leslie, 1b.	Hartnett, c.
Mancuso, c.	Marty, cf.
Whitehead, 2b.	Jurges, ss.
Gumbert, p.	Lee, p.

Umpires—Moran, Magerkurth and Parker.
Attendance—20,000.

FIRST INNING.

Bartell was called out on strikes.

Continued on Page 29.

DODGERS

By HERBERT GOREN.

SPORTSMANS PARK, St. Louis, June 22.—It was Tuberculosis Day here today and about 15,000 fans turned out to see the Dodgers and Cardinals meet in the first of a three-game series, which was coupled by a set of track events that preceded the contest.

Jess Haines hurled for St. Louis and Luke Hamlin for Brooklyn.

Papa Jesse Haines, who pitched a no-hit game for the Cardinals against the Boston Braves on this holiday in 1924, made his first start of the season and his mound opponent was Luke Hamlin.

Hamlin's record for the year showed two victories against five defeats. On the Dodgers' first visit here Hamlin pitched and won a three-hit game against the Cardinals.

N. Y. U. WINS TAX SUIT

Y. M. C. A. Also Victor Over City on Sales Levy.

The Appellate Division ruled against the city today in two cases involving payment of the sales tax. The court ruled that New York University was, according to law, a charitable institution and that it was not compelled to pay the sales tax on goods bought and sold.

A similar ruling was made on the Y. M. C. A. The court found that this organization is a semi-public institution within the meaning of the law and that it should not pay the city tax.

The sum of $10,960 was involved in the university case.

Retired Major Sentenced To Death for Murder

SANTA CRUZ, Cal., June 22 (U. P.).—Allan D. Boggs, fifty-four-year-old retired army major, was sentenced today to die at San Quentin on September 10 for the murder of his wife last April.

In The Sun Today

—(19)—

Entered as Second Class Matter Post Office, New York, N. Y.

U. S. WORKERS IN C. I. O.

Charter Granted to Former A. F. of L. Affiliate.

WASHINGTON, June 22 (A. P.).—John L. Lewis's Committee for Industrial Organization issued a charter today to the United Federal Workers of America, a new union composed of seven Washington locals formerly affiliated with the American Federation of Labor. The organization, claiming to represent 3,200 Federal Government employees, said it would start immediate organization activities among the Government's approximately 700,000 workers.

Jacob Baker, who will resign as Assistant Works Progress Administrator July 1, is president of the U. F. of A.

PLANTS ARE REOPENED

4000 Men Report for Work at North Tarrytown.

The Chevrolet Motor Company and Fisher Body plants in North Tarrytown reopened today after having been closed since June 16 because of a shortage of material due to labor troubles in the company's Western plants.

Officials said that a full force aggregating 4,000 men had reported for work in both plants. They explained that the necessary parts for operation had been received.

The suspension was the third this year. The first was in February, during the General Motors strikes, and the second came earlier in June.

President Shakes Off Cold.

WASHINGTON, June 22 (A. P.).—White House officials said today that President Roosevelt had virtually recovered from the nasal cold which kept him away from his office yesterday.

Today's Home Run Roster.

Dickey, Yankees, 1.
Di Maggio, Bees, 1.
Todd, Pirates, 1.
Weintraub, Reds, 1.
West, Browns, 1.

DUCE REPORTED READY TO RUSH ARMY TO SPAIN

Diplomats in Rome Hear of Plan as London Conference Fails.

BRITISH REJECT GERMAN PLAN

Won't Join in Demonstration of Navies Off Valencia and Meeting Collapses.

ROME, June 22 (U. P.).—Developments indicated tonight that Premier Benito Mussolini is seriously considering sending important new assistance, including regular army divisions, to the aid of Gen. Francisco Franco, chief of the Spanish rebels.

Diplomats, having received word from London that efforts to settle the Leipzig incident had broken down, were greatly perturbed.

Whether Mussolini is preparing for open intervention in Spain or merely taking precautions for such a hypothetical possibility could not be learned.

Nevertheless, several significant signs indicated that Mussolini may seize France's preoccupation with internal political troubles to modify his Spanish policy, using the recent Mediterranean incidents and the breakdown of the London negotiations as a pretext.

Troops Told to Be Ready.

From a trustworthy source, it was learned that at least one if not more generals of regular army divisions had received curt orders to keep their men in constant readiness "for service abroad." The one General's division numbers 15,000 men, who would sail from Vivita Vecchia if and when orders are received.

Although Gen. Franco's need is reported for man power, it is understood that Italy so far has hesitated to send any more "volunteers" but has not stinted in the supply of materials, especially airplanes. Several scores of the newest types of bombing planes have gone to Spain in recent weeks, according to excellent authority.

Regarding the breakdown of the London negotiations, the Italians blame Britain and France, insisting that they will maintain a solid front with Germany, even if Berlin decides on reprisals.

Conference Breaks Up.

LONDON, June 22 (A. P.).—Four-Power negotiations over German demands for a display of naval strength to the Spanish Loyalist Government broke down late today. The break came after Great

Continued on Page 3.

OHIO TROOPS BLOCK MILL REOPENING; 4800 POURING INTO YOUNGSTOWN AREA

Johnstown Chamber Protests Martial Law, Asserting Business Men Are Being Crucified

Earle's Order Is Said to Have Cut Employment 50 Per Cent Locally.

JOBS ARE BEING STAGGERED

State Police Being Reduced, but Commandant Denies Rule Has Been Lifted.

JOHNSTOWN, Pa., June 22 (U. P.).—The Chamber of Commerce charged today that Gov. Earle's order closing the Cambria plant of the Bethlehem Steel Corporation had cut employment in Johnstown, exclusive of steel workers, 50 per cent.

"He is crucifying our business men, already in financial straits as a result of the flood," said Lawrence W. Campbell, executive secretary of the Chamber.

Bethlehem Steel closed on Sunday "under protest" its vast Cambria works, employing 15,000 men, after martial law had been declared by Gov. Earle "to preserve peace and avoid bloodshed." Approximately 70,000 people live in Johnstown and more than 100,000 in the metropolitan area. Steel is the principal industry.

Heads Citizens' Committee.

Mr. Campbell, leader of a citizens' committee seeking re-opening of the plant, asserted that employers have begun to stagger their shifts, dividing their employees and working them alternate weeks.

"The economic conditions are such that income to employers in the commercial field is being rapidly curtailed," he said. "The small business man is suffering a substantial loss as a result of the Governor's sensational order.

"Employment in Johnstown, exclusive of the 15,000 steelworkers and 2,000 miners now on strike, has dropped off 50 per cent because of decreased revenue."

Large department stores are the heaviest sufferers, he said.

He estimated that the loss to steelworkers in wages is between $75,000 and $100,000 daily.

State Police Being Reduced.

Additional withdrawals of State highway patrolmen from Johnstown

Continued on Page 2.

ALONG JOHNSTOWN'S MARTIAL FRONT

Associated Press Photo.

Steel worker Leo Oswald asks cops when C. I. O. will let him start working again.

Regiments Arrive From All Parts of State Under Governor's Order.

STRIKERS QUIETLY GO HOME

Serious Clash Was Looked For—Numerous Arrests Made and Arms Seized.

YOUNGSTOWN, Ohio, June 22 (U. P.).—National Guard troops poured into the Mahoning Valley strike center today to preserve order and prevent the re-opening of closed plants until the Federal Steel Mediation Board makes further efforts to settle the seven-State conflict.

Called out suddenly late last night by Gov. Davey, the 4,800 militiamen began arriving in full force shortly before noon, after advance detachments had prevented the scheduled re-opening of plants of the Republic Steel Corporation and the Youngstown Sheet & Tube Company at 7 A. M.

Gov. Davey mobilized the guardsmen and sent them rumbling across flooded central Ohio roads before dawn today because, he said, a clash threatened between re-doubled picket lines and back-to-work marchers.

Gates Are Not Opened.

When the mill whistles blew at the re-opening hour, only a handful of the militia were in the strike zone, but their presence and the military proclamation proved effective.

The companies' threats to "open the gates" despite the Governor's order failed to materialize. Picket lines, strengthened last night by the arrival of hundreds of C. I. O. sympathizers from other Ohio cities and from nearby States—many of them carrying pistols—faded into skeleton shifts.

The police and deputy sheriffs stopped hundreds of union members in nearby towns and at the city limits. More than 115 were arrested on open charges or because they carried weapons. Seventy-two carloads, however, reached one main gate and sixty-five "invading" cars were counted at another gate.

The Troops Pour In.

By daybreak the word had gone out that the reopening of the mills was postponed and that the troops were en route to the city.

It was almost noon before the main detachment began arriving, however, and taking over the strike zone into which Gov. Davey ordered them when the Federal Steel Mediation Board negotiations at Cleveland had failed to reach a quick agreement that would have permitted the peaceful re-opening of the plants normally employing 32,000 workers.

The first big detachments to arrive were assigned to the Warren area, where 500 militiamen leaped from trucks. They were housed in three school buildings and an American Legion hall. Others were arriving to strengthen that area which is under command of Brig.-Gen. L. S. Conelly of Cleveland. The 145th Infantry and Battery D of the 134th Field Artillery were among the Warren guardsmen.

Columbus guardsmen of the 166th Infantry encamped at Campbell for duty along the picket lines of Youngstown Sheet & Tube plant. Under the general command of Major-Gen. Frank D. Henderson, the forces there numbered 231 enlisted men and twenty-four officers.

The 147th Infantry of Cincinnati was assigned to the Youngstown area and will watch over the Poland avenue main gate of the Republic Steel plant, where two men were killed in last Saturday night's riot. Lieut.-Col. Herman C. Doelling of Marysville commanded.

Gen. Henderson set up headquarters in the Campbell City Hall. Encamped near by, in Gordon Park, were the 166th's headquarters and service companies B, I and K, the medical detachment and the headquarters detachments of the First Battalion and the Thirty-seventh Division.

Protest to Governor.

Meanwhile today Frank Purnell, president of the Youngstown Sheet & Tube Company, protested in a telegram to Gov. Davey against the order sending the troops into the Youngstown and Warren areas.

"It is of the highest importance that the authority of the law should be upheld and that law abiding people who want to go back to work

Continued on Page 2.

Hughes's Son's Firm Named

Dwight, Member of Dissolved Law Company, Accused of Tax Avoidance Deal.

WASHINGTON, June 22 (A. P.).—A Senate-House inquiry committee received testimony today that six New Yorkers bought big insurance policies in a Bahamas company in an effort to reduce income tax payments between 1932 and 1936.

Mason B. Leming, a Treasury attorney, testifying at the congressional investigation into tax evasion and avoidance, explained what he termed "the device of foreign insurance companies" for escaping tax payments.

By this method, he said, taxpayers paid single premiums for large policies, then borrowed on the policies and took interest deductions on the loans.

The six New Yorkers were listed by Mr. Leming as follows:

Richard E. Dwight, attorney, with a $4,000,000 policy.

Winfield Ayres, a doctor, $400,000 policy.

Henry W. Lowe, insurance broker, $2,500,000 policy.

Lawrence Marx, cotton broker, one $2,500,000 policy in 1934, and another $2,500,000 policy in 1936.

Jacob W. Schwab, cotton broker, one $1,500,000 and one $1,000,000 policy.

George Thoms, attorney, $875,000 policy.

Standard Life Named.

Mr. Leming said that the policies all were taken out with the

Continued on Page 14.

Confusion Marks Weighing-in

Champion Jokes With Challenger as Fighters Pose for Pictures.

By FRANK GRAHAM.

CHICAGO, June 22.—James J. Braddock and Joe Louis were weighed in today on the stage of the Auditorium Theater, where once grand opera singers trod the boards and rattled the eaves with their high notes. The principal figures at the weighing in were Braddock, Louis and a red-faced police lieutenant, who kept yelling: "Stand back" and shoving everybody around. Fortunately, he stopped yelling for a few seconds at one period of the ceremonies and, in the lull, it was announced that Braddock weighed 197 pounds and Louis 197¼.

Louis was first to arrive at the scene of the weight taking. A crowd that had come for a glimpse of the fighters jammed Congress street between Michigan Boulevard and Wabash avenue and, peeping into the theater building, lined the lobby to the inner doors. Louis was escorted by policemen through the pack around the entrance and Braddock followed a few minutes later and then the crowd was admitted to the balcony and gallery where they had a view of the action on the stage. Not a very good view. There were too many photographers banked on the apron of the stage for that.

The stage had been arranged with the scales in the center, a table for the examining physicians and another for the members of the Illinois Athletic Commission, Joseph K. Triner and George Getz, and chairs for several hundred newspaper men assigned by papers all

Continued on Page 29.

Senator Norris Taken Suddenly Ill

WASHINGTON, June 22 (A. P.).—Senator Norris, Independent, of Nebraska, seventy-five-year-old leader among Senate liberals, was stricken with an attack of indigestion today. Dr. George W. Calver, Capitol physician, said the illness was not serious.

Valentine Denies Plan To Shift High Officers

Rumors that Police Commissioner Valentine has under consideration the transfer of several high ranking officers were brought to his attention today by reporters.

"I have nothing to say about that," the Commissioner declared. "There is nothing of the sort in immediate prospect, however."

RESULTS AT AQUEDUCT

Race Charts on Page 29. Other Results on Page 29.

	First.	Second.	Third.
First Race	Saint Pierre	Stalagmite	Royal Hobo
Prices	12-1 4-1 8-5	1-2 1-4	4-5
Scratched—Wulfstan, Ravenna, Rocky Margot, Crack Up.			
Second Race	Loughtrea	Yemasee	Greek Idol
Prices	3-5 1-4 —	2-5 1-6	1-1
No scratches.			
Third Race	Pockmantie	Sun Flo	Peggy Byrne
Prices	4-1 8-5 4-5	1-2 1-4	4-5
No scratches.			
Fourth Race	Drawbridge	Night Bud	Rebellion
Prices	13-10 1-4 —	8-5 —	—
Scratched—Idle Miss.			
Fifth Race	Recorder	Godspeed	Alarming
Prices	6-1 2-1 1-1	1-1 1-2	3-5
Scratched—Jack Be Nimble, Crepe.			
Sixth Race	Inscolita	Monument	Veiled Lady
Prices	9-5 1-2 —	3-5 —	—
Scratched—Van Nuys.			

WASHINGTON WINS FRESHMAN RACE

Finishes a Length Ahead of California Eight.

POUGHKEEPSIE, N. Y., June 22 (A. P.).—The University of Washington, picking up where it left off last year, today won the two-mile freshman race, opening event of the Thirty-ninth Intercollegiate Rowing Association regatta.

California was second and Syracuse third.

Washington led from the start and won by a good length. California, a contender all the way, held second place safe from Syracuse's fast closing rush. The Golden Bears, touted in advance calculations as a possible winner of the yearling event, took second place by at least a length.

It was Washington's fourth straight victory in the freshman event and the Huskies' fourth successive triumph in Poughkeepsie

Continued on Page 29.

CITY PAY RISE VOTED

Three Classes of Workers to Benefit by Act.

Three bills increasing the pay of city employees were passed today by the Municipal Assembly. One provides a 10 per cent increase for per diem employees in the Department of Parks, a second giving $120 a year to 6,000 civil service employees earning between $1,800 and $5,000, and the third, $120 a year for ungraded employees for a period of six years to bring their pay up to the maximum.

Yankees Defeat Tigers in 11th, 6-5; Cubs Trip Dodgers, 5-2; Cards Beat Giants in 9th, 9-8

Rolfe's 2-Run Homer Nips Detroit for Ruffing's 13th

League Leaders, Held Hitless by Wade Until DiMaggio Clouts 28th Circuit Blow in Sixth, Triumph After Two Base-Running Lapses

By Arthur E. Patterson

Yankee fans, puzzled over the fluctuating fortunes of their favorites on the recently concluded Western trip, saw how the Bronx Bombers have been losing games and how they have been winning them, too, at the Stadium yesterday.

They saw them throw away one opportunity after another to clinch a bitter battle with the Detroit Tigers and then, just as it seemed the Bengals might celebrate with victory Mickey Cochrane's return to the bench, a single by Frankie Crosetti and a homer into the right-field stands by Red Rolfe brought the champions back to a thrilling triumph, 6 to 5.

It was a trying, although eventually happy, afternoon for the other Yankee redhead, Charlie Ruffing, for not only were rival fielders camping in front of his hard-hit liners which might have turned the tide of battle long before the Rolfe homer, but he also suffered as his mates ran bases in incredible fashion. The victory was his thirteenth.

Saltzgaver Blunders

The worst of several blunders was made by Jack Saltzgaver, inserted as a runner for Bill Dickey in the tenth. Dickey, who had tied the score by slapping a double to right with the bases loaded in the eighth, walked with one out. When Jake Powell bounced a single to center Dickey rushed around to third, where he was lifted in favor of the utility man. Cochrane ordered Jack Russell to pass Tony Lazzeri, filling the bases, and Myril Hoag stepped to the plate with the chance to end it all.

He lifted a high fly in short left. Gerald Walker raced in for it and Billy Rogell sped back. The Tigers called Walker off, but just as the shortstop put his glove up for the ball he staggered and fell on his back. He clutched the ball, however, and, knowing he could not possibly throw the runner out at the plate he handed the ball to Walker as he went down. Saltzgaver, who hadn't tagged third, must have thought there was a fumble on the play, for he raced toward the plate. Walker rifled the ball in and Cliff Bolton fumbled it. Many thought the game was over, but Bolton knew differently. Returning the ball to Marvin Owen, standing on third, he completed a double play and the inning.

How Joe McCarthy raged! And his ire wasn't cooled any when the Tigers came up in the eleventh and made a run. After one out, Charlie Gehringer singled, but was forced at second on Greenberg's grounder. Greenberg stole second, Walker, hitless in five previous trips, singled, and the Tigers were ahead, 5 to 4.

Rolfe's Blow Triumphs

But Yankee power rode over other Yankee faults. Ruffing sent Owen to his heels with a line drive. That was the last out Russell, who entered the game after Dickey's double in the eighth, earned, however. Crosetti singled to left and Rolfe put on the finishing touches.

Earlier the Yankees had been weak at the plate. They were outhit, 15 to 8. Jack Wade had a no-hitter under his control for five and one-third innings, but after Rolfe walked Joe DiMaggio blasted a 400-foot homer, No. 28, far into the left-field seats. This left the Tigers still leading, 3 to 2, for Gehringer hit for the circuit in the first, two singles and a fly brought in another in the third and a base on balls, a single and a fly added one in the third. After two out in the eighth the Tigers scored again on successive singles by Bolton, Wade and Fox.

Then the Yankees came out of their lethargy. Crosetti led off with a single. Rolfe flied out, but DiMaggio singled and Gehrig walked, filling the bases. Dickey shot a hard drive under Greenberg's glove down the right-field line and the game should have been won right there. Two scored and Gehrig had to remain at third because, for some unknown reason, he slowed almost to a halt after rounding second. Russell came in and stopped the Yankees until the eleventh.

Chandler Recalled

The Yankees moved to strengthen their creaking pitching staff when they recalled Spud Chandler from Newark after putting Johnny Broaca, A. W. O. L. hurler, on the ineligibility list.

At the same time it was learned that Tommy Henrich, who hit .477 in the West, will be out of action of a week or ten days with water on the knee he injured in chasing Tony Pie's double Sunday. George Selkirk was in uniform, but the Yankees will have to get along a week, at least, with three outfielders.

Although he has returned to the bench, Cochrane has no hope of playing this season. He tires quickly.

"Maybe next spring," he said wistfully.

Joe Louis, heavyweight champion, sat behind the dugout of his favorite club, Detroit. . . . Gus Mancuso, out of the Giants' line-up with a broken finger, watched from a box seat . . . maybe scouting the Yankees for the World Series? . . . Eldon Auker and Lefty Gomez will be the opposing pitchers today.

The score:

DETROIT (A. L.)	ab	r	h	po	a	e
Fox, rf.	6	1	2	5	0	0
Rogell, ss.	5	1	1	3	4	0
Gehr'ger, 2b	6	1	3	3	3	0
Greenb'g, 1b	6	1	2	4	0	0
Walker, lf.	6	0	1	1	1	0
Owen, 3b.	6	0	2	4	0	0
Laabs, cf.	4	0	1	6	0	0
Bolton, c.	4	1	2	5	2	0
WADE, p.	4	0	1	0	1	0
RUSSELL, p	1	0	0	0	1	0
Totals	48	5	15	*31	12	0

NEW YORK (A. L.)	ab	r	h	po	a	e
Crosetti, ss.	5	2	2	3	1	1
Rolfe, 3b.	4	2	1	2	2	0
DiMaggio, cf	5	2	2	3	0	0
Gehrig, 1b.	3	0	0	3	1	0
Dickey, c.	4	0	2	9	1	0
†Saltzgaver	0	0	0	0	0	0
Glenn, c.	0	0	0	0	0	0
Powell, lf.	4	0	1	4	0	0
Lazzeri, 2b.	4	0	0	5	1	1
Hoag, rf.	3	0	0	2	0	0
RUFFING, p	4	0	0	2	1	0
Totals	36	6	8	33	7	2

*One out when winning run was scored.
†Ran for Dickey in tenth inning.

Detroit	101	010	010	01	—5
New York	000	002	020	02	—6

Runs batted in—Gehringer (2), Greenberg, DiMaggio (2), Fox, Dickey (2), Walker, Rolfe (2). Two-base hits—Dickey (2), Greenberg. Home runs—Gehringer, DiMaggio, Rolfe. Stolen bases—Laabs, Crosetti, Greenberg, DiMaggio. Sacrifice—Laabs. Double plays—Wade, Rogell, Bolton and Owen; Rigell, Gehringer and Greenberg; Rogell, Walker, Bolton and Owen. Left on bases—New York, 10; Detroit, 13. Bases on balls—Off Wade, 7; off Ruffing, 2; off Russell, 4. Struck out—By Ruffing, 9; by Russell, 1; by Wade, 2. Hits—Off Wade, 5 in 7 1-3 innings; off Russell, 3 in 3. Losing pitcher—Russell. Umpires—Quinn, McGowan and Ormsby. Time—2:59.

Leading Five Batsmen In Each Major League

AMERICAN LEAGUE

Player and Club	G.	AB.	R.	H.	Pct.
Gehrigh, New York	85	321	76	121	.377
DiMaggio, New York	80	340	86	126	.371
Travis, Washington	62	239	33	88	.368
Bell, St. Louis	86	366	50	129	.353
West, St. Louis	77	303	51	107	.353

NATIONAL LEAGUE

Player and Club	G.	AB.	R.	H.	Pct.
Medwick, St. Louis	86	343	77	139	.405
Hartnett, Chicago	57	185	24	71	.384
P. Waner, Pitts.	85	342	61	129	.377
Herman, Chicago	71	305	59	109	.358
Vaughan, Pitts.	75	295	44	103	.349

Home Runs	Runs Batted In
DiMaggio, Ynks. 28	Medwick, Cards. 97
Foxx, Red Sox. 24	Greenb'g, Tigers. 97
Greenb'g, Tigers. 23	DiMaggio, Yanks. 92
Trosky, Indians. 23	Dickey, Yanks. 81
Medwick, Cards. 21	Gehrig, Yanks. 78
	Foxx, Red Sox. 78
	Walker, Tigers. 78

Senators Beat White Sox, 6-5, On Myer's Hit

Single in 9th Scores Lewis to Extend Washington's Streak to Five Straight

By The Associated Press

WASHINGTON, July 27.—Buddy Myer's ninth-inning single brought Washington a 6-to-5 victory over the Chicago White Sox today and a fifth consecutive triumph.

Lewis singled to open the ninth. Stone walked after two were out and Kuhel was purposely passed filling the bases. Myer banged a clean hit past third base to score Lewis with the deciding run.

The White Sox hopped on Monte Weaver for two runs in the first, scoring on Walker's single and Bonura's home run but the Senators retaliated in their half with four. Five singles and an error by Appling produced the runs.

Weaver was replaced by Appleton in the second after Luke Appling had tripled and two successive batters had walked. Appling scored on a fly by Hayes.

The Senators got another run in the third on Simmons's double and Kuhel's single, but the Sox tied it up in the sixth on a walk, a fielder's choice, a single and an infield out.

The score:

CHICAGO (A. L.)	ab	r	h	po	a	e
Hayes, 2b.	5	0	0	3	2	0
Kreev'h, cf	5	0	0	3	0	0
Walker, rf.	3	1	2	1	0	0
Bonura, 1b.	4	1	1	11	1	0
Radclif'e, lf	4	0	0	3	0	0
Appling, ss.	2	2	2	2	4	1
Berger, 3b.	2	1	0	0	4	0
Sewell, c.	3	0	1	3	0	0
WHIT'HD, p	0	0	0	0	0	0
RIGN'Y, p.	3	0	0	0	2	0
Totals	31	5	6	*26	13	1

WASHINGTON (A. L.)	ab	r	h	po	a	e
Almada, cf.	4	1	1	3	0	0
Lewis, 2b.	5	2	4	0	2	0
Travis, ss.	5	1	1	1	4	0
Sim'ons, lf	4	2	2	3	0	0
Stone, rf.	3	0	0	2	0	0
Kuhel, 1b.	4	0	2	8	0	0
Myer, 2b.	5	0	2	4	3	0
R.Ferrell, c	3	0	0	6	1	0
WEAV'R, p	0	0	0	0	0	0
APPLE'N, p	3	0	0	0	2	0
Totals	36	6	12	27	12	0

*Two out when winning run was scored.

Chicago	210	002	000	—5
Washington	401	000	001	—6

Runs batted in—Bonura (2), Simmons (2), Stone, Myer (2), Hayes (2), Kuhel, Sewell. Two-base hit—Simmons. Three-base hit—Appling. Home run—Bonura. Sacrifices—Stone, Rigney, Berger, Appleton. Double plays—Berger, Hayes and Bonura; Travis, Myer and Kuhel. Left on bases—Chicago, 7; Washington, 11. Bases on balls—Off Weaver, 2; off Appleton, 4. Struck out—By Appleton, 4; by Rigney, 1. Hits—Off Whitehead, 5 in 1-3 inning; off Weaver, 3 in 1; off Rigney, 7 in 8 1-3; off Appleton, 3 in 8. Passed ball—Sewell. Winning pitcher—Appleton. Losing pitcher—Rigney. Umpires—Geisel, Summers and Basil. Time—2:06.

Pirates Defeat Phils Behind Lucas, 4 to 1

PITTSBURGH, July 27 (AP).—The Pirates celebrated their return home today by defeating Philadelphia, 4 to 1.

Red Lucos limited the Phillies to six hits. In the seventh inning the Phillies collected two of their hits on Scharein's double and Atwood's single.

Bucky Walters, Philadelphia hurler, forced in one run in the second and loosened up again in the eighth to yield two more runs. Todd led the Pirate attack with three hits.

The score:

PHILADELPHIA (N. L.)	ab	r	h	po	a	e
Norris, 2b.	4	0	1	1	7	0
Martin, cf.	3	0	1	0	0	0
Klein, rf.	4	0	0	1	0	0
Arnovich, lf	4	0	0	1	0	0
Camilli, 1b	4	0	0	13	0	0
Whitney, 3b	4	0	1	3	3	0
Atwood, c.	4	1	1	2	0	0
Scharein, ss	3	0	2	3	4	1
W'LT'RS, p	3	0	0	0	2	0
Totals	33	1	6	24	16	1

PITTSBURGH (N. L.)	ab	r	h	po	a	e
L. Waner, cf	4	0	1	3	0	0
Jensen, lf.	4	1	1	2	0	0
P.Waner, rf	3	0	1	5	0	0
Suhr, 1b.	3	.	1	9	0	0
Todd, c.	4	1	3	4	0	0
Br'bak'r, 3b	4	1	1	1	3	1
Young, ss.	3	0	0	0	4	0
Handley, 2b	2	0	0	3	4	0
LUCAS, p.	2	0	1	0	0	0
Totals	29	4	9	27	11	1

Philadelphia	000	000	100	—1
Pittsburgh	020	000	02x	—4

Runs batted in—L. Waner, Scharein, Todd, Brubaker. Two-base hits—Todd, Scharein. Sacrifice—P. Waner. Double plays—Whitney, Camilli and Young; Handley and Suhr; Norris, Scharein and Camilli. Left on bases—Philadelphia, 6; Pittsburgh, 6. Bases on balls—Off Lucas, 1; off Walters, 4. Struck out—By Lucas, 2; by Walters, 2. Umpires—Reardon, Pinelli and Goetz. Time—1:43.

Happy Moments for Tigers in Victory for Yankees

Herald Tribune photo

Mickey Cochrane looks mighty fit again as he returns to manage the Tigers and is thankfully welcomed by Bump Hadley, the New York pitcher whose fast ball fractured the Detroit catcher's skull in a game at Stadium May 26

The Tigers were also cheerful in the third inning yesterday, when Fox scored on Gehringer's sacrifice, but the home team won, 6-5

3 Chicago Double Plays Help Carleton Turn Back Brooklyn

Hack, Demaree, Herman Lead Assault on Hamlin as Grimm Rejoins Club

Special to the Herald Tribune

CHICAGO, July 27.—The hard hitting of Stan Hack, Frank Demaree and Billy Herman, coupled with three Cub double plays, was more than the Dodgers could cope with in today's series opener.

The Cubs won, 5 to 2, lifting their lead to three games and giving much pleasure to Charley Grimm and a crowd of 12,000 fans, 10,941 of whom paid. Grimm was back on the bench for the first time since leaving the club in Boston to consult a doctor in St. Louis.

Tex Carleton allowed nine hits, the same number permitted by Luke Hamlin, to score his eighth victory. Hamlin's support was none too good, an error charged to Joe Stripp paving the way for the Cubs' last two runs in the eighth.

The Cubs scored in the first when Cooney crashed into the left centerfield wall going after Hack's drive. It became a three-bagger, Hack scoring on Collins's fly to Cooney.

Dodgers Take Lead

Heinie Manush drove in the tying run for Brooklyn in the fourth with a line single that followed hits by Joe Stripp and Buddy Hasett, and Jack Winsett put Brooklyn ahead with an infield out that brought Hassett home.

In the sixth the Cubs broke through to take another lead that they held until the end. Hack singled to left and after Collins had grounded out Demaree shot a double to letf, scoring Hack, who had reached third on a wild pitch. Another single to left center by Herman brought Demaree home.

Hack again became the spearhead of the Cubs' attack in the eighth, drawing a pass to start the inning. When Collins bunted toward third Stripp came in fast, feinted a throw to second and then threw to first where Lavagetto was covering. But the ball went past him and the runners advanced to second and third, where they lingered only until Demaree hit Hamlin's first pitch to center for a two-run single.

That sent Hamlin away and brought in Roy Henshaw who, aided by a double play, escaped without further scoring.

Winsett singled with one out in the ninth, but two pinch hitters, Jimmy Bucher and Jake Daniel splashed easy grounders to Herman and Collins.

Winsett Caught at Plate

The Dodgers bungled one chance to tie the score in the third when Hamlin singled to short center with Winsett on second. Andy High, acting manager, sent Winsett home, where he was an easy victim of Cavarretta's throw to O'Dea.

Woody English sprained his ankle in the exhibition game at Clinton last night and will be out for a week or more.

The Cubs' third double play, which came in the eighth, was a heartbreaker for the Dodgers. Hassett opened the inning with a single for his third straight hit. Manush shot a liner toward right. Herman leaped high in the air, got the ball in the web of his glove and doubled Buddy off the bag.

Phelps hit into a double play with none out in the second and Stripp repeated in the fifth.

Another scoring opportunity went awry after the sixth, which Hassett started with a double. He was run down after Herman's sparkling play on Manush's grounder.

Dodgers' Score

* * *

BROOKLYN (N. L.)	ab	r	h	po	a	e
Cooney, cf.	4	0	0	7	0	0
Stripp, 3b.	4	1	1	2	1	1
Hassett, 3b.	4	1	3	9	0	1
Manush, rf.	3	0	1	2	0	0
Phelps, c.	3	0	0	2	1	0
Lav'getto, 2b	3	0	0	1	4	0
Winsett, lf.	4	0	2	0	0	0
Brown, ss.	3	0	0	1	1	0
*Bucher	1	0	0	0	0	0
HAMLIN, p	3	0	2	0	2	0
H'SHAW, p	0	0	0	0	0	0
†Daniel	1	0	0	0	0	0
Totals	33	2	9	24	9	2

CHICAGO (N. L.)	ab	r	h	po	a	e
Galan, lf.	4	0	0	1	0	0
Hack, 3b.	3	3	2	1	4	0
Collins, 1b.	3	1	0	16	0	0
Demaree, rf	4	1	3	1	0	0
Herman, 2b	4	0	2	2	10	0
O'Dea, c.	4	0	0	3	0	0
Jurges, ss.	3	0	[illegible]	2	4	1
Cav'retta, cf	3	0	1	0	1	0
Marty, cf.	1	0	0	0	0	0
C'LETON, p	2	0	1	1	3	0
Totals	31	5	9	27	22	1

*Batted for Brown in ninth inning.
†Batted for Henshaw in ninth inning.

Brooklyn	100	002	02x	—5
Chicago	100	002	02x	—5

Runs batted in—Manush, Winsett, Collins, Demaree (3), Herman. Two-base hits—Hassett, Demaree (2), Carleton. Three-base hit—Hack. Sacrifice—Collins. Double plays—Lavagetto and Hassett; Hack, Herman and Collins; Herman, Jurges and Collins; Herman and Collins. Left on bases—Brooklyn, 7; Chicago, 6. Bases on balls—Off Hamlin, 2; off Henshaw, 1; off Carleton, 3. Struck out—By Hamlin, 2. Hits—Off Hamlin, 9 in 7 innings (none out in eighth); off Henshaw, 0 in 1. Wild pitch—Hamlin. Losing pitcher—Hamlin. Umpires—Klem, Sears and Ballanfant. Time—2:00.

Standings in Major Leagues

* * *

WEDNESDAY, JULY 28, 1937

American League

YESTERDAY'S RESULTS

New York, 6; Detroit, 5 (11 innings)
Philadelphia, 4; Cleveland, 3
St. Louis, 8; Boston, 5
Washington, 6; Chicago, 5

STANDING OF THE CLUBS

	New York	Chicago	Detroit	Boston	Cleveland	Washington	St. Louis	Phila'phia	Won	Lost	Percentage
New York	—	6	10	6	9	7	10	9	57	27	.679
Chicago	8	—	3	7	5	10	11	9	53	35	.602
Detroit	6	7	—	7	7	9	5	9	50	34	.595
Boston	2	6	5	—	6	4	11	11	45	37	.549
Cleveland	4	3	5	7	—	7	6	9	41	41	.500
Wash'gton	3	5	3	5	6	—	10	4	36	46	.439
St. Louis	3	3	3	5	2	5	—	7	28	57	.329
Phila'phia	1	5	5	0	6	4	4	—	25	58	.301
Gms. lost	27	35	34	37	41	46	57	58	—	—	

GAMES TODAY

Detroit at New York, 3:15
Chicago at Washington
St. Louis at Boston
Cleveland at Philadelphia

National League

YESTERDAY'S RESULTS

St. Louis, 9; New York, 8
Chicago, 5; Brooklyn, 2
Pittsburgh, 4; Philadelphia, 1
Cincinnati, 3; Boston, 2

STANDING OF THE CLUBS

	Chicago	New York	Pittsburgh	St. Louis	Boston	Brooklyn	Cincinnati	Phila'phia	Won	Lost	Percentage
Chicago	—	8	5	10	7	10	5	10	55	31	.640
New York	6	—	8	9	5	9	9	7	53	35	.602
Pit'sburgh	6	3	—	5	7	6	10	8	45	40	.529
St. Louis	2	6	4	—	9	7	7	10	45	41	.523
Boston	4	5	7	6	—	8	7	6	43	45	.489
Brooklyn	5	3	8	6	2	—	6	5	35	49	.417
Cincinnati	3	6	1	4	8	4	—	9	35	49	.417
Phila'phia	5	4	7	1	7	5	5	—	34	55	.382
Gms. lost	31	35	40	41	45	49	49	55	—	—	

GAMES TODAY

New York at St. Louis
Brooklyn at Chicago
Boston at Cincinnati
Philadelphia at Pittsburgh

Browns Defeat Red Sox, 8 to 5, Behind Koupal

Foxx Wallops 24th Homer and 2 Doubles, but Boston Drops Series Opener

By The Associated Press

BOSTON, July 27.—The St. Louis Browns opened Jim Bottomley's first eastern invasion today with an 8-to-5 victory over Boston's hapless Red Sox, as Lou Koupal went the route and allowed nine hits.

One of them was Jimmy Foxx's twenty-fourth home run, a drive over the left center field wall in the sixth inning that was followed a minute later by Eric McNair's sixth circuit clout.

Foxx also contributed two doubles to Boston's losing cause for a perfect day at bat. The score:

ST. LOUIS (A. L.)	ab	r	h	po	a	e
Davis, 1b.	5	1	2	15	1	0
West, cf.	5	0	0	2	0	1
Vosmik, lf.	5	2	3	1	0	0
Clift, 3b.	4	3	3	0	4	0
Bell, rf	4	1	1	0	0	0
Kn'k'b'r, ss	5	0	1	2	7	0
Hemsley, c	5	1	3	1	0	0
Lipsco'b, 2b	2	0	2	5	4	0
KOUPAL, p	5	0	0	1	1	0
Totals	40	8	15	27	17	1

BOSTON (A. L.)	ab	r	h	po	a	e
Mills, lf.	4	0	1	0	1	0
Chap'an, rf	3	0	0	4	0	0
Cronin, ss.	4	0	0	5	3	1
Foxx, 1b.	3	2	3	10	1	0
Higgins, 3b	4	0	1	2	0	0
McNair, 2b	4	1	1	2	4	0
Cramer, cf.	4	0	1	1	0	0
Desaut'ls, c	2	1	0	2	0	0
*Dalles'dro	1	0	1	0	0	0
MARC'M, p	1	1	1	0	0	0
OST'M'R, p	2	0	0	1	3	0
†Gaffke	1	0	0	0	0	0
Totals	33	5	9	27	12	1

*Batted for Desautels in ninth inning.
†Batted for Ostermueller in ninth inning.

St. Louis	015	020	000	—8
Boston	012	002	000	—5

Runs batted in—Knickerbocker (2), Hemsley (2), Lipscomb (2), Rosnick, Bell, Foxx (2), McNair (2), Mills. Two-base hits—Clift (2), Davis, Knickerbocker, Lipscomb, Marcum, Foxx. Home runs—Foxx, McNair. Double plays—Knickerbocker and Lipscomb; Clift, Lipscomb and Davis (2); McNair, Cronin and Foxx. Left on bases—St. Louis, 10; Boston, 4. Bases on balls—Off Koupal, 3; off Marcum, 1; off Ostermueller, 4. Struck out—By Koupal, 1; Marcum, 1. Hits—Off Marcum, 8 in 3 innings; off Ostermueller, 7 in 6. Losing pitcher—Marcum. Umpires—Owens, Moriarty and Johnston. Time—1:55.

Dunlap, of Royals, Hurt As Jersey City Wins, 12-7

MONTREAL, July 27 (CP).—Knocked unconscious by a pitched ball, Paul Dunlap, center-fielder of the Montreal Royals, was taken to a hospital tonight during an International League game with the Jersey City Giants.

The heavy-hitting outfielder suffered a possible concussion when he ducked into one of Mike Meketi's fast-breaking curves in the fifth inning. The ball hit him on the side of the head.

Jersey City won the game, 12 to 7, behind Meketi's seven-hit pitching.

The score:

JERSEY CITY (I. L.)	ab	r	h	po	a	e
Smith, ss.	5	1	1	2	1	1
C.Wilson, 3b	5	2	3	1	0	0
Lee, cf.	5	2	3	3	0	0
Weintr'b, 1b	4	2	2	4	0	0
E.Wilson, rf	3	0	0	0	0	0
Dwyer, lf.	4	0	2	2	0	0
King, 2b.	3	3	2	2	3	0
Redm'nd, c	3	1	2	7	0	0
MEK'TI, p.	4	1	0	0	0	0
Totals	36	12	15	21	4	1

MONTREAL (I. L.)	ab	r	h	po	a	e
Bell, 2b.	3	2	1	2	2	0
Jeffries, 3b	3	1	2	0	0	0
Dunlap, cf	1	0	0	1	0	0
Hafey, cf.	0	1	0	2	0	0
Dugas, rf.	4	1	1	0	0	1
Cobb, 1b.	3	1	0	6	2	0
Harris, lf.	3	0	0	1	0	1
Sankey, ss.	4	0	1	3	2	1
Dhandl'r, c	4	0	0	5	0	0
POLLI, p.	0	0	0	1	0	0
PAT'IS'N, p	4	1	2	0	0	0
Totals	27	7	7	21	6	2

Jersey City	251	300	1	—12
Montreal	100	020	4	—7

Runs batted in—Weintraub (2), Cobb, Meketi, C. Wilson (3), Redmond (3), Lee (2), Bell, Harris, Dugas (3), Sankey. Two-base hits—Pattison (2), King, Jeffries, Lee, Sankey. Home runs—Weintraub, Redmond, Dugas. Left on bases—Jersey City, 7; Montreal, 8. Bases on balls—Off Polli, 1; off Meketi, 6; off Pattison, 3. Struck out—By Meketi, 7; by Pattison, 5. Hits—Off Polli, 6 in 1 1-3 innings; off Pattison, 9 in 5 2-3. Hit by pitcher—By Meketi (Dunlap). Passed ball—Chancler. Losing pitcher—Polli. Umpires—Jorda and White. Time—1:59.

Landis Denies He'll Probe Baseball's Horse Players

CHICAGO, July 27 (AP).—Kenesaw Mountain Landis, Commissioner of Baseball, denied emphatically tonight published reports from St. Louis that he was about to launch a wholesale investigation into betting on horse races by major league players. The gambling issue was revived with the dismissal of Rogers Hornsby as manager of the St. Louis Browns last week.

Neither is the American League interested in pursuing the private affairs of Hornsby, said William Harridge, president.

Galento Knocks Out Ettore

NEWARK, N. J., July 27 (AP).—Tony Galento, of Orange, scored an eight-round knockout over Al Ettore, of Philadelphia, in the scheduled twelve-round final bout of the milk fund benefit show at the Nutley Velodrome tonight. Galento weighed 232; Ettore, 191.

Medwick's Homer Downs Smith After Hubbell Gives Up 8 in 4th

Blondy Ryan Rejoins Terry Forces, Gets 2 Hits and Drives In Pair of Runs

By Rud Rennie

ST. LOUIS, July 27.—All sorts of things happened to the Giants this afternoon. They had their famous 1933 telegram-sender, Blondy Ryan, playing shortstop without his shinguards. Carl Hubbell, their best pitcher, was shaken to his heels by an eight-run barrage in the fourth inning. The Giants made up seven runs to tie the score in the eighth, but lost in the ninth when Joe Medwick came up with two out and hit a home run into the left-field bleachers.

This defeat, 9 to 8, put the Giants three games behind the league-leading Cubs and did not lighten Bill Terry's worries about his team.

In desperation Terry acquired Ben Cantwell, a pitcher, from the Jersey City farm and purchased Ryan from Milwaukee. Ryan lost no time getting here. He came by airplane and was in camp before the announcement of his purchase was made. He stepped right into the ball game and made two hits and drove in two runs.

Giants Drop Haslin

Simultaneously, Mickey Haslin was cut off the squad, and it is understood that George Davis, utility outfielder, also is about to be sent away to make room for Cantwell.

It was ladies' day and a crowd of 14,133 saw the Giants, apparently hopelessly beaten, struggle into a tie only to lose.

Leslie hit a long fly with the bases filled to make a run for the Giants in the fourth. But the Cardinals went to work on Hubbell in their part of the inning. Johnny Mize knocked one onto the roof of the right-field pavilion for a two-run homer and the Cardinals went on from there and made six more runs before they were through. Twelve men batted and made eight hits for eight runs. Hubbell was knocked out of the box for the second time in succession.

The Giants, to all intents and purposes, were through after this lusty eight-run inning. Theye were seven runs behind. But Si Johnson, the Cardinal pitcher, lost control in the sixth. The Giants batted all the way around and made four runs and knocked him out. They scored two unearned runs off Sheriff Blake in the seventh after Durocher made a wild throw to first. And they tied the score off Bob Weiland in the eighth.

Moore's Hit Ties Score

Ryan took part in the rallies. Chiozza started the eighth with his second double. Whitehead sacrificed and Moore came through with a single to send Chiozza home with the tying run.

Dick Coffman and Al Smith did fine relief work for the Giants. Smith had the Cardinals shut out with one hit in three and two-thirds innings until Medwick smashed his home run in the ninth inning, winning the game.

Ryan was with the Giants in 1933 and 1934. They sent him to Philadelphia for the 1935 season. The Phils wanted to send him to Baltimore. Ryan refused to go and was out six weeks. Then the Yankees bought him. He finished the season with New York. In 1936 he was with Minneapolis, and this year, along in May the Millers sent him to Milwaukee. Now he is back again with the Giants. Terry hopes Ryan can plug the gap until Bartell is well enough to return to work.

Dizzy Dean limped into Doc Weaver's office looking woeful. "Jerome," said Doc Weaver, solicitously, "let me do something for that toe. You know I've been treating fracture cases for twenty-five years. I think I can help you." "Hell, Doc," said Diz, "this ain't no fracture; this toe is broke."

Chiozza had his eyes open and made a good play in the third. He couldn't do anything with Johnson's slow roller, but he spied Owen rounding second and got him with a quick throw to Whitehead.

Cardinals Get Cake

The Gas House gang received a big frosted cake before the game. The only reason for the presentation seemed to be that a lady had baked it and did not know what else to do with it. Frisch would have been more thankful if she had brought in an experienced catcher.

Medwick and Durocher side-swiped each other in pursuit of Coffman's short fly in the fifth. Durocher was all right, but Medwick rolled over like a whirling log and lay still for a moment. The wind had been knocked out of him. As soon as he got his breath he was ready to play again.

When Ott singled in the sixth it was his first hit in fourteen times at bat.

The score:

NEW YORK (N. L.)	ab	r	h	po	a	e
Chiozza, 3b	4	1	2	1	2	0
Whit'h'd, 2b	4	0	0	4	1	0
J.Moore, lf.	5	1	2	1	0	0
Berger, cf.	5	1	1	3	0	1
Ott, rf.	3	2	2	2	0	0
Leslie, 1b.	5	1	2	11	0	0
Danning, c.	5	1	1	3	1	0
Ryan, ss.	5	1	2	1	2	0
HUB'ELL, p	1	0	0	0	1	0
COFFM'N, p	1	0	1	0	1	0
SMITH, p.	2	0	0	0	3	0
†Ripple	1	0	1	0	0	0
Totals	41	8	14	*26	11	1

ST. LOUIS (N. L.)	ab	r	h	po	a	e
T.Moore, cf	5	1	1	2	0	0
Gut'r'ge, 3b.	5	1	2	2	0	1
Mize, 1b.	5	1	1	9	0	0
Medwick, lf	5	2	2	3	0	0
Padgett, rf	4	1	2	2	0	0
Brown, 2b.	4	1	1	3	2	1
Duroch'r, ss	3	0	0	0	5	1
Owen, c.	2	1	2	6	1	0
JOHNS'N, p	2	1	2	0	1	0
BLAKE, p.	0	0	0	0	1	0
WEIL'ND, p	0	0	0	0	0	0
HAR'ELL, p	0	0	0	0	0	0
‡J. Martin	1	0	0	0	0	0
Totals	36	9	13	27	10	3

*Two out when winning run was scored.
†Batted for Coffman in sixth inning.
‡Batted for Weiland in eighth inning.

New York	000	104	210	—8
St. Louis	000	800	001	—9

Runs batted in—Leslie (2), Mize (2), Padgett, Brown, Johnson, T. Moore, Gutteridge (2), Ryan (2), Ripple, Chiozza (2), J. Moore, Medwick. Two-base hits—Berger, Padgett, T. Moore, Coffman, Chiozza (2). Home runs—Mize, Medwick. Sacrifices—Chiozza, Blake, Whitehead. Double Play—Durocher, Brown and Mize. Left on bases—New York, 10; St. Louis, 5. Bases on balls—Off Hubbell, 1; off Smith, 2; off Johnson, 2. Struck out—By Hubbell, 2; by Johnson, 3; by Harrell, 2. Hits—Off Hubbell, 10 in 3 1-3 innings; off Coffman, 1 in 1 2-3; off Smith, 2 in 3 2-3; off Johnson, 9 in 5 1-3; off Blake, 5 in 2; off Weiland, 0 in 2-3; off Harrell, 0 in 1. Wild Pitch—Hubbell. Winning pitcher—Harrell. Losing pitcher—Smith. Umpires—Parker, Moran and Magerkurth. Time—2:35.

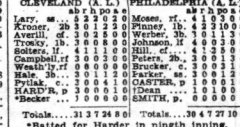

Back With Giants

Blondy Ryan

Grissom Gains Tenth Victory For Reds, 3 to 2

Scarsella's Homer Conquers Bees as Pitcher Fans 11 and Allows Only 4 Hits

By The Associated Press

CINCINNATI, July 27.—Lee Grissom, twenty-four-year-old Cincinnati southpaw, gained his tenth victory of the season today as the Reds defeated Boston 3 to 2, in the ninth inning on Les Scarsella's homer with one on.

Grissom permitted only one hit, walked none and struck out ten up to the ninth frame.

Then Reis batted for Danny MacFayden and singled. Garms doubled and Warstler fanned for the third time and became Grissom's eleventh strikeout.

Vince Dimaggio, whose seventh-inning single made him the only Bee to reach first base in eight innings, then slammed a double and scored Reis and Garms.

Bob Smith then took up the Boston pitching duty. He retired Lombardi and Jordan, but hit Goodman with a pitched ball. Scarsella then hit into the right field bleachers.

The score:

BOSTON (N. L.)	ab	r	h	po	a	e
Garms, lf.	4	1	1	3	0	0
Warstler, ss.	4	0	0	0	1	1
DiMag'io, cf	4	0	2	3	0	0
Cuc'ne'lo, 2b	3	0	0	1	1	0
Moore, rf.	4	0	0	1	1	0
English, 3b.	3	0	0	2	5	0
Fletch'r, 1b	3	0	0	11	1	1
Mueller, c.	3	0	0	4	0	0
M'CF'D'N, p	2	0	0	1	3	0
†Reis	1	1	1	0	0	0
SMITH, p.	0	0	0	0	0	0
Totals	31	2	4	*26	12	2

CINCINNATI (N. L.)	ab	r	h	po	a	e
Jordon, 1b.	5	0	0	9	0	1
Goodman, rf	4	1	1	4	0	0
Scarse'la, lf	5	1	2	0	0	0
Hafey, cf.	4	1	0	1	0	0
V.Davis, c.	3	0	2	10	1	0
Riggs, 3b.	4	0	3	0	1	0
Kamp'is, 2b	4	0	0	2	1	0
Myers, ss.	4	0	0	1	2	0
GRIS'M, p.	1	0	0	0	3	0
‡Lombardi	1	0	0	0	0	0
Totals	35	3	8	27	8	1

*Two out when winning run was scored.
†Batted for MacFayden in ninth inning.
‡Batted for Grissom in ninth inning.

Boston	000	000	002	—2
Cincinnati	000	000	012	—3

Runs batted in—DiMaggio (2), Scarsella (2), Riggs. Two-base hits—Garms, DiMaggio, Davis, Riggs. Home run—Scarsella. Sacrifice—Grissom. Left on bases—Boston, 3; Cincinnati, 10. Bases on balls—Off MacFayden, 2; off Grissom, 1. Struck out—By MacFayden, 2; by Grissom, 11. Hits—Off MacFayden, 7 in 8 innings; off Smith, 1 in 2-3. Hit by pitcher—By Smith (Goodman). Losing pitcher—Smith. Umpires—Stewart, Barr and Stark. Time—2:03.

Athletics Defeat Indians On Werber's Double, 4-3

PHILADELPHIA, July 27 (AP).—Bill Werber's two-bagger, scoring Moses and Finney in the eighth, gave Philadelphia an uphill triumph, 4 to 3, over the Cleveland Indians in the opener of a three-game series today.

The game was a hurling duel between Mel Harder and George Caster, each allowing seven hits. Solters hit a home run with the bags empty in the sixth inning.

Jesse Hill, centerfielder playing in his first home game for the Athletics, batter a single to score Finney in the fourth for the first A's run.

The score:

CLEVELAND (A. L.)	ab	r	h	po	a	e
Lary, ss.	5	2	2	0	2	0
Kroner, 2b	3	0	1	2	2	0
Averill, cf.	3	0	2	5	0	0
Trosky, 1b.	3	0	0	8	0	0
Solters, lf.	4	1	1	1	0	0
Campbell, rf	3	0	0	3	0	0
Weath'ly, rf	0	0	0	0	0	0
Hale, 3b.	3	0	1	1	2	0
Pytlak, c.	3	0	0	4	1	0
HARD'R, p	3	0	0	0	1	0
*Becker	1	0	0	0	0	0
Totals	31	3	7	24	8	0

PHILADELPHIA (A. L.)	ab	r	h	po	a	e
Moses, rf.	4	1	0	3	0	0
Finney, 1b.	4	2	3	10	0	0
Werber, 3b.	3	0	1	1	3	0
Johnson, lf	4	0	0	3	0	0
Hill, cf.	4	1	2	5	0	0
Peters, 2b.	3	0	0	1	3	0
Brucker, c.	3	0	0	3	1	0
Parker, ss.	3	0	0	1	2	0
CASTER, p	1	0	0	0	1	0
†Dean	1	0	1	0	0	0
SMITH, p.	0	0	0	0	0	0
Totals	30	4	7	27	10	0

*Batted for Harder in ningth inning.
†Batted for Caster in eighth inning.

Cleveland	101	001	000	—3
Philadelphia	000	100	12x	—4

Runs batted in—Solters (2), Averill, Hill, Peters, Werber (2). Two-base hits—Averill, Hill, Werber. Home run—Solters. Sacrifices—Kroner, Pytlak. Left on bases—Cleveland, 7; Philadelphia, 4. Bases on balls—Off Harder, 2; off caster, 3; off Smith, 1. Struck out—By Harder, 4; by Caster, 3. Hits—Off Caster, 7 in 8 innings; off Smith, 0 in 1. Wild pitch—Harder. Winning pitcher—Caster. Umpires—Dinneen, Kolls and Hubbard. Time—1:40.

SPORTING FINAL ★★★★★★ RACING CHARTS
Temperatures—Min., 65; Max., 82. (Detailed weather report on page 15.)

The Sun

Copyright, 1937, by The Sun Printing and Publishing Association.

SPORTING FINAL ★★★★★★ 7th RACE RESULT
United States Official Weather Forecast: Partly cloudy tonight and tomorrow.

VOL. CIV—NO. 279—DAILY. NEW YORK, THURSDAY, JULY 29, 1937. PRICE THREE CENTS.

YANKS TOP TIGERS IN 9TH, 7-6, CANTWELL HURLS FOR GIANTS; DODGERS ON SCORING SPREE

YANKEES

DETROIT.

	AB	R	H	PO	A	E
Fox, rf	5	1	1	3	0	0
Rogell, ss	2	0	0	1	1	2
Gelbert, ss	3	0	0	2	2	0
Gehringer, 2b	4	1	1	3	6	0
Greenberg, 1b	5	0	4	8	1	0
Walker, lf	4	0	0	2	0	0
Owen, 3b	4	2	3	2	3	0
Laabs, cf	3	1	2	2	0	0
Bolton, c	4	1	0	3	0	0
Poffenberger, p	2	0	0	0	0	0
Lawson, p	1	0	0	0	0	0
Goslin	1	0	1	0	0	0
Total	38	6	12	*26	13	2

YANKEES.

	AB	R	H	PO	A	E
Crosetti, ss	3	1	0	6	0	0
Rolfe, 3b	3	1	1	0	3	0
DiMaggio, cf	4	1	1	3	0	0
Gehrig, 1b	4	2	1	8	0	0
Dickey, c	5	1	1	3	0	0
Powell, lf	3	1	1	5	0	0
Lazzeri, 2b	3	0	2	0	4	0
Hoag, rf	4	0	0	2	1	0
Pearson, p	1	0	0	0	0	0
Murphy, p	2	0	0	0	5	0
Total	32	7	7	27	13	0

*Two out when winning run was made
Goslin batted for Poffenberger in 5th.

SUMMARY.

Home runs—Laabs, Gehrig, Dickey. Three-base hit—Owens. Two-base hits—Greenberg (2), Owen, Goslin. Double plays—Rogell to Gehringer to Greenberg, Gehringer to Gelbert to Greenberg, Gelbert to Gehringer to Greenberg. Bases on balls—Off Poffenberger 7, off Pearson 1, off Murphy 1, off Lawson 1. Struck out—By Pearson 1. Runs batted in—Greenberg (2), Dickey (2), Laabs (2), Gehrig (2), Bolton, Goslin. Hits—Off Pearson 8 in 4 2-3, off Poffenberger 5 in 5, off Murphy, 4 in 4 1-3, off Lawson 2 in 4. Hit by pitched ball—Crosetti (Poffenberger). Left on bases—Tigers 8, Yankees 7. Umpires—Ormsby, Quinn and McGowan. Attendance—10,962.

By EDWARD T. MURPHY.

YANKEE STADIUM, July 29.—Bill Dickey's seventeenth home run, made in the ninth inning with two out and the bases empty, brought the Yankees a 7 to 6 victory over the Tigers here today to gain the first place New Yorkers two out of three games for the series. The winning blow was made off Roxie Lawson who had relieved Baron Poffenberger and pitched the last four innings. Lou Gehrig made his nineteenth home run in the fourth after Joe DiMaggio had singled.

FIRST INNING.

Fox hit the first ball pitched for

Continued on Page 22.

GIANTS

By WILL WEDGE.

SPORTSMANS PARK, St. Louis, July 29.—The Cardinals opposed the New York Giants in the third and final game of their current series here today.

Right-handed Ben Cantwell, recently brought in from the Jersey City farm team where he had won twelve and lost seven, went to the mound for the Giants. Lefty Bob Weiland started for the home side.

The batting order:

Giants.	Cardinals.
Chiozza, 3b.	T. Moore, cf.
Whitehead, 2b.	S. Martin, 2b.
J. Moore, lf.	Mize, 1b.
Berger, cf.	Medwick, lf.
Ott, rf.	Padgett, rf.
Leslie, 1b.	Gutteridge, 3b.
Danning, c.	Durocher, ss.
Ryan, ss.	Owen, c.
Cantwell, p.	Weiland, p.

Umpires—Magerkurth, Parker and Moran. Attendance—5,000.

FIRST INNING.

Chiozza lined to Mize. Whitehead tapped to Weiland. J. Moore was called out on strikes. No runs, no hits.

In The Sun Today

—(19)—

School News in Home Edition daily.

Entered as Second Class Matter Post Office, New York, N. Y.

BASEBALL

AT YANKEE STADIUM.

										R.	H.	E.
DETROIT	1	2	0	0	1	2	0	0	0—	6	12	2
YANKEES	3	0	0	2	1	0	0	0	1—	7	7	0

Poffenberger, Lawson (6) and Bolton; Pearson, Murphy (5) and Dickey.

AT CHICAGO.

BROOKLYN	4	0	2	0	2	0	1
CHICAGO	0	1	0	0	0	0	

Frankhouse and Phelps; Davis, Shoun (1), Parmelee (5) and O'Dea.

AT ST. LOUIS.

				R.	H.	E.
GIANTS	0	0	0	—		
ST. LOUIS	0	0		—		

Cantwell and Danning; Weiland and Owen.

Giants-St. Louis game starts at 5 P. M., New York daylight time.

AMERICAN LEAGUE

AT BOSTON.

										R.	H.	E.
ST. LOUIS	0	0	0	0	0	0	0	3	0—	3	6	0
BOSTON	0	0	0	0	0	3	2	0	x—	5	9	0

Trotter, Bonetti (8) and Hemsley; McKain, Wilson (8) and Desautels, Berg (9).

AT PHILADELPHIA.

										R.	H.	E.
CLEVELAND	0	1	0	1	0	0	1	0	2—	5	10	1
ATHLETICS	0	0	0	2	0	0	0	2	0—	4	12	3

Galehouse, Andrews (8) and Pytlak; Smith and Brucker, Conway (9).

AT WASHINGTON.

								R.	H.	E.
CHICAGO	0	0	0	0	2	0	0	—		
WASHINGTON	0	0	0	0	0	0	0	—		

Lee and Sewell; W. Ferrell and R. Ferrell.

NATIONAL LEAGUE

AT PITTSBURGH.

										R.	H.	E.
PHILADELPHIA	0	1	1	0	4	0	0	5	0	11	13	0
PITTSBURGH	0	7	0	0	0	0	0	0	0—	7	12	1

Mulcahy, Jorgens (2) and Grace; Blanton, Swift (5) and Todd.

AT CINCINNATI.

										R.	H.	E.
BOSTON	0	0	0	0	0	1	0	0	1—	2	7	1
CINCINNATI	0	0	0	0	1	0	0	0	0—	1	4	0

Turner and Mueller; Derringer and Lombardi.

INTERNATIONAL LEAGUE

AT TORONTO.

										R.	H.	E.
BALTIMORE	0	0	1	0	0	1	0	1	0—	3	12	1
TORONTO	4	0	3	2	0	1	3	0	x—	13	14	1

Winston, Sivess (1), Kimsey (4) and Crouse, Gray (4); Wilson and Hogan.

Syracuse-Buffalo, night game.
Other teams not scheduled.

DODGERS

By HERBERT GOREN.

WRIGLEY FIELD, Chicago, July 29.—The league-leading Cubs went after their third straight victory against the Brooklyn Dodgers with Curt Davis on the mound here today. Fred Frankhouse, right handed curve baller, started for Burleigh Grimes's team in the final game of the series.

The Dodgers knocked out Davis during a four-run attack in the first inning.

The batting order:

Dodgers.	Cubs.
Lavagetto, 2b.	Galan, lf.
Hassett, cf.	Hack, 3b.
Daniel, 1b.	Collins, 1b.
Manush, rf.	Demaree, rf.
Phelps, c.	Herman, 2b.
Winsett, lf.	O'Dea, c.
Stripp, 3b.	Jurges, ss.
Brown, ss.	Cavarretta, cf.
Frankhouse, p.	Davis, p.

Umpires—Ballanfant, Klem and Sears. Attendance—9,000.

FIRST INNING.

Lavagetto walked. Hassett doubled

Continued on Page 22.

REFUSES TO ANSWER

So Woman Tax Witness Is Haled Before U. S. Judge.

Mrs. Moses B. Jasspon of Great Neck, L. I., was taken before Federal Judge Francis G. Caffey today when she refused to answer questions in front of the special Federal Grand Jury which is investigating the income of John Torrio, one time co-boss of the Chicago underworld with Al Capone.

The witness had refused to answer any questions until she had been granted immunity. The court ordered her to return to the jury room to answer any questions which did not tend to incriminate her. He said that he would rule on her claim of privilege if she would name any specific questions of an incriminating nature.

"There is no such thing," commented the judge, "as a general privilege protecting any one being questioned as a witness. The only privilege that exists is that of refusing to answer questions which call for possible incrimination."

WINDSORS TO SEE PLAY

Duke and Bride Get Seats for 'Romeo and Juliet.'

VENICE, July 29 (A. P.).—The Duke and Duchess of Windsor bought seats for that other famous love drama—"Romeo and Juliet."

At the Lido for a week, they will see an outdoor presentation of the play tomorrow. The couple went bathing today.

ADVICE TO WOMEN

Mayor Suggests Public Life and Bars Politicians.

Women should go into public life, but they should not become politicians. This rather enigmatic advice was delivered today by Mayor LaGuardia at a luncheon of the Jackson Heights Merchants Association. To make it all just a little bit more indefinite, the Mayor said: "We could use a few women down at City Hall. I don't know how good they'd be, but they'd be better than what we have now."

This, it was assumed, referred possibly to the Aldermen, who are shortly to be replaced by Councilmen. The Mayor reminded his audience that there can be councilwomen as well as councilmen. All that is needed is a sufficient number of indorsers.

"If you go around to your knitting clubs, all you have to do is get the required number of signatures," the Mayor said.

Government, after all, is extremely simple, the lunchers were told. It is only the politicians who make it appear complicated, according to the Mayor. Those who tried to follow the theories the Mayor was advancing felt they were going right around in a circle to the point that women should be in public life but not in politics because it is politicians who make government seem difficult and therefore that women who go into public life should not become politicians, &c.

THREE DIE IN BLAZE

Victims Are Trapped by Fire in Montreal House.

MONTREAL, July 29 (U. P.).—Three men were burned to death when fire destroyed a rooming house today. A woman was injured.

Firemen believed that others might still be in the burning building, which was still burning.

Lindbergh Flies Across Channel

BOULOGNE, July 29 (U. P.).—Col. Charles A. Lindbergh landed his red and black airplane at St. Inglevert, near here, today after a flight from Lympne, England. Twenty minutes later he took off for Dinant, in Brittany.

Today's Home Run Roster.

Dickey, Yankees, 1.
Gehrig, Yankees, 1.
Brubaker, Pirates, 1.
Foxx, Red Sox, 1.
Grace, Phillies, 1.
Laabs, Tigers, 1.
Lary, Indians, 1.
Weatherly, Indians, 1.
Werber, Athletics, 1.

REQUIEM MASS IS CELEBRATED FOR DOOLING

10,000 Gather in Tribute to Late Leader of Tammany.

ENTIRE BLOCK IS CROWDED

Friends and Political Foes Alike Honor Democratic Leader at Holy Cross Church.

At least 10,000 persons from all walks of life—personal friends and political foes, and the great and the humble of municipal, State and national politics—went to Holy Cross Catholic Church in West Forty-second street today to attend the solemn high mass of requiem for James J. Dooling, the late leader of Tammany Hall.

The large crowd filled the church and overflowed to the street. The sidewalks in Forty-second street from Eighth avenue to Ninth were packed solid by those who were unable to get into the church. Hundreds of others stood on the platform of the Ninth avenue elevated station or leaned from the windows of nearby buildings to catch a glimpse of the funeral cortege and the notables attending the rites.

The crowd laid aside its political differences to pay tribute to Mr. Dooling, who died on Monday after winning the hardest fight of his short career as the leader of Tammany Hall. Among those who entered the church were those who had supported him in that fight and those who fought him bitterly in his determination to designate Senator Royal S. Copeland as Tammany candidate for the Democratic nomination for Mayor.

Senator Copeland was present, as well as Grover A. Whalen, who will be his opponent in the Democratic primary. The service brought together candidates on both Democratic tickets and the men who helped to draw the slates.

Silk Hats and Overalls.

It was a crowd in which the wealthy rubbed elbows with the poor and in which a sprinkling of silk hats contrasted with the overalls of manual workers. A good portion of it was composed of old

Continued on Page 3.

VIGILANTES BEAT HOTEL UNION MEN

Raid Labor Headquarters at Fallsburgh, N. Y.

FALLSBURGH, Sullivan County, N. Y., July 29 (U. P.).—Five persons were severely beaten in a raid on the Hotel, Restaurant and Cafeteria Workers Organization headquarters here today by a group of six self-styled "vigilantes."

The vigilantes arrived in two automobiles carrying out-of-State license plates, entered the union headquarters and beat three union members and two organizers with bats, the police said.

The office was not damaged.

The injured were:

Jay Arnold, Jerry Dale, Emanuel Lopez, Irving Cohen and Mrs. Ernesta Kay. All received cuts and bruises above the head and face during the fight. They were treated at headquarters by a physician.

Dale said a bat was broken over his head. He said one of the raiders remarked: "Here's a sample of what your going to get if you don't stop organizing."

Dale said the raiders pulled weapons from their clothing as they entered headquarters. Mrs. Kay, one of the organizers, was "smacked on the jaw," Dale said, and several of her teeth were loosened.

A dozen deputy sheriffs from nearby Monticello were dispatched to the scene.

A strike called by the union at the Flagler Hotel here was settled on Monday.

Fisher's 60-mile-an-hour Speed Upheld by Court

HILLSIDE, N. J., July 29.—A plea that he had been on official business when he received a summons for driving his automobile at sixty miles an hour won C. Lloyd Fisher dismissal of the charges in police court here today.

Mr. Fisher was a member of the defense staff of Bruno Richard Hauptmann, kidnaper and killer of Charles A. Lindbergh Jr., but now is prosecutor of Hunterdon county, where the trial took place, under appointment by Gov. Harold G. Hoffman.

Four CCC Youths Killed in Truck Crash

RED WING, Minn., July 29 (U. P.).—Four CCC enrollees were reported killed and nine injured, several critically, when a truck on which eighteen youths were riding overturned near here.

GEORGE OPENS SOUTH'S FIGHT ON WAGE BILL

Senator Attacks Powers of Board and Any Link to Secretary of Labor.

AUSTIN ALSO ASSAILS PLAN

Warns Workers and Farmers Are Endangered—Donahey Asks Delay Until Next Year.

WASHINGTON, July 29 (A. P.).—Senator George, Democrat, of Georgia, told the Senate today that the standards provided in the administration's wage-hour bill were "poetry and nothing but poetry."

Senator George, opening a Southern Democratic attack on the measure, criticized powers proposed in the bill for a wage-hour board, the organization of the board and the authority given to the board to use information compiled by the Secretary of Labor.

Senator Austin, Republican, of Vermont, who preceded Mr. George, said that the bill—the Black-Connery measure—would put a strait-jacket on labor and mean an economic loss for agriculture.

Despite this double-barreled attack from opposite sides of the chamber, leaders hoped for a vote late today.

"One thing is very clear," Senator George said, his rich voice roaring through the chamber, "the present Secretary of Labor does not believe in any differential between sections of the country.

"If any differentials are to be allowed, they are inconsequential and wholly inadequate to preserve the great system of agriculture that has grown up under competitive conditions."

Recommitment Urged.

Mr. George demanded that the Senate return the bill to the Labor Committee on the ground that its enactment would result in the crucifixion of Southern industry and the end of State lines.

"It demands the impossible," he exclaimed.

The Labor Committee, he said,

Continued on Page 6.

BRITAIN WARNS TOKIO ON CHINA; AMERICANS IN TIENTSIN AIR RAID

Japanese Planes Endanger Aliens and Start Fires to Expel Chinese.

FOES LOCKED IN DEATH GRIP

Foreigners Huddle in Cellars of Concessions as 3 Armies Strike Tokio Troops.

TIENTSIN, July 29 (A. P.).—Bomb-made flames crackled through sections of this teeming North China commercial mart and many of its outlying villages tonight in the wake of Japanese air raiders.

Chinese troops, holding grimly to positions they won in a three-army assault on vital positions in this Japanese military headquarters, declared that "thousands of non-combatant men, women and children were killed and injured."

The lives of Americans and other foreigners were imperiled. There are 223 United States military personnel and dependents and 403 civilians registered in Tientsin, plus 750 American officers and men.

[A Japanese Domei News Agency dispatch received in Shanghai said that the Chinese at Tientsin had proposed an armistice, but that the Japanese had not replied. Simultaneously, Nanking reported that 1,000 Chinese soldiers had been killed in Japan's onslaught at Nanyuan, Chinese military headquarters south of Peiping. Peiping itself was suddenly peaceful as every Chinese soldier withdrew and a pro-Japanese Chinese General, Chang Tsu-chung, took charge.]

Lieut.-Gen. Kiyoshi Katsuki, Japanese North China commander, told foreign consuls that the bombing of Tientsin was authorized by the thirty-six-year-old Boxer protocol, which, he said, forbade Chinese troops within two miles of the city.

Bridges Burning in Foreign Area.

Ten thousand Japanese live in the Japanese concession, he added, and

Continued on Page 2.

CALLED BY PRESIDENT

Norman H. Davis.

AMERICANS CHARGE 15TH U. S. INFANTRY FAILED TO LEND AID

Missionaries and Others Sheltered by Aliens in Tientsin Bombing.

TIENTSIN, July 29 (U. P.).—Americans, fearing a night of terror, complained angrily tonight that the United States Army authorities refused to aid them.

One group of missionaries called the Chinese police, who provided them with an armed escort which escorted them to the sandbagged, barbed wire Italian concession. From the concession, the Americans telephoned the consulate and the Fifteenth Infantry headquarters.

After a long consultation one consular officer went to the Italian concession and took the missionaries to the British and French concessions. The missionaries indicated that appeals to the army to aid them were vain.

Infantry Remains Inactive.

A consular agent went to the Chinese city, where many Americans were trapped, to see if he could free any. The Fifteenth Infantry, however, took no part in the rescue work except to offer refuge in their barracks to Americans who could find no shelter under the protection of British, French, Italian or other soldiers.

As the threat of trouble became

Continued on Page 2.

Eden Tells Commons That He Opposes Severing More Provinces.

ROOSEVELT CALLS HIS AIDS

Consults Hull and Davis About Tientsin Attack—Hirota Bars Any Interference.

LONDON, July 29 (U. P.).—Great Britain has warned Japan that the British Government does not approve any further attempts to detach Chinese provinces from the Nanking Government, Foreign Secretary Eden revealed in a guarded disclosure today in the House of Commons.

Wedgwood Benn, a Liberal, asked bluntly during the question hour:

"Has the Foreign Secretary made it clear to the Japanese Government that we do not approve of any further attempt to detach provinces from the Nanking Government?"

"Yes," Mr. Eden replied.

Speculation Over League Action.

Then the Foreign Secretary added hastily:

"From your various declarations the honorable member will be able to see that we very much regret the situation, more so as we were hoping for improvement of relations in the Far East generally, which we cannot hope for while present conditions persist."

Mr. Eden's statement led to renewed speculation over whether Britain intended to call a session of the League of Nations council to deal with the Far East crisis.

Questioned in the House yesterday he said that Britain was not prepared at present to take the initiative in summoning the council. He intimated previously that Britain also is disinclined to force the issue by invoking the nine-Power Treaty of China or the Briand-Kellogg anti-war pact.

Mr. Eden was asked again about the league possibilities, however, and replied:

"The Government has no present intention of initiating League of Nations activity, in view of the fact that neither Japan or the United States are members of the league."

Protested About Nationals.

LONDON, July 29 (A. P.).—Foreign Secretary Eden told the House of Commons today that Great Britain had made representatives to Japan about the safety of British subjects in China and that it had received "certain assurances."

"The Japanese Government and local Japanese military authorities," he said, "gave certain assurances (to the British Charge d'Affaires at Tokio) in that respect.

"His Majesty's Charge d'Affaires has also emphasized to the Japanese Government the serious nature of the situation and the grave dangers inherent in it."

Roosevelt Consults Hull.

WASHINGTON, July 29 (U. P.).—President Roosevelt met early today with Secretary of State Hull and the American Ambassador-At-Large, Norman H. Davis, to discuss America's position, in view of new Sino-Japanese developments.

Mr. Hull and Mr. Davis called at the White House and met with the

Continued on Page 2.

LaGuardia Warned by Seabury

Urged to Make Peace With Party Leaders as Uprising Spreads to Brooklyn.

By GEORGE RITCHIE.

Dismayed by an uprising in Republican ranks against the renaming of Mayor LaGuardia, Samuel Seabury's Non-partisan Citizens Executive Committee hastily summoned the Mayor into conference this afternoon in an attempt to stem the tide of revolt.

Mr. Seabury, it is understood, counseled the Mayor to make obeisance before the Republican leaders if he wishes to obtain their primary support. The Mayor was advised, too, to accept the nominees of the Manhattan leader, Kenneth F. Simpson—Joseph D. McGoldrick for Comptroller and Newbold Morris for president of the council—or go down to defeat before the Kings county committee at Kismet Temple tonight.

John R. Crews, Brooklyn boss, and Warren R. Ashmead, Queens leader, stand solidly behind Mr. Simpson in the demand for the McGoldrick-Morris nominations, and for the first time since he won the Republican nomination in 1933, the Mayor will be forced to listen to the demands of the Republican leaders if he wants any part of the 650,000 or more Republican votes that go with the designation.

There was a story prevalent today that the Mayor was going to pass up both the Republican and Democratic primaries and run solely under the aegis of the American Labor party and with the support of the fusion and nondescript groups. It may be that the Mayor already realizes that he might be cut at the elections even if he wins the Republican primary, or that he might be done in by the Manhattan and Brooklyn county committee meetings this week.

Copeland Petitions Out.

Another thing that might have made up his mind for him was the issuance today of designating petitions for Senator Royal S. Copeland by the Independent Republican

Continued on Page 3.

Norway to Nominate Eden for Peace Prize

Special Cable Dispatch to THE SUN.

LONDON, July 29.—Foreign Secretary Eden's efforts to keep Great Britain at peace at almost any price are about to receive the highest recognition available to such diplomacy—nomination for the Nobel peace prize.

Capt. Eden's sponsor is not Benito Mussolini, Adolf Hitler or the Spanish combatants, to whom he has so often turned a charitably blind eye and, when necessary, the other cheek, but the Norwegians.

Motor Blast Fatal.

Robert Koomans, 34 years old, of Moranda, Quebec, one of three men injured when the gasoline tank of the motor boat in which they were cruising in Oyster Bay exploded last Wednesday, died yesterday at North Country Community Hospital at Glen Cove, L. I.

RESULTS AT SARATOGA

Race Charts on Page 22. Other Results on Page 22.

	First.	Second.	Third.
First Race....	Lady Thatcher	Wrenace	Sandstone
Prices....	16-5 6-5 3-5	4-1 2-1	2-1
Scratched—Go Home, Fredrick, Ethel's Choice. Victorious Ann finished second, but was disqualified.			
Second Race..	*Our Trouble	Gay Hill	*Muckledo
Prices....	8-1 2-1 7-10	5-1 2-1	7-10
No scratches. *Perry entry.			
Third Race...	Long Wave	Maxine	Maepop
Prices....	20-1 8-1 4-1	5-2 7-5	1-2
Scratched—Mary Senate, Cindy.			
Fourth Race..	Rehearsal	Evening Shadow	Maeayres
Prices....	13-5 1-1 2-5	1-1 2-5	1-2
Scratched—Rags and Tags.			
Fifth Race...	Gloom Buster	Airflame	Wam
Prices....	30-1 12-1 6-1	6-5 3-5	8-5
Scratched—Advocator.			
Sixth Race....	Count Stone	Chance Ray	Night Bud
Prices....	3-1 6-5 1-2	6-5 1-2	1-2
No scratches.			

NO WORD OF START OF SOVIET FLIGHT

Alaska Expected Takeoff From Moscow Today.

FAIRBANKS, Alaska, July 29 (A. P.).—While refueling plans were virtually completed here, Moscow was silent today on the projected start of a third Soviet airplane dash over the top of the world to the United States.

Daylight around the clock and ideal weather conditions most of the way lay ahead of what possibly may be the first passenger carrying flight over the North Pole, with an American-trained pilot, Sigismund Levaneffsky, "Russia's Lindbergh," at the controls.

The first information here was that he was poised to hop at 8 A. M., Eastern standard time, with from three to five other persons in a huge, four-motored plane, but the morning dragged on with no additional word from Moscow being received by Michael Beliakoff, hydro-meteorologist, and S. A. Smirnoff, radio engineer, here to handle details of the plane's refueling and to aid in transmitting weather reports.

At Victoria, B. C., W. A. Thorn, superintendent of the dominion meteorological station, said he had not yet received any request for weather bulletins to be used in conjunction with the flight. The bureau assisted in gathering weather reports for the two previous flights.

It was Levaneffsky who essayed a flight over the north pole route in August, 1935, but was forced to return to Moscow because of a broken oil feed line when he was well out over the Arctic Ocean.

Three years earlier he and other Russian aviators brought planes here for use in rescuing 101 persons who had been marooned on an ice floe off Cape Karem, on northeast Siberia.

The two previous Soviet non-stop north pole flights were made in single-motored planes.

The first ended June 21 at Vancouver, Wash., about 5,000 miles from Moscow. The second ended in a pasture near San Jacinto, Cal., setting a new non-stop world flight record of 6,262 miles.

2 AMERICANS MISSING

Peiping Authorities Report Their Disappearance.

SHANGHAI, July 20 (U. P.).—It was reported from Peiping today that a Bostonian, Harry S. Martin of the Jefferson Academy, had disappeared on Tuesday and has not been reported at the United States embassy since then.

A mutilated message also indicated that an American named Hunter from Peoria, Ill., is similarly missing.

Slain Infant Found In New Jersey Lot

A female infant, believed to have been not more than three hours old, was found dead in a vacant lot at Dewey avenue and Seventeenth street, West New York, N. J., late last night.

Police believe the infant was murdered. A silk stocking was wrapped around her neck, there was a turkish towel over her mouth, and wads of cotton bearing the odor of ammonia were found stuffed in her ears, nostrils and mouth.

The body was wrapped in two large turkish towels and a rug and then stuffed into a large paper bag. It was discovered by three boys.

DiMaggio Hits No. 31 as Yanks Rout Browns, 14-5; Dodgers Divide; Cubs Beat Giants, 5-4

20,000 Cheer Italian Star, Leading Ruth's Best Pace

Gehrig Parks His 21st Homer, Rolfe Adds Another as Chandler Coasts to Sixth Victory of Year; Heffner Bats in 3 Runs With 2 Singles, Double

By Arthur E. Patterson

They said there never would be another Babe Ruth. And for that indefinite thing called color they may have been right.

But for the Babe's chief stock in trade, home runs, without which his color would have been just so much good copy, there is another Babe at the Yankee Stadium, and this Babe, Joe DiMaggio, right now is ahead of Ruth's pace for the Babe's peak year in homer production.

During a lop-sided 14-to-5 victory over the St. Louis Browns, yesterday, Jolting Joe thrilled 20,000 roaring fans with one of his mightiest slams into the upper left field tier. It was his thirty-first homer of the season, and no matter how you look at it, except in the matter of dates, DiMaggio is ahead of Ruth's rate in 1927, when he broke his own standard by smashing No. 60 the last day of the year.

It was on July 24 that the Babe rode No. 24 into the stands against his old cousin, Alphonse Thomas, out at Comiskey Park in Chicago with 50,000 alien fans looking on. But that was the ninety-third game in the standing of the clubs for the Yankees and the ninetieth game for Ruth, himself. When the Yanks finished their chores with the Browns yesterday they had only eighty-nine contests in the standing and DiMaggio, himself, had been in only eighty-six, including the two ties played to date. Early this season he missed five games because of a tonsillectomy.

DiMaggio Has 65 Games Left

Whether or not the San Francisco slugger will be able to match the Babe's famous tempo through the latter part of the 1927 season—particularly the seventeen homers he hit in September—remains to be seen, but the fact remains that at the current writing DiMaggio, playing his home games in the same park as Ruth, but in one far less suited to his right-handed batting, actually leads the old day-by-day standard. Granted good health and fair weather through the rest of the schedule, he has sixty-five ball games in which to make twenty-nine homers or better. As he is hitting them now the dimensions of the Stadium or any other park will not make much difference.

There just wasn't much to yesterday's ball game except homers and hard hitting. Lou Gehrig parked No. 21 against a right field girder in the first inning and the Yankees batted around in the second for four more runs and a 6-to-1 advantage, chasing Lou Koupal and making the afternoon and his sixth victory easy for Spud Chandler, recently recalled right-hander. The Browns did make it close for a spell when they scored two runs on a single by Joe Vosmik and Harlond Clift's twentieth homer in the fifth, but the Yankees soon broke out in another run-making rash.

Rolfe Also Poles Homer

Red Rolfe slapped one off Beau Bell's glove and into the stands with Don Heffner on base in the sixth and four more tallied in the seventh when Lazzeri and Hoag singled, Chandler sacrificed, Heffner doubled and DiMaggio brought the crowd to its feet with that gigantic upstairs clout. For a few minutes it appeared the ball might pull foul and even DiMaggio waited awhile near the plate, but the umpires waved "fair ball" and Heffner and DiMaggio trotted around, the latter serenely but the former raising his hands aloft like a conquering fighter. You would have thought Heffner did the hitting.

It didn't matter by then, but the teams matched two runs each in the eighth, the Browns on Nig Lipscomb's double and a pinch homer by Ben Huffman, and the Yanks on a base on balls to Lazzeri, Hoag's triple and a long fly by Chandler. By this time one Trotter was doing the St. Louis's flinging.

Knickerbocker, starting shortstop, was chased by Red Ormsby for his violent language concerning a third strike in the fourth. Tom Carey took his place and doubled the next inning.

Frankie Crosetti had to leave the field in the second because of an injured wrist and Heffner came in, hit two singles and a double and drove in three runs.

Powell lost two close running decisions to Harlond Clift's arm. . . . The official paid attendance was 18,924. . . . Chicago will come to the Stadium tomorrow trailing by five games. . . . The White Sox picked up a half-game yesterday by winning twice over the Athletics. . . . DiMaggio batted in three runs and needs one more to drive home an exact 100. . . . In addition to endangering the Babe Ruth record, DiMaggio is almost certain to establish himself as the leading Yankee right-handed slugger of all time. . . . Bob Meusel once hit thirty-three homers, leading the American League in 1925. . . . But DiMaggio should pass that figure this week. . . . Jimmy Foxx's fifty-eight homers is the all-time homer mark for a right-handed batter, but Foxx had the advantage in home parks. . . . He lothes the Stadium.

The score:

ST. LOUIS (A. L.)	ab	r	h	po	a	e	NEW YORK (A. L.)	ab	r	h	po	a	e
Davis, 1b	5	0	1	9	1	0	Crosetti, ss.	1	0	0	0	0	0
West, cf.	5	0	1	0	0	0	Heffner, ss.	4	2	3	2	4	0
Vosmik, lf.	5	1	2	2	1	0	Rolfe, 3b.	5	2	1	0	3	0
Clift, 3b.	3	1	1	2	4	0	DiMaggio, cf	3	3	3	3	0	1
Bell, rf.	5	0	0	2	0	0	Gehrig, 1b.	5	1	4	13	1	0
Kn'ker, ss.	2	0	0	3	2	0	Dickey, c.	2	0	1	1	0	0
Carey, ss.	3	0	1	1	1	0	Powell, lf.	5	0	0	3	0	0
L'comb, 2b.	4	2	3	3	3	0	Lazzeri, 2b.	4	3	2	1	5	0
Heath, c.	1	0	0	1	1	0	Hoag, rf.	4	3	3	2	0	0
Hemsley, c.	2	0	0	1	0	0	CH'LER, p.	3	0	0	2	1	0
TR'TER, p	0	0	0	0	0	0							
KOUPAL, p	1	0	1	0	1	0							
BON'TI, p.	2	0	1	0	1	0							
Huffman, c.	1	1	1	0	0	0							
Totals	39	5	12	24	15	0	Totals	36	14	17	27	14	1

St. Louis	010	020	020	—5
New York	240	002	42x	—14

Runs batted in—Gehrig (3), Koupal, Heffner (3), DiMaggio (3), Clift (2), Rolfe (2), Huffman (2), Hoag, Chandler. Two-base hits—Lipscomb (2), Gehrig, Carey, DiMaggio, Heffner. Three-base hits—Gehrig, Hoag. Home runs—Gehrig, Clift, Rolfe, DiMaggio, Huffman. Sacrifice—Chandler (2). Double plays—Lipscomb, Knickerbocker and Davis; Davis and Carey. Left on bases—New York, 9; St. Louis, 10. Bases on balls—Off Chandler, 3; off Koupal, 3; off Bonetti, 4; off Trotter, 1. Struck out—By Bonetti, 2; by Chandler, 1. Hits—Off Koupal, 6 in 1 2-3 innings; off Bonetti, 10 in 5 1-3; off Trotter, 1 in 1. Hit by pitcher—By Bonetti (DiMaggio). Passed ball—Heath. Losing pitcher—Koupal. Umpires—Ormsby, Quinn and McGowan. Time—2:13.

White Sox Trip A's in 11th, 4-3, Then Score, 5-3

Walker Homer Foils Caster, and 4-Hit Ball of Dietrich and Kennedy Wins Finale

By The Associated Press

PHILADELPHIA, Aug. 1.—An eleventh-inning home run by Dixie Walker and the pitching of Bill Dietrich and Vernon Kennedy brought the Chicago White Sox two victories over the Athletics today.

Walker's hit, one of seven made off George Caster in the first game, provided the winning margin in a 4-to-3 decision. The other three Sox runs were unearned. The game was sent into extra innings when Lynn Nelson, pinch hitter, hit a home run in the ninth.

Dietrich and Kennedy limited the Macks to four hits in capturing the finale, 5 to 3.

The scores:

FIRST GAME

CHICAGO (A. L.)	ab	r	h	po	a	e	PHILADELPHIA (A.L.)	ab	r	h	po	a	e
Hayes, 2b.	4	0	0	3	4	0	Moses, rf.	5	0	2	3	2	0
Kr'vich, cf.	5	0	2	4	0	0	Finney, 1b.	4	1	1	14	0	1
Walker, rf.	5	1	1	0	0	0	Werber, 3b.	5	0	0	2	6	0
Bonura, 1b.	5	0	0	14	0	0	Johnson, lf.	5	1	2	1	0	0
Radcliff, lf.	4	0	1	1	1	0	Hill, cf.	5	0	3	3	0	0
Appling, ss.	5	0	1	3	7	1	Peters, 2b.	3	0	0	3	3	0
Piet, 3b.	4	1	0	1	3	0	Huston, ss.	0	0	0	0	1	0
Shea, c.	4	1	2	7	0	0	P'r, ss, 2b.	4	0	0	4	4	1
LYONS, p.	2	1	0	0	0	0	Brucker, c.	4	0	3	3	0	0
							CASTER, p	4	0	0	0	1	1
							*Nelson	1	1	1	0	0	0
							†Dean	1	0	0	0	0	0
Totals	38	4	7	33	15	1	Totals	41	3	12	33	17	3

*Batted for Peters in ninth inning.
†Batted for Huston in eleventh inning.

Chicago	000	030	000	01	—4
Philadelphia	000	200	001	00	—3

Runs batted in—Werber, Kreevich, Nelson, Walker. Two-base hits—Kreevich, Johnson, Moses. Three-base hits—Finney, Brucker. Home runs—Nelson, Walker. Stolen bases—Piet, Hill. Sacrifices—Lyons, Finney. Double plays—Hayes, Appling and Bonura; Peters, Parker and Finney; Moses and Brucker; Hayes and Bonura. Left on bases—Chicago, 6; Philadelphia, 6. Bases on balls—Off Caster, 3. Struck out—By Caster, 2; by Lyons, 3. Hit by pitcher—By Caster (Piet). Umpires—Kolls, Dinneen and Hubbard. Time—2:03.

SECOND GAME

CHICAGO (A. L.)	ab	r	h	po	a	e	PHILADELPHIA (A.L.)	ab	r	h	po	a	e
Hayes, 2b.	4	1	2	2	5	0	Moses, rf	3	0	0	2	0	0
K'ch, cf, lf	4	1	2	5	0	0	Finney, 1b.	2	0	0	3	0	0
Walker, rf.	4	0	0	1	0	0	Dean, 1b.	2	0	1	9	0	0
Bonura, 1b.	4	0	1	8	0	0	Werber, 3b.	3	1	0	0	5	0
Radcliff, lf.	4	1	1	4	0	0	Johnson, lf.	3	2	1	3	0	0
R'nthal, cf.	0	0	0	0	0	0	Hill, cf.	3	0	1	2	1	0
Appling, ss.	4	1	2	2	4	1	Peters, 2b.	4	0	0	3	5	1
Sewell, c.	4	0	0	2	0	0	Parker, ss.	3	0	0	2	4	0
Piet, 3b.	4	0	0	3	0	1	†Nelson	1	0	0	0	0	0
D'RICH, p.	2	1	0	0	1	0	Brucker, c.	4	0	1	3	0	1
*Haas	1	0	0	0	0	0	ROSS, p.	3	0	0	0	0	0
K'NEDY, p	0	0	0	0	0	0	‡Rothrock	1	0	0	0	0	0
Totals	35	5	8	27	10	2	Totals	32	3	4	27	15	2

*Batted for Dietrich in seventh inning.
†Batted for Parker in ninth inning.
‡Batted for Ross in ninth inning.

Chicago	101	110	001	—5
Philadelphia	000	102	000	—3

Runs batted in—Walker (2), Piet, Kreevich, Peters, Johnson (2), Appling. Two-base hits—Bonura, Hill. Three-base hit—Kreevich. Home runs—Johnson, Appling. Stolen bases—Werber, Hill. Double plays—Parker, Peters and Dean; Appling, Hayes and Bonura. Left on bases—Chicago, 3; Philadelphia, 6. Bases on balls—Off Dietrich, 4. Struck out—By Ross, 3. Hits—Off Dietrich, 3 in 7 innings; off Kennedy, 1 in 2. Winning pitcher—Dietrich. Umpires—Hubbard, Dinneen and Kolls. Time—1:50.

Pirates' Timely Hitting Sends Bees to Defeat, 8-4

PITTSBURGH, Aug. 1 (AP).—Timely hits by Paul Waner and Lee Handley with the bases loaded, coupled with Russ Bauers's relief pitching, gave the Pittsburgh Pirates an 8-to-4 victory over the Boston Bees today.

The game was tied at 4-all in the last half of the seventh when Paul Waner singled to center with three on. In the eighth the sacks again were loaded when Lee Handley doubled off the score board in left. Two runs came in on each of the hits.

The score:

BOSTON (N. L.)	ab	r	h	po	a	e	PITTSBURGH (N. L.)	ab	r	h	po	a	e
Johnson, lf	5	1	1	2	2	0	L. Waner, cf	3	2	2	4	0	0
Warstler, ss	4	1	1	1	6	0	Jensen, lf.	3	1	2	2	0	0
†Mayo	1	0	0	0	0	0	P. Waner, rf	4	1	2	1	0	0
DiMaggio, cf	4	0	0	1	0	0	Suhr, 1b.	3	0	2	7	0	0
Cuccin'lo, 2b	4	1	3	5	2	0	Todd, c.	4	2	2	6	0	0
Moore, rf.	4	0	0	1	0	0	Brubaker, 3b	4	1	0	3	1	0
English, 3b.	4	1	1	1	2	0	Young, ss.	3	0	1	2	5	2
Fletcher, 1b	4	0	1	9	2	0	Handley, 2b	4	0	2	2	4	0
Mueller, c.	4	0	1	4	2	0	LUCAS, p.	2	0	0	0	0	0
M'FAY'N, p	3	0	1	0	2	0	BAUERS, p	2	1	0	0	0	0
HUTCH'N, p	0	0	0	0	0	0							
*Garms	1	0	1	0	0	0							
Totals	38	4	10	24	18	0	Totals	32	8	13	27	10	2

*Batted for Hutchinson in ninth inning.
†Batted for Warstler in ninth inning.

Boston	020	020	000	—4
Pittsburgh	301	000	22x	—8

Runs batted in—Todd (2), Mueller (2), Suhr (2), Cuccinello (2), P. Waner (2), Handley (2). Two-base hits—Handley, Garms. Home run—Todd. Sacrifice—Jensen. Double plays—Warstler, Cuccinello and Fletcher; Fletcher and Cuccinello; Young, Handley and Suhr. Left on bases—Boston, 7; Pittsburgh, 4. Bases on balls—Off MacFayden, 3. Struck out—By MacFayden, 2; by Bauers, 3; by Hutchinson, 1. Hits—Off Lucas, 8 in 4 1-3 innings; off Bauers, 2 in 4 2-3; off MacFayden, 12 in 7 1-3; off Hutchinson, 1 in 2-3. Winning pitcher—Bauers. Losing pitcher—MacFayden. Umpires—Ballanfant, Klem and Sears. Time—2:24.

Standings in Major Leagues

MONDAY, AUGUST 2, 1937

American League

YESTERDAY'S RESULTS

New York, 14; St. Louis, 5
Boston, 11; Detroit, 4 (1st)
Boston, 2; Detroit, 2 (10 ins., 2d, Sunday law)
Chicago, 4; Philadelphia, 3 (11 ins., 1st)
Chicago, 5; Philadelphia, 3 (2d)
Cleveland, 11; Washington, 2

STANDING OF THE CLUBS

	New York	Chicago	Boston	Detroit	Cleveland	Washington	St. Louis	Phila'phia	Won	Lost	Percentage
New York	—	6	6	11	9	7	12	9	60	29	.674
Chicago	8	—	7	3	5	11	11	12	57	36	.613
Boston	2	6	—	8	6	4	13	11	50	37	.575
Detroit	7	7	7	—	7	9	5	9	51	38	.573
Cleveland	4	3	7	5	—	8	6	10	43	44	.494
Wash'ton	3	6	5	3	8	—	10	4	39	48	.448
St. Louis	4	3	5	3	2	5	—	7	29	61	.322
Phila'phia	1	5	0	5	7	4	4	—	26	62	.295
Gms. lost	29	36	37	38	44	48	61	62	—	—	

GAMES TODAY

No games scheduled

National League

YESTERDAY'S RESULTS

Chicago, 5; New York, 4 (11 ins.)
Brooklyn, 7; St. Louis, 3 (1st)
St. Louis, 7; Brooklyn, 1 (2d)
Cincinnati, 5; Philadelphia, 1 (1st)
Philadelphia, 3; Cincinnati, 2 (2d)
Pittsburgh, 8; Boston, 4

STANDING OF THE CLUBS

	Chicago	New York	Pittsburgh	St. Louis	Boston	Brooklyn	Cincinnati	Phila'phia	Won	Lost	Percentage
Chicago	—	11	5	10	7	11	5	10	59	32	.648
New York	6	—	8	10	5	9	9	7	54	39	.581
Pit'sburgh	6	3	—	5	9	6	10	9	48	42	.533
St. Louis	2	7	4	—	9	9	7	10	48	43	.527
Boston	4	5	8	6	—	8	8	6	45	48	.484
Brooklyn	6	3	8	7	2	—	6	5	37	52	.416
Cincinnati	3	6	1	4	9	4	—	10	37	53	.411
Phila'phia	5	4	8	1	7	5	8	—	38	58	.400
Gms. lost	32	39	42	43	48	52	53	57	—	—	

GAMES TODAY

No games scheduled

Lipscomb, of Browns, Sliding for Double Against Yankees

St. Louis second baseman comes into the sack in second inning as Tony Lazzeri covers the base. Quinn is the umpire watching the play. The Yankees won, however, 14 to 5, in game marked by DiMaggio's thirty-first homer — Associated Press photo

Red Sox Third As Tigers Fail By 11-4, Tie, 2-2

Curfew Law Halts 2d in 10th After Wilson Wins 11th as Mates Run String to 5

By The Associated Press

BOSTON, Aug. 1.—The Boston Red Sox today jumped into third place, ousting Detroit by beating the Tigers, 11 to 4, in the first game of a twin bill. The second game was called because of the Massachusetts Sunday sports curfew law, with the teams deadlocked, 2—all, at the end of the tenth inning.

By taking the opener, the Sox swept three from the Tigers and extended their winning streak to five consecutive games. Jack Wilson won his eleventh game of the season as his mates pounded Roxie Lawson and Boots Poffenberger for twelve hits. Detroit made seven hits, two of which were home runs, both coming in the fifth inning. Hank Greenberg poled out his twenty-fourth circuit clout and Chet Laabs blasted a homer into the center-field bleachers a few minutes later for his seventh of the season.

The second game was a hurling duel between Eldon Auker and Buck Newsom. Two of the five hits Boston made off Auker were homers, Eric McNair registering a circuit blow in the fifth and Mike Higgins blasting one as lead-off batter in the ninth.

Both Detroit runs came with two cut. In the fifth Newsom made a bad throw to first on Rogell's grounder and Ray Hayworth galloped from second to score.

With two down in the ninth, Pete Fox doubled, his third hit of the game, and counted on Rogell's single. The scores:

FIRST GAME

DETROIT (A. L.)	ab	r	h	po	a	e	BOSTON (A. L.)	ab	r	h	po	a	e
Fox, rf.	5	1	1	4	0	0	Mills, lf.	3	2	2	3	0	0
Rogell, ss.	2	0	1	1	1	2	Cramer, cf.	5	2	3	4	0	0
*York	1	0	0	0	0	0	Cronin, ss.	4	1	1	0	2	0
Gehr'ger, 2b	5	0	1	1	0	0	Foxx, 1b.	4	1	1	10	0	0
Greenb'g, 1b	4	1	2	7	1	0	Higgins, 3b	3	1	1	0	1	0
Walker, lf.	4	0	0	0	1	0	McNair, 2b	3	2	1	0	4	0
Owen, 3b.	4	1	1	1	2	0	Chapman, rf	5	1	2	5	0	0
Laabs, cf.	3	1	1	3	0	1	Berg, c.	4	1	1	5	0	0
Tebbetts, c.	3	0	0	6	2	0	WILSON, p	3	0	0	0	2	0
LAWSON, p	1	0	0	0	1	0							
POFF'ER, p	1	0	0	1	1	0							
†White	0	0	0	0	0	0							
Totals	33	4	7	24	9	3	Totals	34	11	12	27	9	0

*Batted for Rogell in ninth inning.
†Batted for Poffenberger in ninth inning.

Detroit	100	120	000	—4
Boston	300	230	30x	—11

Runs batted in—Fox, Gehringer, Greenberg, Laabs, Chapman (3), Mills (2), Cramer, Cronin, Foxx, Higgins, McNair, Berg. Two-base hits—Cramer, Higgins. Three-base hit—McNair. Home runs—Greenberg, Laabs. Sacrifices—Tebbetts, Cronin, Higgins. Left on bases—Detroit, 8; Boston, 8. Bases on balls—Off Lawson, 1; off Poffenberger, 5; off Wilson, 5. Struck out—By Lawson, 3; by Poffenberger, 1; by Wilson, 4. Hits—Off Lawson, 6 in 4 innings; off Poffenberger, 6 in 4. Hit by pitcher—By Poffenberger (McNair). Losing pitcher—Lawson. Umpires—Johnston, Owens and Moriarty. Time—1:55.

SECOND GAME

DETROIT (A. L.)	ab	r	h	po	a	e	BOSTON (A. L.)	ab	r	h	po	a	e
Fox, rf.	5	1	3	2	0	0	Mills, lf.	4	0	0	2	0	1
Rogell, ss.	5	0	1	3	2	0	Cramer, cf.	5	0	1	5	0	0
Gehr'ger, 2b	3	0	1	4	2	0	Cronin, ss.	4	0	0	3	2	0
Greenb'g, 1b	5	0	1	9	0	0	Foxx, 1b.	4	0	0	4	1	0
Walker, lf.	4	0	1	3	0	0	Higgins, 3b	4	1	2	1	3	0
Owen, 3b.	5	0	0	1	3	1	McNair, 2b.	4	1	1	7	1	0
Laabs, cf.	4	0	0	3	0	0	Hamp'n, rf.	4	0	0	0	0	0
Hayworth, c	1	1	0	3	2	0	Desautels, c	2	0	1	8	0	0
*Bolton	1	0	0	0	0	0	NEWSOM, p	4	0	0	0	0	1
Tebbetts, c.	0	0	0	2	0	0							
AUKER, p.	4	0	0	0	3	0							
Totals	37	2	7	30	12	1	Totals	35	2	5	30	7	2

*Batted for Hayworth in ninth inning.

Detroit	000	000	101	0	—2
Boston	000	010	001	0	—2

Runs batted in—Rogell, Higgins, McNair. Two-base hits—Fox, Walker. Home runs—Higgins, McNair. Double play—Higgins, McNair and Foxx. Left on bases—Detroit, 11; Boston, 7. Bases on balls—Off Auker, 3; off Newsom, 6. Struck out—By Auker, 5; by Newsom, 7. Hit by pitcher—By Auker (Cronin). Umpires—Owens, Moriarty and Johnston. Time—2:14.

Yates Scores Fourth Ace

ATLANTA, Aug. 1 (AP).—Charlie Yates, former national intercollegiate champion, scored his fourth hole-in-one yesterday at the East Lake No. 1 course.

Cards Win Behind Warneke, 7-1, After Brooklyn Routs Dean, 7-3

Hoyt, Replacing Hurt Hamlin, Gets Credit for Victory, His First With the Team

Special to the Herald Tribune

ST. LOUIS, Aug. 1.—Knocking Dizzy Dean out in the seventh inning, the Dodgers today took the first game of a double-header with the Cardinals, 7 to 3, and then dropped the nightcap, 7 to 1, with Lon Warneke winning his twelfth of the year. The paid attendance was 16,396.

Luke Hamlin, starter against Dean, was forced out in the third by an injury and Waite Hoyt, allowing six hits until the finish, won his first game as a Dodger. He has lost three.

Dean, complaining of a sore arm before the game, threw few fast balls, but still managed to hold the Dodgers to a 1-to-1 tie for six innings.

Max Butcher lasted only one and one-third innings in the second game, retiring with four runs and five hits, one a homer by Don Padgett, charged to him.

The Dodgers drew first blood in the opening game, Hamlin scoring after his opening single (on which he pulled a muscle in his right side), Cookie Lavagetto's sacrifice and Heinie Manush's shot to right. Hamlin pitched to Owen in the Cards' half, then gave up and Hoyt replaced him, making it his own game to win or lose when yielded up a double by Terry Moore and a single by Stu Martin that tied the score.

The deadlock obtained until the seventh, when Manush's third single knocked Dean out and the Dodgers finished the inning with three runs in and a 4-to-1 lead. Red Brown and Lavagetto contributed doubles and Babe Phelps a single, the latter off Harrell.

Don Gutteridge's opening triple and an infield out gave one run back to the Cards in the seventh and they came within one of a tie in the next inning on singles by Terry Moore and Mize and Manush's error of the latter's blow.

In the ninth the Cards didn't support Mike Ryba very well and the Dodgers counted three more runs on two passes, a single by Jake Daniel and errors by Stu Martin and Mize.

The second game started more auspiciously for the Cards. In the first inning Terry Moore walked and, with two out, Joe Medwick tripled off the right field fence to drive in his hundredth run of the year. Don Padgett followed with a home run into the right center stands.

Butcher was knocked out in the second by Brusie Ogrodowski's double and singles by Warneke and Terry Moore, good for another run, and Roy Henshaw replaced Max. Roy did well for an inning, striking out Mize and Medwick, but the fourth saw the Cards take a commanding lead with two more runs on singles by Durocher, Ogrodowski and Terry Moore and Warneke's scoring fly to right.

With only five scattered hits and no runs off Warneke in six innings the Dodgers were no great threat to Lon's peace of mind. Henshaw drove in the first and only Brooklyn run in the seventh, scoring Stripp, who had singled and reached second on an infield out.

Odd play in the third inning of the first game: Gutteridge nabbed Phelps's slow bounder, then ran to second base to force Manush.

Winsett had a tough time trying to get a hit, but he made Gutteridge go a long way for his fouls three times during the afternoon.

Medwick's left hand was hurt when he muffed a low liner from Lavagetto in the seventh of the first game, but apparently not seriously.

The Dodgers left on a 6 o'clock train for Pittsburgh.

Dodgers' Scores

FIRST GAME

BROOKLYN (N. L.)	ab	r	h	po	a	e	ST. LOUIS (N. L.)	ab	r	h	po	a	e
Lavag'to, 2b	3	2	2	1	3	0	T. Moore, cf	4	2	2	3	1	0
Hass't, cf, rf	3	1	0	3	0	0	S.Martin, 2b	4	0	1	1	4	1
Manush, rf	5	1	3	3	0	1	Mize, 1b.	3	0	2	7	1	1
Cooney, cf.	0	0	0	1	0	0	Medwick, lf	4	0	0	2	0	0
Phelps, c.	5	0	1	0	0	0	Padgett, rf.	4	0	0	4	0	0
Winsett, lf.	5	0	0	4	0	0	Gutte'ge, 3b	4	1	1	4	2	0
Daniel, 1b.	5	0	1	11	0	0	Durocher, ss	4	0	0	2	1	0
Stripp, 3b.	5	0	2	2	1	0	Owen, c.	4	0	0	4	4	0
L. Brown, ss	4	1	1	2	2	0	J. DEAN, p	2	0	1	0	0	0
HAMLIN, p	1	1	1	0	1	0	HARR'L, p	0	0	0	0	0	0
HOYT, p.	0	1	0	0	3	0	RYBA, p.	0	0	0	0	0	0
							*Bordag'y	1	0	0	0	0	0
Totals	36	7	11	27	10	1	Totals	34	3	7	27	13	2

*Batted for Harrell in seventh inning.

Brooklyn	001	000	303	—7
St. Louis	001	000	110	—3

Runs batted in—Manush (3), Lavagetto, Phelps, Daniel (2), S. Martin, Durocher. Two-base hits—Mize, T. Moore, L. Brown, Lavagetto. Three-base hit—Gutteridge. Sacrifices—Lavagetto, Hassett (2), Hoyt. Left on bases—Brooklyn, 9; St. Louis, 5. Bases on balls—Off Hoyt, 1; off J. Dean, 1; off Ryba, 2. Struck out—By J. Dean, 2. Hits—Off Hamlin, 1 in 2 1-3 innings; off Hoyt, 6 in 6 2-3; off J. Dean, 9 in 6 1-3; off Harrell, 1 in 2-3; off Ryba, 1 in 2. Winning pitcher—Hoyt. Losing pitcher—J. Dean. Umpires—Barr, Stark and Stewart. Time—1:52.

SECOND GAME

BROOKLYN (N. L.)	ab	r	h	po	a	e	ST. LOUIS (N. L.)	ab	r	h	po	a	e
Lavag'to, 2b	5	0	2	3	3	1	T. Moore, cf	4	1	2	3	0	0
Hassett, cf.	5	0	1	2	0	0	S.Martin, 2b	4	0	0	2	1	0
Manush, rf.	3	0	0	1	0	0	Mize, 1b.	4	0	1	7	1	0
Brack, rf.	1	0	0	0	0	0	Medwick, lf	4	1	2	5	0	0
Phelps, c.	4	0	1	2	0	0	Padgett, rf.	4	2	2	3	0	0
Chervinko, c	0	0	0	0	0	0	Gutte'ge, 3b	4	0	0	1	4	0
Winsett, lf.	4	0	1	3	0	0	Durocher, ss	4	1	1	4	2	0
Daniel, 1b.	4	0	1	8	0	0	Ogrod'ski, c	4	2	2	2	0	0
Stripp, 3b.	4	1	2	2	3	0	WARN'E, p	4	0	2	0	2	0
English, ss.	4	0	1	2	1	0							
BUTCH'R, p	0	0	0	1	0	0							
HENS'W, p.	3	0	2	0	1	0							
*Bucher	1	0	0	0	0	0							
†Frankh'se	0	0	0	0	0	0							
Totals	36	1	11	24	8	1	Totals	36	7	12	27	10	0

*Batted for Henshaw in ninth inning.
†Ran for English in ninth inning.

Brooklyn	000	000	100	—1
St. Louis	310	210	00x	—7

Runs batted in—Medwick, Padgett (2), Warneke (2), T. Moore, Gutteridge, Henshaw. Two-base hits—Ogrodowski, Winsett. Three-base hits—Medwick, Padgett. Home run—Padgett. Double play—Lavagetto and Daniel. Left on bases—Brooklyn, 10; St. Louis, 6. Base on balls—Off Butcher, 1. Struck out—By Henshaw, 2; by Warneke, 2. Hits—Off Butcher, 5 in 1 1-3 innings; off Henshaw, 7 in 6 2-3. Losing pitcher—Butcher. Umpires—Stark, Stewart and Barr. Time—1:50.

Tardiff Wins in Canoeing

George Tardiff, at the helm of Damoesque, led home the Atlantic Division decked-canoe sailing fleet in the weekly divisional series test in Eastchester Bay off City Island yesterday. Rolf Armstrong, sailing Red Cap, placed second and Adam Wahl, in Centaur, took third.

Bears Halt Toronto in 12th, 6-5, Then Clinch Season's Series, 10-2

By The Associated Press

NEWARK, N. J., Aug. 1.—The league-leading Newark Bears clinched their season's series with the Toronto Leafs today by winning both ends of a double-header.

The Bears were forced to travel twelve innings bfore chalking up a 6-to-5 triumph in the opener, but they made short work of the Leafs in the second game, scoring a 10-to-2 decision as Jack Fallon and Joe Beggs gave up four hits between them.

Atley Donald, whose recent victory streak of fourteen games was broken by Montreal, registered his fifteenth triumph of the year in the opener. He yielded eleven blows, but was effective with runners aboard. A single by Bob Seeds in the twelfth with the bases filled broke up the contest.

The scores:

FIRST GAME

TORONTO (I. L.)	ab	r	h	po	a	e	NEWARK (I. L.)	ab	r	h	po	a	e
Madura, 2b	6	2	2	0	7	0	Gordon, 2b.	6	1	3	2	7	1
G'nbein, ss.	5	0	1	2	3	1	Gleeson, lf.	6	0	2	3	0	0
Smith, cf.	5	1	1	4	0	0	McQ'nn, 1b	5	3	0	12	1	0
Pet'skey, lf	4	1	1	0	0	0	D'gren, 3b.	6	1	3	2	2	0
Porter, rf.	5	0	1	6	0	0	Keller, rf.	5	1	2	0	0	0
Ross, 3b.	5	0	2	0	3	0	Seeds, cf.	5	0	2	3	0	0
Walsh, 1b.	4	0	0	14	1	0	H'berger, c	4	0	1	9	0	0
Hogan, c.	4	0	2	3	1	0	Rich'son, ss	4	0	0	5	1	0
†Oliver	0	0	0	0	0	0	§Rosar	1	0	0	0	0	0
Heving, c.	1	0	0	4	1	0	Kel'her, ss.	0	0	0	0	0	0
C'WELL, p.	3	1	0	0	0	0	D'NALD, p.	4	0	0	0	3	0
‡Comorosky	1	0	0	0	0	0							
DAVIS, p.	1	0	0	0	0	0							
Totals	44	5	11	*33	16	1	Totals	46	6	13	36	14	1

*None out when winning run was scored.
†Ran for Hogan in ninth inning.
‡Batted for Caldwell in ninth inning.
§Batted for Richardson in ninth inning.

Toronto	000	104	000	000	—5
Newark	101	000	030	001	—6

Runs batted in—Dahlgren, Madura, Smith, Petoskey, Porter, Ross, Keller, Seeds (2), Hershberger. Two-base hits—Dahlgren, Gordon. Three-base hit—Keller. Home run—Madura. Stolen base—Ross. Sacrifice—Gantenbein. Double plays—Dahlgren and Gordon; Gordon, Richardson and McQuinn; McQuinn, Richardson and McQuinn; Ross, Hogan and Walsh. Left on bases—Toronto, 6; Newark, 12. Bases on balls—Off Donald, 2; off Caldwell, 1; off Davis, 4. Struck out—By Donald, 8; by Caldwell, 2; by Davis, 2. Hits—Off Caldwell, 9 in 8 innings; off Davis, 4 in 3 (none out in twelfth). Losing pitcher—Davis. Umpires—Campbell and Rommel. Time—2:15.

SECOND GAME

TORONTO (I. L.)	ab	r	h	po	a	e	NEWARK (I. L.)	ab	r	h	po	a	e
Madura, 2b.	4	0	1	1	1	0	Gordon, 2b.	4	1	1	2	4	0
Ganten'n, ss	2	1	0	3	2	0	Gleeson, lf.	2	0	1	4	0	0
Smith, cf.	2	1	0	1	0	0	McQuinn, 1b	2	1	0	6	2	0
Petoskey, lf	4	0	2	0	0	0	Dahlgren, 3b	3	1	0	2	1	1
Porter, rf.	2	0	1	2	0	0	Keller, rf.	4	2	1	1	0	0
Ross, 3b.	4	0	0	2	2	1	Seeds, cf.	3	3	2	0	0	0
Walsh, 1b.	3	0	0	5	2	0	Rosar, c.	4	0	3	2	0	0
Hogan, c.	2	0	0	4	0	0	Rich'son, ss	4	1	3	2	2	0
MEOLA, p.	2	0	0	0	1	0	FALLON, p	2	1	1	2	0	1
*Comorosky	1	0	0	0	0	0	BEGGS, p.	1	0	0	0	0	0
MULLI'N, p	0	0	0	0	1	0							
Totals	26	2	4	13	9	1	Totals	29	10	12	21	9	2

*Batted for Meola in sixth inning.

Toronto	000	020	0	—2
Newark	010	414	x	—10

Runs batted in—Rosar (3), Fallon, Gordon (2), Gleeson, Petoskey, Ross, Seeds (3). Two-base hits—Rosar, Gleeson, Petoskey, Keller, Seeds. Three-base hit—Gordon. Stolen base—Gleeson. Double plays—Gantenbein, Walsh and Hogan; Richardson, Gordon and McQuinn. Left on bases—Toronto, 10; Newark, 9. Bases on balls—Off Meola, 4; off Fallon, 6; off Mulligan, 3; off Beggs, 1. Struck out—By Fallon, 1; by Meola, 1; by Mulligan, 1; by Beggs, 1. Hits—Off Fallon, 3 in 4 1-3 innings; off Beggs, 1 in 2 1-3; off Meola, 9 in 5; off Mulligan, 3 in 1. Winning pitcher—Fallon. Losing pitcher—Meola. Umpires—Rommel and Campbell. Time—1:40.

Indians Crush Senators, 11-2, Behind Feller

Young Cleveland Pitcher Allows Only 7 Hits in Second Victory of Season

By The Associated Press

WASHINGTON, Aug. 1.—Bob Feller baffled Washington today with all the speed that earned him a "boy wonder" ranking last season and Cleveland whipped the Senators, 11 to 2.

It was Feller's second victory of the year. He allowed but seven hits and was seldom in trouble. Washington scored one in the fifth on two singles and an error and put across another in the ninth when Bob weakened, filled the bases and then walked in a run.

Bucky Jacobs, former Richmond University ace, opposed Feller in his first starting assignment. After holding the Indians for three innings, he was pounced upon for five straight singles and four runs in the fourth. He was yanked but charged with the defeat.

The score:

CLEVELAND (A. L.)	ab	r	h	po	a	e	WASHINGTON (A. L.)	ab	r	h	po	a	e
Lary, ss.	5	0	2	0	1	0	Almada, cf.	5	0	1	3	0	0
Hughes, 2b	5	1	1	3	1	1	Lewis, 3b.	4	0	0	1	2	0
Averill, cf.	4	1	1	4	0	0	Travis, ss.	4	0	1	3	2	0
Trosky, 1b.	4	2	2	5	0	0	Simmons, lf	4	1	1	3	0	0
Solters, lf.	4	1	1	4	0	0	Stone, rf.	3	0	1	1	0	0
Weathe'y, rf	4	2	1	2	1	1	Kuhel, 1b.	3	0	2	9	1	0
Hale, 3b.	4	3	3	0	0	0	Myer, 2b.	3	0	0	0	4	1
Pytlak, c.	5	1	3	9	0	0	Millies, c.	3	1	1	6	2	0
FELLER, p.	5	0	0	0	0	0	Sabo, c.	0	0	0	1	0	0
							*W. Ferrell	1	0	0	0	0	0
							JACOBS, p.	1	0	0	0	1	0
							COHEN, p.	0	0	0	0	0	0
							†Bluege	1	0	0	0	0	0
							LINKE, p.	0	0	0	0	0	0
							CHASE, p.	1	0	0	0	1	1
							‡Sington	1	0	0	0	0	0
Totals	40	11	14	27	3	2	Totals	34	2	7	27	13	2

*Batted for Sabo in ninth inning.
†Batted for Cohen in fifth inning.
‡Batted for Chase in ninth inning.

Cleveland	000	404	003	—11
Washington	000	010	001	—2

Runs batted in—Weatherly, Hale (2), Pytlak, Feller (2), Lary, Averill, Trosky, Myer. Two-base hits—Lary, Pytlak. Sacrifice—Averill. Left on bases—Cleveland, 8; Washington, 8. Bases on balls—Off Feller, 3; off Cohen, 1; off Chase, 4. Struck out—By Feller, 9; by Jacobs, 2; by Linke, 1; by Chase, 3. Hits—Off Jacobs, 7 in 4 innings; off Cohen, 1 in 1; off Linke, 5 in 1; off Chase, 1 in 3. Wild pitch—Jacobs. Balk—Feller. Losing pitcher—Jacobs. Umpires—Basil, Geisel and Summers. Time—2:37.

Stainback's Hit in 11th Nets Series Sweep, Six-Game Lead

30,326 See Chicago Tie in Eighth on 'Hit' to Ryan; Ott Poles 2, Danning 1

By Rud Rennie

CHICAGO, Aug. 1.—The Giants are now six games out of first place. They lost again today. It was their fourth defeat in succession. The league-leading Cubs beat them, 5 to 4, in eleven innings, and swept the three-game series before a happy crowd of 30,326 persons.

Cliff Melton, gangling left-hander, pitched the entire game for the Giants, and would have won in nine innings if John (Blondy) Ryan, the flame of the 1933 team, had come up with a grounder in the eighth. The tying run scored while Ryan was making a gesture of chagrin.

Bill Terry put Hank Leiber and Dick Bartell into the game in the tenth in an attempt to win. But the attempt failed with the winning run on third and the Cubs won in the eleventh when Tuck Stainback, a pinch hitter, singled with the bases filled.

Charley Root pitched the first seven innings for the Cubs. The Giants made all their hits (six) off him. Half of them were homers. Ott hit two and Danning one. Every Giant run was propelled by a homer.

The Giants landed briefly but forcefully on Root after two were out in the second inning. Leslie rammed a single to right and Danning polled a home run over the inner wall of the uncompleted left-field bleachers. Ryan also hit and Melton walked. But Chiozza ended the attack with a dud to Jurges.

Hack's Single Scores Root

The Cubs got one of their runs back in the third. Root helped. He singled after Marty walked. Hack's one-base smash to left sent Marty home.

Then Ott uncorked a couple of home runs. He opened the fourth with a homer which sailed over the white-shirted people in the right-field bleachers, out of the park onto Sheffield Avenue. Hartnett hit a powerful double, scoring Herman from first in the Cubs' part of the inning. In the sixth, with two out, Ott made his second homer, a line drive over the inner left-field wall.

But again Hartnett came up in the latter part of an inning in which Ott had stroked one out of the park and made a hit which drove in a run. Collins was on third and Herman on first when the jolly Chicago catcher whacked a single to left, sending Collins home. Ryan took Jurges's grounder for a double play that put an end to this rally.

But in the eighth, after Hack looped a single to center and advanced to second on Collins's sacrificial bunt, Ryan did not look so good on a grounder hit by Demaree. They called it a hit, but even Ryan showed embarrassment at not having come up with it. This "hit" let in the tying run, Hack scoring from second.

Double Play Ends Rally

Hartnett failed to improve upon the score in this inning. He came up with men on first and second and hit into a double play which was started by Melton.

Larry French had been sent in to pitch in place of Root in the eighth. Root was tiring. French, fresh from the bullpen, came in with the score tied and shut out the Giants without a hit in four tense innings. He was in trouble in the tenth, when he walked Ryan with one out and Collins fielded Melton's bunt badly to second, getting no one.

Terry promptly made a bid for victory. He sent Hank Leiber to bat for Chiozza. It was Leiber's first appearance in a game since May 3, when he went to a hospital with concussion of the brain. He hit a long fly on which Ryan raced to third. So the Giants had the winning run on third base when Whitehead grounded out to French.

Dick Bartell, another convalescent invalid, was shoved into the game at short stop. He had been out nearly two weeks with a strained muscle in his groin. Ryan moved over to third base. And the Giants held the Cubs at bay through the tenth. But in the eleventh the Cubs crashed through to victory.

Melton walked Herman, the first man up. Berger backed against the center-field wall to catch Hartnett's fly. But Jurges singled to right, Herman went swiftly to third and Jurges took second on the throw. Melton walked Marty purposely, filling the bases, whereupon Grimm sent Stainback to bat for French. It turned out to be a fortunate move. Stainback hit the second pitch into center field and won the game.

Ott, out for a day with a bruised leg, returned to the fray and paddled his twenty-first and twenty-second homers of the year over the garden wall.

Since Ryan joined the club, Leslie has had to be a contortionist and an acrobat to even knock down some of the throws Ryan turns loose in the general direction of first base. By the end of the season, Leslie may be the most spectacular fielding first baseman in either league. If he lives that long.

Giants' Score

NEW YORK (N. L.)	ab	r	h	po	a	e	CHICAGO (N. L.)	ab	r	h	po	a	e
Chiozza, 3b	4	0	0	1	3	0	Galan, lf.	5	0	0	3	0	0
†Leiber	1	0	0	0	0	0	Hack, 3b.	5	1	2	1	3	0
Bartell, ss.	0	0	0	0	1	0	Collins, 1b.	4	1	2	18	0	1
W'head, 2b	5	0	0	6	3	0	Demaree, rf	5	0	3	3	0	0
Moore, lf.	5	0	1	0	0	0	Herman, 2b	3	2	0	1	8	0
Berger, cf.	5	0	0	4	0	0	Hartnett, c	5	0	2	2	0	0
Ott, rf.	5	2	2	0	0	0	Jurges, ss.	5	0	1	1	1	0
Leslie, 1b.	4	1	1	14	2	0	Marty, cf.	2	1	0	3	0	0
Danning, c.	4	1	1	3	0	0	ROOT, p.	2	0	1	1	2	0
R'n, ss, 3b.	3	0	1	3	6	0	‡Bottarini	1	0	0	0	0	0
M'LTON, p.	3	0	0	0	5	0	FRENCH, p	0	0	0	0	3	0
							§Stainback	1	0	1	0	0	0
Totals	39	4	6	*31	20	0	Totals	38	5	12	33	17	1

*One out when winning run was scored.
†Batted for Chiozza in tenth inning.
‡Batted for Root in seventh inning.
§Batted for French in eleventh inning.

New York	020	101	000	00	—4
Chicago	001	101	010	01	—5

Runs batted in—Hack, Demaree, Hartnett (2), Ott (2), Danning (2), Stainback. Two-base hit—Hartnett. Home runs—Ott (2), Danning. Sacrifices—Collins, French. Double plays—Ryan and Leslie; Ryan, Whitehead and Leslie; Melton, Whitehead and Leslie; Bartell, Whitehead and Leslie; Root, Herman and Collins. Left on bases—New York, 4; Chicago, 9. Bases on balls—Off Melton, 5; off Root, 1; off French, 1. Struck out—By Melton, 2; by Root, 1; by French, 1. Hits—Off Root, 6 in 7 innings; off French, 0 in 4. Winning pitcher—French. Umpires—Goetz, Reardon and Pinelli. Time—2:19.

See page 2

66,767 See Yankee Homers Down White Sox Twice, 7-2, 5-3; Reds Subdue Giants in 10th, 3-2

Dickey's Four-Run Wallop Tops Off Lou Gehrig Day

First Baseman, Honored as Most Valuable Player in 1936, Hits for Circuit in His 1,900th Straight Game; DiMaggio Clouts 32d and Lazzeri Poles 2

By J. P. Abramson

Every Yankee run was knocked in by a homer yesterday at the Stadium as the world champions blasted the Chicago White Sox, 7 to 2 and 5 to 3, in a roaring double-header before a crowd of 66,767.

It was Lou Gehrig Day, but not entirely Lou Gehrig's day. He rounded out one more century and started another in his record of durability, playing his 1,900th and 1,901st consecutive league games since he was eased into active duty on June 1, 1925. Because he was voted the most valuable American League player of 1936 he received the "Sporting News" prize, a watch, from the hands of George M. Cohan between games.

The first time up, with two on, Gehrig inaugurated yesterday's home run derby. Tony Lazzeri walloped one, then Joe DiMaggio duplicated the effort of Cap'n Lou. He put the game on ice in the seventh when he socked No. 32 with two on.

Yankees Snap Lee Jinx

The Yankees took the keenest delight in this homer barrage. They made them all off Thornton Lee, the Chicago left-hander whom they could not beat in five earlier engagements, and enabled Red Ruffing to score his first victory over the White Sox.

The second game was more difficult to win. Lazzeri cracked a four-bagger in the fourth inning of this match, but the White Sox got to Lefty Gomez in the eighth, drove him out and led, 3 to 1, when Bill Dickey cleared the bases in the home half with the big homer of the day off Johnny Whitehead.

It was a glorious finish to a glorious Yankee day. There was a World-Series atmosphere about it. The largest mid-week throng in several years turned out to see the league leaders and their No. 1 challengers open the crucial series.

The crowd came early, lunch boxes in hand, at 10 o'clock. Charlie McManus, the Stadium superintendent, who likes to keep ahead of the crowd, opened the gates at 10:30. The 20,000 capacity of the bleachers was filled a half hour before game time, and the bleacher entrances were shut. Thousands milled around outside.

The grandstand and reserved seat wickets were stormed in rousing fashion. There was a line two blocks long at one entrance when Gehrig saluted Lee in the first inning.

Parking Spots Jammed

The latecomers heard the great roar and stampeded up the ramps. Outside, the parking lots and many garages for blocks around were jammed to the last inch, so that late arrivals had to park nearly a mile away and taxi or walk to the scene of all this commotion. And, mind you, on a Tuesday afternoon early in August.

The Yankees, who had been so shaky in Chicago on their recent Western jaunt and dropped three of four games there, were an efficient, confident crew on the home lot. They picked just the perfect spots for their game-wrecking homers. By winning both games they re-established their widest lead of the year, moving out seven games ahead of the Chicago pursuers.

They stopped the White Sox who had come into town with a five-game winning streak. You can't compromise with home runs the way the murdering Yankees were hitting them yesterday, bringing their team total to 122. The champions were outhit, ten to nine, in the first game, and held even in hits, eight all, in the second game, but the lads from Chicago did not have a homer in their system all day. And the Yankees were playing homer or no-count, and paid off on that basis.

Thousands were still on their way in when Frankie Crosetti smote Lee's first pitch for a single to center. Red Rolfe also got a hit on a grounder which Minter Hayes knocked down, but couldn't field.

Gehrig's Homer Nets Three

DiMaggio got an ovation when he went to bat. It was hard to tell whether it was Lou's day or Joe's day. DiMaggio fouled one into the upper stands before flying out, but Gehrig, also greeted with an ovation, proved the showman of the moment. Lee whipped across two strikes on him in a hurry. Then Luke Sewell made a mistake. He called for a fast one. Gehrig bounced it against the last steel pillar in the new right-field stand, the ball dropping into the bullpen.

Ruffing was being hit consistently, but he had his stuff and the Sox didn't score until the fourth when Luke Appling's double to left and Sewell's single gave them a run with two out. Lazzeri got that back in the home half with his eighth homer that just cleared the railing in left.

The Yankees then were quiescent until the seventh when with two out Crosetti and Rolfe singled and DiMaggio made his first hit, on the first pitch, low and inside. He golfed a towering blow into the lower left-field stands.

The Sox picked up their second run in the eighth on singles by Dixie Walker and Zeke Bonura, although touched for ten hits, was never in difficulty. Five of the Sox hits were made after two were out. Red struck out five and did not have much support. It was his fourteenth victory against three defeats, and placed him even in games won with Monte Stratton, of the Sox.

Whitehead Checks Yankees

Whitehead was tougher than Lee. Lazzeri's homer with two out in the second was the only run off him until the eighth. The Yankees made only four other hits until that fateful inning. Gomez also was in fine fettle until the eighth. He retired the first nine men in order, with only one ball hit out of the infield. He had a four-hit game going into the eighth. The Sox had scored with two out in the seventh on singles by Appling and Whitehead, sandwiched around a sacrifice.

Maybe that single by Whitehead was the tipoff that Gomez was getting tired. In the eighth Mike Kreevich and Bonura singled, Rip Radcliff doubled, Appling walked and Sewell made a pinch-hitting single. A fine throw by Hoag and Sewell's inept running helped to keep the damage down to two runs, and Johnny Murphy came in to retire the side.

That was the setting when, with one out, Rolfe singled and DiMaggio got a fluky double to short right. Hayes should have gone for this fly; Walker was backed against the fence and was too far away. So Whitehead intentionally passed Gehrig. It has been proved before that passing Gehrig to get at Dickey is no bargain. Dickey smacked the second pitch into the twelfth row of the right-field stand for his four-run homer, his nineteenth circuit clout of the year, Murphy thus gained credit for his ninth victory, against two defeats.

McCarthy Day Tomorrow

Joe McCarthy will have a "day" for himself, too, tomorrow. He will receive "The Sporting News" scroll from Mayor F. H. LaGuardia as "manager of the year" (1936).

DiMaggio may not touch Babe Ruth's record, but he continues to make the try. The Babe hit his No. 32 in 1927 in his ninety-fourth game, but he also hit No. 33 in the same game.

The mezzanine section in the new right-field annex was opened for customers for the first time yesterday.

Leading Five Batsmen In Each Major League

NATIONAL LEAGUE

Player and club	G.	AB.	R.	H.	Pct.
Medwick, St. Louis..	92	365	80	145	.397
Hartnett, Chicago..	61	196	25	76	.388
P. Waner, Pitts....	92	370	65	138	.373
Herman, Chicago...	77	324	61	116	.358
Mize, St. Louis ...	86	325	53	114	.351
Vaughan, Pitts.....	76	296	44	104	.351

AMERICAN LEAGUE

Player and club	G.	AB.	R.	H.	Pct.
Travis, Washington.	68	267	38	101	.378
Gehrig, New York..	93	347	84	130	.375
DiMaggio, New York	87	366	95	136	.372
Greenberg, Detroit..	91	343	86	122	.356
Gehringer, Detroit..	80	313	72	110	351

Home Runs		Runs Batted In	
DiMaggio, Yanks.	32	Greenb'g, Tigers.	104
Foxx, Red Sox...	26	DiMaggio, Yanks	102
Greenb'g, Tigers.	24	Medwick, Cards..	100
Trosky, Indians..	23	Dickey, Yanks..	91
Ott, Giants......	22	Gehrig, Yanks..	89
Gehrigh, Yanks..	22		

How to Pitch to Medwick

CHICAGO, Aug. 3 (AP).—When some one asked Gabby Hartnett, catcher of the Chicago Cubs, how he has his pitchers toss to slugging Joe Medwick, of the St. Louis Cardinals, Gabby replied: "I just get down on my haunches and tell 'em to fire that ball. Then I run like heck to third base to back up the throw."

Yankees' Scores

FIRST GAME

CHICAGO (A. L.)	ab	r	h	po	a	e
Hayes, 2b..	5	0	1	2	4	0
Kreevich, cf	4	0	1	3	0	0
Walker, rf.	4	1	2	3	0	0
Bonura, 1b.	4	0	1	13	0	0
Radcliff, lf.	4	0	1	0	0	0
Appling, ss.	4	1	1	1	3	0
Sewell, c...	4	0	1	2	0	0
Piet, 3b....	3	0	1	0	3	1
*Rosenthal.	1	0	0	0	0	0
LEE, p....	3	0	1	0	4	0
†Haas.....	1	0	0	0	0	0
Totals...	37	2	10	24	14	1

NEW YORK (A. L.)	ab	r	h	po	a	e
Crosetti ss	4	2	2	3	2	0
Rolfe, 3b..	3	2	2	3	3	0
DiMaggio, cf	3	1	1	3	0	0
Gehrig, 1b.	4	1	1	6	0	0
Dickey, c..	4	0	1	6	0	0
Powell lf..	4	0	0	3	0	0
Lazzeri, 2b.	4	1	2	3	3	0
Hoag, rf...	3	0	0	0	0	0
RUFFING, p	3	0	0	0	1	0
Totals....	32	7	9	27	9	0

*Batted for Piet in ninth inning.
†Batted for Lee in ninth inning.

Chicago..............	000	100	010	—2
New York..........	300	100	30x	—7

Runs batted in—Gehrig (3), Sewell, Lazzeri, DiMaggio (3), Appling. Two-base hit—Appling. Home runs—Gehrig, Lazzeri, DiMaggio. Double plays—Piet, Hayes and Bonura; Hayes, Appling and Bonura. Left on bases—New York, 3; Chicago, 8. Bases on balls—Off Lee, 2. Struck out—By Ruffing, 5; by Lee, 2. Umpires—Moriarty, Johnston and Owens. Time—1:51.

SECOND GAME

CHICAGO (A. L.)	ab	r	h	po	a	e
Hayes, 2b..	5	0	1	5	2	1
Kreevich, cf	5	0	1	3	0	0
Walker, rf.	5	1	1	1	0	0
Bonura, 1b.	3	1	1	9	1	1
Radcliff lf.	4	0	1	0	0	0
Appling, ss.	3	1	1	2	2	0
Piet, 3b....	2	0	0	1	3	0
*Sewell....	1	0	1	0	0	0
Berger, 3b.	0	0	0	0	1	0
Shea, c....	2	0	0	3	2	2
W'HEAD, p	4	0	1	0	2	0
Totals....	34	3	8	24	13	4

NEW YORK (A. L.)	ab	r	h	po	a	e
Crosetti, ss.	3	0	1	2	0	0
Rolfe, 3b..	4	1	2	1	2	0
DiMaggio, cf	4	1	1	2	0	0
Gehrig, 1b.	2	1	0	13	0	0
Dickey, c..	4	1	2	7	1	0
Powell, lf..	4	0	0	1	0	0
Lazzeri, 2b.	3	1	2	0	5	1
Hoag rf...	3	0	0	1	1	0
GOMEZ, p.	3	0	0	0	2	0
MURPHY, p	0	0	0	0	0	0
Totals....	30	5	8	27	11	1

*Batted for Piet in eighth inning.

Chicago............	000	000	120	—3
New York..........	010	000	04x	—5

Runs batted in—Lazzeri, Whitehead, Radcliff, Dickey (4). Two-base hits—Radcliff, DiMaggio. Home runs—Lazzeri, Dickey. Sacrifices—Crosetti, Piet. Double plays—Appling and Bonura; Hayes and Bonura. Left on bases—New York, 6; Chicago, 9. Bases on balls—Off Gomez, 3; off Whitehead, 4; off Murphy, 1. Struck out—By Gomez, 3; by Whitehead, 3; by Murphy, 1. Hits—Off Gomez, 8 in 7 2-3 innings; off Murphy, 0 in 1 1-3. Winning pitcher—Murphy. Umpires—Johnston, Owens and Moriarty. Time—2:10.

Gehrig Is Honored and Proves He Deserves It

Herald Tribune photo—Acme

A near-capacity crowd jammed Yankee Stadium for Lou Gehrig Day yesterday and saw the slugging first baseman receive the American League most valuable player award for 1936 from George M. Cohan, famous actor and song writer

Associated Press photo

Gehrig celebrated his 1900th consecutive game by poling his twenty-second home run of the season with two on base in the first inning of the opener as Yankees defeated Chicago White Sox twice. Red Rolfe and bat boy are greeting him as he crosses the plate

Red Sox Attack Routs Indians For Grove, 13-2

Boston Gets 15 Hits in 6th Straight Victory; 2½ Games Behind Chicago

By The Associated Press

BOSTON, Aug. 3.—Lefty Grove pitched the Boston Red Sox within two and one-half games of second place today as the Fenway Millionaires humbled the Cleveland Indians, 13 to 2, with a fifteen-hit barrage, while the White Sox were losing twice to the Yankees.

It was Boston's sixth straight victory, not counting a 2-to-2 tie game with Detroit Sunday, and Grove's tenth triumph of the season.

The score:

CLEVELAND (A. L.)	ab	r	h	po	a	e
Lary, ss...	4	1	3	1	3	0
Hughes, 2b	4	0	1	4	3	0
Averill, cf.	4	0	0	5	1	1
Trosky, 1b.	4	0	1	7	1	0
Solters lf..	3	0	0	1	0	0
Weath'ly, rf	3	0	0	1	0	0
†Campbell.	1	0	0	0	0	0
Hale, 3b...	4	1	2	4	1	1
Pytlak, c...	4	1	2	4	1	1
HARDER, p	2	0	0	0	1	0
*Becker ...	1	0	0	0	0	0
HEVING, p	0	0	0	0	0	0
WHITH'L, p	0	0	0	0	0	0
‡Sullivan .	1	0	0	0	0	0
Totals...	35	2	8	24	11	2

BOSTON (A. L.)	ab	r	h	po	a	e
Mills, lf....	3	2	0	2	0	0
Cramer cf	4	2	2	2	0	0
Cronin, ss.	3	2	0	1	1	0
Foxx, 1b...	4	2	3	10	1	0
Higgins, 3b	5	3	4	0	2	0
McNair, 2b.	4	1	2	1	5	0
Chapman, rf	4	0	2	1	0	0
Desautels, c	5	1	2	10	1	0
GROVE, p.	3	0	0	0	2	1
Totals	35	13	15	27	12	1

*Batted for Harder in seventh inning.
†Batted for Weatherly in ninth inning.
‡Batted for Whitehill in ninth inning.

Cleveland..........	100	000	100	— 2
Boston..............	310	001	53x	—13

Runs batted in—Lary, Hughes, Higgins (4), Chapman (2), Grove, Foxx, Desautels, McNair (3), Cramer. Two-base hits—Lary, Higgins (2), McNair, Chapman. Three-base hits—Lary, Pytlak. Sacrifices—Grove (2), Cramer, Cronin. Double play—Desautels and Cronin. Left on bases—Cleveland, 8; Boston, 8. Bases on balls—Off Harder, 1; off Heving, 3; off Whitehill, 2; off Grove, 2. Struck out—By Harder, 3; by Whitehill, 1; by Grove, 9. Hits—Off Harder, 10 in 6 innings; off Heving, 2 in 1-3; off Whitehill, 3 in 1 2-3. Losing pitcher—Harder. Umpires—Quinn, McGowan and Ormsby. Time—2:09.

Senators Beat Browns In 12th on Stone's Hit

WASHINGTON, Aug. 3 (AP).—Johnny Stone's single with the bases loaded broke up a twelve-inning pitching battle between Wesley Ferrell and Elon Hogsett today, and brought Washington a 3-to-2 triumph over St. Louis.

The score:

ST. LOUIS (A. L.)	ab	r	h	po	a	e
Davis, 1b..	5	1	0	13	1	0
West, cf....	6	1	3	7	0	0
Vosmik, lf.	5	0	3	2	0	0
Clift, 3b....	4	0	0	0	4	0
Bell, rf....	3	0	0	1	0	0
K'k'b'ker, ss	5	0	0	5	3	0
Hemsley, c.	5	0	1	5	0	0
Lips'mb, 2b	3	0	1	1	5	0
†Huffman .	1	0	0	0	0	0
Carey, 2b..	1	0	0	0	1	0
Hogsett, p..	5	0	0	1	3	1
Totals..	43	2	8	*35	17	1

WASHINGTON (A.L.)	ab	r	h	po	a	e
Almada, cf.	5	1	1	5	0	0
Lewis, 3b..	6	1	2	0	3	0
Travis, ss..	6	0	5	[illegible]	2	0
Simmons, lf	5	0	1	2	0	0
Stone, rf...	6	0	3	2	0	0
Kuhel, 1b..	5	0	2	12	1	0
Myer, 2b...	5	0	2	4	3	0
Millies, c..	4	0	0	10	0	0
‡Bluege....	1	0	0	0	0	0
W.F'R'LL, p	5	1	1	0	2	0
Totals..	48	3	17	36	11	0

*Two out when winning run was scored.
†Batted for Lipscomb in ninth inning.
‡Batted for Millies in twelfth inning.

St. Louis.....	000	010	000	001	—2
Washington...	001	000	000	002	—3

Runs batted in—Lewis (2), Vosmik, Bell, Stone. Two-base hits—Vosmik (2), Travis (2), Lipscomb, W. Ferrell, Almada. Three-base hit—Vosmik. Sacrifices—Almada, Vosmik. Double plays—Lipscomb, Knickerbocker and Davis (3); Hogsett, Lipscomb and Davis. Left on bases—St. Louis, 13; Washington, 12. Bases on balls—Off Hogsett, 1; off W. Ferrell, 6. Struck out—By Hogsett, 4; by W. Ferrell, 7. Hit by pitcher—By W. Ferrell (Clift). Umpires—Dinneen, Kolls and Hubbard. Time2:40.

Standings in Major Leagues

WEDNESDAY, AUGUST 4, 1937

American League

YESTERDAY'S RESULTS

New York, 7; Chicago, 2 (1st)
New York, 5; Chicago, 3 (2d)
Boston, 13; Cleveland, 2
Philadelphia, 2; Detroit, 1
Washington, 3; St. Louis, 2 (12 innings)

STANDING OF THE CLUBS

	New York	Chicago	Boston	Detroit	Cleveland	Washington	St. Louis	Phila'phia	Won	Lost	Percentage
New York.	—	8	6	11	9	7	12	9	62	29	.681
Chicago...	8	—	7	3	5	11	11	12	57	38	.600
Boston....	2	6	—	8	7	4	13	11	51	37	.580
Detroit....	7	7	7	—	7	9	5	9	51	39	.567
Cleveland.	4	3	7	5	—	8	6	10	43	45	.489
Wash'gton	3	6	5	3	8	—	11	4	40	48	.455
St. Louis..	4	3	5	3	2	5	—	7	29	62	.319
Phila'phia	1	5	0	6	7	4	4	—	27	62	.303
Gms. lost.	29	38	37	39	45	48	62	62	—	—	

GAMES TODAY

Chicago at New York, 3:15
St. Louis at Washington
Detroit at Philadelphia
Cleveland at Boston (2)

National League

YESTERDAY'S RESULTS

Cincinnati, 3; New York, 2 (10 ins.)
Pittsburgh, 5; Brooklyn, 4 (1st)
Pittsburgh, 10; Brooklyn, 4 (2d)
Chicago, 4; Philadelphia, 1
St. Louis, 5; Boston, 2

STANDING OF THE CLUBS

	Chicago	New York	Pittsburgh	St. Louis	Boston	Cincinnati	Brooklyn	Phila'phia	Won	Lost	Percentage
Chicago...	—	11	5	10	7	5	11	11	60	32	.652
New York.	6	—	8	10	5	9	9	7	54	40	.574
Pit'sburgh	6	3	—	5	9	10	8	9	50	42	.543
St. Louis..	2	7	4	—	10	7	9	10	49	43	.533
Boston....	4	5	8	6	—	8	8	6	45	49	.479
Cincinnati	3	7	1	4	9	—	4	10	38	53	.418
Brooklyn..	6	3	8	7	2	6	—	5	37	54	.407
Phila'phia	5	4	8	1	7	8	5	—	38	58	.396
Gms. lost.	32	40	42	43	49	53	54	58	—	—	

GAMES TODAY

New York at Cincinnati
Brooklyn at Pittsburgh
Boston at St. Louis
Philadelphia at Chicago

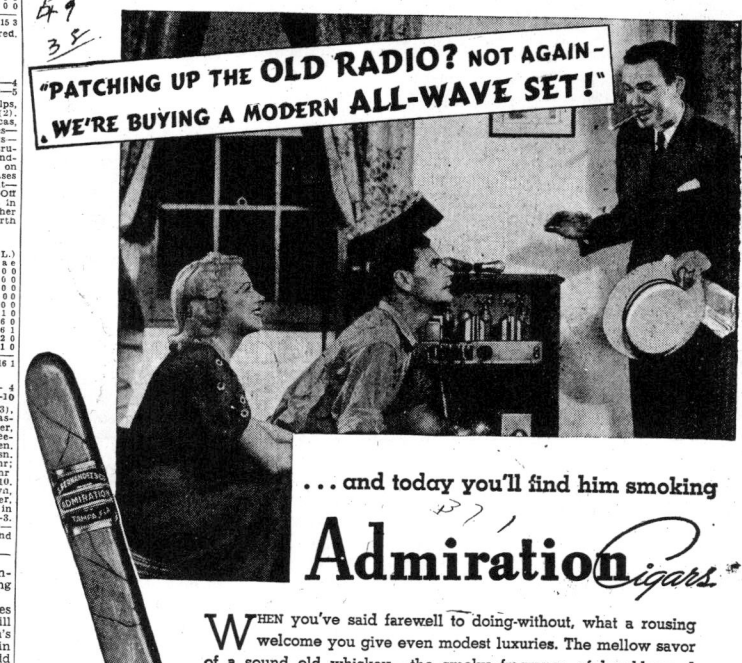

Pirates Beat Dodgers, 5-4, 10-4, Losers Dropping Into 7th Place

Suhr's Ninth-Inning Single Sets Frankhouse Back; Butcher Pelted in Second

Special to the Herald Tribune

PITTSBURGH, Aug. 3.—The Pirates took both ends of a double-header from the Dodgers today, 5 to 4 and 10 to 4, and dropped them into seventh place, a game behind the Cincinnati Reds and only a game and a half out of the cellar.

A two-run rally in the ninth, with a single by Gus Suhr driving in the tying and winning runs, defeated Freddie Frankhouse in the opener. Jim Weaver, third Pirate pitcher in the game, was the winner.

Mace Brown, making his first start of the year, won the second game, although Russ Bauers had to relieve him in the eighth. Max Butcher, going the full eight innings, was hit hard and poorly supported.

Blanton was knocked out in the first inning of the opener after his wild throw on a double-play ball had set up two runs, which Woody English singled home with a line drive to left. Bill Swift gave up a run on singles by Buddy Hassett and Heinie Manush in the third.

Frankhouse Doubles

Swift also was responsible for the fourth and last Brooklyn run in the fourth. English scored it on Frankhouse's double down the right-field foul line.

Buddy Hassett's inexperience as a center fielder allowed the Pirates to get into the game in the fourth, when they scored three times. With one out Buddy misjudged a liner by Floyd Young and muffed it for a two-base error.

Then Lee Handley singled to left on the first pitch and Red Lucas, batting for Swift, doubled off the right-field wall for two runs. Schulte, running for Lucas, scored on Woody Jensen's single off Lavagetto's glove.

The fifth of the double plays the Pirates completed stopped the Dodgers in the ninth after English and Frankhouse's hope of an eighth victory was crushed in the Pirate's half.

Arky Vaughan, still unable to run, batted for Jim Weaver and singled. Both Dickshot, Vaughan's runner, and Lloyd Waner were safe on the latter's sacrifice on Phelps's late throw to second. Paul Waner was purposely passed and, after a long conference by all the Dodgers, including Grimes, Suhr hit the first pitch to right. It was good for two runs and the game.

Pirates Resume Attack

In the second game Hassett's tough breaks continued in the first inning when the Pirates scored twice off Butcher. Lloyd Waner opened with a double to right, moved to third on an infield out and scored on Paul Waner's fly to center. Suhr drew a pass and Al Todd's fly toward right-center went for a triple when Buddy made an unsuccessful attempt at a diving catch.

The Pirates counted four times in the fourth, marked by Bill Brubacker's triple and Jensen's double, and got to Butcher again in the eighth for four more, Todd driving in two with his second triple and fourth hit.

Van Mungo, who had his tonsils removed a week ago in Brooklyn, has lost twenty pounds and has gone to his Pageland, S. C., home for a week.

The Dodger manager had nothing to report as a result of his St. Louis conferences with Branch Rickey.

Dodgers' Scores

FIRST GAME

BROOKLYN (N. L.)	ab	r	h	po	a	e
Lav'getto, 2b	5	0	0	3	4	0
H'ssett, cf, 1b	4	1	2	7	0	1
Manush, rf	4	0	3	1	0	0
Phelps, c..	4	0	0	1	0	0
Winsett, lf.	4	1	1	7	0	0
Daniel, 1b..	2	1	0	3	0	0
Cooney, cf.	2	0	0	1	0	0
Stripp, 3b..	3	0	1	1	2	0
English, ss.	4	1	4	1	3	0
F'HOUSE, p	4	0	3	0	1	0
Totals..	36	4	14	*25	10	1

PITTSBURGH (N. L.)	ab	r	h	po	a	e
L.Waner, cf	4	1	0	3	0	0
Jensen, lf..	3	0	1	0	0	1
P.Waner, rf	4	0	1	1	1	0
Suhr, 1b...	4	0	2	9	1	0
Todd, c....	4	0	1	4	0	1
Brubaker, 3b	4	0	0	1	4	0
Young, ss..	4	1	1	2	4	0
Handley, 2b	4	1	1	7	4	0
BL'NTON, p	0	0	0	0	0	1
SWIFT, p..	1	0	0	0	1	0
†Lucas.....	1	0	1	0	0	0
‡Schulte...	0	1	0	0	0	0
WEAVER, p	1	0	1	0	0	0
§Vaughan..	1	0	1	0	0	0
¶Dickshot..	0	1	0	0	0	0
Totals...	35	5	10	27	15	3

*One out when winning run was scored.
†Batted for Swift in fourth inning.
‡Ran for Lucas in fourth inning.
§Batted for Weaver in ninth inning.
¶Ran for Vaughan in ninth inning.

Brooklyn.............	021	100	000	—4
Pittsburgh..........	000	300	002	—5

Runs batted in—English (2), Phelps, Frankhouse, Lucas (2), Jensen, Suhr (2). Two-base hits—Young, Frankhouse, Lucas, Suhr. Stolen base—English. Sacrifices—Stripp, L. Waner, Jensen. Double plays—Young, Handley and Suhr (2); Swift, Brubaker, Handley and Suhr; Brubaker, Handley and Suhr; Young and Suhr. Left on bases—Brooklyn, 6; Pittsburgh, 10. Bases on balls—Off Frankhouse, 3. Struck out—By Swift, 2; by Weaver, 1. Hits—Off Blanton, 4 in 1 1-3 innings; off Swift, 5 in 2 2-3; off Weaver, 5 in 5. Winning pitcher—Weaver. Umpires—Moran, Magerkurth and Parker. Time—1:59.

SECOND GAME

BROOKLYN (N. L.)	ab	r	h	po	a	e
Lav'getto, 2b	5	0	1	1	2	1
Hassett, cf.	3	1	2	6	0	0
Manush, rf	4	0	1	0	0	0
Phelps, c...	4	0	0	3	0	0
Winsett, lf.	4	0	1	2	0	1
Daniel, 1b.	4	0	1	8	1	0
Stripp, 3b.	4	1	1	1	1	0
English, ss.	4	1	0	2	3	0
B'CHER, p	3	1	2	1	2	0
*Bucher....	0	0	0	0	0	0
Totals....	35	4	9	24	9	2

PITTSBURGH (N. L.)	ab	r	h	po	a	e
L.Waner, cf	4	2	3	2	0	0
Jensen, lf..	4	1	2	5	0	0
P.Waner, rf	4	0	0	1	0	0
Suhr, 1b...	3	2	0	12	0	0
Todd, c....	5	2	4	2	0	0
Brubaker, 3b	4	2	2	0	1	0
Young, ss..	4	0	1	3	6	0
Handley, 2b	4	0	1	2	6	1
BROWN, p	4	1	1	0	2	0
BAUERS, p	0	0	0	0	1	0
Totals..	36	10	14	27	16	1

*Batted for Butcher in ninth inning.

Brooklyn...........	000	030	010	— 4
Pittsburgh.........	200	400	04x	—10

Runs batted in—P. Waner, Todd (3), Brubaker (2), Jensen (2), Lavagetto, Hassett (3). Two-base hits—L. Waner, Butcher, Todd, Jensen, Lavagetto. Three-base hits—Todd (2), Brubaker, Jensen. Stolen base—Handley. Sacrifice—Jenesn. Double plays—Young, Handley and Suhr; Lavagetto and Daniel; Young and Suhr Left on bases—Brooklyn, 6; Pittsburgh, 10. Bases on balls—Off Butcher, 7; off Brown, 1; off Bauers, 1. Struck out—By Butcher, 2; by Brown, 1. Hits—Off Brown, 9 in 7 1-3 innings; off Bauers, 0 in 1 2-3. Passed ball—Phelps. Winning pitcher—Brown. Umpires—Magerkurth, Parker and Moran. Time—2:08.

Hollingsworth Holds New York To 6 Hits as Schumacher Bows

Walker Scores From First on Hafey's Scratch Safety as Terry Shake-Up Fails

By Rud Rennie

CINCINNATI, Aug. 3.—Bill Terry gave the Giants' batting order a violent shake-up for today's game with the Reds. He benched Lou Chiozza, put Mel Ott, the right fielder, at third base and Hank Leiber in right field. All this he did in a desperate effort to pull his team out of a nose-dive toward the second division. But it was no use, the Giants lost again and are now only three games ahead of the third-place Pittsburgh Pirates and seven games back of the league-leading Chicago Cubs.

The Reds won, 3 to 2, in ten innings behind the six-hit pitching of Al Hollingsworth, a left-hander. They beat Hal Schumacher, making two runs in the second and one in the tenth when Hub Walker scored from first on Chick Hafey's pop fly behind second base.

Berger's Throw Wide

Berger certainly should have been able to stop Walker from scoring. But his throw was wide and on the ground. Schumacher tried to cut it off, but it went by him. Walker slid over the plate with the winning run.

So the Giants lost their fifth game in succession. They have now lost six out of seven on this western trip.

Dick Bartell, the ailing shortstop, started the game, but the exercise was too much for him. He had to quit in the sixth after getting two bases on an error by the second baseman and scoring when the third baseman picked up Berger's little hit and flung it against the grandstand.

Bartell was the lead-off man in the new batting order. Moore batted second, and Whitehead was dropped to eighth position.

Ryan took Bartell's place in the last of the sixth and tied the score in the eighth. He drove a triple into center field and scampered home on a fly by Moore.

Hollingsworth had the Giants shut out with three hits until the sixth, when they scored an unearned run on two errors.

Berger's Double Wasted

The Giants' new batting order, designed to lend power, did not function as well as expected. Berger got two hits, but his hardest one, a double in the eighth, was wasted. Leiber, batting after Berger, was handed his second intentional pass in the eighth and Leslie closed the rally with an easy tap to the pitcher.

Ryan drew a base on balls in the tenth and was advanced to second, but Ott was called out on strikes and Berger flied to the center fielder.

It was the Giants' second straight extra inning game. They have been in thirty-two games, which have been decided by one run, and have won nineteen of them and lost thirteen. The opposition is catching up.

One fears that Bartell is not going to be much help to the team. He is willing to play but unable to stand the strain.

Ott did not have much to do at third base, but he handled the job well. He came in fast for Walker's bunt in the tenth and made a fine play to force Cuyler at second.

Gus Mancuso, the first-string catcher, and Clyde Castleman, a starting pitcher, rejoined the team today. Mancuso's broken finger is out of its cast and in a splint, but it may be two weeks before he can play. Castleman says he can pitch, but he does not know how far he can go. He hasn't sciatica. It's his sacroiliac that is bothering him.

Leiber had not started in a ball game since May 3. He was used as a pinch hitter last Sunday.

In addition to doing a neat job of pitching Hollingsworth drove in both his team's runs in the second.

Giants' Score

NEW YORK (N. L.)	ab	r	h	po	a	e
Bartell, ss.	3	1	0	2	5	0
Ryan, ss...	1	1	1	3	0	0
J.Moore, rf	4	0	1	4	0	0
Ott, 3b....	4	0	0	0	2	0
Berger, cf.	5	0	2	1	0	0
Lieber, rf..	2	0	0	2	0	0
Leslie, 7b..	4	0	0	1?	3	1
Danning, c	4	0	1	3	3	0
Whiteh'd, 2b	4	0	1	3	1	0
SCH'KER, p	4	0	0	1	3	0
Totals..	35	2	6	*29	17	1

CINCINNATI (N. L.)	ab	r	h	po	a	e
Cuyler, rf..	5	0	3	1	0	0
Walker, lf..	5	1	2	3	0	0
Scars'la, 1b	5	0	1	12	0	0
Hafey, cf..	4	0	1	2	0	0
Lombardi, c	4	0	1	5	0	1
†Goodman.	0	0	0	0	0	0
Miller, ss..	0	0	0	0	0	0
Riggs, 3b..	3	0	1	2	3	1
K'pouris, 2b	1	1	0	4	4	1
Myers, ss..	3	1	1	0	6	0
V. Davis, c.	1	0	0	1	0	0
H'L'SW'H, p	4	0	1	0		10
Totals..	35	3	11	30	14	3

*Two out when winning run was scored.
†Ran for Lombardi in ninth inning.

New York........	000	001	010	0—2
Cincinnati.......	020	000	000	1—3

Runs batted in—Moore, Hafey, Hollingsworth (2). Two-base hits—Berger, Hollingsworth. Three-base hit—Ryan. Stolen bases—Ott, Walker. Sacrifices—Moore, Riggs, Kampouris. Double plays—Leslie, Bartell and Leslie; Myers, Kampouris and Scarsella. Left on bases—New York, 8; Cincinnati, 8. Bases on balls—Off Schumacher, 3; off Hollingsworth, 4. Struck out—By Schumacher, 3; by Hollingsworth, 5. Umpires—Klem, Sears and Ballanfant. Time—2:15.

Lee's Pitching, 3 Cub Homers Stop Phils, 4-1

Hurler Wins 12th and Gets Four-Bagger; Hartnett, Demaree Hit for Circuit

By The Associated Press

CHICAGO, Aug. 3.—General Bill Lee muffled Philadelphia bats with three-hit pitching today and joined in a home-run assault on Sylvester Johnson to lead the National League pace-making Cubs to a 4-to-1 victory in the opening game of the series.

The triumph, the Cubs' fourteenth in their last seventeen starts, their fourth in a row and Lee's twelfth of the season, combined with New York's defeat at Cincinnati, increased their first place margin over the Giants to seven full games. It was achieved in the jig time of eighty-seven minutes and missed being a shutout for the big righthander when Herschel Martin, center-fielder, belted out a home run in the sixth inning for the Phillies.

The Cub home run drive was handled by Frank Demaree and Gabby Hartnett in addition to Lee. Demaree started it in the first inning after Rip Collins had singled with two out, and Hartnett followed in the fourth. Lee echoed in with his round-tripper in the fifth. Demaree's was his eleventh of the season, and Hartnett's his fifth of the campaign, enabled the big catcher to run his consecutive-game hitting streak to twenty-three.

Outsied of Martin's homer, Lee experienced a minimum of trouble and, except for the home run, the Phillies got only one man past first base. In the eighth, Scharein walked and moved up when Augie Galan muffed Earle Brown's fly. Dolph Camilli collected two singles but was mopped up in a double play on the first one, and was left stranded on the other occasion.

The score:

PHILADELPHIA (N. L.)	ab	r	h	po	a	e
Martin, cf.	4	1	1	2	0	0
Young, 2b.	3	0	0	1	2	0
‡Arnovich..	1	0	0	0	0	0
Norris, 2b..	0	0	0	1	0	0
Moore, rf..	3	0	0	1	0	0
Klein, lf...	4	0	0	4	0	0
Camilli, 1b.	4	0	2	8	3	0
Whitney, 3b	3	0	0	0	2	0
Schar'n, ss	2	0	0	1	5	0
Grace, c...	3	0	0	3	0	0
JOHNS'N, p	2	0	0	3	1	0
*Browne ..	1	0	0	0	0	0
†Kelleher..	0	0	0	0	0	0
JORG'NS, p	0	0	0	0	0	0
Totals...	30	1	3	24	13	0

CHICAGO (N. L.)	ab	r	h	po	a	e
Galan, lf.	3	0	0	2	0	[illegible]
Hack, 3b...	3	0	0	1	3	0
Collins, 1b.	3	1	1	10	2	0
Demaree, rf	4	1	1	3	0	0
Herman, 2b	3	0	1	1	4	0
Hartn't, c..	3	1	1	5	0	0
Jurges, ss..	3	0	0	1	2	0
Cavar'ta, cf	3	0	0	2	0	0
LEE, p.....	3	1	2	2	2	0
Totals...	24	4	6	27	13	1

*Batted for Johnson in eighth inning.
†Ran for Browne in eighth inning.
‡Batted for Young in eighth inning.

Philadelphia.........	000	001	000	—1
Chicago..............	200	110	00x	—4

Runs batted in—Martin, Demaree (2), Hartnett, Lee. Home runs—Martin, Demaree, Hartnett, Lee. Sacrifice—Hack. Double plays—Johnson, Scharein and Camilli; Jurges, Herman and Collins. Left on bases—Philadelphia, 4; Chicago, 3. Bases on balls—Off Johnson, 3; off Lee, 2. Struck out—By Johnson, 1; by Lee, 3. Hits—Off Johnson, 6 in 7 innings; off Jorgens, 0 in 1. Hit by pitcher—By Johnson (Collins). Losing pitcher—Johnson. Umpires—Stewart, Barr and Stark. Time—1:27.

Athletics Beat Tigers, 2-1, on Brucker's Drive

Catcher's Homer in Fifth Defeats Bridges; Mackmen Employ 3 Pitchers

By The Associated Press

PHILADELPHIA, Aug. 3.—Earle Brucker's homer into the left-field stands in the fifth inning gave the Athletics a 2-to-1 victory over Detroit today in a game that saw three Philadelphia hurlers outpitch the veteran Tommy Bridges.

Herman Fink, who twirled the fourth, fifth and sixth innings, received credit for the triumph. He and Lynn Nelson, who pitched the last three innings, gave up one hit apiece. Luther Thomas yielded five hits in the first three innings, three of them in the third, when Hank Greenberg's double scored Bill Rogell with the lone Detroit run.

The score:

DETROIT (A. L.)	ab	r	h	po	a	e
Fox, rf....	5	0	0	0	0	0
Rogell, ss..	4	1	1	1	6	0
Gehr'g'r, 2b	4	0	3	2	6	0
Greenb'g, 1b	3	0	2	10	1	0
Walker, lf.	3	0	0	3	0	0
Owen, 3b...	4	0	0	1	1	0
Laabs, cf...	4	0	1	0	0	0
Bolton, c...	4	0	0	5	0	0
BRIDG'S, p	2	0	0	2	2	0
*Goslin ...	1	0	0	0	0	0
Totals...	34	1	7	24	16	0

PHILADELPHIA (A. L.)	ab	r	h	po	a	e
Moses, lf..	3	1	2	2	0	0
Dean, 1b..	3	0	1	9	[illegible]	0
Werber, 3b.	4	0	0	2	1	0
Johnson, lf	4	0	1	2	0	0
Hill, cf....	4	0	2	3	0	0
Peters, 2b..	4	0	1	3	4	1
Parker, ss..	4	0	1	3	4	1
Brucker, c.	2	1	1	3	1	0
THOMAS, p	0	0	0	0	0	0
†Rothrock ..	1	0	0	0	0	0
FINK, p.	1	0	0	0	0	0
NELSON, p	1	0	0	0	0	0
Totals...	31	2	9	27	10	2

*Batted for Bridges in ninth inning.
†Batted for Thomas in third inning.

Detroit..............	001	000	000	—1
Philadelphia.........	100	010	00x	—2

Runs batted in—Greenberg, Dean, Brucker. Two-base hits—Moses, Johnson, Greenberg. Home run—Brucker. Sacrifice—Brucker. Double plays—Rogell and Greenberg; Parker Peters and Dean. Left on bases—Detroit, 9; Philadelphia, 8. Bases on balls—Off Bridges, 2; off Thomas, 2; off Fink, 1. Struck out—By Bridges, 4; by Fink, 1; by Nelson, 2. Hits—Off Thomas, 5 in 3 innings; off Fink, 1 in 3; off Nelson, 1 in 3. Winning pitcher—Fink. Umpires—Geisel, Summers and Basil. Time—2:00.

Cards Down Bees, 5-2, On Moore's Pinch Hit

ST. LOUIS, Aug. 3 (AP).—Fleet-footed Terry Moore, St. Louis Cardinals' centerfielder, has a batting average of about 2.50, but he's a very good man in a pinch.

With the score tied at 2-all, Mickey Owen on base. He rammed one of Jim Turner's shoots into the left field stands for a home run and a 5-to-2 victory for the Red Birds.

The score:

BOSTON (N. L.)	ab	r	h	po	a	e
RJohns'n, rf	2	0	1	0	0	0
Warstler, ss	4	0	0	0	3	0
Garms, cf..	4	1	1	4	0	0
C'cinello, 2b	4	0	0	1	2	0
E.Moore rf	3	0	1	3	0	0
English, 3b.	4	1	0	1	2	0
Fletcher, 1b	4	0	1	9	0	0
Mueller, c.	4	0	1	5	1	0
Turner, p..	3	0	1	1	1	0
GABLER, p	0	0	0	0	0	0
Totals....	32	2	6	24	9	0

ST. LOUIS (N. L.)	ab	r	h	po	a	e
T.Moore, cf	4	2	2	7	0	0
S.Martin, 2b	4	1	2	1	1	0
Mize, 1b...	4	0	1	7	0	1
Medwick, lf.	4	0	1	0	0	0
Padgett, rf	4	0	0	3	0	0
G't'idge, 3b	4	0	1	2	3	0
Dur'her, ss	2	1	1	0	3	0
Owen, c....	2	1	1	7	0	0
S.J'NS'N, p	3	0	0	0	0	0
Totals...	31	5	9	27	7	1

Boston..............	010	001	000	—2
St. Louis............	000	002	30x	—5

Runs batted in—Turner, English, Medwick, Padgett, T. Moore (3). Two-base hits—Mize, Turner, S. Martin. Three-base hit—R. Johnson. Home run—T. Moore. Stolen base—Durocher. Double plays—Turner and Fletcher; Owen (unassisted). Left on bases—Boston, 6; St. Louis, 4. Bases on balls—Off S. Johnson, 3; off Turner, 2. Struck out—By Turner, 4; by S. Johnson, 4. Hits—Off Turner, 9 in 6 2-3 innings; off Gabler, 0 in 1 1-3. Wild pitch—S. Johnson. Losing pitcher—Turner. Umpires—Reardon, Pinelli and Goetz. Time—1:55.

See pages 6 and 11

Yankees Rout White Sox for Series Sweep

New York Scores 8 Runs in 8th, Winning, 13-8; Gehrig Hits 2; Powell Injured by Pitched Ball

By Arthur E. Patterson

Colonel Jacob Ruppert, who gets a bigger kick out of a home run than his own beer, should have been at the stadium to celebrate his seventieth birthday yesterday. His Yankees put on the sort of ball game he relishes, coming from behind in the eighth inning and battering Clint Brown for eight runs and a 13-to-8 triumph.

Completing a sweep of the four-game series, prolonging a new winning streak through five straight contests, knocking the White Sox out of second place and establishing a lead of nine games over the new "contenders," the Boston Red Sox, the McCarthy maulers once again disproved the old theory that pitching is 70 per cent of a team's strength. In fact, there are few maxims which hold once these Yankees start slugging.

The game would have been a dress parade for Colonel Ruppert had he decided to attend. Before activities began Mayor Fiorello H. LaGuardia presented to Joe McCarthy the "Sporting News" scroll as manager of the year, 1936.

Sixteen Yankees in Game

Then, what with an injury suffered by Jake Powell, the use of three pitchers, one pinch-hitter and various other replacements, sixteen Yankees got into the afternoon's fun.

But of them all, Lou Gehrig was the big man of the afternoon. As his personal gift to the good colonel, his boss, he biffed homers Nos. 24 and 25, driving in Joe DiMaggio with the first and sending home George Selkirk and Red Rolfe with the other, the clinching blow in the high-scoring eighth when ten men came to bat and Gehrig scored twice.

As is customary when Lefty Gomez and Red Ruffing are shackled to the bench, the Yankee pitching was something less than gaudy. Kemp Wicker, the southpaw, was the starter against Monte Stratton. His own two-base error and a single by Tony Piet gave the Sox a run in the second and they whacked in two more in the fourth on a pair of singles, a base on balls and a fly to left which resulted in a double play, but tallied Luke Appling.

Stratton lost his control in the same frame, however, when Crosetti singled and DiMaggio and Dickey walked. He hit Powell on the left ear with a curve ball and sent one runner home and Powell to St. Elizabeth's Hospital, where he joined another ear case, Pat Malone, for a short time.

Stratton Retires in Fourth

This seemed to unnerve Stratton and in the next inning the Yankees got to him for four unearned runs and a temporary lead. With one out, Piet booted Wicker's grounder and Crosetti followed with a single to right. Stratton quit then in favor of Brown, and Jimmy Dykes motioned to the press box that his ace was suffering from a sore arm. Red Rolfe flied to center, scoring Wicker, and Crosetti went to second on Appling's wild relay of the outfielder's return. DiMaggio then tripled to the running track in left center and Gehrig put his first homer in the right-field bleachers.

Wicker couldn't hold the advantage, however. He was nicked for two runs in the sixth, one in the seventh and another in the eighth and finally departed after Minter Hayes made the thirteenth hit against him. Frank Makosky came in, faced one batter, Kreevich, and earned the victory when Dickey took Kreevich's topped shot in front of the plate and threw to Gehrig, while Kreevich waited for George Moriarty, the umpire, to say "Foul."

Here's how the Yankees went to work on Brown in the eighth:

Gehrig started the fans shouting when he walked. Dickey then singled to right and when Dixie Walker juggled the ball, the catcher raced to second. Tom Henrich, inserted for Powell, rammed a double which bounced into the rignt-field seats, tying the score, and Saltzgaver ran for him. Hoag was intentionally passed, and Heffner beat out a bunt, filling the bases.

Rolfe's Hit Scores Two

McCarthy sent Red Ruffing to bat, and he bounced a single to right. Crosetti was the first out, fanning, but Rolfe singled to right for two more runs. After DiMaggio also fanned Gehrig climaxed the clouting with a lofty shot into the right center-field bleachers.

Johnny Murphy was in the box for the third successive game in the ninth and allowed one run, but he didn't have to bear down.

Powell's injury, a badly bruised ear, is not serious. He was in the clubhouse after the game and preparing to witness last night's fight at the Garden.

The Yankees have hit homers in each of the last eight games, seventeen all told. . . . Bob Feller will face the Yankees today in the opener with Cleveland. . . . 500 Buffalo fans will honor Joe McCarthy and Frank Pytlak, home-town boys, Sunday. The score:

CHICAGO (A. L.)	ab	r	h	po	a	e	NEW YORK (A. L.)	ab	r	h	po	a	e
Hayes, 2b..	4	0	2	1	3	0	Crosetti, ss	5	2	2	1	2	0
Kr'vich, cf	5	1	2	5	0	0	Rolfe, 3b...	5	1	1	1	1	0
Walker, rf..	4	0	1	1	0	1	DiMaggio, cf	4	1	1	3	0	0
Radcliff, lf.	5	1	1	1	0	0	Gehrig, 1b.	4	3	2	9	0	0
Appling, ss.	2	3	1	1	2	1	Dickey, c..	4	1	1	3	2	0
Bonura, 1b.	5	2	3	9	0	0	Powell, lf..	1	0	0	2	1	0
Sewell, c....	5	1	1	6	0	0	Henrich, rf.	2	0	1	0	0	0
Piet, 3b....	4	0	2	0	1	1	†Saltzgaver.	0	1	0	0	0	0
ST'TON, p.	2	0	1	0	0	0	Lazzeri, 2b.	0	0	0	0	0	0
BROWN, p.	1	0	0	0	1	0	H'g, rf, lf..	3	1	0	1	0	0
							H'r, 2b, rf.	3	1	1	5	3	0
							WICKER, p	3	1	0	0	3	1
							MA'SKY, p	0	0	0	0	0	0
							*Ruffing ...	1	0	1	0	0	0
							‡Selkirk ...	0	1	0	0	0	0
							M'RPHY, p	0	0	0	0	0	0
Totals....	37	8	14	24	7	3	Totals..	35	13	10	27	11	1

*Batted for Makosky in eighth inning.
†Ran for Henrich in eighth inning.
‡Ran for Ruffing in eighth inning.

Chicago.......... 010 202 111—8
New York.......... 000 140 08x—13

Runs batted in—Piet (3), Bonura (2), Sewell, Powell, DiMaggio, Gehrig (5), Appling, Hayes, Henrich (2), Ruffing, Rolfe (3). Two-base hits—Bonura (2), Kreevich (2), Henrich. Three-base hit—DiMaggio. Home runs—Gehrig (2). Sacrifices—Hayes, Walker, Brown. Double plays—Crosetti and Gehrig; Powell and Heffner. Left on bases—New York, 4; Chicago, 8. Bases on balls—Off Wicker, 2; off Stratton, 2; off Brown, 3; off Murphy, 1. Struck out—By Stratton, 2; by Wicker, 1; by Brown, 3. Hits—Off Stratton, 2 in 4 1-3 innings; off Brown, 8 in 3 2-3; off Wicker, 13 in 7 2-3; off Makosky, 0 in 1-3; off Murphy, 1 in 1. Hit by pitcher—By Stratton (Powell). Winning pitcher—Makosky. Losing pitcher—Brown. Umpires—Moriarty, Johnston and Owens. Time—2:01.

Yankees' Manager Receives Scroll for Leadership

Associated Press photo

It was Joe McCarthy day at the stadium yesterday and Mayor Fiorello H. LaGuardia made the presentation of "The Sporting News" scroll as the outstanding manager of baseball in 1936. Lou Gehrig, captain, looks on and later made the day a memorable one for the manager as he drove out two home runs to help sweep the four-game series with the Chicago White Sox

Red Sox Beat Indians, 5 to 4, Take 2d Place

Newsom Holds Cleveland to Eight Hits for Boston's Ninth Straight Victory

By The Associated Press

BOSTON, Aug. 5.—The Red Sox took over second place in the American League today by whipping the Cleveland Indians, 5 to 4, for their ninth straight victory, not counting a tie game Sunday, a clean-up of the four-game series and the thirty-first triumph in their last thirty-seven home games.

Buck Newsom limited the Indians to eight scattered hits.

The Indians, trailing by two runs entering the seventh, pulled into a 3-to-3 tie when Hale walked and Pytlak drove out a line drive that went for a homer within the grounds.

The Sox went into the lead in their half when Newsom tripled and scored on Mills's long fly, and added what proved to be the winning margin in the next inning when Foxx singled, was sacrificed along by Higgins, and scored on a single by Oscar Melillo, who replaced the lame Eric McNair at second.

The score:

CLEVELAND (A. L.)	ab	r	h	po	a	e	BOSTON (A. L.)	ab	r	h	po	a	e
Lary, ss...	4	0	1	1	6	0	Mills, lf...	4	0	0	3	0	0
Kroner, 2b.	4	0	1	4	3	0	Cramer, cf	4	1	1	4	0	0
Averill, cf.	4	0	1	1	0	0	Cronin, ss.	3	0	2	2	2	0
Trosky, 1b	4	0	1	10	2	0	Foxx, 1b..	4	2	2	6	1	0
Solters, lf.	4	1	1	4	0	0	Higgins, 3b	3	1	2	2	1	0
Campbell, rf	4	0	1	2	0	0	McNair, 2b	3	0	1	2	2	0
Hale, 3b...	3	1	1	0	3	0	Melillo, 2b	1	0	1	0	1	0
Pytlak, c..	3	2	1	1	0	0	Chapman, rf	4	0	1	2	0	0
HUDLIN, p	3	0	0	1	1	0	Desautels, c	4	0	0	6	0	1
							NEWSOM, p	3	1	1	0	0	0
Totals..	33	4	8	24	15	0	Totals...	33	5	11	27	7	1

Cleveland.......... 001 000 201—4
Boston.......... 100 002 11x—5

Runs batted in—Pytlak (2), Campbell, Mills, Foxx, Higgins, McNair, Melillo. Two-base hits—Averill, Trosky, Solters, Higgins. Three-base hits—Campbell, Newsom. Hom run—Pytlak. Stolen bases—Lary, Pytlak. Chapman. Sacrifice—Higgins. Double plays—Hale, Kroner and Trosky; McNair and Foxx; Foxx and Higgins. Left on bases—Cleveland, 4; Boston, 6. Bases on balls—Off Hudlin, 1; off Newsom, 2. Struck out—By Hudlin, 1; by Newsom, 5. Umpires—Quinn, McGowan and Ormsby. Time—2:17.

Browns Rout Appleton, Defeat Senators, 7 to 4

WASHINGTON, Aug. 5 (AP).—The St. Louis Browns hopped on Pete Appleton with a heavy early-inning attack today to defeat the Washington Senator, 7 to 4.

Cecil Travis, the American League batting leader, got three hits in five appearances but failed in the eighth inning, when he flied out with the bases loaded to retire the side and end Washington's biggest rally.

The score:

ST. LOUIS (A. L.)	ab	r	h	po	a	e	WASHINGTON (A. L.)	ab	r	h	po	a	e
Kn'b'k'r, ss	5	0	0	0	1	0	Almada, cf	4	0	0	2	0	0
West, cf...	5	0	0	6	0	0	Sington, rf	1	0	0	1	0	0
Vosmik, lf.	4	1	1	3	0	0	Lewis, 3b...	5	1	4	0	4	0
Clift, 3b...	5	2	2	1	1	0	Travis, ss.	5	0	3	2	1	1
Bell, rf...	4	1	3	6	0	0	Simmons, lf	5	0	0	4	0	0
Hemsley, c	3	1	0	5	0	0	Stone, rf, cf.	4	1	0	0	0	0
Davis, 1b..	2	1	1	5	0	0	Kuhel, 1b.	4	0	2	16	0	0
Carey, 2b..	4	1	1	1	0	0	Myer, 2b..	4	1	1	0	5	0
KOUPAL, p	4	0	1	0	1	0	Millies, c..	4	1	2	2	1	0
HOGSE'T, p	0	0	0	0	0	0	AP'L'T'N, p	1	0	0	0	2	0
							LINKE, p..	2	0	0	0	1	0
							*W. Ferrell.	1	0	1	0	0	0
							CHASE, p	0	0	0	0	0	0
Totals...	36	7	9	27	3	0	Totals..	40	4	13	27	14	1

*Batted for Linke in eighth inning.

St. Louis.......... 041 020 000—7
Washington.......... 000 001 120—4

Runs batted in—Carey (2), Koupal (2), Hemsley, Bell, Davis, Travis (2), Millies, W. Ferrell. Two-base hits—Lewis, Bell. Three-base hits—Clift, Davis, Lewis. Stolen base—Knickerbocker. Sacrifice—Hemsley. Left on bases—St. Louis, 6; Washington, 12. Bases on balls—Off Koupal, 3; off Appleton, 1; off Linke, 1; off Chase, 1. Struck out—By Koupal, 1; by Hogsett, 2; by Chase, 2. Hits—Off Appleton, 9 in 4 2-3 innings; off Chase, 0 in 1; off Linke, 0 in 3 1-3; off Koupal, 11 in 7 1-3; off Hogsett, 2 in 1 2-3. Winning pitcher—Koupal. Losing pitcher—Appleton. Umpires—Hubbard, Kolls and Dinneen. Time—2:04.

Dodgers Pummel Pirates, 9 to 6, As 6 Errors Help Hoyt to Victory

Grimes Men Rout Blanton in 7th; Young Connects for 3-Run Homer in 5th

Special to the Herald Tribune

PITTSBURGH, Aug. 5.—Six Pirate errors, three in the seventh inning, gave the Dodgers the final game with the Pirates, 9 to 6, and evened the series before a Ladies' Day crowd of 3,693.

Waite Hoyt, who has pitched well in previous starts without winning, was fortunate in hanging up his second triumph as a Dodger, since he allowed a dozen hits, including a three-run homer by Floyd Young in the fifth.

Cy Blanton, the losing pitcher, saw the game slip away from him in the seventh when singles by Johnny Cooney and Buddy Hassett and Heinie Manush's double tied the score at 6-all and drove him out.

Todd Starts Error Spree

Ed Brandt came in to pitch to Babe Phelps and Al Todd muffed a high foul back of the plate for the first error of the inning. Lloyd Waner came in for Phleps' short fly and it appeared to have hit him on the head. When Young recovered the ball, he threw to first base with nobody covering and two more runs were in.

Hoyt held the Pirates after the fifth in spite of Cooney's muff of an easy fly in the ninth.

The Dodgers scored in the first on a pass to Lavagetto, Cooney's sacrifice and Manush's double to right. A tie resulted in the same inning on singles by Lloyd and Paul Waner, with Jensen's sacrifice in between.

Again the Dodgers went ahead in the fourth when Young's wild throw with two out set up two runs that Joe Stripp singled home, and the Pirates got another tie in their half on singles by Lloyd Waner and Brubaker and Young's double.

Young's homer in the fifth followed singles by Gus Suhr and Todd. It was a hard drive that cleared the scoreboard in left field.

Score on Handley's Error

The Dodgers came within one of a tie in the sixth on a pass to Phelps, Gibby Brack's double to right center and Handley's error on Winsett's pinch-batting grounder, both runners scoring.

They added the ninth run in the eighth on Stripp's single, Brubaker's wild heave after catching Hoyt's pop bunt and a squeeze-play bunt by Cooney.

Burleigh Grimes and his men started an argument with George Parker, the umpire, in the Pirates' fourth that held up the game ten minutes, but availed them nothing. Grimes thought Stripp had fielded Handley's grounder in fair territory and the umpire called it foul.

Cooney made an extraordinary catch of Brubaker's drive in the fifth. He took the ball over his head while running almost to the center-field flagpole, 450 feet from the plate.

Lavagetto twisted his right ankle coming in for Handley's grounder in the fourth, but was able to continue in the game.

Young's homer was his eighth of the season and makes him the Pirates' leader in that department.

Brack and Manush both turned in a pair of good catches after long runs toward the foul lines in the fifth and eighth. Paul Waner hit one and Red Lucas, batting for Brandt, the other.

Dodgers' Score

BROOKLYN (N. L.)	ab	r	h	po	a	e	PITTSBURGH (N. L.)	ab	r	h	po	a	e
Lavag'to, 2b	3	1	0	3	2	0	L. Waner, cf	5	1	2	2	0	1
Cooney, cf	4	1	2	4	0	1	Jensen, lf..	4	0	1	2	0	0
Hassett, 1b	5	1	3	7	0	0	P. Waner, rf	5	0	1	0	0	0
Manush, rf	5	2	2	5	0	0	Suhr, 1b..	5	1	2	9	0	0
Phelps, c..	4	1	1	3	0	0	Todd, c....	4	1	3	4	1	1
Brack, lf..	4	2	1	4	0	0	Brub'k'r, 3b	4	1	1	3	0	1
English, ss	1	0	0	0	1	0	Young, ss.	4	2	2	2	7	2
*Winsett...	1	0	0	0	0	0	Handley, 2b	4	0	0	5	1	1
Brown, ss.	2	0	0	0	1	0	BL'TON, p.	3	0	0	0	2	0
Stripp, 3b.	5	1	2	1	2	0	BRANDT, p	0	0	0	0	0	0
HOYT, p..	4	0	0	0	2	0	Lucas	1	0	0	0	0	0
							WEAVER, p	0	0	0	0	0	0
Totals...	38	9	11	27	8	1	Totals..	39	6	12	27	12	6

*Batted for English in sixth inning.
†Batted for Brandt in seventh inning.

Brooklyn.......... 100 202 310—9
Pittsburgh.......... 100 230 000—6

Runs batted in—Manush (2), Stripp (2), Handley, P. Waner, L. Waner, Young (3), Winsett, Cooney. Two-base hits—Manush (2), Brack, Young. Home run—Young. Stolen base—Brack. Sacrifices—Cooney, Jensen, Brack. Left on bases—Brooklyn, 8; Pittsburgh, 7. Bases on balls—Off Blanton, 3; off Brandt, 1. Struck out—By Blanton, 1; by Hoyt, 3; by Brandt, 1; by Weaver, 1. Hits—Off Blanton, 8 in 6 1-3 innings; off Brandt, 2 in 1 2-3; off Weaver, 1 in 1. Losing pitcher—Blanton. Umpires—Moran, Magerkurth and Parker. Time—2:17.

Results and Standings In the Minor Leagues

INTERNATIONAL LEAGUE

YESTERDAY'S RESULTS

Newark, 4; Buffalo, 2.
Baltimore, 10; Montreal, 5 (night).
Jersey City, 4; Rochester, 3.
Other clubs not scheduled.

STANDING OF THE CLUBS

	W.	L.	Pct.		W.	L.	Pct.
Newark...	79	29	.731	Toronto....	51	55	.481
Montreal..	54	47	.535	Rochester..	52	59	.468
Syracuse..	56	54	.509	Baltimore.	44	54	.449
Buffalo...	52	53	.495	Jersey City.	36	73	.330

GAMES TODAY

Rochester at Newark, 6:30 p. m.
Montreal at Jersey City
Toronto at Baltimore.
Buffalo at Syracuse.

AMERICAN ASSOCIATION

At Milwaukee— R. H. E.
Toledo...... 330 000 001—7 15 0
Milwaukee.. 300 011 05x—10 14 1

Battries—Sullivan, Johnson and Reiber; Boone, Kimball and Brenzel.

STANDING OF THE CLUBS

	W.	L.	Pct.		W.	L.	Pct.
*Col'bus..	62	47	.569	*Ind'polis.	53	51	.510
*Min'polis	61	47	.565	*Kan. City	51	54	.486
Toledo...	60	49	.550	*St. Paul..	42	64	.396
Milwaukee	56	50	.528	*Louisville	42	64	.396

*Night game.

SOUTHERN ASSOCIATION

At Atlanta— R. H. E.
Nashville...... 100 000 010—2 8 0
Atlanta....... 001 201 00x—4 9 1

Batteries—Johnson, Werk and Leggett; Beekman and Galvin.

At Chattanooga (1st game)— R. H. E.
Knoxville.... 001 010 020—4 7 1
Chattanooga. 210 304 02x—12 22 1

Batteries — Maltzberger, McClure and Wairen; Tinning, Bagner and Livingston.

Second game— R. H. E.
Knoxville........ 000 000 1—1 5 0
Chattanooga..... 010 101 x—3 7 2

Batteries—Chapman and Wairen; Bagner and Livingston.

STANDING OF THE CLUBS

	W.	L.	Pct.		W.	L.	Pct.
*Lit. Rock.	73	37	.664	*N. Orleans	60	55	.522
Nashville..	63	49	.563	*Birm'ham.	56	56	.500
*Memphis.	63	50	.558	Chat'nooga	42	72	.368
Atlanta...	61	52	.540	Knoxville..	34	81	.296

*Night game.

NEW YORK-PA. LEAGUE

At Elmira— R. H. E.
Trenton...... 100 200 000—3 8 1
Elmira....... 110 200 31x—8 12 1

Batteries — Kraukauskas and Pickens; Krausse and Gautreaux.

At Binghamton (first game)— R. H. E.
Scanton...... 010 000 005—6 8 3
Binghamton... 001 140 03x—9 12 1

Batteries—Balas and Wasem; Washburn, La Flamme and Holm.

At Albany (night game)— R. H. E.
Wilkes-Barre. 520 310 000—11 14 9
Albany....... 100 400 000—5 13 1

Batteries—Day and Holden; Callahan, Weafer, McCrory and Goebel.

STANDING OF THE CLUBS

	W.	L.	Pct.		W.	L.	Pct.
Elmira....	61	39	.610	W'msport..	47	50	.485
Hazleton..	60	41	.594	Trenton...	44	56	.440
Wilkes-B..	55	45	.550	Scranton...	43	57	.430
Bing'ton..	52	47	.525	Albany....	36	53	.404

TEXAS LEAGUE

Three night games.

STANDING OF THE CLUBS

	W.	L.	Pct.		W.	L.	Pct.
Okla. City.	76	43	.639	Ft. Worth.	61	58	.513
Beaumont.	62	54	.534	Galveston.	55	63	.466
Tulsa.....	61	55	.526	Houston...	50	67	.427
S. Antonio	63	57	.525	Dallas.....	44	75	.370

PACIFIC COAST LEAGUE

At San Francisco— R. H. E.
Sacramento .. 200 200 100—5 13 1
San Francisco. 200 000 004—6 8 0

Batteries—Newsome, Seats and Cooper; Lamanski and Woodall.

STANDING OF THE CLUBS

	W.	L.	Pct.		W.	L.	Pct.
*San Diego	75	53	.586	*L. Angeles	66	61	.520
Sacramento	73	56	.566	*Oakland..	58	70	.453
*Portland.	67	58	.536	*Seattle...	53	73	.421
San Fran.	69	60	.535	*Missions..	49	79	.383

*Night game.

Standings in Major Leagues

FRIDAY, AUGUST 6, 1937

American League

YESTERDAY'S RESULTS

New York, 13; Chicago, 8
Boston, 5; Cleveland, 4
Detroit, 5; Philadelphia, 3
St. Louis, 7; Washington, 4

STANDING OF THE CLUBS

	New York	Boston	Chicago	Detroit	Cleveland	Washington	St. Louis	Phila'phia	Won	Lost	Percentage
New York.	—	6	10	11	9	7	12	9	64	29	.688
Boston....	2	—	6	8	10	4	13	11	54	37	.593
Chicago...	8	7	—	3	5	11	11	12	57	40	.588
Detroit....	7	7	7	—	7	9	5	11	53	39	.576
Cleveland.	4	7	3	5	—	8	6	10	43	48	.473
Wash'gton	3	5	6	3	8	—	11	4	40	50	.444
St. Louis..	4	5	3	3	2	7	—	7	31	62	.333
Phila'phia	1	0	5	6	7	4	4	—	27	64	.297
Gms. lost.	29	37	40	39	48	50	62	64	—	—	

GAMES TODAY

Cleveland at New York, 3:15
Chicago at Boston
Detroit at Washington
Other clubs not scheduled

National League

YESTERDAY'S RESULTS

New York, 2; Cincinnati, 0 (12 ins.)
Brooklyn, 9; Pittsburgh, 6
Philadelphia, 4; Chicago, 2
Boston, 4; St. Louis, 1

STANDING OF THE CLUBS

	Chicago	New York	Pittsburgh	St. Louis	Boston	Brooklyn	Cincinnati	Phila'phia	Won	Lost	Percentage
Chicago...	—	11	5	10	7	11	5	11	60	34	.638
New York.	6	—	8	10	5	9	11	7	56	40	.583
Pit'sburgh	6	3	—	5	9	8	10	9	50	44	.532
St. Louis..	2	7	4	—	11	9	7	10	50	44	.532
Boston....	4	5	8	7	—	8	8	6	46	50	.479
Brooklyn..	6	3	10	7	2	—	6	5	39	54	.419
Cincinnati	3	7	1	4	9	4	—	10	38	55	.409
Phila'phia	7	4	8	1	7	5	8	—	40	58	.408
Gms. lost.	34	40	44	44	50	54	55	58	—	—	

GAMES TODAY

New York at Pittsburgh
Brooklyn at Cincinnati (night game)
Boston at Chicago (2)
Philadelphia at St. Louis

Phillies Defeat Cubs Again, 4-2, Behind Walters

Philadelphia Ace Allows 4 Hits as Demaree's Homer Scores Both Chicago Runs

By The Associated Press

CHICAGO, Aug. 5.—Backing up Bucky Walters's four-hit pitching with a three-run first-inning flurry off Clyde Shoun, the lowly Philadelphia Phillies again defeated the league-leading Cubs today, 4 to 2. The victory, their second straight here, gave them the series, two games to one.

Frank Demaree's thirteenth home run, his third in as many days over Wrigley Field's new temporary left field partition, scoring Jim Collins, who had singled ahead of him in the fourth inning, accounted for the Cubs' only runs off Walters. He allowed only two other Cubs to pass first base and only one other reached third.

Herschel Martin led the Phillies' ten-hit attack off a trio of Chicago pitchers, starting the first-inning scoring with a double and, after wasting a single in between, hitting a homer off Charley Root in the ninth.

Clay Bryant, who stepped in and stopped the Phils' first-inning rally after Young's safe bunt and an out scored one run and two passes and George Scharein's single scored two more off Shoun, shut out the Phils until excused for a pinch hitter in the seventh.

Gabby Hartnett's twenty-four-game hitting streak was stopped by Walters. The big catcher flied to center and grounded to second in his first two times at bat and then, after being walked in the seventh inning, was retired in favor of a pinch runner. The score:

PHILADELPHIA (N. L.)	ab	r	h	po	a	e	CHICAGO (N. L.)	ab	r	h	po	a	e
Martin, cf.	5	2	3	5	0	0	Galan, cf...	4	0	0	2	0	0
Young, 2b..	5	1	1	4	5	0	Hack, 3b...	4	0	1	1	1	0
Moore, rf...	5	0	0	2	0	0	Collins, 1b.	4	1	1	8	0	0
Arnovich, lf	3	1	1	2	0	0	Demaree, rf	4	1	1	3	0	0
Camilli, 1b.	3	0	0	6	2	0	Herman, 2b	3	0	0	4	2	0
Whitney, 3b	3	0	1	0	0	0	Hartnett, c.	2	0	0	4	0	0
Scharein, ss	4	0	2	4	3	0	*Stainback..	0	0	0	0	0	0
Atwood, c..	4	0	2	4	0	0	ROOT, p...	0	0	0	0	0	0
WAL'RS, p.	3	0	0	0	2	0	†Cavarretta	0	0	0	0	0	0
							Jurges, ss..	3	0	0	3	3	0
							Frey, lf....	3	0	1	1	0	0
							SHOUN, p.	0	0	0	0	1	0
							BRYANT, p	2	0	0	0	3	0
							O'Dea, c....	1	0	0	1	1	0
Totals...	35	4	10	27	12	0	Totals....	30	2	4	27	11	0

*Ran for Hartnett in seventh inning.
†Batted for Root in ninth inning.

Philadelphia........ 300 000 001—4
Chicago............ 000 200 000—2

Runs batted in—Martin, Moore, Scharein (2), Demaree (2). Two-base hits—Martin, Arnovich. Home runs—Martin, Demaree. Stolen bases—Young, Arnovich. Sacrifice—Jurges. Left on bases—Philadelphia, 8; Chicago, 6. Bases on balls—Off Walters, 4; off Shoun, 2; off Bryant, 2. Struck out—By Walters, 4; by Shoun, 1; by Bryant, 2. Hits—Off Shoun, 3 in 2-3 innings; off Bryant, 5 in 6 1-3; off Root, 2 in 2. Losing pitcher—Shoun. Umpires—Stark, Stewart and Barr. Time—1:53.

Greenberg's 25th Homer Beats A's for Tigers, 5-3

PHILADELPHIA, Aug. 5 (AP).—Edgar Smith, southpaw, with the Athletics, almost won his first game of the season today, but with two on and two out in the eighth Hank Greenberg hit a slow ball out of the park that gave Detroit a 5 to 3 victory.

It was the twenty-fifth homer of the year for the slugging Tiger first sacker and gave Elon Auker victory in a close game.

Pete Fox hit a homer off Smith in the first that put the Tigers ahead. In the third, Walker doubled and eventually scored on Gehringer's long fly to Moses. In the fourth, however, the A's tied it up on Bill Werber's single and Bob Johnson's fourteenth homer of the year. In the sixth Werber again singled, went to third on Johnson's one-base smash and scored on Hill's fly to left.

The score:

DETROIT (A. L.)	ab	r	h	po	a	e	PHILADELPHIA (A.L.)	ab	r	h	po	a	e
Walker, lf.	4	1	1	3	0	0	Moses, rf...	4	0	1	1	0	0
Fox, rf.....	3	2	2	1	0	0	Dean, 1b....	3	0	0	12	0	0
Geh'ger, 2b	4	1	1	4	5	0	Werber, 3b.	4	2	2	2	3	0
Gr'berg, 1b	4	1	2	11	1	0	Johnson, lf	4	1	2	2	0	0
Laabs, cf..	4	0	0	1	0	0	Hill, cf....	3	0	0	3	0	0
Owen, 3b...	4	0	0	0	2	0	Peters, 2b..	3	0	0	1	3	0
York, c....	4	0	2	3	0	0	*Finney ...	1	0	0	0	0	0
Rogell, ss..	3	0	0	3	3	0	Parker, ss..	3	0	0	2	5	0
AUKER, p.	3	0	0	1	5	0	†Nelson ...	1	0	1	0	0	0
							Brucker, c..	4	0	2	4	1	0
							SMITH, p.	2	0	1	0	0	0
Totals....	33	5	8	27	16	0	Totals....	32	3	9	27	12	0

*Batted for Peters in ninth inning.
†Batted for Parker in ninth inning.

Detroit............ 101 000 030—5
Philadelphia........ 000 201 000—3

Runs batted in—Fox, Gehringer, Greenberg (3), Johnson (2), Hill. Two-base hits—York, Walker, Moses. Home runs—Fox, Johnson, Greenberg. Sacrifices—Fox, Smith. Double plays—Owen, Gehringer and Greenberg; Gehringer, Rogell and Greenberg; Peters, Parker and Dean; Rogell, Gehringer and Greenberg. Left on bases—Detroit, 3; Philadelphia, 5. Bases on balls—Off Auker, 2; off Smith, 1. Struck out—By Auker, 2; by Smith, 2. Umpires—Basil, Geisel and Summers. Time—1:56.

Newark Trips Buffalo For 7th Straight, 4-2

NEWARK, N. J., Aug. 5 (AP).—Brilliant pitching by Joe Beggs, who was credited with his fifteenth victory of the year, enabled the Newark Bears to increase their winning streak to seven games for the fifth time this season as they defeated the Buffalo Bisons, 1936 champions, 4 to 2, today.

Beggs limited the Herd to five blows, one of which was a home run in the second inning by Eddie Phillips with the bases empty.

The Bears gathered eleven safeties off Ken Ash, who pitched eight innings and was charged with his twelfth defeat of the year and fourth in a row against the league leaders. Joe Gordon, with three singles, led the bombardment.

Babe Dahlgren clouted his sixteenth home run in the fifth frame with Frankie Kelleher aboard.

The score:

BUFFALO (I. L.)	ab	r	h	po	a	e	NEWARK (I. L.)	ab	r	h	po	a	e
McC'k, 1b, cf	4	0	0	7	0	1	Gordon, 2b	5	0	3	1	7	0
Mulleavy, ss	3	1	1	3	6	2	Gleeson, lf..	3	0	0	1	0	0
Tyler, cf...	2	0	1	1	0	0	Kelleher, 3b	2	1	0	1	1	0
Corbett, 1b	1	0	0	5	0	0	Dahlgren, 1b	3	1	2	16	0	0
Carnegie, lf	4	0	1	0	0	0	Keller, rf...	3	0	0	1	0	0
Boland, rf..	4	0	0	0	0	0	Seeds, cf...	3	1	1	2	0	0
Dueker, 3b.	4	0	0	1	2	0	Hershb'r, c	4	0	2	4	0	0
Olson, 2b..	3	0	0	2	7	0	Rich'son, ss	4	1	2	1	4	0
*McGowan..	1	0	0	0	0	0	BEGGS, p.	4	0	1	0	2	0
Phillips, c..	3	1	2	3	0	0							
ASH, p.....	2	0	0	0	0	0							
†Meyers....	1	0	0	0	0	0							
JACOBS, p.	0	0	0	0	0	0							
Totals....	32	2	5	24	16	3	Totals..	32	4	11	27	14	0

*Batted for Olson in ninth inning.
†Batted for Ash in eighth inning.

Buffalo............ 001 100 000—2
Newark............ 000 022 00x—4

Runs batted in—Phillips, Carnegie, Dahlgren (2), Gordon. Two-base hits—Seeds, Dahlgren. Home runs—Phillips, Dahlgren. Double plays—Mulleavy, Olson and McCormick; Olson, Mulleavy and McCormick. Left on bases—Buffalo, 5; Newark, 9. Bases on balls—Off Ash, 5; off Beggs, 1. Struck out—By Beggs, 2; by Ash, 2. Hits—Off Ash, 11 in 7 innings; off Jacobs, 0 in 1. Hit by pitcher—By Beggs (Tyler). Losing pitcher—Ash. Umpires—Jorda and White. Time—1:20.

Jeffcoat Faces Operation

ST. LOUIS, Aug. 5 (AP).—George Jeffcoat, Brooklyn Dodgers pitcher, entered a hospital today to undergo an operation for appendicitis. Jeffcoat first became ill several weeks ago after pitching a game at Brooklyn.

Giants Trip Reds in 12th, 2-0, Castleman Defeating Grissom

New York Pitcher, Encased in Supporting Belt, Cuts Chicago Lead to 5 Games

By Rud Rennie

CINCINNATI, Aug. 5.—Clyde Castleman, fresh from a hospital and making his first appearance since July 21, stepped into a fierce battle with Lee Grissom, of the Reds, this afternoon. The Giants' right hander, encased in a supporting belt, had to pitch shutout ball for twelve innings to win.

Castleman had to do so, because Grissom rode along with him through one scoreless frame after another. Not a run was made until the twelfth when the Giants made two and won, 2 to 0. If there was any question about Castleman's courage, he answered it today.

Sambo Leslie, who made four hits yesterday, got three today and led the winning rally. He opened the twelfth with a double to left. Lou Chiozza ran for him. Then Harry Danning laid down a bunt to the left of the box and Grissom slipped as he came off the mound. Chiozza sped to third and Danning reached first. Blondy Ryan was up.

Scores on Ryan's Single

Away back in the second inning Ryan had come up with the bases filled and had fanned. But now Blondy shortened his grip on his bat and poked a single past Kampouris. Chiozza dashed home with the first run of the game, and Danning took third.

There was none out. But when Castleman was through there were two out. He hit into a double play, erasing Ryan. Danning held third. It looked like a mistake at the time, but it turned out to be a good idea, because Whitehead dumped a single into right and Danning scored. Moore ended the inning with a fly to Kampouris.

Encouraged by this scoring, Castleman fanned Hafey and Virgil Davis in the twelfth and made Riggs pop up.

So the Giants gained another game on the league-leading Cubs. They are now half way between first place and third place—five games behind the Cubs and five ahead of the Pirates.

Grissom, a sturdy left-hander, had pitched five shutouts and thought he had his sixth. He was sure he could outlast and outpitch Castleman, but he was wrong. In the clinch, Grissom was first to weaken.

Reds Held to Eight Hits

Castleman yielded only eight hits. The boys helped him with four double plays. Not a Red reached third base and only three set foot on second.

Grissom was no less effective until the twelfth. Until then he had the Giants shut out with six hits. They made four in the twelfth.

The Cincinnati pitcher was lucky in the second when Leiber singled and Leslie doubled with one out. He walked Danning purposely and fanned Ryan and Castleman.

Only once thereafter until their winning inning did the Giants get a man as far as third base. Ott doubled and reached third in the sixth.

Castleman's toughest inning was the seventh when Virgil Davis doubled with one out and Riggs was walked purposely. This strategy worked. Kampouris hit a double-play ball and Ryan, Whitehead and Leslie made it.

So the Giants won the series two games to one and moved on to Pittsburgh for four games.

After Chiozza ran for Leslie, McCarthy played first base and Ripple took Berger's place in center to strengthen the defense.

George Davis, the Giant outfielder who was sold to the Reds yesterday, reported to his new club today. He would have played against his former teammates if a left-hander had pitched. The Reds now have three Davises, Spud, Peaches and Kiddo.

Ott made a neat play in the first inning to discourage the Reds from bunting at the corseted Castleman. Ott, playing third, sped behind the box and caught Walker's pop bunt and doubled Cuyler off first.

The score:

NEW YORK (N. L.)	ab	r	h	po	a	e	CINCINNATI (N. L.)	ab	r	h	po	a	e
W'head, 2b	6	0	1	2	5	0	Cuyler, rf..	5	0	1	0	0	0
Moore, lf...	6	0	1	2	0	0	Walker, lf..	4	0	0	5	0	0
Ott, 3b....	5	0	1	4	2	0	Sc'sella, 1b	5	0	1	9	0	1
Berger, cf..	5	0	0	2	0	0	Hafey, cf..	4	0	1	0	0	0
Ripple, cf..	0	0	0	1	0	0	W. D'vis, c	5	0	1	7	1	0
Leiber, rf..	5	0	1	3	0	0	Riggs, 3b..	4	0	1	2	0	0
Leslie, 1b..	4	0	3	11	0	0	Kam'ris, 2b	4	0	1	6	7	0
*Chiozza ..	0	1	0	0	0	0	Myers, ss..	4	0	1	7	9	1
McC'y, 1b..	0	0	0	0	0	0	GR'SOM, p	4	0	1	0	0	0
Danning, c.	4	1	2	7	2	0							
Ryan, ss...	4	0	1	4	5	0							
C'MAN, p..	5	0	0	0	0	0							
Totals...	44	2	10	36	14	0	Totals....	39	0	8	36	17	2

*Ran for Leslie in twelfth inning.

New York.... 000 000 000 002—2
Cincinnati.... 000 000 000 000—0

Runs batted in—Whitehead, Ryan. Two-base hits—Ott, Leslie (2), Danning, V. Davis. Double plays—Ott and Leslie; Whitehead, Ryan and Leslie (2); Ryan, Whitehead and Leslie; Myers, Kampouris and Scarsella (2); Kampouris, Myers and Scarsella. Left on bases—New York, 9; Cincinnati, 6. Bases on balls—Off Castleman, 3; off Grissom, 3. Struck out—By Castleman, 6; by Grissom, 7. Umpires—Ballanfant, Klem and Sears. Time—2:37.

Leading Five Batsmen In Each Major League

AMERICAN LEAGUE

Player and club	G.	AB.	R.	H.	Pct.
Travis, Washington.	70	276	40	107	.388
Gehrig, New York.	95	355	89	134	.378
DiMaggio, New York	89	373	99	138	.370
Gehringer, Detroit.	82	322	74	114	.354
Greenberg, Detroit.	93	352	87	124	.352

NATIONAL LEAGUE

Player and club	G.	AB.	R.	H.	Pct.
Medwick, St. Louis	94	374	81	151	.404
Hartnett, Chicago..	63	201	25	78	.388
P. Waner, Pittsb'h	94	380	67	142	.374
Mize, St. Louis....	88	334	55	119	.356
Herman, Chicago..	79	331	67	117	.354
Vaughan, Pittsburgh	77	297	44	105	.354

Home Runs		Runs Batted In	
DiMaggio, Yanks.	32	Greenb'g, Tigers.	108
Foxx, Red Sox..	28	DiMag'o, Yanks.	104
Gehrig, Yanks..	25	Medwick, Cards..	102
Greenb'g, Tigers.	25	Gehrig, Yanks..	98
Trosky, Indians.	23	Dickey, Yanks..	95

Orioles Pound 2 Pitchers, Beating Montreal, 10-5

BALTIMORE, Aug. 5 (AP).—The Baltimore Orioles made a clean sweep of their series with Montreal tonight, jumping on Lisenbee and Polli for a 10-to-5 victory. Carl Fischer, who started for the Orioles and contributed a homer and a single to the attack, was relieved in Montreal's big seventh by Harry Hatuzak, who held the Royals hitless the rest of the way.

Les Powers paced the Birds with a homer and a triple. Ab Wright hit his twenty-sixth home run of the season.

The score by innings:

R. H. E.
Montreal..... 101 000 300—5 10 1
Baltimore.... 111 410 20x—10 11 1

Batteries—Lisenbee, Polli and Kies; Fischer, Matuzak and Crouse.

Cards Connect For 11 Hits, but Bees Win, 4 to 1

Boston's 3 Double Plays Help MacFayden; Vince DiMaggio Gets a Homer

By The Associated Press

ST. LOUIS, Aug. 5.—The St. Louis Cardinals got eleven hits off Danny MacFayden today, but the Boston Bees' right-hander bore down in the tight spots and, aided by three double plays, pitched a 4-to-1 victory.

Pittsburgh lost, too, so the Cardinals remained tied for third place in the National League.

Vince DiMaggio, brother of siege-gun Joe of the New York Yankees, hit a home run for the Bees in the fourth inning. MacFayden put one tally across by laying down a squeeze bunt with Elb Fletcher on third in the seventh inning.

The score:

BOSTON (N. L.)	ab	r	h	po	a	e	ST. LOUIS (N. L.)	ab	r	h	po	a	e
R. J'son, lf.	4	0	0	5	0	0	T. M're, cf	4	0	2	4	1	0
Warstler, ss	5	0	0	5	3	0	S. M'tin, 2b	5	0	2	4	5	1
DiMaggio, cf	4	3	2	3	0	0	Mize, 1b...	4	0	1	10	1	0
C'nello, 2b.	4	0	1	1	4	0	M'wick, lf.	4	0	2	3	0	0
E. M're, rf.	2	0	0	2	0	0	Padgett, rf.	2	0	1	1	0	0
English, 3b	4	0	2	1	1	0	G'ridge, 3b.	4	0	0	2	3	0
Fl'cher, 1b.	4	1	2	8	1	0	Brown, ss..	4	0	0	1	1	1
Mueller, c..	2	0	1	1	0	0	Owen, c....	3	0	2	2	1	0
M'F'DEN, p	2	0	0	1	2	0	HAINES, p.	2	1	0	0	2	0
							H'RELL, p.	0	0	0	0	1	0
							*R. Moore.	1	0	0	0	0	0
							†J. Martin.	1	0	1	0	0	0
							‡Frisch	1	0	0	0	0	0
Totals....	31	4	8	27	11	0	Totals....	35	1	11	27	15	2

*Batted for Haines in seventh inning.
†Batted for Harrell in ninth inning.
‡Batted for T. Moore in ninth inning.

Boston.............. 000 101 110—4
St. Louis............ 000 010 000—1

Runs batted in—DiMaggio, S. Martin, English, MacFayden. Two-base hits—Medwick, Fletcher. Home run—DiMaggio. Sacrifices—Macfayden (2), Mueller (2). Double plays—English, Cuccinello and Fletcher; Cuccinello, Warstler and Fletcher; Warstler and Fletcher; Mize and Gutteridge. Left on bases—Boston, 7; St. Louis, 10. Bases on balls—Off Macfayden, 3; off Haines, 1; off Harrell, 2. Struck out—By Macfayden, 1; by Haines, 2. Hits—Off Haines, 7 in 7 innings; Harrell, 1 in 2. Losing pitcher—Haines. Umpires—Goetz, Reardon and Pinelli. Time—2:07.

Rochester Bows in Final Of Jersey City Series, 4-3

JERSEY CITY, N. J., Aug. 5 (AP).—Don Brennan's effective relief pitching gave the Jersey City Giants a 4-to-3 victory over the Rochester Red Wings in the final of a five-game series today.

The score:

ROCHESTER (I. L.)	ab	r	h	po	a	e	JERSEY CITY (I. L.)	ab	r	h	po	a	e
M'se, 2b, ss	5	0	0	0	2	0	Bluege, ss..	4	1	1	2	2	0
Juelich, 3b.	3	0	0	1	2	0	C. W'n, 3b.	4	1	1	0	1	0
C'lo, 3b, 2b	2	0	1	0	1	0	Lee, cf....	3	1	1	1	0	0
Hopp, rf, cf	3	0	1	3	0	0	W'traub, 1b	4	1	2	10	1	0
C'ee, cf, 3b	3	1	1	1	2	1	E. W'n, rf..	4	0	1	5	0	0
W'd, 1b, rf.	3	1	1	12	1	0	Blakely, lf.	4	0	1	0	0	0
R'ttger, 1b.	0	0	0	1	0	0	King, 2b...	3	0	0	2	3	0
Bl'kerby, lf	3	1	1	1	0	0	R'mond, c.	3	0	1	7	0	0
Poland, c..	3	0	0	5	2	0	BROWN, p.	1	0	0	0	1	0
Marion, ss.	3	1	1	0	1	0	BR'NAN, p.	1	0	0	0	1	0
*Kaufman..	1	0	0	0	0	0							
WHITE, p..	2	0	0	1	2	0							
†Judd	1	0	0	0	0	0							
KL'NKE, p	0	0	0	0	0	0							
‡O'Farrell..	1	0	0	0	0	0							
Totals....	33	3	7	24	11	0	Totals.....	31	4	8	27	9	0

*Batted for White in seventh inning.
†Batted for Marion in eighth inning.
‡Batted for Kleinke in ninth inning.

Rochester.......... 020 000 100—3
Jersey City.......... 200 002 00x—4

Runs batted in—Weintraub (3), Blackerby (2), Blakely, Cuccinello. Two-base hits—Weintraub, Crabtree. Three-base hits—Weintraub, Blakely, Cuccinello. Home run—Blackerby. Sacrifice—Brennan. Left on bases—Rochester, 8; Jersey City, 5. Bases on balls—Off Brennan, 3; off Kleinke, 1. Struck out—By Brown, 1; by White, 3; by Brennan, 4; by Kleinke, 1. Hits—Off Brown, 9 in 3 innings; off Brennan, 3 in 6; off White, 7 in 6; off Kleinke, 1 in 2. Hit by pitcher—By Brown (Hopp). Winning pitcher—Brennan. Losing pitcher—White. Umpires—Swanson, Weafer and Van Grafian. Time—2:02.

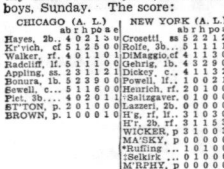

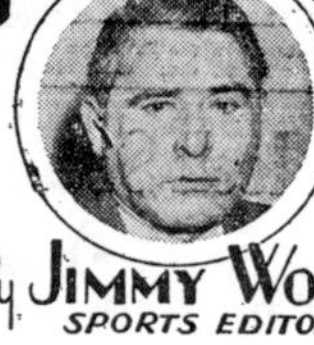

GRIMES TO MILWAUKEE

Latest on the Flatbush Front has it that Burleigh Grimes, probably through as Dodger manager, will manage Milwaukee in the American Association, where he'd succeed Alan Sothoron, if Burly doesn't connect with Montreal.

BROOKLYN EAGLE SPORTS

10 BROOKLYN, N. Y., SATURDAY, OCTOBER 8, 1938 W

MORE WORLD SERIES HISTORY

Much of the talk on the Yankee special that brought the Cubs' tormentors back from Chicago had to do with Lou Gehrig actually shaking Joe DiMaggio's hand after Joe hit that homer in the second game. Scribes who follow the club say it hasn't happened before.

Gordon and Henrich Make Yankees a Nightmare Team

Series Scene Shifts to Stadium

Manager Joe McCarthy of Yankees has right to smile after winning first two games of World Series in Chicago

But the smile on Manager Gabby Hartnett's face seems a bit misplaced with scene of activities moving to Yankee Stadium today

Percentages

The first two games of the current world series classic have been weird workouts for the experts. The Yankees crossed up the press coop by winning the opener on defensive skill. The Fancy Dan didoes of the McCarthymen had the seers all a-twitter. They had expected the Yanks to come out swinging and they came out dancing.

Then the second session found the Yanks reverting to type to confound the experts a second time. These reverse twists put a dent in the prestige of the predictors.

It's not enough to hat pin winners these days. The prediction must carry a blueprint explanation of how it's going to be done. The customers are too smart these days. They can pick as many winners as the experts, the cuties.

Of course, the experts and customers have long conceded that the Yanks are clutch hitters, that they can tee off on opposition pitching when clouts mean runs and runs mean victory.

True, the club was consistently under .280 through the pennant campaign, a sharp dip from the .300 years. But what can be done with a gang of game wreckers that has a Crosetti break up the party when the script calls for a Gehrig or a DiMaggio?

The Yanks of 1938 have proved that percentages run for the eminent Mr. Sweeny in world series play.

Dopey Dope

At best, batting averages make dopey dope. For example——

Since 1903 only four clubs topped .300 in world series play. Eight times in this span of blue ribbon classics teams have slipped under .200.

More emphatic is the fact that world series pitching has had a humiliating effect on batting averages since 1903. Some statistic stabber has calculated that the grand average is .240 for this long stretch, a level lower than that of the weakest club in either league over the last several seasons.

Prof. Connie Mack's Athletics hold the top and bottom batting mark. They dropped to an all-low of .161 against Matty and the Giants in 1905 and zoomed to the top-high of .316 against the Cubs in 1910.

Apparently, it isn't how a team hits, but when it hits, that counts the big test between the major

Cub Background

The Cubs have a colorless background in world series engagements since their last victory in 1908. After that festival of jubilation they won pennants in 1910, 1918, 1929, 1932 and 1935.

In five thrusts at the big money they have missed five times. Indeed, to date they've won only six games in this quintet of world series soirees, while their opposition was collecting 20 victories.

This isn't a sparkling mark of achievement for the citizenry of Chicago to whoop and chortle over, allowing that the Windy City taxpayers go in for whoops and chortles.

Even in the days of the Peerless Frank Chance the Cubs had their moments of despondency. There was that series of 1906, remember? The Cubs were top-heavy favorites to win in the quotations, but Fielder Jones' White Sox of Hitless Wonder fame, crushed them, four games to two.

But—

However, we were talking about percentages before the Cubs world series tale of woe somehow got mixed up in all this.

We started out to prove how little batting and fielding averages mean when the athletes come up to the big showdown.

We apologize fo rthe deviation and our tongue-tied attempt to point out the silliness of dealing with percentages in connection with the classic.

We apologize for the deviation mean as much as they should except that a peek at the composite box score for the first two games shows that the Yankees have batted a .279 against the Cubs .303 and the McCarthymen have fielded .963 against the Cubs .987. But the Yanks have two games in the bag and every one says they should win four straight. According to the figures there must be something askew somewhere.

Hall and Kynaston Clash in Net Final

Hot Springs, Va., Oct. 8 (AP)—J. Gilbert Hall, Manhattan, defending champion, and Percy Kynaston, Brooklyn, 1936 titleholder, meet today in the finals of the men's singles in the annual Hot Springs Fall Invitation Tennis Tournament.

Hall advanced to the finals yesterday by defeating Horace Orser, 6—1, 6—3.

In the finals of the women's singles Mrs. William V. Hester, Glen Cove, L. I., opposed Mary Cooles of Alexandria, Va. Mrs. Hester moved into the finals with a 7—5, 4—6, 8—6 triumph over Virginia Ellis.

Italy's Tax Disbursements

Special to the Brooklyn Eagle

ROME—Tax disbursements for the eight provinces of Italy for the week ending Oct. 8 were as follows, with figures representing thousands:

Naples	.60— 7—21—17—14
Bari	.31—57—66—45—58
Florence	.12—28—58—73— 7
Milan	.65—57— 7—52—61
Palermo	.11—67—65—76— 3
Rome	72—61—74— 4—30
Turin	.39—53—17—18—85
Venice	.82—28—85—46—62

Blues Refuse To Stay Licked

Little World Series With Bears Carried To 7-Game Limit

Kansas City, Oct. 8 (AP)—Because the Kansas City Blues don't know when they are licked, they will play the Newark Bears in the seventh and deciding game of the Little World Series here tonight (8 p.m., C. S. T.)

The Blues were down two games to one to Indianapolis in the American Association semi-final playoffs, then won three straight. They were down three to one to St. Paul in the finals, but again they won three straight.

They were down twice to Newark, International League champions, in the present series, 2 to 1, then 3 to 2, but last night they square dit with a 4 to 2 victory behind the steady pitching of Marvin Breuer.

Prolonging of the series left both Manager Bill Meyer of the Blues and Manager Johnny Neun of Newark somewhat up in the air as to starting hurlers.

Meyer was expected to send Kemp Wicker to the mound and Neun was slated to start Atley Donald, or possibly the steady Joe Beggs.

Wicker gave Kansas City its first victory in the series, 3 to 0, and hurled seven and two-thirds innings in the Blues' 9 to 8 victory Wednesday.

Donald has started twice for the Bears, and has been knocked from the box both times. If Beggs pitches, he will be making his second start in three days. He turned in two of the Newark victories, going the full route in each game.

Breuer's hurling, some timely hitting, and some sensational fielding tell the story of the Blue victory last night. Kansas City drove Jack Haley from the mound and scored three runs in the fourth inning after the Bears had picked up a score in the third. It was a dogfight the rest of the way with Walter Judnich, Blue center fielder, providing a fitting climax with a spectacular one-handed running catch for the final out in the ninth to nip a budding Newark rally.

Kansas City, Oct. 8 (AP)—Attendance and distribution of receipts of the Little World Series:

	6th Game.	Total 6th Game
Attendance	6,304	56,760
Receipts	$4,985.37	$43,887.48
Nat'l Ass'n	149.56	1,316.62
Commission	725.37	6,385.62
Newark Club	2,055.22	8,695.36
Kansas City Club	2,055.22	8,695.37
Player share		18,794.51

Shannon to Head Baseball Writers

Paul Shannon of the Boston Post was elected president of the Baseball Writers' Association of America at the annual World Series meeting today. He succeeds Irving Vaughan of the Chicago Tribune.

Charles J. Doyle of the Pittsburgh Sun-Telegraph was elected vice president and Henry P. Edwards of the American League Service Bureau was re-elected secretary-treasurer.

Four new directors chosen were Tom Swope, Cincinnati Post, J. Roy Stockton, St. Louis Post-Dispatch, John Drohan, Boston Traveler, and Francis Stan, Washington Star.

Writers Name Their Own No. 1 National Heel

Last night was the big night of the year when the ears of our nation's master minds of the sports writing business burned like the great Chicago fire. During every World Series, the boys cease firing their blasts at fellows like Bill Terry and vote to see who among them should be named to the All-America Heel Society.

By mutual agreement of the right guys and the wrong guys, no names are ever given out for you readers of the sports pages to see. It's a secret among those in the profession but the boys feel it's revenue enough to get a pet hate listed among the Heels, who leave the electoral meetings with a crimson blush and fury in their hearts.

Eclipse Dixie Speeches

No campaign speeches down in Dixie can eclipse those of the experts when they arise and nominate so and so of their flock as the All-America wrong guy No. 1. The speeches last from two seconds to an hour and the tabulation of votes is written on a white table cloth, usually signed later by Al Schacht, baseball's clown prince. The chairman of the meeting is the fellow who talks the loudest or gets into the hall first. Finally, a list of ten is made up with the usual rankings.

Qualifications to make the All-America Heel lineup are the same as in your business. There's a Heel in every office, warehouse, big store and country club. Maybe you're it only your best enemies won't come out and put it down in writing on tablecloths like the hardy, outspoken fellows who write sports.

I don't know who thought up the gag of voting on the list, but the three fellows most generally accredited with the idea are Westbrook Pegler and Paul Gallico, who have deserted the field, and Warren Brown, sports editor of the Chicago Herald and Examiner, one of the most popular and able scribes who ever put two and two together.

So far not a single fist fight has resulted from the nominating speeches and voting, though bitter verbal battles have been waged by pals sticking up for pals. There is danger at all times, if you don't stick up for a friend and somebody notices it, you're apt to find yourself on the list somewhere in sixth or seventh place.

Got Himself Nominated

Last year, a prominent sports editor got to his feet and made an eloquent speech nominating a fellow who then worked for him. Right in the middle of it, he was heckled and then stopped by a wit who shouted:

"Any guy who nominates one of his helpers qualifies. I nominate so and so for position No. 1."

Positions 1 to 7 already were filled so he got eighth place by almost unanimous approval. He slinked out of the hall just as quietly as the Cubs left Chicago for New York last night after losing two straight to the Yankees.

Try it some time.

Third Game Lineup

The probable lineup and batting order for the third game of the World Series, which will be played at the Yankee Stadium tomorrow, is as follows:

YANKEES	CUBS
Crosetti, ss	Hack, 3b
Rolfe, 3b	Herman, 2b
Henrich, rf	Demaree, rf
DiMaggio, cf	Marty, cf
Gehrig, 1b	Reynolds, lf
Dickey, c	Hartnett, c
Selkirk, lf	Collins, 1b
Gordon, 2b	Jurgess, ss
Pearson, p	Bryant, p

Umpires—Sears (N. L.), plate; Hubbard (A. L.), first base; Moran (N. L.), second base; Kolls (A. L.), third base.

Crosetti Gets His Due From Joe McCarthy

That Crosetti at shortstop, said Marse Joe McCarthy, is quite a ball player.

There was no one who could disagree with the lantern-jawed manager and master-mind of the Yankees, when he referred thus glowingly to the crack shortstop and backbone of his infield, Frankie Crosetti.

"And," added Marse Joe, "he is undoubtedly the outstanding star of the series so far."

Here again, his listeners agreed unanimously. But it was so unlike McCarthy to single out for praise any one player of the closely-knit unit that is the Yanks, that all concerned were somewhat taken aback.

What Else Could He Say?

Still, when you reconsider, Joe couldn't very well say anything else. There's no secret about the pact that the slim, dark Crosetti was the defensive sparkplug who saved the first game of the current World Series against the Chicago Cubs, and no one can deny that his two-run eighth-inning homer ruined a masterful pitching performance by Dizzy Dean in the second game to put the Yanks two up in the classic as they head into the third tilt today.

So, you inquire around about this Crosetti. Here's a fellow, 28 years old, who has never, in seven years with the Yankees, since coming up from San Francisco, been a dangerous hitter. His lifetime batting average is under .260. He's a swell fellow personally, and all that, but he's the lone member of the Yankee cast who most definitely is lacking in the power hitting that makes the home run almost indispensable to the equipment of all aspirants to membership in the firm of Gehrig & Company.

So the Yankees, who rarely waste time on the lads with nothing on the ball, have kept him around.

Composite Box Score of Series

NEW YORK YANKEES (A. L.)

	G	AB	R	H	2B	3B	HR	RBI	BB	SO	PCT	PO	A	E	PCT
Crosetti, ss.	2	8	1	2	1	0	1	2	0	2	.250	9	9	0	1.000
Rolfe, 3b	2	9	0	1	0	0	0	0	0	2	.111	0	3	2	.600
Henrich, rf.	2	8	2	3	1	0	0	0	0	1	.375	2	0	1	.667
DiMaggio, cf.	2	8	2	2	0	0	1	2	0	0	.250	6	0	0	1.000
Gehrig, 1b	2	6	2	2	0	0	0	0	2	3	.333	16	0	0	1.000
Dickey, c.	2	8	1	4	0	0	0	1	0	0	.500	12	5	0	1.000
Selkirk, lf.	2	7	0	2	0	0	0	1	1	0	.286	1	0	0	1.000
Powell, lf.	1	0	0	0	0	0	0	0	0	0	.000	0	0	0	.000
Gordon, 2b.	2	8	0	3	2	0	0	3	0	2	.375	8	5	0	1.000
Ruffing, p.	1	3	0	0	0	0	0	0	0	0	.000	0	1	0	1.000
Gomez, p.	1	2	0	0	0	0	0	0	0	0	.000	0	1	0	1.000
Murphy, p.	1	0	0	0	0	0	0	0	0	0	.000	0	0	0	.000
xHoag	1	1	1	0	0	0	0	0	0	0	.000	0	0	0	.000
Totals	2	68	9	19	4	0	2	9	3	10	.279	54	24	3	.963

x Batted for Gomez in 8th inning, second game.

CHICAGO CUBS (N. L.)

	G	AB	R	H	2B	3B	HR	RBI	BB	SO	PCT	PO	A	E	PCT
Hack, 3b.	2	9	2	5	0	0	0	1	0	1	.556	1	4	0	1.000
Herman, 2b.	2	8	1	2	0	0	0	0	0	2	.250	3	10	1	.929
Demaree, lf-rf.	2	7	0	1	0	0	0	0	0	2	.143	3	0	0	1.000
xxCavarretta, cf.	2	5	0	3	0	0	0	0	0	1	.600	1	1	0	1.000
Marty, cf.	1	4	0	3	1	0	0	3	0	0	.750	2	0	0	1.000
Reynolds, cf-lf.	2	7	0	0	0	0	0	0	1	1	.000	7	0	0	1.000
Hartnett, c.	2	7	0	1	0	1	0	0	0	1	.143	11	2	0	1.000
Collins, 1b.	2	7	1	2	0	0	0	0	0	1	.286	20	1	0	1.000
Jurges, ss.	2	6	0	1	0	0	0	0	1	2	.167	5	4	0	1.000
Lee, p.	1	2	0	0	0	0	0	0	0	0	.000	1	0	0	1.000
Russell, p.	0	0	0	0	0	0	0	0	0	0	.000	0	0	0	.000
Dean, p.	1	3	0	2	0	0	0	0	0	0	.667	0	2	0	1.000
French, p.	1	0	0	0	0	0	0	0	0	0	.000	0	0	0	.000
xO'Dea	1	1	0	0	0	0	0	0	0	0	.000	0	0	0	.000
Totals	2	66	4	20	1	1	0	4	2	11	.303	54	24	1	.987

x Batted for Lee in 8th inning, first game.
xx Batted for French in 9th inning, second game.

PITCHING RECORDS

	G	CG	IP	H	R	ER	BB	SO	WP	HB	W	L	PCT
YANKEES													
Ruffing	1	1	9	9	1	1	0	5	0	0	1	0	1.000
Gomez	1	0	7	9	3	3	1	5	0	0	1	0	1.000
Murphy	1	0	2	2	0	0	1	1	0	0	0	0	.000
CUBS													
Lee	1	0	8	11	3	3	1	6	0	1	0	1	.000
Russell	1	0	1	1	0	0	0	0	0	0	0	0	.000
Dean	1	0	8	7	6	6	1	2	0	0	0	1	.000
French	1	0	1	0	0	0	1	2	0	0	0	0	.000

COMPOSITE SCORE BY INNINGS:

Yankees	0	4	0	0	0	1	0	2	2—9
Cubs	1	0	3	0	0	0	0	0	0—4

Earned runs—Yankees, 9; Cubs, 4. Stolen base—Dickey. Sacrifices—Ruffing, Demaree. Double plays—Yankees, 4 (Crosetti and Gehrig; Crosetti, Gordon and Gehrig (2); Gordon, Crosetti and Gehrig. Cubs, 3 (Jurges, Herman and Collins; Collins, unassisted; Herman, Jurges and Collins. Left on bases—Yankees, 10; Cubs, 11. Umpires—Moran and Sears (N. L.); Kolls and Hubbard (A. L.). Times of Games—First, 1:53; second, 1:53.

Jimmy Wilson Believed 'In' As Flock Pilot

By BILL McCULLOUGH

The early morning special on the race for the Dodger management is bet Jimmy Wilson to win. But Larry MacPhail still sticks to his policy of saying nothing.

Speaking of Brooklyn managers, Max Carey put in his first appearance of this World Series at the Hotel Commodore last night, blowing in straight from his citrus ranch in Florida.

Joe Marty's three hits and three runs batted in Thursday resulted in the first departure of either team from their ordinary regular lineups. Normally, Marty starts in the Cub outfield only when left-handers throw against the Bruins. But he was to play centerfield today, Gabby Hartnett announced, regardless.

The partially bald dome of slender Frank Crosetti basks in the limelight of heroism for the current baseball campus to date. The San Francisco Italian has been a fine ball player for years, yet World Series heroics are something new for him.

He wore the long ears of a goat back in 1932 when he played in the classic against the Cubs, making four errors in one game to set a World Series record. And last year he produced only one base hit in the five games against the Giants.

Few realize it, but only three Yankee regulars aside from pitchers were regulars on Col. Ruppert's championship team of '32. Lou Gehrig, of course. And Bill Dickey. And the third durable Yankee veteran is Crosetti, who celebrated his 28th birthday on Tuesday, the day before the series started. He has been celebrating it ever since, too.

Patchogue Eleven Nips Huntington

Patchogue, Oct. 8—The Patchogue High Red Raiders nosed out Huntington here last night, 7—0. The Huntington eleven, fighting with its back to the wall during the greater part of the game, showed a marked improvement over last week, when they bowed to Sayville, 13—9.

Patchogue scored in the second quarter when Carter Kyle took one of Butt's punts on his own 45-yard line and fought his way through the entire Huntington eleven to cross the goal line standing up. Mazzotti converted the extra point.

Huntington threatened late in the second half when Butt began heaving passes to Avon for gain after gain. A sure score by Huntington was muffed when a pass from Butt to L'Hommedeau went for naught as the latter was tripped on Patchogue 10-yard line by one of his own men. Patchogue put up a stonewall defense and stopped the march of the North Shore eleven.

Wiffy Cox Retains D. of C. Golf Title

Washington, Oct. 8 (AP)—Wiffy Cox of Washington came from behind to defend his District of Columbia open golf championship yesterday with a 286 total, six over par for the 72 holes at Washington Golf and Country Club.

The early leader, Al Houghton of Old Point Comfort, Va., wound up in second place with 288. Cox shot the last 27 holes in one under par to overhaul the Virginian. His rounds were 72—70 against Houghton's 75—71.

It Hurts Game Gabby to Eat

But He Would Rather Die Than Not Catch For Cubs in Series

Hartnett's hand is so badly banged up that it hurts him to lift a forkful of steak to his lips. But Gabby would rather die than not go behind the plate for the Cubs.

It didn't make the Cubs feel any better that Mr. Marcellus Monte Pearson, the curve ball specialist, was slated to go for the Yankees today, is a native of Oakland, Cal. California Yankees—Crosetti, DiMaggio, Gordon and Gomez—have been poison for the National Leaguers since this thing began.

Extremely satisfied with what has happened so far, Joe McCarthy decided not to practice at the big Bronx stadium yesterday. Hartnett finally decided against it even though the Cubs haven't played there since 1932.

"The rest will do us more good than the workout," said Hartnett. "After all, with that finish in the National League race, we've been under pressure for a long while."

The Dodgers didn't sign a manager yesterday, but a Dodger became a manager. Coach Tom Sheehan signed to handle the Minneapolis ball club and departs with the best of wishes of Larry MacPhail and Co. Sheehand succeeds Donie Bush, who shifted from Minneapolis to Louisville, now a farm of the Red Sox, a couple of weeks ago.

Al Schacht's act, missing in Chicago, will be a welcome feature of the games in New York. Al's only regret is that he didn't know in time enough to arrange an act proving that Gene Tunney is right in his contention that a good man can lick a gorilla.

BILL McCULLOUGH.

Mrs. Untermeyer Wins Jersey Title

Plainfield, N. J., Oct. 8—Playing courageously, despite an injury suffered early in the match, Miss Gail Wild of Baltusrol was defeated, 7 and 5, yesterday in the 36-hole final of the women's New Jersey State golf championship by Mrs. DeWitt Untermeyer of Hollywood.

Miss Wild, daughter of the late Eddie Wild, New Jersey golf immortal, injured herself on the third hole this morning. As she fired a shot from the tee on the par 3 hole, she winced with pain.

Miss Wild played on through the morning round and during the luncheon respite a physician was called to the clubhouse. He said Miss Wild had pulled a tendon over a weak muscle in her side and advised her not to continue with the match.

Mrs. Untermeyer was willing to postpone the final 18, but the officials said it would be impossible to call off the round or to put over the second half.

Champs' Reign Taking Fun Out of Game

Replacements Ready In Minor Leagues Add to the Alarm

By TOMMY HOLMES

It is extremely easy to lose one's self in sheer admiration of the ball team put on the field by the brewery millions of Col. Jacob Ruppert and so shrewdly directed by the broad-beamed Mr. Joe McCarthy. But it is also easy to be disturbed by the might of the merciless Yankees.

Winners of three straight American League flags, two up and two to go in their quest of a third straight world's championship, the free and easy bombers of the Bronx have dominated the game for a long while.

Frightens Common People

For the common people, baseball is going to cease to be fun if the Yankees hold their outstanding position much longer. But what are the common people and the rest of the major leagues going to do about it so long as the Yankees continue to produce young ball players like Joe Gordon and Tommy Henrich?

Gordon and Henrich are the kids of the team. Gordon has just finished his first season in the major leagues. Henrich was with the club last year but sat on the bench while the Yankees were beating the Giants in the World Series. So both youngsters are playing in their first baseball classic. One might add: "And how!"

Before the third series game in the Yankee Stadium this afternoon, both Gordon and Henrich sport batting averages of .375 against Chicago pitching. Defensively, both kids have been impressive with Gordon's second base play verging on the brilliant.

All of which is swell stuff but the trouble is that the Yankees seem likely to produce an endless procession of talented boys. Gordon, the 24-year-old Californian, who has moved in so brilliantly to replace the canny Tony Lazzeri, and Henrich, the curly-haired 22-year-old from Massillon, Ohio, whose left handed batting action at the plate is as smooth a thing as you would care to see, may be only the vanguard.

Keller and Rosar Ready

Suppose McCarthy decides to replace George Selkirk, the veteran left fielder, next year? Probably, King Kong Keller, who for two years the most dreaded slugger in the minors, can move right in and the Yankees will not even falter in their stride. Then there is Joe Gallagher, another red-hot young outfielder at Kansas City.

A great all-around catcher like Bill Dickey would seem irreplaceable. But the Yankees can replace him, although perhaps not entirely. But if Dickey should be injured, the McCarthy men could probably win a pennant with Newark's Buddy Rosar, who led the International League in hitting, behind the plate.

Some one remarked on the Yankee special that no player prominently placed in the Yankee farm organization who shows great promise of being an outstanding big league first baseman. Lou Gehrig hasn't missed a game at first base for the Yankees in more than 13 days. Still, the time may come.

"Well," said Mr. Art Fletcher, "you should see Henrich play first base. He's a big league star at that position if we need him there."

Tinker Arrested In Gambling Raid

Orlando, Fla., Oct. 8 (AP)—Sheriff Frank Karel said he arrested Joe Tinker, former major league baseball star, yesterday, on a charge of operating a bolita gambling house. Karel said Tinker, of the famous "Tinker-to-Evers-to-Chance" combination, was released under $300 bond.

Bolita—Spanish for "little ball"—is a game played in this section of the country by tossing a sack of numbered balls among the participants. The winning ball is selected by grasping it from the outside of the sack.

Nine other persons were arrested with Tinker, Sheriff Karel said. Tinker has been a resident of Orlando for the past several years and has been prominent in local sporting circles. Karel, who led the raid on the establishment, said Tinker had his hand on some bolita tickets resting on a table when officers entered. A quantity of gambling equipment was seized, the sheriff reported.

Budge and Kukuljevic Lose Doubles Match

Berkeley, Cal., Oct. 8 (AP)—Gene Smith, Oakland High School teacher, who eliminated Adrian Quist, Australian star, from the Pacific Coast tennis tournament here, joined Bobbie Harmon of Berkeley yesterday and defeated Don Budge, Oakland, and Franjo Kukuljevic of Yugoslavia, in the doubles.

The score was 6—4, 3—6, 6—0.

Budge, playing in the third round of the men's singles, however, conquered Robert Peacock of Berkeley, 7—5, 6—4, and today meets his first real singles test of the tournament when he plays Ronald Shayes of the English Davis Cup team in a fourth round match.

Joins the Scouts

Baton Rouge, La., Oct. 8 (AP)—A. L. Swanson, coach and scout, has succeeded J. B. (Ears) Whitworth as Louisiana State's flying gridiron spy. Whitworth estimated he traveled 25,000 miles watching Tiger rivals last season. But now he's the line coach and so the job has been turned over to Swanson.

BROOKLYN EAGLE SPORTS

M2 BROOKLYN, N. Y., SUNDAY, OCTOBER 9, 1938 SECTION D

G-Man's Son a Gridder

Washington, Oct. 8 (AP)—Vic Turrou, backfield candidate on George Washington University's football team, is the son of the former G-man, Leon Turrou, who recently resigned from the Federal service after rounding up alleged German spies.

Columbia Tops Army, 20-18 — Dartmouth Drubs Princeton, 22-0

Yanks Take Third Straight, 5 to 2

Roguish Girl, 12 to 1 Shot, Captures the Continental Handicap

Last-Period Score Gives Lions Victory

Luckman Again Stars As Cadets Crumble After Leading, 12-0

By HAROLD PARROTT
Staff Correspondent of the Brooklyn Eagle

West Point, Oct. 8—Army's legions, from brigadier general to the lowliest kitchen swab, had the purple heebee-jeebees tonight at the very thought of the 20-to-18 ball game Columbia snatched from them and the time clock this afternoon in their own Michie Stadium.

The Cadets, looking like one of the country's great teams, had marched to a touchdown in the first three minutes and stunned the embattled Lions with another touchdown nine minutes later for a 12—0 lead. The critics began to compose rave notices as the gold-helmeted herd, striking sharply and defending zealously, compiled an 18—6 lead at the half.

But that was before Brooklyn's Mr. Sid Luckman, who hides a howitzer up his right sleeve, started to blast the Cadets out of their seemingly impregnable position.

Luckman's nose had been rubbed in the dirt thoroughly and ceaselessly through the first half by Army's crashing line, but there was always a smile on his face and fight in his heart. He was there at the finish with the score 18 to 13 against him to hang a third-down pass on a peg for Johnny Siegal to grab on Army's two with exactly five minutes left. Gerry Seidel punched through for the touchdown and Luckman added his second extra point of the afternoon to seal Army's doom.

It was a rip-snorter of a ball game and Columbia's outlook, mighty opaque in spots, never looked blacker than just before the dawn of victory.

Art Radvilas, hard-running Columbia back, took a Luckman pass on Army's 19 with six minutes of the game left and went down with a terrific thump. When he got up he had to leave the game and on the second play following that Johnny Naylor, running in Radvilas' spot, lost five precious yards. Then it seemed that Columbia's last-gasp drive, carrying from its own 20 with unmitigated fury, was doomed to failure. But that was before Luckman loosed that game-changing aerial shot to Siegal.

Today fate did a queer about-face, for the two extra points which Luckman kicked offset the ones Art Walde missed for the Lions last year as they were sunk, 21 to 18.

Frontczak Misses Two

Art Frontczak, Cadet back, missed two place kicks after touchdown today, Charley Long hit the bar with another heartbreaker and then Long, late in the game, failed in a field-goal try from his own 8. When this effort to seal the verdict went awry for the Cadets the Lions, their howl of pain gradually turning to one of conquest, took the ball on their 20 and marched like winners to the clinching score.

Army, running overland for heavy mileage early in the game behind the fiercest blocking an Eastern gridiron has seen in many a moon, shook Woody Wilson, who runs like a scared hare, loose for two touchdowns in the first quarter. Each time Wilson, faking a pass, circled right end. The first time he unwound a 49-yard sprint and the second time it was for ten yards.

The second Army touchdown was a heartbreaker for the Lions. They had just fought themselves out of one nasty hole on their own 13 where Army marched from its own 32, ripping off four first downs on six swift plays by Schwenk, Long and Wilson.

After stalling Army on the 13 and taking the ball, the Lions lost it again when Seidel fumbled on his ten on the first play, Little recovering. Wilson then did his stuff,

Continued on Page 3

Blow That Rocked Bryant

Joe Gordon, Yankee rookie, crossing plate after hitting homer off Bryant in fifth inning to tie score. It was hit of game for Yanks and started Ruppert Rifles on way to third straight World Series victory at Yankee Stadium yesterday, 5 to 2. (Wide World Photo).

Penn Downs Yale by 21-0

Reagan Leads Quaker With 2 Touchdowns Before 50,000

Philadelphia, Oct. 8 (U.P.)—Pennsylvania battered Yale into humiliating defeat, 21-0, before 50,000 fans at Franklin Field today in their traditional gridiron battle.

It was the first time since the Georgia game in 1933 that Yale had been held scoreless. It also was Penn's second victory over the Eli eleven in the 18 times they have met.

Bud Humphrey, Yale's passing star, was bottled up all afternoon by the Penn ends but was outstanding in the backfield. Bill John, the big Blue left tackle, was the sparkplug of the Yale line.

Penn picked up 257 yards by rushing and held Yale to 63 yards. Few passes were thrown by the victors but Yale took to the airways on 31 plays, gaining 132 yards in this department.

Frank Reagan led the Penn scorers with two touchdowns and big Jim Connell tallied the other. Captain Walt Shinn place-kicked all three extra points.

Reagan set up the opening period score by intercepting a Yale pass on the Yale 34 yard line. He carried the ball to the two yard line before he was knocked out of bounds. Connell then plunged over the line. Shinn kicked the point.

Neither team scored in the second session. The breaks set up Penn's third-quarter rally. Crashing ends hit Humphreys as he cocked his passing arm and Penn recovered his fumble on Yale's 29. Connell gained

Continued on Page 3

Esposa Runs Outside As Roguish Girl Wins

By W. C. VREELAND

In a surprising turn over of form, Benjamin Dentch's Roguish Girl, 106 pounds and with Apprentice Yarberry at the reins, held 20,000 racing fans almost speechless by running off with the $8,750 prize of the Continental Handicap, one mile and three sixteenths, at odds of 12 to 1 at the Jamaica track yesterday.

Behind the five-year-old daughter of Roguish Eye, Bull Lea, carrying 119 pounds and Anderson in the saddle, was second, three parts of a length away and a length and a half in front of Idle Miss, 116 pounds, Robertson as her pilot. Idie Miss was favorite at 13 to 5. The time, 1:45, was 2 3-5 seconds behind the record.

Favored with only 106 pounds, a decided contrast to the big weights she had carried in her previous three races, when she was beaten, Roguish Girl practically made all the running. When not in front she was forcing the pace.

Well handled by Yarberry, who put over a "triple" with the victory —he had won the first and second races with Cobe, 5 to 2, and No Ending, 12 to 1, respectively—Roguish Girl, breaking seventh at the start, pinched through a gap next to the rail behind Galapas, the leader, while Anderson was opening up the space that later gave the winning advantage to Roguish Girl.

Galapas did not last long as the pacemaker. Roguish Girl, by fairly hugging the rail, caught and passed him when the backstretch was reached, and gradually gained an advantage till her tail was flicking in front of his nose.

Bull Lea was third, racing under a pull, a length and a half away and four lengths in front of Idle Miss, who was a big gap in front of Can't Wait.

On the turn out of the backstretch Bull Lea moved up fast on the out-

Continued on Page 3

Cornell Wallops Harvard, 20-0

Cambridge, Mass., Oct. 8 (U.P.)—Cornell's rugged eleven continued its bid for high honors by durbbing an improved Harvard team, 20 to 0, before a crowd of 25,000 today.

Three touchdowns were rung up on long runs, the first in the opening quarter when Mal Baker sprinted 75 yards, the second in the third period when Harold McCulough dashed 70 yards, and the final one in the last quarter when George Prek ran 50 yards.

Outweighed 16 pounds to the man, Harvard fought valiantly when their goal line was threatened, only to have its courageous stands nullified by long runs.

Cornell's first touchdown came on the fourth play of the game and on Cornell's first offensive. On a fake reverse, Baker sliced off right tackle, swung toward the sideline and crossed the goal line after thrice shaking off Harvard tacklers.

The second touchdown resulted

Continued on Page 4

Gabby Benches Himself Today

O'Dea to Do Catching For Cubs in Battle With Backs to Wall

By BILL McCULLOUGH

The world champion Yankees took yesterday's 5 to 2 triumph in stride. There was no jubilation in the clubhouse. The Yanks would have been surprised if they had lost.

"Bryant pitched good ball, but I knew we would catch up with him," McCarthy said. "Now that we have won three straight, I'll go with Ruffing today. We want four in a row."

"Pearson was nervous at the start," Dickey said. He was trying too hard. He walked two in the first inning, but after the fifth Monte got mad. He fanned Reynolds and Marty on nine pitches."

"This is a great ball club," Gehrig confided. "Somebody always delivers. Joe Gordon is a star of the first water. When the Cubs knock

Continued on Page 4

Indian Backs Run Wild in Second Half

Hutchinson, MacLeod And Howe Score On Long Gallops

By HAROLD CONRAD
Staff Correspondent of the Brooklyn Eagle

Princeton, Oct. 8—Dartmouth's zephyr-like backfield was too fast and too elusive for Princeton's heavier combination here today as the Indians raced to a 22-0 victory over the Tigers. Some 35,000 turned out for the 19th battle between the two ivy teams which was enhanced by ideal weather.

The Dartmouth backs didn't really get started until the second half, but a field goal by Bill Hutchinson, New York City boy from Monroe High School, in the first few minutes of play gave them an early lead. Tom Mountain's talented toe saved the Princeton forces a lot of embarrassment. Two of his sensational kicks almost led to Tiger touchdowns.

Three minutes after the whistle started the second half Colby Howe dashed through a hole at right tackle, eluded two secondaries and sprinted 55 yards down the right side of the field to score. Hutchinson converted.

Six plays later, Hutchinson found the same opening at right tackle and aided by some perfect blocking, ran 68 yards down the same track Howe made for the second score. This time he missed the kick for the extra point.

Princeton's burly line held the Dartmouth speed merchants at bay for a spell and they went into the final period trailing, 16 to 0, but a few minutes after the teams swapped ends of the field the Indians raised their total to 22.

The Hanoverites went to work on their own 17, ripped to the 28 when Bob McLeod dashed around left end for a first down. An aerial, Cotton to MacLeod, brought Dartmouth up to Princeton's 46. Cotton tried another pass on the next play but it was incomplete. He clicked on the next try, however, MacLeod snaring a 10-yard heave and running the remaining 36 yards to score. Gibson missed the try for the extra point when his kick hit the post.

Princeton claimed MacLeod put one foot out of bounds on his touchdown dash, and it looked very much as though he did, but the officials overruled the complaint.

In the closing minutes of play Coach Tad Wieman rushed Stan Pearson into the game. Pearson, a sophomore, is one of the Tiger's ace passers. He clicked for three short ones but the Tigers bogged down and made no more threats.

Both teams were even on first downs with 10 apiece, but the Indians practically tripled the Tigers' output on rushing with 301 yards to 104. Princeton completed eight passes out of 22 and Dartmouth five out of 12.

Pos.	Princeton	Dartmouth
L.E.	Dahiel	Miller
L.T.	Tierney	Dilkes
L.G.	Herring	Young
C.	Casey	Gibson
R.G.	Worth	Zitrides
R.T.	Bokum	Feeley
R.E.	Stanley	Parks
Q.B.	Jackson	Courter
L.H.	Allerdice	Hutchinson
R.H.	Mountain	MacLeod
F.B.	Lane	Howe

Dartmouht	3	0	13	6	—22
Princeton	0	0	0	0	— 0

Touchdowns: Howe, Hutchinson, MacLeod. Points after touchdowns: Hutchinson. Field goal: Hutchinson. Substitutes: Dartmouth — Ends: Wakelin, Larigan, Weaver, Nissen, Kelley; tackles: Dostal, Somners, Armanini, Guenther, May; guards, Highmark, Mills, Klein; center: Lempke; backs: Nopper, Orr, Kreiger, Cottone, Norton, Bauman, Hayden, Hall. Princeton: Ends: Meyerholz, Longstreth, Aubrey, Raymond; tackles, Cathles, Purnell; guards; Robinson, Tschudy, Cowan; centers: Alger, Newman; backs: Harper, Wells, McCormick, Hinchman, White, Dixon, Pearson, Teirman, Perina, Van Lengen.

Pearson Fans 9 Cubs; Gordon, Dickey, Marty Smash Circuit Clouts

Official Box Score

CHICAGO (N. L.)	AB.	R.	H.	O.	A.
Hack, 3b.	3	1	1	2	0
Herman, 2b.	3	0	0	1	1
Cavarretta, rf.	4	0	1	2	0
Marty, cf.	4	1	3	3	0
Reynolds, lf.	4	0	0	0	0
Hartnett, c.	4	0	0	3	1
Collins, 1b.	4	0	0	8	0
Jurges, ss.	3	0	0	5	3
Lazzeri, xx	1	0	0	0	0
Bryant, p.	2	0	0	0	0
Russell, p.	0	0	0	0	0
Galan, x	1	0	0	0	0
French, p.	0	0	0	0	2
O'Dea, xxx	1	0	0	0	0
Totals	34	2	5	24	7

xBatted for Russell in seventh.
xxBatted for Jurges in ninth.
xxxBatted for French in ninth.

NEW YORK (A. L.)	AB.	R.	H.	O.	A.
Crosetti, ss.	3	0	0	1	0
Rolfe, 3b.	4	0	1	0	1
Henrich, rf.	4	0	0	3	0
DiMaggio, cf.	3	1	1	1	0
Gehrig, 1b.	4	1	1	4	1
Dickey, c.	3	1	1	12	0
Selkirk, lf.	3	0	0	2	0
Gordon, 2b.	4	1	2	2	3
Pearson, p.	3	1	1	2	0
Totals	31	5	7	27	5

Cubs	0	0	0	0	1	0	0	1	0	—2
Yanks	0	0	0	0	2	2	0	1	x	—5

Errors—Crosetti, Gordon, Herman. Runs batted in—Marty 2, Gordon 3, Rolfe, Dickey. Two-base hit—Hack. Home runs—Gordon, Marty, Dickey. Earned runs—Chicago (N. L.), 1; New York (A. L.), 5. Left on bases —Chicago (N. L.), 7; New York (A. L.), 8. Bases on balls—Pearson 2 (Hack, Herman), Bryant 5 (DiMaggio, Dickey, Crosetti 2, Selkirk); Russell 1 (Pearson). Struck out—Pearson 9 (Reynolds 2, Hartnett, Collins, Jurges, Herman 2, Bryant, Hack); Bryant 3 (Crosetti, Selkirk, Gordon). Pitching summary—Off Bryant, 4 runs, 6 hits, in 5 1-3 innings; Russell, 0 runs, 0 hits, in 2-3 innings; French, 1 run, 1 hit, in 2 innings. Losing pitcher—Bryant. Umpires—Sears (N. L.), at plate; Hubbard (A. L.), first; Moran (N. L.), second; Kolls (A. L.), third. Time, 1:57.

Continued From Page One, Main Section

struck out no fewer than seven Chicago batters. Bryant, mixing a fine fast ball with an ocacsional curve and an effective change of pace, had not allowed the Yankees a hit. But, as in the case of Dizzy Dean in Chicago on Thursday, the crowd wondered how long the hard-hitting Yankees could be kept so completely in command. At any moment, the explosion might occur. What professional gamblers call the percentage of the situation was all against the Cubs.

Cubs' Run Arous esaYnks

The Cubs scored a run in the fifth inning. That seemed to be their mistake. Their success merely aroused the Yankees. It especially aroused young Gordon, who nonchalantly erredon an easy ground ball to aid the Chicago score.

Bryant retired the first two New York hitters in the last of the fifth, then Gordon stepped to the plate swinging for the fences. One long flye to left field was just outside the foul line for what the boys call a "loud strike." Then Gordon hit an-

Series Figures

Total for three games:

Attendance	140,986
Receipts	$624,720
Players' pool	318,607
Commissioner's share	93,708
Clubs' and leagues' share	212,404

other and this time the ball was fair, sailing over the distressed head of Left Fielder Carl Reynolds and into theg randstand seats.

That tied the score and the Yankees kept rolling. Pearson singled, rFank Crosetti walked and Red Rolfe singled for another run giving New York a 2 to 1 lead.

The Yankee momentum had not died in the sixth inning when young Gordon, easily the batting hero of the day, came up with the bases filled and pumped two more runs over the plate by slashing a single through the infield to left.

That finished Clay Bryant for the afternoon and made the rest of the game an anti-climax.

Dickey Hits Equalizer

Chicago's batting hero of the series, young Joe Marty, hit a home run high into the left field seats in the eighth inning, but when the Yankees came up a couple of minutes later big Dickey illustrated the futility of that Cub gesture by slamming a home run to right field off the first pitch served him by Larry French, the left-hander, who was on the mound by that time.

Dickey's home run was responsible for a bit of a fuss. The broad-shouldered French slapped the next hitter—George Selkirk—away from the plate with a high, inside pitch. The ball hit Selkirk's bat as he pulled away and rolled into the infield. French threw him out at first.

Selkirk, who had more than a faint suspicion that French had thrown a dust-off ball at his head, said things to the pitcher. French said something in return. Selkirk started out for the box with his bat in his hands. French advanced to meet him.

In two seconds both benches were empty and the center of the diamond was a milling mass of Cubs, Yankees and umpires. The cooler heads got themselves between French and Selkirk, so that there was no actual fistic developments or any one hurt. In a moment or two order was completely restored.

Umpire's Lip Smashed

The only physical casualty of the day—apart from the fan who died of a heart attack in the stands—was Uncle Charley Moran, the veteran National League umpire. Mr. Moran got his face directly in front of a double play throw young Gordon was trying to execute in the fifth inning. That caused a five-minute recess and left Moran tenderly dab-

Continued on Page 5

Minnesota Gains 7-0 Win Over Stubborn Purdue

Minneapolis, Oct. 8 (U.P.)—For three periods under-rated Purdue fought Minnesota to a standstill today but then the mighty Gopher attack began functioning and hammered out a 7-to-0 victory.

The superior Gopher strength was not to be denied. The charging Purdue forwards, weakened under incessant battering, and with Wilbur Moore, Marty Christiansen and Larry Buhler alternating on the ball-carrying, the Gophers moved from their own 30 to a touchdown. Christiansen went over from the two-yard line. Faust converted and the scoring was over for the day.

In the fourth quarter, with Jamnik and Steinbauer, substitute Gopher backs, doing the ball-carrying, Minnesota launched another drive. But the Boilermakers rallied their last strength and held gamely for five plays from within their five-yard line. One down was nullified by a Purdue penalty.

The Boilermakers never threatened. They made only one first down in the entire game, compared to 18 for Minnesota. The attempted but two passes and one of those, a last-minute desperation heave by Lou Brock, was intercepted by Faust.

Minnesota attempted only one pass, and it was incomplete. The Gophers rolled up 289 yards net from rushing, while Purdue got only 82.

Most surprising to experts who had made the Gophers 5-to-1 favorites was the vicious line play and hard tackling of the Purdue line. Time after time they stopped Moore and

Continued on Page 4

N. Y. U. Eleven Routs Rutgers By 25-6 for Second in Row

By CLARENCE GREENBAUM

New Brunswick, N. J., Oct. 8—N. Y. U. power proved too much for the Rutgers eleven at Neilson Field here today as the Violet scored in every period but the third to win, 25 to 6. N. Y. U. opened its season last week with a victory over Maine.

Inaugurating their scoring efforts with a 20-yard flip from Ed Boell to Harry Shorten midway in the first period, the Violets pushed over three more touchdowns by the overland method. Boell, Joe Lamanna and Art Schilling scored the other N. Y. U. touchdowns and a pass from Boell to Shorten accounted for the only Violet conversion.

Before the Violets could sew up the ball game, however, it had a scare thrown into it in the person of Art Gottlieb, Scarlet back, hailing from Brooklyn, who completed a 62-yard pass to Ralph Russo and immediately followed with a 25-yard fling to Parker Staples that was good for the lone Rutgers score in the third period.

Seven fumbles, only two of which were recovered, cut deeply into the efficiency of the Scarlet attack. A Rutgers bobble was followed by N. Y. U.'s first score.

Boell romped 33 yards for the second, three minutes before the half ended, N. Y. U. put on a

Continued on Page 3

Mrs. Mulqueen Wins Canadian Title

Ottawa, Ont., Oct. 8 (AP)—Mrs. F. J. Mulqueen of Toronto won the Canadian women's open golf championship today by defeating Clarrie Tiernan of Dublin, Ireland, on the 36th hole, 1 up.

The Canadian veteran used a superb short game and steady puttin gto offset the longer driving of Miss Tiernan, a member of the British Curtis Cup team. Mrs. Mulqueen was 3 up at the 14th hole of the afternoon round and made that margin last to win. The 22-year-old Irish girl won the 15th and 17th, but the last hole was halved when when Mrs. Mulqueen placed a No. 4 wood shot on the green, instead of playing short, and each got down in two putts.

College Football Results

LOCAL

Fordham	53	Waynesburg	0

EAST

Amherst	34	Tufts	7
Arnold	25	Wagner	0
Berger Jr. Coll.	26	Trenton Tchrs.	7
Boston U.	19	St. Lawrence	14
Brown	20	Lafayette	0
Bowdoin	27	Wesleyan	13
Bucknell	14	Penn State	0
Columbia	20	Army	18
Conn. State	19	Mass. State	0
Cornell	13	Harvard	0
Dartmouth	22	Princeton	0
Dickinson	7	Ursinus	7
Drexel	19	Susquehanna	3
Duke	7	Colgate	0
F. & M.	27	P. M. C.	0
Georgetown	33	Roanoke	6
Gettysburg	7	Albright	0
Hartwick	13	Thiel	0
Haverford	28	Alleghany	0
Holy Cross	19	Manhattan	6
Navy Pl.	51	Valley Forge	2
N. Y. U.	25	Rutgers	6
Maine	21	New Hampshire	0
Marshall	41	Miami	0
Middlebury	7	Coast Guard	0
Montclair Tchrs	3	Hofstra	0
Navy	33	Virginia	0
Northeastern	6	Bates	0
Penn	21	Yale	0
Penn St. Fr.	13	Pitt Fr.	12
Pitt	27	Duquesne	0
Randolf-Macon	27	Delaware	0
R. I. State	31	American Int.	0
Rochester	14	R. P. I.	0
St. Joseph's	27	C. C. N. Y.	7
St. Anselm's	39	Brooklyn Coll.	0
Syracuse	53	Maryland	0
Swarthmore	18	Union	15
Villanova	25	Muhlenberg	7
W. & L.	6	West Virginia	6
Williams	13	Norwich	6
Worcester	12	Trinity	0
West Va. Wes.	6	Davis-Elkins	5
Grove City	15	Hiram	13
Hamilton	13	Hobart	13
Vermont	9	Colby	6
Western Maryland	13	Washington C.	0
Lock Maven Tchrs.	20	Cortl'd Tchs.	13

SOUTH

Alabama	14	No. Car. State	0
Baylor	9	Arkansas	6
Catawba	27	Newbury	14
Clemson	7	V. M. I.	7
Notre Dame	14	Georgia Tech	6
Richmond	26	Hampden-Sydney	0
Tennessee	7	Auburn	0
Tulane	17	No. Carolina.	14
Va. Poly.	27	W. & M.	0
Wake Forest	20	So. Carolina	19
Oklahoma	13	Texas	0
Fisk	12	Tugaloo	12
Tulsa	14	Washington U	0
Miss. State	48	La. Tech.	0
Centenary	6	Southwestern	6

MID-WEST

Carnegie Tech	32	Wittenberg	13
De Pauw	47	Lawrence Tech	6
Illinois	12	Indiana	2
Kansas State	21	Missouri	13
Lehigh	0	Case	0
Michigan	45	Chicago	7
Minnesota	7	Purdue	0
Mich. State	18	Ill. Wesleyan	0
Northwestern	33	Drake	0
So. California	14	Ohio State	7
Toledo	26	Ohio Wes.	0
Western Reserve	26	Ohio U.	14
Xavier	38	Akron	0
Kansas	58	Washburn	14

Continued on Page 4

Munagorri, Pradera Score at Jai-Alai

The fast-moving combination of Munagorri and Pradera, administered a 25—13 defeat to the duo of Kiki and Jose in the feature jai-alai doubles contest at the Hippodrome this afternoon.

In the other two matches played, Tryay and Mugica downed Ulacia and Vizacaya, 20—16, while in the other 25-point match, Ramon and Guisasola beat Eguibar and Epifanio 25—20.

World Series Log

By The Associated Press

THE STANDINGS

	Won	Lost
New York (A. L.)	3	0
Chicago (N. L.)	0	3

FIRST GAME (AT CHICAGO)

	R.	H.	E.
New York (A. L.)	3	12	1
Chicago (N. L.)	1	9	1

Batteries—Ruffing and Dickey; Lee, Russell and Hartnett. Attendance—43,642.

SECOND GAME (AT CHICAGO)

	R.	H.	E.
New York (A. L.)	6	7	2
Chicago (N. L.)	3	11	0

Batteries—Gomez, Murphy and Dickey; Dean, French and Hartnett. Attendance—42,108.

THIRD GAME (AT NEW YORK)

	R.	H.	E.
Chicago (N. L.)	2	5	1
New York (A. L.)	5	7	2

Batteries—Bryant, Russell, French and Hartnett; Pearson and Dickey. Attendance—55,236.

So. California Gridders Top Ohio State, 14-7, Before 62,000

Columbus, O., Oct. 8 (U.P.)—Southern California's Trojans, outplayed in the first half, turned the tables and defeated Ohio State, 14 to 7, in an intersectional game witnessed by 62,578 fans today.

A sideline dash for 82 yards by Grenville Lansdell, triple-threat Trojan quarterback, in the second minute of the game and a third quarter pass for 25 yards from Oliver Day, substitute for Lansdell, to End Al Krueger enabled the Trojans to whip the Buckeyes for the second consecutive year.

The lone Ohio State touchdown came midway in the second period. Joe Aleskus, giant tackle, and Keith Bliss rangy end, broke through a fighting Trojan line to block an attempted punt by Fullback Jimmy Jones. Bliss continued his charge and fell on the ball on the one foot line. Jim Langhurst, Buckeye sophomore fullback, failed to gain on the first play but smashed over his own left tackle on the second try for the touchdown. Charley Maag, sophomore Ohio State center, kicked the extra point.

In the second half, after an exchange of punts, the Trojans took the ball on their own 44, and smashed and passed their way toward the Buckeye goal until stopped by a fumble recovered by Ohio's

Continued on Page 3

BROOKLYN EAGLE SPORTS

CONLAN COMES BACK
Jocko Conlan, former White Sox outfielder, will be back in the American League next year, only this time he will return as an umpire.

McKECHNIE DOG FANCIER
Bill McKechnie, manager of the Reds, is a noted dog fancier and hunter. He possesses a famous collection of guns and all the residents of Wilkinsburg, Pa., are familiar with his dogs. Next to baseball he likes gunning best.

Yanks' Record in World Series Competition Remarkable

ED. HUGHES' COLUMN

New York, the nation's most generous host, observed all the amenities possible with the Cubs at the Yankee Stadium yesterday. For instance, a little thing like torn paper cluttering the diamond might possibly have annoyed the visitors. So, in the eighth inning of yesterday's passage-at-bats with the Chicagoans, the game was interrupted by the clarion voice of the announcer, who chirped:

"Attention, please. In justice to the Chicago club the management asks you to refrain from throwing paper."

This was right thoughtful of the Yankee management, but trifles do not always make the sum of life. In justice to the Chicago club's feelings it must be stated that the bits of paper, which blew over the playing field like flurries of snow, were the very least of their torments. What really discommoded them and lacerated their feelings was the tremendous show of baseball produced by their hosts.

It is a fine thing for a club to earn the right to play in a World Series, indicating, as a rule, the club's exceptional class. It's profitable, too, financially, for the losers will each grab a few thousand dollars for their suffering. Still, there's such a thing as professional pride along with the business acumen. A decent, respectable defeat can be taken gracefully, but humiliation is hard to swallow.

And that is what happened to the Cubs throughout the series. They were humiliated, these proud champions of the National League.

Futility

Although the scores do not indicate it, anyone who witnessed the series will tell you that not many times has a beaten team been so thoroughly outclassed as were the Cubs.

There was a peculiar atmosphere to this series the like of which I've never experienced in baseball. It was an atmosphere of almost complete lack of competition. Outwardly, the Cubs were manifestly ball players. They wore trim uniforms, and they went through the mechanical motions of performers who knew what they were about. They made scintillating plays, tore off respectable hits and they turned in some neat pitching.

Still, they moved in an atmosphere of hopelessness that was downright oppressive to most of the fans. Even when the Cubs rallied in the eighth yesterday and came within a run of tying the score, it gave you no thrill. You were simply numbed, from the start, by the sheer futility of the Cubs trying to lick the Yanks.

Now, ordinarily a home run smash such as O'Dea delivered with Cavarretta on third would have roused expectations of a possible victory for the under dog. But you sensed to the roots of your soul that, although the Cubs had another inning, they wouldn't do anything about it.

Merciless Paw

And there was the uncanny premonition that the Yanks would make them pay dearly for this threatening gesture. It was like a big cat toying with a helpless little mouse, who is permitted to take a few jumps toward safety—only to have the merciless paw crack down on it.

Surely enough, that was what happened, and it didn't surprise you in the least. In their very next turn at the bat the Yanks piled up four runs. They did it with the ease and nonchalance of clouts made in batting practice.

Although the Cubs themselves must have been cockeyed from the drug of despair, still they went through the palsied motions of strategy. After DiMaggio and Gehrig had cut loose with singles, pitcher Page left the box. Maybe he did that instinctively, although I understand Hartnett signalled for him.

Three More

A Mr. French, a left-hander, appeared. French has a bizarre pitching motion. He draws both hands back, brings them forward, stopping with an abrupt jerk in front of him. The elbows are bent stiffly and he presses the ball as if to squeeze the hits from it. Then he lets it go. He made the dangerous Dickey pop-up.

Perhaps he has something, but there's no telling. A left-hander, Hoag is up—and Hartnett decides French can't handle him. French is waved to the bench. Carleton, a right-hander, goes in. His first ball is so freighted with wildness that he almost heaves it into the Cub dugout. Then he cuts loose with a real wild one on which DiMaggio scores. Carleton, soon in trouble, is yanked. The one and only Diz Dean inherits his misery. With the bases full he yields a Texas Leaguer, scoring two runs. Four pitchers in a single inning. That's a World Series record for pitching inefficiency—and typical of the general helplessness of the Cubs before the Yanks.

Yankee Record

The Yankees, already record holders with six world championships, added a seventh against the Cubs yesterday and also became the first team to win three in a row. Winning the last six series in which they competed also is a record, of course, besides taking four series in four straight games.

Their series record:

Year	Winner	Loser
1921	Giants (5)	Yankees (3
1922	Giants (4)	*Yankees (0)
1923	Yankees (4)	Giants (2)
1926	Cardinals (4)	Yankees (3)
1927	Yankees (4)	Pirates (0)
1928	Yankees (4)	Cardinals (0)
1932	Yankees (4)	Cubs (0)
1936	Yankees (4)	Giants (2)
1937	Yankees (4)	Giants (1)
1938	Yankees (4)	Cubs (0)

*One tie game.

Recapitulation

Ten series, seven world championships, 34 victories, 18 defeats, one tie.

The Major Baseball Planet? - - - - - - - - - - By Ed Hughes

Long-Heralded Yank Crackup Not Yet in Sight

There are many today, including eight National League managers, who are viewing with alarm the strangle-hold the Yankees have taken on baseball. They were equally gloomy about the future of the game a year ago, when the Yanks beat the Giants, 4 games to 1. Still, there seems a ray of hope in the fact that the players will divvy up a purse of $434,094.66, which is a record for a four-game affair.

Off their play against the hapless Cubs there is no sign of the long-heralded crackup of Joe McCarthy's great team. Maybe it will go on forever, like a cricket game. Lou Gehrig, the old "iron man" first baseman, is supposed to be on his last legs, but you couldn't detect it by his play the past week. One of his final acts in the ninth inning yesterday was to nearly break his neck diving into the stands after a foul ball.

Never did a club more vividly demonstrate the value of power hitting than did the Yanks this time. They belted five home runs, and three of them virtually were game winners. Tommy Henrich's fourmaster off Charlie Root in the sixth inning was the winning run of yesterday's game, notwithstanding the Cubs' blow-up in the eighth.

The blow-up, incidentally, came just when it looked like the Cubs might get into the ball game. Ken O'Dea, substitute Chicago catcher, had smacked a home run in the first of the eighth with Phil Cavarretta on base, reducing the Yankees' lead to 4 to 3, and the crowd was rooting the visitors on, hoping for at least one thrill in the series.

And that was when the Cubs began using their pitchers in squads and the game became a shambles. Doubles by Hoag and Crosetti, sandwiched between singles by DiMaggio and Gehrig, two walks and a wild pitch by Tex Carleton closed the series on a high, hilarious note.

Box Score of Fourth World Series Game

CHICAGO (N. L.)

	ab.	r.	h.	po.	a.
Hack, 3b	5	0	2	1	0
Herman, 2b	5	0	1	1	3
Cavarretta, rf	4	1	2	1	0
Marty, cf	4	0	0	2	0
Demaree, lf	3	1	0	3	0
O'Dea, c	3	1	1	5	0
Collins, 1b	4	0	0	10	0
Jurges, ss	4	0	2	1	0
Lee, p	1	0	0	0	0
aGalan	1	0	0	0	0
Root, p	0	0	0	0	0
bLazzeri	1	0	0	0	0
Page, p	0	0	0	0	1
French, p	0	0	0	0	0
Carleton, p	0	0	0	0	0
Dean, p	0	0	0	0	0
cReynolds	1	0	0	0	0
Total	36	3	8	24	4

NEW YORK (A. L.)

	ab.	r.	h.	po.	a.
Crosetti, ss	5	0	2	6	1
Rolfe, 3b	5	0	1	0	0
Henrich, rf	4	1	1	1	0
DiMaggio, cf	4	1	1	3	0
Gehrig, 1b	4	1	1	5	2
Dickey, c	4	0	1	7	0
Hoag, lf	4	2	2	1	0
Gordon, 2b	3	2	1	2	4
Ruffing, p	3	1	1	2	3
Total	36	8	11	27	10

aBatted for Lee in fourth.
bBatted for Root in seventh.
cBatted for Dean in ninth.

SCORE BY INNINGS

Cubs	000	100	020	—3
Yankees	030	001	04 .	—8

Errors—Jurges, Gordon.
Runs batted in—Ruffing, Crosetti 4, Henrich, O'Dea 2, Hoag.
Earned runs—Yankees 5, Cubs 2.
Left on bases—Yankees 6, Cubs 8. Struck out—By Ruffing 6, Lee 2, Root 1. Bases on balls—Off Ruffing 2, Carleton 2. Hits—Off Lee 4 in 3 innings, Root 3 in 3, Page 2 in 1 1-3, French 0 in 1-3, Carleton 1 in 0, Dean 1 in 1-3. Wild pitches—Carleton 2. Losing pitcher—Lee. Umpires—Hubbard (A. L.), plate; Moran (N. L.), first base; Kolls (A. L.), third base; Sears (N. L.), third base. Time of game—2:11.

Cubs Soothed By Long Green

4-Game Series Yields Record 'Cut'—Yanks Each Draw $5,815.28

While it doesn't entirely make up for losing the World Series in four straight games, the Chicago Cubs had some consolation today in knowing they would collect $4,674.87 apiece for taking a beating.

The four games of the World Series produced a total "gate" of $851,166 from 200,833 paying customers. Of this, $434,094.66 went into the players' pool, to be split up among the World Series rivals, and the other first division clubs of the two leagues.

The total was a record for a series decided in four games, although in a six-game series, drawing larger crowds to the first four games from which the players' "cut" comes, the Yankees and Giants cut up a $460,002.66 melon in 1936.

The shares of the two clubs also were records for four-game affairs, in which interest generally becomes less as they turn out to be lopsided. They split up 70 percent of the pool on a 60-40 basis.

The Yanks, who gave out $3,500 in cash gifts and split the remainder into 30¾ shares, will get $5,815.28 apiece, while the Cubs will draw down $4,674.87 on each of 25 full shares. The all-time records are $6,544 collected by the Detroit Tigers in 1935, when they beat the Cubs, and $4,656.40, which the Giants got for losing to the Yanks in 1936.

The cuts of the various other clubs are: $32,557.10 each to the second-place Boston Red Sox and Pittsburgh Pirates; $21,704.73 to the third-place Cleveland Indians and New York Giants, and $10,852.37, which the Detroit Tigers and Cincinnati Reds get for finishing fourth.

World Series Log

Standing

	W	L.	Pct.
New York Yankees (A. L.)	4	0	1.000
Chicago Cubs (N. L.)	0	4	.000

Results

First game (at Chicago, Oct. 5)—

		R.	H.	E.
Yankees	0 2 0 0 0 1 0 0 0	—3	12	1
Cubs	0 0 1 0 0 0 0 0 0	—1	9	1

Batteries—Ruffing and Dickey; Lee, Russell and Hartnett.

Second game (at Chicago, Oct. 6)—

		R.	H.	E.
Yankees	0 2 0 0 0 0 0 2 2	—6	7	2
Cubs	0 0 1 0 0 0 0 0 0	—3	11	0

Batteries—Gomez, Murphy and Dickey; Dean, French and Hartnett.

Third game (at New York, Oct. 8)—

		R.	H.	E.
Cubs	0 0 0 0 1 0 0 1 0	—2	5	1
Yankees	0 0 0 0 2 2 0 1 x	—5	7	2

Batteries—Bryant, Russell, French and Hartnett; Pearson and Dickey.

Fourth game (at New York, Oct. 9)—

		R.	H.	E.
Cubs	0 0 0 1 0 0 0 2 0	—3	8	1
Yankees	0 3 0 0 0 1 0 4 x	—8	11	1

Batteries — Lee, Root, Page, French, Carleton, Dean and O'Dea; Ruffing and Dickey.

You must REGISTER this week if you want to vote. Polls open 5 p. m. to 10:30 p. m. Monday through Friday; 7 a. m. through 10:30 p. m. Saturday.

Composite Box Score of Series

NEW YORK YANKEES (A. L.)

Player	G.	AB.	R.	H.	2B.	3B.	HR.	RBI.	BB.	SO.	Pct.	PO.	A.	E.	Pct.
Crosetti, ss	4	16	1	4	2	1	1	6	2	4	.250	16	10	1	.963
Rolfe, 3b	[illegible]	18	0	3	0	0	0	1	0	3	.167	0	4	2	.667
Henrich, rf	4	16	3	4	1	0	1	1	0	1	.250	6	0	1	.857
DiMaggio, cf	4	15	4	4	0	0	1	2	1	1	.267	10	0	0	1.000
Gehrig, 1b	4	14	4	4	0	0	0	0	2	3	.286	25	3	0	1.000
Dickey, c	4	15	[illegible]	[illegible]	[illegible]	0	1	2	1	0	.400	31	5	0	1.000
Selkirk, lf	3	10	0	[illegible]	[illegible]	0	0	1	2	1	.200	3	0	0	1.000
aHoag, lf	2	5	[illegible]	[illegible]	1	[illegible]	0	1	0	0	.400	1	0	0	1.000
Powell, lf	1	0	0	[illegible]	0	0	0	0	0	0	.000	0	0	0	.000
Gordon, 2b	4	15	3	6	[illegible]	[illegible]	1	[illegible]	1	3	.400	12	12	2	.923
Ruffing, p	2	6	1	1	[illegible]	0	[illegible]	[illegible]	1	0	.167	2	4	0	1.000
Gomez, p	1	2	0	0	0	0	0	0	0	0	.000	0	1	0	1.000
Pearson, p	1	3	1	1	0	0	0	0	1	0	.333	2	0	0	1.000
Murphy, p	[illegible]	0	[illegible]	0	[illegible]	[illegible]	0	0	0	0	.000	0	0	0	.000
Totals	4	[illegible]	[illegible]	[illegible]7	6	1	5	21	11	16	.274	108	39	6	.961

aBatted for Gom[illegible] inning, secon[illegible].

CHIC[illegible]BS (N. L.)

Player	G.	AB.	R.	H.	2B.	3B.	HR.	RBI.	BB.	SO.	Pct.	PO.	A.	E.	Pct.
Hack, 3b	4	17	[illegible]	[illegible]	[illegible]	[illegible]	[illegible]	1	1	2	.471	4	4	0	1.000
Herman, 2b	4	[illegible]	[illegible]	[illegible]	0	0	0	[illegible]	1	4	.188	5	14	2	.905
Demaree, lf-rf	3	10	1	1	0	0	0	0	1	2	.100	6	0	0	1.000
bCavaretta, rf	4	13	1	6	1	0	0	0	0	1	.462	4	1	0	1.000
Marty, cf	3	12	1	6	1	0	1	5	0	2	.500	7	0	0	1.000
cReynolds, cf-lf	4	12	0	0	0	0	0	0	1	3	.000	7	0	0	1.000
Hartnett, c	3	11	0	1	0	1	0	0	0	2	.091	14	3	0	1.000
dO'Dea, c	3	5	1	1	0	0	1	2	1	0	.200	5	0	0	1.000
Collins, 1b	4	15	1	2	0	0	0	0	0	3	.133	38	1	0	1.000
Jurges, ss	4	13	0	3	1	0	0	0	1	3	.231	11	7	1	.947
Lee, p	2	3	0	0	0	0	0	0	0	1	.000	1	0	0	1.000
Dean, p	2	3	0	2	0	0	0	0	0	0	.667	0	2	0	1.000
Bryant, p	1	2	0	0	0	0	0	0	0	1	.000	0	0	0	.000
Russell, p	2	0	0	0	0	0	0	0	0	0	.000	0	0	0	.000
French, p	3	0	0	0	0	0	0	0	0	0	.000	0	2	0	1.000
Root, p	1	0	0	0	0	0	0	0	0	0	.000	0	0	0	.000
Page, p	1	0	0	0	0	0	0	0	0	0	.000	0	1	0	1.000
Carleton, p	1	0	0	0	0	0	0	0	0	0	.000	0	0	0	.000
eGalan	2	2	0	0	0	0	0	0	0	1	.000	0	0	0	.000
fLazzeri	2	2	0	0	0	0	0	0	0	1	.000	0	0	0	.000
Totals	4	136	9	33	4	1	2	8	6	26	.243	102	35	3	.979

bBatted for Lee in eighth inning, first game; batted for French in ninth inning, third game.
cBatted for Dean in ninth inning, fourth game.
dBatted for French in ninth inning, second game.
eBatted for Russell in seventh inning, third game; batted for Lee in fourth inning, fourth game.
fBatted for Jurges in ninth inning, third game; batted for Root in seventh inning, fourth game.

PITCHING RECORDS

NEW YORK

	G	CG	IP	H	R	ER	EB	SO	WP	HB	W	L	PCT	ERA
Ruffing	2	2	18	17	4	3	2	11	0	0	2	0	1.000	1.50
Gomez	1	0	7	9	3	3	1	5	0	0	1	0	1.000	3.86
Pearson	1	1	9	5	2	1	2	9	0	0	1	0	1.000	1.00
Murphy	1	0	2	2	0	0	1	1	0	0	0	0	.000	0.00

CHICAGO

	G	CG	IP	H	R	ER	EB	SO	WP	HB	W	L	PCT	ERA
Lee	2	0	11	15	6	3	1	8	0	1	0	2	.000	2.45
Dean	2	0	8⅓	8	6	6	1	2	0	0	0	1	.000	6.75
Bryant	1	0	5⅓	6	4	4	5	3	0	0	0	1	.000	7.20
French	3	0	3⅓	1	1	1	1	2	0	0	0	0	.000	3.00
Russell	2	0	1⅔	1	0	0	1	0	0	0	0	0	.000	0.00
Root	1	0	3	3	1	1	0	1	0	0	0	0	.000	3.00
Page	1	0	1⅓	2	2	2	0	0	0	0	0	0	.000	18.00
Carleton	1	0	0	1	2	2	2	0	2	0	0	0	.000	——

COMPOSITE SCORE BY INNINGS

New York (A. L.)	0 7 0	0 2 4	0 7	2—22
Chicago (N. L.)	1 0 3	1 1 0	0 3	0—.9

Earned runs—New York, 19; Chicago, 7. Stolen bases—Dickey, Rolfe, Gordon. Sacrifices—Ruffing, Demaree. Double plays—New York, 4 (Crosetto and Gehrig; Crosetti, Gordon and Gehrig, 2; Gordon, Crosetti and Gehrig); Chicago, 3 (Jurges, Herman and Collins; Collins, unassisted; Herman, Jurges and Collins). Left on bases—New York, 24; Chicago, 26. Umpires—Moran and Sears, National League; Kolls and Hubbard, American League. Times of games—First, 1:55; second, 1:53; third, 1:57; fourth, 2:11.

Reynolds Seen Series Dunce

Cubs' Outfielder Indisputably Named 'All-American' Out

They'll be remembering Carl Reynolds as the "all-American out" for this World Series.

The ex-American Leaguer, who returned to the big show this year with the Cubs and batted .300 in the regular season, was at bat 12 times in the four games of the series with the Yankees—and failed, completely and entirely, to make a single safe hit.

That is a batting "honor" few have equaled in the history of World Series. In fact, the last time a player went for a line of "goose-eggs" was in 1911, when John Murray of the Giants did it. Only four others did it before Murray.

In a lot of ways Reynolds' work at the plate was more unique in this series than Lefty Gomez's six-game undefeated winning streak for his series career, or Bill Dickey's four singles in the first game, or Stan Hack's seven singles to equal a mark for a four-game series, or the Yankee's' unprecedented feat of winning three world championships in a row.

For instance, Reynolds hit exactly one ball out of the infield in his string of hard luck. He fanned three times, hit into double plays twice.

Generally speaking, however, the 1938 series, short and completely one-sided, showed few important changes in the record books.

Gomez's new mark probably was the most important. Up to this Fall he had been deadlocked among the World Series undefeated pitchers with Jack Coombs, the Athletics' old-time strong man, and Herb Pennock of the Yanks' great ball clubs of the middle 20's.

Hack's .471 batting average, the series leader, is the highest in the National League since Pepper Martin ran wild for .500 for the Cardinals against the Athletics back in 1931 and the highest in both leagues since Lou Gehrig's .529 against the Cubs in '32.

Red Ruffing, turning in two pitching victories, equals the mark for a four-game series. The Cubs, tossing six pitchers into the battle in a futile attempt to stop the Yanks in yesterday's final game, also put one in the books. Bill Lee's two losses is still one more for a four-game series.

Fourth Game Statistics

Attendance (paid)	59,847
Gross receipts	$226,446.00
Commissioner's share	33,966.90
Players' share	115,487.46
Clubs' share	38,495.82
Leagues' share	38,495.82

Total for Four Games

Attendance (paid)	200,833
Gross receipts	$851,166.00
Commissioner's share	127,674.90
Players' share	434,094.66
Clubs' share	144,698.22
Leagues' share	144,698.22

Cubs' Performances Really Not So Bad As May Seem at First

By TOMMY HOLMES

When the late, lamented World Series began last Wednesday the fearful and wonderful Yankees of New York were 1-to-2 favorites to win the thing. They should have been 1 to 20. I don't believe that the Cubs admitted it to themselves, but they had no chance to win. Not only were the National League champions hopelessly outclassed but they weren't in shape for a thing of this sort after the gruelling wear and tear of a terrific pennnt race.

While most of the boys are going around today heaping imprecations upon the Cubs for what has happened to them since 1:30 p.m. last Wednesday, I am inclined to give them a bit of credit. In spite of the fact that they were belted over in four straight games, I thought they put up a better fight than the Giants did last year or the year before. At no time were they beaten by any outlandish scores. Until the eighth inning of the final game they showed no signs of cracking wide open, and by that time, of course, all hope was lost.

It is unfair to Gabby Hartnett's team to blame the Cubs for being outclassed by the Yankees. Any other club in the National League would have been outclassed. Every club in the American League was outclassed during the pennant race. The Cleveland Indians or the Boston Red Sox probably would have been beaten as badly as the Cubs had they faced Joe McCarthy's mighty and merciless men when the chips were down in a World Series. Blaming the Cubs for losing, even blaming them for losing in four straight games is like blaming a man for being run over by a truck.

A Remarkable Achievement

The record of the Yankees in World Series competition is one of the most remarkable achievements in sports. They have won 24 games out of 27 from National League champions. Back in 1927, they beat the Pirates four straight. The next year they won four in succession from the Cardinals. They did not get into another World Series until 1932 and then they won four straight from the Cubs. Two years ago, they won four out of six from the Giants, last year it was four out of five in a nickle World Series and in the slaughter just brought to a close they did not lose a game.

It is worthwhile noting the pitchers who beat the Yankees in the three games in 27 they have lost. Twice Carl Hubbell of the Giants did it. The other flinger was Bill Terry's Hal Schumacher. Hubbell beat them with his screwball, the most highly developed screwball in the business. Schumacher has a sinker ball style all his own. In other words, the only men who could stand out in the box and win from the Yankees in a stretch of games that constitutes more than one-sixth of a regular season were pitchers who served the Yankee hitters something that they could not become accustomed to in their own league because nobody in the American League threw that way. Every pitcher, no matter how good, who depended upon fast balls and curves, was ruthlessly swept aside.

Lesser Stars to Fore

In the final mop-up of the series, it is impossible to select an outstanding hero. A rather surprising development was the fact that Joe Gordon, Frankie Crosetti and Tommy Henrich, who might be called lesser stars of the Yanks, were greater winning factors than Joe DiMaggio, Lou Gehrig and Bill Dickey, more renowned gentlemen of baseball might. Red Ruffing won two games, but Monte Pearson pitched the best game. For the Cubs, Joe Marty was outstanding. A bench-warmer for most of the season, he was on a terrific hitting spree in the World Series that didn't mean anything.

In the goat department, Carl Reynolds, who did not get a hit in 13 times at bat, is a standout. Bill Jurges made a couple of errors for the Cubs in critical moments. Yesterday, in the big Bronx Stadium, Tex Carleton put in a belated bid for the distinction of wearing long curved horns, but nothing mattered by that time.

Jurges' Lapse Fatal

The Yankees laughed their way through the final game. Only one stride away from the unparallelled distinction of a third straight World's Championship, they stepped out before more than 59,000 citizens in the Sabbath finale and won without drawing a deep breath. Big Bill Lee might have given them a battle, but three unearned runs developed from a low Jurges throw in the second inning.

Ruffing experienced a spell of wildness in the fourth and a subsequent dropped throw by Gordon gave the Cubs a run. Henrich hit a home run for the Yanks in the sixth, but in the eighth, Ken O'Dea, playing in place of Manager Hartnett, homered with one on to pull the Cubs to a point only one run behind at 4 to 3. That only seemed to irritate the Yankees, who immediately scored four runs, to make the final score 8 to 3.

Hartnett threw everything into the last half of the eighth inning. Four Chicago pitchers worked in that single frame. Gabby put in Larry French to face Bill Dickey, who hit a homer against French Saturday. French got Dickey out, too. After Carleton messed things up completely, the great man, Dizzy Dean, strode out to take charge with the bases loaded. Nobody was up at the plate but Crosetti, who ruined Dean with a homer on Thursday. Dean fooled Crosetti all right, but nobody could reach the resultant Texas League pop fly over short which fell for a double and drove in the final two runs.

Joe McCarthy First to Win 3 Series in Row

McGraw, Huggins And Mack Failed To Turn This Trick

By BILL McCULLOUGH

Joe McCarthy, manager of the Yankees, was as happy as a lark today. He has accomplished something no other manager could achieve in the history of baseball. When his Yanks, behind Charles (Red) Ruffing, yesterday beat the Cubs for four straight, McCarthy became the first leader to win three World Series in succession.

The Yanks of 1938 beat the Giants in 1936 and 1937. Until this year, Connie Mack, Miller Huggins and John McGraw had won two World Series conquests in a row. Mack failed in 1931, Huggins failed in 1923 and McGraw failed in 191[illegible]

Yanks to Stay Intact

The Yankees' powerful machine, which ran roughshod over the Cubs in four straight games, won't be broken up.

"We are going to fight for our fourth straight pennant and another world championship," Ed Barrow, general manager of the Bombers, said. "Why should we break up? Colonel Ruppert is proud of this year's team."

There was nothing to this series. The Yanks won as they pleased. Ruffing in great form took the first and fourth games. Lefty Gomez grabbed the second, while Monte Pearson won the third. The Yanks just rolled along. They had the pitching, the hitting and the defense. They showed their true worth in this classic.

Winning world championships is not a new wrinkle in the McCarthy makeup. After leaving the National League in 1930, McCarthy went to town with the Yanks. Here is how Marse Joe did it with his Bombers:

1932: Cubs Beaten, 4—0.

This series, which pitted McCarthy against the team he had led from 1926 through 1930, was one of the most one-sided in history. The Cubs never had a chance from the time the Yanks won the opener, 12 to 6, until they took the final, 13 to 6. Chicago used three pitchers in the first game, four in the third game and five in the final tilt.

Lon Warneke, now with the Cardinals, alone went the route against the Bombers, losing the second, 5 to 2, at the Stadium . . . The Yanks slashed eight homers in the four games . . . Lou Gehrig got two hits in each game and batted .525 in the set . . . Gomez and Ruffing went the route in the first two games and George Pipgras, now an umpire in the American League, lasted until the ninth in the third game . . . John Allen was knocked out in the first inning of the final when the Cubs scored four runs, but Wilcy Moore and Herb Pennock did a good relief job between them to save the finale.

1936 Giants Beaten, 4—2

Carl Owen Hubbel started the Giants on the right foot by winning the opener . . . It rained like the dickens, but the Bombers clouted five Giants pitchers for an 18-to-4 triumph in the second game and went on to take the series . . . Bump Hadley made his first World Series start in the third game and allowed one run, a homer by Jimmy Ripple, in eight innings. He was removed for a pinch hitter. Pat Malone finished and the Yanks won, 2 to 1 . . . Fitz was the unlucky loser . . . The winning run was scored on an infield grounder, a blow by Frank Crosetti which Fitz, a great fielding pitcher, misjudged . . . Gomez received plenty of help in scoring two victories, winning the 18-to-4 opener and the 13-to-5 final . . . Jake Powell led the hitters with a .455 mark.

1937: Giants Beaten, 4-1

Lefty Gomez and Carl Hubbell were the pitchers in the opener . . . The Giants were first to score, getting one in the fifth, but the Yanks came back with seven in the sixth and the Giants never caught up with their opponents the rest of the series. Red Ruffing won the second game, 8 to 1.

Cliff Melton was routed. John Murphy came in to Monte Pearson's aid in the third game, won by the Yanks, 5 to 1. . . Hubbell chalked up a 7-to-3 triumph in the fourth, but Gomez won his fifth straight World Series game when he took the final, 4 to 2 . . . Tony Lazzeri, now with the Cubs, was top batsman of the series with .400

Johnstown Takes Wood By 6 Lengths

☆ ☆ ☆ ☆ ☆ ☆ ☆ ☆

DiMaggio Hurt as Nats Topple Yankees By 3-1

CONCERN: Joe DiMaggio is being helped off the field by Dr. Robert E. Walsh, club physician, and trainer Erle Painter after his injury yesterday. The deep concern and worry of the rest of the Yanks over the injury to their ace is vividly pictured here. From left to right can be seen Charley Ruffing, biting his fingernails, George Selkirk, deep in thought, Babe Dahlgren and Billy Knickerbocker with head in hands. Behind Knick is Tommy Henrich. Joe McCarthy i clearly perturbed as Art Fletche (No. 29) clears a way for DiMaggi down the dugout steps. Catcher Bi Dickey is in foreground.

Journal-American Phot

Outfield Ace May Be Out 10 Days; Gomez Outhurled

By Sid Mercer

A shadow fell suddenly over Yankee pennant prospects yesterday when Joe DiMaggio, power hitter in the clean-up spot, collapsed in center field with a leg injury that will deprive the champions of his services for an indefinite period.

Handicapped by the loss of their greatest threat to left-handed pitching, the Yankees went on to a 3 to 1 defeat by the Washington Nationals, their second set-back of the season. Ken Chase thus became the first left-hander to triumph over the Bronx Bombers this Spring. Previously they had averaged nearly a run an inning off the eighteen portsiders who had faced them in exhibition and championship games.

LEG BADLY TORN.

Rushed to St. Elizabeth's Hospital after being assisted from the Yankee Stadium field in the third inning, DiMaggio's injury was diagnosed as a severe tear of the muscles surrounding the fibula and tibia of his right leg. These are the bones back of the shin bone.

At first it was believed that DiMaggio had suffered a fracture just above his ankle. After an examination in the clubhouse, Dr. Emmett Walsh, club physician, rushed DiMaggio to the hospital in his car for further diagnosis and X-ray photographs.

As the game ended it was announced there was no break but that DiMaggio would be out for ten days, possibly longer. The player was taken to his hotel from the hospital.

SERIOUS HANDICAP.

The accident halted DiMaggio for the fourth time in the first month of his four seasons with the Yankees and is a serious handicap to his team for he had made a splendid start and was hitting at a .409 clip up to today's game in which he had delivered a single on his first turn at bat.

Roberto Estalella, Cuban outfielder, was the first Washington batter in the third inning. He fired a line single to center, DiMaggio started in on it but when the ball took a bad bound over his shoulder he attempted to pull up short and turn.

"My foot caught, something cracked and down I went and stayed there," Joe said afterward.

With DiMaggio prone on the grass Jake Powell chased the hit which was good for three bases. Time was called and DiMaggio was assisted from the field by teammates and carried up the steps under the stand to the clubhouse.

KELLER GETS CHANCE.

After a brief examination by Dr. Walsh the injured player took a hot shower, dressed and proceeded to the hospital.

DiMaggio's misfortune provided Charley Keller, Newark rookie, with his first opportunity to face American League pitching. Keller went to left field and Powell moved over to center. Later in the game Buddy Rosar also made

Continued on Page 22.

BOROWY, RAMS, WINS 17TH IN ROW, FANS 13

By David Eisenberg

Hank Borowy, the Fordham U. blazer, once again was whipping them home yesterday. The most important ball athlete to appear at Rose Hill since Frankie Frisch's great days needed little more than to look over New York U.'s battery at Ohio Field yesterday. He had the stuff anyway, more than in any other game this season, and Fordham was a 5-0 winner.

Hank the Blazer pitched with lots of control, a perfect change of pace and even more speed. The 3,000 customers and Yankee scout Paul Kritchell were present at the best college pitching job seen in this area this season.

GIVES 2 HITS; FANS 13.

Borowy set back the Violet sluggers with only two hits. One was Jerry Sasso's third frame single, the other triple off the center field fence by John Fottrell in the sixth.

The Blazer started fanning Violets in the second, and he stirred up those unwelcome breezes for New York thirteen times during the afternoon. George Leavy, the N. Y. U. shortstop, was Borowy's pet fall guy, getting the umpire's thumb three times. Hank's strikeouts for the season now total 66 for 56⅔ innings. He has been nicked for 30 hits over that period, while walking only 21 batters.

Borowy now has won 17 straight games in two years of college hurling, seven this season. He also won five, without a setback, in his freshman season.

(Box Score on Page 21)

Barnes, Bell Win Open Net Crown

WHITE SULPHUR SPRINGS, W. Va., April 29 (AP).—Bruce Barnes of Austin, Tex., and Berkeley Bell of Cresskill, N. J., flashed some fast but erratic tennis today to capture the Greenbrier open doubles title. They defeated Joe Whalen of Memphis, former professional champion, and George Jennings of Chicago, 6—4, 6—4, 4—6, 6—3.

CHICAGO '15' WINS

Chicago Rugby Club defeated the New York Rugby Club, 13—8, at Randalls Island yesterday. This marked Chicago's eighteenth win.

BLOCKADE WINS MARYLAND CUP

BALTIMORE, April 29 (AP).—Mrs. E. Read Beard's veteran timbertopper Blockade won the Maryland Hunt Cup for the second time today, in 9:16 for the four-mile route compared to his course record of 8:44 last year.

Second by half a length was John Strawbridge's Coq Bruyere, third in the Middleburg Hunt Cup two weeks ago. J. C. Leiper's Cherry Brook, an outsider, was third by 20 lengths. Five of the seven starters finished the course, studded with 22 jumps.

A crowd of 10,000 about half that in previous years, braved a chill breeze and overcast skies for the event. The numer of spectators was reduced by parking charges made for the first time on J. W. Y. Martin's estate. There is no admission fee.

Blockade, with J. Fred Colwill up, and the Strawerbridge horse, ridden by R. P. Hamilton, went to the front at the start and passed the lead back and forth throughout.

Hemphill Wins Carolina Golf, 9-3

COLUMBIA, S. C., April 29 (AP).—Kathryn Hemphill of Columbia nursed a morning three-hole advantage through the afternoon round and closed out Jane Cothran of Greenville today at the 33rd hole to win the Carolina woman's golf championship, 4 and 3.

TIGERS BOW, 7 TO 4

COLLEGE PARK, Md., April 29 (AP).—Maryland's lacrosse team scored its sixth straight victory in its bid for the National Open championship as it downed Princeton today, 7 to 4.

Spurns Job

Sutherland Refuses Dental Bureau Job

PHILADELPHIA, April 29 (AP).—Dr. John Bain "Jock" Sutherland, former football coach at the University of Pittsburgh, said today he had decided not to accept a job as director of the dental bureau in the Pennsylvania Department of Health.

"I had intended to accept the job," the "Silent Scout" declared from the stands at Franklin Field, while watching the Penn Relay Carnival. "But when I found I couldn't devote all the time to the work that it required, I changed my mind."

NAVY OARSMEN TOO FAST FOR COLUMBIA

By Paul Gardner

It will take many good beats to beat that Navy crew at Poughkeepsie this year.

The Poughkeepsie winners of 1938, sporting three of the oarsmen that stopped California and Washington last year, took a formidable Columbia eight into camp by a length and a half in the Varsity race of 1¾ miles over the Harlem River course yesterday.

Maintaining a beat of 32 for the larger part of the race, spacing beautifully and generally showing power, Navy went into the lead about 100 yards from the start and from there out was clearly the better crew.

For Columbia there was a measure of solace in that the Lions actually picked up nearly a half length in the closing 250 yards of the race.

Irvin G. Peters, bow, Captain Fred W. Kittler, No. 3, Neal Almgren, No. 3, were the Navy veterans. Tom Walker, junior varsity stroke a year ago, stroked the varsity this time, with Sheldon H. Kenney at No. 2, Guy A. Lucian, No. 4, Louis P. Spear, No. 6, and Virgil Hancock, Jr., stroke.

LION VETERANS.

Columbia's Poughkeepsie leftovers consisted of Henry Wheeler, stroke; Gus Schatzel, No. 6; Captain Henry Remmer, No. 4; John

Continued on Page 21.

Easy Victory Drops Odds On Derby Favorite to 8-5

By Bill Corum.

Anybody who means to win the Kentucky Derby next week had bet sprinkle that old Churchill Downs track, and good. That is, anybody exc Mr. William Woodward, who owns 'The Johnstown Flood'' and therefore l all the water he can use.

For it looks now as if only a muddy track can keep Johnstown—a ho out of a picture book—f romping to victory in the for the Roses in Louisville.

3RD STRAIGHT VICTORY.

At least, he scored his t straight triumph of the Sprin the Wood Memorial at Jam yesterday afternoon, bree home six lengths before a c field and swinging on the bit.

They said maybe he coul run a mile and a quarter u stake weight, but, for the se Saturday in succession, he from horses at a mile and seve yards and was so far in fron the end that the rest of the couldn't have seen him wit television set.

Six lengths seems to be favorite margin of victory. Th as close as any horse has bee him at the judges' stand in three starts of this year. But has never run in mud, or e tried it in a race, though wise, Jim Fitzsimmons, who trains rates him strictly as a fast t horse.

EL CHICO DOUBTFUL START

So Challedon and the rest of horses that oppose him in the D had better start singing "The brella Man." One of those to pose him in the Matt Winn $50 classic probably will not be Chico, the Winter book fav for the race, who tried it in Wood and wound up sixth in field and at the eighth pole.

Although "Chico" was bum in the run for position around first turn, it is extremely dou that Owner William Ziegler, will ship him to Louisville.

It would seem a waste of m with Johnstown in the race, s El Chico can't even "holler" him in their respective pre conditions, much less race him. It was ever thus. El C was unbeaten as a two-year-o 1938. But this is a different y and those juvenile flashes go way. They get burned out babies.

Johnstown's earnings went to $56,945 with the $17,675 he in the Wood, and his victory gave Belair, "Sunny Jim" Jockey Jimmy Stout a s double for the afternoon.

8-5 TO WIN DERBY!

So impressive was Johnsto triumph that he was dropped 8 to 5 in Frank Shannon's fu

Continued on Page 22.

Schumacher Routed as Bees Drub Giants, 8-1

By Garry Schumacher

BOSTON, April 29.—The Giants finally got back into uniform today, after their rain-enforced idleness of the past week, but their working clothes were all that identified them as ball players. They possessed little of the skill the occasion demanded either at the plate or in the field, and so absorbed another defeat as the Boston Bees racked up an 8 to 1 decision.

Practically all the afternoon's action was provided by the Bees, and all that was vital was concentrated into one inning, the fifth, when a four-run splurge knocked Hal Schumacher out of the box. Prince Hal was more sinned against than sinning, but in any case what happened was pretty much the ball game.

That was obvious at the time and became increasingly so as Milkman Jim Turner's dipping curve ball lured the Giant bat swingers into a succession of infield outs. Turner confined them to five hits, spread thinly over the entire journey, and three of these were cancelled by fancy Boston double plays. The Boston infielders contributed a gaudy job.

IN SEVENTH PLACE.

As the third successive Manhattan defeat this one dropped the Giants into seventh place below even the Dodgers: Is that Larry MacPhail's raucous laughter floating over the April breezes?

Schumacher pitched handsomely for four innings but his infield betrayed him in the fifth. Zeke Bonura played one grounder into a base hit and Georgie Myatt kicked another. The erstwhile Glamour Boy doesn't seem able to make it. Later in the game he helped the Bees to three more runs when he failed to intercept a throw from Mel Ott.

The tap from Elbie Fletcher's bat that Bonura knocked into a base hit was the start of Schumacher's misfortunes. Eddie Miller lined a single to left and when Lopez walked the bases became filled. There was a temporary lull while Turner popped out, but Deb Garms' single fetched home two runs and a third scored as Myatt

Continued on Page 22.

PENN CREW BEATS RUTGERS, JASPERS

PHILADELPHIA, April 29 (AP).—Pennsylvania's varsity crew defeated Rutgers and Manhattan today on the placid Schuylkill River before 5,000 rowing followers.

Leading all the way, the Red and Blue varsity covered the Henley course of a mile and five sixteenths in 6:58.2.

The Red and Blue took six out of seven events.

4 Penn Relay Titles to Pitt

By Lewis Burton

PHILADELPHIA, April 29.—Gangling John Woodruff and compact Frank Ohl, the Trylon and Perisphere of foot racing, gave 30,000 spectators at Franklin Field today a thorough presentation of the relay race of tomorrow.

Making the maximum of the greatest concentration of power ever brought to bear at the University of Pennsylvania Relays, with Woodruff and Ohl as its chief factors, Pittsburgh pyramided its strength into the mightiest cleanup in the forty-five years' history of the carnival. Ohl led off and Woodruff finished out two record smashing triumphs in the half-mile and one mile races that gave Pitt a four-victory slam in the two-day meet.

WOODRUFF STANDS OUT.

Woodruff, the six foot two Negro, holder of the Olympic 800-meter championship, topped his farewell carnival performance with a fitting flourish. In the final event he unreeled a 47.4 seconds "440" that brought Pitt's colors to the tape a winner in 3:14.8 for the one mile relay, shattering a carnival record made in 1932 by the Bill Carr anchored Penn team.

In the morning, Pitt's team of Ohl, Al Ferrara, Larry Tregoning and Woodruff won the 880-yard sprint relay championship in 1:25.9, blasting six-tenths of a second off a record set by Cornell in a trial heat. Between Pitt's two par shattering feats, New York University won the two-mile relay, North Texas State took the four miles, Virginia skipped off with the 480-yard shuttle hurdles relay and a succession of minor records fell.

ELLERBE EQUALS MARK.

The day produced seven new marks, all told, and a record was equalled in the 100-yard dash. Mozel Ellerbe, the black thunderbolt from Tuskegee, Ala., Institute, won the century sprint in 9.6 seconds, matching a ten-year-old carnival standard and beating Ken Clapp of Brown, intercollegiate indoor champion, by three yards.

In the record debacle, three interscholastic marks, one Class B college relay mark and one teachers college standard toppled. The only two major college times to go by the boards were those that went to Woodruff, Ohl and their cohorts. Pitt's daily double was opened yesterday with its 440-yard and sprint medley victories, and in every one of its four victories Ohl sent the Panthers away in front or on even terms with the opposition.

For Woodruff, participant in three of the victories, the task was made comparatively easy. Whereas in his solitary race yesterday he had to come from behind with a 1:51.2 half mile, he

Continued on Page 20.

The Cleveland Press

Local Forecast: Occasional showers tonight and Sunday, not much change in temperature.

SCRIPPS—HOWARD

FINAL HOME Complete Stocks

PRICE THREE CENTS

ISSUE NO. 19032—IN TWO SECTIONS—SECTION ONE

CLEVELAND, SATURDAY, MAY 21, 1938

Entered as second-class matter, Post Office, Cleveland, O.

HALF AN HOUR TO PLAY ENDS WITH TRAGEDY

Boy, 8, Fatally Injured by Auto as He Romps in Street Before Bedtime

OVERALLS ARE CLEW

Baggy Attire Brings Identification; Mother Sees Death in Hospital

Pictures on Page Three

The fear that presses hard upon parents when sometimes their children are unaccountably missing came to Mrs. Lillian Steadman, mother of five, about two hours after dinner last night.

Eight-year-old Robert, her youngest, with whom she had joked at the table because his baggy overalls "made him look like Charlie Chaplin," had not come home. He had been allowed to go out to play, "but only for a half-hour."

Taking her oldest son, 16-year-old Harvey, Mrs. Steadman began a search of the neighborhood about her home at 4231 E. 96th street. Robert was not to be found. Then, with premonition dragging heavily at her heart, she went to the Broadway-Jones road police station.

Dies at Hospital

Three hours later, at his bedside in St. Alexis' Hospital, she watched him die, unconscious and with a fractured skull and broken leg.

Robert became Cleveland's fifth child traffic victim of the year when he ran into the path of an automobile in Broadway near the city limits, police said.

The baggy overalls as much as anything led his mother to him before he died. When she mentioned them to police at the precinct station, they knew at once that she was the mother of the unidentified child who had been taken to the hospital not long before.

The overalls were garments necessity forced on Robert. Mrs. Steadman, who is divorced from her husband, has been struggling to keep her family together on relief. Weeping, she said today that Robert would have been 9 in another three weeks.

No Money for Funeral

"I thought I would be able to give him some sort of a little present," she added, "but now I don't even have the money to bury him."

Because 12-year-old Mabel, one of her three daughters, is ill in bed with a severe cold, Mrs. Steadman hadn't had time to remove Robert's roller skates from their habitual resting place.

They stood, mute reminders of another traffic tragedy, on the stair. The other two Steadman children are Marie, 14, and Lila, 10.

DAN MOORE NAMED IN $100,000 SUIT

State Securities Chief Accused of Libel by Ex-Aid

Press State Service

COLUMBUS, O., May 21—Edwin Judy, former attorney examiner in the State Division of Securities, filed suit for $100,000 libel and slander damages today against Dan Moore, chief of the Securities Division. His assistant, James Gruener, Earl Pfitzer of Cincinnati and his wife, Martha.

The suit grew out of the investigation by Mr. Moore into the stock selling activities of Vossler & Vossler Inc., of Cincinnati, in connection with the Ohio Mines Corp.

Mr. Judy charged the defendants with conspiring to libel him by means of the investigation at which Mr. Pfitzer testified before Mr. Moore that Mr. Judy had profited from stock sales. Mr. Pfitzer was a salesman for Vossler & Vossler.

WAGE CUT SOUGHT

PITTSBURGH, May 21—Pittsburgh railways and motor coach companies today asked permission of Federal Courts to cut wages and salaries about 11 per cent pending arbitration of a request for still lower permanent contract wage rates.

HENRY FORD KIN DIES

BOISE, Idaho, May 21—Harry H. Bryant, 66, a brother-in-law of Henry Ford, died today.

THE WEATHER

Complete Report on Page 3

Occasional showers tonight and Sunday, not much change in temperature. Moderate variable winds.

Official temperatures:

Midnight	53	7 a. m.	51
1 a. m.	52	8 a. m.	53
2 a. m.	52	9 a. m.	54
3 a. m.	51	10 a. m.	55
4 a. m.	51	11 a. m.	54
5 a. m.	50	Noon	56
6 a. m.	51	1 p. m.	56

Strikeout Prince Meets Home Run Kings

Joe Di Maggio . . . home run champ

Bob Feller . . . strikeout king

Ken Keltner . . . up he goes

Tom Henrich . . . Massillon star

* * *

60,000 Expected at Stadium Tomorrow to See Tribe and Yankees Open Series

By A. C. DE COLA

An epidemic of pennant fever struck Cleveland and northern Ohio today and was spreading into many towns in neighboring New York and Pennsylvania.

The fever, spread by an army of baseball bugs, will reach its height tomorrow at the Stadium.

Not since the closing days of the 1920 campaign, when the Indians won their only pennant, has the disease struck so severely in this territory.

Sixty thousand or more baseball bugs will gather at the Stadium tomorrow, hoping to raise the fever's temperature.

Baseball diagnosticians gave these reasons today for the spread of the fever:

WORLD CHAMPION New York Yankees open a three-game series here in which first place in the American League will be at stake.

THE INDIANS now are riding the crest of a wave of victories that has returned them to the top rung.

BOB FELLER, the Indians' "boy wonder" hurler, will engage in a pitching battle with the ace of the Yankee staff, Vernon "Lefty" Gomez, the goofy Castilian.

ITALIAN DAY at the Stadium tomorrow in which two enemy stars, Joe Di Maggio, dead-pan home run hitter, and Frankie Crosetti, brilliant shortstop, will be honored by members of the Italo-American National Union.

LEADERSHIP of Manager Oscar Vitt, who has daubed his In-

Turn to Page Two

EVENT: Indians vs. Yankees.
PLACE: Cleveland Stadium.
TIME: 3 p. m. tomorrow.

AT BROOKSIDE

Baseball under the floodlights will make its debut here tomorrow night when the Lyon Tailors and the Poschke Barbecues of Class A clash at Brookside Park Stadium. A crowd of 30,000 is expected. The game will be witnessed by members of the Indians and the Yankees.

BOMB WRECKS NEW CAFE HERE

Police Blame Business Foes as Blast Shatters 100 Windows

A dynamite bomb early today wrecked the new Sunset Cafe at 13407 Miles avenue, smashed more than 100 windows in the neighborhood and awakened residents for blocks around.

It's the worst vandalism outrage in months," said Capt. John Savage of the Vandal Squad. "It's a miracle nobody was hurt."

He said he was convinced labor had no part in the bombing and blamed business competition.

Late this morning the street was still littered with glass and debris and emergency crews hurried to restore broken windows in a dozen business places.

The explosion occurred at 3:50 a. m., an hour after the proprietor of the cafe, Benjamin Kuntz, 10105 Garfield parkway, Garfield Heights, had locked up for the night.

Although the place has been open for a week, tonight was to have been the formal opening.

Just before the bomb went off, John Panek, 4117 E. 137th street, a street car motorman on his way to work, said he saw a dark coupe with two men in it driving back and forth in front of the building.

When he turned to look again the car had moved away and the neigh-

Turn to Page Two

DIVIDES 2 MILLIONS AMONG EMPLOYEES

New York Realtor Thinks One "Ought to Ease Down at 60"

By United Press

NEW YORK, May 21—Charles F. Noyes today distributed among his 165 employees most of his share in the $2,000,000 assets of his realty firm because, he said, "at 60 one ought to turn over to others the management of an enterprise they helped build."

He reduced his holdings of common and preferred stock from 80 per cent to less than 25 and canceled a $1,000,000 life insurance policy to save the firm $42,000 in premiums annually.

The Noyes company, which operates some 2250 buildings, has done $60,000,000 business annually.

METHODISTS OKAY BIRTH CONTROL AID

New Englanders Ask Removal of Restricting Laws

By United Press

LYNN, Mass., May 21—Closing birth control clinics in Massachusetts "is a definite threat against the public good," the New England conference of the Methodist Episcopal Church said in a resolution adopted yesterday.

The conference recommended that national and state laws be changed to remove restrictions on dissemination of birth control information.

Night Club Maps New Town to Fight Dry Law Threat

Press State Service

YOUNGSTOWN, O., May 21—Seeking to eliminate threat of a wet and dry election, employees and entertainers in a night club, near here, have voted to incorporate a town on their own 12-acre plot.

The Mahoning County Board of Elections today announced the official tabulation of the Rendezvous Villa special election. The ballot was 33 to 0 for forming the new town.

The proposed village would contain only the night club and cottages housing the employees.

Opponents of the plan have protested to the Board of Elections which has set June 21 as the date for a hearing against the incorporation.

The 12 acres, which would include the boundaries of the proposed town, are located in Austintown Township where voters are reported considering a local option election in the fall.

Officials in Mahoning County said it was the first time in their knowledge that an attempt was made to organize a town to avoid a wet and dry election in northern Ohio.

STRIKE SETTLED AT NATIONAL ACME CO.

1090 to Return Monday After Pact on Vacations

The strike at the National Acme Co. plant at E. 131st street and Coit road was settled this morning and 1090 men will return to work Monday, it was announced by the management.

"Vacation provisions satisfactory to both sides," was the only comment on details of the agreement.

Members of the Mechanics' Educational Society sat down in the plant 10 days ago when vacations with pay were canceled by the company. They walked out of the plant Thursday after a mediator from the U. S. Department of Labor arrived.

"GRAND OLD MAN" DIES

PITTSBURGH, May 21 — Dr. James M. Hamilton, 88, the "grand old man" who attended the sick of the Allegheny Valley for 62 years and brought more than 4000 babies into the world, died yesterday.

STEALS BASE, DIES

GIRARD, O., May 21—Stealing third base in a neighborhood ball game here today had cost the life of D. A. Wellington, 26, father of three children. Doctors said heart disease was the cause of his death.

CHANGES PHONES

Ohio Bell to Eliminate Republic Exchange by September

Gradual elimination of all Republic telephone exchange numbers and substitution of two-party dial phones for four-party lines was under way today, the Ohio Bell Telephone Co. reported. The change over will be complete by September.

Republic numbers will be changed to Randolph, Cedar or Garfield exchanges.

WPA DIRECTOR GOES ON LEAVE

Joseph Alexander Departs Post for Vacation of Two Months

By ROBERT BORDNER

Joseph H. Alexander, WPA director here for two years, today announced he was starting a two-months' leave of absence, his first vacation since he took the post.

Wheelock H. Cameron, supervisor of operations, becomes acting director, and A. E. Edwards becomes assistant to the director, succeeding W. H. Pinkett who resigned May 1, Mr. Alexander announced.

Other changes announced by Mr. Cameron are:

Frank Miskel, senior field engineer takes Mr. Cameron's post as supervisor of operations, his place being filled by promotion of George H. Jordan, former area engineer.

Mr. Edward's place as supervisor of finance is filled by promotion of H. J. Parker of the finance department.

John Cunningham of the finance department becomes chief payroll

Turn to Page Two

URGES EXTENSION OF CLARK AVE. BUS LINE

Schweid Asks Route Be Pushed to E. 55th Street Crosstown

Extension of the Clark Avenue Bridge bus line from McBride avenue and Broadway to crosstown connections at E. 55th street today was recommended by Edward J. Schweid, traction commissioner.

The recommendation was made after surveys by city traction engineers, Councilman Charles Vanic and Leonard Smith, president of the Manufacturers and Business Men's Association.

As results of Mr. Schweid's independent service studies, the Cleveland Railway Co. this week extended the W. 14th-Brainard bus line to W. 25th street and Hilmden avenue and the western terminus of Clark busses from W. 32d street to Fulton road.

Berea Banks Pay $105,000 to Depositors on Monday

Two Berea banks will pay $105,000 to 2600 depositors Monday, it was announced today by the Bank of Berea Co. and the Commercial & Savings Bank.

Bank of Berea Co. will pay $70,000 to 1500 depositors, while the Commercial & Savings Bank will pay $35,000 to 1100 depositors.

Payment of this sum represents 10 per cent of bank deposits frozen in the two institutions since the bank holiday five years ago. Liquidation of assets, plus receipts of $29,000 from the defunct Union Trust Co., made the payment to depositors possible.

Notices have been sent to depositors that the payment is being made. Depositors must present their participation certificates.

Coming closely on the heels of release of $33,000,000 in frozen deposits of the Union Trust Co., the Berea bank payments are expected to react favorably on Berea business.

When the banks resumed normal business in September, 1934, over $1,000,000 was immediately made available to depositors. The rest was placed in the hands of trustees for liquidation, depositors receiving participation certificates for the amount of withheld deposits.

CZECHS ARM 70,000; TWO NAZIS SLAIN

Shooting of Sudeten Germans by Border Guard Aggravates Bitterness Already Aroused by Pre-Election Clashes

CABINET CALLS OUT ALL RESERVES

German Press Unites in Blast of Criticism; Charge Prague Government Is Failing to Protect Minority Groups

By REYNOLDS PACKARD *(Copyright, 1938, by United Press)*

PRAGUE, Czechoslovakia, May 21—The cabinet, after an extraordinary secret session, decided today to call one year of the army reserve corps to the colors.

An hour after the decision was announced it was admitted officially that two farmers of the German minority population had been killed in the early morning hours in an incident at Eger.

The decision to call to the colors one year of the reserve was announced with the comment that it was decided upon in order to ensure peace and order in a series of municipal elections which start tomorrow and that it was not directed against anyone at all.

Several factors entered into a situation which admission of the killing of two Sudeten Germans made a most dramatic one:

TROOP MOVEMENTS were reported yesterday on the German side of the frontier. Great Britain and Czechoslovakia received assurances that they concerned only the shift of men from winter to summer quarters.

THE SUDETEN German party executive complained to the government that it was not protecting Germans and that there could be no negotiations for a minority statute, granting concessions, until guarantees for safety were given.

THE CABINET late last night suddenly called an emergency council meeting.

THE GERMAN press, closely controlled by the Nazi government, chorused denunciation of conditions in Czechoslovakia as intolerable in their editions today.

Shot at Border

The Germans killed were Niklas Boehm and Georg Hofmann, German farmers of the Sudeten area. Nobody knew whether their names would live in history.

According to circles close to the government the two men were trying to cross the German border illegally and refused to obey a police order to halt. Then, these circles said, the police fired.

Thus the incident was more than a mere election fight.

Sudeten German quarters asserted that Boehm and Hofmann were motorcycling at 2:30 a. m. today and that as they passed the border garrison at Eger, state police fired on them. They said that Hofmann was killed instantly and that Boehm died two hours later in a hospital.

According to German reports Sudeten Germans tried to assist Boehm and Hofmann when they cried for help, but were held back by Czech police.

The sitiuation started to tighten into the crisis stage yesterday.

Cabinet Summoned

After a series of clashes incident to the elections, as the result of which the "Sudeten" German minority party complained that their people were being attacked and that the government was not preserving order, the cabinet met late last night in an extraordinary council meeting.

Then, this morning, came the announcement of the call to the colors of a year's reserves—nominally 70,000 men, men who have had two years' military service and are ranked among the best Europe has.

The call was effective at once, and it was executed with such speed that officers and soldiers were called from their beds at homes or from the

Turn to Page Two

* * *

Fear of New Hitler Coup Stirs Alarm in Europe

By WEBB MILLER, *United Press Staff Correspondent*

LONDON, May 21—Czechoslovakia today called to the colors one year's contingent of its army reserve, and sent a chill of anxiety and alarm to every corner of Europe.

It was asserted officially and emphatically that the reserves were called out to insure peace and order in the municipal elections which start tomorrow, and it was added specifically that their assembly was not aimed against anyone outside the country.

But the fear was immediate in all chancelleries that the situation in Europe had been made even more explosive. The great fear was that the German government might consider the call provocatory and that it might in turn increase German military precautions.

The Czechoslovak government's action hit Europe like an electric shock. It came at a time when fears that Adolf Hitler might be preparing to exert in Czechoslovakia the "protective interest" he asserts in Germans outside Germany's frontiers, already had sent shivers of apprehension through European foreign offices.

Diplomatic tension was at its highest point since Hitler's seizure of Austria. There was serious concern in the British and French foreign offices.

The Czechoslovak municipal elections in 11,000 towns, which have stirred widespread clashes between Czechs and Sudeten minority Germans, suddenly brought the situation to a point approaching that of crisis.

Diplomats feared Hitler might decide to take the opportunity, with France and Italy embroiled over intervention in the Spanish war and with Italian-British relations cooled in consequence, to impose his will upon Czechoslovakia, using the electoral disturbances as an excuse.

A series of incidents which brought German-Czechoslovak relations to a head created an atmosphere exactly reminiscent of that which preceded the exertion of Germany's protective interest in Austria.

FIRST: German troop movements on the Czechoslovak frontier. The German general staff said they involved merely a normal transfer of troops from winter to summer quarters.

SECOND: The Sudeten German minority party's abrupt refusal to negotiate with the Czechoslovak government regarding the proposed minorities statute "so long as terrorism continues." This statute was intended to be the government's olive branch to Konrad Henlein, German minority leader.

THIRD: Henlein's sudden and mysterious departure from Prague three days before election. The Prague right wing newspaper Narodni Politika said he was going from the Austrian Alps to visit Hitler at Berchtesgaden. The Sudeten Germans said merely that he had gone to the "Alps," country unspecified, for a vacation.

FOURTH: The almost unprecedently bitter campaign in the German press against the Czechoslovaks, apparently directly inspired by the government and splashing the newspapers with such banner lines as "intolerable Czech provocation."

FIFTH: Premier Hodza's statement yesterday that "we shall be prepared to defend ourselves if need arises."

SIXTH: The German press charges that the Czechoslovak government was directly responsible for attacks upon the Sudeten Germans. This must be read in the light of Hitler's recent statement that he would not per-

Turn to Page Two

IN THE PRESS

Eject Cutcliffe From Fluker Hearing

AVERAGE TEMPERATURES

Atlanta	84	New Orleans	82
Boston	72	New York	76
Chicago	71	San Francisco	64
Los Angeles	67	Seattle	61
Miami	83	Washington	76

ATLANTA GEORGIAN

COMPLETE MARKETS EARLY BLUE STREAK

TELEPHONE WA. 2500—VOL. XXXVIII. No. 49 ATLANTA, GA., WEDNESDAY, JUNE 21, 1939 FIVE CENTS

Paralysis Ends Gehrig's Play

Oust Cutcliffe From Fluker Case Hearing

Charge of Friendship With Mrs. Guyol Arouses Anger

Walter Cutcliffe, pardoned Atlanta lottery king, Wednesday morning was ejected from the Odie V. Fluker clemency hearing at the State Capitol after he charged that Russell Turner, attorney for Fluker, lied when he made statements charging friendship between Cutcliffe and Mrs. Myrtle Guyol, widow of the man Fluker was found guilty of slaying.

Turner, making an impassioned clemency plea for his client before the State Prison and Parole Commission, charged Cutcliffe and Mrs. Guyol were frequently seen together at baseball games and in other places, that they owned a motorboat on Jackson Lake and a cottage on Lake Blue Ridge.

Cutcliffe jumped from his seat, shouting:

"You're lying, you're lying."

CONTEMPT CHARGED

Clem E. Rainey, chairman of the commission, interrupted with the declaration:

"That's enough, Mr. Cutcliffe. That's enough from you."

The members of the commission immediately retired and came out a few minutes later to order Cutcliffe from the chamber.

"If we had the power of contempt we would fine you for contempt of this body," Judge Rainey said. "But we do not have the power, so all we can do is dispense with your presence."

Cutcliffe then apologized, took his hat and left the room in which the hearing was being held.

Earlier in the hearing Solicitor John A. Boykin examined Francis R. Hoyt, of Decatur, a handwriting and ballistics expert he said testified many times for prosecutors and insurance companies.

Hoyt said that in his "unqualified opinion" Fluker had signed the name of Carl L. Williams on the register of the Edison Hotel in Atlanta on April 10 and 17, 1935. Fluker has introduced evidence to show he was in Birmingham attending a labor conference on the latter date, remaining until after the murder of Eddie Guyol on April 23. Mr. Hoyt said that there were 16 points of similarity between the Williams signature and samples of Fluker's handwriting.

SHOOTING ANGLE

In an effort to show that a woman sitting next to Guyol on the seat of his automobile, parked in his Pelham Road driveway, could not have fired the fatal shot, Solicitor Boykin and Mr. Hoyt sat together and attempted to demonstrate the difficulty of the action.

Turner questioned the expert as to the direction taken by the ejected cartridge which was found between the front seats, and as to whether Mrs. Guyol would have been deafened by the shot which she said was fired over her shoulder by a man standing on the running board.

The Lindbergh kidnaping case was introduced when Boykin asked Mr. Hoyt if, from his study of handwriting, he believed that Bruno Hauptmann had written the ransom notes. The reply was affirmative.

The Cutcliffe episode came shortly before the hearing recessed for lunch. It was revealed recently that Cutcliffe, who received a fine and suspended sentence when he pleaded guilty to lottery operations in 1937, was paroled by Governor Rivers on May 15.

Delaware Results

FIRST RACE—$1,000, claiming, 3-year-olds and up, ¾ mile.
Scarlet O 105 (Friedman) 30.000 12.30 8.30
Sand Cloud 112 (R. Scott) 10.30 6.90
Chance Watch 107 (Stevenson) 3.40
Time 1:16 3-5; off 2:07½.
Elwawa, Walli, Blablah, Remolee, Lina's Son, Nugget, Shindig, Byrds Flight, Kelly Pot also ran.

Legion Warned On Red Danger

Dies Committeeman Tells Perils Of Propaganda in Schools

Legionnaires and hundreds of citizens—who united Tuesday night in a fervent Americanism rally—were told by Congressman Joe Starnes, Dies committee member, that the greatest danger to the nation's future lies in a band of men and women quietly at work in its schools and colleges.

This determined group does not care for acclaim and they wear no uniforms and wave no banners, he said. On the surface they are small in number and their efforts are weak and ineffectual.

"They are master propagandists who have found that more can be gained from working silently, relentlessly and without show."

"They are the Communists."

The rally at which Mr. Starnes spoke, held at the City Auditorium, officially opened the 21st annual convention of the American Legion of Georgia. Lashing out at all un-American elements, he drew the greatest applause from the audience when, speaking as a private citizen, he advocated a four-point program. It was:

4-POINT PROGRAM

1. Deportation of every foreign saboteur and spy.

2. Swift and thorough dissolution of all foreign secret societies that use force to gain their ends.

3. Immediate withdrawal of federal and state funds from all schools or institutions that advocate any "ism" except Americanism.

4. Enactment of legislation, both federal and state, providing that Americans only shall administer the affairs of state.

"I have come to the conclusion," he said, "that we should close the doors to all alien job-seekers until we have found work for every American."

Citing the work of his committee, which has on file thousands of pages of testimony on activities of subversive forces, Congressman Starnes said the group long ago had struck "pay dirt" in its investigation.

'DANGER IS WITHIN'

"When I first heard of the contemplated investigation, I was indifferent because I knew nothing of these subversive activities. I realized later I was

(Continued on Page 8, Col. 1.)

Aqueduct Results

FIRST RACE—$1,000, claiming, maiden 2-year-olds, ⅝ mile:
Air Stream 111 (J. Adams) 8-5 1-2 1-4
aQuaroma 111 (E. Arcaro) 4-1 2-1
Baggrave 117 (Meade) 7-10
Time :59 (off 2:32½).
aHappy Haunt, Spanish Duke, Brown Devil, Aboyne also ran. (aG. B. Travers Stable entry.)

SECOND RACE—$1,000, claiming, maiden 3-year-olds and up, 1 mile.
Claro 109 (R. W. Smith) 7-5 1-2 1-4
Sting Ray 114 (Wagner) 2-1 1-1
Bad Day 105 (Olguin) 5-2
Time 1:41; off 3:00.
Carraigeen, Guitar, Titanium, Tesor Mia, Grandstar, Entour, Galcrest also ran.

THIRD RACE—$1,000, claiming, 4-year-olds and up, 6½ furlongs:
Jim's Niece 111 (S. Renick) 10-1 4-1 2-1
Sky Argo 114 (P. Mills) 2-1 1-1
Devil's Mate 111 (N. Wall) 1-5
Time 1:19 1-5 (off 3:28).
Departed, First Entry, La Charite, Cuckoo, Papa Jack also ran.

Lincoln Fields Results

FIRST RACE—$800, claiming, 4-year-olds and up, ¾ mile:
Sky Cloud 107 (E. Hanke) 7.00 4.80 3.60
Silver Braid 110 (T. P. Martin) 31.20 12.40
Fair So 105 (G. South) 5.80
Time 1:14 2-5 (off 2:18½).
Star Bess, Paulson, Dark Seeker, Sun Erin, Lady Velvet, Heliostat also ran.

Suffolk Downs Results

FIRST RACE—$1,000, claiming, 3-year-olds, one mile:
Double Tough 109 (Berger) 15.00 19.80 7.60
Drosera 104 (F. A. Smith) 6.40 3.60
Post Office 101 (R. Merritt) 3.00
Time 1:43 2-5 (off 2:18).
Royal Upset, Transvine, Sunabell, Tee Tee also ran.

SECOND RACE—$1,000, caliming, 3-year-olds, ¾ mile.
Cordate 111 (Eccard) 16.60 8.60 6.80
Prunay 111 (Krovitz) 12.40 8.20
Questionable 111 (Van Tassel) 16.20
Time 1:15 4-5; off 2:52½.
Charming, General Hay, Martin Boy, Prophecy, Grimes Golden, White Topper, Savant, Regal Link, Selmajack also ran.

THIRD RACE—$2,000, maiden 2-year-olds, ⅝ mile:
Smilin' Jack 116 (Rosen) 9.80 4.80 4.00
High Aim 116 (Fels) 7.80 5.00
Deimos 111 (Dickey) 5.40
Time 1:01 3-5 (off 3:23½).
Dark Palatine, Town Prince, Iron Bar also ran.

Truck Carriers Banned Under Police Order

A general crackdown on unlicensed operators of trucks and other vehicles who have been conducting a flourishing business of hauling hundreds of government relief laborers to and from their work was ordered Wednesday by Assistant Chief A. J. Holcombe.

The order followed the arrest of Rufus Barber, negro, living on Walnut Street, on a charge of "operating a truck for hire without a license" and a subsequent ruling by Assistant City Attorney Charlie Murphy to the effect that vehicles used to haul these workers are subject to city and state regulations governing the operation of buses.

Murphy made his ruling after conferring with J. H. Smith, special investigator for Chief Hornsby, who is out of town, and the police committee of City Council, on the matter. Smith then requested Assistant Chief Holcombe to issue the crackdown order.

Barber was arrested by Motorcycle Officers E. H. Johnson and H. T. Jenkins. His truck was loaded with approximately 30 negro workers.

"There are about 30 or 40 of these trucks operating," Inspector Smith declared. "Most of them are really too dilapidated for any use, much less that of hauling passengers."

In order to comply with city and state bus regulations, each operator would have to post $50,000 bond and each vehicle would have to have seating facilities for 17 or more passengers, it was pointed out.

New Jersey Senator Favors Third Term

WASHINGTON, June 21.—(INS)—New Jersey's 32 delegates will go to the 1940 Democratic National Convention with instructions to draft President Roosevelt for a third term, Senator Smathers (Democrat), of New Jersey, predicted today. He said Mr. Roosevelt is the only Democrat who could carry New York State, and that Mayor La Guardia of New York City would support the President for a third term.

Britain 'Ready To Take Steps' Against Japan

Does Not 'Acquiesce' In Tokio's Action In Far East

By CHARLES A. SMITH, I. N. S. Staff Correspondent.

LONDON, June 21. — Great Britain does not acquiesce to the Japanese blockade of Tientsin "and is prepared to take any steps necessary to insure food supplies" for the British residents, Prime Minister Neville Chamberlain told the House of Commons today.

In reply to a question by former Foreign Secretary Anthony Eden, the Prime Minister made clear that his government has no intention of accepting the Japanese blockade without taking suitable measures to combat it.

Asked whether Japan's failure to formulate her grievances against Great Britain did not make negotiations more difficult, Chamberlain said:

"Yes, it does. But we hope they will formulate their grievances."

The Prime Minister told the House that Britain had not discussed the Tientsin situation with Soviet Russia.

The position of the Tokio government regarding the main issues in the Anglo-Japanese conflict is still "unclear," Chamberlain told the House.

CITES INDIGNITIES

Chamberlain stated four Britons have been stripped and searched while passing the barricades at Tientsin, but said no further incidents have been reported.

The Prime Minister asserted it has not yet been decided whether the issues will be thrashed out at Tientsin or in Tokio, but added that further word on developments was anticipated today or tomorrow.

Japanese Foreign Minister Arita, Chamberlain said, has promised to institute an inquiry into alleged discrimination against and ill-treatment of British residents of Tientsin.

British Ambassador Sir Robert Leslie Craigie has repeatedly called the Japanese government's

(Continued on Page 4, Col. 6.)

Lost 'Baby Clipper' Reports Conflict

PETITE RUCHER, N. B., June 21.—(INS)—Attempts to track down a report that the "Baby Clipper" plane of Thomas Smith, the missing aviator, may have crashed in the heavy woods along the New Brunswick coast during his recent attempt to fly the Atlantic were snagged today in a variety of conflicting statements obtained from residents of the sparsely populated region.

'LARRUPIN' LOU' IS THROUGH

Doctors at Mayo Clinic, Rochester, Minn., looked over Lou Gehrig, "Iron Horse" of the New York Yankees, and Wednesday the decision was made public: "Larrupin' Lou" is through as a baseball player, the victim of a form of infantile paralysis which demands careful treatment and no violent exercise.

International News Picture.

Joe F. Cannon, N. C. Textile Leader, Dies

HOT SPRINGS, Ark., June 21. (INS)—Joe Franklin Cannon, 63, of Concord, N. C., millionaire textile manufacturer, was found dead in his bed in his hotel suite here today. He apparently had died in his sleep.

His physician, Dr. Leonard Ellis, said that Cannon died of apoplexy.

He had come to Hot Springs five weeks ago.

The body will be sent back to his home in Concord this afternoon, it was announced.

NAMED IN SUIT

Cannon several years ago was named defendant in a $250,000 alienation of affections suit which gained nationwide publicity and which was filed against him by his son-in-law, F. Brandon Smith, Jr. Smith charged Cannon with alienating the affections of Smith's wife, Anne Cannon Reynolds Smith, Cannon's daughter.

Smith, a real estate broker, charged that Cannon broke up his marriage to retain custody of Cannon's little granddaughter, Anne Cannon Reynolds, heiress to a large part of the Reynolds tobacco millions. Smith claimed that Cannon refused to let the child live at the Smith home in Charlotte, North Carolina.

The 18 months marriage of Smith and Cannon's daughter, the divorced wife of the late Smith Reynolds, heir to the Reynolds tobacco fortune, ended in May, 1934. They were divorced in Hot Springs.

ILL SEVERAL YEARS

Cannon had been in ill health for several years and had been in Hot Springs since May 16. He was the son of the late J. W. Cannon, founder of the giant Cannon Mills Company of Concord and Kannapolis.

Although Cannon still was connected with a number of textile companies, he had been inactive since 1932.

Husband Swapped By Grandmother

COLUMBIAVILLE, Mich., June 21.—(INS)—Two rural wives, one a grandmother, the other a slim woman of 27, today made a friendly swap of husbands.

They also divided up 14 children, each taking seven.

A cow was moved from one home to the other to assure the younger children of fresh milk.

Here's the lineup:

Mrs. Mildred Davis, 27, mother of four girls, is keeping house in the one-room farmhouse of Clarence June, 42.

Mrs. Edith June, 47, mother of 12, is keeping house in Columbiaville for George Davis, 45.

Mrs. Davis is caring for her four little girls and three of the June children, Clarence, Clair and Herbert, all needed to help work the farm.

Mrs. June is keeping seven of her own children. Two of Mrs. June's daughters are married and don't figure in the deal.

A cow was moved from the June farm to the Davis township home.

Living two miles apart, the two families are maintaining friendly relations.

As yet there has been no divorce, but June and Mrs. Davis plan to file suits and later there will be a double wedding.

Mrs. Davis explained:

"We're all perfectly happy. I love Clarence and that is all there is to it. George, my husband, is perfectly happy, too. It all happened quite suddenly."

Mrs. June said:

"You must understand. My married daughter is living here and everything is as it should be. The neighborhood has been up in arms but there is nothing to get excited about. My friends here need have no fear that we are misbehaving."

AMERICAN LEAGUE

CHICAGO .... 022 0-- --- --- - - -
At NEW YORK .... 000 --- --- --- - - -
Lee and Tresh; Gomez and Dickey.

ST. LOUIS .... 022 00- --- --- - - -
At BOSTON .... 000 00- --- --- - - -
Kramer and Glenn; Heving, Dickman and Peacock.

Detroit at Philadelphia, will be played later date.

NATIONAL LEAGUE

NEW YORK .... 220 --- --- --- - - -
At PITTSBURGH .... 000 --- --- --- - - -
Melton and Danning; Tobin and Mueller.

Brooklyn at Cincinnati, night game.

SOUTHERN LEAGUE

Atlanta at Chattanooga, night game, 9:15.
New Orleans at Birmingham, night game.
Memphis at Little Rock, will be played later date.

TODAY'S INDEX

Baseball Star Remains on Yank Roster

'Have to Take Bitter With Sweet,' Says First Baseman

NEW YORK, June 21.—(INS)—Lou Gehrig is through as a ball player. The "Iron Horse" has been officially disqualified by the Mayo Clinic, of Rochester, Minn., which finds that the veteran Yankee first baseman is suffering from a form of infantile paralysis which calls for careful treatment and abstinence from violent exercise.

Gehrig has lived with this verdict for two days and he put up a brave front after President Edward Barrow, of the New York Yankees, made the official announcement in Manager Joe McCarthy's dressing room this afternoon.

"You have to take the bitter with the sweet," Lou said, as he put on his baseball uniform. "If it's my finish as a player I'll have to take it, but I'm going to give it a fight."

MATES HEAR NEWS

The other Yankees, sympathetically huddled in small groups, heard the news from McCarthy. They were embarrassed and silent, hardly knowing what to say, and one by one they drifted over to Gehrig's locker and tried to put

(Continued on Page 11, Col. 2.)

Clearings Gain 15 Straight Days

Completing the fifteenth successive increase, longest period for the year to date, Atlanta bank clearings Wednesday totaled 11 million dollars, for a gain of $2,200,000 over the same day last year. The previous record was established last month when check transactions increased for 14 consecutive days.

Flying Reporters To Visit Duchess

PARIS, June 21.—(INS)—Newspapermen and women who came to France on the first passenger-carrying flight of the trans-ocean Atlantic Clipper will be received at 6 p. m. today by the Duchess of Windsor at her Paris home.

Market Summary

STOCKS: Steady in sluggish mart; total sales, 466,050 shares.

BONDS: Fractionally higher; total sales, $5,545,100.

CURB STOCKS: Irregular; total sales, 77,000 shares.

COTTON: 1 to 14 points up; Atlanta spots unchanged at 10.05c.

GRAINS: Weak; wheat off 1 cent a bushel.

$70,716 Paid In Job Insurance

Unemployment compensation amounting to $70,716.87 was paid out by the Bureau of Unemployment Compensation last week to unemployed workers of the state, Commissioner of Labor Ben T. Huiet announced Wednesday. The payments represented disposition of 3,454 initial claims and 11,985 continued claims. A total of 11,652 checks were issued.

HOURLY Temperatures

12 Midnight	83	8 A. M.	8[illegible]
1 A. M.	80	9 A. M.	8[illegible]
2 A. M.	78	10 A. M.	84
3 A. M.	78	11 A. M.	87
4 A. M.	76	12 Noon	89
5 A. M.	75	1 P. M.	89
6 A. M.	76	2 P. M.	91
7 A. M.	72	3 P. M.	91

(Forecast on Page Two.)

Wednesday NOT Longest 1939 Day

Atlanta weather conversationalists set out from their homes Wednesday morning, brimming with talk of the summer solstice and canny observations that "this is the longest day of the year."

But, aha, they're wrong!

Stripping the situation of all its technical aspects, the explanation is this, according to the local Weather Bureau:

"We have to throw in an extra day once in a while to straighten the calendar out, and that process occasionally fouls the solstice schedule."

Thus, the summer solstice will occur here at 2:40 a. m. Thursday and June 22 will become the longest day in the year—by the smallest fraction of a second. The sun will rise at 5:27 and set at 7:53, Atlanta time, giving 14.4 hours of daylight.

Stars Defeat Sacs, 6 to 5, in Ninth

Los Angeles Examiner Sports
CHARACTER QUALITY AMERICA FIRST ENTERPRISE ACCURACY
AN AMERICAN PAPER FOR THE AMERICAN PEOPLE — THE GREAT NEWSPAPER OF THE GREAT SOUTHWEST
JUNE 22, 1939 CCC SECTION II

Sports by Al Santoro

Sports Editor of the Examiner

Lou Gehrig was called the Iron Horse. Apparently nothing could run him down. Rain or shine, hot or cold, there was the Old Iron Horse holding down first base for the New York Yankees. As much of a fixture at first as the Statue of Liberty—and he could reach just as high for the overthrows.

Minor league first basemen dreaded graduating to the Yanks. Any other major league club! But not the Yankees. What was the use! There was small hope that when Miller Huggins or Joe McCarthy turned over the daily lineup to the umpire that any rookie first baseman would get the 1000 to 1 chance of breaking in. For though the lineup might change in other positions it was always the same around first base. There was the Old Iron Horse, as mighty a hitter as Babe Ruth, still doing a thriving business at the same old stand.

Lifetime Batting Average .341

Early this year the Old Iron Horse seemed to stumble as they led him from the stable. The keen pair of eyes, which had earned him the lifetime batting average of .341, had dimmed. In the parlance of baseball—Gehrig wasn't hitting the size of his hat, and what with Joe DiMaggio, the youngster, pulling up lame at about the same time, the prospect seemed not too bright for the Yankees.

Now Gehrig was also playing captain of the team, and it behooves the captain, as well as the manager, to put foremost the welfare of the team. The Old Iron horse scratched himself from the lineup—for the first time in 16 years and an understudy—Babe Dahlgren, formerly of the San Francisco Missions of the Pacific Coast League—was the new name fans read in the batting order.

Gehrig's benching of Gehrig brought to an abrupt and rather startling end a consecutive playing record of 2130 games, far in excess of the mark set by Everett Scott, a Yankee shortstop of another day.

It was a glorious record of servitude, but achieved at great cost to a physical and nervous system.

Sixteen Years of Consecutive Play

Sixteen seasons of play! We may assume that Gehrig, though endowed with particularly fine physical endurance, must have, some time during those years, suffered from common colds and ordinary ailments. It would seem apparent that these common ailments have taxed the vitality and taken their toll. For any man to go through as long and as perfect a physical record is nothing short of startling. But these common ailments must have stayed within his system, and when his great vitality ebbed, those stored up minor infections broke through, and now become known.

The End of the Trail

Yesterday Dr. Harold C. Habein at Mayo Clinic gave Ed Barrow, president of the New York Yankees, the bad news. Barrow passed it on to the newspaper men:

"Gehrig is suffering from a mild attack of infantile paralysis."

Good news, if such it may be called, was that Gehrig will remain as he has been doing since earlier this year—on the bench, draw his salary of $35,000.

But for the Old Iron Horse, who insisted he was only temporarily out to baseball pasture, Barrow's announcement means—the end of the trail.

A Few Remarks From the Gallery

Rice Institute will be the only college in the country to boast a line and backfield averaging over 200 pounds. The line averages 203 pounds and the backfield 201. The weights have been checked and you can bet all the Rice in Japan—and in the Institute—they're correct, according to Norman Sper. . . . Major Neyland of Tennessee has a greater percentage of victories than any other football coach in the country. His victories are 89 per cent over a span of 12 years. Sper also predicts that on January 1, 1940, the University of Tennessee will trot into the Pasadena Rose Bowl to oppose—the Trojans.

From New York Frank Tabor writes: "Ceferino Garcia looked like the best middleweight to come along in ages when he flattened Walter (Popeye) Woods the other night in the Garden. Garcia was 3 to 1 short-ender at the time and the "New Yorkels" took the favorite—and a bath. Garcia is signed to box Fred Apostoli in New York, September 7. . . . Tony Galento is 10 to 1 on the short end. Julian Black said at Pompton Lakes the other day:

"These guys are getting more for their 50 cents they pay to watch Joe training than those who'll pay $27.50 at the fight."

In other words—short and sweet for Joseph!

British Net Ace Bows

LONDON, June 21.—(AP)—Handsome Frank Kukuljevic of Yugoslavia eliminated the Wimbledon favorite, veteran Henry Wilfred (Bunny) Austin, in the third round of the London grass courts tennis championships at the Queens Club today, 6-4, 6-4.

At the same time Bobby Riggs of Chicago, second seeded and second choice to Austin in the Wimbledon tourney, went into the quarter-finals by beating A. D. Russell of Argentina, 6-8, 6-3, 6-3. Riggs previously had had a tough three-set fight with New Zealand's champion, N. V. Edwards.

Elwood Cooke of Portland, Ore., also went into the quarter-finals by beating Gene Smith of Berkeley, Calif., 4-6, 6-2, 6-2. Tomorrow he will meet Baron Gottfried von Cramm of Germany, who defeated J. S. Comery of Great Britain, 6-4, 6-1.

Ignac Tlogzynski of Poland, who is seeded eight for the Wimbledon tournament, eliminated Bill Robertson of California, 7-5, 6-3, in the second round, but was beaten in the third by I. G. Collins of Britain, 6-2, 4-6, 6-4.

Rainiers Release Veteran Pickrel

SEATTLE, June 21.—(AP)—The Seattle Rainiers of the Pacific Coast League handed Clarence Pickrel, veteran right-handed pitcher, his release today. Bob Stagg, young Seattle high school catcher, was signed up.

LAST ROUNDUP—Father Time and infantile paralysis caught up with Lou Gehrig, New York Yanks' famous first baseman, and laid him low. An examination yesterday revealed Gehrig's condition, which has caused him to slump this season. At the right is Columbia Lou cracking one high, wide and handsome at the zenith of his career.
—Picture from International News Photograph Service.

Cubs Send Epperly to L. A.

Al Epperly, young right-handed pitcher who has been the property of the Chicago Cubs for several seasons, will report to the Los Angeles Angels on option next week, it was announced yesterday.

Epperly has been with Milwaukee most of the season after spending spring training with the Cubs. He has worked very little for the Brewers, however, winning two and losing two.

Pitching has been the weakest point in the Angel club this season, and Epperly will probably be cast in the role of a starter.

He broke into baseball in 1937 with Moline, winning 14 games and losing six. Epperly is 21 years old, stands 6 feet 2 inches tall and weighs 197 pounds.

N. Y. Saber Stars Arrive at Fair

SAN FRANCISCO, June 21.—(AP)—Dr. John Huffman, six times holder of the national saber championship, and Ralph Marston were here today to represent the New York Athletic Club in the national fencing championships at Treasure Island in San Francisco Bay, June 26 to July 2.

Coast League Standings

	W.	L.	Pct.	*GLB.
LOS ANGELES	49	34	.590	...
Seattle	48	34	.585	½
San Francisco	42	37	.532	5
Oakland	41	41	.500	7½
San Diego	36	43	.456	11
HOLLYWOOD	37	45	.451	11½
Sacramento	34	43	.442	12
Portland	32	42	.423	12½

YESTERDAY'S RESULTS

HOLLYWOOD, 6; Sacramento, 5.

Oakland, 13; San Diego, 0.

LOS ANGELES, 4; Portland, 2.

Seattle, 10; San Francisco, 1.

White Wins When Foe Banned

By Dudley Vernon

Tarzan White won the hard way last night at the Olympic Auditorium, when he was awarded the doctor's decision after the Black Panther, with the aid of his manager, Count Rossi, had fouled White on the ropes.

White took the first fall with his usual vicious flying tackles in 17:11. The second fall was awarded to the Panther on a foul in 6:45.

WHITE CORNERED

Immediately thereafter, White came out and was cornered by the Panther. Rossi then reached into the ring and gouged White in the eyes while the Panther threw some vicious hooks into his mid-section.

With White in apparent agony, Dr. Lloyd Mace pronounced him in no condition to continue.

STEINKE WINS

Lieutenant Manlapig pinned Ivan Mannagoff with a body press in 6:25. Hans Steinke closed the show in 11:21 to subdue Hardboiled Haggerty with a body press.

Dr. "Dropkick" Murphy disposed of Jim Austeri with a single dropkick to win in 8:35. Ed Payson and George Pencheff went 20 minutes to a draw. Casey Columbo put Flash Gordon out of commission in 9:36 with a back body drop. Jose Sevilla, using some very effective rolling headlocks, won over Frank Cutler in 9:26 and Bob Gregory opened the show, going 20 minutes on even terms with Bob Coleman.

Aussies, Mexico Battle June 30

MEXICO CITY, June 21.—(INS)—Australia's Davis Cup team will play a picked squad from the Mexican Lawn Tennis Association in zone matches on June 30 and July 1, it was announced today.

Mako, Lubin Triumph

CHICAGO, June 21.—A group of California netmen, led by Gene Mako and Ronald Lubin of Los Angeles, led the march into the fourth round today in the National Clay Court championships.

Mako, seeded third, made short work of James Evert of Chicago, 6-3, 6-0, and Lubin, rated 12th, defeated John Krietenstein, Chicago, 6-4, 6-4.

Two University of California aces, Douglas Imhoff and Robert Harman of Berkeley, passed third round tests. Imhoff outstroked Robert Jakes, Milwaukee, 6-3, 6-3, and Harman downed a teammate, Tate Coulthard, Berkeley, 2-6, 6-0, 6-0.

In other matches, Harold Surface, Kansas City, defeated James Blade, Ohio, 6-0, 6-0; Henry Prusoff, Seattle, defeated Gordon Reeder, Ohio, 0-6, 7-5, 6-3; Wilbur Coen, Kansas City, defeated Ed Lorfing, Kansas City, 6-3, 6-1.

Williams' Miscue Fatal to Solons

Locals Rally for Triumph

By Bob Hunter

Staging courageous and thrilling eighth and ninth-inning rallies which netted them six runs, the apparently rejuvenated Hollywood Stars pulled another contest from the fire last night, nosing out the Sacramento Solons, 6 to 5, at Gilmore Field.

It was the third straight victory for the Stars, who apparently have snapped out of the lethargy which gripped the club for a couple of weeks and dropped them to sixth place.

For seven innings the Hollywood fans sat back and groaned as the slugging Solons, blasting out two home runs, hung up a seemingly impregnable 5-0 lead.

KAHLE DRIVES IN FOUR

In the eighth, the Stars broke into violent action, however, filling the bases with two out. Bob Kahle hit a homer to end a parade of four runs across the plate.

When the ninth came around, the smoking Stars still were in the same belligerent frame of mind and yanked the contest out of the inferno.

Young Cliff Dapper was sent in to bat for Wayne Osborne and obliged with a single to center. Frankie Morehouse sending Dapper to third.

This blow also sent Al Sherer to the showers. Ira Smith relieved and purposely passed Frenchy Uhalt to fill the bases.

With the count 3-and-2, Bill Cissell fouled off several pitches and the blood-pressure of the excited fans rose steadily with each one. Finally Smith missed the corner with a fast ball, forcing Dapper in with the tying run.

'THROWS GAME AWAY'

Babe Herman hit a roller back to Dib Williams, who threw the ball hurriedly and it kicked up the dirt in front of the plate and rolled away from Catcher Brusie Ogrodowski, permitting Morehouse to score easily with the winning run.

Tonight the clubs play the third game of the series, with Bill Fleming pitching for the Stars and Tony Freitas working for the Sacs.

Sacramento	AB	H	O	A
Marshall.lf	5	2	0	0
Williams.2b	4	1	2	3
Wieczork.rf	1	1	0	0
Garibaldi.3b	3	2	1	5
Barton.1b	4	1	14	0
Scoffic.cf	4	1	1	0
Orengo.ss	3	0	1	4
Ogrodwski.c	3	1	2	1
Sherer.p	4	0	1	3
Winsett.rf	2	1	2	0
Smith.p	0	0	0	0
Totals	33	10	24	16

Hollywood	AB	H	O	A
Morehse.ss	5	1	2	2
Uhalt.cf	2	1	3	0
Cissell.2b	4	0	6	4
Herman.1b	4	0	9	0
Puccinelli.rf	4	1	1	0
Orsatti.lf	3	2	4	0
Kahle.3b	4	1	0	1
Brenzel.c	3	1	2	3
Darrow.p	0	0	0	0
Osborne.p	3	0	0	2
Harris	1	0	0	0
Crandall.c	0	0	0	0
Dapper	1	1	0	0
Totals	34	8	27	12

None out when winning run scored.
Harris batted for Brenzel in 8th.
Dapper batted for Osborne in 9th.

Sacramento	2	0	1	0	0	1	0	1	0	—5
Hollywood	0	0	0	0	0	0	0	4	2	—6

Errors—Williams, Marshall, Morehouse, Puccinelli.

Home runs—Winsett, Garibaldi. Two-base hits—Wieczorek, Uhalt, Orsatti, Williams, Morehouse. Runs batted in—Garibaldi 2, Winsett, Scoffic, Kahle 4, Cissell. Runs—Morehouse, Cissell, Puccinelli, Orsatti, Kahle, Dapper, Garibaldi 2, Williams, Wieczorek, Winsett. Winning pitcher—Osborne. Losing pitcher—Sherer. Innings pitched—Darrow, 1; Sherer, 8 plus. At bat—Off Darrow, 5; Sherer, 33. Hits—Off Darrow, 3; Sherer, 8. Runs scored—Off Darrow, 2; Sherer, 4. Runs responsible for—Darrow, 2; Osborne, 2; Sherer, 3. Strikeouts—Osborne, 2; Sherer, 2. Bases on balls—Off Osborne, 3; Sherer, 3; Smith, 2. Wild pitch—Darrow. Passed ball—Brenzel. Left on bases—Sacramento, 5; Hollywood, 10. Sacrifice—Garibaldi. Stolen base—Garibaldi. Double play—Morehouse to Cissell to Herman. Time—2:15. Umpires—Doran and Engeln.

Coast Track Stars Top Big Ten

BERKELEY, June 21.—(AP)—Pacific Coast track and field athletes demonstrated their superiority over Big Ten rivals late today by winning a 94 1-3 to 36 2-3 victory in the third annual dual meet between picked teams of the two big conferences.

Held on the longest day of the year, the first major twilight meet ever held in the Far West attracted a turnout of 12,000 fans.

They saw a full sized dual competition run off in probably record time of an hour and 25 minutes, during which the Coast athletes snatched 13 first places in the 15 events.

The Coast team also scored a clean sweep in the 100-yard dash.

Bill Dale of Washington State College, took the half mile in 1:51.5, while Louis Zamperini of Southern California came through with a winning mile of 4:11.9.

The Coast mile relay quartet edged out the Big Ten boys, according to official ruling, in the closest race of the meet. Motion pictures were to be studied later to confirm the decision.

Clyde Jeffery of Stanford was the individual high point winner, taking the 100 and 220-yard dashes for 10 tallies. He was clocked in 9.9 and 21.1 seconds respectively.

Bill Watson, Negro star of Michigan, was second high point getter with 9. He took seconds in the discus, shotput and broad jump.

The Big Ten squad won only the two-mile run and the 220-yard low hurdles, in which Roy Cochran of Indiana breasted the tape ahead of Earl Vickery of Southern California in 23.3 seconds.

(Summary on fifth sports page)

'No Baseball Probe' Satisfies Feller

WASHINGTON, June 21.—(AP)—Bob Feller, Cleveland's fireball pitcher, was assured by a member today that the Federal monopoly committee does not intend to investigate baseball.

Feller dropped in on the committee's investigation of life insurance practices and was quickly spied in the audience by Acting Chairman Reece.

"We have Bob Feller with us," Reece interrupted the hearing to [illegible] I will say for him that we have no intention of investigating baseball."

Feller beat a quick retreat.

U. S. Net Queen Seeded No. One

WIMBLEDON, Eng., June 21.—(AP)—United States Champion Alice Marble of San Francisco and Great Britain's Bunny Austin were seeded No. 1 today in the All-England Lawn Tennis Club singles championships starting Monday.

Austin, runnerup to Don Budge in the final last year, was given top place over Bobby Riggs because of the latter's defeat by Don McNeill of Oklahoma City in the final of the French championships last week. McNeill was listed third in the seeded list and Helen Jacobs of Oakland, Calif., second in women's ranking.

Sports Today

HORSE RACING

AT HOLLYWOOD PARK—Eight races. First Post 2:00 p. m.

BASEBALL

AT GILMORE FIELD—Hollywood Stars vs. Sacramento Solons, at 8:15 p. m.

AUTO RACING

AT GILMORE STADIUM—Weekly card of midget auto races, 8:30 p. m.

BOXING

AT JEFFRIES BARN—Regular weekly amateur card, prelims at 8:30 p. m.

SOFTBALL

AT FIEDLER FIELD—Two girls' games at 7:30 p. m.

GOLF

AT LAKESIDE—Invitational tournament at 9:00 a. m. Continuing all day.

Trojan Athlete Quits Gridiron

An unconfirmed report last night stated that Mickey Anderson, Trojan halfback and great sprinter, who has notched many points for the mighty Troy track and field squad this season, will pass up the football squad this year and concentrate on track, in an effort to make the 400-meter relay quartet on the 1940 Olympic Games team.

Gabrielson New Hollywood Star

Len Gabrielson, property of the New York Yankees and who played for the Seattle Rainiers last season, yesterday was purchased by the Hollywood Stars from Baltimore on a conditional basis.

Gabrielson is a towering first baseman. He hits left-handed and has plenty of power.

Walker Polishes Off 'Red' Bush

HAGERSTOWN, Md., June 21.—(AP)—Mickey Walker, in search of a heavyweight white hope, polished off Red Bush of Cumberland, Md., with a knockout in the second round tonight. In the main event, Joey Silver, 129 pounds, of Los Angeles won the decision from Jimmy Lancaster, 131½, of Wilmington, Del.

Yanks' 13 Homers in Two Games Blast Records

ATHLETICS DOWNED BY 23-2 AND 10-0

Yanks Get 8 Homers, New High, in Opener—Two-Game Figure of 13 Also Sets Record

TOTAL-BASE MARK FALLS

Dahlgren, DiMaggio and Gordon Have 3 Circuit Blows Each —Gomez Hurls 3-Hitter

By LOUIS EFFRAT

Special to THE NEW YORK TIMES.

PHILADELPHIA, June 28.—A long distance slugging spree, unparalleled in the 100-year history of the national pastime, carried the world champion Yankees to a pair of new major league records and one American League mark today as the New Yorkers punched the Athletics into submission twice, 23—2 and 10—0, at Shibe Park.

Blasting thirteen home runs, eight in the opening encounter, the McCarthymen shattered the homer standards for a single game and for two consecutive contests. And when in the seventh inning of the curtainer-raiser Babe Dahlgren propelled his second drive into the stands it meant that the Yankees had hit for a total of fifty-three bases, a new junior loop record and only two under the major league mark.

Dahlgren, Joe DiMaggio and Joe Gordon, each with three circuit smashes, paced the Yankees. Tommy Henrich, Bill Dickey, George Selkirk and Frankie Crosetti made one apiece as a banner crowd of 21,612 persons watched with amazement this mighty display of power, which threatened to go on indefinitely.

Gomez in Top Form

When the McCarthymen were not busy hitting four-baggers, they filled in the time with short range blows that took effect just as well. They banged out twenty-seven in the opener and sixteen in the nightcap. All in all, it was quite a day and Monte Pearson and Vernon (Lefty) Gomez, who divided the twirling assignments, enjoyed themselves no end. Pearson yielded seven hits and then El Goofy came on to blank the Athletics with a brilliant three-hitter in the afterpiece.

When it was all over the experts russhed for the record books to determine how much damage the Yankees had done. They learned that the former record for home runs in one game was seven, credited to quite a few clubs, including the Yankees and most recently the Giants.

For most homers by one club in two consecutive games, the previous mark was eleven and belonged to the 1936 Yankees, while the former record for total bases, fifty, was achieved by the Yankees in 1932. The Reds of 1893 set the all-time high of fifty-five. There were one or two records that the champions barely missed, but they were content to rest on their newly won laurels and move on to Washington, where another double-header awaits them tomorrow.

Nine Runs in the Fourth

An inkling of how the Yankee power house mowed down the hapless A's may be gained from a description of the fourth inning of the opener, in which nine big runs crossed the plate.

Rolfe singled, advanced on a passed ball and scored on Henrich's single. DiMaggio then hit one over the left-field roof. Dickey's single was followed by Selkirk's grounder to second for the first out. Then Gordon homered. Dahlgren rolled to third, but Pearson walked and then successive singles by Crosetti and Rolfe and a double by Henrich accounted for the other tallies.

In the previous inning DiMaggio, Selkirk and Dahlgren had clouted homers to sew up the verdict. Thereafter the Yankees were after records and, like most of the things they set out for, they achieved them.

If any one thought that the New Yorkers had punched themselves weary in the first game he was wrong. For as soon as the nightcap started they picked up where they had left off.

Crosetti zoomed one into the left-field stands and before the inning had been completed Gordon had done likewise and the Yankees had five runs, more than enough. In the fifth DiMaggio and Gordon repeated and Dahlgren joined them in the ninth.

One More for the Book

A press-box statistician discovered at a late hour that the Yankees had made a fourth record, that of hitting three homers in one inning ten times. The former mark of nine also belonged to them.

For the sake of the records, the Philadelphia throwers were Lynn Nelson, Bill Beckman and Bob Joyce in the first and George Caster and Chubby Dean in the nightcap.

Unofficially, the Yankees certainly must have created no end of "double-header records." Recapitulation discloses that they scored thirty-three runs and made forty-three hits for eighty-seven bases.

After today's outburst, the season's high, by the way, Yankee homer totals are as follows: Selkirk 12, Gordon 11, Dickey 10, Henrich 7, Dahlgren 7, DiMaggio 6 and Crosetti 3.

Aspirin salesmen would have done a land office business in the press box today. The same holds true in the Philadelphia dugout.

Lou Gehrig, presenting the line-up to the umpires before the second game, received a tremendous ovation. It brought tears to his eyes. Even the venerable Connie Mack, who seldom strays from the bench, came out to home plate to shake his hand.

JOE DIMAGGIO, WHO HIT THREE HOMERS

Yanks' Box Scores

FIRST GAME

NEW YORK (A.)	ab.	r.	h.	po.	a.	e.
Crosetti, ss.	6	1	2	4	7	0
Rolfe, 3b.	7	2	4	0	1	1
Henrich, rf.	7	3	3	2	0	0
DiMaggio, cf	5	4	3	4	0	0
Dickey, c.	5	4	3	2	0	0
Rosar, c.	1	0	0	0	0	0
Selkirk, lf.	7	3	4	3	0	0
Gordon, 2b.	7	3	3	2	5	0
D'hlgren, 1b	6	2	4	10	1	0
Pearson, p.	5	1	1	0	1	0
Total	56	23	27	27	15	1

PHILADELPHIA (A.)	ab.	r.	h.	po.	a.	e.
Lodi'iani, 3b	4	0	1	1	5	1
Ambler, ss.	3	0	0	0	1	0
Newsome, ss.	2	0	1	0	5	0
Miles, rf.	3	1	0	4	0	0
Johnson, cf.	4	0	1	2	1	0
Hayes, c.	3	0	1	2	0	0
Chapman, 1b	3	1	1	11	1	1
Tipton, lf.	4	0	1	3	0	0
Gant'b'n, 2b	3	0	0	4	2	1
Nelson, p.	1	0	1	0	0	0
Beckman, p.	0	0	0	0	0	0
Joyce, p.	2	0	0	0	0	0
aNagel	1	0	0	0	0	0
Total	33	2	7	27	15	3

aBatted for Joyce in ninth.

New York ....0 1 5 9 0 4 4 0 0—23
Philadelphia ....0 1 1 0 0 0 0 0 0— 2

Runs batted in—Dickey, DiMaggio 3, Selkirk 5, Dahlgren 5, Henrich 4, Gordon 3, Rolfe, Nelson, Hayes.

Two-base hits—Chapman, Henrich, Selkirk, Johnson. Three-base hit—Lodigiani. Home runs—Dickey, DiMaggio 2, Selkirk, Dahlgren 2, Gordon, Henrich. Stolen bases—Gordon, Selkirk, Dahlgren. Sacrifice—Hayes. Double play—Gordon, Crosetti and Dahlgren. Left on bases—New York 11, Philadelphia 9. Bases on balls—Off Pearson 4, Nelson 1, Beckman 1, Joyce 3. Struck out—By Pearson 1, Nelson 1. Hits—Off Nelson 9 in 2 2-3 innings, Beckman 7 in 1, Joyce 11 in 5 1-3. Passed balls—Hayes 2. Losing pitcher—Nelson. Umpires—Quinn, McGowan and Pipgras. Time of game—2:27. Attendance—20,000.

SECOND GAME

NEW YORK (A.)	ab.	r.	h.	po.	a.	e.
Crosetti, ss.	6	1	3	2	0	0
Rolfe, 3b.	6	1	1	0	1	0
Henrich, rf.	4	1	1	4	0	0
DiMaggio, cf	5	2	2	4	0	0
Dickey, c.	5	0	1	3	0	0
Selkirk, lf.	3	1	0	5	0	0
Gordon, 2b.	5	3	3	2	3	0
D'hlgren, 1b	4	1	3	6	2	0
Gomez, p.	5	0	2	1	0	0
Total	43	10	16	27	6	0

PHILADELPHIA (A.)	ab.	r.	h.	po.	a.	e.
Lodigi'ni, 3b	3	0	0	4	1	0
Ambler, ss.	4	0	0	3	0	0
Miles, rf.	4	0	0	1	0	0
Johnson, cf.	4	0	1	5	0	0
Brucker, c.	3	0	0	2	0	0
Chapman, 1b	3	0	0	5	0	0
Tipton, lf.	3	0	0	4	0	0
Gant'b'n, 2b	3	0	1	3	2	0
Caster, p.	1	0	0	0	0	0
Dean, p.	2	0	1	0	2	0
Total	30	0	3	27	5	0

New York ....5 0 0 0 2 0 0 1 2—10
Philadelphia ....0 0 0 0 0 0 0 0 0— 0

Runs batted in—Crosetti, Gordon 4, DiMaggio 2, Dahlgren 2, Dickey 1.

Two-base hits—Dahlgren, Gordon, Crosetti. Home runs—Crosetti, Gordon 2, DiMaggio, Dahlgren. Left on bases—New York 11, Philadelphia 4. Bases on balls—Off Gomez 1, Caster 4, Dean 1. Struck out—By Gomez 2, Caster 1. Hits—Off Caster 9 in 5 innings, Dean 7 in 4. Losing pitcher—Caster. Umpires—McGowan, Pipgras and Quinn. Time of game—1:40. Attendance—21,612.

BUXBY LOSES IN UPSET

Bows to Umstaedter, 6-1, 6-2, in New Jersey Tennis

Special to THE NEW YORK TIMES.

ORANGE, N. J., June 28.—William Umstaedter of Millburn, a student at Louisiana State University, scored an upset in the State tennis championship at the Berkeley Club today, defeating Martin Buxby of Miami in the quarter-final round by 6—1, 6—2. Buxby, seeded second, had been a heavy favorite to win the title, since Frank Shields of New York failed to appear. Umstaedter was unseeded.

Frank Bowden of New York, fifth in the draw, who is scheduled to meet William Gillespie tomorrow, is the only seeded player to survive although all eight except Shields saw action.

Richard McKee of Miami Beach gained the semi-final round opposite Umstaedter by defeating Bernard Jacoby of New York, 6—4, 6—2. Awaiting the winner of the Gillespie-Bowden match is Billy McGehee of New Orleans, who triumphed over Louis Brcvnstein of San Diego, Calif., sixth seeded player, in straight sets, 8—6, 6—1.

In the only doubles match of the day, the local team of Donald Hawley and Barclay Kingman, seeded fourth, defeated a Brooklyn pair, Charles Masterson and Nathan Gildstein, 2—6, 6—3, 6—3.

CHESHIRE QUALIFIES FOR YACHTING FINAL

Belmont Hill Crew Also Places in Mallory Cup Series

Special to THE NEW YORK TIMES.

MARION, Mass., June 28.—Typically fine Buzzards Bay racing conditions, with an all-day rail-down southwester blowing and a blue sky aloft, prevailed today as the Beverly Yacht Club staged the remaining four preliminary races of the interscholastic series for the Clifford D. Mallory Cup.

Division A was the center of interest throughout the day's racing as all the crews except one in this group had a chance to qualify for the final series. Trouble at the weather mark proved to be the deciding factor.

The Loomis boat, skippered by Peter Ogilby, and the Hotchkiss crew, headed by Skipper Michael Griggs, had squared around ahead of the trouble, but the Cheshire boat parted its jib stay, dropped from second to fourth, and was on the point of rounding the mark when the Hill School entry, last year's winner, came up on the port tack and forced Cheshire over onto the Tabor and Andover boats.

When the entanglement cleared, Shehire found itself in anchor position. The race committee disqualified Hill and, on the strength of Cheshire's previous showing, which included a first and a third place, the crew qualified for the final.

In Division B, the Belmont Hill School, skippered by Alexander Ellis, made the best showing of all the seventeen entries by amassing a total of 22 points for the preliminary series.

THE SUMMARIES

DIVISION A

SECOND RACE

Course windward-leeward, 4½ miles.

Yacht and School.	Time.	Pts.
Pronto, Westminster	1:01:30	9¼
Poilu, Loomis	1:02:25	10
Sippican, Cheshire	1:02:46	14¼
Massasoit, Andover	1:03:55	9
Maribee, Hotchkiss	1:04:28	9
Awanze, Tabor	1:04:11	10
Polly, Hill	1:07:11	8
Nancy, Gov. Dummer	1:10:02	3

THIRD RACE

Sippican, Loomis	1:03:21	17¼
Nancy, Hotchkiss	1:03:44	15
Awanze, Westminster	1:04:21	14¼
Polly, Andover	1:05:29	12
Ptiloris, Cheshire	1:07:15	17¼
Maribee, Tabor	Disq.	8
Poilu, Tabor	Disq.	10
Pronto, Gov. Dummer	D.N.S.	3

DIVISION B

SECOND RACE

Poilu, Choate	0:55:31	9¼
Massasoit, St. Mark's	1:00:38	12
Polly, St. Paul's	1:00:40	11
Ptiloris, Belmont Hill	1:00:42	14
Awanze, St. George	1:01:58	14¼
Nancy, St. Andrew	1:02:33	7
Poilu, Morristown	1:03:37	5
Maribee, Rye Country School	1:03:50	8
Sippican, Avon Old Farms	1:03:59	6

THIRD RACE

Proto, St. Andrew's	1:01:06	16¼
Massasoit, Belmont Hill	1:01:33	22
Sippican, Morristown	1:02:05	12
Poilu, St. George	1:03:26	20¼
Maribee, St. Paul	1:03:27	18
Awanze, Choate	1:04:00	13¼
Polly, St. Mark's	1:04:21	15
Nancy, Rye Country	1:06:43	10
Ptiloris, Avon Old Farms	1:07:32	7

Honors Given in Two Sports

Varsity letters were given to fourteen members of the baseball squad at Western State Teachers College in Kalamazoo, Mich. Six varsity tennis players also were honored.

Minor League Baseball

By The Associated Press

INTERNATIONAL LEAGUE

Newark 4, Syracuse 2 (night).
Jersey City at Baltimore, rain and cold.

AT ROCHESTER

		R.	H.	E.
Toronto	0 2 2 0 2 0 0 0 0	6	8	0
Rochester	0 0 3 0 3 0 2 0 ..	8	9	1

Batteries—Caldwell and Klimczak, Heath (8); Grodzicki, Roe (3) Ryba and Narron.

AT MONTREAL

(Night Game)

Buffalo	2 0 0 2 0 0 1 4	9	11	2
Montreal	0 0 0 2 1 0 0 0	3	6	5

(Called by agreement).

Batteries—Kowalik and Helf; Grabowski, Duke (1), Nahem (7), Porter (8), Rogers (8) and Hartje.

STANDING OF THE CLUBS

	W.	L.	PC.		W.	L.	PC.
Jersey City	41	28	.594	Buffalo	33	35	.485
Rochester	39	29	.574	Baltimore	31	35	.470
Syracuse	38	34	.528	Montreal	29	38	.433
Newark	37	34	.521	Toronto	26	41	.388

GAMES TODAY

(All Night Games)

Syracuse at Jersey City (9 P. M.).
Newark at Baltimore.
Buffalo at Toronto.
Rochester at Montreal.

AMERICAN ASSOCIATION

(Tuesday Night Game)

AT LOUISVILLE

Toledo	3 0 2 0 0 0 0 0 0	5	9	3
Louisville	0 4 2 4 0 0 6 0 ..	16	18	1

Batteries—Phillips, Pyle (2), McLaughlin (4) and Mackie; Flowers, Schaeffer (1) and Lewis.

STANDING OF THE CLUBS

	W.	L.	PC.		W.	L.	PC.
Kans. City	45	25	.643	Ind'napolis	33	36	.478
Minn'apolis	43	25	.632	St. Paul	31	37	.456
Louisville	33	33	.500	Columbus	30	39	.435
Milwaukee	34	37	.479	Toledo	27	44	.380

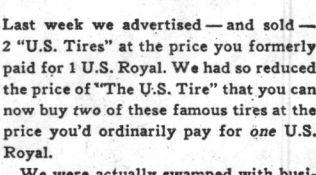

PACIFIC COAST LEAGUE

(Tuesday Night Games)

AT SAN FRANCISCO

		R.	H.	E.
Oakland	0 1 0 0 1 0 0 0 0	2	8	2
San Fran.	0 0 0 0 0 0 0 0 1	1	7	2

Batteries—Cantwell and Raimondi; S. Gibson and Sprinz.

AT SACRAMENTO

Seattle	0 1 0 0 0 0 2 0 0	3	8	0
Sacramento	0 0 0 0 0 0 0 0 0	0	1	0

Batteries—Walker and Hancken; Freitas and Ogrodowski.

AT HOLLYWOOD

L. A.	0 10 2 0 0 0 0 1 0 0 0 2	15	15	2
H'y'd	0 0 0 1 3 0 0 6 3 0 0 0	13	16	2

Batteries—Bonetti, Berry (9), Prim (10) and R. Collins; Ardizoia, Darrow (2), Smith (2), Moncrief (9), Muncrie (10) and Brenzel, Dapper.

AT SAN DIEGO

		R.	H.	E.
Portland	0 1 0 1 0 3 1 0 0	6	10	0
San Diego	0 0 0 1 0 0 0 2 0	3	9	1

Batteries—Thomas and Fernandes; Craghead, Pillette (9) and Starr.

STANDING OF THE CLUBS

	W.	L.	PC.		W.	L.	PC.
L. Angeles	52	37	.584	San Diego	40	46	.465
Seattle	51	37	.580	Hollywood	40	48	.455
S. Fr'cisco	45	40	.529	Portland	36	45	.444
Oakland	44	44	.500	Sacramento	36	47	.434

TEXAS LEAGUE

Shreveport 3, Beaumont 1 (first).
Beaumont 5, Shreveport 0 (second).

STANDING OF THE CLUBS

	W.	L.	PC.		W.	L.	PC.
S. Antonio	47	35	.573	Fort Worth	39	40	.494
Houston	43	34	.558	Tulsa	35	38	.479
Dallas	41	36	.532	Okla. City	35	46	.432
Shreveport	40	40	.500	Beaumont	34	45	.430

Chester Murphy Upsets Harman In U. S. College Tennis, 6-1, 6-2

Guernsey Also Drops Three Games in Beating Fishbach—Lewis and Kamrath Other Victors as Coast Is Shut Out

By ALLISON DANZIG

Special to THE NEW YORK TIMES.

HAVERFORD, Pa., June 28.—The Far West, along with the East, was shut out of the national intercollegiate tennis championship singles today as Rice Institute, the University of Texas, Chicago and Kenyon College of Ohio qualified men for the semi-finals on the clay courts of the Merion Cricket Club.

It is no new experience for the East to find itself relegated to the sidelines in the intercollegiates, in which it has not produced a winner since 1928, but for the Pacific Coast to fail to place a man in the semi-finals is history that neither Los Angeles nor Berkeley will relish reading.

The dire state of affairs came about with the downfall of Robert Harman of the University of California, following upon the defeat of Ronald Lubin of Southern California by Morey Lewis of Kenyon at 7—5, 6—4.

Harman Seeded Third

Harman was placed third in the list of favorites and there were some who thought he should have gone ahead of Robert Kamrath of Texas, as second to Frank Guernsey of Rice, the defending title-holder.

Last year the tall young Californian turned in a thoroughly convincing victory over Joe Hunt in the intercollegiates and on the strength of that performance, as well as his extended experience in tournament competition, he was figured to be Guernsey's most dangerous rival.

Chester Murphy of Chicago ended all such illusions by dispatching Harman by the crushing margin of 6—1, 6—2. Murphy is an earnest young man with an all-round game that is sound and carefully thought out, though lacking in spectacular force. He exercises good judgment in choosing the moment to force.

Kamrath's Stock Rises

All four quarter-final matches were decided in the minimum number of sets and two were as one-sided as Murphy's. Kamrath, in spite of his ailing elbow, overpowered Marvin Wachman of Northwestern, 6—1, 6—2, and played so well that his stock has taken a strong rise.

The blond Texan mixed his game cleverly, employing the drop shot with marked success, and his passing shots from both sides, as well as his sparingly used cannon-ball service, scored for him in vivid fashion.

Guernsey won more easily than had been anticipated from Joe Fishbach of St. John's University of Brooklyn, at 6—2, 6—1. Fishbach played well, though with little confidence, but the little fellow from Texas was so sure in his control and his methods that he always held the upper hand without straining or expending any great amount of energy.

Lewis and Lubin Excel

The best competition of the day was provided in the meeting between Lewis and Lubin. The dark-haired Californian started with a rush, crowding the net behind his service and return of service, to keep Lewis on the defensive.

Not until Lubin had led, at 5—2, did Lewis have a look in. From there on the good-natured, sandy-haired Kenyon College youth came on strongly with his superior ground strokes. His return of service was exceptionally good, and it was his topped back-hand returns of service that ruined Lubin's net excursions.

The No. 1 team in the doubles was eliminated when Guernsey and Dick Morris of Rice lost to Jim Seaver and David Brock of Stanford, 6—2, 6—4. Tomorrow there will be play only in the doubles, the singles semi-finals being scheduled for Friday.

THE SUMMARIES

SINGLES

Quarter-Final Round

Morey Lewis, Kenyon, defeated Ronald Lubin, University of Southern California, 7—5, 6—4; Chester Murphy, Chicago, defeated Robert Harman, University of California, 6—1, 6—2; Frank Guernsey, Rice Institute, defeated Joseph Fishbach, St. John's University, 6—2, 6—1; Robert Kamrath, Texas, defeated Marvin Wachman, Northwestern University, 6—1, 6—2.

DOUBLES

Second Round

William Murphy and Chester Murphy, Chicago, defeated Robert Low and Myron Folsom, Stanford, 6—0, 6—3; Morey Lewis and Gordon Reeder, Kenyon, defeated Leon Everitt and Ronald Lubin, University of Southern California, 6—3, 6—2; Robert Harman and Dan Roberts, California, defeated Douglas Coyle and Art Nielsen, Wisconsin, 6—4, 6—2; George Pero and William Hardie, University of Miami, defeated William Maul and Jack Schlesinger, Wayne, 8—6, 6—4. Robert Kamrath and Warren Christner, Robert Kamrath and Warren Christner, Texas, defeated George Dunkiln, University of Virginia, and Jack Bushman, Louisiana State, 6—3, 6—1; Jim Seaver and David Brock, Sanford, defeated Frank Guernsey and Dick Morris, Rice Institute, 6—2, 6—4; Douglas Imhoff and Robert Peacock, California, defeated Marvin Wachman and Frank Froehling, Northwestern, 6—3, 6—1; William Hoogs and Tate Coulthard, California, defeated Gerald Podesta and John Wendell, Princeton, 6—2, 6—1.

M'HUGH'S REILEEN WINS YACHT TROPHY

Totals 151 Points by Placing Seventh in Final Event

Special to THE NEW YORK TIMES.

NOROTON, Conn., June 28.—Vincent McHugh's Reileen, a Cedar Point Y. C. boat, today won the John Taylor Arms Perpetual Trophy in the final race of the Noroton Yacht Club race-week series. Reileen closed seventh, after some remarkable sailing on the last two legs, finishing 14 minutes 23 seconds behind the winner of the final event, Stanley Turner's Migs, from the Larchmont Y. C.

Reileen was sixteenth when the Stars rounded the windward mark of the five-and-one-half-mile course. She made up a lot of water on the subsequent run and reach. Her point score for the series was 151.

Migs finished 20 seconds ahead of Mr. and Mrs. Gorham Godwin's Hi-Hat, which placed second in the series, with 149 points.

Twenty-seven seconds behind Hi-Hat came B. Gould's and C. Robbins's Nuisance from the New Rochelle Yacht Club. Nuisance was tied for third in the standing with Robert Crane's Silver Mist from the home club, each with 143 points, but the place went to the latter boat because it had finished ahead of nuisance more times than behind. Silver Mist was sixteenth today.

Fifth in the series went to Earl Wicke's Buccaneer of Cedar Point with 136 points. Buccaneer came home sixth in the closing event.

John Taylor Arms, donor of the trophy, presented it to McHugh. The daily prizes and awards for junior and women's races were presented by Commodore Paul Smart.

Major League Leaders

BATSMEN

NATIONAL LEAGUE

	G.	AB.	R.	H.	PC.
Arnovich, Philadelphia	58	222	37	87	.392
Bonura, New York	60	221	49	83	.376
McCormick, Cincinnati	60	237	43	80	.338
Medwick, St. Louis	59	228	39	75	.329
Ott, New York	62	210	50	68	.324

AMERICAN LEAGUE

	G.	AB.	R.	H.	PC.
Foxx, Boston	50	187	48	66	.353
Lewis, Washington	58	226	41	79	.350
McQuinn, St. Louis	60	244	46	85	.349
Dickey, New York	59	222	54	76	.342
Keltner, Cleveland	62	232	28	77	.332

HOME-RUN HITTERS

NATIONAL LEAGUE

Camilli, Brooklyn	14	McCormick, Cinc.	12
Ott, New York	12	Lombardi, Cinc.	11

AMERICAN LEAGUE

Greenberg, Detroit	16	Foxx, Boston	12
Selkirk, New York	12	Gordon, New York	11

RUNS BATTED IN

NATIONAL LEAGUE

McCormick, Cinc.	51	Goodman, Cinc.	47
Bonura, New York	51	Ott, New York	47

AMERICAN LEAGUE

Greenberg, Detroit	57	Dickey, New York	55
Williams, Boston	57		

32,172 See Yankees Trounce Red Sox Twice, 9-1, 19-8, at Stadium; Bees Vanquish Giants, 4-1

Di Maggio's 2 Homers Score 7 In Nightcap Cut to 6½ Innings

Bronx Bombers Amass Total of 27 Hits, Good for 50 Bases, in Double-Header; Russo Limits the Boston Club to Five Safeties in Opening Game

By Arthur E. Patterson

At 7 o'clock last evening the umpires in charge of the Yankee Stadium double-header decided it was time to stop the Yankees. The Red Sox pitchers had the same idea all afternoon, but couldn't do much about it.

With a renewal of their old power the Bronx Bombers mauled six Sox slingers for a total of twenty-seven hits, good for fifty bases and two ball games, 9 to 1 and 19 to 8, while running their streak to five games. The arbiters gave "approaching darkness" as the reason for calling the second at the end of six and one-half innings, but whatever the technical cause, it just seemed like the humane thing to do.

Led by jolting Joe DiMaggio, who has hit in his last ten games and seems intent on regaining some of the old Yankee glory, the champions blasted five home runs, two triples, four doubles and sixteen singles during the afternoon, thrilling a crowd of 32,172. DiMaggio walloped two homers in the nightcap, the first with two aboard and the second with the bases loaded.

DiMaggio Drives in Eight

He also drove in another run with an infield out and, with eight runs batted in, he was only three short of the American League record of eleven set four years ago by Tony Lazzeri. Had the game continued he might have had one and possibly two more chances to add to his afternoon's accomplishments. His second homer was his twenty-fifth.

Joe Gordon opened the Yankees' attack with a circuit clout into the left-field seats, his twenty-second and his second on two successive trips to the plate, for he had broken up Sunday's finale with the A's in the eleventh. Red Rolfe and Babe Dahlgren also poked balls among the customers and Jim Taber, Jimmy Foxx and Ted Williams did likewise for the visiting firemen. It was No. 19 for Tabor, No. 27 for Foxx and No. 15 for Williams, this last being a tremendous lift into the upper right-field boxes where few homers have been hit since the new wing of the Stadium was constructed.

Strange as it may seem after reading about all this fancy slugging, there was some good pitching put on display. Marius Russo, the Ozone Park southpaw, twirled a neat five-hitter in the opener.

Homer Averts Stutout

He lost his shutout on Tabor's homer in the second inning. Time was called twice during this game because of rain—for thirty-five minutes with two out in the Red Sox fourth and for fifteen minutes after Boston had batted in the sixth. Usually such interruptions are troublesome to the pitchers, but Russo seemed to thrive on the added rest.

Neither Red Sox starter got past the first inning. Jim Bagby was charged with four runs and had to be relieved with two out in the first game and the first five Yankees made base hits against Emerson Dickman, Joe Cronin's second starting selection. DiMaggio climaxed this flurry with his three-run homer and before Jack Wilson could retire them the Yankees had sent eleven men to the plate and seven of them over it.

They scored four in the second, also against Wilson, and seven in the fourth when Herb Nash proved to be duck soup for the champions. Hash remained and was done to a crisp when the umpires finally called a halt.

The seven-run assault in the fourth was the outstanding bit of legal murder on the park of the Yankees. All runs came over after two were out. Buddy Rosar singled and stole second. Dahlgren flied to left and Crosetti was hit by a pitched ball. Both runners moved up on Atley Donald's second-out sacrifice.

DiMaggio Hits Grand Slam

Joe Cronin then decided to pass Gordon. Red Rolfe ruined this strategy with a single to left and, after Henrich refilled the bases by waiting and walking, DiMaggio bashed a homer into the Yankee bullpen in left center field.. Doc Cramer sped back hopefully after this drive, but Steve Sundra, of the Yankee relief corps, caught the ball. Keller then tripled and scored on a wild pitch.

With all this second-game hitting, Joe McCarthy needed two pitchers to stow the game away. Marv Brewer was tagged for seven hits and five runs in the third, but Donald hurled five-hit ball thereafter.

The first triumph was even more one-sided. At least the Yankees had good piptching in this one. Two outs followed Gordon's homer. Then DiMaggio singled, Keller walked, Dickey singled, Dahlgren singled and Bagby was motioned to the clubhouse. Joe Heving was greeted by Crosetti's single, which completed the four-run assault.

Rolfe's homer, a base on balls, DiMaggio's double and Dickey's infield out put two more over the plate in the second. Against Yank Terry, Crosetti tripled and scored on a wild pitch in the third, Henrich doubled and went over on DiMaggio's single in the sixth and Gordon singled and tallied on an error, a sacrifice and Henrich's single in the eighth.

The Yankees haven't scored this many runs on the same afternoon since 1939.

Joe Eclipses Brother Dom

Dom DiMaggio may have overshadowed brother Joe in Boston, but his double and safe bunt were insignificant factors yesterday.

Gordon stretched a hitting streak to eight games, all as a lead-off man . . . the Yankees now have 125 homers this season . . . Foxx arrived late after visiting his ill son at Jenkintown, Pa. . . . DiMaggio and Henrich made two great running catches, robbing Terry and Cramer of hits . . . in the last ten games DiMaggio has made twenty-one hits . . . the Yankees yesterday completed the deal for Rinald J. (Rugger) Ardizoia, twenty-year-old right-hander of the Hollywood Stars, strikeout king of the Pacific Coast League. A native of San Francisco, Ardizoia was born in Italy and will be one of the few foreign-born major-leaguers in spring training camps next year.

Yankees Scores

* * *

FIRST GAME

BOSTON (A. L.)	ab	r	h	po	a	NEW YORK (A. L.)	ab	r	h	po	a
D.DiM'gio,cf	4	0	0	2	0	Gordon, 2b	5	2	2	5	3
Cramer, lf	4	0	2	2	0	Rolfe, 3b..	4	1	1	1	1
Cronin, ss.	3	0	0	2	1	Henrich, rf	4	2	2	1	0
Wil'ms, rf	3	0	0	1	0	J.DiM'gio,cf	5	1	3	1	0
Tabor, 3b.	4	1	1	4	2	Keller, lf.	2	1	0	4	0
Finney, 1b	4	0	0	6	1	Dickey, c..	4	1	1	5	0
Doerr, 2b.	2	0	1	0	1	Dahlg'n, 1b	4	0	1	8	0
Peacock, c	2	0	0	7	0	Cros'ti, ss	4	1	2	1	5
†Carey ...	1	0	0	0	0	Russo, p.	3	0	0	1	1
Bagby, p...	0	0	0	0	0						
Heving, p..	0	0	0	0	0						
*Desautels.	0	0	0	0	0						
Terry, p..	2	0	1	0	2						
‡Foxx ...	1	0	0	0	0						
Totals....30		1	5	24	7	Totals..35		9	12	27	10

*Batted for Heving in third inning.
†Batted for Peacock in ninth inning.
‡Batted for Terry in ninth inning.

Boston	010	000	000—1
New York	421	001	01x—9

Error—Cramer. Runs batted in—Gordon, Dickey (2), Dahlgren, Crosetti, Tabor, Rolfe, J. DiMaggio, Henrich. Two-base hits—J. DiMaggio, Henrich. Three-base hit—Crosetti. Home runs—Gordon, Tabor, Rolfe. Stolen base—Keller. Sacrifice—Rolfe. Double plays—Russo and Dahlgren; Rolfe, Gordon and Dahlgren. Left on bases—New York, 8; Boston, 8. Bases on balls—Off Bagby, 1; off Heving, 2; off Russo, 6; off Terry, 2. Struck out—By Russo, 5; by Heving, 1; by Terry, 5. Hits—Off Bagby, 4 in 2-3 inning; off Heving, 3 in 1 1-3; off Terry, 5 in 6. Wild pitch—Terry. Losing pitcher—Bagby. Umpires—Summers, Pipgras and Ormsby. Time—2:55.

SECOND GAME

BOSTON (A. L.)	ab	r	h	po	a	NEW YORK (A. L.)	ab	r	h	po	a
D.DiM'io,cf	5	0	2	1	0	Gordon, 2b	4	2	2	2	2
Cramer, lf	4	1	0	2	0	Rolfe, 3b..	5	3	3	2	2
Cronin, ss	3	2	1	0	0	Henrich, rf	3	2	1	1	0
Carey, ss..	0	0	0	1	0	J.DiM'io,cf	5	3	3	1	0
Foxx, c...	3	2	2	1	1	Keller, lf.	5	3	3	2	0
Peacock, c	1	0	0	1	0	Rosar, c..	4	2	1	6	0
Williams,rf	3	2	2	3	0	D'hlgren,1b	4	2	1	6	0
Finney, 1b	3	0	2	6	1	Crosetti, ss	2	2	1	1	2
Tabor, 3b.	3	0	2	0	4	Breuer, p.	1	0	0	0	2
Doerr, 2b..	3	0	0	2	0	Donald, p.	1	0	0	0	0
Dickman, p	0	0	0	0	0						
Wilson, p.	1	1	1	1	0						
*Spence ..	1	0	0	0	0						
Hash, p..	2	0	0	0	0						
Totals...32		8	12	18	6	Totals..34		19	15	21	8

*Batted for Wilson in third inning.

Boston	005	201	0—8
New York	740	701	x—19

Errors—Tabor, Cronin. Runs batted in—Henrich, J. DiMaggio (8), Crosetti, Gordon (2), Rosar, Dahlgren (3), Foxx (3), Williams (2), Tabor (2), Rolfe (2). Two-base hits—Henrich, Keller, D. DiMaggio. Three-base hit—Keller. Home runs—J. DiMaggio (2), Dahlgren, Foxx, Williams. Stolen bases—Rosar, Rolfe. Sacrifice—Breuer, Donald. Double play—Gordon and Dahlgren. Left on bases—New York, 4; Boston, 8. Bases on balls—Off Breuer, 2; off Hash, 4; off Donald, 3. Struck out—By Donald, 5; by Hash, 1. Hits—Off Dickman, 4 in 0 inning (none out in first); off Wilson, 6 in 2; off Hash, 5 in 4; off Breuer, 7 in 2; off Donald, 5 in 5. Hit by pitcher—By Hash (Crosetti). Wild pitches—Wilson, Hash. Winning pitcher—Donald. Losing pitcher—Dickman. Umpires—Pipgras, Ormsby and Summers. Time—2:15. Attendance—32,172.

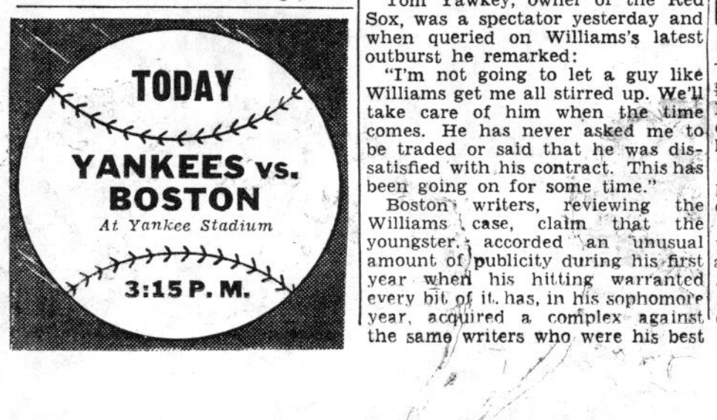

DiMaggio Strikes Mighty Blow in a Big Yankee Inning

Herald Tribune—Acme

New York outfielder completes circuit on first of two homers he hit yesterday as Yankees crushed Red Sox, 9 to 1 and 19 to 8. Wallop came in first inning of second game, scoring Rolfe and Henrich also. Henrich greets DiMaggio as Foxx, Boston catcher, stands by disgusted

Cardinals Win Over Cubs, 5-1, Behind Shoun

Left-Hander Limits Chicago to 7 Hits; Mize Clouts 33d Homer Off French

CHICAGO, Aug. 13 (AP).—The St. Louis Cardinals advanced to within a half game of fifth-place Chicago today when Clyde Shoun set the Cubs down with seven hits for a 5-to-1 victory.

Shoun, a former Cub who went to the Cards two years ago in the Dizzy Dean trade, walked none and allowed only one damaging blow — Hank Leiber's fifth-inning home run.

The Cards nicked Larry French for eleven hits and all their runs in six innings, one of the smashes being Johnny Mize's thirty-third round-tripper of the season. Charley Root and Ken Raffensberger gave up only one hit in the last three innings.

The score:

ST. LOUIS (N. L.)	ab	r	h	po	a	CHICAGO (N. L.)	ab	r	h	po	a
Brown, 3b.	5	1	1	1	1	Hack, 3b..	4	0	2	0	1
Moore, cf.	5	0	0	4	0	Herm'n, 2b	3	0	0	2	2
J.M'rtin, rf.	4	0	1	3	1	Gleeson, lf	4	0	1	1	0
Mize, 1b..	4	1	1	14	0	Nich'ls'n,rf	4	0	1	2	0
Koy, lf ...	4	2	3	2	0	Leiber, cf.	4	1	1	1	1
Orengo, 2b	3	0	1	0	5	Bonura, 1b	4	0	1	10	2
Owen, c..	4	1	3	2	0	Todd, c....	3	0	0	6	0
Marion, ss.	3	0	0	1	2	W'stler, ss	3	0	0	5	5
Shoun, p..	4	0	2	0	2	French, p.	1	0	0	0	1
						*D'l's'ndro.	1	0	1	0	0
						Root, p....	0	0	0	0	0
						†Mattick..	1	0	0	0	0
						†R'f'b'g'r,p	0	0	0	0	0
Totals..36		5	12	27	11	Totals...32		1	7	27	12

*Batted for French in sixth inning.
†Batted for Root in eighth inning.

St. Louis	020	012	000—5
Chicago	000	010	000—1

Errors—None. Runs batted in—Mize, Shoun (2), J. Martin, Owen, Leiber. Two-base hits—Owen (2), Koy. Three-base hit—Brown. Home runs—Mize, Leiber. Sacrifices—Orengo, Herman. Double play—Herman, Warstler and Bonura. Left on bases—St. Louis, 6; Chicago, 5. Base on balls—Off French, 1. Struck out—By Shoun, 2; by French, 5; by Root, 1. Hits—Off French, 11 in 6 innings; off Root, 1 in 2; off Raffensberger, 0 in 1. Losing pitcher — French. Umpires — Ballanfant, Campbell and Klem. Time—1:38. Attendance—7,367.

New York, Detroit Nines Win in Printers' Series

CINCINNATI, Aug. 13 (AP).—The Detroit Typos' crack baseball team blasted out an 11-to-2 victory over Cincinnati in the second round of the International Printers tournament today.

Behind Zaner, who gave up only four hits, New York slapped an 8-to-2 defeat on Indianapolis.

Chicago, Baltimore and the Minneapolis-St. Paul team were defeated for the second time and eliminated.

St. Louis won, 8 ot 4, over Chicago; Washington came from behind to defeat the Twin Cities squad 10 to 7, and Pittsburgh trounced Baltimore, 12 to 5.

Rain Ends Dodger Game With Brooklyn Leading

Rain stopped the Dodgers-Philadelphia game at Ebbets Field yesterday after one inning had been played and Brooklyn was leading, 3 to 0. There will be a double-header today, the first game starting at 1:30 p. m.

The Dodgers got to Clyde Smoll in the first for three hits, which, with a bad throw to second by Warren and a base on balls, resulted in three runs. It was pouring as Coscarart was colled out on strikes for the final out and Tom Dunn called time. The downpour flooded the base paths with puddles.

Ted Williams's Latest 'Pop-off' Ignored by Yawkey and Cronin

Slugger Quoted by Boston Columnist as Declaring He Wants To Be Traded

Ted Williams, the young Boston Red Sox slugger who touched the heights of stardom as an American League freshman last year, but who has been overshadowed by veteran teammates this season, was quoted in an interview with Austen Lake, Boston columnist, yesterday as dissatisfied with his status on the ball club.

According to Lake, Williams wants to be traded, wants more than the $12,500 he is reported to be getting this year and wants to be far, far away from the Boston baseball writers. After flying from the Hub yesterday morning following a rapid recovery from a sacro-iliac ailment, Williams was sent to right field by Joe Cronin. Interviewed by the Boston writers traveling with the club, he denied some phases of the Lake column and confired other angles.

Tom Yawkey, owner of the Red Sox, was a spectator yesterday and when queried on Williams's latest outburst he remarked:

"I'm not going to let a guy like Williams get me all stirred up. We'll take care of him when the time comes. He has never asked me to be traded or said that he was dissatisfied with his contract. This has been going on for some time."

Boston writers, reviewing the Williams case, claim that the youngster, accorded an unusual amount of publicity during his first year when his hitting warranted every bit of it, has, in his sophomore year, acquired a complex against the same writers who were his best friends in 1939 and against the fans. He has threatened to quit on several occasions but no one has taken him seriously.

Joe Cronin didn't put much importance in Williams's latest "pop-off."

"You're not going to worry about what Williams has to say to or about the newspaper men, are you? As long as he produces on the ball field he's my right fielder. He'll be out there today."

ARTHUR E. PATTERSON.

Yawkey's Problem

Ted Williams

Standings in the Major Leagues

WEDNESDAY, AUG. 14, 1940

American League

YESTERDAY'S RESULTS

New York, 9; Boston, 1 (1st).
N. Y., 19; Boston, 8 (2d, 7 ins., dark).
Cleveland, 6; Detroit, 5.
Chicago, 4; St. Louis, 3.
Phila., 6; Wash., 3 (night).

STANDING OF THE CLUBS

	Cleveland	Detroit	Boston	Chicago	New York	Washington	St. Louis	Philadelphia	Won	Lost	Percentage	Games behind
Cleveland.	—	8	10	10	9	9	9	11	66	44	.600	—
Detroit....	5	—	8	7	12	12	13	7	64	46	.582	2
Boston....	6	9	—	9	8	9	10	7	58	51	.532	7½
Chicago....	4	7	8	—	9	9	8	10	55	50	.524	8½
New York.	8	4	8	7	—	8	11	9	55	51	.519	9
Wash'gton	8	5	6	8	2	—	9	9	47	60	.439	17½
St. Louis..	7	3	7	5	5	8	—	11	46	66	.411	21
Phila......	6	10	4	4	6	5	6	—	41	64	.390	22½
Games lost	44	46	51	50	51	60	66	64	—	—	—	

GAMES TODAY

Boston at New York, 3:15.
St. Louis at Detroit.
Chicago at Cleveland (night)
Washington at Philadelphia.

National League

YESTERDAY'S RESULTS

Boston, 4; New York, 1.
Phila. at B'klyn, called end 1st in., rain.
Cincin., 4; Pittsb'gh, 3 (10 ins.).
St. Louis, 5; Chicago, 1.

STANDING OF THE CLUBS

	Cincinnati	Brooklyn	New York	Pittsburgh	Chicago	St. Louis	Boston	Philadelphia	Won	Lost	Percentage	Games behind
Cincinnati	—	11	11	10	10	8	8	9	67	37	.644	—
Brooklyn..	7	—	9	9	9	9	10	9	62	42	.596	5
New York.	5	3	—	10	8	10	8	9	53	47	.530	12
Pittsb'gh..	2	6	5	—	9	10	11	10	53	50	.515	13½
Chicago....	4	8	7	6	—	6	13	10	54	55	.495	15½
St. Louis..	5	8	7	3	7	—	10	10	50	52	.490	16
Boston....	8	5	3	6	5	4	—	9	40	63	.388	26½
Phila......	6	1	5	6	7	5	3	—	33	66	.333	31½
Games lost	37	42	47	50	55	52	63	66	—	—	—	

GAMES TODAY

Phila. at Brooklyn (2), 1st at 1:30.
New York at Boston (2).
Pittsburgh at St. Louis (night).
Cincinnati at Chicago.

Indians Trip Tigers in 9th, 6-5, Increasing Lead to Two Games

Mack Scores Winning Run as Meyer Lets Chapman Drive Go Through Legs

CLEVELAND, Aug. 13 (AP).—Cleveland's battling Indians stretched their league lead to two games over Detroit today with a run in the ninth inning for a 6-to-5 victory over the Tigers.

The Redskins scored when Dutch Meyer, rookie second baseman, allowed Ben Chapman's hot smash to go through his legs. Ray Mack, who had singled and awvanced on a sacrifice and another hit, trotted home with the winning tally.

Cleveland took an uphill course in posting the decision, sweeping the two-game series with the Bengals. Johnny Gorsica, Detroit's starter, limited the Indians to two hits for six innings, but weakened in the seventh and gave way to Al Benton.

The Tigers' ace relief hurler managed to stop the Indians in that session, after two runs had scored, but yielded two tallies in the eighth and was the victim of the winning outburst in the final stanza.

Cleveland used five pitchers, credit for the victory going to the last, Harry Eisenstat. He threw to only one batter, retiring Pete Fox, pinchhitter.

Mel Harder opened for the Indians, but retired for a pinchhitter in th esixth. He was followed by Johnny Humphries, Joe Dobson and Bill Zuber.

Bruce Campbell poled his sixth homer of the season in the fifth inning and tripled to the centerfiled wall in the eighth. Chapman, Mack and Hal Trosky had two hits apiece for the Indians.

Detroit made a desperate bid for the victory in the ninth when Pinky Higgins and Meyer walked. Then Eisenstat replaced Zuber and retired Fox.

The Bengals got nine hits and Cleveland eight.

Cleveland's new-born pennant fever sent 16,128 fans to League Park. The Score:

DETROIT (A. L.)	ab	r	h	po	a	CLEVELAND (A. L.)	ab	r	h	po	a
Bartell, ss	5	0	0	3	3	Ch'pman,lf	5	2	2	0	0
B.C'pbell,rf	5	2	2	0	0	W'therly,cf	3	0	0	3	0
McCosky,cf	4	1	1	1	0	B'dreau, ss	4	0	0	2	3
Gr'nberg,lf	4	1	2	2	0	Trosky, 1b	3	1	2	10	1
York, 1b..	4	0	0	13	2	Bell, rf...	3	1	1	3	0
Higgins, 3b	4	0	2	0	3	Keltner, 3b	4	0	0	1	2
Meyer, 2b.	3	1	1	1	6	Mack, 2b..	4	1	2	1	2
Sullivan, c	3	0	1	4	1	Hemsley, c	2	0	0	5	0
†Fox	1	0	0	0	0	‡Heath ...	1	0	0	0	0
Tebbetts, c	0	0	0	0	0	Pytlak, c..	0	0	0	2	0
Gorsica, p	2	0	0	1	1	Harder, p.	1	0	0	0	2
Benton, p.	1	0	0	0	1	§Hale	1	0	0	0	0
						H'phries, p	0	0	0	0	0
						Dobson, p.	0	0	0	0	0
						¶C. C'pbell.	0	1	0	0	0
						Zuber, p...	0	0	0	0	0
						Eisenstat,p	1	0	1	0	0
Totals..36		5	9	25	*17	Totals...32		6	8	27	10

*One out when winning run was scored.
†Batted for Sullivan in ninth inning.
‡Batted for Hemsley in seventh inning.
§Batted for Harder in sixth inning.
¶Batted for Dobson in eighth inning.

Detroit	010	010	210—5
Cleveland	100	000	221—6

Errors—Mack, Meyer. Runs batted in—Trosky, Gorsica, B. Campbell, Higgins (2), Mack (2), Bell (2). Two-base hit—Greenberg. Three-base hit—B. Campbell. Home run—B. Campbell. Stolen base—Meyer. Sacrifice—Pytlak. Left on bases—Detroit, 12; Cleveland, 6. Bases on balls—Off Gorsica, 1; off Benton, 2; off Harder, 3; off Humphries, 2; off Zuber, 2. Struck out—By Gorsica, 3; by Benton, 1; by Harder, 3; by Dobson, 3; by Zuber, 1. Hits—Off Gorsica, 4 in 6 2-3 innings; off Benton, 4 in 1 2-3; off Harder, 6 in 6; off Humphries, 2 in 1-3; off Dobson, 1 in 1 2-3; off Zuber, 0 in 2-3; off Eisenstat, 0 in 1-3. Hit by pitcher—By Harder (Meyer), by Gorsica (Weatherly). Wild pitch—Dobson. Winning pitcher—Eisenstat. Losing pitcher—Benton. Umpires—Grieve, Geisel, Quinn and Basil. Time—2:39. Attendance—16,128.

Comiskey to Fight Seigel

Bill Daly, manager of Pat Comiskey, heavyweight from Paterson, N. J., said yesterday his youngster had signed to fight Don Seigel, former University of Michigan football player, in Detroit on Aug. 26.

Probable Pitchers For Today's Games

* * *

American League

Boston at New York—Johnson (3-1) vs. Ruffing (10-8).
Washington at Philadelphia — Chase (9-12) vs. Ross (1-0).
St. Louis at Detroit—Whitehead (1-3) vs. Rowe (11-2) or Trout (1-3).
Chicago at Cleveland (night)—Ed. Smith (8-8) vs. Al. Smith (12-5).

National League

New York at Boston (2)—Hubbell (7-6) and Gumbert (9-9) vs. Salvo (7-5) and Errickson (8-8).
Philadelphia at Brooklyn (2)—Si Johnson (2-9) and Pearson (2-9) vs. Fitzsimmons (11-2) and Davis (4-9).
Cincinnati at Chicago—Moore (5-5) vs. Passeau (12-11).
Pittsburgh at St. Louis (night)—Sewell (10-2) vs. McGee (11-7).
Won and lost record in parentheses.

White Sox Beat Browns With 3 in Sixth, 4 to 3

ST. LOUIS, Aug. 13 (AP).—Fred Haney revamped the Browns' line-up, Vern Kennedy pitched out of a couple of bad spots and seemed set for his tenth victory of the year—then the Chicago White Sox ofund the range and came up with a 4-to-3 victory today.

Taft Wright's ninth-inning double, which drove in Luke Appling, was the deciding score, but a three-run rally by the Sox in the sixth pulled them even with St. Louis.

The score:

CHICAGO (A. L.)	ab	r	h	po	a	ST. LOUIS (A. L.)	ab	r	h	po	a
Webb, 2b..	5	0	2	3	4	Heffner, 2b	3	1	0	2	4
Kr'vich, cf	5	0	0	5	0	†Laabs ...	1	0	0	0	0
Kuhel, 1b.	4	0	0	9	1	Grace, rf..	5	0	1	1	0
Appling, ss	2	2	1	1	5	Radcliff, lf.	4	0	1	1	0
Wright, rf.	3	0	1	1	0	Judnich, cf	3	1	2	4	0
R'nthal, lf	3	1	0	3	0	Clift, 3b..	3	0	0	0	3
Tresh, c..	4	1	1	1	1	McQ'nn,1b	4	1	2	13	2
R.K'edy,3b	2	0	1	3	0	B'ardino,ss	3	0	0	2	2
Dietrich, p.	2	0	0	0	0	Swift, c...	3	0	0	3	0
*Silvestri..	1	0	1	0	0	†Cull'nbine	0	0	0	0	0
Appleton, p	0	0	0	1	1	V.K'nedy,p	3	0	2	1	3
Totals...31		4	7	27	12	Totals...32		3	8	27	14

*Batted for Dietrich in sixth inning.
†Batted for Swift in ninth inning.
‡Batted for Heffner in ninth inning.

Chicago	000	003	001—4
St. Louis	200	100	000—3

Errors—None. Runs batted in—Judnich, McQuinn, V. Kennedy, R. Kennedy, Silvestri (2), Wright. Two-base hits—V Kennedy, Radcliff, Silvestri, Wright. Three-base hit—Judnich. Sacrifices—Appling, Appleton, V. Kennedy. Double play—McQuinn and Berardino. Left on bases—Chicago, 11; St. Louis, 8. Bases on balls—Off Dietrich, 3; off Appleton, 2; off V. Kennedy, 9. Struck out—By V. Kennedy, 2; by Appleton, 1. Hits—Off Dietrich, 8 in 5 innings; off Appleton, 0 in 4. Wild pitch—Appleton. Winning pitcher—Appleton. Umpires—Rommel, Moriarty and Hubbard. Time—1:51. Attendance—713.

Toronto Beats Syracuse On Double in 9th, 2 to 1

SYRACUSE, Aug. 13 (AP).—Dario Lodigiani's doube with two out in the ninth inning drove home the run which gave Toronto a 2-to-1 victory in their series final tonight.

The Leafs got only five hits off Jack Tising, who struck out nine, but Kahny's error in the fifth let in the first Toronto run, and Deal slipped in the muddy outfield when it seemed he had Lodigiani's game-winner in his grasp.

The score by innings:

				R.	H.	E.
Toronto	000	010	001	2	5	1
Syracuse	001	000	000	1	6	1

Batteries—McLaughlin and Gray; Tising and Bottarini.

Kennedy's Dad Watches

When the White Sox are playing in Chicago nineteen-year-old Bob Kennedy's dad makes him check in between 9:30 and 10 p. m.

Reds Triumph Over Pirates In 10th, 4 to 3

Frank McCormick's Homer and Single Help League Leaders Halt Pittsburgh

PITTSBURGH, Aug. 13 (AP).—The league-leading Cincinnati Reds spanked the ambitious, red-hot Pittsburgh Pirates, 4 to 3, in ten innings today with the aid of big Frank McCormick's bat and the wildness of Buccaneer flingers.

Joe Bowman was coasting with a 3-to-1 lead going into the ninth. The Bucs had chased Junior Thompson from the mound and seemed headed for their twenty-first victory in twenty-six games.

McCormick lighted the fireworks, blasting the first pitch for his sixteenth homer of the year. Ernie Lombardi singled and when Bowman passed Ival Goodman, Frankie Frisch rushed Johnny Lanning to the mound.

After a sacrifice advanced the two runners, Eddie Joost was given an intentional pass, filling the sacks. Harry Craft, pinch-hitting, flied out, but Bill Werber also drew a pass, forcing home the tying run.

Ken Heintzelman took up the pitching in the tenth for the Pirates. He walked Frey. Frank McCormick singled his mate to third, from where he counted the winning tally on Goodman's long fly to right field.

Maurice Van Robays's single in the first with the bases loaded drove in the first two Pittsburgh runs. Elbie Fletcher drove in his seventy-fourth run in the third and sent Thompson the showers when he singled behind Deb Garms's triple.

Fletcher fell rounding first, so aggravating an injured knee he had to retire, Bill Brubaker replacing him.

For Cincinnati the victory was the tenth in twelve games with Pittsburgh.

The score:

CINCINNATI (N. L.)	ab	r	h	po	a	PITTSBURGH (N.L.)	ab	r	h	po	a
Werber, 3b	4	0	0	4	3	L.Waner,cf	5	1	2	3	0
M.M'C'k,cf	5	0	1	2	0	P.Waner,rf	3	0	1	3	0
Frey, 2b...	4	2	1	2	4	Elliott, rf.	1	0	0	2	0
F.M'C'k,1b	5	1	2	12	1	Garms, 3b	5	2	1	0	1
Lombardi,c	3	0	1	1	0	Vaughan,ss	4	0	0	2	5
*Myers ...	0	1	0	0	0	Fletcher,1b	2	0	1	4	0
Baker, c..	1	0	0	0	0	Brub'k'r,1b	3	0	0	3	2
G'dman, rf	4	0	2	2	0	VanR'ys, lf	3	0	2	3	0
Gamble, lf	3	0	0	1	0	Gustine, 2b	4	0	0	3	1
Arnovich,lf	1	0	0	1	0	Davis, c..	4	0	2	5	2
Joost, ss..	2	0	1	5	4	‡Sewell ...	0	0	0	0	0
Th'mps'n,p	1	0	0	0	0	Lopez, c...	0	0	0	0	0
Shoffner, p	2	0	0	0	0	Bowman, p	3	0	1	2	0
†Craft ...	1	0	0	0	0	Lanning, p	0	0	0	0	0
Beggs, p..	0	0	0	0	1	§Handley..	1	0	0	0	0
						¶Butcher..	0	0	0	0	0
						H'zelman,p	0	0	0	0	0
Totals...36		4	8	30	13	Totals..38		3	10	30	11

*Ran for Lomoardi in ninth inning.
†Batted for Shoffner in ninth inning.
‡Ran for Davis in ninth inning.
§Batted for Lanning in ninth inning.
¶Ran for Handley in ninth inning.

Cincinnati	000	100	002	1—4
Pittsburgh	201	000	000	0—3

Errors—Frey, Elliott. Runs batted in—Van Robays (2), Fletcher, Goodman (2), F. McCormick, Werber. Two-base hits—Frey, Goodman, P. Waner. Three-base hits—Garms, Van Robays. Home run—F. McCormick. Stolen base—Frey. Sacrifice—Gamble. Double plays—Vaughan, Gustine and Fletcher; Werber and Frey; Frey, Joost and F. McCormick; Frey and Joost. Left on bases—Cincinnati, 9; Pittsburgh, 8. Bases on balls—Off Thompson, 3; off Bowman, 3; off Lanning, 2; off Heintzelman, 1. Struck out—By Bowman, 1; by Shoffner, 1. Hits—Off Thompson, 5 in 2 1-3 innings; off Bowman, 7 in 8; off Shoffner, 4 in 5 2-3; off Lanning, 0 in 1; off Beggs, 1 in 2; off Heintzelman, 1 in 1. Winning pitcher—Beggs. Losing pitcher—Heintzelman. Umpires—Goetz, Pinelli and Reardon. Time—2:35. Attendance—6,810.

Athletics Beat Senators With 13-Hit Attack, 6-3

PHILADELPHIA, Aug. 13 (AP).—The revamped Athletics, with Bob Johnson and Benny McCoy on the bench, pounded out thirteen hits tonight to beat Washington, 6 to 3, as Johnny Babich outpitched Dutch Leonard.

Washington got twelve hits off Babich, but the big right-hander was supreme in the pinches to win his ninth game of the season against ten defeats.

Three hits, coupled with a fielder's choice, gave the A.'s three runs in the first inning.

The score:

WASHINGTON (A.L.)	ab	r	h	po	a	PHIL'DELPHIA (A.L.)	ab	r	h	po	a
Case, cf...	5	1	1	3	0	G'nbein, 3b	4	1	2	2	1
Lewis, rf..	5	1	3	1	0	Moses, rf..	4	1	1	2	0
Walker, lf.	5	0	2	0	0	S.C'pm'n,cf	4	2	2	4	0
Travis, 3b.	5	0	2	3	3	W.Miles, lf	4	2	3	3	0
B'worth,1b	4	0	2	9	0	Siebert, 1b	4	0	1	7	1
Myer, 2b..	3	0	0	2	2	Hayes, c..	4	0	1	6	0
Pofahl, ss.	4	0	0	0	2	F.C'pm'n,ss	4	0	0	2	3
Ferrell, c..	4	1	1	6	1	Davis, 2b..	4	0	3	0	3
Leonard, p	3	0	0	0	1	Babich, p.	4	0	0	1	2
*West	1	0	1	0	0						
Totals...39		3	12	24	9	Totals..36		6	13	27	10

*Batted for Leonard in ninth inning.

Washington	001	000	200—3
Philadelphia	300	030	00x—6

Errors—Davis, Leonard. Runs batted in—S. Chapman, Siebert (3), Walker, W. Miles, Lewis, Case. Two-base hits—Davis, Bloodworth, Siebert, Moses, Hayes. Three-base hit—Case. Double plays—Ferrell, Myer and Bloodworth; Pofahl, Myer and Bloodworth. Left on bases—Washington, 10; Philadelphia, 8. Bases on balls—Off Leonard, 2; off Babich, 1. Struck out—By Leonard, 5; by Babich, 5. Umpires—Rue, McGowan and Kolls. Time—2:03. Attendance—7,215.

Young's Poor Throw to Plate Helps Boston Score 4 in 6th

Terry Banished for Dispute With Umpire as Tobin TriumphsOver Lohrman

By Rud Rennie

BOSTON, Aug. 13.—Bill Lohrman has been seeking his tenth victory since July 31. Four times he has tried, but something has happened to foil him. Today, against the humming Bees, it was a blister on his thumb and a bad throw by Babe Young, which let in three unearned runs in a four-run sixth, wherein the Bees won the game from the Giants, 4 to 1.

Lohrman heard about his failure after he had gone, taking his blistered thumb with him. Bill Terry also got a second-hand account of his team's defeat. He was expelled from the proceedings in the fifth for making uncomplimentary remarks to George Magerkurth, umpiring at first base.

The expulsion of the Giants' manager from a ball game is unusual. It has happened only three times in twenty-seven years. Bill Klem gave Terry his first heave-o in 1938. Bick Campbell thumbed him off the bench last year.

Giants Score in Fourth

When Terry departed in the fifth his team was leading, 1 to 0. With two away in the fourth the bottom of the batting order rose up and smote the offerings of Abba Dabba Jim Tobin, a right-hander who was laid up for the greater part of the year with a lame knee.

Nick Witek, Tony Cuccinello and Lohrman tagged Tobin for consecutive singles. Lohrman, driving in the run, gave himself an edge which he kept until the sixth. Then a blister rose on his thumb to distract him. The Bees also rose. And Young gummed up a play at the plate.

Young got Lohrman in trouble to start with by fielding Max West's hit none too well. Chet Ross walked and Eddie Miller came through with a single, tying the score. Buddy Hassett was walked purposely, filling the bases, and then Lohrman, with his blistered thumb, also walked.

Roy Joiner, a left-hander, came in with one out to pitch to Gene Moore, a pinch hitter for Phil Masi. He made Moore hit a grounder to Young, who flung it home. The throw was low. It pulled Hank Danning off the plate. Danning dropped it. Ross was safe at home and the bases were still loaded.

Sisti's Single Scores Two

Tobin eased the situation a little by hitting a line drive to Cuccinello. But with two out Sisti singled sharply to left, knocking in two runs. The Bees batted all the way around in this inning.

Walter Brown stopped the Bees in the last two frames, but Tobin retained his effectiveness and also kept the Giants from scoring. He went the route and chalked up his second victory of the year.

The Bees are going good these days. They have won eleven of their last fifteen games.

This was the Giants' 100th game, and as far as they are concerned the next half hundred are likely to be the hardest.

Asked about the recurrent story that he was going to buy the Boston Bees, Bill Terry chuckled and said: "Yeah; they're giving 'em to me."

Giants Steal Twice

Such speed. Such thievery. Two more Giants stole bases today. That makes four bases the Giants have stolen in their last two games.

Rowell, with one hit out of four times up, took the batting leadership away from Danning, who went four times without a blow.

The score:

NEW YORK (N. L.)	ab	r	h	po	a	BOSTON (N. L.)	ab	r	h	po	a
W'head, 2b	5	0	1	3	3	Sisti, 3b...	4	0	2	0	0
J. Moore, lf	4	0	1	2	0	Cooney, cf	4	0	1	5	1
Demaree,cf	3	0	1	0	0	Rowell, 2b	4	0	1	1	4
Young, 1b.	4	0	0	13	0	West, rf...	4	1	1	1	0
Danning, c	4	0	0	3	0	Ross, lf...	3	1	0	6	0
Ott, rf....	3	0	0	0	0	Miller, ss..	4	1	2	2	1
Witek, ss..	4	1	2	2	3	Hassett, 1b	3	1	1	8	1
C'cinello,3b	4	0	1	1	3	Masi, c...	2	0	0	2	1
Lohrman,p	2	0	1	0	4	‡E. Moore.	1	0	0	0	0
Joiner, p..	0	0	0	0	0	Berres, c..	0	0	0	1	0
*McCarthy	1	0	0	0	0	Tobin, p...	4	0	1	1	0
Brown, p..	0	0	0	0	0						
†Seeds ...	1	0	1	0	0						
Totals...35		1	8	24	13	Totals....33		4	9	27	8

*Batted for Joiner in seventh inning.
†Batted for Brown in ninth inning.
‡Batted for Masi in sixth inning.

New York	000	100	000—1
Boston	000	004	00x—4

Errors—Young, Hassett. Runs batted in—Lohrman, Miller, Sisti (2). Two-base hit—Miller. Stolen bases—Ott, J. Moore. Sacrifice—Berres. Left on bases—New York, 9; Boston, 8. Bases on balls—Off Lohrman, 2; off Tobin, 2. Struck out—By Lohrman, 2; by Brown, 1; by Tobin, 3. Hits—Off Lohrman, 7 in 5 1-3 innings; off Joiner, 1 in 2-3; off Brown, 1 in 2. Losing pitcher—Lohrman. Umpires—Barr, Magerkurth and Stewart. Time—1:54. Attendance—2,434.

Leading Five Batsmen In Each Major League

NATIONAL LEAGUE

Player and club	G.	AB.	R.	H.	Pct.
Rowell, Boston.....	83	288	31	95	.330
Danning, New York	97	369	53	121	.328
F. McCormick, Cin.	104	421	70	135	.321
Walker, Brooklyn..	97	372	49	119	.320
Leiber, Chicago....	80	291	64	93	.320

AMERICAN LEAGUE

Player and club	G.	AB.	R.	H.	Pct.
Radcliff, St. Louis..	107	405	57	142	.351
DiMaggio, New York	86	340	67	119	.350
Finney, Boston....	95	408	59	142	.348
McCosky, Detroit..	103	428	89	148	.346
Appling, Chicago...	101	381	61	130	.341

HOME RUNS

American League	National League
Foxx, Red Sox...27	Mize, Cardinals..33
DiMaggio, Yanks. 25	Nicholson, Cubs..19
Gr'berg, Tigers...23	F. McCor'k, Reds.16

RUNS BATTED IN

American League	National League
Gr'berg, Tigers..101	F. McCor'k, Reds.88
DiMaggio, Yanks 94	Mize, Cardinals..83
Foxx, Red Sox... 85	Fletcher, Pirates.74

Lester Wins Golf Tourney

Special to the Herald Tribune

SOUTHAMPTON, L. I., Aug. 13.—Daniel Lester, of the home club, won the low net prize at the invitation tournament of the Long Island Golf Association at the Southampton Golf Club today. Lester carded an 82—6—76. The low gross prize was taken by Capt. E. F. Cater, of Sands Point, with a 77.

Yankees Defeat Tigers Twice, 4-3, 4-2; Reds Shade Giants, 3-2; Dodgers Lose Two, 3-0, 4-3

30,346 See Champions Climb Back Into Tie for Fourth Place

Ruffing Outpitches Rowe in Opener, Bonham Bests Trout in Nightcap; Selkirk Poles 13th Homer in First Game; Hits Even, 8 and 8, in Each Contest

By Harry Cross

The Yankees ripped a couple of games away from Detroit at the Stadium yesterday, thereby vaulting back into a tie for fourth place with the White Sox. The champions exercised some of their championship authority on the Tigers, winning the first game, 4 to 3, and the nightcap, 4 to 2. A crowd of 30,346 spectators looked on, many of them pleased and others surprised.

Although the Yanks are nine games off the pace being set by Cleveland, innumerable Bronx fans have become so accustomed to seeing the Yankees take everything in sight that they still believe Joe McCarthy's laddiebucks are going to do it again. That isn't strange because there are a lot of people who still thinks the earth is flat.

It was a coincidence that both the Yanks and the Bengals each got eight hits in both games of the double-header. Red Ruffing, however, was better than Schoolboy Rowe in the first game and in the second Tiny Bonham was a superior pitcher to Dizzy Trout. Archie McKain served as relief pitcher in both games for Detroit.

Selkirk Wallops No. 13

George Selkirk embellished the first game with his thirteenth home run of the season and for the Tigers, Pete Fox got his third. The Tigers have a bad habit of running around in a most informal manner. In the second inning of the first game, with Selkirk and Babe Dahlgren on the bases and two out, Frank Crosetti hit a topped ball which spilled in front of the plate for a hit Billy Sullivan, the catcher, and Rowe, the pitcher, both went for the ball and collided head on.

The schoolboy, who was temporarily knocked out, was sprawled along the third base path and Selkirk and Dahlgren scored. Selkirk had to jump over the two Tigers to reach the plate. Sullivan's forehead was cut and it took some time to patch his wound and dispel the stars from Rowe's vision.

The bump didn't help Rowe any, and in the fourth, Dahlgren singled and rode home on Ruffing's double. Selkirk got his homer in the sixth with no one on. The Tigers had tied the score at 2—all in the first of the fourth on Hank Greenberg's double, singles by York and Higgins and a run-scoring fly by Fox.

Yankees Take Two-Run Lead

The Yanks got away to a two-run edge in the first inning of the second game. Trout hit Joe Gordon on the shoulder and Gordon scored on a double by Tom Henrich. Joe DiMaggio's single scored Henrich. Trout also hit Buddy Rosar on the right wrist and the catcher had to leave the game, Bill Dickey taking his place. The ball hit a nerve but fortunately no bones were broken.

Fox's double and a single by Sullivan gave the Bengals their first run in the second. They tied in the first of the fifth. Fox got his second double off Bonham, went to third after Sullivan's long fly and scored on Trout's fly.

The Yankees won it in the last of the fifth. Crosetti singled and was forced by Bonham. After Gordon flied out, Red Rolfe singled and both Bonham and Rolfe scored on Henrich's double, his second of the pastime.

Among the spectators were James A. Farley and George Creel. A. G. Vanderbilt also was down from Saratoga to see the double-header.

The league-leading Cleveland Indians will start a series against the Yankees tomorrow. On Friday the award for the most valuable player in the American League last year will be made to Joe DiMaggio. Mayor LaGuardia has promised to make the presentation.

Dick Bartell has slowed down some at shortstop, but this hasn't slowed up his conversation. He can talk faster than ever.

Bonham struck Rudy York out twice and Ruffing once. Greenberg got two doubles and a single off Ruffing in the first engagement.

Probable Pitchers For Today's Games

* * *

National League

New York at Cincinnati—Schumacher (10-9) vs. Moore (6-5).
Boston at Pittsburgh—Sullivan (9-13) vs. Heintzelman (4-5).
Philadelphia at Chicago—Pearson (2-9) vs. Olsen (8-8).
Brooklyn at St. Louis—Tamulis (7-3) vs. McGee (12-9).

American League

Detroit at New York—Newhouser (8-9) vs. Chandler (7-5).
Cleveland at Boston—Milnar (15-7) vs. Ostermueller (3-5).
Chicago at Philadelphia—Rigney (11-13) vs. Beckman (5-1).
St. Louis at Washington—Mills (0-4) vs. Leonard (12-12).

Keltner Homer With Three on Routs Red Sox

Blow Climaxes Indians' 7-Run Eighth, Saving 22d Victory for Feller, 11-6

BOSTON, Aug. 20 (AP).—Ken Keltner, third baseman of the league-leading Cleveland Indians, went on a batting spree today and helped his team to down the Boston Red Sox, 11 to 6, the victory giving Bobby Feller his twenty-second pitching triumph of the the season.

Keltner poled a round-tripper with the bases loaded in the eighth inning while 20,200 hometown fans looked on.

Feller had left the mound for a pinch hiter just before Keltner contributed to a seven-run outbreak in the eighth, but he was credited with the victory.

When Feller retired, with his teammates on the short end of a 5-to-2 score, it appeared that Jack Wilson, the starting Boston pitcher, was headed for a hero's role.

Then Clarence Campbell, pinch-hitting for Rollie Hemsley, Feller's battery mate, lined out a single and then Jeff Heath, batting for Feller, hit a two-run homer, putting the Indians back on the warpath at 5 to 4.

Ben Chapman, an ex-Bostonian, followed with a single and Wilson gave way to Emerson Dickman. Weatherly forced Chapman at second, but Boudreau singled and Trosky walked, filling the bases. Beau Bell singled Weatherly home with the tying run and left the sacks loaded for Keltner's grand slam homer. Keltner previously had lashed out a triple.

Heath's feat of driving out a pinch-hit homer was duplicated in the ninth by Stan Spence, of the Sox, off Johnny Allen, but the damage had been done.

The score:

CLEVELAND (A. L.)	ab	r	h	po	a	BOSTON (A. L.)	ab	r	h	po	a
Chapm'n,lf	5	1	4	4	0	DiMag'o,cf	5	2	3	5	0
Weath'y,cf	6	2	2	0	0	Cramer,rf.	5	0	3	5	0
Boud'au,ss	4	3	2	1	2	Foxx c...	5	1	1	5	0
Trosky,1b.	3	1	2	10	0	Will'ms,lf	2	1	1	1	0
Bell, rf...	5	1	1	2	0	Finney, 1b	4	0	0	8	1
Keltner,3b.	4	1	2	1	3	Cronin,ss.	4	0	1	1	3
Mack, 2b..	5	0	1	1	2	Doerr, 2b.	4	0	1	1	1
Hemsley,c.	3	0	0	7	2	Tabor, 3b.	4	1	1	1	1
*Campbell.	2	1	1	0	0	Wilson, p..	3	0	0	0	1
Pytlak, c.	0	0	0	1	0	Dickman,p	0	0	0	0	0
Feller, p.	3	0	0	0	3	Hash, p...	0	0	0	0	0
†Heath ...	2	1	1	0	0	‡Spence ..	1	1	1	0	0
Allen, p...	0	0	0	0	1						
Totals	42	11	16	27	13	Totals..	37	6	12	27	7

*Batted for Hemsley in eighth inning.
†Batted for Feller in eighth inning.
‡Batted for Hash in ninth inning.

Cleveland .... 100 000 172—11
Boston .... 103 100 001— 6

Errors—None. Runs batted in—Keltner (6), Heath (2), Bell, Boudreau, Weatherly, Finney (2), DiMaggio, Foxx, Williams, Spence. Two-base hits—Trosky, Foxx. Three-base hits—Weatherly, Keltner, Williams, Tabor. Home runs—Keltner, Heath, Spence. Stolen base—Williams. Left on bases—Cleveland, 13; Boston, 6. Bases on balls—Off Feller, 2; off Wilson, 7; off Dickman, 1; off Nash, 1. Struck out—By Feller, 6; by Allen, 1; by Wilson, 7. Hits—Off Feller, 10 in 7 innings; off Allen, 2 in 2; off Wilson, 10 in 7 (none out in eighth); off Dickman, 3 in 1-3; off Hash, 3 in 1 2-3. Passed balls—Helmley (2). Winning pitcher—Feller. Losing pitcher—Dickman. Umpires—Rommel, Moriarty, Hubbard and Pipgras. Time—2:45. Attendance—20,200.

Yankees Scores

* * *

FIRST GAME

DETROIT (A. L.)	ab	r	h	po	a	NEW YORK (A. L.)	ab	r	h	po	a
Bartell, ss	4	0	0	3	1	Gordon, 2b	4	0	1	2	0
‡Averill ..	1	0	0	0	0	Rolfe, 3b..	4	0	0	3	2
M'C'sky, cf	5	0	0	3	0	Henrich, lf	4	0	0	3	0
Gehr'g'r,2d	3	0	0	2	2	DiM'gio, cf	4	0	2	4	0
Gr'nb'g, lf	4	1	3	4	0	Silkirk, lf	3	2	1	5	0
York, 1b.	4	1	1	4	1	Dickey, c..	3	0	0	5	0
Higgins, 3b	4	0	1	0	1	D'hlg'n, 1b	4	2	2	2	0
Fox, rf ...	4	1	1	3	0	Cros'ti, ss.	3	0	1	3	0
Sullivan, c	3	0	1	4	0	Ruffing, p	3	0	1	0	0
Rowe, p..	1	0	0	1	0						
*Campbell.	1	0	0	0	0						
McKain, p	0	0	0	0	2						
†St'nbach...	1	0	1	0	0						
Totals...	35	3	8	24	7	Totals...	32	4	8	27	2

*Batted for Rowe in seventh inning.
†Batted for McKain in ninth inning.
‡Batted for Bartell in ninth inning.

Detroit .... 000 200 001—3
New York .... 020 101 00x—4

Error—Bartell. Runs batted in—Crosetti (2), York, Fox (2), Ruffing, Selkirk. Two-base hits—Dahlgren, Greenberg (2), Ruffing, Stainback. Home runs—Selkirk, Fox. Stolen base—Rowe. Double play—Gehringer and York. Left on bases—New York, 6; Detroit, 8. Bases on balls—Off Rowe, 1; off Ruffing, 3; off McKain, 1. Struck out—By Ruffing, 4; by Rowe, 1. Hits—Off Rowe, 7 in 6 innings; off McKain, 1 in 2. Passed ball—Dickey. Losing pitcher—Rowe. Umpires—Summers, Basil and Grieve. Time—2:05.

SECOND GAME

DETROIT (A. L.)	ab	r	h	po	a	NEW YORK (A. L.)	ab	r	h	po	a
Bartell, ss	4	0	1	4	2	Gordon, 2b	3	1	1	3	4
M'C'sky, cf	4	0	0	0	0	Rolfe, 3b.	4	1	1	2	1
Gehr'g'r,2b	4	0	2	1	3	H'nrich, rf	4	1	2	1	0
Gr'nb'g. lf	4	0	0	3	0	DiM'gio, cf	4	0	2	4	0
York, 1b..	4	0	1	8	0	Selkirk, lf	3	0	0	3	0
H'gins, 3b	4	0	0	1	1	Roscar, c.	0	0	0	1	0
Fox, rf...	4	2	2	2	0	Dickey, c..	2	0	1	5	0
Sullivan, c	4	0	1	5	1	Dahlg'n, 1b	4	0	0	7	0
Trout, p..	2	0	1	0	5	Cros't, ss.	2	0	1	1	3
*Campbell.	1	0	0	0	0	Bonham, p	3	1	0	0	0
McKain, p	0	0	0	0	0						
Totals...	35	2	8	24	12	Totals...	29	4	8	27	8

*Batted for Trout in seventh inning.

Detroit .... 001 010 000—2
New York .... 200 020 00x—4

Error—Dahlgren. Runs batted in—Henrich (3), DiMaggio, Sullivan, Trout. Two-base hits—Henrich (2), Fox (2), York. Sacrifice—Selkirk. Double plays—Crosetti, Gordon and Dahlgren; Gehringer, Bartell and York. Left on bases—New York, 6; Detroit, 6. Bases on balls—Off Trout, 1; off McKain, 1. Struck out—By Bonham, 5; by Trout, 5. Hits—Off Trout, 7 in 6 innings; off McKain, 1 in 2. Hit by pitcher—By Trout (Gordon, Rosar). Losing pitcher—Trout. Umpires—Basil, Grieve and Summers. Time—2:00. Attendance—30,346.

Auker Baffles Senators As Browns Triumph, 6-3

WASHINGTON, Aug. 20 (AP).—Elden Auker's submarine balls were too much for Washington today and the Senators lost to St. Louis, 6 to 3, their fifth straight defeat.

The Browns hammered the sensational rookie, Sid Hudson, for ten safties, bunching five in the third inning for three runs. Joe Grace knocked in the first St. Louis run with a looping single and Harlond Clift pushed two more across with another.

The Browns got two more in the sixth, one on a squeeze play and the other on Auker's double. Clift batted in St. Louis's final run with a single in the seventh.

The score:

ST. LOUIS (A. L.)	ab	r	h	po	a	WASH'GTON (A. L.)	ab	r	h	po	a
Heffner, 2b	5	0	0	1	3	Case, cf...	5	0	1	3	0
Grace, rf..	5	1	2	2	0	Lewis, rf..	5	0	1	1	0
Radcliff, lf	5	1	1	2	0	Walker, lf	2	0	1	0	0
Laabs, lf.	0	0	0	0	0	Welaj, lf.	2	0	0	1	0
J'dnich, cf	3	2	2	3	0	Travis, 3b	4	0	1	0	3
Clift, 3b..	3	1	2	0	4	Bl'dw'th.1b	4	0	1	14	2
McQ'n, 1b	4	0	1	14	0	Myer, 2b..	4	0	0	1	4
B'n'dino, ss	4	1	1	2	4	Pofahl, ss	4	1	1	3	7
Swift, cf..	1	0	0	0	0	Ferrell, c..	2	1	0	1	1
Susce, c..	2	0	0	2	0	Hudson, c.	2	1	0	1	1
Auker, p..	4	0	1	1	4	*Early ...	1	1	1	0	0
						C'r'sq'l, p	0	0	0	0	0
						†West	1	0	1	0	0
Totals..	36	6	10	27	15	Totals...	37	3	2	27	17

*Batted for Hudson in seventh inning.
†Batted for Carrasquel in ninth inning.

St. Louis .... 003 002 100—6
Washington .... 000 020 100—3

Errors—Hudson, Berardino (2), Grace, Laabs. Runs batted in—Judnich, Clift (3), Pofahl, Susce, Auker, Case. Two-base hit—Auker. Three-base hits—Early, Travis. Home run—Pofahl. Stolen bases—Judnich, Case. Sacrifice—Susce. Double play—Bloodworth, Pofahl and Bloodworth. Left on bases—St. Louis, 6; Washington, 8. Bases on balls—Off Auker, 1; off Hudson, 2. Struck out—By Auker, 2; by Hudson, 2. Hits—Off Hudson, 10 in 7 innings; off Carrasquel, 0 in 2. Balk—Hudson. Losing pitcher—Hudson. Umpires—Rue, McGowan and Kolls. Time—2:01. Attendance—1,500.

Orioles Retain Thomas

BALTIMORE, Aug. 20 (AP).—Alphonse (Tommy) Thomas, serving his first year as manager of the Baltimore Orioles of the International League, today signed a contract to continue for three years "at a substantial raise in salary." The Orioles currently are in third place.

Rowe Knocks Himself Out, but Comes Right Back

Associated Press
Detroit pitcher is rendered unconscious by collision with Sullivan, catcher, as both tried to field ball topped by Crosetti in second inning of first game. Selkirk speeds past fallen hurler to score

Herald Tribune—Acme
One inning after his temporary K. O. Rowe steals second base. Crosetti is taking the throw as Bill Summers calls the play. Yankees won two games, 4 to 3 and 4 to 2

Moses's Steal Of Home Gives Athletics a Split

Dash for Plate in Tenth Wins, 4-3, After White Sox Capture Opener, 6-1

PHILADELPHIA, Aug. 20 (AP).—Wally Moses stole home in the tenth inning of the second game and gave the Athletics a 4-to-3 victory and an even break with the Chicago White Sox in a double-header today.

Chicago won the first game, 6 to 1, when a five-run rally in the ninth inning made a rout of a pitching duel between Ed Smith and Buck Ross. None of Chicago's six runs were earned, the A's committing five errors behind Ross.

Philadelphia's only score came on Al Rubelin's fifth home run of the season.

Nelson Potter pitched shutout ball for eight innings of the second game, then weakened and the Sox tied the score with a three-run attack in the ninth. In the home tenth, Moses singled, advanced on a sacrifice and infield out, and then bolted home as Thornton Lee pitched to Benny McCoy.

The scores:

FIRST GAME

CHICAGO (A. L.)	ab	r	h	po	a	PHILA'PHIA (A. L.)	ab	r	h	po	a
J.Webb, 2b	3	0	0	1	1	Rub'ling,ss	4	1	1	1	0
M.Hay's,2b	0	0	0	1	2	Moses, rf..	4	0	0	4	0
Kr'vich,cf	5	0	1	4	0	S.Ch'p'n,cf	4	0	1	2	0
Kuhel, 1b	3	2	2	9	1	Johnson,lf.	3	0	1	3	0
Solters, lf	3	0	0	0	0	Siebert,1b.	3	0	0	7	2
Ros'n'th'l,lf	1	1	0	2	0	F.Hay's,c.	3	0	0	5	0
Appling,ss.	4	0	1	2	1	Davis, 2b.	3	0	0	3	3
Wright,rf.	4	0	1	3	0	F.Ch'p'n,ss	2	0	0	2	3
Tresh, c..	4	1	1	4	0	Ross, p...	3	0	0	0	1
Ken'edy,3b	4	1	0	0	2						
E.Smith,p.	3	1	1	1	3						
*Sylvestri	1	0	0	0	0						
Totals..	35	6	7	27	10	Totals...	29	1	3	27	9

*Batted for Webb in ninth inning.

Chicago .... 000 001 005—6
Philadelphia .... 000 100 000—1

Errors—Rubeling (3), Davis, Chapman. Runs batted in—Rubeling, Wright, Kreevich, Kuhel, Appling (2). Two-base hits—Smith, Kuhel. Home run—Rubeling. Sacrifice—Webb. Double plays—Davis and Siebert; F. Chapman and Siebert; Appling, M. Hayes and Kuhel. Left on bases—Philadelphia, 3; Chicago, 9. Bases on balls—Off Smith, 2; off Ross, 6. Struck out—By Smith, 3; by Ross, 2. Umpires—Ormsby, Quinn and Geisel. Time—1:59.

SECOND GAME

CHICAGO (A. L.)	ab	r	h	po	a	PHILA. (A. L.)	ab	r	h	po	a
Webb, 2b.	3	0	0	0	2	G't'nb'n,3b	4	1	1	1	4
†Silvestri..	1	0	0	0	0	Moses, rf.	5	1	3	4	0
M.Hayes,2b	1	0	0	2	0	S.Ch'm'n,cf	4	0	1	1	0
Kr'vich, cf	5	0	0	2	0	Johns'n, lf	4	0	0	6	0
Kuhel, 1b.	5	1	3	11	1	S'bert, 1b.	5	1	2	7	0
Solters, lf	3	0	1	2	0	F.Hayes, c	4	0	1	2	0
Ros'th'l lf	1	1	0	1	0	McCoy, 2b	4	0	1	4	2
Appling, ss	4	1	3	1	1	Br'cato, ss	4	0	1	5	4
Wright, rf.	2	0	0	3	0	Potter, p.	3	1	1	0	0
Turner, c..	4	0	0	5	0	‡Simmons.	1	0	0	0	0
K'n'dy, 3b	4	0	0	2	6	Heusser, p	0	0	0	0	0
Lee, p ...	3	0	1	0	1						
Totals..	36	3	8	*29	11	Totals..	38	4	11	30	10

*Two out when winning run was scored.
†Batted for Webb in eighth inning.
‡Batted for Potter in ninth inning.

Chicago .... 000 000 003 0—3
Philadelphia .... 011 000 100 1—4

Errors—Kreevich, Turner, Gantenbein. Runs batted in—S. Chapman (2), Appling. Two-base hits—Kuhel, Gantenbein, S. Chapman, Brancato. Stolen bases—Hayes, Moses. Sacrifice—S. Chapman. Double plays—Brancato and Siebert; Gantenbein, McCoy and Seibert (2). Left on bases—Philadelphia, 9; Chicago, 7. Bases on balls—Off Lee, 3; off Potter, 4. Struck out—By Lee, 5; by Potter, 2. Hits—Off Potter, 8 in 9 innings; off Heusser, 0 in 1. Winning pitcher—Heusser. Umpires—Quinn, Geisel and Ormsby. Time—2:03. Attendance—5,500.

Semi-Pro Baseball

At Wichita

By The Associated Press

Mt. Pleasant, Tex., 5; Wichita Stearmans, 4.
Glendive, Mont., 3; Wilmington, Del., Allieds, 1 (Wilmington eliminated).
St. Louis Naturals, 3; Springfield, Ohio, Colliers, O (Springfield eliminated).

Passeau Yields Phils 3 Hits, Cubs Winning Shutout, 4 to 0

Only Thirty Batsmen Face Chicago Pitcher; Bonura Gets Homer Off Mulcahy

CHICAGO, Aug. 20 (AP).—Claude Passeau racked up his fifteenth victory of the season today, pitching the Chicago Cubs to a 4-to-0 decision over the Phillies.

Only thirty batters faced Passeau as he yielded three hits and issued no walks.

Zeke Bonura contributed the first Cub run when he blasted a home run in the first inning. Chicago added two more in the fourth on three hits of Hugh Mulcahy, the starting and losing pitcher. Passeau's double and Stan Hack's single produced the final run.

The score:

PHILA'PHIA (N. L.)	ab	r	h	po	a	CHICAGO (N. L.)	ab	r	h	po	a
May, 3b..	4	0	1	1	2	Hack, 3b.	4	0	1	0	1
Schulte,2b	3	0	0	2	3	Herman,2b	4	0	0	3	5
Marty, cf.	4	0	0	4	0	Bonura,1b.	3	1	1	16	1
Rizzo, rf.	4	0	1	2	0	Leiber, cf.	3	0	0	2	0
Warren,c.	3	0	0	1	1	Gleeson,rf	2	1	1	1	0
Bragan,ss.	3	0	1	2	6	Dal's'dro,lf	4	1	3	1	0
Mueller,lf.	3	0	0	0	0	Todd, c...	3	0	1	3	1
Mahan, 1b	3	0	0	11	1	Mattick,ss	3	0	0	0	5
Mulcahy,p.	2	0	0	1	0	Passeau,p.	3	1	1	1	3
*Mazzera.	1	0	0	0	0						
Frye, p...	0	0	0	0	1						
Totals..	30	0	3	24	14	Totals..	29	4	8	27	16

*Batted for Mulcahy in eighth inning.

Philadelphia .... 000 000 000—0
Chicago .... 100 200 10x—4

Errors—May, Hack. Runs batted in—Bonura, Dallessandro, Todd. Two-base hits—Gleeson, Todd, Passeau. Home run—Bonura. Stolen base—Dallessandro. Sacrifice—Schulte. Double play—Bragan, Schulte and Mahan. Left on bases—Philadelphia, 4; Chicago, 5. Bases on balls—Off Mulcahy, 3; off Frye, 1. Struck out—By Mulcahy, 1; by Passeau, 2. Hits—Off Mulcahy, 8 in 7 innings; off Frye, 0 in 1. Losing pitcher—Mulcahy. Umpires—Magerkurth, Stewart and Dunn. Time—1:28. Attendance—4,598.

Pirates Buy Infielder For '5-Figure' Price

PITTSBURGH, Aug. 20 (AP).—William E. Benswanger, president of the Pittsburgh Pirates, announced today the purchase of Alfred W. Anderson, infielder, from the Atlanta club of the Southern Association for a "sum of money extending into the five figures and a Pirate player to be agreed upon later."

The twenty-five-year-old former University of Georgia athlete, who has been playing shortstop and batting around .340 for the Atlanta club, will report after Sept. 8. Frankie Frisch, Pirate manager, said the deal would not affect Arky Vaughan, Bucco shortstop.

Leading Five Batsmen In Each Major League

AMERICAN LEAGUE

Player and club	G.	AB.	R.	H.	Pct.
Radcliff, St. Louis	113	431	61	155	.360
Appling Chicago..	108	409	68	142	.347
Williams, Boston..	106	410	100	139	.339
Finney, Boston...	102	435	64	147	.338
DiMaggio,NewYork	94	370	70	125	.338

NATIONAL LEAGUE

Player and club	G.	AB.	R.	H.	Pct.
Rowell, Boston....	91	324	35	107	.330
Walker, Brooklyn..	105	404	56	131	.324
Danning,NewYork	105	396	54	128	.323
Mize, St. Louis...	110	414	85	132	.319
F.McCormick, Cin.	112	450	73	142	.316
Lombardi, Cin....	87	304	39	96	.316

HOME RUNS

American League	National League
Foxx, Red Sox...33	Mize, Cardinals...35
DiMaggio, Yanks.25	Nicholson, Cubs..19
Gr'berg, Tigers...24	Rizzo, Phillies...19

RUNS BATTED IN

American League	National League
Gr'berg, Tigers..104	F. McCor'k, Reds.95
Foxx, Red Sox. 97	Mize, Cardinals...89
DiMaggio,Yanks 97	V.Robays, Pirates 77

Lanahan Routs Bees, 6-3, Ending Skid of Pirates

PITTSBURGH, Aug. 20 (AP).—Although yielding thirteen hits, most of them slow bounders the infield could not handle, Dick Lanahan, southpaw, today pitched Pittsburgh to a 6-to-3 victory over Boston, Fanning six Bees as he broke the Pirates four-game losing streak. Four double plays aided the Buc hurler.

Deb Garms continued his sensational batting streak, getting three hits, including a double and driving in two runs. In hs last twenty-seven games the infielder-outfielder has hit safely in twenty-four for an average of .419, pulling up his average for sixty-two games to .375.

Pittsburgh clinched the game in the eighth with two out and Lanahan on first. Paul Waner's high fly fell safe back of second, Garms doubled and Bob Elliott singled, scoring three runs.

The Buc's catching squad was reduced to one effective man, Virgil Davis, when Eddie Fernandes injured a fifinger. Al Lopez is out for two weeks with a split finger.

The score:

BOSTON (N. L.)	ab	r	h	po	a	PITTSBURGH (N. L.)	ab	r	h	po	a
Sistl. 3b...	4	1	2	3	1	P.Wan'r,1b	5	1	3	11	1
Moore, rf.	5	0	1	4	0	Garms, 3b	5	1	3	1	2
Rowell,2b.	5	1	3	1	3	Elliott,rf..	4	0	2	1	0
Ross, lf..	3	0	1	2	0	Vaugh'n,ss	5	0	1	3	5
Miller ss.	4	0	2	4	1	V.Rob'ys.lf	3	0	1	1	0
West, cf....	4	0	2	1	1	Gustine,3b	4	1	2	4	5
Hassett,1b.	4	0	0	7	0	DiMag'o,cf	4	1	2	0	0
Berres, c..	2	0	0	2	1	Davis, c...	4	0	1	6	1
*Glossop .	1	1	1	0	0	Lanahan,p	4	2	0	0	2
Salvo, p..	3	0	1	0	5						
†Tobin ...	1	0	0	0	0						
Totals.	36	3	13	24	12	Totals.	38	6	15	27	16

*Batted for Berres in ninth inning.
†Batted for Salvo in ninth inning.

Boston .... 000 010 011—3
Pittsburgh .... 020 001 03x—6

Errors—Hassett, Vaughan, Ross, Davis. Runs batted in—Garms (2), Ross, Lanahan, West, Elliott (2), Sisti. Two-base hits—West, Garms. Stolen bases—Miller (2), Glossop. Sacrifice—Elliott. Double plays—Vaughan and P. Waner; Berres and Sisti; Garms and P. Waner; Vaughan, Gustine and P. Waner (2). Left on bases—Boston, 9; Pittsburgh, 10. Bases on balls—Off Lanahan, 3; off Salvo, 1. Struck out—By Lanahan, 6; by Salvo, 1. Umpires—Campbell, Klem and Ballanfant. Time—2:13. Atendance—1,950.

Standings in the Major Leagues

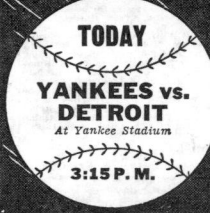

WEDNESDAY, AUG. 21, 1940

American League

YESTERDAY'S RESULTS

New York, 4; Detroit, 3 (1st).
New York, 4; Detroit, 2 (2d).
Chicago, 6; Philadelphia, 1 (1st).
Phila., 4; Chi., 3 (10 ins., 2d).
Cleveland, 11; Boston, 6.
St. Louis, 6; Wash'gton, 3.

STANDING OF THE CLUBS

	Cleveland	Detroit	Boston	New York	Chicago	Washington	St. Louis	Philadelphia	Won	Lost	Percentage	Games behind
Cleveland..	—	8	11	9	12	9	10	11	70	46	.603	—
Detroit....	5	—	8	12	7	12	15	7	66	51	.564	4½
Boston....	7	9	—	9	9	12	10	7	63	53	.543	7
New York..	8	6	9	—	7	8	11	10	59	53	.527	9
Chicago...	4	10	8	9	—	9	8	11	59	53	.527	9
Wash'gton	8	5	6	2	8	—	9	11	49	65	.430	20
St. Louis..	8	3	7	5	5	9	—	11	48	69	.410	22½
Phila......	6	10	4	7	5	6	6	—	44	68	.393	24
Games lost	46	51	53	53	53	65	69	68	—	—		

GAMES TODAY

Detroit at New York, 3:15.
St. Louis at Washington.
Chicago at Philadelphia.
Cleveland at Boston.

National League

YESTERDAY'S RESULTS

Cincinnati, 3; New York, 2.
St. Louis, 3; Brooklyn, 0 (1st).
St. Louis, 4; Brooklyn, 3 (2d).
Pittsburgh, 6; Boston, 3.
Chicago, 4; Philadelphia, 0.

STANDING OF THE CLUBS

	Cincinnati	Brooklyn	New York	St. Louis	Chicago	Pittsburgh	Boston	Philadelphia	Won	Lost	Percentage	Games behind
Cincinnati	—	11	12	8	12	10	8	9	70	41	.631	—
Brooklyn..	7	—	9	9	9	9	12	10	65	47	.580	5½
New York.	6	3	—	10	8	10	9	10	56	52	.519	12½
St. Louis..	7	10	7	—	7	5	10	10	56	53	.514	13
Chicago...	5	8	7	6	—	8	13	11	58	57	.504	14
Pittsb'gh..	2	6	5	11	9	—	12	10	55	55	.500	14½
Boston....	8	6	5	4	5	7	—	9	44	67	.396	26
Phila......	6	3	7	5	7	6	3	—	37	69	.349	30½
Games lost	41	47	52	53	57	55	67	69	—	—		

GAMES TODAY

New York at Cincinnati.
Brooklyn at St. Louis.
Boston at Pittsburgh.
Philadelphia at Chicago.

3-Run Uprising In Ninth Wins For Cincinnati

Lohrman Falters in Final Inning After Holding Foe to 3 Hits for 8 Frames

By Robert B. Cooke

CINCINNATI, Aug. 20.—A gallant effort by the New York Giants to lower the social standing of the Cincinniati Reds ended in catastrophe today when the National League leaders arose in the ninth inning, scored three times after two were out and pocketed a 3-to-2 victory.

For eight innings the Giants seemed intent upon preparing another gift package for Leo Durocher's Dodgres. But the Reds refused to allow the New Yorkers to make such a generous contribution to the Brooklyn cause two days in a row.

Bill Lohrman, a native Brooklyn boy was in charge of the committee sponsoring the welfare of the Dodgers. Given a 2-to-0 lead in the first two rounds he shut out the Reds for eight innings, during which time he pitched to twenty-two men, one over par.

Lohrman Falters in Ninth

Lohrman exhausted all his reserve in those eight innings. When Lew Riggs, batting for Eddie Joost, opened the ninth with a double, the Giant bull-pen crew went to work for the first time during the game. Lohrman lost the contest before Bill Terry had sufficient time to warm up an emergency flinger.

Lee Gamble, pinch hitting for Gene Thompson, flied to Johnny Rucker and Billy Werber grounded to Mickey Witek. The Giants were one out away from victory, but that particular out will never be made.

Lonnie Frey rapped a grounder toward first which bounced underneath Johnny McCarthy's glove, Riggs scoring. Ival Goodman dropped a handle hit into right which fell for a double, Frey reaching third. Frank McCormick, having let one pitch go by, rattled a liner into left, Frey and Goodman tallied and Lohrman headed for the dressing room emptyhanded.

As McCormick's single bounced against the wall in left, 328 feet away from the plate, the Reds emerged from their dugout en masse. Congratulations were passed out in large quantities and the small crowd of 6,360 did its best to lend vehement approval to the Garrison finish.

The Giants picked up a run off Thompson in the first when Joe Moore walked with one away, went to second on an infield out and tallied on McCarthy's double to right-center. Mel Ott's triple down the right-field foul line and Tony Cuccinello's long fly to Mike McCormick produced another run in the second.

3-Hit Effort Wrecked

Thereafter the Cincinnati right-hander kept all runners away from second. But Lohrman, restricting the Reds to three hits in eight innings, seemed a certain winner until the Reds grew resourceful in the final frame and wrecked the pretty picture that he had been painting with his good right arm.

The Reds were on the verge of their longest losing streak of the season until the ninth. They had dropped three in a row.

Rucker expedited Lohrman's labor in the third and fourth when he raced far and wide over a wind-swept outfield to pull down flies off the bats of Ernie Lombardi and Frank McCormick.

Ott has been bolstering his batting average lately. In the last four games, Melvin has connected safely eight times in thirteen chances.

Thompson had Hank Danning's number. He held the Giant catcher hitless in four attempts and the latter's average dropped three points to .323.

The score:

NEW YORK (N. L.)	ab	r	h	po	a	CINCINNATI (N. L.)	ab	r	h	po	a
Rucker,cf.	4	0	2	3	0	Werber, 3b	4	0	2	2	3
Moore, lf.	3	1	0	1	0	Frey, 2b..	4	1	1	2	1
Demaree,rf	4	0	0	2	0	G'dman,rf	4	1	1	1	0
McC'thy,1b	4	0	1	10	1	F.M'C'k,1b	4	0	1	11	1
Danning,c.	4	0	0	5	1	Lombardi,c	3	0	1	7	0
Ott, 3b...	3	1	3	0	2	Arnovich,lf	3	0	0	2	0
Cuc'n'lo,2b	4	0	0	4	0	M.M'C'k,cf	3	0	0	1	0
Witek, ss.	4	0	1	5	7	Joost, ss..	2	0	0	0	7
Loh'man,p	4	0	0	0	1	†Riggs ...	1	1	1	0	0
						Thomp'n,p	2	0	0	1	1
						‡Gamble.	1	0	0	0	0
Totals.	34	2	7	*26	13	Totals..	31	3	7	27	13

*Two out when winning run was scored.
†Batted for Joost in ninth inning.
‡Batted for Thompson in ninth inning.

New York .... 110 000 000—2
Cincinnati .... 000 000 003—3

Errors—None. Runs batted in—McCarthy, Cuccinello, Frey, F. McCormick (2). Two-base hits—McCarthy, Werber, Goodman, Riggs. Three-base hit—Ott. Stolen bases—Ott (2), Witek. Double play—Lohrman, Witek and McCarthy. Left on bases—New York, 7; Cincinnati, 2. Bases on balls—Off Thompson, 2. Struck out—By Lohrman, 2; by Thompson, 7. Passed ball—Lombardi. Umpires—Pinelli, Reardon and Goetz. Time—1:51. Attendance—6,360.

Cards Take Nightcap in Eighth As Casey Walks 3, Forces in Run

Lack of Control Costs Game Tied by Camilli's Homer; Shoun Blanks Brooklyn

By Rud Rennie

ST. LOUIS, Aug. 20.—Having landed safely from their airships, the Dodgers went into a tailspin at Sportsman's Park this afternoon. The red-hot Cardinals beat them in both ends of a double-header, 3 to 0, and 4 to 3, and rose to within half a game of the third-place Giants. The Dodgers, on the other hand, lost a game and a half to the league-leading Reds and are now five and a half games out.

The Cardinals had the Dodgers by only 1 to 0 in the first game until they scored two in the eighth. They won the nightcap in the eighth when Hugh Casey walked three men and forced in a the run which broke a tie established by Dolph Camilli's homer in the sixth.

There were three homers in the second game. Johnny Mize hit his thirty-fifth of the year for the Cards. Pete Coscarart and Camilli connected for the Dodgers, driving in all Brooklyn's runs.

Leo Durocher tried to get by with a couple of uncertain left-handers. He pitched Lee Grissom in the opener and started the rookie, Wesley Flowers, in the nightcap. Grissom twirled nicely; but Clyde Shoun, Cardinal left-hander, was just a little better, winning his third straight.

Warneke Wins Sixth in Row

Lon Warneke weathered the storm and beat the Dodgers in the second game. He has now won six straight and nine of ten since Billy Southworth took over the management of the club.

The Cardinals, incidentally, have won five straight and nine of their last ten.

Both teams made six hits in the first game. The Dodgers, getting three bases on balls, had men on bases in every inning except the first and seventh. But still they could not score. Shoun handcuffed Coscarart, Dixie Walker, Joe Medwick, Gus Mancuso and Durocher, and hung up his first shutout of the year.

Shoun was in trouble in the second, what with a base on balls to Vosmik and a double by Cookie Lavagetto. But after he got Mancuso for the second out, he walked Durocher purposely and made Grissom hit into an out with the bases filled.

Ernie Koy and Pepper Martin made leaping catches against the walls to rub out Medwick and Lavagetto and prevent a score in the sixth. And Shoun fanned Medwick for the third out after Camilli hit for two bases in the eighth.

Most of this happened while the score was 1 to 0 in favor of the Cardinals. They made a run in the second when Grissom walked Mickey Owen and Martin Marion doubled to left center, a good blow which let Owen score from first.

Grissom Weakens

This was the only run in the game until the eighth. Grissom, who failed with the Yankees last spring and who was brought in from Montreal by the Dodgers in July, pitched a capable game until the last inning. Two double plays helped him with the only two men who hit safely between the third and eighth. But in this inning the Cardinals made as many hits as they had in the previous seven, and with three safe blows scored two runs.

Shoun opened the inning with a single to Durocher. Jimmy Brown sacrificed. Then Terry Moore doubled, scoring Shoun, and Martin doubled, scoring Moore. It was Grissom's third start for the Dodgers and his second defeat.

Durocher gave his line-up a shake for the second game, bench Vosmik and Medwich and dropping Coscarart into eighth place. But this didn't help.

The Dodgers went through four more scoreless innings at the start of the second game before they managed to make a run. Warneke had them shut out with one hit and they were trailing, 3 to 0.

Flowers, even though he yielded four hits in the first two innings, got by successfully until the third when, with two away, Mize poled a home run into the right-centerfield pavilion. Then the bottom of the batting order nudged him for two runs in the fourth. Marion knocked in one with a double and Warneke's single drove in the other. It took a double play to get Flowers out of this inning, his last.

Coscarart Hits Homer

After Coscarart poled a home run into the left field bleachers with two out in the fifth to give the Dodgers their first score, Herman Franks was sent to bat for Flowers. He singled, but Peter Reiser ended the rally with a pop fly.

In the sixth, however, the Dodgers tied the score. Walker opened the inning with his first hit of the day. Camilli followed with a home run which struck alongside the right-field foul pole and richochetted along the roof. The Dodgers were back in the ball game.

Tex Carleton held the Cardinals through the fifth and sixth and Joe Gallagher batted for him in the seventh and singled with two out. Reiser also got a hit; but Walker popped up and the rally died. Camilli walked and got as far as third in the eighth.

Then Casey, the current Dodger pitcher, blew up and forced in the winning run with two out. With none out, Mize made his third hit. Enos Slaughter walked. And after Joe Orengo flied out, Casey pitched eight balls without a strike, to Don Padgett, pinch hitting for Owen, and to Stu Martin, pinch hitting for Marion, forcing in Mize. A good play by Coscarart left the Cards with the bases loaded.

Vosmik and Medwick pinch hit in vain for the Dodgers in the ninth, Medwick fanning for the final out amid boos from the 11,888 fans.

Durocher made the only error in the first game. He was too slow getting to second when Camilli threw there for a force play in the sixth and then he threw the ball to the stands, so that the Cards had men on second and hird with one out. But Grissom stopped Martin and Mize and escaped. . . . Grissom made a monkey of Mize, getting him out four times in which he fanned him twice.

Terry Moore, the best center-fielder in the league, made an almost unbelieveable catch of a short fly hit by Walker in the first inning of the second game. He dived and plucked the ball off the grass.

Dodgers' Scores

* * *

FIRST GAME

BROOKLYN (N. L.)	ab	r	h	po	a	ST. LOUIS (N. L.)	ab	r	h	po	a
Cos'cr't,2b	3	0	0	2	1	Brown, 2b	2	0	0	2	3
Walker,cf.	3	0	0	2	0	Moore, cf.	4	1	1	2	0
Camilli,1b.	4	0	1	7	1	J.Mart'n,rf	4	0	1	1	0
Medwick,lf	4	0	0	2	0	Mize, 1b..	4	0	0	13	0
Vosmik,rf.	3	0	2	0	0	Koy, lf...	3	0	1	5	0
*Wasdell .	0	0	0	0	0	Orengo, 2b	3	0	1	0	3
Lavag'o,3b	4	0	2	1	2	Owen, c...	1	1	0	4	0
Manusco,c.	3	0	0	7	0	Ma'ion,ss.	3	0	1	0	1
†Gallagher	1	0	0	0	0	Shoun, p..	3	1	1	0	0
Dur'ch'r,ss	3	0	0	3	1						
Grissom,p.	3	0	1	0	2						
Totals...	31	0	6	24	7	Totals...	27	3	6	27	7

*Ran for Vosmik in ninth inning.
†Batted for Mancuso in ninth inning.

Brooklyn .... 000 000 000—0
St. Louis .... 001 000 02x—3

Error—Durocher. Runs batted in—Marion, Moore, J. Martin. Two-base hits—Lavagetto, Marion, Orengo, Camilli, Moore, J. Martin. Stolen base—J. Martin. Sacrifices—Walker, Orengo, Brown. Double plays—Orengo, Marion and Mize; Coscarart and Durocher; Lavagetto and Camilli. Left on bases—Brooklyn, 8; St. Louis, 6. Bases on balls—Off Grissom, 4; off Shoun, 3. Struck out—By Grissom, 7; by Shoun, 2. Umpires—Sears, Jorda and Barr. Time—1:54.

SECOND GAME

BROOKLYN (N. L.)	ab	r	h	po	a	ST. LOUIS (N. L.)	ab	r	h	po	a
Reiser, rf..	4	0	1	1	0	Bro'n,3b.ss	4	0	0	0	0
Walker,cf.	4	1	1	1	0	Moore, cf.	4	0	0	4	0
Camilli,1b.	3	1	1	10	0	J.Mart'n,rf	2	0	1	1	1
Phelps, c.	3	0	1	4	1	Hopp, lf..	2	0	0	1	0
Wasdell,lf.	4	0	0	5	0	Mize, 1b..	4	2	3	9	0
Lavag'o,3b	4	0	0	0	3	Koy, lf....	1	0	0	0	0
Dur'ch'r,ss	3	0	0	1	2	Slaugh'r,rf	1	0	1	0	0
‡Vosmik ..	1	0	0	0	0	Orengo,2b.	4	1	2	2	6
Cosc'art,2b	4	1	1	2	3	Owen, c...	2	0	1	3	0
Flowers,p.	1	0	0	0	1	Padgett, c.	0	0	0	0	0
*Franks.	1	0	1	0	0	Marion, ss	3	1	1	4	2
Carleton,p.	0	0	0	0	0	S.M'rt'n,3b	0	0	0	0	0
†Gallagher	1	0	1	0	0	Warneke,p.	3	0	1	1	1
Casey, p.	0	0	0	0	0						
§Medwick.	1	0	0	0	0						
Totals..	34	3	7	24	10	Totals..	30	4	10	27	9

*Batted for Flowers in fifth inning.
†Batted for Carleton in seventh inning.
‡Batted for Durocher in ninth inning.
§Batted for Casey in ninth inning.

Brooklyn .... 000 012 000—3
St. Louis .... 001 200 01x—4

Errors—None. Runs batted in—Mize, Marion, Warneke, Coscarart, Camilli (2), S. Martin. Two-base hit—Marion. Home runs—Mize, Coscarart, Camilli. Stolen base—Mize. Sacrifices—Warneke, Owen. Double play—Durocher and Camilli. Left on bases—Brooklyn, 6; St. Louis, 8. Bases on balls—Off Warneke, 2; off Flowers, 2; off Casey, 3. Struck out—By Warneke, 4; by Flowers, 1; by Carleton, 1; by Casey, 2. Hits—Off Flowers, 8 in 4 innings; off Carleton, 1 in 2; off Casey, 1 in 2. Wild pitch—Flowers. Losing pitcher—Casey. Umpires—Jorda, Barr and Sears. Time—1:54. Attendance—9,451.

Section III — SPORTS — NEW YORK Herald Tribune — SPORTS — Section III

EIGHT PAGES — SUNDAY, AUGUST 25, 1940 — EIGHT PAGES

Yankees Beat Feller, 3-2; Dodgers Rout Cubs, 11-3; Giants Win; New World Outfoots Whirlaway in Grand Union at Saratoga

Choice Loses By 1½ Lengths At 6 Furlongs

Victor Leads Throughout and Goes Route in 1:11; Hy-Cop Places Third

Isolater, $17.30, Wins in Handicap

Stout Completes Riding Double on Belair Colt; Your Chance Is Second

By Murray Tynan

SARATOGA SPRINGS, N. Y., Aug. 24.—The two-year-old situation and the weather were knocked high, wide and handsome this afternoon when Alfred Vanderbilt's New World reversed the findings of the Saratoga Special and conquered Warren Wright's Whirlaway in the Grand Union Hotel Stakes before 17,709 overcoated and very chilly race-goers who bet $674,840 on the card. A half hour before William Woodward's Isolater won the Merchants and Citizens Handicap New World took the measure of his arch-rival in 1:11, the fastest time of the meeting for three quarters of a mile.

Considered to be a two-horse race even though four others went away with the two potential champions, this thirty-eighth running of the Grand Union was one of the most interesting races of the meeting. It proved two things, that Whirlaway may not be the world beater he seemed to be in the Saratoga Special and that New World may yet prove to be a stayer. In the Special New World stopped badly and Whirlaway defeated him by a length and a half in 1:11 1-5. This afternoon New World went on and defeated Whirlaway by the same margin, but this time Whirlaway carried 122 pounds and the Vanderbilt colt had a concession of six. Whirlaway was the favorite at 6 to 5 and New World was a shade better than 8 to 5.

New World Goes Into Lead

Six went to the post, and it wasn't long after George Cassidy sent them away that New World went to the top followed by W. E. Boeing's Twinkippy and J. W. Dial's Hy-Cop. Whirlaway, a slow beginner, broke from the inside position, which didn't favor him, and when the field went into the turn it was New World first and Whirlaway. That was the line-up in the Saratoga Special run two weeks ago, but this time Whirlaway was much closer than in the previous race.

It was apparent by this time that Raymond Workman, who rode New World, was restraining the colt just a little to save something for the end, so while the backers of Whirlaway were happy to see him closer up the New World followers were not exactly nervous. Every one knew that the real battle would come in the last furlong when Whirlaway was expected to start his charge toward the front.

Whirlaway was now ready to start his run, but instead of going to the outside as he did two weeks ago, Johnny Longden took the colt between Hy-Cop and Brandywine Stable's Pompion. There wasn't as much room as he thought there would be and the colt's speed might have been retarded a little as he came through.

New World Keeps Going

Some thought that he might have won if Longden had gone to the outside for clear sailing, but that was a matter of opinion. He at least got through in time to start his run at New World, but this time he found a different colt in front of his. Two weeks ago New World tired in the last sixteenth but he just galloped along this time.

Hy-Cop was third, beaten three lengths for the place, and Twinkippy was fourth. New World, which in three races has now won two and been second once, added $10,050 to his earnings. He raced the first quarter in 0:23 and the half in 0:47.

The handicap, like the Grand Union, was a good horse race, and the victory of Isolater, which completed a double for Jimmy Stout, evidently came as a surprise to those who neglected to take into consideration the strong work this son of Blandford had between races this week. Perfectly rated by Stout, he came strongly in the turn, had it out in the stretch with Falaise Stable's War Dog, the early leader, and George D. Widener's Your Chance, and drew off in the last sixteenth of a mile to win by a length and one-half. Your Chance was second, War Dog third and Greentree Stable's Hash fourth. Only six went away.

Your Chance Favored

Being a three-year-old, Your Chance was in this run of one mile and three sixteenths with 116 for Iso- to 119 for Hash and 116 for Isolater, older horses. The crowd made him the favorite, but though he ran a good race and was in close quarters coming around the turn, he wasn't up to the job of beating the fit horse that won. Isolater returned $17.30, and picked up $7,850 for his owner, who is the chairman of The Jockey Club. His time was 1:56 4-5.

With one of the smartest crowds of the season, headed by Woodward and Herbert Bayard Swope, John Hay Whitney and John Sloan, of the racing commission, this next to last

(Continued on page 6, column 3)

California Girls Win Eastern Doubles Title

Miss Pearl Harland, of Santa Monica, Calif., and Miss Patricia Hover, of Hollywood, Calif., won the doubles final in the Eastern girls' invitation grass court tennis tournament yesterday at the Richmond County Country Club in Dongan Hills, Staten Island. Miss Harland and Miss Hover, top-seeded in the draw, defeated Miss Doris Hart, of Miami, Fla., and Miss Nellie Sheer, of Miami Beach, Fla., 7—5, 3—6, 6—2.

Miss Harland had defeated Miss Hart in the singles final a day earlier.

All-Star Team Nets 19 Points In First Test

McLaughry and Nowaski Score Touchdowns in Drill With L. I. Indians

By Al Laney

CORNWALL ON HUDSON, N. Y., Aug. 24.—With the Long Island Indians playing the role of experimental guinea pigs, the Eastern College All-Stars put on a display today the embryonic offense which, when full born, will be thrown against the New York Giants at the Polo Grounds the night of Sept. 4. The experiment was a complete success for, with almost all conceivable combinations of line and backfield men, the All-Stars clicked for two touchdowns, two points after a field goal and a safety, a total of nineteen points. The Indians were on the defensive throughout the hour-and-a-half scrimmage session and, with only one workout behind them, demonstrated that they have a tough team in the making.

Nearly every one of the thirty-one available in camp was used by Tuss McLaughry, All-Star coach, and he could not have been other than well pleased with the way things went. At the end of the workout, in which no All-Star was seriously injured and only one Indian was hurt, the coach had a rather definite idea of what he may demand and expect to get from his squad. His demands will be great and the indications were tonight that the response will be equally great. The first week of training for the annual meeting with the Giants for the Tribune Fresh Air Fund thus ended on a highly optimistic note. The offense is set and the intensive work on defense begins on Monday

McLaughry Goes Over

One All-Star touchdown was scored by John McLaughry, of Brown, who bucked the ball over from the one-yard line after Vito Ananis, of Boston, skirting his own left end behind a wall of blockers, had placed it there at the end of a thirty-yard run. The other was scored by Bob Nowaski, left end from George Washington, who took a long pass from Merlyn Condit, of Carnegie Tech, and stepped into the end zone.

John Rogalla, of Scranton University, kicked the goal from placement, a distance of twenty yards at a difficult angle, and the safety came when the Indians tried to run the ball out from behind their own goal line after McLaughry's quick-kick had rolled over. The ball carrier was nailed in his tracks.

The All-Stars were by no means impressive at the start of the scrimmage and they did not begin to roll until the Indians had forced them to punt several times. With the big Indian forwards crashing through to make violent contact, linemen forgot assignments and backs handled the ball raggedly. But after a few minutes of this sort of thing the boys began to get the feel of things, confidence came to them and with it smoothness and proper timing.

McLaughry sent out first a team which had on the line from left to

(Continued on page 3, column 7)

A Two-Run Homer for the Indians and Ninth-Inning Score Which Beat Them

At left, Ken Keltner crossing the plate after his home run in second inning to receive the congratulations of Heath, who scored ahead of him, and Mack, No. 6. At right, Jake Powell, pinch-runner for Joe DiMaggio, scoring on Knickerbocker's single with run that won for Yankees, 3 to 2

Herald Tribune—Acme

Notre Dame Smashes Records In Speedboat Sweepstakes Race

Detroit Craft Averages 76.14 M.P.H. for First Heat of Test, Runs a 76.923 Lap

By Everett B. Morris

RED BANK, N. J., Aug. 24.—Those members of the speed-boating fraternity who have contended long and loudly that a good 225-cubic-inch hydroplane could blister the paint off the topsides of a Gold Cup boat any time they met in competition were silenced this afternoon when the first heat of the National Sweepstakes race was run under almost perfect conditions on the Shrewsbury.

Herbert Mendelson's Notre Dame argued the question for the Gold Cuppers and did it so well and so thoroughly that there was no rebuttal by the opposition. Notre Dame won the fifteen-mile test from here to there and back again, left the best 225's in the country hull down astern and smashed all sweepstakes records in the process.

Driven cleverly and fearlessly by young Danny Arena, the mahogany-hulled Detroit Yacht Club boat averaged 76.14 miles an hour for the six circuits of the two and one-half-mile oval course. Her fastest trip, the third, was 76.923 m. p. h. Until Notre Dame made the placid Shrewsbury's waters steam in her wake, the sweepstakes heat record stood at 64.439 m. p. h., a figure put on the books in 1937 by Tops II, a 225-cubic inch hydroplane driven by Jack Cooper, the ever youthful grandpop from Kansas City.

Today, in Tops III, a newer and faster 225, Cooper was second to Notre Dame and averaged 67.839 m. p. h. The previous lap record, 65.589 m. p. h., was made in 1936 by the Gold Cup hydroplane, Jay-Dee, with Mrs. Maud Rutherfurd at the wheel.

When the starting gun for the sweepstakes sounded nine 225's and three Gold Cup boats bolted over the line. Upholding Gold Cup class

(Continued on page 5, column 2)

Dean, A's Pitcher, Missing, Says Mack

PHILADELPHIA, Aug. 24 (AP).—Lovill (Chubby) Dean, Athletics pitcher, has disappeared, Connie Mack, manager, said today.

"I have no idea where he is or what has happened to him," said Mack. "I think his failure to pitch as well as he expected to has upset him."

Dean made a poor showing when he relieved John Babich Thursday night in the first game of the current series with St. Louis. Teammates said he had been in depressed spirits for several weeks.

Futurity Taken By Porter's Cap At Chicago Oval

Silvestra Loses in Photo Finish With 13-1 Shot; Swain, Choice, Is Fifth

CHICAGO, Aug. 24 (AP).—Charles S. Howard, of San Francisco, called the luckiest owner on the American turf, sent a little chestnut colt purchased for $1,300 a year ago, to the post in the $43,000 Washington Park Futurity today and the youngster's victory stunned a crowd of 20,000.

The colt was Porter's Cap, which charged through a drizzling rain to beat eight rivals and snare $30,750 as first prize. Porter's Cap, the son of The Porter—The Blonde, finished a neck in front of the speedy filly, Silvestra, with Valdina Groom three-quarters of a length further back in third place.

Struggling another length behind in fourth place was Good Turn, the entry of Alfred G. Vanderbilt, of New York. In fifth place was Cleaveland Putnam's highly touted Swain, which captured the Arlington Park Futurity by five and a half lengths just a month ago.

Porter's Cap, going to the post at odds of 13 to 1, paid $28.40 to win, $13.40 to place and 7.40 to show. The place price on Silvestra, owned by Herbert Woolf, of Kansas City, was $7.20 and the show price $4.80. Valdina Groom, which finished second to Swain in the Arlington, returned $4.20.

First Major Victory

Previous to today's victory Porter's Cap never won an important stake, coming to the Middle West after capturing two allowance races at Hollywood Park with both purses totaling only $1,500.

Porter's Cap, ridden by Carroll Bierman, who guided Gallahadion to victory in the Kentucky Derby, sprinted the six furlongs in 1:12 4-5.

The race was roughly run, with Good Turn, ridden by Basil James, forcing Big Stakes, Silvestra and Valdina Myth to bear out on the back stretch. Good Turn also impeded Valdina Groom and Porter's Cap in the stretch, resulting in James's suspension for the balance of the meeting, and an additional fifty-three days, making sixty in all.

(Continued on page 6, column 2)

Parker-McNeill Bow in Upset In U. S. Tennis

Kramer-Schroeder in Final With Prusoff and Mulloy; Marble, Bundy Duos Win

By Fred Hawthorne

CHESTNUT HILL, Mass., Aug. 24.—A team that was only made up this season gained the final round in the Longwood Cricket Club's fifty-ninth anual national men's doubles lawn tennis championship this afternoon when Jack Kramer, of Montebello, Calif., and Ted Schroeder, of Glendale, Calif., defeated the No. 1 ranking team of the country, Frank A. Parker, of Pasadena, Calif., and Don McNeill, of Oklahoma City, 10—8, 2—6, 7—5, 6—3. In the other semi-final match Henry J. Prusoff, of Seattle, and Gardnar Mulloy, of Miami, Fla., defeated Russell Bobbitt, of Atlanta, and Frank D. Guernsey jr., of Orlando, Fla., 9—7, 4—6, 7—5, 6—4. The final will start at 1:30 p. m. tomorrow.

Miss Alice Marble, of Beverly Hills, Calif., and Miss Sarah Palfrey, of Reno, Nev., defending champions, gained the final in the women's championship by defeating Miss Virginia Wolfenden and Miss Patricia Canning, of California, 6—3, 6—3. The other finalists are Mrs. John Van Ryn, of Austin, Tex., and Miss Dorothy Bundy, of Santa Monica, Calif. They defeated the English Wightman Cup combination of Miss Mary Hardwick and Miss Valerie Scott, 6—3, 9—7, in the other semi-final. Miss Marble and Miss Palfrey will face Mrs. Van Ryn and Miss Bundy at 3 p. m. tomorrow for the title.

Eleonora Sears in Final

The national father-and-son doubles moved into the semi-final round, and G. Colket Caner and C. C Fulton, of Longwood, entered the final of the veterans' doubles by defeating Lawrence A. Baker and Walter Weld, 9—7, 6—2, in the upper half semi-final. In the women's veterans' championship, Miss Eleonora Sears, of Boston, and Mrs. Gretl duPont, of Los Angeles, and Mrs. George W. Wightman and Miss Edith Signourney, of Boston, reached the final. All finals except the mixed doubles, which goes over until Monday, are scheduled for tomorrow.

It was chilly weather for tennis,

(Continued on page 4, column 7)

Davis's Six-Hit Pitching Snaps Brooklyn's Losing Streak at 5

Gallagher Blasts Homer and Double as Durocher Men Score 8 Runs in Second

By Rud Rennie

CHICAGO, Aug. 24.—For the first time in seven games, the Dodgers employed the same starting line-up two days in succession. The players got acquainted with one another and also with the Cub pitchers to the tune of fourteen hits, while Curt Davis held the enemy to six and won the final game here, 11 to 3, as Brooklyn snapped a five-game losing streak.

It was the Dodgers' first victory on the current air-borne western trip. Among other things, they broke the spell, under which left-handers have held them, routing Ken Raffensberger in the second, their biggest scoring inning of the year.

The Dodgers made eight runs in this inning and caused rain. Twelve men batted, but they made only four hits and Joe Gallagher got two of them, a home run with no one on and a double with the bases loaded. One run scored on a wild pitch. Two runs were forced in. And six of the runs were unearned due to an early error by Stanley Hack.

Bryant Ineffective

Raffensberger was taken out after walking Davis with the bases filled, thus forcing in the second run. Clay Bryant, who had pitched only one ball since his return from his cure, started by making a wild pitch letting in another run. He got Harry Lavagetto to pop up for the second out, but he walked Joe Medwick forcing in another run, and then yielded a couple of hits.

Gallagher, who had opened the inning with a home run into the left-field bleachers, came up next time with three on and slammed a double close to the top of the right-field wall, knocking in two runs. Then Joe Vosmik, who had flied to left for the first out, singled to left, scoring Medwick and Gallagher. Dolph Camilli ended the inning with a fly to right.

All this scoring was made possible when Hack missed Coscarart's grounder after Camilli's first time at bat.

For a while it looked as if the rain might deprive the Dodgers of victory. But the Dodgers got a break.

(Continued on page 2, column 4)

Dodgers' Score

* * *

BROOKLYN (N. L.)	ab	r	h	po	a
Reiser, ss..	4	1	2	3	4
Lavag'o, 3b	5	0	0	1	0
Medwick, lf	4	1	1	2	0
Gallag'r, rf	5	2	3	2	0
Vosmik, cf.	5	0	2	2	0
Camilli, 1b	4	1	2	11	1
Co'rt, 2b	5	2	1	2	2
Mancuso, c	5	2	2	3	0
Davis, p....	1	2	1	1	2
Totals..	38	11	14	27	9

CHICAGO (N. L.)	ab	r	h	po	a
Hack, 3b..	4	0	2	0	4
Herman, 2b	4	0	0	6	4
Bonura, 1b	4	1	2	10	2
Leiber, cf..	4	0	0	3	0
Gleeson, rf	4	1	1	2	1
Dal'an'o, lf	4	1	1	2	0
Todd, c....	2	0	0	0	0
Collins, c..	1	0	0	1	0
Mattick, ss	3	0	0	2	2
Raf'b'ger, p	0	0	0	0	0
Bryant, p..	1	0	0	0	1
French, p..	2	0	0	1	0
Totals..	33	3	6	27	14

Brooklyn	081	020	000	—11
Chicago	000	000	300	— 3

Errors—Hack (3), Lavagetto. Runs batted in—Gallagher (3), Davis, Medwick, Vosmik (2), Coscarart, Reiser (3), Dallessandro (3). Two-base hits—Gallagher, Reiser, Davis. Home runs—Gallagher, Coscarart, Dallessandro. Sacrifices—Davis (2). Double plays—Reiser, Coscarart and Camilli; Mattick, Herman and Bonura; Hack, Herman and Bonura (2). Left on bases—Brooklyn, 6; Chicago, 3. Bases on balls—Off Raffensberger, 1; off Bryant, 2. Struck out—By Davis, 3. Hits—Off Raffensberger, 2 in 1 1-3 innings; off Bryant, 9 in 3 2-3; off French, 3 in 4. Hit by pitcher—By French (Camilli). Wild pitch—Bryant. Passed ball—Todd. Losing pitcher—Raffensberger. Umpires—Klem, Ballanfant and Campbell. Time—1:47. Attendance—6,769.

New York Beats Pirates, 7 to 6, On Wild Pitch

Heintzelman's Errant Toss in 9th Enables Hubbell to Register 10th Victory

By Robert B. Cooke

PITTSBURGH, Aug. 24.—A wild pitch by young Kenneth Heintzelman, one of Pittsburgh's untamed left-handers, proved conclusively to the New York Giants today that the best things in life are free.

The Giants and the Pirates were locked in a 6-to-6 tie when Heintzelman appeared bearing gifts in the ninth. With runners on first and second, he heaved the ball beyond the limits of the massive frame of Spud Davis and gave New York a 7-to-6 victory.

Although it was a backhanded way of achieving their objective, the Terrymen were thoroughly satisfied, for it enabled Carl Hubbell to score his tenth victory.

Heintzelman's errant toss provided the finishing touch to a struggle in which the Giants had been compelled to march uphill most of the way.

If the Pirates could pitch the way they can hit, the New Yorkers would have conceded the game long before the ninth. But Frank Frisch has only one ace on his staff, Rip Sewell. The remainder of his hurling corps is composed of deuces, mostly wild.

Unfortunately for the Buccaneers, Sewell had already beaten the Giants in this series and they had to rely on Mace Brown. He was comparatively effective until the Pirates gave him a 5-to-1 lead in the fifth. After that, Brown couldn't stand prosperity and the Giants rocked him for five rune in the next three innings to tie the score at 6-all in the eighth.

Frisch grew tired of Brown's generosity and removed him for an unproductive pinch hitter in the eighth. Heitzelman's first mistake in the next inning occurred when he allowed Joe Moore to open the

(Continued on page 2, column 3)

Standings in the Major Leagues

SUNDAY, AUG. 25, 1940

American League

YESTERDAY'S RESULTS

New York, 3; Cleveland, 2.
Detroit, 12; Boston, 1 (1st).
Boston, 8; Detroit, 7 (2d).
Chicago, 4; Wash'gton, 2 (1st).
Chicago, 2; Wash., 1 (2d).
St. L., 6; Phila., 5 (10 ins.).

STANDING OF THE CLUBS

	Cleveland	Detroit	New York	Boston	Chicago	Washington	St. Louis	Philadelphia	Won	Lost	Percentage	Games behind
Cleveland..	—	8	9	12	12	9	10	11	71	49	.592	—
Detroit....	5	—	12	10	7	12	15	7	68	53	.562	3½
New York.	11	7	—	9	7	8	11	10	63	53	.543	6
Boston....	7	10	9	—	9	12	10	7	64	56	.533	7
Chicago...	4	10	9	8	—	11	8	11	61	55	.526	8
Wash'gton	8	5	2	6	9	—	10	11	51	67	.432	19
St. Louis..	8	3	5	7	5	9	—	13	50	71	.413	21½
Phila......	6	10	7	4	6	6	7	—	46	70	.397	23
Games lost	49	53	53	56	55	67	71	70	—	—		

GAMES TODAY

Chicago at New York (2), 2:05.
St. Louis at Boston (2).
Cleveland at Washington.
Detroit at Philadelphia.

National League

YESTERDAY'S RESULTS

New York, 7; Pittsburgh, 6.
Brooklyn, 11; Chicago, 3.
Cincinnati, 5; Boston, 0.
St. Louis, 1; Philadelphia, 0.

STANDING OF THE CLUBS

	Cincinnati	Brooklyn	St. Louis	New York	Chicago	Pittsburgh	Boston	Philadelphia	Won	Lost	Percentage	Games behind
Cincinnati	—	11	8	12	12	10	10	9	72	43	.626	—
Brooklyn..	7	—	9	9	10	9	12	10	66	50	.569	6½
St. Louis..	7	11	—	7	7	5	10	13	60	53	.531	11
New York.	7	3	10	—	8	12	9	10	59	54	.522	12
Chicago...	5	10	6	7	—	8	13	11	60	59	.504	14
Pittsb'gh..	2	6	11	7	9	—	13	10	58	57	.504	14
Boston....	9	6	4	5	5	7	—	9	45	70	.391	27
Phila......	6	3	5	7	8	6	3	—	38	72	.345	31½
Games lost	43	50	53	54	59	57	70	72	—	—		

GAMES TODAY

New York at Chicago (2).
Brooklyn at Pittsburgh (2).
Boston at St. Louis (2).
Phila. at Cincinnati (2).

2 Hits in Ninth Down Indians Before 50,964

Single by Knickerbocker After DiMaggio Triples Captures Sixth Straight

Rolfe's Two-Bagger Ties Score in 8th

New York, Held Hitless by Youth for 7⅓ Innings, Blasts His Bid for 23d

By Harry Cross

The on-rushing Yankees crushed Cleveland and the fabulous Feller at the Stadium yesterday, 3 to 2, with determined eighth and ninth inning rallies after the great speed-ball pitcher had held the champions hitless for seven and a third innings.

A crowd of 50,964 spectators was keyed to a high pitch at the Stadium's biggest thrill of the season, the crucial victory coming just at the right moment for the tardy Yankees, who have hurled themselves back into the flag fight with unabated fury.

It was the Yankees' sixth straight victory and elevated Joe McCarthy's third-place club to within six games of the league-leading Tribe. The world's titleholders have won thirteen out of their last fifteen games and their uphill fight yesterday in this critical competition puts them in a position to mangle the American League flag race.

Knickerbocker's Hit Wins

The turbulent finish came in the ninth, with the score tied at 2 to 2. Joe DiMaggio thumped a triple off the left-field concrete. He suffered a charleyhorse and limped from second to third, where Jake Powell went in to run for him. Feller passed Selkirk and Dickey intentionally, filling the bases.

Both the Indian infield and outfield were pulled in for a play at the plate. After Babe Dahlgren fanned, Billy Knickerbocker, who had replaced Frank Crosetti at short, walloped a drive to center, scoring Powell for the hard-earned victory. Roy Weatherly was playing close in and made no attempt to chase the ball.

The pitch, with which Knickerbocker brought the coveted triumph, was the 135th thrown by Feller during the momentous engagement. For seven innings it looked as if the mighty strong boy was going to put an end to the menacing advance of the champions. Over that stretch only three Yankees got on base, and these trips to first were gifts. He walked Joe Gordon and Tom Henrich in the first inning and Bill Dickey in the fifth.

Cleveland had presumably sewed up the ball game in the second inning when, with Jeff Heath aboard, Ken Keltner sliced a two-run homer off Atley Donald into the right-field stand.

Dahlgren Gets First Hit

The Yankees were at Feller's mercy until the eighth. With one out, Dahlgren hit a single to center which ruined Feller's chances for a no-hitter. Charle Keller went in as a pinch hitter for Crosetti and walked. Buddy Rosar then went to bat in place of Donald. He blasted a screaming drive to left field. Heath backed up to make the catch and in ramming the stand he dropped the ball. It was close to a home run, but was recorded as a single. The bases were filled. After Gordon struck out, Red Rolfe drove a double to right, scoring Dahlgren and Keller with the tying runs.

Feller was unsteady at the start of the game and walked Gordon. After Rolfe flied to Weatherly, Henrich walked. With a lusty roar, the crowd beseeched DiMaggio to do something valorous. He flied to Chapman and George Selkirk struck out.

After Donald fanned Hal Trosky in the second, Heath walked and Keltner sliced his homer. Donald threw a third strike past Mack, but the ball got by Dickey and rolled to the fence. Mack got to first and the pitch was scored as an error against Donald. Hemsley's single to right sent Mack to third, but the Yankees' discomfort ended when Feller struck out.

The champions seemed a bit nerv-

(Continued on page 2, column 5)

Yankees' Score

* * *

CLEVELAND (A. L.)	ab	r	h	po	a
Ch'man, rf	4	0	0	2	0
Weath'y, cf	4	0	1	4	0
Boud'u, ss.	5	0	0	1	1
Trosky, 1b	5	0	0	3	1
Heath, lf..	4	1	0	1	0
Kelt'r, 3b.	4	1	2	2	1
Mack, 2b..	4	0	3	2	3
Hems'y, c.	3	0	1	9	0
Feller, p..	3	0	0	1	0
Totals...	36	2	7	*25	6

NEW YORK (A. L.)	ab	r	h	po	a
Gordon, 2b	3	0	0	2	2
Rolfe, 3b..	4	0	1	2	4
Henr'h, rf.	3	0	0	2	0
DiMag'o, cf	4	0	1	3	0
§Powell ..	0	1	0	0	0
Selkirk, lf.	3	0	0	1	0
Dickey, c.	2	0	0	8	0
Dahlg'n, 1b	4	1	1	7	0
Crosetti, ss	2	0	0	2	2
†Keller....	0	1	0	0	0
Knick'r, ss	1	0	1	0	0
Donald, p.	2	0	0	0	1
‡Rosar....	1	0	1	0	0
Murphy, p	0	0	0	0	0
Totals....	29	3	5	27	9

*One out when winning run was scored.
†Batted for Crosetti in eighth inning.
‡Batted for Donald in eighth inning.
§Ran for DiMaggio in ninth inning.

Cleveland	020	000	000	—2
New York	000	000	021	—3

Errors—Donald, Dahlgren. Runs batted in—Keltner (2), Rolfe (2), Knickerbocker. Two-base hits—Mack, Rolfe. Three-base hit—DiMaggio. Home run—Keltner. Double play—Boudreau, Mack and Trosky. Left on bases—New York, 7; Cleveland, 12. Bases on balls—Off Feller, 6; off Donald, 5. Struck out—By Feller, 9; by Donald, 6. Hits—Off Donald, 7 in 8 innings; off Murphy, 0 in 1. Passed ball—Dickey. Winning pitcher—Murphy. Umpires—Grieve, Rommel, Summers and Basil. Time—2:35. Attendance—50,961.

Yanks Win Two, 2d in 13th, and Gain Game on Indians; Dodgers, Giants Beaten

CHAMPIONS DOWN BROWNS, 10-3, 6-5

DiMaggio 3-Run Pinch Homer Ties Nightcap in Ninth—Each Side Counts in 11th

CROSETTI BUNT DECIDES

Comes With Bases Loaded and 2 Out in 13th—Yanks Have 10-Run Inning in Opener

By JOHN DREBINGER

Only a game fish, they say, swims against the tide, but yesterday it seemed that the Yankees, continuing their electrifying dash for a fifth straight pennant, practically threshed all the water out of the stream as they sank the Browns in both ends of a double-header at the Stadium.

The opening engagement the Bronx Bombers won, 10 to 3, their entire output of runs crashing home in the fifth inning to give Marius Russo, their youthful left-hander, his eleventh mound triumph of the year against five defeats.

But that wasn't a patch to what had 7,865 hardy onlookers roaring themselves a deep purple as Manager Joe McCarthy's champions came on twice to tie the nightcap and finally win it in the thirteenth, 6 to 5.

With the Yanks trailing Elden Auker by three runs in the ninth they saw Joe DiMaggio hobble to the plate as pinch-hitter for Babe Dahlgren and with two aboard the bases bang the ball into the right-field stand for his twenty-eighth homer of the year. That deadlocked the battle at 4-all.

Brownies Go Ahead

In the eleventh they saw George McQuinn put the Brownies in front again with his fifteenth circuit blow of the year only to have the Yanks draw even once more on Charlie Keller's double and Buddy Rosar's single.

And in the thirteenth, the gathering went into its final frenzy of joy unrestrained as Frankie Crosetti, with the bases full and two out, sent a bunt rolling down the third-base line with the dexterity of a balkline billiard master. That deft stroke gave Frankie his fourth hit of the game and sent Tommy Henrich scampering home with the tally that broke up the conflict before the astonished Browns fully appreciated that it was over.

As a result of these latest twin victories, the Yanks concluded their final home stand of the year against the West with a record of ten victories against one defeat and edged up another full game on the league-leading Indians who, held idle by rain, saw their margin over the onrushing world champions dwindle to four and a half lengths. The Yanks also managed to keep themselves within two and a half games of the second-place Tigers.

Murphy to the Rescue

Fordham Johnny Murphy, once again the Yanks' peerless relief specialist of old, was the winning pitcher of the sizzling nightcap, replacing Steve Sundra in the ninth and holding the Browns to two blows in the last five innings. Auker stepped the entire distance for the St. Louisans.

Sundra, off to a wobbly start, had dropped two runs in the first inning. Another went in the third when Walter Judnich hit his twenty-fourth homer of the campaign and in the fifth Judnich pushed another tally home with a single.

In the meantime, the Yanks had been able to score only once off Auker's tantalizing submarine ball, a Crosetti double paving the way for this one, and the score was still 4—1 as Henrich and Keller opened the last of the ninth with singles.

Agonizing minutes followed as George Selkirk flied out without advancing the runners and Rosar forced Keller at second for the second out. It was a moment that called for drastic action, as the Yanks can ill afford to lose any ball games at this point in the race. But McCarthy was ready to play his remaining trump.

Jolting Joe Connects

He called on DiMaggio to bat for Dahlgren in a daring manoeuvre and it paid a handsome dividend as Jolting Joe sideswiped an outside pitch into the lower right stand.

The game, however, had yet to be won and there was considerable shifting about as the Yanks prepared to go into extra innings. As Jake Powell had been bounced from the bench earlier in the game by Umpire Cal Hubbard, DiMaggio game leg and all, had to continue in the battle in center, while Henrich moved in to cover first base.

After each side had tallied in the eleventh, Henrich launched the final victory drive in the thirteenth with a single and took second on Keller's sacrifice. Selkirk was intentionally passed and after Rosar had flied out DiMaggio also drew an intentional pass. Auker was taking no more chances with Jolting Joe, but he reckoned without Crosetti, whose master poke down the third-base line ended the struggle on the next play. That gave Murphy his sixth victory.

Biggest Inning of Year

The opener promised to remain quite a nerve-throbbing mound duel between Russo and Vernon Kennedy until the fifth, when the Yanks, with scarcely a word of warning, exploded their biggest scoring inning of the year.

Joe Gordon started the rush with a double and presently all nine Yanks in the batting order, from the top to the bottom, crossed the plate. Then, just to run the thing into double figures, Joe the Flash scampered over the plate a second time to make it an even ten.

In the wake of Gordon's double came five singles, five passes and an error, while Manager Fred Haney vainly called on Howie Mills and finally Emil Bildilli to bring the merry-go-round to a full stop. The Yanks sent sixteen batters to the plate and they filled the bases no fewer than nine times.

The Senators move into the Stadium for single games this afternoon and tomorrow and a twin bill Sunday.

A FORCE PLAY AT SECOND BASE AT THE YANKEE STADIUM

Henrich out in the fourth inning of the second game yesterday. Bernardino has the ball, having taken a throw from McQuinn after the latter fielded a grounder by Selkirk. Associated Press

Yankee Box Scores

FIRST GAME

ST. LOUIS (A.)

	ab.	r.	h.	po.	a.	e.
Heffner, 2b	4	0	0	0	5	1
Laabs, rf	3	0	0	2	0	0
Radcliff, lf	4	0	0	3	0	0
Judnich, cf	4	1	1	2	0	0
Clift, 3b	4	1	2	0	0	0
McQuinn, 1b	4	1	1	12	2	0
Berardino, ss	4	[illegible]	3	1	2	0
Swift, c	4	0	2	3	0	0
Kennedy, p	2	0	1	0	1	0
Mills, p	0	0	0	0	0	0
Bildilli, p	0	0	0	1	2	0
aHoag	1	0	0	0	0	0
Coffman, p	0	0	0	0	0	0
bStrange	1	0	0	0	0	0
Total	35	3	10	24	12	1

NEW YORK (A.)

	ab.	r.	h.	po.	a.	e.
Gordon, 2b	6	2	2	4	7	0
Rolfe, 3b	6	1	1	0	0	0
Henrich, cf	3	1	1	3	0	0
Keller, rf	5	1	2	0	0	0
Selkirk, lf	3	1	0	1	0	0
Dickey, c	4	1	1	5	0	0
Dahlgren, 1b	5	1	3	12	0	0
Crosetti, ss	3	1	0	2	4	0
Russo, p	2	1	1	0	3	0
Total	37	10	11	27	14	0

aBatted for Bildilli in seventh.
bBatted for Coffman in ninth.

St. Louis .... 010 000 200—3
New York .... 000 0 10 0 00..—10

Runs batted in—Gordon, Henrich, Keller 3, Selkirk, Dickey, Dahlgren 2, Russo, McQuinn, Swift 2.

Two-base hits—Gordon, Swift. Double plays—Russo, Crosetti and Dahlgren; Gordon and Crosetti. Left on bases—New York 13, St. Louis 6. Bases on balls—Off Russo 1, Kennedy 5, Mills 2, Bildilli 2, Coffman 1. Struck out—By Russo 5, Kennedy 1, Mills 1, Coffman 1. Hits—Off Kennedy 8 in 4 innings (none out in fifth), Mills 1 in 1-3, Bildilli 1 in 1 2-3, Coffman 1 in 2. Losing pitcher—Kennedy. Umpires—Rommel, Hubbard and Moriarty. Time of game—2:03.

SECOND GAME

ST. LOUIS (A.)

	ab.	r.	h.	po.	a.	e.
Heffner, 2b	6	1	1	2	6	0
Laabs, rf	5	1	0	3	0	0
Radcliff, lf	6	1	2	3	0	0
Judnich, cf	4	1	2	5	0	1
Clift, 3b	6	0	1	0	5	0
McQuinn, 1b	6	1	1	18	2	0
Berardino, ss	6	0	1	2	1	0
Swift, c	5	0	1	3	0	0
Auker, p	4	0	0	2	1	0
Total	48	5	9	*38	15	1

NEW YORK (A.)

	ab.	r.	h.	po.	a.	e.
Gordon, 2b	6	0	1	3	2	1
Rolfe, 3b	6	0	1	0	4	0
Henrich, cf, 1b	5	2	2	5	0	0
Keller, rf	5	1	2	3	0	0
Selkirk, lf	5	0	0	9	0	0
Rosar, c	6	1	1	6	1	0
Dahlgren, 1b	3	0	0	10	0	0
DiMaggio, cf	2	1	1	2	0	0
Crosetti, ss	6	1	4	1	5	0
Sundra, p	2	0	1	0	2	0
aDickey	1	0	0	0	0	0
Murphy, p	1	0	0	0	0	0
Total	48	6	13	39	14	1

*Two out when winning run scored.
aBatted for Sundra in eighth.

St. Louis .... 201 010 000 010 0—5
New York .... 000 010 003 010 1—6

Runs batted in—Judnich 3, Clift, Gordon, DiMaggio 3, McQuinn, Rosar, Crosetti.

Two-base hits—Heffner, Clift, Radcliff 2, Crosetti, Keller. Home runs—Judnich, DiMaggio, McQuinn. Sacrifices—Murphy, Keller. Double plays—Sundra, Rosar and Dahlgren; McQuinn (unassisted). Left on bases—New York 9, St. Louis 8. Bases on balls—Off Sundra 4, Auker 3. Struck out—By Sundra 1, Auker 1, Murphy 3. Hits—Off Sundra 7 in 8 innings, Murphy 2 in 5. Wild pitch—Sundra. Winning pitcher—Murphy. Umpires—Hubbard, Moriarty and Romel. Time of game—2:42. Attendance—7,865.

BEES, WITH POSEDEL, TURN BACK CUBS, 3-1

Chicago Is Limited to 5 Hits—Mooty Is Beaten

CHICAGO, Aug. 29 (AP)—Held to five hits by Bill Posedel, the Chicago Cubs lost their second game in a row to the Boston Bees today. The score was 3 to 1.

Posedel retired the first eleven Cubs to face him before Chicago scored in the fourth on singles by Zeke Bonura and Hank Leiber and a double by Jim Gleeson.

The Bees scored in the first on a wild pitch by Jake Mooty, collected another run in the fifth on two hits and clinched the game with another score in the ninth. Mooty allowed nine hits.

The box score:

BOSTON (N.)

	ab.	r.	h.	po.	a.	e.
Glossop, 3b	3	1	0	1	2	0
Cooney, cf	5	2	3	4	0	0
Rowell, 2b	5	0	2	1	2	0
West, 1b	3	0	0	6	2	0
Ross, lf	3	0	2	2	0	0
Miller, ss	4	0	0	2	1	0
Moore, rf	4	0	2	7	0	0
Berres, c	3	0	0	3	0	0
Posedel, p	4	0	0	1	1	0
Total	34	3	9	27	8	0

CHICAGO (N.)

	ab.	r.	h.	po.	a.	e.
Hack, 3b	4	0	0	2	5	0
Herman, 2b	4	0	1	6	2	0
Bonura, 1b	4	1	1	7	0	0
Leiber, cf	3	0	1	2	0	1
Gleeson, rf	3	0	1	2	0	0
Dalles'dro, lf	3	0	0	1	0	0
Collins, c	3	0	0	5	1	0
aNicholson	1	0	0	0	0	0
Warstler, ss	1	0	0	2	2	0
Mattick, ss	2	0	0	0	2	0
Mooty, p	3	0	1	0	0	0
Total	31	1	5	27	12	1

aBatted for Collins in ninth.

Boston .... 100 010 001—3
Chicago .... 000 100 000—1

Runs batted in—Ross, West, Gleeson.

Two-base hit—Gleeson. Double play—Mattick, Herman and Hack. Left on bases—Boston 10, Chicago 6. Bases on balls—Off Posedel 3, Mooty 6. Struck out—By Posedel 3, Mooty 5. Wild pitch—Mooty. Umpires—Dunn, Magerkurth and Stewart. Time of game—1:49. Attendance—7,083.

Giants Shut Out by Cards, 5 to 0, M'Gee Allowing Only Two Hits

St. Louis Pitcher Gains Thirteenth Victory as Schumacher Is Driven From the Box During Five-Run Barrage in First

By JAMES P. DAWSON
Special to THE NEW YORK TIMES.

ST. LOUIS, Aug. 29—The Cardinals gave Fiddler Bill McGee a five-run edge to work on in Sportsman's Park this afternoon, and, since this is tantamount to placing a violin in the hands of the rotund flipper from Batchtown, Ill., the old bow-sweeper went out and pitched his best game of the campaign.

He shut out the Giants on two hits, pitching the Cardinals into undisputed possession of third place in the National League standing, as he carved his thirteenth victory of the year in the Terrymen's farewell appearance here. The count was 5 to 0.

A blistering bombardment of Prince Hal Schumacher in the first inning swept the Dolgeville husky from the scene and the ball game right out of reach of the New Yorkers, notwithstanding some nifty relief hurling by Paul Dean and Japhet Lynn.

Rucker, Cuccinello Single

Encouraged by the five runs with which his mates started, McGee went out and stood the Giants on their heads. The two singles the Fiddler yielded were struck by Johnny Rucker, as the game opened, and by Tony Cuccinello in the eighth.

In between, McGee walked Frank Demaree and Babe Young and they were the only Giants to get on base. None was second, as Rucker died stealing and Cuccinello's blow was erased in a double play. McGee hurled to exactly twenty-nine batters—two over par for the course—in a bit of right-handed flipping that thoroughly thrilled 2,794 cash customers.

Singles by Jimmy Brown and Terry Moore greeted Schumacher, placing runners on first and third. A run trickled over when Mize banged into a double play, but even that didn't loom too menacing—until the blow fell.

Marion's Hit Scores Three

Slaughter singled, Koy doubled, Padgett was intentionally passed and Schumacher forced in a run with an accidental pass to Orengo. Then, with the bases loaded, two out and the count three and two on him and everybody on the run for the plate, Marion lashed a single to center that was good for three more runs before McGee ended the inning by fanning.

Dean checked his old mates with a single hit through the next four innings, when he pitched to exactly twelve Cards, thanks to Mize's hitting into his second double play.

Fans Honor McCarthy

Friends of Johnny McCarthy from his native West Frankfort, Ill., presented a radio to the utility first baseman in a ceremony at the plate before the game. But when Johnny hit for Dean in the sixth he died on a static fly to Slaughter.

Before he struck his lone blow, Cuccinello figured in two double plays, boosting the Giants' total for the season to 103.

And, so, the end of another championship campaign on Western soil. The Giants finished this jaunt with seven victories in thirteen games.

Among the other things that came to an end was Ott's hitting streak. Until today he had connected safely in seven successive contests.

The Box Score

NEW YORK (N.)

	ab.	r.	h.	po.	a.	e.
Rucker, cf	4	0	1	0	0	0
J. Moore, lf	4	0	0	4	0	0
Demaree, rf	2	0	0	1	0	0
Young, 1b	2	0	0	8	1	0
Danning, c	3	0	0	4	0	0
Ott, 3b	3	0	0	1	0	0
Cuc'nillo, 2b	3	0	1	1	4	0
Witek, ss	3	0	0	5	4	0
Schum'her, p	0	0	0	0	0	0
Dean, p	1	0	0	0	1	0
aMcCarthy	1	0	0	0	0	0
Lynn, p	0	0	0	0	1	0
bO'Dea	1	0	0	0	0	0
Total	27	0	2	24	11	0

ST. LOUIS (N.)

	ab.	r.	h.	po.	a.	e.
J. Brown, 3b	4	1	2	1	0	0
T. Moore, cf	4	0	1	3	0	0
Mize, 1b	4	0	1	12	0	0
Slaughter, rf	4	1	1	4	0	0
Koy, lf	3	1	2	0	0	0
Padgett, c	2	1	0	4	1	0
Orengo, 2b	2	1	0	0	4	0
Marion, ss	3	0	1	3	4	0
McGee, p	3	0	0	0	2	0
Total	29	5	8	27	11	0

aBatted for Dean in sixth.
bBatted for Lynn in ninth.

New York .... 000 000 000—0
St. Louis .... 500 000 00..—5

Runs batted in—Orengo, Marion 3.

Two-base hit—Koy. Double plays—Cuccinello, Witek and Young 2; Young, Witek and Young; Orengo, Marion and Mize. Left on bases—New York 2, St. Louis 2. Bases on balls—Off Schumacher 2, McGee 2. Struck out—By Schumacher 1, Dean 1, Lynn 2, McGee 3. Hits—Off Schumacher 5 in 1 inning, Dean 1 in 4, Lynn 2 in 3. Losing pitcher—Schumacher. Umpires—Klem, Ballanfant and Campbell. Time of game—1:28. Attendance—2,794.

TWO TIE IN WOMEN'S GOLF

89s Posted by Mrs. Stevens and Mrs. Beard at Apawamis

Special to THE NEW YORK TIMES.

RYE, N. Y., Aug. 29—Pacing a large field of forty-nine in a Women's Westchester and Fairfield Golf Association one-day tournament over the Apawamis Country Club course today, Mrs. Edward Stevens of Round Hill, who scored 44, 45—89, and Mrs. R. F. Beard of Knollwood, who returned 45, 44—89, tied for low-gross honors. Mrs. Beard, with her handicap of 8 deducted, was the winner of the low net prize, however, so she relinquished her claim to the low-gross award.

A triple tie for second net resulted among Mrs. Robert Heyn of Siwanoy, who had 96, 14—82; Mrs. Leonie Jenkins of Green Meadow, who posted 89, 16—22, and Mrs. H. T. Kilburn of Greenwich, with 103, 21—82. After cards were matched Mrs. Heyn received the second prize, Mrs. Jenkins the third and Mrs. Kilburn the fourth. The putting award went to Mrs. E. F. Morgan of Bonnie Briar, who took 26 strokes on the greens. The leading scores:

Mrs. R. F. Beard, Knollwood ... 89— 8—81
Mrs. Robert Heyn, Siwanoy ..... 96—14—82
Mrs. Leonie Jenkins, Green Meadow .... 98—16—82
Mrs. H. T. Kilburn, Greenwich .103—21—82
Mrs. E. F. Morgan, Bonnie Briar .... 101—18—83
Mrs. Edward Stevens, Round Hill 89— 5—84
Miss aJne Evans, Siwanoy ...... 92— 8—84
Mrs. T. D. F. Haines, Bedford G. & T. .... 94— 9—85
Mrs. Roger Rowe, Wee Burn ... 97—10—87
Mrs. Charles P. Luckey, Lawrence Farms .... 94— 7—87
Mrs. L. H. Spalding, Innis Arden .112—25—87
Mrs. C. H. Gifford, Lawrence Farms .... 106—18—88
Mrs. J. H. Walsh, Innis Arden ..106—17—89
Mrs. Jonathan Moore Jr., Siwanoy .... 102—13—89
Mrs. M. F. Holt, Westchester C. C. .... 110—19—91
Mrs. F. R. Smith, Woodway ....115—23—92
Mrs. Harold Minnott, Lawrence Farms .... 106—12—94

Athletics Get Marchildon

PHILADELPHIA, Aug. 29 (AP)—The Athletics today acquired Phil Marchildon, 23-year-old pitcher with Toronto in the International League, for delivery next year. The purchase price was not disclosed. Marchildon has won nine and lost ten games for Toronto.

Major League Baseball

American League

YESTERDAY'S RESULTS

New York 10, St. Louis 3 (1st).
New York 6, St. Louis 5 (2d) (thirteen innings).
Detroit 3, Washington 2 (1st).
Detroit 6, Washington 0 (2d). (six innings, darkness).
Boston 4, Chicago 3.
Cleveland at Philadelphia (2), rain and wet grounds.

STANDING OF THE CLUBS

	Cleveland	Detroit	New York	Boston	Chicago	Wash'gton	St. Louis	Phila'phia	Won	Lost	Percentage	Games Behind
Cleve.	—	8	9	12	12	10	10	11	72	50	.590	—
Detroit	5	—	12	10	7	14	15	8	71	53	.573	2
N. Y.	11	7	—	9	9	8	13	10	67	54	.554	4½
Boston	7	10	9	—	10	12	12	7	67	58	.536	6½
Chic.	4	10	10	9	—	11	8	11	63	58	.521	8½
Wash.	9	5	2	6	9	—	10	11	52	70	.426	20
St. L.	8	3	5	8	5	9	—	13	51	75	.405	23
Phila.	6	10	7	4	6	6	7	—	46	71	.393	23½
Lost	50	53	54	58	58	70	75	71	—	—		

GAMES TODAY

Washington at New York (3:15 P. M.).
Boston at Philadelphia.
Cleveland at Chicago (night).
Other clubs not scheduled.

National League

YESTERDAY'S RESULTS

St. Louis 5, New York 0.
Cincinnati 9, Brooklyn 3.
Boston 3, Chicago 1.
Pittsburgh 4, Philadelphia 0.

STANDING OF THE CLUBS

	Cincinnati	Brooklyn	St. Louis	New York	Pittsburgh	Chicago	Boston	Phila'phia	Won	Lost	Percentage	Games Behind
Cincin.	—	12	8	12	10	12	10	12	76	44	.633	—
Bklyn.	7	—	9	9	10	10	12	10	67	52	.563	8½
St. L.	7	11	—	8	5	7	12	13	63	56	.529	12½
N. Y.	7	3	11	—	12	10	9	10	62	57	.521	13½
Pitts.	2	7	11	7	—	9	13	13	62	58	.517	14
Chic.	5	10	6	9	8	—	13	11	62	63	.496	16½
Boston	9	6	6	5	7	7	—	9	49	72	.405	27½
Phila.	7	3	5	7	6	8	3	—	39	78	.333	35½
Lost	44	52	56	57	58	63	72	78	—	—		

GAMES TODAY

Brooklyn at Cincinnati.
Philadelphia at Pittsburgh.
Other clubs not scheduled.

Major League Leaders

BATSMEN

AMERICAN LEAGUE

	G.	AB.	R.	H.	PC.
Radcliff, St. Louis	122	472	67	165	.350
Williams, Boston	115	442	111	152	.344
Appling, Chicago	117	441	70	151	.343
DiMaggio, New York	101	391	75	133	.340
McCosky, Detroit	117	489	100	163	.333

NATIONAL LEAGUE

	G.	AB.	R.	H.	PC.
Rowell, Boston	101	365	39	120	.329
Walker, Brooklyn	111	424	58	136	.321
F. McCormick, Cinc.	121	481	77	153	.318
Mize, St. Louis	120	447	90	142	.318
Danning, New York	114	434	58	138	.318

HOME-RUN HITTERS

AMERICAN LEAGUE

Fox, Boston ...... 34 | Greenberg, Detroit 26
DiMaggio, N. Y. ... 28

NATIONAL LEAGUE

Mize, St. Louis ... 37 | Nicholson, Chic. ... 20
Rizzo, Phila 22

RUNS BATTED IN

AMERICAN LEAGUE

Greenberg, Det. ... 111 | Foxx, Boston 106
DiMaggio, N. Y. ... 107

NATIONAL LEAGUE

F. McC'm'k, Cinc. 102 | Fletcher, Pitts. [illegible]

DERRINGER OF REDS TOPS DODGERS, 9-3

Gains 17th Triumph in Rain and Cincinnati Extends Lead to 8½ Games

HOMERS AID MOUND ACE

Lombardi and Myers Account for 5 Runs—Circuit Hit by Medwick Wasted

By ROSCOE McGOWEN
Special to THE NEW YORK TIMES.

CINCINNATI, Aug. 29—Both the Dodgers and their pennant hopes were practically drowned today. Defying the continued rain and soggy field, the champion Reds dragged the Durochers into action and trounced them with ridiculous ease by a 9-3 score.

The defeat dropped Brooklyn eight and one-half games behind the leaders, an advantage that would seem insurmountable with the race so near its end.

A persistent downpour in the early afternoon made the chances of playing appear remote, but General Manager Warren Giles was determined to get the contest out of the way. An hour and three minutes after the scheduled starting time the canvases finally were rolled off the infield amid the cheers of a Ladies Day crowd of 21,680.

The women, numbering 9,912, showed extraordinary patience and disregard for their finery by sitting in the stands throughout and shrieking their approval of the Reds and their complete disapprobation for the Dodgers, especially Pete Coscarart and Whit Wyatt.

Brooklyn Fight Recalled

The latter pair, it will be recalled, was involved in the fight with Lonnie Frey in Brooklyn when the Reds swept a three-game series, and apparently not a single Cincinnati supporter had forgotten this.

There was just one moment of dismay for the crowd in the first inning when Muscles Medwick connected with a Paul Derringer pitch and lined it over the left field wall for his eleventh homer of the campaign and his eighth as a Dodger.

But the Reds erased this lead as soon as they could begin swinging their own bats, and Derringer coasted along to his seventeenth triumph and his fourth, without a loss, over Brooklyn. Wyatt, pitching only two innings, was charged with his fifteenth setback, against the same number of victories. It marked the fifth time this year he has bowed to the champions without beating them once.

Big Cyrano Lombardi contributed a wind-blown home run off Tex Carleton with two aboard in the fifth, and Billy Myers belted another over the same left-field barrier off Hugh Casey with one on in the sixth.

Ripple's Double Helpful

The Reds scored twice in the first on a pass to Bill Werber, Frey's sacrifice and doubles by Frank McCormick and Jimmy Ripple. The latter, whose acquisition by the Reds from Montreal via the waiver route has been a cause of wonder, was making his first start in a Red uniform, playing right field in place of Ival Goodman.

In the second, Mike McCormick doubled off the scoreboard in left center and got around on Myers's sacrifice and an infield out. Frey walked to open the third, with Lee Grissom pitching, and scored on Lombardi's single and Ripple's double play ball that was handled by Grissom only for a forceout.

Singles by Werber and Frey preceded Lombardi's homer in the fifth and a single by Mike McCormick came just ahead of Myers's wallop.

Walker's Hit Scores Head

Wyatt doubled to left center in the third, and Ed Head, running for him, scored on Dixie Walker's single to right. Derringer held the Dodgers scoreless then until the ninth when doubles by Blimp Phelps and Jimmy Wasdell produced the other run.

Tomorrow's game will be started at 2 o'clock to enable the Dodgers to catch a train that will carry them home in plenty of time to keep their engagement with the Giants at Ebbets Field Saturday. Weather conditions, unless they change radically for the better, will cause a cancellation of the air trip.

The box score:

BROOKLYN (N.)

	ab.	r.	h.	po.	a.	e.
Reiser, 3b	3	0	0	0	3	0
Walker, cf	4	0	1	1	0	0
Medwick, lf	4	1	1	3	0	0
Phelps, c	4	1	1	6	0	0
Camilli, 1b	4	0	1	9	0	0
Wasdell, rf	4	0	1	0	0	0
Coscarart, 2b	4	0	0	0	1	0
Durocher, ss	3	0	1	5	1	0
Wyatt, p	1	0	1	0	1	0
aHead	0	1	0	0	0	0
Grissom, p	0	0	0	0	1	0
bVosmik	1	0	0	0	0	0
Carleton, p	0	0	0	0	0	0
Casey, p	0	0	0	0	0	0
cGallagher	1	0	0	0	0	0
Tamulis, p	0	0	0	0	0	0
Total	33	3	7	24	7	0

CINCINNATI (N.)

	ab.	r.	h.	po.	a.	e.
Werber, 3b	4	2	2	2	2	0
Frey, 2b	3	2	1	0	0	0
F. M'C'm'k, 1b	4	1	1	9	1	0
Lombardi, c	4	1	2	3	0	0
Ripple, rf	4	0	1	2	0	0
Craft, cf	4	0	0	2	0	0
M. M'C'm'k, lf	4	2	3	6	0	0
Myers, ss	3	1	1	2	4	0
Derringer, p	4	0	1	1	1	0
Total	34	9	12	27	8	0

aRan for Wyatt in third.
bBatted for Grissom in fifth.
cBatted for Casey in eighth.

Brooklyn .... 101 000 001—3
Cincinnati .... 211 032 00..—9

Runs batted in—Walker, Medwick, Wasdell, F. McCormick 2, Lombardi 2, Ripple 2, Myers 2, Derringer.

Two-base hits—Phelps, Wasdell, Durocher, Wyatt, Werber, F. McCormick, Ripple, M. McCormick, Derringer. Home runs—Medwick, Lombardi, Myers. Sacrifices—Frey, Myers. Double play—Derringer, Myers and F. McCormick. Left on bases—Brooklyn 4, Cincinnati 5. Bases on balls—Off Wyatt 1, Grissom 1, Derringer 1. Struck out—By Grissom 2, Casey 1, Derringer 3. Hits—Off Wyatt 3 in 2 innings, Grissom 1 in 2, Carleton 3 in 1-3, Casey 3 in 2 2-3, Tamulis 2 in 1. Losing pitcher—Wyatt. Umpires—Reardon, Goetz and Pinelli. Time of game—1:41. Attendance—11,768 paid; 9,912 ladies.

Today's Probable Pitchers

By The Associated Press.

American League

Washington at New York—Krakauskas (0-3) vs. Donald (4-2).
Boston at Philadelphia—Ostermueller (3-7) vs, Beckman (6-1).
Cleveland at Chicago (night—Feller (22-7) vs. Lee (9-11).
Other clubs are scheduled.

National League

Brooklyn at Cincinnati—Hamlin (7-7) vs. Thompson (13-7).
Philadelphia at Pittsburgh—Smoll (2-7) vs. Lanning (6-2).
Other clubs not scheduled.

Lavagetto's Appendix Removed; Another Blow to Dodgers' Hopes

Third Baseman Stricken During Night—Reiser Replaces Him—Durocher and Hudson Will Divide Duties at Shortstop

By The Associated Press.

CINCINNATI, Aug. 29—Acute appendicitis struck Harry (Cookie) Lavagetto today and dealt a new stunning blow to pennant hopes of the Brooklyn Dodgers.

As surgeons removed a gangrenous appendix from the 25-year-old veteran third-sacker, Manager Leo Durocher assembled a "scrambled" infield and insisted "We'll carry on."

He conceded, however, that his pennant-hungry charges had experienced another bad break in their injury-plagued battle to wrest the league lead from the champion Reds—currently eight and one-half games ahead.

"A Very Sick Boy"

"Lavagetto is a very sick boy," said Dr. Reed Shank, staff surgeon of the Cincinnati Reds, in a bulletin from the operating room in Christ Hospital.

"The appendix had not ruptured but," he added, "there was a definite gangrenous condition and we took it in the nick of time."

The young Californian was stricken during the night after retiring in apparent good health.

Barring complications, which Dr. Shank said he did not expect, Lavagetto will be confined to the hospital a week or ten days and must rest the remainder of the baseball season.

Reiser at Hot Corner

Rookie Pete Reiser will take over the hot corner and Durocher and Johnny Hudson will divide the shortstop trick where Reiser has been performing in the absence of Harold (Peewee) Reese.

Reese, from Louisville, Ky., and one of the Rookie finds of the year, fractured a bone in his left foot several weeks ago shortly after recovering from the effects of a "beaning."

Other Dodgers have met injury or been otherwise incapacitated:

Whit Wyatt of the hurling staff nursed a bad knee early in the season; Joe Medwick, $150,000 ex-Cardinal outfielder, and Pitcher Hugh Casey were hit with pitched balls; Dolph Camilli, slugging first baseman, was out with a muscular ailment, and Durocher himself has recently complained of a sore throwing arm.

Lavagetto has hit .257 in 118 games, against an even .300 last year. He batted in 41 runs and scored 56, including four circuit blows.

Cookie Lavagetto
Times Wide World

RED SOX TRIUMPH ON CRONIN'S WALK

Winning Run Against White Sox Forced Across in 9th by Rigney—Score Is 4-3

BOSTON, Aug. 29 (AP)—The Red Sox escaped a tumble into the second division today by defeating the Chicago White Sox, 4—3, in the series finale. Johnny Rigney, relief pitcher, gave Boston the game by forcing in the winning run with two out in the ninth.

After uncorking a three-run rally in the sixth, the Red Sox found themselves in a deadlock when they went to bat in the ninth. They loaded the bases with two singles and a pass before Gigney forced in Pitcher Jack Wilson by giving Manager Joe Cronin a base on balls.

Wilson gave the Chisox nine hits while his mates were pounding Jack Knott, who retired in the eighth, and Rigney for eleven safeties.

The box score:

CHICAGO (A.)

	ab.	r.	h.	po.	a.	e.
Hayes, 2b	4	0	1	3	3	0
Ro'thal, cf, lf	5	0	1	2	0	0
Kuhel, 1b	3	1	2	9	0	0
Solters, lf	4	0	1	4	0	0
Kreevich, cf	0	1	0	0	0	0
Appling, ss	4	1	1	1	6	0
Wright, rf	4	0	3	0	0	0
Tresh, c	3	0	0	6	0	0
Kennedy, 3b	4	0	0	1	2	0
Knott, p	3	0	0	0	1	0
Rigney, p	1	0	1	0	1	0
Total	35	3	10	*26	13	0

BOSTON (A.)

	ab.	r.	h.	po.	a.	e.
DiMa'gio, cf	4	2	1	1	0	0
Cramer, rf	4	0	0	1	0	0
Foxx, c	3	1	2	4	2	0
Williams, lf	4	1	1	4	0	0
Cronin, ss	4	0	1	3	8	0
Doerr, 2b	4	0	1	5	1	0
Finney, 1b	4	0	3	8	0	0
Gelbert, 3b	3	0	1	0	0	0
Wilson, p	4	0	1	1	1	0
aCarey	0	0	0	0	0	0
Total	34	4	11	27	12	0

*Two out when winning run scored.
aRan for Wilson in ninth.

Chicago .... 000 100 020—3
Boston .... 000 003 001—4

Runs batted in—Wright 2, Tresh, Doerr 2, Foxx, Cronin.

Two-base hits—DiMaggio, Doerr, Gelbert. Stolen bases—DiMaggio, Finney. Sacrifices—DiMaggio, Cramer. Double play—Appling, Hayes and Kuhel. Left on bases—Chicago 8, Boston 11. Bases on balls—Off Knott 3, Rigney 2, Wilson 3. Struck out—By Knott 4, Wilson 5. Hits—Off Knott 9 in 7 innings (none out in eighth), Rigney 2 in 1 2-3. Losing pitcher—Rigney. Umpires—Basil, Grieve and Summers. Time of game—2:17. Attendance—5,400 paid, 3,200 women.

Valley Stream Signs Naylor

Jack Naylor, Columbia backfield star of 1939 and the Lions' basketball captain last Winter, will play professional football this season with the Valley Stream Red Riders, Long Island independent eleven. In addition to playing, Naylor will help Newt Wilder, another former Columbian and the owner of the club, coach the team.

PIRATES SINK PHILS 8TH STRAIGHT TIME

Macfayden Comes to Brown's Aid in 4-0 Victory—Bucs Do Some Timely Hitting

PITTSBURGH, Aug. 29 (AP)—Doing some timely hitting and turning in three double plays, the Pittsburgh Pirates whitewashed Philadelphia today, 4 to 0, for their eighth straight triumph over the Quakers.

Mace Brown, who has shown a tendency to weaken in the late innings, was summarily yanked by Manager Frankie Frisch in the eighth after Rookie Dan Litwhiler singled and Johnny Rizzo bounced a double off the left-field fence. Danny MacFayden halted the potential rally.

Debs Garms and Bob Elliott gathered three hits apiece. Garms's triple with two out in the third and Elliott's surprise bunt scored the first Pirate run. They clinched the game in the fourth when Arky Vaughan tripled, scoring Fletcher, and came home on Vince DiMaggio's towering fly to center.

The box score:

PHILADELPHIA (N.)

	ab.	r.	h.	po.	a.	e.
May, 3b	4	0	0	1	2	0
Schulte, 2b	4	0	1	1	1	0
Litwhiler, lf	4	0	2	2	0	0
Rizzo, cf	3	0	1	1	0	0
Klein, rf	4	0	0	1	0	0
Warren, c	3	0	1	0	1	0
Millies, c	1	0	0	1	0	0
Bragan, ss	3	0	1	2	[illegible]	0
Mahan, 1b	2	0	0	13	0	0
Mazzera, 1b	1	0	1	2	0	0
Pearson, p	2	0	1	0	2	0
aMueller	1	0	0	0	0	0
Frye, p	1	0	1	0	1	0
Total	33	0	9	24	14	0

PITTSBURGH (N.)

	ab.	r.	h.	po.	a.	e.
Garms, 3b	4	2	3	0	5	0
Elliott, rf	4	0	3	3	0	0
Fletcher, 1b	2	1	0	13	3	0
Vaughan, ss	4	1	1	2	3	0
V. Robays, lf	3	0	0	0	0	0
DiMaggio, cf	3	0	0	1	1	0
Handley, 2b	4	0	1	4	3	1
Davis, c	4	0	0	3	2	0
Brown, p	3	0	0	1	2	0
M'Fayden, p	0	0	0	0	0	0
Total	31	4	8	27	19	1

aBatted for Pearson in seventh.

Philadelphia .... 000 000 000—0
Pittsburgh .... 001 210 00..—4

Runs batted in—Elliott 2, Vaughan, DiMaggio.

Two-base hits—Litwhiler, Garms, Elliott, Rizzo. Three-base hits—Garms, Vaughan. Stolen base—DiMaggio. Double plays—DiMaggio, Fletcher, Davis and Handley; Vaughan, Handley and Fletcher 2. Left on bases—Philadelphia 10, Pittsburgh 7. Bases on balls—Off Pearson 3, Brown 3, Frye 1, MacFayden 1. Struck out—By Brown 2, MacFayden 1. Hits—Off Pearson 5 in 6 innings, Frye 3 in 2, Brown 8 in 7 1-3, MacFayden 1 in 1 2-3. Winning pitcher—Brown. Losing pitcher—Pearson. Umpires—Sears, Jorda and Barr. Time of game—1:53. Attendance—2,239 paid; 3,782 ladies.

Girls' Tennis Postponed

PHILADELPHIA, Aug. 29 (AP)—For the fourth straight day, the start of the junior girls' national tennis tournament was postponed today because of rain.

Minor League Baseball

By The Associated Press.

INTERNATIONAL LEAGUE

(Night Games)

Newark at Baltimore (2), rain.

STANDING OF THE CLUBS

	W.	L.	PC.		W.	L.	PC.
Rochester	84	55	.604	Montreal	69	73	.486
Newark	81	60	.574	Buffalo	68	73	.482
Baltimore	72	67	.518	Syracuse	65	77	.458
Jersey City	71	69	.507	Toronto	51	87	.370

GAMES TODAY

Syracuse at Jersey City (3:15 P. M.).
Newark at Baltimore.
Montreal at Toronto.
Buffalo at Rochester

PACIFIC COAST LEAGUE

(Wednesday Night Games)

AT SEATTLE

		R.	H.	E.
San Diego	000 100 320	6	8	2
Seattle	111 000 100	4	9	2

Batteries—Thomas and Salkeld; Barrett and Kearse.

AT PORTLAND

		R.	H.	E.
Sacramento	000 114 100	7	13	2
Portland	000 000 000	0	1	1

Batteries—Munger and Grilk; Fallon and Adams.

AT OAKLAND

		R.	H.	E.
Los Angeles	010 020 000	3	8	0
Oakland	100 000 000	1	6	0

Batteries—Prim and Holm, Hernande (2); Pippen, Mulligan (9) and Conroy.

AT HOLLYWOOD

		R.	H.	E.
San Fran.	100 000 020	3	9	3
Hollywood	106 500 61..	19	20	1

Batteries—Guay, Kittle (3), Jensen (7), O'Doul (8) and Leonard; Ardioia and Brenel.

STANDING OF THE CLUBS

	W.	L.	PC.		W.	L.	PC.
Seattle	101	55	.647	Hollywood	76	79	.490
L. Angeles	86	68	.558	S'ramento	76	80	.487
Oakland	84	71	.542	San Fran.	69	85	.448
San Diego	80	74	.519	Portland	47	107	.305

EASTERN LEAGUE

Wilkes-Barre at Williamsport, wet grounds.

STANDING OF THE CLUBS

	W.	L.	PC.		W.	L.	PC.
Binghamt'n	75	57	.568	Albany	65	67	.492
Scranton	73	58	.557	Elmira	64	67	.489

AMERICAN ASSOCIATION

AT MILWAUKEE

(First Game.)

		R.	H.	E.
Toledo	001 000 000 00	1	6	0
Milwaukee	000 010 000 01	2	9	2

Batteries—Cox and Grube; Marrow and Hankins.

(Second Game.)

		R.	H.	E.
Toledo	005 000 0	5	6	1
Milwaukee	400 133 ..	11	15	0

Batteries—Marcum, Wagener (5) and Grube; Jungels, Makosky (3), Kramer (6) and Garbark.

(Wednesday Night Game.)

AT KANSAS CITY

		R.	H.	E.
Columbus	000 100 003 000 000	4	8	4
Kan. City	000 300 100 000 001	5	12	2

Batteries—Melton, White (7), Barrett (12) and Cooper; Hendrickson, Reis (9), Gerehauser (10) and Riddle, De Phillips (10).

STANDING OF THE CLUBS

	W.	L.	PC.		W.	L.	PC.
Kan. City	85	47	.644	St. Paul	58	68	.46[illegible]
Min'apolis	72	50	.590	Ind'apolis	54	71	.432
Columbus	76	54	.585	Toledo	53	77	.408
Louisville	64	66	.492	Milwaukee	48	77	.384

SOUTHERN ASSOCIATION

((Wednesday Second Night Game.)

AT LITTLE ROCK

		R.	H.	E.
Knoxville	320 011 1	8	12	2
Little Rock	000 000 0	0	6	0

Batteries—Baker and Fallon; Katz and Rensa.

STANDING OF THE CLUBS

	W.	L.	PC.		W.	L.	PC.
Nashville	89	47	.654	N. Orleans	66	73	.475
Atlanta	87	52	.62[illegible]	Birm'ham	65	75	.464
Memphis	74	63	.540	Little Rock	52	82	.383
Chat'n'ga	66	72	.478	Knoxville	52	87	.374

TEXAS LEAGUE

Tulsa 9, Fort Worth 5.
San Antonio 1, Beaumont 1 (11 innings, darkness).

STANDING OF THE CLUBS

	W.	L.	PC.		W.	L.	PC.
Houston	100	49	.671	Dallas	70	79	.470
S. Antonio	83	66	.557	Tulsa	68	80	.459

TIGERS SET BACK SENATORS, 3-2, 6-0

Climb Within Two Games of Idle Indians as Newsom Hurls No. 17 in Nightcap

GREENBERG SMASHES TWO

Rowe's Long Double Drives Bartell Across to Decide First in Eighth

WASHINGTON, Aug. 29 (AP)—The second-place Tigers today moved up to within two games of the league-leading Indians by virtue of a double victory over the Senators. Detroit won the first game, 3—2, then took the second, a six-inning affair, 6—0. Cleveland was rained out in Philadelphia.

Big Buck Newsom won his seventeenth victory of the campaign in the nightcap, limiting the Senators to four hits, while it was Schoolboy Rowe's hitting as well as pitihing which took the first game.

Long Drives by Greenberg

Hank Greenberg, Detroit left-fielder, was no drawbaik in either iontest. In the first game Hank hit his twenty-fifth homer of the year, a tremendous drive into the left-field bleachers. He also got a double and two singles. In the nightcap he blasted his twenty-sixth round-tripper, which also went into the left-field bleachers.

Rome's hit, however, was the one that spelled victory in the opener. With Dick Bartell on second base in the eighth inning and one out, the Schoolboy hit Ken Chase's first pitch against the right-field fence for a run-scoring double. In the eighth and ninth, Rowe fanned three and allowed no hits.

Tigers Score Early

The second game was a breeze for Newsom, after Detroit scored three times in the first inning on an error, Charley Gehringer's single and Greenberg's round-tripper.

The game was called at the end of the sixth because of darkness, and from the way Newsom was going, the night saved the Senators considerable embarrassment.

The box scores:

FIRST GAME

DETROIT (A.)

	ab.	r.	h.	po.	a.	e.
Fox, rf	5	0	1	1	0	0
McCosky, cf	5	0	0	5	1	0
Higgins, 3b	5	0	2	1	1	0
Greenb'g, lf	5	1	4	1	0	0
York, 1b	1	0	0	10	0	0
Meyer, 2b	4	0	0	1	3	0
Tebbetts, c	4	0	0	5	1	0
Bartell, ss	3	2	1	2	3	1
Rowe, p	4	0	1	1	2	0
Total	36	3	9	27	11	1

WASHINGTON (A.)

	ab.	r.	h.	po.	a.	e.
Case, cf	5	0	1	4	0	0
Lewis, rf	5	1	2	0	0	0
Welaj, lf	3	0	2	1	0	0
Travis, 3b	4	0	0	4	4	0
Myer, 2b	4	1	1	4	1	0
Sanford, 1b	4	0	1	5	1	0
Pofahl, ss	4	0	1	0	1	1
Early, c	2	0	0	8	0	0
Chase, p	3	0	1	1	1	0
aWest	1	0	0	0	0	0
Total	35	2	9	27	8	1

aBatted for Chase in ninth.

Detroit .... 010 010 010—3
Washington .... 001 100 000—2

Runs batted in—Fox, Welaj, Chase, Greenberg, Rowe.

Two-base hits—Greenberg, Bartell, Rowe. Three-base hit—Fox. Home run—Greenberg. Stolen bases—Lewis, Myer. Double play—Travis, Myer and Sanford. Left on bases—Detroit 11, Washington 9. Bases on balls—Off Chase 5, Rowe 3. Struck out—By Chase 6, Rowe 5. Umpires—Geisel, Pipgras and Ormsby. Time of game—2:11. Attendance—4,000.

SECOND GAME

DETROIT (A)

	ab.	r.	h.	po.	a.	e.
Fox, rf	4	1	0	0	0	0
McCosky, cf	3	0	0	3	0	0
Gehr'ger, 2b	4	1	2	1	1	0
Gr'nberg, lf	1	1	1	3	0	0
York, 1b	3	0	0	6	0	0
Higgins, 3b	2	1	0	2	2	0
Sullivan, c	3	2	2	2	0	0
Bartell, ss	1	0	1	1	4	0
Newsom, p	3	0	0	0	1	1
Total	24	6	6	18	8	1

WASHINGTON (A)

	ab.	r.	h.	po.	a.	e.
Case, cf	3	0	2	4	0	0
Lewis, rf	3	0	0	1	0	1
Welaj, lf	3	0	1	1	0	0
Travis, 3b	3	0	0	0	0	0
Bl'dw'th, 2b	3	0	0	2	2	0
Sanford, 1b	2	0	0	5	0	0
Pofahl, ss	2	0	1	2	3	1
Ferrell, c	1	0	0	3	1	0
Hudson, p	0	0	0	0	1	0
aEarly	1	0	0	0	0	0
Carr'quel, p	1	0	0	0	1	0
Total	22	0	4	18	7	2

aBatted for Hudson in second.

Detroit .... 310 002—6
Washington .... 000 000—0

Runs batted in—Gehringer, Greenberg 2, Newsom, Fox.

Two-base hit—Sullivan. Home run—Greenberg. Stolen base—Bartell. Double play—Pofahl, Bloodworth and Sanford. Left on bases—Detroit 6, Washington 5. Bases on balls—Off Newsom 1, Carrasquel 6. Struck out—By Hudson 1, Newsom 2, Carrasquel 1. Hits—Off Hudson 4 in 2 innings, Carrasquel 2 in 4. Losing pitcher—Hudson. Umpires—Pipgras, Ormsby and Geisel. Time of game—1:31. Attendance—4,000.

NEW PLAYS FOR FORDHAM

Rams Also Work on Passing and Kicking in Double Session

The Fordham football squad braved intermittent showers yesterday to take part in morning and afternoon drills on Fordham Field. Vince Dennery was the only player missing from the workouts, but the veteran end is expected to report on Monday.

Both sessions started with calisthenics, followed by signal drills, punting and passing. Jim Blumenstock, who has been shifted to the fullback position from left half, and Steve Filipowicz, a sophomore backfield candidate, were outstanding in the passing drills, while Len Eshmont and Stan Krivik, another sophomore, were particularly effective in punting.

The squad concluded the afternoon practice by rehearsing three plays which were outlined during the morning drill. Coach Jim Crowley announced that only a morning drill would be held tomorrow, but morning and afternoon sessions are listed for Labor Day.

Water Ski Course Open

The course which will be used during the second annual national water ski championships, under the auspices of the American Water Ski Association, tomorrow and Sunday at Zach's Bay, Jones Beach State Park, will be available to out-of-town contestants from 2 to 5 P. M. today, it was announced yesterday by the Long Island State Park Commission.

Gehrig Rites Tomorrow; N. Y. Pays Homage

SPORTS

BY EDWARD W. COCHRANE
Sports Editor.

GONE, BUT NOT FORGOTTEN

By Burris Jenkins Jr.

HERALD CHICAGO AMERICAN
***** TUESDAY, JUNE 3, 1941

White Sox Always K. O.'d by Ill Luck; Rigney Case Latest | Hallett New Hope on Slab Staff to Keep Club in the Race

TEAM WINS ON DYKES' SPIRIT

SOMETHING always happens to the White Sox just when their chances were brightest. They would have won the 1940 pennant if they had not met with the misfortune of losing their star pitcher—Monty Stratton. . . . Would have walked in, as we know now.

EDWARD W. COCHRANE.

Just when they leaped into first place in the present race they are informed that Uncle Sam is grabbing Johnny Rigney, another star pitcher, which is a severe blow.

But if you think they are downhearted and are giving up, you're dead wrong. Not the Sox and not Jimmy Dykes. They still are firmly convinced that they'll go right through to a respectable place in that first division at the finish, and if those Indians and Yanks don't play at least as well as they were expected to do when the season opened, or a shade better, it might come to pass that the Sox will win the pennant.

Stranger things have happened. With Rigney they'd probably win it. Without him they still may win. At least they'll keep right on bearing down and giving all they've got. If that isn't enough it won't be because they didn't give the old college try.

I figured Jimmy Dykes would be very disconsolate when I invaded the Sox clubhouse yesterday to chat with the fiery little manager with the black cigar rolling around in his kisser. Not him. He was as chipper as an expectant bride.

Has High Confidence in Hallett

"Yeah, tough to lose Johnny," Jim said in answer to the question about Rigney joining up with Uncle Sam's forces for defense. "Always tough to lose a swell pitcher like him. But we can't help that. It's all in the game. We'll keep right on fighting to be up there. I don't want to talk about a pennant. We just go from day to day doing the best we can. We get good and bad breaks as they come. That's all in the game."

Asked about who was going to take Rigney's place, he said:

"We will move Jack Hallett in there. He pitched swell ball on the road and a game or two he lost were not his fault. He is big, strong and has a lot of stuff. Pitching regularly he may prove one of the reliables. I believe he will.

"We have four other starters—Smith, Lee, Lyons and Dietrich. Four can win a pennant if they finish often enough. It has been done several times. Of course, we are always on the lookout for another winning pitcher. Hard to get one this time of year and doubt that we will. But we'll grab one if we see the chance. However, I believe the five will do all right, even with Rigney gone."

The reason the Sox are up there is that Dykes knows how to handle his pitchers. Doesn't jerk them out every time the opposition gets three or four hits. In the second game Sunday, Smith started out with the Senators blasting him in the opening inning. A lot of managers might have pulled him. But leaving him in gave him confidence and he hurled a great game after the first inning.

Kennedy Not Suited for Mound

Dykes believes in giving his pitchers confidence by letting them pitch themselves out of trouble if he thinks they can. Smith could and did.

"As for pitchers," said Jimmy, "Muddy Ruel is the boss of our pitchers. He is invaluable to me. He has them ready when they are needed. That has a lot to do with our success. You've got to have pitching. We'll hit in enough runs if we get good pitching. We have had it up to now. The race is a great one. That's because the first six clubs have either pitching or hitting, and none of them has too much of [illegible]

Coach Ruel [illegible] the conversation. I asked him about Bob Kennedy and [illegible] that Dykes might make a pitcher out of [illegible] baseman.

"Sometimes you can [illegible] from another position and make a pitcher out of him," said Ruel, "but not often. Because Bucky Walters left third base to be a winning pitcher, folks think that can be done with most any one. That's not the case. Walters was miscast. He wasn't a good third baseman. He threw such a heavy ball across to first that Jimmy Wilson, then manager of the Phillies, thought he might be able to pitch. So, Jimmy took the chance and it proved all right.

"In the case of Kennedy, that is different. He doesn't throw a heavy ball. In fact, he throws what we call a light, or soft, ball. Sometimes you can make a pitcher out of a man who throws a light ball. But he has to make that ball do certain things. Kennedy hasn't shown that he can. I am sure that if Manager Dykes thought Bob could be a pitcher he would have tried him. Any team can use pitchers.

Club Reflects Dykes' Own Spark

"The reason Jim leaves the pitchers to me is that he can't do everything and he figures I can handle the hurlers. I try to have them in great shape and ready when he needs them. That's my job. Jim has to do a lot of other things. He has other players to manage. He is the boss on the field. He has to direct the attack and the strategy. He has to manage the coaches, too.

"If I can keep four pitchers ready to start who are reasonably sure to also finish most of their games, the Sox will do all right in this race. Maybe we'll have five, even when Rigney has to leave. Like Dykes, I think Hallett is going to be a great pitcher for us. Jim will give him his chance and I will work hard with him to develop Jack into a winner. If he can take Rigney's spot that will help us a lot. That's up to me. The rest is Jim's job and I don't think of saying anything about it. He's the boss."

"There's one thing about the Sox," Muddy smiled as he departed. "Jim is a hustling, fighting type of manager who never knows when he's whipped, and he has instilled the same spirit into his men. If you ask me, that's the real big secret of the Sox. If they have the old Dykes spirit, they'll be up there at the finish."

LOU GEHRIG SET A RECORD OF 2,130 CONSECUTIVE GAMES THAT PROBABLY WILL ENDURE AS LONG AS BASEBALL LIVES
Burris Jenkins Jr.

M'CARTHY FLIES TO FUNERAL

Ex-Yankee Star Dies as Victim of Rare Malady

NEW YORK, June 3.—(AP) From every walk of life tod came the desire to pay homa to Lou Gehrig, the great "Ir Horse" of baseball—the man w played 2,130 consecutive gam and then for two years fought losing fight against a rare a apparently incurable disease.

The big, handsome fellow w for fourteen years held down fi base for the New York Yank died last night from a disea described as hardening of t spinal cord which caused muscles to shrivel.

WILL LIE IN STATE.

The sports world, never one forget its own, so flooded t Yankee office with inquiries garding an opportunity to pay respects that President Ed Ba row announced a change in pla for services after consultati with Mrs. Gehrig and other mem bers of the family.

The funeral services at 9 a. tomorrow will be private but t body will lie in state tonig starting at 7 p. m., at the Chr Episcopal church in the Rive dale section of New York whe Gehrig resided.

Manager Joe McCarthy of t Yankees phoned that he was f ing in from Detroit and Preside Will Harridge of the Americ League notified Barrow he a was enroute.

DICKEY PALLBEARER.

Bill Dickey, veteran catcher w was Gehrig's roommate for ma seasons, also phoned that would fly here for the funer leaving Detroit immediately af today's game. He said he h "promised Lou" to do so.

Mayor LaGuardia headed t list of honorary pallbearers. Ot ers were Manager McCart Dickey, John Kieran of the N York Times; Christy Walsh, pu licist; Parole Commissioner Jo Maher, Parole Commissioner Ma Fraschi, Dr. Caldwell B. Esselst and Drs. Paul O'Leary, He Woltman, Harold C. Harbein a Bayard T. Horton, all of the st of the Mayo Clinic.

FLAG HALF-STAFF.

Flags on public buildings w at half-staff in honor of Lou, w was a member of the Munici Parole commission, a job he w actively engaged in from the of his appointment by Ma La Guardia, Oct. 9, 1939, un a few weeks ago, when he took voluntary leave of absence.

The end came seventeen d before Lou would have been and wrote finis to a fight w disease that was as dramatic courageous as any of his expl on the diamond.

Right up until the time he into a coma yesterday aftern Gehrig never acknowledged t he was licked.

But others knew that he waging a losing fight and w death came his wife and c relatives were gathered at bedside.

IN HALL OF FAME.

Gehrig's place among baseb immortals was assured a year when he was voted into the spo Hall of Fame. Before he vol tarily withdrew from the Yan lineup May 2, 1939, at Detroit set a never approached recor playing in 2,130 consecutive ch pionship games, thirty-four w series contests and countless hibitions.

He started his streak a pinch-hitter on June 1, 1925. next day he replaced Wally at first base and never miss game for fourteen years.

The insidious illness that s out Gehrig was diagnosed "amyotrophic lateral scler Just [illegible] it entered his s never [illegible] known, but it ma

Continued on Next Pa

Sox, Athletics Rained Out

BY WARREN BROWN.

If Jimmy Dykes had any hope of greeting his former boss, Connie Mack, on the field of battle at Comiskey Park today, early morning rains ended all that.

If Jimmy Dykes had any hope of gazing down on Connie Mack from the eminence of first place in the American League standing, that too was ended, before Connie and his Athletics could get here from St. Louis.

FIRST UNDER LIGHTS.

The Washington Senators took care of that yesterday, when they cuffed around Bill Dietrich and Buck Ross.

And now the White Sox, because of today's downpour, will have to wait until tomorrow night, the local season's first game under the lamp light, to let Connie Mack see what kind of a team it was that once led the American League race by five-ten thousandths of a percentage point.

The precarious footing of five-ten thousandths of a percentage point was actually not sufficient for even Dietrich, let alone the rest of the club to stand upon, with comfort. For five innings the White Sox teetered on the five-ten thousandths of a point, and then one wild heave by Luke Appling, the Tired Man, threw them off completely.

LACK TWO REQUISITES.

In their game yesterday the White Sox had all the requisites

Continued on Next Page.

CUBS SHUT OUT; PHIL ROOKIE GIVES 1 HIT

BY FORREST B. MYERS.

SHIBE PARK, Philadelphia, June 3.—The Cubs were the victims of a young hurler from Pennsylvania's coal mines this afternoon—one Tom Hughes, who let them down, 7 to 0, and held them to one hit.

Hughes, a 21-year-old rookie who came up from Baltimore, had a no-hit game for seven frames and no Cub got on the bags until the eighth, when he walked Galan. Lou Novikoff then singled for Chicago's only hit of the game.

The eighth was the only frame in which Hughes was near trouble, and then the farthest advance was second base. He baffled the Bruins throughout with his fast one and fanned six. The others generally hit into infield outs or lifted soft ones for his supporters to pick off.

EVEN SERIES SPLIT.

The Phil victory gave them an even split with the Cubs. The Phils previously had lost five to the Bruins and only yesterday won their first contest of the year from the Wilson crew. As for the Cubs, they were easy victims for the Prothro men. Big Bill Lee had less than nothing on

Continued on Next Page.

Sports Schedule

TODAY.

BOXING.

Weekly amateur card, Savoy A. C., Forty-third and South Parkway. 8:30 p. m.

TOMORROW.

BASEBALL.

White Sox vs. Philadelphia, Comiskey Park, Thirty-fifth and Shields. 8:30 p. m.

HORSE RACING.

Lincoln Fields, Crete, Ill. 2:15 p. m.

WRESTLING.

Weekly card, Marigold Gardens, Broadway and Grace. 8:30 p. m.

Lou's Death Saddens Babe

NEW YORK, June 3.—(AP)—Babe Ruth, the great Bambino of baseball, who, with "Ironhorse" Lou Gehrig, held the sports spotlight as New York Yankee players for more than than a decade, expressed sorrow last night at Gehrig's death and said he believed "the boy hustled too much for his own good." Ruth explained:

"I never knew a fellow who lived a cleaner life. He was a great baseball player and a hustler. I think the boy hustled too much for his own good. He just wanted to win all the time."

Commented Fred Hofmann, coach of the St. Louis Browns and former teammate of Gehrig:

"He was one of the greatest baseball players I ever saw."

At Detroit Joe Di Maggio, the Yankees' brilliant outfielder, said:

"I can't imagine it. I'm simply at a loss for words."

Frankie Frisch, manager of the Pittsburgh Pirates, said:

"Lou and I were very close friends. He always had been a credit to the game and a grand fellow along with it. We're all going to miss him."

Gerry Nugent, president of the Phillies, said Gehrig **"was truly a great player. I'm sorry to hear of his death."**

Manager Doc Prothro, of the Phils, declared:

"It's certainly a shock. He was a remarkable player."

Manager Del Baker of the Detroit Tigers said of Gehrig's death:

"It's baseball's loss. He was one of the best fellows and grandest hustlers I've ever seen in the game."

Lou's Record in Batting

AMERICAN LEAGUE.

Year—	G.	AB.	R.	H.	HR.	RBI.	BA.
1923..	13	26	6	11	1	9	.423
1924..	10	12	2	6	0	6	.500
1925..	126	437	73	129	21	68	.295
1926..	155	572	135	179	16	107	.313
1927..	155	584	149	218	47	175	.373
1928..	154	562	139	210	27	142	.374
1929..	154	553	127	166	35	126	.300
1930..	154	581	143	220	41	174	.379
1931..	155	619	163	211	46	184	.314
1932..	156	596	138	208	34	151	.349
1933..	152	593	138	198	32	139	.334
1934..	154	579	128	210	49	165	.363
1935..	149	535	125	176	30	119	.329
1936..	155	579	167	205	49	152	.354
1937..	157	569	138	200	37	159	.351
1938..	157	576	115	170	29	114	.295
1939..	8	28	2	4	0	1	.143
Tots.	2164	8001	1888	2721	494	1991	.340

WORLD SERIES.

Year—	G.	AB.	R.	H.	HR.	RBI.	BA.
1926..	7	23	1	8	0	3	.348
1927..	4	13	2	4	0	5	.308
1928..	4	11	5	6	4	9	.545
1932..	4	17	9	9	3	8	.529
1936..	6	24	5	7	2	7	.292
1937..	5	17	4	5	1	3	.294
1938..	4	14	4	4	0	0	.286
Totals	34	119	30	43	10	35	.361

ALL-STAR GAMES.

Year—	G.	AB.	R.	H.	HR.	RBI.	BA.
1933.....		2	0	0	0	0	.000
1934.....		4	1	0	0	0	.000
1935.....		3	1	0	0	0	.000
1936.....		2	1	1	1	1	.500
1937.....		4	1	2	1	4	.500
1938.....		3	0	1	0	0	.333
Totals	....	18	4	4	2	5	.222

Brooklyn Wins; Ties for Lead

BROOKLYN, June 3.—(AP)—The Brooklyn Dodgers moved back into a tie with St. Louis for first place in the National League today by crushing the Cardinals 6 to 0 on the six-hit hurling of Whitlow Wyatt and home runs by Dolph Camilli and Pete Reiser. It was Wyatt's ninth triumph of the season.

Carpenter Wins 3d for Giants

NEW YORK, June 3.—(AP)—The New York Giants romped to a 7 to 3 victory over the world champion Cincinnati Reds today, with young Bob Carpenter pitching five-hit ball for his third triumph without defeat this year.

Bill Jurges and Joe Moore hit homers for New York and Jim Gleeson accounted for one Cincinnati run with a circuit blow.

Major League Standings

AMERICAN LEAGUE.

	W.	L.	Pct.	If they Win	If they Lose
Cleveland	30	19	.612	.620	.600
CHICAGO	26	18	.591		
New York	25	20	.556	.565	[illegible]
Boston	22	19	.537	.548	.52[illegible]
Philadelphia	23	21	.523		
Detroit	23	23	.500	.511	.489
Washington	16	29	.356	.370	.348
St. Louis	13	29	.310	.326	.302

NATIONAL LEAGUE.

	W.	L.	Pct.	If they Win
St. Louis	32	12	.727	.733
Brooklyn	31	13	.705	.711
New York	21	19	.525	.537
Cincinnati	21	24	.467	.478
CHICAGO	19	22	.463	.476
Pittsburgh	14	22	.389	.405
Boston	14	24	.368	.385
Philadelphia	13	29	.310	.326

(Winning and losing pitchers indicated by CAPS.)

YESTERDAY'S RESULTS. (American League)

				R.	H.	E.
Washington	000	012	230—	8	13	0
WHITE SOX	001	000	002—	3	10	2

Batteries: DIETRICH, Ross and Tresh; SUNDRA and Pofahl.

				R.	H.	E.
New York	020	100	020—	5	7	1
Cleveland	210	022	00x—	7	10	0

Batteries: RUSSO, Stanceu, Chandler and Rosar; FELLER and HEMSLEY.

				R.	H.	E.
Boston	320	300	100—	9	11	1
Detroit	100	000	000—	1	4	2

Batteries: DOBSON and Pytlak; NEWSOM, Thomas and Tebbetts.

Philadelphia at St. Louis postponed rain.

GAMES TODAY.

Philadelphia at CHICAGO (postponed, rain).
*Washington at St. Louis.
New York at Detroit.
*Boston at Cleveland.
*Night games.

GAMES TOMORROW.

Philadelphia at CHICAGO (night).
Washington at St. Louis.
New York at Detroit.
Boston at Cleveland.

YESTERDAY'S RESULTS. (National League)

				R.
CUBS	000	001	100—	2
Philadelphia	101	001	00x—	3

Batteries: FRENCH and McCul PODGAJNY and Livingston.

				R.
St. Louis	000	130	001—	5
Brooklyn	010	100	020—	4

Batteries: White, Krist, SHOUN Mancuso; Wicker, M. Brown, DAVIS and Owen.

				R.
Cincinnati	000	020	200—	4
New York	000	003	000—	3

Batteries: RIDDLE, Beggs and bardi; McGEE, Melton, Adams and ning.

				R.
Pittsburgh	000	000	000—	0
Boston	001	000	10x—	2

Batteries: LANNING, Wilkie an pez; ERRICKSON and Berres.

GAMES TODAY.

CHICAGO at Philadelphia.
Pittsburgh ta Boston.
St. Louis at Brooklyn.
Cincinnati at New York.

GAMES TOMORROW.

CHICAGO at Brooklyn.
St. Louis at Boston.
Pittsburgh at New York (night).
Cincinnati at Philadelphia (nig

Cobb and Ruth Ready to Play a Third Match for U. S. O. Fund

Babe Evens Golf Series As Both Play Below Form

Ty 3-Putts Extra Hole to Give Foe Victory—Meet Again Next Month

By LAWRENCE ROBINSON.

On the eighteenth tee, after losing the previous hole with an inglorious 6 to Ty Cobb's par 4, squaring the match, Babe Ruth loudly declared that a Detroit match with his illustrious foeman was definitely out as far as he, Ruth, was concerned.

On the nineteenth green, or two holes later, after Ty three-putted to give Babe a one-up victory on this extra hole, the Bambino was all for a third and deciding match and was ready to start for Detroit right from there.

And so the rubber match between these diamond immortals is scheduled some time during the last week in July. Since both Babe and Ty are scheduled to manage rival amateur ball clubs in Ed Bang's annual Cleveland sports party on July 27, they'll be able to get together.

Both are keen for the third match, mainly to redeem themselves for their mediocrity at Fresh Meadow Golf Club yesterday. Out of deference to the glorious baseball past of the heroic veterans, a play-by-play account of their misadventures is hereby glossed over. Babe had an 85, Ty a conceded 84 after picking up on the second hole, still far from home. Babe won the verdict on the first extra hole.

It really was a tremendous battle, sparked by the flaming desire of these two ancients to conquer; even in this match with nothing at stake but prestige. Watching their grim determination and their reactions to good and bad shots, it was obvious that to the competitors at least this was no mere twosome. The world series and the U. S. Open combined in one, couldn't evoke any fiercer effort, even if it was bogeys and buzzards.

As to the crowd, charity also demands that this painful subject be passed over lightly. Less than 500 turned out, and the United Service Organization which sponsored the match now can buy a few bags of peanuts for the soldiers and sailors to use up the microscopic profits. However, it is pointed out that the match, scheduled on a weekday date only a few days before the big July 4th holiday week end was not expected to attract heavy revenue but to draw attention of the sports world to the U. S. O. In this, success was achieved splendidly.

Babe Glad He Brought Cane Seat.

Babe Ruth did as he promised in unveiling a new putter and a cane seat. The putter worked unusually well—for Babe—although he did flub some important three and four footers. Cobb hit a putting streak from the fifth to the seventh, sinking three long ones, that had the Babe worried. But when Ruth came back with a long one on the ninth and another on the 11th, he recovered his equanimity.

The cane seat was just a needle at first, but along toward the end, Babe was mighty glad to use it. The Ruthian dogs were barking loudly.

The match started along the pattern of Wednesday's meeting in Boston, with Babe picking up two holes quickly, then staving off Ty's determined bid. But Cobb got that putting streak and before Babe stemmed the tide with his long putt on the ninth, Ty was 2 up.

Ty went 2 up at the 10th, lost the 11th when Babe dropped a 30-footer and the 12th when Ruth put a nicely punched four iron on while Ty trapped his tee shot for a bogey 4.

They traded misplays to halve the next three, and then Babe's superior directness won him the long 16th. Ty squared it when Babe couldn't stand prosperity on the tee and Cobb made a tremendous recovery from a hooked drive that was a fairway and a half off line to hold Babe even on the 18th.

Ty's tee shot on the first extra hole was another hook and he played his second down the second fairway and pitched nicely over the trees. Babe, on in 3, almost holed his putt for a par 4. Ty, short with his first putt, missed again and it was over.

Contest Trip Winner To Go With Yankees

McGurk to See All-Star Game Also

By LOU MILLER.

It's the Yankees for Bill McGurk, winner of the World-Telegram's 15th annual Most Valuable Baseball Player Contest.

This was the choice of the Montclair (N. J.) High School pitcher when, as a result of his contest victory, he was given his pick of a two weeks' trip West with any one of New York's three major league organizations.

And what a jaunt the 16-year old, 195 pound, 6-foot 2, husky selected. Ordinarily the contest trip lasts 13 days. This time, however, Bill will be on the road 16 days. Also, as an added feature, he will visit Toronto on July 7 for the British War Relief Fund contest, pitting Toronto and Baltimore against the Yanks, and then go to Detroit for the All Star game the next day. All this happens before the tour of the Western circuit actually gets under way.

After moving to St. Louis, on July 10, stopovers are scheduled for Chicago, Cleveland and Detroit. During the journey the most valuable player is expected to room with one of the players, find entertainment in their company and work out during batting practice. The trip will be over July 22.

Bill played varsity ball for two years, starting when he and his schoolmates petitioned school authorities to revive baseball, which had been abandoned for about a decade. Before that, McGurk had played sandlot baseball ever since he could remember.

The boy, who will be 17 on July 27, also was an outstanding end in football and had expected to play on the gridiron for Georgetown, where he plans to enroll in the fall. However, both Joe McCarthy, Yankee manager, and Clary Anderson, Montclair coach who used to be a great blocking back and baseball catcher at Colgate less than 10 years ago, have advised McGurk that football is one of the worst activities in which a prospective big-league pitcher could participate.

Ponzi Winner

Andrew Ponzi, by winning last night's block, 40-34, took his three-cushion billiard match with Frank Copeland by 120-86 at Julian's Academy.

Truly the 'Umblin' Game — by Mullin

Parker Tops Net Field

Many Stars at Jackson Heights

Tennis folk hereabouts will get a first-hand look at Frankie Parker's forehand, 1941 model, in the Eastern clay-court championships that start today at the Jackson Heights Tennis Club.

Parker, fifth ranking United States netman, is one of many outstanding performers signed up by Dick Todd, maestro at Jackson Heights. As defending champion he's seeded first in the men's singles and is followed by Frank Kovacs, Jack Kramer, Ted Schroeder, Ted Olewine, Gene Mako, Gill Hall and Ladislav Hecht.

In the feminine solo division Mrs. Sarah Palfrey Cooke heads the list. She's sixth in the national ranking. The seventh and eighth stars, Virginia Wolfenden and Helen Bernhard, also will perform for the Eastern title. Then come Patricia Cannine, Margaret Osborne, Mrs. Millicent Lang, Barbara Bradley and Mrs. Louise Genzenmuller.

Stevens Named Coach

COLLEGEVILLE, Pa., June 28.—Pete Stevens has been named football coach at Ursinus. He is a former Temple star.

The Roundup — Both League Races Hot

PHILADELPHIA, June 28.—With the ninth annual All-Star game at Detroit in the offing, the baseball spotlight for the time being is being trained on individual achievement. To be sure, those races are hotter than ever, with the Yankees and the Indians clawing at each other's records in the American League and the Dodgers and the Cardinals involved in just as keen and dramatic a battle in the National League. In the American, the new surge of the Red Sox has added thrills to an already pulsating struggle.

Baseball devotees this past week became thoroughly player-conscious through the exploits of Joe Di Maggio. Just how intrigued the customers have become by the batting streak of the Yankee star may be appreciated from the extraordinary attendance here yesterday, and the utter absorption of the Thursday turnout in the Stadium in Giuseppe's efforts, to the neglect of Marius Russo's dazzling one-hitter.

If Joe should continue that streak, he will be quite the featured player in the shindig between the major star teams in Detroit on July 8. He will be a cynosure, in any event. This time the National League is quite likely to find Giuseppe a tougher problem than he has been in the five intercircuit classics in which he has competed since he came from the Pacific Coast in 1936.

In those five contests, Di Maggio has hit National League pitching for the measly average of .143. In two games he got a horse collar and in the other three he ran to uniformity—.250 for each.

Players selected for the All-Star teams will be announced on Tuesday, and some surprises are reported to be in store for the fans—and the players as well.

The week saw Ted Williams of the Red Sox continue to set the batting pace for both majors, with rookie Pete Reiser leading the National. Keener competition for Pete arrived in the return to action of Johnny Mize, home-run slugger of the Cardinals, who had missed 19 games with a fractured thumb.

Bob Feller, standout pitcher of both leagues, made his record for the Cleveland club's Eastern invasion three victories and one defeat, by hanging up his 16th success in Boston on Thursday. The Red Sox took a 5 to 1 lead on Rapid Robert but Joe Cronin's still unsteady slinging bogged down, and the Tribe rallied for an 11 to 8 victory. Feller opened the trip with a beating in New York, but won in Philadelphia, Washington and the Hub.

One of the finest pitched games of the season was Rube Russo's one-hit job for the Bombers against the Browns. The southpaw faced only 28 men, and lost his second shutout because the lone blow was a home run by George McQuinn. It was the sixth one-hitter of the major campaign, with three in each league.

The Yankees seized the lead from the Indians on Wednesday. It was the first time in exactly two months that the Bombers had ousted the Tribe. With that move, the Yankees made it 13 out of 16. They have won 14 out of 18. Against the West they took nine out of 12.

Cleveland's record for the Eastern trip was eight won and five lost. The Yanks figured they had put their rivals in a bad way when they chased them out of the Stadium with three straight defeats, but Peckinpaugh's charges rallied to win eight out of 10.

Against the Western clubs the Red Sox won eight out of 14. Not exactly good, but good enough to push Cronin right into the fight.

In the National League, the Dodgers performed the unexpected when they seized the lead in the West. When they left Flatbush three behind, their admirers figured they would do well to come back with no worse a deficit. But the Superbas carried the fight to the Cardinals by winning 10 out of 14. With Thursday night's triumph over the Braves, the Dodgers were fairly launched on still another winning streak, which has run six straight. The night success over Boston was Whit Wyatt's eleventh and threw the Dodgers into a tie with St. Louis. With Wyatt boasting 11 victories, Kirby Higbe 10 and Hugh Casey nine. Brooklyn has three hurlers with a total of 30 games.

The Cardinals made a disappointing showing against the East on their own lot, winning eight and losing five. Lefty White's two-hit shutout against the Giants was the standout pitching performance of the home stay.

The Giants did mighty well out yonder, winning eight and losing only four, with that Billy Conn broadcast electric light tie in Pittsburgh. Bob Carpenter, who has won five out of six, has been a lifesaver for Terry. As for Fiddler McGee, he was knocked out even by Jersey City on Thursday night.

Sisler Got 78 Hits in Streak

GEORGE SISLER.

When he singled to center in the first inning of the Yankees-Athletics game in Philadelphia yesterday Joe Di Maggio was close on the heels of two great records. He had hit safely in 39 consecutive games and was gunning for the American League mark of 41 set by George Sisler and the all-time major league record of 44 made by Wee Willie Keeler. In these 39 games, Di Maggio has made 59 hits.

Sisler's record was made in 1922 and during that run the St. Louis first sacker hammered out 78 hits. He was finally stopped by Bullet Joe Bush of the Yankees. Sisler finished that season with a batting average of .420.

Before that American League mark was made the record was held by Ty Cobb, who batted safely in 40 games in a row during the season of 1911. Cobb made 77 hits during his streak, and finally was stopped by Ed Walsh of the White Sox and his famous spitball.

Keeler's record of 44 games in which he hit safely was made in 1897 when he was with the Baltimore Orioles of the old National League. He poked out 82 hits during his streak.

Another great consecutive hitting record was made by Bill Dahlen of the Chicago Cubs in 1894. He ran his string to 42, was stopped one day, then went 28 more games without failing to get a hit. This gave him a remarkable mark of hitting safely in 70 out of 71 games.

It must be said, however, that both Keeler and Dahlen had an easier time of it than present-day batters because when they made their records the foul-strike rule was not in vogue.

SATURDAY'S FROTHY FACTS

If Louis Beats Nova in Fall He Will Retire Undefeated

If Joe Louis beats Lou Nova in September he will retire from the ring, yielding to the desire of his people for an undefeated heavyweight champion. Then Billy Conn and Lou Nova will fight next June for the honor of being his successor. . . . When the ownership of the Detroit Tigers passed from the Navins to the Briggses, Owner Walter Briggs had the name of the ball park changed from Navin Field to Briggs Stadium. . . . But when Philadelphia fandom wanted Shibe Park to be renamed Connie Mack Stadium in honor of the grand old man, Connie rebelled and won his point.

Manager Bill McKechnie of the Reds is one of the lightest eaters in baseball, and not merely because the only thing his boys have hit this year is the skids. . . . However, Bill goes in pretty heavily for pastries. . . . This being an age of juvenile precocity, Barbara and Samuel Cohen, aged 8 and 9, respectively, children of Queenboro fight promoter Marty Cohen, can name the champion of every division from flyweight up, even those scrappers recognized by the N. B. A.

Henry Armstrong is refereeing both amateur and professional bouts on the coast. . . . Hollywood Park handled over $9,000,000 for the first 15 days of its meeting, almost $2,000,000 more than last year.

Marquette, which has changed school colors, is looking for a new nickname for its teams. Current name is the Golden Avalanche. . . . Opinion is that Sammy Snead could have avoided his back trouble if he had started treatments earlier.

Young Otto, the referee, watching Joe Louis work out Sunday before the Conn fight, correctly forecast the blow with which Joe would win, a right cross inside Conn's left hook. T. C.

* * *

TEE TOPICS—The oddest golf accident, of minor variety, reported thus far in the Met tournament season was when Billy Dear's putter broke as he holed a 70-footer on the 16th at Baltusrol. . . . A big help in tying for medal honors in the Jersey amateur qualifying round.

A total of 242 private clubs are listed to start competition in the Peter Dawson National Ringer tournament starting next Tuesday and continuing for two months. . . . When Gail Wild, Baltusrol girl golf star, was beaten out by Maureen Orcutt in the final round of the Jersey Women's medal championship, after leading at 36 holes, her mother commented, "I hope Gail isn't going to be like Eddie." . . . Eddie was Gail's father, who held unquestioned title to being the Runner-up Champion of the world. . . . He finished second in about every tournament he started in during his heyday.

An upstate pro greenkeeper named Mike Ontkush hits his wood shots left-handed and his irons from the right side and carries a two-sided putter. . . . He is probably the only switch-hitter in golf.

Jimmy Demaret reports that Ben Hogan, his partner in winning the recent Inverness four-ball tournament, is in a terrible stew because he is hooking his woodshots and pushing his irons. . . . That's covering about all the territory possible.

Senator J. Henry Walters, golf chairman, is tossing a party for Sports Editors and Golf Writers at the Westchester Country Club next Wednesday.

Because of the super-rabbit ball and the extra-heavy turf that the seasonable spring produced, pros are using heavier putters this year than ever before. With Jug McSpaden, Boston pro, topping them all with a 19½-ounce greens blade.

Lewis and Valentine, famous Island horticulturists, golf course architects and operators, are building a new layout near the Veterans' Hospital at Northport, only course to be built in this area in the last ten years. L. R.

* * *

NET NOTES—Wilmer Allison, former U. S. tennis king, now is a captain in the U. S. Army Reserves. . . . An amateur radio expert, Allison entered the signal corps and brought all his own equipment from Texas to Washington.

Johnny Van Ryn, Allison's old doubles partner, may leave his stock-broking business in Austin long enough to play at Seabright. . . . His wife, the former Midge Gladman, will accompany him. . . . Another Gladman coming up in the net world is Ray Gladman, Midge's 18-year-old brother. . . . He lives in Hollywood, but went to Rice Institute just to get coaching from Allison and Midge.

All players in the Jersey championship who have seen the stroke say Frankie Parker's forehand is improved this season. . . . When his service is mentioned, they remain silent.

Don McNeill's greatest enemy, declares Bobby Riggs, is heat. . . . He plays such a vigorous, blasting game that he wilts under a hot sun. J. A. B.

The ★ of the Week . . .

Alvin Martin (Al) Ulbrickson became the star of this week when his Washington varsity crew drove to a convincing triumph at Poughkeepsie. It was the fourth time in six years Ulbrickson's Huskies had carried off the honors and just about convinced the doubtingest Doubting Thomas that the name of Ulbrickson was entitled to top rating among this country's sweep-swinging coaches.

Ulbrickson's fame at Poughkeepsie is twofold. Not only is he outstanding in his chosen field but he's called the handsomest man ever to visit the Hudson for competitive purposes. The movies' loss was rowing's gain, however, and Ulbrickson is perfectly satisfied.

"I'm a family man," Al says. He lives in Seattle, where he was born in 1903, with his wife and son. He was graduated from Washington in 1926, after stroking the varsity three years. Twice he set the pace for Poughkeepsie triumphs in 1924 and '26, and his last effort still is regarded as a classic of courage under fire.

Ulbrickson tore a shoulder muscle a quarter of a mile from the finish mark in '26, when the Huskies were fighting against a great Navy crew stroked by Bob Butler. Washington came through, and nobody knew about Ulbrickson's injury until the following day when he showed up at the train with his arm in a sling.

A couple of years after his graduation, Ulbrickson got his big chance when Rusty Callow went from Washington to Pennsylvania. But he couldn't put over a varsity winner at Poughkeepsie until 1936, when his boats swept the Hudson. Then Al took his No. 1 crew to Berlin to capture Olympic laurels.

Just to make it official, Ulbrickson sent three more crews to Poughkeepsie conquest in 1937, a second clean sweep. This feat probably never will be equaled. The odds, in any book, would be 1000-1 against.

That '37 varsity set the four-mile record of 18:33.3, which was wiped out by California in 1939, a year Washington was relegated to runner-up. But the junior varsity mark for three miles of 13:44, set by Washington in '37, still is unbroken.

Ulbrickson was married while an undergraduate. His son is 9. Naturally, the old man hopes he'll take to an oar, but it's doubtful whether the kid can approach Pop's achievements. When Al first went to Poughkeepsie he made little impression until he sat in a shell. Then, being a long-bodied athlete, he looked a head higher than his mates. And his shoulders drew gasps of wonder.

Pleasant, quiet and a man who prefers to dodge the spotlight when possible, Al still is a psychologist. He's always crying the blues, a la Buck Walsh, but always comes up with a tough boatload of Western mammoths.

On race day at Poughkeepsie Al almost goes quietly crazy. He can't stand being in a launch, so he jumps ashore just before the start of the varsity event and clambers on the observation train. There he perspires and prays. And, as Callow said, "I'd like to get a carbon copy of that prayer."

ASK DANIEL---

Baseball questions are answered here every Saturday. Please do not ask service over telephone. If personal answer is desired inclose self-addressed, stamped envelope.

V. E., Fort Bragg, N. C.—As between Stan Hack and Red Rolfe, lifetime records, Rolfe went into this season hitting .297 and fielding .956. Hack's batting average was .302 and his defense mark .954. There is virtually nothing to hang a choice on. And I'm not dodging.

* * *

R. B., 229 East Kingsbridge Rd.—Landis was not appointed by the President of the United States. The 16 major league clubs chose him and they pay him. His salary and office expenses come out of World Series.

* * *

N. G., Brooklyn—In 1940 Ted Williams hit .344. Camilli has hit a few supers. But day in and day out Joe Di Maggio will put more power into his drive.

* * *

G. K. P., Camp Upton—If Di Maggio had been walked every time up in a game it would not have broken his batting streak.

* * *

I. L., 2373 85th St., Brooklyn—The rule regarding the catcher's position and actions in an intentional pass virtually places no restrictions on the receiver. He seems to be able to stand anywhere and do anything.

* * *

M. B., 1235 Grand Concourse—We do not furnish home addresses of ball players. The Brown of the Pirates you refer to evidently is Mace.

* * *

A. K., 205 W. 80th St.—Consecutive batting records are: Major leagues, Keeler, 44; American League, Sisler, 41; Double A leagues, 61, Joe Di Maggio; organized baseball, Joe Wilhoit, 69, Western League.

* * *

R. J., Camp Upton, L. I.—Jimmy Foxx is supposed to have hit the longest homer in Yankee Stadium, into extreme corner of left upper deck. Joe Jackson hit the longest at the Polo Grounds, into street, over what is now right field wing.

Joe Medwick.

Jimmy Foxx.

* * *

A. L., Fort Dix—Greenberg was drafted. He did not enlist. He is at Camp Custer, Battle Creek, Mich.

* * *

F. F., 313 Seventh Ave., Brooklyn—On Saturday, June 21, Camilli was not among first five hitters. He had 15 home runs. Average, .274.

* * *

N. G., 18 Pitt St.—Hopp certainly is not as valuable as Krist and White, pitchers. Etten looks like best of the new first-sackers. I would not trade Terry Moore for Nicholson.

* * *

M. B., 481 Hinsdale St.—On Thursday morning the Yanks had 84 double plays and the Dodgers 54.

* * *

K. C. A., 2389 West Shore Trail, Lake Mohawk, Sparta, N. J.—Your suggestion that the All-Star game be turned into a double-header, to permit more men to participate, does not strike me as a good one.

* * *

E. B., 505 Ninth St., Brooklyn—It is a foul ball, irrespective of umpire's calling infield fly.

* * *

I. W., 4 Branford Pl., Newark—Nothing but walks in a game would not have broken Di Maggio's batting streak.

N. Y. Batting

YANKEES.			
Rosar	.359	Bordagaray	.261
Di Maggio	.353	Rolfe	.251
Dickey	.333	Henrich	.245
Sturm	.277	Crosetti	.245
Keller	.265	Priddy	.204
Gordon	.264	Selkirk	.167
Rizzuto	.263		
DODGERS.			
Reiser	.356	Wasdell	.291
Durocher	.333	Camilli	.233
Riggs	.322	Franks	.276
Walker	.305	Reese	.248
Herman	.302	Owen	.247
Lavagetto	.301	Vosmik	.220
Medwick	.290	Coscarart	.188
GIANTS.			
O'Dea	.348	Danning	.266
Ott	.304	Hartnett	.265
Bartell	.292	Whitehead	.244
Moore	.290	Young	.229
Rucker	.279	Orengo	.223
Arnovich	.278	Hale	.211
Jurges	.278	Demaree	.167

J. L., Fort Dix—If Di Maggio had made four sacrifices in any game in four times up his batting streak would not have been stopped.

* * *

J. M., 1949 Amsterdam Ave.—Manuel Salvo never pitched for Yankees. Red Sox had him awhile, sent him back to San Diego. Giants bought him and traded Manuel to Braves.

* * *

L. G., 1508 Nelson Ave.—If the outfielder has one foot on the ground when he makes the catch and then falls into the stand it is a legal catch. He cannot dive in for the ball. Ages requested: Doc Cramer, 35; John Murphy, 33; Joe Haynes, 24; Billy Sullivan, 31; Nick Etten, 27; Merrill May, 30; Jack Wilson, 29. When a batter fans the catcher gets the putout.

* * *

L. B., 120 Broadway—I am in no position to settle a bet on a fight in a local ball club's dressing room. I know there have been stories about a battle, but if the club says it was mumps, that's that.

* * *

L. S., New York—Cubs own Los Angeles and have an arrangement with Tulsa.

* * *

H. W., 233 Breeze Court, Brooklyn—Yankee records against other clubs in 1940 were: Detroit 14, New York 8; Cleveland 10, New York 12; Chicago 11, New York 11; Boston 9, New York 13; St. Louis 8, New York 14; Washington 5, New York 17; Philadelphia 9, New York 13.

* * *

M. O., 3266 Hull Ave.—Arlie Latham was utility with Giants in 1909.

Net Title Winner

Judy Atterbury, Great Neck, won the girls' metropolitan tennis championship yesterday at Jackson Heights Tennis Club by beating Betty Grimes, Forest Hills, 6—1, 6—0.

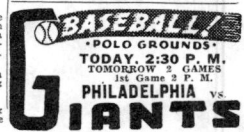

DiMaggio Ties Record as Yanks Take Two Before 52,832

YANKEE STAR HITS 44TH GAME IN ROW

DiMaggio Bats Safely in Two Contests to Equal Keeler's All-Time Major Mark

RED SOX ROUTED, 7-2, 9-2

New Yorkers Add to Lead, but Their Record Homer Streak Ends After 25 Games

By ARTHUR DALEY

The greatest of the present-day ball players drew even with one of the legendary figures of the past yesterday when Joe DiMaggio equaled Wee Willie Keeler's all-time major league record of hitting safely in forty-four consecutive games.

A double-header at the Stadium with the Red Sox gave Jolting Joe the opportunity of overhauling the old Oriole batting artist. And a vast crowd of 52,832, a record for the Stadium this season, wheeled through the turnstiles to see him do it.

This was the Great Man's personal show. No one seemed to care who won the games. The spectators merely wanted to see DiMaggio hit.

Ovation Greets Solid Hit

Twice in the first fray he went out while a pall settled over the stands. In the third trip he scratched a hit that half in the crowd suspected was an error. So when he lined a ringing single to left in his next try roars of delight filled the humid air.

With those hits DiMaggio boosted his modern mark to forty-three straight games. But could he equal Keeler's record of 1897? That was the question uppermost in every one's mind during the intermission.

The crowd did not have long to wait. On his first trip Jolting Joe lined a screaming single to center. He had done it.

Oh, yes. The double-header. The Yankees won both ends with a tremendous display of batting power, cracking out twenty-five hits for 7-to-2 and 9-to-2 victories. By way of lending emphasis to the Bomber clouting the second fray went only five innings before storm clouds and the resultant darkness and rain caused a cessation of play.

For all of the robust slamming of Boston pitchers, the Yankees failed to get a home run in the first game, although Bill Dickey blasted for the circuit in the second one. So the New York record of hitting homers in successive games was halted at 25 contests, in which 40 were hit. Since the old figures, set by the Tigers last year, were 26 four-masters in 17 games, the McCarthymen didn't do a bad job.

Red Sox Appear Lethargic

The Sox looked feeble all afternoon, a dull lethargic club that could not compare with the alert, dashing Yankees who, incidentally, dashed even farther ahead of the second-place Indians, whom they now lead by two and a half games.

The issue was not in doubt long. In the opener five straight hits in the fourth drove Mickey Harris to cover and the score mounted after that. Marius Russo pitched steadily and yielded only six hits in six innings before the heat forced him to retire. Spud Chandler gave only one the rest of the way.

Russo was weakening in the sixth. This was the inning when DiMaggio hit a home run. Unfortunately, however, it was the wrong DiMaggio, Dom instead of Joe. A walk and two more singles drove in another tally, so Joe McCarthy played safe, retiring his left-hander by the pinch-hitter route.

The second game saw Tiny Bonham pitch four-hit ball. A single by Ted Williams and a home run by Manager Joe Cronin provided the Boston tallies, but these came in the fourth after the Yankees had the game tucked away.

They pounced on Jack Wilson in the first, when an error, singles by DiMaggio and Charlie Keller and a double by Dickey provided three tallies. Wilson went out in the third under a four-hit onslaught featured by Dickey's homer into the right field bleachers.

Bonham a Good Omen

It was odd that Bonham was pitching when DiMaggio equaled Keeler's record because the last time Tiny had started was May 15, the very day when Jolting Joe started his streak.

With Buddy Rosar still hobbling around on an injured ankle, Ken Silvestri caught his first game as a Yankee at the Stadium. And he made his first New York hit, a double while batting right-handed against Harris. Then he doubled again, batting left-handed against Mike Ryba.

Tommy Henrich visited some fans in the right-field stands in the sixth inning of the opener when he landed head-first in the box while making a gorgeous gloved-hand catch of Ryba's towering foul.

Nelson Potter, secured from the Athletics on waivers, reported to the Red Sox and promptly saw action as relief pitcher in the opener.

The Yanks are so much on their toes these days that Johnny Sturm raced from first to third on a bunt by Red Rolfe. The Sox neglected to cover the bag.

Lefty Grove, Red Sox veteran, seeking his 299th victory, will oppose Lefty Gomez today.

The box scores:

FIRST GAME

BOSTON (A.)	ab.	r.	h.	po.	a.	e.	NEW YORK (A.)	ab.	r.	h.	po.	a.	e.
D. DiMag., cf	4	1	3	0	0	0	Sturm, 1b	4	0	2	12	0	0
Finney, 1b	3	1	0	5	2	0	Rolfe, 3b	5	2	2	2	2	0
Williams, lf	4	0	1	1	0	0	Henrich, rf	5	0	2	3	1	0
Cronin, ss	4	0	1	1	1	0	J. DiMag., cf	4	0	2	2	0	0
Spence, rf	4	0	1	4	1	0	Gordon, 2b	4	0	0	1	3	1
Tabor, 3b	4	0	1	2	2	1	Keller, lf	5	1	1	0	0	0
Doerr, 2b	4	0	1	0	0	0	Rizzuto, ss	4	1	3	2	7	0
Pytlak, c	3	0	1	7	1	0	Silvestri, c	2	2	2	5	1	0
Harris, p	1	0	0	0	0	0	Russo, p	2	1	1	0	1	0
Ryba, p	1	0	0	0	1	0	aSelkirk	1	0	0	0	0	0
bPeacock	1	0	0	0	0		Chandler, p	1	0	0	0	0	0
Potter, p	0	0	0	1	0	0							
Total	33	2	7	24	8	1	Total	37	7	15	27	15	1

aBatted for Russo in sixth.
bBatted for Ryba in eighth.

Boston	0 0 0	0 0 2	0 0 0	—2
New York	0 0 0	4 0 2	0 1 .	—7

Runs batted in—Silvestri 2, Russo, Sturm, D. DiMaggio, Spence, Rolfe, J. DiMaggio, Gordon.

Two-base hits—Silvestri 2, Russo. Three-base hit—Rizzuto. Home run—D. DiMaggio. Sacrifice—Gordon. Double play—Spence and Pytlak. Left on bases—New York 11, Boston 5. Bases on balls—Off Harris 1, Russo 1, Ryba 1, Potter 2. Struck out—By Russo 4, Ryba 5, Chandler 1. Hits—Off Harris 8 in 3 1-3 innings, Ryba 6 in 3 2-3, Potter 1 in 1, Russo 6 in 6, Chandler 1 in 3. Wild pitch—Potter. Winning pitcher—Russo. Losing pitcher—Harris. Umpires—Summers, Rue, Rommell and Stewart. Time of game—2:32.

SECOND GAME

BOSTON (A.)	ab.	r.	h.	po.	a.	e.	NEW YORK (A.)	ab.	r.	h.	po.	a.	e.
D. DiMag., cf	2	0	0	1	0	0	Sturm, 1b	3	1	0	5	1	0
Finney, 1b	2	0	1	7	1	1	Rolfe, 3b	3	3	2	0	2	0
Williams, lf	2	1	1	1	0	2	Henrich, rf	3	0	0	0	0	0
Cronin, ss	2	1	2	0	4	0	J. DiMag., cf	3	1	1	2	0	0
Spence, rf	2	0	0	0	0	0	Keller, lf	3	2	3	1	0	0
Tabor, 3b	2	0	0	0	1	1	Dickey, c	2	1	2	4	0	0
Doerr, 2b	2	0	0	1	0	0	Gordon, 2b	3	1	1	2	1	0
Peacock, c	2	0	0	4	0	0	Rizzuto, ss	3	0	1	1	1	0
J. Wilson, p	1	0	0	1	1	0	Bonham, p	3	0	0	0	1	0
Dobson, p	1	0	0	0	0	0							
Total	18	2	4	*15	7	3	Total	26	9	10	15	6	0

*Game called at end of fifth, rain and darkness.

Boston	0 0 0	2 0	—2
New York	3 0 4	2 0	—9

Runs batted in—Keller 2, Dickey 3, Rizzuto, Cronin 2, Henrich, J. DiMaggio.

Two-base hits—Keller, Dickey, Rolfe. Home runs—Dickey, Cronin. Double play—Sturm and Rizzuto. Left on bases—New York 4, Boston 1. Bases on balls—Off Dobson 2. Struck out—By Bonham 3, Wilson 2, Dobson 1. Hits—Off Wilson 7 in 2 2-3 innings, Dobson 3 in 2 1-3. Wild pitch—Dobson. Losing pitcher—Wilson. Umpires—Rue, Rommel, Stewart and Summers. Time of game—1:05. Attendance—52,832.

44-YEAR-OLD RECORD TIED

DiMaggio an Opposite of Keeler, Whose Mark He Equaled

Forty-four years passed between the forty-four-game batting streaks of Jolting Joe DiMaggio of the Yankees and Wee Willie Keeler of the Baltimore Orioles. In physical appearance they were marked contrasts—Keeler, 5 feet 4½ inches in height and 138 pounds in weight, who placed his hits; DiMaggio, 6 feet 2 inches tall and a solid 200 pounds, who powders the ball.

Keeler, a left-handed batter, was stopped by Frank Killen, a left-handed pitcher, on June 17, 1897. DiMaggio, a right-handed batter, has a chance to break the old record today.

Here is a comparison of the two forty-four-game hitting streaks:

	AB.	H.	2b.	3b.	HR.	P.C.
Keeler	201	82	11	10	0	.408
DiMaggio	174	66	12	3	12	.379

Pezzella Asbury Park Pro

ASBURY PARK, N. J., July 1 (AP)—Twenty-four-year-old Archie Pezzella was appointed today as pro at the Asbury Park Golf and Country Club, succeeding 74-year-old Joseph I'Anson, who had held the po[illegible] twenty-one years. Pezzella was assistant to Johnny Alberti at Jumping Brook Country Club.

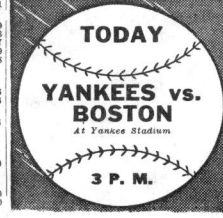

YANKEE SLUGGER CONNECTING TO EQUAL 44-YEAR-OLD MARK

Joe DiMaggio driving a single to center field in the first inning of the nightcap at the Stadium yesterday. The blow ran his consecutive hitting streak to 44, tying Willie Keeler's record, made in 1897. Johnny Peacock is the Red Sox catcher and Joe Rue the umpire.

Manager Joe McCarthy congratulating DiMaggio in the clubhouse after the double-header.

Times Wide World

Yanks' Homer Streak

Date. June—Player.	Pitcher.	Opposing Club.
1—Sturm	Harder,	Cleveland
1—Selkirk	Harder,	Cleveland
2—Henrich	Feller,	Cleveland
2—Henrich	Feller,	Cleveland
3—DiMaggio	Trout,	Detroit
5—Henrich	Newhouser,	Detroit
7—Keller	Muncrief,	St. Louis
8—DiMaggio	Auker,	St. Louis
8—DiMaggio	Auker,	St. Louis
8—Henrich	Auker,	St. Louis
8—Rolfe	Auker,	St. Louis
8—Keller	Bob Harris,	St. Louis
8—Gordon	Bob Harris,	St. Louis
8—DiMaggio	Kramer,	St. Louis
10—Crosetti	Rigney,	Chicago
10—Keller	Rigney,	Chicago
12—Gordon	Lee,	Chicago
12—DiMaggio	Lee,	Chicago
14—Henrich	Feller,	Cleveland
15—DiMaggio	Bagby,	Cleveland
16—Gordon	Milnar,	Cleveland
17—Keller	Rigney,	Chicago
18—Keller	Lee,	Chicago
19—Keller	Edgar Smith,	Chicago
19—DiMaggio	Ross,	Chicago
20—Henrich	Newsom,	Detroit
20—Keller	Newsom,	Detroit
21—Rizzuto	Trout,	Detroit
22—DiMaggio	Newhouser,	Detroit
22—Rolfe	Newsom,	Detroit
24—Rolfe	Muncrief,	St. Louis
24—Henrich	Muncrief,	St. Louis
24—Gordon	Muncrief,	St. Louis
25—DiMaggio	Galehouse,	St. Louis
26—Henrich	Auker,	St. Louis
27—DiMaggio	Dean,	Philadelphia
28—Keller	L. Harris,	Philadel.
29—Henrich	Carrasquel,	Wash.
29—Gordon	Hudson,	Washington
29—Keller	Hudson,	Washington

Johnson, DeMarco to Race

Bob Johnson and Tony DeMarco, the two pilots involved in crack-ups in the last appearance at Thompson Stadium in Staten Island, are scheduled to return to action tomorrow night on the Stapleton track. Johnson and DeMarco, together with Henry Banks, the driver who has been the sensation of the A. R. D. C. circuit this season, will compete in a special forty-lap sweepstakes featuring the midget auto card.

CARDINALS SCORE OVER PIRATES, 11-7

Mize Leads a 17-Hit Attack, Batting In Five on Homer, Double and Two Singles

PITTSBURGH, July 1 (AP)—A pair of "Johns"—Johnny Mize and Johnnny Hopp—gave the Cardinals a hand today which won undisputed possession of first place in the National League stakes with an 11-7 victory over the Pirates.

While the big guns of the Cardinals were blazing in a seventeen-hit attack, the Phillies knocked off the Dodgers, who had shared the lead with St. Louis.

Mize drove in five runs on four hits, including a tremendous three-run homer, his fifth of the season, which put St. Louis in front in the third inning. He also had a double and two singles, missing a perfect day when Bob Elliott backed against the right-field wall to take a hard smash.

Hopp struck out yesterday as a pinch-hitter with the winning run on base, but he made four hits today.

The box score:

ST. LOUIS (N.)	ab.	r.	h.	po.	a.	e.	PITTSBURGH (N.)	ab.	r.	h.	po.	a.	e.
Crespi, 2b	4	3	3	5	5	0	And'rson, ss	5	2	2	2	4	0
Moore, cf	5	0	1	0	0	2	Handley, 3b	5	0	1	3	0	0
Hopp, lf	5	3	4	4	0	0	Fletcher, 1b	3	3	1	10	0	0
Mize, 1b	5	3	4	11	0	0	Elliott, rf	5	2	3	1	0	0
Sl'ughter, rf	5	1	2	3	0	0	V'nR'bays, lf	5	0	3	3	0	0
Marion, ss	5	1	1	0	4	0	DiM'gio, cf	4	0	2	4	1	0
Mancuso, c	4	0	1	3	0	1	Gustine, 2b	3	0	0	3	3	0
Lake, 3b	3	0	0	1	3	0	Baker, c	4	0	1	1	0	0
Krist, p	0	0	0	0	0	0	Sewell, p	2	0	0	0	1	0
Warneke, p	4	0	1	0	0	0	aStewart	1	0	1	0	0	0
							Willkie, p	0	0	0	0	1	0
Total	40	11	17	27	12	3	bMartin	1	0	0	0	0	0
							Total	38	7	14	27	10	0

aBatted for Sewell in sixth.
bBatted for Willkie in ninth.

St. Louis	0 2 3	0 2 1	2 1 0	—11
Pittsburgh	3 0 0	0 1 0	0 0 3	—7

Runs batted in—Van Robays 3, Gustine, Marion 2, Mancuso, Mize 5, Di Maggio, Elliott.

Two-base hits—Mancuso, Hopp, Mize. Three-base hit—Anderson. Home run—Mize. Sacrifice—Mancuso. Double plays—Anderson, Gustine and Fletcher; Mize (unassisted); Marion, Crespi and Mize; Lake, Crespi and Mize. Left on bases—St. Louis 5, Pittsburgh 8. Bases on balls—Off Krist 1, Warneke 3, Sewell 2. Struck out—By Warneke 2, Sewell 1. Hits—Off Krist 3 in 1-3 inning, Warneke 11 in 8 2-3, off Sewell 10 in 6, Willkie 7 in 3. Winning pitcher—Warneke. Losing pitcher—Sewell. Umpires—Jorda, Barr and Sears. Time of game—2:13. Attendance—2,521.

Today's Probable Pitchers

By The Associated Press.

American League

Boston at New York—Grove (5-2) vs. Gomez (5-3).

Washington at Philadelphia—Sundra (6-5) or Chase (3-8) vs. McCrabb (5-6).

Detroit at Chicago (night)—Newsom (5-11) vs. Dietrich (4-4).

Other clubs not scheduled.

National League

Philadelphia at Brooklyn—Hughes (5-7) vs. Higbe (10-6).

New York at Boston (2)—Lohrman (4-5) and Carpenter (5-1) or Wittig (2-0) vs. Johnson (4-5) and Errickson (3-8).

Cincinnati at Pittsburgh—Derringer (7-9) vs. Butcher (6-6).

Other clubs not scheduled.

(Figures in parentheses indicate season's won-and-lost records.)

Major League Baseball

American League

YESTERDAY'S RESULTS

New York 7, Boston 2 (1st).
New York 9, Boston 2 (2d) (five innings, rain).
Detroit 5, Chicago 1.
Philadelphia 10, Washington 1. (night).
Cleveland 10, St. Louis 6 (night).

STANDING OF THE CLUBS

	New York	Cleveland	Boston	Chicago	Detroit	Phila'phia	Wash'gton	St. Louis	Won	Lost	Percentage	Games Behind
N. Y.	—	7	6	5	4	4	8	10	44	26	.629	—
Cleve.	3	—	6	4	6	10	7	7	43	30	.589	2½
Boston	4	3	—	7	7	7	3	5	36	32	.529	7
Chicago	5	6	3	—	6	3	7	6	36	33	.522	7½
Detroit	6	4	6	4	—	8	3	5	36	36	.500	9
Phila.	4	3	3	6	3	—	9	5	33	36	.478	10½
Wash.	2	3	4	5	7	1	—	4	26	43	.377	17½
St. L.	2	4	4	2	3	3	6	—	24	42	.364	18
Lost	26	30	32	33	36	36	43	42	—	—		

GAMES TODAY

Boston at New York (3 P. M.)
Washington at Philadelphia.
Detroit at Chicago (night).
Other clubs not scheduled.

National League

YESTERDAY'S RESULTS

Philadelphia 6, Brooklyn 4 (ten innings).
Boston 6, New York 4.
St. Louis 11, Pittsburgh 7.

Other clubs not scheduled.

STANDING OF THE CLUBS

	St. Louis	Brooklyn	New York	Cincinnati	Pittsburgh	Chicago	Boston	Phila'phia	Won	Lost	Percentage	Games Behind
St. L.	—	5	7	8	9	5	6	8	48	23	.676	—
Bklyn.	6	—	6	8	5	5	7	10	47	24	.662	1
N. Y.	5	4	—	4	3	9	7	5	37	31	.544	9½
Cincin.	4	5	6	—	5	6	6	4	36	33	.522	11
Pitts.	1	3	5	2	—	6	3	8	28	34	.452	15½
Chicago	2	4	3	4	4	—	6	8	31	39	.443	16½
Boston	4	2	2	3	3	5	—	6	25	39	.391	19½
Phila.	1	1	2	4	5	3	4	—	20	49	.290	27
Lost	23	24	31	33	34	39	39	49	—	—		

GAMES TODAY

Philadelphia at Brooklyn (3 P. M.)
New York at Boston (2).
Cincinnati at Pittsburgh.
Other clubs not scheduled.

DODGERS LOSE, 6-4, TO PHILS IN TENTH

Beaten by Quakers First Time This Season, Brooklyn Falls to Second Behind Cards

BENJAMIN'S HIT DECIDES

Single Scores Two to Topple Casey—Herman's Home Run Wasted at Ebbets Field

By ROSCOE McGOWEN

Even the Phillies now and then turn on their tormentors.

Yesterday at Ebbets Field Doc Prothro's stubborn cellar champions outscored the struggling Dodgers, 6-4, in ten innings for their first triumph in eleven starts this year against the Brooklyn forces.

It was an embarrassing setback, too, not only knocking the Brooks out of a first-place tie with the Cardinals but, because of the latters' defeat of the Pirates, dropping Leo Durocher's boys a full game behind the league leaders.

Single Sends in Two

Stan Benjamin took the game away from Hugh Casey and the Dodgers in the final frame when he socked a single through the left side of the closely drawn infield with the bases filled. That scored two runs and the Dodgers failed in their last chance, although getting two on with two away on a pass to Dixie Walker and Harry Marnie's fumble of Jimmy Wasdell's grounder.

Herman Franks then rifled a long foul against the right field screen but finally flied to Joe Marty to end the see-saw affair after 3 hours 11 minutes. It was Casey's fifth loss and second straight, while Ike Pearson, who replaced Lee Grissom in the sixth, received credit for his second success.

Billy Herman walloped his first homer of the campaign off Grissom in the fourth as a prelude to a three-run frame. But nobody else could find the range, although the crowd of 9,550, especially more than 6,000 Knothole Club boys, pleaded for more big Brooklyn blows.

Fitzsimmons Fails to Last

Freddy Fitzsimmons, with three victories and no losses, started and gave two runs in the first inning on one hit, two passes, his fielder's choice on a bunt that filled the bases and Bob Bragan's scoring fly. When Freddy was nailed for a single by Pinky May to start the second, Durocher yanked him and brought in Mace Brown.

The Dodgers got three in the fourth on Herman's homer, singles by Cookie Lavagetto and Pete Reiser, Joe Vosmik's scoring fly and the first of two doubles by Wasdell.

But the Phils got to Brown in the fifth, tying it up on doubles by Danny Litwhiler and Marty and another scoring fly by Bragan.

Lavagetto singled to send Grissom away at the start of the sixth with Pearson pitching, a single by Walker and Wasdell's double sent Cookie around.

The Phils tied it again in the seventh on a double by Benjamin and Bragan's single. The tenth started with a strikeout of Pearson, but Marnie and Litwhiler followed with singles, Marty was purposely passed and Benjamin singled.

Casey Takes Time Out

The heat apparently got Casey in the ninth. He left the mound and went into the dugout for two or three minutes.

Reiser made a great throw in the tenth after fielding Litwhiler's single, almost nipping Marnie going into third. The ball beat the runner, but Lavagetto couldn't hang onto it. Pete nearly got Benjamin at second on Stan's double in the seventh.

The box score:

PHILADELPHIA (N.)	ab.	r.	h.	po.	a.	e.	BROOKLYN (N.)	ab.	r.	h.	po.	a.	e.
Marnie, 2b	5	2	2	2	4	1	Reese, ss	4	0	0	1	3	0
Litwhiler, lf	4	3	2	2	0	0	Herman, 2b	5	1	2	7	1	0
Marty, cf	4	0	1	5	0	0	Lavagetto, 3b	5	2	2	0	4	0
Benjamin, 1b	6	1	3	10	0	0	Medwick, lf	5	0	0	4	0	0
Rizzo, rf	3	0	0	1	0	0	Reiser, cf	4	1	1	2	0	0
Bragan, ss	6	0	1	4	2	0	Vosmick, rf	2	0	0	0	0	0
Warren, c	2	0	1	4	0	0	Walker, rf	2	0	1	1	0	0
aKlein	0	0	0	0	0	0	Wasdell, 1b	5	0	2	11	0	0
Liv'gston, c	0	0	0	0	0	0	Franks, c	4	0	0	3	0	0
May, 3b	5	0	2	2	2	0	Fitzsim'ns, p	0	0	0	0	1	0
Grissom, p	2	0	0	0	2	0	Brown, p	1	0	0	1	3	0
Pearson, p	2	0	0	0	0	0	Casey, p	2	0	0	0	2	0
Total	39	6	12	30	10	1	Total	39	4	8	30	14	0

aBatted for Warren in ninth.

Philadelphia	2 0 0	0 1 0	1 0 0	2	—6
Brooklyn	0 0 0	3 0 1	0 0 0	0	—4

Runs batted in—Benjamin 3, Bragan 3, Herman, Vosmik, Wasdell 2.

Two-base hits—Wasdell 2, Litwhiler, Marty, Benjamin. Home run—Herman. Stolen bases—Benjamin, Bragan. Sacrifices—Marty, Grissom. Double play—Brown and Herman. Left on bases—Philadelphia 15, Brooklyn 10. Bases on balls—Off Grissom 1, Fitzsimmons 2, Brown 4, Pearson 4, Casey 4. Struck out—By Grissom 4, Casey 3. Hits—Off Grissom 5 in 5 innings (none out in 6th), Pearson 3 in 5, Fitzsimmons 2 in 1 (none out in 2d), Brown 3 in 3 2-3, Casey 7 in 5 1-3. Winning pitcher—Pearson. Losing pitcher—Casey. Umpires—Ballanfant, Barlick and Pinelli. Time of game—3:11. Attendance—3,339.

Major League Leaders

BATSMEN

AMERICAN LEAGUE

	G.	AB.	R.	H.	PC.
Williams, Boston	65	219	66	88	.402
Heath, Cleveland	70	268	49	103	.384
Cullenbine, St. Louis	62	199	38	72	.362
Travis, Washington	66	265	46	95	.358
DiMaggio, New York	72	282	67	99	.351

NATIONAL LEAGUE

	G.	AB.	R.	H.	PC.
Mize, St. Louis	52	187	29	69	.369
Reiser, Brooklyn	58	224	56	79	.353
Slaughter, St. Louis	71	276	46	93	.337
Lavagetto, Brooklyn	65	229	41	73	.319
Hack, Chicago	69	264	53	84	.318

HOME-RUN HITTERS

AMERICAN LEAGUE

DiMaggio, N. Y....17 | York, Detroit....16
Keller, N. Y....16 | Johnson, Phila....16

NATIONAL LEAGUE

Ott, New York....18 | Nicholson, Chicago.14
Camilli, Brooklyn..15

RUNS BATTED IN

AMERICAN LEAGUE

Keller, N. Y....68 | York, Detroit....60
DiMaggio, N. Y...62

NATIONAL LEAGUE

Nicholson, Chicago.57 | Slaughter, St. L..50
Ott, New York....51 | Mize, St. Louis...50
Camilli, Brooklyn..50

BRAVES' 6 IN THIRD DEFEAT GIANTS, 6-4

Schumacher Fails in Bid for First Victory in Month as 5 Unearned Runs Cross

YOUNG, O'DEA HIT HOMERS

But Hutchings Protects Lead When Heat Wilts Lamanna After Seven Innings

By LOUIS EFFRAT

Special to THE NEW YORK TIMES.

BOSTON, July 1—Unlucky Hal Schumacher, who hasn't come up with a victory in exactly a month, was the victim of two misplays by Babe Young as the Braves counted six times in the third inning today and handed the Giants a 6-4 setback. Five Boston runs were unearned. Characteristic of how fortune has not been smiling at Prince Hal.

The heat was almost unbearable and to the Giants so were the Braves. The New Yorkers had runners on third and first with none out and the bases loaded with one down in the first, but failed to make the most of the situation against Frank Lamanna. In the second Odell Hale walked, stole second and trotted home on Dick Bartell's single, and it was 1—0 when Boston came up in the third.

On the first play Young booted Sibby Sisti's grounder, whereupon Johnny Cooney singled him to second. Buddy Hassett outraced a fine bunt and the bags were crowded.

Double Play Misses Fire

A line single to right by Max West pushed home two men. Paul Waner then bounded to Young, whose throw to Billy Jurges forced West. Jurges returned a perfect peg to Young for what appeared to be a double play, but the Babe took his foot off the bag, allowing Hassett to score and Waner to reach first.

Bama Rowell doubled and an intentional pass to Eddie Miller filled the bases again. Phil Masi's fly scored Waner and Lamanna's single accounted for another tally. That was enough for Schumacher.

Bob Bowman came on and Sisti, up for the second time in the inning, hit the first pitch for a double to center. At this stage the score was 6—1, with runners at third and second. Except for a great play by Bartell on Cooney's bid for a hit two more would have counted.

With that lead Lamanna pitched a home run ball to Young with none on in the sixth and another with one on to Ken O'Dea in the seventh. Young had failed to hit when the bases were loaded in the first. Because of the heat Lamanna made way for John Hutchings, who hurled the last two stanzas and protected the lead.

The Giants had something to be thankful for and that was the excellent relief work of Fiddler Bill McGee, who twirled the last five innings, yielded only two singles and fanned six.

Melton Gets an Idea

It was so hot Cliff Melton bobbed up with a suggestion. "It's too hot in Boston," he said. "Let's all go to St. Louis."

Schumacher's last triumph was recorded on June 1, when he beat the Reds, 3—2. He now has lost six games, against four victories.

In the ninth, with Harry Danning, who had hit a pinch single, on first, Sisti snared Bartell's hot bounder and started the game-ending double play. It was one of the fielding standouts.

Ott, after a long run, got his glove on Sisti's drive in the third, but couldn't hold the ball.

The box score:

NEW YORK (N.)	ab.	r.	h.	po.	a.	e.	BOSTON (N.)	ab.	r.	h.	po.	a.	e.
Bartell, 3b	4	0	1	0	3	0	Sisti, 3b	5	1	1	2	2	0
Rucker, cf	3	1	1	2	0	0	Cooney, cf	3	1	2	5	0	0
O'Dea, c	4	1	1	7	0	0	Hassett, 1b	4	1	3	11	0	0
Ott, rf	3	0	0	0	0	0	West, lf	4	0	1	1	0	0
Young, 1b	4	1	1	5	2	2	Waner, rf	4	1	0	2	0	0
J. Moore, lf	4	0	0	6	0	0	Rowell, 2b	4	1	2	1	6	0
Hale, 2b	3	1	1	1	2	0	Miller, ss	2	1	0	1	1	0
Jurges, ss	4	0	1	3	2	0	Masi, c	3	0	0	4	0	0
Sch'acher, p	1	0	0	0	0	0	Lamanna, p	3	0	1	0	1	0
Bowman, p	0	0	0	0	0	0	Hutchings, p	1	0	0	0	0	0
aHartnett	1	0	0	0	0	0	Total	33	6	10	27	10	0
McGee, p	1	0	0	0	0	0							
dDanning	1	0	1	0	0	0							
Total	33	4	7	24	9	2							

aBatted for Bowman in fourth.
bBatted for McGee in ninth.

New York	0 1 0	0 0 1	2 0 0	—4
Boston	0 0 6	0 0 0	0 0 .	—6

Runs batted in—Bartell, Young, O'Dea 2, West 2, Masi, Lamanna, Sisti.

Two-base hits—Rowell, Sisti. Home runs—Young, O'Dea. Stolen bases—Hale, Rowell. Double plays—Bartell, Hale and Young; Young, Jurges and Young; Sisti Rowell and Hassett. Left on bases—New York 6, Boston 7. Bases on balls—Off Schumacher 3, McGee 1, Lamanna 4. Struck out—By Schumacher 1, McGee 6, Lamanna 4. Hits—Off Schumacher 7 in 2 2-3 innings, McGee 2 in 5, Bowman 1 in 1-3, Lamanna 6 in 7, Hutchings 1 in 2. Winning pitcher—Lamanna. Losing pitcher—Schumacher. Umpires—Dunn, Magerkurth and Stewart. Time of game—2:30. Attendance—1,580.

Nichols on Long Beach Card

An eight-round bout between Curley Nichols and Aaron Seltzer will feature the boxing card Friday night at the Long Beach Stadium. Another attraction will be a struggle between Harold Valan and Larry McManus. One of the supporting bouts will bring together Tommy Adams and Marty Gordon.

Section III SPORTS NEW YORK Herald Tribune SPORTS Section III

EIGHT PAGES SUNDAY, JULY 6, 1941 EIGHT PAGES

5 Yankee Homers Rout Athletics, 10-5; Dodgers Down Braves, 2-1; Foxbrough Takes Butler Handicap Before 25,043 at Empire City

Victor Beats Tola Rose by Five Lengths

1:58.2 on Muddy Oval for $1\frac{3}{16}$ Miles Is $\frac{4}{5}$ of a Second Shy of Mark

Devil's Crag Third Before Salford II

$1,070,430 Handle Sets Record for Track; Dini Wins Handicap Sprint

By Murray Tynan

William Woodward, chairman of The Jockey Club, and Sunny Jim Fitzsimmons, who trains his horses, came out on top after a smart move yesterday when Foxbrough, full brother to Gallant Fox and Fighting Fox, won the Butler Handicap before 25,043 racegoers who packed Empire City and bet $1,070,430, a new record for the track. After a glance at the rough and muddy track they scratched Fenelon, their ace and top weight in this run with 130 pounds up, and not only won the race but saved their big horse for another day when conditions might be more favorable.

While the withdrawal of Fenelon left the program without a big-name thoroughbred, the horses that ran turned in fine performances, and among them were a dead heat in the third race and a particularly fine effort by W. C. Winfrey's mare Dini when she won the Sting Handicap under top weight of 122 pounds. The band played "The Wearing of the Green" in memory of the late James Butler, in whose honor the handicap was run, and Miss Dorothy Butler, his granddaughter, presented the trophy to Woodward after Foxbrough won the race. The crowd applauded when the presentation was made, which is unusual for racegoers, and left the impression that it was a popular victory, although the winner was not the favorite.

Salford II Favored

There was something of an international angle to this run of one mile and three-sixteenths, because Foxbrough, although bred here, was sent to England as a yearling and was returned to this country last year. His chief rival appeared to be Ralph Beaver Strassburger's Salford II, a refugee from France, which was unbeaten here in three starts during the spring. The crowd liked Foxbrough, and they respected the opinion of Fitzsimmons when he said that he would win the race even with Fenelon scratched, but the majority went against their better judgment and made the French horse a slight favorite over Foxbrough.

Foxbrough, son of Sir Gallahad III from Marguerite, one of the greatest producing mares of all racing history and a daughter of Celt, returned $6.60 to win, $3.20 place and $3.40 to show. He also picked up first money of $19,800 and gave his stable its second straight success in the important handicaps run in New York. Fenelon won the Brooklyn at Aqueduct last Saturday, and for that reason had been assigned the top weight for this run. With Fenelon out Foxbrough shared the honor of carrying top poundage of 118 pounds with Salford II, and while he was winning by five lengths, galloping, the French horse was finishing fourth. The time was 1:58 1-5, which was four-fifths of a second behind the record and was considered to be remarkable for the track. It equalled the track record that Lovely Night erased from the books with only 104 pounds up.

Foxbrough Under Tight Hold

Although only five went away in the Butler it was a pretty race until Foxbrough decided to run away with it. Don Meade, who rode Salford II, took the French horse into a fight with A. J. Sackett's Tola Rose for the lead and while they were at it Jimmy Stout, on Foxbrough, had a firm hold on his horse, trying to keep him from going too fast during the early stages. As the field came down the home stretch for the first time it looked as though Foxbrough might yank Stout right out of the saddle.

The run up the back stretch saw Carroll Bierman win the fight for the lead, but Salford II still had some run left and when Foxbrough and Stout went up to challenge he went with them. Going into the far turn the three of them were abreast, but by that time, Foxbrough had practically pulled the arms out of Stout and the boy had to let him run. They coasted off to a nice lead and had the situation in command the rest of the way. Tola Rose was second, a length and one-half in front of J. B. Partridge's Devil's Crag.

The race was run in 0:24 2-5, 0:49 3-5, 1:13 3-5, 1:39 1-5 for the mile and 1:58 1-5 for the full distance. The time made by Foxbrough and the unquestioned ability of Fenelon leave the stable holding the strongest sort of a hand for the $50,000 Massachusetts Handicap that will be run at Suffolk Downs July 16.

Mrs. Andy Schuttinger's Red Welt and Tower Stable's Two Kick ran the dead heat and there was something of interest there because Nick Coule, who rode Red Welt, never had been on a winner before. This may have been only half a winner

(Continued on page 6, column 4)

Dizzy Dean Will Leave Baseball for Radio Job

PITTSBURGH, July 5 (AP).—Dizzy Dean, who blazed a meteoric trail as a baseball pitcher and who found himself a coach with the Chicago Cubs this year, told newspaper men today that he is leaving baseball for a radio broadcasting job.

Dean said that after tomorrow's double-header he would pack his bags for St. Louis and a new job with a brewing company. He said his contract called for $25,000 for the rest of this year and the next two years—$5,000 for the remainder of 1941 and $10,000 each for 1942 and 1943. In uniform today, Dean coached at first base.

Joe Hunt, Wood Gain Semi-Final At Nassau Nets

Sabin, Segura Also Reach Round of Four in Tennis Tourney at Glen Cove

By Fred Hawthorne

GLEN COVE, L. I., July 5.—Midshipman Joe Hunt, who will graduate from the Naval Academy right onto the deck of a battleship this year; Sidney B. Wood jr., former all-England singles champion; Wayne Sabin, of Reno, Nev., and Francisco Segura, of Ecuador, won their semi-final brackets this afternoon in the twenty-seventh annual invitation tournament of the Nassau Country Club before a record crowd.

Hunt defeated Victor Seixas, of Philadelphia, 6—4, 6—1; Wood vanquished Frank Bowden, of New York, 5—7, 6—1, 6—1; Sabin turned back Gilbert A. Hunt jr., of Washington, 7—5, 6—2, and Segura defeated S. E. Davenport 3d, of Forest Hill, 7—5, 7—5.

Gilbert Hunt, who won the tournament in 1937 and 1938 and was second to the midshipman in the seeded group was the only seeded player eliminated.

Joe Hunt to Meet Wood

Starting tomorrow morning at 10:45, Joe Hunt will play Wood and Sabin will take on Segura. These matches will be staggered and will be for the best of three sets. The final is scheduled to begin at 3 o'clock and unless the semi-finals result in hard three-set battles, will be for the best of five sets. Weather conditions may also affect the number of sets in the final. Threatening skies will sway the committee, headed by Hunt T. Dickinson, chairman, to limit the final to best of three sets.

The morning session was devoted to the playing of the eight matches in the second round. In one of these the gallery saw Frank X. Shields, of New York, former No. 1 ranking player of the United States and Davis Cup star, defeated by Victor Seixas, of Philadelphia, a slim seventeen-year-old stripling, by the score of 2—6, 6—4, 6—3.

In the opening set the giant internationalist was playing about as well as he ever did. His forehand drive was working flawlessly and proved a battering weapon. Shields's services, noted for years as one of the most severe in the game, was an insurmountable obstacle for Seixas. To add to the youngster's difficulties, Shields was forcing ground strokes and dominating the net position. The direct result of this heavy barrage from Shields's side of the net, was to place Seixas on the defensive. He was hurrying his own shots and was obviously nervous.

Youngster Rallies

But Shields these days can apparently go top speed for a limited period, and as soon as he began to slacken in his attack his youthful opponent braced himself and started his fight to regain lost ground. His own service was now under control and his whole game improved. After the first few games of the second set Seixas had taken full control of the match and took the set at 6—4. In the final set it was mainly the internationalist heavy service that kept him in the match.

But when Seixas met Joe Hunt there was a different story. The Naval Academy student is only a youth himself, strong, fast on his feet, and a superb volleyer.

Parker Gains In Clay-Court Net Tourney

Kramer, Schroeder and Mako Also Triumph in Quarter-Final Matches

Virginia Wolfenden At Title Round

Margaret Osborne Loses 3-Set Semi-Final Duel at Jackson Heights Club

By Al Laney

By keeping most of its courts busy nearly all day, the Jackson Heights Tennis Club brought its Eastern clay-court championships into the semi-final round yesterday and will present some attractive matches for the Sunday crowd this afternoon. In the first of these semi-final matches, Frank Parker will meet Frank Kramer and in the other Ted Schroeder will play Gene Mako.

The final, because of Friday's rain, will be played on Monday, along with the women's final. One of the women's finalists will be Miss Virginia Wolfenden, who defeated Miss Margaret Osborne, 5—7, 6—4, 6—4. The other will be either Mrs. Elwood Cooke or Miss Pat Canning, who play their semi-final today.

Schroeder Beats Hecht

The men's semi-final matches were not, with one exception, on the good side. After George Rogers had beaten Gerald Crowther in the morning, Mako beat Rogers, 6—1, 6—3, 6—3, in the afternoon. Ladislav Hecht beat S. E. Davenport before Schroeder beat Hecht, 5—7, 7—5, 6—2, 6—3.

Kramer and Parker already were quarter finalists, so had only one match each. Kramer beat Charles Mattmann, 6—1, 6—2, 6—1, and Parker defeated Ted Olewine, 7—5, 6—1, 6—2. The doubles also reached the semi-final and the field will be reduced to two teams today.

The most notable victory was that of Schroeder over Hecht. The former Czech had given the young [illegible] week in [illegible]sey and Schroeder had apparently been pondering on the reason for that development. This time Schroeder had a best-of-five-set match in which to operate and he was not master of the situation until well into the third. He barely escaped a two-set-to-love deficit but once he had survived that crises he had clear sailing. He is a gifted player and one who should continue to improve from week to week.

Parker Dull but Good

Olewine had a good match with Parker. He is a good player with fine shots all around and he could have won the first set if the umpire had not taken a game away from him with a bad decision. Parker is no different this year in spite of the annual advance reports. He is still a dull and a good player. The forehand is a little changed, but apparently no better. It is as always an ugly push which can fail under pressure. But Parker, as he has been doing for years, is going to beat all but the best players this summer and will rank well up. He might even beat them all. There are no great ones among them.

Mako made quick work of George Rogers, the gangling Irishman, who had beaten Kovacs earlier in the tournament. Mako has brought back from his exile a ridiculous service for a first-rate player. He doesn't take the racket below the

(Continued on page 3, column 3)

Safe on Steal as Slipping Infielder Misses the Ball

Masi, of the Braves, sits on the bag as the ball sails into center field in the second inning of yesterday's game at Ebbets Field. Herman fell and couldn't make the play. Dodgers won, 2 to 1

Herald Tribune—Acme

Wyatt Registers 3-Hit Triumph On His Homer

Brooklyn Boosts Lead to 2 Games as Ace Wins 13th; Camilli Also Connects

By Robert B. Cooke

Whitlow Wyatt, Brooklyn's talented right-hander, who was annoyed when rain prevented him from facing the Giants on Friday, released his pent-up fury against Casey Stengel's innocent Braves yesterday at Ebbets Field. The results enabled the league-leading Dodgers to pull two games away from the faltering Cardinals.

Wyatt not only stifled the Braves, 2 to 1, with a three-hit masterpiece, but also composed part of the home-run music with which the Dodgers won the ball game. With the teams tied at 1-all in the fifth, Wyatt produced the winning run with a four-bagger into the left center-field stands.

Brooklyn had tied the score in the previous inning with the help of Dolph Camilli, who hadn't played since last Saturday. Camilli, who had been afflicted with a touch of the grip, said he was feeling much better before game time. When he rammed his sixteenth homer over the right-field wall in the fourth he proved, beyond question, that his temperature was normal again.

Despite their two homers, the Dodgers weren't certain of victory until Bama Rowell flied to Dixie Walker in left for the final out in the ninth. Stengel started his young right-hander, Tom Earley, who managed to lower many of the Brooklyn batting averages even though his teammates were unable to identify what Wyatt was throwing.

Earley was removed for a pinch hitter in the eighth, and the Braves staged a ninth-inning flurry. After Johnny Cooney had grounded out,

(Continued on page 2, column 2)

Standings in Major Leagues

SUNDAY, JULY 6, 1941

American League

YESTERDAY'S RESULTS

New York, 10; Philadelphia, 5.
Cleveland, 5; Chicago, 3.
Boston, 5; Washington, 0.
St. Louis, 9; Detroit, 3 (1st).

STANDING OF THE CLUBS

	New York	Cleveland	Boston	Chicago	Detroit	Philadelphia	Washington	St. Louis	Won	Lost	Percentage	Games behind
New York	—	7	7	5	4	5	8	10	46	26	.639	—
Cleveland	3	—	6	5	6	10	7	9	46	30	.605	2
Boston	4	3	—	7	7	8	4	5	38	33	.535	7½
Chicago	5	6	3	—	7	3	7	6	37	36	.507	9½
*Detroit	6	4	6	6	—	8	3	5	38	38	.500	10
Phila.	4	3	3	6	3	—	10	5	34	38	.472	12
Wash.	2	3	4	5	7	1	—	4	26	45	.366	19½
*St. Louis	2	4	4	2	4	3	6	—	25	44	.362	19½
Games lost	26	30	33	36	38	38	45	44	—	—		—

*Does not include second game.

GAMES TODAY

Philadelphia at New York (2, 1st at 2:05).
Cleveland at Chicago.
Detroit at St. Louis (2).
Washington at Boston (2).

National League

YESTERDAY'S RESULTS

New York-Philadelphia, wet grounds.
Brooklyn, 2; Boston, 1.
Pittsburgh, 9; Chicago, 6.
Cincinnati, 2; St. Louis, 1.

STANDING OF THE CLUBS

	Brooklyn	St. Louis	New York	Cincinnati	Pittsburgh	Chicago	Boston	Philadelphia	Won	Lost	Percentage	Games behind
Brooklyn	—	6	6	8	5	5	8	11	49	24	.671	—
St. Louis	5	—	7	8	9	5	6	8	48	27	.640	2
New York	4	5	—	4	3	9	8	5	38	32	.543	9½
Cincin.	5	5	6	—	6	6	6	4	38	35	.521	11
Pitts.	3	1	5	4	—	7	3	8	31	35	.470	14½
Chicago	4	5	3	4	4	—	6	8	34	40	.459	15½
Boston	2	4	3	3	3	5	—	9	29	41	.414	18½
Phila.	1	1	2	4	5	3	4	—	20	53	.274	29
Games lost	24	27	32	35	35	40	41	53	—	—		—

GAMES TODAY

Boston at Brooklyn (2, 1st at 2:05).
New York at Philadelphia (2).
Chicago at Pittsburgh (2).
St. Louis at Cincinnati.

Conn Reveals Secret Marriage To Mary Smith Last Tuesday

Newlyweds, at Jacobs Estate, Called 'Scared to Death' of Bride's Father's Wrath

RUMSON, N. J., July 5 (UP).—A frightened pair of newlyweds—Billy Conn and his bride, Mary Louise Smith—were guests today at Mike Jacobs's estate here, where their secret marriage of last Tuesday was announced.

Conn, the handsome Pittsburgh Irishman who braved the dynamite in Joe Louis's fists on June 18 and almost took away Bomber Joe's heavyweight crown, is "scared to death" now, according to Jacobs. "But he isn't half as scared as Mary," Jacobs added.

According to one of Conn's close friends, the bridegroom fears that Mary's father, James Smith, of Pittsburgh—former major league baseball player—will "try to kill him."

Billy and his bride were married Tuesday at St. Patrick's Church in Philadelphia, despite warnings from Smith that he never would permit Conn to be his daughter's husband. But the love of this prizefighter and his lady would not be balked by parental wrath.

They were married at the altar of St. Patrick's—a Catholic church not in use during the summer—by Father Schlindwein, of Brandywine, Pa., who had obtained a special dispensation because of the objections of the girl's father. Mary is only nineteen. Conn's best man was George Ryan, a friend. A maid in the rectory acted as bridesmaid.

Did the couple obtain James Smith's blessing when they notified him of the wedding?

"We got blessed all right," Billy said with a grim smile. "But it was the kind of a blessing you couldn't print. Mary's father was mighty sore. He had been trying to block the wedding, but we managed to sidestep his operatives."

Where have the Conns been since last Tuesday?

"Oh—just hiding out," Billy said.

Smith—who became a wealthy man through various business activities after his major league days—could not be reached today at his summer home in Ocean City, N. J. Smith's brother-in-law said Mary's father probably would refuse to talk to the press.

Smith did not refuse to talk to the press on the day before Billy fought Joe Louis. That was the day when it became known that Conn and Mary had applied for a marriage license. At that time, Smith told reporters, "I'll punch hell out of that fellow if he doesn't stay away from my family. I don't want my daughter to marry a prize-fighter—I know how those people end up."

This marriage, consummating one of the ring's most widely publicized romances was celebrated only four days after Billy's mother, Mrs. Margaret Conn, died at Pittsburgh after a lingering illness.

Billy might have postponed the marriage, but his father and brothers insisted that he go through with it as soon as possible. They told him that his mother would have wanted it that way. The clan of Conn was incensed at Mary's father for trying to raise "the wrong side of the tracks" as a barrier between the greatest of the Conns and his sweetheart.

Billy said that he and Mary will make their home in a Pittsburgh apartment. Meanwhile the newlyweds were ready to leave "at any minute" for Hollywood, Calif., where Billy will begin work on a motion picture in about ten days. He will be the principal in the film version of Octavus Roy Cohen's magazine serial, "Kid Tinsel."

After that picture Billy expects to return to the ring.

"I'm not a movie actor—I'm a fighter. And if I ever get another shot at Louis. I'll be heavyeight champion," he said.

Fighter and Bride in Secret Wedding

Billy Conn and Miss Mary Louise Smith, whose marriage in Philadelphia Tuesday, over the objections of the bride's parents, was disclosed yesterday

Associated Press

Matuszczak, Blocking Back, Selected for College All-Stars

Cornell Ace Accepts Bid to Tackle Giants in Tribune Fresh Air Fund Contest

By Stanley Woodward

Walter J. Matuszczak, Cornell captain and blocking back, is the second man selected for the 1941 Eastern College All-Star football team, according to an announcement made today by Jim Crowley, of Fordham, All-Star coach. Matuszczak joins Lou De Filippo, Fordham captain, in the group which will meet the New York Giants in the sixth annual Tribune Fresh Air Fund game at the Polo Grounds the night of Sept. 3.

Matuszczak stands 6 feet 1 and weighs 212 pounds. He was one of the most popular choices for quarterback on all-America teams selected following last season. His faultless play selection, plus his savage blocking and his tackling behind the defensive line, made him the most valuable player on the Cornell teams of 1939 and 1940. Last fall he played 60 minutes in the games against Pennsylvania, Dartmouth and Ohio State and was relieved only briefly in other games on the Cornell schedule.

Crowley selected Matuszczak for the squad on the recommendation of Carl Snavely, Cornell coach, who was backed up in his judgment by all coaches who had sent teams against Cornell and all players who had come in contact with him in football games.

It is very hard for a blocker to stand out because few people watch any one, but the ball carrier. Matuszczak's work was so outstanding however, that he was spotted as a natural as early as his sophomore year when he made a regular position on the Cornell team. In three years as a varsity player he carried the ball only a few times. Last year he did not carry it once from scrimmage. He did, however, catch seven forward passes for a net gain of seventy-seven yards.

He entered Cornell as an unher-

(Continued on page 4, column 2)

Vander Meer Defeats Cards For Reds, 2 to 1

St. Louis Suffers Fourth Straight Loss, Scoring Unearned Run in Second

CINCINNATI, July 5 (AP).—Johnny Vander Meer pitched and fielded Cincinnati to a 2-to-1 victory over St. Louis today, the first defeat in six starts for young Sammy Nahem and the fourth straight loss for the team sometimes held to be the most likely contender for the pennant.

The Cards' only run, in the second, was unearned, coming after two were out and an argument over a fielding play, as a result of which Mike Gonzales, veteran coach, was ejected from the game.

The inning, which had its other trying moments, went like this: Enos Slaughter walked, Martin Marion fanned, Gus Mancuso was out at first on Bill Werber's off-balance throw from third. The Cards protested. Slaughter took second on the play, advanced on Vandy's wild pitch; Eddie Lake walked and Slaughter scored on a passed ball.

The Reds loaded the bags in the first on Bill Werber's single, one of two Cardinal errors and a sacrifice and fielder's choice and scored their two runs on an infield force play and an outfield liner.

Vander Meer, walking four and striking out as many, turned in six assists and one putout in chalking up his seventh victory against eight setbacks. The score:

ST. LOUIS (N. L.)	ab	r	h	po	a
Crespi, 2b.	3	0	1	6	2
T.Moore, cf	4	0	1	1	0
Triplett, lf	4	0	0	4	0
Mize, 1b..	4	0	1	8	1
Slaug'r, rf.	2	1	1	0	0
Marion, ss.	3	0	1	2	6
Mansuco, c	3	0	0	1	0
*Hopp.....	0	0	0	0	0
Padgett, c.	1	0	0	0	0
Lake, 3b..	2	0	0	1	3
Nahem, p..	2	0	0	1	1
Totals...	28	1	5	24	13

CINCINNATI (N. L.)	ab	r	h	po	a
Werber, 3b	4	1	1	1	5
Waner, cf.	4	1	1	1	0
Frey, 2b..	2	0	0	4	3
F.M'C'k, 1b	4	0	1	13	0
Gleeson, rf	4	0	2	1	0
Lombardi, c	3	0	0	4	1
M.M'C'k, lf	3	0	0	2	0
Joost, ss..	3	0	1	0	2
V. Meer, p	3	0	0	1	6
Totals...	30	2	6	27	17

*Ran for Mancuso in seventh inning.

St. Louis.......... 010 000 000—1
Cincinnati......... 200 000 00x—2

Errors — Crespi, Lake, Werber. Runs batted in—F. McCormick, Gleeson. Two-base hit—T. Moore. Sacrifices—Slaughter, Marion, Nahem, Frey (2). Double plays—Crespi, Marion and Mize; Werber, Frey and F. McCormick (2). Left on bases—St. Louis, 7; Cincinnati, 6. Bases on balls—Off Vander Meer, 4. Struck out—By Nahem, 1; by Vander Meer, 4. Wild pitch—Vander Meer. Passed ball—Lombardi. Umpires—Barr, Sears and Jorda. Time—1:48. Attendance—12,134 paid, 5,255 girls.

DiMaggio's Blast Boosts Streak to 46

Keller Wallops Pair and Rolfe, Sturm One Each in 7th Straight Victory

Ruffing Gets 6th Triumph in Row

Siebert Nicks New York Veteran for 2 Circuit Drives Before 19,977

By Rud Rennie

Five Yankee homers in the Stadium yesterday depressed the visiting Philadelphia Athletics, 10 to 5, while the Bombers continued to zoom along, leading the league with three streaks flaming.

The sensational Joe DiMaggio smote the first pitch on his first time at bat on a line into the left-field bullpen for a two-run homer, his nineteenth of the year, thereby extending his consecutive-game hitting record to forty-six games. It was his only hit, made off Phil Marchildon, a right-hander who went the route for the A's, despite the fact that he was solidly smacked eleven times and scored on in every inning, except the third and fourth.

Charlie Ruffing pitched for the Yankees and has now won six in a row. He has a record of nine and three and has not been charged with a defeat since May 14.

Seventh Straight Victory

And the Yankees are on a seven-game winning streak. They have won twenty-one of their last twenty-five games, and eleven of their last twelve. They are the hottest team in either league.

There were seven home runs all told in the game witnessed by 19,977 persons. Dick Siebert, the Philadelphia first baseman, whacked two solo circuit blows in succession. He was the A's only extra-base batsman. The Yankees outnumbered him. In addition to DiMaggio's homer, Charlie Keller hit two, good for three runs and a tie with DiMaggio for club and league home-run honors. Then Johnny Sturm and Red Rolfe drove consecutive home runs into the right-field stands in the eighth. And between times Ruffing knocked in a run with a double in the sixth.

Marchildon, a well-built fellow with a brisk curve ball, had never faced the Yankees before. It was educational. He found out what happens when the Yankees start bearing down in a tight ball game.

And it was a tight contest until the sixth. Ruffing knocked in an unearned run in the second to give himself a three-run lead. Al Brancato drove in two runs for the A's in the third, and Siebert hit his first homer and started a two-run rally in the fourth which put the A's in front, 4 to 3.

Yankees Regain Lead

Keller's first home run, delivered with two out after DiMaggio had walked, put the Yankees back into the lead in the fifth. Then Siebert's second homer tied the score in the sixth.

It was then that the Yankees really bore down. Ruffing pitched so that the A's scored no more and only two of them made singles. He knocked in a run in a two-run sixth. And then came the homers. Keller plastered his second one into the right-field stands in the seventh. Sturm and Rolfe connected in the eighth and Marchildon bowed to the power of the Yankees. He had won three straight.

DiMaggio's homer went over the railing between the 402 and the 415 foot markers and was caught by John Schulte, the bull-pen catcher. Keller's first homer went into the right centerfield bleachers near the middle exit. After Keller's second homer into the rightfield stands, Bill Dickey also hit one which would have gone in if Eddie Collins had not jumped high and caught it.

The A's hit Ruffing safely in four innings for a total of nine blows and they scored in every inning in which they made hits, except in the ninth when two singles were wasted. They had only four men left on bases.

To Unveil Gehrig Memorial

Today, before a double-header with the A's, the Lou Gehrig Memorial will be unveiled. Tickets

(Continued on page 2, column 5)

Yankees' Score

* * *

PHILA'PHIA (A. L.)	ab	r	h	po	a
Br'ncato, ss	4	0	1	1	2
Collins, rf	4	0	0	3	1
McCoy, 2b.	4	0	0	1	3
Johnson, lf	4	0	0	0	0
Siebert, 1b	4	2	3	6	0
S.C'man, cf	4	1	1	5	0
Hayes, c..	4	1	3	4	0
Suder, 3b.	4	1	1	4	0
March'n, p	2	0	0	0	0
*Moses...	1	0	0	0	0
Totals....	35	5	9	24	6

NEW YORK (A. L.)	ab	r	h	po	a
Sturm, 1b.	4	1	1	5	0
Rolfe, 3b..	5	2	2	1	1
Henrich, rf	3	0	0	2	0
DiMag'o, cf	4	2	1	5	0
Keller, lf..	4	2	2	3	0
Dickey, c.	4	0	0	3	0
Gordon, 2b	4	2	0	6	0
Rizzuto, ss.	3	1	2	2	2
Ruffing, p	4	0	3	0	2
Totals..	35	10	11	27	5

*Batted for Marchildon in ninth inning.

Philadelphia...... 002 201 000—5
New York.......... 210 022 12x—10

Error—Brancato. Runs batted in—DiMaggio (2), Ruffing (2), Brancato (2), Siebert (2), Suder, Keller (3), Henrich, Sturm, Rolfe. Two-base hit—Ruffing. Home runs—DiMaggio, Siebert (2), Keller (2), Sturm, Rolfe. Stolen base—Henrich. Sacrifice—Marchildon. Left on bases—New York, 9; Philadelphia, 4. Bases on balls—Off Marchildon, 7. Struck out—By Ruffing, 2; by Marchildon, 1. Hit by pitcher—By Marchildon (Sturm). Wild pitch — Marchildon. Umpires — Rommell, McGowan, Quinn and Grieve. Time—2:10. Attendance—19,977.

STILL GOING! 51 FOR JOE, YANKS WIN, 7-5

AMERICA FIRST
AN AMERICAN PAPER FOR THE AMERICAN PEOPLE
San Francisco Examiner Sports
Monarch of the Dailies
REG. U.S. PAT. OFF.
CCCC* THE SAN FRANCISCO EXAMINER: SUNDAY, JULY 13, 1941 SPORTS 3

Four Service Teams Battle for Baseball Championship Today

Forts Scott, McDowell Advance With Artillerymen, Moffett Flyers in Examiner Tourney

By Dick Toner

Service baseball champion of the Ninth Corps Area will be Fort Scott . . . or Fort McDowell . . . or Moffett Field . . . or 250th Coast Artillery of Camp McQuaide.

They're the semifinalists in The Examiner Service Men's tournament, which started yesterday with six games on local playgrounds and finishes with a big triple bill in Seals Stadium today.

The big four, which vanquished a total of six rival nines in yesterdays interesting proceedings, will pair off for semi-finals this morning as follows:

Fort Scott vs. Fort McDowell at 9:30 a.m.

Moffett Field vs. 250th Coast Artillery at 12 noon.

And winners in those games, both of which loom absolute toss-ups, will collide at 2:30 p. m. this afternoon in the payoff tilt, with title and Examiner award at stake.

BIG SURPRISE.

The semi-final list includes only one surprise, Fort Scott, which staged yesterday's only surprise by toppling the strong Seventh Division, Fort Ord, club, 6-5, at Club House.

Moffett and Fort McDowell lived up to advance notice by garnering a pair of triumphs apiece. Moffett subdued Fort Funston, 9-3, at Harrison in the morning and dealt Fort Mason a 24-0 trouncing in the afternoon, also at Harrison. The colorful McDowell nine came from behind to clip Letterman General Hospital, 15-4, at Funston No. 1, and then whitewashed McClellan Field of Sacramento, 7-0, on the same field.

13 STRIKE-OUTS.

Powerful 250th Coast Artillery, behind nifty two hit, 13 strikeout pitching by Chet Steengrafe, encountered no trouble in its lone contest, blasting Hamilton Field of Sacramento, 16-0, at Funston No. 2.

Day's classic was the Fort Scott-Fort Ord affair, played before a near capacity crowd. There was tension until the last out, which saw the tying run dying on second.

The Ordmen whacked most of the long blows, collecting two homers and as many triples. But the losers couldn't connect with men on base, which was due in no small part to the "clutch" ability of Fort Scott's flinger, John Chetoskey.

Al Christiansen and Hurler Jerry Soule socked the round trippers. Soule fanned eleven.

HARD PRESSED.

Fort Scott grabbed the lead with three markers in the fourth on a double by Joe Barera, an error and singles by Morrie Levy, Lou Bulman and Walt Miskiewiez. The victors never relinquished the upper hand, but were hard pressed to hold it.

Against Letterman, Fort McDowell trailed until the eighth, when the Indians hit the warpath for nine runs. Tim Sullivan slammed three for three and Jack Falta hammered three for five for McDowell.

Paul Wade twirled five hit ball and whiffed 14 for the Indians against McClellan. Falta and Gordon Chisholm poled homers.

Fort Funston staged a strong stand against Moffett, considering that the losers had only three

(Continued on Page 5, Col. 4)

Seals Set Down by Buxton, 4-0

Oaks Hop on Jansen For 4 Runs in Fifth To Square Series

By Harry Borba

Ralph Buxton, the wiry righthander with the leather arm, had complete charge of everything yesterday in Emeryville including "Lefty" O'Doul's Seals.

His control of the situation was so complete that the Oakland Acorns won a sparkling 4 to 0 victory over the Seals, shutting the locals out for the third time this season.

Buxton outpitched Larry Jansen, the skinny ace of the Seals' mound staff. Larry had one bad inning, the fifth, during which the Acorns put together four hits to make four runs. Larry lost some of his control and was encouraged in his trouble by a bit of skull fielding.

Jansen threw a six hitter which should have been good enough to win, but Buxton outdid him with a five hitter and all the blows were scattered, no two coming in the same inning.

It was a game of sparkling fielding with both centerfielders, Wally Carroll and "Hooks" Devaurs coming up with screaming catches after long runs. "Cocky" Fain produced another one of those double plays that he starts and finishes with such elan. This one was Fain to Fernandez to Fain in the sixth inning to get Gudat who had singled and Devaurs.

Complimented on the play by Manager O'Doul, Cocky said:

"It was nothing. Just like shooting fish."

All of the scoring started and finished in the fifth inning on a mistake. Wally Carroll shouted that he had it when Gudat lofted a Japanese liner behind second

(Continued on Page 4, Col. 3)

It's a Blank!

SEALS Player	AB.	H.	O.	A.	OAKLAND Player	AB.	H.	O.	A.
Holder.rf	4	1	2	0	Dzabou,3b	4	0	2	0
Fain,1b	4	1	6	1	Rigney.ss	4	1	1	5
Carroll,cf	2	1	4	0	Luby,2b	4	1	3	5
Frnndez,ss	4	0	4	1	Chpmn,rf	4	1	1	0
White,lf	4	0	2	0	Gudat.lf	3	2	2	0
Lazzeri,2b	3	1	2	0	Dunn,1b	3	1	13	1
Trower,3b	3	0	1	3	Devaurs.cf	3	0	1	0
Ogrdski.c	3	0	3	0	Conroy,c	2	0	4	0
Jansen,p	3	1	0	1	Buxton,p	2	0	0	2
Stutz,	0	0	0	0					
Totals	30	5	24	6	Totals	29	6	27	13

Stutz ran for Lazzeri in 9th.

Seals	000 000 000—0
Hits	100 100 111—5
Oakland	000 040 00*—4
Hits	010 041 00*—6

Runs—Gudat, Dunn, Conroy, Bruxton. Errors—Duezabou (2), White. Two base hit—Dunn. Runs batted in—Buxton, Duezabou, Rigney (2). Sacrifice—Carroll. Stolen base—Holder. Double plays—Rigney to Luby to Dunne (2), Fain to Fernandez to Fain. Runs responsible for—Jansen, 4. Struck out—By Burton, 4; by Jansen, 1. Bases on balls—Off Burton, 4; off Jansen, 2. Time of game—1 hour 18 minutes. Umpires—Jordan and Engeln.

Gene Sarazen Interested in Leasing Los Angeles Club

DENVER, July 12.—(AP)— Gene Sarazen, one of the most colorful figures in the history of professional golf, disclosed today he was negotiating for the lease of the Midwick Club in Los Angeles.

The golf club was purchased recently at auction by a Los Angeles banana peddler who startled interviewers with the explanation he had taken over the layout in order to become a member.

Sarazen said if the deal is completed, he would operate the course in partnership with Ellsworth Vines, former tennis champion, who has taken up golf seriously.

The little Connecticut farmer already is interested in the Lakeview Club at East Chester, N. Y., serving as its president.

Sarazen said Vines was interested in becoming a professional golfer and if the course was acquired, he probably would serve in that capacity there. "I'll spend my winters in California if the deal goes through," he said.

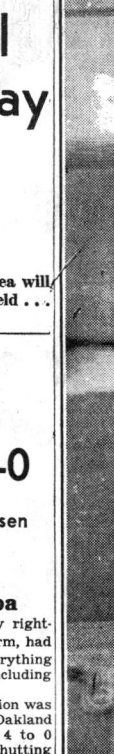

THIS MAD WHIRL—Remarkable sequence shows five movements of a full twisting one and one half dive, performed by the charming and talented Helen Crlenkovich, national senior high diving champion, at Fairmont Plunge. This is a difficult dive to perform correctly. Miss Crlenkovich completes the twist in time to knife the water smoothly—like a champion.

Crlenkovich Seeks Grand Slam

—By Clyde Giraldo—

Curvaceous Helen Crlenkovich, the diving queen, will make the aquatic world sit up and take notice when she scores a grand slam in the national outdoor diving championships August 15 at High Point, N. C.

The authority is Phil Patterson, doting coach of the Fairmont Plunge pretties, who revealed yesterday for the first time that Miss Crlenkovich is going to achieve universal recognition for one of her diving feats at High Point.

She will do a one and a half twister from the high tower—the only girl in the world to attempt this!

"She has been practicing the one and a half twist off the high tower for the past month," Patterson explained. "She will use it as one of her optional dives when she goes after the national outdoor tower and springboard titles. (She holds the indoor title.)

GREAT FEAT.

"Until now this difficult dive has been done off a springboard.

"So far as I know no girl diver has ever accomplished the dive off a high tower, and

(Continued on Page 7, Col. 4.)

Twelfth in Row Puts N.Y. 5 Games Ahead As Cleveland Loses

Di Maggio Cracks Double, Single; Win Sets Season Record; Rizzuto Hits Safely in 15th Straight

ST. LOUIS, July 12.—(AP)—The boys with the slide-rules had to go to work again today as the New York Yankees beat the Browns, 7-5, to sweep their three-game series.

There was Joe Di Maggio, for one, who cracked out a double in the fourth inning and a single in the fifth to make this the fifty-first game in a row in which he has hit safely.

There was the Yankee victory which, combined with Cleveland's loss to Philadelphia, made the New Yorkers' American League lead five full games.

The victory further, as the club's twelfth in succession, established a new 1941 league record for winning streaks. The Indians' eleven straight in the early part of the season had set the previous high.

Like the bombers of old, the Yankees concentrated their fire on one big inning today, and it was Di Maggio's double which touched it off.

Tommy Henrich drew a walk to open the fourth and promptly came racing home on the two-bagger. Before the inning was over the Yanks had four more tallies, on Charley Keller's single; a homer by Bill Dickey, his seventh of the year; errors by Harlond Clift and Roy Cullenbine, and a single by Phil Rizzuto which gave him a record of hitting in fifteen games in a row.

With that much of a working margin Tiny Bonham looked like an easy winner. He was touched for a run in the Browns' half of the fourth but, after the Yanks had picked up two more runs in the sixth on a base on balls, Rizzuto's double and stolen base and an infield out, got into a jam in the seventh, when Chet Laabs clipped him for a three-run homer, and finally was taken out in the eighth.

With one out he walked Walt Judnich, and Cullenbine then smacked a double. Bonham was taken out for Fireman Johnny Murphy, who retired the next two men and got through the ninth at the cost of one run.

NEW YORK. Player.	AB.	H.	O.	A.	ST. LOUIS. Player.	AB.	H.	O.	A.
Sturm.1b	5	1	6	0	Heffner,2b	5	2	2	5
Rolfe,3b	5	0	1	1	Clift,3b	4	0	2	2
Henrich,rf	3	1	1	0	McQuin,1b	5	2	11	2
DiMago.cf	5	2	2	0	Judnich,cf	4	1	3	0
Keller,lf	4	1	7	0	Cullenbn,lf	4	1	1	0
Dickey,c	4	1	5	0	Grace,rf	4	1	3	0
Gordon,2b	3	0	2	1	Ferrell,c	4	0	4	1
Rizzuto,ss	4	2	3	2	Strange,ss	2	0	1	2
Bonham,p	4	0	0	0	Lucadlo,ss	2	2	0	0
Murphy,p	0	0	0	0	Auker,p	1	0	0	0
					Muncrief,p	1	0	0	0
					Laabs	1	1	0	0
					Ostermlr,p	0	0	0	0
					Estalella	1	0	0	0
Totals	37	8	27	4	Totals	38	10	27	1?

Laabs batted for Muncrief in seventh.
Estalella batted for Ostermueller in ninth

New York	000 502 000—7
St. Louis	000 100 301—5

Runs—Henrich, Di Maggio, Keller, Dickey, Gordon 2, Rizzuto, McQuinn, Grace, Lucadello 2, Laabs. Errors — Rizzuto Clift, Cullenbine. Runs batted in—Di Maggio, Keller, Dickey 2, Cullenbine, Rizzuto, Sturm, Laabs 3, McQuinn. Two base hits—Di Maggio, Rizzuto, Henrich, Cullenbine. Home runs—Dickey, Laabs. Stolen base—Ruzzuto. Bases on balls—Off Bonham 2, Auker 2, Muncrief 1. Struck out by—Bonham 3, Murphy 2, Auker 1, Muncrief 1, Ostermueller 1. Hits—Off Auker 5 in 3 innings (none out in fourth; off Muncrief 3 in 4; off Ostermueller 0 in 2; off Bonham 7 in 7 1-3; off Murphy 3 in 1 2-3. Winning pitcher—Bonham. Losing pitcher—Auker.

Joe's New Goal: 61-Game Coast Mark! Anybody Wanna Bet He Doesn't Break It?

ST. LOUIS, July 12.—(AP)— Joe Di Maggio, after hitting safely in fifty-one consecutive games, has a new goal.

He wants to exceed his minor league record of sixty-one straight games, established when he was with the San Francisco Pacific Coast League baseball club in 1933.

And the New York Yankees centerfielder believes he can do it.

"It's up to the pitchers to stop me now. The way I feel now I don't believe I'll be my own undoing. The pressure's completely off now. I go to bat just as relaxed as if there never had been any streak."

The Yankee slugger disclosed today he first felt the strain after hitting in his thirty-third straight game May 16. Since the doubleheader when he tied and surpassed George Sisler's modern major league record of forty-one games the strain has diminished gradually and he feels swell now, Joe says.

His fan mail is keeping pace with his hitting.

"There it is for the last two days, forwarded from New York," he laughed, pointing to a huge sack of unopened letters.

Aided by his wife, Joe answers all fan mail, generally sending a post card with his autograph.

He admits that, of course, the hitting streak can't go on forever.

"It's gotta stop sometime. Then I'll try to break my own record."

A's End Spell, Triumph, 4-2, Over Indians

CLEVELAND, July 12.—(AP)—Connie Mack's scrappy Athletics cast off the Cleveland Indians' spell with a 4 to 2 victory today, pegged on Wally Moses' two run circuit clout and Lester McCrabb's five hit twirling.

The Philadelphia righthander's curve snapped the Tribe's string of eight straight triumphs over the Mackmen. It was McCrabb's seventh win of the season. The victim was Pitcher Al Milnar.

The Indians scored in the first with two out. Roy Weatherly doubled and Jeff Heath scored him with a two bagger.

The lead didn't last. With one down in the third Al Brancato singled, Moses walked and Benny McCoy singled, scoring Brancato. Dick Seibert doubled to tally McCoy.

Relief Pitcher Joe Heving started to warm up, but he didn't replace Milnar until after Brancato looped a Texas League single to center in the fifth stanza and Moses followed with a four bagger.

PHILADELPHIA Player	AB.	H.	O.	A.	CLEVELAND Player	AB.	H.	O.	A.
Brncto,ss	5	2	2	2	Boudru,ss	4	0	1	1
Moses,rf	4	2	3	0	Keltner,3b	3	0	0	4
McCoy,2b	5	2	1	1	Wthrly.cf	3	1	5	0
Johnsn,lf	4	1	4	0	Heath,rf	4	1	1	0
Siebert,1b	4	2	5	1	Cmpbell,lf	4	0	6	0
S.Cpmn,cf	4	2	3	0	Grimes,1b	4	1	8	1
Hayes,c	3	0	6	0	Mack,2b	4	2	3	5
Suder,3b	4	0	2	2	Des'tels,c	2	0	1	0
McCrbb,p	4	0	1	0	Rosenthal	0	0	0	0
					Hemsley,c	0	0	0	0
					Walker	1	0	0	0
					Milnar,p	2	0	1	0
					Trosky	1	0	0	0
					Heving,p	0	0	1	0
					Bell	1	0	0	0
Totals	37	11	27	6	Totals	33	5	27	11

Rosenthal batted for Desautels in 7th.
Trosky batted for Milnar in 7th.
Bell batted for Heving in 9th.
Walker batted for Hemsley in 9th.

Philadelphia	002 020 000—4
Cleveland	100 000 100—2

Runs — Brancato 2, Moses, McCoy, Weatherly, Grimes. Errors—Heath, Brancato. Runs batted in—Heath, McCoy, Siebert, Moses 2, Mack. Two base hits—Weatherly, Heath, Siebert, Grimes. Home run—Moses. Stolen base—Grimes. Double play—Boudreau to Mack to Grimes. Bases on balls—Off McCrabb 3, Milnar 2. Struck out—By McCrabb 4. Hits—Off Milnar 10 in 7 innings; Heving 1 in 2. Losing pitcher—Milnar.

Walters Puts Halt To Brooklyn, 3-2

BROOKLYN, July 12.—(AP)—Bucky Walters slowed up the red hot Brooklyn Dodgers today by pitching a superlative six-hitter to give the stumbling world champion Cincinnati Reds a nerve tingling 3 to 2 victory before 16,022 fans.

In spite of the loss the league leaders remained three and one half games ahead of the St. Louis Cardinals, who were beaten by the New York Giants, 6-4.

The Reds had been blasted by Brooklyn bats for two days, but today Walters weakened in only one inning—the eighth—when the Dodgers pushed across their two tallies.

Jumping on Whitlow Wyatt, the league's top-flight hurler in victories, the Reds jammed over two runs in the first frame. Lloyd Waner beat out an infield hit and Linus Frey was tagged with a pitched ball. After Frank McCormick popped out, Harry Craft singled in Waner and Frey scored when Pete Reiser threw wild past the plate.

Singles by Eddie Joost and Walters and Bill Werber's grounder scored the winning Red run in the seventh.

It was Walters' eleventh win of the year against six losses.

CINCINNATI Player	AB.	H.	O.	A.	BROOKLYN Player	AB.	H.	O.	A.
Werber,3b	4	0	1	2	Walker,rf	4	1	4	1
Waner,rf	4	1	0	0	Herman,2b	4	0	4	2
Frey,2b	3	0	1	3	Reiser,cf	4	3	2	0
F.M'Ck,1b	4	1	11	2	Riggs,3b	3	0	0	0
Craft,cf	3	1	3	0	Camilli,1b	3	0	6	0
M.M'Ck,lf	4	0	3	0	Medwick,lf	4	0	2	0
Joost,ss	4	1	3	3	Reese,cc	3	1	2	1
West.c	3	1	4	0	Owen,c	2	0	6	2
Walters,p	3	1	1	3	Frank,cs	1	0	1	0
					Wyatt,p	2	1	0	2
					Wasdell	1	0	0	0
					Brown,p	0	0	0	0
Totals	32	6	27	13	Totals	31	6	27	8

Wasdell batted for Wyatt in 8th.

Cincinnati	200 000 100—3
Brooklyn	000 000 020—2

Runs—Waner, Frey, Joost, Walker, Reese. Errors—Reiser, Reese 2. Runs batted in—Craft, Werber, Franks, Walker. Two base hits—F. McCormick, Reiser, Reese. Three base hit—Reiser. Home run—Walker. Sacrifices—Craft, West, Riggs. Double plays—Walker to Owen; F. McCormick to Joost. Bases on balls—Off Walters 1. Struck out—By Walters 4, Wyatt 4, Brown 1. Hits—Off Wyatt 6 in 8 innings; Brown 0 in 1. Hit by pitcher—By Wyatt (Frey). Passed ball—West. Losing pitcher—Wyatt.

Chapman Gets Two Singles; Dom Slips, Joe Holds Steady

Joe Di Maggio rung up Number 51 with a double and a single in five trips yesterday and held steady at .365. Joe batted in a run to maintain his major league lead in that department and scored once.

Sammy Chapman continued his climb with two singles in four trips which boosted his average two points to .332.

Dom Di Maggio suffered a six point slump when he collected a lone single in nine appearances during a doubleheader. He batted in one run.

Eddie Joost hit a single and scored a run in three trips; Vince Di Maggio gained a point with a single in three tries and Joe Orengo was idle.

	AB.	R.	H.	HR.	3B.	2B.	RBI.	Pct.
Joe Di Maggio	312	69	114	20	4	22	74	.365
Sam Chapman	268	45	89	9	6	20	41	.332
Dom Di Maggio	307	73	93	4	3	23	26	.303
Eddie Joost	266	27	70	2	1	17	21	.263
Vince Di Maggio	236	30	60	10	1	10	45	.254
Joe Orengo	191	18	43	4	2	3	22	.225

FOUR ACES WIN PENNANT FOR YANKEES—Manager Joe McCarthy, at the right, grins contentedly as he looks at four aces taken from his deck of flag winners. The first three (left to right), Red Ruffing, Lefty Gomez and Bill Dickey, have made comebacks this season, while Joe DiMaggio, who set a 56-game consecutive batting streak, is appropriately pictured as the ace of clubs.

Yanks Cop Flag; Sox Drop to 3d

By MELVILLE WEBB

The Yankees are "in."

Already winning 91 ball games, they now may proceed to lose every remaining engagement and still remain the 1941 champions, even if the White Sox and the Red Sox are not beaten again this year.

The McCarthymen, whose helmsman will not take up the managerial burden again for a few days, slammed Heber Newsome and then Mickey Harris to win over the Red Sox, 6 to 3, at Fenway yesterday. They presented a much broken down team, but it was good enough.

This year's pennant was put in the old bag five days earlier than when the Yanks were the topnotchers, five years ago—as they started on their way to four successive American League pennants.

★ ★ ★

Because they lost to the Yankees yesterday while the Jimmie Dykes Chicagos were not playing, the Cronin Sox today are down in third place.

Out of first money altogether, they now will have more than three weeks battling, against New York and the Western clubs, in hopes of landing the second place purse, which will mean approximately $1200 a man. The purse, however, is still far from the Red Sox' grasp.

Cronin will have to do some tall thinking as he regathers his outfit for the final charge. Jimmie Foxx has a bothersome stiff neck; Pete Fox wrenched his left ankle yesterday chasing a Keller fly and perhaps there is a fracture; Lou Finney received a spike cut over his right eye, in charge at second base—and neither Tex Hughson nor Bob Grove will be available for flinging for the little trip over to the Yankee Stadium which will open tomorrow.

Fans Out to See Williams

Several years ago George Herman Ruth (the "Babe") received from the Yankee management, a purse of $10,000 for "bringing in the crowds."

Wonder if the Fenway management will figure that for the past week. Teddy Williams, more than anyone else on the ball club has kept the turnstiles singing.

In three games with the Macks, two with the Senators and two with the Yankees starting last Saturday, a total of 80,264 ball fans have paid to see the Sox perform on the Jersey-st. grounds.

At only 60 cents per head as the Red Sox' share per customer—and that's putting it low—the Yawkey management has had a yield of more than $48,000 in the last six days—one of them open.

There's just one answer to that patronage—Ted Williams.

Teddy the "Big Show"

With the Sox hopelessly out of first place, and still in a battle even for a first division berth, it has been Williams who has stood out as the big drawing card, and the showman of the Red Sox as well.

In the recent home games with Macks, Senators and Yanks, Ted has been at the plate officially 16 times, and he has turned in a .500 hitting mark with eight hits, no less than five of which have been home runs.

In the seven games, of which the Sox have won four while losing three, Ted has hammered in 10 runs, and has scored four in addition to those produced on his own circuit clouts.

With Ted at bat the crowds have been breathless. They have resented the frequent base-on-ball service; but in only one of the seven games has Teddy missed fire as a hitter.

Braves Home Tomorrow

Rained out in New York yesterday, the Braves will perform at the Giants' Polo Grounds today, and will then return to the Wigwam for a single game with the Phillies tomorrow and a double bill Sunday.

The week-end tuneups will be to prepare for the fourth and final invasion of the National League's western territory, which will start next week.

The Braves will finish at home late in the month, with the Dodgers and Giants coming to the Gaffney-st. yard over the season's last week-end.

Boston fans well may see the World Series contenders in final scheduled action as the Yanks are due here on Sept. 20 and 21 and the Dodgers on Sept. 23, 24 and 25.

HIT AND RUN

Those Yankees won their pennant mainly because of that fine July spurt. . . . "Red" Rolfe is at the Massachusetts General Hospital with reported intestinal grip, and probably will remain under observation until the Yanks return here about 16 days hence. . . . Lou Finney's cut over the right eye did not amount to much, and he will accompany the club to New York at 3 this afternoon. . . . Joe Cronin who finished yesterday's game in left field, says he never before undertook to fill a major league garden berth in his life.

* * *

Playing all the coming World Series games in the New York Stadium in event of the Dodgers being drawn against the Yankees seems definitely "out." . . . Also the Polo grounds, although there's still a chance that the Dodgers will make the late John McGraw's home field their own for the coming series. . . . But one never can tell just how tightly Judge Landis will bolt down the lid. . . . The Commissioner always has frowned on anything favoring just a money-making gag.

* * *

The Yanks won their pennant without much ado. . . . There was a little back-c-back slapping—that was all. . . . The boys however centered on Atley Donald who finished out the necessary string with one finely pitched ball game. . . . Imagine the Sox almost finishing a game with Spence at first base. Carey at second, Newsome at short, Cronin in left and Teddy Williams in right. . . . A. C.—World series tickets are sold in sets of three, with rights to purchase a possible seventh game ticket included.

* * *

The Braves are now dragging up much minor league talent for Fall work. but Rudy Hulswitt thinks a lot of infielder John Dudra from Bridgeport. . . . Hulswitt regards the youngster as very much a potential major league infielder. . . . The boy hit for about a .315 clip this season down in Connecticut. . . . Jack Onslow's in town, looking for somebody to put a new stock on that shotgun of his. . . . Rumors persist that there'll be light for seven night games at the Wigwam another season.

* * *

Braves have won five of the eight home games played against the lowly Phillies this season, and have taken seven of 11 games at Shibe Park. . . . The Tigers, who will be at Fenway the first of the week already have taken six of the nine games played at the Yawkey yard, but have been on the short end of a 6-5 decision out in Detroit. . . . Jimmie Dykes' Chicago gang cost the Sox about $200 a man on the final day of 1940. . . . Now the White Sox again are running neck and neck with the Cronins down the three weeks stretch to the finish

Star of the Month Contest

Yesterday's Points

Mickey Harris	2
Lou Finney	2
L Newsome	1
Johnny Peacock	1

Total to Date

Prev. Total		Sept.	Prev. Total		Sept.
85	Williams	4	55	Tabor	0
16	Dobson	3	41	H Newsome	0
67	Cronin	3	40	Doerr	0
39	Finney	3	31	Grove	0
52	DiMaggio	3	22	Spence	0
31	Wagner	2	18	Pytlak	0
25	Fox	2	18	Ryba	0
27	Harris	2	17	Wilson	0
16	Peacock	1	14	Johnson	0
10	L Newsome	1	13	Hughson	0
63	Foxx	0	1	Potter	0

Major League Baseball

Yesterday's Results

AMERICAN LEAGUE

	R	H	E
New York	6	10	1
Boston	3	5	2
Cleveland	7	12	1
Detroit	6	10	3

Philadelphia-Washington, rain.
Only games scheduled.

NATIONAL LEAGUE

	R	H	E
Chicago (1st game)	3	6	1
St Louis	0	5	2
Chicago (2d game)	4	9	0
St Louis (11 innings)	3	9	5
Pittsburg	4	5	1
Cincinnati (Five innings)	0	1	1

Brooklyn-Philadelphia, rain.
Boston-New York, rain.

League Standings

AMERICAN LEAGUE

G B		Won	Lost	Pct
....	New York	91	45	.669
20	Chicago	70	64	.522
20½	BOSTON	70	65	.519
22½	Cleveland	66	65	.504
26	Detroit	64	70	.478
30½	St Louis	58	73	.443
31	Philadelphia	58	74	.439
33½	Washington	54	75	.419

NATIONAL LEAGUE

G B		Won	Lost	Pct
....	Brooklyn	85	47	.644
1	St Louis	83	47	.638
13	Cincinnati	70	58	.547
13½	Pittsburg	70	59	.543
21	New York	62	66	.484
26	Chicago	60	74	.448
31	BOSTON	52	76	.406
46½	Philadelphia	37	92	.287

Today's Games and Probable Pitchers

(Won-Lost Records in Parentheses)

American League

Cleveland at Detroit—Smith (9-11) vs. Newsom (11-17).
St. Louis at Chicago (night)—Auker (13-13) vs. Ross (3-8).
Only games scheduled.

National League

Cincinnati at Pittsburg (2)—Derringer (10-13) and Turner (5-4) vs. Bucher (15-10) and Dietz (5-1).
Only games scheduled.

FIVE LEADING BATTERS

American League

	G	AB	R	BH	Avg
Williams, Red Sox	124	392	122	161	.411
Travis, Senators	127	514	93	185	.360
DiMaggio, Yanks	124	485	114	172	.355
Heath, Indians	129	499	84	172	.345
McCosky, Tigers	105	407	65	140	.344

National League

	G	AB	R	BH	Avg
Reiser, Dodgers	117	459	100	153	.333
Hopp, Cards	110	353	70	115	.326
Etten, Phillies	126	454	67	146	.322
Mize, Cards	112	430	64	138	.321
Walker, Dodgers	127	443	77	140	.316

HOME RUN STANDING

American League

Williams, Red Sox	34
Keller, Yankees	33
DiMaggio, Yankees	27
Henrich, Yankees	27

National League

Camilli, Dodgers	29
Ott, Giants	27
Nicholson, Cubs	24

RUNS BATTED IN

American League

Keller, Yankees	120
DiMaggio, Yankees	112
Williams, Red Sox	106

National League

Camilli, Dodgers	97
Mize, Cardinals	96
Young, Giants	91

Cards Hand Dodgers Lead by Twin Defeat

By JUDSON BAILEY
Associated Press Sports Writer

Today's best advice for baseball fans is to get your nickels ready for a subway series—the New York Yankees have clinched the American League pennant and the Brooklyn Dodgers have been handed the National League lead on a big, brimming platter.

The Yanks bombed their way to their fifth championship in six years yesterday by smashing the Boston Red Sox, 6—3, with a 10-hit assault on two of Boston's best pitchers, Dick Newsome and Mickey Harris, while Atley Donald was holding the Red Sockers in check on five safeties.

The New Yorkers thus achieved their 91st victory against 45 defeats for a 20-game lead over the Chicago White Sox—who regained exclusive possession of second place through the crumbling of the Red Sox.

Earliest Pennant Verdict

The triumph, which put the Yanks out of reach of all rivals, clinched the pennant at the earliest date in American League history.

All this was no surprise to anyone. The noise like distant thunder heard in the major leagues yesterday was the St. Louis Cardinals crashing in a double-header at Chicago, 3—0 and 4—3.

The Redbirds were presented with the same kind of golden opportunity Brooklyn had fumbled on Wednesday. On that day St. Louis was rained out and the Dodgers had a chance to take charge of the senior circuit by paddling the last-place Phillies in a doubleheader. Brooklyn divided the contests and left the Cards on top of the league.

Yesterday it was Brooklyn that was rained into idleness and the Cardinals who played a double-header with the same huge reward at stake. But they not only muffed the opportunity, their double defeat dropped them one full game back of Brooklyn.

The Cardinals started two of their finest pitchers, Lon Warneke, fresh from his no-hitter at Cincinnati, and the skillful Mort Cooper, but each had to be removed in the fourth inning.

Passeau Blanks Redbirds

Claude Passeau, a great clutch hurler for the sixth-place Cubs, shut out St. Louis, 3—0, on five hits in the opener. Chicago collected one run in the first, one in the second and another in the fourth, and the no-hit relief pitching of Max Lanier and Howard Krist from that point on was not sufficient to change the outcome.

The nightcap was a bitter battle that went 11 innings and was decided by the Cardinals' most glaring weakness—uncertain fielding. The Redbirds made five errors, and on the last outfielder Don Padgett dropped a fly ball to let in the winning run after Stan Hack had walked and gone to third on a single by Lou Stringer. The score was 4-3.

PICTURE OF GLOOM—Manager Billy Southworth appears ready to weep after his Cards dropped two games to Cubs yesterday.

Cooper was wild at the start and let the Cubs score single runs in each of the first three innings. St. Louis again received fine relief pitching to no avail, Howard Pollet and Lanier hurling seven scoreless innings.

Paul Erickson went the rout for the Cubs and, after giving St. Louis two runs in the second, allowed only one other tally—a homer by Johnny Mize in the sixth. Babe Dahlgren hit his 20th of the season in the second for Chicago.

Feller Finally Wins 22d

The Pittsburg Pnrates closed the gap between them and the third-place Reds to a half-game by beating Cincinnati again, 4-0, before rain halted play in the last of the fifth. Rip Sewell held the World Champions to one hit over this abbreviated distance while the Pirates pelted Bucky Walters for five.

Bob Feller finally got his 22d triumph, but it took a three-run rally in the 10th inning by his Cleveland Indians to nose out Detroit, 7-6. The Tigers scored twice in their half of the 10th.

Sports Mirror

By the Associated Press

TODAY A YEAR AGO—Ted Schroeder eliminated Bryan (Bitsy) Grant, 2—6, 6—3, 9—7, 8—6, in fourth round of national singles tennis tourney.

THREE YEARS AGO—Don Bu[illegible]e beat Adrian Quist of Australia, 8—[illegible], 6—1, 6—2, to clinch Davis Cup for United States, three matches to two.

FIVE YEARS AGO—Giants' National League lead cut to 2½ games over St. Louis by double loss to Chicago Cubs, as Cards beat Reds.

Braves Keeping Roberge for '42

By GERRY MOORE

The Braves are back in Boston today, preparing to entertain the Phillies in a three-game week-end series at Allston before the Tribe embarks on its final Western swing of the waning season.

While Prof. Casey Stengel is becoming more determined with each succeeding hour to pursue a New Faces policy as far as is possible for 1942, one youngster who seems certain of being among those present when another season rolls around is Al (Skip) Roberge, the Lowell product. Stengel strongly hinted as much yesterday just before leading his charges back to Boston on a 3 o'clock train when a scheduled twin bill with the Giants was washed out.

★ ★ ★

"One of my plans for the forthcoming western trip calls for Young Roberge to see plenty of action at second base," disclosed Casey. "Although the kid has been with us only about a month he has shown me enough to warrant counting on him for next year. While he may not be able to snag a regular job right off, I think he has the perfect makeup for a valuable utility infielder.

"If you know Al's minor league record, he already has starred at both third and second," went on Casey. "Recently I tried him at shortstop when I decided to give Eddie Miller a little rest and the kid looked good enough there so that you can figure on him playing any one of three positions if needed. Moreover, Al is a fair hitter who may improve more at the bat. Above all, it is easy for him to keep in condition although not playing regularly and that is a most valuable asset for a utility player."

Introducing John Dudra

One of the new Tribal members who may see some action at Allston over the weekend is John Dudra, a 23-year-old infielder who joined the varsity in New York this week after dividing the Summer between the Braves' farms at Hartford and Bridgeport.

Although Dudra comes up with little fanfare, he has compiled a fair record during his four seasons in organized ball. A native of Pana, Ill., the 175-pound, near six-footer, was first recommended to the Owensboro, Ky., club in the Kitty League by the Cubs. Dudra spent two seasons at Owensboro hitting .295 and .316. Last year at York, Penn., he batted .280 and this year after only a brief stay at Hartford swung at a .300 clip for Bridgeport, where he played both second and third.

Dudra's closest pal on the Braves is Lil' Abner Al Javery, since their careers have been strangely linked.

"Some time or another during each of the four years I've been pitching, I've been in the same league with Johnny either as an opponent or teammate," dislosed the North Oxford right-hander.

"That's right," concurred Dudra, "and I hope the same will hold true next year because it looks as if you'll be staying along with the varsity, Jave."

BRAVES BITS

While discussing some of his other minor league prospects, Stengel enthused over the fact that Frank McElyea, the towering first baseman whom the Tribe took to San Antonio last Spring, stole 42 bases for Evansville during the regular Three-I League season. . . . "Bob Coleman told me the big guy could have stolen 65 if Bob had wanted him to," revealed Casey. "According to Coleman, McElyea stole home once without even having to slide. You've got to take another look at a big guy who can run that fast." . . . Another apple of Casey's eye, of course, is Warren Spahn, the 18-year-old Buffalo southpaw who hurled five shutouts and some 18 victories for the pennant-winning Evansville forces this year.

* * *

Although Ole John Cooney is nursing a foot injury that may sideline him for the Philly series, the Cranston veteran continues to prove the big name of the Braves. . . . Two New York writers are readying feature yarns about John for national weeklies. . . . Buddy Hassett also has a sore foot. . . . Buddy spiked himself in Philadelphia. . . . If both Johns are hors de combat for the week-end, Buddy Gremp and Frank Demaree will take over their posts. . . . Jim Tobin goes after his 13th victory in tomorrow's single tilt at Allston, while Roxbury Tom Earley and Manny Salvo will work the Sabbath duet during which Stan Benjamin, the Framingham boy with the Quakers, will be honored by home town friends. . . . As the result of yesterday's postponement, the Braves will be forced to play three double-headers in as many days with the Giants in New York the week of Sept. 20, when the Tribe stops off on the way back from the West. . . . One reason the Giants were not anxious to play off the two games today, which is open date for both clubs, is that Col. Bill Terry is in Memphis, where his son is ill.

Billy McPherson Named Manager of Boston Celts

By GEORGE M. COLLINS

Billy McPherson, former Fall River "great" in the halcyon days when the Marksmen were winning national soccer championships with a regularity that made the opposition dizzy, has been appointed manager of the Boston Celts S. C. of the American League.

This move is expected to reconcile the factions that make up the Irish club and prevent the too

BILLY McPHERSON

many "master minds" from trying to direct the team afield. McPherson also should have the backing of all the Quincy section where many of the players come from.

McPherson hopes to make this the Celts' year. Admitting that the other teams will be strengthened, Billy expects they will do well against all comers once they have scored a few early season wins. He plans to give all the younger players a real chance to make the grade.

Hugh Toner and Jack McPartland will lend their aid on the business end of the club. Now all that is needed is for Secretary W. R. Welch to give the Celts a good opening attraction.

Baseball Brains Discuss Changes in Present Rules

CINCINNATI, Sept. 5 (AP)—Some of the brains of the baseball industry get together today to discuss proposed rule changes for the sport, both in major and minor leagues.

Any recommendations that come out of the all-day conversations will be subject to ratification at the Winter baseball meetings.

Conferees include Ford Frick, president of the National League, and Will Harridge, head of the American; Sam Breadon of the St. Louis Cardinals, Warren C. Giles of the Cincinnati Reds, Clark Griffith of the Washington Senators, George Trautman of the American Association and Maj. Trammell Scott of the Southern Association.

Trautman and Maj. Scott are members of the executive committee of the National Association of Baseball Clubs, which ordered reinstatement as of today of Eddie Mayo of the Los Angeles club in the Pacific Coast League. Mayo was suspended on charges of spitting in an umpire's face, but was cleared.

The committee denied reinstatement to Julio Bonetti of the same club, who was placed on the ineligible list on charges of associating with gamblers.

Toz Dumfounds Skeptics; Keeps Word to Saugus

DAILY BOOST

To the Chicago Cubs for knocking off the Cards twice to tighten up that National League dog fight just that much more.

By HAROLD KAESE

A lot of incredulous skeptics, accustomed to the magnetism of the dollar, the tenor of the times and the practices of football coaches, should have nervous breakdowns trying to figure out this one: Henry Toczylowski of Lynn, great Boston College quarterback and blocker of the last three years, has chosen to coach Saugus High School for $2200 this Fall, rather than play with the Brooklyn Dodgers in the National Football League for $6200.

But while the skeptics are having their breakdowns, the rest of us ordinary mortals who are sufficiently naive to have Faith will be applauding the idealism which must have inspired this sacrifice by Hammering Hank, the quiet and efficient leader who sand-bagged prospective tacklers while the O'Rourkes, Connollys and Montgomerys hot-footed it to fame.

Last evening Toz told Vernon S. Evans, superintendent of schools in Saugus, that he would fulfill his contract calling for him to coach football and teach English at Saugus High. Today he was telling Dan Topping, owner of the Dodgers, that, thanks, he would not play three months of football with the Dodgers for $6200.

This was a mighty decision! Toz never made one to equal it in the heat of conflict. Holovak over right guard, O'Rourke off tackle, a long pass to Currivan, a flat one to Maznicki—grammar school stuff that, compared with this cold-blooded weighing of dollars and cents.

★ ★ ★

What to Do Before Entering Navy

The problem was difficult. It involved principle. These were the leaden facts his conscience wrestled with:

He joined the Naval Reserve only a few weeks ago, after it became clear that he was on the verge of being drafted by the Army, and will go to school at Northwestern University with the intention of becoming a commissioned officer. He leaves in May, if his choice is observed. Otherwise he goes in January. Once in, he will not get out until the war is settled one way or another.

Thus, he was left with only a few months of freedom. How should he spend them? There was the Saugus contract, signed last Jan. 21, when he ignored the $75-a-game offer to play pro football for Brooklyn. He could go through with it and collect part of the $2200 at least. Or he could accept the Dodgers offer which had ballooned to $6200 by the time he left Topping and Jock Sutherland standing in the Polo Grounds dressing room after the All-Star-Giants game Wednesday night.

The Dodgers wanted him badly! They had lost eight or 10 men in the draft. Besides, Sutherland liked his style. They started raising the ante during All-Star preparations at Cornwall-on-the-Hudson. It soared to $6200, and that if he were hurt in the first minute of the first game or played every minute of every game.

This was a magnificent offer. Ace Parker of the Dodgers, most-valuable player in the league last year, received only $6000. It was the kind of money only a super-star like Sammy Baugh could better.

★ ★ ★

Asked 30 People Before Deciding

The Saugus officials made it clear that they would not stand in his way. They understood that Toczylowski's coaching future after this Fall would be problematical at best. They were generous enough not to bar a youngster's chance to grab $6000.

These details dinned through Toczylowski's mind as he trained with the All-Stars, day after day, night after night. The way was open . . . $6200 . . . three months . . . then the Navy . . . only $2200 . . . coaching some kids at a small high school . . . no more headlines . . . no more blocks, and tackles, and passes . . . $6200 . . .

Hammering Hank worried about calling this next play. Comrades knew it at Cornwall-on-the-Hudson. Friends became aware of it in the Polo Grounds dressing room. He consulted the men he respected most, asked their advice.

"I asked at least 30 people what to do," he admitted last night. "They told me what they'd do, but in the end it didn't do any good. One man had to make the decision, and that one man was me."

He made the decision. With the example of dozens of famous coaches before him, men who had broken or been released from contracts on their way up the ladder, Hammering Hank kept a promise. It cost him $4000 to keep this pledge to Saugus High, but for a fellow like Hank that must be a cheap price for a clear conscience.

DAILY KNOCK

To Roy Conacher, glamorous left-winger of the Bruins, for breaking scores of Boston hearts by announcing his engagement to a gal from far-off Saskatchewan.

Cricket Drives

George Bray, Arlington Mills' top-notch bowler, and his teammates will try to do tomorrow what no other team in the State Cricket League has been able to do—defeat West India at Methuen. It will be up to Bray and "Red" Whigham to handcuff Benn, Layne and Co.

* * *

West India is riding high at present in the race because so far Willie Fraser, Keezer, Cox and Roach have been performing like champions. All the boys are fielding likely hits and that's what counts plenty.

* * *

Jack Snowdon, Jim Fletcher and "Slugger" Allfrey of Malden face the rejuvenated Wanderers at Hunting Field, Linden, tomorrow. Doherty, Hickman, Howson and the Normans want to win this clash i[n] the worst way.

* * *

Elliott, Robinson, Cook, Lamy and Jenkinson will experience real opposition when Chandler, Foulks, Callander and Lane get busy with their bats. Wanderers have won their last two games.

* * *

Windsors are due to meet Newton C. C. at Franklin Field. With Kelly, Margerison, Hicks, Simpson and Rev. Dudley Tyng on the field for the visitors, Messrs. Parkes, Evans, Roberts, Allen and Burton can prepare for a battle. This clash looks real good for Dorchester fans.

Yankees Clinch Pennant in Record Time; Idle Dodgers Regain Lead as Cards Lose 2 to Cubs

Players Let Out a Few 'Whoops' After Defeating Red Sox, 6 to 3

McCarthy and DiMaggio Miss Earliest Winning of Major-League Flag; Donald Checks Boston Sluggers as New York's Attack Routs Newsome

By Arthur E. Patterson

BOSTON, Sept. 4.—Perhaps it will come as no surprise to our readers but it's official now at any rate. The Yankees are "in"—champions of the American League for 1941, winners of that crown for the fifth time in six years and the twelfth time in the history of the club.

With Marse Joe McCarthy, recuperating in New York from a recent illness, and Joe DiMaggio, whose great hitting feats in May, June and July spurred the old champions in their comeback also left behind to rest an injured ankle, the other Yankees piloted by Art Fletcher, put over the knockout blow today as Atley Donald beat the Boston Red Sox, 6 to 3.

By clinching the pennant on this date with ninety-one victories the Yankees set an all-time record for runaway triumphs. The 1936 Yankees, who put the title mathematically out of reach on Sept. 9 with an eighteen-game lead, had been the early-birds of baseball history, excepting of course the abbreviated 1918 World War season.

As they put on the finishing touches today the Bronx Bombers led the idle White Sox by twenty lengths.

Triumph After Slow Start

Lowered to third place in 1940 after four straight world championships but re-upholstered by recruits from Kansas City, Phil Rizzuto, shortstop; Johnny Sturm, first baseman, and Gerry Priddy, utility man, the Yankees, after a slow start, zoomed ahead of the favored Cleveland Indians on June 28 and have been adding to their monumental lead ever since.

For more than a month their eventual victory has been a foregone conclusion and so this afternoon, as Rizzuto retired Lamar Newsome for the final out, the Yankees experienced considerable difficulty in mustering a few weak "whoops" as they rushed for the 6 o'clock train.

They were champions. Sure. But they'd known that for sometime. There wasn't much to get excited about.

While this pennant, like all others won by the Yankees under McCarthy, had been accomplished by clear cut dominance it really was the result of one cruising drive which ran concurrently with DiMaggio's fifty-six game hitting streak. During that skein they jumped from fourth place, five and a half games behind Cleveland, to first, six lengths in front of them.

Opposition Paralyzed

In one stretch of fifty-two games they lost only eight and in the full month between June 28, the day they stepped into first place to stay, and July 27 they won thirty out of thirty-three, paralyzing the opposition. That surge included their top consecutive-victory streak — fourteen—from June 28 to July 13.

DiMaggio's hitting havoc, stopped for one night at Cleveland when Ken Keltner robbed him of a hit and helped Jim Bagby and Al Smith halt him, was resumed the next afternoon and continued until he had hit in seventy-two out of seventy-three games. In that overall bombardment by the star slugger, stretched from May 15 to Aug. 2, the Yankees won fifty-five and lost sixteen and they were twelve and a half games in front when DiMag finally was limited to spasmodic slugging.

On Aug. 18 he was injured at Detroit, spraining his left ankle. He has been at bat just once since—in an exhibition game at Kansas City. After a brief slump without him, the Yankees gathered momentum again and moved to their twelfth flag with ten victories in their most recent twelve games.

Despite injuries to DiMaggio, Charlie Keller and Bill Dickey, the ailments of Buddy Rosar and McCarthy and Red Ruffing's stiff neck the Yankees, if not the healthiest were still the best team in the American League at the finish.

Yankees Pound Newsome

The decisive game if such it can be called was an exciting affair with the Sox, battling to defend second place, coming back after Dick Newsome's early ineffectiveness to make it a contest. Newsome, seeking victory No. 17, was bashed for two runs after two out in the first when Tommy Henrich was hit by a pitched ball and Keller followed with a double and Twink Selkirk with a single. A single by Sturm, Rizzuto's safe bunt, Henrich's double and a wild pitch by Mickey Harris, who succeeded Newsome after the Henrich blow, put over two more in the third.

Donald, slipping through a troublesome second, was tagged for two in the third when Dom DiMaggio doubled and, after two out, both Joe Cronin and Ted Williams walked.

With the bases filled, Lou Finney singled two home. The Yankees got those two back in the sixth, thanks to an error by Cronin. After Joe Gordon singled and Priddy walked, Donald hit what should have been an inning-ending double play ball to Skeeter Newsome, but Cronin dropped the throw at second and the bases were thus filled. Rosar batted for Sturm and lofted to center, Gordon scoring after the catch, and Rizzuto's single sent Priddy over.

Then the Sox scored on the third base on balls to Williams, Finney's single and a double-play grounder. Finney was spiked in the head by Gordon during the twin killing, but left the field unaided.

Double Play No. 167

The Sox put on a real threat in the eighth when Cronin and Williams singled, but Bobby Doerr, pinch hitting for Tom Carey, fanned and on the last strike Dickey whipped the ball down to Gordon for Yankee double play No. 167. Even in a clincher one can't forget these little statistics. The Yankees, in their last eighteen games, need twenty twin killings to tie a league record. They haven't much else to do so they'll probably concentrate on it.

Red Rolfe, latest patient in the Yankee infirmary, was left at Phillips House Hospital for a week's observation. He is suffering from an intestinal disorder.

Yankees' Score

* * *

NEW YORK (A. L.)	ab	r	h	po	a	BOSTON (A. L.)	ab	r	h	po	a
Sturm, 1b.	3	1	1	7	0	D.DiM'o,cf	4	1	1	3	0
*Rosar....	1	0	0	0	0	Fox, rf....	2	0	0	0	0
Crosetti,3b	1	0	0	1	1	S'nce,rf,1b	2	0	0	3	0
Rizzuto, ss	5	1	3	2	2	Cro'n,ss, lf	3	1	1	1	1
Henrich,cf	4	1	1	2	0	Wi'ms,lf,rf	1	1	1	2	0
Keller, lf..	4	1	1	0	0	Finney, 1b	3	0	2	6	1
Selkirk, rf	5	0	1	2	0	Carey, 2b.	0	0	0	1	2
Dickey, c..	4	0	0	3	1	Doerr, 2b..	1	0	0	1	0
Gordon, 2b	4	1	2	5	6	Tabor, 3b..	4	0	0	0	3
Pr'dy,3b,1b	3	1	1	5	1	Peacock, c.	4	0	0	5	0
Donald, p.	4	0	0	0	3	L.N'e,2b,ss	4	0	0	5	5
						H. New'e,p	0	0	0	0	0
						Harris, p..	3	0	0	0	1
Totals..	38	6	10	27	14	Totals...	31	3	5	27	13

*Batted for Sturm in sixth inning.

New York........... 202 002 000—6
Boston............. 002 001 000—3

Errors—Gordon, Tabor, Cronin. Runs batted in—Henrich, Keller, Selkirk, Rosar, Rizzuto, Finney (2). Two-base hits—Henrich, Keller, D. DiMaggio. Double plays—Crosetti, Gordon and Priddy; Dickey and Gordon; Cronin, L. Newsome and Finney. Left on bases—New York, 8; Boston, 5. Bases on balls—Off Donald, 4; off Harris, 2. Struck out—By Donald, 3; by Harris, 4. Hits—Off H. Newsome, 6 in 2 innings (none out in third); off Harris, 4 in 7. Wild pitch—Harris. Hit by pitcher—By H. Newsome (Henrich). Losing pitcher—H. Newsome. Umpires—Stewart, Summers and Rue. Time—2:05. Attendance—13,088.

Dodgers Pick Davis to Open Against Giants

Pace Setters, Rained Out in Philadelphia, Prepare for Ebbets Field Series

By Rud Rennie

Brooklyn's Dodgers and the Phillies were in uniform, ready to play yesterday in Shibe Park when the game was called off on account of wet grounds, but really because of a total lack of customers. However, it was a great day for the idle Dodgers. They went back into first place as the Cardinals fell before the Cubs in a double-header.

"I'd like to have got this game out of the way," said Leo Durocher. "Now we'll have five games with the Phillies in three days right on top of the next Western trip."

With no game, the Dodgers caught an early train for New York. They have an open date in their schedule today. Then they play three games with the Giants over the week end before starting on the final and highly important Western trip.

Durocher has his pitching selections all ready for the impending series with the Giants and also the big series with the Cardinals.

Davis to Start Saturday

"I'll start Curt Davis in Saturday's game," he said, "and will go with Kirby Higbe and Whitlow Wyatt in Sunday's double-header. And Fred Fitzsimmons, Wyatt and Davis will pitch in the Cardinal series."

Durocher and the Dodgers were still moaning yesterday about the twist of fate which caused Frank Hoerst to pitch his only good game of the year against them in the nightcap of Wednesday's double-header.

"It looked like a soft touch," said Durocher. "I figure it is a good spot to take a look at my new pitcher, Buster Albosta. If we had not won the first game I would not have started him. But I do, and Hoerst has to be hot for the first time this year. But, despite the fact that he got beat, Albosta showed me enough to satisfy me that I can shove him in when I need help."

Albosta, a six-foot-one rookie from Durham, took his unfortunate debut philosophically. "I was a little nervous at the start," he said, "but I calmed down."

The new pitcher feels more at home on the ball field than he does in the hustle and bustle of New York, which is all new to him. He was born in Saginaw, Mich., and went to high school there.

"I was an outfielder on the baseball team and a center on the basketball team," he said. "I was on the All-Valley team." He smiled self-consciously, adding, "I hit .375."

Was Scouted for Tigers

He started pitching in his senior year in high school and was scouted by Wish Eagan for the Tigers. He also played some semi-pro ball. He could have had a scholarship at Michigan State, but he preferred to start making real money as soon as possible in baseball.

In 1938 he signed with Welch, W. Va. The next year he was with Hot Springs. And that winter he was one of the many Tiger farm hands declared free agents by Judge K. M. Landis.

So he sold himself to Montreal for $1,600 and passed the 1940 season with Dayton. This year he won fifteen and lost five for Durham, fanning 151.

Yankees Whoop It Up in Dressing Room After Clinching Pennant

Beating the Boston Red Sox, 6 to 3, yesterday in Boston, the New York club set the earliest flag-winning date in American League history. Here the players register their joy. At extreme right is Atley Donald, who pitched the deciding game, and second from left is Arthur Fletcher, acting manager in the absence of Joe McCarthy

Herald Tribune—Acme (telephoto)

Feller Wins 22d As Tigers Lose To Indians, 7-6

Tribe's 3 Runs in 10th Boost 4th-Place Margin Over Detroit to 3½ Games

DETROIT, Sept. 4 (AP).—Bob Feller finally won his twenty-second victory today, cashing in on a three-run tenth inning as the Cleveland Indians defeated the Detroit Tigers, 7 to 6. The triumph increased the Indians' margin to three and a half games in their battle with Detroit for fourth place.

Feller yielded ten hits, including Pinky Higgins's tenth home run, and barely survived the tenth inning when Charley Gehringer's two-run pinch double just missed the home-run zone with two out. Feller then retired another pinch hitter, Birdie Tebbetts, ending the game.

Ray Mack opened Cleveland's tenth with a double off Paul Trout, relief pitcher, who was charged with the defeat, but the decisive blow was Lou Boudreau's two-run double. Boudreau scored what proved to be the winning run when he sprinted home on Rudy York's error.

Gerald Walker hit a homer for the Indians with the bases empty in the third.

The score:

CLEVELAND (A. L.)	ab	r	h	po	a	DETROIT (A. L.)	ab	r	h	po	a
Boud'u, ss.	6	1	1	2	2	Perry, ss..	5	0	0	1	3
Weath'y,cf	5	0	1	3	0	‡Tebbetts	1	0	0	0	0
Walker, lf.	5	2	2	5	0	Radcliff, lf	4	0	1	0	0
Heath, rf.	4	2	3	2	0	McCos'y, cf	5	0	1	3	0
Keltner, 3b	5	0	2	1	2	B.C'bell, rf	4	0	1	1	0
Grimes, 1b	5	0	1	7	2	York, 1b..	5	0	0	11	1
Mack, 2b..	3	1	2	2	4	Higgins, 3b	4	2	2	1	4
Des'tels, c.	3	0	0	6	0	Sullivan, c	4	3	2	7	0
Feller, p..	5	1	0	2	1	Meyer, 2b.	3	1	1	6	1
						Newh'ser,p	1	0	1	0	2
						Trout, p..	1	0	0	0	2
						*Gehring'r	1	0	1	0	0
						†Stainback	0	0	0	0	0
Totals..	41	7	12	30	11	Totals..	38	6	10	30	13

*Batted for Trout in tenth inning.
†Ran for Gehringer in tenth inning.
‡Batted for Perry in tenth inning.

Cleveland........ 011 001 100 3—7
Detroit.......... 020 002 000 2—6

Errors—Sullivan, Trout, York, Keltner. Runs batted in—Boudreau (2), Desautels, Walker, Grimes, Keltner, Gehringer (2), Newhouser, Perry, Higgins. Two-base hits—Radcliff, B. Campbell, Sullivan, Gehringer, Keltner, Mack. Home runs—Walker, Higgins. Stolen bases—Heath (2). Sacrifices—Newhouser, Walker, Desautels. Double play—Boudreau, Mack and Grimes. Left on bases—Cleveland, 12; Detroit, 10. Bases on balls—Off Feller, 7; off Newhouser, 4; off Trout, 2. Struck out—By Feller, 6; by Newhouser, 4; by Trout, 3. Hits—Off Newhouser, 9 in 6 1-3 innings; off Trout, 3 in 3 2-3. Wild pitch—Feller. Passed ball—Sullivan. Losing pitcher—Trout. Umpires—Geisel, Hubbard and Pipgras. Time—3:03. Attendance—4,317.

Leading Five Batsmen In Each Major League

AMERICAN LEAGUE

Player, club	G.	AB.	R.	H.	Pct.
Williams, Boston..	124	392	122	161	.411
Travis, Wash.....	127	514	86	185	.360
DiMaggio, N. Y...	123	481	113	171	.356
Heath, Cleveland..	128	495	77	170	.343
Siebert, Phila.....	121	460	62	153	.333

NATIONAL LEAGUE

Player, club	G.	AB.	R.	H.	Pct.
Reiser, Brooklyn..	117	459	100	153	.333
Hopp, St. Louis..	110	353	70	115	.326
Etten, Phila......	126	454	67	146	.322
Mize, St. Louis...	112	430	64	138	.321
Walker, Brooklyn.	127	443	77	140	.316

Home Runs

AMERICAN	NATIONAL
Williams, R. Sox 34	Camilli, Dodgers 29
Keller, Yankees..33	Ott, Giants......27
Henrich, Yanks. 27	Nicholson, Cubs..24
DiMaggio, Yanks 27	

Runs Batted In

AMERICAN	NATIONAL
Keller, Yanks...120	Camilli, Dodgers 97
DiMaggio, Ynks..112	Mize, Cardinals. 96
Williams, R.Sox.106	Young, Giants.. 91

Standing in Major Leagues

FRIDAY, SEPT. 5, 1941

National League

YESTERDAY'S RESULTS

Boston-New York (2), rain
Brooklyn-Philadelphia, wet grounds
Chicago, 3; St. Louis, 0 (1st)
Chicago, 4; St. Louis, 3 (11 innings, 2d)
Pittsburgh, 4; Cincinnati, 0 (5 innings, rain)

STANDING OF THE CLUBS

	Brooklyn	St. Louis	Cincinnati	Pittsburgh	New York	Chicago	Boston	Philadelphia	Won	Lost	Percentage	Games behind
Brooklyn.		9	12	11	11	13	16	13	85	47	.644	—
St. Louis..	10		11	14	13	8	12	15	83	47	.638	1
Cincin.....	7	8	—	6	13	12	12	12	70	58	.547	13
Pitts......	9	4	8		13	12	9	15	70	59	.543	13½
New York.	8	6	6	7		13	10	12	62	66	.484	21
Chicago...	7	8	7	8	7		10	13	60	74	.448	26
Boston....	4	7	8	8	4	9		12	52	76	.406	31
Phila......	2	5	6	5	5	7	7		37	92	.287	46½
Games lost	47	47	58	59	66	74	76	92				

GAMES TODAY

Cincinnati at Pittsburgh (2)
Other clubs not scheduled

American League

YESTERDAY'S RESULTS

New York, 6; Boston, 3
Cleveland, 7; Detroit, 6 (10 innings)
Philadelphia-Washington, rain
Other clubs not scheduled

STANDING OF THE CLUBS

	New York	Chicago	Boston	Cleveland	Detroit	St. Louis	Philadelphia	Washington	Won	Lost	Percentage	Games behind
New York.	—	13	11	13	10	17	13	14	91	45	.669	—
Chicago..	8	—	6	16	9	10	9	12	70	64	.522	20
Boston...	7	13	—	8	9	7	14	12	70	65	.519	20½
Cleveland.	6	5	12	—	10	9	14	10	66	65	.504	22½
Detroit...	9	7	11	9	—	10	12	6	64	70	.478	26
St. Louis.	4	8	13	5	10	—	7	11	58	73	.443	30½
Phila......	7	10	5	6	9	11	—	10	58	74	.439	31
Wash.....	4	8	7	8	13	9	5	—	54	75	.419	33½
Games lost	45	64	65	65	70	73	74	75				

GAMES TODAY

St. Louis at Chicago (night)
Cleveland at Detroit
Other clubs not scheduled

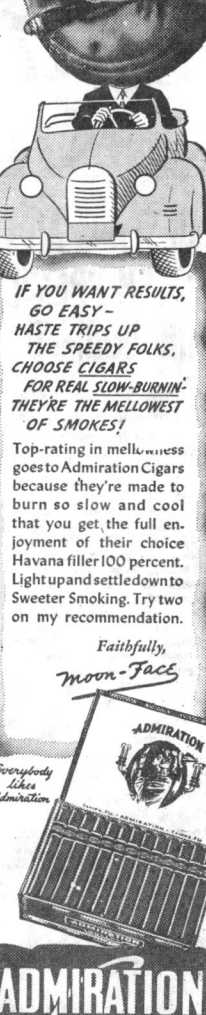

McCarthy Becomes First Pilot To Win 5 Pennants in 6 Years

His 6th Flag for Yankees Equals Team's Number of Titles Under Huggins

By a Staff Correspondent

BOSTON, Sept. 4.—Joe McCarthy, the man behind the Yankees, was at home in his hotel in New York, convalescing from a recent gall-bladder disorder, as his triumphant Yankees marched to their fifth pennant in six years. But his managerial genius is reflected in the great record he has achieved since, let out by the Chicago Cubs, he took over for the late Colonel Jacob Ruppert in 1931 and picked up the thread of success snapped after the death of Miller Huggins.

McCarthy's sixth pennant for the Yankees puts him on even terms with Huggins, who won in 1921-'22-'23-'26-'27-'28—six in eight years—while McCarthy has taken six out of eleven in 1932-'36-'37-'38-'39-'41. No other manager or team in the history of major-league baseball has ever won five pennants in six years.

Inasmuch as Marse Joe had a holdover of one triumph in the National League—he won with the Cubs of 1929—his pennant record of seven is bested only by John J. McGraw's ten with the Giants and Connie Mack's nine with the Philadelphia Athletics. Both, of course, accomplished these record totals for their respective leagues over a longer span of seasons than McCarthy has been at the helm.

Series Record Unequaled

And, in World Series play, the McCarthy record finds no equal. He has won every series into which he led the Bronx Bombers. In 1932 they beat his old Cubs four straight. In 1936 they went six games to top the Giants, the next year only five contests were necessary. Since then the Yankees have swept everything in October classics., trimming the Cubs in four straight in 1938 and the Reds in four in 1939. The Yankees, under the leadership of a man who never played in the major leagues, have won nine straight series games and haven't been stopped since Carl Hubbell prolonged the 1937 interborough clash with a 7-to-3 victory at the Polo Grounds in the fourth game.

In all his victory marches with the Yankees, McCarthy has seen his men crush the opposition. On clinching day he has never had a lead of less than a dozen games. The Yankees were "in" on Sept. 13, 1932, by twelve and a half lengths. They took the 1936 flag on Sept. 9 by eighteen, the 1937 championship on Sept. 23 by twelve, the 1938 title on Sept. 18 by fourteen and the 1939 crown on Sept. 16 by seventeen.

In eleven years with the Yankees, McCarthy has never finished lower than third. That was the standing of the Yankees last year, but the club was only two games below the top when the shooting ceased. In his four other non-pennant years his Yankees were the runner-ups to the team which went over the top in the World Series.

Await Result in National

And now, all the Yankees have to do, for the better part of a month, is sit back and await the result of the red-hot National League race. While they are waiting they may step out to establish new records of dominance. The 1936 Yankees finished nineteen and a half games in front of Detroit, biggest final margin in the American League, while the Pirates of 1902, with a lead of twenty-seven and a half games over Brooklyn, won that circuit's all-time runaway race. Both marks are within the reach of the cannonading Yankees of today, who this evening led the second-place White Sox by twenty games with eighteen engagements remaining on the New York schedule.

McCarthy, of course, belongs in the spotlight as the dugout leader of these continued Yankee triumphs on the field, but there is much credit due, too, to the executive direction of Ed Barrow in the front office, the farm system workings of George Weiss, the able hunting of the big scouting staff headed by Paul Krichell and, far from least, to the late Colonel Ruppert without whose enthusiasm and willingness to spend money this great Yankee dynasty would never have been possible.

Probable Pitchers For Today's Games

* * *

American League

Cleveland at Detroit—Smith (9-11) vs. Newsom (11-17).
St. Louis at Chicago (night)—Auker (13-13) vs. Ross (3-8).
Other clubs not scheduled.

National League

Cincinnati at Pittsburgh (2)—Derringer (10-13) and Turner (5-4) vs. Butcher (15-10) and Dietz (5-1).
Other clubs not scheduled.
(Won-lost records in parentheses).

N. Y. U. Squad Holds Long Drill on Offense

Special to the Herald Tribune

LAKE SEBAGO, N. Y., Sept. 4.—New York University's football squad romped through a three-hour morning workout today as Dr. Marvin A. (Mal) Stevens, coach, stressed offensive maneuvers, particularly forward passing. Joe Frank and Lester Berkowitch, the latter a sophomore, did all the tossing.

A heavy shower in the afternoon kept the boys indoors, where Stevens put them through a blackboard drill and acquainted them with the new rule changes. Jack Barmak, star blocker and pass receiver, arrived this morning. John Garland, guard; John Ryan, tackle, and Herb Chaiten, end, are expected by Saturday. The Violet will hold its first scrimmage tomorrow or Saturday.

Brooklyn College Squad Practices on New Plays

Brooklyn College's football team held two drills yesterday at Brooklyn College Field, walking through a series of new plays in the opening session and running through them in the afternoon. Lou Oshins, head coach, lined up a tentative first-string backfield of Al Sherman, quarterback; Lenny Jordan, fullback; Lou Hurowitz and David Peritz, halfbacks.

Leo Hartman, a sophomore, alternated at one of the halfback posts and Oshins indicated that he may win a starting position.

Results and Standings In the Minor Leagues

* * *

INTERNATIONAL LEAGUE

YESTERDAY'S RESULTS

Rochester, 6; Toronto, 0 (night).
Buffalo, 13; Montreal, 4 (night).
Jersey City-Baltimore (2), rain.
Other clubs not scheduled.

STANDING OF THE CLUBS

	W.	L.	Pct.		W.	L.	Pct.
Newark..	98	52	.653	Jer. City..	70	74	.486
Montreal..	88	63	.583	Syracuse..	68	81	.456
Buffalo....	87	63	.580	Baltimore.	56	90	.384
Rochester.	80	68	.541	Toronto...	47	104	.311

GAMES TODAY

Syracuse at Newark, 8:45 p. m.
Jersey City at Baltimore.
Buffalo at Montreal.
Rochester at Toronto.

AMERICAN ASSOCIATION

At Toledo (1st night game)— R. H. E.
Louisville .... 100 001 000—2 8 0
Toledo .... 100 000 101—3 8 0

Batteries—Butland, Scheetz (7) and Glenn; Biscan, Winegarner (8) and Spindel, Harshany (2).

St. Paul-Milwaukee, rain.

STANDING OF THE CLUBS

	W.	L.	Pct.		W.	L.	Pct.
Columbus	92	56	.622	Toledo...	78	71	.523
Louisville	85	63	.574	India'polis	64	84	.432
Min'polis.	80	67	.544	St. Paul..	61	86	.415
Kan. City	80	67	.544	Milwa'kee	51	97	.345

SOUTHERN ASSOCIATION

All night games.

STANDING OF THE CLUBS

	W.	L.	Pct.		W.	L.	Pct.
Atlanta...	95	54	.638	Birm'ham..	73	75	.486
Nashville.	81	66	.551	Lit. Rock..	67	79	.459
Ch'nooga..	77	73	.513	Memphis..	65	84	.436
N. Orleans	74	74	.500	Knoxville..	60	87	.408

EASTERN LEAGUE

Semi-final Play-offs

Two night games.

STANDING OF THE CLUBS

	W.	L.	Pct.		W.	L.	Pct.
Will'msport	1	0	1.000	Scranton....	0	1	.000
Elmira....	1	0	1.000	Wilkes-Barre	0	1	.000

TEXAS LEAGUE

Four night games.

STANDING OF THE CLUBS

	W.	L.	Pct.		W.	L.	Pct.
Houston.	102	46	.689	Ft. Worth.	74	75	.497
Tulsa...	84	65	.564	Okla. City.	67	82	.450
Shrev'p't	78	69	.531	S. Antonio	58	92	.387
Dallas..	76	74	.507	Beaumont.	56	92	.378

PACIFIC COAST LEAGUE

Six night games.

STANDING OF THE CLUBS

	W.	L.	Pct.		W.	L.	Pct.
Sacr'ento	92	64	.590	San Fran.	72	82	.468
S. Diego..	89	65	.578	Oakland..	69	87	.442
Seattle..	86	64	.573	L. Angeles	65	85	.433
H'llywood	76	78	.494	Portland..	63	87	.420

Pirates Down Reds, 4 to 0, in 5-Inning Game

Sewell Scores Over Walters, Yielding Only One Hit in Contest Halted by Rain

PITTSBURGH, Sept. 4 (AP).—The Pittsburgh Pirates, aided by rain, beat the Cincinnati Reds and their ace pitcher, Bucky Walters, today, 4 to 0, and moved within one-half game of third place now occupied by their opponents.

A sudden downpour of rain in the Pirates half of the fifth inning with one man cut caused the game to be called.

Rip Sewell permitted but one hit, a stinging double by Junior Frey in the first inning, and fanned three.

Walters allowed five hits, one of them a double by Vince DiMaggio in the second inning which scored Stu Martin with the first run. Vince scored on Bill Baker's double and in the next inning knocked in another run with a long fly. Bob Elliott had walked to start the third and was sacrificed to second. After Elbie Fletcher walked, Martin sent Elliott home and Elbie to third with his second single. DiMaggio then sent his long fly to Mike McCormick.

Arky Vaughan, still subject to dizzy spells since he was beaned in an exhibition game last week in London, Ont., was not in uniform. The club phyician ordered him to take a few days' rest.

The score:

CINCINNATI (N. L.)	ab	r	h	po	a	PITTSB'GH (N. L.)	ab	r	h	po	a
Lukon, rf..	2	0	0	1	0	And'son, ss	3	0	0	1	1
Frey, 2b..	2	0	1	0	1	Hand'y, 3b	3	0	0	1	3
Werber, 3b	1	0	0	0	2	Elliott, rf..	1	1	0	2	0
Lombardi,c	2	0	0	1	0	Stewart, lf	2	0	1	2	0
F.M'C'k,1b	2	0	0	8	0	Fletc'r, 1b	1	1	0	4	0
Craft, cf..	2	0	0	0	0	Martin, 2b	2	1	2	2	0
M.M'C'k,lf	2	0	0	3	0	DiMag'o,cf	2	1	1	0	0
Jooset, ss..	2	0	0	0	2	Baker, c..	2	0	1	3	1
Walters, p	1	0	0	0	2	Sewell, p..	2	0	0	0	0
Totals....	16	0	1	13	7	Totals....	18	4	5	15	5

Cincinnati.................. 000 00—0
Pittsburgh.................. 022 0x—4

Errors—Joost, Fletcher. Runs batted in—DiMaggio (2), Baker, Martin. Two-base hits—Frey, DiMaggio, Baker. Stolen base—Werber. Sacrifice—Stewart. Left on bases—Pittsburgh, 5; Cincinnati, 2. Bases on balls—Off Walters, 3; off Sewell, 1. Struck out—By Sewell, 3. Umpires—Barr, Sears and Jorda. Attendance—1,720.

Passeau Baffles St. Louis, 3-0, Then Erickson Wins in 11th, 4-3

Warneke and Cooper Falter on Mound as Red Birds Drop Into Second Place

CHICAGO, Sept. 4 (AP).—The St. Louis Cardinals were knocked out of the National League leadership today by dropping a double-header to the Chicago Cubs, 3 to 0, and 4 to 3. The last game went eleven innings.

The double defeat dropped the Cardinals a full game behind the rained out Brooklyn Dodgers.

The dramatic second game was broken up as shadows were beginning to engulf Wrigley Field and the umpires were considering calling the game because of darkness.

With the score tied at 3 to 3 and one out, Barney Olsen, rookie Cub outfielder, lifted a fly ball to left field which Don Padgett dropped. Stanley Hack, who had walked and reached third on Lou Stringer's single, raced home with the winning run to the cheers of 19,303 spectators, 6,500 of whom were women guests. The rookie, Paul Erickson, went the route for the Cubs.

The double defeat saw the collapse of two of the Cardinals' ace starting pitchers—Lon Warneke and Morton Cooper. Warneke, making his first start after pitching a no-hit game against Cincinnati, failed to survive four innings in the first game, after allowing the Cubs their three runs. He was touched for six hits and gave five bases on balls.

In the first game, the Cubs scored in the opening inning, Hack got a base on balls, was sacrificed to second and crossed the plate on Phil Cavarretta's drive to right field.

Warneke's wildness figured in the Cubs' second run. He walked Dahlgren, who stole second and scored on Stringer's single. The Cubs' third and final run was registered in the fourth when Claude Passeau opened with a single. Hack walked and both runners advanced on Stringer's sacrifice. Passeau came home when Cavarretta singled to center. Hack also tried to score, but was nipped at the plate.

Meanwhile, Passeau had the Cardinals handcuffed under his masterful pitching. He held them to five scattered singles and no Cardinal reached second base until the ninth.

The scores:

FIRST GAME

ST. LOUIS (N. L.)	ab	r	h	po	a	CHICAGO (N. L.)	ab	r	h	po	a
Brown, 3b.	3	0	1	2	0	Hack, 3b..	1	1	0	1	1
Hopp, cf..	4	0	0	1	0	Stringer,2b	2	0	1	2	7
Padgett, lf.	4	0	0	2	0	Cava'ta, cf	4	0	2	2	0
Mize, 1b..	4	0	2	11	0	Nichol'n,rf	3	0	0	3	0
Crabt'e, rf.	4	0	2	0	1	Dalle'ro, lf	4	0	0	0	0
W.Cooper,c	3	0	0	2	0	Dahlg'n,1b	2	1	1	11	0
Crespi, 2b.	3	0	0	5	4	McCul'gh,c	4	0	1	2	0
Marion, ss	2	0	0	1	5	Sturg'n, ss	2	0	0	6	4
Warneke,p	1	0	0	0	1	Passeau, p	3	1	1	0	2
Lanier, p..	1	0	0	0	0						
*Triplett..	1	0	0	0	0						
Krist, p...	0	0	0	0	0						
Totals...	30	0	5	24	11	Totals...	25	3	6	27	14

*Batted for Lanier in eighth inning.

St. Louis............ 000 000 000—0
Chicago............. 110 100 00x—3

Errors—Brown, W. Cooper, Stringer. Runs batted in—Cavarretta (2), Stringer. Stolen bases—Dahlgren, Mize. Sacrifices—Stringer (2). Double plays—Stringer Sturgeon and Dahlgren (2); Crespi, Marion and Mize; Stringer and Dahlgren; Marion, Crespi and Mize. Left on bases—St. Louis, 5; Chicago, 7. Bases on balls—Off Warneke, 6; off Krist, 1; og Passeau, 2. Struck out—By Lanier, 1; by Passeau, 1 Hits—Off Warneke, 6 in 3 2-3 innings; off Lanier, 0 in 3 1-3; off Krist, 0 in 1. Losing pitcher—Warneke. Umpires—Goetz, Reardon and Conlan. Time—1:53.

SECOND GAME

ST. LOUIS (N. L.)	ab	r	h	po	a	CHICAGO (N. L.)	ab	r	h	po	a
Brown, 3b	5	0	1	2	2	Hack, 3b.	3	2	0	2	0
Hopp, cf.	5	0	1	4	0	String'r,2b	5	0	3	0	3
Padgett,lf	5	0	0	2	0	Cavar'a,cf	4	0	0	3	0
Mize, 1b.	4	1	1	10	2	B.Olsen,cf	1	0	0	3	0
Crabtr'e,rf	5	0	1	1	0	Nichol'n,rf	4	0	0	1	0
Crespi, 2b.	3	1	1	3	4	§M'Cul'gh.	1	0	0	0	0
Mario, ss.	4	1	1	2	2	Gilbert,rf.	0	0	0	0	0
Mancuso,c	3	0	1	4	0	Dalles'ro.lf	5	0	1	7	0
†Triplett..	1	0	0	0	0	Dahlg'n,1b	5	1	2	8	0
W.Coop'r,c	1	0	0	2	0	Scheffing,c	5	0	1	5	0
M.Coop'r,p	1	0	0	0	1	Sturge'n,ss	3	0	1	3	2
Pollet, p.	3	0	2	0	1	‡George..	1	0	0	0	0
Lanier, p.	0	0	0	1	0	Hudson,ss.	1	0	0	1	1
Crouch, p.	0	0	0	0	0	Erickson,p	5	1	1	0	1
Totals.	40	3	9	*31	12	Totals..	43	4	9	33	7

*One out when winning run was scored.
†Batted for Mancuso in ninth inning.
‡Batted for Sturgeon in eighth inning.
§Batted for Nicholson in ninth inning.

St. Louis....... 020 001 000 00—3
Chicago......... 111 000 000 01—4

Errors—Marion (3), Crespi, Padgett. Runs batted in—Marion, Mancuso, Mize, Dahlgren. Two-base hits—Marion, Erickson, Pollet, Crespi. Three-base hit—Hopp. Home runs—Dahlgren, Mize. Stolen bases—Hack, Mize. Double plays—Crespi and Mize; Stringer, Sturgeon and Dahlgren (2). Left on bases—St. Louis, 8; Chicago, 13. Bases on balls—Off M. Cooper, 1; off Pollet, 3; off Lanier, 1; off Erickson, 4. Struck out—By M. Cooper, 1; by Pollet, 2; by Lanier, 1; by Erickson, 4. Hits—Off M. Cooper, 3 in 3 innings; off Pollet, 5 in 5 1-3; off Lanier, 1 in 2; off Crouch, 0 in 0. Wild pitches—M. Cooper (2), Erickson. Losing pitcher—Lanier. Umpires—Reardon, Conlan and Goetz. Time—3:03. Attendance—12,803 paid; 6,500 ladies.

WORLD SERIES EXTRA

The San Francisco News

FINAL
Complete N. Y. Stocks
PRICE FIVE CENTS

Local Forecast: Fair and moderately warm today, tonight and tomorrow with early morning clouds. (Complete U. S. Weather Bureau report, Page 20.)

SCRIPPS—HOWARD | Vol. 39 | Entered as second-class matter, San Francisco, Cal., Postoffice. | SAN FRANCISCO, WEDNESDAY, OCTOBER 1, 1941 | c | No. 235

GORDON HOMES, YANKS WIN

Anti-Nazi Revolts Sweep 5 Nations

30 SLAVS AND CZECH PREMIER ARE DOOMED

Greeks Wage 2-Day Uprising; Hundreds Jailed in Bulgaria

War News Inside

By United Press

New anti-Nazi revolts or unrest were reported today to have spread in Bulgaria, Yugo-Slavia, Rumania, Greece and Czecho-Slovakia. The Axis took sweeping retaliations.

Hungary listed 30 persons, "mostly Serbs and Jews," as executed in the Banat area of Yugoslavia on charges of sabotage and communism.

Germans threatened to bomb the former Yugoslav capital of Belgrade to stop spreading resistance, according to British reports. Railroads were wrecked. Thirty-eight "Communists" were seized as hostages.

Greeks in Uprising

Greeks engaged in a two-day armed uprising near Drama, but were suppressed, Sofia reported.

General Alois Elias, premier of the Nazi-dominated state of Bohemia and Moravia, was sentenced to death on charges of plotting a military rebellion, Germany revealed from Prague.

Bulgarian police made a series of raids in an attempt to clean out dangerous elements.

Police were reported to have made a close search of Varna, Bulgaria's chief port, and arrested 844 persons.

The importance of the raid was emphasized by the fact that Varna, Bulgaria's third city, is a main base for ships which Germany is mobilizing, apparently for land, sea and air operations against the Crimea and the Caucasus in Russia.

Berlin admitted that 58 additional persons had been executed in Czechoslovakia and that the total of executions since the German secret police imposed a state of emergency on Czech areas was thus brought to 84, while 256 Czechs were reported turned over to the Gestapo.

Moscow reported that the "national unity" underground radio station in Czechoslovakia had been heard urging the people to organize a general strike in protest against German repression.

FORCE IN ICELAND

By United Press

REYKJAVIK, Iceland, Oct. 1.—Authorities permitted disclosure today that regular United States Army forces have arrived in Iceland to augment the United States Marines who comprised the first forces in the American garrison.

15,000 S. F. GUESTS!
* * * *
You Can Join in Fun

San Francisco put a tassel on its latch string and dusted off the keys to the city today to welcome 15,000 soldiers during a three-day National Defense Pageant, beginning Friday. A provisional battalion of 1000 men from the 78th Coast Artillery at Camp Haan, near Riverside, will be first guests to arrive, going to the Beach Chalet Playground in Golden Gate Park, where a model camp will be set up tomorrow.

Another 9000 men from the Seventh Division at Ft. Ord will follow in a huge caravan of trucks, "jeeps" and scout cars. They will pitch camp at the park polo stadium. Other units from Moffett and Hamilton Fields and other outlying military establishments as well as from the Presidio of San Francisco will be here.

Patriotic Pageants

Under auspices of the Junior Chamber of Commerce, the soldier guests will participate in a program of patriotic pageants, community rallies, mass sings and other activities.

The soldiers will reciprocate by marching in a monster four-hour parade down Market-st Friday night in full war kit with mobile equipment including heavy artillery. Red Cross, State Guard, ROTC and other organizations will join in.

Soldiers in uniform will be admitted at special reduced prices to three football games—Nevada vs. University of San Francisco Friday night at Seals Stadium, St. Mary's vs. Moffett Field Saturday afternoon in Kezar Stadium and Santa Clara vs. Loyola Sunday afternoon, also in Kezar Stadium.

Sunday Dinner Appeal

An appeal to citizens to invite soldiers to dinner Sunday was voiced by Nicholas D. Cline, chairman of the military affairs committee of the Junior Chamber.

Persons wishing to invite soldiers to their homes are asked to stop them in the street and extend invitations or to phone Hospitality House, MArket 8128, or the Chamber office, EXbrook 4511.

Mr. Cline also urged car owners to participate in the caravan of cars taking soldiers on the 49-mile scenic drive around San Francisco. Those offering cars are asked to join the caravan on Polk-st in front of the City Hall

260,000 AXIS TOLL CLAIMED

United Press summary:

Russian counter-attacks gained momentum on two fronts today to offset Axis advances in the far north and toward the Donets Basin.

Leningrad claimed to have inflicted 100,000 casualties on the Nazis on the southern and southwestern sectors alone, while Odessa claimed 160,000 Axis forces killed and wounded.

The Axis Armies took Poltava, the Russians admitted, and advanced eastward to threaten Kharkov and the Crimean peninsula below Perekop.

The Finns reported they had captured the important railroad town of Petrozavodsk on Lake Onega, 185 miles northwest of Leningrad on the route to Murmansk.

But Moscow and London reported that:

The Germans had suffered 100,000 casualties and loss of 400 tanks, 200 big guns and 846 planes on the Leningrad front and 160,000 casualties in the Odessa fighting.

The Ninth Nazi Panzer Division was "annihilated" in the southwest.

The Red Army was attacking on a 200-mile central front in a sweep that seemed to be developing into a counter-offensive.

The Russians killed more than 1800 Germans in a single attack on the central front, which now is reported active from Yartsevo to a point south of Gomel.

An army of some 500,000 Russians has been specially trained for offensive winter operations in the Far North.

$350,000 Fair Fire

POMONA, Oct. 1.—Fire today destroyed the Agricultural Building, largest at the Los Angeles County Fairgrounds, causing loss estimated at $350,000.

Cause was unknown. The blaze swept rapidly through the 800-by-135-foot structure, which had no partitions.

The fair had closed Sunday night.

RAF Sweeps France by Day

By United Press

LONDON, Oct. 1.—The Royal Air Force struck with large bomber squadrons at German continental targets again today and fought the Luftwaffe over the English Channel after making its 11th raid on Stettin and its 79th raid on Hamburg, where big fires were started by heavy explosives.

The Germans admitted that the night attacks were by "great numbers" of planes, causing destruction to dwellings and casualties among civilians.

(The Germans also reported that the Luftwaffe had resumed severe attacks on English targets, chiefly Newcastle, two cities in Scotland and other coastal areas.)

Every Line
GOOD NEWS
To Some One

PAYDAY FOR THE CITY

There were smiles on their faces and cash jingled in the pockets of 13,500 municipal employes today as the controller's office managed to release paychecks on schedule. A "two or three day delay" had been anticipated as result of the Board of Supervisors' inability to pass emergency legislation for the sale of tax anticipation notes a fortnight ago.

* * *

WE SUPPLY THE SEEDS

California is now providing a large part of the world demand for flower and vegetable seeds, according to H. M. Butterfield, specialist of the University of California Agricultural Service. More than 11 million dollars was accrued by the state seed industries in 1940, Mr. Butterfield said.

Inside The News

'JOIN BRITISH IN 10-YR. PACT,' KNOX URGES

Navy Secretary Gives Plan to Rule Seas, Control Aggression

By United Press

INDIANAPOLIS, Ind., Oct. 1.—Secy. of Navy Knox today proposed that the United States and Britain join forces "for 100 years, at least," to produce "by force if need be" an effective system of international law.

He told the 64th annual convention of the American Bar Association that to prevent another World War the seven seas must be controlled for many years to come by the great "peace-minded, justice-loving" powers—the United States and Great Britain—which are "lacking in any desire for selfish aggrandizement."

"To put it bluntly," he said, "we must join our force, our power to that of Great Britain, another great peace-loving nation, to stop new aggression, which might lead to a world disturbance, at its beginnings.

'We Will Come to It'

"We will come to this, I am convinced, by the sheer logic of events. . . . By a gradual recognition of its inevitability.

"We shall have to provide an interregnum in which we shall not only devote ourselves to the pursuit of peaceful aims, but provide the essential might to enforce such a peace on those who are not willing voluntarily to pursue such a course."

Secretary Knox said our safety and prosperity in the world of the future depends upon these three factors:

1.—Stern insistence upon the principle of the freedom of the seas.

2.—The assurance of equal opportunity for world trade.

3.—The proviso that sea power shall not be made the instrument of selfish aggression.

The American people, Secretary Knox said, must be "aroused" to the urgency of the situation and brought to the point of making the necessary sacrifices to defeat Hitler so that the "grander, nobler concept that lies beyond a military victory" can be achieved.

'Victory Insufficient'

"That we shall proceed from one measure to another until we have taken adequate steps to bring defeat to the legions of Hitler and his satellites in Italy and Japan, I have no doubt," he said. "But this is insufficient if we are to do our part to establish a rule of law as contrasted with the rule of men in international affairs. The ultimate defeat of Hitler and the re-establishment of international law go together."

SOLDIERS FIGHT FOREST FIRE

MONTEREY, Oct. 1.—More than 300 soldiers and CCC men were rushed into the rugged country, 10 miles below Big Sur, today to aid in fighting a large forest fire.

WHERE EVERYBODY WENT

—News-Acme Telephoto

The greatest World Series crowd in history—part of the 70,000 that jammed Yankee Stadium in New York for today's opening game. It was more than three hours before game time (see clock at upper right), and every bleacher seat was taken.

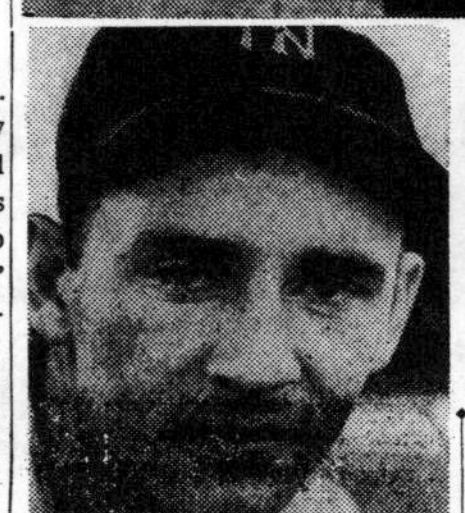

JOC GORDON.
Homes for Yanks.

B. W. Horne, Writer, Dies

Bernard W. Horne, for the past 16 years one of the most widely known newspapermen in Northern California, dropped dead today. He was 45. He had spent most of yesterday and last evening at the City Hall covering last-minute filings by candidates.

B. W. HORNE

With Assessor and Mrs. Russell Wolden, Mr. Horne went to the home of City Atty. O'Toole for dinner. Around midnight he and the Woldens left. They stopped, on the way to Mr. Horne's home, 1673 Eighth-av, for a cup of coffee.

In one corner of the shop Mr. Horne saw a pin-ball machine. Grinning, he left the table, said he guessed he'd try his luck. Suddenly he slumped to the floor, apparently having been instantly killed by a heart attack.

Mr. Horne was born in New York city, attended Cornell University. After serving overseas in the Canadian Expeditionary Force, he worked on newspapers in New York, Chicago, Detroit and Winnipeg. He came to San Francisco in 1925, joined The News staff.

He was a keen student and analyst of local, state and national affairs and soon became The News political writer, continuing that work until a year ago when he joined The Examiner staff as a special writer.

Mr. Horne is survived by his widow, Gladys, and three children, Elizabeth Josephine, 13; Lewis Michael, 10, and Patricia, 9. Funeral services have been tentatively set for Friday.

(Other obituaries on Page 6)

MURDER HINTED IN VET'S DEATH

San Francisco police were confronted today with what appeared to be a murder mystery. The victim was Frank Tierney, 63, Spanish-American War veteran who died at Central Emergency Hospital of a fractured skull after having been found wounded and moaning in his hotel room at 353 Minna-st.

Deputy Coroner Jack Angell, assigned to the case, said it was "probably murder," although there was a possibility the man had fallen and fatally injured himself.

Howard Thomas, clerk at the Minna-st hotel where Mr. Tierney lived, said that Mr. Tierney received a $60 monthly pension check yesterday noon and paid $8 for room rent.

He put the balance, $52, in his wallet, and Mr. Thomas did not see the man until about midnight, when he was attracted to his room by the man's moaning.

Mr. Tierney lay unconscious on his bed, bleeding from the head. He was taken to Central Emergency Hospital and died a few hours later without regaining consciousness.

In the man's pockets was only $1.60. His wallet had disappeared.

Mr. Angell and police investigators believed he had been attacked and robbed after reaching his room. However, they had not the faintest clue as to the identity of the possible assailant.

Commerce Opens With Sacred Heart

The Commerce Bulldogs enter this afternoon's prep football contest a not-too-heavy favorite over the twice victorious Sacred Heart eleven on Commerce Field. Kickoff is set for 3:30 o'clock.

Commerce gets the edge on a stronger, heavier line and superior material in the backfield, but the Irish are by no means a weak eleven this season. Jackie Ryan will lead Sacred Heart's attack, with Ernie Provost engineering the Bulldog offensive.

Play-by-Play First Game

FIRST INNING

DODGERS—Walker walked on four straight pitches. Herman rolled out, Rolfe to Sturm, Walker advancing to second. Reiser flied to Di Maggio on the first pitch, Walker holding second. Camilli fanned, swinging. 0-0-0.

YANKEES—Sturm slashed a single to left on the second pitch. Rolfe forced Sturm at second, Camilli to Reese. Henrich forced Rolfe at second, Herman to Reese. Di Maggio, who was given a tremendous ovation when he came to bat, raised a high fly to Medwick near the leftfield foul line. 0-1-0.

SECOND INNING

DODGERS—The sun went behind the clouds as Medwick came to bat. Medwick took a tremendous cut, fouled off one and then fanned, swinging. Lavagetto grounded out, Rizzuto to Sturm. Reese worked the count to two and two and then flied to Keller, who barely had to move to make the catch. 0-0-0.

YANKEES—Keller flied to Reiser in center. Dickey popped in front of Herman, who threw him out to Camilli. Gordon fouled off four pitches and then, on a two and two count, hit a mighty home run into the lower leftfield boxes about 415 feet from home plate. The crowd gave Gordon a lusty ovation as he circled the bases. Rizzuto flied to Medwick in deep left near the box seats. He misjudged the ball, but untracked himself at the last moment. 1-1-0.

THIRD INNING

DODGERS—The sun came out

(Turn to Page 17, Column 7)

* * *

RECORD CROWD OF 70,000 SEE SERIES OPEN

Joe Di Maggio Is Robbed of Homer By Medwick's Catch

BY TOM LAIRD
The News Sports Editor

YANKEE STADIUM, New York, Oct. 1.—New York's Yankees resumed its old World Series pace today with a victory over Brooklyn in the first game of the 1941 series.

The final score: Yanks, 3; Dodgers, 2.

Gordon of the Yankees slapped a two-and-two ball off Dodger Pitcher Curt Davis in the second inning for a home run and the first run of the series.

Seventy thousand fans, including a huge contingent from baseball-mad Brooklyn, jammed Yankee Stadium to capacity.

New York scored in the fourth on Dicky's double after Keller walked. In the same inning Medwick robbed oe Di Maggio of a hit with a great catch up against the leftfield fence.

Peewee Reese breezed in with a Dodger run in the fifth, on Mickey Owen's slashing triple.

In the sixth inning Ruffing got in trouble with two walks, and Adolf Camilli on base, but he got by without a score.

Keller scored the third Yankee run in the sixth on singles by Dickey and Gordon.

Hugh Casey replaced Davis for Brooklyn and got the side out.

Lew Riggs' pinch hit in the seventh scored Lavagetto, who made base on Rizzuto's error. Wasdell, another pinch hitter, fouled into a double play.

Storm Kills 125

By United Press

MANAGUA, Nicaragua, Oct. 1.—An expedition to hurricane-stricken Cape Gracias found 125 persons known dead and 72 wounded, and it was feared that casualties were much higher, it was reported today.

The town of Cruta was destroyed. The hurricane was still battering Mexico's Isthmus of Tehuantepec.

FOREST FIRE OUT OF CONTROL

MONTEREY, Oct. 1.—A forest fire raced out of control through Los Padres National Forest today. Paul Case, chief of the U. S. Forestry Service, called for help from Ft. Ord and CCC camps. Three hundred fresh fighters were sent to the area.

SPRECKELS SUIT IN SEATTLE

SEATTLE, Oct. 1.—Mrs. Esme Spreckels Dodge filed suit for divorce today from Ben F. Dodge, Seattle realtor. The couple was married in 1934 shortly after Mrs. Dodge was divorced from Adolph B. Spreckels of the San Francisco sugar family.

JOYCE KILMER WIDOW DIES

NEWTON, N. J., Oct. 1.—Mrs. Aline Murray Kilmer, 53, widow of Joyce Kilmer, poet, diet today at her home at Stillwater, N. J., after a long illness.

WORLD SERIES BOX SCORE

FIRST GAME

BR'KLYN	AB	R	H	PO	A	E	NEW YORK	AB	R	H	PO	A	E
Walker,rf	3	0	0	3	0	0	Sturm,1b	3	0	1	7	0	0
Herman,2b	3	0	0	0	5	0	Rolfe,3b	3	0	2	2	3	0
Reiser,cf	3	0	0	4	0	0	Henrich,rf	4	0	1	0	0	0
Camilli,1b	4	0	0	7	2	0	DiMag,cf	4	0	0	5	0	0
Medwick,lf	4	0	1	4	0	0	Keller,lf	2	2	0	4	0	0
Lavgtto,3b	4	1	0	0	0	0	Dickey,c	4	0	2	4	0	0
Reese,ss	4	1	3	4	2	0	Gordon,2b	2	1	2	2	2	0
Owen,c	2	0	1	1	0	0	Rizzuto,ss	4	0	0	3	5	1
Davis,p	2	0	0	1	0	0	Ruffing,p	3	0	0	0	0	0
Casey,p	1	0	0	0	0	0		0	0	0	0	0	0
Riggs	1	0	1	0	0	0		0	0	0	0	0	0
Allen,p	0	0	0	0	0	0		0	0	0	0	0	0
Franks,c	1	0	0	0	1	0		0	0	0	0	0	0
	0	0	0	0	0	0		0	0	0	0	0	0
Totals	32	2	6	24	10	0	Totals	29	3	8	27	10	1

SCORE BY INNINGS

BROOKLYN	000	010	100	2
NEW YORK	010	101	00	3

GETTING AWAY FROM THE WAR

By United Press

DENVER, Oct. 1.—Thomas F. Walsh, 75, goes on trial today for committing assault on an automobile.

He said he was two-thirds across an intersection last night and held up his old blackthorn stick to the driver. But the driver didn't stop for him so Walsh swung twice. He broke out two windows.

"I didn't intend to hit the window with the first swing," he said, "I was aiming at the driver. But on the second swat my Irish was up and I aimed at the window."

"By the way, I had to smack another car a while back."

* * *

HOLLYWOOD, Oct. 1.—Hedy Lamar has invented a remote control device for use in warfare, which is considered "of potential value" by the Government, it was disclosed today.

Colonel L. B. Lent, chief engineer of the National Inventors Council, said that of some 30,000 inventions submitted to the Department of Commerce, about 100 had been turned over to the Army and Navy. Of these, about a dozen are "red hot," he said, and Hedy's invention is one of them. It is of a highly secret nature.

* * *

DENVER, Oct. 1.—Headlights and taillights for horses were ordered today by State Highway Safety Engineers. Horses must be ridden or driven on the right side of highways and streets, and at night reflectors must be fastened "to the bridle in front and the horse's tail behind."

* * *

IMPERIA, Italy, Oct. 1.—Mrs. Pasqualina Stadenni, 43, gave birth to her 21st child today. In January, she gave birth to twins.

* * *

NEW YORK, Oct. 1.—Charles Russo, 25, told police today that he had robbed milkmen to buy a tombstone for his mother.

* * *

SILVER CITY, N. M., Oct. 1.—Mrs. Chase McReynolds, 40, said today that to avoid the flood waters of the Gila River she spent 12 hours in a tree with three rattlesnakes.

She knocked two of them into the water, but they returned to the tree.

"I've lived on a ranch all my life and I'm not afraid of snakes," she said. "I did get a little shaky, though, when it started getting dark, because I was afraid if I wasn't rescued before night came, the snakes might get me."

Flood workers, headed by her husband, rescued her at dusk.

TAX BILL GOING UP?

How much is your home assessed for?

$2500?

Then your tax bill will go up $6.25 a year if Charter Amendment No. 1, the power measure, fails to carry at the Nov. 4 election.

$2000? You'll pay **$5 more a year in taxes.**

$3000? That will cost you **$7.50 more a year.**

$4000? Then defeat of No. 1 will cost you **$10 more a year.**

$5000? Your taxes will go up **$12.50 a year.**

$7500? You'll be out **$18.75 more a year.**

For defeat of No. 1 will boost the city tax rate 25c.

MON FISHING OUTSIDE THE GOLDEN GATE HAS IMPROVED—SEE ED NEAL'S REPORT, PAGE

Yanks Take Opening Victory in Stride; Dodgers Determined to Make Amends

BOMBERS HAPPY, BUT HARDLY NOISY

Yanks' Victory Their 10th in Row, So Clubhouse Demonstration Is Mild One

RUFFING THREW ONE CURVE

Used Fast Balls, Half-Speed Pitches—Chandler or Russo to Take Mound Today

By JAMES P. DAWSON

The Yankees have become so accustomed to these world series conquests that the novelty long since has ceased to exist. The Bombers won the first game of the current classic and, in the slang of the day, "So what?"

That was the impression yesterday in the clubhouse of the American League champions as they trooped off the field after clinching a 3-to-2 victory over the Dodgers as Herman Franks ended the opening game of the 1941 post-season struggle by hitting into a double play.

There was a noisy shout of acclaim on the bench when the twin killing, executed by Joe Gordon, Phil Rizzuto and Johnny Sturm, sealed the verdict. But the clubhouse was not like the corral of a ball club that had just gained its tenth straight world series victory.

Led by Frankie Crosetti, utility infielder, the club trooped into the locker room. There was none of the shouting and hip-hip-hooraying, the emotional outbursts, the kicking of benches, tossing of gloves, dancing of jigs, good-natured trading of playful punches. All the by-play commonly associated with and expected of such an occasion was missing.

Center of Demonstration

The squad, from Manager Joseph Vincent McCarthy right down to the bat boy, Timmy Sullivan, was tickled at the victory. There was hurry and bustle. Charley Ruffing was mobbed. He was the center of the only demonstration. Not a man on the squad but came over to the weary giant and hugged and slapped and cuffed and manhandled the redtop from Nokomis.

Coach Art Fletcher let out a typical "yip-pee." Coach Earle Combs, the old Kentucky Colonel, wore a grin all over his face that bespoke his happiness. For the rest it was as if the Yankees were wearied after the strain of that battle that hung in the balance right down to the finish.

Ruffing was plainly showing the effects. It was a tough game for Red. A cold weather pitcher essentially, he suffered in the sticky, humid weather. His uniform was heavy with perspiration. His forehead was dotted with beads. His hand was wet to the clasp of his mates. He was tired. He had tied the record of Chief Bender, Waite Hoyt and Lefty Gomez with his sixth world series victory. But he was glad it was over.

"I felt fine out there all afternoon save for one spasm of weakness," Ruffing said. "It hit me along about the seventh inning. I felt tired and weary. It was hot and sticky. But it passed quickly and I finished all right.

"Maybe I just got the breaks. But it's great to win. I didn't throw many curves. In fact, I threw just one all afternoon, to Reiser in the eighth inning, I guess. For the rest I gave them fast balls and half-speed pitches.

Fast Balls for Camilli

"I got Camilli on fast balls. But Owen hit my fast one in the fifth, and so did Reese and Riggs in the seventh. Had a lot of trouble with that Reese. Just couldn't seem to get him out."

Manager McCarthy and Catcher Bill Dickey praised Ruffing for a great exhibition of pitching. Dickey said Ruffing was at his best, that he was a master and needed little or no steadying.

"Winning that first game is a great thing because it gives us the edge," said Manager McCarthy from behind a vicious-looking cigar, his spectacles on, with a huge wooden horseshoe inscribed "Good Luck, Bronx Yanks," as a backdrop.

"But the Giants won the first one in 1936 and we came on to win. I mention that merely to show the first game doesn't necessarily decide the series. We got some breaks," McCarthy said. "One of them came when Reese tried to sneak up to third on Wasdell's foul pop in the seventh. That double play helped a lot. But Ruffing was out there pitching a great game all the time, and we managed to get more long hits.

"I'll use Chandler or Russo tomorrow. I won't make up my mind until we see how they shape up on the field."

Examined by Doctor

Marius Russo, a southpaw, is the likely choice. But the Ozone Park hurler was seized with a stomach complaint in the clubhouse and was examined by Dr. Robert Emmet Walsh. The examination revealed no temperature, Dr. Walsh said. Russo attributed his indisposition to a careless diet, and said he hoped to be all right today. Spud Chandler, husky Georgia right-hander, is ready for the call.

Gordon said he hit a fast ball for his second-inning homer. Charley Keller went through the game unharmed, his ailing right ankle heavily taped.

Manager McCarthy got a laugh out of a telegram from Baton Rouge which read: "Can't get game on air. Hope you lose."

AS INTERBOROUGH RIVALS MET IN OPENING GAME OF THE WORLD SERIES AT THE YANKEE STADIUM

Commissioner Landis about to throw out the ball to start the series. With him is Mayor La Guardia.

Rolfe forced at second base in the opening inning after Henrich grounded to Herman. Reese, who took Herman's toss, has just thrown to first in an attempt to double Henrich. Grieve is the umpire.

A view of the jammed bleachers two hours before the game began

Lavagetto safe at home on Riggs's single in the seventh as Umpire McGowan calls the play. Also seen are Dickey, Wasdell (8) and the Dodger batboy.

Joe McCarthy, the Yankee manager, and Leo Durocher, Dodger pilot

New York Times

68,540 SEE YANKS TOP DODGERS, 3-2

Continued From Page One

disheartening double plays that held the remainder of the American League helpless throughout the long Summer.

For the Yanks it marked their tenth successive triumph in a world series game. They suffered their last defeat on Oct. 9, 1937, when Carl Hubbell turned them back in the only game the Giants were to win that year.

On the following day the Bombers clinched that series. In 1938, they polished off the Cubs in four straight and repeated that feat against the Reds in 1939.

For Ruffing, the victory was his sixth, tying a world series record shared by only three other hurlers —Chief Bender, Athletics' star of an almost forgotten era; Waite Hoyt, Yankee ace of more than a decade ago, and Ruffing's present-day colleague, Lefty Gomez. Only once has Big Red tasted defeat in the October classic.

Six Hits for Each Team

It was by no means an overpowering performance which Ruffing put on display in yesterday's mid-summer setting. He yielded six hits, the same number the Yanks clipped off Davis. Hugh Casey and Johnny Allen, who finished on the mound for the Dodgers, gave up no blows.

But the burly, 37-year-old right-hander, popularly known as Big Red, remained master of the situation throughout. Even when his defenses momentarily faltered, as they did in the seventh, when little Phil Rizzuto came up with an annoying and costly error, Ruff never lost his poise or confidence. A little blind base running by the Flatbush Flock at this point also helped and, after that, Big Red scarcely needed anything more than ordinary, perfunctory assistance.

Ruffing kept the Dodgers' mightiest sluggers thoroughly bottled up. Dolph Camilli, the National League's leading home-run clouter, not only got no hits, but struck out three times. Dixie Walker, Pete Reiser and Billy Herman also were held hitless.

Oddly enough, the only two Dodgers who bothered Big Red at all were Brooklyn's two least-feared hitters, Peewee Reese and Mickey Owen. Reese, with three singles, got half of the Flock's output of blows while Owen unfurled a surprise triple in the fifth that gave the Dodgers their first run.

Vaunted Bombers Stopped

Davis, ironically, also kept some of the Yankees' most vaunted bombers at bay. DiMaggio's near home run which Medwick turned into a magnificent out was the closest Jolting Joe came to a safe blow in four tries. Charley Keller, though he walked twice, got no hits. Tommy Henrich also was hitless.

But those jarring wallops by Gordon and Dickey which helped the Yanks to score a run in each of the second, fourth and sixth innings sufficed to carry the day.

The crowd, which topped the former world series mark of 66.669, set at the Stadium on Oct. 4, 1936, when the Yankees faced the Giants, also set a new high for single game receipts with a gate of $265,396. The previous record was $240,591, also set in 1936.

It was, too, a surprisingly orderly gathering. In fact, everything connected with the event went off smoothly and businesslike, in keeping with Yankee efficiency, and perhaps it was this absence of tumult and turmoil which prevented the turbulent Dodgers and their equally boisterous cohorts from ever feeling at home.

Fans Appear at Dawn

The Brooklyn enthusiasts, their "Beloved Bums" in a world series for the first time in twenty-one years, stormed the mighty "House Which Ruth Built" practically at dawn. The gates opened at 8:30 A. M. and by noon the vast bleacher stretch of 14,000 seats and the same number of unreserved seats in the grandstand were blotted out by occupants.

The rest all moved along without fuss or fanfare, with the Brooklyn horde doubtless feeling rather out of place in the roomy reaches of the great arena, so unlike the more homey confines of Ebbets Field where you can almost reach out and pat your favorite on the back or slap down a hated rival.

The Seventh Regiment Band regaled the early arrivals with martial and popular airs while anxious eyes were cast skyward, for a leaden gray sky kept threatening rain nearly all the morning. But as game time arrived the clouds receded and practically all of the game was played under a brilliant sun that provided a day which, with Yankee forethought, must have been picked from the July calendar.

A few minutes before 1:30 the band brought the gathering to its feet with the "Star-Spangled Banner," the white-haired Commissioner, Kenesaw Mountain Landis, dramatically tossed out the first ball, which Dickey, the Yankee catcher, deftly caught, and the battle was on.

Walks First Batsman

Ruffing, appearing in a Yankee world series opener for the fifth time, started by surprisingly tossing four consecutive balls to Walker, the Dodger lead-off hitter, and the Brooklyn contingent sent up a tumultuous cheer. But if the Flatbush denizens accepted this as an omen of good fortune they were soon disillusioned. Ruff quickly snuffed out the next three, with Camilli ending the round with the first of his hree strike-outs. No Dodger got on base in the second, which saw Medwick strike out.

In the meantime, Davis promised to keep pace. Johnny Sturm struck him for a surprise single to open the Yankees' first, but nothing came of this, and when the first two batters were retired in the second, the lean and willowy Brooklyn right-hander seemed to have another round comfortably out of the way.

But it is just at such moments, as most any American League manager knows, that the Yanks are apt to spike their rivals with their deadliest harpoons. Gordon, after running the count to two and two and fouling off three more, caught one on the nose for a towering smash that fell deep in the left wing of the lower grandstand. It was Joe the Flash's second homer of his world series career. He got his first as a freshman sensation against the Cubs in 1938.

It also gave the Yanks the lead and from then on they were never to relinquish it, even though pressed severely a couple of times.

After an uneventful third and also a fourth which saw Ruffing fan Reiser and Camilli in succession, Henrich opened the Yankee half of the fourth round with an easy pop fly. Then DiMaggio sent a lofty shot arching its way toward the left-field stand.

It looked as though it had just enough carry to clear for a second Yankee homer, but Medwick, his back to the stand, timed his leap perfectly and caught the ball in his glove. He came down with a crash but froze to the sphere and the Brooklyn horde let out an ear-splitting roar, in which most every one joined.

Scarcely had the hub-bub subsided than Davis found himself plunged again into trouble. He walked Keller and Dickey followed with a two-base smash that bounced off the bleacher wall in right center. Keller, though his injured right ankle is still heavily taped and bandaged, tore over the ground at his best pace and had ample speed to score on the hit.

The Yankees were now ahead, 2 to 0, while the Dodgers were still seeking their first hit. In the fifth it finally came, and with it came the first Brooklyn tally.

There were two out in the inning when Reese blazed a sharp single to center and, before the Yanks had a chance to recover from the surprise of this, Owen blasted a drive between DiMaggio and Keller in left center, which was good for three bases, Reese scoring on the hit.

The Dodgers were now only one behind, but still the pursuit was to prove as futile as though they were a dozen in arrears. In the sixth Davis got into difficulties again and it was his last inning. Keller walked with one out, and in the wake of this came successive singles by Dickey and Gordon to score King Kong.

Margin Again Two Runs

The Yanks again had a two-run margin while Casey replaced Davis. Round-faced Hugh brought the round to a close without further damage, while Allen blanked the Bombers in the seventh and eighth. But the task of overhauling the Yanks proved a monumental one that eventually ended in failure.

There was a note of Dodger expectancy in the air in the sixth when Ruffing, with one out, walked Herman and Reiser. But, to the consternation of all Brooklyn, Camilli fanned for the third straight time and Medwick ended the threat with an infield grounder to Red Rolfe.

The biggest Dodger chance came in the seventh, and here, for a few minutes, the Flock did look to have Ruffing dangerously close to being down. Harry Lavagetto shot an easy grounder to Rizzuto, who came up neatly with the ball only to throw it into the dirt toward first for an error that put Cookie on base.

Reese followed with a roller that hopped over second, eluded both Rizzuto and Gordon and went to center for a single. Dodger fans were now bellowing with a full throat and the din increased as Lew Riggs, pinch hitting for Owen, lashed a single to center that scored Lavagetto.

One run was in, two runners were on, only one more tally was needed for a tie and, with nobody out, it looked mighty promising.

Third Appears Uncovered

But, the flurry subsided almost as quickly as it had flared up. Jimmy Wasdell, batting for Casey, lifted a foul which Rolfe caught just in front of the Yankee dugout, and with that Reese, on second, thought he had a chance to grab third, which appeared to be uncovered.

The Yanks, however, do not make slips of that kind. While Rolfe was chasing the foul, little Rizzuto was already moving toward third. Perhaps Reese never saw him. But he knew little Philip was there to make the put-out as Peewee slid into the bag. While this was only the second out, it wrecked the rally. Walker ended it a moment later with a grounder to Gordon.

In the ninth came one last Dodger flurry when Medwick, leading off, swung heavily on the ball, topped it for a dribbler down the third-base line and outgalloped it for a hit. Lavagetto fouled out but Reese thrilled the Brooklyn faithful once again with his third successive single, a sharp blow to left.

It was now up to Herman Franks to keep the Dodgers' last-ditch fight alive. But Herman leaned into the first pitch, sent a sharp grounder squarely at Gordon, and folks who have been seeing the Yankees perform all year could have shut their eyes on what happened without missing a thing. Gordon flipped the ball to Rizzuto at second, the mite shortstop hustled it to Sturm at first and another one of those twin killings which only this year had set an American League record had snuffed out a hostile threat.

Today Durocher will make his deferred start with one of his twenty-two-game winners when he sends John Whitlow Wyatt to the mound for the second game. McCarthy, again in the familiar position of worrying the opposition with his wealth of manpower, is letting the Dodgers guess the identity of the pitcher they will have to face. It will be either the right-handed Spud Chandler or the left-handed Marius Russo.

Box Score of the First Game

BROOKLYN DODGERS

	ab.	r.	h.	tb.	2b.	3b.	hr.	bb.	so.	sh.	sb.	po.	a.	e.
Walker, rf	3	0	0	0	0	0	0	1	0	0	0	3	0	0
Herman, 2b	3	0	0	0	0	0	0	1	0	0	0	0	6	0
Reiser, cf	3	0	0	0	0	0	0	1	1	0	0	4	0	0
Camilli, 1b	4	0	0	0	0	0	0	0	3	0	0	7	2	0
Medwick, lf	4	0	1	1	0	0	0	0	1	0	0	4	0	0
Lavagetto, 3b	4	1	0	0	0	0	0	0	0	0	0	0	0	0
Reese, ss	4	1	3	3	0	0	0	0	0	0	0	4	2	0
Owen, c	2	0	1	3	0	1	0	0	0	0	0	1	0	0
aRiggs	1	0	1	1	0	0	0	0	0	0	0	0	0	0
Franks, c	1	0	0	0	0	0	0	0	0	0	0	0	1	0
Davis, p	2	0	0	0	0	0	0	0	0	0	0	1	0	0
Casey, p	0	0	0	0	0	0	0	0	0	0	0	0	0	0
bWasdell	1	0	0	0	0	0	0	0	0	0	0	0	0	0
Allen, p	0	0	0	0	0	0	0	0	0	0	0	0	0	0
Total	32	2	6	8	0	1	0	3	5	0	0	24	11	0

NEW YORK YANKEES

	ab.	r.	h.	tb.	2b.	3b.	hr.	bb.	so.	sh.	sb.	po.	a.	e.
Sturm, 1b	3	0	1	1	0	0	0	0	0	0	0	7	0	0
Rolfe, 3b	3	0	1	1	0	0	0	1	1	0	0	2	2	0
Henrich, rf	4	0	0	0	0	0	0	0	0	0	0	0	0	0
DiMaggio, cf	4	0	0	0	0	0	0	0	0	0	0	5	0	0
Keller, lf	2	2	0	0	0	0	0	2	0	0	0	4	0	0
Dickey, c	4	0	2	3	1	0	0	0	0	0	0	6	0	0
Gordon, 2b	2	1	2	5	0	0	1	2	0	0	0	0	2	0
Rizzuto, ss	4	0	0	0	0	0	0	0	0	0	0	3	5	1
Ruffing, p	3	0	0	0	0	0	0	0	0	0	0	0	0	0
Total	29	3	6	10	1	0	1	5	1	0	0	27	9	1

aBatted for Owen in seventh.
bBatted for Casey in seventh.

SCORE BY INNINGS

Brooklyn Dodgers	0	0	0	0	1	0	1	0	0	—2
New York Yankees	0	1	0	1	0	1	0	0	..	—3

Runs batted in—Gordon 2, Dickey, Owen, Riggs.

Earned runs—Dodgers 1, Yankees 3.

Left on bases—Dodgers 6, Yankees 8. Double plays—Rolfe and Rizzuto; Gordon, Rizzuto and Sturm. Struck out—By Davis 1, Ruffing 5. Bases on balls—Off Davis 3, Allen 2, Ruffing 3. Hit by pitcher—By Allen (Sturm). Pitching summary—Off Davis 6 hits, 3 runs in 5 1-3 innings; Casey 0 runs, 0 hits in 2-3; Allen 0 runs, 0 hits in 2. Losing pitcher—Davis. Umpires—McGowan (A. L.), plate; Pinelli (N. L.), first base; Grieve (A. L.), second base; Goetz (N. L.), third base. Time of game—2:08.

BROOKLYN SQUAD ANGERED BY LOSS

'Beloved Bums,' in Vengeful Mood, Eager to Tie Series Today—Wyatt to Pitch

MISSED SIGN WAS COSTLY

'All My Fault,' Says Wasdell—Camilli, Strikeout Victim, and Reese Disconsolate

By ROSCOE McGOWEN

Nobody was happy in the Dodger clubhouse after yesterday's loss of the world series opener to the Yankees, but neither was anybody in despair.

The boys generally were a bit angry about the whole thing and faced today's contest with a determination to even matters without further delay.

"We blew our chance in the inning that Riggs hit," said Lippy Leo Durocher, meaning the seventh, in which Brooklyn's "Beloved Bums" had the tying run on second, the winning run on first and nobody out. "That's when we should have come through—but we didn't, and all you can go by is the final score."

Wasdell Takes Blame

The unhappiest young man among all the Dodgers was Jimmy Wasdell, whose bat helped to sing a victory tune many times during the terrific race with the Cardinals during the National League season.

"I guess it's all my fault," said Jimmy, standing disconsolate in front of his locker after the boys had trooped grimly into the dressing room.

"I missed the bunt sign," he explained, "and that's just carelessness. I'll take the rap for it. When I came out to bat for Casey," he continued, "Leo told me to 'go on up and hit.' So when Dressen gave the sign to bunt after I had taken one cut, I just didn't see it."

Wasdell was as near to tears as any courageous athlete could be, feeling that he probably had lost the game by not bunting.

"Leo was sore, and he had a right to be," Jimmy went on. "I sure can't blame him. It was my fault."

Durocher Cools Off

But when Durocher was approached some time afterward, when he had cooled off in the shower and was getting into his clothes, his first mood apparently had changed.

"What the heck!" he said, when told that his young utility man was feeling very badly. "It's just one of those things. It's baseball. Sure, it was a tough time to miss a sign like that, but it's not his fault."

Strangely, however, when this information was diplomatically relayed to the unhappy Wasdell, it seemed to make him unhappier than before. Apparently the boss' magnanimity only made Jimmy's sin of omission more enormous in his own eyes.

Peewee Reese, whose own idea it was to attempt to take third base after Red Rolfe's staggering catch of Wasdell's foul pop in the seventh, wasn't in high spirits, despite his three straight hits, his scoring of the first run and the part he played in the second one.

All the Little Colonel wanted was to win the ball game and "to heck with who did it or how it was done." He felt that he had been too ambitious in trying to take third on the play—and yet, had he made it safely, thousands of Dodger fans might be lauding him as the hero of the day.

Camilli Still Swinging

Dolph Camilli, who was struck out three straight times by Red Ruffing and fouled only one pitch during that time, was grinding his teeth as he sat, first here and then there in the clubhouse, gripping a bottle of beer as if it were a bat that he was about to swing.

"We should have beat 'em today," gritted Dolph. "Now we've just gotta go out and get 'em tomorrow."

And Durocher, who announced without any hedging that Whit Wyatt would pitch today, said:

"All I know is that they've got one leg on the trophy. It's a seven-game series unless I am misinformed, and tomorrow is another day."

Curt Davis, in the view of practically every one of his team-mates, "pitched a good game."

Curt said he pitched "a high fast ball" to Flash Gordon, on which the Yankee second baseman hit his homer with two out. Durocher, talked to earlier, seemed to have a different idea.

"Curt threw two low, inside fast balls—one to Gordon and the other to Dickey—which were just the opposite to what he intended to throw, and both of 'em got him into trouble. Gordon hit a homer on one and Bill doubled on the other one."

Muscles Medwick, whose gorgeous leaping catch of Joltin' Joe DiMaggio's bid for a home run into the left field seats in the fourth, saved no end of woe for the Dodgers, wasn't particularly pleased about that, either. Like the rest of the boys, he couldn't find any cause to be happy in defeat.

So these Dodgers all are coming out today to face either Marius Russo or Spud Chandler with a deal of murder and mayhem in their collective hearts. One thing that seemed clear from a general interview with them is that they haven't the remotest notion of lying down and "playing dead" before the McCarthy Bombers.

YANKEES WIN-JOE IN ROW

FINAL NIGHT EDITION
WEATHER: FAIR Details on Page 6

THE CALL-BULLETIN
SAN FRANCISCO — AN INDEPENDENT NEWSPAPER

86TH YEAR CALL AND POST. VOL. 150. NO. 61 THE CALL-BULLETIN, VOL. 170, NO. 61 MONDAY, OCTOBER 6, 1941 5c DAILY

Bonham Beats Dodgers, 3-1, As Series Ends

Today's Box Score

BROOKLYN NATIONALS	AB	R	H	PO	A
Walker, rf	3	0	1	0	0
Riggs, 3b	4	0	1	1	3
Reiser, cf	4	0	1	2	0
Camilli. 1b	4	0	0	9	1
Medwick, lf	3	0	0	0	0
Reese, ss	3	0	0	2	3
Owen, c	3	0	0	9	1
Coscarart, 2b.	2	0	0	3	3
Wyatt, p	3	1	1	1	1
Galan	1	0	0	0	0
Herman, 2b.	0	0	0	0	2
Wasdell	1	0	0	0	0
Totals	31	1	4	27	14

NEW YORK AMERICANS	AB	R	H	PO	A
Sturm, 1b	4	0	1	9	0
Rolfe, 3b	3	0	0	3	0
Henrich, rf	3	1	1	1	0
Di Maggio, cf	4	0	1	6	0
Keller, lf	3	1	0	4	0
Dickey, c	4	1	1	2	0
Gordon, c	3	0	1	0	3
Rizzuto, s	3	0	1	2	2
Bonham, p	4	0	0	0	1
Totals	31	3	6	27	6

Galan batted for Coscarart in seventh inning.
Wasdell batted for Reese in ninth.

SCORE BY INNINGS

	1	2	3	4	5	6	7	8	9	R
New York	0	2	0	0	1	0	0	0	0	3
Brooklyn	0	0	1	0	0	0	0	0	0	1

SUMMARY

Error—Reese. Home run—Henrich. Three base hit—Reiser. Two base hit—Wyatt. Double plays—Owen to Riggs; Reese to Coscarart to Camilli; Herman to Reese to Camilli. Left on base—New York 6, Brooklyn 5. Wild pitch—Wyatt. Struck out—By Wyatt 9 (Di Maggio 2, Bonham 4, Keller, Henrich, Rizzuto); by Bonham 2 (Camilli, Reiser). Bases on balls—Off Wyatt, 5 (Henrich, Keller, Rolfe, Gordon, Rizzuto); off Bonham, 1 (Medwick). Runs batted in—Gordon, Reiser, Henrich. Earned runs—Off Wyatt 3, Bonham 1. Umpires—At plate, McGowan, American League; at first base, Pinelli, National League; at second base, Grieve, American League; at third base, Gomez, National League. Attendance—34,072. Time of game—2:13.

By JACK MAHON
International News Service Sports Writer

EBBETS FIELD, BROOKLYN, Oct. 6 (INS). — The mighty New York Yankees came home to glory here this afternoon.

Pouncing on just two opportunities and with Righthander Ernie Bonham shackling the opposing sluggers when the chips were down, the Titans of the American League beat the Bums of Brooklyn 3 to 1, reached journey's end on their long climb back to the baseball heights, and on the 1941 World Series, their fifth world's championship in the last six years.

DI MAGGIO NEAR FIGHT

Hot tempers flared in the fifth when Joe Di Maggio of the Yankees, irked by the fact that he had been struck out his first two times at bat and angered at several pitches that had made him duck, strode toward Wyatt on the pitching mound ,saying what he thought about it.

Wyatt started to meet him, and instantly both players were surrounded by their hair-trigger teammates, begging for trouble. The umpires tore into the center of the mass to hold Di Maggio and Wyatt apart, and after a moment of uncertainty Di Maggio permitted another Yankee to lead him back to the dugout. There obviously was bad blood between the two teams at the conclusion of the hot intra-city series.

WILD PITCH

There was nothing phony about the Yankee victory today. To win the New Yorkers had to beat Whitlow Wyatt, 33 year old ace of the Bum's—and they did. Two runs in the second inning, helped across by a wild pitch by Wyatt, and a home run over the right field wall by Tommy Henrich, in the fifth, gave the Yankees all the runs they needed.

Bonham saw to that. The big

Continued on Page 13, Column 3

S. F. Bandsman Hurt In Scuffle With Bandit

Lu Watters, orchestra leader at the Dawn Club, in San Francisco, was shot through the left hand early today while scuffling with a petting party bandit on lonely Grizzly Peak, in back of Oakland.

The incident occurred, Watters reported to East Bay police, when an unmasked man stepped from the underbrush by the roadside and demanded his wallet.

Instead of complying, the bandsman said, he jumped from the car and gave fight, wresting the gun from the assailant, who then fled.

With Watters at the time, he reported, was Patricia Joyce, 19, University of California co-ed, living at 700 Alma street, Oakland.

ESCAPED NAZI PRISONERS CAPTURED

TORONTO, Oct. 6 (AP).—Two German prisoners of war were recaptured today a few hours after their escape from a northern Ontario internment camp. Officials anounced that Fritz Fuchs, 33, was caught first "not very far" from the camp, while 27 year old Karl Rudolph was taken a few hours later.

4TH JAMAICA—Easy Blend, won, 11.70, 5.50, 4.00; Count Haste, 2d, 3.00, 2.90; Alca-Gal, 3d, 9.00. Time, 1:14 3-5.

5TH JAMAICA—Speed to Spare, won, 13.00, 5.30, 3.50; Mettlesome, 2d, 8.70, 5.90; Overdrawn, 3d, 3.50. Time, 1:12.

6TH JAMAICA—Here Goes, won, 6.50, 4.10, 3.20; Minee-Mo, 2d, 10.20, 5.40; Dark Imp, 3d, 4.50. Time, 1:45 4-5.

5TH LAUREL—Army Song, won, 4.00, 2.40, 2.20; Roncat, 2d, 2.90, 2.40; Dusky Fox, 3d, 3.50.

6TH LAUREL—Battle Colors, won, 5.20, 3.70, 3.00; Boreale, 2d, 9.00, 5.30; Happy Pilot, 3d, 3.70. Time, 1:42 2-5.

7TH LAUREL—Legal Light, won, 5.30, 3.20, 2.40; Golden Mowlee, 2d, 3.00, 2.10; Dulie, 3d, 2.50. Time, 1:54 1-5.

5TH ROCKINGHAM—Flying Jane, won, 4.00, 2.80, 2.20; Night Tide, 2d, 3.20, 2.40; Reversal, 3d, 2.60. Time, 1:13 2-5.

6TH ROCKINGHAM—Siganar, won, 6.40, 3.80, 2.80; Iron Bar, 2d, 3.60, 3.40; Fancy Free, 3d, 6.00. Time, 1:47 1-5.

7TH ROCKINGHAM—Zaltowna, won, 9.20, 3.20, 2.80; Rebbina, 2d, 2.80, 2.60; Dust Cap, 3d, 4.80. Time, 1:55.

Alameda Recorder Dies

Apparently the victim of a heart attack, Gilman W. Bacon, 77, Alameda County recorder for the last thirty years, was found dead today in the bedroom of his home, at 101 Sunnyside avenue, Piedmont.

The body was discovered by his widow, Mrs. Mabel J. Bacon.

A native of Vermont, Mr. Bacon came to Oakland in 1885. He was employed there for sixteen years by the Oakland Street Railway and, in 1902, he was elected county auditor.

In 1910 he was elected recorder and took office early in 1911

'Deport Bridges:' House

OUSTER BILL PASSED UP TO SENATE

Measure, Like '40 Proposal, Goes Through Without Debate

WASHINGTON, Oct. 6 (AP).—Without a word of debate, the House passed and sent to the Senate today legislation directing the de-portation of Harry Bridges, West Coast C. I. O. leader.

The bill was identical with that passed by the House June 13, 1940, but on which the Senate failed to act.

Bridges' deportation was recommended last week by Charles B. Sears of Buffalo, a retired judge, who made a special investigation of the charges against the labor leader, a native of Australia, for the Justice Department.

Franco Receives U. S. Ambassador at Madrid

MADRID, Spain, Oct. 6 (AP).—Generalissimo Francisco Franco received U. S. Ambassador Alexander Weddell today for a discussion of **"matters of interest to both governments."** No further details of the conversation were given.

Ambassador Phillips Leaves Rome on U. S. Trip

ROME, Oct. 6 (AP).—U. S. Ambassador William Phillips left Rome by plane today for Lisbon en route to the United States.

He intended to take the Clipper from Lisbon Thursday and spend a month in the United States.

SUCH WEATHER!
By Ray Sonde
(The Mechanical Weather Gadget)

"What's up?" the forecaster inquired today

"Well," I radioed down from 55,000 feet, "for one thing, I am."

"Come, come, Sonde," the forecaster snapped back, "you know I meant what's up, meteorologically speaking."

"Here's the forecast," I replied. "Fair and mild today, tonight and tomorrow, with moderate northwest wind in the afternoon."

BRITISH SINK FRENCH SHIP IN ITALY CONVOY

Still Trapped

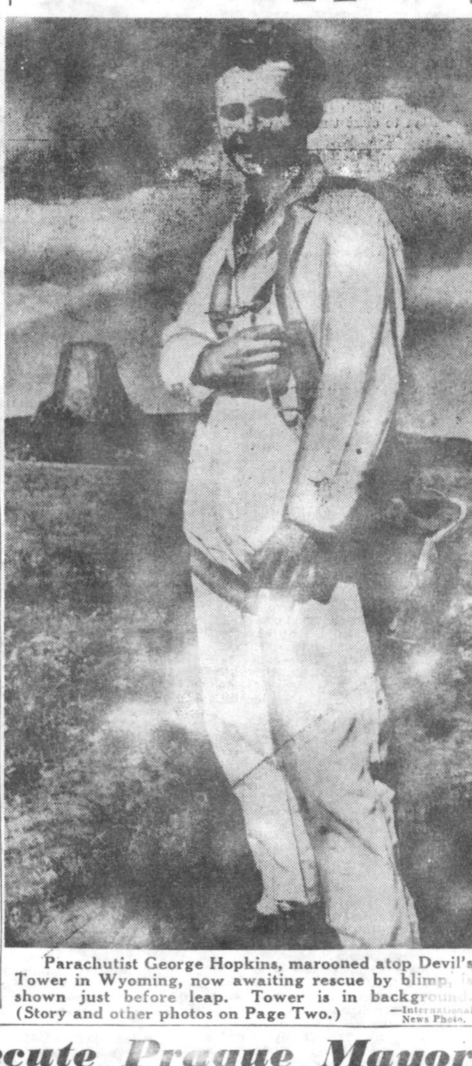

Parachutist George Hopkins, marooned atop Devil's Tower in Wyoming, now awaiting rescue by blimp, is shown just before leap. Tower is in background. (Story and other photos on Page Two.) —International News Photo.

REPORT 2ND BATTLE OFF BRAZIL

One Ship Sunk, Bodies Washed Ashore, Say Maceio Advices

MACEIO, Brazil, Oct. 6 (AP). — Unverified reports along the coast between here and Maragogy indicated today as many as four vessels may have been engaged in a weekend naval battle off the Brazilian coast and that one may have been sunk.

Reports from the Maragogy vicinity said bodies had been washed ashore on the beach of Barra Grande, south of that coast town.

These reports, however, were not confirmed.

HEAVY FIRING HEARD

Sounds of heavy cannonading at sea, reported by fishermen at Maceio over the weekend, led to belief unidentified ships which apparently fought a 30-minute battle off the coast Friday, had come to grips again.

The reports from Maceio, some 60 miles south of Maragogy, said the beams of searchlights were clearly seen stabbing the sky Saturday night as thunder as of gunfire rolled in from the sea.

Residents of Maragogy, many of whom said they saw ships off the coast Friday evening when similar sounds were heard, were convinced a running battle had been fought.

EYEWITNESS REPORT

Former Mayor Ayres Costa, commenting on the Friday incident declared:

"I haven't the slightest doubt that this was a naval combat, as shots characteristic of a cannonade were clearly heard by all of the populace."

Ark Royal Torpedoed, Says Rome

VICHY, Oct. 6 (AP).—The French navy ministry reported tonight that three French merchantmen had been sunk by the British and said that one, the 8,194-ton freighter Theophile Gautier, was part of an Italian convoy when she went down off the east coast of Greece.

ROME, Oct. 6 (AP).—The 22,000-ton British aircraft carrier Ark Royal was damaged seriously by a torpedo from an Italian submarine after the air attack September 27 on a British Mediterranean convoy and has now returned to Gibraltar at slow speed, a special Italian communique announced today.

Three of Britain's biggest battleships, the Rodney, Nelson and King George V, also were in the naval formation against which the Italian submarine attack was reported to have been made last Wednesday.

NELSON TORPEDOED

The 33,900-ton Nelson was declared by the Italians previously to have been hit on the bow by an aerial torpedo in the air-naval battle against the British convoy. She is a sister ship of the Rodney, both being of a type exceeded in the British navy only by the new King George V class of 35,000 ton battleships.

(Editor's Note: The British admiralty admitted on September 30 that an aerial torpedo hit the battleship Nelson and reduced its speed. No casualties were reported.)

SEEKING BATTLE

The announcement said the strength of the British forces indicated the British were seeking a battle against inferior Italian forces.

The convoy of eight or nine merchantmen was too small to justify such a display of force, it was said.

NAZIS OPEN DRIVE ON MOSCOW

Berlin Hints Odessa And Leningrad Siege Will 'Wait'

Associated Press War Summary

NEW YORK, Oct. 6.—A vast new German offensive, with Moscow perhaps as its principal goal and the siege of Leningrad subordinated, appeared to be emerging today on the long eastern front.

Authoritative sources in London, which have been calling the turn of the gigantic struggle, now in its sixteenth week, said the offensive, **"on a very considerable scale,"** had been launched all along the front, with the possible exception of the Leningrad area, where German activity seemed to have dwindled.

GOAL SECRET

The offensive may be the **"gigantic"** operation of which Adolf Hitler hinted in his Sportspalast speech last Friday. At least that was the line taken by German commentators.

Berlin, however, gave no indication of the goal of the new drive, but Dienst Aust Deutschland, a commentary close to official circles, said the operations were so great as to be **"similar to the opening of a new campaign."**

LENINGRAD SUCCESSES

The German offensive was understood to be proceeding in

Cont'd on Page A, Column One

Nazis Execute Prague Mayor

NEW YORK, Oct. 6.—Today's sheaf in the now daily crop of reports on unrest or actual rebellion among the German conquered people of Europe was the Berlin radio's announcement that Otakar Klapka, mayor of Prague, had been executed for plotting a rebellion in the Reich's Czech protectorate of Bohemia-Moravia.

The sentence against him was a sequel to a similar verdict against the protectorate Premier Alois Elias, whose appeal to the mercy of Adolf Hitler, so far as is known, still has not been decided.

JEWS ACCUSED

Dispatches from Prague to Budapest said that synagogues in that protectorate capital had been closed by the Germans on charges that Jews had taken a special part in the wave of Czech unrest. The synagogues were called meeting places for **"aggressive influences."**

In German-occupied France the execution of still another Frenchman, Rene Darreau of Vendome, was announced. Some seventy Frenchmen now have gone before the firing squad, either as hostages or as the principals in military and political offenses against the occupying power.

PRISON TERMS

Darreau was convicted of possessing a revolver and 10 cartridges and it was said he had distributed anti-German leaflets.

A German court martial in Mons, Belgium, sentenced four men to prison terms of from one to six years for possession of forbidden weapons.

Call-Bulletin Today

New Hitler Peace Bid By Jan. 1 Rumored

By Associated Press

CAIRO, Oct. 6.—Adolf Hitler will make a new peace offer to Britain and the United States as well before the year's end, according to information reaching here.

Hitler, according to one American recently arrived from German controlled territory, expects to be able within this time to announce that Russia has been put out of the war and to state that he is going ahead with his "new order" on the continent and ignore England except to carry out reprisals against her for any bombing done to Germany.

PEACE BY STALEMATE

The Germans expect that England after a period of such a stalemate would accept a peace, this informant said.

The peace offer forecast is given considerable credence in both British and American diplomatic quarters here, but both are certain that the offer will be rejected and that the war will go on.

The information comes from various sources. The American

Cont'd on Page A, Column Two

Staid Yankees Stage Wild Dressing Room Scene as Though Series Crown Were Novelty

Durocher Pays Tribute to Foe In Bitter Hour

Bonham Near Tears After Present From DiMaggio; Wyatt Discounts Quarrel

By Robert B. Cooke

A few minutes after they had crowned themselves champions of the baseball world yesterday at Ebbets Field, the New York Yankees staged such a wild celebration in their clubhouse that one might have wondered whether they ever had been champions before.

As the players walked down the runway to their dressing room, Earle Combs lit the spark to the occasion with a loud "Yip-ee-ee!" In another minute all the Yankees were letting off steam with a raucous rendition of "The Sidewalks of New York," the song that is No. 1 on their hit parade.

Joe McCarthy was the last man to reach the dressing room. In his absence Art Fletcher jumped on top of a trunk and gave the athletes the down beat. When their manager finally pushed his way through a group of reporters, the Yankees repeated the song for him before changing their tune to "Roll Out the Barrel."

Durocher Tenders Congratulations

In the hubbub which followed the Yankees had difficulty in shaking hands with each other. Every one was hustling about in a different direction. Photographers' bulbs were flashing and there was a smile on every face. This included the sharp features of a little man who had slipped into the clubhouse unnoticed. It was Leo Durocher, Brooklyn's fiery leader, who had come to congratulate McCarthy and his men.

Durocher, who was stripped down to his underwear, gave McCarthy a slap on the back and shook his hand, saying:

"Well, we gave you a good battle anyway, Joe. Congratulations."

McCarthy, who was in the midst of well wishers, paused to shake Leo's hand and to tell him that "it was a good series."

Then Durocher made the rounds of the various other Yankees. He gave Tiny Bonham an affectionate slap on the cheek and said, "Nice going." He shook hands with Joe Gordon, Charlie Keller and as many others as he could find.

Bonham Claims Priceless Ball

And all the while the pandemanium continued unabated. Bonham was the leading recipient of handshakes. And he also received a priceless gift from Joe DiMaggio, who had made the final putout in center field. DiMaggio carried the ball to the clubhouse and delivered it personally to Bonham.

The big 220-pound right-hander was almost overcome. He was the picture of a man who has realized a life's ambition.

"It's always been my ambition to pitrh a World Series game and win it," he said. "And this is the first time I ever saw a series. You know, it may sound queer, but I wasn't as nervous out there as I have been in some league games.

"When McCarthy told me I was going to pitch the fifth game I was so thrilled that tears came to my eyes. It was what I had always wanted to do.

"I threw one curve all day and used only two fork balls and two change-of-pace balls. The rest were fast balls. Reiser bothered me most of all."

Barrow Pays First Visit

While Bonham was being attended to by the reporters, McCarthy and Ed Barrows, Yankee president, had to pose for the sound films.

"I haven't much to say," said McCarthy as the pair shook hands, "but I think Mr. Barrow has."

"Joe, this is my first visit to the clubhouse all season," Barrow replied. "And I want to congratulate you on a great team and a game team."

"Thank you, Ed," McCarthy answered. "I think we have a great team and a game team, and I think we beat a great team and a game team."

The Yankees were still whooping it up as McCarthy and Barrow were fulfilling their cinema obligations. DiMaggio was discussing the eventful fifth inning, when it looked for a moment that he and Whit Wyatt might come to blows.

"I thought he threw a couple a little too close to my head," said DiMaggio. "As I walked across the field to the dugout, I merely remarked that the series wasn't over yet. When he called me a couple of names, I got sore."

Lefty Gomez Has His Quip

At this point Lefty Gomez broke up the conversation when he was asked how it felt not to have pitched in the World Series.

"McCarthy didn't want to be too tough on them," said Gomez.

Over in the Brooklyn dressing room Wyatt had a different version of the tumultuous fifth inning.

"I heard DiMaggio say something," said Wyatt, "and I yelled back in return. That's all. It happened in the heat of battle. Those things end as quickly as they start. Why should I be angry now? I know DiMaggio and I know a lot of the other Yankees like Charlie Keller and Joe Gordon. They're a fine bunch. There was nothing to the argument."

Although they had just been eliminated from the World Series, the Dodgers were in comparatively good spirits. Losing the series was as nothing compared with dropping the fourth game on Sunday after they actually had subdued the twenty-seventh man.

Wait Until Spring Series!

Freddy Fitzsimmons and Billy Herman were the only Dodgers who showed any signs of Brooklyn's defeat. Fitz was hobbling around on one good leg and Herman was having difficulty drawing breath.

"When I want out to play second in the eighth, I could hardly move," said Herman. "Then I had to start that double play. My side was paining me and when I threw out Dickey for the third out, I could only toss the ball. I'm glad I can rest for awhile."

The Dodgers, like the Yankees, were also doing some handshaking. They were saying good by to each other until next spring. A lot of them were planning hunting trips.

Two Tense Moments in the Final Game, but Neither Proved Serious

Herald Tribune—Acme

Players and umpires rush between Whit Wyatt and Joe DiMaggio after the Yankee outfielder turned to the mound when they exchanged words in the fifth inning. It was all in the heat of the battle and no blows were struck

Associated Press

Bill Dickey is not salaaming to Umpire Bill McGowan, but has doubled up after being hit by a foul tip from Lew Riggs's bat in the first inning. He continued in the game. Buddy Rosar (12), Yankee second-string catcher, is running up to see how badly his teammate is hurt

Composite Score of 5 Games

* * *

Following is the composite box score of the five games of the 1941 World Series:

NEW YORK (A. L.)

	G	AB	R	H	2B	3B	HR	RBI	BB	SO	Pct.	PO	A	E	Pct.
Sturm, 1b	5	21	0	6	0	0	0	2	0	2	.286	48	1	0	1,000
Rolfe, 3b	5	20	2	6	0	0	0	0	2	1	.300	7	8	0	1,000
Henrich, rf	5	18	4	3	1	0	1	1	3	3	.167	6	0	0	1,000
Di Maggio, cf	5	19	1	5	0	0	0	1	2	2	.263	19	0	0	1.000
Keller, lf	5	18	5	7	2	0	0	5	3	1	.389	12	0	0	1.000
Dickey, c	5	18	3	3	1	0	0	1	3	1	.167	24	2	0	1.000
*Bordagary	1	0	0	0	0	0	0	0	0	0	.000	0	0	0	.000
Rosar, c	1	0	0	0	0	0	0	0	0	0	.000	0	0	0	.000
Gordon, 2b	5	14	2	7	1	1	1	5	7	0	.500	6	19	1	.962
Rizzuto, ss	5	18	0	2	0	0	0	0	3	1	.111	12	18	1	.968
Ruffing, p	1	3	0	0	0	0	0	0	0	0	.000	0	0	0	.000
Chandler, p	1	2	0	1	0	0	0	1	0	0	.500	0	0	0	.000
Murphy, p	2	2	0	0	0	0	0	0	0	1	.000	1	0	0	1.000
†Selkirk	2	2	0	1	0	0	0	0	0	0	.500	0	0	0	.000
Russo, p	1	4	0	0	0	0	0	0	0	1	.000	0	4	0	1.000
Donald, p	1	2	0	0	0	0	0	0	0	1	.000	0	1	0	1.000
Breuer, p	1	1	0	0	0	0	0	0	0	0	.000	0	1	0	1.000
Bonham, p	1	4	0	0	0	0	0	0	0	4	.000	0	1	0	1.000
Totals		166	17	41	5	1	2	16	23	18	.247	135	55	2	.990

*Ran for Dickey in eighth inning, second game.
†Batted for Murphy in ninth inning, second game; for Breuer in eighth inning, fourth game.

BROOKLYN (N. L.)

	G	AB	R	H	2B	3B	HR	RBI	BB	SO	Pct.	PO	A	E	Pct.
Walker, rf	5	18	3	4	2	0	0	0	2	1	.222	14	0	0	1.000
Herman, 2b	4	8	0	1	0	0	0	0	2	0	.125	4	13	0	1.000
Coscarart, 2b	3	7	1	0	0	0	0	0	1	2	.000	7	8	0	1.000
Reiser, cf	5	20	1	4	1	1	1	3	1	6	.200	14	1	0	1.000
Camilli, 1b	5	18	1	3	1	0	0	1	1	6	.167	45	5	0	1.000
Medwick, lf	5	17	1	4	1	0	0	0	1	2	.235	8	9	0	1.000
Lavagetto, 3b	3	10	1	1	0	0	0	0	2	0	.100	2	1	0	1.000
Reese, ss	5	20	1	4	0	0	0	2	0	0	.200	13	14	3	.900
Owen, c	5	12	1	2	0	1	0	2	3	0	.167	20	4	1	.960
‡Riggs, 3b	3	8	0	2	0	0	0	1	1	1	.250	1	5	0	1.000
Franks, c	1	1	0	0	0	0	0	0	0	0	.000	0	1	0	1.000
Davis, p	1	2	0	0	0	0	0	0	0	0	.000	1	0	0	1.000
Casey, p	3	2	0	1	0	0	0	0	0	1	.500	0	3	0	1.000
¶Wasdell, lf	3	5	0	1	1	0	0	2	0	0	.200	2	0	0	1.000
Allen, p	3	0	0	0	0	0	0	0	0	0	.000	0	0	0	.000
Wyatt, p	2	6	1	1	1	0	0	0	0	1	.167	1	2	0	1.000
Fitzsimmons, p	1	2	0	0	0	0	0	0	0	0	.000	0	2	0	1.000
French, p	2	0	0	0	0	0	0	0	0	0	.000	0	0	0	.000
§Galan	2	2	0	0	0	0	0	0	0	1	.000	0	0	0	.000
Higbe, p	1	1	0	1	0	0	0	0	0	0	1.000	0	1	0	1.000
Totals		139	11	29	7	2	1	11	14	21	.182	132	60	4	.980

‡Batted for Owen in seventh inning, first game.
¶Batted for Casey in seventh inning, first game; for Reese in ninth inning, fifth game.
§Batted for French eighth inning, third game; for Coscarart seventh inning, fifth game.

PITCHING RECORDS

New York

Pitcher	G	CG	IP	H	R	ER	BB	SO	WP	HB	W	L	Pct.	ERAv
Ruffing	1	1	9	6	2	1	3	5	0	0	1	0	1.000	1.00
Russo	1	1	9	4	1	1	2	5	0	0	1	0	1.000	1.00
Bonham	1	1	9	4	1	1	2	2	0	0	1	0	1.000	1.00
Murphy	2	0	6	2	0	0	1	3	0	0	1	0	1.000	0.00
Chandler	1	0	5	4	3	2	2	2	0	0	0	1	.000	3.60
Donald	1	0	4	6	4	4	3	2	0	0	0	0	.000	9.00
Breuer	1	0	3	3	0	0	1	2	0	0	0	0	.000	0.00

Brooklyn

Pitcher	G	CG	IP	H	R	ER	BB	SO	WP	HB	W	L	Pct.	ERAv
Wyatt	2	2	18	15	5	5	10	14	1	0	1	1	.500	2.50
Davis	1	0	5 1-3	6	3	3	3	1	0	0	0	1	.000	5.40
Casey	3	0	5 1-3	9	6	2	2	1	0	0	0	2	.000	3.60
Fitzsimmons	1	0	7	4	0	0	3	1	0	0	0	0	.000	0.00
Allen	3	0	3 2-3	1	0	0	3	0	0	2	0	0	.000	0.00
French	2	0	1	0	0	0	0	0	0	0	0	0	.000	0.00
Higbe	1	0	3 2-3	6	3	3	2	1	0	0	0	0	.000	6.75

COMPOSITE SCORE BY INNINGS

New York (A. L.)	1	4	1	3	1	1	0	2	4	—17
Brooklyn (N. L.)	0	0	1	2	5	1	1	1	0	—11

Earned runs—New York, 13; Brooklyn, 9. Stolen bases—Sturm, Rizzuto. Sacrifices—None. Double plays—Brooklyn (5): Reese, Herman and Camilli; Reese and Camilli; Owen and Riggs; Reese, Cocarart and Camilli; Herman, Reese and Camilli; New York (7): Gordon, Rizzuto and Sturm (4); Dickey and Gordon; Rolfe and Ruizzuto; Rizzuto and Sturm. Left on bases—Brooklyn, 27; New York, 42. Hit by pitcher—by Allen, 2 (Sturm, Henrich). Umpires—McGowan and Grieve (A. L.), Pinelli and Goetz (N. L.) Times of games—First, 2:08; second, 2:31; third, 2:22; fourth, 2:54; fifth, 2:13. Attendance by games—First, 68,540; second, 66,248; third, 33,100; fourth, 33,813; fifth, 34,092.

Zombrewer Dies at 36, Greyhound's Granddam

LEXINGTON, Ky., Oct. 6 (AP).—The death of Zombrewer, granddam of Greyhound, most famed of trotting horses, was announced today by Warren Wright's Calumet Farm. The mare, aged thirty-six, died yesterday at the farm, and Dan Mahany, business manager of the establishment, said she probably was the oldest horse in the nation. Acquired by Wright's father, the late William Monroe Wright, at the Laurel Hall Farm's dispersal sale in 1925, Zombrewer was the dam of Elizabeth, Greyhound's dam.

Gordon Takes Dodgers Apart In 1-Man Show

(Continued from page twenty-eight)

grand plays he made in the fourth hauled Russo out of what might ehave been a disastrous round. He robbed Billy Herman of a potential hit on a fierce grounder and brought down liners by Pete Reiser and Cookie Lavagetto. Inasmuch as Joe Medwick singled between Reiser and Lavagetto, Gordon's importance here was undeniable.

Furnishes Clincher in Fourth

In the fourth game Gordon really went to town. His single loaded the bases against Kirby Migbe in the fourth and set the stage for Johnny Sturm's two-run slash to left center and itwas Joe's two-tally two-bagger in the ninth which put the game far beyond the Dodgers' grasp at 7 to 4—after the tragic third-strike error by Mickey Owen. Gordon had five chances at second that afternoon but the big one was the D. P. he started on Reiser's hard shot after Walker had opened the seventh inning with a single. And Camilli followed Gordon's play with another single. Get it?

The Dodgers made one run in the last game so the Yankees needed only two—and Gordon, of course, was the batter who produced that second tally. After Keller had walked in the second, Dickey singled and a wild pitch put King Kong over the plate and Dickey at second. Gordon delivered with a poke beyond Pete Coscarart's reach.

Russo pitched a grand game Saturday. Bonham hurled a neat four-hitter yesterday. Keller took the Dodgers apart Sunday. Dickey was dependable as always and handled his pitchers in flawless fashion. Sturm got a hit every day. DiMaggio cut down many a Dodger rally in center field where he made nineteen putouts.

But Joe Gordon was the series hero. ARTHUR E. PATTERSON

Snavely Installs Cushing As First Cornell Center

Special to the Herald Tribune

ITHACA, N. Y., Oct. 6.—A new center play with Cornell's varsity in tonight's workout under the floodlights, Meredith Cushing, of Effertsville, a sophomore. Carl Snavely promoted him as a result of his standout defense play in the Syracuse opener.

Jim Blanchard was at center for the seconds, while Lou Helmick, the No. 3 center was absent because of studies.

Preparations for the Harvard contest began with a light dummy scrimmage, the varsity running plays against the freshmen and defending against a fourth team equipped with Harvard plays.

Register this week if you want to vote in the municipal elections on Nov. 4! Booths will be open from 5 p. m. until 10:30 p. m. today through Friday, and from 7 a. m. until 10:30 p. m. Saturday.

Fourth White Sox-Cubs Game Halted by Rain

CHICAGO, Oct. 6 (UP).—The Chicago White Sox officials peered at a slight drizzle and heavy fog hanging over Comiskey Park today and decided to postpone tonight's fourth game in the city series between the Sox and Chicago Cubs. The game will be played in the Sox park tomorrow night.

The Sox are leading the series with three straight victories.

Oops! No Handles on This Ball, Either

Herald Tribune—Acme

Mickey Owen turns around to pick up the second pitch of the final game as Whit Wyatt's high, hard one jumped out of his glove. Bill McGowan, umpire, stands aside to keep from interfering with ball

DOWN IN FRONT

By RICHARDS VIDMER

Class Will Tell

THE World Series can be summed up by a story that circulated through the press box as the scene shifted to Ebbets Field. At the time the Yankees and Dodgers were tied at one game each. Flatbush was in a frenzy of excitement. And a stranger, according to the tale, wandered into a Brooklyn bar feeling no pain and good will toward all.

He listened attentively to the excited chatter about the Dodgers and their chances for a while. He discreetly waited until there was a lull in the conversations Then with a magnificent gesture he lifted his glass and with a beaming smile, in a loud voice he said:

"May the best team win!"

Whereupon the mob leaped on him with snarls of anger and shouts of "T'row de bum out!" And when he woke up in the hospital he realized that even Brooklyn had no doubts about which was the better team.

Richards Vidmer

The five games were close, but the series was lopsided, for class will tell and the Yankees obviously had the class. The Dodgers might have won the first four contests. They might, too, have won the fifth and last. They were that close. A base hit at the right time, an error avoided, a break here or there could have turned defeat into victory almost anywhere along the line. When a team gets beaten 3 to 2, 2 to 1, 3 to 1, and after the last man has struck out, it certainly can be excused for pointing out what might have happened "if this" and "except for that."

Justice Is Served

AND yet if the little things had been different and the Dodgers had won, the impression would have remained that the better team was beaten. The Dodgers had courage, but the Yankees had the class. When the Yankees were ahead they seemed supremely confident that they would stay there. When the Dodgers were in front they seemed fearful that their lead would be wiped out at any given moment. It was obvious that, facing the Yankees, they realized that the game is never over until the last man is out and, they discovered to their horror, sometimes not even then.

Over the course of the season the Dodgers were more consistent hitters than the American League champions. The Dodgers led their circuit at the bat and were second in the field. The Yankees were third in both departments. The Dodgers had two pitchers who won twenty games. The Yankees had none. But the Yankees won their pennant by a wide margin weeks before the season ended and the Dodgers had to battle right down to the finish line to nose out the Cardinals.

And the series was like that. The Yankees wasted little effort. They didn't overpower the Dodgers in any game, but they won four out of five, Comparing the two teams, game by game, there wasn't a wide margin of difference. Looking at the series as a whole it was lopsided in favor of the Yankees.

Plenty of Pitchers

THEY had the class. Right down the line, from Johnny Sturm through Phil Rizzuto, a threat was at the plate every time a man came to bat. In the field they stifled one Brooklyn cheer after another as they casually scooped up or hauled down potential base hits. And in the box they paraded one winning pitcher after another.

Joe McCarthy, who didn't have a man on his staff who won twenty games over the course of the season, produced five separate pitchers worthy of starting a World Series. The only man he used twice was Johnny Murphy, who serves exclusively in a relief role. Red Ruffing allowed the Dodgers only six hits and two runs in winning the opener. Spud Chandler and Murphy allowed only six between them in the second. Marius Russo let the Dodgers down with four to take the third. And Ernie Bonham allowed just four to win the fifth and final game yesterday. That is pretty fair pitching by a lot of men over the course of the series. Donald, Breuer and Murphy allowed nine hits in the fourth contest, but the Yankees still won.

However, the balance of power could be found in the second-base combinations. All other things being equal, Joe Gordon and Phil Rizzuto still would have been enough to give the Yankees a margin of superiority. Their defensive work was brilliant, sometimes even startling, and Gordon's bat played a pertinent part in every game. He started the Yankees on the road to victory with a home run in the second inning of the opener and he drove in their second, and therefore winning run in the second inning of the finale.

Beaten, but Unbowed

THE Dodgers were game. They battled right down to the finish. They furnished the Yankees with stiffer opposition than any National League team they have met since the Cardinals beat them in 1926. True, the Giants prolonged the series to six games in 1936, but this series also would have gone to six games, or more, if Mickey Owen had held the pitch that struck Tommy Henrich out in the ninth inning on Sunday. And the other scores were much closer.

The Dodgers suffered from the breaks, not the least of which was the line drive that hit Fred Fitzsimmons on the knee and forced him from the box when he was shutting out the Yankees. But great teams, they say, make their own breaks, and class will tell. Many things could have happened to alter the final result, but the stranger who wandered into the Brooklyn bar was beaten to a pulp for what he thought was an innocent remark, got his wish—the better team won.

Tiso and Lantsis's Sub-Par 64 Wins Bonnie Briar Pro-Amateur

Hickory's Assistant Pro's 64 Takes Gross Honors; Maver's 75 Tops Amateurs

Special to the Herald Tribune

LARCHMONT, N. Y., Oct. 6.—Tony Tiso, assistant pro at Hickory, scored a clean sweep in the Westchester P. G. A. one-day tourney at the Bonnie Briar Country Club today, finishing at the tail end of the day's field in semi-darkness with a seven-under-par 32—32—64.

The brilliant round that included eight birdies and one bogey won the pro-amateur best-ball laurels for Tiso and his Fenway partner, Saul Lantzis, by one stroke from the early leaders, Ray Hill and James Maver, of Winged Foot, who had 33—32—65. Maver helped on five holes, three times with his handicap allowance. It was the fourth best-ball victory of the Westchester season for the Tiso Lantzis combine.

Tiso didn't need any assistance from Lantzis for the winning best-ball score. He was driving long and true, but the round was featured by accurate pitching. Nowhere along the line did Tiso need more than an eight-foot putt. He finished with a flourish, birdieing the last three holes, and had he not rimmed two six-foot tries he would have added eagle-3s on the sixteenth and seventeenth. He missed the green at the right on the eighth for his only extra-shot hole.

The Tiso 64 also relegated Lou Barbaro, of Hummocks, to second place in the individual pro flight. The recent Providence open winner playing steadily, had six birdies and one bogey in carding 34—32—66.

The winning card:

Individual Pro Event

Tony Tiso	32—32—64
Louis Barbaro	34—32—66
Joe Rich	36—35—71
Herman Barron	35—37—72
Fred Anunziato	32—40—72

Amateur Handicap Event

James Maver	75— 9—66
Jack Bindamin	83—13—70
John Rago	83—12—71
Jack Gordon	82—11—71

Pro-Amateur

Tony Tiso, Hickory, and Saul Lantzis, Fenway	32—32—64
Ray Hill and James Maver, Winged Foot	33—32—65
Jack Sabol and John Rago, Westchester Hills	32—34—66
Louis Barbaro and Lee Gibson, Hummocks	34—32—66
Fred Anunziato and Howard Schanzer, Metropolis	30—37—67
Joe Rich and Jack Bindamin, Fenway	34—34—68
Arthur Milton, Saxon Woods, and Howard Miller 3d, Wykagyl	35—33—68
Tom Howe and Robert Wilkoc, Carmel	36—32—68
Alex Watson, Hudson River, and Joseph Mitchell, West Hills	36—33—69
Phil Turnesa and Ted Weiler, Elmsford	37—33—70
Herman Barron and Jack Gordon, Fenway	35—35—70
Mike Turnesa and Bernard Davies, Fairview	36—35—71
Charles Warga, Hollow Brook, and Milton Jones, Fenway	33—38—71

Results and Standing Of the World Series

Final Standing

	W.	L.	Pct.
New York Yankees (A. L.)	4	1	.800
Brooklyn Dodgers (N. L.)	1	4	.200

Results

First game (at Yankee Stadium, Oct. 1)—

				R.	H.	E.
Dodgers	000	010	100	—2	6	0
Yankees	010	101	00x	—3	6	1

Batteries—Davis, Casey, Allen and Owen, Franks; Ruffing and Dickey.

Second game (at Yankee Stadium, Oct. 2)—

				R.	H.	E.
Dodgers	000	021	000	—3	6	2
Yankees	011	000	000	—2	9	1

Batteries—Wyatt and Owen; Chandler, Murphy and Dickey, Rosar.

Third game (at Ebbets Field, Oct. 4)—

				R.	H.	E.
Yankees	000	000	020	—2	8	0
Dodgers	000	000	010	—1	4	0

Batteries—Russo and Dickey; Fitzsimmons, Casey, French, Allen and Owen.

Fourth game (at Ebbets Field, Oct. 5)—

				R.	H.	E.
Yankees	100	200	004	—7	12	0
Dodgers	000	220	000	—4	9	1

Batteries—Donald, Breuer, Murphy and Dickey; Higbe, French, Allen, Casey and Owen.

Fifth game (at Ebbets Fields, Oct. 5)—

				R.	H.	E.
Yankees	020	010	000	—3	6	0
Dodgers	001	000	000	—1	4	1

Batteries — Bonham and Dickey; Wyatt and Owen.

Today's Sports

* * *

BOXING

At Broadway Arena, Halsey Street and Broadway, Brooklyn, 8:30 p. m.
At County Center, White Plains, N. Y., 8:30 p. m.

FOOTBALL

Long Island Indians vs. Paterson Panthers, at Municipal Stadium, Valley Stream, L. I., 8:30 p. m.

GOLF

Women's M. G. A. one-day tournament, at Old Oaks Club, Purchase, N. Y., 9 a. m.
Women's senior foursome tournament, at Westchester Country Club, Rye, N. Y., 9 a. m.

RACING

Metropolitan Jockey Club meeting, at Jamaica (L. I.) Racetrack, 2 p. m.

Dodgers Get 3 Hits, Bow to Red Sox, 8-1

Higbe, Chipman and Head Fail on Mound As Hub Rookies Hold Flock Scoreless for Seven Innings—Casey Proves Effective

By TOMMY HOLMES
Staff Correspondent of the Brooklyn Eagle

Sarasota, Fla., March 21—The Dodger batting attack, which flourished to the extent of 19 hits against the Yankees yesterday was a scandal to the Jaybirds here this windy March afternoon. Held to three singles by a couple of over-ripe rookie pitchers, our N. L. champions were beaten, 8 to 1, by Boston's Red Sox before a polite crowd of 750 clients.

The boys blamed it on the wind—a stiff, steady breeze that came in over the center-field fence and directly into the batter's face at home plate. Just why the same wind did not check the 10-hit Red Sox attack goes unexplained, unless you want to call the fact that the Red Sox play in drafty Boston an explanation.

Leo Durocher used four pitchers—Kirby Higbe, Hugh Casey, Bob Chipman and Ed Head. All of them suffered, except Casey.

Dodger Run Forced In

Yank Terry and Oscar Judd were the veteran rookies who humbled the proud Dodgers. Terry is a 29-year-old righthander who learned a trick turntable delivery out at San Diego last season which effectively masks a sneaky, fast ball. He'll probably be a starting pitcher for Joe Cronin this season. Judd, a 32-year-old lefthander, is back from Louisville for another trial

Alex Kampouris got one of the Dodger singles and Lew Riggs got the other two. The final Riggs hit was the only one that figured in the scoring. Reese walked with two out in the Brooklyn eighth and Riggs followed with the hit. Then successive bases on balls to Reiser and Galan forced over the Brooklyn run.

The Red Sox opened up on Higbe in round one by scoring two runs without the aid of a hit. That was largely Higbe's own fault. He gave Dom DiMaggio a base on balls and then threw wild into center field after grabbing the double-play ball Johnny Pesky slapped right back to the box. DiMaggio continued to third on the error, scored while Reese threw out Ulysses Lupien, once baseball captain at fair Harvard. Pesky scored from second when Reese booted Jim Taber's grounder.

Chipman Greeted With Singles

Higbe was untouchable for the rest of his turn and Casey completed three innings without serious trouble. In fact, it was the seventh before the Red Sox broke loose again. Chipman by this time was on the mound.

Johnny Welaj, John Peacock and Judd greeted the Northport, L. I., southpaw with successive singles for one run. Rizzo threw out Peacock trying to reach third on Judd's hit, but then a pass to DiMaggio and Pesky's short single filled the bases. Lupien singled through Galan for another run and Heber Newsome walked, forcing over a third. The fourth run of the inning was Pesky's after Medwick caught Bobby Doerr's fly but the

Continued on Page 2

JUST AN OFF DAY, PALS!

Dodgers	ab	r	h	o	a	Red Sox	ab	r	h	o	a
Reese,ss	3	1	0	3	4	D.DiM'o,cf	3	2	1	0	0
Riggs,3b	4	0	2	2	3	Pesky,ss	5	2	1	2	4
Reiser,cf	3	0	0	3	0	Lupien,1b	4	0	1	10	0
Galan,1b	1	0	0	7	1	Tabor,3b	2	0	1	1	2
Medwick,lf	4	0	0	3	1	L.N's'me,3b	1	0	0	0	3
Rizzo,rf	4	0	0	0	1	Doerr,2b	4	0	0	2	3
Dapper,c	4	0	0	2	0	Finney,rf	4	1	1	1	0
K'pouris,2b	3	0	1	3	3	Welaj,lf	3	2	1	7	0
Higbe,p	1	0	0	0	0	Conroy,c	2	0	1	1	0
Casey,p	0	0	0	1	0	Peacock,c	2	0	2	2	0
Chipman,p	0	0	0	0	0	Terry,p	2	0	0	1	1
Head,p	0	0	0	0	0	Judd,p	2	1	1	0	0
aHerman	1	0	0	0	0						
bPadgett	1	0	0	0	0	Totals	34	8	10	27	13
Totals	29	1	3	24	13						

aBatted for Chipman in eighth inning.
bBatted for Head in ninth inning.

Dodgers ————— 0 0 0 0 0 0 0 1 0—1
Red Sox— ————— 2 0 0 0 0 0 4 2 x—8

Errors—By Higbe, Reese, Riggs. Stolen bases—Lupien. Double plays—Reese, Kampouris and Galan; Pesky, Duerr and Lupien. Bases on balls—Off Higbe 1, Chapman 1, Head 1, Casey 1, Terry 2, Judd 5. Struck out—By Higbe 1, Head 1, Terry 1, Judd 2. Hits—Off Higbe, 1 in 3; Terry, 7 in 6; Casey, 2 in 3; Chipman, 5 in 1.

BROOKLYN EAGLE
SPORTS
CLASSIFIED ADVERTISEMENTS
REAL ESTATE
SUNDAY, MARCH 22, 1942 • SECTIONS C-D

Rangers Drop Cup Clash to Leafs, 3-1

Toronto Takes Playoff Opener As Drillon, Metz and Apps Score

Toronto, March 21 (U.P.)—Toronto's surprising Maple Leafs beat the league-leading New York Rangers, 3 to 1, in the Stanley Cup playoff opener tonight on Toronto ice before 13,313 fans.

Brilliant play by the big Leaf line of Syl Apps, Gordon Drillon and Nick Metz gave Toronto the first victory in the best four-of-seven series. It was a rough clash and the players' blood boiled over. The finish took on the aspect of a brawl and only timely action prevented a general fracas.

Tomorrow night the foes come to grips again in Madison Square Garden.

The Rangers got off to a fast start, but their lead was short-lived. Big Babe Pratt took a pass from Phil Watson at the blue line and broke through the center of the Leafs' defense to light the bulb in 2:26. It was a 20-foot shot and Goalie Broada never had a chance.

Drillon evened the score at 4:15 on a pass from Syl Apps with a low one in close. A little more than a minute later Metz put Toronto in front when he picked up a loose puck and scored on a screened backhand shot from the edge of the crease.

Both teams battled furiously throughout the rest of the period with the Leafs pressing continually. The action was fast and rough, but Bill Henry made a gallant stand in the Rangers' net. Referee King Clancy meted out three penalties, two to the home team.

Leafs Increase Lead

Toronto increased its lead in the second period on Syl Apps' goal at 14:14. The pace slowed somewhat in the middle stanza and the Leafs carried the play to the New Yorkers

Continued on Page 2

Gordon Drillon

NATS RALLY TO NOSE OUT GIANTS, 4-3

Ott Reads Riot Act but Team Suffers Tenth Defeat in 12 Starts

Special to the Brooklyn Eagle

Miami, March 21—Mel Ott read the riot act to his stumbling Giants before today's game with Washington and while the little manager did infuse more life and hustle into the New York play, the result was unchanged. The Giants sustained another defeat, 4 to 3, as the Nats rallied to win. It was their 10th loss in a dozen games.

The Giant regulars played throughout the game. Ott did not substitute a second team as he had hitherto, and the team held Washington even until the ninth when it again ran afoul of the 18-year-old sensation of the Washington camp, Eddie Lyons. This cocky high school rookie from Winston-Salem, N. C., opened the ninth with a stinging double past Billy Weber and rode home on another two-bagger by Stan Spence.

Three days ago, in Orlando, Lyons whipped the Giants with a pinch single for the decisive tally. Senator camp-followers are hailing Lyons as another Pete Reiser.

Adams Finishes Poorly

This time the Giants fielded well enough, despite one unimportant error by the kid second baseman, Connie Ryan, and they hit opportunely. The defeat must be charged to mediocre twirling by Ace Adams, who finished the game after Hal Schumacher had worked the first four innings.

That so-often-fatal faux pas of the Giant staff, walking the first man up, was indulged in by Adams in the seventh when he had a 3—1 lead. Three hits followed and the score was tied. Harry Danning doubled and Bill Jurges drove him in with a single in the fifth off Winn. Werber walked to open the sixth and after two were out, Mize singled. Leiber walked and Danning singled off Bill Zuber, a tall Mennonite from Iowa, for two tallies.

Schumacher had his usual early season trouble with control, filling the bases with free tickets in the second, but he escaped damage. Three singles in the fourth chipped a run off his delivery.

Bob Repass, Senator shortstop, made the fielding gem with a leaping catch of a liner by Ott. Leiber pulled a beauty in center, where he had been shifted to make room for Rookie Willard Marshall in left.

Mize admits his ailing right shoulder is not yet in good condition, but he made two hard throws to second for force plays . . . Ryan's error proved a break for the Giants. He dropped the ball on a force play at second and George Case broke from third for home. Ryan threw him out . . . The last time the Giants won a game Hubbell pitched. And the only two games the club won were on Sunday. Ott is using the lucky combination today, Hubbell on Sunday, against the Senators. Bob Carpenter will share the job with Hub.

The box score:

Senators	ab	r	h	o	a	Giants	ab	r	h	o	a
Case,lf	4	0	2	3	0	Werber,3b	2	1	0	1	3
Spence,cf	5	0	1	1	0	Marshall,lf	4	0	0	4	0
Campb'l,rf	3	0	0	1	0	Ott,rf	4	0	0	1	0
Ortiz,rf	2	0	1	0	0	Mize,1b	4	1	1	6	4
Vernon,1b	5	0	1	14	0	Leiber,cf	3	0	1	3	0
Early,c	4	0	0	4	2	Danning,c	4	1	2	3	1
Galle,3b	3	1	0	0	0	Jurges,ss	4	0	2	4	3
Repass,ss	2	0	1	2	6	Ryan,2b	4	0	1	3	3
Pofahl,2b	2	1	1	2	4	Schum'r,p	1	0	0	2	2
Wynn,p	2	0	0	0	1	Adams,p	1	0	0	0	1
Zuber,p	1	1	1	0	0						
Cathey,p	0	0	0	0	0						
aLyons	1	1	1	0	0						
Totals	34	4	9	27	13	Totals	31	3	7	27	17

aBatted for Zuber in ninth inning.

Senators ————— 0 0 0 1 0 0 2 0 1—4
Giants ————— 0 0 0 0 1 2 0 0 0—3

Errors—Ryan, Pofahl. Runs batted in—Pofahl, Jurges, Mize, Danning, Case, Vernon, Spence. Two-base hits—Danning, Lyons, Spence. Double plays—Repass and Pofahl; Vernon, Early and Repass; Schumacher, Jurges and Mize. Left on bases—Senators, 9; Giants, 5. Bases on balls—Off Wynn, 1; off Schumacher, 3; off Adams, 3; off Zuber, 2. Struck out—By Schumacher, 1; by Wynn, 1; by Zuber, 2; by Adams, 1; by Cathey, 1. Hits—Off Schumacher, 4 in 4 innings; off Adams, 5 in 5; off Wynn, 4 in 5; off Zuber, 3 in 3 Winning pitcher—Zuber. Losing pitcher—Adams. Umpires—Goetz (N. L.) and Summers (A. L.). Time of game—1:58.

N. Y. U. Fencers Bag College Title

New York University won the 49th Intercollegiate Fencing Association tournament at the Salle Santelli last night, copping the three-weapon championship for the eighth time in 10 years.

The Violet duelists retained the epee crown, lost the foils title to Columbia and regained sabre honors for a total of 76½ points.

Army finished second with 72½ points. Columbia was third with 64½, while Penn and Penn State tied for fourth with 56 each. Princeton and Yale deadlocked for sixth with 53½. Navy finished 12th.

Columbia captured foils honors for the first time in two decades. The Lions captured the event with 28 points, Army was second with 25 and N. Y. U., defending champions, took third place honors with 22 tallies.

N. Y. U. won the sabre title by scoring 28 points. Army also took second place in this event with 26 tallies. Princeton was third with 23, Penn fourth with 22, Yale fifth with 20, and Columbia sixth with 19 points.

The Violets won the epee competition with 26½ points.

HERE'S LOOKING AT YOU—The handsome soldier admiring his new outfit is none other than Billy Conn, former light heavyweight champion who is in training for his greatest bout—against the Axis.

HAWKS TO DONATE PROFITS TO WAR FUND

Chicago, March 21 (U.P.)—The Chicago Blackhawks of the National Hockey League will donate their complete profits from the 1942-43 season to a wartime relief agency, Maj. Frederic McLaughlin, president of the club, announced today. The contribution is expected to amount to between $40,000 and $50,000.

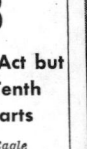

HEADLINERS—Joe DiMaggio, famed Yankee slugger (left), and Hugh Casey, Dodger hurler, turned in neat performances in yesterday's exhibition games. DiMaggio poled out his first home run against Cards, while Casey allowed the Red Sox only two hits in pitching three scoreless innings. Yanks won, but our Dodgers met defeat.

Mioland Sets Track Mark in Tropical Romp

Miami, March 21 (U.P.)—Charles S. Howard's Mioland regained with interest whatever lustre he lost in the Widener Cup as he galloped home a four-length winner in the $7,500 Coral Gables Handicap at Tropical Park today.

The big horse from the West Coast carried high weight in the field of ten starters and was under triple wraps at the wire. Signator who set the pace, was a surprise second, a length and a half before Widener. Our Boots duplicated his Widener performance by finishing a fast closing fourth. The time for a mile and one-eighth was 1:49 2-5, two-fifths off the track record set a year ago by Bonzar.

Stable Jockey Buddy Haas made up most of Mioland's 125 pounds and he waited with his horse while Signator and Sir Marlboro went head and head for six furlongs.

At the far turn Haas let the big fellow go and from there on in the others could never get close. Signator gamely held on for the place award while Llanero closed a little ground for third.

Mioland was a slight favorite and returned $6.50, $4.50 and $3.60. His victory was worth $6,165. Signator paid $10.80 and $6.50, Llanero, $14.40.

Night Tide just managed to get up in time to win the first race, scoring by a nose over Bad Cold. The latter had the lead to the stretch but chucked it in the run for the wire. Arched was third.

Form players were rewarded in the second race when Putitthere stepped down in front at even money. Implicit was second with Mersa Matrush getting in for the short end.

Newcomer Smashes College Swim Record

New Haven, Conn., March 21—A new sprint sensation asserted himself in the Eastern Intercollegiate Swimming championships in the Yale pool today when Ed Hall, sophomore from Massachusetts State, hit a dazzling 51.1 seconds for the 100-yard freestyle. His time not only broke the intercollegiate record, but came within a tenth of a second of Johnny Weissmuller's world mark.

REV. ELLIOTT OF GRID DODGERS NOW IN ARMY

The Rev. Wilson Elliott has notified the Brooklyn football Dodgers he would be unable to play in the National League next Fall, it became known yesterday. Elliott, a six-foot-two, 230-pound tackle from the University of Chattanooga, has enlisted in the army as chaplain. He was Brooklyn's 17th choice in the player draft last December.

WAR'S INROADS TO CHANGE 1942 GRID PICTURE

By JACK GUENTHER

The college football heroes won't report for practice for at least six months more, but you can dust off the little black book and jot down the first new record right now—never before in all the game's history have so many head coaching changes been effected at the major gridiron schools.

Attribute the unprecedented turnover to the war, poor 1941 performances, or even to the natural inclination to seek greener pastures. A United Press survey disclosed today that 15 nationally famed coaches have left their old jobs. Some have joined the army, others the navy and the rest have moved on to bigger fields of operation.

Many Colleges Affected

The roll call is a long one and includes the names of schools from every major conference save one—the Southwest.

Here is the list of switches as it stands today: In the East four schools have been affected. At Fordham—Jim Crowley has joined the navy as a physical instructor and Backfield Coach Earl Walsh will succeed him. At Navy—Major Swede Larson, recalled to active duty, has turned over the Middies to the backfield coach, Commander John Whelchel. At Yale—Spike Nelson joined the army and has not been replaced. At Holy Cross—Joe Sheeketski has resigned.

A similar number of changes have been made on the coast. At Stanford—Clark Shaughnessy resigned today to go to Maryland and Assistant Jim Lawson was elevated to the top job. At Washington—James Phelan's contract was not renewed and Frosh Coach Pest Welch moved up. At Southern California—Sam Barry has joined the navy and Jeff Cravath was recalled from San Francisco to succeed him.

In the Middle West there are four new coaches. At Minnesota—Bernie Bierman joined the marines and Dr. George Hauser, his assistant, will carry on. At Nebraska—Major Biff Jones has returned to West Point as graduate manager and Assistant Glenn Presnell was elevated. At Illinois—Bob Zuppke resigned and Line Coach Ray Eliot was placed in command. At Purdue—Mal Edwards resigned to join the navy and Frosh Coach Elmer Burnham moved up.

The other three switches took place in the South. At Duke—Wallace Wade accepted an army commission and Backfield Coach Eddie Cameron will work in his place for the duration. At Tulane—Red Dawson resigned to become backfield coach at Minnesota and Claude Simon, an assistant, won the job. At Maryland—Shaughnessy will move in and Al Heagy, Al Woods and J. Faber move out.

Gloria Callen Shears Backstroke Record

Miss Gloria Callen broke the world 100-meter indoor backstroke swimming record when she covered the route in 1:14.8 last night in an A. A. U. meet at the New York A. C. The old mark of 1:16.3 was set by Mrs. Eleanor Holm Rose.

COSCARART'S GRAND SLAM HELPS BUCS ROUT A'S, 7-2

Hollywood, Cal., March 21 (U.P.)—Pete Coscarart's fourth inning homer with the bases loaded sparked the Pittsburgh Pirates to a 7—2 triumph over the Philadelphia Athletics today. The score was deadlocked when Coscarart connected, and Vince DiMaggio added another run with a circuit swat in the fifth.

Both teams connected for nine safeties, the A's contributing an error. Ken Heintzelman, Al Butcher and Joe Sullivan hurled for the Pirates, with Newman Shirley and Luman Harris working for the A's.

The score by innings:

		R.	H.	E.
Pittsburgh (N)	0 1 0 4 1 0 0 0 1	7	9	0
Philadelphia (A)	0 1 0 0 0 0 0 0 1	2	9	1

Batteries—Heintzleman, Butcher (4), Sullivan (8) and Baker; Shirley, Harris (5) and Castiglia.

Brown's Rally Wins

Deland, Fla., March 21 (U.P.)—A five-run rally in the sixth inning gave the St. Louis Browns a 5-to-4 triumph over the Braves today. The Braves previously had taken the lead with two in the second and a pair in the fifth.

Three Boston errors aided the Browns as they rapped Manuel Salvo and Dick Errickson for seven hits. The Braves got ten hits off Al Hollingsworth and John Niggeling.

Veteran Outfielder Johnny Cooney, delayed by his wife's illness, made a belated appearance in the Braves' Spring training camp today. Shortstop Eddie Miller makes his playing debut with Boston tomorrow. Outfielder Tommy Holmes of Brooklyn continues to be the best-looking recruit in camp.

The score by innings:

		R.	H.	E.
Boston (N)	0 2 0 0 2 0 0 0 0	4	10	3
St Louis (A)	0 0 0 0 0 5 0 0 x	5	7	1

Batteries—Salvo, Errickson (5) and Lombardi, Montgomery (6); Hollingsworth, Niggeling (6) and Swift, Ferrell (6).

White Sox Defeat Cubs

Los Angeles, Cal., March 21—Behind the five-hit, shutout hurling of veteran Ted Lyons and John Humphries, the White Sox trounced the Cubs, 6—2, today. Bill Lee started for the Cubs and was charged with the defeat.

		R.	H.	E.
Chicago (N)	0 0 0 0 0 0 0 2 0	2	8	2
Chicago (A)	0 0 2 1 1 1 0 1 x	6	9	1

Batteries—Lee, Schmitz (6) and McCullough; Lyons, Humphries (4) and Turner.

Tigers Bow, 3—1

Lakeland, Fla., March 21 (U.P.)—In an exhibition tilt marred by seven errors, the Cleveland Indians topped the Detroit Tigers, 3 to 1, today.

Continued on Page 2

Yankee Homers Top Cards, 4-3

DiMag, Gordon Belt Four-Baggers —Donald Retires 15 Men in Order

Special to the Brooklyn Eagle

St. Petersburg, Fla., March 21—On the spectacular rebound from a trouncing by the Dodgers, the Yankees today clustered a few superlatives. Joe DiMaggio accomplished his first home run of the year, Joe Gordon belted his second in two games with a man on base in the eighth, Charley Keller made an amazing catch in that same session and Swampy Donald turned in five brilliant innings of runless and hitless pitching.

Joe Gordon

The sum total of all this was a 4—3 victory over the Cardinals, who had won three straight from the world champions. Their series of nine meetings now is tied, 3 to 3.

The 18-hit blitz by the Superbas did not agree with Joe McCarthy's tender stomach, so he called a meeting this morning and urged the Bombers to start bombing. In fact, he did more than urge. Tommy Henrich, who has been slow in training and had hit only .220 in a dozen contests, was frowned upon by the management. He was benched in favor of Mike Chartak.

Borowy Yanked in Ninth

With all their achievements and spirit, the Yankees came very near suffering their seventh setback in the Grapefruit League instead of scoring their seventh victory. Hank Borowy, who had not hurled since March 6 because of a finger blister, proved stable-worn and almost spilled the beans. He had to be yanked in favor of Red Branch with two on and nobody out in the ninth.

Branch promptly walked pinch-hitter Crabtree to load the bags, and it took a double play, started by Phil Rizzuto, to keep the damage to one run. With the tie on third, Jimmy Brown ended the game with a foul to Gerry Priddy.

In the eighth inning, with one out and Cardinals on second and third, Keller dashed to the left-field screen, leaped high and clutched Terry Moore's bid for a homer—and the game.

With the best demonstration of pitching seen in Florida this year, Donald was the real hero. Not only did he not allow a hit or a run, but his control never broke. He retired 15 Red Birds in order and only three of them were able to drive a ball out of the infield.

When Borowy got rid of the Cards just as expertly in the sixth, the press box began to wonder about Grapefruit League no-hitters. But with one gone in the seventh, Moore eased a single into left and broke the spell. The Cards got only three more hits.

DiMaggio's homer came off Al Jurisich's first pitch in the second inning.

The losing hurler was the cele-

Continued on Page 2

Snead-Wehrle, Nary-Haas Pairs Gain Golf Final

St. Augustine, Fla., March 21 (U.P.)—Defending champions Sammy Snead and Wilford Wehrle defeated Chandler Harper and Sam Bates today in the semi-finals of the national amateur-professional best-ball golf tournament, one up in 36 holes.

In the other semi-final match Bill Nary, California professional, and Fred Haas, New Orleans, pulled out to win, one up after 37 holes, from medalists Al Brosch, Farmingdale, L. I., and Harry Offutt, St. Petersburg, Fla.

In the morning round Snead birdied the second, sixth and eighth holes, putting the Snead-Wehrle team three up. Harper came back with a birdie four on No. 15 to cut the lead to two up at the end of the round.

In the afternoon Harper came back with three birdies, but Snead birdied two more to win, one up.

Nary and Haas finished even with the Brosch-Offutt team in the morning round. The identical scores

Continued on Page 2

Ruffin Earns Decision Over Parker at Grove

Bobby Ruffin, 136, flashy Astoria lightweight, evened up matters trouncing Morris Parker, 131½, Newark Negro, in the feature eight-round bout at Ridgewood Grove last night before a capacity crowd of 3,000 fans. They had met three previous times. Parker won twice and Ruffin now holds two wins, too.

It was a fast, exciting, hard-fought contest. In the second round Ruffin dropped Parker with a right to the jaw for no count. Despite his defeat, Parker gave a good account of himself against the dancing master.

In two sixes Harold Gibson, 120¼, Harlem, defeated Mario Morales, 122, Havana, and Johnny Greco, 135, Montreal, defeated Joe Torres, 139, Puerto Rico.

In fours, Julie Bort, 132, Brooklyn, defeated Bobby Henderson, 129, Brooklyn; Tommy Marino, 125, Brooklyn, overcame Johnny Price, 130, Montreal; Teddy Delson, 158½, New York, scored over Johnny Landy, 153, New York; Angelo Gonzales, 130½, New York, won from Gregory Costello, 131, Fordham.

By Joe Williams

Bean Ball Makes Laugh of National League

The National League is the bean ballers' paradise. If the skuller is not openly encouraged in that circuit, it is not radically discouraged. At best, the lethal pitch appears to be only lightly regarded.

Just the other day the league was forced to suffer a bizarre and incredible embarrassment when Mr. Larry MacPhail, the distinguished firecracker of Flatbush, actually threatened a more generous use of the leather-covered killer.

"For every ball they throw at our head," roared Mr. MacPhail, with Vesuvian calm, "we'll throw two at theirs."

And to whom did Mr. MacPhail direct these remarks? To his own ball players and in the presence of press box dwellers who had been imperiously summoned to the scene.

Like most gents who are said to be touched with genius, Mr. MacPhail's behaviorisms sometimes verge on madness . . . though there are some gents who insist Mr. MacPhail is merely touched.

In any case there is usually a method in his madness, and the more penetrating observers suspect his newest explosion was shrewdly contrived to keep his delightful Dodgers in a fighting mood; in short, that it was designed to defeat late season complacency.

Whatever the motive, if any, the text and the manner of delivery was scarcely flattering to baseball, the league, or to Mr. MacPhail's concept of the sportsman's credo . . . and, just in passing, it was a swift kick in the pants for Ford Frick, the league president.

In this latter connection we aren't sure that Mr. Frick, a gentle and gracious soul, didn't invite the vulgar hip pocket attack. His handling of the bean ball disgrace in his league has been something less than vigorous. He has encouraged its abuse from the bolos of baseball.

* * *

Bean Ball Rarity in American League.

The bean ball is a rarity in the American League, where the punitive action calls for a $500 fine, immediate eviction from the game and an exile of 10 days. The NL fines both the offender and the club manager, but when you add it up it amounts to little more than milk bottle tops and stifled chuckles. It certainly is nowhere as effective as the AL restraint . . . and now we have the president of the championship club of the National League boasting a reprisal threat of bigger and more brutal beanings and saying, in effect, to hell with the president and his fines.

This is a far cry from the days when Ban Johnson sold baseball to the women by dressing it up, washing it back of the ears and giving the executive hot foot to rowdies. We have heard the colorful and energetic MacPhail compared to Johnson as a baseball influence, and there have been times when we have been happy ourself to subscribe to the comparison, but . . . well, do you know how long Mr. MacPhail would have lasted in baseball if he had gone around rattling the saber in the presence of Johnson and belching fire about throwing at enemy players' skulls? About 20 minutes.

LARRY MacPHAIL.

Of course, things were different in those days. Baseball was younger and the league head had more authority. Frick couldn't be a Johnson today even if he were rigged that way. The executive pattern of the league family makes it impossible. But he can at least go as far as the American League in setting up a sterner restraint. Should, as a matter of fact. The dignity of his office, respect of the game and safety of the players demand all-out policing.

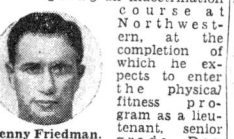

* * *

Why Not Put the Law on Bean Ballers?

And speaking of police, wouldn't it be possible to chase the law on a bean baller, one suspected and charged of deliberately trying to hit a man in the head with what has been proved on certain occasions in the past to be a murderous instrument? Mr. MacPhail has been exposed to Blackstone and would know about that. And how about the man who encourages such an attack, even if it's called a defense? Does that make him an accessory to the fact? We suppose Mr. MacPhail would know about that, too.

Some days ago Bill Klem, the aged umpire, in discussing the noodle torpedo, or bean ball, made a very quaint suggestion; he's the NL's umpire-in-chief and he thought the league's growing shame might be curbed sharply if the sports writers began to put the culprits in the grease.

Why the sports writers? They are always housed far from the scene. Mr. Klem's umpires are right down there on the field. If any neutrals are in a position to perceive the intent of the pitcher they are Mr. Klem's umpires. His failure to demand some sort of co-operation from them has not relieved the situation. And his suggestion that the sports writers do this work for him and his umpires indicates a desire to choose up sides for that grand old game which is known as Passing the Buck.

By the way, we note that the Yankees are bringing Walter Johnson to the Stadium to participate in their war chest double-header Sunday a week.

Wonder if pitchers like Wyatt and Salvo and Erickson and these other skullers ever heard of Walter, ever heard of his cannon ball speed and all the amazing records he made . . . including that one record about which he was proudest of all? Not once in his life did he ever get a ball close to a hitter's head, not even by accident. And he had something to throw, too.

SERVICE MEN and SPORTS

By MAJOR MORALE.

Benny Friedman, who gave up his post as football coach at City College to enter the navy, is undergoing an indoctrination course at Northwestern, at the completion of which he expects to enter the physical fitness program as a lieutenant, senior grade. Dan Grody, who was to have been Benny's assistant, is an air force private at Mitchel Field, where Pvt. John Gudiski of the Dusek wrestling riot squad is answering riot calls as an MP. California Jackie Wilson, welterweight contender, is an acting corporal at Mitchel Field. Corp. Jimmy Keane, ex St. John's U. basketeer and college middleweight boxing champion, feels at home in his present duties as a Mitchel Field physical director. The weather officers' staff there includes First Looey Richard Gill, eight times New England 440 champion, and in the base photo section is Pvt. Norman Elson, national AAU 220 low hurdles titleholder.

Benny Friedman.

Ned Gourdin, intercollegiate broad jump champion at Harvard in the twenties and later Olympic winner, is colonel of a colored regiment and Fritz Pollard, Jr., one of the so-called "black auxiliaries" who was third in the 110-meter high hurdles at the 1936 Olympics, holds the rank of flying lieutenant in the army. . . . Acers at Bayside this week included Ensign H. Robert Reeve, former Dartmouth athlete. The reason Tony Grego, former assistant pro at Bayside, didn't take his accustomed five shots was that he's at an Oaklahoma army camp. Augie Boyd, Tony's associate among the Bayside assistants, was last heard from as an artillery captain in the south Pacific. . . . Jack Miley, the sports writer, joins the navy today as a lieutenant, junior grade.

Jim Nammack, ex-president of the Long Island Golf Assn., has become a lieutenant commander at the naval training school at Cornell.

Ten players of the Missouri Sugar Bowl 11 which met Fordham last New Year are now commissioned officers in the army, including First Looey Darold Jenkins, All-America center, who was with Col. Bob Neyland's army squad practicing at Yale until yesterday, when he was returned to his army post. . . . Sergt. Ken Carson, well known Long Island golfer, has just been assigned to direct military police covering the midtown district. . . . Raymond E. Brooks, former varsity track ace at the University of West Virginia, is a student navigator at the army air forces school in Hondo, Texas.

Darold Jenkins.

Jack Hagerty, Georgetown grid coach, has contributed a flock of players to various services. Here's a rollcall: Art Lemke, lieutenant, Ft. Monmouth; Ben Bulvin and Al Lujack, lieutenants, Ft. Knox; Jim Castiglia and Chris Pavich, privates, army; Jules Koshlap, army air cadet; John Lascari, Marines; Jack Doolan enlisted in the Marine Corps but switched to the Navy pre-Flight School at Athens Ga. Joe Drumm is at Annapolis. Only break the services gave Hagerty was, rejecting 285-pound Ross Sorce because he was overweight, for which small favor Jack says thanks.

Herb Maack, Columbia captain and tackle last year signed by the grid Dodgers, is one of the few players Jimmy Crowley can count on for his pre-Flight School team at Chapel Hill. Jimmy Blumenstock and Jim Lansing, two of Crowley's Rams, are at Pensacola air station, where the football squad will be handled by Potsy Clark, former Dodger coach.

Major Morale can use contributions. It's his pleasure to keep folks informed on what athletes are doing in service. And don't forget to mail this World-Telegram feature to the boys away from home.

Yanks' 7 Double Plays in One Game All-Time Mark

New York World-Telegram
SATURDAY, AUGUST 15, 1942. 15
SPORTS

Help Is Where You Find It — by Mullin

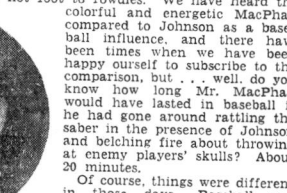

Yanks to Keep Stirnweiss, Says Barrow

Feud Costs McPhail Chance to Get Comet

Special to the World-Telegram.

PHILADELPHIA, Aug. 15.—Conceivably because of the feud which recently developed between Ed Barrow, president of the Yankees, and Larry MacPhail, head of the Dodgers, Brooklyn is not going to be able to purchase George Stirnweiss, the Newark Mercury, to replace the slowing Billy Herman at second base in 1943.

The New York club today announced that Stirnweiss, the Bronx lad who came to the Weiss chain from the University of North Carolina, and who with 62 stolen bases is setting a new record in the International League, had been taken off the market.

Over the telephone, MacPhail said he still was waiting for word from George Weiss concerning the availability of the Newark speedboy. "I don't know whether the lad ever will hit curve-ball pitching, but we are ready to take the chance as he is a splendid fielder," MacPhail added.

At his home in Larchmont, Barrow said: "The Brooklyn club has had a scout following the Bears with particular stress on Stirnweiss. But the second baseman will not go to the Dodgers.

Yankees to Try Out Stirnweiss at Third.

"We have decided to bring Stirnweiss to the Yankees and try him at third base. Obviously he could not hope to give Joe Gordon any competition around second."

Asked if MacPhail's "insulting remarks," as Barrow called them, concerning the Yankees' suggestion that the Dodgers reduce their scheduled double-header with the Giants on Aug. 23 to only one game, had had anything to do with the action on Stirnweiss, Cousin Ed. replied, "That man in Brooklyn has become much too personal. But all I can say is this: Stirnweiss will not be with the Dodgers. He will be with the Yankees."

Barrow still was boiling over the fact that MacPhail had aired details of Ed's suggestion that the Brooklyn club reduce its counter attraction to the Army-Navy double-header with Washington in the Stadium a week from tomorrow. The MacPhail answer was given to the press before Barrow received it.

Whether the Yankees have barred the Dodgers only in the case of Stirnweiss, but have set up a general boycott against MacPhail, soon will be determined, for the second baseman is not the only Yankee farm hand sought by the Brooklyn club.

Giants-Army Grid Tickets Go on Sale

Sale of tickets for the Army Emergency Relief-Tribune Fresh Air Fund football game between the All-Army team and the New York Giants at the Polo Grounds, New York, Saturday, Sept. 12, will open Monday at 9 a. m. in three offices.

Tickets will be sold at the New York Herald Tribune main office, 230 W. 41st St.; at the New York Herald Tribune downtown office, 132 Nassau St., and at the office of the New York Football Giants, 11 W. 42nd St.

Tickets in the lower stand are priced at $2.20 and in the upper stand at $3.30. Mezzanine boxes are $22 for each box of four seats, and 100 patrons' boxes on the field, each containing six seats, are priced at $50.

Open Bean Ball Probe Refused by Frick

Action of Prexy Angers MacPhail

By TIM COHANE.

His wounds still gaping and festering despite that double victory over the Braves, 10-0 and 7-3, Larry MacPhail, president of the Dodgers, had phoned Ford Frick, president of the National League today, and demanded an open hearing on the bean ball situation, which umpires, managers and newspapermen would attend.

Frick refused to hold any such meeting.

"For the good of baseball," explained the president, "I don't want this bean ball discussion to be dragged before the public again, with accusations, charges, counter-charges and who-started-it business. I believe the order to umpires that managers are to be fined $200 when, in their judgment, a pitcher has thrown a deliberate bean ball, is sufficient to handle the situation."

MacPhail, enraged at Frick's refusal, invoked a famous World War I statement by Woodrow Wilson: "Open covenants openly arrived at."

"If that was good enough for Wilson, it's good enough for me, and I don't mean Jimmy Wilson, either," roared Larry. "All the Brooklyn club got out of Frick's decision was a suspicion fostered among citizens that we are responsible for the bean ball throwing.

Ebbets Field Twin Bill Free from Dusting.

"Let's bring the thing out in public; put away the black whiskers. Let's have the umpires read their reports in a meeting and find out who really started this bean ball stuff. I'm not trying to run the league, but I'm going to keep after Frick to hold such a meeting."

The double victory over the Braves was significantly free from dusting. There were a few close ones to drive batters back, but nothing to impel action by the umpires.

Whether or not MacPhail's pep talk Wednesday night had anything to do with it, the fact is the Dodgers were livelier than they had been in a fortnight. They hit the ball hard and fielded briliantly, with four double plays to send their season's total to 111. They provided two errorless games to support the excellent pitching of Curt Davis and Whitlow Wyatt.

Dodgers Snap Out Of Hitting Slump.

Davis' shutout was his fifth of the year and put him one behind Mort Cooper of the Cards. It was the 12th blanking turned in by the Dodger staff. When the Braves finally scored a run off Wyatt in the seventh innings of the nightcap on singles by Cooney and Fernandez and an infield out, it snapped a string of 34 scoreless innings by Dodger pitchers.

More significant than the pitching and fielding, however, were the offensive detonations, definitely indicating that the hitting slump of the last week is over. Capt. Dolph Camilli was the big dynamite with his 18th home run with two on off the hated Manny Salvo in the first inning of the first game, and his 19th with one on in the third inning of the second game off Johnny Sain, who had relieved Tom Early quite early. Dolph also had two singles.

Camilli may do well to finish over .270 in the averages, but he has a strong chance to retain his runs-batted-in and homer crowns. With five tallies driven across he had 70 in that department today, challenging his teammate, Joe Medwick, as well as Johnny Mize and Country Slaughter. And at 19 he was tied with Mize for four-bagger output.

With two singles in the first game and his ninth homer in the nightcap, Pete Reiser showed signs of recovering from his recent lay-off.

N.Y. Batting

DODGERS.			
Reiser	.340	Herman	.253
Medwick	.325	Reese	.231
Riggs	.281	Camilli	.247
Owen	.279	Galan	.244
Vaughan	.275	Bordagaray	.240
Walker	.274	Rizzo	.239
Sullivan	.261	Dahlgren	.173
YANKEES.			
Gordon	.336	Rizzuto	.263
Dickey	.314	Priddy	.261
DiMaggio	.311	Rosar	.253
Hemsley	.304	Crosetti	.242
Hassett	.280	Rolfe	.219
Keller	.271	Selkirk	.143
Henrich	.271		
GIANTS.			
Young	.299	Marshall	.250
Mize	.298	Witek	.249
Jurges	.284	Bartell	.234
Ott	.277	Berres	.227
Maynard	.276	Leiber	.213
Danning	.272	Werber	.201
Barna	.263	Mancuso	.183

Dodger Chief Repeats Demand for Hearing

To Keep Alert—Keep Fit!

Bill Brown Offers World-Telegram Readers Body-Building Program

America's all out in the war now—but not everyone, particularly those men in the late 30s and 40s, feel that they're attuned physically to the times. They'd like to be more fit, more alert.

The World-Telegram believes it can help solve this problem through a series of six articles prepared by Bill Brown, member of the New York State Athletic Commission and famous as squire of his Health Farm at Garrison, N. Y. These articles, to begin Monday, will outline a simple body-building program, designed especially for those who have been inactive.

The exercises, which can be performed in one's home without equipment of any sort, constitute the first step on the road to fitness. Watch for the first article.

Major League Standings

AMERICAN LEAGUE.

Team.	W.	L.	Pct.	G.B.
New York	74	37	.667	—
Boston	60	50	.545	13½
Cleveland	61	53	.535	14½
St. Louis	59	56	.513	17
Detroit	57	61	.483	20½
Chicago	49	59	.454	23½
Washington	46	61	.430	26
Philadelphia	44	73	.376	38

Games Today.

New York at Philadelphia (2).
Washington at Boston (2).
Chicago at Detroit.
St. Louis at Cleveland (night).

Games Tomorrow.

New York at Philadelphia (2).
Washington at Boston (2).
Chicago at Detroit (2).
St. Louis at Cleveland (2).

Yesterday's Results.

New York, 11; Philadelphia, 2 (night).
Detroit, 7; Chicago, 1.
Other clubs not scheduled.

NATIONAL LEAGUE.

Team.	W.	L.	Pct.	G.B.
Brooklyn	78	33	.703	—
St. Louis	69	42	.622	9
New York	60	53	.531	19
Cincinnati	58	52	.527	19½
Pittsburgh	50	57	.467	26
Chicago	52	64	.448	28½
Boston	47	68	.409	33
Philadelphia	31	76	.290	45

Games Today.

Boston at Brooklyn.
Philadelphia at New York (2).
Pittsburgh at Chicago.
Cincinnati at St. Louis.

Games Tomorrow.

Boston at Brooklyn (2).
Philadelphia at New York (2).
Pittsburgh at Chicago.
Cincinnati at St. Louis (2).

Yesterday's Results.

New York, 5; Philadelphia, 2.
Brooklyn, 10; Boston, 0 (1st).
Brooklyn, 7; Boston, 3 (2nd).
Chicago, 7; Pittsburgh, 1.
St. Louis, 4; Cincinnati, 0 (night).

Probable Pitchers

National League.

Philadelphia at New York (2)—Hughes and Podgajny vs. McGee and Lohrman.
Pittsburgh at Chicago (2)—Gornicki and Hamlin vs. Bithorn and Olsen.
Cincinnati at St. Louis—Walters or Starr vs. Krist.
Boston at Brooklyn—Tobin vs. Allen.

American League.

New York at Philadelphia (2)—Breuer and Chandler vs. Fowler and Christopher.
Washington at Boston (2)—Hudson and Masterson vs. Hughson and Dobson.
Chicago at Detroit—Humphries vs. Benton.
St. Louis at Cleveland (night)—Niggeling vs. Dean.

Bombers Run Twin Killing Total to 150 for 111 Tilts

Henrich's Drive Gives Champs League Home-Run Lead with 79

By DANIEL,
World-Telegram Staff Writer.

PHILADELPHIA, Aug. 15.—Having acquired, in other years, virtually all the individual and team records for home runs and other demonstrations of power, the Yankees today stressed their superlative quality in quite another direction. With seven double plays in the nine-inning 11-to-2 triumph over the Athletics under arclights in Shibe Park, the champions of the world established a new all-time high in defensive effectiveness for the major leagues.

When Red Rolfe organized the sixth double play of the game in the eighth inning, the Bombers matched a mark which had been shared by six National League outfits, and the Senators of 1933, who had turned the trick against the Yankees.

But in the ninth the new record was achieved when Billy Knickerbocker grounded sharply to Phil Rizzuto. It was over to Joe Gordon, relayed to Buddy Hassett, and the New York club had the all-time and almost inconceivable standard.

With those seven twin killings, the champions lifted their total for 111 games to 150. It became virtually certain they would better their major league record of 196, established in 1941 in 156 contests.

The carnival of double play fireworks was started in the first inning, and only the second and fourth were devoid of this demonstration of superb Yankee efficiency.

The seven double outs involved Bill Dickey, the catcher, Pitcher Johnny Murphy, who succeeded the victorious Lefty Gomez in the seventh inning, and all of the four infielders.

In the first, Mike Kreevich was doubled at third as Pete Suder struck out. The third inning saw Kreevich a victim at second as Elmer Valo fanned.

Then the Yankees proceeded to jam five double plays into as many innings.

In the fifth, it was Gordon to Rizzuto to Hassett on a ball hit by Kreevich. The sixth saw Knickerbocker's bounder to the Flea start the twin killing, and in the seventh, a feat which was made possible by Rolfe's having booted Dick Siebert's grounder.

The Yankees were sufficiently double play conscious last year. But with the more adroit Hassett in place of Johnny Sturm at first base—and Buddy the best thrower to bases in the American League—the fun really began.

"That guy Gordon hounds me all the time," Rizzuto exulted as the Yanks celebrated the fielding achievement.

"He keeps hollering 'faster' all through the game, and I am starting and pivoting in double plays we would not have made last year. It's a cinch we will go over 200."

DiMaggio and Hassett Keep Streaks Alive.

The Yankees did not put on their great show of defensive skill without a bow to their old specialty of hitting home runs. In the fifth inning Tom Henrich belted his 12th over the right field wall and made the club total 79. This was a particularly significant four-bagger, for it gave the American League lead to the Bombers for the first time this year. The Red Sox were second with 78.

In support of Gomez's sixth victory—with Murphy blanking the A's in the last three heats—the Yankees collected 15 hits for 25 bases off Phil Marchildon and Bob Harris. It was Marchildon's third defeat and second knockout by the Bombers. In accumulating 13 victories he has beaten all the other clubs. But those Bombers have been much too much for the Canadian.

Hitting safely in his 10th consecutive game, Joe DiMaggio got a double and a single and strengthened his position as the Night League champion of the Yankees. Giuseppe has made 14 blows in 36 times at bat in the nine contests the champions have played under the arcs, for an average of .389. He has been stopped in only one night game, by Mel Harder, who made it most emphatic with three strikeouts.

Hassett also poked a two bagger and a single and hit safely in his ninth straight game.

Jurges on Way To All-Time Fielding Mark

Giant Captain Helps Hub Win 7th Straight

By JOE KING.

Casey Stengel, who judges shortstopping by the vaunted Eddie Miller's high standard, gratuitously contributed a rave about Billy Jurges in Boston the other day, and the professor thereby added his voice to a rather substantial yell for the Giant captain. Jurges is scintillating as of old, and when he's in form, there still is no other. Billy is obscured by the notices the Polo Grounds sluggers draw, but if one key guy of the Giants had to be named, the choosers would linger long over the shortstop.

Jurges, incidentally, is on the way to an all-time record fielding average for both leagues. With merely nine errors in 90 games, he's at .982 and only needs to hold that mark to go to the top in the books. Fielding records, it's true, are among the most unreliable of all, but few of the experts would dig behind a figure set by Jurges. He deals only in class stuff.

The Giant infield director is hitting .276, too, in a bid to lead the shortstops at the plate also. Martin Marion's giving him a fight just now, but the others run pretty well behind. Jurges smacked two for three yesterday, drove in a run and scored two, to assist Carl Hubbell to his seventh straight victory, 5-2, over the Phils. The Giant home run power was asleep for the fourth straight game, and Mickey Witek co-operated with Hub and Jurges to win, with his three hits and two RBI.

The Old Master's winning skein is the longest in the league, and it's particularly noteworthy because six of its seven games were nine-inning jobs. Hub put seven together last year, but they weren't so impressive.

Hub Gives Giants Chance To Take Over Third Place.

When Hub whipped the Phils he twirled the Giants into position to soar once more into third place, because that's where they were after the Reds succumbed to the Cards last night. That big chance to win and hold third place follows Mel Ott with the persistence of a panhandler, and it's an opportunity so often rebuffed by the Giants that it really seems a beggar. It's here again today, in the most attractive guise of the season, because the Giants have two week-end double-headers with the Phils, while the Reds wrestle the Cards. Only the New York twin bill record makes the optimist pause, because it is a distressingly unhappy one. Eleven bargain bills have been divided, four won, and six lost. One double-header was dropped to the Phils and two to the Braves. So there is no telling.

But despite a double defeat, the Giant season record against the Phils stood at a very satisfactory 10 won and three lost for today's twin bill. But there was one highly embarrassing angle to the feuding with John Lobert's club. That was homers. The pair struck by Ron Northey and Dan Litwhiler off Hubbell yesterday raised the Philadelphia total to eight off New York hurling. And New York had clouted just two off Philly twirling.

Garden to Get Ice Show Sept 14

The new third edition of Ice Capades, which has its world premiere in Madison Square Garden, Friday night, Sept. 4, has a cast of 110 of the best skaters extant, including several world's champions.

On the roster are Vera Hruba, for five years Czechoslovakian champion and now a citizen of the United States; Lois Dworshak, the rhythm girl and known from coast to coast; Robert Dench and Rosemary Stewart, British gold medalists and champion precision skaters, and Phil Taylor, who has held the stilt skating championship for over 25 years, having originated that style.

Yank Relief Date Stands

Barrow Rejects MacPhail Proposal That Mayor Arbitrate Twin Bill Dispute

Ed Barrow, who's been kept busy this week giving Larry MacPhail the brush-off, turned down another suggestion by the prolific Dodger president today. MacPhail's latest proposal was to call in Mayor La Guardia as arbitrator in the conflict between the Yankee relief fund double-header and the Giant-Dodger twin bill at Ebbets Field on Sunday, Aug. 23.

"Any change now is out of the question," was the Yankee chief's crusher to the MacPhailian scheme. "We have gone far with our plans for the Army-Navy Relief games program and have sold thousands of tickets. It is too late to change."

MacPhail, in a statement issued last night which he said was approved by Horace Stoneham, called for "unity," then continued in part:

"Mr. Stoneham and myself are entirely willing to let the Mayor of New York determine this controversy. If he asks Mr. Barrow to reschedule this game I am very sure Mr. Barrow will agree. If he thinks the New York and Brooklyn National League clubs should arrange another date for Army and Navy Relief, he has Mr. Stoneham's consent and my consent in advance."

Nowhere in the statement was it clearly indicated that MacPhail would be willing to shift the Giant-Dodger double-header in order to make way for the Yankee show.

Dodgers, Cards Win; MacPhail Resigns as Head of Brooklyn Club

FRENCH'S 1-HITTER BLANKS PHILS, 6-0

Single by Etten in the Second Spoils Perfect Game for Veteran Dodger Hurler

LARRY FACES ONLY 27 MEN

He Also Drives Across a Run—Reiser, Camilli and Walker Strike Scoring Blows

By LOUIS EFFRAT

What the Dodgers did against the Phils yesterday at Ebbets Field certainly was not too little, but, all things considered, it may have been too late. Operating on the theory that where there is life there is hope, the Brooks, behind a near-perfect pitching job by Larry French, blanked the visitors, 6—0, and kept alive their chance for the flag, a slim one, even though it was Brooklyn's 100th triumph of the season.

To report that the Dodgers looked great, like the Dodgers of July and August, would be an understatement. They bombarded three hurlers for thirteen hits, wasted few scoring opportunities and generally cavorted like the high-spirited club of the not-too-distant past.

Veteran Inspires Mates

Aside from the tenseness of the pennant race, there was another reason. This was the inspiration furnished by the veteran southpaw in his first start since Aug. 30.

Lefty Larry completely handcuffed the opposition with a one-hit performance that saw him face only twenty-seven men, par for the course. Were it not for a second-inning single by Nick Etten, who was erased a minute later on a double play, French would have matched Charley Robertson's perfect game of 1922.

The 34-year-old portsider was in complete command. His screwball and knuckler never were better and his control magnificent. Add to this the fact that his mates played errorless ball behind him, so that not another Phil reached base. French fanned six, including three of five pinch-hitters called upon by Manager Hans Lobert. The other two failed to hit the ball beyond the infield. Furthermore, only four outfield flies were hit.

It is no secret that French is working under a bonus arrangement with the Dodgers. It was agreed that if Larry pitched a total of 150 innings he would receive an additional $2,500. Including yesterday's game, the southpaw now has twirled 144 1-3 frames. Whether or not he sees action again, he will be paid the extra money. President Larry MacPhail said yesterday French would be paid.

So much for French. His mates virtually clinched matters for him as early as the third inning, when a pass to French, Dixie Walker's double and another two-bagger by Pete Reiser produced a brace of runs against Rube Melton. Nothing mattered after that, but in the fifth Dolph Camilli belted a 400-foot triple, driving home two more tallies. In the sixth, against Ike Pearson, Peewee Reese doubled and French singled him home and, in the eighth, Billy Herman singled, French sacrificed and Walker's clean hit brought Herman around.

Hits a Lazy Liner

Etten's hit was a lazy liner, which Reese almost knocked down.

Aside from his pitching, French did more than his share at bat, as he romped to his fourteenth victory.

Reese was beaned in batting practice. Although a stretcher was rushed out, Peewee returned to the club house under his own steam, and after a short rest was back in action, apparently none the worse for his experience.

The Dodgers have achieved sixteen shut-outs, four by French. That verbal battle between MacPhail and Bill Klem, chief of umpires, the day before was straightened out yesterday and both were on friendly terms. "There's no man in baseball I respect more than the old arbitrator," said MacPhail.

The box score:

PHILADELPHIA (N.)	ab.	r.	h.	po.	a.	e.
May, 3b	3	0	0	2	2	0
Naylor, cf.rf	3	0	0	0	0	0
Northey, rf	2	0	0	1	0	0
Pearson, p	0	0	0	0	0	0
aFreed	1	0	0	0	0	0
Beck, p	0	0	0	0	1	0
Litwhiler, lf	3	0	0	1	0	0
Etten, 1b	2	0	1	10	0	0
Murphy, 1b	1	0	0	1	0	0
Burich, ss	3	0	0	3	2	0
Murtaugh, 2b	2	0	0	1	2	1
bBragan	1	0	0	0	0	0
Livingston, c	2	0	0	5	1	0
cWarren	1	0	0	0	0	0
Melton, p	1	0	0	0	3	0
Koy, rf	2	0	0	0	0	0
Total	27	0	1	24	11	1

BROOKLYN (N.)	ab.	r.	h.	po.	a.	e.
Walker, rf	3	1	3	1	0	0
Vaughan, 3b	4	1	0	1	3	0
Reiser, cf	5	1	3	2	0	0
Camilli, 1b	5	0	2	14	0	0
Galan, lf	3	0	1	1	0	0
Owen, c	4	0	1	6	0	0
Reese, ss	4	1	1	1	4	0
Herman, 2b	4	1	1	1	2	0
French, p	2	1	1	0	2	0
Total	34	6	13	27	11	0

aBatted for Pearson in seventh.
bBatted for Murtaugh in ninth.
cBatted for Livingston in ninth.

Philadelphia .... 0 0 0 0 0 0 0 0 0—0
Brooklyn .... 0 0 2 0 2 1 0 1 ..—6

Runs batted in—Reiser 2, Camilli 2, French, Walker.

Two-base hits—Owen, Walker, Reiser, Reese. Three-base hit—Camilli. Sacrifice—French. Double plays—Reese and Camilli; May and Etten. Left on bases—Philadelphia 0, Brooklyn 9. Bases on balls—Off Melton 3, Pearson 1. Struck out—By Melton 3, French 6. Hits—Off Melton 6 in 5 innings; Pearson 2 in 1; Beck 5 in 2. Losing pitcher—Melton. Umpires—Pinelli, Goetz, Jorda and Stewart. Time of game—1:50. Attendance—4,047.

Oneonta Evens Play-Off Series

ONEONTA, N. Y., Sept. 23 (AP)—Behind Tommy Fine's four-hit pitching and fifteen strike-outs after only one day's rest, the Oneonta Indians tonight evened their Canadian-American League final play-off series with Amsterdam by winning, 4—1. Both teams have won three games in the four-out-of seven set.

THE WINNERS OF THE 1942 PENNANT IN THE AMERICAN LEAGUE

The New York Yankees before the start of yesterday's game at the stadium. Front row, left to right: Buddy Rosar, Charlie Keller, Hank Borowy, Phil Rizzuto, Coach Arthur Fletcher, Manager Joe McCarthy, Coach Earle Combs, Coach John Schulte, Atley Donald, Marvin Breuer. Center row, left to right: Rollie Hemsley, George Stainback, Frank Crosetti, Ernie Bonham, Jim Turner, Paul Schreiber, Marius Russo, Robert Rolfe, Gerry Priddy, Joe Gordon and Trainer Earl Painter. Rear row, left to right: George Selkirk, Vernon Gomez, Joe DiMaggio, Charlie Ruffing, Spurgeon Chandler, Johnny Lindell, Roy Cullenbine, Johnny Murphy and Bill Dickey. Seated in front is Pat O'Doughty, bat boy.

The New York Times Studio

M'PHAIL TO RETAIN ONE DODGER POST

Stays as Director, Resigns as President, General Manager—Will Enter the Army

Larry MacPhail's resignation as president and general manager of the Dodgers was accepted last night by the Brooklyn board of directors, effective at the end of the current season. MacPhail's decision to relinquish these positions was prompted not by any dissension between him and the board, it was said, but because he hopes to report to the Army by the end of this week.

While informing the press, in the presence of the directors, MacPhail, who came from Cincinnati to Brooklyn in 1938 as vice president and general manager and then succeeded the late Stephen W. McKeever as president in May of 1939, said: "I leave here very unhappily. The five years I spent in Brooklyn were indeed happy ones." At this point MacPhail broke down, sobbed, "I don't think I'll have another baseball association other than Brooklyn," and had to leave the Brooklyn office to hide his emotions.

Express Their Regret

The other directors, James A. Mulvey, Joseph A. Gilleaudeau, William L. Hughes and George A. Barnewall, expressed sincere regret that MacPhail had made up his mind to go. They emphasized the harmony that has existed among them and said that no successor has been considered or approached. This put into discard rumors which had had Bill Terry of the Giants and Branch Rickey of the Cardinals, among others, as possible successors. The board was emphatic in saying that the same aggressive policies inaugurated by MacPhail would be continued.

Last Spring, MacPhail, now 52, signed a five-year contract to serve as president and general manager along with acting as a director. MacPhail revealed that he also had tendered his resignation as director but that that had been declined. "I'll continue as a director as long as I am wanted," he stated, thus answering the question of whether he was severing all connections with the club. A director's post, incidentally, is a non-paying one.

Queries Are Invited

The meeting was held at the Brooklyn Club, a fraternal organization in no way connected with the Dodgers. While the session was in progress members of the press were waiting impatiently in the baseball club's offices. MacPhail phoned the writers and asked them to pose six questions, which he, in turn, would refer to the board. He and the directors then came to the offices and invited and answered other queries concerning policy, farm system and future plans.

MacPhail, an alumnus of the University of Michigan and a captain of artillery in the last war, has been connected with organized baseball for fourteen years, in the Michigan State League and with Columbus, Cincinnati and Brooklyn. It was he who introduced night baseball and the broadcasting of games to Brooklyn and he was regarded as the greatest showman in the game.

It was during the first World War that MacPhail, and a few other members of the A. E. F., tried to kidnap the Kaiser after the armistice. Since the start of the present war MacPhail has been eager to get back into uniform. The Brooklyn president may be followed by Leo Durocher, the Dodgers' field manager, who, it is understood, has applied for a naval commission.

Giants Will Admit Fans Who Bring Scrap Metal

The Giants, returning home today, will join the Dodgers in aiding the nation's drive for scrap metal, it was announced yesterday. Starting today and for the remainder of the season, fans may present ten pounds or more of scrap at the 159th Street and Eighth Avenue entrance in exchange for admission to the Polo Grounds.

A similar plan was put into effect at Ebbets Field last Monday. Visiting the Giants this afternoon for a double-header will be the Phils. The first game will get under way at 1:30.

Major League Leaders

BATSMEN

NATIONAL LEAGUE

	G.	AB.	R.	H.	PC.
Lombardi, Boston	102	295	29	97	.329
Reiser, Brooklyn	121	462	87	147	.318
Slaughter, St. Louis	150	582	98	184	.316
Musial, St. Louis	137	455	86	142	.312
Mize, New York	136	518	94	158	.305

AMERICAN LEAGUE

	G.	AB.	R.	H.	PC.
Williams, Boston	149	519	141	185	.357
Pesky, Boston	146	615	105	204	.332
Spence, Washington	149	629	94	203	.323
Gordon, New York	146	535	87	171	.320
Case, Washington	125	515	100	164	.318

HOME RUN HITTERS

NATIONAL LEAGUE

Ott, N. Y. ....28 | Camilli, Bklyn. 25
Mize, N. Y. 25

AMERICAN LEAGUE

Williams, Boston...36 | Keller, N. Y. 26
Laabs, St. Louis...27

RUNS BATTED IN

NATIONAL LEAGUE

Mize, N. Y. ....107 | Slaughter, St. L.. 98
Camilli, Bklyn....101

AMERICAN LEAGUE

Williams, Boston..137 | Keller, N. Y. 109
DiMaggio, N. Y...110

BONHAM OF YANKS TOPS SENATORS, 4-1

Gives Five Hits in Notching 21st Victory as Club Ends Regular Home Season

By ARTHUR DALEY

The Cardinals are the hottest thing in baseball at the moment, but the Yankees hardly have been moving in the frigid zone themselves. They beat the Senators yesterday, 4 to 1, in their final regular appearance at the Stadium this season and this was their thirty-first victory in their last forty-... games. Nothing static about Tiny Bonham, brushing up some chores in the coming ... series, completed his personal campaign with a sterling five hitter as he achieved his twenty-first triumph as against only five reverses. For five innings he pitched perfect ball, losing his no-hitter and his shutout in the sixth.

Make Most of Their Hits

When the Yankees can't overpower a pitcher they are perfectly willing to outslick him. They got only seven safeties from young Rae Scarborough in seven frames, but they were listening almost every time that opportunity knocked.

Red Rolfe opened the fourth with a single and the Washington hurler lost control as he walked Roy Cullenbine, Charlie Keller and Joe Gordon to force in a run. Bill Dickey singled in one more and the third came in on a force play. Another marker arrived in the seventh, and this was opportunism to the hilt.

Phil Rizzuto dropped a blooper in center. Rolfe caromed one off Mickey Vernon at first and stretched it into a double as Scooter scooted home, going to third himself as the outfield throw-in skipped past the catcher. That was a carbon copy of Cardinal base running.

The Senators took their run when Ellis Clary became the first man to reach base on Bonham by way of opening the sixth with a single. Two infield outs moved him to third and George Washington Case singled him home.

Bonham Has Fanned 70

Bonham's record for the year is quite astonishing. He pitched 226 innings, allowed 199 hits, walked only 23 (none yesterday) and fanned 70. . . . This was the end of the Washington season. . . . The Yanks finish at Boston on Sunday, having a complete day off today and practice tomorrow and Saturday. They also will have a Stadium workout on Monday before leaving that night for St. Louis—or is it Brooklyn?

Joe DiMaggio was robbed of two hits, Stan Spence going to the center field wall to haul down a 400-footer and Bobby Estalella spearing a screaming liner and converting it into a double play. No twin killings for the Yanks yesterday, which means that they have little chance to break their old record of 196.

World series portent: Mezzanine seats behind the press box were ripped out to provide temporary press facilities. . . . The Yanks wound up with the Senators as their favorite victims, 17 victories to 5. . . . Rizzuto took too big a lead in the first and was picked off. . . . This cost a run, because Cullenbine doubled in that same frame.

Yankees' Box Score

WASHINGTON (A.)	ab.	r.	h.	po.	a.	e.
Case, lf	4	0	2	2	0	0
Spence, cf	4	0	0	2	0	0
Campbell, rf	4	0	1	1	0	1
Vernon, 1b	4	0	0	11	0	0
Estalella, 3b	4	0	1	3	3	0
Sullivan, ss	3	0	0	3	4	0
Clary, 2b	3	1	1	1	2	0
Early, c	3	0	0	1	0	0
Scarbor'h, p	2	0	0	0	3	0
aCroucher	1	0	0	0	0	0
Kennedy, p	0	0	0	0	0	0
Total	32	1	5	24	12	1

NEW YORK (A.)	ab.	r.	h.	po.	a.	e.
Rizzuto, ss	4	1	2	1	2	0
Rolfe, 3b	4	1	2	0	3	0
Cul'bine, rf	1	1	1	2	0	0
DiMaggio, cf	4	0	0	5	0	0
Keller, lf	3	1	0	6	0	0
Gordon, 2b	3	0	0	0	1	0
Dickey, c	4	0	2	5	0	0
Hassett, 1b	3	0	0	7	1	0
Bonham, p	3	0	0	1	0	0
Total	29	4	7	27	7	0

aBatted for Scarborough in eighth.

Washington .... 0 0 0 0 0 1 0 0 0—1
New York .... 0 0 0 3 0 0 1 0 ..—4

Runs batted in—Gordon, Dickey, Hassett, Case, Rolfe.

Two-base hits—Cullenbine, Rolfe. Double play—Estalella and Vernon. Left on bases—New York 6, Washington 4. Bases on balls—Off Scarborough 5. Struck out—By Bonham 4, Scarborough 1. Hits—Off Scarborough 7 in 7 innings, Kennedy 0 in 1. Losing pitcher—Scarborough. Umpires—Grieve, Rommel, Quinn and McGowan. Time of game—1:34. Attendance—2,198.

National League Race

STANDING OF THE CLUBS

	W.	L.	PC.	Behind.
St. Louis	103	48	.682	..
Brooklyn	100	50	.667	2½

REMAINING GAMES

	St. Louis (3)	Brooklyn (4)
Sept. 24	Cincinnati	Boston
Sept. 25	Open date	Boston
Sept. 26	Chicago	At Philadelphia
Sept. 27	Chicago	At Philadelphia

Major League Baseball

National League

YESTERDAY'S RESULTS

Brooklyn 6, Philadelphia 0.
St. Louis 4, Cincinnati 2. (night).
Other clubs not scheduled.

STANDING OF THE CLUBS

	St. Louis	Brooklyn	New York	Cincinnati	Chicago	Pittsburgh	Boston	Phila'phia	Won	Lost	Percentage	Games Behind
St. L.	—	13	15	14	14	14	16	17	103	48	.682	—
Bkln	9	—	14	15	16	16	14	16	100	50	.667	2½
N. Y.	7	8	—	13	13	15	11	15	82	64	.562	18½
Cinc.	7	7	9	—	9	12	16	16	76	73	.510	26
Chic.	6	6	9	13	—	11	9	14	68	84	.447	35½
Pitts	8	6	7	7	11	—	12	13	64	81	.441	36
Bost.	6	6	7	5	13	7	—	14	58	86	.403	41½
Phila	5	4	3	6	8	6	8	—	40	105	.276	60
Lost.	48	50	64	73	84	81	86	105	—	—		

GAMES TODAY

Philadelphia at New York (2, 1:30 P. M.).
Boston at Brooklyn (3 P. M.).
Cincinnati at St. Louis.
Other clubs not scheduled.

American League

YESTERDAY'S RESULT

New York 4, Washington 1.
Other clubs not scheduled.

STANDING OF THE CLUBS

	New York	Boston	St. Louis	Cleveland	Detroit	Chicago	Wash'gton	Phila'phia	Won	Lost	Percentage	Games Behind
N. Y.	—	10	15	15	15	15	17	16	103	50	.673	—
Bost.	11	—	11	14	15	13	14	14	92	59	.609	10
St. L.	7	11	—	13	11	13	11	16	82	69	.543	20
Clev.	7	8	9	—	7	11	15	16	73	76	.490	28
Det.	7	7	11	13	—	13	9	13	73	79	.480	29½
Chic.	7	8	6	8	9	—	13	12	63	82	.434	36
Wsh.	5	7	11	7	13	7	—	12	62	89	.411	40
Phila	6	8	6	6	9	10	10	—	55	99	.357	48½
Lost.	50	59	69	76	79	82	89	99	—	—		

GAMES TODAY

Chicago at Cleveland (2).
Other clubs not scheduled.

St. Louis Keeps 2½-Game Lead, Beating Reds Under Lights, 4-2

26,514 See Beazley Hurl 2-Hitter for 20th Victory—Cards Need 2 Triumphs for Flag—3 Runs in 3d Trip Walters

By JOHN DREBINGER

Special to THE NEW YORK TIMES.

ST. LOUIS, Sept. 23—Urged on by the joyous shrieks of 26,514 deliriously happy fans, the pennant-bound Cardinals advanced another stride toward their goal tonight when, behind Johnny Beazley's brilliant two-hit pitching, they conquered the redoubtable Bucky Walters and the Reds, 4 to 2.

Thus, despite the Dodgers' victory earlier in the day, Billy Southworth's inspired St. Louisans retained their two-and-a-half-game lead in the National League's seething pennant race.

More important, they advanced to a spot where Brooklyn's position became practically untenable. With only three games to play, one more with Cincinnati and two with the Cubs, the Redbirds need to win only two to clinch the flag even should the Dodgers win all four of their remaining battles.

Combination of Two Needed

One Brooklyn defeat and the Cards need to win only one to clinch, while two Flatbush setbacks would end it regardless of what the St. Louisans did. In other words, any combination of two will turn the trick.

Despite Beazley's superb effort in bagging his twentieth victory against only six defeats, there were some anxious moments when wildness by the freshman star, coupled with an error by the usually reliable Marty Marion, helped the Reds to two runs in the first inning.

Later, as so often has happened during the Cards' electrifying spurt, there again came those fortuitous breaks upon which these alert Redbirds pounce with amazing alacrity, and once they had ripped off three runs in the third they were never headed.

A pass to Eddie Joost started Beazley's troubles in the first. Joost was forced by Gerald Walker, but the latter stole second and then went to third when Max Marshall's grounder got caught in the webbing of Marty Marion's glove. Before the lean shortstop could get the ball on its way to first Marshall had arrived safely on the bag and Marion was charged with an error.

Wild Pitch Lets in Run

A wild pitch scored Walker and when Frank McCormick followed with a single to center, Marshall, who had taken third on the wild heave, also tallied. There was now a deal of activity in the St. Louis bullpen, but Beazley finally found the range.

He snuffed out the next two batters and after that only one Redleg got on base, Bert Haas getting a double to open the fifth but advancing no farther than third.

In the meantime Walters struggled desperately to hold his margin and for two innings succeeded despite one Cincinnati error in the first and two in the second. Walters may hold no deep affection for Brooklyn but he was out to make a fight of it to the end.

In the third luck walked right out on Bucky and ironically it again was Harry Walker, kid brother of the Dodgers' Dixie, who turned the tide of battle in the Cards' favor. He lifted a fly into short center and when Lonnie Frey and Marshall collided in trying for the catch, the ball rolled away for a double.

Enos Slaughter grounded out, but Stan Musial, once again the Redbirds' batting star, singled to drive in one run. Then came the fourth Cincinnati error, this time a costly one, when Frey dropped Joost's throw on Walker Cooper's grounder.

A moment later Ray Sanders, in the line-up in place of Johnny Hopp, whipped a low drive to dead center. Gerald Walker charged the ball in a desperate bid to make a shoestring catch, but missed connections and as the ball rolled out to center, Musial and Cooper scored while Sanders pulled up with a triple.

That was the ball game although the Cards, just to make it more secure, grabbed another run in the seventh on singles by Walker and Slaughter and Musial's third hit, a double to left.

The Box Score

CINCINNATI (N.)	ab.	r.	h.	po.	a.	e.
Joost, ss	3	0	0	2	4	1
G. Walker, cf	4	1	0	1	0	0
Marshall, rf	4	1	0	0	0	0
F. McCork, 1b	4	0	1	0	2	0
Tipton, lf	3	0	0	0	0	0
Lamanno, c	3	0	0	5	0	1
Haas, 3b	3	0	1	2	3	0
Frey, 2b	2	0	0	3	6	1
Walters, p	3	0	0	2	1	1
Total	29	2	2	24	16	4

ST. LOUIS (N.)	ab.	r.	h.	po.	a.	e.
Brown, 2b	5	0	0	3	4	0
H. Walker, cf	4	2	2	3	0	0
Slaughter, rf	4	0	2	0	0	0
Musial, lf	4	1	3	3	0	0
W. Cooper, c	4	1	0	4	1	0
Sanders, 1b	1	0	1	11	0	0
Kurowski, 3b	4	0	0	2	1	0
Marion, ss	4	0	1	1	2	1
Beazley, p	4	0	0	0	3	0
Total	34	4	9	27	11	1

Cincinnati .... 2 0 0 0 0 0 0 0 0—2
St. Louis .... 0 0 3 0 0 0 1 0 ..—4

Runs batted in—F. McCormack, Musial 2, Sanders 2.

Two-base hits—H. Walker, Haas, Musial. Three-base hit—Sanders. Stolen base—G. Walker. Sacrifice—Frey. Double plays—Joost, Frey and F. McCormick; Frey, Joost and F. McCormick. Left on bases—Cincinnati 2, St. Louis 9. Bases on balls—Off Walters 3, Beazley 1. Struck out—By Walters 5, Beazley 3. Wild pitch—Beazley. Umpires—Conlan, Reardon, Barlick and Ballanfant. Time of game—1:43. Attendance—26,514.

Haney Plans to Quit Toledo

TOLEDO, Ohio, Sept. 23 (AP)—Fred Haney, manager of the Toledo American Association Baseball Club, announced today he had informed officials of the parent St. Louis Browns that he wished to resign. Lack of authority to make player deals, Haney said, prompted his action.

Yanks Never Before Met Anybody Like 1942 Cards

BROOKLYN EAGLE
SPORTS
FRIDAY, OCTOBER 2, 1942

BOTH SIDES

By Harold Parrott

WANNA BE AN EGGSPERT, EGBERT?—The second-guess spasm was on today, sure as shootin', and due to reach a climax when the targets, along with the rest of the Yankee-Cardinal circus, hauled into these parts late this p.m.

Targets for today, of course, are Yankee third-base coach, Art Fletcher, and Yank manager, Joe McCarthy, whom the assorted experts allege gummed up a ninth-inning New York counter-attack that should at least have tied the score.

It might be pointed out that the real culprit was Enos Slaughter, the duck-huntin' Carolina kid, whose no-hop throw from right field to third base made Tucker Stainback a dead bird just as sure as the man who gunned it can bring a mallard down on the wing.

Joe McCarthy

Of course this is not meant to detract from the second-guessers' sport. What would a World Series be without a little 100-octane experting?

Our Mr. Leo Durocher was Target No. 1 last year when he opened the World Series with Dodger Curt Davis, flying in the face of the ancient rule that you must always open with your ace. The boys second-guessed Lippy right on down through Owen's classic error, and to the bitter end.

BILLY THE KID FOOLED 'EM — This was no simple second-guess situation. It demanded extraordinary skill, the master-expert's touch. The boys who are always 100 percent right on the rebound were required to reverse their field and make the neatest cut-back you ever saw.

They had been all set, you see, to snipe at Mr. Billy Southworth.

Reason for this was that Billy pitched flighty, easily-upset Johnny Beazley instead of a veteran when the beaten Cards needed somebody to steady the ship.

The smarties all shook their heads sadly and decided in advance that only a change of pace would slow the Yankees up, and that the champs would tee off harder on Beazley's fast stuff than they had on Cooper's.

When the Yanks put on that three-run eighth inning, topped by Keller's homer, the ammunition was already in a thousand typewriters. The kid had blown, hadn't he? Get him out of there, Southworth! Say . . . Billy's leaving him in . . . who's this Southworth think he is? . . . doesn't he know he's playing against men now, not those National League boys?

YANKS COULDN'T SCORE, BUT EXPERTS DID!—Well, when Southworth stuck with Beazley the second-guess boys were just plumb stuck. Because Ernie Bonham blew before the Yankees even got another swing at the ball.

Things looked very, very tough for a time. Could it be that the second-guess boys, now that Southworth had escaped their clutches, were to be left empty handed? What would they fill their columns with?

When Dickey got a life to start the ninth and Stainback ran for him, the boys whipped out their guns, however.

When Hassett singled they started shooting. The second-guess boys from the National League said McCarthy should have called for a sacrifice, because you can't win a ball game until you tie it.

The opposition, however, argued that you've got to play for two runs—play to win—when you're on the other fellow's field. McCarthy had a few of the second-guess boys on his side at this time, you will perceive.

But when Stainback was waved around to third—and into sudden death—the boys really let their big guns go. Didn't Fletcher know about Slaughter's arm? Why take chances with none out—wouldn't the Yanks have been in a grand spot with men on first and second and none out without trying to press their luck and get Stainback into third? McCarthy didn't . . . Fletcher should have . . . Fletcher . . . McCarthy . . . McCarthy, Fletcher, Fletcher, McCarthy——

And so, far into the night . . .

Mom Was Right There At John's Tough Fight

St. Louis, Oct. 2 (U.P.)—Johnny Beazley, whose mother, Mrs. Sue Beazley, was on hand to see her first big league baseball game, when he beat the Yankees in his first World Series start yesterday, said: "I just had to win it for her."

Sprucing up under a shower, he said:

"Mom probably will give me a great big kiss for that ball game. Then she'll just say, 'Nice goin', son,' and that will be that."

Later, as he clutched a rabbit's foot that a pretty feminine fan gave him at the start of the season, he said the Yankees were "pretty tough customers."

President Sam Breadon of the Cards came in the clubhouse to congratulate Beazley personally and to wish the team luck on its trip o New York.

Without predicting what would happen in New York, Manager Billy Southworth said one thing was certain—"we won't be going up there with any defeatism. We're the team they're going to have to beat."

Kurowski, whose triple in the seventh scored Johnny Hopp, and Musial, whose timely single in the eighth gave the Cards their winning run, both said they were "just about due."

The Yankees, refusing to accept the loss as anything but another ball game, had a few gripes, however.

"They got all the breaks," said Manager Joe McCarthy, "Bonham pitched a good game and deserved to win. Did you see that hit of Kurowski's? I thought it was a foul ball."

Bonham, who said he didn't tire or lose his stuff, figured that the Cards "just picked the good balls and hit them."

"Almost all of them were change of pace balls," he claimed.

World Champs Appear Glum As Series Moves East After Hungry Horde Bounces Back

By TOMMY HOLMES
Staff Correspondent of the Brooklyn Eagle

En route to New York, Oct. 2—The traveling baseball circus rolls toward the big town today and even the mighty Yankees seem a little less self assured after a two-day entanglement with a Cardinal club that continues to defy most of the laws of gravity.

The World Series is all tied up at one victory apiece now and perhaps Joe McCarthy's defending champions are suffering the same sort of pixillation that our Dodgers and other assorted National League teams suffered.

At any rate, the Yankees seemed depressed. They usually enjoy steaks on these special trains instead of sitting there in the diner and glowering at them.

A gent who knows the Yankees better than I do, however, assures me that this is the wrong slant. "They're just mad clean through," said he, "because they lost a ball game that should have been a wrap-up. They'll knock the Stadium apart when they get at the Cardinals up in the Bronx tomorrow."

Hit New Series Low

That can be true. Certainly, they are entitled to get mad at themselves. I've never seen a Yankee club play such bad ball in a World Series as they did yesterday when the Cardinals won the second game by a score of 4—3 at Sportsman's Park.

But they sounded exactly like the National League clubs I heard beef about what they should have done to the Cardinals all Summer and do you suppose that this so-called Cardinal luck is going to continue right down to the end?

The Yankees are running into a club the like of which it never saw before. And the notion is slowly beginning to dawn that there never was an outfit like this St. Louis bunch before. Billy Southworth has his lean and hungry champs instilled with the spirit of crusaders.

Wednesday, they had about as much license to put the tying runs on base after going into the ninth trailing by 7—0, as they have to run the U. S. Cabinet. Yesterday, after a 3—0 lead in the eighth inning disappeared to the noise of three successive Yankee explosions, the Cardinals should have been shaken. Instead, they bounced right off the ground and snatched back the victory.

In the first inning, there was no good reason why Tiny Bonham should so far underestimate Cardinal speed that he threw a bunt too late to second base to get anybody out. That meant two runs when Walker Cooper doubled with two out. Cooper's liner went to right center. Playing straight away, Joe Gordon might have caught the ball but for some reason, Gordon was too close to the bag.

It's Uncanny, Pals!

After Johnny Hopp singled in the seventh, the Cards scored their third run when Whitey Kurowski's line triple dropped an inch or two inside the left-field chalk line. All year long, it is uncanny how Cardinal line drives dropped just inside the foul line and never just outside.

Meanwhile, the Yankees had been hitting Johnny Beazley but having a most annoying time. In each of the first five innings they put runners in scoring position and couldn't do themselves any good. In the eighth Cullenbine singled and stole second, DiMaggio singled to drive over a run, then Keller hit a home run to the roof of the right-field pavilion, tying the score.

That should have taught the Cardinals something but it didn't. With two out in the eighth, Slaughter doubled to right. The play at second was close but Rizzuto bobbled Cullenbine's throw and as the ball rolled 15 feet away, Slaughter took off like a rabbit from behind a cabbage and streaked for third.

I thought Slaughter might not have scored from second on Stan Musial's hit but Bill Dickey says that's all wrong and that Musial's hit — through the box and over second — wasn't hard enough for DiMaggio to get the ball to the plate in time.

And then in the ninth the Yanks gummed up the detail again. Dickey opened with a single. Stainback ran for him. Hassett singled to right. Stainback rounded second and tore for third. The Cards needed a perfect throw from Slaughter to get him out.

Slaughter threw a strike and Stainback found the ball waiting for him.

Neither Pilot Set on Starter In Game No. 3

En route to New York, Oct. 2—Leo Durocher and John McDonald of the Dodgers were inhaling ham and eggs this morning when Jimmy Brown of the Cardinals walked into the diner.

"Great stuff, Jimmy," said Leo, beaming broadly, "you've got that hysterical business out of your system now. No more jitters and you fellows will win it."

Can this be the same Durocher who cussed, raged and fought at the Redbirds all Summer?

"Thanks," smiled the St. Louis second baseman. "We feel pretty good about it now."

The Yanks say that it will all be different when Joe Gordon regains his normal World Series form. Gordon has had just one hit in nine times at bat in the two games and has been a strikeout victim five times. Called out on strikes by Bill Summers yesterday, Gordon staged the most un-Yankeelike scene of beefing to the ump.

May be Gordon can get going tomorrow, for Southworth has indicated that his starting pitcher for the third game and the first at the Yankee Stadium, will certainly be a left-hander—either Ernie White or Max Lanier. Joe McCarthy's pitching choice is also problematical. Either Spud Chandler or Hank Borowy will go for the Yanks.

There were two stars in the second game—John Beazley, the 23-year-old Tennessean who out-Coopered Morton Cooper against the Yankees, and Country Slaughter, whose double and alert base running led to the winning run. "I guess the curve I threw to Keller broke a little high," said the quiet Beazley. "He really pickled it, didn't he?"

One thing the Yankees did demonstrate to the St. Louis crowds is that there is another centerfielder in baseball besides Terry Moore. Joe DiMaggio covered a Texas county out there.

The Yankees are slowly becoming aware that National League tales of the Cardinal speed aren't exaggerated.

Johnny Hopp's first World Series hit was a single to right. He rounded first base by 30 feet. Roy Cullenbine heaved the ball to first and violated a National League rule which says never to throw the ball behind anything in a St. Louis uniform. Hopp slid into second base safely on his chest. Cardinal first baseman "Bad" Hopp?

Stan Musial was the last regular on either team to break into the hit column in this series. He certainly picked the spot to give the McCarthy musketeers a headache.

HOLMES.

TRAVELING SCHEDULES MAY BE DISRUPTED

Washington, Oct. 2—The traveling schedules of the World Series teams may be disrupted by the "freezing" of passenger train schedules ordered yesterday by Defense Transportation Director Joseph B. Eastman.

Chartered cars are used by the two clubs. If the series goes beyond five games and the teams return to St. Louis the players and officials may have to travel like any one else.

Eastman can make an exception in this case, but there is some doubt in it.

SLAUGHTER THROWS A STRIKE—This is the beginning of the end for the Yankees in ninth inning of the second World Series game with the Cardinals at Sportsman's Park, St. Louis, yesterday. Tuck Stainback, running for Bill Dickey, is out at third on Enos Slaughter's throw to Whitey Kurowski after Buddy Hassett of the Yankees had singled to right. It was the first out for the Yanks in the inning. Then Ruffing, batting for Bonham flied out, and Rizzuto was thrown out by Marion. The inning ended with one Yankee left stranded and no Yankee runs in, and the series tied at one game each as the Cards won, 4—3.

Fordham-Tennessee Game 6 to 5 and Take Your Pick

Same Odds Quoted on Minnesota, Iowa Cadets in Top Gridiron Test

By OSCAR FRALEY

College football stages its first major weekend carnival starting tonight with public interest diverted from many high-calibred games by the World Series.

Every section of the nation comes up with top games, four dominating tonight's play. These are the Georgia Naval Cadets-North Carolina Cadets, Baylor-Oklahoma Aggies, Georgetown-Mississippi and Temple-VMI tilts, with the first named as the favorites.

JIMMY BROWN of the Cardinals slides safely under Phil Rizzuto of the Yankees in first inning of second game. Brown opened the Cards' half with pass from Ernie Bonham, then made second when Terry Moore bunted to Bonham whose throw was too late.

Feature sectional games tomorrow include:

MIDWEST—Iowa Cadets-Minnesota, Great Lakes-Iowa, Texas-Northwestern, Georgia Tech-Notre Dame.

WEST — Oregon - Washington State, Oregon State-California, Southern California - Washington, Santa Clara-Stanford, California Cadets-Ucla.

SOUTH — Fordham - Tennessee, Purdue-Vanderbilt, South Carolina-North Carolina, Louisiana State-Rice, Mississippi State-Alabama, Auburn-Tulane.

EAST—Penn-Harvard, S. M. U.-Pitt, Duquesne-Holy Cross, Colgate-Cornell, Virginia-Navy.

Mighty Minnesota against Iowa Cadets, coached by former Gopher Mentor Bernie Bierman, rates as tomorrow's game of the day. It's 6—5, and take your pick, with most of the experts holding that the cadets—former pro and college stars—will halt the 1941 national champs.

In other midwestern contests Notre Dame is a 2—1 favorite over Georgia Tech; Texas drew the nod over Northwestern; Great Lakes over Iowa; Wisconsin over Marquette; Nebraska over Iowa State; Illinois over Butler, Ohio State over Indiana, and Michigan over Michigan State.

Washington State, victor over Stanford, draws the nod over Oregon, while Coast selectors believe California, despite a shaky start, has too much all-around strength for Oregon State's Rose Bowlers.

The Fordham-Tennessee tilt is another 6—5 and take your choice. Purdue is the choice over Vanderbilt; Alabama is 7—5 over Mississippi State; Tulane ruled 3—1 over Auburn; T. C. U. over Arkansas; Clemson over North Carolina State; Duke over Wake Forest; Georgia over Furman; South Carolina over North Carolina; William and Mary over V. P. I., and L. S. U. over Rice.

Penn is an 8—5 choice over Harvard, both having lost their first games to service clubs. Pitt draws a shaky nod over S. M. U.; Colgate is 7—5 over Cornell; Army 2—1 over Lafayette; Penn State over Bucknell; Duquesne over Holy Cross; Navy over Virginia; Columbia over Maine; Yale over Lehigh, and Princeton over Williams.

COMPOSITE BOX SCORE

(First Two Games of World Series)

NEW YORK (A. L.)

	g.	ab.	r.	h.	2b.	3b.	hr.	rbi.	so.	bb.	pct.	o.	a.	e.	pct.
Rizzuto, ss.	2	8	0	1	0	0	0	0	1	2	.125	2	5	1	.875
Rolfe, 3b.	2	9	2	3	1	0	0	0	2	0	.333	0	3	0	1.000
Cullenbine, rf.	2	7	2	2	1	0	0	0	1	1	.286	3	0	0	1.000
DiMaggio, cf.	2	9	3	4	0	0	0	2	0	0	.444	10	0	0	1.000
Keller, lf.	2	8	1	2	0	0	1	2	2	1	.250	5	0	0	1.000
Gordon, 2b.	2	9	0	1	1	0	0	0	5	0	.111	2	4	0	1.000
Dickey, c.	2	8	1	4	0	0	0	0	0	1	.500	14	0	0	1.000
Hassett, 1b.	2	8	1	3	1	0	0	2	1	0	.375	14	1	1	.928
Ruffing, p.	2	5	0	1	0	0	0	0	0	0	.200	0	0	0	.000
Chandler, p.	1	0	0	0	0	0	0	0	0	0	.000	1	0	0	1.000
Bonham, p.	1	2	0	0	0	0	0	0	0	1	.000	0	0	0	.000
z-Stainback	0	0	0	0	0	0	0	0	0	0	.000	0	0	0	.000
Totals		73	10	21	4	0	1	6	12	6	.288	51	13	2	.971

Note—Dickey and Hassett scored in eighth of first game on Slaughter's error. Rolfe and Cullenbine scored in ninth of first game on Lanier's error.

ST. LOUIS (N. L.)

	g.	ab.	r.	h.	2b.	3b.	hr.	rbi.	so.	bb.	pct.	o.	a.	e.	pct
Brown, 2b.	2	7	1	1	0	0	0	0	0	2	.143	1	5	1	.833
Moore, cf.	2	7	1	2	0	0	0	1	0	1	.286	3	0	0	1.000
Slaughter, rf.	2	8	1	2	1	0	0	0	1	2	.250	3	1	1	.750
Musial, lf.	2	8	0	1	0	0	0	1	0	1	.125	6	0	0	.000
W. Cooper, c.	2	8	1	2	1	0	0	2	1	0	.250	12	1	0	1.000
Hopp, 1b.	2	7	1	2	1	0	0	0	1	0	.286	22	1	0	1.000
Kurowski, 3b.	2	6	0	1	0	1	0	1	3	0	.167	3	1	0	1.000
Marion, ss.	2	7	1	1	0	1	0	2	1	0	.143	4	6	0	1.000
M. Cooper, p.	1	2	0	0	0	0	0	0	0	0	.000	0	1	0	1.000
Gumbert, p.	1	0	0	0	0	0	0	0	0	0	.000	0	1	0	1.000
Lanier, p.	1	0	0	0	0	0	0	0	0	0	.000	0	1	2	.333
Beazley, p.	1	3	0	0	0	0	0	0	3	0	.000	0	0	0	.000
a-Walker	1	1	0	0	0	0	0	0	1	0	.000	0	0	0	.000
a-Sanders	1	0	1	0	0	0	0	0	0	1	.000	0	0	0	.000
a-O'Dea	1	1	0	1	0	0	0	1	0	0	1.000	0	0	0	.000
z-Crespi	1	0	1	0	0	0	0	0	0	0	.000	0	0	0	.000
Totals		65	8	13	3	2	0	8	11	7	.200	54	18	4	.947

a—Pinch-hitter.
z—Pinch-runner.

Composite score by innings:

NEW YORK	0	0	0	1	1	0	0	6	2	—10
ST. LOUIS	2	0	0	0	0	0	1	1	4	— 8

Earned runs—Yankees, 6; Cardinals, 7. Unearned runs—Yankees, 4; Cardinals, 1. Sacrifices—Yankees, Cullenbine; Cardinals, Moore. Left on bases—Yankees, 16; Cardinals, 13. Stolen bases—Rizzuto, Cullenbine. Bases on balls off—Yankees, Ruffing, 6, Bonham 1; Cardinals, M. Cooper 3, Lanter 1, Beazley 2. Struck out by—Yankees, Ruffing 8, Bonham 3; Cardinals, M. Cooper 7, Lanier 1, Beazley 4. Hits off—Yankees, Ruffing 5 in 8 2-3, Chandler 2 in 1-3, Bonham, 6 in 8; Cardinals, M. Cooper 10 in 7 2-3, Gumbert 0 in 1-3, Lanier 1 in 1, Beazley 10 in 9. Double play—Cardinals, Beazley-Marion-Hopp, Games won—Yankees, Russing; Cardinals, Beazley. Games lost—Yankees, Bonham; Cardinals, M. Cooper. Umpires—First game, Magerkurth (N.), plate; Summers (A.), first base; Barr (N.), second, and Hubbard (A.), third. Second game—Summers (A.), plate; Barr (N.), first base;; Hubbard (A.), second, and Magerkurth (N.), third. Times of games—First game, 2:35; second game, 1:57. Attendances—First game, 34,385; ;second game, 34,255.

BOX SCORE OF SECOND WORLD SERIES GAME

New York (A.L.)	ab.	r.	h.	o.	a.
Rizzuto, ss.	4	0	1	0	3
Rolfe, 3b.	4	0	1	0	2
Cullenbine, rf.	4	1	1	2	0
DiMaggio, cf.	4	1	1	7	0
Keller, lf.	4	1	2	1	0
Gordon, 2b.	4	0	1	0	3
Dickey, c.	4	0	2	5	0
Hassett, 1b.	4	0	1	9	0
Bonham, p.	2	0	0	0	0
z-Stainback	0	0	0	0	0
a-Ruffing	1	0	0	0	0
Totals	35	3	10	24	8

a—Batted for Bonham in 9th.
z—Ran for Dickey in 9th.

St. Louis (N.L.)	ab.	r.	h.	o.	a.
Brown, 2b.	3	1	0	0	3
Moore, cf.	3	1	0	2	0
Slaughter, rf.	4	1	1	2	1
Musial, lf.	4	0	1	5	0
Cooper, c.	4	0	1	4	0
Hopp, 1b.	3	1	2	11	0
Kurowski, 3b.	3	0	1	2	1
Marion, ss.	3	0	0	1	4
Beazley, p.	3	0	0	0	0
Totals	30	4	6	27	9

New York	0	0	0	0	0	0	0	3	0	—3
St. Louis	2	0	0	0	0	0	1	1	x	—4

Errors—Rizzuto, Hassett.

Runs batted in—DiMaggio, Keller (2), Musial, Cooper (2), Kurowski.

Two-base hits—Cooper, Gordon, Rolfe, Hopp, Slaughter.

Three-base hit—Kurowski.

Home run—Keller.

Stolen bases—Rizzuto, Cullenbine.

Sacrifice—Moore.

Left on bases—New York, 7; St. Louis, 4.

Bases on balls—Off Bonham, 1; Beazley, 2.

Struck out—By Bonham, 3; Beazley, 4.

Double play—Beazley-Marion-Hopp.

Winning pitcher—Beazley. Losing pitcher—Bonham.

Umpires—Summers (A.), plate; Barr (N.), first base; Hubbard (A.), second, and Magerkurth (N.), third.

Time—1:57. Attendance—34,255.

Passeau Faces White Sox In Chi Series Tonight

Chicago, Oct. 2 (U.P.)—Claude Passeau, 19-game winner during the regular season, will go to the mound for the Cubs tonight in an attempt to stop the White Sox in the Chicago city series.

The Sox took the first two games at Wrigley Field. As the series moved to their home grounds for two meetings under the lights, Manager Jimmy Dykes announced that Johnny Humphries would oppose Passeau.

Joe Haynes, Sox star relief hurler, rescued Edgar Smith in yesterday's game and held the Cubs scoreless on two hits for six innings while his teammates came from behind to win, 9 to 5.

Lohrman, Not Higbe, to Face Bushwick Club

Black Bill Lohrman, the former Brooklynite, who is now an apple-farmer at New Platz, N. Y., will replace Kirby Higbe as one of the pitchers with Chuck Dressen's Major and Minor League All-Stars when they meet the Bushwicks in a doubleheader at Dexter Park. Higbe has been called out of town and will be unable to make his scheduled appearance.

Once Eyed Bushwick Berth

Lohrman, a bank clerk, who first caught the fancy of big league scouts while pitching in the Queens Alliance once nursed a great ambition to twirl for the Bushwicks. He never joined the Dexter Parkers, however, but eventually the Giants bought him from Baltimore after he had received a brief trial with the Phils.

Johnny Podgjany of the Phils is also slated for mound service against the Bushwicks Sunday. Others in Dressen's lineup are Elbie Fletcher, Pittsburgh first baseman; Bill Jurges, Giants' captain and shortstop; Heinie Majeski, who starred for the Newark Bears; Danny Litwhielr of the Phils, George Case of the Washington Senators, Hal Wagner of the Athletics, Bob Emory and Ed Badke.

Bill Sahlin will be Manager Joe Press' pitching choice for the Bushwicks in one game and either Wally Signer or Bots Nekola will work the other.

SALIENT FACTS ON WORLD SERIES

STANDING	W.	L.	Pct.
New York (A.)	1	1	.500
St. Louis (N.)	1	1	.500

FIRST GAME

										R.	H.	E.
New York (A.)	0	0	0	1	1	0	0	3	2	—7	11	0
St. Louis (N.)	0	0	0	0	0	0	0	0	4	—4	7	4

Batteries—Ruffing, Chandler and Dickey; M. Cooper, Gumbert, Lanier and W. Cooper.

SECOND GAME

										R.	H.	E.
New York (A.)	0	0	0	0	0	0	0	3	0	—3	10	2
St. Louis (N.)	2	0	0	0	0	0	1	1	x	—4	6	0

Batteries—Bonham and Dickey; Beazley and W. Cooper.

SECOND GAME	
Attendance (paid)	34,255
Gross receipts	$150,009.00
Commissioner's share	22,501.35
Players' share	76,504.59
Each club's share	12,750.76
Each league's share	12,750.76
STATISTICS FOR TWO GAMES	
Attendance (paid)	68,640
Gross receipts	$301,806.00
Commissioner's share	45,270.90
Players' share	153,921.06
Each club's share	25,653.51
Each league's share	25,653.51

United Service Organizations receive $100,000 paid for series radio rights. Did not share in gate receipts of the first two games, but will take bulk of receipts from third and fourth games.

SCHEDULE

Third, fourth and fifth games at Yankee Stadium, New York, tomorrow, Sunday and Monday.

Sixth and seventh games (if necessary), at Sportsman's Park, St. Louis, Wednesday, Oct. 7, and Friday, Oct. 9. Thursday, Oct. 8, will be an open date.

LATEST SERIES ODDS

St. Louis, Oct. 2 (U.P.)—**Betting Commissioner James J. Carroll last night announced odds of 2 to 1 on the Yankees and 2 to 1 against the Cardinals to win the World Series.**

Odds on the third game, with Chandler or Borowy against White or Lanier, were posted as Yankees 1 to 2 and Cards 17 to 10.

BASEBALL CLASSIC VIEWED AS TOSS-UP

Yanks Fade as World Series Favorites—Chandler Sure to Hurl Opener Tuesday

CARDS MAY START LANIER

1942 Winners Face Pitching Snarl—Single-Game Record Expected at Stadium

By JOHN DREBINGER

One of the few institutions to survive thus far the ravages of an all-out global war, baseball's world series once again moves into the spotlight.

It will mark the fortieth meeting between the champions of the two major circuits and for the second year in a row it will bring together Joe McCarthy's Yankees, victors in seven of the last eight American League flag races, and Billy Southworth's St. Louis Cardinals, who conquered the New Yorkers in a spectacular five-game upset last fall.

The firing will get under way Tuesday at 1:30 o'clock, when approximately 70,000 will storm the Yankee Stadium. Millions more will listen in throughout the nation and even from the outermost posts of America's far-flung battle lines.

Only one slight alteration has been found necessary to meet wartime needs. The series again will be fought on a basis of four out of seven games, but instead of only the first two encounters being staged in the opening city, the first three will be held here. The second game will be played at the Stadium on Wednesday and the third on Thursday.

Two-Day Interim

That will be the last New York will see of the classic regardless of outcome, as all the remaining games will be played in St. Louis. Friday and Saturday have been left open for travel and next Sunday will see the fourth game played in St. Louis, where the fifth and sixth encounters, if needed, also will be staged the following Monday and Tuesday.

If a seventh game is required, there will be another open date to enable the public to buy the extra tickets and the deciding conflict will be played Thursday, Oct. 14.

As was the case a year ago, war charities will benefit, with the Red Cross and the National War Fund dividing their shares of the receipts equally. They will receive all above the players' share from the third and fourth games and the entire receipts of the sixth and seventh games should these be played.

The prospect is for an all-time world series high in single game attendance and receipts for New York as a result of an unprecedented rush for tickets. All the box and reserved seats were sold out weeks ago. Only the usual 28,000 unreserved seats remain for each of the three Stadium games. Half of these are $3.30 upper grandstand seats. The other half are the $1.10 bleacher tickets. All these will be placed on sale at the park on the morning of each game.

69,902 Set Mark in 1942

The single-game series record was set last October when 69,902 paid $269,409 to see the fourth contest at the Stadium. No series attendance records, of course, can fall in St. Louis, where the capacity of Sportsman's Park is 35,000.

Despite the dramatic manner in which the Cards last October brought the Yanks' phenomenal string of series triumphs to an end—the New Yorkers had won eight, four in a row, with the loss of only four games—New York's sporting element apparently has not lost faith in McCarthy's club. For even with such luminaries as Charlie Ruffing, who pitched the only game won by the McCarthymen last fall; Joe DiMaggio, Phil Rizzuto and Buddy Hassett gone into military service, the Yanks have been quoted favorites for weeks.

However, the odds at first as high as 13 to 20 against the Yanks, have been hammered down to 5 to 6, with the possibility strong that it will be even money before the first pitch on Tuesday. Experts are almost unanimous in regarding the series a toss-up.

New York's hopes rest largely with Spud Chandler, husky right-hander who at 34 years of age has just come through his greatest campaign, winning twenty games and losing only four, with a remarkable earned run average of 1.67. Spud is certain to hurl the opener for McCarthy, with the Yanks' other right bower, Ernie Bonham, slated for game No. 2.

Musial Game's Top Hitter

The Cards, on the other hand, seem hard pressed for mound talent and this alone seriously dims their chances. Such losses as Terry Moore and Enos Slaughter, outfield stars of last fall, the St. Louisans have been able to take in stride, for in Stan Musial they have a player who since has developed into baseball's foremost hitter. And the dazzling Lou Klein has made St. Louis forget all about Jimmy Brown.

But the losses of Johnny Beazley, two-game winner last October, and the brilliant lefty, Howie Pollet, plus Ernie White's ailing arm, have set Manager Southworth a serious problem despite the runaway race he made in the National League this year. He still has Mort Cooper, but the Cards' ace was routed twice by the Yanks last fall, and while earlier in the season Southworth insisted he was still sticking by Cooper as his No. 1 choice for the series, the Card skipper has been strangely silent of late.

Among many observers there is a feeling that on Tuesday, Southworth will switch to Max Lanier, his most experienced left-hander, hold Cooper back for the second game and then stake everything on his two rookie lefties, Alpha Brazle and [illegible]

YANKEE PITCHERS AND CARDINAL INFIELDERS WHO MEET IN SERIES

Hurlers who carry the hopes of New York fans: Bill Zuber, Spud Chandler, Tiny Bonham, Jim Turner, Atley Donald, Johnny Murphy, Charley Wensloff, Hank Borowy, Marius Russo and Marvin Breuer.

Whitey Kurowski, third base; Ray Sanders, first base; Marty Marion, shortstop, and Lou Klein, second base

Associated Press

YANKEES SET BACK BROWNS BY 5-1, 7-6

Continued From Page One

in a season was thirteen, set by the Yanks in 1931 and tied by the McCarthymen in 1941 as well as by the Browns in 1942.

For a time the Yanks promised to gallop off with the nightcap as easily as they had with the opener. They tore into Sundra for three runs in the first inning on hits by Stirnweiss, Bill Johnson and Charlie Keller.

But in the second round Russo was greeted by three straight singles that resulted in a run.

Wensloff took up the hurling in the third, only to be tagged for two more tallies and these tied the score.

The Yanks forged ahead a run in the fourth with the aid of a double by Johnny Lindell only to see Milton Byrnes smack Lefty Byrne for a homer with one on in the sixth to put the Browns ahead.

Gordon's circuit clout with the bases empty tied the score in the sixth, but the Browns were persistent and in the eighth they went ahead once more on a double by Byrnes and Mike Kreevich's single.

However, it was all wasted energy, for in the ninth the Yanks put the game beyond repair while the youthful Byrne notched his second victory of the season.

Muncrief Fails Again

Bob Muncrief, who in three seasons in the American League has yet to score a victory over the Yanks, was the victim in the opener. He lasted less than four rounds, bowing out under a blistering assault that saw Metheny hit a double and single in addition to his homer while Bill Dickey pitched in with two singles and a double.

Metheny's two-bagger and a Dickey single sent the Yanks off to a one-run lead in the first inning. To this margin the McCarthymen added two runs in the third, the Metheny-Dickey combination again leading the attack. This time Bud singled, Dickey doubled and Nick Etten sent both home with a single to center.

In the fourth the Yanks put the finishing touches on the job when Frankie Crosetti singled and jogged home ahead of Metheny's circuit blast. It was Bud's ninth circuit blow of the campaign. After Bill Johnson doubled, Harry Fuchs replaced Muncrief. It marked the fifth time the Yanks had floored Muncrief since Bob came into the loop.

What happened the rest of the way was perhaps not so pleasing to McCarthy. After Fuchs had squirmed out of the fourth without further scoring, Al Hollingsworth came on to demonstrate rather annoyingly that lefties still can be troublesome for the Yanks.

Bonham, who received credit for the victory—his fifteenth of the year against eight setbacks—yielded only two hits in his three innings on the mound. Murphy in the final three gave only one.

Schultz Breaks Finger

The Browns lost the services of their catcher, Joe Schultz, who went out in the second inning of the opener with a broken finger on his right hand, the result of a foul tip off Crosetti's bat.

President Ed Barrow announced that the Stadium gates will open at 10 A. M. Tuesday for the sale of the 28,000 unreserved seats for the first world series game. Half of these are $3.30 tickets for the upper grandstand and the other half are for the bleachers. Barrow points out that never in world series history have the unreserved grandstand and bleacher seats been sold out at the Stadium.

To make certain his Athletes will be in the pink for Tuesday's series opener against the Cards, McCarthy has ordered a final Yankee workout for 11 A. M. tomorrow.

The box scores:

FIRST GAME

ST. LOUIS (A.)	ab.	r.	h.	po.	a.	e.
Clary, 3b	4	0	0	0	1	0
Epps, cf	4	0	1	2	0	0
McQuinn, 1b	4	0	1	4	3	0
Stephens, ss	3	0	1	2	1	1
Byrnes, lf	3	0	0	1	0	0
Chartak, rf	2	1	1	2	0	0
Christm'n 2b	3	0	1	2	1	0
Schultz, c	1	0	0	0	0	0
Ferrell, c	2	0	1	10	0	0
Muncrief, p	1	0	0	0	0	0
Fuchs, p	0	0	0	0	0	0
aLaabs	1	0	0	0	0	0
Hol'sworth, p	1	0	0	1	1	0
Total	29	1	6	24	7	1

NEW YORK (A.)	ab.	r.	h.	po.	a.	e.
Crosetti, ss	5	1	1	2	3	0
Metheny, rf	5	3	3	2	0	1
Johnson, 3b	5	0	2	0	0	0
Keller, lf	4	0	0	4	0	0
Dickey, c	4	1	3	7	1	0
Etten, 1b	3	0	1	5	0	0
Gordon, 2b	4	0	1	2	3	0
Lindell, cf	3	0	1	5	0	0
Bonham, p	1	0	0	0	0	0
bGrimes	1	0	0	0	0	0
Borowy, p	1	0	0	0	0	0
Murphy, p	1	0	0	0	1	0
Total	37	5	12	27	8	1

aBatted for Fuchs in fifth.
bBatted for Bonham in third.

St. Louis	000	010	000	—1
New York	102	200	00..	—5

Runs batted in—Dickey, Etten 2, Metheny 2.

Two-base hits—Epps, Metheny, Dickey, Johnson, Chartak. Three-base hit—Lindell. Home run—Metheny. Double plays—Crosetti, Gordon and Ettene 2; Gordon, Crosetti and Etten; Dickey and Crosetti. Left on bases—St. Louis 2, New York 10. Bases on balls—Off Bonham 1, Muncrief 2. Struck out—By Bonham 3, Hollingsworth 4, Muncrief 2, Borowy 2, Fuchs 2, Murphy 2. Hits—Off Bonham 2 in 3 innings, Borowy 3 in 3, Murphy 1 in 3, Muncrief 10 in 3 (none out in 4th), Fuchs 1 in 1, Hollingsworth 1 in 4. Winning pitcher—Bonham. Losing pitcher—Muncrief. Umpires—Weafer and Hubbard. Time of game—1:35.

SECOND GAME

ST. LOUIS (A.)	ab.	r.	h.	po.	a.	e.
Clary, 3b	2	1	1	1	1	0
Epps, cf	5	1	2	1	0	0
McQuinn, 1b	5	0	1	12	1	0
Stephens, ss	4	2	3	0	3	0
Byrnes, rf	4	2	3	2	0	0
Christm'n, 2b	4	0	1	3	5	0
Kreevich, lf	4	0	1	4	0	0
Hayes, c	3	0	0	1	0	0
Sundra, p	4	0	1	2	3	0
Total	35	6	13	*26	13	0

NEW YORK (A.)	ab.	r.	h.	po.	a.	e.
Stirnw'ss, ss	4	2	2	4	4	0
Metheny, rf	4	1	1	1	0	0
Johnson, 3b	4	1	1	1	1	0
Keller, lf	4	0	1	4	1	0
Sears, c	4	0	0	7	1	0
Gordon, 2b	3	2	2	0	1	0
Lindell, cf	4	0	1	1	0	0
Grimes, 1b	4	1	2	8	1	
Russo, p	1	0	0	0	0	0
Wensloff, p	1	0	0	0	0	0
Byrne, p	2	0	0	1	0	0
Total	35	7	10	27	9	0

*Two out when winning run scored.

St. Louis	012	002	010	—6
New York	300	101	002	—7

Runs batted in—Johnson, Lindell, Keller, Christman, McQuinn, Stephens, Grimes, Byrnes 2, Gordon, Kreevich, Stirnweiss, Metheny.

Two-base hits—Epps, Lindell, Byrnes. Three-base hit—Stirnweiss. Home runs—Byrnes, Gordon. Stolen bases—Stirnweiss, Clary. Sacrifice—Clary. Double plays—Gordon, Stirnweiss and Grimes; Christman and McQuinn; Stirnweiss and Grimes; Sears, Grimes and Stirnweiss. Left on bases—St. Louis 6, New York 5. Bases on balls—Off Sundra 3, Wensloff 1, Byrne 2. Struck out—By Russo 3, Byrne 1, Wensloff 2, Sundra 1. Hits—Off Russo 4 in 2 innings, Wensloff 3 in 3, Byrne 6 in 4. Winning pitcher—Byrne. Umpires—Hubbard and Weafer. Time of game—1:45. Attendance—4,796.

Dickson Gets Furlough To Hurl in World Series

By The Associated Press.

OMAHA, Oct. 2—Seventh Service Command officials said today they had granted Murry Dickson, pitcher for the Cardinals, a ten-day furlough in order to enable him to participate in the world series.

The furlough was granted at the request of Kenesaw M. Landis, commissioner of baseball, and begins today.

Dickson, who has been pitching for the St. Louis Club this season and hurled for the champions part of last season, was to have been inducted at Fort Leavenworth, Kan., his home city. He formerly played for Columbus.

Facts on World Series

Contending Teams — New York Yankees, champions of American League, and St. Louis Cardinals, champions of National League.

Managers—Joseph V. McCarthy, Yankees, and William H. Southworth, Cardinals.

How Series Is Decided—Best four of seven games.

Schedule—The first three games will be played Tuesday, Wednesday and Thursday in the Yankee Stadium. Friday and Saturday will be left open for traveling and all remaining games will be played in St. Louis. The fourth game will be played Sunday. The fifth and sixth, if necessary, will be played Monday and Tuesday. If a seventh game is needed it will be played Thursday, Oct. 14.

In Case of Postponement — The teams will remain booked for the park in which they were scheduled until the game is played. The schedule for the remaining games will be moved up accordingly. A tie, however, will constitute a regularly played game in New York and will cause no shift in the schedule.

Time of Games—New York games will start at 1:30 P. M., EWT. St. Louis games will start 1:30 P. M., CWT (2:30 P. M., EWT).

Seating Capacity—Yankee Stadium, 72,000; Sportsman's Park, St. Louis, 34,000.

Radio—Play-by-play description of each game over station WOR and Mutual network.

Series Eligibles

Yankees—Ernest Bonham, Henry Borowy, Marvin Breuer, Thomas Byrne, Spurgeon Chandler, Atley Donald, John Murphy, Marius Russo, James Turner, Charles Wensloff and William Zuber, pitchers; William Dickey, Ralston Hemsley and Kenneth Sears, catchers; Frank Crosetti, Nicholas Etten, Joseph Gordon, Oscar Grimes, William Johnson and George Stirnweiss, infielders; Charles Keller, Arthur Metheny, George Stainback, John Lindell and Roy Weatherly, outfielders; Arthur Fletcher and Earle Combs, coaches.

Cardinals—Alpha Brazle, Harry Brecheen, Morton Cooper, Murry Dickson, Harry Gumbert, Howard Krist, Max Lanier, George Munger and Ernest White, pitchers; Walker Cooper, Kenneth O'Dea and Sam Narron, catchers; George Fallon, Debs Garms, Louis Klein, George Kurowski, Martin Marion and Ray Sanders, infielders; Frank Demaree, John Hopp, Dan Litwhiler, Stan Musial and Harry Walker, outfielders; Clyde Wares and Miguel Gonzalez, coaches.

Night Game

AMERICAN LEAGUE
At Washington

				R.	H.	E.
Det.	304	202	000	—11	17	0
Wash.	101	001	200	— 5	10	3

Batteries—Trucks and Unser; Newsom, Mertz (5), Carrasquel (9) and Giuliani.

WHITE TRIPS GIANTS FOR CARDINALS, 6-3

Ailing Southpaw, in Test for World Series, Manages to Stagger In a Victor

HOMER BY SANDERS AIDS

Ray Strikes Two-Run Blow in Eighth After Losers Close Gap—Melton Is Beaten

By JAMES P. DAWSON
Special to THE NEW YORK TIMES.

ST. LOUIS, Oct. 2—Viewed on the basis strictly of results, the world series preview of Lefty Ernie White today at Sportsman's Park was a success. He beat the Giants by 6 to 3.

But, for practical purposes, the demonstration which was designed to show whether White, sufferer from bursitis since last May, was ready for another fling at the Yankees, left much to be desired.

White was in his second complete game since last May 13, and he staggered through only because, after being almost rushed out by a 2-run Giant rally in the eighth, Ray Sanders came along with a 2-run homer in the Cards' part of the inning to lengthen the distance between the clubs.

Pulls Down Twisting Fly

White gave every indication of blowing a three-run lead in the eighth until Whitey Kurowski raced out near the stands in left field to pull down Charley Mead's twisting foul fly and turn the tide. That was the second out with a runner on first and two runs across.

Manager Billy Southworth had started out of the dugout when Buster Maynard cracked White for a double, moved along on a wild pitch and scored on Mickey Witek's single. A single by Joe Medwick chased in Witek after White committed another wild pitch.

But the Cardinals' leader, reconsidering, retraced his steps to the dugout, and Sanders' eleventh homer, the seventieth for the Cards this season, carried the ailing southpaw through to the finish.

Cliff Melton suffered his thirteenth defeat in this game, which ended with Ace Adams in on relief for his sixty-ninth appearance of the campaign. It was off Adams that Sanders hit the homer that pulled White through to his fifth victory of the year.

Musial Preserves String

Stan Musial didn't start the game, but he was in as a pinch-hitter, to preserve his unbroken string of 156 games in which he appeared with the Cards this year.

Southworth said his star's ailing ankle is not seriously hurt, but he is taking no chances and intends to rest Musial until the series opens.

Harry Brecheen gave Southworth a scare today when he appeared at the clubhouse running a fever after having a wisdom tooth pulled. The southpaw, who may be called upon to start in the series, was sent home immediately to rest.

The box score:

NEW YORK (N.)	ab.	r.	h.	po.	a.	e.
Maynard, cf	4	1	1	1	0	0
Witek, 2b	3	1	1	3	5	0
Reyes, 1b	4	0	2	11	0	0
Medwick, lf	4	1	2	3	0	0
Mead, rf	3	0	1	3	0	0
Jurges, 3b	4	0	0	0	0	0
Mancuso, c	4	0	1	1	0	0
Kerr, ss	4	0	0	2	2	0
Melton, p	1	0	0	0	6	1
aOtt	1	0	0	0	0	0
Adams, p	0	0	0	0	1	0
bStephenson	1	0	0	0	0	0
Total	33	3	8	24	14	1

ST. LOUIS (N.)	ab.	r.	h.	po.	a.	e.
Klein, 2b	3	2	1	3	2	0
Walker, cf	2	0	0	5	0	0
Demaree, rf	3	1	2	2	0	0
cMusial	1	0	0	0	0	0
Garms, rf	0	0	0	1	0	0
W.Cooper, c	4	0	2	2	0	0
Kurowski, 3b	3	0	1	3	0	0
Litwhiler, lf	4	2	2	1	0	0
Sanders, 1b	4	1	2	9	0	0
Marion, ss	3	0	0	1	4	0
White, p	4	0	1	0	2	0
Total	31	6	11	27	8	0

aBatted for Melton in seventh.
bBatted for Adams in ninth.
cBatted for Demaree in seventh.

New York	000	100	020	—3
St. Louis	200	110	02..	—6

Runs batted in—Demaree 2, W. Cooper, Marion, Sanders 2, Mancuso, Witek, Medwick.

Two-base hits—Medwick, Mancuso, Litwhiler, Maynard. Home run — Sanders. Sacrifices—Walker, Marion. Double plays—Kerr, Witek and Reyes; Marion, Klein and Sanders; Marion and Sanders. Left on bases—New York 6, St. Louis 6. Bases on balls—Off Melton 3, White 3. Struck out—By Melton 1, White 1. Hits—Off Melton 9 in 6 innings, Adams 2 in 2. Wild pitches—White 2. Losing pitcher—Melton. Umpires—Pinelli and Barlick. Time of game—1:49. Attendance—1,516.

Today's Probable Pitchers

By The Associated Press.

American League

St Louis at New York—Potter (10-5) vs. Donald (6-4).

Cleveland at Philadelphia — Harder (8-7) vs. Brown (0-0).

Detroit at Washington — Trout (19-12) vs. Leonard (11-13) or Newsom (13-12).

Chicago at Boston (2)—Ross (11-7) and Humphries (11-11) vs. O'Neill (1-3) and Dobson (7-11).

National League

New York at St. Louis—East (1-2) vs. Byerly (0-0).

Brooklyn at Cincinnati—Wyatt (14-5) vs. Shoun (14-5) or Vander Meer (14-16).

Boston at Chicago (2)—Dagonhard (0-0) and Lindquist (0-1) vs. Bithorn (17-12) and Burrows (0-1).

Philadelphia at Pittsburgh (2)—Barrett (9-13) and Gerheauser (10-19) or McKee (0-0) vs. Gee (4-3) and Klinger (11-8).

Figures in parentheses indicate season's won-and-lost records.

Record of Past Series

Year.	Winner.	Loser.	Games.
1903	Boston (A)	Pittsburgh	5—3
1904	No series.		
1905	New York (N)	Philadelphia	4—1
1906	Chicago (A)	Chicago	4—2
*1907	Chicago (N)	Detroit	4—0
1908	Chicago (N)	Detroit	4—1
1909	Pittsburgh (N)	Detroit	4—3
1910	Phila. (A)	Chicago	4—1
1911	Phila. (A)	New York	4—2
*1912	Boston (A)	New York	4—3
1913	Phila. (A)	New York	4—1
1914	Boston (N)	Philadelphia	4—0
1915	Boston (A)	Philadelphia	4—1
1916	Boston (A)	Brooklyn	4—1
1917	Chicago (A)	New York	4—2
1918	Boston (A)	Chicago	4—2
1919	Cincinnati (N)	Chicago	5—3
1920	Cleveland (A)	Brooklyn	5—2
1921	New York (N)	New York	5—3
*1922	New York (N)	New York	4—0
1923	New York (A)	New York	4—2
1924	Washington (A)	New York	4—3
1925	Pittsburgh (N)	Washington	4—3
1926	St. Louis (N)	New York	4—3
1927	New York (A)	Pittsburgh	4—0
1928	New York (A)	St. Louis	4—0
1929	Phila. (A)	Chicago	4—1
1930	Phila. (A)	St. Louis	4—2
1931	St. Louis (N)	Philadelphia	4—3
1932	New York (A)	Chicago	4—0
1933	New York (N)	Washington	4—1
1934	St. Louis (N)	Detroit	4—3
1935	Detroit (A)	Chicago	4—2
1936	New York (A)	New York	4—2
1937	New York (A)	New York	4—1
1938	New York (A)	Chicago	4—0
1939	New York (A)	Cincinnati	4—0
1940	Cincinnati (N)	Detroit	4—3
1941	New York (A)	Brooklyn	4—1
1942	St. Louis (N)	New York	4—1

INDIANS OVERCOME ATHLETICS, 8-3, 6-2

Take One-Game Lead in Fight With Idle White Sox for Third Position

PHILADELPHIA, Oct. 2 (AP)—The Indians grabbed a one-game lead in their fight for third place in the American League by thumping the Athletics twice, 8—3 in the first game and 6—2 in the second, before 1,358 fans today. The White Sox, tied with Cleveland this morning, were idle.

The box scores:

FIRST GAME

CLEVELAND (A.)	ab.	r.	h.	po.	a.	e.
Hockett, lf	5	1	2	4	0	0
Rocco, 1b	5	0	0	5	0	0
Cull'bine, rf	4	1	2	2	0	0
Keltner, 3b	4	1	1	0	0	0
Edwards, cf	5	2	2	3	0	0
Boudreau, ss	2	1	2	1	1	0
Mack, 2b	3	1	0	1	2	0
Desautels, c	4	1	1	11	2	0
Reynolds, p	4	0	0	0	0	0
Heving, p	0	0	0	0	0	0
Total	36	8	10	27	5	0

PHILADELPHIA (A.)	ab.	r.	h.	po.	a.	e.
Wheaton, cf	3	0	0	1	0	0
Busch, ss	4	1	1	3	2	0
Macki'wicz, rf	5	0	1	6	0	0
Burgo, lf	5	1	2	1	0	0
Skaff, 1b	4	1	1	10	1	0
Rullo, 2b	3	0	1	1	4	0
Hall, 3b	2	0	0	0	1	0
Suder, 3b	2	0	0	1	0	0
Wagner, c	2	0	0	3	0	0
Abernathy, p	0	0	0	0	0	1
Fagan, p	2	0	0	1	3	0
aStaller	0	0	0	0	0	0
Lowry, p	0	0	0	0	0	0
Total	32	3	6	27	11	1

aBatted for Fagan in eighth.

Cleveland	080	000	000	—8
Philadelphia	000	001	020	—3

Runs batted in — Desautels 2, Cullenbine 2, Edwards, Boudreau 2, Rullo, Suder, Wheaton.

Sacrifice—Mack. Double plays—Desautels and Boudreau; Skaff, Rullo and Skaff. Left on bases—Cleveland 6, Philadelphia 11. Bases on balls—Off Reynolds 7, Abernathy 3, Fagan 1. Struck out—By Reynolds 7, Heving 3, Abernathy 2. Hits—Off Abernathy 5 in 1 2-3 innings, Fagan 4 in 6 1-3, Lowry 1 in 1, Reynolds 6 in 7 2-3, Heving 0 in 1 1-3. Hit by pitcher—By Reynolds (Staller, Wheaton). Winning pitcher—Reynolds. Losing pitcher—Abernathy. Umpires—Berry, Rommel and Pipgras. Time of game—2:00.

SECOND GAME

CLEVELAND (A.)	ab.	r.	h.	po.	a.	e.
Hockett, lf	5	0	1	4	1	0
Rocco, 1b	3	0	0	6	3	0
Cullenb'e, rf	4	0	1	0	0	0
Keltner, 3b	4	0	0	0	3	0
Edwards, cf	4	0	2	3	0	1
Boudreau, ss	4	1	1	3	4	0
Mack, 2b	4	3	2	4	3	0
Rosar, c	3	2	1	6	0	0
Smith, p	3	1	2	1	1	0
Heving, p	0	0	0	0	0	0
Total	34	6	10	27	15	1

PHILADELPHIA (A.)	ab.	r.	h.	po.	a.	e.
Wheaton, cf	5	0	1	1	0	0
Busch, ss	4	0	1	4	1	0
Staller, rf	4	0	0	3	1	0
Burgo, lf	3	1	1	3	0	0
Skaff, 1b	4	0	2	10	2	0
Hall, 2b	4	1	1	2	8	1
Suder, 3b	4	0	2	0	0	0
Parisse, c	2	0	0	3	1	0
Bowles, p	4	0	1	1	3	1
aMackiewicz	0	0	0	0	0	0
Total	34	2	9	27	11	2

aRan for Bowles in ninth.

Cleveland	001	023	000	—6
Philadelphia	000	000	002	—2

Runs batted in—Smith 3, Hockett, Mack, Rocco, Burgo, Bowles.

Two-base hits—Rosar, Edwards, Hockett, Boudreau. Stolen base—Mack. Sacrifices—Rocco, Smith. Double plays—Hall and Skaff; Bowles, Hall and Skaff; Mack, Boudreau and Rocco. Left on bases—Cleveland 4, Philadelphia 8. Bases on balls—Off Smith 3, Bowles 1. Struck out—By Smith 3, Bowles 2. Hits—Off Smith 9 in 8 2-3 innings. Heving 0 in 1-3. Winning pitcher—Smith. Umpires—Rommel, Pipgras and Berry. Time of game—1:40. Attendance—1,368.

BRAVES BLANK CUBS, 2-0

Javery Ends Chicago Streak, Gives 3 Hits in 18th Victory

CHICAGO, Oct. 2 (AP)—The Cubs' six-game winning streak struck a snag today in the person of the veteran Al Javery. The right-hander limited Chicago to three scattered hits while the Braves won, 2 to 0, in 1 hour 36 minutes. It was Javery's eighteenth victory of the season against sixteen defeats.

The box score:

BOSTON (N.)	ab.	r.	h.	po.	a.	e.
Holmes, cf	4	0	0	4	0	0
Joost, 2b	4	1	2	2	4	0
Workman, rf	4	0	3	1	0	0
Nieman, lf	4	0	1	1	0	0
Etchison, 1b	4	0	0	11	0	0
Masi, c	4	0	0	5	1	0
W'lmann, ss	3	1	3	1	4	1
Ryan, 3b	4	0	1	2	2	0
Javery, p	3	0	1	0	2	0
Total	34	2	11	27	13	1

CHICAGO (N.)	ab.	r.	h.	po.	a.	e.
Johnson, 2b	4	0	1	4	6	1
Gilbert, lf	3	0	0	1	1	0
Pafko, cf	4	0	0	2	0	0
N'holson, rf	4	0	0	5	0	0
C'rretta, 1b	4	0	1	9	1	0
Ost'wski, 3b	3	0	0	1	2	0
Schuster, ss	3	0	1	3	6	0
Holm, c	2	0	0	2	0	0
aHack	1	0	0	0	0	0
L'ingston, c	0	0	0	0	0	0
Alderson, p	2	0	0	0	1	0
Erickson, p	0	0	0	0	0	0
bDal'ssandro	0	0	0	0	0	0
Prim, p	0	0	0	0	0	0
Total	30	0	3	27	17	1

aBatted for Holm in eighth.
bBatted for Erickson in eighth.

Boston	000	011	000	—2
Chicago	000	000	000	—0

Runs batted in—Ryan, Nieman.

Two-base hits—Schuster, Joost, Wietelmann. Stolen base—Workman. Double plays—Johnson, Schuster and Cavarretta; Schuster, Johnson and Cavarretta; Ostrowski, Johnson and Cavarretta. Left on bases—Boston 6, Chicago 5. Bases on balls—Off Javery 2, Erickson 1. Struck out—By Javery 5, Erickson 2. Hits—Off Alderson 9 in 6 innings, Erickson 1 in 2, Prim 1 in 1. Losing pitcher—Alderson. Umpires—Jorda, Conlan and Barr. Time of game—1:36. Attendance—1,703.

Major League Leaders

BATSMEN

AMERICAN LEAGUE

	G.	AB.	R.	H.	PC.
Appling, Chicago	153	578	62	189	.327
Wakefield, Detroit	153	628	90	197	.314
Hodgin, Chicago	115	401	53	126	.314
Cramer, Detroit	140	606	79	182	.301
Case, Washington	139	605	100	176	.291

NATIONAL LEAGUE

	G.	AB.	R.	H.	PC.
Musial, St. Louis	156	616	107	219	.356
Herman, Brooklyn	152	583	75	193	.331
W. Cooper, St. Louis	122	449	52	143	.319
Elliott, Pittsburgh	154	575	83	182	.316
Witek, New York	152	618	67	194	.314

HOME-RUN HITTERS

AMERICAN LEAGUE

York, Detroit....34 | Stephens, St. L...22
Keller, N. Y.....31

NATIONAL LEAGUE

Nicholson, Chic...28 | Northey, Phila....16
Ott, New York....18

RUNS BATTED IN

AMERICAN LEAGUE

York, Detroit.....115 | Johnson, N. Y.... 94
Etten, N. Y.....107

NATIONAL LEAGUE

Nicholson, Chic..126 | Elliott, Pitts..... 99

Major League Averages

American League

INDIVIDUAL BATTING

	G.	AB.	R.	H.	HR.	RBI.	SB.	PC.
Dickey, N. Y.	83	235	26	80	4	30	2	.340
Appling, Chic.	153	578	62	189	3	78	24	.327
Wood, Det.	58	155	19	49	1	14	2	.316
Wakefield, Det.	153	628	90	197	7	78	4	.314
Hodgin, Chic.	115	401	53	126	1	50	3	.314
Cronin, Bost.	59	79	8	24	5	29	0	.304
Cramer, Det.	140	605	79	182	1	42	3	.301
Wynn, Wash.	38	98	6	29	1	11	0	.296
Staller, Phila.	18	75	13	22	3	11	0	.293
Case, Wash.	139	605	101	176	1	50	56	.291
Fox, Boston	127	489	55	141	2	44	22	.288
Stephens, St. L.	134	501	73	144	22	90	3	.287
Curtright, Chic.	136	479	64	137	3	47	13	.286
Cullenbine, Cle.	135	476	68	136	8	53	3	.286
Sears, N. Y.	57	182	22	52	2	22	1	.286
Boudreau, Clev.	149	528	64	149	3	61	3	.282
Byrnes, St. L.	126	415	57	117	3	48	1	.282
Garrison, Bost.	34	121	13	34	1	11	0	.281
Partee, Boston	96	298	32	83	0	29	0	.279
Hockett, Clev.	138	586	69	163	2	49	13	.278
Johnson, N. Y.	152	579	69	161	5	93	2	.278
Rosar, Clev.	113	374	50	104	1	38	0	.278
Culberson, Bos.	79	309	34	86	3	33	13	.278
Higgins, Det.	138	523	63	145	10	81	2	.277
Priddy, Wash.	148	555	66	153	4	62	5	.276
Christman, St.L.	95	326	31	90	2	32	0	.276
Edwards, Clev.	89	283	35	78	3	27	4	.276
Heath, Clev.	118	424	58	116	18	80	5	.274
York, Detroit	153	563	88	153	34	115	4	.272
Gutteridge, StL.	133	541	79	147	1	35	9	.272
Moore, Wash.	92	254	43	69	2	39	0	.272
Cuccinello, Chi.	34	103	5	28	2	11	2	.272
Outlaw, Det.	18	59	5	16	1	5	0	.271
Doerr, Boston	153	599	78	162	16	72	8	.270
Keller, N. Y.	138	500	95	135	31	85	7	.270
Etten, N. Y.	152	576	77	155	14	105	4	.269
Ross, Detroit	89	247	19	66	0	17	1	.267
Metheny, N. Y.	99	342	47	91	8	32	2	.266
L.Newsome, Bo.	112	441	47	117	1	20	7	.265
Johnson, Wash.	117	438	64	116	7	63	11	.265
Vernon, Wash.	143	553	91	146	7	68	22	.264
Skaff, Phila.	29	53	7	14	1	7	0	.264
Spence, Wash.	147	562	73	148	12	86	7	.263
Keltner, Clev.	107	414	45	109	4	34	2	.263
Clary, Wash-SL.	93	314	50	82	0	25	6	.261
Weatherly, N.Y.	78	284	37	74	7	28	3	.261
Powell, Wash.	34	119	11	31	0	17	3	.261
Radcliff, Det.	70	115	3	30	0	10	1	.261
Stainback, N.Y.	71	231	31	60	0	10	3	.260
Judd, Boston	27	54	2	14	0	0	0	.259
Estalella, Phil.	117	368	43	95	11	62	1	.258
Chandler, N. Y.	28	97	9	25	2	7	0	.258
Early, Wash.	126	424	39	109	5	56	5	.257
Hall, Phila.	148	536	36	137	0	51	10	.256
Zarilla, St. L.	70	227	26	58	2	17	1	.256
Lupien, Bost.	152	601	63	153	4	48	16	.255
Siebert, Phila.	146	554	50	140	1	72	7	.253
Kreevich, St. L.	59	158	25	40	0	9	4	.253
Harris, Det.	112	345	40	87	5	30	5	.252
Laabs, St. L.	149	578	83	144	17	82	5	.249
White, Phila.	139	502	69	125	1	31	11	.249
Metkovich, Bos.	76	313	34	78	5	26	1	.249
Moses, Chic.	148	590	81	146	3	47	56	.248
Rocco, Clev.	105	391	43	97	5	46	0	.248
Grant, Chi-Clev.	73	219	26	54	4	22	4	.247
Turner, Chic.	50	151	16	37	2	10	1	.245
Unser, Det.	37	98	14	24	0	4	0	.245
Hoover, Det.	142	565	76	138	4	37	6	.244
Schultz, St. L.	45	90	6	22	0	8	0	.244
Gordon, N. Y.	149	532	80	129	16	67	4	.243
Tabor, Bost.	135	530	58	129	13	85	7	.243
McQuinn, St.L.	122	437	53	106	12	69	4	.243
Wagner, Phila.	109	284	22	69	1	25	3	.243
Lindell, N. Y.	119	429	53	104	4	50	2	.242
McBride, Bost.	25	95	11	23	0	7	2	.242
Giuliani, Wash.	47	125	5	30	0	20	0	.240
Hemsley, N. Y.	62	180	12	43	2	24	0	.239
Welaj, Phila.	93	281	45	67	0	14	10	.238
Ripple, Phila.	32	126	8	30	0	15	0	.238
Clift, SL-Wash.	113	409	47	97	3	30	5	.237
Bloodworth, Det.	127	467	38	110	6	53	3	.236
Ferrell, St. L.	73	208	12	49	0	17	1	.236
Chartak, St. L.	106	368	36	86	10	33	1	.234
Crosetti, N. Y.	93	339	35	79	2	19	4	.233
Webb, Chic.	56	206	14	48	0	20	4	.233
Tucker, Chic.	137	530	80	123	3	40	28	.232
Robertson, Wash	58	112	21	26	3	12	0	.232
Castino, Chic.	33	103	13	23	2	16	0	.223
Seerey, Clev.	26	72	8	16	1	5	0	.222
Mack, Clev.	150	533	50	118	5	62	7	.221
Lazor, Boston	80	199	20	44	0	13	5	.221
Suder, Phila.	128	464	30	102	3	40	1	.220
Richards, Det.	100	314	32	69	5	32	1	.220
Mayo, Phila.	128	471	49	103	0	28	3	.219
Peters, Clev.	79	215	22	47	1	19	1	.219
Stirnweiss, N.Y.	81	267	32	58	1	23	10	.217
Culler, Chic.	53	148	9	32	0	12	4	.216
Tresh, Chic.	85	276	19	59	0	20	1	.214
Myatt, Wash.	40	47	10	10	0	2	3	.213
Kuhel, Chic.	151	528	54	112	4	47	12	.212
Sullivan, Wash.	133	455	49	95	1	55	5	.209
Kampouris, Wsh.	51	145	24	30	2	13	7	.207
Desautels, Clev.	66	180	13	37	0	17	2	.206
Simmons, Bos.	39	131	8	27	1	12	0	.206
Lake, Boston	75	217	25	44	3	17	2	.203
Peacock, Bos.	48	114	7	23	0	6	1	.202

CLUB BATTING

	G.	R.	H.	2B.	3B.	HR.	RBI.	SB.	PC.
Detroit	153	616	1377	195	44	75	555	36	.260
Cleveland	150	578	1314	233	46	54	530	44	.255
New York	152	652	1315	211	54	98	609	45	.254
Wash'gton	151	649	1309	238	45	47	604	135	.253
St. Louis	150	577	1252	220	36	77	533	35	.247
Boston	153	560	1304	222	41	56	505	87	.246
Chicago	153	566	1278	187	44	34	494	160	.246
Phila.	152	492	1194	168	44	28	455	49	.237

PITCHING RECORDS

	G.	IP.	H.	BB.	SO.	W.	L.	PC.
Chandler, N. Y.	30	253	196	54	134	20	4	.833
Haynes, Chic.	35	109	113	32	31	7	2	.778
Murphy, N. Y.	36	65	42	31	30	12	4	.750
Haefner, Wash.	35	155	119	57	64	11	4	.733
Zuber, N. Y.	19	109	97	70	48	7	4	.636
Smith, Clev.	28	200	178	68	69	16	7	.696
Potter, St. L.	32	167	145	54	78	10	5	.667
Judd, Boston	23	155	131	69	53	11	6	.647
Bonham, N. Y.	27	223	195	48	67	14	8	.636
Maltzberger, Chi.	37	99	86	26	44	7	3	.636
Bridges, Det.	25	192	159	59	126	12	7	.632
Salveson, Clev.	23	86	85	24	17	5	3	.625
Trout, Det.	43	238	195	96	103	19	12	.613
Ross, Chic.	21	149	140	56	41	11	7	.611
Candini, Wash.	28	166	144	67	65	11	7	.611
Carrasquel, Wsh.	38	144	160	58	44	11	7	.611
Grove, Chic.	31	207	188	72	71	14	9	.609
Borowy, N. Y.	28	214	192	72	105	14	9	.609
Wynn, Wash.	37	257	232	83	87	18	12	.600
Trucks, Det.	33	196	161	54	96	15	10	.600
Sundra, St. L.	31	199	202	63	43	15	10	.600
Donald, N. Y.	22	119	134	37	57	6	4	.600
Kennedy, Clev.	28	147	130	58	62	10	7	.588
Ryba, Boston	39	141	140	58	46	7	5	.583
Bagby, Clev.	35	272	244	77	70	17	14	.548
Wensloff, N. Y.	28	220	176	69	104	13	11	.542
Muncrief, St. L.	34	202	201	46	78	13	11	.542
Overmire, Det.	29	147	135	41	44	7	6	.538
Harder, Clev.	18	132	122	58	39	8	7	.533
Dietrich, Chic.	25	178	184	55	50	11	10	.524
Galehouse, St.L.	30	218	205	74	108	11	10	.524
Smith, Clev.	25	188	197	76	59	11	11	.500
Humphries, Chi.	28	188	199	52	47	11	11	.500
Niggeling, St.L.-Wash.	26	201	149	75	95	10	10	.500
Brown, Boston	48	92	70	51	40	6	6	.500
Dean, Clev.	17	76	83	33	29	5	5	.500
Naymick, Clev.	29	69	42	47	40	4	4	.500
Lucier, Boston	15	67	81	32	21	3	3	.500
Flores, Phila.	31	231	208	73	113	12	14	.462
Leonard, Wash.	31	221	219	46	50	11	13	.458
Reynolds, Clev.	33	191	132	108	145	10	12	.455
Woods, Boston	22	99	109	54	30	5	6	.455
Hughson, Bost.	35	266	242	69	110	12	15	.444
Gorsica, Det.	35	96	89	40	44	4	5	.444
Terry, Boston	30	164	147	63	63	7	9	.438
Caster, St. L.	35	79	69	41	41	6	8	.429
Mertz, Wash.	32	113	103	56	52	5	7	.417
Wolff, Phila.	41	221	232	72	90	10	15	.400
Dobson, Boston	25	164	144	56	62	7	11	.389
Christopher, Phil	24	133	120	58	55	5	8	.385
Newsome, Bost.	25	154	166	68	40	8	13	.381
Lee, Chicago	19	126	129	50	34	5	9	.357
White, Detroit	32	178	150	71	59	7	13	.350
Russo, N. Y.	23	100	85	45	39	5	10	.333
Newsom, StL-W.	15	88	97	52	43	4	8	.333
Newhouser, Det.	37	196	162	112	138	8	17	.320
Hollingsw'th, SL.	34	149	168	51	56	6	13	.316
Wade, Chicago	21	84	66	54	41	3	7	.300

National League

INDIVIDUAL BATTING

	G.	AB.	R.	H.	HR.	RBI.	SB.	PC.
Williams, Cin.	29	69	6	26	0	10	0	.377
Musial, St. L.	155	615	107	219	13	77	10	.356
Goodman, Chic.	79	225	31	72	3	43	4	.320
Herman, Bklyn.	151	579	75	193	2	99	3	.333
W.Cooper, St.L.	121	445	52	141	9	78	1	.317
Elliott, Pitts.	154	575	83	182	7	99	3	.316
Waner, Bklyn.	80	219	28	69	1	27	0	.315
Witek, N. Y.	151	615	66	193	6	56	1	.314
Shoun, Cinc.	45	42	3	13	0	5	0	.310
Nicholson, Chic.	151	598	91	184	28	126	6	.308
O'Brien, Pitts.	87	225	35	69	2	23	0	.307
Olmo, Bklyn.	55	229	38	70	4	37	3	.306
McCarthy, Bos.	78	313	32	95	2	33	1	.304
Lombardi, N.Y.	104	296	19	90	10	51	1	.304
McCormick, Cin.	124	467	58	142	8	57	2	.304
Bordagaray, Bkn	88	268	47	81	0	20	6	.302
Vaughan, Bkln.	147	605	114	182	5	63	20	.301
Walker, Bklyn.	136	534	83	161	5	70	3	.301
Rowe, Phila.	82	120	14	36	4	20	0	.300
Kerr, N. Y.	25	90	12	27	2	10	1	.300
Gustine, Pitts.	110	406	40	120	0	45	11	.296
Walker, St. L.	146	559	74	164	2	51	5	.293
Hack, Chic.	142	531	78	154	3	35	5	.290
Lowrey, Chic.	130	479	60	139	1	61	12	.290
Cavarretta, Chi.	140	520	92	150	8	71	4	.288
Dahlgren, Phil.	136	508	54	146	5	56	2	.288
Tipton, Cinc.	139	489	80	141	9	50	1	.288
VanRobays, Pit.	69	236	31	68	1	33	0	.288
Kurowski, St.L.	137	515	70	148	13	67	2	.287
Galan, Bklyn.	139	495	83	142	9	66	7	.287
Sewell, Pitts.	41	105	10	30	0	15	7	.286
O'Dea, St. L.	70	201	15	57	3	25	0	.284
Fletcher, Pitts.	153	541	91	153	9	73	1	.283
Marion, St. L.	127	413	38	117	1	50	2	.283
Klein, St. L.	151	617	87	174	7	63	9	.282
Sanders, St. L.	141	466	68	131	10	71	1	.281
May, Phila.	135	404	31	113	1	45	2	.280
Tobin, Boston	46	107	8	30	2	12	0	.280
Novikoff, Chic.	77	231	21	64	0	29	0	.277
Masi, Boston	78	231	26	64	2	26	6	.277
Demaree, St. L.	38	83	4	23	0	6	1	.277
Medwick, Bkln.-New York	124	489	53	135	5	68	1	.276
Crabtree, Cinc.	94	250	25	69	2	24	1	.276
Baker, Pitts.	63	171	12	47	1	25	3	.275
Holmes, Bost.	149	616	75	169	5	42	7	.274
Northey, Phil.	145	576	71	157	16	66	2	.273
Rucker, N. Y.	131	505	56	138	2	46	3	.273
Bartell, N. Y.	99	337	49	92	5	26	5	.273
Mead, N. Y.	35	139	7	38	1	14	2	.273
Litwhiler, Phil.-St. Louis	114	391	61	106	12	48	3	.271
Mesner, Cinc.	134	496	53	134	0	50	5	.270
Schultz, Bklyn.	43	174	20	47	1	33	2	.270
Farrell, Bost.	85	281	11	75	0	22	0	.267
Bragan, Bklyn.	73	217	17	58	2	24	0	.267
Dickson, St. L.	31	34	1	9	0	5	0	.265
Russell, Pitts.	144	526	80	139	4	46	11	.264
Lopez, Pitts.	117	370	43	98	1	34	2	.264
Hernandez, Chi.	43	125	10	33	0	8	0	.264
Frey, Cinc.	142	578	77	152	2	43	7	.263
Rubeling, Pitt.	47	168	23	44	0	7	0	.262
Wasdell, Pit-Ph.	143	514	57	134	4	66	5	.261
Clay, Cinc.	48	92	18	24	0	8	1	.261
Owen, Bklyn.	104	361	31	94	0	55	4	.260
Triplett, St. L.-Phila.	112	378	45	98	14	55	3	.259
Finley, Phila.	28	81	9	21	1	5	0	.259
Mueller, Cinc.	139	423	49	109	8	50	1	.258
Walters, Cinc.	37	93	11	24	1	12	1	.258
Livingston, Ph.-Chicago	118	371	37	95	7	35	2	.256
Lakeman, Cinc.	22	55	5	14	0	6	0	.255
Garms, St. L.	88	244	26	62	0	20	1	.254
Merullo, St. L.	128	452	34	114	1	26	8	.252
Nieman, Bos.	98	322	40	81	7	43	4	.252
DiMaggio, Pitt.	155	582	67	146	15	88	10	.251
Workman, Bos.	150	599	69	149	10	69	10	.249
Stanky, Chic.	141	508	93	126	0	49	3	.248
Reyes, N. Y.	38	117	12	29	0	13	2	.248
Adams, StL-Ph.	118	423	45	104	4	36	1	.246
Kluttz, Bost.	65	203	12	50	0	18	0	.246
Coscarart, Pit.	131	488	57	118	0	48	5	.242
Walker, Cinc.	112	423	48	102	3	53	6	.241
Ott, New York	124	379	65	90	18	49	7	.238
Barrett, Pitts.	127	286	41	68	1	31	2	.238
Marshall, Cinc.	130	503	54	119	4	37	8	.237
McCullough, Chi.	86	263	20	62	2	24	4	.236
Fallon, St. L.	36	77	10	18	0	5	0	.234
Jurges, N. Y.	134	474	46	108	4	27	2	.228
Miller, Cinc.	152	571	50	129	2	68	9	.226
Hopp, St. L.	91	241	33	54	2	25	8	.224
Dallessandro, Ch	85	177	14	39	1	30	1	.220
Martin, Chic.	64	118	13	26	0	5	1	.220
Ross, Boston	93	284	27	62	6	30	0	.218
Wietelmann, Bos.	150	523	33	112	0	37	9	.214
Burns, Bost.	51	131	12	28	1	5	2	.214
Hamrich, Phil.	42	152	11	32	0	9	0	.211
Ryan, Boston	131	450	51	94	1	23	8	.209
Maynard, N.Y.	119	385	42	80	9	30	3	.208
Stewart, Phila.	108	335	23	69	2	25	1	.206
Mancuso, N. Y.	93	248	11	49	2	20	0	.198
Seminick, Phil.	20	64	7	12	2	5	0	.188
Poland, N. Y.-Boston	47	150	6	27	0	14	0	.180
Berres, N. Y.	21	38	1	4	0	0	0	.143

CLUB BATTING

	G.	R.	H.	2B.	3B.	HR.	RBI.	SB.	PC.
St. Louis	155	668	1495	255	71	69	624	41	.279
Brooklyn	151	714	1441	258	34	39	656	55	.275
Chicago	151	639	1369	201	55	51	559	56	.264
Pittsburgh	155	664	1391	237	72	42	591	63	.263
Cincinnati	153	599	1347	224	46	43	549	50	.255
Phila.	155	560	1299	182	34	65	506	26	.250
New York	154	551	1291	147	31	81	499	34	.248
Boston	150	458	1189	193	37	41	421	50	.233

PITCHING RECORDS

	G.	IP.	H.	BB.	SO.	W.	L.	PC.
Brazle, St. L.	13	87	74	30	26	8	2	.800
Dickson, St. L.	31	116	118	49	45	8	2	.800
Brandt, Pitts.	28	56	51	20	15	4	1	.800
Wyatt, Bklyn.	25	180	139	43	80	14	5	.737
Shoun, Cinc.	44	145	131	44	61	14	5	.737
Cooper, St. L.	37	274	228	79	142	21	8	.724
Sewell, Pitts.	35	265	267	75	66	21	9	.700
Krist, St. L.	34	163	141	62	56	11	5	.688
Lanier, St. L.	32	213	195	75	124	15	7	.682
Gumbert, St. L.	21	132	115	36	40	10	5	.667
Riddle, Cinc.	36	260	233	108	64	21	11	.656
Munger, St. L.	31	89	103	41	46	9	5	.643
Rowe, Phila.	27	199	196	31	53	14	8	.636
Adams, N. Y.	68	136	116	56	46	11	7	.611
Brecheen, St. L.	29	135	99	38	68	9	6	.600
Allen, Bkn-NY.	32	79	78	38	40	6	4	.600
Bithorn, Chic.	38	240	223	63	78	17	12	.586
Klinger, Pitts.	32	195	185	58	63	11	8	.579
Prim, Chic.	27	56	63	13	26	4	3	.571
Gee, Pitts.	14	75	82	27	15	4	3	.571
Heusser, Cinc.	26	91	98	25	28	4	3	.571
Higbe, Bkln.	35	185	190	92	107	13	10	.565
Wyse, Chic.	37	153	155	35	40	9	7	.563
Passeau, Chic.	35	256	245	66	91	15	12	.556
Butcher, Pitts.	33	192	190	54	41	10	8	.556
Hanyzewski, Chi.	33	130	120	52	54	8	7	.533
Starr, Cinc.	36	218	201	90	42	11	10	.524
Javery, Boston	40	294	285	98	123	16	16	.500
Tobin, Boston	33	250	241	66	52	14	14	.500
Beggs, Cinc.	38	108	113	25	28	6	6	.500
Walters, Cinc.	34	246	241	105	80	15	15	.500
Hubbell, N. Y.	12	66	87	24	30	4	4	.500
Hebert, Pitts.	34	183	196	49	37	10	11	.476
Head, Bklyn.	47	109	168	65	81	9	10	.474
VanderMeer, Cin	35	278	224	158	163	14	16	.467
Davis, Bklyn.	30	156	173	35	47	10	12	.455
Warneke, Chic.	20	88	83	18	31	4	5	.444
White, St. L.	13	70	69	32	25	4	5	.444
Melton, N. Y.	33	180	175	66	54	9	12	.429
Derringer, Chi.	32	174	184	41	73	10	14	.417
Salvo, Boston	21	98	99	31	26	5	7	.417
Andrews, Bost.	36	283	254	75	78	14	20	.412
Gornicki, Pitts.	41	147	262	48	61	9	13	.409
Barrett, Chi-Ph.	36	204	182	76	80	9	13	.409
Barrett, Bos.	38	255	240	63	62	12	18	.400
Kraus, Phila.	34	201	198	83	51	10	15	.400
Rescigno, Pitts.	37	131	125	42	38	6	9	.400
Melton, Bklyn.	28	119	106	79	64	5	8	.385
Lohrman, N.Y.-Bklyn	23	108	139	35	19	5	8	.385
Gerhauser, Phil.	38	215	222	72	95	10	19	.345
Fischer, N. Y.	26	131	139	59	51	5	10	.333
Podgajny, Phil.-Pittsburgh	28	97	114	28	20	4	8	.333
Mungo, N. Y.	43	142	134	79	77	3	7	.300
Wittig, N. Y.	39	153	171	72	56	5	15	.250
Chase, N. Y.	21	129	140	74	85	4	12	.250
Lee, Chic.-Phil.	26	139	153	49	34	4	12	.250
Kimball, Bk-Ph.	39	100	95	51	30	2	7	.222

Records include games played Friday, Oct. 1.

BASEBALL'S TOUR OF PACIFIC IS OFF

Continued From Page One

tary experts believed that big military movements were impending in the Pacific. Some others, noting that the trip would have involved about forty persons, expressed a cynical belief that there must have been something else behind the sudden change in plans.

Guessers wondered whether Gen. Douglas MacArthur or some other military leaders in the Pacific had decided, for reasons unknown here, that it would be inadvisable to have the two teams junketing around.

There appeared to be a vague possibility that the tour might be made later in the winter. But it appeared to be exactly that — a vague possibility.

Plans for the trip were announced two weeks ago, after several weeks of conflicting rumors—first that there would be a tour by all-star teams of the Mediterranean, then that there wouldn't be one, and so on.

The teams actually were chosen and announced this week by the presidents of the two major leagues. Each squad numbered eighteen players and a manager—one of American Leaguers, the other of National Leaguers. Each league had assigned an umpire to make the tour. Frankie Frisch, veteran pilot of the Pirates, was to have managed the National League team and Joe Cronin of the Red Sox was to have been his American League counterpart.

Statement by Rickey

Branch Rickey, president of the Dodgers, who fostered the idea of the overseas baseball tour for the benefit of American troops, said yesterday through The United Press that the "war effort must come first 100 per cent of the time," when informed that the War Department had canceled the Pacific trip.

"Of course I regret that it was canceled," he said. "But in times like these we must accept the guidance of the Government. I hope that conditions may permit the trip in the future, but I would favor it only if, as and when it will not interfere with the prosecution of the war."

Frisch Is Disappointed

PITTSBURGH, Oct. 2 (UP)—Frankie Frisch today expressed keen disappointment at the War Department's announcement that the projected baseball tour of the Pacific War theatres has been canceled.

"We sure would have liked to have gone over there and played for those boys," Frisch said, "but we realize that war materials are a lot more important on board ship than baseball players.

"We'll be ready at any time to go over. Just let the War Department tell us when."

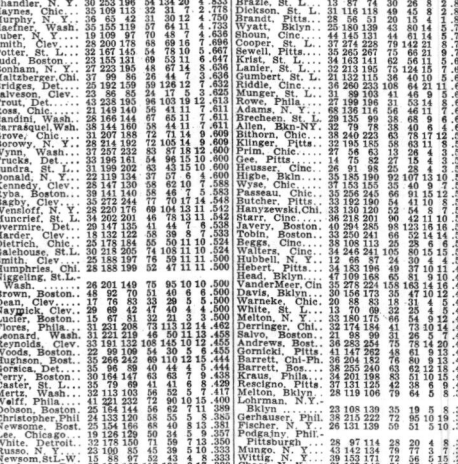

Yankees Send Chandler Against Cooper Today in Attempt to End Classic

M'CARTHY PRAISES PLAY BY CROSETTI

Try for Ball Holding Musial at Second in Eighth Was Key Move, Manager Holds

BUT FRANKIE IS DOWNCAST

Says Error Deprived Russo of Shut-Out—Southworth Curt in Gloomy Clubhouse

By ARTHUR DALEY
Special to THE NEW YORK TIMES.

ST. LOUIS, Oct. 10—The Yankees were happy but not jubilant in the clubhouse after today's victory in the fourth world series game. To them this was no new story but the old pattern being unfolded once again after a year's lapse. One of them remarked exultantly, "Baby, that was the key game." However, they seemed to prefer to talk about Marius Russo rather than the game.

Coach Art Fletcher went saccharine about the performance of the left-hander. "He had a sweet fast ball," he said, "a sweet curve and sweet control."

Bill Dickey, in his blunt way, remarked, "That was as well pitched a game as I ever want to look at."

Russo was swamped by his team-mates the moment Tuck Stainback made the final out. They pounded his back and shook his hand. Everyone had had a turn congratulating him before they reached the seclusion of the clubhouse.

Joe McCarthy didn't have to announce whom he would use in what he hopes is tomorrow's finale. He took care of that this morning when he declared that Spud Chandler would be his choice. For Billy Southworth, it had to be Mort Cooper, and Coop it will be to try to keep the Yanks from ending it tomorrow.

McCarthy Worried by Pause

The Yankee manager declared that he was worried about Russo except when the game was delayed in the seventh inning to permit the clearing of pop bottles from the field. McCarthy admitted that he was momentarily afraid that the pause might chill his left-hander's salary wing. When it didn't, he had no worries.

Frankie Crosetti was downcast that his error had enabled the Cards to score their tally. "Russo should have had a shut-out," he said, "but I spoiled it for him. When that pop fly was hit to me the ball was spinning as it came down and it was still spinning when it hit my glove. Instinctively I knew that I was going to drop it." Russo grinned while Crosetti was talking. "Funny thing about my arm," he remarked. "Some guy on the Giants—I can't remember who — told me that it would take me a year and a half to regain my pitching skill. My arm hurt when I pitched that four-hitter against the Athletics, but it was nice and loose when I pitched the two-hitter against the Tigers. It was really loosey-goosey today."

Analysis by Manager

McCarthy selected as the key play of the game one which most of the experts seemed to have overlooked. In the eighth inning Stan Musial scratched a hit to third, then Walker Cooper drove a grounder over second, a shot that Crosetti knocked down but could not field.

"That was it," said McCarthy. "There was one out at the time, and if Frankie had not knocked down the ball it would have gone out to center field, Musial would have run from first to third and it might very well have been a different ball game. As it was, we were able to make the second out and then get Cooper at second when he overran the bag."

The Cardinals explained the overrunning as due to the fact that Cooper thought he might get an extra base if he didn't slide. So he passed beyond second and the deft Crosetti tagged him out.

All in all, the Cardinals' quarters were gloomy. Manager Southworth was gruff, particularly with one reporter who asked him the wrong question at the wrong time. Billy the Kid exploded on the spot.

Greeting Is Cold

"Ask your questions, boys," was his greeting, "and make them snappy."

The first was as to tomorrow's pitcher. "Cooper," was the crisp answer.

"Is Russo the best pitcher you've seen all year?" was the question which stirred the Southworth wrath.

"That's a silly one," he began. "After looking at fellows like Vander Meer and Riddle all season, you have to think things like that."

When Southworth cooled off, he explained, "The boys aren't hitting." It was obvious that Billy the Kid was not in a merry, conversational mood.

World Series Results

FIRST GAME
At Yankee Stadium

		R.	H.	E.
St. Louis (N.)	0 1 0 0 1 0 0 0 0—2	7	2
N. Y. (A.)	0 0 0 2 0 2 0 0 ..—4	8	2

Batteries—Lanier, Brecheen and W. Cooper; Chandler and Dickey.

SECOND GAME
At Yankee Stadium

		R.	H.	E.
St. Louis (N.)	0 0 1 3 0 0 0 0 0—4	7	2
N. Y. (A.)	0 0 0 1 0 0 0 0 2—3	6	0

Batteries—M. Cooper and W. Cooper; Bonham, Murphy and Dickey.

THIRD GAME
At Yankee Stadium

		R.	H.	E.
St. Louis (N.)	0 0 0 2 0 0 0 0 0—2	6	4
N. Y. (A.)	0 0 0 0 0 1 0 5 ..—6	8	0

Batteries—Brazle, Krist, Breecheen and W. Cooper; Borowy, Murphy and Dickey.

FOURTH GAME
At Sportsman's Park

		R.	H.	E.
N. Y. (A.)	0 0 0 1 0 0 0 1 0—2	6	2
St. Louis (N.)	0 0 0 0 0 0 1 0 0—1	7	1

Batteries — Russo and Dickey; Lanier, Brecheen and W. Cooper.

REMAINING SCHEDULE

Fifth Game—At St. Louis, today.
Sixth Game (if necessary)—At St. Louis, tomorrow.
Seventh Game (if necessary)—At St. Louis, Thursday.

The Fourth Game: It Called for Execution and Examination by the Players

Crosetti falls in his unsuccessful effort to get Cooper's grounder in the eighth inning and Musial reaches second base safely. Gordon is going after the ball.

Lindell (left) inspecting the injury to Kurowski's neck before the teams took the field. They collided at the hot corner in the third game.

YANKS, WITH RUSSO, BEAT CARDS BY 2-1

Continued From Page One

base and into center. It scored Gordon, and the Yanks were ahead, 1 to 0.

That one-run margin Russo brilliantly defended until the seventh. When the Cards finally did break through to draw even, that big moment had to come, ironically enough, when, for strategic purposes, Lanier had to retire for a pinch hitter.

The Cardinals' surge came with two out in the last of the seventh when Crosetti, in trying to pick a pop fly by Ray Sanders out of the glaring sun, wound up dropping the ball for an error.

The crowd, by now in desperate straits to cheer anything that seemed to give rise to a Cardinal hope, set up a mighty roar, which increased to a deafening din when Danny Litwhiler shot a grounder down the first-base line that struck the bag and bounced off at a crazy angle outside the right-field foul line. Before the ball could be retrieved Sanders had scooted around to third and Litwhiler had pulled up at second for a double.

Walks Marion Intentionally

In all this excitement, however, the tall, dark-haired Russo alone seemed utterly unconcerned. He coolly doled out an intentional pass to Marty Marion to fill the bases and then looked over inquiringly toward the Cardinal bench to see what the next development might be from that quarter.

For Manager Southworth the decision was admittedly a tough one. Lanier was pitching a magnificent game, and he was only one run down. But at the same time it was getting along in the battle and before him loomed the inviting set-up of the bases full. The 50-year-old skipper, whom they call Billy the Kid, elected to shoot straight for victory and, without any further hesitation, called upon the veteran outfielder, Frank Demaree, to pinch hit for Lanier.

Demaree, one-time Cub and Giant, hit an awkwardly twisting and rounding grounder down the third-base line toward Johnson, and for the first time in the series the young Yankee third sacker, whose cool playing made him a standout in the series, allowed himself to become a bit flustered. He stepped back for the ball, fumbled it and, as Sanders raced home with the tying run on the error, pandemonium broke out.

So tremendous was the outburst of enthusiasm over this startling turn of events that several of the more virile-minded in the left-field bleachers simply could not express their feelings in any other way than to shower the outfield with pop bottles. It was a demonstration that interrupted play for several minutes while attendants rushed out to clear away the debris.

Bases Still Jammed

When order finally was restored and play resumed Lou Klein stepped into the batter's box, and the bases were still jammed to capacity as was the arena itself. But once again Russo declined to allow himself to become unduly excited.

Klein drove a sharp grounder to the right of second base, but Gordon, leaping into action as though operating on springs, scooped up the ball, flipped it to Crosetti for a force play at second, and the round was over. Southworth had retired his star pitcher in an inviting set-up where just one good shot could have turned the battle upside down.

But all Billy extracted from the situation was a single tally and, though the Cards with this run had pulled themselves back into the conflict, the fans were obviously disappointed.

Their disappointment grew apace when Brecheen, also a left-hander, stepped out for the eighth only to be greeted by Russo's second double of the day which presently was to be converted into what proved to be the deciding tally.

It was in the last of the eighth, however, that the crowd suffered its greatest agony. In this round the Cards, their vaunted speed and assurance deserting them again on the attack, once more made themselves the victims of their own ineptness, a development which by tonight seems to have all the National League cohorts completely stunned.

Scratch Hit for Musial

With one down, Stan Musial, who had come up with one scratch hit in the fourth, bobbed up with another in the eighth when he beat out an infield blow to Johnson. Walker Cooper, back in harness despite an all-night auto ride from Independence, Mo., where he had attended the funeral of his father, also came up with an infield hit, a blow Crosetti knocked down behind second, and the Cards had two on.

Now came Whitey Kurowski to the plate and the crowd, little aware that their plucky third sacker was at that moment a pretty sick boy, implored him for another hit that would tie the score once more. Whitey, only just recovered from the collision he had with Johnny Lindell in New York last Thursday, was taken ill during the night with a recurrence of a gall-gladder ailment and, up to a half hour before game time, was still in the clubhouse receiving medical treatment.

Whitey did connect solidly and, for a moment, hope rose high as the ball soared toward the distant left-field bleachers. But it just lacked sufficient carry and Charlie Keller, Yank left-fielder, hauled it down with his back to the wall.

Then came an even more excruciating play. Sanders hit a hard grounder that skimmed along the ground to the right of second base. Again the acrobatic Gordon collared it but this time, after momentarily juggling the ball, he did not get it to Crosetti, standing on second, quickly enough and as Walker Cooper thundered into the bag Umpire Beans Reardon called him safe.

But it was for only one fleeting fraction that the Cards had the bases filled. For, amid a painful groan from the crowd, Cooper overran the bag and was tagged by Crosetti for the final out of the inning.

Last Ray of Hope

In the ninth came the last faint ray of hope for the crowd. With one down, Marion smashed a double into left and once more the Cards had the tying run on second. But still there was no disturbing the imperturbable Marius Russo. Sam Narron, a third-string catcher, invited to pinch hit for Brecheen, grounded out to Crosetti and a moment later Klein ended it all with a high fly which Stainback smothered in center.

And so, after having a rather daring gamble with the uncertain southpaw pitching arm of Russo, Manager Joe McCarthy tonight stands poised to fire his No. 1 ace, Spud Chandler, into an already badly worsted foe, for the fifth and what may be the final contest tomorrow.

Russo during the past season had won only five engagements against ten defeats, but today he was once again the Brooklyn-born youth who two years ago astounded all Brooklyn by overpowering the Dodgers in the world series. He allowed only seven hits and, up to the Yankee misplays in the seventh, permitted only three Cards to reach first base.

Mort Cooper, who returned during the night with his brother from his father's funeral, will carry the Cards' last hope on the mound tomorrow. He beat the Yanks in the dramatic second game in New York last Wednesday. But in that game he vanquished Ernie Bonham, who inadvertently fed the Cards a couple of home-run balls. Tomorrow brother Mort will have to go against the Yankee star, Chandler, who hurled so effectively to win the first encounter.

36,196 Pay $155,884 At Fourth Series Game

By The Associated Press.

STANDING OF THE TEAMS

	W.	L.	PC.
New York (A.)	3	1	.750
St. Louis (N.)	1	3	.250

Fourth-Game Statistics

Paid attendance	36,196
Gross receipts	$155,884.00
Players' share	79,500.84
*War Relief	76,383.16

Statistics for Four Games

Paid attendance	243,440
Gross receipts	$956,874.00
Players' share	488,005.74
Commissioner's share	79,743.30
Each club's share	45,187.87
Each league's share	45,187.87
*War Relief	208,373.48

*All receipts of the third and fourth games, after deduction of the players' share, and the entire receipts of the sixth and seventh games, if played, go to the War Relief and Service Fund, Inc., which also received the $100,000 paid for radio broadcasting rights.

The players share in the receipts of the first four games only, while the commissioner's office, the competing clubs and the two leagues share in the first and second games and get all receipts of the fifth game.

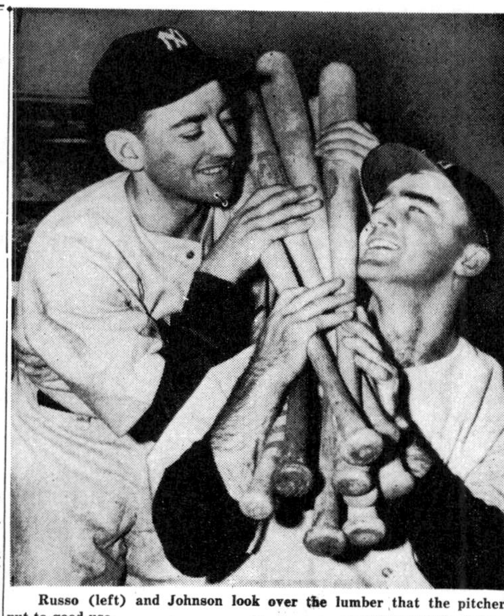

Russo (left) and Johnson look over the lumber that the pitcher put to good use. Associated Press Wirephotos

Box Score of the Fourth Game

NEW YORK YANKEES

	ab.	r.	h.	tb.	2b.	3b.	hr.	bb.	so.	sh.	sb.	po.	a.	e.
Stainback, cf	3	0	0	0	0	0	0	0	0	1	0	1	0	0
Crosetti, ss	4	0	1	1	0	0	0	0	1	0	0	2	2	1
Johnson, 3b	4	0	0	0	0	0	0	0	1	0	0	1	2	1
Keller, lf	4	0	1	1	0	0	0	0	2	0	1	4	0	0
Gordon, 2b	4	1	1	2	1	0	0	0	1	0	0	3	7	0
Dickey, c	3	0	1	1	0	0	0	1	0	0	0	2	0	0
Etten, 1b	4	0	0	0	0	0	0	0	0	0	0	11	0	0
Lindell, rf	3	0	0	0	0	0	0	1	1	0	0	3	0	0
Russo, p	3	1	2	4	2	0	0	1	1	0	0	0	2	0
Total	32	2	6	9	3	0	0	3	7	1	1	27	13	2

ST. LOUIS CARDINALS

	ab.	r.	h.	tb.	2b.	3b.	hr.	bb.	so.	sh.	sb.	po.	a.	e.
Klein, 2d	5	0	0	0	0	0	0	0	0	0	0	1	4	1
Walker, cf	4	0	0	0	0	0	0	0	0	0	0	2	0	0
Musial, rf	4	0	2	2	0	0	0	0	0	0	0	2	1	0
W. Cooper, c	4	0	1	1	0	0	0	0	1	0	0	7	0	0
Kurowski, 3b	4	0	0	0	0	0	0	0	0	0	0	2	1	0
Sanders, 1b	4	1	1	1	0	0	0	0	1	0	0	10	1	0
Litwhiler, lf	4	0	1	2	1	0	0	0	0	0	0	2	0	0
Marion, ss	3	0	2	3	1	0	0	1	0	0	0	1	1	0
Lanier, p	2	0	0	0	0	0	0	0	0	0	0	0	1	0
a Demaree	1	0	0	0	0	0	0	0	0	0	0	0	0	0
b White	0	0	0	0	0	0	0	0	0	0	0	0	0	0
Brecheen, p	0	0	0	0	0	0	0	0	0	0	0	0	1	0
c Narron	1	0	0	0	0	0	0	0	0	0	0	0	0	0
Total	36	1	7	9	2	0	0	1	2	0	0	27	10	1

a Batted for Lanier in seventh.
b Ran for Demaree in seventh.
c Batted for Brecheen in ninth.

SCORE BY INNINGS

New York Yankees	0	0	0	1	0	0	0	1	0	—2
St. Louis Cardinals	0	0	0	0	0	0	1	0	0	—1

Runs batted in—Dickey, Crosetti.

Earned runs—Yankees 2, Cardinals 0.

Left on bases—Yankees 7, Cardinals 9. Struck out—By Russo 2, Lanier 5, Brecheen 2. Bases on balls—Off Russo 1, Lanier 1, Brecheen 2. Hits—Off Lanier 4 in 7 innings, Brecheen 2 in 2. Losing pitcher—Brecheen. Umpires—Stewart (N. L.), plate; Rommel (A. L.), first base; Reardon (N. L.), second base; Rue (A. L.), third base. Time of game—2:06.

Line-Up, Batting Order For Series Game Today

Special to THE NEW YORK TIMES.

ST. LOUIS, Oct. 10—The probable line-up and batting order for tomorrow's fifth world series game, starting at 1:30 P. M. CWT (2:30 EWT), follow:

New York (A.)	St. Louis (N.)
Crosetti, ss	Klein, 2b
Metheny, rf	Walker, cf
Johnson, 3b	Musial, rf
Keller, lf	W. Cooper, c
Dickey, c	Kurowski, 3b
Etten, 1b	Sanders, 1b
Gordon, 2b	Litwhiler, lf
Stainback, cf	Marion, ss
Chandler, p	M. Cooper, p

MAKES 97-YARD RUNBACK

Hill Features 26-to-0 Alameda Victory Over San Francisco

SAN FRANCISCO, Oct. 10 (U.P.)—The Alameda Coast Guard defeated the University of San Francisco by 26—0 today before 3,000.

The winners were sparked by Colin Hill, former San Jose State College star whose 97-yard kick-off run-back in the third period was the highlight of the game.

In the second quarter a 36-yard pass from John Wilborn to Charles McDowell put the ball on the San Francisco 11. A short pass from Dale Halbert to Donald Menicucci was good for the touchdown.

Late in the third period, Gonzales Morales, former St. Mary's player, ran 30 yards for a touchdown. At the opening of the fourth, Wilborn intercepted a pass on the 40-yard line and the Coast Guard drove to another touchdown in six plays.

Russo Was 'Saving' His Arm

ST. LOUIS, Oct. 10 (AP)—Before today's world series game a little boy asked Marius Russo, the Yankee southpaw for his autograph. When Russo wrote his name right-handed, the boy inquired: "What's the matter with your left hand?" Russo smiled: "I'm saving it." Actually he does everything right-handed except throw "and cut bread."

Fans Near Riot at Australia Ball Game; 10,000 See U. S. Navy Nine Top Army, 11-5

By The United Press.

SOMEWHERE IN AUSTRALIA, Oct. 10—A United States Navy baseball team won the southwest Pacific "service men's world series" today, defeating the Army, 11 to 5, before a crowd of 10,000 which became so excited that a riot nearly started when an Australian soldier disagreed with an umpire's decision.

Southpaw P. C. Feakins of Aurora, Ill., who formerly played for Moline, Ill., in the Three-I League, for Hot Springs, Ark, in the Cotton States League and for Dayton, Ohio, in the Middle Atlantic League, pitched his thirty-fourth victory, against eight defeats, since the Navy assigned him to Australia.

The game was the third in a two-out-of-three series. The Navy won the first, 7 to 5, and the Army the second, 6 to 4.

Orlando Rodriquez of Los Angeles, another left-hander, pitched for the Army.

Composed of American and Australian service men, as well as civilians, the crowd took to the game as if it were an Australian football match, providing an enthusiastic backdrop of the Flatbush variety, except for the lack of soda pop and hot dogs.

The fight threatened after the umpire had made a decision against the Navy, but order was quickly restored.

The batting order:

NAVY

H. H. Rogus, East Chicago, Ill., 2b.
Tom Hall, Tacoma, Wash., lf.
Dan Villanon, San Francisco, 3b.
Jim Lorenz, Newport, Ky., c.
G. O. Cox, Cameron, Tex., cf.
Bob DePalma, Milburn, N. J., rf.
E. E. Carter, Dallas, Texas, ss.
D. G. Broker, St. Cloud, Minn., 1b.
P. C. Feakins, p.

ARMY

Robert Teeples, Black River Falls, Wis., ss.
Jack Fidler, Pine Grove, Pa., lf.
James Gagliano, Champaign, Ill., 3b.
Morris Freese, Oklahoma City, Okla., cf.
Carlos Mondragon, Phoenix, Ariz., rf.
Paul Gonzales, Phoenix, Ariz., 2b.
Cliff Blackdeer, Neilsville, Wis., 1b.
Royce Hoard, Sparta, Wis., c.
Orlando Rodriquez, p.

YANKS 4-5 FAVORITES FOR FIFTH CONTEST

St. Louis Commissioner Making No More Series Prices

ST. LOUIS, Oct. 10 (AP)—James J. Carroll, St. Louis Betting Commissioner, made the Yankees 4-to-5 favorites for the fifth game of the sereis tomorrow, with the Cardinals held at even money.

Carroll announced today he was making no more series prices.

Some one in the stands threw an ear of corn to Charlie (King Kong) Keller, the Yankee slugger. If there was a gag intended, Keller missed the point. Considering the shortage of corn for livestock feeding, he might have saved the cob for the hogs down on his farm in Maryland.

Manager Joe McCarthy of the Yankees was in a cheerful mood. Before he retreated to his customary corner in the New York dugout, Joe signed far more than his usual number of autographs. A pretty, young girl brought him three scorecards to decorate and McCarthy asked: "Is that all you have?" But he said it pleasantly

Mrs. Vera Cooper, mother of Morton and Walker Cooper of the Cardinals, came to St. Louis with her sons after her husband's funeral at Independence, Mo., yesterday. She was not at the game and Walker said she would not attend tomorrow, when Morton is scheduled to pitch.

"She's in no condition to come out," Walker said. "She has been in ill health for some time."

NEW HIGH REACHED BY PLAYERS' POOL

$488,005 Sets Series Record Even Though $100,000 for Radio Is Not Included

PREVIOUS TOP IS $474,184

Each Yankee, if Team Defeats the Cardinals in Classic, Will Receive $6,123

ST. LOUIS, Oct. 10 (AP)—The players are cutting up an all-time record financial "pie" from the world series and, if the Yankees win, each man will receive $6,123.

With a 3-1 lead in games and Spud Chandler pitching, the Yanks are odds-on favorites to end the series tomorrow and take the big end of the record $488,005 pool which the two winning teams, and the rest of the first division in both leagues for the regular 1943 season, split up. It's a new record, too, without the $100,000 radio sale price, which ordinarily is included.

The two series teams get 70 per cent—$341,604. The club taking the series gets 60 per cent—$204,962—and the losers, 40 per cent—$136,641.

At the end of the season the Yanks voted to split their end into thirty-two full shares, after taking $9,020 out for cash awards to various assistants, as well as those members of the team who have gone into the armed forces. The Cards ballotted for thirty-one and a half shares.

Of the rest of the players' pool, 50 per cent ($73,200) is divided between the two second-place finishers in the pennant races, the Senators and Reds; 33 1-3 per cent ($48,800) between the third-placers, the Indians and Dodgers, and 16 2-3 per cent ($24,400) between the White Sox and Pirates, who finished fourth.

Although the pool is larger than ever before, eclipsing the previous top of $474,184 on which the Yanks and Dodgers "paid off" two years ago, the individual share, if the Yanks win, will not be a record, because of the number of members of the American League champions' official family who were voted a part of the pot. The all-time high is $6,544 which the Tigers received for beating the Cubs in 1935.

Lincoln High on Top, 21-6

Special to THE NEW YORK TIMES.

JERSEY CITY, N. J., Oct. 10—Lincoln High's eleven took the lead in the Hudson County, N. J., scholastic championship football race today by defeating Ferris High, 21—6, before 6,700 fans. Lloyd Skinner scored two of Lincoln's three touchdowns.

TOMMY HOLMES

It's a Rugged, Hostile Trail

Detroit, Sept. 19

HARD ROAD—If the Yankees should succeed in winning the American League pennant, they'll do it by themselves. Out here in the more or less golden West, they'll find every hand turned against them.

This, of course, is as it should be. And the fire of opposition, stoked by the natural antipathy toward all things New York in this section of the land, could produce some extra curricular excitement in this final, vital voyage of the ball club from the Bronx.

Back in the East the boys are prone to see something admirable and dramatic in the struggle of the Yankees. There have been years when pennants came to Joe McCarthy, but those were the years before Hitler started fouling up the world and gents like DiMaggio, Gordon, Dickey and Keller were around. Remember when they used to write that anybody could manage the Yankees?

Winning with the current club is entirely something else again. His war-ravaged team, shorn of all its super-stars, developed into a contender only by slow and painful degrees, and victory this year would be the supreme achievement in McCarthy's long career of baseball leadership.

DETROIT RED HOT—Out in this country though, that makes no never-mind. All our mid-Western friends know is that the Yankees have won seven flags in the last eight years. That, in the words of their own Josh Billings, is "2 mutch."

Here in Detroit, of course, the turnstile-twirling public needs no anti-Yankee sentiment to drive it into a frenzy. Their beloved Tigers themselves are ripping and tearing toward the pennant.

With the three-game series that starts today, the most important one in which either team has engaged, it isn't safe to predict what course the volatile emotion of a Detroit crowd will take.

There is the famous example of that October afternoon 10 years ago, when the mob spirit ruled over Briggs Stadium. The Cardinal Gashouse Gang was belting the brains out of the Tigers in the seventh and deciding game of the World Series.

RHUBARB—Our old friend, Joe Medwick, slid into third base ahead of a throw. Marvin Owen, Detroit third baseman, took the ball, tossed it to the pitcher, then moved back toward his position. As he stepped over the prostrate Medwick, he "accidently" kicked Joseph, who lashed out with a futile kick of his own that the whole crowd saw.

There was the very devil to pay at the end of the inning, when Medwick went out to play left field. The customers positively refused to permit it. They showered Medwick with empty bottles, tomatoes, oranges, lemons, slightly used sandwiches and gnawed ham-hocks. All entreaties failed and the bleacher supplies seemed inexhaustible.

Under baseball law, the one proper thing would have been to forfeit the game and the series to the Cardinals, but this would have aggravated the riot beyond any manageable bounds. And so, after a conference with the rival managers, Judge Landis gave into the crowd and ordered Medwick out of the game. I often wonder what would have happened if, by some miracle, the Tigers had rallied and won the game.

INDIANS LURK—Cleveland, which is the next Yankee port of call, is another community that can generate unpredictable baseball hysteria. When, back in 1940, the Indians were involved in their famed bit of internal dissension, there was a tremendous to-do in the Forest City.

Cleveland players were taunted with displays of teething rings and three-cornered pants in other cities, and Cleveland fans retaliated by heaving fruit and other throwables at rival contending athletes. The warfare reached its climax when a rooter dropped a whole bushel of fruit, in basket, upon the cruller of Birdie Tebbetts, knocking the Detroit catcher as cold as an iced bluefish.

In Chicago, that lively character, Jimmy Dykes, undoubtedly plans to have some sort of a stew on the stove for the Yankees. It was Mr. Dykes, who wondered out loud this Spring how the Yankees would fare now that McCarthy was unable to "push buttons" to bring ready-made stars up out of Ed Barrow's farm system.

WHITEY WITT—Providing that the final series of the season is a critical one for the Yankees and the Browns, anything might happen. There is that precedent of 1922, when New York and St. Louis teams last clashed with the A. L. pennant at stake.

This was the series made famous by Whitey Witt, the Yankee center fielder, being conked by a pop bottle and landing in a St. Louis hospital. The aftermath was rather amazing. Ban Johnson, then president of the A. L., offered a reward for information leading to the apprehension of perpetrators of this outrage.

The gentleman who collected the reward did so by advancing the novel solution that Witt was not an assault victim. He explained that Whitey, while chasing a fly ball, stepped upon the neck of an empty bottle, which bounced up and knocked him out. It was a clear case of self-defense.

Edwards' 66 Wins With Cox, Klein

Rockville Centre, L. I., Sept. 19—Bert Edwards of Hempstead took the honors in the Long Island P. G. A. amateur-pro tourney at the Rockville Club yesterday. He posted a 66 with Wiffy Cox, Hempstead pro, and duplicated this score with Willie Klein of Wheatley Hills to lead the field.

John Desiderio and R. C. MacDonald of Kissena carded a 67 and tied for third place with Alex Milne Sr., North Hills, and Joe Phillips, Links.

Cox and Klein took pro laurels with 35, 29—64.

Dodgers Send Jarvis To Royals; Sell Osgood

The Dodgers sent Leroy Jarvis, youthful catcher, to Montreal as part of the deal that brought Morrie Anderholt, Stan Andrews and Red Durrett to the Dodgers recently. It was also announced that Charley Osgood, kid pitcher, was sold outright to Newport News, a Brooklyn farm club.

Back at Old Job

Moe (Tubby) Raskin, former City College ace athlete, will again be a member of the staff at Brooklyn College and will coach basketball this season. Raskin, until recently a lieutenant in the Army Air Corps, will soon begin practice with his squad.

Youth Movement Aligned to Lift Flock From Cellar

Westerners Set to Snatch Final 13 Games—407 Hub Fans See Chappy Beaten

By HAROLD C. BURR

The Dodgers, those little men, are back home to stay, a good third in the three-cornered race for sixth place in the National League standing. They fell into Ford Frick's basement again yesterday, when they were nipped by the Braves, 6 to 5, at Boston, not pausing for breath in the seventh slot in their plummetlike plunge.

Now that they must fight their way up again they must do it against the rowdy West in the final 13 games of the schedule with the Pirates, Cubs, Cardinals and Reds. It's up to the junior varsity. The Braves and Phillies will be batting the boys from the badlands, too, but with their regular and more experienced line-ups.

For five innings yesterday it looked as if the Goats of the Gowanus would sink to a new low. Johnny Hutchings, the fattest pitcher in baseball, had a no-hitter in the palm of his pudgy hand for five innings. The 268-pounder grunted and wheezed as he tossed up his screwball. What made it tougher was that he was pitching out of the white background of his own massive shirt front.

407 See Execution

Meanwhile the Brooklyn defense buckled behind Ben Chapman like the Nazis' Westwall. There were only 407 cash customers in the park and young Tom Brown tried to destroy three of 'em with wild heaves from shortstop. Red Durrett perpetrated a fourth Flatbush misplay when a line drive from Butch Nieman's bat spurted out of his rubber glove. Until the tenth inning there was only one earned run off Chapman, Charley Workman's ninth home run of the year.

But Ben wasn't without sin himself. He forced in the first enemy tally and altogether signed eight free tickets to first base. Brownie's trio of errors, however, carried treachery right into the American home. He's Chapman's roomie.

Chapman himself broke through Hutchings' service in the sixth with the first of his pair of hits and the Dodgers went on to score five runs in the last two regulation frames and send the fat man waddling sorrowfully to the showers. Nate Andrews came in to send the ball game into extra innings.

That Holmes Man

Chapman weakened in the final stanza and the Braves set the outfield fences to swaying with the fury of their attack. Phil Masi got the longest single of the year off the left field barrier, started for second and scuttled back to first when he saw he would be a dead pigeon if he kept on his mad flight and Tommy Holmes sent him to third with a double off the right field screen.

The situation called for a fresh pitcher and Tom Sunkel was substituted. The southpaw pitched to only one of the two left-handed hitters coming up. Nieman hit over Durrett's head with the whole Brooklyn infield playing close to cut off the winning run, sending Manager Leo Durocher's strategy haywire. Red couldn't have caught that ball if he had gone back like Joe DiMaggio.

The Braves were offenders against all the laws of decent fielding themselves, chipping in with three errors. There was an animal act under the stands waiting to take over after the ball game. It must have given the hyena a good laugh when told by its trainer about those seven bobbles.

Won Series Over Year

It was the odd game in the five-game set, but the Dodgers won the season's series, 13 combats to nine, thus adding Boston to the Phillies as another team they can beat.

The Dodgers can't expect to make much headway the next three days with the Pirates in town. Manager Frankie Frisch's ball club still has second place to consolidate and Brooklyn has won only four games from the Corsairs all season out of 19 starts, all of the triumphs coming at Ebbets Field.

The Cubs, moreover, have been mean in Brooklyn, too. On their last Ebbets Field invasion they swept the series. The Cards likely will pick a nice, soft spot in Flatbush to snap out of their prolonged slump, and the Reds still have ambitions to displace the Pirates for the runnerup slot.

So that the prospect of our boys winding up sixth with Branch Rickey's Youth Movement once more in full swing is not too gaudy. Yet you never quite know which way a kid is going to jump. They may put on a job drive.

THE SPORTING THING

"He's ticklish!"

Medwick Hopes To Fatten B. A. Against Cubs

By GEORGE COLEMAN

Joe Medwick realizes he has little chance of being the 1944 batting king of the National League. Dixie Walker of the Dodgers has a 20-point edge on Joe with only 14 more contests remaining on the Giants' schedule.

But Medwick will be trying for every point he can get. Even while the Giants hit their low for the year, losing five games to the Phils, Medwick continued to slam the ball at a .316 clip.

Joe set a .486 pace during August, when he faced Western hurlers in 18 tilts and Eastern pitchers in only nine.

Medwick also is interested in his 1945 contract. A high batting mark will give him something to base his likely moneyed fight next year.

In 1937 Joe was king of National League hitters with a .374 average.

Joe expects to add to his batting figures starting tomorrow, when the Cubs call at the Polo Grounds for a four-game series.

A. L. PENNANT GRIND

The American League pennant race at a glance:

Team	W.	L.	Pct.	Games Behind	Games Remaining
Detroit	78	62	.557	—	14
St. Louis	78	63	.553	½	13
New York	76	64	.543	2	14
Boston	74	66	.529	4	14

Games left to play:

Detroit—At home: 3 with New York, 4 with Boston, 3 with Philadelphia, 4 with Washington. Away: None.

St. Louis—At home: 4 with New York, 3 with Boston, 3 with Washington, 3 with Philadelphia. Away: None.

New York—At home: None. Away: 4 at St. Louis, 3 at Detroit, 3 at Cleveland, 4 at Chicago.

Boston—At home: None. Away: 4 at Detroit, 3 at Cleveland, 3 at St. Louis, 4 at Chicago.

BACK IN THE HOLE

Dodgers	ab	r	h	o	a	Braves	ab	r	h	o	a
Miksis,3b,ss	5	1	1	5	0	W'telb'n,ss	5	0	3	2	0
Owen,c	3	0	0	4	2	Masi,1b	5	1	1	13	1
a-Galan	1	0	1	0	0	Holmes,cf	4	2	2	1	0
D'A't'nio,c	1	0	0	1	0	Nieman,lf	5	0	2	3	0
Aderholt,lf	5	0	0	2	1	W'yman,rf	4	2	1	1	0
Durrett,rf	4	1	0	0	0	Hofferth,c	3	1	0	5	0
Rosen,cf	4	1	1	3	0	Phillips,3b	5	0	3	1	3
Schultz,1b	3	0	0	7	2	Drews,2b	4	0	1	3	4
Bolling,1b	1	0	1	0	0	H'tchings,p	3	0	0	1	1
Brown,ss	3	0	0	3	2	Andrews,p	1	0	0	0	1
b-Walker	1	0	0	0	0						
Stanky,2b	0	0	0	0	0						
Basinski,2b	2	1	0	2	3						
B'd'g'r'y,3b	1	0	0	0	0						
Chapman,p	3	1	2	1	2						
Sunkel,p	0	0	0	0	0						
Totals	37	5	6	c28	12	Totals	39	6	13	30	10

a-Singled for Owen in 8th.
b-Lined out for Brown in 9th.
c-One out when winning run scored.

Dodgers	0	0	0	0	0	0	0	3	2	0	—5
Braves	0	1	1	0	1	0	1	1	0	1	—6

Runs batted in—Miksis 2, Galan, Bolling, Bordagaray, Weitelmann, Nieman 2, Workman 2, Phillips. Earned runs—Dodgers 5, Braves 3. Errors—Durrett, Brown 3, Masi, Drews 2. Two-base hits—Wietelmann, Phillips, Miksis, Holmes 2. Home run—Workman. Stolen base—Holmes. Caught stealing—By Owen 2 (Wietelmann, Masi). Sacrifice—Hofferth. Double play—Dodgers 1 (Basinski-Brown-Schultz). Left on bases Dodgers 5, Braves 16. Bases on balls—Off Chapman 7, Hutchings 2, Andrews 1. Struck out—By Chapman 4 (Nieman, Phillips, Masi, Andrews), Hutchings 4 (Durrett 2, Schultz, Brown), Andrews 1 (D'Antonio). Hits—Off Hutchings 4 and 5 runs in 8 innings (pitched to two batters in 9th); Chapman 12 and 6 in 9 1-3; Sunkel 1 and 0 in 0 (pitched to one batter); Andrews 1 and 0 in 2. Passed ball—Hofferth. Winning pitcher—Andrews (14-14). Losing pitcher—Chapman (3-3). Time—2:15. Umpires—Steuart, Magerkurth and Dunn. Attendance—466.

TODAY'S SPORTS

BOXING

Broadway Arena, Broadway and Halsey Sts.—Danny Bartfield vs. Joe Amico, 8 rounds. Other bouts. 8:30 p.m.

HORSE RACING

Belmont Race Track, Elmont, L. I.—1:20 p.m.

TROTTING

Roosevelt Raceway, Westbury, L. I.—8:40 p.m.

AMICO FIGHT RECALLS OLD PHILLY WEIGHT

Joe'll Tip 137 Pounds Against Bartfield At Arena Tonight

By CHARLES VACKNER

The term "Philadelphia lightweight" doesn't apply to Joe Amico. That he comes from Quakertown is true. It is also a fact that he is a legitimate lightweight. Seasons ago when a fighter was billed as a "Philadelphia lightweight" he might have weighed between 133 and 147 pounds. Amico will not weigh more than 137 when he clashes with Danny Bartfield in the top eight at the Broadway Arena tonight.

Amico is the pale-faced bloke who made the phiz of Carmine Fatta extremely red in a recent encounter in Fort Hamilton. Fatta was one of those "name your own odds" choices. At the finish of eight smashing rounds Fatta had to close fast to earn a draw. In addition, Amico has mingled with Frankie Rubino and Morris Reif and turned in creditable performances.

Bartfield Consistent Winner

In close to three dozen battles before he entered the service, Bartfield lost only a pair of decisions. The East Sider will be in there tonight bent on scoring a decisive triumph over the Keystone Stater. There's a good indoor season facing Bartfield and should he take the measure of Amico he will put himself in line for several lucrative bouts.

One of the most willing clouters is blond Johnny Price of Montreal. Price showed in the Halsey St. club late last season and made a favorable impression. This evening the Canadian will square off with Danny Martin of Newark in the eight-round semi-final. Martin fought Harold Green a couple of tough fights and is rated high in welterweight circles. Two sixes and a pair of fours round out the program.

Kochan Vs. LaMotta

The fellow who clipped Ray Robinson's winning string, Jake LaMotta of Bronx County, has been signed to meet Georgie Kochan. Scene of thescrap will be the Detroit Olympia a week from Friday night.

Oma Gets Decision, But Lacks Drive

Lee Oma, 196½, of Detroit, the nation's sixth ranking "duration" heavyweight, made an unimpressive showing last night when he decisioned Teddy Randolph, 171½, New York, in an eight-round bout at the Gueensboro Arena before 4,000 fans.

Oma appeared slow and lazy against his much lighter opponent. Randolph, a light-heavyweight, outboxed Oma through most of the fight. Oma floored Randolph for no count with two stiff rights to the jaw in the second round and Randolph staggered Oma several times with lefts and rights to the chin and opened a cut over Oma's nose.

Doug Carter, 141, Newark, N. J., decisioned Ballessandro Carubia, 147, Astoria (8); Rocco Progano, 131, Stamford, Conn., decisioned Al Bishop, 136, New York (6).

Newark, N. J.—Freddy Schott, 210½, Paterson, N. J., decisioned Johnny Benson, 200½, Indianapolis (10); Louis Long, 191, Chicago, technically knocked out Nate Wright, 211, New York (3).

Baltimore—Curtis Sheppard, 198½, Pittsburgh, decisioned Big Boy Brown, 262, Detroit (10); Roosevelt Thomas, 172½, Philadelphia, drew with Stoney Lewis, 166, Washington (6).

Providence, R. I. — Pat Demers, 132, Brockton, Mass., decisioned Sandiago Riviera, 139, New York (10).

RANGERS AT HOME

Thursday, Nov. 9, Toronto; Saturday, 11, Detroit; Sunday, 12, Boston; Saturday, 18, Detroit; Sunday, 19, Canadiens.

Thursday, Dec. 7, Detroit; Sunday, 10, Chicago; Sunday, 17, Canadiens; Sunday, 24, Chicago; Wednesday, 27, Toronto; Sunday, 31, Boston.

Thursday, Jan. 4, Detroit; Sunday, 7, Chicago; Thursday, 11, Boston; Sunday, 14, Canadiens; Sunday, 28, Toronto.

Sunday, Feb. 11, Canadiens; Thursday, 15, Chicago; Sunday, 18, Boston; Thursday, 22, Detroit; Sunday, 25, Boston.

Thursday, March 1, Chicago; Sunday, 4, Toronto; Sunday, 11, Canadiens; Sunday, 18, Toronto.

HOW DODGERS COMPARE WITH PIRATE PITCHERS

DODGERS' PITCHERS VS. PITTSBURGH

	Lifetime W.	L.	Pct.	1944 W.	L.	Pct.
Wyatt	10	6	.625	0	1	.000
Davis	19	17	.528	1	2	.333
Webber	2	3	.400	0	3	.000
Melton	1	8	.111	0	2	.000
Sunkel	0	1	.000	0	1	.000
Gregg	0	1	.000	0	1	.000
Chapman	0	1	.000	0	1	.000

PIRATES' PITCHERS VS. BROOKLYN

	Lifetime W.	L.	Pct.	1944 W.	L.	Pct.
Roe	2	0	1.000	2	0	1.000
Ostermueller	2	0	1.000	2	0	1.000
Sewell	15	6	.714	4	1	.800
Strincevich	2	1	.667	2	1	.667
Starr	6	5	.545	1	0	1.000
Rescigno	2	2	.500	2	1	.667
Butcher	3	10	.231	2	1	.667

Dodgers' Dungeon May Yield Draft Fruit

Yesterday's final with the Braves at Boston would have been abandoned altogether except for the workings of the baseball draft law. The club that finishes last gets first shot at the draftees. Nobody is anxious to wind up in the booby hatch for that reason. But if the game hadn't been played it might have had a bearing on the final standing of the clubs.

The Dodger defeat may work out to their eventual advantage, if you get what I mean. But it didn't pay to open the park. The 407 paid admissions was the smallest crowd in Boston history.

Manager Leo Durocher flatly contradicted Frank Drews on Morris Alderholt's ground ball in the first inning and got away with it. "I've got it," cried the Braves' second baseman, waving off Phil Masi, playing first instead of the regular custodian, Max Maxon. "No you haven't!" yelled the Lip, as Drews fumbled the ball.

Jack Bolling, spare first baseman and pinch-hitter extraordinary, has received permission to go home to Mobile, Ala., Thursday. He's expecting a blessed event in his family shortly and is going to take a job in a war plant for the Winter, now that he will have to buy shoes for the new baby.

John Dantonio, the new catcher from New Orleans, finally crashed the Dodger lineup when Mickey Owen retired to let Augie Galan hit for him.

"It's the first ball game I've played in three weeks," admitted the stocky Italian.—**BURR.**

YOU PAY YOUR MONEY AND TAKE YOUR CHOICE—Twenty-eight horses entered in the feature race for 2-year-olds at Belmont Park yesterday are thundering down the stretch on the Widener Course. Try and pick a winner. This is how they finished: Pharason, Herb Lindberg up, was first; Sir Francis, jockeyed by Johnny Longden, was second, and Sea Swallow, H. Jones in the saddle, was third. Winner paid $19.

Yanks Need 10 Wins To Wrest Pennant

14-GameStruggle Opens Today in Briggs Stadium

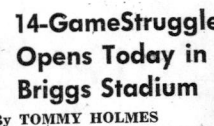

Fred Fitzsimmons

By TOMMY HOLMES

Brooklyn Eagle Staff Correspondent

Detroit, Sept. 19—Grim is the one adjective that fittingly describes the pennant prospects of Joe McCarthy's Yankees today.

It's a case of "they do or they don't" as the champs tear into a three-game series with the Tigers at Briggs Stadium. There is no alternative. The Yankees must win here.

They stand two games behind the league-leading Tigers with the St. Louis Browns in between this morning.

That means the Yankees need three straight to leave this town in first place Thursday night.

If the Yanks win two of the three, they'll be one game out and in not such a bad spot to launch a flag-winning rally from behind.

N. Y. Club on Spot

But if Detroit wins two out of three it will increase the Yankee deficit to three games and render the New York difficulty about twice as desperate as it is today. And should Detroit win three straight, the Yankees will be five games out with only ten games left to play.

You understand that these calculations affect only the comparative positions of the Yankees and Tigers. The Browns must still be considered.

To paraphrase a ballad popular overseas in 1918, the plight of the Yankees shapes up as follows:

"Ashes to ashes and dust to dust;
If the Tigers don't get 'em
Then the Brownies must—"

Need 10 Victories

In a fearful slump over the weekend when Cornelius McGillicuddy's Athletics knocked them off in three straight, the Yankees are faced with the necessity of accomplishing something that has been beyond their ability all season—namely, to inaugurate a whiz-bang of a road trip.

On their first swing through the West, the Yanks won only five out of 13. The next time they toured this country, they won seven out of 17. There are 14 games on this final swing and it's a good bet that the Yanks will need ten victories in order to win. That's a tough order.

More or less dynamic Detroit has piled up woe upon the Yanks so far. In eight games at Briggs Stadium New York has won only once.

Dizzy Trout and Hal Newhouser have beaten the Yanks five times apiece and trust Steve O'Neill to have both of his pitching aces ready for the invaders in this series.

It will be Newhouser in the opener and McCarthy, naturally, counters with Hank Borowy, his strongest pitching bet. This is no time to fool around.

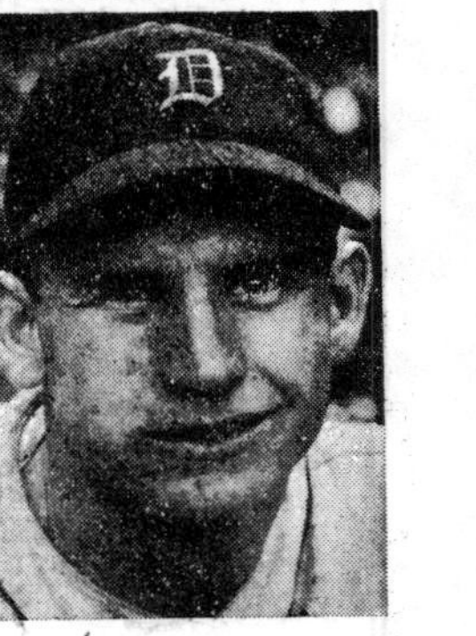

READY FOR YANKS—The Tigers are counting on the pitching of Dizzy Trout (top) and Hal Newhouser (center) and the potent bat of Rudy York (bottom) to cook the world champions' goose in the current pennant fight when they open a three-game "croochal" series in Detroit today.

Phils Predict Improvement in '45 Under Fitz

Philadelphia, Sept. 19 (U.P.)—Freddy Fitzsimmons, whose Phillies have just won five straight ball games to climb out of the National League cellar, yesterday was given another chance to lift the club from their perennial dolrdums. General Manager Herb Pennock said that Fitz would be the manager of the team again next year.

Pennock announced Fitzsimmons had signed a one-year contract to boss the club in 1945, and, at the same time, the front office said without any hesitancy that it never had considered any one else for the post.

Pennock, through a club spokesman, said that both the club president—Sgt. Bob Carpenter, now in Army Service at Atlantic City, N. J.—and he were thoroughly satisfied that Fat Freddy had done as good a job as was possible this year, in view of the talent, and that they were confident that next year he'd do even better.

The trend for better things, Pennock said, lies in the promise and determination of the management that they'll supply him with better ball players if at all possible in 1945, and then it will be up to Fitz to show just what he can do.

The Phillies definitely are satisfied with what Fitz did since he moved over from the Dodgers' active player list in July of 1943 to succeed Bucky Harris as manager. His club finished seventh in 1943, a spot that its ability just about merited.

This year Fitz turned in what the owners thought was a good managerial job that was spoiled in the latter half of the season by the entry of infielder Ray Hamrick into the navy. The business office believes that the recent road trips showed that Fitz could get the most out of his men, but Hamrick's loss took away what Pennock described as half of the team's infield.

Traver, O'Donnell Head Battalion Five

The second Battalion, 13th Regiment, New York Guard, is organizing a basketball team under the direction of Maj. Walter B. Traver and the coaching of Marty O'Donnell, Loughlin High mentor.

Candidates have been called and Major Traver hopes to announce shortly a schedule of games to be played at the armory, Jefferson and Sumner Aves.

The Second Battalion is eager to meet Guard units of the Fifth Brigade, in which the 13th is enrolled and an especial challenge is extended to the 23d Regiment traditional rival.

Major League Standings

NATIONAL LEAGUE

YESTERDAY'S RESULT

Boston 6, Brooklyn 5 (10 innings).
Only game scheduled.

STANDING OF THE CLUBS

	Won	Lost	Pct	G. B.
St. Louis	96	45	.681	—
Pittsburgh	82	58	.586	13½
Cincinnati	79	60	.568	16
Chicago	66	73	.475	29
New York	63	77	.450	32½
Boston	58	82	.414	37½
Philadelphia	57	81	.413	37½
Brooklyn	58	83	.411	38

TODAY'S GAMES

Pittsburgh at Brooklyn postponed.
Cincinnati (Walters 21—8 and Heusser 13—8) at Philadelphia (Raffensberger 12—18 and Schanz 12—13)—Two games; twilight-night.
Only games scheduled.

TOMORROW'S GAMES

Pittsburgh at Brooklyn.
Chicago at New York.
St. Louis at Boston.
Only games scheduled.

AMERICAN LEAGUE

YESTERDAY'S RESULTS

No games scheduled.

STANDING OF THE CLUBS

	Won	Lost	Pct	G. B.
Detroit	78	62	.557	—
St. Louis	78	63	.553	½
New York	76	64	.543	2
Boston	74	66	.529	4
Philadelphia	67	75	.472	12
Cleveland	66	75	.468	12½
Chicago	64	77	.454	14½
Washington	60	81	.426	18½

TODAY'S GAMES

New York (Borowy 17—9) at Detroit (Newhouser 25—8)—3 p.m. EWT.
Philadelphia (Flores 9—9) at Chicago (Humphries 6—9)—Night.
Washington (Leonard 12—13) at St. Louis (Galehouse 7—8)—Night.
Boston (Cecil (3—3) at Cleveland (Gromek 8—7)—Night.
Only games scheduled.

TOMORROW'S GAMES

New York at Detroit.
Boston at Cleveland.
Washington at St. Louis.
Philadelphia at Chicago.

LEADING JOCKEYS

AT BELMONT PARK—First Day

Jockeys	Mts.	1st	2d	3d
D. Meade	6	2	0	0
H. Lindberg	3	1	1	1
E. Arcaro	3	1	1	0
J. Westrope	4	1	1	1
W. Mehrtens	2	1	0	0

REGISTER FROM BROOKLYN WHEN OUT OF TOWN

MAJOR LEAGUE LEADERS

BATSMEN

AMERICAN LEAGUE

	G.	AB.	R.	H.	PC.
Johnson, Boston	130	469	101	153	.3262
Fox, Boston	112	457	67	149	.3260
Doerr, Boston	125	468	93	152	.325
Boudreau, Cleve.	136	528	86	168	.318
Stirnweiss, N. Y.	140	585	114	185	.316

NATIONAL LEAGUE

	G.	AB.	R.	H.	PC.
Walker, Brooklyn	134	486	75	175	.360
Musial, St. Louis	135	520	104	181	.348
Medwick, New York	123	477	63	162	.340
Hepp, St. Louis	128	487	104	162	.333
W. Cooper, St. L.	102	359	51	115	.320
Weintraub, N. Y.	100	341	53	109	.320

HOME RUN HITTERS

AMERICAN LEAGUE

Etten, New York	20	Johnson, Boston	17
Stephens, St. L.	19		

NATIONAL LEAGUE

Nicholson, Chi.	32	Northey, Phila	18
Ott, New York	26		

RUNS BATTED IN

AMERICAN LEAGUE

Stephen, St. L	101	Lindell, New York	91
Johnson, Boston	95		

NATIONAL LEAGUE

Nicholson, Chi.	109	Elliott, Pitts.	94
Sanders, St. L.	101	McCormick, Cin.	94

IL PLAYOFFS

YESTERDAY'S RESULTS

Newark 5, Toronto 4, night.
Buffalo at Baltimore, night, rain.

STANDING OF THE CLUBS

Series A	W.	L.	Pct.	Series B	W.	L.	Pct.
Buffalo	1	0	1,000	Newark	3	0	1,000
Baltimore	0	1	.000	Toronto	0	3	.000

Best four out of seven games.

TONIGHT'S GAMES

Newark at Toronto.
Buffalo at Baltimore.

DODGERS BATTING

Players	G	AB	R	H	2B	3B	HR	RBI	Pct
Wells	7	2	0	1	0	0	0	0	.500
Chapman	14	30	8	11	4	0	0	10	.367
Walker	134	486	75	175	31	7	13	84	.360
Bolling	55	130	21	46	13	1	1	24	.354
Galan	144	509	88	158	38	8	11	77	.310
B'dagaray	123	479	82	132	23	4	6	49	.276
Owen	125	447	43	121	21	3	1	40	.271
Bragan	87	239	23	64	6	4	0	17	.268
Stanky	89	251	32	67	7	4	0	15	.267
Olmo	128	496	64	131	17	5	8	80	.264
Basinski	36	100	12	26	4	1	0	9	.260
Schultz	125	475	54	123	31	3	11	78	.259
Rosen	82	258	35	66	6	3	0	21	.256
Durrett	6	22	2	5	1	0	1	1	.227
Miksis	14	40	4	9	2	0	0	5	.225
Webber	44	38	4	8	1	0	1	3	.211
Koch	30	92	9	19	2	0	0	0	.207
Herring	9	11	3	2	0	0	0	0	.182
Brown	34	110	10	19	2	0	0	5	.173
Wyatt	11	13	1	2	1	0	0	1	.154
Davis	30	59	2	9	1	0	0	3	.153
Melton	33	52	2	7	3	0	0	3	.135
Aderholt	5	21	1	1	0	0	0	-	.048
Andrews	2	6	1	0	0	0	0	0	.000
Zachary	2	2	0	0	0	0	0	0	.000
Hayworth	7	10	1	0	0	0	0	0	.000
Sunkel	9	4	0	0	0	0	0	0	.000
D'Antonio	1	1	0	0	0	0	0	0	.000

Includes games played Sept. 18.

WOMEN IN SPORTS

PACKER INSTITUTE:

Miss Henrietta Strangfeld, the athletic director, said that the Institute will open its sports season with hockey and tennis . . . A tennis tournament will be conducted, with the winners from all grades meeting in a "winner's final" . . . Any one may compete from the seventh grade up . . . Last year's champ was Mary Latson, now a junior at the Institute.

The inter-class hockey games will be played at Prospect Park on Monday, Tuesday, Wednesday and Thursday, if the Park Department approves . . . Anybody who wants to attend is welcome.

There will be swimming at the Y. W. C. A. . . . A badminton teacher and student tournament—incidentally, Mrs. Shafer, the wife of the Head Master, has been a metropolitan champion in badminton—and a ping-ping tournament which will begin immediately.

As a sidelight, Mrs. Jo Dobb, one of the tennis instructors, is a former national champion of Czechoslovakia.

ADELPHI:

Beginning next week, there will be riding, swimming and tennis . . . Miss Gertrude Pullman, head of girls' physical education, announced the names of the athletics association officers . . . They are Margaret Avery, president; Cherie Walford, vice president; Virginia Avery, secretary, and Marvel Morehouse, representative to the student board.

The hockey schedule hasn't been drawn up as yet. However, there will be a varsity and junior varsity team . . . they will probably play four or five games.

PRATT:

Miss Amy Gilbert, head of the department of physical education, was having a busy time . . . There will be hockey, volleyball and swimming until November . . . During the Winter months, basketball, fencing and modern dancing will replace the aforementioned sports.

BERKELEY INSTITUTE

At Berkeley, they will play an "informal schedule" of hockey . . . There will be class teams and an honorary team made up of the best of the class teams . . . Volley ball, tennis, with class tournaments; possibly badminton and battleboard tennis will be played . . . The latter is a comparatively new game, a combination of tennis and handball, developed by Mary K. Brown . . . Miss Gabriella Perrow, head of the physical education department, said that schools will be invited to schedule basketball, bowling, archery and softball teams to compete with their teams . . . Every sport at Berkeley gives the girls points that go toward the 150 needed to get the coveted "B."

BISHOP McDONNELL:

Inter-mural basketball and volleyball are on the schedule . . . There is a bowling team that meets three days a week . . . Usually about 40 or 50 girls bowl . . . They play tennis in the Spring . . . Miss Marie J. Cox, head of the department of physical education, is interested in forming a dance club . . . All sports are run by the girls, who referee, keep score and run the various tournaments . . . In the Spring, there will be about six softball teams.

YANKEES WHIP NATS 6 TO 1

Story on Page 24

HATTEN BEATS GIANTS, 2 TO 1

Story on Page 24

2 CENTS ★★★ FINAL

Daily Mirror

APRIL						
S	M	T	W	T	F	S
	1	2	3	4	5	6
7	8	9	10	11	12	13
14	15	16	17	18	19	20
21	22	23	24	25	26	27
28	29	30				

Vol. 22. No. 259. NEW YORK, MONDAY, APRIL 22, 1946 3c in suburbs 5c Elsewhere in U. S.

BASEBALL BOX SCORES

Yankees, 6; Senators, 1

SENATORS

	AB	R	H	RBI	O	A
Robertson, 3b	4	0	1	0	0	1
Lewis, rf	3	1	0	0	3	0
Spence, cf	3	0	1	0	3	0
Kuhel, 1b	4	0	1	0	9	0
Travis, ss	3	0	1	0	1	3
Binks, lf	4	0	0	1	1	0
Priddy, 2b	4	0	2	0	2	2
Early c	3	0	0	0	5	0
Wolff, p	1	0	0	0	0	0
a-Guerra	1	0	0	0	0	0
Haefner, p	1	0	0	0	0	2
b-Heath	1	0	0	0	0	0
Totals	32	1	6	1	24	8

a-Batted for Wolff in 5th.
b-Batted for Haefner in 9th.

YANKEES

	B.Av.	AB	R	H	RBI	O	A
Gordon, 2b	.158	3	0	1	0	2	7
Stirnweiss, 3b	.143	4	0	0	0	1	1
Henrich, rf	.278	3	0	0	0	2	0
DiMaggio, cf	.304	3	2	2	1	2	0
Keller, lf	.200	4	2	1	1	1	0
Etten, 1b	.227	4	2	1	0	9	0
Dickey, c	.462	4	0	2	0	7	1
Grimes, ss	.286	4	0	0	2	3	2
Chandler, p	W.2-L.0	4	0	1	0	0	2
Totals		33	6	8	4	27	13

SENATORS	000	100	000	—1
YANKEES	030	100	20x	—6

E—Priddy, Robertson, Grimes. HR—DiMaggio, Keller. DP—Priddy, Travis and Kuhel; Chandler, Grimes and Etten. LEFT—Senators 8, Yankees 6. BB—Off Chandler 4, Haefner 2. SO—By Chandler 8, Wolff 3, Haefner 2. HITS—Off Wolff 5 in 4 innings; Haefner 3 in 4. HP—By Wolff (Gordon). WP—Wolff. PB—Early 3. LOSER—Wolff. UMPIRES—Grieve, Weafer, Summers and Paparella. Time—2:10.

Newark, 1, 7; Montreal, 0, 6

(FIRST GAME)

MONTREAL

	ab	r	h	o	a
Rackley, cf	3	0	2	3	0
Robinson, 2b	4	0	1	2	4
Shuba, lf	3	0	0	3	0
Tatum, 1b	4	0	0	8	1
Durrett, cf	2	0	1	0	0
Jorgenson, 3b	3	0	0	1	1
Franks, c	2	0	0	3	2
Breard, ss	3	0	0	3	0
a-Welaj	1	0	0	0	0
Nagy, p	3	0	1	1	1
Totals	28	0	5	24	0

NEWARK

	ab	r	h	o	a
Douglas, rf	4	1	1	3	0
Rabe, cf	2	0	2	3	0
Clark 2b	2	0	0	1	3
Nowak, 1b	4	0	0	11	3
Savage, 3b	4	0	0	0	2
Collins, lf	4	0	0	1	0
Brown, ss	4	0	0	5	4
Fallon, c	2	0	0	2	1
Pitter, p	3	0	1	1	2
Totals	29	1	4	27	15

a-Batted for Breard in 9th.

MONTREAL	0	0	0	0	0	0	0	0	0—0
NEWARK	0	0	0	0	0	0	1	0	x—1

E—Robinson, Breard 2, Jorgenson, Tatum, Savage. RBI—Rabe. 3B—Nagy, Robinson. SB—Rackley, Rabe. Sac.—Franks. DP—Brown, Clark and Nowak; Brown and Nowak; Nowak, Brown and Nowak. Left—Montreal 8, Newark 9. BB—Pitter 6, Nagy 5. SO—Pitter 2, Nagy 3. Ump.—Tatler, Solodare and Zilber. Time—2:05.

(SECOND GAME)

NEWARK

	ab	r	h	o	a
Douglas, rf	3	1	0	1	0
Rabe, cf	2	0	0	1	0
Clark, 2b	3	2	3	1	7
Nowak, 1b	3	2	2	11	1
Savage, 3b	3	1	1	1	2
Collins, lf	3	1	1	1	0
Brown, ss	3	0	0	3	1
Fallon, c	3	0	0	1	0
Davis, p	0	0	0	1	0
Garbett, p	0	0	0	0	0
Mustaikis, p	1	0	0	0	0
Makosky, p	1	0	0	0	0
Totals	25	7	7	21	11

MONTREAL

	ab	r	h	po	a
Rackley, cf	4	0	1	2	0
Robinson, 2b	4	1	2	0	0
Shuba, lf	1	1	1	1	0
Tatum, 1b	4	0	1	4	0
Groat, rf	0	0	0	1	0
Durrett, rf-1b	2	2	1	3	1
Jorgenson, 3b	2	1	0	0	0
Franks, c	4	0	0	6	0
Breard, ss	2	1	1	1	1
Gabbard, p	0	0	0	0	1
a-Pluss	0	0	0	0	0
Fontaine, p	2	0	0	0	1
b-Gallagher	1	0	0	0	0
Totals	26	6	7	18	4

a-Batted for Gabbard in 2nd.
b-Batted for Fontaine in 7th.

MONTREAL	1	3	1	0	0	1	0—6
NEWARK	5	0	0	0	2	0	x—7

E—Breard Mustaikis 2. RBI—Shuba, Collins 3, Clark, Pluss Rackley, Robinson, Breard, Savage, Tatum. 2B—Robinson, Breard, Savage. HR—Collins, Shuba. SB—Rackley. Sac.—Jorgenson. DP—Brown, Clark and Nowak. Left—Montreal 9, Newark 3. BB—Gabbard 1, Davis 4, Garbett 2, Fontaine 4, Mustaikis 3. SO—Gabbard 1, Fontaine 4, Mustaikis 1. Hits—Off Gabbard 3 in 1 inning; Fontaine 4 in 5. Mustaikis 4 in 2 1-3; Garbett 2 in 1 2-3; Davis 1 in 1 1-3; Makosky 0 in 1 2-3. Winner—Makosky. Loser—Fontaine. Umps.—Soldare Zilber and Tatler. Time—1:50.

Dodgers, 2; Giants, 1

GIANTS

	B.Av.	AB	R	H	RBI	O	A
Rigney, ss	.263	4	0	1	0	3	3
Witek, 2b	.429	4	0	2	0	1	2
Ott, rf	.133	4	0	0	0	1	0
Mize, 1b	167	4	1	2	0	10	0
b-Rucker	.500	0	0	0	0	0	0
Cooper, c	.300	4	0	2	0	4	0
Maynard, cf	.000	2	0	0	0	3	0
c-Gordon	.000	1	0	0	0	0	0
Arnovich, lf	.000	3	0	0	0	1	0
Kerr, 3b	.154	2	0	0	0	1	3
Voiselle, p	(W.1,L.1)	2	0	0	0	0	2
a-E. Lombardi	.333	1	0	0	0	0	0
Budnick, p	(W.0,L.0)	0	0	0	0	0	0
Totals		31	1	7	0	24	10

a-Batted for Voiselle in 8th.
b-Ran for Mize in 9th.
c-Batted for Mayard in 9th.

DODGERS

	B.Av.	AB	R	H	RBI	O	A
Whitman, lf	.250	4	1	2	0	1	0
Herman, 2b	.421	4	1	1	0	4	2
Reiser, 3b	.176	4	0	1	1	0	2
Walker, rf	.167	4	0	0	0	3	0
Stevens, 1b	.000	3	0	0	1	9	2
Furillo, cf	.316	4	0	0	0	4	1
Anderson, c	.333	3	0	1	0	2	1
Reese, ss	.375	2	0	2	0	2	4
Hatten, p	(W.1,L.0)	2	0	0	0	2	2
Totals		30	2	7	2	27	14

GIANTS	0	1	0	0	0	0	0	0	0—1
DODGERS	0	0	2	0	0	0	0	0	x—2

E—Stevens, Rigney, Mize, Reese, Maynard. SB—Reiser. Sac.—Maynard, Hatten. DP—Voiselle, Rigney and Mize; Hatten, Reese and Stevens; Rigney, Witek and Mize. Left—Giants 5, Dodgers 7. BB—Voiselle 2, Hatten 1. SO—Voiselle 2, Budnick 1, Hatten 2. Hits—Off Voiselle 7 in 7 innings; Budnick 0 in 1. WP—Hatten. Loser—Voiselle. Ump.—Magerkurth, Stewart, Dunn and Henline. Time—2:03.

Cards, 7; Cubs, 6

ST. LOUIS

	ab	r	h	o	a
Klein, 2b	5	1	2	5	4
Sch'dienst, 3b	5	1	3	1	2
Musial, lf	5	0	0	0	0
Slaughter, rf	5	1	0	2	0
Adams, cf	5	1	2	3	0
Sisler, 1b	4	0	1	6	0
Marion, ss	3	1	1	0	1
Rice, c	2	0	0	3	1
a-Moore	1	0	0	0	0
Wilber, c	0	0	0	3	0
c-Walker	1	1	0	0	0
O'Dea, c	0	0	0	4	0
Barrett, p	2	0	0	0	0
Martin, p	0	0	0	0	0
b-Kurowski	1	1	1	0	0
Dickson, p	0	0	0	0	0
d-Endicott	1	0	1	0	0
e-Cross	0	0	0	0	0
Donnelly, p	0	0	0	0	0
Pollet, p	0	0	0	0	0
Totals	40	7	11	27	8

CHICAGO

	ab	r	h	o	a
Hack, 3b	4	2	2	0	3
Johnson, 2b	4	1	1	0	2
Lowrey, lf	4	0	2	1	0
Cavarretta, 1b	1	1	0	13	1
Pafko cf	5	1	1	3	0
Nicholson, rf	3	0	1	1	0
f-Scheffing	1	0	0	0	0
McCullough, c	5	0	0	7	1
Merullo, ss	5	1	2	1	3
Prim, p	3	0	1	1	3
Wyse, p	0	0	0	0	0
g-Becker	1	0	0	0	0
Schmitz, p	0	0	0	0	0
Totals	36	6	10	27	13

a-Batted for Rice in 7th.
b-Batted for Martin in 7th.
c-Batted for Wilber in 8th.
d-Batted for Dickson in 8th..
e-Ran for Endicott in 8th.
f-Batted for Wyse in 8th.
g-Batted for Nicholson in 9th.

ST. LOUIS	2	0	0	0	0	1	1	3	0—7
CHICAGO	0	0	1	1	3	1	0	0	0—6

E—Sisler 2, Johnson, Merullo 2, Hack. RBI—Musial, Adams 2 Kurowski, Endicott 2, Lowrey, Cavarretta, Pafko Nicholson, McCullough, Prim. 2B—Schoendienst, Endicott, Lowrey, Merullo 2. HR—Adams, Kurowski. Sac.—Lowrey. DP—Schoendienst, Klein and Sisler; Prim, Merullo and Cavarretta. Left—St. Louis 7, Chicago 11. BB—Barrett 3, Martin 1, Donnelly 2, Pollet 1, Wyse 1. SO—Barret 2, Martin 1, Dickson 3, Donnelly 1 Pollet 3, Prim 2, Wyse 1, Schmitz 1. Hits—Off Barrett 8 in 4 1-3 innings; Martin 2 in 1 2-3; Dickson 0 in 1; Donnelly 0 in 1-3; Pollet 0 in 1 2-3; Prim 9 in 7 (none out in 8th); Wyse 2 in 1; Schmitz 0 in 1. Winner—Dickson. Loser—Wyse. Umps.—Goetz, Jorda and Reardon. Time—2:30.

Other Box Scores Inside

JERSEY CITY, 8-1; BUFFALO, 6-7

(FIRST GAME)

BUFFALO

	ab	r	h	po	a
Rogers, ss	4	0	1	2	0
Lurchin, cf	5	0	2	1	0
Antonelli, 3b	5	1	1	3	1
McHale, 1b	3	2	1	8	0
Chipple, lf	5	1	2	1	0
Wertz, rf	4	1	2	0	0
a-Eaton	1	0	1	0	0
Markland, 2b	4	0	0	1	3
b-Reibe	1	0	0	0	0
Tabachek, c	5	1	5	8	0
Horton, p	2	0	1	0	2
Kretlow, p	1	0	0	0	0
c-Clare	1	0	0	0	0
Totals	41	6	16	24	6

JERSEY CITY

	ab	r	h	po	a
Almendro, ss	6	0	2	2	1
Ray, rf	4	1	0	6	0
Robinson 1b	4	0	0	1	0
Thompson, cf	4	3	3	5	2
Miggins, 3b	5	3	2	0	0
Knickerb'ker, lf	5	1	3	1	1
Wein, 2b-ss	1	1	0	4	3
d-Douknight	0	0	0	0	0
Pavich, 2b	0	0	0	0	1
e-Pickell	0	0	0	0	0
Grasso, c	3	0	1	11	0
Sandell, p	4	0	2	0	0
Totals	37	8	13	27	5

a-Batted for Wertz in 9th.
b-Batted for Markland in 9th.
c-Batted for Kretlow in 9th.
d-Batted for Wein in 7th.
e-Ran for Bouknight in 7th.

BUFFALO	0	0	0	3	1	1	0	0	1—6
JERSEY CITY	0	1	2	0	0	0	2	3	x—8

E—Almendro, Rogers. RBI—Sandell (2), Knickerbocker (3), Bouknight, Grasso (2), Chippel (2), Horton, Rogers, Tabachek. 2B—Thomson, McHale. 3B—Thomson, Knickerbocker. HR—Chippel. Sac.—Horton. DP—Markland, McHale. Thomson and Grasso; Thomson Knickerbocker and Almendro. Left—Jersey City 14, Buffalo 12. BB—Sandell 3, Horton 4, Kretlow 4. SO—By Sandell 8 Horton 5, Kretlow 3. Hits—Off Hor[illegible] 6 1-3 innings: Kretlow 4 in 1 2-3. HP—By Horton (Thomson). Balk—Horton. Loser—Kretlow. Umps.—Gore and Robb. Time—2:16.

(SECOND GAME)

BUFFALO

	ab	r	h	po	a
Rogers, ss	2	2	2	4	1
Lurchin, cf	3	1	1	1	0
Rapp, rf	3	0	1	0	0
McHall, 1b	4	0	0	6	1
Boland, lf	4	1	2	1	0
Bero, 3b	2	2	1	1	2
Markland, 2b	3	1	0	1	2
Reibe c	2	0	1	6	0
Eaton, p	3	0	1	1	3
Totals	26	7	9	21	9

JERSEY CITY

	ab	r	h	po	a
Almendro, ss	1	0	0	0	2
Pavich, 2b	3	0	1	3	5
Ray, rf	4	0	0	1	0
Robinson, 1b	3	0	0	8	0
Thomson, cf	3	0	0	3	0
Miggins, 3b	2	0	0	0	1
Knick'bocker, lf	3	0	0	0	1
Wein, 2b-ss	1	0	0	4	3
Grasso, c	2	0	0	2	1
Grissom, p	0	0	0	0	3
a-Austin	1	0	0	0	0
Fisher, p	0	0	0	0	0
b-Kennedy	0	0	0	0	0
Totals	23	1	1	21	16

a-Batted for Grissom in 5th.
b-Batted for Fisher in 7th.

BUFFALO	2	0	3	0	1	1	0—7
JERSEY CITY	0	0	0	0	0	0	1—1

E—Pavich Knickerbocker, Markland. RBI—Pavich, McHale 2, Boland, Reibe 2, Eaton. SB—Rogers. Sac.—Lurchin. DP—Almendro, Wein and Robinson; Wein, Pavich and Robinson. Left—Jersey City 7, Buffalo 6. BB—Grissom 4, Eaton 6, Fisher 2. SO—Eaton 6, Fisher 1. Hits—Off Grissom 8 in 5 innings; Fisher 1 in 2. HP—By Grissom (Bero). Loser—Grissom. Umps.—Robb and Gore. Time—1:50.

(Mirror Photo)

LEFT FOOT. Yank slugger Joe DiMaggio touches plate with left foot to score in 3d inning. Play came when Bill Dickey struck out and ball got away from Washington backstop Early. Wolff, Nats' hurler, covers plate.

(Mirror Photo)

RIGHT FOOT. It's DiMaggio again—this time hooking his right foot into second base as he slides in 2d inning. He advanced from 1st when Nats' Priddy threw low to Travis on Keller's grounder. Ball is on way to Travis, too low—and too late.

Yankees Shade Athletics, 2-1, With 2 Runs in 6th, Before Record Monday Crowd of 23,407

Stadium Unprepared for Mob; 'HotDog,' PeanutFamineResults

Keller Bats In Deciding Run After DiMaggio Is Credited With Triple; Home Run Streak Ends; Many Fans Enter Late Because of Ticket Jam

By Stanley Woodward

Stifled by the pitching of W. Luther (Blimp) Knerr during most of the afternoon, the New York Yankees broke out sufficiently in the sixth inning to put over two runs and beat the Philadelphia Athletics, 2 to 1, in the stadium yeserday.

A record Monday crowd of 23,407 howled delightedly at infield outs and applauded each foul ball, proving that Colonel Leland Stanford MacPhail, the entrepreneur, knows how to make new fans.

The mob scene which developed outside the Stadium at game time startled even such veteran operators as the colonel and the catering Clan Stevens. Hurriedly MacPhail's minions threw open the upper deck and manned twenty-nine ticket windows. Notwithstanding, the tail end of the crowd didn't get in until the second inning. As for the Clan Stevens, it ran out of hotdog rolls and peanuts.

Homer Streak Ends

Though striving to please so flattering and unexpected a crowd. the ankees produced their most pusilanimous batting performance. The consecutive game home-run record which they started with the young season went by the board. There wouldn't have been anything more deadly than a double if Sam Chapman, A's center fielder, had completed a play he alomst made on Joe DiMaggio.

For five innings the Yanks succumbed docilely to the well nourished Knerr's fast ball, curve and blooper, and the As led, 1 to 0, by virtue of a little smart hitting against Floyd Bevins in the first.

Knerr walked George Stirnweiss in the sixth, and veterans among the fans were startled to see Tom Henrich lay down an un-Yankee-like bunt advancing Snuffy. At this juncture DiMaggio came up and the enemy outfielders backed toward the barriers.

DiMaggio whaled a high 400-foot drive into left center. Chapman and Elmer Valo, left fielder, got to the spot and Chapman momentarily had both hands on the ball. It got away from him and rolled toward the fence. The theory was that Valo, who stopped just in time to avoid a crash, bothered him. Stirnweiss trotted home from second and the scorer gave DiMaggio a triple.

Keller Bats in Winning Run

He came home with the winning run when Charley Keller drove a line single, second of three hits, into right field.

After this minor outburst Bevens, who had kept the bases notoriously full of As in the early innings, straightened out and made the victory stick.

Valo, first hitter of the game, scored the enemy run. He walked, advanced on John Wallaese's single to left and came home when Chapman slashed a double over third. The As had men on base in every inning but the eighth, but Bevens got out a long series of clutch hitters.

Phil Rizzuto probably will resume the shortstop role against the Athletics today, which will render the Yankee varsity intact for the first time this year.

Knerr, who had an undistinguished record last year, pitched all winter in Cuba. He now weighs a bare 220 pounds and seems to have more stuff than when he was a heavyweight.

Bevens, Yanks' leading pitcher last year (13—9) was making his first 1946 start. He was fast and slightly wild.

Of the 23,407 persons who attended, 19,915 bought grandstand seats.

Joe McCarthy, the maestro, makes a brief daily appearance in the Stadium Club. He is part of the floor show.

Yankees' Score

PHILADELPHIA (A.L.)	ab	r	h	po	a	NEW YORK (A. L.)	ab	r	h	po	a
Valo lf	4	1	0	3	0	Gordon 2b	4	0	1	3	3
Peck rf	4	0	1	0	0	Stirnweiss 3b	3	1	2	0	0
Wallaesa ss	5	0	1	1	0	Henrich rf	3	0	0	2	0
Chapman cf	3	0	2	7	0	DiMaggio cf	4	1	1	1	0
McQuinn 1b	2	0	0	6	0	Keller lf	4	0	3	4	0
Handley 2b	4	0	1	1	3	Etten 1b	4	0	0	7	0
Kell 3b	4	0	0	1	1	Dickey c	3	0	0	5	0
Desautels c	4	0	1	5	0	Grimes ss	3	0	0	4	4
Knerr p	3	0	1	0	1	Bevens p	3	0	0	1	1
*Konopka	1	0	0	0	0						
Totals	34	1	7	24	5	Totals	31	2	7	27	8

*Batted for Knerr in ninth.

Philadelphia	100	000	000	—1
New York	000	002	00x	—2

Errors—Chapman, Bevens, Etten, Wallaesa. Runs batted in—Chapman, DiMaggio, Keller. Two-base hits—Chapman 2, Keller 2. Three-base hit—DiMaggio. Sacrifice—Henrich. Double plays—Gordon and Etten; Gordon, Grimes and Etten. Left on bases—Philadelphia 11; New York 7. Bases on balls—Bevens 5; Knerr 1. Strikeouts—Bevens 5; Knerr 5. Umpires—Weafer, Summers, Paparella and Grieve. Time—1:44. Attendance—23,407.

Tigers Conquer White Sox, 4-0, Behind Trout

Detroit Righthander Is Touched for Six Hits; Greenberg Slams Triple

CHICAGO, April 22 (AP).—Paul (Dizzy) Trout stopped the Chicago White Sox with six scattered hits today and hurled Detroit to a 4-to-0 shutout victory.

Trout gave a partisan Chicago crowd of 9,933 no chance to shout as he allowed but two White Sox players to reach second base.

Detroit came up with some lusty clouting to get Trout out in front almost at the start, and sharp defensive work by he Tigers kept him out of trouble all the way.

The Tigers scored two runs in the second inning. Dick Wakefield was safe at first on Hal Trosky's error and stole second. Roy Cullenbine walked, then Pinky Higgins slashed a double into left field driving in the two runs.

Hank Greenberg's third-inning triple, his only hit of the game drove in Eddie Lake, who had singled, with another run. The Tigers' final tally came in the sixth when Higgins singled, went to second when Tebbetts walked, reached third on Trout's sacrifice and scored on Eddie Mayo's long fly to center.

Three times the Sox put a man on first to start an inning but never were able to do anything about it. In the seventh, Ralph Hodgin led off with a single, and after Dario Lodigiani flied out, Mike Tresh singled. Trout struck out Wally Moses, pinch-hitter, and Thurman Tucker to end the inning.

The only other time Trout was in any trouble was in the fifth when Lodigiani led off with a double—the only extra-base hit the Sox had. Trout forced Tresh and Eddie Smith to ground out and Tucker lifted a fly to right to end the inning.

The score:

DETROIT (A. L.)	ab	r	h	po	a	CHICAGO (A. L.)	ab	r	h	po	a
Lake ss	3	1	2	2	4	Tucker cf	4	0	1	2	0
Mayo 2b	4	0	0	3	3	Kolloway 2b	4	0	0	3	3
McCosky cf	5	0	0	2	0	Wright rf	3	0	2	3	0
Greenberg 1b	4	0	1	6	0	Appling ss	4	0	0	0	2
Wakefield lf	3	1	1	7	0	Trosky 1b	3	0	0	7	1
Cullenbine rf	3	1	0	1	0	Hodgin lf	4	0	1	1	0
Higgins 3b	4	1	3	1	0	Lodigiani 3b	4	0	1	1	1
Tebbetts c	3	0	0	4	0	Tresh c	3	0	1	10	1
Trout p	3	0	0	0	2	Smith p	2	0	0	0	1
						*Moses	1	0	0	0	0
						Grove p	0	0	0	0	0
Totals	32	4	7	27	9	Totals	32	0	6	27	9

*Batted for Smith in seventh.

Detroit	021	001	000	—4
Chicago	000	000	000	—0

Error—Trosky. Runs batted in—Higgins (2), Greenberg, Mayo. Two-base hits—Higgins (2), Greenberg, Mayo. Two-base hits—Higgins, Lodigiani. Three-base hits—Greenberg, Higgins. Stolen base—Wakefiled. Sacrifices—Mayo, Trout. Double plays—Mayo, Lake and Greenberg; Appling, Kolloway and Trosky. Left on bases—Detroit, 11; Chicago, 7. Bases on balls—Trout, 2; Smith, 6; Grove, 2. Strikeouts—Trout, 4; Smith, 5; Grove, 3. Hits—Off Smith 7 in 7 innings; Grove, 0 in 2. Losing pitcher—Smith. Umpires—Passarella, McGowan and Rue. Time—1:55. Attendance—9,933.

Dykes to Rejoin White Sox

CHICAGO, April 22 (AP).—Jimmy Dykes, ailing manager of the Chicago White Sox, plans to rejoin the club here next Saturday. Dykes, convalescing from a stomach operation, was discharged from a Hollywood, Calif., hospital today. Dykes plans to leave for Chicago on Thursday. Physicians' instructions were for him to take it easy for awhile.

Newark Winning Skein Ended by Montreal, 13-4

NEWARK, N. J. April 22 (AP).—Scoring seven runs in the first three innings and six more in the sixth, the Montreal Royals ended Newark's four-game winning streak today before 3,000 by grinding out a 13-to-4 decision.

Homers by Johnny Jorgenson and Herman Franks, each with one teammate aboard, featured the six-run burst which drove Gene Bergerson, Newark's third pitcher of the game, to the showers. In all, the Royals blasted Norman Branch, Jack Robinson and Hank Perry for twelve safeties. Franks had two singles in additio nto his homer and four R. B. I.'s. Jorgenson also drove in four runs.

The score:

MONTREAL (I. L)	ab	r	h	po	a	NEWARK (I. L)	ab	r	h	po	a
Rackley cf	5	2	1	1	1	Rabe cf	5	0	0	6	0
Robinson 2b	4	2	1	5	2	Selkirk lf	1	1	1	0	0
Shuba lf	3	2	1	2	0	Deininger 1b	2	0	0	6	1
Durrett 1b	6	2	2	9	0	Clark 2b	5	1	2	0	1
Jorgenson 3b	4	2	2	2	3	Nowak 1b lf	4	0	0	4	0
Pluss rf	4	1	1	1	1	Savage 3b	4	0	2	2	0
Franks c	3	1	3	6	0	Collins rf	2	1	1	1	0
Breard ss	5	1	1	1	6	Brown ss	4	1	2	2	3
Paepke p	0	0	0	0	0	Fallon c	3	0	1	6	2
Smolko p	3	0	0	0	2	Branch p	0	0	0	0	1
						Robinson p	0	0	0	0	0
						*Houtz	0	0	0	0	0
						Bergerson p	1	0	0	0	0
						Perry p	1	0	0	0	1
						†Korte	1	0	0	0	0
Totals	37	13	12	27	15	Totals	33	4	9	27	9

*Batted for Robinson in second.
†Batted for Perry in ninth.

Montreal	331	006	000	—13
Newark	120	000	010	—4

Error—Fallon. Runs batted in—Durrett 3, Jorgenson 4, Pluss, Franks 4, Rabe, Savage, Brown, Clark. Two-base hits—Jorgenson, Clark. Three-base hit—Collins. Home runs—Jorgenson, Franks, Clark. Stolen bases—Robinson (Montreal), Rackley. Double plays—Breard, Robinson (Montreal) and Durrett; Brown and Deininger. Left on bases—Montreal 9, Newark 8. Bases on balls—Branch 4, Robinson 2, Bergerson 3, Smolko 6, Perry 3. Strikeouts—Branch 1, Robinson 1, Bergerson 1, Paepke 1, Smolko 2. Hits—Branch 1 in ⅔ innings; Robinson 2 in 1⅓; Bergerson 7 in 3⅓; Perry 1 in 3⅔; Paepke 6 in 1; Smolko 3 in 8. Winning pitcher—Smolko. Losing pitcher—Branch. Umpires—Tatler, Zilber and Solodare. Time—2.30. Attendance—3,000.

Herald Tribune—Kell

SAFE AS HIGH THROW PULLS INFIELDER OFF BAG. Oscar Grimes steps on first as George McQuinn sails into the air for Jack Wallaesa's toss in fifth inning

HE'S OUT AT SECOND: Hal Peck, of Athletics, gets there too late, but Oscar Grimes's throw to catch Jack Wallaesa at first on an attempted double play also was too late. Yankees won, 2 to 1

MEXICO CLAMPS LID

By Rud Rennie

Bang! Jorge Shuts the Door

JORGE PASQUEL, multimillionaire president of the Mexican Baseball League, last night slammed the door in the eager faces of all the second-rate baseball players who either have been, or are about to be, lopped from major-league rosters and sent to the minors.

Rud Rennie

"I do not want players who are not good enough to play in your major leagues," he said over the telephone from Mexico City. He was at home in the Calle Hamburgo. "I want nothing but the best."

One wondered how long Pasquel would continue paying incredible bonuses and salaries to American players of no great distinction. Now it appears evident that he intended to do it only long enough to attract the attention of the baseball world; only until he had established confidence in the integrity of his organization.

He has done both these things. Players in organized baseball no longer doubt that Pasquel keeps all his promises. Every one is interested in the money he is willing to spend. Players who a month ago would not have considered jumping to the Mexican League are now eager to do so.

"I have in my office," he said, "I do not know how many telegrams from players who want to come to Mexico. I have received letters. They telephone. You mention names. I do not know. I cannot remember. I have to look to be able to answer you and the list is in my office. I have not been to the office in a week because it was Holy Week."

He remembered Van Lingle Mungo as one of the applicants.

"I have received bad reports on him," he said. "I do not want him."

Admission by Invitation Only

DOZENS of baseball players will be jolted by Pasquel's decision. Several are known to have been waiting, confident that if their major-league teams did not keep them, they would jump to the Mexican League. It was, from all accounts, a cinch to get into Pasquel's organization, and the bonuses and salaries some of the players thought of demanding were quite interesting. It never occurred to any one that Pasquel would close the gate to the Mexican gold mine.

It is rather obvious now that Jorge (pronounced Hor-gay) did not run the Pasquel fortune up beyond $60,000,000 by being a dope. He is a cute operator with a fine sense of timing.

He worked things so that American players would want to come to Mexico; then, having created the desire, he took down the "welcome" sign and made admission by invitation only.

Early Birds Sitting Pretty

IT MUST be something of a shock to American players who were willing to make the Mexican League a comfy cushion for their declining years in baseball to find that the Mexican League does not want them. They were willing to take five years suspension from organized baseball to make some big, easy dough in three years in Mexico. And now they can't do it.

The early birds—Sal Maglie, George Hausmann, Tom Gorman, Murray Franklin, Mickey Owen and a few more—are in. Now players of the same quality are out.

Pasquel wants only the best. He is ready to pay in a way that will make the magnates shiver.

Nothing to Worry About Now

EXCEPT for saying "How are you?" he asked only one question. He wanted to know if it were true that Commissioner Chandler had declared ineligible all the players who had jumped to the Mexican League.

"Ah," he said, "that is good."

Now he does not have to worry about any of his importations giving him the Vern Stephens treatment, jumping back into organized baseball.

Incidentally, Pasquel says Stephens has not returned the $5,000 he gave him for signing.

Results and Standings In the Minor Leagues

INTERNATIONAL LEAGUE

Yesterday's Results

Montreal, 13; Newark, 4.
Syracuse, 6; Rochester, 3.
Other clubs not schedeuleed.

STANDING OF THE CLUBS

	W.	L.	Pct.		W.	L.	Pct.
Baltimore	3	1	.750	Buffalo	2	3	.400
Syracuse	3	1	.750	Toronto	1	2	.333
Newark	4	2	.667	Jersey City	1	3	.250
Montreal	3	2	.600	Rochester	1	4	.200

GAMES TODAY

Montreal at Newark, 2:30.
Buffalo at Jersey City, 2:30.
Toronto at Baltimore (night).
Rochester at Syracuse.

TEXAS LEAGUE

Yesterday's Results

San Antonio, 8; Beaumont, 4.
Oklahoma City-Dallas, rain.
Tulso-Fort Worth, rain.
Houston-Shreveport, night.

STANDING OF THE CLUBS

	W.	L.	Pct.		W.	L.	Pct.
San Antonio	5	1	.833	Fort Worth	2	4	.333
Tulsa	5	1	.833	Beaumont	2	5	.286
Dallas	4	2	.667	Houston	2	5	.286
Shreveport	4	3	.571	Okla. City	1	5	.167

AMERICAN ASSOCIATION

Yesterday's Results

No games scheduled.

STANDING OF THE CLUBS

	W.	L.	Pct.		W.	L.	Pct.
Minneapolis	4	2	.667	Kansas City	3	3	.500
Indianapolis	4	2	.667	Columbus	2	4	.333
Louisville	4	2	.667	Toledo	2	4	.333
St. Paul	3	2	.600	Milwaukee	1	4	.200

SOUTHERN ASSOCIATION

Yesterday's Results

Little Rock—New Orleans, night.
Nashville—Atlanta, night
Chattanooga—Birmingham, night.
Memphis—Mobile, night.

STANDING OF THE CLUBS

	W.	L.	Pct.		W.	L.	Pct.
New Orleans	7	2	.778	Chattanooga	3	4	.429
Atlanta	6	2	.750	Little Rock	3	5	.375
Memphis	6	2	.750	Birmingham	2	6	.250
Nashville	4	3	.571	Mobile	1	8	.111

PACIFIC COAST LEAGUE

Yesterday's Results

Hollywood-Portland, night game.
Other clubs not scheduled.

STANDING OF THE CLUBS

	W.	L.	Pct.		W.	L.	Pct.
San Fran.	19	6	.760	San Diego	10	14	.417
Los Angeles	18	7	.720	Portland	9	13	.409
Oakland	14	12	.538	Seattle	8	15	.348
Hollywood	10	12	.455	Sacramento	8	17	.320

Red Sox Win On Pellagrini's Homer, 5 to 4

Beaning of Pesky GivesHim First Trip to Big League PlatetoSenators'Chagrin

BOSTON, April 22 (AP).—In his first major league time at bat Eddie Pellagrini today blasted a seventh-inning homer that gave the Boston Red Sox a 5-to-4 victory over the Washington Senators.

Pellagrini, who has been in the Red Sox farm chain for about years, made his first appearance in the game as a runner after Johnny Pesky was struck on the head by one of Sid Hudson's fast pitches in the fifth inning.

Although the ball bounced into the grandstand, Pesky, known as "Hard-Head" to his teammates, did not lost consciousness. After being carried to the clubhouse he remarked, "I've been hit by harder balls than that." His condition was not regarded as serious.

The Red Sox poled out two other four-baggers, by Bobby Doerr and Rudy York, as Mickey Harris, southpaw, won his second decision over the Senators.

The score:

WASHINGTON (A. L.)	ab	r	h	po	a	BOSTON (A. L.)	ab	r	h	po	a
Robertson 3b	5	1	2	2	3	Culberson cf	4	1	0	1	0
Lewis rf	4	0	0	1	0	Pesky ss	2	0	0	2	3
Spence cf	4	0	1	0	0	Pellagrini ss	1	1	1	2	0
Sanford 1b	4	0	0	14	0	Williams lf	4	1	2	4	0
Travis ss	4	1	2	2	5	Doerr 2b	4	1	2	2	1
Priddy 2b	4	1	2	2	3	York 1b	4	1	1	9	0
Evans c	4	1	1	2	0	Metkovich rf	4	0	1	0	0
Goolsby lf	2	0	0	1	0	Andres 3b	2	0	0	0	4
Hudson p	3	0	0	0	2	Pytlak c	3	0	1	7	0
*Gerra	1	0	0	0	0	Harris p	3	0	0	0	1
Totals	35	4	8	24	13	Totals	31	5	8	27	9

*Batted for Hudson in ninth.

Washington	001	300	000	—4
Boston	000	211	10x	—5

Error—Doerr. Runs batted in—Robertson (2), Spence, Evans, Doerr (2), Williams, York, Pellagrini. Two-base hit—Robertson. Three-base hit—Travis. Home runs—Doerr, York, Pellagrini. Sacrifice—Goolsby. Double play—Travis and Sanford. Left on bases—Washington, 6; Boston, 4. Bases on balls—Off Hudson, 1; Harris, 1. Strikeouts—By Hudson, 2; Harris, 7. Hit by pitcher—By Hudon (Pesky). Umpires—Rommel, Boyer and Jones. Time—1:39. Attendance—7,315 paid.

Temple Double in Sixth Defeats N. Y. U., 6 to 5

Special to the Herald Tribune

PHILADELPHIA, April 22.—Howard Cunningham, war veteran, pitched Temple to a 6-to-5 victory over New York University today. The sophomore righthander held the Violets to six scattered hits. Off Arnold Harris, the Owls rolled up thirteen hits, Warren Rozelle and Howard Davis each getting three. Rozelle had two triples and a single.

Temple scored the winning run in the sixth. With two out Joe Chielli was hit by a pitched ball and scored when Ed Rzepski doubled to center, Marty Goldstein losing the ball in the sun.

The score:

N. Y. U.	ab	r	h	po	a	TEMPLE	ab	r	h	po	a
Angelastro 3b	4	0	0	5	5	Chielli lf	3	2	2	2	0
O'Connor ss	4	0	1	1	7	Rzepski 2b	5	1	2	4	4
Medica 2b	3	0	0	2	1	Papaieves 1b	2	0	0	9	0
Simmons lf	3	0	0	1	0	Davis rf	4	1	3	1	0
Wallace 3b	4	2	2	12	1	Rozelle 3b	4	1	3	0	2
Goldstein cf	4	2	1	1	0	Rullo cf	4	1	1	4	0
Autieri rf	2	0	0	0	0	Slosburg ss	2	0	0	2	3
Sarath rf	2	0	0	0	0	Fretz c	3	0	1	5	2
Olsen c	4	1	1	2	2	Cunn'gham p	3	0	1	0	1
Harris p	3	0	1	0	1						
Totals	33	5	6	24	17	Totals	30	6	13	27	12

N. Y. U.	001	202	000	—5
Temple	200	211	00x	—6

Errors—O'Connor, Olsen, Rzepski, Rozelle, Slosburg 2. Two-base hits—Olsen, Davis, Rozelle. Runs batted in—Chielli, Rzepski, Davis, Rozelle, Rullo, Angelastro, Olsen. Three-base hits—Rozelle 2. Sacrifices—Slosburg, Cunningham. Left on bases—N. Y. U., 3; Temple 8. Louble plays—Rozelle, Rzepski and Papaieves; Angelastro and Wallace 2; Slosburg, Rzepski and Papaieves. Stolen base—Rullo. Struck out—Cunningham 4; Harris 1. Base on balls—Cunningham 1, Harris 5. Hit by pitched balls—Harris (Chielli). Cunningham (Simmons). Time—2:05. Umpires—Gilbert and Gillespie.

Cardinals Win Over Reds, 4-1, Behind Lanier

CINCINNATI, April 22 (AP).—Behind the effective six-hit pitching of Max Lanier, the St. Louis Cardinals defeated the Cincinnati Reds, 4 to 1, today for their fifth straight triumph.

Lanier handcuffed Cincinnati until the eighth inning, when a single, two walks and an error by Marty Marion allowed the only Redleg score.

The Cardinals went to work on Johnny Vander Meer in the first inning, scoring three runs on four hits and a walk. Vander Meer settled down in the next six frames but the Cards scored again in the eighth on Stan Musial's walk and two singles.

The Reds loaded the bases in their half of the eighth, after two were out, but Del Rice, catcher, caught Eddie Miller's pop fly, ending the threat.

The score:

ST. LOUIS (N. L)	ab	r	h	po	a	CINCINNATI (N. L)	ab	r	h	po	a
Klein 2b	3	1	1	1	3	Clay cf	4	1	1	4	0
Schoend'st 3b	4	0	0	4	3	R Adams 2b	3	0	2	2	5
Musial lf	3	2	2	1	0	Hatton 3b	3	0	0	0	2
Slaughter rf	4	1	2	2	0	Moss rf	4	0	0	1	0
E Adams cf	4	0	2	3	0	Miller ss	4	0	0	3	6
Sisler 1b	4	0	0	9	0	West lf	4	0	[illegible]	2	0
Marion ss	4	0	2	1	1	Haas 1b	4	0	2	11	1
Rice c	4	0	1	6	0	Mueller c	4	0	0	4	0
Lanier p	4	0	0	0	1	Vander Meer	2	0	0	0	0
						*McCormick	1	0	0	0	0
						Lambert p	0	0	0	0	0
Totals	34	4	10	27	8	Totals	33	1	6	27	14

*Batted for Vander Meer in eighth.

St. Louis	300	000	010	—4
Cincinnati	000	000	010	—1

Error—Marion. Runs batted in—Slaughter, E. Adams 2, Sisler. Two-base hit—Marion. Double plays—Haas, Miller and Haas; Adams, Miller and Haas; Marion, Klein and Sisler; Miller, Adams and Haas. Left on bases—St. Louis 5, Cincinnati 7. Bases on balls—Vander Meer 2, Lanier 2. Strikeouts—Vander Meer 3, Lanier 4. Hits—Vander Meer 10 in 8 innings; Lambert none in 1. Losing pitcher—Vander Meer. Umpires—Barr, Conlan and Boggess. Time—1:39. Attendance—6,868.

Connie Mack, 83, and Wife Separate; A's Owner Transfers Stock to 3 Sons

PHILADELPHIA, April 22 (UP).—Mrs. Cornelius McGillicuddy, wife of the owner-manager of the Philadelphia Athletics Baseball Club, today disclosed that she and Connie Mack have separated.

Mrs. McGillicuddy said the separation followed Mack's distribution of more than half of his stock in the ball club among his three sons, Earle, Roy and Connie jr.

"I learned in October about his transfer of the stock," she said. "I went to St. Petersburg, Fla., in December and asked him about it. He said it would be all straightened out in two or three years. He is 83 and life is too uncertain to anticipate what may happen in the next two or three years.

"I returned here the 1st of January and later he sent word that he was not returning and that he was sending for his clothes. He did so and went to the Mayfair House."

The Mayfair House is in suburban Germantown.

Both she and Mack are living apart at present, Mrs. McGillicuddy said. In New York with his team, Mack told reporters.

"Things will be straightened out in a short time. I have no comment to make. This is a personal matter and I hope people will regard it as private and keep out of it."

Asked if she thought there was any chance of a reconciliation, Mrs. Mack said emphatically: "Not with me."

"I don't know how long I'll stand up, but I'm on my own," she declared.

Mack has two sons by a previous marriage, Earle and Roy. His first wife, the former Margaret Hogan, died in 1892. Connie jr. and his four daughter are children by his present wife, the former Katherine Halloran, whom he married on Oct. 27, 1910.

"The point is," Mrs. Mack told reporters, "that there are nine persons to be considered in this—his eight children and me. And it idn't sound very good when he gave more than half the stock to three of them."

Seven of Mack's eight children are living. Marguerite, a daughter of the first marriage, died several years ago but is survived by her husband, son an grandson.

The Athletics franchise and the real estate, including Shibe Park, are reported valued in the millions. The Macks own controlling interest of the club stock, although large blocks are held by Mrs. Ida Shibe, widow of Thomas Shibe, former club president, and other heirs of Benjamin Shibe, the A's first president.

Mack has managed the As since Philadelphia became a member of the American League in 1901. Prior to that he managed Pittsburgh, of the National League. He celebrated his fiftieth anniversary as a major-league manager on Aug. 4, 1944.

In 1928 Mack created a trust fund for his wife and three oldest children but revoked it a little more than a year later. Hhe trust comprised 747 shares of the club stock. Income accruing from it while it existed was divided as follows: Mrs. McGillicuddy, 62½ per cent; Earle and Roy and Marguerite, 12½ per cent.

The stock reverted to Mack upon his revocation. Its disposition since was not available.

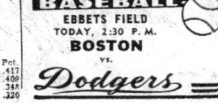

Red Sox Rout Yankees, 12-5, Behind Dobson; Braves Beat Giants in 9th, 5-4; Cooper Hurt

Pesky and Pellagrini Pummel Three of New York's Pitchers

Zuber and Stanceu Pelted After Roser Is Routed in First Inning Before Boston Crowd of 31,150; Gordon Blasts Homer; 3 Singles for DiMaggio

By Stanley Woodward

BOSTON, April 25.—Should you have read how the Yankees walloped the Red Sox, 12 to 5, on Wednesday, you will be in a strong position to comprehend today's development, for the score was the same and the teams were reversed. This time the Boston entry clubbed the whey out of four junior New York pitchers, avenging prior indignities punch for punch and run for run. The Boston triumph helped elevate the Detroit Tigers to the top of the American League and left the Sox and Yankees tied in second placee.

A crowd of 31,150 impassioned clients crowed and whooped as the Boston combatants took the Yankee second-run pitching staff to pieces. The locals rifled the offerings of Emerson (Steve) Roser, Bill Zuber, Charley Stanceu and Bill Wight for thirteen hits and twenty-two bases and made the best of eight bases on balls contributed by these temporary New York residents.

All Bostonese, except the battery men and the reputedly phenomenal Ted Williams, contributed fulsome smites to the barrage. Leading sluggers were John (Hard Head) Pesky, shortstop, who hit two doubles and two singles, and Ed Pellagrini, home-grown third baseman, who hit a triple and single prior to hoisting a monumental home run over the screen in left field.

Three Hits for DiMaggio

Williams walked three times and popped twice. Though comparisons are odious, it is well to note that his hitting rival, the Yankees' Joe DiMaggio, pulled out of his minor slump with three savage singles, two of which nearly carried away Joe Dobson, the full-time Boston pitcher.

As in the previous game of the series, the faithfulness of all hands to the script was downright touching. It has been written that these teams have hitters unsupported by sufficient pitching aplomb and, heaven knows, that's the way it looked. Even Dobson, who went the route, was bumped around by nine solid New York hits, which included Joe Gordon's 1946 home-run debut, a drive into the center-field bleachers.

At the outset Dobson threatened to emulate the efforts of the regrettable Boston heavers of the previous day, for he gave up two hits and walked three men in the first inning, forcing in one of the inning's two Yankee runs.

The restive Boston fans were just getting into good booing fettle when the Sox jumped the Yankee starter, "Blue Boy" Roser, for four in their half of the inning. Items such as two bases on balls, Pesky's first double, Rudy York's single and Pellagrini's clean-up triple to the right-field fence were included in the ana of the inning.

Relief Men Pummeled

After that it was murder. Though Blue Boy was jerked before the end of the inning, the Sox rallied strongly on the successive trails of Zuber and Stanceu, virtually deafening these characters with the clatter of base hits. Wight, who pitched the eighth, escaped damage through a double play Snuffy Stirnweiss started, after yielding a base on balls to York and a single to George Metkovich.

Aside from the enormity of the pitching, the Yankees continued to look like a ball club. They hit enough to win most games and fielded without miscue for the second straight day.

The Yankees now have played to 305,052 paying clients in ten games which is an all-time record. Today's crowd, larger by more than a thousand than that of yesterday was a revelation to the local management.

Stirnweiss passed out cigars in the Hotel Kenmore this morning in celebration of the birth of his third child, a boy weighing nine pounds, three ounces.

The Boston papers appealed to the fans not to boo Ted Williams, and the power of the press never was more graphically illustrated. Even the left-field baiters were stifled.

Yankees' Score

NEW YORK (A. L.)	ab	r	h	po	a	BOSTON (A. L.)	ab	r	h	po	a
Rizzuto ss	4	1	2	1	1	Culberson cf.	3	2	1	2	0
Stirnweiss 3b.	4	1	1	0	4	Pesky ss.	5	2	4	2	0
Henrich rf	3	2	1	2	0	Williams lf.	2	3	0	2	0
J.DiMaggio cf	4	0	3	2	0	Doerr 2b.	5	2	2	1	5
Keller lf	4	0	0	3	0	York 1b.	3	1	2	7	2
Etten 1b	3	0	1	9	0	Metkovich rf	4	0	1	2	0
Gordon 2b	4	1	1	2	3	Pellagrini 3b.	5	2	3	1	1
Robinson c	3	0	0	3	0	Pytlak c.	5	0	0	7	1
Silvestri c	1	0	0	2	0	Dobson p.	4	0	0	3	1
Roser p	0	0	0	0	0						
Zuber p	2	0	0	0	0						
*Metheny	1	0	0	0	0						
Stanceu p	0	0	0	0	2						
†Majeski	1	0	0	0	0						
Wight p	0	0	0	0	0						
Totals	34	5	9	24	10	Totals	36	12	13	27	10

*Batted for Zuber in sixth.
†Batted for Stanceu in eighth.

New York	200	020	010	—5
Boston	432	012	00x	—12

Error—Pellagrini. Runs batted in—Henrich, Etten 2, J. DiMaggio, Gordon, Metkovich, Pytlak, Culberson, Pellagrini 2, Doerr 3, Psky 2. York 2. Two-base hits—Pellagrini, Pesky 2. Three-base hit—Pellagrini. Home runs—Gordon, Pellagrini. Stolen bases—Rizzuto, Culberson. Sacrifice—Stirnweiss. Double plays—Stirnweiss, Gordon and Etten; Pellagrini, Doerr and York. Left on bases—New York 9, Boston 8. Bases on balls—Roser 2, Zuber 2, Stanceu 3, Wight 1, Dobson 6. Strikeouts—Roser 1, Zuber 2, Stanceu 2, Dobson 7. Hits—Roser 3 in ⅔ inning, Zuber 7 in 4⅓, Stanceu 2 in 2, Wight 1 in 1. Wild pitch—Zuber. Passed ball—Robinson. Losing pitcher—Roser. Umpires—Paparella, Weafer, Summers and Grieve. Time—2:25. Attendance—31,150 (paid).

Tigers Defeat Browns, 6 to 5, On Runs in 8th

Newhouser Holds Off Assault by Revamped St. Louis Batting Order in Fourth

ST. LOUIS, April 25 (AP).—A long-range hitting attack against four St. Louis Browns pitchers won a 6-to-5 ball game today for the Detroit Tigers, whose veteran southpaw, Hal Newhouser, staved off a five-run assault in the fourth by a revamped Brownie batting order.

The Browns spotted Detroit four runs in that inning as Johnnie Miller went to the showers. Roy Cullenbine's first homer of the season scored Hank Greenberg with the Tigers' fourth run. Then the Browns hammered Newhouser for six hits in their half to take a 5-to-4 lead.

Greenberg doubled in the eighth and scored the tying run on Dick Wakefield's single. With two out George Tebbett's pop fly dropped behind Babe Dahlgren for a single and Cullenbine scored from second.

The score:

DETROIT (A. L.)	ab	r	h	po	a	ST. LOUIS (A. L.)	ab	r	h	po	a
Lake ss	2	0	0	2	2	Berardino 2b.	5	0	2	4	3
Webb ss	2	0	1	0	1	Dahlgren 1b.	5	0	1	9	2
Mayo 2b	5	1	1	4	4	Stephens ss.	4	0	2	3	2
McCosky cf	5	1	1	2	0	Laabs rf.	5	1	1	1	0
Greenberg 1b.	3	2	3	6	1	McQuillen lf.	4	1	1	0	0
Wakefield lf.	4	0	1	3	0	Judnich cf.	4	0	2	4	0
Cullenbine rf.	4	2	1	1	0	Christman 3b	4	1	0	1	6
Higgins 3b	3	0	1	1	3	Mancuso c.	2	1	1	3	2
Tebbetts c	4	0	1	6	1	Miller p.	1	0	0	2	0
Newhouser p.	4	0	0	2	3	Zoldak p.	0	0	0	0	0
						*Schulte	1	1	1	0	0
						Ferens p.	0	0	0	0	1
						†Lucadello	1	0	0	0	0
						Kramer p.	0	0	0	0	0
Totals	36	6	10	27	15	Totals	36	5	11	27	16

*Batted for Zoldak in fourth.
†Batted for Ferens in eighth.

Detroit	000	400	020	—6
St. Louis	000	500	000	—5

Error—Berardino. Runs batted in—McCosky, Greenberg, Cullenbine 2, Judnich, Mancuso, Schulte 2, Berardino, Wakefield. Two-base hits—Mayo, McCosky, Greenberg 2, Laabs Mancuso, Berardino, Stephens, Judnich. Home run — Cullenbine. Sacrifice — Ferens. Double plays — Newhouser, Webb and Greenberg; Christman and Dahlgren. Left on bases—Detroit 6, St. Louis 8. Bases on balls—Off Newhouser 3, Zoldak 1, Ferens 2. Struck out—By Newhouser 7, Miller 2. Hits—Off Miller 5 in 3⅓ innings, Zoldak 0 in ⅔, Ferens 4 in 4, Kramer 1 in 1. Losing pitcher—Ferens. Umpires—Hubbard, Pipgras and Berry. Time—2:06. Attendance—4,946 (paid).

Syracuse Wins 5th in Row Beating Montreal, 5-4

SYRACUSE, April 25 (AP).—The Syracuse Chiefs tied the score with three runs in the ninth and went on to defeat Montreal in the tenth, 5 to 4, today, for their fifth straight victory.

Dick Sipek delivered the winning blow off Johnny Gabbard, third Royal hurler, singling in Joe Just from second. Just had singled with one away and was sacrificed to second by the winning pitcher, Ken Polivka.

In the ninth inning Just walked, Al Sinton singled and Jack Cassini tripled for two runs. Sipek knotted the count on a deep fly to right.

The score by innings:

						R.	H.	E.
Montreal	000	000	040	0	—4	5	3	
Syracuse	000	000	103	1	—5	10	1	

Batteries—Fontaine, Paepke (8), Gabbard (9) and Franks; Harris, Prendergast (9), Polivka (10) and West, Just (8).

PACIFIC COAST LEAGUE

Four night games.

STANDING OF THE CLUBS

	W.	L.	Pct.		W.	L.	Pct.
San Fran.	19	7	.731	Hollywood	11	14	.440
Los Angeles.	17	9	.654	Portland	11	14	.440
Oakland	16	11	.593	Sacramento	9	17	.346
San Diego.	12	15	.444	Seattle	9	17	.346

Herald Tribune—Frank

OUT AT THE PLATE: Ernie Lombardi tagging Tom Holmes in fourth inning yesterday at the Polo Grounds as Braves edged the Giants, 5 to 4

INSIDE-THE-PARK HOMER: Phil Masi leaping to the plate and completing four-ply blow. Two runners scored ahead of Masi and one of them, Holmes, is congratulating him

SCORING FROM FIRST ON DOUBLE: Ted Williams tearing into the plate on Bobby Doerr's two-base hit at Boston yesterday. The catcher is Aaron Robinson. Red Sox drubbed Yankees, 12 to 5

Associated Press wirephoto

Jersey Giants Beaten By Rochester, 4 to 3

JERSEY CITY, April 25 (AP).—Rochester squared its series with Jersey City at a game apiece today by defeating the Little Giants, 4 to 3, in a game called at the end of seven innings because of rain.

Bud Byerly, although touched for ten hits, managed to avoid trouble except in the second and fourth when home runs by Mickey Grasso accounted for all three Little Giant tallies.

Two bases on balls, a triple and an infield out gave Rochester three runs in the opening inning. The Wings picked up what proved to be the winning marker in the second on successive singles by Ed Joost, Warren Robinson and Byerly.

The score:

ROCHESTER (I. L.)	ab	r	h	po	a	JERSEY CITY (I. L.)	ab	r	h	po	a
Burns 2b	4	1	0	1	2	Maguire 2b.	4	0	0	0	2
Nichols lf	2	1	0	0	0	Ray rf.	4	0	2	2	0
White lf	1	0	0	1	0	Thomson cf.	4	0	1	0	0
Kubski 3b	3	1	2	0	2	Jaeger 1b.	4	0	2	11	2
Rebel rf.	4	0	0	0	0	Miggins 3b.	3	0	0	0	3
Diering cf.	3	0	1	1	0	Austin lf.	3	0	1	1	0
Baron 1b	4	0	0	9	0	Wein ss.	3	1	1	2	2
Joost ss	3	1	1	2	4	Grasso c.	2	2	2	2	0
Robinson c.	2	0	1	7	0	Sandel p.	3	0	1	3	2
Byerly p.	3	0	1	0	1						
Totals	29	4	6	21	9	Totals	30	3	10	21	11

Rochester	310	000	0—4
Jersey City	010	200	0—3

Errors—Maguire, Miggins. Runs batted in—Grasso 3, Kubski 2, Rebel, Byerly. Three-base hit—Kubski. Home runs—Grasso 2. Stolen base—Ray. Double plays—Burns, Joost and Baron; Jaeger and Wein. Left on bases—Jersey City 7, Rochester 9. Bases on balls—Sandel 5, Byerly 1. Strikeouts—Sandel 2, Byerly 7. Umpires—Winters and Tobin. Time—1:31.

TEXAS LEAGUE

Yesterday's Results

Beaumont, 7; Houston, 4 (1st)
Houston, 6; Beaumont, 4 (2d)
Three night games.

STANDING OF THE CLUBS

	W.	L.	Pct.		W.	L.	Pct.
San Antonio	6	1	.857	Ft. Worth	4	4	.500
Dallas	6	2	.750	Beaumont	4	6	.400
Tulsa	5	3	.625	Houston	4	7	.364
Shreveport	4	4	.500	Okla. City	1	7	.125

17 Hits by White Sox Smother Indians, 11 to 2

CLEVELAND, April 25 (AP).—The Cleveland Indians' defense fell apart at the seams today and the Chicago White Sox belted four Tribe hurlers for seventeen hits and a 11-to-2 triumph in the opener of a two-game series.

Allie Reynolds lasted only until the third inning when the Sox pushed across five runs on the combination of five singles, an error and three bases on balls. Reynolds was followed by Pete Center, Vic Johnson and Johnny Podgajny.

Lefty Ed Lopat shut out the Redskins until the eighth as he won his second start of the season.

The score:

CHICAGO (A. L.)	ab	r	h	po	a	CLEVELAND (A. L.)	ab	r	h	po	a
Tucker cf	5	2	1	4	0	Case lf.	5	0	2	3	0
Kolloway 2b.	6	1	2	5	4	Mackiewicz cf	5	0	2	3	0
Wright rf	4	2	1	0	0	Seerey rf.	5	1	2	5	1
Appling ss	5	0	3	2	7	Fleming 1b.	4	0	2	2	0
Trosky 1b	6	2	1	9	0	Keltner 3b.	3	0	0	0	1
Hodgin lf	5	0	2	2	0	Boudreau ss.	4	0	1	4	1
Lodigiani 3b.	5	1	2	2	3	Lollar c.	2	0	0	3	0
Fernandez c.	4	1	2	3	0	Hegan c.	2	0	0	5	0
Lopat p.	4	2	3	0	0	Mack 2b.	4	1	0	2	1
						Reynolds p.	0	0	0	0	0
						Center p.	1	0	0	0	0
						*Monaco	1	0	0	0	0
						Johnson p.	0	0	0	0	1
						†Meyer	1	0	0	0	0
						Podgajny p.	0	0	0	0	0
						‡Brewster	0	0	0	0	0
Totals	44	11	17	27	14	Totals	37	2	9	27	5

*Batted for Center in fifth.
‡Batted for Johnson in seventh.
†Batted for Podgajny in ninth.

Chicago	005	010	113	—11
Cleveland	000	000	011	—2

Errors—Reynolds, Kolloway, Lodigiani, Boudreau, Johnson. Runs batted in—Appling, Hodgin 2, Fernandez 2, Trosky 2, Fleming, Tucker 2, Wright, Mackiewicz. Two-base hits—Seerey, Lodigiani, Fernandez. Three-base hits—Fleming, Tucker. Home run—Trosky. Stolen base—Kolloway. Double plays—Seerey and Hegan; Appling, Kolloway and Trosky. Left on bases—Chicago 12, Cleveland 10. Bases on balls—Reynolds 3, Center 2, Johnson 1, Lapot 2. Strikeouts—Reynolds 3, Johnson 1, Podgajny 3, Lopat 3. Hits—Off Reynolds 6 in 2⅓ innings, Center 2 in 2⅔, Johnson 3 in 2, Podgajny 6 in 2. Passed ball—Fernandez. Losing pitcher—Reynolds. Umpires—Rue, Passarella and McGowan. Time—2:31. Attendance—2,500 (estimated).

Errors by Cubs Pave Reds' Way To 7-5 Victory

Misplays in Seventh Inning Help Cincinnati Score 3 Runs Against Borowy

CHICAGO, April 25 (AP).—The Cincinnati Reds squelched their 1945 nemesis, the Chicago Cubs, for the first time in four 1946 meetings, but needed a fielding blow-up by the Bruins for a 7-to-5 decision before 9,314 shivering fans at today's opener of a two-game series.

Three Cub miscues gave the Reds as many unearned markers in the seventh inning and chased Hank Borowy on the short end of a 6-to-4 score. Johnny Hetki, second of three Redleg hurlers, was the winner.

It was Cincinnati's second triumph in the last twenty-six starts against the Cubs.

After errors by Borowy and Bob Sturgeon helped the Reds fill the bases in the seventh, Mickey Livingston, trying to complete a double play at first, pegged the ball into right field, letting across Cincinnati's fifth and sixth tallies.

Marv Rickert, rookie outfielder of the Cubs, collected five singles in five trips.

CINCINNATI (N. L.)	ab	r	h	po	a	CHICAGO (N. L.)	ab	r	h	po	a
Frey 2b	3	2	3	2	3	Hack 3b.	4	0	0	1	1
McCormick cf	4	2	2	1	0	Johnson 2b.	5	0	0	4	2
Hatton 3b	4	1	0	1	2	Lowrey lf.	3	1	0	1	0
Moss rf	5	0	1	2	0	Cavarretta rf.	4	2	1	0	0
Usher rf	0	0	0	0	0	Rickert cf.	5	2	5	1	1
West lf	3	1	1	2	0	Waitkus 1b.	5	0	3	10	1
Miller ss	5	0	2	2	3	Livingston c.	2	0	2	7	0
Haas 1b	5	0	0	10	0	*Becker	1	0	0	0	0
Mueller c	4	0	1	7	0	Scheffing c.	0	0	0	1	0
Walters p	2	0	0	0	3	Sturgeon ss.	3	0	0	1	2
Hetki p	2	1	0	0	1	†Gilbert	1	0	0	0	0
Lambert p	0	0	0	0	0	Borowy p.	3	0	0	1	3
						Erickson p.	0	0	0	0	1
						‡Dallessandro	0	0	0	0	0
						§Stringer ss.	0	0	0	0	1
						Kush p.	0	0	0	0	0
Totals	37	7	10	27	12	Totals	36	5	11	27	12

*Batted for Livingston in eighth.
†Batted for Sturgeon in eighth.
‡Batted for Erickson in eighth.
§Ran for Dallessandro in eighth.

Cincinnati	200	010	301	—7
Chicago	010	300	010	—5

Errors—Sturgeon, Borowy, Livingston, Usher. Runs batted in—Miller 3, Moss, Waitkus 2, Livingston 2. Two-base hits—Mueller, Waitkus, West. Sacrifices—Hatton, Livingston. Double play—Walters, Miller and Haas. Left on bases—Cincinnati 9, Chicago 10. Bases on balls—Walters 2, Hetki 3, Borowy 5. Strikeouts—Walters 2, Borowy 3, Hetki 3, Erickson 2, Lambert 1. Hits—Off Walters 6 in 4 innings, Borowy 7 in 6⅓, Lambert 1 in 1⅔, Hetki 4 in 3⅔, Erickson 1 in 1⅔, Kush 2 in 1. Passed ball—Scheffling. Winning pitcher—Hetki. Losing pitcher—Borowy. Umpires—Barr, Conlan and Englesss. Time—2:21. Attendance—9,314.

Coleman Blanks Newark For Toronto Leafs, 2 to 0

NEWARK, N. J., April 25 (AP).—Big Joe Coleman, who came down from the Philadelphia Athletics, held the Newark Bears to four singles today and issued one walk while gaining a 2-to-0 victory for the Toronto Leafs in the second game of the series. Only one Newark player reached third.

The Leafs raked young Duane Pillette for seven hits, but a walk and an error played a large part in their scoring. Bob Wilkins drew a pass in the opening frame, then with two out scored Toronto's first run on Ira Houck's double.

The score:

TORONTO (I. L.)	ab	r	h	po	a	NEWARK (I. L.)	ab	r	h	po	a
Wilkins 2b	2	1	1	2	5	Douglas cf.	4	0	0	0	0
Morgan cf	4	1	0	1	0	Brown ss.	4	0	0	1	2
Chapman ss.	4	0	0	1	0	Clark lf.	4	0	0	2	0
Houck lf	4	0	2	3	0	Nowak 1b.	4	0	1	9	2
Yount c	4	0	0	5	1	Savage 3b.	3	0	1	1	4
Gamble rf	4	0	2	2	0	Collins rf.	4	0	0	2	0
Brancato 3b	3	0	1	1	2	Buzas 2b.	3	0	2	4	3
Biassatti 1b	3	0	0	12	0	Fallon c.	3	0	0	7	2
Coleman p	4	0	1	0	1	Pillette p.	2	0	0	1	2
Totals	32	2	7	27	9	Totals	31	0	4	27	15

Toronto	100	010	000	—2
Newark	000	000	000	—0

Errors—Young, Douglas, Chapman. Run batted in—Houck. Two-base hit—Houck. Sacrifices—Wilkins, Pillette. Left on bases—Toronto 7, Newark 6. Bases on balls—Pillette 3, Coleman 1. Strikeouts—Pillette 6, Coleman 4. Umpires—Robb, Gore and Zilber. Time—1:50. Attendance—650.

Probable Pitchers For Game Today

By The Associated Press

National League

Brooklyn at New York—Behrman (1-0) or Lombardi (1-0) vs. Voiselle (1-0).
St. Louis at Pittsburgh—Martin (0-0) vs. Ostermueller (0-0).
Cincinnati at Chicago—Beggs (1-1) vs. Wyse (0-1).
Only games scheduled.

American League

Detroit at St. Louis—Trucks (1-1) vs. Potter (1-1).
Chicago at Cleveland—Lee (0-1) vs Feller (1-1).
New York at Washington—Page (0-0) vs. Hudson (0-1) or Niggeling (0-1).
Boston at Philadelphia—Heflin (0-0) vs. Fowler (0-1).
Won and lost records in parentheses.

Error Helps Boston Snap Tie; Catcher Suffers Broken Finger

Homers by Ryan, Masi Mar Kennedy's Debut; Witek Blasts 4-Bagger Off Lee

By Rud Rennie

The Boston Braves went to extremes to defeat the Giants in the Polo Grounds yesterday, 5 to 4. After making their first four runs with two homers, they made the last one, the winning run, in the ninth without knocking a ball out of the infield, without making a hit. The Giants helped them, and by so doing have now lost six of their last seven games. They also lost the services of their $175,000 catcher, Walker Cooper. The little finger of his right hand was broken.

There were three home runs in the game. It was played in the rain. Even so, there were 9,357 persons present.

The first homer was made by Connie Ryan, first man up. He drove one of Monty Kennedy's pitches against the face of the left-field roof. It was Kennedy's introduction to big-time baseball, if you want to call it that.

Johnny Mize tied it up for the Giants in the last of the same inning with a fly, scoring Mickey Witek who had walked and advanced to third on a single by Willard Marshall.

The second homer was delivered by Witek in the third after Kennedy had singled.

At this stage of the game, the Giants led, 3 to 1.

Marshall threw out Tommy Holmes at the plate in the fourth, and young Kennedy had the lads in the press coop making inquiries about his early life just in case he should turn out to be the second Giant pitcher to go the route.

The Kennedy data were cast aside after the sixth. It was not the pitcher's fault. Babe Young, a converted infielder, came in for Holmes's line drive as hesitantly as if he had a little boy clinging to his sleeve and was afraid to hustle with him. So instead of catching the ball he made a one-handed pick-up and Holmes got a single.

Manny Fernandez batted for Carvel Rowell and pulled a double inside third base. Then Phil Masi came to bat with two on and walloped a long fly to right center.

Marshall went after the ball, but managed to misjudge it so that he had to make a backward turn. He got one hand on it, but dropped it. Then he fell down. The ball rolled to the bull pen and all the base runners rolled home. This was the third homer.

Harry Feldman had to be called in to get the Giants out of this inning. Then the Giants tied the score in the eighth.

Ray Sanders dropped a throw from the shortstop, letting Witek get on for the fourth time. With two away, Ernie Lombardi, who had gone into the game in place of Cooper, slammed a double off the shortstop's foot, sending Witek home for the third time.

Ken Trinkle was pitching for the Giants when the Braves made their winning run. It was unearned.

Trinkle hit Johnny Hopp, the first man up in the ninth, with a pitched ball. Then he made a bad throw with Holmes's bunt, letting Hopp reach third. Then Fernandez squeezed home the run with a bunt. The Braves won the two-game series.

Cooper's finger was broken by a foul tip hit by Rowell in the fourth. It is said that he will be out of action for a month.

Van Lingle Mungo, the Giant pitcher who was suspended a week before the season started for infractions of the club rules, was released unconditionally yesterday.

Giants' Score

BOSTON (N. L.)	ab	r	h	po	a	NEW YORK (N. L.)	ab	r	h	po	a
Ryan 2b	5	1	2	3	2	Rigney ss.	4	0	0	2	4
Hopp cf	4	1	0	0	0	Witek 2b.	3	3	2	2	2
Holmes rf	3	1	3	0	0	Marshall rf.	3	0	1	1	1
Sanders 1b	4	0	0	10	1	Mize 1b.	4	0	0	11	1
Rowell lf	1	0	0	2	0	W. Cooper c.	1	0	0	1	1
Fernandez lf.	2	1	1	0	0	Lombardi c.	3	0	2	6	0
Masi c	4	1	2	1	0	†Maynard	0	0	0	0	0
Roberge 3b	5	0	1	5	3	Kluttz c.	0	0	0	0	0
Wietelm'n ss.	4	0	2	6	4	Young cf.	4	0	0	1	0
Lee p	3	0	1	0	2	Gordon lf.	4	0	0	1	0
						Kerr 3b.	4	0	0	1	2
						Kennedy p.	2	1	1	1	0
						Feldman p.	0	0	0	0	1
						*Pike	0	0	0	0	0
						Trinkle p.	0	0	0	0	2
						‡Ott	0	0	0	0	0
						§Rucker	0	0	0	0	0
Totals	35	5	12	27	12	Totals	32	4	6	27	14

*Batted for Feldman in seventh.
†Ran for Lombardi in eighth.
‡Batted for Trinkle in ninth.
§Ran for Ott in ninth.

Boston	100	003	001	—5
New York	102	000	010	—4

Errors—Wietelmann, Sanders, Trinkle. Runs batted in—Ryan, Mize, Witek 2, Masi 3, Lombardi, Fernandez. Two-base hits—Ryan, Holmes, Fernandez, Lombardi. Home runs—Ryan, Witek, Masi. Sacrifices—Rigney, Lee, Marshall, Holmes, Fernandez. Double play—Sanders and Wietelmann. Left on bases—Boston 11, New York 6. Bases on balls—Kennedy 2, Trinkle 1, Lee 3, Feldman 1. Strikeouts—Kennedy 4, Lee 1, Feldman 1. Hits—Off Kennedy 10 in 5⅓ innings; Feldman 1 in 1⅔; Trinkle 1 in 2. Hit by pitcher—By Trinkle (Hopp). Losing pitcher—Trinkle. Umpires—Barlick, Pinelli and Ballanfant. Time—2:17. Attendance—8, 789 (paid).

Kiner's Homer Helps Pirates Beat Cards, 5-3

Redbirds' Second Setback Gives Idle Dodgers Sole Possession of First Place

PITTSBURGH, April 25 (AP).—Led by Ralph Kiner's home run, the Pittsburgh Pirates handed the St. Louis Cardinals their first defeat in eight games today, 5 to 3, and knocked them out of a first-place tie with the Brooklyn Dodgers.

The Dodgers, also winners of seven consecutive contests, remained in first place as rain forced a postponement of their game at Philadelphia.

Kiner all but stood a crowd of 10,585 on its collective ear as he drove in the Bucs' first run in the first inning and then blasted a tremendous homer in the third that carried 450 feet, clearing the scoreboard in left field. Maurice Van Robays, who had doubled, was aboard. It was Kiner's second roundtripper of the season.

Ken Heintzelman, who handed the Redbirds their other loss on opening day in St. Louis, also was returned the winner today. He had to retire in the seventh, however, because of a blister on the index finger of his pitching hand. Preacher Roe came in and fanned four of the nine batsmen he faced.

Frankie Gustine, with two doubles and a single, paced the Pirates' attack along with Kiner.

The score:

ST. LOUIS (N L)	ab	r	h	po	a	PITTSBURGH (N L)	ab	r	h	po	a
Klein 2b	4	1	0	2	5	Gustine 2b.	5	1	3	2	1
Schoend'st 3b	5	1	2	0	1	VanRobays lf	3	1	1	2	0
Musial lf	5	1	2	1	0	Russell lf.	0	0	0	0	0
Slaughter rf.	5	0	3	1	0	Kiner cf.	4	1	1	3	0
Adams cf	2	0	0	3	0	Gionfriddo cf	0	0	0	1	0
Sisler 1b	4	0	0	10	0	Elliott 3b.	2	0	1	2	0
Marion ss	4	0	0	3	4	Fletcher 1b.	3	0	0	5	1
Rice c	2	0	0	1	0	Cox ss.	4	1	2	0	2
*Moore	1	0	0	0	0	Guintini rf.	2	0	0	1	0
Wilber c	0	0	0	3	0	Barrett rf.	1	1	0	1	0
Brecheen p.	2	0	0	0	1	Smith c.	2	0	0	6	0
†Kurowski	0	0	0	0	0	¶Colman	1	0	0	0	0
‡Cross	0	0	0	0	0	Camelli c.	1	0	0	4	0
Dickson p	0	0	0	0	0	Heintzel'an p	3	0	1	0	0
§Dusak	1	0	0	0	0	Roe p.	1	0	0	0	0
Krist p	0	0	0	0	0						
Totals	35	3	7	24	11	Totals	32	5	9	27	4

*Batted for Rice in sixth.
†Batted for Brecheen in sixth.
‡Ran for Kurowski in sixth.
§Batted for Dickson in eighth.
¶Batted for Smith in sixth.

St. Louis	002	000	100	—3
Pittsburgh	102	002	00x	—5

Errors—Elliott, Kiner. Runs batted in—Kiner 3, Musial, Adams, Gustine 2. Two-base hits—Gustine 2, Van Robays, Schoendienst. Home run—Kiner. Stolen bases—Schoendienst, Slaughter. Sacrifice—Van Robays. Left on bases—St. Louis 10; Pittsburgh 8. Bases on balls—Brecheen 3, Heintzelman 4, Dickson 1, Roe 1. Strikeouts—Heintzelman 3, Dickson 2, Roe 4. Hits—Brecheen 6 in 5 innings, Dickson 3 in 2, Krist 0 in 1, Heintzelman 7 in 6⅓, Roe 0 in 2⅔. Winning pitcher—Heintzelman. Losing pitcher—Brecheen. Umpires—Goetz, Jorda and Reardon. Time—2:11. Attendance—10,585 (517 ladies).

Major League Standings

FRIDAY, APRIL 26, 1946

National League

YESTERDAY'S RESULTS

Boston, 5; New York, 4
Pittsburgh, 5; St. Louis, 3
Cincinnati, 7; Chicago, 5
Brooklyn at Philadelphia, rain

STANDING OF THE CLUBS

	Brooklyn	St. Louis	Boston	Chicago	Pittsburgh	New York	Cincinnati	Philadelphia	Won	Lost	Percentage	Games behind
Brooklyn	—		3			3		1	7	1	.875	—
St. Louis		—		2	2		3		7	2	.778	½
Boston	1		—			2		2	5	4	.556	2½
Chicago		0		—	1		3		4	4	.500	3
Pittsb'gh		2		1	—		1		4	5	.444	3½
New York	0		0			—		3	3	6	.333	4½
Cincinnati		0		1	2		—		3	7	.300	5
Philadel.	0		1			1		—	2	6	.250	5
Games lost	1	2	4	4	5	6	7	6	—	—		

GAMES TODAY

Brooklyn at New York, 2:30 p. m.
St. Louis at Pittsburgh
Cincinnati at Chicago
Other clubs not scheduled

American League

YESTERDAY'S RESULTS

Boston, 12; New York, 5
Detroit, 6; St. Louis, 5
Chicago, 11; Cleveland, 2
Philadelphia at Washington, rain

STANDING OF THE CLUBS

	Detroit	New York	Boston	Cleveland	St. Louis	Chicago	Washington	Philadelphia	Won	Lost	Percentage	Games behind
Detroit	—			2	3	1			6	2	.750	—
New York		—	1				2	4	7	3	.700	—
Boston		1	—				4	2	7	3	.700	—
Cleveland	0			—	1	2			3	3	.500	2
St. Louis	1			0	—	2			3	5	.375	3
Chicago	1			1	1	—			3	5	.375	3
Wash'ton		1	1				—	1	3	6	.333	3½
Philadel.		1	1				0	—	2	7	.222	4½
Games lost	2	3	3	3	5	5	6	7	—	—		

GAMES TODAY

New York at Washington
Boston at Philadelphia
Chicago at Cleveland
Detroit at St. Louis

INTERNATIONAL LEAGUE

Yesterday's Results

Toronto, 2; Newark, 0
Rochester, 4; Jersey City, 3 (7 ins., rain)
Syracuse, 5; Montreal, 4 (10 ins.)
Buffalo-Baltimore, rain

STANDING OF THE CLUBS

	W.	L.	Pct.		W.	L.	Pct.
Syracuse	5	1	.833	Jersey City	3	4	.429
Baltimore	4	2	.667	Buffalo	3	4	.429
Newark	5	4	.556	Toronto	2	4	.333
Montreal	4	4	.500	Rochester	2	5	.286

GAMES TODAY

Toronto at Newark, 2:30.
Rochester at Jersey City, 2:30.
Montreal at Syracuse
Other clubs not scheduled.

AMERICAN ASSOCIATION

Yesterday's Results

Milwaukee, 3; Minneapolis, 0.
St. Paul, 9; Kansas City, 5.
Louisville-Toledo, night.
Indianapolis-Columbus, night.

STANDING OF THE CLUBS

	W.	L.	Pct.		W.	L.	Pct.
Minneapolis.	6	3	.667	Toledo	4	4	.500
Louisville	5	3	.625	Columbus	3	5	.375
St. Paul	5	3	.625	Milwaukee	3	5	.375
Indianapolis.	4	4	.500	Kansas City.	3	6	.333

SOUTHERN ASSOCIATION

Yesterday's Results

Four night games.

STANDING OF THE CLUBS

	W.	L.	Pct.		W.	L.	Pct.
Memphis	8	2	.800	Nashville	4	5	.444
Atlanta	8	3	.727	Little Rock	4	6	.400
New Orleans.	8	3	.727	Birmingham	3	7	.300
Chattanooga.	5	5	.500	Mobile	1	10	.091

FELLER TOPS YANKS WITH NO-HITTER, 1-0

Six Reach Base, 5 on Walks, as the Indians' Ace Hurls Classic for Second Time

38,112 THRILLED BY FEAT

11 New Yorkers Are Struck Out—Home Run by Hayes in Ninth Sets Back Bevens

By LOUIS EFFRAT

They said Bob Feller had lost his fast one. They said the war had taken too much from the right arm of the one-time Iowa farmboy, that, in the parlance of the ball players, he no longer had it. They made all these and other derogatory comments during spring training and when Feller, after winning his first league game this year, proceeded to lose two in a row to the Tigers and White Sox, the dissenters weighed in with lots of "I-told-you-so" snickers.

They'll not say it again!

For, yesterday at the Stadium, the 27-year-old Feller pitched the Indians to a 1—0 victory over the Yankees that afforded 38,112 fans the thrill that only a no-hitter can bring. And that, precisely, was what it was, a no-run, no-hit achievement against a power-packed line-up of pre-war Yankees, any one of whom—except possibly the pitcher—could have wrecked the superb efforts of one of the greatest twirlers of all time. There was drama riding with every pitch of Feller's.

When, with one out in the ninth, Frankie Hayes, Feller's battery-mate propelled one of Floyd Bevens' offerings high into the lower left-field pavilion for his first homer of the year, the Indians had what they had been seeking from the outset, a one-run margin. The way Feller was mowing down the Yankee hitters, it was apparent that one was all Bob would need. He needed no more.

Bears Down All the Way

Obviously, as would be the case in so tightly-waged a contest, in which neither hurler received a comfortable cushion, Feller had to bear down all the way. Bevens, while not quite as overpowering as the Cleveland moundsman, was equally as effective. Only Hayes' round-tripper of the seven safeties he yielded hurt him. There were other spots where the visitors threatened, but on each occasion the big Yankee right-hander pitched his way to safety.

This was not a perfect game for Feller. Six Yankees reached base, five via passes and one on an error by Les Fleming, the Cleveland first-sacker, who booted Snuffy Stirnweiss' drag bunt along the first-base line at the beginning of the bottom half of the ninth. When Fleming miscued, the groan from the stands was a tip-off on how hard the fans were rooting for Feller to succeed in his bid for a second no-hitter. He turned the trick, also by 1—0, against the White Sox on opening day of the 1940 season.

Tommy Henrich added to the tenseness of the situation by sacrificing, his bunt pushing Stirnweiss to second, in scoring position. Feller now had merely to dispose of Joe DiMaggio and Charley Keller—a couple of set-ups. Against DiMaggio, Feller worked the count to 3 and 2. On the next effort, DiMaggio swatted the ball to short, when Playing-Manager Lou Boudreau, a standout shortstop all afternoon, scooped it up and threw out the Jolter.

Keller Ever Dangerous

That Stirnweiss moved down to third on the play meant nothing to Boudreau, Feller and every man in a Cleveland uniform. Nor did anyone in the crowd seem to mind. The most important development was to follow. Would Keller, ever dangerous, play the role of spoiler? He did not, but not because he wasn't trying.

The first pitch to King Kong was called a strike. He swung viciously, vehemently, at the second, but hit nothing. Now Feller was only one strike away from his goal. No one had long to wait before it was all over. For Keller, getting only a piece of the ball, as did all the Yanks throughout the history-making afternoon, bounced meekly to Ray Mack at second. The latter fielded the ball cleanly, easily, flipped to Fleming for the putout at first, and that was that.

Immediately Feller was besieged by his mates and by the fans from every side. Bob made his way to the dugout and was the first to enter the clubhouse, where writers and photographers were at the door, awaiting his arrival. Boudreau gave orders that no one was to enter for five minutes. Then, when the time was up, a swarm of experts rushed in to congratulate and to interrogate the hero, whose war record with the Navy was as great as the one he has compiled on the diamond.

Gives Credit to Hayes

Feller, first of all, credited Hayes for a perfectly caught game, as well as for his game-winning homer. For himself, Bob said he had good stuff, better stuff than won for him in 1940. He praised Boudreau for his great play on the ball Stirnweiss hit through the middle in the first inning, when Boudreau, crossing second, fielded the ball and threw out Snuffy, even while falling flat on his face.

Someone reminded Feller about the deprecatory remarks and rumors that had floated in from the hinterlands concerning his slowing down. "Look," Feller said, apparently perturbed, "when the time comes that I don't have it, I'll be the first to know about it."

Over in the Yankee dressing room all was quiet, as it naturally would be. DiMaggio summed it up best when he said: "Feller was as great as he's ever been. He deserved the no-hitter."

How great Bob was may be gleaned from the fact that he struck out eleven Yankees and permitted only two balls to be hit to the outfield. Boudreau's great play on Stirnweiss in the first was the only really tough one for the Cleveland infield to make. Nevertheless, it was a pulse-stopping contest, one of the greatest ever witnessed here or anywhere. Ask the 38,112 fans, 37,144 of whom paid, exactly how great it was.

Has Six One-Hitters

With this feat, Feller, who also has pitched six one-hitters, joined Johnny Vander Meer of the Reds as the only two still-active pitchers who have hurled two no-hitters. Vander Meer made his in successive outings against the Braves and Dodgers in 1938.

Since Ed Head of the Dodgers came through with a no-hitter a week ago yesterday, one wag was prompted to remark that "it looks like the pitchers are ahead of the hitters."

As if the tension were not high enough, Ken Keltner muffed an easy foul fly hoisted by Phil Rizzuto with two out in the eighth. With this life, the Scooter might have proved troublesome, but Boudreau threw him out on a magnificent play from deep short.

Rizzuto, before the game, revealed that he had been approached by and received an attractive offer from the Mexican League. He turned it down. President Larry MacPhail said he and Rizzuto had been in conference on Monday and that Phil did not receive a raise because of the threat from Mexico. "Rizzuto will receive a bonus, but he was promised that before the season. His 1942 GI contract is unfair," MacPhail declared.

MacPhail disclosed that Stirnweiss, outstanding at third yesterday, and other Yankees have been contacted by Pasquel interests, but that none of his charges had seen fit to do business with them.

Buddy Hassett, veteran first-baseman, was released by the Yankees unconditionally. . . . Charley (Red) Ruffing, late in reporting, is ready to go and Joe McCarthy will send him against Allie Reynolds today. . . . The last time the Yankees were the victims of a no-hitter was in 1919, when Ray Caldwell, also of the Indians, blanked them. . . . Incidentally, yesterday's shut-out was the first suffered by the McCarthymen this season.

When Fleming erred in the ninth, the fans were apprised of the ruling over the public address system. This was the first time such an announcement had been made at the Stadium.

BOB FELLER MAKES 1946 DEBUT AT STADIUM AND PITCHES A NO-HIT GAME

Catcher Hayes has his arm around the hurler as they leave the field. Other members of the team are running to congratulate him and a Yankee player is heading for his own dugout. Associated Press

The speedballer (left) shakes hands with his battery mate, whose homer brought him victory. The New York Times

Letting go with a fast one in the ninth inning. Associated Press

Yanks' Box Score

CLEVELAND (A.)	ab.	r.	h.	po.	a.	e.
Case, lf	4	0	2	1	0	0
Lemon, cf	4	0	1	1	0	0
Edwards, rf	2	0	0	0	0	0
Fleming, 1b	3	0	1	9	0	1
Keltner, 3b	1	0	0	0	3	1
Boudreau, ss	3	0	0	0	4	0
Hayes, c	4	1	2	12	1	0
Mack, 2b	3	0	1	4	2	0
Feller, p	4	0	0	0	1	0
Total	28	1	7	27	11	2

NEW YORK (A.)	ab.	r.	h.	po.	a.	e.
Rizzuto, ss	3	0	0	5	5	1
Stirnweiss, 3b	3	0	0	1	2	0
Henrich, rf	1	0	0	0	0	0
DiMaggio, cf	4	0	0	1	0	0
Keller, lf	3	0	0	3	0	0
Etten, 1b	3	0	0	8	0	0
Gordon, 2b	3	0	0	3	8	0
Dickey, c	2	0	0	6	3	0
Bevens, p	3	0	0	0	2	1
Total	25	0	0	27	15	2

Cleveland .... 000 000 001—1
New York .... 000 000 000—0

Run batted in—Hayes.

Home run—Hayes. Stolen bases—Case, Henrich. Sacrifices—Boudreau, Keltner, Stirnweiss, Edwards, Henrich. Double plays—Gordon, Rizzuto and Etten; Stirnweiss, Rizzuto and Etten; Dickey and Rizzuto. Left on bases—Cleveland 8, New York 5. Bases on balls—Off Bevens 5, Feller 5. Struck out—By Bevens 5, Feller 11. Umpires—Rommel, Byer and Jones. Time of game—2:14. Attendance—38,112.

RED SOX, WITH DOBSON, SHUT OUT TIGERS, 4-0

BOSTON, April 30 (AP)—With right-hander Joe Dobson pitching his third straight victory with a three-hitter, the Red Sox today opened their home stand against Western competition by shutting out the world champion Tigers, 4—0, before a paid crowd of 18,877. As a result, Boston increased its league lead over the Yanks to two games.

While dueling with Hal Newhouser, the Boston flinger got timely hitting from his teammates, including an eighth-inning homer by Bobby Doerr. Each pitcher had nine strike-out while issuing three bases on balls, but Newhouser presented the first run to the Sox with a wild pitch.

After being greeted with a single by lead-off man Eddie Lake, Dobson did not give another hit until he had two out in the ninth. Hank Greenberg slashed a double off the left-field fence, but, after Dick Wakefield had beaten out an infield roller, Dobson ended the game by forcing Pat Mullin to ground out.

Rudy York was first to score. He walked in the second inning, advanced to third on Dom DiMaggio's two-bagger to right center and romped home on Newhouser's wild heave. After Leon Culberson had singled in the third inning, Newhouser passed Ted Williams and both counted on York's double to right center.

The box score:

DETROIT (A)	ab.	r.	h.	po.	a.	e.
Lake, ss	4	0	1	1	4	0
Mayo, 2b	4	0	0	1	0	0
McCosky, cf	4	0	0	1	0	0
Greenb'g, 1b	4	0	1	5	0	0
Wakef'ld, lf	3	0	1	2	0	0
Mullin, rf	4	0	0	1	1	0
Higgins, 3b	3	0	0	1	0	1
Richards, c	1	0	0	11	1	0
Newh'ser, p	2	0	0	0	1	0
Total	29	0	3	24	7	1

BOSTON (A)	ab.	r.	h.	po.	a.	e.
Culb'son, rf	4	1	1	1	0	0
Pesky, ss	4	0	0	1	2	0
Williams, lf	3	1	0	4	0	0
Doerr, 2b	4	1	1	0	0	0
York, 1b	3	1	1	6	1	0
DiM'gio, cf	4	0	3	3	0	0
P'lagrini, 3b	4	0	0	2	1	0
Wagner, c	2	0	1	9	0	0
Dobson, p	3	0	1	1	1	0
Total	31	4	8	27	5	0

Detroit .... 000 000 000—0
Boston .... 012 000 01.—4

Runs batted in—York 2, Doerr.

Two-base hits—Greenberg, York, DiMaggio. Home run—Doerr. Sacrifice—Newhouser. Left on bases—Detroit 6, Boston 6. Bases on balls—Off Newhouser 3, Dobson 3. Struck out—By Newhouser 9, Dobson 9. Wild pitch—Newhouser. Umpires—Paparella, Weafer, Summers and Grieve. Time of game—1:55. Attendance—18,877.

Louis Arrives to Launch Training At Pompton Lakes Today for Conn

By JOSEPH M. SHEEHAN

Heavyweight Champion Joe Louis appeared a lot more interested in baseball than in his impending title defense against Billy Conn yesterday on his arrival here from his preliminary training base at West Baden, Ind.

As soon as he heard that Bobby Feller was slated to pitch for Cleveland against the Yankees, Louis eased toward the exit of the new offices of the Twentieth Century Sporting Club, where the fight reporters were gathered to interview him.

It may have been that he was anxious to see how hard hitters make out against fast throwers at the Yankee Stadium, which also will be the scene of his return rendezvous with Conn on June 19. Or it may have been that he just wanted to make the most of his last fling in society before settling down to hard work. Either way, Louis stood not on the order of his going but up and went as soon as he had satisfied his inquisitors.

Louis Plans to Carry Fight

A little heavier than the Louis of old, but otherwise in apparent good trim, the champion revealed that he weighed 216 pounds. He plans to reduce his poundage to 208 at Pompton Lakes, N. J., where he will start serious training today. He went in at 199½ pounds in his 1941 fight with Conn.

"I'm not worried about my speed, my weight or anything," Louis said. "I plan to carry the fight all the way and if I have anything to say about it, it will be much shorter than last time." It took thirteen rounds for Joe to catch up with Billy, who was leading on points at the time, in their first battle.

Although Louis said that he had been working out at West Baden since March 7, his activities there were confined to hiking through the hills, chopping wood and playing golf. He did not once pull on the gloves.

This matter will be taken care of in short order once he gets settled at Pompton Lakes, where he has trained on several occasions. Half a dozen sparring partners will be in the entourage of twenty that is to accompany the champion to his base.

George Fitch of New Haven, Clint Conway of New York and Jimmy Bell and George Crawford of Washington are among those whose unenviable assignment it will be to sample the speed and punching power of the post-war Louis. The champion is fully confident that he has lost none of this. "My only problems are to sharpen my punching and get my timing back," he confided.

Louis created a minor sensation when he appeared in Promoter Mike Jacobs' royal suite above Madison Square Garden sporting a luxuriant crop of whiskers that set off to striking advantage his snappy brown sports ensemble. However, the beaver was due to be shorn just as soon as he could make his first visit to a barber in two months.

Both the champion and challenger are due to appear at the State Athletic Commission offices Friday to sign official commission contracts and receive preliminary physical examinations. Conn has been training at Greenwood Lake, N. J.

Gillette to Sponsor Television

Exclusive television rights to the Louis-Conn fight have been obtained by the National Broadcasting Company and the Gillette Safety Razor Company, it was announced yesterday by Promoter Jacobs, J. P. Spang, Jr., president of Gillette, and John F. Royal, NBC vice president in charge of television. The event will be broadcast over television station WNBT, which returns to the air on May 9.

NBC and Gillette also have acquired television rights to all other fights promoted by the Twentieth Century Sporting Club at Madison Square Garden and outdoor parks in the New York area from June, 1946, to June, 1947. The three organizations have been cooperating since September, 1944.

Five cameras will be used to cover the fight, three of them equipped with the super-sensitive RCA Image Orthicon. The event will be broadcast to Washington on a closed circuit for the benefit of a selected group of Government officials.

Major League Baseball

Wednesday, May 1, 1946

American League

YESTERDAY'S RESULTS

Cleveland 1, New York 0.
Boston 4, Detroit 0.
Washington 3, Chicago 2.
Philadelphia 12, St. Louis 8.

STANDING OF THE CLUBS

	Boston	New York	Detroit	Cleveland	St. Louis	Chicago	Washington	Phil'delphia	Won	Lost	Percentage
Boston	—	1	1	0	0	0	4	5	11	3	.786
New York	1	—	0	0	0	0	4	4	9	5	.643
Detroit	0	0	—	3	3	1	0	0	7	5	.583
Cleveland	0	1	1	—	1	2	0	0	5	5	.500
St. Louis	0	0	2	0	—	4	0	0	6	7	.462
Chicago	0	0	1	2	2	—	0	0	5	8	.385
Washington	1	2	0	0	0	1	—	1	5	8	.385
Philadelphia	1	1	0	0	1	0	0	—	3	10	.231
Lost	3	5	5	5	7	8	8	10	—	—	

GAMES TODAY

Cleveland at New York (2:30 P. M.).
Detroit at Boston.
St. Louis at Philadelphia.
Chicago at Washington.

National League

YESTERDAY'S RESULTS

New York at St. Louis, wet grounds.
Chicago 2, Brooklyn 1 (11 innings).
Pittsburgh 4, Philadelphia 1.
Boston at Cincinnati, rain.

STANDING OF THE CLUBS

	St. Louis	Brooklyn	Boston	Chicago	New York	Cincinnati	Pittsburgh	Phil'delphia	Won	Lost	Percentage
St. Louis	—	0	0	3	0	3	3	0	9	4	.692
Brooklyn	0	—	3	0	4	0	0	1	8	4	.667
Boston	0	1	—	0	2	0	0	4	7	4	.636
Chicago	2	1	0	—	0	3	1	0	7	5	.583
New York	0	2	0	0	—	0	0	3	5	7	.417
Cincinnati	0	0	0	1	0	—	4	0	5	7	.417
Pittsburgh	2	0	0	1	0	1	—	1	5	8	.385
Philadelphia	0	0	1	0	1	0	0	—	2	9	.182
Lost	4	4	4	5	7	7	8	9	—	—	

GAMES TODAY

New York at St. Louis.
Brooklyn at Chicago.
Philadelphia at Pittsburgh.
Boston at Cincinnati.

GIANTS FAIL IN BID FOR CARD PLAYERS

But Stoneham Plans to Renew Overtures Today—Rain Puts Off First Game of Series

By JOHN DREBINGER
Special to THE NEW YORK TIMES.

ST. LOUIS, April 30—Their ball clubs held idle by a daylong drizzling rain, Horace C. Stoneham and Sam Breadon, owners of the Giants and Cardinals, and their respective managers, Mel Ott and Eddie Dyer, closeted themselves for three hours today in an effort to close a deal supposedly hanging fire ever since the old Polo Grounders made their $175,000 purchase of Walker Cooper last winter.

But the session held in the club offices at Sportsman's Park terminated in another stalemate. Returning to his hotel quarters, Ott said:

"We simply couldn't get anywhere. They wouldn't part with any of the players we would like to have obtained and what they did offer us consisted of players in which we have no particular interest."

On this note the rival factions let the matter rest for at least another twenty-four hours. Stoneham and Breadon said they would meet again tomorrow, but neither appeared optimistic over the outcome.

Adams or Dusek Sought

Although for obvious reasons he would not mention names, Ott admitted that what he wanted most from St. Louis were a right-handed hitting outfielder and a pitcher. So far as the fielder is concerned the general guess is he is either Buster Adams or Erwin Dusek.

As for the hurler, the Giant officials have long made it clear they would consider any one of the Cardinals' topflight flingers. However, in view of the still unsettled character of the St. Louis staff, Dyer apparently hasn't decided what starting pitchers he wants to keep and so means to stall things off a little longer. The Cards have until the June 15 deadline to pare their big squad down to the thirty player limit.

The postponement cut the current series to two games and the contest will not be played off until June 3, originally an open date on the Giants' next visit here. Southpaw Dave Koslo remains at Ott's choice to face the Redbirds tomorrow, but Dyer was undecided whether he would start Fred Martin, a rookie right-hander, or the left-handed Harry Brecheen.

Kraus Reports to Giants

Jack Kraus, southpaw pitcher recently purchased from the Phillies by the Giants, reported to Ott from his home in San Antonio and lost no time signing a New York contract. Kraus had been a hold-out with the Phils this spring.

Gene Thompson, right-hander recently released outright by the Reds, who lives in near-by Decatur, Ill., called on Ott relative to a trial with the Giants. Ott said he was holding the matter under advisement.

Another ball player to confab with the Giants as they lolled around their hotel lobby was Cookie Lavagetto, Dodger third-sacker here getting treatment for a sore arm from Dr. Robert F. Hyland. Cookie will rejoin the Flock here Friday.

BROWNS TURNED BACK BY ATHLETICS, 12 TO 8

PHILADELPHIA, April 30 (AP)—The Athletics took advantage of five bases on balls by St. Louis pitchers to score four runs in the first inning and added eight more tallies today to defeat the Browns, 12 to 8, in the first of a three-game series.

Russ Christopher did not allow the visitors a hit in the first four innings, but was driven out of the box in the sixth, when St. Louis scored five runs. The Browns also chased Lum Harris with three in the eighth.

Sam Chapman hit his third home run of the year in the third inning. The Athletics picked up their final tallies off Steve Sundra.

The box score:

ST. LOUIS (A.)	ab.	r.	h.	po.	a.	e.
Ber'd'o, 2b	5	1	1	2	2	1
Grace, rf	5	0	0	3	0	1
St'ph'ns, ss	5	0	0	0	2	0
McQ'len, lf	0	0	0	1	0	0
Zarilla, lf	3	2	2	3	0	1
Ch'st'n, 3b	1	0	0	0	0	0
Lu'd'o, 3b	3	1	2	1	1	0
Bradley, cf	1	0	0	1	0	0
Judnich, cf	3	1	2	1	0	0
Stevens, 1b	4	1	2	7	0	0
Mancuso, c	1	0	0	4	0	0
Sears, c	1	1	1	1	0	0
Shirley, p	0	0	0	0	1	0
LaM'hia, p	1	0	0	0	0	0
Kinder, p	0	0	0	0	0	0
aSchultz	2	1	1	0	0	0
Sundra, p	0	0	0	0	1	0
bFinney	0	0	0	0	0	0
cDillinger	1	0	0	0	0	0
Hol'g'th, p	0	0	0	0	0	0
Total	36	8	11	24	7	3

PHILADELPHIA (A.)	ab.	r.	h.	po.	a.	e.
Valo, lf	4	2	1	2	0	0
Peck, rf	4	2	2	3	0	0
Wallaesa, ss	4	1	1	2	1	0
Chapman, cf	4	2	1	2	0	0
McQuinn, 1b	4	3	2	7	2	0
Rosar, c	3	1	1	5	0	0
Hall, 2b	4	1	2	2	6	0
Kell, 3b	4	0	0	2	3	0
Christ'her, p	2	0	0	1	0	0
Harris, p	1	0	0	1	0	0
Besse, p	0	0	0	0	0	0
Total	34	12	10	27	12	0

aBatted for Kinder in sixth.
bBatted for Sundra in eighth.
cBatted for Finney in eighth.

St. Louis .... 000 005 030—8
Philadelphia .... 402 201 30.—12

Runs batted in—McQuinn, Rosar, Hall 4, Kell, Chapman 2, Peck, Wallaesa, Lucadello, Sears, Berardino, Zarilla 2, Judnich, Stevens 2.

Two-base hits—McQuinn, Peck, Zarilla, Stevens. Home run—Chapman. Stolen base—Peck. Sacrifices—Peck, Hall, Harris. Double plays—Kell, Hall and McQuinn; Wallaesa, Hall and McQuinn. Left on bases—St. Louis 4, Philadelphia 7. Bases on balls—Off Shirley 4, LaMacchia 1, Christopher 2, Harris 1, Hollingsworth 1. Struck out—By Christopher 4, LaMacchia 1, Kinder 2, Besse 1, Hollingsworth 1. Hits—Off Shirley 0 in 1/3 inning, LaMacchia 5 in 2 2/3, Kinder 0 in 2, Sundra 5 in 2, Christopher 6 in 5 2/3, Harris 5 in 1 2/3, Bess 0 in 1 2/3, Hollingsworth 0 in 1. Passed ball—Mancuso. Winning pitcher—Christopher. Losing pitcher — Shirley. Umpires—McGowan, Rue and Passarella. Time of game—2:19. Attendance—5,192.

Today's Probable Pitchers

By The Associated Press.

American League

Cleveland at New York—Reynolds (1-1) vs. Ruffing (0-0).
Detroit at Boston—Benton (1-1) vs. Ferriss (1-0).
Chicago at Washington — Lee (0-1) vs. Haefner (0-0).
St. Louis at Philadelphia—Potter (2-1) vs. Fowler (0-2).

National League

New York at St. Louis—Koslo (0-1) vs. Martin (1-0) or Brecheen (1-2).
Brooklyn at Chicago — Gregg (1-1) vs. Fleming (0-0).
Philadelphia at Pittsburgh—Judd (1-1) vs. Albosta (0-1).
Boston at Cincinnati—Lee (2-0) vs. Gumbert (0-0).

Figures in parentheses indicate season's won and-lost records.

Dodgers Bow to Cubs in 11th, 2-1, And Yield First Place to Cardinals

Casey, in Relief of Head, Forces Deciding Run Home With Pass—Chicago Ties Score on Fielding Lapses in Ninth Inning

By ROSCOE McGOWEN
Special to THE NEW YORK TIMES.

CHICAGO, April 30—An artistic pitching performance by Ed Head, in his first start since his no-hitter one week ago, became a grotesquery in the eleventh inning today when Hugh Casey pitched four straight balls to Dom Dallesandro with the bases filled to give the Cubs a 2—1 triumph over the Dodgers. The result allowed the idle Cardinals to move into first place, half a game ahead of the Brooks.

For eight innings Head kept Chicago at bay despite threats in four innings, and Brooklyn finally solved the relief offerings of Emil Kush sufficiently to score in the eighth. The run crossed on a long double into the left-field corner by Eddie Stanky, sending Peewee Reese, who had singled, scampering home.

Crowd of 20,234 Present

At this point the 20,234 North Side fans perhaps were almost ready to concede these Dodgers couldn't be beaten, especially after the missed Cub chance in the sixth, when Don Johnson opened with a double.

But the folks were pleasantly surprised in the ninth. After Head had fanned Marvin Rickert, Ed Waitkus slashed a single to right and there followed the first of the chain of events that found the Dodgers a bit wanting. Clyde McCullough slapped a double play ball to Reese, but Peewee's ever so slight juggling of the ball permitted the speedy Waitkus to slide into second ahead of the throw.

Stanky's relay nailed McCullough at first, but the stage was set for the next Dodgerism and the tie score. Heinz Becker batted for Len Merullo and sent a low fly ball into dead center field. Carl Furillo misjudged its trajectory and started in on a trot. He realized his mistake too late, although he made a gallant effort at a diving catch. The blow went for a single and the score was deadlocked.

Reiser's Long Fly Caught

Manager Leo Durocher removed Head in the tenth to let Don Padgett bat vainly for him and, although the bases became filled with two out on passes to Reese, Stanky and Augie Galan, the Cub right-hander escaped when Pete Reiser's fly was pulled down just beyond the curve of the right-field wall by Phil Cavarretta. A few feet toward center field and Pete would have had a long three-run hit.

Came the eleventh and once again it was Waitkus who started the Dodger downfall, this time with a single to left. McCullough bunted and Casey chose to throw to second base when he didn't have a chance to get Waitkus. So Bobby Sturgeon also bunted, and Casey, after going for the ball along the third-base line, backed away and let Ed Stevens handle it.

Result: a hit for Sturgeon and the bases filled with nobody out. Dallesandro stepped up, with the fans yelling themselves hoarse, and Casey never got one ball over the plate, turning away from the mound toward the dugout almost before his final pitch had reached Andy Anderson's glove.

Hank Borowy was Jolly Cholly Grimm's starter and hurled air-tight ball until the start of the fifth, when he walked Furillo. Then Hank took himself out because of a troublesome blister on his right middle finger and young Kush went in, eventually to gain credit for his third straight relief victory.

Cubs Miss Scoring Chance

The Cubs blew a scoring chance in the eighth inning when Stan Hack walked, Johnson sacrificed and Peanuts Lowrey singled to center. Hack, thinking Reese had fielded Lowrey's hit behind him, slid back into second base. Then Head, trying to pick Hack off, threw wild into center field and Hack tried to score, but was cut down, Furillo to Reese to Anderson.

Dixie Walker's seventh-inning line single struck Kush on the pitching hand, but the young fellow stuck it out. . . . First hit off Head to break his no-hit string was a second-inning high bounder by Cavarretta. Head lost the ball in the sun.

The Box Score

BROOKLYN (N.)	ab.	r.	h.	po.	a.	
Stanky, 2b	4	0	1	2	3	0
Whitman, lf	3	0	0	0	0	0
Galan, lf	1	0	0	1	0	0
Reiser, 3b	5	0	1	1	1	0
Walker, rf	5	0	3	2	0	0
Stevens, 1b	5	0	1	13	0	0
Furillo, cf	4	0	0	3	1	0
Anderson, c	4	0	0	6	2	0
Reese, ss	3	1	1	2	5	0
Head, p	3	0	0	0	2	1
cPadgett	1	0	0	0	0	0
Casey, p	0	0	0	0	0	0
Total	38	1	7	*30	14	1

CHICAGO (N.)	ab.	r.	h.	po.	a.	
Hack, 3b	4	0	1	2	0	0
Johnson, 2b	4	0	1	1	3	0
Lowrey, lf	4	0	2	1	0	0
Cavareta, rf	3	0	1	4	0	0
Rickert, cf	4	0	0	6	0	0
Waitkus, 1b	5	2	3	8	1	0
McCulogh, c	4	0	2	8	3	0
Merullo, ss	3	0	0	2	1	0
aBecker	1	0	1	0	0	0
bStringer	0	0	0	0	0	0
Sturgeon, ss	1	0	1	0	0	0
Borowy, p	1	0	0	0	1	0
Kush, p	3	0	0	1	3	0
Dalesndro	0	0	0	0	0	0
Total	37	2	12	33	12	0

*None out when winning run was scored.
aBatted for Merullo in ninth.
bRan for Becker in ninth.
cBatted for Head in tenth.
dBatted for Kush in eleventh.

Brooklyn .... 000 000 010 00—1
Chicago .... 000 000 001 01—2

Runs batted in—Stanky, Becker, Dallessandro.

Two-base hits—Johnson, McCullough, Stanky. Stolen base—Reese. Sacrifices—Lowrey, Johnson, McCullough. Double plays—Johnson, Merullo and Waitkus; Stanky, Reese and Stevens. Left on bases—Brooklyn 8, Chicago 13. Bases on balls—Off Borowy 1, Head 3, Casey 2, Kush 3. Struck out—By Borowy 4, Kush 7, Head 3. Hits—Off Head 9 in 9 innings, Casey 2 in 1 (none out in 11th), Borowy 3 in 4, Kush 4 in 7. Wild pitch—Casey. Passed ball—McCullough. Winning pitcher—Kush. Losing pitcher— Casey. Umpires—Barlick, Pinelli and Ballanfant. Time of game—2:58. Attendance—20,234.

PIRATES DOWN PHILS ON ERROR IN 8TH, 4-1

PITTSBURGH, April 30 (AP)—Tommy Hughes made a wild throw of Frankie Gustine's bunt with two men on in the eighth inning today, giving the Pittsburgh Pirates enough runs to break a 1-1 tie and moving them on to a 4-1 victory over the Phils before 4,970 fans.

Gustine laid down a bunt with Frank Colman on second and Ralph Kiner on first. Hughes pegged the ball far over Jim Tabor's head, Colman and Kiner scoring on the error. Bob Elliott then cracked out a double to bring Gustine across with the third run of the inning.

The box score:

PHILADELPHIA (N)	ab.	r.	h.	po.	a.	e.
Newso'e, ss	3	0	0	6	0	1
Wyr'k, cf-lf	4	0	0	0	0	0
Ennis, lf	3	0	1	0	0	0
DiM'gio, cf	1	0	0	0	0	0
McCor'k, 1b	4	1	1	8	1	0
Northey, rf	3	0	1	1	0	0
Tabor, 3b	3	0	0	1	0	0
Rich'on, 2b	3	0	1	2	6	0
cWasdell	1	0	0	0	0	0
Hemsley, c	3	0	0	6	1	0
T. Hughes, p	3	0	1	0	2	1
Karl, p	0	0	0	0	1	0
Total	31	1	5	24	11	2

PITTSBURGH (N)	ab.	r.	h.	po.	a.	e.
Gionf'do, rf	5	0	2	2	0	0
Russell, lf	3	0	0	2	0	0
Colman, 1b	4	1	1	7	2	1
Kiner, cf	3	1	0	4	0	0
Gustine, 2b	4	1	1	4	3	0
Elliott, 3b	4	0	2	0	1	0
Salkeld, c	2	0	0	2	0	0
aZak	0	1	0	0	0	0
Camelli, c	1	0	0	1	0	0
Cox, ss	3	0	1	5	1	0
Gables, p	1	0	0	0	0	0
bBarrett	1	0	0	0	0	0
Hallett, p	1	0	0	0	0	0
Total	32	4	7	27	7	1

aRan for Salkeld in seventh.
bBatted for Gables in seventh.
cBatted for Richardson in ninth.

Philadelphia .... 000 000 100—1
Pittsburgh .... 000 000 13.—4

Runs batted in—Northey, Gionfriddo, Elliott.

Two-base hits — McCormick, Colman, Elliott. Stolen base—Newsome. Sacrifice—Gables. Double plays—Colman and Cox; Cox, Gustine and Colman. Left on bases—Philadelphia 6, Pittsburgh 9. Bases on balls—Off Gables 2, T. Hughes 3, Karl 1, Hallett 1. Struck out—By T. Hughes 2, Gables 2, Hallett 1. Hits—Off Gables 4 in 7 innings, Hallet 1 in 2, T. Hughes 7 in 7, Karl 0 in 1. Winning pitcher—Hallett. Losing pitcher—T. Hughes. Umpires—Henline, Conlan and Boggess. Time of game—1:51. Attendance—4,970.

SENATORS CONQUER WHITE SOX IN 7TH, 3-2

WASHINGTON, April 30 (AP)—Buddy Lewis' only hit today was a seventh-inning double, but it drove in the run that gave the Senators a 3-2 victory over the White Sox.

With the score standing at 2-all, Al Evans opened Washington's seventh with a single. Ray Scarborough sacrificed and Lewis doubled down the right-field foul line.

The victory was Scarborough's second of the season and lifted Washington into a tie with Chicago for sixth place. Ed Lopat of the White Sox was the fourth southpaw beaten by the left-handed hitting Senators this spring.

Dario Lodigiani, with three out of four, batted in both Chicago runs.

The box score:

CHICAGO (A.)	ab.	r.	h.	po.	a.	e.
Tucker, cf	3	0	0	3	0	0
Kollow'y, 2b	4	0	1	3	3	0
Wright, rf	4	0	0	0	0	0
Appling, ss	3	1	2	3	1	0
Jones, 1b	4	1	1	7	0	0
Hodgin, lf	3	0	1	1	0	0
Lod'iani, 3b	4	0	3	2	0	0
Fernandes, c	4	0	1	5	2	1
Lopat, p	3	0	0	0	5	0
aMoses	1	0	0	0	0	0
Total	33	2	9	24	11	1

WASHINGTON (A.)	ab.	r.	h.	po.	a.	e.
Rob'tson, 3b	4	0	0	0	2	0
Lewis, rf	4	0	1	4	0	0
Binks, lf	4	1	1	7	0	0
Spence, cf	3	0	1	0	0	1
Priddy, 2b	4	0	0	2	5	0
Vernon, 1b	4	1	2	10	3	0
Travis, ss	3	0	1	1	1	0
Evans, c	2	1	1	0	0	0
Scarb'gh, p	2	0	1	3	3	0
Total	30	3	8	27	14	1

aBatted for Lopat in ninth.

Chicago .... 000 011 000—2
Washington .... 000 011 10.—3

Runs batted in—Lodigiani 2, Scarborough, Vernon, Lewis.

Two-base hits—Lewis, Vernon. Sacrifices—Hodgin, Scarborough. Double plays—Robertson, Priddy and Vernon; Scarborough, Travis and Vernon. Left on bases—Chicago 7, Washington 6. Bases on balls—Off Lopat 2, Scarborough 2. Struck out—By Lopat 4. Wild pitch—Lopat. Umpires—Berry, Hubbard and Pipgras. Time of game—1:58. Attendance—4,823.

ADAMS ARRIVES IN MEXICO

Claims More Giants Will Join Him in Mexican League

MEXICO CITY, April 30 (AP)—Ace Adams, former New York Giant pitcher who told friends he would get $10,000 a year to play in the Mexican League, arrived here today and declared "some more Giants" soon would be coming to Mexico.

Adams made the trip by plane, accompanied by Robert Janis, Mexican League scout, and Gerardo and Alfonso Pasquel, brothers of League President Jorge Pasquel.

Harry Feldman, another pitcher who jumped the New York club along with Adams, also was scheduled to arrive but Adams said his teammate stopped off at Tallahassee, Fla., and would come here next week.

Major League Leaders

BATSMEN

AMERICAN LEAGUE

	G.	AB.	R.	H.	PC.
Keller, New York	10	30	11	12	.400
Wagner, Boston	9	24	6	9	.375
Stephens, St. Louis	11	43	3	16	.372
D. DiMaggio, Boston	9	36	8	13	.361
Pesky, Boston	13	50	14	18	.360

NATIONAL LEAGUE

	G.	AB.	R.	H.	PC.
Wietelmann, Boston	9	24	3	10	.417
Herman, Brooklyn	9	36	11	14	.389
Musial, St. Louis	13	54	11	20	.370
Witek, New York	11	46	13	17	.370
Reiser, Brooklyn	12	44	10	16	.364

RUNS BATTED IN

AMERICAN LEAGUE

Doerr, Boston.......17 | Spence, Wash.......12
Etten, New York...12

NATIONAL LEAGUE

Stevens, Brooklyn...12 | Musial, St. Louis...11
Miller, Cincinnati..12

HOME-RUN HITTERS

AMERICAN LEAGUE

J. DiMaggio, N. Y...4 | York, Boston.........2
Chapman, Phila.....3 | Pellagrini, Boston....2
Etten, New York....2 | Keltner, Cleve.......2
Lindell, New York...2

NATIONAL LEAGUE

Walker, Brooklyn....3 | Miller, Cincinnati....2
Witek, New York....2 | Kiner, Pittsburgh....2
Holmes, Boston.......2 | Hatton, Cincinnati...2
Northey, Phila.......2

Section III — SPORTS NEWS — NEW YORK Herald Tribune — CLASSIFIED ADVERTISING MARINE NEWS — Section III

SIXTEEN PAGES — SUNDAY, JUNE 9, 1946 — SIXTEEN PAGES

Indians Defeat Yankees, 2-1; Dodgers Lose, 2-0; Red Sox Win, 15-4; First Flight Takes Astoria Stakes by Three Lengths at Belmont

Whitney Filly Wins $10,750 Under Miller

Daughter of Mahmoud Conquers Miss Kimo in Two-Year-Old Test

Flood Town Victor In Carter Handicap

37,632 Witness Program as Attendance Shows Decrease for Meeting

By Joe H. Palmer

Confirming the form of the Fashion Stakes in most definite style, C. V. Whitney's Mahmoud filly, First Flight, whipped down the Widener course at Belmont yesterday to establish at least a temporary claim to leadership among the season's two-year-old fillies. She was in the fight every step of the way, until the last sixteenth, when it ceased to be a fight, and Paul Miller, apprentice, eased her to the finish three lengths ahead of William Helis's Miss Kimo, which had been considered her most dangerous rival.

This was in the $10,000 Astoria stakes, worth $10,750 to the winner, and it was the third renewal to fall to the Whitney stable, Disdainful winning in 1932 and Mush Mush last year. It was a third victory of the day for Paul Miller, twenty-year-old apprentice who is now leading rider at the Aqueduct-At-Belmont meeting with six winners.

Miller Rides Well

Miller, a West Philadelphia boy, was schooled under V. W. (Buddy) Raines, and until last week his contract was held by Donald Ross's Brandywine stable. Mr. Whitney has apparently made a fortunate purchase, for Miller has been riding excellently, one of his previous victories coming in the Queens County handicap, on Heli-optic. In these stakes events he does not, of course, get the benefit of his apprentice allowance, a fair indication that he will be able to hold his own when the allowance expires.

The Astoria, though it was an excellent race, had no dramatic aspects. Miss Kimo and First Flight in the middle of the track, William La Boyteaux's Pipette on the inside, and John S. Phipps' Dark Venus on the extreme outside, were always on the front end, and though Dark Venus got a temporary lead with a burst of speed near the half-mile pole, First Flight had no trouble when the real racing came.

Miss Kimo, which had been second in the Fashion, met no better fortune yesterday, though this time she was giving only three pounds instead of nine. Dark Venus held on to be second and Pipette was fourth. The winner paid $4.30, and the five and one-half furlongs were run in 1:04⅗.

First Flight is a beautifully made, good-sized bay filly, her only white mark being a star-shape symmetrically like a six-sided shield, shaded at the edges, a most distinctive marking. She has raced three times, winning two and earning $23,600. Her only defeat was engineered by the colt, Eternal War, in the Juvenile stakes, and in this First Flight had to run on the inside in the deep going.

Flood Town Beats King Dorsett

In the five-horse Carter Handicap, Jack Campbell, secretary, made a determined pass at another triple dead heat, such as he weighted the 1944 field into. Edward Lasker's Flood Town, under 113 pounds, lasted by something like two inches to beat John B. Theall's King Dorsett (126), which was rapidly getting up on the inside. Jay D. Acres' Black Swan (112), fighting hard on the far outside, was only a head back of the leaders. Flood Town, a highly promising two-year-old but unable to win a race last year at three, was an upset at $22.10, and was ridden by Warren Mehrtens.

Sir Victor Sassoon, president of the Royal Jockey Club of India, was the guest of Theodore J. Knapp yesterday. Sir Victor, who raced extensively in England, won the 1937 Epsom Oaks with Exhibitionist.

The first week of the Aqueduct-at-Belmont meeting drew 149,244 patrons, including a crowd of 37,632 yesterday. As compared to the first week of Belmont's own meeting a month earlier, this was a drop of about 5,500 daily. The first week at Belmont had a pari-mutuel play of $16,288,523, while last week's total was $13,850,995. The split-up of this was $173,137 to New York City, $519,412 to Nassau County, $893,389 to New York State and $595,592 to the Queens County Jockey Club, the latter at some expense to raise it.

In the last race of the day Wil-

(Continued on page 4, column 3)

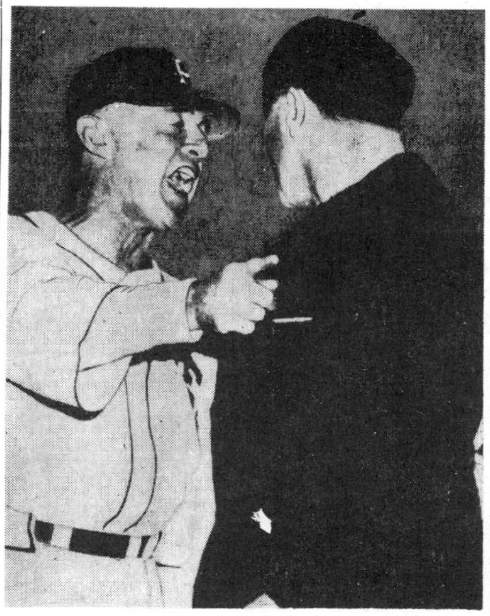

Herald Tribune—Acme telephoto

UMPIRE CALLS STRIKE ON PIRATES: Pittsburgh manager, Frankie Frisch, raucously follows players' lead in calling no strike in game with Giants Friday night, but is outvoted by Tom Dunn, umpire. It was still a strike

Pirates Voted 20-16 for Strike, Averted Only by 2-Thirds Rule

Four More for It Would Have Brought Walkout, Tally Shows; 'We Played a Dirty Trick on Murphy,' Handley Says After Poll

By Rud Rennie

PITTSBURGH, June 8.—The secret "strike" vote taken in the Pirates' clubhouse before last night's game was 20 to 16 in favor of going out on strike. It had been decided, however, that a two-thirds majority would be necessary for the first walkout of its kind in baseball history. Thirty-six players voted. The strike failed for lack of four votes.

Today there was no more talk of a strike among the Pirates. They do feel, however, that an organization of players is necessary. Whether the American Baseball Guild will be the organization remains to be seen. The players would not say whether they would continue with the guild under the leadership of Robert Murphy.

"We played a dirty trick on Murphy," said Lee Handley. "We let him down, and I was one of those who did it. We are not radicals. We don't want to be affiliated with any labor organization.

Thought Given to Fans

"We have no fight with the management of the ball club. We did not go out on strike last night because enough of us thought it was not the thing to do because of Bill Benswanger (club president), who has not hurt us, and the fans who support us.

"But we do think ball players should be organized to correct some of the abuses in baseball. We don't want strikes, but we would like some power to bring about a fair minimum wage, participation by a player in part of his purchase price and some sort of blanket insurance."

There was a growing curiosity among the players as to whether the National Association of Professional Baseball Players, a benevolent organization to which most of them belong, might not be reorganized and revitalized to supply their needs for a bargaining agency.

Murphy, the labor organizer from Boston, met some of the players at his hotel in the wee hours of the morning. There, for the first time, he got a full report of what had happened in the meeting from which he was barred.

He does not consider the defeat of the strike proposition as a de-

(Continued on page 3, column 1)

Fitch's Discus Throw Betters World Record

MINNEAPOLIS, June 8 (AP).—Bob Fitch, of the University of Minnesota, today threw the discus 180 feet 2¾ inches and bettered the world record of 174 feet 10¾ inches, established in 1941 by Adolfo Consolini at Milan, Italy.

Fitch, a Minneapolis boy doing post-graduate work at the university, was competing in the Northwest A. A. U. track and field meet. His toss was made against a moderate wind.

Louis's Timing On Jabs, Hooks Marks Drills

By Jesse Abramson

POMPTON LAKES, N. J., June 8.—Joe Louis shattered a coupe of precedents and legends of long standing today. He broke a training-camp precedent when he sparred seven rounds with a staff of four helpers. This was one round more than he had ever worked before in his ten-year career as heavyweight champion. He cut loose in spots and impressed those of the audience who were in a receptive mood.

The timing of his great left hand was excellent. He jabbed and hooked sharply and explosively, crowding his opposition and battering them and yet keeping under wraps as well. He crossed numerous hard rights and blasted his right to the body with the sort of punches many believe will weaken Billy Conn in their big fight now eleven days off.

The champion also took time out during the customary fanning

(Continued on page 2, column 2)

Major League Standings

SUNDAY, JUNE 9, 1946

National League

YESTERDAY'S RESULTS

New York, 5; Pittsburgh, 3
Chicago, 2; Brooklyn, 0
Cincinnati, 4; Boston, 2
Philadelphia-St. Louis, night

STANDING OF THE CLUBS

	Brooklyn	St. Louis	Chicago	Cincinnati	New York	Boston	Pittsburgh	Philadelphia	Won	Lost	Percentage	Games b'h'nd
Brooklyn	—	0	4	4	5	5	4	8	30	16	.652	—
St. Louis	2	—	5	4	2	5	4	3	25	19	.568	4
Chicago	3	3	—	4	5	5	2	2	24	19	.558	4½
Cincinnati	3	4	2	—	3	1	5	2	20	20	.500	7
New York	3	4	1	1	—	5	4	3	21	25	.457	9
Boston	2	3	3	2	5	—	1	4	20	24	.455	9
Pittsb'gh	3	3	3	2	2	1	—	4	18	24	.429	10
Philadel.	0	2	1	3	3	2	4	—	15	26	.366	12½
Games lost	16	19	19	20	25	24	24	26	—	—		

GAMES TODAY

New York at Pittsburgh (2)
Brooklyn at Chicago (2)
Boston at Cincinnati (2)
Philadelphia at St. Louis (2)

American League

YESTERDAY'S RESULTS

Cleveland, 2; New York, 1
Boston, 15; Detroit, 4
Philadelphia, 9; St. Louis, 3
Washington, 7; Chicago, 6 (1st)
Wash'ton, 7; Chicago, 6 (2d)

STANDING OF THE CLUBS

	Boston	New York	Washington	Detroit	Cleveland	St. Louis	Chicago	Philadelphia	Won	Lost	Percentage	Games b'h'nd
Boston	—	5	6	6	3	6	5	6	37	9	.804	—
New York	3	—	5	4	5	3	5	7	32	18	.640	7
Wash'ton	1	3	—	4	6	0	7	6	27	19	.587	10½
Detroit	1	0	3	—	5	4	5	7	25	22	.532	12½
Cleveland	1	4	2	1	—	5	3	4	20	28	.417	18
St. Louis	1	3	2	3	3	—	4	2	18	28	.391	19
Chicago	1	2	0	3	3	4	—	2	15	29	.341	21
Philadel.	1	1	1	1	3	6	0	—	13	24	.277	24½
Games lost	9	18	19	22	28	28	29	24	—	—		

GAMES TODAY

Cleveland at New York (2, 2:00 p. m.)
Chicago at Washington (2)
St. Louis at Philadelphia (2)
Detroit at Boston (2)

Cubs Subdue Brooklyn for 6th Straight

Chipman Hurls 5-Hitter as Rex Barney Falters in Debut Before 36,229

Rickert Connects For Homer in 4th

Lowrey-Reese Flare-Up in 8th Inning Is Checked as Umpire Intervenes

By Bob Cooke

CHICAGO, June 8.—The Brooklyn Dodgers were reported to be suffering from malnutrition late this afternoon after the Chicago Cubs had stuffed nine zeros down their throats and shut them out for the second time in two days, 2 to 0, for their sixth straight victory.

Despite the fact that they are leading the league, the Dodgers, since their arrival here, have been unable to take in nything except the scenery. Bob Chipman, a Brooklyn alumnus, twirled a five-hitter and spoiled Rex Barney's first start of the 1946 campaign.

Unable to procure any runs off Chipman's tantalizing service, the Dodgers almost lost their tempers as well as the ball game in the eighth. With the Cubs in front, 2 to 0, Peanuts Lowrey slid ferociously into second.

Umpire Separates Them

An exchange of words between Lowrey and Peewee Reese nearly led to a return bout in the Cub-Dodger feud, but Al Barlick, acting in the dual role of first-base umpire and referee, separated the combatants before any blows were struck.

The Reese-Lowrey episode was accompanied by an overwhelming majority of boos from the 36,229 customers, who were attracted to the park more through an intense dislike of the Dodgers than any particular respect for the Cubs.

Immediately following the Reese-Lowrey debate, Phil Cavarretta, Cub captain, couldn't resist a desire to throw another warlike gesture at the Dodgers.

Although Cavarretta was extinguished on an easy force play at second he slid into the bag with his spikes raised on high—shoulder high. Reese, who had taken Stanky's throw and had already stepped off the base after completing the forceout, merely looked at Cavarretta with disgust and walked to the dugout while the crowd yelled like a group of cash customers in the ancient days of Roman gladiators.

No Dodger Reaches Third

Chipman, although he allowed one more hit than Claude Passeau did yesterday, actually pitched a better game. No Brooklyn runner reached third and the left-hander was in danger in only one inning, the seventh, when the Dodgers put men on first and second with one away via a walk and Ferrel Anderson's infield single. Cookie Lavagetto, batting for Barney, gave the customers an undesired thrill by lifting a long fly to Lowrey near the wall and then Stanky flied to center for the third out.

Barney might have won with normal batting support. He permitted one run in the second due to walk and singles by Clyde McCullough and Bob Sturgeon, all of which the Cubs managed after two men were out.

Marvin Rickert gave the Cubs their second run when he plunked a homer into the right center-field stands in the fourth.

Sore Arm Benches Head

Ed Head was scheduled to be Brooklyn's starting pitcher. He warmed up ten minutes before the game, but was scratched at the last moment because of a sore arm.

The Oldtimers' Baseball Asssociation, a local fan club, presented a shotgun to Phil Cavarretta before the game with specific in-

(Continued on page 3, column 1)

Dodgers' Score

BROOKLYN (N. L.)	ab	r	h	po	a
Stanky 2b	3	0	1	3	2
Reese ss	4	0	0	3	2
Herman 3b	3	0	0	0	1
Walker rf	4	0	1	1	0
Furillo cf	3	0	0	3	0
Schultz 1b	3	0	0	9	0
Galan lf	3	0	0	4	2
‡Ramazotti	1	0	0	0	0
Anderson c	3	0	2	7	1
†Rojek	0	0	0	0	0
Sandlock c	1	0	0	0	1
Barney p	2	0	1	0	0
*Lavagetto	1	0	0	0	0
Melton p	0	0	0	0	1
Totals	31	0	5	24	10

CHICAGO (N. L.)	ab	r	h	po	a
Hack 3b	1	0	0	0	1
Johnson 2b	3	0	0	1	3
Lowrey lf	3	0	1	4	0
Cavarretta rf	4	0	0	3	0
Rickert cf	3	1	1	2	0
Waitkus 1b	2	1	0	9	2
McCullough c	3	0	1	4	0
Sturgeon ss	3	0	1	2	4
Chipman p	3	0	0	2	0
Totals	25	2	4	27	10

*Batted for Barney in seventh.
†Ran for Anderson in seventh.
‡Batted for Galan in ninth.

Brooklyn .... 000 000 000—0
Chicago .... 010 100 00x—2

Error—Barney. Runs batted in—Sturgeon, Rickert. Two-base hit—Walker. Home run—Rickert. Sacrifice—Johnson. Double play—Sturgeon, Johnson and Waitkus. Left on bases—Brooklyn 8; Chicago 6. Bases on balls—Barney 5; Melton 1; Chipman 4. Strikeouts—Barney 7; Chipman 3. Hits—Barney 3 in 6 innings; Melton 1 in 2. Losing pitcher—Barney. Umpires—Pinelli, Ballanfant and Barlick. Time—2:08. Attendance—36,229.

Herald Tribune—Frank

FELLER TWICE IN TROUBLE: Above, Charley Keller, of Yankees, scores on homer in third inning off Indians' ace and rates tip of cap from Joe DiMaggio. At right, Feller ducks as throw by George Stirnweiss to Nick Etten nips him at first in second inning. Cleveland won, 2 to 1

Doerr Leads Boston Attack Behind Dobson

Hub Hurler Trims Tigers After Learning of the Death of His Father

BOSTON, June 8 (AP).—Slugging in lusty fashion behind Joe Dobson, whose father died last night, the red hot Red Sox today vanquished Hal Newhouser for the second time this season as they trounced the Detroit Tigers, 15 to 4.

The victory, coupled with New York's loss to Cleveland, lengthened the Boston club's league lead to seven full games over the Yankees.

Newhouser, whose only previous loss of the year was to Dobson and the Boston league-leaders, was found for four hits and five runs in the first inning, the only frame he was allowed to work.

Dobson pitched in fine fashion, scattering most of eleven hits, until the eighth inning when the excessive heat and the emotional strain told on him and Bob Klinger replaced him.

Dobson pitched after a phone conversation with his brother, who notified him of their parent's death.

"You go ahead and work," the brother said. "That's the way Pa'd want it."

Dobson will fly home to Coolidge, Ariz., Monday for the funeral of his father, who died in Arkansas.

Bobby Doerr, with four hits in five trips, one his seventh four-sacker of the year, and Pinky Higgins and Rudy York, both former Tigers, led the Boston attack before 29,543 paid fans.

The paid attendance brought the Boston total for the year to 521,292 for twenty-nine games in twenty-four days, far exceeding that for the first seven weeks of any Boston season.

Doerr, who banged out two doubles and a single in addition to his

(Continued on page 3, column 4)

Koslo Triumphs Over Pirates As Giants End Slump, 5 to 3

Southpaw Beats Pittsburgh for 3d Time in Scoring Fifth Victory of Season

PITTSBURGH, June 8.—Murphy's Mutiny on the Monongahela having backfired, the Pirates continued with the business of baseball today but less lustily than they did last night, fresh from their momentous "no-strike" meeting. Dave Koslo quelled them, 5 to 3. The Giants' southpaw has won five games this year and three of them have been against Pittsburgh.

This New York victory broke an annoying four-game losing streak. Mel Ott, the manager, benched Babe Young and had Johnny Rucker in center field, leading off, and Goodie Rosen in right.

Rucker led off with an infield hit, and the Giants got two runs in the first inning, thanks to a base on balls to Johnny Mize, which filled the sacks, and an error by Jimmy Brown.

The Pirates overtook them in the third, when Hank Camelli and Brown hit singles and Maurice Van Robays tripled and scored on a single by Bob Elliott. But Koslo yielded only three scattered singles thereafter and only one man passed first base.

Giants Regain Lead

The Giants regained the lead in the fifth. Nick Strincevich, the Pirate pitcher, let Koslo get his second hit, a single to left. Rucker got another hit. Then Strincevich threw Rosen's bunt too hard to Brown and the third baseman dropped what would otherwise have been a force-out. Mickey Witek lifted an infield fly. But Johnny Mize slammed a double to center, knocking in two runs.

Strincevich did some nice twirling after that. He walked Walker Cooper purposely and then fanned Blattner and Sid Gordon. The Giants did not score again until the ninth, when Rosen tripled against the right-field screen and Witek singled to center. It was a pleasure to get this strike thing cooled off and to have the Giants come out of their slump.

The Giants, eagerly seeking a right-handed hitting outfielder, have purchased Gayland Lawing from the Cincinnati Reds. Lawing is an ex-service man. Ott said he had received good reports on him as a service player. He is a six-footer, twenty-five years old. He may report here tomorrow.

Frank Frisch has put the club-

(Continued on page 3, column 2)

Giants' Score

NEW YORK (N. L.)	ab	r	h	po	a
Rucker cf	5	2	3	2	0
Rosen rf	4	1	1	3	0
Witek 3b	5	1	2	0	0
Mize 1b	4	0	1	6	0
Cooper c	3	0	0	4	2
Blattner 2b	4	0	1	3	2
Gordon lf	3	0	0	7	0
Kerr ss	4	0	0	2	4
Koslo p	4	1	2	0	1
Totals	36	5	10	27	9

PITTSBURGH (N. L.)	ab	r	h	po	a
Brown 3b	3	1	1	2	0
Van Robays lf	4	1	2	1	0
Gionfriddo lf	0	0	0	0	0
Elliott rf	4	0	1	1	0
Fletcher 1b	3	0	1	13	1
Kiner cf	4	0	0	2	0
Gustine 2b	3	0	1	1	2
Zak ss	2	0	0	1	6
*Baker	1	0	0	0	0
Camelli c	3	1	1	5	2
Strincevich p	3	0	1	1	2
Totals	30	3	8	27	13

*Batted for Zak in ninth.

New York .... 200 020 001—5
Pittsburgh .... 003 000 000—3

Error—Brown. Runs batted in—Cooper, Blattner, Van Robays 2, Elliott, Mize 2, Witek. Two-base hits—Koslo, Mize, Rucker. Three-base hits—Van Robays, Rosen. Stolen base—Blattner. Sacrifices—Zak, Rosen, Brown. Double plays—Kerr, Blattner and Mize; Camelli and Brown; Zak and Fletcher. Left on bases—New York 8, Pittsburgh 4. Bases on balls—Strincevich 3, Koslo 2. Strikeouts—Strincevich 5, Koslo 3. Umpires—Jorda, Stewart, Magerkurth and Dunn. Time—2:11. Attendance—5,785.

Rizzuto Agreed to Jump, Says Mexican; Pasquel Tells of Dinner With Shortstop

Phil Rizzuto, Yankee shortstop, once agreed to join the Mexican League for a $15,000 bonus for signing a five-year contract for $12,000 a season, according to testimony given by Bernardo Pasquel, brother of Jorge Pasquel, president of the Mexican League, in an examination before trial of a suit brought by the New York Yankees to enjoin the Latin-American organization from inducing New York American League players to jump their contracts, it was disclosed yesterday.

Bernardo Pasquel testified in the office of his attorney, Jerome Hess, 74 Trinity Place, according to a transcript of the proceeding. The Mexican, who denied published reports that he is a vice-president of the Mexican League, was examined by Mark F. Hughes, of counsel for the Yankees.

Pasquel's testimony told of a dinner party with Rizzuto in the Waldorf-Astoria on May 1 or 2 and declared that the next day Rizzuto had telephoned to say that if he were given $15,000 for signing a contract he would go to Mexico and was told that he would get that bonus. However, on May 3, according to the transcript, Rizzuto telephoned again to say that he was "undecided." The next day the Yankees filed their suit.

Pasquel said he offered George Stirnweiss, Yankee third baseman and American League batting champion in 1945, $15,000 for signing a contract and $20,000 a season for a five-year agreement. Stirnweiss refused, according to Pasquel's testimony, "because he had a contract for two years," but "Mexico is expecting to see him some day."

Pasquel said that the dinner party took place after he had in-

(Continued on page 3, column 5)

Feller Scores 9th as Seerey Blasts Homer

2-Run Blow Off Marshall Gives Tribe's Ace 5-Hit Victory Over New York

Keller's 4-Bagger Cheered by 50,364

Dickey's Men Fail to Tally in First Inning After Collecting Two Safeties

By Al Laney

Bob Feller pitched against the Yankees in the Stadium again yesterday and the result, while somewhat less spectacular than his no-hitter of a month ago, was practically the same. He pitched the Cleveland Indians to a 2-to-1 victory, giving the Bombers five hits, one of which was Charley Keller's twelfth home run. The two runs that Feller needed were the result of a home run by Pat Seerey, the left fielder, after Hank Edwards had singled in the second inning.

That came in the second inning while Clarence Marshall was pitching and that was all the damage the Indians could do to him, during his six and two-third innings, and to Jake Wade and Randy Gumpert, who followed. Cleveland made seven hits, six of them off Marshall before wildness caused his retirement.

Crowd of 50,364 Hopefuls

It seemed at the beginning that it might be the day that Feller could be beaten and the fact that he was by no means so overpowering as on the no-hit occasion gave hope right through the game to the crowd of 50,364. The closeness of the score, the fact that Keller had teed off in the third, might do so again and that other Yankees could reach the stands, kept hope alive right into the ninth inning, when the Yankees had a base runner on Joe Gordon's infield single.

But the further fact is that Feller dealt with the three potentially dangerous situations which faced him in the most direct way possible.

He fanned the Yankee batters, who might have driven in runs, and his total of strikeouts was eight, making his grand total for the year 126 in 127 innings. The victory was his ninth and he has lost four.

It will be seen from the score that Marshall, who made his major-league debut in the first Stadium night game with Roger Wolff, of Washington, as his opponent, was no sacrificial lamb.

Brilliant Catch by Keller

It was clear that Bill Dickey had hopes of beating Feller with young Cuddles, and but for that one soft pitch to Seerey he could have got away with it. In that case, a catch which Keller made off another ball Seerey hit in the eighth, this one off Gumpert, would have been the most stiffening and significant occurrence of the afternoon.

Seerey hit what could be judged no less than another homer until the moment Keller reached in among the customers and speared it with one hand.

Tommy Henrich, the second batter to face the Tribe's ace, took care of the no-hit tension by banging a single to center. Then, after Keller had gone out, Joe DiMaggio singled into right on a hit-and-run play which sent Henrich to third.

With two hits off Feller in one inning, men on first and third and a power hitter, Nick Etten, at bat, the great man was in trouble. But not much. Etten, who was futile at bat all afternoon, began his lack of effectiveness here with a weak infield tap.

Keller Clouts Homer

In the second inning Dickey got a single with one out, and in the third Keller drove the ball into the right-field bleachers, beyond where the figures read 367 feet. The next ball Feller pitched after that, DiMaggio hit into the top left-field deck, but foul by very

(Continued on page 3, column 2)

Yankees' Score

CLEVELAND (A. L.)	ab	r	h	po	a
Boudreau ss	4	0	0	2	0
Woodling cf	3	0	0	3	0
Fleming 1b	4	0	1	5	1
Edwards rf	4	1	1	1	0
Seerey lf	3	1	2	2	0
Ross 3b	3	0	2	2	0
Hayes c	4	0	1	9	0
Mack 2b	3	0	0	2	4
Feller p	4	0	0	1	0
Totals	32	2	7	27	5

NEW YORK (A. L.)	ab	r	h	po	a
Stirnweiss 3b	4	0	0	0	3
Henrich rf	4	0	1	2	0
Keller lf	4	1	1	2	0
DiMaggio cf	3	0	1	5	0
Etten 1b	4	0	0	5	1
Gordon 2b	4	0	1	3	3
†Souchock	0	0	0	0	0
Dickey c	2	0	1	6	0
Robinson c	1	0	0	2	0
Rizzuto ss	3	0	0	2	2
Marshall p	2	0	0	0	0
Wade p	0	0	0	0	0
*Lindell	1	0	0	0	0
Gumpert p	0	0	0	0	0
Totals	32	1	5	27	9

*Batted for Wade in seventh.
†Ran for Gordon in ninth.

Cleveland .... 020 000 000—2
New York .... 001 000 000—1

Erros—None. Runs batted in—Seerey 2, Keller. Two-base hit—Hayes. Home runs—Seerey, Keller. Sacrfiice—Ross. Double play—Stirnweiss, Gordon and Etten. Left on bases—Cleveland 8; New York 7. Bases on balls—Marshall 4, Feller 3. Strikeouts—Feller 8, Marshall 4, Wade 1, Gumpert 2. Hits—Off Marshall 6 in 6⅔ innings; Wade 0 in ⅓; Gumpert 1 in 2. Losing pitcher—Marshall. Umpires—Grieve, Passarella and Rue. Time—2:35. Attendance—50,364.

Yankees Rout Red Sox, 9-0; Dodgers Beat Phils, 5-4; Giants Win, 8-1, Take Lead

Reynolds Pitches 2-Hitter And Starts 4-Run Attack

His Double Off Dorish With 2 Out in 5th Sparks Surge Capped by Keller's 9th Homer of Year; Stirnweiss Breaks Slump With 3 Singles

By Rud Rennie

In two consecutive games the Yankees shut out the two top teams in the league. Frank Shea blanked the Detroit Tigers with four hits Wednesday night. Allie Reynolds held the champion Boston Red Sox to two hits and beat them, 9 to 0, yesterday afternoon before 25,496 cash clients and 12,000 children in the Stadium.

This was Reynolds's third shutout of the season and his second two-hitter against Boston. The Red Sox have not scored against him this year in two games.

Bill Goodman, a pinch hitter for Harry Dorish, was the only batter to make a clean hit off Reynolds. He singled to center in the sixth. The other hit was made in the eighth when Birdie Tebbetts, the catcher recently acquired from the Tigers, rapped a grounder which took a bad hop and struck Bobby Brown, Yankee third baseman, on the chest.

Williams Walks Three Times

Reynolds walked Ted Williams three times. He passed Rudy York once, but he also fanned him twice. And the Yankee pitcher helped himself by fielding his position with agility, making two putouts and one leaping assist.

The Yankees banged home four runs off Dorish in the fifth, and they got one off Mel Parnell in the sixth and four in the eighth.

Four concentrated hits made the first four scores. Reynolds started it with two away and nobody on base. He doubled to center. George Stirnweiss, who had a good day, followed with his third straight single, sending Reynolds to third and taking second on the throw. Tommy Henrich drove both runners home with a single to right and Charlie Keller slammed his ninth homer of the year into the right-field stands to complete the job.

Scores on Double Play

George McQuinn and Brown hit safely to start the last of the sixth and McQuinn scored while Bobby Doerr and York were making a double play with Johnny Lindell's pinch-hit grounder.

The scoring in the eighth was slightly marvelous. Keller walked and Joe DiMaggio singled. Then McQuinn bunted and the ball hugged the third-base line and rolled that way to the bag with Red Sox players following it in the hope that it would roll foul. The bases were loaded.

Brown took a swing and was hit by the ball and got on base, forcing in a run. Ralph Houk, a substitute catcher, then drove in two runs with a single to left and rounded first and was thrown out coming back to the bag.

Brown Tallies on Error

The fourth run scored when Parnell made a wild pitch and Tebbets retrieved the ball and pegged it into left field so that Brown just kept on running and scored from second.

A meeting of the Yankee players was called yesterday at which they agreed to co-operate with the publicity department in the matter of attending dinners . . . According to the publicity department Bucky Harris, the manager, and twenty-eight players signed a prepared statement saying among other things: "No player on this club has ever been told that he must travel by plane."

Reynolds hustled to first base twice to take tosses from McQuinn for put-outs . . . Keller took two bases in the fourth on a fly ball which fell untouched behind shortstop. P[illegible]grini thought Williams was g[illegible]o take it and Williams just [illegible] thinking.

The [illegible]:

BOSTON (A. L.)	ab	r	h	po	a	NEW YORK (A. L.)	ab	r	h	po	a
Pesky 3b	4	0	0	0	1	Stirnweiss	4	1	3	1	4
D.DiMaggio cf	4	0	0	1	0	Henrich	4	1	1	3	0
Williams lf	1	0	0	1	2	Keller lf	2	2	2	2	0
York 1b	3	0	0	15	0	J.DiMaggio cf	4	1	1	1	0
Doerr 2b	4	0	0	3	6	McQuinn 1b	4	2	2	13	2
Mele rf	4	0	0	1	0	Brown 3b	3	1	1	0	2
Pellagrini ss	3	0	0	1	5	Robinson c	2	0	0	2	0
Tebbetts c	3	0	1	2	0	†Lindell	1	0	0	0	0
Dorish p	1	0	0	0	2	Houk c	1	0	1	2	0
*Goodman	1	0	1	0	0	Rizzuto ss	4	0	0	1	0
Parnell p	1	0	0	0	1	Reynolds p	4	1	1	2	3
Totals	29	0	2	24	17	Totals	33	9	12	27	11

*Batted for Dorish in sixth inning.
†Batted for Robinson in sixth inning.

Boston .... 000 000 000—0
New York .... 000 041 04x—9

Error—Tebbetts. Runs batted in—Henrich 2, Keller 2, Brown, Houk 2. Two-base hits—Keller, Reynolds. Home run—Keller. Double plays—Pellagrini, Doerr and York; Doerr and York. Left on bases—Boston 6, New York 3. Bases on balls—Reynolds 4, Dorish 1, Parnell 1. Strikeouts—Dorish 1, Reynolds 4, Parnell 1. Hits—Off Dorish, 7 in 5 innings; Parnell, 5 in 3. Hit by pitcher—By Parnell (Brown). Wild pitch—Parnell. Losing pitcher—Dorish. Umpires—McGowan, McKinley, Grieve and Jones. Time—2:00. Attendance—25,496.

New Utrecht Hurler Fans 102 in 61 Innings

John Gerace, a fifteen-year-old sophomore at New Utrecht High School, struck out seventeen batters and gave up only one hit and three walks in seven innings as New Utrecht defeated Eastern District, 5 to 0, at the Brooklyn Parade Grounds yesterday.

The seventeen strike-outs increases Gerace's total for eight games and five innings (sixty-one innings) to 102.

Herald Tribune—Acme

TWO-HIT PITCHER: Allie Reynolds, of the Yankees, shows how many hits he allowed the Red Sox in yesterday's 9-0 Yankee victory

New Utrecht Favored to Retain Schoolboy Track Crown Today

Boys', Clinton, Newtown Chief Threats for P.S.A.L. Crown at Randall's Island

By Edward Sinclair

New York's schoolboys, who soon will run out of track meets, get a real fling at racing against the clock and one another today with the holding of the forty-fourth annual public high schools outdoor track and field championships at Randall's Island Stadium.

New Utrecht, the defending champion, is favored to retain its title. Boys' High, Stuyvesant, DeWitt Clinton, Morris and Newton are figured to provide the bulk of competition.

The mile race looms as the best event with Frank Efinger, the national interscholastic mile king from Clinton, making his first start in more than two weeks. After a highly successful winter on the boards, Efinger was ill all spring.

Today he will face Bill Lucas, his old foe from Morris and the current P. S. A. L. outdoor champion who has yet to beat Efinger this year.

New Utrecht's cause will be fought in the main by Isadore Taffel, defending the pole vault; Lou Morelli, who holds the 220-yard low hurdles title; Ed Terranova, a threat in the broad jump, and Larry Fleischman, another pole vaulter.

Roger Montgomery, the Boys' sprinter, is expected to take the 100-yard dash. His teammates, Jim Gathers and Jim Conaway, look good in the 220, while Vinnie Cino stands out in the 440.

The program, starting with the field events, will get under way at 2:00 p. m. Twenty-four events are listed.

Grover Cleveland, City P. S. A. L. baseball titleholder, buttressed its top position in the Queens North Shore Division yesterday with a 3-to-1 victory over Flushing at Farmer's Oval. Bobby Kunze, Cleveland's senior right-hander and star hurler, turned in his second straight one-hit performance for his seventh triumph.

Newtown, the division's second-place squad, stayed up there as Pete Meachini tossed his first no-hitter and defeated Bryant, 4 to 0, at Newtown Field in Elmhurst.

In the Brooklyn division, James Madison downed Brooklyn Tech, 2 to 1, in ten innings at Boys' High Field and retained the runner-up spot. Abraham Lincoln blasted Samuel J. Tilden, 15 to 1, and held third place.

Athletics Beat Senators In Night Game, 8 to 1

PHILADELPHIA, May 23 (AP).—The Philadelphia Athletics, unbeaten under the lights, scored their seventh straight night victory by beating the Washington Senators before 17,429 tonight, 8 to 1. Chet Laabs led the attack on Mickey Haefner with a three-run homer in the fourth, while Elmer Valo also drove in three runs.

The score:

WASHINGTON (A. L.)	ab	r	h	po	a	PHILADELPHIA (A.L.)	ab	r	h	po	a
Grace lf	3	0	0	0	0	Joost ss	4	2	2	2	2
Lewis rf	3	1	1	1	0	Valo rf	3	1	2	1	0
Spence cf	3	0	0	3	0	Laabs lf	4	1	1	2	0
Vernon 1b	4	0	2	9	0	Chapman cf	5	0	1	5	1
Priddy 2b	3	0	0	6	2	Rosar c	4	0	1	8	1
Evans c	3	0	0	4	1	Majeski 3b	4	0	0	2	0
Christman ss	3	0	0	1	3	Handley 2b	3	2	2	2	3
Yost 3b	3	0	0	0	2	Fain 1b	4	1	2	5	0
Haefner p	1	0	0	0	2	Marchildon p	3	1	2	0	0
Scarborough p	1	0	0	0	1						
*Robertson	1	0	0	0	0						
Cary p	0	0	0	0	0						
Totals	27	1	3	24	11	Totals	34	8	13	27	7

*Batted for Scarborough in eighth.

Washington .... 100 000 000—1
Philadelphia .... 110 400 02x—8

Errors—None. Runs batted in—Vernon, Valo 3, Joost, Laabs 3, Marchildon. Two-base hits—Lewis, Joost, Marchildon, Rosar. Home run—Laabs. Sacrifice—Marchildon. Double plays—Priddy and Vernon; Handley, Joost and Fain; Evans Christman and Evans. Left on bases—Washington 3; Philadelphia 8. Base on balls—Off Marchildon 4; Haefner 2, Scarborough 1, Cary 1. Struck out—By Marchildon 4, Scarborough 2, Cary 1. Hits—Off Haefner 8 in 3⅔; Scarborough 1 in 3⅓; Cary 4 in 1. Hit by pitcher—By Haefner (Valo). Losing pitcher—Haefner. Umpires—Papperella, Summers, Hurley and Rue. Time, 2:10. Attendance, 17,429.

Cards Shut Out Pirates Behind Munger, 2 to 0

ST. LOUIS, May 23 (AP).—Big Red Munger shut out Pittsburgh, 2 to 0, with a six-hit performance tonight, giving the St. Louis Cardinals their second straight victory over the Pirates, before 12,722 fans.

The score by innings:

Pittsb'gh 000 000 000—0 6 1
St. Louis 200 000 00x—2 8 1

Batteries—Roe, Bagby (8) and Klutzz; Munger and Rice.

Brooklyn Wins In 7th Inning Without a Hit

Philadelphia Takes 4-Run Lead, Routing Branca; Victors Score 3 in 4th

By Bob Cooke

The Brooklyn Dodgers were so weary after their recent travels in the West last night, at Ebbets Field they let the Phillies force the tying and winning runs down their throats as they won a 5-to-4 victory and ascended into third place.

Behind, 4 to 3 in the seventh inning, the Dodgers stood around without making a hit and let the Phillies push them into the winner's circle. It was a wild inning, due primarily to three Phil hurlers who seemed bent on contributing to the greater Fletbush Fund for the betterment of rBooklyn's pennant chances.

Phils Take Early Lead

For a while it seemed as though the sight of their happy home was such that the Dodgers had forgotten about winning a ball game. The Phils took a 4-to-0 lead in the early innings. They knocked out Ralph Branca in the fourth and bruised Harry Taylor for their final run in that round.

Meanwhile, Dutch Leonard, an ancient right-hander who once toiled in the clothes of a Dodger, had shut out Brooklyn for three innings. In the fourth Leonard eased up and the Dodgers loosened him up for three runs on consecutive singles by Dixie Walker, Gene Hermanski, Bruce Edwards and Arky Vaughan.

Although the evening was pleasantly cool, the Phils were unpleasantly hot in the first inning as far as Branca was concerned. The first three batters hit safely and before the customers or Branca knew what was happening, the Quakers had a 2-to-0 lead.

Skeeter Newsome, leading off, slapped a single to center. Harry Walker, Dixie's kid brother who had been hitting over .400 since he was traded to Phils by the Cards, continued to improve his average with another single to center. Charlie Gilbert drove in one run with a double to right. When Branca walked Andy Seminick, the bases were full. There was still no one out.

But the best the Phils could do was manufacture one more tally. While Johnny Wyrostek was forcing Seminick at second on a grounder to Arky Vaughan, Walker scored from third. Howie Schultz popped to Rojek for the second out and Gilbert was nipped at the plate when the Phils tried [illegible] steal, ending the inning.

Harry Walker and Gilbert proceeded to belabor Branca as soon as they re-appeared at the plate in the third. With one away, they both singled, Walker eventually scoring on Seminick's slow grounder to Rojek. Wyrostek was then passed intentionally and Branca fanned Schultz.

The Phils knocked Branca out in the fourth. Jeep Handley singled to open the inning but Reiser threw him out at second when he attempted to stretch the blow. After Branca walked the next two hitters, Harry Taylor replaced him.

Newsome singled to center driving in Philadelphia's fourth run, Taylor retired the side as Harry Walker hit into a double play.

Dodgers Score Three

Brooklyn pummeled Leonard for three runs in the fourth. With one away Dixie Walker, Gene Hermanski, Edwards and Vaughan slammed singles. Ed Snider, batting for Rojek, fanned. While Taylor was up, Vaughan representing the tying run, took second on a passed ball. Shotton then removed Taylor for Marvin Rackley, a pinch-hitter. Rackley grounded to Leonard for the third out.

The Dodgers finally disposed of Leonard as they took a 5-to-4 lead in the seventh. It was a wild inning, primarily because of the Philadelphia pitchers. Leonard withdrew with the bases full and one away. He walked Eddie Miksis, the first batter, and failed to retire him at second and then at third as the next two batters sacrificed and reached safety via a fielder's choice.

After Leonard reduced Robinson on a pop to Newsome, Ken Heitnzelman relieved and forced in the tying run by walking Reiser. Walker forced a runner at the plate where upon Tommy Hughes, relieving Heittzelman, issued another Brooklyn run and walked home. Edwards fanned leaving three men on basse. The Dodgers didn't make a hit in the inning but they were one run in front as Hugh Casey ambled in to protect them. Casey shut out the Phils in the eighth and ninth.

The score:

PHILA. (N. L.)	ab	r	h	po	a	BROOKLYN (N. L.)	ab	r	h	po	a
Newsome ss	4	1	2	3	2	Reese ss	3	1	0	2	3
†Ennis	1	0	1	0	0	Robinson 1b	4	0	1	9	0
H. Walker cf	5	2	2	2	0	Reiser cf	3	0	1	1	1
Gilbert lf	4	0	2	1	0	F. Walker rf	4	1	1	1	0
Seminick c	2	0	0	6	0	Hermanski lf	3	1	1	2	0
Wyrostek rf	3	0	0	3	0	Furillo lf	0	0	0	0	0
Schultz 1b	4	0	1	7	1	Edwards c	4	1	2	5	2
Handley 3b	4	0	2	0	1	Vaughan 3b	3	0	1	0	5
Verban 2b	3	1	1	2	2	Rojek 2b	1	0	0	5	3
Leonard p	2	0	0	0	2	‡Snider	1	0	0	0	0
Heintzel'n p	0	0	0	0	0	Miksis 2b	1	1	0	2	0
Hughes p	0	0	0	0	0	Branca p	1	0	0	0	0
*Padgett	1	0	0	0	0	Taylor p	0	0	0	0	0
Schanz p	0	0	0	0	1	§Rackley	1	0	0	0	0
						Barney p	0	0	0	0	0
						¶Gionfriddo	0	0	0	0	0
						Casey p	1	0	0	0	0
Totals	33	4	11	24	9	Totals	30	5	7	27	14

*Batted for Hughes in eighth inning.
†Batted for Newsome in ninth inning.
‡Batted for Rojek in fourth inning.
§Batted for Taylor in fourth inning.
¶Batted for Barney in seventh inning.

Philadelphia .... 201 100 000—4
Brooklyn .... 000 300 20x—5

Errors—Seminick, Gilbert. Runs batted in—Gilbert, Wyrostek, Seminick, Newsome, Edwards, Vaughan 2, Reiser, Furillo. Two-base hits—Gilbert, Handley. Sacrifices—Gionfriddo, Reese. Double plays—Verban, Newsome and Schultz; Reese, Rojek and Robinson; Reese and Robinson. Left on bases—Philadelphia 8, Brooklyn 7. Strikeouts—Branca 2, Leonard 3, Barney 1, Hughes 1, Casey 1. Bases on balls—Branca 4, Leonard 2, Barney 1, Heintzelman 1, Hughes 1. Hits—Off Leonard, 7 in 6⅓ innings; Heintzelman, 0 in ⅓; Hughes, 0 in ⅓. Schanz, 0 in 1; Branca, 7 in 3⅓; Taylor, 1 in ⅔; Barney, 1 in 3. Hit by pitcher—Barney (Seminick). Passed balls—Seminick, Edwards. Winning pitcher—Barney. Losing pitcher—Leonard. Umpires—Barr, Boggess, Jorda. Time—2:47. Attendance—33,136.

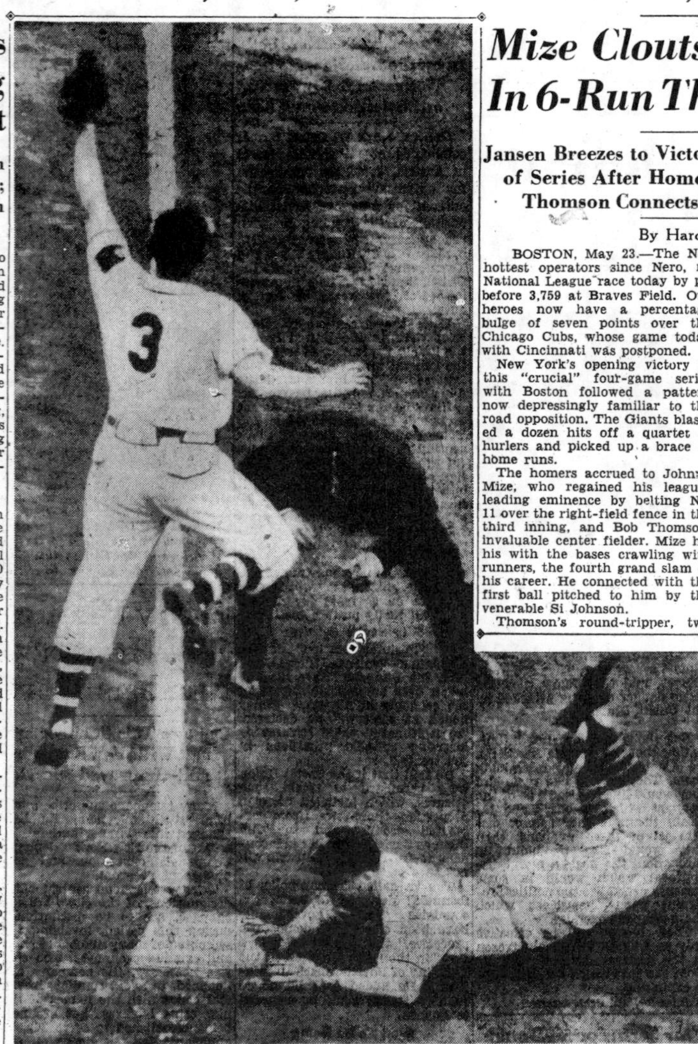

SAFE AT THIRD: Willard Marshall, of the Giants, goes in head first as Bob Elliott, of the Braves, leaps for the ball and Jocko Conlan, umpire, stoops to keep out of the way Associated Press wirephoto

Mize Clouts Grand Slam In 6-Run Third at Boston

Jansen Breezes to Victory Over Braves in Opener of Series After Home-Run Leader Hits 11th; Thomson Connects for 6th of Year in 5th

By Harold Rosenthal

BOSTON, May 23.—The New York Giants, a collection of the hottest operators since Nero, moved back into first place in the National League race today by pulverizing the Boston Braves, 8 to 1, before 3,759 at Braves Field. Our heroes now have a percentage bulge of seven points over the Chicago Cubs, whose game today with Cincinnati was postponed.

New York's opening victory in this "crucial" four-game series with Boston followed a pattern now depressingly familiar to the road opposition. The Giants blasted a dozen hits off a quartet of hurlers and picked up a brace of home runs.

The homers accrued to Johnny Mize, who regained his league-leading eminence by belting No. 11 over the right-field fence in the third inning, and Bob Thomson, invaluable center fielder. Mize hit his with the bases crawling with runners, the fourth grand slam of his career. He connected with the first ball pitched to him by the venerable Si Johnson.

Thomson's round-tripper, two innings later, came as he led off against Johnson's relief [illegible] Ed Wright. Bob's sixth for 1947 cleared the left-field wall.

The Giants' triumph was the eighth in nine games on the road trip, which had its inception almost two weeks ago in St. Louis.

Larry Jansen, the right-hander, appeared in his third winning role. He gave up six hits and never was in a troublesome situation all afternoon, thanks to the Giants' fat third inning, wherein they collected six runs on five hits. This cushion gave him the confidence he had heretofore lacked and he handled the Braves in a cool, workmanlike fashion, striking out five and walking one.

The same can hardly be said for the Boston moundsmen. Johnson, who is alleged to have thrown a slider at Sitting Bull at the Battle of the Little Big Horn, lasted two and a third innings and when Wright came galloping to the rescue Ole Si had given up five runs. Walker Cooper singled off Wright, sending in another run, but Sid Gordon hit into a double play.

Wright Nicked for Two Runs

Eventually Wright gave up two more runs before he was succeeded by Johnny Beazley and Glenn Elliott. Beazley held New York hitless in his two innings and Elliott gave up two singles.

The Braves accounted for their run in the third inning when Earl Torgerson, bespectadled first baseman, hit, singled to right field.

He went to second when Sibby Sisti was thrown out by Buddy Kerr. Wright then lifted a foul near the Giants' dugout and Jansen caught it, but tripped and fell on the gravel patch fronting the dugout and skinned his left elbow. Torgeson went to third, Jansen handed the ball to Cooper, who looked at Torgeson at third and then proceede to throw to the base to make certain Torgeson wouldn't stray.

It was an excellent idea, except that no one was covering the bag. The entire infield had wandered in to look at Jansen's elbow. Torgeson strolled home. It was the only Giant aberration of the afternoon.

Giants Continue Hitting

Every one of the Polo Grounders grabbed himself at least one hit. Bud Blattner, Willard Marshall and Cooper got two apiece. The barrage kept the Giants' per-game average for the road trip close to twelve.

Kerr handled five chances perfectly and boosted his all-time record to 366 in sixty-seven games. He was a little anxious in the third inning in trying for a double-play, and while he beat Torgeson coming down from first base he falied to touch the bag before throwing to Mize.

The last time Si Johnson beat the Giants was two weeks ago in the second game of a Sunday double-header at the Polo Grounds. Today he was seen walking to the showers muttering and glancing over his shoulder. It was quite obvious he was thinking "these guys can't be the Giants."

Leading Five Batsmen In Each Major League

American League

Player and club	G	AB	R	H	Pct.
Mullin, Detroit	27	102	22	37	.363
McQuinn, New York	25	89	10	32	.360
Dillinger, St. Louis	29	124	17	42	.339
Williams, Boston	31	99	27	33	.333
Appling, Chicago	31	121	18	40	.331

National League

Player and club	G	AB	R	H	Pct.
Walker, Philadelphia	27	94	13	38	.404
Mize, New York	27	96	34	34	.354
Lamanno, Cincinnati	21	71	10	25	.352
Elliott, Boston	30	109	18	37	.340
Gustine, Pittsburgh	26	103	19	35	.340

Runs Batted In		Home Runs	
Torgeson, Braves	30	Mize, Giants	11
Williams, Red Sox	25	Williams, Red Sox	10
Marshall, Giants	24	Keller, Yankees	9
Mize, Giants	24	Torgeson, Braves	8
Kennedy, Wh. Sox	23	Miller, Reds	8

Ether Subdues Pratt As Queens Wins, 5-2

Ted Ether gave up eight hits but thwarted threatened rallies with the bases loaded in the first, sixth and ninth innings, as the Queens College nine defeated Pratt Institute, 5 to 2, yesterday at Pratt Field in Brooklyn. Hank Kirchdoefer, who had beaten Queens three times, suffered his first loss to the Knights.

Gene Eliasoth got Queens off to an early lead with a double which drove in two runs in the first inning. John Constantino clinched the game in the sixth with a home-run with one on.

The score by innings:

				R.	H.	E.
Queens	200	102	000	5	6	1
Pratt	100	000	001	2	8	3

Batteries: Ether and Locastro; Kirchdoefer and O'Connor.

Ruth Back From Miami, Too Tired for Interview

Babe Ruth, the ailing former home-run king, was too tired to talk with newsmen upon his return home today from a vacation in Miami, his second since he underwent a neck operation last February.

"Please, not now—I'm a little tired," he said as he entered his apartment building off Riverside Drive. The Babe's plane landed at the Newark Airport. With him were Mrs. Ruth, a nurse and Raymond Kilthau, who was his host at Miami.

Babe was garbed in his favorite manner. He wore a light camel hair peaked cap and a sport suit, a yellow sport shirt, brown and white shoes and carried a camel hair topcoat over his arm.

Cornell Defeats Yale, 2-1, After Losing 1st, 3-1

Turner Holds Blue to 3 Hits; Quinn Strikes Out 10 in Opening Contest

Special to the Herald Tribune

NEW HAVEN, Conn., May 23.—Yale and Cornell split an Eastern Intercollegiate League doubleheader today, 3 to 1 and 2 to 1, the Big Red taking the nightcap. Each contest was seven inings in duration.

Tom Turner silenced the Blue in the second game, spacing three hits, while his mates won the game by bunching a pair of hits with two passes for their runs in the third inning. Yale's run was driven in by Dick Mathews in the first frame.

The scores:

FIRST GAME

CORNELL	ab	r	h	po	a	YALE	ab	r	h	po	a
Arrison lf	4	0	1	2	0	Davis 2b	3	1	0	0	1
Tobey 2b	3	0	2	3	1	Moher ss	2	1	1	0	2
‡Hummer	1	0	0	0	0	Elwell lf	1	0	0	1	0
Dawson rf	3	0	1	1	0	Stanton lf	0	0	0	0	0
McArthur cf	3	0	0	1	0	Mathews 3b	3	0	0	0	1
Farrell c	3	1	1	2	0	Howe rf	3	0	0	0	0
Daukas 1b	2	0	0	5	2	Felske c	3	0	0	11	1
Cordes ss	2	0	0	1	5	Sulliman cf	1	0	1	1	1
Weintraub 3b	2	0	0	2	0	Rosensweig cf	1	0	1	0	0
*McAvoy	1	0	0	0	0	Bush 1b	2	0	0	8	1
Battles p	2	0	0	1	2	Quinn p	1	1	0	0	4
†Willner	0	0	0	0	0						
Totals	26	1	5	18	10	Totals	20	3	3	21	11

*Batted for Weintraub in seventh inning.
†Batted for Battles in seventh inning.
‡Batted for Tobey in seventh inning.

Cornell .... 000 100 0—1
Yale .... 000 120 x—3

Errors—Mathews, Davis, Daukas, Battles. Runs batted in—Howe, Elwell, Mathews. Three-base hit—Dawson. Sacrifices—Bush, Davis, Quinn. Left on bases—Cornell 7, Yale 7. Bases on balls—Battles 4, Quinn 3. Strikeouts—Battles 2, Quinn 10. Umpires—Roche and O'Rourke. Time—1:34.

SECOND GAME

YALE	ab	r	h	po	a	CORNELL	ab	r	h	po	a
Davis 2b	1	0	1	2	2	Arrison lf	3	0	1	1	0
Rosensweig cf	2	1	0	1	0	Tobey 2b	1	1	0	1	2
Howe rf	3	0	1	0	0	Dawson rf	2	0	1	1	0
Stanton lf	0	0	0	0	0	McArthur cf	3	0	1	2	0
Mathews ss	3	0	1	2	3	Tesnow c	1	0	0	3	1
Elwell lf-rf	3	0	0	1	0	Daukas 1b	3	0	0	9	0
Felske c	3	0	0	2	1	Codres ss	3	0	1	1	2
Bush 1b	2	0	0	10	0	Willner 3b	2	0	0	3	4
O'Brien 3b	2	0	0	0	1	Turner p	3	1	1	0	1
Goodyear p	1	0	0	0	3						
*Bracuaro	1	0	0	0	0						
Kemp p	0	0	0	0	0						
†Moher	1	0	0	0	0						
Totals	22	1	3	18	10	Totals	21	2	5	21	10

*Batted for Goodyear in fifth inning.
†Batted for Kemp in seventh inning.

Yale .... 100 000 0—1
Cornell .... 002 000 x—2

Runs batted in—Mathews, Dawson, McArthur. Two-base hit—Arrison. Stolen bases—Rosensweig, Bush. Sacrifices—Rosensweig, Tobey. Left on bases—Yale 6, Cornell 7. Bases on balls—Off Goodyear 3, Kemp 2, Turner 4. Strikeouts—By Goodyear 2, Turner 3. Hits—Off Goodyear, 5 in 4 innings; Kemp, 0 in 2. Wild pitches—Turner 2. Passed ball—Felske. Losing pitcher — Goodyear. Umpires — Roche and O'Rourke. Time—1:29.

Giants' Score

NEW YORK (N. L.)	ab	r	h	po	a	BOSTON (N. L.)	ab	r	h	po	a
Blattner 2b	3	1	2	3	3	Ryan 2b	3	0	0	4	2
Rigney 3b	2	1	1	3	0	Holmes rf	4	0	1	2	0
Thomson cf	5	2	1	1	0	Hopp cf	4	0	1	0	0
Mize 1b	4	2	1	7	2	R. Elliott 3b	4	0	1	2	6
Marshall rf	4	1	2	3	0	Rowell lf	4	0	0	2	0
Cooper c	5	0	2	5	0	Masi c	4	0	0	3	1
Gordon lf	5	0	1	1	0	Torgeson 1b	4	1	1	12	0
Kerr ss	5	0	1	1	4	Sisti ss	3	0	1	2	4
Jansen p	3	1	1	3	2	Johnson p	0	0	0	0	1
						Wright p	1	0	0	0	2
						*M. McCor'k	1	0	1	0	0
						Beazley p	0	0	0	0	0
						†Litwhiler	1	0	0	0	0
						G. Elliott p	0	0	0	0	0
Totals	36	8	12	27	11	Totals	33	1	6	27	16

*Batted for Wright in fifth and doubled.
†Batted for Beazley in seventh and struck out.

New York .... 006 020 000—8
Boston .... 001 000 000—1

Errors—Cooper, Rowell 2. Runs batted in—Mize 4, Thompson 2, Cooper 2. Two-base hit—Marshall, Holmes, M. McCormick. Home runs—Mize 4, Thomson 2, Cooper 2. Two-base hit—plays—Wright, Sisti and Torgeson; R. Elliott, Ryan and Torgeson. Left on bases—New York 9, Boston 6. Bases on balls—Off Jansen 1, Johnson 1, Wright 1, Beazley 2, G. Elliott 3. Strikeouts—By Jansen 5, Johnson 1, Beazley 1. Hits—Off Johnson, 5 in 2⅓ innings; Wright, 5 in 2⅔; Beazley, 0 in 2; G. Elliott, 2 in 2. Losing pitcher—Johnson. Umpires—Reardon, Goetz and Conlan. Time—2:00. Attendance—3,759.

Ch. Deep Haven Warspite Heads Scottish Terriers

Special to the Herald Tribune

WOODCLIFF LAKE, N. J., May 23.—Champion Deep Haven Warspite, Scottie owned by the Marlu Farm Kennels of Mr. and Mrs. Maurice Pollak, of West Long Branch, N. J., won his second best in show of 1947 when he topped forty-seven diehards at the Scottish Terrier Club of America summer specialty show today on the estate of Mr. and Mrs. Charles C. Stalter. The judge was P. K. Groves, retiring president of the Scottish Terrier Club of Chicago.

Best of opposite sex to Warspite was Shieling's Luminous, owned by Mr. and Mrs. T. H. Snethen, of Pittsburgh.

Winner's dog was the Pollasks' Marlu Milady's Beau with reserve going to the Snethens' Shieling's Playboy. Reserve winner's bitch was Mrs. John G. Winant's Edgerstone Orphan.

Ohrbach A. A. Enters Swim

The Ohrbach A. A., which has sponsored men's basketball and track teams, will enter the women's swimming field tomorrow in the first outdoor A. A. U. meet of the season at Raven Hall Bathing Park, Coney Island. The Union Square aggregation will be represented by Leilah MacRobert, daughter of the former Olympic champion, Ethelda Bleibtrey and Pat Wimans.

Major League Standings and Pitchers

SATURDAY, MAY 24, 1947

NATIONAL LEAGUE RESULTS YESTERDAY

New York, 8; Boston, 1
Brooklyn, 5; Philadelphia, 4 (night)
St. Louis, 2; Pittsburgh, 0 (night)
Cincinnati at Chicago, rain

STANDING OF THE CLUBS	New York	Chicago	Brooklyn	Boston	Pittsburgh	Phila.	Cincinnati	St. Louis	WON	LOST	Percentage	Gms behind
New York	—	3	2	3	1	0	2	5	16	11	.593	—
Chicago	0	—	2	0	1	5	5	4	17	12	.586	—
Brooklyn	2	3	—	3	1	5	0	2	16	13	.552	1
Boston	4	1	0	—	3	3	3	2	16	14	.533	1½
Pittsburgh	1	2	2	1	—	2	3	2	13	13	.500	2½
Philadelphia	3	0	3	3	0	—	4	2	15	17	.469	3½
Cincinnati	1	2	2	1	4	1	—	2	13	18	.419	5
St. Louis	0	1	2	3	3	1	1	—	11	19	.367	6½
Games lost	11	12	13	14	13	17	18	19	—	—		

AMERICAN LEAGUE RESULTS YESTERDAY

New York, 9; Boston, 0
Detroit, 5; Chicago, 2
*Washington at Philadelphia, night
*St. Louis at Cleveland, night

STANDING OF THE CLUBS	Detroit	Boston	Cleveland	New York	Chicago	Phila.	Washington	St. Louis	WON	LOST	Percentage	Gms behind
Detroit	—	2	2	1	5	4	2	2	18	11	.621	—
Boston	3	—		3	3	2	2	4	17	13	.567	1½
Cleveland	2	2	—	3	1		1	4	13	10	.565	2
New York	1	4		—	3	3	2	1	14	14	.500	3½
Chicago	2	0	2	3	—	2	5	2	16	16	.500	3½
Philadelphia	1	2	2	1	2	—	2	4	14	15	.483	[illegible]
Washington	0	1	3	2	0	3	—	2	11	15	.423	5½
St. Louis	2	2	1	1	2	1	1	—	10	19	.345	8
Games lost	11	13	10	14	16	15	15	19	—	—		

*Result not included in standing.

National League Games and Pitchers Today

New York (Kennedy, 3-2) at Boston (Spahn, 6-0), night.
Philadelphia (Rowe, 6-0) at Brooklyn (Gregg, 2-1), 2 p. m.
Cincinnati (Blackwell, 5-2) at Chicago (Wyse, 2-3)
Pittsburgh (Ostermuller, 3-1) at St. Louis (Dickson, 0-6, or Brazle, 1-2), night

American League Games and Pitchers Today

Boston (Ferriss, 2-3) at New York (Chandler, 2-3), 2 p. m.
Chicago (Grove, 3-1) at Detroit (Trout, 4-2)
Washington, Newsom, 1-2) at Philadelphia (Coleman, 0-2)
Other clubs not scheduled.

Results in Minor Leagues

International League

Last Night's Results

Baltimore, 10; Jersey City, 2.
Syracuse, 4; Newark, 3 (10 ins.).
Montreal, 13; Buffalo, 3.
Rochester, 8; Toronto, 6.

STANDING OF THE CLUBS

	W.	L.	Pct.		W.	L.	Pct.
Jersey City	18	11	.621	Rochester	15	15	.500
Montreal	15	10	.600	Baltimore	14	16	.467
Syracuse	12	10	.545	Buffalo	11	16	.407
Newark	15	13	.536	Toronto	10	19	.345

Eastern League

Last Night's Results

Scranton, 10; Elmira, 6.
Binghamton, 4; Albany, 3 (10 ins.).
Williamsport, 3; Wilkes-Barre, 2.
Hartford, 5; Utica, 4 (11 ins.).

Pacific Coast League

Thursday's Results

Seattle, 6; San Diego, 4.
Los Angeles, 7; Sacramento, 1
Oakland, 7; San Francisco, 1.
Hollywood, 7; Portland, 5.

Last Night's Games

All night games.

American Association

Thursday's Results

Toledo, 7; Indianapolis, 1 (1st).
Toledo, 7; Indianapolis, 6 (2d, 12 innings).
Columbus, 2; Louisville, 1.
Kansas City, 3; St. Paul, 0.
Minneapolis at Milwaukee, rain.

Last Night's Games

All night games.

Southern Association

Thursday's Results

Atlanta, 1; Mobile, 0 (1st, 10 innings).
Mobile, 6; Atlanta, 1 (2d).
Birmingham, 15; New Orleans, 7.
Little Rock, 7; Chattanooga, 5.
Nashvile, 9; Memphis, 8 (13 ins.).

Last Night's Games

All night games.

Texas League

Thursday's Results

Houston, 1; San Antonio, 0 (1st)
San Antonio, 2; Houston, 1 (2d).
Shreveport, 2; Beaumont, 0.
Dallas, 11; Tulsa, 9.

Last Night's Games

All night games.

The San Francisco News

U. S. WEATHER BUREAU FORECAST: Bay Area—Occasional cloudiness tonight and tomorrow; gentle westerly winds. (Complete forecast on Page 21.)

SCRIPPS-HOWARD — SUNSET — PRICE FIVE CENTS

Vol. 45 Entered as second class matter May 22, 1903, at San Francisco, California, under Act of Congress of March 3, 1879 — SAN FRANCISCO, WEDNESDAY, OCTOBER 1, 1947 — D* — No. 180

YANKEES RUN WILD-10-3

Power Attack Swamps Bums For 2nd Time

Jackie Robinson Stars in Defeat; 69,865 Attend

By Bud Spencer
The News Sports Editor

YANKEE STADIUM, Oct. 1.—A combination of New York extra-base power and high school defense by the collapsing Brooklyn Dodgers added up today to a 10-3 victory for the Yankees for their second straight in the Nickel World Series before a crowd of 69,865.

Lashing out with a 15-hit attack, including three triples to tie a Series record, the Yankees made it easy for Allie Reynolds, pitching his first game in the autumnal classic.

Spacing nine hits, Reynolds, victor in Yankee Stadium 13 out of 15 times during the regular season, had trouble only with Jackie Robinson. The California Comet belted a single and a double and drove home a Dodger run off the Indian righthander.

The Dodgers remained in contention for five innings when Tommy Henrich's towering home-run, the Yankees' first of the Series, gave the residents of the Stadium a 4-2 lead in the fifth.

After that, it was a deluge of runs off four Dodger hurlers, starting with little Vic Lombardi and continuing through Hal Gregg, Hank Behrman and Rex Barney.

YANKS SCORE IN FIRST

The Yanks scored a run in the opening inning—and then tallied in every other but two — when George Stirnweiss and Tommy Henrich singled and Stirnweiss got across while Johnny Lindell was grounding into a double play.

Robinson's single equalized the score in the third when he lashed across Pee Wee Reese, who had drawn a walk and stolen second base.

A pair of triples put the Yanks out in front again in their half of the third. Stirnweiss' line drive flicked Eddie Stanky's glove and rolled deep into the outfield and then Lindell drove a long smash that Pete Reiser failed to handle as Dodger fans booed.

The first circuit belt of the Series, by aging Dixie Walker, brought Dem Bums to 2-2 in the top of the fourth.

TIE BROKEN

Billy Johnson came across with the tie-breaking run in the third when he doubled to center and came home on a cheap double by Phil Rizzuto, which trickled through the "hole" over second base.

The losers made a feeble effort in the ninth to get one run when it was too late. Gene Hermanski walked, raced to third on Reese's single to left and dented the plate when Pinky Jorgensen was forcing Reese out at second.

It was a poor show all way 'round for the Bums, whose sandlot fielding drew raucuous boos.

Manager Bucky Harris has nominated Bobo Newsom as his starter tomorrow when the scene shifts to Ebbetts Field.

His rival, Bert Shotton, was silent, but it is expected he'll counter with Lefty Joe Hatten, an Alameda, Cal., youngster.

(Play by Play, Page 17)

—The News-Acme Radio-telephoto

Out at second is Tommy Henrich of the Yanks on a double-play grounder from the bat of Johnny Lindell in the first inning, as Dodger Ed Stanky completes the toss to first. Umpire is Larry Goetz.

WORLD SERIES BOX SCORE

BROOKLYN—NATIONAL

	AB	R	H	PO	A	E
Stanky,2b	4	0	1	3	2	1
Robinson,1b	4	0	2	5	0	0
Reiser,cf	4	0	1	4	0	1
Walker,rf	4	1	1	1	0	0
Hermanski,lf	3	1	0	3	0	0
Edwards,c	4	0	1	6	1	0
Reese,ss	3	1	2	0	0	0
Jorgensen,3b	4	0	1	2	5	0
Lombardi,p	2	0	0	0	0	0
Gregg,p	0	0	0	0	2	0
Behrman,p	0	0	0	0	0	0
Barney,p	0	0	0	0	0	0
aVaughan	1	0	0	0	0	0
bGinfriddo	1	0	0	0	0	0
Totals	34	3	9	24	10	2

a—Flied out for Gregg in 7th.
b—Forced Jorgensen for Barney in 9th.

NEW YORK—AMERICAN

	AB	R	H	PO	A	E
Stirnweiss,2b	4	2	3	1	2	0
Henrich,rf	4	1	2	3	0	0
Lindell,lf	4	1	2	2	0	0
Di Maggio,cf	4	0	1	4	0	0
McQuinn,1b	5	1	2	6	1	0
W. Johnson,3b	5	2	2	1	2	0
Rizzuto,ss	5	0	1	3	4	0
Berra,c	3	1	0	6	1	1
Reynolds,p	4	2	2	1	0	0
Totals	38	10	15	27	10	1

Score by innings:

Brooklyn (N) 001 100 001— 3 9 2
New York (A) 101 121 40x—10 15 1

Runs batted in: Robinson, Lindell 2, Walker, Rizzuto, Henrich, McQuinn, Reynolds, Johnson, Stirnweiss, Jorgensen. Two-base hits: Rizzuto, Lindell, Robinson. Three-base hits: Stirnweiss, Lindell, Johnson. Home runs: Walker, Henrich. Stolen base: Reese. Sacrifice: Henrich. Left on bases: Brooklyn 6, New York 9. Bases on balls: Off Lombardi 1, Reynolds 2, Gregg 1, Behrman 1, Barney 1. Struck out: By Lombardi 3, Reynolds 6, Gregg 2. Hits: Off Lombardi, 9 in 4 (none out in fifth); Gregg 2 in 2; Behrman 3 in 1-3; Barney 1 in 1 2-3. Wild pitches: Behrman, Barney. Double plays: Jorgensen to Stankey to Robinson, Stirnweiss to Rizzuto to McQuinn. Losing pitcher: Lombardi. Umpires: Pinelli (N.), plate; Rommel (A.), b; Goetz (N.), 2b; McGowan (A.) 3b; foul lines, Magerkurth (N.), Boyer (A.). Time: 2:36. Attendance: 69,865.

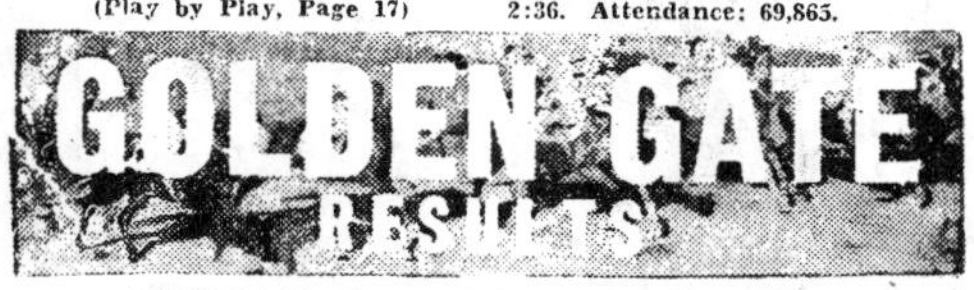

FIRST RACE—Dieppe, $10.30, $4.90, $3.40; Black Chip, $3.60, $2.70; Vain Brother, $4.50. Time—1:13.

SECOND RACE—Moon Dust, $3.80, $2.80, $2.40; Cotopaxi, $6.00, $4.10; Perfectora, $3.80. Time—1:13 4-5.

EASTERN RACE RESULTS

BELMONT—7th—Dockstader, $9.20, $4.70, $3.40; Buffet Supper, $7.30, $4.00; Sir Helix, $5.60. Time—1:45.

HAWTHORNE—4th—Big Casino, $4.60, $4.20, $3.00; Glider Pilot, $14.60, $8.40; Melba Ann, $4.80. Time—1:12 4-5.

NARRAGANSETT—7th—Forward March, $8.60, $4.00, $3.40; Turnabout, $4.20, $3.00; Samanad, $3.00. 1:45 2-5.

Army Transports In From Japan

Two Army transports arrived at Fort Mason from the Pacific today carrying 1306 troops and Army civilians. The U. S. A. T. Fred C. Ainsworth, out of Yokohama, docked at Pier 2 with 407 military and 101 civilians. The Admiral H. T. Mayo brought in 602 troops and 196 civilians from Yokohama and Hongkong.

Aboard the Ainsworth was the body of Maj. Gen. Archer L. Lerch of Oakland, who died Sept. 11 in Korea where he was American military governor.

Court Test Due In Pier Tieup

Court action was scheduled today in an attempt to end a shutdown of the Los Angeles-Long Beach harbor that posed the threat of a coast-wide shipping tieup.

Virtually all activity was halted in the big Southern California port at midnight by the Waterfront Employers Association in a move designed to end the C. I. O. walking bosses' eight-week strike for recognition of the International Longshoremen's & Warehousemen's Union as their bargaining agent.

The Marine Trade Association, an organization of harbor-district businessmen, said their attorney, Mose Lewis Jr., would file an injunction petition in Los Angeles Superior Court today to force the W. E. A. to call off the tieup, United Press reported.

Mr. Lewis said the suit would charge restraint of trade in a labor dispute under provisions of the Taft-Hartley Law.

The walking bosses' coast negotiating committee was to meet today in San Pedro to consider the situation. Harry Bridges, I. L. W. U. president, has charged any port shutdown would amount to cancellation of the coast longshore agreement.

The I. L. W. U. was silent on its strategy but Mr. Bridges' declaration raised the question of whether the union would invoke a previously announced "no contract, no work" policy.

Harbor operations were stopped

(Turn to Page 6, Column 4.)

Chinese Reds Lose Key Port

By United Press

NANKING, Oct. 1.—Chinese Nationalist land, sea and air forces captured the important Communist--held port of Chefoo on the Shantung peninsula today in a victory hailed as the greatest since fall of the one-time Communist capital of Yenan.

Announcement of Chefoo's capture was made here by General Teng Wen-Yi, Nationalist military spokesman. He said the 25th Nationalist Division under Lieut. Gen. Huang Po-Tao fought its way into the strategic port in the climax of a month-long drive up the Shantung peninsula.

Despte this huge success, the Nationalists admitted one column of the Communist New Fourth Army infiltrated deeply into Government territory south of the Lunghai Railway. The column reportedly reached Suhsien station on the Tientsin-Nanking Railway.

Meanwhile, Nationalist naval units entered the battle of Manchuria by shelling Communist forces which crossed the Peiping-Mukden Railway near the Pohai Gulf.

(Map on Page 2.)

Moslems Kill 2000 Refugees

By United Press

NEW DELHI, Oct. 1.—Reliable reports from Amritsar said today nearly 2000 non-Moslem refugees were killed Sept. 26 by Moslem raiders at Tandlianwala in the Pakistan Punjab. The reported mass slaughter was described as the greatest single incident since India was divided into Hindu and Moslem states.

U. S.-Russ Deadlock

By United Press

UNITED NATIONS HALL, Flushing, N. Y.—The United States and the Soviet Union today maintained a bitter deadlock over election of a successor to Poland on the United Nations Security Council and the Assembly failed in eighth and ninth tries to choose between India and Soviet Ukraine.

The Assembly members, locked in the all-out struggle between the United Nation's greatest powers, disclosed in the first ballots after an overnight recess that there had been no break on either side.

TWO MORE BALLOTS

The eighth ballot gave the Soviet Ukraine 31 votes and India 23—virtually the same division which prevailed throughout seven inconclusive ballots yesterday. The ninth ballot gave Ukraine 32 and India 24.

Overnight caucuses brought no change. The Latin Americans, who made a deal with Russia yesterday, were still voting for the most part with the Russians. They agreed to support the Ukraine in return for Russia's vote for Argentina which was elected to the council on the first ballot yesterday.

BIG ISSUE AT STAKE

The United States is trying to repudiate partially and indirectly the Stalin-Roosevelt secret Yalta Agreement which gave the Soviet Union three votes in the United Nations. It would deprive the Ukraine of the right to sit on the Security Council and, in this case, strip Russia of its lone supporter on that body.

Alarmed delegates sat helplessly and almost equally divided while the two giants hurtled head long at each other in a basic struggle over Poland's successor on the Security Council. Many feared it may destroy the United Nations as it now exists.

4000 Volunteers Seek $3,327,000 for Chest

Read editorial, 'We Must Not Fail Again,' and Rodger's cartoon on Page 14.

As of today, it's that time of year again when volunteer solicitors for the Community Chest, San Francisco's unified charity, start ringing doorbells and visiting business offices in a drive to obtain financing for a host of charitable activities for the next year.

Almost 4000 volunteer fund-raisers will sport the red feather, emblem of the chest, as they canvass the city for the more than 3¼ million dollars the chest estimates it will need.

STAGE FOR KICKOFF

Lotta's Fountain at Third and Market-sts was the stage for the campaign kickoff this year, with noon ceremonies today centered around a 30-foot red feather thermometer where the day-by-day progress of the drive will be recorded.

Mayor Roger D. Lapham officially dedicated the thermometer, remarking he was confident "that the residents of this community will give their wholehearted support to this drive."

"All will look forward to seeing the thermometer registering constantly increasing receipts from day to day until the quota is exceeded within the period of this Community Chest drive," the mayor said.

Present at the ceremony were Francis S. Baer, Bank of America vice president and campaign chairman; Harold Winey, Chest executive director, and A. Crawford Greene, president of the San Francisco Community Chest.

The actual goal for this year—$3,327,000—represents the absolute minimum on which the chest estimates its agencies can operate for the coming year.

SERIOUS SITUATION

Chest spokesmen are serious about this. They're faced this year with a tough situation, and to understand their problem, a glance at the nature of the chest and the conditions under which it's now operating is necessary.

The first thing to remember about the Community Chest is that it's not a charitable welfare agency.

It doesn't feed any hungry people. It doesn't rehabilitate any juvenile delinquents. It doesn't find any homes for unwanted children whose parents neglected

(Turn to Page 8, Column 2.)

'Save Food, Cut Prices'--Truman

—The News-Acme Radio-telephoto

Snuffy Stirnweiss slides safely into third, beating the throw to Johnny Jorgensen. Stirnweiss later scored the Yanks' first run in the opening stanza.

S. F. Bars, Builders Protest Sales Tax.

The liquor and building industries protested against the ½ per cent city sales tax at City Hall today as retailers began collecting the new municipal levy with little incident.

Frank E. Tracy, representing the California Federated Institute, a liquor industry organization, declared the decision of Tax Collector Edward F. Bryant to collect the levy on 20 per cent of the gross revenue of bars was "too high."

Liquor itself is exempt from the city tax, being regulated solely by the State and Federal Governments, but mix and non-alcoholic beverages—to say nothing of the cherries, oranges and lemons which go into drinks—are subject to the levy.

HELD ARBITRARY

Mr. Bryant's assumption that non-alcoholic material sold at bars accounted for a fifth of the take was "arbitrary" and contrary to the established practice in Oakland, where a municipal sales tax has been collected for a year, Mr. Tracy said. The Oakland tax collector, he said, assesses the sales levy against only 2 per cent of a tavern's income.

Milton Morris, secretary of the Associated Home Builders, asked that materials used in home construction be exempted from the city sales tax because, when completed, the structures become "real property"—in which form they are exempt from the levy. If building materials are taxed, he warned, the charge will be passd along to the buyer, further increasing the cost of new homes and accentuating the current housing shortage

Both protests were taken under advisement by the three-man board of sales tax review, consisting of Chief Administrative Officer Thomas A. Brooks, Controller Harry Ross, and Assessor Russell Wolden.

UNIFORM POLICY

J. F. Carey, Oakland city treasurer, suggested officials of other Bay Area communities with municipal sales taxes sit with the review board at its twice monthly meetings "with a view to keeping administration and policy uniform."

The San Francisco impost officially went into effect at 12:01 a. m., when merchants added ½ per cent charge to the 2½ per cent

(Turn to Page 6, Column 3)

Railroad Workers Ask 30% Raises

By United Press

CHICAGO, Oct. 1.—Spokesmen for five unions representing 300,000 operating railroad employes said today negotiations with representatives of the nation's railroads for a proposed 30 per cent wage increase would begin next Tuesday.

The brotherhoods served the demands yesterday.

The wage demand would include a minimum increase of $3 per day. Spokesmen for the railroads said the increase would add 400 million dollars annually to rail transportation costs, and said a demand for changes in 44 working rules would cost an additional one billion dollars.

'A Little Rain' Coming—Maybe

A cautious Weather Man looking around to make sure his colleagues weren't listening, said softly out of the side of his mouth today that the Bay Area "might possibly" get a little rain tomorrow evening.

He didn't include the information in his official forecast, though, which said we would have occasional cloudiness today, tonight and tomorrow, with some increase in temperature, and gentle westerly winds.

More Grain for Europe Asked by President

How Much Food Have YOU Saved Today?

REDUCE THAT WASTE-LINE

Now Tell Us, Mr. Truman, How to Do It!

If the average San Franciscan thinks he can comply with President Truman's plea to "save a bushel of grain" within the next few months by eating less bread, cake and pastry, he's sadly mistaken, a survey by The News indicated today.

Here's why: The average person won't consume one bushel of wheat between now and January 1, much less be able to save a bushel.

The average person eats 161 pounds of flour a year, or about 40 pounds every three months.

MORE THAN HE EATS

A 60-pound bushel of wheat produces 45 pounds of flour, and 15 pounds of mill run which could be used, for example, as cattle feed.

Thus, in order to save that bushel of wheat between now and the New Year, the average person would have to eliminate 45 pounds of flour from his diet for the next three months — five pounds more than he eats.

So saving on wheat products alone won't do the job. Mr. San Francisco will have to cut down on corn and its by-products, on rice, macaroni, spaghetti, on rye products, on barley products, on alcohol, on poultry, on eggs, and on meat.

However, Mrs. San Francisco can do her bit, a home economist pointed out, by seeing she tosses no bread, cake and grain products into the garbage can. Make good cake, is the advice, so the family won't refuse it. Serve moderate helpings so some won't be left on the plate. Use leftover hot cereals as fried cakes the next day and breadcrumbs for casserole toppings and for puddings.

MORE GRAIN, LESS MEAT!

As a matter of fact, home economists say the best way to save grain is to eat more actual grain and less items like meat, eggs and poultry, because one pound of grain eaten directly provides a higher caloric and protein content than a pound of beef from a steer fed on grain, or a pound of eggs produced by chickens fed on grain.

It all boils down to this: Mr. San Francisco is going to have to tighten his belt if he wants to feed the starving of the world. And, everything indicates, doing so won't hurt him much — for he already eats more than any one else in any other country.

Old H.C.L. Hits Where It Hurts!

The price of ice cream went up all over town today, following a wholesale price boost of from 15c to 20c a gallon. Dealers added a nickel to the retail price of both pints and quarts. Milkshakes went up 5c in many fountains.

Some ice cream lovers received the news in a cold silence. Others made melting pleas that prices be kept frozen at present levels. Kids, fearing the coming of the 10c ice cream cone, referred bitterly to the high cost of licking.

A few creameries raised their retail prices yesterday.

Inside The News

Text of President Truman's statement on Page 7.

By United Press

WASHINGTON, Oct. 1.—President Truman, calling on the nation to save at least 100 million bushels of grain by wasting less, said today "We must get prices down and help hungry people in other countries at the same time."

He spoke to the first session of the Citizens Food Committee, which met at the White House to plan voluntary food conservation measures.

Mr. Truman pointed out the saving asked of each individual was actually very small.

"One bushel of grain saved by every American in the next few months will do the job," he said.

FEARS HIGH PRICES

Mr. Truman was critical of the continuing effects of increasing prices, saying:

"Failure to check price increases promptly will not only lower the American living standard, but could impair the confidence of business, and thus jeopardize the splendid record we have achieved in the maintenance of high employment, high production and general prosperity."

At the same time, Mr. Truman sent identical letters to the chairmen of the House and Senate foreign relations and appropriations committees, emphasizing "the Congress will soon be called upon to consider the part which the United States should play" in the general economic program for recovery of Europe.

He did not amplify this to say whether this meant he would call a special session.

Mr. Truman estimated 10 per cent of the food purchased by Americans is wasted.

'HELP SIGNIFICANTLY'

"Clearly, by wasting less, American families can help significantly in feeding hungry families abroad," he said. "In addition to cutting down waste, Americans can save by being more selective in the foods they buy."

The President said that under present conditions about 470 million

(Turn to page 7. Column 3)

'Housing Foes Working Fast'

Prediction that public housing opponents would fight to discourage it before the next Congress by making municipal participation in housing programs more costly was voiced here today by Lee Johnson, executive vice president of the National Housing Conference.

At a Women's City Club luncheon meeting of civic groups interested in housing, Mr. Johnson said this opposition probably would demand that cities, which now participate financially in such programs by waiving taxes on housing developments, be forced to contribute more such concessions plus cash.

As far as housing is concerned, the veteran of World War II "is already a forgotten man" in the eyes of Congress, along with "all persons of minor economic status," he declared.

He described as a "complete failure" the recently enacted McCarthy bill, under which housing projects stopped by rising costs, such as the proposed Chinatown project in San Francisco, could be completed through financial assistance from the cities.

Like San Francisco, which has pigeonholed the Chinatown proposal, all other American cities involved have failed to put up the necessary money, Mr. Johnson said.

Young Speeder Gets 6 Months

Arthur E. Pacheco, 19, of 8 North Grant-st, San Mateo, was fined $500 and sentenced to six months in the San Mateo County Jail today by Judge Francis Murphy for speeding at 70 miles an hour on the Bayshore highway. It was his fourth traffic offense in the year.

Raymond W. Lefler, a Greyhound bus driver, was sentenced to five days after a jury convicted him of violating a new state law prohibiting passing on the shoulder of a highway.

Yankees Edge Tigers, 6-5; Giants Down Cardinals, 7-5, in 11th; Dodgers Split

Detroit Loses 9th in Row, Page Saves Game in Ninth

Relief for Drews Fans Mullin With Two Out and Tying Run on First; Berra Hits Homer With 3 On; Johnson's Single in Fifth Nets Victory

By Rud Rennie

With an attack as unexpected and startling as if an order of sirloin steak were suddenly to start singing "Home on the Range," the bedraggled Detroit Tigers made two runs with two out in the ninth in the Stadium yesterday and had the tying run on first.

Those in the crowd of 53,765 persons present who were moving toward the exits stopped and came back to see what was the matter. They saw Karl Drews, who had done such a fine job of relief pitching for eight innings, walking dejectedly off the mound and Joe Page, the Yankees' answer to a manager's prayer, coming in from the bull pen to face Pat Mullin.

Page fanned the Detroit slugger, whizzing a third strike past him and ending the suspense and the game.

The Yankees won, 6 to 5, sweeping the four-game series and improving their position at the top of the league. They have now won four straight and eight of their last nine games.

The poor Tigers, on the other hand, have lost nine in a row. On their current road trip they have lost all eight games played. And they have won only one game in their last twelve.

Gumpert Blasted Early

The Yankees started Randy Gumpert. It was his second start. He fanned two in the first inning, but he could not get the third man out.

Roy Cullenbine and Vic Wertz hit him for singles. Then, with two away, Doc Cramer tripled and George Kell singled, making three runs, and Eddie Mayo singled and Bob Swift walked, filling the bases.

It was then that Drews, a Staten Islander, was brought in. He got the next man out and ended the inning. The Yankees then belted Al Benton for five runs in their half, and Drews went on from there and, with the aid of flashy fielding by Phil Rizzuto, George Stirnweiss and George McQuinn, blanked the Tigers with two hits until the ninth.

Joe DiMaggio knocked in one run with a double in that lusty half of the first Yankee inning, and Yogi Berra came up with two out and the bases loaded and banged a grand-slam homer into the right-field stands.

Tigers Rally in Ninth

McQuinn tripled and scored on a single by Bill Johnson in the fifth. The Yankees got nothing off Johnny Gorsica in their last three turns. So the game went into the ninth inning with the Yankees leading, 6 to 3, and nobody worrying about Drews' ability to keep everything under control.

Drews fanned Swift and Johnny McHale, a pinch hitter for Gorsica. He needed only one more out to complete a nice, orderly job.

Dick Wakefield, limping on a sprained ankle, was sent to bat for Eddie Lake. It looked like a forlorn gesture. But it was electric. Wakefield singled to left and hobbled to first and Skeeter Webb was sent to run for him.

Page Saves Game

Cullenbine, the next hitter, blasted a home run into the right-field stands. The crowd woke up with a roar and looked at their score cards and at the scoreboard. With a tingle, they realized that the Tigers needed only one more run to tie. And that run was on base a moment later when Drews walked Wertz. Jimmy Outlaw was sent to run for Wertz and Pat Mullin was the next hitter.

A roar of approval went up when Page was announced as the incoming pitcher. And another roar went up when he struck Mullin out, putting the Tigers back in their cages for shipment to Boston, their next stop.

Home Fans Honor Shea

In appreciation of Frank Shea's excellent work in his first year as regular Yankee, 7,500 home-town fans from Naugatuck, Conn., came to the stadium and presented an automobile and a gold watch to him. . . . Berra's grand-slam homer was the second such to be made by a Yankee this year. . . . Di Maggio hit the other one in Cleveland, June 1. . . . A delegation from Minooka, Pa., gave Steve O'Neil, the Detroit manager, tokens of their affection.

FOUR-RUN BLOW: Berra crossing the plate after hitting homer

Yankees' Score

* * *

DETROIT (A. L.)	ab	r	h	po	a
Lake ss	3	0	0	1	4
‡Wakefield	1	0	1	0	0
§Webb	0	1	0	0	0
Cullenbine 1b	4	2	2	8	0
Wertz lf	4	1	1	2	0
¶Outlaw	0	0	0	0	0
Mullin rf	5	0	1	3	0
Cramer cf	4	1	2	3	0
Kell 3b	3	0	1	1	4
Mayo 2b	4	0	1	4	1
Swift c	3	0	0	2	1
Benton p	2	0	0	0	1
*Hutchinson	1	0	0	0	0
Gorsica p	0	0	0	0	1
†McHale	1	0	0	0	0
Totals	35	5	9	24	12

NEW YORK (A. L.)	ab	r	h	po	a
Stirnweiss 2b	3	0	0	0	2
Henrich rf	3	1	0	1	0
Lindell lf	4	1	3	2	0
DiMaggio cf	4	1	2	2	0
McQuinn 1b	3	2	1	12	1
W.Johnson 3b	4	0	1	0	3
Berra c	4	1	1	7	0
Rizzuto ss	4	0	1	3	5
Gumpert p	0	0	0	0	0
Drews p	4	0	0	0	1
Page p	0	0	0	0	0
Totals	33	6	9	27	12

*Batted for Benton and grounded out in 6th.
†Batted for Gorsica and fanned in 9th.
‡Batted for Lake and singled in 9th.
§Ran for Wakefield in 9th.
¶Ran for Wertz in 9th.

Detroit .... 300 000 002—5
New York .... 500 010 00x—6

Errors—Cullenbine, McQuinn, Swift. Runs batted in—Cramer 2, Kell, DiMaggio, Berra 4, W. Johnson, Cullenbine 2. Two-base hit—DiMaggio. Three-base hits—Cramer, McQuinn. Home runs—Berra, Cullenbine. Stolen base—Rizzuto. Double plays—McQuinn, Rizzuto and McQuinn; Mayo and Cullenbine; Stirnweiss, Rizzuto and McQuinn. Left on bases—Detroit 8; New York 6. Bases on balls—Gumpert 1, Benton 3, Drews 4. Strikeouts—Gumpert 2, Page 1, Benton 2, Drews 3. Hits—Gumpert 5 in ⅔; Drews 4 in 8; Page 0 in ⅓; Benton 7 in 5; Gorsica 2 in 3. Winning pitcher—Drews. Losing pitcher—Benton. Umpires—McGowan, Grieve, McKinley and Jones. Time—1:58. Attendance—53,765 paid.

Phils Down Pirates, 4-3; Second Game Is Called

PITTSBURGH, June 22 (AP).—The battle of the last-placers—Philadelphia and Pittsburgh—wound up after seventeen innings today with the Pirates more firmly entrenched in the National League cellar. The Phillies took the first game, 4 to 3, in thirteen innings. The nightcap was called at the end of the fourth by a Sunday curfew, with the Phils leading, 8 to 6. The score:

PHILADELPHIA (N.L.)	ab	r	h	po	a
Newsome ss	5	0	1	3	2
Gilbert lf	7	0	1	3	0
Walker cf	6	0	2	1	0
Tabor 3b	5	1	1	1	4
Adams rf	6	1	1	3	0
Lakeman c-1b	5	0	0	8	2
Schultz 1b	6	1	4	15	1
‡Albright	0	0	0	0	0
Mauney p	0	0	0	0	1
Verban 2b	4	0	2	5	5
Hughes p	2	0	0	0	1
*Padgett	1	0	0	0	0
Donnelly p	0	0	0	0	0
†Handley	1	0	0	0	0
Schmidt p	0	0	0	0	0
Judd p	0	0	0	0	0
Jurisich p	0	0	0	0	0
Seminick c	1	1	1	0	0
Totals	49	4	13	39	16

PITTSBURGH (N. L.)	ab	r	h	po	a
Rikard rf	2	1	1	2	0
¶Wietelmann	1	0	0	0	0
Higbe p	0	0	0	1	0
Herman 2b	5	0	1	2	1
Basinski 2b	1	0	0	1	1
Gustine 3b	5	1	2	2	7
Kiner lf	4	0	0	2	0
Cox ss	4	0	0	2	4
Fletcher 1b	5	0	1	14	3
Westlake cf	4	0	0	4	0
Howell c	3	1	3	8	0
Bahr p	2	0	0	1	0
Roe p	0	0	0	0	0
§Sullivan	1	0	0	0	0
Strincevich p	0	0	0	0	0
Russell rf	2	0	0	0	0
Totals	39	3	8	39	16

*Batted for Hughes in 9th.
†Batted for Donnelly in 11th.
‡Ran for Schultz in 13th.
§Batted for Roe in 7th.
¶Batted for Rikard in 11th.

Philadelphia ..... 010 002 000 000 1—4
Pittsburgh .... 100 000 110 000 0—3

Error—Kiner. Runs batted in—Cox, Schultz, Verban, Newsome 2, Rikard, Fletcher. Two-base hits—Howell 2, Adams, Fletcher. Sacrifices—Gustine, Strincevich, Westlake, Verban, Howell. Double plays—Verban, Newsome and Schultz; Basinski, Cox and Fletcher; Verban and Lakeman. Left on bases—Philadelphia 13, Pittsburgh 12. Bases on balls—Hughes 5, Bahr 5, Donnelly 1, Schmidt 2, Higbe 1, Jurisich 2, Mauney 1. Strikeouts—Bahr 4, Hughes 2, Roe 2, Judd 1, Higbe 1, Jurisich 1. Hits—Off Bahr 6 in 5⅔ innings; Strincevich 2 in 4; Donnelly 1 in 2; Judd 0 in ⅔; Mauney 0 in 1; Roe 0 in 1⅓; Hughes 7 in 8; Schmidt 0 in ⅓; Higbe 5 in 2; Jurisich 0 in 1. Winning pitcher—Jurisich. Losing pitcher—Higbe. Umpires—Barlick, Gore and Pinelli. Time—3:44.

Herald Tribune—Rice

RUN DOWN: Rizzuto, of Yankees, is tagged out by Kell, third baseman, after being trapped between home and third in the sixth inning at Yankee Stadium yesterday

Senators Beat Browns, 3 to 2, Then Lose, 9 to 6

St. Louis Snaps 8-Game Losing Streak by 11-Hit Onslaught in Nightcap

WASHINGTON, June 22 (AP).—The St. Louis Browns battered five Washington pitchers for eleven hits and won the second game of a double-header, 9 to 6, today, snapping an eight-game losing streak. Washington won the first game, 3 to 2, before a crowd of 21,863.

Bob Dillinger, with two doubles and a single, sparked the Browns' attack in the nightcap as Sam Zoldak, who was replaced by Ellis Kinder in the eighth, won his first game of the season.

The Browns blasted Sid Hudson for four runs in the third inning when Dillinger doubled with the bases loaded, scoring two runs. The scores:

FIRST GAME

ST. LOUIS (A. L.)	ab	r	h	po	a
Dillinger 3b	4	0	1	1	4
Zarilla rf	3	1	1	1	0
Lehner cf	4	0	1	4	0
Heath lf	3	1	1	2	0
Stephens ss	4	0	0	3	1
Judnich 1b	4	0	2	8	1
Hitchcock 2b	4	0	2	3	2
Moss c	4	0	1	1	1
Kramer p	3	0	0	1	3
*Schultz	1	0	0	0	0
Totals	34	2	9	24	12

WASHINGTON (A. L.)	ab	r	h	po	a
Yost 3b	2	0	2	0	0
Case lf	3	0	0	4	0
Lewis rf	3	0	0	1	0
Vernon 1b	2	1	0	7	0
Spence cf	3	1	1	6	0
Priddy 2b	3	1	1	1	3
Christman ss	3	0	1	2	2
Evans c	3	0	0	6	0
Newsom p	2	0	0	0	0
Ferrick p	1	0	1	0	2
Totals	25	3	6	27	7

*Batted for Kramer and fouled out in ninth.

St. Louis .... 001 001 000—2
Washington .... 030 000 00x—3

Error—Spence. Runs batted in—Priddy, Christman 2, Heath, Hitchcock. Two-base hits—Priddy, Heath. Three-base hit—Moss. Stolen base—Zarilla. Sacrifices—Case, Yost. Double plays—Stephens (unassisted); Priddy, Christman and Vernon; Hitchcock and Judnich; Christman, Priddy and Vernon; Dillinger, Hitchcock and Judnich. Left on bases—St. Louis 7, Washington 3. Bases on balls—Kramer 3, Newsom 2. Strikeouts—Newsom 4, Kramer 2, Ferrick 1. Hits—Newsom 8 in 5⅓ innings; Ferrick 1 in 3⅔. Winning pitcher—Newsom. Umpires—Rue, Paparella and Summers. Time—1:51.

SECOND GAME

ST. LOUIS (A. L.)	ab	r	h	po	a
Dillinger 3b	5	2	3	1	2
Coleman rf	5	0	1	4	0
Heath lf	3	2	1	3	0
Stephens ss	4	2	2	2	4
Judnich 1b	4	0	0	6	0
Zarilla cf	3	0	0	2	0
Hitchcock 2b	5	1	2	3	1
Early c	5	1	1	5	0
Zoldak p	4	1	1	1	1
Kinder p	1	0	0	0	0
Totals	39	9	11	27	8

WASHINGTON (A. L.)	ab	r	h	po	a
Yost 3b	4	0	0	1	1
Travis 3b	1	0	0	0	0
Case rf	3	0	0	2	0
Vernon 1b	5	1	1	8	1
McBride lf	4	1	1	2	0
Spence cf	4	1	1	4	0
Priddy 2b	2	2	1	1	3
Christman ss	4	1	1	3	3
Ferrell c	3	0	2	6	0
Hudson p	2	0	1	0	0
Scarbor'gh p	0	0	0	0	1
Pieretti p	0	0	0	0	0
Cary p	0	0	0	0	1
Candini p	0	0	0	0	0
*Mancuso	1	0	0	0	0
†Evans	1	0	1	0	0
‡Lewis	1	0	0	0	0
§Grace	1	0	0	0	0
Totals	36	6	9	27	10

*Batted for Scarborough in sixth.
†Batted for Cary in eighth.
‡Batted for Case in ninth.
§Batted for McBride in ninth.

St. Louis .... 004 002 102—9
Washington .... 000 201 021—6

Errors—Vernon 2, Stephens, Christman. Runs batted in—Dillinger 2, Coleman 2, Ferrell 3, Stephens, Heath, Hitchcock 2, Evans 2, Zarilla, Grace. Two-base hits—Dillinger 2, Ferrell, Stephens 2. Three-base hit—Vernon. Double play—Christman (unassisted). Left on bases—St. Louis 9, Washington 8. Bases on balls—Zoldak 5, Hudson 1, Pieretti 1, Cary 1, Candini 3. Strikeouts—Hudson 2, Zoldak 2, Cary 1, Kinder 2, Candini 1. Hits—Off Zoldak, 8 in 7⅔; Kinder, 1 in 1⅓; Hudson, 7 in 5⅓; Scarborough, 0 in ⅔; Pieretti, 2 in ⅓; Cary, 1 in 1⅔; Candini, 1 in 1. Passed ball—Ferrell. Winning pitcher—Zoldak. Losing pitcher—Hudson. Umpires—Paparella, Summers and Rue. Tmie—2:32. Attendance—21,863.

Leading Five Batsmen In Each Major League

American League

Player and club	G	AB	R	H	Pct.
Boudreau, Cleveland	50	178	27	61	
McQuinn, New York	56	207	30		
Kell, Detroit	54	204	19		
Spence, Washington	50	166	21	55	
DiMaggio, New York	56	213	39	70	

National League

Player and club	G	AB	R	H	Pct.
Slaughter, St. Louis	57	204	30	70	
Walker, Philadelphia	56	202	26		
Haas, Cincinnati	54	211	31	71	
Elliott, Boston	55	198	31	65	
Furillo, Brooklyn	39	123	16	40	

Runs Batted In		Home Runs	
Mize, Giants	49	Mize, Giants	
Marshall, Giants	46	Keller, Yankees	
W. Cooper, Giants	45	Kiner, Pirates	
Torgeson, Braves	45	Marshall, Giants	
Elliott, Braves	43	Williams, Red Sox	
		Miller, Reds	

Athletics Blank White Sox, 3-0, After Losing, 1-0

First Decided on Unearned Run in Tenth; Scheib Pitches 4-Hit Nightcap

PHILADELPHIA, June 22 (AP)—Carl Scheib, the Philadelphia Athletics' twenty-year-old pitcher, won his third successive start and chalked up his second shutout today, defeating the Chicago White Sox, 3 to 0, in the second game of a double-header after the A's had lost the opener on an unearned run in the tenth inning, 1 to 0. A crowd of 28,852 saw Scheib limit the Sox to four hits.

Bob Gillespie won his fifth game against one loss in the first game. The Chicago run came on Eddie Joost's overthrow on an attempted double play which permitted Bob Kennedy to score from second base. Jesse Flores was the loser.

The scores:

FIRST GAME

CHICAGO (A. L.)	ab	r	h	po	a
Baker 3b	5	0	2	1	3
Philley cf	4	0	1	4	0
Appling ss	4	0	1	1	6
Wallaesa lf	4	0	0	4	0
York 1b	4	0	0	13	0
Kennedy rf	4	1	1	3	1
Michaels 2b	3	0	2	2	4
Dickey c	4	0	1	2	0
Gillespie p	3	0	0	0	1
*Wright	1	0	0	0	0
Caldwell p	0	0	0	0	0
Totals	36	1	8	30	15

PHILADELPHIA (A.L.)	ab	r	h	po	a
Joost ss	5	0	0	3	[illegible]
McCosky lf	5	0	1	5	0
Valo rf	3	0	0	3	0
Adams 1b	4	0	2	11	0
Chapman cf	3	0	2	3	0
Guerra c	4	0	0	5	3
Suder 2b	4	0	0	0	3
Majeski 3b	4	0	1	0	2
Flores p	3	0	1	0	0
†Fain	1	0	0	0	0
Totals	36	0	7	30	9

*Batted for Gillespie and forced Dickey in tenth.
†Batted for Flores and struck out in tenth.

Chicago .... 000 000 000 1—1
Philadelphia .... 000 000 000 0—0

Errors—Joost. Majeski. Runs batted in—Kennedy scored on Joost's error. Two-base hit—Michaels. Double plays—Adams (unassisted); Kennedy and York. Stolen base—Appling. Left on bases—Chicago 6, Philadelphia 8. Base on balls—Flores 1, Gillespie 2. Strikeouts—Flores 3, Gillespie 1, Caldwell 1. Hits—Gillespie 6 in 9 innings; Caldwell 1 in 1. Winning pitcher—Gillespie. Losing pitcher—Flores. Umpires—Hubbard, Berry, Weafer and Hurley. Time—2:04.

SECOND GAME

CHICAGO (A. L.)	ab	r	h	po	a
Baker 3b	4	0	1	0	6
Philley cf	4	0	0	2	0
Appling ss	4	0	0	1	1
Wallaesa lf	2	0	1	9	0
York 1b	3	0	0	8	1
Kennedy rf	2	0	1	0	0
Michaels 2b	3	0	0	2	3
Tresh c	2	0	1	1	0
Dickey c	1	0	0	0	0
Haynes p	1	0	0	0	0
Harrist p	1	0	0	1	0
*Tucker p	1	0	0	0	0
Rigney p	0	0	0	0	0
Totals	29	0	4	24	11

PHILADELPHIA (A.L.)	ab	r	h	po	a
Joost ss	4	0	0	3	6
McCosky lf	4	0	1	6	0
Valo rf	3	0	1	2	0
Adams 1b	4	0	0	11	0
Chapman cf	3	2	2	1	0
Rosar c	3	1	0	2	0
Suder 2b	3	0	1	2	3
Majeski 3b	3	0	1	0	2
Scheib p	3	0	0	0	0
Totals	30	3	6	27	11

*Batted for Harrist in eighth inning.

Chicago .... 000 000 000—0
Philadelphia .... 000 100 20x—3

Error—Appling. Runs batted in—Suder, Majeski (Chapman scored on wild pitch). Two-base hits—Wallaesa, Majeski. Three-base hit—Chapman. Stolen base—Valo. Double plays—Suder, Joost and Adams; Baker, Michaels and York; Majeski, Suder and Adams. Left on bases—Chicago 3, Philadelphia 5. Bases on balls—Off Scheib 1, Harrist 1, Rigney 1. Struck out—By Scheib 2, Harrist 1. Hits—Off Haynes, 3 in 3 innings; Harrist, 3 in 4; Rigney, 0 in 1. Wild pitch—Harrist. Losing pitcher—Harrist. Time—1:36. Umpires—Berry, Weafer, Hurley and Hubbard. Attendance—28,852.

Indians Down Red Sox, 8 to 2, Lose 2d, 6 to 3

34,863 Crowd Sets Mark for 3-Day 4-Game Series, Boosts Total to 100,274

BOSTON, June 22 (AP).—Before the season's largest crowd at Fenway Park, 34,863 paid, the second-place Red Sox and the Cleveland Indians today divided a double-header, the Indians taking the opener, 8 to 2, behind Mel Harder and the defending American League champions winning the second contest, 6 to 3, in back of Larry (Fritz) Dorish.

The three-day, four game series between the two clubs attracted a total of 100,274 cash customers, a record for such a set of games. The previous high was 93,233 who paid to see the New York Yankees here last August in a similar four game battle on three days.

Cleveland's Joe Gordon hit his eleventh home run of the season in the seventh inning, equaling his total output of four baggers in 1946. The scores:

FIRST GAME

CLEVELAND (A. L.)	ab	r	h	po	a
Peck rf	4	1	2	3	0
Keltner 3b	4	1	1	1	4
Edwards lf	4	1	2	2	0
Seerey lf	1	0	0	0	0
Boudreau ss	4	1	1	2	2
Conway ss	1	0	0	1	2
Gordon 2b	5	2	3	0	4
Fleming 1b	4	0	2	7	0
Robinson 1b	1	0	0	5	1
Metkovich cf	4	1	2	3	0
Hegan c	3	0	1	3	0
Harder p	2	1	0	0	0
Totals	37	8	14	27	13

BOSTON (A. L.)	ab	r	h	po	a
Gutt'ge 3b-2b	3	0	0	2	1
Pesky ss	4	0	1	1	2
Moses rf	4	0	1	3	0
Williams lf	3	0	0	4	0
Mele cf	4	0	1	2	0
Doerr 2b	3	1	1	4	3
Russell 3b	1	0	1	1	0
Jones 1b	4	1	1	4	0
Tebbetts c	3	0	0	5	1
Aulds c	1	0	0	1	0
Ferriss p	1	0	0	0	0
Zuber p	1	0	1	0	0
Parnell p	0	0	0	0	0
*DiMaggio	1	0	0	0	0
Murphy p	0	0	0	0	1
Totals	33	2	7	27	8

*Batted for Parnell in seventh.

Cleveland .... 112 100 300—8
Boston .... 000 000 200—2

Errors—Fleming 1, Gutteridge 1. Runs batted in—Edwards 3, Metkovich, Gordon 2, Boudreau, Peck, Jones, DiMaggio. Two-base hit—Peck. Three-base hit—Keltner, Jones. Home run—Gordon. Stolen base—Metkovich. Sacrifice—Harder. Double plays—Boudreau and Fleming; Doerr and Jones; Pesky, Doerr and Jones; Tebbetts and Doerr. Left on bases—Cleveland 7, Boston 6. Bases on balls—Harder 2, Ferriss 1, Zuber 2, Murphy 1. Strikeouts—Harder 3, Ferriss 1, Zuber 4. Hits—Ferriss 5 in 3 innings, Zuber 7 in 3⅔, Parnell 1 in ⅓, Murphy 1 in 2. Losing pitcher—Ferriss. Umpires—Boyer, Rommel and Passarella. Time—2:10.

SECOND GAME

CLEVELAND (A. L.)	ab	r	h	po	a
Peck rf	5	0	1	1	0
Keltner 3b	5	0	0	0	2
Seerey lf	4	1	1	1	0
Boudreau ss	4	0	1	1	8
Gordon 2b	4	1	0	6	2
Fleming 1b	4	0	1	10	1
Metkovich cf	4	0	1	1	0
Hegan c	4	1	2	4	1
Embree p	1	0	0	0	0
Lemon p	1	0	0	0	0
Gromek p	0	0	0	0	0
*Mitchell	1	0	1	0	0
Klieman p	0	0	0	0	0
†Robinson	0	0	0	0	0
Totals	37	3	8	24	14

BOSTON (A. L.)	ab	r	h	po	a
Gutteridge 3b	4	1	0	1	0
Pesky ss	5	1	3	1	4
Williams lf	3	1	1	5	0
Mele rf	3	1	0	1	0
Doerr 2b	3	0	2	2	7
DiMaggio cf	4	0	1	3	0
Jones 1b	4	0	1	11	0
Partee c	4	1	1	3	0
Dorish p	2	1	1	0	1
Johnson p	0	0	0	0	0
Klinger p	0	0	0	0	0
Totals	32	6	10	27	12

*Batted for Gromek in seventh.
†Batted for Klieman in ninth.

Cleveland .... 011 000 100—3
Boston .... 310 200 00x—6

Errors—Gordon, Pesky, Gutteridge 2. Runs batted in—Metkovich, Peck, Seerey, Williams, DiMaggio 2, Doerr, Pesky 2. Two-base hits—Peck, Metkovich, Pesky 2, Dorish, Williams. Three-base hit—Pesky. Home run—Seerey. Sacrifice—Dorish. Double plays—Keltner, Gordon and Hegan, Doerr, Pesky and Jones. Left on bases—Cleveland 8, Boston 9. Bases on balls—Off Embree 1, Lemon 3, Gromek 2, Dorish 1. Strikeouts—By Lemon 1, Gromek 1, Klieman 1, Dorish 2, Johnson 1. Hits—Off Embree, 5 in ⅔ innings; Lemon 2 in 1⅔; Gromek, 3 in 2⅔; Klieman, 0 in 2; Dorish, 8 in 8⅓; Johnson, 0 in ⅓; Klinger, 0 in ⅓. Winning pitcher—Dorish. Losing pitcher—Embree. Umpires—Rommel, Passarella and Boyer. Time—2:26. Attendance—34,863.

Gearhart Ends St. Louis Skein With Home Run

Koslo Chalks Up His Sixth Victory; Dickson, Relief, Is Belted in Final Frame

By Harold Rosenthal

ST. LOUIS, June 22.—Lloyd Gearhart's eleventh-inning home run snapped the Giants' losing road streak and the Cardinals' winning home string this afternoon and gave New York a 7-to-5 victory before 24,703 at Sportsman's Park. It also gave Dave Koslo, the left-hander, his sixth victory of the season and marked the first Giant triumph in four games.

The Cardinals' progression from the bottom of the National League race to a position of contention near the top, came to a temporary halt after a string of nine home triumphs, the best record in the major leagues this season.

Where Murry Dickson, the dour left-hander, had appeared in a winning relief role the day before, he experienced diametrically opposite results in a similar appearance today. He came in late in the Giants' half of the eighth and gave up four hits, three of them in the eleventh inning.

As the Dodgers split with the Reds in Cincinnati, the Giants moved into second place, leading Brooklyn by four points.

Giants Purchase Iott

The Giants purchased Clarence (Hooks) Iott, a left-handed pitcher, from the St. Louis Browns today. Iott, who had a record of ten won and six lost with San Antonia last year, will join the Giants in Chicago tomorrow, where they will open a three-game series with the Cubs.

While the Giant pitching wasn't exactly conducive to causing handsprings among the Polo Grounds faithful, the dynamite appeared in their bats for the first time against St. Louis in the particular series. They registered a total of fifteen hits off Jim Hearn, the starter, his successor, Ted Wilks, and finally Dickson.

Three of these were home runs. In addition to Gearhart's game-winning belt into the left-field stands with Buddy Kerr aboard, Walker Cooper racked up his tenth and eleventh round trippers of the season in consecutive innings.

Musial received the Kenesaw M. Landis plaque in a pre-game ceremony. It is an award made each year by the Baseball Writers Association of America to the previous season's most valuable National League player.

Marion Sidelined

Marty Marion's lame back caught up with him again today and Joffre Cross filled in for the Cardinal at shortstop. Marion played the first two games of the Giant series with a sprained thumb, sustained when he slid home in a game with the Phillies earlier in the week.

The score:

NEW YORK (N. L.)	ab	r	h	po	a
Rigney 2b	6	1	3	5	7
Kerr ss	6	1	3	2	2
Gearhart cf	5	1	1	4	0
Mize 1b	5	0	1	8	3
Marshall rf	6	1	1	5	1
W.Cooper c	5	2	3	4	0
Gordon lf	4	0	1	3	0
Yohrke 3b	5	0	1	1	1
Jansen p	2	0	1	0	1
*Lafata	0	1	0	0	0
Budnick p	1	0	0	0	0
Kolso p	1	0	0	1	1
Totals	46	7	15	33	16

ST. LOUIS (N. L.)	ab	r	h	po	a
Schoend'st 2b	5	1	2	2	7
Moore cf	3	2	3	4	0
Musial 1b	4	2	1	11	0
Slaughter lf	4	0	0	4	0
Northey rf	2	0	0	4	0
†Medwick	1	0	1	0	0
‡Diering	0	0	0	0	0
Rice c	1	0	0	1	0
Kurowski 3b	4	0	0	1	1
Garagiola c	3	0	1	2	0
Dusak rf	2	0	1	1	0
Cross ss	3	0	0	3	5
§Wilbur	1	0	0	0	0
Hearn p	2	0	0	0	0
Wilks p	1	0	0	0	0
Dickson p	2	0	0	0	0
Totals	38	5	9	33	13

*Batted for Jansen in seventh.
†Batted for Northey in eighth.
‡Ran for Medwick in eighth.
§Batted for Cross in eleventh.

New York .... 000 000 320 02—7
St. Louis .... 000 003 020 00—5

Errors—None. Runs batted in—Moore, Musial, Kurowski, Cooper 3, Rigney, Kerr, Medwick 2, Gearhart 2. Two-base hits—Rigney, Schoendienst 2, Moore, Garagiola. Home runs—Cooper 2, Gearhart. Sacrifice—Slaughter. Double plays—Schoendienst, Cross and Musial; Mize and Kerr; Cross, Schoendienst and Musial; Kerr, Rigney and Mize. Left on bases—New York 10, St. Louis 7. Bases on balls—Jansen 3, Hearn 3, Budnich 2, Dickson 1, Koslo 1. Strikeouts—Jansen 2, Hearn 1, Budnich 1, Wilks 1, Dickson 1. Hits—Off Jansen, 6 in 6 innings; Budnich, 0 in 1; Koslo, 3 in 4; Hearn, 7 in 6⅔; Wilks, 4 in 1; Dickson, 4 in 3⅓. Winning pitcher—Koslo. Losing pitcher—Dickson. Umpires—Boggess, Barr, Magerkurth and Jorda. Time—2:47. Attendance—24,703.

Bushwicks Split With Cubans

The Bushwicks string of fifteen straight triumphs was snapped in the second game of the double-header yesterday when the New York Cubans beat them at Dexter Park, 7 to 5. The Bushwicks took the opener, 3 to 2.

The scores by innings:

First game—		R.	H.	E.
N. Y. Cubans	000 010 010	2	5	2
Bushwicks	002 010 00x	3	8	0

Batteries—Scantlebury and Louden; Bittner and White.

Second game—		R.	H.	E.
N. Y. Cubans	140 020 000	7	13	2
Bushwicks	021 020 000	5	10	2

Batteries—Prue, Donosa (3), Santiago (5) and Louden; Moscowitz, Phillips (3), Holborow (6), Nekola (8) and White.

Blackwell Misses No-Hit Game, Reds Win, 4-0, Then Lose, 9-8

Associated Press wirephoto

NO-HIT PITCHERS: After holding the Dodgers to two safeties yesterday Ewell Blackwell (center) got together with Frank (Noodles) Hahn, who piched a no-hitter for the Reds in 1900. and Johnny Vander Meer, who hurled successive no-hit games for the Reds in 1938. Blackwell pitched a no-hitter last week

Stanky and Robinson Single in Ninth Inning With One Away and Spoil Hurler's Bid to Duplicate His Feat in Last Outing

By Bob Cooke

CINCINNATI, June 22.—Folks out here were calling Eddie Stanky a lot of names, including "The Spoiler" tonight. Ewell (The Whip) Blackwell, Cincinnati's spindle-shanked right-hander, was two outs away from his second consecutive no-hitter in the first game of a double-header when Brooklyn's second baseman, who had no desire to fill Blackwell's scrapbook with another page of glory, rammed a single to center.

Stanky's hit, a hard ground ball that scooted between Blackwell's legs and rolled unmolested into center field, broke a hitless string of nineteen innings which the lanky hurler had compiled. Jackie Robinson singled later on in the ninth but Blackwell had little difficulty in registering a two-hit, 4-to-0 victory, his ninth in a row and his eleventh of the season.

Furillo Drives in Seven

The Reds could have used Blackwell in the second game. The Dodgers gained an even break by nipping them, 9 to 8, as Carl Furillo enjoyed a day of plenty by driving in seven runs, four on a grand-slam homer in the fourth.

Joe Hatten was Blackwell's unfortunate rival in th opener. He permitted one harmless hit in five and two-thirds innings but issued four walks in the sixth to permit the Reds to take a one-run lead. Eddie Miller cleared the bases with a double against Hank Behrman in the eighth. Meanwhile the crowd of 31,204 customers sat back to await the Brooklyn ninth.

Not since Johnny Vander Meer, the Red southpaw, had turned in his double no-hit performance in 1938, had a major league pitcher come within such easy reach of two straight no-hitters. Gene Hermanski, the first batter, lifted an easy fly to Angie Galan for the first out. Stanky watched one pitch go by and then lashed his single to center. A more nimble pitcher might have fielded the ball but there was nothing scratchy about the hit. After Al Gionfriddo flied to Galan, Robinson dumped

(Continued on next page)

Dodger Scores

* * *

FIRST GAME

BROOKLYN (N. L.)	ab	r	h	po	a
Stanky 2b	4	0	1	0	3
Grionfr'do lf	4	0	0	0	0
Robinson 1b	4	0	1	8	1
Furillo cf	3	0	0	4	0
Walker rf	1	0	0	3	0
Jorgenson 3b	3	0	0	2	0
Reese ss	2	0	0	3	3
*Vaughan	1	0	0	0	0
Rojek ss	0	0	0	0	0
Hodges c	2	0	0	3	1
†Snider	1	0	0	0	0
Bragan c	0	0	0	1	0
Hatten p	2	0	0	0	0
Behrman p	0	0	0	0	0
‡Hermanski	1	0	0	0	0
Totals	28	0	2	24	8

CINCINNATI (N. L.)	ab	r	h	po	a
Baumholtz rf	2	0	0	3	0
Zientara 2b	4	0	0	1	5
Hatton 3b	4	2	1	0	1
Haas cf	3	1	1	2	0
Young 1b	2	0	0	9	1
Galan lf	2	1	0	4	0
Miller ss	4	0	2	2	1
Lamanno c	2	0	0	6	0
Blackwell p	4	0	0	0	0
Totals	27	4	4	27	8

*Batted for Reese and forced Walker at second in eighth.
†Batted for Hodges and fanned in eighth.
‡Batted for Behrman and flied out in ninth.

Brooklyn .... 000 000 000—0
Cincinnati .... 000 001 03x—4

Runs batted in—Miller 3, Galan. Two-base hits—Miller 2. Double play—Miller, Zientara and Young. Left on bases—Brooklyn 4, Cincinnati 8. Bases on balls—Hatten 6, Behrman 3, Blackwell 3. Hits—Hatten 1 in 5⅔ innings, Behrman 3 in 2⅓. Strikeouts—By Hatten 2, Behrman 1, Blackwell 6. Losing pitcher—Hatten. Umpires—Goetz, Conlan and Reardon. Time—2:13.

SECOND GAME

BROOKLYN (N. L.)	ab	r	h	po	a
Stanky 2b	5	3	3	3	4
Gionfriddo lf	3	1	0	3	0
Robinson 1b	3	2	1	10	1
Furillo cf	5	1	3	2	0
Walker rf	3	0	0	0	0
Jorgenson 3b	4	0	1	0	2
Reese ss	3	1	2	4	0
Miksis ss	1	0	0	0	1
Hodges c	4	0	0	5	2
Barney p	1	0	0	0	0
Lombardi p	3	1	2	0	1
Gregg p	0	0	0	0	0
Totals	35	9	12	27	11

CINCINNATI (N. L.)	ab	r	h	po	a
Baumholtz rf	5	2	2	5	0
Zientara 2b	5	0	1	1	3
Hatton 3b	4	0	1	2	2
Young 1b	5	0	0	5	0
Haase cf	5	1	2	2	1
Galan lf	4	0	0	1	0
Miller ss	4	2	2	7	1
Mueller c	4	1	2	4	2
Walters p	0	0	0	0	1
Riddle p	0	0	0	0	0
Lively p	0	0	0	0	0
*Tatum	1	0	0	0	0
Hetki p	0	0	0	0	1
†Lamanno	1	0	1	0	0
‡Adams	0	1	0	0	0
Erautt p	0	0	0	0	0
§Vollmer	1	1	1	0	0
Gumbert p	0	0	0	0	0
Totals	39	8	12	27	11

*Batted for Lively in fifth and flied out.
†Batted for Hetki in seventh.
‡Ran for Lamanno in seventh.
§Doubled for Erautt in eighth.

Brooklyn .... 201 600 000—9
Cincinnati .... 020 000 240—8

Runs batted in—Furillo 7, Stanky 1, Lombardi, Baumholtz 2, Hatton, Young, Miller, Mueller, Vollmer. Two-base hits—Lombardi, Haas, Miller Vollmer. Three-base hit—Baumholtz. Home run—Furillo. Stolen base—Furillo. Sacrifice—Robinson. Left on bases—Brooklyn 5, Cincinnati 7. Bases on balls—Off Barney 2, Lombardi 1, Walters 1, Riddle 2, Hetki 1, Erautt 1. Strikeouts—By Barney 2, Lombardi 2, Gregg 1, Lively 1, Gumbert 2. Hits—Off Barney, 3 in 1⅓ innings; Lombardi, 8 in 6; Gregg, 1 in 1⅔; Walters, 9 in 3⅓; Riddle, 1 in 0; Lively, 1 in 1⅔; Hetki, 0 in 2; Erautt, 1 in 1; Gumbert, 0 in 1. Passed ball—Mueller. Winning pitcher—Lombardi. Losing pitcher—Walters. Umpires—Conlan, Reardon and Goetz. Time—2:27. Attendance—31,204.

Major League Standings and Pitchers

Monday, June 23, 1947

NATIONAL LEAGUE RESULTS YESTERDAY

New York, 7; St. Louis, 5 (11 inns)
Cincinnati, 4; Brooklyn, 0 (1st)
Brooklyn, 9; Cincinnati, 8 (2d)
Philadelphia, 4; Pittsb'gh, 3 (1st 13 ins)
Second game called in 4th (curfew)
Boston, 8; Chicago, 7 (11 inns)

AMERICAN LEAGUE RESULTS YESTERDAY

New York, 6; Detroit, 5
Cleveland, 8; Boston, 2 (1st)
Boston, 6; Cleveland, 3 (2d)
Chicago, 1; Philadelphia, 0 (1st, 10 inns)
Philadelphia, 3; Chicago, 0 (2d)
Washington, 3; St. Louis, 2 (1st)
St. Louis, 9; Washington, 6 (2d)

STANDING OF THE CLUBS	Boston	New York	Brooklyn	Chicago	St. Louis	Cincin'ti	Phila.	Pittsb'gh	WON	LOST	Percent	Games behind
Boston	—	5	2	5	3	6	4	8	33	24	.579	—
New York	4	—	3	5	7	4	2	5	30	24	.556	1½
Brooklyn	4	4	—	7	3	3	6	5	32	26	.552	1½
Chicago	3	2	2	—	5	6	9	3	30	27	.526	3
St. Louis	5	2	7	2	—	3	6	4	29	29	.500	4½
Cincinnati	2	5	6	3	4	—	3	5	28	32	.467	6½
Philadelphia	4	3	4	1	4	6	—	4	26	34	.433	8½
Pittsburgh	2	3	2	4	3	4	4	—	22	34	.393	10½
Games lost	24	24	26	27	29	32	34	34	—	—		

STANDING OF THE CLUBS	New York	Boston	Phila.	Clevel'd	Detroit	Wash'n	Chicago	St. Louis	WON	LOST	Percent	Games behind
New York	—	7	3	2	8	4	5	6	35	24	.593	—
Boston	3	—	4	5	3	2	7	7	31	24	.564	2
Philadelphia	3	3	—	4	6	3	5	5	29	28	.509	5
Cleveland	3	4	4	—	3	4	3	4	25	25	.500	5½
Detroit	2	3	5	4	—	3	7	3	27	28	.491	6
Washington	3	3	5	6	2	—	1	6	26	28	.481	6½
Chicago	6	1	5	2	3	8	—	3	28	32	.467	7½
St. Louis	4	3	2	2	3	4	4	—	22	34	.393	11½
Games lost	24	24	28	25	28	28	32	34	—	—		

National League Games and Pitchers Today

Boston (Barrett, 6-4) at St. Louis (Munger, 5-1), night.

New York (M. Cooper, 2-6) at Chicago (Erickson, 2-2).

Other clubs not scheduled.

American League Games and Pitchers Today

Cleveland (Black, 4-4) at New York (Johnson, 2-2, or Bevens, 3-8).

Detroit (Hutchinson, 5-3, or Trucks, 3-5) at Boston (Harris, 1-0, or Galehouse, 1-3).

Chicago (Grove, 3-3) at Washington (Wynn, 8-4), night.

Other clubs not scheduled.

AMERICAN ASSOCIATION

Yesterday's Results

Indianapolis, 8; Toledo, 2 (1st).
Indianapolis, 7; Toledo, 0 (2d).
Louisville, 2; Columbus, 0 (1st).
Louisville, 3; Columbus, 2 (2d).
Kansas City, 4; St. Paul, 0 (1st).
Kansas City, 2; St. Paul, 1 (2d).
Minneapolis, 15; Milwaukee, 7 (1st).
Minneapolis, 14; Milwaukee, 5 (2d).

STANDING OF THE CLUBS

	W.	L.	Pct.		W.	L.	Pct.
Kansas City	33	21	.611	Toledo	32	32	.500
Louisville	34	30	.531	Milwaukee	29	30	.492
Indianapolis	33	30	.524	Columbus	28	37	.431
Minneapolis	34	32	.515	St. Paul	27	38	.415

EASTERN LEAGUE

Yesterday's Results

Scranton, 2; Elmira, 1 (1st).
Scranton, 2; Elmira, 1 (2d) 12 inns.
Wilkes-Barre, 9; Williamsport, 7 (1st) 10 inns.
Wilkes-Barre, 7; Williamsport, 2 (2d).
Albany, 9; Binghamton, 7 (1st).
Albany, 6; Binghamton, 4 (2d).
Utica, 3; Hartford, 2 (1st).
Utica, 5; Hartford, 4 (2d) 12 inns.

STANDING OF THE CLUBS

	W.	L.	Pct.		W.	L.	Pct.
Utica	35	18	.660	Williamsport	27	31	.466
Scranton	30	24	.556	Hartford	25	29	.463
Albany	31	25	.554	Elmira	23	31	.426
Wilkes-Barre	31	25	.554	Binghamton	18	37	.327

SOUTHERN ASSOCIATION

Yesterday's Results

New Orleans, 8; Chattanooga, 2 (1st).
New Orleans, 6; Chattanooga, 2 (2d).
Mobile, 3; Nashville, 0 (1st).
Mobile, 4; Nashville, 0 (2d).
Memphis at Atlanta (2, rain).
Little Rock at Birmingham (2, rain).

STANDING OF THE CLUBS

	W.	L.	Pct.		W.	L.	Pct.
Mobile	48	24	.667	Birmingham	35	38	.479
N. Orleans	46	28	.622	Atlanta	33	36	.478
Chattanooga	37	37	.500	Memphis	26	40	.394
Nashville	33	35	.485	Little Rock	25	45	.357

N. C. A. A. Baseball

Western Play-offs at Denver

California 8, Texas 7.

INTERNATIONAL LEAGUE

Yesterday's Results

Jersey City, 6; Syracuse, 1 (1st).
Jersey City, 9; Syracuse, 6 (2d).
Rochester, 15; Newark, 3 (1st).
Rochester, 5; Newark, 2 (2d).
Montreal, 4; Baltimore, 0 (1st).
Baltimore, 2; Montreal, 1 (2d).
Toronto, 3; Buffalo, 2 (1st).
Buffalo, 6; Toronto, 3 (2d).

STANDING OF THE CLUBS

	W.	L.	Pct.		W.	L.	Pct.
Montreal	39	21	.650	Baltimore	27	32	.458
Jer. City	36	26	.581	Buffalo	27	33	.450
Syracuse	31	25	.554	Newark	27	34	.443
Rochester	22	33	.468	Toronto	25	37	.403

Tonight's Games

Jersey City at Montreal.
Syracuse at Toronto.
Baltimore at Buffalo.
Newark at Rochester.

Di Mag Standout Player on Both Clubs: Cobb

DODGER RUN—Peewee Reese is shown sliding across the plate with the Dodgers' final run in the seventh inning of yesterday's World Series inaugural. Reese came in all the way from second after Frank Shea, Yankee pitcher, uncorked a wild throw. Shea is covering the plate while Catcher Yogi Berra (not shown) chases the ball. Umpire is Bill McGowan.

By Bud Spencer
The News Sports Editor

NEW YORK, Oct. 1.—They were setting the stage for the opening game of the World Series in cold windswept Yankee Stadium (a regular Seals Stadium Day) yesterday. A record series crowd of 73,365 was sitting in the stands wrapped in blankets, wearing heavy coats, banging their palms together, and picking dust and bits of paper out of their eyes.

From the brassy throats of the amplifiers came the announcer's voice, giving the names of the starting players.

The announcer didn't get far down the names of the starting before he mentioned a name. It was Joe Di Maggio. In one of the boxes sat a familiar baseball figure of yesteryear.

"The difference between the two ball clubs is Di Maggio," mused Ty Cobb. "This won't be a great major league ball team they'll see out there today. But defensively and offensively Di Maggio is a true major league ballplayer."

As the ball game, a dull uninteresting affair, went along, it became evident that Mr. Cobb looked exceedingly good as a prophet. Di Maggio started the rally in the final half of the fifth that broke Junior Ralph Branca's back. It was a single to deep short that Pee Wee Reese stopped but didn't have a chance to get the runner.

I don't believe a pitcher ever blew the duke, or flipped his lid, as swiftly as Mr. Branca, a powerful citizen of the local suburbs. Mr. Branca had pitched superb ball, no hits in four innings, including five strikeouts, until he faced Di Mag' in this fatal five-run fifth inning. With Di Mag' on base, Brooklyn's top pitcher threw four straight balls to George McQuinn, a jobless free agent last year who got back on the glory road when the Yankee masterminds couldn't find a first sacker. Billy Johnson, up to bunt, took the next Branca wild one on the hand, and there was Branca, gone from superb to worse than worse. You know by this time how it was. The Yankees collected five runs on three hits, the most powerful blow being a line drive by Johnny Lindell that sizzled against the railing in left field for two bases.

The inning was about the only highlight of the ball game. You'd think in an autumn classic between major league ball clubs you might see something exceptionally colorful. But yesterday's opener had nothing—nothing beyond the five-run fifth inning and Cy Young's crack in the seventh inning, "The secret of my success was good old bourbon whisky."

It should be added, of course, that good control didn't hurt, either. Mr. Young won more than 500 games in major league baseball, and I suspect he could tell the boys out there yesterday, including Joe Page, the Yankee relief hurler, who was behind the hitter nine times out of 10, how to make it easy on yourself and tougher on the hitter.

Any records set in this series will be established by the folks who pay the freight, rather than the ballplayers. It is rather generally agreed by competent observers that this year's entries are sub par and that hitting, pitching and fielding standards set by the immortals in bygone days aren't in any serious jeopardy.

There were many great men of yesteryear's World Series scroll on hand for the series. Among them was Stan Coveleskie, who loves the Brooklyns. The first time he looked at the Dodgers was in 1920 and they still look beautiful to him 27 years later. No fooling. Old Stanley stopped the Dodgers three times.

Maybe I ought to take it all back. Mr. Happy Chandler, who is identified as the best commissioner since Landis, got right into the front of things by being the Lincoln of baseball. He beckoned Jackie Robinson over to his box and got his picture taken shaking hands with the Negro star.

Robinson, who plays a baseball boogie woogie, drove Frankie Shea nuts with his dancing on the baselines. His antics were not condemned by Vishinsky as warmongering, but actually it was Robinson who proved Shea's downfall. First of all, our Frankie, who played with Oakland in the third major league (it died like Bugsy Siegel) made the mistake of walking Robinson twice. And the second time, which was the third, the Negro star worked Shea into a frenzy. The result was a papable balk. And this put a thought into the mind of Manager Bucky Harris of the Yankees.

Putting two and two together, which means that Shea was far from right, Mr. Harris used the best judgment of the masterminding in the opener. With the bases loaded in the bombastic Yankee fifth inning, he sent Bobby Brown, golden boy of San Francisco's prep school graduates, up to the plate for Shea. Mr. Harris was playing for the big inning. Three men were on bases, no outs, and Brown, a sound hitter, was just the ticket for smart baseball it proved a wise move. Brown broke Branca's back for sure. He refused to bite at two close pitches and worked out a walk. This is always the difference between a good hitter and an average one.

Flash: Mr. Truman just sent word to the press box that he is too busy to attend this series. Which is just as well, and proves that it takes plenty of work to give away another 19 billion dollars.

Coming back to Ty Cobb's observation, the point is that Di Maggio looks and plays baseball like a big leaguer all the way around. Hardly the ballplayer he was 10 years ago, Di Mag' still stands out. What does that make baseball today? Anyway, he started the rally that ultimately won the ball game, and but for the wind and a magnificent catch by Carl Furillo 415 feet from the plate in deep left center the North Beach favorite would have been the game's real hero. As it was, there was no standout hero.

If you want to get technical, a defensive play by Phil Rizzuto was the stopper that killed the Dodgers. It was the sixth. Stanky singled off Page. Robinson hit a hard grounder that Rizzuto flagged down in deep short, despite a bad hop, and with a lightning underhand toss to Stirnweiss the Yankee shortstop got Stanky by a hair at second. Had this play missed, you can hazard a guess as to what might have happened. I still think Mr. Page was hardly the steady relief twirler he's cracked up to be.

The News Sports

Page 16 SAN FRANCISCO, WEDNESDAY, OCTOBER 1, 1947

Sports-Man About Town

BY JACK ROSENBAUM

Now It Can Be Told Dept. . . .

1.—Dixie Howell's Idaho team apparently came to Palo Alto without any information on Stanford. But the Vandals amazed football followers with their knowledge of Marchy Schwartz' technique. The under-rated visitors anticipated Stanford plays and defensive moves with surprising adeptness. This, we can reveal today, wasn't an accident. The Vandals prepared for the Stanford game from a voluminous report supplied mainly by a San Francisco resident long familiar with the Stanford system. He is Bert (Chick) Stanley, former Notre Dame player under Knute Rockne and professional free-lance scout. (Stanley's most recent assignment carried him to Honolulu to scout St. Mary's for California.)

SCHWARTZ

2.—Joe Scott, new backfield star at University of San Francisco, was a visitor at St. Mary's before he enrolled at USF. He was in the Marine Corps at the time. The strapping young fellow met Coach Jimmy Phelan. They discussed Scott's football experiences at Texas A & M and El Toro Marines. Mr. Phelan, purely by instinct, then painted a glamorous picture of student life in the lush Moraga Valley. Scott listened. He seemed entranced—then entered USF!

* * *

Diss and Data. . . . The Sheridan clan, it seems, put all their biscuits on one number. Both Neill, the Seals' outfielder, and brother Billy, Santa Clara quarterback, wear No. 23. . . . When you speak of the USF Dons as a "fighting" team, be more explicit, chum. At least three members of Coach Ed McKeever's unbeaten eleven are just as adept with their gloved fists as they are playing football. Joe Scott is a heavyweight protege of Billy Newman, noted local manager; Roy Barni was the outstanding ringman on the USF boxing team last season, and Pete Matisi, pudgy fullback, is a brother of Joe Matisi, heavyweight contender from Buffalo, N. Y. . . . Which reminds us that Jess Flores meets stiff opposition when he faces Frankie Moore in Oakland on Oct. 22. Moore's kayo victims include Chalky Wright, Frankie Fernandez, Ritchie Shinn, Bobby Yaeger, Lew Hanbury and Ray Salas. . . . Small World Dept. . . . Those Gallivanting Gaels of St. Mary's sure get around. Their last three games were in Houston, Tex.; Oakland, Cal., and Honolulu, Oahu—and all this year, too. . . . Doc Blanchard and Glenn Davis—Messrs. Inside and Outside—come to town Friday. Not personally, sorry, but in a movie, "The Spirit of West Point," at the Esquire.

* * *

Prediction: Ted Schroeder will turn pro at the same time as his more illustrious tennis partner, Jack Kramer. The two will then tour the country with Don Budge and Bobby Riggs.

TED SCHROEDER

* * *

What They're Doing Today Dept. . . . Billy Hammond, Ex-S. F. State and Coast Guard basketball star, operates a private school on the Peninsula. (Right now Billy and wife, Ruth, are celebrating birth of a son, weight 6 pounds 13 ounces and 20 inches long.) . . . Milo Millicevich, center at St. Mary's under Slip Madigan, plays for the pro Honolulu Warriors by night and is in the steel business by day. . . . And Gus Suhr, who graduated to majors from Seals, is employed by Acme Brewery.

* * *

"The House on Golden Gate-av" is not the title of a forthcoming film. It's a large apartment building directly across the street from the USF practice field and it's causing Messrs. McKeever, Kuharich and Mattock no end of concern. The hedge growing along the street side of the field shields the practice from passersby but tenants in the apartment building have a comfortable, 50-yard line view of everything the Dons do. . . . Last season, we recall, Clipper Smith's life was made miserable by a chap who watched practice every afternoon with a pair of high-powered field glasses. The Clipper was positive he must be in the employ of the enemy.

"With those glasses he can count the freckles on our team," moped Morose Maurice.

We wouldn't be at all surprised if that obnoxious chap hastened the Clipper's departure.

Branca Tried Too Hard in Series Opener

Fifth Inning Lapse Proves Fatal to 21-Year-Old Hurler

By Steve Snider
United Press Sports Writer

NEW YORK, Oct. 1.—A kid who tried too hard lost the series opener.

Struggling to regain his shattered poise before a record World Series crowd of 73,365 at Yankee Stadium, 21-year-old Ralph Branca of the Dodgers came winging in with a fatal pitch to Johnny Lindell and it went screaming into left field for a two-run double that started the Yankee victory parade in the fifth inning.

It was a pitch an older, wiser man might not have thrown, inside to Lindell's strength and high where it could be powered far.

"He's only human," said Manager Burt Shotten in the hushed dressing room of the vanquished Bums. "He's only 21," some one added.

"That's not it," answered the broken-hearted Dodger starter who had won 21 and lost 12 over the National League season.

"I tried too hard," he said. "I wasn't tired, or cold or worried about having the bases loaded. I just tried so hard and I couldn't get the ball over."

Until his strange lapse in the fifth, Branca had pitched one of the true masterpieces of World Series history. He had set down the Yankees in order, toying with that Yankee power. But Joe Di Maggio opened the fifth with a hit and Branca suddenly was a different pitcher. He walked George McQuinn. He beaned Billy Johnson—"I don't see how he got in the way," Ralph said later—and the bases were filled when Lindell strode up.

"I hope you don't think I was scared, do you?" Branca cried after it was all over. "I reared back and let 'er fly with all I had—and tried too hard."

Relief Pitcher Hugh Casey, who finally came in after the Yanks had combed Branca and Hank Behrman for all their five runs, took the youngster aside as the Dodgers were filing out to their bus.

"Next time, boy, just grab the ball and throw like old Hughey. Don't give the hitters time or yourself time to think."

Shotton was unhappy at the defeat but still sure the Bums will win the series. "We've lost games before," he said. "I don't feel any different about winning."

THE YANKS ARE COMING—But Umpire Babe Pinelli just sets his jaw and walks away from the protesting New York Yankee players, who are in hot pursuit of the arbiter after he called Brooklyn's Pete Reiser safe at first when McQuinn missed an attempted tag in the sixth inning. The Yankees claimed Reiser had run out of the baseline. The frowns disappeared by the end of the game, however, as the American Leaguers went on to win the World Series opener, 5-3.

Bears Plan Surprise For Pappy Waldorf

By Jack Rosenbaum

There was a whispered huddle among the undefeated California Bears after a snappy practice last evening. Coach Pappy Waldorf wasn't invited. Indeed, whenever the large man approached the subject changed abruptly. Perhaps we shouldn't give the boys away but shucks, it'll come out sooner or later and we'd kinda like to be first to tell you the Bears are cooking up a little surprise for their popular coach.

It all started when some one thumbed through a California football booklet. He noticed that Pappy was born on Oct. 3, 1902. An idea came into his head. In no time at all the boys agreed he had something.

Pappy's birthday, you see, is Friday. The battle with St. Mary's is Saturday. The plot is to present Pappy with a birthday gift—victory over the Gaels.

Apparently, the wagering folk are sure Waldorf will receive his present. Unofficial odds today list California as a 3 to 1 favorite, with even money the Bears take St. Mary's by 13 points. And from the trend, it may even go to 4-1.

In sharp contrast to the injury complaints from Moraga, California is at full strength for the first time this season. Not a single Bear is under doctor's care. As if to make certain this happy condition remains, Waldorf said he plans little or no body contact for the balance of the week.

"We had quite a bit of contact work against Santa Clara and Navy," he said, "and I have a feeling we'll get plenty from St. Mary's."

We hastily add, however, this doesn't mean the Bears are loafing in practice. Pappy doesn't believe in having his gladiators stand around. He says it dulls them mentally and physically. So, while there was little rough work, the first team spent considerable time in running through their repertoire of plays. Jimmy Phelan at St. Mary's will be interested to know that California didn't show all it's stuff against Navy. In fact, there were a couple of dandy plays in evidence yesterday that were labeled 'touchdown.'

Waldorf still insists he hasn't determined upon a starting lineup but we'd guess his opening backfield will include Erickson at quarter; Fong and Billy Main at halfbacks, Graves at fullback. Ready to spell this quartet will be an equally fearsome foursome of Celeri, Keckley, Swaner and Jensen. The Bears boast two strong lines of almost equal ability, a situation that is allowing Pappy a good night's sleep, which happens to be about five hours during the football season. Huddles with assistant coaches often last until 1 and 2 in the morning.

With the exception of little Spike Cordeiro, St. Mary's will also be able to use its entire squad. However, it isn't at all certain that Wedemeyer, Modrein, Ryan, Flagerman and O'Connor, to mention a few of the better known players who have been under the weather, will be in perfect physical condition.

Glen Bell, who understudied Wedemeyer last year, and Billy Van Heuit, sophomore half from Berkeley, were given special attention from the coaching staff in yesterday's drill. That may be significant. Van Heuit boots the ball a mile high, or so it seemed in Hawaii. He still needs to learn that he can travel farther, if not faster, by following his interference.

Changes At Santa Clara

By Harvey Rockwell

Personnel and strategy are in for rather a thorough going-over down on the Santa Clara campus this week. When the Broncs tripped all over themselves against California, Len Casanova figured a little practice would iron out the rough edges, but when they fought Southern Methodist on almost even terms in one half and fell apart in the second, the SC headman decided action was necessary. With Fresno State next on the list—at Ratcliffe Stadium Saturday night—Casanova is making radical changes.

For one thing, four new faces—all transfers from Menlo Junior College—will be in the lineup that trots onto the turf Saturday.

Billy Sheridan will be at quarterback; Bill Renna at center; Vern Sterling at left guard, and Warner Spindler at left tackle.

Too, with the discovery that Sheridan is better than a fair hand at tossing around the hide—and hitting intended receivers—Casanova intends to develop that arm of his offensive.

* * *

SHERIDAN KEY MAN

Sheridan, Renna and Sterling definitely are regulars as of now. Spindler, a 260-pounder, will start if the Broncs kick off, for his specialty is defense.

It was Sheridan's passes that made the Broncs go when they did roll against SMU, and his smart signal-calling showed that Santa Clara might yet come to life.

Renna, switched from fullback to center just before the UC debacle, was the second best defensive man on the field Saturday. Sterling was top man that day and both were so good Casanova had no choice but to give them regular jobs.

One thing the Broncs still lack is adequate tackling and kicking. Casanova is again stressing tackling this week, and is looking about for a man who can root that hide down the field.

* * *

FRESNO 'TEST CASE'

Bill Crowley, originally tabbed the starting quarterback, is the best kicker on the squad, but injuries have kept him out of action to date this year and it is unlikely he will suit up Saturday.

L'il Fresno, once just a breather on the Santa Clara schedule, surprised the Broncs last year with an upset in the season opener, and this year provided Casanova's men with a "test case."

Down on the Santa Clara campus the word is that the Broncs must lick the Bulldogs to salvage something out of the season. If they get over this, the players feel, they could go on to other conquests.

The bugaboo of injuries is plaguing Casanova, also. Frinstance, Gil McDermid, Jim Buckley, Guy Giacopuzzi and Crowley remain on the injured list. Probably only Giacopuzzi will see action.

Dons Not Yet Ready to Entertain Bowl Bids

By Bill Anderson

Please do not peg us as a chronic carper, killjoy, or a wet-blanket. But we still believe the USF Dons are not ready to entertain Bowl bids off their victories over San Jose State and Nevada. Nor will a rousing triumph over Duquesne Sunday at Kezar Stadium change the opinion.

This may come as an acute surprise to some exuberant undergrads at the Hilltop school, and their equally partisan likenesses in their alumni association. After their lollapaloozin' triumph over Nevada last weekend, it was natural these myriad rooters should let off steam and jabber happily of New Years Day invitations.

And no doubt they fed gluttonously on the lavish praise offered by a scribbler on a local ayem, who stated—but positively—that the Dons today could defeat the California eleven. The fact that the Dons and the Bears are not scheduled may have emboldened the fellow, or it might have been he was just handing a giggle to students of gridology. If so, he succeeded.

Matter of fact, even in the midst of the gayety in the Don's dressing room following Sunday's victory, Coach Ed McKeever stopped praising his youngsters long enough to answer this carping question: "Nevada made quite a few yards through the middle of your line. Were they strong or are you weak there?"

"We're a little weak, and jack reserves," said the man from Texas.

Can you imagine a line weak in the middle and lacking reserves taking the power shots of the Bears, whose two, equally strong forward walls of experienced players ripped up Santa Clara and stopped the mighty Middies?

Would the Bears allow Don Panciera and Jimmy Ryan the time they had to find pass receivers Sunday? The evidence says, "No."

Give the Dons a break. Let them work out their destiny. They should have at least one more happy weekend before running into difficulties. They figure to wallop the Dukes. Even in Pittsburgh the Dons are two-touchdown favorites.

The blunt fact is the Dukes haven't come back to prewar eminence. This is their first team since 1942. And their 7-0, and 6-0 victories over Geneva College and Western Reserve can't be called impressive.

The team may be tough defensively. But it hasn't completed a single pass in 17 attempts. And on the ground they gained but 74 yards against Western Reserve. Nope, this game won't prove the Dons are Bowl bound. It is hoped it will be tough enough to allow them to work out some tricks for the Mississippi State game the following week. And it should provide the line with some badly needed experience.

Negro Promoter Sues Rickey

NEW YORK, Oct. 1.—General Manager Branch Rickey of the Brooklyn Dodgers today faced a $15,427.48 law suit in which a Negro baseball team's promoter charges breach of contract.

The promoter, Joseph Hall of Harrisburg, Pa., complained in Federal Court that Rickey proposed that Hall's Hilldale Club in the United States Baseball League switch its franchise to Ebbets Field in Brooklyn. The idea, Hall said, was to test public sentiment towards Negroes in baseball. This was before, of course, Rickey signed Jackie Robinson as the first Negro in organized baseball.

Hall charged today that he fulfilled his end of the bargain, but that Rickey backed out.

Bruins Face Wildcats

LOS ANGELES, Oct. 1.—Coach Bert LaBrucherie announced Benny Reiges, Skip Rowland, and Cal Rossi were definite UCLA backfield starters against Northwestern Saturday at Evanston.

He added that Jack Meyers, who showed well against Iowa last week, may get the initial call over Jerry Shipkey.

Trojans Stress Pass

LOS ANGELES, Oct. 1.—Coach Newell (Jeff) Cravath today stressed pass defense in preparing his University of Southern California Trojans for their Saturday game against Rice Institute of the Southwest Conference, the "cradle of razzle-dazzle football."

O'Doul Sends Chesnes to Hill For Seals' Goose-Egg Revue

By Bucky Walter

It's up to Bob (Oh, My Aching Arm) Chesnes, the Seals' 22-game winner, to put our bums back on the winning track this evening. But even with a superb effort, the sometimes Rhythm Kid will have his troubles if his mates don't do something—and quickly—about the elementary task of run scoring. Like a wet cake of soap, Lefty O'Doul's guys, appearing thoroughly jaded after a bitter flag drive that ended in frustration, saw their first Governors' Cup Playoff game slip out of their grasp last night when Casey Stengel's Oakies struck suddenly in the ninth inning for a 2-0 victory.

Our bums have now gone 26 innings without denting the plate, counting Monday evening's 5-0 loss to Cliff Chambers as Los Angeles won the "sudden death" pennant playoff in Wrigley Field.

Last night, they succumbed docilely to Stengel's Will Hafey, who won only seven starts during regular season. Will of the numerous Hafeys allowed them only two hits, Roy Nicely's single in the third and Hugh Luby's double in the fourth. Period.

The Oakies didn't exactly tee off on Bob Joyce, but they managed to send Old Reliable down to defeat in the ninth with the help of two broken-bat hits. Dario Lodigiani dropped a single inches behind Nicely and then scored on the pesky Bill Raimondi's looper that arched languidly for two bases into right field. Raimondi counted on a sure-nuff muscular blow when Hafey smashed a two-bagger against the right field screen for the last of eight enemy hits.

Damon (The Demon) Hayes (13-10) will start against Chesnes tonight.

Oaks 2, Seals 0

OAKLAND	AB	R	H	O	A	SAN FRANCISCO	AB	R	H	O	A
Crwfrd,3b	4	0	0	1	1	White,cf	4	0	0	5	0
Wrkman,rf	4	0	1	4	0	Luby,2b	4	0	1	0	4
Holder,lf	4	0	2	1	0	Sheridan,rf	4	0	0	3	0
Etten,1b	4	0	1	11	0	Restelli,lf	4	0	0	1	0
H.Martn,cf	4	0	0	0	0	Orteig,3b	3	0	0	1	1
Ldgiani,2b	4	1	1	3	3	Mathern,1b	3	0	0	8	0
Hamrick,ss	4	0	0	0	7	Nicely,ss	3	0	1	6	2
Raimondi,c	3	1	1	7	0	Gladd,c	2	0	0	2	0
W.Hafey,p	4	0	2	0	1	Joyce,p	3	0	0	0	0
DiMag,cf	0	0	0	0	0						
Totals	35	2	8	27	12	Totals	30	0	2	27	7

Oakland .... 000 000 002—2
San Francisco .... 000 000 000—0

Error: Hamrick. Runs batted in: Raimondi, W. Hafey. Two-base hits: Raimondi, Hafey, Luby, Holder. Official attendance: 3202.

Catcher Drops Ball to Give Angels Victory

By United Press Sports Wire

LOS ANGELES, Oct. 1.—Los Angeles, P. C. L. champions, squeezed across a run in the 11th inning to defeat Portland, 2-1, last night in the opening game of the Governor's Cup playoffs.

Ed Sauer scored the winning run on an error by Catcher Charles Silvera.

The Beavers tallied in the opening stanza when Outfielder Danny Escobar singled and a two-bagger by Dick Wenner sent him home.

The Angels tied it up in the third when Second Sacker Lou Stringer doubled, and a single by Catcher Eddie Malone drove him on in.

Then, Ed Sauer singled to centerfield and Clarence Maddern hit a fly to right field which Escobar failed to reach in time. Silvera caught Escobar's peg to tag out Sauer, but the run counted when he dropped the ball.

Angels 2, Bevos 1

PORTLAND	AB	R	H	O	A	LOS ANGELES	AB	R	H	O	A
Ratto,ss	3	0	1	1	3	Garriott,cf	5	0	0	0	0
Escobar,cf	3	1	1	2	0	Schustr,ss	5	0	1	4	1
Wonner,cf	3	0	1	0	1	Sauer,rf	4	1	2	1	0
Reich,rf	4	0	1	1	0	Maddrn,lf	4	0	1	5	0
Storey,2b	5	0	0	1	1	Ostwski,3b	4	0	0	2	2
Bsinski,2b	5	0	1	5	3	Barton,1b	4	0	1	5	1
Silvera,c	4	0	0	14	2	Stringer,2b	2	1	1	4	2
Vico,1b	3	0	1	8	0	Malone,c	3	0	1	11	4
Bridges,p	4	0	0	0	1	McCall,p	2	0	0	1	0
Lazor,lf	1	0	0	0	0	Dobernic,p	2	0	0	0	0
Mullen,2b	0	0	0	0	1						
Smith,cf	0	0	0	0	0						
Totals	35	1	6	32	12	Totals	35	2	7	23	10

Portland 100 000 000 00—1
Los Angeles 001 000 000 01—2

Error: Basinski. Runs batted in: Wenner, Malone. Two-base hits: Wenner, Stringer. Sacrifices: Stringer, Escobar, Lazor. Struck out: By Bridges 14, McCall 6, Dobernic 3. Bases on balls: Bridges 4, McCall 2, Dobernic 3. Earned runs: Bridges 1, McCall 1. Hits: Off McCall 4 in 7 plus, Dobernic 1 in 3 plus.

Bruns Defeats Lee Henning

Bobby Bruns, Chicago wrestler, won a popular two out of three fall victory over Lee Henning, ex-Pacific Coast champion last night at the Coliseum Bowl.

Fans crowded around the ring at the finish, booing and tossing programs at Henning for rule violations and he had to be escorted to his dressing room by police. Bruns won the first fall with an airplane spin in 17:58. Henning took the second fall with elbow smashes in 6:42, and Bruns the deciding fall with a flying mare and press in 4:12. Jack Wagner refereed.

Other results: Juan Humberto pinned Bobby Roberts, crab hold, 13:23; Ray Eckert used a facelock to beat Gene Bowman, 16:23, and Wilbur Nead and Pat Fraley drew, 20 minutes.

Sulky Drivers Banned for Fix

By United Press Sports Wire

FOXBORO, Mass., Oct. 1.—Two New England harness racing drivers were under a nationwide, one-year suspension today for allegedly conspiring to affect the result of a race at the Bay State Raceway here.

Banned from competing at all U. S. trotting tracks for a year were Howard Parker of White River Junction, Vt., and John Stanley of Somerset, both accused of violating regulations of the U. S. Trotting Association.

A suspension notice posted last night in the racing secretary's office at the track charged Parker and Stanley with "conspiring to fraudulently affect the ultimate result" of last Saturday's sixth race.

Telegraph Hill Cagers in Loss

Ray Rosales tallied 20 points to lead the S. F. Boys Club to a 34-12 victory over Telegraph Hill in a Red Shield-Optimist League 110-pound cage tilt last night.

Bernard Havorka scored seven points as Columbia Park Boys downed Precita Valley, 21-5.

Jack Kramer Scores Twin Win

Jack Kramer, the Babe Ruth of tennis, today led the way in the Pacific Coast tournament, sweeping to a victory over Charles Joplin, 6-1, 6-1, and whipping Cecil Alloo, 6-2, 6-3, yesterday on the Golden Gate Park courts. Jaroslav Drobny, Europe's top racquetteer, Tony Mottram of England and San Francisco's Eddie Moylan each scored twin wins.

Margaret Osborne of San Francisco paced the women stars, downing Barbara Kenny, 6-2, 6-2.

Results yesterday:

MEN'S SINGLES

R. Kavanaugh def. P. Segura; Tony Mottram def. B. Green, 6-2, 6-3; E. Moylan def. L. Jensen, 6-0, 6-3; J. Brink def. J. Peten, 10-8, 6-3; J. Drobny def. K. Colby, 6-0, 6-3; D. Gonzales def. B. Fardin, 6-3, 6-0; D. Slack def. J. Adams, 4-6, 6-2, 6-3; Jack Kramer def. Charles Joplin, 6-1, 6-1; V. Cernik def. G. Rice, 9-11; 6-4, 6-1; M. Ehmke def. J. Murio, 6-3, 6-6, 6-3; J. Heldman def. R. Kavanaugh, 6-3, 6-0; N. Carter def. W. Wright, 6-4, 6-3; J. Drobny def. George Kraft, 6-3, 7-5; D. Gonzales def. D. Slack, 6-1, 6-3; T. Mottram def. M. Mosko, 6-2, 6-4; E. Moylan def. W. Hoepner, 6-2, 6-1; Jack Kramer def. C. Alloo, 6-2, 6-3; Jim Brink def. A. Perlin, 6-0, 6-0; V. Rurac def. K. Briedwell, 6-4, 6-4; H. Roche def. A. Viera, 6-1, 7-5; Sam Match def. Gordon Kocher, 6-2, 6-2.

WOMEN'S SINGLES

B. Caro def. G. Gilmore, 6-0, 6-0; Jean Quertier def. G. Wenger, 7-5, 6-0; B. Krase def. M. Raful, 6-3, 6-2; M. Rurac def. M. Rose, 6-0, 6-0; D. Head def. B. Clark, 6-0, 6-0; N. Bolton def. B. Spiegelman, 6-0, 6-2; B. Rosenquest def. P. Jung, 6-1, 6-1; Jean Quertier def. R. Yokela, 6-1, 6-4; B. Krase def. L. Kugelman, 6-1, 6-0; V. Kovacs def. Joy Gannon, 6-2, 4-6, 6-3; M. Osborne def. Barbara Kenny, 6-0, 6-2; G. Greenlee def. G. Addleman, 6-1, 6-1.

Yankees Hand Shea All Glory For 3d Victory

Harris and Dressen Laud Righ-Hander; Lavagetto Laments Over Strikeout

By Bob Cooke

The Yankees didn't have time to prepare a clubhouse celebration after they had beaten the Dodgers yesterday in the fifth game of the World Series. They didn't even know they were going to win until Frank Shea fanned Cookie Lavagetto for the final out in the ninth.

Less than two minutes later, the New Yorkers began to parade into their dressing room and one by one managed to foment a certain amount of commotion, although they still bore traces of men who had just won an obstacle race by a nose.

Instead of taking their showers immediately, the Yankees whooped it up with particular attention to Frank Shea, the day's pitching hero.

Shea Besieged

Shea, who had toiled tirelessly for nine innings, received no moment of peace in the dressing room and ran the risk of acquiring another sore arm as he willingly shook hands with others in the room.

Bucky Harris, wearing a new coat of smile, wouldn't let any one wish him a word of congratulations. "Better go see Shea," he said. "He's the guy that did it. We got 'em now, I think."

Charlie Dressen, sitting on a stool next to Harris, summed up the confidence the Yankees have in Shea.

"He's got nerve," said Dressen. "That's why we started him in the first game. They may beat him once in a while, but they never beat him bad."

Over in Shea's sitting room, photographers were blocking each other in an effort to catch a picture of his smiling Irish eyes. Joe DiMaggio, whose homer turned out to be the decisive run, was the first to grab Shea's hands.

In the background you could hear Red Patterson, Yankee road secretary, yelling as loud as his hoarse tones can after a season of shouting contests with Larry MacPhail.

Photographers Warned

"Watch where you throw those flash bulbs," cried Patterson at the photographers. "We got another game tomorrow."

The Yankees, bare feet and all, didn't seem to mind walking on a little glass. They had been tightroping on a high wire for nine innings and if it hadn't been for Shea they might have fallen off.

As Shea and DiMaggio embraced each other for a cameraman, Aaron Robinson, Shea's catcher, came over and tossed the last ball to the winning pitcher. Shea made the catch and the ball disappeared into his stock of major-league mementos.

Later on Shea talked about the ninth inning.

"When Lavagetto came up to pinch hit with the tying run on second and two away, I was only interested in one thing. I wanted to see the ball in Robinson's glove. It looked pretty good after that third strike. Why the heck couldn't it have happened to Bevens, too?

Lavagetto was the only one who could answer that one and he was undressing quietly in the Brooklyn chambers.

Lavagetto Laments

"When they send you up as a pinch hitter and you work the count to three and two, you've got to hit the next pitch," said Cookie. "I mean, if it's in there. It was, but I didn't hit it. I had my chance when the count went to three and one. After Shea worked the full count, he had the edge on me."

There was hardly any noise in the Brooklyn dressing room. And Shotton, wearing the strain of a close nine-inning defeat, was busy encouraging his players for the morrow but there were only a few who acted as though they were looking forward to a return trip to the Stadium. The Dodgers, however, have felt this way before during the regular season, without incurring any disaster on the field.

Eddie Stanky and Hugh Casey sat side by side on a bench, not saying much of anything. Someone came up and muttered "tough luck."

"They didn't beat us yet, did they?" said Stanky.

"It was just one of those games," Casey added. "Either team could have won."

Clyde Sukeforth, one of Burt Shotton's aids, was high in praise of Shea.

Didn't Try to Steal

"He pitched a dandy ball game," said Sukeforth. "The Dodgers were taking good balls and swinging at bad ones. We didn't try to steal, because Shea has such a good motion. He can keep a base runner close to the bag."

Shotton said Vic Lombardi might start today's game against Allie Reynolds, Harris's choice. Shotton didn't say for sure and Chuck Dressen, Yankee coach, predicted that Shotton would use Ralph Branca. Meanwhile, Shotton reserved the privilege to sleep on it, although he anticipated a troubled sleep.

Iowa State Eleven Drops Big Six Game to Kansas

LAWRENCE, Kan., Oct. 4 (AP).—Outplayed in the first quarter, the University of Kansas Jayhawks struck back with a rapid-fire attack to defeat the Iowa State Cyclones, 27 to 7, in the opening Big Six Conference football game of the season here today.

Ray Evans, Kansas back, was the standout player of the day, taking a pass from Lynne McNutt for one touchdown and running six yards for another. Approximately 17,500 witnessed the game. (UP).—Harry Forbes, of Wes-

BLOCKED: Tom Henrich, trying to score in the ninth on a passed ball, is blocked off by Hugh Casey, who took the throw from Bruce Edwards Herald Tribune—Frank

WINNERS: Frank Shea and Aaron Robinson, the Yankees' battery, leaving the field after the game

Yankees Win

(Continued from page one)

bases yesterday. Bucky Harris, the Yankee manager, finally had got around to putting Aaron Robinson, his most experienced catcher, in the series.

Lombardi was on second and he stayed there while Henrich gathered in a long fly to right hit by Spider Jorgensen.

Then, with two out, Lavagetto, the thirty-three-year-old veteran who won Friday's game with a double with two out in the ninth, came to bat in place of Casey to try to win this one, or, at least keep the inning alive.

Shea put over a strike. The next three pitches were wide. Lavagetto took a lusty cut at the next one and missed. The count was three and two. Shea put every ounce of his strength in the next pitch and Lavagetto put every ounce of strength in the swing he took at it. But again he missed. Brooklyn's idol had struck out and the game was over.

Shea ran in from the mound and the players hugged him. It had been a hard game. And it might have been so easy if the Yankees had been able to take advantage of the opportunities offered them.

Rex Barney, a refugee from the Brooklyn bullpen who was not a regular starter during the season, was assigned to start the game.

Barney Walks Nine

In four and two-thirds innings he equalled Jack Coombs's record of nine bases on balls in a game in 1910 and he needed only one more to tie the record set Friday by Bill Bevens.

All in all the Dodgers gave the Yankees ten bases on balls, tying the team record for one day's liberality. In addition to this the Yankees had the benefit of two passed balls, one wild pitch, one man hit by a pitched ball, and an error. But they made only five separated hits and left eleven men on bases.

Shea made two of the five hits. He drove in his team's first run with a single in the fourth and he hit a double in the eighth.

The other Yankee run was delivered by Joe DiMaggio in the fifth when he belted a home run into the left-field balcony.

DiMaggio may be said to have won the game with this homer, but he also helped to make the score as close as it was by striking out with the bases filled in the first inning, and by hitting into two double plays.

Barney kept everybody interested and the Dodger bullpen in a constant state of activity. He walked two men in the first around Henrich's double and then fanned DiMaggio, got George McQuinn to hit into an easy force play at the plate, and left the bases filled by striking out Bill Johnson.

Rizzuto Caught Stealing

He walked Phil Rizzuto and made a wild pitch in the second, but was saved when Rizzuto tried to steal third and was thrown out.

He walked two in the third, but Di Maggio hit into a double play.

Out of all this the Yankees got nothing.

There were two out in the fourth when Barney resumed his quest of the base on balls record. He walked Aaron Robinson and Rizzuto. It was then that Shea lined a hit into left field, driving in a run.

Barney also walked Stirnweiss in this inning and the bases were loaded when Henrich rapped a grounder to Ed Stanky.

After DiMaggio whacked the ball into the stands in the next inning, Barney issued his ninth base on balls to Johnson. That was all Shotton could stand. Joe Hatten was brought in and he got Robinson to pop up.

The Yankees led, 2 to 0, going into the sixth. Shea had a no-hit game for four innings. Reese, drawing a pass in the fourth, was the only man to get on base. Gene Hermanski made the first Dodger hit in the fifth.

Scores on Robinson's Single

Then Shea went a little wild. He walked Al Gionfriddo, who led off, batting in place of Hatten in the sixth. He fanned Stanky, but he walked Reese. Then Jackie Robinson cracked a clean single to center, scoring Gionfriddo. The Dodgers had men on second and third when Robinson stretched his single on Di Maggio's throw to catch Reese running to third.

The crowd was clamorous, but Dixie Walker fouled out to the third baseman and Hermanski hit a long fly to DiMaggio.

Hank Behrman, the next Brooklyn pitcher, was tagged for a single by Henrich, but Lindell fanned and, after DiMaggio walked, George McQuinn also fanned. As McQuinn did so the runners advanced on a passed ball. The Yankees had men on second and third when Johnson rapped an easy one back at Behrman for a third out which made the crowd gasp because the throw to Robinson was almost in the dirt.

The Dodgers had their big chance in the seventh. They had the bases filled with two out. Shea walked Edwards. Arky Vaughan, pinch-hitting for Behrman with two away, doubled to right. Pete Reiser, batting for Stanky, was passed purposely amid boos. Then, with the roar of a hostile crowd ringing in his ears, Shea fanned Reese.

The Yankee pitcher hit for two bases in the eighth and went to third on a passed ball. Casey was pitching for Brooklyn then and he fanned Stirnweiss.

There was some concern over Shea's ability to pitch effectively after all the running he had done. But it did not seem to bother him. He got three men out in order in the eighth.

Then the Yankees got nothing out of an error, a hit batsman and a short passed ball in the ninth.

Henrich got on through Miksis's error. Lindell up to bunt, was hit by a pitch. But DiMaggio hit into another double play and when Henrich tried to score on a short passed ball, Casey covered the plate and stopped him, taking the throw from Edwards and practically sitting on Henrich as he came in.

Casey did his part, but Lavagetto was not up to being a hero two days in succession.

Allie Reynolds will pitch for the Yankees today and attempt to end the series. Vic Lombardi probably will pitch for the Dodgers.

ONE FOR THE YANKEES: Aaron Robinson scoring in the fourth inning on Frank Shea's hit

Herald Tribune—Frank

OUT STEALING: Phil Rizzuto is out at third base in the fifth, Edwards to Spider Jorgensen

Dodgers and Yankees Placed on U.N. Agenda

LAKE SUCCESS, N. Y., Oct. 4 (AP).—The following notice was posted today by the United Nations press division on the board telling correspondents of important future events of the world peace organizations:

"Add to agenda—Dodgers-Yankee committee, 1:30 p. m. forum, Ebbets Field."

Minnesota Runners Win

LINCOLN, Neb., Oct. 4 (AP).—The University of Minnesota won the two-mile team race against the University of Minnesota today. Dick Kilty, of Minnesota,, won in the excellent time of 9:55.

Little World Series

Friday's Results

Syracuse (I. L.), 3; Milwaukee (A. A.), 2. Series tied, 3-all.

Dixie Series

Friday's Results

Houston (T. L.), 1; Mobile (S. [illegible] Houston wins seri[illegible], 4-2.

Pacific Coast Leag

SEMI-FINAL SERIES

Friday's Results

Portland, 4; Los Angeles, 2.
Los Angeles leads series, 3-1.
Oakland, 8; San Francisco, 4.
Oakland leads series, 3-1.

Composite Score of 5 Games

Composite box of the first five games of the 1947 World Series by The Associated Press:

By The Associated Press

BROOKLYN (N. L.)

	G	AB	R	H	2B	3B	HR	RBI	BB	SO	Bat. Av.	PO	A	E	Fld. Av.
Stanky, 2b..	5	16	2	3	1	0	0	2	3	2	.188	11	16	1	.964
Rob'son, 1b..	5	18	2	5	1	0	0	2	2	3	.278	39	3	0	1.000
§Reiser, cf, lf	5	8	1	2	0	0	0	0	3	1	.250	7	0	1	.875
Walker, rf...	5	19	1	5	0	0	1	3	2	0	.263	3	1	0	1.000
Hermanski, lf	5	16	3	2	0	0	0	1	2	3	.125	13	0	0	1.000
Furillo, cf...	5	10	1	3	1	0	0	3	3	0	.300	6	0	1	.857
Edwards, c..	5	19	1	3	1	0	0	1	2	6	.158	34	4	1	.974
Jorg'nsen, 3b	5	16	1	3	1	0	0	2	2	4	.188	7	10	1	.944
¶Lavag'to, 3b	3	4	0	1	1	0	0	2	0	2	.350	0	0	0	.000
Reese, ss....	5	16	3	4	0	0	0	2	4	2	.250	6	13	1	.950
Branca, p...	2	3	0	0	0	0	0	0	0	1	.000	0	0	0	.000
Behrman, p.	4	0	0	0	0	0	0	0	0	0	.000	0	3	0	1.000
Casey, p.....	4	1	0	0	0	0	0	0	0	1	.000	2	2	0	.000
‖Lombardi, p	2	2	0	0	0	0	0	0	0	0	.000	0	0	0	.000
Gregg, p....	2	1	0	0	0	0	0	0	1	1	.000	0	3	0	1.000
Barney, p...	2	1	0	0	0	0	0	0	0	0	.000	0	1	0	1.000
Hatten, p...	2	2	1	1	0	0	0	0	0	0	.500	0	0	0	.000
*Miksis, 2b..	3	1	1	0	0	0	0	0	0	1	.000	1	1	1	.667
†Vaughan ..	3	2	0	1	1	0	0	0	1	0	.667	0	0	0	.000
‡Gionfriddo..	2	1	2	0	0	0	0	0	1	0	.000	0	0	0	.000
Totals.....	5	156	19	33	7	0	1	18	26	27	.212	129	57	7	.963

*Batted for Behrman in 7th of first game and struck out; ran for Reiser in 9th of fourth game.

†Batted for Gregg in 7th of second game and flied out; batted for Gregg in 7th of fourth game and walked; batted for Behrman in 7th of fifth game and doubled.

‡Batted for Barney in 9th of second game and forced Jorgensen; ran for Furillo in 9th of fourth game; batted for Hatten in 6th of fifth game and walked.

§Batted for Casey in 9th of fourth game and walked; batted for Stanky in 7th of fifth game and walked.

¶Batted for Stanky in 9th of fourth game and doubled; batted for Casey in 9th of fifth game and fanned.

‖Ran for Edwards in 9th of fifth game.

NEW YORK (A. L.)

	G	AB	R	H	2B	3B	HR	RBI	BB	SO	Bat. Av.	PO	A	E	Fld. Av.
Stirnw'ss, 2b	5	20	3	7	0	1	0	2	4	7	.350	12	11	0	1.000
Henrich, rf..	5	21	1	7	2	0	1	4	2	2	.333	9	0	0	1.000
Berra, c.....	4	13	2	1	0	0	1	1	1	2	.077	19	2	2	.913
DiMaggio, cf.	5	18	3	5	0	0	2	5	5	2	.278	14	0	0	1.000
McQuinn, 1b	5	20	2	3	0	0	0	1	2	7	.150	35	4	0	1.000
Johnson, 3b.	5	18	5	4	0	2	0	1	2	3	.202	9	8	0	1.000
Lindell, lf...	5	16	2	7	3	1	0	6	5	2	.438	11	0	0	1.000
Rizzuto, ss..	5	18	1	4	1	0	0	1	3	0	.222	10	12	0	1.000
Lollar, c.....	1	3	2	2	1	0	0	1	0	0	.667	2	1	0	1.000
A. Rob'son, c	1	3	1	0	0	0	0	0	1	0	.000	7	0	0	1.000
Shea, p.....	2	5	0	2	1	0	0	1	0	2	.400	1	3	0	1.000
Page, p.....	2	2	0	0	0	0	0	0	0	0	.000	1	2	0	1.000
Reynolds, p.	1	4	2	2	0	0	0	1	0	0	.500	1	0	0	1.000
Newsom, p..	1	0	0	0	0	0	0	0	0	0	.000	0	1	0	1.000
Raschi, p....	1	0	0	0	0	0	0	0	0	0	.000	0	0	0	.000
Drews, p....	1	0	0	0	0	0	0	0	0	0	.000	0	2	0	1.000
Chandler, p.	1	0	0	0	0	0	0	0	0	0	.000	0	0	0	.000
Bevens, p...	1	3	0	0	0	0	0	0	0	1	.000	0	1	0	1.000
**Brown ...	2	1	2	1	1	0	0	1	1	0	1.000	0	0	0	.000
††Clark	1	1	1	0	0	0	0	0	0	0	.000	0	0	0	.000
‡‡Phillips ..	1	1	0	0	0	0	0	0	0	0	.000	0	0	0	.000
Totals.....	4	166	27	45	9	4	4	25	27	28	.271	131	47	2	.989

**Batted for Shea in 5th of first game and walked; batted for Chandler in 6th of third game and doubled.

††Batted for Raschi in 3d of third game and walked.

‡‡Batted for Drews in 4th of third game and flied out.

PITCHING RECORDS

DODGERS

	G	CG	IP	H	R	ER	BB	SO	HB	WP	W	L	Pct	ERA
Casey	4	—	7⅓	3	0	0	1	2	1	0	2	0	1.000	0.00
Branca	2	—	6	6	7	7	5	7	1	0	0	1	.000	10.50
Lombardi .	1	—	4	9	5	5	1	3	0	0	0	1	.000	11.25
Barney	2	—	6⅓	4	2	2	10	3	0	2	0	1	.000	2.84
Behrman ..	4	—	4⅔	7	4	4	2	2	0	1	0	0	.000	7.71
Hatten	2	—	5⅔	8	6	6	3	4	0	0	0	0	.000	9.53
Gregg......	2	—	9	6	2	2	4	7	0	0	0	0	.000	2.00
Taylor.....	1	—	0	2	1	0	1	0	0	0	0	0	.000	0.00

YANKEES

	G	CG	IP	H	R	ER	BB	SO	HB	WP	W	L	Pct	ERA
Shea	2	1	14	6	2	2	7	10	0	0	2	0	1.000	1.29
Reynolds ..	1	1	9	9	3	3	2	6	0	0	1	0	1.000	3.00
Bevens	1	1	8⅔	1	3	3	10	5	0	1	0	1	.000	3.12
Newsom ..	1	—	1⅔	5	5	5	2	0	0	0	0	1	.000	27.00
Page	2	—	7	7	2	2	2	5	0	2	0	0	.000	2.57
Raschi	1	—	⅓	2	1	1	0	0	0	0	0	0	.000	27.00
Drews	1	—	1	1	1	1	0	0	1	1	0	0	.000	9.00
Chandler .	1	—	2	2	2	2	3	1	0	0	0	0	.000	9.00

COMPOSITE SCORE BY INNINGS

Brooklyn (N. L.).............	1	6	2	3	0	2	1	0	4	—19
New York (A. L.).............	2	0	4	4	10	2	5	0	0	—27

Earned runs—Brooklyn (N. L.), 19; New York (A. L.), 26. Left on bases—Brooklyn (N. L.), 36; New York (A. L.), 41. Stolen bases—J. Robinson 2, Reese 3, Walker, Rizzuto, Gionfriddo. Sacrifices—Henrich, J. Robinson, Stanky, Bevens, Furillo. Double plays—Johnson and McQuinn; Jorgensen, Stanky and J. Robinson; Stirnweiss, Rizzuto and McQuinn; Reese, Stanky and J. Robinson (4); Stanky and J. Robinson; Gregg, Reese and J. Robinson; Casey, Edwards and J. Robinson. Hit by pitcher—By Branca (Johnson); by Drews (Hermanski); by Casey (Lindell). Balk—Shea. Passed ball—Lollar, Edwards (2). Umpires—McGowan (A. L.), Pinelli (N. L.), Rommel (A. L.), Goetz (N. L.), Magerkurth (N. L.) and Boyer (A. L.). Attendance—First game, 73,365; second game, 69,865; third game, 33,098; fourth game, 33,443; fifth game, 34,379.

Brown Beaten

(Continued from page one)

fine passer but was not today, threw a very bad one on the game's second play and George Franke, the Tiger fullback intercepted it on the Brown 40 and ran to the 17. From there, Franke carried four times from the single wing and was over into the end zone.

Toward the close of the first period Fred Kozak, Brown halfback and a good one, fumbled at midfield and Bob McCormick recovered on the Brown 46 for Princeton. From there the Tigers went on to score in five plays, one a pass, with Sella running 12 yards for the touchdown.

The third score came midway of the second period and was the result of a real drive of seventy yards in which Princeton's line was the dominant factor although Bob McCormick, a new halfback, showed himself a fast and powerful runner. The scoring play this time was a perfectly executed pass from Carl Leibert, left halfback, to Dick West, quarterback, on the 10, with West outrunning the Brown secondary to the end zone. Bob Meyer, starting right end, kicked all three extra points.

Bruins Start to Click

Up to this point Brown had shown something, but comparatively little. It had moved the ball but could not sustain any sort of drive. The main handicap it seemed, was that there was not nearly enough backfield speed. Backs were broken into the Princeton secondary repeatedly but could not go on their own and Finn's passing, pitifully weak at this stage, could not help them by loosening the Tiger defenders.

The Brown touchdown came on the opening play of the last quarter and for it Roger Young, left halfback, ran twenty-eight yards. This was the only occasion all afternoon on which a Brown back really ran away from Nassau's men and Young seemed actually to be the only man in a Bruin uniform with the speed of foot requisite for the T formation attack. Joe Condon, center, kicked the extra point.

From there on Brown had four chances to score touchdowns, recovering a fumble on the Tiger 32 after the following kickoff, intercepting a pass on the enemy 45, taking a punt back to the 20 and taking another punt back to the 10, they were stopped once by a fumble with a first down on the Princeton three-yard line, again by a fumble on the 20, once by a penalty from the 13 and once they were just stopped.

All through this last exciting period Brown was badly in need of accurate passing or a runner who could cut and get away fast or both. With either the Bruins might well have scored once and it is entirely possible they could have tied the game.

The final score leaves Princeton seemingly much the better club but it may not actually be. The Tigers started ten men from last year's team with Sella the only new man in the wing back spot vacated by Ernie Ransome. It seemed to be a team with good speed, adequate passing by Leibert, considerable depth and a fair degree of ruggedness.

Toward the end, however, some of the items were brought slightly into question and, although Brown was unable to make capital of the defect, the Princeton pass defense was shown to be, at least, spotty.

The line-ups:

Pos.	Princeton (21)	Brown (7)
L. E.	Finical	Campbell
L. T.	Williams	Colo
L. G.	Atkinson	Hodosh
C.	Perantoni	Condon
R. G.	B. Robertson	DeAngelis
R. T.	D. Robertson	McLellan
R. E.	Meyer	Pretat
Q. B.	West	Paterno
L. H.	Leibert	Didonemico
R. H.	Sella	Nelson
F. B.	Franke	Green

Scoring

		P	B
FIRST PERIOD			
5:05	Franke (plunge)	6	0
—	Meyer (place-kick)	7	0
14:58	Sella (run)	13	0
—	Meyer (place-kick)	14	0
SECOND PERIOD			
9:05	West (pass from Leibert)	20	0
—	Meyer (place-kick)	21	0
THIRD PERIOD			
	None		
FOURTH PERIOD			
0:09	Young (run)	21	6
—	Condon (place-kick)	21	7

Substitutes

Princeton—Wagner, Cowir, Roulon, Miller, Eastham, McCormick, Collins, Weber, VanDyke, Keuffel, McKenna, Buxton, Cranberry, Brown, Koch, Gallagher, Mead, Smith, Cleveland, Moore, Palin, Sand, Burns, Cohn, Gruber. Brown—Boothby, Flick, Searles, Schuster, Rougvie, Walters, Iacuele, Livingston, Nicholas, D'Angelo, Scott, Bissell, Diehl, Gresh, Kozak, Pastuszok, Rodwig, Young, Finn.

Officials

Referee—John Coles (Westminster). Umpire—Harold Geiges (Temple). Linesman—Charles Eckles (W. & J.). Field judge—Robert Jamieson (F. and M.).

Statistics

	P	B
First downs	6	11
Yards gained rushing (net)	125	191
Yards gained passing	71	3
Passes	13	12
Passes completed	9	5
Punts	8	8
*Average distance of punts	32	35
Runback of punts	57	8
Fumbles	4	5
Ball lost fumbles	2	3
Penalties	4	3
Yards lost penalties	40	25

*Punts averaged from line of scrimmage.

Yanks 1-2 to Win Fourth From Dodgers Today

ST. LOUIS, Oct. 4 (UP).—James Carroll, betting commissioner, ceased quoting odds on the World Series outcome tonight but made the New York Yankees 1-to-2 favorites to win tomorrow's game against Brooklyn at Yankee Stadium.

In tomorrow's contest, the sixth between the two clubs, you risk $2 to win $1 if Allie Reynolds hurls for the Yanks.

With Vic Lombardi pitching for the Dodgers, those betting on Brooklyn will have to put up $5 to win $8.

Section III-IV

SPORTS
FINANCE—BUSINESS

NEW YORK Herald Tribune

MARINE NEWS
STAMPS

Section III-IV

TEN PAGES

SUNDAY, AUGUST 8, 1948

TEN PAGES

Yankees Down Indians, 5-0; Pirates Nip Giants; Dodgers Lose; Cabrera, Argentinian, Wins Olympic Marathon Race on Final Lap

U. S. Runners Disqualified In 400 Meters

Americans Take 1,600-Meter Relay

Mikaelsson, of Sweden, Wins 10,000 Meter Walk Beating Olympic Mark

By Jesse Abramson

LONDON, Aug. 7.—True to the tradition set down by the obscure Greek shepherd boy, Spiridon Loues, who followed the legendary trail of Pheidipppides in winning the first Olympic marathon race in 1896, a son of Argentina just as obscure led home the distance runners of the world in the classic finale to the Olympic track and field games today.

The winner was Delfo Cabrera, a swarthy, smallish twenty-nine-year-old fireman from Buenos Aires, small but well-muscled, with a running style outstanding among men who generally have so little running style.

He was as unknown as an Olympic competitor can be, possibly the least known among the forty-one runners from twenty countries and the five continents who set out from Wembley Empire Stadium amid the roaring cheers of another capacity crowd of 82,000 enthusiasts.

Third-String on Team

Cabrera had never run a marathon race before. He was only the third-string among the three Argentinians. He had won shorter distances in his native land but was not fast enough by far to gain any attention whatever from the athletic world.

This marathon novice ran strongly all the way on the twenty-six mile three-hundred and eighty-five-yard jaunt through every English Middlesex village and farm, up the longest inclines any Olympic course ever had over winding scenic roads. But he was never in the lead until the final lap of 400 meters was run within the packed stadium.

It was a finish reminiscent of the unforgettable end of the famous race won by Johnny Hayes for the United States forty years ago in this same city when Dorando Piertri, of Italy, the Dorando who was taunted as "gooda for not" in the first song published by Irving Berlin, collapsed within the stadium wall.

Once again, forty years later, a runner, faltering, struggling, picking them up and laying them down with unutterable weariness, was the first to show inside the stadium. He was twenty-two-year-old Etienne Gailly, a Belgian cross-country runner who never had run a full distance marathon either.

Unlike Dorando, Gailly was not in complete collapse. He was worn and weary and ready to collapse but collapse he did not until the race was done. Leading them all when he stumbled through the royal tunnel onto the red track, Gailly had only 430 meters to go to win fame and glory.

But an instant after he came through the tunnel Cabrera followed on his heels. And it was evident immediately that Cabrera, strong, fresh, fast, must easily win. He raced past the tall Belgian in half a dozen strides and ran away from him in his one lap tour of triumph.

Tom Richard Second

Sixteen seconds, or a margin of seventy yards back of Cabrera, Tom Richard, of Great Britain, a male nurse in an asylum, finished second evoking an arena shaking roar from the crowd.

Never a winner of the marathon, England provided the runner-up for the third time in successive Olympics. Richard carried on when Britain's hope, Jack Holden, succumbed en route.

Gaily all this while was tottering onward unlike Dorando, who fell and was carried across the finish line by helpful if misguided British officials, the Belgian finished on his own feet in third place, seconds after Richards. Then he passed out cold. Prostrated by heat exhaustion, carted away on a stretcher for treatment and unable to appear on the podium of honor with Cabrera and Richards.

The rest of the runners shuffled or ran in, depending on their finishing condition, at intervals not to be counted in tenth seconds. Johannes Coleman, South Africa policeman, who learned to run chasing ostriches on his farm, finished fourth, complaining he was knocked off the road by a cyclist en route. He had been eighth at Berlin a dozen years ago. Fifth was Eusebio Guinez, the more highly regarded of the Argentin-

(Continued on page 3, column 2)

Herald Tribune—Acme telephotos

PROTEST: Mel Patton (left) listens intently as officials at Wembley rule out the United States' victory in the 400-meter relay, in which Patton ran the anchor leg

EXHAUSTED: John B. Kelly jr., of Philadelphia, is helped to the boat tent by Mickey McLaughlin (left), trainer, and his father, John B. Kelly, after collapsing at the end of a semi-final heat in the Olympic sculls in which he was defeated

American Men Sweep Olympic Swimming and Diving Crowns

By a Staff Correspondent

LONDON, Aug. 7.—A stupendous total sweep of all eight Olympic championships, a sweep unprecedented in Olympic history, was completed by the men swimmers of the United States in the closing session of the eight-day international water carnival today.

Another capacity crowd of 7,000, filling the towering stands on four sides of the fifty-meter course in Wembley Empire Pool, with thousands storming the gates and being shut out, saw seventeen-year-old Jimmy McLane, Andover stripling from Akron, Ohio, win the 1500-meter free style by 25 yards after twenty-two-year-old Joe Verdeur, of La Salle College, Philadelphia, who has been demolishing world records for four years, won the 200-meter breast stroke in Olympic record time in another one-two-three finish for Americans.

To cap the day for the United States Ann Curtis, twenty-two-year-old Californian from San Francisco, scored a smashing victory in the 400-meter free style for women in a race in which the first five broke the Olympic record.

The American male swimmers coached by Bob Kiphuth, of Yale, not only swept the program but put up a world record in the 800-meter relay during the week, demolished Olympic records in four of the six racing events, the relay, 100-meter and 400-meter free style and breast stroke.

The American girls also "won" in their division by taking four of the seven titles, including two races, the 400-meter relay anchored by Miss Curtis and the 400-meter free style, accounting for two of the four Olympic

(Continued on page 2, column 2)

3 American Crews Reach Final as Kelly Is Defeated

* * *

HENLEY-ON-THAMES, England, Aug. 7 (AP).—Three United States crews swept into the finals of the Olympic regatta today on the wind and rain-lashed Thames River but Jack Kelly, of Philadelphia, figured to be as certain as taxes, was eliminated in the single sculls.

Kelly, who has held virtually every major sculling title in the world, was an odds-on choice to take the Olympic Sculls just as his father did twenty years ago. But he collapsed on the finish line and was shunted to the sidelines by unsung Eduardo Risso, of Uruguay. Even without Kelly the United States may improve on its 1932 Olympic record.

California's eight-oared shell slid through 1,900-meters of the abbreviated Olympic course in 6 minutes 36.5 seconds for the fastest time of the division.

The Californians, who provided Olympic winners in this event in 1928 and 1932, are favored to repeat their triumphs in Monday's final. Great Britain, with a 6:38.1 clocking, and Norway, 6:43.9, are the other contenders.

Varsity fours from opposite sides

(Continued on page 2, column 6)

Monmouth's 37,017 Gate Sets Record

$2,494,845 Wagered Last Day of Meeting

Noble Hero Beats First Nighter by 3/4 Length in Choice; Faraway, 3d

By Bill Lauder Jr.

OCEANPORT, N. J., Aug. 7.—Monmouth Park, reveling in the absence of competition from Long Island tracks while the horses are running at Saratoga, closed its meeting today with the largest crowd and largest handle in its three-year history. It presented the $25,000 added Choice Stakes as the piece de resistance and the mile-and-a-quarter run was won by Leo Gerngross's Noble Hero by three-quarters of a length from the favorite, Silas Mason 2d's First Nighter.

Betters Last Year's Record

The program drew a turnstile crowd of 37,017 and surpassed the former high mark of 33,323 set closing day last year. On the impetus of this final week, the first week Monmouth ever has had without competition from Long Island, the track boasted a daily average of 15,885 and became one of the few tracks in the country with a better average this year than last. The 1947 average was 15,598.

The New York bettors who didn't want the long jaunt to Saratoga helped pour $2,494,845 into the mutuels, cracking last year's closing-day and track-record figure of $2,179,860. En route to this total the machines handled a record daily double pool of $158,126, a new high first-race pool, which competes with the double, $187,574, and three times broke the former one-race mark with $335,803 in the feature, $337,056 in the seventh and $343,356 in the last race.

Running over a slow track, Noble Hero covered the route in 2:06 1/5 and, neglected in the betting, returned $18. And Noble Hero, which took the lead at the three-eighths pole, had to have everything that R. J. Martin asked from him down the stretch to hold off the fast-closing First Nighter. Third, five lengths back, was the pacemaker, the Glen Riddle Farms' Faraway, which had a half length on Mrs. John T. Maloney's Big If. Completing the field were Lester Manor Stable's Compliance and C. V. Whitney's Ready Jack.

Faraway Takes Lead

Noble Hero broke on top, but in the run down the stretch the first time Faraway took over the head end and Big If moved into second place a head in front of Noble Hero. First Nighter was trailing in fifth place as they hit the backstretch. Faraway drew out to a four-length margin after six furlongs, with Big If still second ahead of Noble Hero, and by this time First Nighter had begun to move and was fourth.

Going around the bend Noble Hero moved up and collared the tiring Faraway and First Nighter followed. When they straightened out in the stretch for the last three sixteenths Noble Hero had three lengths on First Nighter, with Faraway third. They maintained this order to the finish, First Nighter cutting the margin with every stride, but distance ran out on him.

Faraway just managed to hold off Big If.

Stewards Suspend Martin

The race was worth $19,700 to Noble Hero and was his fifth victory in eleven races. Under 114 pounds, eight less than carried by First Nighter, Noble Hero was reversing the decision of the recent Lamp Lighter Handicap in which he ran fourth and which was won by First Nighter. That time Noble Hero carried 114 and First Nighter 113, so the shift in weights told the story.

After the running of The Choice,

(Continued on page 6, column 6)

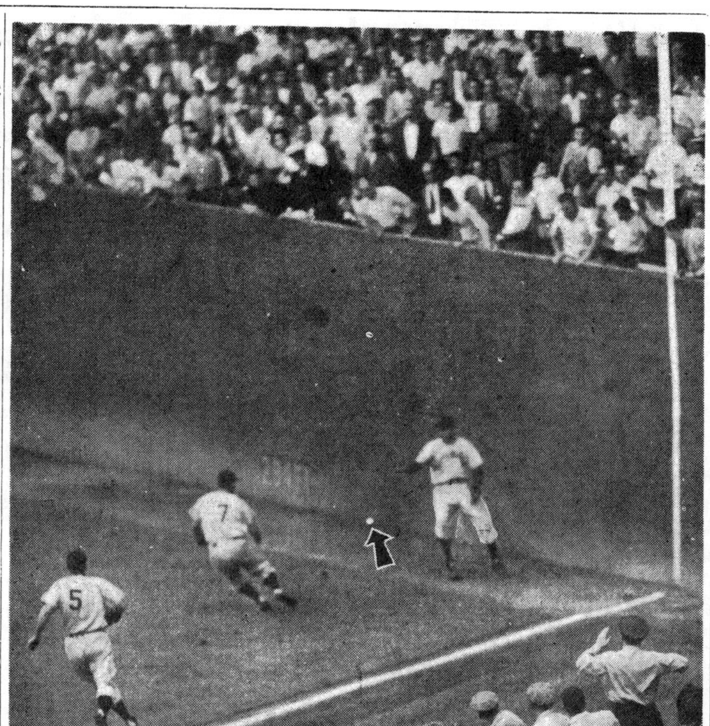

HIT FOR JOHNNY MIZE: Dixie Walker overrunning the ball (arrow) hit by the Giant first baseman at Polo Grounds yesterday. Murtagh (7), second baseman, and Stevens (5), first baseman, are in on the play

Herald Tribune—Frank

Gallorette, The Admiral Win Stakes at Saratoga

By Joe H. Palmer

SARATOGA, Aug. 7.—It took more than two horses could do to stop the Lady from Maryland here today. Natchez spent his speed, and Loyal Legion came on with his finishing burst in the stretch as the Jeffords entry made the old one-two try, but Gallorette dogged the one and outfought the other to win her second stakes of the week, the mile-and-a-quarter Whitney.

It was the reversal of the 1946's story. The Jeffords Stable beat W. L. Brann's great mare in the Whitney that year, at level weight by the scale. This time the Challenger II mare gave the two Jeffords horses weight by the scale and a licking. Meanwhile Arnold Kirkland had switched sides. He rode Pavot in 1946, whistled Gallorette through her drive today.

Loyal Legion gave it a good try but was beaten a long neck, while Natchez, the speedster of the field for a mile, was a distant third. Mill River Stable's Miss Grillo was the other starter, was always fourth.

In the secondary event of the day Ogden Phipps's two-year-old The Admiral, now the ranking juvenile of the meeting, pulled away from the five others in the United States

(Continued on page 6, column 2)

Billows's Team Gains Final in Anderson Golf

Sweeny and Dunphy Lose to Met. Champion and His Partner, Van Benschoten

By Kerr N. Petrie

MAMARONECK, N. Y., Aug. 7.—After hanging on bravely through three rounds, Robert Sweeney and Christopher Dunphy, of Meadow Brook, last year's winners, this afternoon lost their hold on the John G. Anderson Memorial best-ball golf tournament trophy, at the Winged Foot. In the semi-final they were defeated, 1 up in nineteen holes by Ray Billows, and Wesley Van Benschoten, of Poughkeepsie. Billows, winner of the Metropolitan title last week, made the par that won the match as Sweeny and Dunphy both were bunkered.

The other semi-final match, between two Winged Foot teams, went six extra holes. Ed Vaughan and William Schappa winning from Dick Mayor and Charles Mul-

(Continued on page 2, column 8)

Dodger's Rally In 9th Fails as Reds Win, 6-4

VanderMeer Halts Brooklyn for 8 Innings; Gumbert Stops Losers' Late Bid

By Harold Rosenthal

Take a lovely afternoon guaranteed to make every one feel ten years younger including Johnny VanderMeer, venerable left-hander; add a little fielding luck; sprinkle a portion of Dodger over-confidence stemming from the fact that they had beaten the Reds twelve times in fourteen tries this year and what have you got? A 6-to-4 Cincinnati decision over Brooklyn plus Bucky Walters's first victory as a major-league manager before 21,193 disappointed devotees at Ebbets Field yesterday afternoon.

VanderMeer, backed up by capable support in the field and at the plate, had the Dodgers looking sad for eight innings. He restricted them to four hits during this interlude including Roy Campanella's none-on home run in the seventh.

In the ninth, goaded by a five-run deficit, Brooklyn teed off on VanderMeer, but fell short of their objective by a couple of runs. They reached Vandy for four hits in the final frame and routed him after they had nicked him for three runs. It was a spectacle as ineffectual as a pair of chubby fists beating upon a gorilla-like chest. Harry Gumbert, another wheezing gaffer, came in and retired the next two men in order.

Despite the loss Brooklyn managed to cling to second place, because Philadelphia beat St. Louis.

A couple of golden Dodger opportunities offered themselves in the first two innings but the Dodgers turned away. The opportunities weren't there when they went looking for them later.

In the opening frame, VanderMeer gave up two consecutive walks. With two out, Bruce Edwards lined a drive against the

(Continued on page 4, column 2)

Mills, Ill, Cables Niederreiter He Won't Box Gus Lesnevich

By Bob Cooke

The Tournament of Champions, the promtional group which is trying to dislodge Mike Jacobs from absolute powers in the fistic world, lost one of its main attractions yesterday when it was learned that Freddie Mills, light heavyweight titleholder, would be unable to meet Gus Lesnevich because of illness.

Last week Andy Niederreiter, promoter for the Tournament of Champions, announced that Mills, who recently won the light heavywight crown from Lesnevich in a bout in London, would defend the title against Lesnevich at Ebbets Field, with Sept. 23 as a tentative date. The Mills-Lesnevich fight was due to be staged on the same program with the Marcel Cerdan-Tony Zale middleweight title battle.

Niederreiter received the following cablegram yesterday from Ted Broadribb, Mills's manager:

"Mills unwell. Impossible to train. Awaiting medical report Monday. Lesnevich fight must be postponed."

The cablegram spared Niederreiter's backers the annoying bother of putting up a guarantee of $150,000, but it also left them

(Continued on page 6, column 1)

Raschi Holds Tribe Hitters To 4 Singles

DiMaggio Scores 3 With Two Doubles

Bombers Cut Cleveland's Margin to Two Points, 66,693 Witness Game

By Rud Rennie

CLEVELAND, Aug. 7.—Vic Raschi did a professional job of pitching against the Indians this afternoon. He shut them out with four hits—two singles by Dale Mitchell, and two by Larry Doby—while the Yankees whacked Bob Lemon and won, 5 to 0, squaring the series at one-game all before the largest Saturday crowd in Cleveland history, 43,329 paying on a ladies-and-children's day to bring the total attendance to 66,693.

In the hand-to-hand struggle for first place, the Indians held their lead; but the Yankees reduced it to two percentage points. Tomorrow, the teams play a double-header.

Raschi and the old guard—Tommy Henrich, Charlie Kellar and Joe DiMaggio—took charge today. Raschi won his fourteenth game. Henrich, Keller and DiMaggio made six of the Yankees's eight hits and scored four of the five runs.

Raschi Stops Indians

Raschi never looked so strong, throwing the ball with such speed and deception that only two Cleveland batsmen were able to hit it safely. Raschi never let the Indians gang up on him. Never did he let them make more than one hit in any inning. And he was superb in the sixth after Mitchell led off with a single and two of his curves broke into the dirt for wild pitches.

The second wild pitch happened after he had walked Ken Keltner, with two away. He had men on second and third. Joe Gordon, a dangerous man, was at the plate. Raschi struck him out.

The big Yankee right hander fanned seven men and issued only two bases on balls. He whiffed Jim Hegan three times.

Lemon, who had won fourteen

(Continued on page 5, column 3)

Gustine Homer Subdues Giants For Pirates, 5-4

Pittsburgh Infielder's Clout in 11th Wins as Higbe Stops New York Hitters

By Edward Sinclair.

A guy by the name of Frank Gustine fixed New York's Giants, but good, yesterday afternoon. He picked the top of the eleventh inning to stroke his eighth home run of the season, enabling the Pittsburgh Pirates to edge the Giants, 5 to 4, at the Polo Grounds.

A carom shot off the face of the upper left field stands with the bases empty, added a flourishing touch to a fine relief performance by Kirby Higbe. Hig relieved Tiny Bonham, the Buc starter, in the seventh and shut out the Giants with one hit throughout the next five innings.

To the complete embarrassment of 20,408 clients, six pitchers of the local club got into the act. Dave Koslo began the three-hour and nineteen-minute marathon and surrendered the first four Corsair runs in the third. Andy Hansen came on in that inning and gave way to Ken Trinkle in the fourth.

Sheldon (Available) Jones worked the seventh and eighth. Then it was Alex Konikowski in the ninth and tenth and finally Ray Poat in the eleventh. Gustine was the first man Poat faced. It only took two pitches for Poat to receive his sixth loss of the year.

The way things started out it looked as if this one was going

(Continued on page 5, column 4)

Sheridan Mile At Chicago Won By Star Reward

* * *

CHICAGO, Aug. 7 (AP).—Star Reward, at odds of 15 to 1, kept alive the long string of upsets in Chicago Stakes at Washington Park today by sweeping to a four-lengths victory in the $27,350 Sheridan Handicap mile.

Calumet Farm's Fervent, second choice at 7 to 2, finished second, a half a length in front of Augustus and Nahm's Eternal Reward. Fourth place went to Fred W. Hoopers' Colosal by the margin of a head over the 9-to-5 favorite, With Pleasure, thrice the conqueror of the famed Armed last season.

Among the also rans was William Helis's record-breaking Rippey, in a field of eleven.

Star Reward's victory was worth $19,350 to Charles T. Fisher, and his backers in the crowd of 26,389 received $32, $10.80 and $7. Fervent returned $5 and $3.60, and Eternal Reward paid $5.60. Eternal Reward was accompanied to

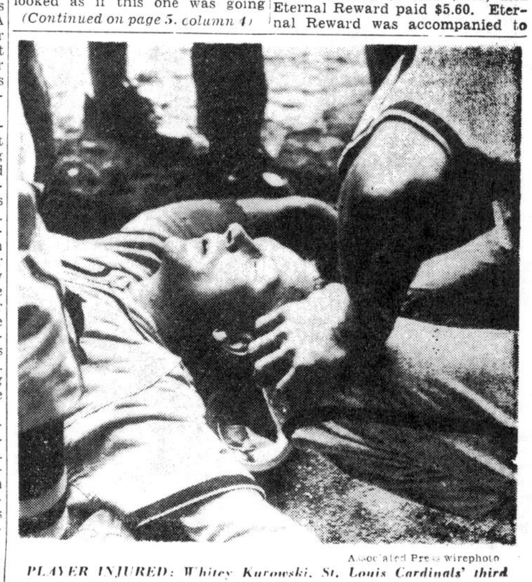

Associated Press Wirephoto

PLAYER INJURED: Whitey Kurowski, St. Louis Cardinals' third baseman, lying on the ground at Shibe Park, Philadelphia, yesterday after being hit in the temple by a ball thrown during practice before the game

Section III-IV | SPORTS · MARINE NEWS | NEW YORK Herald Tribune | FINANCE · BUSINESS | Section III-IV
EIGHT PAGES | SUNDAY, AUGUST 15, 1948 | EIGHT PAGES

Yankees Trounce Athletics 14-3; Giants Vanquish Phillies, 3-1; Ace Admiral Wins Travers, Blue Peter Takes Special at Saratoga

VIEWS OF SPORT

By Red Smith

Peace on Earth

ABOARD S. S. BRITANNIC, Aug. 14.—Well, the first Olympic Games since Hitler are over; the last stout blow for world brotherhood has been struck; the last incompetent boxing referee has been canned; the last infuriated delegate to this council of good will has stomped out in a huff.

Red Smith

"We resign from everything," some French officials screamed as they stormed out of the boxing competition because one of their guys lost a decision. So now that sports have insured the peace of the world, it is time for some summing up.

It has been observed here that the games were well run, in most respects, and were attended by the largest and fairest and most valorous and most generously sportsmanlike crowds assembled since the first discus thrower of ancient Greece skulled his bride with a dinner plate. It must also be confessed that the deportment of the London sports press was as outrageous as that of the customers was exemplary. The blatant provincialism of the Olympic Games coverage would have been deemed scandalous in Columbus, Ohio, at the height of the football season.

Britannia may or may not rule the waves today. She is less than supreme on the cinders. But her domination of movable type is beyond challenging. "McCorquodale Holds U. S. to No. 1," a headline gloated one day. Translated, this meant that the top news of the day was the achievement of Britain's fine sprinter, Alistair McCorquodale, in running second to Barney Ewell in a qualifying heat. Later on when McCorquodale took third in the final behind Bones Dillard and Ewell, one paper paid him the tawdry tribute of describing him as the "World's fastest white human."

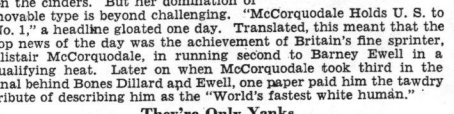

They're Only Yanks

THIS singularly snide sort of voodoo worship is not subscribed to by the British people, whose attitude toward that kind of thing was well stated the other day by two ladies in a fish-market queue. They were talking of President Truman and civil rights. "I don't hold with the color line," said one. "Nor I," said the other. "After all, they're the real Americans. The others are only Yanks."

London's sports fans cheered Mal Whitfield when he broke the Olympic record at 800 meters. But the next morning's headline screamed, "Wint Breaks Record" because the man who finished second was an Empire representative, Art Wint, of Jamaica. When Holland's magnificent mama, Fanny Blankers-Koen, set the only world record established in the games by hitting 11.2 in the 80-meter hurdles, the banner line read, "Maureen Gardner Breaks Record." So it was with Doris Manley, the English typist who was second to Fanny in another race.

So it was, in fact, throughout the competition. The longer England awaited a victory, the more scandalously the press ignored the winners and brayed praise of the home-bred losers. England's sportsmen rejoiced to see justice done when an international jury rejected the improper disqualification of the American 400-meter relay team, but the page 1 streamer wailed: "Our Victory is Victory No Longer; Camera Gives Race to U. S."

The camera, mind you, not Ewell, Dillard, Lorenzo Wright and Mel Patton, who had won the event by seven or eight yards.

Offenders Not on Scene

IN FAIRNESS to individuals, it should be said the worst offenders sat on the copy desk indoors and wrote headlines distorting the reports of the men on the scene. Many London sports writers are competent and honest reporters who produced unbiased and accurate copy although, naturally, they made obeisance to local interest by featuring the best of the British representatives. They couldn't help it, and must have resented it, when some sycophantic slob in the office misrepresented their efforts in the headlines.

Cheaply partisan journalism is not, of course, confined to an Olympic festival nor was it unprecedented. Assorted alibis have been offered for defeats in the past. The most popular device is to blame the austerity diet, whether it's a man or a team or a racehorse that's been licked, and it might be noted in rebuttal that the steak-fed Americans were shut out in all distance races, where stamina is essential.

It Was the Boots

PERHAPS the most piquant excuse yet offered for defeat concerned an Epsom Derby a couple of years ago when the French horse, Pearl Diver, whipped a hot English favorite ridden by Gordon Richards, the champion jockey.

Richards had planned to wear the boots of the late great Steve Donoghue, but when he tried them on before the race they didn't fit. The disappointment, wrote a compassionate chronicler, was more than Gordon could bear.

Maine Chance Horse Scores By 10 Lengths

Winner Pays $25.80 In Stunning Upset

Better Self Second, My Request Out of Money; Crowd Is Spa's Largest

By Joe H. Palmer

SARATOGA, N. Y., Aug. 14.—Just as Saratoga's largest crowd of the season had been lulled by the easy victory of Blue Peter in the Saratoga Special, Maine Chance Farm's three-year-old Ace Admiral put in a stunner and ran off from the seventy-ninth Travers field for a brilliant but highly unexpected victory.

Ace Admiral threw off a couple of lengths at the furlong-pole, apparently shying from the starting gate which had been pulled into the infield, but he had ten left at the finish, with King Ronch's Better Self keeping place by a half length from George Jacobson's Alaiere. Ted Atkinson, getting his second winner of the day, batted Ace Admiral straight and then coasted to the finish line in 2:05 for the mile and a quarter, and those who follow the cerise and white got $25.80.

A race earlier, Blue Peter from J. M. Roebling's New Jersey farm, had won the Special smartly from Woodvale Farm's Sport Page, with William Ziegler's Entrust third.

Crowd of 23,996 Out

Saratoga cut away a considerable part of its deficit in attendance as compared with last year, when the second Saturday drew 23,996. This was up nearly 4,000 over last year's corresponding day, when the count was 20,094, and it was close to 1947's high mark of 24,604.

For the first time this year, the Saratoga handle went over a million, the exact total being $1,122,224. It also beat last year's high mark, $1,110,504, set on closing day.

Ben Whitaker's My Request, starting as odds-on favorite, in the Travers, failed as badly as he had in the class. But this time he had a legitimate excuse. He stumbled leaving the gate and swerved out, grabbing a fore foot with a hind one as he did so. The extent of the injury could not be determined until the colt was cooled out, but it was painful enough that My Request extended himself at no part of the trip and finished as he had started, last, though he picked up a couple of horses meanwhile.

Atkinson had Ace Admiral away winging, and Better Self, hotly in pursuit, cut a nearly three-length advantage to a length rounding the last turn. But once straightened out Ace Admiral began opening. He was running without blinkers, and either the gate or some trick of light through its steel frame scared him, for he ducked suddenly past the middle of the track. But nothing was close enough to profit by the mishap.

Loser Weeper Weakens

Better Self, carrying 124 pounds and giving the winner sixteen, at least ran his race, going steadily for Dave Gorman but never yolking the winner. Loser Weeper, third until the last few strides, weakened a little to lose his position to Alairne.

Ace Admiral was bred in Tennessee, which is supposed to produce walking horse but got a running one today. Miss Mildred Woolwine, who bred him, sold him to Maine Chance at Keeneland in 1946 for $30,000. He had barely won himself out before the Travers, and the $19,650 purse ran his earnings to $52,225.

A son of the English-bred Heliopolis, from the Man o' War mare, War Flower. Ace Admiral has won six of twenty-two starts. The Travers was his first stakes victory, but he placed in five last year, and this season had been third to Mount Marcy and Better Self in the Saranac.

His owner, Mrs. Elizabeth (Arden), Graham, was in Chicago where her unbeaten Mr. Busher was running for the Washington Park Futurity.

Only Four in Special

The Saratoga special, partly because it conflicts with the Sanford on Monday, drew only four starters, with Blue Peter always an odds-on favorite. The War Admiral colt bred by his owner, was quickest at the start and led for every stride of the six-furlong journey. Over a track called fast, but still showing traces of rains on Thursday, he went the distance in 1:13, and paid his backers $2.80.

Entrust was second for the first three furlongs, about a length and a half behind the leader, but as Blue Peter began to draw out, Conn MaCreary began hustling

(Continued on page 5, column 6)

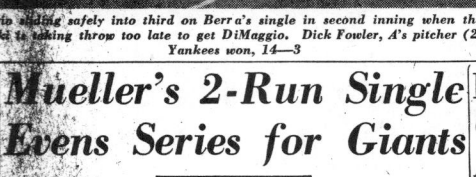

THAT BIG INNING: Joe DiMaggio sliding safely into third on Berra's single in second inning when the Yankees scored eight runs at Stadium yesterday. Hank Majeski is taking throw too late to get DiMaggio. Dick Fowler, A's pitcher (25) is backing up the play. The Yankees won, 14—3

Herald Tribune—Frank

8 Runs in 2d Clinch Game For New York

Raschi Wins 15th On 17-Hit Assault

Harris's Revised Forces Pelt Fowler; DiMaggio Blasts His 25th Homer

By Rud Rennie

The whole thing was accomplished in two shakes. Bucky Harris, the manager, gave the Yankee line-up a shake, and the Yankees gave the Philadelphia Athletics such a shake that all they had left yesterday at the end of nine innings in the Stadium was their breath.

The new Yankee line-up, which had Bobby Brown at third in place of Bill Johnson; Tommy Henrich, the right fielder, at first in place of George McQuinn; Larry Berra, a catcher, in right field; and Gus Niarhos, catching, made seventeen hits and rocked the A's into dizzy defeat, 14 to 3, before 37,036 reanimated rooters.

Every Yankee scored at least once. Each drove in at least one run. Everybody hit safely except George Stirnweiss who went 6 for 0.

Score Eight in One Inning

Twice the Yankees batted all the way around. For the second game in succession they had an eight-run inning against the A's. For the second day in succession they beat the Philadelphia team that has had every one wondering why it was up there in the traffic squeeze at the top of the American League.

Vic Raschi, the Yankee pitcher, had an easy afternoon. With seven hits and two Philadelphia errors which permitted four unearned runs, the Yankees rang up eight tallies in the second inning, all off Dick Fowler, who was allowed to stay in and take it.

They tagged Alex Kellner for four runs in the fourth.

Joe DiMaggio nailed Charlie Harris for a solo homer, his twenty-fifth of the year, in the fifth; and Brown doubled and Henrich knocked him home with a single in the seventh.

The first hit made off Raschi was a home run by Ferris Fain with nobody on in the fourth.

Valo Scores in Fifth

Elmer Valo doubled and Buddy Rosar drove him home in the fifth. Consecutive singles by Barney McCosky, Sam Chapman and Fain accounted for a run in the eighth.

Raschi limited the A's to six hits in winning his fifteenth game of the season.

Twelve men came to bat for the Yankees in the lusty second inning. Four balls batted within the confines of the infield kept the inning going and built up the score.

One run was in and there were men on first and third with none out when Phil Rizzuto bunted and Fain juggled the ball and dropped it. A run scored on this play and a moment later the bases were filled when Niarhos bunted toward third and caught Hank Majeski flat-footed.

When Raschi followed with a hit, which caromed off Fowler's glove past the second baseman, two runs scored. Another came in when Pete Suder fumbled Stirnweiss's grounder.

Brown's Fly Scores Run

Five runs were in before the A's got one out. When Brown flied to Chapman, another run scored.

Then Henrich doubled, putting Stirnweiss on third, and DiMaggio sent both runners home with a single. Berra, up for the second time, got his second hit in the inning, but Keller hit into a double play.

Brown, DiMaggio, Berra and

(Continued on page 2, column 2)

Isa Wins Dash At Atlantic City By 1½ Lengths

Victor Defeats Rampart in 6-Furlong Mermaid Before Record 25,001

By Bill Lauder Jr.

ATLANTIC CITY, N. J., Aug. 14.—An invader from Chicago's Arlington Park, Brookfield Farm's Isa, set the chalk players back on their heels in the $10,000 added Mermaid Handicap today at the Atlantic City Race Track.

The only three-year-old in the field of six fillies and mares and having gone to the post only four times previously, Isa led all the way in the six-furlong event and held off the finishing rush of the even-money favorite, Mrs. H. K. Haggerty's Rampart, by a length and a half.

The crowd of 25,001, which flocked to the seaside course, bettered the former attendance mark of 24,541, set Aug. 9 last year. The throng wasn't able to break the one-day betting mark, but those who thought Rampart, a competitor in top-flight handicap company, was a cinch, lost the $59,540 they bet on the mare to win.

E. K. Bryson's Going Airy was third, nipped by a neck in the last strides by Rampart, and H. S. Horkheimer's Tony's Find was fourth. Completing the field were B. O. Hickman's Valhalla and J. P. Kleis's Sylvia Dear. The victory was worth $8,100 to Isa, which paid $12 for her third victory in five races. She ran the route in 1:12⅘.

Breaking out of the gate Valhalla was the first to show an advantage, but Henri Mora moved Isa up into the lead after a sixteenth. From there on it was a front-running race for the lightweighted filly, which got in under 105 pounds, or fifteen less than toted by Rampart.

Down the backstretch and around the turn the chase after the leader was led by Going Airy, about two lengths back of Isa until they hit the head of the stretch, three-sixteenths from the

(Continued on page 5, column 1)

Mueller's 2-Run Single Evens Series for Giants

By Edward Sinclair

PHILADELPHIA, Aug. 14.—The New York Giants succeeded this afternoon where they failed so miserably last night. Behind Sheldon Jones and his steady hurling, they beat the Phillies, 3 to 1, before a ladies' day crowd of 15,195 at Shibe Park.

Jones yielded seven hits. He gave no more than two in any one inning and that happened only twice. Both times sharp infield work wiped out the threat. The rest of the time he had the Phils hitting just about where he wanted them to hit.

His commendable work in his forty-fifth appearance of the season brought him his eleventh victory as opposed to six defeats. It also boosted the Giants to within a percentage point of the fourth-place Pittsburgh Pirates.

When at bat, the Giants were just as helpful to Jones as they were afield. They pounded Robin Robin Roberts, the $35,000 rookie right-hander, for ten hits, a single by Don Mueller and Walker Cooper's twelfth homer, were the deciding blows.

Mueller's safety came in the fourth inning after Eddie Miller had put the Phils a run in front with a homer into the lower left-field stands in the second inning. Making his first start in the Giant line-up since he came up from Jersey City, Mueller slammed a single to center field with the bases loaded and knocked in two runs.

Two innings later, with two away and the bases empty, Cooper poled one deep into the upper left-field seats. It was the 120th four-bagger for the club this sea-

(Continued on page 2, column 2)

Dodgers Score 6th-Inning Run And Tie Braves

Brooklyn Evens Count on Sturgeon's Two Errors in Third Game of Series

By Harold Rosenthal

BOSTON, Aug. 14.—With their "crucial" series evened off at a game apiece, the Brooklyn Dodgers faced the Boston Braves tonight in the third of a five-game set. Rex Barney, the big right-handed speedballer, was on the mound for Brooklyn, opposing Nelson Potter.

The teams weer tied, 1 to 1, at the end of the sixth inning as this editon went to press.

Barney had a record of ten victories and six losses going into tonight's contest, compared to Potter's two and two since he came up to the Braves late in June. A late afternoon downpour and threatening weather in the evening held the crowd to below capacity figures for the third consecutive night. There were approximately 30,000 customers in the stands when the game started.

Barney had faced the Braves on two previous occasions and dropped both decisions. In both cases he had failed to last the route.

Rackley's Triple Wasted

Marv Rackley opened with a triple into center field, but Potter got the next three batters. Jackie Robinson flied out to Mike McCormick in center, Hermanski was thrown out by Potter on a roller and Duke Snider went down on a grounder to Bob Sturgeon.

Barney set down the Braves in order in their half of the first inning. Holmes rolled out to Robinson, Dark put up a pop fly to Rackley in left field and Robinson handled Torgeson's roller for the third out.

Pee Wee Reese struck out leading off the Dodgers' second. After that Dark threw out Bruce Edwards and Gil Hodges lifted a high fly, which Jeff Heath caught in foul territory in left field.

The Braves picked up one run in the second inning when, with

(Continued on page 2, column 5)

Mrs. Zaharias Paces National Golf With 222

Leader Has 8-Stroke Edge Over Grace Lenczyk After 54 Holes of Play

NORTHFIELD, N. J., Aug. 14 (AP).—Mrs. Mildred Zaharias, of Ferndale, N. Y., had the women's National Open golf tournament in the palm of her hand today after the first fifty-four holes of play at the Atlantic City Country Club.

She set a course record for women with a 72 in a morning round, scoring the tournament's only birdie with a three on the eighteenth hole. Wind slowed down her long ball in the afternoon round, but she finished with a 75 for a 54-hole total of 222.

That gave her an eight-stroke bulge over her nearest rival, Grace Lenczyk, of Newington, Conn., national intercollegiate champion. Miss Lenczyk and Betty Hicks, De-

(Continued on page 3, column 7)

Greiner Takes 1-Stroke Lead In St. Paul Golf

Baltimore Player Cards 67 for 54-Hole Total of 204; Demaret Second

ST. PAUL, Minn., Aug. 14 (AP).—Otto Greiner, of Baltimore, a virtual unknown among professional golfers, boosted himself into the lead of the St. Paul Open at the end of today's third round.

Greiner, twenty-nine-year-old former Navy flyer, fashioned a five-under-par 67 to take a one-stroke lead over Jimmy Demaret, of Ojai, Calif. Demaret started the day with what appeared to be a comfortable three-stroke lead.

But Greiner, shooting excellent golf, particularly with his irons, shot par or better to overtake Demaret. He counted birdies on the fifth and eighth holes, and was two under par on the 519-yard twelfth hole when he dropped his chip shot. He was one over par on the fifteenth hole, but came back with birdies on the sixteenth and eighteenth holes.

Greiner Scores Eagle

Greiner has been playing golf virtually all his life, but has been a professional for but fifteen months. His eagle on the twelfth came when his chip shot hit the green about fifteen feet out, rolled about a foot past the cup and then back in.

Demaret had trouble on the first nine. He took a one-over par 37 going out and had to put in some hard work to finish with a one-under-par 35 coming in.

Greiner, in putting together his 204 total, has played consistent sub-par golf. He shot a 68 the first day, and a 69 yesterday.

Par took a beating from the cut-down field today, nineteen of the contestants bettering par and six others equalling it.

Two strokes behind Demaret at 207 were E. J. (Dutch) Harrison, of Albuquerque, N. M., and George Fazio, Conshohocken, Pa. Harrison

(Continued on page 3, column 5)

Olympics Close With Splendor, Americans Taking 38 Medals

OLYMPIC STADIUM, WEMBLEY, Aug. 14. (AP).—The Olympic games ended late today in golden sunshine and splendor, sixteen days and 1,500,000 spectators after they were opened by Britain's king.

The Olympic torch, which has blazed symbolically through the days and nights of a great sports spectacle was extinguished. The flags of competing nations were paraded as a vast throng of 80,000 stood wth bared heads and sang to the tune of the "Londonderry Air."

"Let us be glad—but not because of winning,
"Let us go home one family today.
"God make our games a glorious beginning,
"And, hand in hand, together guide us on our way."

The music perhaps is better known as that of "Danny Boy."

The music, plus the words, were tremendously moving in today's setting. The words were written especially for the occasion.

England Shows Pride

The British still are the masters of such pageantry. There was a haunting beauty to the closing of the games. A lump was in many a throat when there died upon the sunlit air the final strains of "God Save the King." For a minute the crowd stood still, seemingly not realizing it was over.

Proudest of all, standing there, seemed to be the Americans. For them it had been a glorious two weeks. They were carting away the most gold medals—thirty-eight—and the unofficial team championship with 662 points, compared with 353 for second-place Sweden.

The Olympic Games were such a wondrous success it is difficult to realize tonight that there was great fear less than three weeks ago that they would flop.

The 80,000 and more who climbed the long hill leading to the Olympic Stadium to say goodby to the games might have been there for sixteen days. They looked the same as the sun-baked throng which saw the opening. England has taken a terrific pride in showing the world that, despite its

(Continued on page 3, column 3)

Shillalah Wins Atlantic Coast Star Class Title

* * *

By Everett B. Morris

BAY SHORE, L. I., Aug. 14.—Shillalah, sailed by Mr. and Mrs. E. W. (Skip) Etchells, of the Larchmont Yacht Club, won the Colleen Trophy, emblem of the Atlantic Coast championship of the International Star Class Yacht Racing Association, off here today.

The 1944 winner earned her second leg on the prize by rolling up seventy-three points out of a possible seventy-five in a five-race series conducted under the joint auspices of the Bay Shore Yacht Club and the Great South Bay Star fleet.

Shillalah, which had three firsts and a second to her credit before the final race, finished astern of her clubmate, Wahini, in the last outing. Wahini, with Pat O'Gorman at the helm and Rundelet Blakemore tending sheets and backstays, won the two contests which Shillalah did not and took runner up honors with seventy-one points.

No one was even close to the

(Continued on page 4, column 6)

Jany, French Champion, Beats Americans in Dual Swim Meet

By Jesse Abramson

PARIS, Aug. 14.—While a skeleton task force of the United States Olympic squad was helping to wind up the London games across the Channel, the swimmers inaugurated the post-Olympic invasion of France in the Tourelles swimming stadium today with a succession of reverses in which 200-pound Alex Jany, the deflated darling of France, regained the love of his admirers.

The nineteen-year-old world record holder could not handle the American competition in the United States on his visit there a year and a half ago, and he was soundly beaten by the Americans in all his Olympic races. But in his home waters, ten degrees or more colder than the Wembley pool, and with the aid of home cooking the last week, Jany finally defeated the Americans. He did it twice—in the 100 meter free-style and in the 800-meter relay.

The Americans, to be sure, are barnstorming after unprecedented successes in the Olympics. Wally Ris, Olympic 100-meter free-style champion and record-holder, flew in from Frankfurt last night after giving three days of exhibitions for United States troops.

Enough of such excuses. Jany won, and the capacity crowd of 7,500, jammed on four sides of the fifty-meter pool, went wild over his belated successes. The brawny youngster, off in front and never headed, took the metric century by

(Continued on page 3, column 5)

Mrs. duPont and Miss Brough Win Grass Court Tennis Title

By Fred Hawthorne

SOUTH ORANGE, N. J., Aug. 14.—Mrs. Margaret Osborne duPont, Brough, of Beverly Hills, Calif., won the women's Eastern grass court doubles championship this afternoon by defeating Doris Hart, of Miami, and Mrs. Patricia Canning Todd, of La Jola, Calif., 6—2, 4—6, 6—4, on the courts of the Orange Lawn Tennis Club.

In the semi-final round of the men's singles Frank A. Parker, of Los Angeles, first ranking player in the national listing, defeated Gardnar Mulloy, of Miami Beach, —6, 6—4, 6—3, 6—2, and Ted Schroeder, of La Crescenta, Calif., won from Victor Seixas jr., of North Carolina University, in straight sets, 6—2, 11—9, 8—6.

Parker and Mulloy will start the final round match of the singles at 1:30 o'clock tomorrow afternoon and the final of the women's singles will begin about 3 o'clock. The tournament will end with the final round of the men's doubles, starting at 4 o'clock.

The most thrilling match today was between Schroeder and Seixas, the young collegian who defeated Bill Talbert, third seeded player, and Jim Brink, in the third and fourth rounds earlier this week. Considering that Seixas is No. 10 in the national rating while Schroeder is No. 2, his showing against Schroeder was top class.

In the opening set Schroeder fairly burned up the court as he hammered over furious services, charged in behind these blasting deliveries and also spread-eagled the net when he rushed in behind

(Continued on page 6, column 2)

Dewey And Warren Map Strategy For Campaign

Albany, N.Y., Aug. 16 (UP)—Governor Thomas E. Dewey and his vice-presidential running mate will concentrate on building up Republican strength in the United States Senate as chief objective of their separate but closely co-ordinated campaigns, it was disclosed today.

This was indicated by Herbert Brownell Jr., GOP campaign manager, at a news conference. Dewey and Governor Earl Warren of California were closeted with top Republican strategists.

Brownell said both candidates would conduct "very active campaigns," touching many of the same states but not at the same time. He refused to disclose any definite dates or itineraries.

"WE ARE ALL very happy right now," Brownell said. "We're not overlooking any bets, however, and both candidates will wage vigorous campaigns throughout the country."

He said it was "safe to speculate" that a very important part of the national campaigns will be devoted to increasing the Republican Senate majority.

Brownell said Dewey and Warren probably would make personal appearances in different cities when they visit the same state.

Once Over Lightly

By Walter Seigenthaler

Women like to brag about outstanding things their husbands have done. My wife says mine was sleeping through the "Birth of a Nation." . . . Used to be that they asked Father first. Now they tell him last.

FBI Arrests Deserter Who Fled Fort Knox

Arrest of a 28-year-old Army deserter, inducted once under an alias and again under his real name, was announced yesterday by Harvey G. Foster, special agent in charge of the FBI's Indiana office.

Foster said Hobert B. Rumple was apprehended at his home in the 1200 block of North Oxford Street. Rumple had been sought since June 12, 1946, when he escaped an Army stockade at Fort Knox, Kentucky, where he was serving a three-year term on a previous charge of desertion.

Rumple, Foster said, was inducted in 1944 under the name of Elbert L. Smith, and again in 1945 under his true name. His previous desertion was determined after the latter induction, Foster said.

'Censorship' Bow Wows Out At Dog Pound

It looked for a time yesterday as if even City Dog Pound records are confidential.

Sgt. Thomas Yott, acting pound head, told a reporter they were confidential and could be inspected only on order of the police chief. The reporter was attempting to check a story about two Legionnaires who finally found their lost dog at the pound.

Mayor Al Feeney and Leroy J. Keach, Board of Safety president, quickly overruled Sgt. Yott, who is filling in at the pound during the vacation of Sgt. James Payne.

The Legionnaires turned out to be Ellis E. Campbell, 144 North Alabama Street, and Carl Womack, 121½ North Alabama, who said their dog, Rags, was called out of an ice cream store next door to where Campbell lives by the dog catcher and taken away.

Sgt. Yott said the pound received numerous complaints about Rags being permitted to roam in violation of the quarantine.

Looting Of Safe Inside Job, Belief

A safecracking early yesterday at Stokely-Van Camp, Inc., 2002 South East Street, which netted $660 in cash and $800 in bonds may have been an "inside job," police theorized.

Stanley Short, 58 years old, 1131 East Raymond Street, assistant personnel manager, told police he received a call from Orville Peckinpaugh, 58, 615 Prospect Street, an employe, informing him the safe had been opened and the office ransacked.

Police believed someone familiar with the safe was responsible because it had been opened by working the combination.

Works Board Votes For Paving Of Alley

Paving the alley south of Yoke Avenue from Allen Avenue to Manker Street was authorized yesterday by the Board of Works and ordered advertised for bids. Estimated cost is $5,184.

A complaint from a West Side resident over condition of the intersection at 16th Street and Bellevieu Place brought a promise of action from Mayor Al Feeney and the board.

John A. Weinbrecht, 2447 West 16th Street, wrote the mayor, saying that cuts in the pavement made by the Citizens Gas and Coke Utility have sunk and busses have damaged the pavement and the curb.

Army To Parley On Alaska Plans

Detroit, Mich., Aug. 16 (AP)—The Army Corps of Engineers today mapped a series of conferences to shape up a $65,000,000 air field expansion program for Alaska.

An informal meeting will be held Aug. 24 at Chicago to which construction contractors of that area have been invited. Similar conferences will be held at Seattle, Kansas City and New York.

Col. A. Riani, Detroit district engineer, said the corps plans an 18-months' program to construct housing, warehouses, barracks and air field buildings.

Bids will be asked late this year and early in 1949 on 10 contracts, the largest for about $1,000,000, he added.

Babe Ruth, Idol Of Millions Young And Old, Dies At 53

SCENES IN RUTH'S CAREER—At the left the Babe is shown when he was a great pitcher for the Boston Red Sox early in his career. In the center photo he takes a healthy swing at the ball during an exhibition game in Florida while a member of the New York Yankees. At the right the Bambino poses with his teammate, the late Lou Gehrig (right), in New York during an exhibition game between the Yankees and the Brooklyn Dodgers. (AP Wirephoto.)

RUTH THE SLUGGER—Here is the Babe in his Yankee uniform when he was at the height of his reign as the "Sultan of Swat." One report was that the Babe owed his batting prowess to his excellent eyesight—that Ruth's eye reactions were approximately 12 times faster than the average man's.

RUTH EMBRACES THE GREAT "COLUMBIA LOU" GEHRIG—The two pleasant-faced men above were kingpins of one of the most formidable batting lineups ever brought together in the major leagues. "Truant tears stole bases on his cheeks," one writer said of Lou Gehrig as the Yankee "iron man" heard the thundering cheers of the thousands who attended "Appreciation Day" for the first baseman. However, Lou "bucked up" when Babe Ruth stepped up and embraced him. Lou's baseball career came to a close shortly afterward. He was stricken by a spinal malady. (AP Photo.)

IN HIS HEYDAY—Babe Ruth shows the powerful figure, mighty arms and keen eyes which made him a terror to opposing pitchers. Born Feb. 6, 1895, in a squalid, dock-front section of Baltimore, Md., Ruth became a symbol of the land of opportunity in his rise from poverty to fame and wealth. The Babe was sent as a youngster to a Baltimore industrial home. It was there that the first glimmer of his natural athletic ability appeared.

AUG. 5, 1947—After a siege of 82 days in the hospital, here is Babe Ruth as he left French Hospital in New York City Feb. 15, 1947. This photo shocked millions of baseball fans who remembered the Bambino as a robust, grinning, swashbuckling giant who once, with two strikes on him, pointed out over the outfield wall and then put the next pitch in the exact spot he indicated for a home run. The same grin was still there, but it was hard for many to realize that this was the one and only Babe Ruth. (AP Wirephoto.)

"PRIDE OF THE YANKEES"—Babe Ruth and his wife are shown at the Astor Theater in New York on July 15, 1942, as they attended the world premiere of the movie, "Pride of the Yankees," the story of the life of Lou Gehrig. Babe played himself in the moving picture. (AP Photo.)

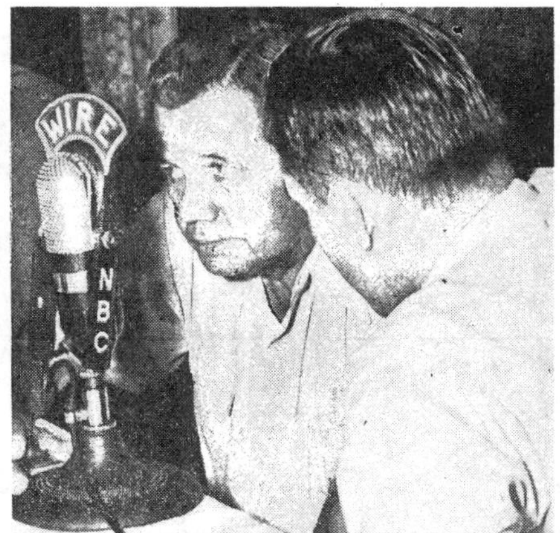

GIVES RADIO INTERVIEW HERE—The Babe gives the lowdown on American Legion junior baseball to Tom Carnegie, WIRE sports commentator, in a radio interview Aug. 5, 1947. The Bambino made two radio broadcasts and appeared at Victory Field during the Legion all-star game that night. He also was guest at a luncheon for press and radio men in Indianapolis. (Star Photo.)

THE BABE AND LOYAL FANS—Here's the way millions of baseball fans, moviegoers and sports addicts remember the Bambino—with a jam of gleeful fans around him. Here he greets them outside his home in New York City. The Babe loved kids and they returned his affection. (AP Wirephoto.)

The Man Who Was Two Men—Babe Ruth

There'll Never Be Another . . .

GEORGE HERMAN RUTH, the immortal Babe of the home-run bat and the timeless king of the baseball diamond, is dead.

A victim of the relentless killer of humanity, cancer, he has died in his fifty-fourth year, and sports-minded America from the mightiest to the most humble mourns his passing.

For Babe Ruth, who rose to fame and wealth from a childhood of extreme obscurity, epitomized the American way of life—the boundless land of opportunity that is this land of ours.

There were two Babes, really.

There was the Babe Ruth of the diamond, a rollicking man of limited education to whom his chosen game had become as natural as eating and breathing.

THIS Babe had a genius for a difficult sport that shone like the star he became. Of him, a great manager once said:

"He never threw to the wrong base. He never made a mental misplay."

His enormous pitching skill was dwarfed and forgotten in his terrific prowess with the bat, which catapulted him into the hall of baseball fame as the Home-Run King of all time.

But there was another Babe Ruth—Babe Ruth the tradition.

In his early, playboy days this second Babe was a-borning, perhaps unknown to the great slugger as he fought for homers and battled his employers for higher and higher pay contracts.

But there came a day when the two were one, and one they were to remain until his death last night.

BABE came to the realization that he belonged to the youth of America—to those humble small boys like the one he had been, and until the last day he did not deny himself to them.

Hand in hand, in kindliness and decency, these two Babes went through life together, the one earning the respect and terror of opposing pitchers, and the other earning the love and undying devotion of all the boys of his native country.

The priest who gave him the last rites of the church told the children assembled outside the hospital:

"He died a beautiful death."

He might have added:

"He lived a beautiful life."

Yes, there were two Babe Ruths—the Slugger and the Tradition.

Only one of them, the Home-Run King, died in New York last night.

The other will live forever.

Going After Business

THAT is an enterprising move which the Baltimore Association of Commerce is making on behalf of this city by establishing a "Port of Baltimore" office in the nation's metropolis and greatest port.

According to Mr. G. H. Pouder, executive vice-president of the association:

"The New York office will develop industrial leads and serve Baltimore business in other ways . . . Much of the control of port business is in New York."

There is much competition for port business and Baltimore does well to be represented in that city where, in the words of Mr. Pouder, so much of the business is controlled. Boston, New Orleans and other cities have offices in New York. Philadelphia, it seems, has a vigilant representative.

During 1947 this port led all the rest in the volume of export tonnage and was second in the total of foreign shipping, export and import. More recently there has been a lull in foreign trade here as in other ports.

Baltimore should be in position to capitalize its advantages in handling such trade, whether there is a lull or a boom, and the Association of Commerce does well in this latest step to promote business.

LISTEN, WORLD!

—By Elsie Robinson

(Registered U. S. Patent Office.)

I am a woman. I admire and have great hopes for my sex, including myself.

But the idea of a woman President gives me the seven-day hiccups.

Why can't women be presidents?

Because women won't pay the price for being presidents.

As long as women are yanked around by every new silly fashion fad . . . as long as women hang and chatter like monkeys from apartment house windows and over the telephones, as long as they decorate themselves with gadgets like the duck-billed natives of the Ubangi, they will never enter the White House.

HAVE SENSE ENOUGH

Haven't women as much intelligence as men?

Maybe.

Aren't they as courageous as men?

Many of them are, and some are more so. And they are endowed with a terrific possessiveness and persistence which we call patience. But they are not trail wise and will not become trail wise, because they are distracted by gadgets and nonessentials.

Yes, men buy fancy neckties, men do silly things, men get tight at conventions. All this is true, but the fact remains that the most chinless wonder of the male sex has a main drive in him which women do not understand.

BOUND BY PAST

For women, even the modern working woman who has taken her place in current life within the last 30 years, are still bound by the old laws of the kitchen and the harem. They still think in personal terms. They still scheme and maneuver to gain their petty ends, as they did when they had to run the house on one dollar per week from their lords and masters.

There is a terrible power in women. Some day that fact will be realized, and this will be a woman's world as well as a man's world. But it is not a woman's world yet, and it will never be as long as she is distracted by a pair of fancy earrings or a hunk of juicy gossip.

Yes, men gossip, but gossip is the froth on a man's life. Underneath that he has learned teamwork. He may be stupid, he may be shallow, but he has learned the main drive from his first job as a newsboy until he takes his seat as a Senator.

DON'T COMPROMISE

And there is another reason why women will not be taken seriously for many a decade. Women do not know how to compromise. They must have life 100 per cent white or it is 100 per cent black.

But compromise is the very essence of the abundant life. You cannot live by your own behavior pattern alone. You must adjust yourself to one hundred and forty million other Americans, and that at present, despite her recent industrial activities, is beyond the average woman's comprehension.

Scales Of Tomorrow

Out in the wasteland of vanishing cheer
Atoms are scarcely the breeders of sorrow;
Science may lurk in a shadow-mind fear
But hatred and love tip the scales of tomorrow.

—Mary O'Connor.

ON THE SIDE

—By E. V. Durling

After pointing out that the author of the best seller, "Live Alone and Like It," hurried into matrimony at the first opportunity offered, I commented:

"Bachelors often live alone and like it. Bachelorettes never do."

From a telegram received from Jean Dalrymple, the brilliant Broadwayite, I quote:

"I am a bachelorette and I live alone and I adore it."

Miss Dalrymple acquires a very fancy income from her efforts as a theatrical producer and public relations expert.

She is domiciled in an elegant duplex apartment and is the possessor of a wardrobe that includes 24 evening gowns and four mink coats.

All that helps make living alone more bearable. But I am prepared to wager that Miss Dalrymple will be married within two years.

Brian Donlevy. Specialist in film portrayals of hard-boiled guys with soft hearts. Brian was born in County Armagh. Ireland, but was brought to this country a babe in arms and reared in Sheboygan Falls, Wis. At the age of thirteen he was a bugler with General Pershing's forces in Mexico. In World War I he fought with the French aviation force. Made his first stage appearance as Corporal Gowdy in "What Price Glory" in 1924.

Estelle Behrens. Song writer. Composer of the touching torch song. "There'll Be Another Spring."

Joe Smith. Veteran comedian. Joe and Charlie Dale have been stage partners for 50 years. That's the record for longevity in stage partnerships, isn't it? All right, name one that lasted longer.

Queries from clients:

Q.—Why is it a dog barks fiercely at the garbage man and wags his tail cordially at the postman and grocery boy? A.—Very simple. A dog figures himself to be chief guardian of his master's property. The garbage man takes something away. The postman and the grocery boy bring things in.

Q.—My father was born in Atlanta, Ga., and loved that city. So he gave me the first name of Atlanta. I don't like it. What do you think? A.—Atlanta isn't such a bad name for a girl. Anyway, be thankful your father wasn't born in Kalamazoo.

South Africa has a higher percentage of millionaire residents than any other country in the world. Most of them live in Capetown, which I understand is a very lively place.

Gailey Bailey of Joplin, Mo., is reported being groomed to run for president of the My-Name-Is-a-Poem Club.

Frank Leonard, Lilian Russell's brother, was a brilliant Christian Science lecturer. So states a Chicagoan who says she knew Frank personally. That's the first time I knew Lilian Russell had a brother. Guess I will have to read her biography again.

Q. And A.

Q.

Brother will vindicate brother,
But who will divulge the reason
For women not loving each other—
Their greatest and stupidest treason?

A.

Well, I—in six words flat:
Men are the cause of that.

—LETA MESTON.

MODEST MAIDENS

Trademark Registered U. S. Patent Office

"WHAT DO YOU SAY WE PLAY HOOKY THIS AFTERNOON AND GO TO A SHOW?"

YOUR AMERICA AND MINE

By HARRY H. SCHLACHT

"BREATHES there the man, with soul so dead,
Who never to himself hath said,
This is my own, my native land!"

"The soul of our America is its freedom of mind and spirit in man."

Thus spoke our only living ex-President Herbert Hoover on the occasion of the celebration of his seventy-fourth birthday in rural Iowa, where he first saw the light of day.

Mr. Hoover lamented that here in America there are those who "never have understood and will never understand what the word America means."

"If the people of our country do not teach its history and perpetuate its spirit and import its moral meaning," declared this great American, "how are the people to know and profit by and enhance their heritage?"

If we love America,
If we love its civilization,
If we love its dream for humanity,
Then let us give young America a thorough knowledge of American history.

Let them know the story and the glory of their country.

Let us organize American history clubs
In all our school houses,
In all our churches,
In all our veteran organizations,
In all our patriotic associations,
In all our public forums.

The Hearst newspapers have advocated for years
The study of American history in all our schools and colleges.

We must be faithful to the ideals
Of our forefathers.

Our forefathers founded our God-given Government.
Our heroes assured its perpetuity to our posterity.

Let us pass our glorious heritage to all future generations—
Not tarnished but made brighter with careful use,
Not diminished but made greater by its
Extension to all people everywhere.

If we meet our duty
We can fulfill our destiny.

May the stars in Old Glory—
Which borrowed its radiance from the Star of Bethlehem—
Send their illuminating rays into the
Spaces of the sea,
Over the mountains, and
Into the valleys of the earth, and
Bring to tired humanity—
PEACE
PROGRESS and
PROSPERITY.

'Memory Now Batting For Babe Ruth'

By ARTHUR (BUGS) BAER

NEW YORK, Aug. 17—(INS)—The living legend that was Babe Ruth now takes its even more vibrant and existing life in the memories of baseball fans.

The Babe typified the dream of American youth in the swish of lumber that propelled the leather comet into the distant bleachers.

Baseball is ins and outs. But the kids snag those flies so they can take their whacks. That's where the Babe stood forth like a lighthouse at low tide, in 22 seasons he took 8,389 official whacks for 2,873 safe pokes.

Every fourth wallop was a home run. That was the Babe's specialty.

When he stood up at the plate with that wand he was his own fairy godmother. He crashed them longer and more often in the clutch than any other player who ever lived.

SHEER POWER

Twenty years ago I compared the Babe with the most scientific batter of baseball history:

"Willie Keeler hits them where they ain't.

"Babe Ruth hits 'em where they're never going to be."

Ruth hit the astounding budget of 714 four-stackers in his big league career. To that you can add an extra 15 picked up in World Series.

His 506 doubles and 136 triples add up the fact that almost every second hit was for extra bases over a span of 22 seasons.

COMPARED WITH COBB

Ty Cobb played 600 more games, but hit 60 fewer home runs. Cobb batted 3,000 more times, but only scored 70 more times.

Cobb played with spikes, teeth, claws and concentrated fury.

The Babe regarded the game as a pastime.

One thing he loved was his whacks. He boosted the four-stacker into a work of surpassing beauty and artistry. I can still see his webbed waddle around the bases to the orchestration of the thunderous cheers that knew no bronx.

In his glorification of the testimonial ankle excursion, the Babe also immortalized the whifferoo—better known to dry statisticians as the strike-out.

Running, throwing and slugging were as natural to the Babe as buttons. But he worked harder striking out than a bird laying a square egg.

MIGHTY SWING

If the Babe had been a couple inches shorter he would have brained himself with that third swing. It was the most vicious thrust I ever gandered.

And the delighted roars of the crowd reverberated through the valleys and echoed from the hills every time the Babe lost his bait.

He was the only man in baseball who actually took bows on a strike-out. When the Babe swung it was whole hog or none.

He built the Yankee Stadium and baseball was good to him. He was a no-tomorrow fellow who never save a dime of the enormous salaries he earned with the smooth shillelah. His annuities were arranged by his eagerly sought commercial endorsements handled by Christy Walsh.

Christy put that money away for the Babe without giving him a swing at it.

INFLUENCED DECISION

It may have been Christy who was also responsible for the decision on the Babe's continuing in baseball. I know he was offered the managerial post in Newark.

I don't know whether I figure it correctly or not, but a job in the minors might have affected the monetary value of the Babe's signature on packaged goods.

Anyway, whether Christy or the Babe turned the job down, the result was the same.

I always find that in order to manage men you first must manage yourself. Probably the Babe didn't rate a million in that department, but he was a perfectionist at the bat.

Baseball paid him $80,000 a season to atomize that apple. Let's hope you and I fulfill our obligations as well.

His last time at bat was a tough and long one. But he went down swinging, even though, for the first time, it was bare-handed.

POLITICAL PARADE

—By George Rothwell Brown

Special to The News-Post.

WASHINGTON, Aug. 17—The possibility of the Presidential election being thrown into the House of Representatives next January, through failure of any candidate to win a majority of votes in the electoral college, will continue to be a hotly debated question from now until the November returns have been tabulated.

In opening full-fledged headquarters in Washington, the Dixiecrats, top-leadered by Governors Thurmond and Wright, have boldly proclaimed their double-jointed purpose to be not only the defeat of President Truman, but a contest in the House from which they could—or so they think—emerge the big winner.

'REBELS' CLAIM 32

They are claiming 32 sure electoral votes, those of Alabama, Mississippi and South Carolina, and a few in Florida, and not counting the 23 of Texas.

They are also hopeful of getting their candidates on the ticket in other States, but this possibility must be counted a remote one.

As President Truman's fortunes sink under the extra load, he has now taken on in minimizing and ridiculing the investigation of Congress of the Communist spy underground, the probability of Governor Dewey's election increases.

The situation is already becoming such in North Carolina and Virginia as to indicate that he will carry at least these two Southern States, and he could bag two or three others.

DEWEY'S CHANCES BRIGHT

Thus Dewey's chances appear brighter than those of any other Republican nominee since Hoover, in 1928.

But this year there are two splinter parties in the field (the Socialist party is not included in this analysis) and the theory that the election could be thrown into the House rests upon the uncertainties growing out of this unusual situation.

The appointment of former Governor Maurice Tobin as Secretary of Labor has aroused waning Democratic hopes of swinging the so-called labor vote to Truman in such States as Michigan, Massachusetts, Pennsylvania, Illinois, West Virginia, Ohio and California.

TOBIN HATES IT

Tobin is an ardent hater of the Taft-Hartley Law and the President's party is pledged to its repeal.

A clean Republican sweep by Dewey, plus the denial of the Southern vote to Truman, might find the President winding up without an electoral vote to his name.

If Truman should carry some of the heavy labor States, the election might be thrown into the House.

In that event the line-up in the electoral college would have to be something as follows:

VOTES ENUMERATED

Dewey—Arizona, 4; Colorado, 6; Connecticut, 8; Delaware, 3; Idaho, 4; Indiana, 13; Iowa, 10; Kansas, 8; Maine, 5; Maryland, 8; Michigan, 19; Minnesota, 11; Montana, 4; Nebraska, 6; Nevada, 3; New Hampshire, 4; New York, 47; North Carolina, 14; North Dakota, 4; Oregon, 6; South Dakota, 4; Tennessee, 12; Vermont, 3; Virginia, 11; Wisconsin, 12. A total of 233.

Truman—California, 25; Illinois, 28; Kentucky, 11; Massachusetts, 16; Missouri, 15; New Jersey, 16; Ohio, 25; Oklahoma, 10; Pennsylvania, 35; Rhode Island, 4; Utah, 4; Washington, 8; West Virginia, 8; Wyoming, 3. A total of 206.

Thurmond—Alabama, 11; Arkansas, 9; Florida, 8; Georgia, 12; Louisiana, 10; Mississippi, 11; South Carolina, 8; Texas, 23. A total of 92.

Since the winner would require 266 votes to have the required majority in the electoral college, the election would be thrown into the House.

WALLACE NOT LISTED

The above figures give Wallace no electoral votes, but they are based on the assumption that in certain States he would run strongly enough to upset the usual normal calculations.

They also indicate that the loss of the Southern seceders would cost Truman the Presidency.

That's what the Dixiecrats want.

But they are blowing their hopes into a mighty thin bubble.

There are no solid indications that Truman will be able to carry any substantial part of the States listed above.

He could easily lose all of them if he persists in all this "red-herring" talk

Nightfall

Finding twilight everywhere
Upon the gentled, blue-mist air,
Day rolls over and with a sigh,
Pulls the blanket of darkness high.

—S. H. Dewhurst.

RUTH TO LIE IN STATE AT YANKEE STADIUM

THE WEATHER

Considerable cloudiness and humid tonight and Wednesday. A few scattered showers likely Wednesday.

Detailed Weather Report Page 20

Read The Baltimore News-Post for complete, accurate news coverage. It is the only Baltimore newspaper possessing the three great wire services—
INTERNATIONAL NEWS SERVICE
ASSOCIATED PRESS
UNITED PRESS

THE BALTIMORE NEWS-POST
AN INDEPENDENT NEWSPAPER
The Largest Evening Circulation in the Entire South

8

VOL. CLIII.—NO. 89 | TUESDAY EVENING, AUGUST 17, 1948 | Entered as second-class matter at Baltimore Postoffice. | PRICE 5 CENTS

Leak In Spy Probe Charged

Lie Detector Information Revealed

BOSTON, Aug. 17—(UP)—Harry Dexter White, fifty-six, Assistant Secretary of the Treasury from 1945 to 1946 and one of the key figures in the current spy hearings in Washington, died of a heart attack at his summer home in Fitzwilliam, N. H., yesterday, his family disclosed today.

By RAYMOND WILCOVE

WASHINGTON, Aug. 17—(INS)—A member of the House Un-American Activities Committee today demanded that the committee be investigated because of a "leak" of secret testimony in the spy probe.

The Congressman, who asked that his name be withheld until he can put his demand before the committee formally, said that the leak was "a violation of an oath by someone on the committee or its staff."

The leak was from the secret session held yesterday to hear Alger Hiss, native Baltimorean and former State Department official and head of the Carnegie Endowment for International Peace.

LIE DETECTOR USE

Published stories said that during the session the possibility of using a lie detector on Hiss and his accuser, Whittaker Chambers, had been discussed. It also was reported that Hiss' wife would be questioned by the committee.

Chambers, a magazine editor, has accused Hiss of being a member of an "elite" Communist underground group. Hiss has denied the charge and said that he never even knew Chambers.

The committee member demanding the probe said:

"It is obvious from reading the papers that someone violated that oath. As soon as the full committee meets again I intend to take this up and find out who is guilty.

"It is a fine thing for a committee questioning the word of witnesses to have an oath violated by someone officially connected with it."

ALL TOOK OATH

Other committee members said they had no comment, but they revealed that all who heard Hiss testify took an oath not to reveal details of his testimony.

Present at the secret session

Continued on Page 2, Column 3.

Scratches At Atlantic City

First Race—Payable, Waterclock.
Second—Battle Scarred, Ice Flow, Zola, Skyway.
Fourth — Count Off, Easter Morning, Combustion, Blunderbuss.
Fifth—Pollys Delay.
Seventh—Miss Fighter, Fagrace.
Eighth—Opening Day, War Sword, Insider, Rough Ordy.
Weather cloudy; track fast.

Pippen Tells Why Babe Ruth Was Baseball Legend

By RODGER H. PIPPEN

Sports Editor, The Baltimore News-Post.

The fabulous Babe Ruth, with his funny mincing walk, his barrel body, toothpick legs, flat nose, high cheeks and his lusty laugh, has gone into the shadow of the dugout to join John McGraw, Hughey Jennings, Willie Keeler, Joe Kelly, Wilbert Robinson, Dan Brouthers, Jack Dunn and other Orioles who helped make Baltimore famous in a baseball way.

It is a pity the new generation will grow up without our Babe, our amazing Babe.

But it is wonderful to know that appreciation of him and his peculiar talents will grow with the years. Even now, before the flowers fade on his grave, he is not merely a man who could hit a baseball farther than any other.

Ruth is a legend.

For 30 years he was as much a part of an era as million-dollar gates, the New Deal, bootleggers, the sugar and butter shortage and two Governors in Georgia.

Although asleep in a pine box, Babe never will vanish altogether from the scene. Drama, in memory, will often stalk the diamond.

This Writer Measured His First Home Run

It so happens this writer has been able, as a reporter, to observe Babe from the first day he came out of St. Mary's Industrial School until he came to the end of the road.

I was the first reporter the Home-Run King ever knew.

I played in the first ball game down in Fayetteville, N. C., in which he participated as an Oriole rookie.

I measured the first home run he hit as a pro.

I roomed with him for three weeks on the first Northern trip of the Orioles that spring.

I wrote his first love letter to the first of his thousand and one sweethearts.

The Peter Pan Of Baseball

After having been in daily contact with him for 60 consecutive days, he didn't know my first or last name. I was "pal" to him. Later he called everybody "kid."

And that's how Babe went through life.

He was the Peter Pan of baseball who never grew up.

Every day, except when he was ill or injured, was a joy and a delight to this lad who came out of St. Mary's with 11 cents in his pocket and who sat in a golden chair on a gilded merry-go-round for a quarter of a century, with his fame world-wide and his admirers unlimited.

Without ever having heard of that Chinese proverb, "Enjoy

Continued on Page 18, Column 7.

City's Flags Dip In Honor Of Ruth

All official city flags were ordered at half-mast today as Baltimore mourned the passing of her great hero, Babe Ruth.

At the same time, at St. Mary's Industrial School, where Ruth started his fabulous career, a few tousled-haired boys joined with the brothers who had know the Babe in childhood, in praying for the repose of his soul.

SENDS TELEGRAM

Mayor D'Alesandro, in ordering the Stars and Stripes placed in the position of mourning on the city's flagstaffs, sent a telegram of condolence to Mrs. Ruth in New York.

The message read:

"We claimed him as our own, for here he first saw the light of day.

"We gloried in his achievements.

"I have ordered the city's flags flown at half mast in his honor.

"On behalf of all our citizens, please accept my most profound sympathy."

DISPLAYS EMOTION

At St. Mary's the boys were unaware of the Babe's death until morning mass, when Brother Charles, superintendent of the institution, stepped into the aisle of the chapel, turned to them and said, in a voice made husky by emotion:

"I want you to remember the soul of Babe Ruth.

"He died last night.

"At one time he sat in these very benches.

"Be generous in your re-

Continued on Page 3, Column 6.

Ruth Memorial On Networks Tonight

NEW YORK, Aug. 17—(AP)—Major radio networks planned memorial services for Babe Ruth on nationwide special programs tonight. The programs:

Mutual—7 to 7.30 P. M. (EST).

NBC—8 to 8.30 P. M. (EST).

ABC—8.30 to 9 P. M. (EST).

BABE RUTH'S LAST APPEARANCE IN UNIFORM

His final farewell to the fans last June 13 at the twenty-fifth anniversary of Yankee Stadium. His famous "No. 3" uniform was then hung in Baseball's Hall of Fame, Cooperstown, N. Y.

BABE RUTH ON LAST VISIT TO BALTIMORE

Baseball's greatest figure returned to his native city last month for the Inter-Faith game. Rain prevented his appearance at the Stadium.

—Picture by News-Post Photographer.

Ruth To Lie In State At Yankee Stadium; Dies Peacefully At 53

By DAVIS J. WALSH

NEW YORK, Aug. 17—(INS)—The thousands who cheered the exploits of Babe Ruth and admirers from every walk of life will have the opportunity to pay final tribute to the baseball immortal in the Yankee Stadium—"the house that Ruth built."

The body of the famed sports hero will lie in state in the rotunda of the Yankee Stadium from 5 o'clock (EDT) this afternoon until tomorrow at 7 P. M.

Then the remains of the Bambino, who died of cancer at 8.01 o'clock last night, will be returned to the Universal Funeral Parlor for private mourning by the family until Thursday morning at 11 when a requiem mass will be celebrated in St. Patrick's Cathedral.

Burial will be at Gate of Heaven Cemetery in Westchester county.

The end came at 8.01 o'clock last night for the man whose ball field deeds and demeanor were such that they captured the heart of a nation and kept it for more than a dozen years after his inevitable withdrawal from the major league scene.

For his was a prodigious talent for sharing his triumphs and occasional sorrows with the huge mass in the stands, unconsciously making them part of his life.

And so it was last night when death came rather suddenly to George Herman Ruth, baseball's most fabulous slugger, at Memorial Hospital.

Its switchboards became clogged with incoming calls for several hours after the news was flashed to the city and nation.

PUBLIC STUNNED

Hospital attaches, in fact, had to be pressed into service in order to handle the volume of inquiries from a stunned public as yet unable or unwilling to believe that this great figure had actually passed from the contemporary scene.

A further announcement was to be made today concerning complete funeral arrangements, including the possibility that Ruth's body might be allowed to lie in state so that a public which so revered him in life might pay its final respects.

It was feared by some that this might bring about a repetition of the abortive rioting which ensued on Upper Broadway in the mid-twenties when Rudolph Valentino, movie idol of an earlier generation, was buried behind a fanfare of havoc and hysterics.

That was only a year before Ruth came to his greatest eminence in 1927 by hitting an all-time record 60 home runs that has withstood all challenges to this day.

Only 32 then, he was still quite a figure of a man—a mite paunchy perhaps, but impelling, compelling and unforgettable.

The torso of a moose set precariously and wondrously upon legs that tapered sharply downward from Chippendale thighs into shins grotesquely like stilts.

But tremendous verve, leverage, vitality and power reposed within that massive shoulder-spread, and between eye and sinew was the flawless co-ordination of a striking copperhead; so that few ever hit a baseball as far—and none as often.

LITTLE RESEMBLANCE

There was pathetically little resemblance between that roaring, swashbuckling character and the feeble, wasted figure that lay spent and drained through yesterday's late afternoon mutely waiting for death.

Only the day before Ruth had been allowed to sit up for a short time in the hope that his great fighting spirit, always so near the

Continued on Page 2, Column 1.

Truman Mourns Death Of Ruth

WASHINGTON, Aug. 17—(INS)—President Truman, an ardent baseball fan, joined the mourners of Babe Ruth's death today.

The President sent a message of condolence to Mrs. Claire Ruth, widow of George Herman Ruth, when he learned of the death.

Only last week Mr. Truman telephoned the Babe and expressed hope for his recovery.

1895—Babe Ruth—1948

THE plaudits of the crowds have turned to tears...
Ten million kids are heart-sick and depressed...
The mightiest bat that baseball ever knew
Is laid away with reverence, to rest.

The Home Run King has joined the higher stars,
But Babe Ruth's inspiration will remain
A constant help and challenge to poor lads
Who cannot see the sunshine for the rain.

The game won't seem the same without the Babe,
But on some diamond where the angels roam
He grins his famous grin and tips his cap
While the umpire gently calls him "safe"... at home.

—NICK KENNY.

VERY LATEST NEWS

(Race Results From Howard Sports Daily, Inc.)

FIRM INDICTED IN GI HOUSING FRAUD

A Federal Grand Jury today returned a 12-count indictment against Chinquapin, Inc., and two of the building firm's officers, Theodore and Frank Julio, in the GI housing fraud investigation. (Details on Page 13.)

24,000 HARVESTER WORKERS STRIKE

CHICAGO, Aug. 17—(AP)—Twenty-four thousand CIO United Auto Workers were called out on strike at seven International Harvester Company plants today under a last-minute change in signals.

Temperatures

Midni't,	.74	7 A. M.,	67
1 A. M.,	73	8 A. M.,	67
2 A. M.,	71	9 A. M.,	69
3 A. M.,	71	10 A. M.,	71
4 A. M.,	69	11 A. M.,	72
5 A. M.,	69	12 Noon,	76
6 A. M.,	67	1 P. M.,	79

JAPS, KOREANS CLASH

TOKYO, Aug. 17—(AP)—Four Koreans were wounded today in a clash with Japanese workmen at an earthquake damage repair job in Kawata Gumma prefecture, the newspaper Asahi reported.

NEWS-POST

Coleman Shuts Out Indians for Athletics, 5 to 0

Cleveland's League Lead Over Mack's Forces Is Reduced to Half a Game

PHILADELPHIA, July 17 (AP).—Using Joe Coleman's sparkling six-hit pitching as a springboard, the amazing Philadelphia Athletics bounced back today and defeated the Cleveland Indians, 5 to 0. Coleman didn't allow any Indian batter to advance past first base.

The victory evened the so-called "crucial series" at two games each and narrowed Cleveland's American League lead over the runner-up A's to a half game.

Cleveland had won the first two games. But, as they have done every time disaster threatened this season, the A's came back—taking the last two of the series.

Hank Majeski started the A's on the victory trail in the first inning, ramming a double off Sam Zoldak and bringing home Don White with the first tally.

The Mackmen completed the game's scoring in the third inning with a four-run splurge. With one out, Barney McCosky and White singled, McCosky scoring when White eluded an attempted rundown.

Ferris Fain doubled and White advanced to third. Majeski was purposely passed, but Elmer Valo upset the strategy with a two-run single. Majeski continued across the plate with the fifth run when Larry Doby fumbled the ball in center field.

After that it was all Coleman, the strong-armed right-hander who pitched three hitless innings in the All-Star game last Tuesday. Coleman's victory was his ninth of the season against six setbacks.

Dale Mitchell and Ken Keltner were the only Cleveland batters to trouble Coleman. Mitchell singled three times and Keltner twice. Lou Boudreau got the only other safety, also a single.

The score:

CLEVELAND (A. L.)	ab	r	h	po	a
Mitchell lf	4	0	3	3	0
Doby cf	4	0	0	2	0
Edwards rf	4	0	0	5	0
Boudreau ss	3	0	1	0	7
Gordon 2b	4	0	0	2	1
Keltner 3b	4	0	2	0	4
Robinson 1b	3	0	0	10	0
Hegan c	3	0	0	2	0
Zoldak p	1	0	0	0	2
*Judnich	1	0	0	0	0
Klieman p	0	0	0	0	0
Totals	31	0	6	24	14

PHILA. (A. L.)	ab	r	h	po	a
Joost ss	4	0	1	8	4
McCosky lf	3	1	1	1	0
White cf	4	2	1	3	0
Fain 1b	4	1	2	8	1
Majeski 3b	3	1	1	1	2
Valo rf	3	0	1	2	0
Rosar c	4	0	0	2	0
Suder 2b	3	0	1	2	7
J. Coleman p	3	0	0	0	1
Totals	31	5	8	27	15

*Batted for Zoldak in eighth and flied out.

Cleveland .... 000 000 000—0
Philadelphia .... 104 000 00x—5

Error—Doby. Runs batted in—Majeski 1, Valo 2. Two-base hits—Majeski, Fain. Double plays—Suder, Joost and Fain, 2. Sacrifice—McCosky. Left on bases—Cleveland 6, Philadelphia 5. Bases on balls—Off J. Coleman 2, Zoldak 1, Klieman 1. Strikeouts—J. Coleman 1, Zoldak 2. Hits—Off Zoldak 8 in 7 innings, Klieman 0 in 1. Losing pitcher—Zoldak. Umpires—McKinley, Hurley, Berry and Grieve. Time—1:36. Attendance—11,432.

Dodgers Win 2

(Continued from page one)

now its three one-thousandths of a percentage point.

Branch Rickey, who was in Cincinnati yesterday, flew to Beaumont, Tex., last night and watched Carl Erskine, a right-hander and one of the more promising of the Dodger farm prospects, pitch a four-hit shutout for Fort Worth. It would not be too surprising to find Bobby Bragan, the new Fort Worth manager, conning railroad schedules on Erskine's behalf very shortly.

Leading Five Batsmen In Each Major League

(200 or more at bats)

American League

Player and club	G.	A.B.	R.	H.	Pct.
Williams, Boston	71	263	66	102	.388
Boudreau, Cleveland	77	287	57	105	.366
Kell, Detroit	58	230	32	76	.330
Evers, Detroit	79	296	41	97	.328
Zarilla, St. Louis	73	267	36	87	.326

National League

Player and club	G.	A.B.	R.	H.	Pct.
Musial, St. Louis	79	309	69	122	.395
Pafko, Chicago	73	274	49	96	.350
Ashburn, Philadel.	78	313	49	106	.339
Holmes, Boston	69	283	46	93	.329
Dark, Boston	64	230	38	75	.326

Runs Batted In — American League: Stephens, RedSox 77; DiMaggio, Yanks 74; Williams, RedSox 72; Gordon, Indians 70; Keltner, Indians 63.

Home Runs — American League: Keltner, Indians 22; DiMaggio, Yanks 19; Stephens, Red Sox 18; Gordon, Indians 17; Williams, Red Sox 16; Doerr, Red Sox 16.

Runs Batted In — National League: Musial, Cardinals 69; Kiner, Pirates 68; Mize, Giants 67; Sauer, Reds 64; Jones, Cardinals 55; Ennis, Phillies 55.

Home Runs — National League: Kiner, Pirates 25; Sauer, Reds 24; Musial, Cardinals 21; Mize, Giants 20; Gordon, Giants 18.

Herald Tribune—Frank

TOM HENRICH DAY: The Yankee outfielder, honored by the fans with a day at the Stadium yesterday, presents orchids to his mother as his father, wife and children look on

Tom bats out a double on his first trip to the plate in appreciation of the gifts of the fans

Yankees Win

(Continued from page one)

Niarhos opened the eighth with his third safety, a double to left. Phil Rizzuto put him on third with a perfect bunt and he scored on Lopat's fly to Kokos.

Friends and admirers gave Tommy Henrich a day. He received an automobile, a movie camera, a luggage set, a rifle, a piano, a suit of clothes and a wrist watch. And he also received nylons, orchids, and wrist watches for his wife and mother, and a ticket for a week's vacation for himself and his wife and children. It was as good as guessing the right answer for a radio program. . . . Henrich played left field and got two hits, but Berra, being in rightfield, had the chance to make the good plays, one on Gerry Priddy's long drive, which he pulled out of the stands, and other a short fly by Kokos.

The score:

ST. LOUIS (A. L.)	ab	r	h	po	a
Dillinger 3b	5	0	3	0	3
Stevens 1b	4	0	0	11	0
Priddy 2b	4	0	1	0	4
Platt lf	4	0	1	3	0
Zarilla cf	3	0	3	3	0
Kokos rf	4	0	1	3	0
Moss, c	4	0	1	4	0
Fannin	0	0	0	0	0
Pellagrini ss	3	0	1	0	1
†Lund	1	0	0	0	0
Biscan p	3	0	0	0	1
‡Anderson	1	0	0	0	0
Totals	36	0	11	24	9

NEW YORK (A. L.)	ab	r	h	po	a
Stirnweiss 2b	5	0	1	1	3
Henrich lf	5	0	2	2	0
Berra rf	5	1	1	4	1
DiMaggio cf	3	0	0	0	0
Johnson 3b	4	2	2	0	2
Souchock 1b	3	0	1	15	0
Niarhos c	4	1	3	5	0
Rizzuto ss	3	0	1	0	2
Lopat p	3	0	0	0	5
Totals	35	4	11	27	13

*Ran for Moss in ninth.
†Batted for Pellagrini in ninth, fanned.
‡Batted for Biscan in ninth, grounded out.

St. Louis .... 000 000 000—0
New York .... 012 000 01x—4

Error—Kokos. Runs batted in—Lopat 2, Johnson. Two-base hits—Henrich, Dillinger, Berra, Priddy, Niarhos. Double plays—Berra, Stirnweiss and Souchock; Souchock (unassited). Left on bases—St. Louis 10, New York 11. Bases on balls—Biscan 4, Lopat 1. Strikeouts—Biscan 2, Lopat 4. Umpires—Stevens, Summers and Jones. Time—1:42. Attendance—15,438 (paid).

Ott's No. 4 Is Retired Permanently by Giants

PITTSBURGH, July 17 (AP).—Horace Stoneham, president of the New York Giants announced today that Mel Ott's uniform with the big No. 4 on its back has been permanently retired. The number is the same as that of Lou Gehrig, of the Yankees, the first major league number retired.

The former Giant manager, in twenty-two seasons with the Giants, hammered out 511 home runs, a National League record.

Leo Durocher, who supplanted Ott at the Giants's helm, asked for and received his old No. 2 uniform. Red Kress, coach, who had worn that number all season, gladly relinquished it.

Dodgers' Scores

(FIRST GAME)

BROOKLYN (N. L.)	ab	r	h	po	a
Reese ss	3	2	0	1	4
Robinson 2b	5	2	2	3	1
Hermanski rf	4	0	2	2	0
Shuba lf	4	0	1	1	0
Reiser cf	4	0	1	4	0
Furillo cf	1	1	0	1	0
Edwards 3b	5	0	1	0	1
Brown 3b	0	0	0	0	0
Campanella c	4	0	0	8	0
Hodges 1b	5	1	2	7	2
Branca p	3	1	2	0	0
*Vaughan	1	1	1	0	0
Palica p	1	0	0	0	0
Totals	40	8	12	27	8

CINCINNATI (N. L.)	ab	r	h	po	a
Baumholtz rf	5	0	3	3	0
Adams 2b	4	0	2	4	2
Wyrostek cf	4	0	0	1	0
Sauer lf	4	1	1	3	0
Kluszewski 1b	4	1	1	10	1
Hatton 3b	3	0	0	0	4
Stallcup ss	4	0	1	4	3
Lamanno c	4	1	1	2	0
Fox p	1	0	0	0	1
†Corbitt	1	0	1	0	0
‡Vander Meer	0	0	0	0	0
Cress p	0	0	0	0	0
§Young	1	1	1	0	0
Gumbert p	0	0	0	0	1
¶Litwhiler	1	0	0	0	0
Totals	36	4	11	27	4

*Batted for Branca in eighth, and singled.
†Batted for Fox in fifth and singled.
‡Ran for Corbitt in fifth.
§Batted for Cress in sixth and singled.
¶Batted for Gumbert in ninth and flied out.

Brooklyn .... 100 020 041—8
Cincinnati .... 010 003 000—4

Errors—Edwards, Kluszewski, Wyrostek, Hatton, Stallcup. Runs batted in—Robinson 4, Hermanski, Hodges, Vaughan, Baumholtz 2, Young. Two-base hits—Hodges 2, Branca, Hermanski, Sauer, Adams. Home run—Robinson. Sacrifice—Adams. Double plays—Reese, Robinson and Hodges; Hodges and Reese; Adams, Stallcup and Kluszewski. Left on bases—Brooklyn 10, Cincinnati 9. Bases on balls—Branca 3, Fox 3, Cress 1, Gumbert 1. Strikeouts—Branca 6, Palica 1, Fox 1, Gumbert 1. Hits—Branca 8 in 7 innings, Palica 3 in 2, Fox 6 in 5, Cress 0 in 1, Gumbert 6 in 3. Wild pitch—Branca. Winning pitcher—Branca. Losing pitcher—Gumbert. Umpires—Barlick, Dascoli and Barr. Time—2:33.

SECOND GAME

BROOKLYN (N. L.)	ab	r	h	po	a
Reese ss	6	0	1	4	5
Robinson 2b	4	2	1	4	4
Hermanski rf	5	0	1	1	0
Shuba lf	4	1	3	0	0
Reiser cf	1	0	0	0	0
Furillo cf	4	0	1	1	0
Brown 3b	5	2	2	1	3
Campanella c	4	2	2	3	1
Hodges 1b	5	1	4	12	2
Taylor p	1	1	1	0	1
*Whitman	1	0	0	0	0
Minner p	2	1	0	1	1
Totals	42	10	16	27	17

CINCINNATI (N. L.)	ab	r	h	po	a
Baumholtz rf	4	2	3	3	1
Adams 2b	4	1	3	2	3
Wyrostek cf	5	0	1	7	0
Sauer lf	5	0	2	2	0
Kluszewski 1b	2	1	2	5	0
Schultz 1b	2	0	0	3	0
Hatton 3b	3	0	1	1	2
Stallcup ss	4	0	0	1	2
Williams c	0	0	0	0	0
Lamanno c	4	0	2	3	1
Wehmeier p	3	0	0	0	0
Hughes p	0	0	0	0	1
†Corbitt	1	0	0	0	0
Peterson p	0	0	0	0	0
Totals	37	4	14	27	10

*Batted for Taylor in fourth.
†Batted for Hughes in eighth.

Brooklyn .... 130 010 041—10
Cincinnati .... 121 000 000—4

Errors—Adams 2, Williams 1. Runs batted in—Reese 2, Shuba 2, Campanella 2, Hodges 1, Wyrostek 2, Kluszewski 2. Two-base hits—Hermanski, Reese, Brown, Shuba, Adams, Wyrostek. Home runs—Shuba, Campenalla, Kluszewski. Stolen base—Campanella. Sacrifices—Stallcup, Schults. Double plays—Hatton and Kluszewski; Robinson, Reese and Hodges; Baumholtz and Lamanno. Left on bases—Brooklyn 10, Cincinnati 12. Bases on balls—Taylor 2, Minner 2, Wehmeier 4, Peterson 1. Strikeouts—Minner 1, Wehmeier 2. Hits—Off Taylor 8 in 3 innings, Minner 6 in 6, Wehmeier 13 in 7⅔, Hughes 0 in ⅓, Peterson 3 in 1. Passed ball—Campanella. Winning pitcher—Minner. Losing pitcher—Wehmeier. Umpires—Dascoli, Barr, Barlick. Time—2:39. Attendance—19,858.

Satchel Paige's Mother Solves Puzzle: He's 44

* * *

MOBILE, Ala., July 17 (AP).—One of baseball's current mysteries—how old is Satchel Paige—was cleared up today.

His mother, a spry, white-haired woman of seventy-eight, says he's forty-four years old.

The ageless cannon-ball chunker of the Cleveland Indians was born here in Mobile, right on the shore of Mobile Bay, in fact.

There are some stories that he got the nickname Satchel from the time he worked as a redcap at the Mobile depot. Mrs. Tula Paige wouldn't know about that.

But she does know about his age.

"I'm sure he's forty-four," she said. "I remember something came up once about changing his age when he left to play ball in Chatanooga back about 1927, but he's really forty-four."

"My boy has always loved baseball," she said. "Why, he'd rather play baseball than eat. It was always baseball, baseball."

She says one of the reasons he made a success was because "he would take advice."

"His greatest ambition was to become a good baseball player and it looks like he's really made good now."

SOUTHERN ASSOCIATION

Friday Night's Results

New Orleans 4; Little Rock, 3.
Nashville, 13; Atlanta, 5.
Birmingham 2; Chattanooga, 1.
Memphis, 9; Mobile, 8.

PACIFIC COAST LEAGUE

Friday Night's Results

Portland, 2; Seattle, 0.
Hollywood, 5; Oakland, 2.
San Diego, 4; Sacramento, 0.
San Francisco 2; Los Angeles, 1.

INTERNATIONAL LEAGUE

Last Night's Games

Newark at Jersey City.
Buffalo at Toronto (2).
Rochester, 2; Montreal, 1.
Syracuse at Baltimore.

AMERICAN ASSOCIATION

Yesterday's Games

Indianapolis at Kansas City.
Toledo at Milwaukee (night).
Columbus at Minneapolis (night).
Louisville at St. Paul (night).

EASTERN LEAGUE

Yesterday's Results

Elmira, 4; Wilkes-Barre, 3.
Other clubs not scheduled.

TEXAS LEAGUE

Friday Night's Results

Dallas, 6; Shreveport, 2.
Fort Worth, 9; Beaumont, 0.
Tulsa, 3; Houston, 1.
San Antonio, 14; Oklahoma City 8.

Hamner Stops Braves, 4 to 1, As Cubs Win

Right-Hander Hurls Four-Hitter for 5th Victory; Pafko Hits 15th Homer

CHICAGO, July 17 (AP).—Ralph Hamner, who was routed by the Boston Braves Thursday before he could get a man out, came back today and hurled a four-hitter against the league leaders to pace the Cubs to a 4-to-1 victory.

The Cubs nailed down the decision by rapping Warren Spahn for three runs in the fourth inning. Andy Pafko smashed out his fifteenth homer to launch the uprising. Bill Nicholson then singled, Hal Jeffcoat walked and both romped home on Bob Scheffing's double. The final Cub run came off Al Lyons in the eighth.

The only run off the right hander was due to a spell of wildness in the sixth. He walked four to give them the tally without a hit. It was Hamner's fifth victory. Spahn lost his seventh against seven victories.

The Score:

BOSTON (N. L.)	ab	r	h	po	a
Holmes rf	5	0	2	2	0
Dark ss	4	0	1	2	2
Torgeson 1b	3	0	0	12	0
Elliott 3b	2	1	1	1	2
Heath lf	3	0	0	1	0
Conatser cf	1	0	0	1	0
Russell cf	1	0	0	0	0
Masi c	4	0	0	3	0
Ryan 2b	3	0	0	1	6
Spahn p	2	0	0	0	2
*F.McC'm'k	1	0	0	0	0
Lyons p	0	0	0	0	1
Shoun p	0	0	0	1	0
†Salkeld	0	0	0	0	0
‡Sturgeon	0	0	0	0	0
Totals	29	1	4	24	13

CHICAGO (N. L.)	ab	r	h	po	a
Schenz 2b	4	1	2	1	3
Waitkus 1b	4	0	1	8	0
Lowrey lf	2	0	0	1	0
Cavarretta lf	2	0	0	2	0
Pafko 3b	3	1	1	1	3
Nicholson rf	4	1	1	1	0
Jeffcoat cf	3	1	0	3	0
Scheffing c	3	0	1	5	0
Smalley ss	2	0	0	4	1
Hamner p	3	0	0	1	3
Totals	30	4	6	27	10

*Batted for Spahn in sixth and struck out.
†Batted for Shoun in ninth and walked.
‡Ran for Salkeld in ninth.

Boston .... 000 001 000—1
Chicago .... 000 300 01x—4

Errors—None. Runs batted in—Pafko, Scheffing 2, Waitkus, Ryan. Two-base hits—Scheffing, Schenz. Home run—Pafko. Double plays—Hamner to Waitkus; Hamner, Smalley and Waitkus. Left on bases—Boston 9, Chicago 5. Base on balls—Off Hamner 8, Spahn 1, Lyons 2. Strikeouts—By Hamner 5, Spahn 2, Lyons 1. Hits—Off Spahn 4 in 5 innings, Lyons 2 in 2⅓, Shoun 0 in ⅔. Losing pitcher—Spahn. Umpires—Reardon, Boggess, Jorda and Goetz. Time—2:13. Attendance—19,166.

Giants Beat

(Continued from page one)

Then came Thomson, hitting for Trinkle, and he rammed Higbe's first pitch to center, scoring Layton and Marshall.

Konikowski took over the pitching and gave up only one hit in the two final innings.

The Giants thus won the shortened series with the Pirates, two games to one. It is the first series the club has taken in more than a month.

A drenching rain all morning flooded the field. Play was possible only because a ground crew worked for hours scooping the water off and by putting the start back to 3 o'clock instead of 1:30.

Of the Giants' fourteen hits, Whitey Lockman made five and Mize three, with a triple beside his homer. Lockman's were well scattered, two to left two to right and one a bunt.

The Giants announced that the No. 4 which Mel Ott, deposed manager, has worn so many years, will be retired and no Giant player ever will be permitted to wear it again.

The score:

NEW YORK (N. L.)	ab	r	h	po	a
Rigney 2b	4	1	1	5	2
Lockman cf	5	1	5	5	0
Gordon lf	5	1	1	3	0
Mize 1b	5	1	3	5	0
Cooper c	3	0	0	3	0
*Layton	0	1	0	0	0
Livingston c	1	0	0	0	0
Marshall rf	3	1	1	3	0
Kerr ss	4	0	2	3	3
Lohrke 3b	1	0	0	0	2
†McCarthy	1	0	0	0	0
Conway 3b	0	0	0	0	0
Jones p	3	0	0	0	1
Trinkle p	0	0	0	0	0
‡Thomson	1	0	1	0	0
Konikowski p	0	0	0	0	1
Totals	36	6	14	27	9

PITTSBURGH (N. L.)	ab	r	h	po	a
Rojek ss	5	1	2	1	4
Gustine 3b	5	0	1	0	5
Hopp cf	5	2	3	1	0
Kiner lf	4	1	1	0	0
Westlake rf	4	0	1	2	1
West 1b	3	0	0	8	2
Stevens 1b	1	0	0	4	0
Murtaugh 2b	3	1	1	4	6
Kluttz c	3	0	0	5	2
FitzGerald c	1	0	0	0	0
Ostermu'ler p	0	0	0	0	0
Gregg p	1	0	1	1	1
§Walker	1	0	1	0	0
Singleton p	0	0	0	1	1
¶Bockman	1	0	0	0	0
Higbe p	0	0	0	0	0
‖Chesnes	1	0	0	0	0
Totals	38	5	11	27	22

*Ran for Cooper in eighth.
†Batted for Lohrke in eighth, grounded out.
‡Batted for Trinkle in eighth, singled.
§Batted for Gregg in fifth, singled.
¶Batted for Singleton in seventh, fanned.
‖Batted for Higbe in ninth, flied out.

New York .... 400 000 020—6
Pittsburgh .... 000 011 300—5

Errors—Rojek 2. Runs batted in—Gordon, Mize 3, Walker, Westlake, Kiner 3, Thomson 2. Two-base hits—Gordon, Murtaugh, Hopp, Lockman. Three-base hit—Mize. Home runs—Mize, Kiner. Stolen base—Lockman. Sacrifice—Lohrke. Double plays—Gregg, Kluttz and West; Gustine, Murtaugh and West; Rojek, Murtaugh and West; Westlake and Rojek; Rojek, Murtaugh and Stevens. Left on bases—New York 8, Pittsburgh 7. Base on balls—Gregg 2, Jones 1, Higbe 2. Strikeouts—Gregg 3, Singleton 1, Jones 2. Hits—Off Ostermueller 5 in ⅓ inning, Gregg 4 in 4⅔, Singleton 2 in 2, Higbe 3 in 2, Jones 9 in 6⅔, Trinkle 1 in ⅓, Konikowski 1 in 2. Winning pitcher—Konikowski. Losing pitcher—Higbe. Umpires—Pinelli, Robb and Gore. Time—2:46. Attendance—16,071.

Major League Averages

* * *

Records below include Friday night baseball

American League

CLUB BATTING

[illegible]

CLUB FIELDING

[illegible]

Triple plays—Philadelphia, Cleveland

INDIVIDUAL BATTING

[illegible]

PITCHING RECORDS

[illegible]

National League

CLUB BATTING

[illegible]

CLUB FIELDING

[illegible]

Triple play—Pittsburgh.

INDIVIDUAL BATTING

[illegible]

PITCHING RECORDS

[illegible]

Trucks Checks Red Sox, 3 to 1, As Tigers Win

Right-Hander Limits Boston to 4 Singles as Mates Pound Kinder for 12 Hits

BOSTON, July 17 (AP).—Virgil (Fire) Trucks, righthander, generally a soft touch for the Boston Red Sox, turned in a sparkling four-hitter, all singles, today to give the Detroit Tigers their first victory in a four-game series with Joe McCarthy's forces, 3 to 1.

It was Trucks's seventh victory of the season against five defeats and the fifth in his total of sixteen starts against the Red Sox.

The Tigers made all twelve of their hits against Ellis Kinder before he was relieved by Tex Hughson in the ninth. The latter, back after nursing his ailing arm in Austin, Tex., for many weeks, set the Tigers down in order in the finale.

Trucks gave only two hits up to the ninth, when the Red Sox filled the bases with two out on singles by Junior Stephens and Bill Goodman and a base on balls to Bobby Doerr. The veteran Wally Moses ended matters, however, by popping out.

The Tigers scored in the second on singles by Hoot Evers, Pat Mullin, George Vico's sacrifice and Bob Swift's long fly to center. The Red Sox pulled into a 1-to-1 tie after filling the bases in the fourth. Dom DiMaggio hit safely and, after Johnny Pesky and Stephens walked, scored on a fly by Doerr.

Dick Wakefield's two-bagger off the left-center wall and Vico's single to right gave the Tigers a second run in the sixth. They added their third in the eighth, when George Kell singled, made third on Wakefield's second hit and was driven in by Evers.

The score:

DETROIT (A. L.)	ab	r	h	po	a
Lipon ss	5	0	1	0	6
Mayo 2b	5	0	1	3	2
Kell 3b	4	1	2	0	0
Wakefield lf	4	1	2	1	0
Evers cf	4	1	2	5	0
Mullin rf	3	0	3	1	0
Vico 1b	3	0	1	9	1
Swift c	4	0	0	7	0
Trucks p	4	0	0	1	0
Totals	36	3	12	27	9

BOSTON (A. L.)	ab	r	h	po	a
DiMaggio cf	4	1	1	4	0
Pesky 3b	3	0	0	3	4
Spence lf	4	0	0	5	0
Stephens ss	3	0	1	3	3
Doerr 2b	3	0	0	2	3
Goodman 1b	4	0	1	9	1
Moses rf	4	0	0	1	0
Batts c	3	0	1	0	1
*Hitchcock	0	0	0	0	0
Tebbetts c	0	0	0	0	0
Kinder p	2	0	0	0	1
†Mele	1	0	0	0	0
Hughson p	0	0	0	0	0
Totals	31	1	4	27	13

*Ran for Batts in eighth.
†Batted for Kinder in eighth, and fanned.

Detroit .... 010 001 010—3
Boston .... 000 100 000—1

Errors—None. Runs batted in—Swift, Vico, Evers, Doerr. Two-base hits—Evers, Wakefield. Sacrifice—Vico. Double plays—Stephens, Doerr and Goodman; Goodman, Batts, Pesky, Batts and Pesky. Left on bases—Detroit 8, Boston 6. Bases on balls—Trucks 3, Kinder 1. Strikeouts—Trucks 6. Hits—Kinder 12 in 8, Hughson 0 in 1. Losing pitcher—Kinder. Umpires—Boyer, Passarella and Rommel. Time—2:02. Attendance—17,477.

White Sox Beat Senators With Twelve Hits, 9 to 7

WASHINGTON, July 17 (AP).—The Chicago White Sox capitalized on pathetic Washington pitching which yielded eight walks and twelve hits to defeat the Senators, 9 to 7, today. Ike Pearson, second of three Chicago pitchers, received credit for the victory.

The White Sox mauled Sid Hudson for three runs in the first inning, but the Senators bounced back to grab a 7-to-4 lead off Al Gettel and Ike Pearson. Chicago clustered four runs off Milo Candini and Forrest Thompson on four walks and two singles in the seventh and added another run in the ninth on Pat Seery's double and Taft Wright's single.

The score:

CHICAGO (A. L.)	ab	r	h	po	a
Kolloway 2b	5	1	3	5	4
Lupien 1b	3	1	1	8	1
Appling 3b	4	2	2	4	2
Seerey lf	2	3	2	1	1
Robinson c	4	1	0	1	2
Wright rf	5	0	3	2	1
Philley cf	5	0	0	4	1
Michaels ss	3	0	1	1	3
Gettel p	1	0	0	0	0
*Baker	1	1	0	0	0
Pearson p	2	0	0	1	0
Caldwell p	0	0	0	0	0
Totals	35	9	12	27	15

WASHINGTON (A. L.)	ab	r	h	po	a
Yost 3b	4	1	1	0	1
Coan lf	5	0	1	3	0
Gillenw'er cf	4	1	2	3	0
Stewart rf	4	1	1	2	0
Christman ss	3	0	0	4	5
Vernon 1b	3	1	0	9	1
Kozar 2b	2	2	0	2	4
Early c	0	0	0	0	0
Evans c	3	1	1	4	1
Hudson p	0	0	0	0	0
†Robertson	1	0	1	0	0
‡Fleitas	0	0	0	0	0
Candini p	2	0	1	0	1
Thompson p	0	0	0	0	0
§McBride	0	0	0	0	0
¶Sullivan	0	0	0	0	0
Totals	31	7	8	27	14

*Batted for Gettell in fourth, hit into force.
†Batted for Hudson in second, doubled.
‡Ran for Robertson in second.
§Batted for Thompson in ninth, walked.
¶Ran for McBride in ninth.

Chicago .... 300 100 401—9
Washington .... 041 101 000—7

Errors—Kolloway, Kozar. Runs batted in—Seerey, Robinson 2, Evans 2, Robertson, Stewart, Kolloway, Coan, Yost 2, Wright 2, Philley. Two-base hits—Seerey 2, Robertson, Gillenwater. Three-base hit—Coan. Stolen base—Kozar. Double plays—Kozar, Christman and Vernon; Philley and Michaels; Vernon, Christman and Vernon; Yost, Christman and Vernon; Wright, Kolloway and Lupien. Left on bases—Chicago 7, Washington 4. Bases on balls—Gettel 3, Candini 7, Thompson 1, Pearson 4. Strike outs—By Hudson 1, Thompson 1. Hits—Off Gettel 4 in 3, Hudson 6 in 2, Pearson 4 in 5, Candini 2 in 4⅓, Caldwell 0 in 1, Thompson 4 in 2⅔. Wild pitch—Hudson. Winning pitcher—Pearson. Losing pitcher—Thompson. Umpires—Paparella, McGowan and Hubbard. Time—2:30. Attendance—2,636.

Major League Standings and Pitchers

Sunday, July 18, 1948

NATIONAL LEAGUE RESULTS YESTERDAY

Brooklyn, 8; Cincinnati, 4 (1st)
Brooklyn, 10; Cincinnati, 4 (2d)
New York, 6; Pittsburgh, 5
Chicago, 4; Boston, 1
Philadelphia, 11; St. Louis, 10

STANDING OF THE CLUBS	Boston	Pittsb'gh	St. Louis	Brooklyn	New York	Phila	Cincin'ti	Chicago	WON	LOST	Percent	Games behind
Boston	—	5	5	5	6	8	8	11	48	32	.600	—
Pittsburgh	6	—	5	6	5	5	6	7	40	37	.519	6½
St. Louis	5	3	—	8	4	10	5	5	40	38	.513	7
Brooklyn	3	5	3	—	8	7	11	2	39	37	.513	7
New York	7	7	6	4	—	5	6	3	38	38	.500	8
Philadelphia	6	5	4	6	3	—	5	9	38	43	.469	10½
Cincinnati	3	6	8	2	6	4	—	8	37	44	.457	11½
Chicago	2	6	7	6	6	4	3	—	34	45	.430	13½

National League Games and Pitchers Today

New York at Cincinnati (2)—Koslo (4-4) and Hartung (4-6) vs. Vander Meer (7-8) and Raffensberger (6-3)

Brooklyn at St. Louis (2)—Roe (4-4) and Behrman (2-1) vs. Dickson (6-7) and Hearn (4-3) or Pollet (6-4)

Philadelphia at Chicago (2)—Rowe (4-5) and Roberts (3-2) vs. Schmitz (8-9) and Meyer (9-6)

Boston at Pittsburgh (2)—Bickford (5-2) and Potter (0-0) vs. Riddle (9-5) and Bonham (3-5)

AMERICAN LEAGUE RESULTS YESTERDAY

New York, 4; St. Louis, 0
Philadelphia, 5; Cleveland, 0
Detroit, 3; Boston, 1
Chicago, 9; Washington, 7

STANDING OF THE CLUBS	Clevel'd	Phila.	New York	Boston	Detroit	Wash'n	St. Louis	Chicago	WON	LOST	Percent	Games behind
Cleveland	—	10	5	6	6	6	6	8	47	30	.610	—
Philadelphia	5	—	6	8	5	8	10	8	50	34	.595	½
New York	6	4	—	5	6	8	11	6	46	33	.582	2
Boston	5	6	7	—	9	4	6	5	42	36	.538	5½
Detroit	5	6	4	4	—	7	5	9	40	40	.500	8½
Washington	4	5	5	5	3	—	5	8	35	44	.443	13
St. Louis	3	2	4	4	6	4	—	6	29	47	.382	17½
Chicago	2	1	2	4	5	7	4	—	25	50	.333	21

American League Games and Pitchers Today

Detroit at New York (2, 2:05 p. m.)—Newhouser (13-6) and Hutchinson (5-4) vs. Raschi (10-3) and Byrne (1-3)

Cleveland at Washington (2)—Feller (9-11) and Bearden (7-3) vs. Wynn (7-9) and Haefner (4-8)

St. Louis at Boston (2)—Stephens (2-4) and Shore (1-1) or Kennedy (1-2) vs. Ferriss (5-2) and Johnson (4-2)

Chicago at Philadelphia (2)—Papish (1-2) and Gillespie (0-2) vs. Scheib (7-4) and McCahan (0-3)

A RUN FOR THE YANKEES: Yogi Berra sliding into the plate, scoring from second on Johnson's hit to right field in the third inning Herald Tribune—Frank

Yankee and Tiger Victories Over Red Sox and Indians Throw Race Into Triple Tie

Johnson's Pinch Homer Beats Boston Rivals, 9-6

Hits for Berra, Slams 3-Run Four-Bagger as Victors Rally in Fifth

(Continued from page one)

place, even though they are sharing it with the Indians and the Red Sox.

No one, whether he was a Boston rooter in Bronx clothing, or a Yankee fan, could have found fault with the way McCarthy handled his team in his old haunts, but Marse Joe, like his athletes, was incapable of finding any fault in Page.

The Red Sox appeared en route to one of their typical slam-bang triumphs when Page sauntered into the game in the fourth with the Yankees trailing by a run. Some folks in the press box thought it was "too early" for Page, since the left-hander does his best work over a short route, but Joe was still out there in the ninth inning with a touch of triumph in his eye and a winning wrinkle on his curve.

In chronological order, the game was sauced with a topsy-turvy twist. Ellis Kinder was pitching for the Sox as the game began, but he became a distant memory by the time the shadows began to stretch themselves over the battlefield.

Brown Delivers Triple

The Yankees had no sooner been introduced to Kinder in the first than they became uncommonly friendly with his offerings. Phil Rizzuto, leading off, beat out an infield hit. Bobby Doerr, despite a severe charleyhorse, made a remarkable scoop of Tommy Henrich's grounder and created a force play at second.

Brown, the next hitter, was careful to keep the ball away from Doerr, about 350 feet away from him. Brown tripled to right center and Henrich scored after a pleasant tour of the bases. Joe DiMaggio sent Brown across with a long liner to his brother Dominic in center.

Vic Raschi, the Yankee starting nominee, held the Sox hitless for two innings. In the third, Raschi lost his controlled touch and walked Birdie Tebbetts as the inning began. Kinder fanned, but Don DiMaggio singled and when Johnny Pesky was hit by a pitched ball, the bases were full. Ted Williams then began waving a bat at Raschi. After two quick strikes, Raschi tried to waste a pitch, but Williams swung and spanked a two-run liner to right for a double, which Yogi Berra touched with his glove, but could not hold.

With men on second and third, Raschi induced Vern Stephens to ground to Brown, while Pesky scored. Then Brown threw out Doerr for the third out.

The Yankees tied it with two away in the third when Brown tripled again, this time to left center, and scored on Joe DiMaggio's line single to left.

Raschi Removed

Came the fourth and away went Raschi. He walked the first two hitters, Stan Spence and Bill Goodman. Birdie Tebbetts forced Spence at third. McCarthy yanked Kinder and sent Wally Moses up as a pinch hitter, but Moses lined to Berra. With two away, Dom DiMaggio sent Goodman home with a single and Page was asked to put an end to the Boston uprising.

With a little better fortune, Page would have retired the side without another run. He induced Pesky to hit a grounder between first and second. Henrich left first base in an effort to grab the ball and when George Stirnweiss eventually picked it up on the edge of the infield grass, there was no one covering first. With the bases loaded, Page walked Williams, forcing in a run which gave Boston a 5-3 lead.

Earl Johnson, a trusted left-hander, was asked to keep the bridge for the Bostonians in the fourth. He managed without much difficulty but in the fifth, Johnson was lifted into the limbo of losing pitchers all because of another fellow named Johnson, Billy of the Yankees.

Johnson Scores Three

With one away in the fifth, Henrich walked and Brown doubled him home. Joe DiMaggio was given an intentional pass whereupon Bill Johnson, batting for Berra, hit his twelfth homer, a high-flying swat which religiously observed traffic regulations by keeping to the right of the left field foul pole.

Armed with a 7-to-5 lead, Page worked easily through the sixth and seventh. In the last half of the seventh the Yankees gave him two more runs. Joe DiMaggio walked with two away. When Hank Bauer tripled to right, DiMaggio mounted his charley horse and hobbled all the way home. Bauer tallied on an infield single by Johnny Lindell.

In the ninth, Spence led off with a single. Goodman doubled him to third. After Page disposed of Tebbetts on a fly to Lindell, Spence scurried home with Boston's sixth run. Page reared up and fanned Bill Hitchcock for the second out but he walked Dom DiMaggio, to preserve a faint Boston hope.

The next hitter was Pesky. If he could get on, Williams was lurking behind him in the batting order. Page took a glance at Williams and decided to work on Pesky. He put over a couple of strikes and then fanned the little third baseman on a called third strike. Pesky stood there, watched the ball rip across the center of the plate and then tiptoed to the dressing room, as though he hoped McCarthy hadn't been watching.

WORLD SERIES FEVER: At the left, Billy Johnson is completing his pinch-hit homer in fifth inning at the Stadium, putting the Yankes ahead, 7 to 5. At right, Gus Niarhos, Yankee catcher, hugging Joe Page after the final Red Sox out Herald Tribune—Frank

Menace of Ted Williams's Bat Keeps Yankee Fans on Edge

By Al Laney

If the Yankees do not win the pennant, and they are certainly no worse than an even bet this morning, they still will have given New York something approximating a World Series in this set of three with the Red Sox. No play-off could be more tense and, at the same time more rewarding and more wearing than yesterday's game. The way the two clubs are constituted it does not seem likely they can play any other kind of game today and tomorrow.

The whole atmosphere of the thing was of the biggest occasion although the crowd, which barely half filled the stands, was surprisingly small. The place was alive with celebrities, mostly movie stars who competed unsuccessfully with the game for attention. Surely no World Series game to come can be more full of the things which make for anxiety and hope and fears of disaster engulfing hope suddenly.

Start Figuring Ahead

It is this way especially when the Yankees are leading the Red Sox and mostly because of one man, Ted Williams. The menace of this gent is simply enormous, even when he is sitting quietly on the bench out of sight. No sooner has he been disposed of in one inning than every one in the place begins to figure ahead on how soon he may be up there again.

The urge to do that is just irresistible and the action developed in such a way yesterday that the mere possibility of his coming to bat in the ninth inning was the most menacing thing imaginable and the most exciting.

Joe Page broke a third strike over on Pesky and so stopped one short of Williams, who would have brought to the plate what is known on the radio as the potential winning run. The relief was so great that the people did not cheer properly Page's feat. They were thinking more of the fact that at least twenty-four hours must pass before Williams can come to bat again.

The other great man of the cast, Joe DiMaggio, also played a big role and, if you want to be sentimental about it, a heroic one. When DiMaggio scored from first on Bauer's triple in the seventh it could plainly be seen by all that he dragged one leg as he ran and that he must have been in pain.

The shifting about of players necessary before the Yanks could win this one was not reassuring because it cost them runs before they got enough themselves. If Henrich had been playing right field, he would no doubt have caught the drive from Williams which Berra just missed and the Sox would have had one run instead of three in the third. And, if McQuinn had been on first, he probably would have made the play which Henrich did not and Boston would have had one run instead of two in the fourth.

Seven to Go

When a team is imperfectly manned right down the line, as the Yanks are, that is what can happen to you if you sacrifice one thing in hopes of getting more of another. It has worked well enough so far, though, that the team is dead level with Boston and Cleveland with only seven to go.

All the grandstand managers seemed to disapprove of Harris's sending Johnson to hit for Berra in the fifth. One swing by Billy and it became a master managerial move, approved by all.

Yankee Score

* * *

BOSTON (A. L.)	ab	r	h	po	a
D. DiMag'o cf	5	1	2	2	0
Pesky 3b	4	1	2	2	1
Williams lf	3	0	2	4	0
Stephens ss	4	0	0	2	3
Doerr 2b	5	0	0	0	1
Spence rf	4	1	2	0	0
Goodman 1b	4	1	2	8	1
Tebbetts c	4	2	1	6	1
Kinder p	1	0	0	0	0
*Moses	1	0	0	0	0
E. Johnson p	1	0	0	0	0
Ferriss p	0	0	0	0	2
‡Hitchcock	1	0	0	0	0
Hughson p	0	0	0	0	1
§Stringer	1	0	0	0	0
Totals	38	6	11	24	10

NEW YORK (A. L.)	ab	r	h	po	a
Rizzuto ss	4	0	1	0	1
Henrich 1b	3	2	0	5	0
Brown 3b	4	3	3	3	2
J. DiMaggio cf	2	2	1	5	0
Berra rf	2	0	1	1	0
†W. Johnson	1	1	1	0	0
Bauer rf	1	1	1	2	0
Keller lf	1	0	0	1	0
Lindell lf	3	0	1	2	0
Niarhos c	4	0	0	7	0
Stirnweiss 2b	4	0	1	1	0
Raschi p	1	0	0	0	1
Page p	3	0	0	0	0
Totals	33	9	10	27	4

*Batted for Kinder in fourth and lined out.
‡Batted for Ferriss in eighth and fanned.
§Batted for Hughson in ninth and fanned.
†Batted for Berra in fifth and hit homer with two on.

Boston .... 003 200 001—6
New York .... 201 040 20x—9

Errors—None. Runs batted in—Brown 2, J. DiMaggio 2, Williams, Stephens, D. DiMaggio, W. Johnson 3, Bauer, Lindell, Tebbetts. Two-base hits—Williams, Brown, Goodman. Three-base hits—Brown 2, Bauer. Home run—W. Johnson. Left on bases—Boston 14, New York 3. Bases on balls—Raschi 4, Page 4, E. Johnson 2, Ferriss 1. Strikeouts—Kinder 1, Raschi 1, E. Johnson 2, Page 6, Hughson 1. Hits—Off Kinder 5 in 3 innings, E. Johnson 3 in 1⅓, Ferriss 2 in 2⅔, Hughson 0 in 1, Raschi 3 in 3⅔, Page 8 in 5⅓. Hit by pitcher—By Raschi (Pesky). Winning pitcher—Page. Losing pitcher—E. Johnson. Umpires—Summers, Rommell, Berry and Paparella. Time—2:31. Attendance—33,609 paid.

Cards Subdue Cubs, 4 to 1, for Brecheen's 19th

Southpaw Limits Losers to Two Hits in 7 Innings; Redbirds Gain on Braves

CHICAGO, Sept. 24 (AP).—With their ace left-hander, Harry Brecheen, limiting the Chicago Cubs to five hits, the St. Louis Cardinals earned a 4-to-1 victory today and moved within six and one-half games of the league leading Boston Braves in the National League.

Brecheen, in collecting his nineteenth victory, was the complete master over the route giving up just two hits until the eighth inning while his teammates pounded two Cub pitchers for eleven.

The Cards, currently embroiled in a bitter battle with Brooklyn for second place, went ahead in the second only to have the Cubs tie it up at 1-to-1 in the third. Stan Musial collected two hits and a walk, boomed out a triple in the sixth to score Brecheen and Marty Marion and put the game away.

Cliff Chambers, whose only victory this season was registered against the Cincinnati Reds, yielded all the runs and eight hits. It was his ninth loss.

The score:

ST. LOUIS (N. L.)	ab	r	h	po	a
Schoend'st 2b	4	0	2	0	4
Marion ss	5	2	1	1	3
Musial lf	3	0	2	3	0
Northey rf	5	0	1	0	0
Dusak rf	0	0	0	1	0
Jones 1b	5	0	1	13	1
Moore cf	4	0	1	1	0
Lang 3b	5	0	2	2	4
Rice c	4	1	1	5	0
Brecheen p	3	1	0	1	1
Totals	38	4	11	27	13

CHICAGO (N. L.)	ab	r	h	po	a
Verban 2b	4	0	0	4	3
Lowrey cf	4	0	1	1	0
Cavarretta 1b	4	0	1	7	2
Pafko 3b	4	0	0	0	1
Scheffing c	1	0	0	1	0
McCullough c	3	0	1	2	0
Nicholson rf	4	0	0	5	0
Maddern lf	2	1	1	2	0
Smalley ss	3	0	1	4	1
Chambers p	1	0	0	1	3
*Lynch	1	0	0	0	0
Hamner p	0	0	0	0	1
†Maugh	1	0	0	0	0
Hacker p	0	0	0	0	0
Totals	32	1	5	27	11

*Batted for Chambers in sixth, grounded out.
†Batted for Hammer in eighth, grounded out.

St. Louis .... 010 012 000—4
Chicago .... 001 000 000—1

Error—Smalley. Runs batted in—Schoendienst, Chambers, Jones, Musial 2. Two-base hits—Smalley, Northey, Maddern. Three-base hit—Musial. Double play—Pafko, Verban and Cavarretta. Left on bases—St. Louis 13, Chicago 5. Bases on balls—Chambers 5. Strikeouts—Chambers 3, Brecheen 5. Hits—Off Chambers 8 in 6 innings, Hamner 3 in 2, Hacker 0 in 1. Hit by pitcher—By Chambers (Breechen), by Brecheen (Maddern). Losing pitcher—Chambers. Umpires—Pinelli, Gore and Robb. Time—1:50. Attendance—5,480.

Leading Five Batsmen In Each Major League

American League

Player and club	G.	A.B.	R.	H.	Pct.
Williams, Boston	129	481	117	178	.370
Boudreau, Clevel'd	144	532	107	188	.353
Mitchell, Cleveland	133	573	76	192	.335
Zarilla, St. Louis	139	513	74	168	.328
McCosky, Philadel.	132	505	94	164	.325

National League

Player and club	G.	A.B.	R.	H.	Pct.
Musial, St. Louis	147	582	130	221	.380
Ashburn, Philadel.	117	463	78	154	.333
Dark, Boston	129	514	81	167	.325
Holmes, Boston	132	556	79	179	.322
Slaughter, St. Louis	146	548	92	176	.321
Pafko, Chicago	135	520	81	167	.321

RUNS BATTED IN		HOME RUNS	
American League		**American League**	
DiMaggio, Yanks	151	DiMaggio, Yanks	39
Stephens, R. Sox	132	Gordon, Indians	30
Williams, R. Sox	122	Keltner, Indians	29
Majeski, Athletics	117	Stephens, R. Sox	28
Gordon, Indians	116	Doerr, R. Sox	25
National League		**National League**	
Mize, Giants	124	Kiner, Pirates	39
Musial, Cardinals	124	Mize, Giants	39
Kiner, Pirates	117	Musial, Cardinals	38
Gordon, Giants	106	Sauer, Reds	35
Pafko, Cubs	100	Gordon, Giants	30
		Ennis, Phillies	30

VIEWS OF SPORT

By Red Smith

Rebirth in the Bronx

ALONG about 3:30 yesterday afternoon, sounds of harsh and strangled breathing could be heard in the Bronx. While authorities debated whether it was (a) the panting of damsels seated near Bob Hope in Yankee Stadium or (b) the death-rattle of the American League pennant race, it was drowned out by the wild, free, hunting cry of 33,609 Yankee fans.

Red Smith

Prodded by Bill Johnson's bat, the moribund Yankees had taken up their beds and jogged—around the bases and into a three-way tie for first place. For the first time since the opening day of the baseball season, they are teetering drunkenly on that eminence this morning, cheek-to-jowl with the Boston Red Sox and Cleveland Indians.

In the opening game of the slightly serious series in the Stadium, the Red Sox achieved a lead of 5 to 3 after four innings. Figures on the scoreboard reported on the plodding progress of the Indians toward a defeat in Detroit. If the status could be preserved at quo, Boston would finish the day one full game ahead of Cleveland, two games in front of New York, and safe from any risk of being passed by the Yankees during the visit here.

Then Bill Johnson batted for Larry Berra, whacked a pitch by Earl Johnson plumb off the reservation and brought three runs home in one chummy cluster. Thus the three leaders passed the night in a situation suspiciously suggestive of bundling.

The Fabulous Invalids

AT FIRST glance, a stranger in the Stadium might have concluded that the New York public was losing interest in the fine old game of rounders, for there were large tracts of unoccupied pews; chances are, however, that the general public took it for granted the park would be sold out, and only the bold and foolish bothered to try for tickets.

This was not the day's only error of judgment. Members of both teams responded nobly to the appeal which a whiff of World Series money invariably makes to a ball player's cupidity. They were all so tight that if you plucked them they would have twanged like guitars.

Mistakes naturally resulted. In the first inning, Boston's ordinarily acute Robert Doerr forgot that the elderly Ellis Kinder was pitching for the Red Sox, and neglected to cover first base for the old gentleman on a bunt by Phil Rizzuto. On a similar play in the fourth, Joe Page took the view that a relief pitcher's job is to pitch, and he declined to invade his infielders' jurisdiction.

As to Doerr, though, it should be mentioned that he is playing with a leg so sore that he wouldn't be in the line-up except for the coarse rewards at stake, and the same is true of Joe DiMaggio. The Yanks have got to have Joe in there, even though he looked like a flat-wheeled trolley scoring from first base on a triple by Hank Bauer.

These are sad days for the old champ. In his weakened state, he was unable to account for even half of the Yankees' runs, batting in only two—that's 151 for the season—and scoring only two more.

A Page From History

THERE was, at the outset, little indication of the course events were to take. The early innings consisted mostly of occasions when the Red Sox had the bases filled and Ted Williams at bat. Indeed, this situation looked practically permanent, like something painted in still life.

In due course, however, Page arrived, and it was like turning back the calendar a year. The large left-hander who was Bucky Harris's pin-up boy in 1947 was sprung from the bullpen in the fourth inning, when Harris's affection for Vic Raschi had cooled.

Joe's appearance aroused even less public enthusiasm, implausible though this sounds, than that of Sugar Robinson in the same park the evening before. Last year the very name of Page revolted batters; this year they've been saying that the guy may not be any Hedy LaMarr, but he has a beautiful soul, and anyhow, the fourth inning seemed perilously early to send Joe to work.

There were two Red Sox on base when Page appeared. An instant later there were three. But after forcing Boston's fifth run home by walking Williams, he went suddenly churlish.

The Rocky Road Ahead

FROM that point on, the Bostons were hitting strictly for height. Joe finished in a common canter, yielding only one consolation run in the ninth inning. Of the sixteen batsmen retired in his five and one-third innings, six struck out and the other ten hit indolent fly balls.

He turned back Boston threats in the fifth, eighth and ninth innings, and gave a final flourish to the performance by shooting a third strike past Johnny Pesky in the ninth while two Red Sox stood on the bases and Pesky stood on his dignity.

This was the big game of the series, and Page saved it. But there's no surcease ahead—the Red Sox play their last five games at home. At home, the Red Sox eat their young.

Three Cleveland Homers Fail as Detroit Wins, 4-3

Hutchinson Yields Six Hits in Snapping Tribe's Streak; Wertz Slams Double Off Lemon With Two Men on Base in 7th to Break 2-All Tie

By Rud Rennie

DETROIT, Sept. 24.—The Tiger jokers who tripped the Yankees and the Red Sox, pulled their biggest trick today when they also knocked off the Cleveland Indians, 4 to 3, thereby contributing to a three-way tie for first place in the American League.

It is thrilling that, at the end of 147 games, three teams, the Yankees, the Red Sox and the Indians, should be all even, just as they were when they opened the season in April. All three teams have won ninety-one games and lost fifty-six, with seven more games to play.

This is fun for the Tigers, in fifth place, sixteen and a half games behind. They hold the key to the gate leading to the pennant because they have five more games with the Indians while the Yankees have four more with the Red Sox. Today the Tigers broke a seven-game Cleveland winning streak in spite of three home runs.

Wertz Slams Double

Freddie Hutchinson, a right-hander, was the winner. He held the Indians to six hits, half of which were homers—one by Larry Doby, one by Ken Keltner and one by Joe Gordon. Freddie outpitched his former Navy bunkmate Bob Lemon and he won when Vic Wertz slammed a double to left with two men on bases in the seventh, breaking a 2-all tie.

It was a keen game, played in cool and breezy weather before 10,464 persons who kept looking at the scoreboard to keep up with what was going on in New York between the Yankees and the Red Sox.

The Tigers were first to score. They got a run in the first inning when Neil Berry singled, took second on a wild pitch and came home after Pat Mullin walked, when Dick Wakefield rifled a single to center. The Tigers then had men on first and third with two out when Eddie Mayo grounded out to Lou Boudreau.

That one run stood up until the fifth. Hutchinson had the Indians shut out with three hits and two away when Doby belted his fourteenth homer of the year into the lower right centerfield stands.

There was one away in the sixth when Keltner socked one into the upper left field stands.

The Indians led, 2 to 1, but Dick Wakefield doubled in the Detroit half of the inning, moved to third on Mayo's sacrifice and came home on George Vico's fly to left.

Lemon Fails to Finish

Then the Tigers routed Lemon who had beaten them three times, once with a no-hitter. For the third time in his last three starts, Lemon failed to finish.

Hutchinson, the first man up in the seventh, socked him for a single. Johnny Lipon sacrificed. Berry walked. The Tigers had men on first and second when Wertz slammed his double to left field, both runners scoring.

Sam Zoldak, a left-hander, was brought in to pitch after that and he walked Mullin. It looked as if the Tigers might be in for a big inning, but Eddie Robinson, the Cleveland first baseman, made a back-handed catch of a line drive hit by Wakefield and doubled Mullin off first.

It was 4 to 2 in favor of the Tigers when Doby opened the eighth with a hit. Then came a double-play which kept the Indians from tying the score.

Boudreau rapped a bouncing grounder to Lipon who fielded it close to second base, stepped on the bag, forcing Doby and threw to first for an easy out on the Cleveland manager. So there was no one on base when Gordon put his thirtieth homer of the year into the lower left field stands.

Hutchinson, angry about these home runs, bore down in the ninth and got Thurman Tucker, Robinson and Hal Peck, a pinch-hitter, out in order. It was this thirteenth victory, his third over the Indians and his first over them here in Detroit.

The Tigers are playing without Hoot Evers, their centerfielder (pneumonia); George Kell, their third baseman (broken jaw), and Eddie Lake, a second baseman, (broken finger).

Yields 31 Home Runs

The Indians enlarged the American League record made by Hutchinson this year. Thirty-one home runs have been hit off the Detroit right-hander, and fourteen of them have been made by the Indians.

Boudreau employed defensive strategy in the late innings, shifting Doby to right in place of Judnich and putting Thurman Tucker in center. . . . And with one out in the seventh he yanked Mitchell and put Bob Kennedy in left field. . . . Hutchinson issued only two passes which got the Indians nowhere and fanned five, striking out Robinson, Hegan and Lemon after Keltner singled and Judnich walked in the second.

The score:

CLEVELAND (A. L.)	ab	r	h	po	a
Mitchell lf	4	0	0	1	0
Kennedy lf	0	0	0	0	0
Doby cf-rf	4	1	2	1	0
Boudreau ss	3	0	0	1	2
Gordon 2b	4	1	1	1	2
Keltner 3b	4	1	3	2	2
Judnich rf	2	0	1	0	0
Tucker rf	1	0	0	1	0
Robinson 1b	4	0	0	12	2
Hegan c	3	0	0	3	1
*Peck	1	0	0	0	0
Lemon p	3	0	0	1	6
Zoldak p	0	0	0	1	0
Totals	33	3	7	24	15

DETROIT (A. L.)	ab	r	h	po	a
Lipon ss	3	0	0	2	3
Berry 2b	2	2	1	0	1
Wertz rf	3	0	1	1	0
Mullin cf	2	0	0	5	0
Wakefield lf	4	1	2	4	0
Mayo 3b	3	0	1	0	0
Vico 1b	3	0	0	8	0
Ginsberg c	4	0	2	7	1
Hutchinson p	4	1	1	0	1
Totals	28	4	8	27	6

*Batted for Hegan in ninth, grounded out.

Cleveland .... 000 011 010—3
Detroit .... 100 001 20x—4

Errors—None. Runs batted in—Doby, Keltner, Gordon, Wakefield, Vico, Wertz 2. Two-base hit—Wakefield. Home runs—Doby, Keltner, Gordon. Sacrifices—Vco, Mayo, Lipon. Double plays—Robinson unassisted. Lipon and Vico. Left on bases—Cleveland 5, Detroit 8. Bases on balls—Lemon 4, Zoldak 1, Hutchinson 2. Strikeouts—Lemon 2, Hutchinson 5. Hits—Off Lemon 7 in 6⅓ innings, Zoldak 1 in 1⅔. Wild pitch — Lemon. Losing pitcher — Lemon. Umpires—Jones, McGowan, Grieve and Stevens. Time—1:51. Attendance—10,464.

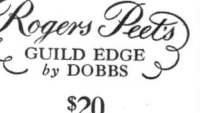

Yankees to Play At Home in Case Of Flag Play-Offs

* * *

CHICAGO, Sept. 24 (AP).—A coin tossing ceremony in the office of Will Harridge, president of the American League, today determined playoffs in event of a tie in the American League race.

If Boston ties New York the playoff will be in New York, Oct. 4.

If Boston ties Cleveland the playoff will be in Boston, Oct. 4.

If New York ties Cleveland, the playoff will be in New York, Oct. 4.

If the three teams tie, New York will meet the winner of the Oct. 4 Boston-Cleveland game at Boston on the home grounds of the winning team, Oct. 5.

Gettel Sets Back Browns For White Sox, 4 to 3

ST. LOUIS, Sept. 24 (AP).—The Chicago White Sox shaded the St. Louis Browns, 4 to 3, tonight behind the effective five-hit pitching of Al Gettel. The White Sox collected eight hits off Ned Garver and one off Bryan Stephens.

The score:

CHICAGO (A. L.)	ab	r	h	po	a
Adams rf	4	1	2	3	0
Delsing cf	5	1	1	3	0
Lupien 1b	3	1	1	8	1
Hodgin lf	5	0	1	1	0
Robinson c	3	1	1	6	1
Kolloway 3b	4	0	2	1	1
Michaels 2b	4	0	1	4	4
Whitman ss	4	0	0	1	2
Gettel p	4	0	0	0	0
Totals	36	4	9	27	9

ST. LOUIS (A. L.)	ab	r	h	po	a
Dillinger 3b	4	0	0	0	0
Lehner cf	4	0	0	5	0
Priddy 2b	4	0	0	4	3
Kokos rf	4	0	0	1	0
Platt lf	4	1	2	1	0
†Lund	0	0	0	0	0
Arft 1b	4	0	0	8	1
Dente ss	4	2	2	6	4
Moss c	3	0	1	2	0
Garver p	1	0	0	0	2
*Zarilla	1	0	0	0	0
Stephens p	0	0	0	0	0
Totals	33	3	5	27	10

*Batted for Garver in seventh, popped out.
†Ran for Platt in ninth.

Chicago .... 100 100 200—4
St. Louis .... 000 010 200—3

Errors—Whitman 3, Priddy 2. Runs batted in—Lupien, Michaels, Moss 3, Robinson, Kolloway. Two-base hits—Adams, Moss. Three-base hit—Dente. Sacrifice—Garver. Double plays—Dente and Arft; Priddy and Arft; Whitman, Michaels and Lupien. Left on bases—Chicago 10, St. Louis 5. Bases on balls—Gettel 1, Garver 5. Strikeouts—Gettel 5, Garver 1, Stephens 1. Hits—Off Garver 8 in 7 innings, Stephens 1 in 2. Losing pitcher—Garver. Umpires—Hurley, Hubbard and McKinley. Time—1:49. Attendance—1,100 (paid).

INTERNATIONAL LEAGUE

Semi-final Playoffs (Best of 7)
Thursday Night's Game

Montreal, 3; Rochester, 0.
Montreal wins series, 4 to 3.

Final Playoffs (Best of 7)

Montreal vs. Syracuse.
No game scheduled last night.

Remaining Games for A.L. Contenders

September	NEW YORK	BOSTON	CLEVELAND
25 (Today)	Boston, at N. Y.	At New York	At Detroit
26 (Sunday)	Boston, at N. Y.	At New York	At Detroit
27 (Mon.)	Open	Open	Open
28 (Tues.)	At Philadelphia	Washington	Chicago (Night)
29 (Wed.)	At Philadelphia	Washington	Chicago
30 (Thurs.)	At Philadelphia	Washington	Open
October			
1 (Fri.)	Open	Open	Detroit
2 (Sat.)	At Boston	New York	Detroit
3 (Sun.)	At Boston	New York	Detroit

Major League Standings and Pitchers

Saturday, Sept. 25, 1948

AMERICAN LEAGUE RESULTS YESTERDAY

New York, 9; Boston, 6
Detroit, 4; Cleveland, 3
Chicago, 4; St. Louis, 3 (night)
Other clubs not scheduled

STANDING OF THE CLUBS	New York	Boston	Clevel'd	Phila	Detroit	St. Louis	Wash'n	Chicago	WON	LOST	Percent	Games behind	G. to Play
New York	—	7	12	10	13	16	17	16	91	56	.619	—	7
Boston	11	—	11	12	15	15	13	14	91	56	.619	—	7
Cleveland	10	11	—	16	10	14	16	14	91	56	.619	—	7
Philadelphia	9	10	6	—	10	18	14	16	83	66	.557	9	5
Detroit	9	7	7	12	—	9	16	14	74	72	.507	16½	8
St. Louis	6	7	8	4	10	—	10	11	56	89	.386	34	9
Washington	5	6	6	6	6	12	—	12	53	95	.358	38½	6
Chicago	6	8	6	6	8	5	9	—	48	97	.331	42	9

American League Games and Pitchers Today

Boston at New York (2 p. m.)—Kramer (16-5) vs. Reynolds (16-6)

Cleveland at Detroit—Bearden (16-7) vs. Trucks (13-12)

Chicago at St. Louis (night)—Haynes (9-9) vs. Kennedy (7-7)

Other clubs not scheduled

NATIONAL LEAGUE RESULTS YESTERDAY

St. Louis, 4; Chicago, 1
Cincinnati, 4; Pittsburgh, 3 (night)
Other clubs not scheduled

STANDING OF THE CLUBS	Boston	St. Louis	Brooklyn	Pittsb'gh	New York	Phila	Cincin'ti	Chicago	WON	LOST	Percent	Games behind	G. to Play
Boston	—	11	12	12	8	14	13	16	86	59	.593	—	8
St. Louis	11	—	10	7	15	17	12	8	80	66	.548	6½	8
Brooklyn	7	12	—	9	11	12	18	11	80	67	.544	7	7
Pittsburgh	10	12	13	—	10	10	9	14	78	68	.534	8½	8
New York	9	7	11	12	—	13	12	11	75	72	.510	12	7
Philadelphia	8	5	6	12	7	—	11	15	64	84	.432	23½	6
Cincinnati	8	10	4	8	10	11	—	11	62	83	.428	24	8
Chicago	6	9	11	8	11	7	8	—	60	86	.411	26½	8

National League Games and Pitchers Today

New York at Boston—Jones (15-8) vs. Sain (22-14)

Brooklyn at Philadelphia (night)—Barney (14-12) vs. Leonard (12-7)

Cincinnati at Pittsburgh—Fox (6-9) vs. Chesnes (13-5)

St. Louis at Chicago—Pollet (13-7) or Dickson (12-14) vs. Lade (4-5)

Cullen and Van Ness Gain Final in N. Y. A. C. Golf

Special to the Herald Tribune

MAMARONECK, N. Y., Sept. 24.—Jimmy Cullen and Frank Van Ness qualified for the final round of the New York Athletic Club golf championships today by winning two matches apiece at the Winged Foot Golf Club. They will met in the final today.

Van Ness, 1946 tourney winner, stopped R. H. Goffe jr., 2 and 1, and Ed Butler, by the same score Cullen defeated Trumbull Richard, 3 and 2, and A. J. Keck, 1 up. Van Ness also took the thirty-six-hole veterans championship with 82—83—165.

AMERICAN ASSOCIATION

Semi-final Playoffs (Best of 7)
Thursday Night's Game

Columbus, 4; Milwaukee, 2.
Columbus wins series, 4 to 3.

Final Playoffs (Best of 7)

Columbus vs. St. Paul.
No game scheduled last night.

Results in College and School Sports

* * *

College

Football

Boston College	26	Wake Forest	9
John Carroll	26	Dayton	18
Lebanon Valley	7	Temple	7
Mayville (N. D.) T.	19	Bottineau	7
Randolph-Macon	19	Newport News	12
Rollins	7	Erskine	0
St. Vincent's	25	Indiana (Pa.) Tchrs.	0
Syracuse	13	Niagara	9
Upsala	0	Montclair State	0
West Chester Tchrs.	14	Rider	0

School

Football

Alumni	19	Garfield	6
Clifton	20	Central (Paterson)	0

Soccer

Bayport	2	Central Islip	1
Bellport	1	Bay Shore	1
Islip	1	Kings Park	0

TEXAS LEAGUE

Final Playoffs (Best of 7)
Thursday Night's Game

Tulsa, 18; Fort Worth, 7.
Teams tied in series, 1-all.

Last Night's Game

Fort Worth at Tulsa.

Yankees Beat Senators in 9th, 2-1, for Third Straight; Giants Check Dodgers, 4-1

Byrne Wins on Bauer's Double In Series Sweep for New York

Outfielder's Blow Snaps Tie After Homer by Lewis Offsets Johnson's Four-Bagger Off Thompson

By Rud Rennie

Another Yankee pitcher, this time Tommy Byrne, went the distance in the Stadium yesterday, and the Yankees swept the three-game series with the Washington Senators, winning in the ninth inning for the second time, 2 to 1. Byrne walked four and hit two, but he yielded only five safeties.

Hank Bauer knocked in the deciding tally with a double after Johnny Lindell opened the inning with a single and Sherry Robertson, newly in the game as the Washington right fielder, dropped Tommy Henrich's line drive.

It was fitting that Bauer should come through with the winning blow, because he had cost the Yankees a run in the fourth by failing to slide to the plate.

He came in on his feet after Clyde Vollmer, the center fielder, caught Larry Barra's short fly, and ran into a put-out for a double play, even though the throw was bad. All the other runs were made with homers. Bill Johnson, one of the Yankee professionals, who was allowed to play yesterday because Forrest Thompson, the Washington hurler, is a southpaw, whacked a home run into the right-field stands in the second inning. Buddy Lewis, Washington's starting right fielder, hit one in the sixth, tying the score.

Escapes Trouble in Seventh

Byrne walked two and hit one and had the bases loaded with two out in the seventh, but he got out of this jam by inducing Sam Dente to rap a grounder at Johnson for a force-out.

Thompson made his second hit in the ninth after Byrne hit another batter, Al Kozar, but again there were two away and Gil Coan was out when he hoisted a foul behind the plate.

The Senators missed another chance to score in the fifth. In this inning the Yankees made two good plays. With one away, Jerry Coleman darted to his left and made a dazzling one-handed stop of Ralph Weigel's grounder. Coleman's throw was low and Jack Phillips, who played first base, missed it. Weigel was credited with a hit.

Thompson followed with a single to left. There were men on first and second with one out when Rizzuto grabbed Gil Coan's grounder, stepped on second and threw to first, where Phillips went into a crowd-pleasing split to get the speedy Coan in a double play.

Two Hits for Johnson

Johnson, a right-handed batsman, made two hits, both into right field.

George Stirnweiss, who strained his left hand opening day, and who has been out of action since then, hopes to be able to play this afternoon when the team opens a three-game series in Boston. . . . Rizzuto felt a little woozy yesterday because of all the drugs injected into him the day before to kill the germs which were inflaming his throat. But he got two hits.

The Senators had gone through seventeen scoreless innings against Yankee pitching when they scored in the sixth. . . . Both the Yankees and the Senators have needed only three pitchers in the three games.

The score:

WASHINGTON (AL)	ab	r	h	po	a	NEW YORK (AL)	ab	r	h	po	a
Coan lf	4	0	1	2	0	Coleman 2b	4	0	1	1	2
Dente ss	4	0	0	1	2	Rizzuto ss	4	0	2	3	5
Lewis rf	3	1	1	4	0	Lindell cf	4	1	1	5	0
Robertson rf	0	0	0	0	0	Henrich rf	3	0	0	0	0
Vollmer cf	4	0	0	2	1	Bauer lf	3	0	1	3	0
Yost 3b	4	0	0	1	0	Johnson 3b	3	1	2	1	0
Robinson 1b	3	0	0	5	0	Berra c	3	0	1	3	1
Kozar 2b	3	0	0	2	2	Phillips 1b	3	0	0	11	0
Weigel c	2	0	1	7	0	Byrne p	3	0	0	0	3
Thompson p	4	0	2	0	2						
Totals	31	1	5*	24	7	Totals	30	2	8	27	11

*None out when winning run was scored.

Washington	000	001	000	—1
New York	010	000	001	—2

Error—Robertson. Runs batted in—Johnson, Lewis, Bauer. Two-base hits—Rizzuto, Bauer. Home runs—Johnson, Lewis. Double plays—Thompson, Dente and Robinson; Vollmer and Weigel; Rizzuto and Phillips. Left on bases—Washington 9, New York 6. Bases on balls—Off Thompson 2, Byrne 4. Struck out—By Thompson 4, Byrne 2. Hit by pitcher—By Byrne (Lewis, Robinson). Winner—Byrne (1-0). Loser—Thompson (0-1). Umpires—Boyer, Hurley, Rommel and Passarella. Time—1:58. Attendance—11,659 (paid).

Duke and Pitt to Renew Football Relations in '50

DURHAM, N. C., April 22 (AP).—Duke University and the University of Pittsburgh will renew football competition in 1950.

First of the two-year series will be played Sept. 30 at Pittsburgh. Site for the second game, to be played Sept. 29, 1951, has not been picked. Both games will be openers for Duke.

Pittsburgh first came to Duke in 1929 and helped dedicate Duke's new stadium, the Panthers handing Duke one of its worst lickings, 52 to 7.

In 1937 Duke held the Panthers to a 10-to-0 score. The next year's game was one of the greatest ever played here. Magnificent punting by Eric Tipton and a punt block by Bolo Perdue gave Duke a 7-to-0 margin.

Herald Tribune—Acme

HIT BY PITCH: Buddy Lewis, of the Senators, is struck by ball thrown by Tommy Byrne, Yankee hurler, in first inning. Catching is Yogi Berra and plate umpire is Jim Boyer

Herald Tribune—Acme

SENATOR DOUBLE PLAY: Sam Dente, Senators' shortstop, fires to first to complete twin killing after retiring Berra at second in second inning. Calling play at second is Umpire Ed Rommel

White Sox Conquer Tigers, 5-2, Holding Groth to One Single

DETROIT, April 21 (AP).—The Chicago White Sox scored their first victory of the American League campaign today when they slowed Johnny Groth, slugging rookie outfielder, and defeated the Detroit Tigers, 5 to 2.

Groth was held to a single in his two official times at bat. On his other appearances, he walked and was hit by the pitcher.

The day's activities left Groth with a record of six hits in nine times at bat in the three-game series. He scored the Tigers' first run today to run his season total in that department to four.

Howard Judson, a right-hander, got credit for the victory, but needed help from Bill Evans, formerly with Muskegon of the Central League, and Matt Surkont.

Surkont did a nice relief job in the eighth after Evans had walked the first two men before being waved to the showers. Surkont forced Dick Wakefield and Pat Mullin, pinch hitters, to fly out. He walked Johnny Lipon to load the bases, but got out of the hole without harm when he got George Kell to fly out.

Herb Adams, Chicago center fielder, came up with three hits to pace the White Sox attack. He also had a busy day defensively, with seven putouts.

Lou Kretlow started for the Tigers but was in hot water in nearly every inning. He gave up all five Chicago runs before Ted Gray and Dizzy Trout finished up the two-hour-forty-minute marathon witnessed by 16,936 fans.

White Sox Score

* * *

CHICAGO (A. L.)	ab	r	h	po	a	DETROIT (A. L.)	ab	r	h	po	a
Adams cf	5	1	3	7	0	Berry 2b	3	0	0	4	2
Philley rf	5	0	0	4	0	†Mullin	1	0	0	0	0
Appling ss	2	2	0	2	3	Lake 2b	0	0	0	0	0
Zernial lf	4	0	2	1	0	Lipon ss	3	1	0	1	2
Tipton c	4	1	0	4	0	Kell 3b	4	0	2	2	2
Michaels 2b	4	0	2	5	2	Wertz rf	4	0	2	2	0
Baker 3b	4	1	1	0	1	Evers lf	4	0	0	0	0
Goldsberry 1b	1	0	1	2	2	Robinson c	4	0	1	4	1
Souchock 1b	2	0	0	1	1	Groth cf	2	1	1	6	1
Judson p	3	0	0	0	1	Vico 1b	2	0	0	8	0
Evans p	0	0	0	0	0	Kretlow p	2	0	0	0	1
Surkont p	1	0	0	1	0	Gray p	1	0	0	0	1
						*Wakefield	1	0	0	0	0
						Trout p	0	0	0	0	1
Totals	35	5	9	27	10	Totals	31	2	6	27	11

*Flied out for Vico in eighth.
†Popped for Berry in eighth.

Chicago	000	212	000	—5
Detroit	010	000	100	—2

Errors—Judson, Groth, Lipon 2, Kell. Runs batted in—Zernial, Adams, Baker, Kell. Sacrifice—Vico. Double plays—Lipon, Berry and Vico; Appling, Michaels and Souchoock; Groth and Berry. Left on bases—Chicago 6, Detroit 13. Bases on balls—Off Judson 5, Evans 3, Surkont 1, Kretlow 3. Strikeouts—By Judson 3, Kretlow 1, Gray 3. Hits—Off Judson, 5 Vico; Appling, Michaels and Souchock; Groth in 2; Kretlow, 8 in 5⅓; Gray, 1 in 2⅔; Trout, 0 in 1. Hit by pitcher—By Judson (Groth). Wild pitches—Judson, Kretlow, Gray. Passed ball—Tipton. Winning pitcher—Judson (1-0). Losing pitcher—Kretlow (0-1). Umpires—Paparella, Hubbard and Berry. Time—2:40. Attendance—16,936.

Edwards to Coach Ends Of Michigan State Team

EAST LANSING, Mich., April 21 (AP).—Appointment of Earl L. Edwards, assistant football coach at Penn State, as Michigan State College end coach was announced today. Edwards will have the title of assistant football coach and associate professor of physical education.

He will fill the position vacated by LaVerne (Kip) Taylor, who left Michigan State to become head coach at Oregon State. Edwards, forty, has been a member of the Penn State coaching staff since 1936.

Italy Wins Saber Crown

CAIRO, April 21 (UP).—Italy won the world saber team championship today beating France in the final by nine bouts to four. Egypt beat Belgium, also by nine bouts to four, to take third place.

Braves Beat Holy Cross, 8–2

WORCESTER, Mass., April 21 (AP).—The Boston Braves, with shortstop Alvin Dark the only regular in the action, pounded two Holy Cross pitchers for eighteen hits and an 8-to-2 victory today in their annual exhibition game.

American Association

Yesterday's Results

St. Paul, 12; Toledo, 11 (11 ins.).
Kansas City at Louisville, rain.
Milwaukee at Columbus (night).
Minneapolis at Indianapolis (night).

Reds Shut Out Cardinals, 5-0, Gain 1st Place

Vander Meer Allows 5 Hits; Sauer and Bloodworth Aid With Round-Trippers

CINCINNATI, April 21 (AP).—Cincinnati poured on the power today, two home runs and three doubles helping Johnny Vander Meer to an easy 5-to0 pitching triumph over the St. Louis Cards. The victory gave Cincinnati undisputed possession of first place in the National League.

Hank Sauer and Jimmy Bloodworth were the homers, and there was a runner on base each time. Howie Pollet was the losing hurler. It was the Reds' second victory in two tries against St. Louis.

Vander Meer, who allowed only five hits—one a double for the first safety of the season for Stan Musial—got stronger as the game progressed, retiring the last eleven batters in order.

Pollet gave up only five hits, but all were for extra bases. Gerald Staley was touched for the other Cincinnati safety.

The score:

ST. LOUIS (N. L.)	ab	r	h	po	a	CINCINNATI (N. L.)	ab	r	h	po	a
Glaviano 3b	4	0	0	1	1	Hatton 3b	3	1	1	0	4
Schoned't 2b	4	0	2	1	2	Wyrostek cf	4	1	1	2	0
Musial cf	4	0	1	5	0	Litwhiler rf	4	1	1	0	0
Slaughter lf	4	0	0	2	0	H. Sauer lf	4	1	1	2	0
Jones 1b	4	0	2	9	0	Bloodworth 2b	3	1	1	1	6
Ed Sauer rf	3	0	0	2	0	Kluszewski 1b	4	0	1	11	0
Marion ss	3	0	0	1	1	Kress 1b	0	0	0	5	0
Rice c	3	0	0	3	0	Corbitt ss	3	0	0	1	3
Pollet p	2	0	0	0	1	Mueller c	2	0	0	5	0
Staley p	0	0	0	0	0	VanderMeer p	3	0	0	0	1
*Kazak	1	0	0	0	0						
Krieger p	0	0	0	0	0						
Totals	32	0	5	24	5	Totals	29	5	6	27	14

*Grounded out for Staley in eighth inning.

St. Louis	000	000	000	—0
Cincinnati	000	302	00x	—5

Error—Vander Meer. Runs batted in—Bloodworth 2, Sauer 2, Litwhiler. Two-base hits—Musial, Wyrostek, Litwhiler, Hatton. Home runs—Bloodworth, H. Sauer. Double plays—Corbitt, Bloodworth and Kluszewski; Glaviano, Schoendienst and Jones. Left—St. Louis 5, Cincinnati 2. Base on balls—Off Kreiger 1. Strikeouts—By Pollet 1, Staley 1, Vander Meer 5. Hits—Off Pollet, 5 in 6 innings; Staley, 1 in 1; Krieger, 0 in 1. Hit by pitcher—By Krieger (Mueller). Wild pitch—Kreiger. Winner—Vander Meer (1-0). Loser—Pollet (0-1). Umpires—Ballanfant, Barlick and Barr. Time—1:52. Attendance—6,429.

Results in College And School Sports

* * *

College

Baseball

Amer. International	6	St. Michael's	15
American U.	3	Loyola (Balt.)	1
C. C. N. Y.	14	Manhattan	8
F. and M.	12	Haverford	2
Howard U.	8	Drew	6
Notre Dame	7	Wisconsin	6
(eleven innings)			
Queens Frosh	8	Columbia Frosh	5
St. Francis	11	Pratt	10
St. John's	8	Kings Point	2
Temple	8	N. Y. U.	2
Villanova	7	Providence	5

Tennis

Seton Hall	5	St. John's	4
William and Mary	9	Maryland	0

Track

Brooklyn Poly	76½	N. Y. Arts Inst.	26½

School

Baseball

Bishop Loughlin	7	Jamaica	3
Browning School	3	Allen Stevenson	2
Cardinal Hayes	5	St. Simon Stock	1
Erasmus	8	Jackson	7
Lincoln	12	Curtis	1
Madison	7	Textile	0
Newtown	6	Brooklyn Prep	5
Power Memorial	7	Xavier	5
Rice	7	De LaSalle	3
St. Ann's	4	LaSalle	3
Seward Park	5	Monroe	4

Lacrosse

Deerfield	[illegible]	Manhasset	3

Tennis

Brooklyn Prep	4	Adelphi	1

Scheffing's Homer Subdues Pirates For Cubs, 4 to 3

* * *

CHICAGO, April 21 (AP).—Bob Scheffing smashed a homer with Andy Pafko aboard in the eighth inning to give the Chicago Cubs a 4-to-3 triumph over the Pittsburgh Pirates before a Ladies' Day crowd of 15,869 today.

It wrecked a seven-hitter for Bob Muncrief, who was making his debut with the Pirates. Walt Dubiel, the ex-Philly making his debut with the Cubs, yielded all the Buc tallies and was lifted for a pinch-hitter after seven rounds. Only one of the runs, however, was earned. The score:

PITTSBURGH (N. L.)	ab	r	h	po	a	CHICAGO (N. L.)	ab	r	h	po	a
Rojek ss	5	1	0	2	5	H. Walker lf	3	1	1	2	0
Hopp 1b	3	0	2	7	0	Gustine 3b	3	0	1	0	4
F. Walker rf	4	1	1	2	0	Cavaretta 1b	4	0	1	11	1
Kiner lf	3	0	1	0	0	Pafko cf	3	1	0	2	0
Westlake cf	4	1	1	4	0	Scheffing c	4	1	1	3	0
Murtaugh 2b	4	0	1	2	0	Jeffcoat rf	4	1	1	2	0
Bockman 3b	3	0	0	0	1	Smalley ss	4	0	1	3	5
Fitzgerald c	4	0	2	7	0	Verban 2b	3	0	0	4	2
Muncrief p	2	0	1	0	3	Dubiel p	2	0	1	0	2
†Fleming	1	0	0	0	0	*A. Walker	1	0	0	0	0
						Kush p	0	0	0	0	0
Totals	33	3	9	24	9	Totals	31	4	7	27	14

†Flied out for Muncrief in ninth inning.
*Struck out for Dubiel in seventh inning.

Pittsburgh	100	101	000	—3
Chicago	100	100	02x	—4

Errors—Smalley, Gustine. Runs batted in—Westlake, Murtaugh, Kiner, Cavarretta, Smalley, Scheffing 2. Two-base hits—Gustine, F. Walker, Hopp. Three-base hit—Jeffcoat. Home run—Scheffing. Stolen base—Gustine. Sacrifice—Muncrief. Double plays—Cavarretta (unassisted); Gustine, Verdan and Cavarretta; Verban, Smalley and Cavarretta. Left on bases—Pittsburgh 7, Chicago 6. Bases on balls—Off Dubiel 3, Muncrief 3. Struck out—By Dubiel 2, Muncrief 4. Hits—Off Dubiel 8 in 7 innings; Kush 1 in 2. Winner—Kush (1-0). Loser—Muncrief (0-1). Umpires—Jorda, Reardon and Goetz. Time—1:55. Attendance—11,599.

Views of Sport

By RED SMITH

Copyright, 1949, New York Herald Tribune Inc.

Angler and Gentleman

"AND my Maudlin," the milkmaid's mother told Izaak Walton and his pupil, "shall sing you one of her best ballads; for she and I both love all anglers, they be such honest, civil, quiet men."

Don Stillman, who wrote the Rod and Gun column for these pages from 1930 until his death this week, was an angler in the classic definition. He was also gentle and gay and charming, as delightful a companion as a man could have on a trout stream or at the dinner table.

When they write a man's obituary for the papers they tell about how well he did at his business. That's generally the yardstick which determines whether his death shall be reported in a paragraph or a couple of columns. Don Stillman did well at life. The possessions he accumulated, and has left as a legacy, are tax-exempt treasures—friendship, humor and memories.

Red Smith

It is said he was a delightful dinner companion. He made joyous company at breakfast, too, through the pieces which he wrote for consumption with the morning coffee. The reference here is not particularly to his reports on how the stripers were running off Montauk, an essential but dull part of the job in this reader's view, nor to his scholarly little essays on the decline of the upland game population.

Knowledge of his subject gave authority to his work along that line, but the pieces where he excelled were those that reflected his own gentle charm. When he wrote of a stroll through the winter woods and the stories he could read in the fresh snow; when he mused over a vista of hills he had known from boyhood; when he reported on a solitary day on a trout stream or told how a small lake had looked at sunset—that was sweet reading, from the typewriter of a sweet guy.

And, Speaking of Gentlemen—

WORD comes from St. Louis that Sam Breadon is seriously ill. He started for a Florida vacation, fell sick and had to return home for treatment. During his illness he has had a lot of mail, much of it from baseball men who knew him, in one capacity or another, when he was president of the Cardinals.

If a fan could read some of these letters, especially from players and former players, the chances are he'd be surprised and bewildered. The sentiments they express would not coincide with the picture of Sam Breadon as it was commonly drawn during his baseball days.

Sports page readers frequently got a distorted notion of the Cardinals' owner, colored by ignorance and provincialism. He was pictured—more often than not by someone who knew the man only casually if at all—as a skinflint sweatshop operator, a bad sport who exploited his stars and then callously discarded them, a nickel-nurser whose guiding business rule was greed.

Even today you hear the statement that if Stan Musial were playing for, say, one of the New York clubs, he would be making twice as much money as the Cardinals give him. Perhaps if a star of Musial's magnitude played in a town where receipts were bigger than in St. Louis, some of that difference might be reflected in his bank account.

The Plain, Dull Facts

BUT the fact is that when Musial was playing first base for Breadon's Cardinals he was, with a single exception, the most highly paid first baseman in the history of the National League. That was the year Hank Greenberg, the single exception, was with the Pirates. And although a superficial reader of the sports pages would have assumed—from the publicity broadcast from Pittsburgh while the Cardinals held their silence—that Hank's wages were at least $50,000 greater than Stan's; the actual difference in base pay provided for in their contracts was $7,500.

Moreover, it has only been in recent seasons that Musial's opposite number in New York, Joe DiMaggio, received more money than Stan has been getting in St. Louis.

A true picture of Sam Breadon would not depict him as a Scrooge or a Lady Bountiful or a sucker. He is, in fact, a smart and able business man whose business situation compelled him to operate on a narrower margin than some other owners, who tried to treat his help fairly, who admires ability and appreciates loyalty, who made friends on all levels of baseball, and has kept them.

He was, of course, incomparably the most able and successful owner the Cardinals ever had. With money he had earned for himself he bought into a bankrupt organization, reorganized and refinanced it, and made it the dominant club of the National League. Under Breadon, the Cardinals were the best team in their League and the chief source from which rivals purchased major-league material.

Some Interests Survive

NATIONAL LEAGUE faces grow pink when modern World Series records are mentioned. They would be purple if it weren't for the clubs Breadon built. In the twenty-three years since 1926, the National League has had eight world champions. Six of them represented St. Louis. In the last eight seasons, the Cardinals have not finished worse than second. This year Breadon is out of baseball and they may drop below that position.

Strictly speaking, though, Sam isn't entirely out of baseball. He still has some personal interests in the game, represented by guys like Mort Cooper. It is, perhaps, worth noting that when big Mort got himself jammed up some months ago, it was not an active baseball man who came to his help and picked up his tab and got a job for him. It was Sam Breadon.

Dillard and Pearman Win In British Guiana Track

GEORGETOWN, British Guiana, April 21 (UP).—American track stars Harrison Dillard and Reggie Pearman scored two victories each today in brilliant performances against local competition.

Pearman, New York University ace, won both the 440-yard run and the 880-yard run, although he gave away large handicaps in each. In the 440 he conceded nineteen yards and sped to victory in 50.2 seconds. In the 880 he overcame a thirty-yard handicap to win in 1:57.2.

Dillard, the Olympic 100-meter champion from Baldwin Wallace, won the 100-meter dash in 10.4 seconds and the 120-yard high hurdles in 14.8 seconds.

International League

Yesterday's Results

Toronto, 8; Newark, 0.
Jersey City, 9; Rochester, 4.
Syracuse, 3; Buffalo, 0.
Montreal, 3; Baltimore, 0.

Homers by Gordon, Livingston Give Hartung Four-Hit Victory

New York Salvages Final of Brooklyn Series on 2-Run Blasts Off Roe in 6th and 7th Innings

By Al Laney

There is a belief that whenever the New York Giants get decent pitching they will hit enough home runs to win the ball game. That is exactly the way it was at Ebbets Field yesterday as the Dodgers were beaten, 4 to 1. It was the season's first victory for the Giants after two straight defeats, and the first setback for the Dodgers.

SID GORDON
Blasts second homer in two days

The home runs were hit by Sid Gordon and Mickey Livingston, each good for a pair of runs, and the pitching was done by Clint Hartung, whose job was so much better than decent it deserves to rank as excellent. The former Phenom limited the Dodgers to four hits and they did not even scare him much after the first inning as, having let them take a one-run lead in the opening frame, he reeled off eight scoreless innings with only three men left on bases.

The Giant home runs were hit off Preacher Roe, Brooklyn's aging if not aged left-hander, Gordon's in the sixth inning with Bobby Rhawn on base and Livingston's in the seventh with Jack Lohrke scoring also.

Banta Finishes

This latter blow was only the fifth hit off Roe, who, aside from the homers, was a wholly effective pitcher. Jack Banta pitched the last two innings.

Leo Durocher, the Giant manager, perhaps a little desperate at the prospect of returning to the Polo Grounds for today's opener with the Braves with three straight losses, redistributed his forces somewhat. He benched Willard Marshall, Walker Cooper and Bill Rigney, sending Gordon to right field, Rhawn to second base, Lohrke to third and Livingston to catch. It worked well, but the big thing was Hartung's pitching, which would have been quite good enough to win with the line-up that lost the first two.

Hartung's work was so good, in fact, it needs to be told in detail. He walked Cal Abrams, the first Brooklyn batter, and Pewee Reese got a single on a half-hit ball that trickled through into right field. From that point on it may be said that Hartung pitched almost, if not quite, perfectly, even though the Dodgers got the run home and led, 1 to 0, through five innings.

Scores on Infield Roller

Abrams reached third when Duke Snider hit a slow roller on which no play was possible elsewhere than at first and scored as Jackie Robinson hit another infield grounder. Carl Furillo was then an easy out and the Dodgers had no runner until Gil Hodges opened the fifth with a single and Roy Campanella walked. That was the first of three successive fairly critical innings for Hartung, but he got out of it easily by fanning Roe and Reese, leaving Hodges on third.

With one out in the sixth, Rhawn booted Robinson's grounder but Hartung promptly caught Jackie off first and that was the end of that. In the seventh Billy Cox opened with a single but Hodges hit into a double play. Then Campanella singled but Gene Hermanski, batting for Roe struck out. That was all. The next six men were easy outs.

Hartung was faster, it seemed, than in any exhibition he had pitched previously and his control was so good that he kept the ball down low around the knees, causing sixteen batters to hit it on the ground. He struck out five and walked only two.

Gordon's Homer His Second

Gordon's homer was his second and his third hit.

The Dodgers also made four hits off a trio of Giant pitchers on Wednesday, bringing the total for two games to eight. But the first four were good for six runs and on opening day eleven hits produced ten runs.

Brooklyn aided the Giants with a pair of errors. One was by Reese in the seventh, and it put Lohrke on base and he scored ahead of Livingston. Roe made the other. It merely advanced Rhawn from second to third so that he had only a short way to go when Gordon hit for the circuit.

The crowd of 22,436 brought the Ebbets Field total to 78,650 for the first three-game series.

Dodgers' Score

* * *

NEW YORK (NL)	ab	r	h	po	a	BROOKLYN (NL)	ab	r	h	po	a
Rhawn 2b	3	1	1	2	5	Abrams lf	3	1	0	2	0
Lockman lf	3	0	1	2	0	Reese ss	4	0	1	4	3
Gordon rf	4	1	2	0	0	Snider cf	4	0	0	4	0
Mize 1b	4	0	0	16	1	Robinson 2b	4	0	0	2	1
Thomson cf	4	0	0	0	0	Furillo rf	4	0	0	4	0
Lohrke 3b	4	1	0	0	2	Cox 3b	4	0	1	0	0
Livingston c	4	1	1	6	0	Hodges 1b	3	0	1	9	0
Kerr ss	4	0	2	1	4	Campanella c	1	0	1	2	0
Hartung p	4	0	0	0	5	Roe p	2	0	0	0	3
						*Hermanski	1	0	0	0	0
						Banta p	0	0	0	0	0
Totals	34	4	7	27	17	Totals	30	1	4	27	7

*Fanned for Roe in seventh inning.

New York	000	002	200	—4
Brooklyn	100	000	000	—1

Errors—Roe, Rhawn, Reese. Runs batted in—Robinson, Gordon 2, Livingston 2. Home runs—Gordon, Livingston. Sacrifice—Lockman. Double play—Kerr, Rhawn and Mize. Left—New York 5, Brooklyn 5. Bases on balls—Off Hartung 3, Roe 1. Strikeouts—By Hartung 7, Roe 1, Banta 1. Hits—Off Roe, 5 in 7 innings; Banta, 2 in 2. Winner—Hartung (1-0). Loser—Roe (0-1). Umpires—Robb, Dascoli, Pinelli and Gore. Time—2:07. Attendance—22,436.

St. Francis Scores Seven In 9th, Beats Pratt, 11-10

St. Francis College rallied for seven runs in the ninth inning and nipped Pratt Institute, 11 to 10, on the loser's field yesterday.

Trailing, 9 to 4, the Terriers combined two doubles, a single, four walks and a dropped third strike to pull out the decision. Ignatius Fazio's double—his third of the game—aided the upsurge.

George Post, loser's center fielder, smashed a homer in the fifth with one on.

The score by innings.

Pratt	100	030	051	—10	9	1
St. Francis	100	001	207	—11	9	1

Sundstrom, Kirchdorfer (9) and Martinez, Goshgarian (8); Kaiven, Parry (6), Johnson (8) and Moran.

Major League Standings and Pitchers

Friday, April 22, 1949

NATIONAL LEAGUE RESULTS YESTERDAY

New York, 4; Brooklyn, 1
Cincinnati, 5; St. Louis, 0
Chicago, 4; Pittsburgh, 3
Other clubs not scheduled

STANDING OF THE CLUBS	Cincin'ti	Boston	Brooklyn	Chicago	New York	Pittsb'gh	Phila	St. Louis	WON	LOST	Percent	Games behind
Cincinnati	—	0	0	0	0	0	0	2	2	0	1.000	—
Boston	0	—	0	0	0	0	3	0	3	1	.750	—
Brooklyn	0	0	—	0	2	0	0	0	2	1	.667	½
Chicago	0	0	0	—	0	2	0	0	2	1	.667	½
New York	0	0	1	0	—	0	0	0	1	2	.333	1½
Pittsburgh	0	0	0	1	0	—	0	0	1	2	.333	1½
Philadelphia	0	1	0	0	0	0	—	0	1	3	.250	2
St. Louis	0	0	0	0	0	0	0	—	0	2	.000	2

National League Games and Pitchers Today

Boston at New York (2:30 p. m.)—Sain (24-15) vs. Jansen (18-12)
Brooklyn at Philadelphia—Barney (15-13) vs. Roberts (7-9)
Cincinnati at Pittsburgh—Wehmeier (11-8) vs. Chesnes (14-6)
Chicago at St. Louis—Schmitz (18-13) vs. Brazle (10-6)

AMERICAN LEAGUE RESULTS YESTERDAY

New York, 2; Washington, 1
Boston, 4; Philadelphia, 0
Cleveland, 8; St. Louis, 2
Chicago, 5; Detroit, 2

STANDING OF THE CLUBS	New York	Clevel'd	Detroit	Phila	Chicago	St. Louis	Boston	Wash'n	WON	LOST	Percent	Games behind
New York	—	0	0	0	0	0	0	3	3	0	1.000	—
Cleveland	0	—	0	0	0	2	0	0	2	1	.667	1
Detroit	0	0	—	0	2	0	0	0	2	1	.667	1
Philadelphia	0	0	0	—	0	0	2	0	2	2	.500	1½
Chicago	0	0	1	0	—	0	0	0	1	2	.333	2
St. Louis	0	1	0	0	0	—	0	0	1	2	.333	2
Boston	0	0	0	1	0	0	—	0	1	2	.333	2
Washington	0	0	0	1	0	0	0	—	1	3	.250	2½

American League Games and Pitchers Today

New York at Boston—Reynolds (16-7) vs. Hughson (3-1)
Philadelphia at Washington (night)—Scheib (14-8) vs. Haefner (5-13)
Detroit at Cleveland—Hutchinson (13-11) vs. Bearden (20-7)
St. Louis at Chicago—Embree (5-3) vs. Pieretti (8-12)

(Won and lost in parentheses are 1948 records)

Section 3-4 | SPORTS NEWS | NEW YORK Herald Tribune | FINANCE—BUSINESS MARINE | Section 3-4

SIX PAGES | SUNDAY, SEPTEMBER 4, 1949 | SIX PAGES

Giants Trip Dodgers, 6-3; Yankees Rout Senators, 6-0; Red Sox Win; Coe Crushes King, 11 and 10, Captures National Amateur Golf Title

Walker Cup Player's Edge Is 2d Highest

Result Surpassed Only by '95 Final

Conqueror of Turnesa Is 5-Down After Morning Round at Rochester

By Doug Kennedy

ROCHESTER, N. Y., Sept. 3.—In a match containing about as much drama as a Sunday School picnic, Charley Coe, Oklahoma City Walker Cup golfer, trounced Rufus King, of Wichita Falls, Tex., 11 and 10, to win the forty-ninth amateur tournament of the United States Golf Association over Oak Hill's splendid course.

One has to turn the pages back to the very first tournament in 1895 at Newport, R. I., to find a precedent for such an horrendous shellacking. That year one C. B. MacDonald defeated C. E. Sands, 12 and 11, for the record as it now stands.

The smooth-stroking Oklahoma stringbean with the picture swing played simply tremendous golf to win the crown so lately worn by Willie Turnesa, who lost to King yesterday. In cold, actual fact he was only even par for the day. he went 4-over in the first three holes this morning. That means he was 4-under par for the twenty-three remaining holes necessary to rout the hapless, but always smiling Texan.

King Never in Contention

King actually never was in contention after the first nine when he was 3-down, and 5-down at the luncheon break. But he was game, and he never lost that grin.

Coe, in contrast, was a cool, methodical man. The blonde twenty-six-year-old insurance broker, winner of the 1947 and '49 Trans-Mississippi titles, only smiled once: that after the match had been won and photographers crowded about the eighth green, actually the twenty-sixth hole of the contest.

It was there that Coe won his title after King had trapped his approach. King blasted weakly out and chipped, weakly again, just past Coe's ball eight feet from the flag. That left King with four blows to Coe's two, and King, with that ever-present grin, walked over to Coe's ball and picked it up, conceding the putt, the birdie, and the match.

That final birdie by Coe was of the conceded variety, but no one in the crowd of about 2,500 believed that he would have missed it had it been necessary to putt it out.

Coe Holes 20-Footer

For this is what Coe did to King when they started off this afternoon. Remember that King was 5-down at the time. On the nineteenth hole Coe went 6-up when he holed a twenty-footer for a birdie. On the twentieth hole he went 7-up when he laid his 120-yard approach eighteen inches from the cup and sank it for another birdie.

On the 201-yard twentieth Coe proved himself temporarily fallible when he trapped his drive, as did King. Coe blasted twenty feet from the cup while King's trap shot ended eight feet away. Coe sank his, King missed and now the margin was 8-up.

On the 533-yard twenty-second Coe placed his No. 1 iron approach seven feet from the pin. He might well have been able to sink the putt for an eagle 3, but it wasn't neces-

(Continued on page 3, column 5)

Herald Tribune—Acme telephoto

NEW CHAMPION: Charley Coe, of Oklahoma City, walloping one out of the rough on ninth hole in final match with Rufus King, whom he beat, 11 and 10, yesterday to win national amateur golf title

U.S. Net Stars Gain National Semi-Finals

Schroeder and Gonzales Extended to Five Sets; Parker and Talbert Win

By Al Laney

The semi-finalists in the National Tennis tournament at Forest Hills are Richard Gonzales, the defending champion, and Frank Parker, survivors in the upper half of the draw, and Ted Schroeder and Billy Talbert in the other. The two matches, Parker against Gonzales and Schroeder against Talbert, will be played this afternoon and indications are that today's crowd of 13,000 will be equaled.

These were the winners of yesterday's quarter-final matches. Gonzales defeated Arthur Larsen, 4—6, 6—1, 6—3, 2—6, 6—1; Parker beat Gardnar Mulloy, 6—4, 6—2, 6—4; Talbert downed Jaroslav Drobny, 6—4, 6—2, 6—2, and Schroeder needed five sets to dispose of Frank Sedgman, 6—3, 0—6, 6—4, 6—8, 6—4.

Schroeder Match Exciting

One of these matches was a fine one, one an interesting and delightful one and the other two more or less disappointing. The presence of two of the four winners in the last round but one is a surprise to those who adhere strictly to the seedings, which said that Drobny and Sturgess, two foreigners, should have been the opponents, of Schroeder and Gonzales, respectively. But Sturgess was beaten by Parker on Friday and Talbert knocked the Czech out of the tournament with very little wasted effort.

The big match of the day, a really exciting one for the crowd, was that between Schroeder and Sedgman. It was their third meeting of the year, their second five-setter and, of course, the third victory for Schroeder. It was a better match than their recent Davis Cup encounter and possibly as exciting as their meeting at Wimbledon, when Sedgman held two match points.

Full of Beautiful Shots

The Australian did not get that close this time, but he actually won more games than Schroeder, twenty-five to twenty-four. In the fifth set, however, where Schroeder had to come to grips with a determined and well equipped opponent, after having lost an opportunity to win earlier, Sedgman could win neither the game that might have given him victory nor the one that would have kept him in the fight. It

(Continued on page 3, column 6)

Leaders Win As Reynolds Hurls 3-Hitter

Stengel Men Cling To 2½-Game Edge

Mole Doubles in 5th for His First Hit in Majors; Woodling Belts Triple

By Ed Sinclair

WASHINGTON, Sept. 3.—Allie Reynolds, the Yankee pitcher who can be counted on to start a game but never to finish one, confounded his critics this afternoon by hurling a three-hit shutout and beating the Senators, 6 to 0, before 13,323 fans in Griffith Stadium.

Easily his best effort of the year, Reynolds's performance earned for him his fourteenth victory against four losses and maintained the Yankees' two-and-a-half game advantage in the American League pennant chase.

There never was any doubt about the New York right-hander's mastery over the Senators. While he struck out only two and walked three, he allowed only one of them to advance as far as second base. That was the most threatening gesture the Senators could muster.

Stewart Singles in First

Just for the record, here is the way the three hits occurred. Ed Stewart singled to right in the first inning and was erased in a double play. In the seventh, Ed Robinson beat out a dribbler toward first with two out, but the next man became the third out. The last hit, in the eighth, could have been an out.

With two away, Sherry Robertson batted for Rae Scarborough, Washington's starter, and sent a bounder down the third-base path. Bobby Brown, thinking it would roll foul, let it go, but the ball hit the bag. By that time there was no chance for a play. The next man forced Robertson at second.

Reynolds completed his assignment, the fourth of twenty-five he has been able to finish, by getting Stewart on a pop to Jerry Coleman, Bob Ortiz on a liner to Coleman and Clyde Vollmer on a fly to Gene Woodling.

Scores on Pitcher's Error

Meanwhile, the Yankees were doing all right against the right-handed services of Scarborough. Joe DiMaggio walked in the second, advanced on Brown's infield hit and scored when Scarborough threw the ball into right field in an attempt to nip Brown off first after catching a pop-up bunt.

Fenton Mole got his first base hit as a Yankee leading off the fifth and scored the second New York run. He sliced the ball between Ed Yost and third base for a double and came home when Charley Silvera singled to right center.

In the sixth, Woodling tripled home a run after Brown walked, and scored himself when Sam Dente booted a grounder hit by Reynolds. DiMaggio doubled in the seventh and crossed the plate on Brown's single to center.

Scarborough retired in the eighth for a pinch batter. Paul

(Continued on page 2, column 3)

Wine List Wins Aqueduct 'Cap, Paying $25.80

Loser Weeper, After Taking 2d Place, Is Disqualified and Riverlane Moved Up

By Joe H. Palmer

In a hard-fought finish, Greentree Stable's three-year-old Wine List turned back a field of older horses to win yesterday's Aqueduct Handicap, with Ted Atkinson hustling him for all he was worth, which at the moment was $16,625 in first money.

It turned out he needn't have hustled quite so hard, for Alfred Vanderbilt's Loser Weeper, which came from last place in the stretch to finish a half-length behind the winner, was disqualified for crossing over and bothering several horses. It was a somewhat unusual circumstance, since the action was initiated by the stewards without a claim of foul being filed.

This moved Joe W. Brown's Riverlane, which ran a surprisingly good race to finish third, beaten another three-fourths of a length, into the official second place, and it pulled C. V. Whitney's Mount Marcy from fourth to third.

Top Crowd for Aqueduct

Aqueduct's crowd of 34,282 — much the largest of the year at this track—could see nothing but My Request in the race, and sent him away at 8 to 5. He beat one horse. Wine List was overlooked at $25.80, Riverlane paid $22.30 to place, and Mount Marcy's show price was $17.80. The time was a moderate 1:46 for the mile and a sixteenth.

The race began with Wine List and Mount Marcy fighting for the lead. The Greentree colt had a bit the best of it to the five-furlong pole where Mount Marcy headed him, and he took the lead back on the far turn and never yielded it again.

Through the early furlongs Royal Governor and Manyunk went along head and head in third place, but neither was in it when the real drive came. River-

(Continued on page 4, column 2)

Jack Frank

FUTILE SLIDE: Bobby Thomson, Giants' centerfielder, slides headlong across home plate in third inning, but Umpire Art Gore had already raised his hands, calling time, thus nullifying the attempted steal. Roy Campanella, Dodgers' catcher, stands by

Cards Attack Vander Meer in 1st for 3 Runs

Musial's Triple Scores 2 as Redbirds Overcome Cincinnati's 1-Run Lead

ST. LOUIS, Sept. 3 (AP).—Back in their own park after a highly successful trip around the circuit, the league-leading St. Louis Cardinals opened a short home stand against the seventh-place Cincinnati Reds tonight.

The Cards led, 3 to 1, in the third inning as this edition went to press.

Cincinnati 1 0
St. Louis 3 0

Vander Meer and Cooper; Brecheen and D. Rice.

Cooper Singles Across Run

The Reds rocked Brecheen for three hits and one run in the first inning. Hatton singled to right. Merriman was called out on strikes but Lowrey singled to right center, Hatton taking third. Cooper singled to left, Hatton scoring, Lowrey stopping at second. Stallcup popped to Glaviano. Litwhiler forced Lowrey at thrid, Glaviano, unassisted, to strand two runners.

The Cards bounced in front in their time at bat as the first four men hit safely. Musial's triple was the big blow.

Diering opened with a single to center. So did Schoendienst, Diering stopping at second. Musial tripled to left center, Diering and Schoendienst scoring. Jones' grounder took a high bounce over Kluszewski's head for a double, Musial scoring. Slaughter lined to Litwhiler. Marion walked. D. Rice flied to Lowrey. Glaviano popped to Kluszewski.

The battig order:

CINCINNATI	ST. LOUIS
Hatton, 3b	Diering cf
Merriman cf	Schoendienst 2b
Lowrey lf	Musial rf
Cooper c	Jones 1b
Stallcup ss	Slaughter lf
Litwhiler rf	Marion ss
Bloodworth 2b	D. Rice c
Kluszewski 1b	Glavlano 3b
Vander Meer p	Breecheen p

Umpires—Jorda, Goetz and Reardon.

Red Sox Crush Athletics, 10 to 3, With 16 Hits; Kinder Wins 18th

Kellner Victim of Boston's Barrage; Williams and Doerr Knock Homers

BOSTON, Sept 3 (AP).—Supported by a lusty sixteen-hit attack, Boston's surprising Ellis Kinder today pitched his eighteenth victory for the Red Sox, who walloped the Philadelphia Athletics, 10 to 3, before 21,269 Fenway Park fans.

The victory, second successive over the A's, kept the runner-up Boston club within two-and-a-half games of the American League-leading New York Yankees, who won, and moved them three games ahead of the third-place Cleveland Indians, who were defeated.

Each of the Red Sox hit at least once. Bob Doerr belted his second homer in two days and his sixteenth of the campaign, a two-run affair into the screen in left in the fourth. Ted Williams rapped his thirty-seventh of the campaign in the eighth.

Williams's drive was lined into the screen in left, the fifth he has hit to that sector this season, three at home and one each in Chicago and St. Louis.

Kinder aided himself to his eighth successive victory by rapping two hits, one a run-scoring double.

Kinder held the A's at bay in all except the fourth inning when the Philadelphians combined three hits with a fielder's choice and two of the six walks he issued.

The Red Sox were held scoreless until the fourth by Alex Kellner, who lost his tenth game against sixteen victories. In that inning Doerr belted his homer with Vern Stephens on first.

TED WILLIAMS

Blasts His 37th Home Run

Red Sox Score

* * *

PHILADELPHIA (A.L.)	ab	r	h	po	a
Fox 2b	4	0	0	1	1
Moses rf	5	0	0	3	1
Valo lf	5	0	2	5	0
Fain 1b	1	1	0	5	0
Chapman cf	4	1	0	3	0
Suder 3b	4	1	1	0	1
Astroth c	4	0	1	5	2
Davis ss	3	0	0	2	2
Kellner p	2	0	0	0	0
*White	0	0	0	0	0
Harris p	0	0	0	0	0
†Wright	0	0	0	0	0
Totals	32	3	4	24	7

BOSTON (A. L.)	ab	r	h	po	a
DiMaggio cf	3	1	1	5	0
Pesky 3b	5	0	2	3	2
Williams lf	4	1	2	4	0
Stephens ss	4	1	1	2	0
Doerr 2b	5	1	1	0	1
Zarilla rf	5	1	2	1	0
Goodman 1b	4	2	2	6	0
‡Tebbetts c	3	2	3	6	1
Kinder p	4	1	2	0	2
Totals	37	10	16	27	6

*Went to bat for Kellner in seventh inning and awarded first base for interference by catcher in seventh inning.
†Walked for Harris in ninth inning.
‡Awarded first base for interference by catcher in sixth inning.

Philadelphia .... 000 300 000—3
Boston .... 000 223 21x—10

E—Astroth, Tebbetts, Doerr. RBI—Suder, Astroth, Kellner, Doerr 2, Pesky 2, Stephens, Kinder, Goodman, Tebbetts, Williams. 2B—Valo 2, Tebbetts, Kinder, Zarilla, Goodman. HR—Doerr, Williams. SB—Valo. DP—Astroth and Davis, Moses and Davis. Left—Philadelphia 9, Boston 8. BB—Kellner 4, Kinder 6. SO—Kellner 3, Harris 1, Kinder 6. HO—Kellner 11 in 6, Harris 5 in 2. WP—Kellner. Winner—Kinder (18—5). Loser—Kellner (16—10). U—Passarella, Rommel, Stevens and Boyer. T—2:31. A—21,269.

Trotter Sold for $100,000

ESSEX JUNCTION, Vt., Sept. 3 (AP).—Nibble Hanover, one of the world's top trotters—now retired to stud—was purchased for $100,-000 today by L. B. Sheppard, owner of Hanover, Pa., Shoe Farms.

Banta Falters As Kennedy Records 11th

New York Clinches Game With 2 in 7th

28,700 at Polo Grounds See Victors Capitalize on Foes' Loose Hurling

By Rud Rennie

The speeding Dodgers, hot in pursuit of the pace-setting St. Louis Cardinals, encountered an unsympathetic traffic cop, a left-hander by the name of Monte Kennedy, in the Polo Grounds yesterday. Kennedy stopped them despite four errors by his partners, and the Giants won, 6 to 3, before a crowd of 28,700.

The Dodgers outhit the Giants, 9 to 8; but Kennedy issued only one base on balls. The three Brooklyn pitchers, Jack Banta, Carl Erskine and Erv Palica issued a total of four bases on balls, Banta hit one batsman, and Palica made a wild pitch.

Therein lay the difference. Every one of those gifts hurt. Three of the four walkers scored and the other forced in a run. The man who was hit by the pitched ball scored. And the man who advanced on the wild pitch also scored.

Errors Figure in Scoring

The Dodgers made two errors and both figured in scoring innings although all the Giants' runs were earned.

The Dodgers simply did not get good pitching yesterday and the Giants did.

Burt Shotton, the Brooklyn manager, started Banta because he went the route for the first time in his career the last time he worked, which was against the Pirates Aug. 29. Shotton hoped he could do it again. Well, he didn't do it again.

Banta walked Whitey Lockman in the first inning and let him get a jump and steal second. When Willard Marshall pulled a hard hit past Gil Hodges, Lockman scored.

In the second inning, Banta hit Henry Thompson with a pitched ball and walked Wes Westrum. Billy Cox fumbled Kennedy's grounder and the bases were filled with one out. Up came Bill Rigney and banged a single to right knocking in two runs.

Banta Through in Third

When Marshall and Bobby Thomson opened the third with singles, Banta was through.

A few minutes later, the Giants filled the bases again when Henry Thompson raced to first on a tap to Hodges and beat the toss to Erskine at first.

Erskine fanned Joe Lafata and got Westrum to pop up, but, with two away, he walked Kennedy forcing in a run. The bases were still loaded when Rigney flied to Luis Olmo.

So the score was 4 to 1 at the end of the third, the Dodgers having picked up a run in their half of the thrid by breaking up two attempts at double plays after Olmo and Banta singled. Cox knocked in the run, scoring Mike McCormick, who had forced Olmo.

An error by Rigney on a broken-bat grounder by Reese in the sixth, let the Dodgers get an unearned run and cut the Giants' lead in half. Again, in this inning, the Dodgers broke up a possible play, Reese taking out Rigney so that Cox was safe, and able to score on singles by Carl Furillo and Jackie Robinson.

Bobby Thomson made an important play in this inning,

(Continued on page 2, column 4)

Ted Kell

MORE WEEPING FOR LOSERS: Wine List (No. 1) swept to a half-length victory over Loser Weeper, on far left, in the Aqueduct Handicap yesterday, but those who had the Vanderbilt colt for place or show did the crying when the horse was disqualified. Riverlane, on the rail, was awarded second place, and Mount Marcy, partially hidden between Wine List and Loser Weeper, took third

My Sweetie Wins Speedboat Heat For Silver Cup

* * *

DETROIT, Sept. 3 (AP)—Horace E. Dodge's My Sweetie ran away with the first heat of the Silver Cup Speedboat Trophy race today.

The heavy-footed Bill Cantrell wheeled the boat around the three-mile course in the Detroit River fifteen times at an average speed of 77.639 miles an hour. He finished nearly two miles ahead of Jack Schafer's Such Crust, of Detroit. In third place at the finish was Miss Pepsi, another Detroit boat, while Guy Lombardo's Tempo VI finished fourth.

Hard luck again pursued the the Canadian contender, Miss Canada IV, of Ingersoll, Ont. The Canadian boat, which failed to get up speed in the recent Harmsworth raced, dropped out in the first three-mile lap of today's heat after losing her propeller.

Twelve boats started the race, but seven of them dropped out or fared so poorly as to furnish no competition at all.

Cantrell shot My Sweetie across the starting line first, only inches ahead of Miss Pepsi, Such Crust and Miss Canada. He pulled away easily from the field, however, and held first place through each lap to the end.

Cantrell's fastest lap was at the rate of 83.475 miles an hour in the second time around the three-mile course. This tops the recognized record of 78.182 miles an hour for a three-mile lap made last year by Stanley Dollar's Skip-A-Long. The average of 77.639 miles an

(Continued on page 3, column 8)

Major League Standings and Pitchers

Sunday, September 4, 1949

NATIONAL LEAGUE RESULTS YESTERDAY

New York, 6; Brooklyn, 3
Philadelphia, 10; Boston, 4
Chicago, 11; Pittsburgh, 7
*Cincinnati at St. Louis (night)

STANDING OF THE CLUBS	St. Louis	Brooklyn	Boston	Phila.	New York	Pittsb'gh	Cincin'ti	Chicago	WON	LOST	Percent.	Games behind
St. Louis	—	11	15	10	13	9	12	9	79	48	.622	—
Brooklyn	8	—	6	9	10	16	15	14	78	51	.605	2
Boston	5	10	—	10	9	10	11	12	67	62	.519	13
Philadelphia	9	9	6	—	7	12	8	15	66	63	.512	14
New York	7	7	8	10	—	10	13	10	65	63	.508	14½
Pittsburgh	9	4	9	8	9	—	8	10	57	70	.449	22
Cincinnati	4	5	9	12	5	5	—	11	51	75	.405	27½
Chicago	6	5	9	4	10	8	8	—	50	81	.382	31

*Night game not in standing.

National League Games and Pitchers Today

Brooklyn at New York (2 p. m.)—Barney (6-8) vs. Jansen (15-12)

Pittsburgh at Chicago—Chesnes (5-10) vs. Muncrief (5-11)

Cincinnati at St. Louis—Raffensberger (14-14) vs. Lanier (1-3)

Boston at Philadelphia (2)—Sain (10-13) and Bickford (14-8) vs. Borowy (12-9) and Donnelly (2-1)

AMERICAN LEAGUE RESULTS YESTERDAY

New York, 6; Washington, 0
Boston, 10; Philadelphia, 3
St. Louis, 4; Cleveland, 3
Detroit, 5; Chicago, 3

STANDING OF THE CLUBS	New York	Boston	Cleveland	Detroit	Phila.	Chicago	St. Louis	Wash'ton	WON	LOST	Percent.	Games behind
New York	—	10	10	9	10	14	15	11	79	47	.627	—
Boston	5	—	6	13	12	16	13	14	79	52	.603	2½
Cleveland	9	14	—	9	9	10	12	12	75	54	.581	5½
Detroit	11	7	5	—	13	11	12	16	75	58	.564	7½
Philadelphia	7	6	12	7	—	15	9	11	67	62	.519	13½
Chicago	6	5	7	8	4	—	10	13	53	77	.408	28
St. Louis	5	7	6	8	10	4	—	8	48	83	.366	33½
Washington	4	3	8	4	4	7	12	—	42	85	.331	37½

American League Games and Pitchers Today

New York at Washington—Lopat (13-6) vs. Harris (3-11)

Chicago at Detroit—Pierce (7-12) vs. Newhouser (14-9)

St. Louis at Cleveland—Papai (4-7) vs. Garcia (11-5)

Philadelphia at Boston—Fowler (12-8) vs. Stobbs (0-4) or McDermott (5-4)

Rossides and Bryant Get All-Stars Award

Gene Rossides, of Columbia, and Goble Bryant, of Army, were the outstanding players in the Eastern All-Stars' 28-to-13 victory over the New York football Giants Thursday night, according to the All-Stars' coaching staff headed by Yale's Herman Hickman.

The coaches, after studying films of the Fresh Air Fund game, voted special awards to the two players for their work on offense and defense, respectively. Rossides, T-formation quarterback, was singled out for his ball-handling, faking and play-calling. Bryant, co-captain and tackle, directed the All-Stars' defense formations.

Voting, along with Hickman, were Harold Kopp, line coach; Harry Jacunski, end coach; Nick Kotys, backfield coach, and Jim Dunn, assistant coach, all of Yale.

COMPLETE FINAL
★★★★★★
CLOSING WALL STREET PRICES

The Sun

Copyright, 1949, by The New York Sun, Inc.

CLOSING
WALL STREET
PRICES

U. S. Weather Bureau Forecast:
Sunny today; fair tonight. Sunny tomorrow.
Temperatures Today—Min., 65; Max., 69.
Sun rises 5:59 A. M. Sun sets 5:28 P. M.
(Detailed weather report on page 7.)

VOL. 117—NO. 32. Entered as Second Class Matter Post Office, New York, N. Y. NEW YORK, SATURDAY, OCTOBER 8, 1949. FIVE CENTS EVERYWHERE

NEWCOMBE TO OPPOSE LOPAT

SHOTTON PICKS MOUND ACE FOR FOURTH GAME

Warm and Mostly Sunny Forecast—Yanks Now Heavy Favorites.

HITTERS FINALLY HAVE DAY

Both Teams Square Off for Tilt That May Prove Critical to Flatbush Men's Hopes.

By WILBUR WOOD,
(Sports Editor of The Sun).

With the spell the pitchers had held over the hitters in the world series until the ninth inning in yesterday's third game finally broken, the New York Yankees and Brooklyn Dodgers squared off today for the fourth game of the baseball classic, at Ebbets Field, with the Yankees on top, two games to one.

With only two full days of rest, Don Newcombe, the powerful rookie right-hander, who lost the dramatic 1—0 decision in Wednesday's series opener, was nominated to pitch for Brooklyn against Ed Lopat of the Yankees in today's game. It is obvious that Manager Burt Shotton is coming back with his best, minimizing as best he can the danger of allowing the Yankees to go two games up.

The weatherman said that the early morning fog and cloudiness would clear away by game time and the day's diamond doings would be carried on under mostly sunny skies. The thermometer was expected to hover between 75 and 80.

When the hitters finally came out of their creeping paralysis yesterday in that tumultuous ninth inning they delivered the sort of fireworks that had been long awaited. They put five runs over the plate in that one inning, more than had been amassed by both teams in the previous twenty-six frames.

Going into the that inning with the count tied at 1—1, the Yankees pushed over three markers, with Johnny Mize, the refugee from the Giants, coming through with the blow that finished Ralph Branca, a smash off the right field screen, with the bases full and two out, that drove over two runs. Jerry Coleman followed with a single that produced still another tally for the Yankees. It was well for them that he did, as

Continued on Page 8.

FOURTH GAME BATTING ORDER

The probable batting order for the fourth game of the world series at Ebbets Field today:

New York.	Brooklyn.
Rizzuto, ss	Reese, ss
Henrich, 1b	Miksis, 3b
Berra, c	Furillo, rf
DiMaggio, cf	Robinson, 2b
Brown, 3b	Hodges, 1b
Woodling, lf	Olmo, lf
Mapes, rf	Snider, cf
Coleman, 2b	Campanella, c
Lopat (15-10), p	Newc'be (17-8),

Umpires—Jorda (N.L.), plate; Hubbard (A. L.), first base; Reardon (N. L.), second base; Passarella (A. L.), third base; Barr (N. L.) right-field foul line; Hurley (A. L.), left-field foul line.

Game Time—1:00 P. M.

In The Sun Today

School News Appears Daily in the Night Edition.

100,000 Will See Army Tackle Michigan in East-West Classic

OPPOSING PITCHERS TODAY

Don Newcombe, Dodgers.

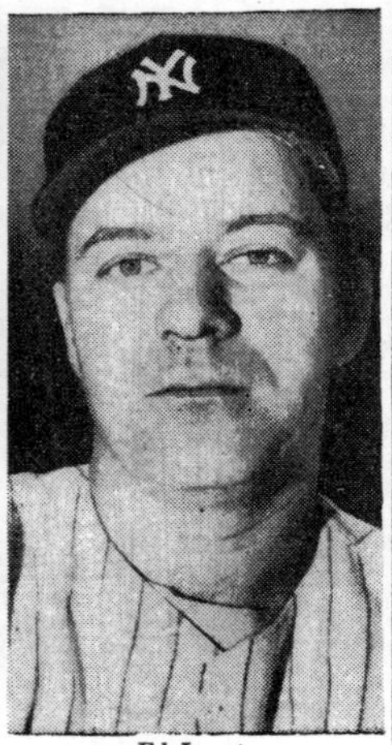

Ed Lopat, Yankees.

HE WAS IN THERE CHEROOTIN'

Associated Press Photo.

Samuel Howard of Newburyport, Mass., is caught in four poses as he observes his beloved Brooklyn Dodgers in their third world series yesterday. The sad pose at bottom, right, tells the story as the Dodgers lost, 4 to 3.

Wolverines Seeking to Tie Modern Record of 26 Consecutive Wins.

'MAKE OR BREAK' FOR CADETS

Ailing Yale Meets Columbia's Sophs Here—Pennsylvania Invades Princeton.

By GEORGE TREVOR.

Ann Arbor, Oct. 8.—This bustling college town of 30,000 is ballooning into a seething metropolis of 130,000 persons as the football fans, who will jam the University of Michigan's remodeled stadium this afternoon to watch Army's gridiron Grenadiers crash head on with the rampant Wolverines, come rolling in by special trains or motor caravan from Detroit, Cleveland, Chicago, Cincinnati, Minneapolis, and points east, west and south.

The "house that Yost built" back in 1927 was a rectangular concrete bowl seating some 79,000 spectators. University of Michigan moguls enlarged the stadium to accommodate 86,000 for the 1943 Notre Dame game. Last

Continued on Page 9.

LEADING FOOTBALL GAMES FOR TODAY

LOCAL.

Yale vs. Columbia, Baker Field, 2 P. M. (WINS, 1:45 P. M.; WCBS-TV, after world series).

Brooklyn College vs. N. Y. U., Polo Grounds, 8:30 P. M.

Fordham vs. Merchant Marine, Kings Point, 2 P. M.

EAST.

City College vs. New Haven State, New Haven, Conn., 2 P. M.

Boston College vs. Penn State, State College, Pa., 2 P. M.

Boston University vs. Colgate, Hamilton, N. Y., 2 P. M.

Cornell vs. Harvard, Cambridge, Mass., 2 p. m. (WGHF, 1:45.)

Holy Cross vs. Dartmouth, Hanover, N. H., 2 P. M.

Duke vs. Navy, Baltimore, 2 P. M.

Pennsylvania vs. Princeton, Princeton, N. J., 2 P. M. (WOR, after world series.)

Pittsburgh vs. West Virginia, Morgantown, W. Va., 2 P. M.

Lehigh vs. Rutgers, New Brunswick, N. J., 2 P. M.

MID-WEST.

Army vs. Michigan, Ann Arbor, Mich., 2 P. M. (WNBC, 1:45; WJZ, 1:45; WMGM, 1:55.)

Illinois vs. Iowa, Iowa City, 3 P. M.

T. C. U. vs. Indiana, Bloomington, Ind., 3 P. M.

Maryland vs. Michigan State, East Lansing, Mich., 2 P. M.

Northwestern vs. Minnesota, Minneapolis, Minn., 3 P. M.

Oklahoma A. and M. vs. Missouri, Columbia, Mo., 3 P. M.

Notre Dame vs. Purdue, Lafayette, Ind., 3 P. M.

California vs. Wisconsin, Madison, Wis., 3 P. M.

SOUTH.

North Carolina vs. South Carolina, Columbia, S. C., 2:30 P. M.

Mississippi vs. Vanderbilt, Nashville, Tenn., 2:30 P. M.

Georgetown vs. Wake Forest, Wake Forest, N. C., 2:30 P. M.

Georgia vs. Kentucky, Lexington, Ky., 9 P. M.

Texas A. and M. vs. L. S. U., Baton Rouge, La., 9:30 P. M.

SOUTHWEST.

Oklahoma vs. Texas, Dallas, Tex., 3 P. M. (WCBS, 2:45 P. M.)

Arkansas vs. Baylor, Waco, Tex., 3 P. M..

FAR WEST.

Ohio State vs. Southern California, Los Angeles, 5:30 P. M.

Oregon University vs. Washington State, Pullman, Wash., 5:30 P. M.

Oregon State vs. Washington University, Seattle, Wash., 5:30

Fan, 10, Makes the Bleachers

While Old Sol made feeble passes at cutting through the light haze which enshrouded Ebbets Field today, 2,750 bleacherites and 2,500 standees flocked inside four hours before game time and their voices were in fine fettle when the curtain went up on the fourth act in the series.

When the gates at the bleachers' entrance were opened at 9 A. M. the tickets—at $1 a head—disappeared like corn in a crowded chicken coop. The last fan to get under the wire on the bleacher line was also the littlest, Tommy Gallagher, 10, of 306 Lincoln Road, Brooklyn. No need to say which team he was rooting for.

Controlling the crush of the crowd and, incidentally, keeping an eye out for the favorite pastime of pickpockets, was a police detail of 250 uniformed men, 220 detectives, twenty-five mounted policemen and sixty traffic patrolmen.

At the other end of the line were four friends who had been waiting since 1 P. M. yesterday. The first two were Leon Felcher, 20, of 156 East 91st street, Brooklyn, who was discharged from the Army only a week ago, and Dannie Solkoff, 19, of 202 East 91st street, also Brooklyn. Felcher lost a bet on the Dodgers one time.

Felcher, Solkoff and their two buddies had come well-prepared for their long vigil with sandwiches, blankets and even a mattress. Many of the others line had blankets or camp chairs, and there was much grumbling when the police prohibited reclining after midnight. (Too hard to count the number in line if they were on the ground, explained members of the 130-man police detail).

The oldest man in line was Bernard J. Dever, 78, of Windber, Pa., who said this was his thirty-second world series. A Brooklyn woman whom he'd met in the bleachers yesterday held a place in line for him until he arrived this morning. Who was he rooting for? Who else could he root for, he asked, when a Dodger fan had been so considerate?

Veteran observers declared that the crowds flocking to Ebbets today were much larger than those which turned out for the subway series in 1947.

Meanwhile, the Hotel Association of New York city reported that a survey of the availability of hotel rooms showed that out-of-town attendance at the series was below early estimates. Rooms were generally available last night and were expected to be during the week end and next week. Hotel men said that this was because the series is "a sub-

SPLIT GERMANY REACHES VITAL PACT ON TRADE

Political Division Ignored in $150,000,000 Accord for Exchanging Goods.

BIG AID TO ECONOMIC UNITY

Both Zones Will Get Needed Commodities—Agreement Runs Until June 30, 1950.

Frankfurt, Oct. 8 (A. P.).—Divided Germany took a step toward economic unity today despite its deep political split. The Eastern and Western zones signed a 600,000,000-mark ($150,000,000) trade agreement in which all political implications were studiously avoided.

The agreement, previously approved by the Western Allied high commissioners, was signed by representatives of economic bodies which were created before establishment of the Soviet Eastern and Allied Western German republics. It cut across political differences created by the formation of the two rival governments.

The German signers of the agreement said it was "vital to Germany's economic life." The pact lasts until June 30, 1950.

Will Get Vital Steel.

The Russian zone will get 335,000 tons of badly needed iron and steel from the Western controlled Ruhr Valley industrial region and thousands of tons of other raw materials and manufactured goods from the West.

In return the Western zones get, among other products, vitally needed pit props for the Ruhr coal mines.

Western Berlin, economically starved by Russian pressure tactics, has some hope of benefiting from the agreement. Dr. Otto Graf, of the Western Economics Administration, proposed in a letter accompanying the agreement that Berlin should engage in one-third of the total trade.

His Eastern counterpart, Joseph Orlopp, replied: "Your proposal will be taken into account in the interests of the Berlin population.

Two-way Trade to Flow.

The agreement calls for the movement of 300,000,000 marks ($75,000,000) worth of trade in each direction across the zonal borders in Germany.

The western zones will export, in addition to iron and steel, manufactured goods, machine tools, chemical products, rubber and textile goods and optical goods.

The eastern zones will send to the west agricultural products, timber, mineral oils, chemical products and brown coal, an inferior grade of coal.

Eastern and western Germany have two difefrent currencies, but there will be no exchange of money. The entire agreement will be on a bookkeeping basis.

POLICEMAN SHOOTS BURGLARY SUSPECT

A 22-year-old burglar suspect, who, the police said, was attempting to steal a television set in order to watch the world series games, was shot and seriously wounded today by a patrolman following an eight-block chase.

The suspect, William Blunt, Negro, of 822 Hewitt Place, the Bronx, was taken to Morrisania Hospital. Patrolman Charles Greutzner, who shot and seized the man after a chase from 586 East 161st street to 784 Melrose avenue, said that Blunt had broken into offices of the Amalgamated Meat Cutters Union at the East 161st street address and moved a television set and a typewriter to the rear yard.

The policeman said that Blunt scrambled over a fence and the patrolman followed, firing a warning shot. The chase continued and the patrolman fired several more times.

When the fugitive reached the Melrose avenue address he collapsed, wounded in the abdomen.

Malta Feels Earth Tremor.

Valletta, Malta, Oct. 8 (A. P.).

VINSON SAYS NAVY AIR ARM IS DUE TO BE CUT IN HALF BY DEFENSE BUREAU ORDER

Sees U. S. Atomic Lead Staving Off War 20 Years

Scientist Fermi Says Russia Won't Permit Inspection—Urges America to Look to Air Defenses.

Rome, Oct. 8 (A. P.).—Enrico Fermi, an atom bomb scientist, predicted today that if the United States maintains atomic supremacy over Russia there will be no war for twenty years.

"American supremacy is predictable up to twenty years if we work hard," he said in an interview. "As for me, I expect to sleep as well as my insomnia permits. I'm a fatalist by nature anyway."

He suggested that the atomic bomb alone might not decide a future war, explaining: "If I were a general I wouldn't want to put all my eggs in one basket. Conventional bombs took heavy tolls of armies and civilians alike in the last war."

Fermi, an Italian-born American scientist and Nobel prize winner in physics, was a leader in the development of the first atomic bomb exploded near Los Alamos, N. M., in 1945. Now a physics professor at the University of Chicago, he is a frequent consultant to the Atomic Energy Commission. He will return to Chicago later this month after physics lectures at the University of Rome and in Milan.

Sees Russia Adamant.

Fermi replied to a series of questions with the following observations:

It is almost a certainty that Russia never will permit regular inspection of her atomic developments by United Nations experts.

American supremacy in atomic research at present seems the only sure guaranty of peace.

America should look to its air defenses. He indicated any attack likely would be launched by enemy bombers.

Danger from atomic rocket attacks is largely a matter of the future.

The smuggling of an enemy bomb into the United States by submarine or other means is possible but not probable.

Large scale attempts to move industry and populace underground are unnecessary. Wide dispersal of factories is impractical.

A so-called preventive war by the United States against Russia is "politically impossible and militarily impractical."

Fermi predicted it will be twenty to thirty years before industrial use of atomic power becomes practical.

Heart Attack Fatal

Senator B. H. Miller.

SENATOR MILLER OF IDAHO, 70, DIES

Washington, Oct. 8 (A. P.).—United States Senator Bert Henry Miller, 70, (D.-Idaho), died of a heart attack at his home here at 8 A. M. today.

Senator Miller, then a justice of the Idaho Supreme Court, was elected to the Senate last November, his victory over Republican Senator Henry C. Dworshak helping to give the Demorcats a 54-to-42 edge in the upper house. Presumably Senator Miller's death will mean the loss of a seat for his party, since Idaho's Gov. C. Robins, who will name a successor, is a Republican.

The Senator had been active recently, casting a vote on the farm bill yesterday, but had not been in good health for some time.

Senator Miller was born at St. George, Utah, on December 15, 1879, educated at Brigham Young University at Provo, Utah, and received his law degree from Cumberland University at Lebanon, Tenn.

After practicing law for many years, he was a prosecuting attorney and then served as Attorney-General of Idaho for four terms.

He was a member of the Senate's District of Columbia, Interior and Insular Affairs and Judiciary Committees.

He is survived by his widow, the former Carolyn Hopkins; a son, Lee S. Miller, and a daughter, Mrs. James Halley Jr.

Jersey Woman Is Dead at 102

Mrs. Henrietta Lord of 301 Larch avenue, Bogota, N. J., died there yesterday at the age of 102.

Born in New York, she moved in 1857 to Edgewater,- N. J., where her family helped to found the Episcopal Church of the Mediator. She was a descendant of the Vreeland family, one of the earliest families in Bergen county.

Tremor in Sicily Empties Homes.

Catania, Sicily, Oct. 8 (A. P.).—An earth tremor which sent residents fleeing from their homes was recorded here early today by university seismographs. The

FINDS DOUBLE TROUBLE

The driver of a stolen truck called attention to himself today by overturning the one-and-a-half-ton machine as he rounded a sharp turn on the East Drive of Central Park, near 95th street and Fifth avenue.

The police said the driver was Edward Griffin, 22, of 23-05 30th street, Astoria, Queens. He suffered a fractured left foot, was charged with grand larceny and taken to City Hospital.

Griffin, a student, told the police he was merely hitching a ride, didn't know the truck was stolen and hadn't been at the wheel. He contended that the driver had escaped uninjured, but the police declared there was no trace of a second man.

Up for Deportation, He Hangs Himself

Eusebio Gallarta, 28-year-old Spaniard who was being held for deportation, hanged himself today in the Federal House of Detention, 427 West street. The police said a keeper found the body hanging from a cell door by a belt and part of a bed sheet. Gallarta, whose home was in Bil-

Declares It Is Plan to Let Force 'Wither on Vine' —Tells of Document.

ADMIRAL TESTIFIES ON FUNDS

Hopwood Before House Unit to Tell of Budget—Johnson May Face Inquiry.

Washington, Oct. 8 (A. P.).—Representative Vinson (D.-Ga.), chairman of the House Armed Services Committee, said today the Department of Defense has decided to cut naval and marine aviation about in half.

Vinson's report of "secret ders" at the Pentagon came as the committee dug grimly into "disturbing" reports that defense chiefs were scuttling the Navy's air arm.

Vinson said further that he has it on reliable authority that the Air Force has taken the position that no large aircraft carriers or their air groups should be kept in the Navy.

Hopwood Before Committee.

He spoke up as his committee started another day's hearing to get to the bottom of friction in the armed services. Before the committee was Rear Admiral Herbert G. Hopwood, Navy budget officer, to explain the Navy's financial position.

Hopwood was called to tell what is happening to funds earmarked by Congress for naval air. That inquiry follows Navy charges yesterday of Air Force bungling and plotting.

Vinson himself reeled off figures from this year's appropriation for the Navy—which Congress has not finally decided. These, he said, show cuts for the naval air arm that indicate "Congress intended to let it wither on the vine by failing to give it enough operating aircraft."

Says He Has Document.

"I have seen a reputable document indicating that decisions have been reached in the (Defense) Department to cut naval and Marine aviation strength about in half and that the Air Force is to be given an expanded role," Vinson said. "The Navy would become a protective convoy to move troops and fight submarines.

"It is my understanding that secret orders to that effect have been issued in the Pentagon."

In addition to reductions being made by Congress in this year's naval funds, Vinson said he understands the Navy is to be cut $353,000,000 more by action of the Department of Defense itself.

Hopwood said: "Yes sir, that is right."

Hopwood was brought into the hearing by Vinson, who said that he was "greatly disturbed" by a report that Secretary of Defense

Continued on Page 2.

'Live' Rod Kills 6 in Succession

Sao Paulo, Brazil, Oct. 8 (A. P.).—Six women were electrocuted in succession here yesterday after an iron rod hit a high-tension wire in a flooded yard.

Mrs. Isoldina Martine had borrowed the rod to open a drain in her flooded back yard. When she touched it against live wires overhead, the current killed her. Three of her daughters ran to save her. Each died when she touched her mother. The same fate met Mrs. Martine's sister and the neighbor who had loaned the rod.

A passerby warned other would-be rescuers away.

Kirk Leaves Moscow by Plane.

Moscow, Oct. 8 (A. P.).—Alan G. Kirk, United States Ambassador, left by plane today for the United States envoys' conference in London. En route, Kirk will

NEW YORK WORLD-TELEGRAM, OCTOBER 8, 1949. 7
SATURDAY SPORTS

Three Doubles for Three Runs Rout Newcombe

By Joe Williams

Page and Mize Accent Yanks' Bench Class

Back in the pressroom before the .game Rogers Hornsby, nibbling daintily on a mess of fresh shrimps, marinara, was saying as how this was the worst Yankee team he had ever seen in a World Series, and he wondered, along with others, how it had ever managed to win the pennant.

Well, this certainly isn't the best team that ever flew Yankee colors in the big fall show and even if it continues to be a mystery to fellows like Hornsby and others how they won the pennant the fact remains that they did—and it isn't often that the best team doesn't win, no matter what you may hear to the contrary.

It is also a fact that as of today this Yankee team is leading Brooklyn—and this is the team B. (For Builder) Rickey boasts is the best he ever put together—in the World Series, two games to one and until the Yankees are beaten there are a number of stubborn diehards who will refuse to believe they can be beaten.

As I've pointed out before the Yanks do not have many genuine stars but they do have an exceptionally large number of very competent players. They have what is known in the trade as a good bench. How and why they won the pennant is or should be no mystery to observing baseball minds. Casey Stengel had more able reserves at his command than any other manager in the league. Only Burt Shotton and his Brooks would come close in the other league.

* * *

What Other Team Has a Joe Page?

In winning the third game of the series at Ebbets Field yesterday the Yanks followed a familiar pattern. They won it with their reserve forces. When Tommy Byrne, the leftie who can be so good, when he can locate the plate, and so slovenly when he can't, had to leave in the fourth with the score tied, the bases full and only one down. The perfectly wonderful Joe Page came in and took complete charge. What other team in baseball has a Joe Page? His presence alone moves the entire Yank staff up two or three points in class.

Going into the ninth the score was still tied at one all. The Brooks' starting pitcher, young Ralph Branca, a product of New York University and a part-time vaudevillian, picking up where his two predecessors, Don Newcombe in the first game and Preacher Roe in the second had left off, was spinning a lustrous two-hitter.

When the right-hander got Tommy Henrich to start the ninth, thanks to a breathless stop by Jackie Robinson, he had retired 14 Yanks in a row. Then Yogi Berra worked him to three and two and walked. This brought up Joe DiMaggio. The Clipper had fanned twice and popped out. Underweight and still weak from a siege of virus infection he has had a rugged time of it. But anytime Joe DiMaggio is able to swing a bat he is a menace to the other side.

His friends in the stands, conversant with his condition and knowing how low he feels emotionally because he realizes he hasn't been able to help the club, or rather to play up to his usually high standard, were desperately pulling for him. But an infield out was the best the Clipper could manage and so there were two down and Berra had not moved from first.

* * *

And How Can Mize's Bat Hurt You?

A single to right by Bobby Brown kept the inning alive, and when Gene Woodling walked the bases were full—the first time they had been full since the series started. Cliff Mapes had walked to the plate when Stengel decided to play it differently. The deferred preference was extended to big Jawn Mize, who had been waived out of the National League and picked up by the Yanks in late August just on the off chance—

"Well, just the off chance that he may be able to help us here and there in spots," explained George Weiss, the Yanks' general manager. "Besides, I have reason to believe the Red Sox want him. If he can help them he can help us, too." My understanding is Weiss paid the Giants $25,000, or thereabouts, for his contract.

Well, that was the situation when Big Jawn, the National League outcast, stood at the plate brandishing his war club and glaring defiance at the young right-handed pitcher. A few moments before there had been a conference in the middle of the diamond and it looked as if Branca might be removed in favor of Joe Hatten, a leftie, who was at that moment throwing in the Brooks' pull pen. It was the routine move to make: A leftie vs. a leftie, but in the end, the dugout decision was to go along with Branca in the crisis—the gravest Brooklyn crisis the game had developed.

In less than it takes to tell, Mize had rocked the right field wall with an explosive single to send two Yanks home, and to all practical intents and purposes, wrap up the ball game, though the dead-game Brooks did come back in their half and with two solo homers make a dogfight of it right down to the final out.

This was another illustration of why the Yanks win ball games—why they won the flag in their league despite the presence of a supposedly superior team, the Boston Red Sox, and why they are one up on the Brooks, another team that supposedly carries too many guns and has too much raw ability and youthful speed for them. How many teams carry a man like Mize as a pinch hitter? Stengel's formula is this: he'll try to beat you with nine men, if he can't he'll throw, if needed, twice nine at you. And what makes this formula stand up more times than not is the fact that Stengel has the men to throw.

Yesterday was a big win for Stengel. If the Yanks had lost it would virtually have amounted to losing two games the same afternoon, for Page had to go five and two-third innings and with that kind of work even this remarkable young man must take time out to recharge his batteries. Stengel could scarcely call on Page for relief today and it is to be doubted that the southpaw would have his sharp stuff even by Sunday. So when the third game was over Stengel had the satisfaction of knowing he hadn't wasted Page—and at this stage of the series a wasted stint by Page is just about the worst thing that can happen to the Yanks.

And Now He's a Wastrel

by Mullin

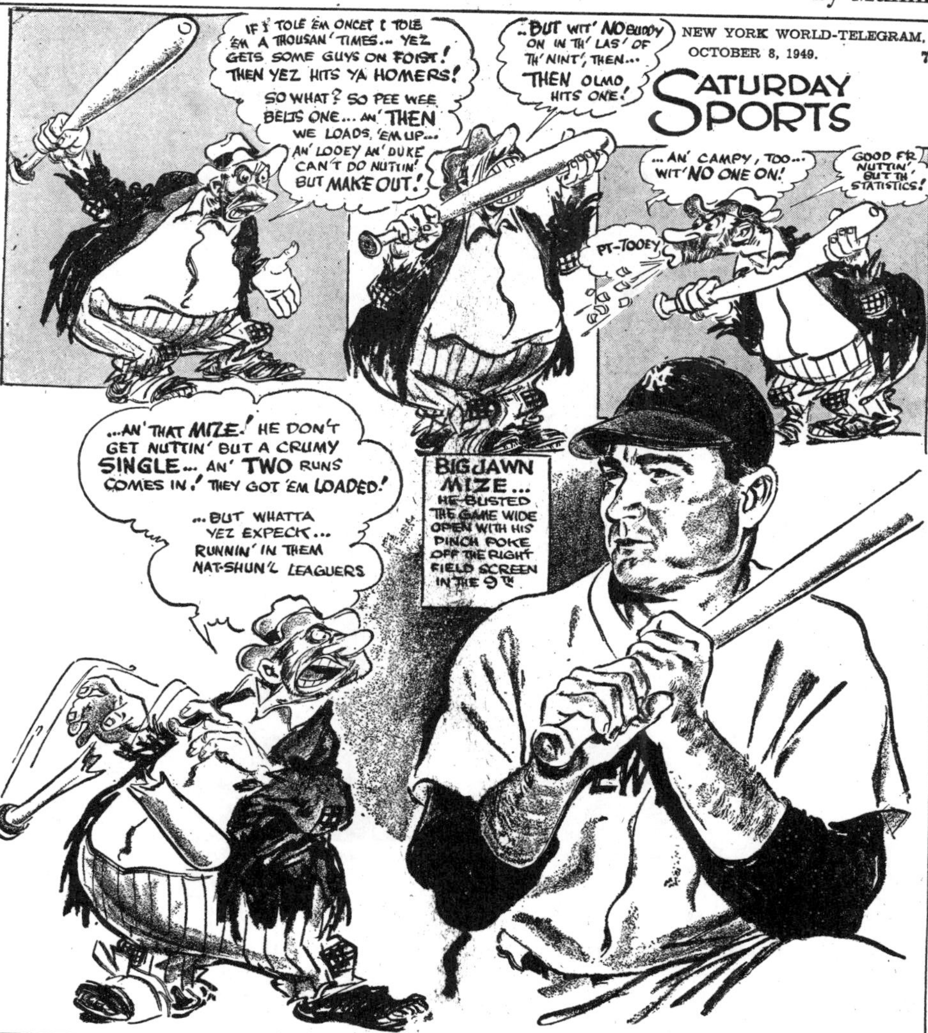

IF I TOLE 'EM ONCET I TOLE 'EM A THOUSAN' TIMES... YEZ GETS SOME GUYS ON FOIST! THEN YEZ HITS YA HOMERS!
SO WHAT? SO PEE WEE BELTS ONE... AN' THEN WE LOADS 'EM UP... AN' LOOEY AN' DUKE CAN'T DO NUTTIN' BUT MAKE OUT!
..BUT WIT' NOBUDDY ON IN TH' LAS' OF TH' NINT', THEN...
THEN OLMO HITS ONE!
... AN' CAMPY, TOO... WIT' NO ONE ON!
GOOD F'R NUTTIN' BUT TH' STATISTICS!
PT-TOOEY
...AN' THAT MIZE! HE DON'T GET NUTTIN' BUT A CRUMY SINGLE... AN' TWO RUNS COMES IN! THEY GOT 'EM LOADED!
...BUT WHATTA YEZ EXPECK... RUNNIN' IN THEM NAT-SHUN'L LEAGUERS
BIG JAWN MIZE... HE BUSTED THE GAME WIDE OPEN WITH HIS PINCH POKE OFF THE RIGHT FIELD SCREEN IN THE 9TH

Brown, Mapes and Lopat Spark Yank Rally in 4th

By DANIEL.

(Continued From Page One.)

took over in right field, batting eighth. Luis Olmo was in left.

As the teams were about to take the field the sun was trying to break through overcast skies. There were about 33,000 in the stands.

The sun was trying desperately to break through the overcast as the Dodgers dashed into the field and Phil Rizzuto came to the plate. Newcombe was pitching for the fourth straight time with only two days of rest and he immediately showed the effects of the ordeal. However, the Bombers failed to score even though they got two hits and a pair of walks.

Rizzuto drove Don's second pitch into center for a single, his second hit of the series. Henrich fouled off eight, then hit the two and two pitch into right, for his second blow of the classic. The Scooter slid into third. It was close as Hermanski made a fine throw. Joe Hatten began to warm up.

Then things got gummed up for the Yankees, but good. Berra grounded to Miksis. Rizzuto was called out for running wide. Henrich was off second, watching developments, ad was doubled by Campanella's alert throw to Reese.

One minute the Yankees were threatening, boldly, now they had a man on first with two out.

DiMaggio walked on five pitches. Newcombe threw three straight balls to Brown and was visited by Clyde Sukerforth, emissary of the manager. Then Bobby walked. The Bombers had five men on base, and still no run.

The bases were loaded, when Woodling stepped to the plate. Gene flied to Snider. It was an inning for the book.

Dodgers Go After Lopat but Fizzle.

Brooklyn started after Lopat with a two bagger, but nothing came of the opportunity.

Reese doubled to left after he had taken a strike. Miksis tapped a ball right in front of the Yogi and was tossed out. Peewee held. Snider was thrown out by Brown, and again Reese lingered at second. He was left when Robinson was thrown out by Rizzuto. Phil made a great play behind second, and his boounce throw was held by Henrich.

The Yankees were retired in order in the second round. Mapes shot a stinger to Newcombe and was tossed out. Coleman fouled to Campanella and Lopat lofted lazily to the Duke.

Brooklyn's second was without incident. Hodges flied to Woodling. So did Olmo. Campanella tapped the ball to Lopat and was heaved out.

New York's third inning was nothing to write about. Miksis tossed out Rizzuto, and Henrich was retired by Hodges and Newcombe. Hermanski caught Berra's fly near the scoreboard.

The clouds were being forced out of the picture and the sky over left field was blue. It was a crowd in shirt sleeves.

The third round ended with the score still 0 to 0. The Dodgers sent only three men to the plate in their half.

Lopat went all the way with Hermanski and struck him out. There was a big hand for Newcombe, but he fanned. Reese popped to Henrich.

Joe Hatten Replaces Newcombe on Mound.

The fourth inning saw Newcombe knocked out and the left-handed Joe Hatten take his place. The Yankees got three doubles and a pass off Don, who had no semblance of the sharpness of his gorgeous performance in the opening game. As Hatten came in, Jack Banta began to warm up. The Bombers scored three runs before they were retired.

DiMaggio lashed at the one and one pitch, and it appeared to be headed for the left field stands. However, Snider got it.

Brown got hold of the two and two pitch for a line double to left center. Woodling walked on four straight pitches, and Newcombe was in hot water again. Hatten started to warm up a second time.

Mapes doubled to the opposite field, into the corner in left. Brown and Woodling scored. Coleman fouled to Olmo but Lopat doubled to left center, scoring Mapes. Lopat came very close to being nipped at second.

Newcombe was relieved by Hatten.

Rizzuto singled to left and when Lopat was sent in by Frankie Crosetti, he was out, Olmo to Campanella.

Dodger Fans Protest Lopat's Easy Stroll.

Lopat took his time going to the mound for Brooklyn's fourth and the home fans protested loudly. However, there was no Dodger at the plate. Finally the pitcher faced Miksis, who took a third strike. Snider flied to Mapes.

Robinson walked on four nonchalant pitches and then Lopat fanned Hodges.

Brown's triple with the bases loaded gave the Yankee three runs in the fifth.

To begin with, Hatten got two strikes on Henrich and then lost him. Old Reliable walked.

Berra singled to right and Tommy stopped at second. However, when Miksis let Hermanski's throw to third get away from him, the runners advanced a base. Hatten walked DiMaggio intentionally, to fill the bases with nobody out. Now Banta and Carl Erskine both were warming up.

ED LOPAT.

Stengel let Brown face the southpaw Hatten, and Bobby hit tthe two and 2 ball off the right field wall, at its base, for a triple, clearing the bases. Woodling flied to Snider in shallow center, and Brown held his base.

Bauer, a righthanded hitter, replaced Mapes at the plate, but Shotton kept Hatten pitching. He uncorked a wild one, but Brown did not try to score. Paul Minner, lefthander, replaced Banta in the warmup exercises.

Reese Recovers Fumble for Out.

Bauer flied to Hermanski in short right. But Brown still did not come in. The throw to the plate was wild and Bob could have made it.

Coleman grounded to Reese, who fumbled, but recovered just in time to retire the batter.

It was announced that the attendance was 33,934 and the net take $167,906.

When Brooklyn came to bat in its fifth, Bauer was in right field for the Bombers. The Dodgers did nothing with Lopat in this round beyond getting a second hit.

Olmo fouled to the Yogi and Rizzuto was spectacular on Campanella's grounder. Hermanski's single to right was Brooklyn's first blow since Reese's opening double.

Tom Brown batted for Hatten and flied to Bauer.

In the sixth inning the Yankees faced Carl Erskine, righthander. Henrich's second hit was the only Bomber incident.

Lopat waited for a three and nothing count, but eventually he popped to Hodges. Rizzuto flied deep to Olmo. Henrich rapped a single off the right-field wall, a homer in the Stadium. Berra popped to Jackie.

Brooklyn scored four runs, all after two out, on seven hits, in the sixth, and knocked Lopat out of the box. But for a double play it would have been a more harrowing round for the Bombers. Reynolds relieved and got Jorgensen on strikes, to end the rally.

Reese opened with a hit in short center. Cox batted for Miksis and topped a hit to Lopat. The pitcher had to take the ball on his wrong side, and it popped out of his grasp.

Snider poked into a double play. Rizzuto stepped on second heaved the ball to Henrich. Now Reese was on third. He dashed home when Robinson rifled a single to left. Nobody was warming up in the Yankee bullpen.

The Game to Win, For Both Sides.

Hodges singled to center and Jackie ran to third. Olmo singled to center, scoring Robinson, with Hodges reaching third. Allie Reynolds began to warm up for the Yankees. Vic Raschi went out to the bullpen. This was the game to win, on both sides.

Campanella hit the first pitch for a single to left, scoring Hodges, with Olmo stopping at second. Everything had happened after two out.

Hermanski singled to right, scoring Olmo and putting Campanella on third. Lopat was removed and Reynolds succeeded him—Reynolds, winner of the opening game, 1 to 0.

Jorgensen batted for Erskine. Wahoo shot over a low strike and the Spider fouled off strike two. Then Jorgensen took strike three, and protested loudly.

When the Yankees came to bat in the seventh, Jack Banta was the Brooklyn pitcher and Billy Cox at third base. Ralph Branca, yesterday's loser, was warming up.

Banta stopped the Bombers cold. DiMaggio went to three and two and then grounded out to Robinson. Brown and Woodling also rolled to Jackie.

The Dodgers subsided in their seventh and were retired in order. Reese flied to Bauer. Cox lined to DiMaggio and Snider fanned.

New York's eighth inning was a tame affair. Banta's grip on the game was tight, but he was two runs behind. Bauer grounded out to Reese, Coleman flied to Hermanski and Reynolds fouled to Campanella.

DiMaggio Draws Cheers For Long Practice Belt

By BILL ROEDER,
World-Telegram Sports Writer.

EBBETS FIELD, Brooklyn, Oct. 8.—The sun favored the Yankee home games, but once the clubs got to Brooklyn, Old Sol got to sulking. The Yankees brought their gray suits and Branch Rickey provided skies to match.

* * *

Today it was hazy, sticky and altogether cheerless as the teams went into rehearsal. Still, there was no rain. All the signs were present, but the rain itself was holding back, in the way of a stubborn sneeze. Meantime, you kept hearing the sun was going to come out any minute.

* * *

The stands filled slowly, but the bleachers were packed when batting practice opened. Two happenings drew roars from the dollar seats. First, Don Newcombe went up to hit in the Brooklyn drill, confirming that he would be the starting pitcher. And when the Yanks took their turn, Joe DiMaggio surprised the onlookers by thumping one into the center-field stands. It used to be a surprise when Joe didn't hit one. But in this series he's been saving his hits for the best seller list.

* * *

Carl Furillo elected to sit this one out, which was all right except that he might have picked a more comfortable seat. Furillo was in the whirlpool bath. This is only the fourth game of the series, but Furillo already has been in the water longer than Shirley May France.

* * *

With Furillo out, the Dodgers had Duke Snider hitting third against a left-hander. As soon as this was announced a representative of the percentage-plus society went to Shotton and demanded that he turn in his card. Casey Stengel had already been expelled. In one of the games Stengel had the audacity to use left handed pinch-hitters against a pitcher of the same persuasion. There was talk of a Congressional investigation after that one.

* * *

Few Cheers for Heroes of 1916 Pennant Crew

Stengel stuck his mug into a microphone at home plate and introduced the old timers. The only names the fans responded to were those of Marquad and Zach Wheat. For all the applause they received, all the other veterans could have been Joe Lafata.

* * *

Phil Rizzuto had to duck the first pitch of the game. But Newcombe had to duck the next one. It screamed right over his head for a single to center. This was so much at odds with the pattern of the series that the Dodgers couldn't believe it. Luis Olmo, for one, thought he was seeing things. As soon as Rizzuto landed on base Olmo had play stopped while he called for his glasses. Rex Barney, who had hoped to pitch the game found himself in the role of office-boy instead. He hustled the specs out to Olmo.

* * *

First Inning Double Play Is Strictly from Flatbush.

Henrich followed with a hit, Rizzuto advancing to third. Then came the first bit of raw Flatbush the series has produced, but with

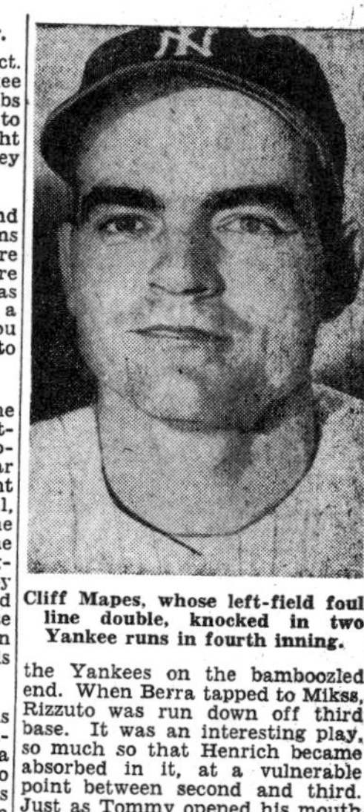

Cliff Mapes, whose left-field foul line double, knocked in two Yankee runs in fourth inning.

the Yankees on the bamboozled end. When Berra tapped to Mikss, Rizzuto was run down off third base. It was an interesting play, so much so that Henrich became absorbed in it, at a vulnerable point between second and third. Just as Tommy opened his mouth to say "Well done," Campanella threw to Robinson to double him up. Tommy opened his mouth again, but not quite as appreciatively.

* * *

In the first inning the Yankees put five men on base and failed to score. The fans hadn't seen this since Babe Herman's day, but at least the Yankees provided a new touch. They used three bases instead of just one.

* * *

Someone suggested the park might prove a little too small for Ed Lopat, with that "gopher" weakness of his. But at first the park seemed a little too big. Reese, the first hitter for the Brooklyns, trained his sights on a stretch of rolling pasture in left center and shot a double out there.

* * *

In the second Mapes chopped a high bouncer that looked dangerous until Newcombe went clamoring after it. The pitcher stuck his paw out so greedily you might have thought the ball was worth several thousand dollars. With his connections, Newcombe ought to be able to get 'em wholesale, $16.50 per dozen.

* * *

Sure enough, by the third inning the sun was shining brightly. At any minute the pessimists of the forenoon expected a sky-writer to buzz the ball park with a message from the weatherman: "I told you." By the way this was the first day no aircraft hovered over the field. The fly boys must have given up hope that DiMaggio would pop one that high.

Dykes Next Senator Pilot According to Grapevine

By JOE KING.

Today's tip is Jimmy Dykes to manage Washington. Griff, Mack and Dykes met yesterday. Dykes recommended Brooklyn farm hand Irv Noren, Hollywood outfielder, to Griff, and the Old Fox got up the dough to help out Rickey. But is that good for Dykes, spending Griff's dough?

* * *

Joe DiMag is going back home to San Francisco, the lucky fellow, when the series ends. Out there his ma, no doubt, will see he inhales enough minestrone and ravioli to stoke and stack the man for next year. Joe is weak. He is going on spirit. But even on crutches, whom would you rather see bat four for New York?

* * *

Weiss and Rickey are running a ticket feud. Weiss sent a long night letter to Branch complaining about Yankee ticket allotments in Ebbets Field. Branch, burned about Dodger allotments in the Stadium, retorted he would never do series business with Georgie excepting before the high commissioner with seat layouts of both parks in evidence. Boys will be boys.

* * *

Happy Chandler speaking: "I've got six umps and when I think they need help from Jackie Robinson I'll let him know." Seven umps? Oh, please, dear commissioner.

* * *

Street scene before Ebbets Field yesterday saw two specs unloading a few six-buck seats for a buck. But shed no tears. One of the young businessmen explained that the pile had been made.

* * *

The Dodgers used to be famous for their ninth-inning finishes. In this series they are noted for the payoff pitches their chuckers chuck in the ninth. Newcombe and Branca did it and only Roe escaped.

* * *

Even in Ebbets Field the series crowds are just rubberneck. They do not have the appreciation nor the enthusiasm of the regular season fans. They are just the tourist, society, cafe society, politician and upper class customers who nab the tickets. Like a charity crowd in the theater. Sitting on their hands.

* * *

Pie Traynor had a hard time figuring why Mize came to bat. "Stengel has done everything upside down all year, so it isn't a surprise when he lifts a regular, Mapes, for another lefty, Mize, with a bad shoulder. But it isn't so upside down when you think Mize is a slugger but one who doesn't go for the bad pitch, a veteran who will try for the walk." Only one guess to a customer, Pie.

* * *

Second guessing? Shotton's getting it. For Branca. But a club official said: "It's a tough situation. What does he do. When he pulled the guy the last time in just such a situation as today, he got hell. So he goes with him today and he gets hell." It's just plain hell.

Billy Morris Dies; Retired Penn Trainer

By the United Press.

PHILADELPHIA, Oct. 8.—William B. (Billy) Morris, 81, University of Pennsylvania athletic trainer for 42 years upon his retirement in 1948, died at his home today. During his service at Penn, Morris also was head trainer for five U.S. Olympic teams.

Right Back Over Newk

Acme Telephoto.

Maybe this was the tip that Don Newcombe didn't have it. Phil Rizzuto is shown belting the Dodger's first pitch over the mound into center field for a single. Don was out in fourth inning.

Army Harriers Romp

WEST POINT, Oct. 8.—The Army cross-country team romped over New York University, 19-42, yesterday for its second straight victory.

Penn Leads at Half

By BILL WALLACE,
World-Telegram Sports Writer.

PRINCETON, Oct. 8.—With an impressive opening 21-0 victory over Dartmouth to its credit, Penn opposed Princeton in Palmer Stadium here today. The Tigers had lost to Navy last week following an opening triumph over Lafayette.

Penn led at the half, 14 to 6.

The Quakers had beaten Princeton two in a row since the Tigers' big upset of 1946, but trail in the 73-year-old series, 32 victories to nine with one tie.

FIRST PERIOD.

Princeton kicked off, Deuber returning to Penn's 25. Penn stalled, Dooney kicking to McCandless, who made a fair catch on Princeton's 33. The Tigers picked up two first downs, McNeil plunging for one, Kazmeier passing to Reed for the other at Penn's 44.

Kazmeier then skirted right end for a score. Reichel's conversion failed. The Tiger drive covered 67 yards in five plays.

Score: Princeton 6, Penn 0.

Deuber returned the kick off to Penn's 44. On third down with 20 to go Dooney kicked to Kazmaier, who was dropped at his 26. Kazmaier passed to Sella and a first at the Tiger 40. McCandless hit Reed for 13 more. Penn held and when Kazmaier attempted to kick, Agocs blocked the punt, the Quakers taking over on Princeton's 35.

Penn could not move, Dooney kicking out on Princeton's 14.

Kazmaier kicked out to Bagnell who returned 21 yards to Princeton's 34. Bagnell's short pass to Dooney carried to Princeton's 18.

On third down Wettlaufer took Bagell's pass on the Tiger 5 and scored. Agocs converted.

Score—Penn 7, Princeton 6.

On the first play after the kick-off, Kazmaier fumbled and Schweder recovered for Penn at the Tiger 36. Dooney bulled through the middle for 20 yards in three plays.

Score at the end of the first period: Penn 7, Princeton 6.

SECOND PERIOD:

Dooney hit Wettlaufer on a jump pass for a Quaker first at the Tiger 5. Deuber cut inside tackle to the 3 and Dooney plunged for the touchdown. Agocs converted.

Score: Penn, 14; Princeton, 6.

Princeton started a drive from its 26 after the kickoff. McNeil bucked two firsts and Kazmeier passed to Reed for 13 to the Penn 40. But the Red and Blue held and Kazmeier corner kicked to the Penn 8.

Deuber streaked 46 yards to the Princeton 46 and Penn was off again. Deuber's pass to Roberts was good for 14 but Sella intercepted on the Tiger 10. Kazmeier kicked to the Princeton 47.

After a punt exchange Kazmaier put Penn in trouble with a 59-yard quick kick to the Quaker 20.

Score at end of the second period: Penn 14, Princeton 6.

The lineups:

Pos.	PRINCETON.	PENN.
L. E.	Bunnell	Roberts
L. T.	Buxton	De Torre
L. G.	Moore	Lemonick
C.	Cohn	Hassler
R. G.	Palin	Schweder
R. T.	Kline	Reichenbach
R. E.	Reed	Wettlaufer
Q. B.	Chandler	Coulson
L. H.	Kazmaier	Deuber
R. H.	Sella	Topchick
F. B.	Powers	Dooney

Referee—William Holloran, Providence. Umpire—John J. Burke. Field Judge—Fred R. Wallace, Washington. Linesman—John F. Kelleher, Boston College.

Facts and Figures On World Series

FIRST GAME (66,224).

				R.	H.	E.
Dodgers	000	000	000—	0	2	1
Yankees	000	000	001—	1	5	0

NEWCOMBE and Campanella. REYNOLDS and Berra.

SECOND GAME (70,053).

				R.	H.	E.
Dodgers	010	000	000—	1	7	2
Yankees	000	000	000—	0	6	1

ROE and Campanella. RASCHI, Page and Silvera, Niarhos.

THIRD GAME (32,788).

				R.	H.	E.
Yankees	001	000	003—	4	5	0
Dodgers	000	100	002—	3	5	0

Byrne, PAGE and Berra. BRANCA, Banta and Campanella.

Third-Game Statistics.

Attendance—32,788.
Receipts (net)—$164,016.71.
Commissioner's share—$24,602.50.
Players' share—$83,648.43.
Club's and leagues' share—$55,765.78.

Three-Game Totals.

Attendance—169,065.
Receipts—$794,556.06.
Commissioner's share—$119,183.40.
Players' share—$405,223.50.
Clubs' and leagues' share—$270,149.16.

Hollywood Victory Evens Coast Series

By the United Press.

HOLLYWOOD, Oct. 8.—The Pacific Coast League champion Hollywood Stars defeated San Diego, 7-4, last night evening the Governor's Cup play-offs at two games each.

Six-Day Cyclists Coming

Sverino Rigoni and Antonio Bevilaqua, the Italian [illegible]sts, and Henri Surbatis, veteran French-Greek favorite, will ride in the International Six-Day bike race that starts here Oct. [illegible] at the 22nd Engineers Armory.

Section 3-4 | SPORTS NEWS STAMPS

NEW YORK Herald Tribune

FINANCE BUSINESS MARINE | Section 3-4

FOURTEEN PAGES | SUNDAY, OCTOBER 9, 1949 | FOURTEEN PAGES

Yankees Defeat Dodgers, 6-4, and Take 3-1 World Series Lead; Army Upsets Michigan, 21-7; Cornell, Yale and Penn Triumph

100,000 See Cadets Score Three Times

Victors Snap String Of Opponent at 25

Winners Drive 89 Yards to First Touchdown in the Tenth Minute

By Jesse Abramson

ANN ARBOR, Mich., Oct. 8.—Football's most extensive all-winning streak of this quarter century became a museum piece today, wrecked by the fire and brilliance, speed and devastating drive of Army's cadets.

Red Blaik, envying the might and power of Michigan, from whom he had borrowed the two-platoon system of operations, turned loose a force that demolished the Colossus of the West, 21 to 7. With an eighty-nine-yard ground and air march in the tenth minute, another touchdown capitalizing a Wolverine fumble early in the second period, and finally with a galloping rush to a third touchdown in the closing minutes, the underdog West Point entry racked up three touchdowns, yielding one score to the Big Ten champions at the outset of the last quarter.

A crowd of 100,000, shirt-sleeved under a cloudless midsummer sky, was stunned by the masterful drive and skill of the enemy through a first half in which their prides were pushed around by Army offense, throttled by Army's equally shattering defense.

Michigan Rallies

The crowd (of which 97,239 paid) saw Michigan rally and put vise-like pressure on Army.

The Maize and Blue stormed back through the third period, bent but could not break the doughty Army defense until the third minute of the last quarter, when a monstrous double break set up the only Ann Arbor tally. And then it was the ball game this vast throng had assembled to see. Michigan kept Army on the run and was striking for the equalizing touchdown when Tom Brown, sophomore safety from Tallahassee, Fla., intercepted a Wolverine pass in his end zone.

That play embodied all that was wrong with Michigan today. The Wolverines, famed for their passers, had no air force to bomb the Army. They couldn't hit a barn door at ten paces, nor could the receivers hold what they got. They completed only three of their twenty-three passes for a meager sixteen yards, threw four passes into Army's loving grasp.

Major General Bryant E. Moore, West Point superintendent and every Army devotee, drew a deep breath after twenty minutes of exquisite strain and tension on the Brown interception. That did for Michigan. It never threatened again, hardly had possession as the West Pointers resumed their first-half control and made it pay off with a cushion score.

Outcome Stuns Nation

The outcome stunned the nation. It terminated Michigan's string at twenty-five straight. Not since Illinois beat the home team, 13 to 9, three years ago has a Michigan team lost. Army balked Michigan from tying Cornell's modern record of twenty-six straight set in 1921-'23, and saw its own defeatless streak flower to fourteen straight (with two ties) and made it three out of three over Michigan.

Frank Fischl, junior right half,

(Continued on page 4, column 5)

Big Red Eleven Subdues Fighting Harvard, 33-14

Dorset, Chollet Spark Powerful Drives of Victors, Overcoming Early Lead Gained by Crimson

By Al Laney

CAMBRIDGE, Oct. 8.—Cornell defeated Harvard, 33 to 14, in the Stadium this afternoon and that was about the way the game figured to go given the relative talents involved and the records of the two teams. What was not looked for was the way in which Harvard, a battered team going into the game and growing steadily more battered, gave it the old spirited try throughout.

The crowd of about 24,000 got a real lift from this prolonged fight against odds that really were overwhelming, and saw the possibility that Harvard, now thrice defeated and without a victory for the season, will be a much better football team from Saturday to Saturday, especialy when injured operatives return to full-time duty.

Harvard scored first, going seventy yards with the opening kick-off, getting Charlie Roche over after relinquishing the ball close up and regaining it on a fumble. The Crimson held this 7-to-0 lead for only a few minutes and then yielded to Cornell's superiority in practically every department of play.

The Big Red went seventy yards to send Lyndon Hull, halfback, over from fifteen yards out at 13:40 of the first period, and eighty yards for Hull's second touchdown midway of the second quarter. Hillary Chollet took a short pass from Pete Dorset to score the third just before the half ended and two more came in the third period.

For the first of these, Bob Haley, fullback, intercepted Bill Henry's pass and ran forty yards. The other was a pass from Dorset to Walt Bruska, right end.

Harvard scored its second touchdown in a drive of sixty-five yards which spanned the third and fourth quarters. The touchdown went to John White, first starting wingback in the absence of Harold Moffie, a badly missed player today.

Cornell's attack was beautifully co-ordinated at times, and it seemed it might carry all the way to the end zone each time the Big-Red got the ball. But sloppy execution cost them dearly and piled up the ground lost by penalties.

(Continued on page 5, column 1)

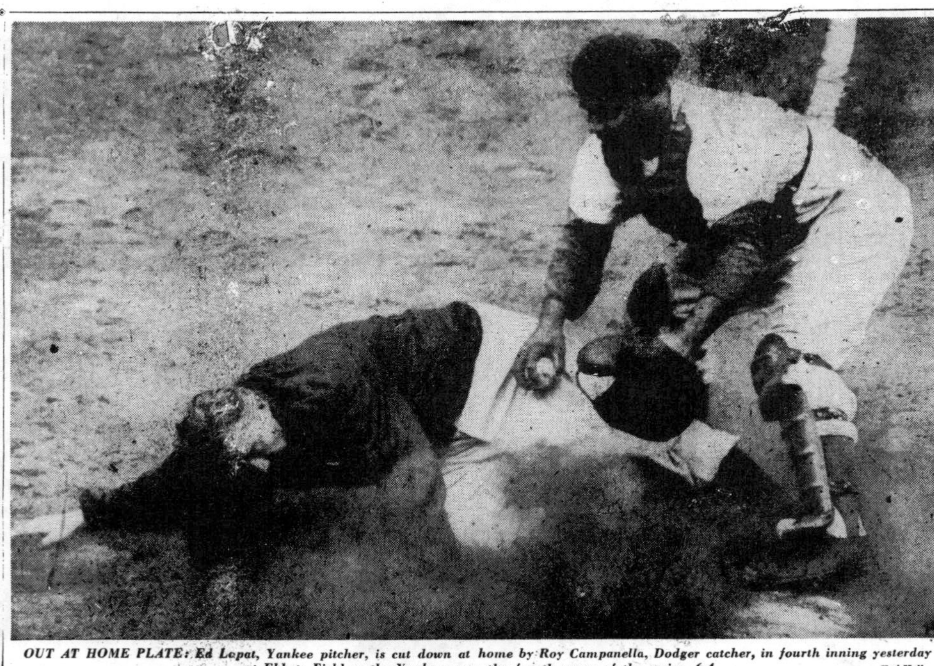

OUT AT HOME PLATE: Ed Lopat, Yankee pitcher, is cut down at home by Roy Campanella, Dodger catcher, in fourth inning yesterday at Ebbets Field as the Yankees won the fourth game of the series, 6-4 Ted Kell

Pair of 3-Run Innings Wins For New York

Reynolds Thwarts Brooklyn in Relief

Newcombe, Lopat Falter; Losers Score 4 in 6th; Brown's Triple Decides

By Harold Rosenthal

Allie Reynolds, strictly a cash-on-the-barrelhead operator slammed the door in the Dodgers' faces yesterday. The Yankee right-hander, responding to a frantic sixth-inning call for help as though he was part St. Bernard rather than part Creek Indian, hurled a perfect three and one-third innings in the Yankees' thrilling 6-to-4 triumph before 33,934 customers at Ebbets Field.

New York now leads, three games to one, in the interborough World Series. The Yankees can clinch it without returning to their own ball park by winning the final game slated for Brooklyn this afternoon.

Eddie Lopat got credit for this one, although the red-headed left-hander was a slightly dazed man when he departed after the Dodgers had clipped him for a record-equaling seven singles in a night-marish sixth inning.

Reynolds Foils Dodgers

Reynolds, who had hurled a two-hitter in the Yankees' opening victory, hustled on stage and forthwith stopped all these Dodger two-out shenanigans. He struck out the pinch-hitting Johnny Jorgensen, then faced the irreducible minimum of nine men in the next three innings.

Burt Shotton, Dodger manager, led with his rookie right-handed ace, Don Newcombe, in a desperate attempt to get back into the Series. Newcombe worked with only two days' rest, and he was about as enigmatic as a limpid pool to the muscle-flexing Yankees. Shotton saw him trumped and routed before the fourth inning had ended. The Yankees racked up half their runs as well as five of their ten hits off big Don.

The Dodgers got some hitting, too, eight singles and a double, but too much of it came in their big sixth inning. Up to that point Lopat, the one-time Radio City usher, was guiding them gently, but firmly toward the nearest exit with a two-hit performance. He gave up a lead-off double to Pee-Wee Reese, then shut the Dodgers out until Gene Hermanski lined a single to right field in the fifth.

Dodgers Pound Lopat

Lopat had everything, including a big six-run lead, and when the Dodgers started to make threatening gestures in the sixth, especially with two out, the Yankee bench didn't gesture frantically toward the bullpen until a couple of runs had crossed the plate.

Casey Stengel was confident Lopat would pull out of the hole, especially with two out. He was anxious to give his pitcher every opportunity to win his first World Series game on his very first try.

But Lopat had run out of gas and the empty gas gauge now showed nothing but five straight singles and Reynolds warming up

(Continued on page 2, column 2)

Navy Conquers Duke, 28-14, in 2d-Half Rally

Zastrow Passes Account for 3 Tallies; Red Devils Sustain Year's 1st Loss

By Bill Lauder Jr.

ANNAPOLIS, Md., Oct. 8.—Navy's revitalized football team, striking back after Duke's Blue Devils surged to touchdowns the first two times they had the ball, remained on the alkaline side at Thompson Stadium today by walloping the visitors from Carolina, 28 to 14, before a howling crowd of 22,000 which included, replete with healthy lungs, the brigade of midshipmen.

Navy, which in the last two seasons had won only one game and tied two, finally broke into the victory column against Princeton last week. All wheed up with that taste of success, the future admirals lidn't let the fact that Duke already had won two this year, and was favored today, phase them. Paced by Bob Zastrow, who brewed their T too strong for the Devils, the midshipmen fought back in the second half after trailing 14 to 7, at intermission.

Complementing Zastrow, who completed ten of fourteen passes for 195 yards, was a mercury-footed demon named Frank Hauff. Operating from left half, this five-nine 170-pound ace starred both on offense and defense. He was in there most of the way and received a rising ovation from the brigade when he came off the field near the end of the game. His pass defense was excellent, he came in fast to stop running plays and he carried the ball for seventy-seven yards rushing.

Duke, with Billy Cox directing the attack from his left halfback spot in Wallace Wade's single wing, scored in three plays after the opening kick-off.

Tom Powers, who paced the Devil's running attack, circled his left end on a reverse on the first play after the kick-off and went

(Continued on page 4, column 3)

Yale's 5-Touchdown Barrage Tumbles Columbia Eleven, 33-7

Lions March 62 Yards for Only Score in 1st Period; Fuchs Boots 24-Yard Field Goal

By Everett B. Morris

The first time Columbia got its hands on the ball in its twenty-seventh football game with Yale yesterday afternoon at Baker Field, the Lions rode sixty-two yards along the air lanes for a touchdown, kicked the extra point and gave the Light Blue section of the Alumni Homecoming Day crowd of 30,000 an idea that this was to be indeed an occasion for celebration.

But that was all for Columbia. The rest of the sultry, summery afternoon was spent in watching the resurgent, if erratic, sons of Elihu scampering into the Lion end zone with such frequency that the New Haven ensemble was able to perpetrate a 33-to-7 hosing of the home forces.

Five touchdowns and a field goal made up the Yale total as the Bulldogs doled out the worst thumping either team has suffered in the modern phase of a rivalry which began back in 1872 when Columbia became Eli's first intercollegiate opponent.

Jackson Runs 19 Yards

Yale passed to its first tally late in the opening period, assumed the lead with another air-borne attack in the second quarter and then swarmed all over the hapless Columbians in the closing chukkers. A pass produced an early score in the third period and in the fourth came the deluge.

A Columbia fumble which did not hit the ground was returned thirty-eight yards for one touchdown: Levi Jackson, two of whose long runs were wasted earlier in the action, sped nineteen yards up the middle for the final six-pointer and, after the Yale running attack had been stalled by a fumble, Jim Fuchs place-kicked a field goal from twenty-four yards out.

Apparently Herman Hickman, the New Haven chieftain, ordered this gesture to give Fuchs some obviously needed kicking practice. He had missed two points after touchdown when they appeared important and, at the end of the

(Continued on page 5, column 2)

Dartmouth Puts Holy Cross to Rout, 31 to 7

Unheralded Roberts Paces Big Green With Dashes of 34, 52, 55 Yards

By Doug Kennedy

HANOVER, N. H., Oct. 8.—Displaying an almost incredible impotence that netted it only four earned first downs, one in the first half, the Holy Cross football team allowed itself to be overrun by Dartmouth's swift but damaged backfield, 31 to 7, this muggy day before 13,000 witnesses at Memorial Stadium.

The Crusaders were never in the contest and only dented the scoring column because Paul Gallo galloped six yards with one of Gil Mueller's mislaid passes early in the fourth period. At that stage Dartmouth was coasting along with a 25-to-0 lead.

The game was a sloppy three-hour affair marred, to a considerable extent, by the decimation of the Crusader forces. After approximately every third play an unhorsed knight in purple could be detected writhing on the turf, a compliment to the decisive and deadly Dartmouth blocking and tackling.

The score would indicate that Dartmouth was a red-hot football team, but the recent memory of the Penn defeat would belie that impression. Rather it was the lack

(Continued on page 5, column 6)

Penn Nips Rally By Princeton And Wins, 14-13

Agocs' Extra Points Decide, Despite Kazmaier's Long Scoring Runs for Tigers

By Irving T. Marsh

PRINCETON, N. J., Oct. 8.—Princeton scored two touchdowns to Pennsylvania's two, outgained the Quakers on the ground, outpassed them in completions and in yardage, out-first-downed them and outfought them, but lost the forty-third imbroglio between these ancient rivals, 14 to 13, at Palmer Stadium this hot, humid afternoon.

By the margin on a bobbled try for the point after the first Nassau touchdown, bobbled mainly because of a poor pass from center, potent Pennsylvania edged the Tigers in a football game that was played to the hilt despite the unseemly weather that reduced the crowd of 32,000 to its shirt-sleeves.

Valentzas's Block Helps

Having scored in its last twenty-nine games, thereby tying the Tiger record for this department, Princeton broke the mark when it went sixty-seven yards in five plays the first time it had the ball for a score in 4 minutes 12 seconds of the first quarter. Little Dick Kazmaier, a 168-pound sophomore who played a whale of a ball game all afternoon, scoring both Tiger touchdowns on long runs, administered the coup de grace with a forty-three-yard run from scrimmage, in which he outsped completely the Pennsylvania defenders. A fine block by Dick Valentzas, tackle, helped him on his way.

Frank Reichel dropped back to attempt the extra point, with Cliff Kurras holding. The snapback however, was a little high. Kurras bobbled the ball and couldn't get it into position. He attempted to throw to Reichel, who ran to his right but Reichel was pounced on after he'd taken a few steps. That point was lost.

For the rest of the first quarter and all of the second and third, that missed point didn't seem important. For Penn came back late in the opening period and pushed across the touchdown, converted the point and then went on to

(Continued on page 5, column 4)

Ponder, Theory Win Features For Calumet Farm at Belmont

Sons of Pensive Take Jockey Club Gold Cup and Champagne Stakes for Total of $58,450

By Joe H. Palmer

The Calumet Collection Agency, which had annoyingly missed a couple of important calls at the Belmont meeting, got itself soundly organized yesterday and doubled The Jockey Club Gold Cup and the Champagne Stakes, for a total of $58,450 as Belmont closed its eighteen-day fall meeting. There were 28,500 witnesses.

Ponder and Theory, both sons of Pensive, did the business. Ponder, winner of the Lawrence Realization here, plugged along steadily for a mile and a quarter, ran into a blind switch as he moved up, got out of that and got through inside and pulled off to win the cup by two and a half lengths from King Ranch's Flying Missel, with Mrs. Ben Whitaker's Miss Request third. This was worth $35,300 to the stable, $3.10 to the customers.

A race earlier Theory, beaten last Saturday in the Futurity, came from fairly close to the early pace to win the Champagne Stakes by two lengths from Greentree's Androcles, with Brookmead Stable's Sunglow four more lengths away third. This was a $23,150 item, and the colt paid $3.30.

200th Victory for Brooks

The Champagne Stakes gave Steve Brooks his two-hundredth riding victory of the year, and the cup started him on his third hundred. For Calumet it was an old story, the stable having won both races three times before, though never in the same year.

Greentree, which had received the Calumet invasion most inhospitably by beating Theory with Guillotine and Coaltown with Capot, had the pacemaker in both

(Continued on page 7, column 4)

N. Y. U. Defeats Brooklyn's Eleven, 39 to 13

Cassowitz, Eisenman, Payne and Novotny Register Touchdowns for Violets

By Leonard Koppett

All the Bronx vs. Brooklyn athletic activity in New York wasn't confined to Ebbets Field yesterday. At the Polo Grounds last night New York University's and Brooklyn College's football teams squared off in the sixth installment of their lately formed Metropolitan rivalry.

Although the Kingsmen had won their one previous start this season while N. Y. U. was losing to Bucknell in its opener, the burden of proof in tonight's clash rested on Ted Rosequist's eleven. Last year the Violets handed Brooklyn one of its two defeats, 21 to 7, and no Brooklyn team had ever defeated N. Y. U. since the series began in 1944. This was the school's sixth meeting.

N. Y. U. won, 39 to 13.

Both teams showed ability to move the ball in the first quarter, but a fumble halted N. Y. U.'s opening drive which got to Brooklyn's 39, and Brooklyn's counter-attack stalled on N. Y. U.'s 30. An exchange of punts gave Brooklyn possession on its own 42.

Then a pass by Gerry Edwards was intercepted on the 47 by Norm Cassowitz, the Violet's defensive right half, and Norm sped unobstructed to the goal line. George Lorentz missed the extra point.

Edwards fumbled the ensuing kickoff and George Starke recovered for the Violets on Brooklyn's 30. Two running plays, a twenty-

(Continued on page 4, column 7)

Score of Fourth Game

* * *

NEW YORK (A)

	ab	r	h	po	a
Rizzuto, ss.	4	0	2	1	4
Henrich, 1b.	4	1	3	10	0
Berra, c.	5	1	1	10	1
DiMaggio, cf.	3	1	0	1	0
R. Brown, 3b.	3	1	2	0	3
Woodling, lf.	3	1	0	2	0
Mapes, rf.	2	1	1	1	0
Bauer, rf.	2	0	0	2	0
Coleman, 2b.	4	0	0	0	0
Lopat, p.	3	0	1	0	1
Reynolds, p.	1	0	0	0	0
Totals	34	6	10	27	9

BROOKLYN (N)

	ab	r	h	po	a
Reese, ss.	4	1	2	0	2
Miksis, 3b.	2	0	0	0	2
Cox, 3b.	2	0	1	1	0
Snider, cf.	4	0	0	4	0
Robinson, 2b.	3	1	1	2	3
Hodges, 1b.	4	1	1	8	1
Olmo, lf.	4	1	1	2	1
Campanella, c.	4	0	1	5	2
Hermanski, rf.	4	0	2	4	0
Newcombe, p.	1	0	0	1	1
Hatten, p.	0	0	0	0	0
*T. Brown	1	0	0	0	0
Erskine, p.	0	0	0	0	0
†Jorgensen	1	0	0	0	0
Banta, p.	0	0	0	0	0
‡Whitman	1	0	0	0	0
Totals	35	4	9	27	12

*Flied out for Hatten in fifth inning.
†Struck out for Erskine in sixth inning.
‡Struck out for Banta in ninth inning.

New York (A)	0	0	0	3	3	0	0	0	0	— 6
Brooklyn (N)	0	0	0	0	0	4	0	0	0	— 4

Error—Miksis. Runs batted in—Mapes 2, Lopat, R. Brown 3, Robinson, Olmo, Campanella, Hermanski. Two-base hits—Reese, R. Brown, Mapes, Lopat. Three-base hit—R. Brown. Double plays—Miksis, Campanella and Robinson; Rizzuto and Henrich. Earned runs—New York (A) 6; Brooklyn (N) 4. Left on base—New York (A) 7; Brooklyn (N) (5). Base on balls—Off Newcombe 3 (DiMaggio, Brown, Woodling); Lopat 1 (Robinson); Hatten 2 (Henrich, DiMaggio); Banta 1 (Rizzuto). Struck out—By Lopat 4 (Hermanski, Newcombe, Miksis, Hodges); Reynolds 5 (Jorgensen, Snider, Olmo, Hermanski, Whitman); Banta 1 (DiMaggio). Hits and runs—Off Newcombe 5 and 3 in 3 2/3 innings; Hatten 3 and 3 in 1 1/3; Erskine 1 and 0 in 1; Banta 1 and 0 in 3; Lopat 9 and 4 in 5 2/3; Reynolds 0 and 0 in 3 1/3. Winner—Lopat. Loser—Newcombe. Umpires—Jorda (N. L.) plate; Hubbard (A. L.) first base; Reardon (N. L.) second base; Passarella (A. L.) third base; Hurley (A. L.) left field foul line; Barr (N. L.) right field foul line. Attendance—33,934 (paid). Time—2:42. Receipts—$167,906.37.

ARMY TOUCHDOWN PLAY: Frank Fischl, Army back, carries ball around own left end to score touchdown from 5-yard line in first period. Michigan player who missed tackle is Bob Erben, center. Michigan back, Walt Teninga (42), also missed Fischl as Jim Cain (45) leads interference. Note players in upper right as lines crashed on play Associated Press wirephoto

College and School Football

* * *

Colleges

East

Alfred	27	Clarkson	0
Allegheny	21	Oberlin	20
Amherst	14	Bowdoin	7
Bates	12	Tufts	7
Bloomsburg Tchrs.	21	Kings College	0
Boston U.	40	Colgate	21
Brown	46	Rhode Island	0
Bucknell	13	Delaware	7
Carnegie Tech	28	St. Francis	19
California Tchrs.	27	Indiana Tchrs.	7
Clarion Tchrs.	47	Rio Grande	0
Concord	13	Davis-Elkins	12
Cornell	33	Harvard	14
Cornell Frosh	19	Wyoming Seminary	0
Dartmouth	31	Holy Cross	7
Dickinson	13	Franklin Marshall	13
Fordham	44	Kings Point	9
Gettysburg	21	Drexel	0
Hofstra	19	Wagner	6
Kutztown Tchrs.	12	Mansfield Tchrs.	12
Lafayette	35	Muhlenberg	21
Maine	26	New Hampshire	13
Middlebury	19	Hamilton	14
Morrisville Frosh	18	Clarkson Frosh	6
National Agricultural	32	New York Aggies	7
Navy	28	Duke	14
New Britain Tchrs.	19	Trenton Tchrs.	0
Nichols Jr. Coll.	33	Mass. Maritime	0
Northeastern	27	Colby	0
P. M. C.	28	Swarthmore	0
Penn State	32	Boston College	7
Pennsylvania	14	Princeton	13
Pittsburgh	20	West Virginia	7
Rutgers	40	Lehigh	27
St. Bonaventure	25	Wayne	7
St. Lawrence	42	Hobart	6
St. Michael's	32	Lowell Textile	0
Slippery Rock	28	Edinboro Tchrs.	6
Springfield	26	Connecticut	7
[illegible]hanna	[illegible]	[illegible]	[illegible]
Trinity	71	Norwich	0
[illegible]	[illegible]	[illegible]	7
Ursinus	14	Haverford	14
Wagner	19	Hofstra	6
Western Maryland	39	Lebanon Valley	7
Wesleyan	12	Coast Guard	6
Williams	35	Rochester	0
Worcester Tech	7	Massachusetts U.	6
Yale	33	Columbia	7

South

Alabama A. and M.	14	Xavier (New Orleans)	2
Alabama Poly	14	Florida	14
Baylor	35	Arkansas	13
Claflin	[illegible]	Georgia Tech	0
Clemson	7	Mississippi State	7
Dillard	[illegible]	Tougaloo	7
Eastern Kentucky	20	Murray	0
Elon College	33	East. Carolina Tchrs.	7
Georgetown	12	Wake Forest	6
Georgia Tech	36	Washington and Lee	0
Grambling	20	Wiley	0
Greensboro	20	Hampton	13
Guilford	36	Randolph-Macon	12
Jackson	37	Campbell	0
Johns Hopkins	19	Washington (Md.)	7
Leland (La.)	20	Rust	6
Maryland State	39	South Carolina State	0
Maryville	28	Centre	25
Morgan State	20	North Carolina Coll.	7
Morris Brown	49	Morehouse	0
North Carolina	28	South Carolina	13

(Continued on page 6, column 7)

Section 3-4

SPORTS NEWS

NEW YORK Herald Tribune

FINANCE—BUSINESS STAMPS

Section 3-4

TWELVE PAGES

SUNDAY, APRIL 16, 1950

TWELVE PAGES

Yankees Vanquish Dodgers, 6-4; Giants Overwhelm Indians, 9-0; Lotowhite, 18-1, Wins Experimental at Jamaica; Hill Prince 9th

41,068 Watch 1-to-2 Favorite Run Into Rail

Colt Then Bounces Against Lights Up

Kentucky Derby Prospect Thrown Off Stride in Mile and Sixteenth Test

By Joe H. Palmer

With C. T. Chenery's Hill Prince hopelessly blocked in away behind him, Hal Price Headley's light-weighted Lotowhite skipped away from the Experimental Free Handicap field in the stretch at Jamaica yesterday, and won by four and a half lengths from another outsider, J. M. Seider's Royal Castle. Sam Boulmetis, the Florida riding sensation, was the rider.

A length and a half farther back, F. N. Phelps's Sturdy One finished third, improving considerably on his effort in the six-furlong version of the Experimental, and it was another length and a half to Mrs. Andy Schuttinger's Ferd, the colt which upset Middleground last Tuesday.

The mile and a sixteenth was run in a fair 1:44 3/5 over a track officially called fast but hardly in its best condition. Lotowhite, which had only one victory to show for eighteen previous starts, was an upset at $37.90, and Royal Castle, which went off at 45 to 1, paid $33.70 to show. Sturdy One wasn't expected either, and his show price was $10.80.

Winner Carries 107 Pounds

It was a clean sweep for the lightweights, Lotowhite carrying 107 pounds, and Royal Castle and Sturdy One going in with 106 each. Hill Prince went off at 1 to 2. He was moving up at the five-sixteenths pole when the horse struck the rail and bounced into Lights Up, on the outside. It threw him off stride, and it was Eddie Arcaro's opinion that he wasn't going anywhere afterwards. But in any case, he was blocked completely at the top of the stretch, and Eddie was forced to stand up and snatch him.

Jamaica drew a crowd of 41,068 for a day which was intermittently sunshine and overcast and a trifle cold. They had a perfectly devilish time with favorites anyway, but Hill Prince struck an almost fatal blow, $357,780 being bet across the board on him.

The race started with Lotowhite breaking first, but Guillotine outran him to the turn, and was joined by Casemate. These two pulled away out, leading Royal Castle down the backstretch by six lengths, with Lotowhite fourth, Sturdy One fifth. Hill Prince had only one horse beaten on the first turn, the outsider Trumpet King.

Sturdy One Responds

There was no material change in the order to the far turn, where Casemate and Guillotine stopped as fast as they had been running, so fast in fact that they made some jamming as they came back to the field. Lotowhite spurted past. Sturdy One went to a drive on the rail, and Royal Castle made one bid.

Sturdy One responded to Herb Lindberg's drive and went to the leader's head at the furlong-pole, but then he was done. Lotowhite

(Continued on page 4, column 2)

Misses Brough, Hart On Wightman Team

The United States Wightman Cup team this year will be composed of the four top ranking women tennis players in the country—Mrs. Margaret Osborne du Pont, of Bellvue, Del.; Louise Brough, of Beverly Hills, Calif.; Doris Hart, of Jacksonville, and Mrs. Pat Todd, of La Jolla, Calif.

Mrs. James W. Moss, of Boston, chairwoman of the U. S. L. T. A. Wightman Cup committee, who made the announcement yesterday, also said that Mrs. Richard A. Buck, of Boston, has been reappointed non-playing captain.

The event will be held at Wimbledon on June 16 and 17. It will be the twenty-second match in the series, and the United States team will be shooting for its eighteenth victory. The last time England won was in 1930.

Sunglow Wins Chesapeake at Havre de Grace

Brookmeade Stable Runs 1-2 as Greek Ship Gains Place; Entry Pays $8.80

HAVRE DE GRACE, Md., April 15 (AP).—Brookmeade Stable's entry of Sunglow and Greek Ship ran one-two today in the Chesapeake Stakes to reverse their finish in the Louisiana Derby.

The two Kentucky Derby candidates beat fourteen three-year-olds, including seven other eligibles for the classic.

Mrs. James Carson's Kinsman, only one of three starters not named for at least one of the three-year-old classics, was third. Mrs. Walter M. Jefford's Suleiman was fourth.

Sunglow was half a length ahead of stablemate Greek Ship at the finish of the mile and sixteenth run in 1:46. Suleiman was a neck behind. The favorite, Palestine Stable's Quiz Show, was way back in eleventh place.

The race was worth $22,725, $18,725 for first, to Brookmeade.

It was the first start for Sunglow and Greek Ship since they dominated the Louisiana Derby on March 11. They paid $8.80 to their backers today.

Sunglow is eligible for the Derby and Preakness and Greek Ship for all three classics, including the Belmont.

An estimated crowd of 18,000 witnessed the race.

Our Hobo Home First In 'Chase in Maryland

BALTIMORE, April 15 (AP).—Our Hobo led a field of eleven over eighteen timber jumps in the rolling hills north of Baltimore today to win the My Lady's Manor point-to-point, traditional opener of Maryland's steeplechase season.

Our Hobo is owned by Mrs. John B. Hannum 3d, and was ridden by her husband. The jumper completed the rugged three-mile test in 6 minutes 23 and six-tenths seconds.

Roxspur, ridden by David Pearce and owned by Laura Franklin, was second. Samuel R. Fry's Identiroon, ridden by Walter Brewster, was third.

R. P. I. Wins in Lacrosse

TROY, N. Y., April 15 (AP).—Les Eustace, of Rensselaer Polytechnic Institute, scored five goals today to lead the Engineers to a 20-to-2 lacrosse victory over Adelphi College.

Jack Frank

BEFORE AND AFTER: Joe DiMaggio (at left) has just connected with Preacher Roe's fast ball in fifth inning and (right) he's completing tour of bases on homer with Yogi Berra (8) greeting him. Umpire is Ed Rommel. In same inning, DiMaggio made spectacular catch that robbed Roy Campanella of a homer. The Yankees beat the Dodgers, 6 to 4

Navy's Crew Defeats Columbia On Harlem for Stevenson Cup

Lion Varsity's Final Sprint Fails to Catch Middie Shell by Tenth of Second in 1¾-Mile Race

By Leonard Koppett

Columbia's varsity crew, seeking its first victory in three years under Coach Walt Raney, missed it by a couple of feet on the Harlem yesterday, as its magnificent last-quarter-mile sprint fell a m... short of Navy's shell in the ... race for Maxwell Stevenson Cup.

The Lions, covering the mile and three-quarter course downstream in 7:51.4, were clocked one-tenth of a second behind Navy, which led all the way but had a half-length lead dwindle in the last 400 yards.

Actually Columbia lost the race on the very first stroke. At the start, the Light Blue's whole port side caught a crab, shaking up the boat and giving the Navy about a quarter-length lead. Although Columbia quickly made this up, it fell behind again, caught up again, and fell behind once more before its final spurt. The pressure of catching up throughout the race, instead of rowing practically even as a good start might have made possible, was a decided factor in Columbia's failure to overtake the Middies at the end.

Navy J. V.'s Wins

Three other races preceded the varsity test, in good smooth water with a moderate quartering wind from the Northwest and cold, partly cloudy weather. Columbia's lightweight varsity defeated the Undine Boat Club in the first event, the Lion heavyweight freshmen followed with a clear-cut triumph over Navy and the Navy junior varsity whipped Columbia.

The freshman race was a wonderful battle. The Middies got off to a slight lead at the start and held it, with margins ranging up to half a length, throughout the first mile. Between the bridges, Columbia pulled even and coming out from under the second bridge, with a little more than half a mile to go, held a four or five-foot advantage. From there to the finish, with both crews rowing at 36, Columbia pulled away strongly to its final length-and-a-third margin. Columbia's time was 8:14.9, Navy's 8:19.4. Particularly impressive was the Lion stroke, Don Fleming, who a year ago rowed on a national championship West Side Boat Club crew in Buffalo, his home town.

Columbia Lightweights Win

In the junior varsity test, Navy got the jump and simply pulled away, winning by four and a half lengths in 8:04.8. Columbia's time was 8:19.6. The lightweight race was over a mile and five-sixteenths course, Columbia covering it in 6:18.4. About a quarter mile from the finish, the Unline shell struck a piece of driftwood, stopped, and came on across the line in 7:10.8.

The varsity race overshadowed the other three. On the traditional side, Columbia and Navy had raced each other twenty-four times previously in dual meets since 1899, Navy winning thirteen

(Continued on page 5, column 2)

Demaret Takes Lead With 204 In Atlanta Golf

Winner of Masters Cards 64 for Course Record; Snead Is 3 Strokes Back

ATLANTA, April 15 (AP).—Jimmy Demaret, who last Sunday won the Augusta Masters, today shot the greatest round of competitive golf ever played at North Fulton—a 7-under-par 64—to sweep to the lead in the North Fulton open.

His three-day total is 204, three strokes better than second-place Sam Snead, who came in with a third-round 69.

Demaret's great round included eight birdies and only one over-par hole. His putter was accurate on the speedy greens and he had no complaints about pin positions, although nearly every other golfer contended that holes were located to penalize putters.

In third place after fifty-four holes on the 6,762-yard course was Jim Ferrier, the big Australian who flubbed the Masters on the last nine holes. Ferrier, now living in San Francisco, was two under par with a 69 for a 208 total.

Clayton Heafner, of Charlotte, N. C., the second-round leader, got a 72 for a 209. Johnny Palmer, of Badin, N. C., co-leader after the first round, took another 71 to slip into a tie for fifth place with 211 stroker. Henry Ransom, of St. Andrews, Ill., got a 69 to join Palmer.

Lloyd Mangrum, of Chicago, the other first-day leader, was in a tie for tenth place after a costly

(Continued on page 5, column 1)

Senators' Scarborough To Face A's in Opener

WASHINGTON, April 15 (AP).—Washington manager Bucky Harris today nominated his ace, Ray Scarborough, to pitch for the Nats on opening day Tuesday.

It will be the second straight year that the righthander has faced the Philadelphia Athletics on opening day. He won last year.

Jack Frank

FIRST HIT: Gil Hodges, of Dodgers, beats out infield single to Scooter Rizzuto, whose throw to Joe Collins at first was short. Coaching at first base for Dodgers is Jake Pitler

Ranger Sextet Seeks to Break Stanley Cup Tie

Red Wing Coach Brings Up 5 Players in Effort to Stop Blue Shirts at Toronto

By Bill Lauder Jr.

TORONTO, April 15.—"Smiling Jack" Adams, manager of Detroit's tired Red Wings, wasn't smiling tonight as his squad took the ice at Maple Leaf Gardens for the third game of the Stanley Cup's final series against the New York Rangers. For, the rip-roaring Broadway Blues skated the legs off his charges last Thursday in beating them, 3 to 1, and deadlocking the series at one game each.

So, Jittery Jack put in a hurry call to Indianapolis and brought up five members of the Detroit farm team which just won the American Hockey League crown. Three of them were scheduled to play against the Rangers in the final "home" game for the Blues at the Maple Leaf Gardens, while two regulars and two replacements from Omaha who had shone in previous cup games, were benched.

Slowinski in Starting Line

Meanwhile Lynn Patrick, coach of the surprising Rangers, was having one real worry—how to keep his boys from again becoming overconfident. He started his line of Don Raleigh, Pentti Lund and Ed Slowinski, the top scoring trio in the play-offs with 21 points among them in seven games.

Edgar Laprade, back in form, centered the line with Tony Leswick and Dunc Fisher, each of whom showed to much better advantage last Thursday. Skating with Buddy O'Connor were Jack Gordon and Nick Mickoski.

Ted Lindsay, Detroit ace who has been a scoreless flop in the play-offs, was a doubtful starter right up to game time. He returned to the line-up Thursday after having missed the opening game in Detroit because of a bad back and the doctor all he showed he might just as well have remained on the sidelines.

Adams said after that game that "Lindsay was terrible." And now he has decided to bench Pete Babando, a hard-hitting forward, and Steve Black, a young rookie who had been doing a good job on the backline.

Marcel Pronovost and Larry Wilson, two recent recruits from

(Continued on page 2, column 6)

Navy Nine Tops Columbia, 8-4, In Ivy Opener

Middies Hand Lions 3d Loss in Row on 13-Hit Attack Behind Hawkins' Hurling

Special to the Herald Tribune

ANNAPOLIS, Md., April 15.—Navy combined a thirteen-hit attack with the four-hit pitching of right-hander Bill Hawkins to win the Eastern Intercollegiate Baseball League's 1950 opener here today, 8 to 4.

It was victory number two for Hawkins this season—he has lost one—and was Navy's third victory in six starts. Columbia's loss was its third straight without winning.

The Midshipmen scored once in the first inning and added two more in the second on third-baseman Pat Corrigan's home run with a mate aboard. Four Navy runs crossed the plate in the fifth frame on four hits, a sacrifice and an error.

Columbia did all of its scoring in the top half of the seventh with two singles, three walks, and a two-base error.

George Smith started on the mound for the Lions but retired for a pinch hitter after giving up thirteen hits and three bases on balls in the six innings he worked. He was relieved by Kermit Tracy

(Continued on page 2, column 7)

Jansen, Koslo, Jones Combine On Two-Hitter

New York Blasts Bearden for 7 Runs in 5th; Now Trails in Series, 9 to 8

By Ed Sinclair

CLEVELAND, April 15.—In the frigid cavern that is Municipal Stadium, the New York Giants whipped the Cleveland Indians, 9 to 0, today, and Larry Jansen proved conclusively his right to be the Giants' opening-day pitcher next Tuesday for the third year in a row.

The ace right-hander of the Polo Grounds entry in the National League pennant race looked his very best as he pitched three near-perfect innings while his teammates mobbed Gene Bearden to end a three-game losing streak.

Janse, working strongly and with his characteristic 'guile, faced only nine men and retired them with dispatch. In his last inning, the third, he walked the lead-off batter, fanned the next one and then induced Luke Easter to hit into a double play which he started himself.

Koslo Jones Also Star

Jansen's performance began a happy day for the Giants in every respect. Dave Koslo, New York's best left-hander, and Sheldon Jones, the No. 2 right-hander, divided the last six innings and allowed but one hit apiece while maintaining the shutout.

Meanwhile, their teammates took all sorts of freedoms with the Cleveland mound staff. They picked a run from Early Wynn in the second inning, persecuted Bearden for seven runs in the fifth and made their final score in the seventh off the services of Mike Garcia.

Wynn and Garcia, two very able right-handers, got along well enough for the Indians, but Bearden was practically helpless. The southpaw, who just two seasons ago was a major factor in the world's championship coming to Cleveland, had one of the worst days in his training.

Yields Five Walks in Fifth

After downing the Giants in the fourth, he went all to pieces. He allowed five bases on balls to which the Giants added four singles. Alvin Dark chased two runs home with a shot into center field, and Eddie Stanky accounted for two more with a blooper over third base.

There wasn't much hope for the Indians after that, especially in the light of Koslo's and Jones's work. Koslo had given up a desultory single in the fourth. In the

(Continued on page 2, column 1)

Anglers Jam Jersey Streams As State Trout Season Opens

NEWARK, N. J., April 15 (AP).—Trout was sizzling in many a New Jersey frying pan tonight.

Fishermen by the thousands flocked to the state's streams and ponds for the opening day of the season.

From reports of official and non-official observers, plenty of trout were caught.

Chief Warden Fred C. Craig said the streams were running high, but in "fishable condition."

The day was sunny but chilly. Ice lined the watersides when fishermen arrived. The air temperature was 38 degrees.

The roads leading to such favorite spots as the Musconetcong, Flatbrook, Rockaway, Pequest and other areas were jammed with cars by sunup.

An hour before the 8 a. m. opening time, one observer said fishermen were driving "bumper to bumper" on Routes 6 and 10 toward the more than 200,000 brook and rainbow trout which were planted in scores of brooks, ponds and rivers.

Newspapermen who ventured into the mass of waving trout rods and nets reported good catches were made. One editor said the crowd this year was at least as good as last year's—with "possibly a few more this year."

Not everyone was able to drive to the fishing spots.

West Orange police reported one of their patrol cars overtook three lads at 3 a. m., hiking to Diamond Mill Pond, Millburn. By 4:30 a. m., the boys had breakfast

(Continued on page 5, column 8)

4 Runs Follow Homer in 5th By DiMaggio

12,632 Electrified By Clipper's Catch

Brooklyn Held to 3 Hits; Lopat, Raschi Impress; Roe Routed; Byrne Wild

By Al Laney

The Yankees and Dodgers played their exhibition game at the Stadium yesterday in weather that was first sunny and cold and then rainy and colder with 12,632 fans sitting it out through a very good and interesting contest. The Yankees won, 6 to 4, by concentrating on the left-handed offerings of Preacher Roe for five runs in the fifth inning after the Preacher had blanked them for four with no hits at all.

But these runs and the others scored by both teams do not constitute the important news about the game. Nor, for that matter, does the excellent pitching of Ed Lopat and Vic Raschi, who shut out Brooklyn with one scratch hit through the first six innings. The big thing is the performance of Joe DiMaggio, who made perhaps one of his greatest catches of a ball hit by Roy Campanella and then started off the big inning by hitting a home run deep into the lower left-field stand.

Proves DiMaggio Ready

DiMaggio's catch, for which he had to run a very long way, almost to the wall in left center-field, showed beyond any possible doubt that this great player is in shape. For, to pull this one down in the old DiMaggio way required perfect judgment.

It was a mighty drive that the catcher hit off Raschi in the fifth and it did not seem possible that the ball could be caught when it left the bat. It began to seem possible only at the very end when DiMaggio's loping stride carried him near a converging point.

He stuck out his glove at the last moment and grabbed it with the grace that he always has had.

The Clipper was the first batter in the next Yankee turn and when he swung on Roe's pitch the Yankees were on their way to their first victory of the spring over the Dodgers. They made another run in the seventh off Willie Ramsdell.

The Dodgers made all their runs off Tommy Byrne, who pitched the last three innings. Byrne walked five. He allowed three runs in the seventh and the other in the eighth. But Byrne gave only two hits to bring the Brooklyn total to three. And his triple was the next longest hit of the game after DiMaggio's homer.

Roe Pounded in Fifth

The big Yankee inning, as noted, began with DiMaggio's blow and did not appear likely to develop much when Berra, who made two of the three outs, hit weakly to second. But then Billy Johnson, John Lindell, Billy Martin and Raschi hit safely and solidly in succession off Roe, and, since Martin's blow was a double, three runs were in, making the total four.

That was all for Roe and Pod-

(Continued on page 2, column 4)

Manhattan Beats St. John's, 1-0, on Lone Hit in 12th

The Manhattan College baseball team, held hitless for eleven innings by Jack Gordon, got its first and only hit in the twelfth inning and defeated St. John's at Dexter Park yesterday in a Metropolitan Collegiate Baseball Conference game.

The Jaspers' tally came with two out in the twelfth after Gordon struck out the first two men, Jack Cassidy and Ray McCourt. However, Howie Kelly was safe at first base when the Redmen's shortstop threw wide to first. Then Regis King slashed a sharp single to right sending Kelly to third. Gordon, unnerved by the hit, walked Don Mortalbano, loading the bags.

Then Jerry Lowe rapped a sharp grounder to short and the shortstop bobbled the ball for his second and miscue of the inning and Kelly scampered across the plate with the clincher.

Jack Meagher, who pitched the route for the Kelly Green gave up three hits, retired the St. John's batters in order and preserved the margin of victory.

The triumph was Manhattan's third in four conference starts this season. St. John's suffered its second setback against a single triumph.

The score by innings:

Manhattan ... 000 000 000 001—1 1 1
St. John's ... 000 000 000 000—0 3 2
Meagher and Pelca (8), Cassidy; Gordon and Tully.

Associated Press wirephoto

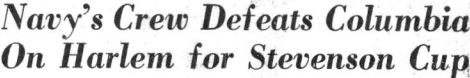

XPERIMENTAL NO. 2 FINISH: Lotowhite, foreground, with Sam Boulmetis up, crosses finish line ahead of Royal Castle (center, rear) and Sturdy One (on rail)

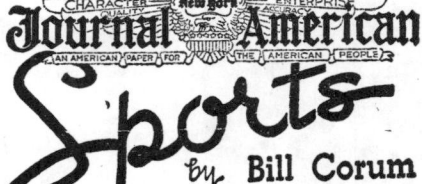

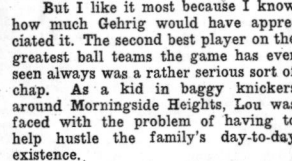

THE BEGINNING . . . The Giants and the Phillies put on some fistic fireworks at Shibe Park with Ed Stanky and Andy Seminick the key figures. Stankey waved arms when Andy was at bat, after Giants had agreed not to attempt strategy." Seminick retaliated by sliding hard into second, knocking down Bill Rigney. Here Seminick and Rigney are being separated by players and umps.

. . . AND THE END . . . Moments later, as Giant and Phil players traded swings, both benches emptied and more than 40 players rushed on the field. Focal points (arrows) show Phil coach Dusty Cooke (32) holding back a Giant while at left the players are gathered around some fighters on the ground. Final result: Stanky, Rigney and Seminick were tossed out of the game, order was restored, but the Giants announced they were playing the game under protest. A triple by Stan Lopata and a long outfield fly by Ed Waitkus brought in the wining run in 11th as Phils won, 5 to 4 and protected their National League lead.

AP Wirephotos

CHARACTER · QUALITY · New York · ACCURACY · ENTERPRISE
Journal-American
AN AMERICAN PAPER FOR THE AMERICAN PEOPLE

Yanks Win; Fists Fly as Giants Bow

Sports by Bill Corum

This Is a 'Natural' And Typical of Mel . . — Are Yanks Near End Of Another Era?

GEHRIG WOULD HAVE LIKED THE IDEA

That's a nice thing that Mel Allen is doing in establishing a Lou Gehrig scholarship at Columbia Univ. out of the proceeds from Mel Allen Day at the Yankee Stadium. It's typical of the sort of fellow that the "Alabama Nightingale" is, and it will add a dignity to the occasion that it would not otherwise have. Not even with the dignified Jim Farley serving as chairman of the event.

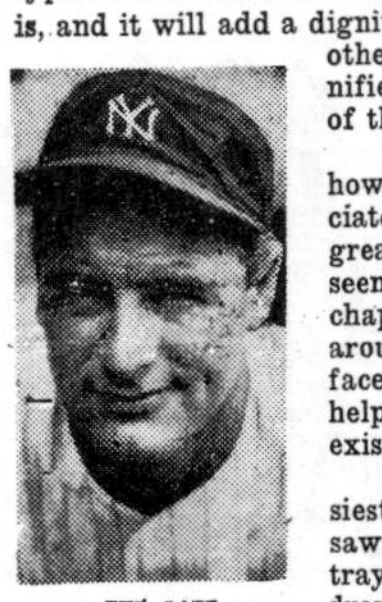

THE LATE LOU GEHRIG

But I like it most because I know how much Gehrig would have appreciated it. The second best player on the greatest ball teams the game has ever seen always was a rather serious sort of chap. As a kid in baggy knickers around Morningside Heights, Lou was faced with the problem of having to help hustle the family's day-to-day existence.

He must have been about the clumsiest waiter on tables that anybody ever saw. But he was in there banging those trays around with a will and trying to drop a few less dishes every day. Which was the way Lou learned everything, including how to hit and play first base.

Just dogged perseverance and the will to do it was what made Gehrig a great ball player. I used to see him doing it in the long Spring twilights on old South Field even before I knew his name. I was about to say, "working at it." But baseball was play for Lou and in those years he never got enough of it.

Night Baseball Without Lights:

When he quit and went home, it was really dark. But the next evening and practically every evening save Sunday, he would be out there swinging a bat and galloping around shagging flies again. I guess that must have been when Coach Andy Coakley and Scout Paul Kritchell, who combed the college diamonds for the Yanks first started noticing him.

I have said that Gehrig was second best of the GREAT YANKEES and that was true. There was only one Ruth. And there won't be another. But there was a period in there when "five o'clock lightning" was wont to strike at the Stadium, when Gehrig was an even more dangerous hitter than Ruth.

Anyhow, when the pair of them came up there back to back, the opposing pitcher wasn't getting any lollipop to quiet his nerves.

And when that disease, somehow to me still unbelievably, struck at Lou, I think he was underneath his smile the first to know that his number was up.

But he never complained. It wouldn't have been in him to do so. I'm sure those who were there will never forget that day in the Stadium when he said: "I'm the happiest man in the world."

So this is a fine thing that Broadcaster Allen, the Yanks and baseball are doing. A "natural," as we say in sports.

My feeling about "Days" for people is that they can easily be overdone. That they are better when they are widely spaced, since there is no escaping that they have, at best, a faint aura of trying to squeeze the orange to the last drop.

The Dog Show Mustn't Wave the Sport:

Give-aways and fat man's races and dog shows, etc., are all well and good up to a certain point. But a little of them can go a long way, it seems to me, if we're not going to come to the place where the dog show is waving the championship baseball.

When the game is no longer the thing in a ball park, then the game is in trouble.

I shall be there on August 23 to add my mite to Brother Allen's afternoon. But it strikes me that the Yanks are just now faced with a far more serious problem than conducting girls' baseball games in their big store.

How about conducting some better and more successfully concluded men's games?

It's not so much that the team isn't making gestures at the moment as if it may be going to win the pennant. Which I don't think it is. That isn't so bad. Surely they have won their share in recent years, so that a change of venue won't do baseball any harm.

But what are they going to do for DiMaggios next year, and in the years just ahead?

An era, the greatest one of all, ended with the passing of Babe and Lou. Then along came the flawless Clipper to take up the slack and make the fans forget. Now the DiMaggio era is drawing to a close. One of the most difficult things about success is that it is so hard to follow.

Where do we go from here? That's the real problem that faces George Weiss and the Yankee organization now. They are not going to solve it by presenting the man on the flying trapeze. When a fellow wants to see the circus, the place to go is the circus.

Reynolds Tops A's

Woodling's Hitting Paces 7-2 Victory

By Hugh Bradley

Operating in the manner of a bunch of big guys stealing candy from a band of babies, our Yankees had a prosperous afternoon at the Stadium yesterday. Socking slingers Carl Scheib and Bobby Shantz for nine hits, when the blows counted, the Stengeleers romped to a 7 to 2 victory over the apathetic Athletics, while taking a 2 to 1 lead in the four game series.

With the Tigers idle, the triumph enabled the Yankees to cut down the first place margin of the Bengals to three lengths. And as the White Sox upended Cleveland, it also moved the Yanks back into second place, half game ahead of the Indians.

DULL GAME.

Witnessed by a ladies' day crowd of 34,460—which included 18,618 full price customers—the game was one of the most uninteresting of the year. Actually the Stengeleers did not have to extend themselves at any time.

Apparently merely going through the motions until the final paychecks arrive at the finish of the season, the Macks performed in a fashion that would have brought salvoes of boos on any sandlot. While making only two errors for the record, the infield and the outfield were listless while failing to go after balls that where scored as base hits.

EASY FOR ALLIE.

Achieving his tenth triumph of the season against a like number of losses, Allie Reynolds had no trouble while going the route for the tenth time this year. Albeit not quite as sharp as usual, while issuing six passes, Wahoo merely toyed with the Athletics at times when hits could have counted if combined with the walks.

In the first, a pass to Eddie Joost was combined with a sacrifice and singles by Paul Lehner and Sam Chapman for the Mack's first tally. The other came in the fourth when little Bobby Shantz, the southpaw slinger, socked a homer into the leftfield stands.

Otherwise Reynolds kept the blows well scattered while also keeping down his mark for extra bases. During the last 39 innings he has permitted 44 hits but only a double and two homers have been included in the lot.

With Gene Woodling starring on the attack with three hits, including his second inside the park homer of the year, the Yankees wrapped up their triumph early.

The second frame was the big one. Doubles by Yogi Berra and Phil Rizzuto, hitting in his sixth straight game, were combined with singles by Reynolds and Woodling to do the damage in that session. Ten men came to the plate, three of them drawing passes, while five runs were being racked up off Schibe.

PHILADELPHIA	ab	r	h	o	a	NEW YORK	ab	r	h	o	a
Joost,ss	4	1	1	2	3	Woodling,lf	5	2	3	3	0
McC'cky,lf	1	0	0	1	0	Rizzuto,ss	4	0	1	1	1
Lehner,rf	5	0	1	1	0	Bauer,rf	4	0	0	3	0
Chapm'n,cf	4	0	3	0	0	Mize,1b	3	0	0	5	0
Fain,1b	4	0	0	11	1	Collins,1b	1	0	0	3	0
Hitchc'k,2b	4	0	0	2	7	Berra,c	4	1	1	4	1
Wahl,3b	4	0	1	2	2	Brown,ss	3	2	1	1	3
Tipton,c	3	0	1	4	0	Mapes,cf	3	0	0	3	0
Scheib,p	1	0	1	0	0	Coleman,2b	3	1	2	4	2
Shantz,p	3	1	1	1	1	Reynolds,p	4	1	1	0	1
Totals	33	2	9	24	14	Totals	34	7	9	27	8

Philadelphia	100	100	000—2
NEW YORK	050	110	00x—7

E—Joos, Hitchcock. RBI—Chapman, Shantz, Reynolds 2, Woodling 2, Rizzuto, Mize, Coleman. 2B—Berra, Rizzuto. 3B—Brown. HR—Shantz, Woodling. S—McCosky, Mapes. DP—Coleman and Collins; Rizzuto, Coleman and Collins. LEFT—Philadelphia 12, New York 8. BB—Scheib 2, Shantz 2, Reynolds 7. SO—Shantz 3, Reynolds 3. HO—Scheib 4, in 1 1-3 innings; Shantz, 5 in 6 2-3 innings. WINNER—Reynolds (1-10). LOSER—Scheib (3-8). U—Rommel, Hurley and McGowan. T—2:28. A—18,618 paid.

Pair For Widener

Travers to Lights Up, Battlefied in Special

By Pat Lynch

SARATOGA SPRINGS, N. Y., Aug. 12.—Before what was problong history, George D. Widener's Lights Up won the 81st edition of ably the largest crowd in the Spa's the Travers Stakes yesterday afternoon by three lengths over Bed O'Roses. Passemson was third in 2:03 for a mile and a quarter, third fastest running of the nation's oldest stake since Man O'War required 2:01 4-5 in 1920.

The sun-drenched throng numbered an unofficial 24,488. This was only 174 short of the record numbered tabulated the following afternoon Aug. 17, 1946.

The handle for this event reached $147,011 while for the eight-race program, a total of $1,-139,924 passed through the mutuel machines.

SPECIAL TO BATTLEFIELD.

It was a gratifying day for Jockey Club Chairman Widener. As an appetizer, he fielded the successful $4 choice, Battlefield, in the Saratoga Special. The East's leading juvenile defeated Northern Star by three parts of a length for a winner take all tab of $11,500.

In this event, George Hettinger's loss of his whip at the head of the stretch aboard Northern Star was a factor in Battlefield's victory.

The same Hettinger contributed compellingly to the $16,350 pickup for Lights Up by a well judged ride in the Travers. The three-year-old son of Eight Thirty collared Passemson inside the final sixteenth, then had enough go left to hold the favored Bed O' Roses safe at the wire.

Lights Up paid $6.30, $2.90 and $3.00. Bed O'Roses was $2.90 and $2.70. Passemson, who cut out the pace, was $6.60 for third.

FIELD REDUCED.

With Middleground and Hill Prince on the side lines, the Travers field was cut to nine when Greek Ship, Dooly and Admiral's Pride were scratched prior to the race. Overnight, Brandywine Stable's Greek Song, winner of the Arlington Futurity by a nose, was withdrawn because of a threatened bow in his right leg. He is through for the year.

A decided factor in Lights Up victory was his comparitively lightweight of 110 pounds. In addition, of course, to the ride given by Hettinger.

Lights Up is the kind of a colt that doesn't give his best when allowed to get free and clear early. It cost him a victory in the Saranac Handicap recently when he moved to the front too soon.

This time Hettinger sat still, content to let Passemson cut out the running. Bed O' Roses, better placed early than normally, was third most of the trip.

TAKES LEAD IN STRETCH.

Passemson had a commanding lead entering the stretch, but with a sixteenth to go, Hettinger set down on Lights Up. The colt drew clear and appeared well on his way home, but Hettinger whacked him stoutly a couple of times for insurance as Bed O' Roses couldn't make it. Mr. Trouble was fourth.

It was Lights Up's fourth victory in 16 starts this season, spent in the main chasing Middleground and Hill Prince. Prior to this afternoon, his most notable performance was a second to Middleground in the Belmont Stakes at scale weights and in his last, was beaten a nose by Greek Ship at Monmouth Park.

Dodgers Bow, 10-2

Braves Coast Home On 7 Flock Errors

By Michael Gaven

BOSTON, Aug. 12.—The Dodgers fell apart completely tonight, committing seven errors that enabled the Boston Braves to rack up an easy 10 to 2 victory before 34,732, largest Braves Field crowd of the season.

Warren Spahn coasted to his 15th victory as every man in the Boston lineup got at least one hit and scored at least one time. Don Newcombe, first of three Dodger hurlers, was the loser, and was followed by Chris Van Cuyk and Billy Loes. The loss left the Brooks seven games out of the lead.

The Braves stepped off in front in the second when Sid Gordon doubled and scored on a single by Willard Marshall and the Dodgers tied it up in the third which saw them woefully miss an opportunity to blow the game wide open.

To be sure, they needed four bases on balls and an error to score one run. After retiring the first six batters, thanks no end to Buddy Kerr's double play stab of a liner by Duke Snider, Spahn walked Campanella and Cox with none out.

Newcombe then struck out after a feeble attempt to bunt and Campanella permitted himself to be picked off second. With one out, Spahn walked Reese and Russell but all this merely loaded the bases. The Dodgers finally got their tally when Hartsfield booted Snider's easy bounder all over the infield.

BRAVES GET LEAD.

The Brooks had tried their best to hand the Braves a run in the first when Reese erred and Campanella was charged with a boot, which should also have gone to Peewee. But two strikeouts by Newcombe offset the errors.

Big Newk wasn't so successful in the home third as the Tribe regained the lead, Hartsfield got a double on a bad hop over Cox's head and took third on an infield out. Campanella seemed to have the runner picked off but the throw got away from Cox and the catcher was again charged with the error, his second.

After having played for more than two seasons without committing more than three errors in a game, the Dodgers ran their total to five in the fourth as a pair of miscues by Furillo handed the Braves two more runs.

Kerr singled with one out and when Spahn followed suit, Furillo fumbled the ball, permitting Kerr to take third. The right fielder then threw the ball into the stands behind third base and the umpires waved Kerr home and Spahn to third. The latter scored on a single by Jethroe with two out.

Newcombe finally gave up a run without any assistance from his supporting cast in the fifth but before the inning was over his mates had chucked the Braves two more on as many more errors. The horrible details follow:

INFIELD FOLDS.

Elliott singled, Cooper doubled and an intentional pass to Gordon loaded the bases. Robinson fielded Marshall's grounder without mishap and forced Elliott at the plate. Newcombe then walked Kerr to force home a run.

But the infield was not to be outdone. Spahn's bounder to Reese should have been an easy double play. But Robinson threw

Continued on Fourth Sports Page

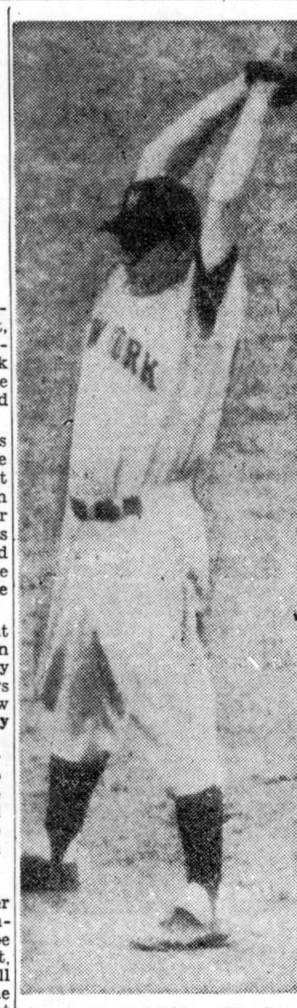

PRECOCIOUS . . . The Brat, Ed Stanky, makes like a prisoner of war as he attempts to bother Seminick at bat. This started the fightin' (above pictures) and put Ed out of the game in fourth inning.

Miss Jahn Upset In Tennis Final

BALTIMORE, Aug. 12 AP).—Patsy Zellmer of San Diego, Calif., upset top-seeded Laura Lou Jahn of Clearwater, Fla., today to win the Middle Atlantic girls tennis tournament.

The third-seeded California girl dropped the first set of the final match 2-6, but recovered to trounce her tiring opponent 6-3, 6-4 in the next two.

PHILS WIN IN 11 AFTER BRAWL, 5-4

Stanky Arm-Waving as Seminick Bats, Touches off Fight; 3 Booted

By Barney Kremenko

PHILADELPHIA, Aug. 12.—In the stormiest free-for-all Philadelphia has seen since Ty Cobb cut Frank (Home Run) Baker with flying spikes 39 years ago, the New York Giants and the Philadelphia Phillies engaged in a wild swinging, hectic Donnybrook before 23,741 Kids' Day onlookers at Shibe Park here this afternoon.

The Phillies won the game, 5-4, in 11 innings, but that was entirely incidental to the other exciting developments.

There has been bitter feeling brewing between the two clubs for some time, but it took a fistic scuffle between Bill Rigney of the Giants and Philly catcher Andy Seminick to touch off the real fireworks.

EVERYBODY SWINGS.

Once they started swining at each other just as the fourth inning ended, every man on both benches came streaming on the field to join the melee.

When the four umpires and four city policemen had finally brought order, Rigney and Seminick were banished from the game and umpire Lee Ballanfant had to talk the police out of taking first baseman Tookie Gilbert of the Giants to jail. They claimed Gilbert directed profane language at them.

OUT GOES STANKY.

Behind it all lurked the figure of Edward Raymond Stanky, the Brat. As a matter of fact, when the big fight broke out he had already been in the dressing room, heaved out of the game some moments earlier.

In the game of the night before, whenever Seminick came to bat, Stanky took a position behind second base, directly in line of Andy's view, and waved his arms just as the pitch was to come over the plate.

This not only incensed Seminick, but owner Bob Carpenter and Manager Eddie Sawyer of the Phillies as well. Carpenter and Sawyer protested to the umpires, claiming it was confusing the batter.

A GOOD BOY.

There is nothing in the rules which says that Stanky's arm-waving is illegal, but the four arbiters—Lon Warneke, Al Barlick, Augie Donatelli and Lee Ballanfant—got together and delegated Barlick to go to the Giants' dressing room before today's game and talk to Leo Durocher.

"Leo was very, very nice about it," reported Barlick, "and agreed to tell Stanky to cut it out until such time that we could get the league president, Ford Frick, to give us a ruling."

Then the game began. The first time Seminick came to the plate, in the second inning, Stanky didn't move. He just folded his arms and stood frozen—and he did it so that everybody in the park could notice that he was being a good boy.

Something happened shortly after, that changed the Giants' attitude.

Seminick walked and the next

Continued on Fourth Sports Page

The Box Score

NEW YORK	ab	r	h	o	a	PHILADELPHIA	ab	r	h	o	a
Stanky,2b	2	0	0	2	4	Waitkus,1b	4	0	1	5	2
L'hrke,3-2b	3	1	2	2	4	Ashburn,cf	4	0	0	6	0
Lockman,lf	5	0	2	1	0	Sisler,lf	5	0	0	3	0
Mueller,rf	6	0	3	1	0	Ennis	5	0	1	2	1
Th'pson,3b	1	0	0	0	1	W. Jones,3b	5	0	0	3	0
Rig'y,3b-2b	1	0	0	1	1	Hamner,ss	5	1	2	2	3
Irvin,3b	2	0	1	1	0	Seminick,c	1	1	0	3	0
Westrum,c	6	0	0	2	0	Lopata,c	3	1	1	5	0
Thomson,cf	6	1	2	2	0	Goliat,2b	4	2	2	3	1
Dark,ss	5	1	1	4	6	Roberts,p	2	0	1	0	1
Gilbert,1b	5	0	2	14	1	b-Nicholson	1	0	1	0	0
S.Jones,p	0	0	0	0	0	c-Caballero	0	0	0	0	0
aWeatherly	1	0	0	0	0	Konstanty,p	0	0	0	1	0
Kramer,p	0	1	0	1	1	d-Bl'dworth	0	0	0	0	0
Koslo,p	1	0	0	0	1	K. Johnson	0	0	0	0	0
Totals	44	4	13	*31	19	Totals	39	5	9	33	8

*One out when winning run scored.
a—Struck out for S. Jones in 4th.
b—Singled for Roberts in 7th.
c—Ran for Nicholson in 7th.
d—Walked for Konstanty in 11th.
e—Ran for Bloodworth in 11th.

NEW YORK	010	002	100	00—4
PHILADELPHIA	030	000	100	01—5

Stanky, Mueller 2, Thomson, Goliat, Roberts, E—Goliat, Dark, Gilbert, Lockman. RBI—Waitkus 2. 2B—Hamner. 3B—Lopata. HR—Thomson. SB—Ashburn. S—S. Jones, Konstanty. DP—Goliat and Waitkus; Dark, Lohrke and Gilbert; Stanky, Dark and Gilbert, Thomson, Stanky and Gilbert. LEFT—New York 14, Philadelphia 9. BB—Roberts 6, Jones 2, Kramer 1, Koslo 3. SO—Roberts 3, Koslo 1. Konustanty 1, Jones 1. HO—Jones, 4 in 3 innings; Kramer, 1 in 3 1-3; Koslo, 4 in 4 1-3; Roberts, 11 in 7; Konstanty, 2 in 4. WP—Roberts. WINNER—Konstanty (10-4) . LOSER—Koslo (11-10). U—Donatelli, Ballanfant, Warneke and Barlik. A—14,955. T—2:55.

Aussie Cuppers Win Doubles For 2 to 1 Lead Over Sweden

By David Eisenberg

RYE, N. Y. Aug. 12—Australia gained a most important point in its Davis Cup Inter-zone tennis final against Sweden here at the Westchester Country Club this afternoon. It won doubles to gain a 2-1 lead.

John Bromwich, the man who scored in the singles yesterday, was the key factor in the doubles as well. He teamed with Frank Sedgman to beat the Swedish pair of Lennart Bergelin, yesterday's Davis Cup hero, and Sven Davidsson 6-1, 7-5, 7-5.

ROMP IN 1ST SET.

Now Australia needs but one more point to qualify for the challenge cup matches against the United States two weeks hence. A victory for Bromwich or Sedgman, in their final singles tussles against Torsten Johansson or Bergelin, respectively, tomorrow, will do the trick .

Bromwich and Sedgman encountered little opposition in the first set. The Swedes, especially the 20-year-old youngster Davidsson, were nervous in that opening set. The Aussies cracked through Davidsson's service in the third game to gain a 2-1 lead and then raced right through the next four for the set.

But the Swedes settled down in the second set and made quite a battle of it.

The break did not come until the 12th game when Davidsson weakened. He was serving. He made one great stand at match-point when he fell as the ball came to him. He managed to get it over the net, rise in time to make another return and then score a point. But he banged a forehand into the net and then Bergelin missed an easy smash for the set.

The Swedes dominated most of the third set. But again they weakened at the end. First they broke through Bromwich in the opening game. They held that margin going right up to a 5—4 score.

But after reaching set-point on Bergelin's service, the Swedes lost out. First Davisson netted one. Then the same youngster hit out twice, losing the game and squaring the set at 5-all.

Sedgman easily held his own service in the next game. Then came the break through Davidsson. The Aussies had a little luck on their side. Twice Bromwich hit the top of the net, the ball each time taking a high bound over Bergelin for a scoring point. The second put the Aussies at match point.

Lone Run

Bobby Brown (at left) scored for the Yankees on Jerry Coleman's fly to left in the fourth inning of the World Series opener. Andy Seminick is the Phils' catcher and Jocko Conlon the plate umpire.

★

Shortstop Granny Hamner of the Phils (below) makes a futile dive for Vic Raschi's line single in the third inning.

★

Raschi, Yankees Win

CHICAGO DAILY NEWS sports
46 ★★★★ WEDNESDAY, OCT. 4, 1950.

Sox Open Way for Hornsby

PHILADELPHIA — (Special) —The way is open for Rogers Hornsby to manage the White Sox in 1951. He hasn't been hired and "Red" Corriden hasn't been fired, but general manager Frank Lane said: "I certainly would not oppose the selection of Hornsby. I regard him as one of the finest baseball men I know."

Of Corriden's work this year, Lane said: "We made a definite improvement when he replaced Onslow, but we have made no arrangements with anybody for next year."

Besides Lane, the Sox party here includes Vice-President Chuck and Mrs. Comiskey, plus other attaches.

"We will get together on a manager for 1951 after the series," said Lane. "The job is open to anybody, including Corriden."

A DAY'S WORK

Yanks Not Steamed Up Over Win

PHILADELPHIA —(AP)— You would have thought the New York Yankees had just lost a World Series game the way they sat lined up on benches facing each other in the narrow, steamy dressing room reserved for visiting clubs.

Vic Raschi, who had just spun the 12th two-hit pitching job in World Series records, was as glum as the rest. He was pale, with his thinning hair pasted down on his forehead.

"Tough? Sure it was tough. They're all tough," he said, and began to smile a little.

* * *

"MY BEST ball? It was my fast ball. That's what I struck out Mike Goliat with in the fifth."

That was the one big Philadelphia threat when singles by Puddinhead Jones and Andy Seminick put men on first and second.

"It was good, though. I was sweating all the way."

The collar of his uniform was wet and there were patches of damp at his shoulders.

* * *

THE FEELING you got from him and the rest of the quiet Yankee team was that they were good, professional workmen who had just done a satisfactory, polished job, and now they were catching their breath.

Was everything all right, someone asked Raschi.

"I hurt my knee in the first inning fielding Richit Ashburn's grounder—twisted it a little, but not bad."

This is the twelfth two hit game in the World Series, someone said proudly.

"Is that right," and Raschi smiled broadly. "Shudda been a one hitter, though. That single Jones got in the fifth—I thought it was hit real hard and got out of the way of it. It was just a dribbler."

* * *

WHAT was your impression of the Phillies?"

"Impression? They're a good ball club." Raschi smiled. "Impression? We gotta play 'em three more times."

Meaning he thinks the Yankees will win the series in four straight.

"Were you relieved when Jones got a hit—I mean, the pressure of pitching a no-hitter in the World Series was off then?"

"Relieved? No." Raschi snapped. "It meant they had a man on base."

* * *

WILL YOU pitch again, he was asked.

"I hope I don't have to come back. I'll be ready as soon as Casey (Stengel) says."

Expert testimony came from catcher Yogi Berra. "Was tsis the best game Raschi pitched all season?"

Yogi, swarthy and solemn, knitted his brows.

"No," he said, "there was a game out in Cleveland. It was a better game, exceptin' this was in the World Series."

BACK TO WALL—Del Ennis, Phillies' right fielder, hits the wall in vain effort to catch foul fly hit by Johnny Mize in third inning of the series opener. Ball is shown dropping to the ground as fans' faces show varying emotions.

Phillies Lose 1-0 On 2 Hits

Continued from first page.

nolds, (16-12) who pitches here tomorrow against Robin Roberts (20-10, bested Don Newcombe with two hits a year ago this time in Yankee Stadium. (Casey Stengel announced that Ed Lopat, the southpaw, will open the third game in New York.)

* * *

KONSTANTY'S experience as a trouble-shooter helped him weather a first-inning in which Woodling walked on five pitches and Ruzzuto singled to left.

Berra, Di Maggio and Mize, the big three of the Yank batting order couldn't get Woodling any further than third and the partisan fans exulted noisily as Ennis galloped under the third out.

The second frame was a breeze. But when Raschi opened the third with a single through Hamner and Woodling again walked, another Phil pitcher began warming up in the bullpen.

Once more Berra failed, this time on a fly to Sisler in short left and Di Maggio was promptly passed to fill the bases, even though it meant that Konstanty had to face the southpaw swinging Mize.

The big guy popped to Jones and the Yanks had left five men stranded out of 14 hitters.

* * *

BUT THE Phils nullified this sterling mound chore by going down in order the first time around, only one man (Goliat) getting the ball out of the infield as Raschi and Berra handled five of the first nine men.

The third Yankee hit was Brown's double to left that opened the fourth and for the third time the defending champions had a men on third with one out when Brown scampered there after Ashburn ran down Bauer's long drive.

Not even Konstanty could get out of this jam and Coleman's long fly to Sisler let Brown score.

* * *

RASCHI RAN his string of hitless innings to four and a third before Jones finally broke the spell with a ground-single past second which Rizzuto couldn't quite reach.

The customers made quite a fuss over this sudden show of life and when Seminick hit safely to left (after Hamner flied for the second out) even the Phil bench began to look alive.

Goliat fouled off the first pitch with such force that the ball got through Berra and hit Umpire Jocke Conlan on the right arm. Time had to be called while Conlan was administered to and then Goliat went down swinging.

* * *

DI MAGGIO hit one into the stands in the sixth but it was foul and he settled for a walk. Once again Mize popped to Jones and although Brown smacked one on the nose the ball sailed into Ennis' hands and Bauer forced Di Maggio.

That lone run was assuming magnified proportions as Konstanty fanned to open the home sixth.

Then Waitkus got the first walk off Raschi but became the third Phil to perish on the bases as Ashburn flied to Di Maggio and Sisler popped to Mize.

Raschi was on base again in the seventh when Jones threw his grounder low for an error after the same Jones had tossed out Coleman. Woodling's first hit was a single to center on which Raschi coasted into second.

* * *

THAT'S as far as anybody got in the wake of Rizzuto's infield fly and Berra's grounder to first.

In the face of this offensive ineptitude, Raschi continued to mow down the opposition. Getting Enuis, Jones and Hamner in the stand-up seventh, although Bauer had to fall against the wall to pick off Hamner's drive.

In that manager Stengel installed Johnny Hopp at first base and Bill Johnson at third for defensive purposes and the move was accomplished in time so that Hopp could dash to the box-seat railing for Seminick's twisting foul in the eighth.

* * *

BEHIND this out, Goliat lined to Coleman and Whitman, batting for Konstanty, pinned Bauer against the wall to retire the side.

The new Phil hurler was Russ Meyer, the ex-Cub, and he got off to a bad start when Bauer's bounder toward third caromed off Jones' bare hand for a hit. But nothing came of it.

Only three men stood between the Yanks and their 56th World Series' victory in this, their 17th appearance. The first was Waitkus, who grounded to Rizzuto. Ashburn shot a sizzler down the first-base line which Hopp corralled in time.

That made the issue a duel between Raschi and Sisler, whose home run clinched the Phil pennant in Brooklyn Sunday. Raschi won, striking out the Phil left-fielder.

Another 'Moose' Boosts Irish

BY HOWARD ROBERTS

From one "Moose" comes word that Notre Dame has another who is destined to keep the nickname prominent in the school's football history.

The new one is James "Moose" Dunlay, an 18-year-old sophomore who'll be at at left tackle on defense Saturday when the Irish meet Purdue at South Bend.

And apparently he is cut from the same pattern as Ed Krause, George Connor and Bill Fischer, who were called by the same descriptive name and who earned All-American honors in the line.

* * *

IT WAS Krause, now athletic director at his alma mater, who sang Dunlay's praise to the Chicago football writers at their weekly luncheon yesterday.

Krause pointed out how the youngster was instrumental in bringing victory to Notre Dame last Saturday in the 14-7 thriller with North Carolina.

Midway of the third quarter North Carolina was in possession of the ball on the Irish 3-yard-line, fourth down. Dick Bunting faded to pass but as he set himself to throw Dunlay tackled him and the pass went wide. Paul Burns intercepted and ran back to midfield.

"That," Krause declared, "was the turning point of the ball game."

* * *

DUNLAY, who is 6 feet 2 inches tall and weighs 205 pounds, has another omen other than his nickname in his favor. He comes from Oakmont, Pa., which is in the Pennsylvania football belt that has contributed Johnny Lujack, Leon Hart, John Masrangelo and Frank Spaniel to Notre Dame.

From this same area comes another sophomore who will see considerable service against Purdue. He is Ralph Paolone.

The Notre Dame offense should be at its peak for the Boilermakers. Billy Barrett has recovered from an ankle injury and Bill Gay's damaged heel has mended to the point where he can run with his old speed.

History Repeats for Coleman

PHILADELPHIA —(AP)— History repeated itself for young Gerry Coleman as the New York Yankees took the opening game of the 1950 World Series from the Philadelphia Phillies, 1-0.

Coleman's outfield fly in the fourth inning drove in the lone run as Vic Raschi's two-hit pitching overcame the fine effort by Jim Konstanty.

It was the third time in the last two years Coleman had a hand in a Yankee World Series victory.

* * *

COLEMAN'S fly to left field came after Bobby Brown opened the fourth inning with a double down the left field foul line and took third on Hank Bauer's fly to center field.

In the Yankee-Dodger classic last fall Coleman drove home the winning run in the ninth inning of the third game, a 4-3 test.

At Ebbets Field in the fifth and final game the Yankee second baseman from San Francisco drove in three runs in a 10-6 Yankee victory that ended the Series, four games to one.

The 26-year-old former Navy air force lieutenant went hitless in four trips today but he never will hit a more important fly ball. The ball was driven so deep to left field that Dick Sisler never had a chance to get Brown at the plate.

JUDSON FAILS DRAFT EXAM

Howie Judson, 24-year-old White Sox hurler, has been notified that he failed to pass his draft physical examination.

A native of Hebron, Ill., the former University of Illinois pitcher was released from service during World War II because of poor eyesight.

Fete Charles At Homecoming

CINCINNATI, Ohio—(AP)—New heavyweight champion Ezzard Charles, quite a fighter himself, has requested that the huge homecoming celebration set for him here this evening observe a moment of silence for the soldiers killed in World War II and the present Korean conflict.

Graziano, Burton Clash

Phil Kids Take Loss Like Men

PHILADELPHIA — (AP) — The Whiz Kids took their heart-breaking 1-to-0 defeat like adults today.

As the Philadelphia Phillies filed into their dressing room, outfielder Dick Sisler set the pace for this group of youngsters who caught the imagination of the baseball public. Sisler said:

"That guy (Vic) Raschi really had it today. We have to hand it to him. There's no use making excuses when you lose a well-played ball game like that."

There were several nods of approval. The Phillies were giving credit where it was due—to the fine Yankee pitcher, Raschi.

* * *

SISLER, the hero of the pennant-winning game in Brooklyn last Sunday, said he had no chance today to duplicate that flag-clinching three-run homer.

"Raschi had good control. He game me nothing good to hit at. Brother, I was really reaching for them. He had my number."

The Phillies were disappointed, not dejected. After all, they had played a good ball game and lost. The Yankees hadn't, as most of the experts predicted, blasted them out of the ball park.

* * *

JIM KONSTANTY, the Phil's surprise starting pitcher in the opener, stood in a corner surrounded by reporters. The bespectacled right hander who starred in the regular season as a premier relief pitcher, was feeling just a little low about the way New York scored the winning run.

"That (Bobby) Brown hit an awfully good pitch in the fourth for his double. It was a slider and I was real surprised when Brown hit it."

Then those two fly balls that "Hank" Bauer and "Gerry" Coleman hit. They were both my pet slider pitches. That's a great way to lose a ball game, one hit and two fly balls. I wouldn't have minded too much if they had scored with solid smashes. Oh well, I guess it just wasn't to be."

Konstanty said he is ready to pitch in relief again tomorrow if skipper Sawyer needs him.

Cards Obtain Swistowicz

The Chicago Cardinals added Mike Swistowicz to the squad today to replace Bob Nussbaumer, injured safety man.

Swistowicz was obtained from the New York Yanks on waivers.

Sunny and Cool For Second Game

PHILADELPHIA—(UP)—Sunny and cool weather was forecast for the second game of the 1950 World Series tomorrow.

Weather Bureau Forecaster Henry Adams said the temperature during game time would be in the lower 60's. Light northern breezes also were expected.

Adams said there was no hint of rain.

The Barber Shop

by JOHN P. CARMICHAEL

PHILADELPHIA—Not since that October day in 1929 when Howard Ehmke warmed up for the Athletics against the Cubs has a World Series crowd been as startled as by the announcement of Jim Konstanty going to the post for the Phillies this afternoon.

HOWARD EHMKE

On that day 21 years ago both George Earnshaw, the present Phil scout, and "Lefty" Grove were hoping for the inaugural assignment. A half hour before the game in Wrigley Field neither man had been nominated by manager Connie Mack. Finally they couldn't stand the strain of waiting. Earnshaw broke the ice by asking Grove: "You going?"

Grove shook his head. "You?" he countered. This time Earnshaw said no. And then the negative aspects of the situation shocked each into silence. If they weren't going to pitch, who was?

★ ★ ★

IT WAS ABOUT that time that Ehmke got up off the bench and shucked his jacket. He called for a warmup ball . . . and down at one end of the bench Al Simmons' eyes almost popped out of his head. Like a guy in a trance Simmons got up and walked down to where Mack was sitting.

"You're not starting him?" he gulped in disbelief. The ramrod figure of the Athletics' patriarch didn't bend. Connie just turned his head and those watery blue eyes regarded Simmons in an impassive stare.

"Yes," said Connie, "I am. If it's all right with you, Al."

★ ★ ★

AS IF THOSE words broke the spell. Simmons blurted out, "Oh yes, Mr. Mack," and stumbled back to his seat. Earnshaw and Grove sat down alongside. Grove couldn't hold his tongue. "The old man must be nutty," he chattered.

The rest, of course, is series history. Ehmke beat the Cubs 3-1 and fanned 13 for a record that still stands.

Big, strong men like Rogers Hornsby, Hack Wilson, Gabby Hartnett, Kiki Cuyler and Riggs Stephenson carried their lumber back to the bench . . . while over in the A's dugout players kept looking at Mack as if he were the Wizard of Oz.

★ ★ ★

EHMKE TRIED TO come back in the same series and was blasted off the hill, but nobody remembers that. He will live forever as the mystery man who stifled, for one awesome afternoon, one of the greatest hitting clubs ever to play in a series, sliding the ball off his right hip against the background of shimmering white shirts in the bleachers.

Picking Ehmke wasn't a Mack whim or snap judgment. Connie planned it that way, not even taking the veteran on the last road trip that year.

"You stay here," said Connie, "and scout the Cubs when they come in. If you've got one good game left in your system, I'll start you . . . but don't tell a soul."

★ ★ ★

THE IMMEDIATE reaction to the naming of Konstanty was varied and explosive. Bill Terry, who used to manage the Giants, didn't like the idea. "Back in 1933 Washington decided to save Earl Whitehill for the second game against us," said Bill. "So they gambled with Walter Stewart in the opener. We beat Stewart. Whitehill shut us out in the second game . . . but he never got to pitch again. We beat 'em four out of five."

Even members of the Phils were flabbergasted when they learned about Konstanty. Young Bob Miller gasped and said: "He is?" And then quickly settled into acceptance of the assignment.

Here, too, the final decision was made by manager Eddie Sawyer and his coaches, with Robin Roberts, the 20-11 winner, and Konstanty also behind the closed door.

Before this day is out Konstanty will have won or lost, but he's already inscribed in the records as the only man ever to pitch the opening game of a World Series in his first start of the season.

SCALPERS GET 'SCALPED'

PHILADELPHIA — (UP) — World Series ticket scalpers got "scalped" today.

They were left holding the bag—a bag of 3,000 World Series tickets worth $6.50 each—a total of $19,500.

They had purchased the tickets, hoping to sell them at a premium, but they found no takers.

As a result the first game of the World Series drew only 30,746—just 3,000 short of capacity.

Rocky Has Nine Pound Weight Edge

Tonight's Card

Rocky Graziano vs. Gene Burton (10), 160 pounds.
Dale Hall vs. Rex Layne (10), heavyweights.
Joe Garza vs. Hal Meredith (6), 147 pounds.
Ralph Schneider vs. Harvey Mack (6), heavyweights.
Chuck Davey vs. Jimmy Campbell (4), 147 pounds.

BY JOE REIN

Rocky Graziano, who has had more trouble outside the prize fight ring than in it, risks his fistic future in a 10-round bout at the Stadium tonight.

The former middleweight champion meets Gene Burton in a bout which can either catapult him back to wealth and prominence or slide him into athletic oblivion. The odds are 3 to 1 on the first possibility.

* * *

THE International Boxing Club, which is promoting the first of a series of 10 shows, expects a crowd of 11,000 people to pay some $35,000 for the privilege of watching the fracas.

Rocky has to win this one. It is his first appearance here in more than three years—years which saw him suspended in New York for failure to report a bribe offer and elsewhere because of disclosure of his bad military record.

Graziano has always been at his best against welterweights. In Burton he is meeting a 151-pounder, which will give him a weight edge of more pounds. Gragiano weighed 160.

Burton is well known to fans here. He is unbeaten in his last 10 starts and boasts victories over such well-known battlers as "Sugar" Costner, Ike Williams and Johnny Bratton.

* * *

A HEAVYWEIGHT number will pair Rex Layne, winner in 26 of 27 starts, against Dale Hall. Layne has built up a reputation on the West Coast and is attempting to crash into the heavyweight title picture.

Chuck Davey, National A.A.U. champion who won 93 of 94 starts as an amateur, will be after his fifth straight pro win when he takes on Jimmy Campbell in a four.

Joe Garza, Detroit bomber, will be after his 17th straight in a six-round bout with Hal Meredith.

The Graziano-Burton bout will be televised over WBKB, channel 4, and will be broadcast over WBBM, starting at 9 o'clock.

Curt Pitches For Phils---in Bat Practice

PHILADELPHIA —(UP)— Curt Simmons pitched 10 minutes of batting practice today and said, "I'd sure like to pitch in this World Series if the boss says so."

But Philadelphia Phillies manager Eddie Sawyer said flatly, "no—he's off the eligible list and he stays off."

The $65,000-bonus left-hander who just received a 10-day furlough from Camp Atterbury, Ind., where he is on active Army duty, also chased flies in the outfield before today's opening game of the series.

Rickey and McKinney In Market for Browns

PHILADELPHIA — (Special) — The newest combination in baseball may be Frank McKinney, former owner of the Pirates, and Branch Rickey, current president of the Dodgers. It was learned here today that the pair may be the new bosses of the St. Louis Browns at a price of something like $1,800,000.

The Browns, under such direction, would be transferred eventually to Los Angeles or Milwaukee.

Bill Veeck, former Indian owner, also is in the running to ... Browns, and he, too, would put them in Los Angeles.

... **that of the Boston Braves, by co-owners Lou and Guido Rugo, is reported imminent.**

ALLIES GET SET FOR BIG PUSH

WARMER

Fair and cool tonight. Light frost in city, heavier in suburbs. Low 38 in city, 30 to 35 in suburbs. Thursday fair and warmer. High 65. Friday fair, warmer. Sunrise 5:51, sunset 5:28.

10 p.m....51	6 a.m....39	10 a.m....49	2 p.m....53
Midn't....49	7 a.m....39	11 a.m....50	3 p.m....51
2 a.m....46	8 a.m....43	Noon......51	4 p.m....51
4 a.m....43	9 a.m....46	1 p.m....52	5 p.m....51

(U.S. official weather report.)

CHICAGO DAILY NEWS

★ An Independent Newspaper ★

75TH YEAR—233 WEDNESDAY, OCT. 4, 1950. 56 PAGES 5 CENTS

MARKETS RED STREAK

Council Battles Over Drury Death Probe

DOWN . . . NOT OUT

Gene Woodling, Yankee left fielder, braces himself as he crashes into a barrier chasing a foul hit by Eddie Waitkus of the Phillies in the first inning of the World Series game in Shibe Park, Philadelphia.

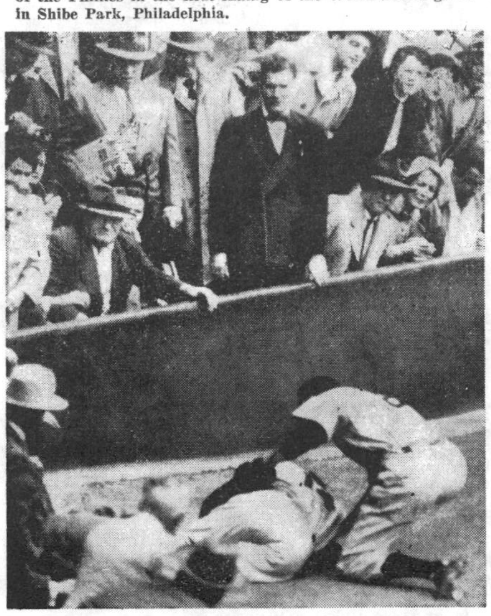

Teammate Bobby Brown, third baseman, bends over Woodling to find out if he's hurt. Woodling resumed play.

Series Telecast Goes P-f-f-f-t!

PHILADELPHIA — (AP) — Power failure at Shibe Park blacked out telecast of the World Series during the early part of the opening game Wednesday.

A spokesman at WPTZ, originating station for the Series TV coverage, said no information was available as to what caused the power failure.

TV coverage of the game was off the air for about 20 minutes of the second and third innings.

There was also a five-minute sound failure.

Envoy

QUITO, Ecuador — (AP) — Dr. Luis Antonio Penaherrera has been named Ecuadorean ambassador to Washington.

You'll Find:

E. Reich Jails Cultists as Spies

BERLIN —(AP)— The Soviet zone's highest court Wednesday condemned two German officials of Jehovah's Witnesses, a religious sect, to life imprisonment for "spying on order of American imperialism."

Seven other officials of the sect, which has been outlawed in Communist-controlled East Germany since last month, received prison sentences of 8 to 15 years.

Race Results

AT HAWTHORNE			
5—At'c Energy	8.20	4.20	3.20
Raffle House		5.40	3.60
Fine Fettle			4.00
AT BELMONT			
8—Fertile Lands	9.80	4.40	3.50
Star Knightess		4.70	3.60
Low and High			5.40
AT ROCKINGHAM			
8—Lucullus	4.40	3.60	2.80
Arklow H.		8.00	4.20
Unapproachable			3.00
AT BOWIE			
7—Sonofun	16.20	5.00	4.40
Laran		2.60	2.40
My Sonny Boy			6.40
8—Pritty Watch			
Flying Mane			
True Dream			
AT DETROIT			
5—Cr's Duchess	8.80	3.80	2.60
Bimont		3.60	2.40
Atoka Lad			2.60

YANKS TOP PHILS 1 TO 0 IN OPENER

ONE FOR NEW YORK

YANKEES	AB.	R.	H.	P.	A.	PHILLIES	AB.	R.	H.	P.	A.
Woodling, lf.	3	0	1	1	0	Waitkus, 1b.	3	0	0	9	2
Rizzuto, ss.	3	0	1	0	2	Ashburn, cf.	4	0	0	2	0
Berra, c.	4	0	0	7	0	Sisler, lf.	4	0	0	3	0
Di Maggio, cf.	2	0	0	3	0	Ennis, rf.	3	0	0	4	0
Mize, 1b.	4	0	0	7	0	Jones, 3b.	3	0	1	4	3
Hopp, 1b.	0	0	0	3	0	Hamner, ss.	3	0	0	0	1
Brown, 3b.	4	1	1	0	0	Seminick, c.	3	0	1	1	1
Johnson, 3b.	0	0	0	0	0	Goliat, 2b.	3	0	0	3	2
Bauer, rf.	4	0	1	5	0	Konstanty, p.	2	0	0	1	0
Coleman, 2b.	4	0	0	1	2	Whitman	1	0	0	0	0
Raschi, p.	3	0	1	0	3	Meyer, p.	0	0	0	0	1
Totals	31	1	5	27	7	Totals	29	0	2	27	10

Whitman flied out for Konstanty in the 8th.

	1	2	3	4	5	6	7	8	9—	R.	H.	E.
YANKEES	0	0	0	1	0	0	0	0	0—	1	5	0
PHILLIES	0	0	0	0	0	0	0	0	0—	0	2	1

Error—Jones. Run batted in—Coleman. Two-base hit—Brown. Sacrifice hits—Rizzuto, Raschi. Left on base—Yankees 9, Phillies 3. Struck out—By Raschi 5. Bases on balls—Off Konstanty 4, Raschi 1. Hits—Off Konstanty 4 in 8 innings; Meyer 1 in 1. Winning pitcher—Raschi. Losing pitcher—Konstanty. Umpires—Conlan (N), plate; McGowan (A), 1b; Boggess (N), 2b; Berry (A), 3b; Barlick (N), lf; and McKinley (A), rf. Time—2:17. Attendance—30.746.

Raschi Allows Two Hits

Brown's Double Leads to Lone Run

Series Facts

PHILADELPHIA —(AP)— Figures on the first game of the World Series:

Attendance—30,746.
Total receipts—$160,130.28.
Commissioner's share—$24.019.54.
Players' share—$81,666.44.
Clubs and league share—$54.444.30.
Series standings—(Four-out-of seven games wins) Yankees 1, Phils 0.

BY JOHN P. CARMICHAEL
Staff Writer

PHILADELPHIA—If you give the Yankees an inch, they don't always take a mile. Sometimes they just protect that inch as they did this crisp afternoon in Shibe Park when they held 30,746 World series fans spellbound with a 1-0 triumph over the first Philly pennant team in 35 years.

There were no home runs and at least half of the five Yankee hits wouldn't have reached either fence if laid end to end. The lone extra-base blow was Bobby Brown's fourth-inning double from which the winning run materialized with the help of two fly balls.

By just such a score did the Yanks beat the Dodgers in the opener one year ago and the Braves nosed out the Indians in the 1948 inaugural at Boston.

* * *

JIM KONSTANTY, who won 16 games and lost seven in 74 relief appearances for the Phils, made his only start in two and a half years and lost it because his teammates couldn't solve the sleight-of-hand with which Vic Raschi mesmerized them on a two-hit performance.

Raschi retired the first 13 Phillies, yielded singles to Willie Jones and Andy Seminick around two outs in the fifth and faced only 13 more men thereafter.

Raschi gave one base on balls, struck out five and, aside from those two hits, allowed only six other balls to be hit past the infield.

In the face of such counter-pitching, Konstanty's own brilliant effort to justify the faith of Manager Eddie Sawyer fell short by the narrowest of margins.

* * *

EVENTUALLY Konstanty had to retire for a pinch hitter (Dick Whitman) in the eighth but by then he had muzzled catcher "Yogi" Berra, Joe DiMaggio and Johnny Mize without a hit although they came up twice as units in the first three innings with two and three men on base.

This was the 12th two-hit game in series history and the third in a row on opening day.

Bob Feller got beat 1-0 on his two-hitter in 1948 and Allie Reyn-

Turn to Page 46, Column 8.

TRIALS WITH NO DEFENSE

Charges Slaughter Of 10,000 at Seoul

SEOUL, Korea — (AP) — A South Korean official estimated Wednesday that the Communists massacred more than 10,000 Seoul residents before being driven from the city by U.S. forces.

"Several thousand more are reported lying in the hills," said Lee Joong Choon, chief of the municipal public information section of Seoul. "Many were dumped into rivers by the Reds."

* * *

"PEOPLE'S COURTS" in Seoul are reported to have been in operation within 10 days after Communist occupation of the capital June 28.

Trials of political prisoners were described this way:

The prisoners were marched to the balcony of the people's theater building.

The charges were read and the crowd below was asked: "Guilty or not guilty?"

Executions followed invariably.

"We were told many skilled persons, such as doctors, engineers, musicians, leading actors and actresses and professors were taken north to enrich the Communist country with needed talent," Lee said.

It's Frost On Pumpkin Time Again

Fall is busting out all over.

The first real frost of the season is expected in the suburbs Wednesday night with temperatures of 30 to 35 forecast.

* * *

THE Weather Bureau forecast a high of about 60 degrees in the city during the day, with a drop to about 38 at night.

Fair weather is expected through Thursday, and probably Friday.

State Relief Rolls Drop 5th Month

SPRINGFIELD, Ill.—(AP)—Relief rolls dropped during August for the fifth sartight month, the Illinois Public Aid Commission reported Wednesday.

Recipients totaled 86,234 or a drop of 41,503 since last March. State-federal assistance totaled $2,553,627 during August.

Today's Chuckle

"I'm glad to find you as you are," said the old friend. "Your wealth hasn't changed you."

"Well," replied the candid millionaire, "it has changed me in one way. I'm now 'eccentric' where I used to be impolite, and 'delightfully witty' where I used to be rude."

THE LINCOLN.

Trolley Kills Mother of Crash Victim

Mrs. Veronica Jankauskis, 55, mother of a girl who burned to death in the streetcar-gas truck collision at 63d and State sts. May 25, was struck and killed by a trolley Wednesday.

Mrs. Jankauskis was struck at 101st st. and Michigan av. while out shopping for the wedding of her son John, which was to be held Oct. 14.

Her daughter Martha, 23, was killed in the streetcar disaster that took 34 lives.

Mrs. Jankauskis lived at 10117 S. State st.

$3,793 Theft

Burglars Tuesday stole a safe containing $3,793 in cash from the office of the Chicago Housing Authority, 4230 W. 79th st.

Famed G.I. Unit In War Zone

3d Infantry in Far East; Allies Gird for Big Push

TOKYO—(UP)—A third South Korean division wheeled into line on Korea's 38th Parallel Wednesday, amid increasing indications that United Nations' forces were getting ready for their big offensive to crush the North Korean Communist army.

The South Korean 6th Division reached Jinran, a village barely one mile south of the parallel.

A source close to Gen. MacArthur said Allied troops would begin their big assault as soon as they are fully regrouped and equipped.

It appeared to be only a matter of days.

* * *

MacARTHUR'S spokesman disclosed that the U.S. 3d Infantry Division, an outfit with a fine record of fighting in North Africa, Italy, France and Germany in World War II, had arrived in the Far Eastern theater. Presumably it will be sent to Korea to join the final battles.

It will be the seventh U.S. division in the U.N. forces.

High Army sources said that British and Australian forces will play an important part in the big push.

* * *

THE ENEMY also was preparing. American Superforts and light bombers, attacking in dirty weather, reported increasing enemy activity along railroads and highways both northeast and northwest of Pyongyang, North Korean capital.

One column of 150 vehicles was reported moving south in the Pakchon area, 50 miles north of Pyongyang.

Pyongyang is expected to be the west coast anchor of the next big Communist defense line, running from there to Wonsan on the east coast.

* * *

THE South Korean 3d Division pushed two miles north of Kosong, on the North Korean east coast, 67 road miles above the parallel. It halted there because American advisers thought it best for it to rest and consolidate.

The 3d Division is only 58 miles from Wonsan.

Stassen Makes Plea To Stalin

WASHINGTON —(UP)— Harold E. Stassen disclosed Wednesday that he has personally appealed to Premier Stalin to change Russia's foreign policy and "stop the drift toward war."

HAROLD STASSEN

Stassen, president of the University of Pennsylvania, also announced his willingness to lead a delegation of private citizens to Moscow to explore avenues to peace.

The former governor of Minnesota said his appeal to Stalin was contained in a letter delivered last Sunday to the Soviet embassy here.

* * *

STASSEN'S announcement ended more than 10 days of speculation. He had said mysteriously that he would have an announcement of major importance.

It had been speculated that he would take a government job.

In a statement released at a news conference, he said he believed the Soviet rulers are reexamining their own world policies and that the greatest danger of another world war would come from Russia miscalculating or underestimating the strength and intentions of the United States.

Stassen suggested it was important that the Soviet rulers get an expression from someone in the political party, that is the Republican party, not in power in the United States.

2,343 Marine War Casualties

WASHINGTON—(UP)—The Marine Corps announced Wednesday that it suffered 2,343 casualties in Korea up to Sept. 25.

The casualties included 412 dead, 1,901 wounded and 30 missing. The Marines have 31,529 men in the Korean struggle.

Are YOU Registered To Vote Nov. 7?

SEE STORY ON PAGE 40

Stocks Reach New Peak

NEW YORK — (AP) — Stocks reached a new 19-year high point on average Wednesday in a bull market movement led by motor shares.

Chrysler was the top buying favorite that started off the forward surge of prices. It reached a new high during the session and closed up $3.37 at $82.37. General Motors was another star performer up $3.37 at $53.37.

Steels joined in the rise along with rails and other key segments of the market.

The Associated Press average of 60 stocks gained 90 cents at $84.50, the highest point since Feb. 27, 1931.

Mayor Joins in Shouting

Plea for U.S. Quiz Sidetracked

A resolution asking a federal grand jury investigation of the Drury-Bas slayings was pigeonholed Wednesday in a stormy City Council session.

Republicans and Democrats, including Mayor Kennelly, sniped at each other.

CHARLES GIOE

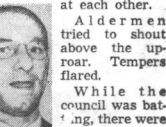

Aldermen tried to shout above the uproar. Tempers flared.

While the council was battling, there were other developments in the slaying investigation.

Charles "Cherry Nose" Gioe, paroled mob boss, surrendered to State's Attorney Boyle for questioning.

He will be held until 10 a.m. Thursday while Boyle checks his account of what he was doing on Sept. 25, night of the slayings.

* * *

MEANWHILE, two of Gioe's associates, Paul Ricca and Louis Campagna, were ordered released after state's attorney's police had checked their alibis in the slayings.

Police said the alibis looked "pretty good."

* * *

IN THE CITY Council battle, the resolution that started the uproar was introduced by Ald. Nicholas Bohling (7th), who is running for county clerk on the Republican ticket.

The resolution called on the Kefauver Senate crime committee to request a federal grand jury investigation into the slayings of William Drury, ousted police lieutenant, and Marvin J. Bas, attorney.

The slayings gave Chicago a black eye before the whole world, the resolution stated.

* * *

AFTER BOHLING'S move was tabled, Mayor Kennelly, who presides at council sessions, took a whack at the aldermen.

"As mayor I have been fighting crime for three and a half years," Kennelly said.

"This is the first time I have seen the alderman express an interest in the matter."

Bohling, his face flushed, cried: "I resent those remarks."

In introducing the resolution, Bohling explained that a federal grand jury probe was needed because the county grand jury is limited to one-month terms, and more time is required.

"The people in my ward are aroused over these murders," Bohling said.

* * *

THE BATTLE against the resolution was led by Aldermen John J. Duffy (19th), George D. Kells (28th), Clarence P. Wagner (14th) and Dorsey Crowe (42d), all Democrats.

They charged that the resolution was out of order and that

Turn to Page 3, Column 1.

Top Spots In Crime Probe News

State's Attorney Boyle reveals plan to ask Kefauver crime investigators to give him income-tax data on Chicago criminals. Page 3.

Crime probe paying its way, committee reports. Page 4.

Life sketch of Sen Kefauver, newest gangbuster. Page 5.

Sen. Kefauver's answer to 10 questions on "who, what, why" of investigation. Page 5.

To avoid delay, please use the specific Chicago Tribune phone number assigned to take care of your needs.

SUperior 7 9260 — For latest sports results, call this number between noon and midnight.
SUperior 7 0200 — For general information, call this number between 8:30 A.M. and 9:00 P.M.
SUperior 7 0100 — For want ads and Tribune, WGN and WGN-TV business, call this number.

Chicago Daily Tribune
THE WORLD'S GREATEST NEWSPAPER
Wed., October 4, 1950 *F Page 1

PART 4 — SPORTS MARKETS WANT ADS

YANKS FACE KONSTANTY IN SERIES TODAY

In the WAKE of the NEWS

BY ARCH WARD
[Chicago Tribune Press Service]

PHILADELPHIA, Oct. 3—The fightin' Phils, who will represent the National league in the world series beginning tomorrow for the first time since 1915, will be followed by more fans than ever before have seen the competition for the championship of major league baseball. . . . More extensive video coverage is the answer. . . . Revenue from television—$800,000—also makes the Phillies-Yankees series the biggest money maker of all time. . . . Video editors estimated that 35,000,000 saw Notre Dame defeat North Carolina Saturday, and at least that many, probably more, will look on when the Yankees come to bat in the first inning tomorrow, despite the fact that it will be played when other millions must stick to their office desks or factory benches.

The tremendous interest and financial aspects of the 1950 series are in sharp contrast to the original playoff between the league champions in 1903. . . . That one brought together the Pittsburgh Pirates, led by the immortal Flying Dutchman, Honus Wagner, and

Honus Wagner — Barney Dreyfuss — Bill Dinneen — Tom Connolly

the Boston Red Sox of the American league. . . . The first world series was arranged by President Henry Killilea of Boston and the Pittsburgh owner, Barney Dreyfuss, when it became apparent in August that their clubs would be pennant winners. . . . Nine games were agreed upon and each club made its own deal with the players. . . . Boston was at a disadvantage because its contracts expired Sept. 30, while the Pirates' ran to Oct. 15. . . . Boston players demanded and received a major share of the club's receipts, each getting $1,182. . . . The Pirates, tho defeated, fared somewhat better, because Dreyfuss tossed in his share. . . . Each Pittsburgh player received $1,316.25.

A baseball scrivener of that day wrote that the series attracted tremendous crowds and more than $50,000 in receipts. . . . Total attendance for the eight games was 100,429. . . . The largest crowd was in Boston, 18,801 for the third game, and the smallest was 7,405, also in Boston, when the Red Sox clinched the title with their fifth victory. . . . The attendance for the opening game of the 1949 series in Yankee stadium was 66,230. . . . There's one world series angle that time hasn't changed—the admiration of the fans for their diamond heroes. . . . The star of the 1903 Pirates was a big right handed pitcher named Deacon Phillippe, who won the first, third, and fourth games for Pittsburgh and lost the seventh and eighth. . . . After his 5 to 4 victory in the fourth game, old timers say that Phillippe was lifted on the shoulders of enthusiasts and escorted to the clubhouse, where for half an hour he was compelled to shake hands with admirers. . . . The Phillies of 1950 had a comparable demonstration when they pulled into Philadelphia's 30th st. station Sunday evening after whipping the Dodgers in the final game of the season.

Cy Young

Hank O'Day

Bill Dinneen, later an American league umpire, was the pitching hero of the first world series with three Boston triumphs, two of them shutouts. . . . His top performance was in the second game when he struck out 11 and allowed only three hits. . . . Cy Young, who still is rated one of baseball's all-time great moundsmen, won the other two games that gave Boston the title. . . . Wagner, like many other prominent stars who followed him, didn't have much luck at bat in the 1903 series. . . . He got only six hits for a percentage of .214. . . . The leading Boston hitter was Chick Stahl, who had a .309 average.

Tommy Connolly, who is attending the current series as umpire in chief of the American league in his 57th year in organized baseball, teamed with Hank O'Day as the 1903 officials. . . . Connolly recalls that he got $450 for his services in the original world series, out of which he had to pay his traveling and living expenses. The competition dragged out from Oct. 1 to Oct. 13. . . . He figures his take home pay was about $275. . . . The umpires in the 1950 series will get $2,500 apiece, plus traveling expenses and $25 a day for food, lodging, and incidentals.

Autumn

Some leaves already hinting
Of burnished brown or gold,
As autumn's muted colorings
Cameleon-like unfold.
Some birds already winging
Their usual southward way,
Forgetful of the singing
Which graced their season's stay.
Some gardens gently offering
Their latest blossoming rows,
The reminiscent story
Which October days disclose.
Some winds already bringing
Faint flickerings of cold,
Foreshadowings of wintriness
As autumn days unfold.
—*Lucille Veneklasen*

* *

Ad Similes

As dead as a witness enjoying police protection.
—Farmer's Boy

* *

Now

All of Now is yours and mine;
Now is all we have of time,
Precious Now to do our part,
Now to work with hand and heart.
—*C Nile*

Never!

No man should be elected
To solve our nation's strife,
If after he's elected
He takes orders from his wife.
—Vic. L.

* *

Free Substitution

Now that they are leaving "and obey" out of the marriage ceremony, don't you think they should add "and get him out of bed in the morning?"
—Moon

* *

Happy Days!

With all the little Hopalong Cassidys back in school, it's awfully quiet around the house and once more it's safe to come home without fear of stumbling over boots, spurs and pistols on the stairs as we try to sneak into the bedroom without waking the wife.
—Skipper

* *

Sign of the Times?

Like my druggist friend, Skid Smith, said, "Doc, I think I'll take another trip to Mexico while my vaccination is still good."
—Doc Richards, Minn. '25

* *

The Wake Depends Upon Its Friends — Help! Help!

Ten Years Ago Today—Fritzie Zivic defeated Henry Armstrong for the world welterweight title. . . . The Brooklyn Dodgers whipped the Philadelphia Eagles, 30 to 17, in a National Football league game.

Graziano, Burton Battle Tonight

10 ROUND BOUT HEADS OPENING STADIUM CARD

Rocky to Hold 14 Pound Edge

Stadium Card

Rocky Graziano, New York, vs. Gene Burton, New York, 10 rounds, 160 pounds.
Rex Layne, Lewiston, Utah, vs. Dale Hall, Los Angeles, 10 rounds, heavyweights.
Joe Garza, Detroit, vs. Hal Meredith, Macon, Ga., 6 rounds, 152 pounds.
Ralph Schneider, Chicago, vs. Herbit Mack, Detroit, 6 rounds, heavyweights.
Chuck Davey, Detroit, vs. Jimmy Campbell, Steubenville, O., 4 rounds, 147 pounds.
TELECAST — WBKB—9 p. m. [Graziano-Burton fight only.]

BY CHARLES BARTLETT

A newly winsome Rocky Graziano and Gene Burton, No. 1 bodyguard for Welterweight Champ Ray Robinson, will sling gloved fists for 10 rounds or less tonight in the opening extravaganza of the International Boxing club's 1950-51 indoor program in Chicago stadium.

Best of the supporting quarrels on the five bout program will bring together Rex Layne, already dubbed the best heavyweight prospect to emerge from Utah since a kid named Jack Dempsey checked into the big time, and Dale Hall, Los Angeles Negro who has been around more than somewhat.

For Graziano and Burton tonight's argument will be a real homecoming.

Scene of Title Triumph

The big west side building was the scene of Rocky's greatest triumph on July 16, 1947, when he dethroned Tony Zale as world middleweight champion. The stadium also has been a good luck house for the clever Burton, who has not been beaten in his last 10 appearances there, winning nine and gaining a draw with Freddie Dawson.

The counting room hands were reluctant to estimate this evening's audience, altho one of them was pressed into confessing that a sudden rush for the less expensive pews might actually bring the attendance to the 10,000 mark. All of the ringside seats have been seized by eager clients who enjoy cheering or booing Graziano.

The Graziano-Burton business will be televised, beginning at 9 o'clock.

Weight Point at Issue

All principals in the cast will weigh in at noon in the offices of the Illinois Athletic commission. Graziano is expected to step off the scales with a record of 161 pounds, against an approximate 147 for Burton. Poundage has been the subject of a deal of prefight bickering, the Burton entourage expressing doubt that Rocky will be able to get down to 161, his agreed weight.

Graziano, who once was wont to snarl and snap at his best friends, is now a man of charm and good fellowship. In his training endeavors, the once careless Rocky has betrayed his detractors by getting 100 in deportment, effort, and concentration. He is, of course, expected to rely on his native bulling tactics tonight with a view to verifying the prophets who have made him a favorite.

Aside from the main event, all of the other bouts tonight rate as promising action a-plenty. Layne, the 22 year old Utahan, has won 26 of his 27 professional fights.

Voigts Alters N.U.'s Platoon Plan for Navy

BY WILFRID SMITH

The Western conference race gets under way Saturday with vital games between Wisconsin and Illinois at Champaign and Indiana and Iowa in Bloomington. All are undefeated, altho the Hoosiers were held to a tie last week by Nebraska.

Regardless of the importance of these games in the percentage columns of the Big Ten, the nonconference contests hold more that usual interest, partly because of opening day defeats. Northwestern, winner over Iowa State, is the only one of the group that was not beaten last week.

Northwestern leaves by plane Friday to play Navy in Baltimore. The other nonconference games are Dartmouth at Michigan, Nebraska at Minnesota, Pittsburgh at Ohio State, and Purdue at Notre Dame.

Voigts Changes Plans

Bob Voigts, Northwestern coach, told members of the Chicago Football Writers' association at luncheon yesterday that the Wildcats will not employ two platoons against Navy.

"From our reports on Navy," Voigts said, "it's apparent we'll need experienced men in the line. That means double duty for some of our veterans. Rudy Cernoch probably will play both offense and defense at tackle." Voigts continued, "Don MacRae likely will do the same at guard, and Ray Wietacha will be used at offensive center and as a line backer."

Northwestern will substitute at least one line backer [possibly two], defensive half backs, and a safety when Navy has the ball. Voigts believes Richie Anderson, regular guard who has a muscle injury, will be ready to play.

Navy "Wins" Statistically

Bob Clifford, Northwestern coach who scouted the midshipmen as they lost to Maryland, 35 to 21, gave the statistics which showed that Navy outgained Maryland, completed more passes, and had a decided advantage in rushing.

Clifford believes Bob Zastrow, junior quarter back from Algoma, Wis., is considerably improved over last season. "He's throwing better because he was coached this spring by Frankie Albert and he completed 60 per cent of his passes against Maryland."

Eddie Erdelatz, in his first year as Navy coach, has installed the T formation he helped teach in 1948 and 1949 as a member of the staff of the San Francisco professional staff. Among the personnel shifts is that of Dave Bannerman. Last year Bannerman was Navy's best ground gainer. Now he is a line backer and his work has greatly improved defensive line play.

Krause Praises Flood

Ed Krause, director of athletics at Notre Dame; Charles Flynn, Illinois; Art Lentz, Wisconsin, and Kenneth L. Wilson, Big Ten commissioner, were other speakers at yesterday's luncheon.

Krause praised North Carolina's line play in Saturday's game which Notre Dame won 14 to 7 principally by passes. He also pointed out the pass interceptions by Dave Flood, Notre Dame defensive right half back, which stopped the Tarheels' attacks.

Billy Barrett and Bill Gay, who have been slowed by injuries, will be ready for the Purdue game, Krause said.

SAWYER'S SURPRISE FOR SERIES OPENER

It will be Jim Konstanty in a new role today as Philadelphia Phillies meet New York Yankees in opening game of world series. Jim has been named starting pitcher for the Phillies in a surprise move by Manager Eddie Sawyer. It will be Konstanty's first start of season. In record 74 appearances in relief role he won 16 and lost 7 during National league campaign. [TRIBUNE Photo]

C. Y. O. RING MEET STARTS TONIGHT

176 Boxers Seek South Section Honors

BY FRANK MASTRO

The 20th Catholic Youth organization amateur boxing tournament will start tonight in C. Y. O. center gymnasium, 31 E. Congress st., with competition among 176 contestants for south section championships. More than 20 bouts will be held in every weight class.

Art Manzy

The event, which will get under way at 7:30 o'clock, will continue tomorrow and be concluded Friday when 16 sectional winners—eight each in the open and novice divisions—will be chosen to represent the south in the championship final in Chicago Stadium Oct. 24.

The north siders will get their chance next Monday, Tuesday, and Wednesday.

12 Finalists Enter

Twelve finalists in the 1949 tourney—six each in the open and novice divisions—are among contestants. The open finalists: Augie Lopez and Jake Marshall, flyweights; Jack Corvino, bantamweight; Art Manzy, featherweight; Nate Morgan, lightweight, and Rufus Johnson, welterweight.

Novice finalists: John Hawes, featherweight; Bill Hartman, welter; Edward Jones and James Rivera, middleweights; Jake Solus, light heavyweight, and Paul Cheung, heavyweight.

Lopez, Manzy, Johnson, Morgan, Hawes, Hartman, Jones, and Solus captured championships. As a result of their successes the novice title holders will fight in the open competition this time.

16 Sailors to Box

Hartman is one of 16 representatives from the Great Lakes naval training station. Other organizations represented include Our Lady of Guadalupe, West Side Community center, St. Elizabeth, St. Francis Assisi, Russell square, St. Rita High school, St. George High, and Leo High. Great Lakes and St. Francis Assisi tied for the team championship in 1949 with 13 points apiece.

Illini Expect 55,000 to See Badger Game

Champaign, Ill., Oct. 3 [Special]—An I Men's day crowd of 55,000 will see the Wisconsin-Illinois game here Saturday, Ticket Manager George Legg of Illinois estimated today. It will be the largest in the history of the Illini-Badger series, Legg added.

Meanwhile, the Illini scrimmaged against the freshmen using Wisconsin plays. Full Back Bill Tate engaged in contact work for the first time since he pulled a groin muscle two weeks ago. He is expected to play Saturday.

BADGERS POLISH DEFENSE

Madison, Wis., Oct. 3 [Special]—Wisconsin went thru one of the longest defensive drills of the season today. No changes were made in the line as coaches concentrated on stopping the running of Johnny Karras. Line Backer Deral Teteak appeared to be in excellent shape and probably will be able to go full time Saturday. Bill Hutchinson, the Chicago sofomore, who ran so well against Marquette, probably will be a starter against Illinois at the right half back.

IOWA STRESSES PASSING

Iowa City, Ia., Oct. 3 [Special]—Upset-happy Iowa began overhauling its pass defense today for its opening Big Ten game against Indiana at Bloomington Saturday. Coach Len Raffensperger also had the Hawkeyes working on their own passing game. Scout Maury Kent warned the Hawkeyes to set up defenses for at least three Hoosiers — Quarter Back and Passer Lou D'Achille, Half Back Bobby Robertson, and End Clifton Anderson.

BIRD DOUBTFUL STARTER

Bloomington, Ind., Oct. 3 [Special]—Bill Bird, 205 pound defensive left tackle, was ruled a doubtful starter for Indiana against Iowa because of failure of a sprained ankle to show satisfactory improvement. Guard Larry Martin and Quarter Back John Zuger also went on the injury list as a result of a rough defensive scrimmage.

Vic Raschi, ace of the Yankee mound staff will be Konstanty's foe. During the season he won 21; lost 8.

Simmons Gets Leave, but He Won't Pitch

[Chicago Tribune Press Service]

Philadelphia, Oct. 3—Curt Simmons, 21, star pitcher with the Philadelphia Phillies until called up for regular army duty, will return to Philadelphia for the opening of the world series tomorrow, but not as a member of the National league champions' mound corps.

Simmons, granted a 10 day leave by the army, was en route to Philadelphia by plane, but Manager Eddie Sawyer of the Phils said he would not seek to use the pitcher against the Yankees.

"Pitch Batting Practice"

"Simmons probably will pitch batting practice," Sawyer said tonight. "He will not sit on the bench during the series. We have reports that Simmons definitely is not in shape to play world series ball. He has had no chance to practice, and we understand he suffered an injury to the index finger of his pitching hand."

Earlier, Commissioner A. B. Chandler indicated that if the Phillies did decide to use Simmons he would give favorable consideration to the request.

SIMMONS WANTS TO HURL

Harrisburg, Pa., Oct. 4 [Wednesday]—(AP)—Curt Simmons, pitching great flying east to the world series, said here that he would be only "too willing to take his place on the mound" with the Philadelphia Phillies.

"I can get ready for the fifth, sixth, or seventh world series games,' said Simmons in a stopoff here while flying from Indianapolis to Newark, N. J.

"I have not talked to Manager Eddie Sawyer about playing in the series," the young hurler said. "I don't understand about the procedure of returning to the active list."

"However, if I think I can do the club some good, I'm only too willing to take my turn on the mound or wherever Manager Sawyer sees fit to use me."

TV Receivers at Tribune to Present Series

Two 19 inch television receivers will be placed in Nathan Hale court in Tribune Square today to enable passersby to view the world series over WGN-TV. Sets will be turned on at 11:45 a. m. daily. This is the third year W-G-N, Inc., has provided this service. Previously, loud speakers were installed for radio broadcasts. Jack Brickhouse of WGN-TV and Jim Britt will announce this year's series for television audiences.

X-RAYS REVEAL CHIPPED BONE IN BAUGH'S ELBOW

Washington, Oct. 3 (AP)—Dick McCann, general manager of the Washington Redskins, said that X-ray pictures taken today revealed a small chipped bone in the right elbow of Quarter Back Sammy Baugh, injured in the game with Pittsburgh last Sunday.

Harry Gilmer, the team's other quarter back, will see physicians tomorrow on whether he'll be able to play Sunday. Gilmer has strained ligaments in his right knee. If neither Gilmer nor Baugh is ready by Sunday, Half Back Bill Dudley probably will be shifted to the signal calling post.

SAWYER PICKS RELIEF HERO FOR OPENER

Stengel Stands By Choice of Raschi

Today's Lineups

NEW YORK	PHILADELPHIA
Woodling, lf [.283]	Waitkus, 1b [.284]
Rizzuto, ss [.324]	Ashburn, cf [.303]
Berra, c [.320]	Sisler, lf [.299]
Di Maggio, cf [.301]	Ennis, rf [.313]
Mize, 1b [.277]	Jones, 3b [.266]
Mapes, rf [.246]	Hamner, ss [.270]
Brown, 3b [.264]	Seminick, c [.288]
Coleman, 2b [.287]	Goliat, 2b [.234]
Raschi, p [21-8]	Konstanty, p [16-7]

BY EDWARD BURNS
[Chicago Tribune Press Service]

Philadelphia, Oct. 3—Jim Konstanty, who pitched in 74 games for the Phillies without starting one, will start for Philadelphia in the opening game of the 1950 world series tomorrow. As announced by the Yankees yesterday, Vic Raschi will pitch for New York.

Manager Eddie Sawyer of the Phillies named his 33 year old relief star shortly before 2 o'clock today. Inasmuch as Konstanty never had started in three years with the Phillies, his selection was a surprise, tho it had been anticipated that the fireman, who set a major league record for the number of relief assignments this season, would be available for heavy duty at his specialty, if called upon.

At the same time he named Konstanty, Sawyer made it known that his 20 game ace, 24 year old Robin Roberts, will pitch the second game Thursday. The Springfield, Ill., lad needed another day of rest, it was believed. Counting his brilliant 10 inning clincher victory over the Brooklyn Dodgers last Sunday, Roberts had pitched in three of the last five Phillies' games.

Yanks Refuse To Panic

Decision to start with Konstanty, it was said, was not sprung as a coup, a la Connie Mack's Howard Ehmke surprise on the Cubs in the opener of the 1929 series. The Cubs had no form charts on Ehmke, whereas the Yankees probably have paid as much attention to advance study of Konstanty's stuff as they have any other pitcher on the Phillies' staff. There are some Yankees who had expected to see Konstanty in every one of the games in the series.

Announcement of Konstanty caused no great panic in the Yankees' camp. Konstanty throws a wide variety of pitches, but his soft stuff is supposed to have won him his greatest fame this season. It is said to be the thought of the Phillies' board of strategy that Joe Di Maggio, Johnny Mize and several other Yankees have thrived only on hard throwing this year and this may have had much to do with the decision to lead with Konstanty.

New York partisans recall that each of the Yankees on occasion this year has whacked all kinds of pitching and may do it again tomorrow.

Last Appearance Unimpressive

Konstanty's last appearance in National league competition was far from being the most impressive of the season, even tho it set the present record. Against the Dodgers in Brooklyn Saturday he rushed to the relief of Bob Miller in the fifth, first scoring inning of the game. Duke Snider banged Jim's first pitch for a two run homer to give the Dodgers a 4 to 0 lead. The Phillies shortened the lead to 4 to 3 in the next inning, and Konstanty stayed on the job. The final score was effected in the eighth when Roy Campanella

[Continued on page 4, column 6]

Series Data

CONTESTANTS—Philadelphia Phillies, National league champions, and New York Yankees, American league champions.

SERIES—Best four of seven games.

GAMES—First two at Shibe park, Philadelphia, starting today; third, fourth, and fifth [if needed], at Yankee stadium, New York; sixth and seventh [if needed] at Shibe park. Play is on successive days with no break for travel.

STARTING TIMES—Noon [Chicago time] for all weekday games; 12:05 p. m. for Sunday game in New York..

ATTENDANCE—Complete sellouts for all games at Shibe park. [Seating capacity, 33,-166] and Yankee stadium [67,000].

BETTING ODDS—Yankees 1-2 favorite for the series, Yankees 11 to 5 to win the opener.

WEATHER PROSPECTS—Cloudy, cool today; temperature in the 70s.

PRICE OF TICKETS—At Shibe park, box seats $8.75, reserved seats $6.50, bleachers $1, no standing room sold; at Yankee stadium, box seats, $8, reserved seats $6, standing room, $4, bleachers $1.

RADIO BROADCAST—Mutual network and W-G-N [11:45 a. m. [Chicago time].

TELEVISION—ABC, NBC, and CBS networks, WGN-TV.

PROBABLE PITCHERS—Yankees, Vic Raschi [21-8]; Phillies, Jim Konstanty [16-7].

UMPIRES—Jocko Conlan [N. L.], plate; Bill McGowan [A. L.], first base; Dusty Boggess [N. L.], second base; Charley Berry [A. L.], third base; Al Barlick [N. L.], left field; Bill McKinley [A. L.] right field.

Today in COLOR!
Souvenir Photos of Both WORLD SERIES TEAMS
Suitable for Framing
See the back page today!

Yankees Beat Phillies in 10th, 2-1, on DiMaggio's Homer and Take 2-0 Series Lead

Clipper's Only Hit in 2 Games Defeats Roberts for Reynolds

32,660 See Four-Bagger Break Tie, Achieved by N. L. Champions in 5th

(Continued from page one)

By Harold Rosenthal

inside slider," recalled DiMaggio.

Up to that point it had been three hours of pushing and tugging, with the Phillies finally managing to end a run-famine record which had extended all the way back to their 1915 series. They did it with a tying run in the fifth. The Yankees had scored easily with a walk and successive singles in the second.

The Yankees had Roberts in trouble with at least one hit in each of the first four innings, but never generated a knockout punch, or for that matter much of a scoring punch. Plugging along with them, the Phillies connected for a triple and two doubles in the first three innings, but couldn't sock a run across during this interlude.

Reynolds then entered upon a four-inning period in which he allowed only two hits. Singles by Mike Goliat and Eddie Waitkus, backed by Richie Ashburn's fly into left added up to the Philadelphia fifth-inning run. It ended a string of nineteen scoreless Philly World Series innings going back to that last game of the pre-World War I series with the Red Sox when the Phillies stopped scoring after the fourth inning.

Yankees Wait for Break

Today they stopped scoring after the fifth, although no one can say they stopped trying. The Yankees, moving along patiently waiting for their break, got it from the talents of an old hand who was playing in World Series games when a good many of the current Whiz Kids were collecting his picture off bubble-gum wrappers.

From the first-inning proceedings it might easily have turned into a Philly rout. The Yankees got runners on first and third on a couple of singles by Gene Woodling and Yogi Berra, but an equal number of pop-ups took care of the New York threat.

In the second, with two out, the Yankees threatened and made good on the threat. Jerry Coleman drew a full-count walk and Reynolds, getting his first and last hit of the game, sliced a single into right field. It moved Coleman to third and Woodling's second single, a bouncer past Willie Jones, the third baseman, brought Coleman home.

Twice after that the Yankees left a couple of runners stranded. In the fourth, Coleman's double and a walk to Reynolds went for naught when Woodling fouled out to Dick Sisler in left field and Scooter Rizzuto sliced one squarely into Del Ennis's glove in right.

Brown Singles Again

In the eighth, Bobby Brown got his second single to left field with one out. Brown went to second on Hank Bauer's single past Jones, who was having a rough afternoon with a lot of tough chances. Then Johnny Hopp ran for Brown and wound up on third on Caleman's roller to Hamner. Reynolds fanned to extinguish the threat.

In the ninth the Yankees failed to get the ball out of the infield, going down in order, but in the tenth the Clipper took charge and drove the telling shot out of the playing area. After that Billy Johnson fanned, Hopp flied to Sisler and Bauer grounded out. It didn't much matter.

The Phillies couldn't do much with their final chance in the tenth. They sent Jack Mayo, the rookie outfielder, up to bat for Roberts, and Mayo drew a walk. Waitkus sacrificed him along to second and there Mayo languished when the game ended.

It ended two batters later when Ashburn fouled out to Hopp and Sisler fanned on three pitches. Reynolds fed him a couple of curves and then let him have the fast one.

Sisler got his bat a foot or two off his shoulder and stood there completely fooled. Bill McGowan, the plate umpire, struck his strike pose, doffed his mask and cap exposing his bald spot to the assemblage of predominantly Philly rooters, who certainly were looking for something better, and the game was over.

The Yankees are now at the half-way point in the effort to sweep their sixth World Series in thirteen tries. They have the pitching to do it in their own park the next two days. If the Phillies manage to circumvent this they'll get another look at Reynolds. What they've seen thus for does not make this an inviting prospect. Reynolds, who saw his sixteen and two-thirds scoreless World Series innings streak come to an end here today might get mad and really go to work on a new one.

Please Call ME 7-1212 ForWorldSeriesScores

Baseball enthusiasts who wish to keep posted on the progress of the World Series games between the Yankees and Phillies may do so by calling ME 7-1212, the telephone time bureau, where scores are announced by operators at 15-second intervals.

The final score will be continued until 6:30 p. m. *Please do not call the Herald Tribune for scores.*

Forty Candidates Report For Columbia Basketball

Coach Gordon Ridings will begin preparation for his fifth Columbia basketball season today when forty candidates for the squad will report to him on the University Hall court for pre-season practice. Two Ridings-coached teams have won Ivy League championships, two have finished second and his 1947-'48 five played in the N. C. A. A. tournament.

Leading nine returnees from last winter's varsity which compiled a 22-7 season record is All-Metropolitan and All-Ivy guard John Azary. Azary, a 6-foot-3 candidate for All-America honors, is also the team captain.

Box Score of Second Game

* * *

NEW YORK (A.)	ab	r	h	po	a
Woodling lf	5	0	2	2	0
Rizzuto ss.	4	0	0	2	1
Berra, c	5	0	1	7	0
DiMaggio cf	5	1	1	3	0
Mize 1b	4	0	1	6	0
Johnson 3b	1	0	0	0	2
Brown 3b	4	0	2	0	0
Hopp 1b	1	0	0	3	0
Bauer rf	5	0	1	1	0
Coleman 2b	3	1	1	5	6
Reynolds p	3	0	1	1	2
Totals	40	2	10	30	11

PHILADELPHIA (N.)	ab	r	h	po	a
Waitkus 1b	4	0	2	8	0
Ashburn cf	5	0	2	4	0
Sisler lf	5	0	0	3	0
Ennis rf	4	0	0	1	0
Jones 3b	4	0	0	3	0
Hamner ss	3	9	2	2	2
Seminick c	2	0	0	5	0
*Caballero	0	0	0	0	0
Silvestri c	0	0	0	1	0
†Whitman	0	0	0	0	0
Lopata, c	0	0	0	1	0
Goliat 2b	4	1	1	2	2
Roberts p	2	0	0	0	0
‡Mayo	0	0	0	0	0
Totals	33	1	7	30	4

*Ran for Seminick in 7th.
†Walked for Silvestri in 9th.
‡Walked for Roberts in 10th.

NEW YORK (A.)	0 1 0	0 0 0	0 0 0	1	—2
PHILADELPHIA (N.)	0 0 0	0 1 0	0 0 0	0	—1

RBI—Woodling, Ashburn, DiMaggio. 2B—Ashburn, Waitkus, Coleman, Hamner. 3B—Hamner. HR—DiMaggio. SB—Hamner. S—Roberts, Waitkus. Winner—Reynolds. Loser—Roberts. Left—New York 11, Philadelphia 8. BB—Off Roberts 8, Reynolds 4. SO—By Reynolds 6, Roberts 5. DP—Johnson-Coleman-Hopp; Rizzuto-Coleman-Hopp.

Umpires—McGowan (A.), plate; Boggess (N.), 1B; Berry (A.), 2B; Conlan (N.), 3B; Barlick (N.) and McKinley (A.), four lines. Time—3:06. Attendance—32,660.

Associated Press wirephoto

CENTER OF ATTRACTION: Joe DiMaggio is surrounded by happy teammates yesterday in the dressing room at Shibe Park after the Clipper had won the second game of the World Series for the Yankees with a home run in the tenth inning. Left to right are Allie Reynolds, who set the Phils down with seven hits; Bobby Brown, DiMaggio, Gene Woodling and Jerry Coleman

Camera Highlights of Second Game of World Series as Yankees Won Again

Herald Tribune—Acme telephoto

FIRST BATTER: Gene Woodling facing Robin Roberts to start second game of World Series yesterday. Umpire is Bill McGowan. Woodling opened the game with an infield single

Associated Press wirephoto

PHILS BREAK ICE: Mike Goliat scoring the Phils' lone run of the two games thus far in the fifth inning yesterday. Teammate Dick Sisler signals no need to slide as Goliat registers tying run on Ashburn's loft to Woodling

Associated Press wirephoto

Joe DiMaggio being greeted by the batboy as he scores on his homer in tenth inning, of second game

San Antonio Triumphs In Dixie Series, 4 to 3

NASHVILLE, Tenn., Oct. 5 (AP).—The San Antonio Missions won their first Dixie Series tonight, clipping five Nashville pitchers for a 9-to-5 victory in the seventh and pay-off game of the series. The Texas Leaguers scored six runs in the sixth inning and three in the eighth to win the last three games in a row from the Southern Association club. The score by innings:

San Antonio	0 0 0	0 0 6	0 3 0	—9	10	0
Nashville	0 2 0	0 1 2	0 0 0	—5	9	3

Sleater, Gibson (2), Hudson (6), Herrera (6) and Baich. Schulz, Flamini (6), Atchley (6), Hollman (8), Modica (8) and Fernandes.

Shreveport Buys Outfielder

BURLINGTON, N. C., Oct. 5 (AP).—The Burlington Bees of the Class B Carolina League today announced the sale of outfielder Bill Evans, the loop's leading hitter this year, to Sheveport, La., of the Class AA Texas league.

Yankees Now 10 to 1 To Win World Series

Winning the first two games has skyrocketed the odds on the New York Yankees' winning the World Series to 10 to 1.

The Yankees had been 3-to-1 choices before the series opened and 4-to-1 after winning the first game. Odds on today's third game listed the Yankees at 12-to-5 favorites.

VIEWS OF SPORT

By RED SMITH

A Game for Boys

PHILADELPHIA, Oct. 5.—After thirty-five years, three hours and fifty-six minutes, the Phillies scored a run off American League pitching today, and such excitement swept this town you'd have thought the British were coming again. They weren't. DiMaggio was.

If the second game of the World Series proved anything to the 32,660 witnesses yeeping and bawling in Shibe Park this afternoon, it demonstrated that baseball is a young man's game. For nine innings the elderly gentlemen who work for the Yankees hit pusillanimous pop-ups against the wonderful pitching of the Phillies' young Robin Roberts.

Red Smith

On fourteen separate occasions the field agents of Casey Stengel tottered up to the plate and gave what Uncle Wilbert Robinson once described as brilliant imitations of men hitting out of a well. It was a bad day for low-flying ducks.

Again and again, feeble little bloopers spiraled skyward and descended into the gloves of Philadelphia infielders. On five occasions, the New York batter missed the ball altogether, striking out.

Doddering Joe DiMaggio, who'll hobble into his thirty-seventh year next month, was the feeblest of them all. On his first time at bat, he popped to the second baseman, on his next, he popped to the second baseman. On his third, he popped to the third baseman and a small cheer went up among a knot of his friends.

"He's pulling the ball now," they exulted. But on his fourth trip Old Joe popped to the first baseman.

An Old Professional Gentleman

THEN he came up again in the tenth inning with the score tied at 1-all, Roberts threw him one pitch. Joe said later that it was a slider, and Roberts said it was a fast ball. There'll be bad blood between them until the issue is settled, so let's not be drawn into the quarrel. Whatever it was coming, it was a fast ball going.

It streaked over second base on a rising line. Richie Ashburn, playing center field for the Phillies, turned and started toward the double-decked bleachers. He ran a few yards, stopped and watched. He saw a customer several rows back in the upper stands rise, catch the ball and sit down.

It was an old gentleman's hit, an old professional gentleman's. The old professional gentleman went creaking around the bases, and the Yankees got ready to catch a train for New York, where they will endeavor to beat the Phillies for the third and fourth time tomorrow and Saturday.

As a matter of fact, Joe may have saved the game in his elderly, professional style a few minutes before hitting the home run that won it. With one out in the ninth inning, Granny Hamner—whose name suggests a sweet old lady smelling of lavendar but who used to rack balls in a pool hall in Richmond, Va.—racked up a ball served by Allie Reynolds.

It was a long line drive that whistled out on a flat trajectory between center and right fields, and if it had got through the New York defense it would surely have been a triple and possibly the home run that would end the game. DiMaggio, starting when the ball did, loped over to his left, fielded the hit like a shortstop, and stopped Hamner at second base.

What followed did not suggest that the Phillies could have scored Hamner, even from third base. But nobody ever can tell about that. The way it went, Professor Eddie Sawyer, the licensed sorcerer of the Phillies, chose Dick Whitman to bat for Ken Silvestri, and Casey Stengel, the Yankees' resident djinn, advised Reynolds to put him on first base. Mike Goliat then grounded into a double play, retiring the side.

Clean, Refined Entertainment

BY CONTRAST with the Phillies' demonstration of how not to hit Vic Raschi in the first game, this was lively entertainment. Philadelphia kept rapping Reynolds for extra bases and managed to tie the score in the fifth inning. Roberts and Reynolds, both pitching elegantly, managed to keep it tied until DiMaggio loosened the stays.

With both teams frequently threatening, excitement grew. At one point Happy Chandler, baseball's little king, came right up out of his box seat and visited the Phillies dugout, presumably to ask the score. His action was generally approved, on the principle that a fellow ought to know the score at least once in five years.

Afterward it was said that the fans who waited since 1915 for their Phils to get into a World Series no longer seemed to care if they had to wait thirty-five years to see it happen again. This was unfair. They were still whooping for their heroes in the home half of the tenth when a walk and sacrifice put the tying run on second base with one out.

Reynolds threw something small, blurred and white to Richie Ashburn, who popped up. He threw more of the same to Dick Sisler, who started to swing at a third strike, checked himself half-way around and learned from Bill McGowan, the umpire, that the game was over.

Mr. Stengel's Last Word

McGOWAN walked toward the dugout. Yogi Berra and the Yankee infielders ran toward the mound to salute Reynolds. Sisler stomped behind McGowan, saying things. Nobody listened. He hurled his bat away and a customer leaped aside, dodging.

Mr. Stengel smiled and spoke behind his hand in the manner of a conspirator. "I am," he confided hoarsely, "getting good work from my help."

Stadium TV Technique to Give All an Umpire's View of Series

A "keep 'em in their seats" technique will be used for telecasts of the World Series when it shifts to the Yankee Stadium here today.

Most of the action will be covered by two matched cameras behind home plate to give "an umpire's view," except from about thirty-five feet up.

One of the cameras will have a Zoomar lens which enables it to shift smoothly and continuously from closeups to panoramic views and back—so you don't have to take your eye off the ball.

Roy Meredith, sports production director of station WOR-TV which will originate Series telecasts from the Stadium for the A. B. C.,C . B. S. and N. B. C. networks, as well as itself, explained that by covering most of the action with the paired cameras "you don't yank the video spectator out of one set and put him in another."

Meredith, one-time movie man, and sports director Bob O'Connor, decided on camera positions for the Stadium after an exhaustive survey. Meredith explained it was a well recognized principle in the movies that the viewer is momentarily thrown for a loss when his vantage point is suddenly shifted over a wide angle.

ReynoldsHears RadioReporton Winning Blow

Allie in Clubhouse When Jolter Connects; Hurler Uses Mostly Fast Balls

By Allie Reynolds
(As told to the United Press)

PHILADELPHIA, Oct. 4 (UP).—I heard about it on the radio. Honest. I heard about DiMag's homer on the radio.

God bless Joe DiMaggio! If he hadn't hit it, I'd probably still be pitching yet.

But I never saw Joe hit it. I had gone into our clubhouse for a few minutes while we were hitting and I heard the radio announcer say DiMaggio hit the ball into the left-field stands. I never felt so good about anything in my life, although I still wanted to go out and see that one run on the score board.

As for my pitching, I had the same trouble out on the mound that Vic Raschi had yesterday. It was so cold that I couldn't get my curve working too well. So I relied mostly on fast balls. Another thing that bothered me was getting a decent grip on the ball. My fingers were so black from resin after the game that it looked like I was digging coal.

Just to keep the Phillies off balance once in a while I mixed in a few sliders. Let me tell you I have plenty of respect for that Philadelphia club, especially Granny Hamner. Hamner got to me for a triple, a double and a walk. They tipped me he was a good high-ball hitter and now I'm really ready to believe it. He hit two high balls pretty good off me. I just couldn't keep the ball down when I was pitching to him.

Already some folks are asking me whether I received a bigger thrill out of beating the Phillies today or beating Brooklyn, 1 to 0, in the opening game of the 1949 World Series. Well, to tell the truth I really don't know which game meant more, although I will say this one was harder to win. You see, my case was something like the case of Philadelphia's pitcher Robin Roberts.

Facts and Figures On World Series

By The Associated Press

Facts and figures on second game of World Series.

Standing

	W.	L.
New York (A.)	2	0
Philadelphia (N.)	0	2

First Game at Philadelphia

New York (AL)	1	5	0
Philadelphia (NL)	0	2	1

Raschi and Berra; Konstanty, Meyer (9) and Seminick.

Second Game at Philadelphia

New York (A.)	2	10	0
Philadelphia (N.)	1	7	0

Reynolds and Berra; Roberts and Seminick, Silvestra (8), Lopata (10).

Remaining Games

Third, fourth and fifth (if necessary) at Yankee Stadium, Oct. 6, 7 and 8.

Sixth and seventh (if necessary) at Philadelphia, Oct. 9 and 10.

Yesterday's Figures

Attendance, 32,660.
Receipts, $171,143.36.
Commissioner's share, $25,671.50.
Players' share, $87,283.12.
Clubs' and leagues' share, $58,-188.74.

Total for Two Days

Attendance, 63,406.
Receipts, $331,273.64.
Commissioner's share, $49,691.04.
Players' share, $168,949.56.
Clubs' and leagues' share, $112,-633.04.

Player Limit Increased

BUFFALO, N. Y., Oct. 5 (AP).—The American Hockey League player limit has been raised from 13 to 14 men, excluding goal-tenders.

To avoid delay, please use the specific Chicago Tribune phone number assigned to take care of your needs.

SUperior 7 0260	SUperior 7 0200	SUperior 7 0100
For latest sports results, call this number between noon and midnight.	For general information, call this number between 8:30 A.M. and 9:00 P.M.	For want ads and Tribune, WGN and WGN-TV business, call this number.

Chicago Daily Tribune
THE WORLD'S GREATEST NEWSPAPER
Saturday, October 7, 1950 **F Page 1

PART 3

SPORTS MARKETS

YANKS WIN 3D; SEND FORD AFTER TITLE TODAY

In the WAKE of the NEWS

BY ARCH WARD
[Chicago Tribune Press Service]

BALTIMORE, Oct. 6—On Sept. 25, 1949, Dale Liechty of Lake Geneva, Wis., full back on Yale's football team, was stricken with polio, causing cancelation of the Yale-Fordham game. . . . One year later, to a day, Sept. 25, Liechty had licked the disease sufficiently to permit his enrollment in Northwestern's medical school, proving again that, even in these changing times, it's difficult to keep a good man down. . . . There's little chance that Golfer Bobby Locke will find the going tough when his tournament days are over. . . . Gordon Collins, president of a $210,000,000 South African banking institution, visiting in Chicago, revealed that the British Open champion already has invested $160,000 in a new apartment building in the Johannesburg area. . . . Illini punting, a problem both this year and last, apparently will be well handled the next three seasons. . . . Among freshmen at Champaign is one Ken Miller from Bloomington, Ill., who is capable of booting 60 yards consistently and once in high school kicked one 80 yards on the fly against Lincoln High. . . . Add to sports' father and son teams Paul Dunham and offspring, Don, who officiate high school football games at Salisbury, N. C. . . . Dunham Sr., a former Tulsa athlete, also is one of the leading officials in the Southern conference. . . . The Belmont Park race meet, which closes Monday has been up 12.5 per cent in handle and 10 per cent in attendance over a year ago. . . . An average of $1,600,000 has passed thru Belmont's betting machines daily since Sept. 18. . . . Frank Clement, one time assistant to athletic publicitor Walter Paulison at Northwestern, has been hired by television sponsors of Coliseum games in Los Angeles to lure fans into the vast expanse of empty seats for which the sponsors, by contract, must reimburse the contending teams. . . . The 26 story tower of the main building overlooking the University of Texas campus is bathed in orange floodlight on nights when Longhorn teams emerge victorious. . . . When Texas loses, the electrician flicks on the white lights, the same as on days when there is no game, just as if nothing had happened.

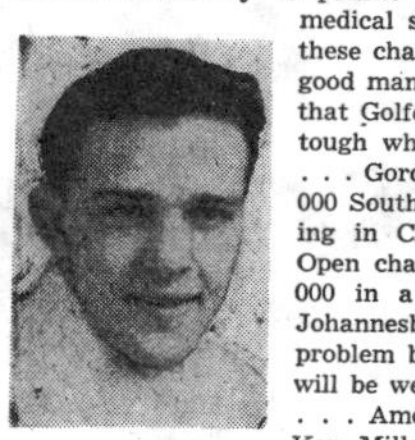

Dale Liechty

Twenty-one of the 50 members of the Southern California freshmen team this fall were captains of their high school teams. . . . Two weeks before the National league season ended, the Phillies were quoted by loop bookies as a 300 to 1 favorite to win the pennant. . . . On the last day of the season, Brooklyn was even money in the books to beat the Whiz Kids out of the flag. . . . Bob Kepler, Ohio State golf coach, is recuperating from a spinal operation. . . . Jim Rhodes, youthful mayor of Columbus, O., and originator of the national caddie tournament, has temporarily abandoned an idea to import a team of British caddies for a match against American lads. . . . Rhodes has discovered that most British caddies are old enough to be fathers, and in some cases grandfathers, of American bag toters. . . . The Ohio State-Southern Methodist game was the longest opening day contest in Buckeye history. . . . It lasted 2 hours and 48 minutes, leading one wag to remark that young Fred Benners, the Mustangs' passing star, used up 2 hours and 17 minutes of the time in the second half selecting receivers.

Leaves Love Me

Brown lives to the south of me,
Smith lives to the north. . . .
Living in between I see
Some work is coming forth.

Soon the leaves from down their trees
Will flutter to my lawn,
Then I, with rake, will venture forth
Until each leaf is gone.

And Smith will smile and so will Brown
At my autumnal labors,
And I will curse the blowing winds
And my leafless neighbors.
—The Iron River Kid

* *

Search Us

The boss asked for the facts and figures in the Blackstone case. I sent 'em over with Miss Arden and Miss Shirley and a note. . . . "Dear Boss: Here are the facts. Miss Arden and Miss Shirley have the figures." Now why do you think he wants to see me in his office? —H. J. L.

* *

Dumbell [?] Pome

The rooster as a timepiece
Is simplest of all.
No setting up in the summer,
No setting back in the fall.
—Paul T. Tomlin

* *

Dusting Off the Old Ones

Judge: Do you mean to tell me that besides taking the money, you also took some jewelry?

Prisoner: Yes, your honor. You see, I was taught that money alone can't bring happiness.
—Bernard Lyons

* *

Newsboy

Out on the street at the first crack of dawn,
He peddles his papers until they are gone.
Bearing the cold and the snow and the rain,
Great his endeavor, and small is his gain.
If he is lucky, a scooter or bike
Will carry his bag; or if not, he must hike
Until he has covered each home on his route,
To carry the news just as soon as it's out.
Big is the task and how little we pay
To learn how the other half lives, every day.
—Lorraine Good

* *

The Wake Depends Upon Its Friends — Help! Help!

"Bathing" Beauties

Speaking of terms ambiguous
And the way they dub our cuties—
If they are seen in bathing garb
Then they've called bathing beauties.

Full many have a perfect right
To be called King Neptune's daughters;
But a whole lot more in bathing suits
Would drown in a foot of water.
—Aunt Matilda

* *

You Can't Say It Again

"If we can hold the Russians off long enough," says Sen. Douglas, "we are going to build an army adequate for our situation." Huh! The alternate certainly is intriguing. —Bob Gordon

* *

Fencetastic

Boy, did we ever get stung. Some glib-tongued gook called and offered to fix the decrepit fence around the barn. He'd do it in the latest style for only fifty bucks. So we said go ahead and what do you think? That's right. All he did was build two little stairs on opposite sides so you can walk over the darned thing.—John Fahrner Jr.

* *

Advice to a Son

Do as your mother says . . . you're no better than I am!
—Carry of Ioway

* *

Sky Writing

Higher education gets higher all the time. Have you noticed tuition figures lately?
—Ting-a-Ling

Ten Years Ago Today—Bucky Walters evened the world series at three games apiece by blanking the Detroit Tigers, 4 to 0.

Illini vs. Badgers; Iowa at Indiana

55,000 WILL SEE EXPECTED SPEED BATTLE

Rain May Hamper Rivals Today

I's Have It

ILLINOIS		WISCONSIN
Klimek	L. E.	Faverty
Ulrich	L. T.	Yderstad
Cahill	L. G.	Kennedy
Vohaska	C.	Hansen
Brown	R. G.	Staiger
Siegart	R. T.	Huxhold
Fox	R. E.	Meyers
Major	Q. B.	Petruska
Piazza	L. H.	Strehlow
Karras	R. H.	Hutchinson
Raklovits	F. B.	Radcliffe

Referee—George Rennis [Minnesota]. Umpire—John Wilson [Ohio State]. Field judge—Joel Burghalter [Heidelberg]. Head Linesman—Cleo Diehl [Northwestern].

Broadcasts—American Broadcasting company, Columbia Broadcasting system, Wisconsin network, Badger network; WJJD, Chicago.

Television — Telecast on screens of State-Lake and Tivoli theaters over WBKB.

Kickoff—1:30 p. m.

BY WILFRID SMITH
[Chicago Tribune Press Service]

Champaign, Ill., Oct. 6—A forecast of showers disturbed Wisconsin and Illinois camps today as they completed preparations for their Western conference football game tomorrow afternoon in Memorial stadium. Illini and Badgers can present two of the fastest teams in the Big Ten and a firm turf is essential for that speed.

Johnny Karras

Fifty-five thousand, it is believed, will gather for the game which is dedicated to Illinois athletes who have received the varsity award and, in particular, to Judge Arthur Hall of Danville, who was head coach of Illinois football from 1907 thru 1912.

Governors on Hand

Judge Hall's 1910 team won seven games, was not scored on, and gave Illinois its first conference title. Illinois letter men honored Hall tonight at dinner.

Gov. Stevenson of Illinois and Gov. Rennebohm of Wisconsin, headliners in the receptions, will watch the first half of the game from the Illinois side of the field and then join Wisconsin's delegation.

Sixty-three players of the Wisconsin varsity and junior varsity squads arrived in two planes at the Illinois airport late this morning. The JV's played the Illini reserves in the afternoon after the Badger varsity had practiced. They remained in town but the Wisconsin varsity continued by bus to Danville for the night.

Platoon Systems

Bob Petruska, Wisconsin's veteran T formation quarter back and forward passer, is principal threat to Illinois. Johnny Karras, Illinois right half back whose open field running is superb, will get primary attention from the Badgers' defensive platoon.

Both squads offer offensive and defensive units. However, Hal Faverty and Bob Radcliffe are scheduled for double duty for Wisconsin. Faverty, 24 year old junior from Evanston, is offensive left end and backs up the left side of Wisconsin's five man defensive line. Radcliffe, 195 pound senior, is offensive full back and right side line backer.

Badger JVs Beat Illini, 20 to 7, in 4th Quarter

Champaign, Ill., Oct. 6 [Special]—Wisconsin's junior varsity handed the Illinois Jayvees their first defeat today, 20 to 7. The Badgers scored early in the first quarter and Illinois tied the score at 7 to 7 in the third after it recovered a fumble on the Wisconsin 11. Bryce Reeve tallied for the Illini. Wisconsin then came back to score twice in the final quarter.

Homecoming for Hoosiers Opens Race

Big Ten Kickoff

INDIANA		IOWA
Anderson	L. E.	Long
Kovatch	L. T.	Johnston
Georgakis	L. G.	Turner
Dolan	C	Towner
Smith	R. G.	Ginsberg
Boask	R. T.	Buntz
Craton	R. E.	Hoff
D'Achille	Q. B.	Drahn
Robertson	L. H.	Commack
Gomory	R. H.	Faske
Tutsie	F. B.	Reichardt

Referee—J. J. Berwanger [Chicago]. Umpire—Carl Rentschler [Ohio]. Field judge—E. C. Krieger [Ohio]. Head linesman — John R. McPhee [Oberlin].
Kickoff—1:30 p. m., Chicago time.

[Chicago Tribune Press Service]

Bloomington, Ind., Oct. 6—Iowa's surprising Hawkeyes, riding high after their 20 to 14 ambushing of Southern California, and Indiana's Hoosiers will come together in their first Big Ten test tomorrow before a homecoming crowd of 30,000.

Indiana, held to a 20 to 20 tie by Nebraska, faces the problem of stopping a potent Iowa running attack that smothered the Trojans.

Big Ten Debut for Coach

The game will mark the debut of Iowa's Leonard Raffensperger in Big Ten competition, opposing Indiana's Clyde Smith, starting his third season with brighter hopes than in the two preceding campaigns.

The principal task confronting the Hoosier defense, which allowed more than 300 yards rushing by Nebraska, will be coping with Half Backs Jerry Faske and Don Commack and Full Back Bill Reichardt, as well as the passing and kicking of Quarter Back Glenn Drahn. Loss of Bill Bird, defensive tackle, by injury will not make it easier.

One Sofomore to Start

Only one sofomore appears likely to crack the otherwise all-veteran lineups. Lou D'Achille, Hoosier quarter back, proved himself against the Huskers and will carry most of those duties for Indiana.

The game will be the 23d between the teams in a rivalry starting in 1912. Iowa holds a 10 to 8 margin in victories, while four games have ended in ties.

Dartmouth and Michigan Clash Today

Just a Start

MICHIGAN		DARTMOUTH
Clark	L. E.	Mariott
Hess	L. T.	Eberle
Jackson	L. G.	Price
Padjen	C.	Staley
Kelsey	R. G.	Morelli
Wahl	R. T.	Bailey
Allis	R. E.	McDonald
Putich	Q. B.	Clayton
Ortmann	L. H.	Tyler
Koceski	R. H.	Isbey
Dufek	F. B.	Roberts

Referee—Mike Layden [Notre Dame]. Umpire—L. Dobbins [Fordham]. Field judge—Ray Barbuti [Syracuse]. Head linesman—C. O. Dollings [Ohio U.]. Fifth official—Mike Lambke [Northwestern].
Broadcasts—WJR and WWJ, Detroit; WPAG and WUOM, Ann Arbor.
Kickoff—1 p. m. [Chicago time].

BY CHARLES BARTLETT
[Chicago Tribune Press Service]

Ann Arbor, Mich., Oct. 6—Michigan and Dartmouth, two of football's long time powers, will meet on the Wolverines' yard tomorrow afternoon for the first time in a contest that truly can be called colorful. The Michiganders will be sporting their traditional maize-and-blue regimentals. The Dartmouths naturally will appear in the verdant jerseys that have earned them the battle name of the Big Green.

These bright hues, however, will be outshone by the scarlet complexions of the contending athletes, brought on by embarrassments of no longer ago than last Saturday. It behooves each squad to get well tomorrow, after Michigan's 14 to 7 defeat by its up-the-road foe, Michigan State, and the 21 to 21 tie that Dartmouth had to sweat for against Dr. Eddie Anderson's Holy Cross Crusaders.

73,000 to Attend

Tomorrow's game crowd will be swelled to 73,000 by high school student guests.

For all that they were in on

[Continued on page 4, column 3]

PURDUE PERILS NOTRE DAME'S VICTORY MARCH

It's 22d Meeting in State Rivalry

Hoosier Battle

PURDUE		NOTRE DAME
Flowers	L. E.	Ostrowski
Janosek	L. T.	Flynn
Jackson	L. G.	Burns
Knitz	C.	Groom
Skibinski	R. G.	Wallner
Beletic	R. T.	Toneff
Brewster	R. E.	Mutscheller
Samuels	Q. B.	Williams
Maccioli	L. H.	Petitbon
Schmidt	R. H.	Barrett
Kerestes	F. B.	Landry

Referee—Rollie Barnum [Wisconsin]. Umpire—Dal Marvil [Northwestern]. Head linesman—Archie Morrow [Fall Rivers]. Field judge—W. E. Farrell [Minnesota]. Fifth official—Elliott Hasan [Illinois].
Broadcasts—WMAQ and WBBM, Chicago; WKJG and WOWO, Fort Wayne; WJOB, Hammond; WBAA, Lafayette; WSBT, South Bend.
Telecast—WGN-TV, 1:50 p. m. Kickoff—2:15 p. m. Chicago time.

BY IRVING VAUGHAN
[Chicago Tribune Press Service]

Notre Dame, Ind., Oct. 6—Notre Dame's Irish and Purdue's Boilermakers, both of whom had an intersectional flavor in their programs a week ago, will get down to some good old fashioned intrastate football brawling here tomorrow before 57,000 stadium patrons. It will mark the 22d meeting of the two Indiana schools.

The Boilermakers made it by bus today from their Lafayette headquarters and the thing uppermost in their minds was No. 40. The number also is of more than ordinary significance for the Irish, but for a different reason. The Irish want it because it will mean that many successive triumphs, interspersed by two ties. And, naturally enough, the Boilermakers would prefer not to be the 40th victim.

Purdue Always a Threat

While Purdue was thrown for a 34 to 26 loss last Saturday against Texas, the outcome didn't cause sparing use of the crying towels hereabouts during the week. Scouts came back singing the blues about the Boilermakers' explosive possibilities, particularly in the air.

In the last three years the Boilermakers have put on their best performances against the Irish. Three years ago the Big Ten members outran Notre Dame but succumbed to the skill of Johnny Lujack. Two years back Purdue outpointed the Irish in every department except in scoring and that final was 28 to 27. Last fall the Boilermakers, while losing 35 to 12, rushed for 282 yards, a total that other Notre Dame foes couldn't match.

Maccioli to Be Ready

Purdue met Texas without the services of Mike Maccioli, its ace breakaway ball carrier, but he is being figured on for full time employment against the Irish defense. The Boilermakers also expect to have Dale Samuels, the sofomore who sparkled at quarter in his debut last Saturday. During the week he suffered a shoulder injury. However, there is doubt about the appearance of Clinton Knitz at center.

College Football

LAST NIGHT'S RESULTS

College of Pacific, 41; Denver, 7.
Drake, 14; Oklahoma A. & M., 14.
Carthage, 20; Eureka, 6.
St. John's [Minn.], 34; St. Mary's [Minn.], 0.
North Western [Tex.], 26; Lamar Col., 0.
N. Texas State, 76; So'western [Okla.], 6.
Ottawa, 27; Bethel, 0.
Potomac State, 44; Newport News, 25.
Parris Island, 40; Fort Lee [Va.], 0.
North Dakota, 26; Bemidji Tchrs., 6.
Platteville Tchrs., 12; Superior Tchrs., 6.
Gannon, 34; Wilmington, 20.
Marietta, 20; Anderson, 7.
Wisconsin B, 20; Illinois B, 7.
Xavier [N. O.], 7; Fisk, 0.
Macalester, 7; Augsburg, 0.
South Carolina, 21; Furman, 6.
Memphis, 26; Chattanooga, 8.
Ithaca, 18; Brockport, 14.
Mount Union, 53; Clarion Teachers, 0.
Geo. Washington, 21; West Virginia, 14.
Miami [Fla.], 18; Villanova, 12.
Wichita, 21; Detroit, 13.
Doane, 20; Iowa Central, 0.
Concordia [Neb.], 13; York, 0.
Buena Vista, 7; Luther, 0.
Rider, 36; Arnold, 6.
Northern Michigan, 13; Northland [Wis.], 7.
Murray [Ky.], 19; Eastern State [Ky.], 0.
Southwest [Mo.] State, 19; Kirksville, 19.
Middle Tennessee, 47; Union [Tenn.], 0.
Kentucky Frosh, 37; Tennessee Frosh, 27.
Central [Mo.], 40; Shurtleff, 6.
Panzer, 14; Montclair, 13.
Bethany [Kas.], 12; Col. of Emporia, 7.

[COLLEGE GAMES TODAY ON P. 4]

DANCE STEP TO VICTORY

Bat boy (right) goes into victory dance as Gene Woodling scores Yankees' winning run in ninth inning on Gerry Coleman's single. New Yorkers took 3 to 0 game lead in world series over Phils thru 3 to 2 triumph yesterday in Yankee stadium.
[Associated Press Wirephoto]

Whiz Kids Run Out of Whiz Again

PHILADELPHIA	AB	R	H	RBI	P	A	E
Waitkus, 1b.	5	0	1	0	8	0	0
Ashburn, cf.	4	0	1	0	0	0	0
Jones, 3b.	3	0	1	0	1	1	0
Ennis, rf.	4	1	1	0	3	0	0
Sisler, lf.	4	0	1	1	2	1	0
Mayo, lf.	0	0	0	0	1	0	0
Hamner, ss.	4	1	3	0	2	2	1
Seminick, c.	2	0	1	0	5	0	1
Goliat, 2b.	3	0	1	1	4	1	0
§Caballero	0	0	0	0	0	0	0
Bloodworth, 2b.	0	0	0	0	0	0	0
Heintzelman, p.	2	0	0	0	0	2	0
Konstanty, p.	0	0	0	0	0	0	0
Meyer, p.	0	0	0	0	0	0	0
	‡32	2	10	2	¶26	7	2

NEW YORK	AB	R	H	RBI	P	A	E
Rizzuto, ss.	3	1	1	0	1	1	0
Coleman, 2b.	4	1	3	2	3	1	0
Berra, c.	2	0	0	0	6	1	0
Di Maggio, cf.	3	0	1	0	1	0	0
Bauer, lf.	3	0	0	0	1	0	0
*Brown	1	0	0	0	0	0	0
†Jensen	0	0	0	0	0	0	0
Ferrick, p.	0	0	0	0	0	0	0
Mize, 1b.	4	0	0	0	9	2	0
Collins, 1b.	0	0	0	0	1	1	0
Johnson, 3b.	4	0	0	0	1	3	0
Mapes, rf.	4	0	0	0	3	0	0
Lopat, p.	2	0	1	0	1	4	0
Woodling, lf.	2	1	1	0	0	0	0
	32	3	7	2	27	13	0

*Safe on error for Bauer in 8th. †Ran for Brown in 8th. ‡Whitman grounded out for Konstanty in 9th. §Ran for Goliat in 9th. ¶Two out when winning run scored.

	1	2	3	4	5	6	7	8	9	
Philadelphia	0	0	0	0	0	1	1	0	0	—2
New York	0	0	1	0	0	0	0	1	1	—3

Sacrifices—Seminick [2], Heintzelman, Jones. Two base hits—Ennis, Hamner. Stolen base—Rizzuto. Double play—Hamner to Waitkus. Left on bases—Philadelphia, 8; New York, 9. Earned runs—Philadelphia, 2; New York, 2.

Pitching summary—Runs and hits—Heintzelman, 2 runs and 4 hits in 7⅔ innings; Konstanty, no runs and no hits in ⅓; Meyer, 1 run and 3 hits in ⅔; Lopat, 2 runs and 9 hits in 8; Ferrick, no runs and 1 hit in 1. Struck out—Heintzelman [3], Johnson, 2; Lopat; Meyer [1], Mapes; Lopat [5], Ashburn 3, Seminick, Jones. Bases on balls—Heintzelman [6], Rizzuto 2, Berra 2, Coleman, Di Maggio; Ferrick [1], Goliat. Winning pitcher—Ferrick. Losing pitcher—Meyer. Time—2:29. Umpires—Boggess [N. L.], plate; Berry [A. L.], first base; Conlan [N. L.], second base; McGowan [A. L.], third base; Barlick [N. L.], left field; McKinley [A. L.], right field. Attendance—64,505.

N. U., Navy Open Football Series Today

Anchors Aweigh!

NORTHWESTERN		NAVY
Stonesifer	L. E.	Wilson
Huizinga	L. T.	Tetreault
Nowicki	L. G.	Fischer
Wietecha	C.	Bryson
Macrae	R. G.	Steele
Cernoch	R. T.	Hunt
Keddie	R. E.	Baldinger
Flowers	Q. B.	Zastrow
Alban	L. H.	Hauff
G. Miller	R. H.	Sindry
Athan	F. B.	France

Referee—David Buchanan [Temple]. Umpire—Arthur Barry [Princeton]. Field judge—Walter Coffee [Rutgers]. Head linesman—Howard Eyth [Carnegie Tech].

Kickoff—1 p. m., Chicago time.

Broadcast — WIND [Chicago]; WNMP [Evanston].

BY ARCH WARD
[Chicago Tribune Press Service]

Baltimore, Oct. 6—A new football rivalry will be inaugurated here tomorrow when Northwestern meets Navy in the newly completed Baltimore memorial stadium. The game not only is the first meeting between the teams, but marks the first appearance of the Wildcats in the east since 1940.

Upon arrival by chartered plane today the Wildcats found themselves established as one touchdown favorite over the Midshipmen, who bowed to Maryland, 35 to 21, Saturday while Northwestern was taking the measure of Iowa State, 23 to 13.

Wildcats Work Out

Altho cast in a favorite's role, the Wildcats were not in an overconfident mood as they settled in their quarters in the Emerson hotel after a brief workout this afternoon. Coach Bob Voigts displayed his respect for Navy by announcing plans to abandon his two platoon system in order to strengthen the Purple defense. At least three linemen will operate on both offense and defense.

This year's Navy team, operating under a new coaching regime headed by Eddie Erdelatz, former line coach with San Francisco's 49ers, flashed a well coördinated attack against Maryland.

Navy probably will be without

[Continued on page 4, column 5]

Series Figures

STANDINGS

	W.	L.	Pct.
New York [A.]	3	0	1.000
Philadelphia [N.]	0	3	.000

First game in Shibe park, Philadelphia:

	R.	H.	E.
New York [A.]	1	5	0
Philadelphia [N.]	0	2	1

Batteries—Raschi and Berra; Konstanty, Meyer [9] and Seminick.

Second game in Shibe park, Philadelphia:

	R.	H.	E.
New York [A.]	2	10	0
Philadelphia [N.]	1	7	0

[10 innings]

Batteries—Reynolds and Berra; Roberts and Seminick, Silvestri [8], Lopata [10].

Third game in Yankee stadium, New York:

	R.	H.	E.
Philadelphia [N.]	2	10	2
New York [A.]	3	7	0

Batteries—Heintzelman, Konstanty [8], Meyer [9], and Seminick; Lopat, Ferrick [9] and Berra.

FINANCIAL FIGURES
Third Game

Attendance, paid	64,505
Receipts	$309,040.35
Commissioner's share	$46,356.05
Players' share	$157,610.58
Clubs' and leagues' shares	$105,073.72

THREE GAME FIGURES

Attendance, paid	127,911
Receipts	$640,313.99
Commissioner's share	$96,047.09
Players' share	$326,560.14
Clubs' and leagues' share	$217,706.76

DRAKE IS TIED BY OKLAHOMA AGGIES, 14 TO 14

Des Moines, Oct. 6 (AP)—Drake battled Oklahoma A. & M. to a 14 to 14 tie tonight in the opening game of the Missouri Valley conference for both teams.

The Aggies drove 58 yards for the deadlock after Drake had taken the lead on a 54 yard pass-run play featuring Half Back Johnny Bright and End Bob Binette early in the fourth period. Bright pushed Drake into a 7 to 7 tie with a 23 yard touchdown sprint in the second quarter.

Pro Football

NATIONAL LEAGUE
NATIONAL CONFERENCE

	W.	L.	T.	Pct.	Pts.	O.P.
Chgo. Bears	2	1	0	.667	77	71
N. Y. Yanks	2	1	0	.667	93	83
Detroit	2	1	0	.667	76	58
Los Angeles	2	1	0	.667	100	66
Green Bay	2	1	0	.667	73	87
San Francisco	0	3	0	.000	1	88
Baltimore	0	3	0	.000	27	124

AMERICAN CONFERENCE

	W.	L.	T.	Pct.	Pts.	O.P.
N. Y. Giants	2	0	0	1.000	24	7
Cleveland	2	1	0	.667	66	16
Philadelphia	1	1	0	.500	55	42
Chgo. Cards	1	1	0	.500	62	58
Washington	1	2	0	.333	66	75
Pittsburgh	1	2	0	.333	40	35

GAMES TONIGHT
Los Angeles at Philadelphia.
Cleveland at Pittsburgh.
[Only Games Scheduled]

PHILS' SHAKY FIELDING AIDS IN 3-2 VICTORY

Miller or Church May Start

BY EDWARD BURNS
[Chicago Tribune Press Service]

New York, Oct. 6—The Philadelphia Phillies forged ahead of the New York Yankees today for the first time in the 1950 world series, but, quite tragically, were unable to protect a 2 to 1 lead they possessed with two out and none on in the eighth, or a 2 to 2 tie they had with two out and none on in the ninth. So the Yankees won their third straight game before 64,505 this afternoon, 3 to 2.

Thus far the Yanks have won, 1 to 0, 2 to 1, and 3 to 2, perhaps indicating they will conclude the series tomorrow by a score of 4 to 3, tho it is problematical just how the National leaguers are going to score three runs against Eddie Ford, the boy wonder lefty, who will start for the Yankees. In his American league debut season, Ford won nine straight before he lost his final decision in relief. Bob Miller, who won his first eight National league games and finished with an 11 to 6 ratio, probably will start for the Phillies. If Miller doesn't go, Bubba Church may draw the assignment.

Can Match 1939 Effort

If the Yankees continue to produce the essential one extra run or more tomorrow, it will be the first swept world series since the Yankees bowled over the Cincinnati Reds in 1939.

Today's game was the first real thriller of the series, the excitement stretching over several innings. Joe Di Maggio's 10th inning victory homer in Philadelphia yesterday was dramatic enough, but it was accomplished in a matter of seconds.

Granny Hamner, generally rated as the best National league shortstop, and heaviest hitter of the day and series, was perhaps the outstanding goat of today's loss. His fumble of an easy grounder, which should have ended the eighth with the Phillies still ahead, 2 to 1, on a run he himself had provided in the seventh inning was a devastating development for mournful Philadelphians, and for underdog sympathizers in general.

Coleman Has Busy Day

The Yankees' first run, like the other two, began to bloom after two were out and, like the winning run, was sent home on a single by Gerry Coleman.

In the third inning, Ken Heintzelman made Cliff Mapes pop to Eddie Waitkus, then struck out Eddie Lopat, the Yankee starter. Phil Rizzuto walked. He stole second and went on to third when Andy Seminick threw low to second. Coleman then singled to left—first Yankee hit—scoring Rizzuto. It was an earned run because Rizzuto would have scored from second had he stopped there after his theft.

Sisler Drives in Ennis

The Phillies tied the score in the sixth. Richie Ashburn executed his third strikeout and Willie Jones also fanned. Then Del Ennis doubled to right, his first hit of the series, and scored on Dick Sisler's single, also his first hit of the series. Sisler was picked off first when Hamner failed to connect on an attempted surprise bunt maneuver.

Hamner, who had wasted a single in the second inning, led off the seventh with a single and moved up on Seminick's sacrifice. Mike Goliat singled, scoring Hamner to put the Phillies ahead for the first time in the series. Heintzelman sacrificed, but the side was out on Waitkus' fly.

Heintzelman, who had receded from the 17 games he won for the Phillies in 1949 to three this season, retired Johnny Mize, Bill Johnson, and Mapes in order in the seventh.

Ashburn Left on Second

Ashburn led off the Phils' eighth with a single and moved up on Jones' sacrifice. But Ennis and Sisler couldn't advance him.

Then came the Yanks' tying eighth. Gene Woodling batted for Lopat and popped to Hamner. Rizzuto supplied the second out with a grounder to Jones. Coleman walked after a three and two count, and this seemed to upset the 35 year old Heintzelman. He walked Yogi Berra and Di Maggio on eight straight wide ones, loading the bases.

Then Manager Eddie Sawyer summoned Jim Konstanty and Manager Casey Stengel sent Bobby Brown to bat for Hank Bauer. Konstanty pitched a ball to Brown. Brown fouled off three, after which he sent a gentle grounder straight to Hamner. Hamner juggled the ball, and Coleman ran home with the one run he didn't drive home. Mize then fouled to Jones and the

[Continued on page 3, column 4]

MOON MULLINS

Woodling Makes Second, Scores in Ninth as Yankees Win Third World Series Game, 3 to 2

[Acme Telephoto]

Granny Hamner scores Phils' second run in seventh inning, giving Philadelphia game lead for first time in series. Yankee Catcher Yogi Berra (right) gets ball too late after Mike Goliat's single. Ed Lopat (30), Yank pitcher, backs up play while Phils' Ed Waitkus (4) watches. Umpire is Dusty Boggess.

[Associated Press Wirephoto]

Granny Hamner, Phillies shortstop, is out trying to score from third in ninth inning on Dick Whitman's bounce to first with two team mates on base. Joe Collins threw to Yogi Berra for out and Yankee catcher turns to check progress of other base runners. Umpire is Dusty Boggess. Whitman was pinch hitting for Jim Konstanty.

[Associated Press Wirephoto]

Gene Woodling (right), Yank left fielder, slides for second in ninth inning as Granny Hamner (left), Phils shortstop, and Jim Bloodworth, second baseman, go for loose ball (arrow) after Bloodworth made diving stop of Phil Rizzuto's liner. Woodling, safe, was driven home with winning run on Gerry Coleman's hit.

[Associated Press Wirephoto]

Phil Rizzuto leaps over Mike Goliat of Phils at second following bunt in seventh inning. Activity was wasted, however, when batted ball was ruled foul.

[TRIBUNE Photo]

Nick Amato (left) takes blow on neck from David Harris in south side finals of Catholic Youth organization boxing tournament in C. Y. O. gym. Harris won bout.

SPARTANS SEEK THIRD STRAIGHT

Tab Maryland as Their Next Victim

Power Test

MICHIGAN STATE		MARYLAND
Carey	L. E.	Karnash
Coleman	L. T.	Pobiak
Yocca	L. G.	O'Connor
Tamburo	C	Cosgrove
Tobin	R. G.	Troha
Horrell	R. T.	Dean
Minarik	R. E.	Augsburger
Dorow	Q. B.	Scarbath
Grandelius	L. H.	Shemonski
Pisano	R. H.	Modzelewski
Crane	F. B.	Fullerton

Referee—Russell Rupp [Lebanon Valley]. Umpire—G. K. Tebell [Wisconsin]. Head linesman—Fk. C. Curtiss [Chicago]. Field judge—D. J. Lutz [St. John's]. Fifth official—C. J. Bauer [Michigan].

Radio broadcasts—CBS network: WILS, Lansing, Mich.; CKLW, Detroit; WJIM, Lansing, Mich., and Michigan network.

Kickoff—1 p. m. [CST].

BY GEORGE STRICKLER

[Chicago Tribune Press Service]

East Lansing, Mich., Oct. 6—Michigan State's Spartans, thoroly enjoying their role as the No. 2 team in the nation, pronounced themselves ready tonight to strengthen their position in Macklin stadium tomorrow by beating University of Maryland.

Two factors contrived to keep Spartan confidence at a lofty pitch. One is the belief, locally, that Michigan State is as good as any team in the country, including, or, if you please, not excepting Notre Dame.

Bob Ciolek Ready

The other is the unexpected return to right half back of big Bob Ciolek, who has been sidelined for three weeks with an injury. Ciolek's presence gives Coach Biggie Munn three capable first string passers, and obviously leaves the Spartans better fortified than they were a week ago at Ann Arbor, where they precipitated riots and severe headaches by toppling Michigan, 14 to 7.

Maryland is viewed as just the type of a victim needed by any team nursing a hankering for top national ranking. The Terrapins have been acclaimed by their own coach, Jim Tatum, as " my best at Maryland."

Georgia Stunned Maryland

The Terrapins, however, were the victims of a sad accident at Georgia two weeks ago. But after the 27to 7 upset by the Bulldogs, Maryland bounced back into stride last week to trounce Navy, 35 to 21.

Michigan State made it four straight over Maryland last year by a score of 14 to 7, but on that occasion the Spartans were not confronted with one John Scarbath, a sofomore quarter back passing wizard who bedeviled Navy from ward room to poop deck.

Composite Box of World Series

THREE GAMES

NEW YORK

	G	AB	R	H	2B	3B	HR	RBI	BB	SO	Bat Av	P	A	E	Fld Av
Woodling, lf	3	10	1	4	0	0	0	1	2	0	.400	3	0	0	1.000
Rizzuto, ss	3	10	1	2	0	0	0	0	2	0	.200	3	4	0	1.000
Berra, c	3	11	0	1	0	0	0	0	3	1	.091	20	1	0	1.000
Di Maggio, cf	3	10	1	2	0	0	1	1	3	0	.200	7	0	0	1.000
Mize, 1b	3	12	0	1	0	0	0	0	0	1	.083	22	2	0	1.000
Hopp, 1b	2	1	0	0	0	0	0	0	0	0	.000	6	0	0	1.000
Collins, 1b	1	0	0	0	0	0	0	0	0	0	.000	1	1	0	1.000
Brown, 3b	3	9	1	3	1	0	0	0	0	0	.333	0	0	0	.000
Johnson, 3b	3	5	0	0	0	0	0	0	0	3	.000	1	5	0	1.000
Bauer, rf-lf	3	12	0	2	0	0	0	0	0	0	.167	7	0	0	1.000
Mapes, rf	1	4	0	0	0	0	0	0	0	1	.000	3	0	0	1.000
Coleman, 2b	3	11	2	4	1	0	0	3	2	0	.364	9	9	0	1.000
*Jensen	1	0	0	0	0	0	0	0	0	0	.000	0	0	0	.000
Raschi, p	1	3	0	1	0	0	0	0	0	0	.333	0	3	0	1.000
Reynolds, p	1	3	0	1	0	0	0	0	1	2	.333	1	2	0	1.000
Lopat, p	1	2	0	1	0	0	0	0	0	1	.500	1	4	0	1.000
Ferrick, p	1	0	0	0	0	0	0	0	0	0	.000	0	0	0	.000
	3	103	6	22	2	0	1	5	13	9	.214	84	31	0	1.000

PHILADELPHIA

	G	AB	R	H	2B	3B	HR	RBI	BB	SO	Bat Av	P	A	E	Fld Av
Waitkus, 1b	3	12	0	3	1	0	0	0	1	0	.250	25	2	0	1.000
Ashburn, cf	3	13	0	3	1	0	0	1	0	3	.231	6	0	0	1.000
Sisler, lf	3	13	0	1	0	0	0	1	0	4	.077	8	1	0	1.000
Ennis, rf	3	11	1	1	1	0	0	0	0	1	.091	8	0	0	1.000
Jones, 3b	3	10	0	2	0	0	0	0	0	2	.200	8	5	1	.929
Hamner, ss	3	10	1	5	2	1	0	0	1	0	.500	4	5	1	.900
Seminick, c	3	7	0	2	0	0	0	0	1	3	.286	11	1	1	.923
†Caballero	2	0	0	0	0	0	0	0	0	0	.000	0	0	0	.000
Silvestri, c	1	0	0	0	0	0	0	0	0	0	.000	1	0	0	1.000
‡Whitman	3	2	0	0	0	0	0	0	1	0	.000	0	0	0	.000
Lopata, c	1	0	0	0	0	0	0	0	0	0	.000	1	0	0	1.000
Goliat, 2b	3	10	1	2	0	0	0	1	1	1	.200	9	5	0	1.000
Bloodworth, 2b	1	0	0	0	0	0	0	0	0	0	.000	0	0	0	.000
Konstanty, p	2	2	0	0	0	0	0	0	0	1	.000	1	0	0	1.000
Meyer, p	2	0	0	0	0	0	0	0	0	0	.000	0	1	0	1.000
Heintzelman, p	1	2	0	0	0	0	0	0	0	0	.000	0	2	0	1.000
Roberts, p	1	2	0	0	0	0	0	0	0	1	.000	0	0	0	.000
§Mayo, lf	2	0	0	0	0	0	0	0	1	0	.000	1	0	0	1.000
	3	94	3	19	5	1	0	3	6	16	.202	83	22	3	.972

*Ran for Brown in 8th inning of 3d game.

†Ran for Seminick in 7th inning of 2d game and for Goliat in 9th of 3d game. ‡Flied out for Konstanty in 8th inning of 1st game, was walked intentionally for Silvestri in 9th inning of 2d game, hit into fielder's choice for Konstanty in 9th inning of 3d game. §Walked for Roberts in 10th inning of 2d game.

COMPOSITE SCORE BY INNINGS

New York	011	100	011	1—6
Philadelphia	000	011	100	0—3

Earned runs—New York, 5; Philadelphia, 3. Runs batted in—Coleman [3], Woodling, Di Maggio, Ashburn, Sisler, Goliat. Sacrifices—Rizzuto, Raschi, Roberts, Waitkus, Seminick [2], Heintzelman, Jones. Stolen bases—Hamner, Rizzuto. Double plays—Johnson to Coleman to Hopp, Rizzuto to Coleman to Hopp, Hamner to Waitkus. Left on bases—New York, 29; Philadelphia, 19. Umpires—Conlan [N.], McGowan [A.], Boggess [N.], Berry [A.], Barlick [N.], McKinley [A.]. Attendances—30,745 [first game]; 32,660 [second game]; 64,505 [third game]. Times—2:17 [first game]; 3:06 [second game]; 2:35 [third game].

PITCHING SUMMARY

NEW YORK

	G	CG	IP	H	R	ER	BB	SO	HB	WP	W	L	Pct.	ER. Av.
Raschi	1	1	9	2	0	0	1	5	0	0	1	0	1.000	0.00
Reynolds	1	1	10	7	1	1	4	6	0	0	1	0	1.000	0.90
Lopat	1	0	8	9	2	2	0	5	0	0	0	0	.000	2.25
Ferrick	1	0	1	1	0	0	1	0	0	0	1	0	1.000	0.00
	3	2	28	19	3	3	6	16	0	0	3	0	1.000	0.93

PHILADELPHIA

	G	CG	IP	H	R	ER	BB	SO	HR	WP	W	L	Pct.	ER. Av.
Konstanty	2	0	8⅓	4	1	1	4	0	0	0	0	1	.000	1.13
Meyer	2	0	1⅔	4	1	1	0	1	0	0	0	1	.000	4.50
Roberts	1	1	10	10	2	2	3	5	0	0	0	1	.000	1.80
Heintzelman	1	0	7⅔	4	2	1	6	3	0	0	0	0	.000	1.13
	3	1	27⅔	22	6	5	13	9	0	0	0	3	.000	1.61

RAMS SEEK 1ST VICTORY OVER EAGLES TONIGHT

Philadelphia, Oct. 6 (AP)—The Los Angeles Rams, seeking their first victory over the Philadelphia Eagles in 11 meetings, will play the injury riddled National Football league champions in Municipal stadium tomorrow night. The Rams have not beaten the Eagles since they moved from Cleveland after winning the league title in 1946.

They'll find several of the Eagles on the injured list. Steve Van Buren, the league's record holding ground gainer, still is a doubtful quantity altho he is listed to start. Half Back Bosh Pritchard and Tackle Al Wistert have not fully recovered from training game injuries.

Today's Events in Chicago

ICE SHOW

Ice Follies in Chicago Arena, Erie, McClurg ct., and Ontario st., 2:30 and 8:30 p. m.

PROFESSIONAL WRESTLING

At Marigold Gardens, Broadway and Grace sts., 8:30 p. m.

BROWNS MEET STEELERS

Pittsburgh, Oct. 6 (AP)—A crowd of 20,000 is expected to watch tomorrow night's National Football league game between the Cleveland Browns and the Pittsburgh Steelers. Coach Johnny Michelosen of the Steelers said his team will be handicapped thru the loss of Half Back Bobby Gage who is sidelined with an injured rib cartilage.

YANKS WIN 3D OVER PHILS, 3-2

Ford Will Seek Final Victory Today

[Continued from first sports page]

game went into the ninth, a 2 to 2 tie.

Hamner Atones for Error

Ferrick was successor to Lopat at the start of the ninth. Hamner greeted him with a double, his fifth hit and third extra base swat in two days. Seminick bunted a high pop which Johnson elected to trap. With Johnson holding the ball and third base uncovered, Hamner ran to third. Johnson still had time to throw out Seminick, and Andy's effort went for a sacrifice. Goliat was given an intentional pass.

Dick Whitman, batting for Konstanty, topped one to Joe Collins, who had supplanted Mize at first base. Collins threw to Berra and Hamner was out at the plate. Ralph Caballero was sent to second to run for Goliat, an unhappy move as things turned out because it brought Jimmy Bloodworth into the game as the second baseman in a fateful role in the Yankee ninth. The Phillie ninth ended when Waitkus flied to Mapes.

Phils' Fielding Collapses

Russ Meyer, former Cub, took over the Phillies' pitching responsibility in the home ninth. Johnson flied out after a three and two count and Mapes struck out. Woodling missed two strikes, then was safe on a carom off Bloodworth's glove, registered as the Yankees' fifth hit, tho many apparently believed Goliat would have made the play. Rizzuto lined one toward center which Bloodworth knocked down but couldn't hold. Woodling was safe at second, Rizzuto at first, credited with a single.

Coleman then sent a high fly between Jack Mayo, who had supplanted Sisler in left, and Ashburn, who has caught many similar flies in his day. Woodling was home with the winning run long before the the fly plunked to the sod.

Hawks, Ontario Amateur All-Stars Play Tonight

OTTAWA, Ont., Oct. 6 [Special]—The Chicago Blackhawks of the National Hockey league will oppose an Ontario All-Star amateur team tomorrow night in an exhibition duel. The Chicagoans have won six exhibitions in a row, the most recent a 6 to 3 decision over the Cleveland Barons of the American league.

Gophers Play Huskers; Seek Rugged Crew

BY EDWARD PRELL

[Chicago Tribune Press Service]

Minneapolis, Oct. 6—The University of Minnesota will be searching for aggressiveness first, and victory second, against Nebraska's Cornhuskers tomorrow afternoon. Chances are that it will take both of these elements to satisfy the anticipated crowd of 45,000. Followers of the Gophers were very unhappy last Saturday evening when the report came in from the west coast that Washington had whipped their favorites, 28 to 13.

Bernie Bierman, the harried Minnesota coach, will go down the line with an all-sofomore offensive lineup looking for a combination with the desire to play rugged football, a hall mark at Minnesota in the veteran's previous 15 seasons.

Hudak Demoted

Among the Minnesota flops of last Saturday was George Hudak, who had been counted on for a sparkling job at tail back in the single wing attack. The junior from Chisholm will be sidelined tomorrow for Larry Esser, a 190 pounder from Madison, Wis. If Bierman carries thru with his all-sofomore battle front, it will be a first in modern Minnesota football.

Nebraska is sofomore conscious, too. In the Huskers' 20 to 20 tie last week with Indiana, Bobby Reynolds scored all three of the touchdowns and kicked two extra points. One of his scoring runs covered 46 yards. The team from the Big Seven conference rushed 309 yards against the Hoosiers, throwing only two passes, both of which were completed, but for only 13 yards.

Nebraska's head coach is Bill Glassford, no stranger to Bierman. Glassford was on the 1933 and 1934 University of Pittsburgh teams, which were beaten for the national collegiate title by Minnesota. This was during a football era dominated by Jock Sutherland's Pitt Panthers and Bierman's Gophers, both exponents of muscle, or single wing, football.

Sofomores Move Up

Bierman has shifted Jack Mertes, 203 pound sofomore, from fourth string tackle to a starting assignment at left guard. Almost as drastic was the promotion of Jim Boo, 215 pound sofomore, to the middle spot in the five man defensive line after scant action at end and tackle.

Bernie's Burned

MINNESOTA		NEBRASKA
French	L. E.	Simon
E. Johnson	L. T.	Twogood
Mertes	L. G.	Spellman
Robinson	C	McGill
Olson	R. G.	Strasheim
Johansen	R. T.	Handshy
Mitchell	R. E.	Regier
Gelle	Q. B.	Nagle
Esser	L. H.	Reynolds
Cochran	R. H.	Mueller
G. Johnson	F. B.	Curtis

Referee—L. A. House [William Jewell]. Umpire—R. W. Finsterwald [Ohio U.]. Field judge—M. J. Delaney [St. Viator]. Head linesman—Richard Sklar [Kansas].

Kickoff—1:30 p. m.

Sports Telecasts

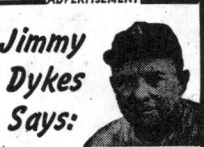

TODAY

12:15 p. m.—WENR-TV—World series.
WNBQ—Harvard vs. Columbia.
12:30 p. m.—WBKB—World series.
12:55 p. m.—WBKB—Army vs. Penn State.
1:30 p. m.—WGN-TV—Notre D. vs. Purdue.
8:15 p. m.—WENR-TV—Browns vs. Steelers.
10:00 p. m.—WGN-TV—Wrestling from Marigold.

SPORTS RESULTS

For the latest sports results, call the Chicago Tribune—SUperior 7-0260. This special Tribune sports telephone service is available from noon to midnight. Please do *not* use this number when you call the Tribune for general information, to place a want ad, or on Tribune or W-G-N business.

CAL.
Today's
GRID-EYE
SCOPE
and
LINEUPS
PENN

BOY DIES AFTER UC HAZING

BLUE STREAK EDITION TELEPHONE YU 6-5151

NEW YORK STOCKS COMPLETE

THE CALL BULLETIN

AN INDEPENDENT NEWSPAPER

CALL AND POST, VOL. 168, NO. 43
THE CALL-BULLETIN, VOL. 188, NO. 43
SATURDAY, OCTOBER 7, 1950 7c DAILY

Ford, Miller Start On Mound

Grid-Eye-Scope Gives Bears Edge

Six positions for California, one for Penn and four even. That's the way The Call-Bulletin Grid-Eye-Scope sizes up today's game at the Memorial Stadium at Berkeley.

The contest starts at 2 o'clock.

PENNSYLVANIA					CALIFORNIA	
No.	Player	Wt.	Position	Wt.	Player	No.
87	Roberts	185	LER	198	Cummings	80

Roberts is a senior who has been on the varsity for three years. He's a fine pass catcher and a good blocker. He runs with the ball so well that he will play safety on defense. Cummings is most improved end on the Bear squad. A senior, he has finally found himself. Not spectacular and just a fair pass receiver, he gets his licks in as a blocker. **POSITION EVEN.**

71	Evans	215	LTR	220	Krueger	73

Evans is a husky sophomore who eastern critics are hailing as one of the best first year men in their section. He's 19 years old and stands 6 feet 2. Krueger is one of the Bear sophomores, big and rugged, but not too fast. **POSITION EVEN.**

68	Lemonick	200	LGR	225	Richter	67

The Penn fellow is the east candidate for All-American and Penn usually gets a man on the team. He is the best Quaker lineman. Richter is California's All-American line candidate. He's rough, tough and big. We'll take him. **EDGE TO CALIFORNIA.**

52	Greenawalt	210	C	200	Harris	54

Greenawalt won a letter as a sophomore last year. He's steady and plays both offense and defense. His dad was a Penn end of the 20's. Harris is a steady and secure guy. Seldom makes a bad pass and does some fine inside blocking. **POSITION EVEN.**

64	Krimmel	200	RGL	210	Edmonston	6

Krimmel is a fast and agile fellow, playing his second yea with the club. Edmonston is up from the Ramblers and one o Pappy Waldorf's finds. He's a good blocker and can play on defense. **POSITION EVEN.**

73	McGinley	200	RTL	220	Karpe	72

McGinley's father was an All-American tackle at Penn and played against Cal in 1924. This McGinley is not quite that good.

Continued on Page 5, Column 1

Phil Rizzuto, Yankee shortstop, leaps in air over sliding Mike Goliat (9) of the Phils in seventh inning of third World Series game at Yankee Stadium. Play began when Phil pitcher Ken Heintzelman tried bunt to push Goliat to second. Ball went foul, but Yank catcher Yogi Berra grabbed it and threw to Rizzuto who was covering second. Umpires ruled no play. Yanks went on to win, 3 to 2. (More photos on Sports pages.)

Whitey Ford (above), 21 year old rookie, will hurl for the Yankees against the Phils today in the fourth World Series game at Yankee Stadium. —Associated Press Wirephoto

Cal-Penn Tops Grid Fare

By ROY CUMMINGS

If we can get your mind off the World Series and those amazing Yankees for a minute or two there is a heck of a lot of important football on tap in our league this afternoon, tonight and tomorrow.

This is the schedule.

TODAY

California vs. Pennsylvania at Berkeley.

Stanford vs. Oregon State at Corvallis.

UCLA vs. Washington at Seattle.

USC vs. Washington State at Pullman.

TONIGHT

Santa Clara vs. San Jose State at San Jose.

TOMORROW

St. Mary's vs. Loyola at Los Angeles.

USF vs. Nevada at Kezar.

Coach Lynn Waldorf's Golden Bears face their first real test of the year against Penn, always one of the top teams of the country despite their Ivy League affiliations. A crowd of 70,000, the biggest of the season in the west is expected for the game, all wanting to find out just how good the Bears are.

MUST BE BETTER

The new Bears, victors over Santa Clara and Oregon in their first two starts, will have to play a lot better football than they have so far to lick the Quakers who beat Virginia in their first game of the season last Saturday.

Stanford is a top heavy favorite to take Oregon State in their first conference game but might find the going rough on what is certain to be a heavy and wet field at Corvalis. It has been raining there since Thursday and slow going could down the Indians' speed and passing attack.

SPARTANS, BRONCOS

Tonight's contest at San Jose between the Spartans and the Broncos looks like a tough one. The Broncos are favored, but might get a surprise from San Jose, which did better than well against Stanford.

USF, still down from the whipping it took from Stanford last week, will be trying to get going again against Nevada tomorrow.

The Sunday game of the week is the St. Mary's clash with Loyola in Los Angeles. The Gaels captured everybody's admiration when they held Georgia to a 7 to 7 tie a week ago and this one will show whether they can keep going or not. Loyola is loaded and Coach Joe Ruetz's gang will have to be high to win.

Back home and to the game at Berkeley, California will face its biggest defensive test of the young season when it goes against Penn's single wing and "L" formations which will be something completely new to them.

WEST'S KOREA PLAN OK'D BY UN

NEW YORK, Oct. 7 (AP).—The United Nations Assembly today approved the eight-nation western plan for Korea which authorizes a final UN drive over the 38th Parallel and writes a master plan for rebuilding Korea. The Assembly vote was 47 to 5. (Earlier details, Page A.)

FOUR S. F. YOUTHS HURT IN CRASH

Four San Francisco youths were injured today, on critically, when their automobile overturned and hit an embankment on Highway 40 in Pinole. Most severely hurt was Ernest E. Soto Jr., 22, of 84 Colgary street.

GUIRINO HIKES PRICES ON IMPORTS

MANILA, Oct. 7 (AP).—President Elpidio Quirino today authorized a general increase in ceiling prices about 10 per cent for coffee, flour and canned meats and up to 15 per cent on other items of import.

MINE FIELD SPOTTED OFF KOREA COAST

WASHINGTON, Oct. 7 (AP).—American destroyers have destroyed two more floating mines off the coast of Korea, the Navy said today. A helicopter also has spotted a field of about 15 moored mines in the same general area, the Navy added.

Gaudy If Not Neat

That's Rube Goldberg's latest invention—for getting a woman out of a telephone booth. It all starts with President Truman jumping out of bed at 6 a. m. See page 3.

CHAMPS SEEK 'CLINCHER' IN 4TH GAME

NEW YORK, Oct. 7.—A pair of rookie pitchers started on the mound today as the New York Yankees pressed to make it a four-straight clean sweep over the Phillies in the 1950 World Series.

Eddie Ford, 21 year old southpaw "golden boy" was Casey Stengel's starting Yank hurler, while Manager Eddie Sawyer, just before game time, assigned 24 year old righthander Bob Miller to pitch.

Both pitchers are in their first World Series.

Ford, from Astoria, Long Island, copped nine in a row before he lost a game on relief.

Miller, troubled by a sore shoulder in mid-September, won 11 and lost six in the season. He started with eight in a row before he was finally beaten in mid-July. Sawyer will have Jim Konstanty ready for action if Miller shows signs of weakening.

Sawyer started the same batting order against Ford as he

Continued on Page 4, Column 8

CALL-BULLETIN TODAY

Freak Mishap Kills Driver On Gate Span Road

(Photo on Page B)

One man was killed early today in a freak auto accident on the Richardson avenue ramp of the Golden Gate Bridge.

Highway Patrol officers said the victim, Ernest Tate, 31, of 3048 Sixteenth street, foreman for a janitorial maintenance company, apparently fell out of his car as the door on the driver's side opened.

Southbound, Tate had passed another car and was pulling in front of it when he toppled. His car smashed into the retaining wall, and the following vehicle, driven by William F. Green, 22, of 686 Sixty-third street, Oakland, passed over his body.

Green and Charles A. Deardorf, 62, of 473 Ellis street, a passenger in Tate's auto, were uninjured when Green's car piled into Tate's.

In an accident last night, Alfred J. Haywood, secretary of the San Francisco Musicians' Union, and his wife, Josephine, both 68, suffered shock and possible leg injuries when their auto hit a tree.

The accident occurred on Sneath lane, between Junipero Serra cutoff and El Camino Real, in San Mateo County. Officers said Haywood, of 540 O'Farrell street, apparently lost control of the car.

The Weather

Bay Area—Fair today, tonight and Sunday. Warmer today. (Details on Page 2.)

U. C. YOUTH, 18, KILLED DURING FRAT STUNT

A University of California sophomore was killed and another student seriously hurt early today in the tragic climax of a U. C. fraternity hazing stunt in Contra Costa County.

The boys were struck by an auto as they walked along a country road where they had been left by their Sigma Pi fraternity brothers to make their way home as part of the fraternity initiation rite.

YOUTH, 18, KILLED

Dead was Gerald Foletta, 18, of San Ardo, near King City.

Theodore Glasnow, 25, a senior of 332 Twenty-seventh street, San Francisco, was taken to Cowell Memorial Hospital, on the Berkeley campus, with a compound fracture of the left leg and other undetermined injuries.

Three other boys escaped injury. They were Robert John Halpin, 22, and Robert L. McNary, 19, both of Compton, and Clyde M. Marquat, 21, of Lompoc.

LEFT ON PEAK

Deputy Coroner Robert W. Cockburn said the survivors told him they had been taken up Mt. Diablo last night and left there, without money.

This is a traditional phase of UC fraternity initiations.

The boys started to walk home and were on the north side of Ygnacio Valley road, just east of

Continued on Page A, Column 3

U. S. Troops Take City Near Parallel

By HOWARD HANDLEMAN
Far Eastern Director, International News Service

TOKIO, Oct. 7 (INS).—The U. S. First Cavalry Division captured the vital city of Kaesong only two miles south of the Thirty-eighth Parallel today and a fourth South Korean division was believed to have pierced the boundary in preparation for an early United Nations general offensive.

American seizure of Kaesong and reported crossing of the parallel by the Republic of Korea Eighth Division means that General Douglas MacArthur's UN forces have taken control of virtually the entire 200 mile length of the vanishing boundary from east to west.

Advances by the Eighth Korean Division were said to mean that four ROK divisions already have all or part of their fighting

Daily Double Specials

By KEY HORSE

Observer to Strike Three
Soon Again to Strike Three
Sea Angel to Strike Three

BAY MEADOWS CONSENSUS

ASSOCIATED PRESS	INS	HERNANDEZ	CONSENSUS
1—Leota W. M. T. Pockets *Gin High	No Selections	Ed Heller Leota V. *Gin High	Leota W. (13) Ed Heller (8) M. T. Pockets (3)
2—Sea Angel Librarian Observer	Sea Angel *Soon Again Observer	Sea Angel Observer Librarian	Sea Angel (18) Observer (10) Librarian (4)
3—Matarrah Slick Pigeon Mimosan	War Adend Matarrah *Jade C.	Slick Pigeon Matarrah Strike Three	Matarrah (11) Slick Pigeon (9) Strike Three (8)
4—Castle Oak Speedmark *Man's Agent	Castle Oak Anayr Speedmark	Castle Oak Anayr Speedmark	Castle Oak (15) Speedmark (6) Anayr (6)
5—Fox Hunt Pepper N' Salt Flying Box	Fox Hunt Flying Box Pepper N' Salt	Fox Hunt Pepper N' Salt Irish Horn	FOX HUNT (20) Pepper N' Salt (10) Flying Box (4)
6—Stirrup Cup Jackstraw Top View	Jackstraw Top View Alibi Kate	Jackstraw Stirrup Cup Alibi Kate	Jackstraw (18) Stirrup Cup (11) Top View (4)
7—REIGHMOYER Rado Kid Phil D.	Reighmoyer Rado Kid Harvest Time	PHIL D. Reighmoyer Rado Kid	Reighmoyer (18) Phil D. (9) Rado Kid (8)
8—Cash Reward Beau Lief Justa Shower	CASH REWARD Beau Lief Heel Stay	Justa Shower Knights Music Cash Reward	Cash Reward (11) Justa Shower (7) Beau Lief (6)
9—Vino Fino Sun State Blue Tiger	Precession Blue Tiger Outotheblue	Blue Tiger Vino Fino Sun State	Blue Tiger (14) Vino Fino (9) Outotheblue (6)
10—Makai King Count Nazina	Class Day One Patch Makai	Makai Shifty Roman Trinket Time	Makai (14) Trinket Time (6) Class Day (5)

*Scratched. Horses listed in capitals are selector's best bets.
Ed Romero's selections are included in consensus figures. Consensus figured five points for first, three for second and one for third.

DiMaggio Lifts Yank Series Hopes

Brass Hats Brew Big Trades During Series

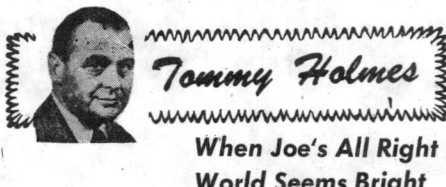

BROOKLYN EAGLE
Sports
Edited by
LOU NISS

Tommy Holmes

When Joe's All Right World Seems Bright

HE BETTER BE GOOD—In the Yankee clubhouse after the fourth game, nobody knew who would be Leo Durocher's next pitching choice. The manager of the Giants had said that he would make his selection right after the game, but word had not yet drifted in from across the hall.

The news caught Casey Stengel as he hustled toward the showers. It was to be Larry Jansen, the great white father of the National League.

"A good pitcher," said Stengel, nodding vigorously. "He showed us that the other day. But we beat one of their good pitchers today, didn't we? That Maglie's nobody's monkey.

"Anyway, Jansen's gotta be good. Leastways, any feller with seven kids better be. But if we've finally learned how to hit, maybe everything will be all right."

This time the Yankee clubhouse was bustling with confidence and spirit. Nothing like a few good hits—and the Yanks had racked up 12 in their 6-to-2 victory—to bring the sunshine out again. Probably the story was Joe DiMaggio. "When Joe's all right, the world seems bright," the Yankees used to sing, and this seemed like old times.

THE CLEAN-UP SPOT—In three games the ancient Clipper had the boys in the pressbox composing his baseball obituary. Eleven times at bat without the slightest sign of a basehit. That was his record.

But Skipper Stengel, who shook his batting order up vigorously before the fourth game, by-passed the fourth spot.

"I ain't goin' to take him out of the clean-up position," said Stengel. "He hasn't been right but he's as likely to explode there as anybody else."

DiMaggio was retired for the 12th time in a row in the first inning when Sal Maglie fooled him with a curve and he took a third strike. But, even in that fruitless time at bat, he looked better. Before he went down, he hit one hard against the upper facade in left field just a few feet foul.

The score was tied at 1 to 1 and two were out when he came up in the fourth. He singled to left for his first hit and a huge roar went up from the crowd. (The majority of fans in this World Series are rooting for the miracle Giants, but practically everybody is rooting for DiMaggio.) Anyway, nothing happened in that inning because Monte Irvin made a spectacular one-handed grab of Gene Woodling's long blast to left center.

EXIT MAGLIE—The Yankees led by 2 to 1 when DiMaggio came up in the fifth and that wasn't much of a lead the way Allie Reynolds had been cat-walking along. This time his appearance was preceded by Yogi Berra's single. With one blast of his bat, the score became 4 to 1. He belted it high and far into the upper left field stands. That finished Maglie, who was taken out for a pinch hitter in the bottom half of that inning. And though a mild eruption occurred in the ninth, the Yankees really weren't in much danger after that.

The Yankees said they were impressed by Maglie's pitching, but this is a World Series in which everybody says nice things about everybody else. In the old days an incident such as occurred Saturday when Eddie Stanky kicked the ball out of Phil Rizzuto's hand to launch a five-run rally would have resulted in fire and brimstone flashing between the benches.

THE BARBER'S STYLE CRAMPED?—But, shucks, Rizzuto and Stanky appeared on a national TV hook-up Sunday night for $1,000 apiece and ribbed each other on the question of whether Stanky has touched second base yet. Maybe, things like that are the reason why the old spirit of diamond violence seems to be disappearing.

The Yankees said that Maglie's stuff was good but that they weren't falling for his outside curves, hitting only his pitches that came in over the plate. This is a trick which few in the National League have been able to learn.

One theory advanced is that Maglie's style may have been cramped by that coast-to-coast TV and radio hook-up. At any rate, he neglected to give hitters that quick-shave with his fast ball that so frequently has seemed to make his outside curves more effective. That might not have looked so good with six umpires on the field and millions looking on.

But the Giants deny this. "That wouldn't have made any difference to Sal," one of them said. "Why do you think we call him the barber?"

A KEY MAN—Reynolds was better than he was in the opening game when the Giants beat him, but still far from razor sharp. He was frequently behind the hitters and had to work hard, but he had better stuff.

His key pitch came in the fourth inning. At that time, the Yanks had just taken a 2-to-1 lead. In the first inning, Al Dark hit the first of his three doubles and scored when the troublesome Irvin singled to left. In the fourth, Dark doubled again and Irvin came up with one out.

The count reached three-and-two and "Superchief" really roared down the middle with a slider that blazed past Irvin's bat.

Even so, Reynolds might have had real trouble had Willie Mays not been so docile at the plate. Allie couldn't get Bob Thomson out at all. The Scot, who wrecked the Dodgers, walked twice and singled twice. But three of these times he was erased when Mays grounded into a double play. The last one sent the Yankees to the clubhouse. The Giants too, only the Giants walked more slowly.

Dodgers Hope To Pry Pitcher From Cincy

There are a number of big player deals bubbling among the baseball men at the Worlds Series, and American League batting champion Ferris Fain of the Philadelphia A's may be involved in them.

It appeared likely that none of the deals now being discussed will be announced this week, because the owners don't want to compete with the World Series for publicity.

But you could be mighty sure that the deals were going on, because there wasn't a club in either major league which finished the season satisfied with its roster. And you could see the executives of the clubs huddling together in the hotels here during the hours they are not at the ball park.

Angle for Cal

The runner-up Dodgers may get that long sought-for starting pitcher from the Cincinnati Reds.

The Reds are hot after a shortstop and a left-fielder. They'd like to have Dodger utility men Bobby Morgan or Rocky Bridges for shortstop, and they think Cal Abrams would become a .300 hitter if he played left field for them regularly. In exchange, the Dodgers would like to get Ewell Blackwell but might be more than happy to settle for Howie Fox or Herman Wehmeier, both strong-armed hurlers.

It was known that the A's, anxious to gain money and talent in an effort to crack the first division, were willing to part with Fain, the slick-fielding first baseman who topped 'em all in his league with .344.

A club doesn't usually trade away a batting king, but the A's know that he is the man who will command the best deal.

One deal the Philadelphians discussed had Fain going to the anxious-to-rebuild Boston Red Sox. In exchange, the A's would get big Walt Dropo, the inconsistent-hitting first baseman; good-field, no-hit infielder Fred Hatfield, and a young pitcher.

On the other hand, Fain also was reportedly offered to the White Sox as part of an even bigger deal. Things were only in the talking stage on this one, which would have Fain and Bobby Shantz, the hottest southpaw in the league in the late weeks of the season, going to the Sox for first-baseman Eddie Robinson, utility man Don Lenhardt, outfielder Al Zarilla, and pitcher Randy Gumpert. The A's would like to deal for young Minnie Minoso, but the Sox reportedly weren't interested.

The White Sox have announced the only deal during the series. Last year, the Chiagoans were the busiest trading team in either league and this time they started by buying third baseman Hector Rodriguez from Montreal, Dodger farm team in the International League.

Rodriguez, 31-year-old Negro, was voted "rookie of the year" in the I. L. His purchase is especially significant since it was in a similar deal the Sox bought Al Carrasquel from the Dodger farm system.

Even those hot Giants weren't satisfied with their team at the end of the most amazing stretch run in history. They're interested in additional outfield and catching strength, and maybe getting a fellow lined up to replace veteran Eddie Stanky at second base.

A WINNING COMBINATION — Slugger Joe DiMaggio (right) and pitcher Allie Reynolds of the New York Yankees embrace each other in victory in the dressing room after yesterdays fourth World Series game at the Polo Grounds. The Chief, Allie Reynolds, Indian-signed the Giant batters to eight scattered hits while the Yankee Clipper, Joe DiMaggio, hitless in 12 previous attempts, singled and smacked a tremendous home run in the fifth with one on, to prod the American Leaguers to victory. They beat the Giants, 6 to 2, to lock the Series in a tie, 2—2.

Baseknocks Bring Back Yank Smiles

By JOE LEE

Whether it be war or baseball, there's nothing more pleasant than a smiling Yankee. And there was a whole gang of 'em wearing broad grins in the dressing rooms at the Polo Grounds yesterday after the boys from across the Harlem River squared the Series count with the Giants.

The American League champions had reason to rejoice. Joe DiMaggio came out of his batting slump of 12 for zero by rapping out a single and a two-run homer and the infield had the Yankee poise of old as they executed four double plays to tie the series record for twin killings.

Casey Stengel, the winking greybeard, who reminded his guys in a pre-game pep talk that they "hadn't done much to be proud of as Yankees," was more than pleased with the balanced rapping of bats for base hits and the slick defensive font of his infield.

"Even in practice we looked alive," Casey remarked, "Joe came out of it and tagged a few. Everybody hit, in fact. The base running looked shabby in a few spots. McDougald shouldn't have been hit by Bauer's drive through second and third and Reynolds getting thrown out rounding first didn't look so good. But Allie pitched much better today. We finally looked like the Yankees."

DiMaggio had a big audience as he explained how he shortened his swing on the advice of Lefty O'Doul and received other tips from Lou Fonseca, former White Sox first baseman, who now directs the World Series movies for both leagues. It was the eighth World Series home run that Joe delivered in his career.

"By shortening my swing, I got my timing back," Joe explained. "It was a curve ball I hit for the homer. It felt mighty good, but the one I hit the best was that foul ball my first time up. That one was really tagged. I've been using a 35-ounce Babe Ruth model bat. Today I used a 34-ounce model."

Over in the Giants dressing quarters, Manager Leo Durocher said he was still playing the Yanks "a game at a time."

Lippy would not say whether he would rest Maglie for another starring role or use them in relief spots. However, Lippy did say he was going to string along with Willie Mays, the rookie outfielder who hit into three double plays.

"Maglie couldn't put the ball where he wanted it and Allie Reynolds had great stuff out there today. That about sums up the ball game." Durocher remarked "We might have gotten Reynolds out of there though, if Whitey Lockman hadn't swung at that bad pitch in the last inning. If he walked, the bases would have been loaded and that would have finished Reynolds."

Willie Mays just doesn't know what's the matter. I hit the ball good," he said, "but it just don't go through, that's all. Maybe I'll use a heavier bat. That may help."

All Squared Away

Yankees (6)	ab	r	h	po	a	Giants (2)	ab	r	h	po	a
Bauer,lf	4	0	2	0	0	Stanky,2b	4	0	1	3	0
Rizzuto,ss	5	1	1	5	5	Dark,ss	4	1	3	2	1
Berra,c	5	1	1	8	1	Thompson,rf	3	0	0	1	0
DiM'gio,cf	5	1	2	2	0	Irvin,lf	4	1	2	3	0
Woodl'g,lf	4	2	1	1	0	Lockman,1b	4	0	0	4	0
McD'd,2,3b	4	0	1	3	2	Thomson,3b	2	0	2	2	3
Brown,3b	4	1	2	0	0	Mays,cf	4	0	0	5	1
Coleman,2b	0	0	0	1	1	Westrum,c	2	0	0	7	1
Collins,1b	3	0	1	7	0	Maglie,p	1	0	0	0	0
Reynolds,p	4	0	1	0	2	aLohrke	1	0	0	0	0
						Jones,p	0	0	0	0	0
						bRigney	1	0	0	0	0
						Kennedy,p	0	0	0	0	0
Totals	38	6	12	27	11	Totals	30	2	8	27	6

aPopped out for Maglie in 5th.
bStruck out for Jones in 8th.

Yankees	0 1 0 1 2 0 2 0 0—6
Giants	1 0 0 0 0 0 0 0 1—2

Errors—Stanky, Thomson. Runs batted in—Irvin, Collins, Reynolds, DiMaggio 2 (Rizzuto scored on Stanky's error in 7th), McDougald, Thomson. Two base hits—Dark 3, Woodling, Brown. Home run—DiMaggio. Left on bases—Yankees 8, Giants 5. Bases on balls off—Reynolds 4, Maglie 2, Jones 1. Struck out by—Reynolds 7, Maglie 3, Jones 2, Kennedy 2. Hits and runs off—Maglie, 8 and 4 in 5 innings; Jones, 4 and 2 in 3; Kennedy, 0 in 1. Double plays—Rizzuto-McDougald-Collins, Reynolds-Rizzuto-Collins (2), Rizzuto-Coleman-Collins. Winning pitcher—Reynolds. Losing pitcher—Maglie. Umpires—Barlick (N.), plate; Summers (A.), 1b; Ballanfant (N.), 2b; Paparella (A.), 3b; Gore (N.), and Stevens (A.) foul lines. Time—2:57. Attendance—49,010.

Veeck, Hornsby Sure to Prove Explosive Mix

Bill Veeck and Rogers Hornsby, guiding geniuses of the St. Louis Browns, may prove the most explosive mix since the unknown hero poured dry vermouth and gin into a glass and made the first martini.

Veeck is baseball's star showman—the tieless and tireless chap who introduced fireworks, a midget and other elaborate sideshows into the game.

Hornsby is the direct opposite—a solid, hard baseball man who likes his baseball straight.

The men are similar, however, in one important respect: each speaks his mind in loud, clear tones, frequently without regard to the consequence.

It is just that fact which has the baseball world buzzing in anticipation of a stormy and wordy three-year sideshow to end all sideshows in St. Louis.

Veeck announced yesterday that the Browns had signed Hornsby to a three-year contract. And no more than three hours later Hornsby was making a few things about the Browns clear.

"There'll be no clowning," the straightforward Hornsby said. "It's going to be straight baseball with no midgets and no clowns."

Just Smiles

Veeck, sitting only about three feet away when Hornsby laid down the new law, just smiled a pleased little smile and said nothing. But there is no one connected with baseball who thinks for a minute that Veeck will be able to go through an entire season without trying to "clown it up a bit."

And there is no one who doesn't believe Hornsby—the old out-spoken rajah — will stand up and tell Mr. Veeck to peddle his sideshows to some travelling circus.

"Three years is a long time," one prominent baseball man said. "It's a long time for two very different type men to live together."

Hornsby has always had a reputation for being a martinet. He tolerates no foolishness from his players and he expects them to drive themselves as hard as he drove himself during his magnificent career.

Joe's Homer Sparks Mates Into Lathering Giants' Sal Maglie

By HAROLD C. BURR

The 1951 World Series began to take on the good old Yankee look at the Polo Grounds yesterday. The Bronx Bombers sholled Sal Maglie from the mound in five heats—the Barber of Seville didn't come out for the sixth round—and went on to even the Series at two games each with a 6-to-2 victory behind a 12-hit attack.

The Yanks realized that this was the one they had to win to stay in the gold-and-glory games and like so many of their key games in the American League race they crashed through.

They had looked stale and listless in the first three games beside the Giants' hustle. But yesterday they went up to hit, grim and tight-lipped. They refused to go after bad balls.

Perhaps it could be traced to Joe DiMaggio's first time at bat in the opening inning. All the Jolter did eventually was to take a third strike. Maglie said it was his best pitch of the ball game. But prior to that DiMaggio racked up a savage drive against the green roof coping in left field that was foul by only a foot or so, and hit a couple of more hot shots before going down.

Joe singled in the third for his first hit of the Series and in the fifth, with Yogi Berra flinging his arms aloft on first base, Joe hit high and deep into the left field upper deck for his eighth World Series home run that gave Allie Reynolds all the tallies he required. Everybody in the crowd of 49,010 impartially cheered Joe as he circled the bases.

If the Clipper continues to hit the chances of the Yankees to take the Series are bright. The world champions must win again today with Ed Lopat going against Larry Jansen to successfully defend their title. It isn't going to be easy, but our neighbors across the bridge have done it before.

Reynolds atoned for his miserable showing in the first fray and held baseball's miracle team to eight hits that the Giants bunched only in the first and ninth innings. But he was often behind the hitter and on his own confession was tiring at the fiinsh. Casey Stengel came out of the dugout in the ninth when the inevitable Giant rally swung into motion.

"I'll take care of these guys," he confidently told the anxious Professor. He did, too, when Willie Mays hit into his third double play of the afternoon.

"My stuff was working good," insisted the Chief. "Yeah, Mays helped," he added frankly.

Maglie said his curve ball was hanging.

"The gopher ball I threw to DiMaggio hung, too—away out and upstairs,' 'Sal said ruefully. "I couldn't get loose all day. Perhaps it as the sudden change in the temperature. But that isn't any alibi."

The Barber wandered around the quiet dressing room at a loose end.

"I guess I might just as well shave this beard off," he muttered, stroking his bristles. "I thought it would bring me luck. But it didn't."

The Yanks hit Maglie hard in the early frames, but either their drives went foul or they were caught by the Giant outfield. Mays made a circus catch on Bobby Brown in the second, losing his cap and falling down in the process. But the first Yankee run in that same second round was set up by Gene Woodling's blooper to left for two bases.

The rally ended with one run when Joe Collins was hit by Hank Bauer's batted ball. Reynolds himself knocked in another with a hard single to center, but was caught between bases on the old cutoff play. Sheldon Jones relieved for the Giants in the sixth. Phil Rizzuto foxed Wes Westrum into throwing to the wrong base and Gil McDougald hit safely to left, which added up to two more runs.

Base running by Yankee pitchers—Vic Raschi Saturday and Reynolds yesterday—hasn't been exactly wide awake, but the American Leaguers' defense has been sharper over the four-game stretch. They caught another Giant stealing yesterday on a pitch out and this time Rizzuto held the ball to tag out Monty Irvin, just after he batted in the first run of the ball game.

It's been the friendliest of Series with the players fraternizing at the bat and in the field. Durocher is the originator of the epigram, "Nnce guys finish last." It could be that his nice guys—Stankey excepted—may finish second.

SAL MAGLIE, Giant pitcher, makes the long walk back to the clubhouse at the end of the fifth inning during which he was tagged for a homer by Joe DiMaggio. Maglie was lifted for a pinch-hitter after completing the rough inning.

Yanks 17-10 Choice In Fifth Clash Today

Reno, Nevada, Oct. 9—(U.P.) The Yankees are in the World Series driver's seat, according to the odds-makers of the Nevada Turf Club.

Going into yesterday's fourth game, the club was quoting the series as an even money bet. But, after the Yankees won, the odds were revised to make the Yankees 12½ to 10 favorites to win the series.

In today's fifth game, the Yankees are favored at 17 to 10 if their Eddie Lopat pitches against Larry Jansen of the Giants.

Cuccinello Quits Post

Tony Cuccinello resigned the job of coach with the Cincinnati Reds today to accept a similar position with another major-league team. In accepting his resignation, the Reds did not reveal the identity of his new team.

FACTS AND FIGURES ON WORLD SERIES

Fifth game—Today at the Polo Grounds.
Standings New York Yankees, won 2, lost 2. New York Giants, won 2 lost 2.
Game time today—1 p.m., EST.
Probable pitchers — Yankees: Ed Lopat (21-9). Giants: Larry Jansen (23-11).
Weather forecast—Fair and cool.
Radio broadcast—Mutual Broadcasting System.
Television—National Broadcasting System.
Remaining games—Sixth at Yankee Stadium, Wednesday; sevents if necessary) at Yankee Stadium, Thursday.
Four-game total atendance—232,736. Receipts—$1,099,141.92. Commissioners share—$164,871.29. Players' share—$560,562.37. Club's and leagues' share—$373,707.86.

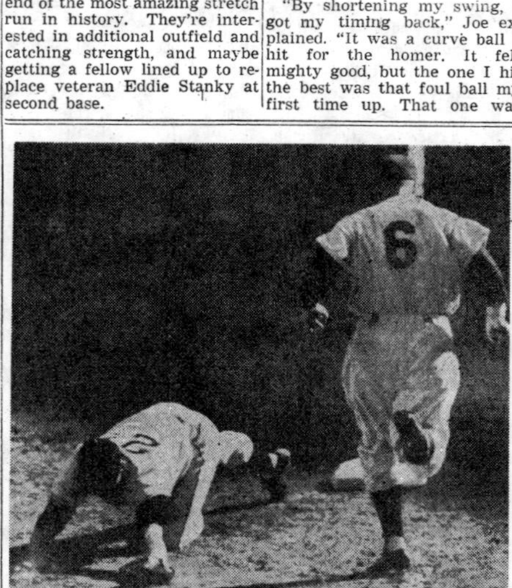

STARTS BALL ROLLING—Yankee third baseman Bobby Brown trots safely into first after beating out a hit in the fourth inning against the Giants at the Polo Grounds yesterday. Dark made a beautiful stop, but his throw to first pulled Lockman off the bag. Brown scored later on Reynolds' single.

Casey Stengel Retirement Story Denied

The Yankees, midway through the fourth World Series game at the Polo Grounds yesterday, denied officially over the press box loud speaker the story that Casey Stengel wouldn't manage the world champions next year.

"There's no truth in it," came blaring over the air. "Stengel signed a two-year contract and it still has a year to run."

Earlier in the day Business Manager George Weiss made the same denial.

Alvin Dark banged out three doubles off Allie Reynolds. This isn't a record. Frank Isbell, second baseman of the 1906 White Sox, hit four against the Chicago Cubs.

But another Giant hitter has a good chance of shattering an old mark. Monty Irvin lashed out two more hits to bring his total for the series up to nine. The record is 12 safeties, set by Sam Rice, Pepper Martin, Buck Herzog and Joe Jackson.

The Yankees equaled the record for double plays with four, held by several clubs.

Poor Willie Mays hit into three of 'em.

"I'm hitting the ball good," muttered the crestfallen Willie. "It just hasn't eyes for me. I can't seem to find the holes in the infield."

The players will whack up $560,562.07 for their share of the gate, which sets a new high for series' spoils.

The mortality on the bases has been high. Each club has left 29 runners stranded.

Phil Rizzuto pulled an old Tony Lazzeri trick on Wes Westrum in the seventh.

The Scooter was on second and deliberately ran halfway down to third. Instead of running out into the infield with the ball to hang up the Yankee shortstop between bases, the Giant catcher pegged to Eddie Stanky, whose throw to third hit Rizzuto on the head and rolled away for a Yankee run.

Rizzuto is taking a physical beating in this series. Both wrists were banged up when Jim Hearn hit him with a pitched ball and Stanky kicked the ball out of his hands. His ankles were cut and slashed by Giant runners going into him, and now he has a bump on his cranium to add to his souvenirs.

Half of the Giants and Yankee players have disconnected their telephones for the duration so they won't be bothered with World Series ticket requests. H. C. B.

THE WEATHER

Today: Fair and cool; moderate west to northwest winds, becoming gentle at night.

Tomorrow: Fair, with somewhat higher afternoon temperatures; northwest winds.

Temperatures Yesterday: Max., 61.8; Min., 49
Today's Probable Range: Max., 60; Min., 45
Humidity at 3 p. m. Yesterday: 43%
Expected Humidity This Afternoon: 40-50%

Detailed Report and Map—Page 39

NEW YORK

Herald Tribune

European Edition Published Daily in Paris

Late City Edition

111th Year VOL. CXI NO. 38,313

TUESDAY, OCTOBER 9, 1951

230 West 41st Street, New York 18, N. Y. Telephone PEnnsylvania 6-4000

FIVE CENTS

Truce Talks This Week Likely as Allies Accept Site Proposed by Reds

Ridgway's Liaison Team to Meet Reds

General Approves Talks at Pan Mun Jom; Won't Broaden Neutral Zone

By Mac R. Johnson

From the Herald Tribune Bureau

TOKYO, Tuesday, Oct. 9.—Early resumption of Korean armistice talks, probably by the week end, seemed likely today, following an exchange of messages by the United Nations and Communist commanders in which both sides agreed to abandon Kaesong in favor of a new conference site in the Pan Mun Jom area.

Gen. Matthew B. Ridgway, the U. N. commander, notified the Communists that he would send liaison officers to Pan Mun Jom to meet the Red liaison officers at 10 a. m. Wednesday to dispose of details preliminary to a conference resumption.

Site Is Farming Village

In a message broadcast from Peking Sunday night, the Communists accepted Gen. Ridgway's invitation to name a new conference site and proposed Pan Mun Jom, a farming village six miles southeast of Kaesong, the city where truce talks have been held in the past.

Gen. Ridgway, in a reply broadcast Monday night by the U. N. radio at Tokyo, did not specifically accept Pan Mun Jom but said he believed "a site in the immediate vicinity of Pan Mun Jom will meet the fundamental condition of equality of movement and control."

A copy of this message was handed to the Communists at 8 a. m. today at Pan Mun Jom by a U. N. liaison officer.

In his reply, Gen. Ridgway rejected, in mild terms, a proposal by North Korean Premier Kim Il Sung and Gen. Peng Teh-huai, the Chinese Communist commander, that the Kaesong neutral zone be expanded to include Munsan, where the U. N. command has an advance camp for the purpose of the truce negotiations.

Stipulates Neutral Zone

"It is my view," Gen. Ridgway said, "that all that is necessary is a small neutral zone around the new conference site, with Kaesong, Munsan and the roads leading to Pan Mun Jom from Kaesong and Munsan free from attack."

He also reiterated a stand which he took in messages to the Communists on Sept. 27 and Oct. 4—that the fundamental condition "which must exist in order to insure equality of movement and control to, from and within the conference site" is that the site must be situated "approximately midway between our respective lines." He said that only then "can each side be expected to discharge its share of responsibility for the security of the approaches to the

(Continued on page 10, column 5)

Stassen Calls Testimony of Jessup False

Asserts State Dept. Considered Red Aid

His Charges Challenged, but He Says Record Will Bear Him Out

By Don Irwin

WASHINGTON, Oct. 8.—Harold E. Stassen, in subsequently challenged testimony, charged today that Ambassador-at-Large Philip C. Jessup had given "absolutely false" testimony to the Senate Foreign Relations subcommittee considering Dr. Jessup's nomination as a delegate to the United Nations.

In reply to a question by Sen. Guy M. Gillette, D., Iowa, Mr. Stassen said Dr. Jessup's testimony under oath before the subcommittee last Thursday had been untrue, "specifically when he said the State Department had never considered or contemplated the recognition of Communist China."

"Simply Wasn't True"

Mr. Stassen, president of the University of Pennsylvania and former Republican Governor of Minnesota, said it "simply wasn't true" that the United States had continuously supported the Nationalist government of China, as Dr. Jessup had testified.

Sen. H. Alexander Smith, R., N. J., noted that Dr. Jessup had emphasized to the subcommittee that he had used the word "considered" in the sense of actually preparing for a course of action.

Later, Sen. John J. Sparkman, D., Ala., the chairman, disputed Mr. Stassen's accusations at length, referring to State Department documents and hitherto secret subcommittee testimony to show that Mr. Stassen had drawn what he called a "completely erroneous conclusion."

Sen. Smith's Stand

Sen. Smith, in questions and statements, undertook to make it clear that he wanted the record to show that a vote against Dr. Jessup's confirmation should not be interpreted as impugning the diplomat's loyalty, despite charges of an "affinity" for Communist causes made before the subcommittee by Sen. Joseph R. McCarthy, R., Wis. Some observers interpreted his insistence on the point to mean that he was paving the way for opposing the nomination.

The Senators may have their first opportunity to vote their sentiments at a closed meeting of the subcommittee set for 10 a. m. tomorrow. Sen. Sparkman declined tonight to predict whether a vote would be taken at the session,

(Continued on page 16, column 2)

Yankees Win, 6 to 2, Tie Series

Don Rice

YANKEE HEROES—Allie Reynolds, who hurled eight-hitter, and Joe DiMaggio, who hit homer

DiMaggio Hits 2-Run Homer Before 49,010

Reynolds Sets Back Giants; Jansen Slated to Face Lopat in Today's Game

By Harold Rosenthal

Allie Reynolds' well pitched eight-hitter, Joe DiMaggio's two-run homer in the fifth, and Willie Mays' unfortunate predelection for bouncing into double plays, carried the New York Yankees to a 6-to-2 victory over the New York Giants before 49,010 yesterday at the Polo Grounds. It squared the World Series at two games apiece and moved the Yankees out of their unfamiliar role of underdog in the fall classic.

With Ed Lopat slated to face Larry Jansen in the last of the three games in the Giants' home park this afternoon, and with Vic Raschi probably opposing Jim Hearn tomorrow when the series moves back to the Yankee Stadium, the defending world champions are once more even money or better to emerge on top again.

A Dozen Hits

They did it yesterday with an outburst of a dozen hits off two of the three Giant pitchers they faced. Sal Maglie, ace of the Polo Grounds staff, went five innings, gave up eight hits, including the circuit blow that Joe DiMaggio drove into the upper left-field seats. DiMaggio's hit was his second of the game. It followed his third-inning single, which in turn, had followed a dozen fruitless appearances at the plate in the three previous games.

DiMaggio teed off on a three-and-one offering and drove it in a screeching arc into the seats. It was his eighth World Series homer. Joe hit his first in this same ball park fifteen years ago. Maglie got the side out after that by getting Gene Woodling on a pop-up and fanning Gil McDougald, but the inning finished him.

It also gave the Yankees a 4-1 edge and furnished Reynolds with enough of a margin to let him work on the hitters. Reynolds, coming back from a series defeat

(Continued on page 27, column 1)

Harriman to Head Foreign Aid With 7.5 Billion Fund for Year

Senate Sends Truman Bill Setting Up New Agency and Stressing Arms Help Above Economic

By Ned Russell

WASHINGTON, Oct. 8. — W. Averell Harriman, President Truman's special assistant for foreign affairs, will direct the Administration's 1951-'52 $7,483,400,000 foreign military-economic aid program, it was learned tonight.

Congressional action on the aid bill, which sets up a new Federal body, the Mutual Security Agency, and is designed to assist the free world in achieving its rearmament goals by the summer of 1954, was completed today and the measure was sent to the White House for the President's signature.

Mr. Truman, it was understood, will send Mr. Harriman's name to the Senate within a few days for confirmation in the dual role of co-ordinator of the aid program and administrator of the Mutual Security Agency. Mr. Harriman, however, will probably not be able to take over active control of the new setup until after Dec. 1.

Mr. Harriman, who has had wide experience in the field of both economic and military policies, flew to Paris Saturday to begin his latest assignment in this field. He is the American representative on the twelve-member temporary committee of the North Atlantic Treaty Organization which was set up at Ottawa last month with instructions to reconcile the military requirements for the defense of Western Europe and the economic capabilities of the European allies to meet them.

Mr. Harriman's background for his next role as administrator of the M. S. A. and co-ordinator of the foreign aid program includes the jobs of chief of the Economic Co-operation Administration in Europe, war-time Ambassador to Russia and later Great Britain as well as various war-time assignments concerning the lend-lease program.

The completion of Congress' action on the foreign military-economic aid bill today came when the Senate approved, by a voice

(Continued on page 41, column 1)

Injured Football Player Wins Disability Pay From Denver U.

By The United Press

DENVER, Oct. 8.—The Colorado State Industrial Commission ruled today that a former University of Denver football player is entitled to disability pay from the university's insurance company for time lost for a gridiron injury.

Industrial Commission Referee David F. How jr. decided that Ernest E. Nemeth, in effect, was hired to play football and was entitled to disability pay for his gridiron injury. The ruling may have nation-wide repercussions in collegiate football circles.

Mr. Nemeth, former Denver University guard, suffered a back injury during spring practice of 1950. In filing his claim with the Industrial Commission the player said he had a part-time job that hinged entirely on his ability to make the varsity football team.

After his injury, Mr. Nemeth asserted, he was unable to perform his duties and lost a $50-a-month job, free training-table meals and a free room. During the Industrial Commission hearing on his claim, Mr. Nemeth testified that sometimes he did nothing to get his pay except play football.

Referee How said he had decided that Mr. Nemeth should be paid about $13 a week from June, 1950, when he underwent an operation for his injury, until his current disability is ended. Mr. Nemeth wears his back in a brace since the injury.

Acording to the referee, evidence at the hearings showed that, in effect, Mr. Nemeth was hired to play football, which makes an injury suffered on the football field one for which he is entitled disability pay.

Mossadegh Here, Assails Stand of U.N.

Asserts Oil Dispute Is Domestic Affair

Indicates Position in U.N. by Laying Iran Poverty to 'Former' Company

By Arch Parsons Jr.

Mohammed Mossadegh, seventy-two-year-old Premier of Iran, flew into New York yesterday and lost no time in asserting that the United Nations Security Council has no business intervening in the oil dispute between his country and, in his view, a company which just happened to be controlled by another sovereign nation—Great Britain.

The Iranian leader — looking healthier than most observers had been led to expect—read a written statement to a mass of U. N. delegates, reporters, camera men and police after his arrival from Tehran at 11:22 a. m. at Idlewild Airport on a KLM Royal Dutch Airlines plane.

Is Sped to Hospital

A police motorcycle escort sped the frail Premier, obviously weary after his long flight, to New York Hospital, at First Ave. and 68th St., where he took up residence for the duration of his visit in a blue-tinted room on the sixteenth floor of the George F. Baker Pavilion.

He had not been there long when Ambassador Ernest A. Gross, deputy United States representative to the U. N., paid a call. It was more than a courtesy visit, for the United States delegation has been in the forefront of those delegations seeking a renewal in New York of negotiations between the British and Iranians.

It was felt that Ambassador Gross, who is maintaining close touch with the British U. N. representative, Sir Gladwyn Jebb, called upon Dr. Mossadegh to see if the latter is ready to sit down with the British in a fresh attempt to reach a permanent settlement in the protracted wrangle over Iran's nationalization of her oil fields.

Gross Sees Jebb

The American delegate was accompanied on his visit at 3 p. m. by George C. McGhee, Assistant Secretary of State in charge of Middle Eastern affairs. Ambassador Gross left the hospital and went immediately to call upon Sir Gladwyn. It was understood that this visit was to prevail upon the British delegate to keep mild any resolution offered to the Council. The British are reported to be drafting a resolution calling for further negotiations on the dispute, possibly under U. N. auspices.

Dr. Mossadegh's statement at the airport contained the essence of what he is expected to say when he goes before the Council—probably on Thursday—to present his nation's case:

"It is unbelievable to me that a group of shareholders of the former Anglo-Iranian Oil Company have been able to take advantage of the existing international organizations for the continuation of their pillage of the national wealth of a poor nation."

Iran Disputes Jurisdictions

Since the dispute first developed, Iran's view has been that neither the International Court of Justice, which ruled in July that both parties to the dispute should allow the company to operate the fields pending a final settlement, nor the Council, which voted on Oct. 8 to hear the dispute, have any jurisdiction over the matter.

Dr. Mossadegh charged in his statement that the role of the British government in the argument is merely that of a "guardian" over the company.

Then, turning to the company itself, he said, "The sole reason for the lack of development, the deprivation and the misfortunes of Iran during the last fifty years are

(Continued on page 31, column 5)

Mossadegh Arrives to Argue Iran's Case

Ira Rosenberg

Premier Mohammed Mossadegh reading statement after arrival at Idlewild Airport yesterday. Nasrollah Entezam, Iran's chief U. N. delegate, is at left; Assadi Mahsen, interpreter, at right

9 Killed, 18 Injured In Destroyer Blast

Explosion on the Small, Off Korea, Laid to Mine

WASHINGTON, Oct. 8 (UP).—The destroyer Ernest G. Small was damaged by an explosion, probably a mine, off Korea Sunday, and nine Navy men were killed and eighteen injured, the Navy announced tonight.

The announcement, first reported United States naval casualty since June 18, brought to nine the number of American ships that have been sunk or damaged by mines and Communist gunfire during the Korean War. Total casualties aboard the nine warships were fifty-six dead, forty missing and 149 injured.

The Navy announcement gave almost no details about the Small's explosion, except to say it was a "probable enemy mine in the Korean area." It added, "the destroyer was able to proceed to Sasebo, Japan, under her own power."

The last report of damage to a warship was on June 18, when the destroyer Frank E. Evans was hit by enemy shore fire, but with no casualties among the men on board.

The last announcement involving casualties was on June 15, when the Navy reported the minesweeper Thompson had been raked by Communist shore batteries on the Korean east coast, with three killed and four wounded.

The Navy had no comment on whether the new mine attack might mean a resumption of the mine barrage that at one time posed a serious threat to American warships and troop ships off Korea.

The list of dead included Edward Kravetz, S03, of 2526 Valentine Ave., the Bronx, New York.

Princess Elizabeth in Canada; Is Hailed at Montreal Airport

Associated Press wirephoto

Canadian Prime Minister Louis St. Laurent greeting Princess Elizabeth and the Duke of Edinburgh in Montreal. The Princess is wearing a fur-felt hat, blue wool suit and mink jacket. The Duke is in uniform of a British Navy lieutenant commander

By Judith Crist

MONTREAL, Oct. 8.—Princess Elizabeth, heiress presumptive to the British throne, and her husband, the Duke of Edinburgh, the first members of the royal family to visit Canada since 1939 and the first in British history to fly the Atlantic Ocean, arrived here today for a thirty-five-day tour of the Dominion.

Tens of thousands of Montrealers delayed their Canadian Thanksgiving dinners to crowd the Montreal Airport at Dorval, eight miles from the city, to greet the royal couple, who appeared in public for forty-five minutes before boarding the royal train which will take them to Quebec, where their visit begins officially at 9:45 a. m. tomorrow.

The Princess, deemed unanimously by press and public to be even prettier than her pictures, and her husband descended from their specially fitted British Overseas Airways Stratocruiser to the sounds of a twenty-one-gun salute, reviewed the honor guard, circled the airport in an open car, then proceeded to a railroad siding two miles away to board their train for Quebec.

The royal couple first touched Canadian soil at 4:50 a. m. when their plane landed for a two-hour stopover at Gander, Newfoundland. They could have landed here at 9:30 a. m., thus completing their journey in twelve hours of actual flight, but the pilot slowed the plane to arrive as scheduled.

With the arrival announced for noon, men, women and children began flocking to the airport three hours beforehand, in spite of a light rain and gray skies. At about 11 a. m. the sun broke through

(Continued on page 14, column 2)

The Forrestal Diaries

James Byrnes in Discussion of Russian-American Policy Says Stalin Told Him He Did Not Like Truman

12. Men and Issues

Forrestal's diary notes through the latter part of 1947 contain many interesting sidelights on men and issues.

18 September 1947 JAMES F. BYRNES

Lunched today with Jimmy Byrnes. We talked about Russia and American policy from 1943 on. He said one of the difficulties, he thought, after Roosevelt's death, was that Stalin did not like Truman and had told him (Byrnes) so. I made the observation that Mr. Truman was the first one who had ever said "no" to anything Stalin asked—that he had good reason for liking FDR because he got out of him the Yalta Agreement, anything he asked for during the war, and finally an opportunity to push Communist propaganda in the United States and throughout the world.

[A few days later Forrestal saw the President in connection with a high-level appointment.

25 September 1947

MEETING WITH PRESIDENT

The President interpolated the remark that the Chief Executive of the United States had to spend most of his time soothing the sensitivities of the people he wanted to get to work for him. He mentioned the fact that he had spent fifteen minutes this morning listening to a man he had asked to head up the Food Conservation program as to where he would rank as to protocol, this matter seeming to the individual concerned to be paramount to the job that he was asked to do. In short, the President said, the President of the United States has to spend a good part of his time saluting the backsides of a large number of people. . . .

Eisenhower and the Presidency

[In October Forrestal was again talking with the President:

6 October 1947 THE PRESIDENT

With regard to Eisenhower's presidential flirtation, [Mr. Truman] said he had been amused to have Ike tell him upon his return from Japan that he thought the President would have to face the prospect of MacArthur's returning here in the spring to launch a campaign for himself; on the other hand, another visitor to MacArthur had returned the message from MacArthur warning the President that Eisenhower would be a candidate for the presidency!

The President remarked that everybody seemed to get either "Potomac fever" or "brass infection."

He remarked that he looked forward with deep misgivings to another four years after 1948 in the White House. And that if it were not his duty to run again in the face of world conditions, the delay in getting the peace treaties with Japan, Germany, Austria, etc., he would like to step aside.

He said he wanted to get a place for Vaughan,

(Continued on page 21, column 5)

Index

News Summaries on Page 2

Yankees Defeat Giants, 6-2, Before 49,010 and Tie World Series at 2 Games Apiece

Reynolds Pitches 8-Hit Victory; DiMaggio Blasts 2-Run Homer

Dark Clouts Three Doubles in a Row; Mays' Hits Into 3 Double Plays

(Continued from page one)

in the opening game last week, operated carefully on each batter and an unusual number of counts went to the full three-and-two. He pitched three-hit ball for the first five innings, then was nicked for hits in the next three innings. He gave up two in the ninth when he was saved from a possibly unpleasant situation. by Mays' grounding to Phil Rizzuto to start the game-ending double play.

3 Doubles for Dark

Mays and Al Dark had reason to remember this day as one on which things came in threes, but for different reasons. Mays came to bat four times and three times he hit into twin killings. Two of these ended innings.

Dark, for a while, seemed to be the only Giant able to hit Reynolds, and he hit him in freakishly consistent fashion. The first three times he came to bat he doubled. After that he must have exchanged trade secrets with Mays because the final time the Giant shortstop came to bat, Dark ended the eighth by grounding to Reynolds to start a double play.

Three doubles in one World Series game is only one off the record which has stood for almost a half-century. Four double plays in a series contest equals the mark in the book. The Giants became the fifth club to do it.

A series record which was broken was the players' pool. It was announced that the sum to be divided up (the contestants share in the proceeds of the first four games only, for obvious reasons) will be $560,562.37.

Through the years the Yankees have come to be known as "money" players. It is barely possible that the fact that a half-million dollars reposed in the pot was—made known to them along about the same time they realized that Maglie wasn't as sharp as Leo Durocher would have liked him to have been.

Maglie was going with a four-day rest instead of three because of Sunday's rain out. The extra day, however, had no visible effect upon the thirty-four-year old right-hander, making his first World Series appearance. If anything, he looked dull.

That first inning, even though the Yankees failed to hit him, might have had a lot to do with divesting Maglie of some of his edge. After Hank Bauer walked on four straight balls in his unusual role of lead-off, Phil Rizzuto fanned, Yogi Berra lined to Mays and DiMaggio looked at a three-and-two-strike. That sounds like a fairly innocuous inning, but both Rizzuto and DiMaggio fouled off a lot of pitches, and no doubt sapped more than a little from Maglie's arm in the process. He had to pitch ten times to DiMaggio alone in that one inning.

After that Maglie was no problem. Two hits and an error by Bobby Thomson added up the first Yankee run in the second, equalizing the Giant run driven in by Monte Irvin's first-inning single. Irvin's hit came with two out, following Dark's first double. After two men on, two out, and the ball hit McDougald and retired the side.

In the fourth the Yankees moved into the lead which they never relinquished. A brace of singles sandwiching a walk did it, with one away. Bobby Brown singled through short, went to second on the pass issued to Joe Collins, and scored on Reynolds' line single Dark scored Irvin was thrown out attempting to steal.

Ball Hits McDougald

The Yankee's first scoring inning ended on a slightly similar note. With apparently a big inning on the verge of getting started, Bauer slashed a single down toward Dark. There were down the middle. Allie was nailed after he had taken too big a turn toward second. When Maglie got Bauer on a infield roller to end the inning, the damages didn't appear too large.

But in the fifth, with one away, the Yankees put Maglie over the barrel, even though he finished up the inning. Yogi slammed a single through the right side, and DiMaggio came through with his circuit sock.

Sheldon Jones, who had previously appeared in relief Saturday when Jim Hearn weakened in the eighth inning of the third game, pitched for the next three innings, and the Yankees got to him for a two-run frame in the seventh.

Eddie Stanky, whose "drop kick" sent the ball out of Phil Rizzuto's glove in the big inning on Saturday, figured in the last of the Giant aberrations. So did little Phil, who played with a couple of bruised wrists.

Rizzuto led off the seventh with a single through the right side. Two outs later he moved along on a walk to Woodling. McDougald came to bat still seeking his first hit. He eventually got it but not before there had been an attempted pick-off by Wes Westrum on Rizzuto, to wit:

Hits Rizzuto in Back

Westrum threw to Stanky and Phil lit out for third. Stanky threw to third and hit Rizzuto in the back. The ball caromed away from Bobby Thomson and Rizzuto scored easily. Woodling moved up to second on the play and scored when McDougald laced the next pitch into left field. After that there was no further hitting except for Bauer's eighth-inning single off Jones. Monte Kennedy retired the Yankees easily and in order in the ninth, fanning the last two batters he faced, DiMaggio and Woodling.

The same description can hardly be applied to Reynolds' ninth. Up to that frame he had permitted a half dozen hits. While his possible shutout went out the window in the very first inning, he looked very much the boss throughout.

Then in the ninth the Giants started to alter his appearance. Hank Thompson led off with a walk, and Irvin got his second single, a line shot into center field. Whitey Lockman lifted a fly to Woodling on a full count. Bob Thomson worked Reynolds up to another full count and then singled home Thompson with a hit to left.

That put it up to Mays, and the jittery twenty-year-old rookie did just what the Yankees had scarcely dared hope he would. He got the count up to three and two, then rolled to Rizzuto, who threw to Jerry Coleman, who whipped the ball to Collins, and the game was over.

Coleman was a seventh-inning replacement when McDougald was moved over to third when Doc Brown was lifted. Jerry was the only member of the Yankee line-up who failed to get a hit, but the reason was fairly obvious. He didn't get a chance to come to bat.

12 Blows for Yankees

The dozen Yankee hits were the highest total they've collected in any of the series games so far. It was the first time in the series, too, they've hit in double figures.

Reynolds, with a record of one and one, is through for the series as a starter unless bad weather comes up, but he is still one of Casey Stengel's aces-up-a-sleeve in relief. Allie has a four-and-one series record, having now scored in each of the Yankees World Series, starting in 1947. The Chief fanned seven and walked four in his latest, and Stengel couldn't have asked for a better man out there when things became threatening in the ninth.

It was a big afternoon for another old pro. DiMaggio, who had been restricted to a starvation diet in his three previous games, finally busted out in his forty-ninth World Series game. His eighth World Series round-tripper gave him a shade more than half of Babe Ruth's fifteen-homer total, but, while DiMaggio will never break Ruth's mark, there's one series record he'll set before the week is over. Barring something unforeseen, this afternoon he'll tie Frankie Frisch's old mark for World Series games played in—fifty.

4th Game Score

* * *

YANKEES

	ab	r	h	po	a
Bauer rf	4	0	2	0	0
Rizzuto ss	5	1	1	5	5
Berra c	5	1	1	8	1
DiMaggio cf	5	1	2	2	0
Woodling lf	4	2	1	1	0
McDgould2b-3b	4	0	1	3	2
Brown 3b	4	1	2	0	0
Coleman 2b	0	0	0	1	1
Collins 1b	3	0	1	7	0
Reynolds p	4	0	1	0	2
Totals	38	6	12	27	11

GIANTS

	ab	r	h	po	a
Stanky 2b	4	0	1	3	0
Dark ss	4	1	3	2	1
Thompson rf	3	1	0	1	0
Irvin lf	4	0	2	3	0
Lockman 1b	4	0	0	4	0
Thomson 3b	2	0	2	2	3
Mays cf	4	0	0	5	1
Westrum c	2	0	0	7	1
Maglie p	1	0	0	0	0
*Lohrke	1	0	0	0	0
Jones p	0	0	0	0	0
†Rigney	1	0	0	0	0
Kennedy p	0	0	0	0	0
Totals	30	2	8	27	6

*Popped out for Maglie in fifth.
†Struck out for Jones in eighth.

YANKEES	010	120	200	—6
GIANTS	100	000	001	—2

E—Thomson, Stanky. RBI—Irvin, Collins, Reynolds, DiMaggio 2, McDougald, Thomson. 2B—Dark 3, Woodling, Brown. HR—DiMaggio. DP — Rizzuto, McDougald and Collins; Reynolds, Rizzuto and Collins 2; Rizzuto, Coleman and Collins. Left — Yankees 8; Giants 5. BB—Maglie 2 (Bauer, Collins); Jones 1 (Woodling); Reynolds 4 (Thomson 2, Westrum, Thompson). SO—Maglie 3 (Rizzuto, DiMaggio, McDougald; Jones 2 (Reynolds, Rizzuto); Kennedy 2 (DiMaggio, Woodling); Reynolds 7 (Lockman, Westrum 2, Maglie, Irvin, Stanky, Rigney). HO—Maglie, 8 in 5 innings; Jones, 4 in 3; Kennedy, 0 in 1. Winner—Reynolds; Loser—Maglie. U—Al Barlick (NL), home plate; Bill Summers (AL), first base; Lee Ballanfant (NL), second base; Joe Paparella (AL), third base; Art Gore (NL), leftfield foul line; John Stevens (AL), rightfield foul line. T—2:57. A—49,010 (PAID). Receipts—$233,887.85.

Jack Frank

PICK-OFF PLAY: Allie Reynolds, Yankee hurler, tries for a pick-off in the fourth inning of yesterday's World Series game at the Polo Grounds. Alvin Dark, Giants' shortstop, beats the throw to Phil Rizzuto, however. Gil McDougald backs up the play as umpire Lee Ballanfant looks on

Jack Frank

WELCOME HOME: Joe DiMaggio crosses the plate after belting his homer in the fifth inning yesterday at the Polo Grounds, scoring Yogi Berra (8). Left to right are Gene Woodling, the next batter; Berra, DiMaggio and the bat boy. Wes Westrum, Giants' catcher, is in background

Composite Score of 4 Games

* * *

Giants

	G	AB	R	H	2B	3B	HR	RBI	BB	SO	Batting Avg	PO	A	E	Fld Avg
Stanky, 2b	4	13	2	2	0	0	0	0	3	2	.154	10	8	1	.947
Dark, ss	4	17	3	7	3	0	1	4	0	1	.412	7	11	0	1.000
Thompson, rf	4	11	3	1	0	0	0	0	4	2	.091	6	0	1	.857
Irvin, lf	4	16	3	9	0	1	0	1	1	1	.563	12	0	0	1.000
Lockman, 1b	4	16	1	3	1	0	1	4	1	2	.188	29	2	2	.939
Thomson, 3b	4	13	1	4	1	0	0	1	4	0	.308	8	12	1	.952
Mays, cf	4	17	0	2	0	0	0	1	0	1	.118	12	1	0	1.000
Westrum, c	4	11	1	2	0	0	0	0	4	2	.182	9	2	1	.955
*Schenz	1	0	0	0	0	0	0	0	0	0	.000	0	0	0	.000
Hartung, rf	1	1	0	0	0	0	0	0	0	0	.000	0	0	0	.000
†Rigney	2	2	0	0	0	0	0	1	0	1	.000	0	0	0	.000
Noble, c	1	1	0	0	0	0	0	0	0	0	.000	0	0	0	.000
Koslo, p	1	3	0	0	0	0	0	0	0	2	.000	2	0	0	1.000
Spencer, p	1	0	0	0	0	0	0	0	0	0	.000	0	0	0	.000
Jansen, p	1	2	0	0	0	0	0	0	0	0	.000	0	0	0	.000
Hearn, p	1	3	0	0	0	0	0	0	0	1	.000	0	2	0	1.000
Jones, p	2	0	0	0	0	0	0	0	0	0	.000	0	1	0	1.000
Maglie, p	1	1	0	0	0	0	0	0	0	1	.000	0	0	0	.000
‡Lohrke	1	1	0	0	0	0	0	0	0	0	.000	0	0	0	.000
Kennedy, p	1	0	0	0	0	0	0	0	0	0	.000	0	0	0	.000
Totals	4	128	14	30	5	1	2	12	17	16	.234	105	39	6	.960

Yankees

	G	AB	R	H	2B	3B	HR	RBI	BB	SO	Batting Avg	PO	A	E	Fld Avg
Mantle, rf	2	5	1	1	0	0	0	0	2	1	.200	4	0	0	1.000
Rizzuto, ss	4	17	2	5	0	0	0	0	0	3	.294	11	14	1	.962
Bauer, lf-rf	4	14	0	2	0	0	0	0	1	0	.143	3	0	0	1.000
DiMaggio, cf	4	16	1	2	0	0	1	2	0	4	.125	13	0	0	1.000
Berra, c	4	15	1	3	0	0	0	0	1	1	.200	20	3	1	.958
McDougald, 3b-2b	4	14	1	5	1	0	0	2	2	2	.357	7	9	1	.941
Coleman, 2b	3	3	0	1	0	0	0	0	1	0	.333	5	3	0	1.000
Collins, 1b	4	12	1	3	0	0	1	3	2	0	.250	32	2	0	1.000
§Mize	2	2	0	0	0	0	0	0	0	0	.000	0	0	0	.000
¶Brown, 3b	4	11	1	3	1	0	0	0	1	1	.273	0	5	0	1.000
‖Woodling, lf	4	12	3	2	1	0	1	1	2	2	.167	8	0	0	1.000
**Martin	1	0	1	0	0	0	0	0	0	0	.000	0	0	0	.000
***Hopp	1	0	0	0	0	0	0	0	1	0	.000	0	0	0	.000
Reynolds, p	2	6	0	2	0	0	0	1	0	1	.333	0	5	0	1.000
Hogue, p	2	0	0	0	0	0	0	0	0	0	.000	0	1	0	1.000
Morgan, p	1	0	0	0	0	0	0	0	0	0	.000	0	1	0	1.000
Lopat, p	1	3	0	1	0	0	0	1	0	1	.333	2	2	0	1.000
Raschi, p	1	1	0	0	0	0	0	0	1	0	.000	0	0	0	.000
Ostrowski, p	1	0	0	0	0	0	0	0	0	0	.000	0	0	0	—
Totals	4	131	12	30	3	0	3	10	14	16	.229	105	45	3	.980

*Ran for Westrum in seventh inning of second game. †Flied out for Thompson in seventh inning of second game;struck out for Jones in eighth inning of fourth game. ‡Popped out for Maglie in fifth inning of fourth game. §Popped out for Collins in ninth inning of first game; flied out for Ostrowski in ninth inning of third game. ¶Struck out for Hogue in eighth inning of first game. ‖Struck out for Morgan in ninth inning of first game. **Ran for Brown in eighth inning of second game. ***Walked for Hogue in seventh inning of third game.

Pitching Summary

Giants

	G	CG	IP	H	R	BB	SO	HB	WP	W	L	Pct	Avg
Koslo	1	1	9	7	1	3	3	0	0	1	0	1.000	1.00
Jansen	1	0	6	4	2	0	5	0	0	0	1	.000	3.00
Spencer	1	0	2	2	1	0	0	0	0	0	0	.000	4.50
Hearn	1	0	7⅔	4	1	8	1	1	0	1	0	1.000	1.12
Jones	2	0	4⅓	5	3	1	2	0	0	0	0	.000	2.25
Maglie	1	0	5	8	4	2	3	0	0	0	1	.000	7.20
Kennedy	1	0	1	0	0	0	2	0	0	0	0	.000	0.00
Totals	4	1	35	30	12	14	16	1	0	2	2	.500	2.57

Yankees

	G	CG	IP	H	R	BB	SO	HB	WP	W	L	Pct	Avg
Reynolds	2	1	15	16	7	11	8	0	0	1	1	.500	4.19
Hogue	2	0	2⅔	1	0	0	0	0	0	0	0	.000	0.00
Morgan	1	0	2	2	0	1	3	0	0	0	0	.000	0.00
Lopat	1	1	9	5	1	2	1	0	0	1	0	1.000	1.00
Raschi	1	0	4⅓	5	6	3	3	1	0	0	1	.000	2.25
Ostrowski	1	0	2	1	0	0	1	0	0	0	0	.000	0.00
Totals	4	2	35	30	14	17	16	1	0	2	2	.500	2.31

Score by Innings

Giants	3	1	0	0	5	3	1	0	1—14
Yankees	1	3	0	1	2	0	2	2	1—12

RBI—Lockman 4, Dark 4, Rigney, Mays, Irvin, Thomson, McDougald 2, Collins 2, Lopat, Woodling, Reynolds, DiMaggio 2. 2B—Lockman, McDougald, Thomson, Dark 3, Woodling, Brown. 3B—Irvin. HR—Dark, Collins, Lockman, Woodling, DiMaggio. SB—Irvin 2. S—Koslo 2. DP—McDougald, Rizzuto and Collins; Rizzuto, McDougald and Collins 2; Reynolds, Rizzuto and Collins 2; Dark, Stanky and Lockman; Stanky, Dark and Lockman; Hearn, Dark, Lockman and Dark. Left—Giants 29; Yankees 29. Umpires—Bill Summers (A); Lee Ballanfant (N); Joe Paparella (A); Al Barlick (N); John Stevens (A); Art Gore (N). Attendance—65,673 (first game); 66,018 (second game); 52,035 (third game); 49,010 (fourth game). Time—2:58 (first game); 2:05 (second game); 2:42 (third game); 2:57 (fourth game) Receipts—$311,477.06 (first game); $310,215.9, (second game); $243,961.10 (third game); $233,887.35 (fourth game).

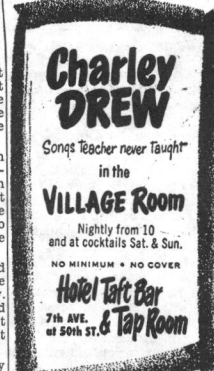

Giants, Embarrassed by Defeat, Agree Maglie Had Nothing

Sal Says He Threw 'Three Good' Pitches; Durocher Will Stick With Mays, Despite Slump

By Ed Sinclair

Some days, it seems, it doesn't pay to appear at the ball park and that's the way the Giants felt yesterday after their defeat by the Yankees at the Polo Grounds. From Leo Durocher's office to that faraway locker of Willie Mays, who had the dubious distinction of hitting into three double plays, there was concern and embarrassment over the team's poor showing.

While the tune, "Take Me Out to The Ball Game" blared from the public address system megaphone overhead, Durocher nervously and abruptly answered the questions of the press which ascertained that Allie Reynolds had good stuff, that Sal Maglie had little of anything and that Joe DiMaggio hit a curve ball for his home run.

Then the big query popped out. Was the Little Shepherd of Coogan's Bluf going to stick with Mays? The question hung there and in its nakedness Durocher found nothing to comfort him. He thought for a moment and then emitted a curt "yes" which underlined his exasperation over the game's proceedings.

Mays Is Puzzled

Mays, the rookie outfielder, was puzzled and hurt by his performance. He likened it to the batting slump which dogged the start of his major league career this year. He said that he wasn't nervous or scared, that he was fighting with every faculty he possessed.

"I don't know what's the matter," he added. "I haven't changed my position in the batter's box at all. I keep trying to snap out of it and I'm hittin' the ball good. It just doesn't go right, that's all. Maybe I'll use a heavier bat. Maybe that'll help."

Maglie, the Giant ace and the loser, was disconsolate over his work. He readily admitted that it was one of his worst jobs, claiming that he threw only three good pitches. To this, Wes Westrum, his catcher, agreed and said that he never has seen the swarthy right-hander so badly off in his control. Durocher did not put all the blame on Maglie, however, although he, too, said that Maglie had no control and that he was behind every batter.

"But nuts," the leader exclaimed "If Lockman doesn't swing at a bad pitch in that last inning he walks. Now the bases are loaded and it's good bye. That guy (Reynolds) is out of there. But now, it's 3-and-2 and he swings at a pitch that's up around his cap, right up at the peak of his cap, and he flies out.

Can't Stop Dark

"I'll tell you one thing, though. As good as that guy (Reynolds again) was, he still hasn't phantomed those two guys, Irvin and Dark. No, sir, and none of those guys (the Yankee staff this time) will either."

Edging out the doorway some one asked Durocher who he was pitching in the fifth series game today. The leader replied that it would be Larry Jansen.

"I want to pitch Larry here," said Leo. "After that it will be Koslo (Dave Koslo, the Giant left-hander who won the first game), and then we'll see what happens."

Majors Turn Over Radio, TV Control To Owners of Clubs

Major league baseball owners yesterday repealed present restrictions on the broadcasting and televising of baseball games and returned full authority to the individual clubs. They had been under league control.

A spokesman for baseball said the action in the long run would help minor leagues because the league agency under which games were sold for nation-wide broadcasting has been ended.

Minor leagues, which suffered heavy attendance losses this year generally, contended the wide broadcasting of big league baseball hit them hard in gate receipts.

Under the action taken here, each big club can sell what it wishes individually subject only to the visiting club's rights.

The big league owners, at the first session presided over by the new commissioner, Ford Frick, decided to hold their annual meeting Dec. 8, 9, and 10 at the Commodore Hotel in New York.

Warren Giles, former president of the Cincinnati Reds, sat in as new president of the National League, succeeding Frick.

Facts and Figures In World Series

* * *

STANDINGS

	W	L	Pct
Giants	2	2	.500
Yankees	2	2	.500

FIRST GAME, THURSDAY, OCT. 4
(At Yankee Stadium)

		R	H	E
Giants	200 003 000	—5	10	1
Yankees	010 000 000	—1	7	1

Koslo and Westrum; Reynolds, Hogue (7), Morgan (8) and Berra.

SECOND GAME, FRIDAY, OCT. 5
(At Yankee Stadium)

		R	H	E
Giants	000 000 100	—1	5	1
Yankees	110 000 01x	—3	6	0

Jansen, Spencer (7) and Westrum; Lopat and Berra.

THIRD GAME, SATURDAY, OCT. 6
(At Polo Grounds)

		R	H	E
Yankees	000 000 011	—2	5	2
Giants	010 050 00x	—6	7	2

Raschi, Hogue (5), Ostrowski (7) and Berra; Hearn, Jones (8) and Westrum.

FOURTH GAME, MONDAY, OCT. 8
(At Polo Grounds)

		R	H	E
Yankees	010 120 200	—6	12	0
Giants	100 000 001	—2	8	2

Reynolds and Berra; Maglie, Jones (6), Kennedy (9) and Westrum.

Fifth game, today, 1 p. m., at Polo Grounds.

Sixth game, tomorrow, at Yankee Stadium.

Seventh game, if necessary, Thursday, Oct. 11, at Yankee Stadium.

FINANCIAL FIGURES
Four-Day Totals

Attendance—232,736.
Receipts—$1,099,141.92.
Players' share (first four games only)—$560,562.37.
Commissioner's share—$164,871.29.
Clubs' and leagues' share—$373,708.26.

Mantle Out of Series; Remains in Hospital

Mickey Mantle, New York Yankee rookie right-fielder injured in the second game of the World Series, is still in the Lennox Hill Hospital and definitely will not see any more action against the New York Giants.

Mantle injured his knee when he apparently stepped into a small hole while going after Willie Mays' fly, which Joe DiMaggio caught.

Yanks Clubhouse Like Old Times: DiMaggio Center of Attraction

Stengel's Three-Minute Meeting Before Game Stirs Players; Rizzuto In on 4 Double Plays

By Rud Rennie

It was like old times in the Yankees' dressing room after their victory in the fourth game of the World Series yesterday. Joe DiMaggio, neglected by photographers and reporters in the first three games because he had not done anything worth photographing or reporting, was once again the center of attraction. The jolter had snapped out of his lamentable batting slump and had hit a single and a two-run homer. Photographers and reporters swarmed around him.

Joe was glad to be talking to people again. He felt good. He sat penned in a corner of the locker room, sipping at a can of beer and answering questions without excitement.

"The best ball I hit," he said, "was that foul in the first inning. That one was really tagged. It was an inside curve, and I hit as good as I've hit any ball all year.

"I hit a low curve for the home run. It felt good; but not as good as the foul. . . . I've been using a 35-ounce Babe Ruth model bat. Today I used a 34-ounce model."

Casey Winks Again

Casey Stengel, the manager, was in a winking mood again for the first time in the series.

"We looked like we're going to do something today," he said. "Before we ever started, in practice, we looked alive. I had a three-minute meeting before the game. I told my men that every one, including myself, had not done well, but that we would do all right if we just went out there and played like we knew how to play.

"Joe come out of it and hit a couple. Everybody hit. We didn't run the bases too good at times. McDougald never should have let himself be hit by that batted ball, and I don't know what happened to Reynolds getting himself thrown out rounding first base. Those two things could have hurt us. As it was, they took us out of two scoring innings. But Reynolds was much better today than he was last time, and we had the chance to make four double plays. (Which tied a record).

"Now it's even up again, and we have a big game tomorrow. I'll pitch Lopat, and we'll see what happens."

Reynolds said he was just missing with his curve.

Dark a Problem

"And," he said, "I couldn't get the ball outside to Dark. I just couldn't (Dark hit him for three consecutive doubles) until the eighth when he hit into a double play."

Reynolds said he grew tired in the ninth. Having to stop suddenly on that pitch in the ninth when Irvin called time did not hurt him any; but he said, "I gave my ankle a little twist, whirling to start that double-play with the ball Dark hit.

"In the ninth I was tired and just missing again. I was three and two on just about everybody. I started on Mays with curves and then switched to fast balls and it was a fast ball he hit for his last double-play (Mays's third).

Reynolds grinned sheepishly about having been caught between bases after he singled in the fourth. "I guess I just don't know my own speed," he said. "I just meant to round the bag just a little bit."

Phil Rizzuto, the shortstop who participated in the four double plays, was under the shower, soaping himself. He had got a hit in the seventh and after going half way from second to third had paused until Westrum threw to Stanky. Then he dashed for third and was able to score when Stanky's throw struck him on the back of the head.

Phil Aches All Over

"Yeah," said the scooter, "the back of the head." "I'm hit all over. I never been so messed up in my life as I have in this series. I got bumps on my wrists from being kicked and hit with a pitched ball. . . . Look at my big toe. It's all raw from where Irvin slid into me today. And look at all them cuts on my ankles. I got all of them in this series from them guys sliding into second base. I ache all over."

The Yankees were much happier yesterday. Everybody made a hit except Jerry Coleman and he never had a chance to bat. They had won and had evened the series at two games all. And they knew that the players' pool, which stops receiving any part of the World Series receipts after the fourth game, was the largest of all time, and that the winners' share would be substantial.

Acker Inducted by Army

FAIR LAWN, N. J., Oct. 8 (AP).—Tom Acker, right-handed pitcher with the Buffalo Bisons, of the International League, reports at Hackensack today for induction into the Army. Acker won ten games while losing thirteen for Buffalo this year. He was the top minor league draft choice at the minor league meetings in St. Petersburg, Fla., last winter.

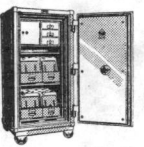

THE WEATHER
Today: Fair, with no important change in temperature; moderate north to northeast winds.
Tomorrow: Fair, with no important change in temperature.
Temperatures Yesterday: Max., 61.2; Min., 44.8.
Today's Probable Range: Max., 62; Min., 45.
Humidity at 3 p. m. Yesterday: 40%.
Expected Humidity This Afternoon: 45-55%.
Detailed Report on Page 29

NEW YORK Herald Tribune

European Edition Published Daily in Paris

Late City Edition

111th Year VOL. CXI NO. 38,314

WEDNESDAY, OCTOBER 10, 1951

230 West 41st Street, New York 18, N. Y. Telephone PEnnsylvania 6-4000

FIVE CENTS

Yanks Rout Giants, 13-1, Need One Game

Jack Frank

GRAND SLAM—Yank's Gil McDougald beams as he crosses plate after his bases-loaded homer in third inning. Scoring ahead of him were Berra, who gives him a hug; Mize (right) and DiMaggio (bottom left). Brown (top left) waits his turn at bat

U. N., Red Officers Meet At Pan Mun Jom to Map Renewal of Truce Talks

Iran Willing To Resume Oil Parleys Here

Says 'Framework' Is Nationalization

British Yield to U. S. Plea to Soften Resolution Against Iran in U. N.

By John G. Rogers

UNITED NATIONS, N. Y., Oct. 9.—Iranian Deputy Premier Hossein Fatemi told a news conference tonight that his country was ready to resume negotiations with Great Britain on the Middle East oil controversy within the framework of Iran's law nationalizing its oil industry.

The qualifications inherent in this declaration implied conditions certain to be unpalatable to the British, but any prospect of renewed British-Iranian negotiations so energetically sought by the United States was the first bright turn in the recent history of the dispute that is costing Western Europe so much oil badly needed for defense machinery.

While Iran thus appeared to be tending in the direction of accepting negotiations, Great Britain took steps toward meeting this position by agreeing in private consultations with the United States and other delegations to temper its demand before the Security Council that the Iranians be ordered to comply with injunctions which they already have rejected.

New British Resolution

Originally, Britain asked the Council to order Iran to fulfill an International Court of Justice injunction proposing joint British-Iranian operation of the Anglo-Iranian Oil Company pending an agreed settlement of the dispute arising out of Iranian nationalization of its oil industry.

However, the British have torn up that resolution and now propose to introduce one which, considering the outraged British temper over recent events in Iran, goes a long way toward conciliation and attempts to leave the way open for resumed negotiations. The exact wording of the document is still being worked out.

During this busy day of behind-scenes U. N. developments in the Iranian oil case, Iranian Premier Mohammed Mossadegh stayed virtually secluded in his hospital quarters, and the infirmity of the seventy-two-year-old diplomat may cause postponement of a scheduled Security Council session from Thursday until Saturday.

Hospital Bulletin

In its 4 p. m. bulletin New York Hospital, York Ave. and 68th St., where Dr. Mossadegh has taken residence, reported that he is "resting comfortably" and was "able to be up and about" in his four-room suite on the sixteenth floor of the George T. Baker Pavilion.

The Premier's son, Dr. Gholem Hossein Mossadegh, said that tests so far show his father to be "in perfect health."

At any rate, the Premier, who arrived here by plane yesterday, was undergoing further medical tests at the hospital today, and so far as could be learned he held political conferences with only one principal diplomat—George McGhee, Assistant Secretary of State for Middle East Affairs.

The United States, filled with anxiety for a non-violent and pro-Western settlement of the British-

(Continued on page 13, column 1)

47,530 Watch McDougald Hit 4-Run Homer

Lopat Gains His 2d Victory in Series With 5-Hitter; Raschi Faces Koslo Today

By Harold Rosenthal

Gil McDougald, a young man with three small children to feed back in 'Frisco, took the bread right out of the mouths of the New York Giants yesterday. His third-inning grand-slam homer off Larry Jansen, first bases-loaded World Series circuit clout since the late Tony Lazzeri also hit one off the Giants' Dick Coffman back in 1936, proved the key wallop in the Yankees' lop-sided 13-1 victory fashioned before 47,530 spectators.

The Yankees now lead, three games to two, and are favored to end the fall classic this afternoon when the scene shifts to the Yankee Stadium. Vic Raschi will face Dave Koslo in the sixth game as the Yankees attempt to rivet their fourteenth triumph in eighteen World Series.

The big blow was McDougald's, his second grand-slammer in his short one-year career in the majors, but the victory was Ed Lopat's. The able left-hander came through with another five-hit performance to go along with the one he inflicted upon the Giants in the second game of the series last Friday. In eighteen innings the Giants were able to reach him for only two runs and if they never see him again the nightmare will probably extend through next July.

Lopat gave up two of his five hits in the first inning. Coupled with an error they led to the Giants one unearned run.

You have to go all the way back to the 1936 series to unearth a score comparable to this one. The Yankees hammered the Giants

(Continued on page 24, column 1)

Mother Tosses 4 Boys to Safety From 3d Story, Then Dies in Fire

Neighbors Catch Them in Her Blanket; Man on Way Up by Ladder as Backdraft Kills Her

A young Brooklyn mother of nine children, trapped on a third-story ledge of her blazing home, calmly directed the rescue of four of her young boys yesterday afternoon and then perished in a backdraft of flames which enveloped her as a neighbor dashed up a ladder in an effort to save her.

More than a thousand horrified spectators watched as Mrs. Irma Randall, thirty-five, tossed her four youngest children one after the other, one of them with his clothing afire, from a thirty-five-foot bay window ledge into a blanket which she had dropped to neighbors to use as a safety net.

But the flash fire which swept the three-story apartment building at 189 Quincy Street in Brooklyn was too fast, and just as a ladder was put up to Mrs. Randall she was engulfed by flames. Many in the throng watching below wept as the heroic mother perished.

One of the four children, James, eight, was the last to be dropped to safety. His clothing was afire and several ribs were broken when he struck the improvised safety net. He was taken to Jewish Hospital, 555 Prospect St., in critical condition.

William Sels, thirty-five, a Board of Transportation employee and a neighbor of the Randalls, made a valiant effort to save Mrs. Randall from her blazing perch with the aid of a forty-foot ladder, but he was driven back when the flames swept over her in the backdraft. He suffered minor burns of the left arm.

The other five Randall children were in school. Mrs. Randall was cooking dinner in her third-floor apartment when the fire broke out shortly before 1 p. m.

(Continued on page 18, column 7)

Senator Seeks Million Truman Library Fund

Anderson Explains Taxes Would Get It Anyway; President Disavows It

By The Associated Press

ST. LOUIS, Oct. 9.—"The Post-Dispatch" reported today that Sen. Clinton P. Anderson, D., N. M., was seeking, by mail, donations for a $1,000,000 Harry S. Truman memorial library from money which he pointed out would go for higher-bracketed taxes anyway.

The newspaper said President Truman quickly disassociated himself from the campaign and took the unusual step of authorizing direct quotation for "The Post-Dispatch," which had brought the Anderson letter to the White House's attention.

"I didn't know anything about the letter," the paper quoted the President as saying, "and if I had known about it, I would have stopped it from being sent."

Sen. Anderson, resting at his home in Albuquerque, declared: "The point is—do something with their money for libraries, universities and institutions rather than spend it on public relations and many other things that can be

(Continued on page 12, column 2)

Bowles, 43-33, Confirmed as Envoy to India

Taft Leads Republicans in Futile Fight, McCarran Only Democrat Opposing

By The Associated Press

WASHINGTON, Oct. 9.—The Senate tonight confirmed Chester Bowles as Ambassador to India over sharp protests by Sen. Robert A. Taft, Ohio, and othe Republicans.

The 43-to-33 vote, largely following party lines, came after Democrats praised Mr. Bowles, former Governor of Connecticut and war-time price administator.

Replying for Republicans, Sen. Taft said he knew of no one "less qualified" to be diplomatic spokesman for the nation in one of the touchiest parts of the world.

Democratic lines held steadier than Republican ranks on the test. Only one Democrat, Sen. Pat McCarran, Nev., voted with thirty-two Republicans against confirmation while favorable votes came from thirty-eight Democrats and five Republicans: George D. Aiken, Vt.; William Langer, N. D.; Henry Cabot Lodge jr., Mass.; Wayne Morse, Ore., and Margaret Chase Smith, Me.

Sen. Taft's criticism of Mr. Bowles came in answer to praise of the nominee from Sen. Brien McMahon, D., Conn., who said Mr. Bowles "fits the picture" better than any man in public life." Sen. McMahon contended that Republicans were opposing the Bowles nomination in a political move.

Sen. Taft said Mr. Bowles, as war-time price czar, "antagonized" both Republicans and Democrats who had to deal with him and

(Continued on page 13, column 3)

British Warn Egypt on Suez Ouster Moves

Troops to Stay, Fight if Necessary; Cairo Gets Allied Defense Talk Bid

By Joseph Newman

From the Herald Tribune Bureau

LONDON, Oct. 9.—Great Britain notified Egypt today that it would not recognize a unilateral denunciation of their 1936 treaty of alliance and their agreement for joint control of the Sudan.

In a statement issued by Foreign Secretary Herbert Morrison, Britain reaffirmed "full rights" under the two agreements.

There was no reference to any measures which Britain would take to uphold these rights, and it is hoped that Egypt will postpone proposed legislation to abrogate the 1936 treaty or refrain from implementing it.

Following its humiliating setback in the Iranian oil dispute, the British government is in no mood to submit to an offense from Egypt.

Unless the Egyptian government is prepared to negotiate a settlement on the basis of a new Middle East defense organization including Egypt, the British government is determined to maintain its troops in the Suez Canal zone, by force if necessary.

While prepared to discuss Egyptian claims to the Sudan, the British government is also intent on maintaining its predominant position there until arrangements are made for the Sudanese themselves to decide whether they want to be independent or to come under the Egyptian crown.

Military Men Called

Mr. Morrison issued his statement after conferring with Marshal of the Air Force Sir John Slessor, chief of the Air Staff; Gen. Sir Brian Robertson, Commander in Chief of the Middle East, and Lt. Gen. Sir Nevil Brownjohn.

It was reported that arrangements are being made to fly in food and other supplies needed by British forces in the canal zone in the event the Egyptians carry out their threat to blockade the troops, numbering roughly 10,,000.

Mr. Morrison also conferred by telephone with Prime Minister Attlee, who was on the second day of his ten-day election tour. It is understood that Mr. Attlee will continue his 1,000-mile tour unless the Egyptian situation becomes more urgent.

Lt. Gen. Sir George Erskine, commander of British troops in Egypt, returned today by plane to the canal zone to carry out the government's decision to hold its position.

Mr. Morrison's statement said that the British government takes "the strongest exception to the action of the Egyptian government in introducing legislation seeking to

(Continued on page 2, column 2)

Gus Hall Arrested At Home in Mexico

Communists Plan to Fight Fugitive's Extradition

MEXICO CITY, Oct. 9 (AP).—The Mexican Communist party said today Gus Hall, fugitive United States Communist leader, had been arrested in Mexico.

Dionisio Encina, general secretary of the party, said he had few details of the arrest. He said Hall, who fled while out on bail in the United States, was arrested early today in Mexico City. There was no confirmation from any official source, but none denied it.

Manuel Terrazas, of the party's executive committee, said "We only know his home was broken into early today and that he is held incomunicado in an unkonwn place."

Hall was one of eleven top Communists convicted in New York of conspiracy to advocate violent overthrow of the government.

Encina said the committee would call a meeting tomorrow to protest the arrest and would ask the government not to return Hall to the United States. He said the appeal would be based on "Mexico's traditional right of asylum for political refugees."

Wallace Denies Red Influence In China Report

Senate Security Inquiry Bars an Open Hearing; He Testifies in Secret

From the Herald Tribune Bureau

WASHINGTON, Oct. 9.—Former Vice-President Henry A. Wallace denied again today that there were Communist influences on his 1944 report on China. The denial came in a statement issued after he failed to obtain assurance of a public hearing to answer charges made before the Senate Internal Security subcommittee.

Mr. Wallace's 2,500-word statement was released tonight by his attorney, George W. Ball, three hours after the former Vice-President had testified in closed session before the subcommittee, headed by Sen. Pat McCarran, D., Nev.

Mr. Ball conceded that Mr. Wallace had agreed during the three-hour hearing to withhold the press statement, which he brought with him. However, Mr. Ball said, his client took the step when Robert Morris, subcommittee counsel, declined to state flatly whether Mr. Wallace would be permitted to testify in open session.

After release of the statement tonight, Mr. Morris expressed surprise that Mr. Wallace had broken an "agreement" not to release the statement until a decision was reached on the matter of the open session. He said Sen. McCarran, who was busy this afternoon with legislation on the Senate floor, had not had time to consider the request.

Later, Sen. McCarran told reporters that Mr. Wallace "undoubtedly was playing to the

(Continued on page 10, column 3)

Reds Accept Ridgway Call For Meeting

Pressure High on Foe; Losses 80,000 Since Kaesong Session Failed

By Mac R. Johnson

From the Herald Tribune Bureau

TOKYO, Wednesday, Oct. 10.—A fresh start in negotiations aimed at ending hostilities in the bloody, fifteen and onet-half-month-old Korean war was assured today. Following receipt of a favorable reply from the Communist commanders, United Nations and Communist liaison officers met at 10 a. m. at Pan Mun Jom to iron out preliminary details for resumption of cease-fire talks by senior delegates.

There were indications from the battle zone that the enemy was under strong military pressure to resume the cease-fire talks. First, Communist casualties were estimated at 80,000 during the seven weeks since Aug. 23 when the Reds broke off negotiations.

Second, the enemy found it necessary to transfer Chinese Red troops to eastern Korea to bolster battered North Korean forces. This was confirmed by the capture of Chinese prisoners on a front where North Koreans previously had opposed the U. N.

Exchange of Messages

The Red commanders' message today, which sent the liaison teams back to work, goes back to developments two days ago. Monday night Gen. Matthew B. Ridgway sent a message to the Reds approving the immediate vicinity of Pan Mun Jom as a substitute truce conference site to Kaesong. The Allied Supreme Commander demanded equal responsibility for both sides on security of the site and its approaches, and suggested that the liaison teams meet today at 10 a. m. at Pan Mun Jom to discuss matters concerning resumption of negotiations.

At 8 a. m. the Communist reply agreeing to the session was delivered to a U. N. liaison officer at the Pan Mun Jom checkpoint.

This reply, broadcast shortly before in English by Radio Peking, also demanded that the two main delegations should immediately resume their armistice negotiations.

Red's Proposal

Premier Kim Il Sung, of North Korea, and Gen. Peng Tehhuai, Chinese Communist commander, who signed the message, also said that the main delegations at their first meeting should "draw up principles extending the scope of the neutral zone and safeguarding the security of the conference site and the setting up of appropriate machinery to solve the various conference questions concerned."

An earlier Red message had proposed extension of the neutral zone to include Communist headquarters at Kaesong along with the U. N. peace camp at Munsan. Pan Mun Jom lies about six miles east of Kaesong and twelve miles west of Munsan. Gen. Ridgway's stand was that only a small neutral zone around the new conference site is needed, with Kaesong and Munsan and the roads to Pan Mun Jom to be immune from attack.

The U. N.-Communist liaison meeting this morning was expected to go into such details as whether to meet in one of Pan Mun Jom's mud-walled thatched-roof huts, or

(Continued on page 6, column 4)

Curb on Sports in TV and Radio Hit by U. S. in Anti-Trust Suit

By The Associated Press

PHILADELPHIA, Oct. 9.—The government today lashed out at controlled television and radio broadcasts of sports events as a violation of the Federal anti-trust laws and instituted a suit against the National Football League in a test case.

H. Graham Morison, Assistant Attorney General in charge of anti-trust activities, said the suit filed here against the league "embodies the basic complaint in all other sports fields."

He said the N. F. L. was singled out because its television and radio control is "the worst in respect to having the greatest restrictions" of any major sports activity.

N. F. L. Commissioner Bert Bell told a reporter "if we are in violation of anti-trust laws, then we want to find out about it. We don't believe it." Furthermore, Mr. Bell argued, "in my opinion the N. F. L. imposes the least restrictions of all major sports on telecasts and broadcasts."

Mr. Bell said the N. F. L. was not notified in advance of the government suit, which asked United States District Court here to enjoin the N. F. L. from restricting television and broadcasting of its football games. The N. F. L. has twenty days in which to file an answer to the complaint.

Mr. Morison released a statement by Mr. McGrath which said:

"This suit has been instituted by the Department of Justice to clarify the position of broadcasting and telecasting in its relation to the sports world. It involves some of the most often-complained-of and aggravated restrictions on the dissemination of athletic events to the public."

Mr. Morison described the suit against the N. F. L. as a test case.

• WHERE IN THE WORLD can you collect a reward for a "Waab"? See interesting "Where in the World" feature, today's Classified Section.

CLASSIFIED AD INDEX..Page 35

The Forrestal Diaries

Futile Attempt to Take Palestine Issue Out of Politics And Retain Arab Friendships for U. S. Security

13. The Palestine Question

Forrestal's activity in the Palestine question—one of the most controversial aspects of his career—sprang at bottom from his sense of the immense strategic significance of the Middle East. It was just after the Republican victory in the Congressional election of 1946 that he first broached the idea that Palestine, with all its explosive implications, might be lifted above the American partisan battle. Yet through 1947 it seemed to become only more deeply entangled in domestic politics, as an example indicates:

4 September 1947 CABINET LUNCH

At the end of the lunch Hannegan [Postmaster General] brought up the question of the President's making a statement of policy on Palestine, particularly with reference to the entrance of a hundred and fifty thousand Jews into Palestine. He said he didn't want to press for a decision one way or the other but simply wanted to point out that such a statement would have a very great influence and great effect on the raising of funds for the Democratic National Committee. He said very large sums were obtained a year ago from Jewish contributors and that they would be influenced in either giving or withholding by what the President did on Palestine. . . . I pointed out that the President's remarks on Palestine of a year ago did not have the expected effect in the New York election. [It was added] that the President was prompted to make the statement by Rabbi [Abba Hillel] Silver, who was neither a Democrat nor friendly to Truman, and said that the net effect of the President's observation was to make the British exceedingly angry.

[Forrestal determined to try his hand.

29 September 1947 CABINET LUNCH

I asked the President whether it would not be possible to lift the Jewish-Palestine question out of politics.

The President said it was worth trying to do although he obviously was skeptical. Anderson asked me what I would do if I were in the other party. I said that if I were in the other party I would listen patiently to the impact of this question on the security of the United States, and if it was dangerous to let it continue to be a matter of barter between the two parties, I felt confident that I would try to put it on a national and bipartisan basis.

[Forrestal opened his campaign with Sen. J. Howard McGrath, the Democratic National Chairman.

26 November 1947 LUNCH—SEN. McGRATH

I said to McGrath that I thought the Palestine question was one of the most important in our

(Continued on page 18, column 6)

Swiss to Try American as 'Spy' For McCarthy on J. C. Vincent

By The Associated Press

GENEVA, Oct. 9.—An American scheduled to go on trial in the Swiss Federal Criminal Court at Lausanne on Monday is charged with conducting illegal political espionage "in supplying information to Sen. McCarthy." The Swiss government charges that the activities of the alleged informant of Sen. Joseph W. McCarthy, R., Wis., violated Swiss sovereignty.

The charge against Charles E. Davis, twenty-four, of Pasadena, Calif., came to light today in the acte d' accusation, comparable to an indictment in United States courts, which has been filed in the Lausanne court.

Mr. Davis is accused specifically of supplying a representative of the Senator in Paris with information concerning John Carter Vincent when Mr. Vincent was United States Minister to Switzerland. The charge says that Mr. Davis was paid for this service.

Mr. Davis, who told United States Consulate officials here that he was correspondent for a Communist newspaper in California, has been in jail for nearly a year since his arrest by Swiss authorities. For the last several months he has been under treatment in the prison ward of a Geneva tuberculosis hospital.

Mr. Vincent was transferred from his post as Minister in Bern to that of Consul-General in Tangier in February. When he was moved, he declined to discuss the background of his transfer, but authorized this statement: "I can't fight back because of financial considerations, but I could fight back on moral grounds."

Mr. Vincent has been a frequent target for Sen. McCarthy's repeated charges of Communist influence in the State Department. The Senator has asserted that Mr. Vincent followed the Communist line particularly when he was serving the State Department in China during the war.

The charge against Mr. Davis

(Continued on page 10, column 4)

Index

News Summaries on Page 2

McDougald grand slams Giants

Durocher goes overboard with Dodger scout reports

By WILLIAM KLEIN

POLO GROUNDS—If the Yankees wrap up the World Series today—and it's going to take the biggest miracle of all to stop them—they should forward their flowers to the Dodgers with a note of thanks. After all, the Giants have been operating on scouting reports turned over by the Brooks.

Smartest move Leo Durocher didn't make, as it turns out, was bolting his door after Dodger scouts Andy High and Jack Sheehan came pounding with everything you have to know to beat the Yankees.

They turned over nothing of definite value, obviously, and we have a sneaking suspicion it was all a hoax. They wanted to see Leo only to get Laraine's autograph.

IS LEO'S FACE RED!

The way Leo praised the reports, it's a cinch no one ever will ask his opinion on such matters again. If the Yankees were the worrying kind, they would have folded in four straight, had they read what he said he knew about them.

Next time Leo receives a 'gift' from the Dodgers he's sure to turn it over to postal authorities to burn or to the FBI for investagation.

If the Dodgers haven't laughed since Bobby Thomson's homer knocked them out of the pennant, they certainly smiled a bit yesterday just thinking what they escaped. After all, they could have been following the same scouting reports to which the Yankees are giving such a lie.

LAUGH WITH SAD HEARTS

Of course they would be laughing with slightly broken hearts. What if the 13-1 thing yesterday doesn't look pretty? The losers still will collect the biggest purse—close to $5,000 per man—in World Series. That would have looked pretty.

The scouting data, which Leo rushed home to burn last night, probably omitted what to do in the event Eddie Lopat pitches and Gil McDougald comes to bat with the bases loaded, and a lot of other things besides.

You can bet on the Lopat omission because the Giants, in two cracks at him, still don't know what to do with his stuff. Steady Eddie probably could come back today without rest and bump 'em out of the series. At least Leo can be thankful that Casey Stengel, when announcing his pitcher for today, didn't give out Lopat's name.

PITCHING TO MCDOUGALD

During the season American League clubs discovered it was a terrible mistake to walk anyone for the purpose of pitching to Joe DiMaggio. The Giants didn't try exactly that yesterday, which was clever, but they attempted a take-off on the idea and what a take-off they got when McDougald fired his grand slam homer!

Gil took a firm grip on the rookie of the year crown with his shot into the upper left field tier. It was the blow that decided the game because the Giants were spiritless after it and easy for Lopat to keep down.

It was quite a year, at that, for McDougald, who though he was in the Yankee spring training camp to chase balls, shine shoes, collect tickets at the gate for exhibition games and run errands for the players.

CLIMAX TO BIG YEAR

The four-in-one-homer, third time it has been accomplished in World Series combat, was a fitting climax to a sensational year for McDougald, whose stance at the plate gives the impression he couldn't hit a Navy blimp if he were standing right next to it.

(That could almost be a quote from the Dodger scouting report on the Yankees.)

Rogers Hornsby, the new Browns' pilot who joined the press box inmates for the series to serve as analyst-correspondent for a Seattle newspaper, wore a big smile as McDougald circled the bases.

Gil is his protege. He had him last in Beaumont and recommended his trial with the Yankees. At first every one thought the Rajah had committed a rare blooper. But McDougald makes him look mighty good, indeed.

The Giants will have a chance today to prove they're miracle men but the betting is they are not. Yankee confidence is kiting—which could mean a hasty conclusion to the series. The players were in a romping mood after the score got slightly lop-sided yesterday, what with Slugger Phil Rizzuto diving head first into a group of teammates in the dugout after he poked his homer.

It's tough to beat a club with that kind of spirit!

IRVIN AND DARK ALERT

The only wide-awake guys in the Giants' lineup seem to be Monte Irvin and Al Dark. The rest seem to have run out of gas—and no wonder. They did come a long way since August. They're learning now how the Phillies felt last fall. There's something about the Yankees you just can't do anything about. It'll surprise no one if the Bombers have their Victory Banquet tonight.

If that should happen a lot of the boys will wait to hear George Weiss speak. Last fall, after the Yankees swept the Phillies, he warned the athletes (jokingly, of course, or so every one thought) not to ask for pay raises because the brief series hadn't done anything for the Yankee treasury.

BEFORE and AFTER

by FRANK CASALE

Yanks' power breaks out at last

POLO GROUNDS—The Giants were bathed in haughty grandeur, eh? They were the "Miracle Team," chosen by Destiny supposedly to fulfill a role of invincibility . . . A flaming spirit, a courageous heart vaulted them past the memorable playoffs into the classic Series . . . And they thundered ahead on the wings of inspiration and skill to deadlock the Yanks in the World Series, at two games each.

Yesterday all the Giants' physical and mental resources were tumbled into the dust as if they were a team as futile and inept as any ever fielded in classic competition . . . Their throbbing, driving spirit was quelled; their aggressiveness was battered out of them and their defensive armor was dented and pierced beyond recognition.

With a burst of all-around belting force, behind an extraordinary defense, the Yanks broke out in all their fury to turn the fifth game into a one-sided slaughter . . . Adding to the Giants' ignominy in the downfall was the fact that they absorbed one of their worst defeats in their own ball yard—the Polo Grounds.

With their withering fire, the Yanks return to their own Stadium with a three-to-two edge and an almost an odds-on chance of clinching the championship today.

You've seen things which had the appearance of authority and of truth suddenly crushed to earth as myths . . . The Giants were crumbled that way yesterday.

In front of the Yanks yesterday the Giants carried on not as inspired, destiny-favored titans of the diamond but were exposed as putrid pushovers; they were not the same team that knocked the Dodgers off in the recent playoffs and held the Yanks even in the first four games of the Series; their identity was the same, but their performance sank to incredibly low level . . . The stunning change-over had to be seen to be believed.

* * *

McDougald sets off attack

THE YANKS STRUCK OUT in traditionally championship quality; theirs was a sustained and diversified attack, such as had enabled the team through the years to achieve a record in competition which may never be equaled.

For some reason, there was a feeling that the Yanks' vaunted power which had been held in some check through the first four games was about due to crash all shackles.

Gil McDougald's grand-slam home run in the third launched the onslaught . . . And from that point onward, the Giants were never in the ball game . . . At the finish you never saw such a beaten, humiliated club.

Ed Lopat came back to the mound for the Yanks and recorded his second victory over the Giants . . . His slow stuff, along with his sharp-breaking curve, placed the Giants completely at his mercy after they wangled a run from him in the first inning . . . During the last three innings he retired the side in one-two-three order . . . He got better as he went along, the Giants learned to their disappointment and sorrow.

Joe DiMaggio, who ended his batting slump with a single and homer in the fourth contest, came through with three more safeties yesterday.

Phil Rizzuto played as fine a game in the field as was ever

(Continued on Page 14)

'Master of Giants,' Rizzuto calls Lopat

By PHIL RIZZUTO

POLO GROUNDS—Steady Eddie, Heady Eddie, call him what you like, I still call him great. If he amazed the Giants last time out, he hypnotized them yesterday. He did it with only three days of rest, too. After yesterday my newspaper friends can call him "Master of the Giants" and point to this Series as proof.

How about that Gil McDougald? He holds the distinction of being the only rookie ever to hit a grand slam home run in a World Series. In addition, he is only the third man to hit one since the World Series began. The other two were Elmer Smith of Cleveland against Brooklyn and Tony Lazzeri the old Yankee against the Giants.

CLIPPER INSPIRES

The Clipper again was the inspiration with his three hits and starting the club to hitting like I knew we could do. Yes sir, I believe we won the crucial game and should take them for sure now.

Another of our conquering heroes is Gene Woodling whose timely hitting and circus catch of Monte Irvin's drive in the ninth had the crowd standing and cheering. Gene has developed into one of the finest fielding left fielders in the game.

I should like to mention briefly of my . . . er . . . home run. I don't believe I would be making a brash statement when I say that I am very happy about it. To be truthful, when I hit the ball I thought I would have to slide into second base. We had the hit and run on and I reached for an outside pitch

(Continued on Page 14)

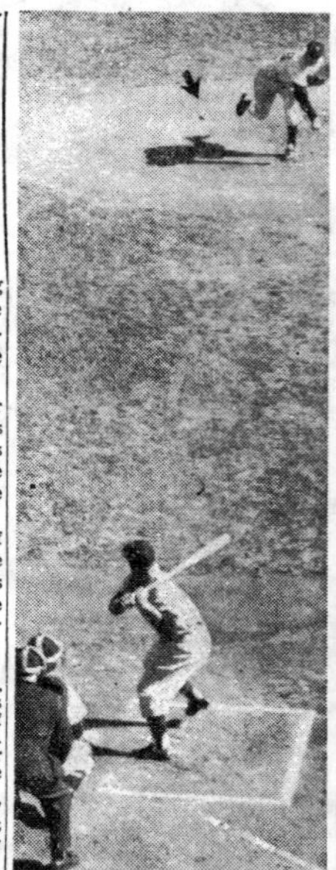

STRIKE — Larry Jansen of Giants starts first pitch of fifth World Series game yesterday. Umpire Bill Summers called it a strike on leadoff Yankee batter Gene Woodling, who struck out. Then came the Yankee deluge! (AP WIREPHOTO)

Series HR not biggest thrill for M'Dougald

By WILL GRIMSLEY

NEW YORK (AP)—The slender, freckle-nosed rookie from San Francisco with the awkward batting stance sat in the glare of exploding flash bulbs, embarrassed by all the attention paid to his grand slam home run yesterday in the fifth World Series game.

"I could tell I got some good wood on it," 22-year-old McDougald said quietly, "but I didn't know it was a home run until I passed second base and saw that Irvin wasn't going back for it."

He didn't know until almost two hours later that his four-run blow, which highlighted the New York Yankees' 13-1 victory over the Giants, was only the third grand slam homer hit in World Series play.

INFORMED LATER

"They told me so when I got back to the dressing room, but, shucks, I didn't care so much about that," commented the modest young father of three children. "I was just glad to give old Lopat that many more runs to work on."

The only other two men to hit grand slam homers in the series were Elmer Smith of Cleveland in 1920 against the Brooklyn Dodgers and Tony Lazzeri, the late Yankee star, who did it in 1936 against these same Giants at the Polo Grounds.

"It was a high, fast pitch," McDougald continued. "I felt that I would meet it solidly—and I did. But as far as being the biggest thrill I ever got that's not necessarily so. I guess I got just a big a kick out of the home run I hit against St. Louis earlier in the season."

HIT ON 6 IN ONE INNING

McDougald hit one with the bases full against the Browns and accounted for six runs in one inning to tie an American League record.

The Yankees showed more post-game animation than anytime during the series yesterday when they trooped into the dressing room with a bulging 3-2 lead over the Giants.

"I wouldn't make any predictions on the series," said manager Casey Stengel, as he quickly changed into civilian clothes. "This is that kind of series. You can't tell about it. But I do think we have the advantage."

Elsewhere, normally dignified world champions whooped and hollered like a bunch of high schoolers on their first out-of-town trip.

They gave the impression of men who felt that today's sixth game at Yankee Stadium would be only a formality.

Almost every man on the team jumped over to run fingers through the mussed red hair of Ed Lopat, the New York lefthander who won his second pitching victory of this series.

"I felt fine out there but I started weakening in the eighth,"

(Continued on Page 14)

TED WILLIAMS REPORTS:

I'll quit if traded

BOSTON (AP)—Boston Herald columnist Bill Cunningham yesterday quoted Ted Williams as saying he would quit baseball if traded or sold by the Boston Red Sox.

In a copyrighted story datelined New York, where Cunningham is covering the World Series, the Herald said:

"In a telephone call from Princeton, Minn., to New York, Williams said he would emulate Bobby Doerr and break with baseball completely and retire to a connection with a manufacturer of fishing tackle if the Red Sox trade or sell him.

"He said," Cunningham continued, "that 'I sincerely mean

seen articles to the effect that the Red Sox are to be broken up and that's he is almost certain to be the first man traded.

Cunningham, quoted Williams as saying:

"I started in Boston and I want to finish in Boston. If I'm traded, or sold, I'll consider that the finish. My other interest is in fishing, as a sport. I consider myself an expert in it, and I have a fine connection waiting in that particular line.

"I'm not trying to dictate to anybody, nor to say what shall or shan't be done to me as a ball player. But I am saying that if the time had come for me to leave Boston, the time

Yanks rip Jansen, 13-1; Lopat wins 2d; Raschi faces Koslo at Stadium today

Star-Ledger Sports

NEWARK, N. J., WEDNESDAY, OCTOBER 10, 1951

STEADY EDDIE YIELDS 5 HITS; DiMAG GETS 3

(Continued from Page One)

long fly in Yankee Stadium. That finished Jansen and ripped the game wide open as the Yanks continued the attack on four relief hurlers.

Lopat spun a brilliant five-hitter as he chalked up his second route-going performance of the series, and the third straight of his career in post season exercises. Steady Eddie did not look too steady at the start but, once he started putting the ball where he wanted it, the Giants frittered away to nothing.

Once again it was Capt. Alvin Dark and Monte Irvin who carried the ball for the Giants' offensive. They each got two hits, their ninth and 11th of the series, respectively, but only Wes Westrum of the other Giants could drop in a safety against the wily little lefthander, who thus put a brilliant climax on the greatest season of his career.

SINGLES LEAD OFF

A pair of Singles by Dark and Irvin intermixed with Gene Woodling's error gave the Giants a 1-0 lead in the first, but thereafter Westrum, who reached second on his double in the fifth, was the only Giant to get that far.

Lopat walked Willie Mays in the second for the only break in his almost impeccable control and turned back three Giants on strikes. Lopat once he got rolling was even more brilliant than in his six hit 3-1 triumph last Friday.

Last week he made 121 pitches, but yesterday only needed 103 to wrap up the decision and, unlike last week, the Giants were never able to get him on the ropes. He merely southpawed them to a slow, painful death as they vainly chased his mystifying assortment of "nothing much."

The rotund little lefty, who had never been able to go nine innings in a Series until last week, has an earned run mark of 0.50 in this one, as the Giants' lone run yesterday was unearned. He is through for the season, unless the unexpected happens and he is needed for a relief job in a seventh game . . . if there is a seventh game.

SMALLEST CROWD

The crowd of 47,530, smallest of the Series so far, was pulling for Irvin to tie the all-time Series high of 12 hits when he batted in the ninth, the crowd booed a little when Lopat got behind 3-0, but Irvin took a strike and then hit what looked like a sure triple to deep left center. Woodling, however, tore after the ball and made a one-handed running catch to make Monte wait at least another day.

Even if Monte does not hit today and the Series ends he can do no worse than tie the record for a six-game Series, which is 11.

Yesterday's defeat was the worst handed out in Series competition since the Yanks beat the Giants 18-4 on Oct. 2, 1936, and the 13 runs were the most scored in a Series since the Yanks ripped the Giants, 13-5, in the sixth game of the 1936 Series on Oct. 6.

Jansen, who to his second defeat of the series was far from the pitcher he was last Friday. His control, which is usually perfect, was far off the beam and got him into trouble in the third inning. With his biting, tearing curves not behaving as directed he could not pitch out of trouble, although the Yanks had only two hits with five runs in the hopper.

KENNEDY GOES IN

Monte Kennedy relieved Jansen and he was followed by George Spencer, Al Corwin and Alex Konikowski, with only the latter escaping unscathed, although giving a ninth inning triple to Woodling. Gene hit the longest ball of the series, a belt over Clint Hartung's head into the Giant bullpen, but a relay from Hartung to Eddie Stanky to Westrum cut Gene down at the plate when he tried for an inside-the-park homer.

Stengel again juggled his lineup and put six left-handed hitters in against the right-handed Jansen, moving Joe Collins to right field and starting Johnny Mize for the first time. Strangely enough, Collins did not handle a single ball in the six innings he played. The outfielder, then moved to first in the seventh.

Phil Rizzuto, his body aching from a variety of blows, was another standout for the now ripping and slashing Yankees. He hit his second World Series homer in the fourth, singled and walked twice and gave a marvelous demonstration of the art of short stopping. Even Giant fans, who try to rate Dark as Rizzuto's equal, had to cheer for the Littlest Yankee of Them All as he scooted all over the infield with a brillinat display of defensive legerdemain.

DiMAGGIO THRILLS 'EM

Perhaps the biggest thrill to the fans, however, was DiMaggio getting a pair of singles and a double in five trips to bat in three runs. The Yankee Clipper is making them forget his fruitless first three games and now is only one run batted in

RIZZUTO SHINES AT BAT, AFIELD; IRVIN, DARK SLUG

behind McDougald, who leads both clubs with six.

The Clipper was hitting the ball well again and his mates are hoping that today's sixth game can be a "DiMaggio Day," for a perfect windup. DiMaggio also pulled off quite a fielding play when Clint Hartung, playing right field in the place of disappointing Henry Thompson, drove a tremendous belt to dead center field. DiMag loped back with his matchless grace and was waiting for it when it came down on the gravel behind the outfield grass. It was a titanic poke, but the old pro was there waiting and made the catch look like an infield pop-up.

Jansen opened the game by whiffing Woodling and making Rizzuto bounce to Stanky, then walked Berra on four pitches before Dark smothered DiMaggio's hot shot and threw to Stanky for the force-out.

STANKY GROUNDS OUT

Stanky grounded out on a 2-2 pitch, then Dark picked up where he left off yesterday with a single to right. Bobby Thomson flied out on a 2-1 pitch, but Irvin drilled a two-strike serve into left field for a single, moving Dark to third, but when Woodling fumbled the ball Dark came in to score and Irvin went to second where he died when Lockman lifted to center.

After Mize missed a homer by three feet he flied to center, to open the second. Then Thomson made a two-base wild throw, after fielding McDougald's rap. Jansen, however, turned back Brown and Collins. Lopat walked Mays, but started a double-play when Hartung hit back to the box, and got Westrum to bounce out.

Lopat made Jansen throw seven pitches in the disastrous three be-

(Continued on Page 14)

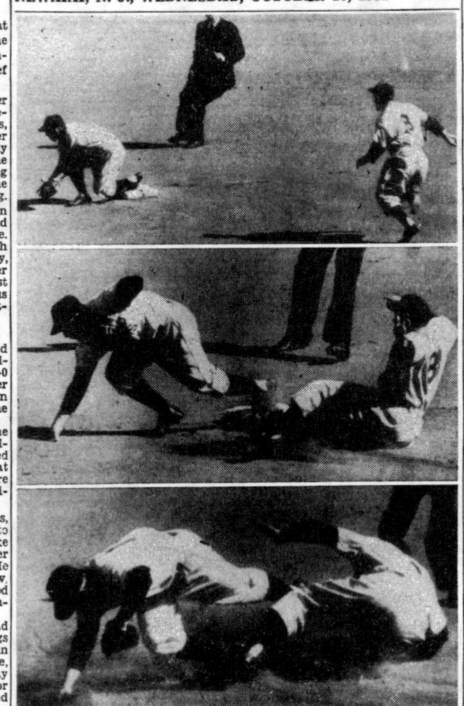

NEAT STANKY PLAY—Ed Stanky (top) kneels to catch low peg from shortstop Al Dark, lunges for ball (center) as Yanks' Yogi Berra slides into second and falls on hand (bottom) but still grips ball for forceout. Joe DiMaggio's grounder to Dark started play. Umpire is Joe Paparella. Happened in first inning. (AP WIREPHOTO)

NEW YORK (A)	ab	r	h	o	a	e
Woodling, lf	3	3	1	5	0	1
Rizzuto, ss	4	3	2	0	6	0
Berra, c	4	2	1	3	0	0
DiMaggio, cf	5	1	3	3	0	0
Mize, 1b	3	1	1	6	0	0
Bauer, rf	1	0	0	0	0	0
McDougald, 2b-3b	5	1	1	2	2	0
Brown, 3b	4	0	2	1	3	0
Coleman, 2b	1	1	0	0	1	0
Collins, rf-1b	5	1	1	7	0	0
Lopat, p	5	0	0	0	2	0
Totals	39	13	12	27	14	1

NEW YORK (N)	ab	r	h	o	a	e
Stanky, 2b	4	0	0	1	4	0
Dark, ss	4	1	2	2	3	0
Thomson, 3b	4	0	0	1	3	1
Irvin, lf	4	0	2	2	0	1
Lockman, 1b	4	0	0	9	3	0
Mays, cf	2	0	0	2	0	0
Hartung, rf	3	0	0	1	1	1
Westrum, c	3	0	1	7	0	0
Jansen, p	0	0	0	1	1	0
a-Lohrke	1	0	0	0	0	0
Kennedy, p	0	0	0	0	1	0
b-Rigney	1	0	0	0	0	0
Spencer, p	0	0	0	0	1	0
Corwin, p	0	0	0	1	0	0
c-Williams	1	0	0	0	0	0
Konikowski, p	0	0	0	0	0	0
Totals	31	1	5	27	17	3

a-Struck out for Jansen in 3rd.
b-Flied out for Kennedy in 5th.
c-Grounded out for Corwin in 8th.

New York (A)	005	202	400—13
New York (N)	100	000	000— 1

RBI—DiMaggio 3, McDougald 4, Rizzuto 3, Mize. 2B—Westrum, Mize, DiMaggio. 3B—Woodling. HR—McDougald, Rizzuto. DP—Lopat, McDougald and Mize. Left—New York (A) 7; New York (N) 4. BB—Jansen 4 (Berra, Woodling, Rizzuto, Mize); Kennedy 1 (Woodling); Spencer 3 (Brown, Woodling, Rizzuto); Lopat 1 (Mays). SO—Jansen 1 (Woodling); Kennedy 2 (Lopat, Collins); Corwin 1 (Coleman); Lopat 3 (Lohrke, Mays, Westrum. HO—Jansen 3 in 3 innings; Kennedy 3 in 2; Spencer 4 in 1¼; Corwin 1 in 1 2-3; Konikowski 1 in 1. WP—Corwin. Winner—Lopat. Loser—Jansen. U—Bill Summers (AL) home plate; Lee Ballanfant (NL) first base; Joe Paparella (AL) second base; Al Barlick (NL) third base; John Stevens (AL) left field foul line; Art Gore (NL) right field foul line. T—2:31. A—47,530. Receipts—$230,389.45.

THE WEATHER
Today: Rain, rather windy and cool; fresh to strong northeast winds.
Tomorrow: Rain in morning, somewhat warmer; north and northwest winds diminishing.
Temperatures Yesterday: Max., 57.3; Min., 48.4.
Today's Probable Range: Max., 57; Min., 51.
Humidity at 3 p. m. Yesterday: 85%.
Expected Humidity This Afternoon: 60-70%.
Detailed Report and Map—Page 37

NEW YORK Herald Tribune

European Edition Published Daily in Paris

Late City Edition

111th Year VOL. CXI NO. 38,315

THURSDAY, OCTOBER 11, 1951

230 West 41st Street, New York 18, N. Y. Telephone PEnnsylvania 6-4000

FIVE CENTS

Yankees Win 3d Series in Row, Beat Giants in 6th Game, 4-3

61,711 See 3 Score On Bauer's Triple

National Leaguers' Bid in 9th Is Checked After Batting 2 Runs Across

By Rud Rennie

In the sixth game of the World Series yesterday, the lordly Yankees expelled the wide-eyed, hard-fighting Giants from the wonderland created for them a week ago by Bobby Thomson's magic bat and left them face to face with the facts of life.

The facts were: The forty-eighth World Series was over, and the Yankees were kings of the realm for their third consecutive year, victorious in the series, four games to two.

The Yankees won, 4 to 3, by dint of a triple by Hank Bauer with the bases loaded in the sixth inning. They left the Giants with the bases loaded and Ray Noble, a pinch hitter, glaring at a third strike in the eighth. And they got the Giants to hit three balls into the air for outs after filling the bases with three hits in their last turn at bat.

Closest of Series

It was the closest game of the series, and it kept the crowd of 61.711 persons glued to their seats until the very end.

The Yankees started the game with Vic Raschi, their best right-hander, but had to call on Johnny Sain and then Bob Kuzava after Ed Stanky, Alvin Dark and Whitey Lockman batted safely in the ninth.

The Giants had the bases loaded and they needed three runs to tie the score and keep the series and their chances of immortality alive.

There was none out when Casey Stengel, the Yankee manager, summoned Kuzava from the bull pen. It seemed odd that Casey should select a left-hander at these tell-tale moments to pitch to right-handed batsmen. But he must have known what he was doing. It worked and gained for the Yankees their fourteenth world championship and their fourth in six tests with the Giants.

The first man to face Kuzava was Monte Irvin, who had already tied the record for most hits in a six-game series even though he had not made one all afternoon. Irvin socked the first pitch far into left field, where Gene Woodling caught the ball.

Stanky Scores

Stanky scored after the catch and Dark and Lockman advanced. The Giants then had men on second and third with one out and a single could tie the score. Thomson, the man whose three-run homer turned the baseball universe upside down a week ago yesterday and landed the Giants in the World Series, had a count of two strikes and two balls when he also poled a fly to left.

Dark scored after Woodling caught this one and the Giants needed only one run to tie and that run was perched on second base.

The crowd was in the greatest excitement it has enjoyed in the series. Sal Yvars, a substitute catcher, was sent to bat in place of Hank Thomson. Sal also is a right-handed hitter. He had been at bat only forty-one times all year, but he had a .317 batting average.

The crowd applauded Yvars. It

(Continued on page 33, column 1)

Herald Tribune—Acme telephoto

CASEY'S HERO—Yankee manager Casey Stengel with Hank Bauer, who batted in three runs

Sanitation Dept. 'Sickness' Up, 987 on Vacation Ordered Back

59 Suspended for 'Feigning Illness'; Mulrain Admits Garbage Collection Is Crippled

By Robert A. Bedolis

The "sickness" wave among sanitation workers increased yesterday, and Commissioner Andrew W. Mulrain, reporting a marked increase in uncollected garbage, ordered 987 employees on vacation to report back to work immediately.

The department said there were 307 new "sickness" cases yesterday and that fifty-nine of the employees were suspended from their jobs for "feigning illness" after examination by department physicians. Four men were suspended in the field for "loitering," bringing the days suspensions to sixty-three and the total since the union-inspired slowdown began on Oct. 1 to 195.

Local 111A of the Building Service Employees International Union, A. F. L., conducting the slowdown to back its demands for a forty-hour, five-day work week for the department's 9,600 workers, said the department's figure was untrue and that 2,700 men reported sick yesterday.

The number of "sicknesses" reported by the department Tuesday was 131, and Sanitation Department representatives said that some of these men returned to work yesterday and others remained out, but gave no figures.

Commissioner Mulrain, who canceled the participation of 3,000 workers in the Columbus Day parade tomorrow, said that 735 truckloads of garbage went uncollected yesterday amounting to 217,000 cans full. This compared with 454 loads uncollected last Wednesday and 200 loads uncollected on Tuesday. The backlog two weeks ago Wednesday, before the slowdown began, was 400 loads.

Stanley Krasowski, Local 111A president, denied the department's figures and said that 1,810 truckloads were not picked up according to the "true but hidden" department figures. The department disdained "crossing swords" with Mr. Krasowski on this.

Acting Mayor Joseph F. Sharkey,

(Continued on page 17, column 2)

Vast Radar Net Set Up in Arctic By U.S., Canada

Long-Range Sets to Guard Against Surprise; Rubber 'Radomes' House Stations

By Ansel E. Talbert

A network of new radar installations capable of detecting enemy aircraft at long range is being completed on the Arctic frontier of North America to protect the United States and Canada from surprise attack, the Air Force disclosed yesterday.

In Ottawa last night, Canada's Department of Defense made public an order in council making it legal for both Canadians and Americans to operate the radar installations. Previously, Canadian law has provided that radio and radar operators in the dominion must be British subjects.

A Canadian defense spokesman said that the installation and operation of the radar network jointly by Canada and the United States was evidence of the close co-operation between the two nations.

Although the exact number of the radar installations now in being was not revealed, the General Electric Company, which built them, described the posts as "the largest and most complex radar systems ever produced."

Each post has the capability of intercepting a large number of enemy air attacks simultaneously

(Continued on page 45, column 8)

30% Commuter Fare Rise Asked By N. Y. Central

Affects Westchester Lines; B. & M. Gets 66% Rise, Southern Roads Get 10%

The New York Central Railroad asked the Public Service Commission yesterday to approve a 30 per cent fare increase on three commuter divisions which would affect 30,000 residents of Westchester County. The railroad said it was losing $2,500,000 a year on its commuter service.

In applying for the fare increase, F. H. Baird, assistant vice-president of the railroad, declared: "Although our application is justified entirely on the basis of increased costs, the adjustments are essential because of the large sums required for commutation equipment." He pointed out that the railroad has spent $11,000,000 for new commuter equipment.

Meanwhile, the Interstate Commerce Commission in Washington authorized southern railroads to increase their passenger fares by 10 per cent and granted the Boston & Maine Railroad a 66 per cent increase in interstate commutation fares.

The I. C. C. said the increase would give the twenty-seven Class I southern carriers a "substantial increase" in annual revenues. It was the first increase granted the southern railroads since 1948. The new schedules will become effective on five days' notice.

Coach fares will be increased from 2.5 to about 2.75 cents a mile and Pullman fares from 3.5 to about

(Continued on page 45, column 6)

Income Tax Rise Of 11¾% Indicated

Conferees Agree on Plan to Break Deadlock

WASHINGTON, Oct. 10 (UP).—House-Senate conferees reached tentative agreement tonight on a proposed increase in personal income taxes, breaking a deadlock that had threatened to hold up action on the huge defense tax bill.

Although the decision was not disclosed, one conferee indicated that the agreement, for most taxpayers at least, called for an increase of 11¾ per cent in individual income tax payments. Another conferee said the agreement was tentative and subject to change tomorrow.

The House-Senate Conference Committee has been working for more than a week to compromise differences between the $5,500,000,000 Senate bill and the $7,200,000,000 House bill. The conferees had agreed previously on a 5 per cent increase in corporation income taxes, which would make the rate 30 per cent on earnings up to $25,000 a year and 52 per cent on all above that.

House conferees surrendered in their fight to apply a 20 per cent withholding tax to payments for dividends, interest and royalties. Because some of these payments are not reported on individual tax returns, the House had estimated that the provision would raise more than $323,000,000 a year.

Billy Rose and Eleanor Holm Separate; She Is Expected to Sue

Billy Rose and his wife, the former Eleanor Holm, have separated permanently, it was learned yesterday. It is expected Mrs. Rose will file suit for divorce.

At Mr. Rose's offices in the Ziegfeld Theater, which he owns and where he has an apartment, it was said that Mr. Rose was "in the country" yesterday. However, there was no answer at his estate in Mount Kisco.

Mrs. Rose was also unavailable. Louis Nizer, a lawyer, of 1501 Broadway, who said he was representing Mrs. Rose, declined to make any statement on the reported break-up of the couple "until certain papers are filed." It was reported that the Roses have been living apart for two weeks.

On July 15, Joyce Mathews, show girl and former wife of Milton Berle, attempted suicide in Mr. Rose's Ziegfeld Theater apartment by slashing her wrists with a razor blade while barricaded behind a locked bathroom door. While police, who had forced the door open, were reviving Miss Mathews, Mr. Rose was reported by police as saying: "Now is the time to have a wife. I'm going to call Eleanor now." He denied that he ever made such a statement.

At the time, Miss Mathews denied any romantic connection with Mr. Rose and Mrs. Rose also denied reports that she was on the verge of separating from him.

Mr. Rose, who is fifty, and his wife, thirty-seven, were married in 1939. She had met Mr. Rose in 1937 and was the star of the Aquacade which he produced at the New York World's Fair. Mrs. Rose, a former Olympic swimmer, was divorced in 1939 from Art Jarrett, orchestra leader. Mr. Rose was married in 1929 to the late Fannie Brice. They were divorced in 1938.

Picture on Page 12.

Where in New York

• **WHERE IN NEW YORK** is the only high school for prospective farmers? Newtown High School, Elmhurst, Queens, has more than 400 boys enrolled in the city's only high school agricultural program. The farmers-to-be, ranging in age from 13 to 18, come from all boroughs, concentrate on agricultural subjects, work on the school's 50-acre farm during the school year, and on private farms during summer vacations.

• **WHERE IN THE WORLD** did a beer shortage make history? See interesting "Where In The World" feature, today's Classified Section.

• **WHERE IN NEW YORK** can you find a better home, job, business opportunity, used car, lost article, etc.? In Herald Tribune Classified. When you have any one of a hundred different items you want to sell, tell it to your most responsive audience through low-cost, result-producing Herald Tribune Classified ads. Simply dial PEnnsylvania 6-4000 and ask for a Classified Ad-taker.

Thanks, Louis Kaufman, New York City. Send your "Where in New York" facts to Dept. WNY, Herald Tribune, 230 W. 41st St., N. Y. 18. $2 paid for each suggestion used.

CLASSIFIED AD INDEX. . Page 45

Acheson Says He Supported China Aid Cut

Denies Jessup Share In 1949 Suggestion

Military Men Proposed It, He Asserts, to Keep Arms From Red Hands

By The Associated Press

WASHINGTON, Oct. 10.—Secretary of State Dean Acheson said today that Ambassador-at-Large Philip C. Jessup was not involved in any way in a 1949 proposal, eventually turned down by President Truman, that American aid to the Chinese Nationalists be suspended.

Mr. Acheson told a news conference it is true that such a step was discussed at a White House meeting on Feb. 5, 1949, and that he supported it. But he said the recommendation came originally not from the State Department but from the military, who feared arms sent to China for the Nationalist forces would fall into Communist hands.

Jessup Not at Meeting

Dr. Jessup did not attend the meeting and was not involved, Secretary Acheson declared.

The question of whether Dr. Jessup was involved has come into Senate controversy over President Truman's nomination of the Ambassador-at-Large to be a United States delegate to the United Nations.

Harold E. Stassen has said the late Sen. Arthur H. Vandenberg, R., Mich., once told him that Secretary Acheson and Dr. Jessup backed at the conference an end to aid to the Chinese Nationalists. Dr. Jessup has said he did not even attend the conference.

Actually, aid was not suspended. President Truman made the decision against stopping it.

In addition to the denials from Secretary Acheson and Dr. Jessup that the Ambassador at Large was there, U. N. records have been brought up to place Dr. Jessup in New York on Feb. 5, 1949. Warren R. Austin, chief United States delegate to the U. N. sent a message to the State Department to that effect last night.

Worried Over Shipments

Mr. Acheson, detailing the circumstances of the White House meeting, said the recommendation to suspend American shipments to the Chinese Nationalists was made by Maj. Gen. David S. Barr, then senior American military representative in China. He said Gen. Barr felt Nationalist resistance was crumbling and that there was danger the arms might fall into Communist hands.

This recommendation, Secretary Acheson said, was supported by the top military and civilian advisers of President Truman. He added that he himself concurred in the recommendations.

He said the matter was brought

(Continued on page 16, column 5)

I. P. R. Records, in Field's Home, Escaped Senate Inquiry Seizure

Holland Tells of Boxes Left Inadvertently in Cellar of House in N. Y.

By Don Irwin

WASHINGTON, Oct. 10.—William L. Holland, secretary-general of the Institute of Pacific Relations, testified under questioning today that "sixteen to twenty cartons" of old I. P. R. records had escaped seizure last February by the Senate Internal Security Subcommittee.

Mr. Holland, appearing at an open hearing before the subcommittee that is investigating the institute as an alleged subversive influence on American foreign policy, said the files had been left inadvertently in the basement of the New York home of Frederick Vanderbilt Field, former I. P. R. trustee, now accused as a Communist.

The witness said existence of the packing boxes was called to his attention by Field on Feb. 12, three days after agents of the subcommittee subpoenaed a large collection of back I. P. R. files that had been stored in a Lee, Mass., barn belonging to Edward C. Carter, retired I. P. R. secretary-general.

Mr. Holland testified that he had looked superficially at the cartons, which he said appeared to contain old bills and "duplicates" of documents in the Lee files. He said he had notified the Federal Bureau of Investigation about the matter two weeks ago, and that agents had been through the cartons and had removed several documents for photostating.

Asked by J. G. Sourwine, Counsel for the Senate Judiciary Committee, of which the subcommittee is a branch, why he had delayed so long, Mr. Holland replied that

(Continued on page 16, column 2)

Herald Tribune—Acme telephoto

William L. Holland testifying yesterday at Senate inquiry

Gus Hall Sped to Prison in Texas; Search Widens for 3 Other Reds

Arrest Spurs Hunt for Thompson, Winston, Green; F.B.I. Is Told, 'Say Nothing, We May Get Break'

By Milton Lewis

Gus Hall, national secretary of the Communist party in the United States, was slapped into jail in Texas yesterday to begin a delayed five-year sentence after he was sumarily deported from Mexico.

With the capture of the fugitive Monday night in Mexico City, the Federal Bureau of Investigation was quietly hopeful of rounding up soon the three other Red leaders who also jumped bail in July.

J. Edgar Hoover, director of the F. B. I., refused to give a single detail as to what led to Hall's trail, and Federal agents working on the case in Mexico and Texas were warned tersely, "Say nothing. If we keep quiet we may get another break shortly."

For the time being, Hall will be held at the Federal Correctional Institution at Texarkana. His prison term should have begun on July 2, when he and his three confederates jumped $20,000 bail each by failing to surrender in United States Court House at Foley Square.

The four, along with seven other top Red leaders who did give up July 2, were convicted of criminally conspiring to teach and advocate the overthrow of the government by force and violence. Only last Monday the United States Supreme Court, which upheld their October, 1949, conviction last June, refused to reconsider its decision.

Late yesterday United States Attorney Myles J. Lane forwarded Hall's commitment papers from New York by air mail to Albert McDonald, warden of the Texas jail. It was uncertain whether the three-month fugitive will remain there. The seven who surrendered July 2 have been sent to various prisons to serve their five-year terms. In view of the circumstances, it was explained, Hall will have no further arraignment in open court in any district.

In addition to continuing their hunt for the three other bail jumpers — Robert Thompson, Henry Winston and Gilbert Green —agents were trying to get a lead on the persons who aided and abetted Hall in his international flight to Mexico, a favorite way

(Continued on page 8, column 2)

The Forrestal Diaries

World Crisis of 1948 Catches Nation Short of Troops; Wedemeyer Critical of Marshall's Work in China

14. "Playing With Fire"

In January, 1948, Gen. Eisenhower, about to resign his office as Chief of Staff, decided to remove himself from further consideration as a presidential candidate. After the War Council on the 22d he showed Forrestal the letter (to Leonard V. Finder, a New Hampshire publisher) which he had prepared to that end.

22 January 1948

CONVERSATION—GENERAL EISENHOWER

[Eisenhower said] that he had spent a great deal of time in the composition of the letter and that his only misgiving had been that a construction could be put upon it of its constituting a refusal to respond to a duty, around which, he said, his entire life had been built. He remarked that there were many youngsters in the country who, whether with reason or not, had made him more or less a symbol of the duties and obligations, as well as the opportunities, open to American youth, and he was truly worried about the responsibility of, in effect, telling them that there was a limit to any man's conception of his obligation to respond to the call of duty. He said that was why he had put in a paragraph about the danger of letting political considerations influence the conduct and actions of men in the high command in the Armed Forces.

I told him that his letter would put him in a position of tremendous influence, above the battle, and that in this role he could still perform a great service to the country. There is no question in my mind as to his complete sincerity or that his letter reflects the outcome of a genuine moral struggle with himself.

He said that he had had the help of nobody in the course of the composition of the letter and had come to me because he didn't know anybody else that he could turn to for advice. I told him that I thought the letter, both in its content and in its style, was splendid, and I would not recommend changing anything in it.

[Eisenhower released the letter the following day, and it had the effect that its author had intended.

Perils Rising on Every Front

[By the latter part of January it was beginning to appear that the nation would be compelled to some reappraisal of its military policies. It was facing perils on every front—in Europe, the Middle East and the Far East—and while the President's $11 billion military budget seemed large by peace-time standards, it was yielding very little actual military strength available for current contingencies. In February Secretary Marshall, reviewing the grave issues before them and renewing his persistent plea for universal military training, remarked "that we are playing with fire while we have nothing with which to put it out."

[The acutely felt want was for currently useful ground forces. At a White House meeting on February 18, Maj. Gen. A. M. Gruenther, the director of the Joint Chiefs' own Joint Staff, gave the President a summary presentation. Total strength of all services was only 1,374,000 against Congressional authorized strength of 1,715,000. The Army had only 140,000 men in the Far East against a "requirement" of 180,000; of these, there were only 20,000 in Korea, where 40,000 were required. They were short in Europe. Of organized Army units in the United States there were but two and one-third under-strength divisions, less than 47,000 men in all and soon to be reduced to 40,000. Beyond a few Marine battalion landing teams there were no other immediately available ground forces. "Gen. Gruenther touched on the possible explosive points in the world, identifying them as Greece, Italy, Korea and Palestine, stating that if a commitment were made in any one of

(Continued on page 26, column 6)

Korean Talks Held Up Over Neutral Zone

Allies Demand Issue Be Ironed Out Now

Reds Want Full Parleys to Decide It; Liaison Teams Meet 2d Time

By Mac R. Johnson
From the Herald Tribune Bureau

TOKYO, Thursday, Oct. 11.—Only one problem—a United Nations demand to discuss the size of the neutral zone now instead of accepting a Communist proposal to defer it until the first full delegation meeting—is holding up resumption of Korean truce negotiations, the Peking radio said in a broadcast today.

The enemy radio said this problem would be discussed at today's meeting of U. N. and Communist liaison officers, which began at 10 a. m. (8 p. m. Wednesday, E. S. T.) at Panmunjom

Gen. Matthew B. Ridgway's headquarters has remained silent on what happened at yesterday's two hour and twenty-five minute meeting of U. N. and enemy liaison teams. But Radio Peking maintained in its version that "in the main" agreement was reached on the date and time for resumption of the truce talks.

Agreed on Other Points

And, the Red station said, "in the main" agreement was obtained on temporary arrangements for joint and responsible protection of the conference site, on the question of a specific location for the conference site and on matters of equipment and facilities for the truce camp.

At Munsan today, the main U. N. truce negotiation delegation said only that the actual ground site of the conference location has not been determined. The delegation said it would be midway between U. N. and Communist lines and in the area of Pan-munjom.

The Peking broadcast quoted a dispatch of a correspondent for the Communist New China News Agency. It expressed no alarm or concern over the development, but seemed to regret that the U. N. liaison officers had tried to open the neutral zone boundary subject, thus delaying a meeting of the main delegations.

In bringing up the matter, the U. N. liaison team said it had not had time to study the Communists' message of Oct. 9, the radio said. "Our liaison officers finally requested that the other side make a careful study of the message of Oct. 9, sent by our commanders, and then agreed to continue the meeting at 10 a. m. on Oct. 11," Peking said.

Reds Proposed Delay on Issue

The message referred to, from Premier Kim Il Sung of North Korea and Gen. Peng Teh-huai, Chinese commander, proposed to Gen. Ridgway that the extension of the neutral zone to include Kaesong and Munsan be discussed by the full delegations.

Marine Col. James C. Murray, Lt. Col. Norman B. Edwards and South Korean Lt. Col. Lee Soo Young spoke for the U. N. This same group made the trip to Panmunjom by helicopter for today's meeting. Col. Chang Chun San was the chief Communist liaison officer.

The U. N. truce team was on hand to enter negotiations as soon as the stage is set. Vice-Adm. C. Turner Joy, chief U. N. delegate, and Air Force Maj. Gen. Lawrence C. Craigie joined Rear Adm. Arleigh Burke in the apple orchard U. N. peace camp at Munsan yesterday afternoon.

The U. N. negotiators remained in seclusion at their camp, which is only fifteen minutes by helicopter from Panmunjom, where a tent city may rise on the sandy

(Continued on page 14, column 5)

Index

News Summaries on Page 2

ALLIE 5-6½ OVER BLACK

Story on Page 20

5 CENTS ★ FINAL

Daily Mirror

OCTOBER						
S	M	T	W	T	F	S
			1	2	3	4
5	6	7	8	9	10	11
12	13	14	15	16	17	18
19	20	21	22	23	24	25
26	27	28	29	30	31	

Vol. 29. No. 86. NEW YORK 17, N. Y., WEDNESDAY, OCTOBER 1, 1952

4c in New York City
5c Elsewhere in U.S.A.

Dodgers' Delivery Dept.

Brooklyn moundsmen line up left to right in the order of their announced appearance in the World Series classic against the Yanks, starting at Ebbets Field today. Photographed at the Stadium yesterday, they're Joe Black, Carl Erskine, Preacher Roe, Billy Loes and John Rutherford.

'LUMBERMEN' Billy Martin (left) and Mickey Mantle get the feel of their bats. Martin's hit won pennant-clinching game for Yanks.

THEY CASE THE PLACE. Walloping Dodgers Shuba (left) and Snider scan the stands.

Bombers' Takeoff Today

Yanks whip up the up-and-at-'em spirit at the Stadium for the Ebbets Field Series opener. Spurting out of the dugout are (l. to r.) Mize, Collins, Woodling, McDougald, Bauer, Rizzuto, Martin, Noren, Berra and Mantle.

(Mirror Photos by Art Sarno)

Yankees Drub Dodgers, 7-1, Behind Raschi's 3-Hitter and Square Series at 1-All

Erskine Routed in 5-Run 6th; Martin Belts Homer With 2 On

NewYork Pitcher Fans 9; Mantle Leads Bombers' 10-Hit Assault With 3

(Continued from page one)

Gene Woodling, back in Casey Stengel's line-up despite a hernia, slashed a long single to center that sent Mantle to second. Reese and Robinson walked to the mound to calm Erskine and Mantle ran to third where umpire Babe Pinelli told him that time had been called and to go back to second. Pinelli needn't have bothered, because while Erskine was walking Yogi Berra he added a wild pitch to his repertoire and both runners advanced.

Erskine left and Loes came in. Joe Collins, up with the bases full, bounced right to Robinson who went for a double play and conceded the run. Robinson tagged Berra on the baseline after Yogi had made a few attempts to dodge and fired a throw right at Hodges' stomach.

McDougald Bunt Messed Up

Hodges let the throw roll off his glove, an out was lost and the big inning was still going strong. Then Gil McDougald pushed a bunt between the mound and first base and Hodges grabbed the ball. By the time the first baseman had finished looking at the plate, thinking and turning there was no play anywhere although Loes had covered first. Then came Martin and the questions that Hodges' misplays created were the ones that held the key to the game.

Would McDougald have bunted with two out?

Was Loes rattled by the bad fielding or did he just seem mad standing at first waiting for a throw that never came?

Would Raschi have found the Dodgers as docile in a game where they had a chance?

It's the stuff that dreams are made of in Brooklyn and ought to provide ample conversational matter until today's game starts at the Stadium.

After Martin's smash Loes went untroubled through the seventh and Ken Lehman, a rookie lefthander, finished. Raschi not only finished, but also was untroubled.

Earlier the contest had been a great deal more exciting as both Erskine and Raschi flirted with trouble and only Erskine was hooked. In each of the first six innings, the first Yankee up reached base. Hank Bauer started the game with a looping single to right center and as Phil Rizzuto swung and missed a second strike, Campanella's perfect throw caught Bauer at second as the hit and run went awry. Then Rizzuto walked, Mantle fanned and with the count two strikes on Woodling, Phil tested Campanella's arm and flunked as badly as Bauer had.

Woodling got another life, worked Erskine for a walk to lead off the second and took third on Berra's long single to right center. Erskine steadied, got Collins to take a curve for strike three, fanned McDougald and Martin was retired on a roller to Reese.

But in the fourth, the Yankees broke through to match Brooklyn's third-inning run. Mantle lined a double off the top of the scoreboard in right and took third on Woodling's grounder to Robinson and scored on Berra's fly to right. The Yankees went ahead for the first time in the series and for the remainder of the afternoon in the fifth.

Scores on Martin's Single

McDougald walked and Stengel played hit and run again, getting a strange but satisfactory result. First McDougald ran and made second when Martin missed a low pitch and the ball glanced off Campanella's glove. Then, a few pitches later, Martin hit a single to left that scored McDougald and offered a fascinating refinement of the pedestrial variety of hit-and-run.

Martin took second on the throw to the plate and after Raschi fanned, Bauer kept things going with a walk. He stopped them with a "rock" immediately. As Erskine was pitching to Rizzuto, Carl bounced a curve in the dirt which Campanella blocked. Bauer ran for second, startling Martin, who saw that the ball was just in front of the catcher, but had to run for third, anyway. He did, motioning Bauer to replace him at second and was retired, Campanella to Billy Cox. Rizzuto ended things with a grounder, but in the sixth things didn't end until the Dodgers were finished.

Brooklyn threatened Raschi in the second when he walked Robinson, Hodges and Carl Furillo, but the crafty Yankee contrived to have Erskine come up with two out and bases full so he was not damaged. Not so in the third when Reese drove Brooklyn's first it, a long single to left center. Snider got the second, a perfect bunt toward third, and Campanella closed the day's batting for the Dodgers with a bounding single through the left side that scored Reese and put Brooklyn ahead, 1 to 0.

In the opener, the Dodgers took a 1-to-0 lead and went on to win. Yesterday they went downhill from there, but then, the team looked completely different than it had, only the uniforms and numbers were the same.

Preacher Roe, who shut the Yankees out for Brooklyn's only victory in the 1949 series, will try to get Dodger triumph No. 2 this afternoon when the show moves to the Stadium. Roe is a thin lefthander who relies on control and guile. His opponent will be Eddie Lopat, a lefthander who differs from Roe only in his size. Lopat is short and squat, but pitches in much the same manner as the Preacher.

World Series Facts, Figures and Standing

* * *

STANDINGS

	W.	L.	Pct.
Brooklyn (N. L.)	1	1	.500
New York (A. L.)	1	1	.500

1ST GAME AT EBBETS FIELD, OCT. 1

	R.	H.	E.
Brooklyn (N. L.)	4	6	0
New York (A. L.)	2	6	2

Reynolds, Scarborough (8) and Berra; Black and Campanella.

2D GAME AT EBBETS FIELD, OCT. 2

	R.	H.	E.
New York (A. L.)	7	10	0
Brooklyn (N. L.)	1	3	1

Raschi and Berra; Erskine, Loes (6), Lehman (8) and Campanella.

Third game, Oct. 3, at Yankee Stadium; fourth game, Oct. 4, at Yankee Stadium; fifth game, Oct. 5, at Yankee Stadium; sixth game, if necessary, Oct. 6, at Ebbets Field; seventh game, if necessary, Oct. 7, at Ebbets Field.

FINANCIAL FIGURES

FIRST GAME

Attendance, 34,861.
Receipts (gross), $209,892.
Receipts (net), $174,845.62.
Players' share, $89,171.27.
Commissioner's share, $26,226.84.
Clubs' and leagues' share, $59,447.51.

SECOND GAME

Attendance—33,792.
Receipts (gross), 05,518.
Receipts (net), $171,279.17.
Players' share—$87,352.37.
Commissioner's share—$25,691.88.
Clubs' and league's share—$58,234.92.

TWO-GAME TOTALS

Attendance—68,653.
Receipts (gross), $415,410.
Receipts (net)—$346,124.79.
Players' share—$176,523.64.
Commissioner's share—$51,918.72.
Clubs' and league's share—$117,682.43.

American League Clubs Buy 3 Cardinal Players

Three St. Louis Cardinals have been sold to American League clubs for the $10,000 waiver price, it was announced yesterday.

Pitcher Bob Habenicht and first baseman Ed Mickelson were sold to the St. Louis Browns and pitcher Bill Werle to the Boston Red Sox.

Werle, obtained from the Pittsburgh Pirates for pitcher George Munger, was on the disabled list during the summer because of a liver ailment.

Habenicht and Mickelson trained with the Cardinals in spring training and rejoined the Red Birds after regular season play with farm clubs.

Call MEridian 7-1212 For World Series Score

Scores by innings of the World Series games between the Yankees and the Dodgers will this year be given every twenty seconds, between each interval of a time announcement at the telephone company's time bureau, Meridian 7-1212. Thus many thousands of fans in the New York metropolitan area will keep posted on the progress of the contests.

A typical announcement will be: "End of — inning, Dodgers —, Yankees —." The final score will be continued in time reports until 6:30 p. m. Any postponement of a game will be included in the announcement before the starting time of the game and for one hour afterwards.

Ted Kell

Billy Martin is trapped between second and third here and was out, Roy Campanella to Billy Cox as umpire Babe Pinelli moves in to call the play. This occurred in fifth inning

Ted Kell

Martin is welcomed home by Joe Collins (41) and Gil McDougald (12) after blasting home run into left field stands in Yankees' big five-run sixth inning. Collins and McDougald both scored on wallop as Yankees won, 7-1, to even the series

James Kavallines

Vic Raschi cools off in Yankee dressing room after cooling off the Dodgers in a three-hit pitching chore

Memphis Leads in Dixie; Drubs Shreveport, 9-1

SHREVEPORT, La., Oct. 2 (AP).—Righthander Tom Hurd pitched the Memphis Chicks within one game of a Dixie Series title tonight, letting the Shreveport Sports down on five nits for a 9-to-1 victory. Memphis has won three games and Shreveport two.

The slight curve baller allowed two hits in the first inning and two in the fourth, when Shreveport scored its lone run on singles by Harry Elliott and Grant Dunlap and a bobble by shortstop Sammy Meeks.

Fred Baczewski was clubbed for eight hits and five runs in the eight innings he worked. Bill Tremel came on to absorb a four-run hiding in the ninth, topped by Al Kozar's grand slam homer.

In all, Memphis garnered a dozen hits, including five by extra-bases.

The score by innings:

Memphis	020	010	114—9	12	1
Shreveport	000	100	000—1	5	0

Hurd and Griffin; Baczewski, Tremel and Livingston.

Dodgers Not Playing Pirates Again—Just Playing Like 'Em

By Rud Rennie

The Brooklyn Dodgers couldn't keep up the deception yesterday. They had been successful Wednesday in the opening game of the World Series, pretending they were playing the Pittsburgh Pirates, who were easy for them all season. But yesterday, in the second game of the series, they could not concentrate. Instead of pretending they were playing the Pirates, they played as if they were the Pirates. So, they lost, 7 to 1.

Vic Raschi, the Yankee pitcher, had a lot to do with disconcerting the National League champions. He let them have three hits, all in one inning. He struck out nine men. The Dodgers had better luck against Raschi when they did not swing. Five walked.

John Carmichael, a Chicago sage, suggests that the Yankees be made to play in World Series games without any insignia to indicate they are Yankees. He thinks it would be fairer to their opponents if they wore plain uniforms, like pajamas, with nothing indicating the identity of the team.

Third to Win Four

Billy Martin probably will start smoking cigars. He's a big man now that he has made his first World Series homer in his first October classic as a regular. . . . He got two hits yesterday and drove in four runs, the first one broke the 1-to-1 tie. The home run in the sixth let the Yankees go the rest of the way in rocking chairs.

Raschi is the third pitcher still active in baseball who has won four World Series games. The others are Allie Reynolds, a teammate, and Harry Brecheen, of the Cardinals.

Criticizes Durocher

Dressen let one go in the direction of Leo Durocher in California. "You'd think," he said, "Durocher would be a good sport and come to the World Series." That is probably the first time Durocher ever has been called a good sport by a good sport.

"Great to be a winner" a friend said to Fresco Thompson, one of the Dodgers vice-presidents before the game. . . . "Especially over the Yankees," responded Thompson. "There aren't many of them, like baseballs autographed by Babe Ruth."

Stengel decided to go with "the other feller" in leftfield today. In this instance "the other feller" was Gene Woodling.

The Dodgers employed the two-platoon system for "Star-Spangled Banner" singers. Everett McCooey sang it Wednesday. Gladys Gooding sang it yesterday.

The Campanella System

Erskine had a great system in the first inning. He let two men reach first and then let Campanella throw them out trying to steal second. . . . In the second inning, he employed a different system. Again the first two men got on base. They were on first and third with none out. This time, he struck out Joe Collins and Gil McDougald and let Reese throw out Martin.

If the series goes more than five games, tickets for the sixth and seventh games will be put on sale at Ebbets Field at 4 o'clock Saturday. . . . This tends to indicate that the Dodgers thought they would lose it in five games, or win it in five games.

Erskine, or "Oiskin" as he is called in Brooklyn, was lucky to last as long as he did. In every one of the first six innings, the first Yankee to bat, got on base, and five times, the second batter also got on base. After the first three men to bat got on base in the sixth, Erskine was taken out.

Billy Loes, the pitcher who inherited Erskine's load of base runners, had less luck getting away from them than Erskine. . . . Loes pitched better after he was able to take his wind-up. He achieved this comfortable condition by throwing a home-run ball to Billy Martin. Then he fanned Raschi and Bauer.

Dressen revealed a shift in his batting order last night. Carl Furillo will supplant Billy Cox as lead-off man, with Cox batting in the No. 8 spot, formerly held down by Furillo. Neither has a hit so far. Duke Snider will be dropped from No. 3 to No. 6 against the left-handed offerings of Ed Lopat, with the other batters moving up.

Who knows, this may have been the Dodgers last appearance in Ebbets Field this season. The Series moves across the river to Yankee Stadium today.

The telephone company yesterday revealed that it had received 212,895 calls for the score on the first day of the series Wednesday. This was a decline over the calls received the same day a year ago, when 247,129 wanted to know.

Topcoats for 3d Game Hinted by WeatherMan

A thunderstorm, accompanied by high winds, struck the city last night and immediately Dodger and Yankee fans wondered if today's game, scheduled for Yankee Stadium, would be played. "You may be in topcoats, but not in raincoats," said the weather man.

Dodger fans, who thought a day's rest might be advantageous, heard that today will be mostly fair and much cooler, with temperature in the 60s. Fresh winds are also predicted. Always willing to prognosticate nature's offerings, the weather man was non-committal on his forecast of today's winner, or which team he rooted for.

Odds on Yankees Soar To 2 to 1 to Win Series

Odds on the New York Yankees to win their fourth straight World Series shifted to 2 to 1 yesterday following a 7-to-1 defeat of the Brooklyn Dodgers in the second game of the post-season baseball classic.

The Yankees also were quoted at 8½ to 5 to win today's game—the first of three to be played at the Yankee Stadium.

Ted Kell

Mickey Mantle slides into second base on his double off the scoreboard in right field in fourth inning. Duke Snider's relay to Pee Wee Reese was not in time. Umpire McKinley calls the play. Mantle moved to third on a fielder's choice and scored on Yogi Berra's long fly

Box Score of 2d Game

* * *

NEW YORK (A)

	ab	r	h	po	a
Bauer rf	4	0	1	3	0
Rizzuto ss	4	0	0	2	2
Mantle cf	5	2	3	2	0
Woodling lf	4	1	1	2	0
Berra c	3	0	2	10	2
Collins 1b	3	1	0	8	1
McDougald 3b	3	2	1	0	1
Martin 2b	4	1	2	0	1
Raschi p	3	0	0	0	0
Totals	33	7	10	27	7

BROOKLYN (N)

	ab	r	h	po	a
Cox, 3b	4	0	0	1	0
Reese, ss	3	1	1	2	5
Snider cf	4	0	1	1	0
Robinson 2b	3	0	0	3	3
Campanella c	4	0	1	7	3
Pafko lf	4	0	0	2	0
Hodges 1b	3	0	0	9	0
Furillo rf	3	0	0	2	0
Erksine p	2	0	0	0	1
Loes p	0	0	0	0	0
*Nelson	0	0	0	0	0
Lehman p	0	0	0	0	1
Totals	30	1	3	27	13

*Walked for Loes in seventh inning.

NEW YORK (A)	000	115	000—7
BROOKLYN (N)	001	000	000—1

E—Hodges. RBI—Campanella, Berra, Martin, 4; McDougald. 2B—Mantle. HR—Martin. SB—McDougald. DP—Reese, Robinson and Hodges. Left—New York, 5; Brooklyn, 7. BB—Erskine 6 (Rizzuto, Woodling, Raschi, McDougald, Bauer, Berra); Raschi 5, (Robinson, Hodges, Furillo, Nelson, Reese); Lehman 1 (Collins). SO—Erskine 4 (Mantle, Collins, McDougald, Raschi); Raschi 9 (Snider 3, Cox, Pafko, Hodges, Reese, Furillo 2); Loes 2 (Raschi, Bauer). HO—Erskine 6 in 5 innings (none out in sixth); Loes 2 in 2; Lehman 2 in 2. R & ER—Erskine 4-4; Loes, 3-2; Lehman, 0-0; Raschi, 1-1. WP—Erskine. Winner—Raschi. Loser—Erskine. U—Passarella (A) plate, Goetz (N) 1B, McKinley (A) 2B, Pinnell (N) 3B, Honochick (A) lf, Boggess (N) rf. T—2:47. A—33,792.

Rochester Wins 5th Game, 10-5, In Little Series

But Kansas City, Yankees' Farm Club, Holds 3-to-2 Edge Over Eastern Team

ROCHESTER, N. Y., Oct. 2 (AP).—Four innings of no-hit, no-run relief pitching by righthander Jack Crimian tonight carried the Rochester Red Wings to a 10 to 5 victory over the sloppy fielding Kansas City Blues in the fifth game of their Little World Series. Kansas City still leads in games, 3 to 2.

The Yankee farm team committed five errors, but managed to score five times on a mere three-hit total, thanks to three miscues and home-run shots by Bill Skowran and starting pitcher Jim Russell.

Trailing, 3 to 0, the Blues took a 5-to-3 lead in the fifth on Russell's homer and a pair of unearned runs. Kansas City reliefer Rex Jones and his mates fell apart in the fifth, as Rochester scored three unearned runs and went on to take the decision before 6,602 chilled fans. The winners committed three errors.

The score:

KANSAS CITY (A. A.)

	ab	r	h	po	a
Wahl ss	5	1	0	1	3
Bollweg 1b	4	1	0	2	1
Cerv rf	2	1	0	1	0
Skowron lf	3	1	1	5	0
Renna cf	3	0	0	2	0
Power 3b	4	0	0	1	0
Segrist 2b	4	0	1	2	1
Owen c	4	0	0	9	1
Russell p	2	1	1	0	0
Jones p	1	0	0	0	0
Gray p	0	0	0	1	1
†Marquis	1	0	0	0	0
Totals	33	5	3	24	7

ROCHESTER (I. L.)

	ab	r	h	po	a
Walker lf	5	1	2	1	0
Richmond 3b.	4	2	1	2	1
Bucha c	4	1	2	7	0
Bilko 1b	0	1	0	4	1
Jablonski ss.	4	1	2	0	4
Repulski cf	4	0	1	5	0
Ciaffone rf	5	0	0	4	0
Ortiz 2b	4	2	1	3	0
Faszholz p	1	0	0	0	0
Hahn p	0	0	0	0	0
*Kahn	1	0	0	0	0
Crimian p	2	2	0	1	0
Totals	34	10	9	27	6

*Bounced out for Hahn in fifth.
†Filed out for Gray in ninth.

Kansas City	000	230	000—5
Rochester	021	023	20x—10

E—Russell, Jablonski 2, Richmond, Cerv, Wahl, Segrist, Power. RBI—Ciaffone, Bucha, Skowron 2, Russell, Renna, Jablonski 3, Walker, Richmond. 2B—Richmond, Bucha. HR—Skowron, Russell. Left—Kansas City 6, Rochester 11. BB—Faszholz 5, Russell 4, Jones 3, Gray 3. SO—Faszholz 3, Russell 6, Crimian 4, Jones 1, Gray 2. HO—Faszholz 3 in 4⅔; Hahn 0 in ⅓; Russell 5 in 4⅔; Jones 3 in 1; Crimian 0 in 4; Gray 1 in 2⅓. HBP—Gray (Repulski). PB—Bucha, Owen. Winner—Crimian. Loser—Jones. U—Mullen, Tatler, O'Connor, Linsalata. T—2:36. A—6,602.

Section 3 | SPORTS NEWS MAIL ORDER

New York Herald Tribune

SPORTS NEWS STAMPS | Section 3

EIGHT PAGES | SUNDAY, OCTOBER 5, 1952 | EIGHT PAGES

Reynolds Blanks Dodgers, 2-0, as Yankees Square Series at 2-All; Navy Beats Cornell; Columbia, Penn, Holy Cross, Princeton Win

Ted Keil

Pee Wee Reese (1), of Dodgers, races for second as Yankees' second baseman, Billy Martin, sprawls on ground after making a bad back-handed flip to shortstop Phil Rizzuto on Duke Snider's grounder in first inning Rizzuto watches ball (left) bound into left field, Reese making third on the play

Midshipmen Romp, 31 to 7, Over Big Red

Gurski, Adorney Each Score Twice

9 Fumbles by Ithacans Make Scoring Easy for Squad From Annapolis

By Jesse Abramson

ITHACA, N. Y., Oct. 4.—Navy's resurgent forces, accepting Cornell's lavish gifts, romped to an easy 31-to-7 victory before 25,000 in Schoellkopf Crescent today in a football game that may easily be the sloppiest of the season.

The jittery Cornellians, who had handed their opener to Colgate last week, dealt the Midshipmen 17 points on two touchdowns and a field goal in the first twelve minutes before Navy earned a first down.

A seventy-one-yard march that was topped off by a fifty-yard pass play from Jack Jaeckel to end Dick Cliggott scored for Cornell early in the second period and hopes flared briefly that the home team might recoup from its early malfeasances and make it a contest.

Capitalizes on Errors

But Navy earned a touchdown by honest sweat and toil later in the same quarter, carried a 24-to-7 margin into the second half and capitalized on another enemy error in the third period.

All but one Navy score accrued from Cornell's bounty. The men of Annapolis scored one touchdown on a blocked punt in the end zone, picked up a field goal after a mental lapse, and scored two more touchdowns on first-down plays following Cornell fumbles. John Gurski, Navy's end and captain, and Frank Adorney, right half, each scored twice, and Ned Snyder contributed seven points, six by kicks and one by running for the extra point when the center pass was bobbled.

Eddie Erdelatz's Crabtown platoons, achieving their second success in two starts and setting full sail for Navy's first winning season in seven years, matched their 31 points of the Yale opener. They gave up their first points of the season when Cliggott got behind all Navy hands for his touchdown.

Franco Races 47 Yards

There was no way of telling whether Navy is as good as its 31-point production in two games suggests. The Midshipmen cashed in on Cornell errors too easily to reveal what they can do on their own. The Sailors made only one march, and that was really only one big run by Fred Franco, who broke off tackle for forty-seven yards to the 12.

Despite the thumping margin, Navy's offense was ragged, Cornell's fumbling must have been contagious. Cornell fumbled nine times and lost the ball six times, but Navy, with five fumbles, was almost as bad, though it never paid for its mistakes.

It was Navy's agile, combative defense which was the star of the day. Led by Steve Eisenhauer, who is naturally called Ike, a guard who plays in and out of the defensive line, and Jack Perkins, a tackle, and an assortment of ends, including Gurski and Herb Tiede, who play both ways. The Midshipmen strangled Cornell's attempts to mount any sort of sustained attacks.

Against the Big Red's ground attack, Navy was invulnerable. The Midshipmen wouldn't let Bob En-

(Continued on page 5, column 4)

U. S. C. Trounces Army, 22-0, With Ground Attack

* * *

LOS ANGELES, Oct. 4 (AP).—A spirited but outmanned Army team held Southern California to a two-point halftime margin today but surrendered a crushing ground attack and miscues in the final stages to give the Trojans a 22-to-0 victory.

A blocked kick that bounded out of the end zone gave U. S. C. an automatic safety, and an Army fumble on its own 7 donated the Trojans a touchdown—more than enough for the one mighty warhorse to subdue the stubborn mule from West Point.

Marching to their third straight victory of the new season and No. 2 in a row over Army, the heavily gunned Trojans managed to travel forty-five yards in eleven plays for their second touchdown. The final score came through the air. The last two tallies came in the fourth quarter.

Scoring hero was tailback Jimmy Sears. He passed for two touchdowns—a ten-yard throw to left end Ron Miller, a seven-yard-

(Continued on page 4, column 6)

Penn Defeats Dartmouth On 56-Yard Air Play, 7-0

Hynoski Passes to Deuber in the Third Quarter; 35,000 Watch Big Green Linemen Star

By Irving T. Marsh

PHILADELPHIA, Oct. 4.—After frittering away four chances in the first half, Pennsylvania's football team connected with one scintillating pass-and-run touchdown play in the twelfth minute of the third quarter and then clung to that slim lead to beat amazing Dartmouth, 7 to 0, before 35,000 at Franklin Field this beautiful football afternoon.

The scoring, and winning, play, which covered fifty-six yards in the air and on the ground, was perpetrated by the young and old of the Penn backfield, Walt Hynoski, sophomore tailback, and Bill Deuber, the senior wingback. It came with electrifying suddenness, for Penn had been no ball of fire in the air—up to then—and had been well contained on the ground by a sturdy Dartmouth line that played its heart out all afternoon.

It came with the ball on Penn's 44-yard line on third down, two plays after Penn had been knocked back eight yards on another attempted pass play. From the 44, Penn went into left formation. Hynoski took the ball directly from center and there was no hipper-dipper about the ball handling. He tossed the ball in a high loop to Deuber on the Dartmouth 40. Deuber took it in easily and behind a perfect block by John Moses, the end, he sped over without being touched. Carl Sempier kicked the extra point and there was the ball game.

But for a long time before that, and for the rest of the game after that, mighty Pennsylvania, heralded as the East's top team, a team that had tied Notre Dame one week ago after completely outplaying the Irish, was held totally in check by that doughty Dartmouth defensive line. Linemen are usually lost in the shuffle of ball carrying. But today those Dartmouth defenders — Clark Murphy, George Rambour, Joe Mesics, Pepe Reich, Emery Pier-

(Continued on page 5, column 5)

Columbia Wins Over Harvard's Eleven, 16 to 7

Lions Outplay the Crimson, Outcome Never in Doubt After the Second Period

By Al Laney

CAMBRIDGE, Mass., Oct. 4.—Columbia's slightly undermanned but efficient and quite rapid football team achieved its first victory of the 1952 season today by defeating Harvard, 16 to 7, in the Stadium here with a rather sparse crowd of 14,000 looking on. Since the Lions were rated a 7½ point favorite over the Crimson, this was a little better than the figures but it was not really a close contest, although there was some excitement in the final period when Harvard, making a brave effort with inadequate forces, threatened twice after scoring a touchdown in the third quarter.

After a scoreless first period, Columbia got nine points in 24 seconds of the second on a safety off a blocked punt and a touch-

(Continued on page 4, column 2)

Yale Crushes Brown Eleven On Passes, 28-0

Molloy, Woodsum Star for Eli; Parsells Place-Kicks All Four Extra Points

By Harold Rosenthal

NEW HAVEN, Conn., Oct. 4.—Yale bounced back from its four-touchdown defeat at the hands of Navy last week, with a 28-to-0 victory over Brown today, before 22,500 in Yale Bowl. The Bruins, making their '52 debut, timed it trifle unfortunately. They ran smack into the best day Yale's pitch-and-catch combination of Ed Molloy and Ed Woodsum have ever enjoyed and the two Eds simply passed them dizzy, with Molloy running the show out of the T formation and hitting Woodsum as though he was swinging at a barn with a bull fiddle.

They scored via the air in every period but the opener. Woodsum then capped matters in the fourth by recovering a punt, fumbled by

(Continued on page 4, column 7)

College and School Results

* * *

College

Football

East

28—Albright	Lafayette— 6
28—Amherst	Union—21
19—Bates	Middlebury—14
28—Brandeis	Northeastern—13
28—California St (Pa)	Indiana St (Pa)—19
16—Columbia	Harvard— 7
26—Connecticut	Massachusetts—13
7—Delaware	Lehigh— 6
28—Denison	Mt. Union—14
18—Dickinson	Allegheny— 0
14—E. Stroudsburg Tchrs.	Kings Coll.— 6
26—Fairmont State	Glenville— 6
19—Franklin & Marshall	Johns Hopkins—13
6—Geneva	Grove City— 0
20—Gettysburg	West. Maryland— 6
52—Hamilton	Brooklyn College— 0
12—Holy Cross	Fordham— 7
7—Kutztown	Cheyney— 0
16—Lincoln (Pa.)	Upsala—13
20—Montclair St. Tch.	Nat. Agricul. Col.— 0
28—Morgan State	Delaware State— 7
7—Morris Harvey	Davis & Elkins— 6

College

Football

East

31—Navy	Cornell— 7
20—N. Y. U.	King's Point—20
13—New Haven Teachers	Champlain— 6
7—Pennsylvania	Dartmouth— 0
12—Penn Military	Drexel— 7
35—Penn State	William & Mary—23
61—Princeton	Rutgers—19
21—Rhode Island	New Hampshire— 7
12—Rochester	Williams— 7
33—Scranton	Adelphi— 6
20—Slippery Rock Tch.	Edinboro Tch.—13
22—Southern Calif.	Army— 0
34—Springfield	Norwich— 7
16—Susquehanna	Ursinus— 0
0—Trenton Teach.	New Britain Teach.— 6
34—Trinity	Hobart— 0
15—Tufts	Worcester Tech—13
14—Vermont	Maine— 6
18—Wagner	Haverford—13
27—Wesleyan	Bowdoin— 7
28—Westminister	Thiel—13

(Continued on page 4, column 4)

Princeton Jolts Rutgers, 61-19, For 24th in Row

Unger, Tryon and Frye Pace Tigers' Attack; Johnson Dreier Excel for Scarlet

By Ed Sinclair

PRINCETON, N. J., Oct. 4.—The undefeated Princeton football team prepped itself for next week's big test with Penn today by running roughshod over an outclassed Rutgers eleven for a 61-to-19 victory, No. 24 in the Tigers's string, before 25,000 at Palmer Stadium.

Starting at 4 minutes and 28 seconds of the first period, Charley Caldwell's masterful unit made a shambles of the forty-fourth renewal of the country's oldest series in which the Orange and Black has conquered the Scarlet forty times.

The Tigers crossed the goal line three times in that first explosive quarter and proceeded to add three more touchdowns in the second period for a 41-to-6 halftime lead. A pair of scores in the third quarter, and another in the final when the reserves were operating, completed the rout.

Rutgers Scores 3 Times

Nevertheless, the boys from New Brunswick gave it a real try. Sustaining drives of forty-two, eighty and eighty-eight yards, Rutgers pierced the Tiger end zone in each of the last three periods.

A glance at the statistics reveals the lopsidedness of the skirmish. Princeton rushed for 395 yards to the Scarlet5s 151, while displaying any number of backfield agents who can do anything Caldwell wants done.

Chief among the Princeton agents were Bob Unger, Bill Tryon and Dick Frye, who had a part in all the Orange and Black scoring. Dick Yaffa and Homer Smith were able conspirators in the offense while Ned Jannotta, Morgan Taylor and Capt. Frank McPhee spearheaded the defense.

Unger, the left halfback, passed eight yards to McPhee for the first touchdown and scored the next two (one on a thirty-eight-yard end run) himself. Tryon passed to Byron Shaffer, Yaffa and Leonard Lyons for the next three.

Frye carried two yards for Princeton's seventh score early in

(Continued on page 5, column 2)

Penn State's Late Surge Beats W. & M., 35 to 23

STATE COLLEGE Pa., Oct. 4 (AP).—Penn State roared back from behind three times and wore down a dangerous William and Mary eleven to score an impressive 35-to-23 triumph before 25,00 here today. Tony Rados passed for one touchdown and directed the Nittany Lions' Winged T faultlessly to lead State to victory.

Giants Win Over Eagles, 31 to 7, In Night Game at Philadelphia

New York Scores in First Quarter, Adds Two in Second and Tallies Another in Third Session

By Bill Lauder Jr.

PHILADELPHIA, Oct. 4.—Two unbeaten squads, each with eyes on the American Conference title in the National Football League—the New York Giants and the Philadelphia Eagles—met tonight at Shibe Park in the second game of the season for each with about 25,000 fans in attendance.

The Giants won, 31 to 7.

The Giants, with five rookies on their offensive starting eleven, showed an explosive offensive thrust in their opening game victory over Dallas last Sunday, 24 to 6, and the Eagles also sparkled offensively as they edged the Steelers in a free-scoring game, 31 to 25.

Steve Owen again went with the same backfield, quarterbacked by Charlie Conerly, with Frank Gifford, the rookie ace, at left half and veteran Joe Scott at right. Eddie Price, as usual, was the fullback.

Coulter Replaces Knight

In the absence of Pat Knight, the linebacker who suffered a broken bone just below the elbow in the Dallas game, Owen decided to use the versatile Tex Coulter defensively—with no guarantee, of course, that the big fellow wouldn't get in on offense as well at either center or tackle if needed.

The Giants broke the ice after the Eagles were unable to move following the opening kick-off. Starting from their 37 they picked up one first down and then Tom Landry punted. Bob Walston took a couple of steps with the punt and then fumbled and George Kennard recovered for the Giants on the Eagle 17. On the next play Frank Gifford took a pitchout, ran to his left and passed to Bob McChesney in the end zone. Ray Poole kicked the point.

The Eagles tied it up, following

(Continued on page 2, column 6)

Gavilan-Graham Bout Put Off Till Tonight

HAVANA, Oct. 4 (AP).—The welterweight championship fight between Kid Gavilan and Billy Graham, scheduled for tonight, was postponed because of a tropical rainstorm. It will be held tomorrow night, weather permitting.

The rain began in the afternoon and was still falling three hours before the 10 p. m. (E.S.T.) starting time. At first the officials decided to wait a while to see if it still was raining when the battle was due to start.

But they decided that even if it stopped the outdoor arena in Grand Stadium would be too wet.

The fight will be held at the same time tomorrow.

Crusaders Beat Fordham, 12-7, On Maloy's Second-Period Pass

By Leonard Koppett

WORCESTER, Mass., Oct. 4.—Holy Cross was leading Fordham, 12 to 7, with about a minute and fifteen seconds to play at Fitton Field this afternoon and Holy Cross had the ball on its own 11-yard line, second down with thirty-six yards to go.

So Chuck Maloy, the Holy Cross quarterback, threw a pass—and got away with it. It was caught by John Carroll for a fourteen-yard gain, a roughing penalty was tacked on, and when the Crusaders finally punted from their own 42 they were out of danger, and made their second victory of the season absolutely official by intercepting Fordham's last pass at mid-field.

Maloy's choice of play was a much better indication of the sort of game this was than the low total of points scored, which reflects neither the philosophies of the two attacks nor the wide-open action seen by 21,895 spectators comprising the first sell-out crowd here since the 1947 opener with Dartmouth.

All the scoring was done in the first half, with a fifty-two-yard punt return by Chick Murphy giving Holy Cross the lead, a sustained drive in the closing minutes of the first period moving Fordham ahead, 7 to 6, and a burst of three short Maloy-to-Carroll passes producing the winning score sixty-seven seconds before the half ended.

But the scoring was only a small part of the excitement produced by Maloy and his opposite number, Fordham's Roger Franz, who called for eighty-one pass plays

(Continued on page 5, column 1)

Gold Cup Race At Belmont Won By One Count

Earns $52,100 in Beating Mark-Ye-Well by Two Lengths as Meet Ends

By Joe H. Palmer

If he never does it again, Dave Gorman outrode Eddie Arcaro at Belmont yesterday afternoon, and for a net purse of $52,100. He had a good deal of horse in Walter Jeffords' One Count, the winner of last spring's Belmont Stakes, but the deciding factor was that, without any violation of the rules, he made Arcaro check on Calumet's Mark-Ye-Well at the half-mile pole, while he went on with One Count.

The Count Fleet colt won the two-mile Jockey Club Gold Cup by two lengths from Mark-Ye-Well, and it was fifteen lengths farther back to Charfran Stable's Crafty Admiral. The only other starter was Gustave Ring's Lone Eagle, which took the lead with a mile and a quarter to go and then dropped steadily back in the last half-mile, against Con Errico's wishes in both cases.

The winner, running the two miles in 3:24 1-5, paid $9.60. A plurality of the 35,089 went wrong

(Continued on page 6, column 4)

Mize Clouts Homer in 4th; Mantle Triples in the 8th, Scores on a Wild Throw

Reynolds Fans 10, Robinson 3 Times

71,787 See Pitcher Hold Foe to 4 Hits in Duel With Black, Rutherford

By Rud Rennie

The hopeful Dodgers, seeking their first world championship and the pretty rings that go with victory as souvenirs, were detoured yesterday by Allie Reynolds, the Yankees' pitcher, and by the aging Johnny Mize, and the youthful Mickey Mantle in the fourth game of the World Series played in Yankee Stadium.

Reynolds pitched a shutout, his second in World Series competition with the Dodgers, and limited them to four separated hits, two by PeeWee Reese and one each by Andy Pafko and Carl Furillo. He struck out ten men, getting Jackie Robinson three times on called strikes and fanning Roy Campanella twice. He walked only two men. He finished strong, facing thirteen men, one over par, in the last four innings.

Mize, starting at first base in place of Joe Collins, broke the scorelessness of the contest with a home run off Joe Black in the fourth inning, and then later hit a double to no purpose.

Mantle made the second run in the eighth, socking Johnny Rutherford for a long triple and scoring when Reese relayed the throw-in over the third baseman's head into the stands behind the Brooklyn dugout.

Series Square at 2-All

So the Yankees won, 2 to 0, and drew even with the Dodgers. Each team has now won two games.

A crowd of 71,787 persons attended the game and thrilled to the job done by Reynolds after he had been defeated in the opening game by the same pitcher who opposed him as a starter yesterday.

Black, the rookie, could not do it twice. It was harder the second time to ignore the Yankees and make believe the uniforms were not champions.

Reynolds' curve did not hang yesterday. He was fast and sure and he took command. It was his fifth World Series victory and his third over the Dodgers. He had shut them out in 1949. Black did not finish. He had to be taken out for a pinch hitter in the eighth.

Even so, the Yankees made only three hits off Black. They got one off Rutherford. And that was all. There were only eight hits in the game; all the Brooklyn hits were singles and all the Yankee hits were for extra bases, two doubles, a triple and a home run.

Reynolds was in trouble only twice, in the first and in the fifth. He fanned his way out of the first inning jam, and Black, missing a bunt in an attempted squeeze play, helped to let him safely out of the fifth.

Today, in the fifth game, Casey Stengel will gamble with Ewell Blackwell, a faded National League star from Cincinnati, acquired on waivers toward the end of the season. Carl Erskine, loser in the second game of the series, will try his luck for the Dodgers.

Starts Without Delay

It was a mild, sunny day and the sun cast the shadow of the rightfield stands and the top-side

(Continued on page 2, column 4)

Box Score of 4th Game

* * *

BROOKLYN (N)

	ab	r	h	po	a
Cox 3b	3	0	0	2	2
†Nelson	1	0	0	0	0
Morgan 3b	0	0	0	0	1
Reese ss	4	0	2	0	3
Snider cf	4	0	0	5	0
Robinson 2b	4	0	0	0	2
Campanella c	3	0	0	4	0
Pafko lf	3	0	1	2	0
Hodges 1b	2	0	0	10	0
Furillo rf	2	0	1	1	0
Black p	1	0	0	0	2
*Shuba	1	0	0	0	0
Rutherford p	0	0	0	0	0
Totals	28	0	4	24	10

NEW YORK (A)

	ab	r	h	po	a
McDougald 3b	3	0	0	0	1
Rizzuto ss	2	0	0	1	3
Mantle cf	3	1	1	4	0
Mize 1b	3	1	2	4	2
‡Collins 1b	0	0	0	1	0
Berra c	4	0	0	12	1
Woodling lf	3	0	1	1	0
Bauer rf	4	0	0	1	0
Martin 2b	3	0	0	2	1
Reynolds p	3	0	0	1	0
Totals	28	2	4	27	8

*Flied out for Black in eighth.
†Struck out for Cox in eighth.
‡Ran for Mize in eighth.

BROOKLYN (N)	0 0 0	0 0 0	0 0 0	—0
NEW YORK (A)	0 0 0	1 0 0	0 1 x	—2

E—Martin, Reese. RBI—Mize. 2B—Woodling, Mize. 3B—Mantle. HR—Mize. S—Furillo. DP—Rizzuto, Martin and Mize. Left—Brooklyn, 5; New York, 8. BB—Black 5 (Mantle, Rizzuto 2, McDougald, Woodling); Rutherford (Mize); Reynolds 3 (Hodges, Black, Campanella). SO—Reynolds 10 (Cox, Robinson 3, Campanella 2, Pafko 2, Black, Nelson); Black (2) (Berra, Reynolds); Rutherford 1 (Bauer). HO—Black 3 in 7 innings; Rutherford 1 in 1. R & ER—Black, 1-1; Rutherford, 1-1; Reynolds, 0-0. Winner—Reynolds. Loser—Black. U—Bill McKinley (A) plate, Babe Pinelli (N) 1b, Art Passarella (A) 2b, Larry Goetz (N) 3b, Jim Honochick (A) lf, Dusty Boggess (N) rf T—2:33. A—71,587 (paid).

Section 3 — SPORTS — BRIDGE—WEATHER
NEW YORK Herald Tribune
SPORTS — MARINE—MAIL ORDER — Section 3
EIGHT PAGES — SUNDAY, SEPTEMBER 7, 1952 — EIGHT PAGES

Giants Top Dodgers, 6-4, 7-3, Trail by 4; Yanks Win, Lead by 2½; Mulloy and Sedgman Gain Title Round in National Tennis

U. S. Star, 38, Eliminates Richardson

Champion Winner Over Rose in 3 Sets

Miss Connelly Defeats Miss Fry, Will Oppose Miss Hart for Crown

By Al Laney

Gardnar Mulloy, the aging veteran whose play has given the National Tennis championships a little something to counteract the devastation caused by the Australians, continued his progress at Forest Hills yesterday by defeating Hamilton Richardson, 10—8, 6—0, 8—6, and became a finalist for the first time in eighteen years of trying.

Along with the match, Mulloy won the doubtful privilege of playing Frank Sedgman, the champion, in today's final. Sedgman dealt wtih his younger Australian teammate Mervyn Rose, about as was to be expected, winning his semi-final, 6—3, 6—3, 6—4, and so entered his second final without having lost a set or having been pressed by any player.

Mulloy's splendid victory, his second such in as many days, delighted a capacity crowd of 13,000 or so but it was Maureen Connolly, the little girl who won the title so sensationally last year, who furnished the thrills. Miss Connolly did so by getting into extreme difficulties in her match with Shirley Fry and coming in sight of what would have been a humiliating defeat before pulling out the match, 4—6, 6—4, 6—1.

Today she will play Doris Hart, the same girl she defeated in last year's final to become champion before she was seventeen. Likewise a year ago she was pressed by Miss Fry in her only really difficult match, so that the pattern is the same and no doubt will continue the same in today's final match. Miss Hart defeated Louise Brough, 9—7, 8—6, in the other semi-final.

Looks Defeat in Face

It is rare that a woman's match can take precedence over the men but in this case it must be discussed first because a champion coming near enough to defeat to look it squarely in the face and then beating it back, is a dramatic thing. Especially when the champion is Miss Connolly, who has caught the imagination of the people as few of her predecessors did and no doubt drew a large part of the big crowd entirely on her own.

But that is the way of champions when they are authentic ones and Miss Connolly is. Few champions have been in tighter corners than she found herself and come out of them. The score of the final set is most deceiving. It was in the second set that Miss Connolly seemed to be and was in extremis.

The crisis was a long one, too, continuing through six games in every one of which it seemed she would go down.

This match was a repetition of the semi-final played by the same two girls last year. Miss Fry, who is a good player and apparently a shrewd one, pursued the same plan again and this time came measurably closer to success. But last year Miss Connolly was just a promising little girl player who might one day become champion. Now she was the champion and, so soon after her dramatic triumph, she was being beaten.

Miss Fry began the match by steering the ball slowly, quietly and cunningly from the base line, waiting for the extravagant or short drive. She offered no pace, nor even crispness. The exchanges

(Continued on page 6, column 3)

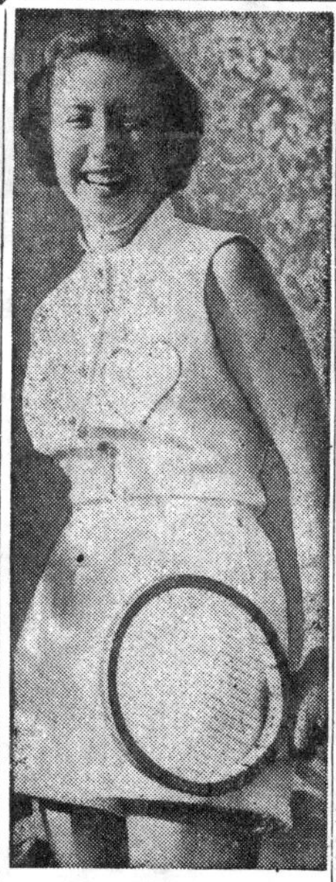

Herald Tribune—United Press
Maureen Connolly

Ferrier Leads By 9 Strokes In Empire Golf

Posts 8-Sub-Par 62 for a 192 Total at End of 54; Snead and Haas Next

ALBANY, N. Y., Sept. 6 (AP).—Big Jim Ferrier fired a record-breaking eight-under-par 62 today to take a nine-stroke lead at the three-quarter mark of the $15,000 Empire State Open golf tournament. The San Francisco pro's scorching round gave him a fifty-four-hole total of 192—eighteen under par.

Deadlocked at second with 201 were Sam Snead, of White Sulphur Springs, W. Va., and Freddie Haas, of New Orleans. Snead shot a 68 and Haas a 67.

Marty Furgol, of Lemont, Ill., was next with 202 after a 65 today.

Bracketed behind him at 204 were Ed Oliver, of Lemont, Mike Homa, of Rye, Armand Farina, of Schenectady, and Mike Turnesa, of White Plains.

Oliver had a 66, Homa a 68, and Farina and Turnesa each had a 71.

Ferrier's blistering round today broke the record 63 he shot Thursday over the 6,178-yard Normanside Country Club course. He needs a 67 in tomorrow's final eighteen holes to tie the P. G. A. all-time tournament record of 259 for seventy-two holes, held by Byron Nelson and Ben Hogan.

Ferrier was out in 33 today, two under par. On the last nine the former Australian birdied the eleventh, twelfth, thirteenth and fourteenth holes. After parring the fifteenth, he knocked a No. 2 iron on the green of the forty-seven

(Continued on page 5, column 1)

Gagliardi Defeats Maber For Winged Foot Crown

Special to the Herald Tribune

MAMARONECK, N. Y., Sept. 6.—Joseph Gagliardi won the club championship at the Winged Foot Golf Club today by beating James D. Maber jr., 6 and 5.

Gagliardi led, 2 up, after the morning round and posted a 75 for the first eighteen holes to Maber's 77. In the afternoon, he moved to a 4-up lead with a 36 on the first nine holes.

Ancestor 1st In Discovery At Aqueduct

Astarita Stake Won By Grecian Queen

Favored Armageddon 9th in $25,000 Handicap; Flaunt Finishes 2d

By Joe H. Palmer

Ancestor, which had two of them and nothing else to recommend him until yesterday afternoon, outran the field for the Discovery Handicap and a net $19,550, and Grecian Queen turned back a field of two-year-old fillies in the Astarita Stakes as 32,764 citizens enjoyed the temperate sunlight and mixed fortunes at Aqueduct.

Ancestor was the major half of the Ogden Phipps entry, and he was ridden by Ted Atkinson, a fair hand at stealing a race if his horse is any sort of accomplice. The two of them opened by four or five lengths in the early stages and then coasted, and when it was time to go get him, he went away. He won by two and a half lengths from Arnold Skjeveland's Flaunt, which was fairly well up all the way, and it was a neck back to Saxon Stable's Marcador, the Golden Gate Derby winner. The time for a mile and a furlong was a good 1:50 4/5.

Grecian Queen, owned by Mrs. Ben F. Whitaker, had a harder time of it. She won under Eric Guerin's furious drive by a half length from Allen Smith's Piedmont Lass, with the favorite, Ogden Phipps' Flirtatious, another half length away third. The six furlongs went in 1:13 3/5 and the horsemen's bookkeeper transferred $8,925 to the Whitaker account.

Ancestor Pays $22

Both races were upsets, with Grecian Queen paying $20.30 and Ancestor worth $22 to his backers, who were few but vocal. In addition to the purse Phipps got a trophy from Alfred Vanderbilt, for whose great handicapper the race was named.

Ancestor is excellently bred, but until yesterday he had shown no signs of being influenced by it. His sire is the fine handicapper, Challedon, and his dam is the Blue Larkspur mare, Bloodroot, which the stable always insisted, without anybody listening, was better than her contemporary, Black Helen. The mare had previously produced stakes winners in Be Faithful, Bimlette, and Bric a Bac, the latter generally unsuccessful in getting the name right.

To this high pedigree Ancestor had added little until the Discovery. He raced three times last year and literally got nothing. This season the colt had been out twenty-three times and had won four overnight races, had ten other placings. The Discovery more than doubled his earnings, which were previously $18,050. Nick Wall had been riding him, but when Great Captain was entered with him, Wall was transferred, because he could make the 104 pounds required, while Atkinson had all he could do to make Ancestor's 107. "He sort of outran himself," Atkinson said afterwards.

The Discovery favorite was Armageddon, which ran fourth much of the way and then faltered back to ninth under his 121 pounds. He doesn't like Aqueduct's sharp turns anyway, preferring the wide sweeps at Belmont, where he has won all three of his stakes victories. Ancestor, on the other hand, was in his own yard, being trained at Aqueduct by the veteran Jim Fitzsimmons, who has been at Aqueduct as long as there has

(Continued on page 4, column 1)

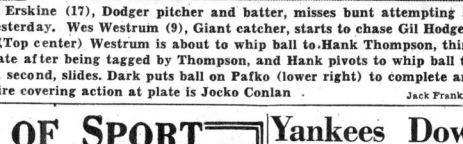

SQUEEZE GOES AWRY: In photo sequence (top left), Carl Erskine (17), Dodger pitcher and batter, misses bunt attempting a squeeze in second inning of first game at Polo Grounds yesterday. Wes Westrum (9), Giant catcher, starts to chase Gil Hodges (14) who, with bases loaded, had come down from third. (Top center) Westrum is about to whip ball to Hank Thompson, third baseman, trapping Hodges. (Top right) Hodges crosses plate after being tagged by Thompson, and Hank pivots to whip ball to Alvin Dark (lower left) as Andy Pafko, coming down from second, slides. Dark puts ball on Pafko (lower right) to complete an unusual double play. The umpire covering action at plate is Jocko Conlan. Jack Frank

49,011 Watch Hearn Pitch 4-Hitter in 2d

His Homer in 4th Is Only Homer of Day

Errors Beat Brooklyn in Opener; Corwin Stops Threats in 8th and 9th

By Harold Rosenthal

The Giants beat the Dodgers in both ends of a lengthy double-header at the Polo Grounds yesterday and contrary to a lot of expectations the earth did not stop turning. It did execute a few flip-flops for the Dodgers, however, and their adherents among the 49,011 spectators who sat through a seven-hour program to watch the league leaders absorb 6-to-4 and 7-to-3 setbacks.

These sliced the Dodgers' once-proud lead to four games, revivified the Giants to the point where they eagerly await today's single game and tomorrow's day-night double-header which will conclude the interborough rivalry for 1952. It is a lead shrunken by almost two-thirds from the ten-and-one-half-game margin enjoyed by Brooklyn as late as Aug. 27.

Playing Time Sets Record

The Dodgers aren't enjoying anything these days. In the first game, a monstrosity that set a record for a regulation nine-inning game of 3 hours and 38 minutes, they committed a season's high of four errors. They blundered this one away and it was destined to stay blundered away.

In the ninth inning of the opener they got back two runs on a pinch walk, a questionable single by Carl Furillo through first base, and a scoring double by Peewee Reese. That put runners on second and third, with the best part of the Dodgers' batting order due to face Al Corwin, the last of three tired Giant pitchers.

Jackie Robinson, who had enjoyed a perfect day with a couple of walks and a couple of singles, hit one hard, and it was lined right into the glove of the slightly startled Hank Thompson who merely had to step on third base to execute the vital double play. After that Roy Campanella ended the marathon by fanning.

There weren't any of these last-ditch dramatics in the second game. The Giants licked them joyfully, getting as many runs in the first frame off Johnny Rutherford as the Dodgers got during the entire game. They pelted the dapper right-hander for eleven hits, including a solo homer by Jim Hearn, who went the route and came up with his first victory and first complete game in more than a month. Hearn's wallop was no cheapie but a solid drive deep into the lower rightfield stands. It was the only round-tripper hit during the long afternoon and supperless fore-evening.

They turned on the lights at the start of the second game but the Dodgers staggered around in darkness from shortly afternoon until Hearn completed his four-hitter. He didn't permit a man to reach base in the last four innings and he was an entirely different fellow from the one who had failed to come up with victory No. 13 in eight previous starts.

Black Merely Warms Up

Hearn was the only solid pitcher in the ball park yesterday, with the possible exception of the Dodgers' ace reliever, Joe Black, who was saved for another day. Black warmed up in the late stages of the opener but his strength was conserved wisely for future action during the second game. This one was gone beyond redemption before the Dodgers could assimilate the 'tween-games pep talk administered by Chuck Dressen following the first-game debacle.

Ordinarily a club with a four-game edge and only twenty-two to play doesn't start looking over its shoulder, but this is no ordinary rivalry. The Giants now have a 13-to-6 margin in the interclub rivalry and there are still three games to play. And a club like the Giants, unpredictable from day to day, under these circumstances

(Continued on page 2, column 5)

Indians Pound Browns, 8-3, as Easter Hits Two

Lemon Captures No. 18 on 5-Hitter as Tribe Wins 3d in Row; Doby Connects

CLEVELAND, Sept. 6 (AP).—The booming home-run bats of big Luke Easter and Larry Doby powered an 8-to-3 victory for the second-place Cleveland Indians over the St. Louis Browns today as Bob Lemon hurled a five-hitter for his eighteenth victory of the season.

The victory, Cleveland's third in a row, still left the Tribe two and a half games behind the Yankees, who won their night game with the Senators.

Big Luke led off the lower half of the second inning with a terrific drive over the centerfield fence. It was his twenty-seventh round trip of the year, and his fourth in succession off lefthand pitching in recent games. The victim this time was Bob Cain, who eventually was charged with today's loss, his ninth against ten triumphs.

In the next inning Easter was on base when Doby smacked one over the rightfield fence for his thirtieth of the season.

And Doby, having walked, was on base when Easter lifted the ball into the rightfield stands for No. 28, in the seventh. The pitcher was Cliff Fannin, the last of three St. Louis hurlers. Easter, who equaled his all-time high for homers, has walloped four in the last three games.

Lemon's eighteenth victory com-

(Continued on page 3, column 1)

Pennant Races At a Glance

* * *

NATIONAL LEAGUE

	W	L	Pct	Games behind	Games left
Brooklyn	84	48	.636	—	22
New York	80	52	.606	4	22

Remaining games:

Brooklyn at Home (16)—Chicago, Sept. 9, 10 (2), 11; St. Louis, Sept. 12, 13; Cincinnati, Sept. 14, 15; Pittsburgh, Sept. 16, 17; Philadelphia, Sept. 23 (2), 24; Boston, 26, 27, 28. Away (6)—New York, Sept. 7, 8 (12); Boston, Sept. 19, 20, 21.

New York at Home (19)—Brooklyn, Sept. 6, 7, 8 (2); Pittsburgh, Sept. 9, 10, 11; Cincinnati, Sept. 12 (2), 13; St. Louis, Sept. 14, 15; Chicago, Sept. 16, 17; Boston, Sept. 23 (2), 24; Philadelphia, Sept. 26, 27, 28. Away (3)—Philadelphia, Sept. 19, 20, 21.

A Year Ago Today

One year ago today the National League pennant race was the following:

	W	L	Pct	Games behind	Games left
Brooklyn	85	47	.644	—	22
New York	81	54	.600	5½	19

AMERICAN LEAGUE

	W	L	Pct	Games behind	Games left
New York	81	56	.591	—	17
Cleveland	78	58	.574	2½	18

Remaining games:

New York at Home (3)—Philadelphia, Sept. 19, 20, 21. Away (14)—Washington, Sept. 7; St. Louis, Sept. 9, 10; Chicago, Sept. 12, 13; Cleveland, Sept. 14; Detroit, Sept. 16, 17; Boston, Sept. 23, 24, 25; Philadelphia, Sept. 26, 27, 28.

Cleveland at Home (16)—St. Louis, Sept. 7 (2); Philadelphia, Sept. 9, 10, 11; Boston, Sept. 12, 13; New York, Sept. 14; Washington, Sept. 16, 17; Detroit, Sept. 19, 20, 21, 22; Chicago, Sept. 23, 24. Away (2)—Detroit, Sept. 27, 28.

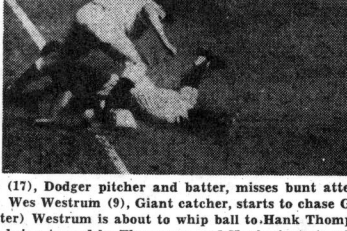

VIEWS OF SPORT

By RED SMITH

They Seem to Glare

IN 1948 an English cricket player named Dennis Compton wrote a book wherein he unburdened a conscience that had oppressed him for eighteen months. He referred to an occasion, a year and a half earlier, when an Australian umpire called him out.

"I wish to take this opportunity of apologizing," Mr. Compton wrote, "if I seemed to stand and glare at him after the decision against me."

Well sir, if everybody around here who has seemed to stand and glare within the last couple of days decides to write a book about it eighteen months hence, the publishing business is heading hell-bent for a boom. Wherever the sports' page reader turned at breakfast yesterday noon, he came upon a report of people who seemed to stand and glare.

Red Smith

There was a photograph of Mr. Steve O'Neill, the keeper of the Phillies, seeming to stand and glare across the greensward of the Polo Grounds. A few minutes before the picture was taken Mr. O'Neill had emerged from the dugout and seemed to stand and glare at August J. Donatelli, an umpire who had just called a strike against a Philadelphian batsman. Mr. Donatelli had recommended that Mr. O'Neill go and seem to stand and glare at the mirror in the clubhouse.

There was a half column about the fines which Warren Giles, president of the National League, assessed against a couple of Dodgers who had seemed to stand and glare at two other umpires during and after a game in Boston. Jackie Robinson said he wouldn't pay until he got a hearing.

Still another item reported that Mr. Casey Stengel had seemed to sit and stare at his Yankee vassals because they were playing an innocent game of "Twenty Questions" in a Pullman dining car after kissing off a ball game in Philadelphia.

Now Necks Grow Warm

TEMPER, temper. The competition and the necks are getting warm in these closing weeks of the baseball season. Maybe there'll be some fun around here, after all, before the pennants are won.

Mr. Stengel may have been justified in dressing down his players. They had lost a game they could have won. Casey was not light-hearted about it. The players would have been well advised to keep their blithe spirits under control in the boss's presence.

Steve O'Neill, of course, could not possibly have been justified in his dispute with Donatelli. It is futile and stupid and annoying for a manager to come off the bench to argue over an umpire's decision on a ball or strike. The practice could be wiped out in one day if the league presidents would establish substantial automatic fines for this offense, to be applied instantly and without exception.

As for the pleasantness involving the Dodgers in Boston—well, here we go again. Last year the Dodgers ran afoul of Frank Dascoli in Braves Field. This time their antagonists were Frank Secory and Larry Goetz. Everybody grows older with the rolling years; some grow wiser.

Moved and Seconded

THE difference of opinion concerned an inside pitch to John Logan of the Braves. The Dodgers said the ball glanced off Logan's bat. Secory said it had first brushed his uniform. He waved Logan to first base and Logan subsequently scored the winning run.

Roy Campanella and Clem Labine were dismissed for arguing. Campanella drew a $100 fine. After the game, Brooklyn's Rocky Nelson asked Secory whether he had shaken Logan's hand in congratulation when he scored. Robinson has said he spoke to Goetz, seconding Nelson's jeer. So Giles fined Robinson for "reviving or condoning an argument after the game."

Robinson is entirely within his rights to insist on a hearing before paying the fine. Anybody accused of any offense in this country has a right to speak in his own defense if he chooses.

By standing on his rights, Robinson can postpone payment of the fine for a few days. Then he will pay, or the Brooklyn club will pay for him. He won't win, and he shouldn't.

A Form of Wit

GILES has been accused of "inconsistency" in dealing more severely with ructious players now than he did earlier in the the season. He is wise to do so. Days and tempers grow shorter in September; special vigilance should be exercised to avert outbreaks which could become disgraceful.

As a matter of fact, Nelson's remark to Secory was more than slightly disgraceful. It was a stupid crack by a man who didn't get his nickname by accident. Robinson has been around longer than Nelson and is supposed to know the house rules. If he concurred with Nelson, he deserves more than a rebuke.

There is an exact parallel between Nelson's implication that

(Continued on page two)

Yankees Down Senators, 5-2; Gorman Stars

Pitcher, in Relief, Checks Washington Bid for Rally After Blackwell Falters

By Rud Rennie

WASHINGTON, Sept. 6.—The Senators greeted the Yankees' "twenty questions" addicts tonight yelling at them "Animal or vegetable?" . . . "Is it alive?"

The Senators were feeling good. They were on a six-game winning streak as they entered tonight's contest, with Connie Marrero pitching for them against Ray Scarborough. They had read about the blast Casey Stengel let off on the train last night, breaking up a noisy "twenty questions" game after the team had blown a contest it should have won. They poured it on "Is it Mineral?".

The Yankees won, 5 to 2, and maintained their two-and-a-half game league lead.

Tom Gorman starred in relief, checking Washington after Elwell Blackwell faltered.

Scarborough was making his first appearance against the Senators as a Yankee after pitching fourteen innings in which he yielded only two runs. Marrero, with a record of ten and six, had beaten the Yankees once and they had defeated him twice.

There were about 22,000 persons present at game-time.

The Yankee quiz kids cooled off their hecklers in the first inning. Gil McDougald drew a base on balls and Joe Collins singled to right. Mickey Mantle struck out. But Yogi Berra shot a single off the second baseman's glove, scoring McDougald and sending Collins to third. Collins scored while Mel Hoderlein was throwing out Gene Woodling. Bauer also grounded out. But the Yankees were off to a two-run lead.

Between innings an impressive group of Yankee pitchers went to the bull pen. They were Vic Raschi, Allie Reynolds, Tom Gorman and Ewell Blackwell.

Scarborough fanned Eddie Yost, the first man to face him. Gil Coan, the next man, knocked a home run over the rightfield wall.

With two out in the third, Mantle socked Marrero for a single,

(Continued on page 2, column 2)

Jacinto Upsets Gottlieb In Junior Tennis Final

SCARBOROUGH, N.Y., Sept. 6.—Joe Jacinto, third seeded player from E. Rockaway, L. I., upset Stephen Gottlieb, Metropolitan junior champion from New York, 7—5, 6—0, 6—2 here today and won the junior boys championship of the annual Hudson Valley Tennis tournament. Gottlieb was top seeded.

Rankings followed form in girls play. Lorrie Lewis, of Yonkers, seeded No. 1, defeated Julia Anne Harmon, 6—3, 6—0. Second-ranked Carl Norguaer, of Yonkers upset defending champion and top seeded George Mandel, of Astoria L. I., 8—6, 3—6, 6—0 in the boys division.

Night Baseball

American League

New York	200	000	102	5	9	0
Wash'ton	100	000	100	2	10	2

SCARBOROUGH, Blackwell (6), Gorman (7) and Berra; MARRERO, Consuegra (8) and Grasso.

National League

Pittsb'gh	301	00
St. Louis.	020	00

Dickson and Garagiola; Haddix and D. Rice.

(Second Game)

Boston	12
Philadel	0

Johnson and Burris; Drews and Burgess.

Major League Standings and Pitchers

Sunday Sept. 7, 1952

NATIONAL LEAGUE RESULTS YESTERDAY

New York, 6; Brooklyn, 4 (1st)
New York, 7; Brooklyn, 3 (2d)
*Philadelphia, 7; Boston, 6 (1st, twilight, 17 ins)
*Boston at Philadelphia (2d, night)
Cincinnati, 3; Chicago, 2
*Pittsburgh at St. Louis (night)

STANDING OF THE CLUBS	B'klyn	N. York	St. Louis	Philadel.	Chicago	Cincinn.	Boston	Pittsb'g.	WON	LOST	Percent	Games Behind
Brooklyn	—	6	10	9	11	16	14	18	84	48	.636	—
New York	13	—	11	9	11	14	10	12	80	52	.606	4
St. Louis	10	9	—	11	9	10	13	15	77	57	.575	8
Philadelphia	10	7	8	—	12	10	11	14	72	61	.541	12½
Chicago	7	9	7	8	—	12	9	14	66	71	.482	20½
Cincinnati	4	5	9	10	9	—	11	12	60	75	.444	25½
Boston	2	9	7	8	11	8	—	13	58	74	.439	26
Pittsburgh	2	7	5	6	8	5	6	—	39	98	.285	47½

*Not included in standings.

National League Schedule and Probable Pitchers

Brooklyn at New York (2:30 p. m., E. D. T.)—Landrum (1-3) vs. Maglie (14-5)
Boston at Philadelphia—Burdette (6-9) vs. Ridzik (2-2)
Cincinnati at Chicago—Raffensberger (15-12) vs. Rush (13-12)
Pittsburgh at St. Louis—Pollet (6-15) vs. Staley (16-12)

AMERICAN LEAGUE RESULTS YESTERDAY

New York, 5; Washington, 2 (night)
Cleveland, 8; St. Louis, 3
Boston, 6; Philadelphia, 4 (1st)
Boston, 10; Philadelphia, 2 (2d)
Chicago, 4; Detroit, 3 (11 ins)

STANDING OF THE CLUBS	N. York	Cleve.	Wash.	Chicago	Boston	Philadel.	St Louis	Detroit	WON	LOST	Percent	Games Behind
New York	—	11	14	12	11	9	13	11	81	56	.591	—
Cleveland	10	—	10	13	12	10	13	10	78	58	.574	2½
Washington	7	10	—	8	10	13	14	10	72	65	.526	9
Chicago	8	7	10	—	8	10	11	17	71	64	.526	9
Boston	8	8	6	12	—	11	10	16	71	64	.526	9
Philadelphia	7	9	8	10	10	—	12	15	71	66	.518	10
St. Louis	7	7	7	5	10	8	—	12	56	80	.412	24½
Detroit	9	6	10	4	3	5	7	—	44	91	3.26	36

American League Schedule and Probable Pitchers

New York at Washington (2:30 p. m., E. D. T.)—Lopat (7-5) vs. Masterson (9-6)
Chicago at Detroit—Grissom (11-7) vs. Gray (11-14)
St. Louis at Cleveland (2)—Byrne (6-13) and Paige (10-9) vs. Garcia (18-9) and Gromek (6-7)
Philadelphia at Boston—Byrd (14-11) vs. Hudson (10-9)

Yankees Win 4th Straight World Series, Downing Dodgers in 7th Game, 4 to 2

Homers by Woodling, Mantle, Martin's Catch Beat Brooklyn

Kuzava, 4th Pitcher for New York, Foils Bid for Late Rally; Black Loser

(Continued from page one)

reached a seventh-inning climax. Then the Yankees led, 4 to 2, just as they did at the finish. It was not as easy as that.

Reynolds had been reached for the fifth-inning run and had not looked strong, so Stengel had Ralph Houk pinch hit and selected Raschi, a winner of two previous games, to clinch yesterday's triumph.

Raschi walked Carl Furillo on five pitches to set the threat in motion. Had Mantle not batted home the fourth run, the Dodgers would have sacrificed to get the tying run to second. As it was, they were down by two and had to play it that way. So Rocky Nelson, who hit for Preacher Roe, Brooklyn's second pitcher, had to swing and popped to Phil Rizzuto at short. Then Raschi threw three straight balls to Billy Cox, worked the count full and Cox lined a single to right that sent Furillo to second.

The pitcher got behind on Reese, too, finally walking the Brooklyn captain, loading the bases. It was a good move for the Yankees because it brought Kuzava in to face the left-handed Duke Snider, star of two of Brooklyn's three victories. Snider got another full count and popped to McDougald. With two out the Dodgers needed a hit and in Robinson they had their best hitter on the spot for the job.

Martin's Catch Ends Rally

Because the wind was strong, Robinson almost came through. He lifted a pop to the right side of the infield that was carried back toward the plate by the wind. Billy Martin, suddenly realizing what was happening, raced in and, going at full speed, caught the ball as he lunged forward.

The crowd, which had been shouting with every pitch, was silent for an instant. Probably the fans were thinking how close the pop had come to falling untouched and how Furillo and Cox would have scored if it had. The thought over, there was a shout and after that no one doubted that the Yankees would win again.

Carl Erskine finished neatly for the Dodgers and McDougald's wild throw allowed Gil Hodges to become the only Dodger base-runner over the last two innings. Coming with one out in the eighth was McDougald's second bad throw of the game and the Yankees' fourth error, but even in that there was little solace for Brooklyn. Andy Pafko pinch hitting for George Shuba and fanned, Furillo flied to Woodling and so nothing was gained by the misplay.

Hodges Goes Hitless in Series

On top of that, Hodges became the first regular in history ever to go hitless in a seven game series. Playing in each of the games, the Brooklyn first baseman batted twenty-one times. Couple of other fellows went twenty-one for 0, in series many years back so Hodges did not set every record for hitting futility, but the other two hitters were blanked in six-game sets.

Futility, in fact, was the keynote of the Brooklyn defeat. In addition to their inability to capitalize on their seventh-inning chance, they flubbed in the fourth.

Ed Lopat started for the Yankees, was not calculated to last long and didn't. In the fourth when the Yankees led, 1 to 0, Snider singled sharply to right, leading off the inning, and Robinson dropped a perfect bunt toward third. Lopat, who reached the ball first did not even try for a play, and Dodgers were on first and second with none out.

It was a possible sacrifice situation, but Roy Campanella swung at the first pitch and fouled it. He bunted the second, picking the spot Robinson had chosen, and although this time Lopat made a play, Campanella beat the throw to first.

Stengel Calls on Reynolds

Lopat had not been hit hard, but Stengel did not intend to wait and see if he would be. The manager brought Reynolds, the ace, from the bullpen. Reynolds fell behind Hodges, throwing two balls, and then Gil lined sharply to Woodling. Snider, who had run as the ball was hit, ran back, tagged third and scored ahead of Woodling's throw which was weak and to the first base side of the plate. Reynolds could not field the throw cleanly and Robinson went to third on the error.

The Yankees were not playing well, Reynolds was not overpoweringly fast and Shuba, a fine left-handed hitter, was up next. But it was then that Reynolds had the something extra and he used it to get Shuba on a swinging third strike. Furillo bounced to McDougald and the bid was ended before it had gotten out of hand.

For a while, in the early going, it looked as if Black was going to conclude the final game of his rookie year on a fittingly successful note. But the twenty-eight-year-old right-hander had pitched hard and brilliantly in two previous World Series games and in fifty-six games during the regular season. The labor took its toll.

Black Weakens in Fourth

Black breezed through the first inning, walked Mize to start the second, but left. Mize at first by getting Yogi Berra, Woodling and Irv Noren on short outfield flies. Then he breezed through the third and weakened in the fourth.

Rizzuto, the Yankee leader, started the fourth with a hard grounder between Cox and third base which carried to the left-field corner for a double. Rizzuto moved to third when Mantle bounced to Hodges, but when Mize, the veteran, crossed up the rookie pitcher, Rizzuto scored. To keep Mize from powering the ball toward right, Black pitched him outside. So Mize passed up the power and tapped an outside pitch to left for a scoring single. Berra then hit into a double play and the Dodgers brought Reynolds into the game as they tied it in the fourth.

They stayed tied only until Woodling had led off the fifth. Gene slammed a one-strike pitch over the rightfield screen, the Yankees led, 2 to 1, but the Dodgers were not through. With one out in their half Cox slammed a long double to right center that carried past Irv Noren. Reese tied the score with a single to left and took second on Woodling's throw which sailed into foul territory to the left of the plate and was scored an error. Snider bounced out to Martin and then Robinson tried to get the Dodgers ahead. Jackie lashed a line drive, but it was badly placed and McDougald reached up and to his left and snared the ball in the top of his glove.

The Yankees promptly finished Black. Rizzuto started the sixth with a liner that Reese backhanded, but no one came close to the ball Mantle hit. Mickey exploded a long high drive that traveled far past the screen in right and got the Yankees ahead to stay. When Mize followed with a single, Chuck Dressen replaced Black with Roe. Berra saw enough of Roe's slow curves to complain to plate umpire Larry Goetz about a call, but he did not see enough

(Continued on page 30, column 3)

Dodgers Find Kuzava As Tough as Giants Did

Lefty Bob Kuzava, who stopped the Dodgers cold when they had the bases loaded in the seventh inning yesterday, also turned the trick on the Giants in the final game of the World Series last year.

The twenty-nine-year-old southpaw relieved Johnny Sain in the ninth inning in '51. The bases were loaded with none out and the Yankees leading, 4 to 1.

He got Monte Irvin on a fly and one run came in. Bobby Thomson also flied out and another run came in to make the score 4 to 3. Pinch-hitter Sal Yvars then lined to Hank Bauer, who made a spectacular catch to end the series.

Box Score of 7th Game

* * *

NEW YORK (A)	ab	r	h	po	a	BROOKLYN (N)	ab	r	h	po	a
McDougald, 3b	5	1	2	2	3	Cox 3b	5	1	2	2	3
Rizzuto ss	4	1	1	1	1	Reese ss	4	0	1	2	2
Mantle cf	5	1	2	1	0	Snider cf	4	1	1	4	0
Mize 1b	3	0	2	6	0	Robinson 2b	4	0	1	0	4
Collins 1b	0	0	0	1	0	Campanella c	4	0	2	2	0
Berra c	4	0	0	7	0	Hodges 1b	4	0	0	13	0
Woodling lf	4	1	2	5	0	Shuba lf	3	0	1	1	0
Noren rf	2	0	0	1	0	§Pafko	1	0	0	0	0
*Bauer rf	1	0	0	0	0	Holmes	0	0	0	0	0
Martin 2b	4	0	1	2	4	Furillo rf	3	0	0	3	0
Lopat p	1	0	0	0	1	Black p	2	0	0	0	0
Reynolds p	1	0	0	1	0	Roe p	0	0	0	0	0
†Houk	1	0	0	0	0	‡Nelson	1	0	0	0	0
Raschi p	0	0	0	0	0	Erskine p	0	0	0	0	0
Kuzava p	1	0	0	0	0	¶Morgan	1	0	0	0	0
Totals	36	4	10	27	9	Totals	36	2	8	27	9

*Safe on error for Noren in sixth.
†Grounded for Reynolds in seventh.
‡Popped out for Roe in seventh.
§Struck out for Shuba in eighth.
¶Flied out for Erskine in ninth.

NEW YORK (A)	0 0 0	1 1 1	1 0 0—4
BROOKLYN (N)	0 0 0	1 1 0	0 0 0—2

E—McDougald, 2; Reynolds, Woodling, Cox. RBI—Mize, Hodges, Woodling, Reese, Mantle 2. 2B—Rizzuto, Cox. HR—Woodling, Mantle. S—Rizzuto. DP—Robinson, Reese and Hodges; Rizzuto, Martin and Mize. Left—New York, 8; Brooklyn, 9. BB—Black 1 (Mize); Erskine 1 (Bauer); Raschi 2 (Furillo, Reese). SO—Black 1 (Mantle); Roe 1 (Berra); Lopat—3 (Cox, Snider, Black); Reynolds 2 (Shuba, Black); Kuzava 2 (Campanella, Pafko). HO—Lopat 4 in 3 innings (none out in 4th); Black 6 in 5 1/3; Reynolds 3 in 3; [illegible]e 3 in 1 2/3; Raschi 1 in 1/3; Erskine 1 in 2; Kuzava 0 in 2 2/3. ER—Lopat, 1-1; Black, 3-3; Reynolds, 1-1; Roe, 1-1; Raschi, [illegible]kine, 0-0; Kuzava, 0-0. Winner—Reynolds. Loser—Black. [illegible] (N) plate, McKinley (A) 1b, Pinelli (N) 2b, Passarella (A) [illegible] (N) lf, Honochick (A) rf. T—2:54. A—33,195 (paid).

Duke Snider crossing plate with Brooklyn's tying run in the fourth on Gil Hodges' fly to left. Yogi Berra is awaiting Gene Woodling's throw, which Allie Reynolds (22) deflected

VIEWS OF SPORT

By RED SMITH

Curtain Calls

EARLY in the game Arthur Patterson, the Yankees' trumpeter, walked through the press box asking, "Will you come to our victory party if we win?" Frank Graham jr., the Dodgers' dean of American literature, came later and his tone was more wistful.

Red Smith

"If we should have a victory party, will you come?" he asked, emphasizing the first part of the sentence.

After all, these celebrations had been going on for forty-nine years and the Dodgers never had tossed one. They still haven't. A couple of citizens named Mickey Mantle and Bob Kuzava saw to that yesterday. Abetted by sundry playmates, this pair won the seventh and deciding game of the World Series, 4 to 2, putting an end to the liveliest baseball show in eighteen years.

Not since the Dean family's brother act in 1934 has there been an entertainment to compare with the one that closed at 3:54 p. m. yesterday in Ebbets Field. It wound up with all the stars and supers on stage taking curtain calls—Joe Black, Preacher Roe, Carl Erskine, Ed Lopat, Allie Reynolds, Vic Raschi and even Kuzava, the specialist whom Casey Stengel keeps around exclusively for pitching in final games of World Series.

The only guy who wasn't there was Ralph Branca, who was invited out by Larry Goetz, the plate umpire, for overdoing eloquence in the Brooklyn dugout. Last year Ralph was invited out by Bobby Thomson, of the Giants.

A Kind of Melon

KUZAVA is a Polish name that sounds like some kind of melon. Anyhow, that's how it sounds to the Yankees, who cut up thirty-four slices worth $6,360 each last night.

A year ago in the final game the Yankees were three putouts short of their third successive world title when the Giants filled the bases with none out. Casey Stengel called in Kuzava to protect Johnny Sain's lead of 4 to 1.

Monte Irvin flied out on Kuzava's first pitch, scoring a run. Bobby Thomson flied out, scoring another. With the Yankee lead reduced to 4 to 3, Sal Yvars lined out and the Series was over.

Yesterday the Yankees were leading, 4 to 2, when the Dodgers filled the bases with one out in the seventh inning. Stengel, who couldn't have visited his pitchers oftener if they'd been rich in-laws, went calling again. With one hand he reached to pat Raschi's lofty bottom consolingly, with the other he beckoned to the bullpen.

Kuzava came in to pitch to Archduke Snider, of Brooklyn's royal family. With the count three balls and two strikes, the best-loved Flatbush entertainer since Henry Ward Beecher popped up. Jackie Robinson got two balls, two strikes. Then he popped up.

The Main Chance

THE ball that Robinson hit bore, in addition to Warren Giles's signature, the name of Joe Collins. It was the Yankee first baseman's to catch but with the sun slanting into his face across the grandstand roof, he couldn't see where it was. He stood gazing curiously aloft, wondering about life. Billy Martin, the second baseman, stood gazing curiously at Collins, wondering about him.

For what seemed a full week, nobody moved. In fact, Collins still hasn't. Martin did, though, and fast. He moved forward, broke into a jog, then stretched into a full run as the wind carried the descending ball away from him toward the plate. He ran harder and harder, ran himself clear out from under his cap, and managed at the last instant to get his glove under the ball.

That closed the inning and put an end to the last real chance the Dodgers ever had to win a world championship. Since Brooklyn got a baseball franchise in 1890, there have been six opportunities to beat a team of American League champions.

The Brooklyn-Cleveland series of 1920 went seven games but in those days a club had to win five and the Dodgers got only two. In 1947 they beat the Yankees three times in another seven-game match. In neither of those years, however, did they play so well or have anything like the opportunities to win that they enjoyed this time.

Man With a Hernia

THIS time they weren't playing Yankees named DiMaggio and Henrich and Keller and Ruffing. They weren't even playing Indians named Smith and Sewell and Wambsganss and Uhle and Speaker or Red Sox named Hooper and Hoblitzel and Lewis.

This was a series in which neither team looked good enough to win more than one game. The Yankees ran off with that game, 7 to 1, but in no other contest was either club able to take charge. A team would get a one-run lead and the opposition would get it back the same inning, or the next.

They pulled and mauled and wrestled around and it took a guy named Kuzava, one of the most obscure of Yankees, to wrap it up. When the last pitch of the series was batted by PeeWee Reese into the glove of Gene Woodling, the whole Yankee squad spewed out of the dugout or rushed in from the field to pelt Kuzava around, mauling him, knocking his hat off, pounding lumps all over him.

Meanwhile Woodling was running in from leftfield, flinging his arms about and leaping like a man with a hernia.

Rolling Rock Hunt Cup Draws Field of 12 Today

LIGONIER, Pa., Oct. 7 (AP).—This southwestern Pennsylvania community plays host tomorrow and Saturday to the annual Rolling Rock Steeplechase races over brush, hurdles and timber.

The opening day feature is the Rolling Rock Hunt Cup $2,500 purse with seventeen horses entered. The top attraction is the $5,000 International Gold Cup race Saturday over 2½ miles of brush.

Suarez Outpoints Wright

NEWARK, N. J., Oct. 7 (AP).—Victor Suarez, 152½, Havana, Cuba, won an eight-round decision over Charley Wright, 145, New York, in the feature bout at Laurel Garden tonight.

Memo for residents of New York City and Westchester County! This is registration week. Registration places are open each night through Friday from 5 to 10:30, and on Saturday from 7 a. m. to 10:30 p. m. Remember! If you don't register, you can't vote!

Herald Tribune—United Press

MARTIN TO THE RESCUE: Billy Martin, Yankee second baseman, about to make the catch that ended the last serious Dodger threat in the last of the seventh. The bases were loaded, two men were out, and Jackie Robinson had popped a wind-blown fly above the infield. Martin, running in from second, made a lunge and caught the ball for the third out. Two Brooklyn runners had already crossed the plate and the score would have been tied at 4-4 if Martin hadn't made catch

Stengel Makes Sure Dodgers Must Wait 'Until Next Year'

By Rud Rennie

Casey Stengel's worries ended at 3:54 p. m. yesterday when PeeWee Reese, the gallant little shortstop and captain of the Brooklyn Dodgers, lifted a fly to Gene Woodling for the final out in the seventh and deciding game of the hard-fought and brilliant World Series. His Yankees were champions of the world for the fourth year in succession, and Stengel had equaled the record for managers set by Joe McCarthy's teams in 1936, '37, '38 and '39.

Stengel, moreover, became the first manager ever to win four world championships in his first four years as manager of a team.

There was, however, one minor difference in the way McCarthy's teams won their four straight titles. They lost only three games in the four series. Stengel's winners lost that many in this series alone.

Dodgers Will Have to Wait

It was the Yankees' fifteenth world championship in nineteen series. They have won the last six series in which they have participated and have not been defeated in World Series play since the Cardinals defeated them in 1942.

So the Yankees, who don't need any more World Series rings, get them again; and the Dodgers, who wanted them so badly because they never had any, once more will have to "wait until next year."

The Dodgers have been in six World Series, but never have won This was the fourth time lost to the Yankees.

Allie Reynolds appeared yesterday for the fourth time as a pitcher in this series and was the winner. It was his second victory. He now has a total of six World Series victories to his credit and is the leading World Series winner among all the pitchers still active.

Stengel had to throw his three stars, Ed Lopat, Reynolds and Vic Raschi into the clinching game; but the one who was patted and pummeled and hugged was Bob Kuzava, who pitched the last two-and-two-thirds innings without yielding a hit.

In the course of a triumph which kept the World Series from being taken over by Brooklyn rooters, the Yankees broke a team record for homers in a seven-game series, and added to the wreckage the two-team record which was broken Monday.

Woodling's homer in the fifth inning was the ninth in this series to be made by a Yankee and it tied the record made by the Yankees of 1928 in four games. . . .

Mickey Mantle's second homer of the series in the sixth was the tenth Yankee homer and gave this year's team the record.

These two home runs, the only ones made in the game, boosted the two-team total for this series to sixteen. The old record was twelve, made by the Pittsburgh Pirates and the Washington Senators in 1925.

Duke Snider, who had a chance to break the record of four homers by an individual in one series which was set by Babe Ruth in 1926 and Lou Gehrig in 1928, got one single yesterday. He needed one homer to outdo Ruth and Gehrig. As it is, he is the first National Leaguer ever to hit four in one series.

Dubious Distinction

Gil Hodges achieved the unwanted distinction of being the only regular ever to go hitless in a seven-game series. Gil went twenty-one times to bat without making a hit. This equals the most times a World Series player ever went hitless. William Sullivan, of the White Sox, did it in 1906, and John Murray, of the Giants, did it in 1911. Both were in six-game series.

The American League has now won thirty-two World Series and the National League has won seventeen.

The Dodgers' six homers in this series was a new high for a National League team. It wasn't enough to win for them.

Joe Black, the Brooklyn starter, is the second rookie ever to start three games in one series. Frank Shea did it for the Yankees in 1947.

Heat on the Dodgers

The Dodgers provide no comfort for the enemy dugout. The Brooklyn dugout is steam heated. The visitors can freeze as far as the Dodgers are concerned. It was cold yesterday.

Ford Frick, the commissioner, impartial in his attitude toward the contending teams, suffered all Monday night because of his broadminded attitude. He ate at the Brooklyn mess hall and the spaghetti and meat balls did something to him. If he were not the

(Continued on page 30, column 5)

Brown Makes N.Y. Debut In Araujo Bout Friday

Joey Brown, New Orleans lightweight, will make his first appearance in a New York ring when he meets George Araujo, of Providence, in a ten-round bout at the St. Nicholas Arena Friday night.

Brown is ranked sixth among the lightweights of the country, while Araujo is the second-ranking lightweight.

Brown has boxed in the South and Middle-West and has scored victories over such men as Luther Rawlings, Arthur King, Virgil Akins and Lester Felton. He knocked out Tommy Campbell and Charley Williams. In sixty fights, he has won forty-two, lost eleven and fought seven draws.

Brown was an all-around athlete in high school in New Orleans. He was a star halfback on the football team, and played baseball and basketball. He is married and has three boys.

Never an amateur, Brown took up fighting after watching and sparring with Johnny Jackson, of Baton Rouge.

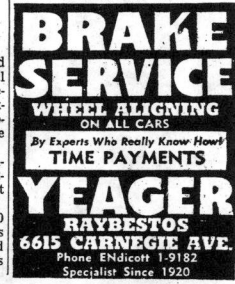

Gil Hodges, Dodgers' first baseman, sits dejectedly in dressing room after the final game of the World Series. Gil went 21 official times at bat in Series without making a hit. Thus he became the first player in World Series history to go seven games without a bingle.

ED McAULEY

Ten Years Later, Scout's Report Looks Excellent

NEW YORK—Old Casey Stengel handed the ball to Bob Kuzava and no one could blame the tall lefthander for neglecting to say "Thank you."

The bases were filled, in the seventh inning at Ebbetts Field Tuesday, and a single would have tied the score. All Kuzava had to do was retire Duke Snider and Jackie Robinson, the third and fourth-place hitters in the Dodgers' batting order.

Thirty minutes and eight putouts later, the grinning pitcher was fighting for his physical well-being. His delirious teammates were punching him in the ribs, pounding him on the back and rubbing their knuckles in his blond, kinky hair.

For Kuzava not only forced both Snider and Robinson to pop up, he went the rest of the distance in full command of this battle of the weary wings. The Yankees always win the big ones, but it would be impossible to say so today if Kuzava had not turned in one of the finest relief jobs in the records of the series.

The former Indian was not precisely a novice at the function indicated. He was in there at the finish last year, when the Yankees beat the Giants. But last year, the Yankees won the top prize in six games. Kuzava could have been belted all over the stadium without depriving his teammates of the chance to win the one they had to win.

OLD SCOUT MENTIONS A NAME

But when he walked in to relieve Vic Raschi Tuesday, Kuzava could have no such comforting reflections. This was it. Some $2,000 a man was riding on his every pitch. And every pitch was thrown at a club which won the National League pennant by murdering southpaws.

Ed Lopat and Allie Reynolds, as well as Raschi, had been used up in this game beyond which there was no tomorrow. Stengel's best pitchers were through. He was reaching into the grab-bag now. Unless Kuzava could pitch as no one in the park expected him to pitch, the Yankees would fail in their quest of their fourth successive championship.

You know what happened. Personally, I got a special kick out of the big fellow's performance. For 10 years ago, almost to the day, I quaffed refreshments in the World Series press room in the pleasant company of an old Cleveland scout named Jack Bracken.

The war was on, but Bracken was looking to the future. He beamed from his bald head to his Adam's apple as he told me about a pitcher I'd be seeing with the Indians.

"Ed," he said, "I think I have a good reputation as a scout. But I'm willing to stake that reputation on one kid. He's in the Navy now, but when he comes out, the Cleveland club can forget its long search for a winning southpaw. Try to remember the name. It's Bob Kuzava."

Remembering names is not one of my brighter tricks, but, for some reason, Bracken's statement came back to me when I met Kuzava for the first time at the Indians' training camp in 1947. I decided to keep a close eye on this youngster who seemed as fast as Lefty Grove and as wild as Grover Lowdermilk.

GETS COMPLIMENT—THEN THE GATE

He looked all right. Early Wynn was with Washington then, and Bob Lemon still was reluctant about learning the pitching trade. Mike Garcia was an unknown youngster somewhere in the farm system. Bob Feller headed the staff, of course, but it seemed to me that there was plenty of room for a big boy who could throw hard with his left hand.

The night we broke camp, I decided to write a little feature on the Cleveland "rookie of the training season." I asked Lou Boudreau to name his candidate.

"No doubt about it," replied the manager. "Kuzava is your man."

I wrote the piece—but before Kuzava's clipping had lost its new look in his pocket he was optioned to Baltimore. It was one of those typical spring occurrences. The club had so many men who could not be optioned. Kuzava could.

Sometime during that 1947 season, I wrote that the Indians had made a serious mistake in sending Kuzava to their farm at Baltimore. I believed that his problems of temperament never would have developed if he had been given the chance he had earned, the chance to pitch in the majors.

Someone evidently sent him a copy of the story, for when he saw me at Tucson the following spring, he thanked me for my attitude.

"It must have taken a lot of courage to write that," he added.

"Courage!" I exclaimed. "What does courage have to do with it?"

"Most reporters," said Kuzava, "are afraid to write anything which they think the club's front office might not like."

I told him he didn't know reporters very well, but I regarded the remark as evidence that the word from Baltimore was accurate. Kuzava had a chip on his shoulder. He had a persecution complex.

Perhaps he did, and perhaps it affected him for years, for the Indians gave up on him, and so did the Chicago White Sox and later the Washington Senators. He joined the Yankees a year ago last June, and while he won 11 games for them that season, he wasn't much help this year, when the champions were desperately in need of help.

But that was no persecution complex. Kuzava was throwing at the Dodgers Tuesday. It was a baseball which whistled and hopped and dived and which made a futile farce of the National Leaguers' last chance for their first world championship.

Ten years is a long time to wait to check an optimistic scouting report, but the probation must have seemed as nothing to Kuzava when his teammates mobbed him in the cool shadows of Ebbets Field. I felt pretty good myself. I still say the Indians should have kept him.

CLEVELAND NEWS SPORTS

It's in the Book—Bums Didn't Have a Chance

HOMER MANTLE —A NATURAL

NEW YORK (INS)—Mickey Mantle, hitting star of the World Series with a .345 average and two important home runs in the last two games, said today his father-in-law has a name all picked out for the baby Mickey and his wife expect next March.

Mickey said:

"He wants to call the baby Homer."

Set 16 New Series Marks

NEW YORK (AP)—The New York Yankees and the Brooklyn Dodgers broke 16 records and tied 17 others in the 1952 World Series. Four of the new marks were set by individuals, while 12 were team records.

Duke Snider of the Dodgers was the outstanding individual batting performer of the series, establishing new records in total bases and extra bases on long hits and equalling four others in runs batted in, home runs, two home runs in a game and long hits.

Records Broken (Based on Seven-Game Series)

Individual

Most total bases—Duke Snider, Brooklyn, 24.

Most extra bases on long hits—Duke Snider, Brooklyn (two 2b, 4HR), 14.

Most chances accepted, catcher—Yogi Berra, New York, 67.

Most putouts, catcher—Yogi Berra, New York, 59.

Team

Lowest batting percentage of club winning series—New York, .216.

Most times at bat, one club, total 19 series—New York, 8,362.

Fewest one-base hits (singles), one club—New York, 33.

Fewest two-base hits (doubles), both clubs—New York (5) vs. Brooklyn (7), 12.

Most home runs, one club—New York, 10.

Most home runs, both clubs—New York (10) vs. Brooklyn (6), 16.

Most strikeouts, one club—Brooklyn 49.

Fewest sacrifice hits, one club—New York, 2.

Fewest assists, one club—New York, 65.

Club playing most series—New York, 19.

Club winning most games—New York 67 (19 series).

Most times winners, total series—New York, 15.

BY CHARLES EINSTEIN

NEW YORK (INS)—No game today. The Yankees done won another one.

They didn't have to play it, really—though millions of fans are glad they did, because it was a memorable World Series, throughout its seven games. But they didn't have to.

The record books could have saved them the trouble, down in the small print where it says the Dodgers don't win World Series and the Yankees do.

That's the way it panned out. Casey Stengel's Yankees—you know, the club that wins the big ones—lost every odd game except the oddest.

In that seventh game Tuesday, Stengel threw his big three pitchers—Ed Lopat, Allie Reynolds and Vic Raschi—and when they couldn't make it, he called in Bob Kuzava and watched him pitch hitless ball the rest of the way, starting with a terrifying situation in the seventh.

But it was still the Yanks. And as the final 4 to 2 score of the final game went up on the board at Ebbets Field, Casey Stengel could count four world championships in his four years as manager.

That tied the record of Joe McCarthy with the 1936-37-38-39 Yankees. It gave the Bombers their 15th triumph in 19 World Series. It gave the American League its sixth straight post-season victory over the Nationals.

It gave Brooklyn a pain, too. The Dodgers, down 4-2, put the Yanks on the ropes in the seventh, routing Raschi as they loaded the bases with one down. Duke Snider and Jackie Robinson were the next hitters.

So this Kuzava, the lefty who protected the Yanks' final-game series win over the Giants a year ago, comes on and gets Snider to pop up. Then he gets Robinson to pop up—a meek little thing that the whole Yankee infield lost in the sun, with Billy Martin making a final despairing clutch of the ball as Dodgers raced madly around the sacks.

The Yanks were hitting Joe Black, Preacher Roe and Carl Erskine—who each had beaten the Bombers once during the series. All three trudged to the hill for Brooklyn Tuesday, in the order mentioned, but the Yanks were in an attacking frame of mind.

Young Mr. Mantle, who batted .345 with 10 series hits, banged in two runs with a single and a homer, the latter being the Yanks' record-breaking tenth of the series.

Gene Woodling homered another run across and John Mize, with a sweet push single over third, batted home the other one.

Snider hit another two homers for the Dodgers to tie the Ruth-Gehrig record of four circuit swats in a series. His total bases—24—set a new record.

Clutch Performance

N. YORK	A	H	O	A	BRKLYN	A	H	O	A
McDougald 3	5	2	2	3	Cox, 3b	5	2	3	3
Rizzuto ss	4	1	1	1	Reese, s	4	1	2	2
Mantle cf	5	2	1	0	Snider, cf	4	1	4	0
Mize, 1b	3	2	6	0	Robinson, 2	4	1	0	4
Collins, 1b	0	0	1	0	C'mpn'lla, c	4	2	2	0
Berra, c	4	0	7	0	Hodges, 1b	4	0	13	0
Woodling, lf	4	2	5	0	Shuba lf	3	1	1	0
Noren, rf	2	0	1	0	§Pafko	1	0	0	0
*Bauer, rf	1	0	0	0	Holmes	0	0	0	0
Martin, 2b	4	1	2	4	Furillo, rf	3	0	3	0
Lopat, p	1	0	0	1	Black, p	2	0	0	0
Reynolds, p	1	0	1	0	Roe, p	0	0	0	0
†Houk	1	0	0	0	‡Nelson	1	0	0	0
Raschi, p	0	0	0	0	Erskine, p	0	0	0	0
Kuzava, p	1	0	0	0	‖Morgan	1	0	0	0
Totals	36	10	27	9	Totals	36	8	27	9

*Safe on error for Noren in sixth.
†Grounded for Reynolds in seventh.
‡Popped out for Roe in seventh.
§Struck out for Shuba in eighth.
‖Flied out for Erskine in ninth.

New York (A)	000	111	100	—4
Brooklyn (N)	000	110	000	—2

R—McDougald, Rizzuto, Mantle, Woodling; Cox, Snider. Errors—McDougald 2, Woodling, Reynolds, Cox. RBI—Mize, Hodges, Woodling, Reese, Mantle 2. 2B—Rizzuto, Cox. HR—Woodling, Mantle. S—Rizzuto. DP—Robinson, Reese and Hodges; Rizzuto, Martin and Mize. Left—New York 8, Brooklyn 9. BB—Black 1 (Mize), Erskine 1 (Bauer), Raschi 2 (Furillo, Reese). SO—Black 1 (Mantle), Roe 1 (Berra), Lopat 3 (Cox, Snider, Black), Reynolds 2 (Shuba, Black), Kuzava 2 (Campanella, Pafko). HO—Lopat, 4 in 3 (none out in 4th); Black, 6 in 5⅓; Reynolds, 3 in 3; Roe, 3 in 1⅔; Raschi, 1 in ⅓; Erskine, 1 in 2; Kuzava, 0 in 2⅔. R-ER—Lopat 1-1, Black 3-3, Reynolds 1-1, Roe 1-1, Raschi 0-0, Erskine 0-0, Kuzava 0-0. Winner—Reynolds. Loser—Black. U—Larry Goetz (N) plate, Bill McKinley (A) first base, Babe Pinelli (N) second base, Art Passarella (A) third base, Dusty Boggess (N) left field, Jim Honochick (A) right field. T—2:54. A—33,195.

Salem Gets TV Bout In Detroit Saturday

Tommy Salem, who won a unanimous eight-round decision over Raoul Prado in Louisville Monday night, will box Dave Rollins in an eight-rounder at Detroit Saturday. The contest will be televised locally by station WEWS.

Also on the Detroit card is Sonny Wilcox, local light heavyweight graduate from Golden Gloves ranks.

FRICK FINES BRANCA $200

NEW YORK (INS)—Baseball Commissioner Ford Frick today fined Pitcher Ralph Branca of the Dodgers $200 for "abusive language" to Umpire Larry Goetz during the final game of the World Series Tuesday.

Goetz, a National League umpire, was working behind the plate. Branca, a benchwarmer most of the season who did not get in any Series game, was vitriolic about Goetz's calls on balls and strikes on the Dodger hitters.

Goetz first warned Branca and then ejected him from the bench.

Greenberg Puts Ban On Winter Baseball

BY HAL LEBOVITZ

The Cleveland Indians will not allow any of its "prospects" to play winter league baseball this year.

The order is from General Manager Hank Greenberg.

Obviously the Tribe's experience with Sam (Tootpick) Jones caused the ban on extra-curricular play for pay.

One of the players who was refused permission to chase flies south of the border this winter was Dave Pope, the American Association batting champ.

Greenberg, however, is making one exception. He has asked Commissioner Ford Frick for permission to allow Dick Weik to pitch in a Winter League. Weik expects to be discharged from the Army and he has asked for this opportunity to earn extra money as well as work himself into shape.

The case of Sam Jones is a sad, strange one. He was the most brilliant pitcher in the minors in 1951. Joe Gordon, the manager of Sacramento, said he was worth at least $100,000 on the open market. Rogers Hornsby, then managing the St. Louis Browns, wanted Jones desperately, calling him a major league pitcher "definitely."

But Jones was not for sale. The Tribe brass predicted he would be the fourth or fifth pitcher—a much needed commodity.

Then, after more brilliant pitching in the Puerto Rico Winter League, Jones reported to spring training. Everyone waited breathlessly for him to pitch. But he didn't. He had a sore arm.

During the season he was a complete flop. Finally he was sent to Indianapolis.

Holmes Is New Milwaukee Pilot

NEW YORK (INS)—General Manager John Quinn of the Boston Braves today announced that Tommy Holmes will manage the Milwaukee club of the American Association in 1953.

Holmes replaces Bucky Walters, manager of Milwaukee's league champs for the past half season. Walters returns as coach for the Braves at his own request.

Nats Release Two

WASHINGTON (INS)—The Washington Senators today announced the unconditional release of Catcher Clyde Kluttz and Pitcher Tom Ferrick and the appointment of a third player, Joe Haynes, as a pitching coach.

Late Start Gives Baron Foes Edge

BY GEOFFREY FISHER
News Staff Writer

OTTAWA, Ont.—The Barons' failure to conquer the Canadian continent in this exhibition series which comes to an end here tonight should not be an indictment of their chances in the regular campaign which opens at Pittsburgh Saturday night.

The club went to the wars too early this season. They had only five actual practice sessions under their skates when they found themselves face-to-face with a program that called for eight games in 12 nights.

That's a muscle-defying menu that General Manager Jim Hendy is not likely to dream up again. He and the rest of the Barons' brain department are convinced the human anatomy requires more conditioning than that.

The fact is that each of the clubs the Barons has met in this exhibition safari had a jump of from one to three weeks on our varsity boys.

The tardy start of the Barons' first-stringers was due in part to a desire of Barons brass to take a good long look at the biggest rookie crop they have ever had in a training camp. At the peak, there were 74 in the drill squadron. Some of the delay in looking this crowd over resulted from the necessity of selecting an entire roster of 14 players to staff the recent New Haven farm acquisition.

The main squad did not take to the ice until all of these details were virtually settled.

Now it had become necessary to play the club into shape and this has come hard. Professional or otherwise, a player can't come off a five-month layoff and turn the jet on like an electric light bulb.

The Barons actually have been progressing steadily in all departments of the game.

But they still lack the co-ordination and split-second timing which makes for a smooth-working machine.

In the great, new Coliesum at Quebec Tuesday night, the Barons dropped their tussle with the Quebec Aces, 4-3. It gave them a record of no victories, two ties and live losses in seven games.

Mrs. Charlie Homenuk, wife of trainer Charley Homenuk, whose two-year-old daughter died from polio last week, became the mother of a baby boy at St. Anne's Hospital in Cleveland Tuesday.

Man in the GRANDSTAND

One-Way Sympathy

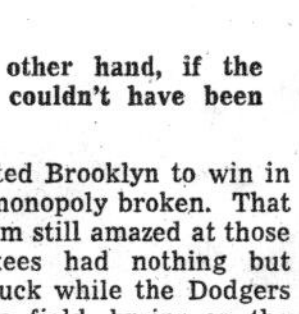

BY HOWARD PRESTON

Apparently I was one of the two or three people in the United States not rooting head over heels for the Brooklyn Dodgers in the World Series (there was a woman in Nashville and a man in Flagstaff who also didn't care which team won).

As far as I can judge, there must been mass hypnotism involved. From the way most people talked, you would have thought the Dodgers had to play with one hand tied behind their backs or else the Yankees were using fourteen players. I've never before heard so much chatter about an underdog as I did about the Dodgers; so much sympathy and so much hope expressed that the Dodgers would beat the bejabbers out of the Yankees.

The Dodgers had more synthetic alumni rooting for them than a Notre Dame football team— and that's saying plenty.

Personally, I didn't care which team won although I figured if the Dodgers took the Series it would make the Indians appear that much worse. On the other hand, if the Yankees won—well, we couldn't have been too bad.

I realize many fans wanted Brooklyn to win in order to have the Yankee monopoly broken. That was all right with me but I'm still amazed at those who contended the Yankees had nothing but brute sluggers and sheer luck while the Dodgers had all the gazelles in the field, brains on the baselines and were as deserving as Little Annie Rooney.

The way I figure it, when two pennant-winning teams meet in a seven-game series, one has about as good a chance to win as the other.

What still bothers me was the lack of pitching. Here were two champs and the Yanks had only Reynolds and Raschi and the Dodgers had only Black and Roe and Erskine as dependable hurlers.

Come to think of it, that gave the Dodgers three pitchers to two, a distinct advantage, but I didn't hear anybody siding with the undermanned Yankees. It was a case of one-way sympathy, all right.

YOGI HOPS A RIDE—Wild with glee Yankee Catcher Yogi Berra jumps on the back of Pitcher Bob Kuzava as the world series ends with a New York victory. Kuzava's relief job put the Dodgers out of their misery and insured the 4-2 clutch victory which meant four series in a row for the Yankees.

Composite Series Data

NEW YORK YANKEES

	G.	AB.	R.	H.	2b	3b	HR.	RBI	BB.	SO.	Bat.	PO.	A.	E.	Fldg.
#Bauer, rf	7	18	2	1	0	0	0	1	4	3	056	10	0	0	1000
Rizzuto, ss	7	27	2	4	1	0	0	0	5	2	148	13	17	1	968
Mantle, cf	7	29	5	10	1	1	2	3	3	4	345	16	0	0	1000
Berra, c	7	28	2	6	1	0	2	3	2	4	214	59	7	1	985
£Collins, 1b	6	12	1	0	0	0	0	0	1	3	000	27	1	0	1000
**Noren, lf-rf	4	10	0	3	0	0	0	1	1	3	300	2	0	0	1000
McDougald, 3b	7	25	5	5	0	0	1	3	5	2	200	4	15	4	826
Martin, 2b	7	23	2	5	0	0	1	4	2	2	217	16	16	2	970
Reynolds, p	4	7	0	0	0	0	0	0	0	2	000	2	1	2	600
*Woodling, lf	7	23	4	8	1	1	1	1	3	3	348	18	0	1	947
Scarborough, p	1	0	0	0	0	0	0	0	0	0	000	0	1	0	1000
Raschi, p	3	6	0	1	0	0	0	1	1	2	167	0	1	0	1000
Lopat, p	2	3	0	1	0	0	0	1	1	1	333	0	1	0	1000
Gorman, p	1	0	0	0	0	0	0	0	0	0	000	0	0	0	000
‡Mize, 1b	5	15	3	6	1	0	3	6	3	1	400	25	3	0	1000
§Sain, p	2	3	0	0	0	0	0	0	0	0	000	0	1	0	1000
Blackwell, p	1	1	0	0	0	0	0	0	0	0	000	0	1	0	1000
Kuzava, p	1	1	0	0	0	0	0	0	0	0	000	0	0	0	000
/Houk	1	1	0	0	0	0	0	0	0	0	000	0	0	0	000
Totals		232	26	50	5	2	10	24	31	32	216	192	65	10	963

BROOKLYN DODGERS

	G.	AB.	R.	H.	2b	3b	HR.	RBI	BB.	SO.	Bat.	PO.	A.	E.	Fldg.
Cox, 3b	7	27	4	8	2	0	0	0	3	4	296	9	14	1	958
//Morgan, 3b	2	1	0	0	0	0	0	0	0	0	000	0	1	0	1000
Reese, ss	7	29	4	10	0	0	1	4	2	2	345	15	18	2	943
Snider fg	7	29	5	10	2	0	4	8	1	5	345	23	0	0	1000
Robinson, 2b	7	23	4	4	0	0	1	2	7	5	174	10	20	0	1000
Campanella, c	7	28	0	6	0	0	0	1	1	6	214	39	5	0	1000
‖Pafko, lf	7	21	0	4	0	0	0	2	0	4	190	12	1	0	1000
Holmes, lf	3	1	0	0	0	0	0	0	0	0	000	2	0	0	1000
Hodges, 1b	7	21	1	0	0	0	0	1	5	6	000	60	5	1	985
Furillo, rf	7	25	1	4	2	0	0	0	3	3	174	13	0	0	1000
Black, p	3	6	0	0	0	0	0	0	1	6	000	1	2	0	1000
Erskine, p	3	6	1	0	0	0	0	0	0	1	000	0	2	0	1000
Loes, p	2	3	0	1	0	0	0	0	0	1	333	0	2	0	1000
†Nelson	4	3	0	0	0	0	0	0	1	2	000	0	0	0	000
Lehman, p	1	0	0	0	0	0	0	0	0	0	000	0	1	0	1000
Roe, p	3	2	0	0	0	0	0	0	0	0	000	1	0	0	1000
¶Shuba, lf	4	10	0	3	1	0	0	0	0	4	300	7	0	0	1000
Rutherford, p	1	0	0	0	0	0	0	0	0	0	000	0	0	0	000
+Amoros	1	0	0	0	0	0	0	0	0	0	000	0	0	0	000
Totals		233	20	50	7	0	6	18	24	49	215	192	71	4	985

*Tripled for Reynolds in eighth inning of first game.
†Walked for Loes in seventh inning of second game, struck out for Cox in eighth inning of fourth game, struck out for Hodges in ninth inning of sixth game, popped out for Roe in seventh inning of seventh game.
‡Homered for Gorman in ninth inning of third game.
§Flied out for Collins in ninth inning of third game.
¶Flied out for Black in eighth inning of fourth game.
£Ran for Mize in eighth inning of fourth game.
**Singled for Blackwell in fifth inning of fifth game.
+Ran for Shuba in eighth inning of sixth game.
‖Popped out for Roe in eighth inning of sixth game, struck out for Shuba in eighth inning of seventh game.
#Safe on error for Noren in sixth inning of seventh game.
/Grounded out for Reynolds in seventh inning of seventh game.
//Flied out for Erskine in ninth inning of seventh game.

PITCHING SUMMARY

NEW YORK YANKEES

	G.	CG.	IP.	H.	R.	ER.	BB.	SO.	HB.	WP.	W.	L.	Pct.	ERA
Reynolds	4	1	20⅓	12	4	4	6	18	0	1	2	1	667	1.80
Scarborough	1	0	1	1	1	1	0	1	0	0	0	0	000	9.00
Raschi	3	1	17	12	3	3	8	18	0	0	2	0	1000	1.59
Lopat	2	0	11⅓	14	6	6	4	3	0	0	0	1	000	4.91
Gorman	1	0	⅔	1	0	0	0	0	0	0	0	0	000	0.00
Blackwell	1	0	5	4	4	4	3	4	0	0	0	0	000	7.20
Sain	1	0	6	6	2	2	3	3	1	0	0	1	000	3.00
Kuzava	1	0	2⅔	0	0	0	0	2	0	0	0	0	000	0.00
Totals		2	64	50	20	20	24	49	1	1	4	3	571	2.81

BROOKLYN DODGERS

	G.	CG.	IP.	H.	R.	ER.	BB.	SO.	HB.	WP.	W.	L.	Pct.	ERA
Black	3	1	21⅓	15	6	6	8	9	0	0	1	2	333	2.57
Erskine	3	1	18	12	9	9	10	10	0	1	1	1	500	4.00
Loes	2	0	10⅓	11	6	5	5	5	0	0	0	1	000	4.50
Lehman	1	0	2	2	0	0	1	0	0	0	0	0	000	0.00
Roe	3	1	11⅓	9	4	4	6	7	1	0	1	0	1000	3.27
Rutherford	1	0	1	1	1	1	1	1	0	0	0	0	000	9.00
Totals		3	64	50	26	25	31	32	1	1	3	4	429	3.52

COMPOSITE SCORE BY INNINGS

New York (A.)	0 1 1	3 7 6	3 4 1	0 0	—26
Brooklyn (N.)	0 2 2	1 5 3	1 3 2	0 1	—20

SB—McDougald, Snider, Reese, Robinson 2, Loes. S—Bauer, Rizzuto, Roe 2, Furillo, Erskine, Cox, Reese. DP—Martin and Collins; Rizzuto and Martin; McDougald and Collins; Rizzuto, Martin and Mize 2; Martin, Rizzuto and Mize; McDougald, Berra and Mize; Cox, Robinson and Hodges; Reese, Robinson and Hodges; Hodges, Reese and Robinson; Robinson, Reese and Hodges. Left—New York 48; Brooklyn 52. PB—Berra. Balk—Loes. Umpires—Babe Pinelli (N.), Art Passarella (A.), Larry Goetz (N.), Bill McKinley (A.), Dusty Boggess (N.), Jim Honochick (A.). Attendance (paid)—34,861 (first game), 33,782 (second game), 66,698 (third game), 71,587 (fourth game), 70,536 (fifth game), 30,037 (sixth game), 33,195 (seventh game). Time—2:21 (first game), 2:47 (second game), 2:56 (third game), 2:33 (fourth game), 3:00 (fifth game), 2:56 (sixth game), 2:54 (seventh game). Receipts (net)—$174,845.62 (first game), $171,279.17 (second game), $311,754.97 (third game), $322,518.84 (fourth game), $308,353.01 (fifth game), $154,733.62 (sixth game), $169,267.78 (seventh game).

Ezz, Reynolds On TV Tonight

CINCINNATI (AP) — Ezzard Charles of Cincinnati, still hopeful of being the first man ever to regain a once-lost heavyweight boxing championship, tries again tonight to get started back on the trail to a title bout.

Charles will meet Bernie Reynolds of Fairfield, Conn., in a 12-round nationally televised bout at the Cincinnati Garden.

The 25-year-old Reynolds has 30 knockouts among his 52 victories but he has been a in-and-outer and the betting boys had made Charles a solid favorite at 2 to 1.

SWEET PATOOTIE, 3-2, VICTOR

Story on Page 20

5 CENTS ★ FINAL

Daily Mirror

OCTOBER						
S	M	T	W	T	F	S
			1	2	3	4
5	6	7	8	9	10	11
12	13	14	15	16	17	18
19	20	21	22	23	24	25
26	27	28	29	30	31	

Vol. 29. No. 93. NEW YORK 17, N. Y., THURSDAY, OCTOBER 9, 1952 4c in New York City 5c Elsewhere in U.S.A.

(Mirror Photos by ArtAbfier)

POST SCRIPT. Dodger Manager Charley Dressen, closing up shop at Ebbets Field for the year, good-naturedly illustrates what his sluggers failed to do in the late lamented Series with the Yanks—wield a "big bat." Chuck said he plans to "get rid of some dead wood" in '53.

MOVING DAY. Brooklyn's Duke Snider, who did right nobly in a losing cause with four Series homers, gets assist from son, Kevin, 3, as he packs in 'til next year. He'll drive back to California home.

(Mirror Photo by Anthony Bernato)

INDIAN SIGN-OFF. Big Chief Allie Reynolds, whom the Dodgers wish they'd never met (he won two games), waves farewell from favorite stamping ground—the Stadium. His home's in Oklahoma City.

(AP Photo)

GOING PLACES. Mickey Mantle, who clouted two game-winning homers for champion Yanks, packs pre-Series photo in car trunk outside hotel before heading for Commerce, Okla.

Giants Divide With Dodgers; Mantle's 565-Foot Home Run Helps Yankees Win

BROOKS SCORE, 12-4, AFTER 6-3 SETBACK

Wilhelm Nips Dodgers' Rally in 9th to Save Giant Home Debut in Afternoon

MAGLIE FALTERS AT END

Hurls Hitless Ball for 6⅔ Innings—6-Run 5th Routs Hearn in Night Game

By JOHN DREBINGER

The Giants finally got around to opening the season at the Polo Grounds yesterday but in an unguarded moment they left the gates open too long. For after bringing down the Dodgers, 6 to 3, in the afternoon, a play-off of Thursday's postponement, Leo Durocher's men came a fearful cropper in the regularly scheduled night game.

Chick Dressen's champions won this one, 12 to 4, to the profound disgust of a majority in a gathering of 29,406, most of whom walked out on the chilly performance when a drizzling rain added to their general misery midway in the struggle.

A crowd of 18,307 turned out for the afternoon engagement in which the Giants deported themselves well enough as they defeated the Dodgers' latest youthful phenom, Johnny Podres. But there wasn't much they could do about young Billy Loes in the night contest, in which their own pitching went completely to pot under a sixteen-hit barrage.

A six-run outburst, with the first three riding in on a Carl Furillo homer, routed Jim Hearn in the fifth and from there on it was just a romp.

The Razor Slips

Taking the afternoon engagement was by no means a soft touch for the Giants even though Sal Maglie, a master at shaving the Flatbush Flock, had a no-hitter going for six and two-thirds innings and as late as the ninth held a commanding 6—1 lead.

For in the top half of the ninth the famed Barber's razor slipped and he almost cut himself as the aroused Brooks lashed back for four singles and two runs with only one out.

But at this point Durocher came up with a long and all too familiar move as far as the Dodgers are concerned. The Giant skipper called on his knuckleballing ace, Hoyt Wilhelm, and though there were a few more anxious moments when a pass filled the bases, the relief star of the Polo Grounds corralled the final out.

Up to this trying moment, it was pretty much all Giant. The Polo Grounders bagged three of their runs off the southpaw Podres, two riding home on a second inning circuit clout by Wes Westrum. Then, after Podres vacated for a pinch-hitter, Jim Hughes came on in the last of the eighth and was himself tagged for three more tallies. That bit of added "insurance" was to pay off handsomely a few minutes later.

Mayor Hurls a Slider

Since Giant-Dodger meetings never need any additional embellishments, the pre-game ceremonies, carried over from Thursday's rained out opener, were to the point. There was the traditional parade to the flagpole; promptly at 1:30 o'clock Mayor Impellitteri unfurled a swift slider that could win him a shutout in City Hall, and a moment later the belligerents were at it.

The first rift in the battle occurred in the second when, with two out, Daryl Spencer, making his formal bow in the championship season at the Polo Grounds, clubbed a triple to left center that cleared all of 440 feet on the fly.

Then the inexperience of youth was to take its toll. Podres, facing Westrum and with Maglie the next batter, chose not to be the least bit discreet. He laid his first pitch in there and the husky Giant backstop whacked it right over the left-field roof.

Something even more astonishing came to pass in the third when the usually flawless Peewee Reese committed misplays on two successive batters. He fumbled Al Dark's grounder, then fired wide of second on Bobby Thompson's bounder, Dark scoring all the way from first on the error.

Spencer Fumbles Grounder

In the meantime, Maglie was mowing down the Brooks. In six innings only one Dodger got on base, Spencer fumbling Don Thompson's sharp grounder in the fifth.

Two were out in the seventh when Jackie Robinson came up with the Brooks' first hit, a pop fly in short left that Monty Irvin couldn't quite reach. Monty added a wild throw-in and Jackie wound up on third. That, however, scarcely was needed as Roy Campanella followed with a mighty three-base blast into right center to score Robbie.

Two were out and only Whitey Lockman on first when throuble overtook Hughes in the Giant eighth. Don Mueller singled, Spencer doubled and one run was in. Following an intentional pass to Westrum, Maglie got an infield hit that Junior Gilliam collared back of second, only to fall asleep. For the hit not only scored Mueller but Spencer as well as the Dodgers' young second sacker nonchalantly tossed the ball to Reese standing on second.

And in the ninth those tallies suddenly became mighty handy as Gilliam opened with a single, grabbing an extra base on Spencer's wide throw to first. Resee singled and Duke Snider's fly drove in Gilliam. Robinson and Campanella singled for another run and that was where Wilhelm came on. He induced Don Thompson to slap into a force play at second, which still left runners on first and third. Then he walked Gil Hodges, filling the sacks. But a moment later the Flock breathed its last as George Shuba fouled out to Spencer back of third.

Furillo's Second Homer

The night game remained a scoreless deadlock for four innings, then blew wide open as Lockman fumbled a grounder to open the fifth. Behind that Hodges singled and Furillo sliced one into the lower right deck for his second homer of the season.

Then all sorts of things happened. Gilliam's blinding speed converted a single into a double and a moment later Junior scored from second base on a wild pitch. Snider singled, stole second and third and when Hearn walked the next two, Frank Hiller came on only to be greeted by Don Thompson's single that drove in two more.

Ruben Gomez was whacked for four more runs on five singles before George Spencer rescued him in the sixth and then George got cuffed for another pair in the eighth. It wasn't until the eighth the Giants finally bestirred themselves to grab two runs and another pair in the ninth. But by then it was all too late.

Robinson, playing third base throughout the day, came to bat nine times and got on base seven times, with five singles and two walks.

Like President Eisenhower in Washington the day before, Mayor Impellitteri sandwiched his opening pitch between speaking engagements. His toss to Westrum, which nicked the outside corner of the imaginery plate, had hardly settled in the catcher's glove before His Honor was off and running to the ... stop.

The Box Scores

AFTERNOON GAME

BROOKLYN (N.)	ab	r	h	po	a	NEW YORK (N.)	ab	r	h	po	a
Gilliam, 2b	4	1	1	1	2	Williams, 2b	4	0	1	1	1
Reese, ss	4	1	1	1	1	Dark, ss	4	1	0	1	4
Snider, cf	4	0	0	1	0	Thomson, cf	3	0	1	6	0
Robinson, 3b	4	1	2	1	4	Irvin, lf	4	0	0	1	0
Campanella, c	4	0	2	3	1	Lockman, 1b	4	1	2	8	1
Thom'n, lf, rf	4	0	0	2	0	Mueller, rf	4	1	2	0	0
Hodges, 1b	3	0	0	12	1	Spencer, 3b	4	2	2	3	2
Furillo, rf	2	0	0	3	0	Westrum, c	3	1	1	6	0
aShuba, lf	2	0	0	0	0	Maglie, p	3	0	1	1	1
Podres, p	2	0	0	0	2	Wilhelm, p	0	0	0	0	0
aWalker	1	0	0	0	0						
Hughes, p	0	0	0	0	0						
Total	34	3	6	24	11	Total	31	6	10	27	9

aGrounded out for Furillo in eighth.
bStruck out for Podres in eighth.

Brooklyn ......0 0 0 0 0 0 1 0 2—3
New York ......0 2 1 0 0 0 0 3 .—6

Errors—Reese 2, Spencer 2, Irvin. Runs batted in—Westrum 2, Campanella 2, Spencer, Maglie 2, Snider. Two-base hit—Spencer. Three-base hits—Spencer, Campanella. Home run—Westrum. Sacrifice hit—Maglie. Double play—Gilliam, Reese and Hodges. Left on bases—Brooklyn 5, New York 7. Bases on balls—Off Podres 3, Hughes 2, Wilhelm 7. Struck out—By Podres 2, Maglie 5. Hits—Off Podres 7 in 7 innings, Hughes 3 in 1, Maglie 6 in 8 1-3, Wilhelm 0 in 2-3. Runs and earned runs—Off Podres 3 and 2, Hughes 3 and 3, Maglie 3 and 3. Winning pitcher—Maglie (1—0). Losing pitcher—Podres (0—1). Umpires—Boggess, Engeln, Stewart and Pinelli. Time of game—2:18. Attendance—18,307.

NIGHT GAME

BROOKLYN (N.)	ab	r	h	po	a	NEW YORK (N.)	ab	r	h	po	a
Gilliam, 2b	6	2	3	4	2	Williams, 2b	4	0	3	1	1
Reese, ss	5	0	0	1	3	Dark, ss	4	0	0	0	1
Snider, cf	5	3	2	2	0	Thomson, cf	4	0	0	2	0
Robinson, 3b	3	3	2	2	2	Irvin, lf	2	0	1	3	0
Cam'nella, c	4	0	2	5	1	Rhodes, lf	1	0	1	0	0
D. Th'son, lf	4	1	2	0	0	Lockman, 1b	4	1	2	10	1
Hodges, 1b	4	1	1	8	0	Mueller, rf	4	1	2	2	0
Furillo, rf	5	2	3	1	0	D. Sp'cer, 3b	4	1	1	1	1
Loes, p	4	0	1	0	1	Westrum, c	1	0	0	5	0
						Calderone, c	2	1	2	1	0
						aThompson	1	0	0	0	0
						Hearn, p	0	0	0	0	4
						Hiller, p	1	0	0	0	0
						bWilson	1	0	0	0	0
						Gomez, p	0	0	0	0	1
						G. Sp'cer, p	0	0	0	0	0
						cGilbert	1	0	0	0	0
						Lanier, p	0	0	0	0	0
						dRigney	1	0	0	0	0
Total	40	12	16	27	10	Total	34	4	9	27	11

aFlied out for Westrum in fifth.
bStruck out for Hiller in fifth.
cFouled out for G. Spencer in eighth.
dGrounded out for Lanier in ninth.

Brooklyn ......0 0 0 0 6 4 0 2 0—12
New York ......0 0 0 0 0 0 0 2 2—4

Error—Lockman. Runs batted in—Furillo 3, D. Thompson 3, Gilliam, Snider, Campanella 3, Williams, Dark, Calderone 2. Two-base hits—Gilliam, Calderone. Home run—Furillo. Stolen bases—Snider 2, Robinson, Campanella. Sacrifices—Loes, Reese. Double plays—Furillo and Hodges; Reese, Gilliam and Hodges. Left on bases—Brooklyn 8, New York 5. Bases on balls—Off Loes 2, Hearn 3, G. Spencer 2. Struck out—By Loes 6, Hearn 5, G. Spencer 1. Hits—Off Hearn 6 in 4 2-3; Hiller 1 in 1-3; Gomez 5 in 2-3, G. Spencer 3 in 2 1-3; Lanier 1 in 1. Runs and earned runs—Off Loes 4 and 4, Hearn 6 and 3, Gomez 4 and 4, G. Spencer 2 and 2, Hiller 0 and 0, Lanier 0 and 0. Wild pitches—By Hearn 3. Winning pitcher—Loes (1—0). Losing pitcher—Hearn (0—1). Umpires—Engeln, Stewart, Pinelli, Boggess. Time of game—2:40. Attendance—29,406.

One Giant Out, Another Scores in Afternoon Game

Lockman of New York is picked off first base on Podres' throw to Hodges in the fourth inning

The New York Times (by Ernest Sisto)

Westrum of the Giants, scoring on his second-inning homer, is congratulated at plate by Spencer (12), who scored ahead of him, and Williams (10), who is waiting for his turn at bat.

BISHOP OF ATHLETICS CHECKS RED SOX, 5-0

PHILADELPHIA, April 17 (AP)—Rookie Charley Bishop, a surprise starter, turned back the Red Sox with a five-hit shutout and drove home a pair of runs as the Athletics won a 5-0 victory today in a game marked by the major league season's first fist fight.

Bishop struck out five and exhibited excellent control by not walking a batter.

The principals in the fight were Sammy White, Boston catcher, and Allie Clark, Philadelphia outfielder. It was a short and brief contest in which Clark landed a good right to White's jaw.

Tempers flared when White blocked Clark's attempt to tally from second on Pete Suder's single in the eighth. Jim Piersall made a great throw to the plate and White blocked the sliding Clark. There was an exchange of words and both players came up swinging.

Umpires jumped between the players and both benches emptied. The plate umpire, Charley Berry, banished White and Clark. It was White's second fight with a Philadelphia player. He and Billy Hitchcock, since traded to Detroit, exchanged punches here last year.

Eddie Joost, A's shortstop, was sidelined because of a charley horse and Joe DeMaestri replaced him.

The box score:

BOSTON (A.)	ab	r	h	po	a	PHILADELPHIA (A.)	ab	r	h	po	a
Goodman, 2b	4	0	2	4	4	DeMaestri, ss	4	0	1	3	3
...tersall, rf	4	0	1	0	1	Philley, cf	4	0	1	1	0
Evers, lf	4	0	0	1	0	Michaels, 2b	4	0	1	5	3
Gernert, 1b	3	0	0	10	0	Robinson, 1b	3	0	0	9	1
Kell, 3b	3	0	0	1	3	Clark, rf	3	0	1	0	0
White, c	3	0	1	6	0	Valo, rf	0	0	0	0	0
Wilber, c	0	0	0	1	0	Zernial, lf	2	2	0	3	0
Umphlett, cf	3	0	1	1	0	Suder, 3b	4	2	3	1	3
Bolling, ss	3	0	0	1	3	Astroth, c	3	1	1	5	1
McDermott, p	1	0	0	0	2	Bishop, p	3	0	1	0	2
Flowers, p	1	0	0	0	0						
aZarilla	1	0	0	0	0						
Delock, p	0	0	0	0	0						
Total	30	0	5	24	11	Total	30	5	9	27	13

aHit into double play for Flowers in eighth.

Boston ......0 0 0 0 0 0 0 0 0—0
Philadelphia ......0 2 0 2 0 0 0 1 .—5

Errors—Goodman, Gernert. Runs batted in—Bishop 2, DeMaestri, Philley. Two-base hit—Philley. Sacrifice—Robinson. Double plays—Astroth and Michaels; Bolling, Goodman and Gernert; Kell, Goodman and Gernert; Bishop, DeMaestri and Robinson. Left on bases—Boston 3, Philadelphia 8. Bases on balls—Off McDermott 2, Flowers 1, Delock 3. Struck out—By McDermott 2, Flowers 3, Delock 1, Bishop 5. Hits—Off McDermott 7 in 4 innings, Flowers 0 in 3, Delock 2 in 1. Runs and earned runs—Off McDermott 4 and 2, Delock 1 and 1. Wild pitch—McDermott. Winning pitcher—Bishop (1—0). Losing pitcher—McDermott (0—1). Umpires—Berry, Hurley, Soar and Rommel. Time of game—2:13. Attendance—2,400.

ETCHELLS TIES FOR LEAD

Equals Star Title Series Total of Knowles, Myers Cup Winner

Special to THE NEW YORK TIMES.

NASSAU, Bahamas, April 17—Durward Knowles of Nassau, sailing Gem III, captured the second race of the Star Class spring championships off Montagu Bay today and tied for first place on total points with E. W. ... Etchells of Greenwich, Conn. Etchells finished third with ... in today's contest. ... Charles ... Jr. of Barnegat ..., with Vega IV, placed second.

Robert Lippincott's Flower of Riverton, N. J., and Jack Price's Commanche of Miami shared third in the series point standing. Lippincott sailed fourth, Price ninth in the race today.

Knowles won the Myers Cup, finishing ahead of Price as George Fleitz of Los Angeles with Wench IV gained third in the three-race Star Class event. The final of the spring title competition is scheduled for tomorrow morning.

Other title race finishers included Charles Knight's Quakeress II, Riverton, N. J., eleventh; Charles Ulmer's Scylla, City Island, N. Y., fourteenth, and Andrew Lawrence's Sonata, Sea Cliff, L. I., twentieth.

REDLEGS' 3 IN 8TH STOP BRAVES, 10-9

Three Walks and Two Singles Off a Milwaukee Rookie Decide Cincinnati Game

CINCINNATI, April 17 (AP)—The Cincinnati Redlegs and the Milwaukee Braves traded hits, runs and the lead freely here today until the Redlegs shattered a 7-all deadlock with a three-run outburst in the eighth inning and then held off th Breaves in the ninth for a 10-9 triumph.

Ed Mathews belted a two-run homer for the losers while Jim Greengrass, Ted Kluszewski and Gus Bell got 4-baggers for the Redlegs. Greengrass connected with two on.

Rookie relief pitcher Bob Buhl's wildness hurt the Braves when he walked three batters in the eighth while getting only one man out on a sacrifice before Johnny Temple and Bobby Adams singled to drive in three runs. Don Liddle replaced Buhl and got Kluszewski to hit into an inning-ending double play, but the damage had been done.

The Braves blended a single, a walk and Andy Pafko's 390-foot double for two runs in the ninth inning before Joe Nuxhall got the side out. Nuxhall was the fourth and last Redleg pitcher to see action, with Frank Smith getting credit for the victory.

The Braves used three hurlers as Cincinnati came up with 10 hits against 12 for Milwaukee. Buhl was charged with the defeat.

Milwaukee made three errors, but only one—Johnny Logan's wide throw on an attempted force out at second in the second—figured in the scoring.

The box score:

MILWAUKEE (N.)	ab	r	h	po	a	CINCINNATI (N.)	ab	r	h	po	a
Bruton, cf	5	2	3	4	1	Temple, 2b	5	0	2	4	3
Logan, ss	5	2	1	2	2	Adams, 3b	5	0	1	0	3
Mathews, 3b	3	2	2	1	1	Marshall, rf	4	1	1	2	0
Gordon, lf	5	0	1	1	0	Klusz'ski, 1b	4	2	1	9	0
dPendleton	0	0	0	0	0	Greengrass, lf	4	2	2	2	0
Pafko, rf	4	0	2	1	0	Bell, cf	3	3	2	4	0
Adcock, 1b	5	0	1	8	1	McMillan, ss	3	0	1	2	3
Cooper, c	3	1	1	3	0	Seminick, c	3	1	0	4	1
eSisti	0	0	0	0	0	Judson, p	1	0	0	0	0
Dittmer, 2b	4	1	1	3	3	bHatton	1	0	0	0	0
fThorpe	1	0	0	0	0	Smith, p	0	0	0	0	0
Wilson, p	2	0	0	1	0	cMarquis	0	1	0	0	0
aKlaus	1	0	0	0	0	Blake, p	0	0	0	0	0
Buhl, p	0	0	0	0	2	Nuxhall, p	0	0	0	0	0
Liddle, p	0	0	0	0	0						
Total	39	9	12	24	10	Total	33	10	10	27	10

aGrounded out for Wilson in sixth.
bFlied out for Judson in sixth.
cWalked for Smith in eighth.
dRan for Gordon in ninth.
eRan for Cooper in ninth.
fFlied out for Dittmer in ninth.

Milwaukee ......2 0 2 0 0 2 1 0 2—9
Cincinnati ......0 2 1 0 4 0 0 3 .—10

Errors—Logan, Mathews, Adcock, Adams. Runs batted in—Bruton, Mathews 3, Gordon, Pafko 3, Klaus, Temple 2, Adams, Kluszewski, Greengrass 3, Bell, Seminick. Two-base hits—Gordon, Pafko. Home runs—Mathews, Kluszewski, Greengrass, Bell. Stolen base—Bruton. Sacrifice—McMillan. Double plays—Mathews, Dittmer and Adcock; Dittmer, Logan and Adcock. Left on bases—Milwaukee 8, Cincinnati 5. Bases on balls—Off Wilson 2, Buhl 3, ... 1, Judson 2, Smith 1, Blake 1, Nuxhall 1. Struck out—By Wilson 2, Buhl 1, Judson 1, Smith 2. Hits—Off Wilson 8 in 5 innings, Buhl 2 in 2 1-3, Liddle 0 in 2-3, Judson 8 in 6, Smith 2 in 2, Blake 1 in 0 (faced two batters), Nuxhall 1 in 1. Runs and earned runs—Off Wilson 7 and 5, Buhl 3 and 3, Judson 6 and 5, Smith 1 and 1, Blake 2 and 2. Winning pitcher—Smith (1—0). Losing pitcher—Buhl (0—1). Umpires—Warneke, Donatelli, Gorman and Conlan. Time of game—2:20. Attendance—1,295.

Pirates Purchase Pellagrini

PITTSBURGH, April 17 (UP)—The Pirates winked at their "youth movement" today by purchasing 34-year-old Eddie Pellagrini from the Cincinnati Redlegs. He will be used as a utility infielder.

Minor Leagues

[From Late Editions of Yesterday's TIMES.]

AMERICAN ASSOCIATION

(Night Games)

Indianapolis 3, Charleston 2.
Minneapolis 16, Kansas City 6.
Toledo 12, Columbus 6.
St. Paul at Louisville, rain.

STANDING OF THE CLUBS

	W.	L.	PC.		W.	L.	PC.
Minneapolis	2	0	1.000	Charleston	0	1	.000
Indianapolis	1	0	1.000	Columbus	0	1	.000
St. Paul	1	0	1.000	Louisville	0	1	.000
Toledo	1	0	1.000	Kansas City	0	2	.000

[From Late Editions of Yesterday's TIMES.]

SOUTHERN ASSOCIATION

(Night Games)

Chattanooga 12, Atlanta 0.
Little Rock 9, New Orleans 1.
... Memphis 7.
... at Nashville, rain.

STANDING OF THE CLUBS

	W.	L.	PC.		W.	L.	PC.
Chattanooga	4	0	1.000	New Orleans	3	3	.500
Little Rock	4	3	.571	Birmingham	2	3	.400
Atlanta	3	3	.500	Memphis	2	3	.400
Nashville	3	3	.500	Mobile	2	5	.286

[From Late Editions of Yesterday's TIMES.]

TEXAS LEAGUE

(Night Games)

Houston 4, Beaumont 0.
Oklahoma City 12, Fort Worth 9.
San Antonio 9, Shreveport 8.
Tulsa 5, Dallas 3.

STANDING OF THE CLUBS

	W.	L.	PC.		W.	L.	PC.
Okla. City	4	1	.800	Shreveport	4	3	.571
San Antonio	5	2	.714	Fort Worth	3	4	.429
Tulsa	4	2	.667	Dallas	1	5	.167
Beaumont	4	3	.571	Houston	1	6	.143

PACIFIC COAST LEAGUE

(Thursday Night Games)

Hollywood 5, Los Angeles 0.
Sacramento at Seattle, rain.
San Diego at Portland, rain.
San Francisco at Oakland, rain.

STANDING OF THE CLUBS

	W.	L.	PC.		W.	L.	PC.
Hollywood	12	6	.667	San Francisco	8	8	.500
Los Angeles	11	6	.647	Sacramento	7	8	.467
Seattle	10	6	.625	San Diego	4	12	.250
Portland	9	6	.600	Oakland	4	13	.235

TIGER RALLY IN 9TH HALTS INDIANS, 6-5

Batts' Triple Routing Feller Is the Key Blow—Delsing Wallops Two Homers

DETROIT, April 17 (AP)—Matt Batts, fighting for the No. 1 catching job on the Detroit Tigers, delivered a triple in the bottom of the ninth inning today to pave the Bengals to a 6-5 victory over the Cleveland Indians.

With the Tigers trailing by one run and a runner on second, Batts drove a run-scoring triple to centerfield and, moments later, his relief runner, Freddie Hatfield, skipped home with the winning tally on Owen Friend's fly ball.

Cleveland had scored once in the top of the ninth on Dale Mitchell's run-producing single. But pinch hitter Johnny Pesky walked to start the Tiger ninth. He reached second on a hit-and-run play when Indian shortstop Ray Boone dropped Catcher Jim Hegan's perfect toss.

Then Batts belted his triple and that knocked Bob Feller, the losing pitcher, from the mound.

Relief Pitcher Lou Brissie walked the next two batters to fill the bases and set up a force play at any base. But Friend, foiled the strategy by belting a long fly to center that sent Hatfield home.

Almost forgotten in the ninth inning excitement was a pair of two-run homers by the Tigers' Jim Delsing. He connected in the second and sixth innings.

Dave Madison, who replaced starter Bill Wight during the Indians' four-run rally, in the third, was the winner. It was Feller's first loss to Detroit since July 7, 1950. He had beaten the Tigers seven straight times.

The box score:

CLEVELAND (A.)	ab	r	h	po	a	DETROIT (A.)	ab	r	h	po	a
Boone, ss	3	1	0	2	6	Kuenn, ss	4	0	2	5	3
Avila, 2b	3	1	0	2	5	Friend, 2b	4	0	0	5	6
Doby, cf	4	1	3	2	0	Sullivan, lf	3	0	0	0	0
Easter, 1b	3	1	2	10	0	Dropo, 1b	4	0	0	9	1
Glynn, 1b	0	0	0	1	1	Nieman, rf	4	2	0	2	1
Rosen, 3b	4	0	1	0	2	Delsing, cf	3	2	2	1	0
Mitchell, lf	4	0	1	1	0	B'gartner, 3b	3	0	0	1	3
Kennedy, lf	0	0	0	0	0	aPesky	0	1	0	0	0
Simpson, rf	4	0	1	3	0	Batts, c	4	0	2	4	0
Hegan, c	4	0	1	2	2	bHatfield	0	1	0	0	0
Feller, p	1	1	0	0	1	Wight, p	1	0	0	0	0
Brissie, p	0	0	0	0	0	Madison, p	2	0	1	0	3
						cMullin	0	0	0	0	0
						dCarswell	0	0	0	0	0
Total	30	5	9	*25	15	Total	30	6	7	27	17

*One out when winning run was scored.
aWalked for Baumgartner in ninth.
bRan for Batts in ninth.
cAnnounced for Madison in ninth.
dWalked for Mullin in ninth.

Cleveland ......0 0 4 0 0 0 0 0 1—5
Detroit ......0 2 0 0 0 2 0 0 2—6

Error—Boone. Runs batted in — Doby, Easter 2, Rosen, Mitchell, Delsing 4, Batts, Friend. Two-base hits—Easter, Hegan, Batts. Three-base hit—Batts. Home runs—Delsing 2. Sacrifices—Feller, Glynn. Double plays—Boone, Avila and Easter; Friend, Kuenn and Dropo 2; Baumgartner, Friend and Dropo. Left on bases—Cleveland 10, Detroit 7. Bases on balls—Off Feller 6, Brissie 2, Wight 4, Madison 6. Struck out—By Feller 2, Wight 1, Madison 2. Hits—Off Feller 7 in 8 innings (none out in ninth), Brissie 0 in 1-3, Wight 3 in 2 1-3, Madison 6 in 6 2-3. Runs and earned runs—Off Feller 6 and 5, Wight 4 and 4, Madison 1 and 1. Winning pitcher—Madison (1—0). Losing pitcher—Feller (0—1). Umpires—Napp, Duffy, Grieve and Passarella. Time of game—2:51. Attendance—2,642.

BROWNS DOWN WHITE SOX

St. Louis Gets Five in Seventh for 6-to-4 Triumph

CHICAGO, April 17 (AP) — The Browns chased 36-year-old Joe Dobson in a five-run seventh to whip the White Sox today, 6—4, before 972 hardy fans who braved the gloomy 36-degree weather.

The big inning broke a 1-1 tie after the Sox scored in the fifth following Vic Wertz' first homer of the season in the top half of the frame.

The box score:

ST. LOUIS (A.)	ab	r	h	po	a	CHICAGO (A.)	ab	r	h	po	a
Groth, cf	5	0	0	3	0	Fox, 2b	5	0	2	3	4
Young, 2b	4	0	2	3	2	Fain, 1b	5	0	1	13	0
Dyck, lf	3	1	0	1	0	Minoso, lf	4	1	0	1	0
Wertz, rf	4	2	2	4	0	Stephens, 3b	4	0	0	0	1
Elliott, 3b	4	0	1	1	1	Rivera, cf	4	1	3	4	0
Sievers, 1b	4	1	2	7	1	Mele, rf	4	1	1	0	0
Moss, c	4	1	2	3	1	C'rasquel, ss	4	0	3	4	8
Hunter, ss	2	0	0	4	3	Wilson, c	2	0	1	2	2
Littlefield, p	3	1	0	1	1	cBoyd	0	1	0	0	0
Paige, p	1	0	0	0	2	Dobson, p	2	0	0	0	2
						Dorish, p	0	0	0	0	0
						aKrsnich	0	0	0	0	0
						bByrne	1	0	0	0	0
						Johnson, p	0	0	0	0	1
						dWright	1	0	1	0	0
Total	34	6	9	27	11	Total	36	4	12	27	18

aAnnounced for Dorish in seventh.
bFlied out for Krsnich in seventh.
cWalked for Wilson in ninth.
dSingled for Johnson in ninth.

St. Louis ......0 0 0 0 1 0 5 0 0—6
Chicago ......0 0 0 0 1 0 1 1 1—4

Errors—Hunter, Wertz, Dobson, Carrasquel. Runs batted in—Wertz, Elliott, Moss 2, Littlefield, Young, Dobson, Wilson, Rivera, Fox. Two-base hits—Moss, Fain. Three-base hit—Rivera. Home run—Wertz. Sacrifice—Wilson. Double plays—Carrasquel, Fox and Fain 2; Young, Hunter and Sievers 2. Left on bases—St. Louis 4, Chicago 8. Bases on balls—Off Dobson 2, Dorish 1, Paige 2. Struck out—By Dobson 2, Littlefield 3. Hits—Off Dobson 6 in 6 1-3 innings, Dorish 2 in 2-3, Johnson 1 in 2, Littlefield 9 in 6 1-3, Paige 3 in 2 2-3. Runs and earned runs—Off Dobson 4 and 4, Dorish 2 and 1, Littlefield 2 and 2, Paige 2 and 2. Winning pitcher—Littlefield (1—0). Losing pitcher—Dobson (0—1). Umpires—Summers, Stevens, Robb and Froese. Time of game—2:28. Attendance—972.

Associated Press Wirephoto

MUSEUM PIECE: If Mickey Mantle didn't quite knock the cover off the ball with that 565-foot home run yesterday in Washington, he gave it a clobbering at any rate. The ball, which Mickey holds, was scuffed in two spots by the time it came to rest in the backyard of a house near Griffith Stadium.

Towering Drive by Yank Slugger Features 7-3 Defeat of Senators

Mantle's 565-Foot Homer at Capital Surpassed Only by Mighty Ruth Wallops

By LOUIS EFFRAT

Special to THE NEW YORK TIMES.

WASHINGTON, April 17—Unless and until contrary evidence is presented, recognition for the longest ball ever hit by anyone except Babe Ruth in the history of major league baseball belongs to Mickey Mantle of the Yankees. This amazing 21-year-old athlete today walloped one over the fifty-five-foot high left-field wall at Griffith Stadium. That ball, scuffed in two spots, finally stopped in the backyard of a house, about 565 feet away from home plate.

This remarkable homer, which helped the Yankees register a 7-3 victory over the Senators, was Mickey's first of the season, but he will have to go some, as will anyone else, to match it.

Chuck Stobbs, the Nat southpaw, had just walked Yogi Berra after two out in the fifth, when Mantle strode to the plate. Batting right-handed, Mickey blasted the ball toward left center, where the base of the front bleachers wall is 391 feet from the plate. The distance to the back of the wall is sixty-nine feet more and then the back wall is fifty feet high.

Bounces Out of Sight

Atop that wall is a football scoreboard. The ball struck about five feet above the end of the wall, caromed off the right and flew out of sight. There was no telling how much farther it would have flown had the football board not been there.

Before Mantle, who had cleared the right-field roof while batting left-handed in an exhibition game at Pittsburgh last week (only Babe Ruth and Ted Beard had ever done that) had completed running out the two-run homer, Arthur Patterson of the Yankees' front-office staff was on his way to investigate the measure.

Patterson returned with the following news:

A 10-year-old lad had picked up the ball. He directed Patterson to the backyard of 434 Oakdale Street and pointed to the place where he had found it, across the street from the park. The boy, Donald Dunaway of 343 Elm Street N. W., accepted an undisclosed sum of money for the prize, which was turned over to Mantle. The Yankee was to send a substitute ball, suitably autographed to the boy.

Until today, when Mantle made it more or less easy for Lefty Ed Lopat, who worked eight innings, to gain his first triumph, no other batter had cleared the left-field wall here. Some years ago, Joe DiMaggio bounced a ball over, but Mickey's accomplishment was on the fly.

Longest Bunt as Well

Later in the contest, Mickey dragged a bunt that landed in front of second base and he outsped it for a single. Thus, in the same afternoon, it would appear, the young man from Commerce, Okla., fashioned one of the longest homers and the longest bunt on record.

Everything else that occurred in this contest was dwarfed by Mantle's round-tripper, which traveled 460 feet on the fly. There was a third-inning homer by Bill Martin, which gave the Yankees' the lead. The Nats tied it against Lopat in the same frame on a single by Wayne Terwilliger, a sacrifice by Stobbs and Eddie Yost's single to left.

However, Hank Bauer doubled and counted on a single by Joe Collins for a 2-1 edge in the fourth then it was that Mickey connected with a fast ball and wrote diamond history. Other things happened, including Tom Gorman's appearance for the last inning, but no one appeared to be interested.

Gone With The Wind

It is true that a strong wind might have helped Mantle, but if the A. A. U. will not recognize the homer, all of baseball will.

Casey Stengel was telling before the game about the great young catching prospect the Yankees have at Kansas City. "Everyone there is raving about Elston Howard," Casey said. Howard is a Negro, who after having come out of the service last summer, played at Muskegon in the Michigan State League.

There is no connection with Stengel's mention of Howard and the fact that Berra, who fanned only a dozen times last season, already has struck out four times this year. Barring injury, it will be quite some time before anyone takes away Yogi's job.

The charley horse in Mantle's left leg did not seem to hamper the lad during batting practice. He put on an electrifying show, hitting against Whitey Ford. Bauer, too, and Jackie Jensen for the Senators smashed long drives into the bleachers.

The Box Score

NEW YORK (A.)	ab	r	h	po	a	WASHINGTON (A.)	ab	r	h	po	a
Martin, 2b	4	1	2	3	4	Yost, 3b	5	0	2	1	4
Rizzuto, ss	5	0	1	3	3	Busby, cf	4	0	1	4	1
Berra, c	4	1	1	2	2	Vernon, 1b	3	0	0	13	1
Mantle, cf	3	1	2	0	0	Jensen, rf	4	0	0	3	0
Bauer, rf	4	2	1	2	0	Runnels, ss	3	1	1	0	2
Woodling, lf	5	1	2	5	0	Wood, lf	4	0	1	2	0
Collins, 1b	4	0	1	11	1	Ter'liger, 2b	4	2	3	2	5
Carey, 3b	4	1	1	1	1	Peden, c	4	0	1	0	1
Lopat, p	4	0	1	0	4	Stobbs, p	1	0	0	2	1
Gorman, p	0	0	0	0	0	aHoderlein	1	0	1	0	0
						Moreno, p	0	0	0	0	0
						bVerble	1	0	0	0	0
Total	37	7	12	27	15	Total	34	3	10	27	15

aSingled for Stobbs in seventh.
bFlied out for Moreno in ninth.

New York ......0 0 1 1 2 0 0 3 0—7
Washington ......0 0 1 0 0 0 1 1 0—3

Errors—None. Runs batted in—Martin 2, Yost, Collins, Mantle 2, Hoderlein, Carey, Woodling, Terwilliger. Two-base hits—Bauer, Terwilliger, Woodling. Home run—Martin, Mantle. Stolen base—Mantle. Sacrifice—Stobbs. Double play—Lopat, Martin and Collins. Left on bases—New York 9, Washington 8. Bases on balls—Off Stobbs 4, Lopat 3, Moreno 2. Struck out—By Lopat 2, Stobbs 3. Hits—Off Lopat 10 in 8 innings, Stobbs 7 in 7, Gorman 0 in 1, Moreno 5 in 2. Runs and earned runs—Stobbs 4 and 4, Lopat 3 and 3, Moreno 3 and 3. Winning pitcher—Lopat (1—0). Losing pitcher—Stobbs (0—1). Umpires—Honochick, McGowan, Paparella and McKinley. Time of game—2:27. Attendance—4,206.

RUTH HIT HOMER 600 FEET

Detroit Scene of 1926 Blast—Exhibition Drive Went 587

Mickey Mantle's home run in Griffith Stadium yesterday failed by about thirty-five feet to match the homer Babe Ruth hit in Briggs Stadium at Detroit in 1926, according to The Associated Press.

Ruth's blow is considered the longest home run ever hit in a major league game. At the time, H. G. Salsinger, sports editor of The Detroit News, obtained an affidavit from several witnesses, who said the ball landed about 600 feet from home plate.

The Babe also is credited with a 587-footer in a 1919 exhibition game at Tampa, Fla., where Ken Silvestri, now with the Phillies, hit one 538 feet in 1941.

Until Mantle's blast yesterday, Ralph Kiner of the Pirates held second place in regular-season competition. He hit one about 560 feet against Cincinnati at Pittsburgh April 22, 1950.

Major League Baseball

Saturday, April 18, 1953

National League

YESTERDAY'S GAMES

New York 6, Brooklyn 3 (aft'noon).
Brooklyn 12, New York 4 (night)
Cincinnati 10, Milwaukee 9.
Philadelphia at Pittsburgh (night), rain.
Other clubs not scheduled.

STANDING OF THE CLUBS

	Brooklyn	Milwaukee	New York	Chicago	St. Louis	Cincinnati	Philadel.	Pittsb'gh	Won	Lost	Perc'tage	Games Behind
Bklyn..	—	0	1	0	0	0	0	2	3	1	.750	—
Milw...	0	—	0	0	1	1	0	0	2	1	.667	½
N. Y....	1	0	—	0	0	0	1	0	2	2	.500	1
Chic....	0	0	0	—	0	1	0	0	1	1	.500	1
St. L...	0	0	0	1	—	0	0	0	1	1	.500	1
Cinc....	0	1	0	0	0	—	0	0	1	2	.333	1½
Phila...	0	0	1	0	0	0	—	0	1	2	.333	1½
Pitts...	0	0	0	0	0	0	1	—	1	2	.333	1½
Lost....	1	1	2	1	1	2	2	2	—	—		

TODAY'S PROBABLE PITCHERS

Brooklyn at New York (1:30 P. M.)—Erskine (0-0) vs. Connelly (0-0).

Chicago at Cincinnati—Rush (1-0) vs. Wehmeier (0-0).

Milwaukee at St. Louis (night)—Antonelli (0-0) vs. Miller (0-0).

Philadelphia at Pittsburgh—Konstanty (0-0) vs. Friend (0-0).

American League

YESTERDAY'S GAMES

New York 7, Washington 3.
Detroit 6, Cleveland 5.
Philadelphia 5, Boston 0.
St. Louis 6, Chicago 4.

STANDING OF THE CLUBS

	New York	Cleveland	St. Louis	Philadel.	Boston	Chicago	Detroit	Wash'gtn	Won	Lost	Perc'tage	Games Behind
N. Y....	—	0	0	1	0	0	0	2	3	1	.750	—
Cleve...	0	—	0	0	0	1	1	0	2	1	.667	½
St. L...	0	0	—	0	0	1	1	0	2	1	.667	½
Phila...	1	0	0	—	1	0	0	0	2	2	.500	1
Bost....	0	0	0	1	—	0	0	0	1	1	.500	1
Chic....	0	0	1	0	0	—	0	0	1	2	.333	1½
Det.....	0	1	0	0	0	0	—	0	1	2	.333	1½
Wash....	0	0	0	0	0	0	0	—	0	2	.000	2
Lost....	1	1	1	2	1	2	2	2	—	—		

TODAY'S PROBABLE PITCHERS

New York at Philadelphia—Blackwell (0-0) vs. Scheib (0-0).

Boston at Washington (night)—Freeman (0-0) vs. Masterson (0-0).

Cleveland at Chicago—Wynn (0-0) vs. Byrne (0-0).

St. Louis at Detroit (2)—Pillette (0-0) and Holloman (0-0) vs. Hoeft (0-0) and Marlowe (0-0).

(Figures in parentheses indicate season's won-and-lost records.)

JERSEY CITY TEAM TAKES MILE RELAY

St. Michael's High Victor in Schoolboy Phase of 7th Seton Hall Competition

By MICHAEL STRAUSS

Special to THE NEW YORK TIMES.

NEWARK, April 17—Absent from the ranks of titleholders since 1948, New Jersey finally emerged with an eastern championship contingent this afternoon when St. Michael's High of Jersey City captured the mile relay at the seventh annual Seton Hall Relays at the Newark Schools Stadium. The triumph was the highlight of a schoolboy prelude to the big college competition tomorrow.

Sharing the honors with the New Jersey team today were two schools from New York City, Boys High and Haaren. Boys won the 880-yard relay while Haaren triumphed in the 440 by beating out New Utrecht, a rival from Brooklyn.

The victory of St. Michael's was scored over highly rated combinations from Mount St. Michael and from St. Augustine's, the national indoor champion. The Lancers from Brooklyn, though handicapped by the absence of Frank Kennedy, put up a strong showing and were in contention until the closing stages.

Maliff Is Anchor Man

The St. Michael's quartet was made up of Jack Heraut, Bill Shyne, Richard Wroblewski and Gene Maliff. Heraut found Bob Martin of St. Augustine's a worthy adversary as the race began and trailed at the completion of the first leg. But Shyne took the lead from Tierny O'Rourke of the Brooklyn team. On the third leg, the Mount's Tom Mackey took command and St. Augustine's colors were in third place. But on the final leg Maliff put on a great sprint and was five yards ahead of Bill Krebs at the finish. The time was 3:30.

Boys High, long a power in eastern schoolboy circles, took the half-mile event as expected, Roy Henry finishing with a fine burst. The time was 1:33.4. In the runner-up berth was Brooklyn Tech, followed by Bishop Loughlin and Ferris of Jersey City. Henry's teammates on the winning contingent were John Sylvester, Lowe Murray and Monzell Price.

New Utrecht and Haaren waged a keen struggle for the pace-setting role during most of the running of the 440, but the Manhattanites proved too strong. The margin at the finish was six yards, Donald Showell clinching the decision with a well-run anchor leg to complete the course in 0:44.2. Strung out behind the two leaders at the end were East New York Vocational and Abraham Lincoln of Brooklyn.

Three Records Are Set

Three new records were set in sectional competition over the mile route.

A Kearny quartet from the Hudson County division was clocked in 3:33.6; St. Cecilia of Englewood registered 3:34.7 in the New Jersey Catholic Schools competition and Tenafly posted 3:35.4 in capturing first place among Bergen County schools.

Adding to the length of the program were events for parochial, grammar and junior high school students. The youngsters went through their heats and finals in a businesslike manner and gave added support to the general feeling that New Jersey has become extremely track conscious. More than 100 schools were represented in today's competition.

The last New Jersey school to win an eastern relay title here was St. Peter's of Jersey City. The Hudson County team took the mile in 1948 with an effort of 3:33.2. Since then Loughlin, New Rochelle and Cardinal Hayes have been the champions.

THE SUMMARIES

EASTERN CHAMPIONSHIPS

440-Yard Relay—1, Haaren (Richard Habersham, Henry Burchett, George Waterman and Donald Showell); 2, New Utrecht; 3, East New York Vocational; 4, Abraham Lincoln. Time—0:44.2.

880-Yard Relay—1, Boys High (John Sylvester, Lowe Murray, Monzell Price and Roy Henry); 2, Brooklyn Technical; 3, Bishop Loughlin; 4, Ferris of Jersey City. Time—1:33.4.

One-Mile Relay—1, St. Michael's of Jersey City (Jack Heraut, William Shyne, Richard Wroblewski and Gene Maliff); 2, Mt. St. Michael; 3, St. Augustine's; 4, Boys High. Time—3:30.

SECTIONAL MILE EVENTS

Hudson County—1, Kearny (C. Rittman, W. Pfeifer, J. McLaren and J. Norton); 2, Bayonne; 3, Memorial of West New York; 4, Snyder of Jersey City. Time—3:33.6 (New record. Old record of 3:34 set by Kearny in 1952).

N. J. Catholic High Schools—1, St. Peter's of Jersey City (John Hanlon, Ted Riordan, George Bednar and Tom Costello); 2, Seton Hall; 3, St. Michael's of Jersey City; 4, St. Cecilia. Time—3:34.7 (New record. Old mark of 3:39.3 set by Seton Hall in 1951).

Central New Jersey—Trenton Central (Melvin Rose, Hy Bronner, Carl Cranmer and William McMillian); 2, Asbury Park; 3, Princeton; 4, Perth Amboy. Time—3:40.8.

Middlesex County—1, Perth Amboy (Cedric Richardson, Arthur Graham, Randolph Grant and Robert Holup); 2, New Brunswick; 3, Metuchen; 4, Highland Park. Time—3:41.

Shore Conference—1, Neptune (Don Harvey, Donald Eckart, Joseph Taylor and Michael Buchanan); 2, Long Branch; 3, Matawan; 4, Asbury Park. Time—3:45.9.

Bergen County—1, Tenafly (Hugh Cameron, Don Schive, William Davis and Arthur Mangels); 2, Englewood; 3, Lyndhurst; 4, St. Mary's of Rutherford. Time—3:35.4 (New record. Old Record of 3:37.2 set by Tenafly in 1951).

City of Newark—1, St. Benedict's (Wayne Letwink, Paul Longua, Ronald Buckingham and John Connolly); 2, West Side; 3, Weequahic; 4, East Side. Time—3:36.4.

Essex County—1, Montclair (Marvin Jones, Lowell Lockett, Peter Johnson and Aubrey Lewis); 2, Columbia; 3, Bloomfield; 4, Orange. Time—3:32.4.

Browns Sell Fannin

ST. LOUIS, April 17 (AP)—The Browns today sold Cliff Fannin, pitcher, to San Diego of the Pacific Coast League for an undisclosed amount. Fannin, who came to the Browns in 1945 from Toledo, is a 28-year-old right hander. He failed to win a game in 1952 while losing two.

Section 3 SPORTS NEWS WEATHER—MAIL ORDER

NEW YORK Herald Tribune

SPORTS NEWS STAMPS—BRIDGE Section 3

EIGHT PAGES v SUNDAY, JUNE 28, 1953 EIGHT PAGES

Yanks Drop 6th in Row; Giants Lose; Tom Fool Equals Record in Carter

Don Rice

Tom Fool gallops to two-length victory in $50,000 added Carter Handicap at Aqueduct yesterday.

VIEWS OF SPORT

By RED SMITH

Strictly Confidential

EARLIER this summer before Gil Hodges started to hit, the Dodgers received a six-page letter advising them not to trade Hodges, Billy Cox and Carl Furillo for Ralph Kiner. The fact that no such deal was contemplated may have helped the office staff to preserve a semblance of calm.

Red Smith

"Personally," the correspondent wrote, "I see young Cox with 3 minor faults to correct, Hodges if he can overcome just 1 big fault you will not be able to touch him on home runs, & Furillo has also 3 minor things to overcome and I believe he would be one of the most talked of baseball player of all times for all round work."

Some paragraphs later came an offer: "If you are interested I would take Young Hodges in Hand and in 10 days time, turn out a boy that Could hit most Anything, I will guarantee to give such delivery or no fee, so all you have to loose is 10 days time and I'm sure it would be worth it. Then you can have the other two boys go for their treatment and have three of the finest ballplayers on any diamond."

"There is only one condition," the letter warned. "That all this must be done without any ballyhoo or publicity, as my work is Strictly Confidential, as I have to protect my private clients to the utmost."

It was signed "Gaby."

Higher Education

WALTER O'MALLEY'S sweet tooth for culture has been throbbing ever since the postman brought this hand-lettered missive:

"Dear President of the Brooklyn Dodgers I am the teacher of a Class of 25 Children and I would like to have a past to come to see the Brooklyn Dodgers in action if you cane I would be grate ful of you. the Schol is a public School Queens."

A wit wrote: "For all the zeal of the average Bklyn fan—for all his loyalty—he is necessarily out of touch with one of the most necessary experiences in baseball. Necessary, that is, if he is to be a competent judge of what is required of a skillful batter. If he knew what big league pitching actually looked like he would appreciate the game and the players all the more.

"If a protective transparent shield could be devised and set up at home plate—removable, of course—and certain fans selected before game time to stand up at home plate with a bat, just to see a curve, a fast ball, a slider and the whole catalogue of pitches that batters face every day, their respect for batting averages and pitchers would surely increase. Their interest in the game and their understanding of the game would be greatly enlarged.

"If any fan should manage to hit the ball out of the infield you could give him or his heirs a box seat for life. Or, a place on the team."

War of the Sexes

A YOUNG lady inquired: "Why isn't there any girls who can be batboys and who take care of the baseball bats? Some people say girls are not strong enough for the job, I myself help my uncle carry beams up a ladder. The people also say that a player doesn't like to get undressed in front of a girl. I'll go along with that, but what if the girl got there earlier? She could get dressed and go tend to the bats and other such things.

"I'm sure if some one would show the girl who to do it and if the girl really liked to do that kind of work with her favorite ball club, the Brooklyn Dodgers, like I would, she would soon show the people she was determined to get the job.

"At the end of a game, while the players are taking their showers, she could put the bats away in the trunk or get them cleaned and ready for the next game. By then the players should be ready to go home. Then she could change and clean up the dressing room, clean the shoes, I'm sure the girls would do a neater job of cleaning up then the boys. They would put everything where the player would find it.

"It would also make baseball history, having the first batgirl to care for bats. Would it be possible to send me individual pictures of the Brooklyn Dodgers?"

Charlotte Dressen

WANT more? This is also from a young lady:

"I will be short and to the point. At present I am fifteen years of age, and at this time I would like to put my name on your file as a future prospect for the position of manager of the Brooklyn Dodgers. I would consider taking the position of assistant manager if you would insure advancement.

"I would appreciate it very much if you would send me an application blank. Please be assured that in the event you consider me for the position, I would be able to furnish excellent references as to educational background, experience and ability.

"Enclose, please find a recent photograph of myself which I hope will meet with your approval."

Ruhe Wins Arlington Race

CHICAGO, June 27 (AP).—Hasty House Farm's Ruhe blunted Hill Gail's 1953 comeback with a driving upset victory today in the $50,000-added Equipoise Mile at Arlington Park.

Ruhe hung back through the early stages but raced up on the outside in the home stretch for a head decision over Sub Fleet, who had taken the lead from Hill Gail, the 1952 Kentucky Derby winner, at the final turn.

Hill Gail finished third, a length back.

The winner, who with stablemate Oil Capital was priced at 6 to 1, paid $15, $5 and $2.60. Sub Fleet paid $9.40 and $4, and Hill Gail $2.40.

The time was 1:35⅖, a full second off the track record set twenty-one years ago by Cornelius V. Whitney's great Equipoise, whose name the race bears.

Colt Does 1:22 Under 135 Pounds

By Bill Lauder jr.

Tom Fool ran 'em down yesterday and beat the daylights out of them. The big Greentree Stable colt, with Ted Atkinson just waving the whip by his head the last furlong, took the long way home around horses on the turn and made them all look like statues in the stretch as he became the first ever to win the Carter Handicap under the back-breaking weight of 135 pounds. And he equaled the track record of 1:22 in doing the job.

The crowd of 30,206 at Aqueduct made Tom Fool the favorite and at the finish he had a margin of two lengths on Mrs. Jan Burke's Squared Away, with Mrs. Al Roberts' Eatontown another two and a half lengths away in third spot. Tom Fool paid $3.30 and picked up a net purse of $41,700 to run his earnings to $436,690—fifteenth on the list of all-time money winners.

Bought for $25,000

The colt was purchased by Greentree as a yearling at private terms, estimated at about $25,000. Despite being ill and missing the classic spring three-year-old races last year, Tom Fool now has run twenty-five times, has won sixteen (eleven of them stakes), been second seven times, third once and out of the money only once.

It was the fifty-third running of the Carter and the only colt ever to get in the money with 135 pounds was Roseben, the 1906 winner, who was given 135 pounds in 1907 and ran second to Glorifier. Two had won previously under 132 pounds—Naturalist in 1919 and Osmand in 1929.

Tom Fool broke alertly as they started the seven-furlong jaunt, but Atkinson let him take it easy down the far side as Squared Away went out for the lead, with Harborvale Stable's Dark Peter, F. A. Clark's Tea-Maker and Eatontown forcing the pace. Tom Fool was fifth and they went into the far turn strung out in this order. And Squared Away was really running. He was clocked the half mile in 0:44 3-5 and after six furlongs, one furlong from the finish, he stopped the watches in 1:09 2-5, just one second faster than the track record for that distance.

Atkinson began to move with Tom Fool as they started around the tight turn. He kept the colt

Continued on page 6, column 5

Jack Frank

Hank Bauer (9) reaching into rightfield stands in vain effort to catch home-run ball hit by Luke Easter, Indians' first baseman, for first Cleveland run in fifth inning. The Indians won, 5 to 0, to hand the Yankees their sixth straight defeat.

44,570 See Tribe Win Again, 5-0

By Rud Rennie

Before a ladies' day crowd of 44,570 persons in the Stadium yesterday afternoon, the world champion league-leading Yankees went to their sixth consecutive defeat and had their lead reduced to seven games. In falling into their longest losing streak since the Yankees of 1945 lost nine in a row, the champions did not even score.

Mike Garcia, a husky righthander, shut them out even though they hit him safely in every inning except the seventh for a total of nine singles, and the Cleveland Indians won again, this time 5 to 0.

Only one other pitcher had blanked the Yanks this year, and that one, Alex Kellner, a left-hander, did it twice in succession. Garcia was the first righthander to turn the trick. It was his ninth victory of the year and his first of the season over the champions. They had beaten him twice.

Ed Lopat, the Yankees senior southpaw, who had not lost a game since July 2, 1952, was the loser. He had won thirteen games in a row, nine this year.

Scoreless for Four Frames

He and Garcia were in a scoreless contest for four innings. The Indians made one hit off Lopat in the fourth, while the Yankees were pecking away at Garcia, making one in every inning.

With one swipe, Big Luke Easter broke the scoreless tie in the fifth. He led off and hoisted his first home run of the season into the rightfield stands, just out of Hank Bauer's leaping reach.

That started it. The Indians scored another run in the sixth and another in the seventh and two in the eighth, all off Lopat. Ray Scarborough finished for him, pitching the ninth.

The Indians made seven hits off Lopat and none off Scarborough. But some of the Cleveland hits fell into place at the right time to promote scoring, and a Yankee error made possible one of the runs.

The Indians got their run in the sixth when Jim Hegan singled and moved to third on a sacrifice by Garcia and an infield out by Dale Mitchell. And he scored with two out when Bob Avila lifted a fly to short left centerfield where Willie Miranda went for it but could not catch it. The ball slid off the tip of his glove.

McDougald Errs

Gil McDougald made a low throw with Easter's grounder in the seventh and his error let the Indians go on and score again. Larry Doby singled and Bob Kennedy walked. The bases were loaded when George Strickland hit into a double play on which Bill Glynn, who was running for Easter, scored.

Garcia opened the seventh with a single and Mitchell tripled and Avila hit a scoring

Continued on page 2, column 1

Dane Upsets Mulloy at Wimbledon

WIMBLEDON, England, June 27 (AP)—Old age and fast tennis overtook Gardnar Mulloy, thirty-nine-year-old physical phenomenon from Coral Gables, Fla., today in the fourth round of the Wimbledon championships.

Frisky Kurt Nielsen, twenty-three-year-old, happy-go-lucky from Copenhagen, whipped the veteran Florida lawyer, 10—8, 6—3, 7—5.

Nielsen played the kind of fast, ground covering tennis that made Mulloy's years weigh heavy. The final point was a clean service ace which Mulloy could not reach in the boiling sunshine.

But even with Mulloy's unexpected defeat, Uncle Sam sent two of his nephews and five of his nieces into the singles quarter-finals, which will be contested Monday. Sunday is an off day because of British blue laws.

Seixas Ousts Worthington

Vic Seixas, of Philadelphia, seeded second behind Australia's young Ken Rosewall, gave an impressive performance in ousting George Worthington, Australian-turned New Zealander, 10—8, 7—5, 6—3. The other United States survivor, lefty Art Larsen, of San Delandro, Calif., advanced yesterday.

Maureen (Little Mo) Connolly, the defending champion, led a party of five Americans into the round of eight in the women's singles division, winning

Continued on page 4, column 1

Coast 'Cap Won By Rejected

INGLEWOOD, Calif., June 27 (AP).—Rejected, a Texas colt, bridged the distance from rags to riches today when he captured the $100,00 Westerner over ten rival three-year-olds at Hollywood Park.

The King Ranch colt, a brown youngster who ran—and won his first race—in an $8,000 claiming race at Tanforan racetrack last May 4, whipped the field at a mile and one quarter and collected $64,500 out of a gross purse of $110,200 for his multi-millionaire owner.

The time was 2.01 2/5 and the winner returned $5.40, $3.60 and $2.90 across the board.

C. C. N. Y. Hurler On All-America

Warren Neuberger, C. C. N. Y.'s fine righthanded pitcher, is one of the two hurlers named to the 1953 All-America college baseball team.

The selection was announced yesterday by the American Association of College Baseball Coaches at East Lansing, Mich.

Neuberger, who was an all-Metropolitan choice, has been signed by the Detroit Tigers.

Miss Rawls, Mrs. Pung Tie in Golf

ROCHESTER, N. Y., June 27 (AP).—Betsy Rawls, a Texan who represents Spartanburg, S. C., in professional golf, and Mrs. Jackie Pung, a 210-pound Hawaiian, w ohregisters from Glasgow, Ky., will clash tomorrow in an eighteen-hole play-off for the United States women's open golf championship.

In a tension-packed finish, they tied at the end of the regulation seventy-two holes with scores of 302, beating out Chicago's Patty Berg, the veteran pro to whom almost every one had conceded the title after only thirty-six holes.

While Miss Berg frittered away a eight-stroke lead, the long-driving Mrs. Pung and steady

Continued on page 2, column 4

Hacker Beats Jansen

Jeffcoat's Homer Gives Cubs Victory by 2 to 1

By Ed Sinclair

CHICAGO, June 27.—Some ridiculous base-running in defiance of Hal Jeffcoat's arm, plus the same Cub outfielder's home run and the six-hit pitching of Warren Hacker and Dutch Leonard, amounted to a 2-to-1 Giant defeat today before 14,975 fans at Wrigley Field. The Bruin victory accomplished four things; it ended Chicago's four-game losing streak and New York's three-game winning streak; it brought Hacker, the artful righthander, his fourth triumph of the campaign and it sent the equally artful Larry Jansen to his sixth defeat.

Hacker's service had the Giants dumbfounded until the ninth when Daryl Spencer walked with two out, Bob Thomson singled off the glove of Ransom Jackson and Bob Hofman's pinch single into left spoiled the shutout. With that, Leonard came on and his one pitch to Davey Williams resulted in a game-ending foul to Dee Fondy behind first base.

Jansen Gives 7 Hits

That one run could have been the difference in the seven-hitter pitched by Jansen over seven innings and preserved by Al Corwin through the eighth, had not Monte Irvin and Henry Thompson tested Jeffcoat's arm earlier.

In the second inning Irvin led off and was safe on an error by Eddie Miksis. Spencer singled to left, moving Irvin to second, and Thomson followed with a fly ball to centerfield. Irvin, whose legs are not the same since his ankle fracture a year ago, attempted to reach third after the catch and was thrown out.

The double play squelched that threat and the Cubs proceeded to take both of their runs from Jansen in the third. Jeffcoat led off with his homer into the left-centerfield bleachers. Hacker and Frankie Baumholtz singled in succession and George Metkovich sacrificed. Bill Serena's long flyball to rightfield got Hacker home with the second run.

Thompson Out at Plate

Hacker, who rarely gets two runs from his teammates, became vulnerable in the fourth when Thompson walked with one away. Irvin then slashed a double against the centerfield wall and Herman Franks made no attempt to hold Thompson at third base.

As Thompson rounded the bag and headed for home, Miksis had taken Jeffcoat's throw behind second base and his relay to the plate caught Thompson by twenty feet. The ensuing fly ball to deep center by Spencer, which would have scored a runner from third, only retired the side.

After that, there wasn't much hope for the Giants, despite the fact that the Cubs made two more errors. And when the New Yorkers finally got around to threatening Hacker for the last

Continued on page 2, column 4

Davis Sets World Jump Mark, 6:11½

By Jesse Abramson

DAYTON, Ohio, June 27.—Ten minutes after Wes Santee romped off with the American mile championship with a mere 4:07.6 that failed to thrill a crowd of 7,500, towering Walt Davis, a Texas oilman, leaped 6 feet 11½ inches for a world high jump record under a blazing sun today.

It was the only world record produced by the cream of America's track and field crop as the two-day meet, deciding twenty-one National A. A. U. championships, concluded in Dayton High School Stadium.

But in five other events today's winners shattered long-standing championship records as the A. A. U. went back to the yardage standard after twenty-one years of that noble experiment—the metric system. They broke records in the mile, 120-yard high hurdles, 220-yard dash, two-mile steeplechase, three-mile run and discus throw. Including last night's opening session, meet records were

Continued on page 4, column 3

Late Baseball

National League

B'klyn. . 0
Milwauk 0

Labine and Campanella; Wilson and Crandall.

(Second Game)

Philadel 1 1 0 0
St. L. . . 1 0 3

R. Miller and Lopata; Haddix and Rice.

American League

Detroit. 1 3 1 0 0 0
Wash. . 0 0 2 0 0 0

Aber and Batts; Shea and FitzGerald.

Major League Standings—Schedules

Sunday, June 28, 1953

NATIONAL LEAGUE RESULTS YESTERDAY

Chicago, 2; New York, 1
*Brooklyn at Milwaukee (night)
Cincinnati, 15; Pittsburgh, 5
St. Louis, 7; Philadelphia, 4 (1st)
*Philadelphia at St. Louis (2d, night)

STANDING OF THE CLUBS	Milw'kee	B'klyn	St. Louis	Phila.	N. York	Cincinn.	Pittsb'h	Chicago	WON	LOST	Percent.	Games Behind
Milwaukee	—	3	3	8	8	6	6	7	41	24	.631	—
Brooklyn	5	—	4	5	5	8	8	5	40	25	.615	1
St. Louis	3	5	—	5	6	7	9	4	39	26	.600	2
Phila.	2	4	4	—	3	5	6	11	35	26	.574	4
New York	4	4	5	1	—	7	6	6	33	32	.508	8
Cincinnati	2	5	4	4	3	—	7	2	27	37	.422	13½
Pittsburgh	5	0	3	3	4	2	—	7	24	48	.333	20½
Chicago	3	4	3	0	3	2	6	—	21	42	.333	19

*Not included in standings.

National League Schedule and Probable Pitchers

New York at Chicago (12:30 p. m., E. D. T.) Hearn (5-4) vs. Klippstein (4-5).

Brooklyn at Milwaukee (3:30 p. m., E. D. T.) —Meyer (5-3) vs. Spahn (8-2).

Pittsburgh at Cincinnati (2)—Bowman (0-2) and Hall (3-3) vs. Baczewski (1-0) and Raffensberger (2-7).

Philadelphia at St. Louis—Drews (5-5) vs. Mizell (7-3).

AMERICAN LEAGUE RESULTS YESTERDAY

Cleveland, 5; New York, 0
Chicago, 6; Boston, 5
St. Louis, 6; Philadelphia, 1
*Detroit at Washington (night)

STANDING OF THE CLUBS	N. York	Cleve.	Chicago	Boston	Wash.	Phila.	St. Louis	Detroit	WON	LOST	Percent.	Games Behind
New York	—	7	4	7	7	4	9	8	46	19	.708	—
Cleveland	2	—	3	4	7	9	7	7	39	26	.600	7
Chicago	7	3	—	7	5	4	7	7	40	28	.588	7½
Boston	2	7	3	—	3	4	10	8	37	33	.529	11½
Wash'ton	2	4	5	5	—	7	6	3	32	35	.478	15
Phila.	2	2	7	5	3	—	6	6	31	37	.456	16½
St. Louis	1	2	3	2	6	4	—	7	25	45	.357	23½
Detroit	3	1	3	3	4	5	0	—	19	46	.292	27

*Not included in standings.

American League Schedule and Probable Pitchers

Cleveland at New York (2:05 p. m., E. D. T.)—Wynn (6-5) vs. Ford (8-1).

Detroit at Washington (2)—Hoeft (5-4) and Gromek (2-1) vs. Marrero (5-3) and Masterson (5-7).

St. Louis at Philadelphia (2)—Larsen (1-5) and Blyzka (2-4) vs. Byrd (8-7) and Scheib (2-5).

Chicago at Boston—Trucks (6-4) vs. Nixon (4-1).

Paced Race

Bannister's 4:02 Mile 3d Fastest on Record

LONDON, June 27 (AP).—Roger Bannister today ran a 4:02 mile—the third fastest on record and only two seconds short of the legendary four-minute mile.

The twenty-four-year-old medical student was clocked in a paced race at Motspur Park.

His time was the fastest ever for a British Empire runner and was only six-tenths of a second off the world record of 4:01.4, set by Gundar Haegg in Sweden in 1945.

Bannister made his unheralded attempt with Don McMillan, of Australia, and Chris Brasher, of Britain.

Bannister's time was the fastest in the world this year. It was exceeded only by Haegg's world mark and Arne Andersson's one-time world record of 4:01.6.

The good-looking Bannister, who finished fifth in the Olympic 1,500-meter race last year, wanted to get his shot at the four-minute mile before Wes Santee, of Kansas, went after it later today at Dayton, Ohio. Santee already has done the distance this year in 4:02.4.

There was no advance notice Bannister would set out on this record attempt. The meet where he ran was a Surrey schoolboys' track and field gathering with about 200 youngsters in attendance.

Section 3 SPORTS NEWS BRIDGE—MARINE

NEW YORK Herald Tribune

SPORTS NEWS WEATHER—MAIL ORDER Section 3

EIGHT PAGES SUNDAY, JULY 5, 1953 EIGHT PAGES

Yanks Win 2; Dodgers, Giants Split; Native Dancer, 1-20, Victor in Dwyer

Associated Press radiophoto from London

Maureen Connolly makes a fancy return during her victorious match with Doris Hart in final of women's singles at Wimbledon yesterday. Miss Connolly won the match, 8—6, 7—5, and her second straight title.

Keeps Wimbledon Title

Miss Connolly Defeats Miss Hart, 8-6 and 7-5

WIMBLETON, England, July 4 (AP).—Maureen Connolly, California's saucy little queen of tennis, won a battle of baseline sharpshooting today from her tradition foe., Doris Hart, to take her second straight Wimbleton singles championship.

Maureen did the job in straight sets, 8—6, 7—5, but the championship didn't come easy. Her Coral Gables, Fla., opponent, senior in experience by about ten seasons, scrapped for every point and placement and got in some beauties of her own.

The victory—on the Fourth of July with 16,000 Britons looking on—was the tenth straight won by an American girl. The last native to take this championship, which practically every player calls "the world's championship," was Dorothy Round in 1937.

Americans in Sweep

The Independence Day motif got started yesterday when Philadelphia's Vic Seixas whipped Denmark's Kurt Nielsen in straight sets for the men's championship.

Except for the men's doubles title which went to the eighteen-year-old Australians, Lewis Hoad and Ken Rosewall, Americans swept everything in sight.

Miss Hart, the world's foremost feminine doubles player, shared in both the women's and mixed doubles championships.

In the doubles she gained a measure of revenge when she and long-time companion Shirley Fry, of Akron, Ohio, trounced Miss Connolly and Julie Sampson, of Pasadena, Calif., 6—0, 6—0. The victory required only 25 minutes. The Hart-Fry team yielded only nine points in the first set and eleven in the second in one of the most one-sided finals ever seen at Wimbleton.

Then the willowy Floridian teamed with Seixas to beat Miss Fry and Argentina's Enrique Morea in the mixed doubles, 9—7, 7—5.

The doubles victory was the third straight at Wimbledon for the Hart-Fry combination. The

Continued on page 5, column 4

Campbell Wins A.A.U. Decathlon

By Jesse Abramson

PLAINFIELD, N. J., July 4.—Before 6,000 of his enthusiastic townsfolk, Local Hero Milton Campbell today won his first National A. A. U. decathlon championship in his third try at the grueling ten-event test of skill, stamina, speed and strength.

On the high school field where he developed his remarkable athletic ability and his chassis of 6-foot 3-inches and 220 pounds, the nineteen-year-old schoolboy giant compiled 7,235 points with a two-day performance that placed him No. 4 in the all-time list of the world's best decathlon men.

The local boy, who made good as the National A. A. U. and Olympic runner-up to the unbeaten Bob Mathias last summer, ran away from all pursuit by a margin of 779 points. Runner-up was the Rev. Bob Richards, the 1951 National decathlon champion, now pastor of the First Brethren Church of Long Beach, Calif., with 6,456 points, the worst score the vaulting vicar had ever made in his half dozen decathlon competitions. It was the first decathlon defeat Richards ever suffered. He never competed against Mathias.

Third was Jim Cooke, of Peekskill, N. Y., a soldier representing

Continued on page 4, column 3

Earns $84,600

Grecian Queen Wins Rich Delaware Race

By Ed Sinclair

WILMINGTON, Del., July 4.—Ben F. Whitaker's Grecian Queen and Ted Atkinson closed out Delaware Park's most successful racing season on this Independence Day with a length victory in the $100,000 added New Castle Handicap, the richest race in the world for fillies and mares.

Before a holiday crowd of 30,770, the three-year-old dark bay filly zipped to the front on the far turn and held off Mrs. John W. Hanes' Devilkin and Bennie Green in the stretch to win $84,600 and increase her lifetime earnings to $259,025.

A 3-to-2 favorite in the betting, the leading money winner of her sex this year returned $5 for $2 and covered the mile and a quarter in 2:02 4/5, just one-fith of a second o f the stake record established by Kiss Me Kate last year, under 114 pounds.

Third to Devilkin, who came up from fifth place in the final stages, was Constance Morabito's My Celeste, a length and a half back, and Martin G. Doherty's Grandma Josie was fourth by a neck. The largest one-race pool in Delaware's history, $303,149, was wagered on the sixteenth running of the track's final program feature.

Leading by a neck, the first time past the grandstand, Grecian Queen fell behind Meyer J. Kaplan's Sunshine Nell around the first turn and contented herself to run in second place down the backstretch. On the far turn, the daughter of Heliopolis responded to Atkinson's encouragement, caught Sunshine Nell, who finished fifth, and won driving.

Atkinson said later that "she

Continued on page 6, column 5

35,865 See Colt Win by 1¾ Lengths

By Bill Lauder Jr.

Native Dancer, the big gray champion of the three-year-olds, added the thirty-sixth running of the Dwyer to his collection yesterday at Aqueduct without undue effort. Sent away at 1 to 20 by the crowd of 35,865, A. G. Vanderbilt's colt won the mile-and-a-quarter race by a length and three-quarters without once tasting the sting of the whip which Eric Guerin carried.

After taking the lead on the turn into the stretch The Dancer just held his field safe. The only real run made at him in the final furlong was by George Auerbach's Dictar, which finished second, but Dictar was disqualified from second place—which would have been worth $10,000 to his owner—for causing interference. He came in on the rail and apparently bothered Mrs. Widener Wichfeld's Guardian II, which finished third, two additional lengths away, but was moved up to second money. Third money then went to the fourth finisher, Mrs. Edward Lasker's By Zeuz, the early pacemaker.

Powhatan Scratched

Native Dancer paid $2.10—the legal minimum in New York—and the disqualification of Dictar had not effect on the betters as there was only win betting on the race. The Dancer turned the route in a comfortable 2:05 1-5 and now is getting richer and richer. But he cost the association $3,332 for a minus pool.

Teh five-horse field—Greentree Stable's Powhatan was a late scratch—made for a gross purse of $56,200 and Native Dancer's share was $38,100. So, having won fifteen of sixteen races, he now has earned $560,845 and passed Oil Capitol, Ponder and On Trust to be sixth on the list of all-time money winners, only $316 back of fifth-place Whirlaway.

It was a race of firsts for Native Dancer. It was the first time he'd been asked to give weight to his rivals—he toted 126 to 114 pounds for each of the other four—it was his first time over the Aqueduct track and it was the first time his owner, who now is in France, missed seeing him run.

The crowd didn't like not being able to bet on any of the Dancer's rivals or The Dancer himself for either second or third but they poured it in on him to win. Of the total pool of $170,674 the sum of $141,338 was wagered on the big grey.

The Dancer Moves

At the break all got away without trouble and as they came down past the stands the first time By Zeus was in the lead with James Cox Brady's Landlocked second and Native Dancer third on the outside. Guardian II was right with them and as they went into the first turn Guerin took back a bit to fourth so that he could get The Dancer on the outside and clear of trouble.

Down the backstretch Native Dancer was about five lengths off the pace as Pete Anderson took By Zeus out front, but the big colt moved to third at the five-and-a-half furlong pole

Continued on page 6, column 3

Jack Frank

Yogi Berra, Yankee catcher, lunges with perfect tag on Carmen Mauro, Athletic outfielder, who attempted to score from second on Alex Kellner's single in fifth inning of first game. The Yankees won, 6-3.

Bucs Lose To Dodgers, 6-5; Win, 5-2

By Leonard Koppett

Acting unfriendly to the Dodgers for the first time in his career, Bob Friend spoiled what could have been a perfect day for Brooklyn yesterday by pitching the Pirates to a 5-to-2 victory in the second game of the holiday double-header which attracted 30,029 customers, biggest crowd of the season at Ebbets Field.

The Dodgers took the opener, 6 to 5, and until the Pirates broke a 2-to-2 tie with a three-run eighth inning, seemed a good bet to sweep the one-day series. After all, the first game was Brooklyn's ninth victory in nine tries against Pittsburgh this year, and Friend started the second game with a career record against the Dodgers that read: ten starts, no complete games, no victories, eight defeats.

However,. the twenty-two-year-old righthander, a Purdue student, took care of all those .000 compilations with one strong performance. He allowed seven hits, fanned six, and issued each of his four walks with two out. His season won-lost record is now only 3-8, but he produced a brand of pitching the Dodgers weren't able to match even in victory.

And because it couldn't, Brooklyn finished the day still in first place on momentous July 4 night, but not by as large a margin as last year's three games, nor as large as seemed likely around the middle of the second game. At this point

Continued on page 2, column 6

Two Aces Made On Same Hole

LARCHMONT, N. Y., July 4.—William R. Kuntz and Joe Di Buono both registered holes-in-one yesterday on the same hole at the Bonnie Briar Country Club in Larchmont. Kuntz scored his with a four-iron and Di Buono with a three-iron on the third hole, a 175-yard uphill drive.

Redlegs Beat Braves in 2, 5-1 and 3-1

MILWAUKEE, July 4 (AP).—A pair of veteran Cincinnati southpaws stymied Milwaukee in both ends of a double-header today, 5 to 1, and 3 to 1, to shove the skidding Braves two full games behind league leading Brooklyn.

The losses, Milwaukee's tenth and eleventh in their last fourteen games at home, left the club only one and a half games ahead of third-place St. Louis which moves in tomorrow for another double-header.

Kenny Raffensberger se the Braves down with six hits in the second game after Harry Perkowski had limited them to seven in the opener. The Braves previously had lost only twice all season to southpaws.

The Redlegs' one-two punch of Gus Bell and Ted Kluszewski took care of Cincinnati's first two runs in the nightcap, Bell doubling and scoring on Kluszewski's line single in both the first and eighth innings. The

Continued on page 2, column 1

Harmon, Nary, Douglas, Burkemo Win in P.G.A.

By Al Laney

BIRMINGHAM, Mich., July 4.—Claude Harmon, the Winged Foot man, kept the metropolitan district's hopes alive in the National Professional Golfers ssAeciation championship today by defeating Ed Furgol, of St. Louis, 5 and 3, after being one down at the halfway mark of their thirty-six-hole match and after Pete Cooper, his neighbor from Century, had been beaten in the third round, 3 and 2, by Walter Burkemo, local pro.

Harmon, twice a semi-finalist in this tournament, entered the quarter-final round for the fourth time by his victory, which was one of a number of fine ones, two of them decided only after extra holes, as the field, devoid now of "name" players, was cut from sixteen to eight.

Harmon's opponent tomorrow wil lbe Bill Nary, Kansas City home pro who was, as they say, as hot as a Fourth of July firecracker today in defeating Jim Browning, of Newton, Mass., by 6 and 5, after a morning round in 65 strokes, six under the course par.

Douglas Extended Again

Dave Douglas, one of only two touring pros left in the running, had to go an extra hole in this third successive match, for a P. G. A. record, to defeat Jackson Bradley, of Chicago, one up at the thirty-seventh.

He will now play Burkemo, finalist two years ago, and a dangerous man rated off his fine recovery to beat Cooper today.

In the lower half of the draw, the two top winners were Felice Torza, of St. Charles, Ill., who defeated Wally Ulrich, of Austin, Minn., one up, at the thirty-eighth after two extra holes and Jimmy Clark, the other touring pro, who played very well to dispose of Henry Williams, of Reading, Pa., 4 and 3. These two are playing in their first P. G. A. tournament. Henry Ransom, the oldest man left in, had a desperate match with Al Smith, of Danville, Va., which the veteran won, one up, with a ten-foot putt for a half on the thirty-sixth green after conceding a putt for a birdie 4.

Ransom's opponent will be Jack Isaacs, Langley Field Air Base pro, who defeated Lebron Harris, Oklahoma A. & M. golf coach, 4 and 3.

Weather Is Perfect

It will be seen from these scores that the golf in the competition in the P. G. A. tournament has lost nothing because of yesterday's orgy of sensations in which all the big names of golf were beaten and departed the scene. Indeed, those occurrances, regarded at the time as catastrophies by the sponors, may even have made it a better tournament.

At any rate the people who pay to see the play did not seem to think that all had been lost. The crowds today were large although certainly somewhat less than the 15,000 "oficially estimated." But there were plenty of people on the course and they had plenty to see. Even the weather co-operated to make it a big day. If the weather at Birmingham took its time about relenting it made a thorough job of it and we have now had two perfect days for playing and watching golf. Play began this morning with cloudless skies, cooling breezes and a course now

Continued on page 3, column 3

Giants Win Opener, 4-2, Lose 2d, 10-4

By Harold Rosenthal

PHILADELPHIA, July 4.—The Giants settled for a split today in their holiday double-header with the Phillies before 23,664 in Connie Mack Stadium. They won the first, 4 to 2, beating Curt Simmons for the first time in three years, and lost the second, 10 to 4, on the unfortunate choice of Larry Jansen for a relief role when the score was tied 3 to 3 in the fourth.

Jansan, who had given up four runs on a brace of homers in the one inning he had worked the day previously, came on after Jim Hearn had loaded the bases with none out. After running the count to three and one on Willie Jones, the Phillies' third baseman, Jansen, served up one which Jones cracked just inside the third base line for a bases-clearing triple. That was the big hit in the game, bigger than Granny Hamner's two-run homer in the first off Hearn, or the sole round-tripper Stan Lopata laced off Hearn in the second.

Hearn, at that, outlasted the Phillies' second-game starter, Karl Drews. The big right-

Continued on page 2, column 5

A's Beaten, 6-3, 4-0, by Bombers

By Roger Kahn

The Yankees, struggling through a depression a few days back, swept a double-header from the Athletics, 6 to 3 and 4 to 0, yesterday, checked the date, the American League standing and discovered that Casey Stengel had never had it so good.

The sweep delighted 33,314 Stadium customers and also stretched the Yankee winning streak to four. It also produced a six-and-a-half-game edge over the second-place White Sox.

Since Stengel launched his all-conquering reign in the Bronx four years ago, the Bombers twice led the league on July 4 and twice were second. Never was their lead more than the four-and-a-half lengths New York enjoyed over the Athletics in 1949, although, of course, Stengel's teams always have held commanding margins in October.

No Support for Kellner

In the opener, Alex Kellner pitched what would have been a shutout if his infield had stopped treating ground balls like cobras.

In the second game, Harry Byrd brought a no-hitter into the sixth inning, when Jim McDonald, his opposing pitcher, singled. The Yankees scored twice before the frame had ended and after that the Athletics went quietly.

McDonald's shutout, his first winning complete game in two seasons with the Yankees, was a five-hitter that looked easy. All the hits were singles, only in the eighth did two come in the same inning and only twice did an Athletic get as far as second. The A's have scored only ten runs in their last eight games, however, so it might be wise to view McDonald's effort in perspective.

Jim set the Bombers straight in more ways than one. Byrd, strong and fast, overpowered the Yankee line-up until McDonald led off the sixth with a sharp poke through the left side. Gil McDougald sacrificed, Irv Noren walked and Byrd hit Bauer, loading the bases. They stayed loaded while Yogi Berra popped out but Don Bollweg lined a two-run single to center.

Two Triples in 8th

The Bombers scored their other two in the eighth when McDougald and Bollweg drove triples in the vicinity of Gus (The Comet) Zernial, a left-fielder who is in considerable peril whenever he lays aside his bat and dons a glove.

In the first game, Zernial was safe because he had no chances. Kellner was ruined by the Athletics' gloves.

Ed Lopat started for the Yankees but left when the A's scored three in the sixth, and Tom Gorman who worked three shutout innings, was the winner. Kellner was the loser, in every sense of the word. Alex assaulted the Bombers with a mysterious assortment of slow curves. The Bombers assaulted the A's with a mysterious assortment of grounders. Both the Yankee hitters and the Athletic infielders were consistently fooled.

With one ou tin the first inning, Kellern walked Bollweg and Bauer—the only passes he allowed. Berra popped out and

Continued on page 2, column 8.

Major League Standings—Schedules

Sunday, July 5, 1953

NATIONAL LEAGUE RESULTS YESTERDAY

Brooklyn, 6; Pittcburgh, 5 (1st)
Pittsburgh, 5; Brooklyn, 2 (2d)
New York, 4; Philadelphia, 2 (1st)
Philadelphia, 10; New York, 4 (2d)
Cincinnati, 5; Milwaukee, 1 (1st)
Cincinnati, 3; Milwaukee, 1 (2d)
St. Louis, 7; Chicago, 3 (1st)
Chicago, 5; St. Louis, 4 (2d)

STANDING OF THE CLUBS	B'klyn	Milw'kee	St. Louis	Phila.	N. York	Cincinn.	Chicago	Pittsb'h	WON	LOST	Percent.	Games Behind
Brooklyn	—	7	4	7	5	8	5	9	45	27	.625	—
Milwaukee	3	—	3	8	8	9	7	6	44	30	.595	2
St. Louis	5	3	—	6	6	7	6	9	42	31	.575	3½
Philad'phia	5	2	5	—	5	5	11	6	39	30	.565	4½
New York	4	4	5	2	—	7	7	6	35	36	.493	9½
Cincinnati	5	6	4	4	3	—	2	9	33	40	.452	12½
Chicago	4	3	7	0	3	2	—	6	25	45	.357	19
Pittsburgh	1	5	3	3	6	2	7	—	27	51	.346	21

National League Schedule and Probable Pitchers

Brooklyn at New York (2 p. m., E. D. T.)—Labine (3-1) vs. Maglie (5-4).

Philadelphia at Pittsburgh (2)—Roberts (12-6) and Miller (0-2) vs. Dickson (7-8) and Waugh (0-0).

St. Louis at Milwaukee (2)—Staley (12-2) and Miller (2-4) vs. Spahn (9-3) and Surkont (9-12).

Cincinnati at Chicago (2)—Collum (2-3) and King (1-3) or Wehmeier (1-5) vs. Pollet (3-3) and Church (4-4)

AMERICAN LEAGUE RESULTS YESTERDAY

New York, 6; Philadelphia, 3 (1st)
New York, 4; Philadelphia, 0 (2d)
Cleveland, 4, Detroit, 1 (1st)
Detroit, 6; Cleveland, 1 (2d)
Boston, 7; Washington, 2 (1st)
Washington, 8; Boston, 4 (2d)
Chicago, 13; St. Louis, 0 (1st)
Chicago, 4; St. Louis, 2 (2d)

STANDING OF THE CLUBS	N. York	Chicago	Cleve.	Boston	Wash.	Phila.	St. Louis	Detroit	WON	LOST	Percent.	Games Behind
New York	—	4	7	8	7	7	9	8	50	22	.694	—
Chicago	7	—	3	8	5	4	10	7	44	29	.603	6½
Cleveland	3	3	—	4	7	9	7	10	43	29	.597	7
Boston	4	3	7	—	4	4	10	8	40	37	.519	12½
Wash'gton	2	5	4	7	—	9	6	5	38	37	.507	13½
Philad'hia	2	7	2	5	3	—	7	6	32	43	.427	19½
St. Louis	1	4	2	2	6	5	—	7	27	49	.355	25
Detroit	3	3	4	3	5	5	0	—	23	51	.311	28

American League Schedule and Probable Pitchers

New York at Washington (2, 1:30 p. m., E. D. T.)—Kuzava (2-1) and Reynolds (6-4) vs. Porterfield (9-7) and Lane (0-0).

Boston at Philadelphia—Parnell (10-4) vs. Scheib (3-5).

Chicago at Cleveland (2)—Pierce (9-4) and Consuegra (3-1) vs. Lemon (10-7) and Chakales (0-1).

Detroit at St. Louis (2)—Weik (0-0) and Gray (3-9) vs. Larsen (2-5) and Cain (3-3) or Holloman (3-5).

R. A. F. Henley Champion

Princeton 150-Pounders Beaten in Semi-Finals

HENLEY ON THAMES, England, July 4 (AP).—After trying for six years a British rowing eight today recovered from America one of the most famous trophies of international rowing—the Thames Challenge Cup.

It was recaptured by a snappy crew of the Royal Air Force which defeated the sturdy 150-pound Princeton University crew on the historic one mile, 550-yard course.

Princeton put up a rugged battle on the Thames which was smooth as a pavement. But they couldn't quite match the R. A. F. power. At the finish line, before a crowd estimated at more than 5,000, Princeton was one-third of a length behind.

It was a semi-final, and in the afternoon the R. A. F. went out to grab the trophy, held last year by the University of Pennsylvania, by defeating the Imperial Boat Club of London by half a length.

The R. A. F. time against Princeton was seven minutes five seconds, considerably slower than the record of six minutes 45 seconds set up by Princeton in a preliminary on Thursday.

"Our boys rowed a good race, with no mistakes visible to the eye, and we were fairly beaten," said Art Sueltz, Princeton coach.

Since 1929, America has held the Thames Challenge Cup twelve years, including six successive years since 1947. It has been held once by the Browne and Nichols school, three times by Tabor, four times by Kent, and twice each by Pennsylvania and Princeton.

Tony Fox, of London, won the Diamond Sculls by trouncing Robert George, twenty-two-year-old Belgian. Fox won by four lengths in 8:12 and more than made up for a beating he took from George over a shorter course at Liege three weeks ago.

Yanks 6-5 to Win Series For Fifth Straight Year

Herald Tribune—United Press

300 Club—This Dodger quintet all finished season with better than .300 batting average. Left to right: Gil Hodges, .302; Roy Campanella, .312; Jackie Robinson, .329; Duke Snider, .336, and Carl Furillo, .344, best in the National League.

Ted Kell

First in line—Crowd outside bleacher entrance to Yankee Stadium last night and they had signs to say that they were ALL Dodger fans.

Erskine Gets Reynolds for A Foe Today

By Rud Rennie

This afternoon at 1:05 o'clock in Yankee Stadium, on the golden anniversary of the World Series, the dauntless Dodgers will begin their endeavor to destroy the lordly Yankees and their hopes of being the first team in the history of baseball to win five world championships in succession, and, coincidentally, put an end to years of waiting and hoping by winning their first World Series for Brooklyn.

Six times the Dodgers have represented the National League in World Series with American League champions and six times they have failed. Now, with what is conceded to be the most power-laden team in Brooklyn's history, the Dodgers meet the Yankees in a World Series for the the fifth time, playing them for the second year in succession, and they figure it is now or never.

But, despite the superior power of the Dodgers, the Yankees, fifteen times world champions and winners four times in a row as they enter this, their twentieth World Series, have been established 6-to-5 favorites to do it again and make Casey Stengel, their manager, the only man who ever guided a team to five successive world championships.

Allie Reynolds, the Yankees' most successful World Series pitcher, with six victories and two defeats in five Series, will start the opening game, needing one victory to tie Charley Ruffing's Series record of seven victories. Reynolds, a righthander, is thirty-five years old. He won thirteen and lost seven this year and was used twenty-six times in relief.

Starting for the Dodgers will be Carl Erskine, a twenty-game winner this season, and the only twenty-game winner in the Series. This will be Carl's third World Series adventure. He pitched one and two-thirds innings in 1949, and was in three games last year, winning one and losing one.

This year Erskine, winning fifteen and losing two after July 1, is the pitcher on whom Charlie Dressen, the Brooklyn manager, is counting most heavily to pitch the Dodgers to their first world championship. Erskine is his No. 1 hurler, assigned for the first time to pitch the opening game of a World Series, and burdened with the further responsibility of starting twice after that, should the need arise. Erskine also is a righthander, less experienced than Reynolds, and younger. He is twenty-six.

Both teams will be at full strength in this record-breaking Series since Gene Woodling, the Yankees' leftfielder, and Carl Furillo, the Brooklyn rightfielder, have tested their injured hands and found them workable.

It will be a record-breaking Series because the prices of the tickets have been increased, and because, no matter which team wins, it will be a record—an all-time major league record for the Yankees, or a Brooklyn record.

Dodger Hitting Strong

The Dodgers are a good, strong, experienced team. It clinched its pennant on Sept. 12, the earliest date in the history of National League pennant races. Its personnel smashed individual records in all directions. The four good batters who performed so ineffectually in last year's Series go into this one with distinguished batting records and accomplishments.

Gil Hodges, the first baseman who did not make a hit in twenty-one times at bat last year, is batting .302 and has hit thirty-one home runs. Jackie Robinson, a leftfielder now, who batted .147, is now hitting .329. Furillo, another .174 hitter in last year's Series, is the champion batsman of the National League with .344. And Roy Campanella, who hit .214, had a tremendous season with forty-one home runs, 142 runs batted in, and a batting average of .312.

The Yankees, defending champions, have no such array of sluggers. Only two of their regulars, Hank Bauer and Woodling, batted .300. Bauer hit .304 and Woodling .306.

But the Yankees are a better double-play team, and they figure to get better pitching than the Dodgers. And they have better reserve players.

Pitching is the Dodgers only weakness; but it could be the weakness that will cause their defeat. Too much depends on Erskine.

Only four pitchers ever have beaten the Yankees twice in a World Series. Jess Barnes and Phil Douglas, of the Giants, did it in 1921; Johnny Beazley, of the Cardinals, did it in 1942; and Hugh Casey, of Brooklyn, did it as a relief pitcher in 1947. Whether Erskine can do it remains to be seen. Obviously, it is not impossible but it is hard to do.

Gilliam a New Face

The Yankees will have the same starting players as last year. The Dodgers will be the same except for Jim Gilliam at second base.

The Yankee pitching staff has been strengthened by the return of Whitey Ford, a lefthander. And the Brooklyn staff has been strengthened by the acquisition of Russ Meyer.

The Yankees were in a slump at the end of the regular season. Three Boston lefthanders beat them and held them to two runs in their last three games. Finishing the season, the team looked bad. But the Yankees always have been tough when the chips were down and now the chips are down.

A crowd of approximately 60,000 is expected to attend the opening game, and every one who has to use the subway as a means of transportation is urged to supply himself with the necessary tokens in advance to avert a mob-scene in the stations after the game. The weather prediction for today is clear and warm.

The bleacher ticket booths will open at 9 a. m. and 14,000 bleacher seats will be put on sale.

The grandstand ticket booths where the $4 standing room tickets will be sold will open at 10 a. m.

Guy Lombardo's Royal Canadians and Major Francis Sutherland's 7th Regiment band will provide pre-game music.

Miss Lucy Monroe will sing the National Anthem after a color guard of United States Marines raises the flag.

Cy Young, eighty-six years old, who pitched and won 511 games in his time and who pitched for the Boston Red Sox in the first World Series in 1903, will throw out the first ball. Bill Dineen, another pitcher from the 1903 Red Sox, will throw out the first ball in tomorrow's game. Friday the series will move to Brooklyn.

Herald Tribune—United Press

Yankee Power—Gene Woodling (left), Mickey Mantle (center) and Hank Bauer, whose bats Stengel is depending upon for Yankee power.

Call ME 7-1212 For Series News

Please do not call the Herald Tribune for scores of World Series games.

Inning-by-inning scores of each World Series game will be announced along with the usual time signals by the New York Telephone Co., starting today, on number MEridian 7-1212.

Final scores will be announced after each game until 6:30 p. m., and postponements or delays because of weather will be covered the same way.

Howard Beats Smith

HALIFAX, N. S., Sept. 29 (CP).—Richard (Kid) Howard, 138, of Halifax, turned in the best fight of his career tonight to win a unanimous decision over Charley Smith, 134, of Newark, N. J., in a ten-round bout.

World Series Scalping

Police Arrest 3 in Raid On Ticket Speculators

Three men were taken into custody yesterday afternoon when police raided a midtown ticket agency and confiscated 141 World Series baseball tickets in connection with alleged excessive charges for the coveted pasteboards. It was reported to be the first raid on scalpers and followed a series of complaints by out-of-twoners and New York business firms.

With reports that speculators were demanding—and getting—four times the face value of the tickets while fans were waiting in line hoping to buy a bleacher seat or a standing-room ticket, police swooped down on the Embassy Theater Ticket Service, Inc., at 234 W. 50th St.

The visit by police raiders followed a telephoned deal to buy two sets of tickets, police said.

Chief Inspector Conrad H. Rothengast assigned Deputy Chief Inspector James Nidds and Acting Captain Louis Sisapel, of the supervising and investigating unit, Office of the Chief Inspector, to investigate complaints from firms that they were being squeezed for exorbitant prices for tickets for out-of-town customers.

Inspector Nidds and Captain Sisapel went to the midtown area with some plainclothes patrolmen.

Captain Sisapel telephoned the Embassy Agency, he said. He asked if any tickets were available for the series, which opens today in Yankee Stadium and shifts on Friday to Ebbets Field.

The games at Yankee Stadium, scheduled to be the first, second, sixth and seventh, must be bought in strips of four—one for each game. The Ebbets Field strips are for three games—Nos. 3, 4 and 5.

Captain Sisapel said he arranged to buy two strips of tickets for Ebbets Field, with a legitimate price of $7 each, for $170. The total face value of the tickets would be $42. Brokers are allowed to charge $1 more than the face value per ticket.

He said he was quoted $150 for four box seats, which have a face value of $10 each. He said he arranged to call at the Embassy Agency and pick up the tickets.

Shortly before one o'clock he arrived there, while the other officers remained outside in an automobile. He said he identified himself as the man who ordered the tickets and received the two sets of three tickets, paying $170 in marked money.

The police said they seized forty-four sets of tickets—thirty-five sets of three for Brooklyn, and nine sets of four for the Stadium. They also seized books of the firm, which, the police said, showed one transaction for tickets running to more than $2,000, and several sales between $400 and $500.

The police took the following to the West 47th St. station:

Walter Bernstein, thirty-five-years old, of 2780 University Ave., the Bronx, secretary-treasurer of the agency.

Abe Spitalnick, thirty-five, of the Beau Arts Apartment, 310 E. 44th St., a clerk; and Bernie Russ, forty-nine, of Manhattan Towers, 76th St. and Broadway, a clerk.

Dixie Series

Dallas at Nashville (Dallas leads best of seven series (3-2).

American Association

Toledo, 4; Kansas City, 2 (Final series tied, 3-3).

How Herald Tribune Will Cover World Series

Five staff writers of the New York Herald Tribune sports department, and three staff photographers, will cover the World Series beginning this afternoon.

Rud Rennie, who traveled with the Yankees throughout the year, will write the lead story. The dressing rooms will be covered by Roger Kahn (Dodgers), and Leonard Koppett (Yankees). Harold Rosenthal will report on the crowd and opening day highlights. Red Smith, Herald Tribune sports columnist, will analyze the opener in his column.

The staff photographers assigned to the opener are Jack Frank, Don Rice and Ted Kell.

The writers, interviewed yesterday, picked the Yankees by a margin of three to two. Their individual forecasts follow: Rud Rennie—Yankees in 6; Roger Kahn—Dodgers in 7; Red Smith—Yankees in 6; Leonard Koppett—Yankees in 5; Harold Rosenthal—Dodgers in 6.

Saxton Whips Giardello in Ten-Rounder

PHILADELPHIA, Sept. 29 (AP).—Johnny Saxton, swift punching New York welterweight, pounded out a unanimous ten-round decision over middleweight Joey Giardello, of Philadelphia, tonight in the first indoor bout of the season at the Arena. Saxton weighed 151; Giardello 155.

Saxton opened cuts under both of Giardello's eyes in winning the nod of Judge Billy Yancey, 5-3-2; Judge Herb Goldman, on the unusual count of 3-1-6 and Referee Joe Sweeney, 5-4-1.

Giardello, who seeks a fight with the winner of the Bobo Olson-Randy Turpin middleweight title bout, appeared lead-footed and out of condition. The swarthy Philadelphian tossed a lot of leather in the first three rounds, all of which he appeared to have won. But from that point on, Saxton took complete charge of the fight.

The New Yorker made his second Philadelphia appearance his forty-first victory in forty-three fights. Only a draw and a defeat here at the hands of welterweight Gil Turner, of Philadelphia, marred the impressive record of the spindly-built welterweight. Saxton is anxious for a crack at Kid Gavilan's 147-pound crown.

Redlegs Name Tebbetts Pilot

George (Birdie) Tebbetts yesterday was named manager of the Cincinnati Redlegs for 1954 and 1955, succeeding the recently fired Rogers Hornsby.

Tebbets, veteran major league catcher managed Indianapolis of the American Association this season. He finished fourth with the Cleveland farm club.

Gabe Paul, general manager of the Cincinnati club, did not announce salary terms. Paul said he had considered Tebbetts for some time but did not discuss the matter with him until today.

Pre-Series Workouts

Yankees Riddle Fences; Furillo Hits 3 'Homers'

By Roger Kahn

To the surprise of practically every one, including manager Casey Stengel and publicity man Arthur (Red) Patterson, the Yankees held a full-scale workout at the Stadium yesterday and did enough hitting to wear out four pitchers.

"I had to meet the commissioner," Stengel said, "I don't know a thing about the workout. I wasn't there and all I said was that anyone who wanted to work out could."

"All that was scheduled," Patterson reported, "was a skull session. We didn't expect a workout."

But there was a workout in the morning after the skull session, and, voluntary or not, every Yankee took part. Lefthanders Bill Miller and Steve Kraly pitched along with righthanded coaches Frank Crosetti and Ralph Houk. Of the hitters, Yogi Berra, Joe Collins and Mickey Mantle were most impressive and Gene Woodling slugged as though his sore left hand has stopped aching.

Casey Visits Frick

"No," Stengel said, "I didn't know about the workout because I was satisfied with what I saw yesterday and I had to meet the commissioner.

"We've got a nice team," he added, "and there's a splendid team over there so it should be a splendid World Series."

Tennis, anyone?

The Dodger workout yesterday morning, which started at 9:30, was so well-planned that manager Charlie Dressen put in an appearance in street clothes before traveling to the commissioner's office.

The star of the drill was Carl Furillo who belted three into the leftfield seats off Bob Milliken who was throwing hard. He'll go into today's game with his injured left hand bandaged and a layer of sponge wrapped around his bat but no injection of novocain will be necessary.

"He's come along much better than I expected," Dr. Harold Wendler, the Dodger trainer said.

The Dodgers held their skull session after the workout and it was unique. The team met in Brooklyn's downtown offices with all the scouts on hand as well as Dressen and the coaches. What transpired was kept secret, except for the Dodgers' book on Willie Miranda.

"For Miranda," Dressen revealed, "our pitchers will throw the ball over the plate."

In order to reduce congestion at the change booths, the New York City Transit Authority has appealed to all baseball fans who will go to the World Series by subway to buy no fewer than two tokens so that none will have to be purchased on the return. This will be the first token series.

On 119 TV Stations

Since World Series inevitably produce the biggest and the best, even the numbers spouted by statisticians, the National Broadcasting Co., which will televise the games, figured the audience for seven games at 525,000,000. This is based on multiplication and is far too complicated to go into here. At any rate, 119 stations, including channels 4 and 9 in New York, blanketing 113 cities will televise the games, creating the largest live network in TV history.

Including Canadian stations, 750 will broadcast the series, which Mutual is carrying for the fifteenth year. WOR is the local outlet, and here the statistic for each game is 55,000,000 listeners, with, presumably, 110,000,000 ears.

The meeting between Commissioner Ford C. Frick and the managers was routine, covering ground rules, conduct on the field and such. Frick advised against abusing umpires, both managers chorused, "Who, me?" and the meeting was adjourned.

Lights for this series will be turned on as needed, Sunday or any other day. The advent of Eastern Standard Time makes darkness a real possibility, particularly on Sunday when the game starts at 2:05 p. m.

Series Weather: Fair and Warm

Perfect baseball weather was forecast last night for the opening game of the World Series this afternoon at Yankee Stadium.

The weather for today was predicted "fair and warm with highest temperatures in the 80s and gentle, variable winds becoming moderate in the afternoon."

Schools

Soccer

1—Islip	Bayport—0
6—Bellport	Northport—0
1—Center Moriches	Central Islip—0
5—Kings Park	Bay Shore—0
5—Grover Cleveland	Erasmus—0
3—Lafayette	Newton—0

Columbia Team Stresses Its Defense Against Passing

Disappointed by Columbia's pass defense against Lehigh last Saturday and concerned over Princeton's potent aerial attack this Saturday, coach Lou Little devoted the major portion of the Lions' football practice yesterday to correcting errors in the defensive secondary. Safety man Bob Mercier, halfbacks Dick Carr and Max Pirner and line backers Keith Krebs and Jerry Hampton drilled against pass plays run out of a simulated Princeton single-wing offense.

Last week, the Lion defenders permitted Lehigh thirteen completions in twenty-eight attempts for 140 yards and a touchdown. Princeton won its game from Lafayette mainly with an aerial offense, completing fourteen of nineteen for 281 yards. Princeton's passing potential and a study of defensive mistakes against Lehigh prompted the long defensive drill during the Lion scrimmage yesterday.

Coach Little was pleased with the improvement shown by the top defenders during the drill. With sophomore quarterback Charles Nations doing the tossing, the Lion defenders stopped most of his thrusts and succeeded in intercepting a few throws.

Brown Drills for Yale

Special to the Herald Tribune

PROVIDENCE, R. I., Sept. 29.—Brown coach Alva Kelley sent his forty-four man squad through a three-hour drill today in preparation for Saturday's encounter with Yale. The Bears concentrated on defensive work.

Rams Test Three Fullbacks

With three senior fullbacks fighting for the starting assignment against the University of Detroit Friday night, the Fordham varsity yesterday held its last scrimmage at Fordham Field in preparation for the Rams' season opener. Charlie Dietlin and Malachy Stafford each scored touchdowns, while John Griffin looked better than he has at any time during training. Coach Ed Danowski still is undecided upon his started at the position.

Harvard in Drill

Special to the Herald Tribune

CAMBRIDGE, Mass., Sept. 29.—John Culver playing his third season as first-team fullback but his first as a defensive back, sparkled on both offense and defense today at Harvard football practice.

Frye in Princeton Drill

PRINCETON, N. J., Sept. 29 (AP).—Princeton coach Charlie Caldwell's hopes of improving on last Saturday's running attack received a big boost this afternoon as tailback Dick Frye returned to heavy duty for the first time in three weeks.

Frye was at first string on both offense and defense, and Caldwell expects him to be in good shape for the Columbia game.

YANKEES DEFEAT DODGERS, 9-5, IN OPENER

BERRA, GILLIAM, HODGES, SHUBA AND COLLINS HIT HOME RUNS

By Bob Broeg
Of the Post-Dispatch Sports Staff.

NEW YORK, Sept. 30—The World Champion New York Yankees, breaking out of their end-of-the-season batting slump, outslugged Brooklyn's National League pennant-winning Dodgers today in the first game of the 1953 World Series at Yankee Stadium, 9 to 5.

Led by Billy Martin, their cocky dead-end kid at second base, the Yanks clobbered four Brooklyn pitchers for 12 hits, routing righthanded ace, Carl Erskine, with a four-run first inning, scoring once off Jim Hughes in the fifth and then finishing strong by tallying three times each against Loser Clem Labine ad Ben Wade in the seventh and eighth frames.

The Dodgers, too, managed 12 hits off Allie Reynolds and Johnny Sain, but were unable to make the most of their opportunities and therefore fell behind in the seventh world series in which they have carried the National League colors. Brooklyn has not won a series while the Yankees have won 15 of 19.

Martin and Gil Hodges, the husby Brooklyn first baseman who was the goat a year ago when he went hitless in seven games, led both sides with three hits apiece. Martin delivered the game's most decisive blow, a three-run triple in the first inning.

Not Quite Homer Record.

Hodges collected one of the game's five home runs, just one short of the record for circuit smashes in a series contest, and also singled twice.

Yogi Berra, the Yankee catcher from the Hill in St. Louis, hit his fifth series homer and a single, Joe Collins also homered for the American League kings, and Hank Bauer of East St. Louis whacked a single and triple.

Junior Gilliam, the Dodgers' rookie second baseman, singled and hit a home run, and George Shuba, pinch-batting, became only the third specialist to homer in world series history.

A crowd of 69,374, cramming Yankee Stadium and contributing record gross and net receipts of $465,267 and $387,574.74, saw the Dodgers overcome deficits of 4-0 and 5-1 by routing Reynolds, only to have Sain check them in relief to record the victory. Collins's homer off Labine in the seventh put the Yanks ahead to stay.

Gilliam Gets First Hit.

The first ball was thrown out by Denton (Cy) Young, the 86-year-old pitching star of the first world series 50 years ago. The famed old right-hander was wide with his toss, and so was Reynolds with the first pitch of the game to switch-hitting Gilliam.

Gilliam ran the count to 3-2 and then singled back through Reynold's legs and into center field. On the second pitch to Reese, Gilliam broke for second—the hit-and-run play was on—but Peewee popped the ball to Bauer in short right and Gilliam had to scurry back to first base. The free-swinging Snider grounded softly to Martin, too softly for a play at second, and Robinson bounced just as easily to Rizzuto to end the inning.

Erskine's first pitch to McDougald, the Yankee lead-off man, was a curved called strike. On the fourth pitch, Mac lifted a short pop-up to Gilliam. Pitching to Collins, Erskine switched to the fast ball and lost the Yankee first baseman on four straight pitches. If the home crowd enjoyed the walk, it was nothing to the roar that followed when Bauer, the East St. Louis athlete, hit a 1-2 curve into right center for a hit. Snider, rushing over, missed a stab at the bounding ball, which rolled past him for a run-scoring triple. Berra, the muscle man from the Hill, whacked a hanging curve into the right-field stands for a long foul that also excited the big throng and then struck out on a full count pitch.

Erskine, still having trouble controlling his breaking stuff, walked Mantle on four pitches. The Brooklyn bullpen under the left-field runway went into action after the first two pitches to Woodling also missed the plate. Gene then drew another four-pitch pass that filled the bases.

Three-Run Triple.

A big inning quickly followed as Martin slammed a high curve into left-center for a three-run triple. Rizzuto, eighth man to bat in the inning, hit an easy grounder to Cox, but it had been a costly frame for Erskine, and the Dodgers—four runs on just two hits.

Opening the Brooklyn second, Reynolds got two strikes on Campanella and then, apparently trying to brush the husky catcher back, hit Campy painfully on the right hand as the Brooklyn slugger fell to the ground trying to avoid a high-and-tight pitch.

Hodges got the Chief in a hole with two wide pitches, but then flied to Woodling close behind the infield. Furillo, batting with a bandaged left hand, was called out on a beautiful sharp-breaking curve. Cox socked the first pitch over third base for a double, Woodling's knowledge of the rebounds holding Campanella at third. Wayne Belardi came up next as the first pinch-hitter of the series, batting for Erskine, but Manager Dressen's hopes of cutting the Yankee lead failed to materialize as Reynolds powdered three fast balls past Belardi. The Brooklyn pitcher in the New York second was Jim Hughes, a strapping righthander who distinguished himself early in the season in relief for the Dodgers and then tailed off.

One-Two-Three Stuff.

Hughes, raring back, had an easy inning. Reynolds struck out, McDougald grounded to Reese, and Collins, after hitting one long foul, sent a broken-bat pop fly to Reese.

The Dodgers came up for the second time around in the third inning. This time Gilliam struck out. Reese walked on five pitches. Snider's king-sized cuts amused the crowd, but not the Duke, who went down swinging. Robinson hit a low and light inning-ending liner to Martin.

Bauer, opening the Yankee third, went down on strikes, taking a low curve that hit the outside corner. Berra, who'll swing at anything, chased a low pitch in the dirt and fanned, but had to be thrown out, Campanella to Hodges. Mantle rapped a line-drive single to right. On a 2-1 pitch taken by Woodling, Mantle was out stealing on Campanella's strong, accurate throw to Reese.

In the Brooklyn fourth, Campanella popped to Rizzuto. Hodges ran the count to the limit, then broke to first too soon on a corner-catching curve and was called out. Furillo had better success in "umpiring," taking a "3-2" fast ball for a base on balls. Cox flied to Bauer in short-right.

'Three-Base' Bunt.

Woodling, leading off the Yankee fourth, lined to Snider, but then the fun began. Martin, roundly applauded for his triple, bunted between home plate and the mound.

While Campaneiia wheeled and argued with plate Umpire Grieve that the tapped ball had hit Martin's bat twice, Hughes came off the hill and fielded the bunt, but threw to first too late—base hit. When Hughes's throw was low, bouncing into right field, Martin took second on the error and reached third on a second misscue as Furillo's return throw to the infield skipped past Cox to the grandstand wall.

No runs resulted though, for Martin held third as Rizzuto grounded to Reese with the infield in, Reynolds walked and McDougald forced Reynolds, Reese to Gilliam. But the crowd had needed the excitement to enliven the slow-moving contest.

There was a murmur of press-box second-guessing as Hughes was permitted to bat for himself at the start of the fifth and was called out, Reynolds's sixth strikeout victim. A cheer followed as Gilliam hit the Chief's first pitch deep into the lower deck of the right field stands for his second hit and the Dodgers' first run, a homer. Reese flied to Bauer in the right field corner, and Snider doubled inside he right field line, again bringing the crowd to life. When Robinson walked on four pitches, the Yankee bullpen swung into action. Campanella ended the inning, however, with a medium-deep fly to Woodling.

Yogi's Fifth Series Homer.

Now the tempo was picking up. Collins, the Yanks' first batter in the sixth, sent Snider back to the cinder track in deep right-center for his drive. Duke was uncertain of his distance from the wall, hesitated and finally leaped to make a glove-hand catch that thrilled the spectators. Bauer flied to Furillo in routine fashion, but Berra picked on an 0-2 pitch and blasted it way back into the lower right field stands for a home run, Yogi's fifth in world series play. Gilliam had to hurry to throw out the fleet Mantle.

When Hodges decided to end his slump, the series goat of '52 came out of it handsomely, for in the sixth the husky Brooklyn first baseman, hitless in 22 trips last year and in his first two this time, hammered a full-count pitch into the left field stands for a home run. It was his second in series competition.

Out in the Yankee bullpen they were up and throwing again as Furillo flied deep to Bauer and Cox singled to center for his second safety. Dressen wasn't waiting any longer and George Shuba batted for Hughes and lined a 3-1 pitch into the right field seats for a two-run homer that put the Dodgers only one behind. Bauer nearly catapulted over the low wall trying for a catch and Manager Stengel rushed as quickly from the dugout to replace Reynolds with Johnny Sain, the former side-wheeling National League righthander.

Sain got out of the inning without further scoring — just barely, that is. Martin juggled Gilliam's grounder, but threw him out. Reese walked and Snider pounded a hot single, past Collins into right field, sending Reese to third. With a stir of expectancy, Robinson hit a pitch off his fists for an inning-ending grounder to McDougald.

Labine Third Dodger Hurler.

Clem Labine, Brooklyn's best 1 eason relief pitcher, was on the firing line in the last of the sixth. Woodling looped a single to short center, kindling Yankee hopes of adding to the slender lead, but Martin forced Woodling, Gilliam to Reese. Billy then went out stealing on a remarkable throw by Campanella, who grabbed a low sweeping curve and pegged out the runner side-armed. Labine knocked down Rizzuto's sharp grounder and retired the Scooter.

The Brooklyn followers stretched traditionally for good luck at the start of the seventh and the Dodgers immediately sampled same as Campanella drew a fortunate single on a high short fly that fell in front of Woodling, who broke late on the ball. Hodges followed with a ground single to Rizzuto's left and off the shortstop's glove, slowing the ball enough to permit Campy to waddle around to third.

The score became tied and excitement at a new high as Furillo drilled a full-count pitch on a line over second base for a single, scoring Campanella, Hodges halting at second. In a sacrifice situation Sain held the runners close and Berra bounded quickly from behind the plate for Cox's bunt, throwing to third, where Umpire Gore's force-out call brought a dance of disgust from Dressen, coaching there, and a howl of protests from the Brooklyn bench. Labine also bunted and this time there was no complaint as Yogi again fielded the ball and achieved a force play at third. Gilliam fouled to Berra to leave the score 5-5.

Bust of '52 Busts One.

Labine's job looked soft in the home seventh when Sain took a called third strike and McDougald flied deep to Snider, but Collins lifted a 1-0 pitch into the right field seats for a homer that put the Yankees ahead again. It was the second in series play for a batting bust of the '52 show. The hit was Collins's first in his last 17 series times at bat.

When Bauer singled to left and Berra to right, each collecting his second hit, Dressen removed Labine and brought in Ben Wade, a strapping righthander. At about the same moment a fan left the park, too. The crowd chuckled as he wandered onto the field and immediately was surrounded by blue-coated policemen. After play was resumed, Mantle was called out on three pitches.

To open the Dodgers' eighth, Reese was brushed back with a pitch, then flied to Woodling. Snider carried the count to the limit and grounded out to Collins. Robinson drove deep to Woodling, and the Yankees were only three outs from victory.

Opening the home club's eighth, Woodling bounced to Gilliam. Martin popped a single to short right for his third hit. In the Yankees' third stolen-base bid and his second, Billy finally made it, beating Campanella's throw. Rizzuto walked. Sain, always a good hitting pitcher, cuffed a 2-2 curve to right-center for a double that scored both Martin and Rizzuto. McDougald lined to Furillo. But Collins hit a fly-ball single in front of Furillo, scoring Sain with the third run of the inning, and the big crowd began to wander away. Bauer struck out.

SCORE BY INNINGS

	1	2	3	4	5	6	7	8	9	T.
DODGERS	0	0	0	0	1	3	1	0	0	5
YANKEES	4	0	0	0	1	0	1	3	X	9

THE BOX SCORE

BROOKLYN DODGERS

	AB	R	H	2B	3B	HR	BB	SO	PO	A	E
Gilliam 2b	5	1	2	0	0	1	0	1	3	3	0
Reese ss	3	0	0	0	0	0	2	0	3	3	0
Snider cf	5	0	2	1	0	0	0	1	3	0	0
Robinson lf	4	0	0	0	0	0	1	0	0	0	0
Campanella c	4	1	1	0	0	0	0	0	6	3	0
Hodges 1b	5	1	3	0	0	1	0	1	7	0	0
Furillo rf	4	0	1	0	0	0	1	1	2	0	1
Cox 3b	5	1	2	1	0	0	0	0	0	1	0
ERSKINE P	0	0	0	0	0	0	0	0	0	0	0
HUGHES P	1	0	0	0	0	0	0	1	0	0	1
LABINE P	1	0	0	0	0	0	0	0	0	1	0
WADE P	0	0	0	0	0	0	0	0	0	0	0
Belardi	1	0	0	0	0	0	0	1	0	0	0
Shuba	1	1	1	0	0	1	0	0	0	0	0
TOTALS	39	5	12	2	0	3	4	6	24	11	2

Belardi, for Erskine, struck out in second.
Shuba, for Hughes, hit 2-run homer in sixth.

NEW YORK YANKEES

	AB	R	H	2B	3B	HR	BB	SO	PO	A	E
McDougald 3b	5	0	0	0	0	0	0	0	3	2	0
Collins 1b	4	2	2	0	0	1	1	0	6	0	0
Bauer rf	5	1	2	0	1	0	0	2	4	0	0
Berra c	4	1	2	0	0	1	0	2	8	2	0
Mantle cf	3	1	1	0	0	0	1	1	0	0	0
Woodling lf	3	1	1	0	0	0	1	0	4	0	0
Martin 2b	4	1	3	0	1	0	0	0	1	2	0
Rizzuto ss	3	1	0	0	0	0	1	0	1	1	0
REYNOLDS P	1	0	0	0	0	0	1	1	0	0	0
SAIN P	2	1	1	1	0	0	0	1	0	0	0
TOTALS	34	9	12	1	2	2	5	7	27	7	0

Umpires—Grieve, Stewart, Hurley and Gore, with Soar and Dascoli on the foul lines.

RBI—Bauer, Martin 3, Gilliam, Berra, Hodges, Shuba 2, Furillo, Collins 2, Sain 2. SB—Martin. Left—Dodgers 12, Yankees 6. BB—Reynolds 3, Sain 1, Erskine 3, Hughes 1, wade 2. SO—Reynolds 6, Erskine 1, Hughes 3, Labine 1, Wade 2. Hits—Off Erskine, 2 in 1; Hughes, 3 in 4; Reynolds, 7 in 5⅓; Labine, 4 in 1⅔; Wade, 3 in 1⅓; Sain, 5 in 3⅔. R and ER—Erskine 4-4, Hughes 1-1, Reynolds 4-4, Labine 1-1, Wade 3-3, Sain 1-1. HBBP—By Reynolds (Campanella). Winner—Sain. Loser—Labine. T— 3h., 10m. A—69,374 (paid). Receipts—(net) $387,574.74.

SERIES FACTS

NEW YORK, Sept. 30 (UP)—Figures on the first game of the World Series at Yankee Stadium today:

Paid attendance—69,374.
Gross receipts (before taxes)—$465,267.00.
Net total receipts (after taxes)—$387,574.74.
Commissioner's share—$58,136.21.
Players' pool—$197,633.12.
Club and league share—$131,775.41.
Federay tax—$77,692.26.

	R.	H.	E.
Brooklyn (NL)	5	12	2
NEW YORK (AL)	9	12	0

Erskine, Hughes (2), Labine (6), Wade (7) and Campanella; Reynolds, Sain (6) and Berra. W.—Sain; L.—Labine.

Club.	W.	L.	Pct.
Yankees	1	0	1.000
Dodgers	0	1	.000

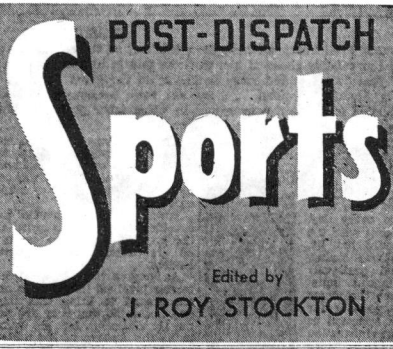

First Run of the Series

—United Press Telephoto.

JOE COLLINS, Yankee first baseman, crosses plate in opening inning for first of four runs for American League champions in first game of world series. Catcher is ROY CAMPANELLA, umpire BILL GRIEVE of the American League, batter coming up YOGI BERRA. Collins, who had walked, got around on triple by Hank Bauer.

Lefty Duel in 2nd Game---Lopat vs. Roe

By a Staff Correspondent of the Post-Dispatch.

NEW YORK, Sept. 30.

Manager Casey Stengel of the Yankees and Chuck Dressen of Brooklyn confirmed pre-series popular selections of second-game pitchers. Ed Lopat of the Yanks and Preacher Roe of the Dodgers will start tomorrow, making it a left-handed duel of veterans.

Advance ticket prices didn't cause any downward trend in attendance at the series opener. There were reports that scalpers were getting more than $100 for two strips of tickets for the three Brooklyn games and correspondingly high prices for the contests scheduled at the Stadium.

Miss Lucy Monroe, as usual, sang the national anthem to conclude pre-game ceremonies. Bleacher fans gawked, thinking it was Marilyn.

Wags were saying as early as last night that there was a rumor that the Baltimore franchise was to be transferred to California. It might as well start early.

Cy Young, one of the great pitchers of long ago, threw out the first ball and Yogi Berra, after catching it, returned it to Cy as a souvenir.

First Game, Play-by-Play

FIRST INNING — DODGERS —Gilliam singled through the box. Reese flied to Bauer in short right. Snider went out, Martin to Collins. Rizzuto threw out Robinson.

YANKEES — McDougald popped to Gilliam. Collins walked on four pitches. Bauer tripled to right-center, scoring Collins. Berra struck out. Mantle walked. Woodling walked, filling the bases. Martin tripled to left-center, scoring Bauer, Mantle and Woodling. Cox threw out Rizzuto. **FOUR RUNS.**

SECOND—DODGERS — Campanella was hit by a pitched ball. Hodges flied to Woodling. Furillo struck out. Cox doubled to left, Campanella stopping at third. Belardi batted for Erskine and struck out.

YANKEES — Hughes pitched for the Dodgers. Reynolds struck out. Reese threw out McDougald. Collins popped to Reese.

THIRD—DODGERS— Gilliam struck out. Reese walked. Snider struck out. Robinson lined to Martin.

YANKEES—Bauer was called out on strikes. Berra struck out and had to be thrown out, Campanella to Hodges. Mantle singled to right. Mantle was out attempting to steal, Campanella to Reese.

FOURTH—DODGERS— Campanella flied to Rizzuto. Hodges was called out on strikes. Furillo walked. Cox flied to Bauer.

YANKEES — Woodling flied to Snider. Martin bunted safely and when Hughes threw wild to first, Martin contined to second and advanced to third on Furillo's wild throw to the infield (errors were charged to both Hughes and Furillo). Rizzuto grounded out to Reese, Martin holding third. Reynolds walked. McDougald forced Reynolds, Reese to Gilliam.

FIFTH—DODGERS— Hughes was called out on strikes. **Gilliam hit into the right field seats for a home run.** Reese flied to Bauer. Snider doubled to right. Robinson walked. Campanella flied to Woodling. **ONE RUN.**

YANKEES—Collins flied deep to Snider, who made a leaping, one-handed catch. Bauer flied to Furillo. **Berra hit into the lower right field stands for a home run.** Gilliam threw out Mantle. **ONE RUN.**

SIXTH—DODGERS— Hodges hit into the lower left field stands for a home run. Furillo flied to Bauer. Cox singled to center. **Shuba batted for Hughes and hit into the lower right field stands for a home run, scoring behind Cox.** Sain replaced Reynolds on the mound for the Yankees. Martin threw out Gilliam. Reese walked. Snider singled to right, sending Reese to third. McDougald threw out Robinson. **THREE RUNS.**

YANKEES — Labine pitched for the Dodgers. Woodling singled to center. Martin forced Woodling, Gilliam to Reese. Martin went out attempting to steal, Campanella to Gilliam. Labine tossed out Rizzuto.

SEVENTH — DODGERS — Campanella singled to left. Hodges singled off Rizzuto's glove, sending Campanella to third. Furillo singled through the box, scoring Campanella, Hodges stopping at second. Cox bunted and forced Hodges at third, Berra to McDougald. Labine bunted and forced Furillo at third, Berra to McDougald. Gilliam fouled to Berra. **ONE RUN.**

YANKEES — Sain was called out on strikes. McDougald flied to Snider. **Collins hit a home run into the right field seats.** Bauer singled to left. Berra singled to right, Bauer stopping at second. Wade replaced Labine on the mound for the Dodgers. Mantle was called out on strikes. **ONE RUN.**

EIGHTH—DODGERS— Reese flied to Woodling. Snider bounced to Collins, unassisted. Robinson flied to Woodling.

YANKEES — Gilliam threw out Woodling. Martin singled to right for his third hit. Martin stole second. Rizzuto walked. Sain doubled to right-center, scoring Martin and Rizzuto. McDougald flied to Furillo. Collins singled to center, scoring Sain. Bauer struck out. **THREE RUNS.**

NINTH — DODGERS — Campanella lined to McDougald. Hodges singled to left. Furillo fouled to Berra. McDougald threw out Cox.

Coast Racing Official Resigns.

DEL MAR, Calif., Sept. 30 (UP)—Phillip B. Cross has resigned as vice president and director of the Del Mar Turf Club. President Alfred Hart announced appointment of Philip L. Gabriel of Whittier, Calif., as vice president and San Diego Attorney Herbert Kunzel as a member of the club's board of directors.

Baltimore Drew 240,000 Fans

BALTIMORE, Md., Sept. 30 (UP).

ELATED Baltimore fans were predicting today that they would smash the first-year attendance showing turned in this year by Milwaukee fans, but that promised to be a tough job.

Milwaukee, in its first season in the majors, set a new National League record this year with an attendance of 1,826,397. This year's attendance for the Baltimore club of the International League was about 240,000. This year's attendance for the Browns, in St. Louis, was 306,728.

POST-DISPATCH Sports

Edited by J. ROY STOCKTON

Tebbetts Signed To Manage the Redlegs 2 Years

NEW YORK, Sept. 30 (AP)—George (Birdie) Tebbetts went shopping today for right-handed pitchers as the new manager of the Cincinnati Redlegs.

Tebbetts, who piloted Indianapolis to fourth place in the American Association this season after 16½ years of major league catching, was signed to a two-year contract late yesterday as the successor to the recently fired Rogers Hornsby.

Facts and Figures

Opponents — New York Yankees, American League champions, vs. Brooklyn Dodgers, National League champions.

Series—Best of seven.

Remaining Schedule— Oct. 1 at Yankee Stadium, Oct. 2, Oct. 3 and Oct. 4 (if necessary) at Ebbets Field; Oct. 5 and Oct. 6 (if necessary) at Yankee Stadium.

Game Time—12:05 p.m. (St. Louis time), Sunday—1:05 (St. Louis time).

Series standings — American League 32, National League 17.

Odds—Yankees 6½ or 6 to 5 favorites.

Series records of opponents—Yankees won 15, lost 4; Dodgers won none, lost six.

Postponed games—To be played on grounds for which originally scheduled before next scheduled game is played.

Tie game—To be played off where originally scheduled on the second day following Game No. 7.

Radio—Mutual Broadcasting System (on KWK in St. Louis).

Television — National Broadcasting System (KSD-TV in St. Louis area).

Umpires—Bill Grieve, Ed Hurley and Hank Soar (alternate) of the American League and Bill Stewart, Art Gore and Frank Dascoli (alternate) of the National League.

Scorers—Joe Cashman, Boston Record; Rud Rennie, New York Herald Tribune, and Dick Young, New York Daily News.

Players pool—Receipts of the first four games only, plus radio and TV money.

37 Writers Favor Yankees, 23 Pick Dodgers to Triumph

NEW YORK, Sept. 30 (AP)—Thirty-seven of the 60 writers polled by the Associated Press selected the New York Yankees to win the world series from the Brooklyn Dodgers.

Of the 37, 22 picked the Yanks in six games, 10 thought they would win in seven and five saw them taking it in five. Nine thought the Yanks would sweep through in four.

Of the 23 who selected the Dodgers, 14 saw it going six games, six like the Brooks in seven, two selected them in five and one Brave soul thinks they are going to take it in four.

Mantle Slam Rocks Brooklyn, 11-7

Reynolds Stops Flock in 9th; 6 HRs Set 1-Game Series Mark

By GUS STEIGER

The big guns, supposedly on the side of the Dodgers, must have been misplaced Sunday for it was the Yankees who accounted for the heavy fire in the free-hitting fifth contest of the 1953 World Series. The American

SMASH OPENING: Gene Woodling, nominated as lead-off man by Casey Stengel Sunday, crosses plate after slamming Podres for first inning homer. Joe Collins congratulates Gene as Ump Bill Grieve stands by. (Mirror Photo)

Leaguers assaulted four Flatbush hurlers for 11 blows that produced 27 total bases to ease the way to an 11-7 triumph at Ebbets Field and a three-two lead in games that placed Manager Casey Stengel and his Yankees one victory away from their fifth consecutive World's Championship.

Included in the New York attack were a pair of doubles, a triple and four lusty homers in chronological order, by Gene Woodling, Mickey Mantle, Billy Martin and Gil McDougald, who also belted a three-bagger.

The quartet of four-baggers accounted for eight of the Yankee tallies. The biggest of these was that by Mantle, who crowned a five-run third inning with the fourth grand-slam of Series history to provide Jim McDonald a substantial lead.

* * *

THIS WAS the third Series slam by a Yankee, for Tony Lazzeri in 1936 and McDougald in 1951 had accounted for two of the blows, with Elmer Smith delivering the first in 1920, wherein the chastened Dodgers also were the victims.

It was the second homer of the current title event for both Mantle and Martin as these young worthies had collaborated in such fashion to encompass the defeat of Preacher Roe in the second game.

Now the Series shifts back to the Yankee Stadium with the defending champions in the driver's seat and in position to end the exercises with another win Monday. The Dodgers, who began the Sabbath on even terms and with such bright prospects of ending Yankee domination. now are in a desperate situation and will come back with their ace. Carl Erskine, in their effort to win today and carry the event into a seventh and deciding contest.

THE DODGERS actually outhit the Yankees, 14-11, but the Bombers got a worthy game out of McDonald, credited with the victory, although Bob Kuzava, who appeared ahead of normal Series schedule and Allie Reynolds got into the affair before it was over. In his two previous Series showings, Kusava didn't show up until the seventh game.

...onald, however, served ...y until Billy Cox came through with a three-run homer to finish off a four-run eighth.

Statistics!

NEW YORK (AL)	3	2	.600
BROOKLYN (NL)	2	3	.400

REMAINING SCHEDULE:

Sixth Game at Yankee Stadium, Monday, Oct. 5; Seventh game (if necessary), at Yankee Stadium, Tuesday, Oct. 6.

FINANCIAL FIGURES
FIFTH GAME

Attendance (paid), 36,775.
Receipts (net), $214,394.33.
Commissioner's share, $32,159.15.

(FIVE-GAME FIGURES)

Attendance (paid), 244,981.
Receipts (net), $1,407,221.00.
Players pool (first 4 games only) $691,-341.61.
Commissioner's share, $211,083.15.
Clubs' and league's share $587,796.24.

This also finished McDonald, but his club was far in front when he left.

Junior Gilliam belted Kuzava for another four-bagger in the ninth and to subdue the Brooks for the day Stengel brought in Reynolds to serve a double-play ball to Jackie Robinson.

Manager Charley Dressen did not have his thinking cap properly adjusted Sunday. He took a flyer to begin with by starting John Podres, who marked his 21st birthday last Wednesday. Only pitcher younger than the rookie southpaw to start a series game was Joe Bush of the Athletics in 1913.

PODRES LACKED control and

Continued on Next Page

ALL YOURS: Charley Dressen hands youthful Johnny Podres ball along with some last minute instructions before fifth Series conflict at Ebbets Field Sunday. Charley kept his pitching selection mum over night and rookie southpaw was in nature of surprise starter, getting call over veteran Russ Meyer. (Mirror Photo)

Cholly Playing Last Ace Again-Erskine!

By KEN SMITH

Ever since Rube Marquard, Sherrod Smith and Jake Pfeffer were thumped by the Red Sox in 1916, the Dodgers have been searching for a pitching staff that can win a World Series and Charley Dressen was down to his last ace again, Carl Erskine, as the Big Tent was pitched again in the Stadium Monday (today).

Casey Stengel, with his 3-2 lead, was in a position to gamble on Whitey Ford transforming himself into a Dr. Jekyl Monday after his Mr. Hyde one-inning performance of last Saturday, same as Erskine had done on Friday. Vic Raschi gets ready for game 7, if necessary, and Ed Lopat also looms handy.

THE AMERICAN LEAGUERS sit pretty at six or six and one-half to five favorites in Game 6 and 2-1 to cop the Series. Once more, the Brooks are on the brink of defeat because they ran short of pitchers when John Podres and Russ Meyer failed, while the Yankees came up with a surprise winner, Jim McDonald, supported by Bob Kuzava, and Allie Reynolds under the late afternoon lights.

But Series history is dotted with stars like Erskine, who have shouldered most of the responsibility, on undermanned staffs and Erskine has the stuff to do it. Seven years ago, Harry Brecheen won three games. Dizzy and Paul Dean each won three in 1934.

A year ago at this time, the Yankees trailed Brooklyn, 3-2 and copped the last two as Raschi and Reynolds came back. Brooklyn has a good chance of doing the same with Erskine and Bill Loes.

MICKEY MANTLE

Nine times teams have been in the same predicament as Brooklyn Monday when the loss of one game meant goodbye to the Series, and swept through to win. The Cards turned this trick three times, the Yankees twice and the Reds, Giants, Pirates and Red Sox each once.

Junior Gilliam's ninth-inning homer was the sixth of the game, tying the record set by the 1932 Yankees and Cubs. It brought the 1953 total to 16, tying last year's record set by the Dodgers and Yankees.

Sunday's 47 total bases were more than any two clubs ever amassed in a Series game.

Snider, Robinson, Berra, Martin and other sluggers flailed away at the fences in practice oblivious to the pitching plotting which dominated Sunday's pregame dugout sceen.

Charley Dressen used Russ Meyer as a decoy, keeping the veteran on the bench instead of letting him roam the outfield with the other twirlers not expected to get into the game. Although it became known early that Podres had been tapped for the starting assignment, the

Continued on Page 40

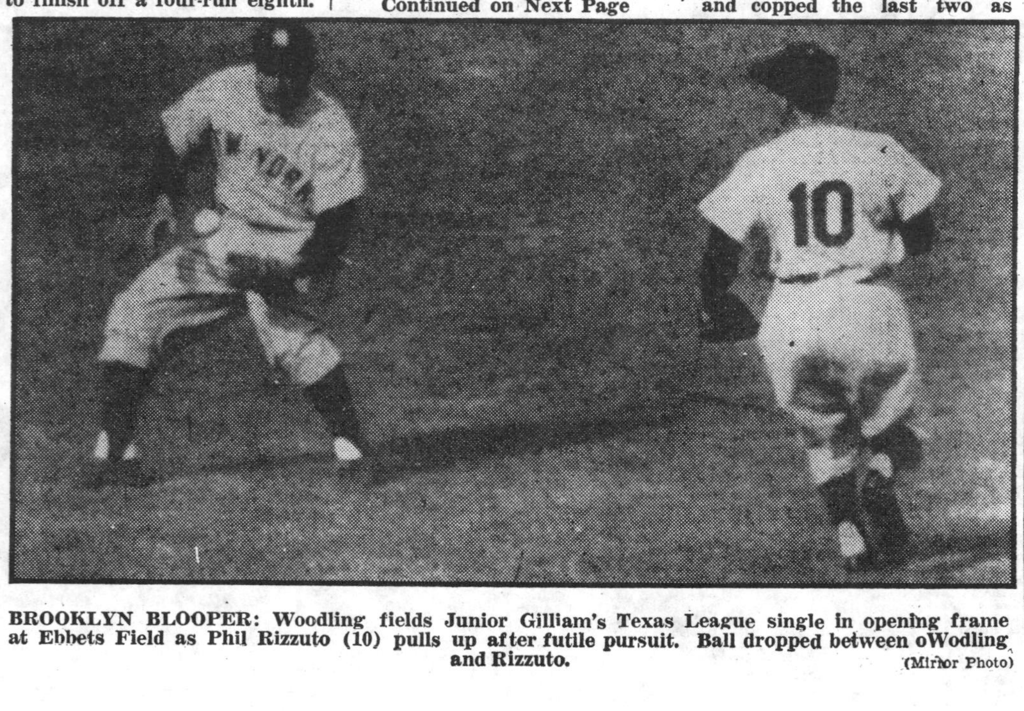

BROOKLYN BLOOPER: Woodling fields Junior Gilliam's Texas League single in opening frame at Ebbets Field as Phil Rizzuto (10) pulls up after futile pursuit. Ball dropped between oWodling and Rizzuto. (Mirror Photo)

SERIES DAY BY DAY.
Sept. 30—Yanks 9, Dodgers 5.
Oct. 1—Yanks 4, Dodgers 2.
Oct. 2—Yanks at Dodgers.
Oct. 3—Yanks at Dodgers.
Oct. 4—Yanks at Dodgers IF
Oct. 5—Dodgers at Yanks IF
Oct. 6—Dodgers at Yanks IF

		RUNS.	HITS.	ERRORS.
YANKEES . . .	000 010	—		
DODGERS . . .	000 011	—		

For Yankees—Raschi and Berra; For Dodgers—Erskine and Campanella.

SERIES STANDING.	W.	L.	Pct.
Yankees	2	0	1.000
Dodgers	0	2	.000

Four victories decide.

New York World-Telegram and The Sun

SCRIPPS-HOWARD

Local Forecast: Clear tonight. Tomorrow sunny, pleasantly warm. Weather Fotocast on Page 32.

7TH SPORTS Wall St. Closing BASEBALL—RACING

VOL. 121—NO. 25— IN TWO SECTIONS SECTION ONE NEW YORK, FRIDAY, OCTOBER 2, 1953 FIVE CENTS

BUMS RALLY, GO AHEAD

Troast Linked To Fay, Pal of Raceway Czar

By WALTER MacDONALD AND FRED J. COOK, *Staff Writers.*

Paul L. Troast, Republican candidate for governor of New Jersey, once appealed for commutation of the prison sentence of labor extortionist Joseph S. Fay, the World-Telegram and Sun learned today.

Mr. Troast headed an impressive gallery of distinguished names appended to letters sent to Gov. Thomas E. Dewey in Albany, begging that Fay be let out of prison because he was such a nice person and had served adequate time for the offense of shaking down Delaware Aqueduct contractors for $368,000.

This was the latest revelation to develop from the spreading harness racing scandal.

Man Behind the Scenes.

In this, Fay has slowly emerged as a behind-the-scenes power, a man with admittedly close relationships with William DeKoning, the AFL labor czar of Long Island, whose regime has shaken down Roosevelt Raceway employees for an estimated $345,000 a year.

Records today disclosed that an intensive campaign was waged in 1951 to spring Fay from Sing Sing through a commutation of his prison term. And it was revealed that Fay, even in prison, was such a power that some of the most distinguished public officials in this state came to visit him.

Lt. Gov. Arthur H. Wicks admitted that he visited Fay four or five times. "I went to see Joe in relation to the labor situation in my district," he said.

Bleakley Saw Him, Too.

Former Supreme Court Justice William F. Bleakley, now counsel for Yonkers Raceway, admitted that he, too, called on Fay, but he said the call had nothing to do with racing matters. He had been asked by a contractor client to see Fay on the latter's drive

Continued on Page Two

One of Gang Seized In Car Loan Fraud

2 Banks Swindled, Queens DA Reveals

District Attorney T. Vincent Quinn of Queens County announced today that he had in custody one of a group of ex-convicts who for a short time had perpetrated a unique swindle upon at least two banks.

The prosecutor said the gang began its operation with the purchase of a new car which they had registered in a fictitious name. Then, he said, they had the registration transferred to another fictitious name through the Motor Vehicle Bureau and they were ready to go to work.

The first victim, he said, was the Franklin National Bank at Franklin Square, L. I., which granted a loan of $1594 on the car. Next came a branch of the Manufacturers Trust Co. at 159-17 Jamaica Ave., Jamaica, which loaned $1594 on the car.

Ex-Forger Seized.

Yesterday the gang made a mistake. Taken into custody was a man who said he was Anthony De Maio, 30, of 8815 Elderts Lane, Bklyn., who only six months ago finished a prison term for a forgery committed in Brooklyn.

De Maio was arrested following suspicions he raised in the mind of Henry L. Fry, manager of the Manufacturers Trust Co. branch at 72-71 Main St., Kew Gardens. He had heard about what happened in the Jamaica branch and when De Maio called at his branch yesterday and asked for a $1600 loan on his car he delayed the transaction and sent for a cop.

De Maio, awaiting arraignment in Felony Court, Ridgewood on charges of forgery and grand larceny, allegedly admitted his part in the swindle and said the group hoped to pick up several thousand dollars and then skip town.

Rented Furnished Room.

Mr. Quinn said the defendant explained that they rented a furnished room on Atlantic Ave., Bklyn., and used a phony business name and address, equipped with phone, with which their loan applicants would associate themselves. Then when the bank called to inquire whether a certain person was employed there, the man at the phone would say he did and point him up as a most reliable person.

Mr. Quinn said he hoped to have three more men in custody within a short time.

Three Indicted In Butcher's Killing

By the United Press.

MONTICELLO, N. Y. Oct. 2.—Three Bronx youths were indicted by a Sullivan County grand jury today for first degree murder in the Labor Day slaying of Israel Present, Brooklyn butcher.

The three, Matthew Terrigno, 22, Raymond Rico, 23, and Thomas O'Hara, 17, will be arraigned here Monday.

Today's Index

Full page of School News daily, Monday through Friday, in the Night Edition.

Motel Men in Hotel

By the Associated Press.

CHATTANOOGA, Tenn., Oct. 2.—An estimated 250 motel owners and operators from a 14-state area today began a convention here—in a hotel.

Racing at Belmont Park

(Charts and Other Race Results in Sports Section.)

FIRST.	1—Heltop (Boland)	15.90	7.00	4.60
	2—P's and Q's (O'Brien)	—	4.50	3.40
	3—Tornabuoni (Atkinson)	—	—	3.50
SECOND.	1—Dash For Cash (Arcaro)	5.60	3.10	2.50
	2—Deep River (Atkinson)	—	3.70	2.90
	3—Outbird (Mayer)	—	—	4.70
	Daily double (9 and 4) paid $60.			
THIRD.	1—Outpoint (Jackson)	4.80	4.30	2.90
	2—Coveted (Schulhofer)	—	4.30	2.90
	3—St. Quill (Riles)	—	—	2.80
FOURTH.	1—Swift Sword (Cole)	9.60	5.50	4.00
	2—Old Glendale (Lane)	—	6.70	4.10
	3—Post Prandial (McCreary)	—	—	8.30

The World-Telegram and Sun Sports Section Leads the Field!

Larceny doesn't pay. Junior Gilliam is tagged out by Phil Rizzuto on his attempted steal of second in the first. Umpire Bill Grieve called it. United Press Telephoto.

BULLETIN

An around-the-clock police guard has been assigned to Joseph P. Ryan, president of the International Longshoremen's Assn., following a report that two gunmen were on their way to New York to murder him. Mr. Ryan is ill in French Hospital. At the same time, John Dwyer, head of the rival group of longshoremen, asked for a bodyguard and a detective was assigned to him. (Earlier details on Page 3.)

Non-Flatbush Fans Also Burned Up

By the Associated Press.

IVANHOE, Ill., Oct. 2.—As the Cecil Pinkous family watched a telecast of yesterday's World Series game, a passerby rushed in and announced that the house was on fire.

Mr. Pinkous, his pregnant wife and their 10 children escaped uninjured. They salvaged only a few belongings.

The house was destroyed.

Ticket Policy Converts 100 Dodger Fans to Yanks

The name of Walter O'Malley was mud today to something more than 100 ex-Dodger fans who couldn't get standing room in the bleachers at Ebbets Field.

"O'Malley's killing the goose that lays the Golden Egg," a spokesman said as he marched among several placard-bearers whose signs spoke equivalent fables.

According to James Thompson, superintendent of the Dodger ballpark, the trouble began at dawn today when fans began to gather for $2 standing room tickets in the bleachers.

They were told, Mr. Thompson said, that the bleachers were sold out, but that $4 standing room tickets were available at another gate.

That did it. Veteran Dodger fans . . . "the regular Bum supporters are bums now" . . . began to mutter. Down with O'Malley, they said. Down with the Dodgers. "I hope the Yankees win," someone said. "They will, brother," another remarked.

Among the disappointed was Ralph J. Belcore, 39, a carnival man out of Chicago. Been a Dodger fan all his life, seen 60 World Series games since 1924. Yankee fan forever now. Mr. Belcore was first in line, got there at 6 p.m. yesterday. He and the hundred-odd Yankee fans said they'll stay. Principle of the thing.

Get Out of Town, Thief! That Car Is Anastasia's

Murder Inc. Executioner Up in Arms Over Stolen Caddy, Even Calls Cops

Here's some advice for a clever car thief. If the car you stole from a midtown parking lot was a black 1949 two-door Cadillac sedan, leave it where it is and GET OUT OF TOWN.

That car belongs to Albert Anastasia, the oldest, toughest and most sinister of the Anastasia brothers.

Albert, chief executioner of Murder, Inc., is said to have killed men with ice picks, shotguns and his bare hands when he wasn't even mad.

And last night when he tried to pick up his car at that lot, the one at 231 W. 50th St., and found you had already claimed it—well, they say he was red hot.

They say he had a few thousand well-chosen words, none printable, to say to the hapless attendant who gave you the car. Then, like any other good citizen, he called the police.

They've been broadcasting city-wide alarms ever since so the car is as hot as you are.

And, police say, Albert is particularly incensed at the sneaky way you operate. Calling up the lot and telling them the owner was sending you over to pick up his car.

So if you're smart you will dye your hair, grow a mustache and go away somewhere—Outer Mongolia maybe.

Payroll Bandits Give Victim Token Sendoff

A pair of holdup men invested a 15-cent transit token today to assure the success of a $2500 payroll robbery in downtown Manhattan.

Jerome Nathanson, 27, of 2225 64th St., Bklyn., told police he was robbed of the payroll of the import-export firm of E. Miltenberg Inc., 43 Great Jones St., shortly after he left the National City Bank at Third St. and Broadway.

The thugs, he said, then walked him to the IRT subway at Bleecker and Lafayette Sts. One of the pair, he added, put a token in the turnstile and bade Mr. Nathanson bon voyage.

Mr. Nathanson rode to Spring St. and reported to police. There was no trace of the holdup men.

13 Fishermen Saved

By the Associated Press.

SINGAPORE, Oct. 2.—Thirteen Indonesian fishermen were rescued by the Panamanian tanker, Stanvac Sumatra, a radio message from the tanker said today. The rescue was made after the fishing boat sank in the Java Sea.

What Did Stengel Tell Lopat in 9th?

It was the last half of the ninth in yesterday's game. Two out, two Brook runners on and Duke Snider at bat. A home run would put the Bums ahead. The famous Stengel brain went into action.

What did he whisper in Lopat's ear when he strode to the mound? Read Joe Williams' column

IN TODAY'S SPORTS PAGES.

Play-by-Play Story Of 3rd Series Game

Special to World-Telegram and Sun.

EBBETS FIELD, Oct. 2.—The play-by-play of today's third game of the World Series between the Yankees and Dodgers:

Yank First—McDougald fanned after fouling off three pitches. Collins fanned on the 2-2 pitch. Bauer worked the count to 3 and 2 and then grounded out, Reese to Hodges.

Dodger First—Gilliam hit the 2-2 pitch to Martin, who couldn't handle it, for a base hit. Gilliam was caught stealing, Berra to Rizzuto. Reese was called out on strikes. Snider rolled behind second but Rizzuto threw him out.

Yank Second—Berra worked the count to 3 and 2 and went all the way to second when the fourth ball was a wild pitch. Mantle was called out on strikes on a 2-2 pitch. Woodling went out, Hodges to Erskine, Berra taking third. Martin walked. Rizzuto was called out on strikes.

Dodger Second—Hodges singled past McDougald. Campanella fanned on a 2-2 count. Furillo hit into a double play, Rizzuto to Martin to Collins.

Yank Third—Raschi was called out on strikes. McDougald hit a short fly to Robinson. Collins went down swinging on the 1-2 pitch.

Dodger Third—Robinson flied to Bauer in right center. Cox hit a one bouncer to McDougald and was thrown out. Erskine bunted out, McDougald to Collins.

Yank Fourth—Bauer was out on a close play, Reese to Hodges. Berra was hit on the right shoulder and went to first. Mantle fanned for the second time for Erskine's seventh strikeout. Woodling popped to Reese.

Dodger Fourth—Gilliam grounded out, Martin to Collins. Reese popped to McDougald. Snider walked on four pitches. Hodges worked the count to 3 and 2 and walked. Campanella forced Hodges, Martin to Rizzuto.

Yank Fifth—Martin beat out a hit to deep short for the first safe blow off Erskine. Rizzuto got an infield single when Gilliam failed to come up with the ball, Martin reaching second. Raschi sacrificed, Erskine to Hodges, the runners advancing. McDougald singled off Cox's glove, scoring Martin. Collins was called out on strikes. Bauer hit an easy chopper to Gilliam. ONE RUN.

Dodger Fifth—Furillo flied to Mantle. Robinson doubled off the right field screen. Raschi committed a balk and Robinson took third. Cox bunted and Robinson scored on the squeeze play, Cox reaching first. Erskine singled to left. Gilliam fouled to McDougald on a 3-2 pitch. Reese out, Martin to Collins. ONE RUN.

Yank Sixth—Berra singled past Hodges. Mantle went down swinging his third whiff and number nine for Erskine. Woodling, swinging, was victim number 10. Martin flied deep to center, Furillo mak ing a great one-handed catch after misjudging it.

Dodgers Sixth—Snider singled to right.

Hodges walked.

Campanella popped to Rashi on an attempted bunt.

Furrillo took a call third strike.

Robinson single to left scoring Snider.

Cox struck out.

Jelke Bail Fixed At $50,000 in Appeal

Bail of $50,000 for Minot F. Mickey) Jelke, convicted procurer, was set today by Supreme Court Justice Joseph A. Cox in advance of Jelke's release from Rikers Island where he is serving an eight-month sentence for possession of two guns, Jelke is eligible for release Tuesday.

Counsel for the oleo heir had asked for bail of $10,000, but the district attorney's office had argued for the higher amount. Jelke will be taken to City Prison on his release.

He still faces a prison term on the procurement convicteion, but Justice Cox has granted a certificate of reasonable doubt to permit the five-judge Appellate Division to review the question whether Jelke's trial was public with the press barred.

Please DON'T Ask Scores

Please don't phone the World-Telegram and Sun to find out how the World Series is going.

This service is being supplied by the New York Telephone Co. Call MEridian 7-1212, and you'll hear inning-by-inning scores, along with the usual time signals. Final scores will be announced after each game until 6:30 p.m.

If Egg Crate Breaks, Sit On Your Dignity, Fans!

By WILLIAM MICHELFELDER, *Staff Writer.*

Duke Snider had just lined a fast ball down the first base line. The gentleman from Ho-Ho-Kus, N. J., sitting three city blocks from home plate on a wicker basket, suddenly collapsed with a tearing sound.

Plucking a straw from herring-bone trousers this man, Sidney Reckman, well-heeled insurance man, bounced back up on his feet saying, "What the hell. For $1.50 I sat down at least 10 minutes."

$1.50 for a Basket.

Mr. Reckman, affable and half-crazed Dodger fan, paid $4 along with some 5000 others for the privilege of standing behind the very last row of seats. The $1.50 he paid to the vendor for his empty wicker basket after the last box of popcorn had been sold.

Egg crates, worn-out clubhouse office chairs, cardboard boxes, a folding chair that said in the back "Martin's Funeral Home" were also in circulation at prices up to $2.50.

"Last time I went to a Series here," went on Mr. Reckman, "there was a guy who somehow sneaked in a dozen beat-up tripods. He threw in a square of cardboard to balance on. All for $2."

DeLuxe Equipment.

Standees at Yankee Stadium are devotees of self-torture and added expense. DeLuxe equipment: $4 to stand; $1.50 to $2 for a body prop; $2 for a pair of toy field glasses; 35 cents for sunshade; 35 cents for beer; 50 cents for pennant; $2.25 for autographed baseball with facsimile autographs. Mr. Reckman had all of these.

"If I had bought a $7.50 seat," he said, "I couldn't have afforded the extras."

Engraved Signs.

Best seats in the joint are the reserved boxes along the first base line. With comparable seats on the third base line, in the hot sun and consequently discomforting, one is able to make a study of how to select a profitable livelihood. The Yankee management has nailed engraved signs to the all-season reserved boxes. On the first base line, where they cost up to 40 percent more, are the banks, railroads, pharmaceutical houses, oil companies, hotel chains and Wall Street firms.

Along the cheaper third base boxes are the small manufacturers, book publishers, wholesale plumbers and family groups. The trouble with the $4 standees far in the rear is that when they pay $1.50 for a wicker basket or egg crate they sit down and can see nothing.

Mr. Reckman had an answer to that. "Then," he said triumphantly, "I turn on my portable radio."

And he did. For an extra $2 he got an old Yankee office chair. "C'mon!" he screamed at the radio, "Whaddya using? A bag for a glove?"

Yankees Score First in Tight Pitching Duel

Raschi Balk Sets Up Brooklyn Comeback

YANKEES.	DODGERS.
McDougald, 3b	Gilliam, 2b
Collins, 1b	Reese, ss
Bauer, rf	Snider, cf
Berra, c	Hodges, 1b
Mantle, cf	Campanella, c
Woodling, lf	Furillo, rf
Martin, 2b	Robinson, lf
Rizzuto, ss	Cox, 3b
Raschi, p (13-6)	Erskine, p (20-6)

Umpires: Plate, Hurley (AL); first base, Gore (NL); Second Base, Grieve (AL); Third Base, Stewart (NL); Left Field, Soar (AL); Right Field, Dascoli (NL).

Game Time: 1:05 P.M.

By DANIEL, *Sports Writer.*

EBBETS FIELD, Oct. 2.—After four scoreless innings, both teams broke through in the fifth in the third World Series game today. The Yankees put together three infield hits and a sacrifice for one run, but the Dodgers came back to tie on a double, a balk and a squeeze bunt.

The first three frames of this tense duel saw six Yankees go down on strikes. Meanwhile, only nine Dodgers came to bat, two who got hits being erased.

Roy Campanella was named to catch Erskine, much to everybody's surprise. The burly receiver's hand had been injured in the first game when he was hit by an Allie Reynolds pitch, and in yesterday's contest he was futile at bat. In four trips he hit slow rollers for easy outs, sometimes at critical moments.

Campanella, after the defeat, had indicated he would step aside for Rube Walker, his slow-footed reserve. Dressen had concurred. But this morning the manager asked Roy if he wanted to play.

Roy declared that he did, that the hand seemed much improved.

Trainer Harold Wendler could offer no explanation for the apparent recovery. Wendler said there would be no attempt to "freeze" the hand through use of drugs.

Dressen, however, revamped his batting order, with Gil Hodges

Continued on Page 31.

Snowsuit or Swim Suit?

By the Associated Press.

HELENA, Mont., Oct. 2.—While Miles City recovered from a record 93-degree autumn heat wave, four other Montana cities received snow today. Weather Bureau officials said wet snow fell at Dillon, Butte, Bozeman and Livingston, melting as it fell.

The Weather

(Official United States Forecast)

New York City and Vicinity, Northern New Jersey and Long Island: Clear tonight with temperatures much the same as last night, lowest about 60 in the city proper and near 45 in northern suburbs. Tomorrow sunny and pleasantly warm again with highest temperatures in the upper 70s. Gentle variable winds tonight, becoming gentle to moderate south to southeasterly tomorrow.

Connecticut: Continued cool tonight. Tomorrow sunny, temperatures about the same as today.

FIVE-DAY FORECAST.

Weather forecast for Middle Atlantic States and Eastern New York, tomorrow through Wednesday: Temperatures will average well above normal, with warmest period Sunday and Monday. Fair and sunny weather with no rain indicated except for a possibility of scattering showers upstate.

TODAY'S READINGS.

	Temp.	Hum.		Temp.	Hum.
Midnight	65	—	8 a.m.	59	54
1 a.m.	62	—	9 a.m.	62	51
2 a.m.	63	—	10 a.m.	70	42
3 a.m.	61	—	11 a.m.	72	35
4 a.m.	60	—	Noon	72	26
5 a.m.	59	—	1 p.m.	74	25
6 a.m.	58	66	2 p.m.	74	26
7 a.m.	55	67	3 p.m.	73	26

Year ago: High, 77. Low, 54.

SANDY HOOK TIDES.

	A.M.	P.M.		A.M.	P.M.
High	3:21	3:38	Low	9:34	10:18

SERIES DAY BY DAY.						RUNS.	HITS.	ERRORS.
Sept. 30—Yanks 9, Dodgers 5.	DODGERS . . .	000	001	002	—	3	8	3
Oct. 1—Yanks 4, Dodgers 2.	YANKEES . . .	210	000	001	—	4	13	0
Oct. 2—Dodgers 3, Yanks 2.								
Oct. 3.—Dodgers 7, Yanks 3.								
Oct. 4—Yanks 11, Dodgers 7.								
Oct. 5—Yankees 4, Dodgers 3.								

For Dodgers—Erskine, Milliken, Labine and Campanella. For Yankees—Ford, Reynolds and Berra.

SERIES STANDING.

	W.	L.	Pct.
Yankees	4	2	.667
Dodgers	2	4	.333

(Four Victories Decide.)

SCRIPPS-HOWARD

New York World-Telegram and The Sun

Local Forecast: Mostly cloudy tonight and tomorrow, chance of light rain. Fotocast on Page 30.

VOL. 121—NO. 27— IN TWO SECTIONS SECTION ONE NEW YORK, MONDAY, OCTOBER 5, 1953 FIVE CENTS

7TH SPORTS
Wall St. Closing
SERIES EXTRA

YANKS WORLD CHAMPS!

Bare 'Loyalty' Review Of Raceway Workers

Former State Senator Had Screening Job

By WALTER MacDONALD and FRED J. COOK, *Staff Writers.*

Former State Sen. S. William N. Conrad admitted today that he had served as vice chairman of the screening committee that passes on all applicants for jobs at Roosevelt Raceway under the regime of Long Island labor czar William C. DeKoning Sr.

Racetrack workers who have run the gauntlet of this committee pictured it to The World-Telegram and Sun as a loyalty review board that has just one standard of patriotism—how faithful has the applicant been in attendance at DeKoning's Mule Club and how much has he kicked into the kitty?

Sen. Conrad gave a different version when reached at his Ridgewood home. He denied he knew anything about pressure on racetrack workers; but he did confirm much that this newspaper had been told by informants.

He admitted he had worked at Roosevelt Raceway until it closed Sept. 26. He volunteered that he is supervisor of the track's Tel-Autograph system—exactly what this newspaper had been told. And he agreed that he had served as vice-chairman of the DeKoning screening committee, just as track workers had said.

It was on the account of what the screening committee did, or didn't do, that the versions of the former Democratic state senator and city councilman diverged from those of the workers who had appeared before him.

Racetrack employees gave a

Continued on Page 10.

Warren Takes Oath, Presides At High Court

By CHARLOTTE G. MOULTON, *United Press Staff Writer.*

WASHINGTON, Oct. 5.—Earl Warren, swearing to "do equal right to the poor and to the rich," became 14th Chief Justice of the United States today and then presided over the opening session of the Supreme Court's 1953-54 term.

The former governor of California took the oath in the marble-pillared chambers of the Supreme Court in the presence of President and Mrs. Eisenhower, Mrs. Warren and other notables.

Critical Cases Pending.

Mr. Warren succeeds Chief Justice Fred M. Vinson, who died of a heart attack Sept. 8.

The new Chief Justice takes over at a time when the tribunal is confronted with some of the most important decisions in its history, including the question of

Continued on Page Two.

Ryan Dockers Vow To Defy Injunction

By JOSEPH ALVAREZ and NORTON MOCKRIDGE, *Staff Writers.*

Although the five-day waterfront strike was expected to come to an official end late today or early tomorrow as a result of a court injunction, there was every indication today that turmoil on the docks would continue.

First, President Eisenhower's special board of inquiry reported to him in Washington that a negotiated settlement of the East

Continued on Page Two

Sixth Game Box Score

DODGERS

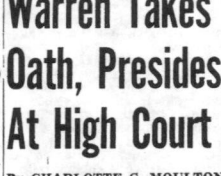

	AB.	R.	H.	RBI.	SO.	BB.	PO.	A.	E.
Gilliam, 2b	4	0	0	0	1	0	4	4	1
Reese, ss	4	0	1	0	0	0	1	4	0
Robinson, lf	4	1	2	0	0	0	3	0	0
Campanella, c	4	0	1	1	2	0	4	0	0
Hodges, 1b	4	0	0	0	0	0	7	0	0
Snider, cf	3	1	0	0	3	1	4	1	0
Furillo, rf	4	1	3	2	0	0	2	0	0
Cox, 3b	0	0	1	0	2	0	0	1	1
Erskine, p	1	0	0	0	1	0	0	0	1
Milliken, p	0	0	0	0	0	0	0	0	0
Labine, p	1	0	0	0	1	0	0	1	0
Williams	0	0	0	0	0	1	0	0	0
Morgan	1	0	0	0	0	0	0	0	0
Totals	34	3	8	3	10	2	25	11	3

YANKEES

	AB.	R.	H.	RBI.	SO.	BB.	PO.	A.	E.
Woodling, lf	4	1	2	1	0	1	1	0	0
Collins, 1b	3	0	1	0	1	1	5	1	0
Bollweg, 1b	0	0	0	0	0	0	0	0	0
Bauer, rf	3	2	1	0	0	2	3	0	0
Berra, c	5	0	2	1	0	0	9	0	0
Mantle, cf	4	0	1	0	0	1	5	0	0
Martin, 2b	5	0	2	2	0	0	1	0	0
McDougald, 3b	4	0	0	0	1	0	0	0	0
Rizzuto, ss	4	1	2	0	0	0	2	2	0
Ford, p	3	0	1	0	0	0	0	1	0
Reynolds, p	1	0	1	0	0	0	0	0	0
Mize	1	0	0	0	0	0	0	0	0
Totals	37	4	13	4	2	5	27	4	0

Umpires—Plate, Stewart (NL); first, Hurley (AL); second, Gore (NL); third, Grieve (AL); foul lines, Dascoli (NL) and Soar (AL). Attendance—62,370.

Today's Index

BULLETIN

By the United Press.

WASHINGTON, Oct. 5.—President Eisenhower today directed the Justice Department to seek a Federal Court injunction to halt the East Coast strike for at least 80 days.

Found Dead, Gas On

August Kravos, 39, an office worker, was found dead of illuminating gas inhalation in his furnished room at 525 W. 123rd St. last night. Police listed the death as suicide.

Racing at Belmont Park

(Charts and Other Race Results in Sports Section.)

FIRST.	1—Queen's Story (Mayer)	27.20	12.70	9.10
	2—Jiggle (Stovall)	—	7.70	5.50
	3—Lecount (Guerin)	—	—	8.00
SECOND.	1—Cloudy (Atkinson)	7.30	4.40	2.80
	2—Hi Chief (Arcaro)	—	6.70	4.50
	3—Brown Dalton (Eccard)	—	—	2.80
	Daily double (6 and 11) paid $125.40.			
THIRD.	1—First Copy (Cangemie)	37.60	12.70	6.10
	2—Capeador (Guerin)	—	3.10	2.60
	3—Honest Bread (Sande)	—	—	5.10
FOURTH.	1—Sea O' Erin (Arcaro)	10.60	5.10	4.20
	2—Gotta Go (Atkinson)	—	4.80	3.70
	3—Indian File (Woodhouse)	—	—	5.00
FIFTH.	1—Williamsburg (Riles)	5.20	4.10	3.10
	2—King Commander (Smith'k)	—	4.10	3.10
	3—Hyvania (Smiley)	—	—	3.50

The World-Telegram and Sun Sports Section Leads the Field!

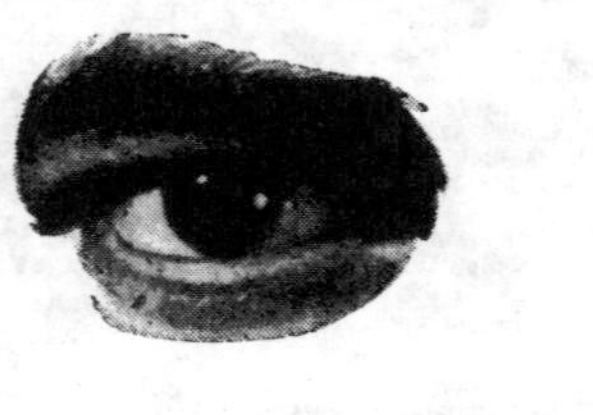

LARGER TYPE TODAY

News stories and features throughout today's World-Telegram and Sun appear in a new, larger, more legible type.

The great clarity of this especially designed type and its benefits to eye health have been heartily indorsed by the New York State Optometrics Assn., leading educators and readers who have previewed it.

The new, easier-to-read type will be used from now on. We hope this improvement will contribute to your daily reading pleasure.

An Early Getaway Helps

Whitey Ford, who made a late start from third on Yogi Berra's fly to center, is tagged out at home by Roy Campanella. Bill Stewart's thumb gives the out signal. This ended the second inning.

United Press Telephoto.

6th Game Detail, Play-by-Play

Special to World-Telegram and Sun.

YANKEE STADIUM, Oct. 5.—The play-by-play of today's sixth game of the World Series between the Yankees and Dodgers:

Dodgers First—Gilliam popped the 2-1 pitch to Collins. Reese singled to left on the 1-1 pitch. Robinson hit to Martin, who tagged Reese on the baseline and both sprawled in the dirt. Stengel came on the field to claim interference with Martin's effort to throw to first. Campanella singled to center, Robinson stopping at second. Hodges lined to Rizzuto.

YANK FIRST—Woodling walked on a full count. Collins fanned, swinging. Bauer singled to left, Woodling stopping at second. Berra lashed the first pitch to right. The ball glanced off Furillo's glove into the stands for a double, Woodling scoring, Bauer taking third. Mantle was purposely passed. Martin reached first, Bauer scored and the runners advanced when Gilliam failed to hold Billy's hard ground ball. McDougald hit into a double play, Cox to Gilliam to Hodges. TWO RUNS.

Dodger Second—Snider, on a full count, fanned. Furillo dropped a single behind first base and was out trying for second, Collins to Rizzuto. Cox fanned.

Yank Second—Rizzuto singled over Reese's head. Ford singled to right, Rizzuto taking third. Woodling flied to Robinson, Rizzuto scoring after the catch. Collins plunked a ball to the left of the mound and reached second when Erskine threw over Hogdes' head, Ford taking third. It was a hit for Collins. Bauer walked, filling the bases. After Berra flied to Snider. Ford made a break for the plate, stopped, then started again and was out, Snider to Gilliam to Campanella. ONE RUN.

Dodger Third—Erskine fanned. Gilliam flied to Woodling. Reese flied to Mantle.

Yank Third—Mantle grounded to Gilliam on the 3-0 pitch. Martin flied to Robinson after a full count. Cox couldn't hold McDougald's hard drive and was charged with an error. Rizzuto fouled to Hodges.

Dodger Fourth — Robinson bounced to Rizzuto. Campanella fanned. Hodges, on a full count, bounced to Ford.

Yank Fourth—Ford flied to Snider. Woodling singled over second on the second pitch. Collins flied to Furillo after a full count. Bauer forced Woodling, Reese to Gilliam.

Dodger Fifth — Snider again fanned on the 3-2 pitch. Furillo doubled off the scoreboard in left. Ford had retired eight men in order. Cox flied to Mantle. Williams batted for Erskine and walked after a full count. Gilliam was called out on strikes.

Yank Fifth—Milliken took the mound for the Dodgers. Berra popped to Gilliam on the first pitch. Mantle flied to Snider after fouling the 3-0 pitch. Martin sliced a drive to right field which bounced into the stands for a ground rule double. It was Martin's 11th hit. McDougald bounced to Reese.

Dodger Sixth—Reese flied to Mantle in deep right center. Robinson doubled down the left-field line. Robinson stole third, drawing no throw. Campanella was tossed out by Rizzuto, Robinson scoring. Hodges bounced to Collins. ONE RUN.

Yank Sixth—Rizzuto popped to Snider. Ford bounced to Reese. Woodling singled off Gilliam's glove. Collins walked on four pitches. Bauer popped to Reese.

Dodger Seventh—Snider fanned for the third time, as leadoff each time. Furillo, on a full count, flied to Mantle. Cox singled to left. Morgan batted for Milliken and flied to Bauer who made a running catch against the fence.

Yank Seventh—Labine replaced Milliken.

Berra singled to left.

Mantle flied to Robinson.

Martin hit into a double play, Labine to Gilliam to Hodges.

Dodger Eighth—Reynolds replaced Ford.

Gilliam flied to Bauer.

Reese flied to Bauer.

Robinson singled to left.

Campanella strike out.

Yank Eighth — McDougald fanned. Rizzuto beat out a hit to short. Reynolds singled to right, Rizzuto reaching third. Woodling grounded to short and Reese threw out Rizzuto at the plate. Mize batted for Collins and grounded to Hodges.

Dodger Ninth—Bollweg played first. Hodges flied to Mantle. Snider walked. Furillo hit a home run into the right field stands, scoring Snider to tie the score. Cox fanned. Labine fanned. TWO RUNS.

Yank Ninth — Bauer walked. Berra flied to Furillo. Mantle singled off Cox's glove, Bauer reaching second. Martin singled to center, scoring Bauer with the winning run. ONE RUN.

Sign Up, Rivals Urge As Registry Begins

Don't forget to register this week if you want to vote in the important Nov. 3 general election.

The registry books were to open at 3:30 p.m. today in polling places in the city and remain open until 10:30 p.m. The same schedule will be followed every day through Friday. On Saturday, the final day for registration, the hours are from 7 a.m. to 10:30 p.m.

Traditionally the first day's turnout is light. Board of Elections officials were expecting the avalanche later in the week. Their suggestion: register early and avoid the rush.

Mayoral candidates were unanimous yesterday in urging New Yorkers to register this week.

Robert F. Wagner, Democratic candidate, said:

"Make New York City's government your government. Do this by voting on Nov. 3 for whomever you think you want to entrust your government to. Please vote. Vote for whomever you wish. But vote."

A special appeal to women voters came from Mrs. Preston Davie, special adviser to Harold Riegelman, Republican candidate. She said:

"Women have tremendous responsibility and power in the

Continued on Page Six.

Bombers Take Title for Fifth Straight Time

Erskine Fails to Stem Stengel Tide

By DANIEL, *Sports Writer.*

YANKEE STADIUM, Oct. 5.—The Yankees today captured their fifth straight world's championship as they defeated the Dodgers again to win the World Series, four games to two.

The score was 4 to 3.

Furillo slammed a home run off Reynolds in the top of the ninth with Snider on base to tie the score at 3-3.

Back in their own park, the Bombers tallied twice in the first when Woodling walked, Bauer si[illegible] Berra doubled and Gil[illegible] by Mar[illegible] scored [illegible]

[illegible] the Dodgers [illegible] their ace pitcher, Carl Erskine, a 20-game winner, who fanned 14 Yankees in capturing the third contest after lasting just one inning in the opener.

The Yankees countered with their young left-hander, Whitey Ford, who started the fourth game Saturday, but gave way after yielding three runs in the first inning.

Casey Stengel, who had used four different Yankee lineups in the first five games, came back today with the batting order that started yesterday. Gene Woodling was leadoff, Billy Martin sixth and Gil McDougald seventh.

The Dodger lineup was the one that opposed Ford at the start of Saturday's game, with Duke

Continued on Page 21

Killed Atop Box Car

Special to World-Telegram and Sun.

MOUNT VERNON, N. Y., Oct. 5.—Edward McKenna, 21, of 150 South Broadway, Yonkers, was found dead early this morning atop a box car in the New York Central Freight Yard. Mount Vernon police theorized that he hopped the car at its New York City starting point and was struck by a low bridge while standing.

McIntyre at Tuckahoe

Special to World-Telegram and Sun.

TUCKAHOE, N. Y., Oct. 5.—A solemn pontifical mass presided over by James Francis Cardinal McIntyre, Archbishop of Los Angeles, highlighted the observance of the 100th anniversary of the Catholic Church of the Immaculate Conception on Winter Hill Rd. here yesterday.

The Weather

(Official United States Forecast)

New York and vicinity, northern New Jersey and Long Island: Mostly cloudy tonight and tomorrow with chance of some light rain; cooler today than yesterday with highest temperatures in upper 60s tomorrow. Cooler tonight with lowest temperatures around 50 degrees and highest tomorrow again in the 60s. Gentle to moderate north to northeast winds tonight, becoming moderate east to southeast early tomorrow and shifting to northwest late tomorrow.

Connecticut: Rain with little change in temperatures tonight. Tomorrow, rain in the morning, followed by clearing in the afternoon, continued cool.

TODAY'S READINGS.

	Temp.	Hum.		Temp.	Hum.
Midnight	66	—	8 a.m.	61	47
1 a.m.	66	—	9 a.m.	61	47
2 a.m.	65	—	10 a.m.	62	54
3 a.m.	64	—	11 a.m.	63	57
4 a.m.	64	—	Noon	63	57
5 a.m.	63	—	1 p.m.	63	61
6 a.m.	62	70	2 p.m.	63	65
7 a.m.	62	48	3 p.m.	60	70
			4 p.m.	60	71

Year ago: High, 75. Low, 55.

SANDY HOOK TIDES.

	A.M.	P.M.		A.M.	P.M.
High	5:56	6:06	Low	—	12:01

Sunrise 5:56 a.m. Sunset 5:33 p.m.

BASEBALL TEN PINS: YANKEES' BOB CERV THROWS SHOULDER BLOCK ON RED SOX' BILLY GOODMAN (No. 10) IN BREAKING UP DOUBLE-PLAY ATTEMPT IN SIXTH INNING.
—Associated Press Wirephoto

Yanks Beat Sox in Night Game, Clinching 6th Pennant In 7 Years

Ford Checks Threat As Larsen Weakens

By F. C. MATZEK
Journal-Bulletin Sports Writer

Boston—The New York Yankees are back again in an old familiar role—champions of the American League.

They applied the clincher last night at Fenway Park with a 3 to 2 conquest of the Red Sox before 25,158 chilled and thrilled customers.

It meant the Yanks' 21st crown in the 55-year history of the junior circuit and their sixth in the seven-year managerial reign of the smart and cagey oldster, Charles Dillon (Casey) Stengel.

The clincher was in the best tradition of Stengel-directed Yankee teams.

Beaten 8 to 4 by the Sox in an afternoon game the Yanks made the night contest one of their "big" game targets and went out and won it in typical Yankee fashion with an opportune attack and good pitching.

The opportune attack started with Gil McDougald's 13th homer as the forerunner of a two-run first inning burst against Boston's best Yankee-tamer of recent years, Willard Nixon.

All They Needed

A third Yank run in the fifth, punched home by big Ed Robinson's pinch-hit single, boosted the Yank advantage to 3-0, which was all the margin Don Larsen and Whitey Ford needed.

Between them they limited the Sox to nine hits but only two runs. Larsen was the starter and winner of his ninth decision and third straight against the Bostons but when he faltered and gave up the first Bosox run in the seventh, Ford moved stolidly to his rescue and did a superb job that included shutting off the seventh inning splurge by getting Ted Williams to rap into a double play.

Winningest of the Yankee hurlers with a 18-7 record, the towheaded southpaw held the Sox to just one hit during his relief chore of two and two-thirds innings. It didn't even matter that the one hit was a lead off homer by Jackie Jensen in the eighth, his 26th of the year and second of the day. He hit No. 25 in the afternoon game.

Matter of fact neither of the Jensen homers had too much effect on the Yankee overall plan, which was to win at least one of their final four games here at the Fens—and thus apply the crown clincher.

Restrained Joy

They did in the nightcap and even then there was merely restrained joy in the Yankee clubhouse when that little title business was accomplished. The Yanks were happy, of course, but in a definitely restrained way.

Most of the exuberance shown in the locker room was for the benefit of the cameramen. Winning pennants is an old custom for quite a contingent of these Yanks. They're not the excitable type.

They didn't get excited one little bit when the Sox snapped an eight-game winning streak in the 8-4 afternoon game, a victory which was cemented for a good Bosox relief pitcher, Ike Delock, when he and his mates exploded against starter Tommy Byrne and the veteran reliefer, Jim Konstanty, for six runs in the third inning.

In the afternoon game, Bob Cerv's leadoff homer in the first plus a second inning tally, scored when Grady Hatton booted Byrne's double play hopper, gave the Yanks a 2-0 lead which was erased in the second as Jerry Coleman let Tommy Brewer's routine grounder skitter past him for a two-run error.

Brewer aggravated a pulled muscle he sustained just a few days ago and retired after he got two out in the third. It was then Delock took over and his five-hit, two-run chucking over the final six and a third innings earned him his ninth victory of the year and third over the Yanks.

It was nailed down in the big third. Jensen's 25th homer, opened that burst and before it was over Sammy White singled for a run, Billy Goodman singled for two, Billy Klaus for one and Jensen, up for the second time, walked with the bases loaded, forcing in the sixth and final tally.

The Sox victory snapped a seven-game losing streak and gave them their seventh triumph in 19 wrangles with the Stengelmen.

But their one triumph wasn't the starter of any new winning sequence. The Yanks saw to that in the nightcap.

Another Quick Start

Again they got away to a quick start. After McDougald's first inning homer, No. 3 of the year for him, Irv Noren doubled into the left field corner, reached third on Yogi Berra's single to right and scored as Joe Collins grounded out.

Cerv's walk after two were out in the fifth got the game's winning rally under way most inauspiciously. The Yank center fielder raced to third as Billy Martin singled off the left field scoreboard and scored as Robinson, batting for Phil Rizzuto, singled into right center.

That was all for the Yanks and it also was enough because Larsen and Ford, the latter particularly, were so efficient.

Larsen had a five-hit shutout going into the seventh. Then Dick Gernert, White and Eddie Joost singled for the first Bosox run, a set of circumstances that brought Ford to Larsen's rescue with two runners still aboard and only one out.

Ford had had to warm up quickly and he was just a trifle wild. He walked Klaus, the first batter he faced, and the bases were loaded.

But the crafty young lefty had the stopper. He ended the rally by getting Williams with his double play pitch.

Jensen's homer in the eighth was young Mr. Ford's only errant action—if you can call a home run pitch errant. Anyway, after that he turned back the next six Bosox in order, three of them on strikeouts.

NEW YORK	AB	H	O	A	BOSTON	AB	H	O	A
Cerv. cf	4	2	1	0	G'dman.2b	5	2	1	1
M'D'al.3b	5	1	0	5	Klaus. ss	4	2	1	1
Bauer. rf	5	1	2	0	Will'ms.lf	3	0	0	0
Berra. c	4	1	4	1	St'ph'ns.lf	1	0	0	0
Collins. 1b	3	0	11	1	Jensen. rf	3	1	2	0
Howar. lf	3	0	3	0	Zauchin.1b	1	0	4	0
Martin. 2b	4	2	2	3	fGern't.1b	3	0	3	0
Byrne. p	1	0	1	0	Hatton. 3b	4	2	2	2
Konst'ty. p	1	0	0	0	Piersall.cf	4	1	3	0
aRob'son	0	0	0	0	White. c	4	2	9	1
bRich'n.ss	1	0	0	1	Brewer. p	1	0	0	1
Col'm'n.ss	2	0	0	2	Delock. p	2	1	0	2
cBerb'et	1	1	0	0					
dCarroll	0	0	0	0					
Wiesler. p	0	0	0	1					
eSkowr'n	1	0	0	0					
St'riv't. p	0	0	0	0					
Totals	35	8	24	14		35	11	27	8

a—Walked for Konstanty in 6th.
b—Ran for Robinson in 6th.
c—Singled for Coleman in 6th.
d—Ran for Berberet in 6th.
e—Lined out for Wiesler in 8th.
f—Ran for Zauchin in 3rd.

New York	110 002 000	—4
Boston	026 000 00x	—8

R—Cerv, Collins, Howard, Richarson, Goodman, Jensen, Gernert, Hatton 2, White 2, Delock. E—Hatton, Coleman. RBI—Cerv 2, Berberet, Jensen 2, White, Goodman 2, Klaus. 2B—White, Goodman, Bauer. HR—Cerv, Jensen. SB—Piersall. DP—Berra, Martin and Collins. Left—New York 9, Boston 9. BB—Byrne 3, Konstanty 2, Sturdivant 1, Brewer 3, Delock 2. SO—Konstanty 1, Wiesler 1, Sturdivant 2, Brewer 4, Delock 5. HO—Byrne 7 in 2 2-3, Konstanty 3 in 2 1-3, Wiesler 1 in 2, Sturdivant 0 in 1, Brewer 3 in 2 2-3, Delock 5 in 6 1-3. R-ER—Byrne 8-6, Konstanty 0-0, Wiesler 0-0, Sturdivant 0-0, Brewer 2-1, Delock 2-2. WP—Brewer. W—Delock (9-7). L—Byrne (16-5). U—Napp, Umont, Rommel, Paparella. T—2:56. A—10,848.

Second Game

NEW YORK	AB	H	O	A	BOSTON	AB	H	O	A
Bauer. rf	4	0	0	0	Joost. 2b	4	2	3	3
M'D'ald.3b	4	3	0	1	Klaus. ss	3	0	5	3
Noren. cf	5	2	0	0	Will'ms.lf	4	2	2	0
Berra. c	5	1	10	0	Jensen. rf	4	1	2	1
Collins.1b	4	1	8	2	Hatton. 3b	4	0	0	1
Cerv. lf	2	1	3	0	Piersall.cf	4	0	1	0
Martin.2b	4	2	1	4	Gernert.1b	4	2	9	2
Rizzuto.ss	1	0	1	1	White. c	3	1	4	0
aRob'son	1	1	0	0	Nixon. p	2	1	1	1
Col'm'n.ss	2	0	3	3	bThr'b'ry	1	0	0	0
Larsen. p	4	0	1	0	Kiely. p	0	0	0	1
Ford. p	0	0	0	1	cMalzone	1	0	0	0
Totals	36	11	27	12	Totals	34	9	27	12

a—Single for Rizzuto in 5th.
b—Popped out for Nixon in 7th.
c—Called out on strikes for Kiely in 9th.

New York	200 010 000	—3
Boston	000 000 110	—2

R—McDougald, Noren, Cerv, Jensen, Gernert. E—Joost, White, Gernert, Hatton. RBI—McDougald, Collins, Robinson, Joost, Jensen. 2B—Noren, Gernert. HR—McDougald, Jensen. SB—Cerv. S—Rizzuto, Cerv. DP—Collins, Rizzuto and Collins; Martin, Coleman and Collins; Klaus, Joost and Gernert. Left—New York 14, Boston 8. BB—Larsen 2, Ford 1, Nixon 4, Kiely 1. SO—Larsen 3, Ford 3, Nixon 3. HO—Larsen 8 in 6 1-3, Ford 1 in 2 2-3, Nixon 10 in 7, Kiely 1 in 2. R-ER—Larsen 1-1, Ford 1-1, Nixon 3-3, Kiely 0-0. HBP—By Nixon (Cerv). W—Larsen (9-2). L—Nixon (12-10). U—Umont, Rommel, Paparella, Napp. T—3:02. A—25,158.

Whooping It Up: Here is how the Yankee dressing room looked last night after the New Yorkers had clinched their 21st American League pennant by beating the Red Sox, 3-2. Yogi Berra hoists Don Larsen on his back and Casey Stengel (left) goes into a swoon. That's co-owner Del Webb in the center of things.
—Associated Press Wirephoto

Rogovin Hurls Phillies Over Giants, 5 to 1

New York—(AP)—Saul Rogovin an American League castoff from Baltimore, limited the New York Giants to five scattered singles yesterday as the Philadelphia Phillies clinched a tie for fourth place in the National League with a 5-1 victory.

PHILADELPHIA	AB	H	O	A	NEW YORK	AB	H	O	A
Ashburn.cf	4	0	2	0	Garn'r.ss	4	0	0	4
Morgan.ss	5	1	3	4	Mueller.rf	4	1	3	0
Hamner.2b	4	2	2	2	Mays. cf	4	0	2	0
Ennis. lf	4	2	1	0	Th'pson.3b	3	2	0	3
Jones. 3b	4	1	3	1	L'kman. lf	2	1	3	0
Lopata. 1b	3	1	6	0	Harris. 1b	3	0	7	1
Blayl'k.1b	0	0	2	0	Hofman.2b	3	0	6	1
Gr'ngr's.rf	3	1	3	0	Katt. c	3	1	6	1
Seminick.c	3	1	5	0	Gomez. p	1	0	0	1
Rogovin. p	3	0	0	0	aRhodes	1	0	0	0
					Giel. p	0	0	0	0
					bTaylor	1	0	0	0
					Wilhelm.p	0	0	0	0
Totals	33	9	27	7	Totals	29	5	27	11

a—Flied out for Gomez in 6th.
b—Grounded out for Giel in 8th.

Philadelphia	200 011 010	—5
New York	000 000 100	—1

R—Morgan, Hamner 2, Lopata, Seminick. Mueller. E—None. RBI—Ennis, Jones 2, Seminick, Lockman, Rogovin. HR—Seminick. S—Seminick, Rogovin. SF—Lockman. DP—Hamner and Lopata; Hamner, Morgan and Lopata. Left—Philadelphia 8, New York 2. BB—Gomez 2, Giel 1. SO—Rogovin 4, Gomez 3, Giel 1, Wilhelm 1. HO—Gomez 8 in 6, Giel 1 in 2, Wilhelm 0 in 1. R-ER—Rogovin 1-1, Gomez 4-4, Giel 1-1, Wilhelm 0-0. HBP—By Gomez (Lopata), by Giel (Greengrass). W—Rogovin (5-3). L—Gomez (9-10). U—Conlan, Dascoli, Gorman, Donatelli. T—2:01. A—1,154.

Inside Out

By Earl Lofquist

A Pair of Tossups . . .

With football going into high gear, Brown and the University of Rhode Island, the only two colleges fielding football around here, are matched with opponents who may be regarded as roughly their peers.

Rhode Island, at home to the University of Maine, has one distinct advantage over the visiting team. It got a game of football under its belt last Saturday, and should be the better for it in this Yankee Conference contest. Although a tie satisfies no one, the Rams showed enough in tying Northeastern to inspire the hope they will do well in their league.

In discussing Rhode Island's prospects in the impending game, Tom Doherty, spokesman for sports as played at the state university, drops a broad hint that Billy Montanaro will bear watching.

Montanaro was the big wheel as Rhode Island defeated Maine, 14-7, at Orono last year. A right halfback, he got into the game only because of an injury experienced by the redoutable Pat Abbruzzi, now of the professional Montreal Alouettes. With his side trailing in the third quarter, Montanaro tied it up with a pass to Dick Cahill, the play covering 81 yards. Shortly later he was on the receiving end, taking a pass for 65 yards and the winning touchdown.

Some Average . . .

Up until he was lost because of a broken leg, Montanaro compiled a pass record which Doherty aptly describes as remarkable. He threw four times, complete all four, three of them for touchdowns.

It should be a good shown down at Kingston this afternoon.

Brown is in New York to play Columbia in the first of the season's Ivy League games. The morning line has Brown favored by a point and a half, whatever that means. Coach Al Kelley has had to rebuild virtually from the ground up. Although he is in position to start a team composed entirely of juniors and seniors, mighty few of them were regulars last season. At Columbia veteran Coach Lou Little has more carryovers, but then his 1954 team enjoyed little success, defeating only Harvard.

Both coaches have their worries, but in different spots.

Kelley: "The end squad . . . was completely decimated by the loss of Harry Josephson, Bianowicz and Bartuska. . . ."

Little: "We should be stronger at end than last fall. . . ."

Kelley: "Tackles—our strongest position. . . ."

Little: "Practically all our tackles graduated last June."

Kelley: "Guards—This position will be completely rebuilt starting with letterman Jim Lohr. . . ."

Little: "Guards should be better than last fall. . . ."

Kelley: "Centers—completely unknown quality and quantity. . . ."

Little: "We hope to be better at center. . . ."

Interesting Challenge . . .

Kelley: "The quarterback responsibility so ably handled the last three seasons by Pete Kohut will fall to one of three senior reserves who have seen little if any game action. . . ."

Little: "Quarterbacks—If Benham doesn't have a recurrence of his shoulder injury (sustained in the Army game) he should do well. . . ."

Kelley: "Halfbacks—Williams, a fine halfback reserve last season, along with Thompson and Cronin, return to head the halfback slot. . . . Fullbacks—a complete rebuilding job is in order. . . ."

Little: "Backs—Wilson, Giampetro, Altman and Spraker should develop and, we hope, be helpful.

Kelley: "The 1955 season offers a real and interesting challenge to Brown football. . . ."

Little: "I expect Columbia to be improved, but since most of opponents will be stronger, it is questionable whether or not we can improve our won-loss record. . . ."

It would be sheer hokum to try and name the winner of this game in the advance of the playing of it. If Baker Field is dry, the scoring should be high, but too much new has been added to both sides to justify any other prediction.

SMITH LEAFS CAPTAIN

Toronto— (AP) —Leftwinger Sid Smith yesterday was named captain of the Toronto Maple Leafs of the National Hockey League. He succeeds Ted Kennedy who retired from play last season.

TOBACCO BOWL GAME

Richmond, Va.—(UP) — The 1956 Tobacco Bowl game will be played in Richmond between the University of Virginia and the University of North Carolina, Oct. 13, during Richmond's annual tobacco festival.

Durocher Out As Giant Pilot, U.P. Reports

By MILTON RICHMAN

New York — (UP) — Manager Leo Durocher and the New York Giants will part company by "mutual consent" within the next few weeks and Bill Rigney of the Minneapolis Millers will be appointed his successor, it was learned reliably yesterday.

The decision was reached after a recent board of directors meeting among Giants' officials but it was decided to wait until the end of the season before making any announcement.

"I have no comment on the story," said Charles (Chub) Feeney, a club vice president, when questioned.

"Horace Stoneham (Giant owner) has said before that no announcement will be made on that situation until the season is over," Feeney said.

Durocher, who has led the Giants to two National League pennants and one world championship since he took them over in midseason of 1948, had no comment to make, either.

"I'm going to have a talk with Mr. Stoneham soon and it will be settled then," he said.

It is known, however, that Durocher is interested in a number of other propositions, including a lucrative television venture in Hollywood.

There is also a strong chance he may wind up managing the St. Louis Cardinals for whom he starred as a shortstop from 1933 through 1937, or that he even may take over the managerial reins at Milwaukee next year, even though Durocher often has said, "When I take off this (the Giants) uniform, I'm through with baseball."

Senators Trip Orioles Twice In 'Cellar' Duel

Washington — (AP)—Trying to escape the American League cellar, Washington defeated Baltimore, 6-4 and 7-3, in a doubleheader last night and moved within a game of the seventh place Orioles. The first game victory snapped a 7-game losing streak for the Senators while ending Baltimore's 7-game winning streak.

First Game

BALTIMORE	AB	H	O	A	WASHINGTON	AB	H	O	A
Diering. cf	5	1	1	0	Yost. 3b	4	1	0	3
Dyck. lf	5	0	2	0	Oravetz.cf	4	2	4	0
Philley. rf	4	2	3	0	Runnels.2b	5	2	4	1
Tri'dos. 1b	5	1	7	0	Vernon. 1b	3	1	5	0
Smith. c	2	1	9	0	Sievers. lf	3	1	3	0
Marsh. 2b	4	2	1	3	Lemon. rf	4	2	6	0
Rob'son.3b	3	0	0	2	Korch'k. c	4	0	4	0
Schall'k. p	0	0	0	1	Valdi'so.ss	3	0	1	3
bSegrist	1	0	0	0	M'Der'tt.p	3	1	0	2
Dorish. p	0	0	0	0	Ramos. p	1	0	0	0
Mir'da. ss	2	1	1	3					
Wilson. p	2	0	0	0					
Brown. p	0	0	0	0					
aAbr'ms.lf	1	0	0	0					
Totals	34	8	24	9	Totals	34	10	27	9

a—Flied out for Brown in 6th.
b—Flied out for Schallock in 8th.

Baltimore	201 000 010	—4
Washington	100 320 00x	—6

R—Diering, Philley, Smith 2, Oravetz, Runnels, Sievers 2, Lemon, McDermott. E—Valdivielso, Philley, Diering, Robinson. RBI—Triandos, Smith, Runnels, Marsh, McDermott, Sievers, Lemon. 2B—Runnels, Smith. 3B—Sievers. S—Oravetz. SF—Smith. DP—Valdivielso, Runnels and Vernon. Left—Baltimore 9, Washington 9. BB—McDermott 5, Wilson 1, Brown 1, Schallock 1, Dorish 1. SO—Wilson 2, McDermott 4, Schallock 3, Dorish 2. HO—Wilson 9 in 4 1-3, Brown 0 in 2-3, Schallock 1 in 2, Dorish 0 in 1, McDermott 7 in 7 2-3, Ramos 1 in 1 1-3. R-ER—Wilson 6-4, Brown 0-0, Schallock 0-0, Dorish 0-0, McDermott 4-3, Ramos 0-0. PB—Korcheck. W—McDermott (10-10). L—Wilson (12-18). U—Honochick, Chylak, Grieve, Hurley. T—2:21.

Second Game

BALTIMORE	AB	H	O	A	WASHINGTON	AB	H	O	A
Diering.3b	5	2	2	3	Yost. 3b	5	0	2	1
Abrams.cf	4	1	1	2	Ump'ett.cf	2	0	5	0
Philley.rf	5	2	2	0	Vernon.1b	4	1	7	0
Tri'os.1b	5	1	8	0	Sievers.lf	4	2	2	0
Dyck. lf	3	0	5	0	Lemon. rf	3	0	1	0
Smith. c	4	1	2	0	Runnels.2b	4	1	6	2
Marsh.2b	4	0	3	4	Fitzg'l.c	4	3	2	0
Mir'a.ss	3	2	1	1	Vali'so.ss	1	1	2	6
Lopat.p	1	0	0	0	Schmitz.p	3	1	0	0
aSegrist	1	1	0	0					
H'rris'n.p	0	0	0	0					
bGastall	1	1	0	0					
Locke. p	0	0	0	2					
cPope	1	1	0	0					
Totals	37	12	24	12	Totals	30	9	27	9

a—Singled for Lopat in 5th.
b—Doubled for Harrison in 7th.
c—Singled for Locke in 9th.

Baltimore	001 000 101	—3
Washington	020 320 00x	—7

R—Abrams, Miranda 2, Umphlett, Vernon, Sievers, Runnels, FitzGerald 2, Valdivielso, Schmitz 3. E—Abrams, Runnels. RBI — FitzGerald, Valdivielso, Philley, Schmitz 3, Sievers 2, Abrams. 2B—Valdivielso, Philley, Vernon, Gastall. 3B—FitzGerald, Sievers. S—Valdivielso. DP—Runnels and Vernon; Yost and Vernon; Diering, Marsh and Triandos. Left—Baltimore 10, Washington 6. BB—Schmitz 3, Harrison 4, Locke 1. SO—Schmitz 2, Locke 1. HO—Lopat 6 in 4; Harrison 3 in 2; Locke 0 in 2. R-ER—Lopat 5-5, Harrison 2-2, Locke 0-0, Schmitz 3-3. HBP—Lopat (Valdivielso). W—Schmitz (7-10). L—Lopat (7-12). U—Chylak, Grieve, Hurley, Honochick. T—2:15. A—766.

MODENA RACE OFF

Modena, Italy— (AP) —Modena's Automobile Club yesterday announced cancellation of Modena's grand prix automobile race. The reason: Not enough entries.

Stengel Says Yanks Will Handle Dodgers

Boston — "We know how to win the pennants in this league," shouted Casey Stengel, manager of the 1955 American League champion New York Yankees, right after the Bombers clinched the pennant with their 3-2 nod over the Red Sox last night at Fenway.

"And," he added joyously and boisterously, "we also know how to win World Series. We know how to take care of those Brooklyn Dodgers.

"And we will!"

Tired as he was, Stengel joyfully announced that Whitey Ford would pitch the opening game of the World Series. "He won that right tonight" exclaimed Casey and added "he'll be well rested."

Ford said he would be very well rested, explaining that he usually only needs three days rest anyway. "I hope the weather stays like this" he added, "I like to pitch when it's cool."

"This will be the first Series Ford has pitched where he had the right amount of rest" Stengel added, "and Tommy Byrne will be rested and so will (Bob) Grim and (Don) Larsen," he concluded.

Not only Stengel but the rest of the Yanks were restrained in their show of joyousness in the Yank clubhouse.

Stengel took time out from posing for cameramen to make the rounds of his players and shake each one's hand and thank him individually for his help in the winning title fight.

Ol' Case is a stickler for details and that was a happy detail.

The cameramen wanted Case to smack Yank owner, Del Webb on the cheek but the Bomber boss bridled at that.

"We're happy," he said, "but not that happy."

Asked prior to last night's game if there was a victory party arranged for after the game Casey noted that if there was one in the offing he had no part in its arrangement.

"I never get involved in arranging these affairs," he said with a wink." They can start by themselves and you can always run into one."

Case and the Yanks ran into one at their hotel, Boston's Kenmore, later last evening.

And about then they decided they had something to celebrate. They are the American League baseball champions of 1955, a worthy achievement.

MATZEK

Braves Win, 4-2, On Home Runs

St. Louis, Mo. —(UP)— The Milwaukee Braves made thier runs one at a time on four homers last night and defeated the St. Louis Cardinals, 4-2.

Southpaw Warren Spahn, who had blanked the Cards on six hits until catcher Dick Rand homered with a man aboard in the ninth inning, hit one of the round-trippers. Eddie Mathews hit one, and George Crowe hit two.

Righthander Tom Poholsky was the victim of all the Braves' long blows and suffered his 11th defeat. Spahn notched his 17th victory.

Mathews smashed his 40th four-bagger in the fourth and Crowe followed with his 13th. Then in the sixth, Crowe hit No. 14.

MILWAUKEE	AB	H	O	A	ST. LOUIS	AB	H	O	A
Bruton. cf	4	1	4	0	Bl'g'me.2b	3	2	1	2
Logan. ss	4	0	2	2	Boyer. 3b	4	1	2	4
M'th'ws.3b	4	1	0	3	Musial. 1b	3	1	11	1
Aaron. rf	4	0	1	0	Alston. 1b	0	0	1	0
Crowe. 1b	3	2	10	1	Rep'ski. lf	4	0	1	0
Tanner. lf	3	0	0	0	Elliott. rf	4	2	3	0
O'Con'll.2b	4	0	2	2	Whis'nt.cf	4	1	3	0
Crandall.c	4	1	8	0	Gram's.ss	3	0	1	1
Spahn. p	3	2	0	5	Schof'l.ss	1	0	0	1
					Rand. c	4	1	3	0
					Poh'lsky.p	1	0	1	4
					aSarni	1	0	0	0
					Arroyo. p	0	0	0	1
					bSch'd'st	1	0	0	0
Totals	33	7	27	13	Totals	33	8	27	14

a—Grounded out for Poholsky in 7th.
b—Fouled out for Arroyo in 9th.

Milwaukee	000 201 100	—4
St. Louis	000 000 002	—2

R—Mathews, Crowe 2, Spahn, Elliott, Rand. E—O'Connell. RBI—Mathews, Crowe 2, Spahn, Rand 2. 2B—Bruton, Musial. HR—Mathews, Crowe 2, Spahn, Rand. S—Poholsky, Tanner. DP—Logan, O'Connell and Crowe. Left—Milwaukee 4, St. Louis 7. BB—Spahn 2, Arroyo 1. SO—Spahn 7, Poholsky 2, Arroyo 1. HO—Poholsky 7 in 7, Arroyo 0 in 2. R-ER—Spahn 2-2, Poholsky 4-4, Arroyo 0-0. W—Spahn (17-14). L — Poholsky (9-11). U—Pinelli, Warneke, Ballanfant, Barlick. T—2:10. A—6,910.

ADIOS HARRY UPSET

Yonkers, N. Y.—(UP)—Meadow Rice, driven by Jimmy Jordan, scored an upset victory in the featured Peekskill pace at Yonkers Raceway last night. Adios Harry, the 1-4 favorite, was third.

FOOTBALL DRILL

The Dexter Lions football team will practice at 9 o'clock tomorrow morning at Dexter Training Grounds. New candidates are welcome.

College Sports

FOOTBALL

Toledo 12	Detroit 7
Maryland State 19	Hofstra 13
Huron 56	Sioux Falls 0
Middle Tennessee 21	East'n Kentucky 14

USC 42, Oregon 15.
Denver 33, Drake 7.
San Jose State 34, Hawaii 0.
Huron (SD) 56, Sioux Falls (SD) College 0.

Major League Baseball

American League

RESULTS YESTERDAY

Cleveland at Detroit, ppd., rain.
Boston 8-2, New York 4-3.
Washington 6-7, Baltimore 4-3.
Chicago 12, Kansas City 4.

STANDING OF THE TEAMS

	W.	L.	P.C.	G.B.
New York	95	57	.625	—
Cleveland	91	60	.603	3½
Chicago	89	63	.587	6
Boston	83	69	.546	12
Detroit	78	73	.517	16½
Kansas City	63	89	.414	32
Baltimore	54	97	.358	40½
Washington	53	98	.351	41½

National League

RESULTS LAST NIGHT

Philadelphia 5, New York 1.
Milwaukee 4, St. Louis 2.
Brooklyn at Pittsburgh, ppd., rain.
Only games scheduled

STANDING OF THE TEAMS

	W.	L.	P.C.	G.B.
Brooklyn	97	53	.647	—
Milwaukee	85	67	.559	13
New York	79	73	.520	19
Philadelphia	76	76	.500	22
Cincinnati	74	78	.487	24
Chicago	71	80	.470	26½
St. Louis	66	86	.434	32
Pittsburgh	58	93	.384	39½

GAMES TODAY AND PROBABLE PITCHERS

Cleveland at Detroit (2)—Score (15-10) and Wynn (17-11) vs. Lary (14-14) and Garver (12-15).
New York at Boston—Kucks (8-7) vs. vs. Susce (8-7).
Baltimore at Washington (2 twi-night)—Moore (9-10) and Wight (5-8) vs. Abernathy (5-8) and Ramos (5-10).
Kansas City at Chicago—Kellner (11-8) vs. Donovan (14-9).

Philadelphia at New York—Dickson (12-11) vs. Hearn (14-15) or Antonelli (14-16).
Brooklyn at Pittsburgh (twi-night)—Loes (10-4) and Newcombe (20-5) vs. Friend (12-9) and Hall (5-6).
Milwaukee at St. Louis (night)—Crone (10-9) or Robinson (3-1) vs. McDaniel (0-0).
Chicago at Cincinnati—Jones (13-20) or Kaiser (0-0) vs. Nuxhall (17-11).

LEADING HITTERS

	G	AB	R	H	P.C.
Kaline, Detroit	149	580	120	198	.341
Power, Kan. City	145	588	90	188	.320
Kell, Chicago	127	426	44	133	.312
Mantle, New York	145	515	121	158	.307
Kuenn, Detroit	142	608	99	186	.306
Smith, Cleveland	151	600	120	182	.304
Fox, Chicago	152	628	97	190	.303
Simpson, Kan. C.	114	393	43	118	.300
Philley, Balt.	123	403	63	120	.298
Vernon, Wash.	148	529	72	157	.297
x-Williams, Bos.	96	318	77	112	.352

x-Fewer than 375 at bats.

	G.	A.B.	R.	H.	P.C.
Ashburn, Phila.	138	526	90	180	.342
Campanella, B'k'n	120	438	81	140	.320
Musial, St. Louis	152	554	96	176	.318
Mays, New York	150	572	120	181	.317
Kluszewski, C'n'ti	151	602	115	190	.316
Aaron, Milwaukee	151	595	105	186	.313
Furillo, Brooklyn	138	516	82	161	.312
Bell, Cincinnati	152	604	87	187	.310
Post, Cincinnati	152	593	115	184	.310
Snider, Brooklyn	145	526	126	162	.308

HOME RUNS

Mantle, New York, 37; Zernial, Kansas City, 30; Williams, Boston, 28; Zauchin, Boston, Kaline, Detroit, and Berra, New York, 27 each.

Mays, New York, 50; Kluszewski, Cincinnati, 47; Banks, Chicago, 44; Snider, Brooklyn, 42; Mathews, Milwaukee, 40.

RUNS BATTED IN

Jensen, Boston, 116; Boone, Detroit, 114; Berra, New York, 108; Sievers, Washington, 106; Kaline, Detroit, 102.

Snider, Brooklyn, 134; Mays, New York, 124; Ennis, Philadelphia, 120; Banks, Chicago, 116; Kluszewski, Cincinnati, 113.

The World Series: The Scenes and the Players

New York Yankees

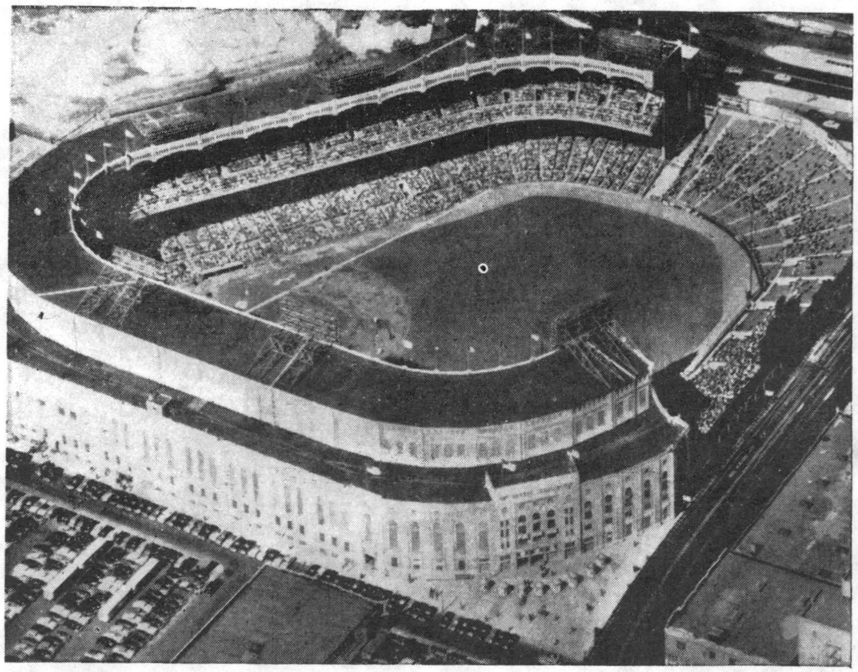

Yankee Stadium: First two games of the series will be played here. The home of the Bronx Bombers seats 67,000.

Top Hurlers: Bob Turley, Whitey Ford and Don Larsen (left to right).

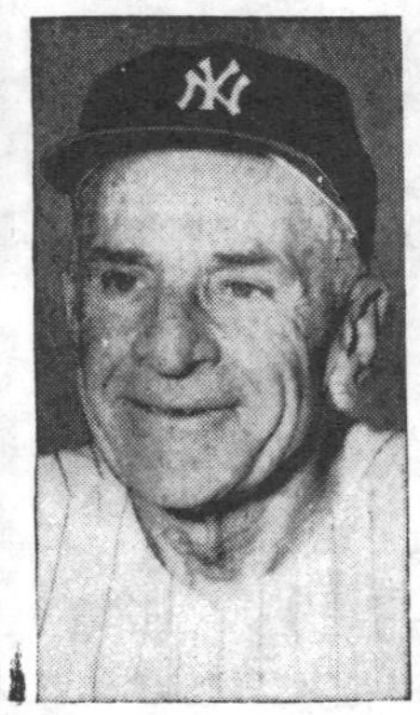

Manager: Casey Stengel.

Byrne Sturdivant Grim Kucks Morgan

Robinson Cerv Mantle Bauer Noren

Carey Silvera Howard Berra Coleman

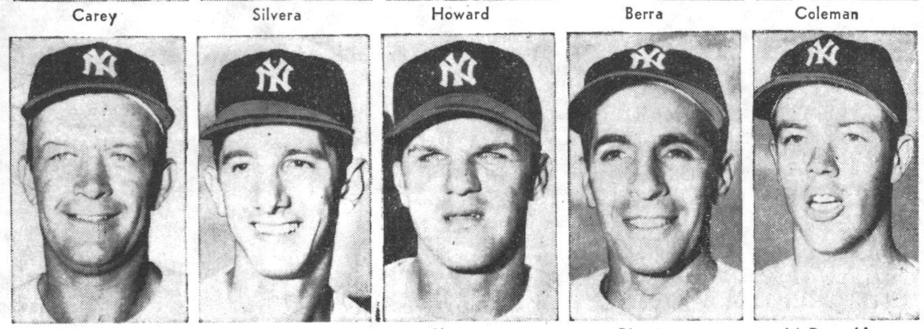

Collins Martin Skowron Rizzuto McDougald

Brooklyn Dodgers

Spooner Amoros Shuba Roebuck Koufax Meyer

Loes Robinson Craig Walker Erskine Bessent

Rhody's pride: Clem Labine, North Smithfield

—Staff Photo by Frank J. Farley

Gilliam Reese Newcombe

Zimmer Podres Huak

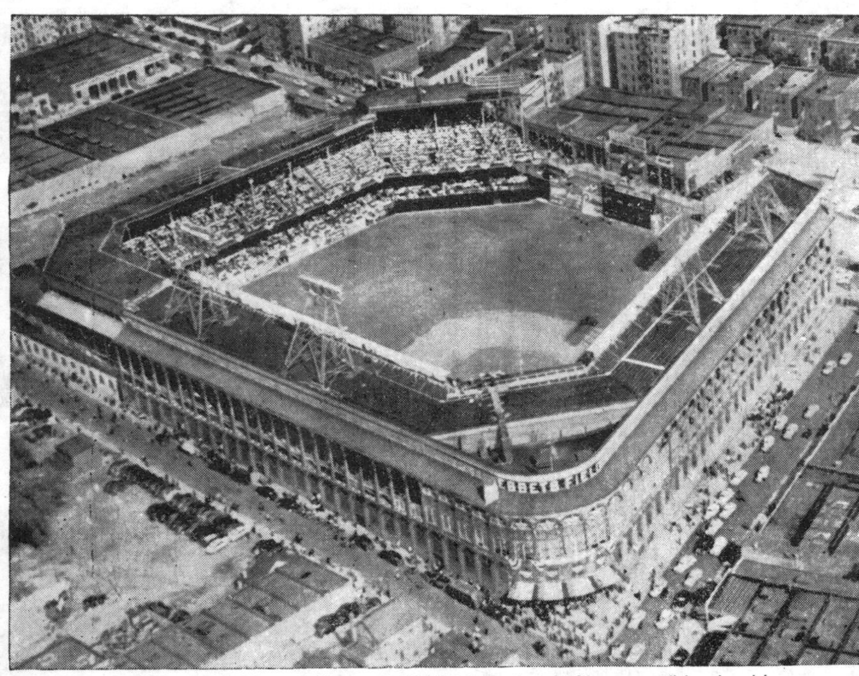

Ebbets Field: The Dodgers' home field seats 32,111. Third, fourth and fifth games will be played here.

Manager: Walter Alston

Top hitters: From left, Carl Furillo, Gil Hodges, Roy Campanella and Duke Snider.

3 Yankee Homers Flatten Newcombe, Dodgers, 6-5

Examiner Sports
LOS ANGELES, THURSDAY, SEPTEMBER 29, 1955
Section Four CCC

ROBINSON SPEEDS HOME, BALL TOO

BERRA HAS BALL AS JACKIE SLIDES

LOOKS LIKE TAG, BUT IS IT?

ROBINSON OVER THE PLATE NOW

JACKIE COMES HOME—Jackie Robinson, Brooklyn third baseman, steals home in eighth inning of opening World Series game yesterday at Yankee Stadium. Robinson was called safe by Umpire Bill Summers which started big argument by Yankee Catcher Yogi Berra. It appears Berra already has ball (Panel 2), but whether Robinson slid away from him, only Summers knows.

—Associated Press wirephoto.

Two Belts by Collins; Ford Wins

(Continued from Page One)

bowl of alphabet soup could spell and took the fine old Celtic handle of Joe Collins.

This fine broth of a boy put the Yanks ahead, 4-3, with a home run in the fourth and stunned Newcombe with a ferocious two-run home run his next time up.

YOGI SCORES——

That second Collins blow pushed home Yogi Berra, who had reached for and hit a ball into right for a simple single with one out in the inning. Collins' blast shook the towering Newcombe from his huge feet to monumental head. Don got Elston Howard out after that, but Billy Martin, a man who seems to be stoked with red pepper, truculently belted a 450-foot triple to left center.

Walter Alston trudged wearily to the hill to give Newcombe the privilege of taking the first shower of the 1955 series. There were some scattered boos for the big pitcher here and there in the crowd of 63,869 as he forlornly headed for the dugout. He was a saddened hulk. For all his power, skill and opportunity he has never been able to win a series game.

The Dodgers, lagging behind at 6-3 in the eighth, got to the tiring Whitey Ford and with the help of Gil McDougald's two-base error, they scored twice and had Ford on the verge of collapse.

Furillo, who was harder to get out today than a singing drunk, started the Dodger eighth with a single to center. Gil Hodges skied out. Then Robinson, whose earlier triple and fine play at third gave evidence that he was going to have a great day, banged a savage grounder through McDougald. Gil might have played the ball a bit better but nothing mattered now except that Furillo was on third and Robinson on second. Furillo scored to shave the Yank lead to 6-4, on Don Zimmer's fly and Jackie moved to third.

From that outpost Robinson brilliantly stole home. Berra, Stengel and half the Yankee team blew their stacks and shouted brazen words through bared fangs at a stout little man named Wilyum Summers, the plate umpire. Mr. Summers is not a man who changes his mind, not even for the Yankees. The score is now 6-5, Mr. Summers said, or words to that effect. He was right, too.

It was the 18th time Robinson has stolen home since he cracked the color barrier and became big league baseball's first Negro player, eight years ago.

LOOPING SINGLE——

Frank Kellert, pinch-hitting, found a hole among Hank Bauer, Collins and Martin, in short right, and deposited a looping single into it after the Robinson steal. Old Casey waddled out of his cement cave and for a time it looked as if he'd given Ford the heav-o. But some mercy or mood moved him to keep him in, and the young man responded by forcing Junior Gilliam to pop up for the third out of the ominous inning.

Ford couldn't pitch the ninth. He spent everything he had buying his way out of the eighth. No southpaw has pitched and won a full nine-inning game againt the Dodgers all season, and Ford wasn't destined to be the boy to do it. Bob Grim, a strong young right-hander, was Stengel's choice to pitch the ninth, even though Snider, a most menacing left-handed hitter, would be second man up.

Grim had never before played in a World Series, but he looked as calm as the flagpole as he bent a great third strike past the astute Brooklyn shortstop, captain Peewee Reese, for the first out. Casey conferred with his boy and clapped him fondly on the back before letting him pitch to Snider. There was a press box report that Casey instructed Grim to hold Snider to a single. Anyway, that's what he did.

Now there was Campanella, as menacing as they come in baseball. Grim got him in trouble with fast breaking stuff. Then Campy reached out and hit a tremendously hard liner to right. It would have knocked

(Continued on Page 4, Col. 3)

JOE-LTER—Here's Joe Collins, the hero of yesterday's first game of the World Series. The part-time New York Yankee first baseman hit two homers.

—Associated Press wirephoto.

Stengel Strategy With Southpaws Pays Off

By Vincent X. Flaherty

NEW YORK, Sept. 28.—When it comes to baseball strategy, weather-beaten and crinkly-faced Casey Stengel, a cagey old customer, is known as a man who moves in mysterious ways. A lot of things he does do not make sense until you sift things apart and take a look at his reasoning.

Then when you behold the ultimate result and find everything has panned out just the vay Casey wanted it, there isn't anything mysterious about his scheming at all.

Take this afternoon in Yankee Stadium, for example. Casey's Yankees won the opening game of the 1955 World Series over the Brooklyn Dodgers by a score of 6 to 5.

And how did Casey do it? He did a thing that made most of the experts wince. He shot a left-hander named Ed "Whitey" Ford in there against the Dodgers and made 'em like it.

Now, everyone knows the Dodgers are holy murder on lefties. No lefthander was able to complete a game against them at any time during the regular season.

As a matter of fact, Ford wasn't there at the finish today, either. Stengel removed him at the end of the eighth inning and put in Bob Grim, a righthander, to finish the job. Nevertheless, Ford came through with everything Stengel expected of him.

ANOTHER LEFTY READY

Stengel's whole battle plan for the series is a simple one. Using Ford today, and calling upon another leftie, Tommy Byrne, to pitch against the Dodgers tomorrow, Casey will be prepared to turn his right-handers loose against Brooklyn when the series moves across the bridge to Ebbets Field Friday.

Stengel figured Brooklyn would give a lefthander a pretty good pasting. Indeed, Ford was cuffed around briskly this afternoon and would have been gone from the picture early had it not been for some superlative fielding by his Yankee teammates.

As a matter of fact, if today's opener had been played in Brooklyn the Dodgers undoubtedly would have won because they belted a number of boisterous drives during the course of the game. The same drives would have crashed against fences, or even cleared them, in Brooklyn. But in the great yawning spaces of Yankee Stadium the outfielders were flitting to and also fro and picking them out of the air like nothing at all.

FORD IN TROUBLE

That's why Stengel is throwing Byrne against the Dodgers in the second game. If they get tough with his number two leftie, Casey again counts upon the long outfield distances to lesson the pain and serve as an equalizer.

Ford had a rough time today. He was as shaky as a palsied jitterbug and was in trouble during six of his eight innings, most of it self-inflicted. Ford was wild and his best pitches were being busted on the nose by the National Leaguers, only to whiz straight into the hands of some Yankee fielder most of the time.

In that respect, this game was reminiscent of last year's opener between the Giants and Indians. The Indians were doing all of the big blasting, but their drives were speeding straight at Giant fielders.

However, if Ford was having a rough time, you should have seen poor Don Newcombe, Brooklyn's starting pitcher. The Yankees' Joe Collins tied into Newcombe's fast balls as if something personal was involved. Collins clouted two home runs and accounted for three Yankee runs in all. The first one came in the fourth inning and it was a 344-foot job into the rightfield seats.

His second one, a massive blast coming in the sixth inning, carried a little better than 400 feet, sped like a Howitzer and shot into the right centerfield. Yogi Berra was on base, and Newcombe's cow-catcher chin fell all the way down to his ample chest as he watched Berra and Collins circle the bases.

It was the beginning of the end for Brooklyn's 20-game winner. An instant later Billy Martin lambasted a triple which rocketed over Junior Gilliam's head in left center and rolled some 430 feet before colliding with the bleacher wall. That was the finisher for Newcombe. When Billy's bat connected with the ball in extremely loud style, Walter Alston, the Brooklyn manager, flew out of the Dodger cave as if a cannon cracker had exploded in this hip pocket.

Alston didn't bother talking things over. He gave Don the old come hitherto with his index finger and waved in a new Don —Don Bessent, a righthander.

But the damage was done then, even though the Dodgers got a pair of unearned runs in the eighth to lessen the humiliation. One of them was scored by Jackie Robinson who stole home while Ford monkeyed around with a slow wind up.

Duke Snider fanned up a flicker of hope for the fading Dodgers in the ninth with one out when he singled to right. But Bob Grim, who had relieved Ford, took up the slack in his suspenders and got Roy

(Continued on Page 4, Cols. 6-8)

Hot Collins Cools Bums

YANKEE STADIUM, New York, Sept. 28.—(AP)—The official box score of the first game of the 1955 World Series:

Brooklyn, (N.)	AB	R	H	O	A
Gilliam, lf	3	0	0	2	0
Reese. ss	5	0	1	2	5
Snider, cf	5	1	2	1	0
Campanella, c	5	0	0	5	1
Furillo, rf	4	2	3	1	0
Hodges, 1b	4	0	1	12	1
J. Robinson, 3b	4	2	1	0	2
Zimmer, 2b	2	0	1	1	3
Newcombe, p	3	0	0	0	1
Bessent, p	0	0	0	0	1
Kellert	1	0	1	0	0
Hoak	0	0	0	0	0
Labine, p	0	0	0	0	0
Totals	36	5	10	24	14

New York (A.)	AB	R	H	O	A
Bauer, rf	4	0	2	3	0
McDougald, 3b	4	0	1	2	1
Noren, cf	4	0	0	4	0
Berra, c	3	1	1	5	0
Collins, 1b	3	3	2	6	1
Howard, lf	3	1	1	1	0
Martin, 2b	3	0	2	2	3
Rizzuto, ss	2	0	0	3	2
E. Robinson	0	0	0	0	0
Coleman, ss	1	0	0	0	0
Ford, p	2	1	0	1	3
Grim, p	0	0	0	0	0
Totals	29	6	9	27	10

E. Robinson batted for Rizzuto in 6th when Martin was out attempting to steal home.

Kellert singled for Bessent in 8th.

Hoak ran for Kellert in 8th.

Brooklyn (N.)	021 000 020—5
New York (A.)	021 102 00x—6

E—McDougald. RBI—Furillo, Zimmer 2, Howard 2, Snider, Noren, Collins 3. 3B—Robinson, Martin. HR—Furillo, Howard, Snider, Collins 2. SB—Robinson. SF—Zimmer. DP—Zimmer and Hodges; Martin, Rizzuto and Collins; Hodges, Reese and Hodges. Left—Brooklyn (N.) 9, New York (A.) 2. BB—Ford 4, (Gilliam 2, Furillo, Zimmer); Newcombe 2 (Collins, Ford); Labine (Berra). SO—Ford 2 (Snider, Robinson); Newcombe 4 (McDougald, Howard, Rizzuto, Ford); Grim 2 (Reese, Furillo). HO—Newcombe, 8 in 5 2/3; Bessent, 0 in 1 1/3; Ford, 9 in 8; Labine, 1 in 1; Grim, 1 in 1. R-ER—Newcombe, 6-6; Bessent, 0-0; Ford, 5-3; Labine, 0-0; Grim, 0-0. W—Ford. L—Newcombe. U—Summers (A.), plate; Ballanfant (N.), first base; Honochick (A.), second base; Dascoli (N.), third base; Flaherty (A.), left field; Donatelli (N.), right field. T—2:31. A—63,869.

Today's Starting Lineups

NEW YORK, Sept. 28.—(AP)—Probably starting lineups for Thursday's World Series game at Yankee Stadium:

BROOKLYN	NEW YORK
Gilliam, lf	Bauer, rf
Reese, ss	McDougald, 3b
Snider, cf	Noren, cf
Campanella, c	Berra, c
Furillo, rf	Collins, 1b
Hodges, 1b	Howard, lf
Robinson, 3b	Martin, 2b
Zimmer, 2b	Rizzuto, ss
Loes, p (10-4)	Byrne, p (16-5)

(Keep Your Own Scoreboard—Page 4)

UMPIRES—Ballanfant (National), plate; Honochick (American), first base; Dascoli (National), second base; Summers (American), third base; Flaherty (American), left field foul line; Donatelli (National), right field foul line.

'BUGS'-EYE VIEW OF SERIES

Bag Limit in Second Guesses for Bums

By Arthur 'Bugs' Baer

(Distributed by International News Service)

NEW YORK, Sept. 28.—(INS)—Both the visiting firemen and the fire were put out today when the Yanks exercised their inalienable whammy over the Bums.

★ ★ ★

They carried over from 1953 with the Brooklyns doing plenty of window-shopping. As usual they got less than the sucker on a badger pull.

★ ★ ★

Whether they start earlier than an Army bugler or later than the graveyard shift the answer is always the same. The Yanks own 'em in the autumn.

★ ★ ★

If you include the Yanks Stadium and the hotel lobbies there was a seating capacity of about 2,000,000. By tomorrow the interest will fall off like ashes on a nickel cigar. The Yanks can trim the Bums for money, marbles or chalk and give 'em a head start in a hat store.

★ ★ ★

If Don Newcombe had copped the opener there would have been a possibility of Brooklyn winning the series. Don could have come back again Saturday or Sunday if they needed him. He requires less rest than the fiddler at a square dance.

But when the Bums get their kite strings tangled with Casey Stengel's they lose their ball of twine.

★ ★ ★

We will be unable to decipher this mysterious whammicker until Alston trades the Bums' bench for a psychiatrist's couch that will hold 25 players.

★ ★ ★

We heard Peewee Reese and Duke Snider talking big last week but it was twitchful thinking. They can't lift the mortgage on the split-level whammy.

We concede the Bums topped the Yanks in the number of hits, 10 to nine. But when it comes time to lift the cup of victory the raisins walk out of the rice pudding.

★ ★ ★

We don't know why this is because we never took a lesson except on visitor's day. All we know is the Bums have had a half-dozen tries at the Yanks in various tournaments and got the bag limit in second guesses.

50 in Night Seat Vigil

NEW YORK, Sept. 28.—(AP)—Fifty hardy baseball fans braved a cold, driving rain outside Yankee Stadium early today, waiting to buy bleacher seats for the opening game of the World Series.

Only four persons were in the line at 9 p. m. but near midnight, others began to arrive. By 2 a. m., 50 had gathered, shielding themsevles from the rain under umbrellas, cardboard cartons and other makeshift shelters.

One of those who braved the rain was 65-year-old John Boykin, an electrical maintenance man for the RKO movie studios in Los Angeles. He said he flew here on his vacation to see the games.

SPORTS TODAY

BOXING
OLYMPIC AUDITORIUM — Weekly card, 8:30 p. m.

HORSE RACING
POMONA FAIRGROUNDS—12 races, 12:30 p. m.

ICE FOLLIES
PAN PACIFIC AUDITORIUM—Show starts 8:15 p. m.

WRESTLING
LONG BEACH AUDITORIUM — Weekly card, 8:30 p. m.

Collins Landed Knockout Blow

By Bob Hunter

NEW YORK, Sept. 28.—One week ago today it was Archie Moore, and this afternoon it was Brooklyn.

The end for both of them came in the ninth round.

A magnificent set of misfits, the New York Yankees, recorded a knockout just as decisively, and just as unexpectedly, as Rocky did right in this same cavernous arena a week ago.

They spotted the dangerous Dodgers leads in two different innings, they let 'em put on the tying run in the ninth, and then—whoppo, you saw Bob Grim strike out Carl Furillo to end it suddenly and decisively.

The referee didn't even have to count.

It was 6 to 5 before 63,869 citizens, who traipsed in from all over the world to watch the Yankees launch a quest for their 17th world's championship against their favorite foils, the Bums from across the river.

They say its the Yankee uniform that wins games and rules the baseball empire, but I saw plenty of muscles smuggled into those uniforms today.

So did you back there in front of your magic glass panels.

The five monumental hits delivered by New York and Brooklyn in this home run jamboree were just one short of a record for a series game, but, of course, it was the Yankees who got the odd one.

COLLINS' BIG ONE

And that was the big one and the final one. Joe Collins' second of the game, with Yogi Berra perched on first base, that made it 6-3 in favor of the Yankee Doodle Dandies.

Collins likes to pull the ball, and you probably noticed, if you were watching carefully at this moment, that Don Newcombe pitched the Yankee first baseman inside.

You don't pitch that way to a pull hitter and stick around long.

Newcombe didn't.

It was supposed to be the Yankees that were to suffer here for their pitching or lack of it this afternoon, but it was Newcombe, the big, broad right-hander who took it on the chin instead.

However, both starting pitchers were uncertain, and the 19 hits, almost half of them for triples or homers, made it an unartistic thing, for sure.

But the series figured all the way, as I reported to you before, to be a slugging series—and it was the Dodgers who hit the deck today.

I would have taken Newcombe out two batters before Walt Alston did, although no more runs were scored on him after Collins' second blast, a crisp 400-foot shot, had put the frosting on the cake.

I would have taken out Whitey Ford after he walked Junior Gilliam in the second inning, with the Dodgers hold

(Continued on Page 8, Cols. 1-2)

TOO HIGH — Duke Snider, Brooklyn rightfielder, goes high off the ground in vain effort to snare Joe Collins' hit in sixth which dropped in stands for his second homer.

—Associated Press wirephoto.

Fine Weather for 2d Game

NEW YORK, Sept. 28.—(AP)—Fine weather for the second day of the World Series was forecast tonight.

The Weather Bureau said it'll be sunny and mild Thursday with the temperatures high as 75. The Bureau, however, said there is a chance of some showers on Friday.

Casey Convinced as Yank Lefties Steal Show

By FRANK GIBBONS
Press Staff Writer

NEW YORK, Oct. 4—Now that he has beaten the Dodgers three times with left-handed pitchers, when their right-handed sluggers are supposed to eat southpaws with just a dash of salt, Casey Stengel is swinging around to the feeling that ballplayers are human, after all. Not chess men and yes men.

"Well, I guess it doesn't matter much about these things (the left vs. right theory) as long as a guy is a good pitcher or a good hitter," Stengel conceded yesterday after Whitey Ford had dazzled the Dodgers again.

"I remember I was out in Oakland one year and I had six left-handed pitchers. They all said: 'Look at that whacky Stengel with all those lefties.' I couldn't get any good righties, so I preferred good lefties."

If Tom Byrne completes the southpaw picture today and wins another championship for Old Case, it certainly should make it official. Two left-handed pitchers winning a series all by themselves has never happened before, particularly against a team loaded to the gunwales with right-handed distance hitters.

Of course, if the Yankees do win it, this must be put down as a series which was decided by the dimensions of the respective parks, more than any other.

Yankee Stadium is a perfect place for the particular wiles of Ford and Byrne, against a team such as the Dodgers. Horses for courses is a theory never proved as definitely on a race track as it has been on these two diamonds.

It is just another baseball theory, but this is one time when the Dodgers would have been better off if the series had opened in their park, giving them a four-game potential there.

Stengel won't buy this completely. He feels certain the Yankees would have done better in Brooklyn with Mickey Mantle and Hank Bauer healthy and available.

"Bauer made a difference today, even on a bum leg, didn't he?' Stengel asked. That he did, with three hits in Ford's 5-1 second victory over the Brooks.

The fact still remains that Stengel used to win in Brooklyn with Allie Reynolds and Vic Raschi. Not Ed Lopat, who was something special here.

If the Yankees win, their almost flawless fielding must get sufficient credit, too. They have made only one error of commission, few of omission.

The Dodgers may have killed themselves in the field yesterday, around second base. In the big Yankee first, they twice had chances to pull young Karl Spooner out of his predicament.

Junior Gilliam was late covering, or Roy Campanella was late throwing, when Phil Rizzuto went down as Billy Martin struck out. The general feeling was Campanella should have thrown the ball, trusting that Gilliam would get there.

Gilliam next failed to come up with a cheap, bounding single by Yogi Berra to start a double play. He didn't and it wasn't long after that Moose Skowron hit a home run and taps sounded. Ford is tough enough in a close game, and he is tougher with an armed guard of five runs.

Franklin Lewis

Casts Vote for Bauer as Yankee Sparkplug

NEW YORK, Oct. 4—Elsewhere you will read that the Yankees got to play in the seventh game of the World Series because of Whitey Ford's fine pitching in the sixth affair, a bruiseless brush in Yankee Stadium. You will read that Karl Spooner, the Brooklyn starter, got the Yankees back in the Series because he hit their bats with terrifying skill. You will read that the Brooklyns, once they were flushed out of their cubicle that is uproariously called a baseball park, got freckles on their courage.

To all these I profess agreement, to a point. But I also profess an affection for baseball players who can act as a crutch for their teams by merely being in the lineup. They communicate to their brothers an intangible yet powerful strengthening of moral fibers.

If I had to pinpoint one reason the Yankees won the sixth game, I'd nail the medal on the broad chest of Hank Bauer. Why? Well, he was in the starting lineup, lukewarm leg and all, for the first time since the second game. He missed all three games in Brooklyn with the exception of the last inning of the Sunday frolic.

Perhaps it is because of his physical appearance that Bauer infuses the Yankees with his fierceness. Perhaps it is because he will challenge walls and enemies and pitchers and situations as he was schooled by the Marines. More likely it is because Bauer knows how to play baseball only one way: Hard. Oh, yes, a second way, with his mouth shut and his muscles flexed.

He didn't make any diving catches to save the game yesterday. He probably couldn't have reached a tantalizing sphere with his leg paining at every step. But he did single sharply in the first inning, smack in the middle of the five-run rally—topped by Moose Skowron's sliced homer into the right field seats—that spelled out a 5-1 Yankee triumph. He singled again in the third and again in the seventh, and now he has six hits in 10 times at bat.

The only time he didn't hit safely yesterday was when he grounded to Jackie Robinson at third base with a runner on first. It was a perfect double-play hopper. But when the relay finally reached first base, Bauer was across the bag. No one thought for a second he could run that hard with his leg wracked. But there was only one thing to do, in this case. Break up the DP. That's how Bauer plays baseball. He broke up the DP and nearly broke his thigh muscle wide open in the process.

"If I can just hang on for one more game . . . well, I can, I have to," he was saying in the post-mortem in the clubhouse. "Man, this leg really gave me fits on that double-play ball."

This Bauer isn't the world's greatest baseball player. Doesn't pretend to be or will be. He's 33 and this is his seventh year as a Yankee regular. He's close to a .300 hitter, over his span, though he dipped to .297 this past season. Still, he hit 30 home runs, more than he'd ever belted in the majors.

He can run very fast and he can throw hard and he has yet to say no to any fly ball within hearing distance. He'll leave his feet or his park, if necessary. He's a rough one, this German from out Kansas way.

He's not always chewing concrete cuds, however. Take yesterday. He'd come in after the game and the Yankees were whooping it up a bit. Not much. They figured all

along they'd put Spooner in the satchel. They figured there'd be a seventh game because Ford would win and, more to the point, the Brooklyns would be away from Brooklyn.

The only thing he wore was a set of clogs and he had a can of beer in one hand. He kept his hurting leg elevated, resting his foot on a stool. He was grinning and answering reporters' questions, though most of the literary lions were gnawing away on Ford. That's the customary tribute to the winning pitcher. There was a time Bauer wanted to be traded to the Indians. Casey Stengel was playing him only part time and Hank thought he should play every day instead of being platooned against southpaws, and so there was talk of a deal of Bauer for a Cleveland pitcher. Early Wynn was mentioned at the time.

I imagine he was satisfied with everything yesterday, because now he has come of baseball age and he plays every day when he is physically able, as he did all this past year. He speaks his piece, and so when we got to talking about pitchers and about speed he grunted an opinion of Spooner.

"They say this guy throws harder than Herb Score," Hank said. "Silly. He can't begin to throw with Score, but do you know who throws harder than Score, or harder than Ray Narleski? That Don Mossi of the Indians. All our players say that Mossi can throw that fast one so hard you can't see it. He throws a great curve, too, and that's why you don't hear much about his fast ball. Man, he's got one."

A broadcaster from Montreal came over to ask if Bauer would say a few words on his tape recorder. It took only a minute. One of the questions was about his leg.

"All I want to do is get by this one more game, then Honolulu and Japan for me," he said into the mike. The Yankees are close to take-off for their celebrated tour of the Orient.

"My wife's making me go," he turned back to me. "It wasn't a question of whether I wanted to go. When the trip was proposed, she said we'd be happy to go. Oh, I don't mind, really."

He grinned and suddenly you forgot his nose. It's indented on the right side, as if a smooth stone the size of a plum had been imbedded there long enough to leave a permanent impression.

You can't see that nose from the seats, only from spike distance. But you can see other things about Hank Bauer from the pews, and what I saw yesterday was enough for me and the Yankees. He's baseball's newest Bloody Mary Cocktail. Instead of vodka and tomato juice, it's Bauer and the base hit.

30 Veterans:

3 Rookies on Browns

By BOB AUGUST

There are only three rookies left on the Browns' squad that this week will be making preparations for its game with the Philadelphia Eagles on Sunday at the Stadium.

Linebacker Sam Palumbo, Defensive End Chuck Weber and Halfback Bob Smith were the only yearlings to survive the final cut that sliced Tackle Tom Jones and Halfback Henry Ford from the roster.

This is one of the smallest rookie crops in recent years. As none of the three are regulars, the major burden will fall on the Browns' veterans for one more year.

On the strength of their smashing victory over the 49rs, the more mature Browns seem capable of holding up for another season. In addition to the three rookies, the Browns will get help from three other players who are new to Cleveland although they had previous experience. They are Halfbacks John Petitbon and Bob White and Fullback Ed Modzelewski.

When Guard John Macerelli gets off the 30-day injured reserve list, one more cut will be made.

The Eagles, who are rated strong rivals to the Browns in the eastern division, show striking similarities to the defending champions. They also are loaded with veterans and they have made only minor additions in rookie personnel this year.

One important new player, however, is Fullback Dick Bielski of Maryland, who is expected to add muscle to the Eagles' running game. Last season the Eagles finished secong in the division, and this year they have plans to go all the way.

Steeler Coach Fined $500

PHILADELPHIA, Oct. 4—(UP)—Walter Kiesling, coach of the Pittsburgh Steelers of the National Football League, was fined $500 today by Commissioner Bert Bell for his altercation with officials following the Pittsburgh-Los Angeles game Sunday.

The commissioner announced his decision in a single sentence statement which said Kiesling "was fined $500 for his behavior to officials in Los Angeles last Sunday."

Kiesling, a soft-spoken and usually easy going football figure, was fined for his actions following Pittsburgh's last seconds 27-26 loss to Los Angeles. He rushed on the field in the direction of the officials after a field goal which followed a penalty against Pittsburgh provided the winning points.

Earlier, he drew a penalty for grabbing Head Linesman James Underhill by the arm as he protested a decision.

Kiesling made gestures toward the officials, but was restrained by his assistants, when a personal foul penalty against Steeler Halfback Richie McCabe put Los Angeles in position for the winning kick.

Robinson Joins Limping Society

NEW YORK, Oct. 4—(UP)—The Yankees have no monopoly on injuries today.

Along with Duke Snider, who was hobbled by a twisted knee, Jackie Robinson reported that he has a very sore right heel.

Big Crutch Game

By Lou Darvas

Yankees 7 to 5 to Win Today

NEW YORK, Oct. 4—(UP)—The Yankees, at one time 19-5 favorites to win the World Series, were a 7-5 choice over the Dodgers today in the final game.

The official bookmakers' spread was "6½-7½." That meant, if you are a Yankee fan, you had to risk $7.50 to win $5. If you bet the Dodgers, you can win $6.50 for a $5 wager.

But in man-to-man betting, the odds were 7-5 in favor of the Yankees.

Rams Sign Bighead

LOS ANGELES, Oct. 4—(UP)—The Los Angeles Rams signed former Baltimore end Jack Bighead as a free agent.

49ers Overhaul Offensive Unit

SAN FRANCISCO, Oct. 4—(UP)—A complete overhaul of the offensive unit of the San Francisco 49ers will be made this week, Coach Red Strader said in a wake of resounding beatings in the first two games of the National Professional Football League season.

"I don't know what's the matter, but it appears to be a complete unit breakdown," said Strader. "We are going to have to start all over."

The 49ers, perennial threats for the Western Division title under Coach Buck Shaw before he was fired after last season, have been beaten 23-14 by the Los Angeles Rams and 38-3 by the Cleveland Browns in their first two league starts this year after a brilliant exhibition record.

All Even!

Dodgers	A	H	O	A	Yankees	A	H	O	A
Gilliam,2b-lf	3	1	0	0	Rizzuto,ss	3	0	1	5
Reese,ss	4	1	3	2	Martin,2b	4	1	4	2
Snider,cf	1	0	1	0	McDougald,3b	3	0	0	5
*Zimmer,2b	2	0	1	1	Berra,c	3	2	8	0
Campanella,c	3	0	5	0	Bauer,rf	4	3	0	0
Furillo,rf	3	1	1	0	Skowron,1b	2	1	6	0
Hodges,1b	3	0	7	1	†Collins,1b	1	0	5	1
J. Robinson,3b	4	0	2	3	Cerv,cf	4	1	2	0
Amoros,lf-cf	4	1	2	0	Howard,lf	4	0	1	0
Spooner,p	0	0	0	0	Noren,lf	0	0	0	0
Meyer,p	2	0	0	1	Ford,p	4	0	0	1
‡Kellert	1	0	0	0					
Roebuck,p	0	0	2	0	Totals	32	8	27	14
Totals	30	4	24	8					

*Struck out for Snider in fourth.
†Walked for Skowron in fifth.
‡Popped out for Meyer in seventh.

DODGERS	000	100	000—1
YANKEES	500	000	00x—5

RUNS: Reese, Rizzuto, McDougald, Berra, Bauer, Skowron. ERROR: J. Robinson. RUNS BATTED IN: Berra, Bauer, Skowron 3, Furillo. HOME RUN: Skowron. STOLEN BASE: Rizzuto. DOUBLE PLAYS: McDougald to Martin to Skowron; J. Robinson to Hodges. LEFT ON BASE: Dodgers 7, Yankees 7. BASES ON BALLS: Off Spooner 2, off Ford 4, off Meyer 2. STRIKEOUTS: By Ford 8, by Spooner 1, by Meyer 4. HITS: Off Spooner, 3 in ⅓ inning; off Meyer, 4 in 5⅔ innings; off Roebuck, 1 in 2 innings. RUNS AND EARNED RUNS: Spooner 5 and 5, Ford 1 and 1. HIT BY PITCHER: Ford (Furillo). WINNER: FORD. LOSER: Spooner. UMPIRES: Ballafant (N), plate; Honochick (A) 1b; Dascoli (N), 2b; Summers (A), 3b; Flaherty (A), left field; Donatelli (N), right field. TIME: 2:36. ATTENDANCE: 64,022.

Packers Cut Pair

GREEN BAY, Wis., Oct. 4—(UP)—Veteran Defensive Halfback Clarence Self and Rookie Offensive End Jim Jennings were released on waivers by the Green Bay Packers today.

Joe Williams Says:

Bums Should Ask "Left-Wing" Probe

By JOE WILLIAMS, *Scripps-Howard Writer*

NEW YORK, Oct. 4—Perhaps the Brooks should have demanded a congressional investigation simply on the basis of prima facie evidence. All left-wing elements are a threat to security. By now there can be no doubt about those connected with the Yankees—particularly, the cell headed by one Whitey Ford, obviously an alias.

It was Ford's left wing that disrupted the Brooklyns' praiseworthy program to bring succor to the underprivileged people of their community, who have been starving for a World Series championship for nearly 40 years.

Ford Sharper Than in First Game

There is reason to suspect the Yankee left-hander was aided by renegade patriots who smuggled hitting secrets out of the Brooklyn clubhouse, for in winning game No. 6, to even the Series, he was infinitely sharper and more knowing than he had been in winning game No. 1, when he failed to finish.

By way of lending credibility to the belief that a monstrous betrayal has been perpetrated, is the fact that only left-wingers have been able to defeat the Brooklyns, Ford twice and Tommy Byrne once, the latter a sinister character who was brought into the Yankee organization late last season under mysterious circumstances.

It is against all the laws of logic, as well as the overwhelming testimony of past performance, for the Brooklyns to lose to left-handed pitching. In fact, any time this rarity is recorded, there is vast consternation among the people, and even Walter Lippman is sorely pressed to rationalize it.

Save for Duke Snider—and it's usually best to save him for Ebbets Field—practically all the gun power in the Brooklyns' attack is right-handed. It naturally follows, then, that any left-hander who dares face them must be prepared to face his Maker shortly thereafter.

Two Different Breeds of Lefties

This has been the most profound surprise in the Series. How do you explain it? Maybe the answer is that there are two different breeds of left-handers—the National League breed, which the Brooklyns eat alive, and the American League, or Yankee breed, which produces ulcers in their digestive tract, but little else.

One of the big guns in the Brooklyn arsenal is Roy Campanella and he has yet to get a hit off a Yankee left-hander in three games. Yesterday's game typically exposed the futility of the Brooklyns' right-handed power against the Yankee left-wing apparatus. Jackie Robinson left four stranded, Gil Hodges three, Carl Furillo two.

None of the Brooklyns' four hits went for an extra base. For the most part, they spent the afternoon bouncing out to the infield, a tribute to Ford's control and his determination to make them hit his pitch. There were only three Yankee outfield catches, one a Little League blooper. In the net, a brilliant pitching job.

Starting Spooner Surprises Dressen

By CHUCK DRESSEN, *Washington Nats' Manager*

NEW YORK, Oct. 4—I was surprised when Karl Spooner started for the Dodgers. He warmed up hard for the two previous games. But that wasn't the main reason. I was looking for the Dodgers' best. In the World Series you got to decide on your best before you go in, and then get him in as often as you can. It's not like the season when you can try them out.

Alston showed us Newcombe, Loes, Podres, Erskine, Craig and then Spooner, as starters. I have to wonder who does he think is his best. When I had Brooklyn I had to figure Erskine was my best one year and I played him in three games. The other year nobody was best, so I got Black ready in a hurry to work three times.

Stengel knew his best, Ford and Byrne, and he got them in first so he could bring them back. Casey must have sat back and relaxed and thought he was lucky when they hit Spooner for five runs in the first inning. Then Casey could forget how he blew one. That was in Ebbets Field, where different thinking could have saved one game.

Stengel had to know Erskine had a gimpy shoulder for a long time and was not much of a bet to pitch nine innings. Everybody else knew it. Casey also knew he had one shot in Brooklyn with Grim, but he failed to match him against Erskine, where he might have paid off. He went away from his best in Brooklyn in the right spot hoping Turley or Larsen might pitch one good game.

Naturally, I thought Newcombe was coming back. And Loes. The Newcombe thing is puzzling. There are a lot of rumors why he isn't pitching. I saw him get up in the bullpen when Spooner slipped, but they told him to sit down again. If he has a sore arm he shouldn't have pitched in the first place.

Series Figures

NEW YORK, Oct. 4—(UP)—Here are the financial figures for the sixth game of the World Series:

Attendance	**64,022**
Net receipts	**$411,090.72**
Commissioner's share	**61,663.61**
Clubs and leagues' share	**349,427.11**

Dumping the Dodger:

Billy Martin, the rough-and-ready little Yankee, throws a block into Shortstop Pee Wee Reese to break up a double play in yesterday's series game. Reese got the ball away but didn't have enough on it to get Yogi Berra at first in the seventh inning. Berra had grounded to First Baseman Gil Hodges. (UP Telephoto)

THE SUN

BALTIMORE, THURSDAY, OCTOBER 9, 1958

Rose Zayne Is Victor
At Hagerstown: Page 24

Ex-Oriole Hurlers Save Respect Of American Loop

Warhead Wins, Clem Third In $57,100 Belmont Race

3-YEAR-OLD LEADS FOR DISTANCE

Beau Diable Is Second, 1¾ Lengths Behind In Driving Finish

New York, Oct. 8 (AP)—Eddie Arcaro sent Warhead to the front at the start today and the 3-year-old colt led all the way to capture the $57,100 Manhattan Handicap at Belmont. Favored Clem finished third under topweight of 126 pounds.

Warhead, a bay son of Battle Morn - Headfirst, beat Laudy Lawrence's Beau Diable by a length and three quarters in a driving finish.

Beau Diable Second

Beau Diable, ridden by Hedley Woodhouse, came up in the final strides to take second money from Clem by a neck. Warhead packed 116 pounds, Beau Diable was the lightweight with only 108.

Clem, who had upset Round Table in three $100,000 races last month, is owned by Mrs. Adele L. Rand, and took third by three quarters of a length over Leroy G. Burns's Eddie Schmidt. The latter was second topweight with 120 pounds.

The tough mile and one half race again proved too tough a nut to crack for the topweight. Only Stymie has been able to win the race carrying 126 pounds. Stymie later failed with 132, as did Whirlaway. Seabiscuit couldn't win with 128, nor could Noor with the same impost.

Clem Chases Warhead

But Clem, ridden by Willie Shoemaker, gave it a good try. They were right on Warhead's heels from the start, and battled right down to the wire.

Warhead was a length and a half in front of Clem entering the backstretch with a little less than a mile to travel. He maintained that margin into the far turn, where the Greentree Stable's Pop Corn dropped back from third and Eddie Schmidt moved up.

In the middle of the final turn, Eddie Schmidt had taken second, with Clem back in third. But Clem came on again as Eddie Schmidt tired in the stretch, only to miss second money right at the wire.

Bolingbroke Has Mark

The time on a fast track was 2.28 3-5, in one of the fastest Manhattans. The stakes record is 2.27 3-5, made by Bolingbroke (115 pounds) when he beat Whirlaway in 1942.

The crowd of 16,624 turned out in showery weather, and bet Clem down to 13-20 favoritism.

Warhead is owned by Mrs. Mabel C. Scholtz, whose husband, Herman, is a retired Army officer. Warhead paid $15.50, $8.00 and $4.00. Beau Diable, a 10-1 shot, paid $14.80 and $5.30, while Clem returned $2.50 to show.

START OF THE END—Bill Skowron starts toward first after socking single that brought Elston Howard (top) home with second—and winning—run of tenth inning.

THE EYES HAVE IT—Pitcher Warren Spahn (right) turns to watch flight of ball as Gil McDougald raps tie-breaking homer off left-hander's second pitch of tenth inning.

JUST NOT HIS DISH—Andy Pafko's attempt to score from third on Johnny Logan's fly to left fails as Yogi Berra, taking Elston Howard's quick peg in time, bars way, tags runner to complete key double play for reliefer Art Ditmar.

2-0 DEFICIT CONCERNED OFFICIALS

But Larsen, Duren And Turley Boost Yanks Into Contention

Yanks beat Braves, 4-3, in ten innings to even series. Page 1

By BOB MAISEL
[*Sun Staff Correspondent*]

Milwaukee, Oct. 8 — Three former Oriole pitchers have not only saved the Yankees in this World Series, but also the respect of the entire American League.

When the Braves tore through the New Yorkers the first two days, it appeared they would wrap up their second straight world championship in 4 or 5 games. And the way the Yankees were playing the American League would have been regarded as strictly second rate.

Some of the league's officials were admittedly worried about it. One pointed out when the Braves were leading two games to none, "this will really hurt us. The Yankees are our big drawing card. I just wonder if they will continue to be if they lose this thing in 4 or 5 games."

Hurl Two Shutouts

Then Don Larsen and Ryne Duren combined for a shutout in the Yanks' first victory, and after Warren Spahn beat Whitey Ford to make it 3 games to 1, Bob Turley came back to pitch a shutout after being knocked from the box in the first inning of his other start.

And there is no doubt that Duren and Turley, along with Gil McDougald, were the big men in today's New York victory which squared the Series.

Now Casey Stengel says he will pitch Larsen or Johnny Kucks tomorrow in the windup against Lew Burdette. Most observers think Larsen will get the call if his arm feels right.

"The arm is a little stiff, but I think I'll be able to pitch tomorrow if Casey says so," commented Larsen after today's game.

Turley Wants To Pitch

"Heck, I can start tomorrow," chimed in Turley. "I feel real good. No aches or pains or stiffness in my arm anywhere. I can pitch without any trouble."

The big question in the Braves' clubhouse today was the play on which Third Base Coach Billy Herman sent Andy Pafko in to attempt to score on Johnny Logan's short fly to left in the second inning.

Herman's version of the play went like this, "with two out you take a chance. I'll admit it wasn't a very good chance, but there was a chance nevertheless. I wasn't going to send him in at first, but at the last second I thought about that bad throw Howard made earlier in this Series, and I decided to try it. It ain't the first man I ever sent in that was thrown out. Our scouting reports said he had a good arm, but not a great one."

Haney Backs Coach

Manager Fred Haney tried to take his coach off the hook. "The angle and perspective were bad from where I was so I can't say too much, but the first man up in the next inning grounded out anyway, so maybe we wouldn't have scored," he said.

Elston Howard admitted he was surprised when he saw Pafko start for home. "I was gettin' in position to throw, but I didn't think he'd go," said Howard. "That ball was pretty short. Then Mickey (Mantle) yelled to me that he was taggin' up and I should throw home. I was ready then. Mickey always yells on plays like that."

The other controversial play involved Umpire John Flaherty's decision that Mantle had trapped Wes Covington's line drive in the second inning in-

(Continued, Page 26, Column 7)

MCDOUGALD WAS NERVOUS

'Pressure Terrific,' Says Yankee Batting Star

Milwaukee, Oct. 8 (AP)—"My goodness, a World Series like this one takes about ten years off your life. I was as nervous as a long-tailed cat in a room full of rocking chairs."

Gil McDougald, who hit the tenth-inning home run that snapped a 2-to-2 tie and led to the New York Yankees' 4-to-3 triumph over the Milwaukee Braves today, was talking about the last play of the game.

Frank Torre was the hitter. The Braves, trailing 4 to 3, had runners on first and third with two out. Torre, a left-handed batter, was hitting for Del Crandall. Bob Turley had just replaced Ryne Duren. A hit would either tie the score or win the game and the Series for the Braves.

Pressure Terrific

"The pressure was terrific," McDougald said. "There's always pressure in a World Series. But this was something extra special. I don't care who you are. I defy anyone to say he was calm at that moment. I know I was sweating out there. I felt the fingers in my glove shaking."

Torre took a called strike, fouled off a pitch, then stroked a soft liner in McDougald's direction that at first looked as if it might go over Gil's head and drop in short right field.

"I had it all the way," the 30-year-old second baseman said. "It was a routine fly, but I played it as if my life depended upon it. Everything in a World Series is magnified, but this was even more so and don't think I wasn't aware of it.

"If I had dropped the ball, it would have been the biggest boo-boo of the series. It sounds funny now, but that's what I was thinking as I waited for the ball."

Home-Run Special

McDougald's catch might have been routine, as he claimed, but the home run he hit to lead off the tenth was something extra special.

It came off a fast ball, knee high, by Warren Spahn, and landed deep in the left field bleachers, 375 feet away.

"I was lucky," McDougald said, "believe me, Spahnie happened to lay it right down the middle. He'd been pitching me

(Continued, Page 27, Column 3)

ENGLISH GOLF TEAM IN LEAD

U.S. Is Second In World Amateur Tourney

St. Andrews, Scotland, Oct. 8 (AP)—An autumn gale from off the roaring North Sea turned the world's first amateur golf tournament today into a fiasco and a freak.

Britain took the lead for the official team championship with 227 strokes. The United States was second with 233.

Reid Jack, of Scotland, more accustomed to playing in violent air movements than anyone else here, took the lead for the unofficial world individual championship with a 36-36-72—almost a par matcher all the way.

Coe Shoots 74

Jack was one of the early starters, playing before the wind reached full fury. So were Charlie Coe, of Oklahoma City, the United States National champion, and left-handed Bob Charles, of New Zealand, who shared the next best individual score, 74.

The team championship is determined on an aggregate of the three best scores daily by players from each country. It is a four-day, 72-hole medal-play competition.

There is no recognition of an individual champion but the best performer will be unofficially hailed the world's best amateur.

Taylor Penalized Twice

Today the accomplishments of the players were secondary to those of the wind.

One thin Filipino, Francisco Reyes, was bodily blown off the seventeenth tee of St. Andrews'

(Continued, Page 27, Column 5)

COLT SAMPLE INJURES HAND

Four Stitches Needed After Pass Defense Mishap

By CAMERON C. SNYDER

The Colts came up with an injury at practice yesterday when Johnny Sample split the webb between two fingers.

Sample, a former Maryland State star, was on defense at the time and stopped a hard pass with his hand. Apparently the ball tried to go between his fingers and something had to give.

The injury required four stitches, but Johnny was back at practice within an hour.

"Should you be out here?" called Coach Weeb Ewbank.

"Why yes," answered Johnny, "it doesn't bother me at all and I need the work."

Team Spirit Good

Sample's attitude is the same as the rest of the squad. Whether the Colts will be in the right frame of mind for their first road game of the sea-

(Continued, Page 27, Column 7)

Bellino May Not Start For Navy On Saturday

By EDWIN H. BRANDT
[*Sun Staff Correspondent*]

Annapolis, Oct. 8—Power football with the personnel to make it work was the description given Michigan today as Navy Coach Eddie Erdelatz revealed more bad news concerning the Middie injury list.

With its toughest game of the season so far slated Saturday in Ann Arbor, Mich., Navy will again be without its giant tackle, Bob Reifsnyder.

Little Progress In Cure

The brace Navy had constructed for Reifsnyder's leg has been of little aid so far, and Reifsnyder has made little progress since first injuring a muscle in his leg four weeks ago.

He's definitely out this week, and it's a heavy blow to Navy chances with the power offense Michigan has played so far. The Wolverines are six-point choices.

Halfback Joe Bellino, out with a sprained knee, is doubtful for Saturday, while Ends Tom Hyde and John Shirreffs each have an infected foot, but are expected to see action.

Erdelatz's problems have been compounded by the Michigan offense. Against Southern Cali-

(Continued, Page 27, Column 6)

Navy-Irish Game Sellout

Annapolis, Oct. 8 (AP)—Navy officials today announced that the Middies' football game with Notre Dame is a sellout.

A capacity crowd of about 57,000 is expected at Baltimore's Memorial Stadium for the November 1 contest. It will be the thirty-second game in a series unbroken since its beginning in 1927.

Capt. Slade Cutter, director of athletics at the Naval Academy, announced that all tickets have been sold. Cutter said plenty of tickets are still available for the Maryland-Navy game in Baltimore the following Saturday, November 8.

11 NEW MARKS SET IN SERIES

Berra Paces Teams With 3; 7 Records Tied

Milwaukee, Oct. 8 (AP)—Eleven World Series records have been broken or extended and seven tied through six games in the 1958 competition between the Milwaukee Braves and the New York Yankees.

Yankee catcher Yogi Berra has done most of the record smashing. He has established new standards for most hits in total series (60), most total bases in the series (99) and most times at bat, total series (219).

Yogi also tied a record for most series participated in, 10—a mark he now shares with Babe Ruth and Joe DiMaggio.

The records broken:

Most games, total series—60,

(Continued, Page 26, Column 4)

Mt. St. Mary's Wins In Soccer

Emmitsburg, Md., Oct. 8 [*Special*] — Western Maryland tied the score late in the final period only to have Mount St. Mary's boot in a goal in the last 43 seconds to take a 2-to-1 soccer victory here today.

Bill McFann was the hero for the Mounts with his winning goal.

Pete Kuhn had given the home team a 1-to-0 lead in the second quarter, but Don Shure tied it for the Green Terrors with five minutes to go in the game.

Western Maryland now has a 1-1 mark and Mount St. Mary's is unbeaten in two starts.

WEST. MD.		MT. ST. MARY'S
Musselman	G.	O'Conor
Waghelstein	R.F.	Miller
Karrer	L.F.	Clark
Kinter	R.H.	Amunn
Lee	C.H.	Bailev
Schatt	L.H.	Szalay
Corbin	O.R.	Neylan
Varga	I.R.	Kuhn
Shure	C.F.	Williams
Silex	I.L.	McFann
Cole	O.L.	Blanford

Western Md.	0	0	0	1—1
Mt. St. Mary's	0	1	0	1—2

Western Md. Goal—Shure.
Mount St. Mary's Goals — Kuhn. McFann.

Tackle Joins Squad

Lawrence, Kan., Oct. 8 (AP)—Senior Tackle Bill Blasi, who has missed Kansas's first three football games because of a preseason hand fracture, was named to the Jayhawks' starting unit today.

Sports Index

Slow-Starting Ray Takes Close Decision Over Cotton

Louisville, Ky., Oct. 8 (AP)—Sunny Ray, a light heavyweight from Chicago, decisioned Eddie Cotton tonight in a ten-round televised fight from the Fairgrounds Coliseum.

Two of the judges gave the fight to Ray, while the third called it a draw.

Cotton, who was making his first start of the season, carried the fight to his 23-year-old opponent through most of the early rounds, but began to tire under a punishing body attack.

Both fighters were bleeding when it ended, Ray from a cut over the left eye and Cotton from the nose.

Ray, who has been impressive in other fights this year, started slowly against Cotton, but began to pick up speed by the sixth round. He forced Cotton, who comes from Seattle, into a defensive position to protect his midsection.

The victory was No. 19 for Ray, who also has drawn five and lost five. For Cotton, the record stands at 35-8-1.

Despite the long layoff, Cotton carried the fight in the early rounds when he worked Ray over with combination rights and lefts to the head. He also kept him off balance with a piercing left hand that opened a gash over Ray's left eye in the fifth round.

From there on out, Ray, who was four pounds heavier than his opponent at 171½, kept belting Cotton with a combination right and left to the chin that had the Seattle boy holding on as the bell sounded.

Judge Tom Knuckles scored the fight 47-45 for Ray; Judge Walter Beck had his 48-47 for Ray and Referee Paul Machuny had it 46-46.

The Associated Press scorecard gave it to Ray, 48-47.

Navy Gridder Back Of Week

New York, Oct. 8 (AP) — Joe Tranchini's passing virtuosity against Boston University last Saturday today earned the Navy quarterback the designation of back of the week in college football.

"He had a real great day," remarked Coach Eddie Erdelatz afterward in a masterpiece of understatement.

Tranchini, who completed only fourteen passes all last season as substitute for Tom Forrestal, pitched 27 against Boston U. and connected on 18 of them for 221 yards. The eighteen completions tied a Navy record set by George Welsh against Army in 1955.

Tranchini, a 6-foot 180-pounder from Clairton, Pa., kept his opposition off balance by mixing his pass patterns and threw them flat-footed, jumping, retreating and running laterally.

B.U.'s Booters Beaten, 2 To 1

Gettysburg, Pa., Oct. 8 [*Special*]—Gettysburg spotted the University of Baltimore a goal in the first quarter, then came on to defeat the visitors, 2 to 1, here today in a soccer game.

Gene Klemkowski scored the opening goal at the sixteen-minute mark of the first period.

Ritter Smith tied it up in the second session and Don Emich put the Bullets in front in the third quarter with his goal.

BALTIMORE U.		GETTYSBURG
Brocklander	G.	Perrine
Barnett	R.F.	Hathaway
Newbert	L.F.	Koven
Johnson	R.H.	Youse
Poetzel	C.H.	B. Smith
Ward	L.H.	Gutekunst
Gore	O.R.	Roberts
Sraurusa	I.R.	R. Smith
Nippard	C.F.	Emich
Crockett	O.L.	Pflug
Beck	I.L.	Baumgardner

Baltimore U.	1	0	0	0—1
Gettysburg	0	1	1	0—2

Stiff Scrimmage Held

Columbia, Mo., Oct. 8 (AP)—The Missouri Tigers staged a stiff scrimmage today in preparation for Saturday's football game with Southern Methodist.

World Series Box

Milwaukee, Oct. 8 (AP)—The official box score of the sixth game of the 1958 World Series:

NEW YORK (A.)

	Ab.	R.	H.	Rbi.	O.	A.	E
Carey, 3b	5	0	0	0	0	1	0
McDougald, 2b	5	1	2	1	6	4	0
Bauer, rf	5	1	2	1	0	0	0
Mantle, cf	5	1	1	0	0	0	0
Howard, lf	5	1	2	0	3	1	0
Berra, c	4	0	2	1	14	1	0
Skowron, 1b	4	0	1	1	6	2	0
Kubek, ss	2	0	0	0	0	1	0
1Slaughter	1	0	0	0	0	0	0
Duren, p	2	0	0	0	0	0	0
Turley, p	0	0	0	0	0	0	0
Ford, p	1	0	0	0	0	0	0
Ditmar, p	1	0	0	0	1	0	1
2Lumpe, ss	1	0	0	0	0	1	0
Totals	41	4	10	4	30	11	1

1Grounded out for Kubek in sixth.
2Struck out for Ditmar in sixth.

MILWAUKEE (N.)

	Ab.	R.	H.	Rbi.	O.	A.	E
Schoendienst, 2b	4	1	2	0	6	2	1
Logan, ss	2	1	0	0	1	3	2
Mathews, 3b	5	0	0	0	1	3	0
Aaron, rf	5	0	3	2	2	0	0
Adcock, 1b	4	0	1	0	6	0	0
3Mantilla	0	0	0	0	0	0	0
Crandall, c	4	0	0	0	7	1	0
4Torre	1	0	0	0	0	0	0
Covington, lf	4	1	2	0	0	0	0
Pafko, cf	2	0	1	0	3	0	0
Bruton, cf	2	0	0	0	3	0	1
Spahn, p	4	0	1	1	1	2	0
McMahon, p	0	0	0	0	0	0	0
Totals	37	3	10	3	30	11	4

3Ran for Adcock in tenth.
4Popped out for Crandall in tenth.

New York (A)	1	0	0	0	0	1	0	0	0	2	—4
Milwaukee (N)	1	1	0	0	0	0	0	0	0	1	—3

Double plays—Howard, Berra; Crandall, Schoendienst. Left on bases—New York (A), 10; Milwaukee (N), 9. Two-base hit—Schoendienst. Home runs—Bauer, McDougald. Sacrifices—Logan (2). Sacrifice fly—Berra.

PITCHING RECORD

	Ip	H	R	Er
Spahn (L)	9⅔	9	4	4
McMahon	⅓	1	0	0
Ford	1⅓	5	2	2
Ditmar	3⅔	2	0	0
Duren (W)	4⅔	3	1	1
Turley	⅓	0	0	0

Base on balls—Spahn, 2 (Skowron, Lumpe); Ford, 1 (Schoendienst); Duren, 2 (Adcock, Logan). Strikeouts—Spahn, 5 (Kubek, Lumpe, Howard, Duren, Carey); McMahon, 1 (Duren); Ford, 2 (Mathews, Crandall); Ditmar, 2 (Crandall, Spahn); Duren, 8 (Adcock, Crandall, Bruton 2, Spahn 2, Covington, Mathews).

Umpires—Berry (A), plate; Gorman (N), first base; Flaherty (A), second base; Barlick (N), third base; Umont (A), left field; Jackowski (N), right field. Time—3.07. Attendance—46,367. Receipts (net)—$277,263.60.

No Rain, Near 70 Due For Series

Milwaukee, Oct. 8 (AP)—The weatherman predicts Milwaukee's foggy, rainy weather tonight will change to partly cloudy conditions tomorrow for the seventh and final game of the World Series.

The official forecast, released late today, predicts: Mostly cloudy and fog, drizzle and possible showers tonight. Partly cloudy tomorrow, with showers likely tomorrow night. Milwaukee's lowest temperature tonight in mid 50s. Highest temperature tomorrow near 70. Southerly to southwesterly winds, increasing to 15-25 miles per hour tomorrow.

'Now We Can Play In National League,' Stengel

Parti Quiz Wins Sharpsburg Purse At Hagerstown

VICTOR PAYS $11.80 UNDER TONY RUSSO

'Achsah Ann Places And Imperial Runs In Third Place

By WILLIAM BONIFACE
[*Sunpapers Racing Editor*]

Hagerstown, Md., Oct. 9 — Louis Sena's Parti Quiz, which had finished last beaten thirteen lengths in his previous start, shocked the form players with a form reversal in the featured Sharpsburg Purse here today when he won with little difficulty. He paid $11.80 straight.

When beaten in dismal efforts at Timonium and Cumberland, Parti Quiz was ridden by Tony Russo and Mason Gordon. Today Larry Reynolds, was back at the controls.

Gaining his fourteenth win of the ten-day-old meeting, Reynolds rode with confidence when he rated Parti Quiz in the early furlongs and then brought the son of Apache forward to win by two and a half lengths.

Parti Quiz Drives

'Achsah Ann, who had set most of the early pace, could not match Parti Quiz's late drive, but held well enough to take second money from Bertram D. Wright's Imperial while Hillside Farm's Tubee was fourth.

Many of the 4,752 fans, present for the well-prepared program, could not pull themselves away from the TV sets, showing the final game of the World Series, long enough to watch the races. This disinterest in the events on hand showed in the mutuel play which totaled only $296,698 for eight races.

Choices Win 3 Races

Although upset by the form reversal of the feature, the students of the past performance sheets were doing quite well when favorites won the first three races and Robert Riley's Bull Sir got home at $5.60 for $2 in the fifth race and secondary attraction.

Under Jay Hause, Bull Sir was rated for the first part of the mile-and-a-sixteenth test and then galloped to the lead to win by five lengths from Top Brass with Fun N' Fancy gaining the show. Bull Sir went the distance in 1.55.

With only two programs remaining, Reynolds holds a five-winner lead in the contest for saddle honors of the meeting. Tony Russo is the present runnerup with nine victories.

La Villate Comes Up

The third consecutive winning favorite, Edward L. Miller's La Villate came up again after dropping the lead to win the third race for a $5.20 straight payoff.

Ridden by John Sollars, La Villate gave up the command to Poor Shah's Dish for a few strides in the homestretch and then outgamed her rival in the last twenty yards to win by a neck. Poor Shah's Dish held well to be second, about two lengths in front of Super Moose.

The first two races were won by the favorites Northern Stream and Diabolic Test and the daily double payoff of $15.20 was the lowest of the meeting. Lucky numbers were 8 and 6.

First Official Win

The first official winner of the short career of apprentice Mason Gordon came in the second race when he drove Cedar Hill stable's Diabolic Test to a six-length victory. A few days ago, Gordon finished first on Limerick, but his mount was disqualified by the stewards.

Gordon rode like a veteran on Diabolic Test. He sent the five-year-old to the front on the first turn and then rated in front of the field before turning the gelding loose for the stretch run. Diabolic Test paid 2 to 1.

A complete standout at $3.60 straight, Northern Stream had little or no trouble winning the first race. The two-year-old, an invader from the milers, was ridden by Freddy Kratz and romped the five furlongs in 1.07 to win by five lengths.

Sports Index

WHAT A RELIEF—Victorious Yankees mob Bob Turley after right-hander set down Braves in ninth to complete smart relief job.

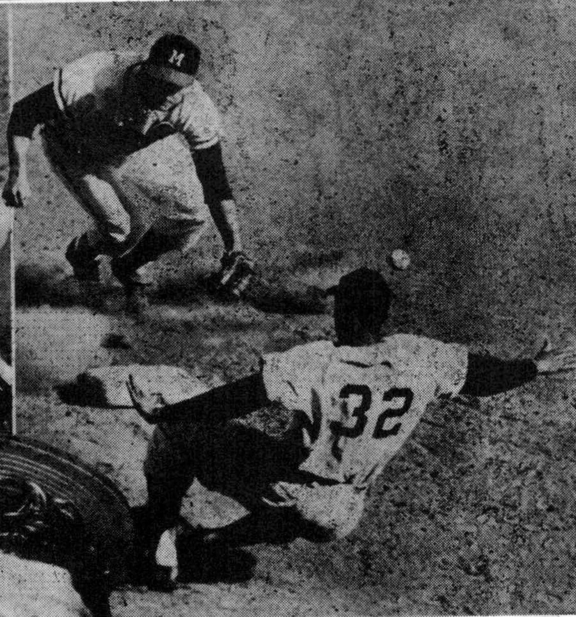

JOHNNY ON THE SPOT—Johnny Logan, Braves shortstop, dashes over to cover too late to handle Del Crandall's peg as Elston Howard steals second base in fourth inning.

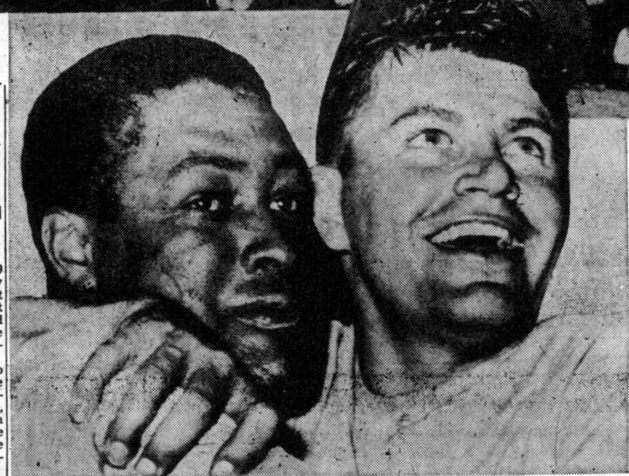

PAIR OF ACES—Elston Howard (left) and Bob Turley, heroes in deciding game over Braves, salute each other in dressing room. Howard singled in go-ahead run for hurler.

NEW ZEALAND GOLFERS GAIN

Move Into Second Behind England; U.S. Third

St. Andrews, Scotland, Oct. 9 (AP) — Great Britain's hardy linksmen faltered today but it was little New Zealand, and not the United States, which moved into stronger contention for the World Amateur Golf Championship.

As icy winds continued to blow over the rolling Old Course of St. Andrews, a New Zealand lefthander, Bob Charles, took the individual lead from Scotland's Reid Jack. And he put his country within one stroke of the front-running British.

England Has 461 Points

Britain's team total after 36 holes was 461. New Zealand was second at 462, followed by the United States with 465.

The competition for the Eisenhower Trophy is a team affair. The scores of the best three players of each country are aggregated daily. The championship will be awarded on the 72-hole aggregate Saturday.

Charles, retaining his putting poise in winds which often reached 35 m.p.h., fired a second straight 74 for a 36-hole score of 148. He overtook Scotland's weather-hardened Jack, who could no no better that 77 after yesterday's opening 72, for 149.

Coe Still In Running

Still strong in the running for unofficial individual honors was Charlie Coe, the reed-thin United States Amateur champion from Oklahoma City. Coe, despite some shaky putting, bracketed a 77 with a previous 74 for 151.

This placed the Oklahoman in third place in the individual race, the victor of which probably will be acclaimed the world's outstanding amateur golfer.

Other Americans fared well, but didn't score well enough to pick up much ground on the British, who led by six strokes after yesterday's round.

Hyndman Scores 77

William Hyndman, of Philadelphia, still looking for his first birdie in the tournament, shot a 77 for 156. Scrambling Billy Joe Patton, of Morganton, N.C., more serious than anyone ever had seen him, added a 78 for 158.

The fourth United States representative, Dr. Frank Taylor, of Pomona, Cal., improved by two strokes with a 79. His 160 total, fourth best among the Yanks, was not counted.

PACKERS HIT BY INJURIES

Quarterbacks Parilli And Starr Both Hurt

By CAMERON C. SNYDER

"There's nothing wrong with the Packers, but what some quarterbacking won't cure," was the way Art Daley, of the Green Bay *Press-Gazette*, summed up their 13-13 tie with the Detroit Lions last Sunday.

Along the same lines he wrote: "The Packers stopped 'em (Lions) with 33 yards and one first down rushing—among other things Detroit's twin 100-touchdown passers, Bobby Layne and Tobin Rote, are capable of much more than 13 points and that's a credit to the Packer defense.

Eye Colt Win

"And speaking of Baltimore, the Packers now get their chance to hand the Colts their first setback in Milwaukee."

But the quarterbacking situation at this time out at Green Bay is in the hands of the Packer trainers.

Babe Parilli is still nursing a rib injury, while Bart Starr played nearly the entire Lion game on a bad ankle. It was reinjured in the last five minutes.

Injured Quarterbacks

Joe Francis, rookie signal caller, was hustled into the breech and nearly presented the Lions with the winning

(Continued, Page 28, Column 2)

Terps Work To Bring Back Scoring Punch

By EDWIN H. BRANDT

Maryland wound up practice for Texas A.&M. yesterday at College Park, with Coach Tommy Mont still concentrating on offense.

Shut out twice in its first three games, Maryland has been able to muster a consistent attack only against N.C. State in a 21-6 victory. The Terps couldn't find the scoring punch against Clemson last week despite 244 yards total offense.

Heartening is the fact Maryland's injury list is virtually cleared up, with Halfback Ted Kershner ready for limited duty against the Aggies, and Vince Scott and Dick Scarbath recovered from sprained ankles.

Terps Favored Slightly

Maryland is a slight favorite for the game tomorrow in Byrd Stadium. A crowd of about 25,000 is expected.

There has been no letup in drills this week, with the Terps working especially hard Tuesday and Wednesday. While the Old Liners worked in sweatsuits yesterday, scrimmaging was in order most of the week.

Mont feels his attack is just about ready to click, and certainly the performances of halfbacks Bob Layman and Dwayne Fletcher last week were encouraging.

Layman Ran 54 Yards

Layman broke away for 54 yards to the Clemson 20 before he stumbled, while Fletcher was a consistent gainer, several times just a step away from going the distance.

The Aggies are still trying to get on their feet after a rocky beginning. They lost to Texas Tech and Houston, but tripped Missouri last week, 12-0.

It may be that Coach Jim Myers has become adjusted to his material and the Aggies have adjusted to his single wing. The Aggies were good enough to go

(Continued, Page 28, Column 3)

Middie Eleven Leaves Today

Navy's football team leaves at noon today for Ann Arbor, Mich., and its game with Michigan tomorrow. About 90,000 are expected for the game.

The Middies held only a light drill yesterday at Annapolis in preparation for their Big Ten opponent, and rate a five-point underdog despite their undefeated status.

Tackle Bob Reifsnyder definitely will be out of the game, while Halfback Joe Bellino will likely see only limited duty in this seventh game of the Michigan-Navy series, which dates back to 1925.

Michigan won the last meeting, 35-0, in 1948, while Navy's last victory was in 1945, 33-7. The Wolverines lead in the series, 3-2, with one tie.

Mrs. Glick Increases Lead In Payne Cup Golf Tourney

Washington, Oct. 9 (AP)—Mrs. Maurice Glick, of Baltimore, maintained her steady pace in the Payne Cup Tournament of the Maryland State Golf Association today, and with a second round 82 increased her lead to two strokes.

With a 36-hole total of 163 Mrs. Glick, four-time winner of this 54-hole medal play event, holds a two-stroke lead over Mrs. Frank Cush, the District champion, with one round remaining.

Miss Schiller Has 83

Mrs. Cush had a 39-42—81, which was tied by Mrs. Claude Richards, of Baltimore, for low round of the day. Mrs. Richards added an 81 to an 89. Mrs. Cush has 84-81—165.

The only player besides Mrs. Cush within seven strokes of Mrs. Glick is Jane Schiller, of Salisbury, Md., who had a second straight 83 for 166.

Today's 81s, and that same score yesterday that gave Mrs. Glick a one-stroke lead, still are low rounds over the Congressional Country Club course that will be the scene of the Women's National Amateur next August.

Mrs. Cush In Second

Most of the players are three-putting several of the huge greens each round. Mrs. Glick three-putted the eighteenth today to lose a chance to break 40 on the back nine.

Mrs. Cush, who is in second place, had a trio of three-putt

(Continued, Page 28, Column 2)

2 Schools Regain N.C.A.A. Rights

Kansas City, Oct. 9 (AP)—Restoration of full rights and privileges of membership to the Universities of Louisville and Washington was announced today by the National Collegiate Athletic Association.

Executive director Walter Byers said the action was taken by the association's officers and the chairman of its committee on infractions after a review of the practices and policies at each of the institutions.

The University of Louisville was placed on probation for two years May 1, 1956, for failure to conform to N.C.A.A. recruiting and financial aid regulations.

The University of Washington was placed on probation for two years August 21, 1956, also for non-conformance to recruiting and financial aid regulations.

Michigan Works On Navy Defense

Ann Arbor, Mich., Oct. 9 (AP). —Michigan has been working overtime this week on its high-stepping, getting ready for its first view of Navy's jitterbug defense.

The Middies are expected to use a perpetual motion defense against the Wolverines Saturday.

Coach Bennie Oosterbaan feels that Navy linemen and line backers will be difficult to block. So the Wolverines have done extra work on offense against the scrubs, who have been jitterbugging just like the Middies.

Oosterbaan said second team guard Tom Jobson, tackle Willie Smith and right halfback Gary McNitt probably will be withheld from the Navy game.

All have been sidelined this week by injuries.

'AIN'T NO JOY IN BUSHVILLE'

'Cause The Braves Has All Made Out'

Milwaukee, Oct. 9 (AP)—"Somewhere the sun is shining," said the poet laureate of Fifth and Wisconsin, "somewhere children shout. But there ain't no joy in Bushville, 'cause the Braves has all made out."

The poet looked sadly and majestically along the cheerless street down which tatters of souvenir pennants were blowing. Several of his listeners, overcome with emotion suiting the occasion, took off their hats.

A man with a large stock of pennants reading "Milwaukee Braves 1958 World Champions," said, without hope, "hey, they're half price."

Back To The Saloon

Then the poet turned and went back to his favorite saloon. Six friends followed him.

Thus the black news that Milwaukee no longer bore the Baseball Championship of the World was received downtown. Actually, the sun was shining brightly. But not through the gloom that pressed down upon that part of the known world which extends for a hundred yards in five directions — East, West, North, South and Up — from the intersection of Fifth street and Wisconsin avenue.

Mayor Frank P. Zeidler telegraphed the ball club that it still had the "undiminished support" of the city. He also telegraphed Mayor Robert F. Wagner of New York city that the Yanks' achievement could be appreciated "even in Milwaukee."

No Wild Outbursts

There were no wild outbursts of grief, you understand. There was nothing like a complete reversal of the wild, sweet frenzy that at the call of the last out a year ago magically jammed the concourse with some hundred thousand or so human beings, from wall to wall and to

(Continued, Page 29, Column 5)

HANEY LAUDS N.Y. PITCHERS

Braves' Manager Has No Alibis After Defeat

Milwaukee, Oct. 9 (AP)—Manager Fred Haney refused to alibi the Braves' World Series collapse today saying, "instead of moaning, let's talk about how good their pitchers were."

Contrary to what might be expected under the circumstances, the Braves, from Haney on down, did not appear to be downhearted over losing their world championship to the Yankees.

The clubhouse was completely relaxed. There even was some horseplay in the showers and wisecracks by individual players.

No Post-Mortems

Haney, corraled by a posse of writers near his cubicle, made it plain there would be no post-mortems on the Braves' 6-to-2 loss to Casey Stengel's Bombers.

"Let's not talk about our batting slump," he said. "Let's talk about their pitching. (Bob) Turley pitched great ball. So did (Whitey) Ford, only he was unlucky.

"I give them all the credit in the world. I have no alibis and neither do my players. We had our chances. They beat us. They deserved to win. To the victor belongs the spoils."

When someone asked Haney to pick a turning point in the Series that saw Milwaukee take a 3-to-1 lead in games and then lose three in a row and the title, he replied:

"The turning point was in our bats. We scored seventeen runs in our first two games and only seven in the last five.

"Yesterday we had our chances. Today we had our chances. If we had some runs, it might have been different, but let's not talk about that. The Yankees were great."

"Only Seven Runs"

"The whole thing in a nutshell," said Warren Spahn, "is that we only scored seven runs in the last five games. We weren't run out of the ball park. Either their pitchers were that

(Continued, Page 30, Column 4)

World Series Box

Milwaukee, Oct. 9 (AP)—The official box score of the seventh game of the 1958 World Series:

MILWAUKEE (N.)

	Ab.	R.	H.	Rbl.	O.	A
Schoendienst, 2b	5	1	1	0	5	3
Bruton, cf	3	0	1	0	1	0
Torre, 1b	2	0	0	0	10	0
Aaron, rf	3	0	1	0	4	0
Covington, lf	4	0	0	1	1	0
Mathews, 3b	1	0	0	0	1	2
Crandall, c	4	1	1	1	4	1
Logan, ss	4	0	0	0	1	5
Burdette, p	3	0	0	0	0	2
McMahon, p	0	0	0	0	0	0
1Adcock	1	0	1	0	0	0
2Mantilla	0	0	0	0	0	0
Totals	30	2	5	2	27	13

NEW YORK (A.)

	Ab.	R.	H.	Rbl.	O.	A
Bauer, rf	5	0	0	0	2	0
McDougald, 2b	5	0	2	0	3	6
Mantle, cf	4	0	0	0	2	0
Berra, c	4	2	1	0	3	1
Howard, lf	3	2	2	1	3	0
Lumpe, 3b	3	0	0	0	0	2
Carey, 3b	1	1	1	0	1	0
Skowron, 1b	4	1	2	4	12	0
Kubek, ss	2	0	0	1	1	2
Larsen, p	1	0	0	0	0	0
Turley, p	2	0	0	0	0	1
Totals	34	6	8	6	27	12

1Singled for McMahon in ninth. 2Ran for Adcock in ninth.

New York (A.)	0	2	0	0	0	0	0	4	0	—6
Milwaukee (N.)	1	0	0	0	0	1	0	0	0	—2

Errors—Torre 2. Double play—McDougald and Skowron. Left on bases—New York (A.), 7; Milwaukee (N.) 8. Two-base hits—McDougald, Berra. Home runs—Crandall, Skowron. Stolen base—Howard. Sacrifices—Torre, Howard, Turley. Sacrifice fly—Kubek.

PITCHING RECORD

	Ip	H	R	Er
Burdette (L.)	8	7	6	4
McMahon	1	1	0	0
Larsen	$2\frac{1}{3}$	3	1	1
Turley (W.)	$6\frac{2}{3}$	2	1	1

Bases on balls—Burdette 2 (Berra, Kubek), McMahon 1 (Mantle), Larsen 3 (Bruton, Aaron, Mathews), Turley 3 (Mathews 2, Torre). Strikeouts—Burdette 3 (Howard, Mantle, Kubek), McMahon 2 (Turley, Bauer), Larsen 1 (Crandall), Turley 2 (Burdette, Bruton). Umpires—Gorman (N.) plate, Flaherty (A.) first base, Barlick (N.) second base, Berry (A.) third base, Umont (A.) left field, Jackowski (N.) right field. Time—2.31. Attendance—46,367.

BURDETTE'S QUOTE CITED BY MANAGER

Casey Claims This Was Greatest Year For Yank Comeback

Yankees defeat Braves, 6-2, to win World Series .. Page 1.

By LOU HATTER
[*Sun Staff Correspondent*]

Milwaukee, Oct. 9—"I'd have to say this was the greatest year to win the pennant and world championship," blurted a jubilant Casey Stengel.

And Casey has led New York to a sockful of them during his ten-year administration as manager of the Yankees — nine American League flags and seven World Series triumphs, tieing Joe McCarthy's all-time record in the post-season classic.

"The reason I say this is for three or four reasons," gloated the 68-year-old boss of the Bronx Bombers in redundant Stengelese.

"Very Good Club"

"First, with a bad start you can't afford to make mistakes. And we came back and won by not making any mistakes," Stengel elaborated.

"More, it showed that our ball club is a very good ball club, even though we faltered the last month and a half of the season.

"And it showed that we have recovered and that now we can play baseball in the National League."

This last declaration, above the bedlam that enveloped the Yankee clubhouse following this afternoon's 6-to-2 New York victory over Milwaukee in the critical seventh game of the 1958 World Series, nearly brought down the house.

Comment Backfires

It was the only occasion on which Stengel took caustic exception to the unwritten law of baseball sportsmanship—never rub it in on a beaten adversary. But there may have been some justification.

Last Thursday, following Milwaukee's 13-to-5 rout of the Yanks that established a 2-to-0 lead for the Braves, Lew Burdette suggested that New York was no better than several of Milwaukee's National League rivals.

Burdette, whom the Bombers blasted for four runs in the eighth inning today, further ventured that he would like to see the Yanks in the National League on a day-to-day basis.

"But, to give them an advantage like the first two games with their kind of pitching . . . well, I wouldn't want to try it again," Stengel hastily amended.

Stengel In High Spirits

Stengel, perhaps never before in such high spirits, was a gracious host when the beaten Milwaukee manager, Fred Haney, visited the riotous Yankee locker room to pay his respects to his conquerors.

"Thanks for coming over, Fred," shouted Stengel. "Tell those boys of yours they played great baseball—a first-class club."

"It was a great Series, Casey," and the rest of the elfish Milwaukee skipper's words were lost in the din, as he took his beating with a smile, shielding his obvious disappointment.

Stengel was lavish in his praise of Bob Turley's clutch pitching that achieved two of the Yankees' three-straight wind-up Series victories and saved a third.

Turley Praised

But nobody expressed the sentiments toward Turley more eloquently than Gil McDougald when the Yankee second baseman strode over, clapped a hand on the broad shoulders of the Lutherville (Md.) resident and said:

"Robert, you were great. You really showed me plenty out there today. Another day of rest, and you ought to be ready to pitch the big one out in Honolulu on Saturday."

Turley was scheduled to fly out of this chastened city of

(Continued, Page 29, Column 1)

Mayor Wagner Lauds Yankees

New York, Oct. 9 (AP)—Mayor Wagner sent the city's "heartiest congratulations" to the New York Yankees today after they won the World Series at Milwaukee.

The telegram, addressed to Manager Casey Stengel, read:

"Heartiest congratulations to all the club from all the people of New York city. We are very proud of our Yankees. Once again, you are the World Champions of the great American sport."

Classified
Comics

St. Louis Globe-Democrat.

Business
Financial

SECTION C — FRIDAY, SEPTEMBER 1, 1961 — PAGES 1 TO 12

Yankees Lose But Set Homer Record

Bow to Twins, 5-4; Mantle, Skowron And Lopez Connect

MINNEAPOLIS-ST. PAUL (AP).—Mickey Mantle clubbed his forty-eighth home run and the New York Yankees set a new American League homer mark Thursday but Minnesota survived the assault and posted a 5-4 victory.

HERB SCORE

★ ★ ★

The triumph gave the Twins the rubber game of this three-game set and made the final record between the two teams 14-4 for the Yankees.

The loss left the Yankees 1½ games ahead of Detroit, 8-2 winners over Chicago.

Mantle's homer, just inside the leftfield foul pole, came off lefty Jack Kralick and left the switch-hitter one game ahead of Babe Ruth's record 60 pace.

Mantle also laced a pair of singles in four trips.

Roger Maris, who has 51 homers and is six games ahead of Ruth, went hitless in four appearances.

After Mantle homered to lead off the fourth, Bill Skowron followed one out later with his 23rd circuit clout to give the Yankees 194 homers for the season. That eclipsed the Al Mark of 193 set by the Yankees in 1960. The Major League record of 221 is held jointly by the 1947 New York Giants and the 1956 Cincinnati Reds.

Hector Lopez added another roundtripper for New York, hitting it with Mantle on base in the sixth.

Minnesota scored five runs before a man was retired in the third inning. Lenny Green walked, went to second on Billy Martin's one-baser and scored on a base hit by Harmon Killebrew. Bob Allison's single scored two more runs and drove Roland Sheldon to the showers.

Jim Lemon then greeted Jim Coates with a two-run homer before the lanky righthander finally retired the side.

Kralick was the winner of his twelfth game and first over the Yankees. He has nine losses.

Clete Boyer committed two errors for the Yanks, both on poor throws, to stop his consecutive-games errorless streak at 41.

NEW YORK	AB.	R.	H.	MINNESOTA	AB.	R.	H.
Rich'on 2b	5	0	1	Green cf-lf	3	1	1
Kubek ss	5	0	3	Martin 2b	3	1	3
Maris rf	4	0	0	Kil'rew 1b	4	1	1
Mantle cf	4	2	3	Allison rf	5	1	1
Howard c	4	0	0	Lemon lf	3	1	1
Sko'ron 1b	4	0	0	Lepcio 3b	0	0	0
Lopez lf	4	1	1	b-Altobelli	1	0	0
Boyer 3b	4	0	1	Vald'so 3b	0	0	0
Sheldon p	1	0	0	Battey c	3	0	1
Coates p	1	0	0	T'tle 3b-cf	4	0	1
a-Cerv	1	0	0	V'salles ss	4	0	1
Reniff p	0	0	0	Kralick p	4	0	0
c-Berra	1	0	0	Totals	34	5	10
Totals	38	4	11				

a-Struck out for Coates in sixth; b-Grounded out for Lepcio in eighth; c-Flied out for Reniff in ninth.

New York 0 0 0 2 0 2 0 0 0—4
Minnesota 0 0 5 0 0 0 0 0 x—5

RBI—Mantle, Skowron, Lopez 2, Killebrew, Allison 2, Lemon 2. E—Boyer 2, Skowron, Lemon. PO-A—New York 24-12, Minnesota 27-10. DP—Sheldon, Richardson and Skowron, Kubek, Richardson and Skowron. LOB—New York 8, Minnesota 12.

2B—Boyer. HR—Lemon, Mantle, Skowron, Lopez. SB—Martin, Mantle. S—Martin.

	IP	H	R	ER	BB	SO
*Sheldon (L, 9-4)	2	5	4	4	1	2
Coates	3	1	1	1	3	4
Reniff	3	4	0	0	2	2
Kralick (W, 12-9)	9	11	4	4	1	7

*Faced four batters in third.

WP—Reniff. U—Stewart, Berry, Linsalata, Umont. T—2:57. A—33,-709.

CHISOX RECALL SCORE, MAY GO AGAINST YANKS

CHICAGO (AP)—Herb Score, once a fireballing mound star, returns to the Chicago White Sox after his San Diego Club finishes its Pacific Coast league season and may get a whirl at the New York Yankees.

Score, one of five players recalled from the Sox farm system Wednesday, is expected to report in time for the home-stand opening against the Yankees.

Since being sent to San Diego May 26, Score has fashioned a 7-5 record.

He had a 1-1 Sox record before Manager Al Lopez sent him to Sa nDiego in hopes that steady work would improve his control.

Others recalled included pitchers Gary Peters and Alan Brice, also from San Diego; outfielder Dean Look from Charleston of the Sally League; and pitcher Ed Drapcho from Mobile of the Southern Association. They will report when their clubs complete their seasons.

2 St. Louis Teams In Softball Meet

Two softball teams, Charlie's and Mayrose, which each won qualifying tournaments in Ellisville in July, will represent St. Louis in the Open and Industrial Slow-Pitch World Softball Tournaments Sept. 1-4.

Charlie's will travel to Louisville, Ky., to compete in the Open Tournament with 40 other teams. Manager Herb Hacker's squad has a 22-5 record.

Mayrose takes a 20-3 mark to the 40-team Industrial Tournament in Toledo, O. The team will be making its fourth consecutive appearance in the tourney.

AMERICAN ASSOCIATION
Houston 1, Omaha 0.
Dallas-Fort Worth 5, Denver 4.
Louisville 5, Indianapolis 4 (12 innings).

Early Start

BUFFALO, N.Y. (AP). — The University of Buffalo football team may get the jump on the rest of the nation's college squads when practice sessions open Friday. The Bulls will start drills at 6 a.m. for the benefit of players attending morning summer school classes.

SPORTS ON THE AIR

RADIO
Baseball
7:55 p.m.—Kmox. St. Louis Cardinals vs. Pittsburgh Piratess.

Cubs Turn on Giants and Post 6-1 Victory

Reaching for Golden Apple

Jackson to Face Bucs Here Tonight

By JACK HERMAN
Globe-Democrat Sports Writer

PHILADELPHIA.—Larry Jackson, who has been Johnny Keane's most reliable pitcher in August, will try to duplicate in the month of September, starting Friday night at St. Louis against the out-going champion Pittsburgh Pirates.

"He still can win 13 or 14 games for us," said the Cardinal manager before Thursday night's series windup with the pesky Phillies.

Of the Cards' remaining 27 games, Jackson figures to start about five or six more. He'll enter the Pirate contest at Busch Stadium with a 10-9 record, including a 4-1 log in August. Not bad for a pitcher out nearly a month with a broken jaw.

Jackson actually has been Keane's most consistent performer on the mound longer than that; in fact, since Keane took over as manager. Starting July 8 at San Francisco, Jackson has lost only once—to Los Angeles—in eight decisions to wipe out the dark memory of a 3-8 personal meeting back on June 26.

In two of his last three starts Jackson has fired three-hit shutouts at the Giants.

Both Jackson and the Red Birds will be happy to resume combat with the stronger clubs in the National League. "We just lay better against the tougher teams," Keane admitted. "The lower clubs bring you down to their level, apparently."

It's certainly been true in the case of the Phillies. The Cards look like world-beaters sweeping the second-place Los Angeles Dodgers and third-place San Francisco Giants for a rollicking six-game run before arriving in the City of Brotherly love.

They lost two of the first three games to the last-place Phils, collecting only 20 hits and 11 runs. The Phils have scored only one more run, but it was enough to give them a 2-1 edge in games.

Major League Standings

NATIONAL LEAGUE

Club.	W.	L.	Pct.	G.B.
Cincinnati	79	53	.599	....
Los Angeles	73	52	.584	2½
San Francisco	69	57	.543	7
Milwaukee	69	57	.548	7
CARDS	**66**	**61**	**.520**	**10½**
Pittsburgh	61	64	.488	14½
Chicago	54	73	.425	22½
Philadelphia	37	91	.289	40

THURSDAY'S RESULTS
Chicago 6 San Francisco 1.
Cardinals at Philadelphia, night.
Los Angeles at Milwaukee, night.

FRIDAY'S SCHEDULE
Pittsburgh at St. Louis, 8 p.m.—Gibbon (10-8) vs. Jackson (10-9).
Los Angeles at Milwaukee, night—Williams (11-10) vs. Buhl (9-10).
San Francisco at Chicago—Jones (8-7) vs. Hobbie (7-12).
Only games scheduled.

AMERICAN LEAGUE

CLUB.	W.	L.	Pct.	G.B.
New York	87	45	.659	....
Detroit	86	47	.647	1½
Baltimore	78	57	.578	10½
Chicago	70	63	.526	17½
Cleveland	66	66	.500	21
Boston	64	72	.471	25
Los Angeles	58	74	.439	29
Minnesota	57	74	.435	29½
Washington	50	79	.388	35½
Kansas City	46	85	.351	40½

THURSDAY'S RESULTS
Minnesota 5, New York 4.
Detroit 8, Chicago 2.
Cleveland at Washington, night.
Kansas City at Los Angeles (2), twi-night.
Only games scheduled.

FRIDAY'S SCHEDULE
Detroit at New York, night—Mossi (14-3) vs. Ford (22-3).
Cleveland at Baltimore, night—Latman (10-4) vs. Estrada (11-7).
Boston at Minnesota, night—Stallard (1-4) vs. Ramos (9-16).
Chicago at Washington (2), twi-night—McLish (9-12) and Pierce (7-7) vs. McClain (7-14) and Sisler (2-7).
Kansas City at Los Angeles—Walker (5-11) vs. Duren (6-11).

COLTS BATTLE DALLAS TONIGHT IN EXHIBITION

By Associated Press

Coach Weeb Ewbank hopes to fit one more piece into the puzzle he's putting together to form the 1961 edition of the Baltimore Colts when the Mustangs run into the Dallas Cowboys at Norman, Ok., Friday nig' in the National Football League's fast-fading exhibition campaign.

Ewbank, whose wizardry at perfecting Colt gridiron puzzles produced world champion teams in 1958 and 1959, hopes to answer at least one bib Colt question against the Cowboys.

Who's going to play fullback?

Ewbank, seeking a successor to the retired Alan Ameche, has four fullback prospects. One is Billy Pricer, Ameche's replacement for four seasons. Another is 12-year veteran Joe Perry, obtained from San Francisco. The others are rookies, Mark Smolinski of Wyoming and Dallas Garber of Marietta, Ohio.

So far, in Baltimore's two exhibition victories and one defeat, the rookies have performed so well that Ewbank doesn't know who will best fit into the starting assignment.

Perry may have the edge. Last week the fellow who has gained 7246 yards in 1451 carries during his NFL career, plunged one yard for the go-ahead touchdown and plucked a 53-yard touchdown pass from Johnny Unitas as the Colts thrashed the Washington Redskins, 41-7.

Only one other NFL game is on Friday night's schedule. The San Francisco 49ers (1-2) visit the Los Angeles Rams (1-1-1) in a battle that could indicate which is the strongest NFL team on the West Coast.

St. Louis, with the ailing Sam Etcheverry ready for action, planned to invade Detroit Friday night but the game was postponed until Saturday night to permit Lion fans to view on television the start of the Detroit Tigers-New York Yankees series in the American League pennant race.

INTERNATIONAL LEAGUE
Toronto 6, Rochester 4.
Buffalo 3, Syracuse 2.
Jersey City 5, Charleston 4.
Richmond 5, Columbus 4.

Rout Marichal As Curtis Flips Neat 7-Hitter

CHICAGO (AP). — The Chicago Cubs turned on their erstwhile tormentors, the San Francisco Giants, Thursday with a 6-1 victory, banging all of their 10 hits in the first three innings to clinch the contest.

Little Jack Curtis spun a well-paced seven-hitter to give the Cubs only their fourth triumph in 17 starts against the third-place Giants this season.

The Giants, who came up with some weird fielding, got excellent relief pitching after starter Juan Marchial left in the third.

Billy O'Dell, who spelled Marichal, yielded one hit and struck out six in four innings, while the third Giant pitcher, Dom Zanni, struck out the side in the Cub seventh.

After the third, O'Dell and Zanni held the Cubs hitless.

Curtis, who notched his ninth decision against 10 defeats, was nicked for a first-inning San Francisco run as Joe Amalfitano tripled and scored on Willie McCovey's sacrifice fly.

After that, the clever lefty kept out of trouble while his Cub mates quickly put Marichal to route.

The Cubs banged four hits for three runs in the first inning. Richie Ashburn, after fouling off 12 pitches, earned a walk. The third hit of the inning was a pop double by Ron Santo which dropped between two Giant fielders.

The Cubs got another run in the second as Ed Bouchee dumped a double between three hesitant Giant fielders and Curtis got a single, looping his hit between the same three Giants.

The Cub scoring was wrapped up in the third on four hits, with O'Dell replacing Marichal after George Altman doubled and Billy Williams and Santo singled to chase the Giant sttrter.

SAN FRANCISCO	AB.	R.	H.	CHICAGO	AB.	R.	H.
Ama'no 2b	4	1	1	Ashb'rn cf	2	1	1
Kuenn rf	3	0	0	Zi'mer 2b	4	1	1
M'Co'y 1b	3	0	2	Banks ss	4	0	0
Mays cf	4	0	1	Altman rf	4	1	1
Cepeda lf	3	0	1	Wi'iams lf	4	2	2
Dave'rt 3b	4	0	0	Santo 3b	3	0	2
Orsino c	3	0	1	Taylor c	4	0	1
Bre'oud ss	4	0	0	Bo'chee 1b	3	1	1
Marichal p	1	0	0	Curtis p	3	0	1
O'Dell p	1	0	1	Totals	31	6	10
a-F.Alou	1	0	0				
Zanni p	0	0	0				
Totals	31	1	7				

a-Struck out for O'Dell in seventh.

San Francisco 1 0 0 0 0 0 0 0 0—1
Chicago 3 1 2 0 0 0 0 0 *—6

RBI—McCovey, Ashburn (2), Altman, Williams (2), Taylor. E—Zimmer. PO-A—San Francisco 24-8, Chicago 27-14. DP—Santo, Zimmer and Bouchee (2); Banks, Zimmer and Bouchee; McCovey, Bressoud and McCovey. LOB—San Francisco 7, Chicago 5.

2B—Santo, Bouchee, Altman. 3B—Amalfitano. SF—McCovey, Ashburn.

PITCHING SUMMARY

	IP.	H.	R.	ER.	BB.	SO.
Marichal (L, 13-9)	*2	9	6	6	1	0
O'Dell	4	1	0	0	1	6
Zanni	2	0	0	0	1	4
Curtis (W, 9-10)	9	7	1	1	3	3

*Faced three batters in third.

PB—Orsino. U—Pelekoudas, Burkhart, Conlan and Steiner. T—2:21. A (paid)—7593.

SOUTH ATLANTIC LEAGUE
Knoxville 8, Charlotte 6.
Greenville 1-1, Jacksonville 0-2.
Portsmouth 19, Asheville 0.
Charleston at Columbia postponed, rain.

NORTHERN LEAGUE
Duluth-Superior 7-3, Winnipeg 0-1.
Grand Forks 6, St. Cloud 4.
Aberdeen 5-5, Eau Claire 0-1.

Tigers, Homers Rip Chisox, 8-2

DETROIT (AP).—The Detroit Tigers awoke from a brief slump Thursday and moved to one and one-half games from first place in the American League with an 8-2 victory over the Chicago White Sox. Billy Bruton and ailing Norm Cash crashed two-run homers for the Tigers.

The second-place Tigers pulled 10 percentage points behind the first-place New York Yankees on the eve of their showdown three-game series starting Friday night in Yankee Stadium.

The Yankees were dropped, 5-4, Thursday by the Minnesota Twins.

The Tigers, who had lost two straight to Chicago, broke out with 14 hits in support of Paul Foytack's strong pitching before 25,504 fans.

BOX SCORE

CHICAGO	AB.	R.	H.	DETROIT	AB.	R.	H.
Robinson rf	4	0	0	Wood 2b	4	1	2
Fox 2b	4	0	0	Bruton cf	5	2	2
Landis cf	4	0	2	Kaline rf	5	2	3
Sievers 1b	4	1	1	Colavito lf	2	0	1
Minoso lf	4	1	3	Cash 1b	4	1	1
Carey 3b	3	0	1	Bertoia 3b	4	0	1
Aparicio ss	4	0	0	Fern dez ss	4	0	1
Lollar c	3	0	0	Roarke c	4	1	3
Baumann p	1	0	0	Foytack p	3	1	1
Kem'rer p	1	0	0	Totals	35	8	14
Hacker p	0	0	0				
a-Martin	1	0	0				
Lown p	0	0	0				
Totals	33	2	7				

a-Popped out for Hacker in seventh.

Chicago 0 0 0 2 0 0 0 0 0—2
Detroit 2 1 1 0 3 1 0 0 x—8

RBI — Carey (2), Wood, Bruton (2), Colavito (2), Cash (2), Bertoia. E—Kemmerer. PO-A—Chicago 24-9, Detroit 27-5. DP—Fox, Aparicio and Sievers; Fernandez and Cash. LOB—Chicago 5, Detroit 7.

2B—Carey, Minoso, Wood, Kaline. HR—Bruton, Cash. SB—Bertoia. S—Foytack, Wood. SF—Colavito.

	IP.	H.	R.	ER.	BB.	SO.
Baum'n (L, 9-11)	2⅔	7	4	4	1	1
*Kemmerer	2⅓	5	4	3	0	0
Hacker	1	1	0	0	0	3
Lown	2	1	0	0	0	1
Foyt'k (W, 10-8)	9	7	2	2	1	7

..*Faced 2 batters in sixth.

WP — Kemmerer. U — Smith, Soar, McKinley, Chylak. T—2:11. A—25,-504.

No. 32 FOR CASH

Bruton got the Tigers ahead in the first inning with his sixteenth homer and Cash belted his thirty-second with Al Kaline on base in a three-run fifth.

Foytack had only one bad inning, the fourth, when Chicago scored both its runs. The righthander, recording his tenth victory against eight losses, yielded six hits and struck out seven.

Foytack now has yielded only four runs in his last three starts.

Cash, leading the league in batting, was back in the linsup after missing Wednesday night's game. He complained of blurred vision and dizziness and was sent home suffering from what doctors diagnosed as flu.

He fainted in the night but reported to Tiger Stadium Thursday fully recovered and manager Bob Sheffing jumped at the chance to restore his left-handed slugger to the batting order.

BAUMANN THE LOSER

Cash's homer struck the facing of the third deck in right and was belted off reliefer Russ Kemmerer.

Bruton's homer was hit off loser Frank Baumann, after Jake Wood had led off with a bunt single.

The Tigers added single runs in the second and third for a 4-0 lead before the Sox got to Foytack for their two runs. Roy Sievers and Minnie Minoso singled with two out and Andy Carey doubled them home.

Bruton led off the Detroit fifth with a bunt single and Kaline followed with his third hit, sending Bruton to third. Rocky Colavito scored Bruton with a short sacrifire fly and Cash's homer brought in Kaline.

Colavito drove in the Tiger's final run in the sixth with a single and stretched his hitting streak to 14 games.

EASTERN LEAGUE
Johnstown 4, Springfield 3.
Williamsport 10, Lancaster 9.
Binghamton 7, Reading 1.

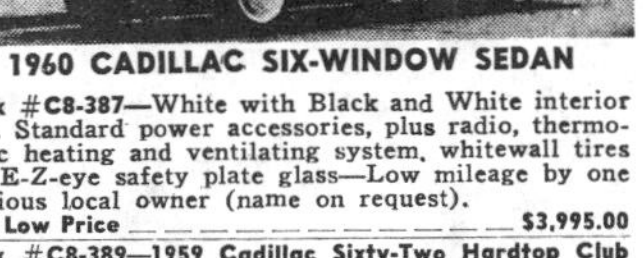

SPORTS **THE INDIANAPOLIS STAR** Section 4 Travel—TV-Radio

SUNDAY MORNING, SEPTEMBER 3, 1961

Maris Clouts Two More Home Runs

★ ★ ★ ★ ★ ★ ★

Osteen Shuts Out Colonels; Only 2 To Go

Indians Return Home Seeking To Clinch Flag

By MAX GREENWALD, Star Sports Writer

Louisville, Ky. — The Indianapolis Indians will return home today for the final series of the season just two victories away from the American Association Pennant.

Claude Osteen last night pitched his first shutout of the year as the Tribe trimmed runner-up Louisville, 5-0. It was the southpaw's 15th triumph.

WITH SIX contests left at Victory Field, the Indians are in possession of a four-game margin over the Colonels. John Tsitouris (9-7) will pitch this afternoon for Indianapolis against Moe Drabowsky (9-6).

Several hundred Indianapolis fans were in the stands to cheer a 12-hit Tribe barrage against three hurlers.

Meanwhile, Osteen allowed just six safeties and had a three-hitter for six stanzas.

The Indians wrapped up the decision with four runs in the fourth.

Cecil Butler, who defeated the Indians with a six-hitter Tuesday night, was routed with none out in that inning with the bases full and two Tribe runs across.

Joe Gaines singled to left and Cliff Cook batted over his 114th RBI on a double to left-center. Cook moved to third on the throw home and, with the infield playing in, Don Pavletich singled through Amado Samuel at short.

HAL BEVAN walked after Bob Uecker permitted his foul to fall and Sandy Valdespino got a bunt hit to load the sacks.

Chi Chi Olivo relieved Butler and Jim Snyder singled to center for two runs. Len Johnston forced Snyder and Valdespino had to scramble back to third after maknig a wide turn. The Colonels bitterly argued with Umpire Tom Bartas that Valdespino had been caught.

Johnston stole second when the peg went to third but Chico Ruiz lined out to left.

Snyder tripled to right center in the sixth and Osteen bounced a single into center for a run.

A Louisville baserunning blunder helped Osteen in the second. With one out, Ron Jackson got the Colonels' first hit and Len Gabrielson singled to center. In trying for a catch of a sinking drive, Valdespino knocked the ball a few steps away from him. Jackson tried for third and easily was out, Valdespino to Cook. Samuel then fanned.

Mack Jones, who hasn't been knifing very many hits since his return from Milwauke, led off the fourth with a single. But Cook handled Mike Krsnich's ground ball to start a double play.

A DOUBLE play got Osteen out of distress in the seventh. After hitting a foul over the leftfield fence, Uecker hit a single which bounced to that barrier. It looked good for a double but Uecker stayed at first although the throw was made to third.

Jackson also singled to left before Gabrielson's ground ball to Ruiz was turned into a double play. Gabrielson rushed out to give his warm opinion to Umpire Serge Schuster about the call at first base. Samuel then popped out to Snyder, leaving Uecker at third, the only Colonel to get that far.

Uecker obtained Louisville's only extra-base hit with two out in the ninth when he slashed a double to left which eluded Johnston. Gaines came in for Jackson's fly to end the game.

HIT-AND-RUN Mike Fandozzi had trouble with Osteen's popup in the third, grabbing the ball before it touched the ground after he didn't hold it the first time.

After Gabrielson walked in the fifth, Manager Cot Deal had a few remarks for Umpire Barney Deary regarding a possible half-swing strike.

The Louisville defense provided some excitement in the seventh. Krsnich ran into foul territory to grab Ruiz' swat and shortstop Samuel knocked down Gaines' hard rap, then pounced on the ball in time for the out.

Osteen hit to left off Connie Grob in the ninth and the ball took a high bounce over Krsnich's head for a double. The Tribe hurler advanced on an infield out but was stranded.

Ruiz made a fine stop of Krsnich's tough bouncer in the ninth and got his man.

INDIANAPOLIS

	AB	R	H	O	A	E
Johnston, lf	5	0	0	3	0	0
Ruiz, ss	5	0	0	0	2	0
Gaines, rf	4	1	2	2	0	0
Cook, 3b	3	1	2	1	3	0
Pavletich, c	4	1	1	5	1	0
Bevan, 1b	3	1	1	7	1	0
Valdespinon, cf	4	0	2	4	1	0
Snyder, 2b	4	1	2	4	4	0
Osteen, p	4	0	2	1	0	0
Totals	36	5	12	27	12	0

LOUISVILLE

	AB	R	H	O	A	E
Fandozzi, 3b	3	0	0	2	0	0
Tate, 2b	3	0	0	4	1	0
Jones, cf	4	0	1	5	0	0
Krsnich, lf	4	0	0	2	0	0
Uecker, c	4	0	2	5	2	1
Jackson, 1b	4	0	2	5	1	0
Gabrielson, rf	2	0	1	1	0	0
Samuel, ss	3	0	0	2	5	0
Butler, p	1	0	0	0	0	0
Olivo, p	1	0	0	0	1	0
[1]Littrell	1	0	0	0	0	0
Grob, p	0	0	0	1	0	0
Totals	30	0	6	27	10	1

[1]Grounded out for Olivo in eighth.

INDIANAPOLIS .... 000 401 000— 5
Louisville .... 000 000 000— 0

RBI—Snyder 2, Cook, Pavletich, Osteen. DP-Cook and Snyder; Ruiz and Snyder; Olivo, Samuel and Jackson. Left-Indianapolis 6; Louisville 6 .2B—Cook, Osteen, Uecker. 3B—Snyder. SB—Gaines, Johnston.

	IP	H	R	ER	BB	SO
Osteen (W, 15-11)	9	6	0	0	3	6
*Butler (L, 9-11)	3	6	4	3	1	1
Olivo	5	5	1	1	1	3
Grob	1	1	0	0	0	0

*Faced five batters in fourth.

U—Deary, Schuster, Bartos. T—2:28. A—3,417.

Tebbetts Replaces Dressen

Milwaukee (AP) — The Milwaukee Braves fired Manager Charlie Dressen and named Executive Vice-President Birdie Tebbetts his successor yesterday for the remainder of the year and the 1962 and '63 seasons.

Dressen was notified that his contract would not be renewed in a meeting with Vice-President and General Manager John McHale after the Braves' 4-0 victory over the Los Angeles Dodgers.

In a quick moving series of news conferences, McHale said Dressen was told of the firing now "to insure him sufficient time in the event other major league managing jobs become available."

TEBBETTS, who left a job as Cincinnati manager to become executive vice-president at Milwaukee three years ago, then met with McHale and newsmen at another conference.

In stepping down from his front office role, Tebbetts said that he "found myself as a baseball man getting farther and farther away from the things I love most."

"I just wasn't happy being so far away from baseball," Tebbetts said. "John McHale has been doing a very fine job. It looked like two fellows doing the same job and only enough work for one.

"It may be hard for some people to believe that a man who could have had the presidency anytime he wanted would take the insecure job of managing. I'm 48 years old and have a family but I do not think there's any insecurity for me."

Tebbetts called the Milwaukee organization "the best in baseball." And he added: "I'm taking over a team which I consider the best in baseball."

McHale said that Birdie made himself available as a field manager at a meeting with owner Lou Perina "a couple of weeks ago."

BIRDIE TEBBETTS
Back In The Cage

WINNING COMBO—Yankee Roger Maris is flanked by pitchers Ralph Terry (left) and Luis Arroyo in the dressing room at Yankee Stadium yesterday after the trio teamed up to beat Detroit, 7-2, and hike the Bombers' league lead to 3½ games. Maris blasted his 52d and 53d home runs and Arroyo saved Terry's 12th win. (AP Wirephoto)

Yankees Whip Tiger Nemesis, Stretch Lead

New York (AP) — Roger Maris, clubbing his way out of a three-week slump, hit his 52nd and 53rd homers and a double yesterday as the New York Yankees whipped nemesis Frank Lary and the Detroit Tigers, 7-2, and stretched their American League lead to 3½ games.

The pair of home runs, coming after Maris had collected only 6 hits in his last 50 at-bats, put the 26-year-old Yankee thumper eight games ahead of the pace Babe Ruth set when he hit a record 60 homers in 1927.

MARIS' FIRST, a high fly into the lower right field stands on a 3-2 pitch off right-hander Lary, broke a 2-all tie in the sixth and put the Yanks into a 3-2 lead. His second, a line drive into the same lower stands off left-hander Hank Aguirre, capped a four-run burst that put it away for New York in the eighth.

Maris' double, a ringing drive to right center, had led to the tying run in the fourth inning—bunted home by Mickey Mantle—after Detroit had jumped to a 2-0 first inning lead on Rocky Colavito's 40th home home run with Al Kaline on base.

Mantle, failing to homer, fell one game behind Ruth's pace. In four times at bats, Mantle walked, sacrificed, grounded out and beat out a bunt. He had 48 home runs.

RALPH TERRY, lanky young right-hander, won his 12th against two losses with four-out relief from Luis Arroyo, the little southpaw relief ace making his 55th appearance of the season.

It was the Yank's second successive success with today's single game left in their showdown three-game series with the runnerup Tigers. New York won Friday night's opener 1-0 on three hits after two were out in the ninth.

Lary, now 26-10 lifetime against New York, was rebuffed in his second attempt at his 20th triumph of the season. He has a 19-8 record.

Arroyo, last of a Yankee trio that blanked the Tigers Friday night, came in with two out in the eighth inning.

Home Run Derby

The following table shows how Roger Maris and Mickey Mantle of New York compare with the record pace of Babe Ruth in 1927:

PLAYER	HOMER	GAMES DECISIONS	DATE HIT
Maris	53	134	Sept. 2
*Mantle	48	134	Aug. 31
Ruth	53	142	Sept. 16

*One behind Ruth's pace.

Detroit	ab	h	rbi	New York	ab	h	rbi
Wood,2	3	1	0	Richardson,2	4	1	0
[2]Osborne	0	0	0	Kubek,ss	4	1	2
[4]Bertoia,2	0	0	0	Maris,rf	4	3	3
Bruton,cf	3	1	0	Mantle,cf	2	1	1
[3]Alusik	1	0	0	Berra,lf	4	0	0
House,c	0	0	0	Howard,c	4	0	0
Kaline,rf-cf	4	1	0	Skowron,1	3	1	1
Colavito,lf	4	2	2	Boyer,3	3	0	0
Cash,1	4	0	0	Terry,p	2	0	0
McAuliffe,3	3	0	0	Arroyo,p	1	1	0
Fernandez,ss	3	0	0	Totals	31	8	7
Roarke,c	2	0	0				
[1]Maxwell	1	0	0				
Morton,rf	0	0	0				
Lary,p	3	1	0				
Aguirre,p	0	0	0	Totals	31	6	2

[1]Fouled out for Roarke in eighth.
[2]Walked for Wood in eighth.
[3]Struck out for Bruton in eighth.
[4]Ran for Osborne in eighth.

Detroit .... 200 000 000— 2
New York .... 010 101 04x— 7

PO-A—Detroit 24-11, New York 27-10. DP—Skowron and Kubek. Left—Detroit 3, New York 2. 2B—Skowron, Maris. HR—Colavito, Maris 2. S—Mantle.

	IP	H	R	ER	BB	SO
Lary (L, 19-8)	7⅓	6	6	6	1	4
Aguirre	⅔	2	1	1	0	0
Terry (W, 12-2)	7⅔	6	2	2	1	[illegible]
Arroyo	1⅓	0	0	0	0	3

PB—Roarke.
U—Runge, Crylak, Drummond and Paparella. T—2:02. A—50,261.

Reds Win 17th Straight From Phils; Lead Is 3½

Philadelphia (AP) — The Cincinnati Reds boosted their National league lead to 3½ games over the second place Los Angeles Dodgers yesterday with a 7-4 victory over their favorite "cousins," the Philadelphia Phillies. Home runs by Vada Pinson, Jerry Lynch and Gene Freese helped the Reds to their 17th straight victory of the season over the last-place Phils.

The victory moved Cincinnati within five games of becoming the first team in major league history to blank an opponent over a season's play. The 1927 New York Yankees won 21 of 22 from the old St. Louis Browns, closest to a seasonal whitewash.

JOEY JAY, Cincinnati's pitching ace, won his 19th against only 8 defeats although the husky right hander wasn't as sharp as usual and several times prompted bullpin action.

He finally needed help on this hot, sultry day—the temperature was in the 90s—when the Phillies rallied for a run in the ninth on a single, a hit batsman and Tony Taylor's double. Bill Henry came on to strike out John Callison for the final out with two men on base.

In earning his sixth decision of the season over the Phillies Jay allowed 9 hits, including Don Demeter's 16th home run, struck out 9 and walked 3.

The Reds started their assault on losing pitcher John Buzhardt in the fourth when Pinson hit his 16th home run, field and bounced onto roof tops across the street. Frank Robinson walked and Lynch lined one over the right field wall for his 11th homer.

The Phillies scored first on a second inning walk to catcher Clay Dalrymple and Ruben Amaro's double.

Cincinnati	ab	h	rbi	Philadelphia	ab	h	rbi
Freese,3	5	1	2	Taylor,2	4	3	1
Chacon,2	5	1	0	Callison,lf	5	0	0
Pinson,cf	4	3	1	Gonzalez,cf	4	0	0
Robinson,rf	2	0	0	Demeter,1	4	1	1
Lynch,lf	2	1	2	Covington,rf	4	1	0
[2]Post,lf	1	0	0	C.Smith,3	3	0	0
[4]Bell,lf	0	0	1	Dalrymple,c	3	1	0
Coleman,1	4	1	0	Amaro,ss	4	2	1
Cardenas,ss	4	0	0	Buzhardt,p	1	0	0
Edwards,c	4	1	0	[1]Valo	1	1	1
Jay,p	4	1	0	Ferrarese,p	0	0	0
Henry,p	0	0	0	[3]Walls	1	0	0
				Baldschun,p	0	0	0
				[5]Herrera	0	0	0
Totals	35	9	6	Totals	34	9	4

[1]Doubled for Buzhardt in fifth.
[2]Grounded out for Lynch in sixth.
[3]Filed out for Ferrarese in seventh.
[4]Safe on error on sacrifice fly for Post in eighth.
[5]Hit by pitch for Baldschun in ninth.

Cincinnati .... 000 320 020— 7
Philadelphia .... 010 110 001— 4

E—Freese, Covington. PO-A—Cincinnati 27-11, Philadelphia 27-10. DP—Robinson and Coleman; Chacon, Cardenas and Coleman; Amaro, Taylor and Demeter. Left—Cincinnati 4, Philadelphia 7. 2B—Amaro, Covington, Valo, Pinson. HR—Pinson, Lynch, Demeter, Freese. SB—Taylor. SF—Bell.

	IP	H	R	ER	BB	SO
Jay (W, 19-8)	8⅔	9	4	4	3	9
Henry	⅓	0	0	0	0	1
Buzhardt (L, 5-15)	5	5	5	5	1	5
Ferrarese	2	0	0	0	0	1
Baldschun	2	4	2	2	1	3

HBP—By Jay (Herrera).
U—Vargo, Crawford, Barlick, Jackowski. T—2:50. A—4,147.

'Extra-Lap' Victory Won By Elmer George

By JEP CADOU JR.
Star Sports Editor

DuQuoin, Ill. — Don Branson of Champaign, Ill., was hurt yesterday during an "extra lap" of a scheduled 25-mile USAC sprint car race here, which was awarded to Elmer George of Indianapolis in a disputed finish.

Branson escaped with cuts on his left hand and face when his Hyneman Special rode up over the right front wheel of George's HOW Special, hit the guard rail on the north turn and overturned.

Branson was taken to the Marshall Browning Hospital here. His condition was not serious.

While George was recovering control after the brush, Parnelli Jones of Torrance, Cal., ducked under him and passed him.

All this happened after the race should have been over. Through failure of the scoring crew to get the word to Starter Pat Vidan at the proper time, George got the white flag (meaning one lap to go), one lap to late — when he actually should have received the checkered flag.

Chief Steward Ike Welch ordered the red flag, stopping the race immediately after the accident.

Joe Pitman, chief mechanic of Jones' Fike Plumbing Special, protested the decision. Another official protest also was filed challenging Branson's receiving 10th place.

After a check of the timing

Turn to Page 2, Column 4

The Standings

AMERICAN ASSOCIATION

	W	L	Pct.	G.B.
INDIANAPOLIS	82	62	.569	..
Louisville	78	66	.542	4
Denver	73	69	.514	8
Houston	69	75	.470	13
Dallas-Ft. Worth	69	75	.479	13
Omaha	60	84	.417	22

AMERICAN LEAGUE

	W	L	Pct.	G.B.
New York	89	45	.664	..
Detroit	86	49	.637	3½
Baltimore	79	59	.572	12
Chicago	72	64	.529	18
Cleveland	69	67	.507	21
Boston	65	73	.471	26
Los Angeles	60	76	.441	30
Minnesota	58	75	.436	30½
Washington	51	82	.383	37½
Kansas City	48	87	.356	41½

NATIONAL LEAGUE

	W	L	Pct.	G.B.
Cincinnati	80	53	.602	...
Los Angeles	74	54	.578	3½
Milwaukee	71	58	.550	7
San Francisco	70	58	.547	7½
St. Louis	68	62	.523	10½
Pittsburgh	62	65	.488	15
Chicago	55	74	.426	23
Philadelphia	37	93	.285	41½

Yesterday's Results

AMERICAN ASSOCIATION

INDIANAPOLIS 5, Louisville 0.
Omaha 2, Houston 1.
Dallas-Fort Worth at Denver, postponed, rain and cold.

NATIONAL LEAGUE

Cincinnati 7, Philadelphia 4.
Milwaukee 4, Los Angeles 0.
Chicago 7, San Francisco 0.
Pittsburgh 5, St. Louis 4.

AMERICAN LEAGUE

New York 7, Detroit 2.
Chicago 12, Washington 7.
Boston 2, Minnesota 1.
Los Angeles 6, Kansas City 3.
Baltimore 3-0, Cleveland 2-6.

Today's Schedule

AMERICAN ASSOCIATION

Louisville at INDIANAPOLIS, 2:30 p.m.

Dallas-Fort Worth at Omaha.
Houston at Denver (2, twi-night).

AMERICAN LEAGUE

Detroit at New York—Bunning (15-10) vs. Stafford (12-7).
Cleveland at Baltimore—Bell (9-14) vs. Barber (15-10).
Boston at Minnesota—Stallard (1-4) vs. Schroll (1-3).
Los Angeles at Kansas City—Moeller (4-8) vs. Archer (8-11).
Chicago at Washington (2)—Pizarro (11-5) and Herbert (9-12) vs. Donovan (9-9) and Gabler (3-7).

NATIONAL LEAGUE

Cincinnati at Philadelphia—Johnson (5-2) vs. Owens (2-9).
Pittsburgh at St. Louis—Friend (12-11) vs. Simmons (8-9).
San Francisco at Los Angeles—McCormick (11-13) vs. Podres (17-4).
Milwaukee at Chicago (2)—Burdette (15-8) and Cloninger (5-2) vs. Brewer (1-6) and Ellsworth (7-9).

Fight Results

Miami Beach—Carlos Ortiz, 139, New York, decisioned Douglas Vaillant, 138, Cuba (10).

Josedale Go Lucky Triumphs In Pace

By BOB COLLINS

Josedale Go Lucky, a colt who had spent his brief career following other horses, could not even find the field at the Indiana State Fair yesterday. It was strung behind him—way behind him.

Josedale was 0-for 6, without so much as a show finish, going into yesterday's Indiana Trotting and Pacing Horse Association two-year-old Pace. But he pranced away from the opposition by six lengths in the first heat and still had enough left to lead from start to finish and win by three in the second.

THE BAY COLT, owned by Oscar A. Jose, Indianapolis, and driven by Russ Bullington Sr., turned in clockings of 2:05.1 and 2:04.2 on the mile track. His two victories were worth $2,110.50 to Jose.

Kenland Lady and Amanola swapped tight finishes in the Two-Year-Old Trot. Amanola won the first heat by a whisker in 2:12.0. They needed a picture to untangle that one. However, Kenland Lady held off another late charge by Amanola in the second heat to win in 2:11.4 and get the trophy on her faster time.

Amkey won both heat in the Three-Year-Old and 25 class Trot, turning in times of 2:06.1 and 2:05.4.

Trim M captured the first heat of the opener, the Three-Year-Old and 25 Class Pace, in 2:04, but couldn't find room soon enough the second time around and finished a length behind Yankee Hanover in 2:04.1. Yankee Hanover was second in the first heat.

JOSEDALE GO Lucky was so far ahead in the first heat of the Two-Year-Old Pace there was reason to suspect he took a short cut through the infield. He was rambling four lengths in front halfway up the backside and was pacing easily with a six-length advantage at the top of the stretch.

The second time around Josedale went for the lead on the first turn. This time, however, he got an argument. The field stayed on his heels with Mountain Connie challenging all the way through the backstretch.

At the three-quarter mark it looked like Josedale was running out of fuel. But the colt cut loose with a great closing effort and moved three lengths in front on the final turn. Success Duke finished fast for second. Tiring Mountain Connie placed fourth.

Kenland Lady, owned by Paul and Pearle Hungerford, Shelbyville, and driven by Paul Hungerford, led almost every inch but the last one in the first heat of the Two-Year-Old trot.

Amanola, owned by Trotter Range, Greenfield, and driven by Ralph Wilfong, made up a lot of distance in a short time down the stretch and won on the last step.

THE SECOND time out Dubble T set a furious pace over the first half-mile but broke stride, allowing Kenland Lady to take a quick four-length lead. And this time, Amanola couldn't catch her.

Amkey ran his victory string to 16 in 26 starts with a pair of head-and-two firsts in the Three-Year-Old and 25 Class Trot.

Amkey was caught in a dandy neck and neck battle with Impetus in the first heat until Impetus went off stride on the way home. In the second heat, Amkey took charge early and held off first Tom Lee and then Impetus.

Amkey is owned by Dr. A. B. Coyner, Lafayette. Robert Willis was the driver.

Trim M. stayed near the pace all the way in the opener. The brown mare, owned by Harold and Gladys Hall, Middletown, and driven by Joe O'Brien, jumped in front at the start, fell back momentarily, then turned on the speed to whip Yankee Honor and Charlie Creed in a close finish.

IN THE SECOND heat, Yankee Hanover, owned by Mrs. K. D. and Dr. E. B. Morgan, Louisville, and driven by Ray Parker, took the lead from Charlie Creed in the stretch and held off a late bid by Trim M.

Attendance yesterday was estimated at 8,500.

There is no racing at the State Fair today. Grand Circuit horses take over tomorrow for four days of racing.

Yesterday's results:

THREE YEAR OLD, 25 CLASS PACE
(Purse $3,075)

Trim M. (Jerry Landess) 1 2
Yankee Honor (Ray Parker) 2 1
Times: 2:04.0, 2:04.1.
Also Started: Success Johnny, 9-3, Charley Creed, 3-12; Purdue Halwyns, 4-4; Mamie's Star, 5-6; Rambling Rose, 6-5; Stanley Mc, 7-7; Filly Hill, 8-9; Suzie Wong, 108; Triple R, 12-10; Good Ways, 14-11; Miss Parker, 11-dr; Charley J. 13-dr.

TWO YEAR OLD TROT
(Purse $3,070)

Kenland Lady (Paul Hungerford ..2 1
Amanola (Ralph Wilfong) 1 2
Times: 2:12.0, 2:11.4.
Also Started: Floral Way, 4-3; Old Ranger, 3-5; Mr. Progress, 5-4; Dubble T., 6-6.

TWO YEAR OLD PACE
(Purse $4,690)

Josedale Go Lucky
(Russ Bullington Sr.) 1 1
Time: 2:05.1, 2:04.2.
Also Started: Success Duke, 2-2; Mountain Connie, 3-4; Eel River, 6-3; Babe Franell, 4-5; Jezebel, 5-8; Mountain Logan, 12-6; Scotty Haven, 8-7; My Dutch Lady, 7-9; Tiger Rag, 9-10; Dr. Masten, 10-12; Donna Truax, 11-11.

THREE YEAR OLD, 25 CLASS TROT
(Purse $3,000)

Amkey (Robert Willis) 1 1
Times: 2:06.1, 2:05.4.
Also Started: Tom Lee 2-3; Impetus 7-2; Lady Diplomat 3-6; Young America 5-4; Bye Bye Dillion 4-5; Truce 6-7; Ohio Demon 8-8; Sunny Sky 9-9; Virginia Mike 10-dr.

YANKEE HONOR UPHELD—Yankee Honor (No. 5) holds off a furious stretch bid by Trim M yesterday to win the second heat of the Three-Year-Old and 25 Class Pace at the State Fairgrounds with a time of 2:04.1. However, Trim M had taken the first heat in 2:04.0 and was declared the over-all winner. (Star Photo)

She's All Even—Yanks Bomb Bums, 5-1

Eggert's Billboard

Faster Speedway Runs Loom

By BILL EGGERT

Smoky Elisian, after buzzing around the "new" Indianapolis Motor Speedway track yesterday at 131 miles an hour, said: "O-o-o-h, m-a-n is that new surface smooth. I didn't know I was going that fast. Boy, don't underestimate these small cars for next year. Not once did the back end want to come around."

Later in the day, Smoky was out again in the Roger Wolcott Special and spun in the southeast turn and slid 300 feet, 150 of it near the infield—second man on the "new" track and first to spin. All but 2,700 feet of the oval now is black-topped.

Possibly an indication of higher speeds for the 1956 500-Mile Race is seen in Pat O'Connor's 140-mph lap late yesterday in the Firestone test car. Pat, who is under six-week contract to test tires for the manufacturer, sees only good in the new racing surface.

"This is it," Pat said, after an earlier run, "hardly any tire wear." After replacing a blown gasket, O'Connor went out late in the afternoon "just to do some running" and whipped up the 140 lap.

Several other cars will test the track later this week. Murrell Belanger plans to bring down his roadster that mechanic Tiny Worley has done over. He hopes to get Art Cross to try it out. The Sumar car also may be tried.

•

NOTICE HOW SEVERAL writers already are doing more accidentally than insiders could do on purpose to arouse Purdue for its homecoming game Saturday with Wisconsin. They have written "after Wisconsin disposes of Purdue." . . . Minnesota sells enough season tickets for home games to till IU's Memorial Stadium . . . . There were big names at the press party the eve of the Minnesota-Purdue game in Minneapolis — Wes Fesler, Bernie Bierman, Harry Struhldreher and Bill Rigney. Rigney, not a football lover, was eager only to talk baseball and especially about Allan Worthington, Minneapolis right-hander who will go with Rigney to the New York Giants.

•

HERE'S THE FIRST glimpse of the new insignia that will identify the United States Auto Club, new governing body of auto racing:

•

UNLESS A BIG TEN team goes through this season untied and unbeaten it won't have a chance of out-balloting Maryland, which now has played its toughest portion of the schedule (13-12 over Missouri, 7-0 over UCLA and 20-6 over Baylor) and can coast through the remainder—Wake Forest, North Carolina, Syracuse, South Carolina, LSU, Clemson and George Washington.

•

CLIFF SIMPSON, once fined $25 for eating pie and breaking training rules when he was playing under Johnny Sorrell for the Indianapolis Caps, is helping Sorrell at the Indianapolis Chiefs' training camp in Aylmer, Ontario. Simpson will coach the Aylmer club this season.

The Chiefs' 14-man squad will return here Oct. 9 for a week of workouts in the Coliseum before opening the season Oct. 16 against Grand Rapids. The rink here will be a challenge for the youngsters who will be used to a skating area 30 feet shorter. The area behind the net in Aylmer is only five feet wide. Here it's 15 feet.

•

A HORRIBLE death for a champion: Twenty years ago tomorrow the original Joe Walcott, former world's welterweight boxing champ around the turn of the century, was run down by a Model A Ford in Dalton, O.—badly mangled, fractured skull, broken arm, fractured legs. He laid in the morgue unidentified and unclaimed and after 10 days was buried in a potter's field. When he was found he had 37 cents in his pocket. The grave today is unmarked and weed-covered.

Afflis, Lisowski In Mat Feature

Dick "Bruiser" Afflis, of Indianapolis, and Reggie Lisowski, Milwaukee heavyweight, will clash in the main event pro wrestling attraction on a three-tilt card booked for the Armory tonight by Indiana Wrestling, Inc.

The bout is signed for two falls out of three with a 90-minute time limit.

In semi-windup action The Mighty Atlas, will go against Maurice Roberre, a French-Canadian, in a meeting billed for one fall or 30-minutes.

Another bout on the same terms will start the card at 8:30 p.m. and pits Mitch Lassen, of Chicago, against John Arjon, Des Moines, Ia. Both matmen are newcomers here.

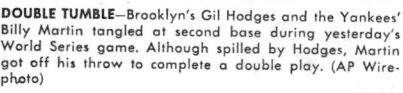

DOUBLE TUMBLE—Brooklyn's Gil Hodges and the Yankees' Billy Martin tangled at second base during yesterday's World Series game. Although spilled by Hodges, Martin got off his throw to complete a double play. (AP Wirephoto)

DODGER KILLERS—Whitey Ford (right) rubs head of Bill Skowron after the Yankees' 5-1 victory yesterday over Brooklyn. Ford gave the Dodgers only four hits while Skowron hit a three-run homer. (AP Wirephoto)

Duke Will Play Today Despite Injured Knee

New York (AP)—Duke Snider, on the very verge of writing his name with baseball's greatest in World Series annals, vowed yesterday he will play today despite his injured left knee — "and it feels pretty good."

The big, handsome Brooklyn Dodger popped a cartilege when he stepped in a hole running for Moose Skowron's fly in the third.

"My knee popped as soon as I started," he said somberly. "I went on running"—and caught the ball—"but it was a leg I hurt earlier in Chicago and so I asked Walt Alston to take me out.

"In Chicago I was so stiff I could hardly walk the next day. But now I'll play even if it's stiff."

SNIDER HAS hit four home runs in this Series, and has a total of nine in Series play—only one behind the great Lou Gehrig of the Yankees. Babe Ruth heads the list with 15.

Manager Alston was as sober and quiet as his big centerfielder. He confirmed what he said Sunday, namely, that he will start John Podres on the mound today. Podres won the third game from the Yankees, 8-3.

Snider spent most of the game in the Dodger dressing room undergoing whirlpool bath treatment.

"It's a knee I first hurt playing baseball back in Compton High School in California and aggravated at Compton Junior College."

Dr. Eugene Zorn, the Dodger physician, said he believed Snider could play.

ALSTON SAID his lineup today for the big final game will depend entirely on Snider's condition. When Snider went out, he shifted Junior Gilliam from second base to left field, moved Sandy Amoros over from left to center field to take Snider's post, and sent Don Zimmer in at second base.

The gloomy Dodgers made much of the fact they might have gotten out of the first inning scoreless except for a few bad breaks. Under normal circumstances catcher Roy Campanella, with his rifle arm, might have caught Phil Rizzuto when he stole second after getting a base on balls. It looked as if Gilliam was slow in covering the bag, and Campanella was slow in getting the throw away.

"I saw Rizzuto when he started to steal, but I didn't break for the bag right away because you're not supposed to leave too fast," said Gilliam. "Anyway the ball caught in the web of Campy's glove."

A moment later, after Gil McDougald had walked, putting two Yankees on base with only one out, Yogi Berra hit a bounding ball just beyond the reach of pitcher Karl Spooner. Gilliam broke for it but could not reach it. If he had it might have been a double play.

"Berra's ball stayed down low," said Gilliam. "I was playing Berra to the right, and I just couldn't get to it."

Manager Alston said that from the dugout he couldn't tell whether Gilliam didn't get over or didn't get the ball.

HURTS KNEE — Brooklyn's Duke Snider yesterday exhibited his bandage-encased injured left knee. (AP Wirephoto)

"IF WE'D have gotten the double play ball we'd have been OK," said Alston. "Spooner had plenty of stuff."

Alston, who was riding the crest Sunday with high hopes of winning the first World Series for the Dodgers, sat back in his little cubicle and answered questions in a low voice.

"Newk wasn't right," he said. "I don't know whether I can use him tomorrow or not."

He was referring, of course, to big Don Newcombe, his 20-game winner in the regular season, but a disappointment in the first game of the Series.

Butler Movies Set

Movies of Butler's 26-to-19 football victory over Indiana State last Saturday will be shown, free of charge and open to the public, tonight at 7:30 p.m. in Atherton Center on the campus. The movies will follow a B-Men's organization meeting at 7 p.m.

Stengel Figures He's In Now

New York (UP)—"We had 'em all the way and we'll make it with Tommy Byrne."

That's the way the Yankees, from Manager Casey Stengel down to the bull-pen catcher, figures the World Series now as it roars down to today's tense finale against the Dodgers with the count squared at three games each.

"We're a confident team now," said Stengel. "We're home. That makes a difference. And Byrne, who pitched the best game of the series up to today, is my man for tomorrow.

"HE'LL START and everybody else will be in the bull pen to come in if necessary."

Whitey Ford, too?

"You're darned right," whooped Ford, whose masterful four-hitter halted a runaway winning streak of three games by the Dodgers. "I've got six weeks to rest up when the ball club tours Japan this winter. I'll be there for as much work as Casey wants from me."

But there was bad news, too, among Casey's Cripples.

"I pulled that leg muscle again running to first in the fifth inning," said Hank Bauer, who celebrated his return as a regular by banging three hits. In the fifth, though, he had to run all out to first base to avoid being caught in a double play.

"I WON'T KNOW until tomorrow whether I can play," he said. "All I know is, it hurts."

Mickey Mantle, also a victim of a pulled thigh muscle, probably will sit out today thereby helping even up for Brooklyn's possible loss of Duke Snider.

"Well, we saw too much of that Snider already," said Stengel. "He may hurt them if he is out but I don't think so."

Casey didn't say so but obviously he isn't going to let his pitchers throw the ball within a city block of The Duke if he gets to the plate again.

Bill Skowron, the Yankee sophomore who blasted a three run homer that climaxed the Yankee first inning rally, was so excited about his hit he couldn't remember what pitch he'd belted.

"It was a fast ball but I don't know whether it was on my hands or outside," he said, "It came in fast and went out fast."

Stengel praised Ford as "better than in the opener" and Whitey agreed.

"I had more control," said Ford. "I had the same stuff but I was getting it just where I wanted it. A sort of a fast sinker to right handers was getting me out of trouble."

Joe Collins, who made a great fielding play to get the Yankees out of a jam in the seventh, was the big man on defense.

"That was the best play for us," said Stengel.

Collins, who pinch hit for Skowron in the fifth, went to his right for a grounder by Pee Wee Reese and pegged to second for a force out that ended a Brooklyn threat.

High School Football

Gary Emerson 13, Gary Wallace 0.
Plainfield Charlton 13, White's Institute 6.
Terre Haute Wiley 43, Linton 0.

Ford Hurls Four-Hitter; Byrne Faces Podres

By BOB CONSIDINE

New York (INS)—Somebody neglected to inform the corpse that he was dead. The poor old fellow, better known as the New York Yankees, was supposed to be put away decently yesterday. But suddenly he let

Other Stories, Picture On Page 28.

out a bellow, stopped the procession, and whaled the tar out of the undertaker, the Brooklyn Dodgers, by a score of 5-1.

Now the World Series of 1955, a thing of violent ebb and flow, is all tied up at 3-3. The Dodgers, so near to but yet so far from the first series title of their long existence, once again are the underdogs.

Today to compound their torment in the final game, they must face the veteran Tommy Byrne, who beat them in the second game. Their top winner for the year, Don Newcombe, complains of many aches and fevers; their slugger Duke Snider is hurt, and the Brooks must depend on Johnny Podres, their surprise winner in the third game.

BUT IT IS of yesterday that the story must be told.

The Yanks fell like a bomb on the Bums. They fell like a bomb that descends without warning, blows things apart, and is no more. They scored all five of their runs in the first inning before the second man was out and never seriously threatened thereafter.

Karl Spooner, who was so confident Brooklyn would win behind him that he made plans before the game to fly to Hudson Bay on a fishing trip this morning, was standing in the way of the bomb when it fell. Yesterday, rather than today, should have been the day when the classy southpaw from Oriskany Falls, N.Y., should have baited his hooks.

Spooner walked little Phil Rizzuto, lead-off man in the shaken-up Yankee lineup. Phil stole second while Karl was striking out Billy Martin. Then Spooner walked Gil McDougald. The fuse was sputtering but none of the 64,022 in the stands at Yankee Stadium this perfect afternoon could comprehend the destruction at hand.

YOGI BERRA shot a crackling single to center to score Rizzuto. Hank Bauer looked as if he had never had a sore leg in his life as he whipped a blazing single to left, scoring McDougald. Bill Skowron, showing absolute contempt of his broken toe, slid a home run into the stands down the right field foul line—and the Yanks had their five runs and a new pitcher, Russ Meyer, to look at.

That was that.

The rest was left up to Whitey Ford, winner of the first game of the series. With the possible exception of Horatius at that bridge, few men have come through as adequately.

Ford held the Dodgers to four hits, struck out eight of them and pitched the first complete series game he has turned in since climbing into Yankee uniform. It was his third such triumph.

THE YOUNG MAN is pitching himself in to halls hitherto reserved in Yankee history for Pennock, Hoyt, Gomez, Ruffing and Reynolds.

He struck out Reese and Snider in the first. Nobody hit the ball out of the infield on him from the time Roy Campanella flied out to center at the start of the second until Carl Furillo singled past Rizzuto in the fourth. He got the menacing Campanella with a great curve-ball called third strike after walking Don Zimmer in the sixth. He struck out Zimmer and Furillo in the eighth and made Campy roll out meekly. And he ended the game by whiffing Sandy Amoros, whose single in the seventh had put Whitey in a bit of trouble.

When he wasn't in complete charge of the Brooks, Ford received more support than Tommy Manville's entire roster of former wives.

For example:

FORD HIT Furillo in the seat of his pants with one out in the second and then walked Gil Hodges. Jackie Robinson, next up and pretty grim about the whole business, slashed a grounder to third that would have pierced most folks. McDougald dug it out of the dirt and shot the ball to Billy Martin. Hodges, trying to break up the double play, hit Martin with a shattering block, but somehow the tough little guy got the ball away in time to catch the straining Robinson at first.

McDougald made a wonderful play off Junior Gilliam in the third. In the fourth, Reese beat out the first Dodger hit, a bounding ball to Martin's right. Ford struck out Zimmer on three pitches. Zimmer was batting for Snider, who had stepped into a hole in center field and hurt his left knee retiring Skowron in the Yankee third.

Following Zimmer, Ford walked Campanella. Furillo's single followed and Reese scored with the first and only Dodger run of the game. Rizzuto took care of things after that, brilliantly turning hard grounders by Hodges and Robinson into forceouts.

McDOUGALD CAME through with another fine play off Roose in the fifth, after Gilliam singled and in the seventh the Yankee defense rose to its peak just when needed. Amoros singled with one out and after pinchhitter Frank Kellert popped up, Ford wild pitched Amoros to third in the course of walking Gilliam.

Into this situation stepped Joe Collins, one of the surest fielders in the business. He went far to his right to make a one-handed stab of Reese's dangerous looking grounder toward right, saw he couldn't catch Reese at first, whipped around like a fine ballet dance and got Gilliam at second by about the width of your hand.

In the ninth, Rizzuto and McDougald were all over that side of the sun-washed diamond, gathering in balls savagely hit by Hodges and Robinson.

Russ Meyer pitched fine ball against the Yankees after relieving Spooner. He gave up only four singles from the first until he disappeared for a pinch-hitter in the seventh. Primarily, he put out the blaze in the first inning.

Brooklyn (N)	AB	R	H	O	A	E
Gilliam, 2, lf	3	0	1	0	0	0
Reese, ss	4	1	1	3	2	0
Snider, cf	1	0	0	1	0	0
[1]Zimmer, 2	2	0	0	1	1	0
Campanella, c	3	0	0	5	0	0
Furillo, rf	3	0	1	1	0	0
Hodges, 1	3	0	0	7	1	0
J. Robinson, 3	4	0	0	2	3	1
Amoros, lf, cf	4	0	1	2	0	0
Spooner, p	0	0	0	0	0	0
Meyer, p	2	0	0	0	1	0
[3]Kellert	1	0	0	0	0	0
Roebuck, p	0	0	0	2	0	0
Totals	30	1	4	24	8	1

New York (A)	AB	R	H	O	A	E
Rizzuto, ss	3	1	0	1	[illegible]	0
Martin, 2	4	0	1	4	2	0
McDougald, 3	3	1	0	0	5	0
Berra, c	3	1	2	8	0	0
Bauer, rf	4	1	3	0	0	0
Skowron, 1	2	1	1	6	0	0
[2]Collins, 1	1	0	0	5	1	0
Cerv, cf	4	0	1	2	0	0
Howard, lf	4	0	0	1	0	0
Noren, lf	0	0	0	0	0	0
Ford, p	4	0	0	0	1	0
Totals	32	5	8	27	14	0

[1]Struck out for Snider in fourth.
[2]Walked for Skowron in fifth.
[3]Popped out for Meyer in seventh.

Brooklyn (N)	000	100	000	—1
New York (A)	500	000	00*	—5

RBI—Berra, Bauer, Skowron 3, Furillo. HR—Skowron. SB—Rizzuto. DP—McDougald, Martin and Skowron; J. Robinson and Hodges. Left—Brooklyn (n) 7, New York (a) 7. BB—Ford 4 (Hodges), Campanella, Zimmer, Gillam), Spooner 2, (Rizzuto, McDougald), Meyer 2, (Berra, Collins). SO—Ford 8 (Reese, Snider, Meler, Zimmer 2, Campanella, Furillo, Amoros), Spooner 1 (Martin), Meyer 4 (Howard 3, Martin). HO—Spooner 3 in 1/3 inning, Meyer 4 in 5 2/3, Roebuck 1 in 2. R and ER—Spooner 5-5, Meyer 0-0, Roebuck 0-0, Ford 1-1. HPB—By Ford (Furillo). WP—Ford. Winner—Ford. Loser—Spooner. U—Ballanfant (N) plate, Honochick (A) first base, Dascoli (N) second base, Summers (A) third base, Flaherty (A) left field, Donatelli (N) right field. T—2:34. A—64,022.

Examiner SPORTS

MELVIN DURSLAG

2d Punch Ruins You

There is an old maxim in football to the effect .t a man who gets into a fight should throw either first punch or the third, but never the second.

The one who throws the second invariably gets penalty.

The thinking on this is that the first punch ually isn't seen—and the third is construed as self-ense, all of which makes the guy who unloads the ond the aggressor and scoundrel in general.

Coach Sid Gillman of the Los Angeles Rams has tured patiently on the subject of retaliation, with etty good results until last Sunday when one of his yers took the second swing.

It got the Rams a 15-yard penalty that touched a chain of misadventures leading to three quick d goals for San Francisco.

Los Angeles had taken command, 7-3, in the st uar. On a third down play, which left the ers 13 ards short of a first down, Larry Morris, e Ram inebacker, put a tackle on John Henry nson of San Francisco.

Johnson has a pretty notorious reputation in e league for being active with his feet once he's en ackled.

Apparently he gave Morris a gentle kick, for rry, ordinarily a peaceable individual, retaliated th a sharp push with his left hand while cocking right as if to throw a grenade.

Well, sir, that was it; the equivalent of a second nch. The 15-yard penalty gave the 49ers a first wn, from whence they ultimately booted a field al to make the score 7-6.

hain Reaction From Incident

As I say, this detonated a chain of explosions. eet Quinlan fumbled the subsequent kickoff and e 49ers soon had another field goal to take the lead, 7.

On the next kickoff, Quinlan fumbled again . . . om . . . field goal . . . and San Francisco was now t there by 12-7.

Mind you, Morris can hardly be held responsible r the Ram loss, because for rock-head football this as what coaches would often describe in victory as team effort.

Other clubs, I am sure, have botched things orse in spots, but for matchless consistency, the rformance by the Rams last Sunday stands un-ralleled.

It's a grim and dismal statistic, but it's still an alterable fact that the Rams booted away all 33 oints in a game which they lost, 33 to 30.

A tasteful mixture of three Los Angeles fumbles, penalty for running into the kicker and Morris' uffle resulted in four field goals for the 49ers in e first half.

Then in the second half, an offside penalty on a ta. hird down play, an interception and a fumble—l working against the Rams—gave the 49ers three uchdowns.

The ams even blocked their own field goal at-mpt. Lining up for a placekick in the second quar-r, someone who could count suddenly discovered at L. A. had only 10 men on the field. An 11th y was summoned, just in time to get hit on the g by the snapback from center.

In watching this, I was somehow reminded of the y Dusty Rhodes was having his customary trouble the outfield. He first fell on his face while chasing fly ball. The next batter then smashed a roller hich Rhodes miscalculated, the ball bouncing hard f his ankle.

When Dusty got to the dugout, he said grimly to anager Leo Durocher, **"Get me out of there, Skip, efore I get killed."**

Ie Tossed a Colossal Right

Returning to retaliation in a football game, you ay recall a week ago when the Rams played the ag's that Buck Lansford, the Philadelphia tackle, so made the grave tactical mistake of throwing the cond punch.

Lansford had tackled Don Burroughs of the Rams ut of bounds after the L. A. back had intercepted a ass. Burroughs rolled on top of Lansford and, with knee in his chest, began to pummel the Eagle line-nan about the face.

Now Buck is a sturdy 230-pounder who comes rom Texas, and I wanna tell you that with the folks own home that stuff jus' don't go. Lansford got p and threw a colossal right at Burroughs, just as ne referree arrived.

Naturally, the Eagles drew a 15-yard penalty, and ld Buck Lansford was tossed out of the game.

Last year, against the Detroit Lions, Don Paul f e Rams kept agitating Leon Hart on pass plays. Don would grab a jersey, or elbow Leon, or stick out foot and trip him.

Hart's patience was soon exhausted. When Paul ried to interfere, Leon turned loose a wicked elbow mash, squarely in front of the head linesman. The ions unhappily were penalized 15 yards.

In behalf of the poor, belabored creatures who hrow the second punch in football, I am contemplat-ng a ca paign which would force officials to examine ll th ience before calling a penalty.

Meanwhile, as a helpful offering to the home unit, it is recommended here that any of the boys vh miss out on the first punch retreat momentarily om the battleground.

The second punch may win you the fight, but ost you the purse.

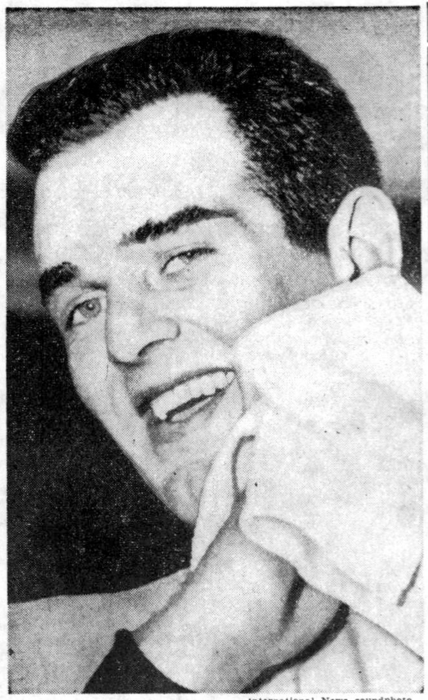

—International News soundphoto.

JUBILANT—And Don Larsen, Yankee pitcher, has a right to be happy as he had just finished tremendous chore of hurling sensational World Series contest.

Larsen Gets 27 in Row, 2-0 No-Hitter

By VINCENT X. FLAHERTY
Los Angeles Examiner Staff Correspondent

NEW YORK, Oct. 8.—They moved the Hall of Fame straight into Yankee Stadium this afternoon and it inclosed a little beige pancake of earth trimly set in an emerald velvet frame. There a San Diego giant named Don Larsen performed a work of art, a masterpiece that shall be talked about as long as baseball is played.

Larsen, a towering, handsome 27-year-old, made imperishable history for himself when he turned in the greatest pitching performance of all time.

He pitched the first no-hit, no-run, no-man-reach-base game since Chicago's Charlie Robertson achieved the distinction when he defeated the Detroit Tigers in a regular season game of 1922 by a score of 2 to 0.

But here this beautiful autumn afternoon, Larsen improved upon perfection as he and his New York Yankees defeated the Brooklyn Dodgers for the third straight day, also by a score of 2 to 0.

The massive black facade of the scoreboard told the story eloquently and properly so in a glowing golden pattern of electric lights.

Larsen achieved a lasting distinction beyond that ever realized by the incomparable Walter Johnson, or Christy Mathewson, or old Cy Young, or any man who ever pitched a no-hit game.

Larsen's was the most perfect of all perfect games. He threw only 97 pitches. But get this, mind you! Only once all day did he throw as many as three balls to any batter.

That happened in the first inning when he pitched against Reese, who ultimately struck out.

None of the other Dodger batters was served more than two balls, and many got no more than one before they grounded out, lofted innocuous flies to the outfield or dribbled grounders into the dirt. The Dodgers were a picture of fantastic futility.

And what a setting Larsen picked to pitch one for posterity.

It shall long be remembered he was the first to pitch a no-hitter of any kind in the entire history of the World Series. Other details will fade into the mists of time and be forgotten. It will be unremembered that he accomplished his superlative craftsmanship in the midst of a tensely contested World Series. Or that his masterpiece, delicately fashioned as it was, was the over-powering blow which broke a two games to two tie between the major league champions.

It was a spectacularly rare privilege to be among the 64,519 persons who watched the writing of this historic chapter in American sports.

It was thrilling to be swept up in the tide of tension which mounted with every pitch in the late innings and engulfed all who sat here this cool and invigorating afternoon of October 8, 1956.

The enormous crowd, in itself, was a rare study in human emotions. strangely silent one instant and bursting with thunderous acclaim the next.

During the eighth and ninth innings Larsen was like a man toiling in a vacant world. Before he started a pitch it was as if the whole universe of the living had deserted him. It was as if the grandstand thousands had suddenly been struck dumb and inanimate; had been frozen by some paralyzing force.

The ninth inning was unbearable. Just three more men to face him; just three more—perhaps a half dozen pitches, or maybe a dozen, and Larsen could make it.

Yes, it was unbearable. The terribly pent-up burden of human emotions had now reached the climactic stage. It had geysered out of all proportions. Adrenalin was coursing through the electric anatomies of the thousand. You knew there was a heart in your body because you felt it pounding so hard you could almost hear it. And most people probably wondered why they should feel this way about a man they didn't know and probably never, never would meet.

So, in that exciting, breathless ninth inning, you felt almost as if you couldn't stand it anymore. You felt all elements of entertainment and drama had been drained from the great spectacle and that it had now become cruelty, not entertainment; and punishment, not drama.

You wanted to help this tall young man from San Diego, and helplessness overcame you and you felt worthless because you didn't know how.

Veteran reporters knew Larsen was doing something different down there, but most just didn't realize what it was until the great game was all over and Larsen made the revelation himself.

He had tried something new. He didn't go into a wind-up of any kind.

"While warming up lately," he said, "I discovered I had better control when I didn't wind up."

His explanation was broken by the surging mob in the Yankee dressing room and between handclasps and back poundings and cacaphony of congratulations, Larsen went on:

"I decided to experiment with it in the first inning," he said, "and when it worked so well (he struck out the first two men to face him) I decided to keep right on doing it."

Larsen usually winds up with his hands high over his head. Today he shot the ball straight from his waist, no wind-up, no gyrations. He guessed the unusual style had faulted the Dodgers' timing. He worked quickly, taking little time between pitches. It was as if the Dodgers were being shot at, not pitched to; shot at by a man shooting from the hip.

He said he had used fast balls and sliders almost exclusively; that he had become aware he was pitching a no-hitter in the seventh inning; that the realization had made him nervous.

Traditionally, when a pitcher is nearing a no-hitter teammates avoid him in the dugout. They do not speak to him. Larsen noticed this. He had heard what Allie Reynolds had said when pitching a no-hitter for the Yankees several years ago. Reynolds broke the dugout silence by shouting: "Look at the scoreboard, boys, I'm pitching a no-hitter!"

Larsen though he might make a jest of the old baseball supersitition and break the silence, as Reynolds had done

Turn to Page 4, Col. 3

Batter Up

BROOKLYN, Oct. 8.—(AP)—Johnny Kucks (18-9) or Bob Turley (8-4) will pitch for New York tomorrow against Clem Labine (10-6) of Brooklyn, the managers said tonight.

Perfect

Brooklyn (N)	AB	R	H	O	A
Gilliam, 2b ...	3	0	0	2	0
Reese, ss	3	0	0	4	2
Snider, cf	3	0	0	1	0
Robinson, 3b ..	3	0	0	2	4
Hodges, 1b	3	0	0	5	1
Amoros, lf	3	0	0	3	0
Furillo, rf	3	0	0	0	0
Campanella, c.	3	0	0	7	2
Maglie, p	2	0	0	0	1
Mitchell	1	0	0	0	0
Totals	27	0	0	24	10
New York (A)	**AB**	**R**	**H**	**O**	**A**
Bauer, rf	4	0	1	4	0
Collins, 1b	4	0	1	7	0
Mantle, cf ...	3	1	1	4	0
Berra, c	3	0	0	7	0
Slaughter, lf ..	2	0	0	1	0
Martin, 2b	3	0	1	3	4
McDougald, ss.	2	0	0	0	2
Carey, 3b	3	1	1	1	1
Larsen, p	2	0	0	0	1
Totals	26	2	5	27	8

Mitchell called out on strikes for Maglie in 9th.

Brooklyn (N)	000 000 000—0
New York (A) ...	000 101 00x—2

E—None. RBI—Mantle, Bauer. HR—Mantle. S—Larsen. DP—Reese and Hodges; Hodges, Campanella, Robinson, Campanella and Robinson. Left—Brooklyn (N) 0, New York (A) 3. BB—Maglie 2 (Slaughter, McDougald). SO—Larsen 7 (Gilliam, Reese, Hodges, Campanella, Snider, Maglie, Mitchell); Maglie 5 (Martin, Collins 2, Larsen, Bauer). R-ER—Larsen 0-0, Maglie 2-2. W—Larsen. L—Maglie. U—Pinelli (N) plate, Soar (A) first base, Boggess (N) second base, Napp (A) third base, Gorman (N) left field, Runge (A). A—64.519. T—2:06.

—Associated Press wirephoto.

TOAST OF THE BIG TOWN is Don Larsen, lanky Yankee righthander, who yesterday flipped his way to baseball immortality as he mowed down the Dodgers to record the first perfect game in World Series history. Only 27 men faced the Yankee twirler. Sparkling defense sparked 2-0 Yankee triumph.

Larsen's Record Mediocre

By DAN HAFNER

Don Larsen is a pitcher with a lifetime major league record of 30 victories and 40 defeats.

The 27-year-old righthander, an occupant of Stengel's doghouse most of his two seasons with the Yankees, was the forgotten man of the pitching staff until the pennant was all but clinched.

On September 3, having been blasted from the mound three straight times and boasting a 7-5 mark, Larsen was given a last chance against the Baltimore Orioles.

He responded with a four-hit shutout, using his now famous no-windup motion.

Larsen's next three starts were just as impressive, two of them four hitters and one a three-hit, seven inning shutout effort.

However, these performances did not indicate that Larsen, who had not been around for the fifth inning in two previous World Series starts, had acquired control because of his new pitching motion.

In 34 innings after emerging from the Stengel doghouse last month Larsen walked 23 batters—quite a contrast from yesterday when he didn't walk a man in nine innings.

DON'S 1956 RECORD

Date	Innings	Hits	Walks	Results
4-17	9*	5	3	W
4-22	4⅔*	5	3	N
4-27	9*	6	4	W
5-3	1⅔*	6	0	N
5-5	2	0	0	N
5-9	5⅓*	3	2	N
5-13	5*	4	3	W
5-18	1⅓	1	2	N
5-21	1⅓*	3	2	N
5-26	2	2	0	N
5-29	1⅔*	3	2	L
5-31	1⅔	3	3	N
6-3	7*	4	5	N
6-9	5*	4	4	N
6-13	1	0	1	N
6-18	6⅓	3	1	W
6-22	2	0	1	N
6-24	7⅔	3	5	N
6-29	⅓	0	0	N
7-4	7⅔*	9	5	W
7-14	3⅔*	5	2	N
7-18	3⅓	5	3	N
7-22	5⅓	5	3	N
7-26	6	5	2	W
7-31	1⅔	0	0	N
8-2	4	2	1	N
8-4	⅔	1	2	L
8-7	10*	4	3	L
8-12	9*	6	4	W
8-16	9*	4	4	L
8-21	2⅓*	5	1	L
8-23	8	9	1	N
8-26	⅓	2	1	N
9-3	9*	4	8	W
9-7	1	0	1	N
9-14	9*	4	3	W
9-22	8⅔*	4	7	W
9-28	7*	3	4	W

*—Starting pitcher.
W—Winner.
L—Loser.
N—Neither won or lost.

Don 'in a Daze'

By WILL GRIMSLEY

NEW YORK, Oct. 8.—(AP)—"I was so weak in the knees out there in the ninth inning, I thought I was going to faint."

Big Don Larsen, admittedly "in a daze," said he also mumbled a little prayer for help before he finally completed his perfect no-hit, no run, no-man-to-first game against the Dodgers in the fifth World Series game.

It was the first no-hit game in World Series history and the first perfect game—no man reaching first—since another obscure pitcher, Charley Robertson of the Chicago White Sox, did it in 1922 against the Detroit Tigers.

Larsen said he realized in the seventh inning that he had a no-hitter going, but added: "I didn't get nervous—my main object was to win the game."

Then, he said, came the ninth, and he felt the full impact of his performance. "The thing I wanted to do was get out of the ninth inning," he said. "Once I mumbled a little prayer to myself. I said, 'Please help me get through this'."

The towering righthander from San Diego, Calif., said nobody on the Yankee bench mentioned that he had a perfect game going.

"The only word said to me was by Yogi Berra," Larsen said. "Yogi hit me in the seat of the pants and said, 'Go out there and let's get the first batter'."

The Yankee dressing room—the dressing room of the "Old Pros"—was bedlam for the first time during the Series.

Yogi grabbed Larsen around the neck. Mickey Mantle, normally quiet and retiring, let out a resounding war whoop. Andy Carey jumped around the room, yelling loudly.

"Beautiful, beautiful," said Casey Stengel, the Yankee manager, his creased face breaking into a broad smile. "This kid is a good pitcher."

Walter O'Malley, the president of the Brooklyn Dodgers, came in.

"You beat us and I'm not happy about that," he said, elbowing his way through the crowd around the beaming pitcher. "I have to congratulate you—do me a favor will you? Sign this ball."

Larsen, who came to the Yankees in December, 1954, as an insignificant part of the 19-player deal with Baltimore which brought the Yankees Bob Turley, said Berra's crafty signal-calling and the Yankees' fine defensive play deserve equal credit for his feat.

"I was pitching fast balls and sliders mostly," he said, "but mainly I had pretty good control. I only shook off a couple of Yogi's signals, but he stuck with them, so I went ahead and pitched what he called. I'm glad of it."

The six-foot-four, 225-pound Californian said his heart sank when Sandy Amoros, the Brooklyn leftfielder, hit that shot in the fifth inning which went foul by inches into the rightfield stands.

"I though sure he had it," Don said, "and I also thought Duke Snider's long foul in the fourth also might have gone in. I was relieved

Turn to Page 4, Col. 1

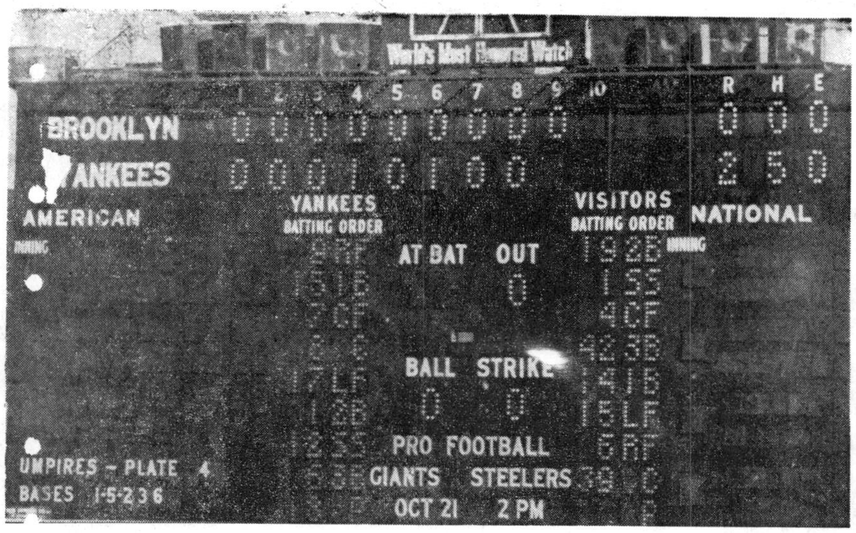

—Associated Press wirephoto.

ZEROED IN—The scoreboard tells the tale of Don Larsen's no-hit, no-run, no-batter-reaches first performance in the fifth game of the World Series yesterday at Yankee Stadium. Of course, Larsen's was the first gem in World Series and first perfect game since 1922. Yankees lead the World Series at 3-2.

Grand Larsen-y

—Associated Press wirephoto.

CLIMB ABOARD—Yogi Berra (8), only 5-8, leaps right into the arms of 6-4 Don Larsen, after the 27-year-old New York Yankee righthander had hurled the first perfect no-hit, no-run game in World Series history yesterday at Yankee Stadium as the Yankees beat Brooklyn, 2-0. Other Yanks join celebration.

CAREY DEFLECTS LINE DRIVE

MC DOUGALD MOVES RIGHT INTO PATH OF BALL

ROBINSON IS GOING ALL OUT

COLLINS STRETCHES AND GEM IS SAVED

—Associated Press wirephoto.

TEAMWORK—Don Larsen's perfect no-hitter could have been ruined on this play in the second inning when Jackie Robinson hit vicious liner toward left. Photos show Third Baseman Andy Carey deflect drive, Gil McDouglald move in position to field it and Joe Collins stretch for putout.

—International News soundphoto.

WHERE'D HE GO?—This bat and cap are symbols of Brooklyn's frustration yesterday. They belong to Duke Snider, who angrily threw down his bat after being called out on strikes in fourth inning. The cap fell off and landed in front of plate. Larsen fanned seven, five of the Dodgers were caught looking at last one.

—International News soundphoto.

ROBBERY—Mickey Mantle, Yankees, who hit his third homer of series in fourth inning for the only run needed, makes a sensational running, back-handed catch of Gil Hodges long drive in fifth inning to save Larsen's gem.

No-Hit Games Alike:

If You've Seen One, You've Seen 'em All

By JOHN LARDNER
North American Newspaper Alliance

YANKEE STADIUM, New York, Oct. 8.—With no wind-up, with his fast ball sneaking over the corners, with his change-up under perfect control, with an outbound breeze of 12 miles per hour, with only two tough chances for his fielders, with a crowd of 64,519 people going nuts in the grandstand, never behind the hitter, cold sober, foursquare, pitching with the right arm only—

Oh, well, these perfect games come along every 34 years these days, and when you've seen one, you've seen 'em all.

But the thing was, practically nobody in the house had ever seen a perfect game, till Don Larsen pitched one today in the rural obscurity of the fifth game of the World Series in the biggest town on earth.

It's said that an old man named Squeers in Section 18 of the stadium today saw Charley Robertson pitch a perfect game for the White Sox in 1922. Squeers refused to give his address. It would be just as well for Larsen if HE concealed his address too, for awhile.

"This guy will be on television every night for the next six days," said a student of human nature in the press box.

"Hell, he'll be on every night for the next six weeks," said another.

Robertson, Cy Young, Addie Joss, and Ernie Shore, the other perfect pitchers, picked their spots better. They worked before the time of TV, and they pitched their perfect games on the sly, in relative privacy.

Larsen was daffy enough to mow down 27 consecutive batters in a World Series. Not only had no one ever done this before—no one had ever thought of doing it before.

When Bill Bevens carried a no-hitter down to the last man in 1947, it was a different kind of game entirely. It was a memorable game, all right, but it was so stained with walks and other flaws that Joe DiMaggio, for instance, playing right behind Bevens, had no idea there had been a no-hit game in progress till someone told him about it in the clubhouse later.

"It surprised me," Joe Says. "It just wasn't that type of a game at all."

No one in the stadium today, in or out of uniform, was thinking of anything but the main issue, right down to the time that Dale Mitchell took the last third strike in the ninth inning. No one was fooled—except the Dodgers. A perfect thing is apt to be a simple thing, and Larsen's game was as simple as a bugle call.

A year ago last spring, Mr. Larsen, while sleeping, as everyone does in St. Petersburg, Fla., at night, wrapped his automobile around a lamppost. True, everyone in St. Petersburg does not sleep at night while driving a car. It was eccentric, and George Weiss and Casey Stengel of the Yankees put their heads together, after ice had been put on Mr. Larsen's.

"The boy had one or two chocolate sodas too many," said Mr. Weiss. "Shall we forgive him?"

"I guess so," said Mr. Stengel. "At least, he hit the post right in the middle. He didn't miss. And when this fella has control, he is quite useful."

Just last Friday, Larsen had no control to speak of, and Mr. Stengel may have rued his good nature. It sounded that way, from the cussing he did. Today Larsen has everything, and his road down the home stretch was paved with shouts and roses.

In the ninth, as Furillo flied straight to Bauer, the crowd screamed with excitement. As Campanella grounded softly to Martin for the second out, the noise could be heard in Hartford, Conn.

As Mitchell took a ball, and then a strike, and then missed a swing, and then fouled one back, the clients were halfway out of their seats. And when the last pitch clipped the corner, there was a cascade of rapture. Not to put too fine a point on it, there was ecstasy.

As I said, it happens every 34 years. But it never happened like this before.

Jurors Open Police Probe Friday—Page 96

ALL STAR LATEST SPORTS

THE EVENING SUN

FINAL CLOSING STOCKS

Vol. 95—No. 149 | PAID CIRCULATION IN SEPTEMBER (Daily—Mon. to Fri.) MORNING, 199,232 EVENING, 214,631 413,863 || SUNDAY 318,158 | BALTIMORE, WEDNESDAY, OCTOBER 9, 1957 | Entered as second-class matter at Baltimore Post Office | 96 Pages | 5 Cents

Eisenhower Sees No Peril In Russ Satellite

YANKS WIN 3-2; TIE SERIES

Late Bulletin

A B-47 BOMBER BLEW UP with four men aboard 700 feet in the air 2 miles northwest of Orlando, Fla., today. The plane was from the 321st Bomber Wing of the Pinecastle Air Force Base, base officials said.

Today's Sports

"BRAVES TO RULE National League for years," Warren Spahn, the distinguished Milwaukee left-handed pitcher said today, pointing out youth and all-around strength as the chief contributing factors (Page 74).

WHAT PROMISES TO BE THE MOST important meeting of the year, D. Eldred Rinehart, chairman of the Maryland Racing Commission, has called a meeting for tomorrow to announce the racing dates for Maryland's 12 race tracks for 1958 (Page 81).

EXPANSION TO TEN OR TWELVE TEAM leagues is the next logical step for further changes in the major-league baseball map, now that the Brooklyn Dodgers and New York Giants are officially headed for the West Coast, National League President Warren Giles said today (Page 75).

FANS GLOATING OVER THE FINE WORK of Gino Marchetti and Art Donovan may tend to overlook the rest of the defensive line, but the camera shows Jack Patera, Big Daddy Lipscomb and Don Joyce are doing their fair share too for the Colts (Page 75).

WINNER OF ALL TWELVE OF HIS PRO FIGHTS, seven of them by knockouts, Alex Miteff, Argentine heavyweight contender, was rated a 4-1 favorite to defeat Mike DeJohn in a ten-rounder tonight at Syracuse, N.Y. (Page 74).

News Summary

National

SPEEDUP OF THE UNITED STATES BALLISTIC MISSILE PROGRAM is being given serious thought, Neil H. McElroy, new Secretary of Defense, said at a news conference held less than five hours after he took office (Page 2).

GOV. ORVAL FAUBUS said that he sees no solution in the Little Rock (Ark.) school integration crisis save the complete withdrawal of the nine Negro students attending Central High School (Page 1).

GHANA'S FINANCE MINISTER was invited to have breakfast at the White House with President Eisenhower tomorrow. The invitation was extended after a Dover (Del.) restaurant refused to serve the official of the Negro republic (Page 1).

PRESIDENT EISENHOWER assured the nation he sees not one iota of reason for concern over national security as a result of Russia's successful launching of an earth satellite (Page 1).

AN F100 SUPERSONIC FIGHTER fired a target rocket at Eglin Air Force Base, Fla., yesterday and swiftly shot it down with a heat-seeking sidewinder missile. Nearly 6,000 persons watched the sudden destruction of the tiny target, representing an enemy plane, at the air-force fire power demonstration (Page 2).

International

A SOVIET BID for direct American-Russian talks to settle major issues involved in control of space missiles was rebuffed by President Eisenhower. He left the door open, however, for a multi-nation study of the problem (Page 2).

THE RUSSIAN EARTH SATELLITE may be smashed out of existence by debris from a comet tonight, a leading British astronomer said in London. The earth crosses the debris left by the comet at about 6 P.M. (E.D.T.). Other British astronomers said the satellite appeared to be changing its course, altitude and speed (Page 1).

THE UNOFFICIAL VATICAN CITY weekly Osservatore Della Domenica today expressed appreciation of the Soviet satellite as a scientific conquest but warned that it is an "artificial island in space" which may lead to a new way of dominating the earth (Page 2).

NIKITA KHRUSHCHEV wants a top-level conference between United States and Soviet leaders because he thinks the two countries must either fight or talk things out, the New York Times said today. Khrushchev indicated that the launching of an earth satellite last week may bring the two countries closer to high-level talks (Page 3).

City and State

THE GRAND JURY INVESTIGATION of allegedly immorality on the part of high-ranking policemen will begin Friday with a special session that will hear two witnesses. The witnesses were identified by J. Harold Grady, State's attorney, as Sergt. Edgar Kirby and Alvin J. T. Zumbrun (Page 96).

BLUE CROSS RATES WILL BE HIGHER next year because of gradually increasing hospital costs. This was predicted today by officials of the Maryland Hospital Service who administer the plan. They said no rate change was planned for Blue Shield medical and surgical care (Page 96).

A FULL MONTH'S BENEFITS ARE PAID new clients on the city's welfare rolls before a representative of the department can visit the applicant's home. Miss Esther Lazarus, welfare director, said the situation prevails because of a shortage of personnel (Page 96).

LAWYERS FOR CONVICTED SLAYER Carl Daniel Kier will ask the Maryland Court of Appeals to upset the guilty verdict handed down yesterday in Frederick County Circuit Court. Kier was sentenced to die in the gas chamber for the slaying of Mrs. John H. Bopst, Jr. (Page 96).

Financial

THE STOCK MARKET had an irregular pattern at the close, but was still apparently ahead on average after many gains won in a brisk rally faded (Page 83).

On Other Pages

Ike Sees No Threat In Satellite

Washington, Oct. 9 (AP)—President Eisenhower assured the nation today that he sees not one iota of reason for concern over national security as a result of Russia's sucessful launching of an earth satellite.

Eisenhower also said in a formal news conference statement that the United States could have beaten Russia to the punch and put up a satellite before now, by merging the satellite and missile programs.

But he said this would have been "to the detriment of scientific goals and military progress."

Eisenhower's news session was given over almost completely to the satellite question and the subject of missiles.

Going Ahead As Planned

All that Eisenhower said added up to the idea that in both fields the United States is going ahead just as it has planned all along, with no special speedup now in the light of the Russian satellite achievement.

Just before Eisenhower's news conference, Government officials had reported the Soviet moon still circling the earth on its original orbit and apparently at about its original speed and altitude.

Some foreign observers had reported the satellite apparently dropping toward the denser lower atmosphere where its life would be short.

But Dr. John P. Hagen, director of Operation Vanguard, the United States satellite project, said, "Our observations do not lead us to believe the U.S.S.R. sattellite is falling into the lower atmosphere."

Confirms Navy Data

That bore out earlier information from the Naval Research Laboratory.

A reporter told Eisenhower the people have confidence in his knowledge and military leadership and asked him to state whether he is more concerned about the nation's security as a result of the Soviet thrust into outer space.

Eisenhower said that so far as the satellite itself is concerned, it doesn't raise his concern one iota.

Eisenhower said the United States plans to launch a first-test vehicle, a small satellite with incomplete instrumentation, in December. He mentioned March, 1958, as the goal for firing the first United States "fully instrumented satellite vehicle."

Priority For Missiles

As for the missile program, Eisenhower said it still has top priority—a priority never accorded the satellite program.

He said it is a great achievement—if done—if the Russians have fired an intercontinental ballistic missile with pinpoint accuracy. But unless there is such accuracy, he said, such a missile has little military value.

The Russians claim they have tested an I.C.B.M. and hit their target area with it. Eisenhower noted that a target area can be any size.

Eisenhower denied that this country ever got into any race to be first up with a satellite. And he said scientists he has talked with have expressed pleasure rather than chagrin at

[Continued, Page 2, Column 6]

Butler Data Is Unknown To President

Washington, Oct. 9 (AP)—President Eisenhower remarked today that Senator Butler (R., Md.) must have more information on the United States earth satellite program than the White House.

The President's remark came during a White House press conference at which he was asked to comment on a prepared statement by Butler, which said:

"I am reliably informed that the Navy, which has been charged with developing our satellite, can launch it whenever the go-ahead is ordered."

Neither Butler nor the President elaborated on their remarks.

A BIG ONE FOR YOGI — Yankee Catcher Yogi Berra is greeted at home plate by Left Fielder Enos Slaughter (partly hidden, right) and batboy after hitting a homer in today's World Series game. Plate Umpire Jocko Conlan and Shortstop Gil McDougald are in the background. It was Yogi's tenth homer in nine Series.

Comet Debris May Wreck Satellite

London, Oct. 9 (AP)—The Soviet earth satellite may be smashed out of existence tonight by debris from a comet, a leading British astronomer said today.

The danger to the earth's first man-made moon lay in the path of the comet Giacobini-Zinner.

The earth crosses the path of this comet about 10 P.M. (6 P.M. E.D.T.) tonight.

Debris scattered by the comet on its journey through space could hit the satellite, Professor A. C. Lovell said.

This debris could deflect the satellite from its course, damage it or wreck it entirely, he added.

He urged all observers of the artificial moon to watch it closely this evening. Its radio signals might tell something of the effects of such a cosmic collision.

Most Important Center

Lovell is head of the Jodrell Bank Radio Astronomy Station the world's most important center of its kind.

Radio telescope exploration of the heavens at Jodrell Bank has produced the theory that debris may be left in patches all along the comet's orbit.

This work has not been publicized, and Lovell said the Russians may not realize the threat to their aluminum moon when the earth spins into the comet's orbit.

Earth Was Bombarded

The records of the Jodrell bank station show that when the earth passed through the orbit of the Giacobini-Zinner comet in 1946 and 1952, the earth was bombarded with vast amount of debris, the London *Times* said.

At other times, however, there was no debris, so there may be none tonight.

None of this debris actually hits the earth's surface. The tiny particles, about the size of grains of sand or smaller, burn up from friction in the earth's atmosphere. These are the meteors, the so-called shooting stars.

But the satellite, whirling around above the denser atmosphere, has no such protection.

Still On Orbit

Washington, Oct. 9 (AP)—Scientists at the Naval Research Laboratory said today their latest calculations indicate the Russian satellite is still whirling around

[Continued, Page 2, Column 6]

Faubus Urges Negro Pupils' Withdrawal

Little Rock, Ark., Oct. 9 (AP)—Gov. Orval Faubus said today that he sees no solution in the Little Rock integration crisis save the complete withdrawal of the nine Negro students attending Central High School.

Faubus was asked at a news conference to explain the "cooling-off" period he has said is needed in the integration deadlock.

He replied: "We need a chance for tenseness to be allayed, time for litigation and time for the people to accept peacefully what is being crammed down their throats at bayonet point."

Asked About Withdrawal

He was asked if this meant the withdrawal of six Negro girls and three boys who have been attending integrated classes at Central High under protection of Federal troops ordered here by President Eisenhow(.

"It's possible," the Governor replied.

Pressed on this point as to whether any solution could be reached while the Negroes are in Central High, Faubus said: "I don't think it is possible at this time with the Negroes in the school."

Says Some Have Power

Faubus said it is within the power of a number of persons, including the courts and the Little Rock School Board, to initiate some break in the deadlock but that he has no suggestions currently under consideration.

Faubus said he was not "closing the door to the possibility of a compromise, because I don't want to appear adamant or arbitrary."

But again he said he had no such move currently under consideration.

Hoping, Says Ike

In Washington, Eisenhower told a news conference he certainly is very hopeful the time may be drawing near when Federal troops can be withdrawn from Little Rock, but he offered no specific information or elaboration.

At the, school, the scene remained quiet. Half a dozen soldiers escorted the nine Negro pupils into the building without incident.

African Gets Ike's Bid After Delaware Snub

New York, Oct. 9 (AP)—K. A. Gbedemah, Ghana's Finance Minister who was refused service in a Dover (Del.) restaurant because of his color, canceled plans to leave for home today in order to breakfast with President Eisenhower in the White House tomorrow.

Washington, Oct. 9 (AP)—President Eisenhower today invited K. A. Gbedemah, Ghana's Finance Minister, to have breakfast at the White House tomorrow.

In response to a question, the White House said that "of course" the invitation to the official of the Negro republic was prompted by an incident in Dover, Del., where a restaurant refused to serve Gbedemah because of his color.

Gbedemah reported he was told by a waitress at the restaurant that "colored people are not allowed to eat in here."

James C. Hagerty, White House press secretary, said in announcing the breakfast engagement that Eisenhower had read about the incident in the newspapers and also was told about it by State Department officials.

Hagerty said Bbedemah had accepted the invitation.

Asked whether the President's invitation was prompted by the episode at Dover, Hagerty replied:

"Of course."

Asked how Eisenhower felt about the refusal to serve Gbedemah, Hagerty replied that Eisenhower's reaction was reflected in his decision to invite the Finance Minister to breakfast.

In reply to another question, Hagerty said Gbedeniah had filed no protest at the State Department.

But even without a protest, the State Department said publicly that it "greatly regrets that this incident has occurred

[Continued, Page 2, Column 5]

Berra, Bauer Blast Homers As Turley Hurls 4-Hitter

By Paul Menton

[*Sports Editor of The Evening Sun*]

New York, Oct. 9—Hank Bauer bounced a home run off the left-field foul pole netting to send the World Series to the seven-game limit as the Yankees nipped the Milwaukee Braves, 3 to 2, behind Bob Turley's four-hit pitching here today.

Four homers accounted for all the runs scored and kept 61,408 fans on the edge of their seats as Turley squeaked through the first series victory of his career—by a matter of inches.

Inches are what kept Bauer's blast fair, in the seventh inning, and inches are what figured in a base on balls given up by the Braves' starter, Bob Buhl, to put Enos Slaughter on the base-paths to set the stage for an earlier, two-run Yankee homer by Yogi Berra.

Bauer's blow, coming with one out and nobody on base in the bottom of the seventh, came off sidearming Ernie Johnson, the second of three Braves pitcher. The last was Don McMahon, who hurled the eighth.

Hits Foul-Pole Mesh

The ball hit the thin strip of mesh that borders the pole, about 10 feet high.

Besides winning the game for the desperate Yankees, the clout also enabled Bauer to tie a series record by hitting safely in his thirteenth consecutive game. The mark had stood the ravages of time for 39 years. After Frank Schulte, of the Cubs, first did it in the 1906-1910 period, Harry Hooper, of the Red Sox matched the mark in 1918.

Turley's strong and supple arm held the fort for the Bombers as much as the power swings of Bauer and Berra. Bullet Bob, the former Oriole, struck out eight men and issued only two walks as he mixed his fast ball with a beautiful changeup curve.

Both Milwaukee runs off him came on lead-off homers.

Frank Torre whacked a 3-2 pitch into the right-field seats, approximately 360 feet away, in the fifth frame to cut the Yankees' lead to 2-1.

Aaron Hits Second Homer

Henry Aaron walloped the other one, in the top of the seventh, to pull the Braves into a short-lived two-all deadlock.

This one was a tremendous 410-foot clout that carried into the Milwaukee bullpen, well out in the left-field sector, where the stadium stands curve deeply.

Turley remained unruffled, though, in sharp contrast to his

[Continued, Page 2, Column 2]

Play By Play

Comment by Paul Menton

FIRST INNING

BRAVES—Mantilla flied to Kubek. Logan struck out. Mathews was retired, Turley to Simpson. No runs; no hits; no errors.

YANKEES—Bauer struck out. Kubek struck out. Slaughter walked. Berra singled, Slaughter stopping at second. Both runners advanced a base on a wild pitch. McDougald struck out. No runs; one hit; no errors.

When Buhl got McDougald to fan on an inside pitch he survived an opening-inning crisis which he failed to do in Milwaukee. He is much faster today, making Bauer and Kubek look bad going after high outside balls. Turley also looks steadier.

SECOND INNING

BRAVES — Aaron struck out. Covington lifted a high fly to Kubek. Torre singled off the handle of his bat into right. Hazle fouled to Berra. No runs; one hit; no errors.

YANKEES — Lumpe singled. Simpson took a third strike and Lumpe was out, trying to steal second, Rice to Logan, Coleman walked. Turley bounced out, Buhl to Torre. No runs; one hit; no errors.

One of the big disappointments of the Series has been Simpson. In the game mainly for his hitting, he has one in ten appearances. He was badly fooled on the three-two pitch and Lumpe, running, an easy out at second.

THIRD INNING

BRAVES—Rice was called out on strikes. Buhl also took a third strike. Mantilla flied deep to Bauer. No runs; no hits; no errors.

YANKEES—Bauer popped to Logan. Kubek grounded out, Mantilla to Torre. Slaughter walked. Berra homered, scoring behind Slaughter. McDougald topped a single past Buhl. Lumpe walked. Johnson replaced Buhl. Simpson struck out. Two runs; two hits; no errors.

The Yankees looked more like themselves with Berra getting his first extra base hit of the series with a line-drive home run to the right-field lower stands. It was his tenth in World Series, tying with Brooklyn's Duke Snider and Lou Gehrig for second place. Of more importance, it started downfall of Buhl.

FOURTH INNING

BRAVES — Logan fouled to Berra. Mathews doubled. Aaron grounded out, Coleman to Simpson, Mathews going to third. Covington fouled to Lumpe. No runs; one hit; no errors.

YANKEES — Coleman hit a Texas-league double to short left. Turley was an automatic strike out victim when he fouled on a third strike bunt attempt. Bauer struck out. Kubek grounded out, Torre to Johnson. No runs; one hit; no errors.

A beautiful slide back to second by Coleman after being caught between second and third on attempted sacrifice was wasted when Turley, Bauer and Kubek were easy outs. It made sixth Yankee left in four innings and keeps pressure on Turley.

FIFTH INNING

BRAVES — Torre homered. Hazle grounded out, Coleman to Simpson. Rice grounded out, Lumpe to Simpson. Johnson called out on strikes. One run; one hit; no errors.

YANKEES — Slaughter was out on a bounce to Torre.

[Continued, Page 2, Column 3]

The Weather

Fair tonight, lows in the 50's. Partly cloudy, a little cooler tomorrow.

Detailed report on Page 2.

Box Score

Sixth Game

MILWAUKEE

	Ab.	R.	H.	O.	A.
Mantilla, 2b	3	0	0	2	1
Logan, ss.	4	0	0	2	1
Mathews, 3b	3	0	1	0	0
Aaron, cf	4	1	1	1	0
Covington, lf	4	0	0	1	1
Torre, 1b	2	1	2	7	1
Hazle, rf	3	0	0	0	0
Rice, c	3	0	0	10	1
Buhl, p	1	0	0	0	1
E. Johnson, p	1	0	0	1	2
aSawatski	1	0	0	0	0
McMahon, p	0	0	0	0	1
Totals	30	2	4	24	9

NEW YORK

	Ab.	R.	H.	O.	A.
Bauer, rf	4	1	1	1	0
Kubek, cf	4	0	0	3	0
Slaughter, lf	2	1	0	0	0
Berra, c	4	1	3	10	0
McDougald, ss	3	0	1	2	2
Lumpe, 3b	3	0	1	1	1
Simpson, 1b	3	0	0	6	0
Collins, 1b	0	0	0	1	1
Coleman, 2b	2	0	1	1	3
Turley, p	3	0	0	2	2
Totals	28	3	7	27	9

Milwaukee (N). 0 0 0 0 1 0 1 0 0—2
New York (A).. 0 0 2 0 0 0 0 1 0 x—3

aStruck out for E. Johnson in 8th. Error—None. Runs Batted In—Berra (2), Torre, Aaron, Bauer. Two-Base Hits—Mathews, Coleman, Berra. Home Runs—Berra, Torre, Aaron, Bauer. Sacrifice—McDougald. Double Plays—Rice and Logan; Covington and Rice; Turley, McDougald and Collins. Left on bases—Milwaukee (N.) 3, New York (A.) 6. Bases on Balls—Turley, 2 (Mantilla, Mathews); Buhl, 4 (Slaughter 2, Coleman, Lumpe). Strikeouts—Turley, 8 (Logan, Aaron 2, Rice 2, Buhl, E. Johnson, Sawatski); Buhl, 4 (Bauer, Kubek, McDougald, Simpson); E. Johnson, 5 (Simpson, Turley 2, Bauer, McDougald). Hits Off—Buhl, 4 in 2 2-3 innings; E. Johnson, 2 in 4 1-3; McMahon, 1 in 1. Runs and Earned Runs—Buhl, 2-2; E. Johnson, 1-1; McMahon, 0-0; Turley, 2-2. Wild Pitch—Buhl. Winning Pitcher—Turley. Losing Piticher—E. Johnson. Umpires—Conlan (N.), home plate; McKinley (A.), first base; Donatelli (N.), second base; Paparella (A.), third base; Secory (N.), left field; Chylak (A.), right field. Time—2.09. Attendance—61,408. Receipts (Net)—$405,784.76.

Mantle Smashes 2, Yankees Win, 8-5

★ ★ ★ ★ ★ ★ ★

Cols Check Tribe Despite 2 Cook Homers

Indians Handed 8-4 Setback; Play 2 Tonight

By MAX GREENWALD

It's still one to tie and two to win for the Indianapolis Indians.

With Cliff Cook slamming home runs in the first and third innings, the Tribe appeared to be headed for a victory yesterday over Louisville.

But the Colonels, outhitting Indianapolis, 13 to six, did some late-inning scoring to conquer the Indians, 8-4. Louisville went ahead with four markers in the seventh, three of them on Ron Jackson's homer.

That outcome left the league-leading Tribe three games ahead of Louisville with five to play. Two of these tilts are booked for tonight along with a between-games firework program.

The Indians started with three tallies in the first. Chico Ruiz walked and Joe Gaines bunted for a hit. Pitcher Moe Drabowsky grabbed the bunt and threw past first base to the pavilion boxes in right. Ruiz scored on the error and Gaines ran to third.

Cook then blasted a high drive over the scoreboard sign.

Cook also connected with a Drabowsky offering in the third for a line drive over the billboard in left. That gave the Indianapolis third baseman 31 homers for the season and 117 RBIs, both highs in the American Association.

BUT THE Indians managed only two hits the rest of the way against relievers Winston Brown and Ken MacKenzie.

The Tribe's best chance for a late threat came on two walks and shortstop Amado Samuel's ground-ball error in the seventh. MacKenzie then relieved Brown and Hal Bevan rapped the lefthander's second pitch into right center where Mack Jones made the catch.

John Tsitouris blanked the Colonels for five innings. A walk, a hit batsman and Samuel's single loaded the sacks in the sixth. Chico Ruiz went to his right for a good play on Brown's sharp grounder and made the force at second as a run scored. It was the first Louisville tally off Tribe pitching in 18 in-

With a 3-0 count on Lee Tate in the seventh, Manager Cot Deal removed Tsitouris, one of the Tribesmen who visited a doctor in Louisville Friday because of the flu.

"He did a good job for us as long as he could go," Deal said, "but he ran out of gas."

Another of the Indians who had been stricken by the bug, southpaw Bob Miller, replaced Tsitouris.

One pitch completed the walk to Tate, who moved up on an infield out. There were two out when Len Gabrielson singled to right center an 0-2 pitch for another tally. After another walk, Jackson lifted his 24th homer which drifted over the sign in left.

In the eighth, a mighty triple almost to the flagpole in center by Jones drove over a run. Ruiz ran into center to take the throw from Sandy Valdespino, then pegged home on the mark to nail Jones sliding in.

Bob Krop yielded two markers in the ninth on a walk, Bob Uecker's double to the scoreboard and MacKenzie's single after Samuel had been given an intentional pass. Cloyd Boyer retired the side with two on.

HIT-AND-RUN—A crowd of 4,737 was on hand yesterday.

Tonight's Tribe pitchers will be John Briggs (2-1) and Don Rudolph (17-9). Denver LeMaster (6-3) will be one of the Louisville hurlers and Manager Ben Geraghty hadn't decided on the other.

Gabrielson had a perfect day at bat with three hits while Jones also had three safeties. Gaines and Cook had two bingles apiece among the Tribe's six. Gaines put his average at .315, high among the Indians at bat enough times to count in official averages.

Gaines singled and Cook walked with one out in the fifth but Don Pavletich and Bevan both flied out.

In the third, Gaines had a solid poke to right center but Gabrielson made a running catch.

Both Brown and Miller made good plays on ground balls.

Tsitouris escaped with the bases full in the fourth. He got Samuel to pop up and fanned Merritt Ranew, a pinch-hitter.

LOUISVILLE

	AB	R	H	O	A	E
Fandozzi,1	5	1	1	0	1	0
Tate,2	4	1	1	3	4	0
Jones,cf	5	0	3	6	0	0
Krsnich,lf	4	1	0	1	0	0
Gabrielson,rf	3	2	3	2	0	0
Uecker,c	3	2	1	2	0	0
Jackson,1	4	1	2	9	2	0
Samuel,ss	4	0	1	3	3	1
Drabowsky,p	1	0	0	0	0	1
[1]Ranew	1	0	0	0	0	0
Brown,p	1	0	0	1	1	0
MacKenzie,p	2	0	1	0	0	0
Totals	37	8	13	27	11	2

INDIANAPOLIS

	AB	R	H	O	A	E
Johnston,lf	4	0	0	3	0	0
Ruiz,ss	4	1	0	1	4	0
Gaines,rf	4	1	2	4	0	0
Cook,3b	4	2	2	1	2	0
Pavletich,c	2	0	0	4	1	0
Bevan,1	3	0	0	11	0	0
Valdespino,cf	3	0	0	2	1	0
[2]Jacobs,cf	1	0	1	0	0	1
Snyder,2b	4	0	1	1	2	0
Tsitouris,p	2	0	0	0	0	0
Miller,p	0	0	0	0	2	0
[3]Boak	1	0	0	0	0	0
Krop,p	0	0	0	0	1	0
Boyer,p	0	0	0	0	0	0
Totals	32	4	6	27	13	1

[1]Struck out for Drabowsky in fourth.
[2]Singled for Valdespino in eighth.
[3]Grounded into double play for Miller in eighth.

Louisville	000	001	412—8
INDIANAPOLIS	301	000	000—4

RBI—Cook 3, Brown, Gabrielson, Jackson 3, Jones, Uecker, MacKenzie (Ruiz scored in first on Drabowsky's error. 2B—Uecker. 3B—Jones. HR—Cook 2, Jackson. SB—Pavletich. S—Tsitouris, Gabrielson. DP—Pavletich and Cook; Samuel, Tate and Jackson. Left—Louisville 11, Indianapolis 9.

	IP	H	R	ER	BB	SO
Drabowsky	3	4	4	4	2	1
Brown (W, 8-11)	3⅔	1	0	0	3	1
MacKenzie	2⅓	1	0	0	1	0
*Tsitouris	6	7	2	2	3	3
Miller (L, 7-6)	2	4	4	4	1	0
Krop	⅔	2	2	2	2	0
Boyer	⅓	0	0	0	0	0

Van Looy Captures World Cycling Crown

Bern, Switzerland (AP)—Rik Van Looy of Belgium won the professional road cycling world championship for the second straight year yesterday.

In a thrilling finish, Van Looy sprinted past Nino Defilippis of Italy over the last 100 meters and won by inches. Van Looy covered the 285.25 kilometer course in 7:46:35. A crowd of about 60,000 watched the race.

Exhibition Football

AMERICAN LEAGUE

San Diego 31, Dallas 10.

SAFE AT THIRD—Amado Samuel of Louisville slides into third base safely during the ninth inning of yesterday's game with Indianapolis. Cliff Cook, Tribe third baseman, was unable to handle the ball as the throw from center skidded in the dirt. (Star Photo by Bob Daugherty)

The Standings

AMERICAN ASSOCIATION

	W	L	Pct.	GB
INDIANAPOLIS	82	63	.566	..
Louisville	79	66	.545	3
Denver	73	69	.514	7½
Dallas-Ft. Worth	70	75	.483	12
Houston	69	75	.479	12½
Omaha	60	85	.414	22

AMERICAN LEAGUE

	W	L	Pct.	GB
New York	90	45	.557	..
Detroit	86	50	.632	4½
Baltimore	80	59	.576	12
Chicago	74	64	.536	17½
Cleveland	69	68	.504	22
Boston	66	73	.475	26
Los Angeles	60	76	.441	30½
Minnesota	58	76	.433	31½
Washington	51	84	.378	39
Kansas City	48	87	.356	42

NATIONAL LEAGUE

	W	L	Pct.	GB
Cincinnati	80	54	.597	..
Los Angeles	75	54	.581	2½
Milwaukee	72	59	.550	6½
San Francisco	70	59	.543	7½
St. Louis	68	63	.519	10½
Pittsburgh	63	65	.492	14
Chicago	56	75	.427	22½
Philadelphia	38	93	.290	40½

Yesterday's Results

AMERICAN ASSOCIATION

Louisville 8, INDIANAPOLIS 4.
Dallas-Fort Worth 3, Omaha 1.
Houston at Denver (2), postponed, snow and cold.

AMERICAN LEAGUE

Boston 8, Minnesota 6.
Chicago 5-4, Washington 4-1.
New York 8, Detroit 5.
Baltimore 1, Cleveland 0 (11 innings).
Los Angeles at Kansas City, postponed, wet grounds.

NATIONAL LEAGUE

Philadelphia 3, Cincinnati 2.
Pittsburgh 8, St. Louis 1.
Los Angeles 5, San Francisco 4.
Chicago 6-2, Milwaukee 5-4 (2d game called after 6 innings, darkness).

Today's Schedule

AMERICAN ASSOCIATION

Louisville at INDIANAPOLIS (2), 6:30 p.m.
Houston at Denver.
Dallas-Fort Worth at Omaha (night).

AMERICAN LEAGUE

Washington at New York (2) – Burnside (1-6) and Daniels (8-9) vs. Sheldon (9-4) and Coates (9-5.

Detroit at Baltimore (2, night) – Foytack (10-8) and Regan 10-7 vs. Fisher (8-11) and Hoeft (4-4).

Los Angeles at Kansas City (2)–Moeller (4-8) and Duren (6-11 vs. Archer (8-11) and Walker (6-11).

Chicago at Minnesota (2, day-night)–Baumann (9-11) and Horlen (0-0) vs. Kaat (7-13) and Kralick (12-9).

Cleveland at Boston–Grant (13-8 vs. Conley (9-1).

NATIONAL LEAGUE

Cincinnati at Philadelphia (2)–Johnson (5-2) and Hunt (9-9) vs. Sullivan (3-13) and Mahaffey (9-18.

Milwaukee at Chicago–Willey (5-9) vs. Curtis (9-10).

San Francisco at Los Angeles (night)–Marichal (13-9) vs. Williams (11-10).

Pittsburgh at St. Louis–Francis (2-5) vs. Sadecki (12-7).

Becky Collins Captures First In Butterfly

Munich, Germany (AP) — About 2,000 Germans turned out in sweltering heat yesterday and watched the U.S. women's swimming team capture five of six events in an international exhibition.

The girls will tour Munich today and leave for home tomorrow from Amsterdam.

The closest event yesterday was the 100-meter backstroke with 15-year-old Nina Harmer of Philadelphia getting the judge's decision over Holland's Corrie Winkel, although each clocked 1:11.4.

Becky Collins, 17, of Indianapolis won the 100 meter butterfly in 1:09.9 with Nancy Kanaby of Portland, Ore., second in 1:11.8.

Robyn Johnson, 15, of Arlington, Va., took the 200 meter freestyle in 2:18.2, followed by Carolyn House in 2:19.0.

The 100 meter breaststroke saw Germany's Martha Hoffmann win with 1:21.7 minutes.

Dale Barnhard of Washington, D.C., was fourth in 1:22.9, followed by Jean Ann Dellekamp of Indianapolis in 1:23.4.

Phils End Reds Jinx, Top Loop Leaders 3 To 2

Philadelphia (UPI) — The Philadelphia Phillies, beaten 17 straight times by Cincinnati, won their first of the season from the league leaders yesterday when pinch batter Wes Covington singled home the winning run in the eighth inning to top the Reds, 3-2.

The loser was Jim Maloney, the $80,000 bonus investment of the Reds, and the winner was Jim Owens, who pitched his first complete game of the season in 13 starts.

MALONEY CAME in as a pinch batter for starter Jim O'Toole in the eighth, after rain caused a 65-minute delay while the Phils were batting in the seventh, and stayed in to be the losing pitcher.

O'Toole had given up five hits, fanned 10 and walked five in the first seven innings.

The 21-year-old Maloney, given a 2-2 ball game, got into immediate trouble when Charlie Smith opened the eighth with a double. Bobby Malkmus went in as a runner. Then Gordie Coleman leaned into the right field stands to gather in Don Demeter's foul, with Malkmus streaking to third when Coleman tumbled over the low fence.

Covington batted for Frank Herrera and singled through the drawn-in infield, scoring Malkmus. Tony Gonzalez also singled and after Reuben Amaro flied out, Bill Henry came in and got Clay Dalrymple to end the inning.

COLEMAN SINGLED with two out in the Reds ninth. Don Blasingame ran for him and took second on a wild pitch while pinch batter Gus Bell was walking, but Eddie Kasko ended it when he flied out.

A triple by Gerry Lynch and Coleman's sacrifice fly gave the Reds one run in the second and the Phils went ahead in the fourth when they loaded the bases on two walks and an infield single. Tony Taylor's double play sent one run home and Callison tripled in the second.

The Reds tied it in the sixth on a double by Elio Chicon and Vada Pinson's third straight single, the 600th hit of his three-year major league career.

Cincinnati

	ab	h	rbi
Frees,3	4	1	0
Chacon,2	4	1	0
Pinson,cf	4	3	1
Roboinson,rf	4	0	0
Lynch,lf	4	1	0
Coleman,1	3	1	1
[6]Blasingame	0	0	0
Cardenas,ss	3	0	0
[5]Bell	0	0	0
Johnson,c	2	0	0
[7]Kasko	1	0	0
O'Toole,p	2	0	0
[1]Maloney,p	1	0	0
Henry,p	0	0	0
Totals	32	7	2

Philadelphia

	ab	h	rbi
Taylor,2	4	0	0
Callison,lf	4	1	1
C.Smith,3	2	1	0
[2]Malkmus,3	0	0	0
Demeter,rf-1	4	0	0
Herrera,1	3	1	0
[3]Covington	1	1	1
[4]Walters,rf	0	0	0
Gonzalez,cf	4	2	0
Amaro,ss	3	1	0
Dalrymple,c	4	1	0
Owens,p	1	0	0
Totals	30	8	2

[1]Grounded out for O'Toole in eighth.
[2]Ran for Smith in eighth.
[3]Singled for Herrera in eighth.
[4]Ran for Covington in eighth.
[5]Walked for Cardenas in ninth.
[6]Ran for Coleman in ninth.
[7]Flied out for Johnson in ninth.

Cincinnati	010	001	000—	2
Philadelphia	000	020	01x—	3

E—None. PO-A—Cincinnati 24-4, Philadelphia 27-10. DP—Cardenas, Chacon and Coleman; Taylor, Amaro and Herrera; Cardenas and Coleman. Left—Cincinnati 6, Philadelphia 8. 2B—Chacon, Freese, C. Smith. 3B—Lynch, Callison. SB—Pinson. SF—Coleman.

	IP	H	R	ER	BB	SO
O'Toole	7	5	2	2	5	10
Maloney (L, 6-6)	⅔	3	1	1	0	0
Henry	⅓	0	0	0	0	0
Owens (W, 3-9)	9	7	2	2	2	3

WP—Owens.
U—Crawford, Barlick, Jackowski, Vargo. T—2:32. A—4,752.

Baseball Leaders

BY THE ASSOCIATED PRESS

AMERICAN LEAGUE

Player and Club	G	AB	R	H	Pct.
Cash Det.	134	449	100	163	.363
Howard, N.Y.	103	360	49	126	.350
Piersall, Clev.	112	449	73	148	.330
Mantle, N.Y.	134	464	117	150	.323

Home Runs		Runs Batted In	
Maris, N.Y.	53	Gentile, Balt.	126
Mantle, N.Y.	50	Colavito, Det.	125
Gentile Balt.	43	Maris, N.Y.	124
Colavito, Det.	40	Mantle, N.Y.	118
Killebrew, Minn.	38	Cash, Det.	112

NATIONAL LEAGUE

Player and Club	G	AB	R	H	PCT.
Clemente, Pittsburgh	126	499	92	181	.363
Pinson, Cincinnati	134	534	94	182	.341
Robinson, Cincinnati	133	472	105	156	.331
Aaron, Milwaukee	132	510	105	166	.325
Moon, Los Angeles	110	377	60	122	.324

Home Runs		Runs Batted In	
Cepeda, S.F.	37	Cepeda, S.F.	120
Robinson, Cincin.	35	Rbnsn, Cincin.	114
Mays, S.F.	34	Aaron, Mlwkee	105
Aaron, Milwaukee	33	Mays, S.F.	102
Mathews, Mlwkee	33	Adcock, Mlwkee	91
Adcock, Mlwkee	29		

AMERICAN ASSOCIATION

Player and Club	G	AB	R	H	Pct.
Bedell, Louisville	134	592	82	194	.328
Wert, Denver	130	496	83	161	.325
LaJoie, Omaha	129	506	68	162	.320
Gaines, Indpls.	139	501	84	158	.31[illegible]
Cook, Indpls.	140	507	101	159	314

Home Runs

Cook, Indpls.	3[illegible]	McKnight, Hous	22
McDaniel, Den.	29	Pavletich, Indp	21
Jackson, Louv.	23		

Runs Batted In

Cook, Indpls	11[illegible]	Krsnich, Louv.	86
McDaniel, Den	10[illegible]	Pavletich, Indp.	7[illegible]
McKnight, Hous	87	Gabrielson, Louv	77

Jones Sets Speed Mark To Win Salem Sprints

Salem, Ind. (Spl.)—Parnelli Jones, almost unbeatable on the high banks this year, won again here yesterday.

Jones whipped a hot field of sprint car drivers in the 100-lap feature with a record time of 32:52.86. Elmer George was second and Chuck Hulse third.

Parnelli collected $1,264 for his day's work. A good crowd of 6,000 was on hand for the accident-free race. The total purse was $7,210.

A. J. Foyt, winner of the 1961 500-Mile race, tied Jones for fastest qualifying time—18:80—but Parnelli started first. However, Foyt was forced out on the 29th lap. He was running third at the time.

Dave Norris set a new track record of 4:03.49 for 12 laps in winning the semifinals. He was followed by Bob Mathouse and Red Renner.

Roger McCluskey won the first heat. Bud Tinglestad was second and Ronnie Duman third. First three finishers in the second heat were Jim Hemmings, Leroy Neumayer and A. J. Shepherd.

Top finishers behind the first three in the feature were: 4th, Jim Hurtubise; 5th, Tinglestad; 6th, Norris; 7th, Neumayer; 8th, Mathauser; 9th, Hemmings; 10th, Leon Clum; 11th, McCluskey; 12th Renner.

Maris Silent; Homer By Howard Wins Tilt

New York (AP) — Mickey Mantle blasted his 49th and 50th home runs yesterday to go two-up on Babe Ruth's 1927 record pace to lead the New York Yankees to an 8-5 victory over the Detroit Tigers and stretch their American League lead to 4½ games.

But Roger Maris failed to connect and fell to seven games ahead of Ruth's record in his chase to break the Babe's mark of 60.

Maris has 53 homers and must hit eight in the next 19 games if he is to break the record.

But while all the attention was riveted on Mantle and

Home Run Derby

The following table shows how Roger Maris and Mickey Mantle of New York compare with the record pace of Babe Ruth in 1927:

PLAYER	HOMER	DECISIONS	DATE HIT
Maris	53	135	Sept. 2
*Mantle	50	135	Sept. 3
Ruth	53	142	Sept. 16

*Two ahead of Ruth's pace.

Maris, the key hit of the game was a towering homer by Elston Howard who nailed down the decision with a ninth-inning homer with two on, after Mantle tied it with his second blast.

The Tigers had trailed right from the first inning until they went ahead in the ninth with two runs on two hits and an error by first baseman Bill Skowron.

That set the stage for the Yanks' rally. Ancient Gerry Staley came in to pitch for the Tigers. With one ball on Mantle, Mickey clouted Staley's next pitch into the right field bleachers to tie it at 5-all.

Then Yogi Berra looped a single into right field and that finished Staley.

Ronnie Kline became the fifth Tiger pitcher. Relief pitcher Luis Arroyo sacrificed Berra to second. Kline purposely passed Moose Skowron to set up a possible double play.

Up came Howard. With one strike on him, he clouted the next pitch into the lower left field stands for three runs and the ball game, enabling the Yanks to sweep the series and deal what could be a fatal blow to the Tigers' chances of overtaking them in the race for the American League pennant.

The Tigers' ninth was a weird one. Bill Stafford and Arroyo, who had taken over in the eighth, had the Bengals pretty well handcuffed.

Dick McAuliffe opened by drawing a pass from Arroyo. Chico Fernandez was called out on strikes. Then Dick Brown dribbled a grounder to the right side. Arroyo scooped it up, but his throw went past Skowron at first, putting McAuliffe on third and Brown on second. It was an error for Skowron.

Pinch hitter Bubba Morton was purposely passed filling the bases, Jake Wood then singled to left, scoring McAuliffe and Rene Bertoia, who was running for Brown. That put the Tigers in front 5-4 until the Yanks opened up again.

The Tigers scored a run in the first. Wood singled but Billy Bruton forced him. Bruton stole second and scored on Rocky Colavito's single.

But the Yanks came right back and scored three runs. Maris singled and scored in front of Mantle's No. 49 homer. Mantle, incidentally, hurt his left forearm in Saturday's game. For a while it was feared that he suffered a torn muscle, but it responded to cold, wet dressings overnight. The final diagnosis was a knotted muscle.

Right after Mantle's homer, Yogi Berra slammed No. 19. That gave Stafford a good working margin. The Yanks scored another in the fifth on a single by Cletus Boyer, Stafford's sacrifice and Bobby Richardson's single.

The Tigers got that one back in the sixth on Norm Cash's 33rd homer and trimmed their deficit to one run in the eighth when Bruton and Al Kaline singled and Colavito hit into a double play. Bruton sneaked home on the play.

Now that Mantle has reached the 50 homer mark, the Yanks have produced another slugging record. It is the first time two players on one team (Mantle and Maris) have hit 50 or more home runs in one season.

Further, Maris and Mantle are only four homers off the all-time two-man record of 107, set by Ruth and Lou Gehrig in 1927.

Arroyo was the winning pitcher, thanks to Mantle and Howard. The decision was his 11th in a row. He also has seven saves along the way. The last time he lost a game was on June 19 to Kansas City.

A crowd of 55,676 was on hand, boosting the three-day total to 171,503.

Detroit

	ab	h	rbi
Wood,2	5	2	2
Bruton,cf	4	1	0
Kaline,rf	5	2	0
Colavito,lf	4	1	1
Cash,1	4	2	1
McAuliffe,3	3	1	0
Fernandez,ss	3	0	0
Roarke,c	2	0	0
[1]Osborne	1	0	0
Brown,c	1	0	0
[6]Bertoia	0	0	0
House,c	0	0	0
Bunning,p	2	0	0
[2]Maxwell	1	0	0
Regan,p	0	0	0
Fox,p	0	0	0
[5]Morton	0	0	0
Staley,p	0	0	0
Kline,p	0	0	0
Totals	35	9	4

New York

	ab	h	rbi
Richardson,2	4	2	1
Kubek,ss	4	0	0
Maris,rf	4	1	0
Mantle,cf	4	2	3
Berra,lf	4	3	1
Blanchard,c	2	0	0
[3]Tresh	0	0	0
Arroyo,p	0	0	0
Skowron,1	3	0	0
Boyer,3	4	1	0
Stafford,p	1	0	0
[4]Howard,c	2	1	3
Totals	32	10	[illegible]

[1]Grounded out for Roarke in seventh.
[2]Struck out for Bunning in seventh.
[3]Ran for Blanchard in seventh.
[4]Struck out for Stafford in seventh.
[5]Walked for Fox in ninth.
[6]Ran for Brown in ninth.

Detroit	100	001	012—5
New York	300	010	004—8

E—Skowron. PO-A—Detroit 26-4 (two out when winning run scored in ninth), New York 27-17. DP—Cash, Fernandez and Cash; Richardson, Kubek and Skowron; Kubek, Richardson and Skowron. Left—Detroit 7, New York 2. 2B—Cash. HR—Mantle 2, Berra, Cash, Howard. SB—Bruton. S—Stafford, Arroyo.

	IP	H	R	ER	BB	SO
Bunning	6	6	4	4	0	7
Regan	0	1	0	0	1	0
Fox	2	0	0	0	0	2
Staley (L, 2-5)	0	2	2	2	0	0
Kline	⅔	1	2	2	1	0
Stafford	7	6	2	2	2	1
Arroyo (W, 13-3)	2	3	3	2	2	2

(Regan pitched to 2 batters in seventh; Staley pitched to 2 batters in ninth).
U — Chylak, Drummond, Paparella, Runge. T—2:47. A—55,676.

THERE GOES NO. 50—New York Yankee outfielder Mickey Mantle completes the swing that led to home run No. 50 yesterday at Yankee Stadium. He got it in the ninth inning to give the Bombers a 5-5 tie with Detroit and Elston Howard sewed up an 8-5 verdict with a three-run blast. Mantle had belted homer No. 49 in the first inning with Roger Maris on base. (AP Wirephoto)

'Snow Ball Game At Denver Park

Denver (AP)—The earliest snow on record forced postponement yesterday of a scheduled American Association baseball doubleheader between Houston and Denver.

A 4-inch snowfall that started late Saturday had melted away by game time, 5:30 p.m. (MST), but the field was soggy and the temperature was in the low 40s.

A doubleheader between the teams Labor Day will begin at 1:30 p.m. (MST).

HAVING PROVED their superiority over the rest of the American Association over the long, hard route in the season which ended last night, our Indianapolis Indians will have to do it all over again beginning tomorrow night.

In case you suspect this is our annual protest against the Shaughnessy playoff system, you're absolutely right.

We have been accused of adopting a "sour grapes" viewpoint in the past when we criticized the playoff system in years when the Tribe missed the playoffs—like last year when Indianapolis finished seventh.

THIS UNDOUBTEDLY is one of the great teams of Indianapolis baseball history and has proved its right to be recognized as Association champion over a 150-game season, playing each of the other five clubs 30 games.

And, the Tribe finished the season in fitting style by standing off the top challenger, Louisville, playing the Colonels in the last 11 games of the season and coming out with a bigger lead than when the head-to-head series began.

We have confidence that Cot Deal and his Indians will win their way through the two rounds of Association playoffs and into the Junior World Series. But, it all seems so unnecessary.

The Tribe first will encounter the fourth-place finisher in a best-of-seven series, then will meet the survivor of a similar series between the second and third-place teams in another best-of-seven.

IT IS SOMEWHAT difficult to understand why the Association and International League cling to the playoffs. If they were financially lucrative, it would be understandable but with the wide-spread geography of the leagues and heavy travel costs, clubs are lucky to make expenses now.

The usual excuse offered is that the playoffs sustain interest in the final weeks of the regular season by keeping the fans wondering whether their team will make it into the post-season competition.

Perhaps that used to be the case, but there is little evidence that it has been in recent years. Certainly, it's rather silly to play all season just to eliminate two clubs from the playoffs.

It appears likely that some sort of consolidation of the Association and the International into one sound, strong minor league will be necessary as the result of the Association losing Houston and the International having several clubs in serious difficulty.

COLUMBUS, formerly an American Association city, already has clinched the International League pennant, but that league won't get its season over until Sunday and will start its playoffs Tuesday.

A sound league could be formed by taking Indianapolis, Louisville and Denver of the Association and Columbus, Toronto, Buffalo, Rochester of the International and adding Atlanta of the Southern Association, a league that appears to be withering on the vine, anyhow.

Then, perhaps we could forget about this silly playoff system and arrange a new "Junior World Series" against the Pacific Coast League champion.

THE NATIONAL Boxing Association, in convention in Hershey, Pa., yesterday, took a big step toward cleaning up the fistic sport when it adopted a rule banning return-bout clauses in NBA states (all except New York, Massachusetts and California.)

The NBA also changed its rules to give the world's heavyweight champion a year instead of six months to defend his title, thereby taking Floyd Patterson "off the hook."

The action came only six days before Patterson's six months were up. He defended March 13 against Ingemar Johansson in Miami Beach.

Patterson's bout with unranked Tom McNeeley at Boston, Nov. 13 won't count as an official defense. He will have to meet some challenger approved by the NBA before next March 13 unless he wants the group to lift his title.

Stanley Goldberg of La Porte, formerly of the Indiana Athletic Commission, was among those nominated for president but both Goldberg and another nominee, Charles P. Mayer of Montreal, withdrew in a harmony move and Dr. Charles P. Larson of Tacoma, Wash., was elected president.

THE MANUAL High School Dads' Club will sponsor its annual fish fry from 4:30 to 7:30 p.m. today in the school cafeteria preceding the Manual-Sacred Heart football game. The public is invited.

DUFFY DAUGHERTY of Michigan State is having his two-a-day football practice sessions at 7 a.m. and 4:30 p.m. Why the long gap between workouts?

"The eight hours enable the squad to snap back almost 100 per cent from the hard morning session," Daugherty explains. "Then we can go full tilt again in the afternoon with a lot less likelihood of injury. We get in two good, sharp drills a day instead of one good one and one loggy one."

COACH GENE CORUM of West Virginia has an unusual complaint — some of his football players have done too good a job of taking off weight. Tackle Steve Edwards is down to 212 and Corum would like to see him 10 pounds heavier. Fullback Glenn Holton weighed in at 193, but Corum thinks he could use 205 on his raw-boned frame.

Maris Still Not Sure Of Record

New York (AP) — "My chances of breaking the record are the same as they were before," Roger Maris of the Yankees said last night after he hit his 55th home run of the season—5 short of Babe Ruth's record 60—against the Cleveland Indians.

"I don't know what my chances are," he said. "I don't know whether I can break it."

Maris said it was a curve ball from left-hander Dick Stigman that he rifled into the right field bleachers in the third inning of the Yanks' 7-3 victory.

"STIGMAN and the others were moving the ball around on me but they were around the plate," he said. "I'm not gonna take any strikes. If it's over, I'm gonna swing at it."

Maris dropped a drag bunt for a single in the first inning, driving in Tony Kubek from third base — sacrificing a chance for a home run to get the run in from third.

"I was up there to get the run in," he said. "That was my job."

Would he change that if and when the Yanks, now 9 games in front, clinch the pennant?

"Yes, I think I might change my mind then and go all out for the home run. But right now, winning is the important thing."

Both Maris and Mickey Mantle thought Mantle's drive to deep right field in the first inning was going in for a home run.

"I thought it was gone when I hit it," Mantle said. "I guess that wind blowing in from right field held it up."

H.S. Football

East Chicago Roosevelt 52, Hammond Tech 0.
Gary Mann 21, Gary Edison 0.
South Bend Washington 13, South Bend St. Joseph's 6.
Evansville Memorial 19, Owensboro (Ky.) Catholic 0.

Maris Bangs 55th As Yanks Win

Joins 4 Great Sluggers

New York (AP)—Roger Maris walloped his 55th home run last night, joining Babe Ruth, Jimmy Foxx, Hank Greenberg and Hack Wilson as the only major league sluggers to hit that many, as the New York Yankees defeated Cleveland, 7-3, for their eighth straight success and a run-away, nine-game lead in the American League race.

Maris, stepping up his pursuit of Ruth's record of 60 homers with his second in two games, stayed seven games ahead of the Babe's record pace of 1927.

The blond clouter needs six in 14 games to break the record within the limit of 154 team decisions set by Baseball Commissioner Ford Frick.

WHILE MARIS was 3-for-3, driving in three runs with his solo homer, a bunt single and a sacrifice fly, teammate Mickey Mantle failed to add to his home run total of 51. The Mick had one hit, a double, in four trips and drove in two run.

Home Run Derby

The following table shows how Roger Maris and Mickey Mantle of New York compare with the record pace of Babe Ruth in 1927:

Player	Homer No.	Team Decisions	Date Hit
Maris	55	140	Sept. 7
xMantle	51	140	Sept. 5
Ruth	55	147	Sept. 21

xTwo games behind Ruth's pace.

With M & M driving in five runs between them and right-hander Ralph Terry winning his 13th with a five-hit pitching performance, the Yankees reduced their pennant-clinching magic number to 14 over second-place Detroit.

The Tigers lost their seventh in a row at Boston, 8-4, and any combination of Yankee victories and Detroit defeats totaling 14 will put away the pennant for New York.

MARIS, after bringing in a first-inning run with a drag bunt, belted his homer in the third off losing left-hander Dick Stigman (2-4).

The shot, on a 1-0 pitch, thundered into the right field bleachers. It was the 12th home run off a left-handed pitcher for Maris, a lefty swinger.

The Yankees, who a week ago last night headed home from a road trip with only a 1½-game lead in the flag race, built a 3-0 lead in three innings, blew it on Tito Francona's three-run, inside-the-park homer in the sixth, and then chopped down the Indians with two-run outbursts in the sixth and seventh.

IT WAS Mantle's double, shooting off the glove of shortstop Woody Held into left field, that broke the tie in the seventh and chased Stigman. It followed a leadoff double by Tony Kubek, who also tripled and singled among the Yankees' 11 hits, and Maris' third hit, a single to right center.

Cleveland	ab	h	rbi	New York	ab	h	rbi
Temple,2	4	1	0	Richardson,2	4	2	0
Francona,lf	4	1	3	Kubek,ss	4	3	0
Power,1	4	0	0	Maris,rf	3	3	3
Kirkland,rf	4	0	0	Mantle,cf	4	1	2
Romano,c	4	1	0	Howard,c	3	1	0
Dillard,cf	3	0	0	Skowron,1	3	0	1
Held,ss	3	0	0	Lopez,lf	4	0	0
Phillips,3	3	1	0	Boyer,3	4	1	0
Stigman,p	2	1	0	Terry,p	3	0	0
Locke,p	0	0	0				
1Bond	1	0	0				
Dailey,p	0	0	0				
Totals	32	5	3	Totals	32	11	6

1Fanned for Locke in eighth.

Cleveland .... 000 003 000—3
New York .... 111 002 20x—7

E—Held. PO-A—Cleveland 24-12, New York 27-13. DP—Held, Temple and Power. Left—Cleveland 2, New York 4. 2B—Romano, Kubek, Mantle. 3B—Kubek, Boyer. HR—Maris, Francona. SF—Maris.

	IP	H	R	ER	BB	SO
xStigman (L, 2-4)	5	9	5	4	0	2
Locke	2	2	2	2	2	1
Dailey	1	0	0	0	0	0
Terry (W, 13-2)	9	5	3	3	0	3

x—Faced three batters in sixth.
WP—Locke. U—Linsalata, Stewart, Berry, Umont. T—2:00. A—18,549.

THERE GOES NO. 55—Roger Maris slams his 55th homer of 1961 last night in third inning against Cleveland in Yankee Stadium. He clouted it off left-hander Dick Stigman. The Yankees won, 7-3. (AP Wirephoto)

HICKS BACK; SIX HIT .300

Tribe Loses 9-3 Finale; Houston Is Playoff Foe

By MAX GREENWALD

The 1961 champion Indianapolis Indians last night prepared for the playoffs by using 18 players in the regular-season finale.

Houston will be the Tribe's opponent in the first-round series with the first three games to be played at Victory Field tomorrow night, Sunday afternoon and Monday night.

LOUISVILLE ended the Indians' four-game winning streak last night, 9-3, but Indianapolis finished six contests ahead of the runnerup Colonels in the final standing.

Six Tribesmen finished with .300 or better batting averages. Joe Gaines is fourth in the American Association list with .315 while Cliff Cook is .311, Sandy Valdespino .302, Jake Jacobs .300, Len Johnston .300 and Hal Bevan .300.

Cook, who received a trophy before last night's game for being voted the Indians' most valuable player, won two titles. He has 119 RBI's and 32 home runs. Cook saw limited duty last night because of a turned ankle but will be ready for the playoffs.

Manager Cot Deal intends to carry only eight pitchers during the playoffs.

This will provide him with additional bench strength and Joe Hicks, outfielder who suffered a broken hand Aug. 1, will return to the active list. Hicks will take special batting practice this morning at Victory Field.

Pitcher-coach Cloyd Boyer and Ted Beard, outfielder-coach, will go off the active roster. Also removed is Sam Ellis, rookie pitcher, who will return to his home at Birmingham, Ala.

THE INDIANS' 1961 attendance totaled 177,861, compared to last year's 158,616.

CLIFF COOK
Named Most Valuable

Tribe fans saw the home club win 52 times while it was losing only 23.

All the Indianapolis runs last night were unearned as they followed drop fly balls by outfielders Mike Krsnich and Mack Jones.

Jones, however, cracked his 11th home run with one on in the fifth, a smash which cleared the 385-foot mark in right center. He also found the range almost at that spot in the ninth for a triple.

Ron Jackson clubbed his 25th homer in the eighth, the drive going over the scoreboard.

Four Tribe pitchers gave up 14 hits with the starter, John Tsitouris, being charged with the defeat.

WINSTON Brown, who hurled the first five frames for the Colonels, was the winner. Hank Fischer fanned three batters in pitching three innings to wind up with 163. However, he lost the strikeout championship by one when Omaha's Charlie Spell whiffed nine Dallas-Fort Worth batters.

Spell struck out the side in the ninth as Omaha won, 5-1, to knock the Rangers out of the playoffs.

The trophy won by Cook was presented by the Indians' Appreciation Committee, a group which also has been active in sponsoring a pre-season banquet for the Tribe. Participating in the vote were baseball writers for the three newspapers and personnel of WTTV who presented 32 games on television.

LOUISVILLE

	AB	R	H	O	A	E
Fandozzi, 3b	5	1	1	1	0	0
Tate, 2b	3	1	1	1	3	0
Samuel, ss	2	0	1	1	2	0
Gabrielson, rf	3	1	1	0	0	0
Krsnich, lf	4	1	1	4	1	1
Ranew, c	5	0	2	5	1	0
Jones, cf	5	1	3	2	0	1
Jackson, 1b	4	2	1	9	1	0
Littrell, ss-2b	5	1	2	3	4	0
Brown, p	3	0	0	0	0	0
Fischer, p	1	1	1	1	0	0
Grob, p	0	0	0	0	0	0
Totals	40	9	14	27	12	2

INDIANAPOLIS

	AB	R	H	O	A	E
Johnston, lf	1	0	1	1	0	0
1Boak, lf	3	0	2	0	0	0
5Beard	1	0	0	0	0	0
Ruiz, ss	5	0	2	1	2	0
Gaines, rf	4	0	1	2	1	0
Hopke, 1b	4	1	1	11	0	0
Pavletich, c	4	0	1	8	3	0
Jacobs, 3b-cf	4	1	1	0	1	0
Valdespino, cf	2	1	0	2	0	0
Bevan, 2b	2	0	2	0	0	0
Snyder, 2b-3b	3	0	0	2	3	0
Tsitouris, p	1	0	0	0	0	0
2Osteen	1	0	0	0	0	0
Jancich, p	0	0	0	0	0	0
3Rippelmeyer	1	0	0	0	0	0
Briggs, p	0	0	0	0	0	0
Miller, p	0	0	0	0	0	0
4Cook	1	0	0	0	0	0
Totals	37	3	11	27	10	0

1Flied out for Johnston in third.
2Grounded into double play for Tsitouris in fifth.
3Struck out for Jancich in seventh.
4Flied out for Miller in ninth.
5Flied out for Boak in ninth.

Louisville .... 003 030 030—9
INDIANAPOLIS .... 000 020 010—3

RBI—Tate, Krsnich 2, Ranew, Jones 2, Boak, Jackson, Fischer, Samuel, Bevan (Jacobs scored in 5th as Osteen grounded into double play). 2B—Johnston, Pavletich, Hopke, Gabrielson. 3B—Fischer, Jones. HR—Jones, Jackson. SB—Hopke. DP—Krsnich and Ranew; Ttate, Littrell and Jackson. Left—Louisville 8, Indianapolis 8.

	IP	H	R	ER	BB	SO
Brown (W, 9-11)	5	6	2	0	1	0
Fischer	3	5	1	0	0	3
Grob	1	0	0	0	0	0
Tsitouris (L, 9-8)	5	7	6	6	3	5
Jancich	2	2	0	0	1	2
Briggs	1	4	3	3	0	1
Miller	1	1	0	0	0	2

PB—Ranew. U—Deary, Schuster and Bartos. T—2:27. A—2,371.

AMERICAN ASSOCIATION (Final)

	W	L	Pct.	GB
*INDIANAPOLIS	86	64	.573	...
Louisville	80	70	.533	6
Denver	75	73	.507	10
Houston	73	77	.487	13
Dallas-Ft. Worth	72	77	.483	13½
Omaha	62	87	.416	23½

*Clinched pennant.

NATIONAL LEAGUE

	W	L	Pct.	GB
Cincinnati	82	56	.594	...
Los Angeles	78	54	.591	1
Milwaukee	74	60	.552	6
San Francisco	70	62	.530	9
St. Louis	70	64	.522	10
Pittsburgh	65	67	.492	14
Chicago	58	77	.430	22½
Philadelphia	39	96	.289	41½

AMERICAN LEAGUE

	W	L	Pct.	GB
New York	95	45	.679	....
Detroit	86	54	.614	9
Baltimore	84	59	.587	12½
Chicago	77	65	.542	19
Cleveland	71	70	.504	24½
Boston	68	75	.476	28
Los Angeles	61	79	.436	34
Minnesota	59	79	.428	35
Kansas City	51	88	.367	43½
Washington	51	89	.364	44

Yesterday's Results

AMERICAN ASSOCIATION

[illegible]

AMERICAN LEAGUE

Boston 8, Detroit 4.
New York 7, Cleveland 3.
Baltimore 6, Washington 3.
Only games scheduled.

NATIONAL LEAGUE

Pittsburgh 7, Chicago 5.
Only game scheduled.

Today's Schedule

AMERICAN ASSOCIATION

Season completed. Playoffs start tomorrow.

AMERICAN LEAGUE

Detroit at Boston (night) – Bunning (15-10) vs. Stallard (2-4).
Cleveland at New York (night)–Grant (14-8) vs. Stafford (12-7).
Washington at Baltimore (2, twi-night) –Kutyna (6-7) and Gabler (3-8) vs. Brown (10-5) and Barber (16-10).
Minnesota at Kansas City (night)–Kaat (7-14) vs. Archer (8-12).
Chicago at Los Angeles (night)–Herbert (9-12) vs. McBride (12-12).

NATIONAL LEAGUE

St. Louis at Cincinnati (night)–Broglio (9-10) vs. O'Toole (14-9).
Pittsburgh at Milwaukee (night) – Friend (13-17) vs. Hendley (5-3).
Philadelphia at Chicago – Mahaffey (10-18) vs. Ellsworth (7-10).

A.A. Linescores

Dallas-Ft. Worth .. 010 000 000— 1 7 1
Omaha .... 200 000 30x— 5 5 0

Pepper, Hernandez (7) and Rodgers; Spell and Camilli. W—Spell. L—Pepper.

FIRST GAME

Houston .... 000 010 0—1 2 0
Denver .... 000 000 0—0 5 2

Nelson, Gerald (1), Guisti (5) and Thacker; Grzenda and Porter. W—Gerard. L—Grzenda.

SECOND GAME

Houston .... 003 001 301— 9 14 1
Denver .... 250 000 003—10 18 2

Mudrock, Lary (2), Nixon (3), Griffin (7), Donnelly (9) and Campbell

Bulky Futurity Goes To Impish

By BOB COLLINS

Impish, a filly who is all business on a race track, raced away and hid from the bulky field yesterday in the Hoosier Futurity for two-year-old trotters.

And the day-late Fox Stake crown was taken by the always early Coffee Break. The run off, between Coffee Break and Meadow Grayson, in this $55,000 event, was rained out Wednesday.

Field for the Hoosier Futurity was so large — 21 entries — it was runoff in two sections. This presented a happy dilemma for Frank Ervin.

HE WON BOTH eliminations, the first with Kindle in 2:07.2, the second with Impish in 2:02.3, a record for the event. The old mark, 2:03, was set last year by Scotch Irish.

Since Ervin obviously couldn't ride the final heat with one foot in each sulky, he chose Impish (this hardly would fall in the category of wild guesses) and raced away from the survivors in 2:05. Impish, one to watch, is owned by the Blue Spruce Farm, Norwich, N.Y.

The Fox Stake Battle was a strategy session between George Sholty on Coffee Break and Jimmy Arthur on Meadow Grayson. That explains the slow time of 2:09.4.

But Coffee Break, leading all the way, was too much horse yesterday. Sholty didn't even use the whip.

NEXT KNIGHT whipped the field twice in a row to take the Hoosier Futurity for two-year-old pacers. The brown colt set a 2:02.1 record for the event in the first heat and had the track to himself the second time around in 2:03.4.

Next Knight was driven by William Haughton and is owned by Dr. Donald Somers, Birmingham, Mich.

Dick Taylor got Bye Bye Dillon home in front in a tough finish to conclude the 22 Class trot and received the prize for the best time of 2:07.2. The first heat was won by Tom Lee in 2:08.4. Tom Lee was third the second time around. Bye Bye Dillon is owned by Everett Byers, West Point.

C. J., a cannonball stretch runner, zoomed past the field on the way home to win both heats in the 22 Class Pace. His times were 2:02.4 and 2.03.

C.J., WAS driven by Ray Parker and is owned by Charles Hurst, Grandall.

Yesterday's events concluded five successful days of harness racing at the State Fairgrounds. The crowd was estimated at 8,000.

FOX STAKE

Two-Year-Old Pace. Purse $55,635.33. (Third heat. First two raced Wednesday)
Coffee Break (G. Sholty) 1
Meadow Grayson (J. Arthur) 2
Times: 2:09⅘.

HOOSIER FUTURITY

Two-Year-Old Pace. Purse $15,261.94.
Next Knight (W. Haughton) 1 1
Emory Hanover (W. Smart) 4 2
Tarport Boy (A. Grant) 2 6
Times: 2:02⅕, 2:03⅘. Also started: Navy Prince, 3-3; Debonnie, 7-4; Ensign Goose, 5-5; King Yankee, 6-7.

HOOSIER FUTURITY

Two-Year-Old Trot. Purse $16,871.94.
Impish (F. Ervin) .... x 1 1
Right Away (W. Smart) .... x 4 2
Apex Hanover (J. Arthur) ...... x 2 3
Times: 2:07⅖, 2:02⅗, 2:05. Also started: Kindle, 1-x-4; American Ace, 5-x-5; Hickory Hill, x-5-6; Highland Hanover, 3-x-7; Chilly Brook, x-3-8; Isaac, 2-x-9; Scott Flash, 4-x-10; Screen Test, 6-x-ro; Happy Newport, x-6-ro; Galcaro, 7-ro; Scotch Ripple, x-7-ro; Winged Star, 8-x-ro; Varlo Hanover, x-8-ro; Sonic Song, 9-x-ro; Gobbler Lind, x-9-ro; Bonnie Laure, 10-x-ro; Cornish Kid, x-10-ro.

22 CLASS PACE

Purse $1,000
C. J. (R. Parker) 1 1
Judy Marie (P. Wagner) 2 2
Flight Rite (W. Trees) 5 3
Times: 2:02⅘, 2:03. Also started: Marie Jay, 3-9; Mamie's Star, 4-4; Linda's Nugget, 6-5; Majesty's Son, 10-6; Star Senator, 7-7; Filly Hill, 8-8; Hanner, 9-10; Miss Beckie, 11-dr.

22 CLASS TROT

Purse $1,000
Bye Bye Dillon (D. Taylor) 2 1
Tom Lee (R. McCord) 1 3
Kimberly Scot (R. Wilfong) 4 2
Times: 2:08⅘, 2:07⅖. Also started: Matthew, 3-4; Sunny Sky, 5-7; Miss Hady, 8-5; Johnne C. W., 6-6; Amosson's Cochise, 7-8; M. May Land, 10-9; Etawah's Boy, 9-dr.

Hoosier-Owned Pacer Breaks World Mark

Yonkers, N.Y. (AP) — The world pacing record for 1½ miles was shattered last night by Stephan Smith, a 5-year-old stallion owned by Harold McGinnis of Franklin, Ind.

Gene Sears drove Stephan Smith past the finish line in the $25,000 Single G. Pace at Yonkers Raceway in 3:03⅖, a full second off the mark held by Adios Harry and Widower Creed.

STEPHAN SMITH, paying $15.10, got up in the last stride to beat Apmat by a head for the $12,500 purse. Right Time, the early pace-setter, was third.

Right time, piloted by Johnny Patterson, shot for the lead and then was battled by the 4-5 favorite, O'Brien Hanover, for 1¼ miles. At the final turn, the favorite started to fade, and Apmat, driven by George Sholty, swept into the lead.

Sears managed to get an opening on the turn and closed down the middle of the track, passing Right Time, and then nailing Apmat at the wire.

The first five finishers, including Tar Boy—who missed fourth by a head after trailing back in seventh most of the way — were under the former record.

SPORTS THE INDIANAPOLIS STAR Section 4 Hobbies
SUNDAY MORNING, SEPTEMBER 10, 1961

Buffs Bop Tribe In Playoff Opener

★ ★ ★ ★ ★ ★ ★

Maris Crashes 56th To Close In On Record

Yankees Win 10th Straight With 4 In 9th

New York (AP) — Roger Maris crashed his 56th home run yesterday—four shy of Babe Ruth's major league home run record—and the Yankees, with four runs in the ninth, rallied for their 10th straight victory, 8-7, over Cleveland.

Four other homers were hit, two by each club, but the biggest cheer from the 37,171 fans came in the seventh when Maris slammed a 2-1 pitch deep into the right centerfield bleachers to stay six games ahead of the pace set by Ruth when the Babe hit his 60 homers for the Yankees in 1927.

With Maris' blow, he and teammate Mickey Mantle established a major league record for home runs in a season

Photo On Page 2

by two players on one team. With Mantle's 52—he went homerless today—the M and M boys have slammed 108 home runs—topping by one the total crashed by Ruth and Lou Gehrig, who hit 47, in 1927.

MARIS, WHO also singled, struck out and grounded out twice, and Mantle, who walked twice, struck out twice and singled, have 12 games to "officially" top Ruth's record under the limit of 154 team decisions set by commissioner Ford Frick.

Home Run Derby

By THE ASSOCIATED PRESS

The following table shows how Roger Maris and Mickey Mantle of New York compare with the record pace of Babe Ruth in 1927:

PLAYER	HOMER NO.	TEAM DECISIONS	DATE HIT
Maris	56	142	Sept. 9
*Mantle	52	142	Sept. 8
Ruth	56	148	Sept. 22

*–Three games behind Ruth's pace.

Johnny Blanchard, who hit his 19th home run earlier, struck the big blow in the first of the ninth rally—a ground rule double with the bases loaded that tied the score 7-7.

After Blanchard's drive bounced into the right field stands, Cleveland reliever Frank Funk walked Elston Howard intentionally to reload the bases. Bill Skowron then delivered the winning run on a sacrifice fly to Willie Kirkland in deep right.

Hector Lopez, batting for winning reliever Luis Arroyo, opened the Yanks' ninth with a triple and scored on Bobby Richardson's bunt single.

Dick Stigman replaced starter Mudcat Grant and Tony Kubek walked on a 3-2 count. Funk took over and the runners moved up a base as Maris tapped out on a roller along the first base line and Mantle was intentionally passed, filling the bases.

THAT BROUGT up Blanchard and moments later the Yanks, making a last-month farce of the American League pennant race, had done it again.

Cleveland	ab	h	rbi	New York	ab	h	rbi
Temple,2	2	1	0	Richardson,2	5	1	1
Piersall,cf	4	0	0	Kubek,ss	4	1	0
Francona,lf	4	2	2	Maris,rf	5	2	1
Kirkland,rf	5	2	2	Mantle,cf	3	1	0
Power,1	5	1	0	Blanchard,lf	5	3	3
Romano,c	4	2	1	Howard,c	3	1	1
Held,ss	4	1	1	Skowron,1	4	1	2
DeLaHoz,3	4	2	0	Gardner,3	4	0	0
Grant,p	2	0	0	Sheldon,p	3	0	0
Stigman,p	0	0	0	Arroyo,p	0	0	0
Funk,p	0	0	0	[1]Lopez	1	1	0
Totals	34	11	6	Totals	37	11	8

[1]Tripled for Arroyo in ninth.

Cleveland	010 001 500– 7
New York	010 101 104– 8

E–Grant, Gardner. PO-A–Cleveland 25-7 (1 out when winning run scored), New York 27-8. DP–Sheldon, Richardson and Skowron. Left–Cleveland 8, New York 9. 2B–Skowron, Blanchard. 3B–Power, Lopez. HR–Blanchard, Kirkland, Power, Howard, Held, Maris. S–Grant 2, Temple. SF–Skowron.

	IP	H	R	ER	BB	SO
Grant	8	10	6	6	2	7
Stigman	0	0	1	1	1	0
Funk (L, 11-10)	⅓	1	1	1	2	0
Sheldon	6	7	5	5	3	1
Arroyo (W, 14-3)	3	4	2	1	2	0

(Grant pitched to two batters in ninth; Stigman pitched to one batter in ninth; Sheldon pitched to three baters in seventh).

WP–Stigman.

U–Berry, Umont, Linsolata, Berry. T–2:41. A–37,161.

Ward Takes Syracuse 100-Miler

Syracuse, N.Y. (Spl.) — Rodger Ward of Indianapolis, the day's fastest qualifier, drove his No. 2 Leader Card race car to a 100-mile victory here yesterday on the state fairgrounds dirt track.

The only driver with a qualifying lap under 36 seconds (35.60), Ward finished 13 seconds in front of Shorty Templeman, also of Indianapolis, in the Bill Forbes Racing Team car. Third was Jim Hurtubise of North Tonawanda, N.Y., in the Sterling Plumbing racer.

FIFTEEN OF the 18 starters, competing for the guaranteed purse of $15,000, were running at the finish. The three dropouts were A. J. Foyt of Houston, Tex., this year's Indianapolis 500-Mile Race winner and current national point leader, Don Branson of Champaign, Ill., and Cotton Farmer of Forth Worth, Tex.

A burned piston in the Bowes Seal Fast car forced Foyt out on the seventh lap. He had started from the 12th position. Branson's Autolite Special had engine trouble af-

Turn to Page 2, Column 4

Reds Down Cards, 4-3, In Twelve

Cincinnati (AP) — Frank Robinson, who has been deep in a hitting slump, singled with two on and two out in the 12th inning yesterday to give the National League-leading Reds a 4-3 victory over St. Louis.

Robinson, who had two hits in Friday night's Cincinnati victory over St. Louis, had batted only .185 in eight games before that. His game-winning blow yesterday was his only hit in five official times at bat.

The single came after reliever Al Cicotte had yielded a double to Leo Cardenas and walked Vada Pinson after fanning Bill Henry and Eddie Kasko.

THE PITCHING credit went to reliever Henry (2-1).

The 3 hour and 47 minute game saw Red's manager Fred Hutchinson use every player on his roster, except pitchers. Ken Johnson was the starter.

Johnson might have had the game won in the regulation nine innings except for shoddy Redleg play in the seventh. The Cards, aided by a pop fly double that never even reached the pitching mound, moved into a 3-2 lead.

The Reds tied it in their half on two walks and a sacrifice fly by Kasko.

That weird seventh inning had everything but good baseball on the part of the Reds.

Ken Johnson got the first two cards out before yielding singles to Charlies James and Carl Sawatski. Then pinch hitter Red Schoendienst got the pop fly double.

Except for Sawatski's home run in the fifth, the Cards didn't threaten Johnson seriously until the seventh.

St. Louis	ab	h	rbi	Cincinnati	ab	h	rbi
Flood,cf	6	0	0	Chacon,2	4	0	0
Javier,2	6	2	0	[7]Bell	1	1	0
White,1	5	0	0	Henry,p	1	0	0
Boyer,3	5	1	0	Kasko,ss-2	5	0	1
Musial,lf	4	1	0	Pinson,cf	5	1	0
Olivares,lf	1	1	0	Robinson,rf	5	1	1
James,rf	4	1	0	Freese,3	5	1	0
Sawatski,c	4	2	1	Post,lf	4	1	0
Schaffer,c	1	0	0	Gernert,1	2	0	0
Lillis,ss	2	1	0	[5]Coleman,1	2	1	0
[1]Schoendienst	1	1	1	Edwards,c	2	0	0
Grammas,ss	2	1	0	Zimmerman,c	0	0	0
Simmons,p	2	0	0	[3]Maloney	0	0	0
[2]Cunningham	1	0	0	D.Johnson,c	2	0	0
Gibson,p	0	0	0	K.Johnson,p	2	1	2
Bauta,p	1	1	0	[4]Blasingame	0	0	0
[9]Jackson	0	0	0	Brosnan,p	0	0	0
Cicotte,p	0	0	0	[6]Lynch	1	0	0
				[8]Cardenas,ss	1	1	0
Totals	45	12	2	Totals	42	8	4

[1]Doubled for Lillis in seventh.
[2]Reached first on passed ball for Simmons in seventh.
[3]Ran for Zimmerman in seventh.
[4]Walked for K. Johnson in seventh.
[5]Singled for Gernert in ninth.
[6]Forced runner for Brosnan in ninth.
[7]Singled for Chacon in ninth.
[8]Ran for Lynch in ninth.
[9]Sacrificed for Bauta in 12th.

St. Louis	000 010 200 000– 3
Cincinnati	000 200 100 001– 4

E–None. PO-A–St. Lolis 35-13 (two out when winning run scored), Cincinnati 36-14. DP–Kasko and Gernert; Cardenas, Kasko and Coleman. Left–St. Louis 8, Cincinnati 10. 2B–Boyer, Schoendienst, Cardenas. HR–Sawatski. SB–Flood, Olivares, Pinson. S–Jackson. SF–Kasko.

	IP	H	R	ER	BB	SO
Simmons	6	4	2	2	3	3
*Gibson	0	0	1	1	2	0
Bauta	5	2	0	0	0	3
Cicotte (L, 2-6)	⅔	2	1	1	1	2
K. Johnson	7	7	3	2	0	3
Brosnan	2	2	0	0	0	0
Henry (W, 2-1)	3	3	0	0	1	0

(*Gibson pitched to two batters in seventh).

PB–Zimmerman.

LOOK HERE, UMP — Manager Cot Deal (right) has a few things to say to umpire Dick Gustavo concerning a decision at first base in the seventh inning of last night. Jim Snyder (left), Deal and some others among the Indianapolis Indians protested after Gustavo called Houston's Moe Thacker safe at first base. Hal Bevan, Tribe first baseman, made a tag try on Thacker and the umpire said he missed. The Indians said he was successful. And the result was that Bob Miller, Indianapolis pitcher, was thumbed from the game. (Star photo by Frank H. Fisse)

McBRIDE TO GO ON GRID TOUR

Twenty-seven sports writers from the midwest and New York City, including Cy McBride of The Indianapolis Star, will make the eighth annual Big Ten Skywriters Tour beginning today.

The week-long flying trip will take them to each of the Big Ten schools and to Notre Dame where they will interview head football coaches and watch practice sessions. Then they'll hit the typewriters to provide colorful, up-to-the-minute preview stories on what to expect in 1961 from the nation's top college football league.

The Star's series will begin Tuesday morning with Northwestern and will continue through Sept. 22 with stories on Iowa, Minnesota, Wisconsin, Michigan State, Michigan, Ohio State, Purdue, Illinois, Indiana and Notre Dame.

BEATS OUT BUNT — Len Johnston, speedy Indianapolis outfielder, beats out a bunt in the first inning against Houston last night. Straining for the throw is Buff first baseman Pidge Browne. (Star Photo)

Houston Hops On Rudolph, Wins 9-7 Tilt

By MAX GREENWALD

There was a slambang contest at Victory Field last night with batted and thrown balls going all over the premises.

And the Indianapolis Indians, newly-crowned American Association champions, didn't do so well when the final figures were assembled.

They showed that Houston had won the opener of the first-round playoff, 9-7.

The second tilt of the series will be played this afternoon with Ray Ripplelmeyer (13-8) pitching against Al Lary (15-9). Game time is 2:30 p.m.

Don Pavletich gave the Indiana a short-lived edge in the third inning last night when he connected with one of Ben Johnson's deliveries for a towering home run over the leftfield wall.

The two-out smash by Pavletich, who had 22 homers during the regular season, followed a walk to Joe Gaines.

At that point the Indians led, 2-1, a sensational play by Jim Snyder having prevented Houston from getting more than one in the top of the third.

WITH RUNNERS on third and second and one out, Pidge Browne rifled a low liner. Snyder dived into the dirt for the catch, then tossed to Chico Ruiz for a double play.

Don Rudolph, the Tribe's 18-game winning southpaw, as usual was surrounded by baserunners but more than the usual number came around to score.

The Buffs got to him for 12 of their 14 hits and all their runs before he departed with none out in the seventh.

Before he left, however, he contributed two of the 11 Indianapolis safeties. Both were long doubles to the same spot in left center and one drove in two markers.

His successor was Bob Miller, another lefthander, and his stay was brief although eventful.

His first pitch was batted by Jim McKnight towards short but the ball suddenly became airborne and went over Ruiz' head for a run-scoring single. Jack Waters provided a sacrifice fly and Moe Thacker then sent a hopper to third.

First Baseman Hal Bevan came off the bag for Cliff Cook's peg for the tag try on Thacker. But Umpire Dick Gustavo ruled that Bevan missed and the Indians protested heatedly. Miller's remarks were regarded as too personal by Gustavo and the pitcher was banished.

BOB KROP was the replacement and he retired the side without further disturbance. Greg Jancich pitched the ninth.

Ruiz singled over a run in the sixth and two more in the eighth.

Jim McKnight and Hank Mitchell had three hits apiece for the Buffs. McKnight, who had 24 regular-season homers, drove one over the fence in left for a tally in the fifth.

He also was involved in a dispute with Rudolph in the fourth, the Tribesman claiming McKnight had blocked his path on the baseline.

STARTER Johnson was routed in the fourth and Phil

Turn to Page 3, Column 1

2 More Indian Stars Honored

Further laurels were gained yesterday by members of the American Association championship Indianapolis squad.

Don Rudolph, southpaw pitcher whose 18-9 standing made him the league's top winner, was chosen player of the month.

Earlier yesterday it was announced that Tribe shortstop Chico Ruiz was named rookie of the year.

Rudolph's record in August was 3-1 to give him the honor over Don Wert, Denver third baseman, whose batting in this period put him in position to win the hitting title by a one-point edge.

Third spot went to Cliff Cook, Indianapolis third baseman, who Saturday won most-valuable-player honors.

Ruiz received the vote from three cities to beat out Wert, who obtained two ballots. The other vote went to Don Pavletich, Indianapolis catcher.

CADOU CALLS 'EM

Most Americans More Absorbed In Big Ms Than Big Ks

ROGER'S BATTING GRIP — This is the batting grip of Roger Maris, the New York slugger who hit his 56th home run yesterday and is just four back of Babe Ruth's record. (AP Wirephoto)

By JEP CADOU JR.
Star Sports Editor

Most red-blooded American males currently are even more absorbed in the daily doings of the Mauling M's (Maris and Mantle) than they are in the muscle maneuvers of the Konferring K's (Kennedy and Khrushchev).

Never in the history of sports has the attention of the nation been glued so firmly on one team and one pair of individuals as it is right now on the New York Yankees' home run twins.

In neighborhood gatherings, in clubs, on the golf course, in taverns, at the office — everywhere sportsmen gather — the conversation eventually turns to the chances of Maris and Mantle (or both) to break Babe Ruth's record of 60 home runs in a 155-game season. (That counts one tie game played by the 1927 Yankees).

THE CURRENT swell of public interest makes it a little surprising to realize that Ruth set the record in what must be termed relative obscurity.

There was none of the current speculation and hysteria surrounding Ruth when he blasted his 60 round-trippers 34 years ago. Undoubtedly, the fact that Ruth was breaking a record he already owned had a lot to do with the lack of fanfare that accompanied his 60th swat.

The Bambino had hit 59 in 1921 to surpass the old American League record of 54, which was set in 1920 by one George Herman Ruth. The previous mark was 29, stroked in 1919 by (you guessed it) a fellow named Ruth.

At any rate, the sportswriters and editors of the era certainly took it in their stride when Ruth clubbed his 60th roundtripper off lefthander Tom Zachary of Washington in Yankee Stadium on Sept. 30, 1927.

You had to do considerable hunting to even find the story in the sports pages of The Star published the morning of Oct. 1, 1927.

Banner headline on the first sports page was devoted to a Junior World Series game not even involving Indianapolis and it read "Mud Hens Trounce International League Champs in Series Opener, 5-2."

THERE WAS nothing on the Ruthian feat on the first sports page. The banner headline on the second sports page was devoted to Shortridge's trouncing of Sheridan, 33-0, in the dedicatory game for the Blue Devil's new football field 'way out on West 43rd Street.

Practically "buried" under a four-column picture of said football game was a modest, one-column head proclaiming, "Bambino's Blow Wins for Yanks."

A five-paragraph story and a box score followed. The story described Ruth's epic-making homer as "a bull-mashie shot into the sun seats of the rightfield stands."

The answer to the relative indifference with which Ruth's feat was treated as compared to the current Maris-Mantle hubbub is, of course, that is the very fact that Ruth's record has withstood all assaults for 34 years that has made it such an object of interest.

Easily the best-known record in all of sports, the 60 homers has taken on an aura of absolute invulnerability down through the years as such greats as Jimmy Foxx, Lou Gehrig, Hank Greenberg, Hack Wilson, Ralph Kiner and Willie Mays fired at it and fell back.

A STUDY OF Ruth's record year contains some interesting facts. For instance:

Ruth hit 32 of his homers on the road and only 28 in the friendly confines of Yankee Stadium.

But, all of his last 11

Turn to Page 2, Column 1

THE RUTHIAN WAY — Babe Ruth, baseball's top home run hitter, displays the grip he used to knock 714 roundtrippers during his illustrious career. (AP Wirephoto)

Maris' 58th Bomb Wrecks Tigers In 12th

HERE'S NO. 58—Roger Maris (9) follows through and the ball (arrow) soars on its way. That became home run No. 58 for the New York outfielder in the 12th inning yesterday at Detroit. The drive was swatted off pitcher Terry Fox. Mike Roarke is the catcher and John Stevens the umpire. (AP Wirephoto)

Detroit (AP) — Roger Maris smashed his 58th homer and missed another by a foot yesterday as he remained a game ahead in his assault on Babe Ruth's home run record. The New York Yankee slugger cracked yesterday's in the 12th inning and it produced a 6-4 victory over the Detroit Tigers.

Maris has three games left

Home Run Derby

By THE ASSOCIATED PRESS

Following table shows how Roger Maris and Mickey Mantle of New York compare with the record pace of Babe Ruth in 1927:

Player	Homer No.	Team Dec.	Date Hit	Games Left
Maris	58	151	Sept. 17	11
*Mantle	53	151	Sept. 10	11
Ruth	58	152	Sept. 27	2

*—Nine games behind Ruth's pace.

in which to get two more homers and match the Babe's mark of 60 in the decreed limit of 154 games.

The victory reduced the Yankees' magic number to two for their 11th pennant in 13 years.

Maris' homer came on a 2-1 pitch with Tony Kubek on base. The ball struck the facing of the upper right-centerfield stands, 400 feet away from home plate, and was hit off reliever Terry Fox.

Maris has played 152 games , in his charge at Ruth's record set in 1927. Ruth smacked his 57th homer in the Yanks' 152d game that year and then hit his 58th and 59th in the 153d game.

This year's Yankees have played one tie which counts in Maris' bid at the record. Commissioner Ford Frick has ruled Maris must make his record bid in 154 decisions, although the American League is playing a 162-game schedule for the first time.

Maris received two extra turns at bat yesterday after the Tigers tied the score 4-4 on Bill Skowron's throwing error in the eighth.

The Yankee right fielder, only the fourth player in major league history to hit as many as 58 homers, drove in the fourth New York run with a line drive triple in the seventh. The ball struck near the top of the nine-foot right center-field screen just over Al Kaline's outstretched glove at the 365-foot mark.

In his other times at bat yesterday, Maris walked twice and struck out once, all on 3-2 pitches, and flied 390 feet to center in the 10th.

The Yankees now move to Baltimore's spacious Memorial Stadium where Maris has failed to hit a homer this season. They open a 4-game series tomorrow night with a doubleheader.

In addition to time running out on Maris at Baltimore, the Yankees will need a combination of two victories or two Detroit defeats to capture the pennant there.

Luis Arroyo earned his 15th victory for the Yankees with 4⅔ innings of relief pitching.

Skowron and Cletus Boyer also hit home runs for New York.

POINTS AT PITCHER—Mickey Mantle (7) points toward Jim Bunning, Detroit pitcher. The New York outfielder claimed that Bunning was throwing at him during the third inning of yesterday's game at Detroit. Dick Brown is the catcher. (AP Wirephoto)

New York	ab	h	rbi
Richardson,2	6	2	0
Kubek,ss	5	2	0
Maris,rf	4	2	3
Mantle,cf	4	0	0
Berra,lf	5	0	0
Blanchard,c	5	0	0
[3]Howard,c	1	0	0
Skowron,1	4	2	1
Boyer,3	5	1	2
Stafford,p	3	0	0
Arroyo,p	2	0	0
Totals	44	9	6

Detroit	ab	h	rbi
McAuliffe,ss	6	2	0
Bruton,cf	6	1	0
Kaline,rf	5	2	0
Colavito,lf	5	3	0
Cash,1	5	2	1
Boros,3	1	0	1
Brown,c	3	0	0
[1]Maxwell	1	1	0
Roarke,c	1	0	0
[4]Wertz	1	0	0
Wood,2	6	1	1
Bunning,p	3	0	0
[2]Morton	1	0	0
Fox,p	1	0	0
Aguirre,p	0	0	0
Regan,p	0	0	0
[5]Osborne	1	0	0
Totals	46	12	3

[1]Doubled for Brown in eighth.
[2]Struck out for Bunning in eighth.
[3]Flied out for Blanchard in 12th.
[4]Flied out for Roarke in 12th.
[5]Hit into force play for Regan in 12th.

New York .... 010 200 100 002— 6
Detroit .... 101 000 020 000— 4

E—Mantle, Skowron. PO-A—New York 36-14, Detroit 36-4. DP—Kubek, Richardson and Skowron; Richardson, Kubek and Skowron. Left—New York 9, Detroit 14. 2B—Maxwell. 3B—Maris. HR—Skowron, Boyer, Maris.

	IP	H	R	ER	BB	SO
Stafford	7⅓	10	4	3	5	2
Arroyo (W, 15-4)	4⅔	2	0	0	3	6
Bunning	8	5	4	4	4	9
Fox (L, 4-2)	3⅔	4	2	2	2	1
*Aguirre	0	0	0	0	0	0
Regan	⅓	0	0	0	0	0

*—Finished walking one batter for Fox in 12th. HBP—By Bunning (Skowron). U—Stevens, Napp, Soar, Chylak. T—3:46. A—44,219.

Tarkenton-Led Vikings Deal Bears 37-13 Loss

Bloomington, Minn. (UPI)—The Minnesota Vikings, paced by rookie quarterback Fran Tarkenton, yesterday scored a major upset in their first National Football League contest by trouncing the Chicago Bears, 37-13.

Tarkenton put on one of the greatest quarterback debuts in pro football history to thrill 32,326 fans at the NFL inaugural.

The former University of Georgia star accounted for five touchdowns — throwing for four and scoring the fifth on a three-yard run.

The Bears, who made easy work of the Vikings during the exhibition season, weren't in the game in the last half.

Minnesota started the day's scoring in the first quarter when a drive was stymied on the Chicago four-yard line. Rookie Mike Mercer booted a field goal to give the Vikings a lead they never surrendered.

TARKENTON THREW touchdown passes to Bob Schnelker, Jerry Reichow, Hugh McElhenny and Dave Middleton.

Schnelker grabbed a 14-yard pass and scored with 1:47 gone in the second quarter. Mercer kicked his first of four conversions to cap a 31-yard drive.

Chicago bounced back to score with Rick Casares plunging over from the three-yard line. The Bears drive covered 66 yards in 13 plays.

But the Vikings came back in the second half to score four touchdowns while completely subduing the Bears.

The Vikings gained a net total of 351 yards—272 yards passing. Tarkenton accounted for 250 yards of the aerial gain by hitting 17 of 23 passes. Minnesota held the Bears to 146 yards through the air and intercepted four Chicago passes.

Chicago .... 0 6 0 7—13
Minnesota .... 3 7 14 13—37

Minn—Mercer 12 field goal.
Minn—Schnelker 14 pass from Tarkenton (Mercer kick).
Chi—Casares 3 run.
Minn—Reichow 29 pass from Tarkenton (Mercer kick).
Minn—McElhenny 3 pass from Tarkenton (Mercer kick).
Minn—Tarkenton 3 run (Mercer kick).
Minn—Middleton 2 pass from Tarkenton (kick blocked).
Chi — Gallimore 10 pass from Wade (Leclerc kick).
Attendance: 32,326.

Conerly Humiliated As Giants Are Upset

New York (UPI)—St. Louis humiliated veteran quarterback Charlie Conerly with a red-dogging defense yesterday and capitalized on mistakes by the Giants to score a 21-10 National Football League upset.

A season-opening crowd of 58,059 watched St. Louis move ahead in the first half when defensive back Willie West recovered a New York fumble in the end zone. The Giants set up two last period St. Louis scores on a feeble field goal try by Pat Summerall and a wayward pass.

Mal Hammack scored a fourth quarter St. Louis touchdown with a 28-yard sweep around right end. Sam Etcheverry, the Canadian League transfer making his NFL debut, passed five yards to Frank Mestnik for the final score.

The huge crowd which had come to watch the Giants make the earliest home start in their history under new coach Al Sherman, directed boos at Conerly in the final quarter.

Conerly, starting his 14th NFL season at the age of 40, spent most of the afternoon on his back. He was rushed off his feet by the St. Louis defense and completed only nine of 21 passing attempts for 75 yards.

New York .... 0 3 7 0—10
St. Louis .... 0 7 0 14—21

StL—West recovered fumble in end zone (Perry kick).
NY—FG Summerall 44.
NY—Hayes recovered blocked punt in end zone (Summerall kick).
StL—Hammack 28 run (Perry kick).
StL—Mestnik 5 pass from Etcheverry (Perry kick).
Attendance—58,059.

Lions Win, Led By Pietrosante

Milwaukee (UP) — The Detroit Lions scored two first-half touchdowns by Nick Pietrosante and then turned on the defense yesterday to beat the defending Western Division champion Green Bay Packers, 17-13, before a record crowd of 44,307.

Two scoring threats by the Packers were turned back in the second half, one on the one-yard line when Green Bay elected to go for a touchdown rather than a field goal on fourth down. The second came on Detroit's 21 with less than two minutes left when Dick Lane intercepted a Bart Starr pass inside the 10-yard line.

Detroit .... 7 7 0 3—17
Green Bay .... 7 3 0 3—13

GB—Taylor, 1 run (Hornung kicked).
Detroit — Pietrosante, 1 run (Martin kick).
Detroit—Pietrosante 15 pass from Morrall (Martin kick).
GB—Hornung 15 field goal.
GB—Hornung 26 field goal.
Detroit—Martin 44 field goal.

Cowboys Win In Last Second

Dallas, Tex. (AP)—Allen Green, the rookie from Mississippi, kicked a field goal from the 27-yard line with one second left yesterday as the Dallas Cowboys beat the Pittsburgh Steelers 27-24 to score their first National Football League victory.

Dallas tallied twice in the final 56 seconds to get the triumph to the delight of a crowd of 23,500 in the Cotton Bowl.

Eddie LeBaron passed Dallas on two magnificent drives to gain the decision. First he engineered a 75-yard surge climaxed with a 17-yard pass to Dick Bielski for a touchdown. He completed five passes for all the yardage in this surge.

Pittsburgh .... 0 14 0 10—24
Dallas .... 7 3 7 10—27

Dal—Clarke 44 pass from Meredith (Green kick).
Pitt—Johnson 1 run (Layne kick).
Pitt—Dial 44 pass from Layne (Layne kick).
Dal—FG Green 15.
Dal—Howton 45 pass from Lebaron (Green kick).
Pitt—FG Michaels 12.
Pitt — Sample 39 pass interception (Layne kick).
Dal — Bielski 17 pass from Lebaron (Green kick).
Dal—FG Green 17.
Attendance—23,500.

Pennsylvania Prep Grid Player Is Dead

Spangler, Pa. (UPI)—Jimmy Salley, 17, a member of the Penns Manor High School football team, died yesterday in a hospital of an intercranial hemorrhage.

Authorities said the youth may have received the injury in a game with Blairsville Saturday. Salley was taken to the hospital after playing part of the game.

Frisco Downs Redskins, 35-3

San Francisco (AP) — With John Brodie passing for four touchdowns, the San Francisco 49ers trounced the young Washington Redskins 35-3 in their National Football League opener yesterday before 43,142 fans.

Brodie, puncturing the Redskin secondary almost at will, threw a pair of touchdown passes for 25 and 4 yards to Monte Stickles, a 34-yarder to J. D. Smith, and a 10-yard scoring heave to Clyde Connor.

Washington .... 3 0 0 0—3
San Francisco .... 7 14 14 0—35

SF — Stickles 25 pass from Brodie (Davis kick).
Wash—FG Aveni 29.
SF—Stickles 4 pass from Brodie (Davis kick).
SF—Smith 34 pass from Brodie (Davis kick).
SF — Connor 10 pass from Brodie (Davis kick).
SF—Smith 3 run (Davis kick).
Attendance: 43,142.

Pro Football

NATIONAL FOOTBALL

Eastern Division

	W	L	T	PCT.
Philadelphia	1	0	0	1.000
St. Louis	1	0	0	1.000
Dallas	1	0	0	1.000
Cleveland	0	1	0	.000
New York	0	1	0	.000
Pittsburgh	0	1	0	.000
Washington	0	1	0	.000

Western Division

	W	L	T	PCT.
Baltimore	1	0	0	1.000
Detroit	1	0	0	1.000
Minnesota	1	0	0	1.000
San Francisco	1	0	0	1.000
Los Angeles	0	1	0	.000
Green Bay	0	1	0	.000
Chicago	0	1	0	.000

Results Yesterday

Philadelphia 27, Cleveland 20
Baltimore 27, Los Angeles 24
St. Louis 21, New York 10
Detroit 17, Green Bay 13
Minnesota 37, Chicago 13
Dallas 27, Pittsburgh 24
San Francisco 35, Washington 3.

AMERICAN LEAGUE

Eastern Division

	W	L	PCT.
Houston	1	0	1.000
New York	1	1	.000
Buffalo	1	1	.500
Boston	1	1	.500

Western Divisions

	W	L	PCT.
San Diego	2	0	1.000
Denver	1	1	.500
Dallas	0	1	.000
Oakland	0	2	.000

Results Yesterday

San Diego 44, Oakland 0
Buffalo 41, New York 31
(Only games scheduled)

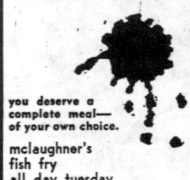

The Standings

NATIONAL LEAGUE

	W	L	Pct.	G.B.
Cincinnati	88	57	.607	..
Los Angeles	83	59	.585	3½
San Francisco	78	64	.549	8½
Milwaukee	76	67	.531	11
St. Louis	76	67	.531	11
Pittsburgh	68	73	.482	18
Chicago	59	85	.410	28½
Philadelphia	44	100	.306	43½

AMERICAN LEAGUE

	W	L	Pct.	G.B.
New York	102	49	.675	....
Detroit	91	59	.607	10½
Baltimore	88	63	.583	14
Chicago	82	70	.539	20½
Cleveland	73	77	.487	28½
Boston	73	79	.480	29½
Minnesota	66	83	.443	35
Los Angeles	66	84	.440	35½
Washington	56	94	.373	45½
Kansas City	55	94	.369	46

Yesterday's Results

AMERICAN ASSOCIATION PLAYOFF

Louisville 2, Houston 0 (Louisville leads best-of-seven final series 2-0).

INTERNATIONAL LEAGUE PLAYOFF

Rochester 1, Columbus 0 (Rochester wins best-of-seven semifinal 4-1).

AMERICAN LEAGUE

New York 6, Detroit 4 (12 innings).
Minnesota 5-5, Cleveland 0-3.
Chicago 8-4, Los Angeles 1-3 (2d game 10 innings).
Kansas City 3, Washington 2.
Boston 1, Baltimore 0.

NATIONAL LEAGUE

Philadelphia 4, Cincinnati 0.
San Francisco 8, Chicago 2.
St. Louis 3, Pittsburgh 0.
Los Angeles 4, Milwaukee 3.

Today's Schedule

AMERICAN ASSOCIATION PLAYOFF

Houston at Louisville.

NATIONAL LEAGUE

St. Louis at Pittsburgh (Night)—Gibson (11-11) vs. Foss (0-0).
Chicago at Los Angeles (Night)—Cardwell (13-12) vs. Golden (1-1) or Ortega (0-0).
Milwaukee at San Francisco (Night)—Hendley (5-5) vs. Duffalo (4-0).
Only games scheduled.

AMERICAN LEAGUE

No games scheduled.

Marr Wins At Seattle In Playoff

Seattle (AP) — Dave Marr of Sun City, Ariz., sank a three-foot birdie putt at the first playoff hole to break a three-way tie yesterday and win the $25,000 Greater Seattle $25,000 Open golf tournament.

Marr went into the sudden-death playoff deadlocked at 265 — 15 strokes under par — with Bob Rosburg of Portland, Ore., and Jacky Cupit of Longview, Tex.

Marr finished with a final round of 63, best 18-hole score of the tournament, seven under par for the 6,328-yard Broadmoor course. Rosburg had a 64, Cupit a 66.

With an excellent chance to make it a four-way deadlock, Gary Player missed a 15-foot birdie putt on the final hole by an inch. Player is the leading money winner of the professional golf tour.

Dave Marr	67-69-66-63—265	$3,500 (won playoff)
Jacky Cupit	66-69-64-66—265	2,050
Bob Rosburg	68-65-68-64—265	2,050
Gary Player	69-64-66-67—266	1,500
Gay Brewer Jr.	69-65-64-69—267	1,300
Doug Sanders	67-69-65-67—268	1,200
Phil Rodgers	68-67-65-69—269	1,050
Jay Herbert	68-65-71-65—269	1,050
Ken Venturi	70-65-65-70—270	925
Bill Collins	64-69-68-69—270	925
Stan Leonard	68-69-65-70—272	775
Jerry Barber	69-69-67-71—272	775
Howie Johnson	71-66-69-66—272	775
Al Balding	66-73-66-67—272	775
Jack Fleck	68-68-68-69—272	610
Marty Furgol	68-68-70-68—273	610
Al Geiberger	70-66-69-68—273	610
Tony Lema	67-71-64-72—274	490
Rod Funseth	69-71-66-68—274	490
Charles Sifford	67-68-69-71—275	390
Gordon Jones	67-70-68-71—275	390
Bob McCallister	71-66-69-68—274	490
Gene Cotchonis	70-68-65-73—276	252
Dave Hill	66-69-67-74—276	252
Jimmy Clark	73-70-65-68—276	252
Bruce Crampton	69-69-72-66—276	252
Art Wall Jr.	72-72-68-64—276	252
E. J. Harrison	70-69-69-69—277	160
Chi Chi Rodriguez	70-70-69-69—278	145
Harry Umbinetti	72-68-69-69—278	145

Amateur Baseball

Lefthander Jerry Seay of the Fall Creek Athletics fanned 22 yesterday beating the First Presbyterian Braves, 8-7, in a 11-inning opener of a doubleheader.

First Game

Braves .... 021 021 000 01— 7 8 3
Fall Creek A's .. 101 310 000 02— 8 10 7

Gaines, Sharp (6) and Haynes; Seay and Simmons, Duke (3).
Home Run—Fall Creek, Ewing.

Second Game

Braves .... 100 002 100— 4 7 1
Fall Creek A's .... 000 000 020— 2 4 3

Dobbs and Haynes; Simmons, Duke (8) and Wendling.

Pinch Rap Helps White Sox Win Pair From L.A.

Chicago (AP) — Billy Goodman's run-scoring pinch single in the 10th inning enabled the White Sox to sweep a doubleheader from Los Angeles yesterday, 8-1 and 4-3.

Goodman's game-winning blow followed a one-out double by Minnie Minoso and an intentional walk to Nellie Fox. Reliever Don Larsen was credited with his eighth victory against one loss.

Al Smith's grand slam homer and the five-hit pitching of Frank Baumann (10-12) were highlights of Chicago's first-game triumph.

FIRST GAME

Los Angeles	ab	h	rbi
Pearson,rf	3	0	0
Duren,p	0	0	0
[3]Averill	1	0	0
Morgan,p	0	0	0
Koppe,ss-2	4	0	0
L.Thomas,1-lf	4	1	0
Hunt,lf-rf	3	1	0
G.Thomas,cf	3	2	1
Rodgers,c	4	0	0
Satriano,3	4	0	0
Bridges,2	1	1	0
Fregosi,ss	1	0	0
Chance,p	0	0	0
[1]Yost	1	0	0
James,p	0	0	0
Fowler,p	0	0	0
[2]Bilko,1	1	0	0
Totals	30	5	1

Chicago	ab	h	rbi
Aparicio,ss	2	1	0
Robinson,rf	5	3	2
Minoso,lf	4	0	1
Sievers,1	3	0	0
Martin,1	0	0	0
Smith,3	4	1	4
Landis,cf	3	0	0
Fox,2	3	2	0
Lollar,c	4	2	0
Baumann,p	4	2	1
Totals	32	11	8

[1]Grounded into double play for Chance in third.
[2]Walked for Fowler in fifth.
[3]Flied out for Duren in eighth.

Los Angeles .... 000 010 000— 1
Chicago .... 040 400 00x— 8

E—Hunt. PO-A—Los Angeles 24-7, Chicago 27-13. DP—Minoso and Sievers; Aparicio, Fox and Sievers; Koppe and L. Thomas. Left—Los Angeles 6, Chicago 7. 2B—G. Thomas, L. Thomas. HR—Smith. SB—Aparicio 2, Landis. SF—Minoso.

	IP	H	R	ER	BB	SO
Chance (L, 0-2)	2	5	4	4	2	1
James	1⅔	3	4	4	2	0
Fowler	⅓	0	0	0	1	0
Duren	3	2	0	0	0	4
Morgan	1	1	0	0	0	0
Baumann (W, 10-11)	9	5	1	1	4	6

HBP—By James (Sievers). PB—Rodgers. U—Drummond, Paparella, Carrigan and Runge. T—2:22.

SECOND GAME

Los Angeles	ab	h	rbi
Yost,3	5	2	0
Koppe,ss	4	0	0
L.Thomas,lf-1	4	1	0
G.Thomas,cf	2	1	3
Hunt,rf-lf	4	1	0
Bilko,1	2	0	0
[1]Pearson,rf	1	0	0
Sadowski,c	3	1	0
[5]Rodgers,c	1	1	0
Bridges,2	3	1	0
[6]Wagner	1	0	0
Grba,p	0	0	0
Moeller,p	2	0	0
Fowler,p	0	0	0
[2]Averill	0	0	0
[3]Ardell	0	0	0
Morgan,p	0	0	0
Donohue,p	0	0	0
Satriano,2	1	0	0
Totals	33	8	3

Chicago	ab	h	rbi
Aparicio,ss	4	1	0
Hershbergr,rf	4	0	0
Landis,cf	5	4	1
Smith,3	5	0	0
Sievers,1	5	1	1
Minoso,lf	5	3	0
Esposito,2	2	0	0
[4]Fox,2	1	0	0
Carreon,c	4	0	1
[8]Goodman	1	1	1
Pierce,p	3	0	0
Hacker,p	0	0	0
Lown,p	0	0	0
[7]Robinson	1	1	0
Larsen,p	0	0	0
Totals	40	11	4

[1]Ran for Bilko in seventh.
[2]Walked for Fowler in eighth.
[3]Ran for Averill in eighth.
[4]Popped out for Esposito in eighth.
[5]Singled for Sadowski in ninth.
[6]Lined into double play for Bridges in ninth.
[7]Singled for Lown in ninth.
[8]Singled for Carreon in 10th.

Los Angeles .... 100 000 020 0— 3
Chicago .... 000 200 010 1— 4

E—Koppe 2. PO-A—Los Angeles 28-10, Chicago 30-8. DP—Carreon and Esposito; Sadowski and Bridges; Sievers unassisted. Left—Los Angeles 5, Chicago 12. 2B—Sadowski, Yost, Hunt, Sievers, Minoso. 3B—Minoso. HR—Landis. SB—Aparicio. S—Koppe. SF—G. Thomas.

	IP	H	R	ER	BB	SO
Moeller	5	5	2	1	2	6
Fowler	1	0	0	0	1	0
Morgan	⅔	2	1	1	0	0
Donohue	⅓	0	0	0	0	0
Grba (L, 10-12)	1⅔	3	1	1	1	2
Pierce	7⅔	6	3	1	1	7
Hacker	1	1	0	0	0	1
Lown	1	0	0	0	0	0
Larsen (W, 8-1)	1	1	0	0	0	1

WP—Moeller.
U—Paparella, Carrigan, Runge and Drummond. T—2:56. A—13,098.

Scoreboard Remains Faithful To Altobelli

Cleveland (AP)—The Cleveland Indians installed an exploding scoreboard earlier this season. It goes off, complete with trumpet fanfare and spouting flames, every time an Indian hits a home run, but remains silent when the opposition socks one.

In the first game of a doubleheader yesterday Minnesota outfielder Joe Altobelli hit a homer. The scoreboard went off.

Embarrassed Tribe officials joshingly explained that Altobelli used to play for the Indians.

Amateur Boxing

The matchmaking committee for the Indiana Fathers and Sons Club television boxing show will meet at Mayer Chapel at 7 p.m. tonight. Coaches are invited.

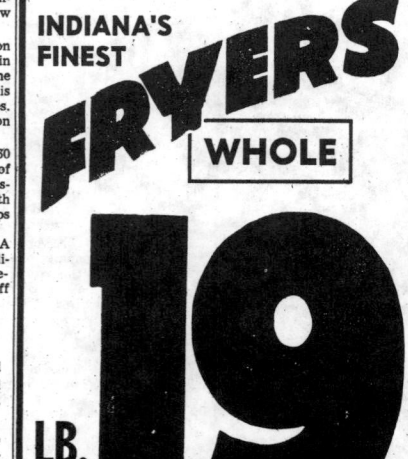

Strong Pitching Gives Twins 2

Cleveland (AP)—The Minnesota Twins got strong pitching performances from Camilo Pascual, Al Schroll and Ray Moore yesterday and swept a doubleheader from Cleveland 5-0 and 5-3.

FIRST GAME

Minnesota	ab	h	rbi
Green,cf-lf	5	2	0
Martin,2	4	2	0
Killebrew,1	3	0	0
Altobelli,lf	4	2	3
Valdivielso,3	0	0	0
Battey,c	4	1	0
Allison,rf	3	1	0
Tuttle,3-cf	4	1	2
Versalles,ss	4	1	0
Pascual,p	3	0	0
Totals	34	10	5

Cleveland	ab	h	rbi
Cline,cf	4	1	0
Francona,lf	3	1	0
Power,2	4	1	0
Luplow,rf	4	0	0
Held,ss	4	0	0
Jones,1	4	1	0
Kubiszyn,3	4	3	0
Thomas,c	4	1	0
Perry,p	2	0	0
Allen,p	0	0	0
[1]Bond	1	0	0
Schaffrnoth,p	0	0	0
Totals	34	8	0

[1]Called out on strikes for Allen in seventh.

Minnesota .... 010 004 000— 5
Cleveland .... 000 000 000— 0

E—None. PO-A—Minnesota 27-12, Cleveland 27-14. DP—Thomas and Power; Perry, Power and Jones; Killebrew, Versalles and Killebrew. Left—Minnesota 5, Cleveland 8. 2B—Power, Martin, Green. HR—Altobelli. SB—Cline. S—Pascual.

	IP	H	R	ER	BB	SO
Pascual (W, 14-15)	9	8	0	0	1	9
Perry (L, 10-15)	5⅔	9	5	5	1	6
Allen	1⅓	0	0	0	0	2
Schaffernoth	2	1	0	0	1	1

WP—Pascual. PB—Thomas.
U—Smith, Schwarts, McKinley and Rice. T—2:37.

SECOND GAME

Minnesota	ab	h	rbi
Green,cf	4	0	0
Martin,2	5	1	0
Killibrew,1	2	0	0
Altobelli,lf	4	1	1
Allison,rf	2	1	0
Naragon,c	4	2	0
Tuttle,3	3	0	1
Valdivielso,ss	4	1	1
Schroll,p	3	0	0
Moore,p	1	0	0
Total	32	6	3

Cleveland	ab	h	rbi
Cline,cf	5	0	0
Francona,lf	2	1	0
Power,2	4	1	0
Romano,c	4	1	0
Held,ss	3	2	1
Luplow,rf	3	0	0
[2]Kirkland,rf	0	0	0
Kubiszyn,3	4	0	0
Jones,1	4	1	2
Grant,p	2	0	0
[1]Dillard	1	0	0
Dalley,p	0	0	0
[3]Bond	1	0	0
Totals	3	6	3

[1]Struck out for Grant in seventh.
[2]Walked for Luplow in eighth.
[3]Struck out for Dalley in ninth.

Minnesota .... 020 001 200—5
Cleveland .... 000 000 210—3

E—Held, Power, Valdivielso. PO-A—Minnesota 27-13, Cleveland 27-8. DP—Valdivielso, Martin and Killibrew; Held, Power and Jones. Left—Minnesota 6, Cleveland 7. 2B—Held.

	IP	H	R	ER	BB	SO
Schroll (W,3-3)	7⅔	6	3	1	3	4
Moore	1⅓	0	0	0	1	2
Grant (L, 14-9)	7	5	5	4	6	5
Dalley	2	1	0	0	0	0

WP—Grant. PB—Romano.
U—Schwarts, McKinley, Rice, Smith. T—2:35. A—6,113.

Pascual racked up his seventh shutout of the season in the opener, scattering eight hits and fanning nine to run his strikeout total to 207.

It was Pascual's 14th victory against 15 losses, but only his third lifetime triumph against the Indians, who have beaten him 14 times in his eight years in the majors. Pascual's three victories over Cleveland have been shutouts.

Schroll and Moore topped Jim Grant (14-9) in the nightcap.

PGA Swingers Tee Off Today

South Bend, Ind. (AP)—Indiana's professional golfers tested the foot-wetting and ball-losing possibilities of the lake sprinkled South Bend Country Club course yesterday in a pro-member preliminary to the annual state PGA tourney.

Eighteen holers of qualifications today will determine pairings for the 64-man championship flight tomorrow through Friday.

Don Street of Muncie won the 1960 Indiana PGA title in a final match with Wayne Timberman of Indianapolis which went the full 36 holes. Street finished eagle-par on the last two.

Entrants also included 1960 semifinalists Paul Gross of Indianapolis and Don Fischesser of Evansville, along with most of the state PGA champs since World War II.

The annual Indiana PGA meeting will precede the qualifying round and the first threesome probably won't tee off until about noon.

Shepherd Critical

Race driver A. J. Shepherd remained in very critical condition last night in Methodist Hospital.

Injured Saturday while qualifying for the Hoosier Hundred, it was learned that Shepherd is suffering from various fractures and dislocations and severe head injuries.

Branson Takes Salem Feature

Salem, Ind. (Spl.) — Don Branson and Bud Tingelstad, each driving a Leader Card Offy, set new midget auto racing records here yesterday.

Branson won the 30-lap feature in record-breaking time of 10 minutes, 50.27 seconds, 11 seconds better than the old mark. Tinklestad was fastest qualifier with a 19.51 lap, which was a new record.

Branson and Tingelstad ran one-two in the feature.

Behind them were: 3, Chuck Rodee; 4, Bob McLean; 5, Ronnie Duman; 6, Leroy Warriner; 7, Tommy Copp, 8, Allen Crowe; 9, Bob Wente; 10, Jimmy Davies; 11, Chuck Marshall; 12, Jim Hemmings; 13, Gene Hartley; 14, Hugh Randall.

Duman, Branson, Warriner and Rodee won heat events and Hemmings took the 12-lap semifinal. Attendance was 3,500 and the payoff was $3,050.

West Is 27-25 Winner In CYO Grid Jamboree

The West scored four times in the first half and then survived a three-touchdown barrage in the second half by the East to score a 27-25 decision in the 10th annual Catholic Youth Organization Cadet Football Jamboree yesterday at CYO Stadium.

A crowd of 7,500 watched 32 Cadet teams play a quarter each. The teams are made up of seventh and eighth graders.

The West held a 27-6 half-time lead.

Summary:

FIRST HALF

West—John Radez (Holy Trinity) 1 run (PAT failed).
West—Chuck Thompson (Holy Trinity) 25 run (PAT by Joe Szakel).
West—Stuart Countryman (Immaculate Heart of Mary) 15 run (PAT by Countryman).
East—Ron Milligan (St. Ann) 6 run (PAT failed).
West—Bob Livingston (St. Anthony) 36 pass from Mike Casey (PAT failed).

SECOND HALF

East—John Mullin (St. Joan of Arc) 20 run (PAT by Kevin Mahern).
East—Steve Budreau (Little Flower) 2 run (PAT failed).
East—Tom Clark (St. Mark) 11 run (PAT failed).

Softball Notes

Douglas Park Tourney — Semifinals: Lee's Garage 9, Hendricks Garage 1; Wagner's Dugout 3, East Side Flashes 0. Consolation: Hendricks 2, E.S. Flashes 1. Championship: Wagner's Dugout 6, Lee's Garage 3. Ray Washington, Lee's Garage, won sportsmanship award.

Rog: Big City Boy Now

'Miracle' Maker Maris

By KEN SMITH

Roger Maris, America's new five-star sports idol with 61 homers to his credit, is a grown-up country boy raised in the Dakota hills and plains, and now a Missourian living on the Kansas border, where there is plenty of room.

Usually, as soon as he can get away from the big cities where he climbed to Babe Ruth's home-run pinnacle—most exciting feat since Roger Bannister broke the four-minute mile—this outdoor man is off for the deer and antelope country, the barbecue pits, horses, wheat, cattle, streams and forests.

This is the Mirror's souvenir edition to mark Roger Maris' historic 61st homer that topped Babe Ruth. Save it and send extra copies to your friends.

Roger Maris . . . the man who finally broke Ruth's mark . . . in overtime.

Giving that up to go into the hero business will be quite a switch for Roger.

MARIS CAUGHT up to Babe by training to keep his shirt on throughout slumps that became annual. Left at the post without a homer until the third week, this season and limited to three in the first month of play, Maris stuck to his calm, rhythmic stroke, instead of trying to fight the ball with overanxious swipes.

Maris' motion will become the rage now. Along the Ruth trail, onlookers' imaginations sometimes get out of line and the true Maris story involves straightening out certain myths. Such as the notion that Maris is a dark horse, a shot-in-the-dark-Cinderella Ruth challenger. As a matter of fact, a directive from the Yankees' intelligence bureau six years ago cautioned operatives to keep steady track of the strong 21year-old Cleveland-owned outfielder, at Reading, Pa., in the Eastern League.

"He seems to be built for the Stadium," said George Weiss, the J. Edgar Hoover of the Yankees at that time. "A left-handed pull hitter."

Spotted by Indians' bird dog, Frank Fahey, in 1953, his education placed in the care of Cyril C. (Cy) Slapnicka, discoverer of Bob Feller, Maris was prepared thoroughly to make the eventual attempt to break the Ruth barrier. At 18, his training was supervised by Jack O'Connor, general manager of the Fargo-Morehead, S. D., Northern League team. Hank Greenberg, 58 HR ace and former Cleveland general manager, gave the young man the personal attention he used to give 54-striped Ralph Kiner and can take a bow as Maris' original producer. Jo Jo White, his manager at Keokuk, Ia., and Reading, taught him to pull.

Unfortunately for the Indians, they weren't sufficiently patient. Frank Lane became GM and to build his fine team, traded Maris with Preston Ward to KC in 1958 in a deal that brought Vic Power and Woody Held to Cleveland. This, of course, brought him nearer New York. Sounded out for Norm Siebern by the late KC owner, Arnold Johnson, after Roger went 65-for-3 in the last half of the 1958 season, Weiss allowed he did not crave Maris that avidly. But when Pittsburgh almost landed him for Don Hoak, Bill Virdon and a pitcher, in the Winter of 1959, Weiss wept as he parted with Siebern and got the man he had eyed since 1955.

They have accused Maris of being surly. Well, if Maris didn't give a tart retort to some of the approaches made to him since becoming a national figure he would be a hypocrite, a description that would no more fit him than the title city slicker. He's surly, all right—to the surly or silly—like strangers who interrupt when he's eating; or, trying to use him to make a buck, have the effrontery to suggest he is jealous of Mickey Mantle or vice versa; or those who want to know why he's surly. Those in the baseball trade are glad he speaks up. Nobody who approaches him as a hard-working ball player finds him not affable. As a matter of fact, Maris likes to talk, on busses, around the park. He is never alone. If he goes 4 for 0 he doesn't smile and sign autographs. If the bus hits a rut and knocks him out of his seat, he cusses. He's surly all right!

MARIS' FATHER, Rudie, an Atchison, Topeka and Santa Fe railroad supervisor and mother, Connie, who looks like Roger's sister, moved from his Hibbing, Minn., birthplace to Fargo, N. D., when he was a toddler and the boy was brought up in rough-and-ready country. His older brother Rudie, Jr., now a RR man, was struck by polio when he was 17. Roger played Little League ball, semi-pro ball and football (with Ken Hunt of the Angels). Bud Wilkinson tried to get him to play football at Oklahoma U. but he signed with the Indians for $15,000. He banged around in the minors and in his early career voiced objection at front office cracks by Lane and disgruntlement at Manager Bob Bragan's badgering. They developed the notion that he wasn't hustling. Long since, it was

Continued on Page S4

Nobody Could Equal Babe!

By GEORGE GIRSCH

Roger Maris—a mere mortal—has hit 61 home runs in his 154 game-plus schedule, to "top" Babe Ruth. But few will dare put Maris in the same class with the immortal Sultan of Swat as a slugger.

And that's no slap at Maris, a mighty man in his own right. After all, there was only one Babe Ruth.

WASN'T HE MARIS, Mickey Mantle and Whitey Ford all rolled into one? Wasn't he Sir Lancelot riding down Broadway wearing a camel's hair coat with a big cigar stuck in his mouth? Didn't he pick baseball up by its bootstraps when it was rocked to the very foundation by the Black Sox Scandal?

Sure, even though the Bambino hit 714 homers during his 22-year major league career, had a lifetime average of .342, and was just about the best southpaw pitcher of his day, he had his faults — like striking out more than anybody else in history; never hitting four homers in a game; and never pitching a no-hit game. Real bad faults.

Ruth had a peculiar build, like a tub on two sticks. He was six feet tall, with most of his 220 pounds seemingly settled in his stomach, chest and shoulders. A wide, flat nose dominated his friendly moon face.

Color just oozed from every pore. People used to say they'd rather see him strike out with that tremendous flourish of his, than see others knock the ball out of the park. And when he popped up, the ball seemed to stay up for eons as infielders staggered around under it.

And who will ever forget those mincing steps as he ran out a homer? Or that booming voice reduced to a whisper by the dread disease that was to claim his life, as he spoke to a hushed Yankee Stadium crowd on "Babe Ruth Day" in April, 1947?

To most players then and now, baseball was strictly business. To the Babe it was fun—just like life was. He was a big flamboyant boisterous kid who enjoyed being the center of attraction. The people loved him and he loved them—especially the kids. He was the idol of every American child—and his dad.

Who else but the Babe could figure in the following little tale:

One afternoon in a late-season contest between the Yankees and Tigers during the 1920s, Fred Haney, curent Los Angeles Angels' general manager, but then a light-hitting third baseman for Detroit, socked a homer. As Haney went to his position he en-

Continued on Page S4

Game-By-Game Log of '60' HR Heroes

ROGER MARIS

Homer No.	Game Played	Date	Opp. Pitcher and Club	Where Made
		April		
1	10	26	Foytack, Detroit	Detroit
		May		
2	16	3	Ramos, Minnesota	Minnesota
3	19	6	Grba, Los Angeles	Los Angeles
4	28	17	Burnside, Wash.	New York
5	29	19	Perry, Cleveland	Cleveland
6	30	20	Bell, Cleveland	Cleveland
7	31	21	Estrada, Baltimore	New York
8	34	24	Conley, Boston	New York
9	37	28	McLish, Chicago	New York
10	39	30	Conley, Boston	Boston
11	39	30	Fornieles, Boston	Boston
12	40	31	Muffett, Boston	Boston
		June		
13	42	2	McLish, Chicago	Chicago
14	43	3	Shaw, Chicago	Chicago
15	44	4	Kemmerer, Chicago	Chicago
16	47	6	Palmquist, Minn.	New York
17	48	7	Ramos, Minnesota	New York
18	51	9	Herbert, K. C.	New York
19	54	11	Grba, Los Angeles	New York
20	54	11	James, Los Angeles	NewYork
21	56	13	Perry, Cleveland	Cleveland
22	57	14	Bell, Cleveland	Cleveland
23	60	17	Mossi, Detroit	Detroit
24	61	18	Casale, Detroit	Detroit
25	62	19	Archer, K. C.	Kansas City
26	63	20	Nuxhall, K. C.	Kansas City
27	65	22	Bass, K. C.	Kansas City
		July		
28	73	1	Sisler, Washington	New York
29	74	2	Burnside, Wash.	New York
30	74	2	Klippstein, Wash.	New York
31	76	4	Lary, Detroit	New York
32	77	5	Funk, Cleveland	New York
33	81	9	Monbouquette, Bost.	N. Y.
34	83	13	Wynn, Chicago	Chicago
35	85	15	Herbert, Chicago	Chicago
36	91	21	Monbouquette, Bost.	Boston
37	94	25	Baumann, Chicago	New York
38	94	25	Larsen, Chicago	New York
39	95	25	Kemmerer, Chicago	New York
40	95	25	Hacker, Chicago	New York
		Aug.		
41	105	4	Pascual, Minnesota	New York
42	113	11	Burnside, Wash.	Washington
43	114	12	Donovan, Wash.	Washington
44	115	13	Daniels, Wash.	Washington
45	116	13	Kutyna, Wash.	Washington
46	117	15	Pizarro, Chicago	New York
47	118	16	Pierce, Chicago	New York
48	118	16	Pierce, Chicago	New York
49	122	20	Perry, Cleveland	Cleveland
50	124	22	McBride, L. A.	Los Angeles
51	128	26	Walker, K. C.	Kansas City
		Sept.		
52	134	2	Lary, Detroit	New York
53	134	2	Aquirre, Detroit	New York
54	139	6	Cheney, Wash.	New York
55	140	7	Stigman, Cleveland	New York
56	142	9	Grant, Cleveland,	New York
57	150	16	Lary, Detroit	Detroit
58	151	17	Fox, Detroit	Deroit
59	154	20	Pappas, Baltimore	Baltimore
60	158	26	Fisher, Baltimore	New York
		Oct.		
61	162	1	Stallard, Boston	New York

("Game Played" figures above are games in the standing (exclusive of tie games)—the yard-stick to be used for home run records according to a ruling by Commissioner Frick.)

BABE RUTH

Homer No.	Game Played	Date	Opp. Pitcher and Club	Where Made
		April		
1	4	15	Ehmke, Phila.	New York
2	11	23	Walberg, Phila.	Philadelphia
3	12	24	Thurston, Wash.	Washington
4	14	29	Harriss, Boston	Boston
		May		
5	16	1	Quinn, Phila.	New York
6	16	1	Walberg, Phila.	New York
7	24	10	Gaston, St. Louis	St. Louis
8	25	11	Nevers, St. Louis	St. Louis
9	29	17	Collins, Detroit	Detroit
10	33	22	Karr, Cleveland	Cleveland
11	34	23	Thurston, Wash.	Washington
12	37	28	Thurston, Wash.	New York
13	39	29	MacFayden, Boston	New York
14	41	30	Walberg, Phila.	Philadelphia
15	42	31	Quinn, Phila.	Philadelphia
16	43	31	Ehmke, Phila.	Philadelphia
		June		
17	47	5	Whitehill, Detroit	New York
18	48	7	Thomas, Chicago	New York
19	52	11	Buckeye, Cleveland	New York
20	52	11	Buckeye, Cleveland	New York
21	53	12	Uhle, Cleveland	New York
22	55	16	Zachary, St. Louis	New York
23	60	22	Wiltse, Boston	Boston
24	60	22	Wiltse, Boston	Boston
25	70	30	Harriss, Boston	New York
		July		
26	73	3	Lisenbee, Wash.	Washington
27	78	8	Hankins, Detroit	Detroit
28	79	9	Holloway, Detroit	Detroit
29	79	9	Holloway, Detroit	Detroit
30	83	12	Shaute, Cleveland	Cleveland
31	94	24	Thomas, Chicago	Chicago
32	95	26	Gaston, St. Louis	New York
33	95	26	Gaston, St. Louis	New York
34	98	28	Stewart, St. Louis	New York
		Aug.		
35	106	5	G. Smith, Detroit	New York
36	110	10	Zachary, Wash.	Washington
37	114	16	Thomas, Chicago	Chicago
38	115	17	Connally, Chicago	Chicago
39	118	20	Miller, Cleveland	Cleveland
40	120	22	Shaute, Cleveland	Cleveland
41	124	27	Nevers, St. Louis	St. Louis
42	125	28	Wingard, St. Louis	St. Louis
43	127	31	Welzer, Boston	New York
		Sept.		
44	128	2	Walberg, Phila.	Philadelphia
45	132	6	Welzer, Boston	Boston
46	132	6	Welzer, Boston	Boston
47	133	6	Russell, Boston	Boston
48	134	7	MacFayden, Boston	Boston
49	134	7	Harriss, Boston	Boston
50	138	11	Gaston, St. Louis	New York
51	139	13	Hudlin, Cleveland	New York
52	140	13	Shaute, Cleveland	New York
53	143	16	Blankenship, Chi.	New York
54	147	18	Lyons, Chicago	New York
55	148	21	Gibson, Detroit	New York
56	149	22	Holloway, Detroit	New York
57	152	27	Grove, Phila.	New York
58	153	29	Lisenbee, Wash.	New York
59	153	29	Hopkins, Wash.	New York
60	154	30	Zachary, Wash.	New York

FINAL ★★★★ 5¢

WEATHER: Cloudy, high in the 70s.

New York Mirror

Vol. 37, No. 86 MONDAY, OCTOBER 2, 1961 O

61 FOR ROG

Souvenir Home-Run Edition

SEE SPECIAL 4-PAGE SECTION IN CENTER; PAGES 1, 3, BACK PAGE, SPORTS PAGES AND CENTERFOLD.

History at the Stadium! After blasting record-making 61st homer, Roger Maris is shown the ball—worth $5,000—by Sal Durante who caught it.

(Mirror Photo by Anthony Bernato)

$2,410 Waiting! Mail Post Position Claims Now!

STORY ON PAGE 5

M-Boys Agree: Whitey Plans, Then Wins the Big Games

Roger Maris and Mickey Mantle are covering the World Series exclusively for The Florida Times-Union. Here is their first post-game report on the opening game, won by the Yankees, 2-0. The Yankee sluggers give the inside report on how Whitey Ford, ace southpaw, was able to blank the Cincinnati Reds in the first Series game.

By MICKEY MANTLE and ROGER MARIS

NEW YORK, Oct. 4 — The first game of the 1961 World Series is the exclusive property of Whitey Ford. Let's start this little rundown right there. When we refer to Whitey as the chairman of the board, the meaning ought to be pretty clear.

Ford wins the big games. You've heard that before. Now we're going to tell you why.

Whitey plans to win. If that sounds crazy, you didn't see Whitey behind closed doors in the Yankee clubhouse an hour before the game started. He was sitting on the rubbing table in Gus Mauch's training room when we walked in on him. And this is what we saw.

Whitey in a 'Trance'

Whitey was in sort of a trance, you might say. He didn't notice us walk in. He was concentrating so hard it was as if we weren't there at all.

He looked up after a while.

"You guys want something?" he asked.

We both shook our heads. This was old stuff, and a good sign. This was the way Whitey behaved before those two shutouts he pitched last fall against the Pittsburgh Pirates. We knew he didn't want to indulge in any small talk.

This was Whitey Ford at work and the first pitch of the game was one hour away.

What was he thinking about? The hitters. He was going over every guy in that batting order, from Don Blasingame right down through Jim O'Toole, the pitcher.

Whitey does this all the time before big games. He is the perfect pitcher to have going for you in a big game because he leaves absolutely nothing to chance. He prepares for his job with the concentration of a chess player.

"That hour before a World Series game I can visualize every characteristic the scouts have told us about the other team," he once said.

Had Right Book

You've got to say he had the right book on the Reds in Yankee Stadium in the first game. That two-hitter was a masterpiece. This was Ford at his very best, and when you see the chairman of the board that way it's a little easier to understand why he's now working on his 28th consecutive scoreless inning. He is just 2 2-3 innings from tying the all-time record for scoreless innings in World Series competition. Don't bet he won't make the grade this weekend in Cincinnati.

Only one of us was in the lineup behind Ford. Maybe this would be a good time for the senior member of this partnership to get something off his chest.

That OK with you, Roger?

Go ahead Mick. But before you do, what's the story on you for the second game?

I won't play, Roger. This leg of mine feels better, but it's crazy for any ball player to play in a World Series when he's not ready. That's silly. Not only that, but when you're playing on one leg you're penalizing your teammates. You're adding a handicap which ought not to be there.

Got you, Mick. That takes care of the second game of the series. How about the third, and the ones after that?

Treatments Help

Roger, I'm hoping and praying I'll be in there when the Series moves to Cincinnati on Saturday. The treatments I've been get-

(Continued on Page 66—Column 1)

—AP Wirephoto

DIVING CLETE BOYER MAKES SENSATIONAL PLAY
. . . Grabs Gernert's Smash, Tosses Him Out at First

Ford's Magic, Yank HRs Top Reds in Opener, 2-0

NEW YORK, Oct. 4 (AP)—Whitey Ford spun his southpaw magic over the Cincinnati Reds with a two-hit, 2-0 opening-game victory for the New York Yankees today and set a World Series record with eight victories.

Once again the Yanks, who hit 240 homers in the regular season, fell back on their familiar weapon with home runs by Elston Howard and Bill Skowron and broke the back of the National League champions.

Jim O'Toole, 24-year-old Cincinnati left-hander, hadn't allowed a home run since July 28 in 16 regular season games. But Howard curled one into the lower right field seats in the fourth and Skowron bombed a 420-footer into the lower stands in left in the sixth.

Boyer's Fielding Sensational

Sensational fielding by third baseman Clete Boyer eased Ford's path as he ran his string of consecutive scoreless innings to 27 over a two-year span.

Boyer thrilled a chilly crowd of 62,387 with a brilliant stop of pinch hitter Dick Gernert's smash in the eighth. Throwing himself into the dirt as he dived to his left, Boyer gloved the ball. Then he threw out Gernert from his knees. In the second inning Boyer made another difficult stop and perfect throw from his knees, nipping Gene Freese.

The Yanks did this without help from the M & M boys. Mickey Mantle was not in the lineup, still hobbled by the effects of minor surgery on an abscess on his right hip. Roger Maris, whose 61 hommers set a new record, failed to hit the ball out of the infield on four trips, striking out once.

Ford Simply Superb

Ford simply was superb on this gray day, spiking the big guns of the Reds' attack, Frank Robinson and Vada Pinson.

Eddie Kasko singled into left field with one out in the first inning and Wally Post lined a single into the left field corner in the fifth. The 32-year-old lefty from Lake Success, N.Y., walked only one man, Robinson in the seventh, and struck out six. The strikeouts boosted his own Series record to 69.

Red Ruffing and Allie Reynolds, a couple of Yanks of former days, each had won seven series games but Ford's brilliant effort made him the top winner of all time in his 15th start

The chunky Yankee pitcher never gave the Reds the ball they wanted. He pitched tight to the plate-crowding Robinson and then made him go after the high outside pitch, striking him out twice.

To Get Record Chance

Only Babe Ruth with 29 2-3 scoreless innings and Christy Mathewson with 28 1-3 (he pitched three shutouts in 1905) have blanked the opposition for as many consecutive innings. Ford undoubtedly will get a chance to top them in the fourth game at Cincinnati Sunday.

Ralph Terry, a 25-year-old right-hander who will be remembered as the fellow who threw the Series-deciding home run ball to Bill Mazeroski in Pittsburgh last October, will pitch for the Yanks in tomorrow's second game. He had a 16-3 record and pitched the pennant clincher.

Joey Jay, a 26-year-old right-hander who was acquired from Milwaukee last winter, will pitch for Cincinnati. Joey, the first Little League grad to make the majors, had a 21-10 season for the Reds.

Blanchard May Play Today

Manager Ralph Houk said he would use Johnny Blanchard in right field tomorrow against Jay if Mantle, still a doubtful starter, is unable to play.

Houk said he had seen Boyer make the same kind of play that he made on Gernert at least four times during the regular season.

The Yanks had O'Toole on the ropes in the first when they loaded the bases on Bobby Richardson's first of three singles and walks to Tony Kubek and Skowron. Yogi Berra popped up for the third out.

Howard, a .348 hitter for the season, hit a 1-1 pitch into the lower seats in right leading off the fourth. He said it was a slider. Whatever it was it curled away from Wally Post who was playing him toward right center. The ball just did make the seats.

Seventh HR for Skowron

Skowron's blast was a homer all the way. It came off an O'Toole curve ball and drilled its way into the eighth row of the

(Continued on Page 67—Column 1)

—AP Wirephoto

FORD MOWS 'EM DOWN
. . . Whip-Like Arm Tames Reds

—AP Wirephoto

REDS' POST WAITS IN VAIN
. . . As Howard Blast (Arrow) Fades Away

Box Score

CINCINNATI (N)	ab	r	h	bi	NEW YORK (A)	ab	r	h	bi
Bl'game 2b	3	0	0	0	Rich'son 2b	4	0	3	0
dLynch	1	0	0	0	Kubek ss	3	0	0	0
Kasko ss	4	0	1	0	Maris cf-rf	4	0	0	0
Pinson cf	4	0	0	0	Howard c	4	1	1	1
Rob'son lf	2	0	0	0	Skowron 1b	3	1	1	1
Post rf	3	0	1	0	Berra lf	2	0	0	0
Freese 3b	3	0	0	0	Lopez rf	2	0	0	0
Coleman 1b	3	0	0	0	cBlanchard	1	0	0	0
D.Johnson c	2	0	0	0	Reed cf	0	0	0	0
aCardenas	1	0	0	0	Boyer 3b	3	0	1	0
Zim'man c	0	0	0	0	Ford p	3	0	0	0
O'Toole p	2	0	0	0					
bGernert	1	0	0	0					
Brosnan p	0	0	0	0					
Totals	29	0	2	0	Totals	29	2	6	2

a—Struck out for D. Johnson in 8th.
b—Grounded out for O'Toole in 8th.
c—Popped out for Lopez in 8th.
d—Popped out for Blasingame in 9th.

Cincinnati (N)	000	000	000—0
New York (A)	000	101	00x—2

E—None. DP—D. Johnson, Kasko and Coleman. LOB—Cincinnati (N) 3, New York (A) 8. HR—Howard, Skowron. PO-A—New York 27-13, Cincinnati 24-6.

	IP	H	R	ER	BB	SO
O'Toole (L)	7	6	2	2	4	2
Brosnan	1	0	0	0	1	1
Ford (W)	9	2	0	0	1	6

U—Runge (A) plate, Conlan (N) first base, Umont (A) second base, Donatelli (N) third base, Crawford (N) left field, Stewart (A) right field. T—2:11. A—62,397.

WORLD SERIES FACTS, FIGURES

By The Associated Press

	W	L	Pct.
New York (AL)	1	0	1.000
Cincinnati (N)	0	1	.000

First game, Oct. 4, at Yankee Stadium.

Cincinnati	000	000	000—0	2	0
New York	000	101	00x—2	6	0

O'Toole, Brosnan (8) and Johnson, Zimmerman (8); Ford and Howard.

Second game, Oct. 5, at Yankee Stadium; third, fourth and fifth games, Oct. 7, 8, 9 at Crosley Field, Cincinnati. Sixth and seventh games, if necessary, Oct. 11 and 12 at Yankee Stadium.

Financial figures:

First game:

Attendance—62,397.
Net receipts—$419,430.83.
Commissioner's share—$62,914.62.
Players' share (60 per cent)—$213,909.73.
Each club's share—$35,651.62.
Each league's share—$35,651.62.

SPORTS The Florida Times-Union
THURSDAY, OCT. 5, 1961 • 65

Baseball's Big Boost

By BILL KASTELZ
SPORTS EDITOR

USUALLY, THE WORLD SERIES has the conversational field all to itself on the local sports scene during the first week in October. Usually—but not this year.

The talk around town yesterday was not only of the American League and the National League, but also of the International League. Although Jacksonville's move into Triple-A baseball had been pushed with varying energies ever since the end of the 1956 Sally League season, and had been anticipated for the past several months, news that it finally had become official was a popular topic of conversation everywhere in the city.

Much of the reaction was along the lines of pleased surprise. The realization that Jacksonville in 1962 will be playing a brand of baseball only one notch below that in the majors took a while to sink in. But, now that the locals have gone and done it, the anticipation is tremendous . . . and so, for that matter, is the advance ticket sale.

Jersey City, whose ball club will be moved here to form a nucleus for our team, along with the players who will be sent here by the Cleveland Indians, drew around 50,000 fans this season. Jacksonville already has sold over 70,000 admissions—and has 11 more months to go toward its total for 1962.

If 100,000 admissions are sold by next Thursday, as is expected, it would not be unreasonable to guess that from 200,000 to 250,000 fans will watch Jacksonville's Triple-A club play next season. In minor league baseball these days, that's a whale of a figure.

Fans' Response Made It Possible

This development appears to bear out a contention often made in this space — that if the attraction is a good one, local fans will support it in fine style.

There's no way of knowing what kind of a club will play here next season, but the mere idea of watching Jacksonville play against teams like Richmond, Columbus, O., Toronto, Buffalo, Rochester, Syracuse and either Atlanta or Charleston, W. Va., seems to have caught on big, judging from the sales.

This is one time the fans themselves can take a deep, deep bow for the way they have responded. Baseball dead here? Not on your life.

Tennis Greats to Play Here

While the baseball buffs are savoring the World Series and the football people look forward to another big weekend, the tennis addicts will have their innings at the Coliseum tomorrow night and Saturday night.

The Southern Professional tournament, a two-night event, will bring to Jacksonville a small but highly-talented field of competitors — laced with a couple of the sport's all-time greats.

Don Budge and Mrs. Pauline Betz Addie head up the list of performers who will appear here. Anyone who hasn't heard of them probably wouldn't be interested in the tournament anyway, so there will be no attempt here to list even a small portion of honors they have won in tennis.

Suffice it to say that they have won just about everything there is to win in competitive tennis, both amateur and pro.

MRS. ADDIE

Mrs. Addie, wife of Washington sports writer Bob Addie, will be one of only two feminine players in the event. Tomorrow night she will play a one-match showdown for the Southern women's professional title with Karol Fageros, a decorative Miami product who also can bat a tennis ball around with the best of them.

In the men's field, besides Budge there will be such standouts as: Jack Arkinstall, former Australian ace who holds victories over Wimbledon champions Jaroslav Drobny, Ken Rosewall and Lew Hoad; Armando Vieira, colorful five-times champion of South America; Jack Rodgers, former national pro doubles champion; hard-hitting Jason Morton, an energetic ball hawk from Tuscaloosa, Ala.; Nat Ritzenberg, the Ormond Beach stylist; Dan Sullivan, former amateur circuit player from St. Petersburg, and Gene Vash, the local pro at San Jose.

In conjunction with the tournament, a clinic, with Budge, Mrs. Addie and Arkinstall teaching will be held from 4 to 6 p.m. tomorrow at the Coliseum. Only admission required, according to Tournament Chairman John Holeman, will be a tennis racket and a pair of sneakers.

The clinic will be for beginners, intermediate players and tournament competitors — juniors and adults alike — and all phases will be developed, starting with grips and fundamentals and right through to tournament tactics.

One set matches will prevail in the tourney, except for the championships.

'MR. FORD AND MR. BOYER'

Houk Describes Game In Five Short Words

NEW YORK, Oct. 4 (UPI)—Somewhat smug, cigar-puffing Ralph Houk said it all in five words — "Mr. Ford and Mr. Boyer!"

The obviously elated New York Yankee manager made sure to put a bit of special emphasis on the word "Mister" in each case today, leaving no doubt whatsoever how he felt about the efforts of southpaw Whitey Ford and third baseman Cletis Boyer.

"Mr. Ford is the guy who did it," were the first words out of Houk's mouth after he had settled himself in his swivel chair, "and don't forget to give Mr. Boyer a big assist, too."

Boyer Draws Attention

Even in the face of Ford's brilliant two-hitter, most of the conversation in the Yankees' clubhouse centered on the two superb defense plays Boyer turned in on Gene Freese's line drive in the second inning and a hard smash by pinch-hitter Dick Gernert in the eighth.

Boyer's play on Gernert in the eighth was one of those things you had to see to believe. The Yankee third baseman made a desperation lunge at the ball, stopped it somehow and then threw out Gernert while still on his knees.

"It was the best play I ever made," Boyer said. "I didn't believe it myself.

"You know what I did? I just pulled that ball out of my ears."

His second inning grab of Freese's line smash was almost as spectacular.

'Found it in Time'

"Actually, I had more trouble on that one," he revealed. "I lost the ball for a second in those flags that drape behind home plate. But I found it in time."

Boyer also was the key figure in what looked like a touchy situation in the fifth when Wally Post barrelled into him coming from second base after Darrell Johnson had bounced back to Clete.

"I would've done the same thing he did," Boyer said, gingerly fingering a small bruise on his upper lip where Post's elbow hit him. "He just tried to knock the ball out of my hand. He's got a right."

Ford, who ran his consecutive World Series scoreless inning

(Continued on Page 67—Column 3)

Fred Hutchinson

Jim O'Toole

BOYER PRAISED, TOO

Glum Reds Laud Ford's Brilliancy

NEW YORK, Oct. 4 (UPI)—"Give Whitey Ford all the credit."

That was Manager Fred Hutchinson's opening remark in the Cincinnati Reds' clubhouse today following the two-hit, 2-0 setback at the hands of Ford and the Yankees.

And his players glumly agreed with Hutch as they sat in front of their stalls and admiringly mulled over Ford's pitching mastery.

"He was as good out there today as I've ever seen him," said Reds' catcher Darrell Johnson, who once handled Ford as a member of the Yankees.

Robinson Lauds Ford

Echoed Frank Robinson, the Reds' top slugger who struck out twice and then drew Ford's only walk of the game: "He's some pitcher. He has about five good

(Continued on Page 68—Column 1)

Darrell Johnson

THE PLAIN DEALER

CLEVELAND, FRIDAY MORNING, OCTOBER 6, 1961

JAY'S 4-HITTER EVENS SERIES, 6-2

SCORES BIG RUN. Reds' Elio Chacon slides right under catcher Elston Howard to score on short passed ball and put Cincinnati ahead to stay, 3-2, in fifth inning. Umpire Jocko Conlon calls the play, on which Chacon came home as Ralph Terry's pitch eluded Howard.

4 LAPSES COSTLY TO YANKEES

By BOB DOLGAN
Staff Correspondent

NEW YORK—The Cincinnati Redlegs won the game they had to win yesterday. They took the second contest of the World Series because the Yankee defense grew knotless, committing four misplays that led to four runs for the National League champions—the margin of difference in a 6-2 decision.

The catalogue of Yankee futility:

Third baseman Clete Boyer failed to handle a hot smash by Frank Robinson that was scored an error. Gordon Coleman, onetime Cleveland Indian, then homered.

Catcher Elston Howard committed a passed ball that let a run score. It was a short passed ball, rolling about 15 feet from the plate, and Elio Chacon might have been caught at the plate had losing pitcher Ralph Terry not been slow getting off the mound. As it was, Chacon easily beat Howard's diving tag.

Jay Hurls 4-Hitter

Relief man Luis Arroyo made a wild throw in the eighth inning, and left fielder Yogi Berra dropped a liner hit by Wally Post in the same round. These boots gave the Reds two more runs and made them as happy especially Joey Jay, the huge right-hander who gave the Yanks only four hits.

So the series is all tied up at a conquest apiece and the teams will have today off before renewing this knickerbockered warfare, which a crowd of 63,083 watched yesterday.

The classic moves to Cincinnati tomorrow and knuckleballing Bob Purkey will pitch for the Reds, opposing Bill Stafford.

If Purkey does as well as Jay did, the people in the Braatwurst belt will be happy. Jay gave the Yanks one good hit, a two-run homer by Berra that tied the score in the fourth inning.

It was the 12th series homer for Berra, who is also known as Ponce De Leon, since he first began participating in these matches 15 autumns ago.

Works Out of Jam

In the next inning Jay worked out of a jam that kept the Reds in business. The frame began with Cincinnati holding a 3-2 lead.

Boyer walked and, after Terry popped, made second safely when second baseman Chacon bungled a double play.

Bobby Richardson hit a perfect double play grounder to shortstop Eddie Kasko, who

Continued on Page 30, Column 7

Yanks Drop to 2-1 for Series

LAS VEGAS, Nev. (AP)—The Yankees dropped to 2 to 1 favorites to take the World Series following their loss yesterday.

The American League champs were 4 to 1 Thursday.

The Yankees are favored among Las Vegas oddsmakers 7 to 5 to win the third game.

REDLEG HEROES. Three standouts in Cincinnati's victory flash winning smiles in clubhouse. Elio Chacon (left) scored on passed ball to put Reds ahead; Joey Jay pitched four-hitter at Yanks, and Gordon Coleman socked two-run homer. AP Wirephotos

Piersall Happy Over Trade

Jim Piersall — Dick Donovan — Jim Mahoney — Gene Green

By BOB DOLGAN

NEW YORK—Jim Piersall was surprisingly calm although his bing-bang talk had not left him. He had just heard that the Indians had traded him to Washington for Dick Donovan, Gene Green and Jim Mahoney and now his voice came over the telephone from his home in Newton, Mass.

"It's a break for me," he said. "Washington has nowhere to go but up and Cleveland will never come back as a baseball town. Besides, I won't have to read your stuff anymore—yours and those two columnists.

"You guys are killing baseball in that town but I like you anyway because you come around and give me a chance to say what I want to your face."

"I bet you're glad I was traded, just like I am."

"That's true, Jim. I am glad to see you go. So are a lot of other people."

"Yeah, well I don't blame you. I'd have made things real rough for you next year. But we're pals, right?"

Good Deal for Tribe

Piersall was asked for his opinion of the trade. "The Cleveland ball club made a helluva deal," he said. "Listen, that Donovan is a great pitcher. Don't worry about centerfield. Ty Cline can do the job. All he needs is a little maturity, so he can lead those other two guys—Kirkland and Francona. The centerfielder has to run the show out there.

"I'm not surprised I was traded. Gabe Paul talked to me a few days ago and told me he might do it. He didn't say it was for any other reason except that he was trying to strengthen the team.

"He's a fine man and he doesn't buy this stuff about me hurting the team even if I hit .300. How can that be? Man, people believe everything they read in the papers. They believe much less what they hear than what they read.

"I try to set 'em straight. Whenever I give a talk I tell 'em about you guys.

"I'll be in Cleveland Oct. 12 for some business. I really liked the fans and they liked me because they know I'm not two-faced. I have no complaints about the Indians' organization, either.

"And we're friends even though I think you're a ...."

"Right, Jim, and the same to you."

Hateful to Fans

So ended one of the more bizarre eras in Cleveland baseball history and it is the contention of some that general manager Gabe Paul should win an award for this deal, which is bound to help the club.

Though Piersall has a following he does not enjoy the universal acceptance Rocky Colavito did. He has been hateful on occasion to the fans and it is characteristic of his chameleon personality that he could be thoroughly charming to the same people.

Besides, good performances from Donovan and Green would make the people forget quickly. Donovan is one of the best pitchers in baseball.

He is 33 years old and he led the league in earned run average this seeason. His ERA was 2.40 and he won 10 and lost 10 for a ninth-place club. A home run by Joe Altobelli deprived Dick of a no-hitter at Minneapolis Sept. 24.

Continued on Page 31, Column 2

Chacon 'on His Own' in Daring Scoring Dash

By HAROLD HARRISON

NEW YORK (AP)—Elio Chacon was running "on his own" when he scored from third base on a passed ball and gave the Reds a lead they maintained as the squared the World Series yesterday.

Chacon, filling in at second base for the ailing Don Blasingame, had singled in the fifth and gone to third on a single by Eddie Kasko. Then, when one of Ralph Terry's pitches got away from Yank catcher Elston Howard, Chacon came barreling in to score and give the Reds a 3-2 lead.

Sees Ball Roll Away

Chacon, who speaks only broken English, said:

"I go because I think I have chance. I see the ball roll away."

Manager Fred Hutchinson confirmed that Chacon didn't wait for any "go" command from third base coach Reggie Otero before making his dash for the plate.

Hutchinson called it perhaps the key play of the game.

The Reds clubhouse had a far different appearance than Wednesday when the Yanks won 2-0. It was packed and the Cincinnatians were grinning.

Joey Jay, who set the Yankees down with four hits, said the pitch Yogi Berra hit for a home run "was not a good pitch."

Slider Best Pitches

"I'm not taking anything away from Berra," he said, "because he might have hit it anyhow but the pitch didn't go where I wanted it to."

Jay said he used mostly sliders and low curves, mixed with the fast ball. Catcher Johnny Edwards, who got two hits and drove in two runs, said the slider was Jay's best pitch.

Over in another corner Gordon Coleman, who hit a two-run homer, was explaining again his "foot in the bucket" batting stance. Coleman pulls away from a pitch with his forward foot.

"As long as I get the job done, that's all that counts," said Coleman. "It's a little too late to change now."

Coleman said the blast was the biggest thrill of his career.

Looking for Pitch

"But I must admit," he laughed, "that I was looking for the pitch Terry threw. It was low and outside and I was waiting. As soon as I hit it, I knew it was going for extra bases."

There was an expression of confidence from Hutchinson about the next games of the Series which will be played in Cincinnati's Crosley Field.

"We'll be playing three games at home and I think that's going to help us," he said.

The Sport Trail

By JAMES E. DOYLE

Happier Days for Reds

Ex-Little Leaguer Joey Jay
R'ared back out there and mowed down
The Yankees in a great big way.
Were those guys ever slowed down!

* * *

And now no Red fan feels too bitter
About sharp Whitey Ford's two-hitter.
—Lank Fellow

* * *

Speaking of Little Leaguers, some of the Yankees performed like such, now and again, as Joey Jay and his swift and smart buddies made what is known as a laugher of that second World Series match yesterday.

* * *

And the New York filberts who were laughing at the Reds throughout and after the opener didn't know what to make of it.

* * *

Red were their faces on this day, though no change of colors had been announced.

He Can Blast 'Em

That Cleveland castoff, Gordon Coleman,
Is now a standout Cincy poleman,
As you know if you saw him haul
Off on Ralph Terry's gopher ball.

* * *

'Twas anything but a Red Chinese homer—the Coleman two-run clout that broke the early 0-0 tie.

* * *

A crash-and-carry sock, it started out as a screamliner, then gained handsome height and distance.

"Subcess" for the Reds

Rookie Catcher John Edwards, a Columbus discovery of the Reds (they found him at dear old Ohio State), broke into action as a sub for the injured Darrell Johnson and broke out with a single and a double for two RBIs . . . And swift Elio Chacon, subbing for injured Second Baseman Don Blansingame, came dashing home with the Reds' large third run while a baffled and bewildered Elston Howard was looking the wrong way after retrieving a passed ball . . . "Nothing succeeds like subcess!" chortled a gleeful Cincinnati rooter.

The Rajah Isn't Rapping

Another rough day for Rajah Maris . . . Hitless once more, he got on base only when he was Jaywalked.

A Strange Sight

Who ever thought that we would see
Famed Yogi earning a goatee?
But that he did earn, sure enough,
With his expensive left-field muff.

* * *

The sun was Yogi's undoing after his homer—no Chinese type, that, either—had fetched the Yankees their only run.

Red Fire and Spirit

Red fire and spirit made an even thing of the series, to put it briefly, with most of the credit going, of course, to that stalwart Red fireman, Joey Jay.

* * *

The new champion of visiting firemen at Yankee Stadium.

Bad Spin, Bad Hops for Yanks

NEW YORK (AP)—"This wasn't our day," Yankee manager Ralph Houk said philosophically as he sat in the clubhouse replaying the defeat to the Cincinnati Reds.

"It was one of those days when a ball that's hit easy has a top spin on it," Houk said. "There were bad hops, and blooper hits and broken bat hits.

"But I wouldn't call our play sloppy. I don't think we did anything to embarrass ourselves."

Houk called Elio Chacon's dash home on a passed ball as the turning point. Ralph Terry's pitch got away from catcher Elston Howard and rolled 15 feet away while Chacon came home to put the Reds ahead to stay.

Dove on Chacon

"I didn't see him (Chacon) right away," said Howard. "When Kasko broke I expected to throw to second, but when I caught Chacon out of the corner of my eye he was starting to slide, so I dove on top of him. It was a close decision.

Houk said he had no intention to pinch hit his ailing ace, Mickey Mantle, once the Yankees fell four runs behind, and

Continued on Page 30, Column 7

Starting All Over Again

CINCINNATI (N)

	AB	R	H	BI	O	A	E
Chacon 2b	4	1	1	0	6	4	0
Kasko ss	5	0	1	0	6	4	0
Pinson cf	5	0	1	0	2	0	0
Rob'son lf	4	2	0	0	0	0	0
Cole'n 1b	5	1	2	2	5	1	0
Post rf	4	2	2	0	0	0	0
Freese 3b	2	0	0	0	1	1	0
Edwards c	4	0	2	2	6	1	0
Jay p	4	0	0	0	1	0	0
Totals	37	6	9	4	27	11	0

NEW YORK (A)

	AB	R	H	BI	O	A	E
Rich's'n 2b	4	0	1	0	2	3	0
Kubek ss	4	0	1	0	1	2	0
Maris cf	3	1	0	0	1	0	0
Berra lf	4	1	2	2	4	0	1
Blan'rd rf	4	0	0	0	0	1	0
Howard c	3	0	0	0	8	0	0
Skow'n 1b	3	0	0	0	8	1	0
Boyer 3b	2	0	0	0	2	1	1
Terry p	2	0	0	0	0	1	0
a-Lopez	0	0	0	0	0	0	0
Arroyo p	0	0	0	0	1	0	1
b-G'dner	1	0	0	0	0	0	0
Totals	30	2	4	2	27	9	3

a—Walked for Terry in 7th.
b—Lined out for Arroyo in 9th.

Cincinnati (N) .... 000 211 020—6
New York (A) .... 000 200 000—2

DP—Chacon, Kasko and Coleman 2. LOB—Cincinnati (N) 8, New York (A) 7. 2B—Post, Edwards, Pinson. HR—Coleman, Berra.

PITCHERS RECORDS

	IP	H	R	ER
Jay (W)	9	4	2	2
Terry (L)	7	6	4	2
Arroyo	2	3	2	1

BB—Jay 6 (Skowron, Maris, Howard, Boyer 2, Lopez), Terry 2 (Chacon, Freese), Arroyo 2 (Robinson, Freese). SO—Jay 6 (Kubek 2, Maris 2, Skowron 2), Terry 7 (Kasko 2, Freese, Post, Jay, Pinson, Coleman), Arroyo 1 (Jay). PB—Howard. U—Conlan (N) plate, Umont (A) first base, Donatelli (N) second base, Runge (A) third base, Crawford (N) left field, Stewart (A) right field. T—2:43. A—63,083.

Plain Dealing

Piersall for Donovan Trade Is Giant Step Forward in Tribe Rebuilding Program

By GORDON COBBLEDICK
Plain Dealer Sports Editor

GORDON COBBLEDICK

NEW YORK—The Cincinnati Reds squared the World Series yesterday by winning an untidy contest in which the Yankees looked for all the world like the married men in their annual game with the single men at an Elks picnic.

But, speaking of married men, the really vital news of the day in Cleveland and other cultural centers was made by James Anthony Piersall.

Paul Was Anxious to Trade Piersall

Like another well-known Boston Democrat, Piersall henceforth will operate out of Washington, D.C. This was arranged early yesterday by Gabe Paul, who thus made himself a leading candidate for the title of Cleveland's man of the year.

For the Indians the trade was, in the quite possibly warped judgment of this observer, a giant step forward. Other steps remain to be taken before our town can hope to regain its place in the baseball sun, and Paul is quite evidently of a mood to take them.

Piersall was first on the list of those whom he believed, with the wholehearted approval of his new team manager, Mel McGaha, would have to go. He said little about it, not wishing to downgrade a piece of merchandise of which he hoped to dispose at a favorable price, but his haste to engineer the deal, less than four days after the season's close, was a measure of his anxiety to make it.

Add to his natural prejudice against outfielders who bat in only 40 runs a predisposition in favor of players who behave like adult professionals without being paid a substantial bonus for doing so, and you have all the explanation needed for Paul's eagerness to do business.

Piersall Called Cleveland Scribes 'Bush'

Moreover, Piersall had made no secret of his desire to leave Cleveland, to whose fans and writers he applied that most biting of baseball epithets, "bush."

When Paul and McGaha saw a chance to dispose of him while strengthening the Indians' shaky pitching staff and increasing their long-ball batting power, they didn't hesitate.

In Dick Donovan they acquired a pitcher of skill and experience and in Gene Green they obtained one of the league's most muscular batsmen.

With them they took on, to be sure, certain problems, not the least of which was that they now must fill a vacancy in center field. Donovan is, by report, not the easiest temperament to get along with and Green has yet to find the spot in a line-up at which his batting strength outweighs his defensive weaknesses.

At Washington he was tried as a catcher and a first baseman. Elsewhere in his career he has attempted the outfield. In no case were the results thoroughly satisfactory. The probability is that in Tucson next spring he'll be given a long trial at first base.

Coleman Adequate First Baseman

The Indians haven't forgotten how apparently hopelessly inept Gordon Coleman was as a first baseman. They worked with him hours on end, trying to teach him to field a ground ball, and the results of their efforts now are apparent. Coleman is the first baseman of a team now in contention with the Yankees for the world's championship, and he is somewhat more than adequate.

Yesterday he supplied the spark that ignited the Reds' dormant batting attack. His two-run homer in the fourth ended a string of 12 scoreless innings for the National League champions, and from that point forward they looked like a club that might make things interesting in what remains of this World Series.

Mel McGaha said the other day that if the Reds won one of the first two games in the Yankee Stadium they'd have something better than a 50-50 chance to win it all.

Now they've won that one game and they're heading for three more in the familiar confines of their own bandbox ball park. Anything can happen there.

N. Y. U. and Kings Point Battle to 20-20 Tie; Wesleyan Conquers Bowdoin, 27-7

Both Teams Fail With Field Goal Tries Near End

Violets Are Outplayed in 2d Half After Scoring Twice in First Quarter

Special to the Herald Tribune

KINGS POINT, L. I., Oct. 4.—A battling band of Kings Point Mariners upset New York University's hopes of winning two football games in a row for the first time since 1946. The Violet was forced to settle for a 20-to-20 tie and was lucky to break even as the Loug Islanders held control throughout the second half and just missed what would have been a tie-breaking field goal with 1:10 left in the last quarter.

What started Kings Point off on its drive to near victory was an N. Y. U. field goal attempt which failed from the thirteen-yard line. Sparked by the running of left halfback Don Carlson, the Mariners moved to the Violet 19 before they were brought to a halt. On N. Y. U.'s first play from scrimmage, Bill Burney fumbled and Kings Point recovered. Unable to make first down in three plays, the Mariners called on Frank Rack to boot the winning three-pointer, but the kick was off to the left.

Di Gaspari Throws Key Block

N. Y. U. scored on the fourth play of the game when Burney took a pitch-out from quarterback Frank Sauchelli, broke through his opposing left tackle, cut to the left and raced sixty-three yards to score. Vince Di Gaspari threw a key block which set Burney free on the Kings Point 19. Sauchelli converted to put the Violets into the lead, 7 to 0.

N. Y. U. scored again when Bob Mautte, defensive halfback, intercepted a Mariner pass and ran thirty-seven yards to set up another touchdown. Sauchelli tallied on a quarterback sneak at 12:30 of the first quarter. He again converted to put the Violets into the lead by 14 to 0.

Kings Point retiated quickly as Mautte fumbled on his 5-yard line and Frank Smith recovered for the home side. At 1:58 of the second period, Charles Allen, the fullback, bucked through the middle and Charles Watson converted to bring the score to 14 to 7.

Following the second-half kick-off, Kings Point moved sixty yards in thirteen plays to score. Smith and Carlson paced this advance with Rodrigo Alvarado scoring on a right-end sweep from the 10-yard line at 6:00. Watson was successful in his second try and the score was deadlocked at 14-all.

An N. Y. U. fumble led to Kings Point's third touchdown when safety man Bob Doherty bobbled a Carlson punt on his 5 and captain Bob Wiechard, a sixty-minute man who played a whale of a game at guard, pounced on the ball. Smith buckled for the score at 11:15 from the 5-yard marker but Watson's conversion attempt was blocked by N. Y. U. captain John Gilligan as the home team took the lead, 20 to 14.

N. Y. U. came back to net the equalizer at 2:30 of the last period on a sauchelli pass to Burney, set up by a Mariner fumble. Doherty made up for his earlier miscue by recovering for N. Y. U. at the Kings Point 40.

James Kavallines

FOURTH-GAME HEROES: Mickey Mantle (left), Allie Reynolds (center) and Johnny Mize, whose combined efforts help pull the Yankees even with the Dodgers at two victories apiece in World Series

Ted Kell

Duke Snider making a one-handed leaping catch of Yogi Berra's long drive to deep right centerfield in fourth inning as Carl Furillo runs up to help. Snider tumbled but held on

Cardinals Gain 2d Victory With Late-Half Surge

Nixon and Brigham Connect on 11 of 28 Passes for 271 Yards for Winners

Special to the Herald Tribune

MIDDLETOWN, Oct. 4.—A late-starting Wesleyan team caught fire in the second half to overwhelm Bowdoin, 27 to 7, before a crowd of 3,500.

Taking to the air after a series of costly fumbles stalled its running attack, Wesleyan scored in each of the last three quarters. Bob Lavin, Wesleyan end who was sidelined since the opener with Middlebury because of an infected elbow, played long enough to catch two scoring passes. The Wesleyan quarterback duo of Dave Nixon and John Brigham completed eleven aerials in twenty-eight tries for a total of 271 yards. Nixon throws right-handed and Brigham is a southpaw.

Bowdoin's lone tally came after an interception on its own 13. They started a scoring drive that went all the way. Quarterback John Cosgrove scored on a sneak through center from the 2.

The longest run of the game was Cardinal halfback John Farese's fifty-four-yard touchdown romp up the sideline after a pitchout from Nixon. Although it outrushed Bowdoin, 156 to 124, Wesleyan never displayed a consistent attack. It scored three times on long penetrations and a thirty-two-yard interception runback by sophomore fullback Dick Sanderson.

The umpire, J. J. Burke, was trapped in the Bowdoin backfield and knocked unconscious late in the game. He sat out half a dozen plays on the Wesleyan bench before returning to action.

The score by periods:

Bowdoin	7	0	0	0—7
Wesleyan	0	7	7	13—27

Bowdoin scoring—Touchdown, Cosgrove. Conversion, Levesque.

Wesleyan scoring—Touchdowns, Farese, Lavin 2, Sanderson. Conversions, Binswanger 3.

Today's Sports and Televised Sports

* * *

BASEBALL

New York Yankees vs. Brooklyn Dodgers in World Series, at Yankee Stadium, River Ave. and 161st St., Bronx, 2 p. m. Herald Tribune staff coverage by Rud Rennie, Roger Kahn, Harold Rosenthal and Edward Sinclair. (Telecast—WOR-TV, Channel 9, 2 p. m., WNBT-TV, Channel 4, 1:45 p. m. Telecasters—Red Barber and Mel Allen.)

GOLF

South Bay Golf Club invitation tourney, North Shore, L. I., 10 a. m.

Pro-member golf tourney, at Rye Wood Country Club, Rye, N. Y., 10 a. m.

GAELIC FOOTBALL

Kerry vs. Mayo at Croke Park, Broadway and 240th St., Bronx, 12:45 p. m.

HURLING

Double-header at Croke Park, Broadway and 240th St., Bronx, 1:45 p. m.

POLO

Bostwick Field, Westbury, L. I., 3:30 p. m.

SOCCER

Double-header at Sterling Oval, Teller Ave. and 165th St., Bronx, 1:15 p. m.

Delaware, 7; Lehigh, 6

Special to the Herald Tribune

BETHLEHEM, Pa., Oct. 4.—The University of Delaware defeated Lehigh University, 7 to 6, before more than 7,000 in Taylor Stadium this afternoon, handing the Engineers their second loss of the season. The victory was the second in a row for the Blue Hens in the seven-game series.

Delaware scored in the first three minutes after Rocco Carzo pounced on Howie Schaefer's fumble on the Lehigh 19.

The score by periods:

Delaware	7	0	0	0—7
Lehigh	0	0	6	0—6

Rochester Topples Williams On Deflected Pass by 12 to 7

WILLIAMSTOWN, Mass., Oct. 4.—Crippled by injuries, Williams College dropped its second game in a row on Weston Field, losing 12 to 7, to the University of Rochester, before a crowd of 3,000. It was Rochester's second consecutive victory.

Williams scored first midway in the first period after end Ted Potter recovered a Rochester fumble on the Rochester 38. The Purple piled up three first downs and ended with halfback Rick Bethune plunging over left guard from the 4-yard line. Al Fletcher's conversion was good.

In the second quarter, Bruce Moses intercepted a Williams pass at midfield and went up to the Williams' 32. Harry Akullian brought the ball to the 7 on an end run and Bill Sharp went through left tackle for the touchdown with forty-five second to go in the half. Sharp's attempted conversion was wide.

Rochester put on a sustained drive in the third quarter with Billy Secor, of Burt, N. Y., and freshman Dick Devereaux, of East Rochester, N. Y., alternating the carries. Two offsides helped bring the ball to the Williams' 25. Mike Rayder, of Williams, then deflected an end zone pass into the hands of Secor.

Williams lost its opener to Headquarters Command U. S. A. F. last week, 28 to 0, and Rochester beat Kings Point Merchant Marine Academy, 20 to 7.

The score by periods:

Williams	7	0	0	0—7
Rochester	0	6	6	0—12

Scoring: Williams—Touchdown, Bethune. Conversion—Fletcher.

Rochester: Touchdowns—Sharp, Secor.

Bates, 19; Middlebury, 14

LEWISTON, Me., Oct. 4.—Bates registered its first victory in two years today, defeating Middlebury, 19 to 14, on a twenty-yard pass play from Dave Harkins to Dan Barrios.

The score by periods:

Bates	0	12	0	7—19
Middlebury	0	0	0	14—14

Brandeis, 28; Northeastern, 13

BOSTON, Oct. 4.—Brandeis University defeated Northeastern University this afternoon, 28 to 13, before 3,500 spectators. It was the first meeting between the two teams.

Tyson, Goldfaber, McKenna and Waldmann each scored touchdowns for the victors with Waldmann adding extra points after each tally. Colverall accounted for all of Northeastern's points, scoring touchdowns in the first and final periods and converting one extra point.

The score by periods:

Brandeis	7	0	14	7—28
Northeastern	6	0	0	7—13

Amherst, 28; Union, 21

AMHERST, Oct. 4.—Amherst scored two touchdowns in the third period today to break a 14-to-14 halftime tie and defeat Union, 28 to 21.

Union tied the score fifteen seconds before the half on a forty-three-yard pass from Lenny Klingberg to Bill Snyder but after intermission the Jeffs drove sixty-five yards with Bob Kisiel going over from the 5. Kisiel went over later in the period from the 13.

The score by periods:

Amherst	7	7	14	0—28
Union	7	7	0	7—21

Amherst scoring: Touchdowns—Kisiel 3, Van Jones. Points after touchdowns—Catlett 4.

Union scoring: Touchdowns—Dickson 2, Snyder. Points after touchdowns—Schappert 3.

Referee—E. R. Gilmartin. Umpire—W. J. Coyle. Field judge—W. D. Ackerly. Head linesman—D. F. Sullivan.

Trinity Crushes Hobart, 34-0, as Del Mastro Stars

* * *

Special to the Herald Tribune

HARTFORD, Oct. 4.—Paced by Umberto Del Mastro, captain, Trinity College crushed Hobart, 34 to 0, before 1,500 here today.

It was Trinity's second triumph in this, its seventy-fifth—diamond jubilee of intercollegiate competition.

Del Mastro, twenty-one-year-old fullback, scored two of the victor's five touchdowns, one on a fifty-seven-yard punt return in the second period.

Trinity hit pay dirt in all four quarters, while staving off Hobart threats in both the third and fourth periods.

Hal Wynkoop, twenty-one-year-old Philadelphia halfback, shared scoring honors with Del Mastro, cracking across from the 4-yard line in the first period and from the 5 in the third.

T-quarterback Jim Logan swept an end from the 11 for the final touchdown. Frank Lentz, Darien, Conn., sophomore, converted four of five times.

The score by periods:

Hobart	0	0	0	0—0
Trinity	7	13	7	7—34

Trinity scoring—Touchdowns: Wynkoop 2, Delmastro 2, Logan. Conversions: Lentz 4.

Rhode Island, 27; N. Hampshire, 7

DURHAM, N. H., Oct. 4.—Brilliant running by Pat Abruzzi and three last-period touchdowns gave the University of Rhode Island Rams a 27-to-7 victory over the University of New Hampshire today in a Yankee Conference tilt before 4,000 fans at Cowell Stadium.

After New Hampshire took a first-period lead after three minutes of play, the Wildcats could do nothing to compare with the attack of Abruzzi. The halfback totaled 306 yards as he outrushed the entire New Hampshire team.

The score by periods:

Rhode Island	0	6	0	21—27
New Hampshire	7	0	0	0—7

Rhode Island Scoring—touchdowns—Abruzzi (3), Gough. Conversion—Dispirito (3).

New Hampshire Scoring—touchdowns—Pappas. Conversions—Kelliher.

Springfield, 34; Norwich, 7

Special to the Herald Tribune

SPRINGFIELD, Mass., Oct. 4.—Springfield College started fast against Norwich University on Pratt Field this afternoon to grind out a 34-to-7 triumph. The Maroons, led by Norm Norris, scored three times in the initial period and twice in the fourth to even its season's record at one and one after an opening loss to Harvard.

The score by periods:

Norwich	0	0	7	0—7
Springfield	20	0	0	14—34

Albright Is 28-6 Victor Over Lafayette Eleven

Special to the Herald Tribune

EASTON, Pa., Oct. 4.—John M. Sudol, 175-pound back from East Rutherford, N. J., paced Albright to a 28-to-6 victory over Lafayette here today.

Sudol scored two of the Lions' four touchdowns, one on a thrilling sixty-two yards run, and the second by hitting center for five yards. Albright marched ninety yards for its first touchdown, Tony D'Apolito, of Peapack, N. J., running the last nine. Mike DePaul scored the fourth touchdown. Lafayette scored in the final period when Joe Callahan passed to Tom McGrail for thirty-five yards.

The score by periods:

Lafayette	0	0	0	6—6
Albright	7	14	0	7—28

Touchdowns—Sudol 2, D'Apolito, DePaul, McGrail, A. M. Powell.

Composite Score of 4 Games

* * *

Dodgers

	G	AB	R	H	2B	3B	HR	RBI	BB	SO	Bat. Avg.	PO	A	E	Fld. Avg.
Cox, 3b	4	12	1	1	0	0	0	0	3	2	.083	4	6	0	1.000
Morgan, 3b	1	0	0	0	0	0	0	0	0	0	.000	0	1	0	.000
Reese, ss	4	16	4	8	0	0	1	2	1	2	.500	7	13	1	.953
Snider, cf	4	17	1	4	1	0	1	2	0	3	.235	11	0	0	1.000
Robinson, 2b	4	13	3	3	0	0	1	2	3	3	.231	6	13	0	1.000
Campanella, c	4	15	0	3	0	0	0	1	1	2	.200	26	4	0	1.000
Pafko, lf	4	15	0	3	0	0	0	1	0	3	.200	9	1	0	1.000
Hodges, 1b	4	11	0	0	0	0	0	0	3	2	.000	34	4	1	.974
Furillo, rf	4	13	1	2	1	0	0	0	1	2	.154	6	0	0	1.000
Black, p	2	4	0	0	0	0	0	0	1	4	.000	1	2	0	1.000
Erskine, p	1	2	0	0	0	0	0	0	0	0	.000	0	1	0	1.000
Loes, p	1	0	0	0	0	0	0	0	0	0	.000	0	0	0	.000
†Nelson	2	1	0	0	0	0	0	0	1	1	.000	0	0	0	.000
Lehman, p	1	0	0	0	0	0	0	0	0	0	.000	0	1	0	1.000
Roe, p	1	2	0	0	0	0	0	0	0	0	.000	1	0	0	1.000
¶Shuba	1	1	0	0	0	0	0	0	0	0	.000	0	0	0	.000
Rutherford, p	1	0	0	0	0	0	0	0	0	0	.000	0	0	0	.000
Totals	4	122	10	24	2	0	3	8	14	24	.197	105	46	2	.987

Yankees

	G	AB	R	H	2B	3B	HR	RBI	BB	SO	Bat. Avg.	PO	A	E	Fld. Avg.
Bauer, rf	4	14	1	1	0	0	0	1	2	3	.071	9	0	0	1.000
Rizzuto, ss	4	14	0	1	0	0	0	0	4	1	.071	9	10	0	1.000
Mantle, cf	4	16	3	6	1	1	0	0	1	2	.375	14	0	0	1.000
Berra, c	4	15	1	5	1	0	1	2	1	1	.333	30	6	1	.973
‖Collins, 1b	4	11	1	0	0	0	0	0	1	2	.000	24	1	0	1.000
Noren, lf	1	3	0	0	0	0	0	0	1	1	.000	1	0	0	1.000
McDougald, 3b	4	12	3	2	0	0	1	2	3	2	.167	1	8	2	.818
Martin, 2b	4	11	1	3	0	0	1	4	2	1	.273	7	6	1	.929
Reynolds, p	2	5	0	0	0	0	0	0	0	2	.000	1	1	1	.667
*Woodling, lf	4	12	2	4	1	1	0	0	2	2	.333	5	0	0	1.000
Scarborough, p	1	0	0	0	0	0	0	0	0	0	.000	0	1	0	1.000
Raschi, p	1	3	0	0	0	0	0	0	1	2	.000	0	0	0	.000
Lopat, p	1	2	0	1	0	0	0	1	1	1	.500	0	0	0	.000
Gorman, p	1	0	0	0	0	0	0	0	0	0	.000	0	0	0	.000
‡Mize, 1b	2	4	2	3	1	0	2	2	1	0	.750	4	2	0	1.000
§Sain	1	1	0	0	0	0	0	0	0	0	.000	0	0	0	.000
Totals	4	123	14	26	4	2	5	12	20	20	.211	105	35	5	.966

*Tripled for Reynolds in eighth inning of first game. †Walked for Loes in seventh inning of second game, struck out for Cox in eighth inning of fourth game. ‡Homered for Gorman in ninth inning of third game. §Flied out for Collins in ninth inning of third game. ¶Flied out for Black in eighth inning of fourth game. ‖Ran for Mize in eighth inning of fourth game.

Pitching Summary

Dodgers

	G	CG	IP	H	R	BB	SO	HB	WP	W	L	Pct.	ER	ER Avg.
Black	2	1	16	9	3	7	8	0	0	1	1	.500	3	1.69
Erskine	1	0	5	6	4	6	4	0	1	0	1	.000	4	7.20
Loes	1	0	2	2	3	0	2	0	0	0	0	.000	2	9.00
Lehman	1	0	2	2	0	1	0	0	0	0	0	.000	0	0.00
Roe	1	1	9	6	3	5	5	1	0	1	0	1.000	3	3.00
Rutherford	1	0	1	1	1	1	1	0	0	0	0	.000	1	9.00
Totals		2	35	26	14	20	20	1	1	2	2	.500	13	3.34

Yankees

	G	CG	IP	H	R	BB	SO	HB	WP	W	L	Pct.	ER	ER Avg.
Reynolds	2	1	16	9	3	5	14	0	1	1	1	.500	3	1.69
Scarborough	1	0	1	1	1	0	1	0	0	0	0	.000	1	9.00
Raschi	1	1	9	3	1	5	9	0	0	1	0	1.000	1	1.00
Lopat	1	0	8 1/3	10	5	4	0	0	0	0	1	.000	5	5.63
Gorman	1	0	2/3	1	0	0	0	0	0	0	0	.000	0	0.00
Totals		2	35	24	10	14	24	0	1	2	2	.500	10	2.57

Score by Innings

BROOKLYN (N)	0	1	2	0	1	2	0	2	2—10
NEW YORK (A)	0	1	1	2	1	5	0	3	1—14

SB—McDougald, Snider, Reese, Robinson. S—Bauer, Roe 2, Furillo. DP—Martin and Collins; Rizzuto and Martin; McDougald and Collins; Rizzuto, Martin and Mize; Cox, Robinson and Hodges; Reese, Robinson and Hodges. Left—Brooklyn 24, New York 26. PB—Berra. Umpires—Babe Pinelli (N); Art Passarella (A); Larry Goetz (N); Bill McKinley (A); Dusty Boggess (N); Jim Honochick (A). Attendance—34,861 (first game); 33,792 (second game); 66,698 (third game); 71,587 (fourth game). Time—2:21 (first game); 2:47 (second game); 2:56 (third game); 2:33 (fourth game). Receipts—$209,892 (first game); $205,518 (second game); $311,754.97 (third game); $322,518.84 (fourth game).

Maris Puts Wood to 61st

Bosox' Stallard Victim

By KEN SMITH

The instant that Tracy Stallard's third pitch in the fourth inning struck Roger Maris' bat, the crowd knew that home run No. 61 was on its way into the right field grandstand at Yankee Stadium yesterday.

Down to the final day of the five and one-half month 162-game schedule, the 27-year-old man from Dakota passed the 60 standard that had lasted since Babe Ruth set it 34 years ago in a 154-game, eight-club league schedule.

THE 23,154 FANS could hear the crack of Roger's bat against Tracy Stallard's third pitch as their eyes followed the arching flight of the white horsehide far over the head of right fielder Lu Clinton, a half-dozen rows back in the lower section, to be seized by gleeful Yankee fan Sal Durante.

A triumphant shout that swelled into a din of cheering worthy of a crowd three times as large accompanied the crew-cut young westerner as he jogged around the same 360-foot trail to fame that the bambino had blazed.

Plainly more relaxed than he had been on the previous afternoon Roger took a reef at Stallard's first pitch in the first inning and flied to left field.

Up again in the fougth, Maris watched a ball sail by, then ball 2, too low for a swing. Finally came the pitch destined for the history books, putting Stallard in the same category with Tom Zachary. Ruth belted No. 60 off Zachary in 1927.

Maris climaxed the most severe spell of pressure ever faced by a home run slugger.

Yogi Berra and batboy Frank Prudento were the first to greet him. A young fan leaped out of the grandstand and got into the act.

In the dugout he was pummeled and the crowd shrieked for a

Continued on Page 36

Have No Regrets—Pitcher

"If I had the ball to throw again I'd throw it the same way." So spoke tall, Tracy Stallard, the man who supplied the pitch for Roger Maris' sizzling, scintillating 61.

"It was a good pitch," Stallard said. "A fast ball, a little away, and little below the waist. I've started to forget about it, already. About 60 other guys threw pitches that he hit."

MANAGER MIKE HIGGINS commented: "A guy pitches a whale of a 1 to 0 game and they forget about that. He got behind on the hitter, that's what set it up, he had to get the next one over.'

In a different mood, Maris pondered all the sweet details of the afternoon he'll never forget.

"I don't know what I was thinking of while I was running around the bases," said the new Rajah of Rap.

"When I came up the next time I told Russ Nixon it would be good to hit another, though afterwards I couldn't care less."

Roger didn't talk with the catcher the next time but in his final scene in the batters' box he talked with the Sox catcher about Sal Durante, the youth who fetched him back his HR ball.

"What do you think of that kid," Maris told Nixon, his former Cleveland teammate. "He is going to get married and could use the money but still he wants to give me the ball. Shows there are some good people in this world."

Maris planned no celebration after the game. "Won't do anything different than usual... Take my wife out to dinner... but I'm not saying where.

"It gives me a pretty good feeling to know I hit more home runs than anybody in the past. Naturally I am happy to have passed Ruth. I would have liked to have hit them in 154 but as long as I didn't, that's OK, too.

"The pressure was more mental than physical. I had to put up with this before and after game, with interviews and pictures every day the last two months. It is bound to affect you."

Handling the bat that propelled the record homer, Maris mused that he would put it away and not use it in the World Series. He thinks he hit No. 59 with the same Roger Maris model lumber. As for the ball that Durante caught Roger said he had not thought what he would do with it after it's returned to him.

Before the game, in the dugout Roger said that he had not received many offers in the banquet league. That will be remedied.

—SMITH

Titans Put Over 37-30 Victory

By FRANK BLAUSCHILD

Al Dorow is ready to pitch the Series' opener for the Yanks if they need him. Knocked cold in the first half, Dorow came back to peg a 13-yarder to Don Maynard in the fourth quarter that dissolved a first-place Eastern tie with the Boston Patriots as the Titans scored a 37-30 win at the Polo Grounds yesterday.

The balding QB tossed two TDs. He needed relief for a while from Bob Scrabis, who came in for three plays and also cashed a scoring flip, two seconds from intermission.

THIS WAS MOST important since it provided the Titans with a 20-9 halftime bulge which offset the free-scoring second half.

Besides the Dorow payoff pitches to Thurlow Cooper (five yards) and Maynard and Scrabis' TD toss, N.Y. got two sixes from Bill Mathis and a field goal off the boot of Bill Shockley, who kicked all the PATs except the final one. Dick Guesman took care of the odd one.

The ability of Mathis to run took a load off Dorow's shoulders and spiced the Titans game. The NY fullback toted the pigskin 12 times for 109 of the club's 157 rushing yards which set up the

Continued on Page 35

Mirror SPORTS

Babe's Widow Is Very Happy—But

"I'm very happy Roger hit 61—but I don't feel that he broke Babe's record."

That was the reaction of Mrs. Babe Ruth, widow of the baseball immortal, last night to Roger Maris' 61st homer.

"I wish Roger the best of luck in the World Series."

Maris' feat, however, brought him a wire from Mayor Wagner voicing the pride of the city and of "every baseball fan in the country." Wishing Maris and his team good luck in the World Series, the Mayor said he was "particularly glad that a Yankee player was the first to hit 61 homers in a season."

Maris proudly displays numerals he'll always be associated with as long as the game is played.

(MIRROR Photo by Frank Mastro)

Tittle Hero as Giants' 2d Half Surge Overcomes Skins, 24-21

By HAROLD WEISSMAN

WASHINGTON, Oct. 1.—In what must pass—and how he had to—as a local pitching performance reminiscent of Walter Johnson, whip-lashing Y. A. Tittle hurled the Giants to a 24-21 cliff-hanger that dedicated the immaculate D.C. Stadium this afternoon.

Hurray Y. A. did it the hard way, slamming his 35-year-old bones into the ponderous Redskin line on three successive sneaks in the fourth quarter from two yards out, thereby preventing the Giants from winding up out—on a limb.

A WEEK AGO against the Steelers, Yelberton Abraham picked up the ball from Charley Conerly and had himself one. But it took a little longer to get the desired results today. Tittle came in after Dale Hackbart whisked 48 yards with a Conerly filch and then yielded an interception that enabled the Skins to open a 21-7 bulge in the first quarter.

And then he went to town. Picking flaws in the Washington defense like a relentless court room prosecutor, Y.A. demolished the Indians with 24-41 315-yard passing that inspired the vaunted New York defenders to clamp a lid on the Skins the rest of the way.

Frustrated in the comebacking second half on Washington's 21 and 30 (Pat Summerall had to settle for a 28-yard field goal on the first drive), Tittle was not to be denied in the closing minutes of the third quarter.

Characteristic was the way he kept it alive in the fourth—with a bold 13-yard strike to Joe Morrisson in a fourth-and-one situation from the 24. Nor did he fold when the Giants were penalized to the 30 when Rosey Brown was detected holding. Yat promptly whipped a blazing pitch to Kyle Rote cutting across the middle to the two and then did the rest himself.

Until he spectacularly extended Washington's losing streak to 11 over two seasons—thereby tying Tommy Manville's record—Tittle had a worthy adversary in Redskin rookie Norman Snead. The Wake Forest rookie who thrilled the sun-splashed crowd of 36,767 with poise and striking power.

However, he didn't have collaborators like Del Shofner (eight for 103 yards), Rote (seven for 105) and Joe Walton (seven for 85). Alex Webster

The PROS

NFL Standings

SUNDAY'S RESULTS

New York, 24; Washington, 21.
St. Louis, 30; Philadelphia, 27.
Cleveland, 25; Dallas, 7.
Baltimore, 34; Minnesota, 33.
San Francisco, 49; Detroit, 0.
Green Bay, 24; Chicago, 0.
Los Angeles, 24; Pittsburgh, 14.

EASTERN DIVISION

	W	L	T	Pct.	PF	PA
New York	**2**	**1**	**0**	**.667**	**51**	**56**
Philadelphia	2	1	0	.667	68	57
Dallas	2	1	0	.667	55	56
St. Louis	2	1	0	.667	68	57
Cleveland	2	1	0	.667	65	51
Pittsburgh	0	3	0	.000	52	68
Washington	0	3	0	.000	31	73

WESTERN DIVISION

	W	L	T	Pct.	PF	PA
Green Bay	2	1	0	.667	67	27
San Francisco	2	1	0	.667	94	33
Baltimore	2	1	0	.667	76	73
Detroit	2	1	0	.667	33	67
Chicago	1	2	0	.333	34	78
Minnesota	1	2	0	.333	77	68
Los Angeles	1	2	0	.333	65	62

NEXT SUNDAY'S GAMES

New York at St. Louis.
Baltimore at Green Bay.
Chicago at Detroit.
Dallas at Minnesota.
Los Angeles at San Francisco.
Pittsburgh at Philadelphia.
Washington at Cleveland.

was a destructive ally on the ground with 98 for 20 running. But in the long run it was all Y.A. The man is simply Tittle-ating. And now are there any bets that he's not No. 1?

THE GIANTS STRUCK so quickly after the opening kickoff that the Skins didn't know what hit them. But after Conerly cashed the fumbled boot for a 7-0 lead everybody in the ball park knew what hit the Giants. It was Snead, bombing out a stunning 21-14 capital advantage.

It looked like a walkover when Summerall's curtain-raising kick-off caromed off Kerr's chest and bounced around loose for Summerall to pick it up on the Washington 24. Conerly capped the break five plays later with a spiral over Scotti's head and into Rote's hands in the right corner of the end zone.

However, the Skins stormed right back behind Snead's demoralizing aerial attack to pull even. Norm covered the 67 necessary yards in eight plays, four of them passes that ate up 49 yards. The payoff was a flanker flip to Bosseler from the three, the first time in his five-year Washington career that the fullback has scored on a pass.

Two minutes later the Tribe leaped to the fore as Hackbart leaped on the NY 48 to spear Conerly's hanging peg intended for Shofner and streaked down the sidelines for a TD. Enroute, he squirmed out of Conerly's grasp on the 35. Hackbart has only been with the club five days, having reported from Green Bay to gain the distinction of being the first Redskin to score with an intercepted pass since Dec. 6, 1953.

THAT WAS ENOUGH to convince Allie Sherman that Conerly didn't have it and he replaced the slumping hero with Tittle. Mean John Paluck promptly cost balding Y.A. a few more precious hairs by batting Tittle's peg skyward and waiting for it to come down into his huge hands on the Giant 42. Snead immediately began exposing the passiveness of the Giants' pass defense with another air strike climaxed by a 29-yard scoring flip to James. Norm had enough time to drink a cup of coffee before releasing the ball that left Patton and Barnes at James' mercy cutting between the goal posts. Aveni's third PAT ran the count to 21-7.

But then Tittle began to fire away with an awesome display of pitching to get the Giants within 21-14 on an 80-yard blitz culminated in the second quarter with an enchanting one-yard scoring flip to Shofner that caught the piled up middle asleep. Y.A. was

Continued on Page 36

Most Humiliating Yankee Defeat, M-Boys Declare

New York Yankee sluggers Mickey Mantle and Roger Maris, who are reporting the 1961 World Series for The Times-Union, give the inside story on yesterday's second game.

By MICKEY MANTLE
and
ROGER MARIS

NEW YORK, Oct. 5—The second game of the 1961 World Series can be described in one word. The word is horrible. That's the way it is if you hang your cap in the Yankee clubhouse.

The 6-2 loss we suffered at the hands of the Cincinnati Reds was the most humiliating defeat any Yankee team we've ever been connected with has ever had to swallow.

The Yankees beat themselves, which is something they don't do very often. Never have they beat themselves the way they did in this game. We played like a bunch of bush leaguers. The hitting was terrible and the fielding was worse than that. About the only consolation is that maybe we've got all that bad baseball out of our systems now.

Wanted 2-0 Edge

We wanted to leave for Cincinnati two games up on the Reds. Now the Series is even. Maybe a look at those short fences in Crosley Field tomorrow will help erase the memories of our stumbling performance in game No. 2.

Despite the terrible time we had at bat and in the field, there's got to be room to say some nice things about the way the Reds took advantage of every opportunity presented them.

They derived the maximum out of the first mistake we made. That was in the fifth inning when Elio Chacon came charging home from third base to score on a short passed ball. That was the key play of the ball game.

Chacon Playing Heads Up

You've got to say Chacon was playing heads up baseball on that maneuver. He had a good lead off third when the ball broke by Elston Howard. Now on a play like that, the element of surprise is everything. Normally, early in the game like that, you won't take that kind of a chance. In this case, you've got to say Chacon was living a little dangerously.

For a play like that to work, two people have to cooperate — the pitcher and the catcher. It was that little bit of indecision by Howard and Ralph Terry that set everything up just dandy for Chacon. The element of surprise was the big factor. There is no other way to describe this play.

That's the kind of a play to turn a Series ball game upside down. We won't go so far as to say it turned the Series upside down. The Yankees are still going to win it, and we're sticking to our original prediction. The Yankees will win in seven games. If it's sooner, so much the better.

No Quick Knockout

We're not counting on a quick knockout, though. These Reds looked dead in the first game of the Series. They weren't dead in the second game. They played a forcing brand of baseball. They hustled and made us pay right through the nose for all our mistakes.

Joey Jay pitched a good ball game. He mixed up his stuff. Most of his out pitches were breaking balls.

Jay had good stuff, but we helped him plenty. This Yankee team swung at more bad balls than they did in the entire seven games of the 1960 World Series. That's what comes of being too eager.

Maris: "I was one of the guiltiest guys on the club as far as swinging at bad pitches was concerned. I've been doing that right along in this series. I'm not hitting the way I should. In fact, I haven't been swinging good since along about the first of September. That may sound strange, because I hit some home runs during the month of September.

'Letting Pitchers Tease Me'

"I think I know the reason for it. I'm letting these pitchers tease me too much. Instead of waiting for my pitch I'm cutting at the one they're putting in the showcase. Most of them aren't good strikes.

"Another thing that ought to be brought up here. I want to give my views on that single Chacon hit in the fifth inning. Maybe some folks think I should have caught that ball. I don't agree with them. I got a good jump on the pitch.

"I'll admit I probably might have caught the ball if I had made a desperation dive for it. I said probably. I maybe had one chance in 100 to catch it. The odds were too high in that situation. We had two outs. There was nobody on base. If I dived and missed, the ball likely would skid by me for extra bases. Trying for a diving, shoestring catch wasn't the percentage play under the circumstances.

"I can understand why there's room for the second guess in this case. Chacon went to third on Eddie Kasko's single, and he scored from there on that passed ball."

Mantle Doesn't Know

Mantle: "The thing to do now is concentrate on Saturday's game. My status regarding the

(Continued on Page 63—Column 1)

The Week's Grid Picks

By BILL KASTELZ
SPORTS EDITOR

NEW ORLEANS, Oct. 5—Nobody's saying too much out loud, but it's no secret that this Tulane game here tomorrow night is being regarded by the Florida coaching staff and a disturbing proportion of Gator fans with more than normal apprehension.

Two factors have triggered this thinking:

(1) Florida being unable to master Florida State, a team the Gators were favored to beat by 13 points, and

(2) The suspicion that Tulane, beaten narrowly by Stanford and Alabama—both undefeated—may be a considerably better football team than the pre-season predictions indicated.

Neither is it a secret that Florida's interior line problems, particularly on offense, have given the coaching staff good reason to worry, not only about the Tulane game, but most of the games left on the schedule.

The more optimistic are inclined to charge off Florida's showing against FSU as "just one of those things," which in itself does an injustice to FSU's inspired performance.

Quite a few others, on the strength of the FSU game, already have abandoned most thoughts about another 8-2 regular season...with opposition like Rice, Georgia Tech, LSU, Auburn and Miami still to be faced.

A personal opinion is that Florida's ultimate record will fall somewhere between the two extremes in thinking: neither brilliant nor mediocre...probably 6-3-1 or 5-4-1.

If the Gators can come lashing back against Tulane, they'll be well on their way to such a record. If they can't, the future may as well be faced realistically.

It's a big, defensively-sharp Tulane team against which Florida will unleash its fleet backs tomorrow night. The guess here is that the Gators...who haven't lost a game since last Oct. 29 when Auburn turned the trick by three points...will edge Tulane by something like three points in a game that's going to be much tougher than a lot of fans suspect.

Ole Miss Is Heavy Favorite

Florida State didn't have much time to celebrate its fine showing of last Saturday, what with Ole Miss to be faced in Oxford on Saturday.

Not even the most optimistic of Seminole fans is picking FSU to topple the mighty Rebs, although, come to think of it, very few thought Florida State could hold its own against Florida.

Bill Peterson's troops will surprise more than one unsuspecting opponent on the balance of their schedule. But, it's hard to see the Seminoles doing anything like this to Ole Miss.

The Rebs rate at least a 15-point edge in this one.

Miami Gets Nod Over Navy

As one who went overboard on Miami on the strength of its showing against Pittsburgh—then chickened out for some odd reason, on the Penn State game last week—I am climbing back on the Hurricane bandwagon for tomorrow night's game with Navy in the Orange Bowl.

The only thing that can stop the 'Canes from having an exceptional season is a possible rash of key injuries.

Unless Miami suffers a tremendous letdown after its superb performance against Penn State, the Hurricanes should take Navy by 14 points.

Penn State Due to Bounce Back

Elsewhere around the nation, this is what things look like this weekend to one who managed a 21-8 record last week and now is 42-14 for a season's percentage of .750.

EAST

Penn State over Boston U.—By about 22 points.
Yale over Brown—The Elis without any strain.
Columbia over Princeton—A toss-up. Columbia by one.
Cornell over Harvard—Cornell's a touchdown better.
Dartmouth over Penn—Another toughie. Dartmouth by two.

SOUTH

Auburn over Kentucky—Tigers look 15 points superior.
Tennessee over Mississippi State—In a tight one.
Alabama over Vanderbilt—Tide keeps rolling along.
Georgia Tech over LSU—Despite Bengals' home field advantage.
South Carolina over Georgia—Anybody's ball game.
North Carolina over Clemson—Tigers' third straight loss.
Duke over Wake Forest—Devils are 10 points better.
N.C. state over Virginia—Wolfpack finally wins one.
Maryland over Syracuse—The upset of the day.

MIDWEST

Michigan State over Stanford—The Spartans have it.
Purdue over Notre Dame—Purdue usually up for this one.
Michigan over Army—Wolverines are on the way back.
Illinois over Northwestern—Going against the odds.
Wisconsin over Indiana—In a battle of "have-nots."
Minnesota over Oregon—The Gophers in a tight game.
Ohio State over UCLA—Bucks are back down to earth.
Missouri over California—To remain undefeated.
Oklahoma over Iowa State—By something like three points.

SOUTHWEST

TCU over Arkansas—Despite some pretty sound advice.
Houston over Boston College—Cougars by seven points.
Texas over Washington State—By three touchdowns.
Texas A&M over Texas Tech—Close, all the way.
SMU over Air Force—Mustangs crash win column.

FAR WEST

Washington over Pittsburgh—Pitt schedule no pushover.
Iowa over Southern California—Two touchdowns better.
Oregon State over Idaho—Not much of a contest.

Weather Outlook Fair for 3rd Tilt

CINCINNATI, Oct. 5 (AP) — The weather outlook for Saturday's third World Series game at Crosley Field is fair and pleasant.

The weatherman would not commit himself on Sunday and Monday.

Hulking Joey Jay Stops Yanks

—AP Wirephoto

REDS' GRUNT, GROAN MAN
... Coleman Slams 2-Run Homer

Reds Win, 6-2; Gain Series Tie

NEW YORK, Oct. 5 (AP)—Hulking Joey Jay, first Little League grad to make the majors, squared the World Series for Cincinnati today with a four-hit 6-2 victory in the second game, while the New York Yankee defense goofed with three errors and costly mental lapses.

Speedy Elio Chacon, subbing for the injured Don Blasingame, scooted home from third with the tie-breaking run in the fifth while a confused Elston Howard hesitated after recovering a passed ball.

Edwards Spoils Strategy

Matters speedily worsened for the proud Yankees when a strategic move by Manager Ralph Houk backfired into a run-scoring single by rookie John Edwards in the sixth.

A wild throw by relief ace Luis Arroyo and a shocking three-base muff on a fly ball by Yogi Berra contributed to two more Cincinnati runs in the eigth.

The teams traded two-run homers in the fourth after Jay and loser Ralph Terry had battled through three scoreless innings. Gordie Coleman slammed a long liner into the bleachers in right center after Frank Robinson's hard shot had bounced off Clete Boyer's chest for an error.

Berra quickly squared matters with his 12th series home run, following a walk to Roger Maris, the home run hero who struck out twice and ran his Series hitless streak to seven at bats. Yogi now trails only Babe Ruth with 15 and Mickey Mantle with 14 in Series homers.

Reds Show Skill, Speed

The Reds, who have been called such uncomplimentary names as "faceless," "castoff" and "misfits" showed fielding dash and speed after yesterday's shutout defeat. The Yanks showed little of the skillful glove work

(Continued on Page 58—Column 1)

Box Score

CINCINNATI (N)	ab	r	h	bi
Chacon 2b	4	1	1	0
Kasko ss	5	0	1	0
Pinson cf	5	0	1	0
Rob'n lf	4	2	0	0
Coleman 1b	5	1	2	2
Post rf	4	2	2	0
Freese 3b	2	0	0	0
Edwards c	4	0	2	2
Jay p	4	0	0	0
Totals	37	6	9	4

NEW YORK (A)	ab	r	h	bi
Richard'n 2b	4	0	1	0
Kubek ss	4	0	1	0
Maris cf	3	1	0	0
Berra lf	4	1	2	2
Blanch'd rf	4	0	0	0
Howard c	3	0	0	0
Skow'n 1b	3	0	0	0
Boyer 3b	2	0	0	0
Terry p	2	0	0	0
aLopez	0	0	0	0
Arroyo p	0	0	0	0
bGardner	1	0	0	0
Totals	30	2	4	2

a—Walked for Terry in 7th.
b—Lined out for Arroyo in 9th.

Cincinnati (N)	000 211 020—6
New York (A)	000 200 000—2

E—Boyer, Arroyo, Berra. DP—Chacon, Kasko and Coleman 2.

LOB—Cincinnati (N) 8, New York (A) 7. 2B—Post, Edwards, Pinson. HR—Coleman, Berra. PO-A—Cincinnati 27-11, New York 27-9.

	IP	H	R	ER	BB	SO
Jay (W)	9	4	2	2	6	6
Terry (L)	7	6	4	2	2	7
Arroyo	2	3	2	1	2	1

PB—Howard U—Conlan (N) plate, Umont (A) first base, Donatelli (N) second base, Runge (A) third base, Crawford (N) left field, Steward (A) right right. T—2:43. A—63,083.

—AP Wirephoto

HOWARD'S PASSED BALL SETS OFF FUTILE CHASE
... He Recovers Ball, But Fails to Stop Sliding Chacon

WASN'T OUR DAY: HOUK

Proud Yanks Admit Kicking Away Game

NEW YORK, Oct. 5 (UPI). Elston Howard and Yogi Berra both blamed themselves for key mistakes today, joining the rest of the depressed New York Yankees in admitting, "We just kicked the ball game away."

Manager Ralph Houk, perhaps, took the 6-2 loss better than most of his players, showing little emotion and absolutely no anger while commenting, "it wasn't our day."

Howard stressed the fact that the fault was "entirely mine"

Howard

Berra

on what could have been the key play of the game in the fifth inning.

The score was tied 2-all at the time, there were two out and Elio Chacon was on third and Eddie Kasko on first. Ralph Terry then came in with a pitch to Vada Pinson, the ball getting past Howard and rolling about 10 feet behind him.

Howard Too Late

Terry started off the mound but didn't get to home plate in time. Howard retrieved the ball, looked at Kasko heading for second, and then was too late when he tried to tag Chacon sliding into the plate.

"I blame myself, not Terry or anyone else," said the Yankee catcher. "I should have caught the ball in the first place.

"The ball hit my glove and popped out. I was looking at second. I didn't see Chacon until it was too late. My job is to look both ways. I didn't, and it cost us."

Berra was just as straightforward as Howard in taking blame for a three-base error he committed on Wally Post's eight-inning liner.

"I didn't lose it in the sun," said Yogi, promptly disdaining any alibi. "I just nonchalanted the ball, that's all. It hit the end of my glove and bounced through my legs."

Berra then surprised most of his listeners by pointing out that

(Continued on Page 60—Column 3)

HEROICS PUT REDS AHEAD TO STAY

Stop! Otero Shouted; Chacon Spurted Home

NEW YORK, Oct. 5 (UPI). Little Elio Chacon, who scooted home with the run that put the Cincinnati Reds ahead to stay in today's World Series game, confessed with a shy smile, "The coach — he tried to stop me, but it was too late."

The tiny Venezuelan, who started the game as the substitute second baseman, was easily among the happiest of a gay bunch of Red players in their dressing room under vast Yankee Stadium.

All square in the series at one game each, the Reds now are headed home for Crosley Field for the next three games of the classic and even dour-faced Manager Fred Hutchinson had to admit, "I got to figure that is going to help us."

Chacon, who had singled and gone to third on Eddie Kasko's single in the fifth inning, raced

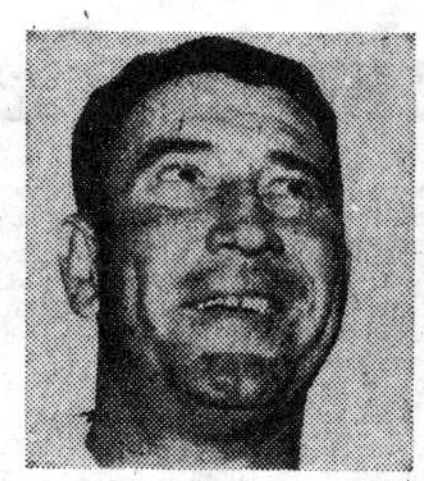

Fred Hutchinson

home with the run that put the Reds ahead, 3-2, when catcher Elston Howard muffed Ralph Terry's low pitch.

"I began to run because I thought I had a chance to score," said Chacon. "The third base coach (Reggie Otero) called to me, 'stop.' But it was too late for me to stop."

Chacon said he thought Howard "had a chance" to get him at the plate if he had thrown to pitcher Terry. But Howard hesitated, then just missed nailing Chacon with a headlong dive.

Joey Jay ,whose four-hit hurling made the Reds' victory possible, was explaining how he retired Roger Maris three times, including striking him out twice with men on base.

"I threw him a lot of breaking pitches — not many fast balls," said the one-time Little League star. "I didn't want to walk him, because the fans don't like that at all. But, on

(Continued on Page 60—Column 1)

GATORS SIX-POINT FAVORITE

Florida Opens SEC Slate Against Tulane Tonight

By BILL KASTELZ
Times-Union Sports Editor

NEW ORLEANS, Oct. 5—With a win and a tie to show for their first two starts, Florida's Gators open the Southeastern Conference phase of their football schedule here tomorrow night, favored by six points over Tulane's overdue Green Wave.

The Gators, who held a final light workout in the Sugar Bowl this afternoon, will be facing a big and beefy, defensively-tough opponent in Tulane, which lost its first two starts, 9-7 to Stanford and 9-0 to Alabama. Both Stanford and Alabama are unbeaten.

Florida, which opened with a 21-17 win over Clemson, had to content itself with a 3-3 tie in last Saturday's game with arch-rival Florida State, and if ever the situation was psychologically right for a rebound, it is this one.

Still, this year's Tulane team, despite its record, seems to be several levels above Green Wave units of recent years.

Against highly-ranked Alabama, the Greenies had a touchdown nullified and actually outgained and outplayed the Crimson Tide in the second half. This moved Coach Andy Pilney to comment later:

Pleased with Defense

"I was pleased with our defensive play against Alabama and our offense in the second half. We found out those sophomores want to play and we're going to use them. One of these days they are going to break loose against someone."

Pilney has yet to beat Florida in three tries, losing, 34-14, in 1958, 30-0 in 1959, and 21-6 a year ago. In the series, which dates back to 1915, Tulane leads, 6-5-2.

Topping the Tulane defenses is 215-pound junior tackle Ernie Colquette, whose 24 tackles in two games and cat-like reactions stamp him as one of the SEC's finest defenders.

The Greenies, who operate from a Winged-T formation, have averaged only 128 yards in their first two starts. But, running frequently from an unbalanced line against Alabama, Tulane managed good chunks of yardage on the sweeps.

Sophs Led Attack

Sophomore halfbacks Larry McIntire, Donnie Cotten, Tommy

Pilney

Graves

Emerson and Russell Galiano, along with soph quarterback Al Burguieres, were standouts in the Alabama game.

Florida has taken note of the fact that Tulane gave up touchdowns to both Stanford and Alabama by passes, and that the Greenies have allowed 18 completions in 37 tries by opponents in the two games.

Coach Ray Graves will go with much the same lineup that started the Florida State game, but it would not surprise anyone here if the Gators threw the ball considerably more against Tulane than they did against Clemson and FSU.

Only hitch in this thinking is that junior quarterback Larry Libertore, the team's top flinger with eight successes in 16 efforts for 156 yards and one touchdown, is still nursing a sore hand, injured against FSU.

Brunt of Florida's defensive chores is expected to fall on Graves' talented end corps, which probably will have a busy evening with Tulane's wide running game.

The game, which is scheduled to start at 9 p.m., Jacksonville time, will be the first of three straight road games for the Gators, who play Rice at Houston on Oct. 14 and Vanderbilt at Nashville on Oct. 21 before returning for a homecoming scuffle with LSU on Oct. 28.

Probable Lineups

FLORIDA	Pos.	Tulane
Smith, 193	LE	Roach, 192
Pearson, 225	LT	Kellum, 217
Travis, 205	LG	Holcombe, 211
Culpepper, 225	C	Chaisson, 201
Entzminger, 188	RG	Gonzales, 228
Beaver, 226	RT	Colquette, 215
Holland, 190	RE	Lasseigne, 224
Libertore, 138	QB	Burguieres, 175
Infante, 178	LH	Oeschsner, 171
Hoover, 197	RH	Cotton, 170
Goodman, 204	FB	Stein, 198

—AP Wirephoto

FORM THAT MADE JAY A WINNER
... Reds' Hurler Rears Back, Unloads Pitch

CLEMSON 27	N. DAME 22	KENTUCKY 14	MARYLAND 22	L.S.U. 10	GEORGIA 17	DUKE 23	ALABAMA 35
N. CAROLINA 0	PURDUE 20	AUBURN 12	SYRACUSE 21	GA. TECH 0	S. CAR. 14	W. FOREST 3	VANDY 6
Page 29	Page 28	Page 27	Page 29	Page 27	Page 29	Page 28	Page 32

Yanks 'Dial M' for Homer to Beat Reds

CINCINNATI, Oct. 7 (AP)—Roger Maris, the "new Babe Ruth," broke out of a shocking 0 for 10 World Series slump with a ninth inning home run today that gave the New York Yankees a 3-2 victory over Cincinnati and a 2-1 edge after three games.

The musuclar blond, who slammed 61 homers during the regular season, had been able to hit only one ball out of the infield until he lashed a long drive into the right field bleachers off Bob Purkey leading off the ninth of a tie ball game.

It was the first time the M and M Boys had shown their power against the National League champs. Mickey Mantle, the other half, finally played after missing the first two games because of an abscess on his right hip, but he went hitless in four trips.

Purkey deserved a better fate. The big right-hander with the butterfly knuckler and wide variety of pitches, had a no-hitter for 4 1-3 innings and a three-hitter for seven innings before the Yanks' power struck with a pinch homer by Johnny Blanchard in the eighth and Maris' blow in the ninth.

Scrappy Cincinnati led at various stages 1-0 and 2-1 and continued to pour on the pressure in the ninth against Luis Arroyo, the winner and last of three Yankee pitchers.

With one out in the home half of the ninth and an enthusiastic Crosley Field crowd of 32,589 yelling for a rally, pinch hitter Leo Cardenas drilled a long double high off the score board in left center field. Three or four feet to the right and it would have sailed out of the park for a tying home run. It was hit off this 51-foot high board instead of over the 18-foot wall that runs the rest of the way in left and center.

Cardenas' ball smashed into the board and bounced back so that Yogi Berra was able to return it in time to hold the Cuban infielder to a double. He died on second when both pinch hitters Dick Gernert and Gus Bell grounded out. Bell bashed a one-hopper at Arroyo who pounced on the ball as it bounced off his glove and threw to first for the final out.

Maris Blasts Homer

The goat's horns were being adjusted to Maris' measurements when he came through with the big blow. He was the only hitless Yankee regular and it appeared the season-long homer pressure had taken its toll. However, he hit a 2-1 pitch about 10 rows back into those right field bleachers, called "The Sundeck" in Cincinnati.

Cincinnati crashed through for a run off Bill Stafford in the third inning with the help of an error. Elio Chacon, the Reds' speed demon second baseman, beat out a bunt to the right of the plate for a single and went to second when Stafford's throw was wild.

Two outs later, Frank Robinson, the Reds' big slugger, snapped out of his batting slump, and rammed a double off the wall in left. Chacon scored easily with the first run on this bright, summery afternoon. It was Robinson's first series hit after seven futile trips.

With Purkey rolling along easily, that run looked bigger and bigger. The Yanks finally got to Purkey for a hit in the fifth, a double by Elston Howard high off the center field fence.

Except for a collision between right fielder Robinson and second baseman Chacon in short right field, Purkey might have had a shutout through seven innings.

Chacon, Robinson Collide

Tony Kubek opened the seventh with a single to center. With one out, Purkey's third pitch to Mantle got away from rookie catcher John Edwards. The ball rolled into the Cincy dugout and Kubek took second.

After Mantle fanned, Berra lofted a fly ball into short right. Robinson came in and Chacon went back beyond the normal range of a second baseman, finally getting his glove on the ball just as Robinson crashed into him. Both went down and the ball rolled on the grass, Kubek scoring the tying run.

Cincinnati bounced right back when Edwards lined a double to the right field corner and scored on Eddie Kasko's single to center. Once again Yankee strategy backfired for Manager Ralph Houk, who ordered pinch hitter Jerry Lynch walked with first base open and chose to have Stafford pitch to Kasko. Lynch, a lefty hitter, had a .404 record as a pinch batter this year.

Following Kasko's hit, Bud Daley replaced Stafford. Arroyo took over after Blanchard hom-

(Continued on Page 30—Column 1)

NEW YORK	ab	r	h	bi	CINCINNATI	ab	r	h	bi
Rich'n 2b	4	0	1	0	Chacon 2b	3	1	1	0
Kubek ss	4	1	1	0	aLynch	0	0	0	0
Maris rf	4	1	1	1	bBlas'g'e 2b	0	0	0	0
Mantle cf	4	0	0	0	fBell	1	0	0	0
Berra lf	3	0	1	1	Kasko ss	4	0	2	1
Howard c	4	0	1	0	Pinson cf	4	0	0	0
Skowron 1b	3	0	0	0	Rob's'n rf	4	0	1	1
Boyer 3b	3	0	0	0	Cole'n 1b	4	0	2	0
Stafford p	2	0	0	0	Post lf	4	0	0	0
Daley p	0	0	0	0	Freese 3b	3	0	0	0
cBlanchard	1	1	1	1	Edwards c	3	1	1	0
Arroyo p	0	0	0	0	dCardenas	1	0	1	0
					Purkey p	3	0	0	0
					eGernert	1	0	0	0
Totals	32	3	6	3	Totals	35	2	8	2

A—Walked intentionally for Chacon in 7th; B—Ran for Lynch in 7th; C—Hit home run for Daley in 8th; D—Doubled for Edwards in 9th; E—Grounded out for Purkey in 9th; F—Grounded out for Blasingame in 9th.

New York	000 000 111—3
Cincinnati	001 000 100—2

E—Stafford. PO-A—New York 27-8, Cincinnati 27-7. DP—Kasko (unassisted). LOB—New York 3. Cincinnati 9.

2B—Robinson, Howard, Edwards, Cardenas. HR—Blanchard, Maris. SB—Richardson.

	IP	H	R	ER	BB	SO
Stafford	6 2-3	7	2	2	2	5
Daley	1-3	0	0	0	0	0
Arroyo (W)	2	1	0	0	0	2
Purkey (L)	9	6	3	2	1	3

PB—Edwards.

U—Umont (AL), Plate; Donatelli (NL), 1B; Runge (AL), 2B; Conlan (NL), 3B; Stewart (AL), LF foul line; Crawford (NL), RF foul line A—32,589. T—2:15.

—AP Wirephotos

Roger, Over and Out in 9th; Chacon, Robinson Miss Berra's RBI Hit in 7th

Powerful Ole Miss Rebs Deflate FSU, 33-0

By RAY CHARLESTON
Times-Union Assistant Sports Editor

UNIVERSITY, Miss., Oct. 7 — Mighty Mississippi's merciless machine meshed with awesome precision to fracture Florida State, 33-0, this afternoon.

The Rebels, rated the nation's No. 2 college football team, played like No. 1, thundering to their third straight win of the season. The feat was accomplished without undue effort.

As expected, Doug Elmore, the Rebs' quality quarterback, was the big show as he guided the

Another Photo on Page 31

talented attack to three touchdowns.

When Elmore wasn't scalping the Seminoles, third string signal-caller Perry Dunn was. Dunn, who could play first string on many college elevens, passed for one touchdown and led the Rebs into position for another.

About the only surprise here today was the size of the crowd. Only 12,500 of the faithful showed up to see the Rebels saunter along the undefeated-untied trail and bounce the Seminoles from the unbeaten ranks.

It didn't take Mississippi long to show who was boss on the field this beautiful football day. The Rebels took the opening kickoff and ate up 77 yards in only seven plays for a touchdown. Right halfback Louis Guy nailed it on a six-yard spurt around left end.

Only the Beginning

That was only the beginning of the end for FSU which caused a

STATISTICS

	Mississippi	Fla State
First downs	28	8
Rushing yardage	351	75
Passing yardage	169	34
Passes	9-19	3-10
Passes intercepted by	1	0
Punts	2-28-5	9-30.5
Fumbles lost	3	0
Yards penalized	46	15

stir in football circles by deadlocking the University of Florida, 3-all, last week.

The Rebs scored again in the opening period and punched the scoreboard with TDs in each of the remaining quarters.

Fullback Billy Ray Adams, Mississippi's bulldozer in football togs, climaxed a 91-yard scoring thrust in 14 plays in the first stanza with a yard blast.

In the second quarter, Dunn flipped 15 yards to Larry Smith for six points, Elmore plowed a foot to pay dirt in the third period and Adams ended the scoring with a yard slam.

Wes Sullivan kicked two extra points and Chuck Tempfer one.

Superb Running Game

Mississippi moved the ball at an astonishing pace, thanks to a superb running game and a lightning-like passing attack. When the final gun ended it, the Rebels had accounted for 520 yards, 351 of them on the ground.

Florida State, which certainly didn't get here first and certainly didn't get here with the most, had a chance to stay in the ball game midway in the first quarter. Mississippi sub fullback Buck Randall fumbled—a rare happening by a Rebel team—and FSU's Jim Daniel pounced on the leather at Mississippi's 30-yard line.

Then the Rebs showed they had it up front as well as in the backfield. Florida State probed the line three times and wound up losing six yards.

91 Breathtaking Yards

Charlie Calhoun kicked the ball out on Mississippi's nine-yard line but it didn't make any difference. The boys in red cranked up and went 91 breathtaking yards in 14 plays for touchdown No. 2.

Florida State, lacking manpower to stay with the rangy and extremely fast opposition, managed to cross into enemy territory only twice the rest of the game. They didn't threaten seriously, getting to the Rebel 38 in the fourth quarter and to the Reb 48 in the final play of the game.

Florida State's only shining light was halfback Keith Kinderman, who managed to dent the Rebel forewall for 59 yards. And, that was a fine feat considering the catlike quickness and leather-popping ability of the Reb linemen.

Costly Penalty Halts Rebels

A costly penalty and an aroused band of Florida State defenders prevented the Rebels' victory margin from being higher. In the second quarter Elmore whipped a strike to Smith in the end zone but an offside assessment wiped out the tally. Florida State jarred Elmore hard on the FSU two-yard stripe in the third quarter, the quarterback losing the ball to FSU's Roy Bickford.

Florida State scouts reported before the game Elmore was a do-anything type of football player. It took the rocket Rebel only a few minutes to prove it was so true. In Mississippi's first touchdown move he kept the drive going with his ground-eating sneaks up the middle, bursts around the ends and deadly passing.

It was more of the same as the Rebs moved for touchdown No. 2. In fact, Elmore was even sharper. Turning from runner to gunner with astonishing ease, Elmore flipped four straight strikes before he missed.

Adams wasn't as highly-touted as Elmore prior to kickoff. He should have been. Before the never-quit fullback ended his daily chores he had churned up 109 yards, most of it between the tackles.

Rebs Impress Peterson

Florida State Head Coach Bill Peterson was impressed with the Rebels. "They were just too good for us," he said. "We didn't see any weaknesses offensively or defensively for Mississippi. Any time a team can move the ball 95 yards they are better than you are."

Peterson praised Kinderman, saying, "he (Kinderman) had a good day running."

Johnny Vaught, head coach of a terrific football team, gave the Rebel linemen credit. "The line did the trick for us," he said.

Vaught, who employed three teams, said this was Mississippi's best game.

That's easy to believe.

FSU	0	0	0	0	—0
Mississippi	13	7	7	6	—33

UM—Guy 6 run (kick failed)
UM—Adams 1 run (Sullivan kick)
UM—Smith 15 pass from Dunn (Tempfer kick)
UM—Elmore 1 run (Sullivan kick)
UM—Adams 1 run (kick failed)
Attendance—12,500.

SPORTS The Florida Times-Union
SUNDAY, OCT. 8, 1961 • 27

BOTTLES UP GANN IN 10-0 WIN

LSU Upsets Jackets

BATON ROUGE, La., Oct. 7 (UPI) — Hard - charging Louisiana State toppled nationally rated Georgia Tech from the unbeaten ranks tonight, winning a 10-0 Southeastern Conference victory.

Louisiana State had Tech's All-America candidate quarterback Stan Gann bottled up. The Tiger line pushed in on Gann each time he dropped back to pass, giving him little time to spot the receiver in the LSU secondary.

The Yellow Jackets got the ball seven times in the first half but could not push past the midfield stripe.

Quarterback Lynn Amedee spearheaded the Tigers' first scoring drive with passes for nine, 18, and seven yards.

Halfback Bo Campbell fumbled

STATISTICS

	LSU	Ga. Tech
First downs	11	9
Rushing yardage	145	86
Passing yardage	66	70
Passes	5-11	6-16
Passes intercepted by	1	1
Punts	8-40	8-37.9
Fumbles lost	2	0
Yards penalized	23	10

16 yards shy of paydirt and the Yellow Jackets recovered.

But four plays later, Tech punter Billy Lothridge fumbled the pass from center, the Tigers recovered, and resumed the drive from the 15.

Fullback Earl Gros punched down the middle for 12 and two plays later, quarterback Jimmie Field dived into the end zone.

Tech moved to the one-foot line on a third-quarter drive that started as it ended, with the Yellow Jackets unable to move.

Lothridge, faking a punt from the Tech 26, flipped a pass to righthalf Billy Williams on the scrimmage line, and Williams raced 18 yards to the LSU 30.

Halfback Wendell Harris booted a 22-yard field goal with seconds remaining in the first half. It ended a drive that began when fullback Buddy Hamic intercepted one of Gann's passes on the Tech 29.

Ga. Tech	0	0	0	0	—0
LSU	0	10	0	0	—10

LSU—Field 1 run (Harris kick)
LSU—FG Harris 22

WOODLUM, HUTCHINSON STAR IN 14-12 SHOCKER

Kentucky's Passing Stuns Auburn

AUBURN, Ala., Oct. 7 (AP). Aroused Kentucky used its great passing combination of Jerry Woolum to Tom Hutchinson to upset Auburn 14-12 today and hand the Tigers their first loss at home in 31 football games.

Only three minutes and 12 seconds were left to play when quarterback Woolum cooly connected with end Hutchinson on a six-yard payoff pitch that made Auburn a loser here for the first time since Mississippi State won in 1952.

Rawson Fumbles

Hutchinson, making a tremendous bid for All-America recognition, got underdog Kentucky in position for its surprise victory by recovering Auburn fullback Larry Rawson's fumble at the Tiger 21. Seven plays later Kentucky scored, shrugging off a 15-yard penalty on the way.

The triumph was Kentucky's first of the season. It came after successive losses to Miami and Mississippi. Auburn, a 24-21 conqueror of Tennessee last week, is now 1-1 for the year.

Auburn took a 6-0 lead in the first quarter when halfback John McGeever blocked a Kentucky

STATISTICS

	Kentucky	Auburn
First downs	11	6
Rushing yardage	115	-11
Passing yardage	74	91
Passes	8-12	6-12
Passes intercepted by	3	1
Punts	7-32.8	4-38.0
Fumbles lost	0	4
Yards penalized	35	55

field goal attempt, grabbed the ball out of the air and raced 82 yards for a touchdown.

Kentucky struck back in the second quarter after end Dave Gash recovered a fumble by Auburn quarterback Bobby Hunt. Starting from the Auburn 26, the Wildcats surged for a touchdown in nine plays and took a 7-6 lead when Clarkie Mayfield converted.

Auburn, restricted to a net of minus 13 yards rushing in the first half, rallied in the third quarter and scored on a 15-yard pass from sophomore quarterback Mailon Kent to senior end Dave Edwards. The Tigers then thrust back a Kentucky drive at their one and seemed to have their 31st consecutive home victory in hand until Rawson's fumble.

Auburn's fumbling tendencies, which almost cost the Tigers their opener against Tennessee, kept them in trouble throughout and eventually turned the course of the bruising game.

Kentucky's hard-charging line, led by tackles Junior Hawthorne and Bob Butler and linebackers Irvin Goode and John Mutchler, blunted every effort at offense by Auburn, a team that had blocked and run extremely well in its opener last week.

Kentucky	0	7	0	7	—14
Auburn	6	0	6	0	—12

AUB—McGeever 82 run after blocking FG attempt (Kick failed)
KY—Bruant 1 run (Mayfield kick)
AUB—Edwards 15 pass from Kent (kick failed)
KY—Hutchinson 6 pass from Wollum (Mayfield kick)
Attendance—32,000.

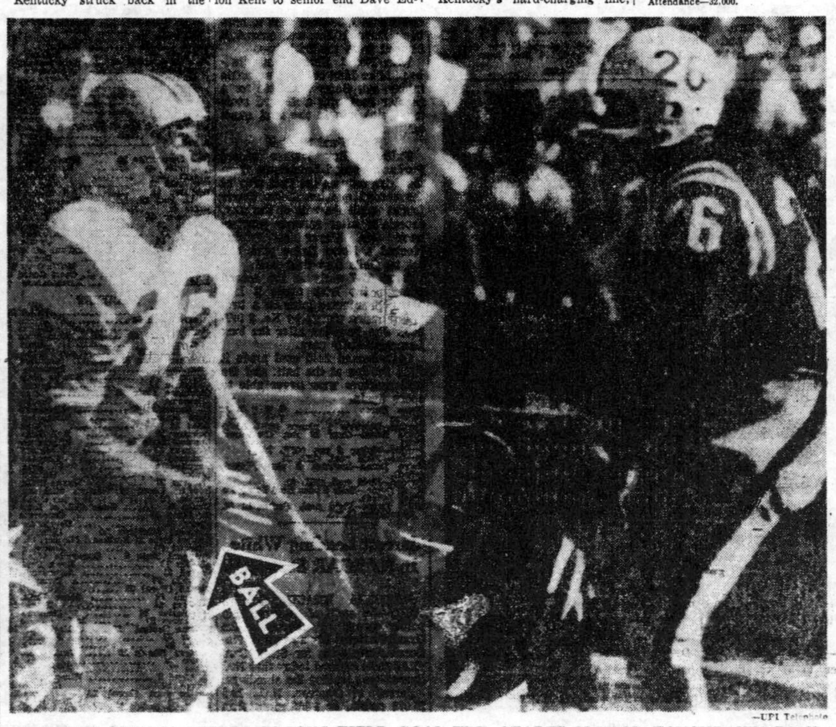

—UPI Telephoto

AUBURN'S JOHN McGEEVER BLOCKS FIELD GOAL TRY, STARTS 82-YARD TOUCHDOWN ROMP
. . . Mayfield of Kentucky's Boot Gobbled Up at Tiger 18; McGeever Caught Ball in Air

PREP FOOTBALL PLAYER DIES

SELIGMAN, Ariz., Oct. 7 (UPI) — A Seligman High School football player died last night after being injured in a game with Ash Fork.

Mike Ortiz, son of Mr. and Mrs. D. C. Ortiz, was injured early in the last quarter of the game. He died en route to the Williams Hospital, 44 miles away.

Dr. John Calley, a spokesman for the hospital, said the 18-year-old youth apparently died from a blow over the heart. He never regained consciousness, although mouth-to-mouth resuscitation was applied for more than a half hour.

Ortiz was injured while tackling a runner. At first, he appeared to have swallowed his tongue. The town's only physician was unavailable and a nurse, Mrs. Paul Chamberlain, had the boy rushed to the Williams Hospital by a highway patrolman.

The game was not resumed after the injury.

'CATS STOMP ILLINI, 28-7

CHAMPAIGN, Ill., Oct. 7 (AP)—High-powered, Northwestern hammered Illinois with sophomore fullback Bill Swingle and an assortment of halfbacks today, grinding out a 28-7 victory on touchdown drives of 75, 64, 55 and 51 yards.

The scoring thrusts totaled 245 yards and were accomplished in 32 plays—an average of 7.6 yards per crack.

Swingle, the 195 - pound Grand Haven, Mich., lad who came out of oblivion by scoring three times in Northwestern's 45-0 route over Boston College last week, twice crossed the goal line today.

Northwestern	7	7	0	14	—28
Illinois	0	7	0	0	—7

NW—Snider 4 run (Damm kick).
NW—Swingle 22 pass from Quinn (Damm kick).
Ill—Wheatland 1 run (Planeknhorn kick).
NW—Swingle 3 run (Damm kick).
NW—Flatley 1 run (Damm kick).
Attendance—40,138.

—AP Wirephoto

HILLABRAND USES HIS HEAD
. . . Seminole Nails Rebel Smith (82)

Wisconsin - 6
Indiana - - 3
—Page 3C

Northwestern 28
Illinois - - 7
—Page 2C

Carroll - - 6
Case - - - 0
—Page 7C

Miami - - 21
Kent State - 0
—Page 6C

Reserve - - 14
W. & J. - - 8
—Page 7C

Maryland - 22
Syracuse - 21
—Page 4C

Princeton - 30
Columbia - 20
—Page 4C

Sport News THE PLAIN DEALER Sport News Section C

CLEVELAND, SUNDAY MORNING, OCTOBER 8, 1961

MARIS' HOMER WINS FOR YANKS, 3-2

Ohio Rallies to Top UCLA, 13-3

WARFIELD, SNELL BAG LATE TD'S

By JOHN DIETRICH
Staff Correspondent

COLUMBUS, O.—Paul Warfield and Matt Snell, sophomore halfbacks, sped for the two touchdowns as Ohio State came from behind in the last quarter to defeat UCLA, 13 to 3, before 82,992 here yesterday.

The passing of Bill Mrukowski, junior quarterback, featured an open-style Buckeye attack. The Elyria boy connected 10 of 11 throws for 86 yards.

The Uclans led, 3 to 0, going into the final period of a field goal place kicked by Bobby Smith, versatile Bruin tailback, in the closing minutes of the first half. The ball was held on the 22 yard line, making the distance 32 yards.

Penalty Helps Ohio

A 15-yard personal foul penalty helped Ohio State's sixty-five yard march to its first touchdown, scored by Warfield, the sophomore speeder from Warren High, on a 13-yard burst off right tackle.

The score came at 46 seconds of the fourth period, and Dick Van Raaphorst, sophomore kicking specialist, booted the conversion to give the Buckeyes a 7-3 lead.

The Bruins sagged after that, and at 5:30 of the period the 203-pound Snell, sophomore right half from Locust Valley, N.Y., breezed through right tackle and galloped 33 yards for touchdown. Van Raaphorst's kick was wide this time, but Ohio State led, 13 to 3, and had command of the game the rest of the way.

Snell played in the first game last week, a 7-7 tie with Texas Christian, but could not be used as a ball carrier because of a leg injury.

UCLA never threw a forward pass until it was behind, 7-3. And its first attempt was nullified by a penalty. After Ohio State had its final lead, the Bruins connected on four of six passes for 53 yards.

Continued on Page 10C, Col. 1

ROGER—AND OUT IT GOES. Yanks' Roger Maris follows through and ball (arrow) sails toward right field bleachers for ninth-inning home run. Cincinnati catcher is John Edwards and the umpire is Frank Umont of the American League. AP Wirephotos

IRISH TRIP PURDUE ON FIELD GOAL

LAFAYETTE, Ind. (AP)—A 28-yard field goal by halfback Joe Perkowski set Notre Dame solidly on the comeback trail yesterday with a 22-20 victory over Purdue's Boilermakers.

Ironically, Purdue led most of the game on a couple of field goals by Skip Ohl. The Irish got ahead for the first time when Perkowski booted the 3-pointer three minutes deep in the final period.

A powerful ground game was a big factor in Notre Dame's first victory over Purdue in their last two meetings, but quarterback Daryl Lamonica also hit with two key passes. He threw 27 yards to end James Kelly to set up one touchdown and tossed Kelly a five-yard scoring pass.

Kelly also distinguished himself by smearing Rom Digravio, Purdue's excellent sophomore

Continued on Page 9-C, Col. 3

Statistics

	Notre Dame	Purdue
First downs	19	18
Rushing yardage	272	184
Passing yardage	77	81
Passes	6-10	6-12
Passes intercepted by	0	0
Punts	4-31.2	5-28
Fumbles lost	1	1
Yards penalized	45	35

Iowa Gets Scare, But Is Victor

LOS ANGELES (AP)—Top-ranked Iowa built up a commanding lead in the early stages, then fought for its life to defeat Southern California yesterday, 35-34, as a last-minute Trojan gamble for two extra points failed in their rousing intersectional game.

The amazing Trojans, two-touchdown underdogs, rallied in the last quarter to score two touchdowns and set the stage for what could have been the shocking upset of the football season.

They went for a two-point pass, but quarterback Bill Nelsen's desperation throw was knocked down in the end zone by Hawkeye Sammie Harris with 48 seconds left, and that was the ball game for Southern Cal.

Iowa's great running attack, coupled with two recovered Trojan fumbles, led to three touchdowns in the first quarter of the nationally televised game.

Hollis' Passes Click

Quarterback Wilburn Hollis, the Hawkeyes' brilliant runner and passer, passed to Joe Williams for 20 yards and a touch-

Continued on Page 8C, Col. 1

GOTHAM BOMBERS CELEBRATE. Maris (left) and John Blanchard flank pitcher Luis Arroyo after sparking Yanks. Maris' homer won game after Blanchard connected in eighth to tie score, while Arroyo hurled two scoreless innings in relief.

Army Is Halted by Michigan

ANN ARBOR, Mich. (AP)—Michigan's bruising line battered Army into submission before halftime and, combined with a devastating ground attack, carried the ninth-ranked Wolverines to a 38-8 victory yesterday.

Some 65,000 persons, many in shirt sleeves in the 80-degree temperature, witnessed the intersectional clash in which undefeated Michigan blistered the previously unbeaten Cadets with a total of 239 yards gained in rushing.

The Wolverines grabbed a 17-0 halftime lead after recovering three Army fumbles, two of them inside the Army 25.

The first set up Michigan's first touchdown scored by Dave Raimey from the 12. Following the kickoff, Army lost the ball again and after the Michigan attack stalled at the four, sophomore Doug Bickle booted an 11-yard field goal.

Michigan's second touchdown came on a 47-yard jaunt by Benny McRae, the Big Ten's hurdles champion, early in the second period.

(Continued on Page 3C)

Big Ten Standings

	W	L	T	Pct	PTS	OP
Michigan State	[illegible]	[illegible]	0	1.000	20	0
Northwestern	1	0	0	1.000	28	7
Wisconsin	1	1	0	.500	6	23
Michigan	0	0	0	.000		
Iowa	0	0	0	.000		
Ohio State	0	0	0	.000		
Purdue	0	0	0	.000	-	-
Minnesota	0	0	0	.000	-	-
Indiana	0	1	0	.000	3	6
Illinois	0	1	0	.000	7	28

(Ties count ½ game won, ½ game lost).

Browns Seek 3d Straight Today

By CHUCK HEATON

The Browns will be aiming at a third straight victory when they meet the Washington Redskins at 2:05 p.m. today at the Stadium.

Bouncing back after an opening loss in Philadelphia, Paul Brown's club squeaked by the St. Louis Cardinals and rolled over the Dallas Cowboys. Those victories put them in a five-way tie for the lead in the National Football League's eastern division.

Cleveland will be without the services of Dick Schafrath at left offensive tackle this afternoon. Since he is in military service, Schafrath needed unanimous league approval to play and George Preston Marshall, owner of the Redskins, refused.

It does not mean that Dick is through for the season. Marshall has indicated that he will switch his vote when another roll call comes up tomorrow.

Ed Nutting gets the call as Schafrath's replacement. The rookie from Georgia has been making progress and may be ready for a sturdy showing.

Back to cheer the home club will be members of the 1950 and 1955 championship teams. Otto Graham and company are slated for a halftime touch

Continued on Page 10C, Col. 4

Clay Stops Miteff for 9th in Row

LOUISVILLE, Ky. (AP)—Cassius Clay, in serious trouble during the early rounds, came back in the sixth last night to score a technical knockout over rugged Alex Miteff in a televised fight from Freedom Hall.

It was the ninth consecutive victory for Clay, who came into the fight 22 pounds lighter than his hard-punching opponent from New York.

Miteff, who had carried the fight to his 19-year-old opponent, dropped his guard as the sixth round opened and Clay poured in a barrage of rights and lefts.

Referee Don Asbury stopped the fight at 1:45 of the sixth.

The officials' cards were split at the end of the fifth round. Two had Clay ahead by a small margin while the other had Miteff in front. Clay was a 2-1 favorite.

Bee Gees Whip Broncos, 21 to 0

By HAL LEBOVITZ
Staff Correspondent

BOWLING GREEN, O.—On the opening kickoff Don Lisbon, Bowling Green's crack senior halfback from Youngstown South, voted the Falcons' most valuable player last season, sprained his right knee and had to be carried off the field. The 7,500 B-G fans in sunny University Stadium groaned.

They needn't have worried. Coach Doyt Perry replaced his star with Al Junior, who coincidentally happens to be a junior and the fleet Elyria substitute proved eminently worthy by scampering for two touchdowns as the Falcons romped over Western Michigan, 21-0, for their second Mid-American Conference victory here yesterday.

The Falcons are now the only unbeaten MAC team and are heavily favored to regain the title they lost to Ohio University last year.

A 21-0 score may not indicate a romp, but that's what it was. The Falcons completely dominated play, grinding out yards when they needed them, completing passes when necessary and stopping Western Michigan's offense so easily one wonders whether the Broncos really had any.

Continued on Page 6C, Col. 5

Blast in 9th Gives N.Y. 2-1 Lead in Series

By BOB DOLGAN
Staff Correspondent

CINCINNATI—This town let its hair down yesterday for its first World Series game in 21 years.

At 3 in the morning, inspired tenors sang songs, a cappella style, about the Yankees and Redlegs.

Gromyko and Kennedy were relegated to Page 2 and a paper ran an eight-column headline on its first page: "This Is the Big Day."

Night-spot comics found that the easiest way to enrapture an audience was to say something disparging about the Yankees.

Every merchant in town had a "fight" sign in the window.

Dawn broke and taxi cabs bulged with extra passengers.

Girls Dance Charleston

A couple of little blonde girls did the Charleston under the stands at Crosley Field before the contest, making the old Dixieland band that accompanied them seem glamorous.

It continued that way as the match progressed and the noise grew until the eighth inning when the Yankee bludgeon suddenly reasserted itself and won this pivotal third game, 3-2.

Cincinnati knuckleballer Bob Purkey took a 2-1 lead into the eighth, whereupon pinch hitter John Blanchard hit a two-out homer into the right field seats to tie it up.

Maris Finally Connects

Roger Maris then made his first hit in 11 series attempts, a home run, which led off the ninth and dropped into almost the same spot Blanchard's had reached.

Both were goodly clouts and sent the Rhinelanders home to cry in their beer.

The standing room crowd of 32,589 saw Purkey throw brilliant, devious baseball most of the way, holding the Yanks hitless until the fifth inning, when Elston Howard doubled off the centerfield wall.

Purkey gave the Yanks only six hits and handled Mickey Mantle easily. Mantle, in the series for the first time, was a caricature of his normal self.

His injured hip prevented him from running hard and the Yanks were fortunate he had only one fielding chance.

At bat he started slowly, then stopped, lifting two routine flies to center before striking out twice.

Continued on Page 10C, Col. 5

Yanks Now 5-1 to Take Series

LAS VEGAS, Nev. (AP)—Las Vegas odds-makers installed the New York Yankees as healthy 5-1 favorites to win the World Series.

The American League champions are 8-5 favorites to take today's game.

'I Knew I Had It,' Says Rog

By TED SMITS

CINCINNATI—Vindication came yesterday for Roger Maris but he took his chance of World Series fortunes calmly, almost glumly.

"I knew I had it," the New York Yankee said.

"I had'nt even hit one out of the park either here or in New York in practice since the series started. Change my swing? I honestly don't know what I'm doing," he said in a whisper.

The other Yankee homer, the pinch hit by John Blanchard in the eighth, was the result of some strategy.

"I made up my mind to go for the first pitch when I noticed Bob Purkey had been getting most of them in, and furthermore he wasn't throwing the knuckleball on the first pitch. So I went for it. It was a slider. I didn't have any intention of hitting it out of the park, but it was good," said Blanchard.

Mickey Mantle, getting into his first game in the series, came in limping, but asserted he felt good.

Whitey Ford, whose stiff neck has been bothering him, said "I'll be all right tomorrow." But he held his head awkwardly.

While Maris said he didn't know what kind of a pitch he stroked out of the park (Purkey said it was a "fast slider"), the handsome, husky Blanchard was sure his came off a slider.

"After two years of going to the plate, thinking I'll do this, or I'll do that," Blanchard explained sardonically, "I now have made up my mind to just go up there and swing at where the ball is, I can't go up there thinking. I guess that's the philosophy a pinch-hitter has to have."

Yankee Homers Do It Again

NEW YORK (A)	AB	R	H	BI	PO	A	E
Richards'n 2b	4	0	1	0	2	2	0
Kubek ss	4	1	1	0	0	1	0
Maris rf	4	1	1	1	2	0	0
Mantle cf	4	0	0	0	1	0	0
Reed cf	0	0	0	0	0	0	0
Berra lf	3	0	1	1	2	0	0
Howard c	4	0	1	0	10	0	0
Skowron 1b	3	0	0	0	9	1	0
Boyer 3b	3	0	0	0	0	3	0
Stafford p	2	0	0	0	1	0	1
Daley p	0	0	0	0	0	0	0
cBlanchard	1	1	1	1	0	0	0
Arroyo p	0	0	0	0	0	1	0
Totals	32	3	6	3	27	8	1

CINCINNATI (N)	AB	R	H	BI	PO	A	E
Chacon 2b	3	1	1	0	2	1	0
aLynch	0	0	0	0	0	0	0
bBlas'g'me 2b	0	0	0	0	0	0	0
fBell	1	0	0	0	0	0	0
Kasko ss	4	0	2	1	3	1	0
Pinson cf	4	0	0	0	4	0	0
Robinson rf	4	0	1	1	1	0	0
Coleman 1b	4	0	2	0	6	3	0
Post lf	4	0	0	0	2	0	0
Freese 3b	3	0	0	0	2	0	0
Edwards c	3	1	1	0	3	0	0
dCardenas	1	0	1	0	0	0	0
Purkey p	3	0	0	0	4	2	0
eGernert	1	0	0	0	0	0	0
Totals	35	2	8	2	27	7	0

a—Intentionally walked for Chacon in 7th.
b—Ran for Lynch in 7th.
c—Homered for Daley in 8th.
d—Doubled for Edwards in 9th.
e—Grounded out for Purkey in 9th.
f—Grounded out for Blasingame in 9th.

New York (A)	000	000	111—3
Cincinnati (N)	001	000	100—2

DP—Kasko (unassisted). LOB—New York (A) 3, Cincinnati (N) 8. 2B—Robinson, Howard, Edwards, Cardenas. HR—Blanchard, Maris. SB—Richardson.

PITCHERS' RECORDS

	IP	H	E	ER
Purkey (L)	9	6	3	2
Stafford	6⅔	7	2	2
Daley	⅓	0	0	0
Arroyo (W)	2	1	0	0

BB—Purkey 1 (Berra), Stafford 2 (Freese, Lynch). SO—Purkey 3 (Berra, Mantle 2), Stafford 5 (Chacon, Robinson, Purkey 3) Arroyo 2 (Robinson, Freese). PB—Edwards.

U—Umont (A) plate, Donatelli (N) first base, Runge (A) second base, Conlan (N) third base, Crawford (N) left field, Stewart (A) right field. T—2:15. A—32,589.

Whitey Ford Sets Series Record; Reds One Step From Elimination

Cincinnati, O. (AP) — Whitey Ford broke Babe Ruth's 43-year-old record by pitching 32 consecutive scoreless innings in World Series play but left with an injured foot in the sixth inning yesterday as the New York Yankees nudged Cincinnati one step from elimination with a 7-0 victory in the fourth game.

The defeat left the underdog Reds in desperate straits, trailing 3-1 in this best-of-seven competition.

Only three clubs, the last being the 1958 Yanks against Milwaukee, ever have come back to win after losing three of the first four.

Ford was injured twice. First he twisted his knee when he stepped into a hole at the side of the mound. Then in the top of the sixth a foul tip hit his foot and the toe turned black and blue. After Elio Chacon opened the Cincinnati sixth with a single to left on which Yogi Berra missed a diving catch, Ford left the game.

JIM COATES, the "long man" in the bullpen, finished up stylishly, allowing one hit in four innings. Ford had yielded only four singles.

For a change the Yankee home run bats were silent. But they went on their biggest batting splurge of the series with 11 hits.

Additional Stories on Page 26
Composite Box on Page 27

The Dixieland bands still tooted away and shapely gals in red dresses still ʻ the Charleston but the crowd of 32,589 had begun to file out of Crosley Field before the bitter end.

Bobby Richardson, a great October hitter led the attack with a double and two singles, bring his 1961 series total to eight hits. He was robbed of a ninth on a leaping catch by Chacon at second base in he eighth. Moose Skowron enjoyed a perfect day with a walk and three singles.

JIM O'TOOLE, a 2-0 loser to Ford in an opening day duel of southpaws, again trailed 2-0 when he left for a pinch hitter in the fifth. It was his second defeat and Ford's ninth series victory, extending his own record.

For today's fifth game, last at Crosley Field and possibly the last of the series, it will be Ralph Terry rematched against Cincinnati's Joey Jay. Jay was the winner of the second game, 6-2, and Terry was the loser.

Mickey Mantle started in center field for the Yanks, although still hobbled by the after-effects of minor surgery for an abscess on his right hip. He grounded out in the first, then singled in the fourth. But he had too much trouble running to first base and manager Ralph Houk immediately replaced him with pinch runner Hector Lopez.

THE YANKS came out of the game with a few cuts and bruises. In addition to Ford's foot injury, Berra was cut over the right eye when he fell trying for the sixth inning catch on Chacon. Richardson was cut on the right foot when taken out of a double play by Frank Robinson in the fourth. Both Berra and Richardson remained in the game.

A walk to Roger Maris, the home run hero of Saturday's game, proved fatal to O'Toole in the fourth inning. Mantle followed with a single and Maris scored when Elston Howard grounded into a double play. As it turned out that one run was all the American League champs needed with the combined five-hit shutout pitching of Ford and Coates.

Despite another double play by the Reds in the fifth, the Yanks still broke through for another run when Ford walked, Richardson singled and Tony Kubek lined a single to right center.

JIM BROSNAN, author of "The Long Season" a year ago, gathered material for a new book on "The Long Innings" when he was racked up for two runs in the sixth and three more in the seventh after replacing O'Toole.

Howard's double to right center started Brosnan's trouble. An intentional walk to Berra and a scratch infield single by Skowron loaded the bases. Clete Boyer picked this moment for his second hit of the series, a long double to the left field corner scoring Howard and Berra.

The Reds' first error of the series helped the Yanks get three more in the seventh, putting the game beyond recall. Richardson singled to center and took second when Vada Pinson let the ball get away from him for an error.

WITH ONE out, Maris was intentionally passed, both runners advanced on a wild pitch and Lopez brought them in with his first hit of the series, a single to center.

Another intentional walk, this time to Berra, and Skowron's single through the middle into center, drove home Lopez with the seventh and final run.

The "big hitters" of the Reds, Frank Robinson and Vada Pinson, have been muffled. Robinson has only one hit in 11 officials trips. Pinson has only one hit in 17 at bats. Gene Freese still is hitless in 12 trips.

The record that Ford broke was set by Ruth in 1916 and 1918. The Babe pitched 13⅓ scoreless innings in the first game for Boston against Brooklyn in 1916 after allowing a homer with two out in the first inning. He then shut out the Chicago Cubs in the 1918 opener and pitched 7⅓ scoreless innings in the fourth game against the Cubs for a total of 29⅔.

Ford shut out Pittsburgh twice last year and blanked the Reds Wednesday in the opener.

THE GAME had one gay moment for Cincinnati fans. With Skowron on third and Boyer on second and one out in the sixth, Ford rolled to Gordy Coleman near first base. Coleman stepped on the bag for the out and then walked across the diamond, faking a throw, while Skowron stood between third and home. Coleman finally touched Moose for the unique unassisted double play.

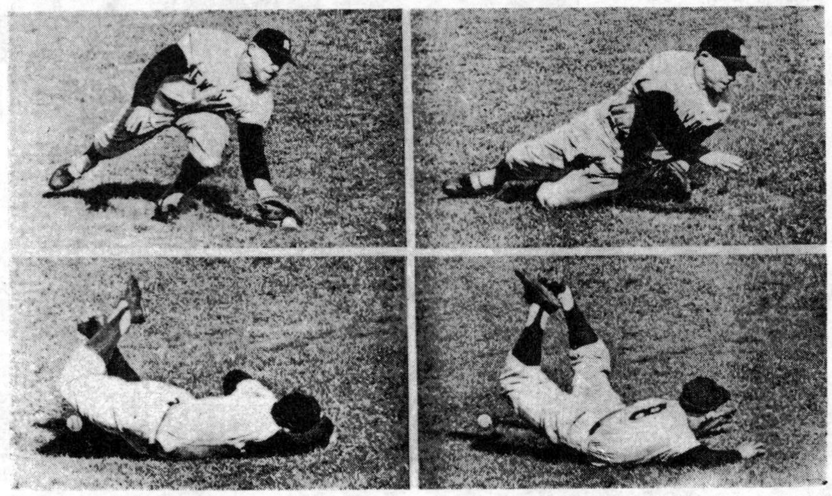

DIVING TRY—Yankee leftfielder Yogi Berra tries for a shoestring catch of Elio Chacon's single of yesterday's World Series game. Berra suffered a cut over the right eye from his sunglasses. He remained in the game after treatment. (AP Wirephoto)

Cincinnati (AP)—The official box score of the fourth game o fthe 1961 World Series:

NEW YORK (A)

	AB	R	H	RBI	O	A
Richardson, 2b	5	1	3	0	4	4
Kubek, ss	5	0	1	1	0	0
Maris, rf-cf	3	2	0	0	3	0
Mantle, cf	2	0	1	0	1	0
[1]Lopez, rf	3	1	1	2	3	0
Howard, c	4	1	1	0	3	0
Berra, lf	2	1	0	0	4	0
Skowron, 1b	3	0	3	1	9	0
Boyer, 3b	4	0	1	2	0	2
Ford, p	2	1	0	0	0	0
Coates, p	1	0	0	0	0	0
Totals	34	7	11	6	27	10

CINCINNATI (N)

	AB	R	H	RBI	O	A
Chacon, 2b	4	0	1	0	4	4
Kasko, ss	4	0	1	0	1	2
Pinson, cf	4	0	0	0	4	1
Robinson, rf	1	0	0	0	2	0
Post, lf	4	0	1	0	1	0
Freese, 3b	4	0	0	0	1	2
Coleman, 1b	4	0	0	0	5	0
D. Johnson, c	2	0	2	0	5	0
[3]Bell	1	0	0	0	0	0
Zimmerman, c	0	0	0	0	3	0
O'Toole, p	1	0	0	0	1	0
[2]Gernert	1	0	0	0	0	0
Brosnan, p	0	0	0	0	0	0
[4]Lynch	1	0	0	0	0	0
Henry, p	0	0	0	0	0	0
Totals	31	0	5	0	27	9

[1]Ran for Mantle in fourth.
[2]Hit into force play for O'Toole in fifth.
[3]Grounded out for D. Johnson in seventh.
[4]Struck out for Brosnan in eighth.

New York (A)	000 112 300–7
Cincinnati (N)	000 000 000–

E–Pinson. DP–Kasko, Chacon and Coleman; Kubek, Richardson and Skowron; Freese, Chacon and Coleman; Coleman (unassisted). Left–New York (A) 6, Cincinnati (N) 7. 2B–Richardson, Howard, Boyer.

	IP	H	R	ER
O' Toole (L)	5	5	2	2
Brosnan	3	6	5	5
Henry	1	0	0	0
*Ford (W)	5	4	0	0
Coates	4	1	0	0

*Faced one batter in sixth.

BB–O'Toole 3 (Skowron, Maris, Ford), Brosnan 3 (Berra 2, Maris), Coates 1 (Robinson). SO–O'Toole 2 (Kubek, Howard), Brosnan 3 (Lopez, Howard, Coates), Henry 2 (Kubek, Maris), Ford 1 (Chacon), Coates 2 (Lynch, Freese). HBP–By Ford (Robinson), by Coates (Robinson). WP–Brosnan. U–Donatelli (N) plate, Runge (A) ifrst base, Conlan (N) second base, Umont (A) third base, Crawford (N) left field, Stewart (A) right field. T–2:27. A–32,589.

MONDAY QUARTERBACKS

Value Of Foot Shown By Irish

Furiously-battling Notre Dame used the field goal to subdue Purdue, 22-20, at West Lafayette Saturday—additional evidence that the kicking game is becoming more and more important in putting together a winning college football team these days.

The Irish, though they outscored Purdue in touchdowns three to two, never were able to get ahead of the Boilermakers until Joe Perkowski booted his 28-yard game-winning three-pointer early in the fourth quarter.

Purdue, on the other hand, held off the charging Greenshirts for 48 minutes with the same tactic—a pair of field goals by Skip Ohl. Ahead 14-7, the Boilermakers pushed their advantage to 10 points on Ohl's 35-yarder. And following a second Notre Dame touchdown, Ohl gave Purdue a 20-13 halftime advantage with a 40-yard field goal just 11 seconds before intermission.

All three of the field goals were kicked over the south crossbar against a stiff wind that held Notre Dame's punting average to 31 yards and Purdue's to 28.

Perkowski had a lot of help from quarterback Daryle Lamonica on his deciding effort. The center snap was poor—almost on the ground—but Lamonica made an infielder's grab and placed the ball perfectly for his kicker. **MAX STULTZ**

I.U. Could Use Passer

Defensively, Indiana University may make it tough for opponents to score this football season, but offensively it doesn't pose much of a threat at the moment.

Holding a team to 163 yards rushing and 60 passing like they did Saturday against Wisconsin is certain to keep the foe from scoring touchdowns, but I.U. couldn't do as well with its own offense and consequently took another loss, 6-3. All points were from field goals.

Now Indiana has to face Iowa, whose backs run like spilled sugar—every direction—and score.

I.U.'s backs have speed. They were quicker than Wisconsin's, but I.U. also could do better with a passing game. In two games thus far it has completed only 9 of 25.

The three yards returned on three Wisconsin punts has been explained by I.U. Coach Phil Dickens as — the punt receivers cut an arc toward the sideline to pick up blockers. Wisconsin's downfield men didn't give Indiana's Marv Woodson a chance to start his arc. **BILL EGGERT**

Blackburn Big Loss

Wabash didn't just lose its homecoming game with Butler Saturday. The Little Giants lost the services of one of their top players and inspirational leaders, blocking back Gene Blackburn, who suffered a critical head injury.

Blackburn, still unconscious and in critical condition at an Indianapolis hospital with a basal skull injury, was a key figure in the single wing attack used by Wabash.

It was his assignment to lead the way on most of the plays and he did a capable job. Much of the yardage tailback Jack McHenry has picked up in the first three games was a direct result of Blackburn's ability to clear a path.

Coach Ken Keuffel heaped praise upon the 178-pound senior Friday night at a pep rally when he said: "I don't know what weight he is listed at on the program, but to me he is 250 pounds of guts."

Keuffel and his staff studied the game movies for hours yesterday but could find no clew to the cause of the injury. Blackburn is in the picture at the start of the play on which he was hurt but he is out of sight toward the end.

Wabash trailed Butler by six points, 13-7, when Blackburn was injured and from that point on the Little Giants weren't the same team that started the game.

Tony Hinkle's Bulldogs once again showed they are the team to beat in the Indiana Collegiate Conference. They have a powerful running attack with five backs that can do a capable job. And, the passing of Phil Long will be hard to stop if he continues to get excellent protection from the forward wall. — **JOHN BANSCH**

CADOU CALLS 'EM

Yankee Pitchers Not That Good, Says Pilot Of Weak-Hitting Reds

By JEP CADOU JR.
Star Sports Editor

Cincinnati, O. — The Queen City's alleged sluggers are hitting like her majesty and the ladies of the royal court but Manager Fred Hutchinson does not attribute the powder-puff performance to Yankee pitching prowess.

Their pitchers are not that good," said the Reds' skipper in the dressing room after yesterday's 7-0 debacle.

"Our big hitters simply aren't hitting. It's definitely a batting slump. And, the unfortunate part of it is that we have had good pitching on the whole and our defense has been good."

As indication of the depths of the diamond doldrums into which the Reds have fallen is the fact that their most potent offensive weapon yesterday was a fellow who got on base twice when he was hit by the pitcher and once when he walked, outfielder Frank Robinson.

THE TRIO of sluggers who provided much of the pennant impetus for the Reds—Robinson, Vada Pinson and Gene Freese—have a frightening aggregate of just two hits in 40 trips to the plate. Robinson is hitting .097, Pinson .059 and Freese a big, fat triple-zero.

At least, it's frightening to Hutch and the Redleg fandom.

"The time is short," Hutchinson said in a classic bit of understatement. "We've simply got to start hitting now. Unfortunately, there's no magic formula for breaking a slump.

"We've had other slumps during the season. In one of them, we lost eight games in a row. But, after those other slumps, we had time to bounce back and always did. Time is running out on us now."

HUTCHINSON expressed confidence that it isn't any lack of desire which is responsible for Cincinnati's anemic stickwork.

"They're trying their best," he said. "They may be trying too hard. Pinson is not swinging like he was during the regular season. Robinson and Freese are swinging like they always have but they're just not hitting."

Hutchinson doesn't plan any shakeup of his lineup for today's fifth game of the series.

"Why should I?," he asked rhetorically, "this is the club that won the pennant for us. I can't take Robinson or Freese or Pinson out of the lineup.

"We have to start getting some breaks. We haven't had many up to now. We've hit a lot of hard fouls that would have made a difference if they had been fair. And, we've had several bloopers hit against us. But they all count."

In the gloom of the slump-ridden Reds' dressing room, Hutchinson summoned up enough of his sense of humor to remark with a touch of irony, "Well, we go into the record books for one thing, anyhow."

He was referring to the new all-time series mark of 32 consecutive scoreless innings hung up by Whitey Ford, who had to be removed from the game after five innings because he had hurt a big toe.

Ford exhibited the baseball with which he got Elio Chacon to ground out from Bobby Richardson to Bill Skowron in the third inning and asked, "I wonder what that fellow in California will give me for this one?"

HE WAS referring to a Fresno, Cal., restaurateur who is going to pay the youth who snagged Roger Maris' 61st home run ball $5,000 for the privilege of presenting it to Maris.

Ford said that he realized he was breaking Ruth's record of 29 and ⅔ scoreless innings (set in the 1916 and 1918 series when Ruth was pitching for Boston's Red Sox.)

"But I really didn't think much about it at the time," he said, "because we still didn't have any runs and I was thinking about winning the game."

Ford went just exactly one inning more than he needed in order to get credit for his World Series victory, another record.

He allowed four of the five hits the Reds got but all of them were singles, two by catcher Darrell Johnson and one each by Chacon and Eddie Kasko.

"Now I think I'll get Wally Moses (Yankee batting coach) to work with me next spring and go after Ruth's other record," Ford said with tongue in cheek.

Ford said he was hit on the big toe of the right foot by his own foul tip in the sixth inning and the injury was exceedingly painful.

WHITEY STAYED in the the game just long enough to ground to Reds' first baseman Gordon Coleman and start one of the weirdest double plays in series history.

Coleman stopped Ford's grounder, ran over and touched first base and then noticed that Skowron was caught between third and home.

Coleman started running toward Skowron with the ball in his hand, alternately feinting throws to third and home. When Skowron would go to his right, Coleman would go to his right and vice versa.

IT WAS like one of those awkward situations when you're walking down the sidewalk and trying to avoid someone coming toward you. And, for Skowron it had the same inevitable conclusion with Coleman and himself finally trying to occupy the same space at the same time.

That unassisted double play gave Redleg rooters their best chance to cheer of the afternoon.

Despite the one-sided nature of the game, however, manager Ralph Houk of the Yanks is taking nothing for granted.

"We looked more normal as far as our hitting was concerned," Houk said, "and it was a big one to win. But that last victory sometimes is the toughest. We still have to win one more game. And, that fourth one is the hardest to get."

"I remember once when it was rather difficult in Milwaukee," Houk added. He was speaking of the series in which the Yanks lost three of the first four games and then came back to win three in a row and capture the classic.

HOUK HAD a somewhat surprising opinion on the turning point of this game. He put his finger on Mickey Mantle's single in the fourth inning which moved Maris to second base.

"That eventually got us that first big run," Houk said.

Trust Yogi Berra to come up with a really unusual injury. Going for a line drive off the bat of Chacon in the sixth, Berra tried a diving catch and went into the ground snoot first.

The generous Berra beak wasn't injured but Yogi's sunglasses dug into his head and cut him above the right eye.

But what hurt more was when umpire Shag Crawford detected him trapping the ball instead of catching it.

Atlanta To Get Club, Is Report

Charleston, W. Va. (AP)—The Charleston club of the International League will be moved to Atlanta, Ga., the Charleston Gazette said last night.

"We just couldn't justify staying another season the way the weather is in Charleston," Owner Bill MacDonald said. "And beside, Atlanta has made us such a fine proposition that we simply can't turn it down."

ON WAY TO RECORD—New York southpaw Whitey Ford pitches in the first inning of yesterday's World Series game at Cincinnati in which he set a record of hurling 32 consecutive scoreless innings. Ford blanked the Reds for five innings yesterday before being relieved as he broke Babe Ruth's old series mark of 29 2/3 straight shutout frames. (AP Wirephoto)

Home Run Bound

CINCINNATI — John Blanchard, New York Yankee right fielder, swings into a home run ball that sank into the right field stands and scored N.Y.'s first two runs of a 13-5 World Series finale romp over Cincinnati. The catcher is John Edwards of the Reds, a former Indianapolis receiver, and the umpire is Ed Runge of the American League.—AP Wirephoto.

Reds' Chacon Goes to Mets in N.L. Draft

By Associated Press

CINCINNATI—The Houston Colts picked Eddie Bressoud, San Francisco shortstop, and Bob Aspromonte, Los Angeles second baseman, as their first two choices in the draft for two new National League teams.

The New York Mets selected, as their first two choices, catcher Hobie Landrith of the Giants, and second baseman Elio Chacon of the National League champion Cincinnati Reds.

Bressoud and Landrith were the first choices as the two new members started to build their rosters for 1962 operations.

President Warren Giles tossed a coin for the first selection and Houston manager Harry Craft won.

General manager Paul Richards of Houston made the first selection of Bressoud. Bressoud, 29, played shortstop four years for the Giants and last season batted .227 in 58 games. He is 6-1, 180 and bats right-handed. His lifetime average is .240.

President George Weiss of the Mets took Landrith as his first selection. The 31-year-old catcher, a left-handed hitter, batted .235 for the Giants in 42 games this year. He is 5.8, 170, and has a lifetime average of .237 and has been around the National League for 10 years, off and on.

Aspromonte, 23-year-old infielder, played third base in most of his games with the Dodgers last season, but he also can play shortstop and second base. He is 6-3, 180 and a right-handed batter. Last season he hit .235 in 45 games. He was a highly-regarded rookie in the Dodger organiation.

Chacon played second base during most of the World Series for Cincinnati. He is a 24-year-old Venezuelan, standing 5.10 and weighing 170. He is a right-handed batter, whose regular season average was .265. He scored the tie-breaking run in Cincinnati's only Series victory in the second game.

The officials at the draft meeting deliberated 45 minutes, discussing military status and physical conditions of the submitted players, before beginning the actual draft.

Opening phase of the draft required each new club to draw a total of 16 players (two from each of the old eight clubs) at $75,000 each, plus a choice of eight more (one from each existing club) at $50,000 each.

12-YEAR SURVEY

Yogi Says Yanks Best He's Seen

By YOGI BERRA for Associated Press

CINCINNATI—This has to be the greatest Yankee team I ever played on and I've now been through 12 World Series.

It had to be. We had six men who hit 21 or more home runs. We had two men—Roger Maris and Mickey Mantle—who hit 115 homers. And we set a home run record of 240 in winning the American League pennant.

Berra

National Leaguers thought we were weak because our league expanded and all we heard all season was how well balanced the other league was. I think we upheld the honor of Joe Cronin's league pretty good.

Other Yankee teams had great players like Joe DiMaggio, Hank Bauer and Phil Rizzuto and pitchers like Allie Reynolds, Vic Raschi, Ed Lopat and Joe Page—but we had team balance.

Ralph Houk, our manager, rebuilt the pitching staff in one season. You can't do that with a so-so team. Fred Hutchinson remade his pitching staff, too.

But we had Whitey Ford. Ralph made him our No. 1 pitcher right from the start, using him with three days rest most of the year and he won 25 games and pitched 14 runless innings in the World Series against the Reds to beat Babe Ruth's pitching record. Whitey always was our No. 1 pitcher with me.

It was a real happy club. Everybody was pulling for everybody. I actually saw Mantle root for Maris and Maris root for Mantle all year. You don't see that on all clubs. Money means so much. But with us it seems to be pride. Money is secondary. We know it's bound to come our way if we put out as hard as we can.

We had great morale on the club this year. Ralph did a wonderful job. I played for three different men on the Yankees but I have to go for this guy. He made us all happy. I can't recall that we had one squabble all year, and goodness knows we've had a few in the past.

I know that at 36 I was mighty proud to be a part of it. Left field was strange to me but I had to give it a whirl because Houk placed so much faith in me. It was a challenge.

SERIES BOX SCORE

NEW YORK (13)

	AB	R	H	RBI	PO	A
Richardson, 2b	6	1	1	0	1	3
Kubek, ss	6	2	2	0	2	1
Maris, cf-rf	5	0	1	1	3	1
Blanchard, rf	4	3	3	2	2	0
Reed, cf	0	0	0	0	0	0
Howard, c	5	3	2	0	4	0
Skowron, 1b	5	2	2	3	7	3
Lopez, lf	4	2	2	5	5	0
Boyer, 3b	3	0	2	1	2	1
Terry, p	1	0	0	0	1	1
Daley, p	1	0	0	1	0	0
	40	13	15	13	27	10

CINCINNATI (5)

	AB	R	H	RBI	PO	A
Blasingame, 2b	4	1	1	0	2	2
eChacon	1	0	0	0	0	0
Kasko, ss	5	1	2	0	0	3
Pinson, cf	5	0	1	0	4	0
Robinson, rf	4	1	2	3	2	0
Coleman, 1b	4	1	1	0	7	0
Post, lf	3	1	2	2	3	0
Freese, 3b	4	0	1	0	1	1
Edwards, c	4	0	1	0	8	0
Jay, p	0	0	0	0	0	0
Maloney, p	0	0	0	0	0	0
K. Johnson, p	0	0	0	0	0	0
aBell	1	0	0	0	0	0
Henry, p	0	0	0	0	0	1
Jones, p	0	0	0	0	0	0
bGernert	1	0	0	0	0	0
Purkey, p	0	0	0	0	0	1
vCardenas	1	0	0	0	0	0
Brosnan, p	0	0	0	0	0	0
dLynch	1	0	0	0	0	0
Hunt, p	0	0	0	0	0	1
	38	5	11	5	27	9

aFouled out for K. Johnson in 2d.
bCalled out on strikes for Jones in 4th.
cFlied out for Purkey in 6th.
dGrounded out for Brosnan in 8th.
eGrounded out for Blasingame in 9th.

New York (A) 510 502 000–13
Cincinnati (N) 003 020 000– 5

E–Coleman, Daley, Kasko, Purkey. LOB–New York (A) 10, Cincinnati (N) 7. 2B–Howard, Boyer, Maris, Freese, Blanchard, Robinson. 3B–Lopez. HR–Blanchard, Robinson, Lopez, Post. S–Terry, Lopez, Daley. SF–Daley.

PITCHING SUMMARY

	IP	H	R	ER
Jay (L)	⅔	4	2	2
Maloney	⅔	2	2	2
K. Johnson	⅔	0	0	0
Henry	1⅓	4	5	5
Jones	⅔	0	0	0
Purkey	2	0	2	0
Brosnan	2	3	0	0
Hunt	1	0	0	0
Terry	2⅓	6	3	3
Daley (W)	6⅔	5	2	0

BB–Maloney 1 (Blanchard), Henry 2 (Boyer, Howard), Purkey 2 (Blanchard, Boyer), Hunt 1 (Maris). SO–Maloney 1 (Terry), Henry 1 (Lopez), Purkey 2 (Maris, Skowron), Brosnan 1 (Maris), Hunt 1 (Howard), Daley 3 (Gernert, Freese, Blasingame). HBP–By Daley (Post). WP–Brosnan. U–Runge (A) plate, Conlan (N) first base, Umont (A) second base, Donatelli (N) third base, Crawford (N) left field, Stewart (A) right field. T–3:05. A–32,589.

Bill Hitchcock Oriole Pilot

By Associated Press

BALTIMORE — Bill Hitchcock today was named to manage the Baltimore Orioles next baseball season.

Lee MacPhail, Oriole president, said Hitchcock's contract will be for one year. The salary was not announced, but it was guessed to be around $30,000.

Hitchcock succeeds Paul Richards, who built the Orioles into a first-division club in the American League. Richards quit after seven years to become general manager of the new Houston member of the National League.

Hitchcock, who lives in Opelika, Ala., is moving into the major leagues after managing Vancouver to second place in the Pacific Coast League this season.

He was player-manager of Buffalo in the International League in 1954 and then coached for Detroit five seasons. Hitchcock was an infielder with Detroit, Washington, St. Louis, Boston and Philadelphia in the American League.

Oscar Will Play at New Castle

Special to The News

NEW CASTLE, Ind.—Oscar Robertson and his Cincinnati Royal teammates will play a National Basketball Association exhibition game at Chryler Fieldhouse tomorrow night.

The St. Louis Hawks will provide the competition for the 8 o'clock game sponsored by the New Castle Jay Cees. Ticekts, priced at $1.50, will be on sale at the door.

Yanks Score 27 Times With Only 2 M&M RBIs

By JERRY LISKA, AP Sports Writer

CINCINNATI—The incredible New York Yankees, with only two RBIs from their fabled M & M flailers, have revived sagging American League prestige with an almost effortless five-game World Series decision over the stunned Cincinnati Reds.

It was true, Roger Maris, the new Babe Ruth, hit a game-winning homer in Saturday's third game, but Maris and the ailing Mickey Mantle otherwise let their less-publicized but highly-talented Yankee mates go about routing the Reds, four games to one.

In yesterday's 13-5 clincher in sun-swathed Crosley Field, such Yankees as John Blanchard, Hector Lopez, Bill Skowron, a former Purdue University athlete, and Clete Boyer cannonaded the Reds into submission.

In this Series, which ended a two-year domination by National League champions—Los Angeles in 1959 and Pittsburgh in 1960—the Yankees won three in a row after Cincinnati's only victory tied the Series 1-all last Thursday.

Many baseball buffs regarded the Reds as a lucky array of castoffs who caught lightning in a bottle by winning the National League pennant after finishing sixth in 1960. However, they also thought the Reds had a fighting chance in the Series after the Maris-Mantle duo which had combined for 115 homers and 270 RBIs almost faded out of the picture—Maris in a slump and Mantle with a painfully infected right hip.

But Cincinnati's big guns never boomed—until a futile salvo in yesterday's anti-climactic finale—and the superbly-balanced Yankees scored 27 times in winning their 19th World Series, handing out the worst Series thumping since 1954 when the New York Giants bounced out the Cleveland Indians in four straight.

This turned out to be a Series of unusual individual performances by the poised and timely-hitting Yankees. Personable Ralph Houk became only the third manager to win a Series title in his freshman year. The other two were by Bucky (Boy Wonder) Harris of Washington in 1924, and Eddie Dyer of the St. Louis Cardinals in 1946.

The Yankee RBI leaders in the Series was utility man Lopez, a .220 regular season hitter, who drove across seven runs with three hits — including a triple and homer yesterday — in 10 times at bat.

Another utility man, rugged Blanchard, finished fast as Mantle's aching hip limited him to only 11 innings of play. Blanchard drove a game-tying pinch homer in Saturday's game, and yesterday, playing right field as Maris switched to center, the 200-pound catcher-outfielder slammed a two-run homer in New York's five-run first and followed with two walks, a double and a single.

Although he figured lightly in Yankee run-production, second baseman Bobby Richardson came through with another spectacular hitting Series, matching a five-game record with nine hits in 23 ABs for a .391 average. However, Babe Ruth once slammed 10 hits in four games.

Although the Reds set a one-team Series record by using eight pitchers, and matched another by employing a total of 21 players yesterday, the most vital statistic was the final financial report.

Based on a distribution, unofficially, of 34 shares for each club from the $271,289 winner's take, each Yankee was tabbed to collect about $8,000. Each Cincinnati player would get $5,200 on the same basis. Exact disbursement will be announced later by Commissioner Ford Frick.

Had the favored Los Angeles Dodgers beaten out the Reds for the National League pennant, as everybody except the inspired Reds was convinced would happen—the Series take would have been approximately doubled—$15,000 for each winning player and around $11,000 for each losing player. This would have resulted because the spacious Los Angeles Coliseum, holds about three times as many people as the Reds' Crosley Field, which drew an average of 32,500 attendance for the three games here.

Cincinnati suffered the first successive three-game blistering on home grounds since the Yankees turned the same trick on the Brooklyn Dodgers in 1949.

The Redlegs didn't get much help from their two heralded stars, Frank Robinson and Vada Pinson, the bulwark of their attack in their amazing drive to the pennant.

Robinson, who had only one hit in 11 trips until yesterday's game, slammed a three-run homer and a double—but hit only .200 for the Series. Pinson collected only two hits in 22 trips. Eddie Kasko, a .271 regular season hitter, led the Reds with seven hits in 22 times at bat.

Yesterday's windup was just about wrapped up in the first inning when Joey Jay, who had given the Reds their only Series triumph with a four-hit, 6-2 victory in the second game, was shelled from the mound in a six-hit attack.

SERIES FACTS

FINAL STANDING

	W	L	Pct.
New York (A)	4	1	.800
Cincinnati (N)	1	4	.200

FIRST GAME, OCT. 4, AT YANKEE STADIUM

Cincinnati 000 000 000–0 2 0
New York 000 101 00x–2 6 0

O'Toole, Brosnan (8) and Johnson, Zimmerman; Ford and Howard.
WP–Ford. LP–O'Toole.
HR–New York: Howard, Skowron.

SECOND GAME, OCT. 5, AT YANKEE STADIUM

Cincinnati 000 211 020–6 9 0
New York 000 200 000–2 4 3

Jay and Edwards: Terry, Arroyo (8) and Howard.
WP-Jay. LP–Terry.
HR–Cincinnati: Coleman; New York: Berra.

THIRD GAME, OCT. 7, AT CROSLEY FIELD

New York 000 000 111–3 6 1
Cincinnati 001 000 100–2 8 0

Stafford, Daley (7), Arroyo (8) and Howard; Purkey and Edwards.
WP–Arroyo. LP–Purkey.
HR–New York: Blanchard, Maris.

FOURTH GAME, OCT. 8, AT CROSLEY FIELD

New York 000 112 300–7 11 0
Cincinnati 000 000 000–0 5 1

Ford, Coates (6) and Howard; O'Toole, Brosnan (6) Henry (9) and Johnson, Zimmerman.
WP–Ford. LP–O'Toole.

FIFTH GAME, OCT .9, AT CROSLEY FIELD

New York 510 502 000–13 15 1
Cincinnati 003 020 000– 5 11 3

Terry, Daley (3) and Howard; Jay, Maloney (1), Johnson (2), Henry (3), Jones (4), Purkey (5), Brosnan (7), Hunt (9) and Edwards.
WP–Daley. LP–Jay.
HR–New York: Blanchard, Lopez; Cincinnati: Robinson, Post.

FINANCIAL FIGURES

Fifth Game

Attendance–32,589.
Net Receipts–$213,533.91.
Commissioner's Share– $32,030.69.
Each Club's and League's Share–$45,375.95.

Five-Game Totals

Attendance–223,247.
Net Receipts–$1,480,059.95.
Commissioner's Share-$222,009.00.
Each Club and League's Share–$153,030.67.
Players' Share (first four games)–$645,928.28.

SERIES BATTING

YANKEES

	AB	R	H	HR	RBI	Pct.
Blanchard	10	4	4	2	3	.400
Richardson	23	2	9	0	0	.391
Skowron	17	3	6	1	5	.353
Lopez	9	3	3	1	7	.333
Berra	11	2	3	1	3	.273
Boyer	15	0	4	0	3	.267
Howard	20	5	5	1	1	.250
Kubek	22	3	5	0	1	.227
Mantle	6	0	1	0	0	.167
Maris	19	4	2	1	2	.105
Reed	0	0	0	0	0	.000
Ford	5	1	0	0	0	.000
Terry	3	0	0	0	0	.000
Arroyo	0	0	0	0	0	.000
Gardner	1	0	0	0	0	.000
Stafford	2	0	0	0	0	.000
Daley	1	0	0	0	1	.000
Coates	1	0	0	0	0	.000
	165	27	42	7	26	.255

REDS

	AB	R	H	HR	RBI	Pct.
D. Johnson	4	0	2	0	0	.500
Edwards	11	1	4	0	2	.364
Post	18	3	6	1	2	.333
Cardenas	3	0	1	0	0	.333
Kasko	22	1	7	0	1	.318
Chacon	12	2	3	0	0	.250
Coleman	20	2	5	1	2	.250
Robinson	15	3	3	1	4	.200
Blasingame	7	1	1	0	0	.143
Pinson	22	0	2	0	0	.091
Freese	16	0	1	0	0	.063
Lynch	3	0	0	0	0	.000
Bell	3	0	0	0	0	.000
Zimmerman	0	0	0	0	0	.000
O'Toole	3	0	0	0	0	.000
Gernert	4	0	0	0	0	.000
Brosnan	0	0	0	0	0	.000
Jay	4	0	0	0	0	.000
Purkey	3	0	0	0	0	.000
Henry	0	0	0	0	0	.000
Maloney	0	0	0	0	0	.000
K. Johnson	0	0	0	0	0	.000
Jones	0	0	0	0	0	.000
Hunt	0	0	0	0	0	.000
	170	13	35	3	11	.206

Ellie Hugs Bud

CINCINNATI—New York catcher Elston Howard lifts pitcher Bud Daley off the mound after Vada Pinson was retired for the final out of the World Series. Daley, a former Indianapolis hurler, was the relief pitcher as the Yankees won the game, 13-5, and the Series, 4-1.—AP Wirephoto.

SERIES PITCHING

YANKEES

	IP	H	BB	SO	W	L	ERA
Ford	14	6	1	7	2	0	0.00
Daley	7	5	0	3	1	0	0.00
Coates	4	1	1	2	0	0	0.00
Arroyo	4	4	2	3	1	0	2.25
Stafford	6⅔	7	2	5	0	0	2.57
Terry	9⅓	12	2	7	0	1	5.00
	45	35	8	27	4	1	1.60

REDS

	IP	H	BB	SO	W	L	ERA
K. Johnson	⅔	0	0	0	0	0	0.00
Jones	⅔	0	0	0	0	0	0.00
Hunt	1	0	1	1	0	0	0.00
Purkey	11	6	3	5	0	1	1.64
O'Toole	12	11	7	4	0	2	3.00
Jay	9⅔	8	6	6	1	1	5.40
Brosnan	6	9	4	5	0	0	7.50
Henry	2⅓	4	2	3	0	0	22.50
Maloney	⅔	4	1	1	0	0	18.00
	44	42	24	25	1	4	4.91

Cooler

Considerable cloudiness and cooler Tuesday with chance of shower or two. Four chances in 10 of showers in a specific location. Low 60 to 65, high in the mid 70s.

ADDITIONAL WEATHER DETAILS, TEMPERATURES—Page 11A.

St. Louis Globe-Democrat.

One Hundred and Nine Years of Public Service

White House Packs the Courts

An Editorial, Page 10A

Vol. 87—No. 8 | St. Louis, Tuesday Morning, October 10, 1961—3 Sections—36 Pages | SEVEN CENTS IN GREATER ST. LOUIS

YANKS BOMB REDS TO WIN SERIES

4 BABIES, 4 FATHERS

Woman on ADC Describes Troubles To Globe Reporter

The number of children on the Aid to Dependent Children program in St. Louis has nearly doubled in the last five years, from 13,400 to 26,400. The cost of ADC in that time has more than doubled, from $4,000,000 a year to almost $9,000,000 last year. Thus, the program is of great concern to all St. Louisans. The Globe-Democrat, believing the taxpayers should know how this money is being spent, has made an exhaustive survey of ADC. We feel it important that serious readers suspend judgment on ADC until they have read all of the series of articles, of which this is the third.

By MARGUERITE SHEPARD
Globe-Democrat Staff Writer

"I have four children,' said the tall young woman. She was barefooted with shell-pink toenails.

"How old are the children?" I asked.

"They're 8, 7, 3 and 2—two boys and two girls."

"And how many fathers have they?"

"Four fathers," answered Mrs. Lula B. "I was married to the first one."

A situation similar to this was frequently encountered in The Globe-Democrat study of the Aid to Dependent Children program.

44.2 Pct. Are BOWs

Of the 26,400 children on ADC rolls in St. Louis city, 44.2 per cent are BOWs—born out of wedlock However, in most of the ADC homes there usually has been at least one marriage.

Mrs. Lula B., like Mrs. Lillian W., the mother of eight described yesterday, is Negro. Ninety-seven per cent of the illegitimate children on ADC rolls here are Negro.

"What happened to your husband?" I asked Mrs. Lula B.

"After the first baby was born, my husband and I didn't get along too good," she said. "I haven't heard from him since he got out of the Army. He didn't come back. My check stopped and I went to the Red Cross.

"They found out he had got discharged in April, 1957. . . . I had two children then."

"And how long have you been on ADC?" I asked.

"Since about then," she said. "Since about a year before the 3-year-old was born."

"Do any of the fathers support their children?"

"I got a little support from two of them," she said. "It's supposed to be $7 every week for each of the two children. That's what the Prosecuting Attorney told them when they were down there. But they're not working."

"What work did they do?"

"One is a construction worker and the other is a bellhop. They're the fathers of the last two.

"The father of the second one, his home was in Alton and they never could get in touch with him. My husband's home is in New Jersey and I don't think they could do anything about him because his home is up there. . . . No, I don't know just where.

"The only thing I want to know about him," she said sharply, "is if he has a divorce because then I would not have to get one. But I don't know where to find out about it.

"The baby's daddy—he's the one who was a bellhop—and I plan on getting married as soon as he gets a steady job and I get a divorce. We are thinking about it."

"Oh," I said. "You see him regularly?"

"I haven't seen him now for three years," she said. "I just decided if I'm going to get married, I would marry him."

Mrs. Lula B. got as far as her senior year in high school but didn't finish. She had her first child when she was 17. She is 26 now.

$101 a Month in ADC

She lives in a six-room West End apartment with her grandmother, a 60-year-old domestic.

She gets $101 a month in ADC.

"I was getting $133 a month (the maximum possible for a mother and four children) till a couple of months ago when they cut it," she said.

"Why?" I asked.

"When the man from welfare was here last year, my grandmother wasn't coming in every night. She was staying on the place she works. This year she's here with me. By her coming in every night, the man said he would have to cut me down."

(Where there is an employable member of the family in the home, except for the mother, that person's income must be taken into consideration in figuring total budget needs, upon which ADC grants are based.)

"Does your welfare worker come by appointment?"

"Last year he made an appointment. This year he did not."

(To be sure of finding the family at home, welfare workers usually make an appointment by telephone or letter. They normally visit the family every six months, but must do so at least two times a year.

A Representative Sample

(I visited a representative sample of ADC families, without making prior appointments. Of 20 homes visited, I found only 13 at home.)

Mrs. Lula B. has never worked. "I can type," she said, "but not 80 words a minute. I took typing in school, then I went to night school and started a course but didn't finish."

She would like to get a divorce and re-marry.

"I have talked to two lawyers," she said. "One told me it would cost $125 and one said it would cost $65. I was thinking of going down and talking to Legal Aid and see how much and what I had to do."

(J. P. Lynes, director of the St. Louis city office of the State Division of Welfare, told me: "We badly need a free Legal Aid Bureau. We have no true free Legal Aid that will go into court and represent people in court. The Health and Welfare Council is interested in getting some group to establish a real free Legal Aid Bureau.)

However, even if Mrs. B. can get a divorce, she still faces a big problem: Will the father of her fourth child marry her and take on support of three other children not his?

Will he get a steady job that will enable him to support a family of six?

Mrs. B. is hopeful.

Mrs. W., described in yesterday's article, was more realistic.

"Not many men will stick by you when you've got a lot of children," she told me.

(Tomorrow: More Babies for More ADC?)

Man Charged With Murder In Tot's Death

Camden Accused After Car Hits Motorcycle

A murder warrant was issued Monday against the driver of a car that crashed into a parked motorcycle Saturday and killed a baby boy.

The warrant charged Ralph E. Camden, 43, with second-degree murder in the death of 11-month-old Michael Strader of 2108 Lafayette ave.

Camden was chadged in a second warrant with assaulting Michael's mother, Mrs. Maureen Strader, 18, with intent to kill.

BROKEN SHOULDER

She suffered a broken shoulder and body cuts when she and the baby were thrown from the motorcycle in the 2200 block of South Jefferson ave. Her husband, Barry, 17, had just parked it and jumped off.

Mr. Strader said Camden made a sudden U-turn on Jefferson, stopped, backed up and then drove forward, hitting the motorcycle and dragging it under the front wheels of the auto.

Camden, who has a lengthy record of arrests for peace disturbance and traffic violations, denied hitting the motorcycle deliberately. He claimed it hit his car first, forcing him into the U-turn.

STORE QUARREL

The two men had quarreled earlier in the day at Camden's confectionery at 2100 Lafayette ave., a few doors from the Strader home.

A coroner's inquest will be held Friday. It had been scheduled for Monday but was postponed at the request of the Circuit Attorney's office so it can study the case.

The warrants were issued by Assistant Circuit Attorney Quentin Gansloser. Camden remained in custody in the Central District police holdover.

The squabble at the confectionary was at 4 p.m. Mr. Strader, a Western Union messenger, said Camden had ranted at him, told him to take his business elsewhere and followed him out of the store.

STORIES DIFFER

Mr. Strader said he reached for a brick in an alley near the store, as if to pick it up, and Mr. Camden backed off.

He said he had had no trouble with Camden before. Camden said the Straders had quarreled

Continued on Page 11A

ACROBATIC REDS lunge desperately for hot smashes off Yankee bats as Cincinnati pitching crumbles in the fifth game o fthe World Series. At left, a grounder by Robby Richardson bounces past shortstop Eddie Kasko for the Yankee second baseman's ninth hit of the series, tieing the record for a five-game classic. The hit opened a five-run first inning rally and the Yankees were never headed. At right, Third baseman Gene Freese makes a spectacular catch of a line drive by New York catcher Elston Howard in the second inning, but his fielding gem merely kept the Reds' 13-to-5 defeat from becoming more humiliating. —A. P. Wirephotos

13-5 Romp Clinches 19th Championship

New York Depth Proves Too Much For Cincinnati

By ROBERT L. BURNES
Globe-Democrat Sports Editor

CINCINNATI. — The world championship of baseball returned on Monday to the city and team where it has rested so long and so often, the New York Yankees, after a three-year absence.

They clinched the championship, the nineteenth in their history and their first since 1958, in an easy 13-5 victory over the pepless, punchless and finally pitcherless Cincinnati Reds to close out the series, four victories to one.

The Yankees did it because they have a depth which few ball clubs possess, but which has always been one of the hallmarks of the Yankees.

POTENT ATTACK

Would you believe that the Yankees could muster a potent attack with both Yogi Berra and Mickey Mantle out of action, with Roger Maris impotent at the plate?

They not only could, but they did and the men who played the stand-in roles for Berra, missing a World Series game for which he was eligible for the first time since 1947, and Mantle delivered the key blows.

John Blanchard, a catcher who was in right field because Maris had to play center for Mantle, put the Yanks in front with a two-run homer in the first, doubled home another run in the fourth and wound up with three hits for the day.

HIGHLIGHT OF CAREER

Hector Lopez, in for Berra who injured his shoulder Sunday in a diving slide into third base, had an even bigger day. He tripled home a run in first, homered over the center field fence for three more in the fourth and climaxed the biggest day of his career by squeezing home a fifth run in the sixth when the Reds' defense collapsed completely.

Between them, Lopez and Blanchard accounted for 11 of the Yankees 13 runs, either in scoring them or driving them home.

While Blanchard and Lopez supplied the fire power, with some help from the rest of the crew, the Yankees themselves were disposed to lionize another unheralded performer, southpaw pitcher Bud Daley, for his top drawer relief work.

FLATTENED IN FIRST

"Once we got the lead," said Manager Ralph Houk after the game, "we wanted to close it out here. If you blow a lead as big as we had in this one, there's no telling what would happen later. It could have given the Reds the lift they needed. But Daley did a great job."

The Yanks had flattened the Reds with a five-run explosion in the first, added another in the second and that should have been enough. But pitcher Ralph Ter-

Continued on Page 2C

Supreme Court Will Review Yellin Case

By EDWARD W. O'BRIEN
Chief of The Globe-Democrat Washington Bureau.

WASHINGTON.—The Supreme Court agreed Monday to review the one-year prison sentence given to Edward Yellin, University of Illinois graduate student, for refusing to answer questions about Communism.

As usual, the court gave no reason in accepting Mr. Yellin's appeal from his conviction on four counts of contempt of Congress.

The conviction resulted from his appearance before the House Committee on Un-American Activities at Gary, Ind., on Feb. 10, 1958. The committee was investigating what it charged was the planting of highly-educated Communist party members in menial factory jobs in 10 cities around the country, including St. Louis.

DECLINES 26 TIMES

Mr. Yellin declined to answer 26 committee questions, including whether he was a Communist when he was hired by a Gary steel mill in 1949.

He gave several reasons for his refusal. One was a claim

Continued on Page 6A

Kennedy Visits Rayburn in Hospital

President Shifts Plans After Report Speaker Feeling Better

By Associated Press

DALLAS.—President Kennedy flew into Texas Monday afternoon to visit Speaker Sam Rayburn, seriously ill with cancer.

It had rained hard earlier in the day, and a light rain was still falling when the big presidential came in.

But President Kennedy came down the ramp without either a hat or ooat, and quickly got into his car for a drive to the hospital.

Originally President Kennedy had intended to go back to Washington from his weekend in Newport, R.I. But Monday morning—possibly because he had been told that Speaker Rayburn was feeling more alert, he changed his plans.

President Kennedy took the long trip to Texas instead for just a few minutes with the politician who has earned the title "Mr. Democrat."

Mr. Kennedy scarcely paused before starting the seven-mile drive from Love Field to Baylor University Medical Center.

There in Room 729 the 79-year-old Rayburn is waging the greatest, hardest fight of his long career.

Cancer has moved through his body so that there is no hope of recovery. Speaker Rayburn began getting daily injections of a drug, "5 Fluoro-Uracil," Sunday, but it can only slow down, or possibly halt, the steady spread of cancer.

On this day of the Presidential visit the medical report was unusually cheering.

Dr. Ralph Tompsett, chief of internal medicine at Baylor, put out this statement Monday afternoon:

"Mr. Sam Rayburn has had his second treatment today with the cancer chemotherapy drug 5 Fluro-Uracil. He has tolerated the drug very well thus far.

"Although Mr. Rayburn's condition remains serious, he seems definitely symptomatically improved today and feels stronger. His menu for lunch today consisted of roast beef, a little gravy, baked potato, asparagus tips, orange bran muffin, iced tea and ice cream.

"When we saw him early this afternoon he was sitting up in bed watching the World Series on television."

U. S. Orders 3 More Air Guard Units to Duty

WASHINGTON (AP). — The Pentagon Monday ordered to active duty three more Air National Guard fighter squadrons and their supporting units.

The squadrons from Arizona, South Carolina and Tennessee will report on Nov. 1 at their home sattions. They will serve for a year.

Called up were the 197th Fighter Interceptor squadron of Phoenix, Ariz., the 157th Fighter Interceptor Squadron, Eastover, S.C., and the 151st Fighter Interceptor Squadron, Knoxville, Tenn.

The squadrons and their sup-

Continued on Page 11A

Trooper Shot Trying to Serve Warrant on Man

BROSELEY, MO. (AP).—A state highway patrolman, who was wounded seven months ago in a gun battle with desperado Douglas Wayne Thompson, was shot and wounded again Monday while trying to serve an insanity warrant on an old man.

Trooper Glen E. Davis, 26, was reported in serious—but not critical—condition in a Poplar Bluff hospital with shotgun pellet wounds of the right arm, right leg and lower abdomen.

Trooper Davis' assailant, Charles S. Brown, 83, barricaded himself in his combination home and tavern and held officers at bay for three hours with shotgun and pistol fire.

Capt. O. L. Wallace, Lt. E. F. Dampf and Trooper Paul Moore stormed the house and took Brown into custody after a barrage of tear gas shells had been fired into the building.

Brown suffered a broken jaw, apparently from being struck by a metal fragment from a tear gas shell.

He was taken to a Poplar Bluff hospital, pending transfer to the Missouri State Hospital at Farmington on the insanity warrant. Neighbors filed a complaint against Brown, claiming he had grow increasingly violent. His liquor license had been revoked a few months ago.

Trooper Davis was wounded by a charge fired through a door as he and Deputy Sheriffs Leo Hodge and Paul Goad tred to take Brown into custody.

The two deputies dragged Trooper Davis out of range and called for reinforcements. They said Brown easily coulld have shot all three of them, but held his fire.

Trooper Davis suffered an arm wound March 17 in a gunfight with Thompson, 27-year-

Continued on Page 6A

SUGGESTS SOVIET AGENTS KILLED DANE

Senate Report Hints Murder In 1959 Death of Bang-Jensen

By Associated Press

WASHINGTON.—A Senate subcommittee raised the question "suicide or murder?" Monday in the mysterious death two years ago of Povl Bang-Jensen, Danish diplomat and former United Nations official.

The Senate Internal Security Subcommittee challenged the New York police verdict of suicide and suggested the possibility that Bang-Jensen might have been killed by Soviet agents.

"There are too many solid arguments against suicide," the subcommittee said, "too many unanswered questions, too many serious reasons for suspecting Soviet motivation and the possibility of Soviet implication."

DIPLOMAT'S ROLE

The 120-page report described the 50-year-old diplomat's role as secretary of the UN special committee investigating the 1956 Hungarian revolution, his subsequent quarrel with UN superiors, and finally the circumstances of his death.

"About the most that can be said on the basis of information available today," the report said, "is that it is still unclear whether it was suicide or murder."

POVL BANG-JENSEN
—A. P. Wirephoto

The report held that the Soviet terror apparatus may have had adequate motivation for the liquidation of Bang-Jensen.

Bang-Jensen left his home on Monday morning, Nov. 23, 1959, for his office. He was employed at the time by CARE, a charitable organization. Three days later, on Thanksgiving morning, his body was found in a Queens park. He had been shot in the right temple with his own gun and there was a suicide note in his pocket.

TIME UNACCOUNTED FOR

There was no satisfactory explanation of what happened between Monday morning, when the diplomat was last seen alive, and Thursday morning when his body was found.

The Soviets, the report said, had good reason to spirit away Bang-Jensen to find out how much he knew about Communist infiltration in the United Nations and in United States intelligence agencies — and how much of this knowledge he had conveyed to American authorities.

"And if Bang-Jensen was taken into custody for such interrogation, his liquidation would have been an inevitable sequel," the report said.

If this theory is correct, it continued, then it can be assumed that the Soviet agents

Continued on Page 11A

Galbraith to Discuss U. S. Aid to Calcutta

CALCUTTA, INDIA (Reuters). —United States Ambassador John K. Galbraith said here Monday he would discuss problems of the development of Calcutta with President Kennedy when he accompanies Prime Minister Jawaharlal Nehru to Washington next month.

Inside Headlines

Important Inside Features